VOLUME 28 • JANUARY 1993-DECEMBER 1993

ISBN 0-87507-049-3

THE CATHOLIC PERIODICAL AND LITERATURE INDEX

Editor
Dana Cernaianu, Ph.D.

Special Project Editor
Arnold Rzepecki

Catholic Library Association
Saint Mary's College of Minnesota #26
700 Terrace Heights
Winona, Minnesota 55987-1399

Indexers:
Margaret A. Bell
Lawrence L. Jaffe, Ph.D.
Elizabeth A. Pitt
Eugene M. Rooney, S.J.

CONTENTS

ABBREVIATIONS OF PERIODICALS INDEXED

AAS - Acta Apostolicae Sedis VC 0001-5199
ABenR - American Benedictine Review US 0002-7650
ACHSR -American Catholic Historical Society Records
US 0002-7790
AFER - African Ecclesial Review KE 0001-1134
Amer J Juris - American Journal of Jurisprudence,
US 00609-8995
America - US 0002-7049
Augustin, Stud - Augustinian Studies
US 0094-5323
Bib Th Bul - Biblical Theology Bulletin US 0146-1079
Bible T - Bible Today US 0006-0836
Cahiers Jos - Cahiers de Josephologie CN 0007-9774
Can Cath Rev - The Canadian Catholic Review
CN 0714-7724
Cathechist - US 0008-7726
Cath Int - Catholic International FR 1153197
Cath Work - Catholic Worker US 0008-8463
Catholica - GW 0008-8501
CBQ - Catholic Biblical Quarterly US 0008-7912
CDgst - Catholic Digest US 0008-7998
CHist - Catholic Historical Reviews US 0008-8080
Christus - Christus (Mexico) MX 0009-5842
ChrWorld - Christ to the World IT 0011-1465
Church - US 0883-5667
Cien Tom - Ciencia Tomista SP 0210-0398
Cist Stud - Cistercian Studies BE 0578-3224
Cithara - US 0009-7527
Civilta - La Civiltà Cattolica IT 0009-8167
CLawyer - Catholic Lawyer US 0008-8137
CLSAP - Canon Law Society of America Prodeedings
US 0277-9889
CLW - Catholic Library World US 0008-820X
Comm - Commonweal US 0010-3330
Communio - Communio: International Catholic Review
US 0094-2065
Crisis - US 0084-1705
Critic - US 0011-149X
CrossCurr - Cross Currents US 0011-1953
Diakonia - US 0012-1959
Doctr Life - Doctrine and Life IE 0012-446X
Ecumen Trends - Ecumenical Trends US 0360-9073
Emmanuel - US 0013-6719
Envoy - US 0013-9408
Eph Theol Lovan - Ephemerides Theologicae
Lovanienses BE 0013-9513
Extensn-Extension
F & R - Faith & Reason US 0098-5449
Franciscanum - Franciscanum: Revista de las
ciencias del espiritu CK 0120-1268
FranStds - Franciscan Studies US 0080-5459
Furrow - IE 0016-3120
Gregorianum - IT 0017-4114 (Abstracts in English)
Health Prog - Health Progress US 0018-5817
Heythrop - Heythrop Journal UK 0018-1196

Horizons (CTS) - Horizons: Journal of the College
Theology Society US 0360-9669
HPR - Homiletic and Pastoral Review US 0018-4268
IPQ - International Philosophical Quarterly
US 0019-0365
J Interdisc St - Journal of Interdisciplinary Studies
US 0890-0132
JEcumen Stds - Journal of Ecumenical Studies
US 0022-0558
LADOC - Latin American Documentation
PE 0360-3350
Laval Theol Phil - Laval Théologique et Philosophique
CN 0023-9054
Liguorian - US 0022-3450
Linacre - Linacre Quarterly US 0024-3639
Listening - US 0024-4414
Liturgy - US 0458-063X
Living Light - US 0024-5275
Living Prayer - US 0890-5568
Louvain Stds - Louvain Studies BE 0024-6964
Lumen - Lumen Vitae BE 0024-7324
Manuscripta - US 0025-2603
Marian Stds - Marian Studies US 0464-9680
Med Stud - Mediaeval Studies CN 0076-5872
Mod Lit - Modern Liturgy US 3263-504X
Mod Schlmn - Modern Schoolman US 0026-8402
Momentum - US 0026-914X
Month - UK 0027-0172
MSR - Mélanges de Science Religieuse FR 0025-8911
(Abstracts in English)
Nat Cath Rep - National Catholic Reporter
US 0027-8939
New Blckfrs - New Blackfriars UK 0028-4289
New Cov - New Covenant US 0744-8589
New Oxford Rev -New Oxford Review US 0149-4244
New Test Stud - New Testament Studies UK 0028-6885
New Theol Rev - New Theology Review US 0896-4297
Notitiae - VC 0029-4306
NRT - Nouvelle Revue Théologique BE 0029-4845
OChr - One in Christ UK 0030-252X
OR(Eng) - L'Osservatore Romano (English)
VC 0030-6312
Origins - US 0093-609X
OSV - Our Sunday Visitor US 0030-6979
OTA - Old Testament Abstracts US 0364-8591
Pacifica - AU 1030-570X
Past Mus - Pastoral Music US 0363-6569
Periodica - Periodica de Re Morali Cannonica Liturgica
IT 0031-529X
Perspectiva - Perspectiva Teologica BL 0102-4469
PhilosTod - Philosphy Today US 0031-8256
Priest - US 0032-8200
Priests & People - UK 0009-8736
REB - Revista Eclesiastica Brasileira BL 0101-8434

Register - National Catholic Register US 0027-8920
Relig Lit. - Religion & Literature US 0029-4500
ReligTJ - Religion Teacher's Journal US 0034-401X
RPhil Louvain - Revue Philosophique de Louvain
BE 0035-3841 (Abstracts in English)
RRel - Review for Religious US 0034-639X
RSocEcon - Review of Social Economy US 0034-6764
RTheol Louvain - Revue Theologique de Louvain
BE 0080-2654
SacM - Sacred Music US 0036-2255
Salt - US 0883-2587
ScriptB - Scripture Bulletin UK 0036-9780
Seminarium - VC 0582-6314 (Abstracts in English)
SIDIC - SIDIC: Service Internationale de Documenta-
tion Judéo-Chrétienne IT 0379-3557
Sisters - Sisters Today US 0037-590X
SocJust - Social Justice Review US 0099-183X
SocThought - Social Thought US 0099-183X
Spir Life - Spiritual Life US 0038-7630
Spir Tod - Spirituality Today US 0162-6760
Spirit - US 0038-7584
St Anth - St. Anthony Messenger US 0036-276X
Stimm Zeit - Stimmen der Zeit GW 0039-1492

Stud Can - Studia Canonica CN 0039-310X
(Abstracts in English)
Stud Form Spir - Studies in Formative Spirituality
US 0193-2478
StudiaM -Studia Missionalia IT 0080-3987
Studies - IE 0039-3495
Supplement - Le Supplément FR 0750-1455
Tablet - Tablet (London) UK 0039-8837
Teilhard Rev - The Teilhard Review (London)
UK 0050-2184
Teol Vida - Teología y Vida CL 0049-3449
TheolDgst - Theology Digest US 0040-5728
TheolStds - Theological Studies US 0040-5639
Thomist - US 0040-6325
Thought - US 0040-6457
Tod Cath Teach - Today's Catholic Teacher
US 0040-8441
Tod Parish - Today's Parish US 0040-8549
TPS - The Pope Speaks US 0032-4353
USCath - US Catholic US 0041-7548
USCath Hist - US Catholic Historian US 0735-8318
Way - UK 0043-1575
Way Suppl - Way Supplement UK 0307-5532
Worship - US 0043-941X

ABBREVIATIONS AND SYMBOLS

Abp........Archbishop	D................December, died	Jb ....*Jahrbuch*	q ....quarterly
abst ....abstract	diag.............diagram	Je ....June	repr ....reprint
Ag ....August	diss ....dissertation	Jl................July	rev ....revised
ann.........annual	doc/s ....document/s	Jr................Junior	rpt............report
anniv ......anniversary	E................East	jt ....joint	S ....September, South
annot ......annotated	ed...............edited, edition, editor	m ....monthly	semi-ann ...semi-annual
Ap ....April	Eng.............England, English	Metr............metropolitan	soc ....society
assoc ......association	F................February	min ....minutes	spec.........special
AT ....*Atles Testament*	facsim...........facsimile	Mr ....March	Spr.........Spring
Aut ....Autumn	fig/s............figure/s	My..............May	Sr ....Senior, Sister
auth........author	fl ....flourished	N..............November, North	Sum ....Summer
bearb ......*bearbeitet*	fr.................from	natl ....national	suppl ....supplement
Beih ....*Beiheft*	Ger ....Germany, German	n.d..............no date given	tr ....translated,
bi-m ....bimonthly	hrsg.............*herausgegeben*	no...............number	translator,
bibliog ....bibliography	il ....illustrated,	ns ....new series	translation
biog........biography	illustration/s	NT..............New Testament	trad ....traduction
Bp ....Bishop	inst ....institute	O................October	translit......transliteration
br ....brother	int,int'l..........international	obit ....obiturary	u ....*und*
cent ....century	introd............introduction	OT..............Old Testament	über.........*übersetzt*
cf...........compare,	ISBN ....Int Standard Book	p,pp ....page, pages	univ........university
comparison	Number	Patr.............Patriarch	v,vol....volume
comm .....committee,	ISSN ....Int Standard Serial	pl/s ....plate/s	W ....West
commission	Number	por..............portrait	Wint ....Winter
comp ......compiled	It.................Italy, Italian	pr ....press	yr ....year
conf.......conference	j.................journal	pseud...........pseudonym	Z,Zs ....*Zeitschrift*
cont........continuation,	Ja ....January	pt ....part	* ....contents, other data
continued	Jahr,Jh ....*Jahrhundert*	pub ....published, publisher	at author entry

USER'S GUIDE

Subject Index

ASYLUM, RIGHT OF
 Europe 1992 and refugees: keeping the world's misery at arm's length. Alt, Jörg. *Month* 25:46-52 F 1992
ATONEMENT
 see also Reconciliation (Theology)
 A theology of atonement and Paul's vision of Christianity. Tambasco, Anthony J. Minnesota: The Liturgical Press, 1991, x, 115p ISBN 0-8146-5679-x LC 91-7112
ATTENTION
 Are you listening? Ranieri, Ralph F. *Liguorian* 80:20-23 F 1992
AUGUSTINE, SAINT, BP OF HIPPO
 The foundations of mysticism. McGinn, Bernard, 1937-, New York: Crossroad, 1991. x, 494p ISBN 0-8245-1121-2 LC 91-23931

- Subject headings with "see" and "see also" references to related headings.

- Personal names as subject headings.

Author and Editor Index

Thomas, David Michael.
 Conversion and family soup. *Mod Lit* 19:8 Mr 1992
Thomas, J.
 Review of: *The moral vision of Dorothy Day: a feminist perspective* by O'Connor, June E. In: *St Anth* 99-52-53 Mr. 1992
 Review of: *The Sabbath in Jewish and Christian traditions* by Eskenazi, Tamara C, et al, eds. In: *St Anth* 99-51 F 1992
Thomas, Leo, and Alkire, Jan.
 Healing as a parish ministry. Notre Dame: Ave Maria Press, 1992. x. 176p ISBN 0-87793-474-6 LC 91-77473

- Entries include authors and editors of articles, books, and reviews.

Book Title Index

The Book of Revelation: the open book of prophecy. Giblin, Charles Homer. Minnesota: The Liturgical Press, 1991. x, 231p ISBN 0-8146-5005-8 LC 91-12958
A bridge to Buddhist-Christian dialogue. Yagi, Seōhi, 1932, and Swidler, Leonard. New York: Paulist Press, 1990. x, 152p ISBN 0-8091-3169-2 LC 90-35653
Catholic social teaching. Henriot, Peter J, et al. Maryknoll: Orbis Books. 1991. x, 164p ISBN 0-88344-8814
Catholic spirituality and the history of religions. Carmody, Denise Lardner, 1935-, and Carmody, John Tully, 1939-. New Jersey: Paulist Press, 1991. x, 179p ISBN 0-8091-3285-0 LC 90-36015

- Entries are arranged alphabetically by the *title* of the book.

Book Review Index

Crosby, Michael II.
 The dysfunctional church: addiction and codependency the the family of Catholicism. Ave Maria Press, 1991.
  Roy, M. *Sisters* 64:140 Mr 1992.
Cross and sword: an eyewitnessed history of Christianity in Latin America.
  Goodpasture, H. McKenzie, ed. Orbis Books, 1989.
   Vercruysse, J. *Eph Theol Lovan* 77:465-466 D 1991.
Crossan, John Dominic.
 The historial Jesus: the life of a Mediterranean Jewish peasant. Harper, n.d.
  Muir, J. *America* 166:198-199 Mr 7 1992.

-Entries are arranged alphabetically by the *author or editor* of the book, or by title when neither of those is given.

Papal documents (texts, translations, and commentaries) appear under the author heading, using the full form of the Pope's name [e.g.: John Paul II, Pope, 1920- (Karol Wojtyla) (elected 1978)] and are listed in chronological order. A full description of the document is given under its subject entry, with a reference to the author entry.

SUBJECT INDEX

A

La secte eglise unie du saint esprit du Congo. Makaya, Jean Florent. *StudiaM* 41:225-239 1992

Theological trends in Africa. Chepkwony, Adam K A. *AFER* 34:2-17 F 1992

Toward an African Christianity: inculturation applied. Hillman, Eugene. New York: Paulist Press, 1993. x, 101p ISBN 0-8091-3381-4 LC 92-39526

AFRICA—SOCIAL CONDITIONS
A Church committed to Africa [editorial]. *Cath Int* 4:150 Ap 1993

John Paul II, Pope, (1993-02-08) Birth of Freedom [English text]. John Paul II, Pope, 1920- (Karol Wojtyla) (elected 1978). *Origins* 22:615-616 F 18 1993*

Le mariage en Afrique. Nothomb, Dominique. *NRT* 114:852-869 N-D 1992

Ministry without borders. *Cath Int* 4:165-168 Ap 1993

Mozambican prelate visits US seeking peacekeepers. Collins, Carole. *Nat Cath Rep* 29:9 Mr 5 1993

AFRICA, EAST—POLITICS AND GOVERNMENT
The social context of the AMECEA countries on the eve of the African Synod. Henriot, Peter F. *AFER* 34:340-363 D 1992

AFRICA, EAST—SOCIAL CONDITIONS
The social context of the AMECEA countries on the eve of the African Synod. Henriot, Peter F. *AFER* 34:340-363 D 1992

AFRICA, NORTH—RELIGION
John Paul II, Pope, (1991-11-26) Allocutiones (Papal address to North African Bishops) [French]. John Paul II, Pope, 1920- (Karol Wojtyla) (elected 1978). *AAS* 84:1143-1147 D 5 1992*

AFRICANS—PSYCHOLOGY
"Am I not a human being and a brother/sister?". Magesa, Laurenti. *AFER* 34:95-114 Ap 1992

AFRO-AMERICAN—AUTHORS
"Malcolm X" di Spike Lee. Fantuzzi, Virgilio. *Civilta* 3:154-161 Jl 17 1993

AFRO-AMERICAN—MUSIC
Wade in the winter: the wisdom of the spirituals. Jones, Arthur C, 1936-. New York: Maryknoll, 1993. x, 182p ISBN 0-88344-923-4 LC 93-7491

AFRO-AMERICAN YOUTH
From Bed-Sty to Israel: black teens on a Kibbutz. McCarthy, Abigail Quigley. *Comm* 120:7-8 Jl 16 1993

Who are their models? Cunningham, Beatrice. *ReligTJ* 27:38-39 O 1993

AFRO-AMERICANS
Ida B Wells. O'Connell-Cahill, Catherine. *Salt* 13:31 Jl-Ag 1993

John Paul II, Pope, (1992-10-12) Defend your identities and values. John Paul II, Pope, 1920- (Karol Wojtyla) (elected 1978). *TPS* 38:103-106 Mr-Ap 1993*

AFRO-AMERICANS—BIOGRAPHY
Catholics look at Malcolm X. Holton, Robert. *OSV* 81:9 F 7 1993

AFRO-AMERICANS—EDUCATION
Celebrating African-American traditions. Inkel, Maxine. *Momentum* 24:71-72 N-D 1993

AFRO-AMERICANS—RELIGION
The black muslims in America. Lincoln, C Eric. Grand Rapids: Eerdmans, 1993. 0-8028-0703-8 ISBN 0-8028-0703-8

Black theology: a documentary history, vol I, 1966-1979. Cone, James H, and Wilmore, Gayraud S, eds. Maryknoll: Orbis Books, 1993. 462p ISBN 0-88344-853-x LC 92-44927

Black theology: a documentary history, vol II, 1980-1992. Cone, James H, and Wilmore, Gayraud S, eds. Maryknoll: Orbis Books, 1993. x, 450p ISBN 0-88344-773-8 LC 79-12747

A change is coming. Hayes, Diana L. *USCath* 58:38-40 S 1993

Shoes that fit our feet: sources for a constructive black theology. Hopkins, Dwight N. Maryknoll, New York: Orbis Books, 1993. x, 242p ISBN 0-88344-848-3 LC 92-38713

Singing the Lord's song in a strange land: the African-American churches and ecumenism. Watley, William D. Grand Rapids: Eerdmans, 1993. 188p ISBN 0-8028-0711-9

AFRO-AMERICANS—SOCIO-ECONOMIC CONDITIONS
The "Brown" decision: 40 years later. Wilkins, Roger, 1932-. *America* 169:4-5 Jl 17-24 1993

AFRO-AMERICANS, CATHOLIC
As black Catholics speak, who will listen? Curry, Adrienne. *USCath* 58:30-31 Ja 1993

AGAPE FEAST
The original "love feast". Ball, Ann. *OSV* 81:8-9 Mr 7 1993

AGATA, GIUDITTA ADELAIDE (GIUSEPPINI VANNINI), 1859-1911
Congregation for the Causes of Saints (1992-03-07) Decree on the heroic virtues. Congregation for the Causes of Saints. *AAS* 84:1080-1083 N 3 1992*

AGE (PSYCHOLOGY)
Soul making and life's second half. Brennan, Anne, and Brewi, Janice. *RRel* 52:220-225 Mr-Ap 1993

AGE DISCRIMINATION IN EMPLOYMENT ACT OF 1967
The Age Discrimination in Employment Act of 1967. Tichy, George J, II. *CLawyer* 34 no 4:373-384 1993

AGED
The Age Discrimination in Employment Act of 1967. Tichy, George J, II. *CLawyer* 34 no 4:373-384 1993

The Catholic way of growing old. Lukefahr, Oscar. *Liguorian* 81:30-35 My 1993

Sacrifice? We wrote the book on it!. Reilly, Robert. *USCath* 58:40-41 N 1993

There is a season. O'Brien, Patricia. *HPR* 93:58-61 Mr 1993

Tips for trips with older travelers [condensed fr *Vibrant Life* Jl/Ag 1992]. Reece, Colleen L. *CDgst* 57:81-91 Jl 1993

Vital options: meeting the elderly's varied needs. Cassidy, Judy, ed. *Health Prog* 74:34-52+ My 1993*

A woman gives a feast: transforming rituals in old age. Simmons, Henry C. *Liturgy* 10:21-30 Wint 1992

AGED—CARE
Autonomy and care for the frail elderly. Szwabo, Peggy, and Stretch, John J. *Health Prog* 74:50-51+ My 1993

Capitation works for long-term care. Hansen, Jennie Chin. *Health Prog* 74:61 Jl-Ag 1993

A change of home. Lyall, Joanna. *Tablet* 247:883 Jl 10 1993

Colorado: American Source Books, 1993. Heath, Angela. Colorado: American Source Books, 1993. 122p ISBN 0-9621333-9-6 LC 92-42895

An effective, efficient elder care program. Gorshe, Nancy. *Health Prog* 74:57-59 Ap 1993

Empowering the frail elderly. Rheinecker, Phil. *Health Prog* 74:23-27 Ja-F 1993

Integrating services for the elderly. Hume, Susan K. *Health Prog* 74:22-25+ O 1993

AGED—ETHICS- ITALY
Considerazioni etico-giuridiche sulle dimissioni. Passano, Paolo Ferrari da. *Civilta* 144:45-50 Ja 2 1993

AGED—HOUSING
Autonomy and care for the frail elderly. Szwabo, Peggy, and Stretch, John J. *Health Prog* 74:50-51+ My 1993

AGED—MEDICAL CARE see Aged—Care

AGED—RELIGIOUS LIFE
Grandparents pass on the faith. Cotter, Theresa. *Church* 9:32-35 Aut 1993

John Paul II, Pope, (1993-09-26) Bring [Orig in Italian]. John Paul II, Pope, 1920- (Karol Wojtyla) (elected 1978). *OR(Eng)* 1311:8 O 13 1993*

AGED WOMEN
The dancing grandmas. Estés, Clarissa Pinkola. *USCath* 58:26-30 N 1993

AGING
Biblical update: the aging process. Hoppe, Leslie J. *BibleT* 30:324-352 N 1992*

Mental healthcare for rural seniors. Smith, Marianne, and Buckwalter, Kathleen C. *Health Prog* 74:52-56+ My 1993

The naked age. Leckie, Judith. *Priests & People* 6:423-425 N 1992

Older? you are a blessing [condensed fr *The Catholic World* N-D 1992]. Fischer, Kathleen. *CDgst* 57:17-18+ F 1993

AGNOSTICISM
A wholesome agnosticism and Christianity's coming dialogue with the world religions. Thornhill, John. *Pacifica* 6:265-277 O 1993

AGORAPHOBIA
A vast confinement. Paige, Harry W, 1922-. *Liguorian* 81:46-50 Jl 1993

AGRICULTURAL SUBSIDIES
GATT: an ethical void. Egan, Eileen. *Cath Work* 60:1+ Je-Jl 1993

Sitting pretty on set-aside [editorial]. *Tablet* 247:1119 S 4 1993

AGRICULTURE
Can nature be a commodity? [fr *The ram's horn*]. Kneen, Brewster. *Cath Work* 60:1+ S 1993

AHAB, KING OF ISRAEL
Josephus' portrait of Ahab. Feldman, Louis H. *Eph Theol Lovan* 78:368-384 D 1992

AIDS (DISEASE)
AIDS and changes in clinical research methods. Hume, Susan K. *Health Prog* 74:17-21 Mr 1993

AIDS and comfort: no one deserves to die alone. Poda, Paula. *Salt* 13:18-21 Ap 1993

AIDS and hospitality. Heuser, Tom. *Cath Work* 60:6 My 1993

AIDS and the media [editorial]. *Register* 69:4 Ja 10 1993

AIDs in the workplace: discrimination by ignorance. Pedreirs, Jorge. *CLawyer* 35 no 2:199-215 1993

AIDS: a worsening crisis challenges church and society. Overberg, Kenneth R, 1944-. *St Anth* 100:22-27 Ja 1993

At the side of the sufferers. *Tablet* 247:650 My 22 1993

A Catholic doctor looks at AIDS in the USA. Barnet, Robert J. *America* 168:6-12 F 6 1993

Extending a hand, soothing a soul. *Origins* 23:65+ Je 17 1993

Group says HIV + priests still stigmatized. Abner, Marchel. *Nat Cath Rep* 29:4 Jl 2 1993

John Paul II, Pope, (1993-02-07) AIDS [Original in English]. John Paul II, Pope, 1920- (Karol Wojtyla) (elected 1978). *Origins* 22:613-614 F 18 1993*

Long-term care survey reveals challenges. Westhoff, Lola J, and Schaefer, Jeffrey C. *Health Prog* 74:38-42 My 1993

"Mom, I have AIDS" [condensed fr *The Family—A Catholic Perspective*, Mr 1993]. Moyer, Sylvia. *CDgst* 57:49-53 Je 1993

Moral leadership needed to respond to AIDS. Fisher, Mary. *Health Prog* 74:55-56 Jl-Ag 1993

Mustering up unconditional parental love. Griffin, Robert F. *OSV* 82:18 My 16 1993

AIDS (DISEASE)—EDUCATION
Extending a hand, soothing a soul. *Origins* 23:65+ Je 17 1993

AIDS (DISEASE)—PATIENTS—EMPLOYMENT
Policy on students and employees affected by AIDS/HIV. *Origins* 23:394-397 N 11 1993

AIDS (DISEASE)—PREVENTION
Abstinence as public policy: a report from New Jersey's schools. Bovenizer, David A. *Crisis* 11:40-41 S 1993

A killer at large. Rice, Judith. *Tablet* 247:232+ F 20 1993

Statement on public schools' condom distribution. *Origins* 22:553-556 Ja 21 1993

AIDS (DISEASE)—PSYCHOLOGICAL ASPECTS
Sida, impuls de vida?: experiencia de Joan Ferrer Sisquella. Bovet, Joan M. Barcelona: Claret, 1993. x, 135p ISBN 84-7263-837-5

AIDS (DISEASE)—RELIGIOUS ASPECTS
Embracing the mystery: prayerful responses to AIDS. Sandys, Sebastian, ed. Minnesota: The Liturgical Press, 1993. x, 105p ISBN 0-8146-2222-4 LC 92-43238

Pastoral care for those living with HIV/AIDS. Paul, John, Bp. *Origins* 23:378-381 N 4 1993

What the Catholic church says about AIDS ministry. *Salt* 13:21-22 Ap 1993

AIDS (DISEASE)—SOCIAL ASPECTS
Extending a hand, soothing a soul. *Origins* 23:65+ Je 17 1993

AIDS (DISEASE)- AFRICA
Papal call for chastity close to AIDS-ravaged Africa bone. McCarthy, Tim. *Nat Cath Rep* 29:11 F 26 1993

AIDS (DISEASE)- LATIN AMERICA
Latin America confronts AIDS. Jeffrey, Paul. *America* 168:10-12 F 13 1993

AIDS (DISEASE)- MEXICO
AIDS silently spreading through Mexico [AIDS epidemic]. Ross, John. *Nat Cath Rep* 29:15 Mr 19 1993

AIDS (DISEASE)- TANZANIA
A circle of death. Goodwin, Gillian. *Tablet* 247:746+ Je 1993

AIDS (DISEASE)- UGANDA
Papal call for chastity close to AIDS-ravaged Africa bone. McCarthy, Tim. *Nat Cath Rep* 29:11 F 26 1993
Pope mingles with AIDS victims. *Tablet* 247:219 F 13 1993

AIDS (DISEASE)- UNDERDEVELOPED AREAS
A killer at large. Rice, Judith. *Tablet* 247:232+ F 20 1993

AIDS (DISEASE) IN CHILDREN
Policy on students and employees affected by AIDS/HIV. *Origins* 23:394-397 N 11 1993

AIRLINES- UNITED STATES
Midflight correction? Reregulation won't work. Kelly, Kevin T. *Comm* 120:6-7 Je 18 1993

ALBANIA—POLITICS
Greek retaliation to priest's expulsion. *Tablet* 247:926 Jl 17 1993

ALBANIA—RELIGION
Albania's legacy of faith. Hurley, Mark Joseph, Bp, 1919-. *OSV* 81:21 Mr 21 1993
Albania, the Church triumphant in ruins. Hurley, Mark Joseph, Bp, 1919-. *America* 168:4-5 F 20 1993
Restoring Albania's social fabric. O'Grady, Desmond. *OSV* 81:21 Ap 18 1993

ALBANIA—SOCIAL CONDITIONS
Albania struggles for its dignity. Blum, Paul Richard. *Register* 69:5 Je 13 1993

ALBANIANS
Albania revisited [interview by J Torrens]. Sinishta, Gjon. *America* 168:20-22 F 20 1993
Orthodox fan flames in Kosovo. *Tablet* 246:1630 D 19-26 1992

ALBERIC OF MONTE CASSINO, ?-1105
Alberic of Monte Cassino. Sitzmann, Marion. *Priest* 49:34-36 Jl 1993

ALBERTUS MAGNUS, SAINT, 1200-1280
Albert the Great in the renaissance: Cristoforo Landino's use of Albert on the soul. McNair, Bruce G. *Mod Schlmn* 70:115-129 Ja 1993

ALCHEMY
Alvaro Alonso Barba's Art of metallurgy: from the poetical to the technological. Soons, Alan. *Cithara* 32:3-12 My 1993

ALCOHOL AND ALCOHOLISM
COAs: behind the masks. Birke, Szifra. *Momentum* 24:54-60 Ap-My 1993
Families of alcoholics: a guide to healing and recovery. Nuechterlein, Anne Marie. Minneapolis: Augsburg, 1993. x, 140p ISBN 0-80662-615-1 LC 92-19156
John Paul II, Pope, (1991-11-23) Allocutiones (Address to a Symposium) [Italian]. John Paul II, Pope, 1920- (Karol Wojtyla) (elected 1978). *AAS* 84:1128-1132 D 5 1992*
Some sober words about grandpa's drinking [interview by B. Dodds]. Martin, Joseph F. *OSV* 82:6 O 24 1993
A story of addiction and co-addiction. Kraft, William F. *RRel* 52:454-460 My-Je 1993

ALCOHOL AND ALCOHOLISM—TREATMENT
Addiction, recovery and God. Mace, Irving B. *Living Prayer* 26:25-26 Ja-F 1993
Alcoholism: a guide to diagnosis, intervention, and treatment. Gallant, Donald M, 1929-. New York: Norton, 1987. x, 256p ISBN 0-39370-043-7 LC 87-23966
The clergy's role in AA's fifth step. O'Neill, Jack. *Priest* 49:19-20 Mr 1993

ALCOHOLICS ANONYMOUS
The clergy's role in AA's fifth step. O'Neill, Jack. *Priest* 49:19-20 Mr 1993

ALEKSIJ II, (ALEKSIJ MIKHALOVICH RIDIGER), PATR OF MOSCOW, 1929-
Church intervenes at moment of crisis. Rich, Vera. *Tablet* 247:1307-1308 O 9 1993
Orthodox takes steps to influence Russia. Hebblethwaite, Peter, 1930-. *Nat Cath Rep* 29:14 O 15 1993
Patriarch Alexis criticises Rome. O'Connell, Gerard. *Tablet* 247:316 Mr 6 1993
Pray for it: religious freedom in Russia. Gaffney, Edward McGlynn, Jr, 1941-. *Comm* 120:5-7 My 7 1993

ALEXANDRIAN SCHOOL, CHRISTIAN
What is new and what is old: patristic exegesis. Barringer, Robert. *Can Cath Rev* 11:7-15 Je 1993

ALIEN LABOR- GERMANY
Fremdenfeindlichkeit. Keller, Albert. *Stimm Zeit* 210:793-794 D 1992
Living in the new Germany. Schonfelder, Kristin. *Cath Work* 60:7 Je-Jl 1993

ALIEN LABOR- UNITED STATES
The Zoe Baird backlash: "Everyone is scared". Acosta, Ana Margarita. *Nat Cath Rep* 29:3 Mr 5 1993

ALIENS
A plea for illegals. *Register* 69:3 O 17 1993

ALIENS- UNITED STATES
The injustice of anti-foreigner sentiment. *Origins* 23:422-423 N 25 1993

ALL AFRICA CONFERENCE OF CHURCHES
All Africa Conference of Churches. *Ecumen Trends* 21:16 D 1992

ALL SAINTS' DAY
Bringing the dead to life. Anderson, Paul. *New Cov* 23:16-17 N 1993
Remembering the dead. Piil, Mary Alice. *Mod Lit* 20:6-7 Ag 1993
Waiting. Ahern, Niall. *Furrow* 43:675-678 D 1992

ALL SOULS' DAY
The Day of the Dead. Schall, James Vincent, 1928-. *Crisis* 10:43-45 N 1992
Death's true meaning. Mangan, Charles M. *Register* 69:4 O 31 1993
Dia de los muertos. *Liturgy* 10:32-33 Wint 1992
Remembering the dead. Piil, Mary Alice. *Mod Lit* 20:6-7 Ag 1993

ALLAMANO, GIUSEPPE
John Paul II, Pope, (1993-06-19) Apostles [Orig in Italian]. John Paul II, Pope, 1920- (Karol Wojtyla) (elected 1978). *OR(Eng)* 1300:7 Jl 21 1993*

ALLAN, WOODY, 1935-
O sole mia the first Nixon prize. Carlin, David Robert, Jr, 1938-. *Comm* 120:9-10 Je 18 1993

ALLEGORY
J R R Tolkien and the art of the parable. Murray, Robert. *Month* 26:35-39 Ja 1993
What is new and what is old: patristic exegesis. Barringer, Robert. *Can Cath Rev* 11:7-15 Je 1993
The whatness of Loulou: allegories of Thomism in Flaubert. Wise, Christopher. *Relig Lit* 25:35-49 Spr 1993

ALOYSIUS GONZAGA, SAINT, 1568-1591
Aloysius. Stevens, Clifford, and McNichols, William Hart, eds. Huntington: Our Sunday Visitor, 1993. x, 160p ISBN 0-87973-528-7
Saint Aloysius Gonzaga: patron of youth. Stamwitz, Alicia von. *Liguorian* 81:26-32 Ag 1993

ALPHONSUS LIGUORI, SAINT, 1696-1787
Alphonsus de Liguori: the Saint of Bourbon Naples, 1696-1787. Jones, Frederick M. Westminster: Christian Classics, 1992. x, 532p ISBN 08-7061-195-x LC 92-73646

ALTARS
Keeping things in place. Santognossi, Ansgar. *Register* 69:5 F 28 1993
Making secular space sacred. Fater, Douglas. *Mod Lit* 20:14-17 My 1993
Ratzinger prefers altar turned around again. Moynihan, Robert. *Nat Cath Rep* 29:7 My 28 1993
"Turned-around" altars [editorial]. Schuler, Richard Joseph, 1920-. *SacM* 120:4-5 Sum 1993

ALTERNATIVE MEDICINE
Ethical issues of unconventional therapies. Callahan, Sidney. *Health Prog* 74:42-43 1993

ALVARADO CARDOZO, LAURA EVANGELISTA, 1875-1967
Congregation for the Causes of Saints (1992-03-07) Decree on the heroic virtues. Congregation for the Causes of Saints. *AAS* 84:1011-1014 O 3 1992*

ALZHEIMER'S DISEASE
In light and shadow. Hallett, Paul. *Register* 69:4 Je 11 1993
When a loved one has Alzheimer's [condensed fr *HomeLife* Ja 1992]. Hawke, Margaret. *CDgst* 58:46-49 N 1993

AMALADOSS, MICHAEL
Gathering together to pray: a special mode of public presence in interreligious dialogue. Kaserow, John. *New Theol Rev* 6:18-29 Ag 1993

AMALIO, BROTHER
John Paul II, Pope, (1993-10-10) Brother Amalio. John Paul II, Pope, 1920- (Karol Wojtyla) (elected 1978). *OR(Eng)* 1311:1 O 13 1993*
Two Spanish Bishops and seven Christian Brothers gave their lives for Catholic faith. *OR(Eng)* 1311:1 O 13 1993

AMBROSE, SAINT, BP OF MILAN
L'effusion de l'Esprit chez les Pères latins. Bentivegua, Giuseppe. *NRT* 115:19-39 Ja-F 1993
In the Catholic tradition. Lenox-Conyngham, Andrew. *Priests & People* 6:467-471 D 1992
The twin legacy of St. Ambrose. McSheffery, Daniel F. *CDgst* 57:120-123 Ag 1993

AMBULATORY MEDICAL CARE
Managing to shift to ambulatory care. Holm, Craig. *Health Prog* 74:62 Jl-Ag 1993
Portal to the community. Warren, Jeffrey A, and Walsh, Julia A. *Health Prog* 74:37-40 Jl-Ag 1993

AMERICA—DISCOVERY AND EXPLORATION
Ak'Kutan, Centro "Bartolomé de Las Casas". Diez, Carlos. *Cien Tom* 120:169-175 Ja-Ap 1993
Hacia el protagonismo de los pueblos indígenas de América. Tapuerca Ceballos, Jesús. *Cien Tom* 120:57-77 Ja-Ap 1993
John Paul II, Pope, (1993-06-14) New World [Orig in Spanish]. John Paul II, Pope, 1920- (Karol Wojtyla) (elected 1978). *OR(Eng)* 1296:8 Je 23 1993*
Os 500 anos e o Nordeste: Resgator as lutas indígenas. Silva, Edson. *REB* 53:174-183 Mr 1993
Report, 1991-92: Western region. Samaha, John M. *Marian Stds* 43:195 1992

AMERICAN LITERATURE
Bearing witness [interview by P Gilmour]. Thornton, Lawrence, 1937-. *Critic* 47:84-94 Wint 1992
From The sun also rises to High noon: the hypervisual great awakening in American literature and film. Meyer, William E H, Jr. *Cithara* 32:39-59 N 1992
Henry James's literary Catholicizing. Fussell, Edwin Sill, 1922-. *New Oxford Rev* 60:8-11 Ja-F 1993
The moral vision of Robert Stone. Finn, James. *Comm* 120:9-14 N 5 1993
Ramblin' Rose. Costello, Gerald M, 1931-. *USCath* 58:48-51 Ja 1993

AMERICAN POETRY
I'm kneeling—still—: A study of Emily Dickinson's siege on the sacred. Rieke, Susan. *ABenR* 44:258-279 S 1993

AMERICANISM (CATHOLIC CONTROVERSY)
Americanist beliefs and papal orthodoxy: 1884-1899. Wangler, Thomas E. *US Cath Hist* 11:37-52 Sum 1993
Bishop Bernard McQuaid: on "true" and "false" americanism. Janus, Glen. *US Cath Hist* 11:53-76 Sum 1993
Conspiracy to commit heresy: The Anti-Americanist Polemic of Canon Henri Delassus, C J T. *US Cath Hist* 11:77-92 Sum 1993
Inculturation as transformation: the case of Americanism revisited. Portier, William J. *US Cath Hist* 11:107-124 Sum 1993
The new Americanism in Catholic historiography. Gleason, Philip. *US Cath Hist* 11:1-18 Sum 1993

ANIMALS
Fido in heaven? Montgomery, John Warwick, 1931-. *New Oxford Rev* 60:20+ O 1993

Learning from animals. Rose, Mary Carman. *Month* 26:331-335 Ag 1993

ANIMALS—(IN RELIGION, FOLKLORE)
Good news for animals?: Christian approaches to animal well-being. Pinches, Charles, and McDaniel, Jay B, eds. Maryknoll, New York: Orbis Books, 1993. x, 258p ISBN 0-88344-866-1 LC 92-41682

ANIMALS IN THE BIBLE
Lilit in Edom (Jes 34, 5-15). Tanghe, Vincent. *Eph Theol Lovan* 69:125-133 Ap 1993

ANIMISM
The faith we have lost. Greeley, Andrew Moran, 1928-. *America* 169:14-16+ O 2 1993

ANNOINTING OF THE SICK
John Paul II, Pope, (1992-04-29) Annointing of the Sick. John Paul II, Pope, 1920- (Karol Wojtyla) (elected 1978). *TPS* 37:364-367 N-D 1992*

Why do we anoint the sick? Boylan, Anthony. *Priests & People* 6:405-408 N 1992

ANNULMENT OF MARRIAGE see Marriage—Annulment

ANOINTING OF THE SICK
Anointing is a sacrament of the living [condensed fr *Catholic Twin Circle* My 16 1993]. Devine, George. *CDgst* 57:106-107 S 1993

ANOINTINGS
The oil of gladness: annointing in the Christian tradition. Dudley, Martin, and Rowell, Geoffrey, eds. Collegeville: Liturgical, 1993. x, 221p ISBN 0-8146-2245-3

ANSELM, SAINT, ABP OF CANTERBURY
Introduction to re-thinking representation: Anselm and visual thinking. Kromm, Jane. *Listening* 28:95-104 Spr 1993

Two medieval soteriologies: Anselm of Canterbury and Julian of Norwich. Nuth, Joan M. *TheolStds* 53:611-645 D 1992

ANTHONY MARY CLARET, SAINT, 1807-1870
A model missionary: episodes in the life of St Anthony Mary Claret. Ramos, Alexis Mary. *ChrWorld* 38:124-134 Mr-Ap 1993

ANTHONY OF PADUA, SAINT, 1195-1231
Charting our second 100 years. Perry, Norman. *St Anth* 101:23 Je 1993

ANTHROPOLOGICAL RESEARCH
Anthropologie et philosophie: un double retour au fondement. Watté, Pierre. *RPhil Louvain* 91:207-227 My 1993

ANTHROPOLOGY
Anthropologie et philosophie: un double retour au fondement. Watté, Pierre. *RPhil Louvain* 91:207-227 My 1993

ANTHROPOLOGY—LAW
Legal anthropology, Australian, Aborigines and natural law. O'Connell, Irene. *Amer J Juris* 37:243-258 1992

ANTHROPOLOGY—METHODOLOGY
Las ensenanzas de Don Carlos: aplicaciones practicas de la obra de Carlos Castaneda. Sanchez, Victor. Madrid: Havilah, 1993. x, 282p ISBN 84-87745-04-0

ANTHROPOLOGY—STUDY
Las ensenanzas de Don Carlos: aplicaciones practicas de la obra de Carlos Castaneda. Sanchez, Victor. Madrid: Havilah, 1993. x, 282p ISBN 84-87745-04-0

Presente y futuro del hombre. Polo, Leonardo. Madrid: Rialp, 1993. x, 208p ISBN 84-321-2977-1

ANTHROPOLOGY AND RELIGION
El hombre es imagen de Dios. Dolby Mugica, Maria del Carmen. Pamplona: Eunsa, 1993. x, 274p ISBN 84-313-1223-8

De Jesús a las antropologías. Meis, Anneliese W. *Teol Vida* 34 no 1-2:39-59 1993

ANTHROPOLOGY AND RELIGION- CHILE
La antropología en las ciencias naturales. Flores, Luis H. *Teol Vida* 34 no 1-2:61-67 1993

Psicoanálisis y reflexión antropológica. Bravo Valdivieso, Luis. *Teol Vida* 34 no 1-2:69-78 1993

ANTICATHOLICISM- IRELAND
Public life in Northern Ireland—another view. Wilson, Desmond. *Furrow* 44:140-147 Mr 1993

ANTICATHOLICISM- UNITED STATES
Anti-Catholicism in the media. Riley, Patrick J, and Shaw, Russell, eds. Huntington: Our Sunday Visitor, 1993. x, 256p ISBN 0-87973-551-1

Church is still fair game. Shaw, Russell. *Register* 69:1+ S 26 1993

Popish plots: Protestant fears in early colonial Maryland, 1676-1689. Graham, Michael. *CHist* 79:197-216 Ap 1993

A prejudice rooted in ignorance. Lockwood, Robert P. *OSV* 82:19 Ag 15 1993

That old-time religion. Johnson, Bud. *Comm* 120:9+ S 10 1993

To the pope-bashers in Denver. Griffin, Robert F. *OSV* 82:14 Ag 8 1993

Tolerating Sinéad. Carigman, Dean M. *Crisis* 10:5-6 N 1992

The unholy ghost: anti-Catholicism in the American experience. Hurley, Mark Joseph, Bp, 1919-. Huntington: Our Sunday Visitor, 1992. 818p ISBN 0-87973-529-5 LC 92-60315

Wolves in sheep's clothing ensnare the faithful. Keating, Karl. *OSV* 82:6-7 Ag 1 1993

ANTINOMY
Tensions in social theory: groundwork for a future moral sociology. Muñoz, Braulio. Chicago: Loyola University Press, 1993. x, 367p ISBN 0-8294-0739-1 LC 92-26436

ANTIOCH (PATRIARCHATE)
The catholicity of the local church in the patriarchate of Antioch after Chalcedon. Halleux, André de. *Jurist* 52 no 1:109-129 1992

ANTIOCHIAN SCHOOL
What is new and what is old: patristic exegesis. Barringer, Robert. *Can Cath Rev* 11:7-15 Je 1993

ANTIQUITIES
'Holy war' and the 'ban' in the Bible [condensed fr *Internationale katholische Zeitschrift: Communio* Mr 1989]. Lohfink, Norbert. *TheolDgst* 38:109-114 Sum 1991

ANTISEMITISM
Christian-Jewish relations in a new Europe. Solomon, Norman. *Month* 26:9-16 Ja 1993

Jacques Maritain and the Jews. Castori, Michael T. *America* 168:18-21 My 29 1993

Looking at the dark side. Miesel, Sandra. *Register* 69:5 O 17 1993

Overcoming fear between Jews and Christians. Charlesworth, James H. New York: Crossroad, 1993. x, 198p ISBN 0-8245-1265-0 LC 92-31262

Pain and polemic: anti-Judaism in the gospels. Smiga, George M. New Jersey: Paulist Press, 1992. x, 210p ISBN 0-8091-3355-5 LC 92-20044

The people to whom Jesus belonged [exc fr *Liturgy: the Christmas cycle*]. *Liturgy* 10:32-33 Spr 1993

Post-holocaust church theology. Williamson, Clark M. Louisville: John Knox, 1993. x, 352p ISBN 0-664-254-54-3

ANTISEMITISM—CONGRESSES
Interwoven destinies: Jews and Christians through the ages. Fisher, Eugene J. New Jersey: Paulist Press, 1993. x, 154p ISBN 0-8091-8363-6 LC 92-37707

ANTISEMITISM- HUNGARY
Statement of the Hungarian Council of Christians and Jews on anti-semitism and nationalism. *SIDIC* 26 no 1:27 1993

ANTITRUST LAW
Antitrust and IDNs: how far can we go? Campbell, Peter. *Health Prog* 74:54-55+ 1993

Antitrust law may be a barrier to collaboration. White, Jane H. *Health Prog* 74:22-24+ Jl-Ag 1993

ANTON, ANGEL
Response to Angel Antón. Pottmeyer, Hermann Joseph. *Jurist* 52 no 1:579-582 1992

ANTONELLI, GIUSEPPE, CARDINAL, 1896-1993
Antonelli, Giuseppe, Cardinal, 1896-1993 [obit]. *OR(Eng)* 1300:2 Jl 21 1993

ANXIETY
Ce qu'être malade veut dire. Jannesse, Alfred. *Supplement* 184:21-32 Mr-Ap 1993

Return to Chile. Cassidy, Sheila. *Tablet* 247:6+ Ja 2 1993

APACHE INDIANS
No easy rewards [photos]. Bartholomew, Marianna. *Extensn* 88:22-27 S-O 1993

APARTHEID see South Africa—Race Relations

APATHY
Indifference turns the modern heart away from heaven. Kreeft, Peter John, 1937-. *Register* 69:1+ My 23 1993

APHORISMS AND APOTHEGMS
Manies i afrodismes. Rubert de Ventos, Xavier. Barcelona: Edicions 62, 1993. x, 107p ISBN 84-297-3651-4

Notebook and candles. Carter, Sydney. *Tablet* 247:465-466 Ap 10-17 1993

APOCALYPSE OF ST JOHN see Bible (NT)- Revelation

APOCALYPTICISM
Apocalypse now in Waco [editorial]. *America* 168:3-4 My 22, 1993

APOCRYPHAL BOOKS (NT)
El desierto delos dioses: teologia e historia en el libro de Oseas. Simian-Yofre, Horacio. Cordoba: Ediciones El Alme, 1993. x, 283p ISBN 84-8005-007-1

Il regno millenario di Cristo e dei suoi (Apos 20, 1-10). Vanni, Ugo. *StudiaM* 42:67-95 1993

APOLOGETICS
Can a scientist pray. Montgomery, John Warwick, 1931-. *New Oxford Rev* 60:22-23 Ap 1993

Christianity for modern pagans. Kreeft, Peter John, 1937-. *Register* 69:5 Ap 11 1993

Death, the unsentimental fact, is our anchor to God's deeper realities. Kreeft, Peter John, 1937-. *Register* 69:1+ My 2 1993

Hey, Catholics, stand up for something!. Marty, Martin E, 1928-. *USCath* 58:36-37 S 1993

Human vanity: it's the wrong path. Kreeft, Peter John, 1937-. *Register* 69:1+ Ap 25 1993

Indirect methods in theology: Karl Rahner as an ad hoc apologist. Healy, Nicholas M. *Thomist* 56:613-633 O 1992

Intellectuals don't need God and other modern myths. McGrath, Alister E. Grand Rapids: Zondervan Publishing House, 1993. x, 256p ISBN 0-310-59091-4

APOLOGETICS—0030-600
Epistle to Diognetus. Firth, Francis. *Can Cath Rev* 11:35-36 Ap 1993

Justin Martyr and the Logos Spermatikos. Osborn, Eric. *StudiaM* 42:143-159 1993

The works of Clement of Alexandria. Firth, Francis. *Can Cath Rev* 11:35 Je 1993

APOPHATIC THEOLOGY
Attributing things to God. Moonan, Lawrence. *Eph Theol Lovan* 78:86-117 Ap 1992

Sinai and Tabor: apophatic and kataphatic symbols in tension. Lane, Belden C. *Stud Form Spir* 14:189-205 My 1993

APOSTLES
An offer they couldn't refuse: the Apostles become fishers of men. Goodman, Richard. *Comm* 120:19-21 O 22 1993

'The twelve apostles were men.'. Raming, Ida. *TheolDgst* 40:21-25 Spr 1993

Who's who in The Last Supper? [condensed fr *Western New York Catholic* Mr 1993]. Kidder, Keith. *CDgst* 57:1-3 Jl 1993

APOSTLES' CREED
The apostles' creed: a faith to live by. Cranfield, C E B. Grand Rapids: Eerdmans, 1993. 72p ISBN 0-8028-0709-7

The Catechism of the Catholic Church in context. Ratzinger, Joseph, Cardinal, 1927-. *Origins* 22:529-532 Ja 14 1993

Credo: the Apostles' Creed explained for today. Kung, Hans, 1928-. New York: Doubleday, 1993. x, 194p ISBN 0-385-47181-5 LC 93-915

APOSTOLATE (THEOLOGY)
The Catechism of the Catholic Church in context. Ratzinger, Joseph, Cardinal, 1927-. *Origins* 22:529-532 Ja 14 1993

A sacred landscape. Wroe, Ann. *Tablet* 247:192-193 F 13 1993

Standing in the light: meditation and the icon. Fohlin, Paul. *Spir Life* 32:73-78 Sum 1993

Visual arts awards. *Mod Lit* 20:5-8 S 1993

What did Jesus really look like? Ramsey, Boniface. *America* 168:16-17 Je 19-26 1993

Women artisans in the service of the church. Abrahamsen, Valerie. *Sisters* 65:96-103 Mr 1993

Worth pondering. O'Connell, Patrick. *Living Prayer* 26:14-15 Jl-Ag 1993

ART, FRENCH

The artist who painted a prayer. Cuevas, Zillah. *CDgst* 57:6-9 Mr 1993

ART, GREEK

'The Greek miracle'. Torrens, James S. *America* 168:18 Ap 3 1993

ART, MODERN

Degenerate moderns. Jones, Michael E. San Francisco: Ignatius Press, 1993. ISBN 0-89810-447-2

Finding a world in a grain of sand: but is it art? Pickstone, Charles. *Month* 26:152-154 Ap 1993

The Oxford guide to classical mythology in the arts, 1300-1990s. Reid, Jane Davidson. New York: Oxford University Press, 1993. ISBN 0-19504-998-5 LC 92-35374

Sacred and profane sex: Edvard Munch at the National Gallery, Eric Gill at the Barbican. Pickstone, Charles. *Month* 26:22-25 Ja 1993

Too high the cornices: the Met's new galleries. Siegel, Lee. *Comm* 120:21-22 O 22 1993

ART, MODERN—19TH CENTURY

The sins of the fathers: decadence and despair in fin-de-siècle France. Pickstone, Charles. *Month* 26:391-395 S-O 1993

ART, RUSSIAN

Russia and the arts of Utopia. Leder, Dennis. *America* 168:16 Ja 2-9 1993

ART AND RELIGION

Art and liturgical environment: an artist's perspective. Malarcher, Patricia. *New Theol Rev* 6:18-26 F 1993

The art of exhibiting the sacred. Arthur, Chris. *Month* 26:281-289 Jl 1993

Art, faith, and wholeness. Adams, Doug. *New Theol Rev* 6:6-17 F 1993

L'arte per la liturgia. *Notitiae* 28:689-692 N-D 1992

Il biennio di formazione all'istituto superiore d'arte sacre beato angelico alla minerva di Roma. Triacca, Achille M. *Notitiae* 28:227-228 Mr 1992

The catechism of the Catholic Church [excerpt and tr by J T Zuhlsdorf]. *SacM* 120:15-16 Spr 1993

Chartres and Ryoan-ji: aesthetic connections and affecting presence. Eusden, John D. *CrossCurr* 43:38-46 Spr 1993

Contemporary art and the expanded death of the human Jesus. Seubert, Xavier John. *New Theol Rev* 6:27-39 F 1993

Faith into art: religion and Vincent van Gogh. Thiessen, Gesa. *Doctr Life* 43:267-274 My-Je 1993

Hidden treasure. Ramsey, David. *Mod Lit* 19:30 D 1992-Ja 1993

Imagination, the poets' God. Madsen, Catherine. *CrossCurr* 43:47-59 Spr 1993

Indian art and Christian faith. *Tablet* 247:615 My 15 1993

John Paul II, Pope, (1993-08-01) Music. John Paul II, Pope, 1920- (Karol Wojtyla) (elected 1978). *OR(Eng)* 1303:12 Ag 18 1993*

Movies: the struggle between art and entertainment. May, John R. *ChrWorld* 236:252-257 N-D 1993

The mutual questioning of ethics and aesthetics. Fuchs, Eric. *CrossCurr* 43:26-37 Spr 1993

On baptizing the visual arts: a friar's meditation on art. Nichols, Aidan. *New Blckfrs* 74:74-84 F 1993

Relazione sulle risposte delle conferenze episcopali circa I patrimoni Artistici e storici della chiesa. *Notitiae* 28:507-527 Ag 1992*

Rethinking religious art. Maksymowicz, Virginia, and Tobia, Blaise. *ChrWorld* 236:244-251 N-D 1993

Some reflections at an art museum. Zimmerman, Paulette. *Sisters* 65:49-52 Ja 1993

Towards a manifesto for art and the sacred. Kennedy, Brian P. *Studies* 82:311-322 Aut 1993

What makes religious art religious? Dixon, John W, Jr. *CrossCurr* 43:5-25 Spr 1993

Willa Cather and the literature of Christian mystery. Murphy, John J. *Relig Lit* 24:39-56 Aut 1992

ART AND RELIGION- CHILE

La necesidad humana del arte. Hernán Errzuriz, Luis. *Teol Vida* 34 no 1-2:79-89 1993

ART AND RELIGION- RUSSIA

Icons, iconoclasm, and the power of images: reflections on art and society in post-Soviet Russia. McPherson, Heather. *Listening* 28:159-171 Spr 1993

ART THERAPISTS

'A window to Annie's world'. Conway, Rose Marie. *New Theol Rev* 6:75-79 F 1993

ART THERAPY

How art heals. Bailey, Judi. *St Anth* 100:36-41 F 1993

'A window to Annie's world'. Conway, Rose Marie. *New Theol Rev* 6:75-79 F 1993

ARTECHE, MIGUEL

La inquietud religiosa en cuatro poetas chilenos contemporáneos (Miguel Arteche, Carlos Bolton, Fidel Sepúlveda y Raúl Zurita). Livacić Gazzano, Ernesto. *Teol Vida* 33 no 3-4:299-314 1992

ARTIFICIAL INSEMINATION

Are contraception and artificial procreation sometimes permissible. Doran, Joseph J. *HPR* 93:48-57 Mr 1993

The disembodiment of parenthood. Grondelski, John M. *HPR* 93:30-31+ F 1993

ARTISTS—INTELLECTUAL LIFE

Degenerate moderns. Jones, Michael E. San Francisco: Ignatius Press, 1993. ISBN 0-89810-447-2

ARTISTS—PSYCHOLOGY ASPECTS

Degenerate moderns. Jones, Michael E. San Francisco: Ignatius Press, 1993. ISBN 0-89810-447-2

ARTS

Arts war likely to continue. Mullen, Peter. *Register* 69:1+ Ja 10 1993

Battle at the BBC. Morris, Colin. *Tablet* 247:942-943 Jl 24 1993

Waldorf education: an innovative tradition. Harrington, Sheila. *Momentum* 24:17-21 F-Mr 1993

ARTS—EDUCATION

Calling a halt to the marginalization of the arts. Mahlmann, John J. *Momentum* 24:25-28 S-O 1993

Let the arts come alive!. Wilgenbusch, Sandra. *Tod Cath Teach* 27:30-33 Ag 1993

ASANTE, MOLEFI KETE

As black Catholics speak, who will listen? Curry, Adrienne. *USCath* 58:30-31 Ja 1993

ASBESTOS—LAW AND LEGISLATION

Funding the asbestos cleanup. Davis, William. *Origins* 23:45-46 Je 3 1993

ASCENSION OF ISAIAH

Isaiah and urban possibility. Brueggemann, Walter. Louisville: Westminster, 1993. x, 96p ISBN 0-664-25460-8

The unity of the Book of Isaiah and its cosmogonic language. Clifford, Richard J. *CBQ* 55:1-17 Ja 1993

ASCETICISM

Christian asceticism and modern culture. Batule, Robert J. *HPR* 93:17-23 F 1993

Mysticism in Islamism and Christianity. McKnight, Peg. *Living Prayer* 26:29-31 Ja-F 1993

Shifting sands: Foucault, Brown and the framework of christian asceticism. Behr, John. *Heythrop* 34:1-21 Ja 1993

ASHE, ARTHUR

The legacy of a life well served. Costello, Gerald M, 1931-. *USCath* 58:48-51 N 1993

ASIA—CHURCH HISTORY

For all the peoples of Asia: documents from 1970-1991. Rosales, Gaudencio B, and Arevalo, Catalino G, eds. Maryknoll, New York: Orbis Books, 1992. x, 356p ISBN 0-88344-837-8 LC 92-5033

ASIA—RELIGION

An Asian paradigm: inter-religious dialogue and theology of religions [repr fr *Qoholet*]. Pieris, Aloysius, 1934-. *Month* 26:129-134 Ap 1993

ASIA—RELIGIOUS LIFE

Asian faces of Jesus. Sugirtharajah, R S, ed. Maryknoll: Orbis Books, 1993. x, 267p ISBN 0-88344-833-5 LC 93-536

ASIAN BISHOPS' CONFERENCES

Root causes of the environmental crisis. *Origins* 22:692-694 Mr 18 1993

ASPIN, LES, 1938-

The 'state' of 'defense'. Hehir, J Bryan, 1940-. *Comm* 120:9-10 Mr 26 1993

ASSASSINATION- CENTRAL AMERICA

The Jesuit assassinations. Kansas City: Sheed and Ward, 1990. x, 158p ISBN 1-55612-409-0

ASSIMILATION (SOCIOLOGY)

The challenge of xenophobia: reflections on the heart of the stranger. Bayfield, Tony. *Month* 26:298-303 Ag 1993

ASSURANCE (THEOLOGY)

Living free in Christ. Anderson, Neil T. Ventura: Gospel Light, 1993. 310p ISBN 0-8307-1604-1 LC 93-7358

ASTRONOMY—HISTORY

Through a daughter's eyes. O'Grady, Desmond. *OSV* 81:16-17 F 14 1993

ASYLUM, RIGHT OF

The church and asylum seekers. Grazer, Walt. *Register* 69:5 Ag 8 1993

John Paul II, Pope, (1992-12-19) Ad limina Apostolorum. John Paul II, Pope, 1920- (Karol Wojtyla) (elected 1978). *TPS* 38:193-200 Jl-Ag 1993*

Refugees: a challenge for solidarity. *TPS* 38:65-77 Mr-Ap 1993

ATHANASIUS, SAINT, PATR OF ALEXANDRIA

Finding God in all things. Garrett, Graeme. *Way* 33:3-11 Ja 1993

ATHEISM- FRANCE

La nouvelle distinction stéréotypes et perceptions respectives des chrétiens et des athées. Traube, Patrick. *Lumen* 47:377-390 D 1992

Sartre's adolescent rejection of God. Santoni, Ronald E. *PhilosTod* 37:62-69 Spr 1993

ATLASES—HISTORY

Historical atlas of the Middle East. Freeman-Grenville, G S P. New York: Simon & Schuster, 1993. x, 144p ISBN 0-13-3-390915-8

ATONEMENT

Adrienne von Speyr and the mystery of the atonement. Nichols, Aidan. *New Blckfrs* 73:542-553 N 1992

Atonement in Judaism and Christianity: toward a rapprochement. Lyden, John C. *JEcumen Stds* 29:47-54 Wint 1992

ATTENTION-DEFICIT HYPERACTIVITY DISORDERS

Every child can learn. Rodriguez, Hector R. *Momentum* 24:51-52 Ap-My 1993

AUDEN, W H, 1907-1973

Who was Didymus? The face behind the pseudonym. *Comm* 120:20-21 Ag 13 1993

AUGUSTINE, SAINT, BP OF HIPPO

Addendum to Boniface Ramsey, 'John Cassian: student of Augustine,' CSQ 28 (1993): 5-15. Ramsey, Boniface. *Cist Stud* 28 no 2:199-200 1993

Augustine on sin. Meredith, Anthony. *Month* 26:367-371 S-O 1993

Augustine today. Neuhaus, Richard John, 1936-, ed. Grand Rapids: Eerdmans, 1993. 168p ISBN 0-8028-0216-8

The 'Confessions:' a sinner's diary. Cameron, Peter John. *Register* 69:1+ O 31 1993

A conversation with Rocco Buttiglione [interview by D Cross]. Buttiglione, Rocco. *Crisis* 10:26-32 D 1992

Culture païenne et foi chrétienne aux racines de l'Europe: La Cité de Dieu d'Augustin. Canévet, Mariette. *Gregorianum* 74 No 1:5-16 1993

El hombre es imagen de Dios. Dolby Mugica, Maria del Carmen. Pamplona: Eunsa, 1993. x, 274p ISBN 84-313-1223-8

John Cassian: student of Augustine. Ramsey, Boniface. *Cist Stud* 28:5-15 1993

Late have I loved you: an interpretation of Saint Augustine on human and divine relationships. Mohler, James Aylward. New Rochelle, New York: New City Press, 1991. 159p ISBN 0-911782-86-9 LC 90-28643

MacIntyre's postmodern Thomism: reflections on Three rival versions of moral enquiry. Hibbs, Thomas S. *Thomist* 57:277-297 Ap 1993

Mixed-up in Milan. Cavnar, Cindy. *New Cov* 23:31 Ag 1993

The religious life according to Saint Augustine. Sage, Athanase. New Rochelle, New York: New City Press, 1990. 240p ISBN 0-911782-81-8 LC 90-47785

"Sacramentum Connubii" et institution nuptiale. Scalco, Eugenio. *Eph Theol Lovan* 69:27-47 Ap 1993

Saint Augustine and Martin Buber as perspectives on John Noonan's persons and masks of the law. Combs, Christopher. *Amer J Juris* 37:145-169 1992

St. Augustine and marriage. Rist, John, and Rist, Anna. *Priests & People* 7:327-334 Ag-S 1993

The sweetness of God. Posset, Franz. *ABenR* 44:143-178 Je 1993

What's so amazing about grace? [interview by editors of US Catholic (Periodical)]. Dreyer, Elizabeth. *USCath* 58:6-13 My 1993

Who are their models? Cunningham, Beatrice. *ReligTJ* 27:38-39 O 1993

AUGUSTINE, SAINT, BP OF HIPPO—ETHICS

"Sacramentum Connubii" et institution nuptiale. Scalco, Eugenio. *Eph Theol Lovan* 69:27-47 Ap 1993

AUGUSTINIAN CANONS

"Sacramentum Connubii" et institution nuptiale. Scalco, Eugenio. *Eph Theol Lovan* 69:27-47 Ap 1993

AUGUSTINIS, EMILIO DE

Ordinazioni Anglicane e Ecclesiologia. I. Rambaldi, Giuseppe. *Gregorianum* 74 no 2:277-307 1993

AUNG, SAN SUU KYI

A light for Asia. *Tablet* 247:686 My 29 1993

Support for Suu Kyi. *Tablet* 247:816 Je 26 1993

AUSCHWITZ (CONCENTRATION CAMP)

John Paul II, Pope, (1993-04-07) Gypsies at Auschwitz. John Paul II, Pope, 1920- (Karol Wojtyla) (elected 1978). *TPS* 38:266-267 S-O 1993*

John Paul II, Pope, (1993-04-09) Letter to Auschwitz nuns. John Paul II, Pope, 1920- (Karol Wojtyla) (elected 1978). *TPS* 38:268-269 S-O 1993*

John Paul II, Pope, (1993-04-09) Letter to the nuns. John Paul II, Pope, 1920- (Karol Wojtyla) (elected 1978). *Origins* 22:795 Ap 29 1993*

Of lingering eyes and talking things: Adorno and Deleuze on philosophy since Auschwitz. Toolan, David S. *PhilosTod* 37:227-246 Aut 1993

Reflections on after virtue after Auschwitz. Chansky, James D. *PhilosTod* 37:247-256 Aut 1993

AUSTIN, JOHN

Why positivism is authoritarian. Dyzenhaus, David. *Amer J Juris* 37:83-112 1992

AUSTRALIA—NATIVE PEOPLE

The hungry heart. Griffiths, Max. Kenthorts, Australia: Kangaroo Press, 1992. 176p ISBN 0-86417-486-1

AUSTRALIA—POLITICS AND GOVERNMENT

A lucky country's last gasp. McGillion, Chris. *Tablet* 247:361 Mr 20 1993

AUSTRALIA—RELIGION

John Paul II, Pope, (1991-12-02) Allocutiones (Reception of ambassadorial credentials from Australia) [English]. John Paul II, Pope, 1920- (Karol Wojtyla) (elected 1978). *AAS* 84:1151-1154 D 5 1992*

AUSTRALIA—SOCIO-ECONOMIC CONDITIONS

A lucky country's last gasp. McGillion, Chris. *Tablet* 247:361 Mr 20 1993

AUSTRALIAN ABORIGINES

The hungry heart. Griffiths, Max. Kenthorts, Australia: Kangaroo Press, 1992. 176p ISBN 0-86417-486-1

AUTHORITY

A neo-Thomist's defense of democracy. Schram, Glenn N. *New Oxford Rev* 60:13-17 Ja-F 1993

AUTHORITY (RELIGION)

Authority in the church: who makes the final call? McClory, Richard J. *USCath* 58:6-13 Mr 1993

Converting the assembly. Pace, Charlotte. *Mod Lit* 20:10-13 F 1993

AUTHORS

E J Oliver. Wall, Barbara. *Tablet* 246:1586 D 12 1992

Friend and teacher: Allan Bloom, 1930-1992. Fortin, Ernest L, 1923-. *Crisis* 11:38-40 Ja 1993

Let us stand together. Vanauken, Sheldon. *Crisis* 11:47-48 Ja 1993

Mary Higgins Clark: queen of suspense. Finley, Mitchel B. *St Anth* 100:28-33 S 1993

AUTHORS, AMERICAN

Haunted by faith. Coulombe, Charles. *Register* 69:3 Je 20 1993

AUTHORS, CATHOLIC see Catholic, Authors

Bernanos: a man of spirit. Celeste, Marie. *Priest* 49:44-46 Je 1993

The Catholic religious poets from Southwell to Crashaw. Cousins, Anthony D. Westminster: Christian Classics, 1993. x, 224p ISBN 0-7220-1570-4

The Christian novelist in an age of transition-a case study. Maher, Eamon. *Studies* 82:140-147 Sum 1993

François Mauriac's "Le cahier noir". O'Connell, David, 1940-. *Comm* 120:22-23 Ap 23 1993

The mixed life of Elizabeth Leseur [condensed fr *Mystic Quarterly* Mr 1993]. Ruffing, Janet K. *CDgst* 57:111-116 Ag 1993

Novel Catholicism: Waugh and Greene [condensed fr *Catholic Twin Circle* D 27 1992-Ja 31 1993]. Vatavuk, William M. *CDgst* 57:42-47 O 1993

Portrait of the artist as a Christian wayfarer. Donohue, John W, 1917-. *America* 168:7-10 Ap 10 1993

Spark of divinity. McInerny, Ralph M. *Crisis* 11:50-51 Jl-Ag 1993

The third career of Sister Mary Pelagia, OP, author. O'Hara, Fred. *CLW* 64:40-42 Jl-S 1993

Thomas Merton still surprises [condensed fr *The Progress* Ap 1 1993]. Dooley, Jerry. *CDgst* 57:57-59 Jl 1993

Walker Percy: pilgrim in our ruins. Finley, Mitchel B. *OSV* 82:16 My 30 1993

AUTHORS, CATHOLIC—BIBLIOGRAPHY

Bibliography of the works of Fr Juniper B Carol, OFM. Fehlner, Peter D. *Marian Stds* 43:48-59 1992

AUTHORS, ENGLISH

Taking a joyride to eternity. Goeglein, Tim. *OSV* 82:10-11 N 7 1993

Top 10 reasons why the devil hates C.S. Lewis. Pieper, Lori. *OSV* 82:10-11 N 7 1993

A voice of his own. *Tablet* 247:884-885 Jl 10 1993

William Golding's vision. Bergonzi, Bernard, 1929-. *Tablet* 247:815 Je 26 1993

AUTHORS, IRISH

Aubrey Gwynn: the person. Hand, Geoffrey, 1931-. *Studies* 81:375-384 Wint 1992

AUTHORS, TURKISH

Death of private soldier. Barchard, David. *Tablet* 247:131-132 Ja 30 1993

AUTHORSHIP

Finding a new way to get a glimpse of God. Nouwen, Henri Josef Machiel, 1932-. *New Oxford Rev* 60:6-8+ Jl-Ag 1993

Larry Woiwode. Block, Ed. *Critic* 47:57-65 Sum 1993

AUTOBIOGRAPHY

Being interested in time: autobiography and repetition. Dupuy, Edward. *Listening* 28:141-157 Spr 1993

I'm Ok, I'm Ok, aren't I. Doyle, Brian. *Comm* 120:9+ S 10 1993

In the heart of the city. Dunne, Sean. *Tablet* 247:944-945 Jl 24 1993

The search for self: a study of the poetic mind. Woolf, James Dudley. New York: Vantage Press, 1993. 320p ISBN 0-533-10364-9 LC 92-90889

The use of memory [excerpt fr the book; 2 parts]. Burns, Tom G. *Tablet* 247:330+ Mr 6; 336-337 Mr 13 1993

AUTOBIOGRAPHY—RELIGIOUS LIFE

A quest for vision [interview by E Wymard]. Hampl, Patricia, 1946-. *Critic* 47:58-64 Spr 1993

The representationj of religious experience in nineteenth-century American women's autobiography. Norman, Rose. *Listening* 28:128-140 Spr 1993

AUTOMOBILES

American addictions [excerpt fr *Around the cragged hill: a personal and political philosophy*]. Kennan, George F, 1904-. *New Oxford Rev* 60:14-25 Je 1993

AUTONOMY

Going, going, gone: the diminution of the self. Carlin, David Robert, Jr, 1938-. *Comm* 120:6-7 S 10 1993

AVARICE

Avarice, a.k.a. greed. Keefe, Jeffrey. *Catechist* 27:4 O 1993

AVERROES, 1126-1198

Averroes, Aristotle, and the Qur'an immortality. Mohammed, Ovey N. *IPQ* 33:37-55 Mr 1993

AVIAT, FRANCOISE DE SALES, 1844-1914

Congregation for the Causes of Saints (1991-12-21) Decree on a miracle . Congregation for the Causes of Saints. *AAS* 84:807-809 Ag 3 1992*

AVICENNA, 980-1037

Instance ontology and Avicenna's arguments. Mertz, Donald W. *Mod Schlmn* 70:189-199 Mr 1993

AVVENIRE (PERIODICAL)

John Paul II, Pope, (1993-05-01) Catholic Journalists [Orig in Italian]. John Paul II, Pope, 1920- (Karol Wojtyla) (elected 1978). *OR(Eng)* 1296:13 Je 23 1993*

AWARDS

Edward Sövik. *Mod Lit* 20:46 N 1993

New Emmys and new season. Stahel, Thomas H, 1938-. *America* 169:24-25 O 16 1993

1993 visual art awards—stained glass. *Mod Lit* 20:4-7 N 1993

AWE

Stewardship and the disposition of reverence. Vandergrift, Nicki Verploegen. *Stud Form Spir* 14:219-231 My 1993

AZERBAIJAN—RELATIONS

Another place, another war. Lieven, Anatol. *Tablet* 247:639-641 My 22 1993

B

BABIUCH, JOLANTA

European Catholics still divided [editorial]. *Tablet* 247:1183 S 18 1993

BABY BOOM GENERATION

The Baby-Boom Catholic [editorial]. *America* 168:3 My 1 1993

A generation of seekers; the spiritual journeys of the baby boom generation. Roof, Wade Clark, 1939-. New York: HarperCollins Publishers, 1993. x, 294p ISBN 0-06-066963-2 LC 92-53920

BAGGIO, SEBASTIANO, CARDINAL, 1913-1993

Bishop-maker Baggio is dead [obit]. Hebblethwaite, Peter, 1930-. *Nat Cath Rep* 29:13 Ap 2 1993

BAHA'I FAITH

The gardeners of God: an encounter with five million Bahá'ís. Gouvion, Colette, and Jouvion, Philippe. Oxford: Oneworld, 1993. x, 223p ISBN 1-85168-052-7

BAKER, JOHN AUSTIN, BP, 1928-

Anglican bishops refine compromise on women priest. *Tablet* 247:867-868 Jl 3 1993

Squaring the Anglican circle [editorial]. *Tablet* 247:839-840 Jl 3 1993

BAKHITA, JOSEPHINE, 1869-1947

Blessed Josephine Bakhita: woman of faith and forgiveness. Stamwitz, Alicia von. *Liguorian* 81:46-53 F 1993

John Paul II, Pope, (1992-05-18) Beatification of Sister Josephine Bakhita. John Paul II, Pope, 1920- (Karol Wojtyla) (elected 1978). *TPS* 37:371-373 N-D 1992*

John Paul II, Pope, (1993-02-10) Innocent victims. John Paul II, Pope, 1920- (Karol Wojtyla) (elected 1978). *TPS* 38:221-225 Jl-Ag 1993*

John Paul II, Pope, (1993-02-17) Vitality of African Christianity. John Paul II, Pope, 1920- (Karol Wojtyla) (elected 1978). *TPS* 38:226-229 Jl-Ag 1993*

John Paul II, Pope, (1993-03-10) Innocent victims [Orig English]. John Paul II, Pope, 1920- (Karol Wojtyla) (elected 1978). *Origins* 22:618-620 F 18 1993*

BALDUCCI, ERNESTO, 1922-
Ernesto Balducci. Del Zanna, Lorenzo. *Civilta* 144:445-458 Mr 6 1993

BALIMA, SERGE THEOPHILE
John Paul II, Pope, (1991-12-20) Allocutiones (Reception of ambassadorial credentials) [French]. John Paul II, Pope, 1920- (Karol Wojtyla) (elected 1978). *AAS* 85:33-35 Ja 7 1993*

BALKAN PENINSULA—HISTORY
Between Dracula and Bovary: Yugoslavia's romantic nationalism. Garvey, John, 1944-. *Comm* 120:7-8 My 21 1993
War at the crossroads: background on the Balkans. Weinberg, Bill, and Wilsnack, Dorie. *Cath Work* 60:1+ Ag 1993

BALKAN PENINSULA—POLITICS AND GOVERNMENT
"On the ground" in Sarajevo [interview by T H Stahel, 1938-]. McCarrick, Theodore Edgar, Abp, 1930-. *America* 168:3-5 F 27 1993
War at the crossroads: background on the Balkans. Weinberg, Bill, and Wilsnack, Dorie. *Cath Work* 60:1+ Ag 1993

BALKAN PENINSULA—RELIGION
Report from the Balkans. *Tablet* 247:180 F 6 1993

BALKAN PENINSULA—WAR
Humanitarian nightmare. *Origins* 23:733+ Ap 8 1993

BALKE, VICTOR H, BP, 1931-
A bishops balk at paying taxes for abortion. Breig, James. *OSV* 82:17 O 31 1993

BALMARY, MARIE
Letture Psicanalitiche Della Bibbia. Rossi, Giacomo. *Civilta* 143:476-487 D 5 1992

BALTHASAR, HANS URS VON, 1905-1988
The beauty of Balthasar. Nemoianu, Virgil, 1940-. *Crisis* 11:42-46 Ap 1993
Carisma e istituzione della chiesa nella teologia di Hans Urs Von Balthasar. Marchesi, Giovanni. *Civilta* 144:14-30 Ja 2 1993
Catholic theology, gender, and the future of Western civilization [editorial]. Schindler, David L. *Communio* 20:200-239 Sum 1993
Christian experience in Hans Urs von Balthasar. Potworowski, Christophe. *Communio* 20:107-117 Spr 1993
Experience as a theological category: Hans Urs von Balthasar on the Christian encounter with God's image. Casarella, Peter. *Communio* 20:118-128 Spr 1993
Hans Urs von Balthasar's anthropology in light of his marian thinking. Roten, Johann G. *Communio* 20:306-333 Sum 1993
How to pray with Elizabeth of the trinity. Barres, John O. *Spir Life* 39:37-43 Spr 1993
Man and woman under God: the dignity of the human being according to Hans Urs von Balthasar. Strukelj, Anton. *Communio* 20:377-388 Sum 1993
Meta-anthropology and Christology: on the philosophy of Hans Urs von Balthasar. Bieler, Martin. *Communio* 20:129-146 Spr 1993
Towards a eucharistic evangelization. Schindler, David L. *Communio* 19:549-575 Wint 1992

BALTIC STATES—RELIGION
Pope speaks of unity on eve of Baltic visit. *Tablet* 247:1140 S 4 1993

BANKS
Bankers and politicians. Keegan, William. *Tablet* 247:781 Je 19 1993
Salt of the earth: Milton Davis [interview by V Anderson]. Davis, Milton. *Salt* 13:4-5 Ap 1993

BANKS—LAW
When the banks went off the rails. Isbell, Harold. *Comm* 120:11-15 F 26 1993

BANNON, KEVIN, -1992
"We who are left"—the death of a clerical student. Sheridan, Daniel. *Furrow* 43:672-675 D 1992

BANZHAF, JOHN, III, 1940-
The man won't stop 'til the world's smoke-free [por]. Mullen, Peter. *Register* 69:1+ S 12 1993

BAPTISISM—HISTORY OF DOCTRINES
Baptists—people of the third way. Dunlop, Robert. *Furrow* 44:226-229 Ap 1993

BAPTISM
Baptism in water and Baptism in the spirit: a biblical, liturgical, and theological exposition. Larere, Philippe. Collegeville: Liturgical, 1993. 94p ISBN 0-8146-2225-9 LC 93-10845
The blind beggar of Jericho [2 parts]. LaVerdiere, Eugene Armand, 1936-. *Emmanuel* 99:86-89+ Mr; 158-166 Ap 1993
Environment [exc fr *Liturgy:* glad shouts and songs; *Liturgy:* dressing the Church; *Liturgy:* languages and metaphor]. Alexander, J Neil, et al. *Liturgy* 10:84-86 Spr 1993
Infant baptism and adult faith. Drumm, Michael. *Furrow* 44:131-139 Mr 1993
Learning from one another [exc fr *Liturgy:* practicing ecumenism]. Henderson, J Frank. *Liturgy* 10:8-9 Spr 1993
The long journey home. Fielding, Ellen Wilson. *Crisis* 11:49-50 Ap 1993
On the baptism of our daughter. Ellsberg, Robert. *Cath Work* 60:6 My 1993
One bread, one cup [exc fr *Liturgy:* putting on Christ; *Liturgy:* covenant with the world]. Stookey, Laurence Hull. *Liturgy* 10:4-6 Spr 1993
Sponsors make the difference. Heller, Chris. *Tod Parish* 25:4+ N-D 1993
Your child's baptism. Dalton, William J. *Furrow* 44:485-489 S 1993

BAPTISM—BIBLICAL TEACHING
Arator on the Acts of the Apostles. Hillier, Richard. New York: Oxford University Press, 1993. x, 224p ISBN 0-814786-4

BAPTISM—CATHOLIC CHURCH
An infant baptism program that works. Heller, Chris. *Tod Parish* 25:13-16 Ap-My 1993
Making the most of it. *Tablet* 247:73 Ja 16 1993
Orthopraxis in the sacramental initiation of unbaptized children of catechetical age: a canonical perspective. Hesch, John B. *Worship* 67:214-225 My 1993

The presider as proclaimer. Bernstein, Eleanor. *Liturgy* 11:78-81 Sum 1993

BAPTISM—CATHOLIC CHURCH- SPAIN
Hispania la iniciación cristiana de los niños no bautizados en edad escolar. Alvarez, Rosendo, Bp, and Rodríguez Plaza, Braulio. *Notitiae* 29:64-75 Ja-F 1993

BAPTISM—HISTORY OF DOCTRINES
Arator on the Acts of the Apostles. Hillier, Richard. New York: Oxford University Press, 1993. x, 224p ISBN 0-814786-4
Baptism. Firth, Francis. *Can Cath Rev* 11:35-36 Mr 1993

BAPTISM, EUCHARIST AND MINISTRY (DOCUMENT)
Reflections by a Pentecostalist on aspects of BEM. Hunter, Harold D. *JEcumen Stds* 29:317-345 Sum-Aut 1992

BAPTISM AND CHRISTIAN UNION
By water and the spirit—a United Methodist understanding of Baptism: a Lutheran response. Nitschke, Beverley A. *Ecumen Trends* 22:3-7 Ja 1993

BAPTISM IN THE HOLY SPIRIT
Towards a new Pentecost: for a new evangelization. McDonnell, Kilian, 1921-, ed. Collegeville: Liturgical, 1993. x, 72p ISBN 0-8146-5846-6 LC 92-46910

BAPTIST UNION OF GREAT BRITAIN AND IRELAND
Baptists—people of the third way. Dunlop, Robert. *Furrow* 44:226-229 Ap 1993

BAPTISTS—HISTORY—SOCIETIES
Baptists—people of the third way. Dunlop, Robert. *Furrow* 44:226-229 Ap 1993

BAR, RONALD PHILIPPE, BP, 1928-
Rumours abound as Bär resigns. Goddijn, Walter, 1921-. *Tablet* 247:413-414 Mr 27 1993

BARAGA, FREDERIC
Frederic Baraga: holiness on showshoes. Convissor, Kate. *CDgst* 57:99-103 Jl 1993

BARBA, ALVARO ALONSO, 1569-1662
Alvaro Alonso Barba's Art of metallurgy: from the poetical to the technological. Soons, Alan. *Cithara* 32:3-12 My 1993

BARBARITO, LUIGI, ABP, 1922-
A personal note. *Tablet* 247:105 Ja 23 1993

BARNABAS
Barnabas. Martin, George. *Liguorian* 81:44-45 O 1993

BARNES, ALBERT C
Idiosyncrasy and genius: the Barnes Foundation on tour. O'Donovan, Leo J. *America* 169:16-18 Jl 17-24 1993

BARNEY, GERALD
Population explosion. Clancy, Paul. *Nat Cath Rep* 29:16-17 My 7 1993

BARON, RAFAEL ARNAIZ, 1911-1938
Congregation for the Causes of Saints (1992-06-13) Decree on a miracle. Congregation for the Causes of Saints. *TPS* 38:19-20 Ja-F 1993*

BARRE, SIAD
Vested interests in Somalia. Stratton, Florence. *Cath Work* 60:3 Ja-F 1993

BARRY, WILLIAM A
Spiritual direction: an ongoing retreat? Finley, Mitchel B. *OSV* 81:6 Ja 31 1993

BARTH, KARL
The Holy Spirit and the Christian life: the library of theological ethics. Barth, Karl, 1886-1968. Louisville: John Knox, 1993. x, 96p ISBN 0-664-25325-3
Humanity in God: on reading Karl Barth in relation to mystical theology. McIntosh, Mark A. *Heythrop* 34:22-40 Ja 1993
Karl Barth et Dostoïevski. Roussel, Jean-François. *Laval Theol Phil* 49:37-55 F 1993
Karl Barth: his life from letters and autobiographical texts. Busch, Eberhard. Grand Rapids: Eerdmans, 1993. 600p ISBN 0-8028-0708-9

BARTH, KARL—ETHICS
The hastening that waits. Biggar, Nigel. New York: Oxford University Press, 1993. x, 208p ISBN 0-826457-7

BARTH, KARL—THEOLOGY—CHRISTOLOGY
Humanity in God: on reading Karl Barth in relation to mystical theology. McIntosh, Mark A. *Heythrop* 34:22-40 Ja 1993

BARTHOLOMEOUS, (DIMITRIOS ARCHONTONIS), PATR
John Paul II, Pope, (1991-10-27) Nuntius Telegraphicus (Telegram) [French]. John Paul II, Pope, 1920- (Karol Wojtyla) (elected 1978). *AAS* 84:871 S 8 1992*

BARTIMAEUS (BIBLICAL CHARACTER)
The blind beggar of Jericho [2 parts]. LaVerdiere, Eugene Armand, 1936-. *Emmanuel* 99:86-89+ Mr; 158-166 Ap 1993

BARTOLI, CECILIA
Listening to Cecilia. Tombes, Jonathan. *Crisis* 11:52-54 Mr 1993

BARZAHGI, CESARE MARIA, 1774-1825
Congregation for the Causes of Saints (1993-07-06) Decree on the heroic virtues. Congregation for the Causes of Saints. *OR(Eng)* 1299:12 Jl 14 1993*

BASIC CHRISTIAN COMMUNITIES
As comunidades edlesiais de base como modelo inspirador da nova evangelização. Barreiro, Álvaro. *Perspectiva* 24:331-356 S-D 1992
The benefits of networking. Bernier, Joan M. *Tod Parish* 25:36-37 O 1993
Catechetics in an at-risk community. Smolich, Thomas H. *Momentum* 24:7-10 Ap-My 1993
A catequese e as CEBs. Cansi, Bernardo. *REB* 52:894-902 D 1992
CEBs e ecumenismo: uma discussão a partir da dimensão ecumênica do oitavo intereclesial. Oliveira Ribeiro, Claudio de. *REB* 52:846-855 D 1992
Christian base communities after Santo Domingo [interview by G Meléndez; fr *Latinoamerica press*]. Richard, Pablo. *LADOC* 24:1-4 S-O 1993
Christian life communities. Rossi, Angela. *Priests & People* 7:238-239 Je 1993
The Church of the future? Bernier, Joan M, and Howard, Barbara, et al. *Tod Parish* 25:26-29 N-D 1993
Church of the poor: the ecclesiology of Gustavo Gutiérrez. Nickoloff, James B. *TheolStds* 54:512-535 S 1993

Communities: new "way of life". Gibeau, Dawn. *Nat Cath Rep* 29:2-3 Ag 27 1993

Congregation-based organizations: a church model for the 90's. Garland, James H. *America* 169:14-16 N 13 1993

Creating small faith communities. Baranowski, Art. *Chicago Stud* 31:182-185 Ag 1992

Faith sharing and new facilitators. Bernier, Joan M. *Tod Parish* 25:36-37 Ja 1993

A Festschrift on small faith communities [symposium, Institute of Pastoral Studies of Loyola University, Jl 1991]. Sweetser, Thomas P, and Forster, Patricia M. *Chicago Stud* 31:173-181 Ag 1992

Five cries of parish. Ventline, Lawrence M. *Priest* 49:17-21 F 1993

Forming a small Christian community: a personal journey. Currier, Richard. Mystic: Twenty-Third Publications, 1992. 178p ISBN 0-89622-511-9 LC 91-68557

Inculturation through small Christian communities. Payeur, Joseph A. *AFER* 35:37-43 F 1993

The Latin American church: balance, tensions and perspectives [fr *Voces*]. Libanio, Joao Batista. *LADOC* 24:16-24 N-D 1993

O oitavo encontro intereclesial de CEBs e a ecologia. Cechin, Irmão Antônio. *REB* 52:856-876 D 1992

One inner city parish community. Tomalak, Ann. *Priests & People* 7:138-144 Ap 1993

Pastoral letter to religious educators. *Living Light* 29:68-80 Spr 1993

The pastoral priorities of the local church in Eastern Africa. Mejia, Rodrigo. *AFER* 34:324-339 D 1992

The practice of theological reflection in small faith communities. Killen, Patricia O'Connell. *Chicago Stud* 31:189-196 Ag 1992

Refounding church—a paradigm shift. Donovan, Vincent. *Chicago Stud* 31: 215-223 Ag 1992

Santo Domingo—an interpretation [excerpt fr *Sedos*]. Secondin, Bruno. *LADOC* 23:1-13 Jl-Ag 1993

Seeking the welfare of the city: the public life of small communities of faith. Cowan, Michael A. *Chicago Stud* 31:205-214 Ag 1992

Seven steps to getting started. Bernier, Joan M. *Tod Parish* 25:36-37 S 1993

Small church communities wax. Vidulich, Dorothy. *Nat Cath Rep* 29:4 Jl 16 1993

Spiritual intimacy and community. English, John. New Jersey: Paulist Press, 1992. x, 207p ISBN 0-8091-3384-9 LC 92-29706

Trabalho, teimosia e esperança (a questão do trabalho no 8 encontro intereclesial das CEBs). Almeida Cunha, Rogério Ignácio de. *REB* 52:877-893 D 1992

VIII encontro intereclesial das CEBS (eventos no evento). Libanio, Joao Batista. *REB* 52:789-800 D 1992

What are basic Christian communities? Marins, José. *Priests & People* 7: 142-144 Ap 1993

BASIC CHRISTIAN COMMUNITIES- BELGIUM
Un dossier "Renouvelons la terre" et ses fruits. Piton, Jacques. *Lumen* 48: 95-104 Mr 1993

BASIC CHRISTIAN COMMUNITIES- BRAZIL
Josiah's passover: sociology and the liberating Bible. Nakanose, Shigeyuki. Maryknoll: Orbis Books, 1993. x, 192p ISBN 0-88344850-5 LC 93-18286

BASIC NEEDS
The necessities of life: drinking and eating [photos]. Pilch, John Joseph, 1936-. *BibleT* 31:231-237 Jl 1993

BASIL, THE GREAT, SAINT
Saint in a soup kitchen: AD 370. Parachin, Victor M. *CDgst* 57:91-93 My 1993

BASILICA DE SANTA MARIA DE GUADALUPE (MEXICO)
Our Lady of Guadalupe: a Liberating interpretation [tr fr *Conciencia Latinoamericana*]. Segundo, Juan Luis. *LADOC* 24:24-27 S-O 1993

Our Lady of Guadalupe: evangelizer of the Americas. McCurry, James E. *Marian Stds* 43:9-16 1992

BASILICA OF NOTRE DAME DE PAIX (IVORY COAST)
A deal with God. Rafferty, Kevin. *Tablet* 247:1003-1004 Ag 7 1993

BASILICAS
John Paul II, Pope (1992-04-25) Litterae Apostolicae (Apostolic Letter establishing a Minor Basilica) [Latin]. John Paul II, Pope, 1920- (Karol Wojtyla) (elected 1978). *AAS* 85:12-13 Ja 7 1993*

John Paul II, Pope, (1992-04-25) Litterae Apostolicae (Apostolic Letter to create Minor Basilica in Raalte) [Latin]. John Paul II, Pope, 1920- (Karol Wojtyla) (elected 1978). *AAS* 85:125 F 3 1993*

John Paul II, Pope, (1992-04-25) Litterae Apostolicae (Apostolic Letters) [Latin]. John Paul II, Pope, 1920- (Karol Wojtyla) (elected 1978). *AAS* 84: 1057-1058 N 3 1992*

John Paul II, Pope, (1992-05-12) Litterae Apostolicae (Apostolic Letter creating Minor Basilica of Church of Nowy Sacz) [Latin]. John Paul II, Pope, 1920- (Karol Wojtyla) (elected 1978). *AAS* 85:126 F 3 1993*

John Paul II, Pope, (1992-05-19) Litterae Apostolicae (Apostolic Letter establishing a Minor Basilica) [Latin]. John Paul II, Pope, 1920- (Karol Wojtyla) (elected 1978). *AAS* 85:13-14 Ja 7 1993*

John Paul II, Pope, (1992-07-03) Litterae Apostolicae (Apostolic Letter) [Latin]. John Paul II, Pope, 1920- (Karol Wojtyla) (elected 1978). *AAS* 85: 15-16 Ja 7 1993*

John Paul II, Pope, (1992-07-06) Litterae Apostolicae (Apostolic Letter) [Latin]. John Paul II, Pope, 1920- (Karol Wojtyla) (elected 1978). *AAS* 85: 16-17 Ja 7 1993*

John Paul II, Pope, (1992-07-23) Litterae Apostolicae (Apostolic Letter) [Latin]. John Paul II, Pope, 1920- (Karol Wojtyla) (elected 1978). *AAS* 85: 18-19 Ja 7 1993*

John Paul II, Pope, (1992-07-23) Litterae Apostolicae (Apostolic Letter) [Latin]. John Paul II, Pope, 1920- (Karol Wojtyla) (elected 1978). *AAS* 85: 19-20 Ja 7 1993*

John Paul II, Pope, (1992-08-28) Litterae Apostolicae (Apostolic Letter) [Latin]. John Paul II, Pope, 1920- (Karol Wojtyla) (elected 1978). *AAS* 85: 21-22 Ja 7 1993*

John Paul II, Pope, (1992-10-15) Litterae Apostolica (Apostolic Letter to create a Minor Basilica of Our Lady in Chile) [Latin]. John Paul II, Pope, 1920- (Karol Wojtyla) (elected 1978). *AAS* 85:127-128 F 3 1993*

John Paul II, Pope, (1992-10-22) Litterae Apostolicae (Apostolic Letter in which cathedral of Kabgayi is made a Minor Basilica) [Latin]. John Paul II, Pope, 1920- (Karol Wojtyla) (elected 1978). *AAS* 85:128-129 F 3 1993*

BATHSHEBA
The story of David and Bathsheba: a different approach. Garsiel, Moshe. *CBQ* 55:244-262 Ap 1993

BATTHYANY-STRATTMANN, LASZLO, 1870-1931
Congregation for the Causes of Saints (1992-07-11) Decree on the heroic virtues. Congregation for the Causes of Saints. *TPS* 38:37-38 Ja-F 1993*

BAUDOUIN ALBERT CHARLES LEOPOLD AXEL MARIE GUSTAVE, KING OF BELGIUM, 1930-1993
King's beatification not ruled out, or in. *Tablet* 247:1140-1141 S 4 1993

Monarchy at its best [editorial]. *Tablet* 247:1031 Ag 14 1993

Baudouin Albert Charles, Leopold Axel Marie Gustave, King of Belguim, 1930-1993 [obit]. *Tablet* 247:1051-1052 Ag 14 1993

BEA, AUGUSTIN, CARDINAL, 1881-1968
Augustin Bea, the Cardinal of unity. Schmidt, Stephen A. New Rochelle, New York: New City Press, 1992. 806p ISBN 1-56548-016-3 LC 92-17612

BEATIFIC VISION
The purification of desire by means of desire in Dante's "Purgatorio". Stratton, Robin. *Spir Life* 39:34-36 Spr 1993

BEATIFICATION
Congregation for the Causes of Saints (1993-07-06) Decree on a miracle. Congregation for the Causes of Saints. *OR(Eng)* 1299:12 Jl 14 1993*

Congregation for the Causes of Saints (1993-07-06) Decree on a miracle. Congregation for the Causes of Saints. *OR(Eng)* 1299:12 Jl 14 1993*

Congregation for the Causes of Saints (1993-07-06) Decree on a miracle. Congregation for the Causes of Saints. *OR(Eng)* 1299:12 Jl 14 1993*

Congregation for the Causes of Saints (1993-07-06) Decree on a miracle. Congregation for the Causes of Saints. *OR(Eng)* 1299:12 Jl 14 1993*

Congregation for the Causes of Saints (1993-07-06) Decree on a miracle. Congregation for the Causes of Saints. *OR(Eng)* 1299:12 Jl 14 1993*

Congregation for the Causes of Saints (1993-07-06) Decree on a miracle. Congregation for the Causes of Saints. *OR(Eng)* 1299:12 Jl 14 1993*

Congregation for the Causes of Saints (1993-07-06) Decree on the heroic virtues. Congregation for the Causes of Saints. *OR(Eng)* 1299:12 Jl 14 1993*

Congregation for the Causes of Saints (1993-07-06) Decree on the heroic virtues. Congregation for the Causes of Saints. *OR(Eng)* 1299:12 Jl 14 1993*

Congregation for the Causes of Saints (1993-07-06) Decree on the heroic virtues. Congregation for the Causes of Saints. *OR(Eng)* 1299:12 Jl 14 1993*

Congregation for the Causes of Saints (1993-07-06) Decree on the heroic virtues. Congregation for the Causes of Saints. *OR(Eng)* 1299:12 Jl 14 1993*

Congregation for the Causes of Saints (1993-07-06) Decree on the heroic virtues. Congregation for the Causes of Saints. *OR(Eng)* 1299:12 Jl 14 1993*

Formal opening of Paul VI's cause. *Tablet* 247:624 My 15 1993

Isabella of Spain—beatification and 1992. Edwards, John. *SIDIC* 25 No 2:8-11 1992

John Paul II, Pope, (1985-08-15) Litterae Apostolicae (Apostolic Letters) [Latin]. John Paul II, Pope, 1920- (Karol Wojtyla) (elected 1978). *AAS* 84: 1112-1115 D 5 1992*

John Paul II, Pope, (1988-09-03). John Paul II, Pope, 1920- (Karol Wojtyla) (elected 1978). *AAS* 84:1115-1117 D 5 1992*

John Paul II, Pope, (1992-05-18) Beatification of Sister Josephine Bakhita. John Paul II, Pope, 1920- (Karol Wojtyla) (elected 1978). *TPS* 37:371-373 N-D 1992*

John Paul II, Pope, (1992-05-18) Blessed Josemaría Excrivá de Balaguer. John Paul II, Pope, 1920- (Karol Wojtyla) (elected 1978). *TPS* 37:368-370 N-D 1992*

John Paul II, Pope, (1992-09-27) Beatification. John Paul II, Pope, 1920- (Karol Wojtyla) (elected 1978). *TPS* 38:57-60 Ja-F 1993*

John Paul II, Pope, (1992-11-22) Ready to confess Christ. John Paul II, Pope, 1920- (Karol Wojtyla) (elected 1978). *TPS* 38:134-137 My-Je 1993*

John Paul II, Pope, (1993-03-21) Authentic witnesses of the Gospel. John Paul II, Pope, 1920- (Karol Wojtyla) (elected 1978). *TPS* 38:245-248 Jl-Ag 1993*

John Paul II, Pope, (1993-05-16). John Paul II, Pope, 1920- (Karol Wojtyla) (elected 1978). *TPS* 38:308-311 S-O 1993*

John Paul II, Pope, (1993-10-10) Hope [Orig in Italian, Spanish]. John Paul II, Pope, 1920- (Karol Wojtyla) (elected 1978). *OR(Eng)* 1311:1+ O 13 1993*

King's beatification not ruled out, or in. *Tablet* 247:1140-1141 S 4 1993

A saint in the making. *Tablet* 246:1568 D 12 1992

A tale of two popes [editorial]. *Tablet* 247:775-776 Je 19 1993

Where does Cardinal Newman's cause stand? Blehl, Vincent Ferrer, 1921-. *America* 169:15-17 S 25 1993

Who is Sister Faustina? Kosicki, George. *Register* 69:4 F 7 1993

BEATITUDES
At pure heart: the window to God. Hummel, Charles, and Hummel, Anne. Grand Rapids: Zondervan Publishing House, 1993. x, 64p ISBN 0-310-59643-2

Eight beatitudes from Qumran [photos]. Viviano, Benedict. *BibleT* 31:219-224 Jl 1993

Joy in suffering: receiving your reward. Lambert, David. Grand Rapids: Zondervan Publishing House, 1993. x, 64p ISBN 0-310-59673-4

Making peace: resolving personal conflicts. Hummel, Charles, and Hummel, Anne. Grand Rapids: Zondervan Publishing House, 1993. x, 64p ISBN 0-310-59653-x

Meekness: claiming your inheritance. Plueddemann, Jim, and Plueddemann, Carol. Grand Rapids: Zondervan Publishing House, 1993. x, 64p ISBN 0-310-59623-8

Mourning: the prelude to laughter. Bruno, Bonnie. Grand Rapids: Zondervan Publishing House, 1993. x, 64p ISBN 0-310-59613-0

Praying with the beatitudes. Buono, Anthony M. *Emmanuel* 99:466-470 O 1993

Revealing happiness. Hanlon, Kevin. *Month* 26:165-167 Ap 1993

Showing mercy: getting what you give. Lambert, David. Grand Rapids: Zondervan Publishing House, 1993. x, 64p ISBN 0-310-59653-x

BECKER, GARY, 1930-
Metaphors of discrimination: a comparison of Gunnar Myrdal and Gary Becker. Shulman, Steven. *RSocEcon* 50:432-452 Wint 1992

BEDAROWSKI, MARY FARRELL
The new consciousness in America. Bryan, Timothy L. *StudiaM* 41:27-47 1992

BEDE, THE VENERABLE, SAINT
Bernard and Bede. Renna, Thomas. *ABenR* 44:223-235 S 1993

Caedmon's hymn and the gebwaernysse (fitness) of things. Abraham, Lenore. *ABenR* 43:331-344 D 1992

The story of Caedmon: Bede's account of the first English poet. O'Hare, Colmán. *ABenR* 43:345-357 D 1992

BEECHING, PAUL Q
The education of an American Catholic. Beeching, Paul Q. Chicago: The Thomas More Press, 1993. x, 405p ISBN 0-88347-275-9

BEGGING
The begging industry. Schall, James Vincent, 1928-. *Crisis* 11:44-45 Je 1993

Cathedral explains its policy on beggars. *Tablet* 247:150 Ja 30 1993

Flea-ing New York: city of inexplicable eructations. Baumann, Paul. *Comm* 120:4-5 S 24 1993

A sedan is not a home. Kirp, David L, 1944-. *Comm* 120:4-6 F 12 1993

BEGUINES
Self-transcendence and the group: the attitude to life of thirteenth and fourteenth century Beguines. Bowie, Fiona. *New Blckfrs* 73:584-598 D 1992

BEINERT, WOLFGANG, 1933-
In Drei Personen—der Trinitarische Schüsselbegriff "Person" in den Entwürfen Jürgen Moltmanns und Walter Kaspers. Radlbeck-Ossmann, Regina. *Catholica* 47:38-51 1993

Response to Wolfgang Beinert. Sullivan, Francis Aloysius. *Jurist* 52 no 1: 484-489 1992

Sensus Fidei: theological reflection since Vatican II: I, 1965-1984. Burkhard, John J. *Heythrop* 34:41-59 Ja; 123-136 Ap 1993

BELANGER, DINA
John Paul II, Pope, (1993-03-21) Authentic witnesses of the Gospel. John Paul II, Pope, 1920- (Karol Wojtyla) (elected 1978). *TPS* 38:245-248 Jl-Ag 1993*

BELGIUM—GOVERNMENT
Monarchy at its best [editorial]. *Tablet* 247:1031 Ag 14 1993

BELIEF AND DOUBT
Doubt in search of understanding. Rees, Frank. *Pacifica* 6:279-296 O 1993

Down the arches of the years, down the labyrinthine ways [interview by J G Deedy, 1923-]. Beeching, Paul Q. *Critic* 47:2-13 Spr 1993

Die Fünfte Weltkonferenz für Glauben und Kirchenverfassung. Radano, John A. *Catholica* 47:20-37 1993

A Jewish pilgrim's progress. Blue, Lionel. *Tablet* 247:1288 O 9 1993

Peeling the onion. Mason, Philip, 1906-. *Tablet* 247:1192 S 18 1993

Pensées pour le temps penitentiel. Schall, James Vincent, 1928-. *Crisis* 11:39-41 F 1993

A quest for vision [interview by E Wymard]. Hampl, Patricia, 1946-. *Critic* 47:58-64 Spr 1993

Reasons for disbelief. Bull, George, 1929-. *Tablet* 247:240-241 F 20 1993

The reformation: too many assumptions? Marius, Richard, 1933-. *Critic* 47: 31-42 Wint 1992

Saved by poetry. Jennings, Elizabeth, 1926-. *Tablet* 247:613-614 My 15 1993

Writing your faith script with God. Auer, Jim. *Liguorian* 81:38-42 O 1993

BELIZE—SOCIAL LIFE AND CUSTOMS
Charting the future of Belize. Holton, Robert. *OSV* 82:5 My 23 1993

BENDIKOVIC, STEFAN
Communism and Catholicism. Hines, Susan C. *Priest* 49:38-40 Mr 1993

BENEDICT, SAINT, ABBOT OF MONTE CASSINO, 480-547
Coming home: encountering the Rule of St. Benedict. Waal, Esther de. *Word Sp* 15:78-86 1993

Get serious! The monastic condemnation of laughter. Russell, Kenneth C. *RRel* 52:371-379 My-Je 1993

The life of St Benedict: Gregory the Great. Vogue, Albert de. Petersham: St Bede's Publications, 1993. x, 186p ISBN 0-932506-77-1 LC 93-420

Liturgy of the hours: a reflection. Zuercher, Suzanne. *RRel* 52:364-370 My-Je 1993

Monastic hospitality and the conversion of the monk. Huerre, Denis. *ABenR* 44:249-257 S 1993

The rule of Benedict: insights for the ages. Chittister, Joan D. New York: The Crossroad Publishing Company, 1992. x, 180p ISBN 0-8245-2503-5 LC 92-17161

The sweetness of God. Posset, Franz. *ABenR* 44:143-178 Je 1993

BENEDICT OF NURSIA, 480-550
The medical world of Hildegard of Bingen. Daaleman, Timothy P. *ABenR* 44:280-289 S 1993

BENEDICT XV, POPE, 1854-1922 (GIACOMO DELLA CHIESA) (ELECTED 1918)
Benedetto XV e il Partito Popolare Italiano. Mellinato, Giuseppe. *Civilta* 3: 271-278 Ag 7-21 1993

BENEDICTINE NUNS
Filipino women: designers of their destiny. Bernas, Mary Bellarmine. *Sisters* 65:175-180 My 1993

BENEDICTINE SISTERS OF CHARITY
Congregation for the Causes of Saints (1992-12-21) Decree on a miracle. Congregation for the Causes of Saints. *OR(Eng)* 1272:4 Ja 6 1993*

BENEDICTINES
And who is my neighbor?. Beaver, William A. *Word Sp* 14:96-104 1992

Benedictine nuns in the United States. Sutera, Judith. *Word Sp* 14:33-40 1992

A conflict of mitres: the diverse polities and Cathedral Abbey of Bishop Leo Haid. Baumstein, Paschal. *Word Sp* 14:76-95 1992

BENEDICTINES—HISTORY- UNITED STATES
Plans for an 18th-century Benedictine settlement in western Pennsylvania: Bishop John Carroll and the English Benedictine Congregation. Kollar, Rene. *Word Sp* 14:3-11 1992

BENEDICTINES—RULE
The achievement of André Borias, exegete of Benedict's rule. Kardong, Terrence G. *ABenR* 44:179-220 Je 1993

Coming home: encountering the Rule of St. Benedict. Waal, Esther de. *Word Sp* 15:78-86 1993

The journey of the heart in the Rule of Benedict. Roberts, Augustine. *Word Sp* 15:74-77 1993

BENEDICTINES- NORTH DAKOTA
Benedictine stability on the North Dakota frontier. Kardong, Terrence G. *Word Sp* 14:53-75 1992

BENEDICTION
Amazing grace: mealtime blessings. Armendariz, Sherry. *Spir Life* 39:137-139 Aut 1993

"Benedetto sia dio che ci ha benedetti" il nuovo rituale delle benedizioni. Ferraro, Giuseppe. *Civilta* 2:238-247 My 1 1993

Blessed art thou, o Lord: a Christian understanding of the Jewish blessing. Sante, Carmine Di. *SIDIC* 26 no 1:10-14 1993

The concept of blessing. Loewe, Herbert, 1882-1940. *SIDIC* 26 no 1:2-9 1993

Eucharist and blessing. Thurian, Max. *SIDIC* 26 no 1:19-20 1993

John Paul II, Pope, (1993-05-23) Heart [Orig in Italian]. John Paul II, Pope, 1920- (Karol Wojtyla) (elected 1978). *OR(Eng)* 1294:8 Je 9 1993*

John Paul II, Pope, (1993-06-20) Nature [Orig in Italian]. John Paul II, Pope, 1920- (Karol Wojtyla) (elected 1978). *OR(Eng)* 1296:1 Je 23 1993*

A reflection on the book of blessings. Frizzell, Lawrence E. *SIDIC* 26 no 1: 15-18 1993

BENEVENUTI, PAUL
"Confortorio" di Paolo Benvenuti. Fantuzzi, Virgilio. *Civilta* 3:394-406 S 4 1993

BENJAMIN, W
Exigencias teólogicas de una filosofía de la historia (la resurrección como teodicea radial). Fernández Del Riesgo, Manuel. *Cien Tom* 119:321-349 My-Ag 1992

BENJAMIN, WALTER, 1892-1940
Walter Benjamin I l'esperit de la modernitat. Barcelona: Barcanova, 1993. x, 421p ISBN 84-7533-851-8

BENTHAUS, JEREMY
Why positivism is authoritarian. Dyzenhaus, David. *Amer J Juris* 37:83-112 1992

BENZIGER, AUGUST, 1867-1955
August Benzinger: international portrait painter. Benzinger, Mariel. Kansas City: Sheed & Ward, 1993. 355p ISBN 1-55612-614-x LC 93-19230

BEREAVEMENT
Becoming a bereavement minister. Curley, Terence P. *Priest* 49:54-55 S 1993

Bereavement: until we meet again. Oberholzer, Felicidad. *Liturgy* 10:47-56 Wint 1992

Christmas mourning: reaching out to the grief stricken. Williams, Donna Reilly. *Mod Lit* 19:14-15 D 1992-Ja 1993

Coming to terms with grief. Hover, Margot. *Tod Parish* 25:20 Ja 1993

The death of dreams: coping with the loss of an unborn child. Wong, Pamela Pearson. *St Anth* 100:36-39 Ja 1993

Helping people avoid bereavement mistakes. Parachin, Victor M. *Priest* 49: 19-20 Ja 1993

Hidden heartache. *Tablet* 247:73 Ja 16 1993

Hospice: death with dignity. Repp, Debbie M. *Liguorian* 81:24-31 Je 1993

A parish plan for bereavement ministry. Schumann, Marge. *Tod Parish* 25: 13-16 Ja 1993

Six steps through grief. Mitchell, Marcia Alice. *CDgst* 57:121-124 Ap 1993

What not to say to a grieving parent. Grimes, Laura M. *USCath* 58:15-18 Ap 1993

When pastoral ministers are grieving. Luther, James B. *Tod Parish* 25:17-19 Ja 1993

BERNADETTE SOUBIROUS, SAINT, 1844-1879
At Lourdes [condensed fr *National Review* Ag 9 1993]. Buckley, William F, Jr. *CDgst* 58:50-55 D 1993

BERNANOS, GEORGES, 1888-1948
Bernanos: a man of spirit. Celeste, Marie. *Priest* 49:44-46 Je 1993

BERNARD OF CLAIRVAUX, SAINT, 1090-1153
Bernard and Bede. Renna, Thomas. *ABenR* 44:223-235 S 1993

Bernard of Clairvaux in the thought of Meister Eckhart. Tamburello, Dennis E. *Cist Stud* 28:73-91 1993

Bernardus Magister: in celebration of the nonacentary of the birth of Saint Bernard of Clairvaux: 1090-1990. Sommerfeldt, John R, ed. Massachusetts: Cistercian Publications, 1992. x, 578p ISBN 0-87907-635-6 LC 92-13334

"Bride" and "Mother" in the Super cantica of St Bernard: an ecclesiology for our time? Kereszty, Roch A, 1933-. *Communio* 20:415-436 Sum 1993

Contemplative action: time in eternity according to Saint Bernard. Dumont, Charles. *Cist Stud* 28 no 2:145-159 1993

The fearless monk. Myers, Rawley. *HPR* 93:44-47 Mr 1993

Saint Bernard's third sermon for the feast of the Annunciation and a play from the N-town cycle. Hufgard, M Kilian. *Cist Stud* 28 no 2:167-178 1993

BERNARDIN, JOSEPH LOUIS, CARDINAL, 1928-
But Father, they're priests! Clerical culture and pedophilia. Greeley, Andrew Moran, 1928-. *Critic* 47:43-51 Wint 1992

Moral methodology and pastoral responsiveness: the case of abortion and the care of children. Whitmore, Todd David. *TheolStds* 54:316-338 Je 1993

Presumed innocent [editorial]. *OSV* 82:2 N 28 1993

Prophetic realism [editorial]. *Cath Int* 4:200 My 1993

Statement supporting Cardinal Bernardin. Keeler, William H, Abp. *Origins* 23:421-422 N 25 1993

Why does the church stand silent while women are abused? Greeley, Andrew Moran, 1928-. *USCath* 58:28-29 S 1993

BERNARDINO, DOMINIC
Activists and charismatics: stronger ties and shared respect. Wood, Charles. *New Cov* 23:8-12 O 1993

BERNARDO, VALERIO
John Paul II, Pope, (1993-10-10) Valerio Bernardo. John Paul II, Pope, 1920- (Karol Wojtyla) (elected 1978). *OR(Eng)* 1311:1 O 13 1993*
Two Spanish Bishops and seven Christian Brothers gave their lives for Catholic faith. *OR(Eng)* 1311:1 O 13 1993

BERNHART, JOSEPH, 1881-1969
Joseph Bernhart. Köhler, Oskar. *Stimm Zeit* 211:376-384 Je 1993

BERTOLUCCI, JOHN
A decade of fireworks. Ferguson, Lisa. *New Cov* 23:20-21 Ag 1993

BETHLEHEM—POLITICS
Dialogue [interview by L Petzvow]. Friej, Elias. *Register* 69:1+ Ap 18 1993

BETHLEHEM UNIVERSITY (WEST BANK)
Bethlehem U: politics is the sport. Pevtzow, Lisa. *Register* 69:1+ Ja 24 1993

BETROTHAL
The Church must stop cheating the engaged. Foley, Gerald. *St Anth* 101:10-13 Je 1993
Engagement: laying a foundation for success. Midgley, John, and Midgley, Sue. *Liguorian* 81:16-20 Je 1993

BETTENCOURT, KATREEN
Katreen Bettencourt. *Mod Lit* 20:46 Je-Jl 1993

BEVILACQUA, ANTHONY JOSEPH, CARDINAL, 1923-
The view from the city of brotherly love [interview by G E Sherry]. *OSV* 82:12 Je 13 1993

BEYENS, HENRI, BARON
John Paul II, Pope, (1991-10-31) Allocutiones (Speech to receive ambassadorial credentials) [French]. John Paul II, Pope, 1920- (Karol Wojtyla) (elected 1978). *AAS* 84:961-963 O 3 1992*

BEYZYM, JAN, 1850-1912
Congregation for the Causes of Saints (1992-12-21) Decree on the heroic virtues. Congregation for the Causes of Saints. *OR(Eng)* 1272:4 Ja 6 1993*

BHARTRHARI, 570?-651?
Revelation in comparative perspective: lessons for interreligious dialogue. Carpenter, David. *JEcumen Stds* 29:175-188 Spr 1992

BHUTAN—POLITICS
Ethnic expulsions from Bhutan. *Tablet* 247:957 Jl 24 1993

BIANCO, FRANK
A father forgets his son [condensed fr *The Providence Visitor* O 8 1992]. Ascoli, E Lynn. *CDgst* 57:118-120 Ja 1993

BIBLE
Disclosure at Emmaus. Roth, Wolfgang. *BibleT* 31:46-51 Ja 1993
Letture Psicanalitiche Della Bibbia. Rossi, Giacomo. *Civilta* 143:476-487 D 5 1992
On cover: based on the new Jerome biblical commentary. Brown, Raymond Edward, et al, eds. London: G Chapman, 1992. x, 456p ISBN 0-22566-642-1 LC 92-44543
A window on the Good Book. Lapin, Daniel. *Crisis* 11:10-11 Jl-Ag 1993

BIBLE—AGRICULTURE
Agricultural imagery in the Gospel of Matthew and the gospel of truth. Cavallo, Jo Ann. *Relig Lit* 24:27-38 Aut 1992

BIBLE—ANTIQUITIES
Holy Land archaeology is source of controversy. Pevtzow, Lisa. *Register* 69:1+ Jl 4 1993
Josephus' portrait of Josiah. Feldman, Louis H. *Louvain Stds* 18:110-130 Sum 1993
Peter's house—the first church. Martin, Geroge. *CDgst* 57:1-3+ S 1993

BIBLE—AUTHORITY
Freedom from the law in early Christianity. Räisänen, Heikki. *TheolDgst* 40:43-48 Spr 1993
Is the Bible true? King, Nicholas. *Priests & People* 7:50-53 F 1993
Scripture, inspiration and the word of God. Garrett, Graeme. *Pacifica* 6:81-99 F 1993

BIBLE—BIBLIOGRAPHY
Literacy-critical approaches to the Bible: an annotated bibliography. Minor, Mark. West Cornwall: Locust Hill Press, 1992. 520p ISBN 0-93395-148-5 LC 92-7469

BIBLE—CANON
Canon and culture: realistic possibilities for the biblical canon. Bossman, David M. *Bib Th Bul* 23:4-13 Spr 1993
The center of the first testament within the canonical process. Christensen, Duane L. *Bib Th Bul* 23:48-53 Sum 1993

BIBLE—CRITICISM, INTERPRETATION
The achievement of André Borias, exegete of Benedict's rule. Kardong, Terrence G. *ABenR* 44:179-220 Je 1993
Addendum to Boniface Ramsey, "John Cassian: student of Augustine," CSQ 28 (1993): 5-15. Ramsey, Boniface. *Cist Stud* 28 no 2:199-200 1993
Algunas cuestiones actuales de escatología. *Teol Vida* 33 no 3-4:193-223 1992
Autore e lettore: il problema della comunicazione nell'ambito dell'esegesi biblica. Grilli, Massimo. *Gregorianum* 74 no 3:447-459 1993
Bílische Dogmatik: vol 3: Theologie als Ökonomic. Mildenberger, Friedrich. Stuttgart: Kohlhammer, 1993. x, 496p ISBN 3-17-011083-7
Catechism presents Scripture as revelation of God's salvific plan. Segalla, Giuseppe. *OR(Eng)* 1294:9-10 Je 9 1993
The confession of the soldiers in Matthew 27:54. Sim, David C. *Heythrop* 34:401-424 O 1993
Creed and criticism: the complementarity of faith and exegesis. Davies, Gordon F. *Can Cath Rev* 11:7-10 O 1993
Esegesi e lettura credente della Scrittura. Costacuria, Bruna. *Gregorianum* 73 No 4:739-745 1992
Essays in memory of John G. Gammie. Perdue, Leo G, et al, eds. Louisville: John Knox, 1993. x, 352p ISBN 0-664-25295-8
Faith seeking understanding: mediaeval exegesis. Boyle, John F. *Can Cath Rev* 11:9-13 Jl-Ag 1993
"A final word" [replay to Boadt, L; N 1991]. Fisher, Eugene J. *New Theol Rev* 6:87-89 F 1993
Incidence de l'exegese sur l'evolution du droit canonique durant la premiere partie du Moyen Age. Pelland, Gilles. *Periodica* 82 no 1:9-25 1993
The interpretation of the Bible in the Church. Fitzmyer, Joseph Augustine, 1920-. *America* 169:12-15 N 27 1993

Interrogantes sobre "Algunas cuestiones actuales de escatología". Noemi Callejas, Juan. *Teol Vida* 33 no 3-4:225-235 1992
Introduction to biblical interpretation. Klein, William Wade, et al, eds. Dallas: Word Publishing, 1993. x, 518p ISBN 0-8499-0774-8 LC 93-20099
Introduction to the history of exegesis [v 3]. Margerie, Bertrand de. Petersham: Saint Bede's Publications, 1991. x, 169p ISBN 0-932506-97-6 LC 93-16067
Is there a Catholic way to read the Bible? Martin, George. *New Cov* 22:11-13 Je 1993
A journey remembered: Catholic biblical scholarship 50 years after Divino afflante spiritu [commentary]. Donahue, John R. *America* 169:6-11 S 18 1993*
El método de Orígenes. Ossandón, Pedro, and Rodríguez, Pedro. *Teol Vida* 33 no 3-4:185-191 1992
Metodi dell'esegesi tra mito, storicità e comunicasione. Lentzen-Deis, Fritz Leo. *Gregorianum* 73 No 4:731-737 1992
Las parábolas; de Jesús: su sentido y adecuada interpreción. Pérez-Cotapos, Eduardo L. *Teol Vida* 33 no 3-4:165-178 1992
Parables stories with double meanings. Hoppe, Leslie J. *St Anth* 101:22-27 O 1993
La *Parola vivente (Eb 4, 12): dallo studio alla vita.* Rasco, Emilio. *Gregorianum* 73 No 4:689-695 1992
The phallacy of Genesis: a feminist and psychoanalytic approach. Rashkow, Ilona N. Louisville: Westminster, 1993. x, 144p ISBN 0-664-25250-8
A quick guide to Christianity. Roberts, David. New York: Vantage Press, 1992. x, 102p ISBN 0-533-10327-4 LC 92-90783
Saint Thomas Aquinas and theological exegesis of sacred scripture. McGuckin, Terence. *New Blckfrs* 74:197-211 Ap 1993
Say it with scripture. Becker, Mary Lee. *ReligTJ* 27:26 O 1993
Taking the Bible seriously. White, Benton J. Louisville: Westminster, 1993. x, 192p ISBN 0-664-25452-7
Telling the Gospel in flesh and blood. Blastic, Michael W. *New Theol Rev* 6:108-112 My 1993
Time and narrative: reflections from Paul Ricoeur. Jasper, David, 1951-. *Heythrop* 34:302-306 Jl 1993
Virtuoso theology: the Bible and interpretation. Young, Frances. Cleveland: The Pilgrim Press, 1993. x, 198p ISBN 0-8298-0948-1 LC 92-43008
What if our only witness happens to be blind? [editorial]. White, Leland J, ed. *Bib Th Bul* 23:90 Aut 1993
What is new and what is old: patristic exegesis. Barringer, Robert. *Can Cath Rev* 11:7-15 Je 1993

BIBLE—CRITICISM, INTERPRETATION—HISTORY
After historical criticism, what? Trends in biblical interpretation and ecumenical, interfaith dialogues. Reumann, John Henry Paul, 1927-. *JEcumen Stds* 29:55-86 Wint 1992
Erlösung durch das Blut—Inhumanität eines gewalttätigen Gottes? Schwager, Raymund. *Stimm Zeit* 211:168-176 Mr 1993
More about the Bible. O'Grady, John F. *Chicago Stud* 31:316-324 N 1992

BIBLE—CRITICISM, LITERARY
After historical criticism, what? Trends in biblical interpretation and ecumenical, interfaith dialogues. Reumann, John Henry Paul, 1927-. *JEcumen Stds* 29:55-86 Wint 1992
The synoptic gospels source criticism and the new literary criticism. Focant, C. *Eph Theol Lovan* 78:494-499 D 1992

BIBLE—CRITICISM, REDACTION
Erlösung durch das Blut—Inhumanität eines gewalttätigen Gottes? Schwager, Raymund. *Stimm Zeit* 211:168-176 Mr 1993

BIBLE—CRITICISM, SOURCE
Let my people go. Lustiger, Jean-Marie, Cardinal, 1926-. *NRT* 115:481-495 Jl-Ag 1993

BIBLE—CRITICISM, TEXTUAL
The etymological origins of the Hebrew nābî: the one who invokes God. Fleming, Daniel E. *CBQ* 55:217-224 Ap 1993

BIBLE—DICTIONARIES
Nelson's quick-reference Bible questions and answers. Nashville: Thomas Nelson Publishers, 1987. x, 374p ISBN 0-8407-6905-9 LC 92-47030
The Oxford companion to the Bible. Metzger, Bruce M, and Coogan, Michael D, eds. New York: Oxford University Press, 1993. x, 874p ISBN 0-19-504645-5 LC 93-19315

BIBLE—ECONOMICS
Bílische Dogmatik: vol 3: Theologie als Ökonomic. Mildenberger, Friedrich. Stuttgart: Kohlhammer, 1993. x, 496p ISBN 3-17-011083-7
A peasant reading of the parable of the talents. Rohrbaugh, Richard L. *Bib Th Bul* 23:32-37 Spr 1993

BIBLE—ETHICS
Don't bully people with the Bible. Hoppe, Leslie J. *USCath* 58:16-21 S 1993
The hastening that waits. Biggar, Nigel. New York: Oxford University Press, 1993. x, 208p ISBN 0-826457-7

BIBLE—GEOGRAPHY
A holy week in a Holy Land. Morrow, Carol Ann. *St Anth* 100:28-33 Ap 1993

BIBLE—HERMENEUTICS *see* Bible—Criticism, Interpretation

BIBLE—HISTORY OF BIBLICAL EVENTS
Chapters into verse: poetry in English inspired by the Bible [vol I: Genesis to Malachi]. Atwan, Robert, and Wieder, Laurence, 1945-, eds. New York: Oxford University Press, 1993. x, 481p ISBN 0-19-506913-7 LC 92-37206
Chapters into verse: poetry in English inspired by the Bible [vol II: Gospels to Revelation]. Atwan, Robert, and Wieder, Laurence, 1945-, eds. New York: Oxford University Press, 1993. x, 391p ISBN 0-19-508305-9 LC 92-37206

BIBLE—HISTORY OF CONTEMPORARY EVENTS
The Collegeville Bible time-line. Payne, David F. Collegeville: Liturgical, 1993. 15p ISBN 0-8146-2275-5 LC 93-19614

BIBLE—INFLUENCE
Don't stop (thinking about the context). Bossman, David M, ed. *Bib Th Bul* 23:46-47 Sum 1993

BIBLE—INSPIRATION
Catechism presents Scripture as revelation of God's salvific plan. Segalla, Giuseppe. *OR(Eng)* 1294:9-10 Je 9 1993

BIBLE—INTERPRETATION *see* Bible—Criticism, Interpretation

BIBLE—LANGUAGE, STYLE

The etymological origins of the Hebrew nābî: the one who invokes God. Fleming, Daniel E. *CBQ* 55:217-224 Ap 1993

The major summaries in Acts. Co, Maria Anicia. *Eph Theol Lovan* 78:49-85 Ap 1992

The sweetness of the Lord: Dulcis and Suavis. Scholl, Edith. *Cist Stud* 27 No 4:359-366 1992

Das Wortfeld der Liebe im Paganen und Biblischen Griechisch. Söding, Thomas. *Eph Theol Lovan* 78:284-330 D 1992

BIBLE—LAW

The background of the Apostolic Decree. Callan, Terrance. *CBQ* 55:284-297 Ap 1993

Was heibt Gottes Gebot? Fuchs, Josef. *Stimm Zeit* 211:435-442 Jl 1993

BIBLE—LITURGICAL USE

Celebration of the word. Deiss, Lucien. Collegeville: Liturgical, 1993. x, 145p ISBN 0-8146-2090-6 LC 93-15193

Other ministries [exc fr *Liturgy: ethics and justice; Strong, loving and wise; Touchstones*]. Gonzalez, Catherine Gunsalus, et al. *Liturgy* 10:77-82 Spr 1993

Proclamation [exc fr *Liturgy: the art of celebration; Liturgy: ethics and justice*, etc]. Harms, Paul W F, et al. *Liturgy* 10:71-76 Spr 1993

L'uso delle versioni della sacra scrittura nella liturgia. Congregation for Divine Worship and Discipline of the Sacraments. *Notitiae* 28:323-331 My 1992

What King James has to say about the new lectionary [editorial]. Callam, Daniel. *Can Cath Rev* 11:2-3 Mr 1993

BIBLE—LITURGY

Preparing for worship: Sundays and feast days. Donovan, Daniel L. Mahwah: Paulist, 1993. x, 211p ISBN 0-8091-3424-1 LC 93-13704

BIBLE—MANUSCRIPTS

"The words are the messengers, the Word is the message": text and translation. Organ, Barbara E. *Can Cath Rev* 11:9-17 Mr 1993

BIBLE—PRAYERS

Why people still put their body and soul into prayer. Cunningham, Lawrence S, 1935-. *USCath* 58:6-13 Jl 1993

BIBLE—PROPHECIES

Discovering prophecy and wisdom: the books of Isaiah, Job, Proverbs, Psalms. Ralph, Margaret Nutting. New York: Paulist, 1993. x, 326p ISBN 08-0913-402-0 LC 93-10245

1944. Camping, Harold. New York: Vantage Press, 1992. x, 551p ISBN 0-533-10368-1 LC 92-90269

BIBLE—READING

Attentive to the word of God. Gustin, Marilyn Norquist. *Liguorian* 81:56-60 Ap 1993

Catechetics in an at-risk community. Smolich, Thomas H. *Momentum* 24:7-10 Ap-My 1993

Conversation with God. Carey, George Leonard, Abp of Canterbury, 1935-. *Tablet* 247:238-240 F 20 1993

An encounter with Christ. Penick, Carol Lacquement. *Living Prayer* 26:29 Jl-Ag 1993

Lectio divina. Schultz, Karl A. *BibleT* 31:197-199 Jl 1993

"Thanks be to God" the Bible and the liturgy. Collins, Thomas. *Can Cath Rev* 11:7-13 Je 20 1993

Transformed by the renewal of the mind. Temple, Katharine. *Cath Work* 60: 3 My 1993

BIBLE—SOCIAL TEACHINGS

A call for pastors without borders. *Origins* 22:589+ F 11 1993

The Ethiopian eunuch and his bible: a social-science analysis. Spencer, F Scott. *Bib Th Bul* 22:155-165 Wint 1992

Helping people cope with Robertson, Ratzinger, et al [editorial]. White, Leland J, ed. *Bib Th Bul* 22:146-148 Wint 1992

Pleasure: a biblical perspective. Lee, Dorothy A. *Way* 33:19-33 Ja 1993

Unterwegs zur interkulturellen Demokratie. Lesch, Walter. *Stimm Zeit* 211: 255-269 Ap 1993

BIBLE—STUDY

An approach to Bible study in one parish. Barbernitz, Peter. *Liturgy* 11:30-33 Sum 1993

At pure heart: the window to God. Hummel, Charles, and Hummel, Anne. Grand Rapids: Zondervan Publishing House, 1993. x, 64p ISBN 0-310-59643-2

The Bible: God's world. Woods, Laurie. Minnesota: The Liturgical Press, 1993. 92p ISBN 0-8146-2276-3

Buried treasures: rediscovering women's roles in the Bible [interview by US Catholic]. *Salt* 13:6-13 Je 1993

Chewing the text: early monastic lectio divina of the Bible. Kardong, Terrence G. *Can Cath Rev* 11:7-10 N 1993

Everything I needed to know about success, I learned in the Bible (and so can you!). Briley, Richard Gaylord. New Hampshire: The publisher-In-The-Glen, 1993. x, 144p ISBN 1-882988-05-1

Facilitating for growth: a guide for Scripture groups and small Christian communities. Fleischer, Barbara J. Collegeville: Liturgical, 1993. 160p ISBN 0-8146-2170-8 LC 93-1341

Group scripture study in the parish. Cameron, Michael. *BibleT* 31:238-243 Jl 1993

The "intellectual" formation of priests. Witherup, Ronald D. *Priest* 49:46-52 Ag 1993

The interpretation of the Bible in the Church. Fitzmyer, Joseph Augustine, 1920-. *America* 169:12-15 N 27 1993

An introduction to the Christian faith: a biblical perspective. Moses, Earl C, Jr. New York: Vantage Press, 1993. 127p ISBN 0-533-10329-0 LC 92-90810

It was good enough for me: teaching that old time religion. Ristow, Kate. *Catechist* 26:14-17 Mr 1993

Journey for the shadowlands: the readings for the Rites of the Cat. Jackson, Pamela E J. Minnesota: The Liturgical Press, 1993. x, 171p ISBN 0-8146-2113-9

Joy in suffering: receiving your reward. Lambert, David. Grand Rapids: Zondervan Publishing House, 1993. x, 64p ISBN 0-310-59673-4

Making peace: resolving personal conflicts. Hummel, Charles, and Hummel, Anne. Grand Rapids: Zondervan Publishing House, 1993. x, 64p ISBN 0-310-59653-x

Meekness: claiming your inheritance. Plueddemann, Jim, and Plueddemann, Carol. Grand Rapids: Zondervan Publishing House, 1993. x, 64p ISBN 0-310-59623-8

Mourning: the prelude to laughter. Bruno, Bonnie. Grand Rapids: Zondervan Publishing House, 1993. x, 64p ISBN 0-310-59613-0

A pastor's vision [interview by G O'Connell]. Martini, Carlo Maria, Cardinal, 1926-. *Tablet* 247:876-878 Jl 10 1993

Showing mercy: getting what you give. Lambert, David. Grand Rapids: Zondervan Publishing House, 1993. x, 64p ISBN 0-310-59653-x

Spiritual living in a secular world: applying the Book of Daniel today. Fernando, Ajith. Grand Rapids: Zondervan Publishing House, 1993. x, 192p ISBN 0-310-59501-0

Theological adult formation in an African diocese. Lobinger, Fritz, Bp. *AFER* 35:209-216 Ag 1993

Ways to approach the Bible. Treston, Kevin. *ReligTJ* 27:8-10 O 1993

BIBLE—STUDY—BIBLIOGRAPHY

ML rates bible study programs. *Mod Lit* 20:20-25 Ap 1993

BIBLE—THEOLOGY

Erlösung durch das Blut—Inhumanität eines gewalttätigen Gottes? Schwager, Raymund. *Stimm Zeit* 211:168-176 Mr 1993

Der Gebrauch der Hl Schrift in der dogmatischen Theologie. Becker, Karl J. *Gregorianum* 73 No 4:671-687 1992

Helping people cope with Robertson, Ratzinger, et al [editorial]. White, Leland J, ed. *Bib Th Bul* 22:146-148 Wint 1992

How to own your own Bible. Costello, Andrew. *USCath* 58:41-43 My 1993

The temple: symbol central to Biblical theology. Meyer, Ben F. *Gregorianum* 74 no 2:223-240 1993

Teología India. Berganza, Carlos. *Cien Tom* 120:79-100 Ja-Ap 1993

Umkämpftes Ja zur Bibelwissenschaft. Kremer, Jacob. *Stimm Zeit* 211:75-94 F 1993

BIBLE—THEOLOGY—METHODOLOGY

Our adversaries are not simpleminded: people need best in biblical scholarship to meet challenge [editorial]. White, Leland J, ed. *Bib Th Bul* 23:2-3 Spr 1993

BIBLE—TRANSLATING

Splitting the faithful: inclusive language is wrong biblically, pastorally, and doctrinally. Sokolwski, Robert, 1934-. *Crisis* 11:24-27 Mr 1993

What King James has to say about the new lectionary [editorial]. Callam, Daniel. *Can Cath Rev* 11:2-3 Mr 1993

"The words are the messengers, the Word is the message": text and translation. Organ, Barbara E. *Can Cath Rev* 11:9-17 Mr 1993

BIBLE—USE

How to own your own Bible. Costello, Andrew. *USCath* 58:41-43 My 1993

BIBLE—VERSIONS

Finland's best-seller. *Tablet* 247:242 F 20 1993

BIBLE—VERSIONS, ENGLISH

Black Bible chronicles: book one: from Genesis to the promised land. New York: African American Family Press, 1993. 190p ISBN 1-56977-000-x LC 93-071549

Let's go to the text: the Gospel without sex. Schroth, Raymond A, 1933-. *Comm* 120:6-7 Ag 13 1993

What King James has to say about the new lectionary [editorial]. Callam, Daniel. *Can Cath Rev* 11:2-3 Mr 1993

BIBLE—VERSIONS, GREEK

The New Testament is in Greek: a short course for exegetes. Countryman, L William. Grand Rapids: Eerdmans, 1993. 205p ISBN 0-8028-0665-1

BIBLE—VERSIONS, JEWISH

"A final word" [replay to Boadt, L; N 1991]. Fisher, Eugene J. *New Theol Rev* 6:87-89 F 1993

BIBLE—VERSIONS, LATIN VULGATE

Journeying with Jerome. Glavich, Kathleen. *ReligTJ* 27:52-53 S 1993

BIBLE—VERSIONS, SPANISH

Biblia de San Vicente convento de San Esteban: Salamanca. Espinel, J Luis. *Cien Tom* 119:521-548 S-D 1992

Biblia del peregrino: vol 1: tento de la Biblia; vol 2; notas exegeticas. Schokel, Luis Alonso. Bilbao: Ege-Mensajero, 1993. x, 2700p ISBN 84-7726-074-5

BIBLE (NT)—BIOGRAPHIES

Who's who in the New Testament. Brownrigg, Ronald. New York: Oxford University Press, 1993. x, 286p ISBN 0-19-521031-x

BIBLE (NT)—CANON

"All who walk by this rule" the canon of the New Testament. Plevnik, Joseph. *Can Cath Rev* 11:12-20 F 1993

BIBLE (NT)—COMMENTARIES

New Testament commentary survey. Carson, D A. Grand Rapids: Baker Book House, 1993. 92p ISBN 0-80102-579-6 LC 93-12051

BIBLE (NT)—CRITICISM, FORM

Life-of-Jesus research and the eclipse of mythology. Evans, Craig A, 1952-. *TheolStds* 54:3-36 Mr 1993

BIBLE (NT)—CRITICISM, INTERPRETATION

The banality of unbelief [excerpt fr *Washington City paper*]. Allen, Charlotte. *Crisis* 11:30-35 Mr 1993

Calvin's New Testament commentaries. Parker, T H L. Louisville: John Knox, 1993. x, 256p ISBN 0-664-25489-6

The future of Christology: essays in honor of Leander E Keck. Malherbe, Abraham J, and Meeks, Wayne A, eds. Minneapolis: Fortress Press, 1993. x, 265p ISBN 0-80062-728-8 LC 92-40265

The Gospels: a source for morality. McIlhone, James P. *BibleT* 31:277-282 S 1993

Incarnation: contemporary writers on the New Testament. Corn, Alfred, ed. New York: Penguin Books, 1991. x, 361p ISBN 0-14011-583-8 LC 90-21991

Introduction to New Testament exegesis. Stenger, Werner. Grand Rapids: Eerdmans, 1993. 240p ISBN 0-8028-0138-2

Journey in dust and light: a modern pilgrimage through the life and letters of Paul. DeMers, John. Minnesota: The Liturgical Press, 1993. x, 112p ISBN 0-8146-5701-x LC 92-40482

Métodos exegéticos en el estudio actual del Nuevo Testamento. Caba, José. *Gregorianum* 73 No 4:611-669 1992

The New Testament world: insights from cultural anthropology. Malina, Bruce J, 1933-. Louisville, Kentucky: John Knox Press, 1993. 224p ISBN 0-664-25456-x

Les Thessaloniciens étaient-ils des paresseux? Romaniuk, Kazimierz. *Eph Theol Lovan* 69:142-144 Ap 1993

BIBLE (NT)—CRITICISM, INTERPRETATION—HISTORY
Life-of-Jesus research and the eclipse of mythology. Evans, Craig A, 1952-. *TheolStds* 54:3-36 Mr 1993

Time travel to ancient Judea. Malina, Bruce J, 1933-. Louisville: Westminster, 1993. x, 208p ISBN 0-664-25457-8

BIBLE (NT)—CRITICISM, TEXTUAL
The major summaries in Acts. Co, Maria Anicia. *Eph Theol Lovan* 78:49-85 Ap 1992

BIBLE (NT)—LANGUAGE, STYLE
The New Testament is in Greek: a short course for exegetes. Countryman, L William. Grand Rapids: Eerdmans, 1993. 205p ISBN 0-8028-0665-1

BIBLE (NT)—POETRY *see* Greek Poetry

BIBLE (NT)—QUOTATIONS FROM OLD TESTAMENT
"In fulfilment of Scripture": Old Testament citations in the New Testament. Duggan, Michael. *Can Cath Rev* 11:5-13 Ap 1993

BIBLE (NT)—RELATION TO OLD TESTAMENT
Beyond the literal sense: the interpretation of Scripture in the Catechism of the Catholic Church. Jensen, Joseph. *Living Light* 29:50-60 Sum 1993

Studying the scriptures. *Liturgy* 10:9-21 Sum 1992

BIBLE (NT)—STUDY
La Biblia Judia y la Biblia Cristiana. Trebolle Barrera, Julio. Madrid: Trotta, 1993. x, 670p ISBN 84-87699-55-3

Métodos exegéticos en el estudio actual del Nuevo Testamento. Caba, José. *Gregorianum* 73 No 4:611-669 1992

BIBLE (NT)—THEOLOGY
"All who walk by this rule" the canon of the New Testament. Plevnik, Joseph. *Can Cath Rev* 11:12-20 F 1993

Conversion. Clark, Michael. *Spir Life* 39:6-10 Spr 1993

Evangelisation and the ghost of Lessing. Turner, Geoffrey. *Month* 25:473-478 D 1992

Jesus, Savior. Kilgallen, John J. *StudiaM* 42:41-65 1993

Los espíritus maléficos en los escritos del Nuevo Testamento. García Cordero, Maximiliano. *Cien Tom* 119:209-249 My-Ag 1992

The ministry of women in the early Church. Gillman, Florence Morgan. *New Theol Rev* 6:89-94 My 1993

New Testament study and ministry of the word. Harrington, Daniel J. *Chicago Stud* 31:117-129 Ag 1992

Reflections on charisma (ta) in the New Testament. Kilgallen, John J. *StudiaM* 41:289-323 1992

The Resurrection, the Church and the Bible. Moore, John C, 1933-. *America* 168:14 Ap 10 1993

A theology of the New Testament. Ladd, George Eldon. Grand Rapids: Eerdmans, 1993. 740p ISBN 0-8028-0680-5

BIBLE (NT)—TRANSLATING
A conversation with scripture scholar Myles M Bourke [interview by T H Stahel, 1938-]. Bourke, Myles M. *America* 168:4-9 Ap 17 1993

Jews or Judeans: a translation challenge. Pilch, John Joseph, 1936-. *Mod Lit* 20:19 Ap 1993

BIBLE (NT)—VERSIONS, ENGLISH
The Bible for today's family. Nashville: American Bible Society, 1991. x, 758p ISBN

A conversation with scripture scholar Myles M Bourke [interview by T H Stahel, 1938-]. Bourke, Myles M. *America* 168:4-9 Ap 17 1993

The message: the New Testament in contemporary English. Peterson, Eugene H. Colorado Springs: NavPress, 1993. 544p ISBN 0-08910-9787 LC 92-63203

BIBLE (NT)—VERSIONS, GREEK
The major summaries in Acts. Co, Maria Anicia. *Eph Theol Lovan* 78:49-85 Ap 1992

BIBLE (NT)- ACTS
Barnabas. Martin, George. *Liguorian* 81:44-45 O 1993

BIBLE (NT)- ACTS—COMMENTARIES
The background of the Apostolic Decree. Callan, Terrance. *CBQ* 55:284-297 Ap 1993

BIBLE (NT)- ACTS—CRITICISM, INTERPRETATION
Acts: a writer's reflections on the church, writing, and his own acts. Woiwode, Larry. San Francisco: HarperSanFrancisco, 1993. 244p ISBN 0-06069-404-1 LC 92-52503

Discussions sur la chronologie paulinienne. Rolland, Philippe. *NRT* 114:870-889 N-D 1992

Luke and Acts. O'Collins, Gerald, 1931-, and Marconi, Gilberto, eds. New York: Paulist Press, 1993. x, 295p ISBN 0-8091-3360-1 LC 92-35226

The major summaries in Acts. Co, Maria Anicia. *Eph Theol Lovan* 78:49-85 Ap 1992

BIBLE (NT)- ACTS—THEOLOGY
Discussions sur la chronologie paulinienne. Rolland, Philippe. *NRT* 114:870-889 N-D 1992

Witnesses. Martin, George. *New Cov* 22:34 F 1993

BIBLE (NT)- ACTS 1-5
The major summaries in Acts. Co, Maria Anicia. *Eph Theol Lovan* 78:49-85 Ap 1992

BIBLE (NT)- ACTS 6-12
The Ethiopian eunuch and his bible: a social-science analysis. Spencer, F Scott. *Bib Th Bul* 22:155-165 Wint 1992

BIBLE (NT)- COLOSSIANS
Clothe yourselves. Martin, George. *New Cov* 22:34 My 1993

BIBLE (NT)- COLOSSIANS—CRITICISM, FORM
The neglected parallelism in Colossians 1, 24-25. Cahill, Michael. *Eph Theol Lovan* 78:142-147 Ap 1992

BIBLE (NT)- COLOSSIANS—THEOLOGY
The neglected parallelism in Colossians 1, 24-25. Cahill, Michael. *Eph Theol Lovan* 78:142-147 Ap 1992

BIBLE (NT)- CORINTHIANS
The concept of charism in Paul. Nardoni, Enrique. *CBQ* 55:68-80 Ja 1993

BIBLE (NT)- CORINTHIANS I 11-14
"The words are the messengers, the Word is the message": text and translation. Organ, Barbara E. *Can Cath Rev* 11:9-17 Mr 1993

BIBLE (NT)- EPHESIANS
Don't bully people with the Bible. Hoppe, Leslie J. *USCath* 58:16-21 S 1993

BIBLE (NT)- EPHESIANS 4-6
Woman church. Shaw, Russell. *Crisis* 11:8-9 Ja 1993

A word on Humanae vitae [fr *New Ilucidations* tr by M T Skerry]. Balthasar, Hans Urs Von, 1905-1988. *Communio* 20:437-450 Sum 1993

BIBLE (NT)- EPISTLES
The birth of the New Testament: the origin and development of the first Christian generation. Collins, Raymond F. New York: Crossroad, 1993. x, 324p ISBN 0-8245-1276-6 LC 93-16647

Controversy and continuity in Romans 1:18-3:20. Tobin, Thomas H. *CBQ* 55:298-318 Ap 1993

The liberation of creation. Sepulveda, Juan. *LADOC* 23:23-27 My-Je 1993

Pelagius on St Paul's Epistle to the Romans. Bruyn, Theodore de, ed. New York: Oxford University Press, 1993. x, 248p ISBN 0-814399-0

Sin and salvation in Romans. Getty, Mary Ann. *BibleT* 31:89-93 Mr 1993

Les Thessaloniciens étaient-ils des paresseux? Romaniuk, Kazimierz. *Eph Theol Lovan* 69:142-144 Ap 1993

BIBLE (NT)- EPISTLES OF PAUL
According to Paul: studies in the theology of the Apostle. Fitzmyer, Joseph Augustine, 1920-. New York: Paulist, 1993. x, 177p ISBN 08-0913-390-3 LC 93-20453

Christian anti-Semitism and Paul's theology. Hall, Sidney G, III. Minneapolis: Fortress, 1993. x, 191p ISBN 0-8006-2654-0 LC 92-30395

The concept of charism in Paul. Nardoni, Enrique. *CBQ* 55:68-80 Ja 1993

The letters of Paul: an introduction. Puskas, Charles B. Collegeville:Liturgical, 1993. x, 216p ISBN 0-8146-5690-0 LC 92-46909

Paul. Martin, George. *Liguorian* 81:56-57 D 1993

Pelagius on St Paul's Epistle to the Romans. Bruyn, Theodore de, ed. New York: Oxford University Press, 1993. x, 248p ISBN 0-814399-0

Postcards from the edge: how Paul dragged Christianity into the first century. Bowe, Barbara E. *USCath* 58:6-13 Ag 1993

Textlinguistics and the integrity of Philippians. Koperski, Veronica. *Eph Theol Lovan* 78:330-367 D 1992

BIBLE (NT)- GALATIANS—CRITICISM, INTERPRETATION
Galatians without tears. Dalton, William J. Collegeville, Minnesota: The Liturgical Press, 1992. 75p ISBN 0-8146-2227-5 LC 93-18782

BIBLE (NT)- GOSPELS
The Alba House Gospels: so you may believe. Wauck, Mark A. New York: Society of St Paul, 1992. x, 92p ISBN 0-8189-0625-1 LC 91-40303

The Christ of faith. Garvey, John, 1944-. *Comm* 120:7-8 Ja 29 1993

Editions of the book of Gospels in English. McManus, Frederick R. *Notitiae* 28:352-356 My 1992

"In fulfilment of Scripture": Old Testament citations in the New Testament. Duggan, Michael. *Can Cath Rev* 11:5-13 Ap 1993

BIBLE (NT)- GOSPELS—COMMENTARIES
Journey with the Fathers: commentaries on the Sunday gospels, Year A. Barnecot, Edith, ed. New Rochelle, New York: New City Press, 1992. 168p ISBN 1-56548-013-9 LC 92-20685

Journey with the Fathers; commentaries on the Sunday gospels, Year B. Barnecut, Edith, ed. New Rochelle: New City Press, 1993. 160p ISBN 1-56548-056-2 LC 92-20685

Paralysis of the heart. McMahon, Michael. *BibleT* 31:85-88 Mr 1993

The prehistory of the Griesbach hypothesis. Lang, Marijke Hélène de. *Eph Theol Lovan* 69:134-139 Ap 1993

Within the outlines of some ancient model. Roth, Wolfgang. *BibleT* 31:103-109 Mr 1993

BIBLE (NT)- GOSPELS—CRITICISM, INTERPRETATION
Jesus ou os pobres? Konings, Johan. *Perspectiva* 25:149-161 My-Ag 1993

Pain and polemic: anti-Judaism in the gospels. Smiga, George M. New Jersey: Paulist Press, 1992. x, 210p ISBN 0-8091-3355-5 LC 92-20044

Presence or absence? the question of women disciples at the Last Supper. Lee, Dorothy A. *Pacifica* 6:1-20 F 1993

Reading the Easter gospels. Swain, Lionel. Collegeville, Minnesota: The Liturgical Press, 1993. 131p ISBN 0-81465-699-4 LC 92-40432

Who do you say that I am? Civba, Edward J. New York: Alba House, 1993. 150p ISBN 0-8189-0638-3 LC 92-37734

BIBLE (NT)- GOSPELS—CRITICISM, SOURCE
The four Gospels 1992. Tuckett, C M. *Eph Theol Lovan* 78:385-396 D 1992

BIBLE (NT)- GOSPELS—PARALLELS
The four Gospels 1992. Tuckett, C M. *Eph Theol Lovan* 78:385-396 D 1992

Outsiders in the Gospels: marginality as a source of knowledge. Kopas, Jane. *Way* 33:117-126 Ap 1993

The prehistory of the Griesbach hypothesis. Lang, Marijke Hélène de. *Eph Theol Lovan* 69:134-139 Ap 1993

BIBLE (NT)- GOSPELS—THEOLOGY
The four Gospels 1992. Tuckett, C M. *Eph Theol Lovan* 78:385-396 D 1992

The prehistory of the Griesbach hypothesis. Lang, Marijke Hélène de. *Eph Theol Lovan* 69:134-139 Ap 1993

BIBLE (NT)- GOSPELS—WOMEN
The feminism of Jesus—women in the gospel [excerpt fr *Accion*]. Munárriz, Jose Miguel. *LADOC* 23:18-23 Jl-Ag 1993

BIBLE (NT)- HEBREWS
The use of rpéreiv and rhetorical propriety in Hebrews 2:10. Mitchell, Alan C. *CBQ* 54:681-701 O 1992

BIBLE (NT)- HEBREWS—AUTHORSHIP
Discursive structure and the unseen Hebrews 2:8 and 11:1: a neglected aspect of the context. Brawley, Robert L. *CBQ* 55:81-98 Ja 1993

BIBLE (NT)- HEBREWS—THEOLOGY
Discursive structure and the unseen Hebrews 2:8 and 11:1: a neglected aspect of the context. Brawley, Robert L. *CBQ* 55:81-98 Ja 1993

Misereor super turbas. Sobrino, John. *Christus* 58:36-38 F 1993

BIBLE (NT)- HEBREWS 10-13
Discoursive structure and the unseen Hebrews 2:8 and 11:1: a neglected aspect of the context. Brawley, Robert L. *CBQ* 55:81-98 Ja 1993

BIBLE (NT)- JAMES—CRITICISM, INTERPRETATION
The Epistle of James for Jews and Christians. McDade, John. *Month* 26: 115-120 Mr 1993
The epistle of James in rhetorical and social scientific perspective holiness-wholeness and patterns of replication. Elliott, John H. *Bib Th Bul* 23:71-81 Sum 1993

BIBLE (NT)- JOHN
The birth of the church: meditations of John 18-21. Speyr, Adrienne von, 1902-1967. San Francisco: Ignatius Press, 1991. 443p ISBN 0-89870-368-9 LC 90-85550
Jesus meets Nicodemus and the Samaritan woman. Stravinskas, Peter. *Register* 69:1+ Mr 7 1993
The promise of Easter. Wallace, James A, 1944-. *Liguorian* 81:4-7 Ap 1993
Understanding the fourth gospel. Ashton, John. New York: Oxford University Press, 1991. x, 599p ISBN 0-19-826353-8 LC 90-43422

BIBLE (NT)- JOHN—COMMENTARIES
The Gospel according to John: a literary and theological commentary. Brodia, Thomas L. New York: Oxford University, 1993. x, 625p ISBN 0-19-505800-3 LC 91-38200
A gospel guide to the season. Stravinskas, Peter. *Register* 69:1+ F 21 1993
The Gospel of John as good news. Kozar, Joseph Vicek. *Catechist* 26:44-50 F 1993
John, the maverick gospel. Kysar, Robert. Louisville: John Knox, 1993. x, 176p ISBN 0-664-25401-2
John, theologian and poet, traces the signs of Christ's divine identity. Stravinskas, Peter. *Register* 69:1+ F 28 1993
Mystical Christianity: a psychological commentary on the Gospel of John. Sanford, John A. New York: Crossroad, 1993. x, 350p ISBN 0-82451-230-8 LC 92-35577
Seeing the light a narrative reading of John 9 [part one]. Holleran, Warren J. *Eph Theol Lovan* 69:5-26 Ap 1993
When we witness Christ's glory, we share His divine life. Stravinskas, Peter. *Register* 69:5 Ap 11 1993

BIBLE (NT)- JOHN—THEOLOGY
The last gospel [condensed fr *Catholic Update* 1992]. Smith, Virginia. *CDgst* 57:137-142 My 1993
Seeing the light a narrative reading of John 9 [part one]. Holleran, Warren J. *Eph Theol Lovan* 69:5-26 Ap 1993
What is John 17 saying to the churches? [exc fr *Liturgy: practicing ecumenism*]. Sloyan, Gerard S. *Liturgy* 10:16-18 Spr 1993
Worship in spirit and in truth. Geraghty, Denis. *New Blckfrs* 74:292-306 Je 1993

BIBLE (NT)- JOHN—THEOLOGY—CHRISTOLOGY
"I have come to bring division". Schall, James Vincent, 1928-. *OR(Eng)* 1301:8-10 Jl 28 1993
Image de Dieu, image de l'homme. Renwart, Léon. *NRT* 115:85-104 Ja-F 1993
John Paul II, Pope, (1993-08-10) Truth [Orig in English]. John Paul II, Pope, 1920- (Karol Wojtyla) (elected 1978). *OR(Eng)* 1303:4 Ag 18 1993*
Möglichkeiten und Grenzen einer Christologie, von unten. Kaiser, Alfred, 1872-1917. Munster: Aschendorff, 1992. x, 334p ISBN 3-402-03161-2

BIBLE (NT)- JOHN 5-12
How saints are relevant. Kreeft, Peter John, 1937-. *New Cov* 22:33 Je 1993
Jesus ou os pobres? Konings, Johan. *Perspectiva* 25:149-161 My-Ag 1993
Seeing the light a narrative reading of John 9 [part one]. Holleran, Warren J. *Eph Theol Lovan* 69:5-26 Ap 1993

BIBLE (NT)- JOHN 1
Dancing Sophia: Rahner's theology of symbols. Clasby, Nancy. *Relig Lit* 25:51-65 Spr 1993

BIBLE (NT)- JOHN 13-21
Hermitage, a metaphor of life. O'Hea, Eileen P. *RRel* 52:503-506 Jl-Ag 1993

BIBLE (NT)- JUDE
Literary statgey in the Epistle of Jude. Daryl, Charles J. Scranton: University of Scranton Press, 1993. 258p ISBN 0-94086-616-1 LC 91-66129

BIBLE (NT)- LUKE
The Annunciation: pivotal moment of history. Yarnold, Edward John, 1926-. *Month* 26:237-239 Je 1993
The ethics of Luke [photos]. Reid, Barbara E. *BibleT* 31:283-291 S 1993
The Gospel of Luke as good news. Kozar, Joseph Vicek. *Catechist* 26:44-49 Ja 1993
Jesus. Martin, George. *Liguorian* 81:44-45 Ap 1993
Mary. Martin, George. *Liguorian* 81:44-45 Jl 1993

BIBLE (NT)- LUKE—CRITICISM, INTERPRETATION
Lucan reflections on aging. Jegen, Carol Frances. *BibleT* 30:335-340 N 1992
Luke and Acts. O'Collins, Gerald, 1931-, and Marconi, Gilberto, eds. New York: Paulist Press, 1993. x, 295p ISBN 0-8091-3360-1 LC 92-35226
The man who was Luke the evangelist. Jefford, Clayton N. *Priest* 49:43-46 O 1993
The ongoing feast: table fellowship and eschatology. Just, Arthur A., Jr. Collegeville: Liturgical, 1993. x, 307p ISBN 0-8146-6013-4 LC 93-595
Les premières Editions de Luc II: l'histoire du texte au IIe siècle. Amphoux, Christian-B. *Eph Theol Lovan* 78:38-48 Ap 1992

BIBLE (NT)- LUKE—THEOLOGY
Exorcismo, evangelização e reino nos escritos Lucanos. Casalegno, Alberto. *Perspectiva* 25:63-76 Ja-Ap 1993

BIBLE (NT)- LUKE-ACTS
In the midst of the highest Christian feast. McDarby, Patrick. *Sisters* 65:206-208 My 1993
Disclosure at Emmaus. Roth, Wolfgang. *BibleT* 31:46-51 Ja 1993

BIBLE (NT)- LUKE 1-4
The Magnificat Mary's canticle of praise. Muckerman, Norman James, 1917-. *Liguorian* 81:4-8 My 1993

BIBLE (NT)- LUKE 10-18
Prayer as relationship. Rohr, Richard, 1943-, and Martos, Joseph. *Living Prayer* 26:28-31 N-D 1993
Prodigal Father. Vanek, Elizabeth-Anne. *Emmanuel* 99:96-100 Mr 1993
Remembering and revelation: a liturgical reflection on Luke 16:19-31. Flanagan, Anne Joan. *Emmanuel* 99:304-307 Jl-Ag 1993

BIBLE (NT)- LUKE 22-24
The Eucharist and the mission of the priest. Schineller, Peter. *Emmanual* 49:364-369 S 1993
Remember me. Martin, George. *New Cov* 22:34 Ap 1993

BIBLE (NT)- MARK
The blind beggar of Jericho [2 parts]. LaVerdiere, Eugene Armand, 1936-. *Emmanuel* 99:86-89+ Mr; 158-166 Ap 1993
Jesus' entry into Jerusalem. LaVerdiere, Eugene Armand, 1936-. *Emmanuel* 99:270-276 Je 1993
The prehistory of the Griesbach hypothesis. Lang, Marijke Hélène de. *Eph Theol Lovan* 69:134-139 Ap 1993
The social location of the Marcan audience. Rohrbaugh, Richard L. *Bib Th Bul* 23:114-127 Aut 1993

BIBLE (NT)- MARK—CRITICISM, INTERPRETATION
'Hiiopei ou 'Eiioiei en mc 6, 20? Romaniuk, Kazimierz. *Eph Theol Lovan* 69:140-141 Ap 1993
Jesus' Temple Act. Seeley, David. *CBQ* 55:262-283 Ap 1993
The persistent sower. Martin, George. *New Cov* 23:34 N 1993
Il Vangelo di Marco: un annuncio di salvezza nel mondo pagano. Riva, Raimondo. *StudiaM* 42:19-40 1993

BIBLE (NT)- MARK—THEOLOGY
'Hiiopei ou 'Eiioiei en mc 6, 20? Romaniuk, Kazimierz. *Eph Theol Lovan* 69:140-141 Ap 1993

BIBLE (NT)- MARK—THEOLOGY—CRISTOLOGY
Jesus' Temple Act. Seeley, David. *CBQ* 55:262-283 Ap 1993

BIBLE (NT)- MARK 10-12
The cursing of the fig tree and the cleansing of the temple Mark 11:12-25. LaVerdiere, Eugene Armand, 1936-. *Emmanuel* 99:440-447 O 1993
Do I really have to sell all I have? Wojcicki, Ed. *USCath* 58:32-33 Je 1993
Hosanna in the highest!. LaVerdiere, Eugene Armand, 1936-. *Emmanuel* 99:322-329+ Jl-Ag 1993
Jesus' Temple Act. Seeley, David. *CBQ* 55:262-283 Ap 1993

BIBLE (NT)- MARK 14-15
Mark's tragic vision: Gethsemane. Ruprecht, Louis A, Jr. *Relig Lit* 24:1-25 Aut 1992

BIBLE (NT)- MARK 16
"The words are the messengers, the Word is the message": text and translation. Organ, Barbara E. *Can Cath Rev* 11:9-17 Mr 1993

BIBLE (NT)- MATTHEW
Agricultural imagery in the Gospel of Matthew and the gospel of truth. Cavallo, Jo Ann. *Relig Lit* 24:27-38 Aut 1992
The Church's handbook. Doohan, Leonard. *Mod Lit* 20:34-35 Je-Jl 1993
Discipleship in Matthew. Doohan, Leonard. *Mod Lit* 20:36 Ag 1993
Home by another way. Temple, Katharine. *Cath Work* 60:1+ Ja-F 1993
The household: a major social component for gender analysis in the gospel of Matthew. Love, Stuart L. *Bib Th Bul* 23:21-31 Spr 1993
Matthew as a Jewish book. Harrington, Daniel J. *Priests & People* 7:240-244 Je 1993
The old news, the daily news, and the good news. Ridge, M D. *Past Mus* 17:26-30 D 1992-Ja 1993
One of the prophets: Matthew's testing narrative as a rite of passage. McVann, Mark. *Bib Th Bul* 23:14-20 Spr 1993
Parables and miracles. Doohan, Leonard. *Mod Lit* 20:34-35 My 1993
The prehistory of the Griesbach hypothesis. Lang, Marijke Hélène de. *Eph Theol Lovan* 69:134-139 Ap 1993
The second commandment in the New Testament: your yes is yes, your no is no. Carrón, Julián. *Communio* 20:5-25 Spr 1993
The storm-tossed Church. Doohan, Leonard. *Mod Lit* 20:40 Mr 1993
The year of Matthew. Doohan, Leonard. *Mod Lit* 19:31 D 1992-Ja 1993

BIBLE (NT)- MATTHEW—COMMENTARIES
The crowds in Matthew's Gospel. Carter, Warren. *CBQ* 55:54-67 Ja 1993
Delegitimation of leaders in Matthew 23. Saldarini, Anthony J. *CBQ* 54:659-680 O 1992
A gospel for a new people: studies in Matthew. Stanton, Graham N. Louisville, Kentucky: John Knox Press, 1993. 424p ISBN 0-664-25499-3
Reading Matthew: a literary and theological commentary on the first Gospel. Garland, David E. New York: The Crossroad Publishing Company, 1993. x, 269p ISBN 0-8245-1275-8 LC 92-38424

BIBLE (NT)- MATTHEW—CRITICISM, LITERARY
The crowds in Matthew's Gospel. Carter, Warren. *CBQ* 55:54-67 Ja 1993

BIBLE (NT)- MATTHEW—THEOLOGY
L'Antigiudaismo nel vangelo di Matteo come problema storico e teologico: uno schizzo. Luz, Ulrich. *Gregorianum* 74 no 3:425-445 1993
The Easter presence. Doohan, Leonard. *Mod Lit* 20:36 Ap 1993
Matthew as a Christian Gospel. Harrington, Daniel J. *Priests & People* 7:284-288 Jl 1993

BIBLE (NT)- MATTHEW 5-7
The Epistle of James for Jews and Christians. McDade, John. *Month* 26:115-120 Mr 1993
In pursuit of holiness. Doohan, Leonard. *Mod Lit* 20:30 F 1993

BIBLE (NT)- MATTHEW 8-10
Sharing the Lord's mission. Doohan, Leonard. *Mod Lit* 20:34-35 S 1993

BIBLE (NT)- MATTHEW 14-17
Qui dis-tu que je suis? (Mt 16, 15). Lecuit, Jean. *Lumen* 48:304-314 S 1993

BIBLE (NT)- MATTHEW 18-25
God's compassion. Martin, George. *New Cov* 22:38 Ja 1993
Investments in the future. Ryan, Patrick J. *America* 169:30-31 N 6 1993
Life-changing verses. Kreeft, Peter John, 1937-. *New Cov* 22:19+ My 1993

BIBLE (NT)- MATTHEW 26-28
The confession of the soldiers in Matthew 27:54. Sim, David C. *Heythrop* 34:401-424 O 1993
Go therefore and make disciples. Doohan, Leonard. *Mod Lit* 20:34-35 O 1993

BIOETHICS
Der Bauplan des Menschen. Reiter, Johannes. *Stimm Zeit* 211:219-231 Ap 1993
A bioethics roundup. Gula, Richard M. *Priest* 49:35-40 Je 1993
Chi E Persona? Persona umana e bioetica. *Civilta* 143:547-559 D 19 1992
Genomanalysen im Versicherungs- und Gerichtswesen. Münk, Hans J. *Stimm Zeit* 211:34-44 Ja 1993
Health care for all: a Catholic perspective. Hehir, J Bryan, 1940-. *Comm* 120:7-9 My 7 1993
It's easier to clone embryo than to figure consequences. Shannon, Thomas A. *Nat Cath Rep* 30:19 N 12 1993
Joseph Fletcher: memoir of an ex-radical: reminiscence and reappraisal. Fletcher, Joseph. Louisville: John Knox, 1993. x, 96p ISBN 0-664-25372-5
Moral theology 2000: four signs and shifts. McCormick, Patrick. *ChrWorld* 236:212-216 S-O 1993
La notion de qualité de la vie dans le champ dela santé. Lamau, Marie-Louise. *MSR* 50:135-150 Ap-Je 1993
Patents encroach upon the body. Kimbrell, Andrew. *Crisis* 11:43-48 My 1993

BIOGRAPHY
Fitting testaments. Coren, Michael. *Can Cath Rev* 11:4-6 F 1993
The legacy of a life well served. Costello, Gerald M, 1931-. *USCath* 58:48-51 N 1993
Saint Evelyn Waugh. McInerny, Ralph M. *Crisis* 10:2-3 N 1992
Witnesses to the tradition: giving flesh to doctrine. Marthaler, Berard L, 1927-. *Living Light* 29:61-70 Sum 1993

BIOMEDICAL ENGINEERING- GERMANY
Der Bauplan des Menschen. Reiter, Johannes. *Stimm Zeit* 211:219-231 Ap 1993

BIOMEDICAL RESEARCH—ETHICAL ASPECTS
John Paul II, Pope, (1993-05-07) Science [Orig in Italian]. John Paul II, Pope, 1920- (Karol Wojtyla) (elected 1978). *OR(Eng)* 1296:14 Je 23 1993*

BIOTECHNOLOGY
Biotechnology and the nature of life. Atwater, Tim. *Cath Work* 60:1+ Ja-F 1993
The priests of cyborg. Reynolds, Peter C, 1943-. *Month* 26:257-266 Jl 1993

BIRT, JOHN, 1944-
Kill or cur at the BBC [editorial]. *Tablet* 247:935-936 Jl 24 1993

BIRTH CONTROL
The adventure of sacramental love. Delaney, Mary Cris. *Crisis* 11:52-53 S 1993
Are contraception and artificial procreation sometimes permissible. Doran, Joseph L. *HPR* 93:48-57 Mr 1993
Beijing and PP affiliate colluding. Meehan, Bridget Mary. *Register* 69:1+ Mr 21 1993
The blessing of children. Mangan, Charles M. *Register* 69:4 Mr 28 1993
The church, population and the environment. Coote, Nicholas. *Priests & People* 7:340-345 Ag-S 1993
The connection between contraception and abortion. Smith, Janet E. *HPR* 93:10-18 Ap 1993
Contraception and the war within the self. DeMarco, Donald. *HPR* 93:29-31+ My 1993
Contraception not banned as a defence against rape. *Tablet* 247:955 Jl 24 1993
The existential isolation of contraception. Klaus, Hanna. *Linacre* 59:29-32 N 1992
Humanae Vitae, +25 [editorial]. *Register* 69:4 Je 13 1993
Impaled upon the horns of faith and reason. Howard, George S. *America* 168:12-15 Mr 6 1993
Inside the commission. Marshall, John. *Tablet* 247:938-939 Jl 24 1993
Minister to raise birth control issue with Vatican. *Tablet* 247:960 Jl 24 1993
My two cents' worth [editorial]. Callam, Daniel. *Can Cath Rev* 11:2-4 N 1993
Natural family planning and family systems theory. Shivanandan, Mary, and Geremia, Marion. *Linacre* 59:57-66 N 1992
Norplant. Hilgers, Thomas W. *Linacre* 60:64-69 F 1993
The prayer of Lady Macbeth: how the contraceptive mentality has neutered religious life. Mankowski, Paul V. *F & R* 19:79-93 Spr 1993
Reaction to the Supreme Court judgement [statement issued Ap 2 1992]. *Doctr Life* 42:346-347 My-Je 1992
Second thoughts on the population bomb. Toolan, David S. *America* 168:16-17 Mr 6 1993
Symposium on the twentieth anniversary of Encyclical Humanae. Smith, Russell, E, ed. Braintree, Massachusetts: The Pope John Center, 1991. x, 384p ISBN 0-935372-30-x LC 91-20331
True meaning of marriage. Marshall, John. *Tablet* 247:1122+ S 4 1993
Who decides how many are too many? Shaw, Russell. *Columbia* 73:5 Jl 1993

BIRTH CONTROL—PAPAL TEACHING
Catholic couples have learned their faith by heart [editorial]. Burns, Robert E, 1924-. *USCath* 58:2 O 1993
Contraception a baby among church's sins [commentary *Veritatis Splendor*]. Greeley, Andrew Moran, 1928-. *Nat Cath Rep* 29:18-21 O 15 1993*
A couple's pilgrimage to Humanae Vitae (commentary: *Humanae Vitae*). Cummings, Richard G, and Cummings, Maureen A. *OSV* 82:10-11 Jl 25 1993*
Encyclical insists intercourse is language of love (commentary: *Humanae Vitae*). Hebblethwaite, Peter, 1930-. *Nat Cath Rep* 29:15-16 Jl 16 1993
Encyclical left church credibility stillborn (commentary: *Humanae Vitae*). Curran, Charles E, 1934-. *Nat Cath Rep* 29:14-15 Jl 16 1993*
An experience of marriage. Smith, Ann. *Tablet* 247:1090 Ag 28 1993
From dissent to acceptance: realizing the full riches of Humanae Vitae. May, William E. *HPR* 94:17-24 N 1993*
Humanae Vitae at 25. Krause, Edward. *Register* 69:5 Mr 28 1993
Humanae Vitae revisited [commentary Humanae Vitae]. Mannion, M Francis. *OSV* 82:19 Ag 1 1993
"Humanae Vitae" 25 years later. McCormick, Richard Arthur, 1922-. *America* 169:6-8+ Jl 17-24 1993
"Humanae Vitae" after 25 years. Schall, James Vincent, 1928-. *Crisis* 11:48-49 Jl-Ag 1993
"Humanae Vitae" and the crisis of dissent. Dulles, Avery Robert, 1918-. *Origins* 22:774-777 Ap 22 1993*

"Humanae Vitae" at 25. Duffy, Shatzi Luisa. *Crisis* 11:15-17 S 1993
"Humanae Vitae": 25th anniversary. McMahon, Kevin. *Origins* 22:768-774 Ap 22 1993*
"Humanae Vitae": the "prophetic" encyclical (commentary: *Humanae Vitae*). Shaw, Russell. *OSV* 82:5 Jl 25 1993*
Humanae Vitae, +25 [commentary]. Dudro, Vivian. *Register* 69:2 My 30 1993
Paul VI was right [reply to "Humanae Vitae" 25 years later by R A McCormick 6-8+ Jl 17 1993; rejoinder]. Flannery, Kevin L, and Koterski, Joseph. *America* 169:7-14 S 25 1993
Reconsidering Humanae Vitae [commentary *Humanae Vitae*]. Balsam, Charles. *Register* 69:5 Ag 1 1993
Reflections on Humanae Vitae's 25th anniversary. Albacete, Lorenzo. *F & R* 19:5-23 Spr 1993
A stumbling-block for many [editorial]. *Tablet* 247:935 Jl 24 1993
Twenty-five years later (commentary: *Humanae Vitae*). *OSV* 82:2 Jl 25 1993
We might all be better off if Paul VI had said nothing (commentary: *Humanae Vitae*). Blackburn, Thomas E. *Nat Cath Rep* 29:17 Jl 16 1993*
Contracepting Humanae Vitae. Shaw, Russell. *Columbia* 73:5 Je 1993*
Human sexuality in God's plan. *OR(Eng)* 1301:3-4 Jl 28 1993
In the heartland, Catholic sexuality celebrated [commentary Humanae Vitae]. Carey, Ann. *OSV* 82:3 Ag 15 1993*
A prophetic document. Daily, Thomas V, Bp., 1927-. *Columbia* 73:6-8 Ag 1993*

BIRTH CONTROL CLINICS—UTILIZATION
CARE for a contraceptive, lady? Sobo, Elizabeth. *Register* 69:2 Mr 21 1993

BIRTH DEFECTS *see* Abnormalities, Human

BIRTH RATE
Population, the Church and the Pope. Schwarz, John C. *America* 168:6-10 Mr 6 1993

BIRTH RATE- EUROPE
Natalità e politiche per la popolazione in Europa. Salvini, Gianpaolo. *Civilta* 144:140-152 Ja 16 1993

BIRTHRIGHT (ORGANIZATION)
Need birthright? call 1-800-LOVE. Jeray, Diane. *Liguorian* 81:26-29 Ja 1993

BISHOP, CLAIRE, -1993
Bishop, Claire, -1993 [obit]. Skillin, Edward S. *Comm* 120:4 Ap 9 1993

BISHOPS
Bishops' Bosnia statement stirs DC waters. Clancy, Paul. *Nat Cath Rep* 29:8 My 28 1993
The bishops' part. Hebblethwaite, Peter, 1930-. *Tablet* 247:609 My 15 1993
John Paul II, Pope, (1992-07-08) Bishops are successors to the Apostles. John Paul II, Pope, 1920- (Karol Wojtyla) (elected 1978). *TPS* 38:34-36 Ja-F 1993*
John Paul II, Pope, (1992-10-28) The apostolic mission of bishops. John Paul II, Pope, 1920- (Karol Wojtyla) (elected 1978). *TPS* 38:107-110 Mr-Ap 1993*
John Paul II, Pope, (1992-12-07) New Catechism is a gift to the Church. John Paul II, Pope, 1920- (Karol Wojtyla) (elected 1978). *TPS* 38:150-154 My-Je 1993*
John Paul II, Pope, (1993-08-04) Bishops [Orig in Italian]. John Paul II, Pope, 1920- (Karol Wojtyla) (elected 1978). *OR(Eng)* 1303:15 Ag 18 1993*
John Paul II, Pope, (1993-08-13) Bishops [Orig in Italian]. John Paul II, Pope, 1920- (Karol Wojtyla) (elected 1978). *Origins* 23:190-191 Ag 26 1993*
John Paul II, Pope, (1993-08-25) Obedience [Orig in Italian]. John Paul II, Pope, 1920- (Karol Wojtyla) (elected 1978). *OR(Eng)* 1305:7 S 1 1993*
John Paul II, Pope, (1993-10-04) Healing [Orig in English]. John Paul II, Pope, 1920- (Karol Wojtyla) (elected 1978). *OR(Eng)* 1311:5 O 13 1993*
"Ken, don't foul up the Church today" [photo]. Desmet, Kate. *Critic* 47:14-29 Spr 1993
"A life of mystery and adventure" Fulton Sheen's reflections on the priesthood. Fields, Kathleen Riley. *US Cath Hist* 11:63-82 Wint 1993
"Mutuae Relationes"—ten years later. Bonfils, Jean. *Con Life* 17 no 2:122-134 1992
The role of auxiliary bishops. Foster, Michael Smith. *Jurist* 51 no 2:423-430 1991
The study of Episcopal conferences: an application of the principle of functionality. Esselman, Thomas. *Jurist* 51 no 2:311-325 1991
Witnesses to the faith: community, infallibility, and the ordinary. Gaillardetz, Richard R. New Jersey: Paulist Press, 1992. x, 238p ISBN 0-8091-3350-4 LC 92-280431

BISHOPS—ELECTION
Papal legates and the appointment of bishops. Metz, René. *Jurist* 52 no 1:259-284 1992
Papal legates and the appointment of bishops. Metz, René. *Jurist* 52 no 1:259-284 1992
Response to René Metz. Corral, Carlos. *Jurist* 52 no 1:285-293 1992
Response to René Metz. Corral, Carlos. *Jurist* 52 no 1:285-293 1992
Troubling shooting [Swiss diocese]. Burke, Greg. *Register* 69:1+ Ap 11 1993

BISHOPS- AFRICA
African holds key to bishops' picks. Burke, Greg. *Register* 69:1+ Ag 22 1993

BISHOPS- AFRICA, NORTH
John Paul II, Pope, (1991-11-26) Allocutiones (Papal address to North African Bishops) [French]. John Paul II, Pope, 1920- (Karol Wojtyla) (elected 1978). *AAS* 84:1143-1147 D 5 1992*

BISHOPS- ALBANIA
Pope to re-establish Catholic hierarchy. *Tablet* 247:521 Ap 24 1993
The resurrection of a Church. *Tablet* 247:556 My 1 1993
Saints Paul and Andrew helped evangelize Albania. Dias, Ivan, Abp. *OR(Eng)* 1272:4 Ja 6 1993

BISHOPS- AUSTRALIA
John Paul II, (1993-10-09) Universality [Orig English]. John Paul II, Pope, 1920- (Karol Wojtyla) (elected 1978). *OR(Eng)* 1312:3 O 20 1993*

BISHOPS- BOLIVIA
Statement of the Bolivian Bishop's Conference. *LADOC* 24:13-15 N-D 1993

BISHOPS- BRAZIL
Converted by the people. *Tablet* 247:368 Mr 20 1993

BISHOPS- CANADA
Brief on native peoples. *Origins* 23:401+ N 18 1993
Canada bishops tackle free market fallout. Lefevere, Patricia. *Nat Cath Rep* 29:12 My 28 1993
Canadian bishops move vigorously on sex abuse problems. Fraze, Barb. *Nat Cath Rep* 29:3 Jl 2 1993
John Paul II, Pope, (1993-09-16) Church's teaching [Orig English, French]. John Paul II, Pope, 1920- (Karol Wojtyla) (elected 1978). *OR(Eng)* 1308:3 S 22 1993*
Our poor bishops [editorial]. Callam, Daniel. *Can Cath Rev* 11:2-3 Je 1993

BISHOPS- CUBA
A call for true dialogue. *Origins* 23:273-279 S 30 1993
The Church in Cuba risks Castro's wrath for sake of reform. Bermudez, Alejandro. *Register* 69:5 O 17 1993
Fidel, Cuban bishops square off. Burke, Greg. *Register* 69:1+ O 31 1993
Is the sun going down on Fidel Castro's Cuba? Holton, Robert. *OSV* 82:17 O 17 1993

BISHOPS- EL SALVADOR
Archbiship Oscar Romero: a shepherd's diary. Romero, Oscar Arnulfo, Abp. Cincinnati: St Anthony Messenger Press, 1993. 542p ISBN 0-86716-170-1

BISHOPS- EUROPE
John Paul II, Pope, (1991-11-28) Allocutiones (Opening address to European Synod of Bishops) [Italian]. John Paul II, Pope, 1920- (Karol Wojtyla) (elected 1978). *AAS* 84:1148-1151 D 5 1992*
John Paul II, Pope, (1993-09-07) Churches [Orig in Italian]. John Paul II, Pope, 1920- (Karol Wojtyla) (elected 1978). *OR(Eng)* 1307:1-2 S 15 1993*
Prague hosts meeting of European bishops. Hebblethwaite, Peter, 1930-. *Nat Cath Rep* 29:8 O 1 1993
The Vatican takes over European bishops. Hebblethwaite, Peter, 1930-. *Nat Cath Rep* 29:11 Mr 5 1993
Will it breathe with two lungs? Hebblethwaite, Peter, 1930-. *Nat Cath Rep* 29:10 S 3 1993

BISHOPS- FRANCE
Le catéchisme de l'Église Catholique. Honoré, Jean, Abp. *NRT* 115:3-18 Ja-F 1993
John Paul II, Pope, (1992-01-13) Allocutiones (Address to French Bishops on Ad Limina visit) [French]. John Paul II, Pope, 1920- (Karol Wojtyla) (elected 1978). *AAS* 85:73-80 Ja 7 1993*
John Paul II, Pope, (1992-01-18) Allocutiones (Exhortation to French Bishops) [French]. John Paul II, Pope, 1920- (Karol Wojtyla) (elected 1978). *AAS* 85:135-140 F 3 1993*
John Paul II, Pope, (1992-01-25) Allocutiones (Homily to French Bishops) [French]. John Paul II, Pope, 1920- (Karol Wojtyla) (elected 1978). *AAS* 85:143-148 F 3 1993*

BISHOPS- HAITI
Joining the comedians: a report from Haiti. Linden, Ian. *Month* 26:308-312 Ag 1993

BISHOPS- HUNGARY
John Paul II, Pope, (1991-08-20) Itinera Apostolica (Apostolic Journey) [Hungarian]. John Paul II, Pope, 1920- (Karol Wojtyla) (elected 1978). *AAS* 84:903-911 S 8 1992*

BISHOPS- IRELAND
Bishops back the enterprise culture. *Tablet* 246:1580-1581 D 12 1992
Bishops oppose repeal of ban on homosexuality. *Tablet* 247:829 Je 26 1993
Faith and work. Kennedy, Finola. *Tablet* 247:330 Mr 13 1993
Forbidden fruit: the true story of my secret love affair with Ireland's most powerful bishop. Murphy, Annie. Boston: Little, Brown and Company, 1993. 358p ISBN 0-31659-090-8 LC 93-3239
"Sailing to the Lowlands low"—the bishops in Brussels, 1-3 February 1993. Devlin, Brendan P. *Furrow* 44:178-181 Mr 1993
The "vagabond friar": Father Mathew's difficulties with the Irish bishops, 1840-1856. Quinn, John F. *CHist* 78:542-556 O 1992

BISHOPS- ITALY
Italian bishops bash "irregular" liaisons. Thavis, John. *Nat Cath Rep* 30:7 O 22 1993
John Paul II, Pope, (1991-10-26) Allocutiones (Papal address to Italian Bishops) [Italian]. John Paul II, Pope, 1920- (Karol Wojtyla) (elected 1978). *AAS* 84:955-958 O 3 1992*
John Paul II, Pope, (1992-01-04) Allocutiones (Homily at visit of some Italian Bishops) [Italian]. John Paul II, Pope, 1920- (Karol Wojtyla) (elected 1978). *AAS* 85:48-52 Ja 7 1993*
John Paul II, Pope, (1992-01-16) Allocutiones (Papal Address to Italian Bishops) [Italian]. John Paul II, Pope, 1920- (Karol Wojtyla) (elected 1978). *AAS* 85:130-135 F 3 1993*

BISHOPS- LATIN AMERICA
Curia faction goes for total control over CELAM IV. MacEoin, Gary. *Nat Cath Rep* 29:14-15 N 6 1992
Curia ignites angry protest at CELAM IV. Wirpsa, Leslie. *Nat Cath Rep* 29:12-13 N 6 1992
Latin American bishops. Palumbo, Gene. *St Anth* 100:10-16 Ap 1993
Santo Domingo foreruns church of next millennium [editorial]. *Nat Cath Rep* 29:1 N 6 1992
What CELAM achieved at Santo Domingo. MacEoin, Gary. *Doctr Life* 43:95-99 F 1993

BISHOPS- LITHUANIA
John Paul II, Pope, (1993-09-06) Clergy [Orig in Lithuanian]. John Paul II, Pope, 1920- (Karol Wojtyla) (elected 1978). *OR(Eng)* 1307:7 S 15 1993*

BISHOPS- MALAWI
Malawi chooses its future. Cullen, Trevor. *Tablet* 247:257-258 F 20 1993

BISHOPS- NETHERLANDS
Raised hopes in Holland. Goddijn, Walter, 1921-. *Tablet* 247:974-975 Jl 31 1993
Rumours abound as Bär resigns. Goddijn, Walter, 1921-. *Tablet* 247:413-414 Mr 27 1993
Worsening crisis in the Dutch Church. Visser, Dirk. *Tablet* 247:797-798 Je 19 1993

BISHOPS- SENEGAL
John Paul II, Pope, (1992-02-21) Itinera Apostolica (On apostolic trip address to Episcopal Conference of Senegal) [French]. John Paul II, Pope, 1920- (Karol Wojtyla) (elected 1978). *AAS* 85:148-153 F 3 1993*

BISHOPS- SICILY
John Paul II, Pope, (1991-11-22) Allocutiones (Conference to Sicilian Bishops) [Italian]. John Paul II, Pope, 1920- (Karol Wojtyla) (elected 1978). *AAS* 84:1123-1127 D 5 1992*

BISHOPS- SPAIN
Bishops take more moderate stance. *Tablet* 247:284 F 27 1993
Conferencia episcopal Catalona, malgrat tot. Bardulet, Salvador. Barcelona: Llibres de L'Index, 1993. x, 99p ISBN 84-87561-46-2
John Paul II, Pope, (1991-10-07) Allocutiones (Papal address to Spanish Bishops) [Spanish]. John Paul II, Pope, 1920- (Karol Wojtyla) (elected 1978). *AAS* 84:863-867 S 8 1992*
John Paul II, Pope, (1991-11-11) Allocutiones (Papal Address to Spanish Bishops) [Spanish]. John Paul II, Pope, 1920- (Karol Wojtyla) (elected 1978). *AAS* 84:969-975 O 3 1992*
John Paul II, Pope, (1991-11-18) Allocutiones (Papal Address to Spanish Bishops) [Spanish]. John Paul II, Pope, 1920- (Karol Wojtyla) (elected 1978). *AAS* 84:1065-1070 N 3 1992*
John Paul II, Pope, (1991-12-16) Allocutiones (Papal Address to Spanish Bishops) [Spanish]. John Paul II, Pope, 1920- (Karol Wojtyla) (elected 1978). *AAS* 85:26-33 Ja 7 1993*

BISHOPS- SUDAN
Bishops plead as civil war goes on. *Tablet* 247:763 Je 1993
Making dialogue work. Wako, Gabriel Zubeir, Abp, et al. *Origins* 23:72-76 Je 17 1993

BISHOPS- SWITZERLAND
Better atmosphere in Chur diocese. *Tablet* 247:487 Ap 10-17 1993
New bishops, new spirit in Chur. Kelly, Robert. *Tablet* 247:798 Je 19 1993
Surprise in Chur as Pope appoints new bishops. *Tablet* 247:347 Mr 13 1993

BISHOPS- UNITED STATES
Ad limina apostolorum. Carroll, William E. *Can Cath Rev* 11:33-34 My 1993
The American bishops and capital punishment. DeCelles, Charles. *SocJust* 84:149-153 S-O 1993
Archbishop James P Lyke: 1939-1992 [obit]. Campion, Owen F. *OSV* 81:3 Ja 10 1993
The bishop was a football hero. Carew, Wally. *Priest* 49:31-32 Ap 1993
Bishops advised on sexual abuse [National Conference of Catholic Bishops' Committee on priestly life and ministry meeting, Kansas City, MO]. Edwards, Robin T. *Nat Cath Rep* 29:5 Mr 5 1993
Bishops and universities: dominion or communion. Orsy, Ladislas, 1921-. *America* 169:11-16 N 20 1993
Bishops take action on a tough, varied agenda. DeMers, John. *Register* 69:1+ Jl 4 1993
Bishops take action on sex abuse. Feuerherd, Peter. *Register* 69:1+ Je 11 1993
Bishops united against population-control efforts. Sobo, Elizabeth. *Register* 69:1+ Ja 3 1993
Bishops' public information campaign. Alvaré, Helen M. *CLawyer* 34 no 4: 385-389 1993
The bishops' role in preserving the ministry's vitality. Bernardin, Joseph Louis, Cardinal, 1928-. *Health Prog* 74:21-22+ Ja-F 1993
"The challenge of peace"—10 years later. Sullivan, Walter Francis, Bp, 1928-. *OSV* 82:23 My 16 1993
The diocesan Bishop's perspective on implementing the Catechism. Wuerl, Donald William, Bp, 1941-. *Living Light* 30:73-78 Aut 1993
Episcopal papers speak a bit on economic justice. Hebblethwaite, Peter, 1930-. *Nat Cath Rep* 29:12 Ap 23 1993
Fight the system!. Royal, Robert. *Crisis* 11:11-12 S 1993
Health care among US bishops' other concerns. Edwards, Robin T. *Nat Cath Rep* 29:3 Jl 2 1993
John Paul II, Pope, (1993-06-05) Spiritual life. John Paul II, Pope, 1920- (Karol Wojtyla) (elected 1978). *OR(Eng)* 1295:3+ Je 16 1993*
John Paul II, Pope, (1993-06-11) Letter [Orig in English]. John Paul II, Pope, 1920- (Karol Wojtyla) (elected 1978). *OR(Eng)* 1297:2 Je 30 1993*
John Paul II, Pope, (1993-06-11) Letter [Orig in English]. John Paul II, Pope, 1920- (Karol Wojtyla) (elected 1978). *TPS* 38:374-376 N-D 1993*
John Paul II, Pope, (1993-10-15) Moral guidance [Orig English]. John Paul II, Pope, 1920- (Karol Wojtyla) (elected 1978). *OR(Eng)* 1312:5 O 20 1993*
John Paul warns of "extreme" feminism. Burke, Greg. *Register* 69:1+ Jl 18 1993
A layman preaches to the bishops. Finley, Mitchel B. *America* 169:10-12 N 13 1993
Looking for answers. Shaw, Russell. *OSV* 82:3 Jl 4 1993
Pathfinder James Lyke dies in Atlanta [obit]. *Nat Cath Rep* 29:2 Ja 8 1993
Pope calls for a new evangelization of America. Shaw, Russell. *OSV* 82:3 Ag 8 1993
The "real Catholic story": U.S. Bishops meet. Stahel, Thomas H, 1938-. *America* 169:4-5 D 4 1993
Resolution on health care reform. *Origins* 23:97+ Jl 1 1993
Response to Hubert Müller. Colombo, Giuseppe. *Jurist* 52 no 1:365-368 1992
The U.S. bishops get a new doctor of doctrine [por]. Mullen, P H, Jr. *OSV* 82:3 O 31 1993
What the Catholic church says about AIDS ministry. *Salt* 13:21-22 Ap 1993
Willing to serve [interview by C Lund and J Sprague]. Gaughan, Norbert Felix, Bp, 1921-. *Critic* 47:46-56 Sum 1993

BISHOPS- ZAMBIA
John Paul II, Pope, (1993-05-31) Citizens [Orig in English]. John Paul II, Pope, 1920- (Karol Wojtyla) (elected 1978). *OR(Eng)* 1294:3 Je 9 1993*

BISHOPS' CONFERENCE OF ENGLAND AND WALES
Arrangements questioned for Anglicans entering Catholic Church. *Origins* 23:37-38 Je 3 1993
On Anglicans approaching the Catholic Church after women's ordination decision. Hume, George Basil, Cardinal, 1923-. *Origins* 23:797+ My 6 1993
Shepherds and pilgrims. *Tablet* 247:1277-1278 O 2 1993

BITTERLICH, GABRIELE
Congregation for the Doctrine of the Faith (1992-06-06) Decretum de doctrina "Opus Angelorum" [Latin]. Congregation for the Doctrine of the Faith. *AAS* 84:805-806 Ag 3 1992*

BLACK MUSLIMS
The black muslims in America. Lincoln, C Eric. Grand Rapids: Eerdmans, 1993. 0-8028-0703-8 ISBN 0-8028-0703-8

BLACK POWER
Black theology: a documentary history, vol I, 1966-1979. Cone, James H, and Wilmore, Gayraud S, eds. Maryknoll: Orbis Books, 1993. 462p ISBN 0-88344-853-x LC 92-44927
Black theology: a documentary history, vol II, 1980-1992. Cone, James H, and Wilmore, Gayraud S, eds. Maryknoll: Orbis Books, 1993. x, 450p ISBN 0-88344-773-8 LC 79-12747

BLACK THEOLOGY
Black theology: a documentary history, vol I, 1966-1979. Cone, James H, and Wilmore, Gayraud S, eds. Maryknoll: Orbis Books, 1993. 462p ISBN 0-88344-853-x LC 92-44927
Black theology: a documentary history, vol II, 1980-1992. Cone, James H, and Wilmore, Gayraud S, eds. Maryknoll: Orbis Books, 1993. x, 450p ISBN 0-88344-773-8 LC 79-12747
Shoes that fit our feet: sources for a constructive black theology. Hopkins, Dwight N. Maryknoll, New York: Orbis Books, 1993. x, 242p ISBN 0-88344-848-3 LC 92-38713

BLACKS—RELIGION
The soul of black worship [exc fr *Liturgy: in daily life*]. Walker, Wyatt Tee. *Liturgy* 10:56-58 Spr 1993

BLACKS—RELIGION—HISTORY
In the beginning, there were black Catholics [interview by the editors of US Catholic (Periodical)]. Davis, Cyprian. *USCath* 58:6-14 Ap 1993

BLACKS- ARGENTINA
A forgotten history: blacks in Argentina. Liboreiro, Cristina. *LADOC* 23:15-22 My-Je 1993

BLACKS- GREAT BRITAIN
The wrong colour. Panzica, Ana. *Tablet* 247:1226-1227 S 25 1993

BLAKE, WILLIAM, 1757-1827
Blake's Milton as kabbalistic vision. Spector, Sheila A. *Relig Lit* 25:19-33 Spr 1993

BLAND, ANTHONY
Debate over Tony Bland ruling. *Tablet* 247:223 F 13 1993
The last days of Tony Bland [editorial]. *Tablet* 247:187 F 13 1993
Law, ethics, and language: the House of Lords and Tony Bland. Walsh, J Leo, and McQueen, Moira M. *Can Cath Rev* 11:6-8 Jl-Ag 1993
A medical and moral dilemma. Kelly, Kevin T. *Month* 26:138-144 Ap 1993
The road to euthanasia. Fisher, Anthony. *Tablet* 247:235-237 F 20 1993

BLESSED—BIOGRAPHY
Blessed Maria Francesca's sisters have brought Gospel of Christ to the world. *OR(Eng)* 1311:2 O 13 1993
Blessed Pedro Poveda devoted life to improving Christian education in Spain. *OR(Eng)* 1311:2 O 13 1993
In mystery of the cross Blessed Maria Crucified lived ardour of seraphic love. *OR(Eng)* 1311:2 O 13 1993
John Paul II, Pope, (1993-06-20) Angela [Orig in Italian]. John Paul II, Pope, 1920- (Karol Wojtyla) (elected 1978). *OR(Eng)* 1298:7 Jl 7 1993*
Teresian spirituality prepared Blessed Victoria Diez to sacrifice her own life. *OR(Eng)* 1311:2 O 13 1993

BLESSING AND CURSING
Bayou blessing. Feister, John Bookser. *St Anth* 100:28-35 F 1993
Broken [excerpt fr *The life of the beloved*]. Nouwen, Henri Josef Machiel, 1932-. *Living Prayer* 26:3-7 Mr-Ap 1993

BLIND—RELIGIOUS LIFE
Listen read: a program for visually handicapped sisters. Logan, Fidelis. *Sisters* 65:53-54 Ja 1993

BLONDEL, MAURICE, 1861-1949
Il centenario de *L'Action* di M. Blondel. Tilliette, Xavier. *Civilta* 3:388-393 S 4 1993
The Christianization of modern philosophy according to Maurice Blondel. Grys, James Le. *TheolStds* 54:455-484 S 1993
Maurice Blondel: 100 years after "L Action". Kerlin, Michael J. *America* 168:12-15 Je 19-26 1993

BLOOM, ALLAN, 1930-1992
Friend and teacher: Allan Bloom, 1930-1992. Fortin, Ernest L, 1923-. *Crisis* 11:38-40 Ja 1993

BLUE, LIONEL
The Baptist and the Rabbi. *Tablet* 247:650-651 My 22 1993

BOBAN, MATE
Croat Catholics divided. Magas, Branka. *Tablet* 247:908-910 Jl 17 1993

BOCCACCIO, GIOVANNI, 1313-1375
Images of paradise. Bull, George, 1929-. *Tablet* 246:1613 D 19-26 1992

BODY, HUMAN
The biblical foundations of the thought of John Paul II on human sexuality. Séguin, Michel. *Communio* 20:266-289 Sum 1993
Patents encroach upon the body. Kimbrell, Andrew. *Crisis* 11:43-48 My 1993

BODY, HUMAN—EDUCATION
Corps et culture. Csepregi, Gabor. *Laval Theol Phil* 49:121-129 F 1993

BODY, HUMAN—RELIGIOUS ASPECTS
"La carne è il cardine della salvezza" la concezione cristiana del corpo umano [editorial]. Salvini, Gianpaolo, ed. *Civilta* 2:3-15 Ap 3 1993
Le corps pour la foi. Domergue, Marcel. *Lumen* 48:263-276 S 1993
Spiritual fitness: everyday exercises for body and soul. Donnelly, Doris. San Francisco: HarperSanFrancisco, 1993. x, 178p ISBN 00-6061-899-x LC 92-53923

BODY AND MIND *see* Mind and Body

BODY AND SOUL
Aquinas concept of the body and out of body situations. Quinn, Patrick. *Heythrop* 34:387-400 O 1993
Body and soul. Young, John. *HPR* 94:60-63+ O 1993

Heart of the matter: what is man? Kreeft, Peter John, 1937. *Register* 69:1+ Ag 29 1993
Persons, souls and embryos. Coghlan, Peter. *Pacifica* 6:165-171 Je 1993

BODY OF CHRIST *see* Jesus Christ—Mystical Body

BOFF, CLODOVIS
Por el camino de emaus en este atardecer neoliberal. Casaldáliga, Pedro, Bp, 1928-. *Christus* 58:66-73 Mr-Ap 1993
Questions d'épistémologie en théologie de la libération, ğ propos de l'ouvrage de Clovdovis Boff. Richard, Jean. *Laval Theol Phil* 49:249-275 Je 1993

BOFF, LEONARDO, 1938-
Boff-an "apostolic and pastoral crisis" [fr *Sal Terrae*]. Sobrino, John. *LADOC* 24:16-23 S-O 1993

BOFILL, JAIME
Persona y amor: el personalismo de Jaime Bofill. Tomar Romero, Francisca. Lleida: PPU, 1993. x, 364p ISBN 84-477-011301

BOHRER, KARL HEINZ
Weder Gold noch Silber. Biser, Eugen. *Stimm Zeit* 211:343-350 My 1993

BOILEAU, DAVID
École Saint-Thomas. Steenberghen, Fernand Van. *RPhil Louvain* 91:1-4 F 1993

BOLEYN, ANNE, 1507-1536
"Break not them then so wrongfully": topical readings of Sir Thomas Wyatt's riddling and bewitched lute and the feminine other. Cunnar, Eugene R. *Cithara* 32:3-30 N 1992

BOLIVIA— SOCIO-ECONOMIC CONDITIONS
Bolivian farmers open market to show coca is not a drug problem. Chauvin, Lucien. *Nat Cath Rep* 29:15 Mr 26 1993
A message from the Bolivian Conference of Catholic Bishops. *LADOC* 23:8-11 Mr-Ap 1993

BOLTON, CARLOS
La inquietud religiosa en cuatro poetas chilenos contemporáneos (Miguel Arteche, Carlos Bolton, Fidel Sepúlveda y Raúl Zurita). Livacić Gazzano, Ernesto. *Teol Vida* 33 no 3-4:299-314 1992

BOMBINGS
Religion a key to terrorist. Pevtzow, Lisa. *Register* 69:1+ Ap 18 1993

BOMBINGS- IRELAND
Church leaders voice disgust and contempt at IRA bombing. *Tablet* 247:416 Mr 27 1993

BOMBINGS- ITALY
Bombings seen as plot to halt regeneration. O'Connell, Gerard. *Tablet* 247:991 Jl 31 1993

BONAVENTURE, SAINT
Revelation in comparative perspective: lessons for interreligious dialogue. Carpenter, David. *JEcumen Stds* 29:175-188 Spr 1992

BONHOEFFER, DIETRICH, 1906-1945
Brautbriefe aus dem Gefängnis. Bleistein, Roman, 1928-. *Stimm Zeit* 211:711-713 O 1993

BOOK COLLECTING
Other men's books. Bovenizer, David A. *Crisis* 11:63-64 Jl-Ag 1993

BOOK OF COMMON PRAYER
Knocking at the papal door. Hamilton, Daniel S. *America* 168:16-17 Ap 24 1993

BOOK REVIEWING
Epistolary advice. Coren, Michael. *Can Cath Rev* 11:5-6 Je 1993
Even in Canada. Coren, Michael. *Can Cath Rev* 11:5-6 Mr 1993

BORAN (AFRICAN PEOPLE)
Dialogue with Waso Boorana traditional religious practices. Aguilar, Mario I. *AFER* 35:101-114 Ap 1993

BORECKY, ISIDORE, BP
Ukrainian bishop fights to hold eparchy. Babych, Art. *Nat Cath Rep* 29:7 S 24 1993

BORELLI, JOHN
The search for common ground. Bole, William. *OSV* 81:3 Ja 17 1993

BORIAS, ANDRE
The achievement of André Borias, exegete of Benedict's rule. Kardong, Terrence G. *ABenR* 44:179-220 Je 1993

BOROWITZ, EUGENE
Borowitz and the postmodern renewal of theology. Ochs, Peter. *CrossCurr* 43:164-183 Sum 1993

BORSELLINO, PAOLO
Battere La Mafia Uiti Si Può. Sorge, Bartolomeo. *Civilta* 143:468-475 D 5 1992

BOSNIA AND HERZEGOVINA
Ancient Macedonia gropes for new paths [photos]. McCarthy, Tim. *Nat Cath Rep* 29:8-10 S 24 1993
Bosnia's tragedy is shame of the West. Muravchik, Joshua. *Register* 69:1+ O 10 1993
Bosnia: couldn't something have been done? Manney, Jim. *OSV* 82:19 Ag 29 1993
Convoy drives hard questions home for peace movment [editorial]. *Nat Cath Rep* 29:20 S 3 1993
Dialogue [interview by Gabriel Meyer]. Ellis, Bernard. *Register* 69:1+ F 14 1993
History won't soon forget our betrayal of ex-Yugoslavia [editorial]. *Nat Cath Rep* 29:28 S 17 1993
In Assisi, religious leaders deplore cruelties. Hebblethwaite, Peter, 1930-. *Nat Cath Rep* 29:14 Ja 22 1993
Moslems in Bosnia face a "genocide" [interview by National Catholic Register (Periodical)]. Ceric, Mustafa. *Register* 69:1+ Ja 3 1993
Mostar man: "Let my son be last sacrifice". Wilkes, Paul, 1938-. *Nat Cath Rep* 29:7-12 Ja 29 1993
Peace crumbles on the way to Sarajevo [photos]. McCarthy, Tim. *Nat Cath Rep* 29:14-16+ Ag 27 1993
Priests: "we are dying: do you understand?" [remarks of Fathers Franjo Rudman and Boze Vuleta]. *Nat Cath Rep* 29:13 Ja 29 1993

BOSNIA AND HERZEGOVINA—POLITICS AND GOVERNMENT
Bishops amend Sermon on Mount: kill the killers. McCarthy, Colman. *Nat Cath Rep* 29:18 Je 4 1993

Bishops entangled in their own Balkans morass. Shaw, Russell. *OSV* 82:3 Je 6 1993

Bosnia. Feuerherd, Peter. *Register* 69:1+ Je 6 1993

Dialogue [interview by J Luxmoore]. Edelman, Mark. *Register* 69:1+ Je 20 1993

Drawing lessons from the slaughter [editorial]. *OSV* 82:2 Je 20 1993

Political quagmire buried in moral morass. Collins, Carole. *Nat Cath Rep* 29: 8 Je 4 1993

A primer for the morally perplexed. Scott, David. *OSV* 82:10-11 Ag 8 1993

War comes to Medjugorje. Manney, Dave. *New Cov* 23:7-11 N 1993

BOSNIA AND HERZEGOVINA—RELIGION
God's peace surpasses understanding. Etchegaray, Roger, Cardinal, 1928-. *OR(Eng)* 1312:6 O 20 1993

Pope keeps in touch, may go to Sarajevo. *Tablet* 247:989 Jl 31 1993

BOSNIA AND HERZEGOVINA—SOCIO-ECONOMIC CONDITIONS
A bishop at bay. McDonagh, Melanie. *Tablet* 247:968+ Jl 31 1993

Dialogue [interview by J Luxmoore and J Babiuch]. Mazowiecki, Tadeusz. *Register* 69:1+ Ap 11 1993

Stupro, aborto e anticoncezionali. Perico, Giacomo. *Civilta* 3:37-46 Jl 3 1993

BOSNIA AND HERZEGOVINA—PEACE
Achieving peace with justice in Bosnia-Herzegovina. Keeler, William H, Abp. *Origins* 22:546-548 Ja 21 1993

BOSTON COLLEGE (MA)
A museum for Catholics over 40. O'Neill, Robert K. *CDgst* 57:59-64 Ja 1993

BOSWELL, JAMES, 1740-1795
A church off the street. Wroe, Ann. *Tablet* 247:262 F 27 1993

BOSWELL, JONATHAN
An essay on Jonathan Boswell's Community and the economy: the theory of public co-operation. Naughton, Michael. *RSocEcon* 51:86-102 Spr 1993

BOUDREAUX, WARREN LOUIS, BP, 1918-
No more bingo on the Bayou. Feister, John Bookser. *St Anth* 100:34-35 F 1993

BOUGAINSVILLE ISLAND (PAPUA NEW GUINEA)—POLITICS
Catholic bishop pleads for help. Freidman, Paul. *Tablet* 247:956-957 Jl 24 1993

BOUNDARIES
Changing unjust borders. Corley, Felix. *Month* 26:71-73 F 1993

BOWMAN, THEA
Who are their models? Cunningham, Beatrice. *ReligTJ* 27:38-39 O 1993

BOYAXHIU, TERESA, MOTHER, 1910-
Calcutta through the eye of the needle. Colson, GiGi. *Liguorian* 81:58-62 Jl 1993

The message of Mother Teresa. McRedmond, Louis. *Tablet* 247:764 Je 1993

Mother Teresa: a life in pictures. Royle, Roger. New York: HarperSanFrancisco, 1992. x, 159p ISBN 0-06-067978-61 LC 92-52654

Mother Teresa: a woman in love. Joly, Edward Le. Indiana: Ave Maria Press, 1993. 190p ISBN 0-877793-7 LC 92-75249

Teresa of Calcutta: a pencil in God's hand. Zambonini, Franca. New York: Alba House, 1993. 189p ISBN 0-8189-0670-7 LC 93-1046

Welcome to Mother Teresa [homily given June 5, 1993]. Cassidy, Joseph, Abp, 1933-. *Furrow* 44:395-398 Jl-Ag 1993

BOYCOTT
How good is good TV? Hart, D G. *Crisis* 11:12-13 S 1993

BOYLE, JOSEPH M, JR
Obstetrical dilemmas and the principle of double effect. Lombardi, Joseph L. *Amer J Juris* 37:197-211 1992

What is included in a means to an end? Flannery, Kevin L. *Gregorianum* 74 no 3:499-513 1993

BRAIN
Chisholm on persons as entia successiva and the brain-microparticle hypothesis. Jacquette, Dale. *Mod Schlmn* 70:99-113 Ja 1993

The sexual brain. LeVay, Simon. Cambridge: MIT Press, 1993. 168p ISBN 0-26212-178-6 LC 92-44691

BRAIN—WOUNDS AND INJURIES
Persistent vegetative state—a medical comment. Poole, Joyce. *Month* 26:226-229 Je 1993

BRAIN DEATH
Morte cerebral e morte cerebral. Lepargneur, Hubert. *REB* 53:87-98 Mr 1993

Persistent vegetative state—a medical comment. Poole, Joyce. *Month* 26:226-229 Je 1993

BRAINWASHING
Cults and cultism. Hughes, Louis. *Furrow* 44:352-358 Je 1993

BRANDSTAETTER, ROMAN
Roman Brandstaetter narratore delle profondità. Castelli, Ferdinando. *Civilta* 2:130-143 Ap 17 1993

BRANHAM, WILLIAM MARION
Prolifération et persistance des sectes dans le milieu urbain de Kinshasa: analyse de quelques cas. Haes, René de. *StudiaM* 41:205-224 1992

BRAZIL—POLITICS AND GOVERNMENT
How US policy trickled down to a Sao Paulo jail. MacEoin, Gary. *Nat Cath Rep* 29:18 Mr 19 1993

BRAZILIAN SOCIETY FOR THE DEFENSE OF TRADITION, FAMILY AND PROPERTY (TFP)
Going all the way. Kepp, Michael. *Register* 69:3 My 23 1993

BRENNAN, BILL
Christ came alive. Harris, King. *New Cov* 23:15-17 O 1993

BRENNAN, HEIDI L
"Discovering Motherhood"—one woman's journey [interview by G Hizer]. *OSV* 81:11 D 20 1992

BREST, UNION OF, 1596
The Union of Brest: a timely topic. Roccasalvo, Joan L. *Diakonia* 26 no 3: 161-183 1993

BREVIARIES
Drinking from the hidden fountain: a patristic breviary. Spidlik, Thomas. London: New City, 1992. 447p ISBN 0-904287-39-4

BRIDGET OF SWEDEN, SAINT, 1302?-1373
John Paul II, Pope, (1991-09-08) St Bridget of Sweden: a Saint of Europe. John Paul II, Pope, 1920- (Karol Wojtyla) (elected 1978). *Con Life* 17 no 2:60-63 1992*

Saint Birgitta. O'Connell-Cahill, Catherine. *Salt* 13:31 Ja 1993

BRITISH BROADCASTING CORPORATION
Battle at the BBC. Morris, Colin. *Tablet* 247:942-943 Jl 24 1993

Kill or cur at the BBC [editorial]. *Tablet* 247:935-936 Jl 24 1993

BROADCAST JOURNALISM
CBS news anchors adrift in shallow waters. Collum, Danny Duncan. *Nat Cath Rep* 29:19 Jl 16 1993

Let the viewer beware: the video camera does lie. Collum, Danny Duncan. *Nat Cath Rep* 29:20 Mr 19 1993

BROADCASTERS
The dangerous Rush Limbaugh. Sobran, Joseph. *Crisis* 11:18-21 My 1993

BROTHERHOODS
The origin of the Penitentes of New Mexico: separating fact from fiction. Espinosa, J Manuel. *CHist* 79:454-477 Jl 1993

BROTHERLINESS
The family: a place of fraternity. Sicari, Antonio. *Communio* 20:290-305 Sum 1993

BROTHERS (RELIGIOUS)
The church still relies on its brothers. Deedy, John G, 1933-. *USCath* 58:33-37 N 1993

F S C vocations today: rediscovering our roots. Hynes, Christian. *Sisters* 65: 293-298 Jl 1993

Vocations among teaching brothers. King, Eleace. *RRel* 52:102-110 Ja-F 1993

BROTHERS AND SISTERS
Desert island choice (1) [winner of the John Harriott Memorial Prize]. Dorrell, Fleur. *Tablet* 247:94 Ja 23 1993

BROTHERS OF THE CHRISTIAN SCHOOLS
La dévotion à Saint Joseph chez les Freres des écoles Chrétiennes [part 2]. Poutet, Yves. *CahiersJos* 41:15-88 Ja-Je 1993

BROWN, PETER
Shifting sands: Foucault, Brown and the framework of christian asceticism. Behr, John. *Heythrop* 34:1-21 Ja 1993

BROWNING, ROBERT, 1812-1889
Incarnational tension in Robert Browning's Karshish. Kass, Thomas G. *ABenR* 44:236-257 S 1993

The Virgin incarnate in Robert Browning's poetry. Johnson, Patricia E. *Listening* 28:118-127 Spr 1993

BROWNSON, ORESTES
Brownson's early christology. Griffioen, Arie J. *ABenR* 44:58-75 Mr 1993

BUBER, MARTIN
Buber and Tillich. Novak, David, 1941-. *JEcumen Stds* 29:159-174 Spr 1992

Judaism: people or religion? some positions in modern Jewish thought. Meir, Ephraim. *SIDIC* 25 No 1:20-25 1992

Saint Augustine and Martin Buber as perspectives on John Noonan's persons and masks of the law. Combs, Christopher. *Amer J Juris* 37:145-169 1992

BUDDHA (THE CONCEPT)
Meditation and prayer (2): sufficiency and satisfaction in Zen Buddhism: recovering an ancient symbolon. Heisig, James W. *Stud Form Spir* 14:57-74 F 1993

BUDDHISM
Monastic formation in Buddhism. Khantipalo, Bhikkhu. *Stud Form Spir* 14: 117-127 F 1993

BUDDHISM—RELATIONS
A bibliographical review of books on spirituality in the Buddhist-Christian dialogue. Mitchell, Donald W. *Stud Form Spir* 14:139-143 F 1993

The Buddha and the Christ: explorations in Buddhist and Christian dialogue. Lefebvre, Leo D. Maryknoll: Orbis, 1993. x, 239p ISBN 0-88344-924-2 LC 93-7972

Il Buddhismo e le altre religioni. Pezzali, Amalia. *StudiaM* 42:347-356 1993

BUDDHISM- FRANCE
Buddhism blossoms in French wine country [photos]. Fox, Thomas C. *Nat Cath Rep* 29:11-13 Jl 16 1993

BUDDHISM- TIBET
Contemplation and action (2): engaged Buddhism from a Thervāda perspective. Sivaraksa, Sulak. *Stud Form Spir* 14:105-116 F 1993

The Karma Kagyupa Tibetan Buddhists. Tiso, Francis V. *StudiaM* 41:145-167 1992

BUDDHISM- UNITED STATES
The Karma Kagyupa Tibetan Buddhists. Tiso, Francis V. *StudiaM* 41:145-167 1992

BUDDHISM AND CHRISTIANITY *see* Christianity and Buddhism

BUDDHISM AND HINDUISM
The Buddhist attitude toward Hinduism. Wayman, Alex. *StudiaM* 42:329-345 1993

BUDGET- UNITED STATES
From arms critic to head of the committee. Clancy, Paul. *Nat Cath Rep* 29: 13 Ja 22 1993

BULGARIA—RELIGION
Schism in the Bulgarian Orthodox Church. Broun, Janice. *Month* 26:290-294 Jl 1993

BULGARIAN ORTHODOX CHURCH *see* Orthodox Eastern Church, Bulgarian

BULGER, JAMES
Anger and anguish over murdered boy. *Tablet* 247:288 F 27 1993

BULTMANN, RUDOLF KARL, 1884-1976
Bultmann. Ferguson, David. Collegeville: The Liturgical Press, 1992. x, 154p ISBN 0-8146-5037-6

BURIAL
The place of the dead: Christian burial and the liturgical environment. Adams, William Seth. *Liturgy* 10:69-73 Wint 1992

BURMA—POLITICS
A light for Asia. *Tablet* 247:686 My 29 1993
Support for Suu Kyi. *Tablet* 247:816 Je 26 1993
BUSH, GEORGE HERBERT WALKER, 1924-
John Paul II, Pope, (1991-10-29) Nuntii Scripto (Written Messages) [English]. John Paul II, Pope, 1920- (Karol Wojtyla) (elected 1978). *AAS* 84:871-872 S 8 1992*
Prolifers and the Reagan/Bush tease [editorial]. *New Oxford Rev* 60:2+ Mr 1993
BUSINESS
The cathedral of business: the fountainhead of values in America today. Lear, Norman, 1922-. *New Oxford Rev* 60:6-13 Ap 1993
Corporate code marries dollars and sense. Gibeau, Dawn. *Nat Cath Rep* 29: 3-4 My 14 1993
God and money. Feuerherd, Peter. *Register* 69:1+ F 28 1993
Oil spill, racism inspired earlier principles. Gibeau, Dawn. *Nat Cath Rep* 29:4 My 14 1993
BUSINESS CYCLES
Income distribution and business cycles. Van Lear, William. *RSocEcon* 50: 316-332 Fall 1992
Structural change in US labor markets. Champlin, Dell. *RSocEcon* 51:40-61 Spr 1993
BUSINESS ETHICS
Ethical risk management: suggestions for an applied risk ethics. Cowell, John. *Teilhard Rev* 28:3-7 Spr 1993
Guideline amendments dramatically change the structure of organizational fines. Fiorelli, Paul E. *CLawyer* 35 no 2:181-197 1993
Moral dilemmas in modern business. Maloney, Oliver. *Furrow* 44:12-20 Ja 1993
Theological trends: business ethics and the pastoral task. Preston, Ronald H. *Way* 33:233-239 Jl 1993
Virtue at work: transforming the heart of business. Bouchard, Charles E. *Liguorian* 81:24-29 O 1993
BUSINESS WOMEN
Faith in the world of business. O'Cathain, Detta. *Priests & People* 7:186-190 My 1993
BYRNE, HARRY J
It's time to conduct civil wars. Costello, Gerald M, 1931-. *USCath* 58:48-51 Ap 1993

C

CADEGAN, UNA
Mary feminism: compatible but challenging. Morrow, Carol Ann. *St Anth* 100:10-15 My 1993
CAHILL, LISA SOWLE
Single Catholics: can we talk about S-E-X? Bearden, Michelle. *USCath* 58: 30-35 Ag 1993
CAKPO-TORO, EDMOND
John Paul II, Pope, (1991-11-25) Allocutiones (Speech to receive Ambassadorial credentials) [French]. John Paul II, Pope, 1920- (Karol Wojtyla) (elected 1978). *AAS* 84:1141-1143 D 5 1992*
CALENDAR
Religion teacher's planning calendar 1993-1994. Costello, Gwen. *ReligTJ* 27: 21-45 S 1993
CALL TO ACTION NATIONAL CONFERENCE, CHICAGO, 1992
Called to action Catholics raise voices from "below". Gibeau, Dawn. *Nat Cath Rep* 29:3-4 N 20 1992
Catholics organize for renewal, reform. *Nat Cath Rep* 29:3 N 20 1992
CALL TO ACTION NATIONAL CONFERENCE, CHICAGO, 1993
Loyalists believe some things worth staying to defend [editorial]. *Nat Cath Rep* 30:24 N 12 1993
Reformed minded Catholics upbeat, active. Fox, Thomas C. *Nat Cath Rep* 30:3+ N 12 1993
CALLAHAN, SIDNEY
Good people get angry, too. Mallowe, Mike. *USCath* 58:14-21 My 1993
CALRE, JOHN
The rustic muse. *Tablet* 247:916 Jl 17 1993
CALVERT, CHARLES, 1637-1715
Popish plots: Protestant fears in early colonial Maryland, 1676-1689. Graham, Michael. *CHist* 79:197-216 Ap 1993
CALVIN, JOHN
Calvin's New Testament commentaries. Parker, T H L. Louisville: John Knox, 1993. x, 256p ISBN 0-664-25489-6
CALVIN, JOHN—CATECHISMS
Das Kirchliche Amt in der Darstellung des Catechismus Romanus. Lülsdorff, Raimund. *Catholica* 47:76-88 1993
CALVIN, JOHN—THEOLOGY
"The truth looks different from here". Soskice, Janet Martin. *New Blckfrs* 73:528-542 N 1992
CAMBODIA—POLITICS
Could Khmer Rouge ever return to power in Cambodia? [editorial]. *Nat Cath Rep* 29:24 My 14 1993
In killing fields, a crying game. Boua, Chanthou. *Nat Cath Rep* 29:14 My 14 1993
Keeping faith with Cambodia's voters [editorial]. *Tablet* 247:675 My 29 1993
A monster revives. Rafferty, Kevin. *Tablet* 247:568+ My 8 1993
CAMBODIA—SOCIAL LIFE AND CUSTOMS
Rice-wine and song. Geach, Catherine. *Tablet* 247:710-711 Je 5 1993
CAMBRIDGE UNIVERSITY
Let us now praise famous men. Duffy, Eamon. *New Blckfrs* 74:337-344 Jl-Ag 1993
CAMEROON—POLITICS
Africa's lost haven. Eppink, Alfons. *Tablet* 247:680-681 My 29 1993

CAMPAIGN FOR HUMAN DEVELOPMENT
Surprising charity has CHD critics seeing red. Bole, William. *Nat Cath Rep* 29:8 N 13 1992
CAMPAIGN FUNDS- GREAT BRITAIN
A party too long in power [editorial]. *Tablet* 247:807-808 Je 26 1993
CAMPBELL, JOSEPH, 1904-1987
American Catholics and the Joseph Campbell phenomenon. Dinges, William D. *America* 168:12-14+ F 20 1993
The Joseph Campbell phenomenon: implications for the contemporary church. Madden, Lawrence J, ed. Washington: The Pastoral Press, 1992. x, 153p ISBN 0-912405-89-9
Valori per il futuro di Malta. Abela, Anthony M. *Civilta* 2:260-269 My 1 1993
CAMPBELL, KATIE, 1942-1993
Campbell, Katie, 1942-1993 [obit]. Roberts, Jo. *Cath Work* 60:7 My 1993
CAMPUS MINISTRY
Forming lay prayer leaders. Arnold, Linda M, and Gallagher, Patricia. *Past Mus* 17:14-15 Je-Jl 1993
Give it that old college try. Macchiarola, Frank J. *Comm* 120:9-12 S 10 1993
CAMUS, ALBERT, 1913-1960
Variations sceptiques sur le thème de la mort. Sansen, Raymond. *MSR* 50: 83-98 Ap-Je 1993
CANAANITES—RELIGION
Caravans, Kenites, and Casus belli: Enmity and Alliance in the Song of Deborah. Schloen, J David. *CBQ* 55:18-38 Ja 1993
CANADA—ECONOMIC POLICY
Canada bishops tackle free market fallout. Lefevere, Patricia. *Nat Cath Rep* 29:12 My 28 1993
CANADA—HISTORY
Exploiting the dead. Coren, Michael. *Can Cath Rev* 11:5-6 N 1993
CANADIAN CONFERENCE OF BISHOPS
La concélébration Repères Théologiques pour une PRatique Renouvelée. *Notitiae* 29:187-243 Ap 1993
CANADIAN CONFERENCE OF CATHOLIC BISHOPS
Brief on native peoples. *Origins* 23:401+ N 18 1993
CANADIAN CONFERENCE OF CATHOLIC BISHOPS—DOCUMENTS
Focus on sexual abuse. Higgins, Michael. *Tablet* 247:194-196 F 13 1993
CANADIAN LITERATURE
Even in Canada. Coren, Michael. *Can Cath Rev* 11:5-6 Mr 1993
Fathers' business: Catholic priests as Canadian writers see them. Kelly, Darlene. *Can Cath Rev* 11:21-29 Ja 1993
The land of the rising Anne. Coren, Michael. *Can Cath Rev* 11:5-6 Jl-Ag 1993
CANCER
The most common skin cancer. Dinolfo, John. *CDgst* 57:12-17 Je 1993
Nun issues warning [breast cancer]. Thompson, Donna. *Register* 69:3 O 24 1993
CANCER—PATIENTS
Liz's 100 bears. Sand, Linda Lee. *St Anth* 100:24-27 F 1993
CANCER—PSYCHOLOGICAL ASPECTS
Face a l'enfant mourant. Hainaut, Hadelin. *Supplement* 184:79-88 Mr-Ap 1993
CANNIBALISM
Passion story. Ahearn, Clare. *Tablet* 247:470 Ap 10-17 1993
CANON LAW
Abortion and the Sacrament of Penance. McAreavey, John. *Furrow* 44:230-235 Ap 1993
Accountability in the church. McDonnell, Dominic. *Priests & People* 6:340-342 Ag-S 1992
Acta tribunalium S Sedis. Navarrete, Urbano. *Periodica* 82 no 2:339-352 1993
Alcuni aspetti della formazione sacerdotale nel diritto canonico. Ghirlanda, Gianfranco. *Civilta* 3:224-237 Ag 7-21 1993
Annulments healing the wounds of divorce. Walden, Mary. *Liguorian* 81:20-26 Mr 1993
Canon law offers flexibility in collaborative relationships. Morrisey, Frank, and Campbell, Peter. *Health Prog* 74:53 Jl-Ag 1993
Canones praeliminares codicis. Urrutia, Francisco J. *Periodica* 81 no 2:179-209 1992
The Church's teaching mission: some aspects of the normative role of episcopal conferences. Green, Thomas J. *Stud Can* 27 no 1:23-57 1993
Common life. McDonough, Elizabeth. *RRel* 52:304-310 Mr-Ap 1993
De curatoris processualis designatione pro mente infirmis. Stankicwicz, Antonius. *Periodica* 81 no 3-4:495-520 1992
Delitti contro il sesto comandamento. Paolis, Velasio De. *Periodica* 82 no 2: 293-316 1993
The Eastern code and the Latin Church. Gallaro, George D. *Can Cath Rev* 11:17-18 O 1993
How to relate theology and Canon Law. Orsy, Ladislas, 1921-. *Origins* 22: 549-552 Ja 21 1993
John Paul II, Pope, (1992-01-23) Allocutiones (Address to Roman Rota) [Italian]. John Paul II, Pope, 1920- (Karol Wojtyla) (elected 1978). *AAS* 85:140-143 F 3 1993*
John Paul II, Pope, (1993-01-29) Interpret law through tradition. John Paul II, Pope, 1920- (Karol Wojtyla) (elected 1978). *TPS* 38:211-214 Jl-Ag 1993*
Law and gospel. Häring, Bernard, 1912-. *Tablet* 247:41-42 Ja 9 1993
New communities. McDonough, Elizabeth. *RRel* 52:140-146 Ja-F 1993
Notes on the canonical status of shrines. Fox, Joseph P. *Notitiae* 28:261-269 Ap 1992
De nullitate sententiae iudicialis propter absolutam iudicis incompetentiam. Stankiewicz, Antonius. *Periodica* 81 no 3-4:535-552 1992
On the letter and the spirit of church law. Walters, Michael. *Register* 69:1+ S 5 1993
One Humanae vitae is enough. *Tablet* 247:30 Ja 9 1993
Optio praecipua pauperum: de ecclesiali pro pauperibus optione tamquam theonomae moralitatis criterio. Pastor, Felix-Alejandro. *Periodica* 81 no 2: 319-346 1992

The new catechism of the Catholic Church. McBride, Alfred. *OSV* 81:14 Mr 7 1993

New catechism prepares church for 21st century. McBride, Alfred. *OSV* 81:9 F 21 1993

The new catechism's audience and uses. McBride, Alfred. *OSV* 81:15 Mr 14 1993

The new Catechism: a first reading. Cunningham, Lawrence S, 1935-. *Comm* 120:8-12 Mr 12 1993

The new universal catechism: a renewed content, traditional form. Stravinskas, Peter. *Register* 69:1+ My 2 1993

The new universal catechism: why it's vitally necessary. Stravinskas, Peter. *Register* 69:1+ Ap 25 1993

On heaven, hell and judgment. Stravinskas, Peter. *Register* 69:1+ O 24 1993

Our bodies will rise!. McBride, Alfred. *OSV* 82:9 S 12 1993

Overview: the catechism of the Catholic Church. Pollard, John E. *Origins* 23: 7-11 My 20 1993

Para renovar la catequesis. *Christus* 58:6-507 Je 1993*

Perspective on the universal catechism. Samaha, John M. *Liguorian* 81:32-34 Je 1993

Playing in Peoria [editorial]. *Register* 69:4 Ap 18 1993

Pope's stern advice to Dutch Catholics. *Tablet* 247:84 Ja 16 1993

Pour une Église en acte d'espérance. Lebeau, Paul. *Lumen* 48:149-159 Je 1993

The priest as catechetical leader [2 pts]. McBride, Alfred. *Priest* 49:15-20 Je 1993; 29-33 Jl 1993

Questions catechists ask and answers that really work. Pfeifer, Carl J, and Manternach, Janaan. Kansas City: Sheed & Ward, 1993. 110p ISBN 1-55612-620-4

Quoting the catechism. Hebblethwaite, Peter, 1930-. *Tablet* 247:71-72 Ja 16 1993

Reflections of a parish priest. Keller, Dan. *Momentum* 24:58-60 S-O 1993

The Resurrection makes credible all Christ taught. McBride, Alfred. *OSV* 82: 12 Je 27 1993

Sfondo "liturgico-vitale" del catechismo della chiesa Cattolica. Triacca, Achille M. *Notitiae* 29:34-47 Ja-F 1993

The spiritual birth of the people of God. McBride, Alfred. *OSV* 82:15 Ag 8 1993*

Still waiting for the new catechism. *Tablet* 247:945-946 Jl 24 1993

The supper of the Lamb. McBride, Alfred. *OSV* 82:16 N 7 1993

La teologia del catecismo de Juan Pablo II. Muñoz, Ronaldo F. *Christus* 58: 32-33 Ag 1993

To reach full knowledge of the truth. Myers, John, Bp. *Origins* 22:593-601 F 11 1993

Trouble with the catechism. *Tablet* 247:206 F 13 1993

Truth reaffirmed about creation and humanity's fall. Stravinskas, Peter. *Register* 69:1+ My 23 1993

Under the influence of the Holy Spirit. McBride, Alfred. *OSV* 82:7 Jl 11 1993

Understanding the catechism. Konstant, David Every, Bp, 1930-. *Priests & People* 7:213-219 Je 1993

La vie dans le Christ. Chapelle, Albert. *NRT* 115:169-185 Mr-Ap 1993

We know not the hour or the day. McBride, Alfred. *OSV* 82:13 Jl 4 1993*

We shall be judged. McBride, Alfred. *OSV* 82:16 S 26 1993

What happens after we die. McBride, Alfred. *OSV* 82:13 S 19 1993

What liturgy is like a party. McBride, Alfred. *OSV* 82:16 O 10 1993

Why a new catechism? Grubb, Geoffrey J. *ReligTJ* 27:40-41 Ap-My 1993

Why the creed is the heart of our faith. Stravinskas, Peter. *Register* 69:1+ My 9 1993

Why virtues are basic to the common good. Bernardin, Joseph Louis, Cardinal, 1928-. *Origins* 23:337+ O 21 1993

Why we need the creeds. Stravinskas, Peter. *Register* 69:1+ My 16 1993

The work of His dying. McBride, Alfred. *OSV* 82:9 O 3 1993

CATECHISMS—CONTROVERSIES

American roadblock: why Rome refused a politically correct translation. *Crisis* 11:35-36 Je 1993

The catechism and inclusive language. Konstant, David Every, Bp, and Law, Bernard Francis, Cardinal, 1931-. *Origins* 22:628-630 F 25 1993

CATECHISMS—HISTORY

El catecismo en la historia de la Iglesia. García Ahumada, Enrique. *Teol Vida* 34 no 1-2:103-117 1993

Historical perspective sheds new light on most recent Catechism. Fernández, Ana Ofelia. *OR(Eng)* 1297:10 Je 30 1993

CATECHISMS—HISTORY- UNITED STATES

The American hierarchy, the propaganda fide, and the composition of hte Baltimore catechism. Malloy, David. *ACHSR* 103:35-46 Aut 1992

CATECHISMS—LANGUAGE

The catechism and inclusive language. Konstant, David Every, Bp, and Law, Bernard Francis, Cardinal, 1931-. *Origins* 22:628-630 F 25 1993

CATECHISMS- BRAZIL

A catequese em 1992. Cansi, Bernardo. *REB* 52:937-946 D 1992

CATECHISMS- SOUTH AFRICA

Synode africain et perspectives d'une nouvelle catéchèse. Kabasele Lumbala, François. *Lumen* 48:217-222 Je 1993

CATECHISMS, FRENCH

The catechism and inclusive language. Konstant, David Every, Bp, and Law, Bernard Francis, Cardinal, 1931-. *Origins* 22:628-630 F 25 1993

CATECHISTS

After the "what," what?. Marthaler, Berard L, 1927-. *Momentum* 24:52-55 S-O 1993

Catechists sound off. Ristow, Kate. *Catechist* 26:22-25 Ap-My 1993

Catechists: you are invaluable. Groome, Thomas H, 1945-. *ReligTJ* 27:4-5 S 1993

For catechists only: a final session. Galvich, Kathleen. *ReligTJ* 27:7 Ap-My 1993

How generous are you? Bowman, Peg. *ReligTJ* 27:7 S 1993

It's time for evaluation. Manternach, Janaan, and Pfeifer, Carl J. *ReligTJ* 27:4-5 Ap-My 1993

John Paul II, Pope, (1992-02-25) Itinera Apostolica (Address to catechists of Guinea during apostolic journey) [French]. John Paul II, Pope, 1920- (Karol Wojtyla) (elected 1978). *AAS* 85:175-178 F 3 1993*

Journeying with Jerome. Glavich, Kathleen. *ReligTJ* 27:52-53 S 1993

Looking back with love. Bowman, Peg. *ReligTJ* 27:13 Ap-My 1993

No saint for catechists? Bowman, Peg. *ReligTJ* 27:11 O 1993

On the road again. Gross, Adela. *ReligTJ* 27:54-55 S 1993

The priest as catechetical leader [2 pts]. McBride, Alfred. *Priest* 49:15-20 Je 1993; 29-33 Jl 1993

Religion teacher's planning calendar 1993-1994. Costello, Gwen. *ReligTJ* 27: 21-45 S 1993

Statement on catechetical ministry. *Living Light* 29:81-84 Spr 1993

Ways to pray with children. Manternach, Janaan, and Pfeifer, Carl J. *ReligTJ* 27:4-7 Mr 1993

We are more than teachers. Bowman, Peg. *ReligTJ* 27:15 F 1993

We are teachers and models. Pearson, Patricia O. *ReligTJ* 27:26-27 F 1993

We are windows to God. MacClennan, Carole. *ReligTJ* 27:47 S 1993

CATECHISTS—EDUCATION

Distance learning: a practical alternative for catechist formation. Schlather, Mary Margaret Ann. *Momentum* 24:73-74 N-D 1993

Feeding your catechists? Paprocki, Joseph. *ReligTJ* 27:63 S 1993

From the director's chair. Johnston, Mary Ann. *Momentum* 24:61-63 S-O 1993

How to care, share, and cooperate. Hennessy, Joan. *ReligTJ* 27:12-13 S 1993

My first incredible year. Mayet, Melva. *ReligTJ* 27:20 S 1993

Recruiting, training, and supporting volunteer catechists for students with challenging needs. Kammer, Kathleen. *Catechist* 27:9-10 N-D 1993

Ways to approach the Bible. Treston, Kevin. *ReligTJ* 27:8-10 O 1993

What should you teach? Treston, Kevin. *ReligTJ* 27:9-11 S 1993

3 great ways to look forward. Inkel, Maxine. *ReligTJ* 27:56-57 S 1993

CATECHISTS- ITALY

Il secondo convegno nazionale dei catechisti Italiani. Giachi, Gualberto. *Civilta* 144:563-570 Mr 20 1993

CATECHUMENS

Blessings and challenges of the RCIA. Griffin, James A, Bp, 1934-. *Origins* 22:565-572 Ja 28 1993

Committed worship: a sacramental theology for converting Christians, v 2. Gelpi, Donald L, 1934-. Minnesota: The Liturgical Press, 1993. x, 312p ISBN 0-8146-5826-1 LC 92-40430

Committed worship: a sacramental theology for converting Christians, v I. Gelpi, Donald L, 1934-. Minnesota: The Liturgical Press, 1993. x, 278p ISBN 0-8146-5825-3 LC 92-40430

Journey for the shadowlands: the readings for the Rites of the Cat. Jackson, Pamela E J. Minnesota: The Liturgical Press, 1993. x, 171p ISBN 0-8146-2113-9

CATEGORIES (PHILOSOPHY)

Actividades de conceptuacion: materiales de didactica de la filosofia sobre supuestos constructivistas. Benavente, Jose W. Madrid: Akal, 1993. x, 136p ISBN 84-460-0166-7

CATHEDRALS

Chartres and Ryoan-ji: aesthetic connections and affecting presence. Eusden, John D. *CrossCurr* 43:38-46 Spr 1993

CATHEDRALS- SPAIN

Almost a million at Mass in Madrid. Tierney, Stephen. *Tablet* 247:828 Je 26 1993

CATHER, WILLA SIBERT, 1873-1947

Willa Cather and the literature of Christian mystery. Murphy, John J. *Relig Lit* 24:39-56 Aut 1992

CATHERINE OF SIENA, SAINT, 1347?-1380

Catherine of Siena—passion for the truth, compassion for humanity: selected spiritual writings. O'Driscoll, Mary, ed. New Rochelle: New City Press, 1993. 144p ISBN 1-56548-058-9 LC 93-2543

In the Catholic tradition: St Catherine of Siena. Ronayne, Mary John. *Priests & People* 7:153-157 Ap 1993

The theological anthropology of Catherine of Siena. Jeremiah, Mary. *Communio* 20:457-462 Sum 1993

CATHOLIC—DOCTRINE

The revolution of the glory; introduction and part I; fundamental theology. Beeck, Frans Jozef van. Collegeville: Liturgical, 1993. x, 360p ISBN 0-8146-5498-3

CATHOLIC, AUTHORS

The forging of a freelance writer [interview by J Deedy]. Wilkes, Paul, 1938-. *Critic* 47:22-30 Wint 1992

The novel as spiritual guide. Sussman, Cornelia Silver, 1914-. *Living Prayer* 26:18-22 Ja-F 1993

Saint Evelyn Waugh. McInerny, Ralph M. *Crisis* 10:2-3 N 1992

Spiritual intimacy and community. English, John. New Jersey: Paulist Press, 1992. x, 207p ISBN 0-8091-3384-9 LC 92-29706

Walker Percy: the man and the movie. Austin, Ronald. *New Oxford Rev* 60: 16-19 O 1993

CATHOLIC ACTION

Catholic laity and social evils: a pre-Vatican II mandate. Kelly, George A. *SocJust* 84:67-76 My-Je 1993

Madonna House: holiness through little things [photos]. Achterhoff, Mary. *OSV* 82:12-13 My 16 1993

Peter Maurin: I am a radical. Hyre, Meg. *Cath Work* 60:1+ My 1993

CATHOLIC BIOGRAPHY

Ernesto Balducci. Del Zanna, Lorenzo. *Civilta* 144:445-458 Mr 6 1993

CATHOLIC CAMPAIGN FOR AMERICA

Catholic Campaign to advance "moral" agenda through media. DeCosse, David E. *Nat Cath Rep* 29:5 N 20 1992

Watch out, America they mean business!. Mullen, Peter. *Register* 69:1+ Ag 8 1993

CATHOLIC CHARISMATIC MOVEMENT see Pentecostalism—Catholic Church

CATHOLIC CHARITIES USA

Creating a new awareness of the adoption option. Barnard, Ann M. *OSV* 82: 17 S 12 1993

CATHOLIC CHURCH

The authority of the Catechism of the Catholic Church. Komonchak, Joseph Andrew, 1939-. *Living Light* 29:39-49 Sum 1993

Choosing a church. Vanauken, Sheldon. *New Oxford Rev* 60:20-22 Ap 1993

The Church as communio. Kasper, Walter. *New Blckfrs* 74:232-244 My 1993

A church is "Catholic" because it's sacramental. McBrien, Richard P. *Nat Cath Rep* 29:26 Ja 15 1993

Courage and the Holy Spirit [speech of Pope John Paul II]. John Paul II, Pope, 1920- (Karol Wojtyla) (elected 1978). *New Cov* 22:29 Je 1993*

Facts, myths and maybes: everything you think you know about Catholicism. Deedy, John G, 1933-. Chicago: The Thomas More Press, 1993. 320p ISBN 0-88347-272-4

God's politician: Pope John Paul II, the Catholic Church, and the new world order. Willey, David. New York: St Martin's Press, 1993. x, 258p ISBN 0-31208-798-5 LC 92-36031

Life's greatest grace: why I belong to the Catholic Church. Miller, J Michael. Huntington: Our Sunday Visitor, 1993. x, 160p ISBN 0-87973-471-9

Many models, one church. Komonchak, Joseph Andrew, 1939-. *Church* 9:12-15 Spr 1993

Observations on healthy sexuality. Griffin-Shelley, Eric. *Priest* 49:29-33 Ja 1993

Participação numa igreja constítuida hierarquicamente. Leites Oares, Alfredo. *Periodica* 82 no 1:139-174 1993

The post-Vatican II Church. Fleming, David L. *RRel* 52:484-485 Jl-Ag 1993

Santo Domingo: doloroso avance de la iglesia de Latinamericano. Gándara, Miguel Alvarez. *Christus* 58:50-55 N-D 1992

A sense of purpose. Miranda, Caroline. *Register* 69:5 Mr 28 1993

Sensus Fidei: theological reflection since Vatican II: I, 1965-1984. Burkhard, John J. *Heythrop* 34:41-59 Ja; 123-136 Ap 1993

A vision for the unity of human kind. Himes, Michael J, and Himes, Kenneth R. *ChrWorld* 236:203-211 S-O 1993

What Catholics really believe [interview by Mitch Finley]. Finley, Mitchel B. *OSV* 81:6-7 F 21 1993

Will the real Catholic Church please stand up. Burns, Robert E, 1919-. *USCath* 58:2 F 1993

CATHOLIC CHURCH—(ARCHDIOCESE) DETROIT
Developing a strategy for the urban parish: the lessons of the church closings in Detroit. Fukuzawa, David. *New Theol Rev* 6:54-65 F 1993

CATHOLIC CHURCH—AUTHORITY
Refounding church—a paradigm shift. Donovan, Vincent. *Chicago Stud* 31:215-223 Ag 1992

CATHOLIC CHURCH—BISHOPS
Stewardship also requires greenbacks, critic says. Vidulich, Dorothy. *Nat Cath Rep* 29:9 Ja 8 1993

CATHOLIC CHURCH—BISHOPS- UNITED STATES
Coming soon to a parish near you. Breig, James. *OSV* 82:12 Ag 8 1993

To support, or not support, Clinton's plan. Shaw, Russell. *OSV* 82:3 My 2 1993

CATHOLIC CHURCH—BYZANTINE RITE
The Elko episcopate an era of conversions. Renoff, Richard. *Diakonia* 26 no 2:99-118 1993

CATHOLIC CHURCH—BYZANTINE RITE—LITURGY
In Byzantine liturgy, heaven is brought down to earth. Ford, Paul, and Daurio, Janice. *Register* 69:1+ O 10 1993

CATHOLIC CHURCH—BYZANTINE RITE, GREEK
Married to priests return to ministry. *Tablet* 247:1108-1109 Ag 28 1993

Remain steadfast in the Catholic faith of our ancestors. *OR(Eng)* 1301:1-2 Jl 28 1993

CATHOLIC CHURCH—BYZANTINE RITE, MELCHITE
The Melkites: Catholicism is Greek to them [interview by C Samra]. Samra, Nicholas J, Bp. *OSV* 82:5 S 26 1993

CATHOLIC CHURCH—BYZANTINE RITE, UKRAINIAN
Cornerstone or stumbling-block? Sorokowski, Andrew. *America* 169:15-17 O 23 1993

Present situation of the Ukrainian Catholic Church in Ukraine. Sulyk, Stephen. *Diakonia* 26 no 3:149-160 1993

Seminary on a shoestring. Johnson, Grove. *Tablet* 247:914-915 Jl 17 1993

The Ukrainian Catholic Church: up from the underground. Widner, Thomas C. *America* 169:12-15 O 23 1993

CATHOLIC CHURCH—CATECHETICS *see* Catechetics—Catholic Church

CATHOLIC CHURCH—CATHOLICITY
The Church and morality: an ecumenical and Catholic approach. Curran, Charles E, 1934-. Minneapolis: Fortress Press, 1993. 126p ISBN 0-8006-2756-3 LC 92-47448

The local church and the church Catholic: the contemporary theological problematic. Komonchak, Joseph Andrew, 1939-. *Jurist* 52 no 1:416-447 1992

Response to Wolfgang Beinert. Sullivan, Francis Aloysius. *Jurist* 52 no 1:484-489 1992

CATHOLIC CHURCH—CLERGY
Ecumenism, sex abuse top CTSA agenda. Jones, Arthur C, 1936-. *Nat Cath Rep* 29:4 Jl 2 1993

CATHOLIC CHURCH—CLERGY—HISTORY
"Sentire cum ecclesia" [2 parts]. Gerhartz, Johannes Günter. *Civilta* 2:227-237 My 1; 313-326 My 15; 227-237 1993

CATHOLIC CHURCH—CONGREGATION FOR BISHOPS—DECREE
Congregation for Bishops (1992-02-28) [Decree]. *AAS* 85:212-213 F 3 1993*

Congregation for Bishops (1992-06-29) [Latin]. *AAS* 85:204-205 F 3 1993*

Congregation for Bishops (1992-09-05). *AAS* 85:205-212 F 3 1993*

Congregation for Bishops (1992-09-19). *AAS* 85:213-214 F 3 1993*

Congregation for Bishops (1992-10-31). *AAS* 85:214-215 F 3 1993*

CATHOLIC CHURCH—CONGREGATION FOR CATHOLIC EDUCATION
Pédagogie du célibat dans les orientations et documents écents de l'église. Marcus, Emile. *Seminarium* 33:15-31 Ja-Mr 1993

CATHOLIC CHURCH—CONGREGATION FOR DIVINE WORSHIP
Congregatio de Culto divino et disciplina sacramentorum. Congregation for Divine Worship and Discipline of the Sacraments. *Notitiae* 28:391-403 Je 1992

Lettera a Mons Johannes Wagner in occasione del suo 85 genetliaco. Javierre, Antonio M, Cardinal, and Angelo, Geraldo M. *Notitiae* 29:28-29 Ja-F 1993

De promissione electorum in ordinatione diaconali iuxta pontificale romanum anni 1990. Ghirlanda, Gianfranco. *Periodica* 81 no 2:211-250 1992

Riti nella chiesa (editorial). *Notitiae* 28:365-368 Je 1992

Riunione della IAG a Salzburg. Fricke, Wolfgang. *Notitiae* 28:290-294 Ap 1992

Santuari (editorial). *Notitiae* 28:233-235 Ap 1992

La Semaine Sainte dans le lectionnaire biennal de l'office de la lecture. Martimorte, Aimé-Georges. *Notitiae* 29:91-93 Mr 1993

Tempus quadragesimae Hebdomada Sancta: Anno I, Liturgia Horarum Supplementum. *Notitiae* 29:94-136 Mr 1993

Tempus quadragesimae Hebdomada sancta: Anno II, Liturgia Horarum Supplementum. *Notitiae* 29:137-168 Mr 1993

When there is no priest. Dubourd, Nancy A. *Mod Lit* 20:14-15 F 1993

CATHOLIC CHURCH—CONGREGATION FOR DIVINE WORSHIP-FRANCE
Gallia: l'activité de la commission épiscopale de liturgie et de pastorale sacramentelle. *Notitiae* 29:285-289 My 1993

CATHOLIC CHURCH—CONGREGATION FOR DIVINE WORSHIP-GERMANY
La revista gottesdienst cuplioó 25 años. Nagel, Eduard, and Palacios, Miguel. *Notitiae* 29:304-306 My 1993

CATHOLIC CHURCH—CONGREGATION FOR DIVINE WORSHIP-ITALY
Italia: La progettazione Di Nuove Chiese. Brandolini, Luca. *Notitiae* 29:290-303 My 1993

CATHOLIC CHURCH—CONGREGATION FOR DIVINE WORSHIP-NIGERIA
Nigeria report of activities of the national liturgy commission. Congregation for Divine Worship and Discipline of the Sacraments. *Notitiae* 28:191-192 Mr 1992

CATHOLIC CHURCH—CONGREGATION FOR DOCTRINE OF THE FAITH
The CDF letter on Communion: reactions and reflections. Rausch, Thomas P. *Ecumen Trends* 22:3-4 Ap 1993

The Church as communion. Yarnold, Edward John, 1926-. *Tablet* 246:1564-1565 D 12 1992

Church unity rooted in Eucharist. *OR(Eng)* 1298:4+ Jl 7 1993*

Gay Christians. Lyons, Kieran. *Furrow* 44:347-351 Je 1993

A glitch or a gulf? Canterbury, Rome and reunion. Nilson, Jon. *Comm* 120:6-8 F 26 1993

The magisterium and morality. Spohn, William C. *TheolStds* 54:95-111 Mr 1993

What about our Church's children? Giurlanda, Paul. *America* 168:12-14 My 8 1993

CATHOLIC CHURCH—CONGREGATION FOR DOCTRINE OF THE FAITH—DECREE
Congregation for the Doctrine of the Faith (1992-06-06) Decretum de doctrina "Opus Angelorum" [Latin]. Congregation for Doctrine of the Faith. *AAS* 84:805-806 Ag 3 1992*

CATHOLIC CHURCH—CONGREGATION FOR INSTITUTES OF CONSECRATED LIFE AND FOR SOCIETIES OF APOSTOLIC LIFE
Activities of the Congregation for Institutes of Consecrated Life and for Societies of Apostolic Life during 1991. *Con Life* 17 no 2:154-166 1992

New communities. McDonough, Elizabeth. *RRel* 52:140-146 Ja-F 1993

CATHOLIC CHURCH—CONGREGATION FOR THE CAUSES OF SAINTS
John Paul II, Pope, (1992-05-31) A faithful servant and perfect friend. John Paul II, Pope, 1920- (Karol Wojtyla) (elected 1978). *TPS* 38:14-18 Ja-F 1993*

CATHOLIC CHURCH—CONGREGATION FOR THE CAUSES OF SAINTS—DECREE
Congregation for the Causes of Saints (1991-12-21) Decree on a miracle . Congregation for the Causes of Saints. *AAS* 84:807-809 Ag 3 1992*

Congregation for the Causes of Saints (1991-12-21) Decree on the heroic virtues Alberto Hurtado Cruchaga [Latin]. Congregation for the Causes of Saints. *AAS* 84:815-818 Ag 3 1992*

Congregation for the Causes of Saints (1991-12-21) Decree on the heroic virtues of Gerardo de San Francisco Sagarduy Salazar [Latin]. Congregation for the Causes of Saints. *AAS* 84:810-814 Ag 3 1992*

Congregation for the Causes of Saints (1991-12-21) Decree on the heroic virtues of Marie Poussepin. Congregation for the Causes of Saints. *AAS* 84:913-916 S 8 1992*

Congregation for the Causes of Saints (1991-12-21) Decree on the heroic virtues of Vincenzo Cimatti [Latin]. Congregation for the Causes of Saints. *AAS* 84:819-822 Ag 3 1992*

Congregation for the Causes of Saints (1992-02-07) Decree on the heroic virtues. Congregation for the Causes of Saints. *AAS* 84:999-1004 O 3 1992*

Congregation for the Causes of Saints (1992-03-07) Decree on a miracle . Congregation for the Causes of Saints. *AAS* 84:924-926 S 8 1992*

Congregation for the Causes of Saints (1992-03-07) Decree on a miracle. Congregation for the Causes of Saints. *AAS* 84:1005-1007 O 3 1992*

Congregation for the Causes of Saints (1992-03-07) Decree on a miracle. Congregation for the Causes of Saints. *AAS* 84:1089-1091 N 3 1992*

Congregation for the Causes of Saints (1992-03-07) Decree on the heroic virtues. Congregation for the Causes of Saints. *AAS* 84:1007-1010 O 3 1992*

Congregation for the Causes of Saints (1992-03-07) Decree on the heroic virtues. Congregation for the Causes of Saints. *AAS* 84:1011-1014 O 3 1992*

Congregation for the Causes of Saints (1992-03-07) Decree on the heroic virtues. Congregation for the Causes of Saints. *AAS* 84:1080-1083 N 3 1992*

Congregation for the Causes of Saints (1992-03-07) Decree on the heroic virtues. Congregation for the Causes of Saints. *AAS* 84:1084-1088 N 3 1992*

Congregation for the Causes of Saints (1992-03-07) Decree on the heroic virtues. Congregation for the Causes of Saints. *AAS* 84:916-923 S 8 1992*

CATHOLIC CHURCH—CONGREGATION FOR THE CLERGY

CATHOLIC CHURCH—CONGREGATION FOR THE EVANGELIZATION OF PEOPLES OR FOR THE PROPAGATION OF THE FAITH

Concili Ecumenic Vatica 2: Constitucions, Decrets, Declaracions. Barcelona: Claret, 1993. x, 495p ISBN 84-7263-839-1

A concise catechism for Catholics. Tolhurst, James. Grand Rapids: Eerdmans, 1993. 80p ISBN 0-8028-0122-6

Current errors and their refutation: respect the charisms God has given Holy Doctors and the Magisterium. Sutton, Alphonsus M. *ChrWorld* 38:144-152 Mr-Ap 1993

Dialogue about Catholic's sexual teaching. Curran, Charles E, 1934-, and McCormick, Richard A, eds. Mahwah: Paulist, 1993. x, 601p ISBN 0-8091-3414-4 LC 93-4370

Dullness of error, splendor of truth. Novak, Michael, 1933-. *Crisis* 11:4-6+ S 1993

"The end of American Catholicism?"—another look. Hegy, Pierre M. *America* 168:4-9 My 1 1993

The Eucharist, our sanctification. Cantalamessa, Raniero. Minnesota: The Order of St Benedict, 1993. x, 89p ISBN 0-8146-2075-2 LC 92-404-433

The Eucharistic mystery: revitalizing the tradition. Power, David Noel. New York: The Crossroad Publishing Company, 1992. x, 370p ISBN 0-8245-1220-0 LC 92-29777

The eucharistic presence of Christ. Cummings, Owen F. *Emmanuel* 99:256-263 Je 1993

European enthusiasm: a bestseller for the hungering faithful. Fumagalli, Armando. *Crisis* 11:31-32+ Je 1993*

Evangelical Kernels: a theological spirituality of the religious life. Billy, Dennis J. New York: Alba House, 1993. ISBN

Everybody has guardian angel: and other lasting lessons I learned in Catholic School. Finley, Mitchel B. New York: The Crossroad Publishing Company, 1993. 188p ISBN 0-8245-1268-5 LC 92-39443

Facts, myths and maybes: everything you think you know about Catholocism. Deedy, John G, 1933-. Chicago: The Thomas More Press, 1993. 320p ISBN 0-88347-272-4

Fullness of faith: the public significance of theology. Himes, Michael J, and Himes, Kenneth R. New York: Paulist Press, 1993. x, 213p ISBN 0-8091-3372-5 LC 92-36140

Gay Catholics divide in approach to church teaching. *Tablet* 247:1023-1024 Ag 7 1993

"Gay gene" forces a rethink on homosexuality. *Tablet* 247:958-959 Jl 24 1993

Hark! it's the sound of protest. Edwards, Robin T. *Nat Cath Rep* 29:5 Ag 27 1993

Horizons for Catholic feminist theology. Conn, Joann Wolski, and Conn, Walter E, eds. Washington, D C: Georgetown University Press, 1992. x, 207p ISBN 0-87840-534-8 LC 92-30435

How to read the church fathers. Hamman, Adalbert. New York: The Crossroad Publishing Company, 1993. x, 132p ISBN 0-8245-1204-9 LC 92-42052

"Humanae Vitae" after 25 years. Schall, James Vincent, 1928-. *Crisis* 11:48-49 Jl-Ag 1993

"Humanae Vitae": 25th anniversary. McMahon, Kevin. *Origins* 22:768-774 Ap 22 1993*

"I'm here" [interview by T H Stahel, 1938-]. Sullivan, Andrew. *America* 168: 5-11 My 8 1993

La identidad eclesial de la teología fundamental. Pié-Ninot, Salvador. *Gregorianum* 74 No 1:75-99 1993

La iglesia local en la inculturación del evangelio. Salado Martinez, Domingo. *Cien Tom* 120:129-152 Ja-Ap 1993

In che senso la dottrina sociale della chiesa è universale? Joblin, Joseph, 1920-. *Civilta* 3:15-28 Jl 3 1993

Interactional morality: a foundation for moral discernment in Catholic pastoral ministry. Poorman, Mark L. Washington: Georgetown University Press, 1993. 157p ISBN 0-87840-536-4 LC 93-3803

Intimate bedfellows: love, sex, and the Catholic Church. Finn, Thomas, and Finn, Donna. Boston: St. Paul Books & Media, 1993. 85p ISBN 0-8198-3667-2 LC 92-42622

John Paul II, Pope, (1993-06-01) Eucharist [Orig in French]. John Paul II, Pope, 1920- (Karol Wojtyla) (elected 1978). *OR(Eng)* 1297:8 Je 30 1993*

Journey of love: God moving in our hearts and lives. Conroy, Maureen. Mahwah: The Paulist Press, 1993. 82p ISBN 0-8091-3413-6 LC 93-979

"Ken, don't foul up the Church today" [photo]. Desmet, Kate. *Critic* 47:14-29 Spr 1993

Life's greatest grace: why I belong to the Catholic Church. Miller, J Michael. Huntington: Our Sunday Visitor, 1993. x, 160p ISBN 0-87973-471-9

Light of faith: the compenduine of theology. Thomas Aquinas, Saint. Manchester: Sophia Institute Press, 1993. x, 412p ISBN 0-918477-15-8 LC 93-6793

Marriage and sacrament: a theology of Christian marriage. Lawler, Michael G. Collegeville: Liturgical, 1993. x, 122p ISBN 0-8146-5051-1 LC 93-22619

Mary and catechesis: there's room for two approaches. Buckley, Francis J. *Catechist* 26:26-29 Ap-My 1993

Near occasions of grace. Rohr, Richard, 1943-. New York: Orbis Books, 1993. x, 118p ISBN 0-88344-852-1 LC 92-33193

The new Catechism: a first reading. Cunningham, Lawrence S, 1935-. *Comm* 120:8-12 Mr 12 1993

The new dictionary of Catholic spirituality. Downey, Michael, ed. Minnesota: The Order of St Benedict, 1993. x, 1083p ISBN 0-8146-5525-4 LC 92-40959

The path to hope: fragments from a theologian's journey. Boff, Leonardo. Maryknoll, New York: Orbis Books, 1993. x, 134p ISBN 0-88344-815-7 LC 92-35823

Population, the Church and the Pope. Schwarz, John C. *America* 168:6-10 Mr 6 1993

A private anguish. Richards, Robin. *Tablet* 247:566 My 8 1993

Razing the bastions: on the church in this age. Balthasar, Hans Urs Von, 1905-1988. San Francisco: Ignatius Press, 1993. ISBN 0-89870-428-6

The real presence through the ages: Jesus adored in the sacrament of the altar. Gaudoin-Parker, Michael L. New York: Alba House, 1993. x, 222p ISBN 0-8189-0662-6 LC 92-42274

Reasons for disbelief. Bull, George, 1929-. *Tablet* 247:240-241 F 20 1993

Reflections of a parish priest. Keller, Dan. *Momentum* 24:58-60 S-O 1993

Safeguarding the faith. Arthadeva, Basil Mary. *ChrWorld* 38:15-23 Ja-F 1993

Tales of the city of God. Valles, Carlos G. Chicago: Loyola University Press, 1993. x, 254p ISBN 0-8294-0750-2 LC 93-8938

Towards a new Pentecost: for a new evangelization. McDonnell, Kilian, 1921-, ed. Collegeville:Liturgical, 1993. x, 72p ISBN 0-8146-5846-6 LC 92-46910

Transforming today's church. Graff, Ann O'Hara. *Chicago Stud* 32:127-142 Ag 1993

A view from Rome: on the eve of the modernist crisis. Schultenover, David G. New York: Fordham University Press, 1993. x, 283p ISBN 0-8232-1358-7 LC 92-23892

The Virgin Mary and the priesthood. Philippe, Pierre Paul, Cardinal, 1905-1984. New York: Alba House, 1993. x, 135p ISBN 0-8189-0668-5 LC 93-6682

What about our Church's children? Giurlanda, Paul. *America* 168:12-14 My 8 1993

Word become flesh: dimensions of Christology. McDermott, Brian O. Minnesota: The Liturgical Press, 1993. x, 302p ISBN 0-8146-5015-5 LC 92-34915

The world made flesh: an overview of the Catholic faith. Marinelli, Anthony. Mahwah: Paulist Press, 1993. 309p ISBN 0-8091-3391-1 LC 92-45629

Wrestling still: twenty-five years and counting. Jordan, Patrick. *Comm* 120: 4-5 Jl 16 1993

CATHOLIC CHURCH—DOCUMENTS
La asamblea y el documento. Trigo, Pedro. *Christus* 58:48-61 Mr-Ap 1993

CATHOLIC CHURCH—EDUCATION
Can higher education foster moral development? Heft, James. *Origins* 22: 557-565 Ja 28 1993

Catholic schools: goals/strategies. *Origins* 23:238-248 S 16 1993

College education/values education. Hagan, Charles H. *Origins* 22:602-604 F 11 1993

Educating in faith. Boys, Mary C. Kansas City: Sheed & Ward, 1989. 230p ISBN 1-55612-668-9

Education for ministry: reform and renewal in theological education. Schner, George P, 1946-. Kansas City: Sheed & Ward, 1993. x, 195p ISBN 15-5612-566-6 LC 92-32958

The Education of American Catholics: shaping the third millenium. Veverka, Fayette Breaux. *Listening* 28:28-40 Wint 1993

Formation of the young as moral agents. Hagan, Charles H. *Origins* 23:430-432 N 25 1993

John Paul II, Pope, (1991-11-23) Allocutiones (Address to Catholic educators) [Italian]. John Paul II, Pope, 1920- (Karol Wojtyla) (elected 1978). *AAS* 84:1132-1138 D 5 1992*

John Paul II, Pope, (1991-11-23) Allocutiones (Address to Catholic educators) [Italian]. John Paul II, Pope, 1920- (Karol Wojtyla) (elected 1978). *AAS* 84:1132-1138 D 5 1992*

John Paul II, Pope, (1993-05-27) Catholic University of America [Orig in English]. John Paul II, Pope, 1920- (Karol Wojtyla) (elected 1978). *OR(Eng)* 1294:10 Je 9 1993*

Keeping a tradtion evergreen. Donahue, John W, 1917-. *America* 168:4 My 29 1993

Morality and youth: fostering Christian identity. DiGiacomo, James J. Kansas City: Sheed & Ward, 1993. x, 156p ISBN 1-55612-652-2 LC 93-938

Parish catechesis: an expanding vision. Humphrey, Robert L, 1923-. *Momentum* 24:31-35 F-Mr 1993

Reflections on World Youth Day: Catholic education. McGuire, Patricia. *Origins* 23:265+ S 30 1993

Religious superiors defend school's Catholic identity. Schaberg, Jane. *Origins* 22:703-704 Mr 25 1993

The soul power a nation needs. Quinn, Francis, Bp. *Origins* 22:605+ F 18 1993

Statement on public schools' condom distribution. *Origins* 22:553-556 Ja 21 1993

To reach full knowledge of the truth. Myers, John, Bp. *Origins* 22:593-601 F 11 1993

Toward effective adult religious education. Dumestre, Marcel. *Origins* 23:24-28 My 27 1993

La vie dans le Christ. Chapelle, Albert. *NRT* 115:169-185 Mr-Ap 1993

Witness and action toward a well-ordered society. Keeler, William H, Abp. *Momentum* 24:6-8 N-D 1993

Women collaborators in Catholic education: nineteenth century America. Donovan, Grace. *ACHSR* 103:23-33 Aut 1992

CATHOLIC CHURCH—EDUCATION- RUSSIA
Catholic seminary opens in Moscow. Mattei, Giampaolo. *OR(Eng)* 1309:6-7 S 29 1993

CATHOLIC CHURCH—EMPLOYEES
Director of volunteer ministries. Ledwig, Frances. *Church* 9:28-30 Sum 1993

Just wages in the church? Almade, Frank D. *Church* 9:41-43 Spr 1993

Study: US dioceses lag in minority hiring. Gibeau, Dawn. *Nat Cath Rep* 29:8 Ja 22 1993

We're all pros now. Feuerherd, Peter. *Register* 69:1+ Mr 28 1993

CATHOLIC CHURCH—ETHIOPIAN RITE
John Paul II, Pope, (1993-06-11) Ethiopian Orthodox Patriarch. John Paul II, Pope, 1920- (Karol Wojtyla) (elected 1978). *OR(Eng)* 1295:5 Je 16 1993*

CATHOLIC CHURCH—FASTS AND FEASTS
The feast of Corpus Christi. Gribble, Richard. *Emmanuel* 99:264-269 Je 1993

The feast of the Chair of Peter. Mangan, Charles M. *OSV* 81:14 F 21 1993

John Paul II, Pope, (1993-06-10) Corpus Christi. John Paul II, Pope, 1920- (Karol Wojtyla) (elected 1978). *OR(Eng)* 1295:2 Je 16 1993*

"O Blessed Mother, a sword has pierced your heart". Gribble, Richard. *OSV* 82:5 S 12 1993

The revision and placement of Marian feasts. Samaha, John M. *Priest* 49:35-39 My 1993

CATHOLIC CHURCH—FINANCE
Accountability in the church. McDonnell, Dominic. *Priests & People* 6:340-342 Ag-S 1992

The bottom line [editorial]. *Register* 69:4 S 26 1993

Catholic giving and the signs of the times. Hofheinz, Fred. *Origins* 22:520-523 Ja 7 1993

Catholics will give when church moves into future. Davis, Charlie. *Nat Cath Rep* 29:13 F 12 1993

Dioceses abhor a vacuum, so offices multiply. Howes, Robert G. *Nat Cath Rep* 29:22 Ja 15 1993

Dollars dried up with move away from tradition. O'Reilly, Stephan J. *Nat Cath Rep* 29:13 F 12 1993

Laity must get involved in dollars and cents. Halloway, George. *Register* 69:7 S 26 1993

What about the finances of the church? Brotherton, Fergus. *Priests & People* 7:191-193 My 1993

What are Catholics holding out for? *USCath* 58:2 Ap 1993

CATHOLIC CHURCH—FINANCE- ITALY

Partecipazione e trasparenza nel sóstegno economico alla chiesa. Giachi, Gualberto. *Civilta* 3:147-153 Jl 17 1993

CATHOLIC CHURCH—GOVERNMENT

A democratic Catholic Church: in a reconstruction of Roman Catholicism. Bianchi, Eugene C, and Ruether, Rosemary Radford, eds. New York: Crossroad, 1993. x, 262p ISBN 0-8245-1186-7 LC 92-7920

"Inside the Vatican:" want a peek? Burke, Greg. *Register* 69:1+ Je 13 1993

John Paul II, Pope, (1992-01-23) Allocutiones (Address to Roman Rota) [Italian]. John Paul II, Pope, 1920- (Karol Wojtyla) (elected 1978). *AAS* 85:140-143 F 3 1993*

CATHOLIC CHURCH—HISTORIOGRAPHY

The Catholic hierarchy in the United States between the Third Plenary Council and the condemnation of Americanism [photos]. Fogarty, Gerald P, 1939-. *US Cath Hist* 11:19-36 Sum 1993

The new Americanism in Catholic historiography. Gleason, Philip. *US Cath Hist* 11:1-18 Sum 1993

CATHOLIC CHURCH—HISTORY

Being Catholic: Commonweal from the seventies to the nineties. Allen, Rodger Van. Chicago: Loyola University Press, 1993. x, 203p ISBN 0-8294-0744-8 LC 92-40701

The catholicity of the church in the New Testament and in the early patristic period. Fahey, Michael A. *Jurist* 52 no 1:44-70 1992

Fray Luis de Granada y Erasmo. Seco, Atilano Rico. *Cien Tom* 119:549-578 S-D 1992

Johann Adam Möhler and worship in Totalitarian society. Franklin, R William. *Worship* 67:2-17 Ja 1993

Response to Michael Fahey. Trevijano, Ramon. *Jurist* 52 no 1:71-78 1992

Who's been sitting in Peter's chair? Pazola, Ron. *USCath* 58:34-39 Jl 1993

The work our era demands of us: the recovery of lay leadership. Sellner, Edward Cletus. *Listening* 28:65-80 Wint 1993

CATHOLIC CHURCH—HISTORY—0030-600

Local churches and catholicity in the first millennium of the Roman tradition. Peri, Vittorio. *Jurist* 52 no 1:79-108 1992

CATHOLIC CHURCH—HISTORY—1500-1600

The Catholic reformation: Savonarola to Ignatius Loyola: reform in the church, 1495-1540. Olin, John C. New York: Fordham University Press, 1992. x, 218p ISBN 0-8232-1477-x LC 92-29865

"Sentire cum ecclesia" [2 parts]. Gerhartz, Johannes Günter. *Civilta* 2:227-237 My 1; 313-326 My 15; 227-237 1993

CATHOLIC CHURCH—HISTORY—1800-1899

The new Americanism in Catholic historiography. Gleason, Philip. *US Cath Hist* 11:1-18 Sum 1993

CATHOLIC CHURCH—HISTORY—1965-

Faith and the human enterprise: a post-Vatican II vision. Weakland, Rembert G, Abp, 1927-. Maryknoll: Orbis Books, 1992. 168p ISBN 0-88344-835-1 LC 92-32884

CATHOLIC CHURCH—INTERNATIONAL COUNCIL FOR CATECHESIS

Para comprender el catecismo. Aguilera, Francisco M. *Christus* 58:37-38 Je 1993

CATHOLIC CHURCH—LITURGY

Advocacy packaged as theology [review article *The new dictionary of sacramental worship* by P Fink, ed]. Boughton, Lynne C. *HPR* 93:56-62 Je 1993

Another "objector". Mullen, Peter. *Register* 69:2 Ap 18 1993

Bodying forth: aesthetic liturgy. Collins, Patrick W, 1936-. New Jersey: Paulist Press, 1992. x, 187p ISBN 0-8091-3352-0 LC 92-28045

Catechumenate for children. Duggan, Robert D. *Church* 9:46-47 Spr 1993

Celebration of the word. Deiss, Lucien. Collegeville: Liturgical, 1993. x, 145p ISBN 0-8146-2090-6 LC 93-15193

Confirmation: the baby in Solomon's court. Turner, Paul. New Jersey: Paulist Press, 1993. x, 188p ISBN 0-8091-3370-9 LC 92-320094

Console one another: a guide for Christian funerals. Curley, Terence P. Kansas City: Sheed & Ward, 1993. 100p ISBN 1-55612-600-x LC 93-3540

Creation and liturgy. McMichael, Ralph N, Jr, ed. Washington: The Pastoral Press, 1993. 320p ISBN 1-562929-001-6

Days of the Lord, vol 5, ordinary time: year B. Collegeville: Liturgical, 1993. 376p ISBN 0-8146-1903-7 LC 90-22253

Days of the Lord: the liturgical year; vol 2. Beaumont, Madeleine. Minnesota: The Liturgical Press, 1990. x, 274p ISBN 0-8146-1900-2 LC 90-22253

Days of the Lord: the liturgical year; vol 3. LaNave, Gred. Minnesota: The Liturgical Press, 1993. x, 364p ISBN 0-8146-1901-0 LC 90-22253

Dialogue [interview by C Allen]. Page, John. *Register* 69:1+ Je 11 1993

Dialogue [interview by P Mullen]. Stravinskas, Peter. *Register* 69:1+ Ja 24 1993

Does the church want adult education? Lundy, Damian. *Priests & People* 7:45-49 F 1993

Eucharist of the assembly. Huck, Gabe. *Church* 9:7-11 Spr 1993

The Eucharistic mystery: revitalizing the tradition. Power, David Noel. New York: The Crossroad Publishing Company, 1992. x, 370p ISBN 0-8245-1220-0 LC 92-29777

Ever old, yet ever new. Walter Scott. *Register* 69:5 F 7 1993

The good fight. Mullen, Peter. *Register* 69:3 Ap 11 1993

Hispanic culture and worship: the process of inculturation. Martínez, Germán. *US Cath Hist* 11:79-91 Spr 1993

In the company of preachers. Minnesota: The Liturgical Press, 1993. x, 227p ISBN 0-8146-2091-4 LC 92-32646

Keeping things in place. Santognossi, Ansgar. *Register* 69:5 F 28 1993

"Let us offer each other the sign of peace"—an enquiry. Woolfenden, Graham. *Worship* 67:239-252 My 1993

Lettera al Prof Balthasar Fischer in occasione del suo 80 genetliaco. Javierre, Antonio M, Cardinal. *Notitiae* 28:584-585 S 1992

The liturgical assembly: review and reassessment. Vincie, Catherine. *Worship* 67:123-144 Mr 1993

Liturgical despots. Trigilio, John P. *HPR* 93:66-69 Ja 1993

Liturgy and personality: the healing power of formal prayer. Hildebrand, Dietrich von. Manchester: Sophia Institute Press, 1993. x, 165p ISBN 0-918477-13-1 LC 29-19821

Liturgy: life-blood of a parish. Clarke, Pauline. *Priests & People* 7:91-93 Mr 1993

Lost in translation: ICEL and the Roman Canon. Pope, Charles E. *HPR* 93:65-73 Ag-S 1993

Making one family out of strangers: re-imagining the Catholic church. Jones, Alan. *Pacifica* 6:249-264 O 1993

A mass at Verdun. Boughton, Willis L. *HPR* 94:55-58 O 1993

Mass confusion [editorial]. *OSV* 81:2 Mr 7 1993

The Mass explained [condensed fr *Eucharistic Minister* S 1992]. McHugh, Joseph F. *CDgst* 57:51-54 F 1993

The Mass explained: part four [condensed fr *Eucharistic Minister* D 1992]. McHugh, Joseph F. *CDgst* 57:47-52 My 1993

The Mass explained: part three [condensed fr *Eucharistic Minister* N 1992]. Mchugh, Joseph F. *CDgst* 57:65-70 Ap 1993

The mass explained: part two [condensed fr *Eucharistic Minister* O 1992]. McHugh, Joseph F. *CDgst* 57:83-87 Mr 1993

Multicultural liturgy. Jordan, Brian J. *Church* 9:11-15 Sum 1993

A museum for Catholics over 40. O'Neill, Robert K. *CDgst* 57:59-64 Ja 1993

Myths and truths about the Eucharist. Beards, Andrew. *HPR* 93:18-26 Ag-S 1993

A necessary revision in competent hands. Field, James A. *Tod Parish* 25:28-30 Ja 1993

A new commandment: toward a renewed rite for the washing of feet. Jeffery, Peter, 1953-. Collegeville, Minnesota: The Liturgical Press, 1992. 80p ISBN 0-81462-004-3 LC 92-17174

Once upon a miracle: dramas for worship and religious education. Moynahan, Michael E. New York: Paulist Press, 1993. x, 210p ISBN 0-8091-3361-x LC 92-41325

Prayer before the Eucharist. Camiré, Bernard. *Emmanuel* 99:184-189 My 1993

The preparatory rites: a case study in liturgical ecology. Foley, Edward, et al. *Worship* 67:17-38 Ja 1993

Preparing for advent. Duggan, Robert D. *Church* 9:36-37 Aut 1993

Preparing the assembly for liturgy. Duggan, Robert D. *Church* 9:36-37 Sum 1993

Preparing the people. Dodds, Bill. *OSV* 81:8 Mr 28 1993

Prier et chanter chacun dans sa propre langue. Speeten, Joseph Van Der. *Notitiae* 28:755-759 N-D 1992

Ratzinger prefers altar turned around again. Moynihan, Robert. *Nat Cath Rep* 29:7 My 28 1993

Rekindling the passion. Jorgensen, Susan S. San Jose: Resource Publications, Inc, 1993. x, 251p ISBN 0-89390-236-5 LC 92-32396

The renewal of liturgical celebrations in the Swedish church. Lindbladh, Nils-Henrik. *Notitiae* 28:492-495 Jl 1992

Le renouveau liturgique au Rwanda. Congregation for Divine Worship and Discipline of the Sacraments. *Notitiae* 28:484-491 Jl 1992

Restoring the sweetness: the liturgical agenda. Collins, Seán. *Doctr Life* 43:130-140 Mr 1993

Seasons and feasts of the church year. Whalon, Michael D. New York: Paulist Press, 1993. 180p ISBN 0-8091-3346-6 LC 92-24215

Shortcuts that short-circuit the liturgy. Grondelski, John M. *Priest* 49:17-18 Ap 1993

Sound the trumpet: reflections on the paschal mystery. Gallagher, Michele T, 1943-. New York: Alba House, 1993. x, 134p ISBN 0-8189-0665-0 LC 92-40309

Untangling the Latin Mass controversy. Carey, Ann. *OSV* 81:12-13 Mr 7 1993

What liturgy is like a party. McBride, Alfred. *OSV* 82:16 O 10 1993

Whiter the mass? Mole, John W. *HPR* 93:46-52 Jl 1993

The witness of the worshiping community. Senn, Frank C. New Jersey: Paulist Press, 1993. x, 177p ISBN 0-8091-3368-7 LC 92-34033

Word wars. Mullen, Peter. *Register* 69:1+ Ap 25 1993

CATHOLIC CHURCH—LITURGY—CONGRESSES

Disciples at the crossroads: perspectives on worship and church leadership. Bernstein, Eleanor, ed. Collegeville:Liturgical, 1993. x, 153p ISBN 0-8146-2146-5 LC 93-591

CATHOLIC CHURCH—MEMBERSHIP

Befriending: a self-guided retreat for busy people. Payne, Joseph A. New Jersey: Paulist Press, 1992. x, 165p ISBN 0-8091-3354-7 LC 92-28398

Committed worship: a sacramental theology for converting Christians, v 2. Gelpi, Donald L, 1934-. Minnesota: The Liturgical Press, 1993. x, 312p ISBN 0-8146-5826-1 LC 92-40430

Committed worship: a sacramental theology for converting Christians, v I. Gelpi, Donald L, 1934-. Minnesota: The Liturgical Press, 1993. x, 278p ISBN 0-8146-5825-3 LC 92-40430

The ministry of consolation: the parish guide for comforting the bereaved. Curley, Terence P. New York: Alba House, 1993. 70p ISBN 0-8189-0651-0 LC 93-10315

No less zeal: a spiritual guide for Catholic lay people. Morin, Douglas J. New York: Alba House, 1993. x, 142p ISBN 0-8189-0631-6 LC 92-34242

Rekindling the passion. Jorgensen, Susan S. San Jose: Resource Publications, Inc, 1993. x, 251p ISBN 0-89390-236-5 LC 92-32396

The sacred world of the Christian: sensed in faith. Wagner, Mary Anthony. Minnesota: The Order of St Benedict, 1993. v, 147p ISBN 0-8146-2102-3 LC 92-40431

CATHOLIC CHURCH—MISSIONS

John Paul II, Pope, (1992-12-22) give thanks for the gift of serving. John Paul II, Pope, 1920- (Karol Wojtyla) (elected 1978). *TPS* 38:172-178 My-Je 1993*

Mission and ministry in the global church. Bellagamba, Anthony. Maryknoll, New York: Orbis Books, 1992. x, 150p ISBN 0-88344-813-0 LC 92-19820

US sources for the Catholic overseas mission movement, 1893-1929. Dries, Angelyn. *US Cath Hist* 11:37-48 Spr 1993

CATHOLIC CHURCH—MISSIONS—CONGRESSES
Papers originally presented at a symposium: the Church: salvation and mission. LaVerdiere, Eugene Armand, 1936-, ed. Collegeville, Minnesota: The Liturgical Press, 1993. 104p ISBN 0-8146-2141-4 LC 93-9678

CATHOLIC CHURCH—MISSIONS- PHILIPPINES
Island of tears, island of hope: living the gospel in a revolutionary situation. O'Brien, Niall. Maryknoll: Orbis, 1993. x, 234p ISBN 0-88344-927-7 LC 73-23776

CATHOLIC CHURCH—MOZARABIC RITE
John Paul II, Pope, (1992-05-28) Santa Messa [Orig Spanish]. John Paul II, Pope, 1920- (Karol Wojtyla) (elected 1978). *Notitiae* 28:404-410 Je 1992*

CATHOLIC CHURCH—PASTORAL LETTERS AND CHARGES
Bishops back the enterprise culture. *Tablet* 246:1580-1581 D 12 1992
"The challenge of peace" revisited. Murray, Pius. *Emmanuel* 99:314-317 Jl-Ag 1993
Choosing our future. *Cath Int* 4:169-174 Ap 1993
The continuing challenge of peace [interview by T Tamberg]. Christiansen, Drew. *OSV* 82:6 Ag 22 1993
Faith and work. Kennedy, Finola. *Tablet* 247:330 Mr 13 1993
In Chancery. Hitchcock, Helen Hull. *Crisis* 11:11-12 Je 1993
Letter on gays draws protest. Lefevere, Patricia. *Nat Cath Rep* 29:5 S 10 1993
Responde la iglesia a los desafios de hoy?: cartas pastorales. Castellanos, Nicholas. Madrid: Grupo Libros, 1993. x, 666p ISBN 84-7906-202-9
Response to pastoral letter called positive. Lefevere, Patricia. *Nat Cath Rep* 29:7 Ja 8 1993
Stewardship also requires greenbacks, critic says. Vidulich, Dorothy. *Nat Cath Rep* 29:9 Ja 8 1993
Two visions with no common ground. Connell, Desmond, Abp. *OR(Eng)* 1300:8 Jl 21 1993
Work is the key [excerpts fr a Pastoral Letter]. Daly, Cahal Brendan, Cardinal, 1917-, et al. *Cath Int* 4:182-189 Ap 1993

CATHOLIC CHURCH—PERIODICALS
Birthday greetings. Coren, Michael. *Can Cath Rev* 11:2 Ja 1993
25 anos: a vida e a história de uma revista [editorial]. Libanio, Joao Batista. *Perspectiva* 25:5-9 Ja-Ap 1993

CATHOLIC CHURCH—POLITICAL ACTIVITY
Murder in the cathedral. Hebblethwaite, Peter, 1930-. *Tablet* 247:713-714 Je 5 1993
On being a Catholic politician in America. Brandl, John E. *Listening* 28:41-51 Wint 1993
What's more important—process or product? Fischer, Mark F. *Tod Parish* 25:21-23 Ja 1993

CATHOLIC CHURCH—POLITICAL ACTIVITY-GERMANY
Katholishe Kirche in der DDR zwischen Staat und Gesellschaft. Haese, Ute. *Stimm Zeit* 211:241-254 Ap 1993
Showdown in Poland. Luxmoore, Jonathan. *Tablet* 247:1190-1191 S 18 1993

CATHOLIC CHURCH—POLITICAL ACTIVITY- TEXAS
The Church and politics in Texas. Cirulli, Carol. *Register* 69:1+ My 30 1993

CATHOLIC CHURCH—PONTIFICAL COUNCIL FOR CULTURE
I beni culturali ecclesiastici. Ferrari da Passano, Paolo. *Civilta* 3:116-128 Jl 17 1993

CATHOLIC CHURCH—PRAYER BOOKS
Backpack meditations for Lent. Schneider, Valerie. New York: Paulist Press, 1990. 57p ISBN 0-8091-3195-1 LC 90-41230
Life after Easter. Smith, Pamela. New Jersey: Paulist Press, 1993. x, 88p ISBN 0-8091-3379-2 LC 92-21195
Sound the trumpet: reflections on the paschal mystery. Gallagher, Michele T, 1943-. New York: Alba House, 1993. x, 134p ISBN 0-8189-0665-0 LC 92-40309

CATHOLIC CHURCH—PRAYERS
The rosary: a prayer for all seasons. Hastings, Joanna. Collegeville:Liturgical, 1993. x, 212p ISBN 0-8146-2134-1 LC 92-43851

CATHOLIC CHURCH—PUBLIC OPINION
Katholishe Kirche in der DDR zwischen Staat und Gesellschaft. Haese, Ute. *Stimm Zeit* 211:241-254 Ap 1993

CATHOLIC CHURCH—RACE RELATIONS
Does the church mishandle its cultural treasures? Windsor, Patricia. *USCath* 58:14-20 F 1993

CATHOLIC CHURCH—RELATIONS
The Church and morality: an ecumenical and Catholic approach. Curran, Charles E, 1934-. Minneapolis: Fortress Press, 1993. 126p ISBN 0-8006-2756-3 LC 92-47448
Der päpstliche rat zur Förderung der Einheit der Christen im Jahre 1992. Cassidy, Edward Idris, 1924-, Cardinal. *Catholica* 47 no 2:89-107 1993
Pentecostal unity: recurring frustration and enduring hopes. Crowe, Terrence Robert. Chicago: Loyola University Press, 1993. x, 282p ISBN 0-8294-0746 LC 93-20683
Pope invited as Church looks to future. *Tablet* 247:381 Mr 20 1993

CATHOLIC CHURCH—RELATIONS—ANGLICAN COMMUNION
Cardinal calls for welcome to Anglicans. *Tablet* 247:523 Ap 24 1993
The Church of England's crisis [editorial]. *Tablet* 247:423 Ap 3 1993
"Communion" in a time of estrangement. Tavard, George Henry. *Ecumen Trends* 22:1+ My 1993
The crisis in Anglo-Catholicism. Caldecott, Stratford. *Crisis* 11:15-16 Je 1993
A glitch or a gulf? Canterbury, Rome and reunion. Nilson, Jon. *Comm* 120:6-8 F 26 1993
Knocking at the papal door. Hamilton, Daniel S. *America* 168:16-17 Ap 24 1993
Laying claim to Newman. Hebblethwaite, Peter, 1930-. *Tablet* 247:834 Je 26 1993
No breakthrough yet in Anglican talks. *Tablet* 247:351-352 Mr 13 1993
No pacts, no deals in talks with Anglicans. *Tablet* 247:255 F 20 1993
No special deal in welcome for Anglicans. *Tablet* 247:558-560 My 1 1993
The real test of conscience [editorial]. *Tablet* 247:535-536 My 1 1993
Roman Catholic bishops of Britain set guidelines for Anglican converts. Solheim, James. *Ecumen Trends* 22:16 My 1993
A tale of two cathedrals. Barnes, Michael R. *Month* 26:I Je 1993

A time for Christian boldness [editorial]. *Tablet* 247:499-500 Ap 24 1993

CATHOLIC CHURCH—RELATIONS—ISLAM
Ecumenism in the wake of terrorism. Holton, Robert. *OSV* 81:21 Mr 28 1993
An Islamic-Roman Catholic "national" dialogue. Borelli, John. *Ecumen Trends* 22:10-13 O 1993
Pope offers olive branch to Islam. Hebblethwaite, Peter, 1930-. *Nat Cath Rep* 29:12 F 19 1993

CATHOLIC CHURCH—RELATIONS—JUDAISM
Catholics, Jews and the state of Israel. Kenny, Anthony John. New York: Paulist Press, 1993. x, 157p ISBN 0-8091-3406-3 LC 93-17833
The church and the Jewish people twenty-five years after the Second Vatican Council (1963-65). Fumagalli, Francesco. *SIDIC* 25 No 2:18-26 1992
Dialog, nicht Proselytenmacherei. Henrix, Hans Hermann. *Stimm Zeit* 211:679-690 O 1993
Dialogue [interview by L Pevtzow]. Dubois, Marcel Jacque. *Register* 69:1+ Ja 3 1993
Seeking the lost Atlantis of Catholics and Jews [por]. Scott, David. *OSV* 82:6-7 S 19 1993
A year of T'shuvah [statement made to Central Conference of American Rabbis (March 26, 1992: Toledo)]. Torrello Cascante, Ramon, Abp. *SIDIC* 25 No 2:28-29 1992
1992: a year of T'shuvah [reply by Joshu O Haberman, p 29]. Haberman, Joshua A. *SIDIC* 25 No 2:29 1992

CATHOLIC CHURCH—RELATIONS—LUTHERAN CHURCH
The one mediator, the saints, and Mary. Anderson, H George, et al, eds. Minneapolis: Augsburg Fortress, 1992. x, 397p ISBN 0-8066-2579-1 LC 91-40822

CATHOLIC CHURCH—RELATIONS—ORTHODOX CHURCH
As Russians and Romans spat, sects surge. Hebblethwaite, Peter, 1930-. *Nat Cath Rep* 29:11 Ap 9 1993
Catholic delegates narrowly escape assassination. *Tablet* 247:865 Jl 3 1993
Communique of the Joint International Commission for Theological Dialogue. *Ecumen Trends* 22:1-2 S 1993
John Paul II, Pope, (1993-07-18) Praying [Orig Italian]. John Paul II, Pope, 1920- (Karol Wojtyla) (elected 1978). *OR(Eng)* 1300:1 Jl 21 1993*
Lebanon meeting statement rejects proselytism. *Origins* 23:166-169 Ag 12 1993
Optimisim from Catholic archbishop in Moscow. *Tablet* 247:178 F 6 1993
Patriarch Alexis criticises Rome. O'Connell, Gerard. *Tablet* 247:316 Mr 6 1993
Pope reaches out to the Orthodox Churches. *Tablet* 247:147-148 Ja 30 1993
The Pope's balancing act. Lieven, Anatol. *Tablet* 247:1208-1209 S 18 1993
The search for common ground. Bole, William. *OSV* 81:3 Ja 17 1993
Statement of the Catholic members of the Consultation. Barringer, Robert, et al. *Ecumen Trends* 22:14-15 Ja 1993
Uniatism, method of union of the past and the present search for full cummunion. *Ecumen Trends* 22:3-7 S 1993
Vatican, Moscow pursue a "delicate" cooperation. Lefevere, Patricia. *Nat Cath Rep* 29:2 Mr 12 1993

CATHOLIC CHURCH—RELATIONS—PROTESTANT CHURCH
English Methodist—RC Committee: can the Roman Catholic and Methodist churches be reconciled? *OChr* 29 no 2:165-169 1993
The one mediator, the saints, and Mary: a Lutheran reflection. Johnson, Maxwell E. *Worship* 67:226-238 My 1993
In-house christies. Patterson, Robert W. *Crisis* 11:13-14 My 1993
John Paul II, Pope, (1992-03-17) Ad limina Apostolorum. John Paul II, Pope, 1920- (Karol Wojtyla) (elected 1978). *TPS* 37:324-328 N-D 1992*
Die katholische Kirche als Medienereignis. Bieger, Erkhard. *Stimm Zeit* 210:855-857 D 1992
Legitimacy of development within the apostolic tradition. Carter, David. *OChr* 29 no 3:226-234 1993
Towards reconciling Reformed and Roman Catholic. Falconer, Alan D. *Doctr Life* 43:274-286 My-Je 1993

CATHOLIC CHURCH—RENEWAL
1993 Conference: fanning the flame (July 9-11, 1993: Seattle, Washington). *New Cov* 23:30 S 1993

CATHOLIC CHURCH—SOCIAL TEACHINGS
Aetatis Novae: pastoral instruction on social communication [a summary]. Faniran, J O. *AFER* 34:364-375 D 1992
The bishops' part. Hebblethwaite, Peter, 1930-. *Tablet* 247:609 My 15 1993
Capital punishment. Langan, John P. *TheolStds* 54:111-124 Mr 1993
Celebrating African-American traditions. Inkel, Maxine. *Momentum* 24:71-72 N-D 1993
The Church in the post-socialist world. Murphy, Séamus. *Studies* 82:87-96 Spr 1993
The Church's social teaching and liberation theologies. Jerez, César. *Month* 26:155-159 Ap 1993
Evangelization and the Church's social teaching. William, Thomas Stafford, Cardinal, 1930-. *Cath Int* 4:210-214 My 1993
Globalization, pluralism, and ecumenics: the old question of Catholicity in a new cultural horizon. Burrows, Mark Stephen. *JEcumen Stds* 29:346-367 Sum-Aut 1992
Health care for all: a Catholic perspective. Hehir, J Bryan, 1940-. *Comm* 120:7-9 My 7 1993
Helping the poor. Mullen, Peter. *Register* 69:1+ Mr 7 1993
Ist Kirche anders? Marx, Reinhard. *Stimm Zeit* 211:123-130 F 1993
John Paul II, Pope, (1993-06-05) Social doctrine [Orig in Italian]. John Paul II, Pope, 1920- (Karol Wojtyla) (elected 1978). *OR(Eng)* 1297:9 Je 30 1993*
Katholische Gesellschaftslehre im Überlick. Kerber, Walter, 1926-, et al, eds. Frankfurt: Knecht, 1993. x, 420p ISBN 3-7820-0623-2
The magisterium and moral theology [condensed fr *Freiburger Zeitschrift für Philosophie und Theologie* (1989)]. Fuchs, Josef. *TheolDgst* 38:103-107 Sum 1991
Remodeling the "domestic church". Hitchcock, Helen Hull. *Crisis* 11:9-10 Ap 1993
Saving children from "a hostile and dangerous place". Hart, Joan. *Momentum* 24:74-75 S-O 1993
The social context of the AMECEA countries on the eve of the African Synod. Henriot, Peter F. *AFER* 34:340-363 D 1992

Tanzanian women peasants: an ethical and theological reflection. Giblin, Marie. *AFER* 34:29-43 F 1992

Ten years after: the bishops (again) on war and peace. Weigel, George. *Crisis* 11:36-41 Mr 1993

That they may converse: voices of Catholic social thought. McCormick, Patrick. *CrossCurr* 42:521-527 Wint 1992-1993

Vatican II: the impact on American society—the pas de deux between rights and responsibilities. Araujo, Robert J. *CLawyer* 35 no 2:109-144 1993

Working with Christ: the Catechism's social teaching. Schall, James Vincent, 1928-. *Crisis* 11:27-30 Je 1993*

CATHOLIC CHURCH—SOCIAL TEACHINGS—HISTORY

Social Catholicism in nineteenth-century Europe: a review of recent historiography. Misner, Paul. *CHist* 78:581-600 O 1992

CATHOLIC CHURCH—WOMEN

Abortion, sex and gender: the Church's public voice. Cahill, Lisa Sowle. *America* 168:6-11 My 22, 1993

Bishops ask priests about women [fr The Pastoral Care of Marriage and Family Life]. *Priests & People* 6:337-340 Ag-S 1992

Bishops at odds over role of women. *Tablet* 247:22 Ja 2 1993

Male and female created he them. Miller, Annabel. *Tablet* 247:839 Jl 3 1993

Mater Angelica. McInerny, Ralph M. *Crisis* 11:19 O 1993

Nature, culture, and the Church. Carroll, William E. *Can Cath Rev* 11:44-47 Ja 1993

On the margin. Thurston, Anne. *Tablet* 247:534 My 1 1993

Ordinary time: cycles in marriage, faith, and renewal. Mairs, Nancy, 1943-. Boston: Beacon Press, 1993. x, 238p ISBN 0-8070-7056-4 LC 92-40421

A pastor's vision [interview by G O'Connell]. Martini, Carlo Maria, Cardinal, 1926-. *Tablet* 247:876-878 Jl 10 1993

The pastoral that wasn't: feminist agenda stalled at Bishops' Conference. Hitchcock, Helen Hull. *Crisis* 11:33-37 Ja 1993

Paul VI and the women [excerpt fr *Paul VI, the first modern pope*]. Hebblethwaite, Peter, 1930-. *Tablet* 247:398-399 Mr 27 1993

Priestertum der Frau. Schiebl, Johanna. *Stimm Zeit* 211:115-122 F 1993

A sister's ministry. Medcalf, John. *Tablet* 247:427 Ap 3 1993

To be black, Catholic, and female. Hayes, Diana L. *New Theol Rev* 6:55-62 My 1993

The vicar-general was a woman. *Tablet* 247:474 Ap 10-17 1993

A way of damaging communion [editorial]. *Tablet* 247:295 Mr 6 1993

What do women want? Thurston, Anne. *Furrow* 43:668-671 D 1992

Women at the crossroads. Noble, Valerie. *Priests & People* 6:312-317 Ag-S 1992

Women in the Church and in Latin American culture [tr and excerpts fr *Boletin CELAM*]. *Cath Int* 4:210-214 My 1993

Women's problems. Soskice, Janet Martin. *Priests & People* 6:301-306 Ag-S 1992

Women's work is never done. Hitchcock, Helen Hull. *Crisis* 11:11-12 My 1993

CATHOLIC CHURCH- AFRICA

Africa's new wind of change [editorial]. *Tablet* 247:1059 Ag 21 1993

African cardinal defends Rome synod site. Hebblethwaite, Peter, 1930-. *Nat Cath Rep* 29:11 Je 18 1993

African synod in Rome sends wrong signal [editorial]. *Nat Cath Rep* 29:24 F 26 1993

African Synod will meet in Rome. *Tablet* 247:252-253 F 20 1993

"Am I not a human being and a brother/sister?". Magesa, Laurenti. *AFER* 34:95-114 Ap 1992

A Church committed to Africa [editorial]. *Cath Int* 4:150 Ap 1993

Church input said to be key to African synod. Collins, Carole. *Nat Cath Rep* 29:15 Jl 30 1993

Climb every mountain. Haynes, A W. *Can Cath Rev* 11:33-35 Je 1993

Cooked in a Roman pot. Shorter, Aylward, 1932-. *Tablet* 247:446-447 Ap 3 1993

Des conditions nouvelles pour l'évangélisation en Afrique. Derroitte, Henri. *NRT* 115:560-576 Jl-Ag 1993

Holding African Synod in Rome miffs Africans. Collins, Carole. *Nat Cath Rep* 29:11 Je 18 1993

John Paul II, Pope, (1993-02-09) The Church in Africa. John Paul II, Pope, 1920- (Karol Wojtyla) (elected 1978). *Origins* 22:653-684 Mr 11 1993*

John Paul II, Pope, (1993-02-17) Vitality of African Christianity. John Paul II, Pope, 1920- (Karol Wojtyla) (elected 1978). *TPS* 38:226-229 Jl-Ag 1993*

Out of repression, life. Burke, Greg. *Register* 69:3 Jl 25 1993

Papal visit proceeding to troubled Africa. Collins, Carole. *Nat Cath Rep* 29:14-15 Ja 15 1993

The Pope in Africa [editorial]. *America* 168:3 Mr 6 1993

Pope names officials for synod. Hebblethwaite, Peter, 1930-. *Nat Cath Rep* 29:15 Jl 30 1993

Racist missionaries: an obstacle to evangelization in Africa. Zvarevashe, Ignatius M. *AFER* 35:115-131 Ap 1993

A vision fades for African Catholics [editorial]. *Tablet* 247:231-232 F 20 1993

CATHOLIC CHURCH- AFRICA, SOUTHERN

Toward an African Christianity: inculturation applied. Hillman, Eugene. New York: Paulist Press, 1993. x, 101p ISBN 0-8091-3381-4 LC 92-39526

CATHOLIC CHURCH- ALBANIA

Albania struggles for its dignity. Blum, Paul Richard. *Register* 69:5 Je 13 1993

Albanian portraits. O'Grady, Desmond. *Tablet* 247:500+ Ap 24 1993

A phoenix rising from the ashes. O'Grady, Desmond. *OSV* 81:21 Ap 4 1993

Pope's visit confirms Albania's new status. Hebblethwaite, Peter, 1930-. *Nat Cath Rep* 29:13 My 7 1993

The resurrection of a Church. *Tablet* 247:556 My 1 1993

CATHOLIC CHURCH- APPALACHIAN REGION

Called to the mountains: the autobiography of Reverend Ralph W. Beiting and the Christian Appalachian project. Beiting, Ralph W. Lancaster: Christian Appalachian Project, 1993. //x, 112p ISBN

CATHOLIC CHURCH- ARGENTINA

Congregation for Bishops (1992-02-28) [Decree]. *AAS* 85:212-213 F 3 1993*

Congregation for Bishops (1992-09-19). *AAS* 85:213-214 F 3 1993*

CATHOLIC CHURCH- ASIA—HISTORY

For all the peoples of Asia: documents from 1970-1991. Rosales, Gaudencio B, and Arevalo, Catalino G, eds. Maryknoll, New York: Orbis Books, 1992. x, 356p ISBN 0-88344-837-8 LC 92-5033

CATHOLIC CHURCH- AUSTRIA

Another crisis over a bishop's style. *Tablet* 247:865-866 Jl 3 1993

CATHOLIC CHURCH- BALTIC STATES

Baltic States. O'Grady, Desmond. *OSV* 82:6-7 S 5 1993

CATHOLIC CHURCH- BELIZE

Charting the future of Belize. Holton, Robert. *OSV* 82:5 My 23 1993

CATHOLIC CHURCH- BOSTON

Boston's cardinal-archbishop [interview by G Sherry; photos]. *OSV* 81:12-13 Ja 31 1993

CATHOLIC CHURCH- BRAZIL

An appeal from the heart. Burke, Greg. *Register* 69:3 Ap 18 1993

Elementos para avaliar o VIII interclesial das CEBS (S Maria, RS Brasil 8-12 Setembro 1992). Marins, José, and Trevisan, Teolide M, et al. *REB* 52:801-813 D 1992

Going all the way. Kepp, Michael. *Register* 69:3 My 23 1993

In Brazil, renewal is thriving. Kepp, Michael. *Register* 69:1+ Mr 7 1993

John Paul II, Pope, (1991-04-29) Constitutiones Apostolicae (Apostolic Constitution) [Latin]. John Paul II, Pope, 1920- (Karol Wojtyla) (elected 1978). *AAS* 85:5-6 Ja 7 1993*

O novo missal para a igrja no Brasil. Congregation for Divine Worship and Discipline of the Sacraments. *Notitiae* 28:221-224 Mr 1992

VIII encontro interclesial das CEBS (eventos no evento). Libanio, Joao Batista. *REB* 52:789-800 D 1992

CATHOLIC CHURCH- BURMA

After six decades, nuns emerge in Burma. Gillotte, Tony. *Nat Cath Rep* 29:12 F 26 1993

CATHOLIC CHURCH- CALIFORNIA

Calendar of documents and related historical materials in the Archival Center, Archdiocese of Los Angeles. Mission Hills: Saint Francis Historical Society, 1993. //x, 79p ISBN

CATHOLIC CHURCH- CAMBODIA

Cambodian Catholics begin rebuilding church. Gillotte, Tony. *Nat Cath Rep* 29:13 My 14 1993

"Killing fields" no more. Mullen, Peter. *Register* 69:3 O 17 1993

CATHOLIC CHURCH- CAMEROON

Africa's lost haven. Eppink, Alfons. *Tablet* 247:680-681 My 29 1993

CATHOLIC CHURCH- CANADA

Canadians told church is not a walled city. Babych, Art. *Nat Cath Rep* 29:12 My 14 1993

Is there a balm in Gilead? Reflections on a Church in need of healing. Paré, U E. *Can Cath Rev* 11:18-21 Ja 1993

CATHOLIC CHURCH- CHILE

John Paul II, Pope, (1992-10-15) Litterae Apostolica (Apostolic Letter to create a Minor Basilica of Our Lady in Chile) [Latin]. John Paul II, Pope, 1920- (Karol Wojtyla) (elected 1978). *AAS* 85:127-128 F 3 1993*

CATHOLIC CHURCH- CHINA

Bishop released to court world opinion. *Tablet* 247:697 My 29 1993

Cardinal looks to the future in hope. Rafferty, Kevin. *Tablet* 247:1203 S 18 1993

The Catholic Church in modern China: perspectives. Tang, Edmond, and Wiest, Jean-Paul, eds. Maryknoll: Orbis, 1993. x, 260p ISBN 0-88344-834-3 LC 93-14944

China calls, Vatican responds. Thavis, John. *Nat Cath Rep* 29:15 S 24 1993

China's loyal church. Dodds, Bill. *OSV* 82:8 My 9 1993

Did Chinese Catholics die for a secondary truth? Zen, Joseph Er-jwun. *Origins* 22:714-716 Mr 25 1993

East meets West. *Tablet* 247:1193 S 18 1993

For Chinese Catholics, a hammering [Kung Foundation]. Feuerherd, Peter. *Register* 69:1+ Mr 21 1993

Growing up in the Church: China and the USA. Shen, Louis. *America* 168:10-12 Ja 16-23 1993

On renewing the church in China. Schreiter, Robert J. *Origins* 22:709-714 Mr 25 1993

CATHOLIC CHURCH- CROATIA

Croat Catholics divided. Magas, Branka. *Tablet* 247:908-910 Jl 17 1993

John Paul II, Pope, (1992-11-09) Vist ad limina. John Paul II, Pope, 1920- (Karol Wojtyla) (elected 1978). *TPS* 38:111-115 Mr-Ap 1993*

CATHOLIC CHURCH- CUBA

Church and state circle warily as faith flourishes. Wirpsa, Leslie. *Nat Cath Rep* 29:13-14 Je 4 1993

The Church in Cuba risks Castro's wrath for sake of reform. Bermudez, Alejandro. *Register* 69:5 O 17 1993

Fidel, Cuban bishops square off. Burke, Greg. *Register* 69:1+ O 31 1993

Is the sun going down on Fidel Castro's Cuba? Holton, Robert. *OSV* 82:17 O 17 1993

CATHOLIC CHURCH- CZECHOSLOVAKIA

Church-State conflict over property. *Tablet* 247:829 Je 26 1993

Communism and Catholicism. Hines, Susan C. *Priest* 49:38-40 Mr 1993

For Czechs, there are tiny signs of progress. O'Grady, Desmond. *OSV* 81:3 F 7 1993

Häring supports married priests. *Tablet* 247:763 Je 1993

John Paul II, Pope, (1992-06-26) Ad limina apostolorum. John Paul II, Pope, 1920- (Karol Wojtyla) (elected 1978). *TPS* 38:29-33 Ja-F 1993*

The long wait. *Tablet* 247:104 Ja 23 1993

Secret ordinations kept Czech church alive. Hebblethwaite, Peter, 1930-. *Nat Cath Rep* 29:9-10 S 10 1993

Slovakia embraces the past. Broun, Janice. *Comm* 120:15 S 24 1993

The vicar-general was a woman. *Tablet* 247:474 Ap 10-17 1993

CATHOLIC CHURCH- DOMINICAN REPUBLIC

Santo Domingo 92 (editorial). *Christus* 57:2-3 O 1992

CATHOLIC CHURCH- EASTERN EUROPE

Tasks of the Church in the new Europe. Hume, George Basil, Cardinal, 1932-. *Origins* 23:341-348 O 21 1993

CATHOLIC CHURCH- EL SALVADOR

A sister's ministry. Medcalf, John. *Tablet* 247:427 Ap 3 1993

Viaje al fondo de la esperanza. Olaizola, Jose Luis. Madrid: Ediciones Rialp, 1993. x, 253p ISBN 84-321-2866-x

What CELAM achieved at Santo Domingo. MacEoin, Gary. *Doctr Life* 43: 95-99 F 1993

What is the church of the poor? A missionary reshapes his theology. Hurteau, Robert. *Comm* 120:13-16 Mr 26 1993

25 anos: a vida e a história de uma revista [editorial]. Libanio, Joao Batista. *Perspectiva* 25:5-9 Ja-Ap 1993

CATHOLIC CHURCH- LATVIA
Church wary of liberal and secular values. *Tablet* 247:1140 S 4 1993

CATHOLIC CHURCH- LEBANON
Pope invited as Church looks to future. *Tablet* 247:381 Mr 20 1993

CATHOLIC CHURCH- LITHUANIA
John Paul II in Lithuania. Krause, Edward. *Register* 69:4 S 19 1993

Lithuania awaits renewal. Luxmoore, Jonathan. *Tablet* 247:1124-1125 S 4 1993

Party on, comrades. Luxmoore, Jonathan. *Register* 69:1+ My 16 1993

The Pope in the role of progressive. Lieven, Anatol. *Tablet* 247:1171 S 11 1993

CATHOLIC CHURCH- MEXICO
Abortive effort to oust bishop puts Vatican on the defensive [por]. Coleman, Bill, and Coleman, Patty. *Nat Cath Rep* 30:7 N 12 1993

Chiapas champion of poor troubles water, church. Ross, John. *Nat Cath Rep* 29:12 My 28 1993

Dialogue [interview by G Burke]. Rodriguez, Tarcisio. *Register* 69:1+ Je 27 1993

John Paul II, Pope, (1992-05-11) Constitutiones Apostolicae (Apostolic Constitution for Ecclesiastical Territory) [Latin]. John Paul II, Pope, 1920- (Karol Wojtyla) (elected 1978). *AAS* 85:6-8 Ja 7 1993*

John Paul II, Pope, (1992-09-21) Litterae Apostolicae (Apostolic Letter to create Apostolic Nuntiature in Mexico) [Latin]. John Paul II, Pope, 1920- (Karol Wojtyla) (elected 1978). *AAS* 85:127 F 3 1993*

Killing of Mexican cardinal raises fears for pope's safety. Ross, John. *Nat Cath Rep* 29:10 Jl 16 1993

Mexican political parties fight for Catholic votes. Smith, Matt. *Nat Cath Rep* 29:5 S 3 1993

A new and definitive path. Zubryn, Emil. *OSV* 81:21 Mr 14 1993

Palabras a Juan Pablo II. Cuxim Caamal, Primitivo. *Christus* 58:44-45 S 1993

Pope's visit to Mexico renews ties severed 130 years ago. Smith, Matt. *Nat Cath Rep* 29:7 Ag 27 1993

Still fit for Greene. Jones, Arthur C, 1936-. *Tablet* 247:1002-1003 Ag 7 1993

Support swells for bishop threatened with removal. Coleman, Bill, and Coleman, Patty. *Nat Cath Rep* 30:16 N 19 1993

CATHOLIC CHURCH- NETHERLANDS
Au nom du Christ, la parole, le sacrament, le ministere et l'ordination (lettre pastorale de la conference episcopales des pays-bas). Simonis, Adrianus. *Notitiae* 28:640-680 O 1992

John Paul II, Pope, (1992-04-25) Litterae Apostolicae (Apostolic Letter to create Minor Basilica in Raalte) [Latin]. John Paul II, Pope, 1920- (Karol Wojtyla) (elected 1978). *AAS* 85:125 F 3 1993*

Pope's stern advice to Dutch Catholics. *Tablet* 247:84 Ja 16 1993

Raised hopes in Holland. Goddijn, Walter, 1921-. *Tablet* 247:974-975 Jl 31 1993

Worsening crisis in the Dutch Church. Visser, Dirk. *Tablet* 247:797-798 Je 19 1993

CATHOLIC CHURCH- NEW YORK
For the record: Pope Leo XIII and the church in New York. Andreassi, Anthony. *Church* 9:46-49 Sum 1993

The poor and the good news: a call to evangelize. Scheuring, Tom, et al, eds. New Jersey: Paulist Press, 1993. x, 162p ISBN 0-8091-3359-8 LC 92-37976

CATHOLIC CHURCH- NICARAGUA
Managua parish combats cardinal over cathedral. Ruether, Rosemary Radford. *Nat Cath Rep* 29:16 F 26 1993

CATHOLIC CHURCH- NIGERIA
Nigeria report of activities of the national liturgy commission. Congregation for Divine Worship and Discipline of the Sacraments. *Notitiae* 28:191-192 Mr 1992

CATHOLIC CHURCH- NORTH CAROLINA
An abbatial diocese in the United States. Baumstein, Paschal. *CHist* 79:217-245 Ap 1993

CATHOLIC CHURCH- PALESTINE
The church in the Holy Land. Martin, George. *New Cov* 22:18-21 Jl 1993

CATHOLIC CHURCH- PERU
"Overcoming evil through good" [interview by M Agama]. Alzamura, Augusto Vargas, Abp. *OSV* 82:21 My 30 1993

CATHOLIC CHURCH- PHILIPPINE ISLANDS
John Paul II, Pope, (1991-07-06) Constitutiones Apostolicae (Apostolic Constitution on Ecclesiastical Territory) [Latin]. John Paul II, Pope, 1920- (Karol Wojtyla) (elected 1978). *AAS* 85:8-9 Ja 7 1993*

John Paul II, Pope, (1991-07-06) Constitutiones Apostolicae (Apostolic Constitution) [Latin]. John Paul II, Pope, 1920- (Karol Wojtyla) (elected 1978). *AAS* 84:1055-1056 N 3 1992*

John Paul II, Pope, (1992-07-06) Constitutiones Apostolicae (Apostolic Constitution to erect Vicariate Apostolic in Philippines) [Latin]. John Paul II, Pope, 1920- (Karol Wojtyla) (elected 1978). *AAS* 85:124 F 3 1993*

John Paul II, Pope, (1992-07-23) Litterae Apostolicae (Apostolic Letter) [Latin]. John Paul II, Pope, 1920- (Karol Wojtyla) (elected 1978). *AAS* 85: 18-19 Ja 7 1993*

CATHOLIC CHURCH- PITTSBURGH (PA)
Though painful, Pittsburgh reorganization draws praise. Wuerl, Donald William, Bp, 1941-. *Register* 69:1+ O 31 1993

CATHOLIC CHURCH- POLAND
Behind the headlines. Luxmoore, Jonathan. *Register* 69:5 O 17 1993

The church and the left. Michnik, Adam. Chicago: University of Chicago Press, 1993. 299p ISBN 0-226-52424-8 LC 92-20503

Dialogue [interview by Jonathan Luxmoore]. Pieronek, Tadeusz, Bp. *Register* 69:1+ Jl 25 1993

Jewish threat to boycott ghetto commemorations. *Tablet* 247:486-487 Ap 10-17 1993

John Paul II, Pope, (1992-05-12) Litterae Apostolicae (Apostolic Letter creating Minor Basilica of Church of Nowy Sacz) [Latin]. John Paul II, Pope, 1920- (Karol Wojtyla) (elected 1978). *AAS* 85:126 F 3 1993*

New church-state concordat in force. Rich, Vera. *Tablet* 247:1019 Ag 7 1993

A new concordat. *Tablet* 247:763-764 Je 1993

Poland's churches lack cash. Luxmoore, Jonathan. *Register* 69:1+ F 7 1993

Poles entrust country's future to Mary. Drazek, Czeslaw. *OR(Eng)* 1305:2 S 1 1993

Polish church may sink government over abortion. Hebblethwaite, Peter, 1930-. *Nat Cath Rep* 29:16 Ja 15 1993

Polish church wary of victory of ex-communists. Luxmoore, Jonathan. *OSV* 82:21 O 10 1993

Résistances aux changements dans la société polonaise. Charytanski, Jan. *Lumen* 47:403-415 D 1992

A revolution not by politics alone. Scott, David. *OSV* 81:15-16 F 28 1993

Seized church property may remain stolen. Luxmoore, Jonathan. *Register* 69:1+ Je 11 1993

A son of Poland. Luxmoore, Jonathan. *Register* 69:2 F 28 1993

Strange twist in Poland. Luxmoore, Jonathan. *Register* 69:1+ S 12 1993

What's a Catholic country to do? The Church's temptation in Poland. Byrnes, Timothy A. *Comm* 120:11-13 S 24 1993

CATHOLIC CHURCH- ROMANIA
John Paul II, Pope, (1992-08-28) Litterae Apostolicae (Apostolic Letter) [Latin]. John Paul II, Pope, 1920- (Karol Wojtyla) (elected 1978). *AAS* 85: 21-22 Ja 7 1993*

John Paul II, Pope, (1993-06-08) Republic of Romania. John Paul II, Pope, 1920- (Karol Wojtyla) (elected 1978). *OR(Eng)* 1297:8 Je 30 1993*

CATHOLIC CHURCH- RUSSIA
The Catholic Church in Russia. Kondrusiewicz, Tadeusz, Abp. *Ecumen Trends* 22:13-15 O 1993

Critical time for the church in Russia. Kondrusiewicz, Tadeusz, Abp. *Origins* 22:695-696 Mr 18 1993

Dialogue [interview by J Luxmoore]. Kondrusiewicz, Tadeusz, Abp. *Register* 69:1+ F 7 1993

The search for common ground. Bole, William. *OSV* 81:3 Ja 17 1993

Storia del pensiero filosofico Russo. Simon, Michele. *Civilta* 144:153-157 Ja 16 1993

CATHOLIC CHURCH- RWANDA
John Paul II, Pope, (1992-03-30) Constitutio Apostolica (Apostolic Constitution) [Latin]. John Paul II, Pope, 1920- (Karol Wojtyla) (elected 1978). *AAS* 84:826-827 S 8 1992*

John Paul II, Pope, (1992-10-22) Litterae Apostolicae (Apostolic Letter in which cathedral of Kabgayi is made a Minor Basilica) [Latin]. John Paul II, Pope, 1920- (Karol Wojtyla) (elected 1978). *AAS* 85:128-129 F 3 1993*

CATHOLIC CHURCH- SENEGAL
John Paul II, Pope, (1992-02-21) Itinera Apostolica (On apostolic journey speech to Diplomatic Corps in Senegal) [French]. John Paul II, Pope, 1920- (Karol Wojtyla) (elected 1978). *AAS* 85:153-157 F 3 1993*

John Paul II, Pope, (1992-02-21) Itinera Apostolica (On apostolic trip address to Episcopal Conference of Senegal) [French]. John Paul II, Pope, 1920- (Karol Wojtyla) (elected 1978). *AAS* 85:148-153 F 3 1993*

John Paul II, Pope, (1992-02-22) Itinera Apostolica (Address to Catholics of Goree Island during apostolic trip) [French]. John Paul II, Pope, 1920- (Karol Wojtyla) (elected 1978). *AAS* 85:157-161 F 3 1993*

CATHOLIC CHURCH- SLOVAKIA
John Paul II, Pope, (1993-06-07) Official visit [original in Slovak]. John Paul II, Pope, 1920- (Karol Wojtyla) (elected 1978). *OR(Eng)* 1295:6 Je 16 1993*

Résistances aux changements dans la Slovaquie actuelle. Pravda, Joseph. *Lumen* 47:417-425 D 1992

CATHOLIC CHURCH- SOUTH AFRICA
From apartheid to democracy. D'Angelo, Pam. *Register* 69:1+ O 17 1993

CATHOLIC CHURCH- SPAIN
Congregation for Bishops (1992-10-31). *AAS* 85:214-215 F 3 1993*

Dominar el pas dels anys. Sobreroca I Ferrer, Lluis Antoni. Barcelona: Scripta, 1993. x, 272p ISBN 84-85205-29-4

Entrevista sobre el fundador del Opus Dei, realizada por Cesare Cavallieri. Portillo, Alvaro del. Madrid: Rialp, 1993. x, 252p ISBN 84-321-2972-0

España: encuentro anual de delegados diocesanos de liturgia. López, Martín, Julián. *Notitiae* 28:425-428 Je 1992

El evangeliario en Castellano. Lopez Martin, Julian. *Notitiae* 28:332-336 My 1992

John Paul II, Pope, (1993-05-15) Spain [Orig in Spanish]. John Paul II, Pope, 1920- (Karol Wojtyla) (elected 1978). *OR(Eng)* 1297:7 Je 30 1993*

John Paul II, Pope, (1993-06-14) Spain [Orig in Italian]. John Paul II, Pope, 1920- (Karol Wojtyla) (elected 1978). *OR(Eng)* 1297:3 Je 30 1993*

CATHOLIC CHURCH- SUDAN
Pope ends trip with call for peace in Sudan. *Nat Cath Rep* 29:11 F 19 1993

Pope sets out for Benin, Uganda and Sudan. *Tablet* 247:147 Ja 30 1993

Pressure continues on Catholic Church after papal visit. Flint, Julie. *Tablet* 247:591 My 8 1993

War-torn Sudan waits for the Pope. Eppink, Alfons. *Tablet* 247:160-161 F 6 1993

CATHOLIC CHURCH- SWITZERLAND
Troubling shooting [Swiss diocese]. Burke, Greg. *Register* 69:1+ Ap 11 1993

CATHOLIC CHURCH- TEXAS
The Catholic Archives of Texas. Scaperlanda, Maria Ruiz. *Columbia* 73:8-10 Jl 1993

CATHOLIC CHURCH- THIRD WORLD
Die Dritte Welt und Europa. Metz, Johann Baptist. *Stimm Zeit* 211:3-9 Ja 1993

CATHOLIC CHURCH- UGANDA
Where catechists build the church. Phelan, Bernard C. *Priests & People* 7: 54-57 F 1993

CATHOLIC CHURCH- UNITED STATE
Handing on the tradition: a Catholic mother laments. Baumer, Patricia Hughes. *New Theol Rev* 6:32-54 My 1993

CENTRO DE ESTUDIOS BRASILENOS
A catequese e as CEBs. Cansi, Bernardo. *REB* 52:894-902 D 1992
CEBs e ecumenismo: uma discussão a partir da dimensão ecumênica do oitavo intereclesial. Oliveira Ribeiro, Claudio de. *REB* 52:846-855 D 1992
Igreja e modernidade: o caminho das CEBs. Ribeiro de Oliveira, Pedro A. *REB* 52:814-820 D 1992
O amadurecimento litúrgico das CEBs e os sinais de uma nova espiritualidade. Murad, Afonso, and Rezende Guimarães, Marcelo. *REB* 52:821-832 D 1992
O oitavo encontro intereclesial de CEBs e a ecologia. Cechin, Irmão Antônio. *REB* 52:856-876 D 1992
Trabalho, teimosia e esperança (a questão do trabaslho no 8 encontro intereclesial das CEBs).·Almeida Cunha, Rogério Ignácio de. *REB* 52:877-893 D 1992

CENTRO ECLESIAL ITALIANO PARA AMERICA LATINA
Una collaborazione ecclesiale tra Italia e America Latina: il ceial-cum. Salvini, Gianpaolo. *Civilta* 2:369-376 My 15 1993

CEREMONIAL OBJECTS
Beyond sentimentality: consciousful design of ceremonial objects. Walton, Rivkah. *CrossCurr* 43:82-91 Spr 1993

CERULLO, MORRIS
Morris Cerullo makes a virtue out of controversy. *Tablet* 247:1023 Ag 7 1993

CEVOLI, FLORIDA (LUCREZIA ELENA), 1685-1767
Congregation for the Causes of Saints (1992-06-13) Decree on a miracle of Servant of God, Florida (Lucrezia Elena Cevoli). Congregation for the Causes of Saints. *AAS* 85:89-91 Ja 7 1993*
Congregation for the Causes of Saints (1992-06-13) Decree on a miracle. Congregation for the Causes of Saints. *TPS* 38:19-20 Ja-F 1993*
John Paul II, Pope, (1993-05-16). John Paul II, Pope, 1920- (Karol Wojtyla) (elected 1978). *TPS* 38:308-311 S-O 1993*

CEZANNE, PAUL
Cézannes Hochamt. Grom, Bernhard. *Stimm Zeit* 211:423-425 Je 1993

CHALCEDON, COUNCIL OF, 451
Contemporary art and the expanded death of the human Jesus. Seubert, Xavier John. *New Theol Rev* 6:27-39 F 1993

CHANDLER, RUSSELL
Sin, evil and death in the New Age. McIntyre, Moni. *Way* 33:210-221 Jl 1993

CHANGE
The Decade of Evangelisation: has Catholicism changed? Sweeney, James. *Month* 25:461-466 D 1992
Thriving on change. Goman, Carol Kinsey. *Health Prog* 74:60 Jl-Ag 1993

CHANGE—RELIGIOUS ASPECTS
Changements et résistances au changement en catéchèse. Fossion, André. *Lumen* 47:391-401 D 1992
Don't be afraid to change. Paprocki, Joseph. *ReligTJ* 27:41 Mr 1993
Faith sharing, trust, and transformation. Bernier, Joan M. *Tod Parish* 25:34-35 Mr 1993
Finding heroes in small community life. Bernier, Joan M. *Tod Parish* 25:34-35 Ap-My 1993
Hoosiers [editorial]. Manney, Jim. *New Cov* 23:5 Ag 1993
Lasting change. Pratt, Lonni Collins. *New Cov* 22:16-17 Je 1993
Ministry in the new South Africa: an intercultural challenge [fr *Entre nous*]. Slattery, Joseph A. *Living Light* 29:49-54 Wint 1992
Pourquoi changer? Pourquoi résister? Rezsohazy, Rudolf. *Lumen* 47:369-376 D 1992
Résistances aux changements dans la Slovaquie actuelle. Pravda, Joseph. *Lumen* 47:417-425 D 1992
Seeking discernment. Wiltshire, Peter. *Living Prayer* 26:24-25 My-Je 1993
Transfiguration and pain in ordinary life. Power, Dermot. *Way* 33:12-18 Ja 1993

CHANGE—RELIGIOUS ASPECTS- LATIN AMERICA
Liberación, inculturación y alteridad. Espeja, Jesús. *Cien Tom* 120:153-167 Ja-Ap 1993

CHANGE (PSYCHOLOGY)
Boundary-dwellers. Ward, Hannah. *Way* 33:97-105 Ap 1993
Jake's castle. Manning, Martha. *USCath* 58:35-37 Je 1993

CHANTS (BUDDHISM)
Authority (2): an essay on the place of the text in Buddhist and Christian formation. Corless, Roger. *Stud Form Spir* 14:31-39 F 1993

CHAOS AND ORDER *see* Order and Chaos

CHAPELS
Chapels on steel wheels [condensed fr *Trains* D 1992 (photos)]. Burghardt, Robert P. *CDgst* 58:66-70 D 1993
The little chapels that could [railroad chapel cars]. Dodds, Bill. *OSV* 82:10-11 S 12 1993

CHAPLAINS
Remembering the Four Chaplains. Crosby, Donald F, 1933-. *CDgst* 57:66-71 F 1993

CHAPLAINS, HOSPITAL
Creative models of spiritual care. Ceronsky, Charles. *Health Prog* 74:58-61 My 1993
Making the rounds with a hospital chaplain. Stefan, Bonaventure. *OSV* 82:12 O 31 1993

CHAPLAINS, MILITARY
Chaplain's assistant. Haynes, A W. *Can Cath Rev* 11:31-32 S 1993
Chaplains under fire in Sicily. Crosby, Donald F, 1933-. *Priest* 49:37-41 Jl 1993
Death comes to the chaplain: Lawrence Lynch of Okinawa. Crosby, Donald F, 1933-. *America* 168:6-12 Ap 24 1993
Desert Storm, 50 years ago: Catholic chaplains in North Africa. Crosby, Donald F, 1933-. *Crisis* 10:33-38 D 1992
The permanent deacon as military chaplain: canonical reflections. Ditewig, William T. *Jurist* 51 no 2:340-363 1991
Zahn, Gordon C. Zahn, Gordon C. *America* 168:5-7 My 15 1993

CHAPLAINS, PRISON
And more than a prophet. Hanley, Boniface. *Stud Form Spir* 14:161-174 My 1993

CHARISMA
Carisma e istituzione della chiesa nella teologia di Hans Urs Von Balthasar. Marchesi, Giovanni. *Civilta* 144:14-30 Ja 2 1993
Charism in the early church since Rudolph Sohm: an ecumenical challenge. Nardoni, Enrique. *TheolStds* 53:646-662 D 1992
Founding charisms: past and present. Hennessy, Paul. *Origins* 23:169-173 Ag 12 1993
Once a charismatic. Hannan, Maryanne. *New Cov* 22:23-24 My 1993
The power is on. Ryan, Ron. *New Cov* 22:26-28 Jl 1993

CHARISMATIC RENEWAL MOVEMENT *see* Pentecostalism

CHARITIES
Catholic relief services. Walsh, Catherine. *St Anth* 100:41 S 1993
A family affair generous beyond measure. McGill, Mary. *Catechist* 27:74-75 S 1993
John Paul II, Pope, (1992-12-19) Ad limina Apostolorum. John Paul II, Pope, 1920- (Karol Wojtyla) (elected 1978). *TPS* 38:193-200 Jl-Ag 1993*
Listening to humanity's heartbeat. *OR(Eng)* 1272:2+ Ja 6 1993
New dimensions of service. Hickey, Tim S. *Columbia* 73:6-7 Jl 1993
Our alms: returning God's love. Shaw, Russell. *Register* 69:1+ Ja 31 1993
Qualms for the poor? [editorial]. Burns, Robert E, 1919-, ed. *USCath* 58:2 Ja 1993
Remember a life to save a life. *Tablet* 247:402-403 Mr 27 1993
Save the children of Croatia. Breslin, Mary. *St Anth* 100:28-35 Mr 1993
Tax exemption threats. *Origins* 23:281+ O 7 1993
Who will speak for the children? Kammer, Fred. *Origins* 22:792-794 Ap 29 1993

CHARITIES- CANADA
Canada's Flying Fathers. Carey, Ann. *OSV* 81:20 Ja 3 1993

CHARITIES- ENGLAND
Refugees of war find help in London. *Tablet* 247:1054 Ag 14 1993

CHARITIES- ITALY
John Paul II, Pope, (1993-06-05) Social doctrine [Orig in Italian]. John Paul II, Pope, 1920- (Karol Wojtyla) (elected 1978). *OR(Eng)* 1297:9 Je 30 1993*

CHARITIES, MEDICAL
Identifying charity care in financial statements. Hoyler, Geraldine M. *Health Prog* 74:13-14 Ap 1993

CHARITY
John Paul II, Pope, (1992-12-20) Charity is an individual and social obligation. John Paul II, Pope, 1920- (Karol Wojtyla) (elected 1978). *TPS* 38:169-171 My-Je 1993*
John Paul II, Pope, (1993-01-01) Lent 1993 [English tr]. John Paul II, Pope, 1920- (Karol Wojtyla) (elected 1978). *Origins* 22:524 Ja 7 1993*
Peter Lynch: applying Wall Street wizardry to Catholic schools. Walsh, Catherine. *St Anth* 100:16-22 My 1993
The sinner against the scoundrels: the ills of doctrine and "schrift" in the Wife of Bath's, Friar's and Summoner's narratives. Kamowski, William. *Relig Lit* 25:1-18 Spr 1993
Whose hand is that? Holton, Robert. *OSV* 81:12-13 Ap 4 1993

CHARLEMAGNE
The Codex Pagesianus: witness to church renewal. Ward, Anthony. *ABenR* 44:308-333 S 1993

CHARLES, ABBOT OF VILLERS, 1197-1209
Four abbots of the golden age of Villers. Cawley, Martinus. *Cist Stud* 27 No 4:299-327 1992

CHASTITY
Abstinence as public policy: a report from New Jersey's schools. Bovenizer, David A. *Crisis* 11:40-41 S 1993
The biblical foundations of the thought of John Paul II on human sexuality. Séguin, Michel. *Communio* 20:266-289 Sum 1993
Chastity as shared strength: an open letter to students. Fouqurean, Mary Patricia Barth. *America* 169:10-15 N 6 1993
Humanae Vitae and some principles for re-evangelization. Cole, Basil. *F & R* 19:95-107 Spr 1993
It's never too late to be chaste. Sepp, E J. *Liguorian* 81:50-53 S 1993
Living chastely. Bucher, Kimberly R. *Crisis* 11:37-39 S 1993
The state, virtue, sex and chastity. Healy, Jack. *Linacre* 60:51-59 My 1993
An undivided heart: making sense of celibate chastity. Sammon, Sean D. New York: Alba House, 1993. x, 160p ISBN 0-8189-0674-x LC 93-3852

CHAUCER, GEOFFREY
The sinner against the scoundrels: the ills of doctrine and "schrift" in the Wife of Bath's, Friar's and Summoner's narratives. Kamowski, William. *Relig Lit* 25:1-18 Spr 1993

CHAVARDES, MAURICE
Lo *J'AccuseDi Maurice Chavardès Contro L'Ipocrisia*. Castelli, Ferdinando. *Civilta* 143:376-381 N 21 1992

CHAVEZ, CESAR, 1927-1993
Cesar Chavez: other words for saintliness [editorial]. *Nat Cath Rep* 29:28 My 7 1993
Chavez, Cesar, 1927-1993 [obit]. *Comm* 120:4 Je 4 1993
Chavez, Cesar, 1927-1993 [obit]. Boyle, Eugene J. *America* 168:4 My 22, 1993
Chavez, Cesar, 1927-1993 [obit]. Moses, Marion. *Cath Work* 60:1+ Je-Jl 1993
Millions reaped what Cesar Chavez sowed [obit]. Jones, Arthur C, 1936-. *Nat Cath Rep* 29:3 My 7 1993
A moment of sorrow, a moment of hope. Burns, Robert E, 1919-. *USCath* 58:2 Ag 1993
The saintliness of Cesar Chavez [editorial]. *Tablet* 247:567 My 8 1993
Thousands mourn non-violent Hispanic activist. *Tablet* 247:590 My 8 1993
What Cesar Chavez believed. Ramirez, Ricardo, Bp. *Origins* 23:17+ My 27 1993

CHENU, MARIE-DOMINQUE
La significacón teológica de los acontecimientos: El estatuto histórico de la teología según Marie-Dominque Chenu. Silva Arévalo, Eduardo. *Teol Vida* 33 no 3-4:269-297 1992

CHESIRE, GEOFFREY LEONARD, 1917-1992
Remember a life to save a life. *Tablet* 247:402-403 Mr 27 1993

CHESTERTON, GILBERT KEITH, 1874-1936
Chesterton and Catholic moments: some reflections on Catholic revivals, past and present. Sparr, Arnold. *ACHSR* 103:11-22 Aut 1992

Homing in on G.K.C. *Tablet* 247:916 Jl 17 1993
In the Catholic tradition: G K Chesterton 1874-1936. Johnson, Luke Timothy, 1943-. *Priests & People* 7:67-69 F 1993
Return to Chesterton. McGovern, Thomas. *HPR* 93:47-55 Je 1993

CHESTO, KATHLEEN O'CONNELL
Why are the dandelions weeds? Chesto, Kathleen O'Connell. Kansas City: Sheed and Ward, 1993. x, 147p ISBN 1-55612-610-7 LC 92-434481

CHIEPPI, AGOSTINO, 1830-1891
Congregation for the Causes of Saints (1992-12-21) Decree on the heroic virtues. Congregation for the Causes of Saints. *OR(Eng)* 1272:4 Ja 6 1993*

CHIESA, MARIO
Quali vie per uscire dal "sistema delle tangenti"? [editorial]. *Civilta* 144:521-534 Mr 20 1993

CHILD ABUSE
Adults should never hit kids. Schlaerth, Katherine. *USCath* 58:24-29 Ja 1993
Against the tide: how to raise sexually pure kids in an "anything-goes" world. Lahaye, Time, and Lahaye, Beverly. Sisters: Questar, 1993. x, 258p ISBN 0-88070-578-7
Becoming whole again. Wolcott, John. *OSV* 81:5 Ja 3 1993
The case of Father X. Castelli, James. *USCath* 58:12-13 S 1993
Dioceses facing up to the fathers' sins. Bole, William. *OSV* 82:6-7 O 31 1993
The fate of priest offenders. Mullen, Peter. *Register* 69:1+ O 3 1993
Healing of scars of childhood sexual abuse. Miles, Adell. *Priest* 49:42-44 Jl 1993
How one diocese responds. Unsworth, Tim. *USCath* 58:14 S 1993
Time of heroism, atmosphere of suspicion. Harrington, Timothy, Bp. *Origins* 22:609-610 F 18 1993
To enable healing. Sipe, A W Richard. *Nat Cath Rep* 29:6-7 S 17 1993

CHILD ABUSE—CONTROVERSIES
Priest and two laymen charge abuse as teens. Hayes, Gary R, and McHugh, James, Bp. *Origins* 23:87-90 Je 24 1993

CHILD CARE
Moral methodology and pastoral responsiveness: the case of abortion and the care of children. Whitmore, Todd David. *TheolStds* 54:316-338 Je 1993

CHILD DEVELOPMENT
A new look at preschool and primary classrooms. Bundy, Blakely Fetridge. *Tod Cath Teach* 27:26-29 O 1993

CHILD MOLESTING
An abused parish. Dunn, Mary. *Tablet* 247:642-643 My 22 1993
Archdiocese admits mistakes over sex abuse case. *Tablet* 247:700 My 29 1993
Bishops speak in public session of sexual abuse. Reese, Thomas Joseph, 1945-. *America* 169:4-6 Jl 3-10 1993
Daring the truth to be told. McLeod, Annmarie. *Sisters* 65:273-275 Jl 1993
A disturbing silence. Faucher, W Thomas, 1945-. *Tablet* 247:706 Je 5 1993
Listening to the survivors: voices of people of God. Berry, Jason. *America* 169:4-9 N 13 1993
Scandals in the Church: reflections at Paschaltide. Quinn, John Raphael, Abp, 1929-. *America* 168:4-6 Ap 10 1993
Sexual abuse in Christian homes and churches. Heggen, Carolyn Holderread, 1946-. Scottdale, Pennsylvania: Herald Press, 1993. 208p ISBN 0-83613-624-1 LC 92-32143
Sins of a father [editorial]. *America* 168:3 Je 19-26 1993
Stale justice. Lawton, Frederick, 1911-. *Tablet* 247:1250 O 2 1993
Stones instead of bread: sexually abusive priests in ministry. Cafardi, Nicholas P. *Stud Can* 27 no 1:145-172 1993

CHILD PSYCHIATRY
Face a l'enfant mourant. Hainaut, Hadelin. *Supplement* 184:79-88 Mr-Ap 1993

CHILD PSYCHOLOGY
Whatever happened to childhood? Elkind, David, 1931-. *Momentum* 24:18-19 Ap-My 1993

CHILD REARING
Searching for the soap: coming clean on gays in the military. Carlin, David Robert, Jr, 1938-. *Comm* 120:11-12 Ap 9 1993

CHILD SUPPORT
Determinants of spells of poverty following divorce. Heath, Julia A, and Kiker, B F, 1937-. *RSocEcon* 50:305-315 Fall 1992

CHILD WELFARE- UNITED STATES
Children first, before and after birth. Casey, Robert P, 1932-. *Origins* 22:696-699 Mr 18 1993
Who will speak for the children? Kammer, Fred. *Origins* 22:792-794 Ap 29 1993

CHILDBIRTH
Brahms' lullaby. Reinart, Leonelle. *Sisters* 65:282 Jl 1993

CHILDREN
CDF advocates say leave no child behind. Clancy, Paul. *Nat Cath Rep* 29:3 Mr 12 1993
Church and rights of the family. Trujillo, López. *OR(Eng)* 1301:6-7 Jl 28 1993
Father Scott's reflections on women, family, and relationships. Scott, John M. Indiana: Our Sunday Visitor, 1993. 139p ISBN 0-87973-530-9 LC 92-61551
John Paul II, Pope, (1993-05-06) Holy Childhood Association's 150th anniversary. John Paul II, Pope, 1920- (Karol Wojtyla) (elected 1978). *TPS* 38:291-294 S-O 1993*
John Paul II, Pope, (1993-08-15) Children. John Paul II, Pope, 1920- (Karol Wojtyla) (elected 1978). *Origins* 23:198-199 Ag 26 1993*
Robert Coles: listening to stories of God in the lives of children. McKenzie, Paula A. *Living Light* 29:65-72 Aut 1992
Saving children from "a hostile and dangerous place". Hart, Joan. *Momentum* 24:74-75 S-O 1993
Social ministers ask Congress to consider families [Social ministry gathering, F 28-Mr 3 1993, Washington, DC]. Vidulich, Dorothy. *Nat Cath Rep* 29:3 Mr 12 1993

CHILDREN—BIBLICAL TEACHING
Jesus and the way of childhood. Tsuchida, Christina. *Living Prayer* 26:19-20 N-D 1993

CHILDREN—CONVERSION
Becoming like children. Douglas, Deborah Smith. *New Cov* 22:23-25 Ja 1993

CHILDREN—DEATH
The children of the world [editorial]. *Month* 26:44-45 F 1993
Face a l'enfant mourant. Hainaut, Hadelin. *Supplement* 184:79-88 Mr-Ap 1993
It hurts so bad: parents grieve the death of their children. Haywood, Christine Curtis. *St Anth* 101:42-45 Je 1993
Mercy home: fighting the horror of infanticide in rural India. Dean, Julia. *OSV* 82:10-11 Jl 18 1993

CHILDREN—EMPLOYMENT—ETHICAL ASPECTS
Free children from exploitation. *OR(Eng)* 1309:7 S 29 1993

CHILDREN—HOSPITAL CARE—ETHICAL ASPECTS
Deciding who lives: fateful choices in the intensive care nursery. Anspach, Renée R. Berkeley: University of California Press, 1993. x, 303p ISBN 0-520-05268-4 LC 91-44245

CHILDREN—RELIGIOUS LIFE
Children's choirs as proclaimers. Brugh, Lorraine. *Liturgy* 11:74-76 Sum 1993
Home-made faith. Lash, Janet. *Priests & People* 6:458-463 D 1992
"Let the little children". Ellsberg, Peggy R. *America* 168:16 Mr 13 1993
Masses with children. Goehring, Raymond. *Priest* 49:45-47 Jl 1993
The spiritual life of children. Thurston, Anne. *Doctr Life* 42:594-599 D 1992
Trailing clouds of glory. Roman, Mary. *Living Prayer* 26:37 Jl-Ag 1993
Why are the dandelions weeds? Chesto, Kathleen O'Connell. Kansas City: Sheed and Ward, 1993. x, 147p ISBN 1-55612-610-7 LC 92-434481

CHILDREN- CROATIA
Save the children of Croatia. Breslin, Mary. *St Anth* 100:28-35 Mr 1993

CHILDREN- SOMALIA
Teaching Somalia's children to sing again. McLoughlin, Marianna. *St Anth* 101:36-41 O 1993

CHILDREN, RUNAWAY see Runaway Children

CHILDREN AND ADULTS
The runaways. McGeady, Mary Rose. *Momentum* 24:33-35 Ap-My 1993
Your children are adults now. Fanning, Marilyn. *New Cov* 22:28-31 My 1993

CHILDREN AND DEATH
Look for me in the rainbow. Johnson, Robert P. *Liguorian* 81:22-23 Je 1993
Talking to children about death. Banta, Margrit. *ReligTJ* 27:29-30 Mr 1993
Through the eyes of children. Clifford, Donald. *ReligTJ* 27:30 Mr 1993

CHILDREN OF ALCOHOLICS
COAs: behind the masks. Birke, Szifra. *Momentum* 24:54-60 Ap-My 1993

CHILDREN OF SINGLE PARENTS
Single-parenthood is okay! And experience says the earth is flat. Carlin, David Robert, Jr, 1938-. *Comm* 120:8-9 O 22 1993

CHILDREN'S DEFENSE FUND
CDF advocates say leave no child behind. Clancy, Paul. *Nat Cath Rep* 29:3 Mr 12 1993

CHILDREN'S LITERATURE
The language police. Aitken, Tom. *Tablet* 247:197 F 13 1993
We are a patchwork quilt. Neuberger, Anne E. *ReligTJ* 27:36-37 O 1993
Which Bible is best? Neuberger, Anne E. *ReligTJ* 27:16-17 Ap-My 1993

CHILDREN'S RIGHTS
A new worldwide commitment to the rights of children. Drinan, Robert Francis, 1920-. *America* 169:22-23 O 16 1993
The rights of the child [editorial]. *Tablet* 247:675 My 29 1993

CHILE—POLITICS AND GOVERNMENT
"I listen, I suspect, later I make poetry" [interview by S Rojas; tr fr *Pastoral Popular*]. Gebara, Ivone. *LADOC* 24:10-15 S-O 1993
Return to Chile. Cassidy, Sheila. *Tablet* 247:6+ Ja 2 1993

CHINA—CHURCH HISTORY
On renewing the church in China. Schreiter, Robert J. *Origins* 22:709-714 Mr 25 1993

CHINA—CHURCH HISTORY—1900-
The Catholic Church in modern China: perspectives. Tang, Edmond, and Wiest, Jean-Paul, eds. Maryknoll: Orbis, 1993. x, 260p ISBN 0-88344-834-3 LC 93-14944

CHINA—INTELLECTUAL LIFE
Did Chinese Catholics die for a secondary truth? Zen, Joseph Er-jwun. *Origins* 22:714-716 Mr 25 1993

CHINA—POLITICS AND GOVERNMENT
China im Wandel. Waldenfels, Hans. *Stimm Zeit* 211:385-394 Je 1993
Journey to Peking. Rafferty, Kevin. *Tablet* 247:1178-1179 S 11 1993
A matter of principle. Smith, Christopher. *Register* 69:4 Jl 18 1993
Public outcry could slow ongoing human-rights violations in China [editorial]. *Nat Cath Rep* 29:28 Jl 16 1993

CHINA—RELIGION
China im Wandel. Waldenfels, Hans. *Stimm Zeit* 211:385-394 Je 1993

CHINA—RELIGION—HISTORY
Chinese religious. Ching, Julia. Maryknoll: Orbis, 1993. x, 275p ISBN 0-88344-875-0 LC 93-2896

CHINA—SOCIAL CONDITIONS
China im Wandel. Waldenfels, Hans. *Stimm Zeit* 211:385-394 Je 1993

CHINA—SOCIAL LIFE AND CUSTOMS
Did Chinese Catholics die for a secondary truth? Zen, Joseph Er-jwun. *Origins* 22:714-716 Mr 25 1993

CHINESE NATIONAL CATHOLIC CHURCH
Catholics in today's China. Cioppa, John. *Origins* 22:704-709 Mr 25 1993

CHISHOLM, RODERICK MILTON, 1916-
Chisholm on persons as entia successiva and the brain-microparticle hypothesis. Jacquette, Dale. *Mod Schlmn* 70:99-113 Ja 1993

CHITWOOD, MICHAEL
Good people get angry, too. Mallowe, Mike. *USCath* 58:14-21 My 1993

CHOICE (PSYCHOLOGY)
A faith perspective on ethical dilemmas: Good decisions and tough choices. Lowry, Douglas. *New Cov* 22:15-16 My 1993
Life-changing choices. Maas, Robin. *Spir Life* 39:140-149 Aut 1993
"Today I put before you life and death": choosing the Body of Christ. Gabriele, Edward F. *Emmanuel* 99:102-106 Mr 1993

CHOMSKY, NOAM, 1928-
Crimes laid bare. Trotta, Carmen. *Cath Work* 60:5 Mr-Ap 1993

CHRIST THE CORNERSTONE CHURCH (MILTON KEYNES, ENGLAND)
A new church in a changing world: Christ the cornerstone, Milton Keynes, England. Farrell, Maureen. *OChr* 29 no 2:170-175 1993
Reserving the sacrament in a shared church. Lewis, Marilyn. *OChr* 29 no 2: 176-184 1993

CHRISTIAN APPALACHIAN PROJECT
Called to the mountains: the autobiography of Reverend Ralph W. Beiting and the Christian Appalachian project. Beiting, Ralph W. Lancaster: Christian Appalachian Project, 1993. //x, 112p ISBN

CHRISTIAN ARABS *see* Arab Christians

CHRISTIAN EDUCATION
Religious education's power to nurture faith. Eklin, Carolyn. *Origins* 23:28-31 My 27 1993

CHRISTIAN EDUCATION—PHILOSOPHY
Road to Emmaus: a new model for catechesis. Ashkar, Dominic. Sant Jose: Resource Publications, 1993. x, 194p ISBN 0-89390-266-7 LC 93-17566

CHRISTIAN EDUCATION—TEXTBOOKS
Teaching the whole child. Chater, Mark. *Tablet* 247:644-646 My 22 1993

CHRISTIAN EDUCATION OF CHILDREN- GREAT BRITAIN
Teaching the whole child. Chater, Mark. *Tablet* 247:644-646 My 22 1993

CHRISTIAN EDUCATION OF CHILDREN- SCOTLAND
Teaching the whole child. Chater, Mark. *Tablet* 247:644-646 My 22 1993

CHRISTIAN ETHICS *see* Ethics, Christian
Autonome Moral oder Moral der Autonomie? Gruber, Hans-Günter. *Stimm Zeit* 211:691-699 O 1993
The magisterium and moral theology [condensed fr *Freiburger Zeitschrift für Philosophie und Theologie* (1989)]. Fuchs, Josef. *TheolDgst* 38:103-107 Sum 1991

CHRISTIAN FAMILY LIFE *see* Family Life, Christian

CHRISTIAN FELLOWSHIP
Bind us together. Weber, Gerard P, and Miller, Robert L. Chicago: ACTA Publications, 1993
Build community or die. Tillard, Jean Marie Roger, 1927-. *Priests & People* 7:129-199 Ap 1993
Concrete koinonia. Tillard, Jean Marie Roger, 1927-. *Tablet* 247:1146-1147 S 4 1993
Faith sharing, trust, and transformation. Bernier, Joan M. *Tod Parish* 25:34-35 Mr 1993
Koinonia: text and context for the church. Fuchs, Lorelei F. *Ecumen Trends* 22:1-2+ F 1993
On the way to fuller koinonia. *Origins* 23:231-232 S 9 1993
On the way to fuller koinonia: message of the Fifth World Conference on Faith and Order. *Ecumen Trends* 22:3-4 O 1993
Parish vs congregation: self-selection isn't the Catholic model. Fichter, Joseph H. *Church* 9:16-19 Sum 1993
"Towards koinonia in faith, life and witness": faith and order's Dublin text, April 1992. *OChr* 28 no 4:357-386 1992
Towards koinonia/communion in faith, life and witness: revised discussion paper for the Fifth World Conference on Faith and Order. Tanner, Mary, et al. *Ecumen Trends* 22:1-24 Je 1993

CHRISTIAN FOUNDATION FOR CHILDREN AND AGING
Guatemala: land of beauty and sorrow. Wintz, Jack Alton, 1936-. *ST Anth* 101:28-34 Jl 1993
Guatemala: land of splendor and sorrow. Weinert, Allan. *Liguorian* 81:12-18 Ap 1993

CHRISTIAN GIVING
Blessings and challenges of the RCIA. Griffin, James A, Bp, 1934-. *Origins* 22:565-572 Ja 28 1993
Catholic giving and the signs of the times. Hofheinz, Fred. *Origins* 22:520-523 Ja 7 1993
Listening to humanity's heartbeat. *OR(Eng)* 1272:2+ Ja 6 1993
Who should get your money? Martin, T R. *America* 169:7-9 Jl 3-10 1993

CHRISTIAN GOSPEL
Acting as Jesus would. Flannery, Kathleen, and Slattery, Marianne. *ReligTJ* 27:28 F 1993
Good news: alive and well. Agnesine, M, and Buschman-Kelly, Mary Ann. *ReligTJ* 27:18-19 F 1993
John Paul II, Pope, (1992-05-14) Church upheld human rights of natives. John Paul II, Pope, 1920- (Karol Wojtyla) (elected 1978). *TPS* 38:9-13 Ja-F 1993*
The meaning of a new evangelization of Europe. Lehmann, Karl, Bp, 1936-. *Communio* 19:541-548 Wint 1992
Il valore storico dei vangeli [editorial]. *Civilta* 144:313-325 F 20 1993

CHRISTIAN GOSPEL- LATIN AMERICA
Proclamación del evangelio en los primeros siglos. Celada, Gregorio. *Cien Tom* 120:33-56 Ja-Ap 1993

CHRISTIAN INITIATION OF ADULTS (CATHOLIC CHURCH) *see* Initiation Rites—Catholic Church

CHRISTIAN LEADERSHIP—CATHOLIC CHURCH
Collaborative ministry: communion, contention, commitment. Cooper, Norman P. New York: Paulist Press, 1993. x, 200p ISBN 0-8091-3376-8 LC 92-38074

CHRISTIAN LEADERSHIP—CATHOLIC CHURCH—CONGRESSES
Disciples at the crossroads: perspectives on worship and church leadership. Bernstein, Eleanor, ed. Collegeville:Liturgical, 1993. x, 153p ISBN 0-8146-2146-5 LC 93-591

CHRISTIAN LIFE
Befilled with the fullness of God: living in the indwelling Trinity. Maloney, George A, 1924-. New Rochelle, New York: New City, Press, 1993. x, 144p ISBN 1-56548-024-4 LC 92-42031
Can I afford this? McNair, J Frank. *Living Prayer* 26:27-28 Mr-Ap 1993
Les Chrétiennes, entre leurs devoirs familiaux et le prestige de l'épiskopè. Dibout, Cécile, and Faivre, Alexandre. *Laval Theol Phil* 49:69-92 F 1993

Divine or distorted?: God as we understand God. Seiden, Jerry. San Diego, California: Recovery Publications, 1993. x, 142p ISBN 0-941405-19-2 LC 92-41854
Do what you have the power to do: studies of six New Testament women. Pearson, Helen Bruch. Nashville: Upper Room Books, 1992. x, 168p ISBN 08-358-0643-x LC 91-65725
Fillin' up: devotional fuel for high performance living. Littleton, Mark. Sisters: Questar, 1993. x, 180p ISBN 0-945564-72-4
Five cries of parish. Ventline, Lawrence M. *Priest* 49:17-21 F 1993
Gott Suchen sich Selbst Erkennen. Cassian, Johannes. Freiburg: Herder, 1993. x, 480p ISBN 3-451-23246-4
Home-made faith. Lash, Janet. *Priests & People* 6:458-463 D 1992
How Christian service is taught in the parish. Dunlap, Judith. *Church* 9:40-42 Aut 1993
Inside the mind of unchurched Harry and Mary. Strobel, Lee. Grand Rapids: Zondervan Publishing House, 1993. x, 224p ISBN 0-310-37561-4
It's time to conduct civil wars. Costello, Gerald M, 1931-. *USCath* 58:48-51 Ap 1993
Jesus: nice ideal but get real!. Auer, Jim. *Liguorian* 81:26-31 Ap 1993
John Paul II, Pope (1993-06-27) Gospel [Orig Italian and English]. John Paul II, Pope, 1920- (Karol Wojtyla) (elected 1978). *OR(Eng)* 1297:1+ Je 30 1993*
John Paul II, Pope, (1992-12-17) Catechism. John Paul II, Pope, 1920- (Karol Wojtyla) (elected 1978). *OR(Eng)* 1272:8 Ja 6 1993*
Leadership in a successful parish. Sweetser, Thomas P, and Holden, Carol M. Kansas City: Sheed & Ward, 1992. x, 203p ISBN 1-55612-564-x LC 92-20718
Martha, Mary, and Jesus: weaving action and contemplation in daily life. Carter, Nancy Corson. Minnesota: The Order of St Benedict, 1992. x, 134p ISBN 0-8146-2119-8 LC 92-23586
Metodologia catequetica. Donzellini, Mary. *Christus* 58:21-25 Je 1993
Richard Rohr: Illuminations of his life and work. Ebert, Andreas, and Brockman, Patricia C, eds. New York: The Crossroad Publishing Company, 1993. x, 200p ISBN 0-8245-1270-7 LC 93-20130
Sexual character: beyond technique to intimacy. Dawn, Marva J. Grand Rapids: Eerdmans, 1993. 192p ISBN 0-8028-0700-3
Something's wrong. O'Connor, Tom. *New Cov* 22:26-28 F 1993
Spiritual living in a secular world: applying the Book of Daniel today. Fernando, Ajith. Grand Rapids: Zondervan Publishing House, 1993. x, 192p ISBN 0-310-59501-0
Tales of the city of God. Valles, Carlos G. Chicago: Loyola University Press, 1993. x, 254p ISBN 0-8294-0750-2 LC 93-8938
Tender warrior: God's intention for a man. Weber, Stu. Sisters: Questar, 1993. x, 224p ISBN 088070-579-5
Themes of the lay life. Keightley, Georgia Masters. *Origins* 22:761-764 Ap 15 1993
Theologian offers Vatican-requested explanations. Guindon, Andre. *Origins* 22:630-636 F 25 1993
A touch of his peace. Stanley, Charles. Grand Rapids: Zondervan Publishing House, 1993. x, 144p ISBN 0-310-54558-7
Toward communion in faith, life and witness. Davis, Kortright. *Ecumen Trends* 22:1-2+ Jl-Ag 1993
The way of the Lord Jesus, volume two, living a Christian life. Grisez, Germain Gabriel, 1929-. Quincy, Illinois: Franciscan Press, 1993. x, 950p ISBN 0-8199-0961-0 LC 83-10508
Where your treasure is: psalms that summon you from self to community. Peterson, Eugene H. Grand Rapids: Eerdmans, 1993. 176p ISBN 0-8028-01153
Working with the Parish Project. Rylands, Paddy. *Priests & People* 7:58-60 F 1993

CHRISTIAN LIFE—BIBLICAL TEACHING
Celebrazione eucaristica e vita cristiana. Galot, Jean. *Civilta* 2:535-547 Je 19 1993
Freedom: the teachings of Jesus. Pierce, Ted M. New York: Vantage Press, 1992. x, 225p ISBN 0-533-10182-4 LC 91-91544
Unity and uniqueness: the perils of consistency. Hoover, Rose. *Chicago Stud* 31:154-172 Ag 1992

CHRISTIAN LIFE—EARLY CHURCH, CA 30-600
Born to write. Davies, Oliver, ed. New Rochelle, New York: New City Press, 1992. 127p ISBN 1-56548-006-6 LC 92-14860

CHRISTIAN LIFE—HISTORY
Shifting sands: Foucault, Brown and the framework of christian asceticism. Behr, John. *Heythrop* 34:1-21 Ja 1993

CHRISTIAN LIFE- BRAZIL
Catequesis y comunidad en la iglesia. *Christus* 58:7-9 Je 1993

CHRISTIAN LITERATURE
Growing pains [editorial]. *New Oxford Rev* 60:2 N 1993
Larry Woiwode. Block, Ed. *Critic* 47:57-65 Sum 1993

CHRISTIAN LITERATURE, EARLY—GREEK AUTHORS
Promise of good things: the Apostolic Fathers. Davies, Oliver, ed. New Rochelle, New York: New City Press, 1993. 115p ISBN 1-56548-019-8 LC 92-42033

CHRISTIAN POETRY *see* Religious Poetry, Christian

CHRISTIAN SAINTS
Claude La Colombiere le sens d'une canonisation. Glotin, Édouard. *NRT* 114:816-838 N-D 1992
Gertrude of Helfta: the herald of divine love. Winkworth, Margaret. New York: Paulist Press, 1993. x, 259p ISBN 0-8091-0458-x LC 92-20663
John Paul II, Pope, (1992-05-29) Litterae Apostolicae (Apostolic Letter) [Latin]. John Paul II, Pope, 1920- (Karol Wojtyla) (elected 1978). *AAS* 85: 14-15 Ja 7 1993*
My child, the saint. Dodds, Bill. *New Cov* 22:21+ Ap 1993
The one mediator, the saints, and Mary. Anderson, H George, et al, eds. Minneapolis: Augsburg Fortress, 1992. x, 397p ISBN 0-8066-2579-1 LC 91-40822
Vincent De Paul and charity. Dodin, André. New Rochelle: New City Press, 1993. 126p ISBN 1-56548-054-6 LC 93-15188
Wisdom of the Celtic saints. Sellner, Edward C. Notre Dame, Indiana: Ave Maria Press, 1993. 207p ISBN 0-87793-492-4 LC 92-74778

CHRISTIAN SAINTS—BIOGRAPHY

Alphonsus de Liguori: the Saint of Bourbon Naples, 1696-1787. Jones, Frederick M. Westminster: Christian Classics, 1992. x, 532p ISBN 08-7061-195-x LC 92-73646

Hildegard of Bingen: mystic healer, companion of the angels. Ulrich, Ingeborg. Collegeville: Liturgical, 1990. 258p ISBN 0-8146-2132-5 LC 93-19848

CHRISTIAN SAINTS- AFRICA

In the beginning, there were black Catholics [interview by the editors of US Catholic (Periodical)]. Davis, Cyprian. USCath 58:6-14 Ap 1993

CHRISTIAN SAINTS- FRANCE

The life of the venerable servant of God Vincent de Paul: founder and first superior general of the Congregation of the Mission (book one). Abelly, Louis. New Rochelle, New York: New City Press, 1993. 403p ISBN 1-56548-052-x LC 93-9446

CHRISTIAN SAINTS- ITALY

The life of St Benedict: Gregory the Great. Vogue, Albert de. Petersham: St Bede's Publications, 1993. x, 186p ISBN 0-932506-77-1 LC 93-420

CHRISTIAN SAINTS, CELTIC

A land of kingdoms, scholars and saints. Miesel, Sandra. OSV 81:18-19 Mr 14 1993

Religious thmes in the work of Patrick Kavanagh: hints of a Celtic tradition. Agnew, Una. Studies 82:257-264 Aut 1993

CHRISTIAN UNION

Directory for the application of the principles and norms of ecumenism. OR(Eng) 1295:I-XIV Je 16 1993

"God unites—in Christ a new creation". Tanner, Mary. OChr 28 no 4:300-306 1992

Historical perspective sheds new light on most recent Catechism. Fernández, Ana Ofelia. OR(Eng) 1297:10 Je 30 1993

"Kenosis": the door to Christian unity. Orsy, Ladislas, 1921-. Origins 23:38-41 Je 3 1993

The state of the ecumenical movement. Rusch, William G. Ecumen Trends 22:3-6 Jl-Ag 1993

Towards Christian unity through the kenosis of the churches. Orsy, Ladislas, 1921-. Ecumen Trends 22:6-10 Jl-Ag 1993

The 1993 directory for ecumenism. Origins 23:129+ Jl 29 1993

CHRISTIANITY

Christian Jungianism: deliverance or danger? Boughton, Jill. HPR 93:54-59 Ja 1993

Christian perspectives on religious knowledge. Evans, C Stephen, and Westphal, eds. Grand Rapids: Eerdmans, 1993. 288p ISBN 0-8028-0679-1

A Christian response to the New Age. Saliba, John A. Way 33:202-232 Jl 1993

Christianisme et Nouvel Âge. Fossion, André. Lumen 48:256-262 S 1993

Christianity for modern pagans. Kreeft, Peter John, 1937-. Register 69:5 Ap 11 1993

Faith without dogma: the place of religion in postmodern societies. Ferrarotti, Franco. New Jersey: Transaction Publishers, 1993. x, 181p ISBN 1-56000-074-0 LC 92-17835

Jews, Christians, and unique revelation. Moran, Gabriel. CrossCurr 42:468-486 Wint 1992-1993

The joy that overcomes everything [editorial]. Tablet 246:1591 D 19-26 1992

Peace and Islam [condensed fr Islam and Christian Muslim Relations Je, 1990]. Tröger, Karl-Wolfgang. TheolDgst 38:115-118 Sum 1991

A quick guide to Christianity. Roberts, David. New York: Vantage Press, 1992. x, 102p ISBN 0-533-10327-4 LC 92-90783

Son of man: a new life of Christ. Drane, John. Grand Rapids: Eerdmans, 1993. 160p ISBN 0-8028-3710-7

CHRISTIANITY—ESSENCE

Le christianisme dans l'histoire. Dagens, Claude. NRT 114:801-815 N-D 1992

John Paul II, Pope, (1993-06-03) Christian hope [Orig in Italian]. John Paul II, Pope, 1920- (Karol Wojtyla) (elected 1978). OR(Eng) 1297:9 Je 30 1993*

Naturalistic humanism. O'Connor, Edward D. HPR 93:19-26 Ap 1993

Only Christianity explains the heart of our human condition. Kreeft, Peter John, 1937-. Register 69:1+ Ap 18 1993

"The truth looks different from here". Soskice, Janet Martin. New Blckfrs 73:528-542 N 1992

CHRISTIANITY—HISTORY see Church History; Church History

CHRISTIANITY—ORIGIN

The birth of the New Testament: the origin and development of the first Christian generation. Collins, Raymond F. New York: Crossroad, 1993. x, 324p ISBN 0-8245-1276-6 LC 93-16647

Le christianisme dans l'histoire. Dagens, Claude. NRT 114:801-815 N-D 1992

Christianity examined at its source. Pevtzow, Lisa. Register 69:1+ Je 13 1993

The emperor and the Gods. Schowalter, Daniel N. Minneapolis: Fortress, 1993. 164p ISBN 0-8006-7082-5 LC 90-40141

The lost gospel: the book of Q and Christian origins. Mack, Burton L. New York: HarperCollins, 1993. x, 275p ISBN 0-06-065374-4 LC 92-53921

"Syncretistic religiosity": the significance of the tautology. Carlson, Jeffrey. JEcumen Stds 29:24-34 Wint 1992

CHRISTIANITY—PHILOSOPHY see Philosophy and Christianity

CHRISTIANITY—PSYCHOLOGY see Psychology and Religion

CHRISTIANITY—STUDY

La nouvelle distinction stéréotypes et perceptions respectives des chrétiens et des athées. Traube, Patrick. Lumen 47:377-390 D 1992

CHRISTIANITY- ASIA

Any room for Christ in Asia? Boff, Leonardo, and Elizondo, Virgil, eds. Maryknoll, New York: Orbis Books, 1993. ISBN 0-88344-870-x

CHRISTIANITY- CHINA

Church and China after Glasnost. Digan, Párig. Furrow 44:493-497 S 1993

CHRISTIANITY- UNITED STATES

Christianity in the twenty-first century: reflections on the challenges ahead. Wuthnow, Robert. New York: Oxford University Press, 1993. x, 251p ISBN 0-19507-957-4 LC 92-39083

A voice crying in America's wilderness [interview by W. Bole, pt 1 of 2]. Feder, Don. OSV 82:6-7 N 28 1993

CHRISTIANITY AND AFRICAN RELIGIONS

African traditional religions and their reactions to other faiths. Tanner, R E S. StudiaM 42:371-394 1993

Les mouvements religieux modernes africains. Bureau, René. StudiaM 41:187-204 1992

Theological trends in Africa. Chepkwony, Adam K A. AFER 34:2-17 F 1992

CHRISTIANITY AND BUDDHISM

The blessings of loving-kindness. Thomas, Janna. Living Prayer 26:20-21 Jl-Ag 1993

The Buddha and the Christ: explorations in Buddhist and Christian dialogue. Lefebvre, Leo D. Maryknoll: Orbis, 1993. x, 239p ISBN 0-88344-924-2 LC 93-7972

Buddhism and Christianity: rivals and allies. Smart, Ninian, 1927-. Honolulu: University of Hawaii Press, 1993. ISBN 0-82481-519-x LC 92-29475

Christian Zen-cum-Ignatian meditation. McCown, Robert. RRel 52:507-518 Jl-Ag 1993

Spiritual formation: a Buddhist-Christian Dialogue [special issue]. Stud Form Spir 14:11-143 F 1993*

World community and religion. Neville, Robert Cummings, 1939-. JEcumen Stds 29:368-382 Sum-Aut 1992

CHRISTIANITY AND CULTURE see Culture and Christianity

Inculturação: um desafio pastoral. Ehle, Paulo. REB 53:167-174 Mr 1993

Liturgical inculturation in multiethnic churches. Chupungco, Anscar J. Past Mus 17:28-29+ F-Mr 1993

Religion aymara y cristianismo. Christus 58:14-21 S 1993

CHRISTIANITY AND CULTURE- LATIN AMERICA

Um projeto cristológico: a colção "Jesus e Jesus Cristo". Palacio, Carlos. Perspectiva 24:375-387 S-D 1992

CHRISTIANITY AND HINDUISM

Christians? Not an issue. Feys, John. StudiaM 42:287-305 1993

Hinduism: what do you know about the world's oldest religion? Whalen, William J. USCath 58:25-29 Ap 1993

John Moffitt: poet from Gorakhpur to America. Samway, Patrick H, 1939-. America 168:17-22 Ap 10 1993

Liberating the unlimited. Gajiwala, Kalpesh. Month 26:135-137 Ap 1993

Revelation in comparative perspective: lessons for interreligious dialogue. Carpenter, David. JEcumen Stds 29:175-188 Spr 1992

CHRISTIANITY AND ISLAM

Christian-Muslim dialogue in a changing world [address, The 36th Annual Robert Cardinal Bellarmarine Lecture, St Louis Univ, S 30 1992]. Michel, Thomas F. TheolDgst 39:303-320 Wint 1992

The Dominican and the dervish: a Christian-Muslim dialogue that might have been between Thomas Aquinas and Jalal ad-Din Rumi. Renard, John. JEcumen Stds 29:189-201 Spr 1992

The flight from Egypt. O'Grady, Desmond. OSV 81:12-13 Mr 28 1993

I Musulmani, che Dio li protegga e li conservi!. Gatta, Secondino. StudiaM 42:271-285 1993

The Incarnation: Muslim objections and the Christian response. Fastiggi, Robert L. Thomist 57:457-493 Jl 1993

Interreligious dialogue today. Fitzgerald, Michael Louis, Bp. Cath Int 4:190-194 Ap 1993

Islam and other faiths. Cragg, Kenneth. StudiaM 42:257-270 1993

Islam and the trialogue of Abrahamic religions. Swidler, Leonard. CrossCurr 42:444-452 Wint 1992-1993

Islamic attitudes to other religions. Watt, William Montgomery. StudiaM 42:245-255 1993

Jesus and Muhammad: Christianity and Islam in dialogue. Bacik, James Joseph, 1936-. Emmanuel 99:13-14+ Ja-F 1993

John Paul II, Pope, (1992-06-26) Christian and Muslim women. John Paul II, Pope, 1920- (Karol Wojtyla) (elected 1978). TPS 38:27-28 Ja-F 1993*

CHRISTIANITY AND JUDAISM

Abraham Joshua Heschel: the inadequacy of the ecumenical perspective. Blumenthal, David Reuben, 1938-. JEcumen Stds 29:249-253 Spr 1992

Atonement in Judaism and Christianity: toward a rapprochement. Lyden, John C. JEcumen Stds 29:47-54 Wint 1992

Christian anti-Semitism and Paul's theology. Hall, Sidney G, III. Minneapolis: Fortress, 1993. x, 191p ISBN 0-8006-2654-0 LC 92-30395

Christian prayer: its relationship with Judaism. Fournier, Marie Hélène. SIDIC 25 No 1:7-10 1992

Christian-Jewish dialogue. Rottenberg, Isaac C, 1925-. JEcumen Stds 29:87-95 Wint 1992

Christian-Jewish dialogue. Sloyan, Gerard S. Living Light 30:93-99 Aut 1993

Christian-Jewish relations in a new Europe. Solomon, Norman. Month 26:9-16 Ja 1993

Christians and Jews: coexistence in the new Europe. Ucko, Hans. JEcumen Stds 29:254-257 Spr 1992

The church and Judaism: questions Catholics ask. Pawlikowski, John T. Chicago Stud 31:244-257 N 1992

Dialogue [interview by L Pevtzow]. Dubois, Marcel Jacque. Register 69:1+ Ja 3 1993

The eclipse of difference: Merton's encounter with Judaism. Plank, Karl A. Cist Stud 28 no 2:179-191 1993

The Epistle of James for Jews and Christians. McDade, John. Month 26:115-120 Mr 1993

Eucharist and blessing. Thurian, Max. SIDIC 26 no 1:19-20 1993

Faith without prejudice: rebuilding Christian attitudes toward Judaism. Fisher, Eugene J. New York: The Crossroad Publishing Company, 1993. x, 208p ISBN 0-8245-1266-9 LC 92-36342

"A final word" [replay to Boadt; L; N 1991]. Fisher, Eugene J. New Theol Rev 6:87-89 F 1993

Homage to the fighters of the Warsaw Ghetto. Luxmoore, Jonathan. Tablet 247:527-529 Ap 24 1993

The interfaith future: from the mind to the heart. Klenicki, Leon. Ecumen Trends 22:9 My 1993

Into the city of faithfulness: negotiating a Jewish-Catholic marriage. Donnelly, Daria. Comm 120:18-20 Je 18 1993

Islam and the trialogue of Abrahamic religions. Swidler, Leonard. CrossCurr 42:444-452 Wint 1992-1993

Israel, fundies share an agenda. Pevtzow, Lisa. Register 69:1+ My 23 1993

Jacques Maritain and the Jews. Castori, Michael T. *America* 168:18-21 My 29 1993

Jewish threat to boycott ghetto commemorations. *Tablet* 247:486-487 Ap 10-17 1993

Let my people go. Lustiger, Jean-Marie, Cardinal, 1926-. *NRT* 115:481-495 Jl-Ag 1993

Letter to Patriarch Sabbah. Roach, John, Abp. *Origins* 23:812 My 6 1993

Lettera a un amico ebreo. Rulli, Giovanni. *Civilta* 3:47-50 Jl 3 1993

Meeting Jacob at the Jabbok: wrestling with a text—a Midrash on Genesis 32:22-32. Knight, Henry F. *JEcumen Stds* 29:451-460 Sum-Aut 1992

My Catholic affair. Blue, Lionel. *Tablet* 247:574 My 8 1993

New visions: historical and theological perspectives on the Jewish-Christian dialogue. McInnes, Val Ambrose. New York: Crossroad, 1993. x, 165p ISBN 0-8245-1246-4 LC 93-4190

The original schism: how Jews and Christians came to a parting of the ways [Interview by the editors of U.S. Catholic (Periodical)]. Pawlikowski, John T. *USCath* 58:15-21 O 1993

Overcoming fear between Jews and Christians. Charlesworth, James H. New York: Crossroad, 1993. x, 198p ISBN 0-8245-1265-0 LC 92-31262

Der päpstliche rat zur Förderung der Einheit der Christen im Jahre 1992. Cassidy, Edward Idris, 1924-, Cardinal. *Catholica* 47 no 2:89-107 1993

A personal note. *Tablet* 247:105 Ja 23 1993

Politics and mystery: the integration of Judaism and Christianity in Edith Stein. Stein, Waltraut J H. *Spir Life* 32:104-110 Sum 1993

Preaching the passion with sensitivity to Judaism. Witherup, Ronald D. *Priest* 49:12-16 Ap 1993

Special Assembly for Europe of the Synod of Bishops. *SIDIC* 25 No 1:26-29 1992

Towards a Jewish-Christian alliance [interview by R Lakind]. Haberman, Joshua A. *Crisis* 11:32-38 F 1993

Two faiths meet on common ground. Gibeau, Dawn. *Nat Cath Rep* 29:5 My 21 1993

Within context: essays on Jews and Judaism in the New Testament. Efroymson, David P, et al, eds. Collegeville, Minnesota: The Liturgical Press, 1993. x, 160p ISBN 0-8146-5033-3 LC 92-34914

CHRISTIANITY AND JUDAISM—CONGRESSES

Interwoven destinies: Jews and Christians through the ages. Fisher, Eugene J. New Jersey: Paulist Press, 1993. x, 154p ISBN 0-8091-8363-6 LC 92-37707

CHRISTIANITY AND JUDAISM—HISTORY

Christianity examined at its source. Pevtzow, Lisa. *Register* 69:1+ Je 13 1993

CHRISTIANITY AND JUDAISM—0030-600

In the midst of the highest Christian feast. McDarby, Patrick. *Sisters* 65: 206-208 My 1993

CHRISTIANITY AND JUDAISM- HUNGARY

Statement of the Hungarian Council of Christians and Jews on anti-semitism and nationalism. *SIDIC* 26 no 1:27 1993

CHRISTIANITY AND JUDAISM- SPAIN

Jews and christians in Spain today. Mihalovici, Ionel. *SIDIC* 25 No 2:12-14 1992

CHRISTIANITY AND JUSTICE

When Christ meets Christ: homilies on the just word. Burghardt, Walter J. New York: Paulist Press, 1993. x, 241p ISBN 0-8091-3373-3 LC 92-46434

CHRISTIANITY AND OTHER RELIGIONS

An Asian paradigm: inter-religious dialogue and theology of religions [repr fr *Qoholet*]. Pieris, Aloysius, 1934-. *Month* 26:129-134 Ap 1993

Christian theology and other religions: an evaluation of John Hick and Paul Knitter. D'Costa, Gavin. *StudiaM* 42:161-178 1993

Christianity and religions of the world. Lefebure, Leo D. *Chicago Stud* 31: 258-270 N 1992

Christology in dialogue. Berkey, Robert F, and Edwards, Sarah A, eds. Cleveland: The Pilgrim Press, 1993. 390p ISBN 0-8298-0956-2 LC 92-47004

The cosmic Christ and world religions. Dhavamony, Mariasusai. *StudiaM* 42: 179-225 1993

Disiplines for Christian living. Ryan, Thomas. New Jersey: Paulist Press, 1993. x, 274p ISBN 0-8091-3380-6 LC 92-42596

Dom Bede Griffiths: symbol of the marriage of East and West (1906-1993). Teasdale, Wayne. *Living Prayer* 26:17-18 S-O 1993

Ecumenical or interfaith? Kessler, Diane C. *Living Light* 30:89-92 Aut 1993

The emperor and the Gods. Schowalter, Daniel N. Minneapolis: Fortress, 1993. 164p ISBN 0-8006-7082-5 LC 90-40141

Evangelisation and the other: response and responsibility. Barnes, Michael R. *Month* 25:479-484 D 1992

Gathering together to pray: a special mode of public presence in inter-religious dialogue. Kaserow, John. *New Theol Rev* 6:18-29 Ag 1993

The human pilgrimage. Boulay, Shirley du. *Tablet* 247:1282 O 9 1993

Interreligious dialogue and theology of religions: an Asian paradigm. Pieris, Aloysius, 1934-. *Horizons (CTS)* 20:106-114 Spr 1993

Interreligious dialogue today. Fitzgerald, Michael Louis, Bp. *Cath Int* 4:190-194 Ap 1993

Interreligious dialogue: a hundred years on. Schreiter, Robert J. *New Theol Rev* 6:6-17 Ag 1993

Missionary service [fr *Yours sincerely*]. Kaut, Bernd. *AFER* 34:376-381 D 1992

Preaching in interreligious contexts. Lefebure, Leo D. *New Theol Rev* 6:64-70 Ag 1993

Remembering Noah [editorial]. Pawlikowski, John T. *New Theol Rev* 6:3-5 Ag 1993

Sinto and Christianity: dialogue for the twenty-first century. Kadowaki, Kakichi. *IPQ* 33:69-89 Mr 1993

Tales of the city of God. Valles, Carlos G. Chicago: Loyola University Press, 1993. x, 254p ISBN 0-8294-0750-2 LC 93-8938

Wrestling with truth. Nicholl, Donald. *Tablet* 247:1291-1292 O 9 1993

CHRISTIANITY AND POLITICS see Politics and Christianity

CHRISTIANS

Christians and their passions. Whitehead, Evelyn Eaton, and Whitehead, James D. *RRel* 52:702-711 S-O 1993

CHRISTIANS—UNIFICATION

John Paul II, Pope, (1993-09-10) Creator [Orig in Estonian]. John Paul II, Pope, 1920- (Karol Wojtyla) (elected 1978). *OR(Eng)* 1308:10 S 22 1993*

CHRISTIANS- AFRICA

Incontro tra Cristiani del sud. Salvini, Gianpaolo. *Civilta* 144:51-54 Ja 2 1993

CHRISTIANS- IRAQ

John Paul II, Pope, (1993-04-28) Christian heritage in Iraq. John Paul II, Pope, 1920- (Karol Wojtyla) (elected 1978). *TPS* 38:280-282 S-O 1993*

CHRISTIANS- ISRAEL

In Israel, Christians "suspect". Pevtzow, Lisa. *Register* 69:1+ Ja 10 1993

Israeli-Arab Christians: a paradox. Pevtzow, Lisa. *Register* 69:1+ My 30 1993

CHRISTIANS- JAPAN

Japan's hidden Christians. Harrington, Ann M. Chicago: Loyola University Press, 1993. x, 110p ISBN 0-8294-0741-3

CHRISTIANS- JORDAN

Jordan faithful eye future. Dennis, Mark. *Register* 69:1+ N 14 1993

CHRISTIANS- LATIN AMERICAN

Incontro tra Cristiani del sud. Salvini, Gianpaolo. *Civilta* 144:51-54 Ja 2 1993

CHRISTIANS- MIDDLE EAST

We are not guests: the exodus of Christians from the Middle East. Samaha, John M. *Can Cath Rev* 11:11-13 N 1993

CHRISTIANS- SOVIET UNION

Candles behind the wall: heroes of the peaceful revolution that shattered communism. Heydt, Barbara von der. Grand Rapids: Eerdmans, 1993. 224p ISBN 0-8028-3722-0

CHRISTIANS- SUDAN

Dialogue [interview by P Mullen]. Gassis, Macram Max, Bp, 1938-. *Register* 69:1+ Je 13 1993

CHRISTIANS- UNITED STATES

The common good: old idea, new urgency. Lynch, Robert, et al. *Origins* 23: 81+ Je 24 1993

The Continuing Kulturkampf [editorial]. Brown, Harold O J. *SocJust* 84:35-39 Mr-Ap 1993

CHRISTIANSEN, DREW

The continuing challenge of peace [interview by T Tamberg]. Christiansen, Drew. *OSV* 82:6 Ag 22 1993

CHRISTMAS

Beyond stable and straw. Svoboda, Melannie. *Liguorian* 81:45-47 D 1993

A carol for Tim. Paffett, Kate. *Liguorian* 81:12-13 D 1993

A Christmas call [a five minute meditation]. Santa, Thomas M. *Liguorian* 81:48-49 D 1993

Christmas in the company of saints. Matz, Terry. *Liguorian* 81:50-55 D 1993

The Christmas story: a gospel enactment. Massion, John Carey. *Catechist* 27:16-18 N-D 1993

The first Christmas. Willie, Caroljean. *Tod Cath Teach* 27:28 N-D 1993

The fleshy way of God [excerpt fr *Sermons for sermon haters* 1992]. Papineau, Andre, 1937-. *Mod Lit* 19:16 D 1992-Ja 1993

Grace under pressure. Manning, Martha. *Salt* 13:45-46 N-D 1993

A hope reborn. Behrens, Jeff. *Liguorian* 81:4-8 D 1993

John Paul II, Pope, (1992-12-24) Light shines [orig Italian]. John Paul II, Pope, 1920- (Karol Wojtyla) (elected 1978). *OR(Eng)* 1272:5 Ja 6 1993*

John Paul II, Pope, (1992-12-25) Come to heal [orig Italian]. John Paul II, Pope, 1920- (Karol Wojtyla) (elected 1978). *OR(Eng)* 1271:1 Ja 6 1993*

The joy that overcomes everything [editorial]. *Tablet* 246:1591 D 19-26 1992

Mystery on the margins. Rockett, Trish. *Furrow* 43:681-682 D 1992

La Nativité et l'Épiphanie dans le dialogue unioniste du VIIe siècle. Halleux, André de. *Eph Theol Lovan* 78:5-37 Ap 1992

The perfect setting. Helgens, Sharon. *Liguorian* 81:60-66 D 1993

Put something different under the tree. Brady, Mary Clare. *USCath* 58:31-33 D 1993

The real St. Nicholas [condensed fr *Again* V 13, no 4]. Bear, Jan, and Gray, Daria. *CDgst* 58:6-10 D 1993

The spirit of Christmas almost here. Auer, Jim. *Liguorian* 81:38-44 D 1993

Starlight: beholding the Christmas miracle all year long. Shea, John B. New York: The Crossroad Publishing Company, 1992. x, 192p ISBN 0-8245-1206-5 LC 92-15952

Towards a Christian Christmas. Mueller, Therese. *Mod Lit* 20:32-33 O 1993

CHRISTMAS—COMPARATIVE STUDIES

Christmas literature from writers ancient and modern. Johnson, Pegram, III, and Troiano, Edna M. Louisville: Westminster, 1993. x, 352p ISBN 0-664-22030-4

CHRISTMAS—REMINISCENCES

A child's Christmas in Roscommon. Scally, John. *Month* 25:491-494 D 1992

CHRISTMAS—SERMONS

John Paul II, Pope, (1991-12-23) Allocutiones (Christmas exhortation to Cardinals and Curial Staff) [Italian]. John Paul II, Pope, 1920- (Karol Wojtyla) (elected 1978). *AAS* 85:37-45 Ja 7 1993*

CHRISTMAS- CHINA

Bethlehem comes to China. Jeffers, Henrietta. *Liguorian* 81:22-27 D 1993

CHRISTOLOGY see Jesus Christ—History of Doctrines

CHRISTOPHER, WARREN, 1925-

The tragedy of Bosnia is not over [editorial]. *America* 169:3 Ag 14-21 1993

CHRONICALLY ILL CHILDREN

Ministry to the chronically ill child. Spinetta, Pat Deasy, and Collins, Denis E. *Momentum* 24:28-30+ Ap-My 1993

CHRONOLOGY

Reply to Smith: on the finitude of the past [reply to Q Smith, 33:109-115 1993]. Craig, William Lane. *IPQ* 33:225-231 Je 1993

CHURCH

"Bride" and "Mother" in the *Super cantica* of St Bernard: an ecclesiology for our time? Kereszty, Roch A, 1933-. *Communio* 20:415-436 Sum 1993

Church in the round: feminist interpretation of the church. Russell, Letty M. Louisville: John Knox Press, 1993. 235p ISBN 0-66425-070-x LC 93-9306

The Church's handbook. Doohan, Leonard. *Mod Lit* 20:34-35 Je-Jl 1993

Church: the human story of God. Schillebeeckx, Edward. New York: Crossroad, 1993. x, 260p ISBN 0-8245-1050-x LC 90-36343

The forest and the trees. Morgan, Winifred. *Sisters* 65:12-19 Ja 1993

Forever faithful: the unfolding of God's promise to creation. Reiser, William, 1943-. Collegeville:Liturgical, 1993. 98p ISBN 0-8146-5849-0 LC 93-15191

Happy the people God has made his own. Higgins, James J. *Liguorian* 81:73 Ja 1993

Mary in the Church [fr *Handmaid of the Lord* tr by E.A. Nelson]. Speyr, Adrienne von, 1902-1967. *Communio* 20:451-456 Sum 1993

CHURCH—AUTHORITY

"All who walk by this rule" the canon of the New Testament. Plevnik, Joseph. *Can Cath Rev* 11:12-20 F 1993

Anglican approaches. *Tablet* 247:560 My 1 1993

Epistola ad Romanos: an open letter to some Roman Catholic friends. Greenacre, Roger. *Month* 26:88-96 Mr 1993

A feminist's path to Rome. Maitland, Sara, 1950-. *Tablet* 247:422 Ap 3 1993

Gender and the will of God. Kreeft, Peter John, 1937-. *Crisis* 11:20-28 S 1993

"Humanae Vitae" 25 years later. McCormick, Richard Arthur, 1922-. *America* 169:6-8+ Jl 17-24 1993

"Humanae vitae": what has it done to us? And what is to be done now? Untener, Kenneth E, Bp. *Comm* 120:12-14 Je 18 1993

Laying claim to Newman. Hebblethwaite, Peter, 1930-. *Tablet* 247:834 Je 26 1993

The limits of infallibility. Hebblethwaite, Peter, 1930-. *Tablet* 247:1036-1037 Ag 14 1993

No bar to entry. Longley, Clifford. *Tablet* 247:1058 Ag 21 1993

No special deal in welcome for Anglicans. *Tablet* 247:558-560 My 1 1993

The real test of conscience [editorial]. *Tablet* 247:535-536 My 1 1993

Sin, power and the Church. Hoose, Bernard. *Month* 26:408-411 S-O 1993

The weakest possible argument [editorial]. Callam, Daniel. *Can Cath Rev* 11:2-4 F 1993

Women priests and Anglo-Catholics. Sutcliffe, Tom. *Month* 26:53-56 F 1993

CHURCH—BIBLICAL TEACHING

see also Bible (NT)—Theology

CHURCH—FOUNDATION

John Paul II, Pope, (1993-07-11) Santo Stefano [Orig in Italian]. John Paul II, Pope, 1920- (Karol Wojtyla) (elected 1978). *OR(Eng)* 1300:3 Jl 21 1993*

CHURCH—INDEFECTIBILITY

When they ask your opinion, give it. Kinast, Robert L. *Emmanuel* 49:402-407 S 1993

CHURCH—MARKS

The Dublin Statement and women's ordination. Baktis, Peter Anthony. *JEcumen Stds* 29:35-46 Wint 1992

John Paul II, Pope, (1993-10-02) Church [Orig in English]. John Paul II, Pope, 1920- (Karol Wojtyla) (elected 1978). *OR(Eng)* 1311:3 O 13 1993*

John Paul II, Pope, (1993-10-02) Structures [Orig in English]. John Paul II, Pope, 1920- (Karol Wojtyla) (elected 1978). *Origins* 23:348-350 O 21 1993*

What is "new" in the new evangelization? Boyack, Kenneth. *Living Light* 30:3-8 Aut 1993

CHURCH—MISSION

Tasks of the Church in the new Europe. Hume, George Basil, Cardinal, 1932-. *Origins* 23:341-348 O 21 1993

CHURCH—TEACHING OFFICE

Ad limina apostolorum. Carroll, William E. *Can Cath Rev* 11:33-34 My 1993

Anglican approaches. *Tablet* 247:560 My 1 1993

Authority in the church: who makes the final call? McClory, Richard J. *USCath* 58:6-13 Mr 1993

The authority of the Catechism of the Catholic Church. Komonchak, Joseph Andrew, 1939-. *Living Light* 29:39-49 Sum 1993

Basil Hume at 70 [interview by J Wilkins]. Hume, George Basil, Cardinal, 1923-. *Tablet* 247:267-268 F 27 1993

The Catechism [commentary]. Johnson, Luke Timothy, 1943-. *Comm* 120:16-18 My 7 1993

The Catholic bind [editorial]. Callam, Daniel. *Can Cath Rev* 11:2-3 Jl-Ag 1993

The Church's teaching mission: some aspects of the normative role of episcopal conferences. Green, Thomas J. *Stud Can* 27 no 1:23-57 1993

Current errors and their refutation: respect the charisms God has given Holy Doctors and the Magisterium. Sutton, Alphonsus M. *ChrWorld* 38:144-152 Mr-Ap 1993

For DREs: challenge and hope. Loughran, Eileen. *Momentum* 24:64-65 S-O 1993

How the church is one. McBride, Alfred. *OSV* 82:13 Ag 15 1993*

"Humanae vitae": what has it done to us? And what is to be done now? Untener, Kenneth E, Bp. *Comm* 120:12-14 Je 18 1993

In the name of Jesus we have confident access to the Father. Corbon, Jean. *OR(Eng)* 1292:10 My 26 1993*

John Paul II, Pope, (1993-03-17) Infallibility. John Paul II, Pope, 1920- (Karol Wojtyla) (elected 1978). *TPS* 38:257-260 S-O 1993*

Ein Kirchen bild für unsere Zeit? Wagner, Marion. *Stimm Zeit* 211:533-546 Ag 1993

The magisterium and morality. Spohn, William C. *TheolStds* 54:95-111 Mr 1993

The marks of the church [commentary]. Stravinskas, Peter. *Register* 69:1+ O 17 1993*

The mystery of the church. McBride, Alfred. *OSV* 82:13 Ag 1 1993*

The new Catechism compared to the "Roman Catechism" of Trent. Lanzetti, Raúl. *OR(Eng)* 1298:9+ Jl 7 1993*

Overview: the catechism of the Catholic Church. Pollard, John E. *Origins* 23:7-11 My 20 1993

Passé et présent de la commission biblique. Vanhoye, Albert. *Gregorianum* 74 no 2:261-275 1993

Pastoral letter to religious educators. *Living Light* 29:68-80 Spr 1993

Praying with Peter [excerpts fr a pastoral letter to the Church of Denver]. Stafford, James Francis, Abp, 1932-. *Crisis* 11:26-31 Jl-Ag 1993

Reception and submission. Pottmeyer, Hermann Joseph. *Jurist* 51 no 2:269-292 1991

The resplendence of truth [editorial]. *Tablet* 247:999-1000 Ag 7 1993

The "secondary object" of infallibility. Sullivan, Francis Aloysius. *TheolStds* 54:536-550 S 1993

The spiritual birth of the people of God. McBride, Alfred. *OSV* 82:15 Ag 8 1993*

A stumbling-block for many [editorial]. *Tablet* 247:935 Jl 24 1993

Teaching Church teaching: theological and pedagogical reflections. Hinsdale, Mary Ann. *Horizons (CTS)* 20:87-98 Spr 1993

Theologian offers Vatican-requested explanations. Guindon, Andre. *Origins* 22:630-636 F 25 1993

Transmisión de la revelación: escritura, tradición, magisterio: (A la luz de la *Dei Verbum del Concilio Vaticano II)*. Sánchez Mielgo, Gerardo. *Cien Tom* 119:251-289 My-Ag 1992

Witnesses to the faith: community, infallibility, and the ordinary. Gaillardetz, Richard R. New Jersey: Paulist Press, 1992. x, 238p ISBN 0-8091-3350-4 LC 92-280431

CHURCH—UNION

Laylines. Mac Réamoinn, Seán. *Doctr Life* 43:108-115 F 1993

CHURCH—UNITY

Catechesis and the relationship of evangelization to ecumenism. Cermak, John. *Living Light* 29:64-68 Wint 1992

The CDF letter on Communion: reactions and reflections. Rausch, Thomas P. *Ecumen Trends* 22:3-4 Ap 1993

"The church as communion": an Anglican response. Hill, Christopher. *OChr* 28 no 4:323-330 1992

Church unity rooted in Eucharist. *OR(Eng)* 1298:4+ Jl 7 1993*

Concepts of division and unity in the ecumenical movement. Tesfai, Yacob. *Ecumen Trends* 22:9-15 Mr 1993

Directory for the application of the principles and norms of ecumenism. *OR(Eng)* 1295:I-XIV Je 16 1993

Ecumenical or interfaith? Kessler, Diane C. *Living Light* 30:89-92 Aut 1993

Ecumenism, spirituality, and the dark night of the soul. Crow, Paula A. *OChr* 29 no 2:100-112 1993

Henri De Lubacs vision of the church. Grace, Madeleine. *Priest* 49:45 F 1993

Impatience and hope as ecumenists meet. *Tablet* 247:1052-1053 Ag 14 1993

John Paul II, Pope, (1993-01-25) Christian unity is our desire. John Paul II, Pope, 1920- (Karol Wojtyla) (elected 1978). *TPS* 38:202-206 Jl-Ag 1993*

John Paul II, Pope, (1993-06-29) Christian unity. John Paul II, Pope, 1920- (Karol Wojtyla) (elected 1978). *OR(Eng)* 1298:2 Jl 7 1993*

John Paul II, Pope, (1993-07-18) Praying [Orig Italian]. John Paul II, Pope, 1920- (Karol Wojtyla) (elected 1978). *OR(Eng)* 1300:1 Jl 21 1993*

"Kenosis": the door to Christian unity. Orsy, Ladislas, 1921-. *Origins* 23:38-41 Je 3 1993

Koinonia: text and context for the church. Fuchs, Lorelei F. *Ecumen Trends* 22:1-2+ F 1993

Major themes and underlying principles of the Catechism of the Catholic Church. Schönborn, Christoph von, Bp. *Living Light* 30:55-64 Aut 1993

Making dialogue work. Wako, Gabriel Zubeir, Abp, et al. *Origins* 23:72-76 Je 17 1993

Das Ökumenismusdekret des Konzils. Suttner, Ernst Chr. *Stimm Zeit* 211:303-317 My 1993

On the way to fuller koinonia: message of the Fifth World Conference on Faith and Order. *Ecumen Trends* 22:3-4 O 1993

Der päpstliche rat zur Förderung der Einheit der Christen im Jahre 1992. Cassidy, Edward Idris, 1924-, Cardinal. *Catholica* 47 no 2:89-107 1993

A pastoral priority. Falardeau, Ernest R, 1928-. *Priest* 49:49-50 Ap 1993

The reception and non-reception of Montreal's call to renewal [speech] to the North American Academy of Ecumenists, S 27 1992. Meyer, Lauree Hersch. *Ecumen Trends* 21:1+ D 1992

Reception—communion. Tillard, Jean Marie Roger, 1927-. *OChr* 28 no 4:307-322 1992

Reconciling unity and plurality. Weakland, Rembert G, Abp, 1927-, and Eastman, Theodore, Bp. *Origins* 22:587-588 F 4 1993

The Roman primacy within the Communion of Churches: French Joint RC-Orthodox Committee. *OChr* 29 no 2:156-164 1993

The Roman principle in the writings of Vladimir Solovyov. Matual, David. *Diakonia* 26 no 1:27-39 1993

The Taizé Community: fifty years of prayer and action. Hicks, Douglas A. *JEcumen Stds* 29:202-214 Spr 1992

Tasks of the Church in the new Europe. Hume, George Basil, Cardinal, 1932-. *Origins* 23:341-348 O 21 1993

The time has come: a vision for the Fifth World Conference on Faith and Order [fr *The Ecumenical review*]. Tanner, Mary. *Cath Int* 4:239-244 My 1993

Towards koinonia/communion in faith, life and witness: revised discussion paper for the Fifth World Conference on Faith and Order. Tanner, Mary, et al. *Ecumen Trends* 22:1-24 Je 1993

True unity: an inspiration for the world. El-Meskeen, Matta. *OChr* 29 no 3:187-198 1993

Unity and uniqueness: the perils of consistency. Hoover, Rose. *Chicago Stud* 31:154-172 Ag 1992

The vision of authentic ecumenism: a Catholic response. Majawa, Clement. *AFER* 35:91-100 Ap 1993

CHURCH ADMINISTRATION

Developing a strategy for the urban parish: the lessons of the church closings in Detroit. Fukuzawa, David. *New Theol Rev* 6:54-65 F 1993

Leadership, liturgy, and identity: parish priorities. Gallagher, Maureen. *Church* 9:17-22 Aut 1993

Let's go back to an open-door policy for our churches. Gannon, Mary-Grace. *OSV* 82:6 Ag 15 1993

Le ministère de présidence du curé: réflexions canoniques et pastorales. Borras, Alphonse. *Stud Can* 27 no 1:59-76 1993

Ministry and the American legal system: a guide for clergy, lay workers, and congregations. Couser, Richard B. Minneapolis: Fortress Press, 1993. 356p ISBN 0-8006-2603-6 LC 92-34214

On the front line: who's minding the door? Walsh, Richard. *Priest* 49:19-20 Jl 1993

A way to evaluate, a way to plan. Iwanowski, Thomas B. *Priest* 49:41-43 Mr 1993

CHURCH AND COMMUNITY

John Paul II, Pope, (1993-10-03) Heart [Origin Italian]. John Paul II, Pope, 1920- (Karol Wojtyla) (elected 1978). *OR(Eng)* 1311:7 O 13 1993*

Pastoral planning for the new millennium. Quinn, John Raphael, Abp, 1929-. *Origins* 22:624-628 F 25 1993

A practical guide to community ministry. Bos, A David. Louisville, Kentucky: John Knox Press, 1993. 112p ISBN 0-694-25405-5

Synod convoked for Charleston Diocese. Thompson, David, Bp. *Origins* 22:509+ Ja 7 1993

CHURCH AND COMMUNITY- BRAZIL
Catequesis y comunidad en la iglesia. *Christus* 58:7-9 Je 1993
CHURCH AND COMMUNITY- GERMANY
Neue Ortskirchen in Deutschland? Zu Schlochtern, Josef Meyter. *Stimm Zeit* 211:617-632 S 1993
CHURCH AND LABOR- UNITED STATES
Organized labor and the Church: reflections of a "labor priest". Higgins, George G, 1916-, and Bole, William. New York: Paulist Press, 1993. x, 245p ISBN 0-8091-3374-1 LC 92-36139
CHURCH AND SOCIAL PROBLEMS
Beyond a theology of development. Peter, C B. *AFER* 35:54-67 F 1993
Just wages in the church? Almade, Frank D. *Church* 9:41-43 Spr 1993
O Mercosul e a integração Latino-Americana. Neutzling, Inácio. *REB* 53:374-389 Je 1993
One-sided Christianity? Uniting the church to heal a loot and broken world. Sider, Ronald J. Grand Rapids: Zondervan Publishing House, 1993. x, 256p ISBN 0-310-58761-1
Religious leaders eye peacemaking. Kezmoh, Heidi Schlumpf. *Register* 69:1+ My 16 1993
There goes the neighborhood: the churches disturb the peace. McCarthy, Abigail Quigley. *Comm* 120:9-10 O 22 1993
World Faith and Order Conference in Spain. *Ecumen Trends* 22:5-6 O 1993
CHURCH AND SOCIAL PROBLEMS—CATHOLIC CHURCH
Appartenance à Église ou itinérance ecclésiale? Borras, Alphonse. *Lumen* 48:161-173 Je 1993
Atividade humana e trabalho na sociedade moderna: uma aproximação ética. Camacho, Ildefonso. *Perspectiva* 25:45-62 Ja-Ap 1993
Catholic stocktaking. Hornsby-Smith, Michael P, 1932-. *Tablet* 247:164-165 F 6 1993
The Church must take sides. McVerry, Peter. *Furrow* 44:78-83 F 1993
Concepts of division and unity in the ecumenical movement. Tesfai, Yacob. *Ecumen Trends* 22:9-15 Mr 1993
Don't let religion get in the way of your faith [interview by editors of US Catholic (Periodical)]. Larsen, Earnie. *USCath* 58:31-35 Mr 1993
The election: hard years ahead. Martin, Ralph. *New Cov* 22:26-31 Ja 1993
Elementos para avaliar o VIII interecclesial das CEBS (S Maria, RS Brasil 8-12 Setembro 1992). Marins, José, and Trevisan, Teolide M, et al. *REB* 52:801-813 D 1992
Environmental degradation and social injustice. Malone, James, Bp. *Origins* 22:685+ Mr 18 1993
European Catholics still divided [editorial]. *Tablet* 247:1183 S 18 1993
Fullness of faith: the public significance of theology. Himes, Michael J, and Himes, Kenneth R. New York: Paulist Press, 1993. x, 213p ISBN 0-8091-3372-5 LC 92-36140
Die katholische Kirche als Medienereignis. Bieger, Erkhard. *Stimm Zeit* 210:855-857 D 1992
Nuova evangelizzazione e dottrina sociale della chiesa. Carrier, Hervé. *Civilta* 144:116-130 Ja 16 1993
Pinpointing the adversary. Kennedy, Frank. *Tablet* 247:930 Jl 17 1993
Un proceso eclesial Latinoamericano. Marins, José, and Chanona, Carolee, et al. *Christus* 58:23-28 Mr-Ap 1993
Quali vie per uscire dal "sistema delle tangenti"? [editorial]. *Civilta* 144:521-534 Mr 20 1993
Reading the signs of the times: resources for social and cultural analysis. Sanks, T Howland, and Coleman, John A, eds. New York: Paulist Press, 1993. x, 232p ISBN 0-8091-33777-6 LC 92-42017
Should the Catholic Church secede from the union? Herrera, Robert A. *F & R* 18:275-285 Aut 1992
Synod convoked for Charleston Diocese. Thompson, David, Bp. *Origins* 22:509+ Ja 7 1993
Universelles Vülkerrecht. García-Mateno, Rogelio. *Stimm Zeit* 210:831-840 D 1992
VIII encontro interecclesial das CEBS (eventos no evento). Libanio, Joao Batista. *REB* 52:789-800 D 1992
CHURCH AND SOCIAL PROBLEMS—CATHOLIC CHURCH- LATIN AMERICA
A Igreja e sua capacidade de satisfazer às demandas religiosas projeto "Construir a Esperança". Libanio, Joao Batista. *Perspectiva* 24:367-374 S-D 1992
CHURCH AND SOCIAL PROBLEMS—EVANGELICALISM
Die Annahme der Gnade als Mitvollzug der Erlösung. Menke, Karl-Heinz. *Catholica* 47:1-19 1993
Ekklesiologische optionen Evangelischer Theologie als Mögliche Leitbilder der Okumene. Wagner, Harald. *Catholica* 47 no 2:124-141 1993
CHURCH AND SOCIAL PROBLEMS—PENTECOSTALISM
Pentecostalismo, governos militares e revolução. Cartaxo Rolim, Francisco. *REB* 53:324-348 Je 1993
CHURCH AND SOCIAL PROBLEMS—PROTESTANT CHURCH
Une vision protestante de l'éthique sociale. Müller, Denis. *Laval Theol Phil* 49:57-67 F 1993
CHURCH AND SOCIAL PROBLEMS- AFRICA
Secular ecumenicity: a challenge to the Church in Africa. Kasenene, Peter. *AFER* 34:44-59 F 1992
CHURCH AND SOCIAL PROBLEMS- BRAZIL
Como ressoou a catequese na 30a AG da CNBB (1992). Cansi, Bernardo. *REB* 52:928-936 D 1992
Teologia, racismo e mestiçagem. Frisotti, Heitor. *REB* 52:833-845 D 1992
CHURCH AND SOCIAL PROBLEMS- CUBA
A call for true dialogue. *Origins* 23:273-279 S 30 1993
CHURCH AND SOCIAL PROBLEMS- GERMANY
Neue Ortskirchen in Deutschland? Zu Schlochtern, Josef Meyter. *Stimm Zeit* 211:617-632 S 1993
CHURCH AND SOCIAL PROBLEMS- THIRD WORLD
Can we really help the third-world poor? Brauder, Bruce. *New Cov* 23:7-10 Ag 1993
CHURCH AND SOCIETY- ITALY
Battere La Mafia Uiti Si Può. Sorge, Bartolomeo. *Civilta* 143:468-475 D 5 1992

CHURCH AND STATE
Archbishop of York defends state link. *Tablet* 247:255 F 20 1993
Church-State conflict over property. *Tablet* 247:829 Je 26 1993
Church-State link under strain [editorial]. *Tablet* 247:127-128 Ja 30 1993
Dear Mr Gummer. Duffy, Eamon, and Lash, Nicholas. *Tablet* 247:602 My 15 1993
"The Knights cannot be admitted": Maltese nationalism, the Knights of St John, and the French occupation of 1798-1800. Castillo, Dennis. *CHist* 79:434-453 Jl 1993
New church-state concordat in force. Rich, Vera. *Tablet* 247:1019 Ag 7 1993
Partners with the poor: an emerging approach to relief and development. Aaker, Jerry. New York: Friendship Press, 1993. x, 158p ISBN 0-377-00252-6 LC 92-35591
Shaking the foundations. Gummer, John Selwyn, 1939-. *Tablet* 247:498 Ap 24 1993
Stuck with a Satanist? religious autonomy in a regulated society [exc fr *The culture of disbelief*]. Carter, Stephen L. *Comm* 120:15-18 Ag 13 1993
The thaw. Mullen, Peter. *Register* 69:1+ Je 11 1993
Towards a Jewish-Christian alliance [interview by R Lakind]. Haberman, Joshua A. *Crisis* 11:32-38 F 1993
Universelles Vülkerrecht. García-Mateno, Rogelio. *Stimm Zeit* 210:831-840 D 1992
CHURCH AND STATE- BULGARIA
Schism in the Bulgarian Orthodox Church. Broun, Janice. *Month* 26:290-294 Jl 1993
CHURCH AND STATE- CHINA
Catholics in today's China. Cioppa, John. *Origins* 22:704-709 Mr 25 1993
CHURCH AND STATE- CUBA
A call for true dialogue. *Origins* 23:273-279 S 30 1993
CHURCH AND STATE- EUROPE
Church, state and theology in the European Community. Nolan, Michael. *Studies* 82:148-159 Sum 1993
CHURCH AND STATE- GERMANY
Katholishe Kirche in der DDR zwischen Staat und Gesellschaft. Haese, Ute. *Stimm Zeit* 211:241-254 Ap 1993
CHURCH AND STATE- ITALY
Nationalists and Catholics in Giolittian Italy: an uneasy collaboration. Cunsolo, Ronald S. *CHist* 79:22-53 Ja 1993
CHURCH AND STATE- POLAND
The church and the left. Michnik, Adam. Chicago: University of Chicago Press, 1993. 299p ISBN 0-226-52424-8 LC 92-20503
CHURCH AND STATE- RUSSIA
Disillusion in Russia. Corley, Felix. *Can Cath Rev* 11:16-17 Ap 1993
Pray for it: religious freedom in Russia. Gaffney, Edward McGlynn, Jr, 1941-. *Comm* 120:5-7 My 7 1993
The shadow of the KGB. Bourdeaux, Michael, 1934-. *Tablet* 247:538-540 My 1 1993
The Union of Brest: a timely topic. Roccasalvo, Joan L. *Diakonia* 26 no 3:161-183 1993
Die Unterdrückung der Ukrainischen Unierten Kirche unter Stalin und das Moskauer Patriarchat. Suttner, Ernst Chr. *Stimm Zeit* 211:560-512 Ag 1993
CHURCH AND STATE- UNITED STATES
Is public education failing God? Unsworth, Tim. *Salt* 13:13-16 O 1993
Is the Supreme Court giving religion a little slack? Shaw, Russell. *OSV* 82:3 Jl 11 1993
Mind the constitution. Royal, Robert. *Register* 69:5 N 14 1993
Ministry and the American legal system: a guide for clergy, lay workers, and congregations. Couser, Richard B. Minneapolis: Fortress Press, 1993. 356p ISBN 0-8006-2603-6 LC 92-34214
Religion, education and the First Amendment. Coughlin, John J. *America* 168:12-15 My 15 1993
A school-board election breeds strange allies. Feuerherd, Peter. *Register* 69:1+ My 23 1993
Separation of church and state. Prosen, Anthony J. *SocJust* 84:57-60 Mr-Ap 1993
The Supreme Court v Religion [adapted fr "The Court's phobia of religion" in *The world and I*]. Hittinger, Russell. *Crisis* 11:22-30 My 1993
We the people: the American transformation of Roman Catholicism. Kress, Robert. *New Theol Rev* 6:63-88 My 1993
CHURCH AND THE POOR see Poor and the Church
Qualms for the poor? [editorial]. Burns, Robert E, 1919-, ed. *USCath* 58:2 Ja 1993
CHURCH AND THE WORLD
Charting our second 100 years. Perry, Norman. *St Anth* 101:23 Je 1993
Faith and the human enterprise: a post-Vatican II vision. Weakland, Rembert G, Abp, 1927-. Maryknoll: Orbis Books, 1992. 168p ISBN 0-88344-835-1 LC 92-32884
I rapporti Nord-Sud dopo i cambiamenti nell'est dell'europa. Salvini, Gianpaolo. *Civilta* 144:326-339 F 20 1993
Kirche in der Fremde. Kehl, Medard. *Stimm Zeit* 211:507-520 Ag 1993
A middle-class church for a working-class people. O'Hanlon, Gerard F. *Furrow* 44:3-11 Ja 1993
New light under the old bushel: what's happening in the French Church? Englund, Steven. *Comm* 120:11-14 Ap 23 1993
On the tasks of Catholic philosophy in our time. Balthasar, Hans Urs Von, 1905-1988. *Communio* 20:147-187 Spr 1993
Reading the signs of the times: resources for social and cultural analysis. Sanks, T Howland, and Coleman, John A, eds. New York: Paulist Press, 1993. x, 232p ISBN 0-8091-33777-6 LC 92-42017
Richard Rohr: Illuminations of his life and work. Ebert, Andreas, and Brockman, Patricia C, eds. New York: The Crossroad Publishing Company, 1993. x, 200p ISBN 0-8245-1270-7 LC 93-20130
Something's wrong. O'Connor, Tom. *New Cov* 22:26-28 F 1993
CHURCH ARCHITECTURE
Designing the post-Vatican II worship space. Habiger, Robert D. *Mod Lit* 20:8-11 N 1993
"Turned-around" altars [editorial]. Schuler, Richard Joseph, 1920-. *SacM* 120:4-5 Sum 1993

What happened to the glory? Menzies, Henry Hardinge. *HPR* 93:27-32 Ap 1993

Why churches shouldn't look like living rooms. Mannion, M Francis. *OSV* 82:23 N 21 1993

CHURCH ATTENDANCE
Are mass stats off? Mullen, Peter. *Register* 69:1+ O 10 1993
"The end of American Catholicism?"—another look. Hegy, Pierre M. *America* 168:4-9 My 1 1993
I like God, but not going to church. Auer, Jim. *Liguorian* 81:30-35 F 1993
Will the churches meet th Europeans? Kerkhofs, Jan, 1924-. *Tablet* 247: 1184-1187 S 18 1993

CHURCH BUILDINGS
Bombings seen as plot to halt regeneration. O'Connell, Gerard. *Tablet* 247: 991 Jl 31 1993
Garden history at Lambeth. *Tablet* 247:615 My 15 1993
Hidden gems. *Tablet* 247:1040 Ag 14 1993
Lament for a gymnasium. Brickley, Rosemarie. *Tod Parish* 25:37-38 Mr 1993
Peter's house—the first church. Martin, Geroge. *CDgst* 57:1-3+ S 1993

CHURCH BUILDINGS—CONSERVATION AND RESTORATION
Work progresses on apse of St. Mary Major. Poletti, Ugo. *OR(Eng)* 1302:3+ Ag 11 1993

CHURCH BUILDINGS—CONSTRUCTION- ITALY
Italia: La progettazione Di Nuove Chiese. Brandolini, Luca. *Notitiae* 29:290-303 My 1993

CHURCH BUILDINGS- ITALY
Americans regain St Susanna Church. O'Grady, Desmond. *OSV* 81:3 F 28 1993
The pilgrim's guide to Rome's principal churches. Tylenda, Joseph N. Minnesota: The Liturgical Press, 1993. x, 380p ISBN 0-8146-5016-3 LC 92-42870

CHURCH COLLEGES
Lamentations. Curry, Dean C, 1952-. *Crisis* 11:9-10 Jl-Ag 1993

CHURCH CONSULTATION
The conciliar passion. Fischer, Mark F. *Tod Parish* 25:23-25 Ap-My 1993

CHURCH DEVELOPMENT, NEW
Kirchenreform. Siller, Hermann Pius. *Stimm Zeit* 211:477-488 Jl 1993
Religious life's charism: transforming life. Brennan, Margaret. *Origins* 23: 207-211 S 2 1993
Transformationen des katholischen Romans. Langenhorst, Georg. *Stimm Zeit* 211:464-476 Jl 1993
What is "new" in the new evangelization? Boyack, Kenneth. *Living Light* 30: 3-8 Aut 1993

CHURCH DEVELOPMENT, NEW—EDUCATION
Catholic secondary schools and the new evangelization. Schenck, Stephen. *Living Light* 30:24-32 Aut 1993

CHURCH FINANCE
Bosnia. Feuerherd, Peter. *Register* 69:1+ Je 6 1993
The bottom line [editorial]. *Register* 69:4 S 26 1993
A challenging, accountable financial program. Champlin, Joseph M. *Church* 9:30-31 Aut 1993
Debt crisis in Glasgow archdiocese. *Tablet* 247:180 F 6 1993
Disquiet at size of Glasgow debt. *Tablet* 247:150-151 Ja 30 1993
Pennies for heaven: Catholic underachievers. Harris, Joseph Claude. *Comm* 120:8-9 Ap 9 1993
The root of all evil. Wilson, Richard. *Priests & People* 7:194-195 My 1993
What about the finances of the church? Brotherton, Fergus. *Priests & People* 7:191-193 My 1993

CHURCH GROUP WORK
Facilitating for growth: a guide for Scripture groups and small Christian communities. Fleischer, Barbara J. Collegeville: Liturgical, 1993. 160p ISBN 0-8146-2170-8 LC 93-1341
A spiritual formation workbook: small group resources for nurturing Christian growth. Smith, James Bryan. New York: HarperSanFrancisco, 1993. 82p ISBN 0-06-066965 LC 92-36860

CHURCH HISTORIANS
John Tracy Ellis. Fogarty, Gerald P, 1939-. *Tablet* 246:1585-1586 D 12 1992
John Tracy Ellis. Unsworth, Tim. *Critic* 47:52-58 Wint 1992

CHURCH HISTORY
After Jesus: the triumph of Christianity. Pleasantville, New York: Reader's Digest, 1993. 352p ISBN 0-89577-9
The apostolic faith: Protestants and Roman Catholics. Norris, Frederick W. Minnesota: The Liturgical Press, 1992. x, 178p ISBN 0-8146-5029-5 LC 92-19536
Backgrounds of early Christianity. Ferguson, Everett. Grand Rapids: Eerdmans, 1993. 608p ISBN 0-8028-0669-4
Boy-bishops. *Tablet* 247:976 Jl 31 1993
The Catholic Church in Russia. Kondrusiewicz, Tadeusz, Abp. *Ecumen Trends* 22:13-15 O 1993
Charism in the early church since Rudolph Sohm: an ecumenical challenge. Nardoni, Enrique. *TheolStds* 53:646-662 D 1992
Choosing a church. Vanauken, Sheldon. *New Oxford Rev* 60:20-22 Ap 1993
Christian experience from the shadow side of history. Murphy, Annie. *Way* 33:127-137 Ap 1993
Le christianisme dans l'histoire. Dagens, Claude. *NRT* 114:801-815 N-D 1992
The church in the nineties: its legacy its future. Hegy, Pierre M. Collegeville, Minnesota: The Liturgical Press, 1993. x, 323p ISBN 0-8146-2098-1 LC 92-45242
Discovering the Real Presence. Shea, Mark P, and Bovenizer, David A. *Crisis* 11:45-48 O 1993
Ekklesiologische optionen Evangelischer Theologie als Mögliche Leitbilder der Okumene. Wagner, Harald. *Catholica* 47 no 2:124-141 1993
The faith we have lost. Greeley, Andrew Moran, 1928-. *America* 169:14-16+ O 2 1993
An introduction to the Christian faith: a biblical perspective. Moses, Earl C, Jr. New York: Vantage Press, 1993. 127p ISBN 0-533-10329-0 LC 92-90810
The reception and non-reception of Montreal's call to renewal [speech] to the North American Academy of Ecumenists, S 27 1992. Meyer, Lauree Hersch. *Ecumen Trends* 21:1+ D 1992

The role of religion in the development of the Znamenny-Rusin Chant. Roccasalvo, Joan L. *Diakonia* 26 no 1:41-66 1993
Sor Juana and evangelization in New Spain. Tavard, George Henry. *US Cath Hist* 11:21-27 Spr 1993
The unfinished agenda of the Church: a critical look at the history of celibacy. Malone, Mary. *Way Suppl* 77:66-75 Sum 1993

CHURCH HISTORY—0030-600
Born to life. Davies, Oliver, ed. New Rochelle, New York: New City Press, 1992. 127p ISBN 1-56548-006-6 LC 92-14860
The catholicity of the church in the New Testament and in the early patristic period. Fahey, Michael A. *Jurist* 52 no 1:44-70 1992
Clement of Alexandria. Firth, Francis. *Can Cath Rev* 11:35-36 My 1993
The emperor and the Gods. Schowalter, Daniel N. Minneapolis: Fortress, 1993. 164p ISBN 0-8006-7082-5 LC 90-40141
Epistle to Diognetus. Firth, Francis. *Can Cath Rev* 11:35-36 Ap 1993
In the tracks of St. Paul. Biddle, Perry H, Jr. *Priest* 49:19-20+ O 1993
John Paul II, Pope, (1992-12-16) Peter ranks first. John Paul II, Pope, 1920- (Karol Wojtyla) (elected 1978). *TPS* 38:165-168 My-Je 1993*
Origen: Christian genius. Firth, Francis. *Can Cath Rev* 11:35-36 O 1993
Preparing for Easter [3 parts]. Rose, John. *Can Cath Rev* 11:36-37 F; 36-37 Mr; 37-38 Ap 1993
Response to Michael Fahey. Trevijano, Ramon. *Jurist* 52 no 1:71-78 1992
The Resurrection, the Church and the Bible. Moore, John C, 1933-. *America* 168:14 Ap 10 1993
Who was Saint Hippolytus? Firth, Francis. *Can Cath Rev* 11:48-49 Ja 1993

CHURCH HISTORY—0600-1500
Christendom and Christianity in the Middle Ages. Bredero, Adriaan H. Grand Rapids: Eerdmans, 1993. 448p ISBN 0-8028-3692-5
History and tradition in eleventh-century Rome. Blumenthal, Uta-Renate. *CHist* 79:185-198 Ap 1993
In the European mainstream: Hungarian churchmen and thirteenth-century synods. Kosztolnyik, Zoltan J. *CHist* 79:413-433 Jl 1993
The laity in the Middle Ages: religious practices and experiences. Vauchez, André. Notre Dame: University of Notre Dame, 1993. x, 350p ISBN 0-268-01297-0 LC 92-53746
Medieval Christendom and the restoration of a Christian society. Tanner, Norman P. *Month* 25:467-472 D 1992

CHURCH HISTORY—1950-
What went wrong in the 'fifties. Hitchcock, James, 1938-. *Crisis* 10:15-19 N 1992

CHURCH HISTORY- LATIN AMERICA
Poder, our, alteridade e evangelho: quinhentos anos de evangelização a partir de uma perspectiva européia. Gonzalez Faus, José Ignacio. *Perspectiva* 24: 313-330 S-D 1992

CHURCH MAINTENANCE AND REPAIR
Inspired partnerships: saving churches and neighborhoods. Copp, Jay. *St Anth* 101:16-20 O 1993

CHURCH MEMBERSHIP
A Church in recession—three national surveys, 1974-1992. Weafer, John A. *Furrow* 44:219-225 Ap 1993
Kirk wrestles with financial crisis. *Tablet* 247:664-665 My 22 1993
Outsiders need not apply. Faucher, W Thomas, 1945-. *Tablet* 246:1566 D 12 1992
Reasons for disbelief. Bull, George, 1929-. *Tablet* 247:240-241 F 20 1993
Three cheers for change. Vallely, Paul. *Tablet* 247:326 Mr 13 1993
A time for listening. *Tablet* 247:159-160 F 6 1993
Why I stay in the Catholic Church. Amlaw, Mary. *Liguorian* 81:4-8 Ag 1993

CHURCH MUSIC
The attack on the church musician. Schuler, Richard Joseph, 1920-. *SacM* 119:3-5 Wint 1992
Conciliar constitution: Sacrosanctum Concilium. Schuler, Richard Joseph, 1920-. *SacM* 119:7-14 Wint 1992
Converting the musician. Winkels, Frank. *Mod Lit* 20:10-11 My 1993
A crisis facing us all. Finn, Peter C. *Past Mus* 17:21-23 Ap-My 1993
A few questions from the Devil's Advocate. Hommerding, Alan J. *Past Mus* 17:34-36 Ag-S 1993
Find versatile service music that works. Lovrien, Peggy. *Past Mus* 17:33-34 Ap-My 1993
The Gospel according to Matthew, Mark, Luke, John and Ringo. Ryan, Dick. *OSV* 81:6-7 F 28 1993
Hospitality for and by musicians: melody and text. Sosa, Juan J. *Past Mus* 17:18-21 F-Mr 1993
How will Cycle A be different and the same? Romeri, John. *Past Mus* 17:35-41 D 1992-Ja 1993
I'd like to say: spare us from unsingable church music. Melaro, Constance L, 1929-. *St Anth* 100:16-20 Mr 1993
III convegno diocesano di musica sacra (Foggia, 28 novembre 1992). Sacco, Antonio. *Notitiae* 28:759-760 N-D 1992
An interview with Professor Joseph Baber. Baber, Joseph, 1910-. *SacM* 120: 9-12 Spr 1993
Let the music grow: in its own time. Faucher, W Thomas, 1945-. *Past Mus* 17:24-25 Ap-My 1993
Letter to a seminarian. Köpe, Károly. *SacM* 120:6-8 Aut 1993
Liturgy and life: an overview. Lackner, Joseph M. *Catechist* 27:86-93 S 1993
Messiah: the Gospel according to Handel's Oratorio. Bullard, Roger A. Grand Rapids: Eerdmans, 1993. 152p ISBN 0-8028-0125-0
Music for liturgies with strangers. Werner, Mary. *Mod Lit* 20:12-14 Je-Jl 1993
Now that we've rearranged the furniture, how do things look? Strusinski, Robert. *Past Mus* 17:30-33 Ag-S 1993
One Lord, one faith, one Baptism; one song? Gibala, Richard P. *Past Mus* 17:22-25 Ag-S 1993
Prier et chanter chacun dans sa propre langue. Speeten, Joseph Van Der. *Notitiae* 28:755-759 N-D 1992
The role of religion in the development of the Znamenny-Rusin Chant. Roccasalvo, Joan L. *Diakonia* 26 no 1:41-66 1993
Selecting music for the year of Matthew. Batastini, Robert J. *Past Mus* 17: 42-45 D 1992-Ja 1993
"Singing pubs and silent churches"—revisited. Flynn, Laurence J. *Furrow* 44: 408-415 Jl-Ag 1993

A sense of the season [exc fr *Liturgy: from ashes to fire—a; Liturgy: the Christmas cycle*]. Lathrop, Gordon, and Torvend, Samuel. *Liturgy* 10:67-68 Spr 1993

Summing up the seasons of faith: the liturgical year. Gustin, Marilyn Norquist. *Liguorian* 81:30-35 D 1993

CHURCH YEAR—MEDITATIONS

Life after Easter. Smith, Pamela. New Jersey: Paulist Press, 1993. x, 88p ISBN 0-8091-3379-2 LC 92-21195

Mary's day—Saturday: meditations for Marian celebrations. Boyer, Mark G. Minnesota: The Liturgical Press, 1993. x, 116p ISBN 0-8146-2092-2 LC 92-39441

CHURCH YEAR—PRAYER BOOKS AND DEVOTIONS

Journey with the Fathers: commentaries on the Sunday gospels, Year A. Barnecot, Edith, ed. New Rochelle, New York: New City Press, 1992. 168p ISBN 1-56548-013-9 LC 92-20685

CIMATTI, SANTINA, 1861-1945

Congregation for the Causes of Saints (1993-07-06) Decree on the heroic virtues. Congregation for the Causes of Saints. *OR(Eng)* 1299:12 Jl 14 1993*

CIMATTI, VINCENZO, 1879-1965

Congregation for the Causes of Saints (1991-12-21) Decree on the heroic virtues of Vincenzo Cimatti [Latin]. Congregation for the Causes of Saints. *AAS* 84:819-822 Ag 3 1992*

CIPITRIA, JUANA JOSEFINA, 1845-1912

Congregation for the Causes of Saints (1993-07-06) Decree on the heroic virtues. Congregation for the Causes of Saints. *OR(Eng)* 1299:12 Jl 14 1993*

CIRCUS PERFORMERS

Finding a new way to get a glimpse of God. Nouwen, Henri Josef Machiel, 1932-. *New Oxford Rev* 60:6-8+ Jl-Ag 1993

Finding the trapeze artist in the priest. Nouwen, Henri Josef Machiel, 1932-. *New Oxford Rev* 60:8-14 Je 1993

CISTERCIANS

Cistercian monastic women: an introduction to Hidden Springs. Nichols, John A. *Cist Stud* 28:59-72 1993

Cistercian scrapbook. Day, Agnes. *Word Sp* 14:118-128 1992

Contemplative action: a review essay on four articles by Charles Dumont. Davis, Thomas X. *Cist Stud* 28 no 2:161-166 1993

Journées d'Études on the mirror of charity of Aelred of Rievaulx, Abbey of Scourmont, October 5-9, 1992. Dumont, Charles. *Cist Stud* 28 no 2:193-197 1993

CISTERCIANS—HISTORY

Bernardus Magister: in celebration of the nonacentary of the birth of Saint Bernard of Clairvaux: 1090-1990. Sommerfeldt, John R, ed. Massachusetts: Cistercian Publications, 1992. x, 578p ISBN 0-87907-635-6 LC 92-13334

Four abbots of the golden age of Villers. Cawley, Martinus. *Cist Stud* 27 No 4:299-327 1992

An introduction to the Exordium Magnum Cisterciense. McGuire, Brian Patrick. *Cist Stud* 27 No 4:278-297 1992

Laybrothers and laysisters in Frisia and Holland: circa 1300-circa 1600. Moor, Geertruida, de. *Cist Stud* 27 No 4:329-339 1992

CISTERCIANS—HISTORY- UNITED STATES

The Cistercians SO in the United States at the 500 mark. Pennington, M Basil, 1931-. *Word Sp* 14:23-32 1992

CISTERCIANS—RELIGIOUS LIFE

Twenty-first conference on Cistercian Studies. Kalamazoo/May 7-10, 1992. Downey, Michael. *Cist Stud* 27 No 4:353-358 1992

CITIES AND TOWNS

Let's not lose the heart of the city. Burns, Robert E, 1919-. *USCath* 58:2 Mr 1993

The virtues of Sarajevo: reflections of a city dweller. Steinfels, Margaret O'Brien, 1941-. *Comm* 120:4-5 Je 18 1993

CITIES AND TOWNS, ANCIENT

The progress of the gospel. Rohrbaugh, Richard L. *BibleT* 31:22-27 Ja 1993

CITIZENSHIP—EDUCATION

The search for integration in the social studies. Schneider, Donald. *Momentum* 24:34-39 S-O 1993

CITIZENSHIP- ISRAEL

When is a Jew not a Jew? Montgomery, John Warwick, 1931-. *New Oxford Rev* 60:25-26 Je 1993

CITY CHURCHES

Catechetics in an at-risk community. Smolich, Thomas H. *Momentum* 24:7-10 Ap-My 1993

Inspired partnerships: saving churches and neighborhoods. Copp, Jay. *St Anth* 101:16-20 O 1993

Ministry goes to work. Droel, William, and Pierce, Gregory F Augustine. *Church* 9:13-16 Aut 1993

CITY CLERGY

The good news for our neighborhood [interview by J Sammon]. Kuhn, George. *Cath Work* 60:1+ Ja-F 1993

Inner-city activism in the 1960s: an oral-history interveiw [interview by B Tucker]. Porter, John, 1930-. *US Cath Hist* 11:101-112 Wint 1993

Los Angeles religious leaders: bridging the gaps that still divide. Mahony, Roger Michael, Cardinal, 1936-, et al. *Origins* 22:781+ Ap 29 1993

CIVICS—STUDY AND TEACHING

Renewing the civic purpose of the schools. Bahmueller, Charles F, 1942-, and Branson, Margaret Stimmann, 1922-. *Momentum* 24:40-43 S-O 1993

CIVIL DISOBEDIENCE see Government, Resistance to

CIVIL LAW—INTERPRETATION AND CONSTRUCTION

La fondation des lois civiles. Goyard-Fabre, Simone. *Laval Theol Phil* 49:105-119 F 1993

CIVIL RELIGION- UNITED STATES

The "Catholic tradition" of Christianity and the "religion of the republic". Wentz, Richard E. *Horizons (CTS)* 20:67-86 Spr 1993

We the people: the American transformation of Roman Catholicism. Kress, Robert. *New Theol Rev* 6:63-88 My 1993

CIVIL RIGHTS- UNITED STATES

Civil rights in the first 100 days. Drinan, Robert Francis, 1920-. *America* 168:14-15 Mr 13 1993

Domestic partnership bills opposed. Bevilacqua, Anthony Joseph, Cardinal, 1923-. *Origins* 23:48 Je 3 1993

Employment issues. Murren, Philip J. *CLawyer* 34 no 4:331-341 1993

CIVILIZATION, CHRISTIAN

Le christianisme dans l'histoire. Dagens, Claude. *NRT* 114:801-815 N-D 1992

John Paul II, Pope, (1991-12-07) Allocutiones (Papal address to Italian Christian Workers) [Italian]. John Paul II, Pope, 1920- (Karol Wojtyla) (elected 1978). *AAS* 84:1154-1158 D 5 1992*

Medieval Christendom and the restoration of a Christian society. Tanner, Norman P. *Month* 25:467-472 D 1992

CIVILIZATION, ISLAMIC

Der fremde Spiegel. Röhrig, Johannes. *Stimm Zeit* 211:10-20 Ja 1993

CIVILIZATION, OCCIDENTAL

The sweetness of God. Posset, Franz. *ABenR* 44:143-178 Je 1993

CLARE OF ASSISI, SAINT, 1194-1253

Christmas in the company of saints. Matz, Terry. *Liguorian* 81:50-55 D 1993

I have kept faith: Clare of Assisi. Karper, Karen. *RRel* 52:275-282 Mr-Ap 1993

Probleme einer Hagiographie heute. Köhler, Oskar. *Stimm Zeit* 211:641-644 S 1993

Shining without a shadow: Clare of Assisi. Baker-Pearce, Cordelia. *Month* 26:323-327 Ag 1993

St Clare of Assisi. Baker-Pearce, Cordella. *Priests & People* 6:334-335 Ag-S 1992

The story of St Clare. Hickey, Rita Marie. *St Anth* 101:33 Ag 1993

Worth pondering. O'Connell, Patrick. *Living Prayer* 26:14-15 Jl-Ag 1993

CLARET Y CLARA, ANTONIO MARIA, SAINT, 1807-1870

Meditation XII-death. Claret, Anthony Maria. *ChrWorld* 38:135-139 Mr-Ap 1993

CLARK, MARY HIGGINS

Mary Higgins Clark: queen of suspense. Finley, Mitchel B. *St Anth* 100:28-33 S 1993

CLARKE, AUSTIN, 1896-1974

The rejection of Yeats: the case of Clarke and O'Faolain. Harmon, Maurice. *Studies* 82:243-256 Aut 1993

CLARKE, KENNETH

Major's little difficulty. Alton, David. *Tablet* 247:779-780 Je 19 1993

CLASSICAL LITERATURE—HISTORY

Heresy and criticism: the search for authenticity in early literature. Grant, Robert McQueen, 1917-. Louisville: John Knox Press, 1993. 180p ISBN 0-66421-971-3 LC 92-20017

CLASSROOM ENVIRONMENT

Self-esteem: from the inside out. Johnson, Christopher. *Momentum* 24:59-62 F-Mr 1993

CLAUDE LA COLOMBIERE, SAINT, 1642-1682

Claude La Colombiere le sens d'une canonisation. Glotin, Édouard. *NRT* 114:816-838 N-D 1992

Congregatio de Culto divino et disciplina sacramentorum. Congregation for Divine Worship and Discipline of the Sacraments. *Notitiae* 28:391-403 Je 1992

John Paul II, Pope, (1992-05-31) A faithful servant and perfect friend. John Paul II, Pope, 1920- (Karol Wojtyla) (elected 1978). *TPS* 38:14-18 Ja-F 1993*

CLAUDINE THEVENET, SAINT

How St Claudine persevered [condensed fr *Catholic Standard* Jl 15 1993]. Zimmerman, Mark. *CDgst* 58:88-91 D 1993

CLEFT PALATE

Understanding cleft palate: a mother's story. Schnatterer, Christine Ruff. *St Anth* 100:36-40 Mr 1993

CLEMENT OF ALEXANDRIA

Advance from faith into knowledge. Firth, Francis. *Can Cath Rev* 11:34-36 S 1993

Clement of Alexandria. Firth, Francis. *Can Cath Rev* 11:35-36 My 1993

Clement's moral teaching. Firth, Francis. *Can Cath Rev* 11:36-38 Jl-Ag 1993

Culture et foi: Clément d'Alexandrie. Crouzel, Henri. *StudiaM* 42:99-121 1993

Les premières Editions de Luc II: l'histoire du texte au IIe siècle. Amphoux, Christian-B. *Eph Theol Lovan* 78:38-48 Ap 1992

The works of Clement of Alexandria. Firth, Francis. *Can Cath Rev* 11:35 Je 1993

CLERGY

Amissio status clericalis. Paolis, Verlasio De. *Periodica* 81 no 2:251-282 1992

As nation discusses pedophilia, even pope admits it's a problem. Fox, Thomas C, and Berry, Jason. *Nat Cath Rep* 29:2-3 Jl 2 1993

Becoming a bereavement minister. Curley, Terence P. *Priest* 49:54-55 S 1993

Being a priest today. Whitehead, James D, et al, eds. Collegeville, Minnesota: The Liturgical Press, 1992. 206p ISBN 0-81465-032-5 LC 92-4819

Bishops and Priests: aspects of a healthy relationship. Bullock, William, Bp. *Origins* 23:226-229 S 9 1993

Collaborative ministry: communion, contention, commitment. Cooper, Norman P. New York: Paulist Press, 1993. x, 200p ISBN 0-8091-3376-8 LC 92-38074

The contribution of the widowed seminarian/priest. Wagner, Roseann. *Priest* 49:53-55 Ag 1993

Dioceses facing up to the fathers' sins. Bole, William. *OSV* 82:6-7 O 31 1993

Fire bearer: evoking a priestly humanity. Dwinell, Michael. Liguori: Triumph Books, 1993. x, 198p ISBN 0-89243-531-3 LC 92-43418

Funding our retired religious. Holton, Robert. *OSV* 81:17 Ja 10 1993

Future of pastors: woe or wonder? Heher, Michael. *Church* 9:32-35 Sum 1993

Group says HIV + priests still stigmatized. Abner, Marchel. *Nat Cath Rep* 29:4 Jl 2 1993

If ministers switched to private practice? White, Leland J. *Nat Cath Rep* 29:17-19 Ja 15 1993

If you ask them, they will come. Carey, Ann. *OSV* 82:18 O 10 1993

John Paul II, Pope, (1993-06-09) Eucharist [original in Italian]. John Paul II, Pope, 1920- (Karol Wojtyla) (elected 1978). *OR(Eng)* 1295:7 Je 16 1993*

Leaders in tomorrow's church: current situation and future challenges. Burns, Camilla, and Elsbernd, Mary. *Chicago Stud* 32:143-155 Ag 1993

Leadership in a successful parish. Sweetser, Thomas P, and Holden, Carol M. Kansas City: Sheed & Ward, 1992. x, 203p ISBN 1-55612-564-x LC 92-20718

The letter carrier. Leonard, William J. Kansas City: Sheed & Ward, 1993. x, 373p ISBN 1-55612-651-4 LC 93-18887

Light in the Lord. Hume, George Basil, Cardinal, 1923-. Minnesota: The Liturgical Press, 1991. x, 174p ISBN 0-8146-2142-2 LC 92-43998

Methodists face split over homosexuals in ministry. *Tablet* 247:594-595 My 8 1993

The ministry of consolation: the parish guide for comforting the bereaved. Curley, Terence P. New York: Alba House, 1993. 70p ISBN 0-8189-0651-0 LC 93-10315

Ministry potential discerner. Wukas, Mark. *Columbia* 73:12-14 Jl 1993

Sex and power issues expand clergy-lay rift [conference sponsored by Victims of Clergy Abuse Link up, O 16-18, 1992, Arlington Heights, Il]. Fox, Thomas C. *Nat Cath Rep* 29:17-19 N 13 1992

Sunday without a priest: what is at stake? [2 parts]. Mannion, M Francis. *Priest* 49:31-36 F 1993; 21-34 Mr 1993

The time of our lives. Casserly, Bernard. *Columbia* 73:9 S 1993

Turning the vocations tide. McMunn, Richard. *Columbia* 73:10-12 S 1993

An undivided heart: making sense of celibate chastity. Sammon, Sean D. New York: Alba House, 1993. x, 160p ISBN 0-8189-0674-x LC 93-3852

The Virgin Mary and the priesthood. Philippe, Pierre Paul, Cardinal, 1905-1984. New York: Alba House, 1993. x, 135p ISBN 0-8189-0668-5 LC 93-6682

De vita consecrata in iure utriusque codicis orientalis et occidentalis. Beyer, Jean. *Periodica* 81 no 2:283-302 1992

When father is burning out. Dickson, Charles. *OSV* 82:23 O 10 1993

When pastoral ministers are grieving. Luther, James B. *Tod Parish* 25:17-19 Ja 1993

A witness to mystery. Buechlein, Daniel M. *Priest* 49:35-37 Mr 1993

Wonderfully, fearfully made. Arpin, Robert L. New York: HarperSanFrancisco, 1992. x, 207p ISBN 0-060075-6 LC 92-53906

CLERGY—CONTINUING EDUCATION
Assembly in Bundoran: the Meath experience. Butler, Eamonn. *Furrow* 43:694-698 D 1992

CLERGY—LEGAL STATUS, LAWS
Ministry and the American legal system: a guide for clergy, lay workers, and congregations. Couser, Richard B. Minneapolis: Fortress Press, 1993. 356p ISBN 0-8006-2603-6 LC 92-34214

Pastoral policy: allegations of clergy sexual misconduct with minors. *Origins* 22:580-582 F 4 1993

CLERGY—MENTAL HEALTH
On screening seminarians. Dyrud, Jarl. *Origins* 23:79-80 Je 17 1993

CLERGY—OFFICE
The crisis in Anglo-Catholicism. Caldecott, Stratford. *Crisis* 11:15-16 Je 1993

Fire bearer: evoking a priestly humanity. Dwinell, Michael. Liguori: Triumph Books, 1993. x, 198p ISBN 0-89243-531-3 LC 92-43418

CLERGY—POLITICAL ACTIVITY
Catholics and Clinton. Jones, Arthur C, 1936-. *Tablet* 247:126 Ja 30 1993

Interference in poll denied by bishops. *Tablet* 247:926 Jl 17 1993

Politicians and the Churches diagnose a social sickness. *Tablet* 247:318-319 Mr 6 1993

Priestly options in a retrenching Church. Standún, Pádraig. *Furrow* 44:84-87 F 1993

CLERGY—PSYCHOLOGY
Scandals in the Church: reflections at Paschaltide. Quinn, John Raphael, Abp, 1929-. *America* 168:4-6 Ap 10 1993

Spiritual wholeness for clergy. Hands, Donald R, and Fehr, Wayne L. Washington: The Alban Institute, 1993. x, 159p ISBN 1-5669-107-2

Time of heroism, atmosphere of suspicion. Harrington, Timothy, Bp. *Origins* 22:609-610 F 18 1993

CLERGY—RELIGIOUS LIFE
John Paul II, Pope, (1993-07-17) Church. John Paul II, Pope, 1920- (Karol Wojtyla) (elected 1978). *OR(Eng)* 1300:11 Jl 21 1993*

Spiritual wholeness for clergy. Hands, Donald R, and Fehr, Wayne L. Washington: The Alban Institute, 1993. x, 159p ISBN 1-5669-107-2

CLERGY—RETIREMENT
Funding our retired religious. Holton, Robert. *OSV* 81:17 Ja 10 1993

How to support the older pastor. Gilbert, Jack. *Tod Parish* 25:38 Ja 1993

CLERGY—SEXUAL BEHAVIOR
Letter after charges involving local priest. Gelineau, Louis E, Bp. *Origins* 23:111-112 Jl 1 1993

CLERGY—SOCIAL ROLE
Time of heroism, atmosphere of suspicion. Harrington, Timothy, Bp. *Origins* 22:609-610 F 18 1993

CLERGY—TRAINING
Rebuilding the Church in Eastern Europe. Mullen, Peter. *Crisis* 11:26-28 F 1993

Scandals in the Church: reflections at Paschaltide. Quinn, John Raphael, Abp, 1929-. *America* 168:4-6 Ap 10 1993

What do women want? Thurston, Anne. *Furrow* 43:668-671 D 1992

CLERGY- GREAT BRITAIN
Chosen: gay Catholic priests tell their stories. Stuart, Elizabeth. New York: Chapman, 1993. / ISBN 02-256-6682-0 LC 92-34966

CLERGY- LITHUANIA
John Paul II, Pope, (1993-09-04) Saint Stanislaus. John Paul II, Pope, 1920- (Karol Wojtyla) (elected 1978). *OR(Eng)* 1306:2 S 8 1993*

CLERGY AND LAITY
Collaborative ministry: not just words. O'Sullivan, Brian. *Tablet* 247:1211-1212 S 18 1993

We are the Church. Hunt, Maire. *Furrow* 44:88-90 F 1993

CLERICALISM
Can laity do more than hunt, shoot and entertain? [comments on book by author, pt 1 of 2]. Shaw, Russell. *OSV* 82:17 N 7 1993

Clericalism and its discontents [comments on book by author, pt 2 of 2]. Shaw, Russell. *OSV* 82:16 N 14 1993

CLINICAL PASTORAL EDUCATION
Catholic secondary schools and the new evangelization. Schenck, Stephen. *Living Light* 30:24-32 Aut 1993

CLINICS
Community clinic offers access to care. Bauer, Susan. *Health Prog* 74:42-44+ O 1993

CLINTON, HILLARY RODHAM, 1947-
Letter to Mrs Clinton: reforming health care. Ricard, John H, Bp. *Origins* 22:783-785 Ap 29 1993

White House guru. McArdle, Thomas. *Register* 69:3 S 12 1993

CLINTON, WILLIAM JEFFERSON, 1946-
An aborted presidency. Novak, Michael, 1933-. *Crisis* 11:2-6 Mr 1993

Activists urge Clinton onward [photos]. Jones, Arthur C, 1936-, and Vidulich, Dorothy. *Nat Cath Rep* 30:4-5 O 22 1993

The age of restraint. Hehir, J Bryan, 1940-. *Comm* 120:8-9 S 24 1993

Bill Clinton's bad start. Neustadt, Richard, 1919-. *Tablet* 247:776+ Je 19 1993

The blood of Bosnia [editorial]. *Comm* 120:3-4 Je 4 1993

Bombs bursting in air [editorial]. *America* 169:3 Jl 31-Ag 7 1993

Can Clinton deliver? Jones, Arthur C, 1936-. *Tablet* 247:296 Mr 6 1993

Catholics and Clinton. Jones, Arthur C, 1936-. *Tablet* 247:126 Ja 30 1993

Clinton abortion moves deplored by Vatican. *Tablet* 247:148 Ja 30 1993

Clinton sounds good: but now a word from scrooge. Baumann, Paul. *Comm* 120:4-5 Ja 15 1993

Clinton speech to United Nations echoes new focus on human rights [editorial]. *Nat Cath Rep* 29:20 O 8 1993

Clinton's change of course [editorial]. *America* 168:3-4 Mr 20-27 1993

Clinton's foreign policy. Hehir, J Bryan, 1940-. *Comm* 120:7-8 N 19 1993

Clinton's new political geography: renewing the language of equality [adapted fr *The election of 1992: reports and interpretations*]. McWilliams, Wilson Carey, 1933-. *Comm* 120:14-18 Ap 23 1993

Correspondence released: abortion and the nominee surgeon general. Keeler, William H, Abp. *Origins* 23:229-230 S 9 1993

The election: hard years ahead. Martin, Ralph. *New Cov* 22:26-31 Ja 1993

Ensoulment in Arkansas. Arkes, Hadley. *Crisis* 11:12-13 Ap 1993

Epistle to the Hoyas. Arkes, Hadley. *Crisis* 11:11-12 Je 1993

Five signatures. Carroll, William E. *Can Cath Rev* 11:33-34 Mr 1993

Give Bill a break, and do something about Saddam, mother of all bullies. Farrell, Michael J. *Nat Cath Rep* 29:22 Jl 16 1993

Handing on the tradition: a Catholic mother laments. Baumer, Patricia Hughes. *New Theol Rev* 6:32-54 My 1993

Hold on, America, it's coming [editorial]. *America* 169:3 N 27 1993

Homosexuals in military service: an issue needing distinctions [editorial]. *America* 168:3-4 F 20 1993

Homosexuals in the military: three issues. Mahony, Roger Michael, Cardinal, 1936-. *Origins* 22:621+ F 25 1993

Hope in the White House. Spaeth, Robert L, 1935-. *Crisis* 11:9 F 1993

L'ingresso di Clinton alla Casa Bianca. Macchi, Angelo. *Civilta* 144:363-369 F 20 1993

Investments in children [editorial]. *America* 168:3 My 29 1993

It could be worse [editorial]. *Comm* 120:3-4 S 10 1993

It doesn't hurt to hope: Clinton is good at comebacks. McCarthy, Abigail Quigley. *Comm* 120:7-8 F 12 1993

John Paul II, Pope, (1993-01-20) Telegram to President Clinton. John Paul II, Pope, 1920- (Karol Wojtyla) (elected 1978). *TPS* 38:201 Jl-Ag 1993*

John Paul II, Pope, (1993-08-12) Arrival [Origin English]. John Paul II, Pope, 1920- (Karol Wojtyla) (elected 1978). *Origins* 23:187-188 Ag 26 1993*

Masculinity and the military. Podles, Leon J. *Crisis* 11:36-40 Jl-Ag 1993

Military hospital personnel who oppose abortion. Dimino, Joseph I, Abp. *Origins* 22:612 F 18 1993

No time for innocents abroad [editorial]. *America* 169:3 N 6 1993

Now for the hard part [editorial]. *Comm* 120:3-4 Mr 1993

Pope woos youth at spiritual Woodstock. Edwards, Robin T. *Tablet* 247:1081-1082 Ag 21 1993

Promised "change" bombed by Clinton's Iraq attack. Scharper, Stephen B. *Nat Cath Rep* 29:22 Jl 16 1993

A short-lived spring. Perko, F Michael. *Month* 26:313-314 Ag 1993

Skepticism softens: can Americans love politics again? Dionne, E J, Jr. *Comm* 120:5-7 Ja 15 1993

Stay focused [editorial]. *Comm* 120:3-4 F 26 1993

That sinking feeling [editorial]. *Comm* 120:3-4 Je 18 1993

A tough start for President Clinton [editorial]. *Tablet* 247:95 Ja 23 1993

The tragedy of Bosnia is not over [editorial]. *America* 169:3 Ag 14-21 1993

The vacuum in God's own country [editorial]. *Tablet* 247:839 Jl 3 1993

Without vision, Clinton's presidency will perish [editorial]. *Nat Cath Rep* 29:28 Je 18 1993

CLONES (BIOLOGY)
Cloning baby. Meehan, Bridget Mary. *Register* 69:1+ N 14 1993

CO-DEPENDENCE (PSYCHOLOGY)—RELIGIOUS ASPECTS
Belongings: bonds of healing and recovery. Linn, Dennis, et al. New Jersey: Paulist Press, 1993. x, 255p ISBN 0-8091-3365-2 LC 92-29855

COALITION OF CONCERNED CANADIAN CATHOLICS CONFERENCE (MAY 1-2, 1993: TORONTO, CANADA)
Canadians told church is not a walled city. Babych, Art. *Nat Cath Rep* 29:12 My 14 1993

COCAINE INDUSTRY- BOLIVIA
Bolivian farmers open market to show coca is not a drug problem. Chauvin, Lucien. *Nat Cath Rep* 29:15 Mr 26 1993

COCAINE INDUSTRY- HAITI
DEA report documents Haitian drug traffic D.C. seems to ignore. Bernstein, Dennis. *Nat Cath Rep* 30:6 N 12 1993

CODEPENDENCE- UNITED STATES
Families of alcoholics: a guide to healing and recovery. Nuechterlein, Anne Marie. Minneapolis: Augsburg, 1993. x, 140p ISBN 0-80662-615-1 LC 92-19156

COFFEY, SHELBY, III
Views exchanged over poll of priests and nuns. Mahony, Roger Michael, Cardinal, 1936-. *Origins* 23:399-400 N 11 1993

COINCAT *see* Consejo International para la Catequesis, 7th, Roma

COIRO, GREGORY
Hollywood calls Father Coiro [condensed fr *Los Angeles Daily News* F 7 1993]. Larsen, Peter. *CDgst* 57:54-56 Jl 1993

COLBERT, DARYL
Darryl Colbert kept his promise. Zimmermann, Mark. *CDgst* 57:24-29 Ja 1993

COLD WAR
The post-cold war agenda for peace. Bernardin, Joseph Louis, Cardinal, 1928-. *Origins* 23:1+ My 20 1993

COLEMAN, GERALD D
Aquinas on disordered pleasures and conditions. Daly, Anthony C. *Thomist* 56:583-612 O 1992

COLES, ROBERT, 1929-
Robert Coles: listening to stories of God in the lives of children. McKenzie, Paula A. *Living Light* 29:65-72 Aut 1992

COLLECTIVE BARGAINING
Labor's metamorphosis? The high stakes at Caterpillar. Kelly, Kevin T. *Comm* 120:7-8 Ja 15 1993

COLLECTS
Patterns for praying always. Hughes, Kathleen. *Past Mus* 17:20-22 Je-Jl 1993

COLLEGE STUDENTS
The baby boomers: here today, gone tomorrow [Commencement Address at the University of Rochester, Spr 1993]. Lasch, Christopher, 1932-. *New Oxford Rev* 60:7-8+ S 1993
Living chastely. Bucher, Kimberly R. *Crisis* 11:37-39 S 1993

COLLEGE STUDENTS—ATTITUDES
All is not lost: an early look at the class of '96. Hunt, Michael J. *Comm* 120:18-21 Ap 9 1993

COLLEGE STUDENTS—SOCIAL NETWORKS
Controversial student organizations. Sasseen, Robert F, and Frank, William F. *Crisis* 11:38-41 O 1993

COLLEGE STUDENTS- GREAT BRITAIN
Students under pressure. Forrester, David. *Tablet* 247:712 Je 5 1993

COLLEGIALITY OF BISHOPS *see* Episcopacy

COLLI, GIEORGIO
Origen y decadencia del logos. Aragay Tusell, Narcis. Barcelona: Anthropos, 1993. x, 284p ISBN 84-7658-383-4

COLLINS, RUSSELL, J
In the church but of the world: pioneer priests on the eve of Vatican II. Appleby, Raphael Scott. *US Cath Hist* 11:83-100 Wint 1993

COLLOQUIUM BIBLICUM LOVANIENSE
The synoptic gospels source criticism and the new literary criticism. Focant, C. *Eph Theol Lovan* 78:494-499 D 1992

COLLOR, FERNANDO MELLO DE, 1949-
A soap too far. O'Shaughnessy, Hugh. *Tablet* 247:397 Mr 27 1993

COLOMBIA—ECONOMIC POLICY
Pope and US juggle agendas. Wirpsa, Leslie. *Nat Cath Rep* 29:16 Jl 30 1993

COLOMBIA—HISTORY
Christopher Columbus and American Catholic identity: 1880-1900. Kauffman, Christopher J. *US Cath Hist* 11:93-110 Spr 1993

COLOMBIA—POLITICS
Colombia confronts the sword [photos]. Wirpsa, Leslie. *Nat Cath Rep* 29:8-9 Ap 9 1993
Colombia's two faces. Linden, Ian. *Tablet* 247:881-882 Jl 10 1993

COLSON, CHARLES WENDELL, 1931-
The Baptist and the Rabbi. *Tablet* 247:650-651 My 22 1993
Teaching right from wrong. Feuerherd, Peter. *Register* 69:3 Ap 25 1993

COLUMBUS, CHRISTOPHER, 1451-1506
"Am I not a human being and a brother/sister?". Magesa, Laurenti. *AFER* 34:95-114 Ap 1992
Christopher Columbus and American Catholic identity: 1880-1900. Kauffman, Christopher J. *US Cath Hist* 11:93-110 Spr 1993
Christopher Columbus, lost biblical sites, and the last crusade. West, Delno C. *CHist* 78:519-541 O 1992
L'Église d'Haiti: histoire d'une naissance. Danroc, Gilles. *NRT* 115:69-84 Ja-F 1993
Is there more to be said? Leeney, Robert. *Columbia* 73:10-13 Ag 1993
John Paul II, Pope, (1992-06-24) Sea was path of Gospel for New World. John Paul II, Pope, 1920- (Karol Wojtyla) (elected 1978). *TPS* 38:24-26 Ja-F 1993*
John Paul II, Pope, (1993-05-14) Huelva [Orig in Spanish]. John Paul II, Pope, 1920- (Karol Wojtyla) (elected 1978). *OR(Eng)* 1296:1+ Je 23 1993*
John Paul II, Pope, (1993-06-14) New World [Orig in Spanish]. John Paul II, Pope, 1920- (Karol Wojtyla) (elected 1978). *OR(Eng)* 1296:8 Je 23 1993*

COMMERCE- LATIN AMERICA
Tratado de libre comercio (TLC) [editorial]. *Christus* 57:2-3 S 1992

COMMITMENT (PSYCHOLOGY)
Integrating the ideas of dissenting economists into a theory of transforamational leadership. Wallis, Joe L. *RSocEcon* 51:14-39 Spr 1993

COMMITMENT (RELIGION)
Confirmation: a grass-roots theological reflection process. Zalewska, Georgette. *Living Light* 29:51-59 Spr 1993

COMMON GOOD
Aligning IDNs' financial interests with communities' best interests. Neale, Ann. *Health Prog* 74:14-15+ O 1993
Apostle of religious freedom [adapted fr *John Courtney Murray and the American civil conversation*]. Canavan, Francis, 1917-. *Crisis* 11:31-35 My 1993
CHA's vision of a redesigned healthcare system. Coreil, Bernice. *Health Prog* 74:12-14 My 1993
The Church in the post-socialist world. Murphy, Séamus. *Studies* 82:87-96 Spr 1993
The conscience of the voter and law-maker [Irish content]. Hannon, Patrick. *Doctr Life* 42:244-252 My-Je 1992
Evolution, Omega and evil. Harris, Errol E, 1908-. *Teilhard Rev* 28:15-22 Spr 1993

Freemen and slaves: justice and equal rights. Jeffery, Peter, 1953-. *Month* 26:57-62 F 1993
Health care for all: a Catholic perspective. Hehir, J Bryan, 1940-. *Comm* 120:7-9 My 7 1993
The health of the nation [editorial]. *Tablet* 247:3 Ja 2 1993
[The lasting contribution of Veritatis splendor]. Cahill, Lisa Sowle. *Comm* 120:15-16 O 22 1993
Maritain on "the common good": reflections on the concept. Kalumba, Kibujjo M. *Laval Theol Phil* 49:93-104 F 1993
Moral dilemmas in modern business. Maloney, Oliver. *Furrow* 44:12-20 Ja 1993
The patient as citizen. Weber, Leonard J. *Health Prog* 74:12-15 Je 1993
We the people: the American transformation of Roman Catholicism. Kress, Robert. *New Theol Rev* 6:63-88 My 1993

COMMONWEAL (PERIODICAL)
Who was Didymus? The face behind the pseudonym. *Comm* 120:20-21 Ag 13 1993

COMMUNICATION
Communicating love to others. Romain, Philip, St. *Liguorian* 81:30-35 Mr 1993
Critica del lenguaje ordinario. Madrid: Libertarias, 1993. x, 780p ISBN 84-7683-252-2
Escaping Hegel. Fritzman, J M. *IPQ* 33:57-68 Mr 1993
Family meetings do work. Light, Judi. *St Anth* 101:10-14 Ag 1993
Is anybody listening? Kollar, Judith Ann. *Tod Parish* 25:4-5 Mr 1993
John Paul II, Pope, (1992-01-24) Message for World Communications Day. John Paul II, Pope, 1920- (Karol Wojtyla) (elected 1978). *AFER* 34:130-133 Je 1992*
Ministry to the chronically ill child. Spinetta, Pat Deasy, and Collins, Denis E. *Momentum* 24:28-30+ Ap-My 1993
Using the media to spread the good news: Sister Angela Ann Zukowski. Ball, Judy. *St Anth* 100:10-16 F 1993
Your children are adults now. Fanning, Marilyn. *New Cov* 22:28-31 My 1993

COMMUNICATION—PSYCHOLOGICAL ASPECTS
Ohne Beziehung keine Kommunikation. Merkert, Rainald. *Stimm Zeit* 211:594-604 S 1993

COMMUNICATION—RELIGIOUS ASPECTS
Adolescent suicide: a minsterial response. McCarty, Robert J. *Momentum* 24:61-65 Ap-My 1993
Aetatis Novae: pastoral instruction on social communication [a summary]. Faniran, J O. *AFER* 34:364-375 D 1992
Getting it back together with God. Auer, Jim. *Liguorian* 81:40-45 Mr 1993
The gods of televangelism. Peck, Janice. Cresskill, New Jersey: Hampton Press, 1993. x, 271p ISBN 1-88130-365-9 LC 92-32476
John Paul II, Pope, (1992-01-24) Nuntii Scripto Dati (Papal message for World Day of Social Communication) [English]. John Paul II, Pope, 1920- (Karol Wojtyla) (elected 1978). *AAS* 84:990-993 O 3 1992*
John Paul II, Pope, (1993-01-24) message for 27th World Communications Day. John Paul II, Pope, 1920- (Karol Wojtyla) (elected 1978). *AFER* 35:66-68 Ap 1993*

COMMUNICATION—SOCIAL ASPECTS
Ohne Beziehung keine Kommunikation. Merkert, Rainald. *Stimm Zeit* 211:594-604 S 1993

COMMUNICATION—THEORY
The trivialization of matter: development of ritual incapacity. Seubert, Xavier John. *Worship* 67:38-53 Ja 1993

COMMUNICATION (THEOLOGY)—BIBLICAL TEACHING
Autore e lettore: il problema della comunicazione nell'ambito dell'esegesi biblica. Grilli, Massimo. *Gregorianum* 74 no 3:447-459 1993

COMMUNICATION IN MEDICINE
Communications technologies: new vistas for integrated care. Ritchey, Woody. *Health Prog* 74:59-60 Jl-Ag 1993

COMMUNION OF SAINTS
Not all saints are canonized. Flathers, Marjorie. *St Anth* 101:22-26 N 1993
A vision for the unity of human kind. Himes, Michael J, and Himes, Kenneth R. *ChrWorld* 236:203-211 S-O 1993

COMMUNISM
Beating the communists was the easy part. Sherry, Gerard E. *OSV* 82:13 O 3 1993
Maritain on "the common good": reflections on the concept. Kalumba, Kibujjo M. *Laval Theol Phil* 49:93-104 F 1993
Report from the Balkans. *Tablet* 247:180 F 6 1993

COMMUNISM AND CHRISTIANITY
Candles behind the wall: heroes of the peaceful revolution that shattered communism. Heydt, Barbara von der. Grand Rapids: Eerdmans, 1993. 224p ISBN 0-8028-3722-0
Philosophy and theology after Kolyma. Chrostowski, Waldemar. *New Theol Rev* 6:102-107 My 1993

COMMUNISM AND CHRISTIANITY—CATHOLIC CHURCH
La rinascita dell'illuminismo dopo il 1989. Mucci, Giandomenico. *Civilta* 144:535-546 Mr 20 1993

COMMUNISM AND CHRISTIANITY—CATHOLIC CHURCH- POLAND
The church and the left. Michnik, Adam. Chicago: University of Chicago Press, 1993. 299p ISBN 0-226-52424-8 LC 92-20503

COMMUNIST ETHICS
What is alive and what is dead in Marx and Marxism a la Elster. Nielsen, Kai. *Laval Theol Phil* 49:277-293 Je 1993

COMMUNITIES, CHRISTIAN *see* Christian Communities

COMMUNITY
Abandoned in a toxic culture: how we failed the new generation. Novak, Michael, 1933-. *Crisis* 10:15-19 D 1992
Bethel Lutheran Church. Scherer-Edmunds, Meinrad. *Salt* 13:6 N-D 1993
But will they ever come running? Reflections on youth ministry. Moore, Joe. *Living Light* 29:45-50 Spr 1993
Church unity rooted in Eucharist. *OR(Eng)* 1298:4+ Jl 7 1993*
Finding the trapeze artist in the priest. Nouwen, Henri Josef Machiel, 1932-. *New Oxford Rev* 60:8-14 Je 1993
How to care, share, and cooperate. Hennessy, Joan. *ReligTJ* 27:12-13 S 1993

Parishes shouldn't be parochial. Hellwig, Monika K, 1929-. *Salt* 13:13 N-D 1993

Saint Augustine and Martin Buber as perspectives on John Noonan's persons and masks of the law. Combs, Christopher. *Amer J Juris* 37:145-169 1992

Single and at home in the Catholic Church. Hudson, Amanda. *Liguorian* 81: 33-35 Jl 1993

St. John student parish. Scherer-Edmunds, Meinrad. *Salt* 13:21 N-D 1993

The trinitarian community. Bruteau, Beatrice, 1930-. *Living Prayer* 26:16-19 Jl-Ag 1993

Your church can be a driving force for justice [interview by the editors of Salt (Periodical)]. Cortes, Ernesto. *Salt* 13:14-19 N-D 1993

COMMUNITY—PHILOSOPHY

The community's absence in Lyotard, Nancy, and Lacoue-Labarthe. May, Todd. *PhilosTod* 37:275-284 Aut 1993

COMMUNITY- LATIN AMERICA

Comunidad y utopia la construccion de nuestra esperanza. Manuel Hurtado, Juan. *Christus* 58:47-49 N-D 1992

La iglesia en America Latina. Roux, Francisco J de. *Christus* 58:38-46 N-D 1992

COMMUNITY (THEOLOGY)

At the heart of the Eucharist. Tetlow, Joseph Allen. *RRel* 52:735-740 S-O 1993

Broken African pots and a mission spirituality. Aguilar, Mario I. *RRel* 52: 202-212 Mr-Ap 1993

Build community or die. Tillard, Jean Marie Roger, 1927-. *Priests & People* 7:129-199 Ap 1993

CEBs e ecumenismo: uma discussão a partir da dimensão ecumênica do oitavo intereclesial. Oliveira Ribeiro, Claudio de. *REB* 52:846-855 D 1992

"The church as communion": an Anglican response. Hill, Christopher. *OChr* 28 no 4:323-330 1992

Concrete koinonia. Tillard, Jean Marie Roger, 1927-. *Tablet* 247:1146-1147 S 4 1993

Finding heroes in small community life. Bernier, Joan M. *Tod Parish* 25:34-35 Ap-My 1993

An historian's perspective: then, now, and then? Killen, Patricia O'Connell. *Listening* 28:14-27 Wint 1993

In the midst of the highest Christian feast. McDarby, Patrick. *Sisters* 65: 206-208 My 1993

Infant baptism and adult faith. Drumm, Michael. *Furrow* 44:131-139 Mr 1993

Koinonia ecclesiology—ecumenical breakthrough? Vandervelde, George. *OChr* 29 no 2:126-142 1993

Koinonia ecclesiology: a response [reply to G. Vandervelde, pp 126-142]. Wingenbach, Gregory C. *OChr* 29 no 2:143-148 1993

Koinonia: text and context for the church. Fuchs, Lorelei F. *Ecumen Trends* 22:1-2+ F 1993

Lettera ai vescovi della chiesa cattolica su alcuni aspetti della chiesa intesa come comunione. Congregation for Doctrine of the Faith. *Notitiae* 28:464-471 Jl 1992

The local church within catholicity. Tillard, Jean Marie Roger, 1927-. *Jurist* 52 no 1:448-454 1992

Local church/regional church: systematic reflections. Antón, Angel. *Jurist* 52 no 1:553-576 1992

Le ministère de présidence du curé: réflexions canoniques et pastorales. Borras, Alphonse. *Stud Can* 27 no 1:59-76 1993

Monasticism and modern culture: I hostility and hospitality—religious community and "the world". Mannion, M Francis. *ABenR* 44:3-21 Mr 1993

An overview of the ecumenical landscape: identifying some signposts. Tesfai, Yacob. *OChr* 28 no 4:342-356 1992

Parish vs congregation: self-selection isn't the Catholic model. Fichter, Joseph H. *Church* 9:16-19 Sum 1993

Pastoral care in context. Patton, John. Louisville: Westminster, 1993. x, 288p ISBN 0-664-22034-7

Postcards from the edge: how Paul dragged Christianity into the first century. Bowe, Barbara E. *USCath* 58:6-13 Ag 1993

Reception—communion. Tillard, Jean Marie Roger, 1927-. *OChr* 28 no 4:307-322 1992

Response to Angel Antón. Pottmeyer, Hermann Joseph. *Jurist* 52 no 1:579-582 1992

Small Christian communities: what parish ministers need to know. Howard, Barbara. *Tod Parish* 25:9-12 Ap-My 1993

Towards koinonia/communion in faith, life and witness: revised discussion paper for the Fifth World Conference on Faith and Order. Tanner, Mary, et al. *Ecumen Trends* 22:1-24 Je 1993

We are more than teachers. Bowman, Peg. *ReligTJ* 27:15 F 1993

COMMUNITY AND CHURCH *see* Church and Commmunity

COMMUNITY HEALTH SERVICES

A blueprint for community benefit. Forschner, Brian, and Troccio, Julie. *Health Prog* 74:34-37 My 1993

Lessons in providing, publicizing community services. Dowling, William, et al. *Health Prog* 74:63-64 Jl-Ag 1993

Retooling for community benefit. Hattis, Paul A. *Health Prog* 74:38-41 1993

COMMUNITY HEALTH SERVICES- PENNSYLVANIA

Women and children first. Marinakos, Plato A. *Health Prog* 74:34-37+ O 1993

COMMUNITY LIFE

Talents for living in community. Svoboda, Melannie. *RRel* 52:131-139 Ja-F 1993

COMMUNITY SCHOOLS

Comunidades de base schools. Ozar, Lorraine A. *Momentum* 24:38-40 F-Mr 1993

An indigenous response to inner-city needs. Ratteray, Joan Davis. *Momentum* 24:28-30 F-Mr 1993

COMPASSION

Clothe yourselves. Martin, George. *New Cov* 22:34 My 1993

Filled with pity. Groeschel, Benedict J. *New Cov* 22:14-15 Je 1993

COMPETITION (PSYCHOLOGY)

Ourselves and others: brokerage, reconciliation and process. O'Connell, James. *Month* 26:355-360 S-O 1993

COMPLAINTS (CRIMINAL PROCEDURE)- CHICAGO

Statement supporting Cardinal Bernardin. Keeler, William H, Abp. *Origins* 23:421-422 N 25 1993

COMPLEXITY (PHILOSOPHY)

Quo Vadis? or evolution and consciousness. Cronin, Francis R. *Teilhard Rev* 27:69-82 Wint 1992

COMPOSERS (MUSIC)

Ernst Krenek's sacred music. Riedel, Johannes. *SacM* 120:15-29 Aut 1993

Licinio Refice [fr *The sacred music of Licinio Refice*]. Siegel, Richard J. *SacM* 120:7-8 Spr 1993

On hearing Dvorak's "Stabat Mater". Schall, James Vincent, 1928-. *Crisis* 11:43-45 Ja 1993

The year of John Tavener: contemporary composer and Christian mystic. Feeney, Joseph J. *America* 168:15-16 Ap 10 1993

COMPULSIVE BEHAVIOR

The first step for people in relationships with addicts. Hunter, Mic. Minneapolis: CompCare Publishers, 1989. x, 122p ISBN 0-89638-163-3 LC 89-15709

COMPUTER ASSISTED INSTRUCTION

Computerized learning in the classroom. Charles, Dorothy. *Momentum* 24:72-73 F-Mr 1993

Connecting with "the real world". Anderson, Peggy. *Momentum* 24:26-27 F-Mr 1993

COMPUTER SECURITY

Computer disasters and how to avoid them. Coburn, Janet. *Tod Cath Teach* 27:34-38 O 1993

COMPUTER SERVICE INDUSTRY

Have you hugged your vendor today? Luther, James B. *Tod Parish* 25:34-35 O 1993

COMPUTER SOFTWARE

Computer bargains and other good deals. Coburn, Janet. *Tod Cath Teach* 27:34-38 N-D 1993

Notes from a computer pusher: improving the worship aid. Bryson, Kathy. *Mod Lit* 20:13-16 Ag 1993

COMPUTER SOFTWARE—EVALUATION

Is this software any good? How to tell. Coburn, Janet. *Tod Cath Teach* 27:40-42 Ag 1993

COMPUTER VIRUSES

Computer disasters and how to avoid them. Coburn, Janet. *Tod Cath Teach* 27:34-38 O 1993

COMPUTERS

The systems blueprint. Zukowski, Angela Ann. *Momentum* 24:77-78 Ap-My 1993

COMPUTERS—RELIGIOUS ASPECTS

An "on-line" Catholic faith. Mallon, John. *Register* 69:3 My 2 1993

CONCELEBRATION

Second thoughts on concelebration. Cosgrave, William. *Furrow* 44:236-239 Ap 1993

CONCENTRATION CAMPS- SOVIET UNION

Philosophy and theology after Kolyma. Chrostowski, Waldemar. *New Theol Rev* 6:102-107 My 1993

CONDUCT OF LIFE

Africa and the return of priestcraft. Nwatu, Felix. *AFER* 35:240-251 Ag 1993

The argument for the bans: combat is no place for women and gays. Reilly, Robert. *Crisis* 11:39-41 Ap 1993

Cardinal Newman on the season of Lent. Oakes, Edward T. *America* 168:7-12 Ap 3 1993

Clement's moral teaching. Firth, Francis. *Can Cath Rev* 11:36-38 Jl-Ag 1993

Culture and the moral sense [fr *The moral sense*]. Wilson, James Q. *Crisis* 11:8+ O 1993

The Epistle of James for Jews and Christians. McDade, John. *Month* 26:115-120 Mr 1993

Homosexuals in the military: three issues. Mahony, Roger Michael, Cardinal, 1936-. *Origins* 22:621+ F 25 1993

La moral como madurez de la persona—Evocando la figura de Antonio Sanchís, OP. Espeja, Jesús. *Cien Tom* 119:391-405 My-Ag 1993

Morals for home, morals for office: the double ethical life of a civil litigator. Rizzo, Patricia L. *CLawyer* 35 no 1:79-96 1993

À propos d'une note roumaine sur le livre d'André Guindon. Couture, Denise. *Laval Theol Phil* 49:321-329 Je 1993

What do I have to do? Barnes, Michael R. *Month* 26:(I) F 1993

CONFERENCE OF EUROPEAN CHURCHES

Bâle et Séoul: générosités, limites et enjeux d'Églises. Briard, Jacques. *Lumen* 48:37-50 Mr 1993

CONFERENCE OF MAJOR SUPERIORS OF MEN RELIGIOUS

Founding charisms: past and present. Hennessy, Paul. *Origins* 23:169-173 Ag 12 1993

Men vowed and sexual conversations about celibate chastity. Sammon, Sean D, and Zielinski, Judith Ann. *RRel* 52:446-453 My-Je 1993

Would that all were prophets. Bergant, Dianne. *RRel* 52:340-349 My-Je 1993

CONFERENCIA NACIONAL DOS BISPOS DO BRASIL

Como ressoou a catequese na 30a AG da CNBB (1992). Cansi, Bernardo. *REB* 52:928-936 D 1992

CONFESSION

The "Confessions:" a sinner's diary. Cameron, Peter John. *Register* 69:1+ O 31 1993

Current errors and their refutation: confessors and spiritual directors. Sutton, Alphonsus M. *ChrWorld* 38:51-55 Ja-F 1993

How long since your last confession? [condensed fr *Catholic Bulletin* Ap 15 1993]. Forliti, John. *CDgst* 57:63-65 Ag 1993

John Paul II, Pope, (1993-03-27) Treat sinners with compassion. John Paul II, Pope, 1920- (Karol Wojtyla) (elected 1978). *TPS* 38:261-265 S-O 1993*

Das Katholische Verständis von Evangelisierung, Konfession und Ökumene. Modesto, Johannes. *Catholica* 47:52-75 1993

Liturgically speaking. Freburger, William J. *Priest* 49:30 Ap 1993

Reconciliation: a meeting place with our loving God. Jeray, Diane. *Liguorian* 81:57-59 Ag 1993

The Sacrament of Reconciliation [repr fr *Vidyajyoti journal of theological reflection*]. Mattam, Joseph. *AFER* 34:293-322 O 1992

Sanctus Pontifex: twenty years later. McSheffery, Daniel F. *HPR* 93:63-67 Mr 1993

The Summae confessorum on the integrity of confession as prolegomena for Luther and Trent. McDonnell, Kilian, 1921-. *TheolStds* 54:405-426 S 1993

Why confess venial sins? Miller, J Michael. *OSV* 81:6 Ja 10 1993

CONFIDENTIAL COMMUNICATIONS
Confidentiality, disclosure, and fiduciary responsibility. Keenan, James F. *TheolStds* 54:142-159 Mr 1993

CONFIRMATION—CATHOLIC CHURCH
The age of Confirmation: a flawed proposal. Duggan, Robert D. *America* 168: 12-14 Je 5-12 1993

Bishops. Turner, Paul. *Mod Lit* 20:6-7 Je-Jl 1993

Confirmation: a grass-roots theological reflection process. Zalewska, Georgette. *Living Light* 29:51-59 Spr 1993

Confirmation: age, sequence, timing [interview]. Gaupin, Linda. *Mod Lit* 20: 8-10 Je-Jl 1993

Confirmation: the baby in Solomon's court. Turner, Paul. New Jersey: Paulist Press, 1993. x, 188p ISBN 0-8091-3370-9 LC 92-320094

Confirmation: what is there to celebrate? Capaldi, Gerard I. *Month* 26:160-164 Ap 1993

The continuing confirmation debate [replies to J Martos, 25:19 Mr 1992; 56-60 Ap/My 1992]. Struckhoff, Charlotte, and Winters, Anne Marie. *Catechist* 26:31-33 F 1993

The continuing confirmation debate [reply to Joseph Martos, 25:19-24 Mr 1992]. Senseman, Rita Burns. *Catechist* 26:37-40 Ja 1993

Creating a hospitable parish for youth: living and celebrating confirmation. Hill, Brennan R,and Riley, David M. *Catechist* 26:34-36 Ja 1993

The gifts of the Spirit. Costello, Gwen. *ReligTJ* 26:39 Ja 1993

La place de la confirmation dans l'initiation chrétienne. Bourgeois, Henri. *NRT* 115:516-542 Jl-Ag 1993

CONFIRMATION—CATHOLIC CHURCH- POLAND
Rinnovamento del sacramento della confermazione. Pierskala, Rudolf. *Notitiae* 28:684-686 O 1992

CONFLICT MANAGEMENT
Getting a grip on stress and conflict. Kinast, Robert L. *Catechist* 27:27-29 S 1993

Negotiation: the art of community living. Misteravich, Daniel. *Past Mus* 17: 17-19 D 1992-Ja 1993

Retaining nurses through conflict resolution. Fowler, Aubrey R, Jr, et al. *Health Prog* 74:25-29 Je 1993

Taming a parish nightmare. Williams, Melvin G. *Tod Parish* 25:12+ N-D 1993

CONFRATERNITIES—HISTORY
The sanctification of their neighbor. Kazanecki, Thaddeus J. *RRel* 52:574-583 Jl-Ag 1993

CONGREGATION FOR THE SACRED HEARTS OF JESUS AND MARY (PICPUS)
Congregation for the Causes of Saints (1992-06-13) Decree on a miracle. Congregation for the Causes of Saints. *TPS* 38:19-20 Ja-F 1993*

CONGREGATION OF CALASANCTIAN SISTERS
Congregation for the Causes of Saints (1992-12-21) Decree on the heroic virtues. Congregation for the Causes of Saints. *OR(Eng)* 1272:4 Ja 6 1993*

CONGREGATION OF MARIAN CLERICS
Congregation for the Causes of Saints (1992-06-13) Decree on the heroic on the heroic virtues. Congregation for the Causes of Saints. *TPS* 38:19-20 Ja-F 1993*

CONGREGATION OF OBLATE SISTERS OF ST ALOYSIUS GONZAGA
Congregation for the Causes of Saints (1992-06-13) Decree on the heroic virtues. Congregation for the Causes of Saints. *TPS* 38:19-20 Ja-F 1993*

CONGREGATION OF SAINTS NICHOLAS AND BERNARD AT MONTE GIOVE
Congregation for the Causes of Saints (1992-07-11) Decree on the martyrdom. Congregation for the Causes of Saints. *TPS* 38:37-38 Ja-F 1993*

CONGREGATION OF SISTERS KNOWN AS THE 'MISERICORDINES' OF SAINT GERARD
Congregation for the Causes of Saints (1992-07-11) Decree on the heroic virtues. Congregation for the Causes of Saints. *TPS* 38:37-38 Ja-F 1993*

CONGREGATION OF THE 'BIGI' BROTHERS OF CHARITY
Congregation for the Causes of Saints (1992-07-11) Decree on a miracle. Congregation for the Causes of Saints. *TPS* 38:37-38 Ja-F 1993

CONGREGATION OF THE 'BIGI' SISTERS OF SAINT ELIZABETH
Congregation for the Causes of Saints (1992-07-11) Decree on a miracle. Congregation for the Causes of Saints. *TPS* 38:37-38 Ja-F 1993

CONGREGATION OF THE DOMINICAN SISTERS OF THE HOLY ROSARY OF SINSINAWA
Congregation for the Causes of Saints (1993-07-06) Decree on the heroic virtues. Congregation for the Causes of Saints. *OR(Eng)* 1299:12 Jl 14 1993*

CONGREGATION OF THE FRANCISCAN SISTER OF THE HOLY CROSS OF LEBANON
Congregation for the Causes of Saints (1992-12-21) Decree on the heroic virtue. Congregation for the Causes of Saints. *OR(Eng)* 1272:4 Ja 6 1993*

CONGREGATION OF THE PASSION OF OUR LORD JESUS CHRIST
Congregation for the Causes of Saints (1992-07-11) Decree on the heroic virtues. Congregation for the Causes of Saints. *TPS* 38:37-38 Ja-F 1993

CONGREGATION OF THE SISTERS OF JESUS AND MARY
Congregation for the Causes of Saints (1992-07-11) Decree on a miracle. Congregation for the Causes of Saints. *TPS* 38:37-38 Ja-F 1993*

CONGREGATION OF THE SISTERS OF JESUS CRUCIFIED OF THE ORDER OF ST BENEDICT
'We believe we are loved by God'. Boughton, Jill. *OSV* 82:5 My 2 1993

CONGREGATION OF THE SISTERS OF ST FELIX OF CANTALICE (FELICIANS)
Congregation for the Causes of Saints (1992-07-11) Decree on a miracle. Congregation for the Causes of Saints. *TPS* 38:37-38 Ja-F 1993*

CONGREGATION OF THE SISTERS OF THE CHILD JESUS
Congregation for the Causes of Saints (1992-12-21) Decree on the heroic virtues. Congregation for the Causes of Saints. *OR(Eng)* 1272:4 Ja 6 1993*

CONGREGATION OF THE SISTERS OF THE SOCIETY OF ST TERESA OF JESUS
Congregation for the Causes of Saints (1992-12-21) Decree on a miracle. Congregation for the Causes of Saints. *OR(Eng)* 1272:4 Ja 6 1993*

CONGREGATION OF THE TERTIARY CAPUCHIN FRIARS OF THE SORROWFUL MOTHER
Congregation for the Causes of Saints (1992-06-13) Decree on the heroic virtues. Congregation for the Causes of Saints. *TPS* 38:19-20 Ja-F 1993*

CONGREGATIONS
Congregation-based organizations: a church model for the 90's. Garland, James H. *America* 169:14-16 N 13 1993

Elements generating catholicity in the local church. *Jurist* 52 no 1:411-415 1992

From reform to renewal. Nijem, Fred. *Mod Lit* 20:6-8 My 1993

'One bishop per city': tensions around the expression of the Catholicity of the local church since Vatican II. Legrand, Hervé. *Jurist* 52 no 1:369-400 1992

Response to Hervé Legrand. Voyé, Liliane. *Jurist* 52 no 1:401-410 1992

CONGRES EUROPEEN DE CATECHESE DE MUNICH
Le congrès européen de catéchèse de Münich (mai 1993). Lobet, Benoît. *Lumen* 48:350-352 S 1993

CONNELLY, CORNELIA, (PEACOCK), 1809-1879
Cornelia Connelly: model of Christian courage. McSheffery, Daniel F. *HPR* 93:57-60 My 1993

Congregation for the Causes of Saints (1992-06-13) Decree on the heroic virtues. Congregation for the Causes of Saints. *AAS* 85:82-85 Ja 7 1993*

Racial integration: did it work in Grand Coteau? Poché, Louis A. *America* 169:16+ N 6 1993

CONNORS, MATTHEW
The gangsters of Greenville meet the brother of love [por]. Holton, Robert. *OSV* 82:6-7 N 21 1993

CONRAD OF URACH
Four abbots of the golden age of Villers. Cawley, Martinus. *Cist Stud* 27 No 4:299-327 1992

CONSCIENCE
Authentic teaching. Knowles, David. *Tablet* 247:939-940 Jl 24 1993

Can the Church reclaim our common conscience? Waters, John. *Furrow* 44: 263-272 My 1993

Conscience as consciousness of the other [condensed fr *Memory and Redemption* Gill and Macmillan, 1993]. McCaughey, Terence P. *Doctr Life* 43:166-178 Mr 1993

La coscienza. Busa, Roberto. *Civilta* 2:339-350 My 15 1993

Interpreting moral doctrine: Newman on conscience and law. Magill, Gerard. *Horizons (CTS)* 20:7-22 Spr 1993

[John Paul II, invoking his authority]. Doyle, Dennis M. *Comm* 120:12-14 O 22 1993

Religious America—threat or blessing? Lapin, Daniel. *Crisis* 11:12-13 My 1993

Respect is not a right. Licht, Robert A. *Crisis* 11:41-47 Jl-Ag 1993

What is a good conscience? Cardinal Ratzinger on moral truth. Callahan, Sidney. *Comm* 120:8-9 O 8 1993

CONSCIENCE, EXAMINATION OF
Forming and following one's conscience. Hogan, Linda. *Doctr Life* 43:402-410 S 1993

The gift of tears in the writings of St Ignatius Loyola and the Eastern Fathers. Maloney, George A, 1924-. *Diakonia* 26 no 1:5-13 1993

The Summae confessorum on the integrity of confession as prolegomena for Luther and Trent. McDonnell, Kilian, 1921-. *TheolStds* 54:405-426 S 1993

Zahn, Gordon C. Zahn, Gordon C. *America* 168:5-7 My 15 1993

CONSCIENTIOUS OBJECTORS
Herald of a renewed Church. Egan, Eileen. *Cath Work* 60:8 My 1993

Zahn, Gordon C. Zahn, Gordon C. *America* 168:5-7 My 15 1993

CONSCIOUSNESS
The fragility of consciousness: Lonergan and the postmodern concern for the other. Lawrence, Fred. *TheolStds* 54:55-94 Mr 1993

The new consciousness [acceptance speech from the John Harriott Memorial Award]. Griffiths, Bede, 1906-. *Tablet* 247:70 Ja 16 1993

Quo Vadis? or evolution and consciousness. Cronin, Francis R. *Teilhard Rev* 27:69-82 Wint 1992

Teilhard today. Stikker, Allerd. *Teilhard Rev* 28:23-27 Spr 1993

Wojtyla and the Council [excerpt from *Il pensiero di Karol Wojtyla*]. Buttiglione, Rocco. *Crisis* 11:21-25 F 1993

CONSECRATION- SPAIN
John Paul II, Pope, (1993-06-15) God [Orgin Spanish]. John Paul II, Pope, 1920- (Karol Wojtyla) (elected 1978). *OR(Eng)* 1297:5 Je 30 1993*

CONSECRATION AT MASS
Catholics should stand at the consecration. Philippart, David. *USCath* 58:20-25 Jl 1993

CONSECRATION OF BISHOPS
The Apostolic tradition. Firth, Francis. *Can Cath Rev* 11:34-36 F 1993

CONSEJO EPISCOPAL LATINOAMERICANO
Santo Domingo, Complejidad Y Riqueza. *Christus* 58:6 F 1993

CONSEJO EPISCOPAL LATINOAMERICANO, MEDELLIN, 1968
Medellín spirit lives, no thanks to Vatican. Wirpsa, Leslie. *Nat Cath Rep* 29: 11-13 O 15 1993

CONSEJO EPISCOPAL LATINOAMERICANO, 4TH, SANTO, DOMINGO, 1992
Partir de la doctrina o partir de la realidad? Mier, Sebastián. *Christus* 58:33-35 F 1993

Un accord tendu autour du 'service de la vie' La IVe Conférence des évêques latino-américains, à Saint-Dominigue. Rodriguez, Gabriel Ignacio. *Lumen* 48:105-111 Mr 1993

CONSEJO INTERNATIONAL PARA LA CATEQUESIS, 7TH, ROMA

CONSENSUS

CONSERVATION OF NATURAL RESOURCES—RELIGIOUS ASPECTS

CONSERVATISM

CONSERVATISM, RELIGIOUS

CONSOLATION

CONSTRUCTIVISM (PHILOSOPHY)

CONSULTATION ON CHURCH UNION

CONSULTATION ON THE PASTORAL CARE OF REFUGEES IN AFRICA (JANUARY 5-9, 1993: LUSAKA, ZAMBIA)

CONTEMPLATION

CONTEMPLATION—COMPARATIVE STUDIES

CONTEMPLATIVE LIFE

CONTINUING EDUCATION

CONTINUUM OF CARE

CONTRACEPTION see Birthcontrol

CONTRADICTION

CONTROL see Firearms

CONTROL (PSYCHOLOGY)

CONVENTS

CONVERSATION

Will it breathe with two lungs? Hebblethwaite, Peter, 1930-. *Nat Cath Rep* 29:10 S 3 1993

COUNCILS AND SYNODS
African Synod will meet in Rome. *Tablet* 247:252-253 F 20 1993

Il celibato sacerdotale al sinodo Dei Vescovi 1990 (Commentary) *Pastores Dabo Vobis.* Caprile, Giovanni. *Civilta* 143:488-501 D 5 1992

Conciliar and postconciliar documents on consecrated life. McDonough, Elizabeth. *RRel* 52:780-786 S-O 1993

Cooked in a Roman pot. Shorter, Aylward, 1932-. *Tablet* 247:446-447 Ap 3 1993

Des conditions nouvelles pour l'évangélisation en Afrique. Derroitte, Henri. *NRT* 115:560-576 Jl-Ag 1993

Did the early Church ordain women to be priests? Most, William G, 1914-. *Can Cath Rev* 11:21-24 F 1993

In the European mainstream: Hungarian churchmen and thirteenth-century synods. Kosztolnyik, Zoltan J. *CHist* 79:413-433 Jl 1993

Interior intelligibility: the use of Scripture in papal and conciliar documents. Miller, J Michael. *Can Cath Rev* 11:9-18 S 1993

Das Kirchliche Amt in der Darstellung des Catechismus Romanus. Lülsdorff, Raimund. *Catholica* 47:76-88 1993

"Pastores dabo vobis": perspectives orientales (Commentary: *Pastores dabo vobis).* Kozah, P Makram. *Seminarium* 32:518-529 O-D 1992

Tiny Vatican office moves mountains [Cor Unum]. Burke, Greg. *Register* 69: 1+ S 5 1993

Toward a new Council of Florence. Nicholas of Cusa, 1401-1464. Washington, DC: Schiller Institute, 1993. x, 577p ISBN 0-9621095-8-4 LC 92-85238

A vision fades for African Catholics [editorial]. *Tablet* 247:231-232 F 20 1993

Das Zweite Vatikanische Konzil. Pesch, Otto Hermann, 1931-. Frieburg: Echter, 1993. x, 444p ISBN 3-429-01533-2

COUNCILS AND SYNODS, ECUMENICAL
La première session du Concile D'Éphèse (22 Juin 431). Halleux, André de. *Eph Theol Lovan* 69:48-87 Ap 1993

COUNSELING
Counseling as a Christian challenge. Monaghan, Andrew. Westminster: Christian Classics, 1993. x, 183p ISBN 0-7171-1831-2

A handbook for coping. Gaddy, Welton C. Louisville: Westminster, 1993. x, 128p ISBN 0-664-25458-6

Helping skills for the nonprofessional counselor. Moore, Joseph. Cincinatti: St Anthony Press, 1993. x, 67p ISBN 0-86716-1744

Spiritual wholeness for clergy. Hands, Donald R, and Fehr, Wayne L. Washington: The Alban Institute, 1993. x, 159p ISBN 1-5669-107-2

COUNTER-REFORMATION
The Catholic reformation: Savonarola to Ignatius Loyola: reform in the church, 1495-1540. Olin, John C. New York: Fordham University Press, 1992. x, 218p ISBN 0-8232-1477-x LC 92-29865

COURAGE—RELIGIOUS ASPECTS
John Paul II, Pope, (1993-05-23) Presence [Orig in Italian]. John Paul II, Pope, 1920- (Karol Wojtyla) (elected 1978). *OR(Eng)* 1294:6+ Je 9 1993*

COUSINS, NORMAN
Laughter is the best medicine. Bragan, Jeris. *New Cov* 22:33-34 Ja 1993

COVENANT HOUSE (NEW YORK, NY)
A covenant kept [condensed fr *Fordham* Wint 1993]. Healey, Michael J. *CDgst* 57:89-93 Ag 1993

I remember Covenant House [condensed fr *Fordham* Wint 1993]. Sullivan, Jay. *CDgst* 57:94-97 Ag 1993

CRANMER, THOMAS, ABP
The background to Archbishop Cranmer's thought on the royal supremacy. Rafferty, Oliver. *Heythrop* 34:288-295 Jl 1993

CREATION
The ascent of love. Nicholl, Donald. *Tablet* 247:845-846 Jl 3 1993

Choirs of millions: a reflection on Thomas Merton and God's creatures. Daggy, Robert E. *Cist Stud* 28:93-107 1993

A contradiction in Saint Thomas's teaching on creation. Kondoleon, Theodore J. *Thomist* 57:51-61 Ja 1993

Creation and liturgy. McMichael, Ralph N, Jr, ed. Washington: The Pastoral Press, 1993. 320p ISBN 1-562929-001-6

Creation or evolution? a call to intellectual conversion. Becker, David R. *HPR* 93:54-61 Ap 1993

Discovering creation. Leese, Mary Sue. *Catechist* 27:72 S 1993

Examining a Manichaean approach to abortion. Shea, Mark P. *New Oxford Rev* 60:13-16+ Ap 1993

Forever faithful: the unfolding of God's promise to creation. Reiser, William, 1943-. Collegeville:Liturgical, 1993. 98p ISBN 0-8146-5849-0 LC 93-15191

Gaia and God: an ecofeminist theology of earth healing. Ruether, Rosemary Radford. San Francisco: HarperSanFrancisco, 1992. 310p ISBN 0-06067-022-3 LC 91-58911

Give me a home. Hinderlider, Sue Ann. *Sisters* 65:198-199 My 1993

God and the pattern of nature [condensed fr *The Christian Century* Jl 29-Ag 5 1992]. Albright, John R. *CDgst* 57:112-117 Ja 1993

Holy ground [condensed fr *Weavings: a Journal of the Christian Spiritual Life* S/O 1992]. Prevallet, Elaine M. *CDgst* 57:33-38 Mr 1993

The liberation of creation. Sepulveda, Juan. *LADOC* 23:23-27 My-Je 1993

Soul: God, self and the new cosmology. Tilby, Angela. New York: Doubleday, 1993. x, 310p ISBN 0-385-47125-4 LC 93-12994

Who doesn't love Francis? Glavich, Kathleen. *ReligTJ* 27:25 O 1993

CREATION—BIBLICAL TEACHING
The biblical foundations of the thought of John Paul II on human sexuality. Séguin, Michel. *Communio* 20:266-289 Sum 1993

Creation in Biblical traditions. Clifford, Richard J, ed. Washington: The Catholic Biblical Association of America, 1992. 151p ISBN 0-915170-23-x LC 92-20268

Pour une théologie à l'école de l'écologie. Peeters, Denise. *Lumen* 48:51-65 Mr 1993

CREATION—COMPARATIVE STUDIES
Freedom and creation in three traditions. Burrell, David B. Notre Dame: University of Notre Dame Press, 1993. x, 224p ISBN 0-268-00987-2 LC 92-53745

CREATIONISM
Boredom and laughter: a visit to the Natural History Museum. Dalzell, Catherine. *Can Cath Rev* 11:11-16 O 1993

CREATIONISM—CONTROVERSIES
Genesis, creation, and creationism. Bailey, Lloyd R. New Jersey: Paulist Press, 1993. x, 259p ISBN 0-8091-3255-9 LC 92-33185

CREATIVITY
Be creative in every class. Salerno, Dorsey Price. *ReligTJ* 27:30-31 O 1993

A creative craft. Howatch, Susan, 1940-. *Tablet* 247:400-401 Mr 27 1993

The creative person [presented as a paper at Conference on Wealth Creation in London, England, in July 1991]. Novak, Michael, 1933-. *Can Cath Rev* 11:14-18 Je 20 1993

How art heals. Bailey, Judi. *St Anth* 100:36-41 F 1993

J R R Tolkien: lover of the logos. Sebanc, Mark, 1941-1992. *Communio* 20: 84-106 Spr 1993

Whiteheadian creativity, the Tao, and the Thomistic act of being. Bracken, Joseph A. *Pacifica* 6:179-188 Je 1993

CREATIVITY—WOMEN
Sexuality: creation's wildcard—sexual energy and feminine creativity. Dwyer, Margretta. *Sisters* 65:276-279 Jl 1993

CREDIBILITY
"Humanae vitae": what has it done to us? And what is to be done now? Untener, Kenneth E, Bp. *Comm* 120:12-14 Je 18 1993

CREDIT—LAW AND LEGISLATION- GREAT BRITAIN
The unacceptable face of credit. Dwyer, Christopher. *Month* 26:40-42 Ja 1993

CREEDS
The apostles' creed: a faith to live by. Cranfield, C E B. Grand Rapids: Eerdmans, 1993. 72p ISBN 0-8028-0709-7

Why we need the creeds. Stravinskas, Peter. *Register* 69:1+ My 16 1993

CRIME AND CRIMINALS
The fall of the prison: biblical perspectives on prison abolition. Griffith, Lee. Grand Rapids: Eerdmans, 1993. 280p ISBN 0-8028-0670-8

People are getting hurt: the rise in gay-bashing. Anderson, George M. *Comm* 120:16+ F 26 1993

Robbing Peter, and Paul, too [Church Vandalism]. Holton, Robert. *OSV* 82:6 O 17 1993

Satanic panic: the creation of a contemporary legend. Victor, Jeffrey S. Chicago: Open Court, 1993. x, 408p ISBN 08-1269-191-1 LC 93-995

When victims and offenders meet face-to-face. Sly, Julie. *OSV* 81:6 F 14 1993

CRIME AND CRIMINALS- HISTORY
Facing the mafia. Burke, Greg. *Register* 69:1+ My 30 1993

CRIME AND CRIMINALS- ITALY
Anti-Mafia priest's death raises questions. Giannantonio, Alfred. *Nat Cath Rep* 29:7 O 8 1993

A dark alliance of forces. Burke, Greg. *Register* 69:5 Ag 15 1993

Scandal in Rome has buffeted the church. Hebblethwaite, Peter, 1930-. *Nat Cath Rep* 29:16 Mr 26 1993

CRIME PREVENTION
What are prisons for? Tuck, Mary. *Tablet* 247:1157-1158 S 11 1993

CRIMES AGAINST HUMANITY
John Paul II, Pope, (1992-12-25) Come to heal [orig italian]. John Paul II, Pope, 1920- (Karol Wojtyla) (elected 1978). *OR(Eng)* 1271:1 Ja 6 1993*

New world, new disorder [fr *Out of control: global turmoil on the eve of the twenty-first century*]. Brzezinski, Zbigniew K, 1928-. *Crisis* 11:39-42 My 1993

CRIMINAL JUSTICE
CNN does it again. Stahel, Thomas H, 1938-. *America* 168:16-17 My 1 1993

Depenalizzazione. Passano, Paolo Ferrari Da. *Civilta* 2:161-164 Ap 17 1993

Malcolm X: what his three lives can teach us [editorial]. Morrow, Carol Ann. *St Anth* 100:17 F 1993

Slovak bishop given three-year sentence. *Tablet* 247:486 Ap 10-17 1993

CRISIS
What's happening to the old magic? finding meaning in family crisis. Gillespie, Joseph P. *Liturgy* 10:35-41 Wint 1992

CRISIS (PSYCHOLOGY)
Boundary-dwellers. Ward, Hannah. *Way* 33:97-105 Ap 1993

Children in crisis in the classroom. Exline, Joseph. *Momentum* 24:12-16 Ap-My 1993

Crisis counseling. Stone, Howard W. Minneapolis: Fortress, 1993. x, 96p ISBN 0-8006-2760-1 LC 92-39489

Crisis counseling: what to do during the first 72 hours. Wright, H Norman. Ventura: Regal Books, 1993. 335p ISBN 0-8307-1611-4 LC 93-10514

CRISIS MANAGEMENT
When you're in trouble. Parachin, Victor M. *CDgst* 57:55-57 Ja 1993

CRITICISM
Historical themes, missionary endeavour and spiritual colonialism in Brian Moore's Black robe. O'Donoghue, Jo. *Studies* 82:131-139 Sum 1993

Scobie's world. Freis, Richard. *Relig Lit* 24:57-78 Aut 1992

"The way we live now": Graham Greene on reading. Kelly, Patrick Hyde. *Can Cath Rev* 11:20-22 Ap 1993

The whatness of Loulou: allegories of Thomism in Flaubert. Wise, Christopher. *Relig Lit* 25:35-49 Spr 1993

Willa Cather and the literature of Christian mystery. Murphy, John J. *Relig Lit* 24:39-56 Aut 1992

Woodstock Catechism Project revisited. Reese, Thomas Joseph, 1945-. *Living Light* 29:71-73 Sum 1993

CRITICISM, REDACTION
Les critères de rédaction du Catéchisme de l'Église catholique. Schönborn, Christoph von, Bp. *NRT* 115:161-168 Mr-Ap 1993

Redaccón y tradicióaon en Ef 2, 11-22. Villegas, Beltrán M. *Teol Vida* 33 no 3-4:179-184 1992

CRITICISM (PHILOSOPHY)
L'idéalisme Allemand face à la raison théologique. Maesschalck, Marc. *Laval Theol Phil* 49:309-320 Je 1993

Wittgenstein's doctrine of silence. McDonough, Richard. *Thomist* 56:695-699 O 1992

CRITICS—LANGUAGE
Holidays. McMahon, John. *Can Cath Rev* 11:38-39 F 1993

CROATIA
Cardinal eyes Croatia struggle [interview by Jonathan Luxmoore]. Kuharic, Franjo, Cardinal, 1919-. *Register* 69:1+ F 21 1993
Croatians welcome offensive. Luxmoore, Jonathan. *Register* 69:1+ F 14 1993
Dialogue [interview by Gabriel Meyer]. Ellis, Bernard. *Register* 69:1+ F 14 1993
Muzzling the dogs of war may be a mistake [photos]. McCarthy, Tim. *Nat Cath Rep* 29:10-11 O 1 1993
Priests: "we are dying: do you understand?" [remarks of Fathers Franjo Rudman and Boze Vuleta]. *Nat Cath Rep* 29:13 Ja 29 1993

CROATIA—POLITICS
Agony of the end-game in Bosnia [eidtorial]. *Tablet* 247:907 Jl 17 1993
Battle for Bosnia. Hastings, Adrian, 1929-. *Tablet* 247:1256-1257 O 2 1993
Croat Catholics divided. Magas, Branka. *Tablet* 247:908-910 Jl 17 1993
Croatia: where guns and roses don't mix [photos]. McCarthy, Tim. *Nat Cath Rep* 29:10-12 O 8 1993
From victim to aggressor. Cviic, Christopher. *Tablet* 247:678-679 My 29 1993
The sins of Croatia [editorial]. *Tablet* 247:603 My 15 1993

CROATIA—SOCIO-ECONOMIC CONDITIONS
Notes from Zagreb. Caldecott, Stratford. *Can Cath Rev* 11:(I)+ Jl-Ag 1993

CRONIN, DANIEL A, ABP, 1927-
Catholic Transcript editors resign in protest. Renner, Gerald. *Nat Cath Rep* 29:6 Mr 26 1993

CROSS
Tree of life and endless mystery: the standard of the cross. Benedict, Therese Francis. *Spir Life* 39:31-33 Spr 1993

CROSS-CULTURAL COUNSELING
Pastoral counseling in a global church: voices from the field. Wicks, Robert J, and Estadt, Barry K, eds. Maryknoll, New York: Orbis Books, 1993. x, 169p ISBN 0-88344-865-3 LC 93-22082

CROWLEY, ALEISTER
Scientology's religious roots. Meldgaard, Helle. *StudiaM* 41:169-185 1992

CRUCIFIXES
The gate of glory. Carey, George Leonard, Abp of Canterbury, 1935-. Grand Rapids: Eerdmans, 1993. 256p ISBN 0-8028-3724-7
A sacred landscape. Wroe, Ann. *Tablet* 247:192-193 F 13 1993
Tree of life and endless mystery: the standard of the cross. Benedict, Therese Francis. *Spir Life* 39:31-33 Spr 1993

CRUCIFIXION
Easter: Christ crucified and raised. Herlong, Theophilus. *Emmanuel* 99:134-137 Ap 1993
What was God doing on the cross? McGrath, Alister E. Grand Rapids: Zondervan Publishing House, 1993. x, 112p ISBN 0-310-59451-0

CRUSADES
Christopher Columbus, lost biblical sites, and the last crusade. West, Delno C. *CHist* 78:519-541 O 1992

CRUZ VARELA, MARIA ELENA
Castro's exhausted angel. Fleming, Thomas, 1927-. *America* 168:14-16 F 6 1993

CUBA—SOCIO-ECONOMIC CONDITIONS
Amid shortage of food, Cuba forages for future. Wirpsa, Leslie. *Nat Cath Rep* 29:11-12 Je 4 1993
Cuba in transition: waking or awakening the socialist economy? Fleming, Thomas, 1927-. *America* 169:12-16 O 30 1993
Cuba—"we manage" despite the blockade. Escandell, Noemi. *Cath Work* 60:8 Mr-Ap 1993
Cuba: "a strange new hybrid" feeling for its roots. Wirpsa, Leslie. *Nat Cath Rep* 29:9-10+ Je 4 1993

CUCKOOS
The messenger. O'Boyle, Patrick J. *Liguorian* 81:24-25 Ag 1993

CUENOT, CLAUDE, 1911-1992
Cuenot, Claude, 1911-1992 [obit]. Cowell, John. *Teilhard Rev* 27:84 Wint 1992

CULTS
Agents of apocalypse [editorial]. *Comm* 120:3-4 My 7 1993
The corruption of faith. Barnes, Michael R. *Month* 26:(I) My 1993
Cults and cultism. Hughes, Louis. *Furrow* 44:352-358 Je 1993
A dangerous pattern. Holton, Robert. *OSV* 81:3 Mr 21 1993
Enforcing the law: consider the Bill of Rights. Gaffney, Edward McGlynn, Jr, 1941-. *Comm* 120:5-6 My 21 1993
Madness, massacre and the millennium. Egan, Anthony. *Month* 26:214-218 Je 1993
One lesson of Waco: it's not just the "wackos". Dodds, Bill. *OSV* 82:17 Je 13 1993
Religious sects and movements. *StudiaM* 41:1-389 1992*
Today's destructive cults and movements. Gesy, Lawrence J. Huntington: Our Sunday Visitor, 1993. 315p ISBN 0-87973-498-1 LC 92-83995

CULTURAL PLURALISM *see* Pluralism, Cultural

CULTURAL RELATIONS
We are a patchwork quilt. Neuberger, Anne E. *ReligTJ* 27:36-37 O 1993

CULTURE
George Steiner and the theology of culture. Ward, Graham. *New Blckfrs* 74:98-105 F 1993
Multi-multiculturalism. Marty, Martin E, 1928-. *Critic* 47:37-45 Sum 1993
Nature, culture, and the Church. Carroll, William E. *Can Cath Rev* 11:44-47 Ja 1993
Pascal, order, and difference. McKenna, Andrew. *Relig Lit* 25:55-75 Sum 1993
The prophetic humanism of John Paul II. Dulles, Avery Robert, 1918-. *America* 169:6-11 O 23 1993

CULTURE—COMMENTARIES
A church historian's odyssey. Davies, Horton. Grand Rapids: Eerdmans, 1993. 218p ISBN 0-8028-0712-7

CULTURE AND CHRISTIANITY
Anvers et son Église diocésaine. Berghe, Paul Van Den. *Lumen* 48:127-134 Je 1993

The beauty of Balthasar. Nemoianu, Virgil, 1940-. *Crisis* 11:42-46 Ap 1993
Bread and wine for the Eucharist: are they negotiable? Silva, Jose' Antunes da. *AFER* 34:258-271 O 1992
Catecismo e inculturacion. Bravo, Gallardo Carlos. *Christus* 58:39-41 Je 1993
The challenge of inculturation. Lane, Dermot A. *Living Light* 29:3-21 Wint 1992
Christology in dialogue. Berkey, Robert F, and Edwards, Sarah A, eds. Cleveland: The Pilgrim Press, 1993. 390p ISBN 0-8298-0956-2 LC 92-47004
Cooked in a Roman pot. Shorter, Aylward, 1932-. *Tablet* 247:446-447 Ap 3 1993
Cultura y evangelizacion. *Christus* 58:7-11 My 1993
La cultura y sus dinamismos. Sweeney, John. *Christus* 58:12-14 My 1993
Culture et foi: Clément d'Alexandrie. Crouzel, Henri. *StudiaM* 42:99-121 1993
Culture païenne et foi chrétienne aux racines de l'Europe: La Cité de Dieu d'Augustin. Canévet, Mariette. *Gregorianum* 74 No 1:5-16 1993
The feast of hospitality. Williams, Joan. *ReligTJ* 27:25 Ap-My 1993
Gesuiti e Bielorussi: ai margini della civiltà o a una svolta culturale? Simon, Constantin. *Civilta* 2:548-562 Je 19 1993
Inculturation through small Christian communities. Payeur, Joseph A. *AFER* 35:37-43 F 1993
En la lucha-In the struggle: a Hispanic women's liberation theology. Isasi-Díaz, Ada María. Minneapolis: Fortress, 1993. x, 226p ISBN 0-8006-2610-9 LC 93-9220
La Madonna a Mosca e a Roma: teologia, arte, devozione popolare. Pfeiffer, Heinrich. *Civilta* 144:370-373 F 20 1993
Nueva evangelizacion promocion humana cultura Cristiana. Taborda, Francisco. *Christus* 58:40-47 Mr-Ap 1993

CULTURE AND CHRISTIANITY—CONGRESSES
Papers originally presented at a symposium: the Church: salvation and mission. LaVerdiere, Eugene Armand, 1936-, ed. Collegeville, Minnesota: The Liturgical Press, 1993. 104p ISBN 0-8146-2141-4 LC 93-9678

CULTURE AND CHRISTIANITY- AFRICA
An African American Catholic rite. Hayes, Diana L. *Living Light* 29:35-48 Wint 1992
The pastoral priorities of the local church in Eastern Africa. Mejia, Rodrigo. *AFER* 34:324-339 D 1992
Toward an African Christianity: inculturation applied. Hillman, Eugene. New York: Paulist Press, 1993. x, 101p ISBN 0-8091-3381-4 LC 92-39526

CULTURE AND CHRISTIANITY- BRAZIL
Cristianismo e culturas indígenas. Taborda, Francisco. *REB* 53:259-282 Je 1993

CULTURE AND CHRISTIANITY- ITALY
La rinascita dell'illuminismo dopo il 1989. Mucci, Giandomenico. *Civilta* 144:535-546 Mr 20 1993

CULTURE AND CHRISTIANITY- LATIN AMERICA
Igreja e modernidade: o caminho das CEBs. Ribeiro de Oliveira, Pedro A. *REB* 52:814-820 D 1992
Procesos culturales y nuevas idenidades. Irarrázaval, Diego. *Christus* 58:15-19 My 1993
Reflections on Santo Domingo. Linden, Ian. *Month* 26:17-21 Ja 1993

CULTURE AND CHRISTIANITY- RWANDA
Changements culturels et lieux d'expériences de la foi au Rwanda. Nkulikiyumukiza, Augustin. *Lumen* 48:195-206 Je 1993

CULTURE AND EDUCATION
Contribución de la universidades católicas a la nueva evangelición. Montealegre, Alberto. *Seminarium* 32:452-462 Jl-S 1992
Cutting through multiculturalism. Hemrick, Eugene F. *Priest* 49:11-16 O 1993
Seminary and religious formation in an African milieu. Kimaryo, Rogath. *AFER* 35:202-208 Ag 1993
Texas university aids migrants [photos]. Vidulich, Dorothy. *Nat Cath Rep* 30:16-17 O 29 1993
Who's afraid of multiculturalism? Hayes, Diana L. *Salt* 13:17 Ap 1993

CULTURE AND RELIGION
Beat his ribs while he is young (Sir 30:12). Pilch, John Joseph, 1936-. *Bib Th Bul* 23:101-113 Aut 1993
Canon and culture: realistic possibilities for the biblical canon. Bossman, David M. *Bib Th Bul* 23:4-13 Spr 1993
Changing structures. Gray, Howard. *Way Suppl* 76:72-84 Spr 1993
Culture and contemplative community. Beha, Marie, 1926-. *RRel* 52:584-595 Jl-Ag 1993
Culture and current practice. Varley, Virginia. *Way Suppl* 76:32-43 Spr 1993
Faith and culture [editorial]. Schuler, Richard Joseph, 1920-. *SacM* 120:3-4 Sum 1993
Global responsibility: in search of a new world ethic. Kung, Hans, 1928-. New York: Crossroad, 1991. x, 158p ISBN 0-8245-1102-6 LC 91-7956
Missionaries and cultures. Berg, Carol. *US Cath Hist* 11:29-36 Spr 1993
Monasticism and modern culture: I hostility and hospitality—religious community and "the world". Mannion, M Francis. *ABenR* 44:3-21 Mr 1993
Monasticism and modern culture: III. the labor of tradition—monasticism as a cultural system. Mannion, M Francis. *ABenR* 44:290-307 S 1993
The new writers: wisdom's response to a changing society. Cox, Dermot. *StudiaM* 42:1-15 1993
O desafio das religiões [editorial]. Libanio, Joao Batista, ed. *Perspevtiva* 25:133-136 My-Ag 1993
La raza cósmica: rediscovering the Hispanic soul. Deck, Allan Figueroa. *Critic* 47:46-53 Spr 1993
Religione, laicismo e postmodernità. Mucci, Giandomenico. *Civilta* 144:131-139 Ja 16 1993
Retorna lo religioso: XX conversaciones de San Esteban. Lago Alba, Luis. *Cien Tom* 119:599-602 S-D 1992
The spirit of the age. Bull, George, 1929-. *Tablet* 247:966 Jl 31 1993
La teologia del XX secolo. Vanzan, Piersandro. *Civilta* 2:566-568 Je 19 1993
Teologia Maya conceptos fundamentales. *Christus* 58:22-27 S 1993
What if our only witness happens to be blind? [editorial]. White, Leland J, ed. *Bib Th Bul* 23:90 Aut 1993
World community and religion. Neville, Robert Cummings, 1939-. *JEcumen Stds* 29:368-382 Sum-Aut 1992

CULTURE AND RELIGION- AFRICA
Shall we dance? religion, culture and movement. Kane, Thomas A. *ChrWorld* 236:265-269 N-D 1993
Theological trends in Africa. Chepkwony, Adam K A. *AFER* 34:2-17 F 1992

CULTURE AND RELIGION- ASIA
Interreligious dialogue and theology of religions: an Asian paradigm. Pieris, Aloysius, 1934-. *Horizons (CTS)* 20:106-114 Spr 1993
Quand le passé ne fascine plus Jeunes aborigènes chrétiens en quête d'identité. Lardinois, Olivier. *Lumen* 48:331-338 S 1993

CULTURE AND RELIGION- BRAZIL
A ambivalência da pastoral popular libertadora face à razão moderna. Gaiger, Luiz Inácio. *Perspectiva* 25:163-180 My-Ag 1993
A condição pós-moderna como desafio à pastoral popular. Carneiro de Andrade, Paulo Fernando. *REB* 53:99-113 Mr 1993

CULTURE AND RELIGION- EUROPE
Weltweite Migrationen als politische Herausforderung Europas. Müller, Johannes. *Stimm Zeit* 210:797-805 D 1992

CULTURE AND RELIGION- FRANCE
Esquisse d'un projet culturel une société performante pour tous. Papeleux, Michel. *Lumen* 47:427-438 D 1992

CULTURE AND RELIGION- GERMANY
Herman Schell and the reform of the Catholic Church in Germany. Griener, George E. *TheolStds* 54:427-454 S 1993

CULTURE AND RELIGION- GREAT BRITAIN
The canon law culture of medieval England. Ferme, Brian. *Periodica* 82 no 1:28-54 1993

CULTURE AND RELIGION- GUATEMALA
500 años sembrando el evangelio. *Christus* 57:49-62 O 1992

CULTURE AND RELIGION- IRELAND
Religion and culture in Irish society. Macken, John. *Studies* 82:123-130 Sum 1993

CULTURE AND RELIGION- ITALY
Nel paese del punto esclamativo: *sette, culti, pseudo-religioni o nuove religioni? Introvigne, Massimo. *StudiaM* 41:1-26 1992

CULTURE AND RELIGION- LATIN AMERICA
Catequesis, cultura religiosidad popular y liberacion. Merlos, Francisco. *Christus* 58:27-31 Ag 1993
Cultura occidental y culturas indígenas. Suazo, Fernando. *Cien Tom* 120:101-115 Ja-Ap 1993
Del imaginario alternativo al imaginario vigente y al revolucionario. Trigo, Pedro. *Christus* 57:23-41 O 1992
La iglesia local en la inculturación del evangelio. Salado Martinez, Domingo. *Cien Tom* 120:129-152 Ja-Ap 1993
Inculturación de la vida religiosa. Garcí Matubuena, Antonio. *Cien Tom* 120:117-128 Ja-Ap 1993
Liberación, inculturación y alteridad. Espeja, Jesús. *Cien Tom* 120:153-167 Ja-Ap 1993
Los vientos que soplaron en Santo Domingo. Sobrino, John. *Christus* 58:29-39 Mr-Ap 1993
Nueva evangelizacion promocion humana cultura cristiana. França Miranda, Mario de. *Christus* 57:18-22 O 1992
La réalité sociale comme point de départ dans la formation pastorale permanente: une perspective latino-américaine. Mejia, Jorge Julio. *Lumen* 48:181-194 Je 1993
Sobre el documento de Santo Domingo. Espeja, Jesús. *Cien Tom* 120:177-185 Ja-Ap 1993

CULTURE AND RELIGION- MIDDLE EAST
Historical atlas of the Middle East. Freeman-Grenville, G S P. New York: Simon & Schuster, 1993. x, 144p ISBN 0-13-3-390915-8

CULTURE AND RELIGION- SOUTH KOREA
Être catholique en Corée du Sud: la mulitple appartenance religieuse. Senécal, Bernard. *Lumen* 48:207-216 Je 1993

CULTURE AND RELIGION- UNITED STATES
The "Catholic tradition" of Christianity and the "religion of the republic". Wentz, Richard E. *Horizons (CTS)* 20:67-86 Spr 1993
Chesterton and Catholic moments: some reflections on Catholic revivals, past and present. Sparr, Arnold. *ACHSR* 103:11-22 Aut 1992
Does the church mishandle its cultural treasures? Windsor, Patricia. *USCath* 58:14-20 F 1993
Hispanic Catholics: does the Church speak your language? [interview by the editors of USCath]. Deck, Allan Figueroa. *USCath* 58:27-30 D 1993
John Paul II on evangelization of culture in the United States. O'Donnell, Robert J. *Living Light* 30:9-22 Aut 1993
Multiculturalism in religious life today. Harmer, Catherine M. *RRel* 52:764-772 S-O 1993
The Supreme Court v Religion [adapted fr "The Court's phobia of religion" in *The world and I*]. Hittinger, Russell. *Crisis* 11:22-30 My 1993

CURIA ROMANA
Curia faction goes for total control over CELAM IV. MacEoin, Gary. *Nat Cath Rep* 29:14-15 N 6 1992
Latin American bishops. Palumbo, Gene. *St Anth* 100:10-16 Ap 1993
Local church and catholicity in the constitution Pastor Bonus. Provost, James H. *Jurist* 52 no 1:299-334 1992
Response to James Provost. Citrini, Tullio. *Jurist* 52 no 1:335-339 1992

CURRAN, CHARLES EDWARD, 1934-
A house divided: what future for American Catholics? D'Souza, Dinesh, 1961-. *Crisis* 10:19-22 D 1992

CURRY, TERRENCE, MSGR
Stealing for lent. Costello, Andrew. *USCath* 58:38-40 Mr 1993

CYPRIAN, SAINT, BP OF CARTHAGE, ?-258
Born to life. Davies, Oliver, ed. New Rochelle, New York: New City Press, 1992. 127p ISBN 1-56548-006-6 LC 92-14860
L'effusion de l'Esprit Saint chez les Pères latins. Bentivegua, Giuseppe. *NRT* 115:19-39 Ja-F 1993

CYRIL, SAINT, BP OF JERUSALEM, 315-386
Cyril of Jerusalem as a postliberal theologian. Cummings, Owen F. *Worship* 67:155-164 Mr 1993

CYRIL, SAINT, PATRIARCH OF ALEXANDRIA, 370?-444
La première session du Concile D'Éphèse (22 Juin 431). Halleux, André de. *Eph Theol Lovan* 69:48-87 Ap 1993

CZECHOSLOVAKIA—FOREIGN RELATIONS
Waters of discord. Bowlby, Chris. *Tablet* 246:1561-1562 D 12 1992

CZECHOSLOVAKIA—POLITICS AND GOVERNMENT
No rest for the travellers. Bowlby, Chris. *Tablet* 247:606+ My 15 1993

CZECHOSLOVAKIA—RELIGION
Growing up or selling out? Czechs face the future. McCarthy, Tim. *Comm* 120:13-16 S 24 1993

CZECHOSLOVAKIA—SOCIAL CONDITIONS
Growing up or selling out? Czechs face the future. McCarthy, Tim. *Comm* 120:13-16 S 24 1993

CZECHOSLOVAKIA—SOCIAL POLICY
For Czechs, there are tiny signs of progress. O'Grady, Desmond. *OSV* 81:3 F 7 1993

D

D'ARCY, JOHN MICHAEL, BP, 1932-
Controversy continues over church renovations. Carey, Ann. *OSV* 82:17 Ag 8 1993

D'ARIENZO, LOU
Always the poor. Dodds, Bill. *New Cov* 22:21-24 Je 1993

DACHAU (CONCENTRATION CAMP)
Innocent at Dachau. Halow, Joseph. Newport Beach, California: Institute for Historical Review, 1993. x, 237p ISBN 0-939482-40-11
A secret hero in Dachau. Finley, Mitchel B. *OSV* 82:9 Ag 15 1993

DAILY, THOMAS VOSE, BP, 1927-
Letter on gays draws protest. Lefevere, Patricia. *Nat Cath Rep* 29:5 S 10 1993
Witnessing the truth [Brooklyn, NY]. Feuerherd, Peter. *Register* 69:3 F 7 1993

DAIRY FARMING
Unnatural growth hormone. Atwater, Tim. *Cath Work* 60:7 Mr-Ap 1993

DAL PRA, M
Coup d'oeil sur la philosophie italienne contemporaine. Rizzerio, Laura. *RPhil Louvain* 90:539-556 N 1992

DALAI LAMA XIV
Learning compassion. Barnes, Michael R. *Month* 26:(I) Ag 1993
A living Buddha. Freeman, Laurence. *Tablet* 247:681-682 My 29 1993
Wisdom with a smile. *Tablet* 247:614-615 My 15 1993

DALY, CAHAL BRENDAN, CARDINAL, 1917-
Irish churches and the Irish media: out of order or out of touch? Collins, Jude. *Studies* 82:185-197 Sum 1993

DAMAS, ARTURO RIVERA, ABP
Salvador archbishop attacks amnesty deal. Palumbo, Gene. *Nat Cath Rep* 29:8 Ap 2 1993

DANCE, RELIGIOUS
Dancing before the Lord. Manternach, Janann, and Pfeifer, Carl J. *ReligTJ* 26:4-6 Ja 1993
Lovely in the dances. Carter, Sydney. *Tablet* 247:1097 Ag 28 1993
Reflective action: a lenten liturgical dance workshop. *Liturgy* 10:37-41 Sum 1992
Shall we dance? religion, culture and movement. Kane, Thomas A. *ChrWorld* 236:265-269 N-D 1993

DANNEELS, GODFRIED, CARDINAL, 1933-
A Christian response to the New Age. Saliba, John A. *Way* 33:202-232 Jl 1993
A diagnosis of Europe's moral malaise. *Tablet* 247:1242-1243 S 25 1993

DANTE ALIGHIERI
Accompanying Dante. Krivak, Andrew J. *America* 169:17-21 O 30 1993
Leaves of light: the textual journeys of Dante and García Márquez. Barciauskas, Jonas. *CrossCurr* 43:212-229 Sum 1993
The purification of desire in Dante's "Purgatorio". Stratton, Robin. *Spir Life* 39:34-36 Spr 1993

DANUBE RIVER
Waters of discord. Bowlby, Chris. *Tablet* 246:1561-1562 D 12 1992

DARWINISM see Evolution

DATING (SOCIAL CUSTOMS)—RELIGIOUS ASPECTS
A father's rules for dating. Dodds, Bill. *New Cov* 22:16+ F 1993

DAUGHTERS OF CHARITY
John Paul II, Pope, (1991-05-27) Poverty today requires authentic charity. John Paul II, Pope, 1920- (Karol Wojtyla) (elected 1978). *Con Life* 17 no 2:31-32 1992*
John Paul II, Pope, (1991-07-03) St Louise, an example to follow and to propose. John Paul II, Pope, 1920- (Karol Wojtyla) (elected 1978). *Con Life* 17 no 2:47-50 1992*

DAUGHTERS OF JESUS
Congregation for the Causes of Saints (1993-07-06) Decree on the heroic virtues. Congregation for the Causes of Saints. *OR(Eng)* 1299:12 Jl 14 1993*

DAUGHTERS OF MARY PIOUS SCHOOLS
Congregation for the Causes of Saints (1992-12-21) Decree on a miracle. Congregation for the Causes of Saints. *OR(Eng)* 1272:4 Ja 6 1993

DAUGHTERS OF MERCY
John Paul II, Pope, (1993-06-21) World. John Paul II, Pope, 1920- (Karol Wojtyla) (elected 1978). *OR(Eng)* 1300:5 Jl 21 1993*

DAUMIER, HONORE, 1808-1879
Temporal but timeless Daumier at the Met. Siegel, Lee. *Comm* 120:20-21 Ap 23 1993

DAVID, KING OF ISRAEL
Find sheds light on David's rule. Pevtzow, Lisa. *Register* 69:1+ Ag 22 1993
The story of David and Bathsheba: a different approach. Garsiel, Moshe. *CBQ* 55:244-262 Ap 1993

The story of David and Goliath the early history of its text. Kooij, Arie van der. *Eph Theol Lovan* 78:118-131 Ap 1992

DAVIDEK, FELIX, -1988
The vicar-general was a woman. *Tablet* 247:474 Ap 10-17 1993

DAVIES, HORTON
A church historian's odyssey. Davies, Horton. Grand Rapids: Eerdmans, 1993. 218p ISBN 0-8028-0712-7

DAY, DOROTHY, 1897-1980
Herald of a renewed Church. Egan, Eileen. *Cath Work* 60:8 My 1993
Light of Day shines yet at Catholic Worker. McCarthy, Tim. *Nat Cath Rep* 29:9-12 My 21 1993
Meeting Dorothy Day [condensed fr *The call of service* 1993]. Coles, Robert, 1929-. *CDgst* 57:90-95 O 1993
Searching for Christ: the spirituality of Dorothy Day. Merriman, Brigid O'Shea. Notre Dame: University of Notre Dame Press, 1992. x, 360p ISBN 0-268-01750-6 LC 93-23827
Sixty years on. *Tablet* 247:614 My 15 1993

DAY CARE CENTERS
Leaving the children at "Mom's house". Barnard, Ann M. *ST Anth* 101:22-27 Jl 1993

DE KLERK, FREDERICK WILLEM, 1936-
South Africa on the edge. Steyn, Richard. *Tablet* 247:1152+ S 11 1993

DEACONS
Between two worlds. Jacquet, Lou. *OSV* 82:8 Je 6 1993
The deacon today. Anderson, Joan Wester, 1938-. *Liguorian* 81:13-17 S 1993
Debating the fate of the diaconate. Jacquet, Lou. *OSV* 82:6 Je 13 1993
Marriage and ministry in the diaconate. Ballweg, John M. *Church* 9:30-32 Sum 1993
The permanent diaconate turns 25. McSheffery, Daniel F. *Priest* 49:12-15 Ag 1993
De promissione electorum in ordinatione diaconali iuxta pontificale romanum anni 1990. Ghirlanda, Gianfranco. *Periodica* 81 no 2:211-250 1992
Religious and the new rite for the ordination of deacons. Egana, Francisco J. *Con Life* 17 no 2:98-121 1992
The survival of permanent deacons. Ellis, Robert F. *HPR* 94:29-32+ O 1993
This is how it was. Pearce, Maurice. *Month* 26:81-84 F 1993

DEAD SEA SCROLLS *see* Qumran Scrolls
What we can learn from the Dead Sea Scrolls [interview by M Finley]. Fitzmyer, Joseph Augustine, 1920-. *OSV* 81:7 Ja 10 1993

DEADLY SINS
Envy: the up-front sin. Keefe, Jeffrey. *Catechist* 27:5 N-D 1993
The seven deadly sins: pride, the number one sin. Keefe, Jeffrey. *Catechist* 27:8 S 1993

DEATH
Being with those who mourn [photographs]. Thompson, Stephanie. *BibleT* 31:95-101 Mr 1993
Bereavement: until we meet again. Oberholzer, Felicidad. *Liturgy* 10:47-56 Wint 1992
Beyond death. Henry, Martin. *Furrow* 43:678-680 D 1992
Bringing the dead to life. Anderson, Paul. *New Cov* 23:16-17 N 1993
The Catholic way of dying. Ball, Ann. *OSV* 82:5 O 31 1993
Catholicism and the "right" to die. Grondelski, John M. *Linacre* 59:50-56 N 1992
Conversations with dying friends [interview by Mitchel B Finley]. Carmody, John Tully. *OSV* 81:6-7 Mr 28 1993
Cramming for your finals: make death a part of life [excerpt fr *The troubled dream of life*]. Callahan, Daniel, 1930-. *Comm* 120:11-15 Jl 16 1993
Dave understanding life through death. Conroy, Bernadette. *St Anth* 100:24-27 My 1993
Death and grief in murals [photographs]. Toomey, Stephana. *Liturgy* 10:58-62 Wint 1992
Death dreams: unveiling mysteries of the unconscious mind. Kramer, Kenneth P. New Jersey: Paulist Press, 1993. x, 288p ISBN 0-8091-3349-0 LC 92-29605
Death, the unsentimental fact, is our anchor to God's deeper realities. Kreeft, Peter John, 1937-. *Register* 69:1+ My 2 1993
Desert island choice (1) [winner of the John Harriott Memorial Prize]. Dorrell, Fleur. *Tablet* 247:94 Ja 23 1993
Direitos de vida numa cultura de morte. Maçaneiro, Marcial. *REB* 53:52-71 Mr 1993
Dying—and see, we are alive. Fitzpatrick, Michael. *RRel* 52:719-730 S-O 1993
The facts of death: some reflections for Lent. Anderson, Paul. *New Cov* 22:26-30 Mr 1993
The fifth commandment. Wuerl, Donald William, Bp, 1941-. *Columbia* 73:19 Ag 1993
Helping Catholics deal with life, death. Gibeau, Dawn. *Nat Cath Rep* 29:6 F 5 1993
Helping the hurting: getting inside another's circle of pain. Pratt, Lonni Collins. *New Cov* 22:15-16 Ap 1993
His brother's keeper: a memorial. Paige, Harry W, 1922-. *Liguorian* 81:18-21 My 1993
It hurts so bad: parents grieve the death of their children. Haywood, Christine Curtis. *St Anth* 101:42-45 Je 1993
John Paul II, Pope, (1992-12-19) Ad limina Apostolorum. John Paul II, Pope, 1920- (Karol Wojtyla) (elected 1978). *TPS* 38:193-200 Jl-Ag 1993*
O Susan!: looking forward with hope after the death of a child. Angell, James W. Pasadena: Hope, 1990. 115p ISBN 0-932727-401-9 LC 90-4699
Pain management. *Health Prog* 74:30-39 Ja-F 1993
The place of the dead: Christian burial and the liturgical environment. Adams, William Seth. *Liturgy* 10:69-73 Wint 1992
The power to act: toward a Christian experience of time. Dalzell, Catherine. *Can Cath Rev* 11:7-11 F 1993
The promise of Easter. Wallace, James A, 1944-. *Liguorian* 81:4-7 Ap 1993
Religion and the moral meaning of euthanasia. Campbell, Courtney S. *Linacre* 59:15-28 N 1993
Reunited with our ancestors. Castel, Pol. *Cath Work* 60:7 Je-Jl 1993
Le sens d'un colloque: moines et moniales devant la mort. Platelle, Henri. *MSR* 50:49-51 Ja-Mr 1993
Talking to children about death. Banta, Margrit. *ReligTJ* 27:29-30 Mr 1993

Thoughts from death and life. Gallagher, Vera, 1917-. *RRel* 52:238-240 Mr-Ap 1993
Through the eyes of children. Clifford, Donald. *ReligTJ* 27:30 Mr 1993
What comes after assisted suicide and legalized euthanasia? Gervais, Marcel, Abp. *Origins* 22:573+ F 4 1993

DEATH—BIBLICAL TEACHING
Death and destiny in the Bible. Wensing, Michael G. Minnesota: The Order of St Benedict, 1993. x, 83p ISBN 0-8146-2093-0 LC 92-27237
Shaping study sessions around Paul's sayings on death. Meeks, Blair Gilmer. *Liturgy* 10:6-9 Wint 1992
What does Paul say to us about death? Bregman, Lucy. *Liturgy* 10:1-5 Wint 1992

DEATH—EDUCATION
Accompagnement des familles et prévention des deuils pathologiques. Vanoverberghe, Arlette. *Supplement* 184:125-144 Mr-Ap 1993

DEATH—ETHICAL ASPECTS
Assisted-suicide ban supported. Maida, Adam, Abp. *Origins* 23:280 S 30 1993
Physician-assisted suicide and euthanasia. *Origins* 23:63-64 Je 10 1993
Pour une éthique de la fin de la vie. Geets, Claude. *Supplement* 184:89-96 Mr-Ap 1993

DEATH—NEAR-DEATH EXPERIENCES
Recognizing God's presence in your life. Froehle, Virginia Ann. *St Anth* 100:10-15 S 1993

DEATH—PSYCHOLOGICAL ASPECTS
Ceremonies of innocence. Paige, Harry W, 1922-. *Liguorian* 81:20-25 F 1993

DEATH—PSYCHOLOGY
Accompagnement des familles et prévention des deuils pathologiques. Vanoverberghe, Arlette. *Supplement* 184:125-144 Mr-Ap 1993

DEATH—THEOLOGY
Death as a hermeneutic. Carmody, John Tully. *Horizons (CTS)* 20:115-117 Spr 1993

DEATH (IN RELIGION, FOLKLORE)
Discouraged? Here's what the Gospel says about it. Anderson, Paul. *New Cov* 23:16-18 Ag 1993

DEATH IN LITERATURE
Variations sceptiques sur le thème de la mort. Sansen, Raymond. *MSR* 50:83-98 Ap-Je 1993

DEATH NOTICES
Fontaine, Gaston, 1921-1992 [obit]. Fauret, Pierre. *Notitiae* 28:428-430 Je 1992
Mendez Arceo, Sergio, [obit] LLaguna Farias, Jose Alberto [obit]. *Christus* 58:59-60 F 1993
A tres años de los mártires de la UCA. Bravo Gallardo, Carlos. *Christus* 58:72-73 N-D 1992

DEATH PENALTY *see* Capital Punishment

DEBT
Debt crisis in Glasgow archdiocese. *Tablet* 247:180 F 6 1993
Disquiet at size of Glasgow debt. *Tablet* 247:150-151 Ja 30 1993
Rich man, poor man. Nicholl, Donald. *Tablet* 247:540-541 My 1 1993
The unacceptable face of credit. Dwyer, Christopher. *Month* 26:40-42 Ja 1993

DEBTS, EXTERNAL
The children of the world [editorial]. *Month* 26:44-45 F 1993
Forgive us our debts. Vallely, Paul. *Tablet* 247:998 Ag 7 1993
The relationship between evangelization and development. Lott, Anastasia. *AFER* 34:66-78 Ap 1992
The social context of the AMECEA countries on the eve of the African Synod. Henriot, Peter F. *AFER* 34:340-363 D 1992

DECADENCE (LITERARY MOVEMENT)
The sins of the fathers: decadence and despair in fin-de-siècle France. Pickstone, Charles. *Month* 26:391-395 S-O 1993

DECISION MAKING
Decision. McMahon, Donal. *Furrow* 44:359-363 Je 1993
Family meetings do work. Light, Judi. *St Anth* 101:10-14 Ag 1993
How democratic should your council be? Fischer, Mark F. *Tod Parish* 25:23-26 O 1993
The Spirit's gift of counsel. Dimock, Giles. *OSV* 81:5 Mr 21 1993

DECISION MAKING—LEGAL ASPECTS
The application of law: some recurring aspects of the process of judicial review and decision making. Feliciano, Florentino P. *Amer J Juris* 37:17-56 1992
Legal argument and decision theory. Klami, Hannu Tapani. *Amer J Juris* 37:171-184 1992

DECISION MAKING—RELIGION
Discernment. Wolff, Pierre. Missouri: Triumph Books, 1993. x, 145p ISBN 0-89243-485-6 LC 93-7922

DECLARATION OF INDEPENDENCE, 1776
Cherishing the sacred. Higgins, James J. *Liguorian* 81:73 Jl 1993

DECONSTRUCTION (CRITICISM)
Derrida and Mādhyamika Buddhism: from linguistic deconstruction to criticism of onto-theologies. Zong-qi, Cai. *IPQ* 33:183-195 Je 1993
Light and metaphor in Plotinus and St Thomas Aquinas. Corrigan, Kevin. *Thomist* 57:187-199 Ap 1993
The voice that keeps reading Evans' strategies of deconstruction. Kates, Joshua. *PhilosTod* 37:318-335 Aut 1993

DEEDY, JOHN G, 1923-
Who was Didymus? The face behind the pseudonym. *Comm* 120:20-21 Ag 13 1993

DEFENSE INDUSTRIES- GREAT BRITAIN
What future for United Kingdom defence industries? Harrison, Roger. *Month* 26:105-106 Mr 1993

DEFENSE MECHANISMS (PSYCHOLOGY)
Who chooses celibacy—and why? Coate, Mary Anne. *Way Suppl* 77:97-105 Sum 1993

DEFILIPPIS, LEONARDO
St. Max on stage. Duin, Julia. *New Cov* 23:22-23 N 1993

DEGRUTTIS, PAOLO, 1826-1905
Congregation for the Causes of Saints (1992-07-11) Decree on the heroic virtues. Congregation for the Causes of Saints. *TPS* 38:37-38 Ja-F 1993

DELASSUS, HENRI
Conspiracy to commit heresy: The Anti-Americanist Polemic of Canon Henri Delassus. Talar, C J T. *US Cath Hist* 11:77-92 Sum 1993

DELEUZE, GILLES
Of lingering eyes and talking things: Adorno and Deleuze on philosophy since Auschwitz. Toolan, David S. *PhilosTod* 37:227-246 Aut 1993

DELILLE, HENRIETTE
Who are their models? Cunningham, Beatrice. *ReligTJ* 27:38-39 O 1993

DELP, ALFRED, 1907-1945
Jesuit presence and the struggle for justice in Nazi Germany. Endean, Philip. *Month* 26:240-246 Je 1993

DEMJANJUK, IVAN
Right or wrong, Demjanjuk may go free. Pevtzow, Lisa. *Register* 69:1+ Ag 15 1993

DEMOCRACY
Capitalism with soul? Novak on the Catholic ethic. Dionne, E J, Jr. *Comm* 120:9-12 My 21 1993
Entre el liberalismo y la socialdemocracia: la sociedad abierta. Perona, Angeles J. Barcelona: Anthropos, 1993. x, 248p ISBN 84-7658-394-x
False democratic dawn. Dowden, Richard. *Tablet* 247:1030 Ag 14 1993
A neo-Thomist's defense of democracy. Schram, Glenn N. *New Oxford Rev* 60:13-17 Ja-F 1993
Victims without tears: democracy and the politics of pity. Amato, Joseph Anthony, 1938-. *Crisis* 11:29-31 F 1993

DEMOCRACY—ETHICAL ASPECTS
John Paul II, Pope, (1993-09-05) Basic values [Orig in Lithuanian]. John Paul II, Pope, 1920- (Karol Wojtyla) (elected 1978). *OR(Eng)* 1306:7-8 S 8 1993*

DEMOCRACY—RELIGIOUS ASPECTS
A democratic Catholic Church: in a reconstruction of Roman Catholicism. Bianchi, Eugene C, and Ruether, Rosemary Radford, eds. New York: Crossroad, 1993. x, 262p ISBN 0-8245-1186-7 LC 92-7920

DEMOCRACY- AFRICA
Africa's new wind of change [editorial]. *Tablet* 247:1059 Ag 21 1993
Choosing our future. *Cath Int* 4:169-174 Ap 1993

DEMOCRACY- CENTRAL AMERICA
"Democracy demands structural change". MacEoin, Gary. *Nat Cath Rep* 30: 10 N 19 1993

DEMOCRACY AND CHRISTIANITY
American spirituality: a distinct contribution? Schall, James Vincent, 1928-. *Living Light* 29:3-13 Aut 1992

DEMOCRACY AND RELIGION
Democracy and its limits: it's wonderful; it's not enough. Garvey, John, 1944- . *Comm* 120:9-10 Ag 13 1993

DEMOGRAPHY
Ethical implications of a people's changing visage. *Origins* 22:758-761 Ap 15 1993

DEMOGRAPHY- NORTHERN IRELAND
Comparisons from the North. Hewitt, Victor. *Studies* 82:24-34 Spr 1993

DEMONSTRATIONS
Public dissent and passive protest. Cummings, Frank P. *SocJust* 84:49-53 Mr-Ap 1993
Stop the killing. McRedmond, Louis. *Tablet* 247:434 Ap 3 1993

DEMONSTRATIONS- GREAT BRITAIN
Irish demonstrate against terrorism. *Tablet* 247:490 Ap 10-17 1993

DEMONSTRATIONS- IRELAND
Irish voices plead for violence to end. *Tablet* 247:444-445 Ap 3 1993

DENNY, REGINALD O
Verdicts and videos [editorial]. *Comm* 120:3-4 N 19 1993

DENOMINATIONS, RELIGIOUS
Approaching "sect" with care. Kydd, Ronald. *Ecumen Trends* 22:3-5 Mr 1993

DEOSZEGI, JUDY
How four artists put the finishing touches on God's creation. Marquardt, Deborah. *USCath* 58:14-21 Ag 1993

DEPORTATION
Commission alleges deportation abuses. *Tablet* 247:1023 Ag 7 1993
Death of a deportee [editorial]. *Tablet* 247:1031 Ag 14 1993

DEPRESSION
And who is my neighbor?. Beaver, William A. *Word Sp* 14:96-104 1992
Memento viva!. Dubruiel, Michael. *New Cov* 23:14-15 Ag 1993
A path through the sea: one woman's journey from depression to wholeness. Grissen, Lillian V. Grand Rapids: Eerdmans, 1993. 240p ISBN 0-8028-0702-x

DEREGULATION
Midflight correction? Reregulation won't work. Kelly, Kevin T. *Comm* 120:6-7 Je 18 1993

DERRIDA, JACQUES, 1930-
Derrida and Mādhyamika Buddhism: from linguistic deconstruction to criticism of onto-theologies. Zong-qi, Cai. *IPQ* 33:183-195 Je 1993
The instant and the living present: Ricoeur and Derrida reading Husserl. Bourgeois, Patrick. *PhilosTod* 37:31-37 Spr 1993
The voice that keeps reading Evans' strategies of deconstruction. Kates, Joshua. *PhilosTod* 37:318-335 Aut 1993

DESCARTES, RENE
Cogito: inference and certainity. Glouberman, Mark. *Mod Schlmn* 70:81-98 Ja 1993
Descartes' discourse. Rudolph, Katherine. *PhilosTod* 37:38-51 Spr 1993
Descartes's three hypothetical doubts. Flage, Daniel E. *Mod Schlmn* 70:201-208 Mr 1993

DESERT FATHERS
A breed apart: the Desert Fathers. Miesel, Sandra. *OSV* 81:10-11 Ap 11 1993

DESERTS- AFRICA
John Paul II, Pope, (1993-01-01) Lent 1993 [English tr]. John Paul II, Pope, 1920- (Karol Wojtyla) (elected 1978). *Origins* 22:524 Ja 7 1993*

DESERTS- AUSTRALIA
John Paul II, Pope, (1993-01-01) Lent 1993 [English tr]. John Paul II, Pope, 1920- (Karol Wojtyla) (elected 1978). *Origins* 22:524 Ja 7 1993*

DESERTS (IN RELIGION, FOLKLORE)
Seers' corner: desert days [photos]. Durken, Daniel. *BibleT* 31:204-205 Jl 1993

DESIRE
The place of desires in the Ignatian exercises. McGrath, Thomas. *Way Suppl* 76:25-31 Spr 1993
The purification of desire by means of desire in Dante's "Purgatorio". Stratton, Robin. *Spir Life* 39:34-36 Spr 1993

DESOLA, CARLA
Carla DeSola. *Mod Lit* 20:46 S 1993

DETECTIVE AND MYSTERY STORIES
Dorothy L Sayers: the centenary celebration. Dale, Alzina Stone. New York: Walker and Co, 1993. 166p ISBN 0-80273-224-0 LC 92-44894

DETERRENCE (STRATEGY)
Interpretations of conflict: ethics, pacificism, and the just-war tradition. Miller, Richard Brian. Chicago: University of Chicago Press, 1991. 294p ISBN 0-22652-795-6 LC 91-3044

DEUSDEDIT, CARDINAL
History and tradition in eleventh-century Rome. Blumenthal, Uta-Renate. *CHist* 79:185-198 Ap 1993

DEUTERO-PAULINE HYPOTHESIS
Textlinguistics and the integrity of Philippians. Koperski, Veronica. *Eph Theol Lovan* 78:330-367 D 1992

DEVEREUX, SEAN, -1993
Devereux, Sean, -1993 [obit]. *Tablet* 247:44-45 Ja 9 1993

DEVEUSTER, DAMIEN, 1840-1889
Congregation for the Causes of Saints (1992-06-13) Decree on a miracle. Congregation for the Causes of Saints. *TPS* 38:19-20 Ja-F 1993*

DEVIL
Good versus evil: beliefs about angels and devils. Ristow, Kate. *Catechist* 26: 34-36 F 1993
La letteratura interpella la teologia. Castelli, Ferdinando. *Civilta* 3:247-255 Ag 7-21 1993

DEVIL—BIBLICAL TEACHING
Los espíritus maléficos en los escritos del Nuevo Testamento. García Cordero, Maximiliano. *Cien Tom* 119:209-249 My-Ag 1992

DEVOTIONAL LITERATURE
The art of meditating on scripture. Toon, Peter. Grand Rapids: Zondervan Publishing House, 1993. x, 176p ISBN 0-310-57761-6
The book of common worship, daily prayer. Louisville: John Knox, 1993. x, 512p ISBN 0-664-22032-0
The book of daily prayers. Webber, Robert. Grand Rapids: Eerdmans, 1993. 544p ISBN 0-8028-3753-0
Devotional classics: selected readings for individuals and groups. Foster, Richard J, and Smith, James Bryan, eds. New York: HarperSanFrancisco, 1993. 353p ISBN 0-06-066966-7 LC 92-53912
Evening devotions. Lane, Wilbur. New York: Vantage Press, 1993. 49p ISBN 0-533-10380-0 LC 92-90962
Fillin' up: devotional fuel for high performance living. Littleton, Mark. Sisters: Questar, 1993. x, 180p ISBN 0-945564-72-4
Life after Easter. Smith, Pamela. New Jersey: Paulist Press, 1993. x, 88p ISBN 0-8091-3379-2 LC 92-21195
Looking for Jesus. Carlisle, Thomas John. Grand Rapids: Eerdmans, 1993. 180p ISBN 0-8028-0667-8
Measuring the days. Eifrig, Gail McGrew. Grand Rapids: Zondervan Publishing House, 1993. x, 400p ISBN 0-06-069248-0
Prayer for daybreak and day's end, vol II: January through June. Taylor, Mary Sue. Cincinnati: St Anthony Messenger Press, 1993. 428p ISBN 0-86716-147-7
Prayer for daybreak and day's end, vol III: July through December. Taylor, Mary Sue. Cincinnati: St Anthony Messenger Press, 1993. 432p ISBN 0-86716-148-5
Promises for the graduate. Richards, Larry. Grand Rapids: Zondervan Publishing House, 1993. x, 128p ISBN 0-310-39700-6
Through the year with Francis of Assisi: daily meditations from his words and life. Francis of Assisi, Saint, 1182-1226. Cincinnati: St Anthony Messenger Press, 1993. 240p ISBN 0-86716-196-5
Time with Jesus. Catucci, Thomas F. Notre Dame: Ave Maria Press, 1993. 158p ISBN 0-87793-499-1 LC 93-71891
A touch of his peace. Stanley, Charles. Grand Rapids: Zondervan Publishing House, 1993. x, 144p ISBN 0-310-54558-7
Wisdom for the graduate. Richards, Larry. Grand Rapids: Zondervan Publishing House, 1993. 128p ISBN 0-310-39710-3

DEVRIES, PETER, 1910-1993
DeVries, Peter, 1910-1993 [obit]. Hunt, George W., 1937-. *America* 169:2 O 23 1993

DIALECTIC
Herméneutique et pneumatologie selon Schleiermacher. Brito, Emilio. *Eph Theol Lovan* 69:88-117 Ap 1993

DIALOGUE—SOCIAL POLITICAL
Diálogo entre Evangelio y Cultura. *Christus* 58:6 My 1993

DIALOGUE (THEOLOGY)
Abraham Joshua Heschel: the inadequacy of the ecumenical perspective. Blumenthal, David Reuben, 1938-. *JEcumen Stds* 29:249-253 Spr 1992
Baltimore and Eisenach [Graymoor Prize Winner]. Banki, Judith Hershcopf. *Comm* 120:11+ Ja 15 1993
Bible truth: a possible dialogue between biblical fundamentalism and Catholic scholarship. Branick, Vincent F. *StudiaM* 41:269-288 1992
A bibliographical review of books on spirituality in the Buddhist-Christian dialogue. Mitchell, Donald W. *Stud Form Spir* 14:139-143 F 1993
Buber and Tillich. Novak, David, 1941-. *JEcumen Stds* 29:159-174 Spr 1992
Catholic delegates narrowly escape assassination. *Tablet* 247:865 Jl 3 1993

Christian-Jewish dialogue. Rottenberg, Isaac C, 1925-. *JEcumen Stds* 29:87-95 Wint 1992

Christian-Jewish dialogue. Sloyan, Gerard S. *Living Light* 30:93-99 Aut 1993

Communique of the Joint International Commission for Theological Dialogue. *Ecumen Trends* 22:1-2 S 1993

Dialogue with Waso Boorana traditional religious practices. Aguilar, Mario I. *AFER* 35:101-114 Ap 1993

Escaping Hegel. Fritzman, J M. *IPQ* 33:57-68 Mr 1993

Evangelisation and the other: response and responsibility. Barnes, Michael R. *Month* 25:479-484 D 1992

The Fifth World Conference and walls of the heart. FitzGerald, Kyriaki Antonia. *Ecumen Trends* 22:1+ Ap 1993

From proclamation to interreligious dialogue. Stoeber, Michael. *Living Light* 30:32-41 Aut 1993

A gathering of the faiths: Chicago 1993. Teasdale, Wayne. *Living Prayer* 26:29-30 My-Je 1993

Gathering together to pray: a special mode of public presence in interreligious dialogue. Kaserow, John. *New Theol Rev* 6:18-29 Ag 1993

Global harmony and public action. Barnes, Michael R. *Month* 26:(I) Mr 1993

Globalization and the autonomy of moral reasoning: an essay in fundamental moral theology. Kopfensteiner, Thomas R. *TheolStds* 54:485-511 S 1993

A great place for dialogue: reflections of a former newspaper editor. Wojcicki, Ed. *America* 168:12-15 F 27 1993

Group asks Lutheran-Roman Catholic talks continue. *Ecumen Trends* 22:8 Mr 1993

In dialogue. *Tablet* 247:306 Mr 6 1993

The interfaith future: from the mind to the heart. Klenicki, Leon. *Ecumen Trends* 22:9 My 1993

Interreligious dialogue and theology of religions: an Asian paradigm. Pieris, Aloysius, 1934-. *Horizons (CTS)* 20:106-114 Spr 1993

Interreligious dialogue today. Fitzgerald, Michael Louis, Bp. *Cath Int* 4:190-194 Ap 1993

Interreligious dialogue: a hundred years on. Schreiter, Robert J. *New Theol Rev* 6:6-17 Ag 1993

An Islamic-Roman Catholic "national" dialogue. Borelli, John. *Ecumen Trends* 22:10-13 O 1993

John Paul II, Pope, (1991-10-14) Meeting the Jewish Community of Brazil. John Paul II, Pope, 1920- (Karol Wojtyla) (elected 1978). *SIDIC* 25 No 1: 30 1992*

Legitimacy of development within the apostolic tradition. Carter, David. *OChr* 29 no 3:226-234 1993

Lutheran-Reformed Committee meets. *Ecumen Trends* 22:8 Mr 1993

Ministry in the new South Africa: an intercultural challenge [fr *Entre nous*]. Slattery, Joseph A. *Living Light* 29:49-54 Wint 1992

Missionary service [fr *Yours sincerely*]. Kaut, Bernd. *AFER* 34:376-381 D 1992

Monks in dialogue with believers from other religions. Béthune, Pierre de. *Stud Form Spir* 14:129-138 F 1993

Mormonism in the twenty-first century. Saliba, John A. *StudiaM* 41:49-67 1992

Opportunities and challenges offered by BEM to the British and Irish churches. Davey, Colin. *OChr* 29 no 3:216-225 1993

A pastor's vision [interview by G O'Connell]. Martini, Carlo Maria, Cardinal, 1926-. *Tablet* 247:876-878 Jl 10 1993

Persons—objects or observers? (A dialogue with Buddhism). Barnes, Michael R. *Way Suppl* 76:98-108 Spr 1993

Pope reaches out to the Orthodox Churches. *Tablet* 247:147-148 Ja 30 1993

Revelation in comparative perspective: lessons for interreligious dialogue. Carpenter, David. *JEcumen Stds* 29:175-188 Spr 1992

Roman Catholics and Episcopalians release statement on 25 years of dialogue. Solheim, James. *Ecumen Trends* 22:16 Mr 1993

Salvation offered by sects (a theological analysis and evaluation). Dhavamony, Mariasusai. *StudiaM* 41:325-352 1992

Three-way games. Lecercle, Jean-Jacques. *PhilosTod* 36:336-350 Wint 1992

Toward communion in faith, life and witness. Davis, Kortright. *Ecumen Trends* 22:1-2+ Jl-Ag 1993

Towards koinonia/communion in faith, life and witness: revised discussion paper for the Fifth World Conference on Faith and Order. Tanner, Mary, et al. *Ecumen Trends* 22:1-24 Je 1993

Tracy in dialogue: mystical retrieval and prophetic suspicion. Barnes, Michael R. *Heythrop* 34:60-64 Ja 1993

Unisichtbar bleibt ihre Frömmigkeit Kritische Begegnung mit Neuen Religiösen Bewegungen. Fuss, Michael. *StudiaM* 41:353-389 1992

DIAZ-PEREZ, VIRIATO, 1875-1958

Modernismo y Teosofia. Larrea Lopez, Juan Felix. Madrid: Libertarias, 1993. x, 400p ISBN 84-7954-122-9

DICKINSON, EMILY, 1830-1886

Emily Dickinson's lectio: wicked as I am, I read my Bible sometimes. Norris, Kathleen. *Sisters* 65:104-108 Mr 1993

I'm kneeling—still—: A study of Emily Dickinson's siege on the sacred. Rieke, Susan. *ABenR* 44:258-279 S 1993

DIEGO, JUAN

Our Lady of Guadalupe: evangelizer of the Americas. McCurry, James E. *Marian Stds* 43:9-16 1992

DIESBOURG, RAYMOND

Single Catholics: can we talk about S-E-X? Bearden, Michelle. *USCath* 58:30-35 Ag 1993

DIEZ Y BUSTOS DE MOLINA, VICTORIA, 1903-1936

John Paul II, Pope, (1993-10-10) Victoria Diez. John Paul II, Pope, 1920- (Karol Wojtyla) (elected 1978). *OR(Eng)* 1311:1 O 13 1993*

Teresian spirituality prepared Blessed Victoria Diez to sacrifice her own life. *OR(Eng)* 1311:2 O 13 1993

DIGNITY—SOCIAL ASPECTS

Left, right, or personalist? Hanink, James G. *New Oxford Rev* 60:14-20 N 1993

DILTHEY, WILHELM, 1833-1911

Phenomenological research as destruktion: the early Heidegger's reading of Dilthey. Bambach, Charles R. *PhilosTod* 37:115-132 Sum 1993

DINOIA, JOSEPH A

The U.S. bishops get a new doctor of doctrine [por]. Mullen, P H, Jr. *OSV* 82:3 O 31 1993

DINOSAURS

Doin' dinosaurs: a schoolwide science project. Cazes, Jo. *Momentum* 24:20-21 S-O 1993

DIOCESES

Diocesan restructuring I. Hurley, Walter A. *CLawyer* 34 no 4:391-402 1993

Diocesan restructuring II. Dusen, Thomas van. *CLawyer* 34 no 4:403-406 1993

De synodo diocesana. Beyer, Jean. *Periodica* 81 no 3-4:381-423 1992

DIRECTORIES

Prolife directory [2 parts]. *Register* 69:5 Ja 17; 5 Ja 24 1993

DIRECTORS OF RELIGIOUS EDUCATION

Biblical charades, anyone? Jesus jeopardy? Davidson, Patricia S. *Tod Parish* 25:6 S 1993

Converting the religious educator. Malone, Miriam. *Mod Lit* 20:18-20 Je-Jl 1993

Don't be afraid to change. Paprocki, Joseph. *ReligTJ* 27:41 Mr 1993

Education: encouraging parish-based programs. Genereux, Susan. *Tod Parish* 25:33 Mr 1993

Evaluating the director of religious education. Hanus, Elaine. *Momentum* 24:72-73 S-O 1993

Feeding your catechists? Paprocki, Joseph. *ReligTJ* 27:63 S 1993

From dream to reality. Paprocki, Joseph. *ReligTJ* 26:41 Ja 1993

From the director's chair. Johnston, Mary Ann. *Momentum* 24:61-63 S-O 1993

Helpful hints for DREs from a DRE. Gilbert, Marjorie. *Catechist* 27:66-67 S 1993

Liturgy and catechesis. Paprocki, Joseph. *ReligTJ* 27:40 F 1993

Open-door religious education. Bishop, Marilyn E. *Momentum* 24:32-36 N-D 1993

This is the army. Parry, Mary. *Tod Parish* 25:23 N-D 1993

When wandering is good. Paprocki, Joseph. *ReligTJ* 27:40-41 O 1993

DIRECTORY FOR ECUMENISM

The 1993 directory for ecumenism. *Origins* 23:129+ Jl 29 1993

DIRR, PETER J

Coming soon to a parish near you. Breig, James. *OSV* 82:12 Ag 8 1993

DISARMAMENT

Mind-blowing nuclear budget is based on fantasy. Drinan, Robert Francis, 1920-. *Nat Cath Rep* 29:6 F 19 1993

Outrageous thoughts on war and peace. Bellah, Robert Neely, 1927-. *New Oxford Rev* 60:15-18+ Mr 1993

A plea to President Clinton: stop the sales of US arms. Drinan, Robert Francis, 1920-. *Nat Cath Rep* 29:16 F 5 1993

Test ban politics proliferate under Clinton. Hunter, Jane. *Nat Cath Rep* 29:3 Jl 30 1993

DISASTER RELIEF

The flood. Kenny, Joe. *Register* 69:1+ Ag 1 1993

Listening to humanity's heartbeat. *OR(Eng)* 1272:2+ Ja 6 1993

DISASTERS

The great flood of 1993 [photos]. Collins, Brad. *Extensn* 88:16-20 O 16 1993

DISCERNMENT

Discernir la historia [editorial]. Valle, Luis del. *Christus* 58:2-3 S 1993

DISCERNMENT—RELIGIOUS ASPECTS

The discernment dilemma. Kreeft, Peter John, 1937-. *New Cov* 22:10-14 My 1993

Seeking discernment. Wiltshire, Peter. *Living Prayer* 26:24-25 My-Je 1993

DISCERNMENT OF SPIRITS

Listening to the music of the spirit: the art of discernment. Lonsdale, David. Notre Dame: Ave Maria Press, 1993. x, 174p ISBN 08-7793-508-4

DISCIPLES

Presence or absence? the question of women disciples at the Last Supper. Lee, Dorothy A. *Pacifica* 6:1-20 F 1993

DISCIPLES, TWELVE

Judas, betrayer or betrayed? Nunes, Danillo. New York: Vantage Press, 1992. x, 319p ISBN 0-533-10065-8 LC 91-912232

"The twelve apostles were men.". Raming, Ida. *TheolDgst* 40:21-25 Spr 1993

DISCIPLESHIP

Being used? By God? Hogan, William Francis, 1930-. *Emmanuel* 99:334-337 Jl-Ag 1993

Celebration, judgment, practice. Warren, Michael, 1935-. *Furrow* 44:199-207 Ap 1993

Christ and the Catholic university. Daley, Brian E. *America* 169:6-14 S 11 1993

The Church of the faithful. O'Malley, William J, 1931-. *America* 168:6-10 Je 19-26 1993

Core of our discipleship [fr *Unity Acres Newsletter*]. McVey, Raymond. *Cath Work* 60:8 Mr-Ap 1993

Dancing feet becoming disciples. Vanden Busch, Roger J. *Emmanuel* 99:432-439 O 1993

Discipleship in Matthew. Doohan, Leonard. *Mod Lit* 20:36 Ag 1993

Dynamic disciples? Hogan, William Francis, 1930-. *Emmanual* 49:374-377+ S 1993

Five cries of parish. Ventline, Lawrence M. *Priest* 49:17-21 F 1993

Jesus. Martin, George. *Liguorian* 81:44-45 Ap 1993

Priestcraft: a how-to guide for everyone. Desiderio, Frank R. *ST Anth* 101:16-21 Jl 1993

Responding to His call. McKenna, Bill. *New Cov* 23:27 S 1993

Sexuality, family, and the life of discipleship: some early Christian perspectives. Hennessey, Lawrence R. *Chicago Stud* 32:19-31 Ap 1993

Sharing the Lord's mission. Doohan, Leonard. *Mod Lit* 20:34-35 S 1993

Stewardship: we reap what we sow [editorial]. Feister, John Bookser. *St Anth* 100:57 Ja 1993

"Today I put before you life and death": choosing the Body of Christ. Gabriele, Edward F. *Emmanuel* 99:102-106 Mr 1993

The women from Galilee. Martin, George. *Liguorian* 81:18-19 S 1993

DISCIPLINE
Adults should never hit kids. Schlaerth, Katherine. *USCath* 58:24-29 Ja 1993
A new look at discipline. Baumgarten, Bruce. *ReligTJ* 27:18-19 Ap-My 1993

DISCRIMINATION
Metaphors of discrimination: a comparison of Gunnar Myrdal and Gary Becker. Shulman, Steven. *RSocEcon* 50:432-452 Wint 1992
Stuck with a Satanist? religious autonomy in a regulated society [exc fr *The culture of disbelief*]. Carter, Stephen L. *Comm* 120:15-18 Ag 13 1993

DISCRIMINATION—RELIGIOUS ASPECTS
On discrimination against homosexual persons. *Origins* 23:359-360 O 28 1993

DISCRIMINATION IN EMPLOYMENT
AIDs in the workplace: discrimination by ignorance. Pedreirs, Jorge. *CLawyer* 35 no 2:199-215 1993
Employment issues. Murren, Philip J. *CLawyer* 34 no 4:331-341 1993
Job discrimination worked in N. Ireland. MacEoin, Gary. *Nat Cath Rep* 30:10-11 O 29 1993
Shattering the glass ceiling. Weiss, Rhoda. *Health Prog* 74:58-59 Mr 1993

DISNEY, WALTER ELIAS, 1901-1966
Walt Disney: he built an empire on a mouse [illus]. Reichman, Theda Kleinhans. *CDgst* 57:91-96 S 1993

DISSENT, POLITICAL
The baby boomers: here today, gone tomorrow [Commencement Address at the University of Rochester, Spr 1993]. Lasch, Christopher, 1932-. *New Oxford Rev* 60:7-8+ S 1993
The March for Life, 1993. Schall, James Vincent, 1928-, et al. *Crisis* 11:28-29 Mr 1993
Now that April's here. Hynes, Brian. *Cath Work* 60:4 Mr-Ap 1993
Public dissent and passive protest. Cummings, Frank P. *SocJust* 84:49-53 Mr-Ap 1993
Sub-versive activity: tip the canoe and Trident, too. Dear, John, 1959-. *Comm* 120:5-7 O 22 1993

DISSENT, RELIGIOUS
[Veritatis splendor belongs to the literary gender]. Curran, Charles E, 1934-. *Comm* 120:14 O 22 1993

DISSENTERS, RELIGIOUS
Autonome Moral oder Moral der Autonomie? Gruber, Hans-Günter. *Stimm Zeit* 211:691-699 O 1993
Die Fünfte Weltkonferenz für Glauben und Kirchenverfassung. Radano, John A. *Catholica* 47:20-37 1993

DISSERTATIONS, ACADEMIC- FRANCE
Maurice Blondel: 100 years after "L Action". Kerlin, Michael J. *America* 168:12-15 Je 19-26 1993

DISTANCE EDUCATION
LIMEX: distance education in intentional learning communities. Lee, Bernard J. *Momentum* 24:7-9 F-Mr 1993

DISTRIBUTION (ECONOMIC THEORY)
Distributing America. Storck, Thomas. *New Oxford Rev* 60:6-10 My 1993

DIVES AND LAZARUS (PARABLE)
Remembering and revelation: a liturgical reflection on Luke 16:19-31. Flanagan, Anne Joan. *Emmanuel* 99:304-307 Jl-Ag 1993

DIVINE MAN
The biblical foundations of the thought of John Paul II on human sexuality. Séguin, Michel. *Communio* 20:266-289 Sum 1993
Celibacy as charism. Schneiders, Sandra M. *Way Suppl* 77:13-25 Sum 1993
Cultivating healthy boundaries. St Romain, Philip. *Liguorian* 81:25-29 S 1993
Image de Dieu, image de l'homme. Renwart, Léon. *NRT* 115:85-104 Ja-F 1993
Loving God [2 pts.]. Anderson, Anthony. *Priest* 49:33-38 O; 40-44 N 1993
The Our Father: the revolutionary prayer of commitment to the Kingdom of God. Mattam, Joseph. *AFER* 35:69-78 Ap 1993
The theological anthropology of Catherine of Siena. Jeremiah, Mary. *Communio* 20:457-462 Sum 1993

DIVINE MESSENGERS *see* Angels

DIVINE OFFICE
Can we revive the prayer of the church? Dean, Stephen. *Priests & People* 7:107-113 Mr 1993
The Catechism [commentary]. Johnson, Luke Timothy, 1943-. *Comm* 120:16-18 My 7 1993
The divine office as personal prayer. Collins, Gregory. *Doctr Life* 42:608-613 D 1992
Liturgy of the hours: a reflection. Zuercher, Suzanne. *RRel* 52:364-370 My-Je 1993
On eagle's wings. Skublics, Ernest. *Can Cath Rev* 11:49-51 Ja 1993
The parish church: a house of prayer. Luka, Ronald, 1937-. *Mod Lit* 20:16-17 F 1993

DIVINE OFFICE—VESPERS
The ancient cathedral office and today's needs. Woofenden, Graham. *Worship* 67:388-405 S 1993
Vespers [editorial]. Schuler, Richard Joseph, 1920-. *SacM* 120:3-4 Aut 1993

DIVORCE
After the royal separation. Dominian, Jack, 1929-. *Tablet* 246:1596 D 19-26 1992
Could a divorced king head the Church? *Tablet* 246:1633-1634 D 19-26 1992
Divorce sometimes "no bad thing", says Carey. *Tablet* 247:736 Je 5 1993
Forgiving an ex-spouse who walked out. Wangler, Joan Norman. *Liguorian* 81:49-51 O 1993
Maritals aids [interview by M Finley]. McManus, Michael J. *OSV* 82:5 Je 6 1993
Marriage? Take it slow [condensed fr *The Catholic Times* Je 18 1993]. Metzger, Richard M. *CDgst* 58:24+ N 1993
The principle of economy a corrective of Christian mercy. Maloney, George A, 1924-. *Diakonia* 26 no 2:119-133 1993

DIVORCE—ECONOMIC CONDITIONS
Accounting for the slowdown in the divorce rate in the 1980s: a bargaining perspective. McCrate, Elaine. *RSocEcon* 50:404-419 Wint 1992

DIVORCE—RELIGIOUS ASPECTS
Parish diary: July. *Tablet* 247:973 Jl 31 1993

DIVORCEES
Determinants of spells of poverty following divorce. Heath, Julia A, and Kiker, B F, 1937-. *RSocEcon* 50:305-315 Fall 1992

DOCTORS OF THE CHURCH
The case for St Thérèse as a doctor of the church. Ahern, Patrick V, Bp, 1919-. *America* 169:12-13+ Ag 28-S 4 1993
St. Jerome: doctor maximus. McSheffery, Daniel F. *HPR* 94:53-57 N 1993

DODD, CHARLES HAROLD
Las parábolas; de Jesús: su sentido y adecuada interpreción. Pérez-Cotapos, Eduardo L. *Teol Vida* 33 no 3-4:165-178 1992

DODD, WESTLEY ALLAN -1993
The hanging of Westley Allan Dodd. Codd, Kevin A. *America* 168:5-6 Ja 30 1993

DOGMA
The Catechism [commentary]. Johnson, Luke Timothy, 1943-. *Comm* 120:16-18 My 7 1993

DOGMA, DEVELOPMENT OF
Partir de la doctrina o partir de la realidad? Mier, Sebastián. *Christus* 58:33-35 F 1993
Reception hermeneutics and the "development" of doctrine: an alternative model. Rush, Ormond. *Pacifica* 6:125-140 Je 1993

DOLAN, JAY
Authority in the church: who makes the final call? McClory, Richard J. *USCath* 58:6-13 Mr 1993

DOLINAY, THOMAS VICTOR, ABP, 1923-1993
Dolinay, Thomas Victor, Abp, 1923-1993 [obit]. *Diakonia* 26 no 2:134 1993

DOMESTIC RELATIONS
Bishops address problems of violence against women. *Nat Cath Rep* 29:28 N 13 1992
Conjugally incorrect. Bright, Kimberly Gustin. *Crisis* 11:43-44 F 1993

DOMESTIC VIOLENCE *see* Family Violence

DOMINICANS
Dominican ideals in early America: the example of Edward Dominic Fenwick. Lisska, Anthony. *New Blckfrs* 74:382-392 S 1993
Dominican nuns in the United States. Jeremiah, Mary. *Word Sp* 14:41-52 1992
The life and teaching of St Thomas Aquinas: a guide for the African Church today. Schineller, Peter. *AFER* 34:18-28 F 1992
Major works/Margaret Ebner. Hindsley, Leonard P, ed. Mahwah: Paulist, 1993. x, 209p ISBN 0-8091-0462-8 LC 92-46650
A passionate mercy. *Tablet* 247:575 My 8 1993
Patores Dabo Vobis [pt 2]. Carey, Michael, and Cole, Basil. *Priest* 49:33-43 Ag 1993
"Saiser Dieu en son vestiaire" L'articulation théologique du sens chez Maître Eckhart. Malherbe, Jean-François. *Laval Theol Phil* 49:201-213 Je 1993
Sisters who cherish the dying [condensed fr *Lear's* F 1993]. Zeitlin, Ariel. *CDgst* 57:64-70 My 1993
The way of the void. Murray, Paul. *New Blckfrs* 74:116-130 Mr 1993

DOMINICANS—HISTORY- SPAIN
Biblia de San Vicente convento de San Esteban: Salamanca. Espinel, J Luis. *Cien Tom* 119:521-548 S-D 1992

DOMINICANS- SPAIN
The Dominican school of Salamanca and the Spanish conquest of America: some bibliographical notes. O'Meara, Thomas Franklin. *Thomist* 56:555-582 O 1992

DONAHUE, WILLIAM
Regaining a Catholic "Voice". Feuerherd, Peter. *Register* 69:3 Je 13 1993

DOOLEY, THOMAS ANTHONY, III, 1927-1961
Tom Dooley's many lives. Fisher, James T. *Comm* 120:6-7 My 21 1993

DORRIE, HEINRICH
Une nouvelle étude surle platonisme antique. Neschke-Hentschke, Ada. *RPhil Louvain* 91:459-465 Ag 1993

DOSTOYEVSKY, FYODOR, 1821-1881
Karl Barth et Dostoïevski. Roussel, Jean-François. *Laval Theol Phil* 49:37-55 F 1993
Perché non si crede? La risposta di Dostoevskij [editorial]. Salvini, Gianpaolo, ed. *Civiltà* 2:209-216 My 1 1993

DOWN'S SYNDROME
Things Danny taught me: a father's story. Maier, Francis X. *Comm* 120:11-12 Mr 26 1993

DOXOLOGY
The concept of blessing. Loewe, Herbert, 1882-1940. *SIDIC* 26 no 1:2-9 1993

DRAGON, EDSON E, 1943-1993
Dragon at the gate. Gibson, Gloria J. *America* 168:12-14 My 22, 1993

DRAMA AND RELIGION
Readers' theater for Lent. Gardiner, Thomas J. *Mod Lit* 20:18-20 Mr 1993
St. Max on stage. Duin, Julia. *New Cov* 23:22-23 N 1993

DRAMA CRITICISM—SINGLE WORKS
Angels in America. Weales, Gerald, *Comm* 120:19-20 Jl 16 1993
Angels in America: millennium approaches. Miracky, James. *America* 168:22-23 My 29 1993
Annie get your gun. Shaw, Roy. *Tablet* 246:1578 D 12 1992
Anthony and Cleopatra. Shaw, Roy. *Tablet* 247:825 Je 26 1993
Arcadia. Shaw, Roy. *Tablet* 247:553 My 1 1993
As you like it. Shaw, Roy. *Tablet* 247:695 My 29 1993
Barnum. Shaw, Roy. *Tablet* 247:52 Ja 9 1993
The beggar's opera. Shaw, Roy. *Tablet* 247:519 Ap 24 1993
Best of friends. Torrens, James S. *America* 168:23 Ap 24 1993
Billy Liar. Shaw, Roy. *Tablet* 247:52 Ja 9 1993
Blood brothers. Torrens, James S. *America* 169:18 S 18 1993
Carousel. Shaw, Roy. *Tablet* 247:20 Ja 2 1993
The changeling. Shaw, Roy. *Tablet* 247:793-794 Je 19 1993
Chatsky. Shaw, Roy. *Tablet* 247:412 Mr 27 1993
City of angels. Shaw, Roy. *Tablet* 247:622 My 15 1993
The comedy of errors. Shaw, Roy. *Tablet* 247:80 Ja 16 1993
A Connecticut Yankee. Shaw, Roy. *Tablet* 247:1106 Ag 28 1993
Crazy for you. Shaw, Roy. *Tablet* 247:379 Mr 20 1993
Cyrano de Bergerac. Shaw, Roy. *Tablet* 247:52 Ja 9 1993

The dearly beloved. Shaw, Roy. *Tablet* 247:760 Je 1993
The deep blue sea. Shaw, Roy. *Tablet* 247:145-146 Ja 30 1993
Don Giovanni. Shaw, Roy. *Tablet* 247:314 Mr 6 1993
Don't fool with love. Shaw, Roy. *Tablet* 247:622 My 15 1993
Dylan Thomas: return journey. Shaw, Roy. *Tablet* 247:20 Ja 2 1993
Elegies for angels, punks and raging queens. Shaw, Roy. *Tablet* 247:216 F 13 1993
Faith healer. Weales, Gerald, 1925-. *Comm* 120:16 Mr 12 1993
Fires in the mirror. Shaw, Roy. *Tablet* 247:484 Ap 10-17 1993
Fool moon. Weales, Gerald, 1925-. *Comm* 120:24 Ap 9 1993
For services rendered. Shaw, Roy. *Tablet* 247:589 My 8 1993
The game of love and chance. Shaw, Roy. *Tablet* 247:113 Ja 23 1993
The ghost train. Shaw, Roy. *Tablet* 246:1626 D 19-26 1992
The gift of the Gorgon. Shaw, Roy. *Tablet* 247:113-114 Ja 23 1993
Godspell. Shaw, Roy. *Tablet* 247:1080 Ag 21 1993
A going concern. Shaw, Roy. *Tablet* 247:1268 O 2 1993
Greasepaint. Shaw, Roy. *Tablet* 247:251 F 20 1993
Hair. Shaw, Roy. *Tablet* 247:1268 O 2 1993
Halcyon days. Weales, Gerald, 1925-. *Comm* 120:20 Ja 15 1993
Hamlet. Shaw, Roy. *Tablet* 247:80 Ja 16 1993
Hay fever. Shaw, Roy. *Tablet* 246:1626 D 19-26 1992
Hysteria. Shaw, Roy. *Tablet* 247:1201 S 18 1993
The importance of being earnest. Shaw, Roy. *Tablet* 247:412 Mr 27 1993
In the summer house. Weales, Gerald, 1925-. *Comm* 120:19-20 S 24 1993
Inadmissible evidence. Shaw, Roy. *Tablet* 247:863 Jl 3 1993
The invisible man. Shaw, Roy. *Tablet* 247:282 F 27 1993
A jovial crew. Shaw, Roy. *Tablet* 247:658 My 22 1993
Juno and the paycock. Shaw, Roy. *Tablet* 247:760-761 Je 1993
King Lear. Shaw, Roy. *Tablet* 247:1238 S 25 1993
King Lear. Shaw, Roy. *Tablet* 247:174 F 6 1993
Kiss of the Spider woman. Torrens, James S. *America* 169:21 N 20 1993
The last Yankee. Shaw, Roy. *Tablet* 247:216 F 13 1993
The last Yankee. Torrens, James S. *America* 168:16 F 27 1993
Lust. Shaw, Roy. *Tablet* 247:1080 Ag 21 1993
Lysistrata. Shaw, Roy. *Tablet* 247:893 Jl 10 1993
Macbeth. Shaw, Roy. *Tablet* 247:519 Ap 24 1993
Mad forest. Weales, Gerald, 1925-. *Comm* 120:20 Ja 15 1993
Madness in Valencia. Shaw, Roy. *Tablet* 247:216 F 13 1993
The madness of George III. Weales, Gerald, 1925-. *Comm* 120:20 N 5 1993
The magic fundoshi. Shaw, Roy. *Tablet* 247:346 Mr 13 1993
Misha's party. Shaw, Roy. *Tablet* 247:1106 Ag 28 1993
Moll Flanders. Shaw, Roy. *Tablet* 247:658-659 My 22 1993
Moonlight. Shaw, Roy. *Tablet* 247:1267-1268 O 2 1993
The mountain giants. Shaw, Roy. *Tablet* 247:1106 Ag 28 1993
Much ado about nothing. Shaw, Roy. *Tablet* 247:953 Jl 24 1993
Murder in the cathedral. Shaw, Roy. *Tablet* 247:1238 S 25 1993
La Musica. Shaw, Roy. *Tablet* 247:251 F 20 1993
The neighbor. Shaw, Roy. *Tablet* 247:553 My 1 1993
The odyssey. Shaw, Roy. *Tablet* 247:1048-1049 Ag 14 1993
Oleanna. Miracky, James J. *America* 168:16 My 15 1993
Oleanna. Shaw, Roy. *Tablet* 247:925 Jl 17 1993
On the ledge. Shaw, Roy. *Tablet* 247:695 My 29 1993
On the piste. Shaw, Roy. *Tablet* 247:346 Mr 13 1993
Orpheus in love. Weales, Gerald, 1925-. *Comm* 120:16-17 F 12 1993
A perfect Ganesh. Torrens, James S. *America* 169:22 Ag 14-21 1993
A perfect Ganesh. Weales, Gerald, 1925-. *Comm* 120:20 S 24 1993
Playland. Shaw, Roy. *Tablet* 247:379 Mr 20 1993
Pope farce wasn't written while slipping on soap. Jones, Arthur C, 1936-. *Nat Cath Rep* 29:24 N 13 1992*
Romeo and Juliet. Shaw, Roy. *Tablet* 247:863 Jl 3 1993
The school of night. Shaw, Roy. *Tablet* 247:589 My 8 1993
Separate tables. Shaw, Roy. *Tablet* 247:952 Jl 24 1993
Shakespeare for my father. Torrens, James S. *America* 169:18 S 18 1993
The showman. Shaw, Roy. *Tablet* 247:760 Je 1993
Sincerity forever. Weales, Gerald, 1925-. *Comm* 120:21 O 8 1993
Someone who'll watch over me. Pilarz, Scott. *America* 168:17 Ap 3 1993
Someone who'll watch over me. Weales, Gerald, 1925-. *Comm* 120:15-16 Mr 12 1993
The song of Jacob Zulu. Torrens, James S. *America* 168:13 Je 19-26 1993
The song of Jacob Zulu. Weales, Gerald, 1925-. *Comm* 120:19 My 7 1993
Starlight express. Shaw, Roy. *Tablet* 246:1578 D 12 1992
Stories from the nerve Bible. Weales, Gerald, 1925-. *Comm* 120:19-20 Je 4 1993
Sunset Boulevard. Shaw, Roy. *Tablet* 247:1048 Ag 14 1993
Sweeney Todd. Shaw, Roy. *Tablet* 247:793 Je 19 1993
Table number seven. Shaw, Roy. *Tablet* 247:952-953 Jl 24 1993
The taming of the shrew. Shaw, Roy. *Tablet* 247:1080 Ag 21 1993
The taming of the shrew. Shaw, Roy. *Tablet* 247:825 Je 26 1993
Three hotels. Shaw, Roy. *Tablet* 247:1201 S 18 1993
Time of my life. Shaw, Roy. *Tablet* 247:1168-1169 S 11 1993
Translations. Shaw, Roy. *Tablet* 247:825 Je 26 1993
Travels with my aunt. Shaw, Roy. *Tablet* 246:1626 D 19-26 1992
Travesties. Shaw, Roy. *Tablet* 247:1305 O 9 1993
Trelawney of the Wells. Shaw, Roy. *Tablet* 247:20 Ja 2 1993
Trelawney of the Wells. Shaw, Roy. *Tablet* 247:281-282 F 27 1993
Wallenstein. Shaw, Roy. *Tablet* 247:1305-1306 O 9 1993
The Who's Tommy. Miracky, James J. *America* 169:17 O 9 1993
The Who's Tommy. Weales, Gerald, 1925-. *Comm* 120:19 Je 4 1993
Wings. Weales, Gerald, 1925-. *Comm* 120:24 Ap 9 1993
The winter's tale. Shaw, Roy. *Tablet* 247:1048 Ag 14 1993
The years. Torrens, James S. *America* 168:16 F 27 1993
The yellow wallpaper. Weales, Gerald, 1925-. *Comm* 120:16-17 F 12 1993
6221, prophecy and tragedy. Weales, Gerald, 1925-. *Comm* 120:19-20 My 7 1993

DRAMA IN CHRISTIAN EDUCATION
Once upon a miracle: dramas for worship and religious education. Moynahan, Michael E. New York: Paulist Press, 1993. x, 210p ISBN 0-8091-3361-x LC 92-41325

DRAMA IN PUBLIC WORSHIP
Once upon a miracle: dramas for worship and religious education. Moynahan, Michael E. New York: Paulist Press, 1993. x, 210p ISBN 0-8091-3361-x LC 92-41325

DRAWING
Learning to see. Russello, Gerald. *Crisis* 11:54-55 Ja 1993

DREAMS
Death dreams: unveiling mysteries of the unconscious mind. Kramer, Kenneth P. New Jersey: Paulist Press, 1993. x, 288p ISBN 0-8091-3349-0 LC 92-29605
From dream to reality. Paprocki, Joseph. *ReligTJ* 26:41 Ja 1993

DREAMS—RELIGIOUS ASPECTS
Dreams and visions. Bar, Shaul. *BibleT* 31:200-203 Jl 1993
The unconscious Christian: images of God in dreams. Hall, James A. Mahwah, New Jersey: Paulist Press, 1993. x, 113p ISBN 0-8091-3353-9 LC 92-26395

DREWERMANN, EUGEN, 1940-
Fido in heaven? Montgomery, John Warwick, 1931-. *New Oxford Rev* 60:20+ O 1993
God and the unconscious mind: the Eugen Drewermann case. St Leger, Moya Frenz. *Doctr Life* 43:323-332 Jl-Ag 1993

DROUGHTS- AFRICA
Africa: road to faith [photos]. Pipkin, Kate. *St Anth* 100:34-40 S 1993

DRUG-FREE WORKPLACE ACT OF 1988
The Drug-Free Workplace Act of 1988. Tichy, George J, II. *CLawyer* 34 no 4:363-371 1993

DRUG ABUSE
Darryl Colbert kept his promise. Zimmermann, Mark. *CDgst* 57:24-29 Ja 1993
The Drug-Free Workplace Act of 1988. Tichy, George J, II. *CLawyer* 34 no 4:363-371 1993
John Paul II, Pope, (1991-11-23) Allocutiones (Address to a Symposium) [Italian]. John Paul II, Pope, 1920- (Karol Wojtyla) (elected 1978). *AAS* 84:1128-1132 D 5 1992*
Parenting well when the other one won't [condensed fr *Christian Parenting Today* Jl/Ag 1991]. Courtney, Anne. *CDgst* 58:103-106 N 1993
Some sober words about grandpa's drinking [interview by B. Dodds]. Martin, Joseph F. *OSV* 82:6 O 24 1993

DRUG ABUSE—PREVENTION
Legalizing drugs is not the solution. Lynch, Gerald W, and Blotner, Roberta. *America* 168:7-9 F 13 1993

DRUG ABUSE—TREATMENT
Addiction, recovery and God. Mace, Irving B. *Living Prayer* 26:25-26 Ja-F 1993
The drug war is a crime: let's try decriminalization. Riga, Peter John, 1933-. *Comm* 120:6-7 Jl 16 1993
Pastor extraordinary. Gilhooley, James. *Tablet* 247:1063-1064 Ag 21 1993

DRUG ABUSE AND CRIME
The drug war is a crime: let's try decriminalization. Riga, Peter John, 1933-. *Comm* 120:6-7 Jl 16 1993
Legalizing drugs is not the solution. Lynch, Gerald W, and Blotner, Roberta. *America* 168:7-9 F 13 1993

DRUG LEGALIZATION
The drug war is a crime: let's try decriminalization. Riga, Peter John, 1933-. *Comm* 120:6-7 Jl 16 1993

DRUG TRAFFIC
Bolivian farmers open market to show coca is not a drug problem. Chauvin, Lucien. *Nat Cath Rep* 29:15 Mr 26 1993
Colombia's two faces. Linden, Ian. *Tablet* 247:881-882 Jl 10 1993

DRUGS
Autonomy and care for the frail elderly. Szwabo, Peggy, and Stretch, John J. *Health Prog* 74:50-51+ My 1993
Recipe for disaster on Moss Side. *Tablet* 247:87 Ja 16 1993

DRUMGOOLD, KATE
The representationj of religious experience in nineteenth-century American women's autobiography. Norman, Rose. *Listening* 28:128-140 Spr 1993

DUALISM
A feminist critique. Dowell, Susan. *Way Suppl* 77:76-86 Sum 1993

DULLES, AVERY
The birth of a new Catholicism. Martin, Ralph. *New Cov* 22:21+ F 1993

DUMONT, CHARLES
Contemplative action: a review essay on four articles by Charles Dumont. Davis, Thomas X. *Cist Stud* 28 no 2:161-166 1993

DUNS SCOTUS, JOHN, 1266?-1308
Analogy and equivocation in thirteenth-century logic: Aquinas in context. Ashworth, E J. *Med Stud* 54:94-135 1992
Blessed John Duns Scotus: champion of Jesus and Mary. Foley, Leonard. *St Anth* 101:10-16 N 1993
John Paul II, Pope, (1993-03-21) Authentic witnesses of the Gospel. John Paul II, Pope, 1920- (Karol Wojtyla) (elected 1978). *TPS* 38:245-248 Jl-Ag 1993*
Method in ethics: a Scotistic contribution. Shannon, Thomas A. *TheolStds* 54:272-293 Je 1993
A saint in the making. *Tablet* 246:1568 D 12 1992

DUTY
An analysis of the use of rights language in pre-modern Catholic social thought. Brady, Bernard V. *Thomist* 57:97-121 Ja 1993
Deontologism and moral weakness. Peterson, John. *IPQ* 33:173-181 Je 1993

DVORAK, ANTONIN, 1841-1904
On hearing Dvorak's "Stabat Mater". Schall, James Vincent, 1928-. *Crisis* 11:43-45 Ja 1993

DWORKIN, RONALD M, 1931-
New light on the abortion controversy? Montgomery, John Warwick, 1931-. *New Oxford Rev* 60:24-26 S 1993
Why positivism is authoritarian. Dyzenhaus, David. *Amer J Juris* 37:83-112 1992

DYSFUNCTIONAL FAMILIES *see* Problem Families

E

EARLY CHILDHOOD EDUCATION
A new look at preschool and primary classrooms. Bundy, Blakely Fetridge. *Tod Cath Teach* 27:26-29 O 1993
Religion in your early childhood program. Pryor, Bonnie. *Tod Cath Teach* 27:30+ O 1993

EARTH
Paolo Foscarini's Letter to Galileo: the search for proofs of the earth's motion. Kelter, Irving A. *Mod Schlmn* 70:31-44 N 1992

EARTH DAY
Musings on Earth Day near Lake Erie. King, Judine. *Sisters* 65:193-197 My 1993

EARTHQUAKES
Spiritual profit from an Indonesian earthquake. Krosnicki, Thomas A. *America* 168:5-6 F 13 1993

EAST AND WEST
Bridging the divide [editorial]. *Month* 26:128 Ap 1993
East and West as dimensions of the Church. Cosgrove, Francis. *Diakonia* 26 no 1:15-25 1993
Pregare Ad Orientem Versus [editorial]. *Notitiae* 29:245-249 My 1993
Sarvepalli Radhakrishnan and religious pluralism. Minor, Robert N. *StudiaM* 42:307-327 1993

EASTER
Celebrate the golden days!. MacClennan, Carole. *ReligTJ* 27:8 Ap-My 1993
Christ the fireman. Cassidy, Sheila. *Tablet* 247:456+ Ap 10-17 1993
Commitment: reflections on women at a tomb. Smith, Patricia. *Sisters* 65: 132-136 Mr 1993
Compost and the paschal mystery. Gonzalez, Paula. *Tod Parish* 25:18-19 Ap-My 1993
Easter in the early church: an anthology of Jewish and early Christian texts. Cantalamessa, Raniero. Collegeville: The Liturgical, 1993. x, 254p ISBN 0-8146-2164-3 LC 92-43999
Easter took over her face. Hanus, Jerome, Bp. *Sisters* 65:121-125 Mr 1993
John Paul II, Pope, (1992-04-19) Nuntii Televisifici (television message) [Italian]. John Paul II, Pope, 1920- (Karol Wojtyla) (elected 1978). *AAS* 84:985-990 O 3 1992*
The promise of Easter. Wallace, James A, 1944-. *Liguorian* 81:4-7 Ap 1993
Reading the Easter gospels. Swain, Lionel. Collegeville, Minnesota: The Liturgical Press, 1993. 131p ISBN 0-81465-699-4 LC 92-40432

EASTER—BIBLICAL TEACHING
Studying the scriptures. *Liturgy* 10:79-90 Sum 1992

EASTER SEASON
A fifty day celebration? Mick, Lawrence E. *Tod Parish* 25:30-33 Ap-My 1993
Life after Easter. Smith, Pamela. New Jersey: Paulist Press, 1993. x, 88p ISBN 0-8091-3379-2 LC 92-21195
Shaping the celebrations. *Liturgy* 10:91-99 Sum 1992
Studying the scriptures. *Liturgy* 10:79-90 Sum 1992
Il tema della "Luce" nella liturgia della quaresima, della pasqua e del tempo pasquale. Ferraro, Giuseppe. *Civilta* 144:547-558 Mr 20 1993

EASTERN CHURCHES, CATHOLIC
Canones praeliminares codicis. Urrutia, Francisco J. *Periodica* 81 no 2:179-209 1992
Canonical interpretation by recourse to "parallel passages": a comparative study of the Latin and Eastern codes. Abbass, Jobe. *Jurist* 51 no 2:293-310 1991
East and West as dimensions of the Church. Cosgrove, Francis. *Diakonia* 26 no 1:15-25 1993
The Eastern code and the Latin Church. Gallaro, George D. *Can Cath Rev* 11:17-18 O 1993
The liturgical dictionary of Eastern Christianity. Day, Peter D. Collegeville: Liturgical, 1993. x, 334p ISBN 0-8146-5848-2 LC 93-20377
Marriage in the Eastern Code. Gallaro, George D. *Priest* 49:41-47 Ja 1993
Uniatism, method of union of the past and the present search for full cummunion. *Ecumen Trends* 22:3-7 S 1993
De vita consecrata in iure utriusque codicis orientalis et occidentalis. Beyer, Jean. *Periodica* 81 no 2:283-302 1992

EASTERN CHURCHES, CATHOLIC—RELATIONS
Eastern Churches topic of discussion. *OR(Eng)* 1300:7 Jl 21 1993

EASTERN ORTHODOX-ROMAN CATHOLIC CONSULTATION (USA)
US Orthodox/Catholic Consultation. *Ecumen Trends* 22:14 Ja 1993

EATING AND MEALS
The ongoing feast: table fellowship and eschatology. Just, Arthur A., Jr. Collegeville: Liturgical, 1993. x, 307p ISBN 0-8146-6013-4 LC 93-595

EBELING, GERHARD
Ekklesiologische optionen Evangelischer Theologie als Mögliche Leitbilder der Okumene. Wagner, Harald. *Catholica* 47 no 2:124-141 1993

ECCLESIASTICAL COURTS
The sinner against the scoundrels: the ills of doctrine and "schrift" in the Wife of Bath's, Friar's and Summoner's narratives. Kamowski, William. *Relig Lit* 25:1-18 Spr 1993

ECCLESIASTICAL GEOGRAPHY
Congregation for Bishops (1992-02-28) [Decree]. *AAS* 85:212-213 F 3 1993*
Congregation for Bishops (1992-06-29) [Latin]. *AAS* 85:204-205 F 3 1993*
Congregation for Bishops (1992-09-05). *AAS* 85:205-212 F 3 1993*
Congregation for Bishops (1992-09-19). *AAS* 85:213-214 F 3 1993*
Congregation for Bishops (1992-10-31). *AAS* 85:214-215 F 3 1993*
John Paul II, Pope, (1991-03-30) Constitutio Apostolica (Apostolic Constitution) [Latin]. John Paul II, Pope, 1920- (Karol Wojtyla) (elected 1978). *AAS* 84:937-938 O 3 1992*
John Paul II, Pope, (1991-04-29) Constitutiones Apostolicae (Apostolic Constitution) [Latin]. John Paul II, Pope, 1920- (Karol Wojtyla) (elected 1978). *AAS* 85:5-6 Ja 7 1993*
John Paul II, Pope, (1991-07-06) Constitutiones Apostolicae (Apostolic Constitution on Ecclesiastical Territory) [Latin]. John Paul II, Pope, 1920- (Karol Wojtyla) (elected 1978). *AAS* 85:8-9 Ja 7 1993*

John Paul II, Pope, (1991-07-06) Constitutiones Apostolicae (Apostolic Constitution) [Latin]. John Paul II, Pope, 1920- (Karol Wojtyla) (elected 1978). *AAS* 84:1055-1056 N 3 1992*
John Paul II, Pope, (1992-03-30) Constitutio Apostolica (Apostolic Constitution) [Latin]. John Paul II, Pope, 1920- (Karol Wojtyla) (elected 1978). *AAS* 84:826-827 S 8 1992*
John Paul II, Pope, (1992-05-11) Constitutiones Apostolicae (Apostolic Constitution for Ecclesiastical Territory) [Latin]. John Paul II, Pope, 1920- (Karol Wojtyla) (elected 1978). *AAS* 85:6-8 Ja 7 1993*
John Paul II, Pope, (1992-05-16) Constitutio Apostolica (Apostolic Constitution) [Latin]. John Paul II, Pope, 1920- (Karol Wojtyla) (elected 1978). *AAS* 84:938-939 O 3 1992*
John Paul II, Pope, (1992-07-06) Constitutiones Apostolicae (Apostolic Constitution to erect Diocese of Accra) [Latin]. John Paul II, Pope, 1920- (Karol Wojtyla) (elected 1978). *AAS* 85:119-120 F 3 1993*
John Paul II, Pope, (1992-07-06) Constitutiones Apostolicae (Apostolic Constitution to erect Vicariate Apostolic in Philippines) [Latin]. John Paul II, Pope, 1920- (Karol Wojtyla) (elected 1978). *AAS* 85:124 F 3 1993*
John Paul II, Pope, (1992-07-06) Constitutiones Apostolicae (Apostolic Constitution to erect Diocese of Koforidua) [Latin]. John Paul II, Pope, 1920- (Karol Wojtyla) (elected 1978). *AAS* 85:120-121 F 3 1993*
John Paul II, Pope, (1992-07-25) Constitutiones Apostolicae (Apostolic Constitution to erect Diocese of Carora) [Latin]. John Paul II, Pope, 1920- (Karol Wojtyla) (elected 1978). *AAS* 85:122-123 F 3 1993*
John Paul II, Pope, (1992-07-25) Constitutiones Apostolicae (Apostolic Constitution) [Latin]. John Paul II, Pope, 1920- (Karol Wojtyla) (elected 1978). *AAS* 85:1053-1055 N 3 1992*
John Paul II, Pope, (1992-09-21) Litterae Apostolicae (Apostolic Letter to create Apostolic Nuntiature in Mexico) [Latin]. John Paul II, Pope, 1920- (Karol Wojtyla) (elected 1978). *AAS* 85:127 F 3 1993*

ECCLESIASTICAL LAW
Les Chrétiennes, entre leurs devoirs familiaux et le prestige de l'épiskopè. Dibout, Cécile, and Faivre, Alexandre. *Laval Theol Phil* 49:69-92 F 1993
How to relate theology and Canon Law. Orsy, Ladislas, 1921-. *Origins* 22: 549-552 Ja 21 1993

ECCLESIASTICAL LAW—WOMEN
Women's role in Church law: past and present. Huels, John M. *New Theol Rev* 6:19-31 My 1993

ECKHART, MEISTER, 1260?-1327
Bernard of Clairvaux in the thought of Meister Eckhart. Tamburello, Dennis E. *Cist Stud* 28:73-91 1993
Meister Eckhart on justice and true obedience. Demkovich, Michael. *Louvain Stds* 18:131-144 Sum 1993
"Saiser Dieu en son vestiaire" L'articulation théologique du sens chez Maître Eckhart. Malherbe, Jean-François. *Laval Theol Phil* 49:201-213 Je 1993
The way of the void. Murray, Paul. *New Blckfrs* 74:116-130 Mr 1993

ECOFEMINISM—RELIGIOUS ASPECTS
Women, earth, and creator spirit. Johnson, Elizabeth A, 1941-. New York: Paulist Press, 1993. x, 79p ISBN 0-8091-3415-2 LC 92-42018

ECOLOGY
La conferenza mondiale di Rio su ambiente e sviluppo. McCarthy, John. *Civilta* 143:560-577 D 19 1992
A critique of Jürgen Moltmann's green theology. Deane-Drummond, Celia. *New Blckfrs* 73:554-565 N 1992
Declaration of the "Mission to Washington". *Living Light* 29:23-25 Aut 1992
L'écologie à l'école. Gilbert, Laure. *Lumen* 48:79-94 Mr 1993
Has the sun set on Rio? Mcdonagh, Sean. *Tablet* 247:749 Je 1993
Make it a Thanksgiving year!. Gonzalez, Paula. *Tod Parish* 25:36-37 N-D 1993
Out of the greenhouse. Milbank, John. *New Blckfrs* 74:4-14 Ja 1993
Progress, evolution and Green theology. Clatworthy, Jonathan. *Teilhard Rev* 28:8-10 Spr 1993
Saving the earth to save life [condensed fr *Pro Mundi Vita Studies* F 1990]. Sebahire, Mbonvinkebe. *TheolDgst* 38:128-129 Sum 1991
The task before us. Harris, Errol E, 1908-. *Teilhard Rev* 28:19-21 Sum 1993
Teilhard today. Stikker, Allerd. *Teilhard Rev* 28:23-27 Spr 1993
Wirtschaft und Umweltschutz aus ethischer Sicht. Schlitt, Michael. *Stimm Zeit* 210:806-818 D 1992

ECOLOGY—RELIGIOUS ASPECTS
Dare ecology use the word "sin"? Echlin, Edward P, 1930-. *Month* 26:206-210 My 1993
Does mother church care for mother nature? Unsworth, Tim. *Salt* 13:12-15 Ap 1993
Nature and grace. Hanink, James G. *Register* 69:5 Ja 10 1993
Population explosion. Clancy, Paul. *Nat Cath Rep* 29:16-17 My 7 1993
"Speciesism": a challenge to theology. Cronin, Kieran. *Doctr Life* 43:357-362 Jl-Ag 1993
Teilhard and ecological spirituality. Sage, Alan. *Teilhard Rev* 28:11-14 Spr 1993
Toward an ecologically informed theology. Peeters, Denise. *TheolDgst* 40: 113-118 Sum 1993

ECOLOGY- BELGIUM
La prise de conscience "verte" et la question du pouvoir. Janssens, Frederick. *Lumen* 48:67-77 Mr 1993

ECOLOGY- CZECHOSLOVAKIA
Life in a face-mask. Bowlby, Chris. *Tablet* 247:266 F 27 1993

ECOLOGY AND CULTURE
Is "sustainable development" sustainable? Echlin, Edward P, 1930-. *Month* 26:402-407 S-O 1993
Root causes of the environmental crisis. *Origins* 22:692-694 Mr 18 1993
Le sommet de Rio: rhétorique et sagesse. McCarthy, John. *Lumen* 48:23-26 Mr 1993

ECOLOGY AND CULTURE—POLITICS
La prise de conscience "verte" et la question du pouvoir. Janssens, Frederick. *Lumen* 48:67-77 Mr 1993

ECOLOGY AND CULTURE- BELGIUM
Un dossier "Renouvelons la terre" et ses fruits. Piton, Jacques. *Lumen* 48: 95-104 Mr 1993

ECOLOGY AND CULTURE- BRAZIL
O oitavo encontro intereclesial de CEBs e a ecologia. Cechin, Irmão Antônio. *REB* 52:856-876 D 1992

ECONOMIC AND SOCIAL COUNCIL OF THE UNITED NATONS (ECOSOC)
No development exists without development of whole person. *OR(Eng)* 1302: 3 Ag 11 1993

ECONOMIC ASSISTANCE
Russia needs more Western help [editorial]. *Tablet* 247:295 Mr 6 1993

ECONOMIC ASSISTANCE, AMERICAN
American foreign aid is now in the condom biz. Sobo, Elizabeth. *Register* 69: 1+ Je 20 1993
It's time to give U.S. foreign aid to those who need it most [editorial]. *Nat Cath Rep* 29:20 O 1 1993
Who really benefits from foreign aid? Unsworth, Tim. *Salt* 13:12-15 Jl-Ag 1993

ECONOMIC ASSISTANCE, BRITISH
Charities contest freeze in overseas aid. *Tablet* 247:1206 S 18 1993

ECONOMIC DEVELOPMENT
No development exists without development of whole person. *OR(Eng)* 1302: 3 Ag 11 1993
Poverty and development: economics and reality. Thanawala, Kishor. *RSocEcon* 50:258-268 Fall 1992

ECONOMIC DEVELOPMENT—ETHICAL ASPECTS
Widespread unemployment: a call to mobilize. *Origins* 22:786-792 Ap 29 1993

ECONOMIC DEVELOPMENT—RELIGIOUS ASPECTS
Faith and the human enterprise: a post-Vatican II vision. Weakland, Rembert G, Abp, 1927-. Maryknoll: Orbis Books, 1992. 168p ISBN 0-88344-835-1 LC 92-32884
John Paul II, Pope, (1991-10-11) Allocutiones (Papal Exhortation) [French]. John Paul II, Pope, 1920- (Karol Wojtyla) (elected 1978). *AAS* 84:868-870 S 8 1992*
Partners with the poor: an emerging approach to relief and development. Aaker, Jerry. New York: Friendship Press, 1993. x, 158p ISBN 0-377-00252-6 LC 92-35591
The relationship between evangelization and development. Lott, Anastasia. *AFER* 34:66-78 Ap 1992

ECONOMIC DEVELOPMENT- GERMANY
Soziale Marktwirtschaft—was ist das? Stegmann, Franz Josef. *Stimm Zeit* 211:291-302 My 1993

ECONOMIC GEOGRAPHY
Creating a trade bloc that won't block justice, freedom [editorial]. *Nat Cath Rep* 29:24 Ap 16 1993

ECONOMIC POLICY
Is a worldly philosophy still possible?: Adolph Lowe as analyst and visionary. Heilbroner, Robert, 1919-. *RSocEcon* 50:374-382 Wint 1992

ECONOMICS
Beyond the self-regulating market society: a critique of Polanyi's theory of the state. Searcy, Dennis R. *RSocEcon* 51:217-231 Sum 1993
Global budgets: a key to Clinton's reform strategy? White, Jane H. *Health Prog* 74:10-12 Ap 1993
Moses, Jesus, and Marx: utopians in search of justice. Soelle, Dorothee. *CrossCurr* 42:528-535 Wint 1992-1993
One leap forward, one step back. Byrnes, Timothy A. *Comm* 120:29-30 N 19 1993
The quest for a just economy in a new Europe: ethical implications of the social market economy. Manenschijn, Gerrit. *Louvain Stds* 18:159-174 Sum 1993
When the banks went off the rails. Isbell, Harold. *Comm* 120:11-15 F 26 1993

ECONOMICS—COMPARATIVE STUDIES
The historical approach to political economy. Sherman, Howard J. *RSocEcon* 51:302-322 Aut 1993

ECONOMICS—ETHICAL ASPECTS
Keynes and conventions. Lawson, Tony. *RSocEcon* 51:174-200 Sum 1993

ECONOMICS—LANGUAGE
Gender and economic ideologies. Nelson, Julie A. *RSocEcon* 51:287-301 Aut 1993

ECONOMICS—RELIGIOUS ASPECTS
Can the Church reclaim our common conscience? Waters, John. *Furrow* 44: 263-272 My 1993
Episcopal papers speak a bit on economic justice. Hebblethwaite, Peter, 1930-. *Nat Cath Rep* 29:12 Ap 23 1993
Religion and the ambiguities of capitalism. Preston, Ronald H. Cleveland: The Pilgrim Press, 1993. x, 192p ISBN 0-8298-0946-5 LC 92-43014

ECONOMICS—SOCIOLOGICAL ASPECTS
Economy and society at the close of the American century: an introduction. Stanfield, James Ronald. *RSocEcon* 50:366-373 Wint 1992
Is there life beyond efficiency? Elements of a social law and economics. Medema, Steven G. *RSocEcon* 51:138-153 Sum 1993
Poverty and development: economics and reality. Thanawala, Kishor. *RSocEcon* 50:258-268 Fall 1992
A review of the troops: social economics in the twentieth century. Waters, William R. *RSocEcon* 51:262-286 Aut 1993

ECONOMICS- ITALY
Partecipazione e trasparenza nel sóstegno economico alla chiesa. Giachi, Gualberto. *Civilta* 3:147-153 Jl 17 1993

ECONOMICS- UNITED STATES
Orthodox investment vs. government spending: two contrasting models for the 1990s. Vatter, Harold Goodhue, 1910-, and Walker, John F. *RSocEcon* 51:154-173 Sum 1993

ECONOMICS AND CHRISTIANITY
The church and the economy some doctrinal perspectives. Simons, Robert G. *Pacifica* 6:311-326 O 1993
What do we mean by consumerism? Murphy, Séamus. *Doctr Life* 43:294-300 My-Je 1993
Without economic justice, there's no wonderful life. McCormick, Patrick. *USCath* 58:18-19 D 1993

ECONOMICS AND CHRISTIANITY—CONGRESSES
John Paul II, Pope, (1991-10-11) Allocutiones (Papal Exhortation) [French]. John Paul II, Pope, 1920- (Karol Wojtyla) (elected 1978). *AAS* 84:868-870 S 8 1992*

ECONOMICS AND RELIGION
Catholic social doctrine and new thinking in economics. Goulet, Denis. *CrossCurr* 42:504-520 Wint 1992-1993
Contemplative businessperson. McNair, J Frank. *Living Prayer* 26:27-28 Ja-F 1993
The economics of religious faith. Lapin, Daniel. *Crisis* 11:12-13 Je 1993

ECONOMICS AND RELIGION- BRAZIL
Podem Passar A Sacolinha. Oro, Ari Pedro. *REB* 53:301-323 Je 1993

ECONOMICS AND RELIGION- ITALY
Un Bilancio del sostentamento economico alla Chiesa Cattolica in Italia. Brunetta, Giuseppe. *Civilta* 3:263-270 Ag 7-21 1993

ECONOMICS AND RELIGION- LATIN AMERICA
El mundo como mercado significado y juicio. Trigo, Pedro. *Christus* 58:25-31 N-D 1992

ECONOMICS TEACHERS- UNITED STATES
American women and the professionalization of economics. Hammond, Claire H. *RSocEcon* 51:347-370 Aut 1993

ECONOMISTS
Is a worldly philosophy still possible?: Adolph Lowe as analyst and visionary. Heilbroner, Robert, 1919-. *RSocEcon* 50:374-382 Wint 1992

ECONOMISTS—WOMEN
American women and the professionalization of economics. Hammond, Claire H. *RSocEcon* 51:347-370 Aut 1993

ECONOMISTS- ENGLAND—1900-
Keynes and conventions. Lawson, Tony. *RSocEcon* 51:174-200 Sum 1993

ECONOMY (THEOLOGY)
The principle of economy a corrective of Christian mercy. Maloney, George A, 1924-. *Diakonia* 26 no 2:119-133 1993

ECUMENICAL MOVEMENT
All together now. *Tablet* 247:717 Je 5 1993
Battlefront ecumenism. Reynolds, Gerry, and Burch, Sam. *Priests & People* 7:14-17 Ja 1993
Catechesis and the relationship of evangelization to ecumenism. Cermak, John. *Living Light* 29:64-68 Wint 1992
Christian unity: no deadline, but a boost in Spain. Lefevere, Patricia. *Nat Cath Rep* 29:13 Ag 27 1993
Church and society: an ecumenical approach. Falconer, Alan D. *Doctr Life* 42:614-618 D 1992
The Church as communio. Kasper, Walter. *New Blckfrs* 74:232-244 My 1993
"The church as communion": an Anglican response. Hill, Christopher. *OChr* 28 no 4:323-330 1992
Church unity rooted in Eucharist. *OR(Eng)* 1298:4+ Jl 7 1993*
The Church—local and Catholic: a Lutheran perspective. Gassmann, Günther. *Jurist* 52 no 1:518-524 1992
Common prayer: an ecumenical bridge. Murdick, Olin J. *Ecumen Trends* 22: 3-6 My 1993
Concepts of division and unity in the ecumenical movement. Tesfai, Yacob. *Ecumen Trends* 22:9-15 Mr 1993
The cutting edge: how churches speak on social and ethical issues. Ellingsen, Mark. Grand Rapids: Eerdmans, 1993. 400p ISBN 0-8028-0710-0
Difficult days for Christian unity [editorial]. *Tablet* 247:63-64 Ja 16 1993
Directory for the application of the principles and norms of ecumenism. *OR(Eng)* 1295:I-XIV Je 16 1993
The ecumenical commitment to human rights. Littell, Franklin H., 1917-. *JEcumen Stds* 29:383-398 Sum-Aut 1992
Ecumenical or interfaith? Kessler, Diane C. *Living Light* 30:89-92 Aut 1993
Ecumenism and evangelization in Christus, Lumen Gentium. Falardeau, Ernest R, 1928-. *Emmanuel* 99:197-200 My 1993
Ecumenism, spirituality, and the dark night of the soul. Crow, Paula A. *OChr* 29 no 2:100-112 1993
The eve of Pentecost. *Liturgy* 10:111-114 Sum 1992
Faith and Order pilgrims. Clements, Keith. *Tablet* 247:1113-1114 Ag 28 1993
The Fifth World Conference and walls of the heart. FitzGerald, Kyriaki Antonia. *Ecumen Trends* 22:1+ Ap 1993
Globalization, pluralism, and ecumenics: the old question of Catholicity in a new cultural horizon. Burrows, Mark Stephen. *JEcumen Stds* 29:346-367 Sum-Aut 1992
"God unites—in Christ a new creation". Tanner, Mary. *OChr* 28 no 4:300-306 1992
A house divided: what future for American Catholics? D'Souza, Dinesh, 1961-. *Crisis* 10:19-22 D 1992
How can we recognize "substantial agreement"? *Origins* 23:41-45 Je 3 1993
John Paul II, Pope, (1992-02-22) Itinera Apostolica (Address to Muslims of Senegal on Apostolic Journey) [French]. John Paul II, Pope, 1920- (Karol Wojtyla) (elected 1978). *AAS* 85:161-165 F 3 1993*
Das Katholische Verständis von Evangelisierung, Konfession und Ökumene. Modesto, Johannes. *Catholica* 47:52-75 1993
"Kenosis": the door to Christian unity. Orsy, Ladislas, 1921-. *Origins* 23:38-41 Je 3 1993
Koinonia ecclesiology—ecumenical breakthrough? Vandervelde, George. *OChr* 29 no 2:126-142 1993
Koinonia ecclesiology: a response [reply to G. Vandervelde, pp 126-142]. Wingenbach, Gregory C. *OChr* 29 no 2:143-148 1993
A new church in a changing world: Christ the cornerstone, Milton Keynes, England. Farrell, Maureen. *OChr* 29 no 2:170-175 1993
One bread, one cup [exc fr *Liturgy*: putting on Christ; *Liturgy*: covenant with the world]. Stookey, Laurence Hull. *Liturgy* 10:4-6 Spr 1993
Opportunities and challenges offered by BEM to the British and Irish churches. Davey, Colin. *OChr* 29 no 3:216-225 1993
Our common calling [exc fr *Liturgy*: Practicing Ecumenism]. Bilheimer, Robert S. *Liturgy* 10:2-3 Spr 1993
Der päpstliche rat zur Förderung der Einheit der Christen im Jahre 1992. Cassidy, Edward Idris, 1924-, Cardinal. *Catholica* 47 no 2:89-107 1993
Parish diary: April. *Tablet* 247:509 Ap 24 1993
A pastor's vision [interview by G O'Connell]. Martini, Carlo Maria, Cardinal, 1926-. *Tablet* 247:876-878 Jl 10 1993

A pastoral priority. Falardeau, Ernest R, 1928-. *Priest* 49:49-50 Ap 1993

The Pontifical Council for Promoting Christian Unity in 1992. Cassidy, Edward Idris, Cardinal, 1924-. *OChr* 29 no 3:199-215 1993

A practical guide to community ministry. Bos, A David. Louisville, Kentucky: John Knox Press, 1993. 112p ISBN 0-694-25405-5

Present state of Anglican-Roman Catholic relations: an assessment. Rausch, Thomas P. *OChr* 29 no 2:118-125 1993

Priest plows, sows ardously in ecumenical field. Jones, Arthur C, 1936-. *Nat Cath Rep* 29:9-10 Ap 2 1993

Protestants are upbeat about impact of encyclical. Gibeau, Dawn. *Nat Cath Rep* 30:12 O 22 1993*

The reception and non-reception of Montreal's call to renewal [speech] to the North American Academy of Ecumenists, S 27 1992. Meyer, Lauree Hersch. *Ecumen Trends* 21:1+ D 1992

Reception—communion. Tillard, Jean Marie Roger, 1927-. *OChr* 28 no 4:307-322 1992

Religious wars and religious peace. McCarthy, Abigail Quigley. *Comm* 120:6-7 Mr 12 1993

Report from the fifth World Conference on Faith and Order. Kinnamon, Michael. *Ecumen Trends* 22:1+ O 1993

Reserving the sacrament in a shared church. Lewis, Marilyn. *OChr* 29 no 2:176-184 1993

Roman Catholic bishops of Britain set guidelines for Anglican converts. Solheim, James. *Ecumen Trends* 22:16 My 1993

The Roman primacy within the Communion of Churches: French Joint RC-Orthodox Committee. *OChr* 29 no 2:156-164 1993

The search for common ground. Bole, William. *OSV* 81:3 Ja 17 1993

Sharing the message. *Liturgy* 10:100-101 Sum 1992

Singing the Lord's song in a strange land: the African-American churches and ecumenism. Watley, William D. Grand Rapids: Eerdmans, 1993. 188p ISBN 0-8028-0711-9

Some responses to attack article. Weiss, Daniel E, et al. *Ecumen Trends* 22:7-8 Mr 1993

The state of the ecumenical movement. Rusch, William G. *Ecumen Trends* 22:3-6 Jl-Ag 1993

Das Studiendokument Kirche und Welt. Scheele, Paul-Werner. *Catholica* 47 no 2:108-123 1993

Taking differences seriously [exc fr *Liturgy: practicing ecumenism*]. White, Susan J. *Liturgy* 10:7 Spr 1993

The time has come: a vision for the Fifth World Conference on Faith and Order [fr *The Ecumenical review*]. Tanner, Mary. *Cath Int* 4:239-244 My 1993

Toward Christian reunity. Holton, Robert. *OSV* 81:6-7 Ja 24 1993

Toward communion in faith, life and witness. Davis, Kortright. *Ecumen Trends* 22:1-2+ Jl-Ag 1993

"Towards koinonia in faith, life and witness": faith and order's Dublin text, April 1992. *OChr* 28 no 4:357-386 1992

Towards koinonia/communion in faith, life and witness: revised discussion paper for the Fifth World Conference on Faith and Order. Tanner, Mary, et al. *Ecumen Trends* 22:1-24 Je 1993

Twelve tales untold: a story guide for ecumenical reception. Ford, John T, and Swan, Darlis J, eds. Grand Rapids: Eerdmans, 1993. 176p ISBN 0-8028-0553-1

The vision of authentic ecumenism: a Catholic response. Majawa, Clement. *AFER* 35:91-100 Ap 1993

Week of prayer for Christian unity. Kriewald, Diedra. *Liturgy* 11:34-37 Sum 1993

Which way for ecumenism? [editorial]. *Tablet* 247:1091 Ag 28 1993

The work of ARC-USA: reflections post-factum. Tavard, George Henry. *OChr* 29 no 3:247-259 1993

100 years of global inter-faith dialogue: 1893-1993. D'Arcymay, John. *Doctr Life* 43:141-146 Mr 1993

ECUMENICAL MOVEMENT—BIBLIOGRAPHY
A bibliographical review of books on spirituality in the Buddhist-Christian dialogue. Mitchell, Donald W. *Stud Form Spir* 14:139-143 F 1993

ECUMENICAL MOVEMENT—CONGRESSES
Ecumenists move from statements to spadework. *Tablet* 247:960 Jl 24 1993

ECUMENICAL MOVEMENT—DOCUMENTS
Koinonia: text and context for the church. Fuchs, Lorelei F. *Ecumen Trends* 22:1-2+ F 1993

New ecumenical directory published. *Tablet* 247:762 Je 1993

Principles and norms of ecumenism. Cassidy, Edward Idris, Cardinal, 1924-. *TPS* 38:321 N-D 1993

The 1993 directory for ecumenism. *Origins* 23:129+ Jl 29 1993

ECUMENICAL MOVEMENT- AFRICA
Secular ecumenicity: a challenge to the Church in Africa. Kasenene, Peter. *AFER* 34:44-59 F 1992

ECUMENICAL MOVEMENT- BRAZIL
CEBs e ecumenismo: uma discussão a partir da dimensão ecumênica do oitavo intereclesial. Oliveira Ribeiro, Claudio de. *REB* 52:846-855 D 1992

ECUMENICAL MOVEMENT- GERMANY
Das Ökumenismusdekret des Konzils. Suttner, Ernst Chr. *Stimm Zeit* 211:303-317 My 1993

Standesamt—Ehe—Kirche. Demel, Sabine. *Stimm Zeit* 211:131-140 F 1993

ECUMENICAL MOVEMENT- GREAT BRITAIN
Oliver Stratford Tomkins, 1908-1992 [address, St. Margaret's Church, London, Ja 21 1993]. *OChr* 29 no 2:93-99 1993

ECUMENICAL MOVEMENT- ITALY
John Paul II, Pope, (1992-01-16) Allocutiones (Papal Address to Italian Bishops) [Italian]. John Paul II, Pope, 1920- (Karol Wojtyla) (elected 1978). *AAS* 85:130-135 F 3 1993*

ECUMENISTS—BIOGRAPHY
Augustin Bea, the Cardinal of unity. Schmidt, Stephen A. New Rochelle, New York: New City Press, 1992. 806p ISBN 1-56548-016-3 LC 92-17612

EDELMAN, MARK
Dialogue [interview by J Luxmoore]. Edelman, Mark. *Register* 69:1+ Je 20 1993

EDMIGIO, BROTHER
John Paul II, Pope, (1993-10-10) Brother Edmigio. John Paul II, Pope, 1920- (Karol Wojtyla) (elected 1978). *OR(Eng)* 1311:1 O 13 1993*

Two Spanish Bishops and seven Christian Brothers gave their lives for Catholic faith. *OR(Eng)* 1311:1 O 13 1993

EDMUND CAMPION, SAINT, 1540-1581
A view of Oxfordshire and St Edmund Campion. Vincent, Francis T. *America* 168:4-5 Ap 24 1993

EDUCATION
Beyond autonomy toward community. Bellah, Robert Neely, 1927-. *Mod Lit* 20:12-16 Mr 1993

Educating for the third millennium [editorial]. McNamee, Catherine. *Momentum* 24:2+ F-Mr 1993

Leaving the children at "Mom's house". Barnard, Ann M. *ST Anth* 101:22-27 Jl 1993

Look out, kids [New York City Rainbows curriculum]. Feuerherd, Peter. *Register* 69:1+ Ja 3 1993

Only cohere [editorial]. *Comm* 120:3-4 Ap 9 1993

Technology and the education renaissance. Milone, Michael. *Tod Cath Teach* 26:14-16+ Mr 1993

EDUCATION—CURRICULA
Educational standards and public policy. McGovern, John E. *Momentum* 24:47 S-O 1993

Rethinking the saber-tooth curriculum [editorial]. *Momentum* 24:4 F-Mr 1993

A victory for parents: New York City's neighborhoods revolt. Marlin, George J. *Crisis* 11:15-20 F 1993

EDUCATION—DATA PROCESSING
Is this software any good? How to tell. Coburn, Janet. *Tod Cath Teach* 27:40-42 Ag 1993

Tips for computerizing your writing program. McGrath, Carol Rito. *Tod Cath Teach* 27:15-16 S 1993

EDUCATION—ETHICAL ASPECTS
Is character education a responsibility of the public schools?: no. Skillen, James W. *Momentum* 24:49+ N-D 1993

Is character education a responsibility of the public schools?: yes. Lickona, Thomas. *Momentum* 24:48+ N-D 1993

EDUCATION—FINANCE
Schools at the crossroads. Walsh, Michael J, 1937-. *Tablet* 247:226 F 13 1993

EDUCATION—LAW AND LEGISLATION
The higher law background of the Notre Dame law school. Kmiec, Douglas W. *Amer J Juris* 37:213-242 1992

EDUCATION—METHODS
Corps et culture. Csepregi, Gabor. *Laval Theol Phil* 49:121-129 F 1993

Discipline: more goals than rules. Svoboda, Melannie. *ReligTJ* 27:4-6 O 1993

Expect great things—and get them. Gargiulo, Barbara. *ReligTJ* 27:7 O 1993

Our parade of saints. Cann, Lorraine, and Quinette, Nancy. *ReligTJ* 27:12-13 O 1993

EDUCATION—PARENT PARTICIPATION
Comunidades de base schools. Ozar, Lorraine A. *Momentum* 24:38-40 F-Mr 1993

Count on Mom: but do it yourself. Byrne, Katharine. *Comm* 120:9-10 Ap 9 1993

EDUCATION—PARENTAL INVOLVEMENT
Get parents involved. Roberto, John. *ReligTJ* 27:26-27 Mr 1993

EDUCATION—PHILOSOPHY
At the top of the class. Walsh, Michael J, 1937-. *Tablet* 247:994-995 Jl 31 1993

Corps et culture. Csepregi, Gabor. *Laval Theol Phil* 49:121-129 F 1993

Newman on the secular need for religious education. Walsh, David. *F & R* 28:359-385 Wint 1992

EDUCATION—STUDY
In search of a new direction in education. Riley, Richard W. *Momentum* 24:9-11 N-D 1993

Psicología y pedagogía de la edad evolutiva según Santo Tomás. Manzanedo, Marcos. *Cien Tom* 119:351-389 My-Ag 1992

EDUCATION- GERMANY
Schule—Bildung—Christlicher Glaube. Ritter, Werner H. *Stimm Zeit* 211:413-421 Je 1993

EDUCATION- RUSSIA
Teaching the nativity. Rich, Vera. *Tablet* 247:27 Ja 2 1993

EDUCATION, CLASSICAL
Study Greek and Latin! Reflections of a housewife. Rist, Anna. *Can Cath Rev* 11:12-15 Ja 1993

EDUCATION, ELEMENTARY
Don't let the learning stop!. Hintz, Walter. *Momentum* 24:46-48 F-Mr 1993

Soaring into the 21st century. Burke, John Francis. *Momentum* 24:40-42 N-D 1993

EDUCATION, HIGHER
Catholic higher education: what happened? Woodward, Kenneth L. *Comm* 120:13-16+ Ap 9 1993

Choosing a college. McCloskey, C. John, III. *Crisis* 11:42-44 O 1993

Do women learn differently from men? Hizer, Gloria. *OSV* 82:6-7 Ag 29 1993

Education a diverse river wide enough for all swimmers [editorial]. *Nat Cath Rep* 30:28 O 29 1993

Flawed jewel in the crown. Pring, Richard. *Tablet* 247:72 Ja 16 1993

Gladly to learn and gladly to teach: why Christians invented the university. Fortin, Ernest L, 1923-. *Crisis* 11:33-38 Ap 1993

Making the best of a bad job? Newman Chaplains between the code and the council. Evans, John Whitney. *US Cath Hist* 11:35-50 Wint 1993

A modest proposal for a class reunion. Davis, Robert Murray, 1934-. *America* 168:5 My 29 1993

National service entangled [editorial]. *America* 169:3-4 Jl 3-10 1993

On teaching. Schall, James Vincent, 1928-. *Crisis* 11:49-50 S 1993

Religion and values: noble lies? Roof, Wade Clark, 1939-. *Critic* 47:35-45 Spr 1993

Second-hand straw. McInerny, Ralph M. *Crisis* 11:15-17 My 1993

A taste for the other: the moral development of college students and young adults. Heft, James L. *Living Light* 29:23-36 Spr 1993

EDUCATION, HIGHER—HISTORY- LATIN AMERICA
Primeras fundaciones de colegios y universidades. Luque Alcaide, Elisa. *Seminarium* 32:404-419 Jl-S 1992

EDUCATION, HIGHER- GREAT BRITAIN
Desperate remedies for education [editorial]. *Tablet* 247:1091 Ag 28 1993
University challenge. Nuttgens, Patrick, 1930-. *Tablet* 247:783-784 Je 19 1993

EDUCATION, HIGHER- LATIN AMERICA
La universidad Ignaciana hoy en America Latina. Mora Lomelí, Raúl H. *Christus* 57:43-51 S 1992

EDUCATION, HUMANISTIC
Catholic higher education: what happened? Woodward, Kenneth L. *Comm* 120:13-16+ Ap 9 1993

EDUCATION, PRESCHOOL
For every child: a head start. Edelman, Marian Wright. *Momentum* 24:37-39 N-D 1993
Preschool playgrounds. Rittner-Heir, Robbin M. *Tod Cath Teach* 27:26-29 O 1993
Preschools bring private schools success. Coburn, Janet. *Tod Cath Teach* 26:17-18+ My-Je 1993

EDUCATION, SECONDARY- IRELAND
Teenagers and religion—reflections on the green paper. Clayton-Lea, Paul. *Furrow* 44:479-484 S 1993

EDUCATION AND CHURCH
John Paul II, Pope, (1991-11-23) Allocutiones (Address to Catholic educators) [Italian]. John Paul II, Pope, 1920- (Karol Wojtyla) (elected 1978). *AAS* 84:1132-1138 D 5 1992*
John Paul II, Pope, (1991-11-23) Allocutiones (Address to Catholic educators) [Italian]. John Paul II, Pope, 1920- (Karol Wojtyla) (elected 1978). *AAS* 84:1132-1138 D 5 1992*

EDUCATION AND CHURCH- ITALY
I docenti dell'Università Cattolica si interrogano. Brovedani, Ennio. *Civilta* 144:340-353 F 20 1993

EDUCATION AND CHURCH- LATIN AMERICA
De seminariis, universitatibus atque scholis Catholicis in America Latina a prima evangelizatione usque ad novam. Laghi, Pio, Cardianl, ed. *Seminarium* 32:369-473 Jl-S 1992*

EDUCATION AND STATE
Mangel an Erziehung? Bleistein, Roman, 1928-. *Stimm Zeit* 211:1-2 Ja 1993

EDUCATION AND STATE- GREAT BRITAIN
All power to the centre. Pring, Richard. *Tablet* 247:201 F 13 1993

EDUCATION FOR PARISH SERVICE PROGRAM
Toward service to the church. Leonhardy, Lee. *OSV* 81:6-7 F 7 1993

EDUCATION IN THE HOME
Home-schooling works. Podles, Mary Elizabeth. *Crisis* 11:27-32 Ap 1993
A profile of US home-schooling families. Morgan, Anne Marie. *Crisis* 11:29 Ap 1993
Tap your heels together three times and repeat after me: there's no place like home. Ristow, Kate. *Catechist* 27:30-33; 29-31 N-D O 1993

EDUCATION OF CHILDREN
Children first, before and after birth. Casey, Robert P, 1932-. *Origins* 22:696-699 Mr 18 1993

EDUCATIONAL CHANGE
Corps et culture. Csepregi, Gabor. *Laval Theol Phil* 49:121-129 F 1993

EDUCATIONAL LAW- GREAT BRITAIN
Controversy over sex education laws. *Tablet* 247:992 Jl 31 1993
Flawed blueprint. Pring, Richard. *Tablet* 247:1062 Ag 21 1993
A man for this season. McLaughlin, T H. *Tablet* 247:198-200 F 13 1993
Schools at the crossroads. Walsh, Michael J, 1937-. *Tablet* 247:226 F 13 1993

EDUCATIONAL LAW- IRELAND
The Green Paper, the Church and the Constitution. Farry, Michael J. *Studies* 82:160-170 Sum 1993

EDUCATIONAL LAW- NORTHERN IRELAND
Fundamentalism by law. Green, Arthur. *Tablet* 247:204-205 F 13 1993

EDUCATIONAL LAW- UNITED STATES
Educational standards and public policy. McGovern, John E. *Momentum* 24:47 S-O 1993
Parental choice in education. McDermott, Edwin J. *America* 169:4-6 O 16 1993

EDUCATIONAL TESTS AND MEASUREMENTS- GREAT BRITAIN
A test too far. Pring, Richard. *Tablet* 247:647 My 22 1993

EDUCATIONAL VOUCHERS
Activist fights for school choice. Mullen, Peter. *Register* 69:1+ S 19 1993
Breaking a monopoly. Ferguson, Lisa. *Register* 69:3 My 9 1993
California gets to vote on school vouchers. Dodds, Bill. *OSV* 82:17 Jl 18 1993
Catholic educators adjust goals. Mullen, Peter. *Register* 69:1+ Mr 14 1993
Choice for America's poor. Roggeveen, Dirk G. *Momentum* 24:26-28 N-D 1993
Educational choice: getting there from here. Quade, Quentin L. *Momentum* 24:19-20 N-D 1993
The growing complexities of school choice. Blackburn, Thomas E. *Nat Cath Rep* 29:25 F 19 1993
A hit on mediocrity [editorial]. *Register* 69:4 O 31 1993
Making parental choice happen. O'Malley, Charles J. *Tod Cath Teach* 26:16-19 F 1993
School choice. Ciotti, Paul. *Register* 69:1+ O 31 1993
School-vouchers forces bowed, but unbeaten. Leary, Mary Ellen. *Nat Cath Rep* 30:6 N 12 1993
Silent money: political persuasion and public policy. McGovern, John E. *Momentum* 24:21-25 N-D 1993
Voters still not vouching for school choice. Dodds, Bill. *OSV* 82:21 N 21 1993
Why school choice is losing [editorial]. *OSV* 82:2 N 21 1993

EDWARD I, KING OF ENGLAND
Aelred, historian: two portraits in Plantagenet myth. Dutton, Marsha L. *Cist Stud* 28 no 2:113-144 1993

EDWARDS, JONATHAN, 1745-1801
Delightful conviction: Jonathan Edwards and the rhetoric of conversion. Yarbrough, Stephen R, and Adams, John C. Westport: Greenwood Press, 1993. x, 208p ISBN 0-313-27582-3
Jonathan Edwards' twelfth sign. Raposa, Michael L. *IPQ* 33:153-162 Je 1993

EFFICIENT MARKET THEORY
Is there life beyond efficiency? Elements of a social law and economics. Medema, Steven G. *RSocEcon* 51:138-153 Sum 1993

EGYPT—CHURCH HISTORY
The word in the desert: scripture and the quest for holiness in early Christian monasticism. Burton-Christie, Douglas. New York: Oxford University Press, 1993. 336p ISBN 0-19-506614-6 LC 91-4150

EGYPT—RELIGION
Egypt's Muslim Brothers. Butt, Gerald. *Tablet* 246:1559-1560 D 12 1992

EICHER, PETER
Habermas e la teologia. Brena, Gian Luigi. *Civilta* 3:51-54 Jl 3 1993

EL ABED, HAMED
John Paul II, Pope, (1992-01-09) Allocutiones (Welcome address to new ambassador from Tunisia) [French]. John Paul II, Pope, 1920- (Karol Wojtyla) (elected 1978). *AAS* 85:52-54 Ja 7 1993*

EL SALVADOR
In El Salvador, two convictions and many questions. Dodds, Bill. *OSV* 81:21 Mr 7 1993

EL SALVADOR—ARMED FORCES
Telling the truth in El Salvador. Hussey, Pamela. *Month* 26:267-271 Jl 1993

EL SALVADOR—CIVIL WAR
Life after death in El Salvador [interview D.S. Toolan]. Guiliano, John. *America* 169:12-14 D 4 1993

EL SALVADOR—FOREIGN RELATIONS
Un rapporto internazionale su El Salvador. Rulli, Giovanni. *Civilta* 2:395-403 My 15 1993

EL SALVADOR—POLITICS AND GOVERNMENT
A birthday party and the Jesuit case. Torrens, James S. *America* 168:3-4 My 15 1993
Hunt begins for stolen children. *Tablet* 247:590-591 My 8 1993
John Paul II, Pope, (1993-06-27) Rome [Orig Italian]. John Paul II, Pope, 1920- (Karol Wojtyla) (elected 1978). *OR(Eng)* 1297:1 Je 30 1993*
Military may strike after Truth Commission report. *Tablet* 247:347 Mr 13 1993
El Mozote: a test of the process of reconciliation in El Salvador. Brown, Michael. *New Theol Rev* 6:74-80 Ag 1993
Peace talks in El Salvador [excerpt fr *Martires de El Salvador*]. *LADOC* 23:24-28 Jl-Ag 1993
Salvador archbishop attacks amnesty deal. Palumbo, Gene. *Nat Cath Rep* 29:8 Ap 2 1993
Salvador nightmare demands further reckoning [editorial]. *Nat Cath Rep* 29:36 Mr 26 1993
Salvadoran reactions to truth report vary. Palumbo, Gene. *Nat Cath Rep* 29:11 Mr 26 1993
Telling the truth in El Salvador. Hussey, Pamela. *Month* 26:267-271 Jl 1993
Truth and its consequences [editorial]. *Comm* 120:4-5 Ap 23 1993
Truth commission points the finger at the armed forces. *Tablet* 247:380 Mr 20 1993
Truth or consequences in El Salvador. *America* 168:3-4 Ap 3 1993
U.S. must use influence for peace in El Salvador [editorial]. *Nat Cath Rep* 30:24 N 19 1993
United States accused of cover-up. *Tablet* 247:413 Mr 27 1993
Virtual coup feared as army make TV broadcast. *Tablet* 247:443 Ap 3 1993

EL SALVADOR—SOCIAL CONDITIONS
Life after death in El Salvador [interview D.S. Toolan]. Guiliano, John. *America* 169:12-14 D 4 1993
El Salvador [photos]. MacEoin, Gary. *Nat Cath Rep* 29:8-9 S 3 1993

ELDERS, JOYCELYN
Correspondence released: abortion and the nominee surgeon general. Keeler, William H, Abp. *Origins* 23:229-230 S 9 1993

ELECTIONS- AFRICA
Africa's new wind of change [editorial]. *Tablet* 247:1059 Ag 21 1993
False democratic dawn. Dowden, Richard. *Tablet* 247:1030 Ag 14 1993

ELECTIONS- CAMBODIA
Keeping faith with Cambodia's voters [editorial]. *Tablet* 247:675 My 29 1993

ELECTIONS- FRANCE
Sacking the Socialists. Woodrow, Alain. *Tablet* 247:395-396 Mr 27 1993

ELECTIONS- GREAT BRITAIN
Britain's angry voters. Alton, David. *Tablet* 247:604-605 My 15 1993

ELECTIONS- MALAWI
Churches hail vote for democracy. Rawlins, Rachel. *Tablet* 247:828-829 Je 26 1993

ELECTIONS- NEW YORK
Alliance for regress [editorial]. *Comm* 120:3-4 My 21 1993

ELECTIONS- POLAND
Showdown in Poland. Luxmoore, Jonathan. *Tablet* 247:1190-1191 S 18 1993

ELECTIONS- UNITED STATES
Clinton's new political geography: renewing the language of equality [adapted fr *The election of 1992: reports and interpretations*]. McWilliams, Wilson Carey, 1933-. *Comm* 120:14-18 Ap 23 1993
The Congress in transition: act II, scene I. Sullivan, George R. *America* 168:6-8 Ja 2-9 1993
Election night in the neighborhood. Marlin, George J. *Crisis* 10:2-3 D 1992
Skepticism softens: can Americans love politics again? Dionne, E J, Jr. *Comm* 120:5-7 Ja 15 1993

ELECTRONIC DATA INTERCHANGE
The ABCs of electronic data interchange. Hoyler, Geraldine M. *Health Prog* 74:13 O 1993

ELIJAH, THE PROPHET
Elijah. Martin, George. *Liguorian* 81:52-53 Je 1993

ELIOT, THOMAS STEARNS, 1888-1965
Lancelot Andrewes and T S Eliot: the making of histories. Timmerman, John H. *ABenR* 44:76-98 Mr 1993
T.S. Eliot and mysticism: a discussion. Williams, Rowan. *Doctr Life* 43:396-401 S 1993

ELIZABETH II, QUEEN OF ENGLAND, 1926-
Diplomatic uses of a cup of tea [editorial]. *Tablet* 247:707 Je 5 1993

In the heartland, Catholic sexuality celebrated [commentary Humanae Vitae]. Carey, Ann. *OSV* 82:3 Ag 15 1993*

Inside the commission. Marshall, John. *Tablet* 247:938-939 Jl 24 1993

No bar to entry. Longley, Clifford. *Tablet* 247:1058 Ag 21 1993

Pastors in a china shop. Hebblethwaite, Peter, 1930-. *Tablet* 247:1159-1160 S 11 1993

Paul VI did more than ban the pill. Costello, Gerald M, 1931-. *USCath* 58: 48-51 O 1993

Populate or perish. Oddie, William. *Crisis* 11:16-17 O 1993

A prophetic document. Daily, Thomas V, Bp., 1927-. *Columbia* 73:6-8 Ag 1993*

Reconsidering Humanae Vitae [commentary *Humanae Vitae*]. Balsam, Charles. *Register* 69:5 Ag 1 1993

Sexual morality's positive goals and the problem of legalism. George, Robert P. *Origins* 22:778-780 Ap 22 1993

Sexualerziehung zwischen Norm und Individualisierung. Bleistein, Roman, 1928-. *Stimm Zeit* 211:521-532 Ag 1993

A stumbling-block for many [editorial]. *Tablet* 247:935 Jl 24 1993

We might all be better off if Paul VI had said nothing (commentary: *Humanae Vitae*). Blackburn, Thomas E. *Nat Cath Rep* 29:17 Jl 16 1993*

A word on Humanae vitae [fr *New Ilucidations* tr by M T Skerry]. Balthasar, Hans Urs Von, 1905-1988. *Communio* 20:437-450 Sum 1993

Wrestling still: twenty-five years and counting. Jordan, Patrick. *Comm* 120: 4-5 Jl 16 1993

ENCYCLICALS, PAPAL—HUMANI GENERIS
École Saint-Thomas. Steenberghen, Fernand Van. *RPhil Louvain* 91:1-4 F 1993

ENCYCLICALS, PAPAL—PASTORES DABO VOBIS
Il celibato sacerdotale al sinodo Dei Vescovi 1990 (Commentary) *Pastores Dabo Vobis*. Caprile, Giovanni. *Civilta* 143:488-501 D 5 1992

Commentaria in ADH Apost Pastores dabo vobis/I. Laghi, Pio, Cardinal, ed. *Seminarium* 32:505-636 O-D 1992*

John Paul II, Pope, (1992-03-25) Pastores Daba Vobis Aspetti Psicologici Nella Formazione al celibato Sacerdotale. John Paul II, Pope, 1920- (Karol Wojtyla) (elected 1978). *Civilta* 3:359-379 S 4 1993*

ENCYCLICALS, PAPAL—REDEMPTORIS MATER
All generations will call her blessed (commentary: *Redemptoris mater*). Collins, Mary Smalara. *USCath* 58:37-40 My 1993*

ENCYCLICALS, PAPAL—REDEMPTORIS MISSIO
Mission before mission: God's mission within us [commentary *Redemptoris Missio*]. Dominic, A Paul. *RRel* 52:119-130 Ja-F 1993*

ENCYCLICALS, PAPAL—RERUM NOVARUM
The American Catholic and Chicago response to Rerum Novarum [commentary *Rerum Novarum*]. Zielinski, Martin. *Chicago Stud* 31:142-153 Ag 1992

Katholische Gesellschaftslehre im Überlick. Kerber, Walter, 1926-, et al, eds. Frankfurt: Knecht, 1993. x, 420p ISBN 3-7820-0623-2

ENCYCLICALS, PAPAL—VERITATIS SPLENDOR
Document begts many legitimate moral questions. McCormick, Richard Arthur, 1922-. *Nat Cath Rep* 29:17 O 15 1993*

Encyclical gets final touches. Burke, Greg. *Register* 69:1+ Je 11 1993

Encyclical not intended to back up Humanae Vitae, says Cardinal. *Tablet* 247:1309 O 9 1993

[Four men taught me moral theology]. Komonchak, Joseph Andrew, 1939-. *Comm* 120:12 O 22 1993

[John Paul II, invoking his authority]. Doyle, Dennis M. *Comm* 120:12-14 O 22 1993

John Paul II, Pope, (1993-10-15) Reflections. John Paul II, Pope, 1920- (Karol Wojtyla) (elected 1978). *Origins* 23:360-362 O 28 1993*

John Paul II, Pope, (19930-10-05) Veritatis Splendor. John Paul II, Pope, 1920- (Karol Wojtyla) (elected 1978). *OR(Eng)* 1310:1 O 6 1993*

[The lasting contribution of Veritatis splendor]. Cahill, Lisa Sowle. *Comm* 120:15-16 O 22 1993

[Many who do not profess]. Smith, Janet E. *Comm* 120:14-15 O 22 1993

The new encyclical [editorial]. *America* 169:3 O 23 1993

Perspectives on "Veritatis Splendor". Quinn, John Raphael, Abp, 1929-. *Origins* 23:398-399 N 11 1993*

The Pope rides out to battle [editorial]. *Tablet* 247:1283 O 9 1993*

The Pope's letter on "the decisive theme of the present day". *Tablet* 247: 1307 O 9 1993

Timeless ethics. Hebblethwaite, Peter, 1930-. *Tablet* 247:1286-1288 O 9 1993*

Veritatis Splendor and moral theology. McCormick, Richard Arthur, 1922-. *America* 169:8-11 O 30 1993*

[Veritatis splendor belongs to the literary gender]. Curran, Charles E, 1934-. *Comm* 120:14 O 22 1993

[Veritatis splendor is unique]. Hauerwas, Stanley Martin, 1940-. *Comm* 120: 16-18 O 22 1993

Veritatis splendor [editorial]. *Comm* 120:3-5 O 22 1993

[Whatever terror may strike the hearts]. Cunningham, Lawrence S, 1935-. *Comm* 120:11-12 O 22 1993

ENCYCLOPEDIAS AND DICTIONARIES
Un valido strumento di lavoro. Rulli, Giovanni. *Civilta* 2:57-60 Ap 3 1993

END OF THE WORLD
The rise and fall of the United States. Farrall, Harold J. New York: Vantage Press, 1992. x, 175p ISBN 0-533-10224-3 LC 92-93307

1944. Camping, Harold. New York: Vantage Press, 1992. x, 551p ISBN 0-533-10368-1 LC 92-90269

ENDS AND MEANS—PHILOSOPHY
Is a worldly philosophy still possible?: Adolph Lowe as analyst and visionary. Heilbroner, Robert, 1919-. *RSocEcon* 50:374-382 Wint 1992

What is included in a means to an end? Flannery, Kevin L. *Gregorianum* 74 no 3:499-513 1993

ENERGY—WOMEN
Sexuality: creation's wildcard—sexual energy and feminine creativity. Dwyer, Margretta. *Sisters* 65:276-279 Jl 1993

ENERGY CONSERVATION
Energy use: where to begin. Gonzalez, Paula. *Tod Parish* 25:22 Mr 1993

Let ther be (green) light!. Gonzalez, Paula. *Tod Parish* 25:32-33 S 1993

ENERGY POLICY
Study, act, vote. Gonzalez, Paula. *Tod Parish* 25:10-11 Ja 1993

ENERGY POLICY- IRELAND
Fuelwood: a crisis in the making. Porter, Neil. *Studies* 82:287-297 Aut 1993

ENGELHARDT, TRISTRAM H, JR
Chi E Persona? Persona umana e bioetica. *Civilta* 143:547-559 D 19 1992

Weltethos oder säkularer Humanismus? Fuchs, Josef. *Stimm Zeit* 211:147-154 Mr 1993

ENGLAND, JOHN, BP
Synod convoked for Charleston Diocese. Thompson, David, Bp. *Origins* 22: 509+ Ja 7 1993

ENGLISH LANGUAGE—COMPUTER-ASSISTED INSTRUCTION
Tips for computerizing your writing program. McGrath, Carol Rito. *Tod Cath Teach* 27:15-16 S 1993

ENGLISH LANGUAGE—EARLY MODERN, 1500-1700—FOREIGN ELEMENTS
What englishness is. Every, George. *New Blckfrs* 74:408-416 S 1993

ENGLISH LANGUAGE—GENDER
American roadblock: why Rome refused a politically correct translation. *Crisis* 11:35-36 Je 1993

A conversation with scripture scholar Myles M Bourke [interview by T H Stahel, 1938-]. Bourke, Myles M. *America* 168:4-9 Ap 17 1993

Freezing the fire: the death of relational language. Montague, George T. *America* 168:5-7 Mr 13 1993

Let's go to the text: the Gospel without sex. Schroth, Raymond A, 1933-. *Comm* 120:6-7 Ag 13 1993

On "Englishing" the Catechism. Clark, Douglas Kent. *Living Light* 29:13-28 Sum 1993

Something fundamental is afoot. Johnson, Luke Timothy, 1943-. *Comm* 120: 17-22 Ja 29 1993

Splitting the faithful: inclusive language is wrong biblically, pastorally, and doctrinally. Sokolwski, Robert, 1934-. *Crisis* 11:24-27 Mr 1993

Stormy weather. Hitchcock, Helen Hull. *Crisis* 11:8-9 Jl-Ag 1993

A theological case for God-She expanding the treasury of metaphor. Johnson, Elizabeth A, 1941-. *Comm* 120:9-14 Ja 29 1993

Trouble with the catechism. *Tablet* 247:206 F 13 1993

Voices of wrath: when words become weapons. Mankowski, Paul V. *Crisis* 10:22-25 D 1992

ENGLISH LANGUAGE—RHETORIC
Connecting with "the real world". Anderson, Peggy. *Momentum* 24:26-27 F-Mr 1993

ENGLISH LITERATURE—STUDY
Teaching narrative prose. Taubitz, Ronald. *Tod Cath Teach* 27:34+ S 1993

ENGLISH LITERATURE—1700-1799
The quotable Johnson. Danckert, Stephen C. San Francisco: Ignatius Press, 1992. x, 148p ISBN 0-89870-415-5 LC 92-71942

ENGLISH LITERATURE—1900-
"As a bee produces honey": William Golding's achievement. Rice, Judith. *Month* 26:382-386 S-O 1993

William Golding (1911-93): lord of horror, lord of awe. Feeney, Joseph J. *America* 169:6-7 Jl 31-Ag 7 1993

William Golding's vision. Bergonzi, Bernard, 1929-. *Tablet* 247:815 Je 26 1993

ENGLISH POETRY
The rustic muse. *Tablet* 247:916 Jl 17 1993

ENLIGHTENMENT
Feminist theology: a proposal. Martin, Francis. *Communio* 20:334-376 Sum 1993

ENNEAGRAM
Enneagram companions: growing in relationships and spiritual direction. Zuercher, Suzanne. Notre Dame: Ave Maria Press, 1993. 181p ISBN 0-87793-510-6 LC 93-71263

ENOMIZA-LASSALLE, HUGO M
Authority (1): the role of the teacher in Buddhist/Christian formation. Hawk, Patrick. *Stud Form Spir* 14:23-29 F 1993

ENTHUSIASM
Dynamic disciples? Hogan, William Francis, 1930-. *Emmanual* 49:374-377+ S 1993

ENVIRONMENTAL ETHICS
"A culture is dying": the timber crisis. Murphy, Thomas Austin, 1911-. *Origins* 22:765+ Ap 22 1993

L'écologie à l'école. Gilbert, Laure. *Lumen* 48:79-94 Mr 1993

Environmental degradation and social injustice. Malone, James, Bp. *Origins* 22:685+ Mr 18 1993

Environmental ethics: preaching or teaching? McCullough, E J. *Can Cath Rev* 11:16-18 Ja 1993

Impaled upon the horns of faith and reason. Howard, George S. *America* 168:12-15 Mr 6 1993

Nature and grace. Hanink, James G. *Register* 69:5 Ja 10 1993

Religion and science: collaboration for the environment. Dalton, Anne Marie. *Living Light* 29:14-22 Aut 1992

Wirtschaft und Umweltschutz aus ethischer Sicht. Schlitt, Michael. *Stimm Zeit* 210:806-818 D 1992

ENVIRONMENTAL POLICY
La conferenza mondiale di Rio su ambiente e sviluppo. McCarthy, John. *Civilta* 143:560-577 D 19 1992

"A culture is dying": the timber crisis. Murphy, Thomas Austin, 1911-. *Origins* 22:765+ Ap 22 1993

Declaration of the "Mission to Washington". *Living Light* 29:23-25 Aut 1992

Environmental degradation and social injustice. Malone, James, Bp. *Origins* 22:685+ Mr 18 1993

John Paul II, (1993-10-22) Rich and poor [Orig in English]. John Paul II, Pope, 1920- (Karol Wojtyla) (elected 1978). *Origins* 23:383-384 N 4 1993*

NGOs' role grows in global environmental diplomacy. Collins, Carole. *Nat Cath Rep* 29:11 Jl 2 1993

Separating fact and fiction. Krause, Edward. *Register* 69:5 Ja 3 1993

Study, act, vote. Gonzalez, Paula. *Tod Parish* 25:10-11 Ja 1993

ENVIRONMENTAL POLICY- ASIA
Root causes of the environmental crisis. *Origins* 22:692-694 Mr 18 1993

The function of the principle of double effect. Keenan, James F. *TheolStds* 54:294-315 Je 1993

Global responsibility: in search of a new world ethic. Kung, Hans, 1928-. New York: Crossroad, 1991. x, 158p ISBN 0-8245-1102-6 LC 91-7956

Globalization and the autonomy of moral reasoning: an essay in fundamental moral theology. Kopfensteiner, Thomas R. *TheolStds* 54:485-511 S 1993

In the end, one thing matters. Hanink, James G. *Register* 69:5 O 31 1993

The incommunicability of human persons [fr *Essay on personal selfhood*]. Crosby, John F, III. *Thomist* 57:403-442 Jl 1993

John Paul II, Pope, (1993-05-08) Faith and science are gifts of God. John Paul II, Pope, 1920- (Karol Wojtyla) (elected 1978). *TPS* 38:295-300 S-O 1993*

Joseph Fletcher: memoir of an ex-radical: reminiscence and reappraisal. Fletcher, Joseph. Louisville: John Knox, 1993. x, 96p ISBN 0-664-25372-5

Légèreté ou gravité de la chair. Lacroix, Xavier. *Supplement* 184:175-191 Mr-Ap 1993

Learning the virtue of justice. Keenan, James F. *Church* 9:38-40 Aut 1993

Malum Vitandum: the role of intentions in first-order morality. Sullivan, Thomas D, and Atkinson, Gary. *IJPS* 1:99-110 Mr 1993

Method in ethics: a Scotistic contribution. Shannon, Thomas A. *TheolStds* 54:272-293 Je 1993

El mite de l'expulsio des paradis o els auguris de l'home boig: cartes a l'academia. Dala Pujolras, Joaquim. Barcelona: Edicions, 1993. x, 222p ISBN 84-297-3609-3

The moral baseline. Habgood, John Stapylton, Abp, 1927-. *Tablet* 247:464 Ap 10-17 1993

Moral fundamental en el nuevo catecismo. Vidal, Marciano. *Christus* 58:42-50 Je 1993

A nation examining its conscience [editorial]. *Tablet* 247:363 F 27 1993

The Notre Dame Law School Commencement Address—three natural law challenges for Notre Dame lawyers. Kmiec, Douglas W. *Amer J Juris* 37:359-361 1992

O sole mia the first Nixon prize. Carlin, David Robert, Jr, 1938-. *Comm* 120:9-10 Je 18 1993

On Sakharov and Rorty. Ratzinger, Joseph, Cardinal, 1927-. *Crisis* 11:36-38 My 1993

Prospects for a common morality. Outka, Gene, and Reeder, John P, Jr, eds. Princeton, New Jersey: Princeton University Press, 1993. x, 302p ISBN 0-69107-418-6 LC 92-5681

Reflections on after virtue after Auschwitz. Chansky, James D. *PhilosTod* 37:247-256 Aut 1993

Religious leaders endorse "new global ethic". Rodenbaugh, Dana. *Nat Cath Rep* 29:3 S 17 1993

Ricoeur's ethics of method. Abel, Olivier. *PhilosTod* 37:23-30 Spr 1993

El rostre de l'altre: passeig filosoficper l'obra d'Emmanuel Levinas. Antich, Xavier. Valencia: Edicions 314, 1993. x, 149p ISBN 84-7502-374-6

De Sade and his progeny. Aeschliman, M D. *Crisis* 11:54-55 S 1993

The self as an other [review artical *Oneselfas Another* by C Reagan]. Reagan, Charles E. *PhilosTod* 37:3-22 Spr 1993

Sexual morality from a social perspective. Sunshine, Edward R. *Chicago Stud* 31:301-315 N 1992

Statement on Boston's clergy sexual misconduct policy. Law, Bernard Francis, Cardinal, 1931-. *Origins* 22:582-583 F 4 1993

Theology, praxis, and ethics in the thought of Juan Luis Segundo, SJ. Zimbelman, Joel. *Thomist* 57:233-267 Ap 1993

Timeless ethics. Hebblethwaite, Peter, 1930-. *Tablet* 247:1286-1288 O 9 1993*

Towards a Jewish-Christian alliance [interview by R Lakind]. Haberman, Joshua A. *Crisis* 11:32-38 F 1993

Truly dishonest. McConnell, Frank, 1942-. *Comm* 120:14-16 Ja 29 1993

Trying to make sense [editorial]. *Month* 26:86-87 Mr 1993

[*Veritatis splendor* is unique]. Hauerwas, Stanley Martin, 1940-. *Comm* 120:16-18 O 22 1993

Weltethos oder säkularer Humanismus? Fuchs, Josef. *Stimm Zeit* 211:147-154 Mr 1993

What do I have to do? Barnes, Michael R. *Month* 26:(I) F 1993

What's your worst moral argument? Keenan, James F. *America* 169:17-18+ O 2 1993

Wirtschaftsethik. Mack, Elke. *Stimm Zeit* 211:713-716 O 1993

World religions seek a global ethic. *Tablet* 247:1172 S 11 1993

ETHICS—CONGRESSES
Tierpatente im Kreuzfeuer der Kritik. Münk, Hans J. *Stimm Zeit* 211:605-616 S 1993

ETHICS—HISTORY
The hastening that waits. Biggar, Nigel. New York: Oxford University Press, 1993. x, 208p ISBN 0-826457-7

ETHICS—STUDY
The Barna report, volume 3, 1993-94: absolute confusion. Beacon, George. Ventura: Regal Books, 1993. x, 309p ISBN 0-8307-1641-6

ETHICS- COLOMBIA
Recherche éthique dans un contexte de violence. Roux, Francisco J de. *Lumen* 48:293-303 S 1993

ETHICS, CHRISTIAN
Les Chrétiennes, entre leurs devoirs familiaux et le prestige de l'épiskopè. Dibout, Cécile, and Faivre, Alexandre. *Laval Theol Phil* 49:69-92 F 1993

Christian ethics: a historical introduction. Wogaman, J Philip. Louisville: John Knox, 1993. x, 352p ISBN 0-664-25163-3

The Church and morality: an ecumenical and Catholic approach. Curran, Charles E, 1934-. Minneapolis: Fortress Press, 1993. 126p ISBN 0-8006-2756-3 LC 92-47448

Fullness of faith: the public significance of theology. Himes, Michael J, and Himes, Kenneth R. New York: Paulist Press, 1993. x, 213p ISBN 0-8091-3372-5 LC 92-36140

Goodness and rightness: Thomas Aquinas' Summa Theologia. Keenan, James F. Washington, D C: Georgetown University Press, 1992. x, 212p ISBN 0-87840-530-5 LC 92-3090

Interactional morality: a foundation for moral discernment in Catholic pastoral ministry. Poorman, Mark L. Washington: Georgetown University Press, 1993. 157p ISBN 0-87840-536-4 LC 93-3803

Is society controllable? Fowler, Thomas B. *F & R* 28:387-413 Wint 1992

Let's be totally honest. Mallowe, Mike. *USCath* 58:20-25 Je 1993

Looking for moral guidance: dilemma and the Bible. Fischer, James A. New York: Paulist Press, 1992. x, 152p ISBN 0-8091-3170-6 LC 92-35933

La moral como madurez de la persona—Evocando la figura de Antonio Sanchís, OP. Espeja, Jesús. *Cien Tom* 119:391-405 My-Ag 1992

Optio praecipua pauperum: de ecclesiali pro pauperibus optione tamquam theonomae moralitatis criterio. Pastor, Felix-Alejandro. *Periodica* 81 no 2:319-346 1992

The question of Christian ethics. McInerny, Ralph M. Washington, D C: Catholic University of America Press, 1990. x, 74p ISBN 0-81320-770-3 LC 92-25511

Unterwegs zur interkulturellen Demokratie. Lesch, Walter. *Stimm Zeit* 211:255-269 Ap 1993

The way of the Lord Jesus, volume two, living a Christian life. Grisez, Germain Gabriel, 1929-. Quincy, Illinois: Franciscan Press, 1993. x, 950p ISBN 0-8199-0961-0 LC 83-10508

ETHICS, JEWISH
Eros and the Jews: from biblical Israel to contemporary America. Biale, David. New York: Basic Books, 1992. 319p ISBN 0-4650-2033-x

Judaism's sexual revolution: why Judaism rejected homosexuality [fr *Ultimate Issues*]. Prager, Dennis. *Crisis* 11:29-34+ S 1993

ETHICS, RELIGIOUS
A faith perspective on ethical dilemmas: Good decisions and tough choices. Lowry, Douglas. *New Cov* 22:15-16 My 1993

Parliament of World Religions' global ethic. *Nat Cath Rep* 29:11-14 S 24 1993

Pouvoir de la singularité: le pathos du visage dans le texte d'Emmanuel Lévinas. Saint-Germain, Christian. *Laval Theol Phil* 49:27-35 F 1993

Religious America—threat or blessing? Lapin, Daniel. *Crisis* 11:12-13 My 1993

ETHICS AND LAW see Law and Ethics

ETHICS AND RELIGION
Die befragte Generation. Belistein, Roman. *Stimm Zeit* 211:232-240 Ap 1993

Ethical self-direction. Fuchs, Josef. *TheolDgst* 39:343-347 Wint 1992

The teleology of law: responsible citizenship and discipleship. Araujo, Robert J. *CLawyer* 35 no 1:57-78 1993

ETHICS AND RELIGION- LATIN AMERICA
O Mercosul e a integração Latino-Americana. Neutzling, Inácio. *REB* 53:374-389 Je 1993

Promoção dos Valores éticos: (PRonunciamento da 31a Assembléia Geral da CNBB, Itaici, SP). Casaldáliga, Pedro, Bp, 1928-. *REB* 53:390-396 Je 1993

ETHIOPIA—RELIGION
Alleluia, Hosanna, and Amen. Haynes, A W. *Can Cath Rev* 11:31-33 My 1993

Awasa. Haynes, A W. *Can Cath Rev* 11:31-33 Ap 1993

ETHNIC RELATIONS- BOSNIA AND HERZEGOVINA
Put an end to "ethnic cleansing". *OR(Eng)* 1305:2 S 1 1993

ETHNIC RELATIONS- GERMANY
Identität und Integration. Friedmann, Friedrich Georg. *Stimm Zeit* 211:270-278 Ap 1993

EUCHARIST
Alberic of Monte Cassino. Sitzmann, Marion. *Priest* 49:34-36 Jl 1993

At the heart of the Eucharist. Tetlow, Joseph Allen. *RRel* 52:735-740 S-O 1993

Battling for the Body of Christ. Luka, Ronald, 1937-. *Mod Lit* 20:13 S 1993

A blend of old and new. Connors, Daniel. *ReligTJ* 27:17 S 1993

Bread and wine for the Eucharist: are they negotiable? Silva, Jose' Antunes da. *AFER* 34:258-271 O 1992

Bringing the priceless gift of the Eucharist. Dodds, Bill. *New Cov* 22:16-18 Ja 1993

Brownson's early christology. Griffioen, Arie J. *ABenR* 44:58-75 Mr 1993

La célébration du mystère chrétien. Gervais, Pierre. *NRT* 115:498-515 Jl-Ag 1993

Can we revive the prayer of the church? Dean, Stephen. *Priests & People* 7:107-113 Mr 1993

A catequese e as CEBs. Cansi, Bernardo. *REB* 52:894-902 D 1992

Celebrazione eucaristica e vita cristiana. Galot, Jean. *Civilta* 2:535-547 Je 19 1993

The centrality of the Eucharist. Mangan, Charles M. *Register* 69:5 Je 20 1993

Christus Lumen Gentium: the Eucharist and evangelization [4 sections]. Vallejo, Carlos Armijo, Abp. *Emmanuel* 99:64-71+ Mr; 138-144 Ap; 190-195+ My; 244-249+ Je 1993

Church, Eucharist and mission. McCormack, William J, Bp., 1924-. *Emmanuel* 99:424-427 O 1993

Committed worship: a sacramental theology for converting Christians, v 2. Gelpi, Donald L, 1934-. Minnesota: The Liturgical Press, 1993. x, 312p ISBN 0-8146-5826-1 LC 92-40430

Communion ministers as proclaimers. Madigan, Shawn. *Liturgy* 11:71-72 Sum 1993

La concélébration Repères Théologiques pour une PRatique Renouvelée. *Notitiae* 29:187-243 Ap 1993

Controversy continues over church renovations. Carey, Ann. *OSV* 82:17 Ag 8 1993

Creation and liturgy. McMichael, Ralph N, Jr, ed. Washington: The Pastoral Press, 1993. 320p ISBN 1-562929-001-6

Deforming the liturgy. Tombes, Jonathan, and Tucker, Jeffrey. *Crisis* 10:20-24 N 1992

"Do this in memory of me". McCarthy, Patricia. *Emmanuel* 99:309-313+ Jl-Ag 1993

Do's and don'ts for eucharistic ministers. Smith, Karen Sue. *Church* 9:38-40 Spr 1993

Ecumenism and evangelization in Christus, Lumen Gentium. Falardeau, Ernest R, 1928-. *Emmanuel* 99:197-200 My 1993

The Eucharist and African culture. Okoye, Chukwuma J. *AFER* 34:272-292 O 1992

Eucharist and blessing. Thurian, Max. *SIDIC* 26 no 1:19-20 1993

Eucharist and christology revisited: the Body of Christ. Collins, Mary Smalara. *TheolDgst* 39:321-332 Wint 1992

The Eucharist and the mission of the priest. Schineller, Peter. *Emmanual* 49:364-369 S 1993

The Eucharist as memory. Freburger, William J. *Priest* 49:28 Je 1993

The Eucharist fount of our joy. Buono, Anthony M. *Emmanuel* 99:146-149 Ap 1993

Eucharist of the assembly. Huck, Gabe. *Church* 9:7-11 Spr 1993

The Eucharist, our sanctification. Cantalamessa, Raniero. Minnesota: The Order of St Benedict, 1993. x, 89p ISBN 0-8146-2075-2 LC 92-404-433

The Eucharist, sacrament at the transformation of the world. LaVerdiere, Eugene Armand, 1936-. *Emmanual* 49:378-385 S 1993

The Eucharist: a holy and living sacrifice. Falardeau, Ernest R, 1928-. *Emmanuel* 98:142-146 Ap 1992

Eucharist: celebrating its rhythms in our lives. Bernier, Paul. Indiana: Ave Maria Press, 1993. 160p ISBN 0-87793-506-8 LC 92-75342

Eucharist: meal or sacrifice? Bernier, Paul. *Emmanuel* 98:64-69+ Mr 1992; 98:136-141+ Ap 1992

The Eucharistic mystery: revitalizing the tradition. Power, David Noel. New York: The Crossroad Publishing Company, 1992. x, 370p ISBN 0-8245-1220-0 LC 92-29777

The eucharistic theologies of Lauda sion and Thomas Aquinas's Summa theologiae. Bell, Thomas J. *Thomist* 57:163-185 Ap 1993

An evangelical who discovered the real presence [interview by B Dodds]. Shea, Mark P. *OSV* 82:7 Je 27 1993

Five ways to put out the welcome mat at mass. Ventline, Lawrence M. *Emmanuel* 99:8-11 Ja-F 1993

Giving thanks. Smith, B F. *Crisis* 10:45-46 N 1992

He is really present. McBride, Alfred. *OSV* 82:9 N 14 1993

Herbert and the Real Presence. Young, Robert V. *Renascence* 45:179-195 Spr 1993

In service of communion: a Trinitarian foundation for Christian ministry. Gaillardetz, Richard R. *Worship* 67:418-433 S 1993

Ein katholischer Vorschlag zur Eucharistiegemeinschaft. Neuner, Peter. *Stimm Zeit* 211:443-450 Jl 1993

'Let the little children'. Ellsberg, Peggy R. *America* 168:16 Mr 13 1993

'Let us offer each other the sign of peace'—an enquiry. Woolfenden, Graham. *Worship* 67:239-252 My 1993

Let's go back to an open-door policy for our churches. Gannon, Mary-Grace. *OSV* 82:6 Ag 15 1993

Lettera ai vescovi della chiesa cattolica su alcuni aspetti della chiesa intesa come comunione. Congregation for Doctrine of the Faith. *Notitiae* 28:464-471 Jl 1992

Liturgy and life: ten things I learned about the Mass. Richstatter, Thomas, 1939-. *Catechist* 27:42-47 N-D 1993

Liturgy: life-blood of a parish. Clarke, Pauline. *Priests & People* 7:91-93 Mr 1993

The local church and the church Catholic: the contemporary theological problematic. Komonchak, Joseph Andrew, 1939-. *Jurist* 52 no 1:416-447 1992

Local church/regional church: systematic reflections. Antón, Angel. *Jurist* 52 no 1:553-576 1992

The local churches and catholicity: an orthodox perspective. Erickson, John H. *Jurist* 52 no 1:490-508 1992

The Lord's Supper: towards an ecumenical understanding of the Eucharist. Larere, Philippe. Collegeville: Liturgical, 1993. x, 94p ISBN 0-8146-2226-7 LC 98-010816

Lucan reflections on aging. Jegen, Carol Frances. *BibleT* 30:335-340 N 1992

Making one family out of strangers: re-imagining the Catholic church. Jones, Alan. *Pacifica* 6:249-264 O 1993

Mass confusion [editorial]. *OSV* 81:2 Mr 7 1993

The Mass explained [condensed fr *Eucharistic Minister* S 1992]. McHugh, Joseph F. *CDgst* 57:51-54 F 1993

The Mass explained: part four [condensed fr *Eucharistic Minister* D 1992]. McHugh, Joseph F. *CDgst* 57:47-54 My 1993

The Mass explained: part three [condensed fr *Eucharistic Minister* N 1992]. Mchugh, Joseph F. *CDgst* 57:65-70 Ap 1993

The mass explained: part two [condensed fr *Eucharistic Minister* O 1992]. McHugh, Joseph F. *CDgst* 57:83-87 Mr 1993

Masses with children. Goehring, Raymond. *Priest* 49:45-47 Jl 1993

Medieval Eucharist theology. Cummings, Owen F. *Emmanuel* 99:72-79 Mr 1993

Myths and truths about the Eucharist. Beards, Andrew. *HPR* 93:18-26 Ag-S 1993

One bread, one cup [exc fr *Liturgy: putting on Christ; Liturgy: covenant with the world*]. Stookey, Laurence Hull. *Liturgy* 10:4-6 Spr 1993

One inner city parish community. Tomalak, Ann. *Priests & People* 7:138-144 Ap 1993

The original 'love feast'. Ball, Ann. *OSV* 81:8-9 Mr 7 1993

Orthopraxis in the sacramental initiation of unbaptized children of catechetical age: a canonical perspective. Hesch, John B. *Worship* 67:214-225 My 1993

Le Parole Eucaristiche di Gesù. Galot, Jean. *Civilta* 2:16-18 Ap 3 1993

A pelican on the altar. Ulmer, Mari W. *Sisters* 65:290-292 Jl 1993

Personale und sakramentale Gegenwart des Herrn in der Eucharistie. Hintzen, Georg. *Catholica* 47 no 3:210-237 1993

Prayer before the Eucharist. Camiré, Bernard. *Emmanuel* 99:184-189 My 1993

Pregare Ad Orientem Versus [editorial]. *Notitiae* 29:245-249 My 1993

The preparatory rites: a case study in liturgical ecology. Foley, Edward, et al. *Worship* 67:17-38 Ja 1993

Preparing the assembly for liturgy. Duggan, Robert D. *Church* 9:36-37 Sum 1993

Repertoire and ritual: the communion rite and the eucharistic prayer. Ciferni, Andrew D, and McMahon, J Michael. *Past Mus* 17:22-27 F-Mr 1993

Reservation of the Blessed Sacrament. Frankovich, Lawrence. *Priest* 49:18-22 S 1993

Restoring the sweetness: the liturgical agenda. Collins, Seán. *Doctr Life* 43:130-140 Mr 1993

The sacraments are meant to celebrate inclusion. Austing, Mary Pat, and Blessing, Marge. *Catechist* 26:22-24 Ja 1993

Second thoughts on concelebration. Cosgrave, William. *Furrow* 44:236-239 Ap 1993

The shape of things to come in liturgy. Hanshell, Deryck. *SacM* 119:15-18 Wint 1992

Sixth-graders host Mass for parents. Mueller, M. Jane. *Catechist* 27:34 O 1993

The spiritual life of the priest. McGovern, Thomas. *HPR* 94:6-15 O 1993

The spirituality of the eucharistic prayer. Miller, Charles E. *Priest* 49:13-18 Ja 1993

A taste of home. Dodds, Bill. *New Cov* 23:32 N 1993

The theme and spirit of the Seville congress. Vallejo, Carlos Armijo, Abp. *Emmanuel* 99:250-254 Je 1993

Through your goodness we have these gift to offer. Gustin, Marilyn Norquist. *Liguorian* 81:28-32 Jl 1993

A timely whack on the head. Field, James A. *Tod Parish* 25:27-29; 31-33 O 13-17 S 1993

Towards a eucharistic evangelization. Schindler, David L. *Communio* 19:549-575 Wint 1992

Untangling the Latin Mass controversy. Carey, Ann. *OSV* 81:12-13 Mr 7 1993

Vinum cui modica aqua miscenda est. Pujol, C. *Periodica* 81 no 2:303-318 1992

We believe in God. Grubb, Geoffrey J. *ReligTJ* 27:18-19 S 1993

What about music as ministry? Brokish, Evelyn. *Past Mus* 17:58-60 Ag-S 1993

Whiter the mass? Mole, John W. *HPR* 93:46-52 Jl 1993

You are invited—with love!. Poppenhagen, Donna. *Catechist* 27:34-35 N-D 1993

EUCHARIST—CONTROVERSIES- UNITED STATES

Handing on the tradition: a Catholic mother laments. Baumer, Patricia Hughes. *New Theol Rev* 6:32-54 My 1993

EUCHARIST—CULTUS

Christus Lumen Gentium: the Eucharist and evangelization [4 sections]. Vallejo, Carlos Armijo, Abp. *Emmanuel* 99:64-71+ Mr; 138-144 Ap; 190-195+ My; 244-249+ Je 1993

John Paul II, Pope, (1993-06-13) International Eucharistic Congress [Orig in Spanish]. John Paul II, Pope, 1920- (Karol Wojtyla) (elected 1978). *OR(Eng)* 1296:6 Je 23 1993*

Ein katholischer Vorschlag zur Eucharistiegemeinschaft. Neuner, Peter. *Stimm Zeit* 211:443-450 Jl 1993

EUCHARIST—ELEMENTS

Communion under both kinds. Magee, Brian. *Furrow* 44:364-368 Je 1993

EUCHARIST—FIRST COMMUNION

A simple sign of service. Perkins, Barbara. *ReligTJ* 27:14 F 1993

EUCHARIST—PAPAL TEACHING

John Paul II, Pope, (1993-05-12) Priests act in the Person of Christ. John Paul II, Pope, 1920- (Karol Wojtyla) (elected 1978). *TPS* 38:304-307 S-O 1993*

John Paul II, Pope, (1993-06-12) Eucharist [Orig in Spanish]. John Paul II, Pope, 1920- (Karol Wojtyla) (elected 1978). *OR(Eng)* 1296:5 Je 23 1993*

Ein katholischer Vorschlag zur Eucharistiegemeinschaft. Neuner, Peter. *Stimm Zeit* 211:443-450 Jl 1993

EUCHARIST—RESERVATION (CANON LAW)

Reservation of the Eucharist in a religious house. Musiol, Jozef. *AFER* 34:115-121 Ap 1992

EUCHARISTIC CONGRESSES

History of eucharistic congresses. McKeon, Thomas. *Emmanuel* 99:288-290 Je 1993

John Paul II, Pope, (1993-06-16) Visit to Spain. John Paul II, Pope, 1920- (Karol Wojtyla) (elected 1978). *OR(Eng)* 1295:1+ Je 16 1993*

EUCHARISTIC PRAYERS

Conducting eucharistic prayer. Schueller, Anthony. *Emmanuel* 99:399-342 Jl-Ag 1993

Institution narratives at the crossroads. Klein, Terrance W. *Worship* 67:407-418 S 1993

John Paul II, Pope, (1993-06-12) God present among us [Orig in Spanish]. John Paul II, Pope, 1920- (Karol Wojtyla) (elected 1978). *OR(Eng)* 1296:4 Je 23 1993*

EUGENICS

Cloning baby. Meehan, Bridget Mary. *Register* 69:1+ N 14 1993

Discredited by Nazis, eugenics quietly lives on. Meehan, Bridget Mary. *Register* 69:1+ Ap 25 1993

Eugenics: abortion's precursor. Meehan, Bridget Mary. *Register* 69:1+ My 16 1993

Eugenics: still alive and well. Meehan, Bridget Mary. *Register* 69:1+ Ag 8 1993

'Genetics' is another word for eugenics. Meehan, Bridget Mary. *Register* 69:1+ Je 6 1993

IPPF links to eugenics uncovered. Meehan, Bridget Mary. *Register* 69:1 Mr 14 1993

Since the '60s, eugenics makes steady progress. Meehan, Bridget Mary. *Register* 69:1+ Mr 28 1993

Value variables in the health-care reform debate. McCormick, Richard Arthur, 1922-. *America* 168:7-13 My 29 1993

EUNUCHS—BIBLICAL TEACHINGS

The Ethiopian eunuch and his bible: a social-science analysis. Spencer, F Scott. *Bib Th Bul* 22:155-165 Wint 1992

EUROPE—CHURCH HISTORY

Dissent and order in the Middle Ages: the search for legitimate authority. Russell, Jeffrey Burton. New York: Twayne Publishers, 1992. x, 128p ISBN 0-80578-603-1 LC 92-5328

EUROPE—EMIGRATION AND IMMIGRATION

Love thy neighbor—except in western Europe. O'Grady, Desmond. *OSV* 81:7 Ja 3 1993

Weltweite Migrationen als politische Herausforderung Europas. Müller, Johannes. *Stimm Zeit* 210:797-805 D 1992

EUROPE—HISTORY

Social Catholicism in nineteenth-century Europe: a review of recent historiography. Misner, Paul. *CHist* 78:581-600 O 1992

EUROPE—POLITICS
Europe's future: is the Maastricht Treaty dead? Bogle, Joanna. *OSV* 81:3 Ap 18 1993

EUROPE—RELIGION
Christian-Jewish relations in a new Europe. Solomon, Norman. *Month* 26:9-16 Ja 1993
Christians and Jews: coexistence in the new Europe. Ucko, Hans. *JEcumen Stds* 29:254-257 Spr 1992
Church, state and theology in the European Community. Nolan, Michael. *Studies* 82:148-159 Sum 1993
Europe under construction: a report from Brussels. Marthaler, Berard L, 1927-. *Living Light* 29:69-76 Wint 1992
Europe's new religions. Walsh, Michael J, 1937-, and Wijngaards, John. *Tablet* 247:448-449 Ap 3 1993

EUROPE—SOCIAL POLICY
European dimensions of the abortion debate. Robinson, William. *Doctr Life* 42:273-281 My-Je 1992

EUROPE—SOCIO-ECONOMIC CONDITIONS
Weltweite Migrationen als politische Herausforderung Europas. Müller, Johannes. *Stimm Zeit* 210:797-805 D 1992

EUROPE, EASTERN—ECONOMIC POLICY
The quest for a just economy in a new Europe: ethical implications of the social market economy. Manenschijn, Gerrit. *Louvain Stds* 18:159-174 Sum 1993

EUROPEAN BISHOPS' CONFERENCE
Prague hosts meeting of European bishops. Hebblethwaite, Peter, 1930-. *Nat Cath Rep* 29:8 O 1 1993
Tasks of the Church in the new Europe. Hume, George Basil, Cardinal, 1932-. *Origins* 23:341-348 O 21 1993

EUROPEAN ECONOMIC COMMUNITY
Action for Bosnia [editorial]. Barnes, Michael R. *Month* 26:2-3 Ja 1993
An angry people. McRedmond, Louis. *Tablet* 247:327-329 Mr 13 1993
Beware the Jesuits. *Tablet* 247:1099 Ag 28 1993
Europe under construction: a report from Brussels. Marthaler, Berard L, 1927-. *Living Light* 29:69-76 Wint 1992
A European diary. Burns, Jimmy. *Tablet* 247:67-69 Ja 16 1993
The European journey. Keegan, William. *Tablet* 246:1592 D 19-26 1992
The golden curtain. Solomon, Jonathan. *Tablet* 247:186 F 13 1993
John Major versus Jacques Delors [editorial]. *Tablet* 247:807 Je 26 1993
The last battle for Maastricht [editorial]. *Tablet* 247:743 Je 1993
Maastricht: dead or alive? Stourton, Edward. *Tablet* 247:936-937 Jl 24 1993
The Prime Minister as scapegoat [editorial]. *Tablet* 247:967 Jl 31 1993
Rescuing the European project [editorial]. *Tablet* 247:635 My 22 1993
A response to unemployment: ten propositions. Quigley, George. *Studies* 82:73-86 Spr 1993
"Sailing to the Lowlands low"—the bishops in Brussels, 1-3 February 1993. Devlin, Brendan P. *Furrow* 44:178-181 Mr 1993
Which way for Europe? Keegan, William. *Tablet* 247:36+ Ja 9 1993
Worse yet to come? Brown, Janice. *Comm* 120:4-5 Ja 29 1993

EUROPEAN ECONOMIC COMMUNITY—ECONOMIC POLICY
The ERM goes on holiday. Keegan, William. *Tablet* 247:1000-1001 Ag 7 1993
The European project in danger [editorial]. *Tablet* 247:999 Ag 7 1993

EUROPEAN LITERATURE
Images of paradise. Bull, George, 1929-. *Tablet* 246:1613 D 19-26 1992

EUTHANASIA
Abortion and the right to life. *Doctr Life* 42:336-344 My-Je 1992
Advising on the ethics of health-care reform. Bole, William. *OSV* 82:3 Je 20 1993
Assisted suicide and legalized euthanasia. Garvais, Marcel. *Doctr Life* 43:308-309 My-Je 1993
Assisted suicide is not the answer [editorial]. Feister, John Bookser. *St Anth* 101:21 O 1993
Can we kill off grandad? Gormally, Luke. *Priests & People* 6:409-414 N 1992
Care of the dying. Cassidy, Sheila. *Tablet* 247:430-431 Ap 3 1993
Care of the dying: a Catholic perspective [4 parts]. *Health Prog* 74:34-38+ Mr; 16-21+ Ap; 22-26+ My; 46-54 Je 1993*
Catholicism and the "right" to die. Grondelski, John M. *Linacre* 59:50-56 N 1992
Churches join forces against euthanasia. *Tablet* 247:899 Jl 10 1993
[Death and dying]. Cassidy, Judy, ed. *Health Prog* 74:34-51 Mr 1993*
Death with dignity. Dudro, Vivian. *Register* 69:4 S 5 1993
Euthanasia, the gentle death: a legal and ethical prospectus on the right to die. Fulk, Kirkland Alan. *CLawyer* 35 no 2:145-168 1993
Kevorkian hasn't got a clue. Meehan, Bridget Mary. *OSV* 82:19 S 19 1993
The last days of Tony Bland [editorial]. *Tablet* 247:187 F 13 1993
The lesson in Ann Humphry's death. Bole, William. *OSV* 82:21 Je 6 1993
The liberalism of fools. Shea, Mark P. *New Oxford Rev* 60:11-13 Ja-F 1993
Mercy and aid. Haynes, A W. *Can Cath Rev* 11:7-8 Mr 1993
Mercy or murder? euthanasia, morality and public policy. Overberg, Kenneth R, 1944-. Kansas City: Sheed and Ward, 1993. x, 278p ISBN 1-55612-609-3 LC 92-43734
Mercy: an insufficient motive for euthanasia. Tuohey, John F. *Health Prog* 74:51-53 O 1993
Murderous euphemisms. Bole, William. *OSV* 82:3 My 16 1993
Nutrition and hydration: moral and pastoral reflections [Committee for Pro-Life Activities, Ap 1992]. *Linacre* 59:33-49 N 1992
On not starving the unconscious. Fisher, Anthony. *New Blckfrs* 74:130-145 Mr 1993
Pastoral reflections: euthanasia, assisted suicide. *Origins* 23:373-378 N 4 1993
Permanently unconscious patients and the ethical controversies surrounding artificial nutrition and hydration: getting the facts straight. Mitchell, Kenneth R, and Lovat, Terence J. *Linacre* 60:75-90 F 1993
Physician-assisted suicide and euthanasia. *Origins* 23:63-64 Je 10 1993
Religion and the moral meaning of euthanasia. Campbell, Courtney S. *Linacre* 59:15-28 N 1992
The road to euthanasia. Fisher, Anthony. *Tablet* 247:235-237 F 20 1993
Slip-sliding away [editorial]. *OSV* 82:2 My 16 1993
U.S., Canada ask: is dying a constitutional right? Dodds, Bill. *OSV* 82:3 N 14 1993

What comes after assisted suicide and legalized euthanasia? Gervais, Marcel, Abp. *Origins* 22:573+ F 4 1993
When truth is more frightening than fiction [editorial]. *OSV* 81:2 F 28 1993
Why doctors are suspicious of "aid in dying" bills. Krause, Edward. *Register* 69:5 Je 13 1993

EUTHANASIA—LAW
Assisted-suicide ban supported. Maida, Adam, Abp. *Origins* 23:280 S 30 1993

EUTHANASIA- CALIFORNIA
The California euthanasia initiative. Rae, Scott B. *Linacre* 59:5-14 N 1992

EUTHANASIA- NETHERLANDS
Like the Nazis, Sgreccia says. *Tablet* 247:284 F 27 1993
A warning from Holland. Krause, Edward. *Register* 69:5 My 9 1993

EVALUATION
Choir festivals: everyone's a winner. Connolly, Michael. *Past Mus* 17:14-15 D 1992-Ja 1993

EVANGELICAL AND REFORMED CHURCH
Die Annahme der Gnade als Mitvollzug der Erlösung. Menke, Karl-Heinz. *Catholica* 47:1-19 1993

EVANGELICAL LUTHERAN CHURCH IN AMERICA
By water and the spirit—a United Methodist understanding of Baptism: a Lutheran response. Nitschke, Beverley A. *Ecumen Trends* 22:3-7 Ja 1993
Lutheran-Reformed Committee meets. *Ecumen Trends* 22:8 Mr 1993

EVANGELICAL LUTHERAN CHURCH IN AMERICA—RELATIONS
Episcopal, Lutheran and Reformed leaders discuss full communion. *Ecumen Trends* 22:14 My 1993

EVANGELICAL LUTHERAN CHURCH OF LATVIA
Women's ordination may be rescinded by Lutheran Church. *Tablet* 247:1171-1172 S 11 1993

EVANGELICALISM
Die Annahme der Gnade als Mitvollzug der Erlösung. Menke, Karl-Heinz. *Catholica* 47:1-19 1993
Ekklesiologische optionen Evangelischer Theologie als Mögliche Leitbilder der Okumene. Wagner, Harald. *Catholica* 47 no 2:124-141 1993
An infant baptism program that works. Heller, Chris. *Tod Parish* 25:13-16 Ap-My 1993
Politics isn't everything. Curry, Dean C, 1952-. *Crisis* 11:10 Mr 1993
Six small syllables [editorial]. Manney, Jim. *New Cov* 22:5 Mr 1993

EVANGELISCHE KIRCHE IN DEUTSCHLAND
Focus on racism at the Kirchentag. Prangemeier, Monika. *Tablet* 247:798 Je 19 1993

EVANGELISCHE KIRCHE IN DEUTSCHLAND—EDUCATION
Schule—Bildung—Christlicher Glaube. Ritter, Werner H. *Stimm Zeit* 211:413-421 Je 1993

EVANGELISTIC CONFERENCES
John Paul II, Pope, (1993-06-15) Church [Orig in Spanish]. John Paul II, Pope, 1920- (Karol Wojtyla) (elected 1978). *OR(Eng)* 1297:4+ Je 30 1993*

EVANGELISTIC WORK
The apostolic faith: Protestants and Roman Catholics. Norris, Frederick W. Minnesota: The Liturgical Press, 1992. x, 178p ISBN 0-8146-5029-5 LC 92-19536
Becoming paschal evangelizers. Kroeger, James H. *Emmanuel* 99:428-431+ O 1993
Catholics should go tell it on the mountain. Johnson, Howard. *OSV* 82:5 O 17 1993
The demands of evangelization [excerpt fr pamphlet written during Vatican Council 2D]. Legrand, F. *ChrWorld* 38:48-50 Ja-F 1993
Don't close inner-city Catholic schools. Davis, Cyprian. *USCath* 58:22-27 My 1993
Ecumenism and evangelization in Christus, Lumen Gentium. Falardeau, Ernest R, 1928-. *Emmanuel* 99:197-200 My 1993
Evangelization for busy parishes. Blum, Susan W. *Tod Parish* 25:8-9 N-D 1993
La formazione missionaria dei sacerdoti alla luce della "Pastores dabo vobis" (commentary: *Pastores dabo vobis*). Saraiva Martins, José. *Seminarium* 32:575-599 O-D 1992
A fundamentalist Nicaragua? Torrens, James S. *America* 168:6-9 Ja 16-23 1993
Hispania sentido evangelizador del domingo y de las fiestas: instrucción pastoral de la Conferencia Episcopal Española. *Notitiae* 28:600-617 S 1992
Inculturação: um desafio pastoral. Ehle, Paulo. *REB* 53:167-174 Mr 1993
Inside the mind of unchurched Harry and Mary. Strobel, Lee. Grand Rapids: Zondervan Publishing House, 1993. x, 224p ISBN 0-310-37561-4
John Paul II, Pope (1991-05-04) Evangelization requires continual profound intellectual formation. John Paul II, Pope, 1920- (Karol Wojtyla) (elected 1978). *Con Life* 17 no 2:41-44 1992*
John Paul II, Pope, (1991-02-02) The witness and fertility of consecrated life. John Paul II, Pope, 1920- (Karol Wojtyla) (elected 1978). *Con Life* 17 no 2:5-7 1992*
John Paul II, Pope, (1991-04-28) Be faithful to your word. John Paul II, Pope, 1920- (Karol Wojtyla) (elected 1978). *Con Life* 17 no 2:19-21 1992*
John Paul II, Pope, (1991-05-16) The Gospel and the world: essential points of reference to your vocation. John Paul II, Pope, 1920- (Karol Wojtyla) (elected 1978). *Con Life* 17 no 2:22-25 1992*
John Paul II, Pope, (1991-09-23) The new evangelization demands love in strict fidelity to the gospel. John Paul II, Pope, 1920- (Karol Wojtyla) (elected 1978). *Con Life* 17 no 2:64-66 1992*
John Paul II, Pope, (1991-12-13) Allocutiones (Address to Special Assembly for Europe of the Synod of Bishops) [Latin]. John Paul II, Pope, 1920- (Karol Wojtyla) (elected 1978). *AAS* 84:1158-1162 D 5 1992*
John Paul II, Pope, (1991-12-14) Allocutiones (Homily to Synod of Bishops for Europe) [Italian]. John Paul II, Pope, 1920- (Karol Wojtyla) (elected 1978). *AAS* 84:1163-1165 D 5 1992*
John Paul II, Pope, (1991-12-23) Allocutiones (Christmas exhortation to Cardinals and Curial Staff) [Italian]. John Paul II, Pope, 1920- (Karol Wojtyla) (elected 1978). *AAS* 85:37-45 Ja 7 1993*
John Paul II, Pope, (1992-01-04) Allocutiones (Homily at visit of some Italian Bishops) [Italian]. John Paul II, Pope, 1920- (Karol Wojtyla) (elected 1978). *AAS* 85:48-52 Ja 7 1993*

EVIL
Black dogs [editorial]. *Month* 26:296-297 Ag 1993
Evil and the experience of God. Elizondo, Virgil. *Way* 33:34-43 Ja 1993
Evolution, Omega and evil. Harris, Errol E, 1908-. *Teilhard Rev* 28:15-22 Spr 1993
[Many who do not profess]. Smith, Janet E. *Comm* 120:14-15 O 22 1993
On the bright side. Wroe, Ann. *Tablet* 247:390 Mr 27 1993
Unless we see the wounds. McMahon, John. *Can Cath Rev* 11:38-39 Je 1993
"The way we live now": Graham Greene on reading. Kelly, Patrick Hyde. *Can Cath Rev* 11:20-22 Ap 1993

EVOLUTION
Boredom and laughter: a visit to the Natural History Museum. Dalzell, Catherine. *Can Cath Rev* 11:11-16 O 1993
Creation or evolution? a call to intellectual conversion. Becker, David R. *HPR* 93:54-61 Ap 1993
Evolution and morality. Shea, Moira C. *Teilhard Rev* 28:9-15 Sum 1993
Evolution today. Leadbetter, Frank. *Teilhard Rev* 28:27 Sum 1993
The fall of the house of Darwin. Banet, Robert A. *HPR* 93:70-73 Ja 1993
Quo Vadis? or evolution and consciousness. Cronin, Francis R. *Teilhard Rev* 27:69-82 Wint 1992

EVOLUTION (TEILHARDIAN)
Ethical risk management: suggestions for an applied risk ethics. Cowell, John. *Teilhard Rev* 28:3-7 Spr 1993
Evolution, Omega and evil. Harris, Errol E, 1908-. *Teilhard Rev* 28:15-22 Spr 1993

EX-NUNS
Leaven—listening to those who have left. Morahan, Justin. *Furrow* 44:154-158 Mr 1993

EX-PRIESTS, CATHOLIC
Leaven—listening to those who have left. Morahan, Justin. *Furrow* 44:154-158 Mr 1993
Politics in the purple kingdom: the derailment of Vatican II. Schlichte, George A. Kansas City: Sheed & Ward, 1993. x, 133p ISBN 1-55612-607-7 LC 92-44098
Vocations in conflict. Castle, Anthony, 1938-. *Tablet* 247:844-845 Jl 3 1993

EXCLUSION, RIGHT OF—CONTROVERSIES
Handing on the tradition: a Catholic mother laments. Baumer, Patricia Hughes. *New Theol Rev* 6:32-54 My 1993

EXEGESIS, BIBLICAL *see* Bible—Criticism, Interpretation

EXISTENCE
Événement et destinée chez Schelling. Maesschalck, Marc. *RPhil Louvain* 91:185-206 My 1993
God and being: the paradox of presence and absence. O'Connell, James. *Month* 26:188-193 My 1993

EXISTENTIAL PSYCHOLOGY
The hiddennes of God. Law, David R. New York: Oxford University Press, 1993. x, 256p ISBN 0-826336-8

EXISTENTIALISM
The art of pain. Pickstone, Charles. *Month* 26:278-280 Jl 1993
Etre et temps et théologie. Berranger, Oliver De. *Gregorianum* 74 no 3:543-561 1993
Variations sceptiques sur le thème de la mort. Sansen, Raymond. *MSR* 50:83-98 Ap-Je 1993

EXODUS, THE
Who can utter the Name of God?—From the holiness of his name to the seriousness of all words. Sales, Michel. *Communio* 20:26-48 Spr 1993

EXORCISM
Possessed: the true story of an exorcism. Allen, Thomas B. New York: Doubleday, 1993. 259p ISBN 0-385-42034-x LC 92-42038

EXPECTATION (PSYCHOLOGY)
Whatever happened to childhood? Elkind, David, 1931-. *Momentum* 24:18-19 Ap-My 1993

EXPERIENCE (RELIGION)
Being interested in time: autobiography and repetition. Dupuy, Edward. *Listening* 28:141-157 Spr 1993
Christian experience from the shadow side of history. Murphy, Annie. *Way* 33:127-137 Ap 1993
Christian experience in Hans Urs von Balthasar. Potworowski, Christophe. *Communio* 20:107-117 Spr 1993
Evil and the experience of God. Elizondo, Virgil. *Way* 33:34-43 Ja 1993
Experience as a theological category: Hans Urs von Balthasar on the Christian encounter with God's image. Casarella, Peter. *Communio* 20:118-128 Spr 1993
"I have experienced God": religious experience in the theology of Karl Rahner. Wiseman, James A. *ABenR* 44:22-57 Mr 1993
In the heart of the city. Dunne, Sean. *Tablet* 247:944-945 Jl 24 1993
A "new" pastoral practice: mystagogy. Regan, David. *Furrow* 44:416-422 Jl-Ag 1993
Sida, impuls de vida?: experiencia de Joan Ferrer Sisquella. Bovet, Joan M. Barcelona: Claret, 1993. x, 135p ISBN 84-7263-837-5
You had to be there. Costello, Andrew. *USCath* 58:38-40 Ap 1993

EXPERIENCE (RELIGION)—WOMEN
Feminism and theology: beyond women's ordination. Cahoy, William J. *Sisters* 65:243-251 Jl 1993
The representationj of religious experience in nineteenth-century American women's autobiography. Norman, Rose. *Listening* 28:128-140 Spr 1993

EXPERIMENTATION ON CHILDREN
Deciding who lives: fateful choices in the intensive care nursery. Anspach, Renée R. Berkeley: University of California Press, 1993. x, 303p ISBN 0-520-05268-4 LC 91-44245

EXPERIMENTATION ON MAN—ETHICAL ASPECTS
Éthique et médecine expérimentale à l'hôpital. Malherbe, Jean-François. *Supplement* 184:107-124 Mr-Ap 1993

EXPLORERS
Is there more to be said? Leeney, Robert. *Columbia* 73:10-13 Ag 1993

EXTINCTION (BIOLOGY)
Teilhard today. Stikker, Allerd. *Teilhard Rev* 28:23-27 Spr 1993

EXTRAORDINARY MINISTERS OF HOLY COMMUNION
John Paul II, Pope, (1993-06-12) Eucharist [Orig in Spanish]. John Paul II, Pope, 1920- (Karol Wojtyla) (elected 1978). *OR(Eng)* 1296:5 Je 23 1993*

EXTRATERRESTRIAL ANTHROPOLOGY
God, ghosts, and UFOs. Auer, Jim. *Liguorian* 81:38-43 Ag 1993

EYRRA, EUSEBIO ALONSO, 1917-1936
Congregation for the Causes of Saints (1992-12-21) Decree on martyrdom. Congregation for the Causes of Saints. *OR(Eng)* 1272:4 Ja 6 1993*

F

FABLES
Fabulous classics. Dreher, Barbara. *Tod Cath Teach* 27:42-45 S 1993

FABLES—RELIGIOUS ASPECTS
Descartes' discourse. Rudolph, Katherine. *PhilosTod* 37:38-51 Spr 1993

FACTS (PHILOSOPHY)
God and the status of facts. Peterson, John. *Thomist* 56:635-646 O 1992
On never reaching Canada. Schall, James Vincent, 1928-. *Crisis* 11:49-50 My 1993

FAHEY, MICHAEL A
Response to Michael Fahey. Trevijano, Ramon. *Jurist* 52 no 1:71-78 1992

FAILURE (CHRISTIAN THEOLOGY)
It's safe to fail. Whitehead, Charles. *New Cov* 22:29 Jl 1993

FAIRY TALES
Good news from Grimm. McDonagh, Melanie. *Tablet* 246:1608 D 19-26 1992

FAITH
Abraham. Martin, George. *Liguorian* 81:44-45 Ja 1993
Breaking the thought barrier. Roman, Mary. *Living Prayer* 26:37 My-Je 1993
Bultmann. Ferguson, David. Collegeville: The Liturgical Press, 1992. x, 154p ISBN 0-8146-5037-6
Der christliche Glaube—unverändert und unverkürzt für die ganze Welt? Feil, Ernst. *Stimm Zeit* 211:579-593 S 1993*
Did faith make a difference this year? Kollar, Judith Ann. *Tod Parish* 25:6 Ap-My 1993
Doubt in search of understanding. Rees, Frank. *Pacifica* 6:279-296 O 1993
Evangelisation and the ghost of Lessing. Turner, Geoffrey. *Month* 25:473-478 D 1992
Experience as a theological category: Hans Urs von Balthasar on the Christian encounter with God's image. Casarella, Peter. *Communio* 20:118-128 Spr 1993
Die Fünfte Weltkonferenz für Glauben und Kirchenverfassung. Radano, John A. *Catholica* 47:20-37 1993
Facing the abusing God: a theology of protest. Blumenthal, David Reuben, 1938-. Louisville: John Knox, 1993. x, 208p ISBN 0-664-25464-0
Faith in the margins: the example of Jean Sulivan. Maher, Eamon. *Doctr Life* 43:147-155 Mr 1993
Faith, conversion and Humanae Vitae. Martin, Ralph. *New Cov* 23:12-14 N 1993
La fede cristiana nell'epoca postmoderna (editorial). *Civilta* 143:329-342 N 21 1992
Good News and old nonsense. O'Collins, Gerald, 1931-. *Tablet* 247:469 Ap 10-17 1993
John Paul II, Pope (1993-06-27) Gospel [Orig Italian and English]. John Paul II, Pope, 1920- (Karol Wojtyla) (elected 1978). *OR(Eng)* 1297:1+ Je 30 1993*
John Paul II, Pope, (1993-09-05) Lithuania [Orig Lithuanian]. John Paul II, Pope, 1920- (Karol Wojtyla) (elected 1978). *OR(Eng)* 1306:1+ S 8 1993*
John Paul II, Pope, (1993-09-06) Holy Spirit [Orig in Lithuanian]. John Paul II, Pope, 1920- (Karol Wojtyla) (elected 1978). *OR(Eng)* 1306:6 S 8 1993*
John Paul II, Pope, (1993-09-15) Baltic [Orig in Estonian]. John Paul II, Pope, 1920- (Karol Wojtyla) (elected 1978). *OR(Eng)* 1308:11 S 22 1993*
On earth as in heaven. Soelle, Dorothee. Louisville: Westminster, 1993. x, 96p ISBN 0-664-25494-2
Radical monotheism and western culture: with supplemental essays. Niebuhr, H Richard. Louisville, Kentucky: John Knox Press, 1993. 112p ISBN 502-569-5043
Rational faith. Osborn, Eric. *Pacifica* 6:297-310 O 1993
Re-informing the faithful: the catechsim that completes the Council. Lawler, Ronald D, 1926-. *Crisis* 11:19-22 Je 1993*
Religious education's power to nurture faith. Eklin, Carolyn. *Origins* 23:28-31 My 27 1993
Resurrection love-life. Dent, Barbara. Mahwah: Paulist, 1993. x, 189p ISBN 0-8091-3405-5 LC 93-11006
Stepping out on faith. Spann, Shirley A. Boston: Deluxe Publications, 1992. 70p ISBN 0-9632239-0-9
Telling the Gospel in flesh and blood. Blastic, Michael W. *New Theol Rev* 6:108-112 My 1993
Weltethos oder säkularer Humanismus? Fuchs, Josef. *Stimm Zeit* 211:147-154 Mr 1993
When the Spirit sweeps over the waters. Canton, Donald R. *Living Prayer* 26:10-14 Ja-F 1993

FAITH—COMPARATIVE STUDIES
Perché non si crede? La risposta di Dostoevskij [editorial]. Salvini, Gianpaolo, ed. *Civilta* 2:209-216 My 1 1993

FAITH AND ORDER MOVEMENT
John Paul II, Pope, (1993-07-21) message to Faith and Order Conference. John Paul II, Pope, 1920- (Karol Wojtyla) (elected 1978). *Ecumen Trends* 22:2 O 1993*
The time has come: a vision for the Fifth World Conference on Faith and Order [fr *The Ecumenical review*]. Tanner, Mary. *Cath Int* 4:239-244 My 1993

FAITH AND REASON
Advance from faith into knowledge. Firth, Francis. *Can Cath Rev* 11:34-36 S 1993
An atheist in the sacristy: why does faith seek intelligence? Schall, James Vincent, 1928-. *F & R* 28:315-334 Wint 1992

Catechesis and religious education. Groome, Thomas H, 1945-. *Living Light* 29:40-46 Aut 1992

Feminist theology: a proposal. Martin, Francis. *Communio* 20:334-376 Sum 1993

Humility is key to knowledge. Gallagher, Michael Paul, 1939-. *OR(Eng)* 1312: 10 O 20 1993

John Paul II, Pope, (1992-05-02) The nobility of science. John Paul II, Pope, 1920- (Karol Wojtyla) (elected 1978). *TPS* 38:5-8 Ja-F 1993*

Rational faith: Catholic responses to reformed epistemology. Zaggelski, Linda Trinkaus, 1946-, ed. Indiana: Notre Dame Press, 1993. x, 290p ISBN 0-268-01643-7 LC 92-537-42

Reason, appropriateness and hope: sketch of a kantian account of a finite rationality. Stratton-Lake, Philip. *IJPS* 1:61-80 Mr 1993

FAITH DEVELOPMENT

Die Fünfte Weltkonferenz für Glauben und Kirchenverfassung. Radano, John A. *Catholica* 47:20-37 1993

Faith in contemporary society. Vaughan, Judy. *Chicago Stud* 31:197-200 Ag 1992

Gott Suchen sich Selbst Erkennen. Cassian, Johannes. Freiburg: Herder, 1993. x, 480p ISBN 3-451-23246-4

Kleines credo fur Verunsicherte. Beinert, Wolfgang, et al. Freiburg: Herder, 1993. x, 144p ISBN 3-451-23245-6

The living water will quench your thirst. Canada, Allie C. New York: Vantage Press, 1993. x, 74p ISBN 0-533-10338-x LC 92-90826

Parish diary: August. *Tablet* 247:1096 Ag 28 1993

The practice of theological reflection in small faith communities. Killen, Patricia O'Connell. *Chicago Stud* 31:189-196 Ag 1992

Religion not dying out around the world. Greeley, Andrew Moran, 1928-. *Origins* 23:49-58 Je 10 1993

Show more faith in your prayers. Szafranski, Richard T. *USCath* 58:36-37 Mr 1993

The soul power a nation needs. Quinn, Francis, Bp. *Origins* 22:605+ F 18 1993

Teenagers: are they losing faith? Moore, Joseph. *ReligTJ* 26:12-14 Ja 1993

FAITH DEVELOPMENT- RWANDA

Changements culturels et lieux d'expériences de la foi au Rwanda. Nkulikiyumukiza, Augustin. *Lumen* 48:195-206 Je 1993

FALL OF MAN

Truth reaffirmed about creation and humanity's fall. Stravinskas, Peter. *Register* 69:1+ My 23 1993

What's in a pedigree? Alcimus Avitus, De Spir Hist Gest 2 50-52, and Juvenal, Sat 8 140-41. Magee, John. *Med Stud* 54:317-326 1992

FAMILY

Defiant hope: spirituality for survivors of family abuse. Leehan, James. Louisville: John Knox, 1993. x, 176p ISBN 0-664-25463-2

The experts are wrong again. Krause, Edward. *Register* 69:5 Mr 7 1993

Families [conference, "Putting Children and Families First: Building Peace, Seeking Justice"]. Mullen, Peter. *Register* 69:1+ Mr 21 1993

The family and the left. Phillips, Melanie. *Tablet* 247:972-973 Jl 31 1993

Family policy in America: a continuing controversy. Stanfield, Jacqueline B. *RSocEcon* 50:420-431 Wint 1992

The family: a place of fraternity. Sicari, Antonio. *Communio* 20:290-305 Sum 1993

Father Scott's reflections on women, family, and relationships. Scott, John M. Indiana: Our Sunday Visitor, 1993. 139p ISBN 0-87973-530-9 LC 92-61551

Home-schooling works. Podles, Mary Elizabeth. *Crisis* 11:27-32 Ap 1993

The Murphy Brown factor at work. Yoest, Charmaine Crouse. *Register* 69:5 S 5 1993

Remodeling the "domestic church". Hitchcock, Helen Hull. *Crisis* 11:9-10 Ap 1993

Some musings on marriage. Myers, Edith. *HPR* 94:47-51 O 1993

Supporting families: a challenge for small Christian communities. Paglia, Donald J. *Tod Parish* 25:7-11 O 1993

Unmask yourself: a family day of reflection. Foley, Anita M, and Hanbury, Kevin M. *Tod Parish* 25:11-13 Mr 1993

What gives a family value? Scott, Charlene. *USCath* 58:32-37 Ja 1993

What's wrong with "family values". Ellsberg, Peggy R. *America* 168:16 Ap 3 1993

Who will speak for the children? Kammer, Fred. *Origins* 22:792-794 Ap 29 1993

FAMILY—BIBLICAL TEACHING

Beyond patriarchy: the images of family in Jesus. Jacobs-Malina, D. Mahwah: Paulist, 1993. x, 211p ISBN 0-8091-3421-7 LC 93-24501

John Paul II, Pope (1992-12-27) The Christian family [orig Italian]. John Paul II, Pope, 1920- (Karol Wojtyla) (elected 1978). *OR(Eng)* 1272:9 Ja 6 1993*

FAMILY—ECONOMIC CONDITIONS

Welfare reform: jobs and families. Ricard, John H, Bp. *Origins* 23:217+ S 9 1993

FAMILY—RELIGIOUS ASPECTS

The family is sanctuary of life. Trujillo, Alfonso López, Cardinal. *OR(Eng)* 1305:4-5 S 1 1993

FAMILY—RELIGIOUS LIFE

Beading a path down the interstate. Coffey, Mary Kean. *Liguorian* 81:26-27 Jl 1993

Becoming married: family living in pastoral perspective. Anderson, Herbert, and Fite, Cotton R. Louisville: Westminster, 1993. x, 160p ISBN 0-664-25126-9

Bringing Jesus back out of the closet. Shannon, Mary L. *St Anth* 100:18-20 Ja 1993

Easter is more than baskets and bunnies. O'Connor, Francine M. *Liguorian* 81:38-42 Ap 1993

Finding the religious dimension in family life. Ziegler, Elena. *Momentum* 24:78-79 F-Mr 1993

Integrating child and adult religious education. Costello, Sydney B. *Momentum* 24:74-76 Ap-My 1993

John Paul II, Pope, (1993-01-30) Promote the family. John Paul II, Pope, 1920- (Karol Wojtyla) (elected 1978). *TPS* 38:215-218 Jl-Ag 1993*

John Paul II, Pope, (1993-08-10) Jamaica. John Paul II, Pope, 1920- (Karol Wojtyla) (elected 1978). *OR(Eng)* 1303:3 Ag 18 1993*

John Paul II, Pope, (1993-09-26) Family [Italian]. John Paul II, Pope, 1920- (Karol Wojtyla) (elected 1978). *OR(Eng)* 1311:9-10 O 13 1993*

Just what can a parent do? DeGidio, Sandra. *St Anth* 100:21 Ja 1993

Lent. Mueller, Therese. *Mod Lit* 20:34-35 N 1993

On eagle's wings. Skublics, Ernest. *Can Cath Rev* 11:49-51 Ja 1993

The season of Advent. Mueller, Therese. *Mod Lit* 20:32-33 S 1993

Spiritual growth in interdenominational families. Lincoln, Timothy D. *Ecumen Trends* 22:7-8 My 1993

Statement on catechetical ministry. *Living Light* 29:81-84 Spr 1993

Towards a Christian Christmas. Mueller, Therese. *Mod Lit* 20:32-33 O 1993

Your child's baptism. Dalton, William J. *Furrow* 44:485-489 S 1993

FAMILY—SOCIAL ASPECTS

The changing face of family. Drennan, Kathleen M. *Catechist* 27:4 N-D 1993

FAMILY- GREAT BRITAIN

Mps welcome focus on the family. *Tablet* 247:352 Mr 13 1993

FAMILY- LATIN AMERICA

A família do documento de Santo Domingo. Guimarães, Almir Ribeiro. *REB* 53:40-51 Mr 1993

FAMILY COUNSELING

Becoming married: family living in pastoral perspective. Anderson, Herbert, and Fite, Cotton R. Louisville: Westminster, 1993. x, 160p ISBN 0-664-25126-9

Gloria Rodriguez [interview by Lillie Rodulfo]. Rodulfo, Lillie. *Salt* 13:4-6 Mr 1993

FAMILY LIFE

Confessions of a perfect parent. Price, W Wayne. Grand Rapids: Eerdmans, 1993. 166p ISBN 0-8028-0676-7

The home front. Finley, Mitchel B, and Finley, Kathy. *Living Prayer* 26:22-23 My-Je 1993

Mangel an Erziehung? Bleistein, Roman, 1928-. *Stimm Zeit* 211:1-2 Ja 1993

Splitting shifts: splitting families. Downs, Peter. *Comm* 120:7-8 Je 4 1993

Take your shoes off my books: negotiating a Hindu-Catholic marriage. McGowan, Joseph. *Comm* 120:15-17 Je 18 1993

TV mothers and fathers. Wallace, James A, 1944-. *Liguorian* 81:45 My 1993

FAMILY LIFE, CHRISTIAN

Because we have children—a mother's reflection [repr fr *The companion magazine*]. O'Brien, Christine. *Furrow* 43:663-667 D 1992

Becoming married: family living in pastoral perspective. Anderson, Herbert, and Fite, Cotton R. Louisville: Westminster, 1993. x, 160p ISBN 0-664-25126-9

Beginnings are never easy. Dodds, Bill. *New Cov* 23:32 S 1993

Building on traditions in Advent and Christmas. McGill, Mary. *Catechist* 27:32-33 N-D 1993

Children first, before and after birth. Casey, Robert P, 1932-. *Origins* 22:696-699 Mr 18 1993

Christian families and today's sexual values. Finley, Mitchel B, and Finley, Kathy. *Living Prayer* 26:21-22 N-D 1993

Christian teaching on family explored. *Tablet* 247:1144 S 4 1993

Church and rights of the family. Trujillo, López. *OR(Eng)* 1301:6-7 Jl 28 1993

The Church must stop cheating the engaged. Foley, Gerald. *St Anth* 101:10-13 Je 1993

Dialogue [interview by Jan Slattery]. Wood, Steve. *Register* 69:1+ Jl 18 1993

Families communities of love and service. Finley, Mitchel B. *Liguorian* 81:38-42 F 1993

Families: signs of God. MacClennan, Carole. *ReligTJ* 26:31 Ja 1993

Family creates peace of the human family. *OR(Eng)* 1300:1 Jl 21 1993

The family is sanctuary of life. Trujillo, Alfonso López, Cardinal. *OR(Eng)* 1305:4-5 S 1 1993

Family meetings do work. Light, Judi. *St Anth* 101:10-14 Ag 1993

Family nonconformists: is there room for wildflowers in your garden? Curran, Dolores. *USCath* 58:14-19 Jl 1993

John Paul II, Pope (1992-12-27) The Christian family [orig Italian]. John Paul II, Pope, 1920- (Karol Wojtyla) (elected 1978). *OR(Eng)* 1272:9 Ja 6 1993*

John Paul II, Pope, (1991-10-04) Allocutiones (Exhortation to Pontifical Council on Family) [Italian]. John Paul II, Pope, 1920- (Karol Wojtyla) (elected 1978). *AAS* 84:851-854 S 8 1992*

John Paul II, Pope, (1993-05-14) Huelva [Orig in Spanish]. John Paul II, Pope, 1920- (Karol Wojtyla) (elected 1978). *OR(Eng)* 1296:1+ Je 23 1993*

John Paul II, Pope, (1993-06-01) Year of the family [Orig in Italian]. John Paul II, Pope, 1920- (Karol Wojtyla) (elected 1978). *OR(Eng)* 1294:1+ Je 9 1993*

Libre de familia: dotze germans I deu escubas. Barcelona: Deriva, 1993. x, 147p ISBN 84-97981-05-4

Salvation and family life. Finley, Mitchel B, and Finley, Kathy. *Living Prayer* 26:23-24 Ja-F 1993

Stringing pearls: making heirlooms of family stories. Kindig, Eileen Silva. *St Anth* 101:10-15 O 1993

What kind of family did Jesus value? McCormick, Patrick. *USCath* 58:36-37 O 1993

What's happening to the old magic? finding meaning in family crisis. Gillespie, Joseph P. *Liturgy* 10:35-41 Wint 1992

Why are the dandelions weeds? Chesto, Kathleen O'Connell. Kansas City: Sheed and Ward, 1993. x, 147p ISBN 1-55612-610-7 LC 92-434481

FAMILY LIFE, JEWISH

Judaism's sexual revolution: why Judaism rejected homosexuality [fr *Ultimate Issues*]. Prager, Dennis. *Crisis* 11:29-34+ S 1993

FAMILY LIFE EDUCATION

Becoming married: family living in pastoral perspective. Anderson, Herbert, and Fite, Cotton R. Louisville: Westminster, 1993. x, 160p ISBN 0-664-25126-9

FAMILY MEDICINE

From assessment to action. Dugas, Nancy. *Health Prog* 74:38-41 O 1993

The "how-to" of integrated delivery. Suh, Young S, and Lee, John P. *Health Prog* 74:48 Jl-Ag 1993

FAMILY PROBLEMS
Shame, dysfunctional families, and lack of due discretion for marriage. Garrity, Robert M. *Jurist* 51 no 2:364-389 1991
FAMILY SIZE
Ethical implications of a people's changing visage. *Origins* 22:758-761 Ap 15 1993
The why of it. Lawlor, Gail M. *Comm* 120:5 Je 18 1993
FAMILY VIOLENCE
Behind closed doors. Hayes, Cathy Cartier. *OSV* 82:10-11 Je 27 1993
Domestic violence. Untener, Kenneth E, Bp. *Origins* 23:357-358 O 28 1993
FAMILY LIFE
Family meetings do work. Light, Judi. *St Anth* 101:10-14 Ag 1993
FAMINES
Africa: road to faith [photos]. Pipkin, Kate. *St Anth* 100:34-40 S 1993
FANATICISM
Bloody Pensacola [editorial]. *Comm* 120:5 Ap 9 1993
Doctor killed at abortion clinic. Smith, John, Bp, et al. *Origins* 22:701+ Mr 25 1993
Fanatics [editorial]. Manney, Jim. *New Cov* 22:5 My 1993
FANTASY
J R R Tolkien: lover of the logos. Sebanc, Mark, 1941-1992. *Communio* 20:84-106 Spr 1993
FARANI, MARIA CONCETTA (ANTONELLA DE SAN MIGUEL ARCANJO), 1906-1963
Congregation for the Causes of Saints (1992-06-13) Decree on the heroic virtues of Antonella de San Miguel Arcanjo. Congregation for the Causes of Saints. *AAS* 84:1184-1188 D 5 1992*
Congregation for the Causes of Saints (1992-06-13) Decree on the heroic virtues. Congregation for the Causes of Saints. *TPS* 38:19-20 Ja-F 1993*
FARLEY, JOHN MURPHY, ABP, 1842-1918
For the record: Pope Leo XIII and the church in New York. Andreassi, Anthony. *Church* 9:46-49 Sum 1993
FARM LIFE- UNITED STATES
Five threats to a rural way of life. Clarke, Kevin. *Salt* 13:6-12 S 1993
Salt of the earth: Ron Rosmann [interview by P Slattery]. Rosmann, Ron. *Salt* 13:4-5 F 1993
FARMER, WILLIAM REUBEN
Methodist minister's ecumenical labor lost. Anderson, David E. *Nat Cath Rep* 30:4 O 29 1993
FARMERS
GATT: an ethical void. Egan, Eileen. *Cath Work* 60:1+ Je-Jl 1993
FARROW, MIA, 1945-
O sole mia the first Nixon prize. Carlin, David Robert, Jr, 1938-. *Comm* 120:9-10 Je 18 1993
FASCISM—CRITICISM, INTERPRETATION
Das Erbe des Gedenkens. Bleistein, Roman, 1928-. *Stimm Zeit* 211:351-352 My 1993
FASTING
Amazing grace. Abiola, Olu. *Tablet* 247:335 Mr 13 1993
Blessings and challenges of the RCIA. Griffin, James A, Bp, 1934-. *Origins* 22:565-572 Ja 28 1993
Breaking the fast. Barnes, Michael R. *Month* 26:(I) Ap 1993
Fasting is the answer in an age hungry for meaning and love. Shaw, Russell. *Register* 69:1+ Ja 24 1993
Fasting: the Bible's spiritual diet. Maller, Allen S. *Spir Life* 39:22-25 Spr 1993
What do they value? Sabatowich, Jerome. *ReligTJ* 27:31 F 1993
FASTS AND FEASTS
Celebrate the golden days!. MacClennan, Carole. *ReligTJ* 27:8 Ap-My 1993
A family affair: the Feast of St. Francis of Assisi. McGill, Mary. *Catechist* 27:20-21 O 1993
Forgotten feast days. McNulty, Maurice F. *CDgst* 57:18+ Je 1993
Just what can a parent do? DeGidio, Sandra. *St Anth* 100:21 Ja 1993
FATE AND FATALISM
Mark's tragic vision: Gethsemane. Ruprecht, Louis A, Jr. *Relig Lit* 24:1-25 Aut 1992
FATHER AND CHILD
Waiting for Lily. Doyle, Brian. *Comm* 119:5-6 D 18 1992
Why have kids? Gudorf, Christine E. *USCath* 58:27-29 F 1993
FATHERHOOD (THEOLOGY)
Freezing the fire: the death of relational language. Montague, George T. *America* 168:5-7 Mr 13 1993
The importance of spiritual fathering. Martos, Joseph. *Liguorian* 81:4-9 Je 1993
FATHERS
Fathers come home: a wake-up call for busy dads. Swindell, Bill. South Bend, Indiana: Greenlawn Press, 1992. x, 101p ISBN 0-937779-23-7 LC 92-75551
FATHERS AND SONS
Father and son retreats: discovering male spirituality. Shimek, Michael. *Catechist* 26:34-36 Ap-My 1993
A father's blessing: it's ours for the asking. Kerner, Robert J. *New Cov* 23:26-27 Ag 1993
A Father's Day requiem. Finley, Mitchel B. *America* 168:4-5 Je 19-26 1993
FATHERS OF THE CHURCH
Christian and eastern mysticism [fr *a new vision of reality: Western science, Eastern mysticism and Christian faith*]. Griffiths, Bede, 1906-. *Living Prayer* 26:3-8 My-Je 1993
Did the early Church ordain women to be priests? Most, William G, 1914-. *Can Cath Rev* 11:21-24 F 1993
Drinking from the hidden fountain: a patristic breviary. Spidlik, Thomas. London: New City, 1992. 447p ISBN 0-904287-39-4
L'effusion de l'Esprit Saint chez les Pères latins. Bentivegua, Giuseppe. *NRT* 115:19-39 Ja-F 1993
Faith seeking understanding: mediaeval exegesis. Boyle, John F. *Can Cath Rev* 11:9-13 Jl-Ag 1993

Journey with the Fathers: commentaries on the Sunday gospels, Year A. Barnecot, Edith, ed. New Rochelle, New York: New City Press, 1992. 168p ISBN 1-56548-013-9 LC 92-20685
Journey with the Fathers; commentaries on the Sunday gospels, Year B. Barnecut, Edith, ed. New Rochelle: New City Press, 1993. 160p ISBN 1-56548-056-2 LC 92-20685
Origen: scripture scholar. Firth, Francis. *Can Cath Rev* 11:36-37 N 1993
What is new and what is old: patristic exegesis. Barringer, Robert. *Can Cath Rev* 11:7-15 Je 1993
Witnesses to the tradition: giving flesh to doctrine. Marthaler, Berard L, 1927-. *Living Light* 29:61-70 Sum 1993
FATIMA FAMILY APOSTOLATE
For Mary, a tireless worker. Dudro, Vivian. *Register* 69:3 Je 6 1993
FEAR
The biological basis of nonviolence. Meyer, Karl. *Cath Work* 60:5 Ja-F 1993
FEAR—RELIGIOUS ASPECTS
Overcoming fear between Jews and Christians. Charlesworth, James H. New York: Crossroad, 1993. x, 198p ISBN 0-8245-1265-0 LC 92-31262
FEAR OF GOD
Focus on feeling. O'Donoghue, Noel D. *Can Cath Rev* 11:16-21 Je 1993
Life-changing verses. Kreeft, Peter John, 1937-. *New Cov* 22:19+ My 1993
The Spirit's gift of fear of the Lord. Dimock, Giles. *OSV* 81:5 Mr 14 1993
FEAST OF THE PRESENTATION OF THE BLESSED VIRGIN MARY
Celebrating the presentation. Gribble, Richard. *OSV* 81:5 Ja 31 1993
FEAST OF THE VISITATION see Mary, Virgin—Visitation
FEASTS see Fasts and Feasts
FEDERAL AID TO EDUCATION- UNITED STATES
Chapter 1 solutions. Brigham, Fred, Jr, and Brandes, Lisa. *Tod Cath Teach* 26:13-15 My-Je 1993
A glimmer of hope for aid to Catholic schools. Drinan, Robert Francis, 1920-. *America* 169:4-5 S 18 1993
FEDERATION OF ASIAN BISHOPS' CONFERENCES
For all the peoples of Asia: documents from 1970-1991. Rosales, Gaudencio B, and Arevalo, Catalino G, eds. Maryknoll, New York: Orbis Books, 1992. x, 356p ISBN 0-88344-837-8 LC 92-5033
FEEDING OF THE MULTITUDE (MIRACLE)
Jesus feeds a hungry multitude and prefigures the life-giving Eucharist. Stravinskas, Peter. *Register* 69:1+ Mr 21 1993
Sharing as sign of Eucharist. Schaller, Jeanne Lound. *Living Prayer* 26:19-20 S-O 1993
FELLINI, FEDERICO, 1920-1993
Arrivederci, Fellini. Blake, Richard A, 1939-. *America* 169:10-11 D 4 1993
La vida Fellini. Austin, Ronald. *Register* 69:2 Mr 14 1993
FELLOWSHIP, CHRISTIAN see Christian Fellowship
FEMININITY—PHILOSOPHY
Advent and psychic birth. Burke, Mariann. New York: Paulist, 1993. x, 164p ISBN 0-8091-3431-4 LC 93-19318
FEMININITY—PSYCHOLOGY
I sit listening to the wind: woman's encounter within herself. Duerk, Judith. San Diego: LuraMedia, 1993. x, 103p ISBN 0-931055-98-9 LC 93-991
FEMININITY OF GOD
Is it okay to call God mother?: considering the feminine face of God. Smith, Paul R. Peabody: Hendrickson Publishers, 1993. 273p ISBN 1-56563-013-0 LC 93-25810
A theological case for God-She expanding the treasury of metaphor. Johnson, Elizabeth A, 1941-. *Comm* 120:9-14 Ja 29 1993
FEMINISM
Amongst women. Kimmerling, Ben. *Furrow* 44:273-282 My 1993
Differences that bind the liberation of women in Africa. Magesa, Laurenti. *AFER* 35:44-53 F 1993
Es geht um mehr als Christa Wolf. Kurz, Paul Konrad. *Stimm Zeit* 211:352-356 My 1993
A feminist critique. Dowell, Susan. *Way Suppl* 77:76-86 Sum 1993
A feminist's path to Rome. Maitland, Sara, 1950-. *Tablet* 247:422 Ap 3 1993
From conception to deception: the nazification of the feminist movement [por]. Sheridan, Ann. *Linacre* 60:31-39 Ag 1993
A good Catholic girl. Gateley, Edwina. *Tablet* 247:851-852 Jl 3 1993
How do I live now? Schmidt, Ruth. *USCath* 58:26-30 Je 1993
La ilustracion olvidada. Condorcet, de Gouges, de Lamberty y Otros. Madrid: Anthropos, 1993. x, 176p ISBN 84-7658-408-3
Mary feminism: compatible but challenging. Morrow, Carol Ann. *St Anth* 100:10-15 My 1993
The misuse of the pen. Cosstick, Vicky. *Tablet* 247:294 Mr 6 1993
Ms Buttons. *Tablet* 247:1099 Ag 28 1993
Newton in drag. D'Souza, Dinesh, 1961-. *Crisis* 11:4-5 Ja 1993
Renewing our love. Mullen, Peter. *Register* 69:2 My 23 1993
What Christopher Columbus has to say about feminism [editorial]. Callam, Daniel. *Can Cath Rev* 11:2-3 Ap 1993
Why feminists and prolifers need each other. Wiley, Juli Loesch. *New Oxford Rev* 60:9-14 N 1993
FEMINISM—ETHICAL ASPECTS
No longer patient: feminist ethics and health care. Sherwin, Susan, 1947-. Philadelphia: Temple University Press, 1992. 286p ISBN 0-87722-889-2 LC 91-14499
FEMINISM—PHILOSOPHY
Alienation, cultura differences, and moral judgment. McLane, Janice. *PhilosTod* 37:78-88 Spr 1993
Edith Stein: essential differences. McAlister, Linda Lopez. *PhilosTod* 37:70-77 Spr 1993
FEMINISM—RELIGIOUS ASPECTS
Discipleship of equals: a critical feminist ecology of liberation. Fiorenza, Elisabeth Schüssler, 1938-. New York: Crossroad, 1993. x, 372p ISBN 0-82451-244-8 LC 92-31264
Gaia and God: an ecofeminist theology of earth healing. Ruether, Rosemary Radford. San Francisco: HarperSanFrancisco, 1992. 310p ISBN 0-06067-022-3 LC 91-58911

John Paul warns of "extreme" feminism. Burke, Greg. *Register* 69:1+ Jl 18 1993

Mysticism and feminism. Proukou, Katherine. *Living Prayer* 26:23-26 S-O 1993

Ordinary time: cycles in marriage, faith, and renewal. Mairs, Nancy, 1943-. Boston: Beacon Press, 1993. x, 238p ISBN 0-8070-7056-4 LC 92-40421

Pope: reject "extreme" feminism. Thavis, John. *Nat Cath Rep* 29:7 Jl 16 1993

FEMINIST THEOLOGY

Are we all feminists now? Steichen, Donna. *SocJust* 84:11-15 Ja-F 1993

Book review [review article *She who is* by E Johnson]. Imbelli, Robert P. *Church* 9:51-56 Aut 1993

But she said: feminist practices of biblical interpretation. Fiorenza, Elisabeth Schüssler, 1938-. Boston: Beacon, 1992. x, 261p ISBN 0-8070-1214-9

Catholic journalism as a chancery bulletin board. Chittister, Joan D. *Nat Cath Rep* 29:14 My 28 1993

Celibacy: a feminist view. Gramick, Jeannine. *Sisters* 65:255-262 Jl 1993

The challenge of inculturation. Lane, Dermot A. *Living Light* 29:3-21 Wint 1992

Christian feminists birth global meeting. Gibeau, Dawn. *Nat Cath Rep* 30:3 N 19 1993

Christian resources for feminist spirituality. Carmody, Denise Lardner. *Stud Form Spir* 14:207-217 My 1993

Church in the round: feminist interpretation of the church. Russell, Letty M. Louisville: John Knox Press, 1993. 235p ISBN 0-66425-070-x LC 93-9306

The day I hated being a man. Schmidt, Stephen A. *USCath* 58:30-31 Je 1993

Discipleship of equals: a critical feminist ecology of liberation. Fiorenza, Elisabeth Schüssler, 1938-. New York: Crossroad, 1993. x, 372p ISBN 0-82451-244-8 LC 92-31264

Feminism and theology: beyond women's ordination. Cahoy, William J. *Sisters* 65:243-251 Jl 1993

Feminist readings, gospel narrative and critical theory. Dewey, Joanna. *Bib Th Bul* 22:167-173 Wint 1992

Feminist theology, evangelisation and the embodiment of truth. Grey, Mary. *Month* 25:485-490 D 1992

Feminist theology: a proposal. Martin, Francis. *Communio* 20:334-376 Sum 1993

Gorgon theology. Montgomery, John Warwick, 1931-. *New Oxford Rev* 60:20-21 Jl-Ag 1993

The gospel according to Mary: a New Testament for women. Winter, Miriam Therese. New York: The Crossroad Publishing Company, 1993. x, 143p ISBN 0-8245-1174-3 LC 92-403531

Horizons for Catholic feminist theology. Conn, Joann Wolski, and Conn, Walter E, eds. Washington, D C: Georgetown University Press, 1992. x, 207p ISBN 0-87840-534-8 LC 92-30435

"I listen, I suspect, later I make poetry" [interview by S Rojas; tr fr *Pastoral Popular*]. Gebara, Ivone. *LADOC* 24:10-15 S-O 1993

Matthew, Mark, Luke, and John. Kunkel, Francis L. *Sisters* 65:283-289 Jl 1993

A middle way for Catholic women. Leifeld, Wendy. *New Cov* 22:7-9 Je 1993

The most adventurous of nuns: Ursulines and the future. Weaver, Mary Jo. *RRel* 52:486-502 Jl-Ag 1993

Re-membering Jesus: women, prophecy, and resistance in the memory of the early churches. D'Angelo, Mary Rose. *Horizons (CTS)* 19:199-218 Fall 1992

"Reproducing the world": Mary O'Brien's theory of reproductive consciousness and implications for feminist incarnational theology. Kaminski, Phyllis H. *Horizons (CTS)* 19:240-262 Fall 1992

The shadow of heaven. Breda, William C Van. *HPR* 93:62-65 Ap 1993

Something fundamental is afoot. Johnson, Luke Timothy, 1943-. *Comm* 120:17-22 Ja 29 1993

A theological case for God-She expanding the treasury of metaphor. Johnson, Elizabeth A, 1941-. *Comm* 120:9-14 Ja 29 1993

The trinity and feminism. Kimel, Alvin F, Jr. *Thomist* 57:509-520 Jl 1993

Women and worship [exc fr *Liturgy: language and metaphor; Liturgy: ethics and justice*]. Buttrick, David G, et al. *Liturgy* 10:34-36 Spr 1993

Women views of Christian life. Long, Grace D Cumming. Louisville: John Knox, 1993. x, 176p ISBN 0-664-25408-x

Women-church: "adrift" from Catholicism? Martinez, Demetria. *Nat Cath Rep* 29:3-4 Ap 16 1993

FEMINISTS FOR LIFE

Supporting prolife women candidates. Ferguson, Lisa. *Register* 69:2 Ap 25 1993

FENWICK, EDWARD DOMINIC, 1768-1832

Dominican ideals in early America: the example of Edward Dominic Fenwick. Lisska, Anthony. *New Blckfrs* 74:382-392 S 1993

FERGUSON, ANN

Alienation, cultura differences, and moral judgment. McLane, Janice. *PhilosTod* 37:78-88 Spr 1993

FERNANDEZ, JORGE A

John Paul II, Pope, (1991-12-21) Allocutiones (Reception of the new Ambassador from Panama) [Spanish]. John Paul II, Pope, 1920- (Karol Wojtyla) (elected 1978). *AAS* 85:35-36 Ja 7 1993*

FERNANDEZ, JOSEPH

The worst of the "Times" some news doesn't fit. Steinfels, Margaret O'Brien, 1941-. *Comm* 120:4-5 Mr 12 1993

FERNANDEZ SOLAR, TERESA DE JESUS DE LOS ANDES (JUANA), 1900-1920

Congregation for the Causes of Saints (1992-07-11) Blessed Teresa de Jesus de los Andes. Congregation for the Causes of Saints. *AAS* 85:201-203 F 3 1993*

Congregation for the Causes of Saints (1992-07-11) Decree on a miracle. Congregation for the Causes of Saints. *TPS* 38:37-38 Ja-F 1993*

FERRARA-FLORENCE, COUNCIL OF, 1438-1439

Toward a new Council of Florence. Nicholas of Cusa, 1401-1464. Washington, DC: Schiller Institute, 1993. x, 577p ISBN 0-9621095-8-4 LC 92-85238

FERRARI, ANDREA, CARDINAL, 1850-1921

John Paul II, Pope, (1987-05-10) Litterae Apostolicae (Apostolic Letters) [Latin]. John Paul II, Pope, 1920- (Karol Wojtyla) (elected 1978). *AAS* 84:832-835 S 8 1992*

FERRER, LUIS AMIGO, BP, 1854-1934

Congregation for the Causes of Saints (1992-06-13) Decree on the heroic virtues. Congregation for the Causes of Saints. *TPS* 38:19-20 Ja-F 1993*

FERRER, VICENTE

Biblia de San Vicente convento de San Esteban: Salamanca. Espinel, J Luis. *Cien Tom* 119:521-548 S-D 1992

FERRY, JEAN-MARC

La personne humaine et son identité morale. Fuchs, Eric. *Supplement* 184:193-203 Mr-Ap 1993

FERTILITY, HUMAN

Ethical implications of a people's changing visage. *Origins* 22:758-761 Ap 15 1993

FERTILIZATION IN VITRO

IVF: it solves very little. Krause, Edward. *Register* 69:5 Je 6 1993

Rachel's lament, Jacob's reply [editorial]. *America* 169:3 N 20 1993

FESTIVALS

Bayou blessing. Feister, John Bookser. *St Anth* 100:28-35 F 1993

FESTS, JOACHIM

Weder Gold noch Silber. Biser, Eugen. *Stimm Zeit* 211:343-350 My 1993

FETAL DEATH

The death of dreams: coping with the loss of an unborn child. Wong, Pamela Pearson. *St Anth* 100:36-39 Ja 1993

FETAL TISSUE—RESEARCH

Baby farming? Ryan, Jim. *SocJust* 84:87-89 My-Je 1993

An ethical look at fetal-tissue research. Shaw, Russell. *OSV* 81:16 Ap 25 1993

Fetal tissue research: the cutting edge? Crutcher, Keith A. *Linacre* 60:10-19 My 1993

Fetal tissue transplantation: an ethical analysis. Roessler, Mark A. *Linacre* 60:60-74 Ag 1993

Fetal-tissue "advances" threaten the unborn. Nanney, Lisa. *OSV* 81:23 F 7 1993

The tissue issue: take it slow on fetal transplants. McCloskey, Liz Leibold. *Comm* 120:5-6 Mr 26 1993

FETUS—ABNORMALITIES

A doctor's dilemma. Lupton, Martin. *Tablet* 247:542 My 1 1993

FETUS—RELIGIOUS ASPECTS

Beratungspflicht und Strafverzicht. Demel, Sabine. *Stimm Zeit* 211:700-710 O 1993

The embryo and the fetus: new moral contexts. Cahill, Lisa Sowle. *TheolStds* 54:124-142 Mr 1993

FICTION

Bearing witness [interview by P Gilmour]. Thornton, Lawrence, 1937-. *Critic* 47:84-94 Wint 1992

The novel as spiritual guide. Sussman, Cornelia Silver, 1914-. *Living Prayer* 26:18-22 Ja-F 1993

FIDELITY

The virtue of fidelity. Keenan, James F. *Church* 9:38-39 Sum 1993

FILM CRITICISM

The Age of Innocence, Orlando. Russell, Kenneth C. *Can Cath Rev* 11:39 N 1993*

Altman goes self-indulgent, and China goes for big time. Cunneen, Joseph. *Nat Cath Rep* 30:16 N 12 1993*

Chasing, searching for and discovering secrets. Cunneen, Joseph. *Nat Cath Rep* 29:13 S 3 1993*

From bard to 'hood, 'tis true, from "Much Ado" to "Menace II". Cunneen, Joseph. *Nat Cath Rep* 29:16 Jl 2 1993*

Growing up is difficult these days. Cunneen, Joseph. *Nat Cath Rep* 29:14 Ap 23 1993*

Hollywood's dirty little secrets. Medved, Michael, 1948-. *Crisis* 11:18-23 Mr 1993

If Clint is best, it's bad news for the rest. Cunneen, Joseph. *Nat Cath Rep* 29:17 Jl 30 1993*

A month at the movies. Cunneen, Joseph. *Nat Cath Rep* 29:22 N 20 1992*

The world of film. Villano, Mark. *ChrWorld* 236:270-275 N-D 1993

FILM CRITICISM—SINGLE WORKS

The adventures of Huck Finn. Russell, Kenneth C. *Can Cath Rev* 11:40 Je 1993

The age of innocence [directed by M Scorses]. Alleva, Richard. *Comm* 120:14-17 N 5 1993

The age of innocence [directed by M. Scorsese]. Arnold, James. *St Anth* 101:4 N 1993

The age of innocence [directed by M. Scorsese]. Blake, Richard A, 1939-. *America* 169:18 O 23 1993

Aladdin. Arnold, James. *St Anth* 100:4 F 1993

Alive [directed by F Marshall]. Arnold, James. *St Anth* 100:4 Ap 1993

Les amants du Pont Neuf. McKevitt, Daniel. *Month* 26:28-29 Ja 1993

Amos and Andrew. Russell, Kenneth C. *Can Cath Rev* 11:40 My 1993

The baby of Mâcon. Darwent, Charles. *Tablet* 247:1238 S 25 1993

Bad lieutenant [directed by A Ferrara]. McKevitt, Daniel. *Month* 26:108 Mr 1993

Bad lieutenant. Allen, Edgar. *Tablet* 247:283 F 27 1993

La bella e la bestia (Beauty and the Beast). Fantuzzi, Virgilio. *Civilta* 2:103-104 Ap 3 1993

Benny and Joon. Russell, Kenneth C. *Can Cath Rev* 11:39-40 Jl-Ag 1993

The bodyguard. Russell, Kenneth C. *Can Cath Rev* 11:40 F 1993

Born yesterday. Russell, Kenneth C. *Can Cath Rev* 11:40 F 1993

Bram Stoker's Dracula. Alleva, Richard. *Comm* 119:17 D 18 1992

Bram Stoker's Dracula. Blake, Richard A, 1939-. *America* 168:16-17 Ja 16-23 1993

Brother's keeper. Blake, Richard A, 1939-. *America* 168:16 Ap 17 1993

Chaplin. Allen, Edgar. *Tablet* 247:20 Ja 2 1993

Chaplin. Alleva, Richard. *Comm* 120:16 F 12 1993

Chaplin. Arnold, James. *St Anth* 100:4 Mr 1993

Chaplin. Austin, Ronald. *Register* 69:5 F 7 1993

Cliffhanger [directed by R Harlin]. Walton, James. *Tablet* 247:864 Jl 3 1993

Cliffhanger. Arnold, James. *St Anth* 101:5 Ag 1993

A complex love-thriller and a whimsical farce. Cunneen, Joseph. *Nat Cath Rep* 29:18 Ja 8 1993*

Soft top, hard shoulder. Allen, Edgar. *Tablet* 247:175 F 6 1993
Sommersby [directed by J Amiel]. Russell, Kenneth C. *Can Cath Rev* 11:39-40 Ap 1993
Sommersby. Allen, Edgar. *Tablet* 247:555 My 1 1993
Sommersby. Arnold, James. *St Anth* 100:5 Ap 1993
Sommersby. McKevitt, Daniel. *Month* 26:230 Je 1993
Sommersby. Wallace, James A, 1944-. *Liguorian* 81:35 Je 1993
Splitting heirs. Allen, Edgar. *Tablet* 247:485 Ap 10-17 1993
Stolen children [directed by G Amelio]. Alleva, Richard. *Comm* 120:20-21 My 7 1993
Stolen children [directed by G Amelio]. Arnold, James. *St Anth* 101:4 Je 1993
The story of Qiu Ju [directed by Zhang Yimou]. McKevitt, Daniel. *Month* 26:230-231 Je 1993
Strictly ballroom. Arnold, James. *St Anth* 100:4-5 My 1993
Swing kids. Coulombe, Charles. *Register* 69:5 Mr 28 1993
Tango. Darwent, Charles. *Tablet* 247:1078 Ag 21 1993
This boy's life [directed by M Caton-Jones]. Alleva, Richard. *Comm* 120:18-19 Je 4 1993
This boy's life. Arnold, James. *ST Anth* 101:4 Jl 1993
Three of hearts. Darwent, Charles. *Tablet* 247:924 Jl 17 1993
Tous les matins du monde [directed by A Corneau]. McKevitt, Daniel. *Month* 26:74-75 F 1993
Tous les matins du monde. Allen, Edgar. *Tablet* 247:52 Ja 9 1993
Toys [directed by B Levinson]. Allen, Edgar. *Tablet* 247:346 Mr 13 1993
Toys. Arnold, James. *St Anth* 100:4-5 Mr 1993
True romance [directed by T. Scott]. Alleva, Richard. *Comm* 120:22-24 O 22 1993
Truly, madly deeply. Wallace, James A, 1944-. *Liguorian* 81:43 F 1993
The unforgiven. Fantuzzi, Virgilio. *Civilta* 2:311-312 My 1 1993
Used people [directed by B Kidron]. Allen, Edgar. *Tablet* 247:485 Ap 10-17 1993
The vanishing. Darwent, Charles. *Tablet* 247:794-795 Je 19 1993
A winter's tale. Allen, Edgar. *Tablet* 247:53 Ja 9 1993
A winter's tale. Bedouelle, Guy. *New Blckfrs* 74:301-306 Je 1993
L 627. Allen, Edgar. *Tablet* 247:81-82 Ja 16 1993

FILMS
From The sun also rises to High noon: the hypervisual great awakening in American literature and film. Meyer, William E H, Jr. *Cithara* 32:39-59 N 1992
Lillian Gish: a passing. Blake, Richard A, 1939-. *America* 168:14 Mr 20-27 1993
Seen any good movies lately? Costello, Gerald M, 1931-. *USCath* 58:48-50 Je 1993
La vida Fellini. Austin, Ronald. *Register* 69:2 Mr 14 1993

FILMS—ETHICAL ASPECTS
Film makers, film viewers: their challenges and opportunities [pastoral letter]. Mahony, Roger Michael, Cardinal, 1936-. Boston: St Paul Books & Media, 1992. 31p ISBN 0-8198-2654-5
Hollywood and violence. Austin, Ronald. *Register* 69:3 Mr 21 1993
A kinder, gentler America. McKevitt, Daniel. *Month* 26:108-109 Mr 1993
Movies: the struggle between art and entertainment. May, John R. *ChrWorld* 236:252-257 N-D 1993
Reel winners: ten good movies that can make you better. Hermes, Joan Garvey. *USCath* 58:6-14 O 1993
Tra cinema e pittura sulle tracce dell'invisibile. Fantuzzi, Virgilio. *Civilta* 144:571-583 Mr 20 1993

FILMS—PHILOSOPHY
Of lingering eyes and talking things: Adorno and Deleuze on philosophy since Auschwitz. Toolan, David S. *PhilosTod* 37:227-246 Aut 1993

FILMS—RELIGIOUS ASPECTS
The Apostle's dialogue with American culture. Jewett, Robert. Louisville: Westminster, 1993. x, 192p ISBN 0-664-25482-9
Hollywood calls Father Coiro [condensed fr *Los Angeles Daily News* F 7 1993]. Larsen, Peter. *CDgst* 57:54-56 Jl 1993
Lungo Il Fiume Di Ermanno Olmi. Fantuzzi, Virgilio. *Civilta* 143:382-393 N 21 1992
Reel power: spiritual growth through film. Sinetar, Marsha. Missouri: Triumph Books, 1993. x, 179p ISBN 0-89243-529-1 LC 92-44676
Saint Paul at the movies: the apostle's dialogue with American culture. Jewett, Robert. Louisville, Kentucky: John Knox Press, 1993. 192p ISBN 0-664-25482-9

FILMS, RELIGIOUS
Theology in the cinema. Pavelin, Alan. *Month* 26:202-205 My 1993

FINANCE
CELAM IV "bottom line" its own statement. Wirpsa, Leslie. *Nat Cath Rep* 29:9 N 20 1992
The great retrenchment and the new industrial state. Dugger, William M. *RSocEcon* 50:453-471 Wint 1992
The Mariological Society of America Financial Report 1 July 1991 to 30 June 1992. Samaha, John M. *Marian Stds* 43:192 1992

FINANCE, PERSONAL
Getting into credit together. Nolan, Margaret. *Priests & People* 7:178-180 My 1993

FINES (PENALTIES)
Guideline amendments dramatically change the structure of organizational fines. Fiorelli, Paul E. *CLawyer* 35 no 2:181-197 1993

FINNIS, JOHN
Basic goods and the human good in recent Catholic moral theology. Porter, Jean. *Thomist* 57:27-49 Ja 1993
Liberty under the moral law: B Hoose's critique of the Grisez-Finnis Theory of human good. George, Robert P. *Heythrop* 34:175-180 Ap 1993

FINNISH LANGUAGE
Finland's best-seller. *Tablet* 247:242 F 20 1993

FIORENZA, FRANCIS SCHUSSLER
Habermas e la teologia. Brena, Gian Luigi. *Civilta* 3:51-54 Jl 3 1993

FIREARMS
Enforcing the law: consider the Bill of Rights. Gaffney, Edward McGlynn, Jr, 1941-. *Comm* 120:5-6 My 21 1993

Only a cultural revolution will end violence [editorial]. *Nat Cath Rep* 29:24 Je 4 1993
The right to bear arms? Settle, Stephen. *Register* 69:5 Jl 25 1993
There's so much folks can do with 60 million handguns [editorial]. *Nat Cath Rep* 29:24 Ja 22 1993

FIREARMS—LAW
Gunfight on Capitol Hill [editorial]. Dangel, Mary Jo. *St Anth* 100:27 Ap 1993

FIRST COMMUNION
"I am with you always". Jeray, Diane. *Liguorian* 81:13-15 Je 1993
We come to your table: DREs talk about first communion. Ristow, Kate. *Catechist* 26:18-21 Ja 1993

FISCHER, ELAINE
A monastic and a firefighter. White, Faye E. *Sisters* 65:30-34 Ja 1993

FISHER, CARL, BP
Youthful churchman dies [obit]. *Register* 69:2 S 19 1993

FISHER, JOHN, BP
Three cheers for John Fisher. Collopy, Anne Marie. *Register* 69:5 Ja 3 1993

FISHERIES
Bayou blessing. Feister, John Bookser. *St Anth* 100:28-35 F 1993

FISHERMEN
An offer they couldn't refuse: the Apostles become fishers of men. Goodman, Richard. *Comm* 120:19-21 O 22 1993

FLAGELLANTS
The origin of the Penitentes of New Mexico: separating fact from fiction. Espinosa, J Manuel. *CHist* 79:454-477 Jl 1993

FLAGS
Flags don't belong in church. Grippo, Dan. *USCath* 58:26-30 Mr 1993

FLATMAN, MARTIN
Asian appeal. *Tablet* 247:44 Ja 9 1993

FLAUBERT, GUSTAVE, 1821-1880
The whatness of Loulou: allegories of Thomism in Flaubert. Wise, Christopher. *Relig Lit* 25:35-49 Spr 1993

FLAY, J
Hegel, Kolb and Flay: foundationalism or anti-foundationalism? Kow, James P. *IPQ* 33:203-218 Je 1993

FLOOD—RELIGIOUS ASPECTS
Between the flood and the rainbow: encountering God in the living community of creation. Smyth, Geraldine Marie. *Doctr Life* 43:216 Ap 1993

FLOODS
The great flood of 1993 [photos]. Collins, Brad. *Extensn* 88:16-20 O 16 1993

FLORENSKY, PAVEL A
The metaphysics of Pan-Unity in Pavel A. Florensky: a world view. Slesinski, Robert, 1950-. *Diakonia* 26 no 3:185-195 1993

FLORIDA—CHURCH HISTORY
The Franciscan Missions of Florida a lost history is found again. Wintz, Jack Alton, 1936-. *St Anth* 101:28-35 Je 1993

FLORIO, JAMES J, 1937-
Just taxation in Catholic social ethics and the Florio plan. Gorrell, Paul J. *SocJust* 84:90-92 My-Je 1993

FLYNN, RAYMOND LEE, 1939-
A Boston politician comes to John Paul's court. O'Grady, Desmond. *OSV* 82:3 Ag 22 1993
Human rights ambassador. *Tablet* 247:785 Je 19 1993
John Paul II, Pope, (1993-09-02) United States [Orig in English]. John Paul II, Pope, 1920- (Karol Wojtyla) (elected 1978). *OR(Eng)* 1306:10 S 8 1993*
Flynn flaps focuses on job's substance, style. McManus, James. *Nat Cath Rep* 29:9 Je 18 1993

FOLIC ACID
Is folic acid a prolife concern? O'Leary, Dale. *Register* 69:5 Jl 4 1993

FOLK LITERATURE
The magic seed. Billy, Dennis J. *Living Prayer* 26:23 N-D 1993

FOLK MUSIC AND SONGS—SPIRITUALS
Wade in the winter: the wisdom of the spirituals. Jones, Arthur C, 1936-. New York: Maryknoll, 1993. x, 182p ISBN 0-88344-923-4 LC 93-7491

FOLK RELIGION- MEXICO
Our Lady of Guadalupe: a Liberating interpretation [tr fr *Conciencia Latinoamericana*]. Segundo, Juan Luis. *LADOC* 24:24-27 S-O 1993

FOLK RELIGION, CHINESE
On renewing the church in China. Schreiter, Robert J. *Origins* 22:709-714 Mr 25 1993

FOLKLORE
Fantastic folklore. Madden, Nora. *Tod Cath Teach* 26:41-42+ Ap 1993
Pennsylvania Dutch. Wentz, Richard E, ed. New York: Paulist Press, 1993. x, 329p ISBN 0-8091-0439-3 LC 92-33184
Pennsylvania Dutch. Wentz, Richard E, ed. New York: Paulist Press, 1993. x, 329p ISBN 0-8091-0439-3 LC 92-33184

FONTAINE, GASTON, 1921-1992
Fontaine, Gaston, 1921-1992 [obit]. Fauret, Pierre. *Notitiae* 28:428-430 Je 1992

FOOD—INTERNATIONAL COOPERATION
John Paul II, Pope, (1992-12-05) basic right to nutrition. John Paul II, Pope, 1920- (Karol Wojtyla) (elected 1978). *TPS* 38:142-146 My-Je 1993*

FOOD FOR THE POOR (ORGANIZATION)
Food for the poor. Weinert, Allan. *Liguorian* 81:4-10 O 1993
Seeking justice for the poor. Schutt, Brian. *Momentum* 24:76-77 F-Mr 1993

FOOD INDUSTRY AND TRADE
GATT: an ethical void. Egan, Eileen. *Cath Work* 60:1+ Je-Jl 1993

FOOD RELIEF
Americans abroad: when good intentions go awry. McCarthy, Abigail Quigley. *Comm* 120:11-12 Je 4 1993
A baby named Luck [editorial]. *Comm* 119:3-4 D 18 1992
Convoys of courage. *Tablet* 247:1009-1010 Ag 7 1993
Hunger. Feuerherd, Peter. *Register* 69:1+ F 21 1993
The limits of the UN [editorial]. *Tablet* 247:775 Je 19 1993
Restoring hope in Somalia [editorial]. *America* 168:3 Ja 2-9 1993

Apostle of religious freedom [adapted fr *John Courtney Murray and the American civil conversation*]. Canavan, Francis, 1917-. *Crisis* 11:31-35 My 1993

The Church learning and the Church teaching: Vatican II and the liberal tradition of religious freedom. O'Donnell, Robert J. *JEcumen Stds* 29:399-417 Sum-Aut 1992

Equal rights for religion [editorial]. *America* 169:3 Jl 17-24 1993

John Paul II, Pope, (1993-04-25) May Albania be equal to the challenge. John Paul II, Pope, 1920- (Karol Wojtyla) (elected 1978). *TPS* 38:275-279 S-O 1993*

Pray for it: religious freedom in Russia. Gaffney, Edward McGlynn, Jr, 1941-. *Comm* 120:5-7 My 7 1993

Religious freedom in the public school setting. Colby, Kimberlee Wood. *Momentum* 24:55-59 N-D 1993

Stuck with a Satanist? religious autonomy in a regulated society [exc fr *The culture of disbelief*]. Carter, Stephen L. *Comm* 120:15-18 Ag 13 1993

FREEDOM, RELIGIOUS- CHINA
The Catholic Church in modern China: perspectives. Tang, Edmond, and Wiest, Jean-Paul, eds. Maryknoll: Orbis, 1993. x, 260p ISBN 0-88344-834-3 LC 93-14944

FREEDOM (THEOLOGY)
Freedom: the teachings of Jesus. Pierce, Ted M. New York: Vantage Press, 1992. x, 225p ISBN 0-533-10182-4 LC 91-91544

Grace and the exercises. Haight, Roger. *Way Suppl* 76:44-52 Spr 1993

The hastening that waits. Biggar, Nigel. New York: Oxford University Press, 1993. x, 208p ISBN 0-826457-7

John Paul II, Pope, (1993-10-05) Veritatis splendor [abridged]. John Paul II, Pope, 1920- (Karol Wojtyla) (elected 1978). *Tablet* 247:1312-1318 O 9 1993*

John Paul II, Pope, (1993-10-05) Veritatis Splendor. John Paul II, Pope, 1920- (Karol Wojtyla) (elected 1978). *Origins* 23:297-334 O 14 1993*

John Paul II, Pope, (19930-10-05) Veritatis Splendor. John Paul II, Pope, 1920- (Karol Wojtyla) (elected 1978). *OR(Eng)* 1310:1 O 6 1993*

Liberación, inculturación y alteridad. Espeja, Jesús. *Cien Tom* 120:153-167 Ja-Ap 1993

Living free in Christ. Anderson, Neil T. Ventura: Gospel Light, 1993. 310p ISBN 0-8307-1604-1 LC 93-7358

FREEDOM (THEOLOGY)—BIBLICAL TEACHING
Morals and the meaning of Jesus: reflections on the hard sayings. Harvey, Nicholas Peter. Cleveland: The Pilgrim Press, 1993. x, 112p ISBN 0-8298-0947-3 LC 94-41216

FREEDOM OF ASSOCIATION
A religion club in the public high school? Marthaler, Berard L, 1927-. *Living Light* 29:11-18 Spr 1993

FREEDOM OF CHOICE ACT
Congresspeak. Arkes, Hadley. *Crisis* 11:11-12 Jl-Ag 1993

Freedom of Choice Act: a great danger. Riga, Peter John, 1933-. *Linacre* 60:83-85 Ag 1993

Is it time? Foster, George P. *OSV* 82:19 Ag 29 1993

FREEDOM OF CONSCIENCE
Conscience clauses offer little protection [excerpt fr *Journal of logal medicine*]. Wardle, Lynn D, 1947-. *Health Prog* 74:79-83 Jl-Ag 1993

Wojtyla and the Council [excerpt fr *Il pensiero di Karol Wojtyla*]. Buttiglione, Rocco. *Crisis* 11:21-25 F 1993

FREEDOM OF SPEECH
The Equal Access Act and the public schools: questions and answers. *Living Light* 29:3-10 Spr 1993

Free speech for whom? D'Souza, Dinesh, 1961-. *Crisis* 10:4 N 1992

FREEDOM OF THE PRESS
The papers protest too much [editorial]. *Tablet* 247:63 Ja 16 1993

FREEMAN, ANTHONY
Anglican priest sacked for unorthodoxy. *Tablet* 247:1111 Ag 28 1993

FREGE, F L GOTTLOB
Frege's error. Ruthrof, Horst. *PhilosTod* 37:306-317 Aut 1993

FREUD, SIGMUND
Degenerate moderns. Jones, Michael E. San Francisco: Ignatius Press, 1993. ISBN 0-89810-447-2

Idols and false images of God: a psychoanalytical perspective. Kelly, Shay. *Doctr Life* 43:13-19 Ja 1993

The phallacy of Genesis: a feminist and psychoanalytic approach. Rashkow, Ilona N. Louisville: Westminster, 1993. x, 144p ISBN 0-664-25250-8

FREYRE, GILBERTO
Teologia, racismo e mestiçagem. Frisotti, Heitor. *REB* 52:833-845 D 1992

FRIARS
Vincent McNabb OP 1868-1943. Ombres, Robert. *New Blckfrs* 74:330-332 Jl-Ag 1993

FRIENDSHIP
Amitiés sacerdotales et célibat. Gaidon, Maurice. *Seminarium* 33:77-87 Ja-Mr 1993

Befriending: a self-guided retreat for busy people. Payne, Joseph A. New Jersey: Paulist Press, 1992. x, 165p ISBN 0-8091-3354-7 LC 92-28398

The eleventh commandment: listen!. Thomas, Ellen Lamar. *CDgst* 57:78-81 Ap 1993

Freya and friendship. Hodgkin, E C. *Tablet* 247:11 Ja 2 1993

How to be friends with your grown children. Callahan, Sidney. *USCath* 58:32-38 Ap 1993

Living as friends. Bonnici, John S. *Priest* 49:39-44 F 1993

Love of friendship. Bonnici, John S. *HPR* 93:31+ Ja 1993

Parish diary: September. *Tablet* 247:1225 S 25 1993

Thomas Aquinas, preacher and friend. Fatula, Mary Ann. Minnesota: The Liturgical Press, 1993. x, 313p ISBN 0-8146-5031-7 LC 92-27552

FRINK, ELISABETH, 1930-1993
Frink, Elisabeth, 1930-1993 [obit]. *Tablet* 247:512-513 Ap 24 1993

FROMM, ERICH
The eclipse of difference: Merton's encounter with Judaism. Plank, Karl A. *Cist Stud* 28 no 2:179-191 1993

FROST, ROBERT
Waiting for a gift from the sea. Foley, Sharon. *Sisters* 65:301-303 Jl 1993

FULL EMPLOYMENT POLICIES
America's silent depression: a challenge to social economics. Peterson, Wallace C, 1921-. *RSocEcon* 51:2-13 Spr 1993

FULL EMPLOYMENT POLICIES- IRELAND
A response to unemployment: ten propositions. Quigley, George. *Studies* 82:73-86 Spr 1993

FUND RAISING
But what shall we sell? McFadden, Sean. *Tod Cath Teach* 26:30+ Ap 1993

Catholic giving and the signs of the times. Hofheinz, Fred. *Origins* 22:520-523 Ja 7 1993

Great fundraising ideas for youth groups. Lynn, David, and Lynn, Kathy. Grand Rapids: Zondervan Publishing House, 1993. x, 208p ISBN 0-310-67171-x

FUNDAMENTALISM
The apostolic faith: Protestants and Roman Catholics. Norris, Frederick W. Minnesota: The Liturgical Press, 1992. x, 178p ISBN 0-8146-5029-5 LC 92-19536

Bible truth: a possible dialogue between biblical fundamentalism and Catholic scholarship. Branick, Vincent F. *StudiaM* 41:269-288 1992

Fondamentalismo e religione. Mertes, Klaus. *Civilta* 2:116-129 Ap 17 1993

Fundamentalism: challenges and dangers. Secondin, Bruno. *TheolDgst* 40:3-7 Spr 1993

Fundamentalismus und Religion. Kunert, Gunther. *Stimm Zeit* 211:53-64 Ja 1993

Secular fundamentalism and secular humanism: value sets for the twenty-first century. Kollar, Nathan R. *Stud Form Spir* 14:233-246 My 1993

When fundamentalism reduces God to a house pet [por]. Sheehan, Jim. *Nat Cath Rep* 30:23 O 29 1993

FUNDAMENTALISM—ISLAM
Dialogue [interview by G Burke]. Borrmans, Maurice. *Register* 69:1+ Ag 29 1993

Egypt's Muslim Brothers. Butt, Gerald. *Tablet* 246:1559-1560 D 12 1992

Islamic fundamentalism. Watt, William Montgomery. *StudiaM* 41:241-252 1992

FUNDAMENTALISM- LATIN AMERICAN
Fundamentalism in Latin America. Galindo, Florencio. *TheolDgst* 40:9-14 Spr 1993

FUNERAL MUSIC
People will sing at funeral vigils and committals. O'Brien, Thomas J. *Past Mus* 17:39-40 Ap-My 1993

FUNERAL RITES
The funeral liturgy communicating peace and hope. Wallace, James A, 1944-. *Liguorian* 81:53 Mr 1993

People will sing at funeral vigils and committals. O'Brien, Thomas J. *Past Mus* 17:39-40 Ap-My 1993

FUNERAL SERMONS
Ann Manganaro, S L. Kavanaugh, John. *Cath Work* 60:7 S 1993

Education was his line. Mitchell, Robert A. *America* 168:4-5 Ja 30 1993

Mass for a dead friend. Crosby, Ned. *Furrow* 44:27-29 Ja 1993

"We who are left"—the death of a clerical student. Sheridan, Daniel. *Furrow* 43:672-675 D 1992

FUNERALS
The Catholic way of dying. Ball, Ann. *OSV* 82:5 O 31 1993

Console one another: a guide for Christian funerals. Curley, Terence P. Kansas City: Sheed & Ward, 1993. 100p ISBN 1-55612-600-x LC 93-3540

The rites of death: celebrating a life. Martin, Joseph F. *Mod Lit* 20:18-20 O 1993

FUNK, VIRGIL C, JR, 1937-
Virgil Funk. *Mod Lit* 20:46 O 1993

FUTURE—BIBLICAL TEACHING
Don't stop (thinking about the context). Bossman, David M, ed. *Bib Th Bul* 23:46-47 Sum 1993

FUTURE LIFE
Eternal life in paradise [tr fr *La Civiltà Cattolica* Ap 4, 1992]. *HPR* 93:7-17 Ag-S 1993

Investments in the future. Ryan, Patrick J. *America* 169:30-31 N 6 1993

Reunited with our ancestors. Castel, Pol. *Cath Work* 60:7 Je-Jl 1993

Thoughts of heaven. Mason, Philip, 1906-. *Tablet* 247:543 My 1 1993

Vigilance! the Lord is coming [tr fr *La Civiltà Cattolica* D 5 1992]. *HPR* 94:7-16 N 1993

Vigilare Nell'Attesa Della Venuta Del Signore (editorial). *Civilta* 143:437-449 D 5 1992

FUTURE LIFE—BIBLICAL TEACHING
Death and destiny in the Bible. Wensing, Michael G. Minnesota: The Order of St Benedict, 1993. x, 83p ISBN 0-8146-2093-0 LC 92-27237

G

GABRIEL, COLUMBA
John Paul II, Pope, (1993-05-16). John Paul II, Pope, 1920- (Karol Wojtyla) (elected 1978). *TPS* 38:308-311 S-O 1993*

GABRIEL, JANINA, 1858-1926
Congregation for the Causes of Saints (1992-12-21) Decree on a miracle. Congregation for the Causes of Saints. *OR(Eng)* 1272:4 Ja 6 1993*

GADAMER, HANS-GEORG, 1900-
Creatures of truth. Bonsor, Jack A. *Thomist* 56:647-668 O 1992

The fragility of consciousness: Lonergan and the postmodern concern for the other. Lawrence, Fred. *TheolStds* 54:55-94 Mr 1993

Raison critique ou raison herméneutique? Aquirre Oraa, José María. *RPhil Louvain* 91:409-440 Ag 1993

GAEBLER, RALPH F
Staggering toward the new Jerusalem of constitutional theory: a response to Ralph F Gaebler. Murphy, Walter F. *Amer J Juris* 37:337-357 1992

GALBRAITH, JOHN KENNETH, 1908-
Does the market create preferred preferences? George, David. *RSocEcon* 51: 323-346 Aut 1993
The great retrenchment and the new industrial state. Dugger, William M. *RSocEcon* 50:453-471 Wint 1992

GALILEI, GALILEO, 1564-1642
Candied limes for Galileo. O'Grady, Desmond. *Tablet* 247:40-41 Ja 9 1993
Dr Frankenstein meets Galileo [editorial]. *OSV* 81:2 F 14 1993
Galileo and the Inquisition. Porter, Neil. *Doctr Life* 43:349-357 Jl-Ag 1993
The leaning tower of truth. Spaeth, Robert L, 1935-. *Comm* 120:6-7 Mr 26 1993
Note in margine al caso Galileo. Gallagher, Michael Paul, 1939-. *Civilta* 144: 424-436 Mr 6 1993
Paolo Foscarini's Letter to Galileo: the search for proofs of the earth's motion. Kelter, Irving A. *Mod Schlmn* 70:31-44 N 1992
A proposito di un recente dibattito su Dio e la scienza. Gallagher, Michael Paul, 1939-. *Civilta* 2:327-338 My 15 1993
The relationship between theology and science [interview by B Dodds]. Jaki, Stanley L. *OSV* 81:8-9 F 14 1993
Sorry about that, Galileo, but it wasn't church's fault. Hebblethwaite, Peter, 1930-. *Nat Cath Rep* 29:21 N 13 1992
Through a daughter's eyes. O'Grady, Desmond. *OSV* 81:16-17 F 14 1993

GALILEI, MARIE CELESTE, 1600-1634
Candied limes for Galileo. O'Grady, Desmond. *Tablet* 247:40-41 Ja 9 1993

GALLAGHER, VERA
Becoming whole again. Wolcott, John. *OSV* 81:5 Ja 3 1993

GAMALIEL II
The Pharisees and the church. Schwartz, G David. *BibleT* 31:301-304 S 1993

GAMBLING—RELIGIOUS ASPECTS
No more bingo on the Bayou. Feister, John Bookser. *St Anth* 100:34-35 F 1993

GAMMIE, JOHN GLENN, 1929-
Essays in memory of John G. Gammie. Perdue, Leo G, et al, eds. Louisville: John Knox, 1993. x, 352p ISBN 0-664-25295-8

GANDHI, MAHATMA
Global harmony and public action. Barnes, Michael R. *Month* 26:(I) Mr 1993
'I can wait 40 or 400 years": Gandhian Satyagraha West and East. Starosta, William J, and Chaudhary, Anju G. *IPQ* 33:163-172 Je 1993

GANGS
Youth gangs: a spreading problem. Martinet, Ken. *Momentum* 24:68-72 Ap-My 1993

GARCIA, SAMUEL RUIZ, BP
Abortive effort to oust bishop puts Vatican on the defensive [por]. Coleman, Bill, and Coleman, Patty. *Nat Cath Rep* 30:7 N 12 1993
Support swells for bishop threatened with removal. Coleman, Bill, and Coleman, Patty. *Nat Cath Rep* 30:16 N 19 1993

GARDENING
The messenger. O'Boyle, Patrick J. *Liguorian* 81:24-25 Ag 1993

GARDENS
A garden of conceptual delights. Podles, Mary Elizabeth. *Crisis* 11:54-60 Je 1993

GARDNER, JOY
Death of a deportee [editorial]. *Tablet* 247:1031 Ag 14 1993

GASPARRI, PIETRO
Ordinazioni Anglicane e Ecclesiologia. I. Rambaldi, Giuseppe. *Gregorianum* 74 no 2:277-307 1993

GASSIS, MACRAM MAX, BP, 1938-
Sudanese bishops decry human-rights abuses. Collins, Carole. *Nat Cath Rep* 29:11 N 6 1992

GATES, JIM
Always the poor. Dodds, Bill. *New Cov* 22:21-24 Je 1993

GAUDIN, JULIETTE
Who are their models? Cunningham, Beatrice. *ReligTJ* 27:38-39 O 1993

GAUNILO OF MARMOUTIER 11TH CENT
Introduction to re-thinking representation: Anselm and visual thinking. Kromm, Jane. *Listening* 28:95-104 Spr 1993

GAZA STRIP—GOVERNMENT
Rabin and Arafat brave radical wrath. Wigoder, Geoffrey Bernard, 1922-. *Tablet* 247:1120-1121 S 4 1993

GEERTZ, CLIFFORD, 1926-
Religion and culture in Irish society. Macken, John. *Studies* 82:123-130 Sum 1993

GENDER
see also English Language—Gender
Catholic theology, gender, and the future of Western civilization [editorial]. Schindler, David L. *Communio* 20:200-239 Sum 1993
Equal gender military: progress or spiritual Nihilism? Chodes, John. *SocJust* 84:40-44 Mr-Ap 1993
Pink or blue: gender roles have colored our view. Unsworth, Tim. *Salt* 13:14-17 Ja 1993
Sex and gender differentiation in Hildegard of Bingen and Edith Stein. Allen, Prudence. *Communio* 20:389-414 Sum 1993

GENERAL CHAPTER OF THE CONSOLATA MISSIONARIES
John Paul II, Pope, (1993-06-19) Apostles [Orig in Italian]. John Paul II, Pope, 1920- (Karol Wojtyla) (elected 1978). *OR(Eng)* 1300:7 Jl 21 1993*

GENEROSITY
Dialogue [interview by J Luxmoore]. Lawson, Doug. *Register* 69:1+ Je 6 1993

GENEROSITY—RELIGIOUS ASPECTS
A family affair generous beyond measure. McGill, Mary. *Catechist* 27:74-75 S 1993

GENET, JEAN, 1910-1986
Killing the cat: sacrifice and beauty in Genet and Mishima. Wyschogrod, Edith. *Relig Lit* 25:107-119 Sum 1993

GENETIC COUNSELING
Prescribing our future: ethical challenges in genetic counseling. Bartels, Dianne M, et al, eds. New York: Aldine de Gruyter, 1993. 186p ISBN 0-20230-452-3 LC 92-21469

GENETIC ENGINEERING
Biotechnology and the nature of life. Atwater, Tim. *Cath Work* 60:1+ Ja-F 1993
Commerce beginning to squeeze genetic science. Meehan, Bridget Mary. *Register* 69:1+ Je 20 1993
Sounding the alarm on sex selection. *Tablet* 247:149 Ja 30 1993
Unnatural growth hormone. Atwater, Tim. *Cath Work* 60:7 Mr-Ap 1993

GENETIC ENGINEERING—ETHICAL ASPECTS
Genomanalysen im Versicherungs- und Gerichtswesen. Münk, Hans J. *Stimm Zeit* 211:34-44 Ja 1993

GENETIC ENGINEERING—RELIGIOUS ASPECTS
Der Bauplan des Menschen. Reiter, Johannes. *Stimm Zeit* 211:219-231 Ap 1993

GENETIC RECOMBINATION—RESEARCH
Der Bauplan des Menschen. Reiter, Johannes. *Stimm Zeit* 211:219-231 Ap 1993

GENNEP, ARNOLD VAN
The transfer and the RCIA: process and ritual. Hughes, Kathleen, and Quinn, Barbara. *RRel* 52:86-101 Ja-F 1993

GENOCIDE
Forgotten holocaust. Luxmoore, Jonathan. *Tablet* 247:842-843 Jl 3 1993
New world, new disorder [fr *Out of control: global turmoil on the eve of the twenty-first century*]. Brzezinski, Zbigniew K, 1928-. *Crisis* 11:39-42 My 1993
Sudan: a grim tragedy. Gassis, Macram Max, Bp, 1938-. *Cath Int* 4:236-237 My 1993

GEOGRAPHY—EDUCATION
Geography for life. Downs, Roger M. *Momentum* 24:12-16 S-O 1993

GEORGETOWN UNIVERSITY—HISTORY
The bicentennials history of Georgetown University: from academy to university, 1789-1982, v1. Curran, Robert. Washington: Georgetown University Press, 1993. 445p ISBN 0-87840-485-6 LC 92-47499

GEORGETOWN UNIVERSITY (WASHINGTON, DC)
Epistle to the Hoyas. Arkes, Hadley. *Crisis* 11:11-12 Mr 1993

GERMAN—NATIONALISM
Fremdenfeindlichkeit. Keller, Albert. *Stimm Zeit* 210:793-794 D 1992

GERMAN AMERICANS
The Catholic parish as a way-station of ethnicity and Americanization: Chicago's Germans and Italians, 1903-1939. Shawn, Stephen Joseph, 1944-. Brooklyn: Carlson Publishers, 1991. 206p ISBN 0-92601-9554 LC 91-26847

GERMAN LITERATURE
Das beschädigte Land. Kurz, Paul Konrad. *Stimm Zeit* 211:663-678 O 1993
Brautbriefe aus dem Gefängnis. Bleistein, Roman, 1928-. *Stimm Zeit* 211: 711-713 O 1993
Hans Carossa und Rupert Mayer. Bleistein, Roman, 1928-. *Stimm Zeit* 211: 105-114 F 1993

GERMAN POETRY
The root of all evil: lessons of an epigram. Harries, Karsten. *IJPS* 1:1-20 Mr 1993

GERMANY—CHURCH HISTORY—1945
Die Annahme der Gnade als Mitvollzug der Erlösung. Menke, Karl-Heinz. *Catholica* 47:1-19 1993

GERMANY—ECONOMIC POLICY
Relevance of social market conditions in the German Health Care System to the United States. Powell, Francis D. *RSocEcon* 50:269-296 Fall 1992

GERMANY—HISTORY
Anniversary letters from Berlin: west side, east side stories. Rodden, John, 1956-. *America* 169:10-15 Jl 3-10 1993
It's not Weimar all over again: the strengths of German democracy. Cooper, Rand Richards. *Comm* 120:11-13 My 7 1993

GERMANY—HISTORY—1933-1945
Jesuit presence and the struggle for justice in Nazi Germany. Endean, Philip. *Month* 26:240-246 Je 1993

GERMANY—INTELLECTUAL LIFE
Germany sobers up. Vallely, Paul. *Tablet* 247:879-880 Jl 10 1993

GERMANY—POLITICS AND GOVERNMENT
It's not Weimar all over again: the strengths of German democracy. Cooper, Rand Richards. *Comm* 120:11-13 My 7 1993

GERMANY—RELIGION
Unisichtbar bleibt ihre Frömmigkeit Kritische Begegnung mit Neuen Religiösen Bewegungen. Fuss, Michael. *StudiaM* 41:353-389 1992

GERMANY—SOCIAL CONDITIONS
Anniversary letters from Berlin: west side, east side stories. Rodden, John, 1956-. *America* 169:10-15 Jl 3-10 1993
Fremdenfeindlichkeit. Keller, Albert. *Stimm Zeit* 210:793-794 D 1992
Germany sobers up. Vallely, Paul. *Tablet* 247:879-880 Jl 10 1993
Living in the new Germany. Schonfelder, Kristin. *Cath Work* 60:7 Je-Jl 1993
Living where the wall was: what still divides the Germans. Brockman, Stephen. *Comm* 120:16-19 S 24 1993
Obdachlosigkeit in Deutschland. Taeubner, Stefan. *Stimm Zeit* 211:187-196 Mr 1993
Soziale Marktwirtschaft—was ist das? Stegmann, Franz Josef. *Stimm Zeit* 211:291-302 My 1993

GERMANY—SOCIAL POLICY
Obdachlosigkeit in Deutschland. Taeubner, Stefan. *Stimm Zeit* 211:187-196 Mr 1993

GERTRUDE, SAINT, 1256-1303
Gertrude of Helfta: the herald of divine love. Winkworth, Margaret. New York: Paulist Press, 1993. x, 259p ISBN 0-8091-0458-x LC 92-20663

GESTURE IN WORSHIP
Catholics should stand at the consecration. Philippart, David. *USCath* 58:20-25 Jl 1993

GIBBONS, JAMES, CARDINAL
A conflict of mitres: the diverse polities and Cathedral Abbey of Bishop Leo Haid. Baumstein, Paschal. *Word Sp* 14:76-95 1992

GIFTS
Put something different under the tree. Brady, Mary Clare. *USCath* 58:31-33 D 1993

Wise guys [excerpt fr *Starlight: beholding the Christmas miracle all yar long*]. Shea, John B. *Comm* 119:10-12 D 18 1992

GIFTS, SPIRITUAL
The breath of life. Santa, Thomas M. *Liguorian* 81:60-61 Ja 1993
Calling forth the talents. Weind, Teresita. *ChrWorld* 236:234-235 S-O 1993
Canonical room for Charisms. Hogan, William Frances, 1930-. *RRel* 52:596-601 Jl-Ag 1993
Charisms and religious life. McDonough, Elizabeth. *RRel* 52:646-659 S-O 1993
Gifts for everyone. Montague, George T. *New Cov* 22:33 Mr 1993
Originalità dei carismi di vita consacrata. Butler, Jean. *Periodica* 82 no 2: 257-292 1993
Reflections on charisma (ta) in the New Testament. Kilgallen, John J. *StudiaM* 41:289-323 1992
Themes of the lay life. Keightley, Georgia Masters. *Origins* 22:761-764 Ap 15 1993

GIFTS, SPIRITUAL—WOMEN
Religious life's charism: transforming life. Brennan, Margaret. *Origins* 23: 207-211 S 2 1993

GIJSEN, JOHANNES BAPTIST MATTHIJS, BP, 1932-
Rumours abound as Bär resigns. Goddijn, Walter, 1921-. *Tablet* 247:413-414 Mr 27 1993

GILES OF ROME, ABP OF BOURGES 1343?-1315
Giles of Rome on natural motion in the void. Trifogli, Cecilia. *Med Stud* 54: 136-161 1992

GILL, ERIC, 1882-1940
Sacred and profane sex: Edvard Munch at the National Gallery, Eric Gill at the Barbican. Pickstone, Charles. *Month* 26:22-25 Ja 1993

GILLESPIE, JOHN BIRKES, 1917-1993
Bebop takes a hard shot: Dizzy Gillespie, RIP. McConnell, Frank, 1942-. *Comm* 120:17-18 F 12 1993

GILLIGAN, CAROL
Celibacy: a feminist view. Gramick, Jeannine. *Sisters* 65:255-262 Jl 1993

GINSBURG, RUTH BADER, 1933-
Courtship. Mullen, Peter. *Register* 69:1+ Jl 4 1993
Dialogue [interview by P Mullen]. Bork, Robert Heron, 1927-. *Register* 69:1+ Ag 1 1993
Going, going, gone: the diminution of the self. Carlin, David Robert, Jr, 1938-. *Comm* 120:6-7 S 10 1993
Justice Ginsburg and the Supreme Court's course [por]. Shaw, Russell. *OSV* 82:17 O 24 1993
The real Judge Ginsburg. Bopp, James, Jr. *Register* 69:5 Ag 1 1993
Stirring a tempest in the pro-choice teapot. Shaw, Russell. *OSV* 82:3 Jl 18 1993

GIRZONE, JOSEPH FRANCIS, 1930-
But is it good theology? ["Joshua" series by Joseph Girzone]. Finley, Mitchel B. *OSV* 81:6 Ap 4 1993

GISH, LILLIAN, 1893-1993
Lillian Gish: a passing. Blake, Richard A, 1939-. *America* 168:14 Mr 20-27 1993

GIVING *see* Generosity

GLEMP, JOZEF, CARDINAL, 1930-
A son of Poland. Luxmoore, Jonathan. *Register* 69:2 F 28 1993

GLOBAL FORUM OF RELIGIOUS (1ST, TAGAYTAY, PHILIPPINES), 1993
"Dangerous" religious forum seeks mission. Chittister, Joan D. *Nat Cath Rep* 30:18 N 19 1993

GLORIEUX, PALEMON
Quaestiones concerning Christ from the first half of the thriteenth century. Principe, Walter H. *Med Stud* 54:1-48 1992

GLOSSOLALIA
The charismatic way. Cooper, Kristina. *Tablet* 247:467-468 Ap 10-17 1993

GNOSTICISM
Agricultural imagery in the Gospel of Matthew and the gospel of truth. Cavallo, Jo Ann. *Relig Lit* 24:27-38 Aut 1992

GOAL (PSYCHOLOGY)
Lou Holtz man with a winning message. Stedman, Rick. *Liguorian* 81:14-17 O 1993
September ministry—and the Garden of Eden. Gilbert, Jack. *Tod Parish* 25: 38 S 1993

GOD
Addiction, recovery and God. Mace, Irving B. *Living Prayer* 26:25-26 Ja-F 1993
The genesis of God: a theological genealogy. Altizer, Thomas J J. Louisville: John Knox, 1993. x, 208p ISBN 0-664-21996-9
God, ghosts, and UFOs. Auer, Jim. *Liguorian* 81:38-43 Ag 1993
Putting some soul into prayer. Imbach, Jeffrey D. *Living Prayer* 26:3-6 Jl-Ag 1993
La raison et le Dieu-trinité. Delesalle, Jacques. *MSR* 50:25-48 Ja-Mr 1993
En relisant l'amour des lettres et le désir de Dieu. Dumont, Camille. *NRT* 114:889-895 N-D 1992

GOD—ATTRIBUTES
Attributing things to God. Moonan, Lawrence. *Eph Theol Lovan* 78:86-117 Ap 1992
Facing the abusing God: a theology of protest. Blumenthal, David Reuben, 1938-. Louisville: John Knox, 1993. x, 208p ISBN 0-664-25464-0
Images of God and the richness of our faith [reply to W Harrington, 42 no 8 467-476 O 1992]. MacCarthy, Thomas. *Doctr Life* 42:629-630 D 1992
Scripture for Christian conversion. Navone, John. *New Blckfrs* 74:21-33 Ja 1993

GOD—BIBLICAL TEACHING
Israel's God, the Psalms, and the city of Jerusalem: life experience and the sacrifice of praise and prayer. Beeck, Frans Jozef van. *Horizons (CTS)* 19: 219-239 Fall 1992
Telling the Gospel in flesh and blood. Blastic, Michael W. *New Theol Rev* 6: 108-112 My 1993
What's God like? Collins, Mary Smalara. *USCath* 58:30-35 S 1993

GOD—COMMANDS
Was heibt Gottes Gebot? Fuchs, Josef. *Stimm Zeit* 211:435-442 Jl 1993

GOD—CREATOR
Not just any old world. Polkinghorne, John. *Tablet* 247:102-103 Ja 23 1993
Religion and science: collaboration for the environment. Dalton, Anne Marie. *Living Light* 29:14-22 Aut 1992
Teilhard and ecological spirituality. Sage, Alan. *Teilhard Rev* 28:11-14 Spr 1993
Trinity and creation in the theology of St. Thomas Aquinas. Walker, David A. *Thomist* 57:443-455 Jl 1993

GOD—FACE
God's human face revealed: a retreat in Wales. Corona, Mary. *RRel* 52:519-531 Jl-Ag 1993
Image de Dieu, image de l'homme. Renwart, Léon. *NRT* 115:85-104 Ja-F 1993
Pouvoir de la singularité: le pathos du visage dans le texte d'Emmanuel Lévinas. Saint-Germain, Christian. *Laval Theol Phil* 49:27-35 F 1993

GOD—FATHERHOOD
Divine or distorted?: God as we understand God. Seiden, Jerry. San Diego, California: Recovery Publications, 1993. x, 142p ISBN 0-941405-19-2 LC 92-41854
The family: a place of fraternity. Sicari, Antonio. *Communio* 20:290-305 Sum 1993
A father's blessing: it's ours for the asking. Kerner, Robert J. *New Cov* 23: 26-27 Ag 1993
The Fatherhood of God. Rutler, George W. *HPR* 93:18-23 Je 1993
Il *Padre Nostro* I. Vanni, Ugo. *Civilta* 3:345-358 S 4 1993

GOD—GOODNESS
One, good, true and beautiful. Lane, Tom. *Doctr Life* 43:411-417 S 1993
Prayer, memories, and God. Mancuso, Theresa. *RRel* 52:541-547 Jl-Ag 1993
Responding to the goodness of God. Wilmer, Gary G. *Momentum* 24:45-47 N-D 1993
St Thomas, God's goodness, and God's morality. Dewan, Lawrence. *Mod Schlmn* 70:45-51 N 1992

GOD—IMMANENCE
The homilies we hear. Costello, Helen. *Furrow* 44:288-291 My 1993
What a coincidence!. Furlong, Monica, 1930-. *Tablet* 247:975 Jl 31 1993

GOD—KNOWABLENESS
Descartes's three hypothetical doubts. Flage, Daniel E. *Mod Schlmn* 70:201-208 Mr 1993
"In the twilight of the twentieth century" on divine sendings. Maurer, Armand A, 1915-. *Can Cath Rev* 11:19-22 Jl-Ag 1993
No night too dark: how God turns defeat into glorious triump. Halliday, Steve. Sisters: Questar, 1993. x, 252p ISBN 0-88070-560-4
"Saiser Dieu en son vestiaire" L'articulation théologique du sens chez Maître Eckhart. Malherbe, Jean-François. *Laval Theol Phil* 49:201-213 Je 1993
Sitting in the dark: a meditation sequence. Gore, Michael. *Living Prayer* 26: 17-21 My-Je 1993
To know God. Martin, George. *New Cov* 22:34 Mr 1993
What's God like? Collins, Mary Smalara. *USCath* 58:30-35 S 1993
What's God like? Collins, Mary Smalara. *USCath* 58:30-35 S 1993
You can know God: Christian spirituality for daily living. Gustin, Marilyn Norquist. Washington, D C: Liguori Publications, 1993. x, 212p ISBN 0-89243-479-1 LC 92-74594
12 ways to know God. Kreeft, Peter John, 1937. *New Cov* 23:33 S 1993

GOD—LAUGHTER
Get serious! The monastic condemnation of laughter. Russell, Kenneth C. *RRel* 52:371-379 My-Je 1993

GOD—LOVE
The ascent of love. Nicholl, Donald. *Tablet* 247:845-846 Jl 3 1993
Author's response [reply to four book reviews *God for us*]. LaCugna, Catherine Mowry (CTS). *Horizons* 20:135-142 Spr 1993
Catherine De'Ricci. Agresti, Domenico di. *New Blckfrs* 74:244-251 My 1993
Christian experience in Hans Urs von Balthasar. Potworowski, Christophe. *Communio* 20:107-117 Spr 1993
Does God have boundaries? Cotter, Jim. *Way* 33:91-96 Ap 1993
Dominion maximum. Imperio, Vic N. New York: Vantage Press, 1992. x, 139p ISBN 0-533-10077-1 LC 91-91242
The Fifth World Conference and walls of the heart. FitzGerald, Kyriaki Antonia. *Ecumen Trends* 22:1+ Ap 1993
God and being: the paradox of presence and absence. O'Connell, James. *Month* 26:188-193 My 1993
God's unexplainable and mysterious love. Pilarczyk, Daniel Edward, Abp, 1934-. *OSV* 82:6 Jl 18 1993
John Paul II, Pope, (1992-12-31) Our generation [orig Italian]. John Paul II, Pope, 1920- (Karol Wojtyla) (elected 1978). *OR(Eng)* 1272:10 Ja 6 1993*
The market place. McNair, J Frank. *Living Prayer* 26:26-27 My-Je 1993
The me God sees: celebrating your true identity. Kuhne, Roberta. Sisters: Questar, 1993. x, 202p ISBN 0-8070-573-6
Meeting the mystics. Giallanza, Joel. *Living Prayer* 26:3-9 Ja-F 1993
An oratory in motion. Huggett, Joyce, 1937-. *Tablet* 247:303-304 Mr 6 1993
The Prodigal Son. Martin, George. *Liguorian* 81:38-39 Mr 1993
Proper and improper partially and the preferential option for the poor. Pope, Stephen J. *TheolStds* 54:242-271 Je 1993
Reflections of a pilgrim [editorial]. Wilkinson, Gertrude A. *Living Prayer* 26: 1 Ja-F 1993
Share the good news. Bertolucci, John. Boston: St Paul Books & Media, 1993. 28p ISBN 0-8198-6885-x
Single parents: building holy families. Finley, Mitchel B. *Liguorian* 81:12-16 Ag 1993
Too good to be true. Grubb, Geoffrey J. *ReligTJ* 27:39 F 1993
The trinitarian community. Bruteau, Beatrice, 1930-. *Living Prayer* 26:16-19 Jl-Ag 1993
Das Wortfeld der Liebe im Paganen und Biblischen Griechisch. Söding, Thomas. *Eph Theol Lovan* 78:284-330 D 1992

GOD—MERCY
Breaking the fast. Barnes, Michael R. *Month* 26:(I) Ap 1993

GOD—MOTHERHOOD
Is it okay to call God mother?: considering the feminine face of God. Smith, Paul R. Peabody: Hendrickson Publishers, 1993. 273p ISBN 1-56563-013-0 LC 93-25810

GOD—NAME
Who can utter the Name of God?—From the holiness of his name to the seriousness of all words. Sales, Michel. *Communio* 20:26-48 Spr 1993

GOD—OMNIPOTENCE
Attributing things to God. Moonan, Lawrence. *Eph Theol Lovan* 78:86-117 Ap 1992
Freedom and creation in three traditions. Burrell, David B. Notre Dame: University of Notre Dame Press, 1993. x, 224p ISBN 0-268-00987-2 LC 92-53745

GOD—OMNIPRESENCE
Author's response [reply to four book reviews *God for us*]. LaCugna, Catherine Mowry, 1952-. *Horizons (CTS)* 20:135-142 Spr 1993
Finding God in all things. Garrett, Graeme. *Way* 33:3-11 Ja 1993

GOD—PHILOSOPHY
Amor y diferencia. Torralba Rossello, Francesc. Barcelona: PPU, 1993. x, 383p ISBN 84-477-0118-2

GOD—PROMISES
Mystery and promise: a theology of revelation. Haught, John F. Collegeville, Minnesota: The Liturgical Press, 1993. 224p ISBN 0-8146-5792-3 LC 92-46908
The power of God's promise [exc fr *Liturgy: rhythms of prayer; Liturgy: the Lord's day*]. Brueggemann, Walter, and Reeder, Rachel. *Liturgy* 10:47-50 Spr 1993
Promises for the graduate. Richards, Larry. Grand Rapids: Zondervan Publishing House, 1993. x, 128p ISBN 0-310-39700-6

GOD—PROOF
God and being: the paradox of presence and absence. O'Connell, James. *Month* 26:188-193 My 1993
A proposito di un recente dibattito su Dio e la scienza. Gallagher, Michael Paul, 1939-. *Civilta* 2:327-338 My 15 1993
Sartre's adolescent rejection of God. Santoni, Ronald E. *PhilosTod* 37:62-69 Spr 1993

GOD—PROOF, ONTOLOGICAL
The status and function of divine simpleness in Summa theologiae Ia, qq 2-13. Burns, Peter. *Thomist* 57:1-26 Ja 1993

GOD—PROOF, TELEOLOGICAL
Who is God for a Hindu, Buddhist or Muslim? Borelli, John. *Origins* 22:769+ Ap 15 1993

GOD—PROVIDENCE
Attributing things to God. Moonan, Lawrence. *Eph Theol Lovan* 78:86-117 Ap 1992

GOD—SIMPLICITY
The status and function of divine simpleness in Summa theologiae Ia, qq 2-13. Burns, Peter. *Thomist* 57:1-26 Ja 1993

GOD—TRANSCENDENCE
Buber and Tillich. Novak, David, 1941-. *JEcumen Stds* 29:159-174 Spr 1992
Pouvoir de la singularité: le pathos du visage dans le texte d'Emmanuel Lévinas. Saint-Germain, Christian. *Laval Theol Phil* 49:27-35 F 1993
Progress, evolution and Green theology. Clatworthy, Jonathan. *Teilhard Rev* 28:8-10 Spr 1993
Revelation and proclamation: shifting paradigms. Hilkert, Mary Catherine. *JEcumen Stds* 29:1-23 Wint 1992

GOD—WILL *see* Will of God

GOD—WORSHIP AND LOVE
The case for St Thérèse as a doctor of the church. Ahern, Patrick V, Bp, 1919-. *America* 169:12-13+ Ag 28-S 4 1993
Forever faithful: the unfolding of God's promise to creation. Reiser, William, 1943-. Collegeville:Liturgical, 1993. 98p ISBN 0-8146-5849-0 LC 93-15191
In search of guidance: developing a conversational relationship with God. Willard, Dallas. New York: HarperSanFrancisco, 1993. x, 247p ISBN 0-06-069520-x LC 92-56406
The journey toward self-esteem. St Romain, Philip. *Liguorian* 81:12-16 My 1993

GOD (BUDDHISM)
Who is God for a Hindu, Buddhist or Muslim? Borelli, John. *Origins* 22:769+ Ap 15 1993

GOD (HINDUISM)
Who is God for a Hindu, Buddhist or Muslim? Borelli, John. *Origins* 22:769+ Ap 15 1993

GOD (ISLAM)
Who is God for a Hindu, Buddhist or Muslim? Borelli, John. *Origins* 22:769+ Ap 15 1993

GOD AND MAN
The Annunciation: pivotal moment of history. Yarnold, Edward John, 1926-. *Month* 26:237-239 Je 1993
Finding God in winter stillness. Barthelemy, Nancy C. *Liguorian* 81:54-55 F 1993
God's passionate and our desire response. Barry, William A. Indiana: Ave Maria Press, 1993. x, 143p ISBN 0-87793-501-7 LC 92-75346
The Gospel is celebration [editorial]. Morvan, Michael Le. *Teilhard Rev* 27:66-68 Wint 1992
The new evangelization: some tasks and risks of the present [address to the Spanish Episcopal Conference Plenary Assembly (May 18, 1992)]. Suquiía, Goicoechea Angel, Cardinal, 1916-. *Communio* 19:515-540 Wint 1992
Through detachment to union. Millette, Adele M. *Living Prayer* 26:22-26 Jl-Ag 1993
Who can utter the Name of God?—From the holiness of his name to the seriousness of all words. Sales, Michel. *Communio* 20:26-48 Spr 1993
Who is God for a Hindu, Buddhist or Muslim? Borelli, John. *Origins* 22:769+ Ap 15 1993

GOD WORSHIP AND LOVE
Hans Urs von Balthasar's anthropology in light of his marian thinking. Roten, Johann G. *Communio* 20:306-333 Sum 1993

GODEL, KURT, 1906-1978
God, the soul and Kurt Godel. Pakaluk, Michael. *Register* 69:1+ F 14 1993

GODPARENTS
Sponsors make the difference. Heller, Chris. *Tod Parish* 25:4+ N-D 1993

GOETHALS, GREGOR
The trivialization of matter: development of ritual incapacity. Seubert, Xavier John. *Worship* 67:38-53 Ja 1993

GOGH, VINCENT VAN
Faith into art: religion and Vincent van Gogh. Thiessen, Gesa. *Doctr Life* 43:267-274 My 1993

GOGOL, NIKOLAI, 1809-1859
"I am that king"—disordered history and delusional writing: the artful derangements of Gogol's "Diary". Ernst, Charles A. *Cithara* 32:39-48 My 1993

GOLAN HEIGHTS—POLITICS
A hill screaming in Golan. Gaffney, James William, 1931-. *America* 169:4-7 N 27 1993

GOLAN HEIGHTS—RELIGIOUS LIFE
A hill screaming in Golan. Gaffney, James William, 1931-. *America* 169:4-7 N 27 1993

GOLDING, WILLIAM, 1911-1993
"As a bee produces honey": William Golding's achievement. Rice, Judith. *Month* 26:382-386 S-O 1993
"I saw a Kingfisher": grace and ruin in Golding's the spire. Yeager, D M. *Horizons (CTS)* 20:44-66 Spr 1993
William Golding (1911-93): lord of horror, lord of awe. Feeney, Joseph J. *America* 169:6-7 Jl 31-Ag 7 1993
William Golding's vision. Bergonzi, Bernard, 1929-. *Tablet* 247:815 Je 26 1993

GOLGOTHA
Piety centered on Jesus' suffering and some eccentric Christian understandings of the mystery of Calvary. Sloyan, Gerard S. *Worship* 67:98-123 Mr 1993

GONZALEZ, BONIFACIR RODRIGUEZ, 1885-1936
Congregation for the Causes of Saints (1992-12-21) Decree on martyrdom. Congregation for the Causes of Saints. *OR(Eng)* 1272:4 Ja 6 1993*

GONZALEZ JUSTO, FRANCISCA (MARIA TERESA), 1921-1967
Congregation for the Causes of Saints (1992-06-13) Decree on the heroic virtues of the Servant of God, Maria Teresa, religious. Congregation for the Causes of Saints. *AAS* 84:1188-1191 D 5 1992*
Congregation for the Causes of Saints (1992-06-13) Decree on the heroic virtues. Congregation for the Causes of Saints. *TPS* 38:19-20 Ja-F 1993*

GOOD AND EVIL
Basic goods and the human good in recent Catholic moral theology. Porter, Jean. *Thomist* 57:27-49 Ja 1993
Goodness and rightness: Thomas Aquinas' Summa Theologia. Keenan, James F. Washington, D C: Georgetown University Press, 1992. x, 212p ISBN 0-87840-530-5 LC 92-3090
Truth reaffirmed about creation and humanity's fall. Stravinskas, Peter. *Register* 69:1+ My 23 1993

GOOD FRIDAY
Good Friday: the passion of the earth. Keevey, Thomas. *Emmanuel* 99:129-134 Ap 1993
The Good Fridays in every week. Power, Dermot. *Priests & People* 7:94-96 Mr 1993

GOOD SAMARITAN (PARABLE)
An incident on the Jericho Road—some correspondence. Draper, Anthony. *Furrow* 44:99-102 F 1993

GOOD WORKS (THEOLOGY)
Forming a circle of love: a profile of Judy Harris. Schaller, Jeanne Lound. *Liguorian* 81:54-58 S 1993

GORE, ALBERT, JR, 1948-
John Paul II, Pope, (1993-08-15) Gore. John Paul II, Pope, 1920- (Karol Wojtyla) (elected 1978). *Origins* 23:200 Ag 26 1993*

GOROSTIAGA, XABIER
"Democracy demands structural change". MacEoin, Gary. *Nat Cath Rep* 30:10 N 19 1993
Rigoberta Menchú Tum, Doctora en justicia. Mencú Tum, Rigoberta. *Christus* 58:74-79 N-D 1992

GOVERNMENT, RESISTANCE TO
Active and messy personalism. Cordaro, Frank. *Cath Work* 60:6 My 1993
Bad consciences on abortion [editorial]. *Tablet* 247:423 Ap 3 1993
Live the revolution now!. True, Michael, 1933-. *Cath Work* 60:8 Ag 1993
Worth pondering. O'Connell, Patrick. *Living Prayer* 26:13-14 My-Je 1993

GRACE
Amazing grace: mealtime blessings. Armendariz, Sherry. *Spir Life* 39:137-139 Aut 1993
Grace and the exercises. Haight, Roger. *Way Suppl* 76:44-52 Spr 1993
Grace under pressure. Manning, Martha. *Salt* 13:45-46 N-D 1993
John Cassian: student of Augustine. Ramsey, Boniface. *Cist Stud* 28:5-15 1993
Revelation and proclamation: shifting paradigms. Hilkert, Mary Catherine. *JEcumen Stds* 29:1-23 Wint 1992
Too good to be true. Grubb, Geoffrey J. *ReligTJ* 27:39 F 1993

GRACE—BIBLICAL TEACHING
Enough is enough: grace for the restless heart. Westfall, John F. New York: HarperSanFrancisco, 1993. x, 165p ISBN 0-06-069289-8 LC 91-58990

GRACE—COMPARATIVE STUDIES
Grace that amazes. Daley, Barbara Carter. *Spir Life* 39:11-21 Spr 1993
What's so amazing about grace? [interview by editors of US Catholic (Periodical)]. Dreyer, Elizabeth. *USCath* 58:6-13 My 1993

GRADING AND MARKING (STUDENTS)
Grades: gods or ghouls? Auer, Jim. *Liguorian* 81:38-43 Ja 1993

GRANADA, LUIS DE
Fray Luis de Granada y Erasmo. Seco, Atilano Rico. *Cien Tom* 119:549-578 S-D 1992

GRANDPARENTING
When the grandchildren visit. Schneider, Mary Jane. *CDgst* 57:26+ Ag 1993

GRANDPARENTS
Aging becomes them. Anderson, Chris. *Comm* 120:5-6 Ag 13 1993
Grandparents pass on the faith. Cotter, Theresa. *Church* 9:32-35 Aut 1993
Mountain memories endure. Olsen, Mary B. *Liguorian* 81:60-61 S 1993

GRANZOTTO, CLAUDIO, 1900-1947
Congregation for the Causes of Saints (1993-07-06) Decree on a miracle. Congregation for the Causes of Saints. *OR(Eng)* 1299:12 Jl 14 1993*

GRAPHOLOGY
Graphoanalysis: reading the word from within. Doyle, Mary E. *Sisters* 65:25-29 Ja 1993

GRATITUDE
Giving thanks. Scanlan, Michael. *New Cov* 22:26-27 My 1993
Giving thanks. Smith, B F. *Crisis* 10:45-46 N 1992
John Paul II, Pope, (1992-12-31) Our generation [orig Italian]. John Paul II, Pope, 1920- (Karol Wojtyla) (elected 1978). *OR(Eng)* 1272:10 Ja 6 1993*
The loving tree. Perry, John D. *Living Prayer* 26:8-10 S-O 1993
Real gratitude. Mangan, Charles M. *New Cov* 23:14-15 S 1993

GRAY, GORDON JOSEPH, CARDINAL, 1910-1993
Gray, Gordon J., Cardinal, 1910-1993 [obit]. *OR(Eng)* 1301:2 Jl 28 1993
Gray, Gordon Joseph, Cardinal, 1910-1993 [obit]. McOwan, Rennie. *Tablet* 247:961-962 Jl 24 1993

GREAT BRITAIN—CHURCH HISTORY
Touching base. *Tablet* 247:306 Mr 6 1993

GREAT BRITAIN—ECONOMIC CONDITIONS
The European journey. Keegan, William. *Tablet* 246:1592 D 19-26 1992
Scandal of the two-thirds society [editorial]. *Tablet* 247:127 Ja 30 1993
Which way for Europe? Keegan, William. *Tablet* 247:36+ Ja 9 1993

GREAT BRITAIN—ECONOMIC POLICY
Bankers and politicians. Keegan, William. *Tablet* 247:781 Je 19 1993
Choices for the Chancellor. Keegan, William. *Tablet* 247:298-299 Mr 6 1993
The flaw in the budget. Keegan, William. *Tablet* 247:358 Mr 20 1993
What future for United Kingdom defence industries? Harrison, Roger. *Month* 26:105-106 Mr 1993

GREAT BRITAIN—FOREIGN RELATIONS
Diplomatic uses of a cup of tea [editorial]. *Tablet* 247:707 Je 5 1993

GREAT BRITAIN—FOREIGN RELATIONS- IRELAND
While Ulster burns. McRedmond, Louis. *Tablet* 247:1094 Ag 28 1993

GREAT BRITAIN—HISTORY—1400-1499
Aelred, historian: two portraits in Plantagenet myth. Dutton, Marsha L. *Cist Stud* 28 no 2:113-144 1993

GREAT BRITAIN—KINGS AND RULERS
Could a divorced king head the Church? *Tablet* 246:1633-1634 D 19-26 1992

GREAT BRITAIN—MORAL CONDITIONS
Trying to make sense [editorial]. *Month* 26:86-87 Mr 1993

GREAT BRITAIN—PARLIAMENT
Legislation for women priests reaches Parliament. *Tablet* 247:524 Ap 24 1993

GREAT BRITAIN—POLITICS AND GOVERNMENT
A beacon of hate [editorial]. *Tablet* 247:1219-1220 S 25 1993
Britain's angry voters. Alton, David. *Tablet* 247:604-605 My 15 1993
The last battle for Maastricht [editorial]. *Tablet* 247:743 Je 1993
Looking to Christian socialism [editorial]. *Tablet* 247:391 Mr 27 1993
Major's little difficulty. Alton, David. *Tablet* 247:779-780 Je 19 1993
The other face of Millwall. *Tablet* 247:1293 O 9 1993
Party leaders take the stage [editorial]. *Tablet* 247:1251 O 2 1993
A party too long in power [editorial]. *Tablet* 247:807-808 Je 26 1993
The Prime Minister as scapegoat [editorial]. *Tablet* 247:967 Jl 31 1993
There should be an alternative [editorial]. *Tablet* 247:603 My 15 1993

GREAT BRITAIN—RACE RELATIONS
Playing with fire on race [editorial]. *Tablet* 247:707 Je 5 1993

GREAT BRITAIN—RELIGION
Shepherds and pilgrims. *Tablet* 247:1277-1278 O 2 1993

GREAT BRITAIN—SOCIAL CONDITIONS
Family values. Field, Frank, 1942-. *Tablet* 247:1034 Ag 14 1993
A nation examining its conscience [editorial]. *Tablet* 247:363 F 27 1993
On the bright side. Wroe, Ann. *Tablet* 247:390 Mr 27 1993
Some cows are sacred, some are not [editorial]. *Tablet* 247:907-908 Jl 17 1993
Trying to make sense [editorial]. *Month* 26:86-87 Mr 1993

GREAT BRITAIN—SOCIO-ECONOMIC CONDITIONS
The family and the left. Phillips, Melanie. *Tablet* 247:972-973 Jl 31 1993

GREECE—FOREIGN RELATIONS—ALBANIA
Greek retaliation to priest's expulsion. *Tablet* 247:926 Jl 17 1993

GREEK DRAMA (TRAGEDY)
Mark's tragic vision: Gethsemane. Ruprecht, Louis A, Jr. *Relig Lit* 24:1-25 Aut 1992

GREEK LANGUAGE
Study Greek and Latin! Reflections of a housewife. Rist, Anna. *Can Cath Rev* 11:12-15 Ja 1993

GREEK LANGUAGE—TERMS
The major summaries in Acts. Co, Maria Anicia. *Eph Theol Lovan* 78:49-85 Ap 1992

GREEK MYTHOLOGY—PSYCHOLOGICAL ASPECTS
Le regard de Méduse: adolescence et fascination. Brouwer, Didier de. *Lumen* 48:324-330 S 1993

GREEK POETRY
Chapter and verse: the life of Christ in poetry. Rooney, William R. New York: Vantage Press, 1993. x, 89p ISBN 0-533-10319-3 LC 92-90788
Religion, poésie et philosophie: Les Grecs et la quête du divin. Motte, André. *RPhil Louvain* 91:366-382 Ag 1993

GREELEY, ANDREW MORAN, 1928-
'The end of American Catholicism?'—another look. Hegy, Pierre M. *America* 168:4-9 My 1 1993
Religious belief remains vital around the world, study says. Gibeau, Dawn. *Nat Cath Rep* 29:4-5 My 28 1993

GREEN, ALLAN, 1935-
The tragic death of Eva Green. Kenny, Mary, 1936-. *Tablet* 247:158 F 6 1993

GREEN, EVA
The tragic death of Eva Green. Kenny, Mary, 1936-. *Tablet* 247:158 F 6 1993

GREEN, JULIAN, 1900-
A medal for Green. *Tablet* 247:434 Ap 3 1993

GREEN HOUSE EFFECT, ATMOSPHERE
Root causes of the environmental crisis. *Origins* 22:692-694 Mr 18 1993

GREENE, GRAHAM, 1904-1991
Graham Greene: an appreciation from Haiti. Farmer, Paul. *America* 168:17-21 F 6 1993
In the end, one thing matters. Hanink, James G. *Register* 69:5 O 31 1993
The novel as spiritual guide. Sussman, Cornelia Silver, 1914-. *Living Prayer* 26:18-22 Ja-F 1993
Novel Catholicism: Waugh and Greene [condensed fr *Catholic Twin Circle* D 27 1992-Ja 31 1993]. Vatavuk, William M. *CDgst* 57:42-47 O 1993
Scobie's world. Freis, Richard. *Relig Lit* 24:57-78 Aut 1992
'The way we live now': Graham Greene on reading. Kelly, Patrick Hyde. *Can Cath Rev* 11:20-22 Ap 1993

GREGORY, SAINT, BP OF NYSSA
Le Traité de la virginité de Grégoire de Nysse. Huybrechts, Paul. *NRT* 115:227-242 Mr-Ap 1993

GREGORY I, POPE, 540?-604
The life of St Benedict: Gregory the Great. Vogue, Albert de. Petersham: St Bede's Publications, 1993. x, 186p ISBN 0-932506-77-1 LC 93-420

GREGORY OF NAZIANZUS, SAINT, 329-389
Pastoral care in patristic times. Grace, Madeleine. *Priest* 49:49-53 S 1993

GREMILLION, JOSEPH
In the church but of the world: pioneer priests on the eve of Vatican II. Appleby, Raphael Scott. *US Cath Hist* 11:83-100 Wint 1993

GRIEF
Being with those who mourn [photographs]. Thompson, Stephanie. *BibleT* 31:95-101 Mr 1993
Beyond tears. Santa, Thomas M. *Liguorian* 81:24-25 Ap 1993
Coming to terms with grief. Hover, Margot. *Tod Parish* 25:20 Ja 1993
Dave understanding life through death. Conroy, Bernadette. *St Anth* 100:24-27 My 1993
Death and grief in murals [photographs]. Toomey, Stephana. *Liturgy* 10:58-62 Wint 1992
The gift of tears in the writings of St Ignatius Loyola and the Eastern Fathers. Maloney, George A, 1924-. *Diakonia* 26 no 1:5-13 1993
Helping people avoid bereavement mistakes. Parachin, Victor M. *Priest* 49:19-20 Ja 1993
It hurts so bad: parents grieve the death of their children. Haywood, Christine Curtis. *St Anth* 101:42-45 Je 1993
Lament and light: embodying our grief. Schroeder, Celeste N. *Mod Lit* 20:14-16 S 1993
Six steps through grief. Mitchell, Marcia Alice. *CDgst* 57:121-124 Ap 1993
The songs we would have sung to him [fr *The family worker*]. Tierney, Michael. *Cath Work* 60:4 Mr-Ap 1993
What not to say to a grieving parent. Grimes, Laura M. *USCath* 58:15-18 Ap 1993

GRIFFIN, MICHAEL
Be fair to Michael Griffin. Gronceski, Mark. *Register* 69:5 Je 27 1993

GRIFFITHS, AMBROSE, BP, 1928-
Politicians and the Churches diagnose a social sickness. *Tablet* 247:318-319 Mr 6 1993

GRIFFITHS, BEDE, 1906-1993
Benedictine Fr Bede Griffiths, 86, dies in India [obituary]. McCarthy, Tim. *Nat Cath Rep* 29:8 My 21 1993
Dom Bede Griffiths: symbol of the marriage of East and West (1906-1993). Teasdale, Wayne. *Living Prayer* 26:17-18 S-O 1993
Griffiths, Bede, 1906-1993 [obit]. Freeman, Laurence. *Tablet* 247:667-668 My 22 1993
Griffiths, Bede, 1906-1993 [obit]. Stout, James. *Cath Work* 60:7 Ag 1993
Griffiths, Bede, 1906-1993 [obit]. Toolan, David S. *America* 168:3-4 Je 5-12 1993
Griffiths, Bede, 1907-1993 [obit]. Freeman, Laurence. *Can Cath Rev* 11:(I+) Je 1993

GRISEZ, GERMAIN GABRIEL, 1929-
Basic goods and the human good in recent Catholic moral theology. Porter, Jean. *Thomist* 57:27-49 Ja 1993
The importance of being Germain Grisez [por]. Shaw, Russell. *OSV* 82:8-9 N 21 1993
Liberty under the moral law: B Hoose's critique of the Grisez-Finnis Theory of human good. George, Robert P. *Heythrop* 34:175-180 Ap 1993
Moral living in a non-Christian world [review article *Living a Christian Life* by G. Grisez]. Hanink, James G. *OSV* 82:9 N 21 1993
Obstetrical dilemmas and the principle of double effect. Lombardi, Joseph L. *Amer J Juris* 37:197-211 1992
What is included in a means to an end? Flannery, Kevin L. *Gregorianum* 74 no 3:499-513 1993

GRODI, MARCUS
Showing the way home. Wilson, Chip. *Register* 69:2 Je 27 1993

GROER, HANS HERMANN, CARDINAL
John Paul II, Pope, (1992-03-12) Nuntius Gratulatorius (Congratulatory Message) [Latin]. John Paul II, Pope, 1920- (Karol Wojtyla) (elected 1978). *AAS* 84:911-912 S 8 1992*

GROSZ, EDWARD M, BP
Report, 1991-92: New England region of the Mariological Society of America. Morry, Matthew F. *Marian Stds* 43:193-194 1992

GROUP DYNAMICS
Compartamiento social y dinamica de groupos. Tous Ral, Jose M. Barcelona: PPU, 1993. x, 379p ISBN 84-477-0140-9
Ourselves and others: brokerage, reconciliation and process. O'Connell, James. *Month* 26:355-360 S-O 1993

GROUP MINISTRY
Pastoral associates guidelines. Hanus, Jerome, Bp. *Origins* 22:699-700 Mr 18 1993

HANDICAPPED CHILDREN—EDUCATION—LAW AND LEGISLATION
Are profoundly handicapped children in Catholic schools entitled to government assistance?. Drinan, Robert Francis, 1920-. *America* 168:16-18 Ja 30 1993

HANDICAPPED STUDENTS—RELIGIOUS ASPECTS
Persons with disabilities. Maida, Adam, Abp. *Origins* 23:353+ O 28 1993

HANI, CHRIS
A Catholic element in the wider story. *Tablet* 247:521 Ap 24 1993
South Africa: can the centre hold? Vallely, Paul. *Tablet* 247:504 Ap 24 1993

HAPPINESS
Revealing happiness. Hanlon, Kevin. *Month* 26:165-167 Ap 1993

HARDEY, ALOYSIA
Racial integration: did it work in Grand Coteau? Poché, Louis A. *America* 169:16+ N 6 1993

HARING, BERNARD, 1912-
Häring supports married priests. *Tablet* 247:763 Je 1993

HARMONY OF THE SPHERES
Reply to Craig: the possible infinitude of the past [reply to W L Craig, 31 no 4:387-410 1991]. Smith, Quentin. *IPQ* 33:109-115 Mr 1993

HARRIOTT, JOHN F X, 1933-1990
Three winners. *Tablet* 247:104-105 Ja 23 1993

HARRIS, JUDY
Forming a circle of love: a profile of Judy Harris. Schaller, Jeanne Lound. *Liguorian* 81:54-58 S 1993

HART, H L A
The actual validity of law. Sellers, Mortimer. *Amer J Juris* 37:283-290 1992

HATE
"Contro l'odio, la forza dell'amore". Borgomeo, Pasquale. *Civilta* 144:539-562 Mr 20 1993
Exclusion and embrace: theological reflections in the wake of "ethnic cleansing". Volf, Miroslav. *JEcumen Stds* 29:230-248 Spr 1992

HAUCH, PAUL A
Good people get angry, too. Mallowe, Mike. *USCath* 58:14-21 My 1993

HAVEL, VACLAV, 1936-
Communications and the religious development of peoples. Zukowski, Angela Ann. *Momentum* 24:75-76 N-D 1993
Jan Patovcka et le phénomène de l'écriture littéraire. Declève, Henri. *Laval Theol Phil* 49:3-26 F 1993

HAYDEN, JOSEPH
Finding growth through chronic pain. Jacquet, Lou. *OSV* 81:5 Ja 24 1993

HAYES, DIANA
She teaches American liberation theology. Szczepanowski, Richard. *Nat Cath Rep* 30:18 O 29 1993

HEAD START PROGRAMS
Investments in children [editorial]. *America* 168:3 My 29 1993

HEALERS
Morris Cerullo makes a virtue out of controversy. *Tablet* 247:1023 Ag 7 1993

HEALING
Considering healing. Sheridan, Stephen. *New Cov* 22:14-16 Mr 1993
Healing is real. Monahan, Jim. *New Cov* 22:26-27 Je 1993
How storytelling heals. Baldwin, Robert F. *New Cov* 23:11-13 Ag 1993

HEALING—RELIGIOUS ASPECTS
Documentary ignores Christian healing tradition. Samra, Cal. *OSV* 82:19 Jl 4 1993
How Christians can receive healing. Ash, Marion F. *New Cov* 23:13-14 O 1993
The purpose of healing [address, 61st Annual Meeting of the National Federation of Catholic Physicians' Guilds O 1992]. Jaki, Stanley L. *Linacre* 60:5-15 F 1993
Should the healing begin at Christmas. McDonagh, Enda. *Furrow* 43:651-655 D 1992

HEALING, SPIRITUAL
Comment faire Église aujourd'hui (à l'hôpital)? Martou, Jean-Marie. *Supplement* 184:145-166 Mr-Ap 1993
Don't let religion get in the way of your faith [interview by editors of US Catholic (Periodical)]. Larsen, Earnie. *USCath* 58:31-35 Mr 1993
Earls Court miracle show. Rice, Judith. *Tablet* 247:1037 Ag 21 1993
From victim to Victor: a biblical guide for turning hurting into healing. Martinez, Yvonne. San Diego: Recovery Publications, 1993. x, 127p ISBN 0-941405-24-9 LC 93-13946
The joy of forgiving [excerpt fr *Swimming in the sun*]. Haase, Albert. *St Anth* 101:28-35 O 1993
Morris Cerullo makes a virtue out of controversy. *Tablet* 247:1023 Ag 7 1993
The spiritual healing of post-traumatic stress disorder at the Menlo Park Veteran's Hospital. Jiménez, Manuel J, Jr. *Stud Form Spir* 14:175-187 My 1993

HEALING BEHAVIOR
Recovering connections. Grant, Richard D, Jr, and Miller, Andrea Wells. New York: HarperCollins, 1992. x, 205p ISBN 0-06-063386-7 LC 91-70707

HEALING OF THE LAME MAN (MIRACLE)
Jesus and a paralytic: the lesson. Stravinskas, Peter. *Register* 69:1+ Mr 14 1993

HEALING OF THE MAN BORN BLIND (MIRACLE)
Our Lord cures the blind man. Stravinskas, Peter. *Register* 69:1+ Mr 28 1993
Seeing and believing. Madden, Michael. *HPR* 93:48-53 F 1993

HEALTH
The purpose of healing [address, 61st Annual Meeting of the National Federation of Catholic Physicians' Guilds O 1992]. Jaki, Stanley L. *Linacre* 60:5-15 F 1993
Wellness: the bridge between body, mind, and spirit. Cassidy, Judy, ed. *Health Prog* 74:33-52+ 1993*

HEALTH—EDUCATION
Parish nurses: pioneers in healthcare. Anderson, Joan Wester, 1938-. *Liguorian* 81:48-52 Mr 1993
Reaching for a healthy tomorrow. Shalala, Donna E. *Momentum* 24:29-31 N-D 1993

A scientific approach to morality. Blase, Mary. *Momentum* 24:23-24 S-O 1993

HEALTH AND RELIGION
"Access to health care and allocation of health care resources: a Jewish perspective". Rudin, A James. *New Theol Rev* 6:80-86 F 1993
Parish nurses: pioneers in healthcare. Anderson, Joan Wester, 1938-. *Liguorian* 81:48-52 Mr 1993

HEALTH CARE
Board members with a mission. Santos, Yolanda M, and Zipprich, John L. *Health Prog* 74:32-36 Jl-Ag 1993
Body and soul. Mullen, Peter. *Register* 69:1+ My 2 1993
The Catholic contribution. *Register* 69:4 O 10 1993
Dialogue [interview by P. Mullen]. Curley, John E, Jr. *Register* 69:1+ O 24 1993
Health-care reform: a Catholic prescription. Dangel, Mary Jo. *St Anth* 101:14-18 Je 1993
Six good reasons why the health-care system needs reform [photos]. Humphrey, Kelly Norton. *Salt* 13:7-13 F 1993

HEALTH CARE—ETHICAL ASPECTS
Living will and proxy for health care decisions. *Origins* 23:161+ Ag 12 1993
Reflections on health care ethics. Poel, Cornelius J van der. *Chicago Stud* 32:166-176 Ag 1993

HEALTH CARE—POLITICS
Fight the "prophets of doom". Rockefeller, John D, 1937-. *Health Prog* 74:43-44 Jl-Ag 1993

HEALTH CARE—RELIGIOUS ASPECTS
Documentary ignores Christian healing tradition. Samra, Cal. *OSV* 82:19 Jl 4 1993
Health care rationing: a theologian's perspective. Smith, Russell, E. *Linacre* 60:20-29 Ag 1993

HEALTH CARE- FLORIDA
Florida health reform may offer model. Saunders, Kathy. *Register* 69:1+ Je 13 1993

HEALTH CARE- UNITED STATES
"Access to health care and allocation of health care resources: a Jewish perspective". Rudin, A James. *New Theol Rev* 6:80-86 F 1993
Alternative health care looks beyond body. Piccolino, Alberta. *Nat Cath Rep* 29:6 Je 18 1993
Antitrust immunity granted in a far-reaching peer review case. Kadzielski, Mark A. *Health Prog* 74:19+ Ja-F 1993
Assessment in action. Hey, Michelle. *Health Prog* 74:54-57 Ja-F 1993
The big blue van and the little children. Stempsey, William E. *America* 168:8-12 Mr 13 1993
Bishops speak in public session of sexual abuse. Reese, Thomas Joseph, 1945-. *America* 169:4-6 Jl 3-10 1993
The bishops' role in preserving the ministry's vitality. Bernardin, Joseph Louis, Cardinal, 1928-. *Health Prog* 74:21-22+ Ja-F 1993
Buzz words or principles? Ethics and health-care reform. McCloskey, Liz Leibold. *Comm* 120:10 S 24 1993
CARE for a contraceptive, lady? Sobo, Elizabeth. *Register* 69:2 Mr 21 1993
Catholic health-care experts meet. DeMers, John. *Register* 69:1+ Je 27 1993
Catholics offer a second opinion on health plan. Barnard, Ann M. *OSV* 82:3 O 10 1993
CHA's vision of a redesigned healthcare system. Coreil, Bernice. *Health Prog* 74:12-14 My 1993
The Clinton election: implications for healthcare. Cox, William J. *Health Prog* 74:16-18 Ja-F 1993
Converting a unit to patient-focused care. Farris, Bain J. *Health Prog* 74:23-25 Ap 1993
Cutting through the confusion of managed competition. White, Jane H. *Health Prog* 74:10-12+ Mr 1993
Educating the community about healthcare reform. Weiss, Rhoda. *Health Prog* 74:60-61+ Ap 1993
An effective, efficient elder care program. Gorshe, Nancy. *Health Prog* 74:57-59 Ap 1993
Fatal coercion. *OSV* 82:1-2 O 24 1993
Fight the system!. Royal, Robert. *Crisis* 11:11-12 S 1993
Forging a future for Catholic healthcare. Coreil, Bernice. *Health Prog* 74:20+ Ja-F 1993
Free clinics deliver basic care with a vision. Gibeau, Dawn. *Nat Cath Rep* 29:6-7 Jl 30 1993
Global budgets: a key to Clinton's reform strategy? White, Jane H. *Health Prog* 74:10-12 Ap 1993
Health and the other Hillary. Royal, Robert. *Crisis* 11:11-12 O 1993
Health care for all: a Catholic perspective. Hehir, J Bryan, 1940-. *Comm* 120:7-9 My 7 1993
Health care reform: now for the hard part!. Torrens, Paul R. *America* 168:14-15 Ap 3 1993
Health decisions or Majoritarian Health Care? Cataldo, Peter J. *Linacre* 60:70-73 F 1993
Health reform at risk [editorial]. *Comm* 120:3 Jl 16 1993
Health-care reform: a Catholic prescription. Dangel, Mary Jo. *St Anth* 101:14-18 Je 1993
Health. Feuerherd, Peter. *Register* 69:1 Mr 14 1993
How Catholic will the Clinton health-care plan be? Shaw, Russell. *OSV* 82:17 S 19 1993
IDN development: issues to resolve. Karst, Philip J. *Health Prog* 74:24-25+ Mr 1993
In the best interest of the patient. Trau, Jane Mary, and McCartney, James J. *Health Prog* 74:50-56 Ap 1993
The leadership challenge: imagine new relationships. Coyle, Maryanna. *Health Prog* 74:16+ Jl-Ag 1993
Let the buyer beware! [editorial]. *Register* 69:1+ N 14 1993
Letter to Mrs Clinton: reforming health care. Ricard, John H, Bp. *Origins* 22:783-785 Ap 29 1993
Living will and proxy for health care decisions. *Origins* 23:161+ Ag 12 1993
Mission integration preserves sponsor's values. Keith, Judith Marie. *Health Prog* 74:38-40 Ap 1993
National health care legislation and the funding of abortion. Mahoney, Hildegarde Marie. *America* 169:8-9 O 16 1993

Of many things. Torrens, James S. *America* 169:2 Jl 3-10 1993

An open letter: four things to keep in mind. Koller, Christopher F. *Comm* 120:5-6 Ap 23 1993

Oregon's health-care plan gets a "yes". Koenig-Bricker, Woodeene. *OSV* 81:17 Ap 11 1993

The patient as citizen. Weber, Leonard J. *Health Prog* 74:12-15 Je 1993

A plea for illegals. *Register* 69:3 O 17 1993

A postelection look at healthcare reform. White, Jane H. *Health Prog* 74:12-15 Ja-F 1993

The potential health-care nightmare. Shaw, Russell. *OSV* 81:3 Mr 7 1993

The price of helping the poor. Vidulich, Dorothy. *Nat Cath Rep* 29:4 Ap 9 1993

Primary care program improves reimbursement. Fahey, Thomas M, and Gallitano, Dennis G. *Health Prog* 74:26-28+ Mr 1993

Reaction to health care reform plan. Ricard, John H, Bp. *Origins* 23:284-285 O 7 1993

Reform and the family [rpt fr Family Research Council]. Daniels, Scott. *Register* 69:3 N 14 1993

Resolution on health care reform. *Origins* 23:97+ Jl 1 1993

Sponsorship networks. Gillis, Virginia. *Health Prog* 74:34-37+ Ap 1993

A system develops values-based reform policy. Kramer, Richard, and Vickers, Susan. *Health Prog* 74:56 Jl-Ag 1993

Technology framework. Stempien, Theresa L. *Health Prog* 74:58-62 Ja-F 1993

Technology: a moral evaluation. Lappetito, Joanne. *Health Prog* 74:48-49+ Ja-F 1993

The time for healthcare reform is now. Davidson, Richard J. *Health Prog* 74:44-45 Jl-Ag 1993

The time to act is now. Myers, Nancy. *Register* 69:5 Ap 25 1993

Two collaborative organizations improve care delivery. Cassidy, Judy. *Health Prog* 74:22-23+ Mr 1993

Value variables in the health-care reform debate. McCormick, Richard Arthur, 1922-. *America* 168:7-13 My 29 1993

What role for surrogate decision makers? Hubbard, Howard, Bp. *Origins* 22:576-579 F 4 1993

HEALTH FACILITIES—AFFILIATIONS

Canon law offers flexibility in collaborative relationships. Morrisey, Frank, and Campbell, Peter. *Health Prog* 74:53 Jl-Ag 1993

Integrated delivery challenges sponsors, systems. Pelham, Judith C. *Health Prog* 74:52 Jl-Ag 1993

Meeting mission challenges in IDNs. Stanley, Teresa. *Health Prog* 74:28-31+ Jl-Ag 1993

Transformation to integrated delivery requires a shared culture. Brennan, Donald A. *Health Prog* 74:58 Jl-Ag 1993

HEALTH FACILITIES—FINANCE

Identifying charity care in financial statements. Hoyler, Geraldine M. *Health Prog* 74:13-14 Ap 1993

HEALTH RISK COMMUNICATION

Wellness in the healing ministry. Burke, Barbara K. *Health Prog* 74:34-37 1993

HEALTH SERVICES ACCESSIBILITY

Board members with a mission. Santos, Yolanda M, and Zipprich, John L. *Health Prog* 74:32-36 Jl-Ag 1993

Catholic providers will play a central role in healthcare reform. Clinton, Hillary Rodham, 1947-. *Health Prog* 74:42-43 Jl-Ag 1993

HEALTH SERVICES ADMINISTRATION

Transformation to integrated delivery requires a shared culture. Brennan, Donald A. *Health Prog* 74:58 Jl-Ag 1993

HEALTH SERVICES ADMINISTRATORS

CHA task force helps managers make values-based decisions. Lappetito, Joanne. *Health Prog* 74:14-16 1993

HEALTH SERVICES ADMINISTRATORS—TRAINING OF

An investment in leadership. Ryan, Mary Jean, and Barney, Steven M. *Health Prog* 74:56-58 Je 1993

HEALY, TIMOTHY S, 1923-1992

Education was his line. Mitchell, Robert A. *America* 168:4-5 Ja 30 1993

HEART

How much can you help your heart? [condensed from *Harvard Health New Letter* S 1992]. Thomas, Patricia. *CDgst* 57:10-13 Mr 1993

HEATH-STUBBS, JOHN, 1918-

A voice of his own. *Tablet* 247:884-885 Jl 10 1993

HEAVEN

Thoughts of heaven. Mason, Philip, 1906-. *Tablet* 247:543 My 1 1993

HECKER, ISAAC THOMAS, 1819-1888

Evangelizing America: transformations in Paulist mission. Robichaud, Paul. *US Cath Hist* 11:61-78 Spr 1993

Inculturation as transformation: the case of Americanism revisited. Portier, William J. *US Cath Hist* 11:107-124 Sum 1993

Ralph Waldo Emerson on Isaac Hecker: a manuscript with commentary. Johnson, Glen M. *CHist* 79:54-64 Ja 1993

HEFT, JAMES L

Mary feminism: compatible but challenging. Morrow, Carol Ann. *St Anth* 100:10-15 My 1993

HEGEL, GEORG WILHELM FRIEDRICH, 1770-1831

Deux théories de l'esprit: Hegel et Schleiermacher. Brito, Emilio. *RPhil Louvain* 91:31-65 F 1993

Escaping Hegel. Fritzman, J M. *IPQ* 33:57-68 Mr 1993

Exigencias teológicas de una filosofía de la historia (la resurrección como teodicea radial). Fernández Del Riesgo, Manuel. *Cien Tom* 119:321-349 My-Ag 1992

Hegel's original insight. Pippin, Robert B. *IPQ* 33:285-295 S 1993

Hegel, des années de jeunesse à la fondation du premier système [two parts]. Depré, Olivier. *RPhil Louvain* 91:111-125 F; 259-274 My 1993

Hegel, idealism, and Robert Pippin. Westphal, Kenneth R. *IPQ* 33:263-272 S 1993

Hegel, Kolb and Flay: foundationalism or anti-foundationalism? Kow, James P. *IPQ* 33:203-218 Je 1993

Le médiation philosophique des valeurs. Henrici, Peter. *Gregorianum* 74 no 3:515-541 1993

Marxa I Sentit especulatius de la historia: comentaris a Hegel. Mayos Solsona, Goncal. Barcelona: PPU, 1993. x, 297p ISBN 84-477-0058-5

Pippin on Hegel's critique of Kant. Sedgwick, Sally. *IPQ* 33:273-283 S 1993

HEIDEGGER, JOHANN HEINRICH, 1633-1698

The root of all evil: lessons of an epigram. Harries, Karsten. *IJPS* 1:1-20 Mr 1993

HEIDEGGER, MARTIN, 1889-1976

Being interested in time: autobiography and repetition. Dupuy, Edward. *Listening* 28:141-157 Spr 1993

The community's absence in Lyotard, Nancy, and Lacoue-Labarthe. May, Todd. *PhilosTod* 37:275-284 Aut 1993

Creatures of truth. Bonsor, Jack A. *Thomist* 56:647-668 O 1992

Etre et temps et théologie. Berranger, Oliver De. *Gregorianum* 74 no 3:543-561 1993

Finitude et altérité dans l'esthétique transcendantale. Giovannangeli, Daniel. *RPhil Louvain* 91:14-30 F 1993

The hermeneutics of the technological world: the Heidegger-Heisenberg dispute. Pöggeler, Otto. *IJPS* 1:21-48 Mr 1993

Phenomenological research as destruktion: the early Heidegger's reading of Dilthey. Bambach, Charles R. *PhilosTod* 37:115-132 Sum 1993

The root of all evil: lessons of an epigram. Harries, Karsten. *IJPS* 1:1-20 Mr 1993

The sign over the barber shop: annotations on the problems of interpretation. Schmitz, Heinz-Gerd. *IPQ* 33:197-202 Je 1993

Why Heidegger's Godot might not be worth the wait. Bruin, John. *Mod Schlmn* 70:143-152 Ja 1993

HEISENBERG, WERNER

The hermeneutics of the technological world: the Heidegger-Heisenberg dispute. Pöggeler, Otto. *IJPS* 1:21-48 Mr 1993

HELL

The "fire" of hell: symbol and reality. *HPR* 94:16-23 O 1993

The hell, you say. Farrell, Michael J. *Nat Cath Rep* 29:14-15 Ap 2 1993

Preaching about hell today [repr fr *La Civiltà Cattolica* Ap 18 1992]. *HPR* 93:20-28 Mr 1993

HELLDORFER, MARTIN

Waiting for a gift from the sea. Foley, Sharon. *Sisters* 65:301-303 Jl 1993

HELMHOLZ, RICHARD H

Roman canon law in Reformation England: a review [review article *Roman canon law in Reformation England* by R Helmholz]. Sunderland, Edwin S S. *Jurist* 51 no 2:415-422 1991

HENNACY, AMMON, 1893-1970

Live the revolution now!. True, Michael, 1933-. *Cath Work* 60:8 Ag 1993

HENRICI, PETER, BP

New bishops, new spirit in Chur. Kelly, Robert. *Tablet* 247:798 Je 19 1993

HENRY VIII, KING OF ENGLAND

"Break not them then so wrongfully": topical readings of Sir Thomas Wyatt's riddling and bewitched lute and the feminine other. Cunnar, Eugene R. *Cithara* 32:3-30 N 1992

The reformation: too many assumptions? Marius, Richard, 1933-. *Critic* 47:31-42 Wint 1992

HERALDRY

The reform of ecclesiatical heraldry revisited. Galles, Duane L C M. *ABenR* 43:414-428 D 1992

HERBERT, GEORGE, 1593-1633

Heaven in ordinary. Beckett, Lucy. *Tablet* 247:1227-1228 S 25 1993

Preaching and poetry: George Herbert. Morneau, Robert F, Bp, 1938-. *Emmanuel* 49:386-391 S 1993

The quatercentenary of George Herbert, 1593-1993. Young, Robert V. *Renascence* 45:131-204 Spr 1993*

Worth pondering. O'Connell, Patrick. *Living Prayer* 26:14-15 Mr-Ap 1993

HERESIES AND HERETICS (CHRISTIANITY)

Heresy and criticism: the search for authenticity in early literature. Grant, Robert McQueen, 1917-. Louisville: John Knox Press, 1993. 180p ISBN 0-66421-971-3 LC 92-20017

HERESIES AND HERETICS (CHRISTIANITY)—1500-1599

The leaning tower of truth. Spaeth, Robert L, 1935-. *Comm* 120:6-7 Mr 26 1993

HERMENEUTICS

Beyond the literal sense: the interpretation of Scripture in the Catechism of the Catholic Church. Jensen, Joseph. *Living Light* 29:50-60 Sum 1993

Bultmann. Ferguson, David. Collegeville: The Liturgical Press, 1992. x, 154p ISBN 0-8146-5037-6

The challenge of inculturation. Lane, Dermot A. *Living Light* 29:3-21 Wint 1992

Death as a hermeneutic. Carmody, John Tully. *Horizons (CTS)* 20:115-117 Spr 1993

Grace in the end: a study in Deuteronomic theology. McConville, J Gordon. Grand Rapids: Zondervan Publishing House, 1993. x, 176p ISBN 0-310-51421-5

Herméneutique et pneumatologie selon Schleiermacher. Brito, Emilio. *Eph Theol Lovan* 69:88-117 Ap 1993

The hermeneutics of the technological world: the Heidegger-Heisenberg dispute. Pöggeler, Otto. *IJPS* 1:21-48 Mr 1993

Interprétation et vérité. Ladrière, Jean. *Laval Theol Phil* 49:189-199 Je 1993

Liberating the unlimited. Gajiwala, Kalpesh. *Month* 26:135-137 Ap 1993

The place of Phronesis in postmodern hermeneutics. Gallagher, Shaun. *PhilosTod* 37:298-305 Aut 1993

Raison critique ou raison herméneutique? Aquirre Oraa, José María. *RPhil Louvain* 91:409-440 Ag 1993

Tracy in dialogue: mystical retrieval and prophetic suspicion. Barnes, Michael R. *Heythrop* 34:60-64 Ja 1993

Weder Gold noch Silber. Biser, Eugen. *Stimm Zeit* 211:343-350 My 1993

HERMENEUTICS—COMPARATIVE STUDIES

The sign over the barber shop: annotations on the problems of interpretation. Schmitz, Heinz-Gerd. *IPQ* 33:197-202 Je 1993

HERMENEUTICS—HISTORY

Kierkegaard's place in the hermeneutic project. Martinez, Roy. *Laval Theol Phil* 49:295-308 Je 1993

HERMITS
The call of the wild. Slattery, Pat. *Register* 69:2 My 2 1993
The hermit archetype within the monastic spiritual journey. Belisle, Peter-Damian. *Word Sp* 15:41-50 1993
Hermits at the bottom of the garden. Hebblethwaite, Margaret, 1951-. *Tablet* 247:782-783 Je 19 1993

HERNANDEZ GUTIERREZ, MANUEL A
John Paul II, Pope, (1991-11-19) Allocutiones (Speech to receive Ambassador of Costa Rica) [Spanish]. John Paul II, Pope, 1920- (Karol Wojtyla) (elected 1978). *AAS* 84:1070-1072 N 3 1992*

HEROD I, THE GREAT
Home by another way. Temple, Katharine. *Cath Work* 60:1+ Ja-F 1993

HEROES
Is God in the grandstands? Auer, Jim. *Liguorian* 81:38-43 Jl 1993
Let's not lose our taste for heroes. Burns, Robert E, 1919-, ed. *USCath* 58:2 Jl 1993

HESCHEL, ABRAHAM JOSHUA, 1907-1972
Abraham Joshua Heschel: the inadequacy of the ecumenical perspective. Blumenthal, David Reuben, 1938-. *JEcumen Stds* 29:249-253 Spr 1992
The eclipse of difference: Merton's encounter with Judaism. Plank, Karl A. *Cist Stud* 28 no 2:179-191 1993

HESYCHASM
The Name of God in Byzantine tradition: from hesychasm to imyaslavie. Slesinski, Robert, 1950-. *Communio* 20:49-62 Spr 1993

HICK, JOHN
Christian theology and other religions: an evaluation of John Hick and Paul Knitter. D'Costa, Gavin. *StudiaM* 42:161-178 1993

HIERARCHIES (PHILOSOPHY)
Participação numa igreja constítuida hierarquicamente. Leites Oares, Alfredo. *Periodica* 82 no 1:139-174 1993

HIGH SCHOOL STUDENTS—RELIGIOUS LIFE
A religion club in the public high school? Marthaler, Berard L, 1927-. *Living Light* 29:11-18 Spr 1993

HIGH SCHOOLS
The Equal Access Act and the public schools: questions and answers. *Living Light* 29:3-10 Spr 1993

HILARY, SAINT, BP OF POITIERS, -367
L'effusion de l'Esprit Saint chez les Pères latins. Bentivegua, Giuseppe. *NRT* 115:19-39 Ja-F 1993

HILDEBRANDE, WALTER
After marx. Ferguson, Lisa. *New Cov* 22:25 Je 1993

HILDEGARD OF BINGEN, SAINT, 1098-1179
Hildegard of Bingen: mystic healer, companion of the angels. Ulrich, Ingeborg. Collegeville: Liturgical, 1990. 258p ISBN 0-8146-2132-5 LC 93-19848
Sex and gender differentiation in Hildegard of Bingen and Edith Stein. Allen, Prudence. *Communio* 20:389-414 Sum 1993

HILLENBRAND, REYNOLD
When Chicago Catholics were second to none. Costello, Gerald M, 1931-. *USCath* 58:48-51 Jl 1993

HINDUISM
Has ecumenism made evangelism irrelevant? Jindal, Bobby. *America* 169:8-13 Jl 31-Ag 7 1993
Hinduism: what do you know about the world's oldest religion? Whalen, William J. *USCath* 58:25-29 Ap 1993
Sarvepalli Radhakrishnan and religious pluralism. Minor, Robert N. *StudiaM* 42:307-327 1993

HINDUISM—PHILOSOPHY
L'induità e la nascita della filosofia Indiana. Desmet, Richard. *Civilta* 3:29-36 Jl 3 1993

HINDUISM—RELATIONS
Christians? Not an issue. Feys, John. *StudiaM* 42:287-305 1993

HIPPOLYTUS, SAINT, 3D CENT
The Apostolic tradition. Firth, Francis. *Can Cath Rev* 11:34-36 F 1993
Baptism. Firth, Francis. *Can Cath Rev* 11:35-36 Mr 1993
L'effusion de l'Esprit Saint chez les Pères latins. Bentivegua, Giuseppe. *NRT* 115:19-39 Ja-F 1993
Who was Saint Hippolytus? Firth, Francis. *Can Cath Rev* 11:48-49 Ja 1993

HIRKA, JAN, BP
Married to priests return to ministry. *Tablet* 247:1108-1109 Ag 28 1993

HIROAKA, KIMITAKE, 1925-1970
Killing the cat: sacrifice and beauty in Genet and Mishima. Wyschogrod, Edith. *Relig Lit* 25:107-119 Sum 1993

HISPANIC AMERICAN CATHOLICS
Hispanic Catholics: does the Church speak your language? [interview by the editors of USCath]. Deck, Allan Figueroa. *USCath* 58:27-30 D 1993
Hospitality for and by musicians: melody and text. Sosa, Juan J. *Past Mus* 17:18-21 F-Mr 1993
La raza cósmica: rediscovering the Hispanic soul. Deck, Allan Figueroa. *Critic* 47:46-53 Spr 1993
Strangers and aliens no longer, part one: the Hispanic presence in the church of the United States. Hemrick, Eugene F. Washington: United States Catholic Conference, 1993. 133p ISBN 1-55586-594-1
U.S. Hispanic Catholics and liturgical reform. Matovina, Timothy M. *America* 169:18-19 N 6 1993
What Anglos can learn from Hispanic Catholics [condensed fr *The Critic* Sp 1993]. Deck, Allan Figueroa. *CDgst* 57:50-53+ S 1993
When parents are upset. Sedano, Maruja. *ReligTJ* 26:17 Ja 1993

HISPANIC AMERICANS
Breaking away. Podsiadlo, Jack. *Momentum* 24:36-37 F-Mr 1993
The journey of Richard Rodriguez. Stavans, Ilan. *Comm* 120:20-22 Mr 26 1993

HISPANIC AMERICANS—RELIGION
US Latinos and religion [interview by J S Torrens]. Maduro, Otto. *America* 169:16-19 Ag 14-21 1993

HISTORIANS
Aubrey Gwynn—the scholar. Walsh, Katherine. *Studies* 81:385-392 Wint 1992

The canon of Irish cultural history: some questions concerning Roy Foster's Modern Ireland. Murphy, Brian P. *Studies* 82:171-184 Sum 1993

HISTORIC BUILDINGS
Homing in on G.K.C. *Tablet* 247:916 Jl 17 1993

HISTORICAL RESEARCH—METHODOLOGY
Historical research, theological inquiry, and the reality of Jesus: reflections on the method of J P Meier. Kereszty, Roch A, 1933-. *Communio* 19:576-600 Wint 1992

HISTORICAL THEOLOGY see Theology, Doctrinal—History

HISTORY
Candles behind the wall: heroes of the peaceful revolution that shattered communism. Heydt, Barbara von der. Grand Rapids: Eerdmans, 1993. 224p ISBN 0-8028-3722-0
What is new age spirituality? Woods, Richard. *Way* 33:176-188 Jl 1993

HISTORY—PHILOSOPHY
Exigencias teólogicas de una filosofía de la historia (la resurrección como teodicea radial). Fernández Del Riesgo, Manuel. *Cien Tom* 119:321-349 My-Ag 1992
On history, charm, and grief. Petricek, Miroslav. *PhilosTod* 36:304-308 Wint 1992
La tesis de Calatayud. Pou i Puigserver, Bartomeu. Barcelona: PPU, 1993. x, 173p ISBN 84-477-0037-2

HISTORY—PHILOSOPHY- RUSSIA
Storia del pensiero filosofico Russo. Simon, Michele. *Civilta* 144:153-157 Ja 16 1993

HISTORY—STUDY
The reformation: too many assumptions? Marius, Richard, 1933-. *Critic* 47:31-42 Wint 1992

HISTORY, ANCIENT
Introduction to the ancient world. Soden, Wolfram von. Grand Rapids: Eerdmans, 1993. 256p ISBN 0-8028-0142-0

HISTORY (THEOLOGY)
L'Antigiudaismo nel vangelo di Matteo come problema storico e teologico: uno schizzo. Luz, Ulrich. *Gregorianum* 74 no 3:425-445 1993
The cosmotheandric experience: emerging religious consciousness. Panikkar, Raimundo, 1918-. Maryknoll, New York: Orbis Books, 1993. x, 160p ISBN 0-88344-862-9 LC 92-46195
Eternity and the special theory of relativity. Padgett, Alan G. *IPQ* 33:219-223 Je 1993
The power to act: toward a Christian experience of time. Dalzell, Catherine. *Can Cath Rev* 11:7-11 F 1993
Reply to Smith: on the finitude of the past [reply to Q Smith, 33:109-115 1993]. Craig, William Lane. *IPQ* 33:225-231 Je 1993
La significacón teológica de los acontecimientos: El estatuto histórico de la teología según Marie-Dominque Chenu. Silva Arévalo, Eduardo. *Teol Vida* 33 no 3-4:269-297 1992

HITCHCOCK, JAMES
How conservative Catholics keep the faith. Pazola, Ron. *USCath* 58:14-19 Je 1993

HITLER, ADOLF, 1889-1945
Hell on earth Hannah Arendt in the face of Hitler. Rogozinski, Jacob. *PhilosTod* 37:257-274 Aut 1993

HNILICA, PAVEL, BP, 1921-
Slovak bishop given three-year sentence. *Tablet* 247:486 Ap 10-17 1993

HOBBS, THOMAS
Why positivism is authoritarian. Dyzenhaus, David. *Amer J Juris* 37:83-112 1992

HODEL, REBECCA
Around the land in 80 days. *Tablet* 247:1129 S 4 1993

HOENEN, PIETRO
Il mio itinerario filosofico. Selvaggi, Filippo. *Gregorianum* 74 no 2:309-329 1993

HOLIDAYS
Christmas mourning: reaching out to the grief stricken. Williams, Donna Reilly. *Mod Lit* 19:14-15 D 1992-Ja 1993
We all have a dream. Fanning, Jim, and Schumacher, Stacy. *ReligTJ* 26:29-30 Ja 1993

HOLINESS
Holiness for everyone. Martin, George. *New Cov* 23:18-20 N 1993
Holiness takes practice [condensed fr *Gleanings* 1991]. Shea, Mark P. *CDgst* 57:40-42 F 1993
In pursuit of holiness. Doohan, Leonard. *Mod Lit* 20:30 F 1993
What makes a family holy? Dominian, Jack, 1929-. *Priests & People* 6:455-D 1992

HOLINESS—BIBLICAL TEACHING
The epistle of James in rhetorical and social scientific perspective holiness-wholeness and patterns of replication. Elliott, John H. *Bib Th Bul* 23:71-81 Sum 1993

HOLINESS—COMPARATIVE STUDIES
Das Problem der Heiligkeit in unserer Zeit. Stelzmann, Rainulf A. *Stimm Zeit* 211:489-500 Jl 1993

HOLISTIC HEALTH see Health Care

HOLISTIC MEDICINE
Holistic approach will transform healthcare services. Drummond, Thomas B, and Przybilla, Carla. *Health Prog* 74:64-65 Jl-Ag 1993
The value of spiritual health. Seidl, Lawrence G. *Health Prog* 74:48-50 1993
Wellness in the healing ministry. Burke, Barbara K. *Health Prog* 74:34-37 1993

HOLOCAUST, JEWISH (1939-1945)
Because it could happen again. Costello, Gerald M, 1931-. *USCath* 58:48-51 F 1993
Descent into hell. Sweeney, Jim. *OSV* 82:10-11 Ag 15 1993
Dialogue [interview by J Luxmoore]. Edelman, Mark. *Register* 69:1+ Je 20 1993
The eclipse of difference: Merton's encounter with Judaism. Plank, Karl A. *Cist Stud* 28 no 2:179-191 1993
My dream for the Pope. Nicholl, Donald. *Tablet* 247:230 F 20 1993
Taking issue with the revisionists. Griffin, Robert F. *OSV* 82:18 My 30 1993

Prejudice or disagreement? Homosexuals in the military. Garvey, John, 1944-. *Comm* 120:9-10 F 26 1993

A private anguish. Richards, Robin. *Tablet* 247:566 My 8 1993

Searching for the soap: coming clean on gays in the military. Carlin, David Robert, Jr, 1938-. *Comm* 120:11-12 Ap 9 1993

Sexually challenged. Sobran, Joseph. *Crisis* 11:41-43 Je 1993

Therapist says gay ministries subvert doctrine [interview by T Ryland, repr fr *San Diego News Notes*]. Nicolòsi, Joseph. *Nat Cath Rep* 29:16-17 My 7 1993

Tom Dooley's many lives. Fisher, James T. *Comm* 120:6-7 My 21 1993

What about our Church's children? Giurlanda, Paul. *America* 168:12-14 My 8 1993

What's the military so afraid of? Burns, Robert E, 1919-. *USCath* 58:2 Je 1993

When words shape reality. Starr, Bill. *SocJust* 84:80-83 My-Je 1993

HOMOSEXUALITY—LAW
On discrimination against homosexual persons. *Origins* 23:359-360 O 28 1993

HOMOSEXUALITY—RELIGIOUS ASPECTS
The church and the homosexual. McNeill, John J. Boston: Beacon, 1993. x, 266p ISBN 0-8070-7931-6 LC 93-7088

Homosexual people in the church. Williamson, David. *Priests & People* 7: 335-339 Ag-S 1993

Homosexuality and world religions. Swidler, Arlene. Philadelphia: Trinity Press International, 1993. 232p ISBN 1-56338-051-x LC 93-6848

Jesus acted up: a gay and lesbian manifesto. Goss, Robert. New York: HarperSanFrancisco, 1993. x, 240p ISBN 0-06-063318-2 LC 92-56415

There's nothing holy about homophobia. Unsworth, Tim. *Salt* 13:12-14 Je 1993

HOMOSEXUALITY—STUDY
Sorry, the numbers were cooked. Wagner, David. *Register* 69:5 Ap 25 1993

HOMOSEXUALS—DISCCRIMINATION
Homosexuals in the military: three issues. Mahony, Roger Michael, Cardinal, 1936-. *Origins* 22:621+ F 25 1993

HONDURAS—BOUNDARIES- EL SALVADOR
Peace talks in El Salvador [excerpt fr *Martires de El Salvador*]. *LADOC* 23: 24-28 Jl-Ag 1993

HONECKER, ERLICH
Befreiung von Knechtschaft. Ehlen, Peter. *Stimm Zeit* 211:21-33 Ja 1993

HONESTY
The dilemma of being nice. Klimoski, Victor J. *Church* 9:44-46 Spr 1993

Let's be totally honest. Mallowe, Mike. *USCath* 58:20-25 Je 1993

HOOD, ROBIN ADRIAN, -1993
Hood, Robin Adrian, -1993 [obit]. Rafferty, Robin. *Tablet* 247:1275-1276 O 2 1993

HOPE
Hope in loneliness. Martin, James Alfred. *RRel* 52:236-237 Mr-Ap 1993

A hope reborn. Behrens, Jeff. *Liguorian* 81:4-8 D 1993

HOPE—BIBLICAL TEACHING
The hope which empowers. McLoughlin, David. *Priests & People* 6:447-451 D 1992

Pour une Église en acte d'espérance. Lebeau, Paul. *Lumen* 48:149-159 Je 1993

HOPE—RELIGIOUS ASPECTS
John Paul II, Pope, (1993-05-23) Presence [Orig in Italian]. John Paul II, Pope, 1920- (Karol Wojtyla) (elected 1978). *OR(Eng)* 1294:6+ Je 9 1993*

John Paul II, Pope, (1993-06-12) Love and hope [Orig in Spanish]. John Paul II, Pope, 1920- (Karol Wojtyla) (elected 1978). *OR(Eng)* 1296:3 Je 23 1993*

HOPE, DAVID MICHAEL, BP, 1940-
Bishop Hope seeks to square the circle on women priests. *Tablet* 247:735-736 Je 5 1993

Rosary to the rescue. Gledhill, Ruth. *Tablet* 247:1037 Ag 14 1993

HOPKINS, GERARD MANLEY, 1844-1889
Gerard Manley Hopkins annual 1993. Sundermeier, Michael, and Egan, Desmond, eds. Omaha: Creighton University Press, 1993. x, 123p ISBN 1-881871-07-x

Gerard Manley Hopkins: the incarnational work of priest and poet. Bouchard, Gary M. *ABenR* 44:115-124 Je 1993

Musings on Earth Day near Lake Erie. King, Judine. *Sisters* 65:193-197 My 1993

Preaching and poetry: Gerard Manley Hopkins. Morneau, Robert F, Bp, 1938-. *Emmanuel* 99:460-464 O 1993

HORKHEIMER, MAX
Exigencias teológicas de una filosofía de la historia (la resurrección como teodicea radial). Fernández Del Riesgo, Manuel. *Cien Tom* 119:321-349 My-Ag 1992

HOSOKAWA, MORIHIRO
Tokyo rumours. *Tablet* 247:1259 O 2 1993

HOSPICES
Care of the dying: a Catholic perspective [4 parts]. *Health Prog* 74:34-38+ Mr; 16-21+ Ap; 22-26+ My; 46-54 Je 1993*

The holiness of death. Coffey, Kathy. *OSV* 81:6 Ap 11 1993

The hospice demystified. Cassidy, Sheila. *Priests & People* 6:415-422 N 1992

Hospice: death with dignity. Repp, Debbie M. *Liguorian* 81:24-31 Je 1993

John Paul II, Pope, (1992-12-19) Ad limina Apostolorum. John Paul II, Pope, 1920- (Karol Wojtyla) (elected 1978). *TPS* 38:193-200 Jl-Ag 1993*

Mercy and aid. Haynes, A W. *Can Cath Rev* 11:7-8 Mr 1993

Midwife for souls: spiritual care for the dying. Magno, Josefina B. Bosston: St Paul Books & Media, 1993. 111p ISBN 0-8198-4769-0 LC 93-32153

HOSPITAL-PHYSICIAN JOINT VENTURES
Hospital-Physician integration takes varied forms. Fox, Wende L, et al. *Health Prog* 74:49-50 Jl-Ag 1993

HOSPITAL-PHYSICIAN RELATIONS
Hospital-physician relationships: a hurdle on the road to reform. White, Jane H. *Health Prog* 74:12-13+ 1993

HOSPITAL TRUSTEES
Board members with a mission. Santos, Yolanda M, and Zipprich, John L. *Health Prog* 74:32-36 Jl-Ag 1993

HOSPITAL UTILIZATION—LENGTH OF STAY
Long-term care and hospital collaboration. Hume, Susan K. *Health Prog* 74: 16-20 Je 1993

HOSPITALITY
God in many disguises. Kirwan, Michael. *Cath Work* 60:7 My 1993

Hospitality, reverence, and talking in church. Mick, Lawrence E. *Tod Parish* 25:20-22 O 1993

Monastic hospitality and the conversion of the monk. Huerre, Denis. *ABenR* 44:249-257 S 1993

A pastor's holiday. Carroll, L Patrick. *America* 169:14+ Ag 28-S 4 1993

Perfect welcome in Lent. Ellsberg, Peggy R. *America* 168:23 F 20 1993

HOSPITALITY—BIBLICAL TEACHING
Man, woman, and hospitality - 2 Kings 4:8-36. Hobbs, T R. *Bib Th Bul* 23: 91-100 Aut 1993

HOSPITALS
Assessment in action. Hey, Michelle. *Health Prog* 74:54-57 Ja-F 1993

Developing a model for technology assessment. Fox, Frank, and Barron, Ellen. *Health Prog* 74:50-53 Ja-F 1993

Health. Feuerherd, Peter. *Register* 69:1 Mr 14 1993

Long-term care and hospital collaboration. Hume, Susan K. *Health Prog* 74: 16-20 Je 1993

Technology decision making. Berkowitz, David A, and Swan, Melanie M. *Health Prog* 74:42-47 Ja-F 1993

Technology framework. Stempien, Theresa L. *Health Prog* 74:58-62 Ja-F 1993

Troubled voices: stories of ethics and illness. Zaner, Richard M. Cleveland: Pilgrim Press, 1993. x, 161p ISBN 0-8298-0964-3 LC 93-3823

Utah bishop asks Rome to halt hospitals' sale [photos]. Carey, Ann. *OSV* 82: 3 N 28 1993

HOSPITALS—ACCOUNTING
The ABCs of electronic data interchange. Hoyler, Geraldine M. *Health Prog* 74:13 O 1993

HOSPITALS—CASE MANAGEMENT
Nurse case managers reduce admissions, stays. Weyant, Jennie, and Swindle, Donna. *Health Prog* 74:61-62 Jl-Ag 1993

On the right path. London, Judy. *Health Prog* 74:36-38 Je 1993

HOSPITALS—ETHICAL ASPECTS
Hôpital et respect des personnes. Geets, Claude, et al, eds. *Supplement* 184: 5-203 Mr-Ap 1993*

Questions d'un gestionnaire d'hôpital. Tassin, Paul. *Supplement* 184:7-19 Mr-Ap 1993

HOSPITALS—HISTORY
Religious women and welfare. Elvins, Mark. *Priests & People* 6:320-322 Ag-S 1992

HOSPITALS—PSYCHOLOGICAL ASPECTS
Hôpital et respect des personnes. Geets, Claude, et al, eds. *Supplement* 184: 5-203 Mr-Ap 1993*

Pour une éthique de la fin de la vie. Geets, Claude. *Supplement* 184:89-96 Mr-Ap 1993

HOSPITALS—RELIGIOUS ASPECTS
Comment faire Église aujourd'hui (à l'hôpital)? Martou, Jean-Marie. *Supplement* 184:145-166 Mr-Ap 1993

HOSPITALS—STUDY
The price of helping the poor. Vidulich, Dorothy. *Nat Cath Rep* 29:4 Ap 9 1993

HOSTAGES
Waite's ordeal. *Tablet* 247:1229 S 25 1993

HOURANI, ALBERT, -1993
Hourani, Albert, -1993 [obit]. Owen, Roger. *Tablet* 247:152-153 Ja 30 1993

HOURS OF LABOR
Accounting for the slowdown in the divorce rate in the 1980s: a bargaining perspective. McCrate, Elaine. *RSocEcon* 50:404-419 Wint 1992

A response to unemployment: ten propositions. Quigley, George. *Studies* 82: 73-86 Spr 1993

Splitting shifts: splitting families. Downs, Peter. *Comm* 120:7-8 Je 4 1993

HOUSEHOLD DUTIES—BIBLICAL TEACHING
The household: a major social component for gender analysis in the gospel of Matthew. Love, Stuart L. *Bib Th Bul* 23:21-31 Spr 1993

HOUSING
The other face of Millwall. *Tablet* 247:1293 O 9 1993

HOVDA, ROBERT W, 1920-1992
Robert Hovda. *Mod Lit* 20:46 Mr 1993

HOWARD, DICK, 1943-
Review essay the possibility of post-socialist politics. Bohman, James. *Mod Schlmn* 70:217-224 Mr 1993

HOWATCH, SUSAN, 1940-
An attack of scientism. Cornwell, John. *Tablet* 247:462-464 Ap 10-17 1993

On the frontier. *Tablet* 247:402 Mr 27 1993

HOWELL, CLIFFORD
The gospel according to Clifford. Ghezzi, Bert. *New Cov* 22:7-8 F 1993

HOXHA, ENVER, 1908-1985
Albania, the Church triumphant in ruins. Hurley, Mark Joseph, Bp, 1919-. *America* 168:4-5 F 20 1993

HUBBARD, RON, 1911-1986?
Scientology's religious roots. Meldgaard, Helle. *StudiaM* 41:169-185 1992

HUMAN DEVELOPMENT
Human development and reconsideration of ensoulment. Kischer, Clayton Ward. *Linacre* 60:57-63 F 1993

In defense of human development. Kischer, Clayton Ward. *Linacre* 59:68-75 N 1992

John Paul II, Pope, (1992-02-11) Nuntii Scripto Dati (Written Papal Message) [French]. John Paul II, Pope, 1920- (Karol Wojtyla) (elected 1978). *AAS* 84:994-996 O 3 1992*

The moral status of the embryo. May, William E. *Linacre* 59:76-83 N 1992

Note per uno sviluppo umano. Salvini, Gianpaolo. *Civilta* 3:491-501 S 18 1993

Pastores dabo vobis—reflections on a conference. Atherton, John. *Furrow* 44: 440-443 Jl-Ag 1993

Scientific and philosophical expertise: an evaluation of the arguments on "personhood". Irving, Diane Nutwell. *Linacre* 60:18-46 F 1993

UN reports on minorities: US not measuring up. Collins, Carole. *Nat Cath Rep* 29:9 Je 18 1993

The urgency of ongoing formation. McGarry, Cecil. *AFER* 34:134-145 Je 1992

Will the real me please stand up? Maas, Robin. *Living Light* 29:37-44 Spr 1993

Writing your faith script with God. Auer, Jim. *Liguorian* 81:38-42 O 1993

HUMAN ECOLOGY—RELIGIOUS ASPECTS
The body of God: an ecological theology. McFague, Sallie. Minneapolis: Fortress Press, 1993. x, 274p ISBN 0-8006 LC 93-6584

Gaia and God: an ecofeminist theology of earth healing. Ruether, Rosemary Radford. San Francisco: HarperSanFrancisco, 1992. 310p ISBN 0-06067-022-3 LC 91-58911

The green Bible. Scharper, Stephen B, and Cunningham, Hilary, eds. Maryknoll, New York: Orbis Books, 1993. x, 113p ISBN 0-85244-230-0 LC 92-35593

Hellfire and lighting rods: liberating science, technology, and religion. Ferré, Frederick. Maryknoll, New York: Orbis Books, 1993. 92-39488 ISBN 0-88344-856-4 LC 92-39488

John Paul II, (1993-10-22) Rich and poor [Orig in English]. John Paul II, Pope, 1920- (Karol Wojtyla) (elected 1978). *Origins* 23:383-384 N 4 1993*

Population, the Church and the Pope. Schwarz, John C. *America* 168:6-10 Mr 6 1993

The promise of nature: ecology and cosmic purpose. Haught, John F. New York: Paulist Press, 1993. x, 156p ISBN 0-8091-3396-2 LC 92-41353

We are home: a spirituality of the environment. Jung, Shannon. New Jersey: Paulist Press, 1993. x, 170p ISBN 0-8091-3364-4 LC 92-37876

Women, earth, and creator spirit. Johnson, Elizabeth A, 1941-. New York: Paulist Press, 1993. x, 79p ISBN 0-8091-3415-2 LC 92-42018

HUMAN EMBRYO see Embryo, Human
The embryo and the fetus: new moral contexts. Cahill, Lisa Sowle. *TheolStds* 54:124-142 Mr 1993

Human development and reconsideration of ensoulment. Kischer, Clayton Ward. *Linacre* 60:57-63 F 1993

The moral status of the embryo. May, William E. *Linacre* 59:76-83 N 1992

Persons, souls and embryos. Coghlan, Peter. *Pacifica* 6:165-171 Je 1993

HUMAN REPRODUCTION
Contraception and the war within the self. DeMarco, Donald. *HPR* 93:29-31+ My 1993

The disembodiment of parenthood. Grondelski, John M. *HPR* 93:30-31+ F 1993

"Reproducing the world": Mary O'Brien's theory of reproductive consciousness and implications for feminist incarnational theology. Kaminski, Phyllis H. *Horizons (CTS)* 19:240-262 Fall 1992

HUMAN REPRODUCTIVE TECHNOLOGY
What price parenthood?: ethics and assisted reproduction. Campbell, Courtney S. Brookfield: Ashgate Publishing Company, 1992. 127p ISBN 1-8552-1224-2

HUMAN RIGHTS
Abortion and the law. Whyte, Gerry. *Doctr Life* 42:253-272 My-Je 1992

The advance of liberty. Patten, Christopher. *Tablet* 247:1025-1027 Ag 7 1993

An analysis of the use of rights language in pre-modern Catholic social thought. Brady, Bernard V. *Thomist* 57:97-121 Ja 1993

ANC not to take action on torture report. Rickard, Carmel. *Tablet* 247:1141 S 4 1993

Clinton speech to United Nations echoes new focus on human rights [editorial]. *Nat Cath Rep* 29:20 O 8 1993

Death of private soldier. Barchard, David. *Tablet* 247:131-132 Ja 30 1993

Dragon in the toy factory: workers' rights in Asian plants. Senser, Robert A, 1921-. *Comm* 120:11-13 O 8 1993

East and West dissent over human rights. *Tablet* 247:797 Je 19 1993

The ecumenical commitment to human rights. Littell, Franklin H., 1917-. *JEcumen Stds* 29:383-389 Sum-Aut 1992

Harden not your hearts [editorial]. *America* 169:3 Ag 28-S 4 1993

"Help us while it is not too late!". Komarica, Franjo, Bp, 1946-, et al. *Cath Int* 4:230-231 My 1993

Human rights and the new society. Shea, John B. *SocJust* 84:100-104 Jl-Ag 1993

Human rights as land rights in the Pacific. May, John D'Arcy. *Pacifica* 6:61-80 F 1993

In difesa dei diritti del bambino. Caprile, Giovanni. *Civilta* 144:165-172 Ja 16 1993

John Paul II, Pope, (1993-09-05) Freedom [Orig in French]. John Paul II, Pope, 1920- (Karol Wojtyla) (elected 1978). *OR(Eng)* 1306:5+ S 8 1993*

Just war, pacifism and humanitarian intervention. Himes, Kenneth R. *America* 169:10-15+ Ag 14-21 1993

Left, right, or personalist? Hanink, James G. *New Oxford Rev* 60:14-20 N 1993

[Many who do not profess]. Smith, Janet E. *Comm* 120:14-15 O 22 1993

A moment of sorrow, a moment of hope. Burns, Robert E, 1919-. *USCath* 58:2 Ag 1993

Over there. Mullen, Peter. *Register* 69:1+ Jl 25 1993

The Prolife Movement: dead or alive? Hanink, James G. *New Oxford Rev* 60:10-14+ My 1993

Prophetic realism [editorial]. *Cath Int* 4:200 My 1993

Refugees: a challenge for solidarity. *TPS* 38:65-77 Mr-Ap 1993

Repression in the Sudan. Barbier, Hubert. *Cath Int* 4:234-236 My 1993

Respect human rights. *Cath Int* 4:237-238 My 1993

The social context of the AMECEA countries on the eve of the African Synod. Henriot, Peter F. *AFER* 34:340-363 D 1992

Sudan: a grim tragedy. Gassis, Macram Max, Bp, 1938-. *Cath Int* 4:236-237 My 1993

Truth commission points the finger at the armed forces. *Tablet* 247:380 Mr 20 1993

UN rights conference avoids meat on bones of contention. Collins, Carole. *Nat Cath Rep* 29:11 Jl 2 1993

Verso una ristesura dei diritti fondamentali dell'uomo? (Recoaro Terme, 11-13 settembre 1992). Rulli, Giovanni. *Civilta* 143:602-611 D 19 1992

World Conference on Human Rights June 14-25, 1993. Drinan, Robert Francis, 1920-. *America* 168:15-16 Je 5-12 1993

HUMAN RIGHTS—CONGRESSES
A triumph for rights. Drinan, Robert Francis, 1920-. *Tablet* 247:870-871 Jl 3 1993

HUMAN RIGHTS—RELIGIOUS ASPECTS
World cannot survive without justice, peace and development. Tauran, Jean-Louis, Abp. *OR(Eng)* 1301:4 Jl 28 1993

HUMAN RIGHTS- ASIA
Asia's new-style tyranny. Himmelfarb, Anne. *Crisis* 11:46-48 S 1993

HUMAN RIGHTS- CHINA
Journey to Peking. Rafferty, Kevin. *Tablet* 247:1178-1179 S 11 1993

A matter of principle. Smith, Christopher. *Register* 69:4 Jl 18 1993

Public outcry could slow ongoing human-rights violations in China [editorial]. *Nat Cath Rep* 29:28 Jl 16 1993

HUMAN RIGHTS- COLOMBIA
Colombia confronts the sword [photos]. Wirpsa, Leslie. *Nat Cath Rep* 29:8-9 Ap 9 1993

Colombia's two faces. Linden, Ian. *Tablet* 247:881-882 Jl 10 1993

HUMAN RIGHTS- EL SALVADOR
Hunt begins for stolen children. *Tablet* 247:590-591 My 8 1993

Military may strike after Truth Commission report. *Tablet* 247:347 Mr 13 1993

El Salvador [photos]. MacEoin, Gary. *Nat Cath Rep* 29:8-9 S 3 1993

HUMAN RIGHTS- GUATEMALA
Nun identifies site of detention. Francke, Caitlin. *Nat Cath Rep* 29:7 Ap 9 1993

HUMAN RIGHTS- LATIN AMERICA
Direitos de vida numa cultura de morte. Maçaneiro, Marcial. *REB* 53:52-71 Mr 1993

HUMAN RIGHTS- MALAWI
Malawi in crisis. *Cath Int* 4:174 Ap 1993

Under the eye of Big Brother. *Tablet* 247:403 Mr 27 1993

HUMAN RIGHTS- MEXICO
Free trade with an unfree land [map, photos]. Jones, Arthur C, 1936-. *Nat Cath Rep* 29:10-12 Ap 16 1993

HUMAN RIGHTS- SOVIET UNION
Philosophy and theology after Kolyma. Chrostowski, Waldemar. *New Theol Rev* 6:102-107 My 1993

HUMAN RIGHTS- SUDAN
A deadly silence: faint voices on Sudan. Jordan, Patrick. *Comm* 120:4-5 My 7 1993

John Paul II, Pope, (1993-02-10) Civil War [English text]. John Paul II, Pope, 1920- (Karol Wojtyla) (elected 1978). *Origins* 22:617-618 F 18 1993*

HUMANISM
Naturalistic humanism. O'Connor, Edward D. *HPR* 93:19-26 Ap 1993

Renaissance humanism. Kelley, Donald R, 1931-. Boston: Twayne Publishers, 1991. x, 176p ISBN 0-80578-606-6 LC 91-4776

Secular fundamentalism and secular humanism: value sets for the twenty-first century. Kollar, Nathan R. *Stud Form Spir* 14:233-246 My 1993

HUMANISM, RELIGIOUS
The human person: contemporary theology and the exercises. Callahan, Annice. *Way Suppl* 76:85-97 Spr 1993

The prophetic humanism of John Paul II. Dulles, Avery Robert, 1918-. *America* 169:6-11 O 23 1993

El taller de mi. Giralt, Joan J. Barcelona: Ser Editorial, 1993. x, 315p ISBN 84-8860-401-7

HUMANISTIC ETHICS
Weltethos oder säkularer Humanismus? Fuchs, Josef. *Stimm Zeit* 211:147-154 Mr 1993

HUMANITIES
John Paul II, Pope, (1993-01-16) Diplomats [Origin French]. John Paul II, Pope, 1920- (Karol Wojtyla) (elected 1978). *Origins* 22:583-587 F 4 1993*

HUMANITY
From matter to mind to meaning. Higgins, James J. *Liguorian* 81:73 Mr 1993

John Paul II, Pope, (1992-12-24) Light shines [orig Italian]. John Paul II, Pope, 1920- (Karol Wojtyla) (elected 1978). *OR(Eng)* 1272:5 Ja 6 1993*

Male and female he created them: a summary of the teaching of Genesis chapter one. Martin, Francis. *Communio* 20:240-265 Sum 1993

Strangers to ourselves. Reilly, Patrick. *New Blckfrs* 74:146-152 Mr 1993

HUME, GEORGE BASIL, CARDINAL, 1923-
An agenda for Europe: Cardinal Hume's address at Prague. *Tablet* 247:1177-1178 S 11 1993

Cardinal calls for action against Balkan war. *Tablet* 246:1583 D 12 1992

Cardinal calls for welcome to Anglicans. *Tablet* 247:523 Ap 24 1993

Encyclical not intended to back up Humanae Vitae, says Cardinal. *Tablet* 247:1309 O 9 1993

"Gay gene" forces a rethink on homosexuality. *Tablet* 247:958-959 Jl 24 1993

Irish voices plead for violence to end. *Tablet* 247:444-445 Ap 3 1993

A lead from Cardinal Hume [editorial]. *Tablet* 247:1151-1152 S 11 1993

Mps welcome focus on the family. *Tablet* 247:352 Mr 13 1993

No breakthrough yet in Anglican talks. *Tablet* 247:351-352 Mr 13 1993

No pacts, no deals in talks with Anglicans. *Tablet* 247:255 F 20 1993

No special deal in welcome for Anglicans. *Tablet* 247:558-560 My 1 1993

Politicians and the Churches diagnose a social sickness. *Tablet* 247:318-319 Mr 6 1993

Stop nuclear tests, church leaders say. *Tablet* 247:319 Mr 6 1993

Touching base. *Tablet* 247:306 Mr 6 1993

Westminster archbishop has good sense of Hume. Hebblethwaite, Peter, 1930-. *Nat Cath Rep* 29:17 Mr 19 1993

HUMILITY
God hides His presence to instruct us in humility. Kreeft, Peter John, 1937-. *Register* 69:1+ My 30 1993

Humility and cosmology. Hodgson, Peter. *New Blckfrs* 74:252-262 My 1993

Humility. Cooney, Arthur. *New Cov* 23:19 Ag 1993

Spiritual adventurers. Hebblethwaite, Margaret, 1951-. *Tablet* 247:1066-1067 Ag 21 1993

The "Spiritual excercises" and spiritual direction. Mohler, James Aylward. *Priest* 49:38-46 S 1993

Spiritual intimacy and community. English, John. New Jersey: Paulist Press, 1992. x, 207p ISBN 0-8091-3384-9 LC 92-29706

Vision and meditation in neoclassical English hymnody: notes toward sources and implications. Murray, Douglas. *Listening* 28:105-117 Spr 1993

ILLEGITIMATE CHILDREN- ITALY
Sacrificed for honor: Italian infant abandonment and the politics of reproductive control. Kertzer, David I. Boston: Beacon Press, 1993. x, 252p ISBN 0-8070-5604-9 LC 92-35169

ILLIG, ALVIN
Evangelizing America: transformations in Paulist mission. Robichaud, Paul. *US Cath Hist* 11:61-78 Spr 1993

ILLITERACY
The broken dream of illiteracy [editorial]. *America* 169:4 O 2 1993

ILLITERACY- AFRICA
John Paul II, Pope, (1993-02-08) Birth of Freedom [English text]. John Paul II, Pope, 1920- (Karol Wojtyla) (elected 1978). *Origins* 22:615-616 F 18 1993*

IMAGE (THEOLOGY)
Introduction to re-thinking representation: Anselm and visual thinking. Kromm, Jane. *Listening* 28:95-104 Spr 1993

Picture that!. Kopek, Robert. *BibleT* 31:225-230 Jl 1993

What did Jesus really look like? Ramsey, Boniface. *America* 168:16-17 Je 19-26 1993

IMAGE OF GOD
Attributing things to God. Moonan, Lawrence. *Eph Theol Lovan* 78:86-117 Ap 1992

The compassion of God the Father in western art. Boespflug, François. *CrossCurr* 42:487-503 Wint 1992-1993

Examining a Manichaean approach to abortion. Shea, Mark P. *New Oxford Rev* 60:13-16+ Ap 1993

Experience as a theological category: Hans Urs von Balthasar on the Christian encounter with God's image. Casarella, Peter. *Communio* 20:118-128 Spr 1993

Gender and the will of God. Kreeft, Peter John, 1937-. *Crisis* 11:20-28 S 1993

Idols and false images of God: a psychoanalytical perspective. Kelly, Shay. *Doctr Life* 43:13-19 Ja 1993

Images of God and the richness of our faith [reply to W Harrington, 42 no 8 467-476 O 1992]. MacCarthy, Thomas. *Doctr Life* 42:629-630 D 1992

Leaves of light: the textual journeys of Dante and García Márquez. Barciauskas, Jonas. *CrossCurr* 43:212-229 Sum 1993

Male and female he created them: a summary of the teaching of Genesis chapter one. Martin, Francis. *Communio* 20:240-265 Sum 1993

Robert Coles: listening to stories of God in the lives of children. McKenzie, Paula A. *Living Light* 29:65-72 Aut 1992

A theological case for God-She expanding the treasury of metaphor. Johnson, Elizabeth A, 1941-. *Comm* 120:9-14 Ja 29 1993

The unconscious Christian: images of God in dreams. Hall, James A. Mahwah, New Jersey: Paulist Press, 1993. x, 113p ISBN 0-8091-3353-9 LC 92-26395

What's God like? Collins, Mary Smalara. *USCath* 58:30-35 S 1993

IMAGINATION
A garden of conceptual delights. Podles, Mary Elizabeth. *Crisis* 11:54-60 Je 1993

Imagination, the poets' God. Madsen, Catherine. *CrossCurr* 43:47-59 Spr 1993

Meditation and prayer (1):creative imagination in the lives of Ignatius Loyola and Khapa: visualization in Catholic and Buddhist practice. Urubshurow, Victoria Kennick. *Stud Form Spir* 14:41-56 F 1993

Preaching the Word [excerpts fr *Bodying forth: aesthetic liturgy*]. Collins, Patrick W, 1936-. *Emmanuel* 99:278-285 Je 1993

IMAGINATION—PSYCHOLOGICAL ASPECTS
Los sentidos internos. Rodriguez, Victorino. Barcelona: PPU, 1993. x, 158p ISBN 84-477-0066-6

IMITATION
Violence, difference, sacrifice [interview by R. Adams]. Girard, René, 1923-. *Relig Lit* 25:11-33 Sum 1993

IMMACULATE CONCEPTION
Blessed John Duns Scotus: champion of Jesus and Mary. Foley, Leonard. *St Anth* 101:10-16 N 1993

IMMIGRATION AND EMIGRATION *see* Emigration and Immigration- California

IMMORTALITY
Averroes, Aristotle, and the Qur'an immortality. Mohammed, Ovey N. *IPQ* 33:37-55 Mr 1993

The Day of the Dead. Schall, James Vincent, 1928-. *Crisis* 10:43-45 N 1992

A deeper clerical problem than sex. Freburger, William J. *Nat Cath Rep* 29: 17 Ap 16 1993

Eternal life in paradise [tr fr *La Civiltà Cattolica* Ap 4, 1992]. *HPR* 93:7-17 Ag-S 1993

Fido in heaven? Montgomery, John Warwick, 1931-. *New Oxford Rev* 60:20+ O 1993

The human person: animal and spirit [by D Braine, review article]. Kerr, Fergus. *New Blckfrs* 74:333-337 Jl-Ag 1993

Immortality and the soul. Selman, F J. *New Blckfrs* 73:566-571 N 1992

The immortality of the soul and the resurrection of the dead. *HPR* 93:9-18 Jl 1993

Vigilance! the Lord is coming [tr fr *La Civiltà Cattolica* D 5 1992]. *HPR* 94: 7-16 N 1993

IMMORTALITY—BIBLICAL TEACHING
The Garden of Eden and the hope of immortality. Barr, James. Minneapolis: Fortress Press, 1993. 146p ISBN 0-80062-744-x LC 92-27037

IMMUNIZATION
Community clinic offers access to care. Bauer, Susan. *Health Prog* 74:42-44+ O 1993

IMPETUS THEORY
Impulsus and impetus in the Liber Jordani de Ratione Ponderis. Giannetto, E, et al. *Med Stud* 54:162-185 1992

IMPRESSIONIST ARTISTS- FRANCE
Cézannes Hochamt. Grom, Bernhard. *Stimm Zeit* 211:423-425 Je 1993

The city as a stage for time: Camille Pissaro's serial cityscapes. O'Donovan, Leo J. *America* 168:18-22 Ap 24 1993

IMPULSE
Impulsus and impetus in the Liber Jordani de Ratione Ponderis. Giannetto, E, et al. *Med Stud* 54:162-185 1992

IN VITRO FERTILIZATION *see* Fertilization, In Vitro

INCARNATION
The challenge of inculturation. Lane, Dermot A. *Living Light* 29:3-21 Wint 1992

Examining a Manichaean approach to abortion. Shea, Mark P. *New Oxford Rev* 60:13-16+ Ap 1993

The Incarnation: Muslim objections and the Christian response. Fastiggi, Robert L. *Thomist* 57:457-493 Jl 1993

Incarnational tension in Robert Browning's Karshish. Kass, Thomas G. *ABenR* 44:236-257 S 1993

Liturgy and life: an overview. Lackner, Joseph M. *Catechist* 27:86-93 S 1993

Woman church. Shaw, Russell. *Crisis* 11:8-9 Ja 1993

INCENSE
Incense: a user's guide. Yoshida, Gregory. *Mod Lit* 20:16-18 Ap 1993

INCEST
The reality, fact, and fantasy of incest. Zuercher, Suzanne. *RRel* 52:712-718 S-O 1993

INCOME DISTRIBUTION
America's silent depression: a challenge to social economics. Peterson, Wallace C, 1921-. *RSocEcon* 51:2-13 Spr 1993

Income distribution and business cycles. Van Lear, William. *RSocEcon* 50: 316-332 Fall 1992

INDEPENDENT CHURCHES
The new churches. Willey, Eldred. *Tablet* 247:165-166 F 6 1993

INDEPENDENT CHURCHES- AFRICA
African independent churches and religious life. O'Reilly, Martin. *AFER* 35: 217-221 Ag 1993

The interaction of African independent churches with traditional religions in Nigeria. Olayiwola, David O. *StudiaM* 42:357-370 1993

INDIA—HISTORY
Recovering a nation: who controls the past. Smith, Brian. *Comm* 120:5-6 Jl 16 1993

INDIA—POLITICS
Reaping the whirlwind [editorial]. *Tablet* 246:1559 D 12 1992

INDIA—RELIGION
Bhagwan Shri Rajneesh. Dolcini, Donatella. *StudiaM* 41:127-143 1992

L'induità e la nascita della filosofia Indiana. Desmet, Richard. *Civilta* 3:29-36 Jl 3 1993

Leave the temple: Indian paths to human liberation. Wilfred, Felix. Maryknoll, New York: Orbis Books, 1992. x, 199p ISBN 0-88344-794-0 LC 92-20801

Recovering a nation: who controls the past. Smith, Brian. *Comm* 120:5-6 Jl 16 1993

INDIANS OF CENTRAL AMERICA—MISSIONS
The life of a parish priest in Guatemala. Urbanski, Liz. *OSV* 82:12-13 My 2 1993

INDIANS OF CENTRAL AMERICA—RELIGION
Teología India. Berganza, Carlos. *Cien Tom* 120:79-100 Ja-Ap 1993

INDIANS OF NORTH AMERICA—CHURCH HISTORY
Kino apostolo degli indiani del Nordamerica. Mellinato, Giuseppe. *Civilta* 144:472-478 Mr 6 1993

INDIANS OF NORTH AMERICA—CIVIL RIGHTS
Apology to native Americans for past mistakes. Kolvenbach, Peter Hans. *Origins* 23:36-37 Je 3 1993

INDIANS OF NORTH AMERICA—MISSIONS
Apology to native Americans for past mistakes. Kolvenbach, Peter Hans. *Origins* 23:36-37 Je 3 1993

No easy rewards [photos]. Bartholomew, Marianna. *Extensn* 88:22-27 S-O 1993

INDIANS OF NORTH AMERICA—RELIGION
American Indians, panel discuss religious laws. Specktor, Mordecai. *Nat Cath Rep* 29:4 Mr 26 1993

Apology to native Americans for past mistakes. Kolvenbach, Peter Hans. *Origins* 23:36-37 Je 3 1993

Native American religions: an introduction. Carmody, Denise Lardner, and Carmody, John Tully. Mahwah: Paulist, 1993. 270p ISBN 0-8091-3404-7 LC 93-15547

INDIANS OF NORTH AMERICA—RELIGIOUS LIFE
Brief on native peoples. *Origins* 23:401+ N 18 1993

INDIANS OF SOUTH AMERICA
The Dominican school of Salamanca and the Spanish conquest of America: some bibliographical notes. O'Meara, Thomas Franklin. *Thomist* 56:555-582 O 1992

Los justos derechos de los pueblos indios. *Christus* 57:6 S 1992

Rigoberta Menchu: the voice of resistance [repr and tr fr Madres de la Plaza de Mayo]. *LADOC* 23:18-22 Mr-Ap 1993

South and Meso-American native spirituality: from the cult of the feathered serpent to the theology of liberation. New York: Crossroad, 1993. x, 563p ISBN 08-2451-224-3 LC 92-40180

INDIANS OF SOUTH AMERICA—MISSIONS
The ethics of conquest: the European background of Spain's mission in the New World. Olsen, Glenn Warren, 1938-. *Communio* 19:619-364 Wint 1992

INDIANS OF SOUTH AMERICA—RELIGION
Complexities of conversion: Latin American and European encounter—500 years. Kirk, Pamela. *Living Light* 29:22-34 Wint 1992

Warriors in Eden. Gagnon, Mariano, et al. New York: William Morrow and Company, 1993. 296p ISBN 0-688-11796-1

INTELLECT—RELIGIOUS ASPECTS
Mente y conducta: ensayos de psicologia cognitiva. Garcia-Albea, Jose E. Madrid: Trotta, 1993. x, 218p ISBN 84-87699-57-x

INTELLECTUAL LIFE
Collegium and the futures of Catholic higher education. Kelly, James R, 1937-. *America* 169:15-17 S 11 1993

INTELLECTUAL LIFE- LATVIA
John Paul II, Pope, (1993-09-09) Conscience [Orig in Latvian]. John Paul II, Pope, 1920- (Karol Wojtyla) (elected 1978). *OR(Eng)* 1307:11+ S 15 1993*

INTELLECTUALS
The decline from authority: Kierkegaard on intellectual sin. Aiken, David W. *IPQ* 33:21-35 Mr 1993

INTELLECTUALS, RUSSIA
And the demons entered into the swine: the Russian intelligentsia and post-Soviet religious thought. Emerson, Caryl. *CrossCurr* 43:184-202 Sum 1993

INTENSIVE CARE, NEONATAL *see* Neonatal Intensive Care

INTENTION
Malum Vitandum: the role of intentions in first-order morality. Sullivan, Thomas D, and Atkinson, Gary. *IJPS* 1:99-110 Mr 1993

Martha, Mary, and Jesus: weaving action and contemplation in daily life. Carter, Nancy Corson. Minnesota: The Order of St Benedict, 1992. x, 134p ISBN 0-8146-2119-8 LC 92-23586

Mercy: an insufficient motive for euthanasia. Tuohey, John F. *Health Prog* 74:51-53 O 1993

The Prolife Movement: dead or alive? Hanink, James G. *New Oxford Rev* 60:10-14+ My 1993

INTER-CHURCH COMMITTEE ON HUMAN RIGHTS
Colombia confronts the sword [photos]. Wirpsa, Leslie. *Nat Cath Rep* 29:8-9 Ap 9 1993

INTERCESSION *see* Prayer—Biblical Teaching

INTERCOMMUNION
Ein katholischer Vorschlag zur Eucharistiegemeinschaft. Neuner, Peter. *Stimm Zeit* 211:443-450 Jl 1993

The Lord's Supper: towards an ecumenical understanding of the Eucharist. Larere, Philippe. Collegeville: Liturgical, 1993. x, 94p ISBN 0-8146-2226-7 LC 98-010816

INTERCULTURAL EDUCATION
Multiculturalism is here: so enjoy it. Burke, John Francis. *Comm* 120:5-6 N 5 1993

INTERDENOMINATIONAL COOPERATION
Difficult days for Christian unity [editorial]. *Tablet* 247:63-64 Ja 16 1993

Parish diary: April. *Tablet* 247:509 Ap 24 1993

Quiet beginnings. *Tablet* 247:816 Je 26 1993

The state of the ecumenical movement. Rusch, William G. *Ecumen Trends* 22:3-6 Jl-Ag 1993

United at table. *Tablet* 247:104 Ja 23 1993

Whitby and Kleve [Graymoor Prize Winner]. Dove, Anthea. *Comm* 120:11-13 Ja 15 1993

INTERDISCIPLINARY STUDY
Art comes to life at St Ann School. Walthall, Barbara. *Momentum* 24:56-57 F-Mr 1993

An attack of scientism. Cornwell, John. *Tablet* 247:462-464 Ap 10-17 1993

Doin' dinosaurs: a schoolwide science project. Cazes, Jo. *Momentum* 24:20-21 S-O 1993

INTEREST AND USURY
Getting into credit together. Nolan, Margaret. *Priests & People* 7:178-180 My 1993

Rich man, poor man. Nicholl, Donald. *Tablet* 247:540-541 My 1 1993

Teach anew that interest is immoral. Carota, Estelle, and Carota, Mario. *Cath Work* 60:3 Ag 1993

Usury is a sin. *Cath Work* 60:8 Mr-Ap 1993

INTEREST AND USURY—RELIGIOUS ASPECTS
Does it matter what we do with our money? Ruston, Roger. *Priests & People* 7:171-177 My 1993

INTEREST RATES- IRELAND
The causes of Irish unemployment: trends and explanations. Browne, Frank, and McGettigan, Donal. *Studies* 82:35-52 Spr 1993

INTERNATIONAL CATHOLIC-JEWISH LIASON COMMITTEE MEETING (14TH: MAY 4-7, 1992: BALTIMORE, MARYLAND)
Baltimore and Eisenach [Graymoor Prize Winner]. Banki, Judith Hershcopf. *Comm* 120:11+ Ja 15 1993

INTERNATIONAL COMMISSION ON ENGLISH IN THE LITURGY
Another "objector". Mullen, Peter. *Register* 69:2 Ap 18 1993

Bishops speak in public session of sexual abuse. Reese, Thomas Joseph, 1945-. *America* 169:4-6 Jl 3-10 1993

The catechetical role of the liturgy and the quality of liturgical texts: the current ICEL translation. Leiva-Merikakis, Erasmo. *Communio* 20:63-83 Spr 1993

Deforming the liturgy. Tombes, Jonathan, and Tucker, Jeffrey. *Crisis* 10:20-24 N 1992

Dialogue [interview by C Allen]. Page, John. *Register* 69:1+ Je 11 1993

Dialogue [interview by P Mullen]. Stravinskas, Peter. *Register* 69:1+ Ja 24 1993

Ever old, yet ever new. Walter Scott. *Register* 69:5 F 7 1993

The good fight. Mullen, Peter. *Register* 69:3 Ap 11 1993

The introductory rites: a chance to refocus. Marchal, Michael. *Mod Lit* 20:18-19 My 1993

Lost in translation: ICEL and the Roman Canon. Pope, Charles E. *HPR* 93:65-73 Ag-S 1993

More trouble from ICEL [editorial]. Schuler, Richard Joseph, 1920-. *SacM* 120:5-6 Spr 1993

Preparing the people. Dodds, Bill. *OSV* 81:8 Mr 28 1993

Word wars. Mullen, Peter. *Register* 69:1+ Ap 25 1993

INTERNATIONAL CONFERENCE ON NUTRITION, ROME, 1992
John Paul II, Pope, (1992-12-05) basic right to nutrition. John Paul II, Pope, 1920- (Karol Wojtyla) (elected 1978). *TPS* 38:142-146 My-Je 1993*

INTERNATIONAL COUNCIL OF CHRISTIANS AND JEWS MEETING (JULY 12-16, 1992: EISENACH, GERMANY)
Baltimore and Eisenach [Graymoor Prize Winner]. Banki, Judith Hershcopf. *Comm* 120:11+ Ja 15 1993

INTERNATIONAL ECONOMIC RELATIONS
Doing social economics in a postmodern world. Brown, Doug. *RSocEcon* 50:383-403 Wint 1992

GATT: an ethical void. Egan, Eileen. *Cath Work* 60:1+ Je-Jl 1993

Poverty and development: economics and reality. Thanawala, Kishor. *RSocEcon* 50:258-268 Fall 1992

The relationship between evangelization and development. Lott, Anastasia. *AFER* 34:66-78 Ap 1992

Trade put first. Keegan, William. *Tablet* 247:913 Jl 17 1993

INTERNATIONAL EUCHARISTIC CONGRESS, 45TH, SEVILLE, 1993
John Paul II, Pope, (1993-06-13) International Eucharistic Congress [Orig in Spanish]. John Paul II, Pope, 1920- (Karol Wojtyla) (elected 1978). *OR(Eng)* 1296:6 Je 23 1993*

John Paul II, Pope, (1993-06-16) Visit to Spain. John Paul II, Pope, 1920- (Karol Wojtyla) (elected 1978). *OR(Eng)* 1295:1+ Je 16 1993*

John Paul II, Pope, (1993-06-23) Seville [Orig in Italian]. John Paul II, Pope, 1920- (Karol Wojtyla) (elected 1978). *OR(Eng)* 1297:11 Je 30 1993*

INTERNATIONAL JEWISH-CHRISTIAN DOCUMENTATION SERVICE (SIDIC)
Dialogue group given Sternberg Award for promoting Christian-Jewish relations. *OR(Eng)* 1292:2 My 26 1993

INTERNATIONAL LAW
Even warfare has its rules [editorial]. *Tablet* 247:1119 S 4 1993

A triumph for rights. Drinan, Robert Francis, 1920-. *Tablet* 247:870-871 Jl 3 1993

World Conference on Human Rights June 14-25, 1993. Drinan, Robert Francis, 1920-. *America* 168:15-16 Je 5-12 1993

INTERNATIONAL PLANNED PARENTHOOD FEDERATION
Beijing and PP affiliate colluding. Meehan, Bridget Mary. *Register* 69:1+ Mr 21 1993

IPPF links to eugenics uncovered. Meehan, Bridget Mary. *Register* 69:1 Mr 14 1993

INTERNATIONAL RELATIONS
Action for Bosnia [editorial]. Barnes, Michael R. *Month* 26:2-3 Ja 1993

Bosnian crisis brings "right and duty" to intervene. *Tablet* 247:54 Ja 9 1993

A challenge of peace: North-South dialogue. Weakland, Rembert G, Abp, 1927-. *Origins* 23:292-296 O 7 1993

Clinton on the world stage: some clues to his perspective. Hehir, J Bryan, 1940-. *Comm* 120:5-7 Ja 29 1993

Evolution, Omega and evil. Harris, Errol E, 1908-. *Teilhard Rev* 28:15-22 Spr 1993

Just war, pacifism and humanitarian intervention. Himes, Kenneth R. *America* 169:10-15+ Ag 14-21 1993

Lest we forget. Cviic, Christopher. *Tablet* 247:1092-1093 Ag 28 1993

Maastricht: dead or alive? Stourton, Edward. *Tablet* 247:936-937 Jl 24 1993

A necessary balance. Cahill, Kevin Michael, 1936-. *America* 169:6-10 Ag 28-S 4 1993

No right choice [editorial]. *Comm* 120:3-4 Mr 26 1993

"On the ground" in Sarajevo [interview by T H Stahel, 1938-]. McCarrick, Theodore Edgar, Abp, 1930-. *America* 168:3-5 F 27 1993

One cheer, or less, for Bosnian "Peace" plan [editorial]. *America* 168:3 Ja 30 1993

Pope sees duty to disarm aggressors. *Tablet* 247:115 Ja 23 1993

Ten years after: the bishops (again) on war and peace. Weigel, George. *Crisis* 11:36-41 Mr 1993

That old "ancient hatreds" rag [editorial]. *America* 168:3 Ap 24 1993

Too reasonable by half. McDonagh, Melanie. *Tablet* 247:774 Je 19 1993

The tragedy of Bosnia is not over [editorial]. *America* 169:3 Ag 14-21 1993

Trick or treaty: can nations learn to get along? Unsworth, Tim. *Salt* 13:14-17 F 1993

War games. *Month* 26:212-213 Je 1993

The West as a paper tiger [editorial]. *Tablet* 247:391 Mr 27 1993

INTERNATIONAL RELATIONS AND CHURCH
I rapporti Nord-Sud dopo i cambiamenti nell'est dell'europa. Salvini, Gianpaolo. *Civilta* 144:326-339 F 20 1993

INTERNATIONAL RELIEF
A necessary balance. Cahill, Kevin Michael, 1936-. *America* 169:6-10 Ag 28-S 4 1993

Rights and wrongs of intervention. O'Connell, Gerard. *Tablet* 246:1629 D 19-26 1992

Seeking justice for the poor. Schutt, Brian. *Momentum* 24:76-77 F-Mr 1993

INTERNATIONAL TEILHARD CONFERENCE (12TH:APRIL 24-26, 1992: LONDON, ENGLAND)
World without frontiers. Woodcock, Evelyn. *Teilhard Rev* 27:85-87 Wint 1992

INTERNATIONAL TRADE
NAFTA spawns a diverse union of critics. Zon, Calvin G. *Nat Cath Rep* 29:5 Ja 29 1993

INTERNATIONAL YOUTH FORUM
International Youth Forum's message to youth. *Origins* 23:181-182 Ag 26 1993

INTERNSHIP PROGRAMS
Misericordia Hospital. Hey, Michelle. *Health Prog* 74:66-67 1993

INTERPERSONAL CONFRONTATION
Retaining nurses through conflict resolution. Fowler, Aubrey R, Jr, et al. *Health Prog* 74:25-29 Je 1993

INTERPERSONAL RELATIONS
Accompagnement des familles et prévention des deuils pathologiques. Vanoverberghe, Arlette. *Supplement* 184:125-144 Mr-Ap 1993

Being used? By God? Hogan, William Francis, 1930-. *Emmanuel* 99:334-337 Jl-Ag 1993

Catechesis for conversion [excerpt fr the book]. O'Malley, William J, 1931-. *Living Light* 29:55-63 Wint 1992

Christ and the transformation of relationships. Bacik, James Joseph, 1936-. *Emmanuel* 99:318-321+ Jl-Ag 1993

Christian and eastern mysticism [fr *a new vision of reality: Western science, Eastern mysticism and Christian faith*]. Griffiths, Bede, 1906-. *Living Prayer* 26:3-8 My-Je 1993

Converting the liturgist. Wagner, Nick. *Mod Lit* 20:12-14 N 1993

Converting the parish staff. Pace, Charlotte. *Mod Lit* 20:6-9 Mr 1993

Cultivating healthy boundaries. St Romain, Philip. *Liguorian* 81:25-29 S 1993

Dancing in my chair. Lobdell, Maryann Artzer. *St Anth* 100:18-21 Ap 1993

Finding the religious dimension in family life. Ziegler, Elena. *Momentum* 24:78-79 F-Mr 1993

The first step for people in relationships with addicts. Hunter, Mic. Minneapolis: CompCare Publishers, 1989. x, 122p ISBN 0-89638-163-3 LC 89-15709

Forgiving an ex-spouse who walked out. Wangler, Joan Norman. *Liguorian* 81:49-51 O 1993

Getting a grip on stress and conflict. Kinast, Robert L. *Catechist* 27:27-29 S 1993

Getting it back together with God. Auer, Jim. *Liguorian* 81:40-45 Mr 1993

"Good riddance!" said grandma: love: the fruit of marriage, not the cause. Houghton, William. *Comm* 120:21-22 Je 18 1993

Hôpital et respect des personnes. Geets, Claude, et al, eds. *Supplement* 184:5-203 Mr-Ap 1993*

The home front. Finley, Mitchel B, and Finley, Kathy. *Living Prayer* 26:22-23 My-Je 1993

Mae: touched by sanctity's wing. Hicks, Thomas H. *America* 169:6-7 O 30 1993

Put intimacy back in your marriage. Bodmer, Judy. *St Anth* 100:22-26 S 1993

Saved by the Holy Ghost. Barnes, Trevor. *Tablet* 246:1603 D 19-26 1992

A survivor's tale. Toolan, David S. *Way Suppl* 77:55-65 Sum 1993

The three r's: relationships, risk and responsibility. Richardson, Carol. *SocJust* 84:55-57 Mr-Ap 1993

We are created to love. St Romain, Philip. *Liguorian* 81:54-59 Ja 1993

Will the real me please stand up? Maas, Robin. *Living Light* 29:37-44 Spr 1993

Women in the Church and in Latin American culture [tr and excerpts fr *Boletin CELAM*]. *Cath Int* 4:210-214 My 1993

INTERPERSONAL RELATIONS IN ADOLESCENCE
Youth gangs: a spreading problem. Martinet, Ken. *Momentum* 24:68-72 Ap-My 1993

INTERPRETATIONS *see* Hermeneutics

INTIMACY (PSYCHOLOGY)
Celibacy and intimacy. Kimmerling, Ben. *Way Suppl* 77:87-96 Sum 1993
Going all the way. Bartlett, Bob. *Momentum* 24:36-39 Ap-My 1993
Put intimacy back in your marriage. Bodmer, Judy. *St Anth* 100:22-26 S 1993

INTROVERSION
Celibacy in another tradition. Woodgate, Michael. *Way Suppl* 77:106-112 Sum 1993

INVESTMENTS—MORAL AND ETHICAL ASPECTS
When social responsibility pays. Torrens, Paul R. *America* 169:5 Jl 17-24 1993

IRAQ—POLITICS AND GOVERNMENT
Give Bill a break, and do something about Saddam, mother of all bullies. Farrell, Michael J. *Nat Cath Rep* 29:22 Jl 16 1993
Holy See agrees to intervene for Iraq at United Nations. *Tablet* 247:115 Ja 23 1993
Iraq and the United Nations [interview by T H Stahel, 1938-]. Ekéus, Rolf. *America* 169:4-5 Ag 14-21 1993
Promised "change" bombed by Clinton's Iraq attack. Scharper, Stephen B. *Nat Cath Rep* 29:22 Jl 16 1993
Religious leaders criticise strikes against Iraq. *Tablet* 247:119-120 Ja 23 1993

IRAQ—REMINISCENCES
"American-Salaam-Iraqi". Storey, Eileen. *Cath Work* 60:8 Ja-F 1993

IRAQ—SOCIAL CONDITIONS
Gratuitous suffering. Trotta, Carmen. *Cath Work* 60:8 Ja-F 1993

IRELAND—CHURCH HISTORY
Aubrey Gwynn—the scholar. Walsh, Katherine. *Studies* 81:385-392 Wint 1992

IRELAND—ECONOMIC CONDITIONS
Bishops back the enterprise culture. *Tablet* 246:1580-1581 D 12 1992
Job discrimination worked in N. Ireland. MacEoin, Gary. *Nat Cath Rep* 30:10-11 O 29 1993

IRELAND—ECONOMIC POLICY
Ideals without strategy—a response to Work is the key. Dorr, Donal, 1935-. *Furrow* 44:472-478 S 1993
Ireland's record—last in the class? Johns, Christopher. *Studies* 82:9-23 Spr 1993
A response to unemployment: ten propositions. Quigley, George. *Studies* 82:73-86 Spr 1993
Solutions and political implications. McAleese, Dermot. *Studies* 82:61-72 Spr 1993

IRELAND—EDUCATION
To quench the thirst for knowledge. Ciarrocchi, Maura. *OSV* 81:8 Mr 14 1993

IRELAND—FOREIGN OPINION
Irish attitudes towards USA foreign policy. Dempsey, G T. *Studies* 82:265-275 Aut 1993

IRELAND—FOREIGN RELATIONS
Diplomatic uses of a cup of tea [editorial]. *Tablet* 247:707 Je 5 1993

IRELAND—HISTORY
The canon of Irish cultural history: some questions concerning Roy Foster's Modern Ireland. Murphy, Brian P. *Studies* 82:171-184 Sum 1993

IRELAND—HISTORY—1800-1899
The "vagabond friar": Father Mathew's difficulties with the Irish bishops, 1840-1856. Quinn, John F. *CHist* 78:542-556 O 1992

IRELAND—POLITICS AND GOVERNMENT
Abortion and the law. Whyte, Gerry. *Doctr Life* 42:253-272 My-Je 1992
Bishops oppose repeal of ban on homosexuality. *Tablet* 247:829 Je 26 1993
Change in Ireland, maybe. McRedmond, Louis. *Tablet* 247:9+ Ja 23 1993
"I don't support the IRA, but" semantic and psychological ambivalence. Murphy, Séamus. *Studies* 82:276-286 Aut 1993
Reform of local government. O'Connor, Tom. *Studies* 82:323-332 Aut 1993
Stop the killing. McRedmond, Louis. *Tablet* 247:434 Ap 3 1993

IRELAND—RELIGION
Conscience as consciousness of the other [condensed fr *Memory and Redemption* Gill and Macmillan, 1993]. McCaughey, Terence P. *Doctr Life* 43:166-178 Mr 1993
Gospel values in Irish life today. O'Hanlon, Gerard F. *Doctr Life* 42:619-628 D 1992
Religion and culture in Irish society. Macken, John. *Studies* 82:123-130 Sum 1993
Values and attitudes in a changing Ireland. Finucane, Marian. *Doctr Life* 43:333-342 Jl-Ag 1993

IRELAND—SOCIAL CONDITIONS
An angry people. McRedmond, Louis. *Tablet* 247:327-329 Mr 13 1993
Faith and work. Kennedy, Finola. *Tablet* 247:330 Mr 13 1993

IRELAND—SOCIAL ECONOMIC CONDITIONS
Work is the key [excerpts fr a Pastoral Letter]. Daly, Cahal Brendan, Cardinal, 1917-, et al. *Cath Int* 4:182-189 Ap 1993

IRENAEUS, SAINT
Transmisión de la revelación: escritura, tradición, magisterio: (A la luz de la *Dei Verbum del Concilio Vaticano II*). Sánchez Mielgo, Gerardo. *Cien Tom* 119:251-289 My-Ag 1992

IRISH DRAMA
Living with Lughnasa. Friel, Judy. *Critic* 47:2-15 Sum 1993

IRISH LITERATURE
Living with Lughnasa. Friel, Judy. *Critic* 47:2-15 Sum 1993
The rejection of Yeats: the case of Clarke and O'Faolain. Harmon, Maurice. *Studies* 82:243-256 Aut 1993

IRISH LITERATURE—COMPARATIVE STUDIES
The rushing up of Synge's buried fire. Krause, David. *Studies* 82:298-310 Aut 1993

IRISH POETRY—COMPARATIVE STUDIES
Religious thmes in the work of Patrick Kavanagh: hints of a Celtic tradition. Agnew, Una. *Studies* 82:257-264 Aut 1993

IRVING, JOHN
Fondamentalismo e religione. Mertes, Klaus. *Civilta* 2:116-129 Ap 17 1993

ISABELLA I, LA CATOLICA, QUEEN OF SPAIN, 1451-1504
Isabella of Spain—beatification and 1992. Edwards, John. *SIDIC* 25 No 2:8-11 1992

ISLAM
Islam and the west: the making of an image. Daniel, Norman. Oxford: Oneworld, 1993. x, 467p ISBN 1-85168-043-8
A Muslim primer: beginner's guide to Islam. Zepp, Ira G, Jr. Westminster, Maryland: Wakefield Editions, 1992. x, 292p ISBN 0-87061-188-7 LC 91-73300
Peace and Islam [condensed fr *Islam and Christian Muslim Relations* Je, 1990]. Tröger, Karl-Wolfgang. *TheolDgst* 38:115-118 Sum 1991

ISLAM—DOCTRINES
On the synergism of gender and class exploitation: theory and practice under Islamic Rule. Parvin, Manoucher. *RSocEcon* 51:201-216 Sum 1993

ISLAM—ECONOMIC POLICY
On the synergism of gender and class exploitation: theory and practice under Islamic Rule. Parvin, Manoucher. *RSocEcon* 51:201-216 Sum 1993

ISLAM—RELATIONS—CHRISTIANITY *see* Christianity and Islam

ISLAM-EGYPT
Egypt's Muslim Brothers. Butt, Gerald. *Tablet* 246:1559-1560 D 12 1992
Note sull'Islamismo in Egitto. Martin, Maurice-Pierre. *Civilta* 3:373-381 S 4 1993

ISLAM-UNITED STATES
Islam. Mullen, Peter. *Register* 69:1+ My 23 1993

ISLAMIC LAW
Repression in the Sudan. Barbier, Hubert. *Cath Int* 4:234-236 My 1993

ISLAMIC LITERATURE
Der fremde Spiegel. Röhrig, Johannes. *Stimm Zeit* 211:10-20 Ja 1993

ISLAMIC SECTS
Muslim mystics. *Tablet* 247:206-207 F 13 1993

ISLAMIC THEOLOGY
An alternative to Islamism: the evolutionary thought of Mahmud Taha. Duran, Khalid. *CrossCurr* 42:453-467 Wint 1992-1993
Islamic attitudes to other religions. Watt, William Montgomery. *StudiaM* 42:245-255 1993
Islamic fundamentalism. Watt, William Montgomery. *StudiaM* 41:241-252 1992
Riflessioni sull'Islam oggi. Amoretti, Biancamaria Scarcia. *StudiaM* 41:253-267 1992

ISRAEL
"Holy war" and the "ban" in the Bible [condensed fr *Internationale katholische Zeitschrift: Communio* Mr 1989]. Lohfink, Norbert. *TheolDgst* 38:109-114 Sum 1991

ISRAEL—ANTIQUITIES
Find sheds light on David's rule. Pevtzow, Lisa. *Register* 69:1+ Ag 22 1993
Urbanization in ancient Israel. Frick, Frank S. *BibleT* 31:4-12 Ja 1993

ISRAEL—EDUCATION
Israeli government helps fund Christian schools. Pevtzow, Lisa. *Register* 69:1+ Jl 25 1993

ISRAEL—EMIGRATION AND IMMIGRATION
When is a Jew not a Jew? Montgomery, John Warwick, 1931-. *New Oxford Rev* 60:25-26 Je 1993

ISRAEL—FOREIGN RELATIONS
Bilateral talks to be productive [interview by L Pevtzow]. Jaeger, David. *Register* 69:1+ Ja 3 1993

ISRAEL—FOREIGN RELATIONS—PAPACY
Vatican-Israel diplomatic relations. Stransky, Thomas F. *America* 169:4-9 N 6 1993

ISRAEL—FOREIGN RELATIONS—VATICAN
Israel, Rome near accord. Pevtzow, Lisa. *Register* 69:1+ O 3 1993
Vatican slows talks with Israel. Pevtzow, Lisa. *Register* 69:1+ Mr 28 1993
Waiting for John Paul [Israel visit]. Pevtzow, Lisa. *Register* 69:2 F 14 1993

ISRAEL—HISTORY
The pre-deuteronomistic story of King Saul and its historical significance. Na'Aman, Nadav. *CBQ* 54:638-658 O 1992

ISRAEL—HISTORY—BIBLICAL TEACHING
Antico Testamento e culture coeve: dal rifiuto illusorio all'assimilazione vitale. Prato, Gian Luigi. *Gregorianum* 73 No 4:697-717 1992

ISRAEL—MILITARY POLICY
Christians in Jewish army on rise. Pevtzow, Lisa. *Register* 69:1+ Ag 8 1993

ISRAEL—POLITICS AND GOVERNMENT
After the handshake. Wigoder, Geoffrey Bernard, 1922-. *Tablet* 247:1220-1221 S 25 1993
Tabernacles of peace. Rogers, Terry. *Cath Work* 60:4 Je-Jl 1993

ISRAEL—RELIGION
Greek clergy, Arab laity in dispute. Pevtzow, Lisa. *Register* 69:1+ F 7 1993
In Israel, Christians "suspect". Pevtzow, Lisa. *Register* 69:1+ Ja 10 1993
Israel, fundies share an agenda. Pevtzow, Lisa. *Register* 69:1+ My 23 1993

ISRAEL- EMIGRATION AND IMMIGRATION
Israeli welcome cool to non-Jews. Pevtzow, Lisa. *Register* 69:1+ Mr 7 1993

ISRAELITES, ANCIENT
Aging according to wisdom literature. Bjornard, Reidar B. *BibleT* 30:330-334 N 1992
The rise and fall of the United States. Farrall, Harold J. New York: Vantage Press, 1992. x, 175p ISBN 0-533-10224-3 LC 92-93307

ITALIAN AMERICANS
The Catholic parish as a way-station of ethnicity and Americanization: Chicago's Germans and Italians, 1903-1939. Shawn, Stephen Joseph, 1944-. Brooklyn: Carlson Publishers, 1991. 206p ISBN 0-92601-9554 LC 91-26847

ITALIAN SOCIETY OF GYNECOLOGY AND OBSTETRICS—CONGRESSES
John Paul II, Pope, (1992-12-05) serve life at its birth. John Paul II, Pope, 1920- (Karol Wojtyla) (elected 1978). *TPS* 38:147-149 My-Je 1993*

ITALY—HISTORY
Un'epoca nuova nella storia del mondo e dell'Italia [editorial]. Salvini, Gianpaolo, ed. *Civilta* 3:3-14 Jl 3 1993

ITALY—HISTORY—1900
Nationalists and Catholics in Giolittian Italy: an uneasy collaboration. Cunsolo, Ronald S. *CHist* 79:22-53 Ja 1993

ITALY—POLITICS AND GOVERNMENT
All change in Italy. Willey, David. *Tablet* 247:808+ Je 26 1993
Blows fall on Catholic movement. *Tablet* 247:381 Mr 20 1993
Church and State, Italian-style. O'Grady, Desmond. *OSV* 81:21 Ap 25 1993
Un'epoca nuova nella storia del mondo e dell'Italia [editorial]. Salvini, Gianpaolo, ed. *Civilta* 3:3-14 Jl 3 1993
Finita la commedia: the fix is out. Wollemborg, Leo J. *Comm* 120:7-9 Je 18 1993
Italy at the cleaners. Willey, David. *Tablet* 247:360-361 Mr 20 1993
Italy will never be the same. Burke, Greg. *Register* 69:1+ My 9 1993
Italy's Andreotti, friend of the Church, may have Mafia link. Burke, Greg. *Register* 69:1+ Ap 18 1993
Key Italian voter bloc unraveling. Burke, Greg. *Register* 69:1+ Je 6 1993
Nationalists and Catholics in Giolittian Italy: an uneasy collaboration. Cunsolo, Ronald S. *CHist* 79:22-53 Ja 1993
A new kid on the block [Lega Nord]. Burke, Greg. *Register* 69:3 Jl 4 1993
Pope, talking pluralism, lights path to polls. Hebblethwaite, Peter, 1930-. *Nat Cath Rep* 29:12 Je 18 1993

ITALY—RELIGION
Nel paese del punto esclamativo: *sette, culti, pseudo-religioni o nuove religioni? Introvigne, Massimo. *StudiaM* 41:1-26 1992
Religion in the ratings. O'Grady, Desmond. *Tablet* 247:101 Ja 23 1993

ITALY—SOCIAL CONDITIONS
L'Italia in un difficile periodo di transizione. Salvini, Gianpaolo. *Civilta* 3:449-461 S 18 1993

ITALY—SOCIO-ECONOMIC CONDITIONS
A dark alliance of forces. Burke, Greg. *Register* 69:5 Ag 15 1993

ITINERANCY (CHURCH POLITY)
Appartenance à Église ou itinérance ecclésiale? Borras, Alphonse. *Lumen* 48:161-173 Je 1993

IVORY COAST—CHURCH HISTORY
Secretariat of State (1992-05-20) Conventio (Treaty of Agreement with Ivory Coast) [French]. *AAS* 84:840-844 S 8 1992*

J

JACOB
If God attacks, don't let him get away with it. Peatman, Bill. *Nat Cath Rep* 29:2 Mr 19 1993
Rachel's lament, Jacob's reply [editorial]. *America* 169:3 N 20 1993

JACOBS, HARRIET, 1813-1897
The representationj of religious experience in nineteenth-century American women's autobiography. Norman, Rose. *Listening* 28:128-140 Spr 1993

JAEGERSTAETTER, FRANZ, 1904-1943
He wouldn't fight for the Nazis. Copp, Jay. *CDgst* 57:136-140+ Ag 1993
A martyr's witness. *Tablet* 247:1009 Ag 7 1993
Worth pondering. O'Connell, Patrick. *Living Prayer* 26:11-12 S-O 1993

JALAL AL-DIN RUMI, MAULANA, 1207-1273
The Dominican and the dervish: a Christian-Muslim dialogue that might have been between Thomas Aquinas and Jalal ad-Din Rumi. Renard, John. *JEcumen Stds* 29:189-201 Spr 1992

JAMAICA—SOCIAL CONDITIONS
A papal visit, a troubled island. Landy, Thomas. *America* 169:6-8 Ag 14-21 1993

JAMES, HENRY, 1843-1916
Henry James's literary Catholicizing. Fussell, Edwin Sill, 1922-. *New Oxford Rev* 60:8-11 Ja-F 1993

JAMES, WILLIAM
Grace that amazes. Daley, Barbara Carter. *Spir Life* 39:11-21 Spr 1993

JANE DE CHANTAL, SAINT, 1572-1641
A developmental view of Salesian spirituality. Conn, Joann Wolski. *RRel* 52:56-68 Ja-F 1993

JAPAN—CHURCH HISTORY
Inculturation and adaptation in Japan before and after Vatican Council II. Takagi, Takako Frances. *CHist* 79:2467-267 Ap 1993

JAPAN—CONSTITUTION
To arm or not to arm: rethinking the constitution. Carraro, Robert J. *Comm* 120:5-6 F 26 1993

JAPAN—FOREIGN RELATIONS
To arm or not to arm: rethinking the constitution. Carraro, Robert J. *Comm* 120:5-6 F 26 1993

JAPAN—POLITICS AND GOVERNMENT
A Japanese rainbow. Rafferty, Kevin. *Tablet* 247:1032-1033 Ag 14 1993

JAPAN—RELIGION
Bishops caution on fashionable weddings. *Tablet* 247:55-56 Ja 9 1993
Japan's hidden Christians. Harrington, Ann M. Chicago: Loyola University Press, 1993. x, 110p ISBN 0-8294-0741-3
The universal attitude of Shinto as expressed in the Shinto sect Kurozumikyō. Stoesz, Willis. *JEcumen Stds* 29:215-229 Spr 1992

JAPANESE LITERATURE
Seeds in the heart: Japanese literature from earliest times to the late sixteenth century. Keene, Donald. New York: Henry Holt and Company, 1993. x, 1265p ISBN 0-8050-1999-5 LC 93-1082

JARAMILLO, JAIME
Hero of the sewers. Traylen, Maryanne. *Tablet* 247:1290 O 9 1993

JAVOUHEY, ANNE-MARIE, 1779-1851
Anne-Marie Javouhey. O'Connell-Cahill, Catherine. *Salt* 13:31 Je 1993

JEFFERSON, THOMAS, 1743-1826
A Jeffersonian Catholicism? McDonald, John S. *New Oxford Rev* 60:17-18 Ja-F 1993
Madison's dilemma, and ours. Goldwin, Robert Allen, 1922-. *Crisis* 10:25-31 N 1992
Why Crisis cannot address the crisis. Craycroft, Kenneth R, Jr. *Crisis* 11:17 Je 1993

JEPSEN, DEE
A Protestant celebrates Mary [interview by M Finley]. Jepsen, Dee. *OSV* 82:5 My 9 1993

JEREMIAS, JOACHIM
Las parábolas; de Jesús: su sentido y adecuada interpreción. Pérez-Cotapos, Eduardo L. *Teol Vida* 33 no 3-4:165-178 1992

JEROME, SAINT, 340?-420
Journeying with Jerome. Glavich, Kathleen. *ReligTJ* 27:52-53 S 1993
St. Jerome: doctor maximus. McSheffery, Daniel F. *HPR* 94:53-57 N 1993

JERUSALEM
The spiritual significance of Jerusalem. *Ecumen Trends* 22:14-15 S 1993
The stones will cry out. Roman, Mary. *Living Prayer* 26:29-31 Mr-Ap 1993

JERUSALEM—HISTORY
Isaiah and urban possibility. Brueggemann, Walter. Louisville: Westminster, 1993. x, 96p ISBN 0-664-25460-8

JERUSALEM—POLITICS AND GOVERNMENT
Palestine Christians vent steam. Pevtzow, Lisa. *Register* 69:1+ Jl 18 1993
Voices: Teddy Kolleck, Jerusalem's outspoken mayor [interview by L Pevtzow]. Kollack, Theodore, 1911-. *Register* 69:1+ Ag 1 1993

JERUSALEM—RELIGION
The always-new forms of suffering in the Holy Land. Sabbah, Michael. *Origins* 23:811 My 6 1993

JERUSALEM (LATIN PATRIARCHATE)
The always-new forms of suffering in the Holy Land. Sabbah, Michael. *Origins* 23:811 My 6 1993

JERUSALEM IN THE BIBLE
Jerusalem in the Bible. Bakke, Raymond. *BibleT* 31:13-16 Ja 1993
Une prière pour le renouveau de Jérusalem le Psaume 51. Vermeylen, Jacques R. *Eph Theol Lovan* 78:257-283 D 1992

JESUIT REFUGEE SERVICE (JRS)
Der Flüchtlingsdienst der Jesuiten. Raper, Mark. *Stimm Zeit* 211:45-52 Ja 1993

JESUITS
Aloysius. Stevens, Clifford, and McNichols, William Hart, eds. Huntington: Our Sunday Visitor, 1993. x, 160p ISBN 0-87973-528-7
Der Flüchtlingsdienst der Jesuiten. Raper, Mark. *Stimm Zeit* 211:45-52 Ja 1993
Gesuiti e Bielorussi: ai margini della civiltà o a una svolta culturale? Simon, Constantin. *Civilta* 2:548-562 Je 19 1993
How I pray now [a conversation with Thomas H. Stahel]. Whelan, Joseph P. *America* 169:17-20 N 20 1993
Jesuits under Kolvenbach face a changed world [por]. Corley, Felix. *OSV* 82:3 N 21 1993
John Paul II, Pope, (1991-04-22) Live your consecration in an exemplary and austere manner. John Paul II, Pope, 1920- (Karol Wojtyla) (elected 1978). *Con Life* 17 no 2:11-15 1992*
Keeping a tradtion evergreen. Donahue, John W, 1917-. *America* 168:4 My 29 1993
Le R P Jacques Coret (1631-1721) et la devotion á Saint Joseph à l'âge classique. Dehon, Gilbert. *MSR* 50:117-133 Ap-Je 1993
Religious life's spirit of solidarity. Gray, Howard. *Origins* 23:173-176 Ag 12 1993
Their eminences SJ. *Tablet* 247:716-717 Je 5 1993
La universidad Ignaciana hoy en America Latina. Mora Lomelí, Raúl H. *Christus* 57:43-51 S 1992

It is the best of times, to be a priest. Quinn, John Raphael, Abp, 1929-. *America* 169:16-17 S 18 1993

Jesus: nice ideal but get real!. Auer, Jim. *Liguorian* 81:26-31 Ap 1993

The market place. McNair, J Frank. *Living Prayer* 26:27-28 S-O 1993

Ministries and the servant community. Matovina, Timothy M. *Worship* 67:351- Jl 1993

Missio ad gentes. Hearne, Brian. *AFER* 35:2-12 F 1993

New models of mission. Hearne, Brian. *Furrow* 44:91-98 F 1993

On getting punched in the face. Webb-Mitchell, Brett. *New Oxford Rev* 60:18-20 Jl-Ag 1993

The sacramentality of the world. Martos, Joseph. *Emmanuel* 99:4-7+ Ja-F 1993

The Samaritan woman. Gossé, Joe. *Living Prayer* 26:31 My-Je 1993

The sign of the star; the sign of the cross. Wysocki, Paul. *Emmanuel* 99:51-52 Ja-F 1993

A tolerance for ambiguity. O'Malley, William J, 1931-. *America* 169:7-13 O 2 1993

The way of the Lord Jesus, volume two, living a Christian life. Grisez, Germain Gabriel, 1929-. Quincy, Illinois: Franciscan Press, 1993. x, 950p ISBN 0-8199-0961-0 LC 83-10508

When good things happen to "bad" people. Magesa, Laurenti. *AFER* 35:79-90 Ap 1993

JESUS CHRIST—FAMILY

Fix your gaze [pilgrim icon]. Hickey, Tim S. *Columbia* 73:16-18 Ag 1993

Le R P Jacques Coret (1631-1721) et la devotion á Saint Joseph à l'âge classique. Dehon, Gilbert. *MSR* 50:117-133 Ap-Je 1993

JESUS CHRIST—HINDU INTERPRETATION

Liberating the unlimited. Gajiwala, Kalpesh. *Month* 26:135-137 Ap 1993

JESUS CHRIST—HISTORICITY

L'Antigiudaismo nel vangelo di Matteo come problema storico e teologico: uno schizzo. Luz, Ulrich. *Gregorianum* 74 no 3:425-445 1993

The banality of unbelief [excerpt fr *Washington City paper*]. Allen, Charlotte. *Crisis* 11:30-35 Mr 1993

Can the Dead Sea Scrolls teach us about the living Jesus? Pazola, Ron. *USCath* 58:13-20 N 1993

Coping with hypotheses: a strategy in regard to the historical Jesus. Cahill, Michael. *Chicago Stud* 31:130-141 Ag 1992

Uma cristologia suspeita? Palacio, Carlos. *Perspectiva* 25:181-196 My-Ag 1993

Gesù nella storia: una vita che non si chiude con la morte [editorial]. Salvini, Gianpaolo, ed. *Civilta* 2:105-115 Ap 17 1993

Life-of-Jesus research and the eclipse of mythology. Evans, Craig A, 1952-. *TheolStds* 54:3-36 Mr 1993

O evangelho segundo Dona Lauricena. Mori, Geraldo Luis De. *Perspectiva* 25:197-227 My-Ag 1993

Parish councils: Jesus never sought consensus. Fischer, Mark F. *Tod Parish* 25:23-26 Mr 1993

Il valore storico dei vangeli [editorial]. *Civilta* 144:313-325 F 20 1993

JESUS CHRIST—HISTORY OF DOCTRINES

Image de Dieu, image de l'homme. Renwart, Léon. *NRT* 115:85-104 Ja-F 1993

Indirect methods in theology: Karl Rahner as an ad hoc apologist. Healy, Nicholas M. *Thomist* 56:613-633 O 1992

Jesus: der neue Mensch. Borg, Marcus J. Frieburg: Herder, 1993. x, 240p ISBN 3-451-23093-3

Meta-anthropology and Christology: on the philosophy of Hans Urs von Balthasar. Bieler, Martin. *Communio* 20:129-146 Spr 1993

Narrative christology in the apocalypse. Boring, M Eugene. *CBQ* 54:702-723 O 1992

JESUS CHRIST—HISTORY OF DOCTRINES—0030-600

Christology in dialogue. Berkey, Robert F, and Edwards, Sarah A, eds. Cleveland: The Pilgrim Press, 1993. 390p ISBN 0-8298-0956-2 LC 92-47004

The future of Christology: essays in honor of Leander E Keck. Malherbe, Abraham J, and Meeks, Wayne A, eds. Minneapolis: Fortress Press, 1993. x, 265p ISBN 0-80062-728-8 LC 92-40265

Re-membering Jesus: women, prophecy, and resistance in the memory of the early churches. D'Angelo, Mary Rose. *Horizons (CTS)* 19:199-218 Fall 1992

JESUS CHRIST—HISTORY OF DOCTRINES—1300-1400

Quaestiones concerning Christ from the first half of the thriteenth century. Principe, Walter H. *Med Stud* 54:1-48 1992

JESUS CHRIST—HISTORY OF DOCTRINES—1900-

Asian faces of Jesus. Sugirtharajah, R S, ed. Maryknoll: Orbis Books, 1993. x, 267p ISBN 0-88344-833-5 LC 93-536

Christology in dialogue. Berkey, Robert F, and Edwards, Sarah A, eds. Cleveland: The Pilgrim Press, 1993. 390p ISBN 0-8298-0956-2 LC 92-47004

Moltmann's post-modern messianic christology: a review discussion. Molnar, Paul D. *Thomist* 56:669-693 O 1992

The present state of Christology. O'Grady, John F. *Chicago Stud* 32:77-91 Ap 1993

JESUS CHRIST—HUMANITY

Did the word of God become a human person? Mertens, Herman-Emiel. *Louvain Stds* 18:175-180 Sum 1993

Good people get angry, too. Mallowe, Mike. *USCath* 58:14-21 My 1993

El método de Orígenes. Ossandón, Pedro, and Rodríguez, Pedro. *Teol Vida* 33 no 3-4:185-191 1992

Quieting the inner noises. Donahue, Lois M. *Liguorian* 81:66-67 Je 1993

To share in the priesthood of suffering: a biblical reflection on the death of Our Lord. Rosica, Thomas M. *Can Cath Rev* 11:14-16 Ap 1993

You had to be there. Costello, Andrew. *USCath* 58:38-40 Ap 1993

JESUS CHRIST—INCARNATION

The everlasting man. Chesterton, Gilbert Keith, 1874-1936. San Francisco: Ignatius Press, 1993. ISBN 0-89870-444-8

El hombre Jesús. Villegas, Beltrán M. *Teol Vida* 34 no 1-2:29-38 1993

A human Christ. Dugan, Irene. *Way Suppl* 76:61-71 Spr 1993

De Jesús a las antropologías. Meis, Anneliese W. *Teol Vida* 34 no 1-2:39-59 1993

The mystery of the incarnation. Schönborn, Christoph von, Bp. San Francisco: Ignatius Press, 1992. x, 67p ISBN 0-89870-393-x LC 92-73690

Roman Brandstaetter narratore delle profondità. Castelli, Ferdinando. *Civilta* 2:130-143 Ap 17 1993

JESUS CHRIST—INTELLECTUAL LIFE

The wisdom and wit of Rabbi Jesus. Phipps, William E. Louisville: Westminster, 1993. x, 272p ISBN 0-664-25232-x

JESUS CHRIST—INTERCESSION

"In the twilight of the twentieth century" on divine sendings. Maurer, Armand A, 1915-. *Can Cath Rev* 11:19-22 Jl-Ag 1993

JESUS CHRIST—ISLAMIC INTERPRETATIONS

The Incarnation: Muslim objections and the Christian response. Fastiggi, Robert L. *Thomist* 57:457-493 Jl 1993

JESUS CHRIST—JEWISH INTERPRETATIONS

A rabbi talks with Jesus: an intermillennial interfaith exchange. Neusner, Jacob. New York: Doubleday, 1993. x, 154p ISBN 0-385-42466-31 LC xs92-16395

JESUS CHRIST—KENOSIS

Soulscape of a journey to spiritual being. Howe, Jean Marie. *Word Sp* 15:1-11 1993

JESUS CHRIST—KINGDOM

Il regno millenario di Cristo e dei suoi (Apos 20, 1-10). Vanni, Ugo. *StudiaM* 42:67-95 1993

JESUS CHRIST—KNOWABLENESS

Simplicity in the midst of complexity: religious education in the twenty-first century. DeBoy, James J, Jr, 1942-. *ChrWorld* 236:227-232 S-O 1993

Why Catholics find it so hard to evangelize. Weinandy, Thomas. *New Cov* 23:18-19 O 1993

JESUS CHRIST—MESSIAHSHIP

Christian-Jewish dialogue. Rottenberg, Isaac C, 1925-. *JEcumen Stds* 29:87-95 Wint 1992

Jesus, Savior. Kilgallen, John J. *StudiaM* 42:41-65 1993

What should you teach? Treston, Kevin. *ReligTJ* 27:9-11 S 1993

JESUS CHRIST—MINISTRY

La asamblea y el documento. Trigo, Pedro. *Christus* 58:48-61 Mr-Ap 1993

Come down, Zacchaeus!. McTighe, John P. *Liguorian* 81:56-60 F 1993

Jesus the Galilean. Martin, George. *Liguorian* 81:60-61 Ag 1993

Jesus y la mentira. González Faus, José Ignacio. *Christus* 58:48-54 My 1993

Responding to His call. McKenna, Bill. *New Cov* 23:27 S 1993

JESUS CHRIST—MIRACLES

The blind beggar of Jericho [2 parts]. LaVerdiere, Eugene Armand, 1936-. *Emmanuel* 99:86-89+ Mr; 158-166 Ap 1993

The innkeeper's tale. Brown, George Mackayu, 1921-. *Tablet* 247:471-473 Ap 10-17 1993

Jesus and a paralytic: the lesson. Stravinskas, Peter. *Register* 69:1+ Mr 14 1993

Jesus feeds a hungry multitude and prefigures the life-giving Eucharist. Stravinskas, Peter. *Register* 69:1+ Mr 21 1993

John Paul II, Pope, (1992-04-29) Annointing of the Sick. John Paul II, Pope, 1920- (Karol Wojtyla) (elected 1978). *TPS* 37:364-367 N-D 1992*

Life-of-Jesus research and the eclipse of mythology. Evans, Craig A, 1952-. *TheolStds* 54:3-36 Mr 1993

Our Lord cures the blind man. Stravinskas, Peter. *Register* 69:1+ Mr 28 1993

Parables and miracles. Doohan, Leonard. *Mod Lit* 20:34-35 My 1993

Peter and the ghost. Walsh, John E. *HPR* 93:24-28 My 1993

Seeing and believing. Madden, Michael. *HPR* 93:48-53 F 1993

Sharing as sign of Eucharist. Schaller, Jeanne Lound. *Living Prayer* 26:19-20 S-O 1993

The wisdom and wit of Rabbi Jesus. Phipps, William E. Louisville: Westminster, 1993. x, 272p ISBN 0-664-25232-x

JESUS CHRIST—MYSTICAL BODY

Eucharist and christology revisited: the Body of Christ. Collins, Mary Smalara. *TheolDgest* 39:321-332 Wint 1992

"I am with you always". Jeray, Diane. *Liguorian* 81:13-15 Je 1993

John Paul II, Pope, (1993-07-11) Santo Stefano [orig Italian]. John Paul II, Pope, 1920- (Karol Wojtyla) (elected 1978). *OR(Eng)* 1300:3 Jl 21 1993*

JESUS CHRIST—MYSTICAL UNION

Humanity in God: on reading Karl Barth in relation to mystical theology. McIntosh, Mark A. *Heythrop* 34:22-40 Ja 1993

JESUS CHRIST—NAME

East and West as dimensions of the Church. Cosgrove, Francis. *Diakonia* 26 no 1:15-25 1993

First-name basis. Costello, Andrew. *USCath* 58:38-40 Je 1993

Jesus' entry into Jerusalem. LaVerdiere, Eugene Armand, 1936-. *Emmanuel* 99:270-276 Je 1993

Il problema di Gesù [editorial]. *Civilta* 144:105-115 Ja 16 1993

The sweetness of the Lord: Dulcis and Suavis. Scholl, Edith. *Cist Stud* 27 No 4:359-366 1992

This is the Lamb of God. Inman, Anne. *New Blckfrs* 74:191-197 Ap 1993

JESUS CHRIST—NATIVITY

Christmas literature from writers ancient and modern. Johnson, Pegram, III, and Troiano, Edna M. Louisville: Westminster, 1993. x, 352p ISBN 0-664-22030-4

Grace has appeared. Schall, James Vincent, 1928-. *Crisis* 10:44-45 D 1992

The historical event of Christ's birth. McBride, Alfred. *OSV* 82:9 My 30 1993

John Paul II, Pope, (1992-12-24) Light shines [orig Italian]. John Paul II, Pope, 1920- (Karol Wojtyla) (elected 1978). *OR(Eng)* 1272:5 Ja 6 1993*

John Paul II, Pope, (1992-12-25) Come to heal [orig italian]. John Paul II, Pope, 1920- (Karol Wojtyla) (elected 1978). *OR(Eng)* 1271:1 Ja 6 1993*

La Nativité et l'Épiphanie dans le dialogue unioniste du VIIe siècle. Halleux, André de. *Eph Theol Lovan* 78:5-37 Ap 1992

Starlight: beholding the Christmas miracle all year long. Shea, John B. New York: The Crossroad Publishing Company, 1992. x, 192p ISBN 0-8245-1206-5 LC 92-15952

Teaching the nativity. Rich, Vera. *Tablet* 247:27 Ja 2 1993

JESUS CHRIST—NATURES

All loves excelling. O'Collins, Gerald, 1931-. *Tablet* 246:1606 D 19-26 1992

"Bride" and "Mother" in the Super cantica of St Bernard: an ecclesiology for our time? Kereszty, Roch A, 1933-. *Communio* 20:415-436 Sum 1993

The cosmic Christ and world religions. Dhavamony, Mariasusai. *StudiaM* 42:179-225 1993

Gesù una personalità sorprendente [editorial]. Salvini, Gianpaolo, ed. *Civilta* 2:521-534 Je 19 1993

Moltmann's post-modern messianic christology: a review discussion. Molnar, Paul D. *Thomist* 56:669-693 O 1992

Who will they be saying that I am? Reiser, William, 1943-. *ChrWorld* 236: 217-222 S-O 1993

JESUS CHRIST—PARABLES

How storytelling heals. Baldwin, Robert F. *New Cov* 23:11-13 Ag 1993

J R R Tolkien and the art of the parable. Murray, Robert. *Month* 26:35-39 Ja 1993

Las parábolas; de Jesús: su sentido y adecuada interpreción. Pérez-Cotapos, Eduardo L. *Teol Vida* 33 no 3-4:165-178 1992

Parables and miracles. Doohan, Leonard. *Mod Lit* 20:34-35 My 1993

A peasant reading of the parable of the talents. Rohrbaugh, Richard L. *Bib Th Bul* 23:32-37 Spr 1993

Youth formation. Doyle, Katherine. *Mod Lit* 19:28 D 1992-Ja 1993

JESUS CHRIST—PASSION

As I see it—Holy Week meditations. Waldron, Thomas. *Furrow* 44:215-218 Ap 1993

The Good Fridays in every week. Power, Dermot. *Priests & People* 7:94-96 Mr 1993

Mark's tragic vision: Gethsemane. Ruprecht, Louis A, Jr. *Relig Lit* 24:1-25 Aut 1992

Mount Royal players: Montreal's living stations. Brown, John J. *Liguorian* 81:20-23 Ap 1993

La pasion de nuestro senor Jesucristo. Suarez, Federico. Madrid: Rialp, 1993. x, 311p ISBN 84-321-3001-x

Piety centered on Jesus' suffering and some eccentric Christian understandings of the mystery of Calvary. Sloyan, Gerard S. *Worship* 67:98-123 Mr 1993

Praying the passion: living the Gospel-scriptual reflections for adult believers. Cornwell, Malcolm. Collegeville:Liturgical, 1993. 76p ISBN 0-8146-2220-8 LC 92-40656

Preaching the passion with sensitivity to Judaism. Witherup, Ronald D. *Priest* 49:12-16 Ap 1993

Preparing for Easter [3 parts]. Rose, John. *Can Cath Rev* 11:36-37 F; 36-37 Mr; 37-38 Ap 1993

Why a redeemer? Why a cross? Billy, Dennis J. *Living Prayer* 26:8-13 Mr-Ap 1993

JESUS CHRIST—PERSON AND OFFICES

Asian faces of Jesus. Sugirtharajah, R S, ed. Maryknoll: Orbis Books, 1993. x, 267p ISBN 0-88344-833-5 LC 93-536

In the presence of the wise and gentile Christ. McNamara, James M. New York: Paulist Press, 1993. x. 156p ISBN 0-8091-3375-x LC 92-36141

Jesus and the Dead Sea Scrolls. Charlesworth, James H. New York: Doubleday, 1992. x, 370p ISBN 0-385-24863-6 LC 92-2617

The one mediator, the saints, and Mary. Anderson, H George, et al, eds. Minneapolis: Augsburg Fortress, 1992. x, 397p ISBN 0-8066-2579-1 LC 91-40822

Talking about Jesus today. Reiser, William, 1943-. New York: Paulist Press, 1993. x, 223p ISBN 0-8091-3358-x LC 92-33240

Word become flesh: dimensions of Christology. McDermott, Brian O. Minnesota: The Liturgical Press, 1993. x, 302p ISBN 0-8146-5015-5 LC 92-34915

JESUS CHRIST—PRAYERS

Jesus and the way of childhood. Tsuchida, Christina. *Living Prayer* 26:19-20 N-D 1993

With Christ in the school and ministry of praying. Fomum, Zacharias Tanee. New York: Vantage Press, 1992. x, 235p ISBN 0-533-09575-1 LC 91-90888

JESUS CHRIST—PRESENCE

The Easter presence. Doohan, Leonard. *Mod Lit* 20:36 Ap 1993

The experience of the divine. Del Colle, Ralph. *Chicago Stud* 31:290-300 N 1992

Jesus the Galilean. Martin, George. *Liguorian* 81:60-61 Ag 1993

Thus shall you prayer. Donze, Mary Terese, 1911-. *Living Prayer* 26:15-16 My-Je 1993

JESUS CHRIST—PRIESTHOOD

Il celibato di Gesù e la verginità di Maria. Marzotto, Damiano, Msgr. *Seminarium* 33:32-47 Ja-Mr 1993

Der Zölibat: Formkraft priesterlicher existenz und priesterlichen dienstes. Scheffczyk, Leo, Msgr. *Seminarium* 33:48-59 Ja-Mr 1993

JESUS CHRIST—RELATION TO JUDAISM

Time travel to ancient Judea. Malina, Bruce J, 1933-. Louisville: Westminster, 1993. x, 208p ISBN 0-664-25457-8

JESUS CHRIST—RELATION TO OLD TESTAMENT

La pasion de nuestro senor Jesucristo. Suarez, Federico. Madrid: Rialp, 1993. x, 311p ISBN 84-321-3001-x

JESUS CHRIST—RELATIONS WITH CONTEMPORARIES

At Jacob's well. Randazzo, Anthony J. *Mod Lit* 20:17 Mr 1993

In the presence of the wise and gentile Christ. McNamara, James M. New York: Paulist Press, 1993. x. 156p ISBN 0-8091-3375-x LC 92-36141

JESUS CHRIST—RESURRECTION

Christ and the transformation of relationships. Bacik, James Joseph, 1936-. *Emmanuel* 99:318-321+ Jl-Ag 1993

Commitment: reflections on women at a tomb. Smith, Patricia. *Sisters* 65: 132-136 Mr 1993

Discouraged? Here's what the Gospel says about it. Anderson, Paul. *New Cov* 23:16-18 Ag 1993

Exploring the resurrection of Jesus. Perry, John Michael. Kansas City: Sheed & Ward, 1993. x, 145p ISBN 1-55612-670-0 LC 93-29160

Forever faithful: the unfolding of God's promise to readers. Reiser, William, 1943-. Collegeville:Liturgical, 1993. 98p ISBN 0-8146-5849-0 LC 93-15191

From Good Friday to Easter: a call for metanoia. Collins, Raymond F. *Emmanuel* 98:125-129 My 1992

Good News and old nonsense. O'Collins, Gerald, 1931-. *Tablet* 247:469 Ap 10-17 1993

He is risen!. Kreeft, Peter John, 1937-. *Register* 69:1+ Ap 11 1993

The Lord is risen! [editorial]. *America* 168:3 Ap 10 1993

Memento viva!. Dubruiel, Michael. *New Cov* 23:14-15 Ag 1993

The new best-sellers: resurrection skeptics [interview by Desmond O'Grady]. O'Collins, Gerald, 1931-. *OSV* 81:5 Ap 11 1993

Of heartwounds and hope. Kokolus, Cait. *Living Prayer* 26:13-16 S-O 1993

Preparing for Easter [3 parts]. Rose, John. *Can Cath Rev* 11:36-37 F; 36-37 Mr; 37-38 Ap 1993

Reading the Easter gospels. Swain, Lionel. Collegeville, Minnesota: The Liturgical Press, 1993. 131p ISBN 0-81465-699-4 LC 92-40432

The Resurrection, the Church and the Bible. Moore, John C, 1933-. *America* 168:14 Ap 10 1993

Risen indeed: a Christian philosophy of resurrection. Davis, Stephen T. Grand Rapids: Eerdmans, 1993. 232p ISBN 0-8028-0126-9

Studying the scriptures. *Liturgy* 10:79-90 Sum 1992

Thoughts from death and life. Gallagher, Vera, 1917-. *RRel* 52:238-240 Mr-Ap 1993

Witnesses. Martin, George. *New Cov* 22:34 F 1993

JESUS CHRIST—ROYAL OFFICE

The Easter presence. Doohan, Leonard. *Mod Lit* 20:36 Ap 1993

The right and the left. Ryan, Patrick J. *America* 169:23 N 13 1993

JESUS CHRIST—SECOND ADVENT

The dream of the seventh-day ark for sores and burns, for soul and body. Smith, Joyce L. New York: Vantage Press, 1993. 97p ISBN 0-533-09090-3

The return of Christ and the general judgment [repr and tr fr *La Civiltà* O 17 1992]. *HPR* 93:24-32 Je 1993

The second coming of Jesus: meditation and commentary on the Book of Revelation. McBride, Alfred. Huntington: Our Sunday Visitor, 1993. 180p ISBN 0-87973-526-0 LC 92-61979

Second coming. Doyle, Joan. *Sisters* 65:126-127 Mr 1993

Vigliare Nell'Attesa Della Venuta Del Signore (editorial). *Civilta* 143:437-449 D 5 1992

JESUS CHRIST—SELF-UNDERSTANDING

Did Jesus know he was God? DeCelles, Charles. *Priest* 49:33-38 Ap 1993

"Did Jesus know he was God?" revisited. Zimmerman, Anthony. *Priest* 49: 11-14 S 1993

JESUS CHRIST—SIGNIFICANCE

The Christ of faith. Garvey, John, 1944-. *Comm* 120:7-8 Ja 29 1993

JESUS CHRIST—TEACHINGS

Freedom: the teachings of Jesus. Pierce, Ted M. New York: Vantage Press, 1992. x, 225p ISBN 0-533-10182-4 LC 91-91544

"I have come to bring division". Schall, James Vincent, 1928-. *OR(Eng)* 1301:8-10 Jl 28 1993

The importance of forgiveness. Pilarczyk, Daniel Edward, Abp, 1934-. *OSV* 82:5 Jl 4 1993

Inner peace—a presence. Hogan, William Francis, 1930-. *Emmanuel* 99:232-235 My 1993

L'insegnamento di gesù [editorial]. Salvini, Gianpaolo, ed. *Civilta* 3:105-115 Jl 17 1993

Medjugorje day by day: a daily meditation book based on the messages of Our Lady of Medjugorje. Beyer, Richard J. Indiana: Ave Maria Press, 1993. [265] leaves ISBN 0-87793-494-0 LC 92-74779

The Pope came to Denver, preaching life against death. Scott, David. *OSV* 82:17 S 5 1993

Praying with the beatitudes. Buono, Anthony M. *Emmanuel* 99:466-470 O 1993

Qoheleth and Jesus. Malchow, Bruce V. *BibleT* 31:110-115 Mr 1993

Revealing happiness. Hanlon, Kevin. *Month* 26:165-167 Ap 1993

Sexuality, family, and the life of discipleship: some early Christian perspectives. Hennessey, Lawrence R. *Chicago Stud* 32:19-31 Ap 1993

The three r's: relationships, risk and responsibility. Richardson, Carol. *SocJust* 84:55-57 Mr-Ap 1993

The wisdom and wit of Rabbi Jesus. Phipps, William E. Louisville: Westminster, 1993. x, 272p ISBN 0-664-25232-x

Within the outlines of some ancient model. Roth, Wolfgang. *BibleT* 31:103-109 Mr 1993

JESUS CHRIST—TRANSFIGURATION

Rosary to the rescue. Gledhill, Ruth. *Tablet* 247:1037 Ag 14 1993

Seeking transfiguration amid disfiguration. Zimmerman, Paulette. *Nat Cath Rep* 29:2 F 26 1993

Transfiguration and pain in ordinary life. Power, Dermot. *Way* 33:12-18 Ja 1993

JESUS CHRIST—WORDS

Morals and the meaning of Jesus: reflections on the hard sayings. Harvey, Nicholas Peter. Cleveland: The Pilgrim Press, 1993. x, 112p ISBN 0-8298-0947-3 LC 94-41216

Le Parole Eucaristiche di Gesù. Galot, Jean. *Civilta* 2:16-18 Ap 3 1993

JESUS CHRIST IN LITERATURE

Jesus im modernen Roman. Langenhorst, Georg. *Stimm Zeit* 210:819-830 D 1992

JESUS CHRIST THE KING, FEAST OF

Who says Christ is King? Jorgensen, Susan S. *Mod Lit* 20:15 N 1993

JESUS PRAYER

The Name of God in Byzantine tradition: from hesychasm to imyaslavie. Slesinski, Robert, 1950-. *Communio* 20:49-62 Spr 1993

Probing Russian Orthodox spirituality. Vinh, Alphonse. *New Oxford Rev* 60: 17-20 My 1993

JEWISH-ARAB RELATIONS

After the handshake. Wigoder, Geoffrey Bernard, 1922-. *Tablet* 247:1220-1221 S 25 1993

Can there be peace in Israel? Wigoder, Geoffrey Bernard, 1922-. *Tablet* 247: 840-841 Jl 3 1993

Hope, at last, in the Middle East [editorial]. *Nat Cath Rep* 29:24 S 10 1993

Israel/P L O: a clock, not a bomb, is now ticking [editorial]. *America* 169:3 O 2 1993

Jewel without a crown. Glass, Charles. *Tablet* 247:1188 S 18 1993

Local Xian anger high for Israel. Pevtzow, Lisa. *Register* 69:1+ Je 6 1993

Not yet the promised land, but closer to peace. *OSV* 82:3 S 19 1993

On the road [editorial]. *Comm* 120:3-4 S 24 1993

The poet as diplomat: optimism isn't enough [interview by M.P. Kelly]. Mikhail-Ashrawi, Hanan. *Comm* 120:4-6 O 8 1993

Pope gives thanks for peace accord, but foresees hard road. O'Connell, Gerard. *Tablet* 247:1203 S 18 1993

JOHN PAUL II, POPE, 1920- (KAROL WOJTYLA) (ELECTED 1978)—HOMILIES

JOHN PAUL II, POPE, 1920- (KAROL WOJTYLA) (ELECTED 1978)—LETTERS

Subject Index 107 John Paul II, Pope, 1920- (Karol

John Paul II, Pope, (1983-01-25) Litterae Apostolicae (Apostolic Letters) [Latin]. John Paul II, Pope, 1920- (Karol Wojtyla) (elected 1978). *AAS* 84: 828-830 S 8 1992*
John Paul II, Pope, (1984-04-14) Litterae Apostolicae (Apostolic Letters) [Latin]. John Paul II, Pope, 1920- (Karol Wojtyla) (elected 1978). *AAS* 84: 830-832 S 8 1992*
John Paul II, Pope, (1985-08-15) Litterae Apostolicae (Apostolic Letters) [Latin]. John Paul II, Pope, 1920- (Karol Wojtyla) (elected 1978). *AAS* 84: 1112-1115 D 5 1992*
John Paul II, Pope, (1985-11-17) Litterae Apostolicae (Apostolic Letters) [Latin]. John Paul II, Pope, 1920- (Karol Wojtyla) (elected 1978). *AAS* 84: 942-945 O 3 1992*
John Paul II, Pope, (1987-05-10) Litterae Apostolicae (Apostolic Letters) [Latin]. John Paul II, Pope, 1920- (Karol Wojtyla) (elected 1978). *AAS* 84: 832-835 S 8 1992*
John Paul II, Pope, (1988-09-03). John Paul II, Pope, 1920- (Karol Wojtyla) (elected 1978). *AAS* 84:1115-1117 D 5 1992*
John Paul II, Pope, (1990-05-06) Litterae Apostolicae (Apostolic Letter for Beatification process) [Latin]. John Paul II, Pope, 1920- (Karol Wojtyla) (elected 1978). *AAS* 85:9-12 Ja 7 1993*
John Paul II, Pope, (1990-06-18) Litterae Apostolicae (Apostolic Letters) [Latin]. John Paul II, Pope, 1920- (Karol Wojtyla) (elected 1978). *AAS* 84: 835-838 S 8 1992*
John Paul II, Pope, (1991-03-30) Constitutio Apostolica (Apostolic Constitution) [Latin]. John Paul II, Pope, 1920- (Karol Wojtyla) (elected 1978). *AAS* 84:937-938 O 3 1992*
John Paul II, Pope, (1991-04-29) Constitutiones Apostolicae (Apostolic Constitution) [Latin]. John Paul II, Pope, 1920- (Karol Wojtyla) (elected 1978). *AAS* 85:5-6 Ja 7 1993*
John Paul II, Pope, (1991-06-05) Litterae Apostolicae (Apostolic Letters) [Latin]. John Paul II, Pope, 1920- (Karol Wojtyla) (elected 1978). *AAS* 84: 945-946 O 3 1992*
John Paul II, Pope, (1991-07-03) St Louise, an example to follow and to propose. John Paul II, Pope, 1920- (Karol Wojtyla) (elected 1978). *Con Life* 17 no 2:47-50 1992*
John Paul II, Pope, (1991-07-06) Constitutiones Apostolicae (Apostolic Constitution on Ecclesiastical Territory) [Latin]. John Paul II, Pope, 1920- (Karol Wojtyla) (elected 1978). *AAS* 85:8-9 Ja 7 1993*
John Paul II, Pope, (1991-07-06) Constitutiones Apostolicae (Apostolic Constitution) [Latin]. John Paul II, Pope, 1920- (Karol Wojtyla) (elected 1978). *AAS* 84:1055-1056 N 3 1992*
John Paul II, Pope, (1991-07-14) Litterae Apostolicae (Apostolic Letter) [Latin]. John Paul II, Pope, 1920- (Karol Wojtyla) (elected 1978). *AAS* 84: 947-949 O 3 1992*
John Paul II, Pope, (1991-07-14) Litterae Apostolicae (Apostolic Letters) [Latin]. John Paul II, Pope, 1920- (Karol Wojtyla) (elected 1978). *AAS* 84: 949-951 O 3 1992*
John Paul II, Pope, (1991-09-08) St Bridget of Sweden: a Saint of Europe. John Paul II, Pope, 1920- (Karol Wojtyla) (elected 1978). *Con Life* 17 no 2:60-63 1992*
John Paul II, Pope, (1991-10-27) Nuntius Telegraphicus (Telegram) [French]. John Paul II, Pope, 1920- (Karol Wojtyla) (elected 1978). *AAS* 84:871 S 8 1992*
John Paul II, Pope, (1991-10-29) Nuntii Scripto (Written Messages) [English]. John Paul II, Pope, 1920- (Karol Wojtyla) (elected 1978). *AAS* 84:871-872 S 8 1992*
John Paul II, Pope, (1991-10-29) Nuntii Scripto (Written Messages) [French]. John Paul II, Pope, 1920- (Karol Wojtyla) (elected 1978). *AAS* 84:872-873 S 8 1992*
John Paul II, Pope, (1992-01-24) Nuntii Scripto Dati (Papal message for World Day of Social Communication) [English]. John Paul II, Pope, 1920- (Karol Wojtyla) (elected 1978). *AAS* 84:990-993 O 3 1992*
John Paul II, Pope, (1992-02-11) Nuntii Scripto Dati (Written Papal Message) [French]. John Paul II, Pope, 1920- (Karol Wojtyla) (elected 1978). *AAS* 84:994-996 O 3 1992*
John Paul II, Pope, (1992-03-06) Constitutio Apostolica (Apostolic Constitution) [Latin]. John Paul II, Pope, 1920- (Karol Wojtyla) (elected 1978). *AAS* 84:825-826 S 8 1992*
John Paul II, Pope, (1992-03-12) Nuntius Gratulatorius (Congratulatory Message) [Latin]. John Paul II, Pope, 1920- (Karol Wojtyla) (elected 1978). *AAS* 84:911-912 S 8 1992*
John Paul II, Pope, (1992-03-25) Pastores Daba Vobis Aspetti Psicologici Nella Formazione al celibato Sacerdotale. John Paul II, Pope, 1920- (Karol Wojtyla) (elected 1978). *Civilta* 3:359-379 S 4 1993*
John Paul II, Pope, (1992-03-25) Pastores Dabo Vobis (Part II). John Paul II, Pope, 1920- (Karol Wojtyla) (elected 1978). *TPS* 37:329-363 N-D 1992*
John Paul II, Pope, (1992-03-25) Pastores Dabo Vobis. John Paul II, Pope, 1920- (Karol Wojtyla) (elected 1978). *AAS* 84:657-804 Ag 3 1992*
John Paul II, Pope, (1992-03-30) Constitutio Apostolica (Apostolic Constitution) [Latin]. John Paul II, Pope, 1920- (Karol Wojtyla) (elected 1978). *AAS* 84:826-827 S 8 1992*
John Paul II, Pope, (1992-03-30) Litterae Apostolicae (Apostolic Letters) [Latin]. John Paul II, Pope, 1920- (Karol Wojtyla) (elected 1978). *AAS* 84: 1056-1057 N 3 1992*
John Paul II, Pope, (1992-03-30) Litterae Apostolicae (Apostolic Letters) [Latin]. John Paul II, Pope, 1920- (Karol Wojtyla) (elected 1978). *AAS* 84: 838-839 S 8 1992*
John Paul II, Pope, (1992-04-14) Litterae apostolicae (Apostolic Letters) [Latin]. John Paul II, Pope, 1920- (Karol Wojtyla) (elected 1978). *AAS* 84: 1117-1118 D 5 1992*
John Paul II, Pope, (1992-04-25) Litterae Apostolicae (Apostolic Letter to create Minor Basilica in Raalte) [Latin]. John Paul II, Pope, 1920- (Karol Wojtyla) (elected 1978). *AAS* 85:125 F 3 1993*
John Paul II, Pope, (1992-04-25) Litterae Apostolicae (Apostolic Letters) [Latin]. John Paul II, Pope, 1920- (Karol Wojtyla) (elected 1978). *AAS* 84: 1057-1058 N 3 1992*
John Paul II, Pope, (1992-05-11) Constitutiones Apostolicae (Apostolic Constitution for Ecclesiastical Territory) [Latin]. John Paul II, Pope, 1920- (Karol Wojtyla) (elected 1978). *AAS* 85:6-8 Ja 7 1993*
John Paul II, Pope, (1992-05-12) Litterae Apostolicae (Apostolic Letter creating Minor Basilica of Church of Nowy Sacz) [Latin]. John Paul II, Pope, 1920- (Karol Wojtyla) (elected 1978). *AAS* 85:126 F 3 1993*
John Paul II, Pope, (1992-05-16) Constitutio Apostolica (Apostolic Constitution) [Latin]. John Paul II, Pope, 1920- (Karol Wojtyla) (elected 1978). *AAS* 84:938-939 O 3 1992*
John Paul II, Pope, (1992-05-17) Litterae Apostolicae (Apostolic Letters) [Latin]. John Paul II, Pope, 1920- (Karol Wojtyla) (elected 1978). *AAS* 84: 1058-1060 N 3 1992*
John Paul II, Pope, (1992-05-19) Litterae Apostolicae (Apostolic Letter establishing a Minor Basilica) [Latin]. John Paul II, Pope, 1920- (Karol Wojtyla) (elected 1978). *AAS* 85:13-14 Ja 7 1993*
John Paul II, Pope, (1992-05-29) Litterae Apostolicae (Apostolic Letter) [Latin]. John Paul II, Pope, 1920- (Karol Wojtyla) (elected 1978). *AAS* 85: 14-15 Ja 7 1993*
John Paul II, Pope, (1992-06-01) Litterae Apostolicae (Apostolic Letters) [Latin]. John Paul II, Pope, 1920- (Karol Wojtyla) (elected 1978). *AAS* 84: 1060-1061 N 3 1992*
John Paul II, Pope, (1992-07-03) Litterae Apostolicae (Apostolic Letter) [Latin]. John Paul II, Pope, 1920- (Karol Wojtyla) (elected 1978). *AAS* 85: 15-16 Ja 7 1993*
John Paul II, Pope, (1992-07-06) Constitutiones Apostolicae (Apostolic Constitution to erect Diocese of Accra) [Latin]. John Paul II, Pope, 1920- (Karol Wojtyla) (elected 1978). *AAS* 85:119-120 F 3 1993*
John Paul II, Pope, (1992-07-06) Constitutiones Apostolicae (Apostolic Constitution to erect Vicariate Apostolic in Philippines) [Latin]. John Paul II, Pope, 1920- (Karol Wojtyla) (elected 1978). *AAS* 85:124 F 3 1993*
John Paul II, Pope, (1992-07-06) Constitutiones Apsotolicae (Apostolic Constitution to erect Diocese of Koforidua) [Latin]. John Paul II, Pope, 1920- (Karol Wojtyla) (elected 1978). *AAS* 85:120-121 F 3 1993*
John Paul II, Pope, (1992-07-06) Litterae Apostolicae (Apostolic Letter) [Latin]. John Paul II, Pope, 1920- (Karol Wojtyla) (elected 1978). *AAS* 85: 16-17 Ja 7 1993*
John Paul II, Pope, (1992-07-08) Litterae Apostolicae (Apostolic Letter) [Latin]. John Paul II, Pope, 1920- (Karol Wojtyla) (elected 1978). *AAS* 85: 17-18 Ja 7 1993*
John Paul II, Pope, (1992-07-23) Litterae Apostolicae (Apostolic Letter) [Latin]. John Paul II, Pope, 1920- (Karol Wojtyla) (elected 1978). *AAS* 85: 18-19 Ja 7 1993*
John Paul II, Pope, (1992-07-23) Litterae Apostolicae (Apostolic Letter) [Latin]. John Paul II, Pope, 1920- (Karol Wojtyla) (elected 1978). *AAS* 85: 19-20 Ja 7 1993*
John Paul II, Pope, (1992-07-25) Constitutiones Apostolicae (Apostolic Constitution to erect Diocese of Carora) [Latin]. John Paul II, Pope, 1920- (Karol Wojtyla) (elected 1978). *AAS* 85:122-123 F 3 1993*
John Paul II, Pope, (1992-07-25) Constitutiones Apostolicae (Apostolic Constitution) [Latin]. John Paul II, Pope, 1920- (Karol Wojtyla) (elected 1978). *AAS* 84:1053-1055 N 3 1992*
John Paul II, Pope, (1992-08-04) Litterae Apostolicae (Apostolic Letter) [Latin]. John Paul II, Pope, 1920- (Karol Wojtyla) (elected 1978). *AAS* 85: 20-21 Ja 7 1993*
John Paul II, Pope, (1992-08-28) Litterae Apostolicae (Apostolic Letter) [Latin]. John Paul II, Pope, 1920- (Karol Wojtyla) (elected 1978). *AAS* 85: 21-22 Ja 7 1993*
John Paul II, Pope, (1992-09-08) Litterae Apostolicae (Apostolic Letter) [Italian]. John Paul II, Pope, 1920- (Karol Wojtyla) (elected 1978). *AAS* 84:1033-1053 N 3 1992*
John Paul II, Pope, (1992-09-21) Litterae Apostolicae (Apostolic Letter to create Apostolic Nuntiature in Mexico) [Latin]. John Paul II, Pope, 1920- (Karol Wojtyla) (elected 1978). *AAS* 85:127 F 3 1993*
John Paul II, Pope, (1992-10-08) Litterae Apostolicae (Apostolic Letter) [Latin]. John Paul II, Pope, 1920- (Karol Wojtyla) (elected 1978). *AAS* 85: 22-23 Ja 7 1993*
John Paul II, Pope, (1992-10-15) Litterae Apostolica (Apostolic Letter to create a Minor Basilica of Our Lady in Chile) [Latin]. John Paul II, Pope, 1920- (Karol Wojtyla) (elected 1978). *AAS* 85:127-128 F 3 1993*
John Paul II, Pope, (1992-10-22) Litterae Apostolicae (Apostolic Letter in which cathedral of Kabgayi is made a Minor Basilica) [Latin]. John Paul II, Pope, 1920- (Karol Wojtyla) (elected 1978). *AAS* 85:128-129 F 3 1993*
John Paul II, Pope, (1992-11-17) Statue of the Litterae Apostolicae (Apostolic Letter for coronation of the Virgin Mary in Halcnow) [Latin]. John Paul II, Pope, 1920- (Karol Wojtyla) (elected 1978). *AAS* 85:129-130 F 3 1993*
John Paul II, Pope, (1993 08-03) God [Orig in English]. John Paul II, Pope, 1920- (Karol Wojtyla) (elected 1978). *OR(Eng)* 1303:14 Ag 18 1993*
John Paul II, Pope, (1993-01-20) Telegram to President Clinton. John Paul II, Pope, 1920- (Karol Wojtyla) (elected 1978). *TPS* 38:201 Jl-Ag 1993*
John Paul II, Pope, (1993-01-24) message for 27th World Communications Day. John Paul II, Pope, 1920- (Karol Wojtyla) (elected 1978). *AFER* 35: 66-68 Ap 1993*
John Paul II, Pope, (1993-02-02) Change violence into acceptance. John Paul II, Pope, 1920- (Karol Wojtyla) (elected 1978). *TPS* 38:219-220 Jl-Ag 1993*
John Paul II, Pope, (1993-03-10) Letter to UN on refugees. John Paul II, Pope, 1920- (Karol Wojtyla) (elected 1978). *TPS* 38:240-242 Jl-Ag 1993*
John Paul II, Pope, (1993-03-11) Letter to UN Secretary General. John Paul II, Pope, 1920- (Karol Wojtyla) (elected 1978). *TPS* 38:243-244 Jl-Ag 1993*
John Paul II, Pope, (1993-04-07) Gypsies at Auschwitz. John Paul II, Pope, 1920- (Karol Wojtyla) (elected 1978). *TPS* 38:266-267 S-O 1993*
John Paul II, Pope, (1993-04-09) Letter to Auschwitz nuns. John Paul II, Pope, 1920- (Karol Wojtyla) (elected 1978). *TPS* 38:268-269 S-O 1993*
John Paul II, Pope, (1993-04-09) Letter to the nuns. John Paul II, Pope, 1920- (Karol Wojtyla) (elected 1978). *Origins* 22:795 Ap 29 1993*
John Paul II, Pope, (1993-05-30) Hungary [Orig in Latin]. John Paul II, Pope, 1920- (Karol Wojtyla) (elected 1978). *OR(Eng)* 1294:2 Je 9 1993*
John Paul II, Pope, (1993-06-11) Letter [Orig in English]. John Paul II, Pope, 1920- (Karol Wojtyla) (elected 1978). *OR(Eng)* 1297:2 Je 30 1993*
John Paul II, Pope, (1993-06-11) Letter [Orig in English]. John Paul II, Pope, 1920- (Karol Wojtyla) (elected 1978). *TPS* 38:374-376 N-D 1993*
John Paul II, Pope, (1993-07-21) message to Faith and Order Conference. John Paul II, Pope, 1920- (Karol Wojtyla) (elected 1978). *Ecumen Trends* 22:2 O 1993*

Subject Index 109 John Paul II, Pope, 1920- (Karol

John Paul II, Pope, (1992-01-10) Allocutiones (Audience to welcome the new ambassador from Bangladesh) [English]. John Paul II, Pope, 1920- (Karol Wojtyla) (elected 1978). *AAS* 85:54-56 Ja 7 1993*
John Paul II, Pope, (1992-01-11) Allocutiones (Address to Diplomatic Corps accredited to the Holy See) [French]. John Paul II, Pope, 1920- (Karol Wojtyla) (elected 1978). *AAS* 85:62-73 Ja 7 1993*
John Paul II, Pope, (1992-01-13) Allocutiones (Address to French Bishops on Ad Limina visit) [French]. John Paul II, Pope, 1920- (Karol Wojtyla) (elected 1978). *AAS* 85:73-80 Ja 7 1993*
John Paul II, Pope, (1992-01-16) Allocutiones (Papal Address to Italian Bishops) [Italian]. John Paul II, Pope, 1920- (Karol Wojtyla) (elected 1978). *AAS* 85:130-135 F 3 1993*
John Paul II, Pope, (1992-01-18) Allocutiones (Exhortation to French Bishops) [French]. John Paul II, Pope, 1920- (Karol Wojtyla) (elected 1978). *AAS* 85:135-140 F 3 1993*
John Paul II, Pope, (1992-01-23) Allocutiones (Address to Roman Rota) [Italian]. John Paul II, Pope, 1920- (Karol Wojtyla) (elected 1978). *AAS* 85:140-143 F 3 1993*
John Paul II, Pope, (1992-01-25) Allocutiones (Homily to French Bishops) [French]. John Paul II, Pope, 1920- (Karol Wojtyla) (elected 1978). *AAS* 85:143-148 F 3 1993*
John Paul II, Pope, (1992-02-21) Itinera Apostolica (On apostolic journey speech to Diplomatic Corps in Senegal) [French]. John Paul II, Pope, 1920- (Karol Wojtyla) (elected 1978). *AAS* 85:153-157 F 3 1993*
John Paul II, Pope, (1992-02-21) Itinera Apostolica (On apostolic trip address to Episcopal Conference of Senegal) [French]. John Paul II, Pope, 1920- (Karol Wojtyla) (elected 1978). *AAS* 85:148-153 F 3 1993*
John Paul II, Pope, (1992-02-22) Itinera Apostolica (Address to Catholics of Goree Island during apostolic trip) [French]. John Paul II, Pope, 1920- (Karol Wojtyla) (elected 1978). *AAS* 85:157-161 F 3 1993*
John Paul II, Pope, (1992-02-22) Itinera Apostolica (Address to Muslims of Senegal on Apostolic Journey) [French]. John Paul II, Pope, 1920- (Karol Wojtyla) (elected 1978). *AAS* 85:161-165 F 3 1993*
John Paul II, Pope, (1992-02-23) Itinera Apostolica (Address to priests and religious of Zambia) [English]. John Paul II, Pope, 1920- (Karol Wojtyla) (elected 1978). *AAS* 85:165-170 F 3 1993*
John Paul II, Pope, (1992-02-25) Itinera Apostolica (Address to catechists of Guinea during apostolic journey) [French]. John Paul II, Pope, 1920- (Karol Wojtyla) (elected 1978). *AAS* 85:175-178 F 3 1993*
John Paul II, Pope, (1992-02-25) Itinera Apostolica (Homily at ordination in Guinea during apostolic journey) [French]. John Paul II, Pope, 1920- (Karol Wojtyla) (elected 1978). *AAS* 85:171-175 F 3 1993*
John Paul II, Pope, (1992-04-17) Nuntii Televisifici (television message) [Italian]. John Paul II, Pope, 1920- (Karol Wojtyla) (elected 1978). *AAS* 84:984-985 O 3 1992*
John Paul II, Pope, (1992-04-19) Nuntii Televisifici (television message) [Italian]. John Paul II, Pope, 1920- (Karol Wojtyla) (elected 1978). *AAS* 84:985-990 O 3 1992*
John Paul II, Pope, (1992-08-15) Message to the youth of the world. John Paul II, Pope, 1920- (Karol Wojtyla) (elected 1978). *Living Light* 29:19-22 Spr 1993*
John Paul II, Pope, (1992-10-11) America, open your doors to Christ. John Paul II, Pope, 1920- (Karol Wojtyla) (elected 1978). *TPS* 38:78-83 Mr-Ap 1993*
John Paul II, Pope, (1992-10-12) Challenges facing the Latin American Church. John Paul II, Pope, 1920- (Karol Wojtyla) (elected 1978). *TPS* 38: 84-102 Mr-Ap 1993*
John Paul II, Pope, (1992-10-12) Defend your identities and values. John Paul II, Pope, 1920- (Karol Wojtyla) (elected 1978). *TPS* 38:103-106 Mr-Ap 1993*
John Paul II, Pope, (1992-10-28) The apostolic mission of bishops. John Paul II, Pope, 1920- (Karol Wojtyla) (elected 1978). *TPS* 38:107-110 Mr-Ap 1993*
John Paul II, Pope, (1992-11-09) Vist ad limina. John Paul II, Pope, 1920- (Karol Wojtyla) (elected 1978). *TPS* 38:111-115 Mr-Ap 1993*
John Paul II, Pope, (1992-11-21) the inalienable rights of the disabled. John Paul II, Pope, 1920- (Karol Wojtyla) (elected 1978). *TPS* 38:129-133 My-Je 1993*
John Paul II, Pope, (1992-11-22) Ready to confess Christ. John Paul II, Pope, 1920- (Karol Wojtyla) (elected 1978). *TPS* 38:134-137 My-Je 1993*
John Paul II, Pope, (1992-12-01) Europe's signs of the times. John Paul II, Pope, 1920- (Karol Wojtyla) (elected 1978). *TPS* 38:138-141 My-Je 1993*
John Paul II, Pope, (1992-12-05) basic right to nutrition. John Paul II, Pope, 1920- (Karol Wojtyla) (elected 1978). *TPS* 38:142-146 My-Je 1993*
John Paul II, Pope, (1992-12-05) serve life at its birth. John Paul II, Pope, 1920- (Karol Wojtyla) (elected 1978). *TPS* 38:147-149 My-Je 1993*
John Paul II, Pope, (1992-12-07) New Catechism is a gift to the Church. John Paul II, Pope, 1920- (Karol Wojtyla) (elected 1978). *TPS* 38:150-154 My-Je 1993*
John Paul II, Pope, (1992-12-08) If you want peace, serve the poor. John Paul II, Pope, 1920- (Karol Wojtyla) (elected 1978). *TPS* 38:155-161 My-Je 1993*
John Paul II, Pope, (1992-12-16) Peter ranks first. John Paul II, Pope, 1920- (Karol Wojtyla) (elected 1978). *TPS* 38:165-168 My-Je 1993*
John Paul II, Pope, (1992-12-19) Ad limina Apostolorum. John Paul II, Pope, 1920- (Karol Wojtyla) (elected 1978). *TPS* 38:193-200 Jl-Ag 1993*
John Paul II, Pope, (1992-12-20) Charity is an individual and social obligation. John Paul II, Pope, 1920- (Karol Wojtyla) (elected 1978). *TPS* 38: 169-171 My-Je 1993*
John Paul II, Pope, (1992-12-22) give thanks for the gift of serving. John Paul II, Pope, 1920- (Karol Wojtyla) (elected 1978). *TPS* 38:172-178 My-Je 1993*
John Paul II, Pope, (1993 06 05) Parishes. John Paul II, Pope, 1920- (Karol Wojtyla) (elected 1978). *TPS* 38:369-373 N-D 1993*
John Paul II, Pope, (1993-00-00) Genuine Spiritual renewal. John Paul II, Pope, 1920- (Karol Wojtyla) (elected 1978). *New Cov* 23:16-17 S 1993
John Paul II, Pope, (1993-01-04) Moral responsibilities of psychiatrists. John Paul II, Pope, 1920- (Karol Wojtyla) (elected 1978). *TPS* 38:179-180 My-Je 1993*
John Paul II, Pope, (1993-01-25) Christian unity is our desire. John Paul II, Pope, 1920- (Karol Wojtyla) (elected 1978). *TPS* 38:202-206 Jl-Ag 1993*
John Paul II, Pope, (1993-01-27) Bishop of Rome is Peter's successor. John Paul II, Pope, 1920- (Karol Wojtyla) (elected 1978). *TPS* 38:207-210 Jl-Ag 1993*
John Paul II, Pope, (1993-01-29) Interpret law through tradition. John Paul II, Pope, 1920- (Karol Wojtyla) (elected 1978). *TPS* 38:211-214 Jl-Ag 1993*
John Paul II, Pope, (1993-01-30) Promote the family. John Paul II, Pope, 1920- (Karol Wojtyla) (elected 1978). *TPS* 38:215-218 Jl-Ag 1993*
John Paul II, Pope, (1993-01-9) Discurso a los indigenas Latino Americanos. John Paul II, Pope, 1920- (Karol Wojtyla) (elected 1978). *Christus* 58:46-48 S 1993*
John Paul II, Pope, (1993-02-10) Innocent victims. John Paul II, Pope, 1920- (Karol Wojtyla) (elected 1978). *TPS* 38:221-225 Jl-Ag 1993*
John Paul II, Pope, (1993-02-17) Vitality of African Christianity. John Paul II, Pope, 1920- (Karol Wojtyla) (elected 1978). *TPS* 38:226-229 Jl-Ag 1993*
John Paul II, Pope, (1993-02-24) Pope exercises supreme jurisdiction. John Paul II, Pope, 1920- (Karol Wojtyla) (elected 1978). *TPS* 38:232-235 Jl-Ag 1993*
John Paul II, Pope, (1993-02-26) Sharing clergy. John Paul II, Pope, 1920- (Karol Wojtyla) (elected 1978). *TPS* 38:236-239 Jl-Ag 1993*
John Paul II, Pope, (1993-03-17) Infallibility. John Paul II, Pope, 1920- (Karol Wojtyla) (elected 1978). *TPS* 38:257-260 S-O 1993*
John Paul II, Pope, (1993-03-21) Authentic witnesses of the Gospel. John Paul II, Pope, 1920- (Karol Wojtyla) (elected 1978). *TPS* 38:245-248 Jl-Ag 1993*
John Paul II, Pope, (1993-03-27) Treat sinners with compassion. John Paul II, Pope, 1920- (Karol Wojtyla) (elected 1978). *TPS* 38:261-265 S-O 1993*
John Paul II, Pope, (1993-04-15) Europe needs solidarity. John Paul II, Pope, 1920- (Karol Wojtyla) (elected 1978). *TPS* 38:270-274 S-O 1993*
John Paul II, Pope, (1993-04-25) May Albania be equal to the challenge. John Paul II, Pope, 1920- (Karol Wojtyla) (elected 1978). *TPS* 38:275-279 S-O 1993*
John Paul II, Pope, (1993-04-28) Christian heritage in Iraq. John Paul II, Pope, 1920- (Karol Wojtyla) (elected 1978). *TPS* 38:280-282 S-O 1993*
John Paul II, Pope, (1993-04-29) New Catechism is basis for local catechisms. John Paul II, Pope, 1920- (Karol Wojtyla) (elected 1978). *TPS* 38:283-286 S-O 1993*
John Paul II, Pope, (1993-05-01) Catholic Journalists [Orig in Italian]. John Paul II, Pope, 1920- (Karol Wojtyla) (elected 1978). *OR(Eng)* 1296:13 Je 23 1993*
John Paul II, Pope, (1993-05-05) Priests sanctify through sacraments. John Paul II, Pope, 1920- (Karol Wojtyla) (elected 1978). *TPS* 38:287-290 S-O 1993*
John Paul II, Pope, (1993-05-06) Help [Orig in French]. John Paul II, Pope, 1920- (Karol Wojtyla) (elected 1978). *OR(Eng)* 1292:3 My 26 1993*
John Paul II, Pope, (1993-05-06) Holy Childhood Association's 150th anniversary. John Paul II, Pope, 1920- (Karol Wojtyla) (elected 1978). *TPS* 38:291-294 S-O 1993*
John Paul II, Pope, (1993-05-07) Science [Orig in Italian]. John Paul II, Pope, 1920- (Karol Wojtyla) (elected 1978). *OR(Eng)* 1296:14 Je 23 1993*
John Paul II, Pope, (1993-05-08) Faith and science are gifts of God. John Paul II, Pope, 1920- (Karol Wojtyla) (elected 1978). *TPS* 38:295-300 S-O 1993*
John Paul II, Pope, (1993-05-09) Faith. John Paul II, Pope, 1920- (Karol Wojtyla) (elected 1978). *OR(Eng)* 1292:6 My 26 1993*
John Paul II, Pope, (1993-05-09) Get up [Orig in Italian]. John Paul II, Pope, 1920- (Karol Wojtyla) (elected 1978). *OR(Eng)* 1292:4+ My 26 1993*
John Paul II, Pope, (1993-05-09) Healthy business. John Paul II, Pope, 1920- (Karol Wojtyla) (elected 1978). *OR(Eng)* 1292:5 My 26 1993*
John Paul II, Pope, (1993-05-09) Repent! God will judge you. John Paul II, Pope, 1920- (Karol Wojtyla) (elected 1978). *TPS* 38:301-303 S-O 1993*
John Paul II, Pope, (1993-05-10) Ethical training [Orig in Italian]. John Paul II, Pope, 1920- (Karol Wojtyla) (elected 1978). *OR(Eng)* 1292:8 My 26 1993*
John Paul II, Pope, (1993-05-10) Sicily. John Paul II, Pope, 1920- (Karol Wojtyla) (elected 1978). *OR(Eng)* 1292:7 My 26 1993*
John Paul II, Pope, (1993-05-12) Priests act in the Person of Christ. John Paul II, Pope, 1920- (Karol Wojtyla) (elected 1978). *TPS* 38:304-307 S-O 1993*
John Paul II, Pope, (1993-05-14) Huelva [Orig in Spanish]. John Paul II, Pope, 1920- (Karol Wojtyla) (elected 1978). *OR(Eng)* 1296:1+ Je 23 1993*
John Paul II, Pope, (1993-05-14) Life [Orig in Italian]. John Paul II, Pope, 1920- (Karol Wojtyla) (elected 1978). *OR(Eng)* 1292:9+ My 26 1993*
John Paul II, Pope, (1993-05-15) Spain [Orig in Spanish]. John Paul II, Pope, 1920- (Karol Wojtyla) (elected 1978). *OR(Eng)* 1297:7 Je 30 1993*
John Paul II, Pope, (1993-05-15) Spirit [Orig in English]. John Paul II, Pope, 1920- (Karol Wojtyla) (elected 1978). *OR(Eng)* 1292:2 My 26 1993*
John Paul II, Pope, (1993-05-16). John Paul II, Pope, 1920- (Karol Wojtyla) (elected 1978). *TPS* 38:308-311 S-O 1993*
John Paul II, Pope, (1993-05-19) Priest [Orig in Italian]. John Paul II, Pope, 1920- (Karol Wojtyla) (elected 1978). *OR(Eng)* 1292:11+ My 26 1993*
John Paul II, Pope, (1993-05-22) Mary. John Paul II, Pope, 1920- (Karol Wojtyla) (elected 1978). *OR(Eng)* 1292:1 My 26 1993*
John Paul II, Pope, (1993-05-23) Heart [Orig in Italian]. John Paul II, Pope, 1920- (Karol Wojtyla) (elected 1978). *OR(Eng)* 1294:8 Je 9 1993*
John Paul II, Pope, (1993-05-23) Presence [Orig in Italian]. John Paul II, Pope, 1920- (Karol Wojtyla) (elected 1978). *OR(Eng)* 1294:6+ Je 9 1993*
John Paul II, Pope, (1993-05-23) Sacraments [Orig Italian]. John Paul II, Pope, 1920- (Karol Wojtyla) (elected 1978). *OR(Eng)* 1294:7 Je 9 1993*
John Paul II, Pope, (1993-05-23) Social dimension [Orig in Italian]. John Paul II, Pope, 1920- (Karol Wojtyla) (elected 1978). *OR(Eng)* 1294:5 Je 9 1993*
John Paul II, Pope, (1993-05-24) Charism [Orig in Italian]. John Paul II, Pope, 1920- (Karol Wojtyla) (elected 1978). *OR(Eng)* 1300:9 Jl 21 1993*
John Paul II, Pope, (1993-05-27) Catholic University of America [Orig in English]. John Paul II, Pope, 1920- (Karol Wojtyla) (elected 1978). *OR(Eng)* 1294:10 Je 9 1993*
John Paul II, Pope, (1993-05-28) God [Orig in Italian]. John Paul II, Pope, 1920- (Karol Wojtyla) (elected 1978). *OR(Eng)* 1294:4 Je 9 1993*
John Paul II, Pope, (1993-05-31) Citizens [Orig in English]. John Paul II, Pope, 1920- (Karol Wojtyla) (elected 1978). *OR(Eng)* 1294:3 Je 9 1993*

John Paul II, Pope, 1920- (Karol 110 **Subject Index**

John Paul II, Pope, (1993-06-01) Eucharist [Orig in French]. John Paul II, Pope, 1920- (Karol Wojtyla) (elected 1978). *OR(Eng)* 1297:8 Je 30 1993*
John Paul II, Pope, (1993-06-01) Year of the family [Orig in Italian]. John Paul II, Pope, 1920- (Karol Wojtyla) (elected 1978). *OR(Eng)* 1294:1+ Je 9 1993*
John Paul II, Pope, (1993-06-02) Priest [Orig in Italian]. John Paul II, Pope, 1920- (Karol Wojtyla) (elected 1978). *OR(Eng)* 1294:11 Je 9 1993*
John Paul II, Pope, (1993-06-03) Christian hope [Orig in Italian]. John Paul II, Pope, 1920- (Karol Wojtyla) (elected 1978). *OR(Eng)* 1297:9 Je 30 1993*
John Paul II, Pope, (1993-06-05) Parishes. John Paul II, Pope, 1920- (Karol Wojtyla) (elected 1978). *Origins* 23:127-128 Jl 15 1993*
John Paul II, Pope, (1993-06-05) Social doctrine [Orig in Italian]. John Paul II, Pope, 1920- (Karol Wojtyla) (elected 1978). *OR(Eng)* 1297:9 Je 30 1993*
John Paul II, Pope, (1993-06-05) Spiritual life. John Paul II, Pope, 1920- (Karol Wojtyla) (elected 1978). *OR(Eng)* 1295:3+ Je 16 1993*
John Paul II, Pope, (1993-06-07) Official visit [original in Slovak]. John Paul II, Pope, 1920- (Karol Wojtyla) (elected 1978). *OR(Eng)* 1295:6 Je 16 1993*
John Paul II, Pope, (1993-06-08) Marriage and Holy Orders [Orig in English]. John Paul II, Pope, 1920- (Karol Wojtyla) (elected 1978). *OR(Eng)* 1296:11 Je 23 1993*
John Paul II, Pope, (1993-06-08) Republic of Romania. John Paul II, Pope, 1920- (Karol Wojtyla) (elected 1978). *OR(Eng)* 1297:8 Je 30 1993*
John Paul II, Pope, (1993-06-09) Church [Orig Italian]. John Paul II, Pope, 1920- (Karol Wojtyla) (elected 1978). *OR(Eng)* 1298:5 Jl 7 1993*
John Paul II, Pope, (1993-06-09) Eucharist [original in Italian]. John Paul II, Pope, 1920- (Karol Wojtyla) (elected 1978). *OR(Eng)* 1295:7 Je 16 1993*
John Paul II, Pope, (1993-06-10) Corpus Christi. John Paul II, Pope, 1920- (Karol Wojtyla) (elected 1978). *OR(Eng)* 1295:2 Je 16 1993*
John Paul II, Pope, (1993-06-11) Ethiopian Orthodox Patriarch. John Paul II, Pope, 1920- (Karol Wojtyla) (elected 1978). *OR(Eng)* 1295:5 Je 16 1993*
John Paul II, Pope, (1993-06-12) Eucharist [Orig in Spanish]. John Paul II, Pope, 1920- (Karol Wojtyla) (elected 1978). *OR(Eng)* 1296:5 Je 23 1993*
John Paul II, Pope, (1993-06-12) God present among us [Orig in Spanish]. John Paul II, Pope, 1920- (Karol Wojtyla) (elected 1978). *OR(Eng)* 1296:4 Je 23 1993*
John Paul II, Pope, (1993-06-12) Love and hope [Orig in Spanish]. John Paul II, Pope, 1920- (Karol Wojtyla) (elected 1978). *OR(Eng)* 1296:3 Je 23 1993*
John Paul II, Pope, (1993-06-13) International Eucharistic Congress [Orig in Spanish]. John Paul II, Pope, 1920- (Karol Wojtyla) (elected 1978). *OR(Eng)* 1296:6 Je 23 1993*
John Paul II, Pope, (1993-06-14) New World [Orig in Spanish]. John Paul II, Pope, 1920- (Karol Wojtyla) (elected 1978). *OR(Eng)* 1296:8 Je 23 1993*
John Paul II, Pope, (1993-06-14) Spain [Orig in Italian]. John Paul II, Pope, 1920- (Karol Wojtyla) (elected 1978). *OR(Eng)* 1297:3 Je 30 1993*
John Paul II, Pope, (1993-06-15) Church [Orig in Spanish]. John Paul II, Pope, 1920- (Karol Wojtyla) (elected 1978). *OR(Eng)* 1297:4+ Je 30 1993*
John Paul II, Pope, (1993-06-15) God [Orgin Spanish]. John Paul II, Pope, 1920- (Karol Wojtyla) (elected 1978). *OR(Eng)* 1297:5 Je 30 1993*
John Paul II, Pope, (1993-06-16) "art of arts" [Orig in Spanish]. John Paul II, Pope, 1920- (Karol Wojtyla) (elected 1978). *OR(Eng)* 1297:6 Je 30 1993*
John Paul II, Pope, (1993-06-16) Baptism, [Orig in Spanish]. John Paul II, Pope, 1920- (Karol Wojtyla) (elected 1978). *OR(Eng)* 1296:1-2 Je 23 1993*
John Paul II, Pope, (1993-06-16) Visit to Spain. John Paul II, Pope, 1920- (Karol Wojtyla) (elected 1978). *OR(Eng)* 1295:1+ Je 16 1993*
John Paul II, Pope, (1993-06-19) Apostles [Orig in Italian]. John Paul II, Pope, 1920- (Karol Wojtyla) (elected 1978). *OR(Eng)* 1300:7 Jl 21 1993*
John Paul II, Pope, (1993-06-19) Human Life [Orig in Italian]. John Paul II, Pope, 1920- (Karol Wojtyla) (elected 1978). *OR(Eng)* 1298:6 Jl 7 1993*
John Paul II, Pope, (1993-06-20) Angela [Orig in Italian]. John Paul II, Pope, 1920- (Karol Wojtyla) (elected 1978). *OR(Eng)* 1298:7 Jl 7 1993*
John Paul II, Pope, (1993-06-20) Nature [Orig in Italian]. John Paul II, Pope, 1920- (Karol Wojtyla) (elected 1978). *OR(Eng)* 1296:1 Je 23 1993*
John Paul II, Pope, (1993-06-21) World. John Paul II, Pope, 1920- (Karol Wojtyla) (elected 1978). *OR(Eng)* 1300:5 Jl 21 1993*
John Paul II, Pope, (1993-06-23) Seville [Orig in Italian]. John Paul II, Pope, 1920- (Karol Wojtyla) (elected 1978). *OR(Eng)* 1297:11 Je 30 1993*
John Paul II, Pope, (1993-06-27) Rome [Orig Italian]. John Paul II, Pope, 1920- (Karol Wojtyla) (elected 1978). *OR(Eng)* 1297:1 Je 30 1993*
John Paul II, Pope, (1993-06-29) Christian unity. John Paul II, Pope, 1920- (Karol Wojtyla) (elected 1978). *OR(Eng)* 1298:2 Jl 7 1993*
John Paul II, Pope, (1993-06-29) Church. John Paul II, Pope, 1920- (Karol Wojtyla) (elected 1978). *OR(Eng)* 1298:1-2 Jl 7 1993*
John Paul II, Pope, (1993-06-29) Prayer [Orig in Italian]. John Paul II, Pope, 1920- (Karol Wojtyla) (elected 1978). *OR(Eng)* 1298:1-2 Jl 7 1993*
John Paul II, Pope, (1993-06-30) Priests [Orig in Italian]. John Paul II, Pope, 1920- (Karol Wojtyla) (elected 1978). *OR(Eng)* 1298:11 Jl 7 1993*
John Paul II, Pope, (1993-07-02) Ministry. John Paul II, Pope, 1920- (Karol Wojtyla) (elected 1978). *OR(Eng)* 1298:3+ Jl 7 1993*
John Paul II, Pope, (1993-07-02) Women. John Paul II, Pope, 1920- (Karol Wojtyla) (elected 1978). *Origins* 23:124-126 Jl 15 1993*
John Paul II, Pope, (1993-07-11) Santo Stefano [Orig in Italian]. John Paul II, Pope, 1920- (Karol Wojtyla) (elected 1978). *OR(Eng)* 1300:3 Jl 21 1993*
John Paul II, Pope, (1993-07-17) Church. John Paul II, Pope, 1920- (Karol Wojtyla) (elected 1978). *OR(Eng)* 1300:11 Jl 21 1993*
John Paul II, Pope, (1993-07-18) Praying [Orig Italian]. John Paul II, Pope, 1920- (Karol Wojtyla) (elected 1978). *OR(Eng)* 1300:1 Jl 21 1993*
John Paul II, Pope, (1993-07-19) Pius XII [Orig in Italian]. John Paul II, Pope, 1920- (Karol Wojtyla) (elected 1978). *OR(Eng)* 1300:1 Jl 21 1993*
John Paul II, Pope, (1993-07-21) Model [Orig in Italian]. John Paul II, Pope, 1920- (Karol Wojtyla) (elected 1978). *OR(Eng)* 1301:11 Jl 28 1993*
John Paul II, Pope, (1993-07-25) Youth [Orig in Italian]. John Paul II, Pope, 1920- (Karol Wojtyla) (elected 1978). *OR(Eng)* 1301:1+ Jl 28 1993*
John Paul II, Pope, (1993-07-28) Priests. John Paul II, Pope, 1920- (Karol Wojtyla) (elected 1978). *OR(Eng)* 1302:7 Ag 11 1993*
John Paul II, Pope, (1993-08-01) Music. John Paul II, Pope, 1920- (Karol Wojtyla) (elected 1978). *OR(Eng)* 1303:12 Ag 18 1993*
John Paul II, Pope, (1993-08-01) Peace [Orig in Italian]. John Paul II, Pope, 1920- (Karol Wojtyla) (elected 1978). *OR(Eng)* 1302:1 Ag 11 1993*
John Paul II, Pope, (1993-08-04) Bishops [Orig in Italian]. John Paul II, Pope, 1920- (Karol Wojtyla) (elected 1978). *OR(Eng)* 1303:15 Ag 18 1993*
John Paul II, Pope, (1993-08-09) Church [Orig in English]. John Paul II, Pope, 1920- (Karol Wojtyla) (elected 1978). *OR(Eng)* 1303:1+ Ag 18 1993*
John Paul II, Pope, (1993-08-10) Christ's love [Orig in English]. John Paul II, Pope, 1920- (Karol Wojtyla) (elected 1978). *OR(Eng)* 1303:2 Ag 18 1993*
John Paul II, Pope, (1993-08-10) Hearts [Orig in English]. John Paul II, Pope, 1920- (Karol Wojtyla) (elected 1978). *OR(Eng)* 1303:5 Ag 18 1993*
John Paul II, Pope, (1993-08-10) Jamaica. John Paul II, Pope, 1920- (Karol Wojtyla) (elected 1978). *OR(Eng)* 1303:3 Ag 18 1993*
John Paul II, Pope, (1993-08-10) Truth [Orig in English]. John Paul II, Pope, 1920- (Karol Wojtyla) (elected 1978). *OR(Eng)* 1303:4 Ag 18 1993*
John Paul II, Pope, (1993-08-11) Jamaica's ideals [Orig in English]. John Paul II, Pope, 1920- (Karol Wojtyla) (elected 1978). *OR(Eng)* 1303:5 Ag 18 1993*
John Paul II, Pope, (1993-08-12) Arrival [Origin English]. John Paul II, Pope, 1920- (Karol Wojtyla) (elected 1978). *Origins* 23:187-188 Ag 26 1993*
John Paul II, Pope, (1993-08-12) Denver. John Paul II, Pope, 1920- (Karol Wojtyla) (elected 1978). *OR(Eng)* 1303:6 Ag 18 1993*
John Paul II, Pope, (1993-08-12) Life. John Paul II, Pope, 1920- (Karol Wojtyla) (elected 1978). *OR(Eng)* 1303:7+ Ag 18 1993*
John Paul II, Pope, (1993-08-12) Young people [Orig in English]. John Paul II, Pope, 1920- (Karol Wojtyla) (elected 1978). *Origins* 23:188-190 Ag 26 1993*
John Paul II, Pope, (1993-08-13) Bishops [Orig in English]. John Paul II, Pope, 1920- (Karol Wojtyla) (elected 1978). *Origins* 23:190-191 Ag 26 1993*
John Paul II, Pope, (1993-08-13) Cross. John Paul II, Pope, 1920- (Karol Wojtyla) (elected 1978). *Origins* 23:191-192 Ag 26 1993*
John Paul II, Pope, (1993-08-14) Christ [Orig English]. John Paul II, Pope, 1920- (Karol Wojtyla) (elected 1978). *OR(Eng)* 1303:8-9 Ag 18 1993*
John Paul II, Pope, (1993-08-14) Colorado [Origin in English]. John Paul II, Pope, 1920- (Karol Wojtyla) (elected 1978). *Origins* 23:194-195 Ag 26 1993*
John Paul II, Pope, (1993-08-14) Forum. John Paul II, Pope, 1920- (Karol Wojtyla) (elected 1978). *Origins* 23:192-194 Ag 26 1993*
John Paul II, Pope, (1993-08-14) Prayer [Origin English]. John Paul II, Pope, 1920- (Karol Wojtyla) (elected 1978). *Origins* 23:182-186 Ag 26 1993*
John Paul II, Pope, (1993-08-15) Celebration [Origin in English]. John Paul II, Pope, 1920- (Karol Wojtyla) (elected 1978). *Origins* 23:177+ Ag 26 1993*
John Paul II, Pope, (1993-08-15) Cherry Creek [Orig in English]. John Paul II, Pope, 1920- (Karol Wojtyla) (elected 1978). *Origins* 23:196 Ag 26 1993*
John Paul II, Pope, (1993-08-15) Children. John Paul II, Pope, 1920- (Karol Wojtyla) (elected 1978). *Origins* 23:198-199 Ag 26 1993*
John Paul II, Pope, (1993-08-15) Church [Orig in English]. John Paul II, Pope, 1920- (Karol Wojtyla) (elected 1978). *Origins* 23:197-198 Ag 26 1993*
John Paul II, Pope, (1993-08-15) Farewell [Origin in English]. John Paul II, Pope, 1920- (Karol Wojtyla) (elected 1978). *Origins* 23:196-197 Ag 26 1993*
John Paul II, Pope, (1993-08-15) Gore. John Paul II, Pope, 1920- (Karol Wojtyla) (elected 1978). *Origins* 23:200 Ag 26 1993*
John Paul II, Pope, (1993-08-15) Manila. John Paul II, Pope, 1920- (Karol Wojtyla) (elected 1978). *OR(Eng)* 1303:11 Ag 18 1993*
John Paul II, Pope, (1993-08-15) Talents. John Paul II, Pope, 1920- (Karol Wojtyla) (elected 1978). *OR(Eng)* 1303:1+ Ag 18 1993*
John Paul II, Pope, (1993-08-25) Obedience [Orig in Italian]. John Paul II, Pope, 1920- (Karol Wojtyla) (elected 1978). *OR(Eng)* 1305:7 S 1 1993*
John Paul II, Pope, (1993-08-29) Baltic. John Paul II, Pope, 1920- (Karol Wojtyla) (elected 1978). *OR(Eng)* 1305:1 S 1 1993*
John Paul II, Pope, (1993-09-01) Cooperation [Orig in Italian]. John Paul II, Pope, 1920- (Karol Wojtyla) (elected 1978). *OR(Eng)* 1306:11 S 8 1993*
John Paul II, Pope, (1993-09-02) United States [Orig in English]. John Paul II, Pope, 1920- (Karol Wojtyla) (elected 1978). *OR(Eng)* 1306:10 S 8 1993*
John Paul II, Pope, (1993-09-04) Baltic nations [Orig Lithuanian]. John Paul II, Pope, 1920- (Karol Wojtyla) (elected 1978). *OR(Eng)* 1306:1+ S 8 1993*
John Paul II, Pope, (1993-09-04) Mary [Orig in Lithuanian]. John Paul II, Pope, 1920- (Karol Wojtyla) (elected 1978). *OR(Eng)* 1306:3 S 8 1993*
John Paul II, Pope, (1993-09-04) Saint Stanislaus. John Paul II, Pope, 1920- (Karol Wojtyla) (elected 1978). *OR(Eng)* 1306:2 S 8 1993*
John Paul II, Pope, (1993-09-05) Basic values [Orig in Lithuanian]. John Paul II, Pope, 1920- (Karol Wojtyla) (elected 1978). *OR(Eng)* 1306:7-8 S 8 1993*
John Paul II, Pope, (1993-09-05) Beyond. John Paul II, Pope, 1920- (Karol Wojtyla) (elected 1978). *Origins* 23:235-237 S 16 1993*
John Paul II, Pope, (1993-09-05) Freedom [Orig in French]. John Paul II, Pope, 1920- (Karol Wojtyla) (elected 1978). *OR(Eng)* 1306:5+ S 8 1993*
John Paul II, Pope, (1993-09-05) Independence. John Paul II, Pope, 1920- (Karol Wojtyla) (elected 1978). *Origins* 23:233 S 16 1993*
John Paul II, Pope, (1993-09-05) Lithuania [Orig Lithuanian]. John Paul II, Pope, 1920- (Karol Wojtyla) (elected 1978). *OR(Eng)* 1306:1+ S 8 1993*
John Paul II, Pope, (1993-09-05) People [Orig in Polish]. John Paul II, Pope, 1920- (Karol Wojtyla) (elected 1978). *OR(Eng)* 1307:3 S 15 1993*
John Paul II, Pope, (1993-09-05) The power of love [Orig in Lithuanian]. John Paul II, Pope, 1920- (Karol Wojtyla) (elected 1978). *OR(Eng)* 1306:8 S 8 1993*
John Paul II, Pope, (1993-09-06) Clergy [Orig in Lithuanian]. John Paul II, Pope, 1920- (Karol Wojtyla) (elected 1978). *OR(Eng)* 1307:7 S 15 1993*
John Paul II, Pope, (1993-09-06) Future [Orig in Lithuanian]. John Paul II, Pope, 1920- (Karol Wojtyla) (elected 1978). *OR(Eng)* 1307:4+ S 15 1993*
John Paul II, Pope, (1993-09-06) Holy Spirit [Orig in Lithuanian]. John Paul II, Pope, 1920- (Karol Wojtyla) (elected 1978). *OR(Eng)* 1306:6 S 8 1993*
John Paul II, Pope, (1993-09-07) Cross [Orig in Lithuanian]. John Paul II, Pope, 1920- (Karol Wojtyla) (elected 1978). *OR(Eng)* 1307:5 S 15 1993*
John Paul II, Pope, (1993-09-07) Mary [Orig in Lithuanian]. John Paul II, Pope, 1920- (Karol Wojtyla) (elected 1978). *OR(Eng)* 1307:6 S 15 1993*
John Paul II, Pope, (1993-09-08) Estonians [Orig in Estonian]. John Paul II, Pope, 1920- (Karol Wojtyla) (elected 1978). *OR(Eng)* 1307:15 S 15 1993*
John Paul II, Pope, (1993-09-08) Grace [Orig in Latvian]. John Paul II, Pope, 1920- (Karol Wojtyla) (elected 1978). *OR(Eng)* 1307:10 S 15 1993*

KOCH, WERNER, 1923-1992
Jesus im modernen Roman. Langenhorst, Georg. *Stimm Zeit* 210:819-830 D 1992

KOINONIA *see* Community (Theology)

KOLB, DIETER
Hegel, Kolb and Flay: foundationalism or anti-foundationalism? Kow, James P. *IPQ* 33:203-218 Je 1993

KOLBE, MAXIMILLIAN, SAINT, 1894-1941
The Holy Spirit and Mary. Campbell, Dwight P. *HPR* 93:12-23 My 1993

KOLBERG, LAWRENCE
Celibacy: a feminist view. Gramick, Jeannine. *Sisters* 65:255-262 Jl 1993

KOLVENBACH, PETER-HANS
Jesuits under Kolvenbach face a changed world [por]. Corley, Felix. *OSV* 82: 3 N 21 1993

KOLYMA (CONCENTRATION CAMP)
Philosophy and theology after Kolyma. Chrostowski, Waldemar. *New Theol Rev* 6:102-107 My 1993

KOMARICA, FRANJO, BP, 1946-
A bishop at bay. McDonagh, Melanie. *Tablet* 247:968+ Jl 31 1993
Humanitarian nightmare. *Origins* 23:733+ Ap 8 1993
More death threats against bishop. *Tablet* 247:414 Mr 27 1993

KONDRUSIEWICZ, TADEUSZ, ABP
Archbishop, condemns new law, appeals to West. Luxmoore, Jonathan. *Tablet* 247:990 Jl 31 1993
Optimisim from Catholic archbishop in Moscow. *Tablet* 247:178 F 6 1993

KOPLING, ADOLF, 1813-1865
John Paul II, Pope, (1991-10-27) Homilia (Sermon on Adolph Kolping) [Italian and German]. John Paul II, Pope, 1920- (Karol Wojtyla) (elected 1978). *AAS* 84:844-848 S 8 1992*

KORDEL, MICHAEL, 1892-1936
Professor Burkhard Neunheuser, OSB: Doctor Honoris Causa of the Pontifival Academy of Theology in Kraków. Reder, Violetta. *Notitiae* 29:81-83 Ja-F 1993

KORESH, DAVID
Agents of apocalypse [editorial]. *Comm* 120:3-4 My 7 1993
Madness, massacre and the millennium. Egan, Anthony. *Month* 26:214-218 Je 1993

KOSOVO (SERBIA)—POLITICS AND GOVERNMENT
Serbia's holy land. Seddon, Catharine. *Tablet* 247:536-538 My 1 1993
Worse yet to come? Brown, Janice. *Comm* 120:4-5 Ja 29 1993

KOSOVO (SERBIA)—SOCIAL CONDITIONS
Aliens in their own land. McDonagh, Melanie. *Tablet* 247:392-394 Mr 27 1993

KOVAC, MICHAL
John Paul II, Pope, (1993-06-07) Official visit [original in Slovak]. John Paul II, Pope, 1920- (Karol Wojtyla) (elected 1978). *OR(Eng)* 1295:6 Je 16 1993*

KOVACEVIC, MIROSLAV
Save the children of Croatia. Breslin, Mary. *St Anth* 100:28-35 Mr 1993

KOVACS, GEORGE, 1935-
Why Heidegger's Godot might not be worth the wait. Bruin, John. *Mod Schlmn* 70:143-152 Ja 1993

KOWALCZYK, JOZEF, ABP
New era of cooperation begins. *OR(Eng)* 1302:2 Ag 11 1993

KOWALSKA, MARIA FAUSTINA (ELENA), 1905-1938
Congregation for the Causes of Saints (1992-03-07) Decree on the heroic virtues. Congregation for the Causes of Saints. *AAS* 84:926-929 S 8 1992*
Congregation for the Causes of Saints (1992-12-21) Decree on a miracle. Congregation for the Causes of Saints. *OR(Eng)* 1272:4 Ja 6 1993
Who is Sister Faustina? Kosicki, George. *Register* 69:4 F 7 1993

KREISKY, BRUNO
Befreiung von Knechtschaft. Ehlen, Peter. *Stimm Zeit* 211:21-33 Ja 1993

KRENEK, ERNST, 1900-
Ernst Krenek's sacred music. Riedel, Johannes. *SacM* 120:15-29 Aut 1993

KRENN, KURT, ABP, 1936-
Another crisis over a bishop's style. *Tablet* 247:865-866 Jl 3 1993

KRISHNA CONSCIOUSNESS MOVEMENT
The Hare Krishna movement. Smith, Richard F. *StudiaM* 41:107-126 1992

KUHARIC, FRANJO, CARDINAL, 1919-
Croat Catholics divided. Magas, Branka. *Tablet* 247:908-910 Jl 17 1993
Desperate appeals as the slaughter goes on and on. *Tablet* 247:661-662 My 22 1993

KUNDERA, MILAN
Kundera, Nietzsche, and politics on the questions of eternal return and responsibility. Parens, Erik. *PhilosTod* 37:285-297 Aut 1993

KUNERT, GUNTER
Fondamentalismo e religione. Mertes, Klaus. *Civilta* 2:116-129 Ap 17 1993

KUNG, HANS, 1928-
Giant among theologians. Bowden, John. *Tablet* 247:364-365 Mr 20 1993

KUNG PIN-MEI, IGNATIUS, CARDINAL, 1901-
China's loyal church. Dodds, Bill. *OSV* 82:8 My 9 1993
For Chinese Catholics, a hammering [Kung Foundation]. Feuerherd, Peter. *Register* 69:1+ Mr 21 1993

KUROZUMIKYO (RELIGIOUS ORGANIZATION)
The universal attitude of Shinto as expressed in the Shinto sect Kurozumikyō. Stoesz, Willis. *JEcumen Stds* 29:215-229 Spr 1992

KUWAIT—POLITICS AND GOVERNMENT
After Kuwait the deluge. Wicker, Brian. *New Blckfrs* 74:85-98 F 1993

L

LABOR ECONOMICS- UNITED STATES
Structural change in US labor markets. Champlin, Dell. *RSocEcon* 51:40-61 Spr 1993

LABOR LAWS- IRELAND
The causes of Irish unemployment: trends and explanations. Browne, Frank, and McGettigan, Donal. *Studies* 82:35-52 Spr 1993

LABOR SUPPLY
A Northern perspective. Borooah, Vani K, and Ackah, Carol. *Studies* 82:53-60 Spr 1993

LABOR SUPPLY—STATISTICS
Ireland's record—last in the class? Johns, Christopher. *Studies* 82:9-23 Spr 1993

LABOR UNIONS
Cesar Chavez: other words for saintliness [editorial]. *Nat Cath Rep* 29:28 My 7 1993
Labor's metamorphosis? The high stakes at Caterpillar. Kelly, Kevin T. *Comm* 120:7-8 Ja 15 1993
A look at holy role models: John Corridan, S.J. O'Connell-Cahill, Catherine. *Salt* 13:47 N-D 1993
Millions reaped what Cesar Chavez sowed [obit]. Jones, Arthur C, 1936-. *Nat Cath Rep* 29:3 My 7 1993
The pain and sacrifice of birthing a union. Jones, Arthur C, 1936-. *Nat Cath Rep* 29:5-6 Ja 22 1993
Reclaiming our daily work. Antonides, Harry. *Can Cath Rev* 11:18-23 My 1993
Wobblies win at bingo!. Flank, Lenny, Jr. *Cath Work* 60:3 S 1993

LABOR UNIONS—HISTORY
In the shell of the old. Mastrodonato, David. *Cath Work* 60:7 Mr-Ap 1993

LABORING CLASSES
Lost strike? No such thing. Mastrodonato, David. *Cath Work* 60:7 Ja-F 1993
Splitting shifts: splitting families. Downs, Peter. *Comm* 120:7-8 Je 4 1993

LACOUE-LABARTHE, PHILLIPE
The community's absence in Lyotard, Nancy, and Lacoue-Labarthe. May, Todd. *PhilosTod* 37:275-284 Aut 1993

LACUGNA, CATHERINE MOWRY
Feminism and theology: beyond women's ordination. Cahoy, William J. *Sisters* 65:243-251 Jl 1993
What's God like? Collins, Mary Smalara. *USCath* 58:30-35 S 1993

LAITY
Accountability in the church. McDonnell, Dominic. *Priests & People* 6:340-342 Ag-S 1992
American Catholic laity in a changing church. D'Antonio, William V, et al. Kansas City: Sheed and Ward, 1989. x, 193p ISBN 1-55612-247-0 LC 88-60114
An American in Rome. O'Grady, Desmond. *OSV* 81:13 Ja 3 1993
Catholic League gets a fighter at the helm. Holton, Robert. *OSV* 82:17 Jl 4 1993
The Catholic moment (address at the National Center for the Laity, 11-1-92, Chicago). O'Brien, David J, 1938-. *ACHSR* 103:1-10 Aut 1992
Challenges for the Christian layperson in the coming millenium [repr and tr fr *Mensaje*]. Etchegaray, Alberto. *LADOC* 23:12-16 Mr-Ap 1993
Collaborators, informers and secret service. Watkins, Clare. *New Blckfrs* 74:263-279 My 1993
Crisi Dei Valori: Una Terapia Comune Tra Laici E Cattolici? Mucci, Giandomenico. *Civilta* 143:450-457 D 5 1992
Deep river: the Christian vocation of the laity. Hayes, Diana L. *Spir Life* 39:131-136 Aut 1993
Evangelization through institutional sponsorship. Hauke, Mary C. *Health Prog* 74:48-50+ O 1993
The freedom and responsibility of the laity. Burke, Cormac. *HPR* 93:19-27 Jl 1993
John of the Cross and the laity. Doohan, Leonard. *Spir Life* 39:164-172 Aut 1993
Laity in the Year 2000. *Listening* 28:6-90 Wint 1993*
Light in the Lord. Hume, George Basil, Cardinal, 1923-. Minnesota: The Liturgical Press, 1991. x, 174p ISBN 0-8146-2142-2 LC 92-43998
New world laity casts off chains of command. D'Antonio, William V. *Nat Cath Rep* 29:11-12 N 20 1992
No less zeal: a spiritual guide for Catholic lay people. Morin, Douglas J. New York: Alba House, 1993. x, 142p ISBN 0-8189-0631-6 LC 92-34242
Priests welcome lay participation. *Tablet* 247:1175 S 11 1993
Quaestiones de officiis ecclesiasticis laicorum. Erdö, Peter. *Periodica* 81 no 2: 179-209 1992
Quaestiones de officiis ecclesiasticis laicorum. Erdö, Peter. *Periodica* 81 no 2: 179-209 1992
Razing the bastions: on the church in this age. Balthasar, Hans Urs Von, 1905-1988. San Francisco: Ignatius Press, 1993. ISBN 0-89870-428-6
Religione, laicismo e postmodernità. Mucci, Giandomenico. *Civilta* 144:131-139 Ja 16 1993
The religious strain. Mac Conghail, Muriris. *Furrow* 44:292-296 My 1993
Themes of the lay life. Keightley, Georgia Masters. *Origins* 22:761-764 Ap 15 1993
Toward service to the church. Leonhardy, Lee. *OSV* 81:6-7 F 7 1993
Towards Christian unity through the kenosis of the churches. Orsy, Ladislas, 1921-. *Ecumen Trends* 22:6-10 Jl-Ag 1993
A vocation for lay persons [interview by Lou Jacquet]. Coppinger, John. *OSV* 82:6 My 2 1993

LAITY—CONGRESSES
Called to action Catholics raise voices from "below". Gibeau, Dawn. *Nat Cath Rep* 29:3-4 N 20 1992

LAITY—HISTORY
Cistercian laybrothers in the twelfth and twentieth centuries. Greenia, Conrad. *Cist Stud* 27 No 4:341-351 1992
An historian's perspective: then, now, and then? Killen, Patricia O'Connell. *Listening* 28:14-27 Wint 1993
The laity in the Middle Ages: religious practices and experiences. Vauchez, André. Notre Dame: University of Notre Dame, 1993. x, 350p ISBN 0-268-01297-0 LC 92-53746
Ministry: lay ministry in the Catholic Church, its history and theology. Osborne, Kenan B. New Jersey: Paulist Press, 1993. x, 722p ISBN 0-8091-3371-7 LC 92-40299

LAITY—HISTORY—1300-1600
Laybrothers and laysisters in Frisia and Holland: circa 1300-circa 1600. Moor, Geertruida, de. *Cist Stud* 27 No 4:329-339 1992

LAMB, MATTHEW L
Habermas e la teologia. Brena, Gian Luigi. *Civilta* 3:51-54 Jl 3 1993

LAMB OF GOD
This is the Lamb of God. Inman, Anne. *New Blckfrs* 74:191-197 Ap 1993

LAMENT, BOLESLAWA MARIA, 1862-1946
John Paul II, Pope, (1991-06-05) Litterae Apostolicae (Apostolic Letters) [Latin]. John Paul II, Pope, 1920- (Karol Wojtyla) (elected 1978). *AAS* 84: 945-946 O 3 1992*

LAMENTS
Lament and light: embodying our grief. Schroeder, Celeste N. *Mod Lit* 20:14-16 S 1993

LAMONT, NORMAN, 1942-
The flaw in the budget. Keegan, William. *Tablet* 247:358 Mr 20 1993

LAND
Human rights as land rights in the Pacific. May, John D'Arcy. *Pacifica* 6:61-80 F 1993

LAND (THEOLOGY)- LATIN AMERICA
La tierra. *Christus* 58:45-47 My 1993

LAND REFORM
Reflections on Santo Domingo. Linden, Ian. *Month* 26:17-21 Ja 1993

LANDINO, CRISTOFORO
Albert the Great in the renaissance: Cristoforo Landino's use of Albert on the soul. McNair, Bruce G. *Mod Schlmn* 70:115-129 Ja 1993

LANGEAC, AGNES DE JESUS GALAND DE, 1602-1634
Congregation for the Causes of Saints (1992-12-21) Decree on a miracle. Congregation for the Causes of Saints. *OR(Eng)* 1272:4 Ja 6 1993

LANGUAGE
Dancing Sophia: Rahner's theology of symbols. Clasby, Nancy. *Relig Lit* 25: 51-65 Spr 1993
Talking dirty. Finley, Mitchel B. *OSV* 82:6 S 26 1993
When words fail us. Paige, Harry W, 1922-. *Liguorian* 81:52-56 Ag 1993
Who can utter the Name of God?—From the holiness of his name to the seriousness of all words. Sales, Michel. *Communio* 20:26-48 Spr 1993

LANGUAGE—PHILOSOPHY
The crisis of the subject: from Baroque to postmodern. Reijen, Willem van. *PhilosTod* 36:310-323 Wint 1992
Le discours théologique et son objet: perspectives neo-pragmatistes. Viau, Marcel. *Laval Theol Phil* 49:233-248 Je 1993
Eliminative naturalism and artistic meaning. Pylkkö, Pauli. *PhilosTod* 37: 183-200 Sum 1993
Frege's error. Ruthrof, Horst. *PhilosTod* 37:306-317 Aut 1993
Logica, Plenguatge i matematica. Graell i Deniel, Ferran. Barcelona: Anthropos, 1993. x, 377p ISBN 84-7658-399-0
Of medicine and metaphor: significant findings from Walker Percy. Allsopp, Michael E. *Linacre* 60:48-55 F 1993
The place of Phronesis in postmodern hermeneutics. Gallagher, Shaun. *PhilosTod* 37:298-305 Aut 1993
The search for implicit axioms behind doctrinal texts. Ritschl, Dietrich. *Gregorianum* 74 no 2:207-221 1993
Weder Gold noch Silber. Biser, Eugen. *Stimm Zeit* 211:343-350 My 1993

LANGUAGE—STUDY
Critica del lenguaje ordinario. Madrid: Libertarias, 1993. x, 780p ISBN 84-7683-252-2
Manies i afrodismes. Rubert de Ventos, Xavier. Barcelona: Edicions 62, 1993. x, 107p ISBN 84-297-3651-4

LANGUAGE AND CULTURE
Critica del lenguaje ordinario. Madrid: Libertarias, 1993. x, 780p ISBN 84-7683-252-2

LANGUAGE AND RELIGION
The catechetical role of the liturgy and the quality of liturgical texts: the current ICEL translation. Leiva-Merikakis, Erasmo. *Communio* 20:63-83 Spr 1993
The Catechism [commentary]. O'Brien, Dennis. *Comm* 120:15-16 My 7 1993
Preaching and poetry: Gerard Manley Hopkins. Morneau, Robert F, Bp, 1938-. *Emmanuel* 99:460-464 O 1993
The sweetness of the Lord: Dulcis and Suavis. Scholl, Edith. *Cist Stud* 27 No 4:359-366 1992
La théologie comme science et la voction de savant d'après Max Weber. Gendron, Pierre. *Laval Theol Phil* 49:215-222 Je 1993
Weder Gold noch Silber. Biser, Eugen. *Stimm Zeit* 211:343-350 My 1993

LANGUAGE ARTS
The computer: it isn't just for math anymore. Coburn, Janet. *Tod Cath Teach* 27:46+ S 1993
Fabulous classics. Dreher, Barbara. *Tod Cath Teach* 27:42-45 S 1993
Kindling a love for reading and reasoning. Pankiewicz, Mary Ann. *Momentum* 24:44-46 S-O 1993

LAROCHELLE, GILBERT
That which resists, after all [conversation between cited authors]. Lyotard, Jean-François, and Larochelle, Gilbert. *PhilosTod* 36:402-417 Wint 1992

LAS CASAS, BARTOLOME DE, 1474-1566
Ak'Kutan, Centro "Bartolomé de Las Casas". Diez, Carlos. *Cien Tom* 120: 169-175 Ja-Ap 1993
Bartolomé de Las Casas en el V Centenario: revisión de su figura y de su doctrina moral. Osuna, Antonio. *Cien Tom* 119:459-498 S-D 1992
Las Casas und seine Gegner. Delgado, Mariano. *Stimm Zeit* 210:841-854 D 1992
The Dominican school of Salamanca and the Spanish conquest of America: some bibliographical notes. O'Meara, Thomas Franklin. *Thomist* 56:555-582 O 1992
Francisco de Vitoria y Bartolomé de Las Casas. Hernández, Ramón. *Cien Tom* 119:433-457 S-D 1992

LAST SUPPER
Presence or absence? the question of women disciples at the Last Supper. Lee, Dorothy A. *Pacifica* 6:1-20 F 1993

LATIN AMERICA—CHURCH HISTORY
Complexities of conversion: Latin American and European encounter—500 years. Kirk, Pamela. *Living Light* 29:22-34 Wint 1992

LATIN AMERICA—RELIGION
Articulaciones Ante la llegada del v centenario. *Christus* 57:24-28 S 1992
500 anos: história e evangelização. Beozzo, Josús Oscar. *Perspectiva* 24:291-312 S-D 1992

LATIN AMERICA—SOCIAL CONDITIONS
John Paul II, Pope, (1992-10-11) America, open your doors to Christ. John Paul II, Pope, 1920- (Karol Wojtyla) (elected 1978). *TPS* 38:78-83 Mr-Ap 1993*
500 anos: história e evangelização. Beozzo, Josús Oscar. *Perspectiva* 24:291-312 S-D 1992

LATIN AMERICA—SOCIAL ECONOMIC CONDITIONS
La iglesia en America Latina. Roux, Francisco J de. *Christus* 58:38-46 N-D 1992

LATIN LANGUAGE
Don't fight. Just ignore. [editorial]. Schuler, Richard Joseph, 1920-. *SacM* 120:4-5 Aut 1993
A mass at Verdun. Boughton, Willis L. *HPR* 94:55-58 O 1993
"Missa Latina," yes. Bowman, Jim. *Comm* 120:6-7 O 8 1993
The shape of things to come in liturgy. Hanshell, Deryck. *SacM* 119:15-18 Wint 1992
Study Greek and Latin! Reflections of a housewife. Rist, Anna. *Can Cath Rev* 11:12-15 Ja 1993

LATIN LITERATURE
What's in a pedigree? Alcimus Avitus, De Spir Hist Gest 2 50-52, and Juvenal, Sat 8 140-41. Magee, John. *Med Stud* 54:317-326 1992

LATIN LITERATURE, MEDIEVAL AND MODERN
Evidence for the use of Adam of Buckfield's writings at Paris: a note on New Haven, Yale University, Historical-Medical Library 12. Noone, Timothy B. *Med Stud* 54:308-316 1992

LATVIA—RELIGION
Latvia growing stronger, but struggles remain. O'Grady, Desmond. *OSV* 82:6-7 S 12 1993

LAUGHTER
Get serious! The monastic condemnation of laughter. Russell, Kenneth C. *RRel* 52:371-379 My-Je 1993
Laughter is the best medicine. Bragan, Jeris. *New Cov* 22:33-34 Ja 1993

LAURICENA, DONA
O evangelho segundo Dona Lauricena. Mori, Geraldo Luis De. *Perspectiva* 25:197-227 My-Ag 1993

LAW
The ethics of conquest: the European background of Spain's mission in the New World. Olsen, Glenn Warren, 1938-. *Communio* 19:619-364 Wint 1992
A window on the Good Book. Lapin, Daniel. *Crisis* 11:10-11 Jl-Ag 1993

LAW—CASES
Verdicts and videos [editorial]. *Comm* 120:3-4 N 19 1993

LAW—HISTORY
The structure of legal systems. Barton, Thomas D. *Amer J Juris* 37:291-317 1992

LAW—PHILOSOPHY
La fondation des lois civiles. Goyard-Fabre, Simone. *Laval Theol Phil* 49: 105-119 F 1993
The philosophy of air law. Abeyratne, R I R. *Amer J Juris* 37:135-144 1992
Rechtsphilosophie. Brieskorn, Norbert. *Stimm Zeit* 211:318-330 My 1993
The structure of legal systems. Barton, Thomas D. *Amer J Juris* 37:291-317 1992

LAW- ITALY
Considerazioni giuridiche sulla chiamata di correo. Passano, Paolo Ferrari Da. *Cívilta* 2:29-43 Ap 3 1993

LAW- PHILIPPINES
The application of law: some recurring aspects of the process of judicial review and decision making. Feliciano, Florentino P. *Amer J Juris* 37:17-56 1992

LAW- SOUTH AFRICA
Why positivism is authoritarian. Dyzenhaus, David. *Amer J Juris* 37:83-112 1992

LAW- UNITED STATES
The limits of natural law: Thomas Rutherforth and the American legal tradition. McDowell, Gary L. *Amer J Juris* 37:57-81 1992

LAW, BERNARD FRANCIS, CARDINAL, 1931-
Boston's cardinal-archbishop [interview by G Sherry; photos]. *OSV* 81:12-13 Ja 31 1993

LAW AND ETHICS
The actual validity of law. Sellers, Mortimer. *Amer J Juris* 37:283-290 1992
The ethical foundations of judicial decision-making. Grib, Philip J. *CLawyer* 35 no 1:1-55 1993
Interpreting moral doctrine: Newman on conscience and law. Magill, Gerard. *Horizons (CTS)* 20:7-22 Spr 1993
Is there a natural law right to privacy? Gaebler, Ralph F. *Amer J Juris* 37: 319-336 1992
Rechtsphilosophie. Brieskorn, Norbert. *Stimm Zeit* 211:318-330 My 1993
Sexual morality's positive goals and the problem of legalism. George, Robert P. *Origins* 22:778-780 Ap 22 1993

LAW AND RELIGION
Abortion and the right to life. *Doctr Life* 42:336-344 My-Je 1992
La fondation des lois civiles. Goyard-Fabre, Simone. *Laval Theol Phil* 49: 105-119 F 1993
Freedom from the law in early Christianity. Räisänen, Heikki. *TheolDgst* 40: 43-48 Spr 1993
The teleology of law: responsible citizenship and discipleship. Araujo, Robert J. *CLawyer* 35 no 1:57-78 1993

LAWRENCE, STEPHEN
Tablet couple witness racist tragedy. *Tablet* 247:831-832 Je 26 1993

LAWRENCE OF THE RESURRECTION, 1614-1691
The conversion of Brother Lawrence. Beaufort, Joseph De. *Spir Life* 39:4-5 Spr 1993

LAWYERS

Law as ministry: a perspective from the Judaeo-Christian tradition. Enman, Fred M. *CLawyer* 35 no 1:97-107 1993

Morals for home, morals for office: the double ethical life of a civil litigator. Rizzo, Patricia L. *CLawyer* 35 no 1:79-96 1993

LAWYERS—COSTUME

Will balder heads prevail? Bruel, John S. *Crisis* 10:6-7 N 1992

LAY APOSTOLATE *see* Catholic Action

LAY MINISTRY

Aging becomes them. Anderson, Chris. *Comm* 120:5-6 Ag 13 1993

Are all Christian ministers? Collins, John N. Collegeville: The Liturgical Press, 1992. x, 168p ISBN 0-8146-2168-6 LC 92-9599

Bringing the priceless gift of the Eucharist. Dodds, Bill. *New Cov* 22:16-18 Ja 1993

Can laity do more than hunt, shoot and entertain? [comments on book by author, pt 1 of 2]. Shaw, Russell. *OSV* 82:17 N 7 1993

The Church must stop cheating the engaged. Foley, Gerald. *St Anth* 101:10-13 Je 1993

Clericalism and its discontents [comments on book by author, pt 2 of 2]. Shaw, Russell. *OSV* 82:16 N 14 1993

Collaborative ministry: communion, contention, commitment. Cooper, Norman P. New York: Paulist Press, 1993. x, 200p ISBN 0-8091-3376-8 LC 92-38074

Converting the youth minister. Reicher, Chris. *Mod Lit* 20:8-12 Ag 1993

An example of substantial lay responsibility [Minnesota Parish]. Wood, Charles. *Priest* 49:42-45 My 1993

"Faith is strengthened when it is given to others!" [photos]. Cosgrove, Jim, and Brankin, Patrick. *Extensn* 88:8-15 Jl 1993

Forming lay prayer leaders. Arnold, Linda M, and Gallagher, Patricia. *Past Mus* 17:14-15 Je-Jl 1993

The freedom and responsibility of the laity. Burke, Cormac. *HPR* 93:19-27 Jl 1993

Horizons of the charism of an institute: the "new" participation of the lay faithful. Secondin, Bruno. *Con Life* 17 no 2:83-97 1992

How much is lay ministry worth? Kinast, Robert L. *Origins* 23:287-292 O 7 1993

It's time for some Holy Name changes. Holton, Robert. *OSV* 82:13 S 26 1993

John Paul II, Pope, (1993-07-02) Women. John Paul II, Pope, 1920- (Karol Wojtyla) (elected 1978). *Origins* 23:124-126 Jl 15 1993*

Lay partners. Kelly, Joseph F. *AFER* 34:382-384 D 1992

Leaders in tomorrow's church: current situation and future challenges. Burns, Camilla, and Elsbernd, Mary. *Chicago Stud* 32:143-155 Ag 1993

Mary Mauren healer of hearts. Thiele, Gloria. *St Anth* 100:40-43+ Ja 1993

Ministry: lay ministry in the Catholic Church, its history and theology. Osborne, Kenan B. New Jersey: Paulist Press, 1993. x, 722p ISBN 0-8091-3371-7 LC 92-40299

New parish ministers: laity & religious on parish staffs. Murnion, Philip J, 1938-. New York: National Pastoral Life Center, 1992. 131p ISBN 1-88130-701-8

Preparing for the future church. McDermott, Philomena. *Priests & People* 7:61-64 F 1993

Priests and laity promote renewal. Miller, Annabel. *Tablet* 247:1205-1206 S 18 1993

Reaching out—honey vs vinegar. Ganss, Karl, and Fuller, Kathleen. *Tod Parish* 25:7-8 Ap-My 1993

Small Christian communities: what parish ministers need to know. Howard, Barbara. *Tod Parish* 25:9-12 Ap-My 1993

"To form an elite body of laymen" Terence J Shealy, SJ, and the laymen's league, 1911-1922. McShane, Joseph M, 1949-. *CHist* 78:557-580 O 1992

Waiting in the wings: will laypeople take a leading role in the church? [a reader's survey]. Smith, Karen Sue. *USCath* 58:6-13 F 1993

We are all called to be missionaries. John Paul II, Pope, 1920- (Karol Wojtyla) (elected 1978). *Extensn* 88:16 Jl 1993

8 hands-on ministries that promote justice. Humphrey, Kelly Norton. *Salt* 13:7-12 N-D 1993

LAY MINISTRY- GUYANA

Lay ministry transforms a parish in Guyana. Connors, Patrick. *America* 168:14-15 F 13 1993

LAY MINISTRY- NIGERIA

Nigeria report of activities of the national liturgy commission. Congregation for Divine Worship and Discipline of the Sacraments. *Notitiae* 28:191-192 Mr 1992

LAY READERS

From reform to renewal. Nijem, Fred. *Mod Lit* 20:6-8 My 1993

Proclamation primer. Klarner, Anne. *Mod Lit* 20:12-13 My 1993

LAZARUS, RAISING OF (MIRACLE) *see* Raising of Lazarus (Miracle)

LEADERSHIP

A credible, effective force for Catholic healthcare. Curley, John E, Jr. *Health Prog* 74:14-15+ Jl-Ag 1993

Developing leadership among urban youth. Brown, A J, Jr. *Momentum* 24:46-47+ Ap-My 1993

Integrating the ideas of dissenting economists into a theory of transformational leadership. Wallis, Joe L. *RSocEcon* 51:14-39 Spr 1993

Leadership for mission: a key agenda for the 1990s. Hinojosa, Juan Lorenzo. *Health Prog* 74:62-63+ O 1993

A short-lived spring. Perko, F Michael. *Month* 26:313-314 Ag 1993

You need more than good technique. Fischer, Mark F. *Tod Parish* 25:23-26 13-17 S 1993

LEADERSHIP, RELIGIOUS

Christians prepare to monitor electoral process. Rickard, Carmel. *Tablet* 247:732+ Je 5 1993

Church leaders react to NATO's threat. *Tablet* 247:1053-1054 Ag 14 1993

Church leaders voice disgust and contempt at IRA bombing. *Tablet* 247:416 Mr 27 1993

Churches tackle London's racism. *Tablet* 247:1310-1311 O 9 1993

Conflicting styles of parish leadership: two responses. Rosinski, Geri, and Mannion, M Francis. *New Theol Rev* 6:95-101 My 1993

The laity and the leadership crisis. Steinfels, Margaret O'Brien, 1941-. *Comm* 120:8+ S 10 1993

Leadership, authority, and religious government. Linscott, Mary. *RRel* 52:166-193 Mr-Ap 1993

The ministry of women in the early Church. Gillman, Florence Morgan. *New Theol Rev* 6:89-94 My 1993

Religious-leadership competencies. Nygren, David J. *RRel* 52:390-417 My-Je 1993

Ritual leave-taking. Foley, Edward. *RRel* 52:691-701 S-O 1993

Take the lead. Costello, Andrew. *USCath* 58:40-42 Jl 1993

When Chicago Catholics were second to none. Costello, Gerald M, 1931-. *USCath* 58:48-51 Jl 1993

Word faiths for peace. Willey, David. *Tablet* 247:1276-1277 O 2 1993

LEADERSHIP CONFERENCE OF WOMEN RELIGIOUS

Leadership, authority, and religious government. Linscott, Mary. *RRel* 52:166-193 Mr-Ap 1993

Would that all were prophets. Bergant, Dianne. *RRel* 52:340-349 My-Je 1993

LEARNING, PSYCHOLOGY OF

Homework: a fresh approach to a perennial problem. Marino, Joseph F. *Momentum* 24:69-71 F-Mr 1993

Ten hints for adult educators. McHugh, Thomas. *Priests & People* 7:65-66 F 1993

LEARNING AND SCHOLARSHIP

Archives: disposition of personal papers. Baumstein, Paschal. *CLW* 64:20-21 Jl-S 1993

Cooperative learning: go for it!. Hennessy, Joan. *ReligTJ* 27:32-33 O 1993

An invitation to dance: towards a spirituality of education. Stoecklin, Carol. *Living Light* 29:58-64 Aut 1992

LEBANON—PEACE

John Paul II, Pope, (1993-08-01) Peace [Orig in Italian]. John Paul II, Pope, 1920- (Karol Wojtyla) (elected 1978). *OR(Eng)* 1302:1 Ag 11 1993*

LEBANON—RELIGION

Goodbye Lebanon. Butt, Gerald. *Tablet* 247:460-461 Ap 10-17 1993

LEBANON—SOCIAL CONDITIONS

Goodbye Lebanon. Butt, Gerald. *Tablet* 247:460-461 Ap 10-17 1993

LECLERCQ, JACQUES

En relisant l'amour des lettres et le désir de Dieu. Dumont, Camille. *NRT* 114:889-895 N-D 1992

LECTIONARIES

The birth and growth of the lectionary. Krosnicki, Thomas A. *Past Mus* 17:23-25 D 1992-Ja 1993

The lectionary: a resource for general intercessions. Boisclair, Regina A. *Liturgy* 11:9-13 Sum 1993

"Thanks be to God" the Bible and the liturgy. Collins, Thomas. *Can Cath Rev* 11:7-13 Je 20 1993

LEE, SPIKE

"Malcolm X" di Spike Lee. Fantuzzi, Virgilio. *Civilta* 3:154-161 Jl 17 1993

LEGAL ETHICS

Moral debate and social change. Edmondson, Ricca. *Doctr Life* 42:233-243 My-Je 1992

LEGION OF MARY

Father Faber and the Legion's concluding prayer [fr *Maria Legionis* v 34, no 2, 1991]. Nolan, Herman. *ChrWorld* 37:372-375 N-D 1992

LEGRAND, HERVE

Response to Hervé Legrand. Voyé, Liliane. *Jurist* 52 no 1:401-410 1992

LEHMANN, KARL, BP, 1936-

Mass rape revealed by German TV. *Tablet* 246:1579 D 12 1992

LEIBOVITCH, ISAIAH

Judaism: people or religion? some positions in modern Jewish thought. Meir, Ephraim. *SIDIC* 25 No 1:20-25 1992

LEISURE

Waiting for a gift from the sea. Foley, Sharon. *Sisters* 65:301-303 Jl 1993

LENT

Among ourselves. Weinert, Allan. *Liguorian* 81:1 F 1993

Backpack meditations for Lent. Schneider, Valerie. New York: Paulist Press, 1990. 57p ISBN 0-8091-3195-1 LC 90-41230

Cardinal Newman on the season of Lent. Oakes, Edward T. *America* 168:7-12 Ap 3 1993

The cross: a sign of love. Glavich, Kathleen. *ReligTJ* 27:12-13 F 1993

The facts of death: some reflections for Lent. Anderson, Paul. *New Cov* 22:26-30 My 1993

Good news: alive and well. Agnesine, M, and Buschman-Kelly, Mary Ann. *ReligTJ* 27:18-19 F 1993

A gospel guide to the season. Stravinskas, Peter. *Register* 69:1+ F 21 1993

In the mood for lent. Gardner, M Judith. *New Cov* 22:14-15 F 1993

In touch with Jesus. Becker, Mary Lee. *ReligTJ* 27:14-15 Mr 1993

John, theologian and poet, traces the signs of Christ's divine identity. Stravinskas, Peter. *Register* 69:1+ F 28 1993

Lent and Lazarus. Dodds, Bill. *New Cov* 22:18+ Mr 1993

Lent and the seven gifts of the Holy Spirit. Dimock, Giles. *OSV* 81:5 F 21 1993

Lent is a time for giving. Neuberger, Anne E. *ReligTJ* 27:34 F 1993

Lent. Mueller, Therese. *Mod Lit* 20:34-35 N 1993

Lent: a time for what? Mick, Lawrence E. *Tod Parish* 25:31-32+ Ja 1993

Lenten box projects. Inkel, Maxine. *ReligTJ* 27:19 Mr 1993

Mardi Gras leads to lent. Fanning, Jim, and Schumacher, Stacy. *ReligTJ* 27:24-30 F 1993

Praying the passion: living the Gospel-scriptual reflections for adult believers. Cornwell, Malcolm. Collegeville:Liturgical, 1993. 76p ISBN 0-8146-2220-8 LC 92-40656

Reaching into the past. Gillie, Joyce. *ReligTJ* 27:38 F 1993

Reflective action: a lenten liturgical dance workshop. *Liturgy* 10:37-41 Sum 1992

Shaping the celebrations. *Liturgy* 10:22-32 Sum 1992

The Spirit's gift of wisdom. Dimock, Giles. *OSV* 81:5 F 28 1993

Stealing for lent. Costello, Andrew. *USCath* 58:38-40 Mr 1993

Il tema della "Luce" nella liturgia della quaresima, della pasqua e del tempo pasquale. Ferraro, Giuseppe. *Civilta* 144:547-558 Mr 20 1993

What do they value? Sabatowich, Jerome. *ReligTJ* 27:31 F 1993

Il tema della "Luce" nella liturgia della quaresima, della pasqua e del tempo pasquale. Ferraro, Giuseppe. *Civilta* 144:547-558 Mr 20 1993

LIGONDE, FRANCOISE-WOLFF
Haitian Archbishop Ligonde back from exile. Slavin, J P. *Nat Cath Rep* 29:9 N 20 1992

LILLI, SALVATORE, 1853-1895
John Paul II, Pope, (1982-10-03) Litterae Apostolicae (Apostolic Letters) [Letters]. John Paul II, Pope, 1920- (Karol Wojtyla) (elected 1978). *AAS* 84:940-942 O 3 1992*

LIMBAUGH, RUSH, 1951-
The dangerous Rush Limbaugh. Sobran, Joseph. *Crisis* 11:18-21 My 1993
It's not hell, just Limbaugh: excellence in bombast. McConnell, Frank, 1942-. *Comm* 120:20+ Je 4 1993

LIMBURG STIRUM, ROLAND HUGH VAN
John Paul II, Pope, (1991-09-30) Allocutiones (Speech for reception of credentials) [French]. John Paul II, Pope, 1920- (Karol Wojtyla) (elected 1978). *AAS* 84:848-850 S 8 1992*

LIMINALITY
Boundary-dwellers. Ward, Hannah. *Way* 33:97-105 Ap 1993

LINCOLN, ABRAHAM
A birthday tribute to Father Abraham. Griffin, Robert F. *OSV* 81:18 F 21 1993

LINDBERGH, ANN MORROW
Waiting for a gift from the sea. Foley, Sharon. *Sisters* 65:301-303 Jl 1993

LINGUISTIC ANALYSIS (LINGUISTICS)
Textlinguistics and the integrity of Philippians. Koperski, Veronica. *Eph Theol Lovan* 78:330-367 D 1992

LISTENING
Amongst women. Kimmerling, Ben. *Furrow* 44:273-282 My 1993
Authority (2): an essay on the place of the text in Buddhist and Christian formation. Corless, Roger. *Stud Form Spir* 14:31-39 F 1993
Feminist theology, evangelisation and the embodiment of truth. Grey, Mary. *Month* 25:485-490 D 1992
Giving emotional support. Fry, Patricia L. *St Anth* 101:38-41 N 1993
"I am the Messiah and you're not". Ganss, Karl, and Fuller, Kathleen. *Tod Parish* 25:18-19 O 1993
Is anybody listening? Kollar, Judith Ann. *Tod Parish* 25:4-5 Mr 1993
Listening and liturgy. MacCarthy, Peter T. *SacM* 120:34-38 Aut 1993
Listening. Wilkinson, Gertrude A. *Living Prayer* 26:1 Mr-Ap 1993
The lure of honey. Cassidy, Sheila. *Tablet* 247:1068-1069 Ag 21 1993
Saints know how to listen. MacClennan, Carole. *ReligTJ* 27:34-35 O 1993

LITERARY MOVEMENTS
Schlesien in der polnischen Gegenwartsliteratur. Zybura, Marek. *Stimm Zeit* 211:197-209 Mr 1993

LITERATURE
Lo *J'AccuseDi Maurice Chavardès Contro L'Ipocrisia.* Castelli, Ferdinando. *Civilta* 143:376-381 N 21 1992
La literatura mesopotámica antigua. Moreno Garrido, Jaime. *Teol Vida* 33 no 3-4:237-254 1992
Plain beauty. Costello, Gerald M, 1931-. *USCath* 58:48-51 My 1993

LITERATURE—ETHICAL ASPECTS
Sobre virtudes y vicios: tres ejercicios literario filosoficos. Garcia Bacca, Juan David. Madrid: Anthropos, 1993. x, 87p ISBN 84-7658-396-6

LITERATURE—PSYCHOLOGY
La locura compartida. Rendueles Olmedo, Guillermo. Asturias: Belladona, 1993. x, 1993 ISBN 84-604-5959-4

LITERATURE—STUDY AND TEACHING
Peter Wimsey—Ein Lord braucht seinen Mord. Steinacker, Hans. *Stimm Zeit* 211:403-412 Je 1993

LITERATURE—THEMES
Jesus im modernen Roman. Langenhorst, Georg. *Stimm Zeit* 210:819-830 D 1992
Karl Barth et Dostoïevski. Roussel, Jean-François. *Laval Theol Phil* 49:37-55 F 1993

LITERATURE- FRANCE
Un arbre en plein vent. Joassart, Bernard. *NRT* 115:243-245 Mr-Ap 1993

LITERATURE, COMPARATIVE
Das beschädigte Land. Kurz, Paul Konrad. *Stimm Zeit* 211:663-678 O 1993
Jesus im modernen Roman. Langenhorst, Georg. *Stimm Zeit* 210:819-830 D 1992
Karl Barth et Dostoïevski. Roussel, Jean-François. *Laval Theol Phil* 49:37-55 F 1993

LITERATURE, GERMAN
Das Erbe des Gedenkens. Bleistein, Roman, 1928-. *Stimm Zeit* 211:351-352 My 1993
Es geht um mehr als Christa Wolf. Kurz, Paul Konrad. *Stimm Zeit* 211:352-356 My 1993
Peter Wimsey—Ein Lord braucht seinen Mord. Steinacker, Hans. *Stimm Zeit* 211:403-412 Je 1993
Das Problem der Heiligkeit in unserer Zeit. Stelzmann, Rainulf A. *Stimm Zeit* 211:489-500 Jl 1993

LITERATURE, JEWISH
The search for original sin. Stuhlmueller, Carroll. *BibleT* 31:73-78 Mr 1993

LITERATURE, MEDIEVAL
Saint Bernard's third sermon for the feast of the Annunciation and a play from the N-town cycle. Hufgard, M Kilian. *Cist Stud* 28 no 2:167-178 1993

LITERATURE, MODERN—1900-
Schlesien in der polnischen Gegenwartsliteratur. Zybura, Marek. *Stimm Zeit* 211:197-209 Mr 1993
Three good stories that didn't make the list. Costello, Gerald M, 1931-. *USCath* 58:48-51 S 1993

LITERATURE AND CHRISTIANITY
Investigating Herbert criticism. Stewart, Stanley. *Renascence* 45:131-158 Spr 1993
"Me thoughts I heard one calling, child!": Herbert's *The Collar*. Roberts, John R. *Renascence* 45:196-204 Spr 1993
Oscar Wilde E Il Suo Cristo Romantico. Castelli, Ferdinando. *Civilta* 144:31-44 Ja 2 1993

Willa Cather and the literature of Christian mystery. Murphy, John J. *Relig Lit* 24:39-56 Aut 1992

LITERATURE AND CHRISTIANITY- BRAZIL
O evangelho segundo Dona Lauricena. Mori, Geraldo Luis De. *Perspectiva* 25:197-227 My-Ag 1993

LITERATURE AND MORALS- GERMANY
Von realer Gegenwart. Kurz, Paul Konrad. *Stimm Zeit* 211:547-559 Ag 1993

LITERATURE AND RELIGION
Emily Dickinson's lectio: wicked as I am, I read my Bible sometimes. Norris, Kathleen. *Sisters* 65:104-108 Mr 1993
Hans Carossa und Rupert Mayer. Bleistein, Roman, 1928-. *Stimm Zeit* 211:105-114 F 1993
"I saw a Kingfisher": grace and ruin in Golding's the spire. Yeager, D M. *Horizons (CTS)* 20:44-66 Spr 1993
Karl Barth et Dostoïevski. Roussel, Jean-François. *Laval Theol Phil* 49:37-55 F 1993
La letterature interpella la teologia. Castelli, Ferdinando. *Civilta* 3:247-255 Ag 7-21 1993
Myth and culture in theology and literature [interview by R. Adams]. Dunne, John S, 1929-. *Relig Lit* 25:79-104 Sum 1993
Racconta il tuo Dio. Castelli, Ferdinando. *Civilta* 2:563-565 Je 19 1993
Roman Brandstaetter narratore delle profondità. Castelli, Ferdinando. *Civilta* 2:130-143 Ap 17 1993
The synoptic gospels source criticism and the new literary criticism. Focant, C. *Eph Theol Lovan* 78:494-499 D 1992
Tragedy as subclause: George Steiner's dialogue with Donald MacKinnon. Ward, Graham. *Heythrop* 34:274-287 Jl 1993
L'uomo e il suo destino. Salvini, Gianpaolo. *Civilta* 3:256-262 Ag 7-21 1993
Von realer Gegenwart. Kurz, Paul Konrad. *Stimm Zeit* 211:547-559 Ag 1993

LITHUANIA—POLITICS AND GOVERNMENT
Party on, comrades. Luxmoore, Jonathan. *Register* 69:1+ My 16 1993

LITHUANIA—RELIGIOUS LIFE
John Paul II, Pope, (1993-09-05) Independence. John Paul II, Pope, 1920- (Karol Wojtyla) (elected 1978). *Origins* 23:233 S 16 1993*
Pope visits Baltics amid promise, perils. Hebblethwaite, Peter, 1930-. *Nat Cath Rep* 29:11-12 S 17 1993

LITHUANIA—SOCIAL CONDITIONS
Lithuania awaits renewal. Luxmoore, Jonathan. *Tablet* 247:1124-1125 S 4 1993

LITTLE SISTERS OF JESUS
A meeting of elders. Little Sister Beatrice. *Sisters* 65:181-182 My 1993

LITTLE SISTERS OF THE POOR
The first Little Sister [condensed fr *The Word Amoung Us* N 1992]. *CDgst* 57:47-50 F 1993
Little sisters who beg [condensed fr *Catholic Standard* O 15 1992]. Zimmermann, Mark. *CDgst* 57:43-46 F 1993

LITURGICAL ADAPTION
In heaven there are no thunderstorms: celebrating the liturgy with developmentally disabled people. Okhuijsen, Gijs. Collegeville:Liturgical, 1992. 136p ISBN 0-81461-999-1 LC 91-41-4407

LITURGICAL LANGUAGE
What englishness is. Every, George. *New Blckfrs* 74:408-416 S 1993

LITURGICAL LANGUAGE- ENGLISH
Splitting the faithful: inclusive language is wrong biblically, pastorally, and doctrinally. Sokolowski, Robert, 1934-. *Crisis* 11:24-27 Mr 1993

LITURGICAL YEAR *see* Church Year

LITURGIES
Book of common worship, pastoral edition. Louisville: John Knox, 1993. x, 368p ISBN 0-664-22033-9
Women at worship: interpretations of North American diversity. Proctor-Smith, Marjorie, and Walton, Janet R. Louisville, Kentucky: John Knox Press, 1993. 272p ISBN 0-664-25253-2

LITURGY
Advice for liturgical orphans. Mankowski, Paul V. *America* 169:15+ Ag 28-S 4 1993
The assembly as proclaimer. Senn, Frank C. *Liturgy* 11:14-15 Sum 1993
At least two words: the liturgy as proclamation. Lathrop, Gordon. *Liturgy* 11:1-4 Sum 1993
Congregatio de Culto divino et disciplina sacramentorum. Congregation for Divine Worship and Discipline of the Sacraments. *Notitiae* 28:391-403 Je 1992
Credibilità della riforma liturgica. *Notitiae* 28:625-628 O 1992
The distortion of Christian ritual. Darragh, Neil. *Pacifica* 6:21-47 F 1993
Does your justice liturgy do justice to liturgy? Hutchinson, Robert. *Salt* 13:28-32 N-D 1993
Ecumenicity in Lake Wobegon [exc fr *Liturgy: the church and culture*]. Ugolnik, Anthony. *Liturgy* 10:14-15 Spr 1993
Encountering the holy [exc fr *Liturgy: the art of celebration; Liturgy: in daily life*]. Angell, Jeannette L, and Bower, Richard Allen. *Liturgy* 10:51-55 Spr 1993
España: encuentro anual de delegados diocesanos de liturgia. López, Martín, Julián. *Notitiae* 28:425-428 Je 1992
The eucharistic prayer. Gustin, Marilyn Norquist. *Liguorian* 81:46-50 Ag 1993
A fifty day celebration? Mick, Lawrence E. *Tod Parish* 25:30-33 Ap-My 1993
From reform to renewal. Nijem, Fred. *Mod Lit* 20:6-8 My 1993
Here's a catechetical resource waiting to be used. Ostdiek, Gilbert. *Past Mus* 17:28-30 Je-Jl 1993
Hermeneutics in the study of liturgical performance. Kelleher, Margaret Mary. *Worship* 67:292-318 Jl 1993
In Byzantine liturgy, heaven is brought down to earth. Ford, Paul, and Daurio, Janice. *Register* 69:1+ O 10 1993
John Paul II, Pope, (1992-12-17) Catechism. John Paul II, Pope, 1920- (Karol Wojtyla) (elected 1978). *OR(Eng)* 1272:8 Ja 6 1993*
Learning from one another [exc fr *Liturgy: practicing ecumenism*]. Henderson, J Frank. *Liturgy* 10:8-9 Spr 1993
Letter to a seminarian. Köpe, Károly. *SacM* 120:6-8 Aut 1993
Lettera al Prof Balthasar Fischer in occasione del suo 80 genetliaco. Javierre, Antonio M, Cardinal. *Notitiae* 28:584-585 S 1992

Differend and agonistics: a transcendental argument? Ruthrof, Horst. *PhilosTod* 36:324-335 Wint 1992
Just between us. Melville, Stephen. *PhilosTod* 36:367-376 Wint 1992
The place of Phronesis in postmodern hermeneutics. Gallagher, Shaun. *PhilosTod* 37:298-305 Aut 1993
That which resists, after all [conversation between cited authors]. Lyotard, Jean-François, and Larochelle, Gilbert. *PhilosTod* 36:402-417 Wint 1992

M

MAASAI (AFRICAN PEOPLE) *see* Masai (African People)
MAASTRICHT TREATY
Europe's future: is the Maastricht Treaty dead? Bogle, Joanna. *OSV* 81:3 Ap 18 1993
MACCARRONE, MICHELE-1993
Maccarrone, Michele, -1993 [obit]. *CHist* 79:600-601 Jl 1993
MACE, DAVID
Marriage and daily life: adult learning that really matters. Thomas, David M. *Tod Parish* 25:20-22 Ap-My 1993
MACEDONIA
Ancient Macedonia gropes for new paths [photos]. McCarthy, Tim. *Nat Cath Rep* 29:8-10 S 24 1993
MACEDONIA—POLITICS AND GOVERNMENT
Worse yet to come? Brown, Janice. *Comm* 120:4-5 Ja 29 1993
MACH, ELIZABETH
Lay missioner nurses victims of Sudan war [por]. Jones, Arthur C, 1936-. *Nat Cath Rep* 30:9 N 19 1993
MACHA, KAREL HYNEK, 1810-1836
Jan Patocka et le phénomène de l'écriture littéraire. Declève, Henri. *Laval Theol Phil* 49:3-26 F 1993
MACINTYRE, ALASDAIR C, 1929-
MacIntyre's postmodern Thomism: reflections on Three rival versions of moral enquiry. Hibbs, Thomas S. *Thomist* 57:277-297 Ap 1993
Reflections on after virtue after Auschwitz. Chansky, James D. *PhilosTod* 37:247-256 Aut 1993
MACKEY, STANISLAS, 1916-1989
The shooting of Sister Stan [condensed fr *Catholic Health World* D 1 1992]. Farren, Suzy. *CDgst* 57:112-117 My 1993
MACKILLOP, MARY HELEN, 1842-1902
Congregation for the Causes of Saints (1992-06-13) Decree on the heroic virtues. Congregation for the Causes of Saints. *TPS* 38:19-20 Ja-F 1993*
Congregation for the Causes of Saints (1992-06-13) Decree on the heroic virtues. Congregation for the Causes of Saints. *AAS* 85:85-89 Ja 7 1993*
Congregation for the Causes of Saints (1993-07-06) Decree on a miracle. Congregation for the Causes of Saints. *OR(Eng)* 1299:12 Jl 14 1993*
MACKINNON, DONALD
Tragedy as subclause: George Steiner's dialogue with Donald MacKinnon. Ward, Graham. *Heythrop* 34:274-287 Jl 1993
MADHYAMIKA (BUDDHIST SCHOOL)
Derrida and Mādhyamika Buddhism: from linguistic deconstruction to criticism of onto-theologies. Zong-qi, Cai. *IPQ* 33:183-195 Je 1993
MADISON, JAMES, 1751-1836
Madison's dilemma, and ours. Goldwin, Robert Allen, 1922-. *Crisis* 10:25-31 N 1992
MADONNA HOUSE (CANADA)
Madonna House: holiness through little things [photos]. Achterhoff, Mary. *OSV* 82:12-13 My 16 1993
MADONNAS
Our Lady of the chiseled heart [photo]. Gadoua, Renée K. *OSV* 82:12-13 N 21 1993
MAFIA- ITALY
Battere La Mafia Uiti Si Può. Sorge, Bartolomeo. *Civilta* 143:468-475 D 5 1992
Facing the mafia. Burke, Greg. *Register* 69:1+ My 30 1993
Italy's Andreotti, a former friend of the Church, may have Mafia link. Burke, Greg. *Register* 69:1+ Ap 18 1993
John Paul II, Pope, (1993-05-09) Repent! God will judge you. John Paul II, Pope, 1920- (Karol Wojtyla) (elected 1978). *TPS* 38:301-303 S-O 1993*
Pope passionately denounces Mafia. *Tablet* 247:624 My 15 1993
MAGALLANES, CRISTOBAL, 1869-1927
Congregation for the Causes of Saints (1992-02-07) Decree on the heroic virtues. Congregation for the Causes of Saints. *AAS* 84:999-1004 O 3 1992*
MAGI
Home by another way. Temple, Katharine. *Cath Work* 60:1+ Ja-F 1993
Wise guys [excerpt fr *Starlight: beholding the Christmas miracle all yar long*]. Shea, John B. *Comm* 119:10-12 D 18 1992
Wise Men from afar. Fielding, Ellen Wilson. *Crisis* 11:45-46 Ja 1993
MAHONY, ROGER MICHAEL, CARDINAL, 1936-
America again a player in population issues. Clancy, Paul. *Nat Cath Rep* 29:3 F 5 1993
Hollywood blues. Jones, Arthur C, 1936-. *Tablet* 247:849-850 Jl 3 1993
Mahony is a big man in the church [photos]. Jones, Arthur C, 1936-. *Nat Cath Rep* 30:8-14 N 12 1993
Mahony, public TV make peace. Feuerherd, Peter. *Register* 69:1+ Ja 10 1993
MAIMONIDES, MOSES
Il posto della metafisica nel sapere umano Il pensiero di Maimonide e il suo influsso su S Tommaso d'Aquino. Pangallo, Don Mario. *Gregorianum* 74 no 2:331-352 1993
MAIN, JOHN, -1982
A monk for today. Freeman, Laurence. *Tablet* 246:1604-1605 D 19-26 1992
MAIRS, NANCY
Nancy Mair's book of hours. Mason, Alane Salierno. *Comm* 120:22-24 N 5 1993

MAJOR, JOHN, 1943-
John Major versus Jacques Delors [editorial]. *Tablet* 247:807 Je 26 1993
Major's little difficulty. Alton, David. *Tablet* 247:779-780 Je 19 1993
Party leaders take the stage [editorial]. *Tablet* 247:1251 O 2 1993
The Prime Minister as scapegoat [editorial]. *Tablet* 247:967 Jl 31 1993
There should be an alternative [editorial]. *Tablet* 247:603 My 15 1993
While Ulster burns. McRedmond, Louis. *Tablet* 247:1094 Ag 28 1993
MALAWI—POLITICS AND GOVERNMENT
Choosing our future. *Cath Int* 4:169-174 Ap 1993
Churches hail vote for democracy. Rawlins, Rachel. *Tablet* 247:828-829 Je 26 1993
Made in England. Coates, Ken, 1930-. *Month* 26:315 Ag 1993
Malawi chooses its future. Cullen, Trevor. *Tablet* 247:257-258 F 20 1993
Malawi in crisis. *Cath Int* 4:174 Ap 1993
Opposition's hopes in struggle for democracy. *Tablet* 247:253 F 20 1993
MALCOLM X, 1927-1965
Catholics look at Malcolm X. Holton, Robert. *OSV* 81:9 F 7 1993
Malcolm after Mecca: East Africa, 1964. Snyder, Margaret. *Comm* 119:6-7 D 18 1992
"Malcolm X" di Spike Lee. Fantuzzi, Virgilio. *Civilta* 3:154-161 Jl 17 1993
Malcolm X: what his three lives can teach us [editorial]. Morrow, Carol Ann. *St Anth* 100:17 F 1993
Of many things. Stahel, Thomas H, 1938-. *America* 168:2 Ja 2-9 1993
MALLINCKRODT, PAULINE VON, 1817-1881
John Paul II, Pope, (1984-04-14) Litterae Apostolicae (Apostolic Letters) [Latin]. John Paul II, Pope, 1920- (Karol Wojtyla) (elected 1978). *AAS* 84: 830-832 S 8 1992*
MALTA—HISTORY
"The Knights cannot be admitted": Maltese nationalism, the Knights of St John, and the French occupation of 1798-1800. Castillo, Dennis. *CHist* 79: 434-453 Jl 1993
The Maltese cross. Castillo, Dennis. *Priest* 49:41-43 Je 1993
MALTA—SOCIAL CONDITIONS
Valori per il futuro di Malta. Abela, Anthony M. *Civilta* 2:260-269 My 1 1993
MAMMAN, YARO YUSUF
John Paul II, Pope, (1992-01-04) Allocutiones (Reception of the new Ambassador of Nigeria) [English]. John Paul II, Pope, 1920- (Karol Wojtyla) (elected 1978). *AAS* 85:45-47 Ja 7 1993*
MAN
Discussion: soul, rational soul and person in Thomism. Plante, Harry La. *Mod Schlmn* 70:209-216 Mr 1993
Evolution and morality. Shea, Moira C. *Teilhard Rev* 28:9-15 Sum 1993
Horsepower, machines and human beings. Ringwald, Christopher. *Cath Work* 60:4 S 1993
MAN—ETHICAL ASPECTS
Chi È Persona? Persona umana e bioetica. *Civilta* 143:547-559 D 19 1992
MAN—RELATION TO NATURE
Challenges for the Christian layperson in the coming millenium [repr and tr fr *Mensaje*]. Etchegaray, Alberto. *LADOC* 23:12-16 Mr-Ap 1993
Christianity and the survival of creation. Berry, Wendell. *CrossCurr* 43:149-163 Sum 1993
"A culture is dying": the timber crisis. Murphy, Thomas Austin, 1911-. *Origins* 22:765+ Ap 22 1993
Dare ecology use the word "sin"? Echlin, Edward P, 1930-. *Month* 26:206-210 My 1993
Declaration of the "Mission to Washington". *Living Light* 29:23-25 Aut 1992
Is "sustainable development" sustainable? Echlin, Edward P, 1930-. *Month* 26:402-407 S-O 1993
Learning from animals. Rose, Mary Carman. *Month* 26:331-335 Ag 1993
Liberté et vérité selon K Wojtyla. Guggenheim, Antoine. *NRT* 115:194-210 Mr-Ap 1993
Progress, evolution and Green theology. Clatworthy, Jonathan. *Teilhard Rev* 28:8-10 Spr 1993
Teilhard and ecological spirituality. Sage, Alan. *Teilhard Rev* 28:11-14 Spr 1993
Troutlilies for Mother's Day. Giordan, Alma Roberts, 1917-. *America* 168:4 My 8 1993
1993 UN focus: indigenous people. FitzMaurice, Eileen Claire. *Momentum* 24:79-80 Ap-My 1993
MAN (ISLAM)
Der fremde Spiegel. Röhrig, Johannes. *Stimm Zeit* 211:10-20 Ja 1993
MAN (PHILOSOPHY)
Anthropologie et philosophie: un double retour au fondement. Watté, Pierre. *RPhil Louvain* 91:207-227 My 1993
El mite de l'expulsio des paradis o els auguris de l'home boig: cartes a l'academia. Dala Pujolras, Joaquim. Barcelona: Edicions, 1993. x, 222p ISBN 84-297-3609-3
Presente y futuro del hombre. Polo, Leonardo. Madrid: Rialp, 1993. x, 208p ISBN 84-321-2977-1
MAN (THEOLOGY)
Body and soul. Young, John. *HPR* 94:60-63+ O 1993
The cosmotheandric experience: emerging religious consciousness. Panikkar, Raimundo, 1918-. Maryknoll, New York: Orbis Books, 1993. x, 160p ISBN 0-88344-862-9 LC 92-46195
Hans Urs von Balthasar's anthropology in light of his marian thinking. Roten, Johann G. *Communio* 20:306-333 Sum 1993
Heart of the matter: what is man? Kreeft, Peter John, 1937. *Register* 69:1+ Ag 29 1993
The human person: animal and spirit [by D Braine, review article]. Kerr, Fergus. *New Blckfrs* 74:333-337 Jl-Ag 1993
Legal anthropology, Australian, Aborigines and natural law. O'Connell, Irene. *Amer J Juris* 37:243-258 1992
Reflections on Humanae Vitae's 25th anniversary. Albacete, Lorenzo. *F & R* 19:5-23 Spr 1993
Somebodyness: Martin Luther King, Jr., and the theory of dignity. Baker-Fletcher, Garth. Minneapolis: Fortress, 1993. x, 193p ISBN 0-8006-7087-6 LC 93-19847

The theological anthropology of Catherine of Siena. Jeremiah, Mary. *Communio* 20:457-462 Sum 1993

L'uomo e il suo destino. Salvini, Gianpaolo. *Civilta* 3:256-262 Ag 7-21 1993

MANAGED CARE PLANS (MEDICAL CARE)

Aligning IDNs' financial interests with communities' best interests. Neale, Ann. *Health Prog* 74:14-15+ O 1993

Antitrust and IDNs: how far can we go? Campbell, Peter. *Health Prog* 74:54-55+ 1993

Antitrust law may be a barrier to collaboration. White, Jane H. *Health Prog* 74:22-24+ Jl-Ag 1993

Creating the future. Araujo, Marianne D, and Carballo, Suzanne M. *Health Prog* 74:22-24+ Je 1993

The "how-to" of integrated delivery. Suh, Young S, and Lee, John P. *Health Prog* 74:48 Jl-Ag 1993

MANAGEMENT

An essay on Jonathan Boswell's Community and the economy: the theory of public co-operation. Naughton, Michael. *RSocEcon* 51:86-102 Spr 1993

MANANZAN, MARY JOHN

Women's stuggle in the Third World. *Tablet* 247:753 Je 1993

MANCINI, ITALO

Italo Mancini: un profeta sotto la toga dell'accademico. Vanzan, Piersandro. *Civilta* 2:351-364 My 15 1993

MANDELA, NELSON, 1918-

Mandela in waiting. Steyn, Richard. *Tablet* 247:811-812 Je 26 1993

South Africa on the edge. Steyn, Richard. *Tablet* 247:1152+ S 11 1993

MANGANARO, ANN, -1993

Ann Manganaro, S L. Kavanaugh, John. *Cath Work* 60:7 S 1993

MANICHAEISM

Examining a Manichaean approach to abortion. Shea, Mark P. *New Oxford Rev* 60:13-16+ Ap 1993

MANION, CLARENCE

The higher law background of the Notre Dame law school. Kmiec, Douglas W. *Amer J Juris* 37:213-242 1992

MANISCALCO, FRANCIS J

Speaking for the bishops. Ryan, Dick. *OSV* 82:16 My 16 1993

MANNERS AND CUSTOMS

The amen corner. Mitchell, Nathan D. *Worship* 67:164-173 Mr 1993

A child's Christmas in Roscommon. Scally, John. *Month* 25:491-494 D 1992

MANNION, M FRANCIS

Are we all feminists now? Steichen, Donna. *SocJust* 84:11-15 Ja-F 1993

MANUFACTURES- UNITED STATES

America's silent depression: a challenge to social economics. Peterson, Wallace C, 1921-. *RSocEcon* 51:2-13 Spr 1993

Choices for the Chancellor. Keegan, William. *Tablet* 247:298-299 Mr 6 1993

Structural change in US labor markets. Champlin, Dell. *RSocEcon* 51:40-61 Spr 1993

MANUSCRIPTS, GREEK

The concept of charism in Paul. Nardoni, Enrique. *CBQ* 55:68-80 Ja 1993

MANUSCRIPTS, LATIN

Addenda to Codices Latini Antiquiores (II). Bischoff, Bernhard, et al. *Med Stud* 54:286-307 1992

Three previously unpublished chapters from St Thomas Aquinas's commentary on Aristotle's Meteora: Sentencia Super Meteora 2 13-15. White, Kevin. *Med Stud* 54:49-93 1992

Virgil's Eclogues, Nicholas Trevet, and the harmony of the spheres. Lord, Mary Louise. *Med Stud* 54:186-273 1992

MANZANARES, JULIO

Response to Julio Manzanares. Feliciani, Giorgio. *Jurist* 52 no 1:255-258 1992

MARCH MESA, NAZARIA IGNACIA, 1889-1943

Congregation for the Causes of Saints (1992-03-07) Decree on a miracle . Congregation for the Causes of Saints. *AAS* 84:924-926 S 8 1992*

MARCH OF DIMES

Catholics and the March of Dimes. Meehan, Bridget Mary. *Register* 69:1+ S 19 1993

A different take on the March of Dimes. Meehan, Bridget Mary. *Register* 69:1+ Ag 29 1993

MARCION, OF SINOPE

Hacia la doctrina marcionítica de la redención. Órbe, Antonio. *Gregorianum* 74 No 1:45-74 1993

Les premières éditions de Luc II: l'histoire du texte au IIe siècle. Amphoux, Christian-B. *Eph Theol Lovan* 78:38-48 Ap 1992

MARELLO, GIUSEPPE, BP, 1844-1895

John Paul II, Pope, (1993-09-25) Church [Orig in Italian]. John Paul II, Pope, 1920- (Karol Wojtyla) (elected 1978). *OR(Eng)* 1309:1-2 S 29 1993*

MARGINALITY, SOCIAL

Outsiders in the Gospels: marginality as a source of knowledge. Kopas, Jane. *Way* 33:117-126 Ap 1993

MARGUERITE, D'YOUVILLE 1701-1771

Saint Marguerite d'Youville. Lefevre, Marie Cecilia. *Sisters* 65:183-186 My 1993

MARIA, AURELIO

John Paul II, Pope, (1993-10-10) Aurelia Maria. John Paul II, Pope, 1920- (Karol Wojtyla) (elected 1978). *OR(Eng)* 1311:1 O 13 1993*

Two Spanish Bishops and seven Christian Brothers gave their lives for Catholic faith. *OR(Eng)* 1311:1 O 13 1993*

MARIAM, HAILE, 1895-1934

Congregation for the Causes of Saints (1992-12-21) Decree on the heroic virtues. Congregation for the Causes of Saints. *OR(Eng)* 1272:4 Ja 6 1993*

MARIE DE FRANCE

Eliduc and the iconography of love. Coolidge, Sharon. *Med Stud* 54:274-285 1992

MARIGNATIUS ZAKKA I, PATRIARCH OF ANTIOCH

Syrian Orthodox Patriarch visits the Pope. *OR(Eng)* 1309:12 S 29 1993

MARINO, VITTORIO MARIA DE, 1831-1925

Congregation for the Causes of Saints (1992-12-21) Decree on the heroic virtues. Congregation for the Causes of Saints. *OR(Eng)* 1272:4 Ja 6 1993*

MARION, JEAN-LUC, 1946-

Costly giving: on Jean-Luc Marion's theology of the gift. Moss, David. *New Blckfrs* 74:393-399 S 1993

The God of love. Schmitz, Kenneth L. *Thomist* 57:495-508 Jl 1993

MARISCAL, FERNANDO

How four artists put the finishing touches on God's creation. Marquardt, Deborah. *USCath* 58:14-21 Ag 1993

MARITAIN, JACQUES, 1882-1973

Jacques Maritain and the Jews. Castori, Michael T. *America* 168:18-21 My 29 1993

Jacques Maritain and the Jews. Royal, Robert, ed. Notre Dame: University of Notre Dame Press, 1993. 264p ISBN 0-268-01193-1 LC 93-4633

Maritain on "the common good": reflections on the concept. Kalumba, Kibujjo M. *Laval Theol Phil* 49:93-104 F 1993

MARKETING

Give it that old college try. Macchiarola, Frank J. *Comm* 120:9-12 S 10 1993

MARLIN, GEORGE

The Marlin factor in New York. Schall, James Vincent, 1928-. *Crisis* 11:49 O 1993

MARONS, MONIKA

Das beschädigte Land. Kurz, Paul Konrad. *Stimm Zeit* 211:663-678 O 1993

MARQUEZ, GABRIEL GARCIA

Leaves of light: the textual journeys of Dante and García Márquez. Barciauskas, Jonas. *CrossCurr* 43:212-229 Sum 1993

MARRIAGE

After the royal separation. Dominian, Jack, 1929-. *Tablet* 246:1596 D 19-26 1992

How to spell success in marriage [condensed fr *The Tennessee Register* N 9 1992]. Griffin, Kathy, and Griffin, John. *CDgst* 57:67-69 Mr 1993

John Paul II, Pope, (1993-09-24) Christian [Orig in English]. John Paul II, Pope, 1920- (Karol Wojtyla) (elected 1978). *OR(Eng)* 1309:3+ S 29 1993*

Nurturing black marriages [interview by C Wood]. Lyke, Terri, and Lyke, Andrew. *OSV* 82:6 Je 20 1993

Put intimacy back in your marriage. Bodmer, Judy. *St Anth* 100:22-26 S 1993

Searching for the soap: coming clean on gays in the military. Carlin, David Robert, Jr, 1938-. *Comm* 120:11-12 Ap 9 1993

Some musings on marriage. Myers, Edith. *HPR* 94:47-51 O 1993

Speaking of family values. Higgins, James J. *Liguorian* 81:73 F 1993

Until death do they part? Thunder, James. *Register* 69:5 F 14 1993

Your wedding workbook. Belting, Natalia, and Hine, James R. Danville: Interstate Publishers, 1993. 121p ISBN 0-8134-2953-6

MARRIAGE—ANNULMENT

The annulment process and pastoral care. Curley, Terence P. *Priest* 49:39-41 O 1993

Annulment: do you have a case? Tierney, Terrence E. New York: Alba House, 1993. x, 142p ISBN 0-8189-0667-7 LC 93-7090

Annulments healing the wounds of divorce. Walden, Mary. *Liguorian* 81:20-26 Mr 1993

Catechumens: addressing a failed marriage. Laird, William. *Origins* 23:358-359 O 28 1993

Church courts weigh the history of a marriage. Walters, Michael. *Register* 69:1+ S 19 1993

Church tribunals look after the supreme good of souls. Walters, Michael. *Register* 69:1+ S 26 1993

Conformity of sentence in marriage nullity cases. McGrath, Aidan. *Stud Can* 27 no 1:5-22 1993

Marital failure: the church's response. Place, Michael D, and Maletta, Sammie L, Jr. *Chicago Stud* 31:271-281 N 1992

On the letter and the spirit of church law. Walters, Michael. *Register* 69:1+ S 5 1993

One Humanae vitae is enough. *Tablet* 247:30 Ja 9 1993

Publish and be damned: one practitioner's experience. Nau, Dale. *Jurist* 51 no 2:442-450 1991

Shame, dysfunctional families, and lack of due discretion for marriage. Garrity, Robert M. *Jurist* 51 no 2:364-389 1991

Spanish language cases and canon 1673, 4. Lagges, Patrick R. *Jurist* 51 no 2:431-441 1991

Take a closer look. Feuerherd, Peter. *Register* 69:1+ Je 27 1993

What God has joined. Walters, Michael. *Register* 69:1+ S 12 1993

"You want an annulment?"—the work of an auditor. Lawrence, Susan. *Priests & People* 6:323-326 Ag-S 1992

MARRIAGE—RELIGIOUS ASPECTS

Couples who pray together [condensed fr *Home Life* F 1993]. Iijima, Geneva Cobb. *CDgst* 57:64-66 Je 1993

Creating a marriage. Greteman, James. New York: Paulist, 1993. x, 106p ISBN 0-8091-3393-8 LC 92-42927

A perfect giving of self. Cameron, Peter John. *Register* 69:5 O 10 1993

Refusal to make a promise in a mixed marriage. Coriden, James A. *New Theol Rev* 6:72-74 F 1993

Three pastoral challenges for family ministers. McCord, H Richard, Jr. *Origins* 23:61-63 Ag 19 1993

Turning wine into vinegar: pre-Cana needs work. McCloskey, Liz Leibold. *Comm* 120:7-8 N 5 1993

MARRIAGE, MIXED

The Elko episcopate an era of conversions. Renoff, Richard. *Diakonia* 26 no 2:99-118 1993

Into the city of faithfulness: negotiating a Jewish-Catholic marriage. Donnelly, Daria. *Comm* 120:18-20 Je 18 1993

Pastoral care for interfaith couples—a beginning. Borelli, John. *New Theol Rev* 6:30-42 Ag 1993

Refusal to make a promise in a mixed marriage. Coriden, James A. *New Theol Rev* 6:72-74 F 1993

Spiritual growth in interdenominational families. Lincoln, Timothy D. *Ecumen Trends* 22:7-8 My 1993

Take your shoes off my books: negotiating a Hindu-Catholic marriage. McGowan, Joseph. *Comm* 120:15-17 Je 18 1993

MARRIAGE (CANON LAW)

Acta tribunalium S Sedis. Navarrete, Urbano. *Periodica* 82 no 2:339-352 1993

MARY, VIRGIN

Advent and psychic birth. Burke, Mariann. New York: Paulist, 1993. x, 164p ISBN 0-8091-3431-4 LC 93-19318

'Bride' and 'Mother' in the Super cantica of St Bernard: an ecclesiology for our time? Kereszty, Roch A, 1933-. *Communio* 20:415-436 Sum 1993

Catholic theology, gender, and the future of Western civilization [editorial]. Schindler, David L. *Communio* 20:200-239 Sum 1993

Il celibato di Gesù e la verginità di Maria. Marzotto, Damiano, Msgr. *Seminarium* 33:32-47 Ja-Mr 1993

Challenges refuted about Mary. Manelli, Stefano M. *ChrWorld* 38:165-172 Mr-Ap 1993

Christus Lumen Gentium: the Eucharist and evangelization [4 sections]. Vallejo, Carlos Armijo, Abp. *Emmanuel* 99:64-71+ Mr; 138-144 Ap; 190-195+ My; 244-249+ Je 1993

For Mary, a tireless worker. Dudro, Vivian. *Register* 69:3 Je 6 1993

The Hail Mary: a verbal icon of Mary. Ayo, Nicholas. Notre Dame: University of Notre Dame Press, 1994. x, 256p ISBN 0-268-01101-x LC 93-24743

Hans Urs von Balthasar's anthropology in light of his marian thinking. Roten, Johann G. *Communio* 20:306-333 Sum 1993

The Holy Spirit and Mary. Campbell, Dwight P. *HPR* 93:12-23 My 1993

How Mary became my mother. White, Patricia A. *Liguorian* 81:46-48 O 1993

Man and woman under God: the dignity of the human being according to Hans Urs von Balthasar. Strukelj, Anton. *Communio* 20:377-388 Sum 1993

Mary and catechesis: there's room for two approaches. Buckley, Francis J. *Catechist* 26:26-29 Ap-My 1993

Mary and obedience. Knoblach, Thomas. *HPR* 93:64-70 My 1993

Mary and the unremembered past. Flanagan, Donald. *Doctr Life* 43:260-266 My-Je 1993

Mary in the Church [fr *Handmaid of the Lord* tr by E.A. Nelson]. Speyr, Adrienne von, 1902-1967. *Communio* 20:451-456 Sum 1993

Mary, faithful disciple. Buby, Bertrand. *Emmanuel* 99:214-221 My 1993

Mary. Martin, George. *Liguorian* 81:44-45 Jl 1993

Mary: yesterday, today, tomorrow. Halkes, Catharina J M, et al. New York: Crossroad, 1993. 88p ISBN 0-8245-1371-1 LC 93-19852

Meditations on Mary. Cooke, Terence. New York: Alba House, 1993. x, 132p ISBN 0-8189-0683-9 LC 93-26373

Medjugorje day by day: a daily meditation book based on the messages of Our Lady of Medjugorje. Beyer, Richard J. Indiana: Ave Maria Press, 1993. [265] leaves ISBN 0-87793-494-0 LC 92-74779

'O Blessed Mother, a sword has pierced your heart'. Gribble, Richard. *OSV* 82:5 S 12 1993

The one mediator, the saints, and Mary. Anderson, H George, et al, eds. Minneapolis: Augsburg Fortress, 1992. x, 397p ISBN 0-8066-2579-1 LC 91-40822

Piety, purity, and Mary Immaculate. Cameron, Peter John. *HPR* 93:61-63 My 1993

Proceedings of the forty-third National Convention of the Mariological Society of America held in Houston, Texas, My 28 and 29, 1992. McCurry, James E, et al. *Marian Stds* 43:9-189 1992*

A Protestant celebrates Mary [interview by M Finley]. Jepsen, Dee. *OSV* 82:5 My 9 1993

Renewing our love. Mullen, Peter. *Register* 69:2 My 23 1993

Revisionist history of virgin birth a misconception [review article *A Bishop Rethinks the Birth of Jesus* by J Spong]. Ruether, Rosemary Radford. *Nat Cath Rep* 29:27 Ja 15 1993

The rosary, arm of peace [fr *The Laity: Journal of Christian Thought* O-N, 1992]. Leite, P. *ChrWorld* 38:160-164 Mr-Ap 1993

Time to search for Mary between the lines. Drinan, Robert Francis, 1920-. *Nat Cath Rep* 29:2 My 14 1993

The Virgin Mary and the priesthood. Philippe, Pierre Paul, Cardinal, 1905-1984. New York: Alba House, 1993. x, 135p ISBN 0-8189-0668-5 LC 93-6682

Will the real me please stand up? Maas, Robin. *Living Light* 29:37-44 Spr 1993

MARY, VIRGIN—ANNUNCIATION

The Annunciation: pivotal moment of history. Yarnold, Edward John, 1926-. *Month* 26:237-239 Je 1993

Walsingham: Mary's message for rich and poor [photo]. Allen, Peter. *Priests & People* 7:197-201 My 1993

MARY, VIRGIN—APPEARANCES

Fatima's consecration: the Soviet collapse. Smolenski, Stanley. *HPR* 93:8-16 Ja 1993

The high price of spiritual complacency. Campbell, Michael. *New Cov* 23:11 N 1993

Is there a balm in Gilead? Reflections on a Church in need of healing. Paré, U E. *Can Cath Rev* 11:18-21 Ja 1993

Mary, mad as hell, at Medjugorje—now. McBrien, Richard P. *Nat Cath Rep* 29:18 Je 4 1993

Our Lady of Bellevue [editorial]. Ward, Donald. *Can Cath Rev* 11:2-4 O 1993

To Jesus through Mary. Feuerherd, Peter. *Register* 69:3 N 14 1993

War comes to Medjugorje. Manney, Dave. *New Cov* 23:7-11 N 1993

MARY, VIRGIN—ART

The Dormition of the Mother of God. McNichols, William Hart. *America* 169:20 Ag 14-21 1993

Guadalupe icon comes to US. Smith, Matt. *Nat Cath Rep* 29:3 Ja 29 1993

MARY, VIRGIN—ASSUMPTION

Assumptions about Mary [condensed fr *This Rock* My-Je 1992]. Frazier, T L. *CDgst* 57:82-88 Ag 1993

The Dormition of the Mother of God. McNichols, William Hart. *America* 169:20 Ag 14-21 1993

The fifteen mysteries in image and word. Pennington, M Basil, 1931-. Huntington: Our Sunday Visitor, 1993. 165p ISBN 0-87973-499-x LC 92-61553

The liturgy and the Assumption. Duggan, Paul E. *Priest* 49:16-18 Ag 1993

Mary's bodily assumption. Meyer, Gabriel. *Register* 69:5 Ag 15 1993

MARY, VIRGIN—BIBLICAL TEACHING

Mary in ordinary time: Biblical references. Turro, James C. *Marian Stds* 43:60-71 1992

MARY, VIRGIN—CULT

Catechism points to Mary as the mother and example of the faithful. Archideo, Lila B. *Heythrop* 34:65-69 Ja 1993

The cult of the saints in Anglo-Saxon England. Cubitt, Catherine. *Heythrop* 34:65-69 Ja 1993

John Paul II, Pope, (1992-03-30) Litterae Apostolicae (Apostolic Letters) [Latin]. John Paul II, Pope, 1920- (Karol Wojtyla) (elected 1978). *AAS* 84:1056-1057 N 3 1992*

John Paul II, Pope, (1992-05-29) Litterae Apostolicae (Apostolic Letter) [Latin]. John Paul II, Pope, 1920- (Karol Wojtyla) (elected 1978). *AAS* 85:14-15 Ja 7 1993*

John Paul II, Pope, (1992-07-08) Litterae Apostolicae (Apostolic Letter) [Latin]. John Paul II, Pope, 1920- (Karol Wojtyla) (elected 1978). *AAS* 85:17-18 Ja 7 1993*

John Paul II, Pope, (1992-08-04) Litterae Apostolicae (Apostolic Letter) [Latin]. John Paul II, Pope, 1920- (Karol Wojtyla) (elected 1978). *AAS* 85:20-21 Ja 7 1993*

John Paul II, Pope, (1992-10-08) Litterae Apostolicae (Apostolic Letter) [Latin]. John Paul II, Pope, 1920- (Karol Wojtyla) (elected 1978). *AAS* 85:22-23 Ja 7 1993*

John Paul II, Pope, (1992-11-17) Statue of the Litterae Apostolicae (Apostolic Letter for coronation of the Virgin Mary in Halcnow) [Latin]. John Paul II, Pope, 1920- (Karol Wojtyla) (elected 1978). *AAS* 85:129-130 F 3 1993*

John Paul II, Pope, (1992-12-30) Marian devotion [orig Italian and French]. John Paul II, Pope, 1920- (Karol Wojtyla) (elected 1978). *OR(Eng)* 1272:11 Ja 6 1993*

John Paul II, Pope, (1993-06-14) Spain [Orig in Italian]. John Paul II, Pope, 1920- (Karol Wojtyla) (elected 1978). *OR(Eng)* 1295:3 Je 30 1993*

John Paul II, Pope, (1993-06-19) Human Life [Orig in Italian]. John Paul II, Pope, 1920- (Karol Wojtyla) (elected 1978). *OR(Eng)* 1298:6 Jl 7 1993*

John Paul II, Pope, (1993-06-20) Nature [Orig in Italian]. John Paul II, Pope, 1920- (Karol Wojtyla) (elected 1978). *OR(Eng)* 1296:1 Je 23 1993*

John Paul II, Pope, (1993-09-07) Mary [Orig in Lithuanian]. John Paul II, Pope, 1920- (Karol Wojtyla) (elected 1978). *OR(Eng)* 1307:6 S 15 1993*

Keeping Mary in balance (but not in check). Ullrich, Coralie. *New Cov* 23:20-22 O 1993

Learning from Mary. Reimers, Adrian J. *New Cov* 23:28-29 S 1993

The Marian movement. Scanlan, Michael. *New Cov* 22:23-24 Mr 1993

Mary feminism: compatible but challenging. Morrow, Carol Ann. *St Anth* 100:10-15 My 1993

Theological reflection: from Marialis Cultus to mission. Brennan, Walter T. *Marian Stds* 43:132-159 1992

MARY, VIRGIN—FEASTS

A letting go like rain: the Mary mystery of presentation and purification. Weber, Christin Lore. *Sisters* 65:116-120 Mr 1993

A letting go like rain: the Mary mystery of presentation and purification. Weber, Christin Lore. *Sisters* 65:116-120 Mr 1993

Mary's day—Saturday: meditations for Marian celebrations. Boyer, Mark G. Minnesota: The Liturgical Press, 1993. x, 116p ISBN 0-8146-2092-2 LC 92-39441

The revision and placement of Marian feasts. Samaha, John M. *Priest* 49:35-39 My 1993

MARY, VIRGIN—HISTORY OF DOCTRINES

Catechism points to Mary as the mother and example of the faithful. Archideo, Lila B. *OR(Eng)* 1295:4 Je 16 1993

Fr Juniper B Carol, OFM: his mariology and scholarly achievement. Fehlner, Peter D. *Marian Stds* 43:17-47 1992

The one mediator, the saints, and Mary: a Lutheran reflection. Johnson, Maxwell E. *Worship* 67:226-238 My 1993

Triduo mariano: 500 años de evangelizacion fiesta patronal del inmaculado Corazon de Maria Col Guerrero, D F. *Christus* 58:51-56 Je 1993

MARY, VIRGIN—IN LITERATURE

The Virgin incarnate in Robert Browning's poetry. Johnson, Patricia E. *Listening* 28:118-127 Spr 1993

MARY, VIRGIN—MIRACLES

Catechism points to Mary as the mother and example of the faithful. Archideo, Lila B. *OR(Eng)* 1295:4 Je 16 1993

John Paul II, Pope, (1992-12-30) Marian devotion [orig Italian and French]. John Paul II, Pope, 1920- (Karol Wojtyla) (elected 1978). *OR(Eng)* 1272:11 Ja 6 1993*

MARY, VIRGIN—PRAYER BOOKS

John Paul II, Pope, (1993-06-30) Priests [Orig in Italian]. John Paul II, Pope, 1920- (Karol Wojtyla) (elected 1978). *OR(Eng)* 1298:11 Jl 7 1993*

John Paul II, Pope, (1993-09-04) Mary [Orig in Lithuanian]. John Paul II, Pope, 1920- (Karol Wojtyla) (elected 1978). *OR(Eng)* 1306:3 S 8 1993*

MARY, VIRGIN—VIRGINITY

Born of a virgin. Daley, Brian E. *Tablet* 246:1598-1603 D 19-26 1992

MARY, VIRGIN—VISITATION

The Magnificat Mary's canticle of praise. Muckerman, Norman James, 1917- . *Liguorian* 81:4-8 My 1993

MARY, VIRGIN, AND CHRISTIAN UNION

All generations will call her blessed (commentary: *Redemptoris mater*). Collins, Mary Smalara. *USCath* 58:37-40 My 1993*

La Madonna a Mosca e a Roma: teologia, arte, devozione popolare. Pfeiffer, Heinrich. *Civilta* 144:370-373 F 20 1993

Mary's blood. Kreeft, Peter John, 1937. *New Cov* 23:33 N 1993

MARY, VIRGIN, IN LITERATURE

A survey of recent Mariology. Carroll, Eamon R. *Marian Stds* 43:160-189 1992

MARY, VIRGIN, IN THE LITURGY

Catechism points to Mary as the mother and example of the faithful. Archideo, Lila B. *OR(Eng)* 1295:4 Je 16 1993

John Paul II, Pope, (1993-06-20) Nature [Orig in Italian]. John Paul II, Pope, 1920- (Karol Wojtyla) (elected 1978). *OR(Eng)* 1296:1 Je 23 1993*

Mary in ordinary time: Biblical references. Turro, James C. *Marian Stds* 43:60-71 1992

Mary in the mysteries of Christ during Ordinary Time: Liturgical references. Joncas, Jan Michael. *Marian Stds* 43:72-131 1992

MAURIN, ARISTIDE PETER, 1877-1949
Do not conform yourselves to this age. Sammon, Jane. *Cath Work* 60:3 My 1993
Peter Maurin: I am a radical. Hyre, Meg. *Cath Work* 60:1+ My 1993
Transformed by the renewal of the mind. Temple, Katharine. *Cath Work* 60: 3 My 1993

MAURINA, MARY
The adventures of Sister Maurina [condensed fr *The Philadelphia Inquirer* Ap 11 1993]. O'Brien, Ellen. *CDgst* 57:44-49 Ag 1993

MAXIM, PATRIARCH
A church at a standoff. Corley, Felix. *OSV* 81:21 Ja 31 1993

MAXIMILLIAN KOLBE, SAINT, 1894-1941
A secret hero in Dachau. Finley, Mitchel B. *OSV* 82:9 Ag 15 1993
St. Max on stage. Duin, Julia. *New Cov* 23:22-23 N 1993

MAXIMUS, CONFESSOR, SAINT, CA 580-662
Maximus the Confessor: a precursor to Teilhard? Pomerai, David de. *Teilhard Rev* 28:16-18 Sum 1993

MAYAS
Guatemala: land of beauty and sorrow. Wintz, Jack Alton, 1936-. *ST Anth* 101:28-34 Jl 1993
Mayan Indians seek U.S. help. Martinez, Demetria. *Nat Cath Rep* 30:5 O 29 1993

MAYAS—RELIGION
John Paul II, Pope, (1993-01-9) Discurso a los indigenas Latino Americanos. John Paul II, Pope, 1920- (Karol Wojtyla) (elected 1978). *Christus* 58:46-48 S 1993*
Teologia Maya conceptos fundamentales. *Christus* 58:22-27 S 1993

MAYER, RUPERT EMIL, 1876-1945
Hans Carossa und Rupert Mayer. Bleistein, Roman, 1928-. *Stimm Zeit* 211: 105-114 F 1993
Jesuit presence and the struggle for justice in Nazi Germany. Endean, Philip. *Month* 26:240-246 Je 1993
Rupert Mayer: der verstummte Prophet. Bleistein, Roman, 1928-. Frankfurt: Knecht, 1993. x, 480p ISBN 3-7620-0664-x

MAYS, KARL
Karl May im katholischen Verlagswesen während des Kulturkampfs. Hoffmann, Fernand. *Stimm Zeit* 211:177-186 Mr 1993

MAZZUCHELLI, CHARLES SAMUEL, 1806-1864
Congregation for the Causes of Saints (1993-07-06) Decree on the heroic virtues. Congregation for the Causes of Saints. *OR(Eng)* 1299:12 Jl 14 1993*

MCBRIDE, MARY
The world's funniest mom. Fixmer, Audrey Mettel. *OSV* 82:16 My 9 1993

MCCALL, CINDY
McCall, Cindy [obit]. Boagni, Annie, and Hynes, Brian. *Cath Work* 60:6 Mr-Ap 1993

MCCARTHY, ANN
Activists and charismatics: stronger ties and shared respect. Wood, Charles. *New Cov* 23:8-12 O 1993

MCCARTHY, ROBERT J
Carny priest. Thoren, Ken. *OSV* 82:10-11 Je 13 1993

MCCARTHY, TERENCE BARRY
John Paul II, Pope, (1991-12-02) Allocutiones (Reception of ambassadorial credentials from Australia) [English]. John Paul II, Pope, 1920- (Karol Wojtyla) (elected 1978). *AAS* 84:1151-1154 D 5 1992*

MCCORMACK, ARTHUR, 1911-1992
Father Mac remembered. Reilly, Ruth Norrington. *Tablet* 247:89-90 Ja 16 1993
McCormack, Arthur, 1911-1992 [obit]. *Tablet* 246:1636 D 19-26 1992

MCCORMICK, RICHARD
Feminism and theology: beyond women's ordination. Cahoy, William J. *Sisters* 65:243-251 Jl 1993

MCCOY, CHARLES N R, -1989
Transcendent man in the limited city: the political philosophy of Charles N R McCoy. Schall, James Vincent, 1928-. *Thomist* 57:63-95 Ja 1993

MCCREADY, WILLIAM C
"The end of American Catholicism?"—another look. Hegy, Pierre M. *America* 168:4-9 My 1 1993

MCGANN, DIARMUID
God's human face revealed: a retreat in Wales. Corona, Mary. *RRel* 52:519-531 Jl-Ag 1993

MCGILLICUDDY, FRANCES LEE
Ms Buttons. *Tablet* 247:1099 Ag 28 1993

MCGINN, JOHN T
Evangelizing America: transformations in Paulist mission. Robichaud, Paul. *US Cath Hist* 11:61-78 Spr 1993

MCKENZIE, JOHN L
Authority in the church: who makes the final call? McClory, Richard J. *USCath* 58:6-13 Mr 1993

MCKNIGHT, AL
Does the church mishandle its cultural treasures? Windsor, Patricia. *USCath* 58:14-20 F 1993

MCNABB, VINCENT, 1868-1943
Vincent McNabb OP 1868-1943. Ombres, Robert. *New Blckfrs* 74:330-332 Jl-Ag 1993

MCNAMARA, DESMOND ARTHUR
John Paul II, Pope, (1991-10-28) Allocutiones (Speech of reception of credentials) [English]. John Paul II, Pope, 1920- (Karol Wojtyla) (elected 1978). *AAS* 84:959-961 O 3 1992*

MCQUAID, BERNARD, BP, 1823-1909
Bishop Bernard McQuaid: on "true" and "false" americanism. Janus, Glen. *US Cath Hist* 11:53-76 Sum 1993

MCSORLEY, JOSEPH, 1874-1963
Phantom heresy: A Twice-Told Tale. Reher, Margaret M. *US Cath Hist* 11: 93-105 Sum 1993

MEANING
The catechetical role of the liturgy and the quality of liturgical texts: the current ICEL translation. Leiva-Merikakis, Erasmo. *Communio* 20:63-83 Spr 1993
The Catholic university and its inherent promise. Buckley, Michael J, 1931-. *America* 168:14-16 My 29 1993
Cramming for your finals: make death a part of life [excerpt fr *The troubled dream of life*]. Callahan, Daniel, 1930-. *Comm* 120:11-15 Jl 16 1993
From matter to mind to meaning. Higgins, James J. *Liguorian* 81:73 Mr 1993
On making sense of the universe. Schall, James Vincent, 1928-. *Crisis* 11:47-48 Ap 1993
The sacraments and evangelisation. Woolfenden, Graham. *Month* 26:121-126 Mr 1993

MEDIATION—PHILOSOPHY
Le médiation philosophique des valeurs. Henrici, Peter. *Gregorianum* 74 no 3:515-541 1993

MEDICAID
Primary care program improves reimbursement. Fahey, Thomas M, and Gallitano, Dennis G. *Health Prog* 74:26-28+ Mr 1993

MEDICAL—ETHICS
Obstetrical dilemmas and the principle of double effect. Lombardi, Joseph L. *Amer J Juris* 37:197-211 1992

MEDICAL CARE
Network unites payers, physicians, hospitals. Cassidy, Judy. *Health Prog* 74: 18-21 My 1993
The politics of health-care ethics [interview by Ann Carey]. Anderson, Carl. *OSV* 81:21 F 28 1993

MEDICAL CARE—FINANCE
Basic health benefits: deciding what to cover. White, Jane H. *Health Prog* 74:8-10 Je 1993
A Catholic doctor looks at AIDS in the USA. Barnet, Robert J. *America* 168:6-12 F 6 1993
Catholic health care: a changing field [interview by J S Torrens]. Bader, Diana. *America* 169:12-15 S 18 1993
Catholic providers will play a central role in healthcare reform. Clinton, Hillary Rodham, 1947-. *Health Prog* 74:42-43 Jl-Ag 1993
Clinton's change of course [editorial]. *America* 168:3-4 Mr 20-27 1993
Controlling health costs. Reilly, Jeremiah P. *Comm* 120:5-6 Mr 12 1993
A framework for comprehensive healthcare reform. *Health Prog* 74:20-23 1993
Genomanalysen im Versicherungs- und Gerichtswesen. Münk, Hans J. *Stimm Zeit* 211:34-44 Ja 1993
Making capitation work. Kirschner, Leonard, and Willert, Joan St. *Health Prog* 74:57-58 Jl-Ag 1993
Meeting mission challenges in IDNs. Stanley, Teresa. *Health Prog* 74:28-31+ Jl-Ag 1993
Questions d'un gestionnaire d'hôpital. Tassin, Paul. *Supplement* 184:7-19 Mr-Ap 1993
Relevance of social market conditions in the German Health Care System to the United States. Powell, Francis D. *RSocEcon* 50:269-296 Fall 1992
What will healthcare reform cost? White, Jane H. *Health Prog* 74:15-17+ My 1993

MEDICAL CARE—NEEDS ASSESSMENT
From assessment to action. Dugas, Nancy. *Health Prog* 74:38-41 O 1993

MEDICAL CARE- ARIZONA
Making capitation work. Kirschner, Leonard, and Willert, Joan St. *Health Prog* 74:57-58 Jl-Ag 1993

MEDICAL CARE, COST OF
A double mugging: defender of the faith gets maced. Jordan, Patrick. *Comm* 120:4-5 N 5 1993
Health care: your money or your life [interview by J.S. Torrens]. Roberts, Marc J. *America* 169:6-9 D 4 1993

MEDICAL CARE, COST OF—LAW AND LEGISLATION
Hold on, America, it's coming [editorial]. *America* 169:3 N 27 1993

MEDICAL COLLEGES
Does Catholic medical education have a future? [presentation given during 1992 100th birtday of Creighton University's Medical Schools]. Heaney, Robert P. *Health Prog* 74:67 Ja-F 1993
The fullness of life. Sulmasy, Daniel P. *Health Prog* 74:76-78 Ja-F 1993
Preserving a presence in medical education. Byron, William J, 1927-. *Health Prog* 74:68-69 Ja-F 1993

MEDICAL ECONOMICS
An open letter: four things to keep in mind. Koller, Christopher F. *Comm* 120:5-6 Ap 23 1993

MEDICAL ETHICS
Advising on the ethics of health-care reform. Bole, William. *OSV* 82:3 Je 20 1993
A bioethics roundup. Gula, Richard M. *Priest* 49:35-40 Je 1993
The birth lottery: prenatal diagnosis and selective abortion. Boss, Judith A. Chicago: Loyola University Press, 1993. 326p ISBN 0-8294-0740-5 LC 92-49738
Brave new medicine. Charles, J Daryl. *SocJust* 84:59-60 Mr-Ap 1993
Buzz words or principles? Ethics and health-care reform. McCloskey, Liz Leibold. *Comm* 120:10 S 24 1993
The California euthanasia initiative. Rae, Scott B. *Linacre* 59:5-14 N 1992
Can we kill off grandad? Gormally, Luke. *Priests & People* 6:409-414 N 1992
Catholicism and the "right" to die. Grondelski, John M. *Linacre* 59:50-56 N 1992
Commerce beginning to squeeze genetic science. Meehan, Bridget Mary. *Register* 69:1+ Je 20 1993
Il consenso informato in medicina. Cuyás, Manuel. *Civilta* 2:61-67 Ap 3 1993
Death with dignity. Dudro, Vivian. *Register* 69:4 S 5 1993
Debate over Tony Bland ruling. *Tablet* 247:223 F 13 1993
Decision tree. Meeker, Tobias. *Health Prog* 74:48-51 Mr 1993
The disembodiment of parenthood. Grondelski, John M. *HPR* 93:30-31+ F 1993
A doctor's dilemma. Lupton, Martin. *Tablet* 247:542 My 1 1993

Does compassion include Euthanasia? Hooyman, Nancy W. *Health Prog* 74:
44-47 Mr 1993
The embryo and the fetus: new moral contexts. Cahill, Lisa Sowle.
TheolStds 54:124-142 Mr 1993
An ethical look at fetal-tissue research. Shaw, Russell. *OSV* 81:16 Ap 25
1993
Ethics, gag rules, and title X. Grondelski, John M. *Linacre* 60:20-24 My 1993
Éthique et médecine expérimentale à l'hôpital. Malherbe, Jean-François.
Supplement 184:107-124 Mr-Ap 1993
Fetal tissue research: the cutting edge? Crutcher, Keith A. *Linacre* 60:10-19
My 1993
Fetal tissue transplantation: an ethical analysis. Roessler, Mark A. *Linacre*
60:60-74 Ag 1993
From conception to deception: the nazification of the feminist movement
[por]. Sheridan, Ann. *Linacre* 60:31-39 Ag 1993
Health decisions or Majoritarian Health Care? Cataldo, Peter J. *Linacre* 60:
70-73 F 1993
Helping Catholics deal with life, death. Gibeau, Dawn. *Nat Cath Rep* 29:6 F
5 1993
It's a high price to pay. Valko, Nancy Guilpoy. *Register* 69:5 My 9 1993
It's easier to clone embryo than to figure consequences. Shannon, Thomas
A. *Nat Cath Rep* 30:19 N 12 1993
IVF: it solves very little. Krause, Edward. *Register* 69:5 Je 6 1993
The last days of Tony Bland [editorial]. *Tablet* 247:187 F 13 1993
Law, ethics, and language: the House of Lords and Tony Bland. Walsh, J
Leo, and McQueen, Moira M. *Can Cath Rev* 11:6-8 Jl-Ag 1993
A license to kill. Carroll, William E. *Can Cath Rev* 11:33-35 Ap 1993
A medical and moral dilemma. Kelly, Kevin T. *Month* 26:138-144 Ap 1993
Mercy or murder? euthanasia, morality and public policy. Overberg, Kenneth
R, 1944-. Kansas City: Sheed and Ward, 1993. x, 278p ISBN 1-55612-609-3
LC 92-43734
Murderous euphemisms. Bole, William. *OSV* 82:3 My 16 1993
No longer patient: feminist ethics and health care. Sherwin, Susan, 1947-.
Philadelphia: Temple University Press, 1992. 286p ISBN 0-87722-889-2 LC
91-14499
La notion de qualité de la vie dans le champ dela santé. Lamau, Marie-
Louise. *MSR* 50:135-150 Ap-Je 1993
Nutrition and hydration: moral and pastoral reflections [Committee for Pro-
Life Activities, Ap 1992]. *Linacre* 59:33-49 N 1992
On dying poorly: the gracelessness of euthanasia. Meehan, Bridget Mary.
Crisis 11:37-40 Je 1993
On not starving the unconscious. Fisher, Anthony. *New Blckfrs* 74:130-145
Mr 1993
Permanently unconscious patients and the ethical controversies surrounding
artificial nutrition and hydration: getting the facts straight. Mitchell, Ken-
neth R, and Lovat, Terence J. *Linacre* 60:75-90 F 1993
The politics of health-care ethics [interview by Ann Carey]. Anderson, Carl.
OSV 81:21 F 28 1993
"A pro-life RSVP". Alvaré, Helen M. *America* 168:7-10 Ja 30 1993
Rest for Tony Bland. Kelly, Kevin T. *Tablet* 247:332-334 Mr 13 1993
The road to euthanasia. Fisher, Anthony. *Tablet* 247:235-237 F 20 1993
Slip-sliding away [editorial]. *OSV* 82:2 My 16 1993
Sounding the alarm on sex selection. *Tablet* 247:149 Ja 30 1993
Troubled voices: stories of ethics and illness. Zaner, Richard M. Cleveland:
Pilgrim Press, 1993. x, 161p ISBN 0-8298-0964-3 LC 93-3823
Value variables in the health-care reform debate. McCormick, Richard Ar-
thur, 1922-. *America* 168:7-13 My 29 1993
A warning from Holland. Krause, Edward. *Register* 69:5 My 9 1993
What comes after assisted suicide and legalized euthanasia? Gervais, Marcel,
Abp. *Origins* 22:573+ F 4 1993
What price parenthood?: ethics and assisted reproduction. Campbell, Court-
ney S. Brookfield: Ashgate Publishing Company, 1992. 127p ISBN 1-8552-
1224-2
Why doctors are suspicious of "aid in dying" bills. Krause, Edward. *Register*
69:5 Je 13 1993
Why we should not legalize euthanisa. Place, Michael D. *Health Prog* 74:39-
43+ Mr 1993

MEDICAL ETHICS—CONGRESSES
John Paul II, Pope, (1993-05-07) Science [Orig in Italian]. John Paul II,
Pope, 1920- (Karol Wojtyla) (elected 1978). *OR(Eng)* 1296:14 Je 23 1993*

MEDICAL ETHICS- BRAZIL
O paciente terminal nos códigos brasileiros de ética médica. Martin, Leonard
M. *REB* 53:72-86 Mr 1993

MEDICAL GENETICS—ETHICAL ASPECTS
Genomanalysen im Versicherungs- und Gerichtswesen. Münk, Hans J.
Stimm Zeit 211:34-44 Ja 1993

**MEDICAL INSTRUMENTS AND APPARATUS—LAW AND LEGIS-
LATION**
Facilities strive to comply with new act. Schuster, Debra K, and Butler,
Kathy H. *Health Prog* 74:53-57 My 1993

MEDICAL PERSONNEL
Conscience clauses offer little protection [excerpt fr *Journal of logal medicine*]. Wardle, Lynn D, 1947-. *Health Prog* 74:79-83 Jl-Ag 1993

MEDICAL POLICY
Catholic healthcare ministry's key role in healthcare reform. Coreil, Bernice.
Health Prog 74:18-19+ 1993
Lessons from abroad on healthcare reform. Weil, Thomas P. *Health Prog* 74:
74-78 Jl-Ag 1993

MEDICAL PROTOCOLS
Practice parameters benefit all. Rothschild, Richard D. *Health Prog* 74:24-29
1993

MEDICAL RECORDS
Strategies for successful information system development. Rheinecker, Phil.
Health Prog 74:18-21+ Jl-Ag 1993

MEDICAL RESEARCH
AIDS researcher wields tools of evolution to meet challenge. Jones, Arthur
C, 1936-. *Nat Cath Rep* 29:7 N 20 1992
John Paul II, Pope, (1993-02-07) AIDS [Original in English]. John Paul II,
Pope, 1920- (Karol Wojtyla) (elected 1978). *Origins* 22:613-614 F 18 1993*

Weakened research protections for unborn child opposed. Quinn, Gail. *Origins* 22:610-611 F 18 1993

MEDICAL RESEARCH—COMMENTARIES
Éthique et médecine expérimentale à l'hôpital. Malherbe, Jean-François.
Supplement 184:107-124 Mr-Ap 1993

MEDICAL RESEARCH—ETHICS
Tierversuche und Tierethik. Reiter, Johannes. *Stimm Zeit* 211:451-463 Jl
1993

MEDICAL TECHNOLOGY
New angles on technology assessment. *Health Prog* 74:42-62 Ja-F 1993*
Patents encroach upon the body. Kimbrell, Andrew. *Crisis* 11:43-48 My 1993

MEDICALLY UNDERSERVED AREAS
Health care and the rural poor. Anderson, George M. *America* 169:16-18 Jl
3-10 1993

MEDICARE
Hospital-physician relationships: a hurdle on the road to reform. White,
Jane H. *Health Prog* 74:12-13+ 1993
Primary care program improves reimbursement. Fahey, Thomas M, and
Gallitano, Dennis G. *Health Prog* 74:26-28+ Mr 1993

MEDICATION ERRORS
Medicines that don't mix [condensed fr *The Catholic Standard and Times* Jl
16 1992]. Catanzaro, Ana Maria. *CDgst* 57:105-107 F 1993

MEDICINE
Médecine générale et sciences humaines. Breton, David Le, and Broussier,
Jean. *Supplement* 184:167-173 Mr-Ap 1993
Truth at the sickbed [condensed fr *Stimmen der Zeit* D 1989]. Schmitz,
Philip. *TheolDgst* 38:141-145 Sum 1991

MEDICINE—HISTORY
The medical world of Hildegard of Bingen. Daaleman, Timothy P. *ABenR*
44:280-289 S 1993

MEDICINE—RESEARCH
John Paul II, Pope, (1992-12-05) serve life at its birth. John Paul II, Pope,
1920- (Karol Wojtyla) (elected 1978). *TPS* 38:147-149 My-Je 1993*

MEDICINE—STUDY
Médecine générale et sciences humaines. Breton, David Le, and Broussier,
Jean. *Supplement* 184:167-173 Mr-Ap 1993

MEDICINE- AFRICA
John Paul II, Pope, (1993-02-07) AIDS [Original in English]. John Paul II,
Pope, 1920- (Karol Wojtyla) (elected 1978). *Origins* 22:613-614 F 18 1993*

MEDICINE, EXPERIMENTAL
Der Bauplan des Menschen. Reiter, Johannes. *Stimm Zeit* 211:219-231 Ap
1993

MEDICINE, PREVENTIVE
Accompagnement des familles et prévention des deuils pathologiques.
Vanoverberghe, Arlette. *Supplement* 184:125-144 Mr-Ap 1993

MEDICINE, STATE- CANADA
Lessons from abroad on healthcare reform. Weil, Thomas P. *Health Prog* 74:
74-78 Jl-Ag 1993

MEDICINE, STATE- GERMANY
Lessons from abroad on healthcare reform. Weil, Thomas P. *Health Prog* 74:
74-78 Jl-Ag 1993

MEDICINE AND RELIGION
Comment faire Église aujourd'hui (à l'hôpital)? Martou, Jean-Marie. *Supple-
ment* 184:145-166 Mr-Ap 1993
Pastoral reflections: euthanasia, assisted suicide. *Origins* 23:373-378 N 4 1993

MEDICINE AND THE HUMANITIES
Der Bauplan des Menschen. Reiter, Johannes. *Stimm Zeit* 211:219-231 Ap
1993

MEDINA, JOHN
Examining a Manichaean approach to abortion. Shea, Mark P. *New Oxford
Rev* 60:13-16+ Ap 1993

MEDINA OLMOS, MANUEL, BP
John Paul II, Pope, (1993-10-10) Manuel Medina Olmos. John Paul II, Pope,
1920- (Karol Wojtyla) (elected 1978). *OR(Eng)* 1311:1 O 13 1993*
Two Spanish Bishops and seven Christian Brothers gave their lives for
Catholic faith. *OR(Eng)* 1311:1 O 13 1993

MEDITATION
Elizabeth Ann Seton: a woman of prayer. Celeste, Marie. New York: Alba
House, 1993. 134p ISBN 0-8189-0650-2 LC 92-44978
An encounter with Christ. Penick, Carol Lacquement. *Living Prayer* 26:29
Jl-Ag 1993
God's passionate and our desire response. Barry, William A. Indiana: Ave
Maria Press, 1993. x, 143p ISBN 0-87793-501-7 LC 92-75346
Just a moment: life matters with Father Tom. Hartman, Thomas. Liguori:
Triumph Books, 1993. 222p ISBN 0-89243-530-5 LC 92-43420
Measuring the days. Eifrig, Gail McGrew. Grand Rapids: Zondervan Publish-
ing House, 1993. x, 400p ISBN 0-06-069248-0
Meditation and prayer (1):creative imagination in the lives of Ignatius
Loyola and Khapa: visualization in Catholic and Buddhist practice. Urub-
shurow, Victoria Kennick. *Stud Form Spir* 14:41-56 F 1993
Meditation and prayer (3): the way of devotion: pure land Buddhism. Bragt,
Jan van. *Stud Form Spir* 14:75-89 F 1993
Meditation XII-death. Claret, Anthony Maria. *ChrWorld* 38:135-139 Mr-Ap
1993
Meditations on Mary. Cooke, Terence. New York: Alba House, 1993. x, 132p
ISBN 0-8189-0683-9 LC 93-26373
A monk for today. Freeman, Laurence. *Tablet* 246:1604-1605 D 19-26 1992
Prayer made easy [adapted fr *Prayers for a planetary pilgrim*]. Hays, Ed-
ward. *St Anth* 100:10-14 Mr 1993
Quieting the inner noises. Donahue, Lois M. *Liguorian* 81:66-67 Je 1993
Recover and heal: meditations on the twelve steps. Albertus, Karen. Cin-
cinatti: St Anthony Press, 1993. x, 308p ISBN 0-86716-1531
Sitting in the dark: a meditation sequence. Gore, Michael. *Living Prayer* 26:
17-21 My-Je 1993
Through the year with Francis of Assisi: daily meditations from his words
and life. Francis of Assisi, Saint, 1182-1226. Cincinnati: St Anthony Messenger Press, 1993. 240p ISBN 0-86716-196-5

Time with Jesus. Catucci, Thomas F. Notre Dame: Ave Maria Press, 1993. 158p ISBN 0-87793-499-1 LC 93-71891

Why orthodox Catholics look to Zen. Gawronski, Raymond T. *New Oxford Rev* 60:13-16 Jl-Ag 1993

MEDITERRANEAN AREA
Journey in dust and light: a modern pilgrimage through the life and letters of Paul. DeMers, John. Minnesota: The Liturgical Press, 1993. x, 112p ISBN 0-8146-5701-x LC 92-40482

MEDVED, MICHAEL
Movies: the struggle between art and entertainment. May, John R. *ChrWorld* 236:252-257 N-D 1993

Seen any good movies lately? Costello, Gerald M, 1931-. *USCath* 58:48-50 Je 1993

MEIER, JOHN P
Historical research, theological inquiry, and the reality of Jesus: reflections on the method of J P Meier. Kereszty, Roch A, 1933-. *Communio* 19:576-600 Wint 1992

MEISNER, JOACHIM, CARDINAL, 1933-
Charge and counter-charge over church informers. *Tablet* 247:956 Jl 24 1993

MEMORY
His brother's keeper: a memorial. Paige, Harry W, 1922-. *Liguorian* 81:18-21 My 1993

Memories are made of this. Burleigh, Anne Husted, 1941-. *Crisis* 11:45-46 Je 1993

The memory lingers on. Gittins, Anthony J, 1943-. *New Theol Rev* 6:81-85 Ag 1993

Prayer, memories, and God. Mancuso, Theresa. *RRel* 52:541-547 Jl-Ag 1993

Trial by memory. Paige, Harry W, 1922-. *Liguorian* 81:4-8 Ja 1993

MEMORY—PSYCHOLOGICAL ASPECTS
Los sentidos internos. Rodriguez, Victorino. Barcelona: PPU, 1993. x, 158p ISBN 84-477-0066-6

MEMORY—RELIGIOUS ASPECTS
Putting out roots to the stream: on reading the monastic story. Belsole, Kurt. *Word Sp* 14:129-138 1992

MEN
Male and female he created them: a summary of the teaching of Genesis chapter one. Martin, Francis. *Communio* 20:240-265 Sum 1993

Our fathers, ourselves healing men's brokenness. Martos, Joseph. *Liguorian* 81:52-57 O 1993

MEN—PSYCHOLOGY
The wild man's journey: reflections on male spirituality. Rohr, Richard, 1943-, and Martos, Joseph. Cincinnati: St Anthony Messenger Press, 1993. ISBN 0-86716-1280

MEN—RELIGIOUS LIFE
Tender warrior: God's intention for a man. Weber, Stu. Sisters: Questar, 1993. x, 224p ISBN 088070-579-5

The wild man's journey: reflections on male spirituality. Rohr, Richard, 1943-, and Martos, Joseph. Cincinnati: St Anthony Messenger Press, 1993. ISBN 0-86716-1280

MENCHU TUM, RIGOBERTA
Rigoberta Menchú Tum, Doctora en justicia. Mencú Tum, Rigoberta. *Christus* 58:74-79 N-D 1992

Rigoberta Menchu: the voice of resistance [repr and tr fr Madres de la Plaza de Mayo]. *LADOC* 23:18-22 Mr-Ap 1993

MENDOZA, JUSTO ZARIQUIEGUI, 1886-1936
Congregation for the Causes of Saints (1992-12-21) Decree on martyrdom. Congregation for the Causes of Saints. *OR(Eng)* 1272:4 Ja 6 1993*

MENTAL HEALTH AND RELIGION
Religion and prevention in mental health: research, vision, and action. Pargament, Kenneth I, et al. New York: The Haworth Press, 1992. 92-5887/x, 333p ISBN 1-56024 LC 225-6

MENTAL HEALTH SERVICES
Linking individual and organizational wellness. Canosa, James F, and Lewandowski, Leonard M. *Health Prog* 74:44-47 1993

Mental healthcare for rural seniors. Smith, Marianne, and Buckwalter, Kathleen C. *Health Prog* 74:52-56+ Mr 1993

MENTAL ILLNESS
The growing dialogue of church and couch [interview by D Scott]. English, Joseph. *OSV* 82:12 Jl 4 1993

Our society is still giving mental illness a bum rap. Heffern, Rich. *Nat Cath Rep* 29:8 Jl 2 1993

Priests' treatment facility rocked by suits. Martinez, Demetria. *Nat Cath Rep* 29:5 F 26 1993

MENTALLY HANDICAPPED
In heaven there are no thunderstorms: celebrating the liturgy with developmentally disabled people. Okhuijsen, Gijs. Collegeville:Liturgical, 1992. 136p ISBN 0-81461-999-1 LC 91-41-4407

MENTALLY HANDICAPPED CHILDREN
Things Danny taught me: a father's story. Maier, Francis X. *Comm* 120:11-12 Mr 26 1993

MENTORS IN EDUCATION
Connecting with "the real world". Anderson, Peggy. *Momentum* 24:26-27 F-Mr 1993

MEOSKA, JOHN
The call of the wild. Slattery, Pat. *Register* 69:2 My 2 1993

MERCIER, EVANGELINE, -1993
Mercier, Evangeline, -1993 [obit]. Moore, Nina Polcyn. *Cath Work* 60:7 S 1993

MERCY
Filled with pity. Groeschel, Benedict J. *New Cov* 22:14-15 Je 1993

Justice isn't enough. Kosicki, George. *Register* 69:4 Mr 7 1993

The Name of God in Byzantine tradition: from hesychasm to imyaslavie. Slesinski, Robert, 1950-. *Communio* 20:49-62 Spr 1993

MERCY—BIBLICAL TEACHING
Streams of justice and mercy. Martin, George. *New Cov* 23:34 S 1993

MERKAVA
Blake's Milton as kabbalistic vision. Spector, Sheila A. *Relig Lit* 25:19-33 Spr 1993

MERLEAU-PONTY, MAURICE, 1908-1961
Merleau-Ponty's logos: the sens-ing of flesh. Stenstad, Gail. *PhilosTod* 37:52-61 Spr 1993

MERTON, THOMAS, 1915-1968
Choirs of millions: a reflection on Thomas Merton and God's creatures. Daggy, Robert E. *Cist Stud* 28:93-107 1993

The eclipse of difference: Merton's encounter with Judaism. Plank, Karl A. *Cist Stud* 28 no 2:179-191 1993

Jesus saves; but how? Appleby, Raphael Scott. *USCath* 58:30-36 F 1993

Song for nobody: a memory of Thomas Merton. Seitz, Ron. Liguori: Triumph Books, 1993. 188p ISBN 0-89243-486-4 LC 92-43419

Swimming in the sun: discovering the Lord's prayer with Francis of Assisi and Thomas Merton. Haase, Albert. Cincinnati: St Anthony Messenger Press, 1993. 216p ISBN 0-86716-193-0

Thomas Merton still surprises [condensed fr *The Progress* Ap 1 1993]. Dooley, Jerry. *CDgst* 57:57-59 Jl 1993

Thomas Merton: monk and mystic. Wilkins, Sally. *Liguorian* 81:14-20 D 1993

Thomas Merton: the vigilance of desire. Albert, John. *Word Sp* 14:105-117 1992

Worth pondering [commentary on Thomas Merton]. O'Connell, Patrick. *Living Prayer* 26:11-12 N-D 1993

MESOPOTAMIA—ANTIQUITIES
La literatura mesopotámica antigua. Moreno Garrido, Jaime. *Teol Vida* 33 no 3-4:237-254 1992

MESSALIANS
Le Traité de la virginité de Grégoire de Nysse. Huybrechts, Paul. *NRT* 115: 227-242 Mr-Ap 1993

MESTRI, GUIDO DEL, CARDINAL, 1911-193
Del Mestri, Guido, Cardinal, 1911-1993 [obit]. *OR(Eng)* 1303:12 Ag 18 1993

METALLURGY
Alvaro Alonso Barba's Art of metallurgy: from the poetical to the technological. Soons, Alan. *Cithara* 32:3-12 My 1993

METANOIA *see* Conversion

METAPHOR
Feminist theology: a proposal. Martin, Francis. *Communio* 20:334-376 Sum 1993

Light and metaphor in Plotinus and St Thomas Aquinas. Corrigan, Kevin. *Thomist* 57:187-199 Ap 1993

Metaphor for life. Costello, Andrew. *USCath* 58:39-41 F 1993

Metaphorical theology. Begley, John. *Pacifica* 6:49-60 F 1993

Metaphors of discrimination: a comparison of Gunnar Myrdal and Gary Becker. Shulman, Steven. *RSocEcon* 50:432-452 Wint 1992

A theological case for God-She expanding the treasury of metaphor. Johnson, Elizabeth A, 1941-. *Comm* 120:9-14 Ja 29 1993

METAPHYSICS
Le concept de philosophie première chez Aristote. Fallon, Jacques. *RPhil Louvain* 91:5-13 F 1993

Deontologism and moral weakness. Peterson, John. *IPQ* 33:173-181 Je 1993

Document: le concept mégarique et aristotélicien de possibilité. Hartmann, Nicolaï. *Laval Theol Phil* 49:131-146 F 1993

De l'ontologie à la théologie. Gérard, Gilbert. *RPhil Louvain* 90:445-485 N 1992

The metaphysics of higher spiritual conciousness. Sherrill, Julian F, Sr. New York: Vantage Press, 1992. x, 264p ISBN 0-533-10214-6 LC 92-90684

The metaphysics of Pan-Unity in Pavel A. Florensky: a world view. Slesinski, Robert, 1950-. *Diakonia* 26 no 3:185-195 1993

Metaphysics: what we believe about reality. Kreeft, Peter John, 1937. *Register* 69:1+ Ag 22 1993

Our longest lie: irreligious thoughts on the relation between metaphysics and politics. Kramer, Matthew. *PhilosTod* 37:89-109 Spr 1993

Person, being, and St Thomas. Clarke, W Norris. *Communio* 19:601-618 Wint 1992

Physique et métaphysique chez Aristote. Destrée, Pierre. *RPhil Louvain* 90: 422-444 N 1992

Platon, l'École de Tübingen et Giovanni Reale. Rizzerio, Laura. *RPhil Louvain* 91:90-110 F 1993

Il posto della metafisica nel sapere umano Il pensiero di Maimonide e il suo influsso su S Tommasso d'Aquino. Pangallo, Don Mario. *Gregorianum* 74 no 2:331-352 1993

Reply to Craig: the possible infinitude of the past [reply to W L Craig, 31 no 4:387-410 1991]. Smith, Quentin. *IPQ* 33:109-115 Mr 1993

Resistance to the rule of time or a "post-metyphysical metaphysics": Michael Theunissen's Negative Theology of Time. Penta, Leo J. *PhilosTod* 37:211-224 Sum 1993

Ser y conocer. Garcia Del Muro Solans, Juan. Barcelona: PPU, 1993. x, 580p ISBN 84-477-0017-8

Le statut de l'un dans la Métaphysique. Couloubaritsis, Lambros. *RPhil Louvain* 90:497-522 N 1992

La stylométrie et la question de Métaphysique K. Rutten, Christian. *RPhil Louvain* 90:486-496 N 1992

METAPHYSICS—STUDY
Discusiones sobre la metafisica. Armesto, Indalecio. Santiago: Universidad, 1993. x, 360p ISBN 84-7191-968-0

METHODIST CHURCH (GREAT BRITAIN)
Methodists face split over homosexuals in ministry. *Tablet* 247:594-595 My 8 1993

METHODIST CHURCHES—CLERGY
Preacher on Tower Hill. Griffiths, Leslie. *Tablet* 247:135-136 Ja 30 1993

METHODIST CHURCHES—RELATIONS—CATHOLIC CHURCH
Methodist minister's ecumenical labor lost. Anderson, David E. *Nat Cath Rep* 30:4 O 29 1993

METHODIST CHURCHES- GREAT BRITAIN
Methodists aim for compromise in debate on homosexuality. *Tablet* 247:868-869 Jl 3 1993

METROPOLITAN MUSEUM OF ART (NEW YORK, NY)
Too high the cornices: the Met's new galleries. Siegel, Lee. *Comm* 120:21-22 O 22 1993

METTE, NORBERT
Habermas e la teologia. Brena, Gian Luigi. *Civilta* 3:51-54 Jl 3 1993

MEXICAN AMERICANS—SOCIAL CONDITIONS
What Cesar Chavez believed. Ramirez, Ricardo, Bp. *Origins* 23:17+ My 27 1993

MEXICO—POLITICS AND GOVERNMENT
Dialogue [interview by G Burke]. Rodriguez, Tarcisio. *Register* 69:1+ Je 27 1993
Mexican political parties fight for Catholic votes. Smith, Matt. *Nat Cath Rep* 29:5 S 3 1993
Outsider who would be Mexican president [interview by Arthur Jones]. Cárdenas, Cuauhtémoc. *Nat Cath Rep* 29:12-13 Jl 30 1993
Still fit for Greene. Jones, Arthur C, 1936-. *Tablet* 247:1002-1003 Ag 7 1993

MEXICO—SOCIAL CONDITIONS
Free trade with an unfree land [map, photos]. Jones, Arthur C, 1936-. *Nat Cath Rep* 29:10-12 Ap 16 1993

MICHELANGELO BUONARROTI, 1475-1564
Michelangelo's Four Pieta's [photos]. Thiele, Gloria. *CDgst* 57:1-6 Ag 1993

MICHIGAN CATHOLIC CONFERENCE
Physician-assisted suicide and euthanasia. *Origins* 23:63-64 Je 10 1993

MICROECONOMICS
The Church in the post-socialist world. Murphy, Séamus. *Studies* 82:87-96 Spr 1993

MIDDLE AGE—PSYCHOLOGICAL ASPECTS
Soul making and life's second half. Brennan, Anne, and Brewi, Janice. *RRel* 52:220-225 Mr-Ap 1993

MIDDLE AGE—RELIGIOUS ASPECTS
Out of control. Costello, Andrew. *USCath* 58:38-40 Ja 1993

MIDDLE AGES
Medieval Christendom and the restoration of a Christian society. Tanner, Norman P. *Month* 25:467-472 D 1992
Sexuality and spirituality in the European Middle Ages. Gross-Diaz, Theresa. *Chicago Stud* 32:32-42 Ap 1993
Sin in the Middle Ages. Tanner, Norman P. *Month* 26:372-375 S-O 1993

MIDDLE AGES—CHURCH HISTORY
Christendom and Christianity in the Middle Ages. Bredero, Adriaan H. Grand Rapids: Eerdmans, 1993. 448p ISBN 0-8028-3692-5

MIDDLE AGES—CONGRESSES
Do North Americans understand the Middle Ages better than Europeans? Tanner, Norman P. *America* 169:5-6 O 2 1993

MIDDLE AGES—RELIGION
Magic in the age of faith. Greeley, Andrew Moran, 1928-. *America* 169:8-14 O 9 1993

MIDDLE EAST—HISTORY
Historical atlas of the Middle East. Freeman-Grenville, G S P. New York: Simon & Schuster, 1993. x, 144p ISBN 0-13-3-390915-8

MIDDLE EAST—POLITICS AND GOVERNMENT
Dialogue [interview by L Petzvow]. Friej, Elias. *Register* 69:1+ Ap 18 1993
Hope is scarce as water in the Middle East. Schroth, Raymond A, 1933-. *Nat Cath Rep* 29:11-12 S 3 1993
Hope, at last, in the Middle East [editorial]. *Nat Cath Rep* 29:24 S 10 1993
The other peace process. Goodman, Daniel. *Register* 69:4 O 24 1993
That my people will live in a peaceful home [address, Christian Culture Series, D 6 1992]. Sabbah, Michael. *Can Cath Rev* 11:14-18 N 1993

MIDDLE EAST—RELIGION
We are not guests: the exodus of Christians from the Middle East. Samaha, John M. *Can Cath Rev* 11:11-13 N 1993

MIDDLE EAST STUDIES
Historical atlas of the Middle East. Freeman-Grenville, G S P. New York: Simon & Schuster, 1993. x, 144p ISBN 0-13-3-390915-8

MIDDLE SCHOOL STUDENTS
A scientific approach to morality. Blase, Mary. *Momentum* 24:23-24 S-O 1993

MIDDLE SCHOOLS—CURRICULA
Playing Shakespeare. Bashian, Kathleen Ryniker. *Momentum* 24:67-68 F-Mr 1993

MIDRASH
Meeting Jacob at the Jabbok: wrestling with a text—a Midrash on Genesis 32:22-32. Knight, Henry F. *JEcumen Stds* 29:451-460 Sum-Aut 1992

MIGRANT LABOR
On the road again. Gross, Adela. *ReligTJ* 27:54-55 S 1993
The saintliness of Cesar Chavez [editorial]. *Tablet* 247:567 My 8 1993

MIGRATION, INTERNAL
Comparisons from the North. Hewitt, Victor. *Studies* 82:24-34 Spr 1993

MIGRATIONS OF NATIONS—ETHICAL ASPECTS
Ethical implications of a people's changing visage. *Origins* 22:758-761 Ap 15 1993

MIGUEZ, MANUEL, 1831-1925
Congregation for the Causes of Saints (1992-12-21) Decree on the heroic virtues. Congregation for the Causes of Saints. *OR(Eng)* 1272:4 Ja 6 1993*

MILAN, DIEGO VENTAJA, 1880-1936
Congregation for the Causes of Saints (1992-12-21) Decree on martyrdom. Congregation for the Causes of Saints. *OR(Eng)* 1272:4 Ja 6 1993*

MILBANK, JOHN
(En)countering the (post)modern. Lakeland, Paul. *Month* 26:63-70 F 1993

MILITARY ASSISTANCE
Between Dracula and Bovary: Yugoslavia's romantic nationalism. Garvey, John, 1944-. *Comm* 120:7-8 My 21 1993

MILITARY CHAPLAINS see Chaplains, Military

MILITARY ETHICS
Homosexuals in the military: three issues. Mahony, Roger Michael, Cardinal, 1936-. *Origins* 22:621+ F 25 1993

MILITARY GOVERNMENT- LATIN AMERICA
Pentecostalismo, governos militares e revolução. Cartaxo Rolim, Francisco. *REB* 53:324-348 Je 1993

MILITARY POLICY
Military hospital personnel who oppose abortion. Dimino, Joseph I, Abp. *Origins* 22:612 F 18 1993

MILITARY RELIGIOUS ORDERS
The templar order: a failed ideal? Menache, Sophia. *CHist* 79:1-21 Ja 1993

MILITARY SERVICE- UNITED STATES
The argument for the bans: combat is no place for women and gays. Reilly, Robert. *Crisis* 11:39-41 Ap 1993
Homosexuals in the military: policy and morality. Coleman, Gerald D. *Church* 9:20-23 Sum 1993
Homosexuals in the military: three issues. Mahony, Roger Michael, Cardinal, 1936-. *Origins* 22:621+ F 25 1993

MILK PRODUCTION
Unnatural growth hormone. Atwater, Tim. *Cath Work* 60:7 Mr-Ap 1993

MILLENNIALISM
Apocalypse now in Waco [editorial]. *America* 168:3-4 My 22, 1993

MILLER, PEGGY, -1993
Miller, Peggy, -1993 [obit]. *Tablet* 247:816 Je 26 1993

MILLET, JEAN FRANCOIS, 1814-1875
The artist who painted a prayer. Cuevas, Zillah. *CDgst* 57:6-9 Mr 1993

MILOSEVIC, SLOBODAN
Lest we forget. Cviic, Christopher. *Tablet* 247:1092-1093 Ag 28 1993
Will the Balkans burn? Lukovic, Petar. *Tablet* 247:32+ Ja 9 1993

MILTON, JOHN, 1608-1674
"Conversing, looking, loving": the discourse of reason in Paradise lost. Cacicedo, Al. *Cithara* 32:13-28 My 1993

MIND AND BODY
Chisholm on persons as entia successiva and the brain-microparticle hypothesis. Jacquette, Dale. *Mod Schlmn* 70:99-113 Ja 1993
The value of spiritual health. Seidl, Lawrence G. *Health Prog* 74:48-50 1993

MINIHAN, JEREMIAH FRANCIS, BP
The bishop was a football hero. Carew, Wally. *Priest* 49:31-32 Ap 1993

MINISTRY
AIDS and hospitality. Heuser, Tom. *Cath Work* 60:6 My 1993
Airport priest [condensed fr *Chicago Tribune* Ap 4 1993]. Hutchcraft, Chuck. *CDgst* 57:66-70 O 1993
A breakthrough for ministry. Brennan, Noel. *AFER* 35:27-36 F 1993
Calling forth the talents. Weind, Teresita. *ChrWorld* 236:234-235 S-O 1993
Checklist for collaborative ministry. Kinast, Robert L. *Tod Parish* 25:13-16, 13-17 O S 1993
The contemplative pastor: returning to the art of spiritual direction. Peterson, Eugene H. Grand Rapids: Eerdmans, 1993. 192p ISBN 0-8028-0114-5
Converting the liturgist. Wagner, Nick. *Mod Lit* 20:12-14 N 1993
Directory for the application of the principles and norms of ecumenism. *OR(Eng)* 1295:I-XIV Je 16 1993
The future of the Church and its ministries: imperatives for the twenty-first century. McBrien, Richard P. *New Theol Rev* 6:43-52 Ag 1993
The good news for our neighborhood [interview by J Sammon]. Kuhn, George. *Cath Work* 60:1+ Ja-F 1993
Happy in his work. *Tablet* 247:1193 S 18 1993
"I am the Messiah and you're not". Ganss, Karl, and Fuller, Kathleen. *Tod Parish* 25:18-19 O 1993
"I'm here" [interview by T H Stahel, 1938-]. Sullivan, Andrew. *America* 168: 5-11 My 8 1993
If ministers switched to private practice? White, Leland J. *Nat Cath Rep* 29: 17-19 Ja 15 1993
"Make the best of the present time" [repr fr *Crossroads*]. Wermter, Oskar. *AFER* 34:183-187 Je 1992
Parish diary: February. *Tablet* 247:270 F 27 1993
A parish plan for bereavement ministry. Schumann, Marge. *Tod Parish* 25: 13-16 Ja 1993
Priestcraft: a how-to guide for everyone. Desiderio, Frank R. *ST Anth* 101: 16-21 Jl 1993
Reflections of a parish priest. Keller, Dan. *Momentum* 24:58-60 S-O 1993
September ministry—and the Garden of Eden. Gilbert, Jack. *Tod Parish* 25: 38 S 1993
Sharing the Lord's mission. Doohan, Leonard. *Mod Lit* 20:34-35 S 1993
A sister's ministry. Medcalf, John. *Tablet* 247:427 Ap 3 1993
Sponsorship networks. Gillis, Virginia. *Health Prog* 74:34-37+ Ap 1993
Three pastoral challenges for family ministers. McCord, H Richard, Jr. *Origins* 23:61-63 Je 10 1993
Towards koinonia/communion in faith, life and witness: revised discussion paper for the Fifth World Conference on Faith and Order. Tanner, Mary, et al. *Ecumen Trends* 22:1-24 Je 1993
Tradition and transformation. Arghittu, Mary, et al. *Health Prog* 74:28-33 Ap 1993

MINISTRY—CONTROVERSIES
Handing on the tradition: a Catholic mother laments. Baumer, Patricia Hughes. *New Theol Rev* 6:32-54 My 1993

MINISTRY—EDUCATION
LIMEX: distance education in intentional learning communities. Lee, Bernard J. *Momentum* 24:7-9 F-Mr 1993

MINISTRY—SOCIAL POLICY
Pastoral ministers and persons with disabilities. Bevilacqua, Anthony Joseph, Cardinal, 1923-. *Origins* 22:518-520 Ja 7 1993

MINISTRY—WOMEN
The ministry of women in the early Church. Gillman, Florence Morgan. *New Theol Rev* 6:89-94 My 1993

MINISTRY TO PRIESTS PROGRAMME
Priestly development for collaboration in ministry. Kilroy, Bernard. *Doctr Life* 43:287-294 My-Je 1993

MINORITIES
Changing unjust borders. Corley, Felix. *Month* 26:71-73 F 1993
Minority museum: fighting hatred, instilling dignity. Whitney, Sally. *St Anth* 100:34-39 Ap 1993

MINORITY STUDENTS
Of many things. Donohue, John W, 1917-. *America* 169:2 S 18 1993

John Paul II, Pope, (1993-10-05) Veritatis Splendor. John Paul II, Pope, 1920- (Karol Wojtyla) (elected 1978). *Origins* 23:297-334 O 14 1993*

John Paul II, Pope, (19930-10-05) Veritatis Splendor. John Paul II, Pope, 1920- (Karol Wojtyla) (elected 1978). *OR(Eng)* 1310:1 O 6 1993*

Key query: what must I do to be saved? McInerny, Ralph M. *Register* 69:1+ N 14 1993*

The lesson of Lent. Novak, Michael, 1933-. *Crisis* 11:4-7 Ap 1993

Liberty under the moral law: B Hoose's critique of the Grisez-Finnis Theory of human good. George, Robert P. *Heythrop* 34:175-180 Ap 1993

"Listening" to nature: the significance of Leon Kass for Catholic moral theology. Torraco, Stephen F. *Linacre* 60:40-55 Ag 1993

Living in Christ: the catechism reunites morality and spirituality. Ashley, Benedict M. *Crisis* 11:23-26 Je 1993*

The magisterium and morality. Spohn, William C. *TheolStds* 54:95-111 Mr 1993

A medical and moral dilemma. Kelly, Kevin T. *Month* 26:138-144 Ap 1993

Method in ethics: a Scotistic contribution. Shannon, Thomas A. *TheolStds* 54:272-293 Je 1993

Models of the person in moral theology. Rigali, Norbert J. *Chicago Stud* 32:177-185 Ag 1993

La moral como madurez de la persona—Evocando la figura de Antonio Sanchís, OP. Espeja, Jesús. *Cien Tom* 119:391-405 My-Ag 1992

Moral living in a non-Christian world [review article *Living a Christian Life* by G. Grisez]. Hanink, James G. *OSV* 82:9 N 21 1993

Moral reason is basis of virtue. Stafford, J Francis, Abp, 1939-. *OR(Eng)* 1311:10 O 13 1993*

Moral theology 2000: four signs and shifts. McCormick, Patrick. *ChrWorld* 236:212-216 S-O 1993

The new Catechism compared to the "Roman Catechism" of Trent. Lanzetti, Raúl. *OR(Eng)* 1298:9+ Jl 7 1993*

The new encyclical [editorial]. *America* 169:3 O 23 1993

New papal letter seeks to strengthen moral teaching. *Tablet* 247:1019 Ag 7 1993

On dying poorly: the gracelessness of euthanasia. Meehan, Bridget Mary. *Crisis* 11:37-40 Je 1993

On sex and sexuality: the challenge of André Guindon. Selling, Joseph A. *Doctr Life* 43:31-41 Ja 1993

Perspectives on "Veritatis Splendor". Quinn, John Raphael, Abp, 1929-. *Origins* 23:398-399 N 11 1993*

The Pope dissents from America. Pfaff, William. *OSV* 82:23 N 14 1993

Pope's new encyclical has little to do with real world. McCarthy, Colman. *Nat Cath Rep* 30:22 O 29 1993*

Presentation of the Encyclical Letter "Veritatis Splendor". Ratzinger, Joseph, Cardinal, 1927-. *OR(Eng)* 1310:1-2 O 6 1993*

Proportionalism and a text of the young Aquinas: Quodlibetum IX, Q 7, A 2. Johnson, Mark A. *TheolStds* 53:683-699 D 1992

À propos d'une note romaine sur le livre d'André Guindon. Couture, Denise. *Laval Theol Phil* 49:321-329 Je 1993

The resplendence of truth [editorial]. *Tablet* 247:999-1000 Ag 7 1993

Sexual morality's positive goals and the problem of legalism. George, Robert P. *Origins* 22:778-780 Ap 22 1993

The sources of morality: function, conformity and aesthetics. O'Connell, James. *Heythrop* 34:160-170 Ap 1993

A Southern Baptist view. Heimbach, Daniel R. *Crisis* 11:23 O 1993

Suicide in the Bible. Lenzen, Verena. *TheolDgst* 40:37-42 Spr 1993

Tierpatente im Kreuzfeuer der Kritik. Münk, Hans J. *Stimm Zeit* 211:605-616 S 1993

Tres ensayos sobre Kelsen. Bocardo, Enrique. Sevilla: Universidad Sevilla, 1993. x, 135p ISBN 84-7405-977-1

Unofficial glimpse of encyclical on morals. *Tablet* 247:926 Jl 17 1993

Vatican's marked cards can give "dissenters" a raw deal. Hebblethwaite, Peter, 1930-. *Nat Cath Rep* 30:9 O 29 1993*

Veritatis Splendor and moral theology. McCormick, Richard Arthur, 1922-. *America* 169:8-11 O 30 1993*

Veritatis Splendor draws cheers and jeers. *Nat Cath Rep* 29:15 O 15 1993*

[Veritatis splendor is unique]. Hauerwas, Stanley Martin, 1940-. *Comm* 120:16-18 O 22 1993

Veritatis splendor [editorial]. *Comm* 120:3-5 O 22 1993

Veritatis Splendor [excerpts]. John Paul II, Pope, 1920- (Karol Wojtyla) (elected 1978). *Register* 69:2 O 17 1993*

La vie dans le Christ. Chapelle, Albert. *NRT* 115:169-185 Mr-Ap 1993

Weltethos oder säkularer Humanismus? Fuchs, Josef. *Stimm Zeit* 211:147-154 Mr 1993

What bishop might tell her people about encyclical. Ruether, Rosemary Radford. *Nat Cath Rep* 30:18 N 12 1993*

Wirtschaftsethik. Mack, Elke. *Stimm Zeit* 211:713-716 O 1993

You can't keep a good theory down: the just war, the Gulf War and beyond. Pope, J Stephen. *Comm* 120:9-12 F 12 1993

MORAL THEOLOGY- EUROPE

European enthusiasm: a bestseller for the hungering faithful. Fumagalli, Armando. *Crisis* 11:31-32+ Je 1993*

MORAL THEOLOGY- GERMANY

Sexualerziehung zwischen Norm und Individualisierung. Bleistein, Roman, 1928-. *Stimm Zeit* 211:521-532 Ag 1993

MORAL THEOLOGY- ITALY

An Italian view of the debate on virtue. Kennedy, Terence. *Thomist* 57:123-130 Ja 1993

MORE, THOMAS, SAINT, 1478-1535

Worth pondering. O'Connell, Patrick. *Living Prayer* 26:11-12 S-O 1993

MORMON CHURCH

Are the Moonies Latter-Day Mormons? Miller, Timothy. *StudiaM* 41:67-83 1992

MORMON CHURCH—DOCTRINE

Mormonism in the twenty-first century. Saliba, John A. *StudiaM* 41:49-67 1992

MORMON CHURCH—HISTORY

Mormonism in the twenty-first century. Saliba, John A. *StudiaM* 41:49-67 1992

MORON HIDALGO, JOAQUIN

John Paul II, Pope, (1992-07-25) Constitutiones Apostolicae (Apostolic Constitution) [Latin]. John Paul II, Pope, 1920- (Karol Wojtyla) (elected 1978). *AAS* 84:1053-1055 N 3 1992*

MOSCOW—DESCRIPTION AND TRAVEL

How to be an alien in Moscow. *Tablet* 247:575 My 8 1993

MOSES (BIBLICAL LEADER)

Moses and Matthew. Roth, Wolfgang. *BibleT* 30:362-366 N 1992

Moses, Jesus, and Marx: utopians in search of justice. Soelle, Dorothee. *CrossCurr* 42:528-535 Wint 1992-1993

Moses. Martin, George. *Liguorian* 81:44-45 F 1993

MOSES THE BLACK, SAINT, 330?-405?

Saint Moses the Black. O'Connell-Cahill, Catherine. *Salt* 13:31 Ap 1993

MOTHER AND CHILD

A mother's prayer. Jeray, Diane. *Liguorian* 81:46-48 S 1993

MOTHERHOOD

"Discovering Motherhood"—one woman's journey [interview by G Hizer]. *OSV* 81:11 D 20 1992

Father Scott's reflections on women, family, and relationships. Scott, John M. Indiana: Our Sunday Visitor, 1993. 139p ISBN 0-87973-530-9 LC 92-61551

From Eve to Mary: mothers in God's plan. Donahue, Lois M. *Liguorian* 81:56-61 My 1993

"Non c'è amore piu grande" [editorial]. *Civilta* 144:417-423 Mr 6 1993

Plush lawns: here comes the baby. McCloskey, Liz Leibold. *Comm* 120:8-9 Ap 23 1993

Ramblin' Rose. Costello, Gerald M, 1931-. *USCath* 58:48-51 Ja 1993

"Reproducing the world": Mary O'Brien's theory of reproductive consciousness and implications for feminist incarnational theology. Kaminski, Phyllis H. *Horizons (CTS)* 19:240-262 Fall 1992

MOTHERHOOD—PHILOSOPHY

A theology for mother church. Gallagher, Rosemary. *Priests & People* 7:301-305 Ag-S 1993

MOTHERS

Count on Mom: but do it yourself. Byrne, Katharine. *Comm* 120:9-10 Ap 9 1993

MOTHERS (IN RELIGION, FOLKLORE)

Five mothers who found time to be saints. Hermes, Joan Garvey. *USCath* 58:28-33 My 1993

From Eve to Mary: mothers in God's plan. Donahue, Lois M. *Liguorian* 81:56-61 My 1993

MOTHERS AND DAUGHTERS

Journey with my daughter. Maitland, Sara, 1950-. *Tablet* 247:1065-1066 Ag 21 1993

"Things my mother taught me" [interview by J A Wintz, 1936-]. Shields, Brooke, 1965-. *St Anth* 100:28-32 My 1993

MOTION PICTURE AUTHORSHIP

Writing for the screen [interview by J G Deedy, 1923-]. Hume, Edward. *Critic* 47:16-25 Sum 1993

MOTION PICTURE PRODUCERS AND DIRECTORS

Arrivederci, Fellini. Blake, Richard A, 1939-. *America* 169:10-11 D 4 1993

Eric Rohmer: the charm of the real. Cunneen, Joseph. *Critic* 47:83-90 Spr 1993

MOTION PICTURES—SINGLE WORKS

Made in America. Prizer, John. *Register* 69:5 Je 20 1993

MOTION PICTURES- ITALY

Arrivederci, Fellini. Blake, Richard A, 1939-. *America* 169:10-11 D 4 1993

MOUNTAINS (IN RELIGION, FOLKLORE)

Sinai and Tabor: apophatic and kataphatic symbols in tension. Lane, Belden C. *Stud Form Spir* 14:189-205 My 1993

MOURNING CUSTOMS

Musicians as mourners. Keyl, Timothy J. *Liturgy* 10:63-67 Wint 1992

MOVING, HOUSEHOLD

Moving days. Cullen, Paul. *Columbia* 73:14-15 Je 1993

MOVING PICTURES see Films—Religious Aspects

MOYLAN, JOSEPH

A good judge meets a bad choice on abortion. Sheehan, Pete. *OSV* 82:3 O 3 1993

MOYNIHAN, ROBERT

"Inside the Vatican:" want a peek? Burke, Greg. *Register* 69:1+ Je 13 1993

MOZAMBIQUE

Mozambican prelate visits US seeking peacekeepers. Collins, Carole. *Nat Cath Rep* 29:9 Mr 5 1993

MUGGING- NEW YORK

A double mugging: defender of the faith gets maced. Jordan, Patrick. *Comm* 120:4-5 N 5 1993

MUHAMMAD, THE PROPHET

I Musulmani, che Dio li protegga e li conservi!. Gatta, Secondino. *StudiaM* 42:271-285 1993

Islam and other faiths. Cragg, Kenneth. *StudiaM* 42:257-270 1993

Islamic attitudes to other religions. Watt, William Montgomery. *StudiaM* 42:245-255 1993

Jesus and Muhammad: Christianity and Islam in dialogue. Bacik, James Joseph, 1936-. *Emmanuel* 99:13-14+ Ja-F 1993

MULHERN, MARTHA

Sister Martha's second calling [condensed fr *C S J Focus* F 1993]. Anderson, Norm. *CDgst* 57:57-59 Ag 1993

MULLER, HUBERT

Response to Hubert Müller. Colombo, Giuseppe. *Jurist* 52 no 1:365-368 1992

MULLIGAN, CYRIL, -1992

Mass for a dead friend. Crosby, Ned. *Furrow* 44:27-29 Ja 1993

MUMCU, UGUR, -1992

Death of private soldier. Barchard, David. *Tablet* 247:131-132 Ja 30 1993

MUNARRIZ, FELIPE DE JESUS, 1875-1936

Congregation for the Causes of Saints (1992-03-07) Decree on the heroic virtues. Congregation for the Causes of Saints. *AAS* 84:916-923 S 8 1992*

MYSTICISM—HISTORY
Angela of Foligno: complete works. Angela, of Foligno, 1248?-1309. New York: Paulist Press, 1993. x, 424p ISBN 0-8091-0460-1 LC 92-38830
Complete works. Angela, of Foligno, 1248?-1309. New York: Paulist Press, 1993. x, 424p ISBN 0-80910-460 LC 92-38830

MYSTICISM—ISLAM
Mysticism in Islamism and Christianity. McKnight, Peg. *Living Prayer* 26: 29-31 Ja-F 1993

MYSTICISM AND LITERATURE
Blake's Milton as kabbalistic vision. Spector, Sheila A. *Relig Lit* 25:19-33 Spr 1993
T.S. Eliot and mysticism: a discussion. Williams, Rowan. *Doctr Life* 43:396-401 S 1993

MYSTICS
Gertrude of Helfta: the herald of divine love. Winkworth, Margaret. New York: Paulist Press, 1993. x, 259p ISBN 0-8091-0458-x LC 92-20663
Meeting the mystics. Giallanza, Joel. *Living Prayer* 26:3-9 Ja-F 1993

MYTH
American Catholics and the Joseph Campbell phenomenon. Dinges, William D. *America* 168:12-14+ F 20 1993
The Joseph Campbell phenomenon: implications for the contemporary church. Madden, Lawrence J, ed. Washington: The Pastoral Press, 1992. x, 153p ISBN 0-912405-89-9
Myth and culture in theology and literature [interview by R. Adams]. Dunne, John S, 1929-. *Relig Lit* 25:79-104 Sum 1993
Une nouvelle approche de la philosophie d'Ernst Cassirer. Lofts, Steve. *RPhil Louvain* 90:523-538 N 1992

MYTHOLOGY
Life-of-Jesus research and the eclipse of mythology. Evans, Craig A, 1952-. *TheolStds* 54:3-36 Mr 1993

MYTHOLOGY—INFLUENCE
Sports: shaping our stories and our myths. Fisher, Doug. *ChrWorld* 236:282-285 N-D 1993

MYTHOLOGY, CLASSICAL
The Oxford guide to classical mythology in the arts, 1300-1990s. Reid, Jane Davidson. New York: Oxford University Press, 1993. ISBN 0-19504-998-5 LC 92-35374

MYTHOLOGY IN LITERATURE
Jan Patovcka et le phénomène de l'écriture littéraire. Declève, Henri. *Laval Theol Phil* 49:3-26 F 1993

N

NA'MAAT, JOSEPH
God's human face revealed: a retreat in Wales. Corona, Mary. *RRel* 52:519-531 Jl-Ag 1993

NAGARJUNA, 150?-250
Derrida and Mādhyamika Buddhism: from linguistic deconstruction to criticism of onto-theologies. Zong-qi, Cai. *IPQ* 33:183-195 Je 1993

NAILATIKAU, RATU EPELI
John Paul II, Pope, (1991-11-15) Allocutionhes (Papal reception of ambassadorial credentials) [English]. John Paul II, Pope, 1920- (Karol Wojtyla) (elected 1978). *AAS* 84:982-984 O 3 1992*

NANCY, JEAN-LUC
The community's absence in Lyotard, Nancy, and Lacoue-Labarthe. May, Todd. *PhilosTod* 37:275-284 Aut 1993

NARCISSISM see Self-Love

NARRATION IN THE BIBLE
Das Wortfeld der Liebe im Paganen und Biblischen Griechisch. Söding, Thomas. *Eph Theol Lovan* 78:284-330 D 1992

NARRATIVE (THEOLOGY)
Metaphorical theology. Begley, John. *Pacifica* 6:49-60 F 1993
Time and narrative: reflections from Paul Ricoeur. Jasper, David, 1951-. *Heythrop* 34:302-306 Jl 1993

NATIONAL BLACK CATHOLIC CONGRESS, NEW ORLEANS, 1992
Highlights of the National Black Catholic Congress VII. Chipungu, Sandra S. *Momentum* 24:64-65 F-Mr 1993

NATIONAL CATHOLIC EDUCATIONAL ASSOCIATION CONVENTION
Educators meet to share good news, ideas. *Nat Cath Rep* 29:2 Ap 23 1993
Toward effective adult religious education. Dumestre, Marcel. *Origins* 23:24-28 My 27 1993

NATIONAL CONFERENCE OF CATECHETICAL LEADERSHIP
Overview: the catechism of the Catholic Church. Pollard, John E. *Origins* 23: 7-11 My 20 1993
Religious education's power to nurture faith. Eklin, Carolyn. *Origins* 23:28-31 My 27 1993

NATIONAL CONFERENCE OF CATHOLIC BISHOPS
see also United States Catholic Conference
The age of Confirmation: a flawed proposal. Duggan, Robert D. *America* 168: 12-14 Je 5-12 1993
Bishops speak in public session of sexual abuse. Reese, Thomas Joseph, 1945-. *America* 169:4-6 Jl 3-10 1993
The Bishops' Symposium on the Catechism. Carotta, Mike. *Momentum* 24: 70 S-O 1993
Bishops. Turner, Paul. *Mod Lit* 20:6-7 Je-Jl 1993
"The challenge of peace" revisited. Murray, Pius. *Emmanuel* 99:314-317 Jl-Ag 1993
"The challenge of peace"—10 years later. Sullivan, Walter Francis, Bp, 1928-. *OSV* 82:23 My 16 1993
A challenge of peace: North-South dialogue. Weakland, Rembert G, Abp, 1927-. *Origins* 23:292-296 O 7 1993
Child sexual abuse: think tank recommendations. *Origins* 23:108-111 Jl 1 1993
Confirmation: age, sequence, timing [interview]. Gaupin, Linda. *Mod Lit* 20: 8-10 Je-Jl 1993

Correspondence released: abortion and the nominee surgeon general. Keeler, William H, Abp. *Origins* 23:229-230 S 9 1993
Health care among US bishops' other concerns. Edwards, Robin T. *Nat Cath Rep* 29:3 Jl 2 1993
In Chancery. Hitchcock, Helen Hull. *Crisis* 11:11-12 Je 1993
Miles to go [editorial]. Pawlikowski, John T. *New Theol Rev* 6:3-5 My 1993
Moral methodology and pastoral responsiveness: the case of abortion and the care of children. Whitmore, Todd David. *TheolStds* 54:316-338 Je 1993
Nature, culture, and the Church. Carroll, William E. *Can Cath Rev* 11:44-47 Ja 1993
NCCB establishes committee on sexual abuse. Kinney, John, Bp. *Origins* 23: 104-105 Jl 1 1993
The pastoral that wasn't: feminist agenda stalled at Bishops' Conference. Hitchcock, Helen Hull. *Crisis* 11:33-37 Ja 1993
Sexuality education—forward or backward? Miller, Patricia F. *Momentum* 24:49-52 F-Mr 1993
Stewardship: we reap what we sow [editorial]. Feister, John Bookser. *St Anth* 100:57 Ja 1993
Stormy weather. Hitchcock, Helen Hull. *Crisis* 11:8-9 Jl-Ag 1993
Subcommittee head introduces think tank recommendations. Connors, Canice. *Origins* 23:105-107 Jl 1 1993
Ten years after: the bishops (again) on war and peace. Weigel, George. *Crisis* 11:36-41 My 1993
Women's work is never done. Hitchcock, Helen Hull. *Crisis* 11:11-12 My 1993

NATIONAL CONFERENCE OF CATHOLIC BISHOPS MEETING, NEW ORLEANS, 1993
Bishops take action on a tough, varied agenda. DeMers, John. *Register* 69:1+ Jl 4 1993
Bishops take action on sex abuse. Feuerherd, Peter. *Register* 69:1+ Je 11 1993
Looking for answers. Shaw, Russell. *OSV* 82:3 Jl 4 1993

NATIONAL CONFERENCE OF CATHOLIC BISHOPS', KANSAS CITY, 1993
Bishops advised on sexual abuse [National Conference of Catholic Bishops' Committee on priestly life and ministry meeting, Kansas City, MO]. Edwards, Robin T. *Nat Cath Rep* 29:5 Mr 5 1993

NATIONAL CONFERENCE OF PRIESTS ANNUAL MEETING, BIRMINGHAM, ENGLAND, 1993
Collaborative ministry: not just words. O'Sullivan, Brian. *Tablet* 247:1211-1212 S 18 1993
Priests and laity promote renewal. Miller, Annabel. *Tablet* 247:1205-1206 S 18 1993
Priests welcome lay participation. *Tablet* 247:1175 S 11 1993

NATIONAL CONGRESS ON CATHOLIC SCHOOLS FOR THE 21ST CENTURY, WASHINGTON, 1991
Responding to the goodness of God. Wilmer, Gary G. *Momentum* 24:45-47 N-D 1993

NATIONAL CONVENTION OF THE MARIOLOGICAL SOCIETY OF AMERICA, 43RD, HOUSTON
Proceedings of the forty-third National Convention of the Mariological Society of America held in Houston, Texas, My 28 and 29, 1992. McCurry, James E, et al. *Marian Stds* 43:9-189 1992*
The secretary's report. Thompson, Thomas L. *Marian Stds* 43:190-191 1992

NATIONAL COUNCIL OF CATHOLIC WOMEN
"On the wings of change?". Hitchcock, Helen Hull. *Register* 69:3 O 24 1993

NATIONAL COUNCIL OF CHURCHES IN THE USA
The common good: old idea, new urgency. Lynch, Robert, et al. *Origins* 23: 81+ Je 24 1993
National Council of Churches denies observer status to UFMCC. Solheim, James. *Ecumen Trends* 22:13 Ja 1993

NATIONAL ENDOWMENT OF THE ARTS (NEA)
Arts war likely to continue. Mullen, Peter. *Register* 69:1+ Ja 10 1993

NATIONAL HEALTH SERVICE (GREAT BRITAIN)
No joy for Jerry. Stanford, Peter. *Tablet* 247:1257-1258 O 2 1993
The rights of the child [editorial]. *Tablet* 247:675 My 29 1993

NATIONAL PASTORAL LIFE CENTER
How much is lay ministry worth? Kinast, Robert L. *Origins* 23:287-292 O 7 1993

NATIONAL RIGHT TO LIFE COMMITTEE
Doctor killed at abortion clinic. Smith, John, Bp, et al. *Origins* 22:701+ Mr 25 1993

NATIONAL SERVICE
Goodfellows: reinventing government. McCarthy, Abigail Quigley. *Comm* 120: 9-10 My 7 1993
Linking the new communitarians. Byron, William J, 1927-. *America* 168:11-13 Mr 20-27 1993
National service entangled [editorial]. *America* 169:3-4 Jl 3-10 1993

NATIONAL SOCIALISM- GERMANY
L'Apostolato e i Nazisti in Russia nel 1941. Graham, Robert A. *Civilta* 144: 437-444 Mr 6 1993
Fede e amore nei *Lager* Nazisti. Marchesi, Giovanni. *Civilta* 2:144-152 Ap 17 1993
Hell on earth Hannah Arendt in the face of Hitler. Rogozinski, Jacob. *PhilosTod* 37:257-274 Aut 1993
Reflections on after virtue after Auschwitz. Chansky, James D. *PhilosTod* 37:247-256 Aut 1993

NATIONALISM
Salvaging patriotism from the narrow nationalist. Elshtain, Jean Bethke, 1941-. *New Oxford Rev* 60:6-8+ O 1993
We are all foreigners: religion, nation and race. Garvey, John, 1944-. *Comm* 119:8-9 D 18 1992

NATIONALISM- HUNGARY
Statement of the Hungarian Council of Christians and Jews on anti-semitism and nationalism. *SIDIC* 26 no 1:27 1993

NATIONALISM- YUGOSLAVIA
Between Dracula and Bovary: Yugoslavia's romantic nationalism. Garvey, John, 1944-. *Comm* 120:7-8 My 21 1993

NATIONALISM AND RELIGION
Achieving peace with justice in Bosnia-Herzegovina. Keeler, William H, Abp. *Origins* 22:546-548 Ja 21 1993

Christian-Jewish relations in a new Europe. Solomon, Norman. *Month* 26:9-16 Ja 1993

Nationalismus und Multikulturalismus. Brieskorn, Norbert. *Stimm Zeit* 211:651-662 O 1993

NATIVE AMERICAN CHURCH
Brief on native peoples. *Origins* 23:401+ N 18 1993

Committee gives voice, hand to South's poor. Garrison, Greg. *Nat Cath Rep* 29:5 N 20 1992

NATURAL FAMILY PLANNING
Final declaration on family planning. Bernard, Catherine, et al. *TPS* 38:162-164 My-Je 1993

"Humanae Vitae" at 25. Duffy, Shatzi Luisa. *Crisis* 11:15-17 S 1993

Paul VI was right [reply to "Humanae Vitae" 25 years later by R A McCormick 6-8+ Jl 17 1993; rejoinder]. Flannery, Kevin L, and Koterski, Joseph. *America* 169:7-14 S 25 1993

NATURAL LAW
Abortion and the law. Whyte, Gerry. *Doctr Life* 42:253-272 My-Je 1992

An analysis of the use of rights language in pre-modern Catholic social thought. Brady, Bernard V. *Thomist* 57:97-121 Ja 1993

Authentic teaching. Knowles, David. *Tablet* 247:939-940 Jl 24 1993

Does the "incommensurability thesis" imperil common sense moral judgments? George, Robert P. *Amer J Juris* 37:185-195 1992

The higher law background of the Notre Dame law school. Kmiec, Douglas W. *Amer J Juris* 37:213-242 1992

Is there a natural law right to privacy? Gaebler, Ralph F. *Amer J Juris* 37:319-336 1992

[The lasting contribution of Veritatis splendor]. Cahill, Lisa Sowle. *Comm* 120:15-16 O 22 1993

Legal anthropology, Australian, Aborigines and natural law. O'Connell, Irene. *Amer J Juris* 37:243-258 1992

The limits of natural law: Thomas Rutherforth and the American legal tradition. McDowell, Gary L. *Amer J Juris* 37:57-81 1992

Natural law as a form of legal studies. Grazin, Igor. *Amer J Juris* 37:1-16 1992

The Notre Dame Law School Commencement Address—three natural law challenges for Notre Dame lawyers. Kmiec, Douglas W. *Amer J Juris* 37:359-361 1992

On Leo Strauss's understanding of the natural law theory of Thomas Aquinas. Kries, Douglas. *Thomist* 57:215-232 Ap 1993

The Prolife Movement: dead or alive? Hanink, James G. *New Oxford Rev* 60:10-14+ My 1993

Ratzinger and the terrorists. Caldecott, Stratford. *Crisis* 11:13-14 Jl-Ag 1993

Staggering toward the new Jerusalem of constitutional theory: a response to Ralph F Gaebler. Murphy, Walter F. *Amer J Juris* 37:337-357 1992

NATURAL THEOLOGY
Biblical faith and natural theology. Barr, James. New York: Oxford University Press, 1993. x, 256p ISBN 0-826205-1

Rational faith: Catholic responses to reformed epistemology. Zaggelski, Linda Trinkaus, 1946-, ed. Indiana: Notre Dame Press, 1993. x, 290p ISBN 0-268-01643-7 LC 92-537-42

NATURALISM
Eliminative naturalism and artistic meaning. Pylkkö, Pauli. *PhilosTod* 37:183-200 Sum 1993

Nietzsche as anti-naturalist. Matthis, Michael J. *PhilosTod* 37:170-182 Sum 1993

NATURE—RELIGIOUS ASPECTS
The earth as a gift. Willey, Petroc, and Willey, Eldred. *New Blckfrs* 74:60-74 F 1993

The green Bible. Scharper, Stephen B, and Cunningham, Hilary, eds. Maryknoll, New York: Orbis Books, 1993. x, 113p ISBN 0-85244-230-0 LC 92-35593

Nature, culture, and the Church. Carroll, William E. *Can Cath Rev* 11:44-47 Ja 1993

The promise of nature: ecology and cosmic purpose. Haught, John F. New York: Paulist Press, 1993. x, 156p ISBN 0-8091-3396-2 LC 92-41353

The sacramentality of the world. Martos, Joseph. *Emmanuel* 99:4-7+ Ja-F 1993

Simple prayers, common miracles. Canton, Donald R. *Living Prayer* 26:9-12 My-Je 1993

Women, earth, and creator spirit. Johnson, Elizabeth A, 1941-. New York: Paulist Press, 1993. x, 79p ISBN 0-8091-3415-2 LC 92-42018

NATURE (THEOLOGY)
Choirs of millions: a reflection on Thomas Merton and God's creatures. Daggy, Robert E. *Cist Stud* 28:93-107 1993

Give me a home. Hinderlider, Sue Ann. *Sisters* 65:198-199 My 1993

Out of the greenhouse. Milbank, John. *New Blckfrs* 74:4-14 Ja 1993

Pour une théologie à l'école de l'écologie. Peeters, Denise. *Lumen* 48:51-65 Mr 1993

Seeds in the muck [editorial]. Manney, Jim, ed. *New Cov* 23:5 S 1993

Ways to celebrate Earth Day. Fanning, Jim, and Schumacher, Stacy. *ReligTJ* 27:28-29 Ap-My 1993

NATURE (THEOLOGY)- BELGIUM
Un dossier "Renouvelons la terre" et ses fruits. Piton, Jacques. *Lumen* 48:95-104 Mr 1993

NECESSITIES OF LIFE *see* Basic Needs

NEEDS, BASIC *see* Basic Needs

NEEDS ASSESSMENT
A spiritual tool. Kerrigan, Ruth, and Harkulich, Joan T. *Health Prog* 74:46-49 My 1993

NEGOTIATION
Negotiation: the art of community living. Misteravich, Daniel. *Past Mus* 17:17-19 D 1992-Ja 1993

NEIBUHR, REINHOLD
A prayer for all seasons. Seethaler, Scott. *New Cov* 23:22-26 S 1993

NEIGHBORHOOD
Is there room for justice in your backyard? Vogel, Carl. *Salt* 13:6-11 Ap 1993

NENGAPETA, MARIA CLEMENTINA ANWARITE, -1964
John Paul II, Pope, (1985-08-15) Litterae Apostolicae (Apostolic Letters) [Latin]. John Paul II, Pope, 1920- (Karol Wojtyla) (elected 1978). *AAS* 84:1112-1115 D 5 1992*

NEOCLASSICAL SCHOOL OF ECONOMICS
Gender and economic ideologies. Nelson, Julie A. *RSocEcon* 51:287-301 Aut 1993

The historical approach to political economy. Sherman, Howard J. *RSocEcon* 51:302-322 Aut 1993

NEONATAL INTENSIVE CARE
Deciding who lives: fateful choices in the intensive care nursery. Anspach, Renée R. Berkeley: University of California Press, 1993. x, 303p ISBN 0-520-05268-4 LC 91-44245

NEOPLATONISM
The metaphysical aspect of tenses in Proclus. Plass, Paul. *IPQ* 33:143-151 Je 1993

Platon, l'École de Tübingen et Giovanni Reale. Rizzerio, Laura. *RPhil Louvain* 91:90-110 F 1993

NEOSCHOLASTICISM
Living in ambiguity: a paradigm shift experienced by the sister formation movement. Dries, Angelyn. *CHist* 79:478-487 Jl 1993

NEPAL—SOCIAL CONDITIONS
Ethnic expulsions from Bhutan. *Tablet* 247:957 Jl 24 1993

NESTORIUS
La première session du Concile D'Éphèse (22 Juin 431). Halleux, André de. *Eph Theol Lovan* 69:48-87 Ap 1993

NEUHAUS, JOHN
Chesterton and Catholic moments: some reflections on Catholic revivals, past and present. Sparr, Arnold. *ACHSR* 103:11-22 Aut 1992

NEUNHEUSER, BURKHARD
Professor Burkhard Neunheuser, OSB: Doctor Honoris Causa of the Pontifival Academy of Theology in Kraków. Reder, Violetta. *Notitiae* 29:81-83 Ja-F 1993

NEUROPSYCHOLOGY
The sexual brain. LeVay, Simon. Cambridge: MIT Press, 1993. 168p ISBN 0-26212-178-6 LC 92-44691

NEUROSIS
A vast confinement. Paige, Harry W, 1922-. *Liguorian* 81:46-50 Jl 1993

NEVES, LUCAS MOREIRA, CARDINAL, 1925-
A soap too far. O'Shaughnessy, Hugh. *Tablet* 247:397 Mr 27 1993

NEVIN, JOHN WILLIAMSON
The "Catholic tradition" of Christianity and the "religion of the republic". Wentz, Richard E. *Horizons (CTS)* 20:67-86 Spr 1993

NEW AGE MOVEMENT
A Christian response to the New Age. Saliba, John A. *Way* 33:202-232 Jl 1993

Christianisme et Nouvel Âge. Fossion, André. *Lumen* 48:256-262 S 1993

Christians and the New Age. Williams, Alison. *Teilhard Rev* 27:88-94 Wint 1992

New age guru. *Tablet* 247:512 Ap 24 1993

New age spiritualities: how are we to talk of God? Woods, Richard. *New Blckfrs* 74:76-191 Ap 1993

The new consciousness in America. Bryan, Timothy L. *StudiaM* 41:27-47 1992

Pourquoi le Nouvel Âge fascine-t-il? Raemdonck, André van. *Lumen* 48:247-255 S 1993

Theological trends: beyond familiar shores: New Age spirituality. Angle, Siddika. *Way* 33:138-147 Ap 1993

What is new age spirituality? Woods, Richard. *Way* 33:176-188 Jl 1993

NEW AGE MOVEMENT—ETHICAL ASPECTS
Sin, evil and death in the New Age. McIntyre, Moni. *Way* 33:210-221 Jl 1993

NEW AGE MOVEMENT—HISTORY
Whither the New Age? Melton, J Gordon. *Way* 33:199-209 Jl 1993

NEW AGE MOVEMENT—RITUAL
New Age rites: the recovery of ritual. Northcott, Michael S. *Way* 33:189-198 Jl 1993

NEW DEAL, 1933-1939
Catholic clergymen, Franklin D Roosevelt, and the New Deal. Billington, Monroe Lee, 1928-, and Clark, Cal. *CHist* 79:65-82 Ja 1993

NEW JERSEY—ECONOMIC CONDITIONS
Just taxation in Catholic social ethics and the Florio plan. Gorrell, Paul J. *SocJust* 84:90-92 My-Je 1993

NEW MEXICO—CHURCH HISTORY
The origin of the Penitentes of New Mexico: separating fact from fiction. Espinosa, J Manuel. *CHist* 79:454-477 Jl 1993

NEW RIGHT (CHRISTIANITY)
The rise and rise of the Christian Right. Appleby, Raphael Scott. *Tablet* 247:847-848 Jl 3 1993

NEW YORK, NY—POLITICS AND GOVERNMENT
The Marlin factor in New York. Schall, James Vincent, 1928-. *Crisis* 11:49 O 1993

NEW YORK TIMES
The worst of the 'Times' some news doesn't fit. Steinfels, Margaret O'Brien, 1941-. *Comm* 120:4-5 Mr 12 1993

NEWMAN, JOHN HENRY, CARDINAL, 1801-1890
Cardinal Newman on the season of Lent. Oakes, Edward T. *America* 168:7-12 Ap 3 1993

Catechesis and religious education. Groome, Thomas H, 1945-. *Living Light* 29:40-46 Aut 1992

Education a diverse river wide enough for all swimmers [editorial]. *Nat Cath Rep* 30:28 O 29 1993

For want of a miracle, Newman's cause is help up [por]. Hebblethwaite, Peter, 1930-. *Nat Cath Rep* 30:15 N 12 1993

Founding charisms: past and present. Hennessy, Paul. *Origins* 23:169-173 Ag 12 1993

Interpreting moral doctrine: Newman on conscience and law. Magill, Gerard. *Horizons (CTS)* 20:7-22 Spr 1993

John Henry Newman: heart to heart. Giese, Vincent. New York: New City Press, 1993. x, 96p ISBN 1-56548-023-6 LC 92-42030

Laying claim to Newman. Hebblethwaite, Peter, 1930-. *Tablet* 247:834 Je 26 1993

Newman on the secular need for religious education. Walsh, David. *F & R* 28:359-385 Wint 1992

Where does Cardinal Newman's cause stand? Blehl, Vincent Ferrer, 1921-. *America* 169:15-17 S 25 1993

NEWMAN CLUBS
Making the best of a bad job? Newman Chaplains between the code and the council. Evans, John Whitney. *US Cath Hist* 11:35-50 Wint 1993

NEWSPAPER PUBLISHING- GREAT BRITAIN
Rupert Murdoch's responsibilities [editorial]. *Tablet* 247:1183-1184 S 18 1993

NEWSPAPERS
The "Observer's SOS". Keegan, William. *Tablet* 247:573-574 My 8 1993

NEWSPAPERS—RELIGIOUS ASPECTS
Coverage of religion isn't all bad. Dart, John A. *Register* 69:5 O 31 1993
The media elite and issues of faith. Riley, Patrick. *Register* 69:5 O 31 1993

NICARAGUA—POLITICS AND GOVERNMENT
Cardinal mediates in hostage crisis. *Tablet* 247:1108 Ag 28 1993
What is the church of the poor? A missionary reshapes his theology. Hurteau, Robert. *Comm* 120:13-16 Mr 26 1993

NICARAGUA—RELIGION
A fundamentalist Nicaragua? Torrens, James S. *America* 168:6-9 Ja 16-23 1993

NICENE CREED
We profess what we believe. Gustin, Marilyn Norquist. *Liguorian* 81:48-53 My 1993

NICHOLAS, SAINT, BP OF MYRA, 4TH CENT
Nikolaus von Kues Skize einer Biographie. Meuthen, Erich. Münster: Aschendorff, 1992. x, 139p ISBN 3-402-03492-1
The real St. Nicholas [condensed fr *Again* V 13, no 4]. Bear, Jan, and Gray, Daria. *CDgst* 58:6-10 D 1993

NICHOLAS OF CUSA, 1401-1464
Toward a new Council of Florence. Nicholas of Cusa, 1401-1464. Washington, DC: Schiller Institute, 1993. x, 577p ISBN 0-9621095-8-4 LC 92-85238

NICHOLAS TREVET, 1265-1334?
Virgil's Eclogues, Nicholas Trevet, and the harmony of the spheres. Lord, Mary Louise. *Med Stud* 54:186-273 1992

NICHOLS, AIDAN
The panther and the hind. Matthews, Melvyn. *New Blckfrs* 74:417-422 S 1993

NICODEMUS
Jesus meets Nicodemus and the Samaritan woman. Stravinskas, Peter. *Register* 69:1+ Mr 7 1993

NIETZSCHE, FRIEDRICH WILHELM, 1844-1900
Dioniso dormido sobre un tigre: a traves de Nietzchey su teoria del lenguaje. Lynch, Enrique. Barcelona: Destino, 1993. x, 400p ISBN 84-233-2269-6
Friederich Nietzsche: una biografia. Morey, Miguel. Madrid: Archipielago, 1993. x, 126p ISBN 84-88595-00-x
Kundera, Nietzsche, and politics on the questions of eternal return and responsibility. Parens, Erik. *PhilosTod* 37:285-297 Aut 1993
Mark's tragic vision: Gethsemane. Ruprecht, Louis A, Jr. *Relig Lit* 24:1-25 Aut 1992
Nietzsche as anti-naturalist. Matthis, Michael J. *PhilosTod* 37:170-182 Sum 1993
Nietzsche's earliest essays: translation of and commentary on "Fate and History" and "Freedom of Will and Fate". Stack, George J. *PhilosTod* 37:153-169 Sum 1993
Religious pluralism: a missiological approach. Newbigin, Lesslie. *StudiaM* 42:227-244 1993
Ressentiment and the preferential option for the poor. Byrne, Patrick H. *TheolStds* 54:213-241 Je 1993
Robert Musil: da Nietzsche alla mistica. Sommavilla, Guido. *Civilta* 3:129-142 Jl 17 1993
Voluntad de lo tragico: el concepto nietzscheano de voluntad a partir de el nacimiento de la tradgedia. Barrios Casares, Manuel. Sevilla: A Er, Revista de Filosofia, 1993. x, 190p ISBN 84-604-5347-2

NIGERIA—RELIGION
The interaction of African independent churches with traditional religions in Nigeria. Olayiwola, David O. *StudiaM* 42:357-370 1993

NIKODIM, METROPOLITAN, 1929-1978 *see* Rotov Boris Georgievich (Nikodim), Metr, 1929-1978

NIMBY SYNDROME
Is there room for justice in your backyard? Vogel, Carl. *Salt* 13:6-11 Ap 1993

NIREBI Y DIEZ, EZEQUIEL, 1848-1906
Congregation for the Causes of Saints (1992-03-07) Decree on a miracle. Congregation for the Causes of Saints. *AAS* 84:1089-1091 N 3 1992*

NOLAN, TIMOTHY
A prayerful parish. Wood, Charles. *New Cov* 22:8-10 Mr 1993

NON-FORMAL EDUCATION
Breaking away. Podsiadlo, Jack. *Momentum* 24:36-37 F-Mr 1993
Something old, something new. Pergler, Bonnie Schwartz. *Momentum* 24:10-12 F-Mr 1993

NONVERBAL COMMUNICATION
The biological basis of nonviolence. Meyer, Karl. *Cath Work* 60:5 Ja-F 1993
Celibacy and intimacy. Kimmerling, Ben. *Way Suppl* 77:87-96 Sum 1993
Lament and light: embodying our grief. Schroeder, Celeste N. *Mod Lit* 20:14-16 S 1993
The sacred game of conversation. Cowan, Michael A. *Furrow* 44:30-34 Ja 1993

NONVIOLENCE
The biological basis of nonviolence. Meyer, Karl. *Cath Work* 60:5 Ja-F 1993
Charles Alphin [interview by T Jarvis]. Alphin, Charles. *Salt* 13:4-6 Ja 1993
In this 25th-anniversary year of the death of Dr King [editorial]. *America* 168:3 Ja 16-23 1993
On getting punched in the face. Webb-Mitchell, Brett. *New Oxford Rev* 60:18-20 Jl-Ag 1993

Overcome evil by good: Eileen Egan and her ilk. Jordan, Patrick. *Comm* 120:4-5 Mr 26 1993
"Small cells of people doing good". Humphrey, Marj. *Cath Work* 60:5 Ag 1993
Wisdom with a smile. *Tablet* 247:614-615 My 15 1993
Worth pondering. O'Connell, Patrick. *Living Prayer* 26:13-14 My-Je 1993

NOONAN, JOHN
Saint Augustine and Martin Buber as perspectives on John Noonan's persons and masks of the law. Combs, Christopher. *Amer J Juris* 37:145-169 1992

NORMS
Malum Vitandum: the role of intentions in first-order morality. Sullivan, Thomas D, and Atkinson, Gary. *IJPS* 1:99-110 Mr 1993
Sexual morality's positive goals and the problem of legalism. George, Robert P. *Origins* 22:778-780 Ap 22 1993
Wirtschaftsethik. Mack, Elke. *Stimm Zeit* 211:713-716 O 1993

NORTH AMERICAN FREE TRADE AGREEMENT (NAFTA)
Catholics divided on NAFTA. Mullen, Peter. *Register* 69:1+ O 17 1993
Free trade slurping jobs around the world. Blackburn, Thomas E. *Nat Cath Rep* 29:15 My 21 1993
Life-form patents are "shady aspect" of NAFTA. Wirpsa, Leslie. *Nat Cath Rep* 29:16 Mr 19 1993
The light and dark side of NAFTA. Kenny, Joe. *Register* 69:1+ Ag 15 1993
NAFTA south of the border: high stakes, big hopes, real fears. Meyers, William K. *Comm* 120:5-7 S 24 1993
NAFTA spawns a diverse union of critics. Zon, Calvin G. *Nat Cath Rep* 29:5 Ja 29 1993
South of the border, free trade? [editorial]. *America* 169:3 S 18 1993
Trading up or down? [editorial]. *Comm* 120:3-4 O 8 1993
US Catholics ask if trade pact is a good deal. Ringwald, Christopher. *OSV* 82:3 S 12 1993
What's in NAFTA for us? [editorial]. *America* 169:3 O 30 1993
While a NAFTA is needed, this is not NAFTA we need [editorial]. *Nat Cath Rep* 30:28 O 29 1993

NORTH AND SOUTH
Les rapports Nord-Sud après la chute du deuxième monde. Herr, Édouard. *NRT* 114:837-851 N-D 1992
The role of the religious in evangelization. Kalilombe, Patrick Augustine, Bp, 1933-. *AFER* 34:163-169 Je 1992

NORTH ATLANTIC TREATY ORGANIZATION
The golden curtain. Solomon, Jonathan. *Tablet* 247:186 F 13 1993

NORTH CAROLINA—CHURCH HISTORY
An abbatial diocese in the United States. Baumstein, Paschal. *CHist* 79:217-245 Ap 1993

NORTHERN IRELAND—CHURCH HISTORY
An Irish priest in England. Lally, John. *Priests & People* 7:22-26 Ja 1993
The origins of the troubles. Duffy, Eamon. *Priests & People* 7:3-9 Ja 1993

NORTHERN IRELAND—ECONOMIC CONDITIONS
Comparisons from the North. Hewitt, Victor. *Studies* 82:24-34 Spr 1993
A Northern perspective. Borooah, Vani K, and Ackah, Carol. *Studies* 82:53-60 Spr 1993

NORTHERN IRELAND—HISTORY
Public life in Northern Ireland—another view. Wilson, Desmond. *Furrow* 44:140-147 Mr 1993

NORTHERN IRELAND—POLITICS
Self-help in Ulster. Burns, Jimmy. *Tablet* 247:133-134 Ja 30 1993
A strategy for Northern Ireland [2 parts]. *Tablet* 247:327 Mr 13; 359-360 Mr 20 1993
The two minorities. Gordon, Robert. *Priests & People* 7:10-13 Ja 1993
What makes a republican? McDonagh, Melanie. *Tablet* 247:636-638 My 22 1993

NORTHERN IRELAND—POLITICS AND GOVERNMENT
An English view of the Irish question. Johnson, Marigold. *Priests & People* 7:18-21 Ja 1993
The impasse in Northern Ireland [editorial]. Rafferty, Oliver. *Month* 26:254-256 Jl 1993
Mood music for Ulster. Burns, Jimmy. *Tablet* 247:813-815 Je 26 1993
No alternative talks. *Tablet* 247:159 F 6 1993
Northern Ireland. MacEoin, Gary. *Nat Cath Rep* 30:8-9 O 22 1993
Public life in Northern Ireland—another view. Wilson, Desmond. *Furrow* 44:140-147 Mr 1993
Public life in Northern Ireland. White, Barry. *Furrow* 43:656-662 D 1992

NORTHERN IRELAND—RELIGION
Battlefront ecumenism. Reynolds, Gerry, and Burch, Sam. *Priests & People* 7:14-17 Ja 1993

NORTHERN IRELAND—SOCIAL CONDITIONS
Mood music for Ulster. Burns, Jimmy. *Tablet* 247:813-815 Je 26 1993
A strategy for Northern Ireland [2 parts]. *Tablet* 247:327 Mr 13; 359-360 Mr 20 1993

NOSTRA AETATE (DOCUMENT) *see* Vatican Council, 2D, 1962-1965—non-Christians

NOTHINGNESS
Empty room, empty tomb. Firestone, Denise Fainberg. *Spir Life* 39:26-30 Spr 1993

NOTRE DAME UNIVERSITY (NOTRE DAME, IN)
Notre Dame debates need for Catholic faculty. Carey, Ann. *OSV* 82:3 Je 13 1993

NOVITIATE
Journal of a novice director. Svoboda, Melannie. *RRel* 52:602-609 Jl-Ag 1993

NUCLEAR WARFARE
"The challenge of peace" revisited. Murray, Pius. *Emmanuel* 99:314-317 Jl-Ag 1993

NUCLEAR WARFARE—RELIGIOUS ASPECTS—CATHOLIC CHURCH
The new demands of global security. Martino, Renato, Abp. *Origins* 23:381-383 N 4 1993

O

Youthful churchman dies [obit]. *Register* 69:2 S 19 1993
2,000 gather to mourn activist Father Olivares [obituary]. Fox, Thomas C. *Nat Cath Rep* 29:2 Ap 2 1993

OBLATES OF MARY IMMACULATE
John Paul II, Pope, (1991-04-26) Your vocation is to respond to the missionary needs of the Church. John Paul II, Pope, 1920- (Karol Wojtyla) (elected 1978). *Con Life* 17 no 2:16-18 1992*

OBSCENITY (LAW)
La obscenidad. Castilla del Pino, Carlos. Madrid: Alianza, 1993. x, 156p ISBN 84-206-2744-5

OBSERVER (PERIODICAL)
The "Observer's SOS". Keegan, William. *Tablet* 247:573-574 My 8 1993

OBSESSIVE-COMPULSIVE NEUROSIS
There's help for the sexual addict. Olert, Stephen, and Williams, Ruthann. *Sisters* 65:263-271 Jl 1993

OCAMPO, JUAN JESUS POSADAS, CARDINAL
Dialogue [interview by G Burke]. Rodriguez, Tarcisio. *Register* 69:1+ Je 27 1993
Slain cardinal was conservative power in Mexico. *Nat Cath Rep* 29:8 Je 4 1993

OCCUPATIONAL TRAINING
Vocational and professional training for religious: a crucial need in Africa today. Mejia, Rodrigo. *AFER* 34:158-162 Je 1992

OCCUPATIONS
What do you want to be? Auer, Jim. *Liguorian* 81:38-43 S 1993

ODONE, CRISTINA
Lorenzo's sister edits Catholic paper. Hebblethwaite, Peter, 1930-. *Nat Cath Rep* 29:17 F 26 1993

OESTERREICHER, JOHN, 1904-1993
Oesterreicher, John M, 1904-1993 [obit]. *Crisis* 11:16 Jl-Ag 1993
Oesterreicher, John, 1904-1993 [obit]. Hotchkin, John, et al. *Origins* 22:796 Ap 29 1993

OFFERINGS (IN RELIGION, FOLKLORE)
Through your goodness we have these gift to offer. Gustin, Marilyn Norquist. *Liguorian* 81:28-32 Jl 1993

OGORODNIKOV, ALEXANDER
Comrades in crosses: Christian Democracy comes to Russia. Bole, William. *America* 168:4-5 Ja 16-23 1993

OLIVARES, LUIS A
A moment of sorrow, a moment of hope. Burns, Robert E, 1919-. *USCath* 58:2 Ag 1993
2,000 gather to mourn activist Father Olivares [obituary]. Fox, Thomas C. *Nat Cath Rep* 29:2 Ap 2 1993

OLIVER, E J, 1911-1992
E J Oliver. Wall, Barbara. *Tablet* 246:1586 D 12 1992

OLMI, ERMANNO
Lungo Il Fiume Di Ermanno Olmi. Fantuzzi, Virgilio. *Civilta* 143:382-393 N 21 1992

OLMOS, MANUEL MEDINA, 1869-1936
Congregation for the Causes of Saints (1992-12-21) Decree on martyrdom. Congregation for the Causes of Saints. *OR(Eng)* 1272:4 Ja 6 1993*

ONTOLOGY
Buber and Tillich. Novak, David, 1941-. *JEcumen Stds* 29:159-174 Spr 1992
Catechesis and religious education. Groome, Thomas H, 1945-. *Living Light* 29:40-46 Aut 1992
Catholic theology, gender, and the future of Western civilization [editorial]. Schindler, David L. *Communio* 20:200-239 Sum 1993
Costly giving: on Jean-Luc Marion's theology of the gift. Moss, David. *New Blckfrs* 74:393-399 S 1993
Discusiones sobre la metafisica. Armesto, Indalecio. Santiago: Universidad, 1993. x, 360p ISBN 84-7191-968-0
Document: le concept mégarique et aristotélicien de possibilité. Hartmann, Nicolaï. *Laval Theol Phil* 49:131-146 F 1993
Événement et destinée chez Schelling. Maesschalck, Marc. *RPhil Louvain* 91:185-206 My 1993
Finding God in all things. Garrett, Graeme. *Way* 33:3-11 Ja 1993
The God of love. Schmitz, Kenneth L. *Thomist* 57:495-508 Jl 1993
Instance ontology and Avicenna's arguments. Mertz, Donald W. *Mod Schlmn* 70:189-199 Mr 1993
De l'ontologie à la théologie. Gérard, Gilbert. *RPhil Louvain* 90:445-485 N 1992
Merleau-Ponty's logos: the sens-ing of flesh. Stenstad, Gail. *PhilosTod* 37:52-61 Spr 1993
Meta-anthropology and Christology: on the philosophy of Hans Urs von Balthasar. Bieler, Martin. *Communio* 20:129-146 Spr 1993
A new ontology? A response to a recent suggestion [reply to J Honner]. Kelly, Tony. *Pacifica* 6:189-209 Je 1993
Ser y conocer. Garcia Del Muro Solans, Juan. Barcelona: PPU, 1993. x, 580p ISBN 84-477-0017-8
Le statut de l'un dans la Métaphysique. Couloubaritsis, Lambros. *RPhil Louvain* 90:497-522 N 1992
La stylométrie et la question de Métaphysique K. Rutten, Christian. *RPhil Louvain* 90:486-496 N 1992
Wojtyla and the Council [excerpt fr *Il pensiero di Karol Wojtyla*]. Buttiglione, Rocco. *Crisis* 11:21-25 F 1993

OPEN MARKET OPERATIONS
The evolution of the "investment system": Keynes' theory of employment and money revisited. McDermott, Karl A. *RSocEcon* 51:62-85 Spr 1993

OPERA
In the midst of life. Mawdesley, Anthony. *Month* 26:150-151 Ap 1993
Listening to Cecilia. Tombes, Jonathan. *Crisis* 11:52-54 Mr 1993

OPERA—CLASSICAL INFLUENCES
Opera: the creative expression of Italy. Navone, John. *New Blckfrs* 74:400-407 S 1993

OPERA- ITALY
Opera: the creative expression of Italy. Navone, John. *New Blckfrs* 74:400-407 S 1993

OPERATION RESCUE
Klan act offers no shelter to abortion clinics. McCarthy, Colman. *Nat Cath Rep* 29:2 F 5 1993

OPIELA, STANISLAW
A Jesuit looks at the religious scene. *Tablet* 247:55 Ja 9 1993
Jesuits fighting for freedom in Russia. Corley, Felix. *OSV* 82:17 Ag 22 1993

OPTIMISM
Die befragte Generation. Belistein, Roman. *Stimm Zeit* 211:232-240 Ap 1993

OPUS DEI
Entrevista sobre el fundador del Opus Dei, realizada por Cesare Cavallieri. Portillo, Alvaro del. Madrid: Rialp, 1993. x, 252p ISBN 84-321-2972-0
El Opus Dei en la Iglesia. Rodriguez, Pedro. Madrid: Ediciones Rialp, 1993. x, 346p ISBN 84-321-2969-0
Prayers for busy people. Kreeft, Peter John, 1937-. *New Cov* 22:17+ F 1993
Prelatura personale: problemi e dubbi [2 parts]. Celeghin, Adriano. *Periodica* 82 no 2:95-138: 82 no 1; 213-256: 82 no 2, 1993
What is Opus Dei? [interview]. Hirtle, Walter. *Can Cath Rev* 11:6-8 S 1993

OPUS DEI- LATIN AMERICA
Viaje al fondo de la esperanza. Olaizola, Jose Luis. Madrid: Ediciones Rialp, 1993. x, 253p ISBN 84-321-2866-x

ORAL TRADITION
The Catechism [commentary]. O'Brien, Dennis. *Comm* 120:15-16 My 7 1993

ORATOIRE DE FRANCE
The sanctification of their neighbor. Kazanecki, Thaddeus J. *RRel* 52:574-583 Jl-Ag 1993

ORATORIES
Reservation of the Eucharist in a religious house. Musiol, Jozef. *AFER* 34:115-121 Ap 1992

ORDER AND CHAOS
The future is now: from chaos to cosmos. McCarthy, Tim. *Nat Cath Rep* 29:5-6 Ap 16 1993

ORDER OF AUGUSTINIAN RECOLLECTS
Congregation for the Causes of Saints (1992-06-13) Decree on the heroic virtues. Congregation for the Causes of Saints. *TPS* 38:19-20 Ja-F 1993*

ORDER OF CANONS REGULAR OF ST AUGUSTINE
Congregation for the Causes of Saints (1992-07-11) Decree on the martyrdom. Congregation for the Causes of Saints. *TPS* 38:37-38 Ja-F 1993*

ORDER OF DISCALCED CARMELITES
Congregation for the Causes of Saints (1992-07-11) Decree on a miracle. Congregation for the Causes of Saints. *TPS* 38:37-38 Ja-F 1993*

ORDINATION—ANGLICAN COMMUNION
A way past Apostolicae Curae. Yarnold, Edward John, 1926-. *Tablet* 247:874 Jl 10 1993

ORDINATION—CATHOLIC CHURCH
John Paul II, Pope, (1992-02-25) Itinera Apostolica (Homily at ordination in Guinea during apostolic journey) [French]. John Paul II, Pope, 1920- (Karol Wojtyla) (elected 1978). *AAS* 85:171-175 F 3 1993*
John Paul II, Pope, (1993-06-12) Eucharist [Orig in Spanish]. John Paul II, Pope, 1920- (Karol Wojtyla) (elected 1978). *OR(Eng)* 1296:5 Je 23 1993*
Our own idea of time [repr fr *Crossroads*]. Zvarevashe, Ignatius M. *AFER* 34:188-192 Je 1992
Priestertum der Frau. Schiebl, Johanna. *Stimm Zeit* 211:115-122 F 1993
A priesthood continued. Hughes, John Jay, 1928-. *Tablet* 247:903 Jl 10 1993
Religious and the new rite for the ordination of deacons. Egana, Francisco J. *Con Life* 17 no 2:98-121 1992
"Whatever is original, spare, strange". Sylva, Douglas. *America* 168:4 Je 5-12 1993

ORDINATION OF WOMEN
Bishop Hope seeks to square the circle on women priests. *Tablet* 247:735-736 Je 5 1993
"Communion" in a time of estrangement. Tavard, George Henry. *Ecumen Trends* 22:1+ My 1993
A conversation with scripture scholar Myles M Bourke [interview by T H Stahel, 1938-]. Bourke, Myles M. *America* 168:4-9 Ap 17 1993
Four Anglo-Catholic variations. *Tablet* 247:1144-1145 S 4 1993
Gender and the priesthood of Christ: a theological reflection. Ashley, Benedict M. *Thomist* 57:343-379 Jl 1993
Gender and the will of God. Kreeft, Peter John, 1937-. *Crisis* 11:20-28 S 1993
Hear this [editorial]. *Comm* 120:3 Ja 29 1993
In defense of the "Declaration". Healy, Jack. *HPR* 93:67-70 Jl 1993
Its principles will stand, but the church shall challenge. West, Morris L. *Nat Cath Rep* 29:14 F 12 1993
Legislation for women priests reaches Parliament. *Tablet* 247:524 Ap 24 1993
Miles to go [editorial]. Pawlikowski, John T. *New Theol Rev* 6:3-5 My 1993
The ministries of women [editorial]. McDade, John. *Month* 25:458-460 D 1992
On the one hand, women and ordination—time for dialogue? St Leger, Moya Frenz. *Priests & People* 6:327-329 Ag-S 1992
On the other hand, the priesthood—a conservative view. Lee, Martin. *Priests & People* 6:330-333 Ag-S 1992
Women's ordination: tradition and inculturation. Børresen, Kari Elisabeth. *TheolDgst* 40:15-19 Spr 1993
Yet another look at the question of ordination of women. Coll, Regina. *Sisters* 65:110-115 Mr 1993

ORDINATION OF WOMEN—CATHOLIC CHURCH
Asian appeal. *Tablet* 247:44 Ja 9 1993
Did the early Church ordain women to be priests? Most, William G, 1914-. *Can Cath Rev* 11:21-24 F 1993
Divided we stand: "forward in faith" on the march. Hebblethwaite, Margaret, 1951-. *Tablet* 247:597-598 My 8 1993
The Dublin Statement and women's ordination. Baktis, Peter Anthony. *JEcumen Stds* 29:35-46 Wint 1992
Epistola ad Romanos: an open letter to some Roman Catholic friends. Greenacre, Roger. *Month* 26:88-96 Mr 1993
The ministry of women: gift or threat to the churches? Thurston, Anne. *Doctr Life* 43:387-395 S 1993
The pastoral that wasn't: feminist agenda stalled at Bishops' Conference. Hitchcock, Helen Hull. *Crisis* 11:33-37 Ja 1993

A handbook for coping. Gaddy, Welton C. Louisville: Westminster, 1993. x, 128p ISBN 0-664-25458-6
Pain management. *Health Prog* 74:30-39 Ja-F 1993
Praying our pain. McGrane, Janice. *Spir Life* 32:87-90 Sum 1993
Should the healing begin at Christmas. McDonagh, Enda. *Furrow* 43:651-655 D 1992

PAINTING
Hunt the painting. *Tablet* 247:474-475 Ap 10-17 1993

PALESTINE
The stones will cry out. Roman, Mary. *Living Prayer* 26:29-31 Mr-Ap 1993

PALESTINE—ANTIQUITIES
Jesus and the forgotten city: new light on Sepphoris and the urban world of Jesus. Batey, Richard A. Grand Rapids: Baker Book House, 1991
The new encyclopedia of archaeological excavations in the Holy Land. Stern, Ephraim, ed. New York: Simon & Schuster, 1993. 64p ISBN 0-13-276288-9

PALESTINE—CHURCH HISTORY
No peace for reds and whites. Pevtzow, Lisa. *Register* 69:1+ Mr 21 1993

PALESTINE—GEOGRAPHY
A holy week in a Holy Land. Morrow, Carol Ann. *St Anth* 100:28-33 Ap 1993

PALESTINE LIBERATION ORGANIZATION
A rumor of peace. Pevtzow, Lisa. *Register* 69:1+ S 19 1993

PALESTINIANS
Christmas message for those in fear and pain. *Tablet* 247:22 Ja 2 1993
The end of Zionism. Cantor, Norman F. *Comm* 120:11-13 N 19 1993
On the road [editorial]. *Comm* 120:3-4 S 24 1993
Palestine Christians vent steam. Pevtzow, Lisa. *Register* 69:1+ Jl 18 1993
The poet as diplomat: optimism isn't enough [interview by M.P. Kelly]. Mikhail-Ashrawi, Hanan. *Comm* 120:4-6 O 8 1993
Rabin and Arafat brave radical wrath. Wigoder, Geoffrey Bernard, 1922-. *Tablet* 247:1120-1121 S 4 1993
Voices in the wilderness. White, Patrick. *Tablet* 246:1594-1596 D 19-26 1992
West Bank settlers won't go. Pevtzow, Lisa. *Register* 69:1+ Je 27 1993

PALMENTIERI, LUDOVICO OF CASORIA (ARCANGELO), 1814-1885
Congregation for the Causes of Saints (1992-07-11) Decree on a miracle. Congregation for the Causes of Saints. *TPS* 38:37-38 Ja-F 1993
Congregation for the Causes of Saints (1992-07-11) Ludovico of Casoria (Palmentieri Arcangelo). Congregation for the Causes of Saints. *AAS* 85:199-201 F 3 1993*

PALMER-BUCKLE, GABRIEL
John Paul II, Pope, (1992-07-06) Constitutiones Apsotolicae (Apostolic Constitution to erect Diocese of Koforidua) [Latin]. John Paul II, Pope, 1920- (Karol Wojtyla) (elected 1978). *AAS* 85:120-121 F 3 1993*

PANAMA
Film blasts Panama invasion myths. Rodulfo, Lillie. *Nat Cath Rep* 29:7 N 6 1992

PANNENBERG, WOLFHART, 1928-
Creatures of truth. Bonsor, Jack A. *Thomist* 56:647-668 O 1992

PAPACY
Apostolic See in the new Oriental Canonical Legislation. Abbass, Jobe. *Stud Can* 27 no 1:173-215 1993
I Gesuiti e il Papato storia di un voto di obbedienza. Salvini, Gianpaolo. *Civilta* 2:44-56 Ap 3 1993
Papal reservation and Recognitio: considerations and proposals. Manzanares, Julio. *Jurist* 52 no 1:228-254 1992
The Pope's bodyguards [photos]. Gordon, Lucy. *OSV* 82:12-13 O 10 1993
Ratzinger comments on changing papacy. Hebblethwaite, Peter, 1930-. *Nat Cath Rep* 29:16 F 26 1993

PAPACY—HISTORY
The Holy See and the promotion of an indigenous clergy from Leo XIII to Pius XII. Soetens, Claude. *Jurist* 52 no 1:162-182 1992
Der Papst im Spannungsfeld zwischen Vorgänger und Nachfolger. Corsten, Angela. *Stimm Zeit* 211:425-427 Je 1993
Who's been sitting in Peter's chair? Pazola, Ron. *USCath* 58:34-39 Jl 1993

PAPACY—RELATIONS (DIPLOMATIC)
Accord with Vatican comes nearer. *Tablet* 247:1239 S 25 1993
Holy See agrees to intervene for Iraq at United Nations. *Tablet* 247:115 Ja 23 1993
John Paul II, Pope, (1992-01-11) Allocutiones (Address to Diplomatic Corps accredited to the Holy See) [French]. John Paul II, Pope, 1920- (Karol Wojtyla) (elected 1978). *AAS* 85:62-73 Ja 7 1993*
Vatican forced to rethink Mideast policy. Irani, George Emile. *Nat Cath Rep* 29:17 Mr 12 1993

PAPACY—RELATIONS (DIPLOMATIC)- AUSTRALIA
John Paul II, Pope, (1991-12-02) Allocutiones (Reception of ambassadorial credentials from Australia) [English]. John Paul II, Pope, 1920- (Karol Wojtyla) (elected 1978). *AAS* 84:1151-1154 D 5 1992*

PAPACY—RELATIONS (DIPLOMATIC)- BANGLADESH
John Paul II, Pope, (1992-01-10) Allocutiones (Audience to welcome the new ambassador from Bangladesh) [English]. John Paul II, Pope, 1920- (Karol Wojtyla) (elected 1978). *AAS* 85:54-56 Ja 7 1993*

PAPACY—RELATIONS (DIPLOMATIC)- BELGIUM
John Paul II, Pope, (1991-10-31) Allocutiones (Speech to receive ambassadorial credentials) [French]. John Paul II, Pope, 1920- (Karol Wojtyla) (elected 1978). *AAS* 84:961-963 O 3 1992*

PAPACY—RELATIONS (DIPLOMATIC)- BENIN
John Paul II, Pope, (1991-11-25) Allocutiones (Speech to receive Ambassadorial credentials) [French]. John Paul II, Pope, 1920- (Karol Wojtyla) (elected 1978). *AAS* 84:1141-1143 D 5 1992*

PAPACY—RELATIONS (DIPLOMATIC)- BOLIVIA
John Paul II, Pope, (1991-11-22) Allocutiones (Papal address to President of Bolivia) [Spanish]. John Paul II, Pope, 1920- (Karol Wojtyla) (elected 1978). *AAS* 84:1075-1078 N 3 1992*

PAPACY—RELATIONS (DIPLOMATIC)- BURKINA FASO
John Paul II, Pope, (1991-12-20) Allocutiones (Reception of ambassadorial credentials) [French]. John Paul II, Pope, 1920- (Karol Wojtyla) (elected 1978). *AAS* 85:33-35 Ja 7 1993*

PAPACY—RELATIONS (DIPLOMATIC)- CHINA
Cardinal in China: nothing doing. McGurn, William. *Register* 69:1+ O 24 1993

PAPACY—RELATIONS (DIPLOMATIC)- COSTA RICA
John Paul II, Pope, (1991-11-19) Allocutiones (Speech to receive Ambassador of Costa Rica) [Spanish]. John Paul II, Pope, 1920- (Karol Wojtyla) (elected 1978). *AAS* 84:1070-1072 N 3 1992*

PAPACY—RELATIONS (DIPLOMATIC)- ESTONIA
John Paul II, Pope, (1993-09-28) Ambassador [Orig in German]. John Paul II, Pope, 1920- (Karol Wojtyla) (elected 1978). *OR(Eng)* 1306:9 S 8 1993*

PAPACY—RELATIONS (DIPLOMATIC)- FIJI
John Paul II, Pope, (1991-11-15) Allocutionhes (Papal reception of ambassadorial credentials) [English]. John Paul II, Pope, 1920- (Karol Wojtyla) (elected 1978). *AAS* 84:982-984 O 3 1992*

PAPACY—RELATIONS (DIPLOMATIC)- INDONESIA
John Paul II, Pope, (1991-11-07) Allocutiones (Speech to received ambassadorial credentials) [English]. John Paul II, Pope, 1920- (Karol Wojtyla) (elected 1978). *AAS* 84:963-966 O 3 1992*

PAPACY—RELATIONS (DIPLOMATIC)- IRELAND
John Paul II, Pope, (1991-12-16) Allocutiones (Speech to received ambassadorial credentials) [English]. John Paul II, Pope, 1920- (Karol Wojtyla) (elected 1978). *AAS* 85:23-25 Ja 7 1993*

PAPACY—RELATIONS (DIPLOMATIC)- ISRAEL
Bilateral talks to be productive [interview by L Pevtzow]. Jaeger, David. *Register* 69:1+ Ja 3 1993
Chief Rabbi meets Pope and invites him to Jerusalem. *Tablet* 247:1270+ O 2 1993
Israel and the Vatican: "the process must go on". *OSV* 81:21 Ja 24 1993
Israel, Rome near accord. Pevtzow, Lisa. *Register* 69:1+ Mr 28 1993
Vatican slows talks with Israel. Pevtzow, Lisa. *Register* 69:1+ Mr 28 1993
Waiting for John Paul [Israel visit]. Pevtzow, Lisa. *Register* 69:2 F 14 1993

PAPACY—RELATIONS (DIPLOMATIC)- MEXICO
John Paul II, Pope, (1992-09-21) Litterae Apostolicae (Apostolic Letter to create Apostolic Nuntiature in Mexico) [Latin]. John Paul II, Pope, 1920- (Karol Wojtyla) (elected 1978). *AAS* 85:127 F 3 1993*
Still fit for Greene. Jones, Arthur C, 1936-. *Tablet* 247:1002-1003 Ag 7 1993

PAPACY—RELATIONS (DIPLOMATIC)- NAURU
John Paul II, Pope, (1992-06-01) Litterae Apostolicae (Apostolic Letters) [Latin]. John Paul II, Pope, 1920- (Karol Wojtyla) (elected 1978). *AAS* 84:1060-1061 N 3 1992*

PAPACY—RELATIONS (DIPLOMATIC)- NETHERLANDS
John Paul II, Pope, (1991-09-30) Allocutiones (Speech for reception of credentials) [French]. John Paul II, Pope, 1920- (Karol Wojtyla) (elected 1978). *AAS* 84:848-850 S 8 1992*

PAPACY—RELATIONS (DIPLOMATIC)- NIGERIA
John Paul II, Pope, (1992-01-04) Allocutiones (Reception of the new Ambassador of Nigeria) [English]. John Paul II, Pope, 1920- (Karol Wojtyla) (elected 1978). *AAS* 85:45-47 Ja 7 1993*

PAPACY—RELATIONS (DIPLOMATIC)- PANAMA
John Paul II, Pope, (1991-12-21) Allocutiones (Reception of the new Ambassador from Panama) [Spanish]. John Paul II, Pope, 1920- (Karol Wojtyla) (elected 1978). *AAS* 85:35-36 Ja 7 1993*

PAPACY—RELATIONS (DIPLOMATIC)- PARAGUAY
John Paul II, Pope, (1991-11-11) Allocutiones (Speech to receive credentials) [Spanish]. John Paul II, Pope, 1920- (Karol Wojtyla) (elected 1978). *AAS* 84:966-969 O 3 1992*

PAPACY—RELATIONS (DIPLOMATIC)- POLAND
New era of cooperation begins. *OR(Eng)* 1302:2 Ag 11 1993
Polish concordat hits roadblock. Luxmoore, Jonathan. *Register* 69:1+ O 3 1993

PAPACY—RELATIONS (DIPLOMATIC)- ROMANIA
John Paul II, Pope, (1993-06-08) Republic of Romania. John Paul II, Pope, 1920- (Karol Wojtyla) (elected 1978). *OR(Eng)* 1297:8 Je 30 1993*

PAPACY—RELATIONS (DIPLOMATIC)- SANTA LUCIA
John Paul II, Pope, (1991-10-28) Allocutiones (Speech of reception of credentials) [English]. John Paul II, Pope, 1920- (Karol Wojtyla) (elected 1978). *AAS* 84:959-961 O 3 1992*

PAPACY—RELATIONS (DIPLOMATIC)- SENEGAL
John Paul II, Pope, (1992-02-21) Itinera Apostolica (On apostolic journey speech to Diplomatic Corps in Senegal) [French]. John Paul II, Pope, 1920- (Karol Wojtyla) (elected 1978). *AAS* 85:153-157 F 3 1993*

PAPACY—RELATIONS (DIPLOMATIC)- SPAIN
Keeping the Pope out. *Tablet* 247:753 Je 1993

PAPACY—RELATIONS (DIPLOMATIC)- THAILAND
Allocutiones (Speech to received Ambassador of Thailand) [English]. John Paul II, Pope, 1920- (Karol Wojtyla) (elected 1978). *AAS* 84:1073-1075 N 3 1992*

PAPACY—RELATIONS (DIPLOMATIC)- TUNISIA
John Paul II, Pope, (1992-01-09) Allocutiones (Welcome address to new ambassador from Tunisia) [French]. John Paul II, Pope, 1920- (Karol Wojtyla) (elected 1978). *AAS* 85:52-54 Ja 7 1993*

PAPACY—RELATIONS (DIPLOMATIC)- UNITED NATIONS
John Paul II, Pope, (1991-11-14) Allocutiones (Address to United Nations' FAO meeting) [English]. John Paul II, Pope, 1920- (Karol Wojtyla) (elected 1978). *AAS* 84:978-981 O 3 1992*

PAPACY—RELATIONS (DIPLOMATIC)- UNITED STATES
A dream come true [editorial]. Lawler, Philip F. *Register* 69:4 Ap 11 1993
Flynn flaps focuses on job's substance, style. McManus, James. *Nat Cath Rep* 29:9 Je 18 1993
Getting the facts straight. Pauley, Michael. *Register* 69:5 F 21 1993
Human rights ambassador. *Tablet* 247:785 Je 19 1993
John Paul II, Pope, (1993-09-02) United States [Orig in English]. John Paul II, Pope, 1920- (Karol Wojtyla) (elected 1978). *OR(Eng)* 1306:10 S 8 1993*
Relations between the church in the United States and the Holy See. Fogarty, Gerald P, 1939-. *Jurist* 52 no 1:210-227 1992

Working with the Parish Project. Rylands, Paddy. *Priests & People* 7:58-60 F 1993

Your church can be a driving force for justice [interview by the editors of Salt (Periodical)]. Cortes, Ernesto. *Salt* 13:14-19 N-D 1993

PARISHES—HISTORY

How churches build the kingdom, one parish at a time. Unsworth, Tim. *Salt* 13:22-25 N-D 1993

PARLIAMENT OF THE WORLD'S RELIGIONS (AUGUST 28-SEPTEMBER 5, 1993: CHICAGO, IL)

Unique parliament of world religions celebrates diversity. Rodenbaugh, Dana. *Nat Cath Rep* 29:4+ S 10 1993

PAROCHIAL SCHOOLS *see* Church Schools

PARSONS, TALCOTT, 1902-

Poder y sociedad: la sociologia en Talcott Parsons. Garcia Ruiz, Pablo. Pamplona: Eunsa, 1993. x, 280p ISBN 84-313-1196-7

PARTICIPATION

"Am I not a human being and a brother/sister?". Magesa, Laurenti. *AFER* 34:95-114 Ap 1992

Are kids telling us something about the Mass? Finley, Mitchel B, and Finley, Kathy. *Living Prayer* 26:23-24 Mr-Ap 1993

Conciliar constitution: Sacrosanctum Concilium. Schuler, Richard Joseph, 1920-. *SacM* 119:7-14 Wint 1992

A crisis facing us all. Finn, Peter C. *Past Mus* 17:21-23 Ap-My 1993

Music in Church. MacNamara, Frank. *Furrow* 44:148-153 Mr 1993

The Sacramentary's introductory materials: worth a second look. Francis, Mark R. *Past Mus* 17:17-19 Je-Jl 1993

Should the Mass be televised? Zukowski, Angela Ann. *America* 168:13-15 Ap 17 1993

Singing at the rites begins with Sunday. Quinn, Mary Jo. *Past Mus* 17:35-37 Ap-My 1993

"Singing pubs and silent churches"—revisited. Flynn, Laurence J. *Furrow* 44: 408-415 Jl-Ag 1993

Tanzanian women peasants: an ethical and theological reflection. Giblin, Marie. *AFER* 34:29-43 F 1992

Why I stay in the Catholic Church. Amlaw, Mary. *Liguorian* 81:4-8 Ag 1993

The work of the faithful. Kane, Mortimer. *AFER* 34:122-123 Ap 1992

PARTICULARISM (THEOLOGY)

Instance ontology and Avicenna's arguments. Mertz, Donald W. *Mod Schlmn* 70:189-199 Mr 1993

PASCAL, BLAISE, 1623-1662

Christianity for modern pagans. Kreeft, Peter John, 1937-. *Register* 69:5 Ap 11 1993

Death, the unsentimental fact, is our anchor to God's deeper realities. Kreeft, Peter John, 1937-. *Register* 69:1+ My 2 1993

God hides His presence to instruct us in humility. Kreeft, Peter John, 1937-. *Register* 69:1+ My 30 1993

Human vanity: it's the wrong path. Kreeft, Peter John, 1937-. *Register* 69:1+ Ap 25 1993

Indifference turns the modern heart away from heaven. Kreeft, Peter John, 1937-. *Register* 69:1+ My 23 1993

Only Christianity explains the heart of our human condition. Kreeft, Peter John, 1937-. *Register* 69:1+ Ap 18 1993

Pascal, order, and difference. McKenna, Andrew. *Relig Lit* 25:55-75 Sum 1993

Time: why we don't have any. Kreeft, Peter John, 1937-. *Register* 69:1+ My 16 1993

We should fear sin far more than death. Kreeft, Peter John, 1937-. *Register* 69:1+ My 9 1993

PASCHAL MYSTERY

Becoming paschal evangelizers. Kroeger, James H. *Emmanuel* 99:428-431+ O 1993

Cruciform dialogue in mission. Kroeger, James H. *AFER* 35:13-19 F 1993

Life after Easter. Smith, Pamela. New Jersey: Paulist Press, 1993. x, 88p ISBN 0-8091-3379-2 LC 92-21195

The paschal triduum. *Liturgy* 10:43-52 Sum 1992

Preparing for Easter [3 parts]. Rose, John. *Can Cath Rev* 11:36-37 F; 36-37 Mr; 37-38 Ap 1993

Shaping the celebrations. *Liturgy* 10:53-66 Sum 1992

Sound the trumpet: reflections on the paschal mystery. Gallagher, Michele T, 1943-. New York: Alba House, 1993. x, 134p ISBN 0-8189-0665-0 LC 92-40309

PASCHAL MYSTERY—HISTORY

A sense of the season. *Liturgy* 10:1-4 Sum 1992

PASSION-PLAYS

Mount Royal players: Montreal's living stations. Brown, John J. *Liguorian* 81:20-23 Ap 1993

PASSIVE RESISTANCE

"I can wait 40 or 400 years": Gandhian Satyagraha West and East. Starosta, William J, and Chaudhary, Anju G. *IPQ* 33:163-172 Je 1993

PASSIVITY (PSYCHOLOGY)

Passivity in the first stage toward union: learning to depend on God's love. Simsic, Wayne. *Spir Life* 32:96-103 Sum 1993

PASSOVER

A sense of the season. *Liturgy* 10:1-4 Sum 1992

PASTORAL ASSOCIATIONS

Pastoral associates guidelines. Hanus, Jerome, Bp. *Origins* 22:699-700 Mr 18 1993

XVIII Encontro Nacional de Pastoral Liturgica. *Notitiae* 28:686-688 O 1992

PASTORAL ASSOCIATIONS- ITALY

Associazione Italiana dei professori e cultori di liturgia. *Notitiae* 29:75-80 Ja-F 1993

PASTORAL CARE *see* Pastoral Theology

PASTORAL COUNSELING

Belongings: bonds of healing and recovery. Linn, Dennis, et al. New Jersey: Paulist Press, 1993. x, 255p ISBN 0-8091-3365-2 LC 92-29855

Crisis counseling. Stone, Howard W. Minneapolis: Fortress, 1993. x, 96p ISBN 0-8006-2760-1 LC 92-39489

Crisis counseling: what to do during the first 72 hours. Wright, H Norman. Ventura: Regal Books, 1993. 335p ISBN 0-8307-1611-4 LC 93-10514

Domestic violence. Untener, Kenneth E, Bp. *Origins* 23:357-358 O 28 1993

Helping skills for the nonprofessional counselor. Moore, Joseph. Cincinatti: St Anthony Press, 1993. x, 67p ISBN 0-86716-1744

Is spiritual direction losing its bearings? Leech, Kenneth, 1939-. *Tablet* 247: 634 My 22 1993

Leaven—listening to those who have left. Morahan, Justin. *Furrow* 44:154-158 Mr 1993

A minister's handbook of mental disorders. Ciarrocchi, Joseph W. Mahwah: Paulist, 1993. x, 221p ISBN 0-8091-3403-9 LC 93-11092

Parish diary: June. *Tablet* 247:812 Je 26 1993

Pastoral associates guidelines. Hanus, Jerome, Bp. *Origins* 22:699-700 Mr 18 1993

Pastoral counseling in a global church: voices from the field. Wicks, Robert J, and Estadt, Barry K, eds. Maryknoll, New York: Orbis Books, 1993. x, 169p ISBN 0-88344-865-3 LC 93-22082

Pastoral ministers and persons with disabilities. Bevilacqua, Anthony Joseph, Cardinal, 1923-. *Origins* 22:518-520 Ja 7 1993

What about our Church's children? Giurlanda, Paul. *America* 168:12-14 My 8 1993

PASTORAL COUNSELORS

Pastoral care in context. Patton, John. Louisville: Westminster, 1993. x, 288p ISBN 0-664-22034-7

PASTORAL PSYCHOLOGY

A feminist model for pastoral psychology. DeMarinis, Valerie M. Louisville: John Knox, 1993. x, 208p ISBN 0-664-22041-x

A minister's handbook of mental disorders. Ciarrocchi, Joseph W. Mahwah: Paulist, 1993. x, 221p ISBN 0-8091-3403-9 LC 93-11092

On screening seminarians. Dyrud, Jarl. *Origins* 23:79-80 Je 17 1993

PASTORAL THEOLOGY

Family ministry: preparing a parish pastoral plan. Meehan, Bridget Mary. *Tod Parish* 25:9-10 Mr 1993

PASTORAL THEOLOGY—CATHOLIC CHURCH

Abortion and the Sacrament of Penance. McAreavey, John. *Furrow* 44:230-235 Ap 1993

Appartenance à Église ou itinérance ecclésiale? Borras, Alphonse. *Lumen* 48: 161-173 Je 1993

Are all Christian ministers? Collins, John N. Collegeville: The Liturgical Press, 1992. x, 168p ISBN 0-8146-2168-6 LC 92-9599

Care of the dying: a Catholic perspective [4 parts]. *Health Prog* 74:34-38+ Mr; 16-21+ Ap; 22-26+ My; 46-54 Je 1993*

The contemplative pastor: returning to the art of spiritual direction. Peterson, Eugene H. Grand Rapids: Eerdmans, 1993. 192p ISBN 0-8028-0114-5

Converting the pastor. Moudry, Richard P. *Mod Lit* 20:6-8 Ap 1993

Creative models of spiritual care. Ceronsky, Charles. *Health Prog* 74:58-61 My 1993

Directory for the application of the principles and norms of ecumenism. *OR(Eng)* 1295:I-XIV Je 16 1993

Formulas should be adapted to needs and capacity of audience. Martinelli, Raffaello. *OR(Eng)* 1296:10+ Je 23 1993

Gay Christians. Lyons, Kieran. *Furrow* 44:347-351 Je 1993

Hard cases and hard teaching [editorial]. *Tablet* 247:31-32 Ja 9 1993

Interactional morality: a foundation for moral discernment in Catholic pastoral ministry. Poorman, Mark L. Washington: Georgetown University Press, 1993. 157p ISBN 0-87840-536-4 LC 93-3803

An interview with Bernard Häring, influential moral theologian [interview by J Tobin and W Bueche]. Häring, Bernard, 1912-. *Liguorian* 81:46-51 Je 1993

Is spiritual direction losing its bearings? Leech, Kenneth, 1939-. *Tablet* 247: 634 My 22 1993

John Paul II, Pope, (1993-06-16) "art of arts" [Orig in Spanish]. John Paul II, Pope, 1920- (Karol Wojtyla) (elected 1978). *OR(Eng)* 1297:6 Je 30 1993*

John Paul II, Pope, (1993-10-15) Moral guidance [Orig English]. John Paul II, Pope, 1920- (Karol Wojtyla) (elected 1978). *OR(Eng)* 1312:5 O 20 1993*

Leadership in a successful parish. Sweetser, Thomas P, and Holden, Carol M. Kansas City: Sheed & Ward, 1992. x, 203p ISBN 1-55612-564-x LC 92-20718

Light in the Lord. Hume, George Basil, Cardinal, 1923-. Minnesota: The Liturgical Press, 1991. x, 174p ISBN 0-8146-2142-2 LC 92-43998

Living with the less-than-perfect pastor. Gilbert, Jack. *Tod Parish* 25:38-39 Ap-My 1993

Marche vers la splendeur—ton Dieu marche avec toi [I congrès mondial des pastorale des sanctuaries et des Pèlerinages]. Calimé, Pierre. *Notitiae* 28: 294-296 Ap 1992

Metodi dell'esegesi tra mito, storicità e comunicasione. Lentzen-Deis, Fritz Leo. *Gregorianum* 73 No 4:731-737 1992

Le ministère de présidence du curé: réflexions canoniques et pastorales. Borras, Alphonse. *Stud Can* 27 no 1:59-76 1993

Moral methodology and pastoral responsiveness: the case of abortion and the care of children. Whitmore, Todd David. *TheolStds* 54:316-338 Je 1993

New parish ministers: laity & religious on parish staffs. Murnion, Philip J, 1938-. New York: National Pastoral Life Center, 1992. 131p ISBN 1-88130-701-8

The non-ordained pastor: a paradigm for future church leadership. Gilmour, Peter. *Listening* 28:81-90 Wint 1993

Parish diary: February. *Tablet* 247:270 F 27 1993

Parish diary: July. *Tablet* 247:973 Jl 31 1993

Parish diary: March. *Tablet* 247:401 Mr 27 1993

Pastoral care for interfaith couples—a beginning. Borelli, John. *New Theol Rev* 6:30-42 Ag 1993

Pastoral care for those living with HIV/AIDS. Paul, John, Bp. *Origins* 23: 378-381 N 4 1993

Pastoral care in context. Patton, John. Louisville: Westminster, 1993. x, 288p ISBN 0-664-22034-7

Pastoral inculturada entre refugiados [interview by the editors of Christus] (Periodical). Falla, Ricardo. *Christus* 58:39-44 My 1993

Pastoral planning for the new millennium. Quinn, John Raphael, Abp, 1929-. *Origins* 22:624-628 F 25 1993

Pastoral reflections: euthanasia, assisted suicide. *Origins* 23:373-378 N 4 1993

Pastoral response to sexual ethics. Arnold, William V. Louisville, Kentucky: John Knox, 1993. 176p ISBN 0-66425420-0

Spokesmen for the spiritual dimension of the world order. Muller, Robert. *Sisters* 65:202-205 My 1993

A stumbling-block for many [editorial]. *Tablet* 247:935 Jl 24 1993

A tale of two popes [editorial]. *Tablet* 247:775-776 Je 19 1993

Twenty-five years later (commentary: *Humanae Vitae*). *OSV* 82:2 Jl 25 1993

PAULIST FATHERS
Evangelizing America: transformations in Paulist mission. Robichaud, Paul. *US Cath Hist* 11:61-78 Spr 1993

PAULIST FATHERS—HISTORY
John Paul II, Pope (1993-06-27) Gospel [Orig Italian and English]. John Paul II, Pope, 1920- (Karol Wojtyla) (elected 1978). *OR(Eng)* 1297:1+ Je 30 1993*

PAULOS, ABUNA, PATRIARCH
John Paul II, Pope, (1993-06-11) Ethiopian Orthodox Patriarch. John Paul II, Pope, 1920- (Karol Wojtyla) (elected 1978). *OR(Eng)* 1295:5 Je 16 1993*

PAX CHRISTI INTERNATIONAL
Delcaração da dlegação de Pax Christi Internacional para a IV Conferência Geral do Episcopado Latino-Americano. Ven, Joao Henrique Van de. *REB* 53:163-166 Mr 1993

A paixão de Cristo na tradicço luso-Brasileira. Azzi, Riolando. *REB* 53:114-149 Mr 1993

PAX CHRISTI USA
Activists and charismatics: stronger ties and shared respect. Wood, Charles. *New Cov* 23:8-12 O 1993

Haiti, Sarajevo, peacemaking among topics at Pax Christi USA's assembly. Tekippe, Patricia. *Nat Cath Rep* 29:2 Ag 27 1993

Somalia strains Pax Christi. Bole, William. *Nat Cath Rep* 29:10 Ja 8 1993

PAX CHRISTI'S USA NATIONAL ASSEMBLY (AG 6-8, 1993: SOUTH BEND, IN)
Haiti, Sarajevo, peacemaking among topics at Pax Christi USA's assembly. Tekippe, Patricia. *Nat Cath Rep* 29:2 Ag 27 1993

PAZ ZAMORA, JAIME
John Paul II, Pope, (1991-11-22) Allocutiones (Papal address to President of Bolivia) [Spanish]. John Paul II, Pope, 1920- (Karol Wojtyla) (elected 1978). *AAS* 84:1075-1078 N 3 1992*

PEACE
Catechism fails to convey pope's passion for peace. Hebblethwaite, Peter, 1930-. *Nat Cath Rep* 29:16 Ja 29 1993

Catholic peacemakers: a documentary history [VI]. Musto, Ronald G. New York: Garland Publishing, 1993. x, 818p ISBN 0-8153-0604-0 LC 92-42658

"The challenge of peace" revisited. Murray, Pius. *Emmanuel* 99:314-317 Jl-Ag 1993

"The challenge of peace"—10 years later. Sullivan, Walter Francis, Bp, 1928-. *OSV* 82:23 My 16 1993

A challenge of peace: North-South dialogue. Weakland, Rembert G, Abp, 1927-. *Origins* 23:292-296 O 7 1993

The continuing challenge of peace [interview by T Tamberg]. Christiansen, Drew. *OSV* 82:6 Ag 22 1993

For peace reach to the poor, Pope says. *Tablet* 246:1629-1630 D 19-26 1992

Gorbachev calls for "moral impetus". *Tablet* 247:1239 S 25 1993

Gumbleton: push just peace, not just war [address, University of Dayton, Dayton, Ohio, Jl 6 1993]. *Nat Cath Rep* 29:3 Jl 30 1993

John Paul II, Pope, (1992-01-09) we pray for peace. John Paul II, Pope, 1920- (Karol Wojtyla) (elected 1978). *TPS* 38:181-183 My-Je 1993*

John Paul II, Pope, (1992-12-08) If you want peace, serve the poor. John Paul II, Pope, 1920- (Karol Wojtyla) (elected 1978). *TPS* 38:155-161 My-Je 1993*

John Paul II, Pope, (1993-01-01) God wants [orig Italian]. John Paul II, Pope, 1920- (Karol Wojtyla) (elected 1978). *OR(Eng)* 1272:3 Ja 6 1993*

John Paul II, Pope, (1993-01-01) Peace through helping poor. John Paul II, Pope, 1920- (Karol Wojtyla) (elected 1978). *Nat Cath Rep* 29:12-13 Ja 8 1993*

John Paul II, Pope, (1993-01-01) Poverty and peace [abridged]. John Paul II, Pope, 1920- (Karol Wojtyla) (elected 1978). *Tablet* 247:25-26 Ja 2 1993*

John Paul II, Pope, (1993-01-16) Diplomats [Origin French]. John Paul II, Pope, 1920- (Karol Wojtyla) (elected 1978). *Origins* 22:583-587 F 4 1993*

Outrageous thoughts on war and peace. Bellah, Robert Neely, 1927-. *New Oxford Rev* 60:15-18+ Mr 1993

Peace and Islam [condensed fr *Islam and Christian Muslim Relations* Je, 1990]. Tröger, Karl-Wolfgang. *TheolDgst* 38:115-118 Sum 1991

The post-cold war agenda for peace. Bernardin, Joseph Louis, Cardinal, 1928-. *Origins* 23:1+ My 20 1993

Religious wars and religious peace. McCarthy, Abigail Quigley. *Comm* 120:6-7 Mr 12 1993

The spiritual significance of Jerusalem. *Ecumen Trends* 22:14-15 S 1993

Ten years after: the bishops (again) on war and peace. Weigel, George. *Crisis* 11:36-41 Mr 1993

Word faiths for peace. Willey, David. *Tablet* 247:1276-1277 O 2 1993

PEACE (THEOLOGY)
Abortion and peace. Lang, David P. *HPR* 93:10-19 Mr 1993

Inner peace—a presence. Hogan, William Francis, 1930-. *Emmanuel* 99:232-235 My 1993

PEACE MOVEMENT
Activists debate tactics for new world wars. O'Grady, Jim. *Nat Cath Rep* 29:6 Ja 29 1993

Convoy drives hard questions home for peace movment [editorial]. *Nat Cath Rep* 29:20 S 3 1993

Fired up: Cantonsville files plus nine hearts. Clancy, Paul. *Nat Cath Rep* 29:3 My 21 1993

Peace crumbles on the way to Sarajevo [photos]. McCarthy, Tim. *Nat Cath Rep* 29:14-16+ Ag 27 1993

A quantum leap [editorial]. *Register* 69:5 S 19 1993

PEACOCK, CORNELIA, 1809-1879
Congregation for the Causes of Saints (1992-06-13) Decree on the heroic virtues. Congregation for the Causes of Saints. *TPS* 38:19-20 Ja-F 1993*

PEARCE, JOSEPH CHILTON
Christian families and today's sexual values. Finley, Mitchel B, and Finley, Kathy. *Living Prayer* 26:21-22 N-D 1993

PEASANTS
Magic in the age of faith. Greeley, Andrew Moran, 1928-. *America* 169:8-14 O 9 1993

PEDOPHILIA—CLERGY
Abuse of faith. Castelli, James. *USCath* 58:6-15 S 1993

An archdiocese's healing process. Sheehan, Michael, Abp. *Origins* 23:285-287 O 7 1993

Bishops speak in public session of sexual abuse. Reese, Thomas Joseph, 1945-. *America* 169:4-6 Jl 3-10 1993

Breach of faith. Costello, Gerald M, 1931-. *USCath* 58:48-51 Mr 1993

But Father, they're priests! Clerical culture and pedophilia. Greeley, Andrew Moran, 1928-. *Critic* 47:43-51 Wint 1992

The case of Father X. Castelli, James. *USCath* 58:12-13 S 1993

Child sexual abuse: think tank recommendations. *Origins* 23:108-111 Jl 1 1993

Focus on sexual abuse. Higgins, Michael. *Tablet* 247:194-196 F 13 1993

How one diocese responds. Unsworth, Tim. *USCath* 58:14 S 1993

How serious is the problem of sexual abuse by clergy? Greeley, Andrew Moran, 1928-. *America* 168:6-10 Mr 20-27 1993

Letter after charges involving local priest. Gelineau, Louis E, Bp. *Origins* 23: 111-112 Jl 1 1993

Moving beyond denial, sex abuse examination begins [editorial]. *Nat Cath Rep* 29:24 Jl 2 1993

NCCB establishes committee on sexual abuse. Kinney, John, Bp. *Origins* 23: 104-105 Jl 1 1993

On screening seminarians. Dyrud, Jarl. *Origins* 23:79-80 Je 17 1993

Pastoral policy: allegations of clergy sexual misconduct with minors. *Origins* 22:580-582 F 4 1993

A plea for pruning. Leonard, George. *Priests & People* 7:30-31 Ja 1993

The priesthood in the third millennium. Hemrick, Eugene F. *Priest* 49:22-24 Ag 1993

Priests who stray. Harvey, John F, 1921-. *Crisis* 10:37-42 N 1992

The reassignment of a cleric who has been professionally evaluated and treated for sexual misconduct with minors: canonical considerations. Griffin, Bertram F. *Jurist* 51 no 2:326-339 1991

Rebuilding trust: clergy sexual abuse. Connors, Canice. *Church* 9:5-10 Sum 1993

The search for answers. Conners, Canice. *USCath* 58:8-11 S 1993

The see-no-problem, hear-no-problem, speak-no-problem problem sex abuse. Kennedy, Eugene. *Nat Cath Rep* 29:5+ Mr 19 1993

Statement on Boston's clergy sexual misconduct policy. Law, Bernard Francis, Cardinal, 1931-. *Origins* 22:582-583 F 4 1993

Subcommittee head introduces think tank recommendations. Connors, Canice. *Origins* 23:105-107 Jl 1 1993

Telling the whole truth [interview by W Bole]. Rossetti, Stephen. *OSV* 82:6 Jl 11 1993

Time of heroism, atmosphere of suspicion. Harrington, Timothy, Bp. *Origins* 22:609-610 F 18 1993

PEIRCE, CHARLES SANDERS, 1839-1914
Jonathan Edwards' twelfth sign. Raposa, Michael L. *IPQ* 33:153-162 Je 1993

PELAGIA, MARY
The third career of Sister Mary Pelagia, OP, author. O'Hara, Fred. *CLW* 64: 40-42 Jl-S 1993

PELAGIANISM
What went wrong in the 'fifties. Hitchcock, James, 1938-. *Crisis* 10:15-19 N 1992

PELAGIUS, 360-420
Pelagius on St Paul's Epistle to the Romans. Bruyn, Theodore de, ed. New York: Oxford University Press, 1993. x, 248p ISBN 0-814399-0

What's so amazing about grace? [interview by editors of US Catholic (Periodical)]. Dreyer, Elizabeth. *USCath* 58:6-13 My 1993

PENANCE
Abortion and the Sacrament of Penance. McAreavey, John. *Furrow* 44:230-235 Ap 1993

Christianity and the "eminent good works". Shaw, Russell. *Register* 69:1+ Ja 10 1993

Conversion: a lifelong journey. Connolly, Hugh G. *Furrow* 44:159-166 Mr 1993

Current errors and their refutation: confessors and spiritual directors. Sutton, Alphonsus M. *ChrWorld* 38:51-55 Ja-F 1993

John Paul II, Pope, (1993-03-27) Treat sinners with compassion. John Paul II, Pope, 1920- (Karol Wojtyla) (elected 1978). *TPS* 38:261-265 S-O 1993*

John Paul II, Pope, (1993-05-23) Social dimension [Orig in Italian]. John Paul II, Pope, 1920- (Karol Wojtyla) (elected 1978). *OR(Eng)* 1294:5 Je 9 1993*

John Paul II, Pope, (1993-06-02) Priest [Orig in Italian]. John Paul II, Pope, 1920- (Karol Wojtyla) (elected 1978). *OR(Eng)* 1294:11 Je 9 1993*

Liturgically speaking. Freburger, William J. *Priest* 49:30 Ap 1993

Penance (again)!. Freburger, William J. *Priest* 49:28 Mr 1993

Penance is more than penalty: it's the wellspring of authentic Christian life. Cameron, Peter John. *Register* 69:1+ F 28 1993

The penance of inconvenience. Svoboda, Melannie. *Liguorian* 81:26-29 F 1993

The power is the Lord's. Foley, James S. *HPR* 94:24-28 O 1993

Reconciliation: restored to full health and grace. Wallace, James A, 1944-. *Liguorian* 81:4-9 Mr 1993

The Sacrament of Reconciliation [repr fr *Vidyajyoti journal of theological reflection*]. Mattam, Joseph. *AFER* 34:293-322 O 1992

Seeing sin for what it is. Cameron, Peter John. *Register* 69:1+ Mr 14 1993

The sinner against the scoundrels: the ills of doctrine and "schrift" in the Wife of Bath's, Friar's and Summoner's narratives. Kamowski, William. *Relig Lit* 25:1-18 Spr 1993

PENITENTS
Piety centered on Jesus' suffering and some eccentric Christian understandings of the mystery of Calvary. Sloyan, Gerard S. *Worship* 67:98-123 Mr 1993

PENNSYLVANIA—POLITICS AND GOVERNMENT
Governor Robert P Casey: Pro-life Democrat fights party line. Hillenmeyer, Kathleen. *St Anth* 100:28-34 Ja 1993

PENNSYLVANIA—RELIGION
Pennsylvania Dutch. Wentz, Richard E, ed. New York: Paulist Press, 1993. x, 329p ISBN 0-8091-0439-3 LC 92-33184

PENNY, SAMUEL
Archdiocese admits mistakes over sex abuse case. *Tablet* 247:700 My 29 1993

PENSIONS
John Paul II, Pope, (1992-09-08) Litterae Apostolicae (Apostolic Letter) [Italian]. John Paul II, Pope, 1920- (Karol Wojtyla) (elected 1978). *AAS* 84:1033-1053 N 3 1992*

Secretariat of State (1992-10-02) Decretum (Decree on Norms of Pensions) [Italian]. *AAS* 84:1079 N 3 1992*

PENTECOST
The eve of Pentecost. *Liturgy* 10:111-114 Sum 1992

Fanning the parish flame. Ginter, Mark. *New Cov* 22:12-13 Mr 1993

The feast of hospitality. Williams, Joan. *ReligTJ* 27:25 Ap-My 1993

Like a fire within us. Glavich, Kathleen. *ReligTJ* 27:32-33 Ap-My 1993

Mary in ordinary time: Biblical references. Turro, James C. *Marian Stds* 43: 60-71 1992

Pentecost message from The World Council of Churches. Aagaard, Anna Marie, et al. *Ecumen Trends* 22:2 Ap 1993

Searching for spirit. Richards, Dennis. *ReligTJ* 27:35-36 Ap-My 1993

PENTECOSTAL CHURCHES- BRAZIL
Podem Passar A Sacolinha. Oro, Ari Pedro. *REB* 53:301-323 Je 1993

PENTECOSTALISM
Bridge builders. Winter, Harry. *New Cov* 22:7-9 My 1993

Fanning the parish flame. Ginter, Mark. *New Cov* 22:12-13 Mr 1993

Giving thanks. Scanlan, Michael. *New Cov* 22:26-27 My 1993

Healing is real. Monahan, Jim. *New Cov* 22:26-27 Je 1993

Lessons from evangelicals. Heron, Benedict. *Tablet* 247:674 My 29 1993

New charismatic leader has two crosses to bear. Carey, Ann. *OSV* 82:17 Je 27 1993

Once a charismatic. Hannan, Maryanne. *New Cov* 22:23-24 My 1993

A prayerful parish. Wood, Charles. *New Cov* 22:8-10 Mr 1993

Reflections by a Pentecostalist on aspects of BEM. Hunter, Harold D. *JEcumen Stds* 29:317-345 Sum-Aut 1992

The song of the Church. Weakland, Rembert G, Abp, 1927-. *Origins* 23:12-16 My 20 1993

They have life in the spirit. Sabatowich, Jerome. *ReligTJ* 26:36-37 Ja 1993

Where in the world is the Catholic charismatic renewal? Metz, Kenneth. *New Cov* 22:8-10 Ja 1993

PENTECOSTALISM—CATHOLIC CHURCH
Activists and charismatics: stronger ties and shared respect. Wood, Charles. *New Cov* 23:8-12 O 1993

The birth of a new Catholicism. Martin, Ralph. *New Cov* 22:21+ F 1993

The charismatic way. Cooper, Kristina. *Tablet* 247:467-468 Ap 10-17 1993

Christ came alive. Harris, King. *New Cov* 23:15-17 O 1993

A decade of fireworks. Ferguson, Lisa. *New Cov* 23:20-21 Ag 1993

The disturbing charismatic renewal. Whitehead, Charles. *New Cov* 23:29 N 1993

Dreams of renewal. Ryan, Ron. *New Cov* 23:25 Ag 1993

Holiness for everyone. Martin, George. *New Cov* 23:18-20 N 1993

Keeping Mary in balance (but not in check). Ullrich, Coralie. *New Cov* 23: 20-22 O 1993

Mainstreaming. Wilson, Chip. *Register* 69:1+ Je 20 1993

The Marian movement. Scanlan, Michael. *New Cov* 22:23-24 Mr 1993

"Most Holy Father: I hope to avoid the shock that your decision would cause" [Letter to PP VI to protect the infant charismatic renewal]. Suenens, Leo-Jozef, Cardinal, 1904-. *New Cov* 22:7-9 Ap 1993

Pentecostal unity: recurring frustration and enduring hopes. Crowe, Terrence Robert. Chicago: Loyola University Press, 1993. x, 282p ISBN 0-8294-0746 LC 93-20683

Pope encourages Catholic charismatics. Cooper, Kristina. *Tablet* 247:1239-1240 S 25 1993

Towards a new Pentecost: for a new evangelization. McDonnell, Kilian, 1921-, ed. Collegeville:Liturgical, 1993. x, 72p ISBN 0-8146-5846-6 LC 92-46910

1993 Conference: fanning the flame (July 9-11, 1993: Seattle, Washington). *New Cov* 23:30 S 1993

PEOPLE OF GOD
The forest and the trees. Morgan, Winifred. *Sisters* 65:12-19 Ja 1993

What sort of people do the exercises foster? Chadwick, Graham. *Way Suppl* 76:109-116 Spr 1993

Will the real Catholic Church please stand up. Burns, Robert E, 1919-. *USCath* 58:2 F 1993

PERCEPTION
The fragility of consciousness: Lonergan and the postmodern concern for the other. Lawrence, Fred. *TheolStds* 54:55-94 Mr 1993

Merleau-Ponty's logos: the sens-ing of flesh. Stenstad, Gail. *PhilosTod* 37:52-61 Spr 1993

PERCY, WALKER, 1916-1990
Of medicine and metaphor: significant findings from Walker Percy. Allsopp, Michael E. *Linacre* 60:48-55 F 1993

Walker Percy: the man and the movie. Austin, Ronald. *New Oxford Rev* 60: 16-19 O 1993

PEREZ DE CUELLAR, JAVIER
John Paul II, Pope, (1991-11-25) Allocutiones (Reception of UN Secretary General) [French]. John Paul II, Pope, 1920- (Karol Wojtyla) (elected 1978). *AAS* 84:1138-1141 D 5 1992*

PEREZ FLORIDO, ANA JOSEFINA, 1884-1936
Congregation for the Causes of Saints (1993-07-06) Decree on a miracle. Congregation for the Causes of Saints. *OR(Eng)* 1299:12 Jl 14 1993*

PERFECTION
Perfection without God: a view from the Pāli Canon. Katz, Nathan. *Stud Form Spir* 14:11-22 F 1993

PERFORMANCE
The market place. McNair, J Frank. *Living Prayer* 26:30-31 Jl-Ag 1993

PERFORMANCE—LAW—HISTORY
Is there life beyond efficiency? Elements of a social law and economics. Medema, Steven G. *RSocEcon* 51:138-153 Sum 1993

PERIODICALS
Growing pains [editorial]. *New Oxford Rev* 60:2 N 1993

PERIODICALS- GERMANY
La revista gottesdienst cuplioó 25 años. Nagel, Eduard, and Palacios, Miguel. *Notitiae* 29:304-306 My 1993

PERIODICALS, RELIGIOUS
How I use Today's Parish. Goessl, Celine. *Tod Parish* 25:31 S 1993

"Inside the Vatican:" want a peek? Burke, Greg. *Register* 69:1+ Je 13 1993

Vivifying the parish. *Tablet* 247:545 My 1 1993

PERSECUTION
Christian-Jewish relations in a new Europe. Solomon, Norman. *Month* 26:9-16 Ja 1993

Forgotten holocaust. Luxmoore, Jonathan. *Tablet* 247:842-843 Jl 3 1993

Growing up in the Church: China and the USA. Shen, Louis. *America* 168: 10-12 Ja 16-23 1993

"Help us while it is not too late!". Komarica, Franjo, Bp, 1946-, et al. *Cath Int* 4:230-231 My 1993

More death threats against bishop. *Tablet* 247:414 Mr 27 1993

No rest for the travellers. Bowlby, Chris. *Tablet* 247:606+ My 15 1993

The resurrection of a Church. *Tablet* 247:556 My 1 1993

PERSECUTION- ALBANIA
Albania, the Church triumphant in ruins. Hurley, Mark Joseph, Bp, 1919-. *America* 168:4-5 F 20 1993

John Paul II, Pope, (1993-04-25) May Albania be equal to the challenge. John Paul II, Pope, 1920- (Karol Wojtyla) (elected 1978). *TPS* 38:275-279 S-O 1993*

PERSECUTION- ASIA
Asia's new-style tyranny. Himmelfarb, Anne. *Crisis* 11:46-48 S 1993

PERSECUTION- SUDAN
Sudan: a grim tragedy. Gassis, Macram Max, Bp, 1938-. *Cath Int* 4:236-237 My 1993

War-torn Sudan waits for the Pope. Eppink, Alfons. *Tablet* 247:160-161 F 6 1993

PERSIAN GULF WAR, 1991
After Kuwait the deluge. Wicker, Brian. *New Blckfrs* 74:85-98 F 1993

Desert Storm revisited: bombs, hatred for Iraq. Schroth, Raymond A, 1933-. *Nat Cath Rep* 29:17 F 5 1993

Statement on the morality of the war in the Persian Gulf. *Horizons (CTS)* 20:118-126 Spr 1993

You can't keep a good theory down: the just war, the Gulf War and beyond. Pope, J Stephen. *Comm* 120:9-12 F 12 1993

PERSONAL FINANCE see Finance, Personal

PERSONALISM
Die Annahme der Gnade als Mitvollzug der Erlösung. Menke, Karl-Heinz. *Catholica* 47:1-19 1993

Para una ciencia del sujeto: investigacion de la persona. Fierro, Alfredo. Barcelona: Anthropos, 1993. x, 494p ISBN 84-7658-387-7

Poder y sociedad: la sociologia en Talcott Parsons. Garcia Ruiz, Pablo. Pamplona: Eunsa, 1993. x, 280p ISBN 84-313-1196-7

PERSONALITY
Liturgy and personality: the healing power of formal prayer. Hildebrand, Dietrich von. Manchester: Sophia Institute Press, 1993. x, 165p ISBN 0-918477-13-1 LC 29-19821

PERSONALITY—ETHICAL ASPECTS
La personne humaine et son identité morale. Fuchs, Eric. *Supplement* 184: 193-203 Mr-Ap 1993

PERSONNEL MANAGEMENT
Quality management of human resources. Blair, Carol S, et al. *Health Prog* 74:16-21 O 1993

PERSONS (PHILOSOPHY)
The incommunicability of human persons [fr *Essay on personal selfhood*]. Crosby, John F, III. *Thomist* 57:403-442 Jl 1993

Para una ciencia del sujeto: investigacion de la persona. Fierro, Alfredo. Barcelona: Anthropos, 1993. x, 494p ISBN 84-7658-387-7

Person, being, and St Thomas. Clarke, W Norris. *Communio* 19:601-618 Wint 1992

Scientific and philosophical expertise: an evaluation of the arguments on "personhood". Irving, Diane Nutwell. *Linacre* 60:18-46 F 1993

PERSONS (THEOLOGY)
Man and woman under God: the dignity of the human being according to Hans Urs von Balthasar. Strukelj, Anton. *Communio* 20:377-388 Sum 1993

Persons, souls and embryos. Coghlan, Peter. *Pacifica* 6:165-171 Je 1993

PERU—POLITICS AND GOVERNMENT
What is the church of the poor? A missionary reshapes his theology. Hurteau, Robert. *Comm* 120:13-16 Mr 26 1993

PESCI, VINCENZO, 1853-1929
Congregation for the Causes of Saints (1993-07-06) Decree on the heroic virtues. Congregation for the Causes of Saints. *OR(Eng)* 1299:12 Jl 14 1993*

PETER, SAINT, APOSTLE
The feast of the Chair of Peter. Mangan, Charles M. *OSV* 81:14 F 21 1993

John Paul II, Pope, (1992-12-16) Peter ranks first. John Paul II, Pope, 1920- (Karol Wojtyla) (elected 1978). *TPS* 38:165-168 My-Je 1993*

John Paul II, Pope, (1993-01-27) Bishop of Rome is Peter's successor. John Paul II, Pope, 1920- (Karol Wojtyla) (elected 1978). *TPS* 38:207-210 Jl-Ag 1993*

John Paul II, Pope, (1993-06-29) Prayer [Orig in Italian]. John Paul II, Pope, 1920- (Karol Wojtyla) (elected 1978). *OR(Eng)* 1298:1-2 Jl 7 1993*

Peter and the ghost. Walsh, John E. *HPR* 93:24-28 My 1993

Peter's house—the first church. Martin, Geroge. *CDgst* 57:1-3+ S 1993

Praying with Peter [excerpts fr a pastoral letter to the Church of Denver]. Stafford, James Francis, Abp, 1932-. *Crisis* 11:26-31 Jl-Ag 1993

Reconciliation: a meeting place with our loving God. Jeray, Diane. *Liguorian* 81:57-59 Ag 1993

Santo Domingo desde dentro. Arizmendi Esquivel, Felipe, Bp. *Christus* 58: 15-22 Mr-Ap 1993

Should Paul once again oppose Peter to his face? Dunn, James D G. *Heythrop* 34:425-428 O 1993

Who's been sitting in Peter's chair? Pazola, Ron. *USCath* 58:34-39 Jl 1993

PHILOSOPHY, ITALIAN
Thomas the thinker [review article *The thought of Thomas Acquinas* by B Davies]. Walsh, Liam G. *Doctr Life* 43:156-161 Mr 1993

PHILOSOPHY, MEDIEVAL
La fondation des lois civiles. Goyard-Fabre, Simone. *Laval Theol Phil* 49:105-119 F 1993

PHILOSOPHY, MODERN
Between foundationalism and nihilism: is phronēsis the via media for theology? Guarino, Thomas. *TheolStds* 54:37-54 Mr 1993

Categorias, intencionalidad y numeros: introduccion a la filosofia primera y a los origens del pensamiento fenomenologico. Garcia-Baro, Miguel. Madrid: Teconos, 1993. x, 198p ISBN 84-309-2329-2

Coup d'oeil sur la philosophie italienne contemporaine. Rizzerio, Laura. *RPhil Louvain* 90:539-556 N 1992

La fondation des lois civiles. Goyard-Fabre, Simone. *Laval Theol Phil* 49:105-119 F 1993

The hiddennes of God. Law, David R. New York: Oxford University Press, 1993. x, 256p ISBN 0-826336-8

Jan Patovcka et le phénomène de l'écriture littéraire. Declève, Henri. *Laval Theol Phil* 49:3-26 F 1993

Marxa I Sentit especulatius de la historia: comentaris a Hegel. Mayos Solsona, Goncal. Barcelona: PPU, 1993. x, 297p ISBN 84-477-0058-5

On the tasks of Catholic philosophy in our time. Balthasar, Hans Urs Von, 1905-1988. *Communio* 20:147-187 Spr 1993

That which resists, after all [conversation between cited authors]. Lyotard, Jean-François, and Larochelle, Gilbert. *PhilosTod* 36:402-417 Wint 1992

Voluntad de lo tragico: el concepto nietzscheano de voluntad a partir de el nacimiento de la tradgedia. Barrios Casares, Manuel. Sevilla: A Er, Revista de Filosofia, 1993. x, 190p ISBN 84-604-5347-2

PHILOSOPHY, MODERN—1900-
The community's absence in Lyotard, Nancy, and Lacoue-Labarthe. May, Todd. *PhilosTod* 37:275-284 Aut 1993

PHILOSOPHY, SPANISH
Geographia de l'absurd. Torralba Rossello, Francesc. Lerida: Pages, 1993. 149p ISBN 84-7935-132-2

PHILOSOPHY AND CHRISTIANITY
Amitié, attirance et amour chez S. Thomas d'Aquin. McEnvoy, James. *RPhil Louvain* 91:383-408 Ag 1993

Un arbre en plein vent. Joassart, Bernard. *NRT* 115:243-245 Mr-Ap 1993

L'attitude d'Oridène face aux philosophies et religions païennes. Fédou, Michel. *StudiaM* 42:123-142 1993

The Christianization of modern philosophy according to Maurice Blondel. Grys, James Le. *TheolStds* 54:455-484 S 1993

Contemporary art and the expanded death of the human Jesus. Seubert, Xavier John. *New Theol Rev* 6:27-39 F 1993

El dios de los dioses: ciencia del arte. Galan, Ilia. Madríd: Líbertarias, 1993. x, 237p ISBN 84-7954-116-4

For Christians, faith and reason are partners. Kreeft, Peter John, 1937. *Register* 69:1+ Ag 8 1993

Hegel, des années de jeunesse à la fondation du premier système [two parts]. Depré, Olivier. *RPhil Louvain* 91:111-125 F; 259-274 My 1993

Jonathan Edwards' twelfth sign. Raposa, Michael L. *IPQ* 33:153-162 Je 1993

Kundera, Nietzsche, and politics on the questions of eternal return and responsibility. Parens, Erik. *PhilosTod* 37:285-297 Aut 1993

Il mio itinerario filosofico. Selvaggi, Filippo. *Gregorianum* 74 no 2:309-329 1993

On Leo Strauss's understanding of the natural law theory of Thomas Aquinas. Kries, Douglas. *Thomist* 57:215-232 Ap 1993

Peter Singer on famine, affluence, and morality: a Christian response. Spoerl, Joseph S. *Amer J Juris* 37:113-133 1992

Rational faith: Catholic responses to reformed epistemology. Zaggelski, Linda Trinkaus, 1946-, ed. Indiana: Notre Dame Press, 1993. x, 290p ISBN 0-268-01643-7 LC 92-537-42

El retorno a la experiencia en teología: Ernst Troeltsch redivivo. García Prada, José María. *Cien Tom* 119:585-592 S-D 1992

PHILOSOPHY AND CHRISTIANITY—GREEK PHILOSOPHY
Le concept de philosophie première dans la Métaphysique d' Aristote. Destrée, Pierre. *RPhil Louvain* 90:387-421 N 1992

Culture et foi: Clément d'Alexandrie. Crouzel, Henri. *StudiaM* 42:99-121 1993

PHILOSOPHY AND SOCIAL SCIENCES
Entre el liberalismo y la socialdemocracia: la sociedad abierta. Perona, Angeles J. Barcelona: Anthropos, 1993. x, 248p ISBN 84-7658-394-x

PHILOSOPHY AND THEOLOGY
Athens and Jerusalem: the role of philosophy in theology. Bonsor, Jack A. Mahwah: Paulist Press, 1993. 192p ISBN 0-8091-3398-9

Hans Urs von Balthasar's anthropology in light of his marian thinking. Roten, Johann G. *Communio* 20:306-333 Sum 1993

"Humanae Vitae": 25th anniversary. McMahon, Kevin. *Origins* 22:768-774 Ap 22 1993*

L'idéalisme Allemand face à la raison théologique. Maesschalck, Marc. *Laval Theol Phil* 49:309-320 Je 1993

Implicazioni filosofiche e teologiche delle nuove cosmologie. Coyne, George V. *Civilta* 143:343-352 N 21 1992

Italo Mancini: un profeta sotto la toga dell'accademico. Vanzan, Piersandro. *Civilta* 2:351-364 My 15 1993

Jonathan Edwards' twelfth sign. Raposa, Michael L. *IPQ* 33:153-162 Je 1993

Ludere est contemplari: on the unseriousness of human affairs. Schall, James Vincent, 1928-. *ABenR* 44:99-111 Mr 1993

MacIntyre's postmodern Thomism: reflections on Three rival versions of moral enquiry. Hibbs, Thomas S. *Thomist* 57:277-297 Ap 1993

Meta-anthropology and Christology: on the philosophy of Hans Urs von Balthasar. Bieler, Martin. *Communio* 20:129-146 Spr 1993

On the tasks of Catholic philosophy in our time. Balthasar, Hans Urs Von, 1905-1988. *Communio* 20:147-187 Spr 1993

Philosophy and theology after Kolyma. Chrostowski, Waldemar. *New Theol Rev* 6:102-107 My 1993

Il posto della metafisica nel sapere umano Il pensiero di Maimonide e il suo influsso su S Tommasso d'Aquino. Pangallo, Don Mario. *Gregorianum* 74 no 2:331-352 1993

La tesis de Calatayud. Pou i Puigserver, Bartomeu. Barcelona: PPU, 1993. x, 173p ISBN 84-477-0037-2

Thomas Aquinas' double metaphysics of simplicity and infinity. Sweeney, Eileen C. *IPQ* 33:297-317 S 1993

PHILOSOPHY OF MIND
Science, knowledge and mind: a study in the philosophy of C S Peirce. Delaney, Cornelius F, 1938-. Indiana: University of Notre Dame Press, 1993. x, 183p ISBN 0-268-01748-4 LC 92-53743

Transforming light: intellectual conversion in the early Lonergan. Liddy, Richard M. Collegeville: Liturgical, 1993. x, 225p ISBN 0-8146-5839-3 LC 93-22620

PHOTOGRAPHS
A Protestant consideration of icons. Koyzis, David T. *New Oxford Rev* 60:24-25 Mr 1993

PHOTOGRAPHY—EXHIBITIONS
"The waking dream" photography's first century. Torrens, James S. *America* 168:18-19 My 22, 1993

PHYSICIAN AND PATIENT
Care of the dying: a Catholic perspective [4 parts]. *Health Prog* 74:34-38+ Mr; 16-21+ Ap; 22-26+ My; 46-54 Je 1993*

Controlling health costs. Reilly, Jeremiah P. *Comm* 120:5-6 Mr 12 1993

Euthanasia, the gentle death: a legal and ethical prospectus on the right to die. Fulk, Kirkland Alan. *CLawyer* 35 no 2:145-168 1993

Hôpital et respect des personnes. Geets, Claude, et al, eds. *Supplement* 184:5-203 Mr-Ap 1993*

A license to kill. Carroll, William E. *Can Cath Rev* 11:33-35 Ap 1993

La notion de qualité de la vie dans le champ dela santé. Lamau, Marie-Louise. *MSR* 50:135-150 Ap-Je 1993

Vérité et mensonge dans la relation au malade. Geets, Claude. *Supplement* 184:56-77 Mr-Ap 1993

PHYSICIANS
Antitrust immunity granted in a far-reaching peer review case. Kadzielski, Mark A. *Health Prog* 74:19+ Ja-F 1993

Doctor killed at abortion clinic. Smith, John, Bp, et al. *Origins* 22:701+ Mr 25 1993

Of medicine and metaphor: significant findings from Walker Percy. Allsopp, Michael E. *Linacre* 60:48-55 F 1993

Primum non nocere. Morgan, Anne Marie. *Crisis* 11:17-25 Jl-Ag 1993

The purpose of healing [address, 61st Annual Meeting of the National Federation of Catholic Physicians' Guilds O 1992]. Jaki, Stanley L. *Linacre* 60:5-15 F 1993

The rock from which living water springs. Callahan, Sidney. *Health Prog* 74:74-75+ Ja-F 1993

PHYSICIANS (GENERAL PRACTICE)
Lack of primary care physicians: Achilles' heel of reform? Keller, Gerald C, and Blankenbaker, Ronald G. *Health Prog* 74:48-49 Jl-Ag 1993

PHYSICIANS (GENERAL PRACTICE)—SUPPLY AND DEMAND
Health care and the rural poor. Anderson, George M. *America* 169:16-18 Jl 3-10 1993

PHYSICS
Essays on science and faith. Pannenbert, Wolfhart. Louisville: Westminster, 1993. x, 208p ISBN 0-664-25384-9

Positions in the cage: toward a Christian experience of space. Dalzell, Catherine. *Can Cath Rev* 11:18-25 Mr 1993

Relativity, relativism: they're not the same!. Pakaluk, Michael. *Register* 69:1+ F 7 1993

PHYSICS—1300-1400
Giles of Rome on natural motion in the void. Trifogli, Cecilia. *Med Stud* 54:136-161 1992

PIANISTS- FRANCE
French pianism: an historical perspective. Timbrell, Charles. White Plains: Pro/Am Music Resources, 1992. x, 288p ISBN 0-912483-89-x

PIANO
French pianism: an historical perspective. Timbrell, Charles. White Plains: Pro/Am Music Resources, 1992. x, 288p ISBN 0-912483-89-x

PICASSO, PABLO
Degenerate moderns. Jones, Michael E. San Francisco: Ignatius Press, 1993. ISBN 0-89810-447-2

PIERONEK, TADEUSZ, BP
Dialogue [interview by Jonathan Luxmoore]. Pieronek, Tadeusz, Bp. *Register* 69:1+ Jl 25 1993

PIETA
Michelangelo's Four Pieta's [photos]. Thiele, Gloria. *CDgst* 57:1-6 Ag 1993

PIETY
The gift of piety. Dimock, Giles. *OSV* 81:5 Ap 4 1993

Icons for liturgy. Lefchick, Basil. *Mod Lit* 19:10-11 D 1992-Ja 1993

La raza cósmica: rediscovering the Hispanic soul. Deck, Allan Figueroa. *Critic* 47:46-53 Spr 1993

Restless for him. Ford, Paul, and Daurio, Janice. *Register* 69:1+ S 26 1993

Sanctifying the ordinary. Ford, Paul, and Daurio, Janice. *Register* 69:1+ O 17 1993

Towards a hermeneutics of piety for the ecumenical movement. Gros, Jeffrey, 1938-. *Ecumen Trends* 22:1-2+ Ja 1993

PILATE, PONTIUS
Pontius Pilate: Book II [novel]. Babb, Charles E. New York: Vantage Press, 1992. x, 369p ISBN 0-533-10149 LC 91-91527

PILGRIMS AND PILGRIMAGES
Around the land in 80 days. *Tablet* 247:1129 S 4 1993

God's path to peace. Barnes, Michael R. *Month* 26:(I) Jl 1993

Have faith, will travel. Scherer, Scott. *Register* 69:1+ Ag 22 1993

The heart in pilgrimage. Furlong, Monica, 1930-. *Tablet* 247:305 Mr 6 1993

Heaven's road. Coulombe, Charles. *Register* 69:3 Je 11 1993

High expectations: Denver, World Youth Day and the Pope [editorial]. Morrow, Carol Ann. *St Anth* 101:15 Ag 1993

A holy week in a Holy Land. Morrow, Carol Ann. *St Anth* 100:28-33 Ap 1993

John Paul II, Pope, (1992-05-18) Blessed Josemaría Excrivá de Balaguer. John Paul II, Pope, 1920- (Karol Wojtyla) (elected 1978). *TPS* 37:368-370 N-D 1992*

Libyan "pilgrims" a fiasco. Pevtzow, Lisa. *Register* 69:1+ Je 20 1993

Message from Medjugorje. Brown, Andrew. *Tablet* 247:1155-1156 S 11 1993

My pilgrimage to Lourdes. Malcolm, Catherine. *Liguorian* 81:32-35 O 1993

Pilgrim. Murphy, Jim. *New Cov* 22:21-22 My 1993

Pilgrimage: accept the invitation. Grace, Madeleine. *OSV* 81:6 Mr 21 1993

The stones will cry out. Roman, Mary. *Living Prayer* 26:29-31 Mr-Ap 1993

To be a pilgrim: journeys for the coming months. *Tablet* 247:321 Mr 6 1993

Towards a hermeneutics of piety for the ecumenical movement. Gros, Jeffrey, 1938-. *Ecumen Trends* 22:1-2+ Ja 1993

Visiting Fatima. Wells, Joel F, 1930-. *Critic* 47:66-70 Sum 1993

PINTER, HAROLD, 1930-
Madness in Harold Pinter's plays and filmscripts: the public consequences of private madness. Prentice, Penelope. *Cithara* 32:31-38 N 1992

PIO, PADRE, 1887-1968
Mary's house: Mary Pyle: under the spiritual guidance of Padre Pio. Gaudiose, Dorothy M. New York: Society of St Paul, 1993. x, 189p ISBN 0-8189-0646-4 LC 92-21401

PIPPIN, ROBERT B
Hegel, idealism, and Robert Pippin. Westphal, Kenneth R. *IPQ* 33:263-272 S 1993

PISSARRO, CAMILLE, 1830-1903
The city as a stage for time: Camille Pissaro's serial cityscapes. O'Donovan, Leo J. *America* 168:18-22 Ap 24 1993

PITTAVINO, MATTEO (ANGELICO DA NONE), 1875-1953
Congregation for the Causes of Saints (1992-03-07) Decree on the heroic virtues. Congregation for the Causes of Saints. *AAS* 84:1084-1088 N 3 1992*

PIUS IX, POPE, 1792-1878 (GIOVANNI MARIA MASTAI-FERRETTI) (ELECTED 1846)
De scholae catholicae libertatis exercitio in saeculo XIX et XX ineunte. Lasala, Fernando de. *Periodica* 81 no 3-4:425-467 1992

PIUS XII, POPE, 1876-1958 (EUGENIO PACELLI) (ELECTED 1939)
École Saint-Thomas. Steenberghen, Fernand Van. *RPhil Louvain* 91:1-4 F 1993

El encuentro '92 de la sociedad Argentina de liturgia. Muñoz, Héctor. *Notitiae* 28:424-425 Je 1992

John Paul II, Pope, (1993-07-19) Pius XII [Orig in Italian]. John Paul II, Pope, 1920- (Karol Wojtyla) (elected 1978). *OR(Eng)* 1300:1 Jl 21 1993*

A journey remembered: Catholic biblical scholarship 50 years after Divino afflante spiritu [commentary]. Donahue, John R. *America* 169:6-11 S 18 1993*

PLANNED COMMUNITIES
Ecological sustainability at Bamberton [fr the *Bamberton News*]. Dauncey, Guy. *Teilhard Rev* 28:22-24 Sum 1993

PLANNED PARENTHOOD see Birth Control
Blinded by its own propaganda [editorial]. *OSV* 82:2 Jl 11 1993

PLANNING
A response to unemployment: ten propositions. Quigley, George. *Studies* 82:73-86 Spr 1993

PLANTS IN THE BIBLE
Seeds of faith. Ciarrocchi, Maura. *OSV* 82:5 Je 27 1993

PLATO
Diagrams: Socrates and Meno's slave. Giaquinto, Marcus. *IJPS* 1:81-97 Mr 1993

Une nouvelle étude surle platonisme antique. Neschke-Hentschke, Ada. *RPhil Louvain* 91:459-465 Ag 1993

Platon, l'École de Tübingen et Giovanni Reale. Rizzerio, Laura. *RPhil Louvain* 91:90-110 F 1993

Provoking today's students [excerpt fr *The Republic of Plato*]. Bloom, Allan, 1930-1992. *Crisis* 11:25-26 My 1993

Le statut de l'un dans la Métaphysique. Couloubaritsis, Lambros. *RPhil Louvain* 90:497-522 N 1992

PLATONISTS
Une nouvelle étude surle platonisme antique. Neschke-Hentschke, Ada. *RPhil Louvain* 91:459-465 Ag 1993

PLAY
Let us play. Roman, Mary. *Living Prayer* 26:37 N-D 1993

PLAYGROUNDS
Preschool playgrounds. Rittner-Heir, Robbin M. *Tod Cath Teach* 27:26-29 O 1993

PLEASURE
Aquinas on disordered pleasures and conditions. Daly, Anthony C. *Thomist* 56:583-612 O 1992

Pleasure: a biblical perspective. Lee, Dorothy A. *Way* 33:19-33 Ja 1993

PLOTINUS
Light and metaphor in Plotinus and St Thomas Aquinas. Corrigan, Kevin. *Thomist* 57:187-199 Ap 1993

PLURALISM, CULTURAL
The health of the nation [editorial]. *Tablet* 247:3 Ja 2 1993

Let them eat cake: a love letter to multiculturalists. Carlin, David Robert, Jr, 1938-. *Comm* 120:9-10 Ap 23 1993

Liturgical inculturation in multiethnic churches. Chupungco, Anscar J. *Past Mus* 17:28-29+ F-Mr 1993

Martians and their place at Notre Dame. Griffin, Robert F. *OSV* 81:14 Mr 21 1993

Ministry in the new South Africa: an intercultural challenge [fr *Entre nous*]. Slattery, Joseph A. *Living Light* 29:49-54 Wint 1992

Multi-multiculturalism. Marty, Martin E, 1928-. *Critic* 47:37-45 Sum 1993

Multiculturalism is here: so enjoy it. Burke, John Francis. *Comm* 120:5-6 N 5 1993

Nationalismus und Multikulturalismus. Brieskorn, Norbert. *Stimm Zeit* 211:651-662 O 1993

Religion and values: noble lies? Roof, Wade Clark, 1939-. *Critic* 47:35-45 Spr 1993

PLURALISM, RELIGIOUS
Apostle of religious freedom [adapted fr *John Courtney Murray and the American civil conversation*]. Canavan, Francis, 1917-. *Crisis* 11:31-35 My 1993

Buddhism and Christianity: rivals and allies. Smart, Ninian, 1927-. Honolulu: University of Hawaii Press, 1993. ISBN 0-82481-519-x LC 92-29475

Christian theology and other religions: an evaluation of John Hick and Paul Knitter. D'Costa, Gavin. *StudiaM* 42:161-178 1993

Creating options: shattering the "exclusivist, inclusivist, adn pluralist" paradigm [reply by Gavin D'Costa, pp 41-47]. Markham, Ian. *New Blckfrs* 74:33-34 Ja 1993

Globalization, pluralism, and ecumenics: the old question of Catholicity in a new cultural horizon. Burrows, Mark Stephen. *JEcumen Stds* 29:346-367 Sum-Aut 1992

O desafio das religiões [editorial]. Libanio, Joao Batista, ed. *Perspevtiva* 25:133-136 My-Ag 1993

Proportionalism and a text of the young Aquinas: Quodlibetum IX, Q 7, A 2. Johnson, Mark A. *TheolStds* 53:683-699 D 1992

Religious pluralism: a missiological approach. Newbigin, Lesslie. *StudiaM* 42:227-244 1993

A response to Chris Barrigar's social theory, language, and the crisis in Anglican pluralism. Whalon, Pierre W. *JEcumen Stds* 29:461-465 Sum-Aut 1992

Sarvepalli Radhakrishnan and religious pluralism. Minor, Robert N. *StudiaM* 42:307-327 1993

Social theory, language, and the crisis in Anglican pluralism. Barrigar, Chris. *JEcumen Stds* 29:461-465 Sum-Aut 1992

POEMS
Boots; Old summer; Temptation; Love song in black. Schuster, Marc. *Spirit* 57:54-56 Spr-Sum 1992

Cautionary tale; Cousins travelling; By return mail; A sentence; An onion. Cochran, Leonard. *Spirit* 57:21-23 Spr-Sum 1992

Children; Estinguished; Her family; Friends. Heine, Heinrich, 1797-1856. *Spirit* 58:28-31 1993

Cutting the strings; An Easter fire; The Resurrection; The return. Gray, Cecile. *Spirit* 57:50-53 Spr-Sum 1992

Deaf at the beach; after the ballet; four years; Saffo on the east side. McCrorie, Edward. *Spirit* 58:3-6 1993

Dogs in the sheep; Green Father; Corn Maiden. Rader, Judith. *Spirit* 57:39-41 Spr-Sum 1992

The end of the welfare state; Premonition of passage; Spectator sport; The right reader; Poeme trouve; The art center; Moving apart. Edkins, Anthony. *Spirit* 58:11-14 1993

Entelechy just happens; Chardin and the new filioque. Cervo, Nathan. *Spirit* 58:32-34 1993

Having come this way; Dog Island; transcriptions; advice from further up; a poem from Borges; Sunyatta. Donovan, Laurence. *Spirit* 57:1-9 Spr-Sum 1992

Influences; Influences Flood; International Folk Sing. Wilcox, Patricia. *Spirit* 57:18-20 Spr-Sum 1992

Myths; Night snow. Merziak, Regina. *Spirit* 58:26-27 1993

The night he came. Scarbrough, George. *Spirit* 58:1-2 1993

Night piece; Woman bathing. Ahr, Katherine. *Spirit* 58:8-9 1993

Puppet to puppeteer; Puppet show. Cochran, Leonard. *Spirit* 58:7 1993

Sandor Woeres; Solidarity; Boston; St Petersburg; Summer house, Winter house; Katyn Forest; Prague; Gulag; Budapest; 1944; Lenin; Vilnius. Niditch, B Z. *Spirit* 57:26-38 Spr-Sum 1992

The sickening smile of Jesus; the jetty. Sullivan, James A. *Spirit* 58:23-25 1993

Sunyatta; On Powder Bridge Road death everlasting' Golgotha; Golden Market Revisited; the Eternal Bustiwaker; The River. Cervo, Nathan. *Spirit* 57:10-17 Spr-Sum 1992

Three fragments of Pindar; Antigone, Act II; Oedipus at Colonus; Greece. Hölderlin. *Spirit* 58:17-20 1993

To be continued; Kid's day; Murphy's law; Writer's block. Niditch, B Z. *Spirit* 58:36-39 1993

Trick or treat; Cnut's day out; Flood warning; Revisiting Luarka. Edkins, Anthony. *Spirit* 57:42-46 Spr-Sum 1992

The universal waste basket; Bleak thought. Nathan, Norman. *Spirit* 58:40 1993

Untitled; Children in a storm; An azure shadowed room. Cleve, Emerald. *Spirit* 58:15-16 1993

Winter journey; New Year's Day; Watching you; Lost Kingdom; The Swans. Cleve, Emerald. *Spirit* 57:23-26 Spr-Sum 1992

The world faces Johnny Tripod. Millett, John. *Spirit* 58:42-44 1993

POETRY
A celebration of Denise Levertov's comings and goings. Thorpe, Doug. *CrossCurr* 43:247-252 Sum 1993

Saved by poetry. Jennings, Elizabeth, 1926-. *Tablet* 247:613-614 My 15 1993

POETRY—RELIGIOUS ASPECTS
Religion, poésie et philosophie: Les Grecs et la quête du divin. Motte, André. *RPhil Louvain* 91:366-382 Ag 1993

POETRY—STUDY AND TEACHING
Teaching poetry. Schrankel, Catherine. *Tod Cath Teach* 27:38+ S 1993

POETRY—TRANSLATING
Accompanying Dante. Krivak, Andrew J. *America* 169:17-21 O 30 1993

POETS, AMERICAN
John Moffitt: poet from Gorakhpur to America. Samway, Patrick H, 1939-. *America* 168:17-22 Ap 10 1993

POETS, CATHOLIC
The Catholic religious poets from Southwell to Crashaw. Cousins, Anthony D. Westminster: Christian Classics, 1993. x, 224p ISBN 0-7220-1570-4

POETS, CUBAN
Castro's exhausted angel. Fleming, Thomas, 1927-. *America* 168:14-16 F 6 1993

POETS, ENGLISH—CRITICISM, INTERPRETATION
"Break not then them so wrongfully": topical readings of Sir Thomas Wyatt's riddling and bewitched lute and the feminine other. Cunnar, Eugene R. *Cithara* 32:3-30 N 1992

Gerard Manley Hopkins annual 1993. Sundermeier, Michael, and Egan, Desmond, eds. Omaha: Creighton University Press, 1993. x, 123p ISBN 1-881871-07-x

The quatercentenary of George Herbert, 1593-1993. Young, Robert V. *Renascence* 45:131-204 Spr 1993*

The Virgin incarnate in Robert Browning's poetry. Johnson, Patricia E. *Listening* 28:118-127 Spr 1993

Worth pondering. O'Connell, Patrick. *Living Prayer* 26:14-15 Mr-Ap 1993

POETS, SPANISH
La inquietud religiosa en cuatro poetas chilenos contemporáneos (Miguel Arteche, Carlos Bolton, Fidel Sepúlveda y Raúl Zurita). Livacić Gazzano, Ernesto. *Teol Vida* 33 no 3-4:299-314 1992

POINT OF VIEW (LITERATURE)
Scobie's world. Freis, Richard. *Relig Lit* 24:57-78 Aut 1992

POLAND—CHURCH HISTORY
The church and the left. Michnik, Adam. Chicago: University of Chicago Press, 1993. 299p ISBN 0-226-52424-8 LC 92-20503

POLAND—FOREIGN RELATIONS—PAPACY
Polish concordat hits roadblock. Luxmoore, Jonathan. *Register* 69:1+ O 3 1993

POLAND—POLITICS
Behind the headlines. Luxmoore, Jonathan. *Register* 69:5 O 17 1993

POLAND—POLITICS AND GOVERNMENT
Interference in poll denied by bishops. *Tablet* 247:926 Jl 17 1993

A parting of the ways. Luxmoore, Jonathan. *Register* 69:2 Jl 25 1993

Polish church wary of victory of ex-communists. Luxmoore, Jonathan. *OSV* 82:21 O 10 1993

Polish visitor. *Tablet* 247:338 Mr 13 1993

Résistances aux changements dans la société polonaise. Charytanski, Jan. *Lumen* 47:403-415 D 1992

A revolution not by politics alone. Scott, David. *OSV* 81:15-16 F 28 1993

POLAND—SOCIAL CONDITIONS
Controversial law on abortion. Rich, Vera. *Tablet* 247:381-382 Mr 20 1993

Poland at the crossroads (again). Gawronski, Raymond T. *America* 168:15-17 My 22, 1993

Showdown in Poland. Luxmoore, Jonathan. *Tablet* 247:1190-1191 S 18 1993

POLAND—SOCIO-ECONOMIC CONDITIONS
Strange twist in Poland. Luxmoore, Jonathan. *Register* 69:1+ S 12 1993

POLANYI, KARL, 1886-1964
Beyond the self-regulating market society: a critique of Polanyi's theory of the state. Searcy, Dennis R. *RSocEcon* 51:217-231 Sum 1993

A review of the troops: social economics in the twentieth century. Waters, William R. *RSocEcon* 51:262-286 Aut 1993

POLARITY (PHILOSOPHY)
Herméneutique et pneumatologie selon Schleiermacher. Brito, Emilio. *Eph Theol Lovan* 69:88-117 Ap 1993

POLICE
Charles Alphin [interview by T Jarvis]. Alphin, Charles. *Salt* 13:4-6 Ja 1993

POLISH LITERATURE
Schlesien in der polnischen Gegenwartsliteratur. Zybura, Marek. *Stimm Zeit* 211:197-209 Mr 1993

POLITICAL ACTION COMMITTEES
Silent money: political persuasion and public policy. McGovern, John E. *Momentum* 24:21-25 N-D 1993

POLITICAL ETHICS
Nel crepuscolo della probabilità etica e politica. Cultrera, Francesco. *Civilta* 2:153-160 Ap 17 1993

POLITICAL PARTIES- CANADA
The Tories say goodby. *Comm* 120:4-5 N 19 1993

POLITICAL PARTIES- ITALY
All change in Italy. Willey, David. *Tablet* 247:808+ Je 26 1993

POLITICAL PARTIES- NEW YORK
Make Gotham, governable. Katz, Wallace. *Comm* 120:5-7 N 19 1993

POLITICAL PRISONERS
A wall of silence. Kerness, Bonnie. *Cath Work* 60:1+ Mr-Ap 1993

POLITICAL PRISONERS- CHILE
Return to Chile. Cassidy, Sheila. *Tablet* 247:6+ Ja 2 1993

POLITICAL SCIENCE
Befreiung von Knechtschaft. Ehlen, Peter. *Stimm Zeit* 211:21-33 Ja 1993

Mr. Conservative. Wilhelmsen, Frederick D, 1923-. *Crisis* 11:28 O 1993

Nationalismus und Multikulturalismus. Brieskorn, Norbert. *Stimm Zeit* 211:651-662 O 1993

Our longest lie: irreligious thoughts on the relation between metaphysics and politics. Kramer, Matthew. *PhilosTod* 37:89-109 Spr 1993

La Reconquista del Paraiso. Tamames, Ramon. Barcelona: Temas de Hoy, 1993. x, 220p ISBN 84-7880-231-2

Review essay the possibility of post-socialist politics. Bohman, James. *Mod Schlmn* 70:217-224 Mr 1993

They've stolen my name. Carlin, David Robert, Jr, 1938-. *Comm* 120:7-9 Ag 13 1993

Utopias y anarquismo. Garcia, Victor. Madrid: Madre Tierrra, 1993. x, 220p ISBN 84-86864-08-9

POLITICAL SCIENCE—HISTORY
El concejo y consejeros del principe. Furio Ceriol, Fadrique. Madrid: Tecnos, 1993. x, 178p ISBN 84-309-2278-4

POLITICAL SCIENCE—HISTORY- UNITED STATES
After 26 years: Murray's public argument. Novak, Michael, 1933-. *Crisis* 11:4-10 My 1993

Why Crisis cannot address the crisis. Craycroft, Kenneth R, Jr. *Crisis* 11:17 Je 1993

POLITICAL SCIENCE—PHILOSOPHY
On Leo Strauss's understanding of the natural law theory of Thomas Aquinas. Kries, Douglas. *Thomist* 57:215-232 Ap 1993

Transcendent man in the limited city: the political philosophy of Charles N R McCoy. Schall, James Vincent, 1928-. *Thomist* 57:63-95 Ja 1993

POLITICAL SCIENCE- UNITED STATES
Catholic makers of America: biographical sketches of Catholic statesmen and political thinkers in America's first century, 1776-1876. Krason, Stephen

M. Front Royal, Virginia: Christendom Press, 1993. 260p ISBN 0-931888-44-2

POLITICS—ETHICAL ASPECTS
Politische Ethik und Politikverdrossenheit. Wiemeyer, Joachim. *Stimm Zeit* 211:363-375 Je 1993

POLITICS- EUROPE
John Paul II, Pope, (1993-09-10) Estonia [Orig in Estonia]. John Paul II, Pope, 1920- (Karol Wojtyla) (elected 1978). *OR(Eng)* 1307:14 S 15 1993*

POLITICS, PRACTICAL
Congresspeak. Arkes, Hadley. *Crisis* 11:11-12 Jl-Ag 1993

Credit where credit is due [pro-abortion candidates]. Hoffman, Julie. *Register* 69:5 Ja 31 1993

Election night in the neighborhood. Marlin, George J. *Crisis* 10:2-3 D 1992

L'ingresso di Clinton alla Casa Bianca. Macchi, Angelo. *Civilta* 144:363-369 F 20 1993

Priestly options in a retrenching Church. Standún, Pádraig. *Furrow* 44:84-87 F 1993

The rise and rise of the Christian Right. Appleby, Raphael Scott. *Tablet* 247:847-848 Jl 3 1993

A short-lived spring. Perko, F Michael. *Month* 26:313-314 Ag 1993

Ten ways to wake up city hall. Scott, David. *Salt* 13:6-11 Je 1993

POLITICS, PRACTICAL—TERMINOLOGY
The politicization of language. Lang, David P. *SocJust* 84:106-107 Jl-Ag 1993

POLITICS AND CHRISTIANITY
A Christian take on politics. Kreeft, Peter John, 1937. *Register* 69:1+ S 19 1993

Politicians and the Churches diagnose a social sickness. *Tablet* 247:318-319 Mr 6 1993

Politics isn't everything. Curry, Dean C, 1952-. *Crisis* 11:10 Mr 1993

The politics of God: Christian theologies and social justice. Tanner, Kathryn, 1957-. Minneapolis: Fortress Press, 1992. 262p ISBN 0-80062-613-3 LC 92-19360

Quali vie per uscire dal "sistema delle tangenti"? [editorial]. *Civilta* 144:521-534 Mr 20 1993

Questions d'épistémologie en théologie de la libération, g propos de l'ouvrage de Clovdovis Boff. Richard, Jean. *Laval Theol Phil* 49:249-275 Je 1993

The rise and rise of the Christian Right. Appleby, Raphael Scott. *Tablet* 247:847-848 Jl 3 1993

POLITICS AND CHRISTIANITY—CATHOLIC CHURCH
Catholics and Clinton. Jones, Arthur C, 1936-. *Tablet* 247:126 Ja 30 1993

The Church in the post-socialist world. Murphy, Séamus. *Studies* 82:87-96 Spr 1993

The evangelical's political dilemma. Hart, D G. *Crisis* 11:11-12 Ap 1993

Faith and the human enterprise: a post-Vatican II vision. Weakland, Rembert G, Abp, 1927-. Maryknoll: Orbis Books, 1992. 168p ISBN 0-88344-835-1 LC 92-32884

Network: a Catholic political ministry. Drinan, Robert Francis, 1920-. *America* 168:14-15 Ap 24 1993

Transformationen des katholischen Romans. Langenhorst, Georg. *Stimm Zeit* 211:464-476 Jl 1993

Verso una ristesura dei diritti fondamentali dell'uomo? (Recoaro Terme, 11-13 settembre 1992). Rulli, Giovanni. *Civilta* 143:602-611 D 19 1992

POLITICS AND CHRISTIANITY- EUROPE
Natalità e politiche per la popolazione in Europa. Salvini, Gianpaolo. *Civilta* 144:140-152 Ja 16 1993

POLITICS AND CHRISTIANITY- MALTA
Valori per il futuro di Malta. Abela, Anthony M. *Civilta* 2:260-269 My 1 1993

POLITICS AND CHRISTIANITY- MEXICO
En que pais vivimos? [editorial]. Bravo, Gallardo Carlos. *Christus* 58:2-3 Ag 1993

POLITICS AND CHRISTIANITY- SAN SALVADOR
Amnistía o amnesia en el Salvador? [editorial]. *Christus* 58:2-3 My 1993

POLITICS AND CHRISTIANITY- SOUTH AFRICA
Prayer and work, mostly in South Africa. Stanton, Timothy. *RRel* 52:553-565 Jl-Ag 1993

POLITICS AND JUDAISM
All the Jewish positions. Lapin, Daniel. *Crisis* 11:9 Mr 1993

Why are so many Jews liberal? Lapin, Daniel. *Crisis* 11:10-11 Ap 1993

POLITICS AND RELIGION
After 26 years: Murray's public argument. Novak, Michael, 1933-. *Crisis* 11:4-10 My 1993

Alliance for regress [editorial]. *Comm* 120:3-4 My 21 1993

L'antigiuridismo di Max Stirner. Sbardella, Agapito. *Civilta* 2:248-251 My 1 1993

Benedetto XV e il Partito Popolare Italiano. Mellinato, Giuseppe. *Civilta* 3:271-278 Ag 7-21 1993

Edith Stein. Cavnar, Cindy. *New Cov* 22:24 F 1993

Evangelization and the Church's social teaching. William, Thomas Stafford, Cardinal, 1930-. *Cath Int* 4:210-214 My 1993

Flags don't belong in church. Grippo, Dan. *USCath* 58:26-30 Mr 1993

The paradox of Catholics in Congress. Shaw, Russell. *OSV* 81:3 Ja 24 1993

Politische Ethick und Politikverdrossenheit. Wiemeyer, Joachim. *Stimm Zeit* 211:363-375 Je 1993

Reaping the whirlwind [editorial]. *Tablet* 246:1559 D 12 1992

What is alive and what is dead in Marx and Marxism a la Elster. Nielsen, Kai. *Laval Theol Phil* 49:277-293 Je 1993

What's a Catholic country to do? The Church's temptation in Poland. Byrnes, Timothy A. *Comm* 120:11-13 S 24 1993

POLKINGHORNE, JOHN
Can a scientist pray. Montgomery, John Warwick, 1931-. *New Oxford Rev* 60:22-23 Ap 1993

POLLUTION
Life in a face-mask. Bowlby, Chris. *Tablet* 247:266 F 27 1993

Toxins and other hazards stalk receding Mississippi [editorial]. *Nat Cath Rep* 29:28 S 17 1993

What did '93 flood leave behind? Jones, Arthur C, 1936-. *Nat Cath Rep* 29:5 S 17 1993

John Paul II, Pope, (1993-05-14) Huelva [Orig in Spanish]. John Paul II, Pope, 1920- (Karol Wojtyla) (elected 1978). *OR(Eng)* 1296:1+ Je 23 1993*
John Paul II, Pope, (1993-05-15) Spain [Orig in Spanish]. John Paul II, Pope, 1920- (Karol Wojtyla) (elected 1978). *OR(Eng)* 1297:7 Je 30 1993*
John Paul II, Pope, (1993-06-12) Eucharist [Orig in Spanish]. John Paul II, Pope, 1920- (Karol Wojtyla) (elected 1978). *OR(Eng)* 1296:5 Je 23 1993*
John Paul II, Pope, (1993-06-12) God present among us [Orig in Spanish]. John Paul II, Pope, 1920- (Karol Wojtyla) (elected 1978). *OR(Eng)* 1296:4 Je 23 1993*
John Paul II, Pope, (1993-06-14) New World [Orig in Spanish]. John Paul II, Pope, 1920- (Karol Wojtyla) (elected 1978). *OR(Eng)* 1296:8 Je 23 1993*
John Paul II, Pope, (1993-08-29) Baltic. John Paul II, Pope, 1920- (Karol Wojtyla) (elected 1978). *OR(Eng)* 1305:1 S 1 1993*
John Paul II, Pope, (1993-09-04) Baltic nations [Orig Lithuanian]. John Paul II, Pope, 1920- (Karol Wojtyla) (elected 1978). *OR(Eng)* 1306:1+ S 8 1993*
John Paul II, Pope, (1993-09-05) Beyond. John Paul II, Pope, 1920- (Karol Wojtyla) (elected 1978). *Origins* 23:235-237 S 16 1993*
John Paul II, Pope, (1993-09-05) Independence. John Paul II, Pope, 1920- (Karol Wojtyla) (elected 1978). *Origins* 23:233 S 16 1993*
John Paul II, Pope, (1993-09-05) People [Orig in Polish]. John Paul II, Pope, 1920- (Karol Wojtyla) (elected 1978). *OR(Eng)* 1307:3 S 15 1993*
John John Paul II, Pope, (1993-09-08) Grace [Orig in Latvian]. John Paul II, Pope, 1920- (Karol Wojtyla) (elected 1978). *OR(Eng)* 1307:10 S 15 1993*
John Paul II, Pope, (1993-09-08) Problems [Orig in Latvian]. John Paul II, Pope, 1920- (Karol Wojtyla) (elected 1978). *OR(Eng)* 1307:8 S 15 1993*
John Paul II, Pope, (1993-09-10) Estonia [Orig in Estonian]. John Paul II, Pope, 1920- (Karol Wojtyla) (elected 1978). *OR(Eng)* 1308:5 S 22 1993*
Papal visit proceeding to troubled Africa. Collins, Carole. *Nat Cath Rep* 29:14-15 Ja 15 1993
Pope asks help for Africa, and religious tolerance. Collins, Carole. *Nat Cath Rep* 29:11 F 26 1993
The Pope becomes a voice for the voiceless. Bragotti, Joseph. *Tablet* 247:252 F 20 1993
Pope ends trip with call for peace in Sudan. *Nat Cath Rep* 29:11 F 19 1993
The Pope in Africa [editorial]. *America* 168:3 Mr 6 1993
The Pope in Denver. Higgins, James J. *Liguorian* 81:73 Ag 1993
Pope John Paul's tenth African tour. *Tablet* 247:177 F 6 1993
Pope mingles with AIDS victims. *Tablet* 247:219 F 13 1993
Pope sets out for Benin, Uganda and Sudan. *Tablet* 247:147 Ja 30 1993
Pope visits Baltics amid promise, perils. Hebblethwaite, Peter, 1930-. *Nat Cath Rep* 29:11-12 S 17 1993
Pope visits Catholic minority in Jamaica. Slavin, J P. *Nat Cath Rep* 29:6 Ag 27 1993
The Pope's balancing act. Lieven, Anatol. *Tablet* 247:1208-1209 S 18 1993
Pope's visit confirms Albania's new status. Hebblethwaite, Peter, 1930-. *Nat Cath Rep* 29:13 My 7 1993
Pope's visit to Mexico renews ties severed 130 years ago. Smith, Matt. *Nat Cath Rep* 29:7 Ag 27 1993
Pope's witness against "culture of death". *Tablet* 247:1051 Ag 14 1993
Restoring Albania's social fabric. O'Grady, Desmond. *OSV* 81:21 Ap 18 1993
Upon this rock star. *Comm* 120:4 S 10 1993
Waiting for John Paul [Israel visit]. Pevtzow, Lisa. *Register* 69:2 F 14 1993

POPPER, KARL RAIMUND, 1902-
Entre el liberalismo y la socialdemocracia: la sociedad abierta. Perona, Angeles J. Barcelona: Anthropos, 1993. x, 248p ISBN 84-7658-394-x

POPS—INFALLIBILITY
The limits of infallibility. Hebblethwaite, Peter, 1930-. *Tablet* 247:1036-1037 Ag 14 1993

POPULAR CULTURE
Hollywood's dirty little secrets. Medved, Michael, 1948-. *Crisis* 11:18-23 Mr 1993
An incoherent culture life after "Ozzie and Harriet". Garvey, John, 1944-. *Comm* 120:10-11 Je 18 1993

POPULAR MUSIC—JAZZ
Bebop takes a hard shot: Dizzy Gillespie, RIP. McConnell, Frank, 1942-. *Comm* 120:17-18 F 12 1993

POPULAR MUSIC—ROCK MUSIC
How I got stung. Bright, Kimberly J. *Crisis* 11:63-64 O 1993
U2 is a rock band on a mission. Pike, Lori. *Register* 69:5 Ag 29 1993

POPULATION
America again a player in population issues. Clancy, Paul. *Nat Cath Rep* 29:3 F 5 1993
At Dakar conference "fix was in" [UN regional conference on population control, D 5-12, 1992, Dakar, Senegal]. Sobo, Elizabeth. *Register* 69:1+ Ja 17 1993
CARE for a contraceptive, lady? Sobo, Elizabeth. *Register* 69:2 Mr 21 1993
Ethical implications of a people's changing visage. *Origins* 22:758-761 Ap 15 1993
Impaled upon the horns of faith and reason. Howard, George S. *America* 168:12-15 Mr 6 1993
McCormack, Arthur, 1911-1992 [obit]. *Tablet* 246:1636 D 19-26 1992
Populate or perish. Oddie, William. *Crisis* 11:16-17 O 1993
Second thoughts on the population bomb. Toolan, David S. *America* 168:16-17 Mr 6 1993
Separating fact and fiction. Krause, Edward. *Register* 69:5 Ja 3 1993
A sign and a challenge. Kuharski, Mary Ann, and Fleming, Dorothy. *Register* 69:5 Je 27 1993
Who decides how many are too many? Shaw, Russell. *Columbia* 73:5 Jl 1993

POPULATION—RELIGIOUS ASPECTS
Bishops united against population-control efforts. Sobo, Elizabeth. *Register* 69:1+ Ja 3 1993
Church must confront world's population problem now [editorial]. *Nat Cath Rep* 29:28 Jl 30 1993
The church, population and the environment. Coote, Nicholas. *Priests & People* 7:340-345 Ag-S 1993
Minister to raise birth control issue with Vatican. *Tablet* 247:960 Jl 24 1993
Population explosion. Clancy, Paul. *Nat Cath Rep* 29:16-17 My 7 1993
Population, the Church and the Pope. Schwarz, John C. *America* 168:6-10 Mr 6 1993

POPULATION DENSITY
Population density: a hands-on geography activity. Miles, Adell. *Momentum* 24:14-15 S-O 1993

PORNOGRAPHY
Pornography: cancer in print and on screen. Auer, Jim. *Liguorian* 81:38-44 My 1993
Rediscovering the sacred in human sexuality [editorial]. *Nat Cath Rep* 29:24 Jl 2 1993

PORTER, H BOONE
Creation and liturgy. McMichael, Ralph N, Jr, ed. Washington: The Pastoral Press, 1993. 320p ISBN 1-562929-001-6

PORTILLO, MICHAEL, 1953-
Portillo's gospel of self-reliance. *Tablet* 247:1243 S 25 1993

PORTRAIT PAINTERS- SWITZERLAND
August Benzinger: international portrait painter. Benzinger, Mariel. Kansas City: Sheed & Ward, 1993. 355p ISBN 1-55612-614-x LC 93-19230

POSADAS OCAMPO, JUAN JESUS, 1926-
Killing of Mexican cardinal raises fears for pope's safety. Ross, John. *Nat Cath Rep* 29:10 Jl 16 1993

POSITIVISM
Le choix du métier: sur le "rationalisme" de Husserl. Benoist, Jocelyn. *RPhil Louvain* 91:66-89 F 1993

POSITIVISM—LAW
Why positivism is authoritarian. Dyzenhaus, David. *Amer J Juris* 37:83-112 1992

POST-TRAUMATIC STRESS DISORDER
Horrific traumata: a pastoral response to the post-traumatic stress disorder. Sinclair, N Duncan. Binghamton, New York: The Haworth Pastoral Press, 1993. x, 118p ISBN 1-56024-294-9 LC 92-4194

POSTMODERNISM
La atrición universal del viejo mundo XII Congreso internacional de estética: "La modernidad como estética". Perez Gago, Santiago. *Cien Tom* 119:593-597 S-D 1992
The crisis of the subject: from Baroque to postmodern. Reijen, Willem van. *PhilosTod* 36:310-323 Wint 1992
El dios de los dioses: ciencia del arte. Galan, Ilia. Madríd: Líbertarias, 1993. x, 237p ISBN 84-7954-116-4
Doing social economics in a postmodern world. Brown, Doug. *RSocEcon* 50:383-403 Wint 1992
(En)countering the (post)modern. Lakeland, Paul. *Month* 26:63-70 F 1993
The fragility of consciousness: Lonergan and the postmodern concern for the other. Lawrence, Fred. *TheolStds* 54:55-94 Mr 1993
Kierkegaard and post-modernity: Judas as Kierdegaard's only disciple. Manning, Robert John Scheffler. *PhilosTod* 37:133-152 Sum 1993
Nots. Taylor, Mark C, 1945-. Chicago: University of Chicago Press, 1993. x, 275p ISBN 02-2679-130-0 LC 92-38702
Over the ashes. Loughlin, Gerard. *New Blckfrs* 73:605-613 D 1992
Postmodernism and "The end of philosophy". Cooper, David E. *IJPS* 1:49-59 Mr 1993

POSTMODERNISM—RELIGIOUS ASPECTS
Between foundationalism and nihilism: is phronēsis the via media for theology? Guarino, Thomas. *TheolStds* 54:37-54 Mr 1993
Bishops, religious face postmodern world era. Brennan, Margaret. *Origins* 23:120-124 Jl 15 1993
Faith without dogma: the place of religion in postmodern societies. Ferrarotti, Franco. New Jersey: Transaction Publishers, 1993. x, 181p ISBN 1-56000-074-0 LC 92-17835
La fede cristiana nell'epoca postmoderna (editorial). *Civilta* 143:329-342 N 21 1992
Hellfire and lighting rods: liberating science, technology, and religion. Ferré, Frederick. Maryknoll, New York: Orbis Books, 1993. 92-39488 ISBN 0-88344-856-4 LC 92-39488
Kirche in der Fremde. Kehl, Medard. *Stimm Zeit* 211:507-520 Ag 1993
Religione, laicismo e postmodernità. Mucci, Giandomenico. *Civilta* 144:131-139 Ja 16 1993
Religious pluralism: a missiological approach. Newbigin, Lesslie. *StudiaM* 42:227-244 1993

POSTMODERNISM- LATIN AMERICA
Que queda de la opcion por los pobres? Vigil, José María. *Christus* 58:7-19 Ag 1993

POSTMODERNISM CATHOLIC CHURCH- BRAZIL
A condição pós-moderna como desafio à pastoral popular. Carneiro de Andrade, Paulo Fernando. *REB* 53:99-113 Mr 1993

POUSSEPIN, MARIE, 1653-1744
Congregation for the Causes of Saints (1991-12-21) Decree on the heroic virtues of Marie Poussepin. Congregation for the Causes of Saints. *AAS* 84:913-916 S 8 1992*

POVEDA CASTROVERDE, PEDRO, 1874-1936
Blessed Pedro Poveda devoted life to improving Christian education in Spain. *OR(Eng)* 1311:2 O 13 1993
John Paul II, Pope (1993-10-10) Pedro Poveda. John Paul II, Pope, 1920- (Karol Wojtyla) (elected 1978). *OR(Eng)* 1311:1 O 13 1993*

POVERTY
Determinants of spells of poverty following divorce. Heath, Julia A, and Kiker, B F, 1937-. *RSocEcon* 50:305-315 Fall 1992
John Paul II, Pope, (1992-12-08) If you want peace, serve the poor. John Paul II, Pope, 1920- (Karol Wojtyla) (elected 1978). *TPS* 38:155-161 My-Je 1993*
Poverty as the embrace of insecurity. DeMaria, Richard J. *RRel* 52:432-445 My-Je 1993

POVERTY—BIBLICAL TEACHING
Priestly poverty. Carville, John. *Priest* 49:17-18 O 1993

POVERTY- ITALY
Terzo rapporto sulla povertà in Italia. Salvini, Gianpaolo. *Civilta* 3:55-62 Jl 1993

POWER (SOCIAL SCIENCES)
Moral dilemmas in modern business. Maloney, Oliver. *Furrow* 44:12-20 Ja 1993

POWERS, JESSICA

An experience of God: reflections of a poet's journey. Mourneau, Robert F, Bp, 1938-. *Living Prayer* 26:3-7 S-O 1993

The sublime quest of Jessica Powers [condensed fr *Wisconsin* Ap 11, 1993]. Hendrickson, Dave. *CDgst* 57:50-56 Ag 1993

POWERS (THEOLOGY)

Tra cinema e pittura sulle tracce dell'invisibile. Fantuzzi, Virgilio. *Civilta* 144:571-583 Mr 20 1993

PRACTICE (THEOLOGY)

Selbstverständnis und Praxis des kirchlichen Lehramts. Koch, Kurt. *Stimm Zeit* 211:395-402 Je 1993

PRAGMATISM—COMPARATIVE STUDIES

Le discours théologique et son objet: perspectives neo-pragmatistes. Viau, Marcel. *Laval Theol Phil* 49:233-248 Je 1993

PRAISE OF GOD

The catechism of the Catholic Church [excerpt and tr by J T Zuhlsdorf]. *SacM* 120:15-16 Spr 1993

Conversation with God. Carey, George Leonard, Abp of Canterbury, 1935-. *Tablet* 247:238-240 F 20 1993

The eucharistic prayer. Gustin, Marilyn Norquist. *Liguorian* 81:46-50 Ag 1993

I want to know if you love my Lord (includes a photo essay by Steven P Smith). Wood, Charles. *USCath* 58:26- Jl 1993

"Music" [fr *Dictionary of the Church*]. Staunton, William. *SacM* 120:13-14 Spr 1993

Prayers of penitence and praise. Gustin, Marilyn Norquist. *Liguorian* 81:56-60 Mr 1993

Preaching and poetry: George Herbert. Morneau, Robert F, Bp, 1938-. *Emmanuel* 49:386-391 S 1993

Priesthood and sacrifice. Falardeau, Ernest R, 1928-. *Emmanual* 49:370-373+ S 1993

Wrestling with angels. Mason, Philip, 1906-. *Tablet* 247:271 F 27 1993

PRAYER

Amazing grace. Abiola, Olu. *Tablet* 247:335 Mr 13 1993

The art of meditating on scripture. Toon, Peter. Grand Rapids: Zondervan Publishing House, 1993. x, 176p ISBN 0-310-57761-6

Beading a path down the interstate. Coffey, Mary Kean. *Liguorian* 81:26-27 Jl 1993

The book of common worship, daily prayer. Louisville: John Knox, 1993. x, 512p ISBN 0-664-22032-0

Can we revive the prayer of the church? Dean, Stephen. *Priests & People* 7:107-113 Mr 1993

The charismatic way. Cooper, Kristina. *Tablet* 247:467-468 Ap 10-17 1993

Christians, prayer and the "three good works". Shaw, Russell. *Register* 69:1+ Ja 17 1993

Common prayer: an ecumenical bridge. Murdick, Olin J. *Ecumen Trends* 22:3-6 My 1993

Converted by the Psalms [exc fr *Liturgy: in spirit and truth*]. Chamberlain, Gary. *Liturgy* 10:27-28 Spr 1993

Couples who pray together [condensed fr *Home Life* F 1993]. Iijima, Geneva Cobb. *CDgst* 57:64-66 Je 1993

A creative craft. Howatch, Susan, 1940-. *Tablet* 247:400-401 Mr 27 1993

The divine office as personal prayer. Collins, Gregory. *Doctr Life* 42:608-613 D 1992

Embracing the mystery: prayerful responses to AIDS. Sandys, Sebastian, ed. Minnesota: The Liturgical Press, 1993. x, 105p ISBN 0-8146-2222-4 LC 92-43238

The eucharistic prayer. Gustin, Marilyn Norquist. *Liguorian* 81:46-50 Ag 1993

The family rosary in the real world [condensed fr *The Family—a Catholic Perspective* O 1992]. Rosser, Donna Colwell. *CDgst* 57:109-111 Ja 1993

Few Orthodox likely to attend prayers for peace. O'Connell, Gerard. *Tablet* 247:54-55 Ja 9 1993

A gift for others. Martin Israel, 1927-. *Tablet* 247:362-363 Mr 20 1993

Guided prayer in parishes. Purnell, A Patrick. *Way Suppl* 75:39-48 Aut 1992

The Hail Mary: a verbal icon of Mary. Ayo, Nicholas. Notre Dame: University of Notre Dame Press, 1994. x, 256p ISBN 0-268-01101-x LC 93-24743

Hermitage, a metaphor of life. O'Hea, Eileen P. *RRel* 52:503-506 Jl-Ag 1993

How I pray now [a conversation with Thomas H. Stahel]. Whelan, Joseph P. *America* 169:17-20 N 20 1993

How should we pray? Costello, Gwen. *ReligTJ* 27:16-17 Mr 1993

How to pray the Psalms [interview by A Winter, condensed fr *Praying* My-Je 1993]. Nowell, Irene. *CDgst* 57:121-126 O 1993

Institution narratives at the crossroads. Klein, Terrance W. *Worship* 67:407-418 S 1993

An interview with Father Thomas Keating [interview by A Vest]. Keating, Thomas. *Liguorian* 81:12-17 Ja 1993

John Paul II, Pope, (1992-01-09) we pray for peace. John Paul II, Pope, 1920- (Karol Wojtyla) (elected 1978). *TPS* 38:181-183 My-Je 1993*

John Paul II, Pope, (1992-09-09) Prayer as essential as breathing. John Paul II, Pope, 1920- (Karol Wojtyla) (elected 1978). *TPS* 38:44-45 Ja-F 1993*

John Paul II, Pope, (1992-09-10) prayer, message for peace. John Paul II, Pope, 1920- (Karol Wojtyla) (elected 1978). *TPS* 38:46-48 Ja-F 1993*

John Paul II, Pope, (1992-09-16) Prayer's dialogue with God. John Paul II, Pope, 1920- (Karol Wojtyla) (elected 1978). *TPS* 38:49-50 Ja-F 1993*

Julian of Norwich, Mary Magdalene, and the drama of prayer. Koenig, Elisabeth K J. *Horizons (CTS)* 20:23-43 Spr 1993

Just do it: how to jump start your prayer life [interview by the editors of US Catholic (Periodical)]. Foster, Richard J. *USCath* 58:21-26 F 1993

The lectionary: a resource for general intercessions. Boisclair, Regina A. *Liturgy* 11:9-13 Sum 1993

Let my prayer rise like incense before you. Mancuso, Theresa. *Living Prayer* 26:7-13 Jl-Ag 1993

Let us play. Roman, Mary. *Living Prayer* 26:37 N-D 1993

Living in Christ: the catechism reunites morality and spirituality. Ashley, Benedict M. *Crisis* 11:23-26 Je 1993*

Meditation and prayer (1):creative imagination in the lives of Ignatius Loyola and Khapa: visualization in Catholic and Buddhist practice. Urubshurow, Victoria Kennick. *Stud Form Spir* 14:41-56 F 1993

Meditation and prayer (3): the way of devotion: pure land Buddhism. Bragt, Jan van. *Stud Form Spir* 14:75-89 F 1993

A mother's prayer. Jeray, Diane. *Liguorian* 81:46-48 S 1993

The mystery of unanswered prayer. Seethaler, Scott. *New Cov* 23:25-27 N 1993

Not all saints are canonized. Flathers, Marjorie. *St Anth* 101:22-26 N 1993

Notebook and candles. Carter, Sydney. *Tablet* 247:465-466 Ap 10-17 1993

"Oh God, help!" a conversation about prayer with Richard Foster [interview by Mitch Finley for New Covenant (periodical)]. Foster, Richard J. *New Cov* 22:9-13 F 1993

On eagle's wings. Skublics, Ernest. *Can Cath Rev* 11:49-51 Ja 1993

Open door retreats. Morley, Winifred. *Way Suppl* 75:49-55 Aut 1992

Origen's On Prayer: a reflection and appreciation. Cunningham, Lawrence S, 1935-. *Worship* 67:332-339 Jl 1993

Our father: the inner sacrament. Turner, Peter. *ReligTJ* 27:12-13 Mr 1993

A painful accident reveals God's love. Finley, Mitchel B, and Finley, Kathy. *Living Prayer* 26:21-22 S-O 1993

Politics and prayer [exc fr *Liturgy: teaching prayer; Liturgy: teaching prayer*]. Kellerman, Bill, and Grindel, Garcia. *Liturgy* 10:29-31 Spr 1993

A powerhouse of prayer for peace in Europe. O'Connell, Gerard. *Tablet* 247:83 Ja 16 1993

Pray at fixed times, pray always: patterns of monastic prayer. Timko, Philip. *ABenR* 43:395-413 D 1992

Prayer and work, mostly in South Africa. Stanton, Timothy. *RRel* 52:553-565 Jl-Ag 1993

Prayer as relationship. Rohr, Richard, 1943-, and Martos, Joseph. *Living Prayer* 26:28-31 N-D 1993

Prayer before the Eucharist. Camiré, Bernard. *Emmanuel* 99:184-189 My 1993

A prayer for all seasons. Seethaler, Scott. *New Cov* 23:22-26 S 1993

Prayer for daybreak and day's end, vol II: January through June. Taylor, Mary Sue. Cincinnati: St Anthony Messenger Press, 1993. 428p ISBN 0-86716-147-7

Prayer for daybreak and day's end, vol III: July through December. Taylor, Mary Sue. Cincinnati: St Anthony Messenger Press, 1993. 432p ISBN 0-86716-148-5

A prayer for healing. Weinert, Allan. *Liguorian* 81:27-29 Mr 1993

Prayer in the household [exc fr *Liturgy: rhythms of prayer; Liturgy: Lent*]. Vance-Welsh, Mary C, and Huck, Gabe. *Liturgy* 10:59-62 Spr 1993

Prayer made easy [adapted fr *Prayers for a planetary pilgrim*]. Hays, Edward. *St Anth* 100:10-14 Mr 1993

Prayer made simple. Catoir, John T. *CDgst* 57:43+ S 1993

Prayer of the heart. Foster, Richard J. *New Cov* 22:12-13 F 1993

Prayer rider. Schaller, Jeanne Lound. *Liguorian* 81:54-55 My 1993

Prayer that "works" [editorial]. Manney, Jim, ed. *New Cov* 22:5 Je 1993

Prayer, memories, and God. Mancuso, Theresa. *RRel* 52:541-547 Jl-Ag 1993

Prayer: discouragement and its antidotes. Hassel, David. *Sisters* 65:20-24 Ja 1993

Prayer: just do it!. Kreeft, Peter John, 1937-. *New Cov* 22:19-20 Ap 1993

Prayer: letting go, letting God. Singelis, William. *Emmanuel* 99:212-213+ My 1993

Prayer: our everyday encounter with God. Santa, Thomas M. *Liguorian* 81:4-7 F 1993

Praying in times of stress. Neuman, Matthias. *Living Prayer* 26:29-31 S-O 1993

Praying on the run. Seethaler, Scott. *New Cov* 22:18-20 Je 1993

Praying our pain. McGrane, Janice. *Spir Life* 32:87-90 Sum 1993

The present moment. Cotter, Jim. *Tablet* 247:432-433 Ap 3 1993

Putting some soul into prayer. Imbach, Jeffrey D. *Living Prayer* 26:3-6 Jl-Ag 1993

Recognizing God's presence in your life. Froehle, Virginia Ann. *St Anth* 100:10-15 S 1993

Repertoire and ritual: the communion rite and the eucharistic prayer. Ciferni, Andrew D, and McMahon, J Michael. *Past Mus* 17:22-27 F-Mr 1993

A rose is a rose is a rose. Wyneken, Cherise. *Spir Life* 39:47-48 Spr 1993

Rules for prayer. Paulsell, William O. New York: Paulist Press, 1993. 151p ISBN 0-8091-3410-1 LC 93-4387

Seeking the heart of God: reflections on prayer. Boyaxhiu, Teresa, Mother, 1910-. New York: HarperCollins, 1992. x, 100p ISBN 0-06-068238-8 LC 92-54257

Show more faith in your prayers. Szafranski, Richard T. *USCath* 58:36-37 Mr 1993

Simple prayers, common miracles. Canton, Donald R. *Living Prayer* 26:9-12 My-Je 1993

Speaking to God. Benvenga, Nancy. Indiana: Ave Maria Press, 1993. x, 144p ISBN 0-87793-502-5 LC 92-97150

Spirituality in ecumenical perspective. Hinson, Glenn E. Louisville: Westminster, 1993. x, 160p ISBN 0-664-25385-7

The spirituality of the eucharistic prayer. Miller, Charles E. *Priest* 49:13-18 Ja 1993

The Taizé Community: fifty years of prayer and action. Hicks, Douglas A. *JEcumen Stds* 29:202-214 Spr 1992

Talking to God? mind your manners. McLaughlin, Dorothy. *CDgst* 57:30+ My 1993

Thus shall you prayer. Donze, Mary Terese, 1911-. *Living Prayer* 26:15-16 My-Je 1993

Ways to pray with children. Manternach, Janaan, and Pfeifer, Carl J. *ReligTJ* 27:4-7 Mr 1993

Where your treasure is: psalms that summon you from self to community. Peterson, Eugene H. Grand Rapids: Eerdmans, 1993. 176p ISBN 0-8028-01153

You hear us when we call upon you. Gustin, Marilyn Norquist. *Liguorian* 81:54-58 Je 1993

PRAYER—BIBLICAL TEACHING

Prayer in the New Testament. Doohan, Helen. Collegeville: Liturgical, 1992. 143p ISBN 0-81465-007-4 LC 91-35750

The prayer of foreigners: evidence of the biblical tradition. Frizzell, Lawrence E. *SIDIC* 25 No 1:11-17 1992

With Christ in the school and ministry of praying. Fomum, Zacharias Tanee. New York: Vantage Press, 1992. x, 235p ISBN 0-533-09575-1 LC 91-90888

What now? Pro-Life strategy for the Clinton era. Forsythe, Clarke. *Crisis* 11: 24-27 Ja 1993

Why has the truth not prevailed? Odell, William. *OSV* 81:23 Ja 17 1993

PRO-LIFE MOVEMENT- EUROPE
European dimensions of the abortion debate. Robinson, William. *Doctr Life* 42:273-281 My-Je 1992

PRO-LIFE MOVEMENT- FLORIDA
Bloody Pensacola [editorial]. *Comm* 120:5 Ap 9 1993

PRO-LIFE MOVEMENT- GREAT BRITAIN
Pro-life activists target Britain. *Tablet* 247:445 Ap 3 1993
Pro-life and pro-choice after Reagan-Bush. Kelly, James R, 1937-. *America* 168:11-15 Ja 30 1993

PRO-LIFE MOVEMENT- POLAND
New Polish abortion law pleases no one. Luxmoore, Jonathan. *Register* 69: 1+ Jl 18 1993

PRO-LIFE MOVEMENT- RUSSIA
Russia's prolifers. Meehan, Bridget Mary. *Register* 69:2 Jl 18 1993

PRO-LIFE MOVEMENT- ST LOUIS, MO
Can abortion be curbed? A report from Saint Louis. Wagner, David. *Crisis* 11:18-19 Ap 1993

PROBABILITY
Nel crepuscolo della probabilità etica e politica. Cultrera, Francesco. *Civilta* 2:153-160 Ap 17 1993

PROBLEM SOLVING
Chinese rice problem intrigues students. Brahier, Daniel J. *Momentum* 24: 10-11 S-O 1993

PROCLUS, 410?-485
The metaphysical aspect of tenses in Proclus. Plass, Paul. *IPQ* 33:143-151 Je 1993

PROCREATION *see* Reproduction

PRODIGAL SON (PARABLE)
Prodigal Father. Vanek, Elizabeth-Anne. *Emmanuel* 99:96-100 Mr 1993
The Prodigal Son. Martin, George. *Liguorian* 81:38-39 Mr 1993

PRODUCER COOPERATIVES
Minding their own business: worker ownership. Scott, David. *St Anth* 100: 16-21 S 1993

PROFESSIONAL EDUCATION
By their fruits you shall assess them. Donohue, John W, 1917-. *America* 168: 4-5 F 13 1993
Flawed jewel in the crown. Pring, Richard. *Tablet* 247:72 Ja 16 1993
University challenge. Nuttgens, Patrick, 1930-. *Tablet* 247:783-784 Je 19 1993

PROFESSIONAL ETHICS
Ethics in the everyday practice of law. Paprocki, Thomas J. *CLawyer* 35 no 2:169-180 1993

PROFIT
Moral dilemmas in modern business. Maloney, Oliver. *Furrow* 44:12-20 Ja 1993

PROMISE AND FULFILLMENT
The cosmic Christ and world religions. Dhavamony, Mariasusai. *StudiaM* 42: 179-225 1993

PROPAGANDA
Will the Balkans burn? Lukovic, Petar. *Tablet* 247:32+ Ja 9 1993

PROPAGANDA, RELIGIOUS
The American hierarchy, the propaganda fide, and the composition of hte Baltimore catechism. Malloy, David. *ACHSR* 103:35-46 Aut 1992

PROPERTY
An analysis of the use of rights language in pre-modern Catholic social thought. Brady, Bernard V. *Thomist* 57:97-121 Ja 1993
The Church's social teaching and liberation theologies. Jerez, César. *Month* 26:155-159 Ap 1993
Distributing America. Storck, Thomas. *New Oxford Rev* 60:6-10 My 1993

PROPHECY (CHRISTIANITY)
The problem with prophecy. Kurz, William S. *New Cov* 23:11-13 S 1993
Prophecy or restorationism in religious life. Arbuckle, Gerald A. *RRel* 52: 326-339 My-Je 1993

PROPHETS
Prophetic teaching on sin. Tambasco, Anthony J. *BibleT* 31:79-84 Mr 1993
Quodlibetalia biblica. Tambasco, Anthony J. *Chicago Stud* 31:282-289 N 1992
Would that all were prophets. Bergant, Dianne. *RRel* 52:340-349 My-Je 1993

PROPHETS IN THE NEW TESTAMENT
One of the prophets: Matthew's testing narrative as a rite of passage. McVann, Mark. *Bib Th Bul* 23:14-20 Spr 1993

PROPHETS IN THE OLD TESTAMENT
The etymological origins of the Hebrew nābî: the one who invokes God. Fleming, Daniel E. *CBQ* 55:217-224 Ap 1993
Why prophets won't leave well enough alone [interview by the editors of US Catholic (Periodical)]. Brueggemann, Walter. *USCath* 58:6-13 Ja 1993

PROSTITUTION
Freedom and slavery. Cavanaugh-O'Keefe, John. *Register* 69:5 Je 11 1993
A killer at large. Rice, Judith. *Tablet* 247:232+ F 20 1993

PROSTITUTION—RELIGIOUS ASPECTS
A good Catholic girl. Gateley, Edwina. *Tablet* 247:851-852 Jl 3 1993
An unique ministry in Michigan. Carey, Ann. *OSV* 82:21 My 16 1993

PROTECTIONISM
Trade put first. Keegan, William. *Tablet* 247:913 Jl 17 1993

PROTEST, POLITICAL *see* Dissent, Political

PROTESTANT CHURCHES- NORTHERN IRELAND
A Northern perspective. Borooah, Vani K, and Ackah, Carol. *Studies* 82:53-60 Spr 1993

PROTESTANT CHURCHES- UNITED STATES
What do Southern Baptists believe? Whalen, William J. *USCath* 58:22-27 S 1993

PROTESTANTISM
A Protestant celebrates Mary [interview by M Finley]. Jepsen, Dee. *OSV* 82: 5 My 9 1993

PROULX, RICHARD
Richard Proulx. *Mod Lit* 20:46 Ag 1993

PRUDENCE
A bridge between knowing truth and acting on it. Cameron, Peter John. *Register* 69:1+ Mr 21 1993
Confidentiality, disclosure, and fiduciary responsibility. Keenan, James F. *TheolStds* 54:142-159 Mr 1993
The function of the principle of double effect. Keenan, James F. *TheolStds* 54:294-315 Je 1993

PSYCHIATRIC HOSPITALS—ETHICS
Quelques questions sur l'éthique en psychiatrie. Cassiers, Léon. *Supplement* 184:97-106 Mr-Ap 1993

PSYCHIATRY
The denaturalization of the profession of psychiatry. Nigro, Samuel A. *SocJust* 84:104-106 Jl-Ag 1993

PSYCHIATRY—ETHICAL ASPECTS
John Paul II, Pope, (1993-01-04) Moral responsibilities of psychiatrists. John Paul II, Pope, 1920- (Karol Wojtyla) (elected 1978). *TPS* 38:179-180 My-Je 1993*
Quelques questions sur l'éthique en psychiatrie. Cassiers, Léon. *Supplement* 184:97-106 Mr-Ap 1993

PSYCHIATRY AND ART
"A window to Annie's world". Conway, Rose Marie. *New Theol Rev* 6:75-79 F 1993

PSYCHIATRY AND RELIGION
The growing dialogue of church and couch [interview by D Scott]. English, Joseph. *OSV* 82:12 Jl 4 1993
On screening seminarians. Dyrud, Jarl. *Origins* 23:79-80 Je 17 1993
A path through the sea: one woman's journey from depression to wholeness. Grissen, Lillian V. Grand Rapids: Eerdmans, 1993. 240p ISBN 0-8028-0702-x

PSYCHOANALYSIS AND RELIGION
Letture Psicanalitiche Della Bibbia. Rossi, Giacomo. *Civilta* 143:476-487 D 5 1992
The phallacy of Genesis: a feminist and psychoanalytic approach. Rashkow, Ilona N. Louisville: Westminster, 1993. x, 144p ISBN 0-664-25250-8
Psicoanalisis y literatura. Guimon, Joes. Barcelona: Kairos, 1993. x, 329p ISBN 84-7245-259-x
The unconscious Christian: images of God in dreams. Hall, James A. Mahwah, New Jersey: Paulist Press, 1993. x, 113p ISBN 0-8091-3353-9 LC 92-26395

PSYCHOANALYSIS AND RELIGION- CHILE
Psicoanálisis y reflexión antropológica. Bravo Valdivieso, Luis. *Teol Vida* 34 no 1-2:69-78 1993

PSYCHOLINGUISTICS
The search for implicit axioms behind doctrinal texts. Ritschl, Dietrich. *Gregorianum* 74 no 2:207-221 1993

PSYCHOLOGICAL HERMENEUTICS
The hermeneutics of the technological world: the Heidegger-Heisenberg dispute. Pöggeler, Otto. *IJPS* 1:21-48 Mr 1993

PSYCHOLOGY
The journey toward self-esteem. St Romain, Philip. *Liguorian* 81:12-16 My 1993
Psychology as a human science and the human science of transcendent formation. Kaam, Adrian L Van, 1920-. *Stud Form Spir* 14:247-270 My 1993

PSYCHOLOGY—STUDY
Compartamiento social y dinamica de groupos. Tous Ral, Jose M. Barcelona: PPU, 1993. x, 379p ISBN 84-477-0140-9

PSYCHOLOGY—STUDY AND TEACHING
Quodlibets: reflexions escrites en Veu Alta. Patuel I Puig, Jaume. Barcelona: L'Aixernador Ed, 1993. x, 249p ISBN 84-8632-99-0

PSYCHOLOGY, DEVELOPMENTAL
The Catechism in context. Kelly, Francis D. *Living Light* 29:29-38 Sum 1993
Catholic schools: mirror or leaven in the 21st century? Gorman, Margaret. *Momentum* 24:42-45 F-Mr 1993
Psicología y pedagogía de la edad evolutiva según Santo Tomás. Manzanedo, Marcos. *Cien Tom* 119:351-389 My-Ag 1992
The tasks and pitfalls of growing up. Andrews, Paul. *Studies* 81:408-416 Wint 1992
"The tragic experience of consciousness": psychological reflections on sin and guilt. Callaghan, Brendan. *Month* 26:396-401 S-O 1993
The urgency of ongoing formation. McGarry, Cecil. *AFER* 34:134-145 Je 1992
Whatever happened to childhood? Elkind, David, 1931-. *Momentum* 24:18-19 Ap-My 1993

PSYCHOLOGY, PATHOLOGICAL
Aquinas on disordered pleasures and conditions. Daly, Anthony C. *Thomist* 56:583-612 O 1992
La locura compartida. Rendueles Olmedo, Guillermo. Asturias: Belladona, 1993. x, 1993 ISBN 84-604-5959-4

PSYCHOLOGY, PHILOSOPHICAL
Deux théories de l'esprit: Hegel et Schleiermacher. Brito, Emilio. *RPhil Louvain* 91:31-65 F 1993
Los sentidos internos. Rodriguez, Victorino. Barcelona: PPU, 1993. x, 158p ISBN 84-477-0066-6

PSYCHOLOGY AND RELIGION
La coscienza. Busa, Roberto. *Civilta* 2:339-350 My 15 1993
Divine or distorted?: God as we understand God. Seiden, Jerry. San Diego, California: Recovery Publications, 1993. x, 142p ISBN 0-941405-19-2 LC 92-41854
Personal growth and the Ignatian spiritual exercises. Meadow, Mary Jo. *Way Suppl* 76:13-24 Spr 1993
Quodlibets: reflexions escrites en Veu Alta. Patuel I Puig, Jaume. Barcelona: L'Aixernador Ed, 1993. x, 249p ISBN 84-8632-99-0
Religion and prevention in mental health: research, vision, and action. Pargament, Kenneth I, et al. New York: The Haworth Press, 1992. 92-5887/x, 333p ISBN 1-56024 LC 225-6

Q

R

RACHEL (BIBLICAL CHARACTER)
Rachel's lament, Jacob's reply [editorial]. *America* 169:3 N 20 1993
RACISM
A beacon of hate [editorial]. *Tablet* 247:1219-1220 S 25 1993
Church must use its power to fight racism [editorial]. *Nat Cath Rep* 29:28 Mr 19 1993
Churches tackle London's racism. *Tablet* 247:1310-1311 O 9 1993
Does the church mishandle its cultural treasures? Windsor, Patricia. *USCath* 58:14-20 F 1993
Focus on racism at the Kirchentag. Prangemeier, Monika. *Tablet* 247:798 Je 19 1993
Malcolm X: what his three lives can teach us [editorial]. Morrow, Carol Ann. *St Anth* 100:17 F 1993
Minority museum: fighting hatred, instilling dignity. Whitney, Sally. *St Anth* 100:34-39 Ap 1993
Priest deplores Catholic racism. *Tablet* 247:1242 S 25 1993
Racism hits home. Dodds, Bill. *New Cov* 22:20+ Ja 1993
Racism: a problem we must address. Campion, Owen F. *Priest* 49:3 O 1993
Racist missionaries: an obstacle to evangelization in Africa. Zvarevashe, Ignatius M. *AFER* 35:115-131 Ap 1993
Tablet couple witness racist tragedy. *Tablet* 247:831-832 Je 26 1993
We are all foreigners: religion, nation and race. Garvey, John, 1944-. *Comm* 119:8-9 D 18 1992
Welcoming the stranger in Europe. McTernan, Oliver. *Month* 26:304-307 Ag 1993
RADCLIFFE, TIMOTHY
A passionate mercy. *Tablet* 247:575 My 8 1993
RAFOLS, MARIA, 1781-1853
Congregation for the Causes of Saints (1993-07-06) Decree on a miracle. Congregation for the Causes of Saints. *OR(Eng)* 1299:12 Jl 14 1993*
RAHNER, KARL, 1904-1984
The Catholic moment (address at the National Center for the Laity, 11-1-92, Chicago). O'Brien, David J, 1938-. *ACHSR* 103:1-10 Aut 1992
The content of faith. Lehmann, Karl, Bp, 1936-, et al, eds. New York: The Crossroad Publishing Company, 1993. x, 668p ISBN 0-8245-1221-9 LC 92-27765
Dancing Sophia: Rahner's theology of symbols. Clasby, Nancy. *Relig Lit* 25:51-65 Spr 1993
Development of a theology of the local church from the first to the Second Vatican Council. Cardedal, Olegario González de. *Jurist* 52 no 1:11-42 1992
Do we believe in a church of sinners. Kelly, Kevin T. *Way* 33:106-116 Ap 1993
God's human face revealed: a retreat in Wales. Corona, Mary. *RRel* 52:519-531 Jl-Ag 1993
The heart in Rahner's philosophy of mysticism. Tallon, Andrew. *TheolStds* 53:700-728 D 1992
"I have experienced God": religious experience in the theology of Karl Rahner. Wiseman, James A. *ABenR* 44:22-57 Mr 1993
Indirect methods in theology: Karl Rahner as an ad hoc apologist. Healy, Nicholas M. *Thomist* 56:613-633 O 1992
Symbols in Rahner: a note on translation. Liberatore, Albert. *Louvain Stds* 18:145-158 Sum 1993
The wit and whimsy of Karl Rahner [por]. Finley, Mitchel B. *OSV* 82:6 N 7 1993
RAILROADS- UNITED STATES
American addictions [excerpt fr *Around the cragged hill: a personal and political philosophy*]. Kennan, George F, 1904-. *New Oxford Rev* 60:14-25 Je 1993
RAINBOW—RELIGIOUS ASPECTS
Between the flood and the rainbow: encountering God in the living community of creation. Smyth, Geraldine Marie. *Doctr Life* 43:216 Ap 1993
RAISER, KONRAD
Raiser and Keshishian address Faith and Order Conference. *Ecumen Trends* 22:16 O 1993
RAISING OF LAZARUS (MIRACLE)
The innkeeper's tale. Brown, George Mackayu, 1921-. *Tablet* 247:471-473 Ap 10-17 1993
Lent and Lazarus. Dodds, Bill. *New Cov* 22:18+ Mr 1993
RAJNEESH, BHAGWAN SHRI
Bhagwan Shri Rajneesh. Dolcini, Donatella. *StudiaM* 41:127-143 1992
RAMOS, CELINA
A tres años de los mártires de la UCA. Bravo Gallardo, Carlos. *Christus* 58:72-73 N-D 1992
RAMOS, ELBA
A tres años de los mártires de la UCA. Bravo Gallardo, Carlos. *Christus* 58:72-73 N-D 1992
RAMOS, JOAQUIN, BP
Suspicion lingers in wake of Salvadoran bishop's murder. Palumbo, Gene. *Nat Cath Rep* 29:10 Jl 16 1993
RAMSEY, MICHAEL, ABP OF CANTERBURY, 1904-1988
Radical questioning. *Tablet* 247:402 Mr 27 1993
RAPE
Contraception not banned as a defence against rape. *Tablet* 247:955 Jl 24 1993
The day I hated being a man. Schmidt, Stephen A. *USCath* 58:30-31 Je 1993
Guidelines for Catholic hospitals treating victims of sexual assault. *Origins* 23:810 My 6 1993
How do I live now? Schmidt, Ruth. *USCath* 58:26-30 Je 1993
Rape protocol. Diamond, Eugene F. *Linacre* 60:8-14 Ag 1993
RAPE—PSYCHOLOGICAL ASPECTS
Guidelines for Catholic hospitals treating victims of sexual assault. *Origins* 23:810 My 6 1993
RAPE—RELIGIOUS ASPECTS
John Paul II, Pope, (1993-02-02) Change violence into acceptance. John Paul II, Pope, 1920- (Karol Wojtyla) (elected 1978). *TPS* 38:219-220 Jl-Ag 1993*
RAPE- BOSNIA AND HERZEGOVINA
Stupro, aborto e anticoncezionali. Perico, Giacomo. *Civilta* 3:37-46 Jl 3 1993

RAPTURE (CHRISTIAN ESCHATOLOGY)
Aquinas concept of the body and out of body situations. Quinn, Patrick. *Heythrop* 34:387-400 O 1993
The rapture: biblical fact or wishful thinking? Engleman, Dennis. *New Cov* 22:28-31 Ap 1993
1944. Camping, Harold. New York: Vantage Press, 1992. x, 551p ISBN 0-533-10368-1 LC 92-90269
RARE BOOKS *see* Bibliography S Bibliography—Rare Books
RATIONALISM
Le choix du métier: sur le "rationalisme" de Husserl. Benoist, Jocelyn. *RPhil Louvain* 91:66-89 F 1993
Reason, appropriateness and hope: sketch of a kantian account of a finite rationality. Stratton-Lake, Philip. *IJPS* 1:61-80 Mr 1993
Secularization, rationalism, and sectarianism: essays in honour of Bryan R Wilson. Barker, Eileen, et al, eds. New York: Oxford University Press, 1993. x, 322p ISBN 0-19-827721-0 LC 92-41458
RATZINGER, JOSEPH, CARDINAL, 1927-
Le catéchisme de l'Église Catholique. Honoré, Jean, Abp. *NRT* 115:3-18 Ja-F 1993
Dalla presentazione del catechismo della chiesa Cattolica da parte del Cardinal Joseph Ratzinger. *Notitiae* 29:30-33 Ja-F 1993
Helping people cope with Robertson, Ratzinger, et al [editorial]. White, Leland J, ed. *Bib Th Bul* 22:146-148 Wint 1992
John Paul II, Pope, (1992-06-25) Universal Catechism approved. John Paul II, Pope, 1920- (Karol Wojtyla) (elected 1978). *TPS* 37:377-378 N-D 1992*
Para renovar la catequesis. *Christus* 58:6-507 Je 1993*
The Pope's letter on "the decisive theme of the present day". *Tablet* 247:1307 O 9 1993
Ratzinger and the terrorists. Caldecott, Stratford. *Crisis* 11:13-14 Jl-Ag 1993
Ratzinger comments on changing papacy. Hebblethwaite, Peter, 1930-. *Nat Cath Rep* 29:16 F 26 1993
Ratzinger prefers altar turned around again. Moynihan, Robert. *Nat Cath Rep* 29:7 My 28 1993
Rome prepares to launch encyclical. O'Connell, Gerard. *Tablet* 247:1270 O 2 1993
We the people: the American transformation of Roman Catholicism. Kress, Robert. *New Theol Rev* 6:63-88 My 1993
What is a good conscience? Cardinal Ratzinger on moral truth. Callahan, Sidney. *Comm* 120:8-9 O 8 1993
RAZ, JOSEPH
The actual validity of law. Sellers, Mortimer. *Amer J Juris* 37:283-290 1992
RAZAFIMAHATRATRA, VICTOR, 1921-1993
Razafimahatratra, Victor, 1921-1993 [obit]. *OR(Eng)* 1311:6 O 13 1993
RCIA *see* Rite of Christian Initiation of Adults
READER'S DIGEST (PERIODICAL)
Letter from WCC head on attack by magazine. Raiser, Konrad. *Ecumen Trends* 22:7 My 1993
The Reader's Digest and the World Council of Churches. Gill, Theodore A Gill, Jr. *Ecmen Trends* 22:1+ Mr 1993
READING
The written word in an aural age. Callam, Daniel. *Can Cath Rev* 11:4-6 Ja 1993
READING IN PUBLIC WORSHIP
Proclamation primer. Klarner, Anne. *Mod Lit* 20:12-13 My 1993
Readers as proclaimers of the word. Trost, Louise, and Trost, Frederick. *Liturgy* 11:45-46 Sum 1993
REALISM IN ART- GREAT BRITAIN
The virtuosity of detachment: Walter Sickert. Hackett, Peter. *Month* 26:26-27 Ja 1993
REALITY
Kierkegaard's place in the hermeneutic project. Martinez, Roy. *Laval Theol Phil* 49:295-308 Je 1993
REASON
Between foundationalism and nihilism: is phronēsis the via media for theology? Guarino, Thomas. *TheolStds* 54:37-54 Mr 1993
"Conversing, looking, loving": the discourse of reason in Paradise lost. Cacicedo, Al. *Cithara* 32:13-28 My 1993
The Dominican and the dervish: a Christian-Muslim dialogue that might have been between Thomas Aquinas and Jalal ad-Din Rumi. Renard, John. *JEcumen Stds* 29:189-201 Spr 1992
Rational faith. Osborn, Eric. *Pacifica* 6:297-310 O 1993
REASONING
Warden for a week. O'Malley, William J, 1931-. *Living Light* 29:60-67 Spr 1993
RECONCILIATION
Conversion: a lifelong journey. Connolly, Hugh G. *Furrow* 44:159-166 Mr 1993
Exclusion and embrace: theological reflections in the wake of "ethnic cleansing". Volf, Miroslav. *JEcumen Stds* 29:230-248 Spr 1992
Getting it back together with God. Auer, Jim. *Liguorian* 81:40-45 Mr 1993
The mission of Taizé [repr fr *Etudes*]. Lena, Marguerite. *Month* 26:46-52 F 1993
The path back. Ash, Lucy. *Liguorian* 81:12-16 Jl 1993
Pilgrim. Murphy, Jim. *New Cov* 22:21-22 My 1993
Reconciliation in 12 (not so easy) steps. Roll, Susan K. *Doctr Life* 43:69-76 F 1993
Reconciliation renewal: healing for today's church. O'Connell, Timothy E. *Chicago Stud* 32:114-126 Ag 1993
Reconciliation: restored to full health and grace. Wallace, James A, 1944-. *Liguorian* 81:4-9 Mr 1993
The Sacrament of Reconciliation [repr fr *Vidyajyoti journal of theological reflection*]. Mattam, Joseph. *AFER* 34:293-322 O 1992
The storm-tossed Church. Doohan, Leonard. *Mod Lit* 20:40 Mr 1993
To find real, inner peace, we must wash clean in Christ's blood. Cameron, Peter John. *Register* 69:1+ Ap 11 1993

RECONCILIATION- EL SALVADOR
El Mozote: a test of the process of reconciliation in El Salvador. Brown, Michael. *New Theol Rev* 6:74-80 Ag 1993

RECREATION
Entertain us. McMahon, John. *Can Cath Rev* 11:38-39 S 1993

REDEMPTION
Hacia la doctrina marcionítica de la redención. Órbe, Antonio. *Gregorianum* 74 No 1:45-74 1993

REDUCTIONISM
Scientists, God and "chaos" theory. Pakaluk, Michael. *Register* 69:1+ F 21 1993

REFERENCE BOOKS
Un valido strumento di lavoro. Rulli, Giovanni. *Civilta* 2:57-60 Ap 3 1993

REFICE, LICINIO, 1883-1954
Licinio Refice [fr *The sacred music of Licinio Refice*]. Siegel, Richard J. *SacM* 120:7-8 Spr 1993

REFLECTION (THEOLOGY)
Aspectos y visión global de una teología de la salvación. Arias Reyero, Maximino. *Teol Vida* 34 no 1-2:91-102 1993
Reflexiones metodologicas en Santo Domingo. Valle, Luis del. *Christus* 58: 29-32 F 1993

REFORMATION
Beyond charity: Reformation initiations for the poor. Lindberg, Carter. Minneapolis: Fortress Press, 1993. x, 235p ISBN 0-8006-2569-2 LC 92-29963
The reformation: too many assumptions? Marius, Richard, 1933-. *Critic* 47: 31-42 Wint 1992

REFORMATION- SPAIN
Counting on statistics [review article *The Phoenix and the Flame* by H. Kamen]. Freburger, William J. *Priest* 49:32 Ag 1993

REFORMED CHURCHES—DOCTRINES
Meeting each other in doctrine, liturgy, and government. Meeter, Daniel. Grand Rapids: Eerdmans, 1993. 240p ISBN 0-8028-0717-8

REFORMED CHURH IN AMERICA
Lutheran-Reformed Committee meets. *Ecumen Trends* 22:8 Mr 1993

REFORMED CISTERCIAN ORDER
Congregation for the Causes of Saints (1992-06-13) Decree on a miracle. Congregation for the Causes of Saints. *TPS* 38:19-20 Ja-F 1993*

REFUGEE CAMPS- HONG KONG
Children in the camps [photos]. Reynolds, Brad. *America* 168:6-11 F 20 1993

REFUGEE CHILDREN
Children in the camps [photos]. Reynolds, Brad. *America* 168:6-11 F 20 1993

REFUGEES
Intervene to protect innocent. Tabet, Paul F. *OR(Eng)* 1309:10 S 29 1993
John Paul II, Pope, (1991-10-05) Allocutiones (Address to Congress) [Italian]. John Paul II, Pope, 1920- (Karol Wojtyla) (elected 1978). *AAS* 84:860-863 S 8 1992*
John Paul II, Pope, (1993-03-10) Letter to UN on refugees. John Paul II, Pope, 1920- (Karol Wojtyla) (elected 1978). *TPS* 38:240-242 Jl-Ag 1993*
John Paul II, Pope, (1993-08-06) Migrant family [Orig in Italian]. John Paul II, Pope, 1920- (Karol Wojtyla) (elected 1978). *OR(Eng)* 1309:4 S 29 1993*
The never up-to-date map of refugees. Etchegaray, Roger, Cardinal, 1922-. *Origins* 22:755-757 Ap 15 1993
Refugees and hospitality. Zwick, Mark, and Zwick, Louise. *Cath Work* 60:7 My 1993
Refugees in the limelight. Torrens, James S. *America* 168:6 Ap 3 1993
Refugees of war find help in London. *Tablet* 247:1054 Ag 14 1993
Refugees: a challenge for solidarity. *TPS* 38:65-77 Mr-Ap 1993
Welcoming the stranger in Europe. McTernan, Oliver. *Month* 26:304-307 Ag 1993
What Christopher Columbus has to say about feminism [editorial]. Callam, Daniel. *Can Cath Rev* 11:2-3 Ap 1993

REFUGEES- AFRICA
A call for pastors without borders. *Origins* 22:589+ F 11 1993

REFUGEES- BHUTAN
Ethnic expulsions from Bhutan. *Tablet* 247:957 Jl 24 1993

REFUGEES- BOSNIA AND HERZEGOVINA
Humanitarian nightmare. *Origins* 23:733+ Ap 8 1993

REFUGEES- CROATIA
Life in limbo. McDonagh, Melanie. *Tablet* 247:458-459 Ap 10-17 1993

REFUGEES- EUROPE, EASTERN
Church is a godsend to refugees. Luxmoore, Jonathan. *Register* 69:1+ Mr 14 1993

REFUGEES- SERBIA
Serbia's holy land. Seddon, Catharine. *Tablet* 247:536-538 My 1 1993

REFUGEES- SUDAN
"Faith, hope—but please, no charity": a visit to the Sudan. Chitnis, Paul. *Month* 26:328-330 Ag 1993

REFUGEES- UNITED STATES
Church immigration view: "countercultural". Jones, Arthur C, 1936-. *Nat Cath Rep* 29:11 S 10 1993

REFUGEES, AFRICAN
The flight to and from Thika. Martin, James Alfred. *America* 168:14-15 Ja 16-23 1993
Ministry without borders. *Cath Int* 4:165-168 Ap 1993

REFUGEES, GUATEMALAN
Guatemalan refugees return. *Cath Work* 60:1+ Je-Jl 1993
Refugees return. *Tablet* 247:487-488 Ap 10-17 1993

REFUGEES, HAITIAN
Courts rule on Haitians. Sammon, Jane. *Cath Work* 60:3 Ag 1993

REFUGEES, LATIN AMERICAN
Rocking the boat in Miami. Slavin, J P. *Nat Cath Rep* 29:3-5+ Ja 15 1993
Salt of the earth: Donna Thompson [interview by M Ervin]. Thompson, Donna. *Salt* 13:4-5 Je 1993

REFUGEES, MUSLIM
Appeal to Croats and Muslims: stop fighting each other. Kuharic, Franjo, Cardinal, 1919-. *Origins* 23:33+ Je 3 1993

REFUGEES, PERUVIAN
Refugees blaze more hopeful shining path in Peru. Wirpsa, Leslie. *Nat Cath Rep* 29:12 O 1 1993

REFUGEES, POLITICAL
The church and asylum seekers. Grazer, Walt. *Register* 69:5 Ag 8 1993

REFUGEES, VIETNAMESE
Children in the camps [photos]. Reynolds, Brad. *America* 168:6-11 F 20 1993

REGIONAL MEDICAL PROGRAMS
Network unites payers, physicians, hospitals. Cassidy, Judy. *Health Prog* 74: 18-21 My 1993

REHABILITATION
Priests who stray. Harvey, John F, 1921-. *Crisis* 10:37-42 N 1992

RELATION (PHILOSOPHY)
Saint Augustine and Martin Buber as perspectives on John Noonan's persons and masks of the law. Combs, Christopher. *Amer J Juris* 37:145-169 1992

RELATION (THEOLOGY)
Conversation with God. Carey, George Leonard, Abp of Canterbury, 1935-. *Tablet* 247:238-240 F 20 1993
Knowledge, and our position regarding God. Baxter, Anthony. *Heythrop* 34: 137-159 Ap 1993
Living with the less-than-perfect pastor. Gilbert, Jack. *Tod Parish* 25:38-39 Ap-My 1993
"Mutuae Relationes"—ten years later. Bonfils, Jean. *Con Life* 17 no 2:122-134 1992
Our deepening relationships. Walgenbach, Mary David. *Sisters* 65:2-7 Ja 1993
Person, being, and St Thomas. Clarke, W Norris. *Communio* 19:601-618 Wint 1992
Saint Augustine and Martin Buber as perspectives on John Noonan's persons and masks of the law. Combs, Christopher. *Amer J Juris* 37:145-169 1992
"They shall become one flesh". Naughton, Michael. *Sisters* 65:252-254 Jl 1993
We are created to love. St Romain, Philip. *Liguorian* 81:54-59 Ja 1993

RELATIONS
Peace and Islam [condensed fr *Islam and Christian Muslim Relations* Je, 1990]. Tröger, Karl-Wolfgang. *TheolDgst* 38:115-118 Sum 1991

RELATIVITY
Eternity and the special theory of relativity. Padgett, Alan G. *IPQ* 33:219-223 Je 1993
Relativity, relativism: they're not the same!. Pakaluk, Michael. *Register* 69: 1+ F 7 1993

RELAXATION
Time: why we don't have any. Kreeft, Peter John, 1937-. *Register* 69:1+ My 16 1993

RELGIOUS OF THE SACRED HEART
An American miracle [condensed fr *Extension* N 1992]. Bartholomew, Marianna. *CDgst* 57:1-3+ Ap 1993

RELICS
The real story on relics [condensed fr *This Rock* 1993]. Frazier, T L. *CDgst* 58:114-118 D 1993

RELIGION
The cosmotheandric experience: emerging religious consciousness. Panikkar, Raimundo, 1918-. Maryknoll, New York: Orbis Books, 1993. x, 160p ISBN 0-88344-862-9 LC 92-46195
Dominar el pas dels anys. Sobreroca I Ferrer, Lluis Antoni. Barcelona: Scripta, 1993. x, 272p ISBN 84-85205-29-4
Modernity and religion. McInerny, Ralph M, ed. Notre Dame: University of Notre Dame Press, 1994. x, 168p ISBN 0-268-01408-6
New visions: historical and theological perspectives on the Jewish-Christian dialogue. McInnes, Val Ambrose. New York: Crossroad, 1993. x, 165p ISBN 0-8245-1246-4 LC 93-4190
Religion not dying out around the world. Greeley, Andrew Moran, 1928-. *Origins* 23:49-58 Je 10 1993
Religiosi e liturgia (editorial). *Notitiae* 28:497-499 Ag 1992

RELIGION—HISTORY
The everlasting man. Chesterton, Gilbert Keith, 1874-1936. San Francisco: Ignatius Press, 1993. ISBN 0-89870-444-8
El Opus Dei en la Iglesia. Rodriguez, Pedro. Madrid: Ediciones Rialp, 1993. x, 346p ISBN 84-321-2969-0

RELIGION—PHILOSOPHY
Christian perspectives on religious knowledge. Evans, C Stephen, and Westphal, eds. Grand Rapids: Eerdmans, 1993. 288p ISBN 0-8028-0679-1
Faith without dogma: the place of religion in postmodern societies. Ferrarotti, Franco. New Jersey: Transaction Publishers, 1993. x, 181p ISBN 1-56000-074-0 LC 92-17835
Hellfire and lighting rods: liberating science, technology, and religion. Ferré, Frederick. Maryknoll, New York: Orbis Books, 1993. 92-39488 ISBN 0-88344-856-4 LC 92-39488
Indirect methods in theology: Karl Rahner as an ad hoc apologist. Healy, Nicholas M. *Thomist* 56:613-633 O 1992
Nots. Taylor, Mark C, 1945-. Chicago: University of Chicago Press, 1993. x, 275p ISBN 02-2679-130-0 LC 92-38702
Zur Klassifikation religionstheologischer Modelle. Schmidt-Leukel, Perry. *Catholica* 47 no 3:163-183 1993

RELIGION—RESEARCH
Catholic stocktaking. Hornsby-Smith, Michael P, 1932-. *Tablet* 247:164-165 F 6 1993
Historical research, theological inquiry, and the reality of Jesus: reflections on the method of J P Meier. Kereszty, Roch A, 1933-. *Communio* 19:576-600 Wint 1992
Religious belief remains vital around the world, study says. Gibeau, Dawn. *Nat Cath Rep* 29:4-5 My 28 1993

RELIGION—STUDY AND TEACHING
Commitment, theology, and the dilemma of religious studies at the state university. Hann, Robert R. *Horizons (CTS)* 19:263-276 Fall 1992
Religion and values: noble lies? Roof, Wade Clark, 1939-. *Critic* 47:35-45 Spr 1993

The family and religious life linked. Kezmoh, Heidi Schlumpf. *Register* 69:1+ My 2 1993

Galloping nun. *Tablet* 247:1129 S 4 1993

New communities. McDonough, Elizabeth. *RRel* 52:140-146 Ja-F 1993

Religious life: a time for assessing mission. Nygren, David J, and Ukeritis, Miriam D. *Health Prog* 74:55 Jl-Ag 1993

Seminary and religious formation in an African milieu. Kimaryo, Rogath. *AFER* 35:202-208 Ag 1993

RELIGIOUS INSTITUTES—WOMEN

Almost empty: religious life as many seekers see it. Huddleston, Mary Anne. *Sisters* 65:40-48 Ja 1993

RELIGIOUS INSTITUTIONS—SEALS

The reform of ecclesiatical heraldry revisited. Galles, Duane L C M. *ABenR* 43:414-428 D 1992

RELIGIOUS LIFE

Activities of the Congregation for Institutes of Consecrated Life and for Societies of Apostolic Life during 1991. *Con Life* 17 no 2:154-166 1992

Almost empty: religious life as many seekers see it. Huddleston, Mary Anne. *Sisters* 65:40-48 Ja 1993

Aubrey Gwynn: the Jesuit. O'Donoghue, Fergus. *Studies* 81:393-398 Wint 1992

Charisms and religious life. McDonough, Elizabeth. *RRel* 52:646-659 S-O 1993

A creative craft. Howatch, Susan, 1940-. *Tablet* 247:400-401 Mr 27 1993

Galilean perspectives on religious life. Hennessy, Anne. *RRel* 52:247-258 Mr-Ap 1993

Hermits at the bottom of the garden. Hebblethwaite, Margaret, 1951-. *Tablet* 247:782-783 Je 19 1993

John Paul II, Pope, (1991-02-02) The witness and fertility of consecrated life. John Paul II, Pope, 1920- (Karol Wojtyla) (elected 1978). *Con Life* 17 no 2:5-7 1992*

Multiculturalism in religious life today. Harmer, Catherine M. *RRel* 52:764-772 S-O 1993

The pebble in my pocket. Taylor, Terri. *Liguorian* 81:58-59 O 1993

The prayer of Lady Macbeth: how the contraceptive mentality has neutered religious life. Mankowski, Paul V. *F & R* 19:79-93 Spr 1993

Prophecy or restorationism in religious life. Arbuckle, Gerald A. *RRel* 52:326-339 My-Je 1993

Psalms in the city. Mancuso, Theresa. *Living Prayer* 26:16-22 Mr-Ap 1993

Religious life and evanglization. Hamer, Jerome, Cardinal. *Con Life* 17 no 2:77-81 1992

Religious life in Africa today. Nwagwu, Gerard M. *AFER* 35:222-239 Ag 1993

Religious life in Nigeria today. Nwagwu, Gerard M. *RRel* 52:259-274 Mr-Ap 1993

Religious life's spirit of solidarity. Gray, Howard. *Origins* 23:173-176 Ag 12 1993

Religious life—mystery or mistake? Pelletier, Annette M. *RRel* 52:773-779 S-O 1993

Religious-leadership competencies. Nygren, David J. *RRel* 52:390-417 My-Je 1993

Some ruminations on the identity of religious. O'Connor, David F. *RRel* 52:418-427 My-Je 1993

Talents for living in community. Svoboda, Melannie. *RRel* 52:131-139 Ja-F 1993

Thirty-two days without bread. Schroth, Raymond A, 1933-. *America* 169:4-6 O 30 1993

A witness marked by love and humility. Quinn, John Raphael, Abp, 1929-. *Origins* 23:113+ Jl 15 1993

RELIGIOUS LIFE- EUROPE

Religious life at the Synod of Bishops on Europe. Cabra, Pier Giordana. *Con Life* 17 no 2:135-147 1992

RELIGIOUS LIFE- EUROPE, EASTERN

Activities of the Council of the "16" during 1991: religious life in the countries of Eastern Europe. Hamer, Jerome, Cardinal. *Con Life* 17 no 2:149-153 1992

RELIGIOUS LIFE- WEST AFRICA

Religious life in West Africa 1966-1990. O'Reilly, Martin. *RRel* 52:566-573 Jl-Ag 1993

RELIGIOUS LITERATURE

La literatura mesopotámica antigua. Moreno Garrido, Jaime. *Teol Vida* 33 no 3-4:237-254 1992

RELIGIOUS MOVEMENTS, POPULAR

Religious sects and movements. *StudiaM* 41:1-389 1992*

US Latinos and religion [interview by J S Torrens]. Maduro, Otto. *America* 169:16-19 Ag 14-21 1993

Whither the New Age? Melton, J Gordon. *Way* 33:199-209 Jl 1993

RELIGIOUS MOVEMENTS, POPULAR- EUROPE

Europe's new religions. Walsh, Michael J, 1937-, and Wijngaards, John. *Tablet* 247:448-449 Ap 3 1993

Les sectes, nouveaux mouvements religieux, et la nouvelle religiosité en Europe. Vernette, Jean. *Lumen* 47:439-450 D 1992

RELIGIOUS MOVEMENTS, POPULAR- UNITED STATES

Religious right eyes Clinton feast. Jones, Arthur C, 1936-. *Nat Cath Rep* 29:3 S 24 1993

RELIGIOUS MUSIC *see* Church Music

RELIGIOUS PLURALISM *see* Pluralism, Religious

RELIGIOUS POETRY

Chapters into verse: poetry in English inspired by the Bible [vol I: Genesis to Malachi]. Atwan, Robert, and Wieder, Laurence, 1945-, eds. New York: Oxford University Press, 1993. x, 481p ISBN 0-19-506913-7 LC 92-37206

Chapters into verse: poetry in English inspired by the Bible [vol II: Gospels to Revelation]. Atwan, Robert, and Wieder, Laurence, 1945-, eds. New York: Oxford University Press, 1993. x, 391p ISBN 0-19-508305-9 LC 92-37206

An experience of God: reflections of a poet's journey. Mourneau, Robert F, Bp, 1938-. *Living Prayer* 26:3-7 S-O 1993

Gerard Manley Hopkins: the incarnational work of priest and poet. Bouchard, Gary M. *ABenR* 44:115-124 Je 1993

Heaven in ordinary. Beckett, Lucy. *Tablet* 247:1227-1228 S 25 1993

The quatercentenary of George Herbert, 1593-1993. Young, Robert V. *Renascence* 45:131-204 Spr 1993*

Vision and meditation in neoclassical English hymnody: notes toward sources and implications. Murray, Douglas. *Listening* 28:105-117 Spr 1993

Windows in heaven. Burton, Grace Oakes. New York: Vantage Press, 1993. 58p ISBN 0-533-10339-8 LC 92-90825

Worth pondering. O'Connell, Patrick. *Living Prayer* 26:14-15 Mr-Ap 1993

RELIGIOUS POETRY- CHILE

La inquietud religiosa en cuatro poetas chilenos contemporáneos (Miguel Arteche, Carlos Bolton, Fidel Sepúlveda y Raúl Zurita). Livacić Gazzano, Ernesto. *Teol Vida* 33 no 3-4:299-314 1992

RELIGIOUS POETRY, CHRISTIAN

Looking for Jesus. Carlisle, Thomas John. Grand Rapids: Eerdmans, 1993. 180p ISBN 0-8028-0667-8

RELIGIOUS REFORM

Bishops, religious face postmodern world era. Brennan, Margaret. *Origins* 23:120-124 Jl 15 1993

RELIGIOUS SURVEYS

American culture key to understanding lay shifts. O'Brien, David J, 1938-. *Nat Cath Rep* 29:30-31 O 8 1993

Catholic stocktaking. Hornsby-Smith, Michael P, 1932-. *Tablet* 247:164-165 F 6 1993

Catholics remain committed as they accommodate change [tables]. D'Antonio, William V. *Nat Cath Rep* 29:26-27 O 8 1993

A Church in recession—three national surveys, 1974-1992. Weafer, John A. *Furrow* 44:219-225 Ap 1993

"The end of American Catholicism?"—another look. Hegy, Pierre M. *America* 168:4-9 My 1 1993

Generational differences among Catholics emerge. Davidson, Jim. *Nat Cath Rep* 29:29-30 O 8 1993

Listening to Jewish women. *Tablet* 247:1085-1086 Ag 21 1993

Poll raises questions about future Catholic identity. Hoge, Dean. *Nat Cath Rep* 29:26 O 8 1993

Poll-arization. *Crisis* 11:9-10 S 1993

U.S. Catholics loyal, choose moral terms [charts]. Fox, Thomas C. *Nat Cath Rep* 29:22-23 O 8 1993

Views exchanged over poll of priests and nuns. Mahony, Roger Michael, Cardinal, 1936-. *Origins* 23:399-400 N 11 1993

RELIGIOUS THOUGHT—HISTORY

Geschichte der religiösen Ideen: 5 vols. Eliade, Mircea, 1907-1985. Freiburg: Herder, 1993. x, 2200p ISBN 3-451-04200-2

RELIGIOUS THOUGHT—1700-1799

Delightful conviction: Jonathan Edwards and the rhetoric of conversion. Yarbrough, Stephen R, and Adams, John C. Westport: Greenwood Press, 1993. x, 208p ISBN 0-313-27582-3

REMARRRIAGE

The principle of economy a corrective of Christian mercy. Maloney, George A, 1924-. *Diakonia* 26 no 2:119-133 1993

REMEDIAL TEACHING

Computerized learning in the classroom. Charles, Dorothy. *Momentum* 24:72-73 F-Mr 1993

RENAISSANCE

Renaissance humanism. Kelley, Donald R, 1931-. Boston: Twayne Publishers, 1991. x, 176p ISBN 0-80578-606-6 LC 91-4776

RENO, JANET, 1938-

Reno's death-penalty ethic mocks consistency. McCarthy, Colman. *Nat Cath Rep* 29:17 Ap 2 1993

RENZI, ELISABETTA, 1786-1859

John Paul II, Pope, (1990-06-18) Litterae Apostolicae (Apostolic Letters) [Latin]. John Paul II, Pope, 1920- (Karol Wojtyla) (elected 1978). *AAS* 84:835-838 S 8 1992*

REPENTANCE

Atonement in Judaism and Christianity: toward a rapprochement. Lyden, John C. *JEcumen Stds* 29:47-54 Wint 1992

Hope for the human family [editorial]. *Tablet* 247:455 Ap 10-17 1993

Prayers of penitence and praise. Gustin, Marilyn Norquist. *Liguorian* 81:56-60 Mr 1993

Repent and believe. Grubb, Geoffrey J. *ReligTJ* 27:19 O 1993

The Sacrament of Reconciliation [repr fr *Vidyajyoti journal of theological reflection*]. Mattam, Joseph. *AFER* 34:293-322 O 1992

We're free people. Manney, Jim. *New Cov* 22:5 F 1993

REPENTANCE—BIBLICAL TEACHING

The aesthetics of repentance: re-reading the phenomenon of Job. Dailey, Thomas F. *Bib Th Bul* 23:64-70 Sum 1993

REPETITION

What matters is that our song comes from the heart. Bunbury, Richard R. *Past Mus* 17:58-60 Ap-My 1993

REPETITION—EDUCATION

To memorize or not to memorize? Massion, John Carey. *ReligTJ* 26:27-28 Ja 1993

REPETITION—PHILOSOPHY

Being interested in time: autobiography and repetition. Dupuy, Edward. *Listening* 28:141-157 Spr 1993

REPRODUCTIVE TECHNOLOGY

What price parenthood?: ethics and assisted reproduction. Campbell, Courtney S. Brookfield: Ashgate Publishing Company, 1992. 127p ISBN 1-8552-1224-2

RESEARCH

Universities at risk. Dummett, Michael. *Tablet* 247:1095-1096 Ag 28 1993

RESEARCH—ETHICAL ASPECTS

Le dimensioni etiche della ricerca scientifico-tecnologica. Brovedani, Ennio. *Civilta* 3:382-387 S 4 1993

RESOURCE ALLOCATION

The Catholic Church, resource allocation and the priest shortage. Zech, Charles E. *RSocEcon* 50:297-304 Fall 1992

The patient as citizen. Weber, Leonard J. *Health Prog* 74:12-15 Je 1993

RESPECT
The moral baseline. Habgood, John Stapylton, Abp, 1927-. *Tablet* 247:464 Ap 10-17 1993
Respect is not a right. Licht, Robert A. *Crisis* 11:41-47 Jl-Ag 1993

RESPONSIBILITY
But Father, they're priests! Clerical culture and pedophilia. Greeley, Andrew Moran, -. *Critic* 47:43-51 Wint 1992
The crisis of the welfare state. Novak, Michael, 1933-. *Crisis* 11:4-7 Jl-Ag 1993
I think you should be responsible. Marino, Gordon D. *Comm* 120:13-15 F 12 1993
Portillo's gospel of self-reliance. *Tablet* 247:1243 S 25 1993
Scobie's world. Freis, Richard. *Relig Lit* 24:57-78 Aut 1992

RESTORATIONISM
Prophecy or restorationism in religious life. Arbuckle, Gerald A. *RRel* 52: 326-339 My-Je 1993

RESURRECTION
Exigencias teológicas de una filosofía de la historia (la resurrección como teodicea radial). Fernández Del Riesgo, Manuel. *Cien Tom* 119:321-349 My-Ag 1992
The immortality of the soul and the resurrection of the dead. *HPR* 93:9-18 Jl 1993
Mary Magdalene. Walters, Hugh. *Doctr Life* 43:363-365 Jl-Ag 1993
On making sense of the universe. Schall, James Vincent, 1928-. *Crisis* 11:47-48 Ap 1993
Our Easter hope and my priesthood. Storey, Tony. *Priests & People* 7:145-147 Ap 1993
Risen indeed: a Christian philosophy of resurrection. Davis, Stephen T. Grand Rapids: Eerdmans, 1993. 232p ISBN 0-8028-0126-9
Who killed Stutz Bearecat?: stories of finding faith after loss. Ingram, Kristen Johnson. San Jose: Resource Publications, 1993. 90p ISBN 0-89390-264-0 LC 93-23775

RESURRECTION—BIBLICAL TEACHING
The Garden of Eden and the hope of immortality. Barr, James. Minneapolis: Fortress Press, 1993. 146p ISBN 0-80062-744-x LC 92-27037

RETIREMENT
I'm retiring in the morning. Schneider, Mary Jane. *CDgst* 57:117-119 Jl 1993

RETIREMENT COMMUNITIES
A little help, a lot of independence. Paul, Mary. *Health Prog* 74:43-45 My 1993

RETREATS
Father and son retreats: discovering male spirituality. Shimek, Michael. *Catechist* 26:34-36 Ap-My 1993
Holistic retreats. Garvin, Margaret L, et al. *Health Prog* 74:51-52+ 1993
The lure of honey. Cassidy, Sheila. *Tablet* 247:1068-1069 Ag 21 1993
My at-home retreat. Banner, Charla Leibenguth. *CDgst* 57:137-139 Mr 1993
Retreat yourself to solitude. Finley, Mitchel B. *USCath* 58:37-38 F 1993
Retreats in daily life. *Way Suppl* 75:3-84 Aut 1992*
Spiritual adventurers. Hebblethwaite, Margaret, 1951-. *Tablet* 247:1066-1067 Ag 21 1993
Tis a gift to be simple [interview]. Toolan, Suzanne. *Mod Lit* 19:6-9 D 1992-Ja 1993
"To form an elite body of laymen" Terence J Shealy, SJ, and the laymen's league, 1911-1922. McShane, Joseph M, 1949-. *CHist* 78:557-580 O 1992

RETREATS FOR MEMBERS OF RELIGIOUS ORDER- WALES
God's human face revealed: a retreat in Wales. Corona, Mary. *RRel* 52:519-531 Jl-Ag 1993

REVELATION
Between foundationalism and nihilism: is phronēsis the via media for theology? Guarino, Thomas. *TheolStds* 54:37-54 Mr 1993
The Catechism in context. Kelly, Francis D. *Living Light* 29:29-38 Sum 1993
Jews, Christians, and unique revelation. Moran, Gabriel. *CrossCurr* 42:468-486 Wint 1992-1993
Mystery and promise: a theology of revelation. Haught, John F. Collegeville, Minnesota: The Liturgical Press, 1993. 224p ISBN 0-8146-5792-3 LC 92-46908
No bar to entry. Longley, Clifford. *Tablet* 247:1058 Ag 21 1993
The rapture: biblical fact or wishful thinking? Engleman, Dennis. *New Cov* 22:28-31 Ap 1993
Revelation and proclamation: shifting paradigms. Hilkert, Mary Catherine. *JEcumen Stds* 29:1-23 Wint 1992
Revelation in comparative perspective: lessons for interreligious dialogue. Carpenter, David. *JEcumen Stds* 29:175-188 Spr 1992

REVELATION—HISTORY OF DOCTRINES
Der Gebrauch der Hl Schrift in der dogmatischen Theologie. Becker, Karl J. *Gregorianum* 73 No 4:671-687 1992
Principios para una catequesis renovada. *Christus* 58:26-36 Je 1993
Transmisión de la revelación: escritura, tradición, magisterio: (A la luz de la *Dei Verbum del Concilio Vaticano II*). Sánchez Mielgo, Gerardo. *Cien Tom* 119:251-289 My-Ag 1992

REVIVALS
Chesterton and Catholic moments: some reflections on Catholic revivals, past and present. Sparr, Arnold. *ACHSR* 103:11-22 Aut 1992

REVOLUTIONS (THEOLOGY)
Del imaginario alternativo al imaginario vigente y al revolucionario. Trigo, Pedro. *Christus* 57:23-41 O 1992

REWARDS (PRIZES, ETC)
The Baptist and the Rabbi. *Tablet* 247:650-651 My 22 1993
Carla DeSola. *Mod Lit* 20:46 S 1993
Eugene Walsh, SS. *Mod Lit* 20:46 Ap 1993
Frank Kacmarcik. *Mod Lit* 20:46 My 1993
John Harriott awards. *Tablet* 247:73-74 Ja 16 1993
Katreen Bettencourt. *Mod Lit* 20:46 Je-Jl 1993
A medal for Green. *Tablet* 247:434 Ap 3 1993
Richard Proulx. *Mod Lit* 20:46 Ag 1993
Robert Hovda. *Mod Lit* 20:46 Mr 1993
Second-hand straw. McInerny, Ralph M. *Crisis* 11:15-17 My 1993
Three winners. *Tablet* 247:104-105 Ja 23 1993
Virgil Funk. *Mod Lit* 20:46 O 1993

Visual arts awards. *Mod Lit* 20:5-8 S 1993
The 1993 Jerome Award. Jastrab, Kathy. *CLW* 64:18-19 Jl-S 1993

REYNOLDS, ALBERT, 1935-
Change in Ireland, maybe. McRedmond, Louis. *Tablet* 247:9+ Ja 23 1993

RHETORIC
Delightful conviction: Jonathan Edwards and the rhetoric of conversion. Yarbrough, Stephen R, and Adams, John C. Westport: Greenwood Press, 1993. x, 208p ISBN 0-313-27582-3

RHYTHM
Find versatile service music that works. Lovrien, Peggy. *Past Mus* 17:33-34 Ap-My 1993

RICARD, JOHN H, BP, 1940-
Africa: road to faith [photos]. Pipkin, Kate. *St Anth* 100:34-40 S 1993

RICARDO, EVENCIO
John Paul II, Pope, (1993-10-10) Evencio Ricardo. John Paul II, Pope, 1920- (Karol Wojtyla) (elected 1978). *OR(Eng)* 1311:1 O 13 1993*
Two Spanish Bishops and seven Christian Brothers gave their lives for Catholic faith. *OR(Eng)* 1311:1 O 13 1993

RICCI, CATHERINE DE'
Catherine De'Ricci and the will of God [pt 2 of 3]. Agresti, Domenico di. *New Blckfrs* 74:307-316 Je 1993
Catherine De'Ricci [pt 3 of 3]. Agresti, Domenico di. *New Blckfrs* 74:355-363 Jl-Ag 1993
Catherine De'Ricci. Agresti, Domenico di. *New Blckfrs* 74:244-251 My 1993

RICE, ANNE, 1941-
Haunted by faith. Coulombe, Charles. *Register* 69:3 Je 20 1993

RICH MAN AND LAZARUS (PARABLE) *see* Dives and Lazarus

RICOEUR, PAUL
Historical research, theological inquiry, and the reality of Jesus: reflections on the method of J P Meier. Kereszty, Roch A, 1933-. *Communio* 19:576-600 Wint 1992
The instant and the living present: Ricoeur and Derrida reading Husserl. Bourgeois, Patrick. *PhilosTod* 37:31-37 Spr 1993
Ricoeur's ethics of method. Abel, Olivier. *PhilosTod* 37:23-30 Spr 1993
The self as an other [review artical *Oneselfas Another* by C Reagan]. Reagan, Charles E. *PhilosTod* 37:3-22 Spr 1993
Time and narrative: reflections from Paul Ricoeur. Jasper, David, 1951-. *Heythrop* 34:302-306 Jl 1993

RIGHT AND LEFT (POLITICAL SCIENCE)
Boff-an "apostolic and pastoral crisis" [fr *Sal Terrae*]. Sobrino, John. *LADOC* 24:16-23 S-O 1993
The family and the left. Phillips, Melanie. *Tablet* 247:972-973 Jl 31 1993
Review essay the possibility of post-socialist politics. Bohman, James. *Mod Schlmn* 70:217-224 Mr 1993

RIGHT AND WRONG
Goodness and rightness: Thomas Aquinas' Summa Theologia. Keenan, James F. Washington, D C: Georgetown University Press, 1992. x, 212p ISBN 0-87840-530-5 LC 92-3090

RIGHT TO DIE
Care of the dying: a Catholic perspective [4 parts]. *Health Prog* 74:34-38+ Mr; 16-21+ Ap; 22-26+ My; 46-54 Je 1993*
Churches join forces against euthanasia. *Tablet* 247:899 Jl 10 1993
Helping Catholics deal with life, death. Gibeau, Dawn. *Nat Cath Rep* 29:6 F 5 1993
The liberalism of fools. Shea, Mark P. *New Oxford Rev* 60:11-13 Ja-F 1993
A license to kill. Carroll, William E. *Can Cath Rev* 11:33-35 Ap 1993
Mercy and aid. Haynes, A W. *Can Cath Rev* 11:7-8 My 1993
Persistent vegetative state—a medical comment. Poole, Joyce. *Month* 26:226-229 Je 1993
Rest for Tony Bland. Kelly, Kevin T. *Tablet* 247:332-334 Mr 13 1993

RIGHT TO HEALTH CARE
Church brings rich resources to healthcare debate. Hehir, J Bryan, 1940-. *Health Prog* 74:51-52 Jl-Ag 1993
A framework for comprehensive healthcare reform. *Health Prog* 74:20-23 1993
Health care: your money or your life [interview by J.S. Torrens]. Roberts, Marc J. *America* 169:6-9 D 4 1993
Keeping the debate in focus. Reinhardt, Uwe E. *Health Prog* 74:44 Jl-Ag 1993
States pursue reform initiatives. Merritt, Dick E, et al. *Health Prog* 74:45 Jl-Ag 1993

RIGHT TO LIFE
Beratungspflicht und Strafverzicht. Demel, Sabine. *Stimm Zeit* 211:700-710 O 1993
Welcome to Mother Teresa [homily given June 5, 1993]. Cassidy, Joseph, Abp, 1933-. *Furrow* 44:395-398 Jl-Ag 1993

RIGHT TO WORK
Work is the key [excerpts fr a Pastoral Letter]. Daly, Cahal Brendan, Cardinal, 1917-, et al. *Cath Int* 4:182-189 Ap 1993

RIGHTEOUSNESS
Dangerous waters of justice and righteousness: Amos 5:18-27. Berquist, Jon L. *Bib Th Bul* 23:54-63 Sum 1993

RILEY, RICHARD
Catholic educators adjust goals. Mullen, Peter. *Register* 69:1+ Mr 14 1993

RINPOCHE, KALU
The Karma Kagyupa Tibetan Buddhists. Tiso, Francis V. *StudiaM* 41:145-167 1992

RIOTS- CALIFORNIA
Looting democratic capitalism. Redpath, Peter A. *Crisis* 10:8+ N 1992

RISK—ETHICAL ASPECTS
Ethik in der Risikogesellschaft. Höhn, Hans-Joachim. *Stimm Zeit* 211:95-104 F 1993

RISK ASSESSMENT
Ethik in der Risikogesellschaft. Höhn, Hans-Joachim. *Stimm Zeit* 211:95-104 F 1993

RISK MANAGEMENT
Ethical risk management: suggestions for an applied risk ethics. Cowell, John. *Teilhard Rev* 28:3-7 Spr 1993

SACRAMENTS—UNITED STATES
Reconciliation renewal: healing for today's church. O'Connell, Timothy E. *Chicago Stud* 32:114-126 Ag 1993
SACRED BOOKS
An anthology of sacred texts by and about women. Young, Serinity, ed. New York: Crossroad, 1993. x, 452p ISBN 0-8245-1143-3 LC 92-36343
SACRED HEART
A paixão de Cristo na tradicço luso-Brasileira. Azzi, Riolando. *REB* 53:114-149 Mr 1993
SACRED PLACES see Space, Sacred
Between the flood and the rainbow: encountering God in the living community of creation. Smyth, Geraldine Marie. *Doctr Life* 43:216 Ap 1993
The heart in pilgrimage. Furlong, Monica, 1930-. *Tablet* 247:305 Mr 6 1993
Making secular space sacred. Fater, Douglas. *Mod Lit* 20:14-17 My 1993
There is no outer without inner space. Panikkar, Raimundo, 1918-. *CrossCurr* 43:60-81 Spr 1993
SACRIFICE
"Ain't nobody clean": the liturgy of violence in Glory. Culbertson, Diana. *Relig Lit* 25:37-52 Sum 1993
Atonement in Judaism and Christianity: toward a rapprochement. Lyden, John C. *JEcumen Stds* 29:47-54 Wint 1992
The Eucharist and African culture. Okoye, Chukwuma J. *AFER* 34:272-292 O 1992
The eucharistic theologies of Lauda sion and Thomas Aquinas's Summa theologiae. Bell, Thomas J. *Thomist* 57:163-185 Ap 1993
Killing the cat: sacrifice and beauty in Genet and Mishima. Wyschogrod, Edith. *Relig Lit* 25:107-119 Sum 1993
On the other hand, the priesthood—a conservative view. Lee, Martin. *Priests & People* 6:330-333 Ag-S 1992
Priesthood and sacrifice. Falardeau, Ernest R, 1928-. *Emmanual* 49:370-373+ S 1993
Sacrifice? We wrote the book on it!. Reilly, Robert. *USCath* 58:40-41 N 1993
SADE, MARQUIS DE, 1740-1814
De Sade and his progeny. Aeschliman, M D. *Crisis* 11:54-55 S 1993
SADOLETO, JACOPO, CARDINAL, 1477-1547
"The truth looks different from here". Soskice, Janet Martin. *New Blckfrs* 73:528-542 N 1992
SAFE SEX IN AIDS PREVENTION
The principle of double effect and safe sex in marriage: reflections on a suggestion. Johnson, Mark A. *Linacre* 60:82-89 My 1993
SAGARDUY SALAZAR, GERARDO DE SAN FRANCISCO, 1881-1962
Congregation for the Causes of Saints (1991-12-21) Decree on the heroic virtues of Gerardo de San Francisco Sagarduy Salazar [Latin]. Congregation for the Causes of Saints. *AAS* 84:810-814 S 3 1992*
SAGHEDDU, MARIA GABRIELLA, 1914-1939
John Paul II, Pope, (1983-01-25) Litterae Apostolicae (Apostolic Letters) [Latin]. John Paul II, Pope, 1920- (Karol Wojtyla) (elected 1978). *AAS* 84:828-830 S 8 1992*
SAINT, VINCENT DE PAUL, SOCIETY OF
A vocation for lay persons [interview by Lou Jacquet]. Coppinger, John. *OSV* 82:6 My 2 1993
SAINT EXUPERY, ANTOINE DE, 1900-1944
Au revoir, Saint Ex. Mooney, Philip. *America* 169:14-16 Jl 31-Ag 7 1993
SAINTS—BIOGRAPHY
Aloysius. Stevens, Clifford, and McNichols, William Hart, eds. Huntington: Our Sunday Visitor, 1993. x, 160p ISBN 0-87973-528-7
At Lourdes [condensed fr *National Review* Ag 9 1993]. Buckley, William F, Jr. *CDgst* 58:50-55 D 1993
The autobiography of St. Ignatius Loyola. Ignatius, of Loyola, Saint, 1491-1556. New York: Fordham University Press, 1992. x, 113p ISBN 0-8232-1480-x LC 92-32959
Becket, the martyred shepherd. Miesel, Sandra. *Register* 69:4 Ja 3 1993
Bishop, saint, journalist. Parachin, Victor M. *OSV* 81:3 F 7 1993
Elizabeth Bayley Seton: an American saint. Stone, Elaine Murray. New York: Paulist Press, 1993. 86p ISBN 0-8091-6609-7 LC 92-42020
A European hero. Miesel, Sandra. *Register* 69:14 O 17 1993
The fearless monk. Myers, Rawley. *HPR* 93:44-47 Mr 1993
The first school teacher. Miesel, Sandra. *Register* 69:4 Ja 24 1993
A holy couple. Miesel, Sandra. *Register* 69:4 S 26 1993
How St. Claudine persevered [condensed fr *Catholic Standard* Jl 15 1993]. Zimmerman, Mark. *CDgst* 58:88-91 D 1993
In the Catholic tradition. Lenox-Conyngham, Andrew. *Priests & People* 6:467-471 D 1992
In the Catholic tradition: St Catherine of Siena. Ronayne, Mary John. *Priests & People* 7:153-157 Ap 1993
A litany of saints. Ball, Ann. Indiana: Our Sunday Visitor, 1993. 244p ISBN 0-879973 LC 92-61546
A model missionary: episodes in the life of St Anthony Mary Claret. Ramos, Alexis Mary. *ChrWorld* 38:124-134 Mr-Ap 1993
Nikolaus von Kues Skize einer Biographie. Meuthen, Erich. Münster: Aschendorff, 1992. x, 139p ISBN 3-402-03492-1
Of sanctity and saints. McCann, Deborah. *ReligTJ* 27:14-15 O 1993
Of sin and sanctity. Miesel, Sandra. *Register* 69:4 F 21 1993
The one mediator, the saints, and Mary: a Lutheran reflection. Johnson, Maxwell E. *Worship* 67:226-238 My 1993
Our parade of saints. Cann, Lorraine, and Quinette, Nancy. *ReligTJ* 27:12-13 O 1993
Probleme einer Hagiographie heute. Köhler, Oskar. *Stimm Zeit* 211:641-644 S 1993
The real Mary Magdalene. Cummings, Owen F. *Priest* 49:47-49 F 1993
Rescuing St Al [condensed fr *National Jesuit News*, D 1992/Ja 1993]. Martin, James Alfred. *CDgst* 57:20+ My 1993
Saint Birgitta. O'Connell-Cahill, Catherine. *Salt* 13:31 Ja 1993
Saint Frances of Rome. O'Connell-Cahill, Catherine. *Salt* 13:31 My 1993
Saint in a soup kitchen: AD 370. Parachin, Victor M. *CDgst* 57:91-93 My 1993

A saint in psycho-analysis [review article *Ignatius of Loyola: the psychology of a saint* by W Meissner]. Jones, Frederick M. *Doctr Life* 43:208-215 Ap 1993
Saint Moses the Black. O'Connell-Cahill, Catherine. *Salt* 13:31 Ap 1993
The Saint of reason [condensed fr *The Providence Visitor* Ja 28 1993]. Lennon, Joseph L. *CDgst* 57:139-141 Je 1993
Saint of the devout life [condensed fr *Spirit and Life* Ja/F 1993]. Dowling, Dolores. *CDgst* 57:58-61 Ap 1993
Saints know how to listen. MacClennan, Carole. *ReligTJ* 27:34-35 O 1993
Saints riding stand by. O'Grady, Desmond. *OSV* 82:10-11 O 31 1993
Saints speak volumes. Kenny, Mary, 1936-. *Tablet* 247:911-913 Jl 17 1993
St Clare of Assisi. Baker-Pearce, Cordella. *Priests & People* 6:334-335 Ag-S 1992
Tomb of St Francis. Thiele, Gloria. *CDgst* 57:1-2+ O 1993
The twin legacy of St. Ambrose. McSheffery, Daniel F. *CDgst* 57:120-123 Ag 1993
Two Thomases, twins in sanctity [condensed fr *Lay Witness* D 1992]. Dorman, Regina. *CDgst* 58:30-35 N 1993
SAINTS—CULT
The cult of the saints in Anglo-Saxon England. Cubitt, Catherine. *Heythrop* 34:65-69 Ja 1993
SAINTS—INFLUENCE
Five mothers who found time to be saints. Hermes, Joan Garvey. *USCath* 58:28-33 My 1993
How saints are relevant. Kreeft, Peter John, 1937-. *New Cov* 22:33 Je 1993
SAINZ, ADRIAN, 1907-1936
Congregation for the Causes of Saints (1992-12-21) Decree on martyrdom. Congregation for the Causes of Saints. *OR(Eng)* 1272:4 Ja 6 1993*
SAKHAROV, ANDREI D, 1921-1989
On Sakharov and Rorty. Ratzinger, Joseph, Cardinal, 1927-. *Crisis* 11:36-38 My 1993
SALAMEH, MOHAMMED
Religion a key to terrorist. Pevtzow, Lisa. *Register* 69:1+ Ap 18 1993
SALAWA, ANGELA, 1881-1922
John Paul II, Pope, (1991-08-13) Itinera Apostolica (Apostolic Journey) [Polish]. John Paul II, Pope, 1920- (Karol Wojtyla) (elected 1978). *AAS* 84:873-878 S 8 1992*
SALEEBY, CALEB WILLIAMS
Evolution and morality. Shea, Moira C. *Teilhard Rev* 28:9-15 Sum 1993
SALES, EUGENIO DE ARAUJO, CARDINAL, 1920-
Street children slaughtered in the night. Pimentel-Pinto, Francis. *Tablet* 247:990 Jl 31 1993
SALESIANS
A developmental view of Salesian spirituality. Conn, Joann Wolski. *RRel* 52:56-68 Ja-F 1993
Rinnovamento liturgico in Polonia: a proposito di sette simposi a Lad. Durak, Adam. *Notitiae* 28:229-230 Mr 1992
SALINAS DE GORTARI, CARLOS, 1948-
NAFTA south of the border: high stakes, big hopes, real fears. Meyers, William K. *Comm* 120:5-7 S 24 1993
SALISBURY CATHEDRAL
A vision at Salisbury. Howatch, Susan, 1940-. *Tablet* 247:1007-1008 Ag 7 1993
SALVATION
Aspectos y visión global de una teología de la salvación. Arias Reyero, Maximino. *Teol Vida* 34 no 1-2:91-102 1993
"Bride" and "Mother" in the Super cantica of St Bernard: an ecclesiology for our time? Kereszty, Roch A, 1933-. *Communio* 20:415-436 Sum 1993
Creating options: shattering the "exclusivist, inclusivist, adn pluralist" paradigm [reply by Gavin D'Costa, pp 41-47]. Markham, Ian. *New Blckfrs* 74:33-34 Ja 1993
The death of Jesus and sin. McDade, John. *Month* 26:340-347 S-O 1993
Have you been saved? Grubb, Geoffrey J. *ReligTJ* 27:34 Mr 1993
Henri de Lubac—evangeliser. McPartlan, Paul. *Priests & People* 6:343-346 Ag-S 1992
"In the twilight of the twentieth century" on divine sendings. Maurer, Armand A, 1915-. *Can Cath Rev* 11:19-22 Jl-Ag 1993
Jesus saves; but how? Appleby, Raphael Scott. *USCath* 58:30-36 F 1993
Jovem, família e áfetividade: pecado e salvação. Chisleni, Maria Agusta. *REB* 53:412-419 Je 1993
The liberation of creation. Sepulveda, Juan. *LADOC* 23:23-27 My-Je 1993
The mystery of Christ and why we don't get it. Capon, Robert Farrar. Grand Rapids: Eerdmans, 1993. 192p ISBN 0-8028-0121-8
Responding to His call. McKenna, Bill. *New Cov* 23:27 S 1993
Salvation offered by sects (a theological analysis and evaluation). Dhavamony, Mariasusai. *StudiaM* 41:325-352 1992
"The truth looks different from here". Soskice, Janet Martin. *New Blckfrs* 73:528-542 N 1992
Two medieval soterologies: Anselm of Canterbury and Julian of Norwich. Nuth, Joan M. *TheolStds* 53:611-645 D 1992
Who can be saved? Martin, George. *New Cov* 22:34 Mr 1993
SALVATION—BIBLICAL TEACHING
Sin and salvation in Romans. Getty, Mary Ann. *BibleT* 31:89-93 Mr 1993
Il Vangelo di Marco: un annunico di salvezza nel mondo pagano. Riva, Raimondo. *StudiaM* 42:19-40 1993
SALVATION ARMY
Onward Christian soldier. Aitken, Tom. *Tablet* 247:598 My 8 1993
SAMARITANS
The Samaritan woman. Prest, Loring A. *BibleT* 30:367-371 N 1992
SAMSON
A model for Israel. Schaafsma, Roberta. *BibleT* 31:208-212 Jl 1993
SAN SALVADOR—POLITICS AND GOVERNMENT
Suspicion lingers in wake of Salvadoran bishop's murder. Palumbo, Gene. *Nat Cath Rep* 29:10 Jl 16 1993
SAN XAVIER DEL BLANC MISSION (ARIZONA)
Mission to the desert [photos]. Sherry, Gerard E. *OSV* 82:10-11 S 19 1993

SERMONS

Beyond death. Henry, Martin. *Furrow* 43:678-680 D 1992

Fifty years a priest [fr his sermon]. Lavery, Hugh. *Tablet* 247:544 My 1 1993

The fleshy way of God [excerpt fr *Sermons for sermon haters* 1992]. Papineau, Andre, 1937-. *Mod Lit* 19:16 D 1992-Ja 1993

The great church year: the best of Karl Rahner's homilies, sermons, and meditations. Rahner, Karl, 1904-1984. New York: Crossroad, 1993. 396p ISBN 0-8245-1220-6 LC 93-3930

Guiding principles behind the bad homilies. Pilch, John Joseph, 1936-. *Nat Cath Rep* 29:18 Ap 2 1993

The homilies we hear. Costello, Helen. *Furrow* 44:288-291 My 1993

John Paul II, Pope, (1992-09-27) Beatification. John Paul II, Pope, 1920- (Karol Wojtyla) (elected 1978). *TPS* 38:57-60 Ja-F 1993*

John Paul II, Pope, (1993-05-09) Repent! God will judge you. John Paul II, Pope, 1920- (Karol Wojtyla) (elected 1978). *TPS* 38:301-303 S-O 1993*

Lancelot Andrewes and T S Eliot: the making of histories. Timmerman, John H. *ABenR* 44:76-98 Mr 1993

Priests should make preaching thier number one job. Greeley, Andrew Moran, 1928-. *USCath* 58:13-17 D 1993

The religious strain. Mac Conghail, Muriris. *Furrow* 44:292-296 My 1993

"Thanks be to God" the Bible and the liturgy. Collins, Thomas. *Can Cath Rev* 11:7-13 Je 20 1993

Waiting. Ahern, Niall. *Furrow* 43:675-678 D 1992

Welcome to the table [sermon for a first communion Mass]. Iwanowski, Thomas B. *ReligTJ* 26:16 Ja 1993

When Christ meets Christ: homilies on the just word. Burghardt, Walter J. New York: Paulist Press, 1993. x, 241p ISBN 0-8091-3373-3 LC 92-46434

SERMONS—ILLUSTRATIONS

The sixth Sunday of Easter. Shanahan, Thomazine. *Liturgy* 11:47-49 Sum 1993

The third Sunday of Advent. Notebaart, James. *Liturgy* 11:5-8 Sum 1993

Twenty-first Sunday after Pentecost. Harms, Paul W F. *Liturgy* 11:60-64 Sum 1993

SERMONS, CHURCH YEAR

Texts for preaching. Brueggemann, Walter, et al, eds. Louisville: Westminster, 1993. x, 704p ISBN 0-664-21970-5

SERMONS, MEDIEVAL

Saint Bernard's third sermon for the feast of the Annunciation and a play from the N-town cycle. Hufgard, M Kilian. *Cist Stud* 28 no 2:167-178 1993

SERRANO, JORGE

Beware the demons loosed by Guatemala's coup. McConahay, Mary Jo. *Nat Cath Rep* 29:6 Je 4 1993

SERVANTS OF THE PARACLETE

Priests' treatment facility rocked by suits. Martinez, Demetria. *Nat Cath Rep* 29:5 F 26 1993

SERVICE (THEOLOGY)

Active and messy personalism. Cordaro, Frank. *Cath Work* 60:6 My 1993

Christ and the Catholic university. Daley, Brian E. *America* 169:6-14 S 11 1993

The Eucharist and the mission of the priest. Schineller, Peter. *Emmanual* 49:364-369 S 1993

John Paul II, Pope, (1992-02-25) Itinera Apostolica (Homily at ordination in Guinea during apostolic journey) [French]. John Paul II, Pope, 1920- (Karol Wojtyla) (elected 1978). *AAS* 85:171-175 F 3 1993*

Kingship of service. Doohan, Leonard. *Mod Lit* 20:36 N 1993

Learning through service. Bowman, Peg. *ReligTJ* 27:33 Mr 1993

New kid on the block. Gilbert, Jack. *Tod Parish* 25:38 O 1993

The permanent diaconate turns 25. McSheffery, Daniel F. *Priest* 49:12-15 Ag 1993

Service calls. Murphy, Jim. *New Cov* 23:30 Ag 1993

Single and at home in the Catholic Church. Hudson, Amanda. *Liguorian* 81:33-35 Jl 1993

Young people and religion growing out of the Church in the 1960s and 1990s. Kennedy, Finola. *Studies* 81:417-425 Wint 1992

The youth's response to God's call to love one another. Chidothi, Charles L D. *AFER* 34:79-94 Ap 1992

SERVICE BOOKS (MUSIC)

One Lord, one faith, one Baptism; one song? Gibala, Richard P. *Past Mus* 17:22-25 Ag-S 1993

SEX

The existential isolation of contraception. Klaus, Hanna. *Linacre* 59:29-32 N 1992

Living with compulsory celibacy. O'Keefe, James. *Way Suppl* 77:37-45 Sum 1993

Love of friendship. Bonnici, John S. *HPR* 93:31+ Ja 1993

On sex and sexuality: the challenge of André Guindon. Selling, Joseph A. *Doctr Life* 43:31-41 Ja 1993

The sexual brain. LeVay, Simon. Cambridge: MIT Press, 1993. 168p ISBN 0-26212-178-6 LC 92-44691

Sexuality: creation's wildcard—sexual energy and feminine creativity. Dwyer, Margretta. *Sisters* 65:276-279 Jl 1993

The state, virtue, sex and chastity. Healy, Jack. *Linacre* 60:51-59 My 1993

SEX—BIBLICAL TEACHING

The Bible talks about sex. Collins, Raymond F. *Priests & People* 7:306-311 Ag-S 1993

SEX—RELIGIOUS ASPECTS

The biblical foundations of the thought of John Paul II on human sexuality. Séguin, Michel. *Communio* 20:266-289 Sum 1993

Does the church's teaching on sex make sense? Fisher, Anthony. *Priests & People* 7:317-322 Ag-S 1993

Eros and the Jews: from biblical Israel to contemporary America. Biale, David. New York: Basic Books, 1992. 319p ISBN 0-4650-2033-x

Homosexuals in the military: three issues. Mahony, Roger Michael, Cardinal, 1936-. *Origins* 22:621+ F 25 1993

Human sexuality from God's perspective. *Origins* 23:164-166 Ag 12 1993

Human sexuality: an all-embracing gift. Coleman, Gerald D. New York: Alba House, 1992. x, 441p ISBN 0-81890-643-x LC 92-20661

Intimate bedfellows: love, sex, and the Catholic church. Finn, Thomas, and Finn, Donna. Boston: St. Paul Books & Media, 1993. 85p ISBN 0-8198-3667-2 LC 92-42622

Living as friends. Bonnici, John S. *Priest* 49:39-44 F 1993

Man and woman under God: the dignity of the human being according to Hans Urs von Balthasar. Strukelj, Anton. *Communio* 20:377-388 Sum 1993

Mixed-up in Milan. Cavnar, Cindy. *New Cov* 23:31 Ag 1993

NCCB establishes committee on sexual abuse. Kinney, John, Bp. *Origins* 23:104-105 Jl 1 1993

Pastoral policy: allegations of clergy sexual misconduct with minors. *Origins* 22:580-582 F 4 1993

Preaching and teaching sexuality: the dilemmas and possibilities. Cameli, Louis J. *Chicago Stud* 32:54-63 Ap 1993

Sex and gender differentiation in Hildegard of Bingen and Edith Stein. Allen, Prudence. *Communio* 20:389-414 Sum 1993

Sex and the adult Christian. Cosstick, Vicky. *Priests & People* 7:311-316 Ag-S 1993

Sexual abuse in Christian homes and churches. Heggen, Carolyn Holderread, 1946-. Scottdale, Pennsylvania: Herald Press, 1993. 208p ISBN 0-83613-624-1 LC 92-32143

Sexualerziehung zwischen Norm und Individualisierung. Bleistein, Roman, 1928-. *Stimm Zeit* 211:521-532 Ag 1993

Sexuality and spirituality in the European Middle Ages. Gross-Diaz, Theresa. *Chicago Stud* 32:32-42 Ap 1993

The world's wisdom [editorial]. *Register* 69:4 Ag 29 1993

Yes to life [extract fr pastoral letter *human life is sacred*]. *Doctr Life* 42:326-335 My-Je 1992

SEX (PSYCHOLOGY)

La ilustracion olvidada. Condorcet, de Gouges, de Lamberty y Otros. Madrid: Anthropos, 1993. x, 176p ISBN 84-7658-408-3

There's help for the sexual addict. Olert, Stephen, and Williams, Ruthann. *Sisters* 65:263-271 Jl 1993

SEX —RELIGIOUS ASPECTS

Theologian offers Vatican-requested explanations. Guindon, Andre. *Origins* 22:630-636 F 25 1993

SEX ABUSE

O'Connor: abuse is a sin, too. Feuerherd, Peter. *Register* 69:1+ Ag 1 1993

Priest offenders and the saga of the Paracletes. Chittister, Joan D. *Nat Cath Rep* 29:20 Jl 30 1993

SEX ADDICTION

Sexual addiction. Keefe, Jeffrey. *Catechist* 26:11 Mr 1993

SEX ADDICTS- UNITED STATES

There's help for the sexual addict. Olert, Stephen, and Williams, Ruthann. *Sisters* 65:263-271 Jl 1993

SEX AND LAW

Privacy and the law. Arkes, Hadley. *Crisis* 11:14-15 My 1993

The sexual revolution, explained. Canavan, Francis, 1917-. *New Oxford Rev* 60:21-24 N 1993

SEX CRIMES (CANON LAW)

Stones instead of bread: sexually abusive priests in ministry. Cafardi, Nicholas P. *Stud Can* 27 no 1:145-172 1993

SEX CUSTOMS

A circle of death. Goodwin, Gillian. *Tablet* 247:746+ Je 1993

Going all the way. Bartlett, Bob. *Momentum* 24:36-39 Ap-My 1993

Sexual morality from a social perspective. Sunshine, Edward R. *Chicago Stud* 31:301-315 N 1992

Sexual morality's positive goals and the problem of legalism. George, Robert P. *Origins* 22:778-780 Ap 22 1993

The sexual revolution aftershock. Kezmoh, Heidi Schlumpf. *Register* 69:1+ My 2 1993

Sexually challenged. Sobran, Joseph. *Crisis* 11:41-43 Je 1993

SEX DIFFERENCES

Sex and gender differentiation in Hildegard of Bingen and Edith Stein. Allen, Prudence. *Communio* 20:389-414 Sum 1993

Sounding the alarm on sex selection. *Tablet* 247:149 Ja 30 1993

SEX DIFFERENCES (PSYCHOLOGY)

Celibacy: a feminist view. Gramick, Jeannine. *Sisters* 65:255-262 Jl 1993

Male and female created he them. Miller, Annabel. *Tablet* 247:839 Jl 3 1993

SEX EDUCATION

Against the tide: how to raise sexually pure kids in an "anything-goes" world. Lahaye, Time, and Lahaye, Beverly. Sisters: Questar, 1993. x, 258p ISBN 0-88070-578-7

Controversy over sex education laws. *Tablet* 247:992 Jl 31 1993

The infusion approach to sexuality education. Ryan, Ellen. *Momentum* 24:53-55 F-Mr 1993

Sexuality education—forward or backward? Miller, Patricia F. *Momentum* 24:49-52 F-Mr 1993

Statement on public schools' condom distribution. *Origins* 22:553-556 Ja 21 1993

What Catholic teens need to know about sex. Stafford, Geraldine. *HPR* 94:52-54 O 1993

SEX IN MARRIAGE

The principle of double effect and safe sex in marriage: reflections on a suggestion. Johnson, Mark A. *Linacre* 60:82-89 My 1993

SEX IN MOTION PICTURES

Hollywood blues. Jones, Arthur C, 1936-. *Tablet* 247:849-850 Jl 3 1993

SEX IN THE BIBLE

"Male and female he created them". Collins, Raymond F. *Chicago Stud* 32:9-18 Ap 1993

SEX INSTRUCTION FOR YOUTH- NEW JERSEY

Abstinence as public policy: a report from New Jersey's schools. Bovenizer, David A. *Crisis* 11:40-41 S 1993

SEX ROLE

The argument for the bans: combat is no place for women and gays. Reilly, Robert. *Crisis* 11:39-41 Ap 1993

I sit listening to the wind: woman's encounter within herself. Duerk, Judith. San Diego: LuraMedia, 1993. x, 103p ISBN 0-931055-98-9 LC 93-991

A role of one's own. Garvey, John, 1944-. *Comm* 120:8-9 Mr 26 1993

SEXISM—RELIGIOUS ASPECTS

Bishops ask priests about women [fr The Pastoral Care of Marriage and Family Life]. *Priests & People* 6:337-340 Ag-S 1992

The homilies we hear. Costello, Helen. *Furrow* 44:288-291 My 1993

Is it okay to call God mother?: considering the feminine face of God. Smith, Paul R. Peabody: Hendrickson Publishers, 1993. 273p ISBN 1-56563-013-0 LC 93-25810

Should the healing begin at Christmas. McDonagh, Enda. *Furrow* 43:651-655 D 1992

SEXUAL ETHICS

Abortion, sex and gender: the Church's public voice. Cahill, Lisa Sowle. *America* 168:6-11 My 22, 1993

Body and soul. Dunstan, Petà. *Priests & People* 7:323-326 Ag-S 1993

Dialogue about Catholic's sexual teaching. Curran, Charles E, 1934-, and McCormick, Richard A, eds. Mahwah: Paulist, 1993. x, 601p ISBN 0-8091-3414-4 LC 93-4370

Encyclical insists intercourse is language of love (commentary: *Humanae Vitae*). Hebblethwaite, Peter, 1930-. *Nat Cath Rep* 29:15-16 Jl 16 1993

Encyclical left church credibility stillborn (commentary: *Humanae Vitae*). Curran, Charles E, 1934-. *Nat Cath Rep* 29:14-15 Jl 16 1993*

Eros and the Jews: from biblical Israel to contemporary America. Biale, David. New York: Basic Books, 1992. 319p ISBN 0-4650-2033-x

Going all the way. Bartlett, Bob. *Momentum* 24:36-39 Ap-My 1993

A great pleasure [review article *The body in context* by G Moore]. Kelly, Kevin T. *Priests & People* 7:361-365 Ag-S 1993

Human sexuality: an all-embracing gift. Coleman, Gerald D. New York: Alba House, 1992. x, 441p ISBN 0-81890-643-x LC 92-20661

Humanae Vitae revisited [commentary Humanae Vitae]. Mannion, M Francis. *OSV* 82:19 Ag 1 1993

"Humanae Vitae": the "prophetic" encyclical (commentary: *Humanae Vitae*). Shaw, Russell. *OSV* 82:5 Jl 25 1993*

In the heartland, Catholic sexuality celebrated [commentary Humanae Vitae]. Carey, Ann. *OSV* 82:3 Ag 15 1993*

Légèreté ou gravité de la chair. Lacroix, Xavier. *Supplement* 184:175-191 Mr-Ap 1993

Men vowed and sexual conversations about celibate chastity. Sammon, Sean D, and Zielinski, Judith Ann. *RRel* 52:446-453 My-Je 1993

NCCB establishes committee on sexual abuse. Kinney, John, Bp. *Origins* 23:104-105 Jl 1 1993

Privacy and the law. Arkes, Hadley. *Crisis* 11:14-15 My 1993

Reconsidering Humanae Vitae [commentary Humanae Vitae]. Balsam, Charles. *Register* 69:5 Ag 1 1993

The rights of the child [editorial]. *Tablet* 247:675 My 29 1993

The sexual revolution, explained. Canavan, Francis, 1917-. *New Oxford Rev* 60:21-24 N 1993

Single Catholics: can we talk about S-E-X? Bearden, Michelle. *USCath* 58:30-35 Ag 1993

The sins of the flesh. Wilson, Richard. *Priests & People* 7:346-347 Ag-S 1993

Society needs sexual evolution. Callahan, Sidney. *Nat Cath Rep* 29:19 Je 4 1993

Theologian offers Vatican-requested explanations. Guindon, Andre. *Origins* 22:630-636 F 25 1993

Theological trends—sexual ethics: some recent developments. Hoose, Bernard. *Way* 33:54-62 Ja 1993

Veritatis splendor [commentary]. Patrick, Anne E. *Comm* 120:18 O 22 1993

SEXUAL ETHICS—CLERGY

Candidates with difficulties in celibacy: discernment, admission, formation. Kiely, Bartholomew. *Seminarium* 33:107-118 Ja-Mr 1993

SEXUAL ETHICS FOR TEENAGERS

Chastity as shared strength: an open letter to students. Fouqurean, Mary Patricia Barth. *America* 169:10-15 N 6 1993

SEXUAL HARASSMENT OF WOMEN

The roots of violence against women. Mejia, Jorge Julia, Bp. *Origins* 23:369+ N 4 1993

SEXUALLY ABUSED CHILDREN

A moral emergency: breaking the cycle of child sexual abuse. Angelica, Jade C, 1952-. Kansas City: Sheed & Ward, 1993. x, 161p ISBN 15-5612-617-4 LC 93-939

Muckrakers. Breig, James. *OSV* 82:3 Jl 25 1993

Sexual abuse in Christian homes and churches. Heggen, Carolyn Holderread, 1946-. Scottdale, Pennsylvania: Herald Press, 1993. 208p ISBN 0-83613-624-1 LC 92-32143

SEXUALLY TRANSMITTED DISEASES

Abstinence as public policy: a report from New Jersey's schools. Bovenizer, David A. *Crisis* 11:40-41 S 1993

SHAKERS

Lovely in the dances. Carter, Sydney. *Tablet* 247:1097 Ag 28 1993

SHAKERSPEARE, WILLIAM

Playing Shakespeare. Bashian, Kathleen Ryniker. *Momentum* 24:67-68 F-Mr 1993

SHAME

The depleted self: sin in a narcissistic age. Capps, Donald. Minneapolis: Fortress Press, 1993. x, 176p ISBN 0-80062-587-0 LC 92-7931

Shame, dysfunctional families, and lack of due discretion for marriage. Garrity, Robert M. *Jurist* 51 no 2:364-389 1991

SHAME—RELIGIOUS ASPECTS

Shame and grace. Smedes, Lewis, B. New York: HarperCollins, 1993. x, 170p ISBN 0-06-067521-7 LC 92-53897

SHAPIRO, DAVID

Minority museum: fighting hatred, instilling dignity. Whitney, Sally. *St Anth* 100:34-39 Ap 1993

SHARING

Faith sharing, trust, and transformation. Bernier, Joan M. *Tod Parish* 25:34-35 Mr 1993

Sharing as sign of Eucharist. Schaller, Jeanne Lound. *Living Prayer* 26:19-20 S-O 1993

Sharing the message. *Liturgy* 10:33-36 Sum 1992

SHARWIN, BYRON

Seeking the lost Atlantis of Catholics and Jews [por]. Scott, David. *OSV* 82:6-7 S 19 1993

SHEALY, TERENCE J, 1863-1922

"To form an elite body of laymen" Terence J Shealy, SJ, and the laymen's league, 1911-1922. McShane, Joseph M, 1949-. *CHist* 78:557-580 O 1992

SHEEN, FULTON, JOHN, BP, 1895-1979

"A life of mystery and adventure" Fulton Sheen's reflections on the priesthood. Fields, Kathleen Riley. *US Cath Hist* 11:63-82 Wint 1993

SHINTO

Sinto and Christianity: dialogue for the twenty-first century. Kadowaki, Kakichi. *IPQ* 33:69-89 Mr 1993

The universal attitude of Shinto as expressed in the Shinto sect Kurozumikyō. Stoesz, Willis. *JEcumen Stds* 29:215-229 Spr 1992

SHORT STORIES

Collected works of G K Chesterton VI 14: short stories, fairytales, mystery, and illustrations. Chesterton, Gilbert Keith, 1874-1936. San Francisco: Ignatius Press, 1993. ISBN 0-89870-401-4

SHRINES

The heart in pilgrimage. Furlong, Monica, 1930-. *Tablet* 247:305 Mr 6 1993

John Paul II, Pope, (1993-09-07) Cross [Orig in Lithuanian]. John Paul II, Pope, 1920- (Karol Wojtyla) (elected 1978). *OR(Eng)* 1307:5 S 15 1993*

The miracle of San Luis. Stevens, Barbara. *OSV* 81:10-11 Ja 10 1993

Newest Marian shrine dedicated. Paradis, Steve. *OR(Eng)* 1307:2 S 15 1993

Notes on the canonical status of shrines. Fox, Joseph P. *Notitiae* 28:261-269 Ap 1992

Our Lady of Siluva. Zalatorius, Genevieve. *Register* 69:2 Mr 28 1993

SHRINES- CUBA

Shrine a giant tribute to bishop and his devout Cuban parishioners. Slavin, J P. *Nat Cath Rep* 29:7 Ja 15 1993

SHRINES- EASTERN EUROPE

Eastern Europe's Marian shrines bask in freedom. Luxmoore, Jonathan. *Register* 69:1+ Ag 22 1993

SHRINES- ENGLAND

England's White Friars. Dickie, Amanda. *Tablet* 247:122 Ja 23 1993

Walsingham: Mary's message for rich and poor [photo]. Allen, Peter. *Priests & People* 7:197-201 My 1993

SHRINES- ITALY

John Paul II, Pope, (1993-08-15) Loreto. John Paul II, Pope, 1920- (Karol Wojtyla) (elected 1978). *OR(Eng)* 1308:6-7 S 22 1993*

A visit to Mary's house [Holy House of Loreto Shrine, Italy]. Burke, Greg. *Register* 69:3 Ja 31 1993

SHRINES- NORTH CAROLINA

In North Carolina they trust [photos]. Crawford, Don. *OSV* 82:5 O 24 1993

SHRINES- POLAND

Poles entrust country's future to Mary. Drazek, Czeslaw. *OR(Eng)* 1305:2 S 1 1993

SICILY (ITALY)—CHURCH HISTORY

The Italo-Greeks and Melkite Antioch. Gallard, George D, and Messina, A. *Diakonia* 26 no 2:89-98 1993

SICILY (ITALY)—CIVILIZATION—GREEK

The Italo-Greeks and Melkite Antioch. Gallard, George D, and Messina, A. *Diakonia* 26 no 2:89-98 1993

SICK

Ce qu'être malade veut dire. Jannesse, Alfred. *Supplement* 184:21-32 Mr-Ap 1993

If I were Pope [winner of John Harriott Memorial Prize]. Kapusnak, Pat. *Tablet* 247:62 Ja 16 1993

What's good about being sick? Johnson, Richard P. *Liguorian* 81:20-25 Jl 1993

SICK—ETHICAL ASPECTS

Vérité et mensonge dans la relation au malade. Geets, Claude. *Supplement* 184:56-77 Mr-Ap 1993

SICK—PSYCHOLOGY

La maladie comme expérience et comme condition. Geets, Claude. *Supplement* 184:33-55 Mr-Ap 1993

SICK—PSYCHOLOGY ASPECTS

Ce qu'être malade veut dire. Jannesse, Alfred. *Supplement* 184:21-32 Mr-Ap 1993

SICK—RELIGIOUS LIFE

Praying our pain. McGrane, Janice. *Spir Life* 32:87-90 Sum 1993

A spirituality for the chronically ill. Russell, Kenneth C. *Spir Life* 32:79-86 Sum 1993

SICK, CARE OF

Converting a unit to patient-focused care. Farris, Bain J. *Health Prog* 74:23-25 Ap 1993

My father's left hand: a death he did not deserve. Gorman, Geraldine. *Comm* 120:16+ Jl 16 1993

St Joseph's Hospital. Yablonka, Marc Phillip. *Sisters* 65:209-211 My 1993

SICK, CARE OF—SOCIAL ASPECTS

Questions d'un gestionnaire d'hôpital. Tassin, Paul. *Supplement* 184:7-19 Mr-Ap 1993

SICKERT, WALTER

The virtuosity of detachment: Walter Sickert. Hackett, Peter. *Month* 26:26-27 Ja 1993

SIGNS AND SYMBOLS

Christian and eastern mysticism [fr *a new vision of reality: Western science, Eastern mysticism and Christian faith*]. Griffiths, Bede, 1906-. *Living Prayer* 26:3-8 My-Je 1993

Flags don't belong in church. Grippo, Dan. *USCath* 58:26-30 Mr 1993

Gender and the will of God. Kreeft, Peter John, 1937-. *Crisis* 11:20-28 S 1993

"Ordinary" symbols and rituals. Becker, Mary Lee. *ReligTJ* 26:34-35 Ja 1993

Religious symbols belong in your home. Tuohy, Patrice J. *USCath* 58:19-24 Ap 1993

The sacraments and evangelisation. Woolfenden, Graham. *Month* 26:121-126 Mr 1993

Seeds in the muck [editorial]. Manney, Jim, ed. *New Cov* 23:5 S 1993

SIGOURNEY, LYDIA, 1791-1865

The representationj of religious experience in nineteenth-century American women's autobiography. Norman, Rose. *Listening* 28:128-140 Spr 1993

SILENCE

The lure of honey. Cassidy, Sheila. *Tablet* 247:1068-1069 Ag 21 1993

When words fail us. Paige, Harry W, 1922-. *Liguorian* 81:52-56 Ag 1993

Why orthodox Catholics look to Zen. Gawronski, Raymond T. *New Oxford Rev* 60:13-16 Jl-Ag 1993

SILESIAN LITERATURE
Schlesien in der polnischen Gegenwartsliteratur. Zybura, Marek. *Stimm Zeit* 211:197-209 Mr 1993

SILVA CENCIO, JORGE
John Paul II, Pope, (1991-11-14) Allocutiones (Speech to receive Ambassadorial credentials) [Spanish]. John Paul II, Pope, 1920- (Karol Wojtyla) (elected 1978). *AAS* 84:975-977 O 3 1992*

SILVESTRINI, ACHILLE, CARDINAL
Silvestrini's red hat in ring for nex pope [por]. Hebblethwaite, Peter, 1930-. *Nat Cath Rep* 30:11 N 19 1993

SIMON, YVES R, 1903-1961
A neo-Thomist's defense of democracy. Schram, Glenn N. *New Oxford Rev* 60:13-17 Ja-F 1993

SIMON COMMUNITY (LONDON)
Beggars for beggars. Rice, Judith. *Tablet* 247:1126-1127 S 4 1993

SIMONIS, ADRIANUS JOHANNUS, CARDINAL, 1931-
Rumours abound as Bär resigns. Goddijn, Walter, 1921-. *Tablet* 247:413-414 Mr 27 1993

SIN
Beyond the darkness, into the light: thinking about sin and forgiveness today. Caserta, Thomas G. Boston: St Paul Books & Media, 1993. 67p ISBN 0-8198-1142 LC 93-19167

Cardinal Newman on the season of Lent. Oakes, Edward T. *America* 168:7-12 Ap 3 1993

A day without sin. Kreeft, Peter John, 1937-. *New Cov* 23:33 Ag 1993

Delitti contro il sesto comandamento. Paolis, Velasio De. *Periodica* 82 no 2: 293-316 1993

The depleted self: sin in a narcissistic age. Capps, Donald. Minneapolis: Fortress Press, 1993. x, 176p ISBN 0-80062-587-0 LC 92-7931

Exclusion and embrace: theological reflections in the wake of "ethnic cleansing". Volf, Miroslav. *JEcumen Stds* 29:230-248 Spr 1992

The gift of tears in the writings of St Ignatius Loyola and the Eastern Fathers. Maloney, George A, 1924-. *Diakonia* 26 no 1:5-13 1993

The importance of forgiveness. Pilarczyk, Daniel Edward, Abp, 1934-. *OSV* 82:5 Jl 4 1993

Jovem, família e áfetividade: pecado e salvação. Chisleni, Maria Agusta. *REB* 53:412-419 Je 1993

The lesson of Lent. Novak, Michael, 1933-. *Crisis* 11:4-7 Ap 1993

Moral fundamental en el nuevo catecismo. Vidal, Marciano. *Christus* 58:42-50 Je 1993

Reconciliation renewal: healing for today's church. O'Connell, Timothy E. *Chicago Stud* 32:114-126 Ag 1993

Reconciliation: a meeting place with our loving God. Jeray, Diane. *Liguorian* 81:57-59 Ag 1993

Sin and how to cope with it. Fahey, John H. *HPR* 94:62-65 N 1993

Sin in the Middle Ages. Tanner, Norman P. *Month* 26:372-375 S-O 1993

Sin is a matter of broken relationship, not legalisms. Cameron, Peter John. *Register* 69:1+ Mr 7 1993

Sin is real. Pilarczyk, Daniel Edward, Abp, 1934-. *OSV* 82:9 Jl 11 1993

The sinner against the scoundrels: the ills of doctrine and "schrift" in the Wife of Bath's, Friar's and Summoner's narratives. Kamowski, William. *Relig Lit* 25:1-18 Spr 1993

Think wrongly and judge rashly. Fahey, John H. *HPR* 94:58-61 N 1993

To find real, inner peace, we must wash clean in Christ's blood. Cameron, Peter John. *Register* 69:1+ Ap 11 1993

We should fear sin far more than death. Kreeft, Peter John, 1937-. *Register* 69:1+ My 9 1993

When a Christian sins. Kreeft, Peter John, 1937-. *New Cov* 22:19-20 Mr 1993

Why confess venial sins? Miller, J Michael. *OSV* 81:6 Ja 10 1993

Worshiping at the shrine of self conquering pride. Anderson, Joan Wester, 1938-. *Liguorian* 81:46-50 Ja 1993

SIN—BIBLICAL TEACHING
The Bible on sin. Hoppe, Leslie J, ed. *BibleT* 31:68-93 Mr 1993*

Do we believe in a church of sinners. Kelly, Kevin T. *Way* 33:106-116 Ap 1993

Early Judaism looks at Adam. Levison, John R. *BibleT* 30:372-377 N 1992

Seeing sin for what it is. Cameron, Peter John. *Register* 69:1+ Mr 14 1993

Sin in biblical and rabbinic thought. Cooper, Howard. *Month* 26:348-354 S-O 1993

SIN, ORIGINAL
Augustine on sin. Meredith, Anthony. *Month* 26:367-371 S-O 1993

The biblical foundations of the thought of John Paul II on human sexuality. Séguin, Michel. *Communio* 20:266-289 Sum 1993

Gifts from our brokenness: gifts from our unity. Grove, William Boyd, Bp. *Ecumen Trends* 22:12-14 S 1993

The long journey home. Fielding, Ellen Wilson. *Crisis* 11:49-50 Ap 1993

Eine Minute Unsinn. DeMello, Anthony, 1931-. Frieburg: Herder, 1993. x, 224p ISBN 3-451-23053-4

Original sin: a residue of some primal crime? Coyle, Kathleen. *Doctr Life* 43: 83-94 F 1993

Le péché originel chez Philon d'Alexandrie. Baudry, Gérard-Henry. *MSR* 50: 99-115 Ap-Je 1993

Le péché originel dans les écrits de Qoumrân. Baudry, Gérard-Henry. *MSR* 50:7-22 Ja-Mr 1993

The search for original sin. Stuhlmueller, Carroll. *BibleT* 31:73-78 Mr 1993

Trying to make sense [editorial]. *Month* 26:86-87 Mr 1993

SINAI, MOUNT
Sinai and Tabor: apophatic and kataphatic symbols in tension. Lane, Belden C. *Stud Form Spir* 14:189-205 My 1993

SINGER, PETER
Peter Singer on famine, affluence, and morality: a Christian response. Spoerl, Joseph S. *Amer J Juris* 37:113-133 1992

SINGERS
Listening to Cecilia. Tombes, Jonathan. *Crisis* 11:52-54 Mr 1993

SINGING
In hospice work, music is our great ally. Burns, Sharon. *Past Mus* 17:11-13 F-Mr 1993

"Music" [fr *Dictionary of the Church*]. Staunton, William. *SacM* 120:13-14 Spr 1993

A season for glad songs. Fanning, Jim, and Schumacher, Stacy. *ReligTJ* 27: 36-37 Mr 1993

Sing to the Lord a sturdy song. Moleck, Fred. *Past Mus* 17:26-28 Ap-My 1993

Singing at the rites begins with Sunday. Quinn, Mary Jo. *Past Mus* 17:35-37 Ap-My 1993

Today's singing child, tomorrow's singing adult. Gwozdz, Lee. *Past Mus* 17: 15-17 F-Mr 1993

What matters is that our song comes from the heart. Bunbury, Richard R. *Past Mus* 17:58-60 Ap-My 1993

SINGKAI, GREGORY, BP, 1935-
Catholic bishop pleads for help. Freidman, Paul. *Tablet* 247:956-957 Jl 24 1993

SINGLE-PARENT FAMILY
Determinants of spells of poverty following divorce. Heath, Julia A, and Kiker, B F, 1937-. *RSocEcon* 50:305-315 Fall 1992

Single parents: building holy families. Finley, Mitchel B. *Liguorian* 81:12-16 Ag 1993

Single-parenthood is okay! And experience says the earth is flat. Carlin, David Robert, Jr, 1938-. *Comm* 120:8-9 O 22 1993

SINGLE PARENTS
Leaving the children at "Mom's house". Barnard, Ann M. *ST Anth* 101:22-27 Jl 1993

Prolifers who seek to do more. Meehan, Bridget Mary. *Register* 69:1+ Ja 31 1993

SINGLE PEOPLE
What are single people called to do? Brady, Mary Clare. *USCath* 58:32-33 Jl 1993

SINGLE PEOPLE—RELIGIOUS LIFE
Single people in the church. *Origins* 23:801-804 My 6 1993

Singles in the Church of the nineties. Canty, Anne P. *Liguorian* 81:30-34 Ja 1993

SINGLE PEOPLE—SOCIAL ASPECTS
Single people in the church. *Origins* 23:801-804 My 6 1993

SIPE, CRESCENZIO, ABP
The celibacy question. Sipe, A W Richard. *Tablet* 247:737-738 Je 5 1993

SISTERS, RELIGIOUS *see* Nuns

SISTERS OF 'CATECHESI TRADENDAE DOLORES SOPENA' INSTITUTE
Congregation for the Causes of Saints (1992-07-11) Decree on the heroic virtues. Congregation for the Causes of Saints. *TPS* 38:37-38 Ja-F 1993*

SISTERS OF JESUS AND MARY, CONGREGATION OF
Congregation for the Causes of Saints (1992-07-11) Blessed Marie de Saint-Ignace (Thevenet). Congregation for the Causes of Saints. *AAS* 85:189-191 F 3 1993*

SISTERS OF LIFE
These are sisters for life [photos]. Ryan, Dick. *OSV* 82:10-11 O 3 1993

SISTERS OF PROVIDENCE
A sign of God's presence. Lambert, Jean M, and Laboure, M Catherine. *Health Prog* 74:62+ Ap 1993

SISTERS OF PROVIDENCE OF ST MARY-OF-THE-WOODS
Congregation for the Causes of Saints (1992-07-11) Decree on the heroic virtues of Theodore (Anna Therese Guerin). Congregation for the Causes of Saints. *AAS* 85:185-189 F 3 1993*

Congregation for the Causes of Saints (1992-07-11) Decree on the heroic virtues. Congregation for the Causes of Saints. *TPS* 38:37-38 Ja-F 1993*

SISTERS OF ST FELIX OF CANTALICE
Congregation for the Causes of Saints (1992-07-11) Decree on the heroic virtues of Mary Angela (Sofia Camilla Truszkowska). Congregation for the Causes of Saints. *AAS* 85:183-185 F 3 1993*

SISTERS OF ST JOSEPH
Congregation for the Causes of Saints (1993-07-06) Decree on a miracle. Congregation for the Causes of Saints. *OR(Eng)* 1299:12 Jl 14 1993*

SISTERS OF THE GOOD SHEPHERD
An unique ministry in Michigan. Carey, Ann. *OSV* 82:21 My 16 1993

SISTERS OF THE HOLY FAMILY OF NAZARETH
Commemoration for 11 martyred sisters. *OR(Eng)* 1301:5 Jl 28 1993

SIXTUS, V, POPE, 1531-1590 (FELICE PEROTTI) (ELECTED 1585)
Five years that changed Rome. O'Grady, Desmond. *OSV* 82:5 Je 20 1993

SJARIF, ACHJADI ACHID
John Paul II, Pope, (1991-11-07) Allocutiones (Speech to received ambassadorial credentials) [English]. John Paul II, Pope, 1920- (Karol Wojtyla) (elected 1978). *AAS* 84:963-966 O 3 1992*

SLAVE TRADE
"Am I not a human being and a brother/sister?". Magesa, Laurenti. *AFER* 34:95-114 Ap 1992

A forgotten history: blacks in Argentina. Liboreiro, Cristina. *LADOC* 23:15-22 My-Je 1993

Pope's witness against "culture of death". *Tablet* 247:1051 Ag 14 1993

SLAVERY
John Paul II, Pope, (1992-02-22) Itinera Apostolica (Address to Catholics of Goree Island during apostolic trip) [French]. John Paul II, Pope, 1920- (Karol Wojtyla) (elected 1978). *AAS* 85:157-161 F 3 1993*

John Paul II, Pope, (1992-10-12) Defend your identities and values. John Paul II, Pope, 1920- (Karol Wojtyla) (elected 1978). *TPS* 38:103-106 Mr-Ap 1993*

SLAVERY—BIBLICAL TEACHING
Slavery in the second testament world. Osiek, Carolyn. *Bib Th Bul* 22:174-179 Wint 1992

SLAVERY AND THE CHURCH
"Am I not a human being and a brother/sister?". Magesa, Laurenti. *AFER* 34:95-114 Ap 1992

John Paul II, Pope, (1992-01-25) Allocutiones (Homily to French Bishops) [French]. John Paul II, Pope, 1920- (Karol Wojtyla) (elected 1978). *AAS* 85:143-148 F 3 1993*

Katholishe Kirche in der DDR zwischen Staat und Gesellschaft. Haese, Ute. *Stimm Zeit* 211:241-254 Ap 1993

Ein Kirchen bild für unsere Zeit? Wagner, Marion. *Stimm Zeit* 211:533-546 Ag 1993*

Responde la iglesia a los desafios de hoy?: cartas pastorales. Castellanos, Nicholas. Madrid: Grupo Libros, 1993. x, 666p ISBN 84-7906-202-9

SOCIETY AND CHURCH- LATIN AMERICA
La modernidad en America Latina. Araujo de Oliveira, Manfredo. *Christus* 58:20-25 My 1993

SOCIETY OF CATHOLIC SOCIAL SCIENTISTS
Catholic scholars seek new impact. Fox, Jim. *Register* 69:1+ Ap 11 1993

SOCIETY OF FRIENDS
What friends believe. Jacob, Philip. *Furrow* 44:490-492 S 1993

SOCIETY OF FRIENDS- GREAT BRITAIN
Traditions of spiritual guidance. The real presence a Quaker perspective on spiritual direction. Kolp, Alan. *Way* 33:240-247 Jl 1993

SOCIETY OF MISSIONARIES OF AFRICA
John Paul II, Pope, (1992-06-15) Live the spirit of Cardinal Lavigerie. John Paul II, Pope, 1920- (Karol Wojtyla) (elected 1978). *TPS* 38:21-23 Ja-F 1993*

SOCIETY OF SISTERS FOR THE CHURCH
The Society of Sisters for the Church: a contemporary Diaconal model. Meehan, Bridget Mary. *Sisters* 65:8-11 Ja 1993

SOCIETY OF THE HOLY CHILD JESUS
Congregation for the Causes of Saints (1992-06-13) Decree on the heroic virtues. Congregation for the Causes of Saints. *TPS* 38:19-20 Ja-F 1993*

Cornelia Connelly: model of Christian courage. McSheffery, Daniel F. *HPR* 93:57-60 My 1993

SOCIO-ECONOMICS—HISTORY
A review of the troops: social economics in the twentieth century. Waters, William R. *RSocEcon* 51:262-286 Aut 1993

SOCIOLINGUISTICS
Voices of wrath: when words become weapons. Mankowski, Paul V. *Crisis* 10:22-25 D 1992

SOCIOLOGICAL JURISPRUDENCE- GERMANY
Rechtsphilosophie. Brieskorn, Norbert. *Stimm Zeit* 211:318-330 My 1993

SOCIOLOGICAL JURISPRUDENCE- ITALY
Considerazioni giuridiche sulla chiamata di correo. Passano, Paolo Ferrari Da. *Civilta* 2:29-43 Ap 3 1993

SOCIOLOGY
Tensions in social theory: groundwork for a future moral sociology. Muñoz, Braulio. Chicago: Loyola University Press, 1993. x, 367p ISBN 0-8294-0739-1 LC 92-26436

SOCIOLOGY—HISTORY
La théologie comme science et la voction de savant d'après Max Weber. Gendron, Pierre. *Laval Theol Phil* 49:215-222 Je 1993

SOCIOLOGY, BIBLICAL
Beat his ribs while he is young (Sir 30:12). Pilch, John Joseph, 1936-. *Bib Th Bul* 23:101-113 Aut 1993

Josiah's passover: sociology and the liberating Bible. Nakanose, Shigeyuki. Maryknoll: Orbis Books, 1993. x, 192p ISBN 0-88344850-5 LC 93-18286

Les Thessaloniciens étaient-ils des paresseux? Romaniuk, Kazimierz. *Eph Theol Lovan* 69:142-144 Ap 1993

SOCIOLOGY, CHRISTIAN
The Catholic ethic and the spirit of capitalism. Novak, Michael, 1933-. New York: Macmillan International, 1993. x, 334p ISBN 0-02923-235-x LC 92-32151

Faith without dogma: the place of religion in postmodern societies. Ferrarotti, Franco. New Jersey: Transaction Publishers, 1993. x, 181p ISBN 1-56000-074-0 LC 92-17835

Fullness of faith: the public significance of theology. Himes, Michael J, and Himes, Kenneth R. New York: Paulist Press, 1993. x, 213p ISBN 0-8091-3372-5 LC 92-36140

The politics of God: Christian theologies and social justice. Tanner, Kathryn, 1957-. Minneapolis: Fortress Press, 1992. 262p ISBN 0-80062-613-3 LC 92-19360

Reading the signs of the times: resources for social and cultural analysis. Sanks, T Howland, and Coleman, John A, eds. New York: Paulist Press, 1993. x, 232p ISBN 0-8091-33777-6 LC 92-42017

Unterwegs zur interkulturellen Demokratie. Lesch, Walter. *Stimm Zeit* 211:255-269 Ap 1993

SOCIOLOGY, URBAN
Let's not lose the heart of the city. Burns, Robert E, 1919-. *USCath* 58:2 Mr 1993

SOCIOLOGY, URBAN—ANTIQUITIES
Isaiah and urban possibility. Brueggemann, Walter. Louisville: Westminster, 1993. x, 96p ISBN 0-664-25460-8

SOCIOLOGY, URBAN- ISRAEL
Jesus and the forgotten city: new light on Sepphoris and the urban world of Jesus. Batey, Richard A. Grand Rapids: Baker Book House, 1991

SOCIOLOGY AND RELIGION
Approaching "sect" with care. Kydd, Ronald. *Ecumen Trends* 22:3-5 Mr 1993

"The end of American Catholicism?"—another look. Hegy, Pierre M. *America* 168:4-9 My 1 1993

Madness, massacre and the millennium. Egan, Anthony. *Month* 26:214-218 Je 1993

Person and society in the exercises. Clarke, Thomas E. *Way Suppl* 76:53-60 Spr 1993

Religion and values: noble lies? Roof, Wade Clark, 1939-. *Critic* 47:35-45 Spr 1993

Secularization, rationalism, and sectarianism: essays in honour of Bryan R Wilson. Barker, Eileen, et al, eds. New York: Oxford University Press, 1993. x, 322p ISBN 0-19-827721-0 LC 92-41458

Soziologie und Theologie in Nachbarschaft. Köhler, Oskar. *Stimm Zeit* 211:210-212 Mr 1993

La théologie comme science et la voction de savant d'après Max Weber. Gendron, Pierre. *Laval Theol Phil* 49:215-222 Je 1993

Troeltsch's treatment of the Thomist synthesis in The Social Teacing as a signal of his view of a new cultural synthesis. Dietrich, Wendell S. *Thomist* 57:381-401 Jl 1993

SOCIOLOGY AND RELIGION- INDIA
Leave the temple: Indian paths to human liberation. Wilfred, Felix. Maryknoll, New York: Orbis Books, 1992. x, 199p ISBN 0-88344-794-0 LC 92-20801

SOCIOLOGY AND RELIGION- LATIN AMERICA
La Desigualdad Creciente Entre Sur y Norte [editorial]. *Christus* 58:2-3 F 1993

Tres maneras de articular fe y analisis. Morales, José. *Christus* 58:34-52 Ag 1993

SOCRATES
Diagrams: Socrates and Meno's slave. Giaquinto, Marcus. *IJPS* 1:81-97 Mr 1993

Malum Vitandum: the role of intentions in first-order morality. Sullivan, Thomas D, and Atkinson, Gary. *IJPS* 1:99-110 Mr 1993

SODANO, ANGELO, CARDINAL, 1927-
Bosnian crisis brings "right and duty" to intervene. *Tablet* 247:54 Ja 9 1993

Tourism must respect the earth. Calimé, Pierre. *OR(Eng)* 1309:9 S 29 1993

SOFTWARE COMPATIBILITY
Notes from a computer pusher: improving the worship aid. Bryson, Kathy. *Mod Lit* 20:13-16 Ag 1993

SOHM, RUDOLPH
Charism in the early church since Rudolph Sohm: an ecumenical challenge. Nardoni, Enrique. *TheolStds* 53:646-662 D 1992

SOLAR ENERGY INDUSTRY
Fuelwood: a crisis in the making. Porter, Neil. *Studies* 82:287-297 Aut 1993

SOLDIERS
Der Soldat, sein Gewissen und die Tradition. Dillmann, Robert. *Stimm Zeit* 211:65-68 Ja 1993

SOLIDARITY
An agenda for Europe: Cardinal Hume's address at Prague. *Tablet* 247:1177-1178 S 11 1993

The love called solidarity. Rohr, Richard, 1943-, and Martos, Joseph. *SocJust* 84:23-24 Ja-F 1993

A middle-class church for a working-class people. O'Hanlon, Gerard F. *Furrow* 44:3-11 Ja 1993

Proper and improper partially and the preferential option for the poor. Pope, Stephen J. *TheolStds* 54:242-271 Je 1993

A vision for the unity of human kind. Himes, Michael J, and Himes, Kenneth R. *ChrWorld* 236:203-211 S-O 1993

SOLIDARITY—RELIGIOUS ASPECTS
Challenges for the Christian layperson in the coming millenium [repr and tr fr *Mensaje*]. Etchegaray, Alberto. *LADOC* 23:12-16 Mr-Ap 1993

John Paul II, Pope, (1992-02-21) Itinera Apostolica (On apostolic journey speech to Diplomatic Corps in Senegal) [French]. John Paul II, Pope, 1920- (Karol Wojtyla) (elected 1978). *AAS* 85:153-157 F 3 1993*

John Paul II, Pope, (1993-04-15) Europe needs solidarity. John Paul II, Pope, 1920- (Karol Wojtyla) (elected 1978). *TPS* 38:270-274 S-O 1993*

Religious life's spirit of solidarity. Gray, Howard. *Origins* 23:173-176 Ag 12 1993

SOLIDARITY UNION (POLAND)
A parting of the ways. Luxmoore, Jonathan. *Register* 69:2 Jl 25 1993

SOLITUDE
Celibacy in another tradition. Woodgate, Michael. *Way Suppl* 77:106-112 Sum 1993

Retreat yourself to solitude. Finley, Mitchel B. *USCath* 58:37-38 F 1993

SOLOVYOV, VLADIMIR SERGEEVICH, 1853-1900
The Roman principle in the writings of Vladimir Solovyov. Matual, David. *Diakonia* 26 no 1:27-39 1993

SOMALIA
Somalia pressing policy issues. Collins, Carole. *Nat Cath Rep* 29:15 Ja 8 1993

Somalia strains Pax Christi. Bole, William. *Nat Cath Rep* 29:10 Ja 8 1993

Somalia: a land of nomads, anarchists and poets. Farrell, Michael J. *Nat Cath Rep* 29:16 Ja 22 1993

Update on Somalia. Hempel, Tricia. *OSV* 81:3 F 21 1993

SOMALIA—POLITICS AND GOVERNMENT
Attacks by warlord Aidid: the U.N. and U.S. respond. *St Anth* 101:39 O 1993

The limits of the UN [editorial]. *Tablet* 247:775 Je 19 1993

The other Somalia. Reyes-Manzo, Carlos. *Month* 26:5-8 Ja 1993

Restoring hope in Somalia [editorial]. *America* 168:3 Ja 2-9 1993

So far, so good as the food gets through. *Tablet* 247:177 F 6 1993

Support for armed intervention. *Tablet* 246:1579-1580 D 12 1992

Vested interests in Somalia. Stratton, Florence. *Cath Work* 60:3 Ja-F 1993

The view from Baidoa: Somalia is no Vietnam. Dodds, Bill. *OSV* 82:3 O 24 1993

SOMALIA—SOCIAL CONDITIONS
A baby named Luck [editorial]. *Comm* 119:3-4 D 18 1992

The other Somalia. Reyes-Manzo, Carlos. *Month* 26:5-8 Ja 1993

Planting the seeds of hope in Somalia. Gallagher, Joseph. *OSV* 82:3 My 30 1993

SOMALIS
Nagaa: the forgotten quest for peace in modern Kenya. Aguilar, Mario I. *Month* 26:183-187 My 1993

SON OF GOD
Gesù una personalità sorprendente [editorial]. Salvini, Gianpaolo, ed. *Civilta* 2:521-534 Je 19 1993

SONG OF DEBORAH
Caravans, Kenites, and Casus belli: Enmity and Alliance in the Song of Deborah. Schloen, J David. *CBQ* 55:18-38 Ja 1993

Candidates with difficulties in celibacy: discernment, admission, formation. Kiely, Bartholomew. *Seminarium* 33:107-118 Ja-Mr 1993

Challenges facing women religious in the evangelization of Africa. Nwagwu, Gerard M. *AFER* 34:146-157 Je 1992

The cloistered heart. Shuman, Nancy. *RRel* 52:68-85 Ja-F 1993

Communities of memory: the formative role of liturgy and catechesis. Gabriele, Edward F. *Emmanual* 49:396-401 S 1993

Converting the assembly. Pace, Charlotte. *Mod Lit* 20:10-13 F 1993

A developmental view of Salesian spirituality. Conn, Joann Wolski. *RRel* 52: 56-68 Ja-F 1993

Disiplines for Christian living. Ryan, Thomas. New Jersey: Paulist Press, 1993. x, 274p ISBN 0-8091-3380-6 LC 92-42596

Graphoanalysis: reading the word from within. Doyle, Mary E. *Sisters* 65:25-29 Ja 1993

Images of Jesus: ten invitations to intimacy. McBride, Alfred. Cincinnati: St Anthony Messenger Press, 1993. x, 239p ISBN 0-86716-180-9

Inner journeying: the hero's quest. Vanek, Elizabeth-Anne. *Emmanuel* 98: 158-163 Ap 1992

John Paul II, Pope (1991-05-04) Evangelization requires continual profound intellectual formation. John Paul II, Pope, 1920- (Karol Wojtyla) (elected 1978). *Con Life* 17 no 2:41-44 1992*

John Paul II, Pope, (1991-09-21) In continuing formation your vocation is dynamically renewed. John Paul II, Pope, 1920- (Karol Wojtyla) (elected 1978). *Con Life* 17 no 2:58-59 1992*

John Paul II, Pope, (1992-03-25) Pastores Daba Vobis Aspetti Psicologici Nella Formazione al celibato Sacerdotale. John Paul II, Pope, 1920- (Karol Wojtyla) (elected 1978). *Civilta* 3:359-379 S 4 1993*

Journal of a novice director. Svoboda, Melannie. *RRel* 52:602-609 Jl-Ag 1993

The journal of a soul. Johnson, Richard P. *Liguorian* 81:18-23 Ag 1993

Kleines credo fur Verunsicherte. Beinert, Wolfgang, et al. Freiburg: Herder, 1993. x, 144p ISBN 3-451-23245-6

Lettera agli arcivescovi e vescovi residenziali della chiesa universale. Rabitti, Paolo. *Notitiae* 28:714-731 N-D 1992

The living water will quench your thirst. Canada, Allie C. New York: Vantage Press, 1993. x, 74p ISBN 0-533-10338-x LC 92-90826

Parish diary: August. *Tablet* 247:1096 Ag 28 1993

Pastoral letter to religious educators. *Living Light* 29:68-80 Spr 1993

La "Pastores dabo vobis" alla luce del pensiero conciliare sul sacerdozio e sulla formazione sacerdotale (commentary on: *Pastores daba vobis*). Rypar, Francesco. *Seminarium* 32:530-549 O-D 1992

Pastores dabo vobis—reflections on a conference. Atherton, John. *Furrow* 44: 440-443 Jl-Ag 1993

Pedagogia formativa del celibato sacerdotale. Gianola, Pietro. *Seminarium* 33:60-76 Ja-Mr 1993

Philosophy and spirituality: cultivating a virtue. Dewan, Lawrence. *HPR* 94: 25-30 N 1993

Priests for our time. Danneels, Godfried, Cardinal, 1933-. *Furrow* 44:331-440 Je 1993*

Psychology as a human science and the human science of transcendent formation. Kaam, Adrian L Van, 1920-. *Stud Form Spir* 14:247-270 My 1993

Religion not dying out around the world. Greeley, Andrew Moran, 1928-. *Origins* 23:49-58 Je 10 1993

The "Spiritual excercises" and spiritual direction. Mohler, James Aylward. *Priest* 49:38-46 S 1993

A spiritual formation workbook: small group resources for nurturing Christian growth. Smith, James Bryan. New York: HarperSanFrancisco, 1993. 82p ISBN 0-06-066965 LC 92-36860

Spiritual formation: a Buddhist-Christian Dialogue [special issue]. *Stud Form Spir* 14:11-143 F 1993*

Spirituality in ecumenical perspective. Hinson, Glenn E. Louisville: Westminster, 1993. x, 160p ISBN 0-664-25385-7

Stepping out on faith. Spann, Shirley A. Boston: Deluxe Publications, 1992. 70p ISBN 0-9632239-0-9

Traditions of spiritual guidance: St John of the Cross: spiritual guide. Culligan, Kevin. *Way* 33:63-74 Ja 1993

The transfer and the RCIA: process and ritual. Hughes, Kathleen, and Quinn, Barbara. *RRel* 52:86-101 Ja-F 1993

The use of psychology as an aid to priestly formation. Costello, Timothy J. *Seminarium* 32:629-636 O-D 1992

Value archetypes: a multi-faceted spirituality. Dolan, Patrick. *Emmanuel* 99: 203-209 My 1993

When anomalies consistently appear at the interface between learning and experience we must act. Whelan, Michael. *Stud Form Spir* 14:271-285 My 1993

The wild man's journey: reflections on male spirituality. Rohr, Richard, 1943-, and Martos, Joseph. Cincinnati: St Anthony Messenger Press, 1993. ISBN 0-86716-1280

Your life story: self-discovery and beyond. O'Heron, Edward J. Cincinnati: St Anthony Messenger Press, 1992. x, 181p ISBN 0-86716-177-9

SPIRITUAL LIFE

Abandonment to divine providence. Caussade, Jean Pierre de, -1751. New York: Doubleday, 1975. x, 119p ISBN 0-385-24937-3 LC 74-2827

Adding up 75 years. Gallagher, Vera, 1917-. *RRel* 52:548-552 Jl-Ag 1993

Aelred, historian: two portraits in Plantagenet myth. Dutton, Marsha L. *Cist Stud* 28 no 2:113-144 1993

Befriending: a self-guided retreat for busy people. Payne, Joseph A. New Jersey: Paulist Press, 1992. x, 165p ISBN 0-8091-3354-7 LC 92-28398

Being "church". King, Sue. *Way Suppl* 75:62-66 Aut 1992

Blessings and challenges of the RCIA. Griffin, James A, Bp, 1934-. *Origins* 22:565-572 Ja 28 1993

Body and soul. Dunstan, Petà. *Priests & People* 7:323-326 Ag-S 1993

Born to shine. Costello, Andrew. *USCath* 58:38-40 Ag 1993

Broken, blessed. Legere, Thomas. *Emmanuel* 99:450-451 O 1993

Catherine of Siena—passion for the truth, compassion for humanity: selected spiritual writings. O'Driscoll, Mary, ed. New Rochelle: New City Press, 1993. 144p ISBN 1-56548-058-9 LC 93-2543

The changing state of spirituality: 1968 and 1993. Hamma, Robert M. *America* 169:8-10 N 27 1993

Chiara Lubich: life for unity. Lubich, Chiara. New York: New City Press, 1992. x, 181p ISBN 0-904287-45-91

The child and me. Magers, Stella. *Sisters* 65:299-300 Jl 1993

Christian resources for feminist spirituality. Carmody, Denise Lardner. *Stud Form Spir* 14:207-217 My 1993

The Christian's call to grow. Keenan, James F. *Church* 9:48-49 Spr 1993

The cloud of unknowing: learning to love Him alone. Cameron, Peter John. *Register* 69:1+ N 14 1993

Contemplative action: time in eternity according to Saint Bernard. Dumont, Charles. *Cist Stud* 28 no 2:145-159 1993

A corporate experience. Jeff, Gordon, and Nicholson, Dorothy. *Way Suppl* 75:30-38 Aut 1992

The cosmotheandric experience: emerging religious consciousness. Panikkar, Raimundo, 1918-. Maryknoll, New York: Orbis Books, 1993. x, 160p ISBN 0-88344-862-9 LC 92-46195

Cum Petro et sub Petro. Rego, Richard J. *HPR* 94:31-32+ N 1993

Damian of Molokai. Cavnar, Cindy. *New Cov* 22:25+ My 1993

Dark nights and hard days: a view of marital spirituality. McDonald, Patrick J, and McDonald, Claudette. *Spir Life* 39:150-159 Aut 1993

Deep river: the Christian vocation of the laity. Hayes, Diana L. *Spir Life* 39: 131-136 Aut 1993

Deepening our spiritual life. Hollings, Michael. *Priests & People* 7:87-90 Mr 1993

A descent into peace. Rushen, Karen. *Living Prayer* 26:13-16 N-D 1993

Disiplines for Christian living. Ryan, Thomas. New Jersey: Paulist Press, 1993. x, 274p ISBN 0-8091-3380-6 LC 92-42596

Don't waste religious education on the young. Fournier, Raymond. *USCath* 58:28-29 Ag 1993

The emergence of an American Catholic spirituality. Tetlow, Joseph Allen. *TheolDgst* 40:27-36 Spr 1993

Encountering God in the third Christian millennium: a spirituality of contradiction and mystery. Wicks, Robert J. *ChrWorld* 236:223-226 S-O 1993

Ernesto Balducci. Del Zanna, Lorenzo. *Civilta* 144:445-458 Mr 6 1993

Evangelical Kernels: a theological spirituality of the religious life. Billy, Dennis J. New York: Alba House, 1993. ISBN

Fede e amore nei *Lager* Nazisti. Marchesi, Giovanni. *Civilta* 2:144-152 Ap 17 1993

Five mothers who found time to be saints. Hermes, Joan Garvey. *USCath* 58:28-33 My 1993

The fount of spirituality. Ford, Paul, and Daurio, Janice. *Register* 69:1+ O 3 1993

Francis de Sales: finding God wherever you are. Power, Joseph F. New York: New City Press, 1993. 159p ISBN 1-56548-021-x LC 92-44973

Francisco de Vitoria y Bartolomé de Las Casas. Hernández, Ramón. *Cien Tom* 119:433-457 S-D 1992

Gerard Manley Hopkins: the incarnational work of priest and poet. Bouchard, Gary M. *ABenR* 44:115-124 Je 1993

The gospel according to Clifford. Ghezzi, Bert. *New Cov* 22:7-8 F 1993

Hermitage, a metaphor of life. O'Hea, Eileen P. *RRel* 52:503-506 Jl-Ag 1993

History: a school of humility and a source of hope. Maruca, Dominic. *Seminarium* 33:96-106 Ja-Mr 1993

Horizons of the charism of an institute: the "new" participation of the lay faithful. Secondin, Bruno. *Con Life* 17 no 2:83-97 1992

How to pray with Elizabeth of the trinity. Barres, John O. *Spir Life* 39:37-43 Spr 1993

How to stay sane in a crazy world [interview by M. Finley]. Leipert, Jack. *OSV* 82:13 O 17 1993

I have kept faith: Clare of Assisi. Karper, Karen. *RRel* 52:275-282 Mr-Ap 1993

If grain could talk. Marie, Virginia. *RRel* 52:731-734 S-O 1993

The Ignatian exercises in daily life: some problematic issues. Peloso, Barbara. *Way Suppl* 75:56-61 Aut 1992

In search of guidance: developing a conversational relationship with God. Willard, Dallas. New York: HarperSanFrancisco, 1993. x, 247p ISBN 0-06-069520-x LC 92-56406

Jesuits, Carmelites; warriors and mystics. Ford, Paul, and Daurio, Janice. *Register* 69:1+ O 31 1993

John Paul II, Pope, (1991-04-22) Renounce all in order to give all. John Paul II, Pope, 1920- (Karol Wojtyla) (elected 1978). *Con Life* 17 no 2:8-10 1992*

John Paul II, Pope, (1991-05-31) Harmonious unity between spiritual life and the apostolate. John Paul II, Pope, 1920- (Karol Wojtyla) (elected 1978). *Con Life* 17 no 2:33-34 1992*

John Paul II, Pope, (1991-06-03) The Church has a great need today of your spirit of sacrifice. John Paul II, Pope, 1920- (Karol Wojtyla) (elected 1978). *Con Life* 17 no 2:35-40 1992*

John Paul II, Pope, (1993-06-09) Eucharist [original in Italian]. John Paul II, Pope, 1920- (Karol Wojtyla) (elected 1978). *OR(Eng)* 1295:7 Je 16 1993*

John Paul II, Pope, (1993-09-01) Cooperation [Orig in Italian]. John Paul II, Pope, 1920- (Karol Wojtyla) (elected 1978). *OR(Eng)* 1306:11 S 8 1993*

Journey of love: God moving in our hearts and lives. Conroy, Maureen. Mahwah: The Paulist Press, 1993. 82p ISBN 0-8091-3413-6 LC 93-979

Lasting change. Pratt, Lonni Collins. *New Cov* 22:16-17 Ja 1993

Leadership for mission: a key agenda for the 1990s. HInojosa, Juan Lorenzo. *Health Prog* 74:62-63+ O 1993

Listening to the music of the spirit: the art of discernment. Lonsdale, David. Notre Dame: Ave Maria Press, 1993. x, 174p ISBN 08-7793-508-4

The little red house. Stasiak, Susan A. *Spir Life* 39:160-163 Aut 1993

The market place. McNair, J Frank. *Living Prayer* 26:26-27 N-D 1993

The market place. McNair, J Frank. *Living Prayer* 26:27-28 S-O 1993

May I love you, Lord: a modern Psalm. Savonarola, Girolamo. *RRel* 52:241-246 Mr-Ap 1993

Meeting the mystics. Giallanza, Joel. *Living Prayer* 26:3-9 Ja-F 1993

Mendicants keep it simple. Ford, Paul, and Daurio, Janice. *Register* 69:1+ O 24 1993

Metaphor for life. Costello, Andrew. *USCath* 58:39-41 F 1993

The metaphysics of higher spiritual conciousness. Sherrill, Julian F, Sr. New York: Vantage Press, 1992. x, 264p ISBN 0-533-10214-6 LC 92-90684

Eine Minute Unsinn. DeMello, Anthony, 1931-. Frieburg: Herder, 1993. x, 224p ISBN 3-451-23053-4

Near occasions of grace. Rohr, Richard, 1943-. New York: Orbis Books, 1993. x, 118p ISBN 0-88344-852-1 LC 92-33193

The new dictionary of Catholic spirituality. Downey, Michael, ed. Minnesota: The Order of St Benedict, 1993. x, 1083p ISBN 0-8146-5525-4 LC 92-40959

No less zeal: a spiritual guide for Catholic lay people. Morin, Douglas J. New York: Alba House, 1993. x, 142p ISBN 0-8189-0631-6 LC 92-34242

No salvation outside the world? praying in place. Sheldrake, Philip. *Way Suppl* 75:3-11 Aut 1992

'Oh God, help!' a conversation about prayer with Richard Foster [interview by Mitch Finley for New Covenant (periodical)]. Foster, Richard J. *New Cov* 22:9-13 F 1993

Ordinary time: cycles in marriage, faith, and renewal. Mairs, Nancy, 1943-. Boston: Beacon Press, 1993. x, 238p ISBN 0-8070-7056-4 LC 92-40421

Parish directed retreat reflections: *Non MultaSed Multum*. Ganley, Natalie T. *Way Suppl* 75:76-84 Aut 1992

The path back. Ash, Lucy. *Liguorian* 81:12-16 Jl 1993

The path to hope: fragments from a theologian's journey. Boff, Leonardo. Maryknoll, New York: Orbis Books, 1993. x, 134p ISBN 0-88344-815-7 LC 92-35823

PB, SV, HB and Bal. Blue, Lionel. *Tablet* 247:880 Jl 10 1993

Perché non si crede? La risposta di Dostoevskij [editorial]. Salvini, Gianpaolo, ed. *Civiltà* 2:209-216 My 1 1993

Place and retreat. Stoney, Brian. *Way Suppl* 75:12-19 Aut 1992

The power is the Lord's. Foley, James S. *HPR* 94:24-28 O 1993

Prayer: discouragement and its antidotes. Hassel, David. *Sisters* 65:20-24 Ja 1993

Praying our pain. McGrane, Janice. *Spir Life* 32:87-90 Sum 1993

A priest's prayer life. Bertolucci, John. *New Cov* 23:6 Ag 1993

Radical optimism: rooting ourselves in reality. Bruteau, Beatrice, 1930-. New York: The Crossroad Publishing Company, 1993. x, 119p ISBN 0-8245-1354 LC 92-39444

Reel power: spiritual growth through film. Sinetar, Marsha. Missouri: Triumph Books, 1993. x, 179p ISBN 0-89243-529-1 LC 92-44676

Religious life's spirit of solidarity. Gray, Howard. *Origins* 23:173-176 Ag 12 1993

Reporting religion: holiness in the ordinary. Moses, Paul. *America* 168:12-15 My 1 1993

Restless for him. Ford, Paul, and Daurio, Janice. *Register* 69:1+ S 26 1993

Resurrection love-life. Dent, Barbara. Mahwah: Paulist, 1993. x, 189p ISBN 0-8091-3405-1 LC 93-11006

Retreat yourself to solitude. Finley, Mitchel B. *USCath* 58:37-38 F 1993

Richard Rohr: Illuminations of his life and work. Ebert, Andreas, and Brockman, Patricia C, eds. New York: The Crossroad Publishing Company, 1993. x, 200p ISBN 0-8245-1270-7 LC 93-20130

Robert Coles: listening to stories of God in the lives of children. McKenzie, Paula A. *Living Light* 29:65-72 Aut 1992

A rose is a rose is a rose. Wyneken, Cherise. *Spir Life* 39:47-48 Spr 1993

Rules for prayer. Paulsell, William O. New York: Paulist Press, 1993. 151p ISBN 0-8091-3410-1 LC 93-4387

The sacred world of the Christian: sensed in faith. Wagner, Mary Anthony. Minnesota: The Order of St Benedict, 1993. v, 147p ISBN 0-8146-2102-3 LC 92-40431

A search for God in story and time. Elwood, J. Murray. *America* 169:10-12+ O 16 1993

A solitary life. Ristine, John D. *New Cov* 22:21-22 Mr 1993

Soul making and life's second half. Brennan, Anne, and Brewi, Janice. *RRel* 52:220-225 Mr-Ap 1993

Spiritual fatigue. Martin, George. *New Cov* 23:34 O 1993

Spiritual fitness: everyday exercises for body and soul. Donnelly, Doris. San Francisco: HarperSanFrancisco, 1993. x, 178p ISBN 00-6061-899-x LC 92-53923

The spiritual life of children. Thurston, Anne. *Doctr Life* 42:594-599 D 1992

A spiritual tool. Kerrigan, Ruth, and Harkulich, Joan T. *Health Prog* 74:46-49 My 1993

A spirituality for the chronically ill. Russell, Kenneth C. *Spir Life* 32:79-86 Sum 1993

A spirituality of aging. Moga, Michael D. *RRel* 52:213-219 Mr-Ap 1993

Stealing for lent. Costello, Andrew. *USCath* 58:38-40 Mr 1993

Super powers of the mind: transform your life through the twelve powers. Jones, Cody L. Commerce Twp: Quinten Publishing, 1993. 195p ISBN 1-878040-07-03 LC 92-34528

The sweetness of God. Posset, Franz. *ABenR* 44:143-178 Je 1993

Tales of the city of God. Valles, Carlos G. Chicago: Loyola University Press, 1993. x, 254p ISBN 0-8294-0750-2 LC 93-8938

El taller de mi. Giralt, Joan J. Barcelona: Ser Editorial, 1993. x, 315p ISBN 84-8860-401-7

Thomas Aquinas, preacher and friend. Fatula, Mary Ann. Minnesota: The Liturgical Press, 1993. x, 313p ISBN 0-8146-5031-7 LC 92-27552

Thomas Merton: the vigilance of desire. Albert, John. *Word Sp* 14:105-117 1992

Through detachment to union. Millette, Adele M. *Living Prayer* 26:22-26 Jl-Ag 1993

Traditions of spiritual guidance: John Ruusbroec as spiritual guide. Wisemann, James A. *Way* 33:148-155 Ap 1993

Understanding secular institutes. *Origins* 23:410-416 N 18 1993

La 'Vita' de María Magdalena. Moreno Garrido, Jaime. *Teol Vida* 34 no 1-2:119-143 1993

Vulnerability and strength: the paradox of spiritual maturity. Mancuso, Theresa. *Living Prayer* 26:6-10 N-D 1993

Waiting for a gift from the sea. Foley, Sharon. *Sisters* 65:301-303 Jl 1993

A warm, moist, salty God: women journeying towards wisdom. Gateley, Edwina. Trabuco Canyon: Source Books, 1993. x, 107p ISBN 0-940147-26-2 LC 93-11919

We are home: a spirituality of the environment. Jung, Shannon. New Jersey: Paulist Press, 1993. x, 170p ISBN 0-8091-3364-4 LC 92-37876

What is new age spirituality? Woods, Richard. *Way* 33:176-188 Jl 1993

What is Opus Dei? [interview]. Hirtle, Walter. *Can Cath Rev* 11:6-8 S 1993

What trouble is. Dunne, Tad. *RRel* 52:532-540 Jl-Ag 1993

Who killed Stutz Bearcat?: stories of finding faith after loss. Ingram, Kristen Johnson. San Jose: Resource Publications, 1993. 90p ISBN 0-89390-264-0 LC 93-23775

Who says soul doesn't sell? Costello, Gerald M, 1931-. *USCath* 58:48-51 Ag 1993

Woman to woman: an anthology of women's spiritualities. Zagano, Phyllis. Collegeville: Liturgical, 1993. x, 115p ISBN 0-8146-5025-2 LC 93-18865

The work our era demands of us: the recovery of lay leadership. Sellner, Edward Cletus. *Listening* 28:65-80 Wint 1993

You can know God: Christian spirituality for daily living. Gustin, Marilyn Norquist. Washington, D C: Liguori Publications, 1993. x, 212p ISBN 0-89243-479-1 LC 92-74594

SPIRITUAL LIFE—BIBLICAL TEACHINGS

Ezekiel and the covenant of friendship. Sloan, Ian B. *Bib Th Bul* 22:149-154 Wint 1992

SPIRITUAL LIFE—ORTHODOX EASTERN CHURCH

Probing Russian Orthodox spirituality. Vinh, Alphonse. *New Oxford Rev* 60:17-20 My 1993

SPIRITUAL LIFE—0600-1500

Major works/Margaret Ebner. Hindsley, Leonard P, ed. Mahwah: Paulist, 1993. x, 209p ISBN 0-8091-0462-8 LC 92-46650

SPIRITUAL LIFE (BUDDHISM)

Healing breath: Zen spirituality for a wounded earth. Habito, Ruben L.F. Maryknoll: Orbis, 1993. x, 166p ISBN 0-88344-919-0 LC 93-5125

Persons—objects or observers? (A dialogue with Buddhism). Barnes, Michael R. *Way Suppl* 76:98-108 Spr 1993

SPIRITUAL LIFE (JUDAISM)

Dialog, nicht Proselytenmacherei. Henrix, Hans Hermann. *Stimm Zeit* 211:679-690 O 1993

Knock, knock, wink, wink. Blue, Lionel. *Tablet* 247:752 Je 1993

SPONG, JOHN SHELBY, BP, 1931-

Revisionist history of virgin birth a misconception [review article *A Bishop Rethinks the Birth of Jesus* by J Spong]. Ruether, Rosemary Radford. *Nat Cath Rep* 29:27 Ja 15 1993

SPORTS

Is God in the grandstands? Auer, Jim. *Liguorian* 81:38-43 Jl 1993

Sports: shaping our stories and our myths. Fisher, Doug. *ChrWorld* 236:282-285 N-D 1993

SPRING, RICHARD, 1950-

Change in Ireland, maybe. McRedmond, Louis. *Tablet* 247:9+ Ja 23 1993

ST EDWARD UNIVERSITY (AUSTIN, TX)

Texas university aids migrants [photos]. Vidulich, Dorothy. *Nat Cath Rep* 30:16-17 O 29 1993

ST JOSEPH'S CHURCH (LOWELL, MA)

Police remove protesters, but battle for parish continues. Bole, William. *Nat Cath Rep* 29:3 Jl 16 1993

ST JOSEPH'S SEMINARY (NY)

The history of St. Joseph's Seminary, New York. Shelley, Thomas J. Westminster: Christian Classics, 1993. x, 480p ISBN 0-87061-198-4

ST MARY'S SEMINARY (BALTIMORE, MD)

Bicentennial hopes for America's first seminary. Leavitt, Robert F. *US Cath Hist* 11:119-122 Wint 1993

ST MUNGO MUSEUM OF RELIGIOUS LIFE AND ART (GLASGOW, SCOTLAND)

The art of exhibiting the sacred. Arthur, Chris. *Month* 26:281-289 Jl 1993

ST PATRICK'S SEMINARY (MENLO PARK CA)

When Menlo became a bastion of Catholicism. Coleman, Gerlad D. *US Cath Hist* 11:123-125 Wint 1993

ST SUSANNA CHURCH (ROME, ITALY)

Americans regain St Susanna Church. O'Grady, Desmond. *OSV* 81:3 F 28 1993

STALIN, IOSIF, 1879-1953

Die Unterdrückung der Ukrainischen Unierten Kirche unter Stalin und das Moskauer Patriarchat. Suttner, Ernst Chr. *Stimm Zeit* 211:560-512 Ag 1993

STANFIELD J RON, 1945-

A review of the troops: social economics in the twentieth century. Waters, William R. *RSocEcon* 51:262-286 Aut 1993

STARK, FREYA MADELINE, 1893-

Freya and friendship. Hodgkin, E C. *Tablet* 247:11 Ja 2 1993

STATE, THE

Just war, pacifism and humanitarian intervention. Himes, Kenneth R. *America* 169:10-15+ Ag 14-21 1993

Mangel an Erziehung? Bleistein, Roman, 1928-. *Stimm Zeit* 211:1-2 Ja 1993

The state as already withered away. Cowles, David T, Jr. *SocJust* 84:25-28 Ja-F 1993

STATE, THE—PHILOSOPHY

A Christian take on politics. Kreeft, Peter John, 1937. *Register* 69:1+ S 19 1993

STATE AND RELIGION

Abortion, gay rights and the social contract. Carlin, David Robert, Jr, 1938-. *America* 168:6-10 F 27 1993

Working with Christ: the Catechism's social teaching. Schall, James Vincent, 1928-. *Crisis* 11:27-30 Je 1993*

STATE AND SOCIETY

A conversation with Rocco Buttiglione [interview by D Cross]. Buttiglione, Rocco. *Crisis* 10:26-32 D 1992

Mangel an Erziehung? Bleistein, Roman, 1928-. *Stimm Zeit* 211:1-2 Ja 1993

STATESMEN—BIOGRAPHIES

Catholic makers of America: biographical sketches of Catholic statesmen and political thinkers in America's first century, 1776-1876. Krason, Stephen M. Front Royal, Virginia: Christendom Press, 1993. 260p ISBN 0-931888-44-2

STATICS AND DYNAMICS (SOCIAL SCIENCES)

Does the market create preferred preferences? George, David. *RSocEcon* 51:323-346 Aut 1993

STATIONS OF THE CROSS

Mount Royal players: Montreal's living stations. Brown, John J. *Liguorian* 81:20-23 Ap 1993

New Stations of the Cross? Martin, George. *CDgst* 57:53-55 Mr 1993

Praying the stations. Beilman, J Brian. *ReligTJ* 27:15 Mr 1993

Readers' theater for Lent. Gardiner, Thomas J. *Mod Lit* 20:18-20 Mr 1993

STEIN, EDITH, 1891-1942
Edith Stein's conversion: how a Jewish philosopher became a Catholic saint. Dougherty, Jude P, 1930-. *Crisis* 10:39-43 D 1992
Edith Stein. Cavnar, Cindy. *New Cov* 22:24 F 1993
Edith Stein: essential differences. McAlister, Linda Lopez. *PhilosTod* 37:70-77 Spr 1993
Etre et temps et théologie. Berranger, Oliver De. *Gregorianum* 74 no 3:543-561 1993
Politics and mystery: the integration of Judaism and Christianity in Edith Stein. Stein, Waltraut J H. *Spir Life* 32:104-110 Sum 1993
Sex and gender differentiation in Hildegard of Bingen and Edith Stein. Allen, Prudence. *Communio* 20:389-414 Sum 1993

STEINER, GEORGE
George Steiner and the theology of culture. Ward, Graham. *New Blckfrs* 74:98-105 F 1993
Tragedy as subclause: George Steiner's dialogue with Donald MacKinnon. Ward, Graham. *Heythrop* 34:274-287 Jl 1993

STEINER, RUDOLF, 1861-1925
Waldorf education: an innovative tradition. Harrington, Sheila. *Momentum* 24:17-21 F-Mr 1993

STEPFAMILIES
Secrets of successful stepfamilies. Fry, Patricia L, and Mize, Judith. *ST Anth* 101:10-15 Jl 1993

STEPPE, MARY
Always the poor. Dodds, Bill. *New Cov* 22:21-24 Je 1993

STEREOTYPE (PSYCHOLOGY)
Fathers' business: Catholic priests as Canadian writers see them. Kelly, Darlene. *Can Cath Rev* 11:21-29 Ja 1993
La nouvelle distinction stéréotypes et perceptions respectives des chrétiens et des athées. Traube, Patrick. *Lumen* 47:377-390 D 1992
Women in the Church and in Latin American culture [tr and excerpts fr *Boletin CELAM*]. *Cath Int* 4:210-214 My 1993

STEWARDSHIP, CHRISTIAN
Do I really have to sell all I have? Wojcicki, Ed. *USCath* 58:32-33 Je 1993
No more bingo on the Bayou. Feister, John Bookser. *St Anth* 100:34-35 F 1993
Pennies for heaven. Novak, Francis A. *OSV* 82:12 Je 20 1993
Pennies for heaven: Catholic underachievers. Harris, Joseph Claude. *Comm* 120:8-9 Ap 9 1993
Stewardship also requires greenbacks, critic says. Vidulich, Dorothy. *Nat Cath Rep* 29:9 Ja 8 1993
Stewardship and the disposition of reverence. Vandergrift, Nicki Verploegen. *Stud Form Spir* 14:219-231 My 1993
Stewardship: we reap what we sow [editorial]. Feister, John Bookser. *St Anth* 100:57 Ja 1993
Synod convoked for Charleston Diocese. Thompson, David, Bp. *Origins* 22:509+ Ja 7 1993

STIEGLITZ, RICHARD
Haitian adoption leads to priest's ouster [photos]. Lemmon, Michele. *Nat Cath Rep* 29:10 O 15 1993

STIGMATIZATION
Il fenomeno delle stimmate. Mucci, Giandomenico. *Civilta* 2:217-226 My 1 1993

STIRNER, MAX
L'antigiuridismo di Max Stirner. Sbardella, Agapito. *Civilta* 2:248-251 My 1 1993

STOCK, FRANZ, 1904-1948
And more than a prophet. Hanley, Boniface. *Stud Form Spir* 14:161-174 My 1993

STOCKHOLDERS
Don't turn back the clock on corporate responsibility [editorial]. Feister, John Bookser. *St Anth* 100:33 My 1993

STOFFMAN, JUDY
Epistolary advice. Coren, Michael. *Can Cath Rev* 11:5-6 Je 1993

STOJAR, ANDREW
A good shepherd [Andrew Stojar]. Schaefer, Vernon J. *HPR* 93:75-76 Ag-S 1993

STONE, ROBERT, 1937-
The moral vision of Robert Stone. Finn, James. *Comm* 120:9-14 N 5 1993

STORYTELLING
A search for God in story and time. Elwood, J. Murray. *America* 169:10-12+ O 16 1993
Stringing pearls: making heirlooms of family stories. Kindig, Eileen Silva. *St Anth* 101:10-15 O 1993

STORYTELLING—RELIGIOUS ASPECTS
How storytelling heals. Baldwin, Robert F. *New Cov* 23:11-13 Ag 1993
The rock that is higher: story as truth. L'Engle, Madeleine. Wheaton, Illinois: H Shaw Publishers, 1993. 296p ISBN 0-87788-726-8 LC 92-24204

STRAUSS, LEO, 1899-1973
On Leo Strauss's understanding of the natural law theory of Thomas Aquinas. Kries, Douglas. *Thomist* 57:215-232 Ap 1993

STRAVINSKAS, PETER
Dialogue [interview by P Mullen]. Stravinskas, Peter. *Register* 69:1+ Ja 24 1993

STREET CHILDREN- BRAZIL
Mass for the slain street children. O'Gorman, Frances. *Tablet* 247:1082-1083 Ag 21 1993
Street children slaughtered in the night. Pimentel-Pinto, Francis. *Tablet* 247:990 Jl 31 1993

STREET CHILDREN- COLOMBIA
Hero of the sewers. Traylen, Maryanne. *Tablet* 247:1290 O 9 1993

STRESS (PSYCHOLOGY)
Adolescent suicide: a minsterial response. McCarty, Robert J. *Momentum* 24:61-65 Ap-My 1993
Getting a grip on stress and conflict. Kinast, Robert L. *Catechist* 27:27-29 S 1993

Praying in times of stress. Neuman, Matthias. *Living Prayer* 26:29-31 S-O 1993
The spiritual healing of post-traumatic stress disorder at the Menlo Park Veteran's Hospital. Jiménez, Manuel J, Jr. *Stud Form Spir* 14:175-187 My 1993
Students under pressure. Forrester, David. *Tablet* 247:712 Je 5 1993

STRIKES
Lost strike? No such thing. Mastrodonato, David. *Cath Work* 60:7 Ja-F 1993

STRUCTURALISM (LITERARY ANALYSIS)
After historical criticism, what? Trends in biblical interpretation and ecumenical, interfaith dialogues. Reumann, John Henry Paul, 1927-. *JEcumen Stds* 29:55-86 Wint 1992

STUDENT-FACULTY RELATIONSHIPS
The camouflaged at-risk student: white and wealthy. Metz, Elinor D. *Momentum* 24:40-44 Ap-My 1993
Children in crisis in the classroom. Exline, Joseph. *Momentum* 24:12-16 Ap-My 1993
Miss Brodie on the prairies or what a novel says about teaching [fr *The voice*]. Kelly, Darlene. *Can Cath Rev* 11:19-22 O 1993
Teachers love their students. Kealey, Robert J. *Tod Cath Teach* 27:6 O 1993

STUDENT ACTIVITIES
A religion club in the public high school? Marthaler, Berard L, 1927-. *Living Light* 29:11-18 Spr 1993

STUDENTS
The use of memory [excerpt fr the book; 2 parts]. Burns, Tom G. *Tablet* 247:330+ Mr 6; 336-337 Mr 13 1993

STUDENTS—CONDUCT OF LIFE
Can higher education foster moral development? Heft, James. *Origins* 22:557-565 Ja 28 1993

STUDENTS—RELIGIOUS LIFE
Can higher education foster moral development? Heft, James. *Origins* 22:557-565 Ja 28 1993
Looking for higher education on campus [interview by W Bole]. Hunt, Michael J. *OSV* 82:5 Ag 29 1993

STUDENTS—REMINISCENCES
Stonyhurst remembered. Burns, Jimmy. *Tablet* 247:648-649 My 22 1993

SUAREZ, FRANCISCO, 1548-1617
An analysis of the use of rights language in pre-modern Catholic social thought. Brady, Bernard V. *Thomist* 57:97-121 Ja 1993

SUBEV CHRISTOFOR, BP
A church at a standoff. Corley, Felix. *OSV* 81:21 Ja 31 1993

SUBSIDIARITY
An African American Catholic rite. Hayes, Diana L. *Living Light* 29:35-48 Wint 1992

SUBSTANCE (PHILOSOPHY)
Platon, l'École de Tübingen et Giovanni Reale. Rizzerio, Laura. *RPhil Louvain* 91:90-110 F 1993

SUBSTANCE ABUSE
Darryl Colbert kept his promise. Zimmermann, Mark. *CDgst* 57:24-29 Ja 1993
The Drug-Free Workplace Act of 1988. Tichy, George J, II. *CLawyer* 34 no 4:363-371 1993
Is someone you love addicted? [condensed fr *Our Family* Ap 1992]. Johnson, Jan. *CDgst* 57:118-123 My 1993
Reconciliation in 12 (not so easy) steps. Roll, Susan K. *Doctr Life* 43:69-76 F 1993
Recovering connections. Grant, Richard D, Jr, and Miller, Andrea Wells. New York: HarperCollins, 1992. x, 205p ISBN 0-06-063386-7 LC 91-70707
A story of addiction and co-addiction. Kraft, William F. *RRel* 52:454-460 My-Je 1993

SUCCESS
Everything I needed to know about success, I learned in the Bible (and so can you!). Briley, Richard Gaylord. New Hampshire: The publisher-In-The-Glen, 1993. x, 144p ISBN 1-882988-05-1

SUCHOCKA, HANNA
Polish visitor. *Tablet* 247:338 Mr 13 1993

SUDAN
Sudan cries for help [repr fr *Catholic International* D 1-14 1992]. *Register* 69:1+ Ja 10 1993
Sudanese bishops decry human-rights abuses. Collins, Carole. *Nat Cath Rep* 29:11 N 6 1992

SUDAN—POLITICS AND GOVERNMENT
Bishops plead as civil war goes on. *Tablet* 247:763 Je 1993
Cold war forces called to clean up Sudan mess [editorial]. *Nat Cath Rep* 30:24 N 19 1993
A deadly silence: faint voices on Sudan. Jordan, Patrick. *Comm* 120:4-5 My 7 1993
Respect human rights. *Cath Int* 4:237-238 My 1993
Sudan opposition debates war. Collins, Carole. *Nat Cath Rep* 30:9 N 19 1993
Sudan: a grim tragedy. Gassis, Macram Max, Bp, 1938-. *Cath Int* 4:236-237 My 1993
War-torn Sudan waits for the Pope. Eppink, Alfons. *Tablet* 247:160-161 F 6 1993

SUDAN—RELIGION
Dialogue [interview by P Mullen]. Gassis, Macram Max, Bp, 1938-. *Register* 69:1+ Je 13 1993
The Pope becomes a voice for the voiceless. Bragotti, Joseph. *Tablet* 247:252 F 20 1993

SUDAN—SOCIAL CONDITIONS
"Faith, hope—but please, no charity": a visit to the Sudan. Chitnis, Paul. *Month* 26:328-330 Ag 1993
John Paul II, Pope, (1993-02-10) Civil War [English text]. John Paul II, Pope, 1920- (Karol Wojtyla) (elected 1978). *Origins* 22:617-618 F 18 1993*
John Paul II, Pope, (1993-02-10) Innocent victims. John Paul II, Pope, 1920- (Karol Wojtyla) (elected 1978). *TPS* 38:221-225 Jl-Ag 1993*
John Paul II, Pope, (1993-03-10) Innocent victims [Orig English]. John Paul II, Pope, 1920- (Karol Wojtyla) (elected 1978). *Origins* 22:618-620 F 18 1993*

There are no safe corridors for the people of Sudan. Humphrey, Marj. *Cath Work* 60:5 Je-Jl 1993

SUENENS, LEO JOZEF, CARDINAL, 1904-
Behind the scenes. *Tablet* 247:945 Jl 24 1993
The memoirs of Cardinal Leo Jozef Suenens. Murphy, Francis Xavier, 1914-. *America* 168:17-18 Je 5-12 1993

SUFFERING—BIBLICAL TEACHING
Dance for joy. Cuzzola, Theresa. *Emmanuel* 99:80-84 Mr 1993

SUFFERING—RELIGIOUS ASPECTS
Agony as advertisement. Arthur, Chris. *Month* 26:97-104 Mr 1993
Broken [excerpt fr *The life of the beloved*]. Nouwen, Henri Josef Machiel, 1932-. *Living Prayer* 26:3-7 Mr-Ap 1993
Christ the fireman. Cassidy, Sheila. *Tablet* 247:456+ Ap 10-17 1993
Dying—and see, we are alive. Fitzpatrick, Michael. *RRel* 52:719-730 S-O 1993
Finding growth through chronic pain. Jacquet, Lou. *OSV* 81:5 Ja 24 1993
From victim to Victor: a biblical guide for turning hurting into healing. Martinez, Yvonne. San Diego: Recovery Publications, 1993. x, 127p ISBN 0-941405-24-9 LC 93-13946
Gratuitous suffering. Trotta, Carmen. *Cath Work* 60:8 Ja-F 1993
A handbook for coping. Gaddy, Welton C. Louisville: Westminster, 1993. x, 128p ISBN 0-664-25458-6
How to handle trouble. Carmody, John Tully. New York: Doubleday, 1993. x, 226p ISBN 0-385-47120-3 LC 93-16848
John Paul II, Pope, (1993-01-01) Lent 1993 [English tr]. John Paul II, Pope, 1920- (Karol Wojtyla) (elected 1978). *Origins* 22:524 Ja 7 1993*
The liberation of creation. Sepulveda, Juan. *LADOC* 23:23-27 My-Je 1993
Of heartwounds and hope. Kokolus, Cait. *Living Prayer* 26:13-16 S-O 1993
Religion and the moral meaning of euthanasia. Campbell, Courtney S. *Linacre* 59:15-28 N 1992
Thoughts from death and life. Gallagher, Vera, 1917-. *RRel* 52:238-240 Mr-Ap 1993
To share in the priesthood of suffering: a biblical reflection on the death of Our Lord. Rosica, Thomas M. *Can Cath Rev* 11:14-16 Ap 1993
Why a redeemer? Why a cross? Billy, Dennis J. *Living Prayer* 26:8-13 Mr-Ap 1993

SUFISM
Muslim mystics. *Tablet* 247:206-207 F 13 1993

SUICIDE
Assisted suicide and legalized euthanasia. Garvais, Marcel. *Doctr Life* 43:308-309 My-Je 1993
Assisted suicide is not the answer [editorial]. Feister, John Bookser. *St Anth* 101:21 O 1993
Care of the dying: a Catholic perspective [4 parts]. *Health Prog* 74:34-38+ Mr; 16-21+ Ap; 22-26+ My; 46-54 Je 1993*
Clergy suicides tip of depression iceberg. Unsworth, Tim. *Nat Cath Rep* 29:13-14 O 1 1993
Confronting depression. Campion, Owen F. *OSV* 82:10 My 16 1993
Does compassion include Euthanasia? Hooyman, Nancy W. *Health Prog* 74:44-47 Mr 1993
A Father's Day requiem. Finley, Mitchel B. *America* 168:4-5 Je 19-26 1993
Slip-sliding away [editorial]. *OSV* 82:2 My 16 1993
Students under pressure. Forrester, David. *Tablet* 247:712 Je 5 1993
The tragic death of Eva Green. Kenny, Mary, 1936-. *Tablet* 247:158 F 6 1993
U.S., Canada ask: is dying a constitutional right? Dodds, Bill. *OSV* 82:3 N 14 1993

SUICIDE—RELIGIOUS ASPECTS
Suicide in the Bible. Lenzen, Verena. *TheolDgst* 40:37-42 Spr 1993

SULIVAN, JEAN, 1913-1980
The Christian novelist in an age of transition-a case study. Maher, Eamon. *Studies* 82:140-147 Sum 1993
Faith on the margins: the example of Jean Sulivan. Maher, Eamon. *Doctr Life* 43:147-155 Mr 1993

SULPICIANS
The Americanization of St Sulpice; context and charism. Kauffman, Christopher J. *US Cath Hist* 11:21-34 Wint 1993

SUNDAY LEGISLATION
Blue-light specials driving blue laws out of business. Bole, William. *OSV* 82:21 N 28 1993

SUNDAY LEGISLATION- GREAT BRITAIN
Moral victory for Sunday Bill. *Tablet* 247:665 My 22 1993

SUPERNATURAL
The Christianization of modern philosophy according to Maurice Blondel. Grys, James Le. *TheolStds* 54:455-484 S 1993

SUPPLY AND DEMAND
Does the market create preferred preferences? George, David. *RSocEcon* 51:323-346 Aut 1993

SURGERY
Journey with my daughter. Maitland, Sara, 1950-. *Tablet* 247:1065-1066 Ag 21 1993

SUSTAINABLE DEVELOPMENT
Ecological sustainability at Bamberton [fr the *Bamberton News*]. Dauncey, Guy. *Teilhard Rev* 28:22-24 Sum 1993

SVIDERCOSCHI, GIAN FRANCO
Lettera a un amico ebreo. Rulli, Giovanni. *Civilta* 3:47-50 Jl 3 1993

SWAGGART, JIMMY
The gods of televangelism. Peck, Janice. Cresskill, New Jersey: Hampton Press, 1993. x, 271p ISBN 1-88130-365-9 LC 92-32476

SWEARING
Talking dirty. Finley, Mitchel B. *OSV* 82:6 S 26 1993

SWEENEY, DAVID F, -1993
Sweeney, David F, -1993 [obit]. Lynch, Cyprian J. *CHist* 79:598-600 Jl 1993

SYMBOLISM
Une nouvelle approche de la philosophie d'Ernst Cassirer. Lofts, Steve. *RPhil Louvain* 90:523-538 N 1992

SYMBOLISM, CHRISTIAN
African independent churches and religious life. O'Reilly, Martin. *AFER* 35:217-221 Ag 1993

The blind beggar of Jericho [2 parts]. LaVerdiere, Eugene Armand, 1936-. *Emmanuel* 99:86-89+ Mr; 158-166 Ap 1993
Converting the artist. Woeger, William. *Mod Lit* 20:10-11 S 1993
Gender and the priesthood of Christ: a theological reflection. Ashley, Benedict M. *Thomist* 57:343-379 Jl 1993
The little red house. Stasiak, Susan A. *Spir Life* 39:160-163 Aut 1993
A pelican on the altar. Ulmer, Mari W. *Sisters* 65:290-292 Jl 1993
Religious symbols belong in your home. Tuohy, Patrice J. *USCath* 58:19-24 Ap 1993
Sacred symbol sacred ceremony. Gustin, Marilyn Norquist. *Liguorian* 81:12-17 F 1993
The temple: symbol central to Biblical theology. Meyer, Ben F. *Gregorianum* 74 no 2:223-240 1993
When there is no priest. Dubourd, Nancy A. *Mod Lit* 20:14-15 F 1993

SYMBOLISM, JEWISH
The challenge of Auschwitz today. Krajewski, Stanislaw. *SIDIC* 26 no 1:21-22 1993

SYMBOLISM IN LITERATURE
'I saw a Kingfisher': grace and ruin in Golding's the spire. Yeager, D M. *Horizons (CTS)* 20:44-66 Spr 1993

SYMBOLISM IN RELIGION
American Catholics and the Joseph Campbell phenomenon. Dinges, William D. *America* 168:12-14+ F 20 1993
Deep river: the Christian vocation of the laity. Hayes, Diana L. *Spir Life* 39:131-136 Aut 1993
The Eucharist and African culture. Okoye, Chukwuma J. *AFER* 34:272-292 O 1992
The forest and the trees. Morgan, Winifred. *Sisters* 65:12-19 Ja 1993
Not just an art: spiritual significance of iconography. Angell, Jeannette L, and Squires, Susan E. *Spir Life* 32:67-72 Sum 1993
The roots of the Jesse Tree. Zyromski, Page. *Catechist* 27:21-22 N-D 1993
Words, symbols, experience, and the naming of the divine. Shinn, Larry Dwight, 1942-. *JEcumen Stds* 29:418-431 Sum-Aut 1992

SYMBOLISM IN RELIGION—HISTORY
Geschichte der religiösen Ideen: 5 vols. Eliade, Mircea, 1907-1985. Freiburg: Herder, 1993. x, 2200p ISBN 3-451-04200-2

SYMPATHY
Victims without tears: democracy and the politics of pity. Amato, Joseph Anthony, 1938-. *Crisis* 11:29-31 F 1993

SYMPOSIUM OF EPISCOPAL CONFERENCES OF AFRICA AND MADAGASCAR (SECAM)
West Africans hold congress on applying Church's social doctrine. *OR(Eng)* 1302:8 Ag 11 1993

SYNAGOGUE COUNCIL OF AMERICA
The common good: old idea, new urgency. Lynch, Robert, et al. *Origins* 23:81+ Je 24 1993

SYNCRETISM (RELIGION)
'Syncretistic religiosity': the significance of the tautology. Carlson, Jeffrey. *JEcumen Stds* 29:24-34 Wint 1992
Theological trends in Africa. Chepkwony, Adam K A. *AFER* 34:2-17 F 1992
US Latinos and religion [interview by J S Torrens]. Maduro, Otto. *America* 169:16-19 Ag 14-21 1993

SYNCRETISM (RELIGION)- SOUTH KOREA
Être catholique en Corée du Sud: la mulitple appartenance religieuse. Senécal, Bernard. *Lumen* 48:207-216 Je 1993

SYNERGISM
On the synergism of gender and class exploitation: theory and practice under Islamic Rule. Parvin, Manoucher. *RSocEcon* 51:201-216 Sum 1993

SYNGE, J M, 1871-1909
The rushing up of Synge's buried fire. Krause, David. *Studies* 82:298-310 Aut 1993

SYNOD OF BISHOPS
African synod in Rome sends wrong signal [editorial]. *Nat Cath Rep* 29:24 F 26 1993
The Church's teaching mission: some aspects of the normative role of episcopal conferences. Green, Thomas J. *Stud Can* 27 no 1:23-57 1993
Katholishe Kirche in der DDR zwischen Staat und Gesellschaft. Haese, Ute. *Stimm Zeit* 211:241-254 Ap 1993
Quibus enim communis est cura, communis etiam debet esse oratio [editorial]. *Notitiae* 29:169-172 Ap 1993
Religious life at the Synod of Bishops on Europe. Cabra, Pier Giordana. *Con Life* 17 no 2:135-147 1992
The synod of consecrated life. McDonough, Elizabeth. *RRel* 52:626-621 Jl-Ag 1993
De synodo diocesana. Beyer, Jean. *Periodica* 81 no 3-4:381-423 1992
Understanding secular institutes. *Origins* 23:410-416 N 18 1993

SYNOD OF BISHOPS, SPECIAL ASSEMBLY FOR AFRICA
Church input said to be key to African synod. Collins, Carole. *Nat Cath Rep* 29:15 Jl 30 1993
Holding African Synod in Rome miffs Africans. Collins, Carole. *Nat Cath Rep* 29:11 Je 18 1993
Out of repression, life. Burke, Greg. *Register* 69:3 Jl 25 1993
Pope names officials for synod. Hebblethwaite, Peter, 1930-. *Nat Cath Rep* 29:15 Jl 30 1993

SYNTHESIZER (MUSICAL INSTRUMENT)
Buying a church synthesizer. Gagliano, Joseph R, Jr. *Past Mus* 17:47 Ag-S 1993
Is it time to buy a church synthesizer? Gagliano, Joseph R, Jr. *Past Mus* 17:43-44 Ap-My 1993

SYNTHESIZER MUSIC
Is it time to buy a church synthesizer? Gagliano, Joseph R, Jr. *Past Mus* 17:43-44 Ap-My 1993

SYRIAN ORTHODOX CHURCH (NON-CHALCEDONIAN)
The catholicity of the local church in the patriarchate of Antioch after Chalcedon. Halleux, André de. *Jurist* 52 no 1:109-129 1992
Response to De Halleux and Van Esbroeck. Wickham, Lionel. *Jurist* 52 no 1:130-137 1992

SYSTEMS THEORY
Logica, Plenguatge i matematica. Graell i Deniel, Ferran. Barcelona: Anthropos, 1993. x, 377p ISBN 84-7658-399-0

SZOKA, EDMUND CASMIR, CARDINAL, 1927-
An evangelical who discovered the real presence [interview by B Dodds]. Shea, Mark P. OSV 82:7 Je 27 1993

T

TAIZE COMMUNITY
The mission of Taizé [repr fr Etudes]. Lena, Marguerite. Month 26:46-52 F 1993
The secret of Taizé [photos]. Emile, Brother, and John, Brother. Priests & People 7:278-282 Jl 1993
The Taizé Community: fifty years of prayer and action. Hicks, Douglas A. JEcumen Stds 29:202-214 Spr 1992

TALAMONI, LUIGI, 1848-1926
Congregation for the Causes of Saints (1992-07-11) Decree on the heroic virtues. Congregation for the Causes of Saints. TPS 38:37-38 Ja-F 1993*
Congregation for the Causes of Saints (1992-07-11) Luigi Talamoni. Congregation for the Causes of Saints. AAS 85:191-194 F 3 1993*

TAMAR, DAUGHTER OF DAVID
Kinship in 2 Samuel 13, Propp, William H. CBQ 55:39-53 Ja 1993

TANZANIA—RELIGION
Toward an African Christianity: inculturation applied. Hillman, Eugene. New York: Paulist Press, 1993. x, 101p ISBN 0-8091-3381-4 LC 92-39526

TANZANIA—SOCIAL CONDITIONS
Tanzanian women peasants: an ethical and theological reflection. Giblin, Marie. AFER 34:29-43 F 1992

TAOISM
Whiteheadian creativity, the Tao, and the Thomistic act of being. Bracken, Joseph A. Pacifica 6:179-188 Je 1993

TAVENER, JOHN, 1944-
The year of John Tavener: contemporary composer and Christian mystic. Feeney, Joseph J. America 168:15-16 Ap 10 1993

TAVRIS, CAROLE
Good people get angry, too. Mallowe, Mike. USCath 58:14-21 My 1993

TAX CREDITS
Panel: pro education tax credits. Feuerherd, Peter. Register 69:1+ Jl 4 1993

TAX EXEMPTIONS
Challenges to tax exemption growing. Connell, Richard E. Health Prog 74:58-59 Jl-Ag 1993

TAXATION
Now that April's here. Hynes, Brian. Cath Work 60:4 Mr-Ap 1993
Now, here's a dollar source! [liquor]. Jacobson, Michael. Register 69:2 O 3 1993
Reflections and points for discussion: Mammon vs God. James, Lawrence. Living Light 29:38-39 Aut 1992
A theological approach toward taxation. Nash, James L. Living Light 29:27-37 Aut 1992

TAXATION—RELIGIOUS ASPECTS
Just taxation in Catholic social ethics and the Florio plan. Gorrell, Paul J. SocJust 84:90-92 My-Je 1993

TAXATION- UNITED STATES
America's silent depression: a challenge to social economics. Peterson, Wallace C, 1921-. RSocEcon 51:2-13 Spr 1993

TEACHERS
Friend and teacher: Allan Bloom, 1930-1992. Fortin, Ernest L, 1923-. Crisis 11:38-40 Ja 1993
Sexuality education—forward or backward? Miller, Patricia F. Momentum 24:49-52 F-Mr 1993
Teaching as a vocation in the public school. Whitehead, Sharon. Momentum 24:22-25 F-Mr 1993

TEACHERS—CERTIFICATION
Teachers: identifying the best and the brightest. Shapiro, Barbara C. Momentum 24:29-32 S-O 1993

TEACHERS—POLITICAL ACTIVITY
A test too far. Pring, Richard. Tablet 247:647 My 22 1993

TEACHERS—RATING OF
Teachers: identifying the best and the brightest. Shapiro, Barbara C. Momentum 24:29-32 S-O 1993

TEACHERS, TRAINING OF
Great teachers of faith. Glavich, Kathleen. ReligTJ 26:15-16 Ja 1993
How to learn to teach. Pring, Richard. Tablet 247:918 Jl 17 1993
Warden for a week. O'Malley, William J, 1931-. Living Light 29:60-67 Spr 1993

TEACHERS IN LITERATURE
Miss Brodie on the prairies or what a novel says about teaching [fr The voice]. Kelly, Darlene. Can Cath Rev 11:19-22 O 1993

TEACHING
Discipline: more goals than rules. Svoboda, Melannie. ReligTJ 27:4-6 O 1993
An invitation to dance: towards a spirituality of education. Stoecklin, Carol. Living Light 29:58-64 Aut 1992
Learning compassion. Barnes, Michael R. Month 26:(I) Ag 1993
Looking back with love. Bowman, Peg. ReligTJ 27:13 Ap-My 1993
On teaching. Schall, James Vincent, 1928-. Crisis 11:49-50 S 1993
Seven common mistakes—and how to fix them. Svoboda, Melannie. Catechist 27:65-66 S 1993

TEACHING—METHODOLOGY
Mind forming and manductio in Aquinas. George, Marie I. Thomist 57:201-213 Ap 1993
Rebuilding broken lives. Sorensen, Kathleen M. Momentum 24:20-25 Ap-My 1993

TECHNOLOGY
The final decade? McMahon, John. Can Cath Rev 11:51-53 Ja 1993
The future now. McMahon, John. Can Cath Rev 11:38-39 My 1993
Technology and the education renaissance. Milone, Michael. Tod Cath Teach 26:14-16+ Mr 1993
The wave of the future. Prizer, John. Register 69:2 Je 11 1993

TECHNOLOGY—MORAL AND ETHICAL ASPECTS
The hermeneutics of the technological world: the Heidegger-Heisenberg dispute. Pöggeler, Otto. IJPS 1:21-48 Mr 1993

TECHNOLOGY—RELIGIOUS ASPECTS
Aetatis Novae: pastoral instruction on social communication [a summary]. Faniran, J O. AFER 34:364-375 D 1992
Hellfire and lighting rods: liberating science, technology, and religion. Ferré, Frederick. Maryknoll, New York: Orbis Books, 1993. 92-39488 ISBN 0-88344-856-4 LC 92-39488

TECHNOLOGY—RISK ASSESSMENT
Ethik in der Risikogesellschaft. Höhn, Hans-Joachim. Stimm Zeit 211:95-104 F 1993

TEILHARD DE CHARDIN, PIERRE, 1881-1955
The cosmic Christ and world religions. Dhavamony, Mariasusai. StudiaM 42:179-225 1993
Decision. McMahon, Donal. Furrow 44:359-363 Je 1993
Evolution today. Leadbetter, Frank. Teilhard Rev 28:27 Sum 1993
Father Pierre Teilhard de Chardin and I [excerpt fr The story of Peking Man]. Lampo, Jia, and Weiwen, Huang. Teilhard Rev 27:82-84 Wint 1992
Maximus the Confessor: a precursor to Teilhard? Pomerai, David de. Teilhard Rev 28:16-18 Sum 1993
Quo Vadis? or evolution and consciousness. Cronin, Francis R. Teilhard Rev 27:69-82 Wint 1992
Teilhard and ecological spirituality. Sage, Alan. Teilhard Rev 28:11-14 Spr 1993
Teilhard today. Stikker, Allerd. Teilhard Rev 28:23-27 Spr 1993
Undergraduates discover Pierre Teilhard De Chardin. Ballweg, John M. Horizons (CTS) 19:277-287 Fall 1992

TELECOMMUNICATION IN EDUCATION
New initiatives for a new year. Zukowski, Angela Ann. Momentum 24:71 S-O 1993

TELEPHONE MINISTRY
Parish diary: June. Tablet 247:812 Je 26 1993

TELEVISION
The cathedral of business: the fountainhead of values in America today. Lear, Norman, 1922-. New Oxford Rev 60:6-13 Ap 1993
Hollywood and violence. Austin, Ronald. Register 69:3 Mr 21 1993
Let the viewer beware: the video camera does lie. Collum, Danny Duncan. Nat Cath Rep 29:20 Mr 19 1993
A nation of standups: starring in our own scripts. McConnell, Frank, 1942-. Comm 120:20-21 F 26 1993
Process and product. McMahon, John. Can Cath Rev 11:38-39 O 1993
The roots of tv violence. Rocchio, Vincent. Register 69:3 Ag 15 1993
Why murder in May brings good things to life for networks. Collum, Danny Duncan. Nat Cath Rep 29:18 Je 18 1993

TELEVISION—INFLUENCE
Broadcast and be saved. Woodrow, Alain. Tablet 247:9-10 Ja 2 1993

TELEVISION—RELIGIOUS ASPECTS
Italy's newest television star: the Pope. O'Grady, Desmond. OSV 82:6 My 16 1993

TELEVISION—SOCIAL ASPECTS
TV's iconic imagery in a secular society. Goethals, Gregor T. New Theol Rev 6:40-53 F 1993

TELEVISION- GERMANY
Die Messe im Fernsehen als Medienspektakel und Geschft. Rolfes, Helmuth. Stimm Zeit 211:331-342 My 1993

TELEVISION AND CHILDREN
Children and television. Zukowski, Angela Ann. ChrWorld 236:258-264 N-D 1993
Kids and television. Dodds, Bill. New Cov 22:18+ My 1993
TV sweeps and stats. Wallace, James A, 1944-. Liguorian 81:51 Ag 1993
Warning: TV violence is hazardous to our children [editorial]. Dangel, Mary Jo. St Anth 101:17 N 1993

TELEVISION AND FAMILY
Media education at home. Wallace, James A, 1944-. Liguorian 81:49 S 1993

TELEVISION AUTHORSHIP
Writing for the screen [interview by J G Deedy, 1923-]. Hume, Edward. Critic 47:16-25 Sum 1993

TELEVISION BROADCASTING OF NEWS
CNN does it again. Stahel, Thomas H, 1938-. America 168:16-17 My 1 1993

TELEVISION CRITICISM
CBS news anchors adrift in shallow waters. Collum, Danny Duncan. Nat Cath Rep 29:19 Jl 16 1993
Coming this fall, the same old violent television shows. Breig, James. OSV 82:3 S 26 1993
Enough is enough!. Mullen, Peter. Register 69:1+ S 5 1993
The final decade? McMahon, John. Can Cath Rev 11:51-53 Ja 1993
Holidays. McMahon, John. Can Cath Rev 11:38-39 F 1993
How good is good TV? Hart, D G. Crisis 11:12-13 S 1993
It's not hell, just Limbaugh: excellence in bombast. McConnell, Frank, 1942-. Comm 120:20+ Je 4 1993
Manufacturing reality. McMahon, John. Can Cath Rev 11:38-39 Ap 1993
Media get complaints on coverage. Mullen, Peter. Register 69:1+ Ap 11 1993
New Emmys and new season. Stahel, Thomas H, 1938-. America 169:24-25 O 16 1993
Of new programs and other matters, like well, you know. Stahel, Thomas H, 1938-. America 168:24-25 F 20 1993
Smart, hip and real: Bochco's "NYPD Blue". McConnell, Frank, 1942-. Comm 120:20-21 O 8 1993
Television as service: asking the right questions. Stahel, Thomas H, 1938-. America 169:22-23 Jl 3-10 1993
TV mothers and fathers. Wallace, James A, 1944-. Liguorian 81:45 My 1993

Warning: television may endanger your health!. Feuerherd, Peter. *Register* 69:1+ Jl 25 1993

When the spark is gone. Hynes, Joseph. *Comm* 120:14 My 21 1993

The yellowing of "60 Minutes" [editorial]. *America* 168:4 Ap 3 1993

TELEVISION PROGRAMS

Celibacy in fashion. *Tablet* 247:1040-1041 Ag 14 1993

TEMPERANCE

The "vagabond friar": Father Mathew's difficulties with the Irish bishops, 1840-1856. Quinn, John F. *CHist* 78:542-556 O 1992

TEMPLARS

The templar order: a failed ideal? Menache, Sophia. *CHist* 79:1-21 Ja 1993

TEMPTATION

Tempted? God may be knocking!. Cameron, Peter John. *Register* 69:1+ Mr 28 1993

TEN COMMANDMENTS

Delitti contro il sesto comandamento. Paolis, Velasio De. *Periodica* 82 no 2: 293-316 1993

Ethics in the everyday practice of law. Paprocki, Thomas J. *CLawyer* 35 no 2:169-180 1993

The fifth commandment. Wuerl, Donald William, Bp, 1941-. *Columbia* 73:19 Ag 1993

The fourth commandment. Wuerl, Donald William, Bp, 1941-. *Columbia* 73: 15 Jl 1993

The second commandment in the New Testament: your yes is yes, your no is no. Carrón, Julián. *Communio* 20:5-25 Spr 1993

The sixth commandment. Wuerl, Donald William, Bp, 1941-. *Columbia* 73:13 S 1993

The third commandment. Wuerl, Donald William, Bp, 1941-. *Columbia* 73:21 Je 1993

Was heibt Gottes Gebot? Fuchs, Josef. *Stimm Zeit* 211:435-442 Jl 1993

Who can utter the Name of God?—From the holiness of his name to the seriousness of all words. Sales, Michel. *Communio* 20:26-48 Spr 1993

TENSE (LOGIC)

The metaphysical aspect of tenses in Proclus. Plass, Paul. *IPQ* 33:143-151 Je 1993

TERMINAL CARE

Decision tree. Meeker, Tobias. *Health Prog* 74:48-51 Mr 1993

Does compassion include Euthanasia? Hooyman, Nancy W. *Health Prog* 74: 44-47 Mr 1993

Helping the hurting: getting inside another's circle of pain. Pratt, Lonni Collins. *New Cov* 22:15-16 Ap 1993

The holiness of death. Coffey, Kathy. *OSV* 81:6 Ap 11 1993

Hospice: death with dignity. Repp, Debbie M. *Liguorian* 81:24-31 Je 1993

In hospice work, music is our great ally. Burns, Sharon. *Past Mus* 17:11-13 F-Mr 1993

My father's left hand: a death he did not deserve. Gorman, Geraldine. *Comm* 120:16+ Jl 16 1993

O paciente terminal nos códigos brasileiros de ética médica. Martin, Leonard M. *REB* 53:72-86 Mr 1993

Pour une éthique de la fin de la vie. Geets, Claude. *Supplement* 184:89-96 Mr-Ap 1993

What comes after assisted suicide and legalized euthanasia? Gervais, Marcel, Abp. *Origins* 22:573+ F 4 1993

TERMINAL CARE—PSYCHOLOGICAL ASPECTS

La maladie comme expérience et comme condition. Geets, Claude. *Supplement* 184:33-55 Mr-Ap 1993

TERMINAL CARE—RELIGIOUS ASPECTS

Care of the dying. Cassidy, Sheila. *Tablet* 247:430-431 Ap 3 1993

Care of the dying: a Catholic perspective [4 parts]. *Health Prog* 74:34-38+ Mr; 16-21+ Ap; 22-26+ My; 46-54 Je 1993*

Midwife for souls: spiritual care for the dying. Magno, Josefina B. Bosston: St Paul Books & Media, 1993. 111p ISBN 0-8198-4769-0 LC 93-32153

TERMINALLY ILL

Dragon at the gate. Gibson, Gloria J. *America* 168:12-14 My 22, 1993

A private anguish. Richards, Robin. *Tablet* 247:566 My 8 1993

TERRAVADA BUDDHISM

Perfection without God: a view from the Pāli Canon. Katz, Nathan. *Stud Form Spir* 14:11-22 F 1993

TERRORISM

Church leaders voice disgust and contempt at IRA bombing. *Tablet* 247:416 Mr 27 1993

Religion a key to terrorist. Pevtzow, Lisa. *Register* 69:1+ Ap 18 1993

TERRORISM—PHILOSOPHY

Of lingering eyes and talking things: Adorno and Deleuze on philosophy since Auschwitz. Toolan, David S. *PhilosTod* 37:227-246 Aut 1993

TERTIARY CAPUCHIN SISTERS OF THE HOLY FAMILY

Congregation for the Causes of Saints (1992-06-13) Decree on the heroic virtues. Congregation for the Causes of Saints. *TPS* 38:19-20 Ja-F 1993*

TERTULLIAN

Hacia la doctrina marcionítica de la redención. Órbe, Antonio. *Gregorianum* 74 No 1:45-74 1993

TESTS AND MEASUREMENTS IN EDUCATION

Educational standards and public policy. McGovern, John E. *Momentum* 24: 47 S-O 1993

Whose standards? Whose measure? [editorial]. McNamee, Catherine. *Momentum* 24:3-4 S-O 1993

TETTAMANZI, DIONIGI

XXVI congresso nazionale ceciliano (Bologna, 16-20 settembre 1992). Zaccaria, Sante. *Notitiae* 28: 736-740 N-D 1992

TEXTBOOKS

The future of textbooks in Catholic Schools. *Tod Cath Teach* 26:25+ Ja 1993

Textbooks that teach truth. Daly, Mary. *Register* 69:5 Jl 25 1993

THANKSGIVING DAY

Make it a Thanksgiving year!. Gonzalez, Paula. *Tod Parish* 25:36-37 N-D 1993

Through the ages: a Thanksgiving Day play. Gerth, Mary E. *Tod Cath Teach* 27:21-22 N-D 1993

Unhappy Thanksgiving. Ganss, Karl, and Fuller, Kathleen. *Tod Parish* 25: 10-11 N-D 1993

THANT, U, 1909-1974

Spokesmen for the spiritual dimension of the world order. Muller, Robert. *Sisters* 65:202-205 My 1993

THE LOCAL CHURCH AND CATHOLICITY COLLOQUIUM (APRIL 2-7, 1991: SALAMANCA, SPAIN)

The local church and catholicity. Legrand, Hervé. *Jurist* 52 no 1:7-586 1992*

THEOLOGIANS

The magisterium and morality. Spohn, William C. *TheolStds* 54:95-111 Mr 1993

[Whatever terror may strike the hearts]. Cunningham, Lawrence S, 1935-. *Comm* 120:11-12 O 22 1993

THEOLOGIANS—BIOGRAPHY

The beauty of Balthasar. Nemoianu, Virgil, 1940-. *Crisis* 11:42-46 Ap 1993

Giant among theologians. Bowden, John. *Tablet* 247:364-365 Mr 20 1993

Karl Barth: his life from letters and autobiographical texts. Busch, Eberhard. Grand Rapids: Eerdmans, 1993. 600p ISBN 0-8028-0708-9

THEOLOGIANS, AFRO-AMERICAN

A change is coming. Hayes, Diana L. *USCath* 58:38-40 S 1993

THEOLOGIANS, BELGIUM

Schillebeeckx. Kennedy, Philip. Collegeville: Liturgical, 1993. x, 144p ISBN 0-8146-5502-5

THEOLOGIANS, CATHOLIC

At the service of the church: Henri de Lubac reflects on the circumstances that occasioned his writings. Lubac, Henri De, Cardinal. San Francisco: Ignatius Press, 1993. x, 411p ISBN 08-9870-414-6

Cyril of Jerusalem as a postliberal theologian. Cummings, Owen F. *Worship* 67:155-164 Mr 1993

In the Catholic tradition: G K Chesterton 1874-1936. Johnson, Luke Timothy, 1943-. *Priests & People* 7:67-69 F 1993

Karl May in katholischen Verlagswesen während des Kulturkampfs. Hoffmann, Fernand. *Stimm Zeit* 211:177-186 Mr 1993

Mascall, Eric Lionel, 1905-1993 [obit]. Smythe, Harry. *Tablet* 247:256-257 F 20 1993

An observation on Robert Lauder's review of G A McCool, SJ [reply to "On being or not being a Thomist," 55:301-319 by R Lauder]. Cessario, Romanus. *Thomist* 56:701-710 O 1992

El Opus Dei en la Iglesia. Rodriguez, Pedro. Madrid: Ediciones Rialp, 1993. x, 346p ISBN 84-321-2969-0

The wit and whimsy of Karl Rahner [por]. Finley, Mitchel B. *OSV* 82:6 N 7 1993

THEOLOGIANS, FRENCH

Paradoxe et mystère logique théologique chez Henri de Lubac. Chantraine, Georges. *NRT* 115:543-559 Jl-Ag 1993

THEOLOGIANS, GERMAN

Joseph Bernhart. Köhler, Oskar. *Stimm Zeit* 211:376-384 Je 1993

Karl Adam's blind spot. *Tablet* 247:272 F 27 1993

"Saiser Dieu en son vestiaire" L'articulation théologique du sens chez Maître Eckhart. Malherbe, Jean-François. *Laval Theol Phil* 49:201-213 Je 1993

THEOLOGIANS, SPANISH

Juan de Zumarraga y su "Regla Cristiana breve". Alejos-Grau, Carmen Jose. Vitoria: Gobierno Vasco, 1993. x, 242p ISBN 84-457-0129-0

THEOLOGIANS, WOMEN

Catholic feminist theologians on Catholic women in the Church. Graff, Ann O'Hara. *New Theol Rev* 6:6-18 My 1993

"I listen, I suspect, later I make poetry" [interview by S Rojas; tr fr *Pastoral Popular*]. Gebara, Ivone. *LADOC* 24:10-15 S-O 1993

Miles to go [editorial]. Pawlikowski, John T. *New Theol Rev* 6:3-5 My 1993

On the one hand, women and ordination—time for dialogue? St Leger, Moya Frenz. *Priests & People* 6:327-329 Ag-S 1992

THEOLOGIANS, WOMEN—CONGRESSES

Women in theology. Hebblethwaite, Margaret, 1951-. *Tablet* 247:1115 Ag 28 1993

THEOLOGIANS, WOMEN- UNITED STATES

To be black, Catholic, and female. Hayes, Diana L. *New Theol Rev* 6:55-62 My 1993

THEOLOGICAL EDUCATION- AFRICA

Minor seminaries: the need to animate them. Ciampa, Pio. *AFER* 34:124-126 Ap 1992

THEOLOGICAL EDUCATION- UNITED STATES

The diocesan seminary and the community of faith: reflections from the American experience [photos]. White, Joseph M. *US Cath Hist* 11:1-20 Wint 1993

THEOLOGICAL SEMINARIES

I seminaristi provenienti dalle nuove realtà aggregative (commentary: *Pastores dabo vobis*). Camisasca, Massimo. *Seminarium* 32:622-628 O-D 1992

Minor seminaries: the need to animate them. Ciampa, Pio. *AFER* 34:124-126 Ap 1992

De seminario dioecesano recentiora quaedam quaesita. Beyer, Jean. *Periodica* 82 no 1:55-93 1993

Il seminario maggiore (commentary: *Pastores dabo vobis*). Coletti, Diego. *Seminarium* 32:561-574 O-D 1992

Seminary on a shoestring. Johnson, Grove. *Tablet* 247:914-915 Jl 17 1993

Willing to serve [interview by C Lund and J Sprague]. Gaughan, Norbert Felix, Bp, 1921-. *Critic* 47:46-56 Sum 1993

THEOLOGICAL SEMINARIES—CURRICULUM

Amitiés sacerdotales et célibat. Gaidon, Maurice. *Seminarium* 33:77-87 Ja-Mr 1993

Candidates with difficulties in celibacy: discernment, admission, formation. Kiely, Bartholomew. *Seminarium* 33:107-118 Ja-Mr 1993

Focus on sexual abuse. Higgins, Michael. *Tablet* 247:194-196 F 13 1993

The use of psychology as an aid to priestly formation. Costello, Timothy J. *Seminarium* 32:629-636 O-D 1992

THEOLOGICAL SEMINARIES—FIELD WORK

Field education for Catholic rural life. Balke, Victor H, Bp, 1931-. *America* 168:8-11 My 15 1993

THEOLOGICAL SEMINARIES—INTELLECTUAL LIFE
Seminary trains students for life shaped by word and sacrament. Hillenbrand, Karl. *OR(Eng)* 1305:3-4 S 1 1993*

THEOLOGICAL SEMINARIES- BRAZIL
Seminário Nacional de Pastoral Litúrgica. *REB* 53:420-427 Je 1993

THEOLOGICAL SEMINARIES- LATIN AMERICA
Los seminarios Iberoamericanos en el período Hispano-Portugues. Cardenas, P Eduardo. *Seminarium* 32:369-403 Jl-S 1992

THEOLOGICAL SEMINARIES- UNITED STATES
The history of St. Joseph's Seminary, New York. Shelley, Thomas J. Westminster: Christian Classics, 1993. x, 480p ISBN 0-87061-198-4
Quigley seminary. Unsworth, Tim. *Nat Cath Rep* 30:17 O 22 1993

THEOLOGICAL SEMINARIES, CATHOLIC- UNITED STATES
The Americanization of St Sulpice; context and charism. Kauffman, Christopher J. *US Cath Hist* 11:21-34 Wint 1993
Bicentennial hopes for America's first seminary. Leavitt, Robert F. *US Cath Hist* 11:119-122 Wint 1993
Dialogue [interview by Peter Mullen]. Wister, Robert J. *Register* 69:1+ F 28 1993
The diocesan seminary and the community of faith: reflections from the American experience [photos]. White, Joseph M. *US Cath Hist* 11:1-20 Wint 1993
When Menlo became a bastion of Catholicism. Coleman, Gerlad D. *US Cath Hist* 11:123-125 Wint 1993

THEOLOGY
Between foundationalism and nihilism: is phronēsis the via media for theology? Guarino, Thomas. *TheolStds* 54:37-54 Mr 1993
Bultmann. Ferguson, David. Collegeville: The Liturgical Press, 1992. x, 154p ISBN 0-8146-5037-6
The changing state of spirituality: 1968 and 1993. Hamma, Robert M. *America* 169:8-10 N 27 1993
Church unity rooted in Eucharist. *OR(Eng)* 1298:4+ Jl 7 1993*
Church, state and theology in the European Community. Nolan, Michael. *Studies* 82:148-159 Sum 1993
The city: center of early Christian life. Osiek, Carolyn. *BibleT* 31:17-21 Ja 1993
Commitment, theology, and the dilemma of religious studies at the state university. Hann, Robert R. *Horizons (CTS)* 19:263-276 Fall 1992
Consciousness and transcedence: the theology of Eric Voegelin. Morrisey, Michael P. Notre Dame: University of Notre Dame Press, 1994. x, 384p ISBN 0-268-00793-4 LC 92-50159
The content of faith. Lehmann, Karl, Bp, 1936-, et al, eds. New York: The Crossroad Publishing Company, 1993. x, 668p ISBN 0-8245-1221-9 LC 92-27765
The distortion of Christian ritual. Darragh, Neil. *Pacifica* 6:21-47 F 1993
Down the arches of the years, down the labyrinthine ways [interview by J G Deedy, 1923-]. Beeching, Paul Q. *Critic* 47:2-13 Spr 1993
The genesis of God: a theological genealogy. Altizer, Thomas J J. Louisville: John Knox, 1993. x, 208p ISBN 0-664-21996-9
Habermas e la teologia. Brena, Gian Luigi. *Civilta* 3:51-54 Jl 3 1993
How to relate theology and Canon Law. Orsy, Ladislas, 1921-. *Origins* 22:549-552 Ja 21 1993
The human person: contemporary theology and the exercises. Callahan, Annice. *Way Suppl* 76:85-97 Spr 1993
Humanity in God: on reading Karl Barth in relation to mystical theology. McIntosh, Mark A. *Heythrop* 34:22-40 Ja 1993
Intellectuals don't need God and other modern myths. McGrath, Alister E. Grand Rapids: Zondervan Publishing House, 1993. x, 256p ISBN 0-310-59091-4
Julian's way: a practical commentary on Julian of Norwich. Bradley, Ritamary. London: HarperCollins Religious, 1992. x, 231p ISBN 0-00-599275-3
Law, change and revolution: a theological note on the finality of capitalist resurgence. Moss, David. *New Blckfrs* 73:614-622 D 1992
Liturgy and life: ten things I learned about the Mass. Richstatter, Thomas, 1939-. *Catechist* 27:42-47 N-D 1993
My work: in retrospect. Balthasar, Hans Urs Von, 1905-1988. San Francisco: Ignatius Press, 1993. ISBN 0-89870-435-9
Post-holocaust church theology. Williamson, Clark M. Louisville: John Knox, 1993. x, 352p ISBN 0-664-254-54-3
El retorno a la experiencis en teología: Ernst Troeltsch redivivo. García Prada, José María. *Cien Tom* 119:585-592 S-D 1992
Sacramental theology liturgical theology primary theology. Skublics, Ernest. *Can Cath Rev* 11:36-37 My 1993
Soziologie und Theologie in Nachbarschaft. Köhler, Oskar. *Stimm Zeit* 211:210-212 Mr 1993
"Speciesism": a challenge to theology. Cronin, Kieran. *Doctr Life* 43:357-362 Jl-Ag 1993
Symbols in Rahner: a note on translation. Liberatore, Albert. *Louvain Stds* 18:145-158 Sum 1993
Toward an ecologically informed theology. Peeters, Denise. *TheolDgst* 40:113-118 Sum 1993
Unity through theology. Hayes, Doris K. *Priests & People* 7:27-29 Ja 1993
What if there were no theology? Skublics, Ernest. *Can Cath Rev* 11:37-38 Je 1993
A wholesome agnosticism and Christianity's coming dialogue with the world religions. Thornhill, John. *Pacifica* 6:265-277 O 1993
Why Heidegger's Godot might not be worth the wait. Bruin, John. *Mod Schlmn* 70:143-152 Ja 1993

THEOLOGY—CONTROVERSIES
Las Casas und seine Gegner. Delgado, Mariano. *Stimm Zeit* 210:841-854 D 1992
In Drei Personen—der Trinitarische Schüsselbegriff "Person" in den Entwürfen Jürgen Moltmanns und Walter Kaspers. Radlbeck-Ossmann, Regina. *Catholica* 47:38-51 1993

THEOLOGY—HISTORY
The body of God: an ecological theology. McFague, Sallie. Minneapolis: Fortress Press, 1993. x, 274p ISBN 0-8006 LC 93-6584
Costly giving: on Jean-Luc Marion's theology of the gift. Moss, David. *New Blckfrs* 74:393-399 S 1993

Juan de Zumarraga y su "Regla Cristiana breve". Alejos-Grau, Carmen Jose. Vitoria: Gobierno Vasco, 1993. x, 242p ISBN 84-457-0129-0
Paradoxe et mystère logique théologique chez Henri de Lubac. Chantraine, Georges. *NRT* 115:543-559 Jl-Ag 1993
Universelles Vülkerrecht. García-Mateno, Rogelio. *Stimm Zeit* 210:831-840 D 1992

THEOLOGY—HUMOR
Wild creatures discovering the theological plain. Johnson, Ken, and Coe, John. Grand Rapids: Zondervan Publishing House, 1993. x, 112p ISBN 0-310-57681-4

THEOLOGY—METHODOLOGY
Deux paradigmes pour penser le rapport de la théologie aux sciences humaines: herméneutique et narratologie. Fortin-Melkevik, Anne. *Laval Theol Phil* 49:223-231 Je 1993
Metaphorical theology. Begley, John. *Pacifica* 6:49-60 F 1993
À propos d'une note romaine sur le livre d'André Guindon. Couture, Denise. *Laval Theol Phil* 49:321-329 Je 1993
Zur Klassifikation religionstheologischer Modelle. Schmidt-Leukel, Perry. *Catholica* 47 no 3:163-183 1993

THEOLOGY—STUDY
John Cassian: student of Augustine. Ramsey, Boniface. *Cist Stud* 28:5-15 1993
En relisant l'amour des lettres et le désir de Dieu. Dumont, Camille. *NRT* 114:889-895 N-D 1992

THEOLOGY—TERMINOLOGY
Le discours théologique et son objet: perspectives neo-pragmatistes. Viau, Marcel. *Laval Theol Phil* 49:233-248 Je 1993

THEOLOGY—0030-0060
Gateway to paradise: Basil the Great. Davies, Oliver, ed. New Rochelle, New York: New City Press, 1992. 125p ISBN 1-56548-0023 LC 91-34259

THEOLOGY—0600-1500
Faith seeking understanding: mediaeval exegesis. Boyle, John F. *Can Cath Rev* 11:9-13 Jl-Ag 1993

THEOLOGY—1500-
The reformation: too many assumptions? Marius, Richard, 1933-. *Critic* 47:31-42 Wint 1992

THEOLOGY—1900-
The college student's introduction to theology. Rausch, Thomas P, ed. Collegeville: Liturgical, 1993. 216p ISBN 0-8146-5841-5 LC 93-1263
La teologia del XX secolo. Vanzan, Piersandro. *Civilta* 2:566-568 Je 19 1993
Troeltsch's treatment of the Thomist synthesis in The Social Teacing as a signal of his view of a new cultural synthesis. Dietrich, Wendell S. *Thomist* 57:381-401 Jl 1993

THEOLOGY—1950-
La significacón teológica de los acontecimientos: El estatuto histórico de la teología según Marie-Dominque Chenu. Silva Arévalo, Eduardo. *Teol Vida* 33 no 3-4:269-297 1993

THEOLOGY- GERMANY
Robert Musil: da Nietzsche alla mistica. Sommavilla, Guido. *Civilta* 3:129-142 Jl 17 1993

THEOLOGY, CATHOLIC
Building the free society: democracy, capitalism, and Catholic Social Teaching. Weigel, George, and Royal, Robert, eds. Grand Rapids: Eerdmans, 1993. 232p ISBN 0-8028-0129-x
Catholicity as a property of the Church. Beinert, Wolfgang. *Jurist* 52 no 1:455-483 1992
The church—one and diverse—in service to mission. Suquiía, Goicoechea Angel, Cardinal, 1916-. *Jurist* 52 no 1:7-10 1992
Crisi e recupero del teocentrismo trinitario. Vanzan, Piersandro. *Civilta* 3:143-146 Jl 17 1993
Development of a theology of the local church from the first to the Second Vatican Council. Cardedal, Olegario González de. *Jurist* 52 no 1:11-42 1992
Do whales have souls? Jones, David Albert. *New Blckfrs* 73:598-605 D 1992
Have you been saved? Grubb, Geoffrey J. *ReligTJ* 27:34 Mr 1993
How to read the church fathers. Hamman, Adalbert. New York: The Crossroad Publishing Company, 1993. x, 132p ISBN 0-8245-1204-9 LC 92-42052
Inculturation as transformation: the case of Americanism revisited. Portier, William J. *US Cath Hist* 11:107-124 Sum 1993
Karl May im katholischen Verlagswesen während des Kulturkampfs. Hoffmann, Fernand. *Stimm Zeit* 211:177-186 Mr 1993
"Listening" to nature: the significance of Leon Kass for Catholic moral theology. Torraco, Stephen F. *Linacre* 60:40-55 Ag 1993
Mary's bodily assumption. Meyer, Gabriel. *Register* 69:5 Ag 15 1993
Mary: yesterday, today, tomorrow. Halkes, Catharina J M, et al. New York: Crossroad, 1993. 88p ISBN 0-8245-1371-1 LC 93-19852
Mysterium paschale: the mystery of Easter. Balthasar, Hans Urs Von, 1905-1988. Grand Rapids: Eerdmans, 1993. 168p ISBN 0-8028-0216-8
Return to Chesterton. McGovern, Thomas. *HPR* 93:47-55 Je 1993
Teaching Church teaching: theological and pedagogical reflections. Hinsdale, Mary Ann. *Horizons (CTS)* 20:87-98 Spr 1993
Theological trends—sexual ethics: some recent developments. Hoose, Bernard. *Way* 33:54-62 Ja 1993
A theology for mother church. Gallagher, Rosemary. *Priests & People* 7:301-305 Ag-S 1993
What are the theologians saying now? Hellwig, Monika K, 1929-. Westminster: Christian Classics, 1993. x, 170p ISBN 0-87061-194-1
Who will they be saying that I am? Reiser, William, 1943-. *ChrWorld* 236:217-222 S-O 1993

THEOLOGY, CATHOLIC—CONGRESSES
John Paul II, Pope, (1991-08-15) Itinera Apostolica (Apostolic Journey) [Polish]. John Paul II, Pope, 1920- (Karol Wojtyla) (elected 1978). *AAS* 84:885-892 S 8 1992*

THEOLOGY, CONTEXTUAL
Questions d'épistémologie en théologie de la libération, ǵ propos de l'ouvrage de Clovdovis Boff. Richard, Jean. *Laval Theol Phil* 49:249-275 Je 1993

THEOLOGY, DOCTRINAL
Bartolomé de Las Casas en el V Centenario: revisión de su figura y de su doctrina moral. Osuna, Antonio. *Cien Tom* 119:459-498 S-D 1992

Uma cristologia suspeita? Palacio, Carlos. *Perspectiva* 25:181-196 My-Ag 1993

L'esegesi e l'evangelizzazione della nuova Europa. Marchesi, Giovanni. *Gregorianum* 73 No 4:719-730 1992

Evangelical Kernels: a theological spirituality of the religious life. Billy, Dennis J. New York: Alba House, 1993. ISBN

Il fenomeno delle stimmate. Mucci, Giandomenico. *Civilta* 2:217-226 My 1 1993

Der Gebrauch der Hl Schrift in der dogmatischen Theologie. Becker, Karl J. *Gregorianum* 73 No 4:671-687 1992

In che senso la dottrina sociale della chiesa è universale? Joblin, Joseph, 1920-. *Civilta* 3:15-28 Jl 3 1993

L'insegnamento di gesù [editorial]. Salvini, Gianpaolo, ed. *Civilta* 3:105-115 Jl 17 1993

Interpreting moral doctrine: Newman on conscience and law. Magill, Gerard. *Horizons (CTS)* 20:7-22 Spr 1993

Introduction to systematic theology. Slavens, Thomas Paul. Maryland: University Press of America, 1992. x, 71p ISBN 0-8191-8228-1 LC 91-10147

Let's hear it for doctrine. Walsh, Richard. *ReligTJ* 27:38-39 Ap-My 1993

Light of faith: the compenduine of theology. Thomas Aquinas, Saint. Manchester: Sophia Institute Press, 1993. x, 412p ISBN 0-918477-15-8 LC 93-6793

The revolution of the glory; introduction and part I; fundamental theology. Beeck, Frans Jozef van. Collegeville: Liturgical, 1993. x, 360p ISBN 0-8146-5498-3

The search for implicit axioms behind doctrinal texts. Ritschl, Dietrich. *Gregorianum* 74 no 2:207-221 1993

THEOLOGY, DOCTRINAL—HISTORY

Augustine today. Neuhaus, Richard John, 1936-, ed. Grand Rapids: Eerdmans, 1993. 168p ISBN 0-8028-0216-8

Las Casas und seine Gegner. Delgado, Mariano. *Stimm Zeit* 210:841-854 D 1992

Medieval Eucharist theology. Cummings, Owen F. *Emmanuel* 99:72-79 Mr 1993

THEOLOGY, DOCTRINAL—0030-600

Late have I loved you: an interpretation of Saint Augustine on human and divine relationships. Mohler, James Aylward. New Rochelle, New York: New City Press, 1993. 159p ISBN 0-911782-86-9 LC 90-643

Pastoral care in patristic times. Grace, Madeleine. *Priest* 49:49-53 S 1993

THEOLOGY, DOCTRINAL- ASIA

Emerging trends in Asian theology. Chandrakanthan, A J V. *TheolDgst* 39:339-341 Wint 1992

THEOLOGY, DOCTRINAL- AUSTRALIA

Are there really angels in Carlton? Australian literature and theology. Rowe, Noel. *Pacifica* 6:141-164 Je 1993

THEOLOGY, DOCTRINAL- BRUSSELS

Trois brefs témoignages. Aitken, Ann-Marie, and Lalawne, Stanislas, et al. *Lumen* 48:175-178 Je 1993

THEOLOGY, DOCTRINAL- FRANCE

Deux paradigmes pour penser le rapport de la théologie aux sciences humaines: herméneutique et narratologie. Fortin-Melkevik, Anne. *Laval Theol Phil* 49:223-231 Je 1993

THEOLOGY, DOCTRINAL- GERMANY

Herman Schell and the reform of the Catholic Church in Germany. Griener, George E. *TheolStds* 54:427-454 S 1993

Carisma e istituzione della chiesa nella teologia di Hans Urs Von Balthasar. Marchesi, Giovanni. *Civilta* 144:14-30 Ja 2 1993

In Drei Personen—der Trinitarische Schüsselbegriff "Person" in den Entwürfen Jürgen Moltmanns und Walter Kaspers. Radlbeck-Ossmann, Regina. *Catholica* 47:38-51 1993

Möglichkeiten und Grenzen einer Christologie, von unten. Kaiser, Alfred, 1872-1917. Munster: Aschendorff, 1992. x, 334p ISBN 3-402-03161-2

Personale und sakramentale Gegenwart des Herrn in der Eucharistie. Hintzen, Georg. *Catholica* 47 no 3:210-237 1993

THEOLOGY, DOCTRINAL- GREECE

De l'ontologie à la théologie. Gérard, Gilbert. *RPhil Louvain* 90:445-485 N 1992

THEOLOGY, DOCTRINAL- IRELAND

Religious thmes in the work of Patrick Kavanagh: hints of a Celtic tradition. Agnew, Una. *Studies* 82:257-264 Aut 1993

THEOLOGY, DOCTRINAL- LATIN AMERICA

Il documento de pastoral indígena. *Cien Tom* 120:5-31 Ja-Ap 1993

Teología India. Berganza, Carlos. *Cien Tom* 120:79-100 Ja-Ap 1993

THEOLOGY, ECUMENICAL

Entering ecumenism's reception phase. Staalsett, Gunnar. *Origins* 23:744-746 Ap 8 1993

The ex cathedra status of the encyclical Humanae Vitae. Harrison, Brian W. *F & R* 19:25-78 Spr 1993

The measure of Catholic ecumenical commitment. Cassidy, Edward Idris, Cardinal, 1924-. *Origins* 23:736-744 Ap 8 1993

Principles and norms of ecumenism. Cassidy, Edward Idris, Cardinal, 1924-. *TPS* 38:321 N-D 1993

The 1993 directory for ecumenism. *Origins* 23:129+ Jl 29 1993

THEOLOGY, FUNDAMENTAL

La identidad eclesial de la teología fundamental. Pié-Ninot, Salvador. *Gregorianum* 74 No 1:75-99 1993

Indirect methods in theology: Karl Rahner as an ad hoc apologist. Healy, Nicholas M. *Thomist* 56:613-633 O 1992

Taking the Bible seriously. White, Benton J. Louisville: Westminster, 1993. x, 192p ISBN 0-664-25452-7

THEOLOGY, FUNDAMENTAL- CHILE

Lobre la dimensión política de la escatología cristiana; una aproximación teológico-fundamental. Noemi Callejas, Juan. *Teol Vida* 34 no 1-2:145-152 1993

THEOLOGY, GERMANY

God and the unconscious mind: the Eugen Drewermann case. St Leger, Moya Frenz. *Doctr Life* 43:323-332 Jl-Ag 1993

THEOLOGY, JEWISH *see* Jewish Theology

THEOLOGY, LUTHERAN

The Church—local and Catholic: a Lutheran perspective. Gassmann, Günther. *Jurist* 52 no 1:518-524 1992

THEOLOGY, PRACTICAL

Las Casas und seine Gegner. Delgado, Mariano. *Stimm Zeit* 210:841-854 D 1992

The mystery of Christ and why we don't get it. Capon, Robert Farrar. Grand Rapids: Eerdmans, 1993. 192p ISBN 0-8028-0121-8

Selbstverständnis und Praxis des kirchlichen Lehramts. Koch, Kurt. *Stimm Zeit* 211:395-402 Je 1993

The song of the Church. Weakland, Rembert G, Abp, 1927-. *Origins* 23:12-16 My 20 1993

Theology, praxis, and ethics in the thought of Juan Luis Segundo, SJ. Zimbelman, Joel. *Thomist* 57:233-267 Ap 1993

THEOLOGY, PROTESTANT

Taking the Bible seriously. White, Benton J. Louisville: Westminster, 1993. x, 192p ISBN 0-664-25452-7

THEOLOGY, REFORMED

A Presbyterian viewpoint. Thompson, John. *Furrow* 44:399-402 Jl-Ag 1993

THEOLOGY OF ARISTOTLE (NEOPLATONIC TEXT)

De l'ontologie à la théologie. Gérard, Gilbert. *RPhil Louvain* 90:445-485 N 1992

THEOSOPHY—RELIGIOUS ASPECTS

Modernismo y Teosofia. Larrea Lopez, Juan Felix. Madrid: Libertarias, 1993. x, 400p ISBN 84-7954-122-9

THERESA OF LISIEUX, SAINT, 1873-1897

The case for St Thérèse as a doctor of the church. Ahern, Patrick V, Bp, 1919-. *America* 169:12-13+ Ag 28-S 4 1993

Christmas in the company of saints. Matz, Terry. *Liguorian* 81:50-55 D 1993

John Paul II, Pope, (1993-04-09) Letter to Auschwitz nuns. John Paul II, Pope, 1920- (Karol Wojtyla) (elected 1978). *TPS* 38:268-269 S-O 1993*

John Paul II, Pope, (1993-04-09) Letter to the nuns. John Paul II, Pope, 1920- (Karol Wojtyla) (elected 1978). *Origins* 22:795 Ap 29 1993*

Life-changing choices. Maas, Robin. *Spir Life* 39:140-149 Aut 1993

The market place. McNair, J Frank. *Living Prayer* 26:26-27 My-Je 1993

My child, the saint. Dodds, Bill. *New Cov* 22:21+ Ap 1993

THEVENET, MARIE DE SAINT-IGNACE (CLAUDINE), 1744-1837

Congregation for the Causes of Saints (1992-07-11) Blessed Marie de Saint-Ignace (Thevenet). Congregation for the Causes of Saints. *AAS* 85:189-191 F 3 1993*

Congregation for the Causes of Saints (1992-07-11) Decree on a miracle. Congregation for the Causes of Saints. *TPS* 38:37-38 Ja-F 1993*

THIRD WORLD—RELATIONS- EUROPE

Die Dritte Welt und Europa. Metz, Johann Baptist. *Stimm Zeit* 211:3-9 Ja 1993

THIRD WORLD—RELIGION

Die Dritte Welt und Europa. Metz, Johann Baptist. *Stimm Zeit* 211:3-9 Ja 1993

THIRD WORLD—SOCIO-ECONOMIC CONDITIONS

Die Dritte Welt und Europa. Metz, Johann Baptist. *Stimm Zeit* 211:3-9 Ja 1993

THOMAS AQUINAS, SAINT.

Amitié, attirance et amour chez S. Thomas d'Aquin. McEnvoy, James. *RPhil Louvain* 91:383-408 Ag 1993

Analogy and equivocation in thirteenth-century logic: Aquinas in context. Ashworth, E J. *Med Stud* 54:94-135 1992

An analysis of the use of rights language in pre-modern Catholic social thought. Brady, Bernard V. *Thomist* 57:97-121 Ja 1993

Aquinas concept of the body and out of body situations. Quinn, Patrick. *Heythrop* 34:387-400 O 1993

Aquinas on disordered pleasures and conditions. Daly, Anthony C. *Thomist* 56:583-612 O 1992

Aquinas on punishment and the death penalty. Calvert, Brian. *Amer J Juris* 37:259-281 1992

A contradiction in Saint Thomas's teaching on creation. Kondoleon, Theodore J. *Thomist* 57:51-61 Ja 1993

Discussion: soul, rational soul and person in Thomism. Plante, Harry La. *Mod Schlman* 70:209-216 Mr 1993

The Dominican and the dervish: a Christian-Muslim dialogue that might have been between Thomas Aquinas and Jalal ad-Din Rumi. Renard, John. *JEcumen Stds* 29:189-201 Spr 1992

École Saint-Thomas. Steenberghen, Fernand Van. *RPhil Louvain* 91:1-4 F 1993

The eucharistic theologies of Lauda sion and Thomas Aquinas's Summa theologiae. Bell, Thomas J. *Thomist* 57:163-185 Ap 1993

Goodness and rightness: Thomas Aquinas' Summa Theologia. Keenan, James F. Washington, D C: Georgetown University Press, 1992. x, 212p ISBN 0-87840-530-5 LC 92-3090

The human person: animal and spirit [by D Braine, review article]. Kerr, Fergus. *New Blckfrs* 74:333-337 Jl-Ag 1993

Israel's God, the Psalms, and the city of Jerusalem: life experience and the sacrifice of praise and prayer. Beeck, Frans Jozef van. *Horizons (CTS)* 19:219-239 Fall 1992

Light and metaphor in Plotinus and St Thomas Aquinas. Corrigan, Kevin. *Thomist* 57:187-199 Ap 1993

Mind forming and manductio in Aquinas. George, Marie I. *Thomist* 57:201-213 Ap 1993

Natural law as a form of legal studies. Grazin, Igor. *Amer J Juris* 37:1-16 1992

Nova et vetera: "Le fondement de la morale" de Mgr A Léonard. Rosemann, Philipp W. *RPhil Louvain* 91:126-136 F 1993

On Leo Strauss's understanding of the natural law theory of Thomas Aquinas. Kries, Douglas. *Thomist* 57:215-232 Ap 1993

Person, being, and St Thomas. Clarke, W Norris. *Communio* 19:601-618 Wint 1992

Philosophy and spirituality: cultivating a virtue. Dewan, Lawrence. *HPR* 94:25-30 N 1993

Il posto della metafisica nel sapere umano Il pensiero di Maimonide e il suo influsso su S Tommaso d'Aquino. Pangallo, Don Mario. *Gregorianum* 74 no 2:331-352 1993

Proportionalism and a text of the young Aquinas: Quodlibetum IX, Q 7, A 2. Johnson, Mark A. *TheolStds* 53:683-699 D 1992

Psicología y pedagogía de la edad evolutiva según Santo Tomás. Manzanedo, Marcos. *Cien Tom* 119:351-389 My-Ag 1992

Sacraments and women's experience. Ross, Susan A. *Listening* 28:52-64 Wint 1993

The Saint of reason [condensed fr *The Providence Visitor* Ja 28 1993]. Lennon, Joseph L. *CDgst* 57:139-141 Je 1993

Saint Thomas Aquinas and theological exegesis of sacred scripture. McGuckin, Terence. *New Blckfrs* 74:197-211 Ap 1993

The status and function of divine simpleness in Summa theologiae Ia, qq 2-13. Burns, Peter. *Thomist* 57:1-26 Ja 1993

Thomas Aquinas's' double metaphysics of simplicity and infinity. Sweeney, Eileen C. *IPQ* 33:297-317 S 1993

Thomas Aquinas, preacher and friend. Fatula, Mary Ann. Minnesota: The Liturgical Press, 1993. x, 313p ISBN 0-8146-5031-7 LC 92-27552

Thomas the thinker [review article *The thought of Thomas Acquinas* by B Davies]. Walsh, Liam G. *Doctr Life* 43:156-161 Mr 1993

Transcendent man in the limited city: the political philosophy of Charles N R McCoy. Schall, James Vincent, 1928-. *Thomist* 57:63-95 Ja 1993

THOMAS AQUINAS, SAINT—ETHICS
Nova et vetera: "Le fondement de la morale" de Mgr A Léonard. Rosemann, Philipp W. *RPhil Louvain* 91:126-136 F 1993

THOMAS AQUINAS, SAINT—INFLUENCE
The life and teaching of St Thomas Aquinas: a guide for the African Church today. Schineller, Peter. *AFER* 34:18-28 F 1992

The whatness of Loulou: allegories of Thomism in Flaubert. Wise, Christopher. *Relig Lit* 25:35-49 Spr 1993

THOMAS AQUINAS, SAINT—THEOLOGY
St Thomas, God's goodness, and God's morality. Dewan, Lawrence. *Mod Schlmn* 70:45-51 N 1992

Three previously unpublished chapters from St Thomas Aquinas's commentary on Aristotle's Meteora: Sentencia Super Meteora 2 13-15. White, Kevin. *Med Stud* 54:49-93 1992

Trinity and creation in the theology of St. Thomas Aquinas. Walker, David A. *Thomist* 57:443-455 Jl 1993

THOMAS BECKET, SAINT, ABP OF CANTERBURY
Becket, the martyred shepherd. Miesel, Sandra. *Register* 69:4 Ja 3 1993

Two Thomases, twins in sanctity [condensed fr *Lay Witness* D 1992]. Dorman, Regina. *CDgst* 58:30-35 N 1993

THOMAS MORE, SAINT, 1478-1535
Ethics and the mandarins. Hunt, John Dixon. *Priests & People* 7:224-227 Je 1993

Prayers for busy people. Kreeft, Peter John, 1937-. *New Cov* 22:17+ F 1993

The reformation: too many assumptions? Marius, Richard, 1933-. *Critic* 47:31-42 Wint 1992

Saint Thomas More. Novak, Michael, 1933-. *Crisis* 11:5-10 Je 1993

Two Thomases, twins in sanctity [condensed fr *Lay Witness* D 1992]. Dorman, Regina. *CDgst* 58:30-35 N 1993

THOMISM
École Saint-Thomas. Steenberghen, Fernand Van. *RPhil Louvain* 91:1-4 F 1993

MacIntyre's postmodern Thomism: reflections on Three rival versions of moral enquiry. Hibbs, Thomas S. *Thomist* 57:277-297 Ap 1993

Nova et vetera: "Le fondement de la morale" de Mgr A Léonard. Rosemann, Philipp W. *RPhil Louvain* 91:126-136 F 1993

An observation on Robert Lauder's review of G A McCool, SJ [reply to "On being or not being a Thomist," 55:301-319 by R Lauder]. Cessario, Romanus. *Thomist* 56:701-710 O 1992

Second-hand straw. McInerny, Ralph M. *Crisis* 11:15-17 My 1993

Troeltsch's treatment of the Thomist synthesis in The Social Teacing as a signal of his view of a new cultural synthesis. Dietrich, Wendell S. *Thomist* 57:381-401 Jl 1993

Whiteheadian creativity, the Tao, and the Thomistic act of being. Bracken, Joseph A. *Pacifica* 6:179-188 Je 1993

THOUGHT AND THINKING
Breaking the thought barrier. Roman, Mary. *Living Prayer* 26:37 My-Je 1993

L'idéalisme Allemand face à la raison théologique. Maesschalck, Marc. *Laval Theol Phil* 49:309-320 Je 1993

TIBET (CHINA)
A living Buddha. Freeman, Laurence. *Tablet* 247:681-682 My 29 1993

TIBETAN BUDDHISM
Authority (2): an essay on the place of the text in Buddhist and Christian formation. Corless, Roger. *Stud Form Spir* 14:31-39 F 1993

Meditation and prayer (1):creative imagination in the lives of Ignatius Loyola and Khapa: visualization in Catholic and Buddhist practice. Urubshurow, Victoria Kennick. *Stud Form Spir* 14:41-56 F 1993

TILLARD, JEAN MARIE ROGER, 1927-
The Church as communion. Yarnold, Edward John, 1926-. *Tablet* 246:1564-1565 D 12 1992

The Holy Spirit and the church in Catholic theology: a study in the ecclesiology of J-M R Tillard. O'Connor, Michael. *OChr* 28 no 4:331-341 1992

TILLICH, PAUL JOHANNES OSKAR, 1886-1965
Buber and Tillich. Novak, David, 1941-. *JEcumen Stds* 29:159-174 Spr 1992

TILLSLEY, BRAMWELL
Onward Christian soldier. Aitken, Tom. *Tablet* 247:598 My 8 1993

TIME
The instant and the living present: Ricoeur and Derrida reading Husserl. Bourgeois, Patrick. *PhilosTod* 37:31-37 Spr 1993

"Make the best of the present time" [repr fr *Crossroads*]. Wermter, Oskar. *AFER* 34:183-187 Je 1992

The metaphysical aspect of tenses in Proclus. Plass, Paul. *IPQ* 33:143-151 Je 1993

Our own idea of time [repr fr *Crossroads*]. Zvarevashe, Ignatius M. *AFER* 34:188-192 Je 1992

Reply to Smith: on the finitude of the past [reply to Q Smith, 33:109-115 1993]. Craig, William Lane. *IPQ* 33:225-231 Je 1993

TIME—RELIGIOUS ASPECTS
The liturgical year: mainspring of Christian life. Joncas, Michael, et al. *Past Mus* 18:25-31 O-N 1993

The power to act: toward a Christian experience of time. Dalzell, Catherine. *Can Cath Rev* 11:7-11 F 1993

TIME (THEOLOGY)
Contemplative action: time in eternity according to Saint Bernard. Dumont, Charles. *Cist Stud* 28 no 2:145-159 1993

Etre et temps et théologie. Berranger, Oliver De. *Gregorianum* 74 no 3:543-561 1993

Time to do nothing: why I don't worry about wasting time. Bauer, Catherine Lazers. *Spir Life* 39:173-175 Aut 1993

TIME MANAGEMENT
Helpful hints for DREs from a DRE. Gilbert, Marjorie. *Catechist* 27:66-67 S 1993

TIMOR ISLAND (INDONESIA)—POLITICS
Resistance leader shows his defiance. *Tablet* 247:697 My 29 1993

TIMOR ISLAND (INDONESIA)—POLITICS AND GOVERNMENT
"Propaganda" and "lies" after capture of guerrilla leader. McGillian, Chris. *Tablet* 246:1580 D 12 1992

TIPITAKA
Perfection without God: a view from the Pāli Canon. Katz, Nathan. *Stud Form Spir* 14:11-22 F 1993

TITHES
Bosnia. Feuerherd, Peter. *Register* 69:1+ Je 6 1993

Catholics will give when church moves into future. Davis, Charlie. *Nat Cath Rep* 29:13 F 12 1993

Dollars dried up with move away from tradition. O'Reilly, Stephan J. *Nat Cath Rep* 29:13 F 12 1993

Our alms: returning God's love. Shaw, Russell. *Register* 69:1+ Ja 31 1993

TOBACCO
Churches are strangely quiet in the fight against tobacco. Drinan, Robert Francis, 1920-. *Nat Cath Rep* 29:25 Ja 15 1993

TOCQUEVILLE, ALEXIS DE, 1805-1859
American spirituality: a distinct contribution? Schall, James Vincent, 1928-. *Living Light* 29:3-13 Aut 1992

The crisis of the welfare state. Novak, Michael, 1933-. *Crisis* 11:4-7 Jl-Ag 1993

TODD, JOHN M, 1918-1993
Todd, John M, 1918-1993 [obit]. Moore, Sebastian, and O'Collins, Gerald, 1931-. *Tablet* 247:801-802 Je 19 1993

TOLERATION
The Catholic case for inclusion. DeCosse, David E. *America* 168:15-16 My 8 1993

Is it ideology? The agenda of real-life gays. Hoyt, Robert G. *Comm* 120:4-5 My 21 1993

Prejudice or disagreement? Homosexuals in the military. Garvey, John, 1944-. *Comm* 120:9-10 F 26 1993

Respect is not a right. Licht, Robert A. *Crisis* 11:41-47 Jl-Ag 1993

They call themselves liberals. Carlin, David Robert, Jr, 1938-. *Comm* 120:8-9 F 26 1993

TOLERATION, RELIGIOUS
Attention verses distraction: beyond the Quincentennial of Columbus. Starkloff, Carl. *TheolDgst* 40:119-131 Sum 1993

TOLKIEN, J R R, 1892-1973
J R R Tolkien and the art of the parable. Murray, Robert. *Month* 26:35-39 Ja 1993

J R R Tolkien: lover of the logos. Sebanc, Mark, 1941-1992. *Communio* 20:84-106 Spr 1993

TOMBS
The graveyard of Jesus. Martin, George. *CDgst* 57:7-11 Ap 1993

TOMBSTONES
Beauty in natural stone. O'Hagan, Daniel. *Cath Work* 60:2 Je-Jl 1993

TOMKINS, OLIVER STRATFORD, 1908-1992
Oliver Stratford Tomkins, 1908-1992 [address, St. Margaret's Church, London, Ja 21 1993]. *OChr* 29 no 2:93-99 1993

TOOLAN, DAVID
A Christian response to the New Age. Saliba, John A. *Way* 33:202-232 Jl 1993

TORNAY, MAURICE, 1910-1949
Congregation for the Causes of Saints (1992-07-11) Decree on the heroic virtues of Maurice Tornay. Congregation for the Causes of Saints. *AAS* 85:180-181 F 3 1993*

Congregation for the Causes of Saints (1992-07-11) Decree on the martyrdom. Congregation for the Causes of Saints. *TPS* 38:37-38 Ja-F 1993*

John Paul II, Pope, (1993-05-16). John Paul II, Pope, 1920- (Karol Wojtyla) (elected 1978). *TPS* 38:308-311 S-O 1993*

TORRAS Y BAGES, JOSE, BP, 1846-1916
Congregation for the Causes of Saints (1992-06-13) Decree on the heroic virtues. Congregation for the Causes of Saints. *TPS* 38:19-20 Ja-F 1993*

Congregation for the Causes of Saints (1992-06-13) Decree on the heroic virtues of Servant of God, Jose Torras y Bages. Congregation for the Causes of Saints. *AAS* 85:97-100 Ja 7 1993*

TORTURE
Friendly house rehabilitates torture victims. Gibeau, Dawn. *Nat Cath Rep* 29:6 Ap 23 1993

TOTALITARIANISM
John Paul II, Pope, (1993-09-05) Beyond. John Paul II, Pope, 1920- (Karol Wojtyla) (elected 1978). *Origins* 23:235-237 S 16 1993*

Maritain on "the common good": reflections on the concept. Kalumba, Kibujjo M. *Laval Theol Phil* 49:93-104 F 1993

TOULMIN, ROGER, ?-1993
Toulmin, Roger, ?-1993 [obit]. *Tablet* 247:1009 Ag 7 1993

TOUVIER, PAUL
New light under the old bushel: what's happening in the French Church? Englund, Steven. *Comm* 120:11-14 Ap 23 1993

On never reaching Canada. Schall, James Vincent, 1928-. *Crisis* 11:49-50 My 1993

The sign over the barber shop: annotations on the problems of interpretation. Schmitz, Heinz-Gerd. *IPQ* 33:197-202 Je 1993

Truth and freedom. Bedell, Gary. *Mod Schlmn* 70:53-62 N 1992

Truth-telling and marriage. Gillespie, Joseph P. *New Theol Rev* 6:71-73 Ag 1993

TRUTH—RELIGIOUS ASPECTS
Truth at the sickbed [condensed fr *Stimmen der Zeit* D 1989]. Schmitz, Philip. *TheolDgst* 38:141-145 Sum 1991

TRUTH, THEOLOGY
Vérité et mensonge dans la relation au malade. Geets, Claude. *Supplement* 184:56-77 Mr-Ap 1993

Feminist theology, evangelisation and the embodiment of truth. Grey, Mary. *Month* 25:485-490 D 1992

How we know truth; considering the source. Kreeft, Peter John, 1937. *Register* 69:1+ Ag 15 1993

John Paul II's truths sacrifice tradition of pastoral concern [editorial *Veritatis Splendor*]. *Nat Cath Rep* 29:28 O 15 1993*

John Paul II, (1993-10-05) Veritatis splendor [abridged]. John Paul II, Pope, 1920- (Karol Wojtyla) (elected 1978). *Tablet* 247:1312-1318 O 9 1993*

John Paul II, Pope, (1993-10-05) Veritatis Splendor. John Paul II, Pope, 1920- (Karol Wojtyla) (elected 1978). *Origins* 23:297-334 O 14 1993*

John Paul II, Pope, (1993-10-15) Reflections. John Paul II, Pope, 1920- (Karol Wojtyla) (elected 1978). *Origins* 23:360-362 O 28 1993*

John Paul II, Pope, (19930-10-05) Veritatis Splendor. John Paul II, Pope, 1920- (Karol Wojtyla) (elected 1978). *OR(Eng)* 1310:1 O 6 1993*

Pope John Paul answers the big questions in life. Shaw, Russell. *OSV* 82:3 O 17 1993*

The second commandment in the New Testament: your yes is yes, your no is no. Carrón, Julián. *Communio* 20:5-25 Spr 1993

[Veritatis splendor belongs to the literary gender]. Curran, Charles E, 1934-. *Comm* 120:14 O 22 1993

TRUTHFULNESS AND FALSEHOOD
Jesus y la mentira. González Faus, José Ignacio. *Christus* 58:48-54 My 1993

TSCHIDERER, GIOVANNI NEOPMUCENO DE, 1777-1860
Congregation for the Causes of Saints (1992-12-21) Decree on a miracle. Congregation for the Causes of Saints. *OR(Eng)* 1272:4 Ja 6 1993*

TUITION TAX CREDITS
In New York, a new model for Catholic schools. Bole, William. *OSV* 82:17 Ag 29 1993

Panel: pro education tax credits. Feuerherd, Peter. *Register* 69:1+ Jl 4 1993

TURKEY—ECONOMIC CONDITIONS
Turkey's unlikely hero. Barchard, David. *Tablet* 247:506-507 Ap 24 1993

TURKEY—FOREIGN RELATIONS
Another place, another war. Lieven, Anatol. *Tablet* 247:639-641 My 22 1993

TURKEY—POLITICS AND GOVERNMENT
Death of private soldier. Barchard, David. *Tablet* 247:131-132 Ja 30 1993
Turkey's unlikely hero. Barchard, David. *Tablet* 247:506-507 Ap 24 1993

TURNER, EDITH
Boundary-dwellers. Ward, Hannah. *Way* 33:97-105 Ap 1993

TURNER, VICTOR
Boundary-dwellers. Ward, Hannah. *Way* 33:97-105 Ap 1993

TWELVE-STEP PROGRAMS—RELIGIOUS ASPECTS
Belongings: bonds of healing and recovery. Linn, Dennis, et al. New Jersey: Paulist Press, 1993. x, 255p ISBN 0-8091-3365-2 LC 92-29855

Recover and heal: meditations on the twelve steps. Albertus, Karen. Cincinatti: St Anthony Press, 1993. x, 308p ISBN 0-86716-1531

TWENTIETH CENTURY
La teologia del XX secolo. Vanzan, Piersandro. *Civilta* 2:566-568 Je 19 1993

TWENTY-FIRST CENTURY—FORECASTS
Christianity in the twenty-first century: reflections on the challenges ahead. Wuthnow, Robert. New York: Oxford University Press, 1993. x, 251p ISBN 0-19507-957-4 LC 92-28689

Preparing for the twenty-first century. Kennedy, Paul M, 1945-. New York: Random House, 1993. x, 428p ISBN 0-39458-443-0 LC 91-52668

TYLER, ANNE
Das Problem der Heiligkeit in unserer Zeit. Stelzmann, Rainulf A. *Stimm Zeit* 211:489-500 Jl 1993

TZU, CHUANG, 369 BC-?
What-being: Chuang Tzu versus Aristotle. Li, Chenyang. *IPQ* 33:341-353 S 1993

U

UKRAINIAN CATHOLIC CHURCH
Ukrainian bishop fights to hold eparchy. Babych, Art. *Nat Cath Rep* 29:7 S 24 1993

The Ukrainian Catholic Church: up from the underground. Widner, Thomas C. *America* 169:12-15 O 23 1993

UKRAINIAN CATHOLIC CHURCH- UKRAINE
Present situation of the Ukrainian Catholic Church in Ukraine. Sulyk, Stephen. *Diakonia* 26 no 3:149-160 1993

ULTRASONIC IMAGING
Other abortion providers. Morgan, Anne Marie. *Crisis* 11:18-19 Jl-Ag 1993

UMANA, JOAQUIN RAMOS, BP
John Paul II, Pope, (1993-06-27) Rome [Orig Italian]. John Paul II, Pope, 1920- (Karol Wojtyla) (elected 1978). *OR(Eng)* 1297:1 Je 30 1993*

UNBORN CHILDREN (LAW)- GERMANY
Beratungspflicht und Strafverzicht. Demel, Sabine. *Stimm Zeit* 211:700-710 O 1993

UNDERDEVELOPED AREAS
Poverty and development: economics and reality. Thanawala, Kishor. *RSocEcon* 50:258-268 Fall 1992

UNDERDEVELOPED AREAS—THEOLOGY
Beyond a theology of development. Peter, C B. *AFER* 35:54-67 F 1993

UNEMPLOYED
Eight ways to help the people you know. Koenig-Bricker, Woodeene. *Salt* 13:12-13 Ja 1993

A Gospel for the unemployed. O'Collins, Gerald, 1931-. *Tablet* 247:1182 S 18 1993

How to really help the unemployed. Koenig-Bricker, Woodeene. *Salt* 13:8-12 Ja 1993

Work Is the Key: a view from the dole queue. Owens, John Joseph. *Doctr Life* 43:227-231 Ap 1993

UNEMPLOYED- GREAT BRITAIN
Hope on the dole. Miller, Annabel. *Tablet* 247:38-39 Ja 9 1993

UNEMPLOYMENT
America's silent depression: a challenge to social economics. Peterson, Wallace C, 1921-. *RSocEcon* 51:2-13 Spr 1993

Bishops back the enterprise culture. *Tablet* 246:1580-1581 D 12 1992

Can Clinton deliver? Jones, Arthur C, 1936-. *Tablet* 247:296 Mr 6 1993

Faith and work. Kennedy, Finola. *Tablet* 247:330 Mr 13 1993

Scandal of the two-thirds society [editorial]. *Tablet* 247:127 Ja 30 1993

Sitting pretty on set-aside [editorial]. *Tablet* 247:1119 S 4 1993

UNEMPLOYMENT—EFFECT OF UNEMPLOYMENT INFLATION ON- IRELAND
The causes of Irish unemployment: trends and explanations. Browne, Frank, and McGettigan, Donal. *Studies* 82:35-52 Spr 1993

UNEMPLOYMENT—EFFECT OF UNEMPLOYMENT INSURANCE ON- IRELAND
The causes of Irish unemployment: trends and explanations. Browne, Frank, and McGettigan, Donal. *Studies* 82:35-52 Spr 1993

UNEMPLOYMENT—REGIONAL DISPARITIES
Comparisons from the North. Hewitt, Victor. *Studies* 82:24-34 Spr 1993

UNEMPLOYMENT- CANADA
Our poor bishops [editorial]. Callam, Daniel. *Can Cath Rev* 11:2-3 Je 1993

Widespread unemployment: a call to mobilize. *Origins* 22:786-792 Ap 29 1993

UNEMPLOYMENT- EUROPE
Ireland's record—last in the class? Johns, Christopher. *Studies* 82:9-23 Spr 1993

John Major versus Jacques Delors [editorial]. *Tablet* 247:807 Je 26 1993

UNEMPLOYMENT- GREAT BRITAIN
Family values. Field, Frank, 1942-. *Tablet* 247:1034 Ag 14 1993

UNEMPLOYMENT- IRELAND
Can the Church reclaim our common conscience? Waters, John. *Furrow* 44:263-272 My 1993

Ideals without strategy—a response to Work is the key. Dorr, Donal, 1935-. *Furrow* 44:472-478 S 1993

Unemployment in the Republic and Northern Ireland. Barber, Noel, and Rea, Desmond, eds. *Studies* 82:9-96 Spr 1993*

Work is the key [excerpts fr a Pastoral Letter]. Daly, Cahal Brendan, Cardinal, 1917-, et al. *Cath Int* 4:182-189 Ap 1993

UNEMPLOYMENT- SPAIN
In the steps of Christopher Columbus. *Tablet* 247:796-797 Je 19 1993

UNIFICATION CHURCH
Are the Moonies Latter-Day Mormons? Miller, Timothy. *StudiaM* 41:67-83 1992

UNITARIANS AND UNITARIANISM
A Jeffersonian Catholicism? McDonald, John S. *New Oxford Rev* 60:17-18 Ja-F 1993

UNITATIS REDINTEGRATIO (DOCUMENT) *see* Vatican Council, 2D, 1962-1965—Ecumenism

UNITED CHURCH OF CHRIST
Lutheran-Reformed Committee meets. *Ecumen Trends* 22:8 Mr 1993

UNITED FARM WORKERS' UNION
Thousands mourn non-violent Hispanic activist. *Tablet* 247:590 My 8 1993

UNITED METHODIST CHURCH
By water and the spirit—a United Methodist understanding of Baptism: a Lutheran response. Nitschke, Beverley A. *Ecumen Trends* 22:3-7 Ja 1993

UNITED NATIONS
At 50, the United Nations needs some remodeling. Drinan, Robert Francis, 1920-. *Nat Cath Rep* 29:13 Ap 30 1993

Give Bosnia a chance. Hastings, Adrian, 1929-. *Tablet* 247:64+ Ja 16 1993

Holy See agrees to intervene for Iraq at United Nations. *Tablet* 247:115 Ja 23 1993

Iraq and the United Nations [interview by T H Stahel, 1938-]. Ekéus, Rolf. *America* 169:4-5 Ag 14-21 1993

Refugees in the limelight. Torrens, James S. *America* 168:6 Ap 3 1993

Refugees: a challenge for solidarity. *TPS* 38:65-77 Mr-Ap 1993

The task before us. Harris, Errol E, 1908-. *Teilhard Rev* 28:19-21 Sum 1993

UN double standard meand double trouble for hot spots [editorial]. *Nat Cath Rep* 29:28 Jl 16 1993

1993 UN focus: indigenous people. FitzMaurice, Eileen Claire. *Momentum* 24:79-80 Ap-My 1993

UNITED NATIONS—ARMED FORCES
Attacks by warlord Aidid: the U.N. and U.S. respond. *St Anth* 101:39 O 1993

The blood of Bosnia [editorial]. *Comm* 120:3-4 Je 4 1993

The end of the road. Williams, Shirley, 1930-. *Tablet* 247:676 My 29 1993

The limits of the UN [editorial]. *Tablet* 247:775 Je 19 1993

The morality of caution [editorial]. *Month* 26:170-171 My 1993

A necessary balance. Cahill, Kevin Michael, 1936-. *America* 169:6-10 Ag 28-S 4 1993

Religious leaders criticise strikes against Iraq. *Tablet* 247:119-120 Ja 23 1993

Support for armed intervention. *Tablet* 246:1579-1580 D 12 1992

UNITED NATIONS—CHILDREN
The children of the world [editorial]. *Month* 26:44-45 F 1993

A new worldwide commitment to the rights of children. Drinan, Robert Francis, 1920-. *America* 169:22-23 O 16 1993

UNITED NATIONS—COMMISSION ON HUMAN RIGHTS
Respect human rights. *Cath Int* 4:237-238 My 1993

UNITED STATES—FOREIGN RELATIONS- MEXICO
A call to reassess Operation Blockade. Pena, Raymundo, Bp. *Origins* 23:372-373 N 4 1993

UNITED STATES—FOREIGN RELATIONS- PERU
Refugees blaze more hopeful shining path in Peru. Wirpsa, Leslie. *Nat Cath Rep* 29:12 O 1 1993

UNITED STATES—FOREIGN RELATIONS- RUSSIA
Whither Holy Russia? [editorial]. *America* 168:3 F 13 1993

UNITED STATES—FOREIGN RELATIONS- RUSSIA (FEDERATION)
Thinking about Russia [editorial]. *America* 168:3 My 8 1993

UNITED STATES—FOREIGN RELATIONS- SUDAN
Cold war forces called to clean up Sudan mess [editorial]. *Nat Cath Rep* 30:24 N 19 1993

UNITED STATES—FOREIGN RELATIONS- VATICAN
A Boston politician comes to John Paul's court. O'Grady, Desmond. *OSV* 82:3 Ag 22 1993

UNITED STATES—FOREIGN RELATIONS- VIETNAM
Asia's new-style tyranny. Himmelfarb, Anne. *Crisis* 11:46-48 S 1993

UNITED STATES—FOREIGN RELATIONS- ZAIRE
US waives ban on Zairean visits; incites Mobutu critics. Collins, Carole, and Askin, Steve. *Nat Cath Rep* 29:10 Jl 30 1993

UNITED STATES—GOVERNMENT
It doesn't hurt to hope: Clinton is good at comebacks. McCarthy, Abigail Quigley. *Comm* 120:7-8 F 12 1993

UNITED STATES—HISTORY
The essential elements of and conditions for a "Democratic Republic": the view prevalent at the founding and in Early American History. Krason, Stephen M. *F & R* 18:235-274 Aut 1992

UNITED STATES—HISTORY—1861-1865 (CIVIL WAR)
"Ain't nobody clean": the liturgy of violence in Glory. Culbertson, Diana. *Relig Lit* 25:37-52 Sum 1993

UNITED STATES—HISTORY—1900
Bill Clinton's bad start. Neustadt, Richard, 1919-. *Tablet* 247:776+ Je 19 1993

UNITED STATES—INTELLECTUAL LIFE
The Catholic as Conservative: Russell Kirk's Christian humanism. Wolfe, Gregory. *Crisis* 11:25-32 O 1993

UNITED STATES—MILITARY POLICY
Equal gender military: progress or spiritual Nihilism? Chodes, John. *SocJust* 84:40-44 Mr-Ap 1993
An open letter to the federal government [editorial]. Krason, Stephen M. *SocJust* 84:131-132 S-O 1993
Pentagon best kept secret of U.S. waste, inefficiency [editorial]. *Nat Cath Rep* 29:20 O 1 1993

UNITED STATES—MINORITIES
Civil rights in the first 100 days. Drinan, Robert Francis, 1920-. *America* 168:14-15 Mr 13 1993
E pluribus unum? Chavez, Linda. *Crisis* 11:12-13 Mr 1993

UNITED STATES—MORAL CONDITIONS
Abandoned in a toxic culture: how we failed the new generation. Novak, Michael, 1933-. *Crisis* 10:15-19 D 1992
Penance, 1993. Burleigh, Anne Husted, 1941-. *Crisis* 11:44-45 Mr 1993
The vacuum in God's own country [editorial]. *Tablet* 247:839 Jl 3 1993

UNITED STATES—NATIONAL SECURITY
The "state" of "defense". Hehir, J Bryan, 1940-. *Comm* 120:9-10 Mr 26 1993

UNITED STATES—OFFICIALS AND EMPLOYEES
Goodfellows: reinventing government. McCarthy, Abigail Quigley. *Comm* 120:9-10 My 7 1993

UNITED STATES—POLITICAL PARTIES
Lessons from November. Carlin, David Robert, Jr, 1938-. *Comm* 119:7-8 D 18 1992

UNITED STATES—POLITICS
An aborted presidency. Novak, Michael, 1933-. *Crisis* 11:2-6 Mr 1993
Bill Clinton's bad start. Neustadt, Richard, 1919-. *Tablet* 247:776+ Je 19 1993
Clinton sounds good: but now a word from scrooge. Baumann, Paul. *Comm* 120:4-5 Ja 15 1993
Clinton's new political geography: renewing the language of equality [adapted fr *The election of 1992: reports and interpretations*]. McWilliams, Wilson Carey, 1933-. *Comm* 120:14-18 Ap 23 1993
Lessons from November. Carlin, David Robert, Jr, 1938-. *Comm* 119:7-8 D 18 1992
Religious right eyes Clinton feast. Jones, Arthur C, 1936-. *Nat Cath Rep* 29:3 S 24 1993
The rise and rise of the Christian Right. Appleby, Raphael Scott. *Tablet* 247:847-848 Jl 3 1993
Skepticism softens: can Americans love politics again? Dionne, E J, Jr. *Comm* 120:5-7 Ja 15 1993
Supporting prolife women candidates. Ferguson, Lisa. *Register* 69:2 Ap 25 1993
That sinking feeling [editorial]. *Comm* 120:3-4 Je 18 1993

UNITED STATES—POLITICS—RELIGIOUS ASPECTS
Catholics and politics in post-world war II America: some key questions. Varacalli, Joseph A. *SocJust* 84:78-83 My-Je 1993

UNITED STATES—POPULATION
A sign and a challenge. Kuharski, Mary Ann, and Fleming, Dorothy. *Register* 69:5 Je 27 1993

UNITED STATES—RACE RELATIONS
Church must use its power to fight racism [editorial]. *Nat Cath Rep* 29:28 Mr 19 1993

UNITED STATES—RELIGION
A call to arms. Flannery, Tom. *SocJust* 84:83-85 My-Je 1993
Communication and change in American religious history. Sweet, Leonard I, ed. Grand Rapids: Eerdmans, 1993. 400p ISBN 0-8028-0682-1
The Continuing Kulturkampf [editorial]. Brown, Harold O J. *SocJust* 84:35-39 Mr-Ap 1993

A generation of seekers; the spiritual journeys of the baby boom generation. Roof, Wade Clark, 1939-. New York: HarperCollins Publishers, 1993. x, 294p ISBN 0-06-066963-2 LC 92-53920
Our wake-up call. Hallsted, Bill D. *SocJust* 84:86 My-Je 1993
Ralph Waldo Emerson on Isaac Hecker: a manuscript with commentary. Johnson, Glen M. *CHist* 79:54-64 Ja 1993
Reading the signs of the times: resources for social and cultural analysis. Sanks, T Howland, and Coleman, John A, eds. New York: Paulist Press, 1993. x, 232p ISBN 0-8091-33777-6 LC 92-42017
Towards a Jewish-Christian alliance [interview by R Lakind]. Haberman, Joshua A. *Crisis* 11:32-38 F 1993
Tremors in the foundation of the US Catholic Church. Green, Bernard D. *New Oxford Rev* 60:11-16 O 1993

UNITED STATES—SOCIAL CONDITIONS
A baby named Luck [editorial]. *Comm* 119:3-4 D 18 1992
The Baby-Boom Catholic [editorial]. *America* 168:3 My 1 1993
The Barna report, volume 3, 1993-94: absolute confusion. Beacon, George. Ventura: Regal Books, 1993. x, 309p ISBN 0-8307-1641-6
The future ain't what it used to be [interview by Salt editors]. Theobald, Robert. *Salt* 13:6-11 Jl-Ag 1993
Let them eat cake: a love letter to multiculturalists. Carlin, David Robert, Jr, 1938-. *Comm* 120:9-10 Ap 23 1993
No surprise. Dilsaver, G C. *HPR* 93:54-57 F 1993
A passion for the possible: a message to U.S. churches. Coffin, William Sloane. Louisville: John Knox, 1993. x, 96p ISBN 0-664-25428-4
The rise and fall of the United States. Farrall, Harold J. New York: Vantage Press, 1992. x, 175p ISBN 0-533-10224-3 LC 92-93307
Stay focused [editorial]. *Comm* 120:3-4 F 26 1993
They've stolen my name. Carlin, David Robert, Jr, 1938-. *Comm* 120:7-9 Ag 13 1993
A wall of silence. Kerness, Bonnie. *Cath Work* 60:1+ Mr-Ap 1993

UNITED STATES—SOCIAL POLICY
Broadening welfare reform's context. Kammer, Fred. *Origins* 23:221-224 S 9 1993
Family policy in America: a continuing controversy. Stanfield, Jacqueline B. *RSocEcon* 50:420-431 Wint 1992
Investments in children [editorial]. *America* 168:3 My 29 1993

UNITED STATES—SOCIO-ECONOMIC CONDITIONS
Hope in the White House. Spaeth, Robert L, 1935-. *Crisis* 11:9 F 1993
Immigration debate [editorial]. *America* 169:3 O 9 1993
Mr Clinton, make them rare. Flynn, Raymond L. *Comm* 120:4 F 26 1993
Some cause for hope. McCarthy, Abigail Quigley. *Comm* 120:8-9 Ja 15 1993
What's happening to America? Boyd, John F. *SocJust* 84:15 Ja-F 1993

UNITED STATES—SUPREME—DECISIONS
Religion, education and the First Amendment. Coughlin, John J. *America* 168:12-15 My 15 1993

UNITED STATES—SUPREME COURT
Are profoundly handicapped children in Catholic schools entitled to government assistance?. Drinan, Robert Francis, 1920-. *America* 168:16-18 Ja 30 1993
Courtship. Mullen, Peter. *Register* 69:1+ Jl 4 1993
Dialogue [interview by P Mullen]. Bork, Robert Heron, 1927-. *Register* 69:1+ Ag 1 1993
Film-flam and treachery [editorial]. *Register* 69:4 Jl 4 1993
Is the Supreme Court giving religion a little slack? Shaw, Russell. *OSV* 82:3 Jl 11 1993
Justice Ginsburg and the Supreme Court's course [por]. Shaw, Russell. *OSV* 82:17 O 24 1993
The real Judge Ginsburg. Bopp, James, Jr. *Register* 69:5 Ag 1 1993
Shifting the weight. Shaw, Russell. *OSV* 81:3 Ap 11 1993

UNITED STATES—SUPREME COURT—DECISIONS
The abortion controversy: seeking a common ground. Bernardin, Joseph Louis, Cardinal, 1928-. *Cath Int* 4:210-214 My 1993
The "Brown" decision: 40 years later. Wilkins, Roger, 1932-. *America* 169:4-5 Jl 17-24 1993
A close call. Hittinger, Russell. *Crisis* 11:8+ F 1993
Dred Scott, again. Casey, Robert P, 1932-. *Crisis* 11:16-23 Ap 1993
Equal rights for religion [editorial]. *America* 169:3 Jl 17-24 1993
First Amendment watch. Ball, William Bentley. *Crisis* 11:42-45 S 1993
A glimmer of hope for aid to Catholic schools. Drinan, Robert Francis, 1920-. *America* 169:4-5 S 18 1993
A religion club in the public high school? Marthaler, Berard L, 1927-. *Living Light* 29:11-18 Spr 1993
The Supreme Court v Religion [adapted fr "The Court's phobia of religion" in *The world and I*]. Hittinger, Russell. *Crisis* 11:22-30 My 1993
The thaw. Mullen, Peter. *Register* 69:1+ Je 11 1993

UNITED STATES BISHOP'S COMMITTEE FOR ECUMENICAL AND INTERRELIGIOUS AFFAIRS
Reconciling unity and plurality. Weakland, Rembert G, Abp, 1927-, and Eastman, Theodore, Bp. *Origins* 22:587-588 F 4 1993

UNITED STATES CATHOLIC CONFERENCE
Bishops entangled in their own Balkans morass. Shaw, Russell. *OSV* 82:3 Je 6 1993
The common good: old idea, new urgency. Lynch, Robert, et al. *Origins* 23:81+ Je 24 1993
Funding the asbestos cleanup. Davis, William. *Origins* 23:45-46 Je 3 1993
No more business as usual? Royal, Robert. *Crisis* 11:8 Mr 1993
Planning the implementation of the Catechism of the Catholic Church. Pollard, John E. *Living Light* 29:74-77 Sum 1993
Rebuilding the Church in Eastern Europe. Mullen, Peter. *Crisis* 11:26-28 F 1993

UNITED STATES HOLOCAUST MEMORIAL MUSEUM (WASHINGTON, DC)
No ordinary museum. McCloskey, Liz Leibold. *Comm* 120:10-11 Je 4 1993
This museum is not a metaphor: confronting the hard facts of the Holocaust. Gediman, Paul. *Comm* 120:13-15 Je 4 1993

UNITY AND PLURALITY
Liturgical inculturation in multiethnic churches. Chupungco, Anscar J. *Past Mus* 17:28-29+ F-Mr 1993

UNIVERSAL FELLOWSHIP OF METROPOLITAN COMMUNITY CHURCHES
National Council of Churches denies observer status to UFMCC. Solheim, James. *Ecumen Trends* 22:13 Ja 1993

UNIVERSAL PRIESTHOOD see Priesthood of all Believers

UNIVERSALISM
Attention verses distraction: beyond the Quincentennial of Columbus. Starkloff, Carl. *TheolDgst* 40:119-131 Sum 1993
The Roman principle in the writings of Vladimir Solovyov. Matual, David. *Diakonia* 26 no 1:27-39 1993

UNIVERSITIES AND COLLEGES—CURRICULUM- CHILE
Dos años de labor del programa "fe, ciencia, universidad". Silva, Sergio G. *Teol Vida* 34 no 1-2:3-27 1993

UNIVERSITIES AND COLLEGES—FACULTY
Aubrey Gwynn: the person. Hand, Geoffrey, 1931-. *Studies* 81:375-384 Wint 1992
Can a university be both great and Christian? Lent, Craig S. *New Oxford Rev* 60:10-14 S 1993
The fourth centenary of Trinity College Dublin: reflections of a Jesuit ecumenist. Hurley, Michael. *Studies* 81:399-407 Wint 1992

UNIVERSITIES AND COLLEGES—HISTORY
Gladly to learn and gladly to teach: why Christians invented the university. Fortin, Ernest L, 1923-. *Crisis* 11:33-38 Ap 1993

UNIVERSITIES AND COLLEGES—LAW
The higher law background of the Notre Dame law school. Kmiec, Douglas W. *Amer J Juris* 37:213-242 1992

UNIVERSITIES AND COLLEGES- GREAT BRITAIN
On the move. *Tablet* 247:816 Je 26 1993
Universities at risk. Dummett, Michael. *Tablet* 247:1095-1096 Ag 28 1993

UNIVERSITIES AND COLLEGES, CATHOLIC
Bishops and universities: dominion or communion. Orsy, Ladislas, 1921-. *America* 169:11-16 N 20 1993
Catholic higher education: what happened? Woodward, Kenneth L. *Comm* 120:13-16+ Ap 9 1993
Catholic identity in medical schools. Pellegrino, Edmund D. *Health Prog* 74: 70-73 Ja-F 1993
The Catholic university and its inherent promise. Buckley, Michael J, 1931-. *America* 168:14-16 My 29 1993
Christ and the Catholic university. Daley, Brian E. *America* 169:6-14 S 11 1993
A collegiate conversation. O'Brien, David J, 1938-, and Buckley, Michael J, 1931-. *America* 169:18-23 S 11 1993
Collegium and the futures of Catholic higher education. Kelly, James R, 1937-. *America* 169:15-17 S 11 1993
Controversial student organizations. Sasseen, Robert F, and Frank, William F. *Crisis* 11:38-41 O 1993
Dialogue [interview by P Mullen]. Lopez, Benito. *Register* 69:1+ S 19 1993
Ex corde ecclesiae and its ordinances. Curran, Charles E, 1934-, et al. *Comm* 120:14+ N 19 1993
From ghetto to hilltop: our colleges, our selves. Carlin, David Robert, Jr, 1938-. *Comm* 120:6-7 F 12 1993
John Paul II, Pope, (1992-02-29) Be proud of the name "Catholic". John Paul II, Pope, 1920- (Karol Wojtyla) (elected 1978). *TPS* 37:321-323 N-D 1992*
Keeping colleges Catholic. Scanlan, Michael. *Crisis* 11:33-37 O 1993
More bang for the buck. Feuerherd, Peter. *Register* 69:1+ S 19 1993
Newman on the secular need for religious education. Walsh, David. *F & R* 28:359-385 Wint 1992
Notre Dame debates need for Catholic faculty. Carey, Ann. *OSV* 82:3 Je 13 1993
Preserving a presence in medical education. Byron, William J, 1927-. *Health Prog* 74:68-69 Ja-F 1993
Returning Gospel values to nursing education. Lane, Julia A. *Health Prog* 74:30-35 Je 1993
Second-hand straw. McInerny, Ralph M. *Crisis* 11:15-17 My 1993
The supernatural vision of life (an address given by Timothy O'Donnell on his installation as president of Christendom College: 11 O 1992). O'Donnell, Timothy. *F & R* 18:229-233 Aut 1992
Values that offer a running start on life. Mohan, Robert Paul. *Origins* 23:31-32 My 27 1993

UNIVERSITIES AND COLLEGES, CATHOLIC—INTELLECTUAL LIFE
Can a university be both great and Christian? Lent, Craig S. *New Oxford Rev* 60:10-14 S 1993

UNIVERSITIES AND COLLEGES, CATHOLIC- ITALY
I docenti dell'Università Cattolica si interrogano. Brovedani, Ennio. *Civilta* 144:340-353 F 20 1993

UNIVERSITY OF DETROIT MERCY (MICHIGAN)
Religious superiors defend school's Catholic identity. Schaberg, Jane. *Origins* 22:703-704 Mr 25 1993

UNMARRIED COUPLES
Cohabitation: a perplexing pastoral problem. Finley, Mitchel B. *America* 169: 16-17 Jl 31-Ag 7 1993

UNMARRIED MOTHERS
Family values. Field, Frank, 1942-. *Tablet* 247:1034 Ag 14 1993
Gimme shelter: a house can be a home. McCarthy, Abigail Quigley. *Comm* 120:10-11 Ap 9 1993
The Murphy Brown factor at work. Yoest, Charmaine Crouse. *Register* 69:5 S 5 1993

UNTENER, KENNETH E, BP, 1937-
Homeless bishop speaks for the poor. Schaller, Jeanne Lound. *St Anth* 100: 22-27 Mr 1993
"Ken, don't foul up the Church today" [photo]. Desmet, Kate. *Critic* 47:14-29 Spr 1993

URBAN POOR
An opportunity for positive change. Sullivan, Joseph M, Bp, 1930-. *Health Prog* 74:56-59+ 1993

URBAN RENEWAL
Enterprise zones have negligible history of success. McClure, Laura. *Nat Cath Rep* 29:9 N 13 1992

URBAN SCHOOLS
An indigenous response to inner-city needs. Ratteray, Joan Davis. *Momentum* 24:28-30 F-Mr 1993
Something old, something new. Pergler, Bonnie Schwartz. *Momentum* 24:10-12 F-Mr 1993

URBAN SCHOOLS- NEW YORK
Schools worthy of kids: Saint Angela's needs help. Kelly, Patrick F. *Comm* 120:6-8 Ap 9 1993

URBAN VIII, POPE, 1568-1644 (MAFFEO BARBERINI) (ELECTED 1623)
Urban VIII and the revision of the Latin Hymnal. Lenti, Vincent A. *SacM* 120:30-33 Aut 1993

URBANIZATION—RELIGIOUS ASPECTS
The city: center of early Christian life. Osiek, Carolyn. *BibleT* 31:17-21 Ja 1993
Urbanization in ancient Israel. Frick, Frank S. *BibleT* 31:4-12 Ja 1993
Using God's resources wisely: Isaiah and urban possibility. Brueggemann, Walter. Louisville, Kentucky: John Knox Press, 1993. 96p ISBN 0-664-25460-8

URBANIZATION—RELIGIOUS ASPECTS- CHILE
"A Religiosidade Urbana". Parker Gumucio, Christán. *REB* 53:283-300 Je 1993

URSULINE COLLEGE (PEPPER PIKE, OH)
Do women learn differently from men? Hizer, Gloria. *OSV* 82:6-7 Ag 29 1993

URSULINES—HISTORY
The most adventurous of nuns: Ursulines and the future. Weaver, Mary Jo. *RRel* 52:486-502 Jl-Ag 1993

USURY see Interest and Usury—Religious Aspects

UTOPIAS
Befreiung von Knechtschaft. Ehlen, Peter. *Stimm Zeit* 211:21-33 Ja 1993
La Reconquista del Paraiso. Tamames, Ramon. Barcelona: Temas de Hoy, 1993. x, 203p ISBN 84-7880-231-2
Utopias y anarquismo. Garcia, Victor. Madrid: Madre Tierrra, 1993. x, 220p ISBN 84-86864-08-9

UTOPIAS- LATIN AMERICA
Comunidad y utopia la construccion de nuestra esperanza. Manuel Hurtado, Juan. *Christus* 58:47-49 N-D 1992

V

VACATIONS
A tale of shells. Burns, Jimmy. *Tablet* 247:1098 Ag 28 1993

VALADIER, PAUL
New light under the old bushel: what's happening in the French Church? Englund, Steven. *Comm* 120:11-14 Ap 23 1993

VALDEZ, PATRICK M
The miracle of San Luis. Stevens, Barbara. *OSV* 81:10-11 Ja 10 1993

VALENTINUS, 2D CENT
Agricultural imagery in the Gospel of Matthew and the gospel of truth. Cavallo, Jo Ann. *Relig Lit* 24:27-38 Aut 1992

VALTORTA, MARIA, 1897-1961
Looking at the dark side. Miesel, Sandra. *Register* 69:5 O 17 1993

VALUES
Die befragte Generation. Belistein, Roman. *Stimm Zeit* 211:232-240 Ap 1993
The cathedral of business: the fountainhead of values in America today. Lear, Norman, 1922-. *New Oxford Rev* 60:6-13 Ap 1993
Catholic identity in cooperative ventures. DeSilva, Joseph, and Place, Michael D. *Health Prog* 74:53-54 Jl-Ag 1993
CHA task force helps managers make values-based decisions. Lappetito, Joanne. *Health Prog* 74:14-16 1993
Choosing a college. McCloskey, C. John, III. *Crisis* 11:42-44 O 1993
College education/values education. Hagan, Charles H. *Origins* 22:602-604 F 11 1993
Crisi Dei Valori: Una Terapia Comune Tra Laici E Cattolici? Mucci, Giandomenico. *Civilta* 143:450-457 D 5 1992
Deontologism and moral weakness. Peterson, John. *IPQ* 33:173-181 Je 1993
A diagnosis of Europe's moral malaise. *Tablet* 247:1242-1243 S 25 1993
Dialogue [interview by P Mullen]. Kristol, William. *Register* 69:1+ S 12 1993
Integrating the ideas of dissenting economists into a theory of transformational leadership. Wallis, Joe L. *RSocEcon* 51:14-39 Spr 1993
Is society controllable? Fowler, Thomas B. *F & R* 28:387-413 Wint 1992
John Paul II, Pope (1992-12-27) The Christian family [orig Italian]. John Paul II, Pope, 1920- (Karol Wojtyla) (elected 1978). *OR(Eng)* 1272:9 Ja 6 1993*
John Paul II, Pope, (1993-06-03) Christian hope [Orig in Italian]. John Paul II, Pope, 1920- (Karol Wojtyla) (elected 1978). *OR(Eng)* 1297:9 Je 30 1993*
Public education: a fertile field for religious educators. Doyle, Michelle L. *Momentum* 24:14-16 F-Mr 1993
Ratzinger and the terrorists. Caldecott, Stratford. *Crisis* 11:13-14 Jl-Ag 1993
La raza cósmica: rediscovering the Hispanic soul. Deck, Allan Figueroa. *Critic* 47:46-53 Spr 1993
Ressentiment and the preferential option for the poor. Byrne, Patrick H. *TheolStds* 54:213-241 Je 1993
Returning Gospel values to nursing education. Lane, Julia A. *Health Prog* 74:30-35 Je 1993
Schools for the real world. Pring, Richard. *Tablet* 247:394 Mr 27 1993
Secular fundamentalism and secular humanism: value sets for the twenty-first century. Kollar, Nathan R. *Stud Form Spir* 14:233-246 My 1993
Seen any good movies lately? Costello, Gerald M, 1931-. *USCath* 58:48-50 Je 1993
Ser y conocer. Garcia Del Muro Solans, Juan. Barcelona: PPU, 1993. x, 580p ISBN 84-477-0017-8
The sinfulness of normality. Arthur, Chris. *Month* 26:361-366 S-O 1993

La stylométrie et la question de Métaphysique K. Rutten, Christian. *RPhil Louvain* 90:486-496 N 1992

A system develops values-based reform policy. Kramer, Richard, and Vickers, Susan. *Health Prog* 74:56 Jl-Ag 1993

Theology, praxis, and ethics in the thought of Juan Luis Segundo, SJ. Zimbelman, Joel. *Thomist* 57:233-267 Ap 1993

"Things my mother taught me" [interview by J A Wintz, 1936-]. Shields, Brooke, 1965-. *St Anth* 100:28-32 My 1993

Value variables in the health-care reform debate. McCormick, Richard Arthur, 1922-. *America* 168:7-13 My 29 1993

What gives a family value? Scott, Charlene. *USCath* 58:32-37 Ja 1993

What kind of family did Jesus value? McCormick, Patrick. *USCath* 58:36-37 O 1993

Will the churches meet th Europeans? Kerkhofs, Jan, 1924-. *Tablet* 247:1184-1187 S 18 1993

Youth formation. Doyle, Katherine. *Mod Lit* 19:28 D 1992-Ja 1993

VALUES—LAW

Does the "incommensurability thesis" imperil common sense moral judgments? George, Robert P. *Amer J Juris* 37:185-195 1992

VALUES—PHILOSOPHY

Le médiation philosophique des valeurs. Henrici, Peter. *Gregorianum* 74 no 3:515-541 1993

VALUES—RELIGIOUS ASPECTS

A witness marked by love and humility. Quinn, John Raphael, Abp, 1929-. *Origins* 23:113+ Jl 15 1993

VALUES- MALTA

Valori per il futuro di Malta. Abela, Anthony M. *Civilta* 2:260-269 My 1 1993

VALUES, SOCIAL

Capital punishment. Langan, John P. *TheolStds* 54:111-124 Mr 1993

College education/values education. Hagan, Charles H. *Origins* 22:602-604 F 11 1993

The conscience of the voter and law-maker [Irish content]. Hannon, Patrick. *Doctr Life* 42:244-252 My-Je 1992

GATT: an ethical void. Egan, Eileen. *Cath Work* 60:1+ Je-Jl 1993

Moral debate and social change. Edmondson, Ricca. *Doctr Life* 42:233-243 My-Je 1992

New world, new disorder [fr *Out of control: global turmoil on the eve of the twenty-first century*]. Brzezinski, Zbigniew K, 1928-. *Crisis* 11:39-42 My 1993

Penance, 1993. Burleigh, Anne Husted, 1941-. *Crisis* 11:44-45 Mr 1993

Trying to make sense [editorial]. *Month* 26:86-87 Mr 1993

VAN ESBROECK, M

Response to De Halleux and Van Esbroeck. Wickham, Lionel. *Jurist* 52 no 1:130-137 1992

VANDALISM

Robbing Peter, and Paul, too [Church Vandalism]. Holton, Robert. *OSV* 82:6 O 17 1993

VANITY *see* Pride and Vanity

VANUNU, MORDECHAI

Time to let out the secret. Torrens, James S. *America* 169:4 O 23 1993

VASARI, GIORGIO, 1511-1574

Images of paradise. Bull, George, 1929-. *Tablet* 246:1613 D 19-26 1992

VATICAN

Tiny Vatican office moves mountains [Cor Unum]. Burke, Greg. *Register* 69:1+ S 5 1993

VATICAN—ECONOMIC CONDITIONS

Awash in a sea of red ink [2nd of 2 pts]. O'Grady, Desmond. *OSV* 82:10-11 Jl 4 1993

Deficit buster [1st of two parts]. O'Grady, Desmond. *OSV* 82:6 Je 27 1993

VATICAN CITY

John Paul II, Pope, (1992-09-08) Litterae Apostolicae (Apostolic Letter) [Italian]. John Paul II, Pope, 1920- (Karol Wojtyla) (elected 1978). *AAS* 84:1033-1053 N 3 1992*

John Paul II, Bujak, Adam. Krakow: Parol Company, 1992. x, 111p ISBN 0-89870-424-3 LC 92-71934

Secretariat of State (1992-10-02) Decretum (Decree on Norms of Pensions) [Italian]. *AAS* 84:1079 N 3 1992*

VATICAN COUNCIL, 2D, 1962-1965

Abandoned in a toxic culture: how we failed the new generation. Novak, Michael, 1933-. *Crisis* 10:15-19 D 1992

Anno propedeutico: vera novità del Concilio Vaticano II (commentary: *Pastores dabo vobis*). Negro, Donato. *Seminarium* 32:600-621 O-D 1992

The attack on the church musician. Schuler, Richard Joseph, 1920-. *SacM* 119:3-5 Wint 1992

The challenge of inculturation. Lane, Dermot A. *Living Light* 29:3-21 Wint 1992

Committed Christian secularity. Philibert, Paul J. *RRel* 52:350-362 My-Je 1993

Continuing summons to renewal and reorientation. Gray, Howard. *Origins* 23:115-120 Jl 15 1993

A Council betrayed. Novak, Michael, 1933-. *Crisis* 11:6-7 O 1993

La cuestion institucional. Dussel, Enrique. *Christus* 58:62-65 Mr-Ap 1993

Designing the post-Vatican II worship space. Habiger, Robert D. *Mod Lit* 20:8-11 N 1993

Deutsche evangeliare. *Notitiae* 28:348-351 My 1992

Entering ecumenism's reception phase. Staalsett, Gunnar. *Origins* 23:744-746 Ap 8 1993

John Paul II, Pope, (1992-05-22) Canon Law should renew ecclesial life. John Paul II, Pope, 1920- (Karol Wojtyla) (elected 1978). *TPS* 37:374-376 N-D 1992*

John Paul II, Pope, (1992-12-22) give thanks for the gift of serving. John Paul II, Pope, 1920- (Karol Wojtyla) (elected 1978). *TPS* 38:172-178 My-Je 1993*

John Paul II, Pope, (1992-12-22) Give thanks [orig Italian]. John Paul II, Pope, 1920- (Karol Wojtyla) (elected 1978). *OR(Eng)* 1272:6-7 Ja 6 1993*

Man and woman are loved by the Lord and desired for one another. Cànopi, Anna Maria. *OR(Eng)* 1300:10+ Jl 21 1993

The memoirs of Cardinal Leo Jozef Suenens. Murphy, Francis Xavier, 1914-. *America* 168:17-18 Je 5-12 1993

Politics in the purple kingdom: the derailment of Vatican II. Schlichte, George A. Kansas City: Sheed & Ward, 1993. x, 133p ISBN 1-55612-607-7 LC 92-44098

The post-Vatican II Church. Fleming, David L. *RRel* 52:484-485 Jl-Ag 1993

Remember Vatican II? [condensed fr *Catholic Update* Mr 1993]. Foley, Leonard. *CDgst* 57:86-92 Je 1993

Sensus Fidei: theological reflection since Vatican II: I, 1965-1984. Burkhard, John J. *Heythrop* 34:41-59 Ja; 123-136 Ap 1993

Shifting paradigm: layleadership in the Year 2000. Roy, Lucien. *Listening* 28:6-13 Wint 1993

A tale of two popes [editorial]. *Tablet* 247:775-776 Je 19 1993

Vatican II perspectives. McRedmond, Louis. *Doctr Life* 42:298-304 My-Je 1992

VATICAN COUNCIL, 2D, 1962-1965—BISHOPS

John Paul II, Pope, (1992-10-28) The apostolic mission of bishops. John Paul II, Pope, 1920- (Karol Wojtyla) (elected 1978). *TPS* 38:107-110 Mr-Ap 1993*

VATICAN COUNCIL, 2D, 1962-1965—CHURCH

The local church and the church Catholic: the contemporary theological problematic. Komonchak, Joseph Andrew, 1939-. *Jurist* 52 no 1:416-447 1992

Reception and submission. Pottmeyer, Hermann Joseph. *Jurist* 51 no 2:269-292 1991

Teaching Church teaching: theological and pedagogical reflections. Hinsdale, Mary Ann. *Horizons (CTS)* 20:87-98 Spr 1993

VATICAN COUNCIL, 2D, 1962-1965—CHURCH IN THE MODERN WORLD

Catholic giving and the signs of the times. Hofheinz, Fred. *Origins* 22:520-523 Ja 7 1993

Catholic megatrends. Upton, Julia. *ChrWorld* 236:197-202 S-O 1993

Função dos pais e padrinhos nos sacramentos da iniciação Cristã. Feracine, Luiz. *REB* 52:903-916 D 1992

La identidad problematica. Palacio, Carlos. *Christus* 58:26-38 My 1993

The search for original sin. Stuhlmueller, Carroll. *BibleT* 31:73-78 Mr 1993

Transforming today's church. Graff, Ann O'Hara. *Chicago Stud* 32:127-142 Ag 1993

Vatican II: the impact on American society—the pas de deux between rights and responsibilities. Araujo, Robert J. *CLawyer* 35 no 2:109-144 1993

Wojtyla and the Council [excerpt fr *Il pensiero di Karol Wojtyla*]. Buttiglione, Rocco. *Crisis* 11:21-25 F 1993

VATICAN COUNCIL, 2D, 1962-1965—CONGRESSES

The church in the nineties: its legacy its future. Hegy, Pierre M. Collegeville, Minnesota: The Liturgical Press, 1993. x, 323p ISBN 0-8146-2098-1 LC 92-45242

VATICAN COUNCIL, 2D, 1962-1965—DOCUMENTS

Concili Ecumenic Vatica 2: Constitucions, Decrets, Declaracions. Barcelona: Claret, 1993. x, 495p ISBN 84-7263-839-1

Re-informing the faithful: the catechsim that completes the Council. Lawler, Ronald D, 1926-. *Crisis* 11:19-22 Je 1993*

VATICAN COUNCIL, 2D, 1962-1965—EASTERN CHURCHES, CATHOLIC

Apostolic See in the new Oriental Canonical Legislation. Abbass, Jobe. *Stud Can* 27 no 1:173-215 1993

VATICAN COUNCIL, 2D, 1962-1965—ECUMENISM

Das Ökumenismusdekret des Konzils. Suttner, Ernst Chr. *Stimm Zeit* 211:303-317 My 1993

Der päpstliche rat zur Förderung der Einheit der Christen im Jahre 1992. Cassidy, Edward Idris, 1924-, Cardinal. *Catholica* 47 no 2:89-107 1993

The 1993 directory for ecumenism. *Origins* 23:129+ Jl 29 1993

VATICAN COUNCIL, 2D, 1962-1965—INFLUENCE

Das Zweite Vatikanische Konzil. Pesch, Otto Hermann, 1931-. Frieburg: Echter, 1993. x, 444p ISBN 3-429-01533-2

VATICAN COUNCIL, 2D, 1962-1965—LAITY

Collaborators, informers and secret service. Watkins, Clare. *New Blckfrs* 74:263-279 My 1993

Ministry: lay ministry in the Catholic Church, its history and theology. Osborne, Kenan B. New Jersey: Paulist Press, 1993. x, 722p ISBN 0-8091-3371-7 LC 92-40299

Quaestiones de officiis ecclesiasticis laicorum. Erdö, Peter. *Periodica* 81 no 2:179-209 1992

Themes of the lay life. Keightley, Georgia Masters. *Origins* 22:761-764 Ap 15 1993

VATICAN COUNCIL, 2D, 1962-1965—LITURGY

The catechetical role of the liturgy and the quality of liturgical texts: the current ICEL translation. Leiva-Merikakis, Erasmo. *Communio* 20:63-83 Spr 1993

Conciliar constitution: Sacrosanctum Concilium. Schuler, Richard Joseph, 1920-. *SacM* 119:7-14 Wint 1992

Converting the assembly. Pace, Charlotte. *Mod Lit* 20:10-13 F 1993

Eucharist of the assembly. Huck, Gabe. *Church* 9:7-11 Spr 1993

Hispanic culture and worship: the process of inculturation. Martínez, Germán. *US Cath Hist* 11:79-91 Spr 1993

Hospitality and by musicians: melody and text. Sosa, Juan J. *Past Mus* 17:18-21 F-Mr 1993

Liturgy and catechesis: two sides of the same coin. Moynahan, Michael E. *Living Light* 29:47-57 Aut 1992

One heart and voice: Musicam Sacram and liturgical unity. Joncas, Michael. *Past Mus* 17:19-21 Ag-S 1993

Sacraments: Jesus is the starting point. Richstatter, Thomas, 1939-. *St Anth* 101:22-27 Ag 1993

They're wrong! [editorial]. Schuler, Richard Joseph, 1920-. *SacM* 120:3-5 Spr 1993

L'uso delle versioni della sacra scrittura nella liturgia. Congregation for Divine Worship and Discipline of the Sacraments. *Notitiae* 28:323-331 My 1992

VATICAN COUNCIL, 2D, 1962-1965—MISSIONS

Mission and Church. Furioli, Anthony. *AFER* 34:170-182 Je 1992

VATICAN COUNCIL, 2D, 1962-1965—NON-CHRISTIANS
Christian-Muslim dialogue in a changing world [address, The 36th Annual Robert Cardinal Bellarmarine Lecture, St Louis Univ, S 30 1992]. Michel, Thomas F. *TheolDgst* 39:303-320 Wint 1992

VATICAN COUNCIL, 2D, 1962-1965—PRIESTS
Pastores Dabo Vobis and priestly formation [pt 1]. Carey, Michael, and Cole, Basil. *Priest* 49:10-18 Jl 1993

Pastores Dabo Vobis and priestly formation [pt 1]. Carey, Michael, and Cole, Basil. *Priest* 49:10-18 Jl 1993

La "Pastores dabo vobis" alla luce del pensiero conciliare sul sacerdozio e sulla formazione sacerdotale (commentary: *Pastores daba vobis*). Rypar, Francesco. *Seminarium* 32:530-549 O-D 1992

Patores Dabo Vobis [pt 2]. Carey, Michael, and Cole, Basil. *Priest* 49:33-43 Ag 1993

Women's role in Church law: past and present. Huels, John M. *New Theol Rev* 6:19-31 My 1993

VATICAN COUNCIL, 2D, 1962-1965—RELIGIOUS FREEDOM
Apostle of religious freedom [adapted fr *John Courtney Murray and the American civil conversation*]. Canavan, Francis, 1917-. *Crisis* 11:31-35 My 1993

The Church learning and the Church teaching: Vatican II and the liberal tradition of religious freedom. O'Donnell, Robert J. *JEcumen Stds* 29:399-417 Sum-Aut 1992

Liberación, inculturación y alteridad. Espeja, Jesús. *Cien Tom* 120:153-167 Ja-Ap 1993

VATICAN COUNCIL, 2D, 1962-1965—RELIGIOUS LIFE
John Paul II, Pope, (1991-05-25) Evangelize by charity. John Paul II, Pope, 1920- (Karol Wojtyla) (elected 1978). *Con Life* 17 no 2:28-30 1992*

Leadership, authority, and religious government. Linscott, Mary. *RRel* 52: 166-193 Mr-Ap 1993

The religious life futures project: executive summary. Nygren, David J, and Ukeritis, Miriam D. *RRel* 52:6-55 Ja-F 1993

The synod of consecrated life. McDonough, Elizabeth. *RRel* 52:626-621 Jl-Ag 1993

VATICAN COUNCIL, 2D, 1962-1965—REMINISCENCES
Vatican II diary. Hebblethwaite, Peter, 1930-. *Tablet* 247:750-751 Je 1993

VATICAN COUNCIL, 2D, 1962-1965—REVELATION
New Testament study and ministry of the word. Harrington, Daniel J. *Chicago Stud* 31:117-129 Ag 1992

Transmisión de la revelación: escritura, tradición, magisterio: (A la luz de la *Dei Verbum del Concilio Vaticano II*). Sánchez Mielgo, Gerardo. *Cien Tom* 119:251-289 My-Ag 1992

Umkämpftes Ja zur Bibelwissenschaft. Kremer, Jacob. *Stimm Zeit* 211:75-94 F 1993

VATICAN COUNCIL, 2D, 1962-1965—STUDY AND TEACHING
Das Zweite Vatikanische Konzil. Pesch, Otto Hermann, 1931-. Frieburg: Echter, 1993. x, 444p ISBN 3-429-01533-2

VATICAN LIBRARY (VATICAN CITY)
Rome reborn: the Vatican library and Renaissance culture. Gratton, Anthony, ed. Washington, DC: Library of Congress, 1993. x, 323p ISBN 0-300-05442-4 LC 92-62275

Rome reborn: the Vatican library and renaissance culture. Sweeney, Jim. *OSV* 81:12-13 F 7 1993

The Vatican library goes to Washington [condensed fr *Rome reborn: the Vatican library and Renaissance Culture*]. Grafton, Anthony. *CDgst* 57:1-8 F 1993

VAZ, JOSEPH, 1651-1711
Congregation for the Causes of Saints (1993-07-06) Decree on a miracle. Congregation for the Causes of Saints. *OR(Eng)* 1299:12 Jl 14 1993*

VEGETARIANISM—RELIGIOUS ASPECTS
Good news for animals?: Christian approaches to animal well-being. Pinches, Charles, and McDaniel, Jay B, eds. Maryknoll, New York: Orbis Books, 1993. x, 258p ISBN 0-88344-860-1 LC 92-41682

VENTAJA MILAN, DIEGO, BP
John Paul II, Pope, (1993-10-10) Diego Ventaja Milan. John Paul II, Pope, 1920- (Karol Wojtyla) (elected 1978). *OR(Eng)* 1311:1 O 13 1993*

Two Spanish Bishops and seven Christian Brothers gave their lives for Catholic faith. *OR(Eng)* 1311:1 O 13 1993

VEUSTER, DAMIEN DE, 1840-1889
Congregation for the Causes of Saints (1992-06-13) Decree on a miracle of Servant of God, Damien de Veuster. Congregation for the Causes of Saints. *AAS* 84:1174-1176 D 5 1992*

Damian of Molokai. Cavnar, Cindy. *New Cov* 22:25+ My 1993

VICTIMS OF CRIME
Listening to the survivors: voices of people of God. Berry, Jason. *America* 169:4-9 N 13 1993

People are getting hurt: the rise in gay-bashing. Anderson, George M. *Comm* 120:16+ F 26 1993

VICUNA, LAURA, 1891-
John Paul II, Pope, (1988-09-03). John Paul II, Pope, 1920- (Karol Wojtyla) (elected 1978). *AAS* 84:1115-1117 D 5 1992*

VIDEO ART
Diving in. McMahon, John. *Can Cath Rev* 11:38-39 Jl-Ag 1993

VIDEO TAPES
The final decade? McMahon, John. *Can Cath Rev* 11:51-53 Ja 1993

VIDEO TAPES IN EDUCATION
Stay tuned!. Hendricks, Kathleen. *Tod Parish* 25:27-28 O 1993

VIETNAMESE WAR, 1957-1975—VETERANS
The spiritual healing of post-traumatic stress disorder at the Menlo Park Veteran's Hospital. Jiménez, Manuel J, Jr. *Stud Form Spir* 14:175-187 My 1993

VILLANOVA UNIVERSITY (PA)—HISTORY
Ever ancient, ever new: Villanova University, 1842-1992 [photos]. Contosta, David R, and Gallagher, Dennis J. Virginia Beach: The Donning Company, 1992. 120p ISBN 0-89865-870-0 LC 92-24373

VINCENT DE PAUL, SAINT
Vincent De Paul and charity. Dodin, André. New Rochelle: New City Press, 1993. 126p ISBN 1-56548-054-6 LC 93-15188

VINCENT DE PAUL, SAINT, 1581-1660
The life of the venerable servant of God Vincent de Paul: founder and first superior general of the Congregation of the Mission (book one). Abelly, Louis. New Rochelle, New York: New City Press, 1993. 403p ISBN 1-56548-052-x LC 93-9446

Vincent de Paul's charism in today's church. Luttenberger, Gerard H. *RRel* 52:660-683 S-O 1993

VINCENTIANS
Always the poor. Dodds, Bill. *New Cov* 22:21-24 Je 1993

VINCI, LEONARD DA, 1452-1519
Who's who in The Last Supper? [condensed fr *Western New York Catholic* Mr 1993]. Kidder, Keith. *CDgst* 57:1-3 Jl 1993

VIOLENCE
An antidote to violence? Lascaris, Andrew. *New Blckfrs* 74:345-355 Jl-Ag 1993

Bad consciences on abortion [editorial]. *Tablet* 247:423 Ap 3 1993

Beyond the myth of dominance: an alternative to a violent society. McMahon, Edwin M, 1930-. Kansas City: Sheed & Ward, 1993. x, 271p ISBN 15-5612-563-1

Enough is enough!. Mullen, Peter. *Register* 69:1+ S 5 1993

Hollywood and violence. Austin, Ronald. *Register* 69:3 Mr 21 1993

Light in a culture of violence. Higgins, James J. *Liguorian* 81:73 D 1993

Media violations. Malloy, Richard G. *America* 168:4-5 F 6 1993

A neighbourhood in ruins. Jabusch, Willard. *Tablet* 247:1128 S 4 1993

No alternative talks. *Tablet* 247:159 F 6 1993

The roots of tv violence. Rocchio, Vincent. *Register* 69:3 Ag 15 1993

Self-help in Ulster. Burns, Jimmy. *Tablet* 247:133-134 Ja 30 1993

Times of violence, dreams of peace. Cameli, Louis J. *Priest* 49:12-18 Mr 1993

Warning: television may endanger your health!. Feuerherd, Peter. *Register* 69:1+ Jl 25 1993

VIOLENCE—RELIGIOUS ASPECTS
Gaia and God: an ecofeminist theology of earth healing. Ruether, Rosemary Radford. San Francisco: HarperSanFrancisco, 1992. 310p ISBN 0-06067-022-3 LC 91-58911

The roots of violence against women. Mejia, Jorge Julia, Bp. *Origins* 23:369+ N 4 1993

VIOLENCE- BRAZIL
Street children slaughtered in the night. Pimentel-Pinto, Francis. *Tablet* 247:990 Jl 31 1993

VIOLENCE- COLOMBIA
Recherche éthique dans un contexte de violence. Roux, Francisco J de. *Lumen* 48:293-303 S 1993

VIOLENCE- GREAT BRITAIN
Recipe for disaster on Moss Side. *Tablet* 247:87 Ja 16 1993

VIOLENCE- HAITI
A poisoned chalice. Griffiths, Leslie. *Tablet* 247:1254 O 2 1993

VIOLENCE- LEBANON
Catholic delegates narrowly escape assassination. *Tablet* 247:865 Jl 3 1993

VIOLENCE- NORTHERN IRELAND
Irish demonstrate against terrorism. *Tablet* 247:490 Ap 10-17 1993

VIOLENCE- SOMALIA
The flight to and from Thika. Martin, James Alfred. *America* 168:14-15 Ja 16-23 1993

VIOLENCE- SOUTH AFRICA
ANC not to take action on torture report. Rickard, Carmel. *Tablet* 247:1141 S 4 1993

Sunday—day of murder by gun and grenade. Pickard, Carmel. *Tablet* 247:989-990 Jl 31 1993

VIOLENCE IN HOSPITALS- PENSACOLA, FLORIDA
Doctor killed at abortion clinic. Smith, John, Bp, et al. *Origins* 22:701+ Mr 25 1993

VIOLENCE IN MASS MEDIA
Hollywood blues. Jones, Arthur C, 1936-. *Tablet* 247:849-850 Jl 3 1993

VIOLENCE IN TELEVISION
TV sweeps and stats. Wallace, James A, 1944-. *Liguorian* 81:51 Ag 1993

Violence on the home screen. Gardella, Kay. *America* 169:4 S 11 1993

Warning: TV violence is hazardous to our children [editorial]. Dangel, Mary Jo. *St Anth* 101:17 N 1993

VIOLENT DEATHS
Doctor killed at abortion clinic. Smith, John, Bp, et al. *Origins* 22:701+ Mr 25 1993

VIRGIL
The Roman principle in the writings of Vladimir Solovyov. Matual, David. *Diakonia* 26 no 1:27-39 1993

VIRGIN BIRTH
Born of a virgin. Daley, Brian E. *Tablet* 246:1598-1603 D 19-26 1992

John Paul II, Pope, (1992-12-30) Marian devotion [orig Italian and French]. John Paul II, Pope, 1920- (Karol Wojtyla) (elected 1978). *OR(Eng)* 1272:11 Ja 6 1993*

The mystery of the incarnation. Schönborn, Christoph von, Bp. San Francisco: Ignatius Press, 1992. x, 67p ISBN 0-89870-393-x LC 92-73690

VIRTUE
Can virtue be taught? Darling-Smith, Barbara. Notre Dame: University of Notre Dame Press, 1993. x, 224p ISBN 0-268-00799-3 LC 93-4578

An essay on Jonathan Boswell's Community and the economy: the theory of public co-operation. Naughton, Michael. *RSocEcon* 51:86-102 Spr 1993

The state, virtue, sex and chastity. Healy, Jack. *Linacre* 60:51-59 My 1993

VIRTUES
Die befragte Generation. Belistein, Roman. *Stimm Zeit* 211:232-240 Ap 1993

An Italian view of the debate on virtue. Kennedy, Terence. *Thomist* 57:123-130 Ja 1993

Seeing anew: beauty, the arts, and Christian faith [editorial]. Pawlikowski, John T. *New Theol Rev* 5:3-5 F 1993

What's good about being sick? Johnson, Richard P. *Liguorian* 81:20-25 Jl 1993

Why virtues are basic to the common good. Bernardin, Joseph Louis, Cardinal, 1928-. *Origins* 23:337+ O 21 1993

Working with Christ: the Catechism's social teaching. Schall, James Vincent, 1928-. *Crisis* 11:27-30 Je 1993*

VISINTAINER, PAULINE OF THE HEART OF JESUS IN AGONY (AMABILIS), 1865-1942

John Paul II, Pope, (1991-07-14) Litterae Apostolicae (Apostolic Letters) [Latin]. John Paul II, Pope, 1920- (Karol Wojtyla) (elected 1978). *AAS* 84: 949-951 O 3 1992*

VISITATION NUNS

A developmental view of Salesian spirituality. Conn, Joann Wolski. *RRel* 52: 56-68 Ja-F 1993

Escape to Eden. McLoughlin, Marianna. *Register* 69:2 O 31 1993

VISITATIONS (CHURCH WORK)

Parish diary: March. *Tablet* 247:401 Mr 27 1993

VISUAL PERCEPTION

From The sun also rises to High noon: the hypervisual great awakening in American literature and film. Meyer, William E H, Jr. *Cithara* 32:39-59 N 1992

VITORIA, FRANCISCO DE, 1486?-1546

An analysis of the use of rights language in pre-modern Catholic social thought. Brady, Bernard V. *Thomist* 57:97-121 Ja 1993

Francisco de Vitoria y Bartolomé de Las Casas. Hernández, Ramón. *Cien Tom* 119:433-457 S-D 1992

VLADIMIR, SAINT, 956-1015

From first to third millennium: the social Christianity of St Vladimir of Kiev. Obolensky, Alexander P. *CrossCurr* 43:203-211 Sum 1993

VLAUN, JAMES

The Gospel according to Matthew, Mark, Luke, John and Ringo. Ryan, Dick. *OSV* 81:6-7 F 28 1993

VLK, MIROSLAV, ABP

Reorganized council tilts to the East. *Tablet* 247:1020 Ag 7 1993

VOCAL REGISTERS

Find versatile service music that works. Lovrien, Peggy. *Past Mus* 17:33-34 Ap-My 1993

VOCATION

F S C vocations today: rediscovering our roots. Hynes, Christian. *Sisters* 65: 293-298 Jl 1993

Moses. Martin, George. *Liguorian* 81:44-45 F 1993

Teaching as a vocation in the public school. Whitehead, Sharon. *Momentum* 24:22-25 F-Mr 1993

The time of our lives. Casserly, Bernard. *Columbia* 73:9 S 1993

Turning the vocations tide. McMunn, Richard. *Columbia* 73:10-12 S 1993

Understanding secular institutes. *Origins* 23:410-416 N 18 1993

What are single people called to do? Brady, Mary Clare. *USCath* 58:32-33 Jl 1993

VOCATION, ECCLESIASTICAL

Discerning vocations. Klein, Terrance W. *America* 168:10-11 My 1 1993

How to relate theology and Canon Law. Orsy, Ladislas, 1921-. *Origins* 22: 549-552 Ja 21 1993

John Paul II, Pope, (1993-02-26) Sharing clergy. John Paul II, Pope, 1920- (Karol Wojtyla) (elected 1978). *TPS* 38:236-239 Jl-Ag 1993*

Living with compulsory celibacy. O'Keefe, James. *Way Suppl* 77:37-45 Sum 1993

Parish diary: May. *Tablet* 247:685 My 29 1993

The pastoral priorities of the local church in Eastern Africa. Mejia, Rodrigo. *AFER* 34:324-339 D 1992

Priests for our time. Danneels, Godfried, Cardinal, 1933-. *Furrow* 44:331-440 Je 1993*

En relisant l'amour des lettres et le désir de Dieu. Dumont, Camille. *NRT* 114:889-895 N-D 1992

Saint Aloysius Gonzaga: patron of youth. Stamwitz, Alicia von. *Liguorian* 81: 26-32 Ag 1993

Towards what kind of priest? Duffy, Eugene. *Furrow* 44:208-214 Ap 1993

Vocation: it's not just for priest anymore. Shaw, Russell. *Columbia* 73:6-8 S 1993

Vocations in conflict. Castle, Anthony, 1938-. *Tablet* 247:844-845 Jl 3 1993

A witness to mystery. Buechlein, Daniel M. *Priest* 49:35-37 Mr 1993

VOCATION (IN RELIGIOUS ORDERS)

Boosting vocations: time to refocus. Myers, John, Bp. *Register* 69:1+ O 10 1993

Discerning vocations. Klein, Terrance W. *America* 168:10-11 My 1 1993

The good news about vocations. Mallon, John. *Register* 69:1+ O 10 1993

If you ask them, they will come. Carey, Ann. *OSV* 82:18 O 10 1993

Inside a high school seminary [condensed fr *Vocations and Prayer* Jl/S 1993]. Martini, Dick. *CDgst* 58:108-111+ D 1993

Ministry potential discerner. Wukas, Mark. *Columbia* 73:12-14 Jl 1993

The monastic journey. Merton, Thomas, 1915-1968. Kalamazoo: Cistercian Publications, 1992. x, 186p ISBN 0-87907-5333

The priest and the guerillas [interview]. Falla, Ricardo. *Month* 26:219-225 Je 1993

Religious vocations: new signs of the times. DiIanni, Albert. *RRel* 52:745-763 S-O 1993

They heard a second call [condensed fr *Catholic Courier* Ap 29 1993]. Strong, Lee. *CDgst* 57:120-124 S 1993

The urgency of ongoing formation. McGarry, Cecil. *AFER* 34:134-145 Je 1992

Vocations among teaching brothers. King, Eleace. *RRel* 52:102-110 Ja-F 1993

VOEGELIN, ERIC

Consciousness and transcedence: the theology of Eric Voegelin. Morrisey, Michael P. Notre Dame: University of Notre Dame Press, 1994. x, 384p ISBN 0-268-00793-4 LC 92-50159

VOLLMAR, PAUL, BP

New bishops, new spirit in Chur. Kelly, Robert. *Tablet* 247:798 Je 19 1993

VOLUNTARISM

Called, gifted, and burned out. Ganss, Karl, and Fuller, Kathleen. *Tod Parish* 25:7-8 Ja 1993

Families communities of love and service. Finley, Mitchel B. *Liguorian* 81: 38-42 F 1993

Invitation to altruism. Coffey, Kathy. *Momentum* 24:73 Ap-My 1993

The search for personal justice. Aiken, William. *Living Prayer* 26:17 Ja-F 1993

A taste for the other: the moral development of college students and young adults. Heft, James L. *Living Light* 29:23-36 Spr 1993

VOLUNTEER SERVICE

Director of volunteer ministries. Ledwig, Frances. *Church* 9:28-30 Sum 1993

Needed: volunteer policies. Shaughnessy, Mary Angela. *Momentum* 24:62-64 N-D 1993

VOLUNTEERS

Volunteers: just say "no". Dodds, Bill. *New Cov* 23:32 Ag 1993

VOLUNTEERS—RECRUITING

The resourceful recruiter. Connolly, Theresa. *Catechist* 27:70-71 S 1993

VON SPEYR, ADRIENNE

Adrienne von Speyr and the mystery of the atonement. Nichols, Aidan. *New Blckfrs* 73:542-553 N 1992

VOTING—RESEARCH

Interpreting the Catholic vote in 1992. Prendergast, William B. *America* 169: 15+ O 16 1993

VOTING- IRELAND

The conscience of the voter and law-maker [Irish content]. Hannon, Patrick. *Doctr Life* 42:244-252 My-Je 1992

VOUCHERS, EDUCATIONAL see Educational Vouchers

VOYAGES AND TRAVELS

Dutch treat. Blue, Lionel. *Tablet* 247:1039 Ag 14 1993

John Paul II, Pope, (1993-09-10) Gospel. John Paul II, Pope, 1920- (Karol Wojtyla) (elected 1978). *OR(Eng)* 1307:13 S 15 1993*

Malcolm after Mecca: East Africa, 1964. Snyder, Margaret. *Comm* 119:6-7 D 18 1992

"Sailing to the Lowlands low"—the bishops in Brussels, 1-3 February 1993. Devlin, Brendan P. *Furrow* 44:178-181 Mr 1993

Thirty-two days without bread. Schroth, Raymond A, 1933-. *America* 169:4-6 O 30 1993

W

WAGES

Income distribution and business cycles. Van Lear, William. *RSocEcon* 50: 316-332 Fall 1992

Quality management of human resources. Blair, Carol S, et al. *Health Prog* 74:16-21 O 1993

WAGNER, JOACHIM

Our Lady of the chiseled heart [photo]. Gadoua, Renée K. *OSV* 82:12-13 N 21 1993

WAGNER, JOHANNES

Lettera a Mons Johannes Wagner in occasione del suo 85 genetliaco. Javierre, Antonio M, Cardinal, and Angelo, Geraldo M. *Notitiae* 29:28-29 Ja-F 1993

WAGNER, ROGER

Roger Wagner, R I P. Skeris, Robert A. *SacM* 120:26-29 Sum 1993

WAITE, TERENCE HARDY, 1939-

Waite's ordeal. *Tablet* 247:1229 S 25 1993

WAKE SERVICES

The rites of death: celebrating a life. Martin, Joseph F. *Mod Lit* 20:18-20 O 1993

WALDORF METHOD OF EDUCATION

Waldorf education: an innovative tradition. Harrington, Sheila. *Momentum* 24:17-21 F-Mr 1993

WALESA, LECH, 1943-

A parting of the ways. Luxmoore, Jonathan. *Register* 69:2 Jl 25 1993

WALLICH-CLIFFORD, ANTON, 1923-

Beggars for beggars. Rice, Judith. *Tablet* 247:1126-1127 S 4 1993

WALSH, EUGENE

Eugene Walsh, SS. *Mod Lit* 20:46 Ap 1993

WALZER, MICHAEL

Rechtsphilosophie. Brieskorn, Norbert. *Stimm Zeit* 211:318-330 My 1993

WAPNICK, KENNETH

Sin, evil and death in the New Age. McIntyre, Moni. *Way* 33:210-221 Jl 1993

WAR

New world, new disorder [fr *Out of control: global turmoil on the eve of the twenty-first century*]. Brzezinski, Zbigniew K, 1928-. *Crisis* 11:39-42 My 1993

The post-cold war agenda for peace. Bernardin, Joseph Louis, Cardinal, 1928-. *Origins* 23:1+ My 20 1993

War comes to Medjugorje. Manney, Dave. *New Cov* 23:7-11 N 1993

WAR—ETHICAL ASPECTS

Even warfare has its rules [editorial]. *Tablet* 247:1119 S 4 1993

Interpretations of conflict: ethics, pacifism, and the just-war tradition. Miller, Richard Brian. Chicago: University of Chicago Press, 1991. 294p ISBN 0-22652-795-6 LC 91-3044

Just war, pacifism and humanitarian intervention. Himes, Kenneth R. *America* 169:10-15+ Ag 14-21 1993

Put an end to "ethnic cleansing". *OR(Eng)* 1305:2 S 1 1993

Statement on the morality of the war in the Persian Gulf. *Horizons (CTS)* 20:118-126 Spr 1993

You can't keep a good theory down: the just war, the Gulf War and beyond. Pope, J Stephen. *Comm* 120:9-12 F 12 1993

WAR—PSYCHOLOGICAL ASPECTS

War makes people feel so alive. Farrell, Michael J. *Nat Cath Rep* 29:4-5 F 19 1993

WAR—RELIGIOUS ASPECTS

Achieving peace with justice in Bosnia-Herzegovina. Keeler, William H, Abp. *Origins* 22:546-548 Ja 21 1993

Appeal to Croats and Muslims: stop fighting each other. Kuharic, Franjo, Cardinal, 1919-. *Origins* 23:33+ Je 3 1993

God's peace surpasses understanding. Etchegaray, Roger, Cardinal, 1928-. *OR(Eng)* 1312:6 O 20 1993

John Paul II, Pope, (1993-01-01) God wants [orig Italian]. John Paul II, Pope, 1920- (Karol Wojtyla) (elected 1978). *OR(Eng)* 1272:3 Ja 6 1993*

John Paul II, Pope, (1993-01-01) Poverty and peace [abridged]. John Paul II, Pope, 1920- (Karol Wojtyla) (elected 1978). *Tablet* 247:25-26 Ja 2 1993*

Der Soldat, sein Gewissen und die Tradition. Dillmann, Robert. *Stimm Zeit* 211:65-68 Ja 1993

WAR- AZERBAIJAN
Another place, another war. Lieven, Anatol. *Tablet* 247:639-641 My 22 1993

WAR- BALKAN PENINSULA
Cardinal calls for action against Balkan war. *Tablet* 246:1583 D 12 1992

Exclusion and embrace: theological reflections in the wake of "ethnic cleansing". Volf, Miroslav. *JEcumen Stds* 29:230-248 Spr 1992

Lest we forget. Cviic, Christopher. *Tablet* 247:1092-1093 Ag 28 1993

Life in limbo. McDonagh, Melanie. *Tablet* 247:458-459 Ap 10-17 1993

A powerhouse of prayer for peace in Europe. O'Connell, Gerard. *Tablet* 247:83 Ja 16 1993

WAR- BOSNIA AND HERZEGOVINA
Action for Bosnia [editorial]. Barnes, Michael R. *Month* 26:2-3 Ja 1993

Agony of the end-game in Bosnia [eidtorial]. *Tablet* 247:907 Jl 17 1993

Appeal to Croats and Muslims: stop fighting each other. Kuharic, Franjo, Cardinal, 1919-. *Origins* 23:33+ Je 3 1993

Battle for Bosnia. Hastings, Adrian, 1929-. *Tablet* 247:1256-1257 O 2 1993

Between Dracula and Bovary: Yugoslavia's romantic nationalism. Garvey, John, 1944-. *Comm* 120:7-8 My 21 1993

Between two armies. McDonagh, Melanie. *Tablet* 247:1284-1286 O 9 1993

The blood of Bosnia [editorial]. *Comm* 120:3-4 Je 4 1993

Bosnian crisis brings "right and duty" to intervene. *Tablet* 247:54 Ja 9 1993

Bridging the divide [editorial]. *Month* 26:128 Ap 1993

Carnage in the Balkans. Walsh, Catherine. *St Anth* 100:32-33 Mr 1993

Chief Rabbi's red alert for Bosnia. *Tablet* 247:149-150 Ja 30 1993

Church leaders react to NATO's threat. *Tablet* 247:1053-1054 Ag 14 1993

Croat Catholics divided. Magas, Branka. *Tablet* 247:908-910 Jl 17 1993

Decision time for Bosnia [editorial]. *Tablet* 247:31 Ja 9 1993

Desperate appeals as the slaughter goes on and on. *Tablet* 247:661-662 My 22 1993

The end of the road. Williams, Shirley, 1930-. *Tablet* 247:676 My 29 1993

From victim to aggressor. Cviic, Christopher. *Tablet* 247:678-679 My 29 1993

Give Bosnia a chance. Hastings, Adrian, 1929-. *Tablet* 247:64+ Ja 16 1993

"Help us live or watch us die" [editorial]. *Tablet* 247:967 Jl 31 1993

"Help us while it is not too late!". Komarica, Franjo, Bp, 1946-, et al. *Cath Int* 4:230-231 My 1993

John Paul II, Pope, (1993-01-16) Diplomats [Origin French]. John Paul II, Pope, 1920- (Karol Wojtyla) (elected 1978). *Origins* 22:583-587 F 4 1993*

John Paul II, Pope, (1993-02-02) Change violence into acceptance. John Paul II, Pope, 1920- (Karol Wojtyla) (elected 1978). *TPS* 38:219-220 Jl-Ag 1993*

John Paul II, Pope, (1993-03-11) Letter to UN Secretary General. John Paul II, Pope, 1920- (Karol Wojtyla) (elected 1978). *TPS* 38:243-244 Jl-Ag 1993*

The lost city. Mostyn, Trevor, 1946-. *Tablet* 247:1222-1223 S 25 1993

Message from Medjugorje. Brown, Andrew. *Tablet* 247:1155-1156 S 11 1993

The morality of caution [editorial]. *Month* 26:170-171 My 1993

My dream for the Pope. Nicholl, Donald. *Tablet* 247:230 F 20 1993

No right choice [editorial]. *Comm* 120:3-4 Mr 26 1993

Now the Muslims commit atrocities. *Tablet* 247:1082 Ag 21 1993

One cheer, or less, for Bosnian "Peace" plan [editorial]. *America* 168:3 Ja 30 1993

A pair of shoes. Wroe, Ann. *Tablet* 247:538 My 1 1993

Pope keeps in touch, may go to Sarajevo. *Tablet* 247:989 Jl 31 1993

Pope sees duty to disarm aggressors. *Tablet* 247:115 Ja 23 1993

Raising a monster in the Balkans [editorial]. *Tablet* 247:499 Ap 24 1993

Sarajevo is like a "concentration camp", bishop says. *Tablet* 247:1051 Ag 14 1993

Too reasonable by half. McDonagh, Melanie. *Tablet* 247:774 Je 19 1993

Towards a Switzerland in the Balkans. Cviic, Christopher. *Tablet* 247:162-163 F 6 1993

The tragedy of Bosnia is not over [editorial]. *America* 169:3 Ag 14-21 1993

Unholy war. *Tablet* 247:785 Je 19 1993

The virtues of Sarajevo: reflections of a city dweller. Steinfels, Margaret O'Brien, 1941-. *Comm* 120:4-5 Je 18 1993

War games. *Month* 26:212-213 Je 1993

The West as a paper tiger [editorial]. *Tablet* 247:391 Mr 27 1993

WAR- CROATIA
John Paul II, Pope, (1992-11-09) Vist ad limina. John Paul II, Pope, 1920- (Karol Wojtyla) (elected 1978). *TPS* 38:111-115 Mr-Ap 1993*

WAR- LEBANON
Goodbye Lebanon. Butt, Gerald. *Tablet* 247:460-461 Ap 10-17 1993

WAR- NAGASAKI (JAPAN)—WAR
Nagasaki's loss. *Tablet* 247:1040 Ag 14 1993

WAR- SUDAN
A deadly silence: faint voices on Sudan. Jordan, Patrick. *Comm* 120:4-5 My 7 1993

John Paul II, Pope, (1993-02-10) Innocent victims. John Paul II, Pope, 1920- (Karol Wojtyla) (elected 1978). *TPS* 38:221-225 Jl-Ag 1993*

John Paul II, Pope, (1993-03-10) Innocent victims [Orig English]. John Paul II, Pope, 1920- (Karol Wojtyla) (elected 1978). *Origins* 22:618-620 F 18 1993*

Repression in the Sudan. Barbier, Hubert. *Cath Int* 4:234-236 My 1993

There are no safe corridors for the people of Sudan. Humphrey, Marj. *Cath Work* 60:5 Je-Jl 1993

WAR AND LITERATURE
The moral vision of Robert Stone. Finn, James. *Comm* 120:9-14 N 5 1993

WAR CRIMES
Put an end to "ethnic cleansing". *OR(Eng)* 1305:2 S 1 1993

Right or wrong, Demjanjuk may go free. Pevtzow, Lisa. *Register* 69:1+ Ag 15 1993

WAR IN LITERATURE
Hans Carossa und Rupert Mayer. Bleistein, Roman, 1928-. *Stimm Zeit* 211:105-114 F 1993

WAR VICTIMS
Intervene to protect innocent. Tabet, Paul F. *OR(Eng)* 1309:10 S 29 1993

WAR VICTIMS- BALKANS
In God's name, stop the war in the Balkans!. Kuharic, Franjo, Cardinal, 1919-. *OR(Eng)* 1292:1+ My 26 1993

WAR VICTIMS- BOSNIA AND HERZEGOVINA
God's peace surpasses understanding. Etchegaray, Roger, Cardinal, 1928-. *OR(Eng)* 1312:6 O 20 1993

WARD, MARY, 1585-1646
Galloping nun. *Tablet* 247:1129 S 4 1993

WARSAW (POLAND)—UPRISING OF 1943
Homage to the fighters of the Warsaw Ghetto. Luxmoore, Jonathan. *Tablet* 247:527-529 Ap 24 1993

1943 ghetto uprising is remembered. Luxmoore, Jonathan. *Register* 69:1+ My 2 1993

WASHINGTON (DC)—POLITICS AND GOVERNMENT
Election day hope stirs DC's hardest hit. McCarthy, Tim. *Nat Cath Rep* 29:18-21 N 20 1992

WATTS, FRASER
Hot seat. *Tablet* 247:1070 Ag 21 1993

WAUGH, EVELYN, 1903-1966
Novel Catholicism: Waugh and Greene [condensed fr *Catholic Twin Circle* D 27 1992-Ja 31 1993]. Vatavuk, William M. *CDgst* 57:42-47 O 1993

Portrait of the artist as a Christian wayfarer. Donohue, John W, 1917-. *America* 168:7-10 Ap 10 1993

Saint Evelyn Waugh. McInerny, Ralph M. *Crisis* 10:2-3 N 1992

WEAKLAND, REMBERT G, ABP, 1927-
Bishops at odds over role of women. *Tablet* 247:22 Ja 2 1993

Hear this [editorial]. *Comm* 120:3 Ja 29 1993

WEALTH
The camouflaged at-risk student: white and wealthy. Metz, Elinor D. *Momentum* 24:40-44 Ap-My 1993

WEALTH- BIBLICAL TEACHING
Who can be saved? Martin, George. *New Cov* 22:34 Mr 1993

WEBER, MAX, 1864-1920
The Decade of Evangelisation: has Catholicism changed? Sweeney, James. *Month* 25:461-466 D 1992

La théologie comme science et la voction de savant d'après Max Weber. Gendron, Pierre. *Laval Theol Phil* 49:215-222 Je 1993

Une vision protestante de l'éthique sociale. Müller, Denis. *Laval Theol Phil* 49:57-67 F 1993

WEDDINGS
Bishops caution on fashionable weddings. *Tablet* 247:55-56 Ja 9 1993

"I do". Smith, B F. *Crisis* 11:41-42 F 1993

Your wedding workbook. Belting, Natalia, and Hine, James R. Danville: Interstate Publishers, 1993. 121p ISBN 0-8134-2953-6

WEEK OF PRAYER FOR CHRISTIAN UNITY
John Paul II, Pope, (1993-01-25) Christian unity is our desire. John Paul II, Pope, 1920- (Karol Wojtyla) (elected 1978). *TPS* 38:202-206 Jl-Ag 1993*

Pope John Paul II and "Faith and Order". Radano, John A. *Ecumen Trends* 22:3-6 F 1993

WEEK OF PRAYER FOR CHRISTIAN UNITY—HISTORY
The Week of Prayer for Christian Unity: a look back and ahead. Fuchs, Lorelei F. *Ecumen Trends* 21:2 D 1992

WEHRLE, VINCENT
Benedictine stability on the North Dakota frontier. Kardong, Terrence G. *Word Sp* 14:53-75 1992

WEIGAND, WILLIAM KEITH, BP, 1937-
Utah bishop asks Rome to halt hospitals' sale [photos]. Carey, Ann. *OSV* 82:3 N 28 1993

WEIST, EDELTRUD
Our deepening relationships. Walgenbach, Mary David. *Sisters* 65:2-7 Ja 1993

WELFARE STATE
The crisis of the welfare state. Novak, Michael, 1933-. *Crisis* 11:4-7 Jl-Ag 1993

WELLS, (GEORGE) ORSON, 1915-1985
Il Ritorno di Orson Welles. Fantuzzi, Virgilio. *Civilta* 144:55-63 Ja 2 1993

WELLS, IDA B
Ida B Wells. O'Connell-Cahill, Catherine. *Salt* 13:31 Jl-Ag 1993

WERBLOWSKY, ZWI
The eclipse of difference: Merton's encounter with Judaism. Plank, Karl A. *Cist Stud* 28 no 2:179-191 1993

WEST (UNITED STATES)—CHURCH HISTORY
Cultura occidental y culturas indígenas. Suazo, Fernando. *Cien Tom* 120:101-115 Ja-Ap 1993

WEST BANK
Can there be peace in Israel? Wigoder, Geoffrey Bernard, 1922-. *Tablet* 247:840-841 Jl 3 1993

Voices in the wilderness. White, Patrick. *Tablet* 246:1594-1596 D 19-26 1992

West Bank settlers won't go. Pevtzow, Lisa. *Register* 69:1+ Je 27 1993

WESTMINSTER CATHEDRAL (LONDON, ENGLAND)
Cathedral explains its policy on beggars. *Tablet* 247:150 Ja 30 1993

WHALEY, DOTTIE, -1993
Whaley, Dottie, -1993 [obit]. Noel, Jeannette. *Cath Work* 60:7 My 1993

WHITE, JAMES BOYD
Is there life beyond efficiency? Elements of a social law and economics. Medema, Steven G. *RSocEcon* 51:138-153 Sum 1993

WHITEHEAD, ALFRED NORTH, 1861-1947
University challenge. Nuttgens, Patrick, 1930-. *Tablet* 247:783-784 Je 19 1993

Whiteheadian creativity, the Tao, and the Thomistic act of being. Bracken, Joseph A. *Pacifica* 6:179-188 Je 1993

WIERTZ, FRANZ, BP
Raised hopes in Holland. Goddijn, Walter, 1921-. *Tablet* 247:974-975 Jl 31 1993

WILDE, OSCAR, 1854?-1900
Oscar Wilde E Il Suo Cristo Romantico. Castelli, Ferdinando. *Civilta* 144:31-44 Ja 2 1993

WILKES, PAUL, 1938-
Sins of a father [editorial]. *America* 168:3 Je 19-26 1993

WILL
Augustine on sin. Meredith, Anthony. *Month* 26:367-371 S-O 1993
De sensu clausulae dummodo non determinet voluntatem Can 1099. Navarrete, Urbano. *Periodica* 81 no 3-4:469-493 1992

WILL OF GOD
Catherine De'Ricci and the will of God [pt 2 of 3]. Agresti, Domenico di. *New Blckfrs* 74:307-316 Je 1993
Catherine De'Ricci [pt 3 of 3]. Agresti, Domenico di. *New Blckfrs* 74:355-363 Jl-Ag 1993
Discipleship in Matthew. Doohan, Leonard. *Mod Lit* 20:36 Ag 1993
"I saw a Kingfisher": grace and ruin in Golding's the spire. Yeager, D M. *Horizons (CTS)* 20:44-66 Spr 1993
In search of guidance: developing a conversational relationship with God. Willard, Dallas. New York: HarperSanFrancisco, 1993. x, 247p ISBN 0-06-069520-x LC 92-56406
Out of control. Costello, Andrew. *USCath* 58:38-40 Ja 1993
Vincent de Paul's charism in today's church. Luttenberger, Gerard H. *RRel* 52:660-683 S-O 1993

WILLEBRANDS, JAN, CARDINAL
Theology in an ecumenical context: on Catholic attitudes to the decision of the general synod of the Church of England. Merrigan, Terrence. *Heythrop* 34:171-175 Ap 1993

WILLIAM OF OCKHAM
William of Ockham andAdam Wodeham. White, Graham. *Heythrop* 34:296-302 Jl 1993 ·

WILLIAM OF SAINT THIERRY, 1085?-1148
Julian of Norwich, Mary Magdalene, and the drama of prayer. Koenig, Elisabeth K J. *Horizons (CTS)* 20:23-43 Spr 1993

WILLIAMS, BRUCE
Aquinas on disordered pleasures and conditions. Daly, Anthony C. *Thomist* 56:583-612 O 1992

WILLS
Living wills and religious communities. Carr, William F. *Linacre* 60:72-77 My 1993

WILSON, A N, 1950-
The banality of unbelief [excerpt fr *Washington City paper*]. Allen, Charlotte. *Crisis* 11:30-35 Mr 1993
Good News and old nonsense. O'Collins, Gerald, 1931-. *Tablet* 247:469 Ap 10-17 1993

WILSON, BRYAN
TV's iconic imagery in a secular society. Goethals, Gregor T. *New Theol Rev* 6:40-53 F 1993

WILSON, MARY
An American miracle [condensed fr *Extension* N 1992]. Bartholomew, Marianna. *CDgst* 57:1-3+ Ap 1993

WIMMER, BONIFACE
And who is my neighbor?. Beaver, William A. *Word Sp* 14:96-104 1992

WISDOM—BIBLICAL TEACHING
The Spirit's gift of wisdom. Dimock, Giles. *OSV* 81:5 F 28 1993

WISDOM LITERATURE
Aging according to wisdom literature. Bjornard, Reidar B. *BibleT* 30:330-334 N 1992

WIT AND HUMOR
The dangerous Rush Limbaugh. Sobran, Joseph. *Crisis* 11:18-21 My 1993
The world's funniest mom. Fixmer, Audrey Mettel. *OSV* 82:16 My 9 1993

WITNESS BEARING (CHRISTIANITY)
Catechesis and the relationship of evangelization to ecumenism. Cermak, John. *Living Light* 29:64-68 Wint 1992
The Catechism [commentary]. O'Brien, Dennis. *Comm* 120:15-16 My 7 1993
Christus Lumen Gentium: the Eucharist and evangelization [4 sections]. Vallejo, Carlos Armijo, Abp. *Emmanuel* 99:64-71+ Mr; 138-144 Ap; 190-195+ My; 244-249+ Je 1993
Down at the pub. *Tablet* 247:976 Jl 31 1993
Evangelization and the Church's social teaching. William, Thomas Stafford, Cardinal, 1930-. *Cath Int* 4:210-214 My 1993
Faith sharing and new facilitators. Bernier, Joan M. *Tod Parish* 25:36-37 Ja 1993
Has ecumenism made evangelism irrelevant? Jindal, Bobby. *America* 169:8-13 Jl 31-Ag 7 1993
Inside the mind of unchurched Harry and Mary. Strobel, Lee. Grand Rapids: Zondervan Publishing House, 1993. x, 224p ISBN 0-310-37561-4
Is the Irish Church in crisis? O'Donoghue, Helena. *Furrow* 44:67-77 F 1993
John Paul II, Pope, (1991-07-14) Bear witness gratuitiously and enthusiasitcally. John Paul II, Pope, 1920- (Karol Wojtyla) (elected 1978). *Con Life* 17 no 2:45-46 1992*
John Paul II, Pope, (1992-01-24) Message for World Communications Day. John Paul II, Pope, 1920- (Karol Wojtyla) (elected 1978). *AFER* 34:130-133 Je 1992*
John Paul II, Pope, (1992-05-14) Church upheld human rights of natives. John Paul II, Pope, 1920- (Karol Wojtyla) (elected 1978). *TPS* 38:9-13 Ja-F 1993*
John Paul II, Pope, (1993-04-15) Europe needs solidarity. John Paul II, Pope, 1920- (Karol Wojtyla) (elected 1978). *TPS* 38:270-274 S-O 1993*
John Paul II, Pope, (1993-05-06) Holy Childhood Association's 150th anniversary. John Paul II, Pope, 1920- (Karol Wojtyla) (elected 1978). *TPS* 38:291-294 S-O 1993*
The meaning of a new evangelization of Europe. Lehmann, Karl, Bp, 1936-. *Communio* 19:541-548 Wint 1992
Pope John Paul evangelist [editorial]. *America* 169:3 S 11 1993
Preaching the Word [excerpts fr *Bodying forth: aesthetic liturgy*]. Collins, Patrick W, 1936-. *Emmanuel* 99:278-285 Je 1993
The promulgation of the Catechism of the Catholic Church. Law, Bernard Francis, Cardinal, 1931-. *Living Light* 29:5-6 Sum 1993

Why Catholics should witness verbally to the Gospel. Weinandy, Thomas. *New Oxford Rev* 60:16-18 Jl-Ag 1993
Witnesses. Martin, George. *New Cov* 22:34 F 1993

WITNESSES
The first witness. Martin, George. *New Cov* 23:34 Ag 1993

WITNESSING
John Paul II, Pope, (1992-10-12) Challenges facing the Latin American Church. John Paul II, Pope, 1920- (Karol Wojtyla) (elected 1978). *TPS* 38:84-102 Mr-Ap 1993*

WITTGENSTEIN, LUDWIG JOSEPH JOHANN, 1889-1951
Acerca de Wittgenstein. Sanfelix, Vidarte, ed. Valencia: Pre-Textos, 1993. x, 202p ISBN 84-87101
Wittgenstein's doctrine of silence. McDonough, Richard. *Thomist* 56:695-699 O 1992

WODEHAM, ADAM
William of Ockham andAdam Wodeham. White, Graham. *Heythrop* 34:296-302 Jl 1993

WOIWODE, LARRY, 1941-
Larry Woiwode. Block, Ed. *Critic* 47:57-65 Sum 1993

WOLF, CHRISTA
Es geht um mehr als Christa Wolf. Kurz, Paul Konrad. *Stimm Zeit* 211:352-356 My 1993

WOMEN
Equal dignity [Speech, assembly on equality of women, Rome, O 21-22 1993]. Majía, Jorge María, Bp, 1923-. *Register* 69:2 N 14 1993
Male and female he created them: a summary of the teaching of Genesis chapter one. Martin, Francis. *Communio* 20:240-265 Sum 1993
Praying with Peter [excerpts fr a pastoral letter to the Church of Denver]. Stafford, James Francis, Abp, 1932-. *Crisis* 11:26-31 Jl-Ag 1993
The role of women in the evolutionary process. Ward, Sheila. *Teilhard Rev* 28:25-26 Sum 1993

WOMEN—CONGRESSES
Bang the drum—not: Women-Church in the desert. Walsh, Catherine. *Comm* 120:6-7 Je 4 1993
Celebrating diversity of Catholic women. Martinez, Demetria. *Nat Cath Rep* 29:5 Ap 30 1993

WOMEN—EMPLOYMENT
A Northern perspective. Borooah, Vani K, and Ackah, Carol. *Studies* 82:53-60 Spr 1993
Shattering the glass ceiling. Weiss, Rhoda. *Health Prog* 74:58-59 Mr 1993

WOMEN—HEALTH
No longer patient: feminist ethics and health care. Sherwin, Susan, 1947-. Philadelphia: Temple University Press, 1992. 286p ISBN 0-87722-889-2 LC 91-14499

WOMEN—HISTORY—0600-1500
Saints speak volumes. Kenny, Mary, 1936-. *Tablet* 247:911-913 Jl 17 1993

WOMEN—INTELLECTUAL LIFE
Man and woman are loved by the Lord and desired for one another. Cànopi, Anna Maria. *OR(Eng)* 1300:10+ Jl 21 1993

WOMEN—PSYCHOLOGY
I sit listening to the wind: woman's encounter within herself. Duerk, Judith. San Diego: LuraMedia, 1993. x, 103p ISBN 0-931055-98-9 LC 93-991
Questions women ask in private. Wright, H Norman. Ventura, California: Regal Books, 1993. 426p ISBN 0-8307-1522-3 LC 93-913

WOMEN—RELIGIOUS LIFE
Bang the drum—not: Women-Church in the desert. Walsh, Catherine. *Comm* 120:6-7 Je 4 1993
The Church and women. O'Connor, John, Cardinal, and Weakland, Rembert G, Abp, 1927-. *Origins* 22:532-536 Ja 14 1993
Internationality: intentional or accidental. Harmer, Catherine M. *RRel* 52:111-118 Ja-F 1993
Lesbian identity: how to explain it all? Gramick, Jeannine. *Sisters* 65:58-59 Ja 1993
A monastic and a firefighter. White, Faye E. *Sisters* 65:30-34 Ja 1993
Questions women ask in private. Wright, H Norman. Ventura, California: Regal Books, 1993. 426p ISBN 0-8307-1522-3 LC 93-913
Religious life's charism: transforming life. Brennan, Margaret. *Origins* 23:207-211 S 2 1993
Seasons of the feminine divine: Christian feminist prayers for the liturgical cycle. Schmitt, Mary Kathleen Speegle. New York: The Crossroad Publishing Company, 1993. 129p ISBN 0-8245-1279-0 LC 93-588
Women artisans in the service of the church. Abrahamsen, Valerie. *Sisters* 65:96-103 Mr 1993

WOMEN—RELIGIOUS LIFE- UNITED STATES
Women collaborators in Catholic education: nineteenth century America. Donovan, Grace. *ACHSR* 103:23-33 Aut 1992

WOMEN—RELIGIOUS LIFE- WEST AFRICA
2,000 pack cathedral for nuns' memorial. McDonagh, Mary Ellen. *Nat Cath Rep* 29:6 N 20 1992

WOMEN—RIGHTS
Abortion, sex and gender: the Church's public voice. Cahill, Lisa Sowle. *America* 168:6-11 My 22, 1993
Pope supports women's rights, criticises feminist ideology. *Tablet* 247:896-897 Jl 10 1993
Women in the Church and in Latin American culture [tr and excerpts fr *Boletin CELAM*]. *Cath Int* 4:210-214 My 1993

WOMEN—SOCIAL LIFE AND CUSTOMS
Man and woman are loved by the Lord and desired for one another. Cànopi, Anna Maria. *OR(Eng)* 1300:10+ Jl 21 1993

WOMEN- AFRICA
Differences that bind the liberation of women in Africa. Magesa, Laurenti. *AFER* 35:44-53 F 1993

WOMEN- EUROPE, EASTERN
East Europe's second sex. Luxmoore, Jonathan. *Tablet* 247:188+ F 13 1993

WOMEN- LATIN AMERICA
Women in the Church and in Latin American culture [tr and excerpts fr *Boletin CELAM*]. *Cath Int* 4:210-214 My 1993

WOMEN- PHILIPPINES
Women's stuggle in the Third World. *Tablet* 247:753 Je 1993

WOMEN- TANZANIA
Tanzanian women peasants: an ethical and theological reflection. Giblin, Marie. *AFER* 34:29-43 F 1992

WOMEN, CATHOLIC
Amongst women. Kimmerling, Ben. *Furrow* 44:273-282 My 1993
Bishops ask priests about women [fr The Pastoral Care of Marriage and Family Life]. *Priests & People* 6:337-340 Ag-S 1992
Catholic feminist theologians on Catholic women in the Church. Graff, Ann O'Hara. *New Theol Rev* 6:6-18 My 1993
Catholic women more open to change than Catholic men. Wallace, Ruth A. *Nat Cath Rep* 29:28 O 8 1993
Celebrating diversity of Catholic women. Martinez, Demetria. *Nat Cath Rep* 29:5 Ap 30 1993
A good Catholic girl. Gateley, Edwina. *Tablet* 247:851-852 Jl 3 1993
Handing on the tradition: a Catholic mother laments. Baumer, Patricia Hughes. *New Theol Rev* 6:32-54 My 1993
Horizons for Catholic feminist theology. Conn, Joann Wolski, and Conn, Walter E, eds. Washington, D C: Georgetown University Press, 1992. x, 207p ISBN 0-87840-534-8 LC 92-30435
If underground, women's press mulitiplies. Vidulich, Dorothy. *Nat Cath Rep* 29:2 Ja 15 1993
John Paul warns of "extreme" feminism. Burke, Greg. *Register* 69:1+ Jl 18 1993
Like bread, their voices rise! Global women challenge the Church. O'Connor, Bernard. Notre Dame: Ave Maria Press, 1993. 204p ISBN 0-87793-509-2 LC 93-77734
Miles to go [editorial]. Pawlikowski, John T. *New Theol Rev* 6:3-5 My 1993
The ministry of women: gift or threat to the churches? Thurston, Anne. *Doctr Life* 43:387-395 S 1993
"On the wings of change?". Hitchcock, Helen Hull. *Register* 69:3 O 24 1993
Saints speak volumes. Kenny, Mary, 1936-. *Tablet* 247:911-913 Jl 17 1993
To be black, Catholic, and female. Hayes, Diana L. *New Theol Rev* 6:55-62 My 1993
Women at the crossroads. Noble, Valerie. *Priests & People* 6:312-317 Ag-S 1992
Women's problems. Soskice, Janet Martin. *Priests & People* 6:301-306 Ag-S 1992
Women-church: "adrift" from Catholicism? Martinez, Demetria. *Nat Cath Rep* 29:3-4 Ap 16 1993

WOMEN, CATHOLIC—RELIGIOUS LIFE
Woman to woman: an anthology of women's spiritualities. Zagano, Phyllis. Collegeville: Liturgical, 1993. x, 115p ISBN 0-8146-5025-2 LC 93-18865

WOMEN, CATHOLIC—SOCIAL ASPECTS
Religious: evangelizers in a new context. Luna, Anita de. *Origins* 23:201+ S 2 1993

WOMEN, JEWISH
Listening to Jewish women. *Tablet* 247:1085-1086 Ag 21 1993

WOMEN, POOR
"I listen, I suspect, later I make poetry" [interview by S Rojas; tr fr *Pastoral Popular*]. Gebara, Ivone. *LADOC* 24:10-15 S-O 1993

WOMEN (IN RELIGION, FOLKLORE)
Matthew, Mark, Luke, and John. Kunkel, Francis L. *Sisters* 65:283-289 Jl 1993
Mythological woman: contemporary reflections on ancient religious stories. Carmody, Denise Lardner. New York: The Crossroad Publishing Company, 1992. x, 160p ISBN 0-8245-1217-0 LC 92-26086

WOMEN (THEOLOGY)
Frauen und Ökumene. Harles, Sabine. *Stimm Zeit* 210:857-860 D 1992
St Paul: promoter of the ministry of women. O'Connor, Jerome Murphy. *Priests & People* 6:307-311 Ag-S 1992

WOMEN (THEOLOGY)—BIBLICAL TEACHING
The household: a major social component for gender analysis in the gospel of Matthew. Love, Stuart L. *Bib Th Bul* 23:21-31 Spr 1993

WOMEN AND RELIGION
Priestertum der Frau. Schiebl, Johanna. *Stimm Zeit* 211:115-122 F 1993

WOMEN IN BUSINESS
Faith in the world of business. O'Cathain, Detta. *Priests & People* 7:186-190 My 1993

WOMEN IN CHRISTIANITY
Church in the round: feminist interpretation of the church. Russell, Letty M. Louisville: John Knox Press, 1993. 235p ISBN 0-66425-070-x LC 93-9306
The spiritual journey: the way of Christian womanhood. Muto, Susan. *Word Sp* 15:95-104 1993
A warm, moist, salty God: women journeying towards wisdom. Gateley, Edwina. Trabuco Canyon: Source Books, 1993. x, 107p ISBN 0-940147-26-2 LC 93-11919
Women views of Christian life. Long, Grace D Cumming. Louisville: John Knox, 1993. x, 176p ISBN 0-664-25408-x
Women, earth, and creator spirit. Johnson, Elizabeth A, 1941-. New York: Paulist Press, 1993. x, 79p ISBN 0-8091-3415-2 LC 92-42018

WOMEN IN CHRISTIANITY—EARLY CHURCH
Did the early Church ordain women to be priests? Most, William G, 1914-. *Can Cath Rev* 11:21-24 F 1993
The ministry of women in the early Church. Gillman, Florence Morgan. *New Theol Rev* 6:89-94 My 1993

WOMEN IN CHURCH WORK
Catholic feminist theologians on Catholic women in the Church. Graff, Ann O'Hara. *New Theol Rev* 6:6-18 My 1993
The Church and women. O'Connor, John, Cardinal, and Weakland, Rembert G, Abp, 1927-. *Origins* 22:532-536 Ja 14 1993
East Europe's second sex. Luxmoore, Jonathan. *Tablet* 247:188+ F 13 1993
John Paul II, Pope, (1993-07-02) Women. John Paul II, Pope, 1920- (Karol Wojtyla) (elected 1978). *Origins* 23:124-126 Jl 15 1993*
The ministries of women [editorial]. McDade, John. *Month* 25:458-460 D 1992
On the margin. Thurston, Anne. *Tablet* 247:534 My 1 1993

WOMEN IN CHURCH WORK—HISTORY
Women's role in Church law: past and present. Huels, John M. *New Theol Rev* 6:19-31 My 1993

WOMEN IN COMBAT
Brave new world. Chavez, Linda. *Crisis* 11:14-15 Jl-Ag 1993

WOMEN IN ISLAM
Der fremde Spiegel. Röhrig, Johannes. *Stimm Zeit* 211:10-20 Ja 1993

WOMEN IN LITERATURE
The Virgin incarnate in Robert Browning's poetry. Johnson, Patricia E. *Listening* 28:118-127 Spr 1993

WOMEN IN RELIGION
An anthology of sacred texts by and about women. Young, Serinity, ed. New York: Crossroad, 1993. x, 452p ISBN 0-8245-1143-3 LC 92-36343
Man and woman are loved by the Lord and desired for one another. Cànopi, Anna Maria. *OR(Eng)* 1300:10+ Jl 21 1993
Miles to go [editorial]. Pawlikowski, John T. *New Theol Rev* 6:3-5 My 1993
On Anglicans approaching the Catholic Church after women's ordination decision. Hume, George Basil, Cardinal, 1923-. *Origins* 23:797+ My 6 1993
Women at worship: interpretations of North American diversity. Proctor-Smith, Marjorie, and Walton, Janet R. Louisville, Kentucky: John Knox Press, 1993. 272p ISBN 0-664-25253-2

WOMEN IN THE BIBLE
Buried treasures: rediscovering women's roles in the Bible [interview by US Catholic]. *Salt* 13:6-13 Je 1993
Do what you have the power to do: studies of six New Testament women. Pearson, Helen Bruch. Nashville: Upper Room Books, 1992. x, 168p ISBN 08-358-0643-x LC 91-65725
Man, woman, and hospitality - 2 Kings 4:8-36. Hobbs, T R. *Bib Th Bul* 23: 91-100 Aut 1993
Presence or absence? the question of women disciples at the Last Supper. Lee, Dorothy A. *Pacifica* 6:1-20 F 1993
Where are the women? Durken, Daniel. *Sisters* 65:109 Mr 1993
The women from Galilee. Martin, George. *Liguorian* 81:18-19 S 1993
Women in the Bible: friends or foes? Bergant, Dianne. *TheolDgst* 40:103-112 Sum 1993
Women of the gospel. Powers, Isaias. Mystic, Connecticut: Twenty-Third Publications, 1993. x, 153p ISBN 0-89622 LC 92-81796

WOMEN MINISTERS
Frauen und Ökumene. Harles, Sabine. *Stimm Zeit* 210:857-860 D 1992
Reconciling unity and plurality. Weakland, Rembert G, Abp, 1927-, and Eastman, Theodore, Bp. *Origins* 22:587-588 F 4 1993
Some of the best priests I know are women. Malloy, Richard G. *USCath* 58: 30-31 Ap 1993
Women's role in Church law: past and present. Huels, John M. *New Theol Rev* 6:19-31 My 1993

WOMEN MINISTERS—CONTROVERSIES
Conflicting styles of parish leadership: two responses. Rosinski, Geri, and Mannion, M Francis. *New Theol Rev* 6:95-101 My 1993

WOMEN MISSIONARIES
Priestertum der Frau. Schiebl, Johanna. *Stimm Zeit* 211:115-122 F 1993

WOMEN MYSTICS
Major works/Margaret Ebner. Hindsley, Leonard P, ed. Mahwah: Paulist, 1993. x, 209p ISBN 0-8091-0462-8 LC 92-46650

WOMEN NOVELISTS
Live, on stage with Amy Tan [interview by E Wymard]. Tan, Amy, 1952-. *Critic* 47:77-83 Wint 1992

WOMEN PRISONERS
Women in prison. Johnston, Rosemary. *Nat Cath Rep* 29:5-7 My 14 1993

WOMEN'S RIGHTS
Anti-abortion racketeers? Gaffney, Edward McGlynn, Jr, 1941-. *Comm* 120: 6-7 N 5 1993
Why feminists and prolifers need each other. Wiley, Juli Loesch. *New Oxford Rev* 60:9-14 N 1993

WOMEN'S RIGHTS—SPIRITUAL ASPECTS
Why feminists and prolifers need each other. Wiley, Juli Loesch. *New Oxford Rev* 60:9-14 N 1993

WOMEN'S WORLD DAY OF PRAYER
Palestinian women's prayers under attack. *Tablet* 247:831 Je 26 1993

WONDER
Focus on feeling. O'Donoghue, Noel D. *Can Cath Rev* 11:16-21 Je 1993
Simple prayers, common miracles. Canton, Donald R. *Living Prayer* 26:9-12 My-Je 1993

WONG-STAAL, FLOSSIE T
AIDS researcher wields tools of evolution to meet challenge. Jones, Arthur C, 1936-. *Nat Cath Rep* 29:7 N 20 1992

WOOLF, JAMES DUDLEY, 1914-
The search for self: a study of the poetic mind. Woolf, James Dudley. New York: Vantage Press, 1993. 320p ISBN 0-533-10364-9 LC 92-90889

WOOLLEN, RUSSELL
How four artists put the finishing touches on God's creation. Marquardt, Deborah. *USCath* 58:14-21 Ag 1993

WORD AND SACRAMENT
What if there were no theology? Skublics, Ernest. *Can Cath Rev* 11:37-38 Je 1993

WORD OF GOD
Creed and criticism: the complementarity of faith and exegesis. Davies, Gordon F. *Can Cath Rev* 11:7-10 O 1993
Inculturar la palabra. Lenkersdorf, Carlos. *Christus* 58:36-59 S 1993
The "intellectual" formation of priests. Witherup, Ronald D. *Priest* 49:46-52 Ag 1993
John Paul II, Pope, (1991-09-20) In your missionary service the Gospel message is ever new. John Paul II, Pope, 1920- (Karol Wojtyla) (elected 1978). *Con Life* 17 no 2:53-54 1992*
Lectio divina. Schultz, Karl A. *BibleT* 31:197-199 Jl 1993
Scripture, inspiration and the word of God. Garrett, Graeme. *Pacifica* 6:81-99 F 1993
Sit down and be quiet!. Connors, Daniel. *ReligTJ* 27:28-29 O 1993
Word from the Lord?. Haggith, David. *New Cov* 22:14-15 Jl 1993

X

Y

YELTSIN, BORIS N, 1931-
Boris Yeltsin's gamble [editorial]. *Tablet* 247:1219 S 25 1993
Desperate straits for Russia's reformers. Lieven, Anatol. *Tablet* 247:424+ Ap 3 1993
High noon in Moscow [editorial]. *America* 169:3 O 16 1993
So far so good for Boris Yeltsin [editorial]. *Tablet* 247:535 My 1 1993
Storia del pensiero filosofico Russo. Simon, Michele. *Civilta* 144:153-157 Ja 16 1993
Thinking about Russia [editorial]. *America* 168:3 My 8 1993
Yeltsin takes charge. Lieven, Anatol. *Tablet* 247:1252-1253 O 2 1993

YEPES, JUAN DE
John of the Cross and the laity. Doohan, Leonard. *Spir Life* 39:164-172 Aut 1993

YERMO Y PARES, JOSE MARIA, 1851-1904
John Paul II, Pope, (1990-05-06) Litterae Apostolicae (Apostolic Letter for Beatification process) [Latin]. John Paul II, Pope, 1920- (Karol Wojtyla) (elected 1978). *AAS* 85:9-12 Ja 7 1993*

YOUNG, BRIGHAM
Mormonism in the twenty-first century. Saliba, John A. *StudiaM* 41:49-67 1992

YOUTH
Catechesis for conversion [excerpt fr the book]. O'Malley, William J, 1931-. *Living Light* 29:55-63 Wint 1992
The church and the American teenager: what works and doesn't work in youth ministry. Campolo, Tony. Grand Rapids: Zondervan Publishing House, 1993. x, 224p ISBN 0-310-52471-7
Teens can offer your parish more than car washes. Wood, Charles. *USCath* 58:6+ D 1993
What Catholic teens need to know about sex. Stafford, Geraldine. *HPR* 94:52-54 O 1993

YOUTH—CONDUCT OF LIFE
Formation of the young as moral agents. Hagan, Charles H. *Origins* 23:430-432 N 25 1993
In praise of teenagers. Dodds, Bill. *New Cov* 23:32 O 1993
John Paul II, Pope, (1993-05-23) Sacraments [Orig Italian]. John Paul II, Pope, 1920- (Karol Wojtyla) (elected 1978). *OR(Eng)* 1294:7 Je 9 1993*
John Paul II, Pope, (1993-08-12) Denver. John Paul II, Pope, 1920- (Karol Wojtyla) (elected 1978). *OR(Eng)* 1303:6 Ag 18 1993*
John Paul II, Pope, (1993-08-13) Cross. John Paul II, Pope, 1920- (Karol Wojtyla) (elected 1978). *Origins* 23:191-192 Ag 26 1993*
John Paul II, Pope, (1993-08-15) Celebration [Origin in English]. John Paul II, Pope, 1920- (Karol Wojtyla) (elected 1978). *Origins* 23:177+ Ag 26 1993*
A taste for the other: the moral development of college students and young adults. Heft, James L. *Living Light* 29:23-36 Spr 1993
Youth gangs: a spreading problem. Martinet, Ken. *Momentum* 24:68-72 Ap-My 1993

YOUTH—CONGRESSES
Instituto de Pastoral da Juventude/Leste II. Maçaneiro, Marcial. *REB* 53:409-411 Je 1993
John Paul II, Pope, (1992-08-15) Christ offers abundant life. John Paul II, Pope, 1920- (Karol Wojtyla) (elected 1978). *TPS* 38:39-43 Ja-F 1993*
John Paul II, Pope, (1992-08-15) Message to the youth of the world. John Paul II, Pope, 1920- (Karol Wojtyla) (elected 1978). *Living Light* 29:19-22 Spr 1993*

YOUTH—INTELLECTUAL LIFE
John Paul II, Pope, (1993-07-25) Youth [Orig in Italian]. John Paul II, Pope, 1920- (Karol Wojtyla) (elected 1978). *OR(Eng)* 1301:1+ Jl 28 1993*

YOUTH—POLITICAL ACTIVITY
International Youth Forum's message to youth. *Origins* 23:181-182 Ag 26 1993

YOUTH—RELIGIOUS LIFE
A Catholic in the cafeteria. Dowling, Regina Plunkett. *Comm* 120:11 S 10 1993
College education/values education. Hagan, Charles H. *Origins* 22:602-604 F 11 1993
Converting the youth minister. Reicher, Chris. *Mod Lit* 20:8-12 Ag 1993
Cults and cultism. Hughes, Louis. *Furrow* 44:352-358 Je 1993
Denver fits the larger picture. Burke, Greg. *Register* 69:1+ Ag 1 1993
Faith in students. Radcliffe, Fabian. *Priests & People* 7:273-277 Jl 1993
John Paul II, Pope, (1992-08-15) Christ offers abundant life. John Paul II, Pope, 1920- (Karol Wojtyla) (elected 1978). *TPS* 38:39-43 Ja-F 1993*
John Paul II, Pope, (1992-08-15) Message to the youth of the world. John Paul II, Pope, 1920- (Karol Wojtyla) (elected 1978). *Living Light* 29:19-22 Spr 1993*
John Paul II, Pope, (1993-05-23) Sacraments [Orig Italian]. John Paul II, Pope, 1920- (Karol Wojtyla) (elected 1978). *OR(Eng)* 1294:7 Je 9 1993*
John Paul II, Pope, (1993-08-12) Life. John Paul II, Pope, 1920- (Karol Wojtyla) (elected 1978). *OR(Eng)* 1303:7+ Ag 18 1993*
John Paul II, Pope, (1993-09-17) Christ [Orig in Italian]. John Paul II, Pope, 1920- (Karol Wojtyla) (elected 1978). *OR(Eng)* 1308:2 S 22 1993*
John Paul II, Pope, (1993-09-21) Youth. John Paul II, Pope, 1920- (Karol Wojtyla) (elected 1978). *Origins* 23:271-273 S 30 1993*
John Paul II, Pope, (1993-09-26) Never [Orig in Italian]. John Paul II, Pope, 1920- (Karol Wojtyla) (elected 1978). *OR(Eng)* 1311:9 O 13 1993*
Looking for higher education on campus [interview by W Bole]. Hunt, Michael J. *OSV* 82:5 Ag 29 1993
Mapping the land of the young. Felzmann, Vladimir. *Priests & People* 7:264-268 Jl 1993
The mission of Taizé [repr fr *Etudes*]. Lena, Marguerite. *Month* 26:46-52 F 1993
Nine youth ministry principles. Wenke, Leonard. *Origins* 23:350-352 O 21 1993
Resonate Christ with Roman heart. Noè, Virgilio, Cardinal. *OR(Eng)* 1300:6 Jl 21 1993
Rocky mountain high. Myers, David. *Register* 69:1+ Ag 8 1993
Sharing the enrichments of World Youth Day. Jones, Charlotte. *Priest* 49:23 S 1993
Showing the way home. Wilson, Chip. *Register* 69:2 Je 27 1993

"So much depends on you!" [ed homily, World Youth Day, Ag 15 1993]. John Paul II, Pope, 1920- (Karol Wojtyla) (elected 1978). *OSV* 82:4 Ag 29 1993
A time for listening. *Tablet* 247:159-160 F 6 1993
Why are young people leaving the Church? Appleby, Raphael Scott. *Priests & People* 7:255-251 Jl 1993
Why work with young people? Kennedy, Anne. *Priests & People* 7:269-272 Jl 1993
Young people and religion growing out of the Church in the 1960s and 1990s. Kennedy, Finola. *Studies* 81:417-425 Wint 1992
A young person's view. Toner, Roisin. *Priests & People* 7:251-268 Jl 1993
A young pilgrim's notebook. Yound, York. *OSV* 82:9 S 5 1993

YOUTH—SOCIAL ASPECTS
Denver is a mirror of the future [interview by S P Lovett]. Stafford, Francis J, Abp. *OR(Eng)* 1301:5 Jl 28 1993

YOUTH—SOCIAL CONDITIONS
John Paul II, Pope, (1993-08-14) Prayer [Origin English]. John Paul II, Pope, 1920- (Karol Wojtyla) (elected 1978). *Origins* 23:182-186 Ag 26 1993*

YOUTH—SUICIDAL BEHAVIOR
Adolescent suicide: a minsterial response. McCarty, Robert J. *Momentum* 24:61-65 Ap-My 1993
The camouflaged at-risk student: white and wealthy. Metz, Elinor D. *Momentum* 24:40-44 Ap-My 1993

YOUTH- JAMAICA
John Paul II, Pope, (1993-08-10) Hearts [Orig in English]. John Paul II, Pope, 1920- (Karol Wojtyla) (elected 1978). *OR(Eng)* 1303:5 Ag 18 1993*

YOUTH IN CHURCH WORK
Youth evangelization and counter-evangelization. Warren, Michael, 1935-. *Living Light* 30:42-52 Aut 1993

YOUTH IN THE ECUMENICAL MOVEMENT
Youth evangelization and counter-evangelization. Warren, Michael, 1935-. *Living Light* 30:42-52 Aut 1993

YWAHOO, DHYANI
Sin, evil and death in the New Age. McIntyre, Moni. *Way* 33:210-221 Jl 1993

Z

ZACCHAEUS
Come down, Zacchaeus!. McTighe, John P. *Liguorian* 81:56-60 F 1993

ZAIRE—POLITCS AND GOVERNMENT
US waives ban on Zairean visits; incites Mobutu critics. Collins, Carole, and Askin, Steve. *Nat Cath Rep* 29:10 Jl 30 1993
Church groups planning new era, official says. Askin, Steve. *Nat Cath Rep* 29:14 Mr 19 1993
Economic strain could help topple Mobutu. Askin, Steve. *Nat Cath Rep* 29:14 Mr 19 1993
Zaire's democracy struggle tests church, Clinton. Collins, Carole. *Nat Cath Rep* 29:9 F 12 1993

ZAMPETTI, ENRICO
Fede e amore nei *Lager* Nazisti. Marchesi, Giovanni. *Civilta* 2:144-152 Ap 17 1993

ZANGARA, MARIA ROSA
John Paul II, Pope, (1993-06-21) World. John Paul II, Pope, 1920- (Karol Wojtyla) (elected 1978). *OR(Eng)* 1300:5 Jl 21 1993*

ZEN BUDDHISM
Authority (1): the role of the teacher in Buddhist/Christian formation. Hawk, Patrick. *Stud Form Spir* 14:23-29 F 1993
Christian Zen-cum-Ignatian meditation. McCown, Robert. *RRel* 52:507-518 Jl-Ag 1993
Contemplation and action (1): engaged Buddhism from a Zen perspective. Aitken, Robert. *Stud Form Spir* 14:91-104 F 1993
Healing breath: Zen spirituality for a wounded earth. Habito, Ruben L.F. Maryknoll: Orbis, 1993. x, 166p ISBN 0-88344-919-0 LC 93-5125
Meditation and prayer (2): sufficiency and satisfaction in Zen Buddhism: recovering an ancient symbolon. Heisig, James W. *Stud Form Spir* 14:57-74 F 1993
Why orthodox Catholics look to Zen. Gawronski, Raymond T. *New Oxford Rev* 60:13-16 Jl-Ag 1993

ZEROMSKI, STEFAN
Schlesien in der polnischen Gegenwartsliteratur. Zybura, Marek. *Stimm Zeit* 211:197-209 Mr 1993

ZIMBABWE—CHURCH HISTORY
Jesuit presence and the struggle for freedom. Buckland, Stephen. *Month* 26:174-182 My 1993

ZIONISM
The end of Zionism. Cantor, Norman F. *Comm* 120:11-13 N 19 1993
Judaism: people or religion? some positions in modern Jewish thought. Meir, Ephraim. *SIDIC* 25 No 1:20-25 1992

ZUBEIR WAKO, GABRIEL, ABP, 1941-
War-torn Sudan waits for the Pope. Eppink, Alfons. *Tablet* 247:160-161 F 6 1993

ZUKOWSKI, ANGELA ANN
Using the media to spread the good news: Sister Angela Ann Zukowski. Ball, Judy. *St Anth* 100:10-16 F 1993

ZULINSKI, TADEUSZ
Ombudsman under fire for being anti-Catholic. *Tablet* 247:732 Je 5 1993

ZUMARRAGA, JUAN DE
Juan de Zumarraga y su "Regla Cristiana breve". Alejos-Grau, Carmen Jose. Vitoria: Gobierno Vasco, 1993. x, 242p ISBN 84-457-0129-0
Our Lady of Guadalupe: evangelizer of the Americas. McCurry, James E. *Marian Stds* 43:9-16 1992

ZURITA, RAUL
La inquietud religiosa en cuatro poetas chilenos contemporáneos (Miguel Arteche, Carlos Bolton, Fidel Sepúlveda y Raúl Zurita). Livacic Gazzano, Ernesto. *Teol Vida* 33 no 3-4:299-314 1992

AUTHOR
AND
EDITOR
INDEX

A

Aagaard, Anna Marie, et al.
Pentecost message from The World Council of Churches. *Ecumen Trends* 22:2 Ap 1993

Aaker, Jerry.
Partners with the poor: an emerging approach to relief and development. New York: Friendship Press, 1993. x, 158p ISBN 0-377-00252-6 LC 92-35591

Abastoflor Montero, Edmundo.
Que caminhos segue a igreja na América Latina? *REB* 53:158-162 Mr 1993

Abbass, Jobe.
Apostolic See in the new Oriental Canonical Legislation. *Stud Can* 27 no 1: 173-215 1993
Canonical interpretation by recourse to "parallel passages": a comparative study of the Latin and Eastern codes. *Jurist* 51 no 2:293-310 1991

Abein, Reinhard. *see* Balling, Adalbert Ludwig, jt auth

Abel, Olivier.
Ricoeur's ethics of method. *PhilosTod* 37:23-30 Spr 1993

Abela, Anthony M.
Review of: *Bible translation and language. Essays into the history of Bible translation in Maltese* by Sant, Carmel. In: *Gregorianum* 74 no 3:567-568 1993
Valori per il futuro di Malta. *Civilta* 2:260-269 My 1 1993

Abelly, Louis.
The life of the venerable servant of God Vincent de Paul: founder and first superior general of the Congregation of the Mission (book one). New Rochelle, New York: New City Press, 1993. 403p ISBN 1-56548-052-x LC 93-9446

Abeln, Reinhard. *see* Balling, Adalbert Ludwig, jt auth

Abeyratne, R I R.
The philosophy of air law. *Amer J Juris* 37:135-144 1992

Abiola, Olu.
Amazing grace. *Tablet* 247:335 Mr 13 1993

Abner, Marchel.
Group says HIV + priests still stigmatized. *Nat Cath Rep* 29:4 Jl 2 1993

Abraham, Lenore.
Caedmon's hymn and the gebwaernysse (fitness) of things. *ABenR* 43:331-344 D 1992

Abrahamsen, Valerie.
Women artisans in the service of the church. *Sisters* 65:96-103 Mr 1993

Abrogi, Thomas E.
Darkness visible: South Africa en route to rebirth. *Nat Cath Rep* 29:9 Jl 16 1993

Achterhoff, Mary.
Madonna House: holiness through little things [photos]. *OSV* 82:12-13 My 16 1993

Ackah, Carol. *see* Borooah, Vani K, jt auth

Acosta, Ana Margarita.
The Zoe Baird backlash: "Everyone is scared". *Nat Cath Rep* 29:3 Mr 5 1993

Acton, Charles.
Review of: *Born before all time?* by Kuschel, Karl-Josef. In: *Priests & People* 7:126 Mr 1993

Adam, Andrew K M.
Review of: *The promise and practice of Biblical theology* by Reumann, John Henry Paul, ed. In: *CBQ* 55:417-418 Ap 1993
Review of: *The son of man tradition* by Hare, Douglas R A. In: *CBQ* 54:782-783 O 1992

Adams, Doug.
Art, faith, and wholeness. *New Theol Rev* 6:6-17 F 1993

Adams, John C. *see* Yarbrough, Stephen R, jt auth

Adams, Michael.
Review of: *Death plus ten years* by Cooper, Roger. In: *Tablet* 247:756 Je 1993
Review of: *Medieval Tuscany and Umbria* by McIntyre, Anthony Osler. In: *Tablet* 247:1076-1077 Ag 21 1993
Review of: *Original sins: reflections on the history of Zionism and Israel* by Beit-Hallahmi, Benjamin. In: *Tablet* 247:309 Mr 6 1993

Adams, William Seth.
The place of the dead: Christian burial and the liturgical environment. *Liturgy* 10:69-73 Wint 1992

Adler, Mortimer Jerome.
The angels and us. New York: Macmillan, 1982. x, 205p ISBN 0-02-030065-4 LC 93-1377

Adler, William.
Review of: *Lobgesänge der Armen: Studien zum Magnifikat, den HJodajot von Qumran und einigen späten Psalmen* by Lohfink, Norbert. In: *CBQ* 55:380-381 Ap 1993

Adnès, Pierre.
Review of: *Saint Jean de la Croix* by Longchamp, Max Huot de. In: *Gregorianum* 74 No 1:172 1993

Aeschliman, M D.
De Sade and his progeny. *Crisis* 11:54-55 S 1993

Agnelo, Geraldo, Abp.
XXV Anniversario della fondazione della rivista "Gottesdienst". *Notitiae* 28: 712-713 N-D 1992

Agnesine, M, and Buschman-Kelly, Mary Ann.
Good news: alive and well. *ReligTJ* 27:18-19 F 1993

Agnew, Una.
Religious thmes in the work of Patrick Kavanagh: hints of a Celtic tradition. *Studies* 82:257-264 Aut 1993

Agresti, Domenico di.
Catherine De'Ricci and the will of God [pt 2 of 3]. *New Blckfrs* 74:307-316 Je 1993
Catherine De'Ricci [pt 3 of 3]. *New Blckfrs* 74:355-363 Jl-Ag 1993
Catherine De'Ricci. *New Blckfrs* 74:244-251 My 1993

Aguilar, Mario I.
Broken African pots and a mission spirituality. *RRel* 52:202-212 Mr-Ap 1993
Dialogue with Waso Boorana traditional religious practices. *AFER* 35:101-114 Ap 1993
Nagaa: the forgotten quest for peace in modern Kenya. *Month* 26:183-187 My 1993

Aguilera, Francisco M.
Para comprender el catecismo. *Christus* 58:37-38 Je 1993

Ahearn, Clare.
Passion story. *Tablet* 247:470 Ap 10-17 1993

Ahern, Niall.
Waiting. *Furrow* 43:675-678 D 1992

Ahern, Patrick V, Bp, 1919-.
The case for St Thérèse as a doctor of the church. *America* 169:12-13+ Ag 28-S 4 1993

Ahr, Katherine.
Night piece; Woman bathing. *Spirit* 58:8-9 1993

Aichele, George.
Review of: *Imitating Paul: a discourse of power* by Castelli, Elizabeth A. In: *CrossCurr* 43:130 Spr 1993
Review of: *Let the reader understand* by Fowler, Robert M. In: *CrossCurr* 43:130 Spr 1993
Review of: *Literary criticism and the gospels: the theoretical challenge* by Moore, Stephen D. In: *CrossCurr* 42:558-561 Wint 1992-1993
Review of: *The book and the text: the Bible and literary theory* by Schwartz, Regina, ed. In: *CrossCurr* 42:558-561 Wint 1992-1993

Aiken, David W.
The decline from authority: Kierkegaard on intellectual sin. *IPQ* 33:21-35 Mr 1993

Aiken, William.
The search for personal justice. *Living Prayer* 26:17 Ja-F 1993

Ainley, Alison.
Review of: *Hipparchia's choice, an essay concerning women, philosophy, etc* by Doeuff, Michèle Le. In: *IJPS* 1:137-140 Mr 1993

Aitken, Ann-Marie, and Lalawne, Stanislas, et al.
Trois brefs témoignages. *Lumen* 48:175-178 Je 1993

Aitken, M Beverly.
The monastic journey in John of Forde. *Word Sp* 15:69-73 1993

Aitken, Robert.
Contemplation and action (1): engaged Buddhism from a Zen perspective. *Stud Form Spir* 14:91-104 F 1993

Aitken, Tom.
The language police. *Tablet* 247:197 F 13 1993
Onward Christian soldier. *Tablet* 247:598 My 8 1993
Review of: *Ensign in Italy: a platoon commander's story* by Brutton, Philip. In: *Tablet* 247:759 Je 1993
Review of: *Grandchildren of Albion* by Horovitz, Michael, ed. In: *Tablet* 247: 51 Ja 9 1993
Review of: *If you want my opinion* by Levin, Bernard. In: *Tablet* 247:77-78 Ja 16 1993
Review of: *Memories of the Ford administration* by Updike, John, 1932-. In: *Tablet* 247:694 My 29 1993
Review of: *Operation Shylock: a confession* by Roth, Philip. In: *Tablet* 247: 552 My 1 1993
Review of: *The official politically correct dictionary and handbook* by Beard, Henry, and Cerf, Christopher. In: *Tablet* 247:406-407 Mr 27 1993
Review of: *War in Italy 1943-45: a brutal story* by Lamb, Richard. In: *Tablet* 247:920 Jl 17 1993

Albacete, Lorenzo.
Reflections on Humanae Vitae's 25th anniversary. *F & R* 19:5-23 Spr 1993

Alberg, Jeremiah L.
Review of: *Die gnade vollendeter endlichkeit: zur transzendental-theologischen auslegung der thomanischen anthropologie* by Schenk, Richard. In: *Thomist* 57:321-323 Ap 1993

Albert, John.
Thomas Merton: the vigilance of desire. *Word Sp* 14:105-117 1992

Albertus, Karen.
Recover and heal: meditations on the twelve steps. Cincinatti: St Anthony Press, 1993. x, 308p ISBN 0-86716-1531

Albright, John R.
God and the pattern of nature [condensed fr *The Christian Century* Jl 29-Ag 5 1992]. *CDgst* 57:112-117 Ja 1993

Alejos-Grau, Carmen Jose.
Juan de Zumarraga y su "Regla Cristiana breve". Vitoria: Gobierno Vasco, 1993. x, 242p ISBN 84-457-0129-0

Alesandro, John A.
Review of: *Congregatio plenaria diebus 20-29 Octobris 1981 habita*. In: *Jurist* 51 no 2:504-507 1991

Alexakos, Panos D.
Review of: *Nietzsche on truth and philosophy* by Clark, Maudemarie. In: *IPQ* 33:127-128 Mr 1993

Alexander, J Neil, et al.
Environment [exc fr *Liturgy: glad shouts and songs*; *Liturgy: dressing the Church*; *Liturgy: languages and metaphor*]. *Liturgy* 10:84-86 Spr 1993

Alfred, Joseph R.
Review of: *A brief history of Christian worship* by White, James F. In: *Mod Lit* 20:37 O 1993
Review of: *Caring evangelism: a visitation program for congregations* by Braden, Suzanne G, and Clement, Shirley F. In: *Mod Lit* 20:36 My 1993
Review of: *Leader's guide* by Braden, Suzanne G, and Clement, Shirley F. In: *Mod Lit* 20:36 My 1993
Review of: *Once upon a time: story sermons for children* by Timmer, John. In: *Mod Lit* 20:40-41 Je-Jl 1993
Review of: *Participant's workbook* by Braden, Suzanne G, and Clement, Shirley F. In: *Mod Lit* 20:36 My 1993

Alkire, Jan.
Too shy to evangelize? [condensed fr *Evangelism: sharing God's good news*]. *CDgst* 57:28-30 Ap 1993 see Thomas, Leo, jt auth

Allard, G.
Review of: *Femmes et pouvoir dans la cité philosophique: relire l'Utopie de Thomas More* by Bouchard, Gary M. In: *Laval Theol Phil* 49:175-176 F 1993

Allen, Charlotte.
The banality of unbelief [excerpt fr *Washington City paper*]. *Crisis* 11:30-35 Mr 1993
Review of: *Jesus* by Wilson, A N, 1950-. In: *Crisis* 11:30-35 Mr 1993

Allen, Christine.
True fasting: sheltering homeless people. *Priests & People* 7:97-101 Mr 1993

Allen, Diogenes.
Review of: *Metaphysics as a guide to morals* by Murdoch, Iris. In: *Comm* 120:24-25 Ap 23 1993

Allen, Edgar.
Bad lieutenant. *Tablet* 247:283 F 27 1993
Chaplin. *Tablet* 247:20 Ja 2 1993
The cutter. *Tablet* 247:217 F 13 1993
Deep cover. *Tablet* 247:175 F 6 1993
The distinguished gentleman [directed by J Lynn]. *Tablet* 247:441 Ap 3 1993
The end of the golden weather. *Tablet* 247:217-218 F 13 1993
A few good men. *Tablet* 247:52-53 Ja 9 1993
A heart in winter [directed by J Amiel]. *Tablet* 247:555 My 1 1993
Home alone 2: lost in New York. *Tablet* 246:1628 D 19-26 1992
Indochini [directed by R Wargnier]. *Tablet* 247:441 Ap 3 1993
Into the west. *Tablet* 246:1628 D 19-26 1992
The last days of chez nous. *Tablet* 247:283 F 27 1993
Leap of faith. *Tablet* 247:520 Ap 24 1993
Leon the pig farmer [directed by G Sinyor and V Jean]. *Tablet* 247:315 Mr 6 1993
Lorenzo's oil [directed by G Miller]. *Tablet* 247:314-315 Mr 6 1993
Malcolm X [directed by S Lee]. *Tablet* 247:346 Mr 13 1993
Man bites dog. *Tablet* 247:112 Ja 23 1993
Night and the city. *Tablet* 247:174-175 F 6 1993
Olivier, Olivier. *Tablet* 247:251 F 20 1993
Orlando [directed by S Potter]. *Tablet* 247:377-378 Mr 20 1993
The ox [directed by S Nykvist]. *Tablet* 247:520 Ap 24 1993
Raising Cain. *Tablet* 247:82 Ja 16 1993
Reservoir dogs. *Tablet* 247:82 Ja 16 1993
A river runs through it. *Tablet* 247:283 F 27 1993
Scent of a woman. *Tablet* 247:378 Mr 20 1993
Shadows and fog. *Tablet* 247:251 F 20 1993
Sherlock Junior. *Tablet* 247:250-251 F 20 1993
The silent touch [directed by K Zanussi]. *Tablet* 247:485 Ap 10-17 1993
Soft top, hard shoulder. *Tablet* 247:175 F 6 1993
Sommersby. *Tablet* 247:555 My 1 1993
Splitting heirs. *Tablet* 247:485 Ap 10-17 1993
Tous les matins du monde. *Tablet* 247:52 Ja 9 1993
Toys [directed by B Levinson]. *Tablet* 247:346 Mr 13 1993
Used people [directed by B Kidron]. *Tablet* 247:485 Ap 10-17 1993
A winter's tale. *Tablet* 247:53 Ja 9 1993
L 627. *Tablet* 247:81-82 Ja 16 1993

Allen, Gary Gene. see Allen, Karen Lawrence, jt auth

Allen, Juanita.
Review of: *The gift of Christmas* by Winkler, Jude. In: *Mod Lit* 20:40 N 1993

Allen, Peter.
Walsingham: Mary's message for rich and poor [photo]. *Priests & People* 7: 197-201 My 1993

Allen, Prudence.
Sex and gender differentiation in Hildegard of Bingen and Edith Stein. *Communio* 20:389-414 Sum 1993

Allen, Rodger Van.
Being Catholic: Commonweal from the seventies to the nineties. Chicago: Loyola University Press, 1993. x, 203p ISBN 0-8294-0744-8 LC 92-40701

Allen, Thomas B.
Possessed: the true story of an exorcism. New York: Doubleday, 1993. 259p ISBN 0-385-42034-x LC 92-42038

Allessandri, M.
Review of: *Alla ricerca di nostri predecessori: compendio di paleoantropologia* by Marcozzi, Vittorio. In: *Civilta* 143:523-524 D 5 1992

Alleva, Richard.
The age of innocence [directed by M Scorses]. *Comm* 120:14-17 N 5 1993
Bram Stoker's Dracula. *Comm* 119:17 D 18 1992
Chaplin. *Comm* 120:16 F 12 1993
The crying game. *Comm* 120:19-20 F 26 1993
Dave [directed by I Reitman]. *Comm* 120:20-21 Jl 16 1993
Falling down [directed by J Schumacher]. *Comm* 120:21+ Ap 9 1993
Groundhog Day. *Comm* 120:16+ Mr 26 1993
Hoffa. *Comm* 120:15-16 F 12 1993
Jurassic park. *Comm* 120:18-19 Ag 13 1993
The last action hero [directed by J McTiernan]. *Comm* 120:19-20 Ag 13 1993
The last of the Mohicans. *Comm* 119:16-17 D 18 1992
Lorenzo's oil. *Comm* 120:14-15 Mr 12 1993

Alleva, Richard. *(cont'd)*
Mad dog and glory [directed by J McNaughton]. *Comm* 120:19 Ap 23 1993
Malcolm X. *Comm* 120:18-20 Ja 15 1993
El mariachi. *Comm* 120:21 Jl 16 1993
Much ado about nothing [directed by K Branagh]. *Comm* 120:23-24 Je 18 1993
Passion fish. *Comm* 120:18-19 Ap 23 1993
Scent of a woman. *Comm* 120:12+ Mr 12 1993
The secret garden [directed by A. Holland]. *Comm* 120:17-19 O 8 1993
Stolen children [directed by G Amelio]. *Comm* 120:20-21 My 7 1993
This boy's life [directed by M Caton-Jones]. *Comm* 120:18-19 Je 4 1993
True romance [directed by T. Scott]. *Comm* 120:22-24 O 22 1993

Allison, Dale C. see Davies, W D, jt auth

Allitt, Patrick.
Review of: *Mission to rural America: the story of W Howard Bishop, founder of Glenmary* by Kauffman, Christopher J. In: *ChrWorld* 236:236+ S-O 1993

Allsopp, Michael E.
Of medicine and metaphor: significant findings from Walker Percy. *Linacre* 60:48-55 F 1993
Review of: *A feminist ethic of risk* by Welch, Sharon D. In: *Month* 26:233-234 Je 1993
Review of: *In good conscience: reason and emotion in moral decision making* by Callahan, Sidney. In: *Month* 26:376-377 S-O 1993

Almade, Frank D.
Just wages in the church? *Church* 9:41-43 Spr 1993

Almeida Cunha, Rogério Ignácio de.
Trabalho, teimosia e esperança (a questão do trabaslho no 8 encontro intereclesial das CEBs). *REB* 52:877-893 D 1992

Aloysia, M.
Review of: *Life of the beloved* by Nouwen, Henri Josef Machiel, 1932-. In: *Sisters* 65:141-142 Mr 1993

Alphin, Charles.
Charles Alphin [interview by T Jarvis]. *Salt* 13:4-6 Ja 1993

Althann, Robert.
Review of: *El Creciente fértil y la Biblia* by Echegaray, Joaquín González. In: *CBQ* 55:110-111 Ja 1993
Review of: *Guida allo studio dell'Ebraico biblico* by Deiana, Giovanni, and Spreafico, Ambrogio. In: *CBQ* 54:743-744 O 1992
Review of: *The prayers of David (Psalms 51-72): Studies in the Psalter, II* by Goulder, Michael. In: *Heythrop* 34:186-187 Ap 1993

Altizer, Thomas J J.
The genesis of God: a theological genealogy. Louisville: John Knox, 1993. x, 208p ISBN 0-664-21996-9

Alton, David.
Abortion politics. *Tablet* 247:508-509 Ap 24 1993
Britain's angry voters. *Tablet* 247:604-605 My 15 1993
Major's little difficulty. *Tablet* 247:779-780 Je 19 1993
Review of: *Reclaiming the ground* by Smith, John, et al. In: *Tablet* 247:549 My 1 1993

Altschuler, Glenn C.
Review of: *Rethinking social policy: race, poverty, and the underclass* by Jencks, Christopher. In: *CrossCurr* 42:545-549 Wint 1992-1993
Review of: *The new politics of poverty* by Mead, Lawrence M. In: *CrossCurr* 42:545-549 Wint 1992-1993
Review of: *Two nations* by Hacker, Andrew. In: *CrossCurr* 42:545-549 Wint 1992-1993

Alvaré, Helen M.
Bishops' public information campaign. *CLawyer* 34 no 4:385-389 1993
"A pro-life RSVP". *America* 168:7-10 Ja 30 1993
What abortion advocates really want. *OSV* 82:19 Je 20 1993

Alvarez, Rosendo, Bp, and Rodríguez Plaza, Braulio.
Hispania la iniciación cristiana de los niños no bautizados en edad escolar. *Notitiae* 29:64-75 Ja-F 1993

Alvez de Lima, Luiz.
Renovacion catequistica Bracileña. *Christus* 58:10-20 Je 1993

Alzamura, Augusto Vargas, Abp.
"Overcoming evil through good" [interview by M Agama]. *OSV* 82:21 My 30 1993

Amato, Joseph Anthony, 1938-.
Victims without tears: democracy and the politics of pity. *Crisis* 11:29-31 F 1993

Amis, John.
Review of: *Elisabeth Schumann* by Puritz, Gerd. In: *Tablet* 247:585 My 8 1993
Review of: *Henry Purcell—glory of his age* by Campbell, Margaret. In: *Tablet* 247:585 My 8 1993
Review of: *Music and the mind* by Storr, Anthony. In: *Tablet* 246:1624 D 19-26 1992
Review of: *Pablo Casals* by Baldock, Robert. In: *Tablet* 247:172-173 F 6 1993
Review of: *Reggie* by Lucas, John. In: *Tablet* 247:585 My 8 1993
Review of: *Rutland Boughton and the Glastonbury Festivals* by Hurd, Michael. In: *Tablet* 247:585 My 8 1993
Review of: *The new guide to classical music* by Swafford, Jan. In: *Tablet* 247:585 My 8 1993
Review of: *True artist and true friend* by Fifield, Christopher. In: *Tablet* 247: 585 My 8 1993

Amlaw, Mary.
Why I stay in the Catholic Church. *Liguorian* 81:4-8 Ag 1993

Amoretti, Biancamaria Scarcia.
Riflessioni sull'Islam oggi. *StudiaM* 41:253-267 1992

Amos, Thomas.
Review of: *Authentic witnesses: approaches to Medieval texts and manuscripts* by Rouse, Mary A, and Rouse, Richard H. In: *CHist* 79:313-314 Ap 1993

Amphoux, Christian-B.
Les premières Editions de Luc II: l'histoire du texte au IIe siècle. *Eph Theol Lovan* 78:38-48 Ap 1992

Amprimoz, A.
Review of: *Muslims under Latin rule, 1100-1300* by Powell, James M, ed. In: *Can Cath Rev* 11:33 Ja 1993

Amspaugh, Linda. see Drake, Bob M, jt auth

Anderson, Anthony.
Loving God [2 pts.]. *Priest* 49:33-38 O; 40-44 N 1993

Anderson, Carl.
The politics of health-care ethics [interview by Ann Carey]. *OSV* 81:21 F 28 1993

Anderson, Chris.
Aging becomes them. *Comm* 120:5-6 Ag 13 1993

Anderson, David E.
Methodist minister's ecumenical labor lost. *Nat Cath Rep* 30:4 O 29 1993

Anderson, Denise.
Review of: *A place for Baptism* by Kuehn, Regina. In: *Past Mus* 17:41-42 F-Mr 1993

Anderson, Gary.
Review of: *Numbers* by Milgrom, Jacob. In: *CBQ* 55:122-123 Ja 1993

Anderson, George M.
Health care and the rural poor. *America* 169:16-18 Jl 3-10 1993
People are getting hurt: the rise in gay-bashing. *Comm* 120:16+ F 26 1993
Review of: *Last one over the wall: the Massachusetts experiment in closing reform schools* by Miller, Jerome G. In: *America* 168:19-20 F 13 1993

Anderson, H George, et al, eds.
The one mediator, the saints, and Mary. Minneapolis: Augsburg Fortress, 1992. x, 397p ISBN 0-8066-2579-1 LC 91-40822

Anderson, Herbert, and Fite, Cotton R.
Becoming married: family living in pastoral perspective. Louisville: Westminster, 1993. x, 160p ISBN 0-664-25126-9

Anderson, Joan Wester, 1938-.
The deacon today. *Liguorian* 81:13-17 S 1993
Parish nurses: pioneers in healthcare. *Liguorian* 81:48-52 Mr 1993
Worshiping at the shrine of self conquering pride. *Liguorian* 81:46-50 Ja 1993

Anderson, Neil T.
Living free in Christ. Ventura: Gospel Light, 1993. 310p ISBN 0-8307-1604-1 LC 93-7358

Anderson, Norm.
Sister Martha's second calling [condensed fr *C S J Focus* F 1993]. *CDgst* 57:57-59 Ag 1993

Anderson, Paul.
Bringing the dead to life. *New Cov* 23:16-17 N 1993
Discouraged? Here's what the Gospel says about it. *New Cov* 23:16-18 Ag 1993
The facts of death: some reflections for Lent. *New Cov* 22:26-30 Mr 1993

Anderson, Peggy.
Connecting with "the real world". *Momentum* 24:26-27 F-Mr 1993

Anderson, Robert A.
Review of: *The living Psalms* by Westermann, Claus. In: *Pacifica* 6:100-101 F 1993

Anderson, Ted.
Review of: *Catholic social teaching: our best kept secret* by Henriot, Peter J, et al. In: *Living Light* 29:91-92 Aut 1992

Andre, Lorayne.
Review of: *Forming a small Christian community* by Currier, Richard, and Gram, Frances. In: *Sisters* 65:138-139 Mr 1993

Andreassi, Anthony.
For the record: Pope Leo XIII and the church in New York. *Church* 9:46-49 Sum 1993

Andrews, Paul.
Review of: *Ignatius of Loyola* by Meissner, William W. In: *Studies* 82:198-206 Sum 1993
Le tappe e le insidie del crescere. *Civilta* 2:569-578 Je 19 1993
The tasks and pitfalls of growing up. *Studies* 81:408-416 Wint 1992

Angela, of Foligno, 1248?-1309.
Angela of Foligno: complete works. New York: Paulist Press, 1993. x, 424p ISBN 0-8091-0460-1 LC 92-38830
Complete works. New York: Paulist Press, 1993. x, 424p ISBN 0-80910-460 LC 92-38830

Angelica, Jade C, 1952-.
A moral emergency: breaking the cycle of child sexual abuse. Kansas City: Sheed & Ward, 1993. x, 161p ISBN 15-5612-617-4 LC 93-939

Angell, James W.
O Susan!: looking forward with hope after the death of a child. Pasadena: Hope, 1990. 115p ISBN 0-932727-401-9 LC 90-4699

Angell, Jeannette L, and Bower, Richard Allen.
Encountering the holy [exc fr *Liturgy: the art of celebration; Liturgy: in daily life*]. *Liturgy* 10:51-55 Spr 1993

Angell, Jeannette L, and Squires, Susan E.
Not just an art: spiritual significance of iconography. *Spir Life* 32:67-72 Sum 1993

Angelo, Geraldo M. see Javierre, Antonio M, Cardinal, jt auth

Angle, Siddika.
Theological trends: beyond familiar shores: New Age spirituality. *Way* 33:138-147 Ap 1993

Angue, Jean-Louis.
Un évangéliaire pou notre temps: L'evangeliaire en langue Française. *Notitiae* 28:337-347 My 1992

Anspach, Renée R.
Deciding who lives: fateful choices in the intensive care nursery. Berkeley: University of California Press, 1993. x, 303p ISBN 0-520-05268-4 LC 91-44245

Antall, Richard C.
Latin America's newest civil war. *OSV* 82:5 Ag 22 1993
A one-way ticket and a restless farewell. *OSV* 82:12 O 24 1993

Antich, Xavier.
El rostre de l'altre: passeig filosoficper l'obra d'Emmanuel Levinas. Valencia: Edicions 314, 1993. x, 149p ISBN 84-7502-374-6

Antoci, Peter.
Review of: *Theology without boundaries: encounter of Eastern Orthodoxy and Western tradition* by Calian, Carnegie Samuel. In: *Living Light* 29:89-90 Wint 1992

Antón, Angel.
Local church/regional church: systematic reflections. *Jurist* 52 no 1:553-576 1992

Antoniazzi, Alberto.
Interrogações em forma de respostas: observações sobre a Conferência e as conclusões de Santo Domingo. *Perspectiva* 25:90-98 Ja-Ap 1993

Antonides, Harry.
Reclaiming our daily work. *Can Cath Rev* 11:18-23 My 1993

Apathy, Andy.
Review of: *Roots and wings* by Allen, Karen Lawrence, and Allen, Gary Gene. In: *Nat Cath Rep* 29:16 S 24 1993
Review of: *Your family in focus* by Finley, Mitchel B. In: *Nat Cath Rep* 29:16 S 24 1993

Apczynski, John V.
Review of: *The new universalism: foundations for a global theology* by Krieger, David J. In: *JEcumen Stds* 29:492 Sum-Aut 1992

Appleby, George W.
Review of: *Ignatius of Loyola: the psychology of a saint* by Meissner, William W. In: *New Oxford Rev* 60:30-31 Je 1993

Appleby, Raphael Scott.
In the church but of the world: pioneer priests on the eve of Vatican II. *US Cath Hist* 11:83-100 Wint 1993
Jesus saves; but how? *USCath* 58:30-36 F 1993
The rise and rise of the Christian Right. *Tablet* 247:847-848 Jl 3 1993
Why are young people leaving the Church? *Priests & People* 7:255-251 Jl 1993

Appleyard, Joseph A.
Review of: *Genre choices, gender questions* by Gerhart, Mary. In: *America* 169:27-28 S 11 1993

Aquirre Oraa, José María.
Raison critique ou raison herméneutique? *RPhil Louvain* 91:409-440 Ag 1993

Aragay Tusell, Narcis.
Origen y decadencia del logos. Barcelona: Anthropos, 1993. x, 284p ISBN 84-7658-383-4

Arakal, Joseph J.
The Psalms in inclusive language. Minnesota: The Liturgical Press, 1993. x, 150p ISBN 0-8146-2024-8 LC 92-32647

Araujo, Marianne D, and Carballo, Suzanne M.
Creating the future. *Health Prog* 74:22-24+ Je 1993

Araujo, Robert J.
The teleology of law: responsible citizenship and discipleship. *CLawyer* 35 no 1:57-78 1993
Vatican II: the impact on American society—the pas de deux between rights and responsibilities. *CLawyer* 35 no 2:109-144 1993

Araújo, Serfim Fernandes de.
Jesus Cristo ontem, hoje e sempre (Homilia na celebração eucarística de abertura da Primeira Semana Teológica do CES). *Perspectiva* 24:287-290 S-D 1992

Araujo de Oliveira, Manfredo.
La modernidad en America Latina. *Christus* 58:20-25 My 1993

Arbery, Glenn.
Review of: *The guns of the South: a novel of the Civil War* by Turtledove, Harry. In: *Crisis* 11:58-59 Jl-Ag 1993

Arbuckle, Gerald A.
Prophecy or restorationism in religious life. *RRel* 52:326-339 My-Je 1993

Archard, David.
Review of: *The good polity: normative analysis of the state* by Hamlin, Alan, and Petit, Philip, eds. In: *IJPS* 1:146-148 Mr 1993

Archideo, Lila B.
Catechism points to Mary as the mother and example of the faithful. *OR(Eng)* 1295:4 Je 16 1993

Ardito, Mary Frances.
Review of: *Intimacy and the hungers of the heart* by Collins, Patrick W, 1936-. In: *Cist Stud* 28:[5]-[7] 1993

Arevalo, Catalino G. see Rosales, Gaudencio B, jt ed

Arghittu, Mary, et al.
Tradition and transformation. *Health Prog* 74:28-33 Ap 1993

Arias Reyero, Maximino.
Aspectos y visión global de una teología de la salvación. *Teol Vida* 34 no 1-2:91-102 1993

Arinze, Francis, Cardinal.
Priestly celibacy and association with women. *Seminarium* 33:88-95 Ja-Mr 1993

Aristide, Jean-Bertrand, 1953-.
Aristide: an autobiography. Maryknoll, New York: Orbis Books, 1993. 205p ISBN 0-88344-845-9 LC 92-34558
Communion in exile [interview by K DeSmet]. *Critic* 47:2-8 Wint 1992

Arizmendi Esquivel, Felipe, Bp.
Santo Domingo desde dentro. *Christus* 58:15-22 Mr-Ap 1993

Arkes, Hadley.
Congresspeak. *Crisis* 11:11-12 Jl-Ag 1993
Ensoulment in Arkansas. *Crisis* 11:12-13 Ap 1993
Epistle to the Hoyas. *Crisis* 11:11-12 Mr 1993
Have argument, will travel. *Crisis* 11:14-15 Je 1993
The party of abortion finds its limit. *Crisis* 11:13-14 S 1993
Privacy and the law. *Crisis* 11:14-15 My 1993
A season for turning. *Crisis* 11:14-15 O 1993

Arkins, Brian.
Review of: *John Henry Newman—Theology and reform* by Allsopp, Michael E, and Burke, R R, eds. In: *Studies* 82:347-350 Aut 1993
Review of: *The relationship between neoplatonism and Christianity* by Finan, T, and Toomey, V, eds. In: *Studies* 82:351-354 Aut 1993

Arledler, G.
Review of: *La musica e la Bibbia: atti del Convegno Internazionale di Studi (Siena 24-26 agosto 1990)* by Troia, Pasquale, ed. In: *Civilta* 144:100 Ja 2 1993
Review of: *Mozart* by Ballola, Giovanni Carli, and Parenti, Roberto. In: *Civilta* 143:639 D 19 1992

Armando, G.
Review of: *Clero e società nell'Italia contemporanea* by Rosa, Mario. In: *Civilta* 3:318-319 Ag 7-21 1993

Armendariz, Sherry.
Amazing grace: mealtime blessings. *Spir Life* 39:137-139 Aut 1993

Armesto, Indalecio.
Discusiones sobre la metafisica. Santiago: Universidad, 1993. x, 360p ISBN 84-7191-968-0

Arnold, James.
The age of innocence [directed by M. Scorsese]. *St Anth* 101:4 N 1993
Aladdin. *St Anth* 100:4 F 1993
Alive [directed by F Marshall]. *St Anth* 100:4 Ap 1993
Chaplin. *St Anth* 100:4 Mr 1993
Cliffhanger. *St Anth* 101:5 Ag 1993
The crying game [directed by N Jordan]. *St Anth* 100:5 Ap 1993
Dave. *St Anth* 101:4 Jl 1993
Falling down. *St Anth* 100:4 My 1993
A few good men. *St Anth* 100:4 F 1993
The firm [directed by S Pollack]. *St Anth* 100:4 S 1993
Free Willy. *St Anth* 101:4 O 1993
The fugitive [directed by A. Davis]. *St Anth* 101:4 N 1993
Groundhog Day. *St Anth* 100:4 My 1993
Heart and soul [directed by R. Underwood]. *St Anth* 101:4 O 1993
Hoffa. *St Anth* 100:5 Mr 1993
Home alone 2: lost in New York. *St Anth* 100:4 F 1993
In line of fire [directed by W Petersen]. *St Anth* 100:4 S 1993
Indecent proposal. *St Anth* 101:4 Je 1993
Jack the bear. *St Anth* 101:4-5 Je 1993
Jennifer 8. *St Anth* 100:5 Ja 1993
Jurassic park. *St Anth* 101:4 Ag 1993
The last action hero. *St Anth* 101:4 Ag 1993
Leap of faith. *St Anth* 100:4 F 1993
Life with Mikey. *St Anth* 101:4-5 Ag 1993
Lorenzo's oil [directed by G Miller]. *St Anth* 100:4-5 Ap 1993
Lost in Yonkers [directed by M Coolidge]. *ST Anth* 101:4 Jl 1993
Made in America [directed by R Benjamin]. *St Anth* 101:5 Ag 1993
Malcolm X. *St Anth* 100:4 Ja 1993
The man without a face [directed by M. Gibson]. *St Anth* 101:4 N 1993
Manhattan murder mystery [directed by W. Allen]. *St Anth* 101:4 N 1993
Married to it. *St Anth* 101:4 Je 1993
Night and the city. *St Anth* 100:5 Ja 1993
Passion fish [directed by J Sayles]. *St Anth* 100:4 My 1993
Poetic justice. *St Anth* 101:4 O 1993
Rich in love [directed by B Beresford]. *ST Anth* 101:4 Jl 1993
Rising sun. *St Anth* 101:4 O 1993
A river runs through it. *St Anth* 100:4-5 Ja 1993
Scent of a woman. *St Anth* 100:4 Mr 1993
Searching for Bobby Fischer [directed by G. Zaillian]. *St Anth* 101:4-5 N 1993
The secret garden [directed by A. Holland]. *St Anth* 101:4 O 1993
Sleepless in Seattle [directed by N Ephron]. *St Anth* 100:4 S 1993
Sliver [directed by P Noyce]. *St Anth* 101:5 Ag 1993
Sommersby. *St Anth* 100:5 Ap 1993
Stolen children [directed by G Amelio]. *St Anth* 101:4 Je 1993
Strictly ballroom. *St Anth* 100:4-5 My 1993
This boy's life. *ST Anth* 101:4 Jl 1993
Toys. *St Anth* 100:4-5 Mr 1993

Arnold, Linda.
Review of: *They call her pastor* by Wallace, Ruth A. In: *Living Light* 29:81-82 Wint 1992

Arnold, Linda M, and Gallagher, Patricia.
Forming lay prayer leaders. *Past Mus* 17:14-15 Je-Jl 1993

Arnold, William V.
Pastoral response to sexual ethics. Louisville, Kentucky: John Knox, 1993. 176p ISBN 0-66425420-0

Arnold-Foster, Val.
Review of: *An autobiography: part 1* by Frost, David. In: *Tablet* 247:1197-1198 S 18 1993

Arnstein, Walter L.
Review of: *The Protestant crusade in Great Britain, 1829-1860* by Wolffe, John. In: *CHist* 79:120-122 Ja 1993

Aronowicz, Annette.
Review of: *Judaism, Christianity, and liberation—an agenda for dialogue* by Maduro, Otto, ed. In: *CrossCurr* 43:125-127 Spr 1993

Arpin, Robert L.
Wonderfully, fearfully made. New York: HarperSanFrancisco, 1992. x, 207p ISBN 0-060075-6 LC 92-53906

Arteaga Manieu, Andrés.
Review of: *Breve teología fundamental* by Imbach, Jeffrey D. In: *Teol Vida* 34 no 1-2:160 1993
Review of: *Tomás de Aquino* by Pesch, Otto Hermann, 1931-. In: *Teol Vida* 34 no 1-2:159-160 1993

Arthadeva, Basil Mary.
Safeguarding the faith. *ChrWorld* 38:15-23 Ja-F 1993

Arthur, Chris.
Agony as advertisement. *Month* 26:97-104 Mr 1993
The art of exhibiting the sacred. *Month* 26:281-289 Jl 1993
The sinfulness of normality. *Month* 26:361-366 S-O 1993
Utility, understanding and creativity in the study of religions. *New Blckfrs* 74:14-20 Ja 1993

Artuso, P.
Review of: *Enciclopedia delle scienze fisiche, vol I.* In: *Civilta* 2:407-408 My 15 1993

Ascoli, E Lynn.
A father forgets his son [condensed fr *The Providence Visitor* O 8 1992]. *CDgst* 57:118-120 Ja 1993

Ash, Lucy.
The path back. *Liguorian* 81:12-16 Jl 1993

Ash, Marion F.
How Christians can receive healing. *New Cov* 23:13-14 O 1993

Ashkar, Dominic.
Road to Emmaus: a new model for catechesis. Sant Jose: Resource Publications, 1993. x, 194p ISBN 0-89390-266-7 LC 93-17566

Ashley, Benedict M.
Gender and the priesthood of Christ: a theological reflection. *Thomist* 57:343-379 Jl 1993
Living in Christ: the catechism reunites morality and spirituality. *Crisis* 11:23-26 Je 1993
Catechism of the Catholic Church (Commentary).

Ashton, Dianne. see Umansky, Ellen M, jt ed

Ashton, John.
Review of: *Structure and message of the epistle to the Hebrews* by Vanhoyne, Albert. In: *Heythrop* 34:77-78 Ja 1993
Review of: *The epistle to the Hebrews: a commentary on the Epistle to the Hebrews* by Attridge, Harold W. In: *Heythrop* 34:77-78 Ja 1993
Review of: *The shepherd discourse of John 10 and its context: studies by members of the Johannine writings seminar* by Beutler, Johannes, and Fortna, Robert T, eds. In: *Heythrop* 34:76-77 Ja 1993
Understanding the fourth gospel. New York: Oxford University Press, 1991. x, 599p ISBN 0-19-826353-8 LC 90-43422

Ashworth, E J.
Analogy and equivocation in thirteenth-century logic: Aquinas in context. *Med Stud* 54:94-135 1992

Askin, Steve.
Church groups planning new era, official says. *Nat Cath Rep* 29:14 Mr 19 1993
Economic strain could help topple Mobutu. *Nat Cath Rep* 29:14 Mr 19 1993
see Collins, Carole, jt auth

Askonas, Peter.
Review of: *Business ethics: the state of the art* by Freeman, Edward R, ed. In: *Heythrop* 34:466-468 O 1993

Asma, Lawrence F.
Review of: *Who knows what is good?* by Farmer, Kathleen A. In: *CBQ* 54:745-746 O 1992

Aspinwall, Bernard.
Review of: *Revivalism and social change: Christianity, nation building and the market in the nineteenth-century United States* by Thomas, George M. In: *Heythrop* 34:345-346 Jl 1993

Astarita, Tommaso.
Review of: *Heavenly supper: the story of Maria Janis* by Tomizza, Fulvio. In: *CHist* 79:114-115 Ja 1993

Astrain, Ricardo Salas.
Review of: *Cosmología, religión y política en el Renacimiento* by Granada, Miguel. In: *RPhil Louvain* 91:466-467 Ag 1993

Atherton, John.
Pastores dabo vobis—reflections on a conference. *Furrow* 44:440-443 Jl-Ag 1993

Atkin, Nicholas. see Tallert, Frank, jt ed

Atkins, Anselm.
Review of: *Humanists and Protestants, 1500-1900* by Hall, Basil. In: *JEcumen Stds* 29:112-113 Wint 1992
Review of: *Reclaiming the high ground: a Christian response to secularism* by Montefiore, Hugh. In: *JEcumen Stds* 29:112-113 Wint 1992

Atkinson, Gary. see Sullivan, Thomas D, jt auth

Attarian, John.
Review of: *Hollywood vs America* by Medved, Michael, 1948-. In: *Crisis* 11:55-57 S 1993
Review of: *Inside American education: the decline, the deception, the dogmas* by Sowell, Thomas. In: *Crisis* 11:52-54 Ap 1993

Attridge, Harold W.
Review of: *A key to the Peshitta Gospels: vol 1, Ālaph-Dālath* by Falla, Terry C. In: *CBQ* 55:146-147 Ja 1993

Atwan, Robert, and Wieder, Laurence, 1945-, eds.
Chapters into verse: poetry in English inspired by the Bible [vol I: Genesis to Malachi]. New York: Oxford University Press, 1993. x, 481p ISBN 0-19-506913-7 LC 92-37206
Chapters into verse: poetry in English inspired by the Bible [vol II: Gospels to Revelation]. New York: Oxford University Press, 1993. x, 391p ISBN 0-19-508305-9 LC 92-37206

Ballweg, John M.
Marriage and ministry in the diaconate. *Church* 9:30-32 Sum 1993
Undergraduates discover Pierre Teilhard De Chardin. *Horizons (CTS)* 19: 277-287 Fall 1992

Balsam, Charles.
Reconsidering Humanae Vitae [commentary *Humanae Vitae*]. *Register* 69:5 Ag 1 1993

Balthasar, Hans Urs Von, 1905-1988.
Explorations in theology, VI III: creator spirit. San Francisco: Ignatius Press, 1993. ISBN 0-89870-437-5
My work: in retrospect. San Francisco: Ignatius Press, 1993. ISBN 0-89870-435-9
Mysterium paschale: the mystery of Easter. Grand Rapids: Eerdmans, 1993. 168p ISBN 0-8028-0216-8
On the tasks of Catholic philosophy in our time. *Communio* 20:147-187 Spr 1993
Razing the bastions: on the church in this age. San Francisco: Ignatius Press, 1993. ISBN 0-89870-428-6
A word on Humanae vitae [fr *New Ilucidations* tr by M T Skerry]. *Communio* 20:437-450 Sum 1993

Balycomb, John.
Review of: *Faith without the church? Nominalism in Australian Christianity* by Bentley, Peter, et al. In: *Pacifica* 6:359-361 O 1993

Bambach, Charles R.
Phenomenological research as destruktion: the early Heidegger's reading of Dilthey. *PhilosTod* 37:115-132 Sum 1993

Bancroft, Nancy.
Review of: *Human rights: Christians, Marxists, and others in dialogue* by Swidler, Leonard, ed. In: *JEcumen Stds* 29:493 Sum-Aut 1992
Review of: *Marxian and Christian utopianism* by Marsden, John Joseph. In: *JEcumen Stds* 29:492-493 Sum-Aut 1992

Bandera, Armando.
Review of: *De gratia Dei: in I-II Summae theologiae divi Thomae expositio* by Ramírez, Iacobus M. In: *Cien Tom* 120:191-193 Ja-Ap 1993
Review of: *Diccionario teológico: El Dios cristiano* by Pikaza, Xavier, and Silanes, Nereo, eds. In: *Cien Tom* 120:190 Ja-Ap 1993
Review of: *Evangelische ARmut und Kirche: Thomas von Aquin und die Armutskontroversen des 13 und gebinnenden 14 Jahrhunderts* by Horst, Ulrich. In: *Cien Tom* 120:195-196 Ja-Ap 1993
Review of: *Evolución de la Iglesia según J González Arintero* by Rodríguez, Valentín. In: *Cien Tom* 120:190-191 Ja-Ap 1993
Review of: *Iglesia de iglesias: Eclesiología de comunión* by Tillard, Jean Marie Roger, 1927-. In: *Cien Tom* 119:613-614 S-D 1992
Review of: *Iglesia sacerdotal, Iglesia profõaetica* by Martínez, Felícismo. In: *Cien Tom* 119:420-421 My-Ag 1992
Review of: *Iglesias locales y catolicidad* by Legrand, Hervé, et al, eds. In: *Cien Tom* 119:610-611 S-D 1992
Review of: *Juan de la Cruz: un caso límite* by Javierre, J M. In: *Cien Tom* 119:624-625 S-D 1992
Review of: *La eucaristía misterio de comunión* by Gesteira, Manuel. In: *Cien Tom* 119:414-415 My-Ag 1992
Review of: *Le Cristologie contemporanee e le loro posizioni fondamentali al vaglio della dottrina di San Tommaso* by Ols, Daniel. In: *Cien Tom* 120: 187-188 Ja-Ap 1993
Review of: *Obras completas, a cargo de Maximiliano Herráiz* by Juan De La Cruz, San. In: *Cien Tom* 119:420 My-Ag 1992

Banet, Robert A.
The fall of the house of Darwin. *HPR* 93:70-73 Ja 1993

Banker, James R.
Review of: *Albertanus of Brescia: the pursuit of happiness in the early thirteenth century* by Powell, James M. In: *CHist* 79:321-322 Ap 1993

Banki, Judith Hershcopf.
Baltimore and Eisenach [Graymoor Prize Winner]. *Comm* 120:11+ Ja 15 1993

Bankston, Carl L, III.
Review of: *American Catholic arts and fictions* by Giles, Paul. In: *Comm* 120:28-30 F 26 1993
Review of: *Power and persuasion in late antiquity: towards a Christian empire* by Brown, Peter Robert Lamont. In: *Comm* 120:28-29 Ap 9 1993

Banner, Charla Leibenguth.
My at-home retreat. *CDgst* 57:137-139 Mr 1993

Banta, Margrit.
Talking to children about death. *ReligTJ* 27:29-30 Mr 1993

Bar, Shaul.
Dreams and visions. *BibleT* 31:200-203 Jl 1993

Baragli, Enrico.
Review of: *Communicazione: crisi della Chiesa* by Cappelli, Piero. In: *Civilta* 3:337-338 Ag 7-21 1993
Review of: *Da 6 a 11 anni: Sviluppo dell intelligenza, maturazione affettiva, scoperta della vita sociale, confronti familiari* by Galimard, Pierre. In: *Civilta* 144:102 Ja 2 1993
Review of: *Dizionario dei nomi geografici italiani e stranieri* by Rudoni, Antonio. In: *Civilta* 144:616-617 Mr 20 1993
Review of: *Ethique et communication, Actes du Colluque.* In: *Civilta* 2:201-202 Ap 17 1993
Review of: *I mezzi di comunicazione di massa* by Olmi, Massimo. In: *Civilta* 2:204-205 Ap 17 1993
Review of: *Il linguaggio giovanile degli anni Novanta* by Banfi, Emanuele, and Sobrero, Alberto A, eds. In: *Civilta* 3:334-335 Ag 7-21 1993
Review of: *Il mercante e l'inquisitiore. Apologia della televisione commerciale* by Debbio, Paolo Del. In: *Civilta* 2:202-203 Ap 17 1993
Review of: *Il sistema dell'informazione e la deontologia, Vol II* by Faustini, Gianni. In: *Civilta* 2:201-202 Ap 17 1993
Review of: *Il villaggio globale. XXI secolo* by McLuhan, Marshall, and Powers, Bruce R. In: *Civilta* 3:335 Ag 7-21 1993
Review of: *Illusioni necessarie: mass media e democrazia* by Chomsky, . Noam. In: *Civilta* 3:336 Ag 7-21 1993

Baragli, Enrico. *(cont'd)*
Review of: *In punta di lingua* by Marchi, Cesare. In: *Civilta* 3:334-335 Ag 7-21 1993
Review of: *Informatica e diritti umani* by Silva, Custódio Augusto Ferreira, da. In: *Civilta* 144:103-104 Ja 2 1993
Review of: *Isegnare TV a scuola* by Moro, Walter. In: *Civilta* 2:102-103 Ap 3 1993
Review of: *L'arte di communicare* by Majello, Carlo. In: *Civilta* 2:203 Ap 17 1993
Review of: *L'arte di persuadere* by Prezzolini, Giuseppe. In: *Civilta* 3:207 Jl 17 1993
Review of: *La comunicazione nella storia* by Bautier, Robert Henri, and Piemontese, Angelo Michele. In: *Civilta* 3:338 Ag 7-21 1993
Review of: *La felicità eterna: la rappresentazione della morte nella TV e nei media* by Abruzzese, Alberto, and Scalamonti, Antonio Cavicchia, eds. In: *Civilta* 3:336-337 Ag 7-21 1993
Review of: *La grande maestra: la Tv tra politica e società* by Radi, Luciano. In: *Civilta* 144:102-103 Ja 2 1993
Review of: *La lingua come strumento di libertà* by Nadin, Lucia, and Serra, Michele, eds. In: *Civilta* 143:639 D 19 1992
Review of: *La lingua degli studenti universitari* by Lavinio, Cristina, and Sobrero, Alberto A. In: *Civilta* 2:203 Ap 17 1993
Review of: *La lingua filmata: Didascalie e dialoghi nel cinema italiano* by Raffaelli, Sergio. In: *Civilta* 144:102 Ja 2 1993
Review of: *Lettura e didattica del racconto visivo* by Moro, Walter. In: *Civilta* 2:102-103 Ap 3 1993
Review of: *Manto nero (Blackrobe)* by Moore, Brian. In: *Civilta* 2:307 My 1 1993
Review of: *Manuale di diritto internazionale della comunicazione sociale* by Fragola, Augusto. In: *Civilta* 3:333 Ag 7-21 1993
Review of: *Miscellanea della storia della carta* by Castagnari, Giancarlo, and Grégoire, Reginald, et al. In: *Civilta* 3:319-320 Ag 7-21 1993
Review of: *Per una storia dei media* by Ortoleva, Peppino. In: *Civilta* 3:333-334 Ag 7-21 1993
Review of: *Quale preghiera per l'uomo d'oggi?* by Insolera, Vincenzo. In: *Civilta* 144:198 Ja 16 1993
Review of: *Storia della scrittura* by Février, James G. In: *Civilta* 2:203-204 Ap 17 1993
Review of: *Storia e potere della scrittura* by Martin, Henry-Jean. In: *Civilta* 2:203-204 Ap 17 1993

Baranowski, Art.
Creating small faith communities. *Chicago Stud* 31:182-185 Ag 1992

Barber, Hugh R K.
A crisis of conscience: a Catholic doctor speaks out for reform. New York: Carol Publishing Group, 1993. 22p ISBN 1-55972-162-6 LC 92-39827

Barber, Michael D.
Review of: *Correlations in Rosenzweig and Levinas* by Gibbs, Robert. In: *Mod Schlmn* 70:234-236 Mr 1993

Barber, Noel, and Rea, Desmond, eds.
Unemployment in the Republic and Northern Ireland. *Studies* 82:9-96 Spr 1993
Ireland's record last in the class?, by C Johns. Comparisons from the North, by V Hewitt. The causes of Irish unemployment: trends and explanations, by D McGittigan, and F Browne. A Northern perspective, by V K Borooah, and C Ackah. Solutions and political implications, by D McAleese. Response to unemployment: ten propositions, by G Quigley. The Church in the post-socialist world, by S Murphy.

Barbernitz, Peter.
An approach to Bible study in one parish. *Liturgy* 11:30-33 Sum 1993

Barbier, Hubert.
Repression in the Sudan. *Cath Int* 4:234-236 My 1993

Barbour, Brian.
Review of: *The panther and the hind: a theological history of Anglicanism* by Nichols, Aidan. In: *New Oxford Rev* 60:22-23 O 1993

Barchard, David.
Death of private soldier. *Tablet* 247:131-132 Ja 30 1993
Turkey's unlikely hero. *Tablet* 247:506-507 Ap 24 1993

Barciauskas, Jonas.
Leaves of light: the textual journeys of Dante and García Márquez. *CrosssCurr* 43:212-229 Sum 1993

Bardulet, Salvador.
Conferencia episcopal Catalona, malgrat tot. Barcelona: Llibres de L'Index, 1993. x, 99p ISBN 84-87561-46-2

Barenbaum, M.
Review of: *A fundamental practical theology: descriptive and strategic proposals* by Browning, Don S. In: *TheolStds* 53:772-775 D 1992

Barker, Bede M.
Review of: *Homilies on the Gospels, 2 vols* by Bede, the Venerable, Saint. In: *Cist Stud* 28:[23]-[25] 1993
Review of: *La Vierge Marie: homélies des Pères Cisterciens* by Thomas, Robert. In: *Cist Stud* 28:[32]-[34] 1993
Review of: *Medieval texts and images: studies of manuscripts from the Middle Ages* by Manion, Margaret, and Muir, Bernard, eds. In: *Cist Stud* 27 No 4:[105]-[108] 1992

Barker, Eileen, et al, eds.
Secularization, rationalism, and sectarianism: essays in honour of Bryan R Wilson. New York: Oxford University Press, 1993. x, 322p ISBN 0-19-827721-0 LC 92-41458

Barker, Felix.
Review of: *Panoramas of London* by Moore, Rowan, and Lloyd, Sampson. In: *Tablet* 247:1076 Ag 21 1993
Review of: *The London encyclopaedia* by Weinreb, Ben, and Hibbert, Christopher, eds. In: *Tablet* 247:1076 Ag 21 1993
Review of: *Walks in old London* by Jackson, Peter. In: *Tablet* 247:1076 Ag 21 1993

Barker, Margaret.
Review of: *Idolatry* by Halbertal, Moshe, and Margalit, Avishai. In: *Month* 26:196-197 My 1993

Barnard, Ann M.
Catholics offer a second opinion on health plan. *OSV* 82:3 O 10 1993
Creating a new awareness of the adoption option. *OSV* 82:17 S 12 1993
Leaving the children at "Mom's house". *ST Anth* 101:22-27 Jl 1993

Barnecot, Edith, ed.
Journey with the Fathers: commentaries on the Sunday gospels, Year A. New Rochelle, New York: New City Press, 1992. 168p ISBN 1-56548-013-9 LC 92-20685

Barnecut, Edith, ed.
Journey with the Fathers; commentaries on the Sunday gospels, Year B. New Rochelle: New City Press, 1993. 160p ISBN 1-56548-056-2 LC 92-20685

Barnes, Michael R.
Action for Bosnia [editorial]. *Month* 26:2-3 Ja 1993
Breaking the fast. *Month* 26:(I) Ap 1993
The corruption of faith. *Month* 26:(I) My 1993
Evangelisation and the other: response and responsibility. *Month* 25:479-484 D 1992
Face to faith in 1993. *Tablet* 247:2 Ja 2 1993
Global harmony and public action. *Month* 26:(I) Mr 1993
God's path to peace. *Month* 26:(I) Jl 1993
Learning compassion. *Month* 26:(I) Ag 1993
On being good news. *Month* 25:I D 1992
Persons—objects or observers? (A dialogue with Buddhism). *Way Suppl* 76:98-108 Spr 1993
Review of: *Christian theology and inter-religious dialogue* by Wiles, Maurice. In: *Way* 33:168-169 Ap 1993
Review of: *Loosing the chains* by Kirk, Andrew. In: *Way* 33:169 Ap 1993
Review of: *Metaphysics as a guide to morals* by Murdoch, Iris. In: *Month* 26:272-273 Jl 1993
Review of: *Pilgrimage of hope* by Braybrooke, Marcus. In: *Way* 33:168 Ap 1993
Review of: *Radical pluralism and truth: David Tracy and the hermeneutics of religion* by Jeanrond, Werner G, and Rike, Jennifer L, eds. In: *Horizons (CTS)* 20:161-162 Spr 1993
Review of: *The ancient wisdom of Origen* by Smith, John Clark. In: *TheolStds* 54:554-561 S 1993
A tale of two cathedrals. *Month* 26:I Je 1993
Tracy in dialogue: mystical retrieval and prophetic suspicion. *Heythrop* 34:60-64 Ja 1993
What do I have to do? *Month* 26:(I) F 1993

Barnes, Michel R.
Review of: *Platonism in late antiquity* by Gersh, Stephen, and Kannengiesser, Charles, eds. In: *Cist Stud* 28 no 2:[48]-[49] 1993

Barnes, Robert. *see* Prickett, Stephen, jt auth

Barnes, Trevor.
Saved by the Holy Ghost. *Tablet* 246:1603 D 19-26 1992

Barnet, Robert J.
A Catholic doctor looks at AIDS in the USA. *America* 168:6-12 F 6 1993
Review of: *Human experimentation: a guided step into the unknown* by Silverman, William A. In: *Linacre* 60:90-92 My 1993
Review of: *Rationing America's medical care: the Oregon plan and beyond* by Strosbert, Martin, et al, eds. In: *Linacre* 60:92-94 My 1993
Review of: *What kind of life: the limits of medical progress* by Callahan, Daniel, 1930-. In: *Linacre* 60:93-94 Ag 1993

Barney, Steven M. *see* Ryan, Mary Jean, jt auth

Barr, David L.
John's apocalypse as good news. *Catechist* 26:50-54 Ap-My 1993

Barr, James.
Biblical faith and natural theology. New York: Oxford University Press, 1993. x, 256p ISBN 0-826205-1
The Garden of Eden and the hope of immortality. Minneapolis: Fortress Press, 1993. 146p ISBN 0-80062-744-x LC 92-27037

Barrado, G.
Review of: *Los dominicos y la evangelización del Uruguay* by Esponera Cerdán, Alfonso. In: *Cien Tom* 119:424-425 My-Ag 1992

Barrado, J.
Review of: *El Cardenal Fr Manuel García y Gil, OP Obispo de Badajoz y Arzobispo de Zaragoza (1802-1881)* by Gómez García, Vito Tomás. In: *Cien Tom* 119:425-426 My-Ag 1992
Review of: *La oración, experiencia liberadora* by Herraiz García, Maximiliano. In: *Cien Tom* 120:204 Ja-Ap 1993
Review of: *Pío IX: profilo spirituale* by Bogliolo, Luigi. In: *Cien Tom* 120:194-195 Ja-Ap 1993
Review of: *XVI Centenario: 589-1989.* In: *Cien Tom* 119:423-424 My-Ag 1992

Barré, Michael L.
"My strength and my song" in Exodus 15:2. *CBQ* 54:623-637 O 1992

Barreiro, Álvaro.
As comunidades edlesiais de base como modelo inspirador da nova evangelização. *Perspectiva* 24:331-356 S-D 1992

Barres, John O.
How to pray with Elizabeth of the trinity. *Spir Life* 39:37-43 Spr 1993

Barrigar, Chris.
Social theory, language, and the crisis in Anglican pluralism. *JEcumen Stds* 29:461-465 Sum-Aut 1992

Barringer, Robert, et al.
Statement of the Catholic members of the Consultation. *Ecumen Trends* 22:14-15 Ja 1993

Barringer, Robert.
What is new and what is old: patristic exegesis. *Can Cath Rev* 11:7-15 Je 1993

Barrins, Aine.
Review of: *For the sake of the Kingdom* by Delizy, Bernadette. In: *Furrow* 44:387-388 Je 1993
Review of: *Reweaving religious life* by Leddy, Mary Jo. In: *Furrow* 44:387-388 Je 1993
Review of: *The Bible and counselling* by Hurding, Roger. In: *Furrow* 44:515-516 S 1993
Review of: *What about me?* by Mullarney, Máire. In: *Furrow* 44:449-450 Jl-Ag 1993

Barrios, Marciano.
Review of: *Historia de la Iglesia contemporanea* by Schatz, Klaus. In: *Teol Vida* 33 no 3-4:330 1992
Review of: *Memorias* by Silva Henriquez, Raul. In: *Teol Vida* 33 no 3-4:325-326 1992

Barrios Casares, Manuel.
Voluntad de lo tragico: el concepto nietzscheano de voluntad a partir de el nacimiento de la tradgedia. Sevilla: A Er, Revista de Filosofia, 1993. x, 190p ISBN 84-604-5347-2

Barrios Villegos, Marciano.
Review of: *Esbozo de un Santoral latinoamericano* by Mathei, Mauro. In: *Teol Vida* 34 no 1-2:162 1993
Review of: *Historia de la evangelización de América: Trayectoria, identidad y esperanza de continente.* In: *Teol Vida* 34 no 1-2:163 1993
Review of: *Juan Diego y la Santísma Virgen María de Guadalupe* by Medina, Jorge. In: *Teol Vida* 34 no 1-2:162-163 1993
Review of: *Mariano o la fuerza de Dios* by Cabre, Agustin. In: *Teol Vida* 34 no 1-2:161-162 1993

Barron, Ellen. *see* Fox, Frank, jt auth

Barruffo, A.
Review of: *La vita consacrata, Le varie forme dalle origini ad oggi* by López Amat, Alfredo. In: *Civilta* 144:200 Ja 16 1993

Barry, Kevin.
Review of: *The great melody: a thematic biography of Edmund Burke* by O'Brien, Conor Cruise. In: *Studies* 82:333-339 Aut 1993

Barry, R.
Review of: *The giving and taking of life: essays ethical* by Burtchaell, James Tunstead. In: *Thomist* 56:733-738 O 1992

Barry, William A.
God's passionate and our desire response. Indiana: Ave Maria Press, 1993. x, 143p ISBN 0-87793-501-7 LC 92-75346

Barta, Karen A.
Review of: *The revelatory text: interpreting the New Testament as sacred scripture* by Schneiders, Sandra M. In: *TheolStds* 54:165-166 Mr 1993

Bartelme, Elizabeth.
Review of: *Dakota: a spiritual geography* by Norris, Kathleen. In: *Comm* 120:23-24 My 7 1993
Review of: *Gospel* by Barnhardt, Wilton. In: *Comm* 120:26-27 O 8 1993

Bartels, Dianne M, et al, eds.
Prescribing our future: ethical challenges in genetic counseling. New York: Aldine de Gruyter, 1993. 186p ISBN 0-20230-452-3 LC 92-21469

Barth, Karl, 1886-1968.
The Holy Spirit and the Christian life: the library of theological ethics. Louisville: John Knox, 1993. x, 96p ISBN 0-664-25325-3

Barthelemy, Nancy C.
Finding God in winter stillness. *Liguorian* 81:54-55 F 1993

Bartholomew, Marianna.
An American miracle [condensed fr *Extension* N 1992]. *CDgst* 57:1-3+ Ap 1993
Father Tom lives Matthew 25 [photos]. *Extensn* 88:9-15+ O 16 1993
No easy rewards [photos]. *Extensn* 88:22-27 S-O 1993

Bartlett, Bob.
Going all the way. *Momentum* 24:36-39 Ap-My 1993

Barton, Ellen L.
Review of: *Grand rounds on medical malpractice* by Campion, Francis X. In: *Health Prog* 74:68 Mr 1993

Barton, John.
Review of: *Creative Biblical exegesis: Christian and Jewish hermeneutics through the centuries* by Uffenheimer, Benjamin, and Reventlow, Henning Graf, eds. In: *Heythrop* 34:313 Jl 1993

Barton, Thomas D.
The structure of legal systems. *Amer J Juris* 37:291-317 1992

Bashian, Kathleen Ryniker.
Playing Shakespeare. *Momentum* 24:67-68 F-Mr 1993

Basler, Howard B.
Review of: *Reading the signs of the times* by Sanks, T Howland, and Coleman, John A, eds. In: *Church* 9:56 Aut 1993

Bast, Robert J.
Review of: *The European Reformation* by Cameron, Euan. In: *CHist* 79:331-332 Ap 1993

Batastini, Robert J.
Selecting music for the year of Matthew. *Past Mus* 17:42-45 D 1992-Ja 1993
Why don't our presiders chant? *Past Mus* 17:23-25 Je-Jl 1993

Batey, Richard A.
Jesus and the forgotten city: new light on Sepphoris and the urban world of Jesus. Grand Rapids: Baker Book House, 1991

Battaglia, Anthony.
Review of: *Faith and faithfulness* by Meilaender, Gilbert C. In: *Horizons (CTS)* 20:179-181 Spr 1993

Batto, Bernard F.
Review of: *Old Testament parallels* by Matthews, Victor H, and Benjamin, Don C. In: *CBQ* 54:754-755 O 1992

Batule, Robert J.
Christian asceticism and modern culture. *HPR* 93:17-23 F 1993

Baudry, Gérard-Henry.
Le péché originel chez Philon d'Alexandrie. *MSR* 50:99-115 Ap-Je 1993
Le péché originel dans les écrits de Qoumrân. *MSR* 50:7-22 Ja-Mr 1993
Review of: *Pythagore* by Gobry, Ivan. In: *MSR* 50:72-73 Ja-Mr 1993

Bauer, Catherine Lazers.
Time to do nothing: why I don't worry about wasting time. *Spir Life* 39:173-175 Aut 1993

Bauer, Susan.
Community clinic offers access to care. *Health Prog* 74:42-44+ O 1993

Bauknecht, James R.
Rachel. *SocJust* 84:113-115 Jl-Ag 1993

Baum, Gregory.
Review of: *Christian mission and interreligious dialogue* by Mojzes, Paul, and Swidler, Leonard, eds. In: *JEcumen Stds* 29:491-492 Sum-Aut 1992
Review of: *Culture dialogue, and the Church* by Manathodath, Jacob. In: *JEcumen Stds* 29:491-492 Sum-Aut 1992

Baumann, Paul.
Clinton sounds good: but now a word from scrooge. *Comm* 120:4-5 Ja 15 1993
Easter Sunday, 1944: escape to Berlin. *Comm* 120:5-6 Je 4 1993
Flea-ing New York: city of inexplicable eructations. *Comm* 120:4-5 S 24 1993
Review of: *The subversive family: an alternative history of love and marriage* by Mount, Ferdinand. In: *Comm* 120:28 Je 18 1993
Sodom and Begorra: it rained on the parade. *Comm* 120:5-6 Ap 9 1993

Baumer, Patricia Hughes.
Handing on the tradition: a Catholic mother laments. *New Theol Rev* 6:32-54 My 1993

Baumgarten, Bruce.
Adolescence: a gray area. *ReligTJ* 27:35 F 1993
How important is content? *ReligTJ* 27:50-51 S 1993
A new look at discipline. *ReligTJ* 27:18-19 Ap-My 1993

Baumstein, P.
Review of: *'Stewardship and the kingdom in RB 31-33'* by Sutera, Judith. In: *Cist Stud* 27 No 4:[95]-[96] 1992

Baumstein, Paschal.
An abbatial diocese in the United States. *CHist* 79:217-245 Ap 1993
Archives: disposition of personal papers. *CLW* 64:20-21 Jl-S 1993
A conflict of mitres: the diverse polities and Cathedral Abbey of Bishop Leo Haid. *Word Sp* 14:76-95 1992

Baxendale, Janet.
Spiritual potential of the Liturgy of the Hours. *Origins* 23:385-394 N 11 1993

Baxter, Anthony.
Knowledge, and our position regarding God. *Heythrop* 34:137-159 Ap 1993

Bayer, Richard C.
Review of: *Doing well and doing good* by Neuhaus, Richard John, 1936-. In: *TheolStds* 54:187-189 Mr 1993
Review of: *The Catholic ethic and the spirit of capitalism* by Novak, Michael, 1933-. In: *TheolStds* 54:592-593 S 1993

Bayfield, Tony.
The challenge of xenophobia: reflections on the heart of the stranger. *Month* 26:298-303 Ag 1993

Bazyn, Barbara.
Review of: *Orwell* by Sheldon, Michael. In: *New Oxford Rev* 60:28-30 Ap 1993

Beacon, George.
The Barna report, volume 3, 1993-94: absolute confusion. Ventura: Regal Books, 1993. x, 309p ISBN 0-8307-1641-6

Bear, Jan, and Gray, Daria.
The real St. Nicholas [condensed fr *Again* V 13, no 4]. *CDgst* 58:6-10 D 1993

Bearden, Michelle.
Single Catholics: can we talk about S-E-X? *USCath* 58:30-35 Ag 1993

Beards, Andrew.
Myths and truths about the Eucharist. *HPR* 93:18-26 Ag-S 1993

Beaufort, Joseph De.
The conversion of Brother Lawrence. *Spir Life* 39:4-5 Spr 1993

Beaumont, Madeleine.
Days of the Lord: the liturgical year; vol 2. Minnesota: The Liturgical Press, 1990. x, 274p ISBN 0-8146-1900-2 LC 90-22253

Beaver, William A.
And who is my neighbor?. *Word Sp* 14:96-104 1992

Becker, David R.
Creation or evolution? a call to intellectual conversion. *HPR* 93:54-61 Ap 1993

Becker, Karl J.
Der Gebrauch der Hl Schrift in der dogmatischen Theologie. *Gregorianum* 73 No 4:671-687 1992

Becker, Mary Lee.
In touch with Jesus. *ReligTJ* 27:14-15 Mr 1993
'Ordinary' symbols and rituals. *ReligTJ* 26:34-35 Ja 1993
Say it with scripture. *ReligTJ* 27:26 O 1993

Beckett, Lucy.
Heaven in ordinary. *Tablet* 247:1227-1228 S 25 1993

Beckford, J.
Review of: *The social dimensions of Sectarianism: sects and new religious movements in contemporary society* by Wilson, Bryan. In: *Heythrop* 34:120-121 Ja 1993

Beckman, Joseph F.
Haiti at the crossroads. *St Anth* 101:36-43 Ag 1993

Bedard, Mariette.
Review of: *A northern nativity. Christmas dreams of a prairie boy* by Kurelek, William. In: *CahiersJos* 41:141-142 Ja-Je 1993
Review of: *L'Évangile de Marie* by Balquière, Georgette. In: *CahiersJos* 41:139 Ja-Je 1993

Bedard, Mariette. *(cont'd)*
Review of: *Paroisse St-Joseph. 100 ans 1892-1992* by Gauvreau, Gustave. In: *CahiersJos* 41:132-133 Ja-Je 1993
Review of: *Saint Joseph* by Galot, Jean. In: *CahiersJos* 41:137-138 Ja-Je 1993
Review of: *St. Joseph, quiet man of God* by Leonard, Seán, and Tuffy, Edward. In: *CahiersJos* 41:133-134 Ja-Je 1993
Review of: *Sur les litanies de saint Joseph.* In: *CahiersJos* 41:135 Ja-Je 1993
Review of: *The purpose of the Biblical genealogies with special reference to the setting of the genealogies of Jesus* by Johnson, Marshall D. In: *CahiersJos* 41:139-140 Ja-Je 1993
Review of: *Une belle église. Deusxième édition* by Gauvreau, Gustave. In: *CahiersJos* 41:131-133 Ja-Je 1993

Bedell, Gary.
Truth and freedom. *Mod Schlmn* 70:53-62 N 1992

Bedford, William J.
Review of: *Being a priest today* by Goergen, Donald J, ed. In: *Church* 9:60-61 Spr 1993

Bedouelle, Guy.
A winter's tale. *New Blckfrs* 74:301-306 Je 1993

Bedouelle, Thierry.
Review of: *Résurrection et expérience morale* by O'Donovan, Oliver. In: *RPhil Louvain* 91:507-509 Ag 1993
Review of: *Saint Bernard et la philosophie* by Brague, Rémi. In: *RPhil Louvain* 91:318-319 My 1993

Beeching, Paul Q.
Down the arches of the years, down the labyrinthine ways [interview by J G Deedy, 1923-]. *Critic* 47:2-13 Spr 1993
The education of an American Catholic. Chicago: The Thomas More Press, 1993. x, 405p ISBN 0-88347-275-9

Beeck, Frans Jozef van.
Israel's God, the Psalms, and the city of Jerusalem: life experience and the sacrifice of praise and prayer. *Horizons (CTS)* 19:219-239 Fall 1992
The revolution of the glory; introduction and part I; fundamental theology. Collegeville: Liturgical, 1993. x, 360p ISBN 0-8146-5498-3

Beenaert, P. Mourlon.
Review of: *Au nom des Pères. La Bible pour la prière* by Legarde, Claude. In: *Lumen* 48:231 Je 1993
Review of: *Credo. Méditations sur le Symbole des Apôtres* by Balthasar, Hans Urs Von, 1905-1988. In: *Lumen* 48:232-233 Je 1993
Review of: *Jean, de l'exégèse à la prédication, Vol I: carême et Pâques* by Gourgues, Michel. In: *Lumen* 48:231 Je 1993
Review of: *L'Église-Fraternité, vol I* by Dujarier, Michel. In: *Lumen* 48:232 Je 1993

Beentjes, Pancratius C.
'You have given a road in the sea'. *Eph Theol Lovan* 78:137-141 Ap 1992

Begg, Christopher T.
Review of: *A beginner's guide to the Old Testament* by Davidson, Robert. In: *OTA* 16:157-158 F 1993
Review of: *A handbook on lamentations* by Reyburn, William D. In: *OTA* 16:432 Je 1993
Review of: *A handbook on the Book of Job* by Rayburn, William D. In: *OTA* 16:424 Je 1993
Review of: *Abraham Kuenen* by Dirksen, P B, and Kooij, A Van Der, eds. In: *OTA* 16:394 Je 1993
Review of: *Abrahams historie:en historisk-kritisk kommentar til Genesis 11, 26-25, 11* by Nielsen, Eduard. In: *OTA* 16:419 Je 1993
Review of: *Aegyptiaca-Biblica: Notizen und Beiträge zu den Beziehungen zwischen Ägypten und Israel* by Görg, Manfred. In: *OTA* 15:472-473 O 1992
Review of: *Alttestamentliche Glaube und Biblische Theologie* by Hausmann, Jutta, and Zobel, Hans-Jürgen, eds. In: *OTA* 16:153 F 1993
Review of: *Beyond form criticism: essays in Old Testament literary criticism* by House, Paul R, ed. In: *OTA* 16:154 F 1993
Review of: *David and his God: religious ideas as reflected in Biblical historiography and literature* by Gelander, Shamai. In: *OTA* 15:498 O 1992
Review of: *David, Saul und die Propheten* by Dietrich, Walter. In: *OTA* 16:173 F 1993
Review of: *DBSup 11, 1057-1420* by Briend, Jacques, and Cothenet, E, eds. In: *OTA* 16:403 Je 1993
Review of: *DBSup 12, 1-256* by Briend, Jacques, and Cothenet, E, eds. In: *OTA* 16:403 Je 1993
Review of: *Deuteronomium II* by Braulik, Georg. In: *OTA* 16:171 F 1993
Review of: *Die deuteronomischen Gesetze und der Dekalog* by Braulik, Georg. In: *OTA* 16:171 F 1993
Review of: *Die Einheit der Schrift: Gesammelte Aufsätze* by Lubsczyk, Hans. In: *OTA* 15:474-475 O 1992
Review of: *Die groben Religionen des Alten Orients und der Antike* by Brunner-Traut, Emma, ed. In: *OTA* 16:403-404 Je 1993
Review of: *Die Priesterschrift und die vorexilische Zeit* by Krapf, Thomas M. In: *OTA* 16:416-417 Je 1993
Review of: *Die Sünde im Alten Testament* by Koch, Robert. In: *OTA* 16:187 F 1993
Review of: *Die Selbstbehauptung Israels in der Welt des Alten Orients* by Nordheim, Eckhard von. In: *OTA* 16:156 F 1993
Review of: *Dieu dans l'Ecriture* by Briend, Jacques. In: *OTA* 16:184-185 F 1993
Review of: *Discovering Old Testament origins* by Ralph, Margaret Nutting. In: *OTA* 16:164 F 1993
Review of: *Divine disclosure: an introduction to Jewish apocalyptic* by Russell, David Syme. In: *OTA* 16:439-440 Je 1993
Review of: *Een magisch Ritueel in Jahwistisch Perspectief* by Becking, Bob. In: *OTA* 16:422 Je 1993
Review of: *El códice de profetas de el Cairo* by Castro, F Pérez. In: *OTA* 16:177-178 F 1993
Review of: *Ernten was man sät* by Daniels, Dwight R, et al, eds. In: *OTA* 16:151 F 1993

Belsole, Kurt.
Putting out roots to the stream: on reading the monastic story. *Word Sp* 14: 129-138 1992

Belting, Natalia, and Hine, James R.
Your wedding workbook. Danville: Interstate Publishers, 1993. 121p ISBN 0-8134-2953-6

Ben-Ze'ev, Aaron.
Envy and pity. *IPQ* 33:3-19 Mr 1993

Benavente, Jose W.
Actividades de conceptuacion: materiales de didactica de la filosofia sobre supuestos constructivistas. Madrid: Akal, 1993. x, 136p ISBN 84-460-0166-7

Benavidas, Gustavo.
Review of: *Buddhist emptiness and Christian trinity: essays and explorations* by Corless, Robert, and Knitter, Paul F, eds. In: *Horizons (CTS)* 20:194-196 Spr 1993
Review of: *The emptying God: a Buddhist-Jewish-Christian conversation* by Cobb, John B, Jr, and Ives, Christopher, eds. In: *Horizons (CTS)* 20:194-196 Spr 1993

Bench, Jeannie.
Why I understand Mary Magdalene. *Sisters* 65:128-129 Mr 1993

Benedict, Philip.
Review of: *Civic Calvinism in Northwestern Germany and the Netherlands: sixteenth to nineteenth centuries* by Schilling, Heinz. In: *CHist* 79:530-532 Jl 1993

Benedict, Therese Francis.
Tree of life and endless mystery: the standard of the cross. *Spir Life* 39:31-33 Spr 1993

Benestad, J Brian.
Review of: *Act of compassion* by Wuthnow, Robert. In: *America* 168:20+ My 22, 1993
Review of: *Catholic bishops in American politics* by Byrnes, Timothy A. In: *CHist* 78:691-693 O 1992
Review of: *Just doctoring: medical ethics in the United States* by Brennan, Troyen. In: *America* 168:20+ My 22, 1993

Benjamin, Don C. see Matthews, Victor H, jt auth

Benko, S.
Review of: *Called to be saints: Christian living in first-century Rome* by Mullins, Michael. In: *CHist* 78:627-628 O 1992

Benoist, Jocelyn.
Le choix du métier: sur le "rationalisme" de Husserl. *RPhil Louvain* 91:66-89 F 1993

Bense, Walter F. see Adams, James Luther, jt ed

Bent, Ans J van der.
Review of: *Gott ist Christus der Sohn der Maria* by Risse, Günter. In: *JEcumen Stds* 29:489 Sum-Aut 1992
Review of: *My ecumenical journey: 1947-1975* by Thomas, M M. In: *JEcumen Stds* 29:105-106 Wint 1992

Bentivegua, Giuseppe.
L'effusion de l'Esprit Saint chez les Pères latins. *NRT* 115:19-39 Ja-F 1993

Bentué, Antonio.
Rasionalidad científica y teología. *Teol Vida* 33 no 3-4:255-267 1992
Review of: *Breve Diccionario Teológico Latinoamericano* by Rosales, Raul, and De Ferari, Jose Manuel, eds. In: *Teol Vida* 34 no 1-2:158 1993
Review of: *Diccionario de teología fundamental* by Latourelle, Rene, et al, eds. In: *Teol Vida* 34 no 1-2:161 1993
Review of: *Tratado de teología fundamental* by Pie I Minot, Salvador. In: *Teol Vida* 34 no 1-2:160-161 1993

Benvenga, Nancy.
Speaking to God. Indiana: Ave Maria Press, 1993. x, 144p ISBN 0-87793-502-5 LC 92-97150

Benzinger, Mariel.
August Benzinger: international portrait painter. Kansas City: Sheed & Ward, 1993. 355p ISBN 1-55612-614-x LC 93-19230

Beozzo, Jesús Oscar.
Compromisos eclesiales con una nueva evangelizacion. *Christus* 57:32-42 S 1992
Evangelizacion y v centenario. *Christus* 57:7-14 S 1992
500 años de evangelizacion en America Latina. *Christus* 58:7-24 N-D 1992

Beozzo, Josús Oscar.
500 anos: história e evangelização. *Perspectiva* 24:291-312 S-D 1992

Berbusse, Edward J.
Review of: *Catholics and the New Age* by Pacwa, Mitch. In: *F & R* 28:419-424 Wint 1992

Berenbaum, Michael.
Review of: *Disinheriting the Jews: Abraham in early Christian controversy* by Siker, Jeffrey S. In: *JEcumen Stds* 29:485-486 Sum-Aut 1992
Review of: *Maimonides' ethics: the encounter of philosophic and religious morality* by Weiss, Raymond L. In: *TheolStds* 54:387 Je 1993
Review of: *Renewing the covenant: a theology for the postmodern Jew* by Borowitz, Eugene B. In: *TheolStds* 53:774-775 D 1992

Berendes, M Benedicta.
Review of: *Instrumentation and the liturgical ensemble* by Haugen, Marty. In: *Mod Lit* 20:39-40 S 1993

Berg, Carol.
Missionaries and cultures. *US Cath Hist* 11:29-36 Spr 1993

Bergant, Dianne.
Review of: *A time for war: a study of warfare in the Old Testament* by Hobbs, T R. In: *New Theol Rev* 6:114-115 My 1993
Review of: *Biblical hermeneutics of liberation: modes of reading the Bible in the South African context* by West, Gerald O. In: *CBQ* 55:189-190 Ja 1993
Review of: *But she said* by Fiorenza, Elisabeth Schüssler, 1938-. In: *TheolStds* 54:344-345 Je 1993

Bergant, Dianne. *(cont'd)*
Review of: *The feminine unconventional: four subversive figures in Israel's tradition* by LaCocque, André. In: *Horizons (CTS)* 19:310-311 Fall 1992
Review of: *Voices from the margin: interpreting the Bible in the Third World* by Sugirtharajah, R S. In: *New Theol Rev* 6:90-91 F 1993
Women in the Bible: friends or foes? *TheolDgst* 40:103-112 Sum 1993
Would that all were prophets. *RRel* 52:340-349 My-Je 1993

Berganza, Carlos.
Teología India. *Cien Tom* 120:79-100 Ja-Ap 1993

Berger, Petra. see Berger, Thomas, jt auth

Berghe, Paul Van Den.
Anvers et son Église diocésaine. *Lumen* 48:127-134 Je 1993

Bergin, Martin J, Jr.
Review of: *On divorce* by Bonald, Louis de. In: *CHist* 79:344-345 Ap 1993

Bergonzi, Bernard, 1929-.
Review of: *Aimed at nobody* by Graham, W S. In: *Tablet* 247:170-171 F 6 1993
Review of: *Dance with a shadow* by Ratushinskaya, Irina. In: *Tablet* 247:170-171 F 6 1993
Review of: *Eye of the camera: a life of Christopher Isherwood* by Fryer, Jonathan. In: *Tablet* 247:1074-1075 Ag 21 1993
Review of: *Lawrence's women: the intimate life of D H Lawrence* by Feinstein, Elaine. In: *Tablet* 247:246 F 20 1993
Review of: *Mass for hard times* by Thomas, R S. In: *Tablet* 247:170-171 F 6 1993
Review of: *Time and Seasons* by Jennings, Elizabeth, 1926-. In: *Tablet* 247:170-171 F 6 1993
Review of: *Wilfred Owen: the last year* by Hibberd, Dominic. In: *Tablet* 247:17-18 Ja 2 1993
William Golding's vision. *Tablet* 247:815 Je 26 1993

Bergren, Theodore A.
Review of: *Power and politics in Palestine: the Jews and the governing of their land, 100 BC-AD 70* by McLaren, James S. In: *CBQ* 55:384-385 Ap 1993
Review of: *The authenticity of the Pauline Epistles in the light of stylostatistical analysis* by Neumann, Kenneth J. In: *CBQ* 54:795-796 O 1992

Berkey, Robert F, and Edwards, Sarah A, eds.
Christology in dialogue. Cleveland: The Pilgrim Press, 1993. 390p ISBN 0-8298-0956-2 LC 92-47004

Berkowitz, David A, and Swan, Melanie M.
Technology decision making. *Health Prog* 74:42-47 Ja-F 1993

Bermudez, Alejandro.
The Church in Cuba risks Castro's wrath for sake of reform. *Register* 69:5 O 17 1993

Bernard, Catherine, et al.
Final declaration on family planning. *TPS* 38:162-164 My-Je 1993

Bernard, G W.
Review of: *The stripping of the altars* by Duffy, Eamon. In: *Heythrop* 34:452-455 O 1993

Bernard, J.
Review of: *Apparitions et miracles* by Dierkens, Al, ed. In: *NRT* 115:608-609 Jl-Ag 1993
Review of: *L'Église et l'Argent sous l'"Ancien Régime"* by Michaud, C. In: *NRT* 114:920-921 N-D 1992
Review of: *L'ancienne hagiographie byzantine* by Delehaye, H, -1941. In: *NRT* 114:919 N-D 1992

Bernardin, Joseph Louis, Cardinal, 1928-.
The abortion controversy: seeking a common ground. *Cath Int* 4:210-214 My 1993
The bishops' role in preserving the ministry's vitality. *Health Prog* 74:21-22+ Ja-F 1993
The post-cold war agenda for peace. *Origins* 23:1+ My 20 1993
Why virtues are basic to the common good. *Origins* 23:337+ O 21 1993

Bernas, Casimir.
Review of: *Faith under fire: how the Bible speaks to us in times of suffering* by Simundson, Daniel J. In: *Cist Stud* 28:[20] 1993
Review of: *In the beginning: a humorous survey of the Bible* by Lambin, Helen Reichert. In: *Cist Stud* 28 no 2:[47]-[48] 1993
Review of: *L'apocalittica giudaica e la sua storia* by Sacchi, Paolo. In: *CBQ* 55:203-204 Ja 1993
Review of: *Revelation, vision of a just world* by Fiorenza, Elisabeth Schüssler, 1938-. In: *Cist Stud* 27 No 4:[84]-[85] 1992

Bernas, Mary Bellarmine.
Filipino women: designers of their destiny. *Sisters* 65:175-180 My 1993

Bernier, Joan M.
The benefits of networking. *Tod Parish* 25:36-37 O 1993
Faith sharing and new facilitators. *Tod Parish* 25:36-37 Ja 1993
Faith sharing, trust, and transformation. *Tod Parish* 25:34-35 Mr 1993
Finding heroes in small community life. *Tod Parish* 25:34-35 Ap-My 1993
Seven steps to getting started. *Tod Parish* 25:36-37 S 1993

Bernier, Joan M, and Howard, Barbara, et al.
The Church of the future? *Tod Parish* 25:26-29 N-D 1993

Bernier, Paul.
Eucharist: celebrating its rhythms in our lives. Indiana: Ave Maria Press, 1993. 160p ISBN 0-87793-506-8 LC 92-75342
Eucharist: meal or sacrifice? *Emmanuel* 98:64-69+ Mr 1992; 98:136-141+ Ap 1992

Bernstein, Dennis.
DEA report documents Haitian drug traffic D.C. seems to ignore. *Nat Cath Rep* 30:6 N 12 1993

Bernstein, Eleanor.
The presider as proclaimer. *Liturgy* 11:78-81 Sum 1993

Bernstein, Eleanor, ed.
Disciples at the crossroads: perspectives on worship and church leadership. Collegeville:Liturgical, 1993. x, 153p ISBN 0-8146-2146-5 LC 93-591

Berquist, Jon L.
Dangerous waters of justice and righteousness: Amos 5:18-27. *Bib Th Bul* 23: 54-63 Sum 1993

Berranger, Oliver De.
Etre et temps et théologie. *Gregorianum* 74 no 3:543-561 1993

Berridge, Elizabeth.
Review of: *Make believe* by Athill, Diana. In: *Tablet* 247:621 My 15 1993
Review of: *Wartime and aftermath: English literature and its background, 1939-1960* by Bergonzi, Bernard, 1929-. In: *Tablet* 247:822-823 Je 26 1993

Berridge, John M.
Review of: *A redaction history of Jeremiah 2:1-4:2* by Biddle, Mark E. In: *CBQ* 55:323-324 Ap 1993

Berry, Jason.
Listening to the survivors: voices of people of God. *America* 169:4-9 N 13 1993
Nun writes of wrongs in throes of death row. *Nat Cath Rep* 29:9 Jl 2 1993
see Fox, Thomas C, jt auth

Berry, Thomas. see Swimme, Brian, jt auth

Berry, Wendell.
Christianity and the survival of creation. *CrossCurr* 43:149-163 Sum 1993

Berthelot, M.
Review of: *Celebrating the rites of adult initiation: pastoral reflections* by Tufano, Victoria M. In: *Mod Lit* 20:39 F 1993

Berthold, George C.
Review of: *Broken lights and mended lives: theology and common life in the Church* by Greer, Rowan A. In: *Thomist* 57:328-330 Ap 1993

Bertier de Sauvigny, G de.
Review of: *Austria and the Papacy in the Age Metternich, volume 2: revolution and reaction, 1830-1838* by Reinerman, Alan J. In: *CHist* 79: 546-547 Jl 1993

Bertolucci, John.
A priest's prayer life. *New Cov* 23:6 Ag 1993
Share the good news. Boston: St Paul Books & Media, 1993. 28p ISBN 0-8198-6885-x

Bertone, T.
Review of: *Materia e spirito* by Cicchitti, Mario. In: *Civilta* 2:613-614 Je 19 1993

Beseda, David.
Review of: *America: what went wrong* by Barlett, Donald, and Steele, James. In: *Cath Work* 60:6 Je-Jl 1993

Best, E.
Review of: *The greening of the Church* by McDonagh, Sean. In: *Emmanuel* 98:174-176 Ap 1992

Béthune, Pierre de.
Monks in dialogue with believers from other religions. *Stud Form Spir* 14: 129-138 F 1993

Beuken, W A M.
Review of: *A study of Job 4-5 in the light of contemporary literary theory* by Cotter, David W. In: *Eph Theol Lovan* 69:165-166 Ap 1993
Review of: *Josia* by Dorp, Jacob van. In: *Eph Theol Lovan* 78:414-415 D 1992
Review of: *The cosmic covenant* by Murray, Robert. In: *Eph Theol Lovan* 69:167-168 Ap 1993
Review of: *Wealth and poverty in the Book of Proverbs* by Whybray, R N. In: *Eph Theol Lovan* 78:424-425 D 1992

Bevans, Stephen.
Review of: *Faith on the edge: religion and marginalized existence* by Boff, Leonardo. In: *New Theol Rev* 6:118-119 F 1993
Review of: *Must God remain Greek? Afro cultures and God-talk* by Hood, Robert E. In: *New Theol Rev* 6:95-96 Ag 1993
Review of: *Sacramental theology* by Vorgrimler, Herbert. In: *CLW* 64:33 Jl-S 1993
Review of: *Spiritual guides for today* by Callahan, Annice. In: *CLW* 64:36 Jl-S 1993
Review of: *Transforming mission* by Bosch, David J. In: *New Theol Rev* 6: 106-108 F 1993

Bevans, Stephen B. see Scherer, James A, jt ed

Beverly, Elizabeth.
Review of: *Curriculum vitae* by Spark, Muriel, 1918-. In: *Comm* 120:13+ My 21 1993

Bevilacqua, Anthony Joseph, Cardinal, 1923-.
Domestic partnership bills opposed. *Origins* 23:48 Je 3 1993
Parish and schools reorganization. *Origins* 22:767-768 Ap 22 1993
Pastoral ministers and persons with disabilities. *Origins* 22:518-520 Ja 7 1993

Beyer, Jean.
De seminario dioecesano recentiora quaedam quaesita. *Periodica* 82 no 1:55-93 1993
De synodo dioecesana. *Periodica* 81 no 3-4:381-423 1992
De vita consecrata in iure utriusque codicis orientalis et occidentalis. *Periodica* 81 no 2:283-302 1992

Beyer, Richard J.
Medjugorje day by day: a daily meditation book based on the messages of Our Lady of Medjugorje. Indiana: Ave Maria Press, 1993. [265] leaves ISBN 0-87793-494-0 LC 92-74779

Bhaldraithe, E.
Review of: *Rites of religious profession: pastoral introduction and complete text* by Foley, Edward. In: *Cist Stud* 27 No 4:[108] 1992

Bharanikulangara, Kuriakose.
New major archbishop enthroned at solemn ceremonies in Ernakulam. *OR(Eng)* 1302:6 Ag 11 1993

Biale, David.
Eros and the Jews: from biblical Israel to contemporary America. New York: Basic Books, 1992. 319p ISBN 0-4650-2033-x

Biallas, Leonard J.
Review of: *Christian uniqueness reconsidered* by D'Costa, Gavin, ed. In: *Horizons (CTS)* 19:346-347 Fall 1992
Review of: *Who's who of world religions* by Hinnells, John R, ed. In: *Horizons (CTS)* 20:192-193 Spr 1993

Bianchi, Eugene C, and Ruether, Rosemary Radford, eds.
A democratic Catholic Church: in a reconstruction of Roman Catholicism. New York: Crossroad, 1993. x, 262p ISBN 0-8245-1186-7 LC 92-7920

Bibbi, Giacomo.
Le celebrazioni diocesane a Bologna del centario della nascita del Cardinale Giacomo Lercaro (1891-1991). *Notitiae* 28:286-289 Ap 1992

Biddle, Mark E.
Review of: *Klagender Gott—klagende Menschen* by Bak, Dong Hyun. In: *CBQ* 55:108-109 Ja 1993
Review of: *Life "Anew": a literary-theological study of Jer 30-31* by Bozak, Barbara A. In: *CBQ* 55:324-325 Ap 1993

Biddle, Perry H, Jr.
In the tracks of St. Paul. *Priest* 49:19-20+ O 1993

Biecheler, James E.
Review of: *Opera omnia. XVI: Sermones I (1430-1441)* by Nicholas of Cusa, 1401-1464. In: *JEcumen Stds* 29:272-273 Spr 1992

Biechler, James E.
Review of: *Die Herausforderung des Islam* by Italiaander, Rolf, ed. In: *JEcumen Stds* 29:131-132 Wint 1992
Review of: *Die theologischen Beziehungen des Islams zu Judentum und Christentum* by Busse, Heribert. In: *JEcumen Stds* 29:131-132 Wint 1992

Bieger, Erkhard.
Die katholische Kirche als Medienereignis. *Stimm Zeit* 210:855-857 D 1992

Bieler, Martin.
Meta-anthropology and Christology: on the philosophy of Hans Urs von Balthasar. *Communio* 20:129-146 Spr 1993

Biesinger, J.
Review of: *Die christliche Arbeiterbewegung in Bayern vom Ersten Weltkrieg bis 1933* by Krenn, Dorit-Maria. In: *CHist* 78:673-675 O 1992

Bietenholz, Peter G.
Review of: *Patristic scholarship: the edition of St Jerome* by Brady, James F, and Olin, John C, eds. In: *CHist* 79:336-337 Ap 1993

Biggar, Nigel.
The hastening that waits. New York: Oxford University Press, 1993. x, 208p ISBN 0-826457-7

Bilaniuk, Petro B T.
Review of: *Imperial unity and Christian divisions: the Church 450-680 A.D* by Meyendorff, John. In: *CHist* 79:510-511 Jl 1993

Bilheimer, Robert S.
Our common calling [exc fr *Liturgy: Practicing Ecumenism*]. *Liturgy* 10:2-3 Spr 1993

Billington, Monroe Lee, 1928-, and Clark, Cal.
Catholic clergymen, Franklin D Roosevelt, and the New Deal. *CHist* 79:65-82 Ja 1993

Billington, Rachel, 1942-.
Review of: *Folly* by Minot, Susan. In: *Tablet* 247:892 Jl 10 1993
Review of: *Maqroll* by Mutis, Alvaro. In: *Tablet* 247:892 Jl 10 1993
Review of: *Perspectives on marriage* by Scott, Kieran, and Warren, Michael, 1935-. In: *Tablet* 247:1232-1233 S 25 1993
Review of: *The end of marriage: why monogamy isn't working* by Hafner, Julian. In: *Tablet* 247:1232-1233 S 25 1993
Review of: *The story of a single woman* by Chiyo, Uno. In: *Tablet* 247:19 Ja 2 1993
Review of: *Uno Chiyo: the sound of the wind: a biography with three novellas* by Copeland, Rebecca. In: *Tablet* 247:19 Ja 2 1993

Billy, Dennis J.
Evangelical Kernels: a theological spirituality of the religious life. New York: Alba House, 1993. ISBN
The magic seed. *Living Prayer* 26:23 N-D 1993
Why a redeemer? Why a cross? *Living Prayer* 26:8-13 Mr-Ap 1993

Binder, M. see Strolz, M K, jt ed

Bird, Christopher. see Tompkins, Peter, jt auth

Birke, Szifra.
COAs: behind the masks. *Momentum* 24:54-60 Ap-My 1993

Bischoff, Bernhard, et al.
Addenda to Codices Latini Antiquiores (II). *Med Stud* 54:286-307 1992

Biser, Eugen.
Weder Gold noch Silber. *Stimm Zeit* 211:343-350 My 1993

Bishop, Marilyn E.
Open-door religious education. *Momentum* 24:32-36 N-D 1993
Some beginning basics. *Catechist* 27:6-7 S 1993

Bitel, L.
Review of: *Pilgrimage in Ireland: the monuments and the people* by Harbison, Peter. In: *CHist* 78:625-626 O 1992

Bitton, Davis. see Arrington, Leonard J, jt auth

Bjornard, Reidar B.
Aging according to wisdom literature. *BibleT* 30:330-334 N 1992

Black, Clifton C.
Review of: *The past of Jesus in the gospels* by Lemcio, Eugene E. In: *CBQ* 55:378-379 Ap 1993

Blackburn, Thomas E.
Free trade slurping jobs around the world. *Nat Cath Rep* 29:15 My 21 1993
The growing complexities of school choice. *Nat Cath Rep* 29:25 F 19 1993
Let Catholics cast cold eye on city on hill. *Nat Cath Rep* 30:18 O 22 1993

Bohman, James.
Review essay the possibility of post-socialist politics. *Mod Schlmn* 70:217-224 Mr 1993

Boisclair, Regina A.
The lectionary: a resource for general intercessions. *Liturgy* 11:9-13 Sum 1993
Review of: *Jewish prayer: the origins of Christian liturgy* by Sante, Carmine Di. In: *JEcumen Stds* 29:486-487 Sum-Aut 1992
Review of: *Paul the Convert: the apostolate and apostasy of Saul the Pharisee* by Segal, Alan F. In: *JEcumen Stds* 29:276-277 Spr 1992
Review of: *The Gospel in a pluralist society* by Newbigin, Lesslie. In: *JEcumen Stds* 29:282-283 Spr 1992
Review of: *The pre-Christian Paul* by Hengel, Martin. In: *JEcumen Stds* 29:276-277 Spr 1992
Review of: *What should we teach?* by Palmer, Martin. In: *JEcumen Stds* 29:493-494 Sum-Aut 1992

Boissinot, Christian.
Review of: *Actualiser la morale, mélanges offerts à René Simon* by Bélanger, Rodrigue, and Plourde, Simonne. In: *Laval Theol Phil* 49:331-334 Je 1993
Review of: *L'éthique du don* by Rabaté, J-M, and Wetzel, M, eds. In: *Laval Theol Phil* 49:339-342 Je 1993
Review of: *Le principe responsabilité, une éthique pour la civilisation technologique* by Jonas, Hans. In: *Laval Theol Phil* 49:334-339 Je 1993

Bole, William.
Advising on the ethics of health-care reform. *OSV* 82:3 Je 20 1993
Blue-light specials driving blue laws out of business. *OSV* 82:21 N 28 1993
Comrades in crosses: Christian Democracy comes to Russia. *America* 168:4-5 Ja 16-23 1993
Dioceses facing up to the fathers' sins. *OSV* 82:6-7 O 31 1993
Fashioning a better workplace. *OSV* 82:5 S 5 1993
In New York, a new model for Catholic schools. *OSV* 82:17 Ag 29 1993
The lesson in Ann Humphry's death. *OSV* 82:21 Je 6 1993
Murderous euphemisms. *OSV* 82:3 My 16 1993
Police remove protesters, but battle for parish continues. *Nat Cath Rep* 29:3 Jl 16 1993
The search for common ground. *OSV* 81:3 Ja 17 1993
Somalia strains Pax Christi. *Nat Cath Rep* 29:10 Ja 8 1993
Surprising charity has CHD critics seeing red. *Nat Cath Rep* 29:8 N 13 1992
"Zero tolerance" for clergy child abuse. *OSV* 82:5 Jl 18 1993 *see* Higgins, George G, 1916-, jt auth

Bonfils, Jean.
"Mutuae Relationes"—ten years later. *Con Life* 17 no 2:122-134 1992

Bonnici, John S.
Living as friends. *Priest* 49:39-44 F 1993
Love of friendship. *HPR* 93:31+ Ja 1993

Bonsor, Jack A.
Athens and Jerusalem: the role of philosophy in theology. Mahwah: Paulist Press, 1993. 192p ISBN 0-8091-3398-9
Creatures of truth. *Thomist* 56:647-668 O 1992

Booth, Philip.
Love among the ruins: music's eternal epiphanies. *ChrWorld* 236:276-278 N-D 1993

Booth, Tim.
Liturgical music for teens. *Mod Lit* 20:16-17 O 1993

Booty, John. *see* Sykes, Stephen, jt ed

Bopp, James, Jr.
The real Judge Ginsburg. *Register* 69:5 Ag 1 1993

Borelli, John.
An Islamic-Roman Catholic "national" dialogue. *Ecumen Trends* 22:10-13 O 1993
Pastoral care for interfaith couples—a beginning. *New Theol Rev* 6:30-42 Ag 1993
Review of: *The diversity of religions* by DiNoia, J A. In: *Living Light* 29:93-94 Spr 1993
Who is God for a Hindu, Buddhist or Muslim? *Origins* 22:769+ Ap 15 1993

Borg, Marcus J.
Jesus: der neue Mensch. Frieburg: Herder, 1993. x, 240p ISBN 3-451-23093-3

Borges, Pedro.
Catholicity and the local church in Latin America. *Jurist* 52 no 1:189-209 1992

Borgia, Francis.
Review of: *A woman styled bold: the life of Cornelia Connelly, 1809-1879* by Flaxman, Radegunde. In: *Studies* 81:466-469 Wint 1992
Review of: *Esteem builders for children's ministry* by Rowland, Beth, ed. In: *Mod Lit* 20:41 O 1993
Review of: *Family rituals and celebrations* by Roberto, John, ed. In: *Mod Lit* 20:38 Ap 1993
Review of: *Living scripture (Cycle A): reproducible lectioanry-based reflections on Sunday scriptures* by Finley, Mitchel B. In: *Mod Lit* 20:39 Je-Jl 1993
Review of: *Prayers for dawn and dusk* by Gabriele, Edward F. In: *Mod Lit* 19:41 D 1992-Ja 1993
Review of: *Praying in the Catholic tradition* by Schineller, Peter. In: *Mod Lit* 20:39 My 1993
Review of: *Psalm services for group prayer* by Cleary, William. In: *Mod Lit* 20:41 My 1993
Review of: *The sacred world of the Christian* by Wagner, Mary Anthony. In: *Mod Lit* 20:37-38 O 1993

Borgomeo, Pasquale.
"Contro l'odio, la forza dell'amore". *Civilta* 144:539-562 Mr 20 1993

Boring, Eugene M.
Review of: *Jesus and the oral gospel tradition* by Wansbrough, Henry, ed. In: *CBQ* 55:422-423 Ap 1993

Boring, M Eugene.
Narrative christology in the apocalypse. *CBQ* 54:702-723 O 1992

Bork, Robert Heron, 1927-.
Dialogue [interview by P Mullen]. *Register* 69:1+ Ag 1 1993

Borooah, Vani K, and Ackah, Carol.
A Northern perspective. *Studies* 82:53-60 Spr 1993

Borras, Alphonse.
Appartenance à Église ou itinérance ecclésiale? *Lumen* 48:161-173 Je 1993
Le ministère de présidence du curé: réflexions canoniques et pastorales. *Stud Can* 27 no 1:59-76 1993

Børresen, Kari Elisabeth.
Women's ordination: tradition and inculturation. *TheolDgst* 40:15-19 Spr 1993

Borrmans, Maurice.
Dialogue [interview by G Burke]. *Register* 69:1+ Ag 29 1993

Bortone, G.
Review of: *Atti del XIV Congresso Nazionale di Studi Manzoniani (Lecco, 10-14 ottobre 1990) tomo I* by Grossi, Manzoni. In: *Civilta* 3:539-540 S 18 1993
Review of: *Dal Manzoni alla Scapigliatura* by Farinelli, Giuseppe. In: *Civilta* 143:633-34 D 19 1992

Bos, A David.
A practical guide to community ministry. Louisville, Kentucky: John Knox Press, 1993. 112p ISBN 0-694-25405-5

Boss, Judith A.
The birth lottery: prenatal diagnosis and selective abortion. Chicago: Loyola University Press, 1993. 326p ISBN 0-8294-0740-5 LC 92-49738

Boss, Sarah.
Review of: *In a chariot drawn by lions: the search for the female deity* by Long, Asphodel P. In: *Tablet* 247:1297-1299 O 9 1993

Bossman, David M.
Canon and culture: realistic possibilities for the biblical canon. *Bib Th Bul* 23:4-13 Spr 1993
Review of: *Judaism, Christianity, and liberation—an agenda for dialogue* by Maduro, Otto, ed. In: *Horizons (CTS)* 19:339-340 Fall 1992
Review of: *Satire and the Hebrew prophets* by Jemielity, Thomas. In: *Cithara* 32:50-51 My 1993

Bossman, David M, ed.
Don't stop (thinking about the context). *Bib Th Bul* 23:46-47 Sum 1993

Boua, Chanthou.
In killing fields, a crying game. *Nat Cath Rep* 29:14 My 14 1993

Bouchard, Charles E.
Virtue at work: transforming the heart of business. *Liguorian* 81:24-29 O 1993

Bouchard, Gary M.
Gerard Manley Hopkins: the incarnational work of priest and poet. *ABenR* 44:115-124 Je 1993
Review of: *Les droits des femmes* by Dumais, Monique. In: *Laval Theol Phil* 49:174-175 F 1993

Boudens, R.
Review of: *À la veille du Concile Vatican II* by Lamberigts, Matthieu, and Soetens, Claude, eds. In: *Eph Theol Lovan* 78:487-488 D 1992
Review of: *Archivalia over de Aartsbisschoppen van Mechelen* by Wiel, Constant Van de. In: *Eph Theol Lovan* 78:486-487 D 1992
Review of: *De stomme duivelen: het anti-missinair syndroom in de westerse Kerk* by Neckebrouck, Valeer. In: *Eph Theol Lovan* 78:184-185 Ap 1992
Review of: *Italia meridionale e PUglia paleocristiane* by Otranto, Giorgio. In: *Eph Theol Lovan* 78:449-450 D 1992
Review of: *Thomas Müntzer e la rivoluzione dell'uomo comune* by Rocca, Tommaso La, ed. In: *Eph Theol Lovan* 78:172-173 Ap 1992

Boughton, Jill.
Christian Jungianism: deliverance or danger? *HPR* 93:54-59 Ja 1993
"We believe we are loved by God". *OSV* 82:5 My 2 1993

Boughton, Lynne C.
Advocacy packaged as theology [review article *The new dictionary of sacramental worship* by P Fink, ed]. *HPR* 93:56-62 Je 1993

Boughton, Willis L.
A mass at Verdun. *HPR* 94:55-58 O 1993

Bouillette, Antonia C.
Review of: *No contest: the case against competition* by Kohn, Alfie. In: *Momentum* 24:80 S-O 1993

Boulay, Shirley du.
The human pilgrimage. *Tablet* 247:1282 O 9 1993

Boulding, Mary Cecily.
Review of: *The Holy Eucharist* by Nichols, Aidan. In: *New Blckfrs* 73:574-576 N 1992
Review of: *The morals of Jesus* by Harvey, Nicholas Peter. In: *New Blckfrs* 73:624-625 D 1992

Bourdeaux, Michael, 1934-.
Look to the East. *Tablet* 247:3-4 Ja 2 1993
Review of: *Religious policy in the Soviet Union* by Ramet, Sabrina Petra, ed. In: *Tablet* 247:3-4 Ja 2 1993
The shadow of the KGB. *Tablet* 247:538-540 My 1 1993

Bourdua, Louise.
Review of: *Episcopal power and Florentine society, 1000-1320* by Dameron, George W. In: *Heythrop* 34:326-327 Jl 1993

Bourgeois, Henri.
La place de la confirmation dans l'initiation chrétienne. *NRT* 115:516-542 Jl-Ag 1993

Bourgeois, Patrick.
The instant and the living present: Ricoeur and Derrida reading Husserl. *PhilosTod* 37:31-37 Spr 1993

Bourgeois, Patrick L. *see* Rosenthal, Sandra B, jt auth

Bourgeois, Roy, and Imerman, Vicky.
Lessons in terror at the School of the Americas. *Cath Work* 60:1+ S 1993

Bourke, Myles M.
A conversation with scripture scholar Myles M Bourke [interview by T H Stahel, 1938-]. *America* 168:4-9 Ap 17 1993

Bourke, Vernon J.
Review of: *Le monde naturel et le mouvement de l'existence humaine* by Patocka, Jan. In: *Mod Schlmn* 70:68-70 N 1992
Review of: *William of Ockham and the divine freedom* by Klocker, Harry. In: *Mod Schlmn* 70:160-162 Ja 1993

Bourque, Edgar.
A place of grace for all. *Register* 69:5 Ag 22 1993

Bouyer, Louis.
Review of: *The foundations of mysticism* by McGinn, Bernard John, 1937-. In: *CHist* 79:93 Ja 1993

Bovée, David S.
Review of: *"Some seed fell on good ground": the life of Edwin V O'Hara* by Dolan, Timothy Michael. In: *CHist* 79:373-374 Ap 1993

Bovenizer, David A.
Abstinence as public policy: a report from New Jersey's schools. *Crisis* 11:40-41 S 1993
Other men's books. *Crisis* 11:63-64 Jl-Ag 1993
Review of: *Chesterton* by Crowther, Ian. In: *Crisis* 11:61-63 S 1993 *see* Shea, Mark P, jt auth

Bovet, Joan M.
Sida, impuls de vida?: experiencia de Joan Ferrer Sisquella. Barcelona: Claret, 1993. x, 135p ISBN 84-7263-837-5

Bowden, John.
Giant among theologians. *Tablet* 247:364-365 Mr 20 1993

Bowe, Barbara E.
Postcards from the edge: how Paul dragged Christianity into the first century. *USCath* 58:6-13 Ag 1993
Review of: *Conflict at Rome: social order and hierarchy in early Christianity* by Jeffers, James S. In: *CBQ* 55:372-374 Ap 1993
Review of: *Frühjüdische briefe: die paulinischen Briefe im Rahmen der offiziellen religiösen Briefe des Frühjudentums* by Taatz, Irene. In: *CBQ* 55:185-186 Ja 1993

Bower, Bobbie. *see* Johnson, Evelyn M R, jt auth

Bower, Richard Allen. *see* Angell, Jeannette L, jt auth

Bowes, Keith.
Review of: *Evangelistically yours* by Fung, Raymond. In: *Pacifica* 6:363-365 O 1993

Bowie, Fiona.
Review of: *Evelyn Underhill: artist of infinite life* by Greene, Dana. In: *Heythrop* 34:347-348 Jl 1993
Self-transcendence and the group: the attitude to life of thirteenth and fourteenth century Beguines. *New Blckfrs* 73:584-598 D 1992

Bowlby, Chris.
Life in a face-mask. *Tablet* 247:266 F 27 1993
No rest for the travellers. *Tablet* 247:606+ My 15 1993
Waters of discord. *Tablet* 246:1561-1562 D 12 1992

Bowman, Jim.
"Missa Latina," yes. *Comm* 120:6-7 O 8 1993

Bowman, Peg.
How generous are you? *ReligTJ* 27:7 S 1993
Learning through service. *ReligTJ* 27:33 Mr 1993
Looking back with love. *ReligTJ* 27:13 Ap-My 1993
No saint for catechists? *ReligTJ* 27:11 O 1993
We are more than teachers. *ReligTJ* 27:15 F 1993
When do we know enough? *ReligTJ* 26:19 Ja 1993

Boyack, Kenneth.
What is "new" in the new evangelization? *Living Light* 30:3-8 Aut 1993 *see* DeSiano, Frank, jt auth

Boyaxhiu, Teresa, Mother, 1910-.
Seeking the heart of God: reflections on prayer. New York: HarperCollins, 1992. x, 100p ISBN 0-06-068238-8 LC 92-54257

Boyd, John F.
What's happening to America? *SocJust* 84:15 Ja-F 1993

Boyea, Earl.
Review of: *The Polish experience in Detroit* by Wytrwal, Joseph A. In: *CHist* 79:367-368 Ap 1993

Boyer, Mark G.
Breathing deeply of God's new life. Cincinnati: St Anthony Messenger Press, 1993. x, 170p ISBN 0-86716-163-9
Mary's day—Saturday: meditations for Marian celebrations. Minnesota: The Liturgical Press, 1993. x, 116p ISBN 0-8146-2092-2 LC 92-39441

Boylan, Anthony.
Why do we anoint the sick? *Priests & People* 6:405-408 N 1992

Boyle, John F.
Faith seeking understanding: mediaeval exegesis. *Can Cath Rev* 11:9-13 Jl-Ag 1993

Boyle, John P.
Review of: *Quality of life: the new medical dilemma* by Walter, James J, and Shannon, Thomas A, eds. In: *Horizons (CTS)* 20:177-178 Spr 1993

Boys, Mary C.
Educating in faith. Kansas City: Sheed & Ward, 1989. 230p ISBN 1-55612-668-9
Review of: *Jesus and politics* by Kealy, Sean P, 1937-. In: *CBQ* 54:786-787 O 1992
Review of: *Jesus and the marginalized in John's Gospel* by Karris, Robert J. In: *CBQ* 54:786-787 O 1992
Review of: *She who is* by Johnson, Elizabeth A, 1941-. In: *CrossCurr* 43:269-272 Sum 1993
Review of: *Stages of faith and religious development: implications for church, education, and society* by Fowler, James W, and Nipkow, Karl, et al. In: *Horizons (CTS)* 20:176-177 Spr 1993

Braaten, Jane.
Review of: *Between Freiburg and Frankfurt: toward a critical ontology* by Dallmayr, Fred. In: *IPQ* 33:246-249 Je 1993

Brachlow, S.
Review of: *John Smyth's congregation: English Separatism, Mennonite influence, an d the elect nation* by Coggins, James Robert. In: *CHist* 78:659-660 O 1992

Bracken, Joseph A.
Review of: *Divine infinity in Greek and medieval thought* by Sweeney, Leo. In: *TheolStds* 54:365-366 Je 1993
Review of: *History and the triune God: contributions to trinitarian theology* by Moltmann, Jürgen. In: *TheolStds* 53:765 D 1992
Review of: *The promise of Trinitarian theology* by Gunton, Colin E. In: *Horizons (CTS)* 19:321-322 Fall 1992
Whiteheadian creativity, the Tao, and the Thomistic act of being. *Pacifica* 6:179-188 Je 1993

Braconier-d'Alcantara, Anne de.
Les jeunes et la fascination. *Lumen* 48:315-316 S 1993

Bradley, Gerard V.
Homosexuality and public policy. *SocJust* 84:132-139 S-O 1993
Review of: *Moral absolutes: tradition, revision and truth* by Finnis, John. In: *New Oxford Rev* 60:30-31 S 1993

Bradley, James.
Review of: *Russell, idealism and the emergence of analytical philosophy* by Hylton, Peter. In: *Heythrop* 34:218-220 Ap 1993

Bradley, Ritamary.
Julian's way: a practical commentary on Julian of Norwich. London: Harper-Collins Religious, 1992. x, 231p ISBN 0-00-599275-3
Review of: *Evelyn Underhill: artist of the infinite life* by Greene, Dana. In: *Relig Lit* 24:79-84 Aut 1992
Review of: *The ways of the spirit* by Underhill, Evelyn, 1875-1941. In: *Relig Lit* 24:79-84 Aut 1992

Bradley, Rtiamary.
Review of: *Modern guide to the ancient quest for the holy* by Underhill, Evelyn, 1875-1941. In: *Relig Lit* 24:79-84 Aut 1992

Brady, Bernard V.
An analysis of the use of rights language in pre-modern Catholic social thought. *Thomist* 57:97-121 Ja 1993

Brady, Mary Clare.
Put something different under the tree. *USCath* 58:31-33 D 1993
What are single people called to do? *USCath* 58:32-33 Jl 1993

Brady, Michael. *see* Trainor, Michael, jt auth

Brady, Ray.
Review of: *Being a priest today* by Goergen, Donald J, ed. In: *Furrow* 44:381-383 Je 1993
Review of: *Silent lamp: the Thomas Merton story* by Shannon, William Henry, 1917-. In: *Furrow* 44:325-326 My 1993

Bragan, Jeris.
Laughter is the best medicine. *New Cov* 22:33-34 Ja 1993

Bragotti, Joseph.
The Pope becomes a voice for the voiceless. *Tablet* 247:252 F 20 1993

Bragt, Jan van.
Meditation and prayer (3): the way of devotion: pure land Buddhism. *Stud Form Spir* 14:75-89 F 1993

Brahier, Daniel J.
Chinese rice problem intrigues students. *Momentum* 24:10-11 S-O 1993

Bramlett, Bruce R.
Review of: *Double belonging: interchurch families and Christian unity* by Kilcourse, George. In: *JEcumen Stds* 29:478-479 Sum-Aut 1992
Review of: *The convent at Auschwitz* by Bartoszewski, Wladyslaw T. In: *JEcumen Stds* 29:279-280 Spr 1992

Brand, P. *see* Yancey, P, jt auth

Brander, Bruce R.
Looking for love: a romantic cruise from eros to philia to agape. *New Cov* 22:12-14 Ap 1993

Brandes, Lisa. *see* Brigham, Fred, Jr, jt auth

Brandl, John E.
On being a Catholic politician in America. *Listening* 28:41-51 Wint 1993

Brandolini, Luca.
Italia: La progettazione Di Nuove Chiese. *Notitiae* 29:290-303 My 1993

Branick, Vincent F.
Bible truth: a possible dialogue between biblical fundamentalism and Catholic scholarship. *StudiaM* 41:269-288 1992
Studying the letters of Paul. *Catechist* 26:44-48 Mr 1993

Brankin, Patrick. *see* Cosgrove, Jim, jt auth

Branson, Margaret Stimmann, 1922-. *see* Bahmueller, Charles F, 1942-, jt auth

Bratt, J.
Review of: *A transforming faith: explorations of twentieth-century American evangelicalism* by Watt, David Harrington. In: *CHist* 78:690-691 O 1992

Brauder, Bruce.
Can we really help the third-world poor? *New Cov* 23:7-10 Ag 1993

Bravo, Gallardo Carlos.
Catecismo e inculturacion. *Christus* 58:39-41 Je 1993
En que pais vivimos? [editorial]. *Christus* 58:2-3 Ag 1993
Review of: *Fe y politica* by Mardones, José Ma. In: *Christus* 58:62 S 1993
Reflexiones en torno a Santo Domingo. *Christus* 58:67-71 N-D 1992
Review of: *Espiritualidad de la liberación* by Casaldáliga, Pedro, Bp, 1928-, and Vigil, José María. In: *Christus* 58:59 My 1993
A tres años de los mártires de la UCA. *Christus* 58:72-73 N-D 1992

Bravo Valdivieso, Luis.
Psicoanálisis y reflexión antropológica. *Teol Vida* 34 no 1-2:69-78 1993

Brawley, Robert L.
Discoursive structure and the unseen Hebrews 2:8 and 11:1: a neglected aspect of the context. *CBQ* 55:81-98 Ja 1993
Review of: *Bursting the bonds? A Jewish-Christian dialogue on Jesus and Paul* by Swidler, Leonard, et al, eds. In: *JEcumen Stds* 29:277-278 Spr 1992

Braybrooke, Neville.
Review of: *A crash of rhinoceroses* by Collings, Rex. In: *Tablet* 247:374 Mr 20 1993
Review of: *A mouthful of air* by Burgess, Anthony. In: *Tablet* 247:48 Ja 9 1993
Review of: *Amazing buildings.* In: *Tablet* 247:374 Mr 20 1993
Review of: *Catholic trivia* by Elvins, Mark. In: *Tablet* 247:374 Mr 20 1993
Review of: *Epitaphs* by Rees, Nigel. In: *Tablet* 247:374 Mr 20 1993
Review of: *Hindsights* by Heath-Stubbs, John. In: *Tablet* 247:982-983 Jl 31 1993
Review of: *In a dictionary of idioms* by Flavell, Linda, and Flavell, Roger. In: *Tablet* 247:583 My 8 1993
Review of: *Irish cottages* by Shaffrey, Maura. In: *Tablet* 247:583 My 8 1993
Review of: *Keepers of the flame* by Hamilton, Ian. In: *Tablet* 247:311-312 Mr 6 1993
Review of: *Literary essays and reviews* by Whitehead, John. In: *Tablet* 247:582 My 8 1993
Review of: *On foot in Snowdonia* by Allen, Bob. In: *Tablet* 247:583 My 8 1993
Review of: *Pet poems* by Fisher, Robert. In: *Tablet* 247:374 Mr 20 1993
Review of: *Seaside houses* by Darblay, Jerome, and D'Arnoux, Alexandra. In: *Tablet* 247:583 My 8 1993
Review of: *Stephen's history of saints* by Pepler, Stephen. In: *Tablet* 247:374 Mr 20 1993
Review of: *The body atlas* by Parker, Steve. In: *Tablet* 247:582 My 8 1993
Review of: *The coastlines of Britain* by Muir, Richard. In: *Tablet* 247:583 My 8 1993
Review of: *The Easter craft book* by Berger, Thomas, and Berger, Petra. In: *Tablet* 247:374 Mr 20 1993
Review of: *The encyclopaedia of seashells.* In: *Tablet* 247:374 Mr 20 1993
Review of: *The essential Easter book* by MacDonald, Alan. In: *Tablet* 247:374 Mr 20 1993
Review of: *The temple* by Lundquist, John M. In: *Tablet* 247:790 Je 19 1993
Review of: *The things that matter* by Neuberger, Julia. In: *Tablet* 247:374 Mr 20 1993
Review of: *The ubiquitous pig* by Nissenson, Marilyn. In: *Tablet* 247:374 Mr 20 1993
Review of: *Victorian cottages* by Clayton-Payne, Andrew. In: *Tablet* 247:582-583 My 8 1993
Review of: *Walt Whitman* by Callow, Philip. In: *Tablet* 247:213-214 F 13 1993

Breda, William C Van.
The shadow of heaven. *HPR* 93:62-65 Ap 1993

Bredero, Adriaan H.
Christendom and Christianity in the Middle Ages. Grand Rapids: Eerdmans, 1993. 448p ISBN 0-8028-3692-5

Breen, Laurie.
Review of: *Law and legality in China* by Ladany, Laszlo. In: *Tablet* 247:49 Ja 9 1993

Breen, Lawrie.
Review of: *Black hands of Beijing: lives of defiance in China's democracy movement* by Black, George, and Munro, Robin. In: *Tablet* 247:1132-1133 S 4 1993
Review of: *The Catholic Church in modern China* by Tang, Edmond, and Wiest, Jean-Paul, eds. In: *Tablet* 247:1262-1263 O 2 1993

Breen, Michael. see McEntee, Seán, jt auth

Bregman, Lucy.
What does Paul say to us about death? *Liturgy* 10:1-5 Wint 1992

Breig, James.
An animated faith. *OSV* 82:2 My 23 1993
A bishops balk at paying taxes for abortion. *OSV* 82:17 O 31 1993
Coming soon to a parish near you. *OSV* 82:12 Ag 8 1993
Coming this fall, the same old violent television shows. *OSV* 82:3 S 26 1993
Muckrakers. *OSV* 82:3 Jl 25 1993

Breitling, JoAnn.
Matthew. *Liguorian* 81:52-53 Ja 1993

Brena, Gian Luigi.
Habermas e la teologia. *Civilta* 3:51-54 Jl 3 1993
Review of: *Habermas e La Teologia* by Arens, E, ed. In: *Civilta* 3:51-54 Jl 3 1993
Review of: *Il mito in Platone* by Ceccarini, Luigi. In: *Civilta* 2:410 My 15 1993

Brennan, Anne, and Brewi, Janice.
Soul making and life's second half. *RRel* 52:220-225 Mr-Ap 1993

Brennan, Dermot.
Review of: *Grief ministry* by Williams, Donna Reilly, and Sturzl, Jo Ann. In: *Doctr Life* 43:447-448 S 1993
Review of: *The Bible on human suffering* by McDermott, John M. In: *Doctr Life* 43:447-448 S 1993

Brennan, Donald A.
Transformation to integrated delivery requires a shared culture. *Health Prog* 74:58 Jl-Ag 1993

Brennan, Jim.
Review of: *Science and language links classroom implications* by Scott, Johanna. In: *Momentum* 24:77 N-D 1993

Brennan, Margaret.
Bishops, religious face postmodern world era. *Origins* 23:120-124 Jl 15 1993
Religious life's charism: transforming life. *Origins* 23:207-211 S 2 1993

Brennan, Noel.
A breakthrough for ministry. *AFER* 35:27-36 F 1993

Brennan, Patrick J, and Melendez, Dawn Mayer.
Long gone—returning home: re-involving inactive Catholics. *Chicago Stud* 32:100-113 Ag 1993

Brennan, Walter T.
Review of: *Journey in the risen Christ—the "Little Mandate" of Catherine de Hueck Doherty* by Wild, Robert A. In: *CLW* 64:38 Jl-S 1993
Review of: *Mary in the mystery of the covenant* by Potterie, Ignace de la. In: *CLW* 64:38-39 Jl-S 1993
Theological reflection: from Marialis Cultus to mission. *Marian Stds* 43:132-159 1992

Brenner, Athalya. see Radday, Yehuda T, jt ed

Brenner, Susan W.
Review of: *The Christian foundations of criminal responsibility: a philosophical study of legal reasoning* by Crawford, J M B, and Quinn, J F. In: *Amer J Juris* 37:367-371 1992

Breslin, John B.
Review of: *College Catholics: a new counter-culture* by Hunt, Michael J. In: *Comm* 120:25-26 S 10 1993

Breslin, Mary.
Save the children of Croatia. *St Anth* 100:28-35 Mr 1993

Breton, David Le, and Broussier, Jean.
Médecine générale et sciences humaines. *Supplement* 184:167-173 Mr-Ap 1993

Breton, Jean-Claude.
Review of: *Sermons* by Tauler, Jean. In: *Laval Theol Phil* 49:170-171 F 1993

Bretzke, J.
Review of: *Following Christ in a consumer society: the spirituality of cultural resistance* by Kavanaugh, John F. In: *Gregorianum* 73 No 4:763-764 1992

Bretzke, James T.
Review of: *Reading in communion: Scripture and ethics in Christian life* by Fowl, Stephen E, and Jones, L Gregory. In: *Gregorianum* 74 no 2:375-376 1993
Review of: *The primacy of love* by Wadell, Paul J. In: *Gregorianum* 74 no 2: 376-378 1993

Breuning, Klaus. see Trutwin, Werner, jt ed

Brewi, Janice. see Brennan, Anne, jt auth

Briard, Jacques.
Bâle et Séoul: générosités, limites et enjeux d'Églises. *Lumen* 48:37-50 Mr 1993

Brickley, Rosemarie.
Lament for a gymnasium. *Tod Parish* 25:37-38 Mr 1993

Brieskorn, Norbert.
Nationalismus und Multikulturalismus. *Stimm Zeit* 211:651-662 O 1993
Rechtsphilosophie. *Stimm Zeit* 211:318-330 My 1993
Review of: *Conquista und Evangelisation* by Sievernich, Michael, et al, eds. In: *Stimm Zeit* 211:430-431 Je 1993
Review of: *Fürstinnen und Städterinnen* by Beyreuther, Gerald, and Pätzold, Barbara, et al, eds. In: *Stimm Zeit* 211:717-718 O 1993

Brigham, Fred, Jr, and Brandes, Lisa.
Chapter 1 solutions. *Tod Cath Teach* 26:13-15 My-Je 1993

Bright, Kimberly Gustin.
Conjugally incorrect. *Crisis* 11:43-44 F 1993

Bright, Kimberly J.
How I got stung. *Crisis* 11:63-64 O 1993

Briley, Richard Gaylord.
Everything I needed to know about success, I learned in the Bible (and so can you!). New Hampshire: The publisher-In-The-Glen, 1993. x, 144p ISBN 1-882988-05-1

Brings, Allen.
On being called. *New Oxford Rev* 60:24-26 N 1993

Brinkman, B.R.
Review of: *Beauty and revelation in the thought of Saint Augustine* by Harrison, Carol. In: *Heythrop* 34:316-318 Jl 1993
Review of: *Born before all time* by Kuschel, Karl-Josef. In: *Heythrop* 34:437-440 O 1993
Review of: *Christ, ethics and tragedy essays in honor of Donald MacKinnon* by Surin, Kenneth. In: *Heythrop* 34:437-438 O 1993
Review of: *Grace, politics and desire* by Meynell, Hugo, ed. In: *Heythrop* 34: 316-318 Jl 1993
Review of: *Heresy and mysticism in Sixteenth-Century Spain: the Alumbrados* by Hamilton, Alastair. In: *Heythrop* 34:333-334 Jl 1993
Review of: *La correzione fraterna in s. Agostino* by Clerici, Agostino. In: *Heythrop* 34:316-318 Jl 1993
Review of: *William of Ockham and the divine freedom* by Klocker, Harry. In: *Heythrop* 34:470-472 O 1993

Brinkman, B R.
Review of: *Freedom in the modern world: Maritain, Simon, Adler* by Torre, Michael D, ed. In: *Heythrop* 34:470-472 O 1993

Brito, Emilio.
Deux théories de l'esprit: Hegel et Schleiermacher. *RPhil Louvain* 91:31-65 F 1993
Herméneutique et pneumatologie selon Schleiermacher. *Eph Theol Lovan* 69: 88-117 Ap 1993
Review of: *Barth and Rahner in dialogue* by Highfield, Ron. In: *Eph Theol Lovan* 78:471-472 D 1992
Review of: *Christian uniqueness reconsidered* by D'Costa, Gavin, ed. In: *Eph Theol Lovan* 78:446-468 D 1992
Review of: *Ermeneutica et cristologia in Walter Kasper* by Madonia, Nicolò. In: *Eph Theol Lovan* 78:473-474 D 1992
Review of: *Filosofia, teologia, religione* by Raspanti, Antonino. In: *Eph Theol Lovan* 78:460 D 1992
Review of: *Jésus: Christ universel?* by Petit, Jean-Claude. In: *Eph Theol Lovan* 78:474-475 D 1992
Review of: *L'essence de la religion selon Schleiermacher* by Demange, Pierre. In: *RPhil Louvain* 91:479-481 Ag 1993

Brito, Emilio. *(cont'd)*
Review of: *La semaine Sainte des philosophes* by Tilliette, Xavier. In: *RPhil Louvain* 91:156-159 F 1993
Review of: *La théologie après Wittgenstein* by Kerr, Fergus. In: *Eph Theol Lovan* 78:469-470 D 1992
Review of: *Le Christ de la philosophie* by Tilliette, Xavier. In: *RPhil Louvain* 91:154-156 F 1993
Review of: *Liebe—das Geheimnis der Welt* by Paulus, Engelbert. In: *Eph Theol Lovan* 78:473 D 1992
Review of: *Lonergan workshop* by Lawrence, Fred, ed. In: *Eph Theol Lovan* 78:470 D 1992
Review of: *Penser la religion* by Greisch, Jean, ed. In: *Eph Theol Lovan* 78:463-464 D 1992
Review of: *Systematische theologie, vol I* by Pannenberg, Wolfhart. In: *Eph Theol Lovan* 78:462-463 D 1992
Review of: *Teologia sistematica, vol 1* by Pannenberg, Wolfhart. In: *Eph Theol Lovan* 78:462-463 D 1992
Review of: *The immutability of God in the theology of Hans Urs von Balthasar* by O'Hanlon, Gerard F. In: *Eph Theol Lovan* 78:470-471 D 1992
Review of: *Theology after Wittgenstein* by Kerr, Fergus. In: *Eph Theol Lovan* 78:469-470 D 1992

Britt, John.
Review of: *Desperately seeking Mary: a feminist appropriation of a traditional religious symbol* by Maeckelberghe, Els. In: *Horizons (CTS)* 20:155-156 Spr 1993

Brittan, Steve.
Who needs Catholic schools? [excerpts from a speech given to Knights of Columbus, Burgettstown]. *Tod Cath Teach* 27:6 N-D 1993

Broadhurst, John.
A difficult pilgrimage. *Tablet* 247:806 Je 26 1993

Brock, James W. see Adams, Walter, jt auth

Brocke, Rita.
A song of the city. *Sisters* 65:188-190 My 1993

Brockman, Patricia C. see Ebert, Andreas, jt ed

Brockman, Stephen.
Living where the wall was: what still divides the Germans. *Comm* 120:16-19 S 24 1993

Broderick, John J.
Review of: *Beyond borders* by Ferris, Elizabeth G. In: *Nat Cath Rep* 29:31 S 10 1993

Brodia, Thomas L.
The Gospel according to John: a literary and theological commentary. New York: Oxford University, 1993. x, 625p ISBN 0-19-505800-3 LC 91-38200

Broek, Lyle D Vander. see Bailey, James L, jt auth

Brogan, Jacqueline Vaught.
Review of: *American Catholic arts and fictions* by Giles, Paul. In: *America* 168:19 My 15 1993

Brogan, John J.
Review of: *The New Testament text of Gregory of Nyssa* by Brooks, James A. In: *CBQ* 55:143-145 Ja 1993

Brokish, Evelyn.
What about music as ministry? *Past Mus* 17:58-60 Ag-S 1993

Bromberg, Judith.
Review of: *Discipleship of equals* by Schussler, Elisabeth. In: *Nat Cath Rep* 30:27 N 19 1993
Review of: *Fraud* by Brookner, Anita. In: *Nat Cath Rep* 29:28 My 28 1993
Review of: *Living in the lap of the goddess* by Eller, Cynthia. In: *Nat Cath Rep* 30:27 N 19 1993
Review of: *The Catholic woman: difficult choices in a modern world* by Pieper, Jeanne. In: *Nat Cath Rep* 30:27 N 19 1993
Review of: *The myth of the goddess* by Baring, Anne, and Cashford, Jules. In: *Nat Cath Rep* 30:27 N 19 1993
Review of: *The spirit of community* by Bromberg, Judith. In: *Nat Cath Rep* 29:27 S 10 1993
Review of: *Where silence speaks* by Erickson, Victoria Lee. In: *Nat Cath Rep* 30:27 N 19 1993
Review of: *Woman to woman* by Zagano, Phyllis. In: *Nat Cath Rep* 30:27 N 19 1993

Bromberg, L.
Review of: *Modern esoteric spirituality: world spirituality: an encyclopdic history of the Religious quest* by Faivre, Antoine, and Needleman, Jacob, eds. In: *Nat Cath Rep* 29:35 F 5 1993

Brotherton, Fergus.
What about the finances of the church? *Priests & People* 7:191-193 My 1993

Broun, Janice.
Schism in the Bulgarian Orthodox Church. *Month* 26:290-294 Jl 1993
Slovakia embraces the past. *Comm* 120:15 S 24 1993

Broussier, Jean. see Breton, David Le, jt auth

Brouwer, Didier de.
Le regard de Méduse: adolescence et fascination. *Lumen* 48:324-330 S 1993

Brovedani, Ennio.
Le dimensioni etiche della ricerca scientifico-tecnologica. *Civilta* 3:382-387 S 4 1993
I docenti dell'Università Cattolica si interrogano. *Civilta* 144:340-353 F 20 1993

Brown, A J, Jr.
Developing leadership among urban youth. *Momentum* 24:46-47+ Ap-My 1993

Brown, Andrew.
Message from Medjugorje. *Tablet* 247:1155-1156 S 11 1993

Brown, Anne.
Review of: *The complete guide to religious educational vouchers* by Ratcliff, Donald E, and Neff, Blake J. In: *Momentum* 24:78 N-D 1993

Brown, Catherine D.
Review of: *Jean Gerson and De consolatione theologiae (1418)* by Burrows, Mark Stephen. In: *TheolStds* 53:754-755 D 1992

Brown, Daniel A.
Review of: *Confirmation* by Turner, Paul. In: *Mod Lit* 20:36 S 1993
Review of: *Documents of Christian worship* by White, James F. In: *Mod Lit* 20:36 My 1993
Review of: *Fire and light in the Western Triduum: their use at Tenebrae and at the Paschal Vigil* by MacGregor, A J. In: *Mod Lit* 20:40 Ag 1993
Review of: *Foundations of liturgy* by Adam, Adolf. In: *Mod Lit* 20:36 My 1993
Review of: *History of the Mass* by Cabie, Robert. In: *Mod Lit* 20:37 Je-Jl 1993
Review of: *Journey with the fathers, Year A* by Barnecut, Edith, ed. In: *Mod Lit* 20:38 My 1993
Review of: *Living with wisdom: a life of Thomas Merton* by Forest, Jim. In: *New Theol Rev* 6:111-112 F 1993
Review of: *Shaping the Easter Feast* by Chupungco, Anscar J. In: *Mod Lit* 20:39 My 1993
Review of: *The Byzantine Rite* by Taft, Robert F. In: *Mod Lit* 20:36 S 1993

Brown, David O.
Review of: *Channels of healing prayer* by Heron, Benedict. In: *Mod Lit* 20:40 F 1993
Review of: *Healing as a parish ministry: mending body, mind, and spirit* by Thomas, Leo, and Alkire, Jan. In: *Mod Lit* 19:42 My 1993-Ja 1993
Review of: *Liturgical inculturation: sacramentals, religiosity, and catechesis* by Chupungco, Anscar J. In: *Mod Lit* 20:37 Je-Jl 1993
Review of: *Liturgy models* by Gilbert, Ann, et al. In: *Mod Lit* 20:36 My 1993
Review of: *Ordained to preach* by Miller, Charles E. In: *Mod Lit* 20:37 My 1993
Review of: *Reading the signs of the times* by Sanks, T Howland, and Coleman, John A, eds. In: *Mod Lit* 20:37 O 1993
Review of: *Seasons and feasts of the Church Year* by Whalen, Michael D. In: *Mod Lit* 20:39 S 1993
Review of: *The rites of people* by Pottebaum, Gerard A. In: *Mod Lit* 20:42 Ag 1993
Review of: *Worship* by Stevenson, Kenneth W. In: *Mod Lit* 20:39 F 1993

Brown, Doug.
Doing social economics in a postmodern world. *RSocEcon* 50:383-403 Wint 1992

Brown, Douglas.
Review of: *Here and now: a spirituality for the redeemed* by Leonard, George. In: *Tablet* 247:1102 Ag 28 1993 see Pasco, Rowanne, jt auth

Brown, George Mackayu, 1921-.
The innkeeper's tale. *Tablet* 247:471-473 Ap 10-17 1993

Brown, Harold O J.
The Continuing Kulturkampf [editorial]. *SocJust* 84:35-39 Mr-Ap 1993

Brown, Janice.
Worse yet to come? *Comm* 120:4-5 Ja 29 1993

Brown, John J.
Mount Royal players: Montreal's living stations. *Liguorian* 81:20-23 Ap 1993

Brown, Kerry. see Batchelor, Martine, jt ed

Brown, Marvin L, Jr.
Review of: *Paul de Cassagnac and the authoritarian tradition in nineteenth-century France* by Offen, Karen. In: *CHist* 79:549-550 Jl 1993

Brown, Michael.
El Mozote: a test of the process of reconciliation in El Salvador. *New Theol Rev* 6:74-80 Ag 1993

Brown, Raymond Edward, et al, eds.
On cover: based on the new Jerome biblical commentary. London: G Chapman, 1992. x, 456p ISBN 0-22566-642-1 LC 92-44543

Brown, Raymond Edward.
Review of: *The temptation and the passion: the Markan soteriology, second edition* by Best, Ernest. In: *Heythrop* 34:73-74 Ja 1993
Review of: *Understanding the fourth gospel* by Ashton, John. In: *TheolStds* 53:744-746 D 1992

Brown, Robert McAfee, 1920-.
Liberation theology: an introductory guide. Louisville: John Knox Press, 1993. x, 143p ISBN 0-66425-424-1 LC 92-30934

Brown, Roselee.
The greatest gift of all. *ReligTJ* 26:18 Ja 1993

Brown, Susan Mader.
Review of: *Modern Catholicism: Vatican II and after* by Hastings, Adrian, 1929-, ed. In: *Can Cath Rev* 11:25-26 Ap 1993

Brown, William S.
Review of: *Ecocide in the USSR* by Feshbach, Murray, and Friendly, Alfred, Jr. In: *RSocEcon* 51:244-246 Sum 1993

Browne, Frank, and McGettigan, Donal.
The causes of Irish unemployment: trends and explanations. *Studies* 82:35-52 Spr 1993

Browning, Tatiana. see FitzLyon, Kyril, jt auth

Brownrigg, Ronald.
Who's who in the New Testament. New York: Oxford University Press, 1993. x, 286p ISBN 0-19-521031-x

Bruce, Colin John. see Smithers, Edward, jt auth

Brueggemann, Walter, et al, eds.
Texts for preaching. Louisville: Westminster, 1993. x, 704p ISBN 0-664-21970-5

Brueggemann, Walter.
Isaiah and urban possibility. Louisville: Westminster, 1993. x, 96p ISBN 0-664-25460-8
Narrative coherence and theological intentionality in 1 Samuel 18. *CBQ* 55:225-243 Ap 1993

Brueggemann, Walter. *(cont'd)*
Review of: *The Book of Genesis, Chapters 1-17* by Hamilton, Victor P. In: *CBQ* 55:113-115 Ja 1993
Using God's resources wisely: Isaiah and urban possibility. Louisville, Kentucky: John Knox Press, 1993. 96p ISBN 0-664-25460-8
Why prophets won't leave well enough alone [interview by the editors of US Catholic (Periodical)]. *USCath* 58:6-13 Ja 1993

Brueggemann, Walter, and Reeder, Rachel.
The power of God's promise [exc fr *Liturgy: rhythms of prayer; Liturgy: the Lord's day*]. *Liturgy* 10:47-50 Spr 1993

Bruel, John S.
Will balder heads prevail? *Crisis* 10:6-7 N 1992

Brugh, Lorraine.
Children's choirs as proclaimers. *Liturgy* 11:74-76 Sum 1993

Bruin, John.
Why Heidegger's Godot might not be worth the wait. *Mod Schlmn* 70:143-152 Ja 1993

Brummel, M.
Review of: *The prophetic imagination* by Brueggemann, Walter. In: *USCath* 58:6-13 Ja 1993

Brundage, James A.
Review of: *La institucion matrimonial en la Hispania Cristiana bajo-medieval (1215-1563)* by Gil, Federico R Aznar. In: *Jurist* 51 no 2:515-517 1991
Review of: *La parola all'accusato* by Vigueur, Jean-Claude Maire, and Bagliani, Agostino Paravicini, eds. In: *CHist* 79:319-320 Ap 1993

Brunet, Louis. *see* Morin, Lucien, jt auth

Brunetta, Giuseppe.
Un Bilancio del sostentamento economico alla Chiesa Cattolica in Italia. *Civilta* 3:263-270 Ag 7-21 1993
Review of: *L'istruzione religiosa nelle scuole italiane* by Gianni, Andrea. In: *Civilta* 2:206-207 Ap 17 1993

Brungs, Robert.
Confronting the brave new world of science [interview by B. Dodds]. *OSV* 82:14 N 28 1993

Bruno, Bonnie.
Mourning: the prelude to laughter. Grand Rapids: Zondervan Publishing House, 1993. x, 64p ISBN 0-310-59613-0

Bruns, Edgar J.
Review of: *The secret identity of the beloved disciple* by Grassi, Joseph A. In: *CBQ* 55:367-368 Ap 1993

Bruns, William R.
Guiding your parish through the Christian initiation process: a handbook for leaders. Cincinnati: St Anthony Messenger Press, 1993. 152p ISBN 0-86716-188-4

Brusselmans, A.
Review of: *Faith in Catholic classrooms* by Fahy, Patrick S. In: *Lumen* 48: 354 S 1993

Bruteau, Beatrice, 1930-.
Radical optimism: rooting ourselves in reality. New York: The Crossroad Publishing Company, 1993. x, 119p ISBN 0-8245-1354 LC 92-39444
The trinitarian community. *Living Prayer* 26:16-19 Jl-Ag 1993

Bruyn, P-H De.
Review of: *Jésus-Christ à la rencontre des religions* by Dupuis, Jacques. In: *NRT* 115:595-596 Jl-Ag 1993
Review of: *Jeuscristo al encuentro de las religiones* by Dupuis, Jacques. In: *NRT* 115:595-596 Jl-Ag 1993

Bruyn, Severyn T.
Review of: *Haves without have-nots: essays for the 21st century on democracy and socialism* by Adler, Mortimer Jerome. In: *RSocEcon* 51:105-108 Spr 1993

Bruyn, Theodore de, ed.
Pelagius on St Paul's Epistle to the Romans. New York: Oxford University Press, 1993. x, 248p ISBN 0-814399-0

Bryan, Timothy L.
The new consciousness in America. *StudiaM* 41:27-47 1992

Bryson, Kathy.
Notes from a computer pusher: improving the worship aid. *Mod Lit* 20:13-16 Ag 1993

Brzezinski, Zbigniew K, 1928-.
New world, new disorder [fr *Out of control: global turmoil on the eve of the twenty-first century*]. *Crisis* 11:39-42 My 1993

Buby, Bertrand.
Mary, faithful disciple. *Emmanuel* 99:214-221 My 1993

Buchanan, George Wesley.
Review of: *The continuing voice of Jesus* by Boring, M Eugene. In: *CBQ* 55: 141-143 Ja 1993

Bucher, Kimberly R.
Living chastely. *Crisis* 11:37-39 S 1993

Buckland, Stephen.
Jesuit presence and the struggle for freedom. *Month* 26:174-182 My 1993

Buckley, Francis J.
Mary and catechesis: there's room for two approaches. *Catechist* 26:26-29 Ap-My 1993

Buckley, L.
Review of: *The end of ancient Christianity* by Markus, R A. In: *Can Cath Rev* 11:36-37 Ja 1993

Buckley, Michael J, 1931-.
The Catholic university and its inherent promise. *America* 168:14-16 My 29 1993
Church of the loaves and fishes. *CDgst* 57:1-5 Mr 1993 *see* O'Brien, David J, 1938-, jt auth

Buckley, William F, Jr.
At Lourdes [condensed fr *National Review* Ag 9 1993]. *CDgst* 58:50-55 D 1993

Buckwalter, Kathleen C. *see* Smith, Marianne, jt auth

Buechlein, Daniel M.
A witness to mystery. *Priest* 49:35-37 Mr 1993

Buggert, Donald W.
Review of: *Dynamics of theology* by Haight, Roger. In: *New Theol Rev* 6:93-95 Ag 1993

Buijs, Joseph A.
Review of: *Faith seeking understanding: learning and the Catholic tradition* by Berthold, George C, ed. In: *Can Cath Rev* 11:30 Jl-Ag 1993

Bujak, Adam.
John Paul II. Krakow: Parol Company, 1992. x, 111p ISBN 0-89870-424-3 LC 92-71934

Bull, George, 1929-.
Images of paradise. *Tablet* 246:1613 D 19-26 1992
Reasons for disbelief. *Tablet* 247:240-241 F 20 1993
Review of: *The final martyrs* by Endo, Shusaku, 1923-. In: *Tablet* 247:1077 Ag 21 1993
Review of: *The great melody: a thematic biography of Edmund Burke* by O'Brien, Conor Cruise. In: *Tablet* 247:618-619 My 15 1993
Review of: *The use of memory: publishing and further pursuits* by Burns, Tom G. In: *Tablet* 247:341-342 Mr 13 1993
The spirit of the age. *Tablet* 247:966 Jl 31 1993

Bullard, Roger A.
Messiah: the Gospel according to Handel's Oratorio. Grand Rapids: Eerdmans, 1993. 152p ISBN 0-8028-0125-0

Bullert, Gary.
Review of: *Utopia against the family: the problems and politics of the American family* by Christensen, Bryce J. In: *SocJust* 84:92-93 My-Je 1993

Bullock, William, Bp.
Bishops and Priests: aspects of a healthy relationship. *Origins* 23:226-229 S 9 1993

Bunbury, Richard R.
What matters is that our song comes from the heart. *Past Mus* 17:58-60 Ap-My 1993

Bundy, Blakely Fetridge.
A new look at preschool and primary classrooms. *Tod Cath Teach* 27:26-29 O 1993

Bundy, David.
Review of: *A tale of two cities: Sodom and Gomorrah in the Old Testament, early Jewish and early Christian traditions* by Loader, J A. In: *CBQ* 54: 752-753 O 1992
Review of: *Prudens dispensator verbi: Romani 5, 12-21 nell' esegesi di Clemente Alessandrino e Origene* by Mascellani, Elisa. In: *Eph Theol Lovan* 78:171-172 Ap 1992
Review of: *Translatio Religionis: die Paulusdeutung des Origenes* by Heither, Theresia. In: *Eph Theol Lovan* 78:170-171 Ap 1992
Review of: *Vangelo Arabo aprocrifo dell'Apostolo Giovanni da un manuscrito della Biblioteca Ambrosiana* by Moraldi, Luigi. In: *Eph Theol Lovan* 78: 168-169 Ap 1992

Bundy, Lester I.
Review of: *The ecumenical movement today* by Cavatas, Natale. In: *JEcumen Stds* 29:472 Sum-Aut 1992
Review of: *The sense of ecumenical tradition* by Bria, Ion. In: *JEcumen Stds* 29:472 Sum-Aut 1992

Bunson, Matthew. *see* Bunson, Margaret, jt auth

Buono, Anthony M.
The Eucharist fount of our joy. *Emmanuel* 99:146-149 Ap 1993
Praying with the beatitudes. *Emmanuel* 99:466-470 O 1993

Burbank, James.
New Mexico reels in wake of sex allegations against Sante Fe prelate. *Nat Cath Rep* 29:5+ Mr 19 1993

Burch, Sam. *see* Reynolds, Gerry, jt auth

Bureau, René.
Les mouvements religieux modernes africains. *StudiaM* 41:187-204 1992

Buren, Paul Matthews van, 1924-.
Review of: *The covenant never revoked: biblical reflections on Christian-Jewish dialogue* by Lohfink, Norbert. In: *JEcumen Stds* 29:122 Wint 1992

Burgaleta, Claudio.
Review of: *Nuestro clamor por la vida: teología Latinoamericana desde la perspectiva de la mujer* by Aquino, Mariá Pilar. In: *RRel* 52:295-296 Mr-Ap 1993

Burghardt, Robert P.
Chapels on steel wheels [condensed fr *Trains* D 1992 (photos)]. *CDgst* 58:66-70 D 1993

Burghardt, Walter J, et al.
The American Catholic heritage: reflections on the growth and influence of the Catholic Church in the United States. Rome: Pontifical North American College, 1992. 131p ISBN 1-55586-544-5

Burghardt, Walter J.
When Christ meets Christ: homilies on the just word. New York: Paulist Press, 1993. x, 241p ISBN 0-8091-3373-3 LC 92-46434

Burke, Barbara K.
Wellness in the healing ministry. *Health Prog* 74:34-37 1993

Burke, Christine E.
Review of: *Common journey, different paths: spiritual direction in cross-cultural perspective* by Rakoczy, Susan, ed. In: *Pacifica* 6:357-359 O 1993

Burke, Cormac.
The freedom and responsibility of the laity. *HPR* 93:19-27 Jl 1993

Byles, Mary.
Review of: *Jews and Christians in a pluralistic world* by Bockenförde, Ernst-Wolfgang, and Shils, Edward, eds. In: *CrossCurr* 42:562 Wint 1992-1993

Byrne, Brendan.
Review of: *The Romans debate* by Donfried, Karl P. In: *Pacifica* 6:216-218 Je 1993

Byrne, Harry M.
Review of: *Freedom for ministry* by Neuhaus, Richard John, 1936-. In: *RRel* 52:630-631 Jl-Ag 1993

Byrne, Katharine.
Count on Mom: but do it yourself. *Comm* 120:9-10 Ap 9 1993

Byrne, N.
Review of: *James Duhig* by Boland, T P. In: *CHist* 78:700-701 O 1992

Byrne, Pat.
Review of: *Ministry in the Church* by Bernier, Paul. In: *Mod Lit* 20:38 Je-Jl 1993
Review of: *The liturgy of the world: Karl Rahner's theology of worship* by Skelley, Michael. In: *Mod Lit* 20:39 S 1993
Review of: *The witness of the worshipping community: liturgy and the practice of evangelism* by Senn, Frank C. In: *Mod Lit* 20:36 S 1993

Byrne, Patrick H.
Ressentiment and the preferential option for the poor. *TheolStds* 54:213-241 Je 1993

Byrnes, J P. *see* Gelman, S A, jt ed

Byrnes, Timothy A.
One leap forward, one step back. *Comm* 120:29-30 N 19 1993
Review of: *A flock of shepherds* by Reese, Thomas Joseph, 1945-. In: *Comm* 120:28-29 Ja 29 1993
Review of: *Poland's jump to the market economy* by Sachs, Jeffrey. In: *Comm* 120:29-31 N 19 1993
What's a Catholic country to do? The Church's temptation in Poland. *Comm* 120:11-13 S 24 1993

Byron, William J, 1927-.
Linking the new communitarians. *America* 168:11-13 Mr 20-27 1993
Preserving a presence in medical education. *Health Prog* 74:68-69 Ja-F 1993

C

Caba, José.
Métodos exegéticos en el estudio actual del Nuevo Testamento. *Gregorianum* 73 No 4:611-669 1992

Cabra, Pier Giordana.
Religious life at the Synod of Bishops on Europe. *Con Life* 17 no 2:135-147 1992

Cacicedo, Al.
"Conversing, looking, loving": the discourse of reason in Paradise lost. *Cithara* 32:13-28 My 1993

Cadwallader, Alan H.
Review of: *Mary for all Christians* by Macquarrie, John. In: *Pacifica* 6:349-352 O 1993

Cafardi, Nicholas P.
Stones instead of bread: sexually abusive priests in ministry. *Stud Can* 27 no 1:145-172 1993

Cafone, James M.
Celibacy: a talk to seminarians. *Priest* 49:31-34 My 1993

Cahalan, John C.
Review of: *Covenant community and Church* by Clark, Stephen B. In: *New Oxford Rev* 60:28-29 Mr 1993

Cahill, F.
Review of: *Partners in faith: a programme of adult faith development* by Earley, C, and McKenna, G. In: *Furrow* 44:56-57 Ja 1993
Review of: *Walking together in faith: a handbook for sponsors of Christian initiation* by Morris, Thomas H. In: *Furrow* 44:56-57 Ja 1993

Cahill, Kevin Michael, 1936-.
A necessary balance. *America* 169:6-10 Ag 28-S 4 1993

Cahill, Lisa Sowle.
Abortion, sex and gender: the Church's public voice. *America* 168:6-11 My 22, 1993
The embryo and the fetus: new moral contexts. *TheolStds* 54:124-142 Mr 1993
[The lasting contribution of Veritatis splendor]. *Comm* 120:15-16 O 22 1993
Review of: *Interpretations of conflict: ethics, pacifism, and the just-war tradition* by Miller, Richard Brian. In: *Horizons (CTS)* 20:184-186 Spr 1993

Cahill, Michael.
Coping with hypotheses: a strategy in regard to the historical Jesus. *Chicago Stud* 31:130-141 Ag 1992
The neglected parallelism in Colossians 1, 24-25. *Eph Theol Lovan* 78:142-147 Ap 1992
Review of: *A christological catechism: New Testament answers* by Fitzmyer, Joseph Augustine, 1920-. In: *CBQ* 54:776-777 O 1992

Cahoy, William J.
Feminism and theology: beyond women's ordination. *Sisters* 65:243-251 Jl 1993

Caldecott, Stratford.
The crisis in Anglo-Catholicism. *Crisis* 11:15-16 Je 1993
Notes from Zagreb. *Can Cath Rev* 11:(I)+ Jl-Ag 1993
Ratzinger and the terrorists. *Crisis* 11:13-14 Jl-Ag 1993
Review of: *Christianity, wilderness, and wildlife: the original desert solitaire* by Bratton, Susan Power. In: *Tablet* 247:1233-1234 S 25 1993
Review of: *Coming of age: an exploration of Christianity and the New Age* by Palmer, Martin. In: *Tablet* 247:790-791 Je 19 1993

Caldecott, Stratford. *(cont'd)*
Review of: *Covenant of the heart: meditations of a Christian hermeticist on the mysteries of tradition* by Tomberg, Valentin. In: *Tablet* 247:790-791 Je 19 1993
Review of: *The duty of mercy: and the sin of cruelty to brute animals* by Primatt, Humphry. In: *Tablet* 247:1233-1234 S 25 1993

Calimé, Pierre.
Marche vers la splendeur—ton Dieu marche avec toi [I congrès mondial des pastorale des sanctuaries et des Pèlerinages]. *Notitiae* 28:294-296 Ap 1992
Tourism must respect the earth. *OR(Eng)* 1309:9 S 29 1993

Callaghan, Brendan.
Review of: *Chosen: gay Catholic priests tell their stories* by Stuart, Elizabeth. In: *Tablet* 247:550 My 1 1993
"The tragic experience of consciousness": psychological reflections on sin and guilt. *Month* 26:396-401 S-O 1993

Callahan, Annice.
The human person: contemporary theology and the exercises. *Way Suppl* 76:85-97 Spr 1993

Callahan, Daniel, 1930-.
Cramming for your finals: make death a part of life [excerpt fr *The troubled dream of life*]. *Comm* 120:11-15 Jl 16 1993
Review of: *Holy entrepreneurs: Cistercians, knights, and economic exchange in twelfth-century Burgundy* by Bouchard, Constance Brittain. In: *CHist* 78:636-640 O 1992
Review of: *Life's dominion* by Dworkin, Ronald. In: *Comm* 120:23-24 S 24 1993
Review of: *Medieval agriculture, the southern French countryside, and the early Cistercians* by Berman, Constance Hoffman. In: *CHist* 78:636-640 O 1992
Review of: *The politics of virtue: is abortion debatable?* by Mensch, Elizabeth, and Freeman, Alan. In: *Comm* 120:23-24 S 24 1993

Callahan, Nelson J.
Review of: *Sister Ignatia: angel of Alcoholics Anonymous* by Darrah, Mary C. In: *CHist* 79:143-144 Ja 1993

Callahan, Sidney.
Ethical issues of unconventional therapies. *Health Prog* 74:42-43 1993
How to be friends with your grown children. *USCath* 58:32-38 Ap 1993
The rock from which living water springs. *Health Prog* 74:74-75+ Ja-F 1993
Society needs sexual evolution. *Nat Cath Rep* 29:19 Je 4 1993
Virtue by the numbers. *Comm* 120:8-9 N 19 1993
What is a good conscience? Cardinal Ratzinger on moral truth. *Comm* 120:8-9 O 8 1993

Callahan, William J.
Review of: *Iglesia y sociedad zaragozanas a mediados del s XVIII: la visita pastoral del arzobisop D Francisco Añnoa a su diócesis* by Colomina, Pilar Pueyo. In: *CHist* 79:545-546 Jl 1993
Review of: *J A Llorente, un ideal de burguesía: su vida y su obra hasta el exilio en Francia (1756-1813)* by Cerceda, Enrique de la Lama. In: *CHist* 79:118-119 Ja 1993

Callam, Daniel.
The Catholic bind [editorial]. *Can Cath Rev* 11:2-3 Jl-Ag 1993
My two cents' worth [editorial]. *Can Cath Rev* 11:2-4 N 1993
Our poor bishops [editorial]. *Can Cath Rev* 11:2-3 Je 1993
Review of: *Are all Christians ministers?* by Collins, John N. In: *Can Cath Rev* 11:23-24 N 1993
Review of: *Dead wrong* by Kienzle, William X. In: *Can Cath Rev* 11:27 Jl-Ag 1993
Review of: *Ethics for high schools* by Kennedy, Leonard A. In: *Can Cath Rev* 11:28-29 F 1993
Review of: *How to keep your university Catholic* by Kennedy, Leonard A. In: *Can Cath Rev* 11:28-29 F 1993
Review of: *Human immortality and the redemption of death* by Tugwell, Simon. In: *Can Cath Rev* 11:42 Ja 1993
Review of: *Saint Thomas Aquinas: his importance today* by Kennedy, Leonard A. In: *Can Cath Rev* 11:28 F 1993
Throwing out the bath water [editorial]. *Can Cath Rev* 11:2-3 S 1993
The weakest possible argument [editorial]. *Can Cath Rev* 11:2-4 F 1993
What Christopher Columbus has to say about feminism [editorial]. *Can Cath Rev* 11:2-3 Ap 1993
What King James has to say about the new lectionary [editorial]. *Can Cath Rev* 11:2-3 Mr 1993
The written word in an aural age. *Can Cath Rev* 11:4-6 Ja 1993

Callan, Terrance.
The background of the Apostolic Decree. *CBQ* 55:284-297 Ap 1993

Calvert, Brian.
Aquinas on punishment and the death penalty. *Amer J Juris* 37:259-281 1992

Camacho, Fernando. *see* Mateos, Juan, jt auth

Camacho, Ildefonso.
Atividade humana e trabalho na sociedade moderna: uma aproximação ética. *Perspectiva* 25:45-62 Ja-Ap 1993
Review of: *La Encíclica "centesimus annus" en la nueva evangelización de América Latina* by Antoncich, Ricardo. In: *Perspectiva* 24:406-407 S-D 1992

Cameli, Louis J.
Preaching and teaching sexuality: the dilemmas and possibilities. *Chicago Stud* 32:54-63 Ap 1993
Times of violence, dreams of peace. *Priest* 49:12-18 Mr 1993

Cameron, A.
Review of: *Holy city, holy places: Christian attitudes to Jerusalem and the Holy Land in the fourth century* by Walker, Peter W L. In: *Heythrop* 34:114-116 Ja 1993

Cameron, Michael.
Group scripture study in the parish. *BibleT* 31:238-243 Jl 1993

Cameron, Peter John.
A bridge between knowing truth and acting on it. *Register* 69:1+ Mr 21 1993
The cloud of unknowing: learning to love Him alone. *Register* 69:1+ N 14 1993
The "Confessions:" a sinner's diary. *Register* 69:1+ O 31 1993
Penance is more than penalty: it's the wellspring of authentic Christian life. *Register* 69:1+ F 28 1993
A perfect giving of self. *Register* 69:5 O 10 1993
Piety, purity, and Mary Immaculate. *HPR* 93:61-63 My 1993
Seeing sin for what it is. *Register* 69:1+ Mr 14 1993
Sin is a matter of broken relationship, not legalisms. *Register* 69:1+ Mr 7 1993
Tempted? God may be knocking!. *Register* 69:1+ Mr 28 1993
To find real, inner peace, we must wash clean in Christ's blood. *Register* 69:1+ Ap 11 1993

Camiré, Bernard.
Prayer before the Eucharist. *Emmanuel* 99:184-189 My 1993

Camisasca, Massimo.
I seminaristi provenienti dalle nuove realtà aggregative (commentary: *Pastores dabo vobis*). *Seminarium* 32:622-628 O-D 1992

Cammarata, Joan F.
Review of: *Teresa of Avila and the rhetoric of femininity* by Weber, Alison. In: *CrossCurr* 43:113-114 Spr 1993

Campbell, Charles M.
Review of: *Reawakenings* by Keating, Thomas. In: *St Anth* 100:53 Mr 1993

Campbell, Courtney S.
Religion and the moral meaning of euthanasia. *Linacre* 59:15-28 N 1992
What price parenthood?: ethics and assisted reproduction. Brookfield: Ashgate Publishing Company, 1992. 127p ISBN 1-8552-1224-2

Campbell, Dwight P.
The Holy Spirit and Mary. *HPR* 93:12-23 My 1993

Campbell, James.
Review of: *A new handbook of Christian theology* by Musser, Donald W, and Price, Joseph L, eds. In: *Month* 26:34 Ja 1993
Review of: *A snail in my prime* by Durcan, Paul. In: *Month* 26:381 S-O 1993
Review of: *A use of gifts: the Newman Association 1942-1992*. In: *Month* 26:80 F 1993
Review of: *Basic is beautiful* by Hebblethwaite, Margaret, 1951-. In: *Month* 26:235-236 Je 1993
Review of: *Christian faith and the world economy today: a study document from the World Council of Churches*. In: *Month* 26:80 F 1993
Review of: *Equal partners? Theological training and racial justice* by Patel, Raj, et al. In: *Month* 26:34 Ja 1993
Review of: *How I pray* by Wilkins, John, ed. In: *Month* 26:381 S-O 1993
Review of: *I have my doubts: how to become a Christian without being a fundamentalist* by Kuitert, H M. In: *Month* 26:149 Ap 1993
Review of: *Knowing Jesus* by Alison, James. In: *Month* 26:198 My 1993
Review of: *May the Lord in his mercy be kind to Belfast* by Parker, Tony. In: *Month* 26:275 Jl 1993
Review of: *Ragman and other cries of faith* by Wanger, Walter. In: *Month* 26:381 S-O 1993
Review of: *Religion and culture in a dialogue* by Lane, Dermot A, ed. In: *Month* 26:381 S-O 1993
Review of: *Religion in public life* by Cohn-Sherbok, Dan, and McLellan, David. In: *Month* 26:114 Mr 1993
Review of: *Roget's thesaurus of the Bible* by Day, A Colin. In: *Month* 26:34 Ja 1993
Review of: *Silent lamp: the Thomas Merton story* by Shannon, William Henry, 1917-. In: *Month* 26:198 My 1993
Review of: *Teresa of Avila* by O'Brien, Kate. In: *Month* 26:381 S-O 1993
Review of: *The Catholic fact book* by Deedy, John G, 1933-. In: *Month* 26:34 Ja 1993
Review of: *The concise dictionary of early Christianity* by Kelly, Joseph F. In: *Month* 26:236 Je 1993
Review of: *The fount book of prayer* by Weyer, Robert Van de. In: *Month* 26:236 Je 1993
Review of: *The placing of T S Eliot* by Brooker, Jewel Spears, ed. In: *Relig Lit* 24:107-108 Aut 1992
Review of: *The Satanic verses: Bradford resonds* by Bowen, David G, ed. In: *Month* 26:322 Ag 1993
Review of: *The use of memory* by Burns, Tom G. In: *Month* 26:198 My 1993
Review of: *Verbum caro: an encyclopedia on Jesus the Christ* by Carroll, Michael O. In: *Month* 26:236 Je 1993
Review of: *What is God like?* by Schall, James Vincent, 1928-. In: *Month* 26:149 Ap 1993
Review of: *What will give us happiness?* by Poupard, Paul, Cardinal, 1930-. In: *Month* 26:80 F 1993

Campbell, Joe.
Review of: *A time to choose life: women, abortion, and human rights* by Gentles, Ian, ed. In: *Can Cath Rev* 11:26 F 1993
Review of: *Breach of trust/breach of faith: child sexual abuse in the Church and society*. In: *Can Cath Rev* 11:30-31 My 1993
Review of: *From pain to hope*. In: *Can Cath Rev* 11:30-31 My 1993
Review of: *Human sexuality: a Catholic perspective for education and life-long learning*. In: *Can Cath Rev* 11:30-31 My 1993

Campbell, Michael.
The high price of spiritual complacency. *New Cov* 23:11 N 1993

Campbell, Patrick J.
Review of: *Fr Mathew and the Irish temperance movement 1838-1849* by Kerrigan, Colm. In: *Furrow* 43:703-704 D 1992
Review of: *The victory of the cross* by O'Grady, Desmond. In: *Furrow* 44:123 F 1993

Campbell, Peter.
Antitrust and IDNs: how far can we go? *Health Prog* 74:54-55+ 1993
Review of: *Health care and antitrust law* by Miles, John J. In: *Health Prog* 74:68-69 My 1993 see Morrisey, Frank, jt auth

Campbell-Johnson, Michael.
Review of: *Popular voices in Latin American Catholicism* by Levine, Daniel H. In: *Month* 26:379-380 S-O 1993

Campbell-Johnston, Michael.
Review of: *The eye of the storm* by Leech, Kenneth, 1939-. In: *Tablet* 247:110 Ja 23 1993

Camping, Harold.
1944. New York: Vantage Press, 1992. x, 551p ISBN 0-533-10368-1 LC 92-90269

Campion, Owen F.
Abortion victimizes all. *OSV* 81:10 F 7 1993
Archbishop James P Lyke: 1939-1992 [obit]. *OSV* 81:3 Ja 10 1993
Confronting depression. *OSV* 82:10 My 16 1993
A look at the worldwide Catholic press. *OSV* 81:8 F 28 1993
Racism: a problem we must address. *Priest* 49:3 O 1993

Campolina Martins, Antonio Henrique.
Review of: *Caminhos de Minas: apresentação de Francisco Iglésias* by Martins, Sebastião. In: *REB* 53:238-239 Mr 1993

Campolo, Tony.
The church and the American teenager: what works and doesn't work in youth ministry. Grand Rapids: Zondervan Publishing House, 1993. x, 224p ISBN 0-310-52471-7

Camps, Victoria.
Paradojas del individualismo. Barcelona: Critica, 1993. x, 201p ISBN 84-7423-591-x

Canada, Allie C.
The living water will quench your thirst. New York: Vantage Press, 1993. x, 74p ISBN 0-533-10338-x LC 92-90826

Canavan, Francis, 1917-.
Apostle of religious freedom [adapted fr *John Courtney Murray and the American civil conversation*]. *Crisis* 11:31-35 My 1993
The sexual revolution, explained. *New Oxford Rev* 60:21-24 N 1993

Candon, Cyprian.
Review of: *Being a priest today* by Goergen, Donald J, ed. In: *Doctr Life* 43:375-376 Jl-Ag 1993

Canévet, Mariette.
Culture païenne et foi chrétienne aux racines de l'Europe: La Cité de Dieu d'Augustin. *Gregorianum* 74 No 1:5-16 1993

Cann, Lorraine, and Quinette, Nancy.
Our parade of saints. *ReligTJ* 27:12-13 O 1993

Cannon, Howard.
Review of: *Gregory the Gret: the life of Saint Benedict*. In: *Word Sp* 15:105-106 1993
Review of: *Saint Benedict, a Rule for beginners* by Stead, Julian. In: *Word Sp* 15:105-106 1993

Cannuyer, Christian.
Review of: *Juifs et chrétiens d'hier à demain* by Yohanan, Frère. In: *MSR* 50:154-156 Ap-Je 1993
Review of: *The Babi and Baha'i religions: from messianic shicism to a world religion* by Smith, Peter. In: *MSR* 50:156-157 Ap-Je 1993

Cànopi, Anna Maria.
Man and woman are loved by the Lord and desired for one another. *OR(Eng)* 1300:10+ Jl 21 1993

Canosa, James F, and Lewandowski, Leonard M.
Linking individual and organizational wellness. *Health Prog* 74:44-47 1993

Cansi, Bernardo.
A catequese e as CEBs. *REB* 52:894-902 D 1992
A catequese em 1992. *REB* 52:937-946 D 1992
Como ressoou a catequese na 30a AG da CNBB (1992). *REB* 52:928-936 D 1992

Cantalamessa, Raniero.
Easter in the early church: an anthology of Jewish and early Christian texts. Collegeville: The Liturgical, 1993. x, 254p ISBN 0-8146-2164-3 LC 92-43999
The Eucharist, our sanctification. Minnesota: The Order of St Benedict, 1993. x, 89p ISBN 0-8146-2075-2 LC 92-404-433

Canton, Donald R.
Simple prayers, common miracles. *Living Prayer* 26:9-12 My-Je 1993
When the Spirit sweeps over the waters. *Living Prayer* 26:10-14 Ja-F 1993

Cantor, Norman F.
The end of Zionism. *Comm* 120:11-13 N 19 1993

Canty, Anne P.
Singles in the Church of the nineties. *Liguorian* 81:30-34 Ja 1993

Capaldi, Gerard I.
Confirmation: what is there to celebrate? *Month* 26:160-164 Ap 1993

Capizzi, Carmelo.
La meritata fortuna di una collana di "testi-patristici". *Civilta* 144:459-467 Mr 6 1993
Review of: *Acta Eugenii papae IV (1431-1447) e Vaticanis aliisque regestis collegit notisque illustravit* by Fedalto, Giorgio. In: *Civilta* 144:193-194 Ja 16 1993
Review of: *Alle origini di Soriano Calabro* by Ferrari, Giuseppe. In: *Civilta* 144:410-411 F 20 1993
Review of: *Basilica Patriarcale in Venezia San Marco: I mosaici; vol I*. In: *Civilta* 3:329-330 Ag 7-21 1993
Review of: *Calabria bizantina: testimonianze d'arte e strutture di territori*. In: *Civilta* 143:538-539 D 5 1992
Review of: *Descrizione Topografica dello Stato Presente di Costantinopoli arricchita di figure* by Carbognano, Cosimo Comidas De. In: *Civilta* 2:97-98 Ap 3 1993
Review of: *Dizionario della lingua italiana* by Palazzi, Fernando, and Folena, Gianfranco. In: *Civilta* 2:194-195 Ap 17 1993
Review of: *Il primato del vescovo di Roma nel primo millennio: Ricerche e testimonianze: Atti del Symposium storico-teologico, Roma 9-13 ottobre 1989* by Maccarone, Michele, ed. In: *Civilta* 144:407-408 F 20 1993

Capizzi, Carmelo. *(cont'd)*
Review of: *La Certosa di S Stefano del Bosco a Serra S Bruno* by Gritella, Gianfranco. In: *Civilta* 3:321-322 Ag 7-21 1993
Review of: *La fiera dei ricordi: Cortometraggi su Mussomeli e mussomelesi* by Giannino, Alfonso. In: *Civilta* 2:618-619 Je 19 1993
Review of: *Rufino di Concordia tra Oriente e Occidente* by Fedalto, Giorgio. In: *Civilta* 143:636 D 19 1992
Review of: *Va e grida: le prediche del Ven. Domenico Lentini* by Cantisani, Antonio. In: *Civilta* 3:324-325 Ag 7-21 1993
Il 75 annniversario del Pontificio Istituto Orientale. *Civilta* 144:158-164 Ja 16 1993

Capon, Robert Farrar.
The mystery of Christ and why we don't get it. Grand Rapids: Eerdmans, 1993. 192p ISBN 0-8028-0121-8

Capps, Donald.
The depleted self: sin in a narcissistic age. Minneapolis: Fortress Press, 1993. x, 176p ISBN 0-80062-587-0 LC 92-7931

Caprile, Giovanni.
Il celibato sacerdotale al sinodo Dei Vescovi 1990 (Commentary) *Pastores Dabo Vobis. Civilta* 143:488-501 D 5 1992
In difesa dei diritti del bambino. *Civilta* 144:165-172 Ja 16 1993
Review of: *Aborto e Politica* by Schooyans, Michel. In: *Civilta* 3:204-205 Jl 17 1993
Review of: *Bibliografia della Massoneria in Italia* by Simoni, Enrico. In: *Civilta* 3:95 Jl 3 1993
Review of: *Chiesa e sport: Un percorso etico* by Mazza, Carlo, ed. In: *Civilta* 144:206 Ja 16 1993
Review of: *De Gasperi e la scelta occidentale: La strategia del Centrismo; Vol; XVV: 1950-1953.* In: *Civilta* 143:531-532 D 5 1992
Review of: *Dieci comandamenti* by John Paul II, Pope, 1920- (Karol Wojtyla) (elected 1978). In: *Civilta* 2:305-306 My 1 1993
Review of: *Documenti Pontifici sullo scautismo* by Morello, Giovanni, and Pieri, Francesco. In: *Civilta* 144:207 Ja 16 1993
Review of: *Enchiridion Vaticanum, vol 12.* In: *Civilta* 144:415-416 F 20 1993
Review of: *Gennaro, il Santo di Napoli* by Grieco, Gianfranco, and Del Preite, Mariano. In: *Civilta* 3:323 Ag 7-21 1993
Review of: *Homo imago et amicus Dei.* In: *Civilta* 2:614-615 Je 19 1993
Review of: *I congressi Eucaristici Internazionali per una nuova evangelizzazione* by Pratzner, Ferdinand, ed. In: *Civilta* 143:638 D 19 1992
Review of: *I rapporti tra i cattolici e gli ortodossi nella Bosnia ed Erzegovina dal 1878 al 1903: uno studio storico-teologico* by Vukšić, Tomo. In: *Civilta* 2:298-299 My 1 1993
Review of: *Il cardinale Pericle Felici.* In: *Civilta* 3:95-96 Jl 3 1993
Review of: *Il caso Lefebvre* by Perrin, Luc. In: *Civilta* 143:434-435 N 21 1992
Review of: *Il Centrismo dopo De Gasperi: Da Pella a Loli; Vol XVIII, 1959-1963.* In: *Civilta* 143:531-532 D 5 1992
Review of: *Il Centrismo: Apogeo e caduta di DeGasperi Vol XVII: 1954-1958.* In: *Civilta* 143:531-532 D 5 1992
Review of: *Il Figlio dell'Uomo* by Cascioli, Lino. In: *Civilta* 143:642 D 19 1992
Review of: *Il mondo di Giovanni Paolo II* by Frossard, André. In: *Civilta* 3:101 Jl 3 1993
Review of: *Il Parlamento italiano 1861-198, vol XV: 1948-1949.* In: *Civilta* 143:531-532 D 5 1992
Review of: *Il Presepe napoletano* by Piccoli Catello, Marisa. In: *Civilta* 143:636 D 19 1992
Review of: *Il vento che li portò a Gaeta* by Capobianco, Paolo. In: *Civilta* 3:93 Jl 3 1993
Review of: *Insegnamenti di Giovanni Paolo II, vol XIII, 2 parts.* In: *Civilta* 2:616 Je 19 1993
Review of: *Interventi nella Commissione Centrale Preparatoria del Concilio Ecumenico Vaticano II (gennaio-Giugno 1962)* by Montini, Giovanni Battista. In: *Civilta* 3:317 Ag 7-21 1993
Review of: *L'amministrazione communale di Cuneo dal Settecento ai giorni nostri* by Mola, Aldo A. In: *Civilta* 3:102-103 Jl 3 1993
Review of: *L'islàm fra noi: conoscere una realtà vicina e lontana* by Ianari, Vittorio, ed. In: *Civilta* 144:517-518 Mr 6 1993
Review of: *La crisi jugoslava: Posizione e azione della Santa Sede (1991-1992).* In: *Civilta* 143:434 N 21 1992
Review of: *La diocesi di Roma 1991-92.* In: *Civilta* 143:640-641 D 19 1992
Review of: *La Franc-Maçonnerie italienne devant la guerre et devant le fascisme* by Rygier, Maria. In: *Civilta* 143:537-538 D 5 1992
Review of: *La Massoneria oggi* by Benimeli, José A Ferrer, and Mola, Aldo A, eds. In: *Civilta* 2:207 Ap 17 1993
Review of: *La Salette* by Stern, Jean. In: *Civilta* 143:544-545 D 5 1992
Review of: *Lettere dalla Sicilia a S Alfonso* by Giammusso, Salvatore. In: *Civilta* 143:539-540 D 5 1992
Review of: *Libero pensiero e Massoneria* by Álvarez Lázaro, Pedro. In: *Civilta* 2:610-611 Je 19 1993
Review of: *Maria nel pensiero dei Padri della Chiesa* by Gambero, Luigi. In: *Civilta* 144:202-203 Ja 16 1993
Review of: *Maria, stella sul nostro commino* by Magrassi, Mariano. In: *Civilta* 3:201-202 Jl 17 1993
Review of: *Monasteri italiani* by Bosi, Roberto. In: *Civilta* 3:101-102 Jl 3 1993
Review of: *Parole feriali* by Fanti, Aldo. In: *Civilta* 3:201-202 Jl 17 1993
Review of: *Paul VI et la vie internationale.* In: *Civilta* 3:327-328 Ag 7-21 1993
Review of: *Per conoscere l'islàm: Cristiani e musulmani nel mondo di oggi* by Liegro, Luigi Di, and Pittau, Franco. In: *Civilta* 144:413-414 F 20 1993
Review of: *Per la storia del monastero di Santa Chiara in Napoli* by Dell'Aja, Gaudenzio. In: *Civilta* 3:94 Jl 3 1993
Review of: *Per me vivere è Cristo* by Magrassi, Mariano. In: *Civilta* 3:201-202 Jl 17 1993
Review of: *Pompei città non città* by Maggi, Giuseppe. In: *Civilta* 2:617-618 Je 19 1993
Review of: *Posso darti del tu, Signore? Note di Catechesi sulla preghiera, vol I* by Quattrocchi, Paolino Beltrame. In: *Civilta* 2:198-199 Ap 17 1993
Review of: *Pregare per le vocazioni* by Sapienza, Leonardo. In: *Civilta* 2:199-200 Ap 17 1993

Caprile, Giovanni. *(cont'd)*
Review of: *Preghiere di marito e moglie.* In: *Civilta* 2:198-199 Ap 17 1993
Review of: *Quando Karol aveva 18 anni.* In: *Civilta* 2:612-613 Je 19 1993
Review of: *Quel che passava il convento: Tavola e cucina dei monasteri femminili nei secoli XVI-XVIII in Romagna* by Zannini, Gian Ludovico Masetti. In: *Civilta* 144:205-206 Ja 16 1993
Review of: *Ritrovare le radici* by Baracco, Lino. In: *Civilta* 2:198-199 Ap 17 1993
Review of: *San Ignacio de Loyola por dentro* by Arnaiz, Francisco. In: *Civilta* 2:612 Je 19 1993
Review of: *Signore Gesù insegnami a pregare. Corso di preghiera personale in sette settimane* by Rooney, Lucy, and Faricy, Robert. In: *Civilta* 2:198-199 Ap 17 1993
Review of: *Souvenirs et espérances* by Suenens, Leo Jozef, Cardinal, 1904-. In: *Civilta* 3:91-92 Jl 3 1993
Review of: *Un cartografo in età barocca* by Spagnolo, Gilberto. In: *Civilta* 3:94-95 Jl 3 1993
Review of: *Un'amicizia massonica: Carteggio Lemmi-Carducci con documenti inediti* by Pipino, Cristina. In: *Civilta* 2:101 Ap 3 1993
Review of: *Una difficile transizione Verso il Centro-Sinistra.* In: *Civilta* 143:531-532 D 5 1992
Review of: *Vangelo secondo Rembrandt* by Baudiquey, Paul. In: *Civilta* 3:328-329 Ag 7-21 1993

Carabine, Deirdre.
Review of: *The philosophical theology of St Thomas Aquinas* by Elders, Leo J. In: *IJPS* 1:164 Mr 1993

Carballo, Suzanne M. *see* Araujo, Marianne D, jt auth

Carbonell De Masy, Rafael.
Review of: *La contabilidad en las Reducciones guaranies* by Blumes, Teresa. In: *Gregorianum* 74 no 3:592 1993

Carcia Calvo, Agustin.
Contra el tiempo. Zamora: Lucina, 1993. x, 302p ISBN 84-85708-5

Cardedal, Olegario González de.
Development of a theology of the local church from the first to the Second Vatican Council. *Jurist* 52 no 1:11-42 1992

Cárdenas, Cuauhtémoc.
Outsider who would be Mexican president [interview by Arthur Jones]. *Nat Cath Rep* 29:12-13 Jl 30 1993

Cardenas, P Eduardo.
Los seminarios Iberoamericanos en el período Hispano-Portuges. *Seminarium* 32:369-403 Jl-S 1992

Carelli, Rocco. *see* Fizzotti, Eugenio, jt auth

Carew, Wally.
The bishop was a football hero. *Priest* 49:31-32 Ap 1993

Carey, Ann.
Bishops and politicans: a sensitive situation. *OSV* 81:3 Ap 25 1993
Canada's Flying Fathers. *OSV* 81:20 Ja 3 1993
Controversy continues over church renovations. *OSV* 82:17 Ag 8 1993
If you ask them, they will come. *OSV* 82:18 O 10 1993
In the heartland, Catholic sexuality celebrated [commentary Humanae Vitae]. *OSV* 82:3 Ag 15 1993
Humanae Vitae, on the regulation of birth [1968 07 27].
Kindling Christ's light of hope in the poor. *OSV* 82:5 N 14 1993
New charismatic leader has two crosses to bear. *OSV* 82:17 Je 27 1993
Notre Dame debates need for Catholic faculty. *OSV* 82:3 Je 13 1993
Religious orders: defining their role in the church. *OSV* 82:17 Jl 11 1993
Rumors of the nuns' demise are premature. *OSV* 82:6 O 10 1993
A season of soul-searching for pro-lifers. *OSV* 82:6-7 O 3 1993
An unique ministry in Michigan. *OSV* 82:21 My 16 1993
Untangling the Latin Mass controversy. *OSV* 81:12-13 Mr 7 1993
Utah bishop asks Rome to halt hospitals' sale [photos]. *OSV* 82:3 N 28 1993

Carey, George Leonard, Abp of Canterbury, 1935-.
Conversation with God. *Tablet* 247:238-240 F 20 1993
The gate of glory. Grand Rapids: Eerdmans, 1993. 256p ISBN 0-8028-3724-7

Carey, Michael, and Cole, Basil.
Pastores Dabo Vobis and priestly formation [pt 1]. *Priest* 49:10-18 Jl 1993
Patores Dabo Vobis [pt 2]. *Priest* 49:33-43 Ag 1993

Carey, Patrick W.
The Roman Catholics. Westport: Greenwood Press, 1993. x, 375p ISBN 0-313-25439-7 LC 93-20125

Cargas, Harry James.
Gypsies in terror as European fascism grows. *Nat Cath Rep* 29:24 N 13 1992

Carigman, Dean M.
Tolerating Sinéad. *Crisis* 10:5-6 N 1992

Carignan, Dean M.
Review of: *Can't we make moral judgements?* by Midgley, Mary. In: *Crisis* 10:53-54 D 1992

Carlin, David Robert, Jr, 1938-.
Abortion, gay rights and the social contract. *America* 168:6-10 F 27 1993
Bishops and generals institutional identities. *Comm* 120:9-10 Ja 15 1993
From ghetto to hilltop: our colleges, our selves. *Comm* 120:6-7 F 12 1993
Going, going, gone: the diminution of the self. *Comm* 120:6-7 S 10 1993
Lessons from November. *Comm* 119:7-8 D 18 1992
Let them eat cake: a love letter to multiculturalists. *Comm* 120:9-10 Ap 23 1993
O core mia the first Nixon prize. *Comm* 120:9-10 Je 18 1993
Paying for abortion. *America* 169:6-10 N 20 1993
Searching for the soap: coming clean on gays in the military. *Comm* 120:11-12 Ap 9 1993
Single-parenthood is okay! And experience says the earth is flat. *Comm* 120:8-9 O 22 1993
They call themselves liberals. *Comm* 120:8-9 F 26 1993
They've stolen my name. *Comm* 120:7-9 Ag 13 1993

Carlini, G.
Review of: *La biblioteca dei cappuccini di Livorno* by Laurentini, Giuliano. In: *Civilta* 3:320-321 Ag 7-21 1993

Carlisle, Thomas John.
Looking for Jesus. Grand Rapids: Eerdmans, 1993. 180p ISBN 0-8028-0667-8

Carlson, Jeffrey.
"Syncretistic religiosity": the significance of the tautology. *JEcumen Stds* 29:24-34 Wint 1992

Carmody, Denise Lardner.
Christian resources for feminist spirituality. *Stud Form Spir* 14:207-217 My 1993
Mythological woman: contemporary reflections on ancient religious stories. New York: The Crossroad Publishing Company, 1992. x, 160p ISBN 0-8245-1217-0 LC 92-26086 *see* Carmody, John Tully, jt auth

Carmody, Denise Lardner, and Carmody, John Tully.
Native American religions: an introduction. Mahwah: Paulist, 1993. 270p ISBN 0-8091-3404-7 LC 93-15547

Carmody, John Tully.
Conversations with dying friends [interview by Mitchel B Finley]. *OSV* 81:6-7 Mr 28 1993
Death as a hermeneutic. *Horizons (CTS)* 20:115-117 Spr 1993
How to handle trouble. New York: Doubleday, 1993. x, 226p ISBN 0-385-47120-3 LC 93-16848
Review of: *Fullness of faith* by Himes, Michael J, and Himes, Kenneth R. In: *Nat Cath Rep* 29:19 Jl 30 1993
Review of: *The wild man's journey: reflections on male spirituality* by Rohr, Richard, 1943-, and Martos, Joseph. In: *Horizons (CTS)* 20:167-168 Spr 1993 *see* Carmody, Denise Lardner, jt auth

Carneiro de Andrade, Paulo Fernando.
A condição pós-moderna como desafio à pastoral popular. *REB* 53:99-113 Mr 1993

Carota, Estelle, and Carota, Mario.
Teach anew that interest is immoral. *Cath Work* 60:3 Ag 1993

Carota, Mario. *see* Carota, Estelle, jt auth

Carotta, Mike.
The Bishops' Symposium on the Catechism. *Momentum* 24:70 S-O 1993

Carpenter, David.
Revelation in comparative perspective: lessons for interreligious dialogue. *JEcumen Stds* 29:175-188 Spr 1992
Review of: *Hinduism and Christianity* by Brockington, J L. In: *TheolStds* 54:607-608 S 1993

Carr, David.
Review of: *Announcements of Plot in Genesis* by Turner, Laurence A. In: *CBQ* 55:133-134 Ja 1993

Carr, William F.
Living wills and religious communities. *Linacre* 60:72-77 My 1993

Carraro, Robert J.
To arm or not to arm: rethinking the constitution. *Comm* 120:5-6 F 26 1993

Carrier, Hervé.
Nuova evangelizzazione e dottrina sociale della chiesa. *Civilta* 144:116-130 Ja 16 1993

Carro Celada, Esteban. *see* Palmero Ramos, Rafael, jt auth

Carroll, Denis.
Review of: *Creation and history* by Trigo, Pedro. In: *Furrow* 44:385-386 Je 1993
Review of: *Reconciliation. Essays in honour of Michael Hurley* by Rafferty, Oliver, ed. In: *Furrow* 44:514-515 S 1993
Review of: *The analogy between God and the world in St Thomas Aquinas and Karl Barth* by Chavannes, Henry. In: *Furrow* 44:256-258 Ap 1993

Carroll, Eamon R.
A survey of recent Mariology. *Marian Stds* 43:160-189 1992

Carroll, Elizabeth.
La casa de la Mujer: symbol of hope. *Sisters* 65:162-164 My 1993

Carroll, L Patrick.
A pastor's holiday. *America* 169:14+ Ag 28-S 4 1993

Carroll, Sidney. *see* Inhaber, Herbert, jt auth

Carroll, William E.
Ad limina apostolorum. *Can Cath Rev* 11:33-34 My 1993
Biology, parents, and the law. *Can Cath Rev* 11:34-35 N 1993
Five signatures. *Can Cath Rev* 11:33-34 Mr 1993
A license to kill. *Can Cath Rev* 11:33-35 Ap 1993
Nature, culture, and the Church. *Can Cath Rev* 11:44-47 Ja 1993
Two cultures. *Can Cath Rev* 11:33-35 O 1993

Carrón, Julián.
The second commandment in the New Testament: your yes is yes, your no is no. *Communio* 20:5-25 Spr 1993

Carson, D A.
New Testament commentary survey. Grand Rapids: Baker Book House, 1993. 92p ISBN 0-80102-579-6 LC 93-12051

Cartaxo Rolim, Francisco.
Pentecostalismo, governos militares e revolução. *REB* 53:324-348 Je 1993

Carter, David.
Legitimacy of development within the apostolic tradition. *OChr* 29 no 3:226-234 1993

Carter, Nancy Corson.
Martha, Mary, and Jesus: weaving action and contemplation in daily life. Minnesota: The Order of St Benedict, 1992. x, 134p ISBN 0-8146-2119-8 LC 92-23586

Carter, Paul. *see* Highfield, Roger, jt auth

Carter, Stephen L.
Stuck with a Satanist? religious autonomy in a regulated society [exc fr *The culture of disbelief*]. *Comm* 120:15-18 Ag 13 1993

Carter, Sydney.
Lovely in the dances. *Tablet* 247:1097 Ag 28 1993
Notebook and candles. *Tablet* 247:465-466 Ap 10-17 1993

Carter, Sydney. *(cont'd)*
Review of: *Noel and Cole: the sophisticates* by Citron, Stephen. In: *Tablet* 247:891 Jl 10 1993

Carter, Warren.
The crowds in Matthew's Gospel. *CBQ* 55:54-67 Ja 1993

Carville, John.
Priestly poverty. *Priest* 49:17-18 O 1993

Cary, Diana Serra.
My friend the tin woodman. *CDgst* 57:106-111 O 1993

Casaldáliga, Pedro, Bp, 1928-.
On the road to Emmaus in the neoliberal twilight [fr *Utopias (Colombia)*]. *LADOC* 24:5-9 S-O 1993
Pelo caminho del Emaús Neste Crepúsculo neoliberal. *REB* 53:397-408 Je 1993
The poor and God we have always with us [fr *Crie*]. *LADOC* 24:25-28 N-D 1993
Por el camino de emaus en este atardecer neoliberal. *Christus* 58:66-73 Mr-Ap 1993
Promoção dos Valores éticos: (PRonunciamento da 31a Assembléia Geral da CNBB, Itaici, SP). *REB* 53:390-396 Je 1993

Casalegno, Alberto.
Exorcismo, evangelização e reino nos escritos Lucanos. *Perspectiva* 25:63-76 Ja-Ap 1993

Casanovas, Domingo.
Teoria del conocimiento. Barcelona: Universitat Autonoma de Barcelona, 1993. x, 237p ISBN 84-7929-656-9

Casanovas, J.
Review of: *Galileo la Chiesa, ossia il diritto ad errare* by Brandmüller, Walter. In: *Civilta* 3:310-311 Ag 7-21 1993

Casarella, Peter.
Experience as a theological category: Hans Urs von Balthasar on the Christian encounter with God's image. *Communio* 20:118-128 Spr 1993

Casebolt, Carl J. *see* Robb, Carol S, jt ed

Caserta, Thomas G.
Beyond the darkness, into the light: thinking about sin and forgiveness today. Boston: St Paul Books & Media, 1993. 67p ISBN 0-8198-1142 LC 93-19167

Casey, Gerard.
Review of: *Aristotle's first principles* by Irwin, T H. In: *IJPS* 1:166-167 Mr 1993
Review of: *Educating the virtues* by Carr, David. In: *IJPS* 1:163 Mr 1993
Review of: *Logical forms* by Sainsbury, Mark. In: *IJPS* 1:168 Mr 1993

Casey, Michael.
Review of: *Spirit of the world: the moral basis of Christian spirituality* by Brown, Neil. In: *Pacifica* 6:224-225 Je 1993

Casey, Robert P, 1932-.
Children first, before and after birth. *Origins* 22:696-699 Mr 18 1993
Dred Scott, again. *Crisis* 11:16-23 Ap 1993

Casey, Stephen J.
Review of: *Social Catholicism in Europe: from the onset of industrialization to the First World War* by Misner, Paul. In: *Horizons (CTS)* 20:151-152 Spr 1993
Review of: *Technology, theology, and the idea of progress* by Hopper, David H. In: *Horizons (CTS)* 19:341-342 Fall 1992

Casey, Thomas F.
Review of: *From generation to generation II: stories in Catholic history from the archives of the Archdiocese of Boston* by Patkus, Ronald D, ed. In: *CHist* 79:575-576 Jl 1993

Cashford, Jules. *see* Baring, Anne, jt auth

Casper, Kathryn.
Review of: *Woman, why do you weep? Spirituality for survivors of childhood sexual abuse* by Flaherty, Sandra M. In: *Sisters* 65:221-222 My 1993

Cassady, Marsh. *see* Sturkie, Joan, jt auth

Casserly, Bernard.
The time of our lives. *Columbia* 73:9 S 1993

Cassian, Johannes.
Gott Suchen sich Selbst Erkennen. Freiburg: Herder, 1993. x, 480p ISBN 3-451-23246-4

Cassidy, Edward Idris, 1924-, Cardinal.
Der päpstliche rat zur Förderung der Einheit der Christen im Jahre 1992. *Catholica* 47 no 2:89-107 1993

Cassidy, Edward Idris, Cardinal, 1924-.
The measure of Catholic ecumenical commitment. *Origins* 23:736-744 Ap 8 1993
The Pontifical Council for Promoting Christian Unity in 1992. *OChr* 29 no 3:199-215 1993
Principles and norms of ecumenism. *TPS* 38:321 N-D 1993

Cassidy, Joseph, Abp, 1933-.
Welcome to Mother Teresa [homily given June 5, 1993]. *Furrow* 44:395-398 Jl-Ag 1993

Cassidy, Judy.
Network unites payers, physicians, hospitals. *Health Prog* 74:18-21 My 1993
Two collaborative organizations improve care delivery. *Health Prog* 74:22-23+ Mr 1993

Cassidy, Judy, ed.
Beyond the paradigm. *Health Prog* 74:28-40 Ap 1993
Tradition and transformation, by A Arghittu, et al. Sponsorship networks, by V. Gillis. Mission integration preserves sponsor's values, by J Keith.
[Death and dying]. *Health Prog* 74:34-51 Mr 1993
Contents: Care of the dying: a Catholic perspective (Part I), by CHA. Why we should not legalize euthanasia, by M Place. Does compassion include euthanasia?, by N Hooyman. Decision tree, by T Meeker.

Cassidy, Judy, ed. *(cont'd)*
Nursing in a new context. *Health Prog* 74:21-45+ Je 1993
Creating the future, by M D Araujo. Retaining nurses through conflict resolution, by A R Fowler, Jr, et al. Returning Gospel values to nursing education, by J A Lane. On the right path, by J London. The pace of change.
Vital options: meeting the elderly's varied needs. *Health Prog* 74:34-52+ My 1993
A blueprint for community benefit, by B Forschner, and J Trocchio. Long-term care survey reveals challenges, by L J Westhoff, and J C Schaeffer. A little help, a lot of independence, by M Paul. A spiritual tool, by R Kerrigan, and J T Harkulich. Autonomy and care for the frail elderly, by P A Szvabo, and J J Stretch.
Wellness: the bridge between body, mind, and spirit. *Health Prog* 74:33-52+ 1993
Wellness in the healing ministry, by B K Burke. Retooling for community benefit, by P A Hattis. Ethical issues of unconventional therapies, by S Callahan. Linking individual and organizational wellness, by J F Canosa, and L M Lewandowski. The value of spiritual health, by L G Seidl. Holistic retreats, by M L Garvin, et al.

Cassidy, Mary.
Review of: *Rekindling the passion* by Jorgensen, Susan S. In: *Furrow* 44:518-519 S 1993

Cassidy, Sheila.
Care of the dying. *Tablet* 247:430-431 Ap 3 1993
Christ the fireman. *Tablet* 247:456+ Ap 10-17 1993
The hospice demystified. *Priests & People* 6:415-422 N 1992
The lure of honey. *Tablet* 247:1068-1069 Ag 21 1993
Return to Chile. *Tablet* 247:6+ Ja 2 1993

Cassiers, Léon.
Quelques questions sur l'éthique en psychiatrie. *Supplement* 184:97-106 Mr-Ap 1993

Casteel, John L.
Review of: *Convergence: a reconciliation of Judaism and Christianity in the life of one woman* by Bruder, Judith. In: *RRel* 52:631-632 Jl-Ag 1993

Castel, Pol.
Reunited with our ancestors. *Cath Work* 60:7 Je-Jl 1993

Castellanos, Nicholas.
Responde la iglesia a los desafios de hoy?: cartas pastorales. Madrid: Grupo Libros, 1993. x, 666p ISBN 84-7906-202-9

Castelli, Ferdinando.
Lo *J'AccuseDi Maurice Chavardès Contro L'Ipocrisia*. *Civilta* 143:376-381 N 21 1992
La letteratura interpella la teologia. *Civilta* 3:247-255 Ag 7-21 1993
Oscar Wilde E Il Suo Cristo Romantico. *Civilta* 144:31-44 Ja 2 1993
Racconta il tuo Dio. *Civilta* 2:563-565 Je 19 1993
Review of: *Fonti di diritto nella perdonanza aquilana* by Cervelli, Amedeo. In: *Civilta* 2:99 Ap 3 1993
Review of: *I Gesuiti e la Calabria. Atti del Convegno: Reggio Calabria, 27-28 febbraio 1991* by Sibilio, Vincenzo. In: *Civilta* 3:547 S 18 1993
Review of: *Racconta il too Dio* by Panzeri, F, and Righetto, R, eds. In: *Civilta* 2:563-565 Je 19 1993
Roman Brandstaetter narratore delle profondità. *Civilta* 2:130-143 Ap 17 1993

Castelli, James.
Abuse of faith. *USCath* 58:6-15 S 1993
The case of Father X. *USCath* 58:12-13 S 1993

Castilla del Pino, Carlos.
La obscenidad. Madrid: Alianza, 1993. x, 156p ISBN 84-206-2744-5

Castillo, Dennis.
"The Knights cannot be admitted": Maltese nationalism, the Knights of St John, and the French occupation of 1798-1800. *CHist* 79:434-453 Jl 1993
The Maltese cross. *Priest* 49:41-43 Je 1993

Castle, Anthony, 1938-.
Vocations in conflict. *Tablet* 247:844-845 Jl 3 1993

Castori, Michael T.
Jacques Maritain and the Jews. *America* 168:18-21 My 29 1993

Castronovo, David.
Review of: *Loose canons* by Gates, Henry Louis, Jr. In: *Comm* 119:22-23 D 18 1992
Review of: *The sixties: the last journal, 1960-72* by Wilson, Edmund. In: *Comm* 120:29-30 O 22 1993

Cataldo, Peter J.
Health decisions or Majoritarian Health Care? *Linacre* 60:70-73 F 1993

Catanzaro, Ana Maria.
Medicines that don't mix [condensed fr *The Catholic Standard and Times* Jl 16 1992]. *CDgst* 57:105-107 F 1993

Catoir, John T.
Father Catoir: "God delights in you" [interview by B Dodds]. *New Cov* 22:9-11 Jl 1993
Prayer made simple. *CDgst* 57:43+ S 1993

Cattaneo, E.
Review of: *Didimo il cieco: Lo Spirito Santo* by Noce, Celestino. In: *Civilta* 144:404-405 F 20 1993

Catucci, Thomas F.
Time with Jesus. Notre Dame: Ave Maria Press, 1993. 158p ISBN 0-87793-499-1 LC 93-71891

Caussade, Jean Pierre de, -1751.
Abandonment to divine providence. New York: Doubleday, 1975. x, 119p ISBN 0-385-24937-3 LC 74-2827

Cavadini, John C.
Review of: *The presence of God: a history of Western Christian mysticism* by McGinn, Bernard John, 1937-. In: *Horizons (CTS)* 20:146-149 Spr 1993

Cavalcanti, Tereza.
Review of: *O segredo feminino do Mistério* by Bingemer, Maria Clara L. In: *REB* 52:1002-1003 D 1992

Cavallo, Jo Ann.
Agricultural imagery in the Gospel of Matthew and the gospel of truth. *Relig Lit* 24:27-38 Aut 1992

Cavanaugh-O'Keefe, John.
Freedom and slavery. *Register* 69:5 Je 11 1993

Cavnar, Cindy.
Damian of Molokai. *New Cov* 22:25+ My 1993
Edith Stein. *New Cov* 22:24 F 1993
Mixed-up in Milan. *New Cov* 23:31 Ag 1993

Cawley, Martinus.
Four abbots of the golden age of Villers. *Cist Stud* 27 No 4:299-327 1992

Cazes, Jo.
Doin' dinosaurs: a schoolwide science project. *Momentum* 24:20-21 S-O 1993

Cechin, Irmão Antônio.
O oitavo encontro intereclesial de CEBs e a ecologia. *REB* 52:856-876 D 1992

Celada, Gregorio.
Proclamación del evangelio en los primeros siglos. *Cien Tom* 120:33-56 Ja-Ap 1993
Review of: *Historia de la teología cristiana, vol III: Siglos XVIII, XIX, XX* by Vilanova, Evangelista. In: *Cien Tom* 120:200-202 Ja-Ap 1993
Review of: *La predicación cristiana antigua* by Olivar, Alexandre. In: *Cien Tom* 119:421-423 My-Ag 1992

Celeada, Gregorio.
Review of: *Diccionario patristico y de la Antigüedad Cristiana*. In: *Cien Tom* 119:418-420 My-Ag 1992

Celeghin, Adriano.
Prelatura personale: problemi e dubbi [2 parts]. *Periodica* 82 no 2:95-138: 82 no 1; 213-256: 82 no 2, 1993
Review of: *Le prelature personali. Profili giurdici* by Castro, Gaetano Lo. In: *Gregorianum* 74 no 2:386-388 1993

Celeste, Marie.
Bernanos: a man of spirit. *Priest* 49:44-46 Je 1993
Elizabeth Ann Seton: a woman of prayer. New York: Alba House, 1993. 134p ISBN 0-8189-0650-2 LC 92-44978

Celio, Mary Beth.
Catholics: who, how many and where? *America* 168:10-14 Ja 2-9 1993

Cerf, Christopher. see Beard, Henry, jt auth

Ceric, Mustafa.
Moslems in Bosnia face a "genocide" [interview by National Catholic Register (Periodical)]. *Register* 69:1+ Ja 3 1993
Save Sarajevo! *Tablet* 247:971 Jl 31 1993

Cermak, John.
Catechesis and the relationship of evangelization to ecumenism. *Living Light* 29:64-68 Wint 1992

Ceronsky, Charles.
Creative models of spiritual care. *Health Prog* 74:58-61 My 1993

Cervo, Nathan.
Entelechy just happens; Chardin and the new filioque. *Spirit* 58:32-34 1993
Sunyatta; On Powder Bridge Road death everlasting' Golgotha; Golden Market Revisited; the Eternal Bustiwaker; The River. *Spirit* 57:10-17 Spr-Sum 1992

Cesareo, Francesco C.
Review of: *Marcello Cervini and ecclesiastical government in Tridentine Italy* by Hudon, William V. In: *CHist* 79:338-339 Ap 1993

Cessario, Romanus.
An observation on Robert Lauder's review of G A McCool, SJ [reply to "On being or not being a Thomist," 55:301-319 by R Lauder]. *Thomist* 56:701-710 O 1992

Chadwick, Graham.
What sort of people do the exercises foster? *Way Suppl* 76:109-116 Spr 1993

Chadwick, Henry.
Local and universal: an Anglican perspective. *Jurist* 52 no 1:509-517 1992
Review of: *One in 2000? Towards Catholic-Orthodox unity: agreed statements and parish papers* by McPartlan, Paul, ed. In: *Tablet* 247:1135-1136 S 4 1993
Review of: *The Eucharist makes the Church: Henri de Lubac and John Zizioulas join in dialogue* by McPartlan, Paul. In: *Tablet* 247:1135-1136 S 4 1993
Review of: *The panther and the hind: a theological history of Anglicanism* by Nichols, Aidan. In: *Tablet* 247:342-343 Mr 13 1993

Chalupa, V.
Review of: *The road from paradise* by Meštrović, Stjepan G, et al. In: *SocJust* 84:154-157 S-O 1993

Chamberlain, Gary.
Converted by the Psalms [exc fr *Liturgy: in spirit and truth*]. *Liturgy* 10:27-28 Spr 1993

Chamberlain, Guy. see Howell, Patrick J, jt ed

Chambers, Francis E.
A priest reflects: walking with the downtrodden. *America* 168:6 Ap 10 1993

Champlin, Dell.
Structural change in US labor markets. *RSocEcon* 51:40-61 Spr 1993

Champlin, Joseph M.
A challenging, accountable financial program. *Church* 9:30-31 Aut 1993

Chandrakanthan, A J V.
Emerging trends in Asian theology. *TheolDgst* 39:339-341 Wint 1992

Chanona, Carolee, et al. see Marins, José, jt auth

Chansky, James D.
Reflections on after virtue after Auschwitz. *PhilosTod* 37:247-256 Aut 1993

Ciappi, M L.
Review of: *Art and the Word of God: arte e la Parola di dio* by Zarlenga, Angelico Rinaldo. In: *Civilta* 144:414-415 F 20 1993

Ciaramelli, Fabio.
Review of: *Filosofie del soggetto e diritto del senso* by Masullo, Aldo. In: *RPhil Louvain* 91:330-333 My 1993

Ciarlò, Canon John. *see* Galea, Michael, jt ed

Ciarrocchi, Joseph W.
A minister's handbook of mental disorders. Mahwah: Paulist, 1993. x, 221p ISBN 0-8091-3403-9 LC 93-11092

Ciarrocchi, Maura.
Seeds of faith. *OSV* 82:5 Je 27 1993
To quench the thirst for knowledge. *OSV* 81:8 Mr 14 1993

Ciferni, A.
Review of: *Sacraments alive: their history, celebration and significance* by DeGidio, Sandra. In: *New Theol Rev* 6:109-111 F 1993

Ciferni, Andrew D, and McMahon, J Michael.
Repertoire and ritual: the communion rite and the eucharistic prayer. *Past Mus* 17:22-27 F-Mr 1993

Cinnici, Rosemary.
Review of: *Generous lives* by Redmont, Jane. In: *America* 168:18-19 Ap 17 1993

Cioppa, John.
Catholics in today's China. *Origins* 22:704-709 Mr 25 1993

Ciotti, Paul.
School choice. *Register* 69:1+ O 31 1993

Cirulli, Carol.
The Church and politics in Texas. *Register* 69:1+ My 30 1993

Citrini, Tullio.
Response to James Provost. *Jurist* 52 no 1:335-339 1992

Civba, Edward J.
Who do you say that I am? New York: Alba House, 1993. 150p ISBN 0-8189-0638-3 LC 92-37734

Clague, Julie.
Review of: *The wisdom of fools?* by Grey, Mary. In: *Tablet* 247:1301-1302 O 9 1993

Clancy, Finbarr G.
Review of: *Beauty and revelation in the thought of Saint Augustine* by Harrison, Carol. In: *Month* 26:197-198 My 1993

Clancy, Paul.
America again a player in population issues. *Nat Cath Rep* 29:3 F 5 1993
Bishops' Bosnia statement stirs DC waters. *Nat Cath Rep* 29:8 My 28 1993
CDF advocates say leave no child behind. *Nat Cath Rep* 29:3 Mr 12 1993
Clinton faces long legacy of substandard housing. *Nat Cath Rep* 29:6 Mr 5 1993
Fired up: Cantonsville files plus nine hearts. *Nat Cath Rep* 29:3 My 21 1993
From arms critic to head of the committee. *Nat Cath Rep* 29:13 Ja 22 1993
Population explosion. *Nat Cath Rep* 29:16-17 My 7 1993

Clancy, Thomas H.
Review of: *John Gee's "Foot out of the snare" (1624)* by Harmsen, T H B M, ed. In: *CHist* 79:113-114 Ja 1993

Claret, Anthony Maria.
Meditation XII-death. *ChrWorld* 38:135-139 Mr-Ap 1993

Clark, Anthony.
Review of: *How adult is adult religious education? Gabriel Moran's contribution to adult religious education* by Devitt, Patrick M. In: *Heythrop* 34: 201-202 Ap 1993

Clark, Cal. *see* Billington, Monroe Lee, 1928-, jt auth

Clark, Douglas Kent.
On "Englishing" the Catechism. *Living Light* 29:13-28 Sum 1993

Clark, Mary T.
Review of: *Augustine's love of wisdom* by Bourke, Vernon J. In: *IPQ* 33:376-377 S 1993
Review of: *Beauty and revelation in the thought of Saint Augustine* by Harrison, Carol. In: *New Blckfrs* 74:283-285 My 1993

Clark, Michael.
Conversion. *Spir Life* 39:6-10 Spr 1993

Clark, Neal, and Ristine, John.
The answer at last. *New Cov* 23:22-24 Ag 1993

Clarke, Kevin.
Actions speak louder than words. *Salt* 13:34-39 N-D 1993
Five threats to a rural way of life. *Salt* 13:6-12 S 1993
Who's hungry now? *Salt* 13:7-12 Mr 1993 *see* Guarino, Mark, jt auth

Clarke, Pauline.
Liturgy: life-blood of a parish. *Priests & People* 7:91-93 Mr 1993
Review of: *Liturgical theology: a primer* by Irwin, Kevin W. In: *Priests & People* 7:251-252 Je 1993
Review of: *The Mass* by Deiss, Lucien. In: *Priests & People* 7:168 Ap 1993

Clarke, Thomas E.
Person and society in the exercises. *Way Suppl* 76:53-60 Spr 1993
Review of: *Prayerful responsibility: prayer and social responsibility in the religious thought of Douglas Steere* by Copenhaver, John D, Jr. In: *Horizons (CTS)* 20:169-170 Spr 1993

Clarke, W Norris.
Person, being, and St Thomas. *Communio* 19:601-618 Wint 1992
Review of: *Plotinus: the experience of unity* by Gurtler, Gary M. In: *IPQ* 33: 123-124 Mr 1993
Review of: *The perfection of the universe according to Aquinas: a theological cosmology* by Blanchette, Oliva. In: *TheolStds* 54:167-168 Mr 1993

Clarot, B.
Review of: *Ainsi priaient les luthériens* by Driancourt-Ginod, J. In: *NRT* 115:613-614 Jl-Ag 1993

Clarot, B. *(cont'd)*
Review of: *J'aime mon Église* by Manaranche, A. In: *NRT* 115:583-584 Jl-Ag 1993
Review of: *Nous avons rendez-vous avec l'Europe* by Lustiger, Jean-Marie, Cardinal, 1926-. In: *NRT* 115:120-121 Ja-F 1993
Review of: *Teologia spirituale* by Bernard, Charles-André, ed. In: *NRT* 115: 133 Ja-F 1993
Review of: *Una vita per l'unita* by Thurian, Max. In: *NRT* 114:937 N-D 1992

Clasby, Nancy.
Dancing Sophia: Rahner's theology of symbols. *Relig Lit* 25:51-65 Spr 1993

Clatworthy, Jonathan.
Progress, evolution and Green theology. *Teilhard Rev* 28:8-10 Spr 1993

Clayton-Lea, Paul.
Review of: *How to teach with the lectionary* by McBrien, Philip J. In: *Furrow* 44:124-125 F 1993
Review of: *Mozart: traces of transcendence* by Küng, Hans, 1928-. In: *Furrow* 44:58 Ja 1993
Review of: *Parish project* by O'Shea, John, et al, eds. In: *Furrow* 44:124-125 F 1993
Review of: *Strategic planning for pastoral ministry* by Balhoff, Michael J. In: *Furrow* 44:124-125 F 1993
Review of: *The Columba lectionary for masses with children—Year B and C* by McEntee, Seán, and Breen, Michael. In: *Furrow* 44:124-125 F 1993
Teenagers and religion—reflections on the green paper. *Furrow* 44:479-484 S 1993

Cleary, Edward L.
Review of: *A violent evangelism: the political and religious conquest of the Americas* by Rivera, Luis N. In: *America* 169:19+ O 23 1993
Review of: *Frontiers of Hispanic theology in the United States* by Deck, Allan Figueroa. In: *America* 169:19+ O 23 1993
Review of: *Latinos* by Shorris, Earl. In: *Comm* 120:23-24 Mr 26 1993
Review of: *The Catholic Church in Peru, 1821-1985* by Klaiber, Jeffrey L. In: *America* 169:19+ O 23 1993

Cleary, W.
Review of: *Free priests* by Powers, William F. In: *Nat Cath Rep* 29:38 F 5 1993

Cleese, John. *see* Skynner, Robin, jt auth

Clement, Shirley F. *see* Braden, Suzanne G, jt auth

Clements, Keith.
Faith and Order pilgrims. *Tablet* 247:1113-1114 Ag 28 1993

Cleve, Emerald.
Untitled; Children in a storm; An azure shadowed room. *Spirit* 58:15-16 1993
Winter journey; New Year's Day; Watching you; Lost Kingdom; The Swans. *Spirit* 57:23-26 Spr-Sum 1992

Cliath, Baile Átha. *see* Ó Riagáin, Pádraig, jt auth

Clifford, Donald.
Through the eyes of children. *ReligTJ* 27:30 Mr 1993

Clifford, Richard J.
Review of: *Amos* by Paul, Shalom M. In: *TheolStds* 53:737-739 D 1992
Review of: *Wisdom and worship* by Davidson, Robert. In: *CBQ* 54:742-743 O 1992
The unity of the Book of Isaiah and its cosmogonic language. *CBQ* 55:1-17 Ja 1993

Clifford, Richard J, ed.
Creation in Biblical traditions. Washington: The Catholic Biblical Association of America, 1992. 151p ISBN 0-915170-23-x LC 92-20268

Clinton, Hillary Rodham, 1947-.
Catholic providers will play a central role in healthcare reform. *Health Prog* 74:42-43 Jl-Ag 1993

Clinton, William Jefferson, 1946-.
John Paul II's arrival in Denver. *Origins* 23:186-187 Ag 26 1993

Clowes, Brian.
Anti-life maneuvers. *SocJust* 84:123-125 Jl-Ag 1993

Co, Maria Anicia.
The major summaries in Acts. *Eph Theol Lovan* 78:49-85 Ap 1992

Coate, Mary Anne.
Who chooses celibacy—and why? *Way Suppl* 77:97-105 Sum 1993

Coates, Ken, 1930-.
Made in England. *Month* 26:315 Ag 1993

Cobb, John B, Jr.
Review of: *Mahāyāna: Buddhism for a post-modern world* by Akizuki, Ryōmin. In: *JEcumen Stds* 29:285-286 Spr 1992

Cobe, Patricia. *see* Plotch, Batia, jt auth

Coburn, Janet.
Computer bargains and other good deals. *Tod Cath Teach* 27:34-38 N-D 1993
Computer disasters and how to avoid them. *Tod Cath Teach* 27:34-38 O 1993
The computer: it isn't just for math anymore. *Tod Cath Teach* 27:46+ S 1993
Is this software any good? How to tell. *Tod Cath Teach* 27:40-42 Ag 1993
Preschools bring private schools success. *Tod Cath Teach* 26:17-18+ My-Je 1993

Cochran, Clarke E.
Review of: *Church, state, morality, and law* by Hannon, Patrick. In: *Comm* 120:25-27 Jl 16 1993
Review of: *No longer exiles: the Religious New Right in American politics* by Cromartie, Michael, ed. In: *Comm* 120:25-27 Jl 16 1993
Review of: *Religion and radical politics* by Craig, Robert H, 1942-. In: *Comm* 120:25-27 Jl 16 1993

Cochran, Leonard.
Cautionary tale; Cousins travelling; By return mail; A sentence; An onion. *Spirit* 57:21-23 Spr-Sum 1992
Puppet to puppeteer; Puppet show. *Spirit* 58:7 1993

Codd, Kevin A.
The hanging of Westley Allan Dodd. *America* 168:5-6 Ja 30 1993

Codina, Victor.
Crônica de Santo Domingo. *Perspectiva* 25:77-89 Ja-Ap 1993

Cody, Aelred.
Review of: *Die lateinischen Evangelien bis zum 10. Jahrhundert* by Fischer, Bonifatius. In: *CBQ* 55:366-367 Ap 1993
Review of: *Leviticus 1-16* by Milgrom, Jacob. In: *OTA* 15:494-495 O 1992

Coe, John. see Johnson, Ken, jt auth

Coffey, Kathy.
The holiness of death. *OSV* 81:6 Ap 11 1993
Invitation to altruism. *Momentum* 24:73 Ap-My 1993
Ministry in the public schools. *Momentum* 24:70 N-D 1993
Review of: *The Gospel according to Mary* by Winter, Miriam Therese. In: *Momentum* 24:76 S-O 1993
Review of: *The house on Mango St* by Cisneros, Sandra. In: *Momentum* 24:75 F-Mr 1993

Coffey, Mary Kean.
Beading a path down the interstate. *Liguorian* 81:26-27 Jl 1993

Coffin, David R.
Review of: *"Il Gran Cardinale": Alessandro Farnese, patron of the arts* by Robertson, Clare. In: *CHist* 79:108-109 Ja 1993

Coffin, William Sloane.
A passion for the possible: a message to U.S. churches. Louisville: John Knox, 1993. x, 96p ISBN 0-664-25428-4

Cogan, Patrick.
Review of: *Independent bishops: an international directory* by Ward, Gary L, and Persson, Bertil, et al, eds. In: *Stud Can* 27 no 1:263-264 1993

Coghlan, Peter.
Persons, souls and embryos. *Pacifica* 6:165-171 Je 1993

Cohalan, F.
Review of: *Opus Dei* by Walsh, Michael J, 1937-. In: *HPR* 94:67-71 O 1993

Cohen, Thomas V.
Review of: *Jerome Nadal, SJ, 1507-1580* by Bangert, William V. In: *TheolStds* 54:567-569 S 1993

Cohn, Mary Ellen.
Hold us in Your mercy. *Tod Parish* 25:5 S 1993
We are the work of your hands: a prayer for Advent. *Tod Parish* 25:25 N-D 1993

Colapietro, Vincent M.
Review of: *America's philosophical vision* by Smith, John E. In: *IPQ* 33:356-364 S 1993
Review of: *Antifoundationalism old and new* by Rockmore, Tom, and Singer, Beth J, eds. In: *IPQ* 33:251-254 Je 1993

Colby, Kimberlee Wood.
Religious freedom in the public school setting. *Momentum* 24:55-59 N-D 1993

Cole, Basil.
Humanae Vitae and some principles for re-evangelization. *F & R* 19:95-107 Spr 1993
Music and morals. New York: Alba House, 1993. x, 158p ISBN 0-8189-0660-x LC 92-36135 see Carey, Michael, jt auth

Cole, Dan P. see Shanks, Hershel, jt ed

Coleman, Bill, and Coleman, Patty.
Abortive effort to oust bishop puts Vatican on the defensive [por]. *Nat Cath Rep* 30:7 N 12 1993
Support swells for bishop threatened with removal. *Nat Cath Rep* 30:16 N 19 1993

Coleman, Gerald D.
Homosexuals in the military: policy and morality. *Church* 9:20-23 Sum 1993
Human sexuality: an all-embracing gift. New York: Alba House, 1992. x, 441p ISBN 0-81890-643-x LC 92-20661

Coleman, Gerlad D.
When Menlo became a bastion of Catholicism. *US Cath Hist* 11:123-125 Wint 1993

Coleman, John A. see Sanks, T Howland, jt ed

Coleman, Patty. see Coleman, Bill, jt auth

Coles, Robert, 1929-.
Meeting Dorothy Day [condensed fr *The call of service* 1993]. *CDgst* 57:90-95 O 1993

Coletti, Diego.
Il seminario maggiore (commentary: *Pastores dabo vobis*). *Seminarium* 32:561-574 O-D 1992

Coll, Regina.
Review of: *But she said* by Fiorenza, Elisabeth Schüssler, 1938-. In: *Nat Cath Rep* 29:27 F 5 1993
Review of: *Gaia and God: an ecofeminist theology of earth healing* by Reuther, Rosemary Radford. In: *Nat Cath Rep* 29:27 F 5 1993
Yet another look at the question of ordination of women. *Sisters* 65:110-115 Mr 1993

Collinge, William J.
Review of: *A concise dictionary of theology* by O'Collins, Gerald, 1931-, and Farrugia, Edward G. In: *Living Light* 29:85 Wint 1992

Collings, Ross.
A dark God. *Way* 33:44-53 Ja 1993

Collins, Adela Yarbro.
Review of: *New Testament Apocrypha* by Schneemelcher, Wilhelm, ed. In: *CBQ* 55:180-182 Ja 1993

Collins, Brad.
The great flood of 1993 [photos]. *Extensn* 88:16-20 O 16 1993

Collins, Carole.
Church input said to be key to African synod. *Nat Cath Rep* 29:15 Jl 30 1993

Collins, Carole. *(cont'd)*
Holding African Synod in Rome miffs Africans. *Nat Cath Rep* 29:11 Je 18 1993
Mozambican prelate visits US seeking peacekeepers. *Nat Cath Rep* 29:9 Mr 5 1993
NGOs' role grows in global environmental diplomacy. *Nat Cath Rep* 29:11 Jl 2 1993
Papal visit proceeding to troubled Africa. *Nat Cath Rep* 29:14-15 Ja 15 1993
Political quagmire buried in moral morass. *Nat Cath Rep* 29:8 Je 4 1993
Pope asks help for Africa, and religious tolerance. *Nat Cath Rep* 29:11 F 26 1993
Somalia pressing policy issues. *Nat Cath Rep* 29:15 Ja 8 1993
Sudan opposition debates war. *Nat Cath Rep* 30:9 N 19 1993
Sudanese bishops decry human-rights abuses. *Nat Cath Rep* 29:11 N 6 1992
UN reports on minorities: US not measuring up. *Nat Cath Rep* 29:9 Je 18 1993
UN rights conference avoids meat on bones of contention. *Nat Cath Rep* 29:11 Jl 2 1993
War shackles a nation founded by free slaves. *Nat Cath Rep* 29:3-4 N 13 1992
Zaire's democracy struggle tests church, Clinton. *Nat Cath Rep* 29:9 F 12 1993

Collins, Carole, and Askin, Steve.
US waives ban on Zairean visits; incites Mobutu critics. *Nat Cath Rep* 29:10 Jl 30 1993

Collins, Clare.
Review of: *The dork of Cork* by Raymo, Chet. In: *Comm* 120:23-24 Jl 16 1993

Collins, Denis E. see Spinetta, Pat Deasy, jt auth

Collins, Gregory.
The divine office as personal prayer. *Doctr Life* 42:608-613 D 1992

Collins, John N.
Are all Christian ministers? Collegeville: The Liturgical Press, 1992. x, 168p ISBN 0-8146-2168-6 LC 92-9599

Collins, Jude.
Irish churches and the Irish media: out of order or out of touch? *Studies* 82:185-197 Sum 1993

Collins, Mary Smalara.
All generations will call her blessed (commentary: *Redemptoris mater*). *USCath* 58:37-40 My 1993
Redemptoris Mater (The Mother of the Redeemer) on the Blessed Virgin Mary, in the life of the Pilgrim Church, [1987 02 25]: encyclical of His Holiness Pope John Paul II.
Eucharist and christology revisited: the Body of Christ. *TheolDgst* 39:321-332 Wint 1992
What's God like? *USCath* 58:30-35 S 1993

Collins, Patrick W, 1936-.
Bodying forth: aesthetic liturgy. New Jersey: Paulist Press, 1992. x, 187p ISBN 0-8091-3352-0 LC 92-28045
Preaching the Word [excerpts fr *Bodying forth: aesthetic liturgy*]. *Emmanuel* 99:278-285 Je 1993
Priests: problem and solution [ex fr *Bodying forth: aesthetic liturgy*]. *Emmanuel* 99:448+ O 1993

Collins, Phil. see Stevens, R. Paul, jt auth

Collins, Raymond F.
The Bible talks about sex. *Priests & People* 7:306-311 Ag-S 1993
The birth of the New Testament: the origin and development of the first Christian generation. New York: Crossroad, 1993. x, 324p ISBN 0-8245-1276-6 LC 93-16647
From Good Friday to Easter: a call for metanoia. *Emmanuel* 98:125-129 Ap 1992
'Male and female he created them'. *Chicago Stud* 32:9-18 Ap 1993
Review of: *Jesucristo, su persona y su obra, en la carta a los Hebreos* by Franco Martínez, César Augusto. In: *Eph Theol Lovan* 69:194 Ap 1993
Review of: *Jesus and the samaritan woman* by Botha, J Eugene. In: *Louvain Stds* 18:187-188 Sum 1993
Review of: *Priesthood today* by Rausch, Thomas P. In: *Louvain Stds* 18:190 Sum 1993
Review of: *Sacred space* by Isaacs, Marie E. In: *Eph Theol Lovan* 69:193 Ap 1993
Review of: *The four gospels 1992: Festschrift Frans Neirynck* by Segbroeck, F Van, et al, eds. In: *Louvain Stds* 18:186-187 Sum 1993

Collins, Seán.
Restoring the sweetness: the liturgical agenda. *Doctr Life* 43:130-140 Mr 1993

Collins, Thomas.
Review of: *As ministers of Christ: the Christological dimension of ministry in the New Testament* by Forestell, J T. In: *Can Cath Rev* 11:26-27 My 1993
'Thanks be to God' the Bible and the liturgy. *Can Cath Rev* 11:7-13 Je 20 1993

Collopy, Anne Marie.
Three cheers for John Fisher. *Register* 69:5 Ja 3 1993

Collum, Danny Duncan.
CBS news anchors adrift in shallow waters. *Nat Cath Rep* 29:19 Jl 16 1993
Let the viewer beware: the video camera does lie. *Nat Cath Rep* 29:20 Mr 19 1993
Why murder in May brings good things to life for networks. *Nat Cath Rep* 29:18 Je 18 1993

Colombo, Giuseppe.
Response to Hubert Müller. *Jurist* 52 no 1:365-368 1992

Colombo, J.A.
Review of: *The liberation of dogma* by Segundo, Juan Luis. In: *Living Light* 30:108-109 Aut 1993

Colson, GiGi.
Calcutta through the eye of the needle. *Liguorian* 81:58-62 Jl 1993

Combs, Christopher.
Saint Augustine and Martin Buber as perspectives on John Noonan's persons and masks of the law. *Amer J Juris* 37:145-169 1992

Condorcet, de Gouges, de Lamberty y Otros.
La ilustracion olvidada. Madrid: Anthropos, 1993. x, 176p ISBN 84-7658-408-3

Cone, James H, and Wilmore, Gayraud S, eds.
Black theology: a documentary history, vol I, 1966-1979. Maryknoll: Orbis Books, 1993. 462p ISBN 0-88344-853-x LC 92-44927
Black theology: a documentary history, vol II, 1980-1992. Maryknoll: Orbis Books, 1993. x, 450p ISBN 0-88344-773-8 LC 79-12747

Conn, Joann Wolski.
A developmental view of Salesian spirituality. *RRel* 52:56-68 Ja-F 1993
Review of: *Spirituality and history* by Sheldrake, Philip. In: *Horizons (CTS)* 20:173-174 Spr 1993

Conn, Joann Wolski, and Conn, Walter E, eds.
Horizons for Catholic feminist theology. Washington, D C: Georgetown University Press, 1992. x, 207p ISBN 0-87840-534-8 LC 92-30435

Conn, Walter E.
Review of: *Handbook of religious conversion* by Malony, H Newton, and Southard, Samuel, eds. In: *Living Light* 29:87-88 Sum 1993 *see* Conn, Joann Wolski, jt ed

Connell, Desmond, Abp.
Two visions with no common ground. *OR(Eng)* 1300:8 Jl 21 1993

Connell, Richard E.
Challenges to tax exemption growing. *Health Prog* 74:58-59 Jl-Ag 1993

Conners, Canice.
The search for answers. *USCath* 58:8-11 S 1993

Connolly, Hugh G.
Conversion: a lifelong journey. *Furrow* 44:159-166 Mr 1993

Connolly, Michael.
Choir festivals: everyone's a winner. *Past Mus* 17:14-15 D 1992-Ja 1993

Connolly, Theresa.
The resourceful recruiter. *Catechist* 27:70-71 S 1993

Connors, Canice.
Rebuilding trust: clergy sexual abuse. *Church* 9:5-10 Sum 1993
Subcommittee head introduces think tank recommendations. *Origins* 23:105-107 Jl 1 1993

Connors, Daniel.
A blend of old and new. *ReligTJ* 27:17 S 1993
Sit down and be quiet!. *ReligTJ* 27:28-29 O 1993

Connors, Joseph.
Dialogue [interview by M Meehan]. *Register* 69:1+ Ja 17 1993

Connors, Patrick.
Lay ministry transforms a parish in Guyana. *America* 168:14-15 F 13 1993
Priest worker. *America* 169:4-5 Ag 28-S 4 1993

Conolly, William J. *see* Barry, William A, jt auth

Conroy, Bernadette.
Dave understanding life through death. *St Anth* 100:24-27 My 1993

Conroy, Charles.
Reflections on the present state of Old Testament studies. *Gregorianum* 73 No 4:597-609 1992
Review of: *Amos* by Paul, Shalom M. In: *Gregorianum* 74 no 2:358-362 1993
Review of: *Guida allo studio dell'Ebraico biblico* by Deiana, Giovanni, and Spreafico, Ambrogio. In: *Gregorianum* 74 No 1:191-192 1993
Review of: *Reading Isaiah* by Conrad, Edgar W. In: *Gregorianum* 74 No 1: 146-148 1993

Conroy, Maureen.
The discerning heart: discovering a personal God. Chicago: Loyola University Press, 1993. x, 272p ISBN 0-8294-0752-9 LC 93-12508
Journey of love: God moving in our hearts and lives. Mahwah: The Paulist Press, 1993. 82p ISBN 0-8091-3413-6 LC 93-979

Contosta, David R, and Gallagher, Dennis J.
Ever ancient, ever new: Villanova University, 1842-1992 [photos]. Virginia Beach: The Donning Company, 1992. 120p ISBN 0-89865-870-0 LC 92-24373

Contreni, J.
Review of: *Hinkmar von Reims als Verwalter von Bistum und Kirchenprovinz* by Stratmann, Martina. In: *CHist* 78:632-633 O 1992

Convissor, Kate.
Feed my lambs. *St Anth* 101:16-21 Ag 1993
Frederic Baraga: holiness on showshoes. *CDgst* 57:99-103 Jl 1993

Conway, John S.
Review of: *Die Vereinigung der evangelischen Kirchen in Deutschland* by Heckel, Martin. In: *JEcumen Stds* 29:473-474 Sum-Aut 1992
Review of: *Gelähmte Ökumene* by Koch, Kurt. In: *JEcumen Stds* 29:473-474 Sum-Aut 1992
Review of: *Germania e Santa Sede: le nunziature di Pacelli fra la Grande guerra e la Repubblica di Weimar* by Fattorini, Emma. In: *CHist* 79:555-557 Jl 1993
Review of: *The Vatican and Zionism: conflict in the Holy Land, 1895-1925* by Minerbi, Sergio I. In: *JEcumen Stds* 29:279 Spr 1992

Conway, Pierre.
Review of: *Galileo, Bellarmine and the Bible* by Blackwell, Richard J. In: *HPR* 93:76-79 My 1993
Review of: *Religion in an age of science: the Gifford lectures, vol I* by Barbour, Ian. In: *HPR* 93:77-79 F 1993

Conway, Rose Marie.
"A window to Annie's world". *New Theol Rev* 6:75-79 F 1993

Coogan, Michael D. *see* Metzger, Bruce M, jt ed

Cook, Michael L.
Review of: *Christology and spirituality* by Thompson, William M. In: *Horizons (CTS)* 20:154-155 Spr 1993

Cooke, Bernard.
Review of: *A flock of shepherds* by Reese, Thomas Joseph, 1945-. In: *America* 169:20-21 Jl 17-24 1993
Review of: *The craft of theology* by Dulles, Avery Robert, 1918-. In: *America* 168:19+ Ja 16-23 1993

Cooke, Judy.
Review of: *Daphne du Maurier* by Forster, Margaret. In: *Tablet* 247:437-438 Ap 3 1993
Review of: *In a hotel garden* by Josipovici, Gabriel. In: *Tablet* 247:985 Jl 31 1993
Review of: *Josiah Wedgwood* by Reilly, Robin. In: *Tablet* 247:277-278 F 27 1993
Review of: *Letters from Menabilly* by Maurier, Daphne du, 1907-1989. In: *Tablet* 247:437-438 Ap 3 1993

Cooke, Terence.
Meditations on Mary. New York: Alba House, 1993. x, 132p ISBN 0-8189-0683-9 LC 93-26373

Coolidge, Sharon.
Eliduc and the iconography of love. *Med Stud* 54:274-285 1992

Coombs, Marie Theresa. *see* Nemeck, Francis Kelly, jt auth

Cooney, Arthur.
Humility. *New Cov* 23:19 Ag 1993

Cooper, Alan.
Review of: *Four approaches to the Book of Pslams: from Saadia Gaon to Abraham Ibn Ezra* by Simon, Uriel. In: *CBQ* 55:353-354 Ap 1993

Cooper, Austin.
Review of: *An anthology of Christian mysticism* by Egan, Harvey. In: *Pacifica* 6:243-244 Je 1993

Cooper, David E.
Postmodernism and "The end of philosophy". *IJPS* 1:49-59 Mr 1993

Cooper, Howard.
Sin in biblical and rabbinic thought. *Month* 26:348-354 S-O 1993

Cooper, Kristina.
The charismatic way. *Tablet* 247:467-468 Ap 10-17 1993
Pope encourages Catholic charismatics. *Tablet* 247:1239-1240 S 25 1993

Cooper, Michael.
Review of: *Japan's encounter with Christianity: the Catholic mission in premodern Japan* by Fujita, Neil S. In: *Heythrop* 34:334-335 Jl 1993

Cooper, Norman P.
Collaborative ministry: communion, contention, commitment. New York: Paulist Press, 1993. x, 200p ISBN 0-8091-3376-8 LC 92-38074

Cooper, Rand Richards.
It's not Weimar all over again: the strengths of German democracy. *Comm* 120:11-13 My 7 1993
Review of: *A complicated war: the harrowing of Mozambique* by Finnegan, William. In: *Comm* 119:18-20 D 18 1992
Review of: *Body and soul* by Conroy, Frank. In: *Comm* 120:33-34 N 5 1993

Coote, Mary P. *see* Coote, Robert B, jt auth

Coote, Nicholas.
The church, population and the environment. *Priests & People* 7:340-345 Ag-S 1993

Copleston, Frederick C.
Memoirs of a philosopher. Kansas City: Sheed & Ward, 1993. 228p ISBN 1-55612-570-4 LC 93-7810

Copp, Jay.
He wouldn't fight for the Nazis. *CDgst* 57:136-140+ Ag 1993
How Harry and Alice made a difference [photos]. *CDgst* 57:97-102 S 1993
Inspired partnerships: saving churches and neighborhoods. *St Anth* 101:16-20 O 1993

Coppa, Frank J.
Review of: *Gioacchino Ventura e il pensiero politico d'ispirazione cristiana dell'Ottocento* by Guccione, Eugenio, ed. In: *CHist* 79:348-349 Ap 1993

Coppens, Christian.
Review of: *Index d'Anvers, 1569, 1570, 1571* by Bujanda, Jesus M de, ed. In: *CHist* 79:532-534 Jl 1993

Coppinger, John.
A vocation for lay persons [interview by Lou Jacquet]. *OSV* 82:6 My 2 1993

Corbett, Thomas.
Review of: *Theology as hermeneutics* by Putti, Joseph. In: *Furrow* 44:126 F 1993

Corbon, Jean.
In the name of Jesus we have confident access to the Father. *OR(Eng)* 1292: 10 My 26 1993
The new Catechism of the Catholic Church conforms to the genuine tradition of the Church, especially to the teachings of the second Vatican Council (December 17, 1993, Commentary).

Corcoran, Donald.
Reflections on the monastic spiritual journey. *Word Sp* 15:12-28 1993

Cordaro, Frank.
Active and messy personalism. *Cath Work* 60:6 My 1993

Corecco, Eugenio, Bp.
Charity and pardon heal divisions. *OR(Eng)* 1300:4 Jl 21 1993

Coreil, Bernice.
Catholic healthcare ministry's key role in healthcare reform. *Health Prog* 74: 18-19+ 1993
CHA's vision of a redesigned healthcare system. *Health Prog* 74:12-14 My 1993
Forging a future for Catholic healthcare. *Health Prog* 74:20+ Ja-F 1993

Coren, Michael.
Birthday greetings. *Can Cath Rev* 11:2 Ja 1993
Bomber command. *Can Cath Rev* 11:5-6 S 1993
Epistolary advice. *Can Cath Rev* 11:5-6 Je 1993
Even in Canada. *Can Cath Rev* 11:5-6 Mr 1993

Coren, Michael. *(cont'd)*
Exploiting the dead. *Can Cath Rev* 11:5-6 N 1993
Fitting testaments. *Can Cath Rev* 11:4-6 F 1993
The land of the rising Anne. *Can Cath Rev* 11:5-6 Jl-Ag 1993
Review of: *Archibald Macleish* by Donaldson, Scott. In: *Can Cath Rev* 11:4-6 F 1993
Review of: *Cleese encounters* by Margolis, Jonathan. In: *Can Cath Rev* 11:3-4 Ja 1993
Review of: *Darwin: the life of a tormented evolutionist* by Desmond, Adrian, and Moore, James. In: *Can Cath Rev* 11:4-6 F 1993
Review of: *Frank Lloyd Wright* by Secrest, Meryle. In: *Can Cath Rev* 11:4-6 F 1993
Review of: *Gertrude and Alice* by Souhami, Diana. In: *Can Cath Rev* 11:4-6 F 1993
Review of: *Hadley* by Diliberto, Gioia. In: *Can Cath Rev* 11:4-6 F 1993
Review of: *Hot breakfast for sparrows: my life with Harold Town* by Nowell, Iris. In: *Can Cath Rev* 11:4-6 F 1993
Review of: *Marlene Dietrich: life and legend* by Bach, Steven. In: *Can Cath Rev* 11:4-6 F 1993
Review of: *Prism of the night: a biography of Anne Rice* by Ramsland, Katherine. In: *Can Cath Rev* 11:4-6 F 1993
Review of: *The English Bible and the seventeenth-century revolution* by Hill, Christopher. In: *Can Cath Rev* 11:5-6 Je 20 1993
Review of: *Trollope* by Glendinning, Victoria. In: *Can Cath Rev* 11:4-6 F 1993
Review of: *You see, I haven't forgotten* by Hamon, Herve, and Rotman, Patrick. In: *Can Cath Rev* 11:4-6 F 1993
Simply to British. *Can Cath Rev* 11:3-4 Ap 1993

Coriden, James A.
Refusal to make a promise in a mixed marriage. *New Theol Rev* 6:72-74 F 1993

Corish, Patrick J.
Review of: *St Patrick's world* by Paor, Liam de, 1926-. In: *Furrow* 44:386 Je 1993

Corkery, James.
Review of: *The craft of theology* by Dulles, Avery Robert, 1918-. In: *Studies* 82:97-100 Spr 1993

Corless, Roger.
Authority (2): an essay on the place of the text in Buddhist and Christian formation. *Stud Form Spir* 14:31-39 F 1993

Corless, Roger J.
Review of: *Spirituality and emptiness: the dynamics of spiritual life in Buddhism and Christianity* by Mitchell, Donald W. In: *TheolStds* 54:607 S 1993

Corley, Felix.
Anglican vote is met with mixed response. *OSV* 81:21 D 20 1992
Changing unjust borders. *Month* 26:71-73 F 1993
A church at a standoff. *OSV* 81:21 Ja 31 1993
Disillusion in Russia. *Can Cath Rev* 11:16-17 Ap 1993
Jesuits fighting for freedom in Russia. *OSV* 82:17 Ag 22 1993
Jesuits under Kolvenbach face a changed world [por]. *OSV* 82:3 N 21 1993
Meet the new boss, same as the old boss? *OSV* 82:5 Je 13 1993
Review of: *The final revolution* by Weigel, George. In: *Can Cath Rev* 11:25-26 N 1993

Corn, Alfred, ed.
Incarnation: contemporary writers on the New Testament. New York: Penguin Books, 1991. x, 361p ISBN 0-14011-583-8 LC 90-21991

Cornell, Tom.
With the down and out in Waterbury. *New Oxford Rev* 60:19-24 S 1993

Cornwell, John.
An attack of scientism. *Tablet* 247:462-464 Ap 10-17 1993

Cornwell, Malcolm.
Praying the passion: living the Gospel-scriptural reflections for adult believers. Collegeville:Liturgical, 1993. 76p ISBN 0-8146-2220-8 LC 92-40656

Cornwell, Peter.
Review of: *A church for the nation? Essays on the future of Anglicanism* by Warren, Allen, ed. In: *Tablet* 247:619-620 My 15 1993
Review of: *Celibacy: gift or law?* by Vogel, Heinz-Jurgen. In: *Tablet* 247:1073-1074 Ag 21 1993

Corona, Mary.
God's human face revealed: a retreat in Wales. *RRel* 52:519-531 Jl-Ag 1993

Corral, Carlos.
Response to René Metz. *Jurist* 52 no 1:285-293 1992

Corrigan, Kevin.
Light and metaphor in Plotinus and St Thomas Aquinas. *Thomist* 57:187-199 Ap 1993

Corry, Emmett.
Review of: *Catholic school education in the United States* by Grant, Mary C, and Hunt, Thomas C. In: *CLW* 64:30-32 Jl-S 1993

Corsten, Angela.
Der Papst im Spannungsfeld zwischen Vorgänger und Nachfolger. *Stimm Zeit* 211:425-427 Je 1993

Cort, John C.
Review of: *Organized labor and the Church* by Higgins, George G, 1916-. In: *Comm* 120:26-27 Ag 13 1993
Review of: *The CIO's left-led unions* by Rosswurm, Steve, ed. In: *Comm* 120:26-27 Ag 13 1993

Cortes, Ernesto.
Your church can be a driving force for justice [interview by the editors of Salt (Periodical)]. *Salt* 13:14-19 N-D 1993

Cosgrave, William.
Second thoughts on concelebration. *Furrow* 44:236-239 Ap 1993

Cosgrove, Francis.
East and West as dimensions of the Church. *Diakonia* 26 no 1:15-25 1993

Cosgrove, Jim, and Brankin, Patrick.
"Faith is strengthened when it is given to others!" [photos]. *Extensn* 88:8-15 Jl 1993

Cosstick, Vicky.
The misuse of the pen. *Tablet* 247:294 Mr 6 1993
Sex and the adult Christian. *Priests & People* 7:311-316 Ag-S 1993

Costa, Ruy O. *see* Getz, Lorine M, jt ed

Costa Silva, Carlo Albeta da.
Orações, Bênçãos e a Bíblia. *REB* 53:428-435 Je 1993

Costacuria, Bruna.
Esegesi e lettura credente della Scrittura. *Gregorianum* 73 No 4:739-745 1992

Costello, Andrew.
Born to shine. *USCath* 58:38-40 Ag 1993
First-name basis. *USCath* 58:38-40 Je 1993
How to own your own Bible. *USCath* 58:41-43 My 1993
Metaphor for life. *USCath* 58:39-41 F 1993
Out of control. *USCath* 58:38-40 Ja 1993
Stealing for lent. *USCath* 58:38-40 Mr 1993
Take the lead. *USCath* 58:40-42 Jl 1993
You had to be there. *USCath* 58:38-40 Ap 1993

Costello, Gerald M, 1931-.
Because it could happen again. *USCath* 58:48-51 F 1993
Breach of faith. *USCath* 58:48-51 Mr 1993
It's time to conduct civil wars. *USCath* 58:48-51 Ap 1993
The legacy of a life well served. *USCath* 58:48-51 N 1993
Paul VI did more than ban the pill. *USCath* 58:48-51 O 1993
Plain beauty. *USCath* 58:48-51 My 1993
Ramblin' Rose. *USCath* 58:48-51 Ja 1993
Review of: *All the pretty horses* by McCarthy, Cormac. In: *USCath* 58:48-51 My 1993
Review of: *Broken Covenant* by Sennott, Charles M. In: *USCath* 58:48-51 Mr 1993
Review of: *Care of the soul* by Moore, Thomas. In: *USCath* 58:48-50 Ag 1993
Review of: *Healing of the mind* by Moyers, Bill. In: *USCath* 58:48-50 Ag 1993
Review of: *Holywood vs America* by Medved, Michael, 1948-. In: *USCath* 58:48-50 Je 1993
Review of: *Lead us not into temptation* by Berry, Jason. In: *USCath* 58:48-51 Mr 1993
Review of: *Paul VI* by Hebblethwaite, Peter, 1930-. In: *USCath* 58:48-51 O 1993
Review of: *Perpetrators victims bystanders; the Jewish catastrophe 1933-1945* by Hilberg, Raul. In: *USCath* 58:48-51 F 1993
Review of: *The devil's card* by Maher, Mary. In: *USCath* 58:49-50 S 1993
Review of: *The fifties* by Halberstam, David. In: *USCath* 58:40-43 D 1993
Review of: *The heather blazing* by Toibin, Colm. In: *USCath* 58:50-51 S 1993
Review of: *The patron Saint of Liars* by Patchett, Ann. In: *USCath* 58:48-51 Ja 1993
Review of: *This confident church: Catholic leadership and life in Chicago, 1940-1965* by Anella, Steven. In: *USCath* 58:48-51 Jl 1993
Review of: *Uncommon decency: Christian civility in an uncivil world* by Mouw, Richard D. In: *USCath* 58:48-51 Ap 1993
Review of: *Virgin time* by Hampl, Patricia, 1946-. In: *USCath* 58:48-49 S 1993
Seen any good movies lately? *USCath* 58:48-50 Je 1993
Three good stories that didn't make the list. *USCath* 58:48-51 S 1993
When Chicago Catholics were second to none. *USCath* 58:48-51 Jl 1993
Who says soul doesn't sell? *USCath* 58:48-51 Ag 1993
The 1950s: the nation's frame of reference. *USCath* 58:40-43 D 1993
Review of: *Days of grace: a memoir* by Asche, Arthur, and Rampersad, Arnold. In: *USCath* 58:48-51 N 1993

Costello, Gwen.
The gifts of the Spirit. *ReligTJ* 26:39 Ja 1993
How should we pray? *ReligTJ* 27:16-17 Mr 1993
Religion teacher's planning calendar 1993-1994. *ReligTJ* 27:21-45 S 1993
Sacraments of God for those we teach (editorial). *ReligTJ* 26:7 Ja 1993

Costello, Helen.
The homilies we hear. *Furrow* 44:288-291 My 1993

Costello, Peter.
Review of: *The James Joyce—Paul Leon papers* by Fahy, Catherine, comp. In: *Studies* 81:452-454 Wint 1992
Review of: *Tolstoy and education* by Murphy, Daniel. In: *Studies* 81:478-482 Wint 1992

Costello, Sydney B.
Integrating child and adult religious education. *Momentum* 24:74-76 Ap-My 1993

Costello, Timothy J.
The use of psychology as an aid to priestly formation. *Seminarium* 32:629-636 O-D 1992

Costigan, Richard F.
Review of: *La science catholique: L'"Encyclopédie théologique" de Migne (1844-1873) entre apologétique et vulgarisation* by Langlois, Claude, and Laplanche, François, eds. In: *CHist* 79:351-352 Ap 1993

Côté, Antoine.
Review of: *Le cose, il pensiero, l'essere* by Ruffinengo, Pier Paolo. In: *RPhil Louvain* 91:333-336 My 1993

Cothenet, E. *see* Briend, Jacques, jt ed

Cottage, Joyce.
When are they ready for the rites? *Tod Parish* 25:29-30 O 1993

Cotter, Jim.
Does God have boundaries? *Way* 33:91-96 Ap 1993
The present moment. *Tablet* 247:432-433 Ap 3 1993

Cotter, Theresa.
Grandparents pass on the faith. *Church* 9:32-35 Aut 1993

Coughlin, Edward.
Review of: *The promise of partnership: leadership and ministry in an adult church* by Whitehead, James D, and Whitehead, Evelyn Eaton. In: *New Theol Rev* 6:110-112 Ag 1993

Coughlin, John J.
Religion, education and the First Amendment. *America* 168:12-15 My 15 1993

Couliano, Ioan P. *see* Eliade, Mircea, 1907-1985, jt auth

Coulombe, Charles.
Crying game. *Register* 69:5 My 9 1993
Haunted by faith. *Register* 69:3 Je 20 1993
Heaven's road. *Register* 69:3 Je 11 1993
Review of: *The Church, community of salvation* by Tavard, George Henry. In: *New Oxford Rev* 60:28 Mr 1993
Swing kids. *Register* 69:5 Mr 28 1993

Couloubaritsis, Lambros.
Le statut de l'un dans la Métaphysique. *RPhil Louvain* 90:497-522 N 1992

Countryman, L William.
The New Testament is in Greek: a short course for exegetes. Grand Rapids: Eerdmans, 1993. 205p ISBN 0-8028-0665-1

Courtney, Anne.
Parenting well when the other one won't [condensed fr *Christian Parenting Today* Jl/Ag 1991]. *CDgst* 58:103-106 N 1993

Courtney, Mark E. *see* Specht, Harry, jt auth

Couser, Richard B.
Ministry and the American legal system: a guide for clergy, lay workers, and congregations. Minneapolis: Fortress Press, 1993. 356p ISBN 0-8006-2603-6 LC 92-34214

Cousins, Anthony D.
The Catholic religious poets from Southwell to Crashaw. Westminster: Christian Classics, 1993. x, 224p ISBN 0-7220-1570-4

Couture, André.
Review of: *Instant et cause: le discontinu dans la pensée philosophique de l'Inde* by Silburn, Lilian. In: *Laval Theol Phil* 49:168 F 1993
Review of: *Jouer avec le feu: pratique et théorie du rituel védique* by Staal, Frits. In: *Laval Theol Phil* 49:169-170 F 1993
Review of: *Vāc, the concept of the word in selected Hindu Tantras* by Padoux, André. In: *Laval Theol Phil* 49:168-169 F 1993

Couture, Denise.
À propos d'une note romaine sur le livre d'André Guindon. *Laval Theol Phil* 49:321-329 Je 1993
Review of: *The sexual creators* by Guindon, Andre. In: *Laval Theol Phil* 49:321-329 Je 1993

Cover, Charles. *see* Charles, Prince of Wales, 1948-, jt auth

Covino, Paul.
Review of: *A world at prayer: the new ecumenical prayer cycle* by Carden, John. In: *Past Mus* 17:49 Ap-My 1993
Review of: *Documents of Christian worship* by White, James F. In: *Past Mus* 17:51-52 Ag-S 1993
Review of: *Eco-Church* by Fritsch, Albert. In: *Past Mus* 17:52 Ag-S 1993
Review of: *Silent voices, sacred lives: women's readings for the liturgical year* by Bowe, Barbara E, et al, eds. In: *Past Mus* 17:52-53 Ag-S 1993
Review of: *The religious potential of the child* by Cavalletti, Sofia. In: *Past Mus* 17:49-50 Ap-My 1993
Review of: *Worship: reforming tradition* by Talley, Thomas J. In: *Past Mus* 17:48-49 Ap-My 1993

Cowan, Marion, and Futrell, John Carroll.
Companions in grace: a handbook for directors of the spiritual exercises of St. Ignatius of Loyola. Kansas City: Sheed & Ward, 1993. x, 246p ISBN 1-55612-667-0 LC 93-6194

Cowan, Michael A.
The sacred game of conversation. *Furrow* 44:30-34 Ja 1993
Seeking the welfare of the city: the public life of small communities of faith. *Chicago Stud* 31:205-214 Ag 1992 *see* Lee, Bernard J, jt auth

Cowdrey, H E J.
Review of: *Peter Damiani: Letters 61-90* by Damiani, Peter. In: *CHist* 79:315-316 Ap 1993

Cowell, John.
Cuenot, Claude, 1911-1992 [obit]. *Teilhard Rev* 27:84 Wint 1992
Ethical risk management: suggestions for an applied risk ethics. *Teilhard Rev* 28:3-7 Spr 1993

Cowles, David T, Jr.
The state as already withered away. *SocJust* 84:25-28 Ja-F 1993

Cox, Dermot.
The new writers: wisdom's response to a changing society. *StudiaM* 42:1-15 1993

Cox, John D.
Review of: *A theater of envy: William Shakespeare* by Girard, René, 1923-. In: *Relig Lit* 24:85-90 Aut 1992
Review of: *Last things and last plays: Shakespearan eschatology* by Marshall, Cynthia. In: *Relig Lit* 24:85-90 Aut 1992
Review of: *Theater and Incarnation* by Harris, Max. In: *Relig Lit* 24:85-90 Aut 1992

Cox, William J.
The Clinton election: implications for healthcare. *Health Prog* 74:16-18 Ja-F 1993

Coyle, Kathleen.
Original sin: a residue of some primal crime? *Doctr Life* 43:83-94 F 1993

Coyle, Maryanna.
The leadership challenge: imagine new relationships. *Health Prog* 74:16+ Jl-Ag 1993

Coyne, George V.
Implicazioni filosofiche e teologiche delle nuove cosmologie. *Civilta* 143:343-352 N 21 1992

Crabtree, Penni.
Review of: *The children of men* by James, P D. In: *Nat Cath Rep* 29:23 My 28 1993

Craft, Carolyn M.
Review of: *Here all dwell free: stories to heal the wounded feminine* by Nelson, Gertrude Mueller. In: *CrossCurr* 42:554-558 Wint 1992-1993
Review of: *Mother church: what the experience of women is teaching her* by Cunneen, Sally. In: *CrossCurr* 42:554-558 Wint 1992-1993
Review of: *Returning words to flesh: feminism, psychoanalysis, and the resurrection of the body* by Goldenberg, Naomi R. In: *CrossCurr* 42:554-559 Wint 1992-1993
Review of: *To be human against all odds* by Franck, Frederick. In: *CrossCurr* 42:554-558 Wint 1992-1993
Review of: *Women and Church: the challenge of ecumenical solidarity in an age of alienation* by May, Melanie A, ed. In: *CrossCurr* 42:554-558 Wint 1992-1993

Cragg, Kenneth.
Islam and other faiths. *StudiaM* 42:257-270 1993

Craghan, John F.
Review of: *Introducing the cultural context of the New Testament, vol II* by Pilch, John Joseph, 1936-. In: *Bib Th Bul* 22:180 Wint 1992
Review of: *Introducing the cultural context of the Old Testament, vol I* by Pilch, John Joseph, 1936-. In: *Bib Th Bul* 22:180 Wint 1992
Review of: *Old Testament theology: basic issues in the current debate* by Hasel, Gerhard. In: *Bib Th Bul* 23:40 Spr 1993
Sin, cleansing, and restoration. *BibleT* 31:68-71 Mr 1993

Craig, Kenneth M, Jr.
Review of: *Power, providence, and personality: biblical insight into life and ministry* by Brueggemann, Walter. In: *CBQ* 54:741-742 O 1992
Review of: *The Jewish Bible after the Holocaust* by Fackenheim, Emil L. In: *JEcumen Stds* 29:127-128 Wint 1992

Craig, Mary.
Review of: *In the scales of fate: an autobiography* by Peterkiewicz, Jerzy. In: *Tablet* 247:1235-1236 S 25 1993
Review of: *Joyce's Ockenden* by Watkin, Pamela. In: *Tablet* 247:1104 Ag 28 1993
Review of: *Protestors for paradise: the story of Christian reformers fromthe thirteenth to the twenty-first century* by Gumley, Frances, and Redhead, Brian. In: *Tablet* 247:517-518 Ap 24 1993
Review of: *The dancing sun: jouneys to the miracle shrines* by Seward, Desmond. In: *Tablet* 247:820 Je 26 1993

Craig, William Lane.
Reply to Smith: on the finitude of the past [reply to Q Smith, 33:109-115 1993]. *IPQ* 33:225-231 Je 1993

Crampsey, James A.
Review of: *Responses to 101 questions on the Dead Sea Scrolls* by Fitzmyer, Joseph Augustine, 1920-. In: *Month* 26:146-147 Ap 1993
Review of: *The Dead Sea Scrolls uncovered* by Eisenman, Robert H, and Wise, Michael. In: *Month* 26:146-147 Ap 1993

Cranfield, C E B.
The apostles' creed: a faith to live by. Grand Rapids: Eerdmans, 1993. 72p ISBN 0-8028-0709-7

Crawford, Alan.
Review of: *Edward Barnsley and his workshop: arts and crafts in the twentieth century* by Carruthers, Annette. In: *Tablet* 247:214 F 13 1993

Crawford, Barry S.
Review of: *Eschatology and the covenant: a comparison of 4 Ezra and Romans 1-11* by Longenecker, Bruce W. In: *CBQ* 55:167-169 Ja 1993

Crawford, Don.
In North Carolina they trust [photos]. *OSV* 82:5 O 24 1993

Craycroft, Kenneth R, Jr.
Why Crisis cannot address the crisis. *Crisis* 11:17 Je 1993

Creegan, Joseph.
How do we renew our people? *Priests & People* 7:134-137 Ap 1993

Cremascoli, G.
Review of: *Inno Acatisto in onore della Madre di Dio* by Donadeo, Maria. In: *Civilta* 3:308-310 Ag 7-21 1993
Review of: *L'antropologia di Gregorio Nisseno* by Castelluccio, Giuseppe. In: *Civilta* 144:402-403 F 20 1993
Review of: *La Vergine Maria in s cromazio* by Trettel, Giulio. In: *Civilta* 144:95-96 Ja 2 1993

Cremins, Robert.
Review of: *Ghosts* by Banville, John. In: *Studies* 82:370-374 Aut 1993

Cresko, Anthony R.
Review of: *A translator's handbook on the Book of Psalms* by Bratcher, Robert G, and Reyburn, William D. In: *CBQ* 54:738-740 O 1992

Cresko, John F.
Review of: *Il libro del Profeta Osea: Edizione critica del testo ebraico* by Borbone, Pier Giorgio. In: *CBQ* 54:737-738 O 1992

Crews, Clyde F.
On a different trolley: the priesthood of E Harold Smith. *US Cath Hist* 11:51-62 Wint 1993
Review of: *American Catholic heritage: stories of growth* by Faherty, William Barnaby. In: *ACHSR* 103:55-56 Aut 1992
Review of: *Faith and fraternalism: the history of the Knights of Columbus* by Kauffman, Christopher J. In: *Living Light* 30:109-110 Aut 1993

Crilly, Oliver.
Review of: *The Gospel of Matthew: a spiritual commentary* by Yeomans, William. In: *Doctr Life* 43:314-315 My-Je 1993

Crilly, Scholastica.
Review of: *Opus Dei* by Walsh, Michael J, 1937-. In: *Register* 69:4 My 2 1993
Review of: *The end of the 20th century and the end of the modern age* by Lukacs, John, 1923-. In: *Register* 69:4 Je 27 1993

Crocker, H W, III.
Review of: *A nation of victims* by Sykes, Charles J. In: *Crisis* 11:50-51 Mr 1993

Cronin, Blaise. *see* Vakkari, Pertti, jt ed

Cronin, Francis R.
Quo Vadis? or evolution and consciousness. *Teilhard Rev* 27:69-82 Wint 1992

Cronin, Kieran.
"Speciesism": a challenge to theology. *Doctr Life* 43:357-362 Jl-Ag 1993

Crosby, Barbara C. *see* Bryson, John M, jt auth

Crosby, Donald F, 1933-.
Chaplains under fire in Sicily. *Priest* 49:37-41 Jl 1993
Death comes to the chaplain: Lawrence Lynch of Okinawa. *America* 168:6-12 Ap 24 1993
Desert Storm, 50 years ago: Catholic chaplains in North Africa. *Crisis* 10:33-38 D 1992
Remembering the Four Chaplains. *CDgst* 57:66-71 F 1993

Crosby, John F, III.
The incommunicability of human persons [fr *Essay on personal selfhood*]. *Thomist* 57:403-442 Jl 1993

Crosby, Ned.
Mass for a dead friend. *Furrow* 44:27-29 Ja 1993

Crout, Robert Rhodes.
Review of: *The political philosophy of Thomas Jefferson* by Sheldon, Garrett Ward. In: *Cithara* 32:63-65 N 1992

Crouzel, Henri.
Culture et foi: Clément d'Alexandrie. *StudiaM* 42:99-121 1993 *see* Brésard, Luc, jt ed

Crow, Paula A.
Ecumenism, spirituality, and the dark night of the soul. *OChr* 29 no 2:100-112 1993

Crowe, Terrence Robert.
Pentecostal unity: recurring frustration and enduring hopes. Chicago: Loyola University Press, 1993. x, 282p ISBN 0-8294-0746 LC 93-20683

Crutcher, Keith A.
Fetal tissue research: the cutting edge? *Linacre* 60:10-19 My 1993

Cryan, Marie Thérèse.
Review of: *What are the theologians saying now?* by Hellwig, Monika K, 1929-. In: *Doctr Life* 43:315-316 My-Je 1993

Csepregi, Gabor.
Corps et culture. *Laval Theol Phil* 49:121-129 F 1993

Cubitt, Catherine.
The cult of the saints in Anglo-Saxon England. *Heythrop* 34:65-69 Ja 1993

Cudahy, R.
Review of: *The nonviolent coming of God* by Douglass, James W. In: *Cist Stud* 27 No 4:[116]-[118] 1992

Cuevas, Zillah.
The artist who painted a prayer. *CDgst* 57:6-9 Mr 1993

Culbertson, Diana.
"Ain't nobody clean": the liturgy of violence in Glory. *Relig Lit* 25:37-52 Sum 1993
Glory. *Relig Lit* 25:37-52 Sum 1993

Cullen, Paul.
Blood money. *OSV* 81:6-7 Ap 18 1993
Bringing children into the church. *OSV* 81:8 Ap 4 1993
Moving days. *Columbia* 73:14-15 Je 1993

Cullen, Trevor.
Malawi chooses its future. *Tablet* 247:257-258 F 20 1993

Culley, Robert C.
Review of: *On humour and the comic in the Hebrew Bible* by Radday, Yehuda T, and Brenner, Athalya, eds. In: *CBQ* 55:201-202 Ja 1993

Culligan, Kevin.
Traditions of spiritual guidance: St John of the Cross: spiritual guide. *Way* 33:63-74 Ja 1993

Culpepper, Gary.
Review of: *God for us: the Trinity and Christian life* by LaCugna, Catherine Mowry. In: *Living Light* 29:85-87 Wint 1992

Cultrera, Francesco.
Nel crepuscolo della probabilità etica e politica. *Civilta* 2:153-160 Ap 17 1993
Review of: *Al fiume del silenzio* by Doucet, Hubert. In: *Civilta* 3:203-204 Jl 17 1993
Review of: *Amare il prossimo: corso di etica* by Trutwin, Werner, and Breuning, Klaus, eds. In: *Civilta* 144:192-193 Ja 16 1993
Review of: *Cristianesimo ed economia, vol II* by Guzzetti, Giovanni Battista. In: *Civilta* 143:529-530 D 5 1992
Review of: *Etica teologica del nuovo testamento* by Lohse, Eduard. In: *Civilta* 143:631-633 D 19 1992
Review of: *Etica y ecología* by Gafo, Javier, ed. In: *Civilta* 144:508-509 Mr 6 1993
Review of: *Fecondazione artificiale: una scelta etica?* by Bruguès, Jean-Louis. In: *Civilta* 143:423-425 N 21 1992
Review of: *Il suicidio: Vuoto esistenziale e ricerca di senso* by Fizzotti, Eugenio, and Gismondi, Angelo. In: *Civilta* 143:427-428 N 21 1992
Review of: *Il volto morale dell'uomo* by Privitera, Salvatore. In: *Civilta* 3:89-91 Jl 3 1993
Review of: *L'etica cristiana* by Vidal, Marciano. In: *Civilta* 2:192-193 Ap 17 1993
Review of: *L'etica nei comitati di bioetica: atti del 3 seminario di etica professionale: 4-8 giugno 1990.* In: *Civilta* 2:303-304 My 1 1993
Review of: *L'insegnamento sociale della chiesa: L'insegnamento socioeconomico* by Guzzetti, Giovanni Battista. In: *Civilta* 143:529-530 D 5 1992
Review of: *La parola e la coscienza* by Pinckaerts, Servais. In: *Civilta* 144:610-611 Mr 20 1993

Cultrera, Francesco. *(cont'd)*
Review of: *Mannuale di bioetica e deontologia medica* by Lega, Carlo. In: *Civilta* 144:91-92 Ja 2 1993
Review of: *Novitas et veritas vitae: Aux sources du renouveau de la morale chrétienne.* In: *Civilta* 2:304-305 My 1 1993
Review of: *Oltre le sabbie mobili* by Mattai, Giuseppe. In: *Civilta* 3:202-203 Jl 17 1993

Cummings, Charles.
Review of: *Letters to contemplatives* by Johnston, William. In: *Cist Stud* 28:[1] 1993
Review of: *The farewell of the word: the Johannine call to abide* by Segovia, Fernando F. In: *Cist Stud* 28:[18]-[19] 1993

Cummings, Frank P.
Public dissent and passive protest. *SocJust* 84:49-53 Mr-Ap 1993

Cummings, G C L. *see* Hopkins, D N, jt ed

Cummings, Maureen A. *see* Cummings, Richard G, jt auth

Cummings, Owen F.
Cyril of Jerusalem as a postliberal theologian. *Worship* 67:155-164 Mr 1993
The eucharistic presence of Christ. *Emmanuel* 99:256-263 Je 1993
Medieval Eucharist theology. *Emmanuel* 99:72-79 Mr 1993
The real Mary Magdalene. *Priest* 49:47-49 F 1993
Review of: *Why do we suffer? new ways of understanding* by Liderbach, Daniel. In: *Living Light* 30:107 Aut 1993

Cummings, Raymond L.
Review of: *Between two amnesties: former political prisoners and exiles in the Roman revolution of 1848* by Glueckert, Leopold G. In: *CHist* 79:145 Ja 1993

Cummings, Richard G, and Cummings, Maureen A.
A couple's pilgrimage to Humanae Vitae (commentary: *Humanae Vitae*). *OSV* 82:10-11 Jl 25 1993
Humanae Vitae, on the regulation of birth [1968 07 25].

Cunliffe, C R A.
Review of: *Chosen: gay Catholic priests tell their stories* by Stuart, Elizabeth. In: *Priests & People* 7:366-367 Ag-S 1993

Cunnar, Eugene R.
"Break not them then so wrongfully": topical readings of Sir Thomas Wyatt's riddling and bewitched lute and the feminine other. *Cithara* 32:3-30 N 1992

Cunneen, Joseph.
African, ethnic, high society—take your pick. *Nat Cath Rep* 29:15 O 8 1993
Film reviewed: *Guelwaar, Samba Traoré, The Age of Innocence, The Joy Luck Club, Household Saints, Into the West.*
Altman goes self-indulgent, and China goes for big time. *Nat Cath Rep* 30:16 N 12 1993
Films reviewed: *Short Cuts, Ruby in Paradise, Fairwell My Concubine.*
Chasing, searching for and discovering secrets. *Nat Cath Rep* 29:13 S 3 1993
Films reviewed: *The Fugitive, Searching for Bobby Fischer, The Secret Garden.*
A complex love-thriller and a whimsical farce. *Nat Cath Rep* 29:18 Ja 8 1993
Films reviewed: *The Crying Game, The Distinguished Gentleman.*
Eric Rohmer: the charm of the real. *Critic* 47:83-90 Spr 1993
Festival captured power, beauty of African films. *Nat Cath Rep* 29:13 My 21 1993
Films reviewd *Guelwaar, Samba Traore, Yeelen, Niwan, Rabi, The Voice in the Wood, etc.*
From bard to 'hood, 'tis true, from "Much Ado" to "Menace II". *Nat Cath Rep* 29:16 Jl 2 1993
Films reviewed: *Much Ado, Menace II Society.*
Growing up is difficult these days. *Nat Cath Rep* 29:14 Ap 23 1993
Films reviewed:*Just another girl on the IRT, Mac, Il Ladro di Bambini.*
If Clint is best, it's bad news for the rest. *Nat Cath Rep* 29:17 Jl 30 1993
Films reviewed: *In the Line of Fire, Sleepless in Seattle.*
A month at the movies. *Nat Cath Rep* 29:22 N 20 1992
Films reviewed: *Van Gogh Strangers in Good Company.*
Movies for Lent have a groundhog, passion fish, ashes and an oak tree. *Nat Cath Rep* 29:19 Mr 12 1993
Films reviewed: *Groundhod Day, Passion Fish, The Oak.*
You take some "Lorenzo's Oil," make a leap of faith, and voilà. *Nat Cath Rep* 29:15 F 5 1993
Films reviewed: *Lorenzo's Oil, Leap of Faith, Tous les Matin du Monde.*

Cunneen, Sally.
Review of: *Desperately seeking Mary: a feminist appropriation of a traditional religious symbol* by Maeckelberghe, Els. In: *CrossCurr* 43:134-135 Spr 1993
Review of: *Generous lives* by Redmont, Jane. In: *CrossCurr* 43:128-129 Spr 1993
Vulnerable sharers, peaceful wrecks. *America* 169:4-6 O 9 1993

Cunningham, A.
Review of: *Women and evil* by Noddings, Nel. In: *Can Cath Rev* 11:40-41 Ja 1993

Cunningham, Beatrice.
Who are their models? *ReligTJ* 27:38-39 O 1993

Cunningham, David S.
Review of: *Rhetoric, power and community* by Jasper, David, 1951-. In: *TheolStds* 54:602-603 S 1993

Cunningham, Hilary. *see* Scharper, Stephen B, jt ed

Cunningham, Lawrence S, 1935-.
The new Catechism: a first reading. *Comm* 120:8-12 Mr 12 1993
Origen's On Prayer: a reflection and appreciation. *Worship* 67:332-339 Jl 1993
Review of: *A democratic Catholic Church* by Bianchi, Eugene C, and Ruether, Rosemary Radford, eds. In: *Comm* 120:28-29 Mr 26 1993
Review of: *A history of Christianity in Asia, Vol I* by Moffett, Samuel Hugh. In: *Comm* 120:27-28 Je 4 1993
Review of: *A legend of holy women* by Delany, Sheila. In: *Comm* 120:29-30 My 7 1993

Cunningham, Lawrence S, 1935-. *(cont'd)*
Review of: *Alphonsus de Liguori; the Saint of Bourbon Naples* by Jones, Frederick M. In: *Comm* 120:28-29 My 7 1993
Review of: *Anchoritic spirituality* by Savage, Anne, et al, eds. In: *Comm* 120:30 Ag 13 1993
Review of: *Catholic spirituality and the history of religions* by Carmody, John Tully, and Carmody, Denise Lardner. In: *Cist Stud* 28 no 2:[40] 1993
Review of: *Dorothy Day* by Ellsberg, Robert, ed. In: *Comm* 120:26 F 12 1993
Review of: *Frontiers of Hispanic theology in the United States* by Figuerora, Allan, ed. In: *Comm* 120:30-31 O 8 1993
Review of: *Ignatius of Loyola: the psychology of a saint* by Meissner, William W. In: *Comm* 120:27 Mr 26 1993
Review of: *Julian's way: a practical commentary on Julian of Norwich* by Bradley, Ritamary. In: *Comm* 120:29-30 Ag 13 1993
Review of: *Karl Adam: Catholicism in German culture* by Krieg, Robert Anthony. In: *Comm* 120:28 My 7 1993
Review of: *Losing God* by Gallagher, Michael Paul, 1939-. In: *Comm* 120:26 Mr 26 1993
Review of: *Martyr of brotherly love* by Balling, Adalbert Ludwig, and Abeln, Reinhard. In: *Comm* 120:28 Je 4 1993
Review of: *Mysticism and language* by Katz, Steven T, ed. In: *Comm* 120:28 Ag 13 1993
Review of: *Peasant fires: the drummer of Niklashausen* by Wunderli, Richard. In: *Comm* 120:28-29 Je 4 1993
Review of: *Prayer: finding the heart's true home* by Foster, Richard J. In: *Comm* 120:26-27 Mr 26 1993
Review of: *Responses to 101 questions on the Dead Sea Scrolls* by Fitzmyer, Joseph Augustine, 1920-. In: *Comm* 120:30 O 8 1993
Review of: *Sainted women of the Dark Ages* by McNamara, Jo Ann, et al, eds. In: *Comm* 120:26 F 12 1993
Review of: *Sainted women of the dark ages.* In: *TheolStds* 54:385-386 Je 1993
Review of: *Salt, leaven and light* by Sanks, T Howland. In: *Comm* 120:29 Mr 26 1993
Review of: *Silent lamp: the Thomas Merton story* by Shannon, William Henry, 1917-. In: *Comm* 120:24 F 12 1993
Review of: *Silent voices, sacred lives: women's readings for the liturgical year* by Bowe, Barbara E, et al, eds. In: *Comm* 120:29-30 O 8 1993
Review of: *Simone Weil: protrait of a self-exiled Jew* by Nevin, Thomas R. In: *Comm* 120:25 F 12 1993
Review of: *The archaeology of the New Testament* by Finegan, Jack. In: *Comm* 120:27 Je 4 1993
Review of: *The Catholic Church and American culture: reciprocity and challenge* by Yuhaus, Cassian, ed. In: *Cist Stud* 28 no 2:[39] 1993
Review of: *The Creed: the Apostolic faith in contemporary theology* by Marthaler, Berard L, 1927-. In: *Comm* 120:29 O 8 1993
Review of: *The divine romance: Teresa of Avila's narrative theology* by Chorpenning, Joseph F. In: *Comm* 120:24-25 F 12 1993
Review of: *The early Reformation in Europe* by Pettegre, Andrew, ed. In: *Comm* 120:29 Je 4 1993
Review of: *The education of an archbishop* by Wilkes, Paul, 1938-. In: *Comm* 120:27-28 Mr 26 1993
Review of: *The land called Holy: Palestine in Christian history and thought* by Wilken, Robert L. In: *Comm* 120:29 Ag 13 1993
Review of: *The mystic fable: v I: the sixteenth and seventeenth centuries* by Certeau, Michel de. In: *Comm* 120:30 My 7 1993
Review of: *The text as thou* by Keppes, Steven. In: *Comm* 120:28 O 8 1993
Review of: *The way of a pilgrim* by Bacovcin, Helen. In: *Comm* 120:26 Mr 26 1993
Review of: *The Word in the desert: scripture and the quest for holiness in early Christian monasticism* by Burton-Christie, Douglas. In: *Comm* 120:28-29 Ag 13 1993
Review of: *Theological investigations XXII* by Rahner, Karl, 1904-1984. In: *Cist Stud* 28:[2]-[3] 1993
Review of: *Theological investigations XXIII* by Rahner, Karl, 1904-1984. In: *Cist Stud* 28:[2]-[3] 1993
Review of: *Who's who in theology* by Bowden, John. In: *Comm* 120:25-26 F 12 1993
[Whatever terror may strike the hearts]. *Comm* 120:11-12 O 22 1993
Why people still put their body and soul into prayer. *USCath* 58:6-13 Jl 1993

Cunningham, Lawrence S., 1935-.
Review of: *The Eucharistic mystery* by Power, David Noel. In: *Comm* 120:28-29 O 8 1993

Cunsolo, Ronald S.
Nationalists and Catholics in Giolittian Italy: an uneasy collaboration. *CHist* 79:22-53 Ja 1993

Curley, John E, Jr.
A credible, effective force for Catholic healthcare. *Health Prog* 74:14-15+ Jl-Ag 1993
Dialogue [interview by P. Mullen]. *Register* 69:1+ O 24 1993

Curley, Terence P.
The annulment process and pastoral care. *Priest* 49:39-41 O 1993
Becoming a bereavement minister. *Priest* 49:54-55 S 1993
The Catechism of the Catholic Church. *Priest* 49:12-14 Je 1993
Catechism of the Catholic Church (Commentary).
Console one another: a guide for Christian funerals. Kansas City: Sheed & Ward, 1993. 100p ISBN 1-55612-600-x LC 93-3540
The ministry of consolation: the parish guide for comforting the bereaved. New York: Alba House, 1993. 70p ISBN 0-8189-0651-0 LC 93-10315

Curran, Charles E, 1934-, et al.
Ex corde ecclesiae and its ordinances. *Comm* 120:14+ N 19 1993

Curran, Charles E, 1934-.
The Church and morality: an ecumenical and Catholic approach. Minneapolis: Fortress Press, 1993. 126p ISBN 0-8006-2756-3 LC 92-47448
Encyclical left church credibility stillborn (commentary: *Humanae Vitae*). *Nat Cath Rep* 29:14-15 Jl 16 1993
Humanae Vitae, on the regulation of birh [1968 O7 25].
Review of: *New directions in moral theology* by Kelly, Kevin T. In: *Heythrop* 34:198 Ap 1993

Curran, Charles E, 1934-. *(cont'd)*
[Veritatis splendor belongs to the literary gender]. *Comm* 120:14 O 22 1993

Curran, Charles E, 1934-, and McCormick, Richard A, eds.
Dialogue about Catholic's sexual teaching. Mahwah: Paulist, 1993. x, 601p ISBN 0-8091-3414-4 LC 93-4370

Curran, Dolores.
Family nonconformists: is there room for wildflowers in your garden? *USCath* 58:14-19 Jl 1993
What's the statute of limitations on blaming your parents? *USCath* 58:14-17 Mr 1993

Curran, R Emmett.
Review of: *American Catholic preaching and piety in the time of John Carroll* by Kupke, Raymond J, ed. In: *CHist* 79:567-568 Jl 1993

Curran, Robert.
The bicentennials history of Georgetown University: from academy to university, 1789-1982, v1. Washington: Georgetown University Press, 1993. 445p ISBN 0-87840-485-6 LC 92-47499

Currier, Richard.
Forming a small Christian community: a personal journey. Mystic: Twenty-Third Publications, 1992. 178p ISBN 0-89622-511-9 LC 91-68557

Curry, Adrienne.
As black Catholics speak, who will listen? *USCath* 58:30-31 Ja 1993

Curry, Dean C, 1952-.
Lamentations. *Crisis* 11:9-10 Jl-Ag 1993
Politics isn't everything. *Crisis* 11:10 Mr 1993

Curtin, Joan.
The Diocesan Catechetical Office perspective on implementing the Catechism. *Living Light* 30:79-82 Aut 1993

Cusack, P.
Review of: *Gregory the Great: perfection in imperfection* by Straw, Carole. In: *Cist Stud* 27 No 4:[93]-[95] 1992

Cutrone, Emmanuel J.
Review of: *The Eucharistic prayer of Addai and Mari* by Gelston, Anthony. In: *Worship* 67:282-284 My 1993

Cuxim Caamal, Primitivo.
Palabras a Juan Pablo II. *Christus* 58:44-45 S 1993

Cuyás, Manuel.
Il consenso informato in medicina. *Civilta* 2:61-67 Ap 3 1993

Cuzzola, Theresa.
Dance for joy. *Emmanuel* 99:80-84 Mr 1993

Cviic, Christopher.
From victim to aggressor. *Tablet* 247:678-679 My 29 1993
Lest we forget. *Tablet* 247:1092-1093 Ag 28 1993
Review of: *The Catholic ethic and the spirit of capitalism* by Novak, Michael, 1933-. In: *Tablet* 247:1012-1013 Ag 7 1993
Review of: *The final revolution* by Weigel, George. In: *Tablet* 247:1012-1013 Ag 7 1993
Review of: *The Vatican in the age of the Cold War 1945-1980* by Rhodes, Anthony. In: *Tablet* 247:1012-1013 Ag 7 1993
Towards a Switzerland in the Balkans. *Tablet* 247:162-163 F 6 1993

Cylwicki, Albert.
Review of: *All eyes and blind: parable stories for Sunday Scripture—Cycle B* by Sullivan, Francis P. In: *Can Cath Rev* 11:30 S 1993
Review of: *Dare to be Christ: homilies for the nineties* by Burghardt, Walter J. In: *Can Cath Rev* 11:29 My 1993

Czuma, Hanna.
Review of: *Faith under fire and the revolutions in Eastern Europe* by Hedberg, Augustin. In: *Can Cath Rev* 11:25-26 My 1993

D

D'Amécourt, Joseph.
Review of: *La doctrine de la revelation divine de Saint Thomas D'Aquin: actes du symposium sur la pensée de Saint Thomas d'Aquin.* In: *Thomist* 57:141-146 Ja 1993

D'Angelo, Mary Rose.
Re-membering Jesus: women, prophecy, and resistance in the memory of the early churches. *Horizons (CTS)* 19:199-218 Fall 1992

D'Angelo, Pam.
From apartheid to democracy. *Register* 69:1+ O 17 1993

D'Antonio, William V, et al.
American Catholic laity in a changing church. Kansas City: Sheed and Ward, 1989. x, 193p ISBN 1-55612-247-0 LC 88-60114

D'Antonio, William V.
Catholics remain committed as they accommodate change [tables]. *Nat Cath Rep* 29:26-27 O 8 1993
New world laity casts off chains of command. *Nat Cath Rep* 29:11-12 N 20 1992

D'Arcy, Fergus.
Review of: *A man called Hughes, the life and times of Seamus Hughes, 1881-1943* by Morrissey, Thomas. In: *Studies* 81:482-484 Wint 1992

D'Arcymay, John.
100 years of global inter-faith dialogue: 1893-1993. *Doctr Life* 43:141-146 Mr 1993

D'Arnoux, Alexandra. see Darblay, Jerome, jt auth

D'Costa, Gavin.
Christian theology and other religions: an evaluation of John Hick and Paul Knitter. *StudiaM* 42:161-178 1993
Review of: *An apology for apologetics: a study in the logic of interreligious dialogue* by Griffiths, Paul J. In: *Thomist* 56:719-723 O 1992

D'Costa, Gavin. *(cont'd)*
Review of: *God—his and hers* by Moltmann-Wendel, Elisabeth, and Moltmann, Jürgen. In: *New Blckfrs* 73:627-628 D 1992
Review of: *Jesus Christ at the encounter of world religions* by Dupuis, Jacques. In: *Thomist* 56:719-723 O 1992
Review of: *The diversity of religions* by DiNoia, J A. In: *Thomist* 57:524-528 Jl 1993

D'Souza, Dinesh, 1961-.
Free speech for whom? *Crisis* 10:4 N 1992
A house divided: what future for American Catholics? *Crisis* 10:19-22 D 1992
Newton in drag. *Crisis* 11:4-5 Ja 1993

D'Souza, M O.
Review of: *Catholic education: transforming our world a Canadian perspective* by Higgins, Michael, et al, eds. In: *Can Cath Rev* 11:23-24 S 1993

Da Passano, P.
Review of: *Enti e beni religiosi in Italia* by Berlingò, Salvatore. In: *Civilta* 144:99-100 Ja 2 1993

Daaleman, Timothy P.
The medical world of Hildegard of Bingen. *ABenR* 44:280-289 S 1993

Dagens, Claude.
Le christianisme dans l'histoire. *NRT* 114:801-815 N-D 1992

Daggy, Robert E.
Choirs of millions: a reflection on Thomas Merton and God's creatures. *Cist Stud* 28:93-107 1993

Dailey, Thomas F.
The aesthetics of repentance: re-reading the phenomenon of Job. *Bib Th Bul* 23:64-70 Sum 1993

Daily, Thomas V, Bp., 1927-.
A prophetic document. *Columbia* 73:6-8 Ag 1993
Humanae Vitae, on the regulation of birth [1968 07 25] Commentary.

Dala Pujolras, Joaquim.
El mite de l'expulsio des paradis o els auguris de l'home boig: cartes a l'academia. Barcelona: Edicions, 1993. x, 222p ISBN 84-297-3609-3

Dale, Alzina Stone.
Dorothy L Sayers: the centenary celebration. New York: Walker and Co, 1993. 166p ISBN 0-80273-224-0 LC 92-44894

Daley, Barbara Carter.
Grace that amazes. *Spir Life* 39:11-21 Spr 1993

Daley, Brian E.
Born of a virgin. *Tablet* 246:1598-1603 D 19-26 1992
Christ and the Catholic university. *America* 169:6-14 S 11 1993

Dallen, James.
Review of: *Christian Initiation and Baptism in the Holy Spirit* by McDonnell, Kilian, 1921-, and Montague, George T. In: *JEcumen Stds* 29:270-271 Spr 1992
Review of: *Fanning the flame: what does Baptism in the Holy Spirit have to do with Christian Initation?* by McDonnell, Kilian, 1921-, and Montague, George T, eds. In: *JEcumen Stds* 29:270-271 Spr 1992
Review of: *The distancing of God: the ambiguity of symbol in history and theology* by Cooke, Bernard J. In: *JEcumen Stds* 29:109-110 Wint 1992

Dalton, Anne Marie.
Religion and science: collaboration for the environment. *Living Light* 29:14-22 Aut 1992

Dalton, William J.
Galatians without tears. Collegeville, Minnesota: The Liturgical Press, 1992. 75p ISBN 0-8146-2227-5 LC 93-18782
Review of: *Parish councils on missin: coresponsibility and authority among pastors and parishioners* by Se-Mang, Peter Kim. In: *Furrow* 44:125-126 F 1993
Your child's baptism. *Furrow* 44:485-489 S 1993

Daly, Anthony C.
Aquinas on disordered pleasures and conditions. *Thomist* 56:583-612 O 1992

Daly, Bernard M.
Review of: *The Church, community of salvation* by Tavard, George Henry. In: *Can Cath Rev* 11:29 Je 1993

Daly, Cahal Brendan, Cardinal, 1917-, et al.
Work is the key [excerpts fr a Pastoral Letter]. *Cath Int* 4:182-189 Ap 1993

Daly, K A.
Irish Society of St Cecilia. *SacM* 120:15-25 Sum 1993

Daly, Mary.
Textbooks that teach truth. *Register* 69:5 Jl 25 1993

Dalzell, Catherine.
Boredom and laughter: a visit to the Natural History Museum. *Can Cath Rev* 11:11-16 O 1993
Positions in the cage: toward a Christian experience of space. *Can Cath Rev* 11:18-25 Mr 1993
The power to act: toward a Christian experience of time. *Can Cath Rev* 11:7-11 F 1993

Damasceno, Raimundo, et al.
Para comprender Santo Domingo. *Christus* 58:7-28 F 1993

Danckert, Stephen C.
The quotable Johnson. San Francisco: Ignatius Press, 1992. x, 148p ISBN 0-89870-415-5 LC 92-71942

Daneels, Frans.
The right of defence [commentary to John Paul II address given on Ja 26 1989: Rome]. *Stud Can* 27 no 1:77-95 1993

Dangel, Mary Jo.
Gunfight on Capitol Hill [editorial]. *St Anth* 100:27 Ap 1993
Health-care reform: a Catholic prescription. *St Anth* 101:14-18 Je 1993
Review of: *Celebrate-your-womanhood therapy* by Katafiasz, Karen. In: *St Anth* 100:52-53 Mr 1993
A teaching and healing ministry. *St Anth* 101:16-17 Je 1993
Warning: TV violence is hazardous to our children [editorial]. *St Anth* 101:17 N 1993

Daniel, Norman.
Islam and the west: the making of an image. Oxford: Oneworld, 1993. x, 467p ISBN 1-85168-043-8

Daniels, Scott.
Reform and the family [rpt fr Family Research Council]. *Register* 69:3 N 14 1993

Danker, Frederick.
Review of: *Conflict in Luke: Jesus, authorities, disciples* by Kingsbury, Jack Dean. In: *CBQ* 54:790-791 O 1992

Danneels, Godfried, Cardinal, 1933-.
Priests for our time. *Furrow* 44:331-440 Je 1993
Apostolic Exhortation, Pastores Dabo Vobis (I will give you shepherds), to the bishops, clergy and faithful on the formation of priests in the circumstances of the present day (commentary).

Danner, Peter L.
Review of: *The good stewards* by Naughton, Michael. In: *RSocEcon* 51:122-123 Spr 1993

Danroc, Gilles.
L'Église d'Haiti: histoire d'une naissance. *NRT* 115:69-84 Ja-F 1993

Darling-Smith, Barbara.
Can virtue be taught? Notre Dame: University of Notre Dame Press, 1993. x, 224p ISBN 0-268-00799-3 LC 93-4578

Darragh, Neil.
The distortion of Christian ritual. *Pacifica* 6:21-47 F 1993

Dart, John A.
Coverage of religion isn't all bad. *Register* 69:5 O 31 1993

Darwent, Charles.
The baby of Mâcon. *Tablet* 247:1238 S 25 1993
Equinox. *Tablet* 247:1018 Ag 7 1993
The fencing master. *Tablet* 247:894 Jl 10 1993
The fugitive [directed by A Davis]. *Tablet* 247:1306 O 9 1993
In the line of fire [directed by W Peterson]. *Tablet* 247:1139 S 4 1993
Innocent blood. *Tablet* 247:826-827 Je 26 1993
Jurassic park. *Tablet* 247:987-988 Jl 31 1993
Made in America [directed by R Benjamin]. *Tablet* 247:1106 Ag 28 1993
Passion fish [directed by J Sayles]. *Tablet* 247:1168 S 11 1993
A place in the world. *Tablet* 247:1201 S 18 1993
Sleepless in Seattle [directed by N Ephron]. *Tablet* 247:1268 O 2 1993
The snapper. *Tablet* 247:1049 Ag 14 1993
Tango. *Tablet* 247:1078 Ag 21 1993
Three of hearts. *Tablet* 247:924 Jl 17 1993
The vanishing. *Tablet* 247:794-795 Je 19 1993

Daryl, Charles J.
Literary stategy in the Epistle of Jude. Scranton: University of Scranton Press, 1993. 258p ISBN 0-94086-616-1 LC 91-66129

Dash, Millicent A.
Review of: *Godly play: a way of religious education* by Berryman, Jerome. In: *Living Light* 29:84-85 Aut 1992

Dauncey, Guy.
Ecological sustainability at Bamberton [fr the *Bamberton News*]. *Teilhard Rev* 28:22-24 Sum 1993

Daurio, Janice.
Review of: *Faith and faithfulness: basic themes in Christian ethics* by Meilaender, Gilbert C. In: *New Oxford Rev* 60:29+ Mr 1993 see Ford, Paul, jt auth

Davey, Colin.
Opportunities and challenges offered by BEM to the British and Irish churches. *OChr* 29 no 3:216-225 1993

Davey, Theodore.
Review of: *Theology and Canon Law* by Orsy, Ladislas M, 1921-. In: *Month* 26:232-233 Je 1993

Davidson, Jim.
Generational differences among Catholics emerge. *Nat Cath Rep* 29:29-30 O 8 1993

Davidson, Patricia S.
Biblical charades, anyone? Jesus jeopardy? *Tod Parish* 25:6 S 1993

Davidson, Peter.
Review of: *The Catholic religious poets from Southwell to Crashaw* by Cousins, Anthony D. In: *Heythrop* 34:456-458 O 1993

Davidson, Richard J.
The time for healthcare reform is now. *Health Prog* 74:44-45 Jl-Ag 1993

Davies, Alan.
Review of: *A legacy of hatred: why Christians must not forget the Holocaust* by Rausch, David A. In: *JEcumen Stds* 29:126-127 Wint 1992
Review of: *Toward a definition of Antisemitism* by Langmuir, Gavin I. In: *JEcumen Stds* 29:126-127 Wint 1992

Davies, Brian.
Review of: *Aquinas on human action* by McInerny, Ralph M. In: *IPQ* 33:239-240 Je 1993
Review of: *At the heart of the real* by O'Rourke, Fran. In: *New Blckfrs* 74:425-426 S 1993
Review of: *Biblical faith and natural theology* by Barr, James. In: *New Blckfrs* 74:367-369 Jl-Ag 1993
Review of: *Perceiving God* by Alston, William P. In: *IPQ* 33:124-127 Mr 1993
Review of: *Pseudo-Dionysius and the metaphysics of Aquinas* by O'Rourke, Fran. In: *New Blckfrs* 74:223-225 Ap 1993 see Walsh, Michael J, 1937-, jt auth

Davies, Gordon F.
Creed and criticism: the complementarity of faith and exegesis. *Can Cath Rev* 11:7-10 O 1993

Davies, Horton.
A church historian's odyssey. Grand Rapids: Eerdmans, 1993. 218p ISBN 0-8028-0712-7

Davies, James A. see Ratcliff, Donald E, jt ed

Davies, Julian A.
Review of: *Imagination: a future for religious life* by Thomasis, Louis De. In: *Sisters* 65:306 Jl 1993

Davies, Meg.
Review of: *What are the Gospels?* by Burridge, Richard A. In: *New Blckfrs* 74:109-110 F 1993

Davies, Oliver.
Review of: *Matins, Lauds, and Vespers for St David's Day* by Edwards, Owain Tudor. In: *Heythrop* 34:327-328 Jl 1993

Davies, Oliver, ed.
Born to life. New Rochelle, New York: New City Press, 1992. 127p ISBN 1-56548-006-6 LC 92-14860
Gateway to paradise: Basil the Great. New Rochelle, New York: New City Press, 1992. 125p ISBN 1-56548-0023 LC 91-34259
Promise of good things: the Apostolic Fathers. New Rochelle, New York: New City Press, 1993. 115p ISBN 1-56548-019-8 LC 92-42033

Davies, Thomas X.
Review of: *Source book of self-discipline: a synthesis of moralia* by Gildea, Joseph. In: *Cist Stud* 28 no 2:[51]-[52] 1993

Davis, Brian.
Review of: *Saint Anselm* by Southern, R W. In: *Heythrop* 34:208-209 Ap 1993 see Walsh, Michael J, 1937-, jt ed

Davis, Charlie.
Catholics will give when church moves into future. *Nat Cath Rep* 29:13 F 12 1993

Davis, Cyprian.
Don't close inner-city Catholic schools. *USCath* 58:22-27 My 1993
In the beginning, there were black Catholics [interview by the editors of US Catholic (Periodical)]. *USCath* 58:6-14 Ap 1993

Davis, Derek. see Wood, James E, Jr, jt ed

Davis, Kenneth.
Review of: *Frontiers of Hispanic theology in the United States* by Deck, Allan Figueroa. In: *RRel* 52:298 Mr-Ap 1993
Review of: *Prophetic vision: pastoral reflections on the national pastoral plan for Hispanic ministry* by Galerón, Soledad, et al, eds. In: *RRel* 52:299 Mr-Ap 1993
US Hispanic Catholics: trends and works 1992. *RRel* 52:283-295 Mr-Ap 1993

Davis, Kortright.
Toward communion in faith, life and witness. *Ecumen Trends* 22:1-2+ Jl-Ag 1993

Davis, Leo Donald.
Review of: *Christian unity* by Alberigo, Giuseppe, ed. In: *TheolStds* 54:351-354 Je 1993

Davis, Milton.
Salt of the earth: Milton Davis [interview by V Anderson]. *Salt* 13:4-5 Ap 1993

Davis, Robert Murray, 1934-.
A modest proposal for a class reunion. *America* 168:5 My 29 1993

Davis, Rose Marie. see Strasser, Stephen, jt auth

Davis, Stephen T.
Risen indeed: a Christian philosophy of resurrection. Grand Rapids: Eerdmans, 1993. 232p ISBN 0-8028-0126-9

Davis, Thomas X.
Contemplative action: a review essay on four articles by Charles Dumont. *Cist Stud* 28 no 2:161-166 1993
Review of: *Monk and mason on the Tigris frontier* by Palmer, Andrew. In: *Cist Stud* 28:[36]-[37] 1993
Review of: *Peter of Waltham, remediarium conversorum* by Gildea, Joseph, ed. In: *Cist Stud* 28 no 2:[51]-[52] 1993
Review of: *The broken covenant* by Bellah, Robert Neely, 1927-. In: *Cist Stud* 28 no 2:[60]-[62] 1993
Review of: *The luminous eye: the spiritual world vision of Saint Ephrem the Syrian* by Brock, Sebastian. In: *Cist Stud* 28:[38] 1993

Davis, William.
Funding the asbestos cleanup. *Origins* 23:45-46 Je 3 1993

Dawn, Marva J.
Sexual character: beyond technique to intimacy. Grand Rapids: Eerdmans, 1993. 192p ISBN 0-8028-0700-3

Day, Agnes.
Cistercian scrapbook. *Word Sp* 14:118-128 1992

Day, John.
Review of: *Divine disclosure: an introduction to Jewish apocalyptic* by Russell, David Syme. In: *New Blckfrs* 74:170-172 Mr 1993
Review of: *The England of Piers Plowman: William Langland and his vision of the fourteenth century* by Boulay, F R H Du. In: *TheolStds* 53:785 D 1992

Day, Peggy L.
Review of: *Text and tradition: the Hebrew Bible and folklore* by Niditch, Susan. In: *CBQ* 55:198-199 Ja 1993

Day, Peter D.
The liturgical dictionary of Eastern Christianity. Collegeville: Liturgical, 1993. x, 334p ISBN 0-8146-5848-2 LC 93-20377

Day, Thomas.
Chant: music of our past, and our future. *Past Mus* 17:26-29 Ag-S 1993

De Ferari, Jose Manuel. see Rosales, Raul, jt ed

De Luis Carballada, R.
Review of: *Veröhnung: Versuche zu ihrer Geschichte und Zukunft* by Eggensperger, T, et al, eds. In: *Cien Tom* 119:412-413 My-Ag 1992

De Rosa, G.
Review of: *Dermi divini nelle religioni: Induismo, Buddhismo, Religiostà cinese, Islam* by Dilenge, Giovanni. In: *Civilta* 144:101-102 Ja 2 1993

Dean, Julia.
Mercy home: fighting the horror of infanticide in rural India. *OSV* 82:10-11 Jl 18 1993

Dean, Stephen.
Can we revive the prayer of the church? *Priests & People* 7:107-113 Mr 1993
Review of: *Fountain of life* by Austin, Gerard, ed. In: *Priests & People* 6:356-357 Ag-S 1993

Deane-Drummond, Celia.
A critique of Jürgen Moltmann's green theology. *New Blckfrs* 73:554-565 N 1992

Dear, John, 1959-.
Sub-versive activity: tip the canoe and Trident, too. *Comm* 120:5-7 O 22 1993

Dearman, J Andrew.
Review of: *Isaiah, Ahaz, and the Syro-Ephraimitic crisis* by Irvine, Stuart A. In: *CBQ* 54:748-749 O 1992
Review of: *The fabric of history* by Edelman, Diana Vikander, ed. In: *CBQ* 55:411-413 Ap 1993

Debarge, Louis.
Review of: *Conférence européene des catéchuménats.* In: *MSR* 50:61-63 Ja-Mr 1993
Review of: *Histoire de la pensée, v I* by Chevalier, Jacques. In: *MSR* 50:161-163 Ap-Je 1993
Review of: *L'antisémitisme* by Chevalier, Yves. In: *MSR* 50:66-68 Ja-Mr 1993
Review of: *L'union chrétienne à Fontenay-Le-Comte* by Debouté, Eugénie. In: *MSR* 50:63-64 Ja-Mr 1993
Review of: *La menace idéologique* by Madelin, Henri. In: *MSR* 50:74-75 Ja-Mr 1993
Review of: *Les Mormons* by Introvigne, Massimo. In: *MSR* 50:64-65 Ja-Mr 1993
Review of: *Les témoins de Jéhovah* by Blandre, Bernard. In: *MSR* 50:65-66 Ja-Mr 1993
Review of: *Mirages du masque* by Pernet, Henry. In: *MSR* 50:73-74 Ja-Mr 1993

Debarger, Louis.
Review of: *Aux risques de l'autre* by Ibal, Bernard. In: *MSR* 50:71-72 Ja-Mr 1993
Review of: *Jeunesses chrétiennes au XXe siècle* by Cholvy, Gérard, et al. In: *MSR* 50:59-61 Ja-Mr 1993

DeBoy, James J, Jr, 1942-.
Review of: *An introduction to Canon Law* by Coriden, James A. In: *Living Light* 29:82-84 Wint 1992
Simplicity in the midst of complexity: religious education in the twenty-first century. *ChrWorld* 236:227-232 S-O 1993

DeCelles, Charles.
The American bishops and capital punishment. *SocJust* 84:149-153 S-O 1993
Did Jesus know he was God? *Priest* 49:33-38 Ap 1993

Deck, Allan Figueroa.
Hispanic Catholics: does the Church speak your language? [interview by the editors of USCath]. *USCath* 58:27-30 D 1993
La raza cósmica: rediscovering the Hispanic soul. *Critic* 47:46-53 Spr 1993
Review of: *Politics and the Catholic Church in Nicaragua* by Kirk, John M. In: *America* 169:24-26 N 20 1993
What Anglos can learn from Hispanic Catholics [condensed fr *The Critic* Sp 1993]. *CDgst* 57:50-53+ S 1993

Decker, Christopher W.
Review of: *Uncommon decency: Christian civility in an uncivil world* by Mouw, Richard J. In: *New Oxford Rev* 60:28-29 Jl-Ag 1993

Declève, Henri.
Jan Patovcka et le phénomène de l'écriture littéraire. *Laval Theol Phil* 49:3-26 F 1993

DeCock, M.
Review of: *Ungodly rage: the hidden face of Catholic feminism* by Steichen, Donna. In: *Can Cath Rev* 11:41-42 Ja 1993

DeCosse, David E.
Catholic Campaign to advance "moral" agenda through media. *Nat Cath Rep* 29:5 N 20 1992
The Catholic case for inclusion. *America* 168:15-16 My 8 1993
Review of: *Organized labor and the Church* by Higgins, George G, 1916-. In: *America* 169:18-20 S 25 1993

DeCoursey, Drew.
Pro-lifers are not "wasting time". *OSV* 82:19 Ag 15 1993

DeCoursey, Vincent W, Jr.
Review of: *Japan's hidden Christians* by Harrington, Ann M. In: *Nat Cath Rep* 29:19 Je 18 1993
Review of: *Last oasis: facing water scarcity* by Postel, Sandra. In: *Nat Cath Rep* 29:18 Mr 12 1993
Review of: *No pity* by Shapiro, Joseph P. In: *Nat Cath Rep* 29:22 O 15 1993

Deedy, John G, 1933-.
The church still relies on its brothers. *USCath* 58:33-37 N 1993
Facts, myths and maybes: everything you think you know about Catholocism. Chicago: The Thomas More Press, 1993. 320p ISBN 0-88347-272-4
Locke's proposal for semiotic adn the scholastic doctrine of species. *Mod Schlmn* 70:165-188 Mr 1993

Deehan, John.
Review of: *Divorce in the New Testament* by Collins, Raymond F. In: *Priests & People* 7:368 Ag-S 1993

Deeley, Mray Katherine.
Review of: *Every promise fulfilled: contesting plots in Joshua* by Hawk, L Daniel. In: *OTA* 16:172-173 F 1993

Deen, Leonard.
Review of: *Marvelous possessions: the wonder of the New World* by Greenblatt, Stephen. In: *Comm* 120:25-26 O 8 1993

DeGidio, Sandra.
Just what can a parent do? *St Anth* 100:21 Ja 1993

Dehon, Gilbert.
Le R P Jacques Coret (1631-1721) et la devotion á Saint Joseph à l'âge classique. *MSR* 50:117-133 Ap-Je 1993

Deiss, Lucien.
Celebration of the word. Collegeville: Liturgical, 1993. x, 145p ISBN 0-8146-2090-6 LC 93-15193

Deitering, Carolyn.
Advent bear. *Living Prayer* 26:3-5 N-D 1993

Del Colle, Ralph.
The experience of the divine. *Chicago Stud* 31:290-300 N 1992

Del Preite, Mariano. see Grieco, Gianfranco, jt auth

Del Zanna, Lorenzo.
Ernesto Balducci. *Civilta* 144:445-458 Mr 6 1993

Delaney, Cornelius F, 1938-.
Science, knowledge and mind: a study in the philosophy of C S Peirce. Indiana: University of Notre Dame Press, 1993. x, 183p ISBN 0-268-01748-4 LC 92-53743

Delaney, Hubert.
Review of: *Metaphysics as a guide to morals* by Murdoch, Iris. In: *Studies* 82:339-346 Aut 1993

Delaney, Mary Cris.
The adventure of sacramental love. *Crisis* 11:52-53 S 1993

Delaney, William K.
Cultivating joy. *New Cov* 22:22-23 Jl 1993

Delay, Jill.
Review of: *A family romance* by Brookner, Anita. In: *Tablet* 247:951 Jl 24 1993
Review of: *Angels and insects* by Byatt, A. S. In: *Tablet* 247:79 Ja 16 1993
Review of: *Dora's room* by Hines, Joanna. In: *Tablet* 247:759 Je 1993
Review of: *Pillion riders* by Taylor, Elisabeth Russell. In: *Tablet* 247:922 Jl 17 1993
Review of: *Present from the past* by Dilke, Annabel. In: *Tablet* 247:248 F 20 1993

DeLeeuw, Patricia Allwin.
Review of: *Faith to creed* by Heim, S Mark, ed. In: *JEcumen Stds* 29:476-477 Sum-Aut 1992

Delesalle, Jacques.
La raison et le Dieu-trinité. *MSR* 50:25-48 Ja-Mr 1993

Delgado, Mariano.
Las Casas und seine Gegner. *Stimm Zeit* 210:841-854 D 1992

Dell, Mary Lynn.
Review of: *Sharing the darkness: the spirituality of caring* by Cassidy, Sheila. In: *New Theol Rev* 6:102-104 Ag 1993

DeLong, Allen.
Review of: *A still small voice* by Groeschel, Benedict J. In: *RRel* 52:636-637 Jl-Ag 1993

DeMarco, Donald.
Contraception and the war within the self. *HPR* 93:29-31+ My 1993

DeMaria, Richard J.
Poverty as the embrace of insecurity. *RRel* 52:432-445 My-Je 1993

DeMarinis, Valerie M.
A feminist model for pastoral psychology. Louisville: John Knox, 1993. x, 208p ISBN 0-664-22041-x

DeMassi, Sandra.
New styles of catechesis. *Mod Lit* 20:9-11 Ap 1993

Demel, Sabine.
Beratungspflicht und Strafverzicht. *Stimm Zeit* 211:700-710 O 1993
Standesamt—Ehe—Kirche. *Stimm Zeit* 211:131-140 F 1993

DeMello, Anthony, 1931-.
Eine Minute Unsinn. Frieburg: Herder, 1993. x, 224p ISBN 3-451-23053-4

DeMers, John.
Bishops take action on a tough, varied agenda. *Register* 69:1+ Jl 4 1993
Catholic health-care experts meet. *Register* 69:1+ Je 27 1993
Journey in dust and light: a modern pilgrimage through the life and letters of Paul. Minnesota: The Liturgical Press, 1993. x, 112p ISBN 0-8146-5701-x LC 92-40482

Demeulenaere, R. see Utyfanghe, M van, jt ed

Demkovich, Michael.
Meister Eckhart on justice and true obedience. *Louvain Stds* 18:131-144 Sum 1993

DeMolen, Richard L.
Review of: *Man on his own: interpretations of Erasmus, c 1750-1920* by Mansfield, Bruce. In: *CHist* 79:502-505 Jl 1993

Dempsey, Deirdre A.
Review of: *Biblical Hebrew: an introductory grammar* by Kelley, Page H. In: *OTA* 16:160-161 F 1993
Review of: *Ezechielstudien* by Pohlmann, Karl-Friedrich. In: *OTA* 16:181 F 1993

Dempsey, G T.
Irish attitudes towards USA foreign policy. *Studies* 82:265-275 Aut 1993

Deneen, Patrick J.
Review of: *Democracy* by Dunn, John, ed. In: *Comm* 120:35-36 Ap 9 1993

Dennis, A-M.
Review of: *Graphic concordance to the Dead Sea Scrolls* by Charlesworth, James H. In: *NRT* 115:262-263 Mr-Ap 1993

Dennis, George T.
Review of: *Rome and the Eastern Churches* by Nichols, Aidan. In: *CHist* 79:302-303 Ap 1993
Review of: *The Oxford dictionary of Byzantium 1-3* by Kazhdan, Alexander P. In: *TheolStds* 53:749-752 D 1992

Dennis, Mark.
Jordan faithful eye future. *Register* 69:1+ N 14 1993

Denniston, Robin.
Review of: *Delusions of grandeur* by Rae, John. In: *Tablet* 247:479-480 Ap 10-17 1993
Review of: *The night manager* by Carré, John le. In: *Tablet* 247:1014-1015 Ag 7 1993

Dent, Barbara.
Resurrection love-life. Mahwah: Paulist, 1993. x, 189p ISBN 0-8091-3405-5 LC 93-11006

Denton, David.
Review of: *What does the Lord require?* by Hart, Stephen. In: *New Oxford Rev* 60:31 My 1993

Depré, Olivier.
Hegel, des années de jeunesse à la fondation du premier système [two parts]. *RPhil Louvain* 91:111-125 F; 259-274 My 1993
Review of: *Einleitung in die Philosophie* by Schelling, Friedrich Wilhelm Joseph. In: *RPhil Louvain* 90:570-571 N 1992
Review of: *Nachgelassene Schriften 1804-1805* by Fichte, Johann Gottlieb. In: *RPhil Louvain* 90:564-570 N 1992
Review of: *Zwischen Revolution und Orthodoxie?* by Jacobs, Wilhelm G. In: *RPhil Louvain* 90:571-574 N 1992

Derousseaux, Louis.
Review of: *L'essere come atto nel tomismo essenziale di Cornelio Fabro* by Pangallo, Don Mario. In: *MSR* 50:158-161 Ap-Je 1993

Derroitte, Henri.
Des conditions nouvelles pour l'évangélisation en Afrique. *NRT* 115:560-576 Jl-Ag 1993 see Pirotte, Jean, jt auth

Deschepper, Jean Pierre.
Review of: *Allgemeiner politischer und historischer Briefwechsel* by Leibniz, Gottfried Wilhelm. In: *RPhil Louvain* 90:560-564 N 1992
Review of: *Correspondance générale et confessions* by Comte, Auguste. In: *RPhil Louvain* 90:574-576 N 1992

Deseure, Benôit.
Review of: *Christianisme et culture en Europe.* In: *MSR* 50:166-167 Ap-Je 1993

Desiderio, Frank R.
Priestcraft: a how-to guide for everyone. *ST Anth* 101:16-21 Jl 1993

DeSilva, Joseph, and Place, Michael D.
Catholic identity in cooperative ventures. *Health Prog* 74:53-54 Jl-Ag 1993

Desjardins, Michel.
Review of: *Concordance des textes de Nag Hammadi* by Charron, Régine. In: *Laval Theol Phil* 49:376-377 Je 1993

Deskins, Daniel R.
Footwashing as a sacrament of friendship. *Mod Lit* 20:12-15 Ap 1993

Desmangles, Leslie Gèrald.
The faces of the gods: vodou and Roman Catholicism in Haiti. Chapel Hill: The University of North Carolina Press, 1992. 218p ISBN 0-80782-059-8 LC 92-53625

Desmet, Huguette. see Pourtois, Jean-Pierre, jt auth

Desmet, Kate.
"Ken, don't foul up the Church today" [photo]. *Critic* 47:14-29 Spr 1993

Desmet, Richard.
L'induità e la nascita della filosofia Indiana. *Civilta* 3:29-36 Jl 3 1993

Destrée, Pierre.
Le concept de philosohie première dans la Métaphysique d' Aristote. *RPhil Louvain* 90:387-421 N 1992
Physique et métaphysique chez Aristote. *RPhil Louvain* 90:422-444 N 1992
Review of: *La physique d'Aristote et les conditions d'une science de la nature* by Gandt, François de, et Souffrin, Pierre, eds. In: *RPhil Louvain* 91:143-145 F 1993
Review of: *La sagezza di Aristotele* by Natali, Carlo. In: *RPhil Louvain* 91:142-143 F 1993
Review of: *Tel un dieu parmi les hommes* by Salem, Jean. In: *RPhil Louvain* 91:145-146 F 1993
Review of: *The fragility of goodness* by Nussbaum, Martha Craven. In: *RPhil Louvain* 91:138-140 F 1993
Review of: *The origins of democratic thinking* by Farrar, Cynthia. In: *RPhil Louvain* 91:140-141 F 1993
Review of: *Traité des premiers principes, vol I* by Damascius. In: *RPhil Louvain* 91:148-150 F 1993
Review of: *Traité des premiers principes, vol II* by Damascius. In: *RPhil Louvain* 91:148-150 F 1993
Review of: *Traité des premiers principes, vol III* by Damascius. In: *RPhil Louvain* 91:148-150 F 1993
Review of: *Traité des vertus* by Pléthon, Georges Gémiste. In: *RPhil Louvain* 91:150-151 F 1993
Review of: *Traité sur la liberté et la volonté de 'Un* by Plotin. In: *RPhil Louvain* 91:146-148 F 1993

Detienne, P.
Review of: *Newman and heresy* by Thomas, Stephen. In: *NRT* 114:911-912 N-D 1992
Review of: *Sermons 1824-1843* by Newman, John Henry, Cardinal, 1801-1890. In: *NRT* 114:912-913 N-D 1992

Deutsch, S.
Review of: *Protestantism in the Sangre de Cristos, 1850-1920* by Walker, Randi Jones. In: *CHist* 78:685-686 O 1992

Deutscher, Thomas.
Review of: *The dawn of the Reformation* by Oberman, Heiko A. In: *Can Cath Rev* 11:22-23 N 1993

Deutscher, Thomas. *(cont'd)*
Review of: *The imaginative landscape of Christopher Columbus* by Flint, Valier I J. In: *Can Cath Rev* 11:31-32 Mr 1993

Devine, George.
Anointing is a sacrament of the living [condensed fr *Catholic Twin Circle* My 16 1993]. *CDgst* 57:106-107 S 1993

Devine, James.
Review of: *The falling rate of profit in the postwar United States economy* by Moseley, Fred. In: *RSocEcon* 51:387-392 Aut 1993

Devine, Philip E.
Review of: *Beyond the culture wars: how teaching the conflicts can revitalize American education* by Graff, Gerald. In: *New Oxford Rev* 60:22-24 My 1993
Review of: *The ethics of authenticity* by Taylor, Charles, 1931-. In: *New Oxford Rev* 60:32 O 1993
Review of: *Valuing life* by Kleinig, John. In: *New Oxford Rev* 60:29-30 Jl-Ag 1993

Devlin, Brendan P.
Review of: *Alphonsus de Liguori, the Saint of Bourbon Naples, 1696-1787* by Jones, Frederick M. In: *Furrow* 43:704-706 D 1992
"Sailing to the Lowlands low"—the bishops in Brussels, 1-3 February 1993. *Furrow* 44:178-181 Mr 1993

DeWaal, E.
Review of: *The art of spiritual guidance* by Gratton, Carolyn. In: *Cist Stud* 27 No 4:[83]-[84] 1992

Dewan, Lawrence.
Philosophy and spirituality: cultivating a virtue. *HPR* 94:25-30 N 1993
St Thomas, God's goodness, and God's morality. *Mod Schlmn* 70:45-51 N 1992

Dewey, Joanna.
Feminist readings, gospel narrative and critical theory. *Bib Th Bul* 22:167-173 Wint 1992

Dexter, Caroline E.
Pompeii: life in the first century. *BibleT* 31:28-39 Ja 1993

Dhavamony, Mariasusai.
The cosmic Christ and world religions. *StudiaM* 42:179-225 1993
Review of: *Cultura e società in India.* In: *Civilta* 2:615-616 Je 19 1993
Salvation offered by sects (a theological analysis and evaluation). *StudiaM* 41:325-352 1992

Dhondt, U.
Review of: *Vatican II, theophany and the phenomenon of man* by Kobler, John F. In: *Can Cath Rev* 11:29 O 1993

Dhôtel, J-C. see Marty, F, jt ed

Di Domizio, Daniel.
Review of: *Covenant for a new creation: ethics, religion, and public policy* by Robb, Carol S, and Casebolt, Carl J, eds. In: *Living Light* 29:87-88 Aut 1992
Review of: *Human life in the balance* by Thomasma, David C. In: *Living Light* 29:87-88 Aut 1992

Di Giacomo, J.
Review of: *Becoming a catechist* by O'Malley, William J, 1931-. In: *America* 168:22-23 Ja 16-23 1993

Di Lella, Alexander A.
Review of: *A Greek-English lexicon of the Septuagint* by Lust, Johan, et al, eds. In: *OTA* 16:162 F 1993
Review of: *Israel in Egypt: reading Exodus 1-2* by Davies, Gordon F. In: *OTA* 16:169-170 F 1993
Review of: *Text history of the Greek Exodus* by Wevers, John William. In: *OTA* 16:170-171 F 1993
Review of: *Textual criticism of the Hebrew Bible* by Tov, Emanuel. In: *OTA* 16:413-414 Je 1993
Review of: *The world of Biblical literature* by Alter, Robert. In: *OTA* 15:478 O 1992
Review of: *Translation technique in the Peshitta to Job* by Szpek, Heidi M. In: *OTA* 16:424 Je 1993
Review of: *When time shall be no more* by Boyer, Paul S. In: *OTA* 16:429 Je 1993

Diamond, Eugene F.
Rape protocol. *Linacre* 60:8-14 Ag 1993
Review of: *Challenging children to chastity* by Sattler, H Vernon. In: *Linacre* 60:96 Ag 1993

Diamond, Pete.
Review of: *Tor der Hoffnung: Vergleichsformen und ihre Funktion in der Sprache der Psalmen* by Jauss, Hannelore. In: *OTA* 16:425-426 Je 1993

Dias, Ivan, Abp.
Saints Paul and Andrew helped evangelize Albania. *OR(Eng)* 1272:4 Ja 6 1993

Díaz Mateos, Manuel.
Jesucristo Ayer, Hoy Y Siempre. *Christus* 58:39-45 F 1993
Teu Irmão Pobre (Dt 15, 7). *Perspectiva* 25:137-148 My-Ag 1993

Dibout, Cécile, and Faivre, Alexandre.
Les Chrétiennes, entre leurs devoirs familiaux et le prestige de l'épiskopè. *Laval Theol Phil* 49:69-92 F 1993

Dickie, Amanda.
England's White Friars. *Tablet* 247:122 Ja 23 1993

Dickson, Charles.
Long-distance salvation. *OSV* 82:19 S 5 1993
When father is burning out. *OSV* 82:23 O 10 1993

Dickson, David.
Review of: *Journals and memoirs of Thomas Russell 1791-5* by Woods, C J, ed. In: *Studies* 81:460-463 Wint 1992

Diener, Paul W.
Review of: *Episcopacy: Lutheran-United Methodist dialogue II* by Tuell, Jack M, and Fjeld, Roger W, eds. In: *JEcumen Stds* 29:268 Spr 1992

Dietrich, Donald J.
Review of: *Deutsche Katholiken, 1918-1945* by Hürten, Heinz. In: *CHist* 79:557-559 Jl 1993
Review of: *The church and Jewish people* by Willebrands, Johannes, Cardinal. In: *America* 169:15-17 D 4 1993
Review of: *The moral core of Judaism and Christianity* by Maguire, Daniel C. In: *America* 169:15-17 D 4 1993

Dietrich, Jeff.
Authentic alternatives have always been pretty rare. *Nat Cath Rep* 29:11 My 21 1993

Dietrich, Wendell S.
Troeltsch's treatment of the Thomist synthesis in The Social Teacing as a signal of his view of a new cultural synthesis. *Thomist* 57:381-401 Jl 1993

Diez, Carlos.
Ak'Kutan, Centro "Bartolomé de Las Casas". *Cien Tom* 120:169-175 Ja-Ap 1993

Digan, Párig.
Church and China after Glasnost. *Furrow* 44:493-497 S 1993

DiGiacomo, James J.
Morality and youth: fostering Christian identity. Kansas City: Sheed & Ward, 1993. x, 156p ISBN 1-55612-652-2 LC 93-938
Review of: *Baseball in the afternoon* by Smith, Robert. In: *America* 168:17 Ap 17 1993
Review of: *Birth of a fan* by Fimrite, Ron, ed. In: *America* 168:17 Ap 17 1993
Review of: *Coming apart at the seams* by Sands, Jack, and Gammons, Peter. In: *America* 168:17 Ap 17 1993
Review of: *The man in the dugout: baseball's top managers and how they got that way* by Koppett, Leonard. In: *America* 168:17-18 Ap 17 1993

DiGiovanni, Stephen M.
Review of: *Scritti editi e inediti* by Bosco, Giovanni. In: *CHist* 79:350 Ap 1993

DiIanni, Albert.
Religious vocations: new signs of the times. *RRel* 52:745-763 S-O 1993

Dillmann, Robert.
Der Soldat, sein Gewissen und die Tradition. *Stimm Zeit* 211:65-68 Ja 1993

Dillon, John.
Review of: *Psychology* by Everson, Stephen, ed. In: *IJPS* 1:140-142 Mr 1993

Dilsaver, G C.
No surprise. *HPR* 93:54-57 F 1993

Dimino, Joseph I, Abp.
Military hospital personnel who oppose abortion. *Origins* 22:612 F 18 1993

Dimock, Giles.
The gift of fortitude. *OSV* 81:5 Mr 28 1993
The gift of piety. *OSV* 81:5 Ap 4 1993
The gifts of understanding and knowledge. *OSV* 81:5 Mr 7 1993
Lent and the seven gifts of the Holy Spirit. *OSV* 81:5 F 21 1993
The Spirit's gift of counsel. *OSV* 81:5 Mr 21 1993
The Spirit's gift of fear of the Lord. *OSV* 81:5 Mr 14 1993
The Spirit's gift of wisdom. *OSV* 81:5 F 28 1993

Dinges, William D.
American Catholics and the Joseph Campbell phenomenon. *America* 168:12-14+ F 20 1993

DiNoia, J A.
Review of: *Christian uniqueness and Catholic spirituality* by Carmody, John Tully, and Carmody, Denise Lardner. In: *Living Light* 29:85-86 Aut 1992
Review of: *One Christ—many religions: toward a revised christology* by Samartha, S J. In: *Living Light* 29:85-86 Aut 1992

Dinolfo, John.
The most common skin cancer. *CDgst* 57:12-17 Je 1993

Dinter, Paul E.
Review of: *Opus Dei: an investigation into the secret society struggling for power within the Roman Catholic Church* by Walsh, Michael J, 1937-. In: *Comm* 120:22+ Mr 12 1993

Dionne, E J, Jr.
Capitalism with soul? Novak on the Catholic ethic. *Comm* 120:9-12 My 21 1993
Review of: *The Catholic ethic and the spirit of capitalism* by Novak, Michael, 1933-. In: *Comm* 120:9-12 My 21 1993
Skepticism softens: can Americans love politics again? *Comm* 120:5-7 Ja 15 1993

Dipple, Geoffrey L.
Review of: *The radical Reformation* by Baylor, Michael G, ed. In: *CHist* 79:526-527 Jl 1993

Discepolo, S.
Review of: *Tessuto nel grembo: Guida alla preghiera per genitori in attesa* by Macnutt, Francis, and Macnutt, Judith. In: *Civilta* 144:201 Ja 16 1993

Dister, John E.
A new introduction to the Spiritual exercises of St. Ignatius. Collegeville: Liturgical, 1993. x, 114p ISBN 0-8146-5844-x LC 93-20553

Ditewig, William T.
The permanent deacon as military chaplain: canonical reflections. *Jurist* 51 no 2:340-363 1991

Dixon, John W, Jr.
What makes religious art religious? *CrossCurr* 43:5-25 Spr 1993

Dodd, Thomas.
Review of: *A violent evangelism: the political and religious conquest of the Americas* by Rivera, Luis N. In: *TheolStds* 54:569-571 S 1993

Dodds, Bill.
Always the poor. *New Cov* 22:21-24 Je 1993
Beginnings are never easy. *New Cov* 23:32 S 1993
Bringing the priceless gift of the Eucharist. *New Cov* 22:16-18 Ja 1993
California gets to vote on school vouchers. *OSV* 82:17 Jl 18 1993
California's doors not so wide open. *OSV* 82:17 Je 20 1993

Donohue, John W, 1917-. *(cont'd)*
Review of: *Evelyn Waugh: the later years 1939-1966* by Stannard, Martin. In: *America* 168:8-10 Ap 10 1993

Donohue, Patricia.
Review of: *Edith Stein* by Herbstrith, Waltraud. In: *Crisis* 11:61-63 O 1993

Donovan, Daniel.
Review of: *Women towards priesthood: ministerial politics and feminist praxis* by Field-Bibb, Jacqueline. In: *TheolStds* 54:379-381 Je 1993
Review of: *Yves Congar* by Nichols, Aidan. In: *Can Cath Rev* 11:33 Jl-Ag 1993
Preparing for worship: Sundays and feast days. Mahwah: Paulist, 1993. x, 211p ISBN 0-8091-3424-1 LC 93-13704

Donovan, Grace.
Women collaborators in Catholic education: nineteenth century America. *ACHSR* 103:23-33 Aut 1992

Donovan, Kevin.
Review of: *The awakening church* by Madden, Lawrence J, ed. In: *Month* 26:112-113 Mr 1993

Donovan, Laurence.
Having come this way; Dog Island; transcriptions; advice from further up; a poem from Borges; Sunyatta. *Spirit* 57:1-9 Spr-Sum 1992

Donovan, M.
Review of: *She who is* by Johnson, Elizabeth A, 1941-. In: *America* 168:18-20 Ja 2-9 1993
Review of: *Virgin time* by Hampl, Patricia, 1946-. In: *America* 168:18-20 Ja 2-9 1993

Donovan, Mary Ann.
Review of: *God for us: the Trinity and Christian life* by LaCugna, Catherine Mowry. In: *Horizons (CTS)* 20:132-133 Spr 1993

Donovan, Vincent.
Refounding church—a paradigm shift. *Chicago Stud* 31:215-223 Ag 1992

Donze, Mary Terese, 1911-.
Thus shall you prayer. *Living Prayer* 26:15-16 My-Je 1993

Donzellini, Mary.
Metodologia catequetica. *Christus* 58:21-25 Je 1993

Doohan, Helen.
Prayer in the New Testament. Collegeville: Liturgical, 1992. 143p ISBN 0-81465-007-4 LC 91-35750

Doohan, Leonard.
The Church's handbook. *Mod Lit* 20:34-35 Je-Jl 1993
Discipleship in Matthew. *Mod Lit* 20:36 Ag 1993
The Easter presence. *Mod Lit* 20:36 Ap 1993
Go therefore and make disciples. *Mod Lit* 20:34-35 O 1993
In pursuit of holiness. *Mod Lit* 20:30 F 1993
John of the Cross and the laity. *Spir Life* 39:164-172 Aut 1993
Kingship of service. *Mod Lit* 20:36 N 1993
Parables and miracles. *Mod Lit* 20:34-35 My 1993
Sharing the Lord's mission. *Mod Lit* 20:34-35 S 1993
The storm-tossed Church. *Mod Lit* 20:40 Mr 1993
The year of Matthew. *Mod Lit* 19:31 D 1992-Ja 1993 *see* Doohan, Helen, jt auth

Dooley, B.
Review of: *Alfonso M de'Liguori e la società civile del suo tempo: Atti del Convegno internazionale per il Bicentenario della morte del santo* by Giannantonio, Pompeo, ed. In: *CHist* 78:664-665 O 1992

Dooley, Jerry.
Thomas Merton still surprises [condensed fr *The Progress* Ap 1 1993]. *CDgst* 57:57-59 Jl 1993

Dooley, Katherine.
Review of: *Seasons and feasts of the Church Year* by Whalen, Michael D. In: *Living Light* 29:92 Sum 1993

Doran, Joseph L.
Are contraception and artificial procreation sometimes permissible. *HPR* 93:48-57 Mr 1993

Doran, Robert.
Review of: *'Women like this': new perspectives on Jewish women in the Greco-Roman world* by Levine, Amy-Jill, ed. In: *CBQ* 54:827-828 O 1992

Dorgan, Dennis L.
Review of: *Creating relevant rituals* by Harris, Chris. In: *Can Cath Rev* 11:26-27 N 1993

Dorman, Regina.
Two Thomases, twins in sanctity [condensed fr *Lay Witness* D 1992]. *CDgst* 58:30-35 N 1993

Dorr, Donal, 1935-.
Ideals without strategy—a response to Work is the key. *Furrow* 44:472-478 S 1993
Review of: *The God of life* by Gutiérrez, Gustavo. In: *Furrow* 43:706-708 D 1992
Review of: *Theology and the option for the poor* by O'Brien, John. In: *Furrow* 43:706-708 D 1992

Dorrell, Fleur.
Desert island choice (1) [winner of the John Harriott Memorial Prize]. *Tablet* 247:94 Ja 23 1993
Review of: *Isolina [tr S. Williams]* by Maraini, Dacia. In: *Tablet* 247:1266 O 2 1993

Doss, Joe Morris. *see* Vincie, Catherine, jt auth

Dotson, Beth.
Battered women: when home is not a shelter. *Salt* 13:18-22 S 1993
Sisters' farmland being revitalized. *Sisters* 65:191-192 My 1993

Dotterweich, Kass.
Review of: *Families exploring faith: a parent's guide to the older adolescent years* by Taylor, Joe, and Taylor, Audrey. In: *Liguorian* 81:68-69 S 1993

Dotterweich, Kass. *(cont'd)*
Review of: *Loving and learning: a guide to practical parenting* by Kenny, James. In: *Liguorian* 81:69 S 1993
Review of: *Quicksilvers: ministering with junior high youth* by Goodwin, Carole. In: *Liguorian* 81:68 S 1993

Dougherty, Edward.
Review of: *The figure of Joseph in post-biblical Jewish literature* by Niehoff, Maren. In: *TheolStds* 54:383-384 Je 1993

Dougherty, Josephine.
Review of: *Hymns to Christ and a concert of miniatures* by Berselli, Constante, ed. In: *Can Cath Rev* 11:31 N 1993

Dougherty, Jude P, 1930-.
Edith Stein's conversion: how a Jewish philosopher became a Catholic saint. *Crisis* 10:39-43 D 1992
Review of: *Jewish social ethics* by Novak, David, 1941-. In: *Crisis* 11:52-55 O 1993
Review of: *On justice: an essay in Jewish philosophy* by Goodman, Lenn. In: *Crisis* 11:52-55 O 1993

Douglas, Deborah Smith.
Becoming like children. *New Cov* 22:23-25 Ja 1993

Douglass, R Bruce.
Review of: *What it means to be an American* by Walzer, Michael. In: *Comm* 120:32-33 Ap 9 1993

Dove, Anthea.
Whitby and Kleve [Graymoor Prize Winner]. *Comm* 120:11-13 Ja 15 1993

Dow, Donald M.
St Joseph House. *Cath Work* 60:2 Mr-Ap 1993

Dowd, John D.
Review of: *Theological hermeneutics* by Jeanrond, Werner G. In: *New Theol Rev* 6:91-93 Ag 1993

Dowd, Mark.
The place of celibacy. *Tablet* 247:906 Jl 17 1993

Dowden, Richard.
False democratic dawn. *Tablet* 247:1030 Ag 14 1993

Dowell, Susan.
A feminist critique. *Way Suppl* 77:76-86 Sum 1993

Dowling, Dolores.
Saint of the devout life [condensed fr *Spirit and Life* Ja/F 1993]. *CDgst* 57:58-61 Ap 1993

Dowling, Katherine.
Seniors should still do their fair share. *USCath* 58:23-27 Ag 1993

Dowling, Regina Plunkett.
A Catholic in the cafeteria. *Comm* 120:11 S 10 1993

Dowling, William, et al.
Lessons in providing, publicizing community services. *Health Prog* 74:63-64 Jl-Ag 1993

Downey, Michael.
Review of: *Creation spirituality: liberating gifts for the peoples of the earth* by Fox, Matthew. In: *Horizons (CTS)* 19:333-335 Fall 1992
Review of: *Heightened consciousness: the mystical difference* by Granfield, David. In: *Horizons (CTS)* 20:170-172 Spr 1993
Review of: *Silence on fire: the prayer of awareness* by Shannon, William Henry, 1917-. In: *Cist Stud* 28:[11]-[12] 1993
Review of: *Spiritual guides for today* by Callahan, Annice. In: *Cist Stud* 28 no 2:[41]-[42] 1993
Review of: *Spirituality and history* by Sheldrake, Philip. In: *TheolStds* 53:778-780 D 1992
Review of: *The nonviolent coming of God* by Douglass, James W. In: *Spir Life* 32:117-119 Sum 1993
Twenty-first conference on Cistercian Studies. Kalamazoo/May 7-10, 1992. *Cist Stud* 27 No 4:353-358 1992

Downey, Michael, ed.
The new dictionary of Catholic spirituality. Minnesota: The Order of St Benedict, 1993. x, 1083p ISBN 0-8146-5525-4 LC 92-40959

Downs, Peter.
Splitting shifts: splitting families. *Comm* 120:7-8 Je 4 1993

Downs, Roger M.
Geography for life. *Momentum* 24:12-16 S-O 1993

Doyle, Áilín.
Review of: *Jesus* by Wilson, A N, 1950-. In: *Furrow* 44:455-456 Jl-Ag 1993

Doyle, B Rod.
Review of: *Matthew's Gospel and formative Judaism* by Overman, J Andrew. In: *Pacifica* 6:335-337 O 1993

Doyle, Brian.
Catholics ought to do with less. *USCath* 58:22-27 O 1993
Everybody loves letters [condensed fr *Portland Magazine* Wint 1992]. *CDgst* 58:62-65 D 1993
I'm Ok, I'm Ok, aren't I. *Comm* 120:9+ S 10 1993
Waiting for Lily. *Comm* 119:5-6 D 18 1992

Doyle, Dennis M.
The Catechism [commentary]. *Comm* 120:14-15 My 7 1993
[John Paul II, invoking his authority]. *Comm* 120:12-14 O 22 1993
Review of: *Faith and the human enterprise: a post-Vatican II vision* by Weakland, Rembert G, Abp, 1927-. In: *Comm* 120:18-20 Mr 12 1993
Review of: *Ministry* by Osborne, Kenan B. In: *Comm* 120:26-28 S 10 1993

Doyle, James J.
Review of: *A case for peace in reason and faith* by Hellwig, Monika K, 1929-. In: *Sisters* 65:219 My 1993

Doyle, Joan.
Second coming. *Sisters* 65:126-127 Mr 1993

Doyle, Katherine.
Youth formation. *Mod Lit* 19:28 D 1992-Ja 1993

Doyle, Mary E.
Graphoanalysis: reading the word from within. *Sisters* 65:25-29 Ja 1993

Doyle, Michelle L.
Public education: a fertile field for religious educators. *Momentum* 24:14-16 F-Mr 1993

Dozeman, Thomas B.
Review of: *Das Bundesbuch (Ex 20, 22-23, 33): Studien zu seiner Enstehung und Theologie* by Schwienhorst-Schönberger, Ludger. In: *CBQ* 54:765-766 O 1992

Drake, Bob M, and Amspaugh, Linda.
Writing to teach mathematics. *Tod Cath Teach* 27:29-31 N-D 1993

Drake, H A.
Review of: *Helena Augusta: the mother of Constantine the Great and the legend of her finding the True Cross* by Drijvers, Jan Willem. In: *CHist* 79: 508-509 Jl 1993

Drane, John.
Son of man: a new life of Christ. Grand Rapids: Eerdmans, 1993. 160p ISBN 0-8028-3710-7

Draper, Anthony.
An incident on the Jericho Road—some correspondence. *Furrow* 44:99-102 F 1993
Review of: *Foundations of theological study: a sourcebook* by Viladesau, Richard, and Massa, Mark, eds. In: *Doctr Life* 43:248-249 Ap 1993
Review of: *Systematic theology, Roman Catholic perspective* by Fiorenza, Francis Schüssler, 1938-, and Galvin, John P, 1944-, eds. In: *Doctr Life* 43: 56-58 Ja 1993

Drazek, Czeslaw.
Poles entrust country's future to Mary. *OR(Eng)* 1305:2 S 1 1993

Dreher, Barbara.
Fabulous classics. *Tod Cath Teach* 27:42-45 S 1993

Drennan, Kathleen M.
The changing face of family. *Catechist* 27:4 N-D 1993

Dreyer, Elizabeth.
Review of: *The divine romance: Teresa of Avila's narrative theology* by Chorpenning, Joseph F. In: *Spir Life* 39:176-177 Aut 1993
What's so amazing about grace? [interview by editors of US Catholic (Periodical)]. *USCath* 58:6-13 My 1993

Dries, Angelyn.
Living in ambiguity: a paradigm shift experienced by the sister formation movement. *CHist* 79:478-487 Jl 1993
US sources for the Catholic overseas mission movement, 1893-1929. *US Cath Hist* 11:37-48 Spr 1993

Drinan, Robert Francis, 1920-.
Are profoundly handicapped children in Catholic schools entitled to government assistance?. *America* 168:16-18 Ja 30 1993
At 50, the United Nations needs some remodeling. *Nat Cath Rep* 29:13 Ap 30 1993
Churches are strangely quiet in the fight against tobacco. *Nat Cath Rep* 29: 25 Ja 15 1993
Civil rights in the first 100 days. *America* 168:14-15 Mr 13 1993
A glimmer of hope for aid to Catholic schools. *America* 169:4-5 S 18 1993
Lay group adds muscle to death-penalty fight. *Nat Cath Rep* 29:15 My 28 1993
Mind-blowing nuclear budget is based on fantasy. *Nat Cath Rep* 29:6 F 19 1993
Network: a Catholic political ministry. *America* 168:14-15 Ap 24 1993
A new worldwide commitment to the rights of children. *America* 169:22-23 O 16 1993
A plea to President Clinton: stop the sales of US arms. *Nat Cath Rep* 29:16 F 5 1993
Review of: *Undermined establishment: church-state relations in America, 1880-1920* by Handy, Robert T. In: *Horizons (CTS)* 20:152 Spr 1993
Time to search for Mary between the lines. *Nat Cath Rep* 29:2 My 14 1993
A triumph for rights. *Tablet* 247:870-871 Jl 3 1993
What if America were not military machine? *Nat Cath Rep* 29:17 Jl 2 1993
World Conference on Human Rights June 14-25, 1993. *America* 168:15-16 Je 5-12 1993

Driscoll, Michael S.
Review of: *Fountain of life* by Austin, Gerard, ed. In: *Worship* 67:184-186 Mr 1993

Droel, William.
Review of: *Upon this rock: the miracles of a black church* by Freedman, Samuel. In: *St Anth* 100:52-53 S 1993

Droel, William, and Pierce, Gregory F Augustine.
Ministry goes to work. *Church* 9:13-16 Aut 1993

Drumm, Michael.
Infant baptism and adult faith. *Furrow* 44:131-139 Mr 1993

Drummond, Richard H.
Review of: *Nihon no shingaku* by Furuya, Yasua, and Ohki, Hideo. In: *JEcumen Stds* 29:115-116 Wint 1992

Drummond, Thomas B, and Przybilia, Carla.
Holistic approach will transform healthcare services. *Health Prog* 74:64-65 Jl-Ag 1993

Dubois, Marcel Jacque.
Dialogue [interview by L Pevtzow]. *Register* 69:1+ Ja 3 1993

Dubourd, Nancy A.
When there is no priest. *Mod Lit* 20:14-15 F 1993

Dubruiel, Michael.
Memento viva!. *New Cov* 23:14-15 Ag 1993

Dudley, Martin, and Rowell, Geoffrey, eds.
The oil of gladness: annointing in the Christian tradition. Collegeville: Liturgical, 1993. x, 221p ISBN 0-8146-2245-3

Dudro, Vivian.
Death with dignity. *Register* 69:4 S 5 1993
For Mary, a tireless worker. *Register* 69:3 Je 6 1993
Humanae Vitae, +25 [commentary]. *Register* 69:2 My 30 1993

Duerk, Judith.
I sit listening to the wind: woman's encounter within herself. San Diego: LuraMedia, 1993. x, 103p ISBN 0-931055-98-9 LC 93-991

Duffy, Eamon.
Let us now praise famous men. *New Blckfrs* 74:337-344 Jl-Ag 1993
The origins of the troubles. *Priests & People* 7:3-9 Ja 1993

Duffy, Eamon, and Lash, Nicholas.
Dear Mr Gummer. *Tablet* 247:602 My 15 1993

Duffy, Eugene.
Towards what kind of priest? *Furrow* 44:208-214 Ap 1993

Duffy, Hugh P.
Review of: *Irish writers and religion* by Welch, Robert, ed. In: *Studies* 81: 443-446 Wint 1992

Duffy, Joseph.
Review of: *The letters of Saint Patrick* by Conneely, Daniel. In: *Furrow* 44: 444-446 Jl-Ag 1993

Duffy, Regis A.
Review of: *Early Christian Baptism and the catechumenate* by Finn, Thomas Macy. In: *Worship* 67:181-182 Mr 1993
Review of: *Sacramental theology* by Vorgrimler, Herbert. In: *TheolStds* 54: 585 S 1993

Duffy, Shatzi Luisa.
"Humanae Vitae" at 25. *Crisis* 11:15-17 S 1993

Dufner, Andrew J.
The Ignatian spiritual exercises and the new world-view. *Way Suppl* 76:3-12 Spr 1993

Dufner, Delores.
Review of: *Psalms for feasts and seasons: revised and augmented full music edition* by Willcock, Christopher. In: *Sisters* 65:142 Mr 1993
Review of: *Psalms for the journey* by Willcock, Christopher. In: *Sisters* 65:60 Ja 1993

Dufresne, Bethe.
Review of: *Cry me a river* by Pearson, T R. In: *Comm* 120:37-38 Ap 9 1993

Dugan, Irene.
A human Christ. *Way Suppl* 76:61-71 Spr 1993

Dugas, Nancy.
From assessment to action. *Health Prog* 74:38-41 O 1993

Duggan, Michael.
"In fulfilment of Scripture": Old Testament citations in the New Testament. *Can Cath Rev* 11:5-13 Ap 1993

Duggan, Paul E.
The liturgy and the Assumption. *Priest* 49:16-18 Ag 1993

Duggan, Robert D.
The age of Confirmation: a flawed proposal. *America* 168:12-14 Je 5-12 1993
Catechumenate for children. *Church* 9:46-47 Spr 1993
Preparing for advent. *Church* 9:36-37 Aut 1993
Preparing the assembly for liturgy. *Church* 9:36-37 Sum 1993

Dugger, William M.
The great retrenchment and the new industrial state. *RSocEcon* 50:453-471 Wint 1992
Review of: *Antitrust economics on trial: a dialogue on the New Laissez-Faire* by Adams, Walter, and Brock, James W. In: *RSocEcon* 50:346-348 Fall 1992
Review of: *The culture of contentment* by Galbraith, John Kenneth, 1908-. In: *RSocEcon* 51:108-111 Spr 1993

Duguid, Iain M.
Review of: *A new heart: a commentary on the Book of Ezekiel* by Vawter, Bruce, and Hoppe, Leslie J. In: *CBQ* 54:770 O 1992

Duin, Julia.
St. Max on stage. *New Cov* 23:22-23 N 1993

Duitt, Amitava Krishna.
Review of: *Reconstructing Keynesian economics with imperfect competition* by Marris, Robin. In: *RSocEcon* 51:393-395 Aut 1993

Dulles, Avery Robert, 1918-.
The four faces of American Catholicism. *Louvain Stds* 18:99-109 Sum 1993
"Humanae Vitae" and the crisis of dissent. *Origins* 22:774-777 Ap 22 1993
Humanae Vitae, on the regulation of birth (commentary). *Origins*
The prophetic humanism of John Paul II. *America* 169:6-11 O 23 1993

Dulles.
Review of: *Believing three ways in one God* by Lash, Nicholas. In: *Tablet* 247:1296-1297 O 9 1993
Review of: *Explorations in theology 2: spouse of the word* by Balthasar, Hans Urs Von, 1905-1988. In: *TheolStds* 53:763-765 D 1992
Review of: *The idea of the university: a reexamination* by Pelikan, Jaroslav. In: *IPQ* 33:240-241 Je 1993

Dumestre, Marcel.
Toward effective adult religious education. *Origins* 23:24-28 My 27 1993

Dummett, Michael.
Universities at risk. *Tablet* 247:1095-1096 Ag 28 1993

Dumont, Camille.
La charité pastorale et la vocation au presbytérat. *NRT* 115:211-226 Mr-Ap 1993
En relisant l'amour des lettres et le désir de Dieu. *NRT* 114:889-895 N-D 1992

Dumont, Charles.
Contemplative action: time in eternity according to Saint Bernard. *Cist Stud* 28 no 2:145-159 1993
Journées d'Études on the mirror of charity of Aelred of Rievaulx, Abbey of Scourmont, October 5-9, 1992. *Cist Stud* 28 no 2:193-197 1993

Dunklee, Larry.
Review of: *Life on the line* by Kilner, John F. In: *Health Prog* 74:70-71 O 1993

Dunlap, Judith.
End-of-the-year evaluations. *Church* 9:50-51 Spr 1993
How Christian service is taught in the parish. *Church* 9:40-42 Aut 1993
Meeting people's needs. *Church* 9:40-41 Sum 1993

Dunlop, Robert.
Baptists—people of the third way. *Furrow* 44:226-229 Ap 1993
Review of: *Through the year with George Otto Simms* by Whiteside, Lesley, ed. In: *Furrow* 44:194 Mr 1993

Dunn, Dennis J.
Review of: *Religious liberty in Eastern Europe and the USSR before and after the great transformation* by Mojzes, Paul. In: *CHist* 79:354-355 Ap 1993

Dunn, James D G.
Should Paul once again oppose Peter to his face? *Heythrop* 34:425-428 O 1993

Dunn, Mary.
An abused parish. *Tablet* 247:642-643 My 22 1993

Dunne, George M.
Review of: *Capitalism and Christians: tough gospel challenges in a troubled world economy* by Jones, Arthur C, 1936-. In: *Nat Cath Rep* 29:16 Ap 2 1993

Dunne, John S, 1929-.
Love's mind: an essay on contemplative life. Notre Dame: University of Notre Dame Press, 1993. x, 208p ISBN 0-268-01303-9 LC 93-13910
Myth and culture in theology and literature [interview by R. Adams]. *Relig Lit* 25:79-104 Sum 1993

Dunne, Sean.
In the heart of the city. *Tablet* 247:944-945 Jl 24 1993

Dunne, Tad.
What trouble is. *RRel* 52:532-540 Jl-Ag 1993

Dunstan, G R.
Review of: *Religious belief and ecclesiastical careers in late Medieval England* by Harper-Bill, Christopher, ed. In: *Heythrop* 34:451-452 O 1993
Review of: *The Papacy, 1073-1198: continuity and innovation* by Robinson, I R. In: *Heythrop* 34:205-208 Ap 1993

Dunstan, Petà.
Body and soul. *Priests & People* 7:323-326 Ag-S 1993

Dupleix, A. *see* Carles, J, jt auth

Dupré, Louis.
Review of: *The foundations of mysticism* by McGinn, Bernard John, 1937-. In: *Thomist* 57:133-135 Ja 1993

Dupuis, J. *see* Neusner, Jacob, jt ed

Dupuis, Jacques.
Review of: *A christological catechism: New Testament answers* by Fitzmyer, Joseph Augustine, 1920-. In: *Gregorianum* 74 No 1:158-159 1993
Review of: *An apology for apologetics: a study in the logic of interreligious dialogue* by Griffiths, Paul J. In: *Gregorianum* 74 No 1:175 1993
Review of: *Asian Christian spirituality: reclaiming traditions* by Fabella, Virginia, et al, eds. In: *Gregorianum* 74 no 3:589-590 1993
Review of: *Bursting the bonds? A Jewish-Christian dialogue on Jesus and Paul* by Swidler, Leonard, et al, eds. In: *Gregorianum* 74 no 2:367-369 1993
Review of: *Chi dite che io sia?* In: *Civilta* 3:103 Jl 3 1993
Review of: *Chiesa e cultura* by Luzbetak, Louis J. In: *Civilta* 3:208 Jl 17 1993
Review of: *Christ at the centre: selected issues in Christology* by Lane, Dermot A. In: *Gregorianum* 73 No 4:758 1992
Review of: *Faces of Jesus in Africa* by Schreiter, Robert J, ed. In: *Gregorianum* 74 No 1:159-160 1993
Review of: *Gandhi on Christianity* by Ellsberg, Robert, ed. In: *Gregorianum* 74 No 1:193 1993
Review of: *Interreligious dialogue: Catholic perspectives* by Kroeger, James H, ed. In: *Gregorianum* 74 No 1:192-193 1993
Review of: *Knowing Christ Jesus: a Christological Soucebook* by Kroeger, James H. In: *Gregorianum* 74 No 1:192 1993
Review of: *Nessun altro nome? Un esame critico degli atteggiamenti cristiani verso le religioni mondiali* by Knitter, Paul. In: *Gregorianum* 74 No 1:175-176 1993
Review of: *New evangelization* by Boff, Leonardo. In: *Gregorianum* 74 no 2:383-384 1993
Review of: *Rediscovering Jesus: challenge of discipleship* by Bredin, Eamonn. In: *Gregorianum* 74 No 1:192 1993
Review of: *Teologia della missione* by Müller, Karl. In: *Civilta* 3:206-207 Jl 17 1993
Review of: *The covenant never revoked: biblical reflections on Christian-Jewish dialogue* by Lohfink, Norbert. In: *Gregorianum* 73 No 4:750 1992
Review of: *The Galilean Jewishness of Jesus: retrieving the Jewish origins of Christianity* by Lee, Bernard J. In: *Gregorianum* 73 No 4:757-758 1992
Review of: *The God of Christians* by Muñoz, Ronaldo. In: *Gregorianum* 74 no 2:382-383 1993
Review of: *The immutability of God in the theology of Hans Urs von Balthasar* by O'Hanlon, Gerard F. In: *Gregorianum* 74 No 1:160-161 1993
Review of: *Trends in mission toward the third millenium* by Jenkinson, William, and O'Sullivan, Helene, eds. In: *Gregorianum* 74 no 2:397-398 1993
Review of: *Voices from the margin: interpreting the Bible in the Third World* by Sugirtharajah, R S. In: *Gregorianum* 74 no 3:566-567 1993
Review of: *World religion and human liberation* by Cohn-Sherbok, Dan, ed. In: *Gregorianum* 74 no 2:384-385 1993

Dupuy, Edward.
Being interested in time: autobiography and repetition. *Listening* 28:141-157 Spr 1993

Durak, Adam.
Rinnovamento liturgico in Polonia: a proposito di sette simposi a Lad. *Notitiae* 28:229-230 Mr 1992

Duran, Khalid.
An alternative to Islamism: the evolutionary thought of Mahmud Taha. *CrossCurr* 42:453-467 Wint 1992-1993

Durbin, J.
Review of: *The eye of the storm* by Leech, Kenneth, 1939-. In: *Sisters* 65:66-67 Ja 1993

Durka, Gloria.
Review of: *Renewing the old school* by McCall, Jack. In: *Living Light* 29:90-91 Spr 1993

Durkan, John.
Review of: *The Gospel of Matthew* by Harrington, Daniel J. In: *Furrow* 44:519-520 S 1993

Durken, Daniel.
Review of: *So you mean to read the Bible!* by Sloyan, Gerard S. In: *Sisters* 65:64-65 Ja 1993
Seers' corner: desert days [photos]. *BibleT* 31:204-205 Jl 1993
Where are the women? *Sisters* 65:109 Mr 1993

Dusen, Thomas van.
Diocesan restructuring II. *CLawyer* 34 no 4:403-406 1993

Dussel, Enrique.
La cuestion institucional. *Christus* 58:62-65 Mr-Ap 1993

Dutka, Joanna.
Review of: *Lay ministry: a theological, spiritual, and pastoral handbook* by Rademacher, William J. In: *Can Cath Rev* 11:29-30 Jl-Ag 1993
Review of: *The English patient* by Ondaatje, Michael. In: *Can Cath Rev* 11:19-20 S 1993

Dutney, Andrew.
Review of: *Through aboriginal eyes* by Pattel-Gray, Anne. In: *Pacifica* 6:119-120 F 1993

Dutton, Marsha L.
Aelred, historian: two portraits in Plantagenet myth. *Cist Stud* 28 no 2:113-144 1993
Review of: *The life of Saint Edward King and Confessor* by Elred of Rievaulx. In: *Cist Stud* 28 no 2:[53]-[57] 1993

Dwinell, Michael.
Fire bearer: evoking a priestly humanity. Liguori: Triumph Books, 1993. x, 198p ISBN 0-89243-531-3 LC 92-43418

Dwyer, Christopher.
The unacceptable face of credit. *Month* 26:40-42 Ja 1993

Dwyer, Margretta.
Sexuality: creation's wildcard—sexual energy and feminine creativity. *Sisters* 65:276-279 Jl 1993

Dych, William V.
Review of: *The graced horizon* by Duffy, Stephen J. In: *TheolStds* 54:375-376 Je 1993

Dyrud, Jarl.
On screening seminarians. *Origins* 23:79-80 Je 17 1993

Dyzenhaus, David.
Why positivism is authoritarian. *Amer J Juris* 37:83-112 1992

E

Eady, Robert.
Review of: *The war against the family* by Gairdner, William D. In: *Can Cath Rev* 11:25-26 S 1993

Eastman, Theodore, Bp. *see* Weakland, Rembert G, Abp, 1927-, jt auth

Ebaugh, Helen Rose Fuchs.
Women in the vanishing cloister: organizational decline in Catholic religious orders in the United States. New Brunswick: Rutgers University Press, 1993. 191p ISBN 0-81351-865-2 LC 92-8035

Ebert, Andreas, and Brockman, Patricia C, eds.
Richard Rohr: Illuminations of his life and work. New York: The Crossroad Publishing Company, 1993. x, 200p ISBN 0-8245-1270-7 LC 93-20130

Ebrom, John Martin.
Review of: *Christ is coming: celebrating Advent, Christmas and Epiphany* by Cotter, Theresa. In: *Mod Lit* 20:41 N 1993
Review of: *Lenten guide for parish leaders* by Craghan, John Francis, 1936-. In: *Mod Lit* 20:39 My 1993

Echeverría, Loreto. *see* Petry, Nicholas, jt auth

Echlin, Edward P, 1930-.
Dare ecology use the word "sin"? *Month* 26:206-210 My 1993
Is "sustainable development" sustainable? *Month* 26:402-407 S-O 1993

Edelman, Diana V.
Review of: *Archaeology and the Bible: the best of BAR* by Shanks, Hershel, and Cole, Dan P, eds. In: *OTA* 15:475-476 O 1992
Review of: *Burial patterns and cultural diversity in late Bronze Age* by Gonen, Rivka. In: *OTA* 16:406 Je 1993
Review of: *Converting the past: studies in ancient Israelite and Moabite historiography* by Smelik, Klaas A D. In: *OTA* 15:476 O 1992
Review of: *Early history of the Israelite people: from the written and archaeological sources* by Thompson, Thomas L. In: *OTA* 16:413 Je 1993
Review of: *Fictional Akkadian autobiography: a generic and comparative study* by Longman, Tremper. In: *OTA* 16:409-410 Je 1993
Review of: *Judahite burial practices and beliefs about the dead* by Bloch-Smith, Elizabeth. In: *OTA* 15:478 O 1992
Review of: *Les relations entre les cités de la côte phenicienne et les royaumes d'Israël et de Juda* by Briquel-Chatonnet, F. In: *OTA* 16:394 Je 1993

Edelman, Diana V. *(cont'd)*
Review of: *Lower Galilee during the Iron Age* by Gal, Zvi. In: *OTA* 16:406 Je 1993
Review of: *The archaeology of Ancient Israel* by Ben-Tor, Amnon. In: *OTA* 16:157 F 1993
Review of: *The archaeology of Israelite Samaria, vol. 1* by Tappy, Ron E. In: *OTA* 16:412 Je 1993
Review of: *The sociology of pottery in ancient Palestine* by Wood, Bryant G. In: *OTA* 15:491 O 1992

Edelman, Marian Wright.
For every child: a head start. *Momentum* 24:37-39 N-D 1993

Edelman, Mark.
Dialogue [interview by J Luxmoore]. *Register* 69:1+ Je 20 1993

Edkins, Anthony.
The end of the welfare state; Premonition of passage; Spectator sport; The right reader; Poeme trouve; The art center; Moving apart. *Spirit* 58:11-14 1993
Trick or treat; Cnut's day out; Flood warning; Revisiting Luarka. *Spirit* 57:42-46 Spr-Sum 1992

Edmondson, Ricca.
Moral debate and social change. *Doctr Life* 42:233-243 My-Je 1992

Edwards, David L.
Review of: *Believing* by O'Collins, Gerald, 1931-, and Venturini, Mary. In: *Tablet* 247:859-860 Jl 3 1993

Edwards, John.
Isabella of Spain—beatification and 1992. *SIDIC* 25 No 2:8-11 1992

Edwards, M J.
Review of: *A history of Gnosticism* by Filoramo, Giovanni. In: *Heythrop* 34:204-205 Ap 1993
Review of: *Hellenic and Christian studies* by Armstrong, A H. In: *Heythrop* 34:203-204 Ap 1993
Review of: *The anatomy of neoplatonism* by Lloyd, A C. In: *Heythrop* 34:217-218 Ap 1993

Edwards, Mark U, Jr.
Review of: *Communal reformation: the quest for salvation in sixteenth-century Germany* by Blickle, Peter. In: *CHist* 79:332-333 Ap 1993

Edwards, Robin T.
Bishops advised on sexual abuse [National Conference of Catholic Bishops' Committee on priestly life and ministry meeting, Kansas City, MO]. *Nat Cath Rep* 29:5 Mr 5 1993
Hark! it's the sound of protest. *Nat Cath Rep* 29:5 Ag 27 1993
Health care among US bishops' other concerns. *Nat Cath Rep* 29:3 Jl 2 1993
Pope woos youth at spiritual Woodstock. *Tablet* 247:1081-1082 Ag 21 1993

Edwards, Sarah A. *see* Berkey, Robert F, jt ed

Edwards, Tilden.
Developing leaders for contemplative groups. *Way Suppl* 75:67-75 Aut 1992

Efroymson, David P, et al, eds.
Within context: essays on Jews and Judaism in the New Testament. Collegeville, Minnesota: The Liturgical Press, 1993. x, 160p ISBN 0-8146-5033-3 LC 92-34914

Egan, Anthony.
Review of: *Kissinger* by Isaacson, Walter. In: *Month* 25:497-499 D 1992
Review of: *Nixon, Kissinger and moral "pragmatism" Nixon: ruin and recovery 1973-1990* by Ambrose, Stephen E. In: *Month* 25:497-499 D 1992
Madness, massacre and the millennium. *Month* 26:214-218 Je 1993
Review of: *The politics of God: Christian theologies and social justice* by Tanner, Kathryn, 1957-. In: *Month* 26:234 Je 1993

Egan, Desmond.
My moment of truth. *Tablet* 247:1038-1039 Ag 14 1993
Review of: *Near Calvary: selected poems 1959-1970* by Lafitte, Nicholas. In: *Tablet* 247:248 F 20 1993
Review of: *Translations from the natural world* by Murray, Les. In: *Tablet* 247:949 Jl 24 1993
Review of: *Tulips in the prison yard* by Berrigan, Daniel. In: *Tablet* 247:248 F 20 1993 *see* Sundermeier, Michael, jt ed

Egan, Eileen.
GATT: an ethical void. *Cath Work* 60:1+ Je-Jl 1993
Herald of a renewed Church. *Cath Work* 60:8 My 1993
Review of: *Prayers of the women mystics* by Chervin, Ronda De Sola, ed. In: *Cath Work* 60:6 Mr-Ap 1993

Egan, Harvey D.
Review of: *Heightened consciousness: the mystical difference* by Granfield, David. In: *TheolStds* 54:394-395 Je 1993

Egan, Kathleen. *see* Egan, Eileen, jt ed

Egan, Keith J.
Review of: *God speaks in the night: the life, times, and teaching of St John of the Cross* by Kavanaugh, Kieran. In: *Horizons (CTS)* 19:315 Fall 1992
Review of: *Historia del Carmelo Español, vol 1: Desde los orígenes hasta finalizar el concilio de Trento, c 1265-1563* by Bayon, Balbino Velasco. In: *CHist* 78:644-645 O 1992
Review of: *Medieval Carmelite heritage: early reflections on the nature of the order* by Staring, Adrianus, ed. In: *CHist* 78:641-642 O 1992
Review of: *Teresa of Avila* by Williams, Rowan. In: *Horizons (CTS)* 19:314 Fall 1992

Egan-Buffet, Maire.
Review of: *Music and the Church* by Gillen, Gerard, and White, Harry, eds. In: *Furrow* 44:321-322 My 1993

Egana, Francisco J.
Religious and the new rite for the ordination of deacons. *Con Life* 17 no 2:98-121 1992

Ehle, Paulo.
Inculturação: um desafio pastoral. *REB* 53:167-174 Mr 1993

Ehlen, Peter.
Befreiung von Knechtschaft. *Stimm Zeit* 211:21-33 Ja 1993

Eifrig, Gail McGrew.
Measuring the days. Grand Rapids: Zondervan Publishing House, 1993. x, 400p ISBN 0-06-069248-0

Eisenman, Robert H.
The Dead Sea Scrolls uncovered: the first complete translation and interpretation of 50 key documents withheld for over 35 years. Rockport: Element, 1992. 286p ISBN 1-85230-368-9

Ekéus, Rolf.
Iraq and the United Nations [interview by T H Stahel, 1938-]. *America* 169:4-5 Ag 14-21 1993

Eklin, Carolyn.
Religious education's power to nurture faith. *Origins* 23:28-31 My 27 1993

El-Meskeen, Matta.
True unity: an inspiration for the world. *OChr* 29 no 3:187-198 1993

Elborn, Geoffrey.
Review of: *A suitable boy* by Seth, Vikram. In: *Tablet* 247:518 Ap 24 1993
Review of: *Morgan: a biography of E M Forster* by Beauman, Nicola. In: *Tablet* 247:1013-1014 Ag 7 1993

Elder, John C. *see* Rockefeller, Steven C, jt auth

Eliade, Mircea, 1907-1985.
Geschichte der religiösen Ideen: 5 vols. Freiburg: Herder, 1993. x, 2200p ISBN 3-451-04200-2

Elie, Paul, 1965-.
Review of: *No other life* by Moore, Brian. In: *Comm* 120:25-26 N 5 1993
Review of: *Temptations* by Wilkes, Paul, 1938-. In: *Comm* 120:24-26 Je 18 1993

Elizondo, Virgil.
Evil and the experience of God. *Way* 33:34-43 Ja 1993 *see* Boff, Leonardo, jt ed

Elkind, David, 1931-.
Whatever happened to childhood? *Momentum* 24:18-19 Ap-My 1993

Elkins, Sharon.
Review of: *The Rule of the Templars: the French text of the Rule of the Order of the Knights Templar*. In: *TheolStds* 54:386 Je 1993

Ellens, J P.
Review of: *Law, politics and the Church of England: the career of Stephen Lushington, 1782-1873* by Waddams, S M. In: *CHist* 79:346-347 Ap 1993

Ellinger, Gerard H.
Review of: *The Origenist controversy* by Clark, Elizabeth Ann. In: *TheolStds* 54:561-563 S 1993

Ellingsen, Mark.
The cutting edge: how churches speak on social and ethical issues. Grand Rapids: Eerdmans, 1993. 400p ISBN 0-8028-0710-0
Review of: *After Patriarchy: feminist transformations of the world religions* by Cooey, Paula M, et al, eds. In: *JEcumen Stds* 29:470-472 Sum-Aut 1992
Review of: *Ecumenism in transition* by Raiser, Konrad. In: *JEcumen Stds* 29:470-472 Sum-Aut 1992

Elliot, John E.
Review of: *Socialism revised and modernized: the case for pragmatic market socialism* by Yunker, James A. In: *RSocEcon* 51:241-244 Sum 1993

Elliot, John H.
Review of: *Christ's proclamation to the spirits: a study of 1 Peter 3:18-4:6* by Dalton, William J. In: *Bib Th Bul* 23:135 Aut 1993
The epistle of James in rhetorical and social scientific perspective holiness-wholeness and patterns of replication. *Bib Th Bul* 23:71-81 Sum 1993
Review of: *Host, guest, enemy and friend: portraits of the Pharisees in Luke and Acts* by Gowler, David B. In: *Bib Th Bul* 23:42-43 Spr 1993
Review of: *Tradition und Theologie neutestamentlicher Haustafelethik* by Gielen, Marlis. In: *CBQ* 54:779-780 O 1992

Elliott, Michael.
Why the homeless don't have homes and what to do about it. Cleveland: Pilgrim Press, 1993. x, 123p ISBN 0-8298-0965-1 LC 93-4208

Elliott, Niel.
Review of: *Revelation and redemption at Colossae* by Sappington, Thomas J. In: *CBQ* 55:395-396 Ap 1993

Ellis, Bernard.
Dialogue [interview by Gabriel Meyer]. *Register* 69:1+ F 14 1993

Ellis, Robert F.
The survival of permanent deacons. *HPR* 94:29-32+ O 1993

Ellsberg, Peggy R.
'Let the little children'. *America* 168:16 Mr 13 1993
Perfect welcome in Lent. *America* 168:23 F 20 1993
What's wrong with "family values". *America* 168:16 Ap 3 1993

Ellsberg, Robert.
On the baptism of our daughter. *Cath Work* 60:6 My 1993

Elsbernd, M.
Review of: *The Catholic peace tradition* by Musto, Ronald G. In: *Cist Stud* 27 No 4:[118]-[119] 1992
Review of: *The social justice agenda: justice, ecology, power, and the church* by Dorr, Donal, 1935-. In: *Cist Stud* 27 No 4:[115]-[116] 1992

Elsbernd, Mary. *see* Burns, Camilla, jt auth

Elshtain, Jean Bethke, 1941-.
Review of: *The anatomy of antiliberalism* by Holmes, Stephen. In: *Comm* 120:30-32 N 5 1993
Review of: *The politics of virtue: is abortion debatable?* by Mensch, Elizabeth, and Freeman, Alan. In: *Comm* 120:24-25 S 24 1993
Salvaging patriotism from the narrow nationalist. *New Oxford Rev* 60:6-8+ O 1993

Elvins, Mark.
Religious women and welfare. *Priests & People* 6:320-322 Ag-S 1992

Elwood, J. Murray.
A search for God in story and time. *America* 169:10-12+ O 16 1993

Emerson, Caryl.
And the demons entered into the swine: the Russian intelligentsia and post-Soviet religious thought. *CrossCurr* 43:184-202 Sum 1993

Emile, Brother, and John, Brother.
The secret of Taizé [photos]. *Priests & People* 7:278-282 Jl 1993

Empereur, James L.
Review of: *What is liturgical theology?* by Fagerberg, David W. In: *TheolStds* 54:589-590 S 1993

Endean, Philip.
Jesuit presence and the struggle for justice in Nazi Germany. *Month* 26:240-246 Je 1993
Review of: *Hans Urs von Balthasar* by O'Donnell, John J. In: *Heythrop* 34: 440-442 O 1993
Review of: *Ignatius of Loyola: the psychology of a saint* by Meissner, William W. In: *Way* 33:249-250 Jl 1993
Review of: *Karl Rahner* by Dych, William V. In: *Month* 26:76-77 F 1993
Review of: *Karl Rahner* by Dych, William V. In: *Heythrop* 34:440-442 O 1993
Review of: *Salvation outside the Church* by Sullivan, Francis Aloysius. In: *Way* 33:249 Jl 1993
Review of: *Science and the soul* by Tilby, Angela. In: *Way* 33:248 Jl 1993
Review of: *St Irenaeus of Lyons: against the heresies, vol 1* by Unger, Dominic J. In: *Way* 33:249 Jl 1993
Review of: *The Christlike God* by Taylor, John V, Bp. In: *Way* 33:248 Jl 1993
Review of: *The early poetic manuscripts and note-books of Gerard Manley Hopkins in facsimile* by MacKenzie, Norman H, ed. In: *Month* 26:148-149 Ap 1993
Review of: *The later poetic manuscripts of Gerard Manley Hopkins in facsimile* by MacKenzie, Norman H, ed. In: *Month* 26:148-149 Ap 1993
Review of: *The puzzle of evil* by Vardy, Peter. In: *Way* 33:248 Jl 1993
Review of: *Theological investigations, vol XXIII* by Rahner, Karl, 1904-1984. In: *Month* 26:76-77 F 1993

Endean, Philip, and Lonsdale, David.
Review of: *Ignatius Loyola: spiritual exercises* by Tetlow, Joseph Allen. In: *Way* 33:251 Jl 1993
Review of: *Jerome Nadal, S.J., 1507-1580* by Bangert, William V, and McCoog, Thomas M. In: *Way* 33:250-251 Jl 1993
Review of: *Praying with Ignatius of Loyola* by Bergan, Jacqueline Syrup, and Schwan, Marie. In: *Way* 33:250 Jl 1993
Review of: *Spiritual intimacy and community* by English, John. In: *Way* 33: 251-252 Jl 1993

Endres, John C.
Review of: *Of scribes and scrolls: studies on the Hebrew Bible, Inter-testamental Judaism, and Christian Origins* by Attridge, Harold W, et al, eds. In: *CBQ* 54:814-815 O 1992
Review of: *The Old Testament of the Old Testament: patriarchal narratives and Mosaic Yahwism* by Moberly, R W L. In: *TheolStds* 54:381-382 Je 1993
Review of: *Wildmen, warriors, and kings: masculine spirituality and the Bible* by Arnold, Patrick M. In: *Horizons (CTS)* 20:166-167 Spr 1993

Engleman, Dennis.
The rapture: biblical fact or wishful thinking? *New Cov* 22:28-31 Ap 1993

English, Isobel.
Review of: *Ottoline Morrell* by Seymour, Miranda. In: *Tablet* 246:1573 D 12 1992
Review of: *The case of Anna Kavan* by Callard, David. In: *Tablet* 247:694 My 29 1993

English, John.
Spiritual intimacy and community. New Jersey: Paulist Press, 1992. x, 207p ISBN 0-8091-3384-9 LC 92-29706

English, Joseph.
The growing dialogue of church and couch [interview by D Scott]. *OSV* 82: 12 Jl 4 1993

Englund, Steven.
New light under the old bushel: what's happening in the French Church? *Comm* 120:11-14 Ap 23 1993

Enman, Fred M.
Law as ministry: a perspective from the Judaeo-Christian tradition. *CLawyer* 35 no 1:97-107 1993

Eno, Robert B.
Review of: *Desire and delight: a new reading of Augustine's confessions* by Miles, Margaret R. In: *CHist* 79:312-313 Ap 1993

Eppink, Alfons.
Africa's lost haven. *Tablet* 247:680-681 My 29 1993
War-torn Sudan waits for the Pope. *Tablet* 247:160-161 F 6 1993

Ercolessi, Maria Cristina. *see* Marchi, Vichi De, jt auth

Erdö, Peter.
Quaestiones de officiis ecclesiasticis laicorum. *Periodica* 81 no 2:179-209 1992
Quaestiones de officiis ecclesiasticis laicorum. *Periodica* 81 no 2:179-209 1992

Erickson, John H.
The local churches and catholicity: an orthodox perspective. *Jurist* 52 no 1: 490-508 1992

Erickson, Joyce Quiring.
On being at home. *CrossCurr* 43:235-246 Sum 1993

Erlandson, Greg.
A modest proposal: "outing" pro-lifers. *OSV* 81:23 F 14 1993

Ernst, Charles A.
"I am that king"—disordered history and delusional writing: the artful derangements of Gogol's "Diary". *Cithara* 32:39-48 My 1993

Escandell, Noemi.
Cuba—"we manage" despite the blockade. *Cath Work* 60:8 Mr-Ap 1993

Escol, R.
Review of: *Augustine, the harvest, and theology (1200-1650)* by Hagen, K, ed. In: *NRT* 114:909-910 N-D 1992
Review of: *Bibliografia Filosofica Italiana: 1989 and 1990* by Scalabrin, C, ed. In: *NRT* 115:277-278 Mr-Ap 1993
Review of: *Dictionnaire de théologie fondamentale* by Latourelle, Rene, et al, eds. In: *NRT* 115:286-287 Mr-Ap 1993
Review of: *Dios es padre.* In: *NRT* 114:898-899 N-D 1992
Review of: *Foi et philosophies* by Léonard, André. In: *NRT* 115:303 Mr-Ap 1993
Review of: *Introduction à l'étude de la théologie* by Doré, Joseph, ed. In: *NRT* 114:897-898 N-D 1992
Review of: *Introduction à l'étude de la théologie* by Doré, Joseph, ed. In: *NRT* 115:577 Jl-Ag 1993
Review of: *Salvation outside the Church* by Sullivan, Francis Aloysius. In: *NRT* 115:584 Jl-Ag 1993
Review of: *Was ist Scholastik?* by Schönberger, R. In: *NRT* 115:302 Mr-Ap 1993
Review of: *Biblia y Cristología: unidad y diversidad en la Iglesia* by Val-divieso, R Sanz. In: *NRT* 115:298 Mr-Ap 1993
Review of: *Fragments et Témoignages* by Anaximandre. In: *NRT* 115:303-304 Mr-Ap 1993
Review of: *OEuvres complètes* by Maritain, R. In: *NRT* 115:304-305 Mr-Ap 1993

Esler, Philip F.
Review of: *What are they saying about Luke?* by Powell, Mark Allan. In: *Bib Th Bul* 23:84-85 Sum 1993

Espeja, Jesús.
La Evangelización en el mundo obrero. *Cien Tom* 119:499-519 S-D 1992
Liberación, inculturación y alteridad. *Cien Tom* 120:153-167 Ja-Ap 1993
La moral como madurez de la persona—Evocando la figura de Antonio Sanchís, OP. *Cien Tom* 119:391-405 My-Ag 1992
Review of: *La Iglesia de los pobres en Nicaragua: Historia y perspectivas* by Aragón, R, and Löschcke, E. In: *Cien Tom* 120:187 Ja-Ap 1993
Review of: *Vivir como Cristo: antropología teológica* by Gelabert Ballester, Martín. In: *Cien Tom* 119:610 S-D 1992
Sobre el documento de Santo Domingo. *Cien Tom* 120:177-185 Ja-Ap 1993

Espinel, J Luis.
Biblia de San Vicente convento de San Esteban: Salamanca. *Cien Tom* 119: 521-548 S-D 1992
Review of: *El Señor de la vida: lectura cristológica del Apocalipsis* by Contreras Molina, Francisco. In: *Cien Tom* 119:407 My-Ag 1992
Review of: *Jésus-Christ en écriture d'images* by Cottin, Jérôme. In: *Cien Tom* 119:408 My-Ag 1992
Review of: *The dwelling of God: the tabernacle in the Old Testament, intertestamental Jewish literature, and the New Testament* by Koester, Craig R. In: *Cien Tom* 119:410 My-Ag 1992
Review of: *The Fourth Gospel and its predecessor: from narrative source to present Gospel* by Fortna, Robert Tomson. In: *Cien Tom* 119:408-409 My-Ag 1992

Espinosa, J Manuel.
The origin of the Penitentes of New Mexico: separating fact from fiction. *CHist* 79:454-477 Jl 1993
Review of: *By force of arms: the journals of Don Diego de Vargas, New Mexico, 1691-1693* by Kessell, John L, and Hendricks, Rick, eds. In: *CHist* 79:360-362 Ap 1993
Review of: *Manipulating the saints: religious brotherhoods and social integration in post-conquest Latin America* by Meyers, Albert, and Hopkins, Diane Elizabeth, eds. In: *CHist* 78:696-698 O 1992

Esselman, Thomas.
The study of Episcopal conferences: an application of the principle of functionality. *Jurist* 51 no 2:311-325 1991

Estadt, Barry K. *see* Wicks, Robert J, jt ed

Estés, Clarissa Pinkola.
The dancing grandmas. *USCath* 58:26-30 N 1993

Estin, C. *see* Mukherjee, Pr, jt auth

Etchegaray, Alberto.
Challenges for the Christian layperson in the coming millenium [repr and tr fr *Mensaje*]. *LADOC* 23:12-16 Mr-Ap 1993

Etchegaray, Roger, Cardinal, 1922-.
The never up-to-date map of refugees. *Origins* 22:755-757 Ap 15 1993
God's peace surpasses understanding. *OR(Eng)* 1312:6 O 20 1993
Haitian people urgently need to feel touch of universal solidarity. *OR(Eng)* 1311:10 O 13 1993

Étienne, Jacques.
Review of: *Adequately considered: an American perspective on Louis Janssens' personalist morals* by Christie, Dolores. In: *Eph Theol Lovan* 78:186-187 Ap 1992
Review of: *Bergson* by Viellard-Baron, Jean-Louis. In: *RPhil Louvain* 90:586-587 N 1992
Review of: *Bonhoeffer's ethics: old Europe and new frontiers* by Carter, Guy, and Eyden, René van, et al, eds. In: *Eph Theol Lovan* 78:483-484 D 1992
Review of: *Christliche Moral zwischen Vernunft und Offenbarung* by Angel, Hans-Gerd. In: *Eph Theol Lovan* 69:215-216 Ap 1993
Review of: *L'État moderne non-confessionnel et le message chrétien* by Thils, Gustave. In: *Eph Theol Lovan* 78:484 D 1992
Review of: *La communion ecclésiale dans le cadre juridique de l'État moderne* by Thils, Gustave. In: *Eph Theol Lovan* 69:216-217 Ap 1993
Review of: *Leçons de morale, psychologie et métaphysique au lycée Henri-IV* by Bergson, Henri. In: *RPhil Louvain* 90:583-586 N 1992
Review of: *Si tu connaissais* by Guelluy, Robert. In: *Eph Theol Lovan* 78: 185-186 Ap 1992
Review of: *Teologia morale e mentalità scientifica* by Targonski, Francesco. In: *Eph Theol Lovan* 78:482-483 D 1992

F

Farrell, Maureen.
A new church in a changing world: Christ the cornerstone, Milton Keynes, England. *OChr* 29 no 2:170-175 1993

Farrell, Michael J.
Give Bill a break, and do something about Saddam, mother of all bullies. *Nat Cath Rep* 29:22 Jl 16 1993
The hell, you say. *Nat Cath Rep* 29:14-15 Ap 2 1993
If more serious Jesus has failed to fix world, is laughing the way. *Nat Cath Rep* 29:2 Mr 26 1993
Pretty isn't enough; art aims to fix earth. *Nat Cath Rep* 30:13-14 O 22 1993
Review of: *North of the border* by Gairdner, William D. In: *Register* 69:5 Mr 21 1993
Review of: *The first dissident: the book of Job in today's politics* by Safire, William. In: *Nat Cath Rep* 29:25-26 F 5 1993
Science screws up world while it blows your mind. *Nat Cath Rep* 29:14-15 Jl 2 1993
Somalia: a land of nomads, anarchists and poets. *Nat Cath Rep* 29:16 Ja 22 1993
War makes people feel so alive. *Nat Cath Rep* 29:4-5 F 19 1993

Farrell, Regina.
Review of: *"Pro-Choice vs prolife: abortion and the courts in Canada"* by Morton, F L. In: *Register* 69:5 Jl 25 1993
Review of: *"The real Anita Hill: the untold story"* by Brock, David. In: *Register* 69:5 Je 20 1993

Farren, Suzy.
The shooting of Sister Stan [condensed fr *Catholic Health World* D 1 1992]. *CDgst* 57:112-117 My 1993
Sister Anne's five years in America [condensed fr *Catholic Health World* Ag 15 1992]. *CDgst* 57:66-70 Ja 1993

Farris, Bain J.
Converting a unit to patient-focused care. *Health Prog* 74:23-25 Ap 1993

Farrugia, E G.
Review of: *St. Paul in Malta* by Galea, Michael, and Ciarlò, Canon John, eds. In: *Civilta* 3:196-197 Jl 17 1993

Farrugia, Edward G. *see* O'Collins, Gerald, 1931-, jt auth

Farry, Michael J.
The Green Paper, the Church and the Constitution. *Studies* 82:160-170 Sum 1993

Fastiggi, Robert L.
The Incarnation: Muslim objections and the Christian response. *Thomist* 57:457-493 Jl 1993

Fater, Douglas.
Making secular space sacred. *Mod Lit* 20:14-17 My 1993

Fattori, Marta. *see* Hamesse, Jacqueline, jt ed

Fatula, Mary Ann.
Thomas Aquinas, preacher and friend. Minnesota: The Liturgical Press, 1993. x, 313p ISBN 0-8146-5031-7 LC 92-27552

Faucher, W Thomas, 1945-.
A disturbing silence. *Tablet* 247:706 Je 5 1993
Let the music grow: in its own time. *Past Mus* 17:24-25 Ap-My 1993
Outsiders need not apply. *Tablet* 246:1566 D 12 1992

Fauci, Christine.
Review of: *Edith Stein* by Herbstrith, Waltraud. In: *ChrWorld* 38:152+ Mr-Ap 1993

Fauret, Pierre.
Fontaine, Gaston, 1921-1992 [obit]. *Notitiae* 28:428-430 Je 1992
Réunion des évêques présidents et des secrétaires des commissions nationales de liturgie des pays francophones. *Notitiae* 28:740-751 N-D 1992

Feder, Don.
An overdue Exodus: breaking the bonds of liberalism. *Crisis* 11:32-35 Jl-Ag 1993
A voice crying in America's wilderness [interview by W. Bole, pt 1 of 2]. *OSV* 82:6-7 N 28 1993

Fedoryka, Damian.
What happens to the victims of compromise abortion laws? *SocJust* 84:115-123 Jl-Ag 1993

Fédou, Michel.
L'attitude d'Oridène face aux philosophies et religions païennes. *StudiaM* 42:123-142 1993

Fedwick, Paul J.
Review of: *Spuren der alten liebe: studien zum kirchenbegriff des Basilius von caesarea* by Koschorke, Klaus. In: *TheolStds* 54:345-347 Je 1993

Fee, Joan Flynn.
Can basic training make better parents? *Salt* 13:18-23 My 1993

Feeney, Joseph J.
Review of: *Hopkins: a literary biography* by White, Norman. In: *America* 168:26-27 F 20 1993
Review of: *Spirit and beauty: an introduction to theological aesthetics* by Sherry, Patrick. In: *TheolStds* 54:603-605 S 1993
William Golding (1911-93): lord of horror, lord of awe. *America* 169:6-7 Jl 31-Ag 7 1993
The year of John Tavener: contemporary composer and Christian mystic. *America* 168:15-16 Ap 10 1993

Fehlner, Peter D.
Bibliography of the works of Fr Juniper B Carol, OFM. *Marian Stds* 43:48-59 1992
Fr Juniper B Carol, OFM: his mariology and scholarly achievement. *Marian Stds* 43:17-47 1992

Fehr, Wayne L. *see* Hands, Donald R, jt auth

Fehringer, Clara.
Review of: *Step spirit: the 12 steps as a spiritual program* by Chapman, Catherine. In: *Sisters* 65:313 Jl 1993
Review of: *The shadow side of community and the growth of the self* by Wolff-Salin, Mary. In: *Sisters* 65:61-62 Ja 1993

Fehringer, Clara. *(cont'd)*
Review of: *Using the 12 steps to grow spiritually* by Wallace, Patricia F, and Winifred, Mary. In: *Sisters* 65:313 Jl 1993

Feil, Ernst.
Der christliche Glaube—unverändert und unverkürzt für die ganze Welt? *Stimm Zeit* 211:579-593 S 1993
The new Catechism of the Catholic Church conferms to the genuine tradition of the Church, especially to the teachings of the second Vatican Council, 12-07 1992 (commentary).

Feister, John Bookser.
Assisted suicide is not the answer [editorial]. *St Anth* 101:21 O 1993
Bayou blessing. *St Anth* 100:28-35 F 1993
Don't turn back the clock on corporate responsibility [editorial]. *St Anth* 100:33 My 1993
No more bingo on the Bayou. *St Anth* 100:34-35 F 1993
Review of: *Fritz Eichenberg* by Ellsberg, Robert, ed. In: *St Anth* 101:50 Je 1993
Review of: *Joshua in the Holy Land* by Girzone, Joseph F. In: *Nat Cath Rep* 29:37 My 28 1993
Review of: *The son of laughter* by Buechner, Frederick. In: *Nat Cath Rep* 29:37 My 28 1993
Stewardship: we reap what we sow [editorial]. *St Anth* 100:57 Ja 1993

Feldman, Louis H.
Josephus' portrait of Ahab. *Eph Theol Lovan* 78:368-384 D 1992
Josephus' portrait of Josiah. *Louvain Stds* 18:110-130 Sum 1993
Review of: *Jewish historiography and iconography in early and medieval Christianity* by Schreckenberg, Heinz, and Schubert, Kurt. In: *OTA* 16:449-450 Je 1993
Review of: *Judaism: practice and belief* by Sanders, E P. In: *CBQ* 55:393-394 Ap 1993

Feliciani, Giorgio.
Response to Julio Manzanares. *Jurist* 52 no 1:255-258 1992

Feliciano, Florentino P.
The application of law: some recurring aspects of the process of judicial review and decision making. *Amer J Juris* 37:17-56 1992

Feliciano, Teo.
Review of: *Vision profetica/prophetic vision* by Galerón, Soledad, et al, eds. In: *Church* 9:61 Spr 1993

Fellhauer, David E.
Review of: *Marriage annulment in the Catholic church* by Brown, Ralph. In: *Jurist* 51 no 2:524-525 1991

Felzmann, Vladimir.
Mapping the land of the young. *Priests & People* 7:264-268 Jl 1993

Femminis, A.
Review of: *Per una scuola che funzioni: dal mito delle riforme alla ricerca dell'efficacia* by Paracone, Corrado, and Mola, Aldo A, eds. In: *Civilta* 2:415 My 15 1993

Fenton, Norman.
Review of: *Being and knowing: reflections of a Thomist* by Wilhelmsen, Frederick D, 1923-. In: *Thomist* 57:153-154 Ja 1993

Fera, Eileen.
Living with infertility when motherhood doesn't happen. *Liguorian* 81:24-28 My 1993

Feracine, Luiz.
Função dos pais e padrinhos nos sacramentos da iniciação Cristã. *REB* 52:903-916 D 1992

Ferguson, Arthur B.
Review of: *Richard Mulcaster (c 1531-1611) and educational reform in the Renaissance* by DeMolen, Richard L. In: *CHist* 79:534 Jl 1993

Ferguson, David.
Bultmann. Collegeville: The Liturgical Press, 1992. x, 154p ISBN 0-8146-5037-6

Ferguson, Everett.
Backgrounds of early Christianity. Grand Rapids: Eerdmans, 1993. 608p ISBN 0-8028-0669-4

Ferguson, Lisa.
After marx. *New Cov* 22:25 Je 1993
Breaking a monopoly. *Register* 69:3 My 9 1993
A decade of fireworks. *New Cov* 23:20-21 Ag 1993
Supporting prolife women candidates. *Register* 69:2 Ap 25 1993

Fergusson, David.
Review of: *Bible and belief* by Houlden, J L. In: *New Blckfrs* 74:50-51 Ja 1993
Review of: *The Bible's authority; a portrait gallery of thinkers from Lessing to Bultmann* by O'Neill, J C. In: *New Blckfrs* 73:632-633 D 1992

Ferme, Brian.
The canon law culture of medieval England. *Periodica* 82 no 1:28-54 1993
Review of: *Problems of authority in the Reformation debates* by Evans, G R. In: *New Blckfrs* 74:333-334 Je 1993

Fernández, Ana Ofelia.
Historical perspective sheds new light on most recent Catechism. *OR(Eng)* 1297:10 Je 30 1993

Fernández-Calienes, Raúl.
Review of: *Cry for justice: the aborginal and islander contribution to the World Council of Churches 7th Assembly* by Pattel-Gray, Anne. In: *Pacifica* 6:120-121 F 1993

Fernández Del Riesgo, Manuel.
Exigencias teólogicas de una filosofía de la historia (la resurrección como teodicea radial). *Cien Tom* 119:321-349 My-Ag 1992

Fernando, Ajith.
Spiritual living in a secular world: applying the Book of Daniel today. Grand Rapids: Zondervan Publishing House, 1993. x, 192p ISBN 0-310-59501-0

Finley, Mitchel B. *(cont'd)*
Review of: *A christological catechism: New Testament answers* by Fitzmyer, Joseph Augustine, 1920-. In: *St Anth* 100:12-13 Ja 1993
Review of: *Addiction and grace* by May, Gerald G. In: *St Anth* 100:12 Ja 1993
Review of: *Fall from grace* by Greeley, Andrew Moran, 1928-. In: *St Anth* 101:53 N 1993
Review of: *Joshua in the Holy Land* by Girzone, Joseph F. In: *St Anth* 100:14 Ja 1993
Review of: *Listening to your life: daily meditations with Frederick Buechner* by Connor, George. In: *St Anth* 100:52 S 1993
Review of: *Love affair: a prayer journal* by Greeley, Andrew Moran, 1928-. In: *St Anth* 100:52-53 F 1993
Review of: *The Catholic myth: the behavior and beliefs of American Catholics* by Greeley, Andrew Moran, 1928-. In: *St Anth* 100:12 Ja 1993
Review of: *The Catholic vision* by O'Connor, Edward C. In: *St Anth* 100:53 Ja 1993
Review of: *The last priests in America* by Unsworth, Tim. In: *St Anth* 100:14 Ja 1993
Review of: *The seven deadly sins: stories on human weakness and virtue* by Stanford, Peter. In: *St Anth* 100:52 My 1993
Review of: *Wages of sin* by Greeley, Andrew Moran, 1928-. In: *St Anth* 100:52-53 F 1993
Review of: *Why Catholics can't sing* by Day, Thomas. In: *St Anth* 100:15 Ja 1993
Review of: *Wildmen, warriors, and kings: masculine spirituality and the Bible* by Arnold, Patrick M. In: *St Anth* 100:14-15 Ja 1993
A secret hero in Dachau. *OSV* 82:9 Ag 15 1993
Seven influential Catholic books. *St Anth* 100:10-15 Ja 1993
Single parents: building holy families. *Liguorian* 81:12-16 Ag 1993
Spiritual direction: an ongoing retreat? *OSV* 81:6 Ja 31 1993
Talking dirty. *OSV* 82:6 S 26 1993
Walker Percy: pilgrim in our ruins. *OSV* 82:16 My 30 1993
What Catholics really believe [interview by Mitch Finley]. *OSV* 81:6-7 F 21 1993
The wit and whimsy of Karl Rahner [por]. *OSV* 82:6 N 7 1993

Finley, Mitchel B, and Finley, Kathy.
Are kids telling us something about the Mass? *Living Prayer* 26:23-24 Mr-Ap 1993
Christian families and today's sexual values. *Living Prayer* 26:21-22 N-D 1993
The home front. *Living Prayer* 26:22-23 My-Je 1993
The home front. *Living Prayer* 26:27-28 Jl-Ag 1993
A painful accident reveals God's love. *Living Prayer* 26:21-22 S-O 1993
Salvation and family life. *Living Prayer* 26:23-24 Ja-F 1993

Finn, Donna. *see* Finn, Thomas, jt auth

Finn, James.
The moral vision of Robert Stone. *Comm* 120:9-14 N 5 1993

Finn, Molly.
Review of: *The children of men* by James, P D. In: *Comm* 120:26-27 Ap 23 1993

Finn, Peter C.
A crisis facing us all. *Past Mus* 17:21-23 Ap-My 1993

Finn, Thomas, and Finn, Donna.
Intimate bedfellows: love, sex, and the Catholic Church. Boston: St. Paul Books & Media, 1993. 85p ISBN 0-8198-3667-2 LC 92-42622

Finn, Thomas Macy.
Review of: *Ascetic behavior in Greco-Roman antiquity: a sourcebook* by Wimbush, Vincent L, ed. In: *CBQ* 54:808-810 O 1992

Finn, Tim.
Review of: *Gone tomorrow* by Indiana, Gary. In: *Nat Cath Rep* 29:26 My 28 1993

Finucane, Marian.
Values and attitudes in a changing Ireland. *Doctr Life* 43:333-342 Jl-Ag 1993

Fiore, Benjamin.
Review of: *The secretary in the letters of Paul* by Richards, E Randolph. In: *CBQ* 55:391-392 Ap 1993
Review of: *What are the Gospels?* by Burridge, Richard A. In: *TheolStds* 53:780-781 D 1992

Fiorelli, Paul E.
Guideline amendments dramatically change the structure of organizational fines. *CLawyer* 35 no 2:181-197 1993

Fiorenza, Elisabeth Schüssler, 1938-.
But she said: feminist practices of biblical interpretation. Boston: Beacon, 1992. x, 261p ISBN 0-8070-1214-9
Discipleship of equals: a critical feminist ecology of liberation. New York: Crossroad, 1993. x, 372p ISBN 0-82451-244-8 LC 92-31264

Fiorenza, Francis Schüssler, 1938-. *see* Browning, Don S, jt ed

Firestone, Denise Fainberg.
Empty room, empty tomb. *Spir Life* 39:26-30 Spr 1993

Firth, Francis.
Advance from faith into knowledge. *Can Cath Rev* 11:34-36 S 1993
The Apostolic tradition. *Can Cath Rev* 11:34-36 F 1993
Baptism. *Can Cath Rev* 11:35-36 Mr 1993
Clement of Alexandria. *Can Cath Rev* 11:35-36 My 1993
Clement's moral teaching. *Can Cath Rev* 11:36-38 Jl-Ag 1993
Epistle to Diognetus. *Can Cath Rev* 11:35-36 Ap 1993
Origen: Christian genius. *Can Cath Rev* 11:35-36 O 1993
Origen: scripture scholar. *Can Cath Rev* 11:36-37 N 1993
Who was Saint Hippolytus? *Can Cath Rev* 11:48-49 Ja 1993
The works of Clement of Alexandria. *Can Cath Rev* 11:35 Je 1993

Fischer, James A.
Looking for moral guidance: dilemma and the Bible. New York: Paulist Press, 1992. x, 152p ISBN 0-8091-3170-6 LC 92-35933

Fischer, Kathleen.
Older? you are a blessing [condensed fr *The Catholic World* N-D 1992]. *CDgst* 57:17-18+ F 1993

Fischer, Mark F.
The conciliar passion. *Tod Parish* 25:23-25 Ap-My 1993
How democratic should your council be? *Tod Parish* 25:23-26 O 1993
Parish council members made or born? *Tod Parish* 25:17+ N-D 1993
Parish councils: Jesus never sought consensus. *Tod Parish* 25:23-26 Mr 1993
What's more important—process or product? *Tod Parish* 25:21-23 Ja 1993
You need more than good technique. *Tod Parish* 25:23-26 13-17 S 1993

Fisher, Anthony.
Does the church's teaching on sex make sense? *Priests & People* 7:317-322 Ag-S 1993
On not starving the unconscious. *New Blckfrs* 74:130-145 Mr 1993
Review of: *Catholics and sex* by Saunders, Kate, and Stanford, Peter. In: *Priests & People* 6:354-356 Ag-S 1992
Review of: *Reading in communion: scripture and ethics in Christian life* by Fowl, Stephen E, and Jones, L Gregory. In: *New Blckfrs* 73:629-630 D 1992
The road to euthanasia. *Tablet* 247:235-237 F 20 1993

Fisher, Doug.
Sports: shaping our stories and our myths. *ChrWorld* 236:282-285 N-D 1993

Fisher, Eugene J.
Faith without prejudice: rebuilding Christian attitudes toward Judaism. New York: The Crossroad Publishing Company, 1993. x, 208p ISBN 0-8245-1266-9 LC 92-36342
"A final word" [replay to Boadt; L; N 1991]. *New Theol Rev* 6:87-89 F 1993
Interwoven destinies: Jews and Christians through the ages. New Jersey: Paulist Press, 1993. x, 154p ISBN 0-8091-8363-6 LC 92-37707
Review of: *The Catholic-Jewish dialogue and the state of Israel* by Kenny, Anthony John. In: *SIDIC* 25 No 1:32-33 1992
Review of: *World religions: beliefs behind today's headlines* by Catoir, John T. In: *CLW* 64:36-37 Jl-S 1993

Fisher, Eugene J, and Bemporad, Jack.
Review of: *Judaism* by Küng, Hans, 1928-. In: *Comm* 120:29-30 Ja 29 1993

Fisher, James T.
Review of: *Conduct unbecoming: gays and lesbians in the US military* by Shilts, Randy. In: *Comm* 120:6-7 My 21 1993
Tom Dooley's many lives. *Comm* 120:6-7 My 21 1993

Fisher, Mary.
Moral leadership needed to respond to AIDS. *Health Prog* 74:55-56 Jl-Ag 1993

Fisichella, Rino.
Review of: *Einsicht und Bekehrung. Ausgangspunkt der Fundamentaltheologie bei Bernard Longergan* by Dobroczyński, Grzegorz. In: *Gregorianum* 74 no 2:366-367 1993
Review of: *Hans Urs von Balthasar: uno stile teologico* by Scola, Angelo. In: *Gregorianum* 74 no 3:581-582 1993
Review of: *Homo creatus est* by Balthasar, Hans Urs Von, 1905-1988. In: *Gregorianum* 74 No 1:157-158 1993
Review of: *Pensare il bello* by Trombino, Mario, et al. In: *Gregorianum* 74 no 2:408-409 1993
Review of: *The modern theologians: an introduction to Christian theology in the twentieth century, 2 vols* by Ford, David F. In: *Gregorianum* 73 No 4:755-756 1992
Review of: *Theologie der drei Tage* by Balthasar, Hans Urs Von, 1905-1988. In: *Gregorianum* 73 No 4:756 1992

Fite, Cotton R. *see* Anderson, Herbert, jt auth

Fitzgerald, Aloysius.
Review of: *"Jahwe und seine Aschera"* by Dietrich, Manfried, and Loretz, Oswald. In: *OTA* 16:185-186 F 1993
Review of: *Arts et industries de la pierre* by Yon, Marguerite, ed. In: *OTA* 15:469 O 1992
Review of: *Astrological reports to Assyrian kings* by Hunger, Hermann. In: *OTA* 16:408 Je 1993
Review of: *Das Recht der Bilder gesehen zu werden* by Keel, Othmar. In: *OTA* 16:407 Je 1993
Review of: *Die hebräischen Präpositionen* by Jenni, Ernst. In: *OTA* 16:159 F 1993
Review of: *Hebrew and Aramaic incantation texts from the Cairo Genizah* by Schiffman, Lawrence H, and Swartz, Michael D. In: *OTA* 16:165-166 F 1993
Review of: *Imperial administrative records* by Fales, F M, and Postgate, J N. In: *OTA* 16:408 Je 1993
Review of: *La trouvaille épigrapique de l'Ougarit, v II* by Cunchillos, Jesús-Luis. In: *OTA* 15:480 O 1992
Review of: *Legal transactions of the royal court of Nineveh* by Kwasman, Theodore, and Parpola, Simo. In: *OTA* 16:408 Je 1993
Review of: *Masada III: the Yigael Yadin excavations 1963-65, final reports* by Netzer, Ehud. In: *OTA* 16:164 F 1993
Review of: *Scarab seals from a middle to late Bronze Age tomb at Pella in Jordan* by Richards, Fiona V. In: *OTA* 16:165 F 1993
Review of: *The Amarna letters* by Moran, William L, ed. In: *OTA* 16:163 F 1993
Review of: *The Damascus document reconsidered* by Broshi, Magen, ed. In: *OTA* 15:469 O 1992
Review of: *Vorderasiatische Stempelsiegel* by Keel-Leu, Hildi. In: *OTA* 16:160 F 1993

FitzGerald, Barbara.
Review of: *An evil cradling* by Keenan, Brian. In: *Furrow* 44:119 F 1993

FitzGerald, Kyriaki Antonia.
The Fifth World Conference and walls of the heart. *Ecumen Trends* 22:1+ Ap 1993

Fitzgerald, Michael Louis, Bp.
Interreligious dialogue today. *Cath Int* 4:190-194 Ap 1993

Fitzgerald, Penelope.
Review of: *The vicar of sorrows* by Wilson, A N, 1950-. In: *Tablet* 247:1266 O 2 1993

FitzLyon, April.
Review of: *Anastasia, the lost princess* by Lovell, James Blair. In: *Tablet* 246:1622-1623 D 19-26 1992
Review of: *Nicholas II, Emperor of all the Russias* by Lieven, Dominic. In: *Tablet* 247:820-821 Je 26 1993
Review of: *The gingerbread race* by Nayrozov, Andrei. In: *Tablet* 247:1263-1264 O 2 1993
Review of: *The last station, a novel of Tolstoy's last year* by Parini, Jay. In: *Tablet* 247:481 Ap 10-17 1993

Fitzlyon, April.
Review of: *The long shadow: inside Stalin's family* by Richardson, Rosamond. In: *Tablet* 247:920-921 Jl 17 1993

FitzLyon, April.
Review of: *The Russian heart: days of crisis and hope* by Turnley, David C. In: *Tablet* 247:76-77 Ja 16 1993
Review of: *The Victorians and Renaissance Italy* by Fraser, Hilary. In: *Tablet* 247:656-657 My 22 1993

FitzMaurice, Eileen Claire.
1993 UN focus: indigenous people. *Momentum* 24:79-80 Ap-My 1993

Fitzmyer, Joseph Augustine, 1920-.
According to Paul: studies in the theology of the Apostle. New York: Paulist, 1993. x, 177p ISBN 08-0913-390-3 LC 93-20453
The interpretation of the Bible in the Church. *America* 169:12-15 N 27 1993
Review of: *An annotated translations of Miqṣāt Ma'aseh ha-ha-Torâ* by Dombrowski, Bruno W W. In: *OTA* 16:191 F 1993
Review of: *An Aramaic Bibliography* by Fitzmyer, Joseph Augustine, 1920-, and Kaufman, Stephen A. In: *OTA* 15:481-482 O 1992
Review of: *Der "Sitz im Leben" in den Josuafluch-Texten, in 4 Q 379 22 II und 4 Q Testimonia* by Burgmann, Hans. In: *OTA* 16:190 F 1993
Review of: *Graphic concordance to the Dead Sea Scrolls* by Charlesworth, James H. In: *CBQ* 55:328-329 Ap 1993
Review of: *Jewish civilization in the Hellenistic-Roman period* by Talmon, Shemaryahu, ed. In: *OTA* 16:451-452 Je 1993
Review of: *Moral y conducta en Qumrán* by Olmos, Santiago Ausín. In: *OTA* 16:190 F 1993
Review of: *New Testament Apocrypha* by Schneemelcher, Wilhelm, ed. In: *TheolStds* 54:554-556 S 1993
Review of: *Qumran and Apocalyptic: studies on the Aramaic texts from Qumran* by Martínez, Florentino García. In: *OTA* 16:190 F 1993
Review of: *Qumran Cave IV and MMT* by Kapera, Zdzislaw J. In: *OTA* 16:192-193 F 1993
Review of: *Textos de Qumrán* by Martinez, Florentino García. In: *OTA* 16:444 Je 1993
Review of: *The Dead Sea Scrolls after forty years* by Shanks, Hershel, et al. In: *OTA* 16:194 F 1993
Review of: *The Scrolls and the New Testament* by Stendahl, Krister, and Charlesworth, James H, eds. In: *OTA* 15:520 O 1992
What they found in the caves. *Comm* 119:13-16 D 18 1992
What we can learn from the Dead Sea Scrolls [interview by M Finley]. *OSV* 81:7 Ja 10 1993

Fitzpatrick, Joseph P, 1913-.
Doth the left hand know what the right hand doeth? *America* 169:5-6 S 25 1993

Fitzpatrick, Michael.
Dying—and see, we are alive. *RRel* 52:719-730 S-O 1993

Fixmer, Audrey Mettel.
The world's funniest mom. *OSV* 82:16 My 9 1993

Fjeld, Roger W. see Tuell, Jack M, jt ed

Flage, Daniel E.
Descartes's three hypothetical doubts. *Mod Schlmn* 70:201-208 Mr 1993

Flanagan, Anne Joan.
Remembering and revelation: a liturgical reflection on Luke 16:19-31. *Emmanuel* 99:304-307 Jl-Ag 1993

Flanagan, Donald.
Mary and the unremembered past. *Doctr Life* 43:260-266 My-Je 1993
Review of: *Mary, mirror of the Church* by Cantalamessa, Raniero. In: *Furrow* 44:189 Mr 1993
Review of: *The immutability of God in the theology of Hans Urs von Balthasar* by O'Hanlon, Gerard F. In: *Doctr Life* 43:252-254 Ap 1993
Review of: *Theology for the third millennium* by Küng, Hans, 1928-. In: *Doctr Life* 43:190-191 Mr 1993

Flank, Lenny, Jr.
IWW organizes small shops. *Cath Work* 60:1+ Mr-Ap 1993
Wobblies win at bingo!. *Cath Work* 60:3 S 1993

Flannery, Kathleen, and Slattery, Marianne.
Acting as Jesus would. *ReligTJ* 27:28 F 1993

Flannery, Kevin L.
Traditional teaching on abortion. *Linacre* 60:67-71 My 1993
What is included in a means to an end? *Gregorianum* 74 no 3:499-513 1993

Flannery, Kevin L, and Koterski, Joseph.
Paul VI was right [reply to "Humanae Vitae" 25 years later by R A McCormick 6-8+ Jl 17 1993; rejoinder]. *America* 169:7-14 S 25 1993

Flannery, Tom.
A call to arms. *SocJust* 84:83-85 My-Je 1993

Flathers, Marjorie.
Not all saints are canonized. *St Anth* 101:22-26 N 1993

Flatman, Frances.
A view from both sides. *Priests & People* 6:317-319 Ag-S 1992

Flavell, Roger. see Flavell, Linda, jt auth

Flay, Joseph C.
Review of: *Hegel, freedom, and modernity* by Westphal, Merold. In: *IPQ* 33:365-366 S 1993

Fleischer, Barbara J.
Facilitating for growth: a guide for Scripture groups and small Christian communities. Collegeville: Liturgical, 1993. 160p ISBN 0-8146-2170-8 LC 93-1341

Fleming, Daniel E.
The etymological origins of the Hebrew nābî: the one who invokes God. *CBQ* 55:217-224 Ap 1993

Fleming, David L.
The post-Vatican II Church. *RRel* 52:484-485 Jl-Ag 1993

Fleming, Dorothy. see Kuharski, Mary Ann, jt auth

Fleming, Thomas, 1927-.
Castro's exhausted angel. *America* 168:14-16 F 6 1993
Cuba in transition: waking or awakening the socialist economy? *America* 169:12-16 O 30 1993

Fletcher, Joseph.
Joseph Fletcher: memoir of an ex-radical: reminiscence and reappraisal. Louisville: John Knox, 1993. x, 96p ISBN 0-664-25372-5

Flew, Antony. see Miethe, Terry, jt auth

Flint, Julie.
Pressure continues on Catholic Church after papal visit. *Tablet* 247:591 My 8 1993

Flood, Edmund. see Dominian, Jack, 1929-, jt auth

Flores, Luis H.
La antropología en las ciencias naturales. *Teol Vida* 34 no 1-2:61-67 1993

Flumeri, E.
Review of: *Diario del carcere* by Rinser, Luise. In: *Civilta* 144:617-618 Mr 20 1993
Review of: *Diario profetico (1942-1944)* by Flinker, Moshe. In: *Civilta* 3:99-100 Jl 3 1993
Review of: *Domenica da Paradiso: Profezia e politica in una mistica del Rinascimento* by Valerio, Adriana. In: *Civilta* 144:203-204 Ja 16 1993
Review of: *Donne del deserto* by Ward, Benedicta. In: *Civilta* 2:205 Ap 17 1993
Review of: *Dostoevskij: creatore di uomini e cercatore di Dio* by Raudive, Zenta Maurina. In: *Civilta* 3:341-342 Ag 7-21 1993
Review of: *Due felicissimi anni* by Cassola, Mimmi. In: *Civilta* 3:206 Jl 17 1993
Review of: *Gesù Cristo nella narrativa italiana del'900* by Brambilla, Rosa. In: *Civilta* 2:308 My 1 1993
Review of: *I giorni del mondo* by Artom, Guido. In: *Civilta* 143:637-638 D 19 1992
Review of: *Io ho un sogno. Scritti e discorsi che hanno cambiato il mondo* by King, Martin Luther. In: *Civilta* 3:542-543 S 18 1993
Review of: *La scala a chiocciola. Paura, horror, finzioni. Dal romanzo gotico a Dylan Dog* by Beseghi, Emi, and Faeti, Antonio, eds. In: *Civilta* 3:543-544 S 18 1993
Review of: *La vita di J R R Tolkien* by Carpenter, Humphrey. In: *Civilta* 143:431-432 N 21 1992
Review of: *Maschio-femmina: nuovi padri e nuove madri* by Melchiorre, Virgilio, ed. In: *Civilta* 144:614-615 Mr 20 1993
Review of: *Nella giungla di Salgari* by Leonardi, Ruggero. In: *Civilta* 144:409-410 F 20 1993
Review of: *Storie e leggende di 100 Paesi* by Marcolini, Egidio. In: *Civilta* 2:613 Je 19 1993
Review of: *Venerina* by Ronsisvalle, Vanni. In: *Civilta* 3:338-339 Ag 7-21 1993

Flumieri, E.
Review of: *La storia commune: funzioni, forma e generi della fiction televisiva* by Casetti, Francesco, and Villa, Federica, eds. In: *Civilta* 2:415-416 My 15 1993

Flynn, Laurence J.
"Singing pubs and silent churches"—revisited. *Furrow* 44:408-415 Jl-Ag 1993

Flynn, Raymond L.
Mr Clinton, make them rare. *Comm* 120:4 F 26 1993

Focant, C.
The synoptic gospels source criticism and the new literary criticism. *Eph Theol Lovan* 78:494-499 D 1992

Fogarty, Gerald P, 1939-.
The Catholic hierarchy in the United States between the Third Plenary Council and the condemnation of Americanism [photos]. *US Cath Hist* 11:19-36 Sum 1993
John Tracy Ellis. *Tablet* 246:1585-1586 D 12 1992
Relations between the church in the United States and the Holy See. *Jurist* 52 no 1:210-227 1992
Review of: *Militant and triumphant: William Henry O'Connell and the Catholic Church in Boston, 1859-1944* by O'Toole, James M, 1950-. In: *America* 168:19-21 Ap 3 1993
Review of: *Paul VI* by Hebblethwaite, Peter, 1930-. In: *Tablet* 247:436-437 Ap 3 1993

Fogarty, Tom.
Review of: *Major John MacBride* by Jordan, Anthony J. In: *Studies* 82:229-230 Sum 1993

Fohlin, Paul.
Standing in the light: meditation and the icon. *Spir Life* 32:73-78 Sum 1993

Fois, M.
Review of: *Popolo e clero in Sicilia nella dialettica socio-religiosa fra cinqueseicento* by Cucinotta, Salvatore. In: *Gregorianum* 73 No 4:767-768 1992

Foisson, A.
Review of: *Traversées* by Reding, José. In: *Lumen* 48:112-113 Mr 1993

Folena, Gianfranco. see Palazzi, Fernando, jt auth

Foley, Anita M, and Hanbury, Kevin M.
Unmask yourself: a family day of reflection. *Tod Parish* 25:11-13 Mr 1993

Foley, Edward, et al.
Extending the dialogue. *Past Mus* 18:32-39 O-N 1993
The preparatory rites: a case study in liturgical ecology. *Worship* 67:17-38 Ja 1993

Foley, Edward.
Review of: *The first rites* by Stevenson, Kenneth W. In: *New Theol Rev* 6: 108-109 Ag 1993
Review of: *The spirituals and the blues* by Cone, James H. In: *Worship* 67: 385-386 Jl 1993
Ritual leave-taking. *RRel* 52:691-701 S-O 1993

Foley, Gerald.
The Church must stop cheating the engaged. *St Anth* 101:10-13 Je 1993
Love is willing to love day after day. *Nat Cath Rep* 29:2 N 6 1992

Foley, James S.
The power is the Lord's. *HPR* 94:24-28 O 1993

Foley, Leonard.
Blessed John Duns Scotus: champion of Jesus and Mary. *St Anth* 101:10-16 N 1993
Remember Vatican II? [condensed fr *Catholic Update* Mr 1993]. *CDgst* 57: 86-92 Je 1993

Foley, Sharon.
Waiting for a gift from the sea. *Sisters* 65:301-303 Jl 1993

Follon, Jacques.
Review of: *Vocabulaire technique et critique de la philosophie* by Lalande, André. In: *RPhil Louvain* 91:512-513 Ag 1993

Fomum, Zacharias Tanee.
With Christ in the school and ministry of praying. New York: Vantage Press, 1992. x, 235p ISBN 0-533-09575-1 LC 91-90888

Fonk, P.
Review of: *Christliche Umweltehik [Eine Einführung]* by Irrgang, Bernhard. In: *Stimm Zeit* 211:502-503 Jl 1993

Fonner, Michael G.
Jesus' death by crucifixion in the Qur'an: an issue for interpretation and Muslim-Christian relations. *JEcumen Stds* 29:432-450 Sum-Aut 1992

Ford, J Massynbaerde.
Bookshelf on prostitution. *Bib Th Bul* 23:128-134 Aut 1993
Review of: *John Henry Newman, sermons 1824-1843, volume I: sermons on the liturgy and sacraments on Christ the mediator* by Murray, Placid. In: *Worship* 67:84-85 Ja 1993

Ford, John T, and Swan, Darlis J, eds.
Twelve tales untold: a story guide for ecumenical reception. Grand Rapids: Eerdmans, 1993. 176p ISBN 0-8028-0553-1

Ford, Liam.
A school to teach the life of faith. *Cath Work* 60:8 S 1993

Ford, Paul, and Daurio, Janice.
The fount of spirituality. *Register* 69:1+ O 3 1993
In Byzantine liturgy, heaven is brought down to earth. *Register* 69:1+ O 10 1993
Jesuits, Carmelites; warriors and mystics. *Register* 69:1+ O 31 1993
Mendicants keep it simple. *Register* 69:1+ O 24 1993
Restless for him. *Register* 69:1+ S 26 1993
Sanctifying the ordinary. *Register* 69:1+ O 17 1993

Forestell, Terence.
Review of: *Der erste Johannesbrief* by Klauck, Hans-Josef. In: *CBQ* 55:374-375 Ap 1993

Foret, Gregory.
On building parish bridges [reply to H Winter, 22:7-9, and P Kreeft, 22:10-14, My 1993]. *New Cov* 23:28 Ag 1993

Forliti, John.
How long since your last confession? [condensed fr *Catholic Bulletin* Ap 15 1993]. *CDgst* 57:63-65 Ag 1993

Forlizzi, G.
Review of: *Dio Amore nell'esperienza e nel pensiero di Chiara Lubich* by Cerini, Marisa. In: *Civilta* 3:197-198 Jl 17 1993
Review of: *Dio, l'uomo e la preghiera* by Ballestero, Anastasio. In: *Civilta* 2: 201 Ap 17 1993
Review of: *Giovanni Battista de La Salle* by Fiévet, Michel. In: *Civilta* 2:310-311 My 1 1993
Review of: *I fioretti* by Francis of Assisi, Saint, 1182-1226. In: *Civilta* 2:198 Ap 17 1993
Review of: *La gnosi; Il volto oscuro della storia* by Benelli, Gian Carlo. In: *Civilta* 144:509-511 Mr 6 1993
Review of: *Senza vaotarsi indietro: vita di S Agnese d'Assisi* by Garzonio, Ghiara Lucia. In: *Civilta* 143:534 D 5 1992
Review of: *Tracce di umanità nei lager nazisti: testimonianze raccolte dal Centro Culturale P M Kolbe di Venezia-Mestre* by Ruffato, Francesco, ed. In: *Civilta* 143:540 D 5 1992
Review of: *Un uomo dalla valle di Spoleto: Francesco tra i suoi contemporanei* by Nolthenius, Helene. In: *Civilta* 143:535-536 D 5 1992
Review of: *Vita di Chiara da Montefalco* by Donadio, Berengario di. In: *Civilta* 143:534-535 D 5 1992
Review of: *Vita di S Bernardo* by Thomas, Robert. In: *Civilta* 2:309-310 My 1 1993

Forrest, Denys.
Review of: *Highgrove: portrait of an estate* by Charles, Prince of Wales, 1948-, and Cover, Charles. In: *Tablet* 247:1103-1104 Ag 28 1993
Review of: *Hodge and his masters* by Jefferies, Richard. In: *Tablet* 247:1200 S 18 1993
Review of: *Honey* by Style, Sue. In: *Tablet* 247:173 F 6 1993
Review of: *Napoleon's children* by Normingotn, Susan. In: *Tablet* 247:1200 S 18 1993
Review of: *The Astors* by Wilson, Derek. In: *Tablet* 247:343 Mr 13 1993
Review of: *The coalminers of Durham* by Emery, Norman. In: *Tablet* 246: 1622 D 19-26 1992
Review of: *The railway builders* by Burton, Anthony. In: *Tablet* 247:173 F 6 1993

Forrest, Denys. *(cont'd)*
Review of: *The world of Fanny Burney* by Farr, Evelyn. In: *Tablet* 247:1200 S 18 1993
Review of: *War at sea* by Smithers, Edward, and Bruce, Colin John. In: *Tablet* 247:173 F 6 1993

Forrester, David.
Review of: *A layman looks at the Love of God: a devotional study of 1 Corinthians 13* by Keller, Philip. In: *Tablet* 247:728 Je 5 1993
Review of: *And so to God* by Zeller, Hubert Van. In: *Tablet* 247:586 My 8 1993
Review of: *Blessed are you: Mother Teresa and the Beatitudes* by Egan, Eileen, and Egan, Kathleen, eds. In: *Tablet* 247:728 Je 5 1993
Review of: *Candles in the dark: seven modern martyrs* by Craig, Mary. In: *Tablet* 247:728 Je 5 1993
Review of: *Forty days and forty nights: a guide for spending time alone with God* by Ramon, Brother. In: *Tablet* 247:586 My 8 1993
Review of: *Glimpses of God: prayer for young adults* by Appleby, Raphael Scott. In: *Tablet* 247:728 Je 5 1993
Review of: *How I pray* by Wilkins, John, ed. In: *Tablet* 247:1304 O 9 1993
Review of: *Love heals: prayers in a violent world* by Hollings, Michael. In: *Tablet* 247:586 My 8 1993
Review of: *Meditations from the road* by Peck, M Scott. In: *Tablet* 247:1304 O 9 1993
Review of: *Prayer: finding the heart's true home* by Foster, Richard J. In: *Tablet* 247:728 Je 5 1993
Review of: *The Catholic Charismatic Renewal* by Heron, Benedict M. In: *Tablet* 247:1304 O 9 1993
Review of: *The desert journal* by Carretto, Carlo. In: *Tablet* 247:728 Je 5 1993
Review of: *The quality of mercy: fresh look at the sacrament of reconciliation* by Arnold, John. In: *Tablet* 247:586 My 8 1993
Review of: *The wind from the stars: through the year with George MacDonald* by Reid, Gordon. In: *Tablet* 247:728 Je 5 1993
Review of: *Through the year with Joyce Huggett* by Bertodano, Teresa de, and Wood, Derek. In: *Tablet* 247:728 Je 5 1993
Review of: *Word made flesh* by Main, John. In: *Tablet* 247:1304 O 9 1993
Review of: *Your sins are forgiven* by Petit, Ian. In: *Tablet* 247:586 My 8 1993
Students under pressure. *Tablet* 247:712 Je 5 1993

Forschner, Brian, and Troccio, Julie.
A blueprint for community benefit. *Health Prog* 74:34-37 My 1993

Forster, Patricia M. *see* Sweetser, Thomas P, jt auth

Forster, Patricia M, and Sweetser, Thomas P.
Transforming the parish: molds for the future. Kansas City: Sheed & Ward, 1993. x, 241p ISBN 1-55612-654-9 LC 93-24332

Forsythe, Basil.
Review of: *Mozart: traces of transcendence* by Kung, Hans, 1928-. In: *Can Cath Rev* 11:31 N 1993

Forsythe, Clarke.
What now? Pro-Life strategy for the Clinton era. *Crisis* 11:24-27 Ja 1993

Fortin, Ernest L, 1923-.
Friend and teacher: Allan Bloom, 1930-1992. *Crisis* 11:38-40 Ja 1993
Gladly to learn and gladly to teach: why Christians invented the university. *Crisis* 11:33-38 Ap 1993

Fortin-Melkevik, Anne.
Deux paradigmes pour penser le rapport de la théologie aux sciences humaines: herméneutique et narratologie. *Laval Theol Phil* 49:223-231 Je 1993

Fortna, Robert T. *see* Beutler, Johannes, jt ed

Fossion, André.
Changements et résistances au changement en catéchèse. *Lumen* 47:391-401 D 1992
Christianisme et Nouvel Âge. *Lumen* 48:256-262 S 1993
Du bon usage du catéchisme de l'Église catholique de 1992. *Lumen* 48:5-20 Mr 1993
Review of: *Becoming a catechist* by O'Malley, William J, 1931-. In: *Lumen* 48:354 S 1993
Review of: *Nicodème-Annuel formation chrétienne des adultes.* In: *Lumen* 47:465 D 1992

Foster, Charles R. *see* Price, Elizabeth Box, jt ed

Foster, George P.
Is it time? *OSV* 82:19 Ag 29 1993

Foster, Michael Smith.
The role of auxiliary bishops. *Jurist* 51 no 2:423-430 1991

Foster, Richard J.
Just do it: how to jump start your prayer life [interview by the editors of US Catholic (Periodical)]. *USCath* 58:21-26 F 1993
"Oh God, help!" a conversation about prayer with Richard Foster [interview by Mitch Finley for New Covenant (periodical)]. *New Cov* 22:9-13 F 1993
Prayer of the heart. *New Cov* 22:12-13 F 1993

Foster, Richard J, and Smith, James Bryan, eds.
Devotional classics: selected readings for individuals and groups. New York: HarperSanFrancisco, 1993. 353p ISBN 0-06-066966-7 LC 92-53912

Fouqurean, Mary Patricia Barth.
Chastity as shared strength: an open letter to students. *America* 169:10-15 N 6 1993

Fournier, Jude Dennis. *see* Wezeman, Phyllis Vos, jt auth

Fournier, Marie Hélène.
Christian prayer: its relationship with Judaism. *SIDIC* 25 No 1:7-10 1992

Fournier, Raymond.
Don't waste religious education on the young. *USCath* 58:28-29 Ag 1993

Fowler, Aubrey R, Jr, et al.
Retaining nurses through conflict resolution. *Health Prog* 74:25-29 Je 1993

Fowler, Thomas B.
Is society controllable? *F & R* 28:387-413 Wint 1992

Fox, Christina.
Review of: *Introduction to eastern patristic and Orthodox theology* by Tsirpanlis, Constantine N. In: *Pacifica* 6:343-344 O 1993

Fox, Frank, and Barron, Ellen.
Developing a model for technology assessment. *Health Prog* 74:50-53 Ja-F 1993

Fox, Jim.
Catholic scholars seek new impact. *Register* 69:1+ Ap 11 1993

Fox, Joseph P.
Notes on the canonical status of shrines. *Notitiae* 28:261-269 Ap 1992
Panama: introducion general al directorio de pastoral liturgica [conferenza Episcopale Panamense]. *Notitiae* 28:270-285 Ap 1992

Fox, Thomas C.
Buddhism blossoms in French wine country [photos]. *Nat Cath Rep* 29:11-13 Jl 16 1993
Reformed minded Catholics upbeat, active. *Nat Cath Rep* 30:3+ N 12 1993
Sex and power issues expand clergy-lay rift [conference sponsored by Victims of Clergy Abuse Link up, O 16-18, 1992, Arlington Heights, Il]. *Nat Cath Rep* 29:17-19 N 13 1992
U.S. Catholics loyal, choose moral terms [charts]. *Nat Cath Rep* 29:22-23 O 8 1993
2,000 gather to mourn activist Father Olivares [obituary]. *Nat Cath Rep* 29:2 Ap 2 1993

Fox, Thomas C, and Berry, Jason.
As nation discusses pedophilia, even pope admits it's a problem. *Nat Cath Rep* 29:2-3 Jl 2 1993

Fox, Wende L, et al.
Hospital-Physician integration takes varied forms. *Health Prog* 74:49-50 Jl-Ag 1993

Fragomeni, Richard. see Downey, Michael, jt ed

França Miranda, Mario de.
Um catolicismo plural? A proposito da "evangelização inculturada" de Santo Domingo. *Perspectiva* 25:31-44 Ja-Ap 1993
Nueva evangelizacion promocion humana cultura cristiana. *Christus* 57:18-22 O 1992

France, J.
Review of: *In quest of the kingdom: ten papers on Medieval monastic spirituality* by Härdelin, Alf, ed. In: *Cist Stud* 27 No 4:[89]-[91] 1992

Francesconi, Gianni. see Trutwin, Werner, jt ed

Francis, Leslie. see Astley, Jeff, jt ed

Francis, Louis.
Review of: *Christians and pagans in Roman Britain* by Watts, Dorothy. In: *Heythrop* 34:448-450 O 1993

Francis, Mark R.
Review of: *Communications and cultural analysis* by Warren, Michael, 1935-. In: *Worship* 67:478-480 S 1993
The Sacramentary's introductory materials: worth a second look. *Past Mus* 17:17-19 Je-Jl 1993

Francis of Assisi, Saint, 1182-1226.
Through the year with Francis of Assisi: daily meditations from his words and life. Cincinnati: St Anthony Messenger Press, 1993. 240p ISBN 0-86716-196-5

Franck, Robert, and Leonardy, Heinz.
Bibliographie sélective des ouvrages et articles consacrés à l'enseignement de la philosophie en milieu scolaire. *RPhil Louvain* 91:229-248 My 1993

Francke, Caitlin.
Church still a target of Guatemalan army. *Nat Cath Rep* 29:9 F 26 1993
Nun identifies site of detention. *Nat Cath Rep* 29:7 Ap 9 1993

Frange, Jonathan De.
Review of: *Francis Janssens, 1843-1897: a Dutch-American prelate* by Kasteel, Annemarie. In: *CHist* 79:365-366 Ap 1993

Frank, Sue.
Review of: *Early Christian texts on Jews and Judaism* by MacLennan, Robert S. In: *JEcumen Stds* 29:124-125 Wint 1992
Review of: *Jews and Christians: the myth of a common tradition* by Neusner, Jacob. In: *JEcumen Stds* 29:124-125 Wint 1992
Review of: *The ascents of James: history and theology of a Jewish-Christian community* by Voors, Robert E Van. In: *JEcumen Stds* 29:124-125 Wint 1992

Frank, William F. see Sasseen, Robert F, jt auth

Franke, Chris.
Review of: *Discovering Eve: ancient Israelite women in context* by Meyers, Carol. In: *OTA* 16:162-163 F 1993
Review of: *Isaiah and his audience* by Gitay, Yehoshua. In: *OTA* 16:178 F 1993
Review of: *No longer be silent: first century Jewish portraits of biblical women* by Brown, Cheryl Anne. In: *OTA* 16:442 Je 1993

Franklin, R William.
Johann Adam Möhler and worship in Totalitarian society. *Worship* 67:2-17 Ja 1993

Frankovich, Lawrence.
Reservation of the Blessed Sacrament. *Priest* 49:18-22 S 1993

Franzmann, Majella.
Review of: *Hymnus: Materialen zu einer Geschichte der antiken Hymnologie* by Lattke, Michael. In: *Pacifica* 6:210-212 Je 1993

Fratto, A.
Review of: *I problemi del concordato preventivo* by Gravio, Dario Di. In: *Civilta* 3:545 S 18 1993

Fraze, Barb.
Canadian bishops move vigorously on sex abuse problems. *Nat Cath Rep* 29:3 Jl 2 1993

Frazier, Jim.
Buying an organ on a small budget. *Mod Lit* 20:15-17 Je-Jl 1993

Frazier, T L.
Assumptions about Mary [condensed fr *This Rock* My-Je 1992]. *CDgst* 57:82-88 Ag 1993
The real story on relics [condensed fr *This Rock* 1993]. *CDgst* 58:114-118 D 1993
Review of: *Roget's thesaurus of the Bible* by Day, A Colin. In: *New Oxford Rev* 60:30-31 My 1993

Freburger, William J.
Counting on statistics [review article *The Phoenix and the Flame* by H. Kamen]. *Priest* 49:32 Ag 1993
A deeper clerical problem than sex. *Nat Cath Rep* 29:17 Ap 16 1993
The Eucharist as memory. *Priest* 49:28 Je 1993
Liturgically speaking. *Priest* 49:30 Ap 1993
Pastoral rigorism. *Priest* 49:30 F 1993
Penance (again)!. *Priest* 49:28 Mr 1993

Freed, John B.
Review of: *Das Zisterzienserinnenkloster Wald* by Kuhn-Rehfus, Maren. In: *CHist* 79:507-508 Jl 1993

Freedman, D N. see Anderson, F I, jt auth

Freeh, John.
Crossing the communication gap. *OSV* 82:12-13 N 14 1993

Freeman, Alan. see Mensch, Elizabeth, jt auth

Freeman, Eileen Elias.
Touched by angels. New York: Warner Books, 1993. 1993 ISBN 0-446-51769-0

Freeman, Laurence.
A living Buddha. *Tablet* 247:681-682 My 29 1993
A monk for today. *Tablet* 246:1604-1605 D 19-26 1992
Review of: *John Main by those who knew him* by Harris, Paul, ed. In: *Tablet* 246:1604 D 19-26 1992
Review of: *The new creation in Christ* by Griffiths, Bede, 1906-. In: *Tablet* 246:1604 D 19-26 1992

Freeman-Grenville, G S P.
Historical atlas of the Middle East. New York: Simon & Schuster, 1993. x, 144p ISBN 0-13-3-390915-8

Freidman, Paul.
Catholic bishop pleads for help. *Tablet* 247:956-957 Jl 24 1993

Freis, Richard.
Scobie's world. *Relig Lit* 24:57-78 Aut 1992

Freske, Pam.
Insights of a Maryknoll lay missioner. *Sisters* 65:165-172 My 1993

Fretheim, Terence E.
Review of: *The cosmic covenant* by Murray, Robert. In: *TheolStds* 54:341-342 Je 1993

Frick, Frank S.
Urbanization in ancient Israel. *BibleT* 31:4-12 Ja 1993

Fricke, Wolfgang.
Riunione della IAG a Salzburg. *Notitiae* 28:290-294 Ap 1992

Friedman, Greg.
What the priesthood is really like [condensed fr *Youth Update* Ap 1993]. *CDgst* 57:120-124 Jl 1993

Friedmann, Friedrich Georg.
Identität und Integration. *Stimm Zeit* 211:270-278 Ap 1993

Friedrichs, Richard M.
Review of: *Thomas Merton: spiritual master, the essential writings* by Cunningham, Lawrence S, 1935-, ed. In: *Louvain Stds* 18:183-184 Sum 1993

Friej, Elias.
Dialogue [interview by L Petzvow]. *Register* 69:1+ Ap 18 1993

Friel, Judy.
Living with Lughnasa. *Critic* 47:2-15 Sum 1993

Friendly, Alfred, Jr. see Feshbach, Murray, jt auth

Friesen, John.
Review of: *Catholicity and secession* by Zwaanstra, Henry. In: *JEcumen Stds* 29:475-476 Sum-Aut 1992

Friesen, Jon.
Review of: *Baptism, peace, and the state in the Reformed and Mennonite traditions* by Bender, Ross T, and Sell, Alan P, eds. In: *JEcumen Stds* 29:475-476 Sum-Aut 1992

Frisotti, Heitor.
Teologia, racismo e mestiçagem. *REB* 52:833-845 D 1992

Fritzman, J M.
Escaping Hegel. *IPQ* 33:57-68 Mr 1993

Frizzell, Lawrence E.
The prayer of foreigners: evidence of the biblical tradition. *SIDIC* 25 No 1:11-17 1992
A reflection on the book of blessings. *SIDIC* 26 no 1:15-18 1993
Review of: *So that your values live on: ethical wills and how to prepare them* by Rumer, Jack, and Sampfer, Nathaniel, eds. In: *SIDIC* 25 No 2:11 1992

Froehle, Virginia Ann.
A Chinese Catholic tells his story. *CDgst* 57:114-121 Je 1993
Recognizing God's presence in your life. *St Anth* 100:10-15 S 1993
Review of: *Learn your story, find your power: using emotional awareness to enrich your self and your relationships* by Harshman, Nancy Floyd. In: *St Anth* 101:49-50 O 1993

Frohnhofen, H.
Review of: *Origenes* by Sieben, Hermann-Josef. In: *Stimm Zeit* 211:142 F 1993

Frost, Kathie.
Remembering with rocks. *ReligTJ* 27:35 Mr 1993

Fry, Patricia L.
Giving emotional support. *St Anth* 101:38-41 N 1993

Fry, Patricia L, and Mize, Judith.
Secrets of successful stepfamilies. *ST Anth* 101:10-15 Jl 1993

Fuchs, Eric.
The mutual questioning of ethics and aesthetics. *CrossCurr* 43:26-37 Spr 1993
La personne humaine et son identité morale. *Supplement* 184:193-203 Mr-Ap 1993
Review of: *Les puissances de l'expérience* by Ferry, Jean-Marc. In: *Supplement* 184:193-203 Mr-Ap 1993

Fuchs, Josef.
Ethical self-direction. *TheolDgst* 39:343-347 Wint 1992
The magisterium and moral theology [condensed fr *Freiburger Zeitschrift für Philosophie und Theologie* (1989)]. *TheolDgst* 38:103-107 Sum 1991
Was heibt Gottes Gebot? *Stimm Zeit* 211:435-442 Jl 1993
Weltethos oder säkularer Humanismus? *Stimm Zeit* 211:147-154 Mr 1993

Fuchs, Lorelei F.
Koinonia: text and context for the church. *Ecumen Trends* 22:1-2+ F 1993
The Week of Prayer for Christian Unity: a look back and ahead. *Ecumen Trends* 21:2 D 1992

Fuchs, Lucy. see Horgan, James J, jt ed

Fuerst, J S.
Public housing can work: small is better. *Comm* 120:6-8 Ap 23 1993

Fuerth, Patrick W.
Review of: *Priest: identity and ministry* by Wister, Robert J, ed. In: *Can Cath Rev* 11:34 Jl-Ag 1993

Fueyo Suárez, Bernardo.
Review of: *Epistemología e instrumentación en ciencias humanas* by Pourtois, Jean-Pierre, and Desmet, Huguette. In: *Cien Tom* 119:627-628 S-D 1992
Review of: *Teoría y terapia de las neurosis: iniciación a la logoterapia y al análisis existencial* by Frankl, Viktor E. In: *Cien Tom* 119:627 S-D 1992
Review of: *Un maître en théologie* by Labourdette, Marie-Michel. In: *Cien Tom* 119:616-617 S-D 1992

Fukuzawa, David.
Developing a strategy for the urban parish: the lessons of the church closings in Detroit. *New Theol Rev* 6:54-65 F 1993

Fulco, William F.
Review of: *Lettura sintattica della prosa ebraico-biblica: principi e applicazioni* by Niccacci, Alviero. In: *CBQ* 55:125 Ja 1993

Fulco, William J.
Review of: *Archaic features of Canaanite personal names in the Hebrew Bible* by Layton, Scott C. In: *CBQ* 54:749-751 O 1992

Fulk, Kirkland Alan.
Euthanasia, the gentle death: a legal and ethical prospectus on the right to die. *CLawyer* 35 no 2:145-168 1993

Fuller, Kathleen. see Ganss, Karl, jt auth

Fumagalli, Armando.
European enthusiasm: a bestseller for the hungering faithful. *Crisis* 11:31-32+ Je 1993
Catechism of the Catholic Church (Commentary).

Fumagalli, Francesco.
The church and the Jewish people twenty-five years after the Second Vatican Council (1963-65). *SIDIC* 25 No 2:18-26 1992

Furey, Robert J.
The joy of kindness. New York: The Crossroad Publishing Company, 1993. x, 155p ISBN 0-8245-1269-3 LC 92-38935

Furio Ceriol, Fadrique.
El concejo y consejeros del principe. Madrid: Tecnos, 1993. x, 178p ISBN 84-309-2278-4

Furioli, Anthony.
Mission and Church. *AFER* 34:170-182 Je 1992

Furlong, Monica, 1930-.
The heart in pilgrimage. *Tablet* 247:305 Mr 6 1993
Review of: *My pilgrim way* by Priestland, Gerald. In: *Tablet* 247:1265-1266 O 2 1993
What a coincidence!. *Tablet* 247:975 Jl 31 1993

Fuss, Michael.
Unisichtbar bleibt ihre Frömmigkeit Kritische Begegnung mit Neuen Religiösen Bewegungen. *StudiaM* 41:353-389 1992

Fussell, Edwin, 1922-.
Review of: *American Catholic higher education: essential documents, 1967-1990* by Galin, Alice, ed. In: *New Oxford Rev* 60:26-30 S 1993

Fussell, Edwin Sill, 1922-.
Henry James's literary Catholicizing. *New Oxford Rev* 60:8-11 Ja-F 1993

Futato, Mark D.
Review of: *God saves: lessons from the Elisha stories* by Moore, Rick Dale. In: *CBQ* 55:342-343 Ap 1993

Futrell, John Carroll. see Cowan, Marion, jt auth

G

Gaál, E.
Review of: *An introduction to Canon Law* by Coriden, James A. In: *HPR* 93:73-74 F 1993

Gabriele, Edward F.
Communities of memory: the formative role of liturgy and catechesis. *Emmanual* 49:396-402 S 1993
Holy Thursday: table protocol. *Emmanuel* 99:124-127+ Ap 1993
"Today I put before you life and death": choosing the Body of Christ. *Emmanuel* 99:102-106 Mr 1993

Gaddy, Welton C.
A handbook for coping. Louisville: Westminster, 1993. x, 128p ISBN 0-664-25458-6

Gadoua, Renée K.
Our Lady of the chiseled heart [photo]. *OSV* 82:12-13 N 21 1993

Gaebler, Ralph F.
Is there a natural law right to privacy? *Amer J Juris* 37:319-336 1992

Gaffney, Edward McGlynn, Jr, 1941-.
Anti-abortion racketeers? *Comm* 120:6-7 N 5 1993
Enforcing the law: consider the Bill of Rights. *Comm* 120:5-6 My 21 1993
Pray for it: religious freedom in Russia. *Comm* 120:5-7 My 7 1993
Review of: *Exiles from Eden: religon and the academic vocation in America* by Schwehn, Mark R. In: *Comm* 120:26-28 Ap 9 1993

Gaffney, James William, 1931-.
Among the Copts. *America* 169:15-16 O 9 1993
A hill screaming in Golan. *America* 169:4-7 N 27 1993

Gaffney, Maureen.
Adolescence and family conflict. *Studies* 81:426-439 Wint 1992

Gaggney, J Patrick.
Review of: *Mary for all Christians* by Macquarrie, John. In: *JEcumen Stds* 29:271-272 Spr 1992

Gagliano, Joseph A.
Review of: *Religion in the Andes: vision and imagination in early colonial Peru* by MacCormack, Sabine. In: *CHist* 79:139-140 Ja 1993

Gagliano, Joseph R, Jr.
Buying a church synthesizer. *Past Mus* 17:47 Ag-S 1993
Is it time to buy a church synthesizer? *Past Mus* 17:43-44 Ap-My 1993

Gagnon, Mariano, et al.
Warriors in Eden. New York: William Morrow and Company, 1993. 296p ISBN 0-688-11796-1

Gaidon, Maurice.
Amitiés sacerdotales et célibat. *Seminarium* 33:77-87 Ja-Mr 1993

Gaiger, Luiz Inácio.
A ambivalência da pastoral popular libertadora face à razão moderna. *Perspectiva* 25:163-180 My-Ag 1993

Gaillardetz, Richard R.
In service of communion: a Trinitarian foundation for Christian ministry. *Worship* 67:418-433 S 1993
Review of: *What are they saying about the ministerial priesthood?* by Donovan, Daniel L. In: *TheolStds* 54:200-201 Mr 1993
Witnesses to the faith: community, infallibility, and the ordinary. New Jersey: Paulist Press, 1992. x, 238p ISBN 0-8091-3350-4 LC 92-280431

Gajiwala, Kalpesh.
Liberating the unlimited. *Month* 26:135-137 Ap 1993

Gal, Patrick Le. see Bedouelle, Guy, jt ed

Galan, Ilia.
El dios de los dioses: ciencia del arte. Madríd: Líbertarias, 1993. x, 237p ISBN 84-7954-116-4

Galindo, Florencio.
Fundamentalism in Latin America. *TheolDgst* 40:9-14 Spr 1993

Gallagher, Dennis J. see Contosta, David R, jt auth

Gallagher, Joseph.
Planting the seeds of hope in Somalia. *OSV* 82:3 My 30 1993

Gallagher, Kathleen M.
A desperate attempt to silence pro-lifers. *OSV* 82:19 O 17 1993

Gallagher, Maureen.
Leadership, liturgy, and identity: parish priorities. *Church* 9:17-22 Aut 1993

Gallagher, Michael Paul, 1939-.
Humility is key to knowledge. *OR(Eng)* 1312:10 O 20 1993
Note in margine al caso Galileo. *Civilta* 144:424-436 Mr 6 1993
A proposito di un recente dibattito su Dio e la scienza. *Civilta* 2:327-338 My 15 1993
Review of: *A new guide to the debate about God* by Prozesky, Martin. In: *Tablet* 247:823-824 Je 26 1993
Science with prayer. *Tablet* 247:630 My 15 1993

Gallagher, Michele T, 1943-.
Sound the trumpet: reflections on the paschal mystery. New York: Alba House, 1993. x, 134p ISBN 0-8189-0665-0 LC 92-40309

Gallagher, Miriam J.
Review of: *All God's children: ministry with disabled persons* by Newman, Gene, and Tada, Joni Eareckson. In: *Mod Lit* 20:38 O 1993
Review of: *Building a great children's ministry* by Johnson, Evelyn M R, and Bower, Bobbie. In: *Mod Lit* 20:41 Je-Jl 1993
Review of: *How to teach with the lectionary* by McBrien, Philip J. In: *Mod Lit* 20:42 Mr 1993
Review of: *Leading public prayer* by Phillips, Sara Webb, and Phillips, L Edwards. In: *Mod Lit* 20:41-42 My 1993
Review of: *The practical youth ministry* by Warden, Michael. In: *Mod Lit* 20:40 O 1993

Gallagher, Patricia. see Arnold, Linda M, jt auth

Gallagher, Peter.
Review of: *Believing three ways in one God* by Lash, Nicholas. In: *Month* 26:318-319 Ag 1993
Review of: *The Christlike God* by Taylor, John V, Bp. In: *Month* 26:318-319 Ag 1993

Gallagher, Rosemary.
A theology for mother church. *Priests & People* 7:301-305 Ag-S 1993

Gallagher, Shaun.
The place of Phronesis in postmodern hermeneutics. *PhilosTod* 37:298-305 Aut 1993

Gallagher, Vera, 1917-.
Adding up 75 years. *RRel* 52:548-552 Jl-Ag 1993
Thoughts from death and life. *RRel* 52:238-240 Mr-Ap 1993

Gallant, Donald M, 1929-.
Alcoholism: a guide to diagnosis, intervention, and treatment. New York: Norton, 1987. x, 256p ISBN 0-39370-043-7 LC 87-23966

Gallard, George D, and Messina, A.
The Italo-Greeks and Melkite Antioch. *Diakonia* 26 no 2:89-98 1993

Gallaro, George D.
The Eastern code and the Latin Church. *Can Cath Rev* 11:17-18 O 1993
Marriage in the Eastern Code. *Priest* 49:41-47 Ja 1993

Galleguillos Guzmán, Juan.
Review of: *Canto a lo divino y religión del oprimido en Chile* by Salinas, Maximiliano. In: *Teol Vida* 33 no 3-4:327 1992

Galles, Duane L C M.
The reform of ecclesiatical heraldry revisited. *ABenR* 43:414-428 D 1992
Review of: *University of Navarre-Saint Paul University, Code of Canon Law annotated: Latin-English edition of the Code of Canon Law* by Caparros, E, et al, eds. In: *SacM* 120:39-40 Aut 1993

Gallitano, Dennis G. *see* Fahey, Thomas M, jt auth

Gallotta, Nino. *see* Volpi, Claudio, jt auth

Galot, Jean.
Celebrazione eucaristica e vita cristiana. *Civilta* 2:535-547 Je 19 1993
L'Esprit Saint et la spiration. *Gregorianum* 74 no 2:241-259 1993
Le Parole Eucaristiche di Gesù. *Civilta* 2:16-18 Ap 3 1993
Review of: *Antropologia del hombre caido* by Sayes, José Antonio. In: *Gregorianum* 74 No 1:165 1993
Review of: *Black theology of liberation: Twentieth Anniversary Edition* by Cone, James H. In: *Gregorianum* 74 No 1:167 1993
Review of: *Christology and spirituality* by Thompson, William M. In: *Gregorianum* 74 no 2:369 1993
Review of: *Dieu sans l'être* by Marion, Jean-Luc. In: *Gregorianum* 74 no 3:577 1993
Review of: *Eucharistie. Geschichte, Theologie, pastoral* by Meyer, Hans Bernhard. In: *Gregorianum* 74 no 2:407 1993
Review of: *Genèse de l'écriture chrétienne* by Bovon, François, and Koester, Helmut. In: *Gregorianum* 74 no 2:363 1993
Review of: *Il mistero dell'uomo in Cristo* by Gozzelino, Giorgio. In: *Gregorianum* 74 no 3:577-578 1993
Review of: *L'Épître de Saint Paul aux Ephésiens* by Bouttier, Michel. In: *Gregorianum* 73 No 4:753-754 1992
Review of: *L'Eglise-Fraternité, vol I* by Dujarier, Michel. In: *Gregorianum* 74 no 2:407 1993
Review of: *L'Eucaristia: La Cena de Signor nella comunità cristiana* by Colombo, Gianni. In: *Gregorianum* 74 No 1:163 1993
Review of: *La Mariologia nella catechesi dei Padri* by Felici, Sergio. In: *Gregorianum* 74 no 2:369-370 1993
Review of: *Le Cristologie contemporanee e le loro posizioni fondamentali al vaglio della dottrina di S Tommaso* by Ols, Daniel. In: *Gregorianum* 74 No 1:160 1993
Review of: *Le premier jour* by Blanquart, Fabien. In: *Gregorianum* 74 no 2:365-366 1993
Review of: *Livre de la consolation d'Israël Is XL-LV* by Beaucamp, Evode. In: *Gregorianum* 73 No 4:752-753 1992
Review of: *Prier au Moyen Age* by Bériou, Nicole, et al, eds. In: *Gregorianum* 74 no 3:589 1993
Review of: *Progrès de la théologie: a quelles conditions?* by Gaboriau, Florent. In: *Gregorianum* 74 No 1:167 1993
Review of: *Sainte Julienne de Cornillon, promotrice de la Fête-Dieu* by Cottiaux, Jean. In: *Gregorianum* 74 No 1:176-177 1993
Review of: *Sentido del dolor en Job* by García-Moreno, Antonio. In: *Gregorianum* 74 no 2:406 1993
Review of: *Stephanos: histoire et discours d'Etienne dans les Actes des Apôtres* by Légasse, Simon. In: *Gregorianum* 73 No 4:753 1992
Review of: *Systematic theology* by Fiorenza, Francis Schüssler, 1938-, and Galvin, John P, 1944-, eds. In: *Gregorianum* 74 no 3:579-580 1993
Review of: *Teologie della liberazione* by Gibellini, R, and Rizzi, A, et al. In: *Gregorianum* 74 no 2:408 1993
Review of: *Virgo liber verbi* by Besutti, P Giuseppe M. In: *Gregorianum* 74 no 2:370-371 1993

Galvich, Kathleen.
For catechists only: a final session. *ReligTJ* 27:7 Ap-My 1993

Galvin, John P, 1944-.
Review of: *Church and culture: German Catholic theology, 1860-1914* by O'Meara, Thomas Franklin. In: *TheolStds* 54:169-171 Mr 1993
Review of: *The real Jesus* by Edwards, David L. In: *Tablet* 246:1575 D 12 1992
Review of: *The word and the Christ: an essay in analytic Christology* by Sturch, Richard. In: *Heythrop* 34:190-191 Ap 1993
Review of: *Towards a contemporary wisdom Christology: a study of Karl Rahner and Norman Pittenger* by Lefebure, Leo D. In: *Heythrop* 34:191-192 Ap 1993 *see* Fiorenza, Francis Schüssler, 1938-, jt ed

Gamble, Clive. *see* Stringer, Christopher, jt auth

Gambra, Irene.
Review of: *Conscience in Newman's thought* by Grave, S A. In: *RPhil Louvain* 90:577-581 N 1992

Gammons, Peter. *see* Sands, Jack, jt auth

Ganley, Natalie T.
Parish directed retreat reflections: *Non MultaSed Multum. Way Suppl* 75:76-84 Aut 1992

Gannon, Mary-Grace.
Let's go back to an open-door policy for our churches. *OSV* 82:6 Ag 15 1993

Ganss, Karl, and Fuller, Kathleen.
Called, gifted, and burned out. *Tod Parish* 25:7-8 Ja 1993
'I am the Messiah and you're not'. *Tod Parish* 25:18-19 O 1993
Maintenance or mission? *Tod Parish* 25:11-12 S 1993
Reaching out—honey vs vinegar. *Tod Parish* 25:7-8 Ap-My 1993
Supporting families: practicing what we preach. *Tod Parish* 25:7-8 Mr 1993
Unhappy Thanksgiving. *Tod Parish* 25:10-11 N-D 1993

Ganzi, I M.
Review of: *Agape: Un cammino sulla carità alla scuola del Nuovo Testamento* by Masseroni, Enrico. In: *Civilta* 144:200-201 Ja 16 1993
Review of: *Cristianesimo quotidiano* by Maggioni, Bruno. In: *Civilta* 2:199 Ap 17 1993
Review of: *Edith Stein* by Croce, Giovanna Della. In: *Civilta* 2:310 My 1 1993
Review of: *L'esperienza spirituale di Itala Mela* by Piccinelli, Aldo. In: *Civilta* 3:200-201 Jl 17 1993
Review of: *La passione del Nome di Dio nella storia della salvezza* by Luzi, Pietro. In: *Civilta* 2:200-201 Ap 17 1993
Review of: *Paola pio Perazzo: Il ferroviere santo* by Racca, Giorgio. In: *Civilta* 143:536 D 5 1992
Review of: *Passer de soi-même à Dieu, Sainte-Foy* by Thomas, Robert. In: *Civilta* 144:199-200 Ja 16 1993
Review of: *Pregare con Ignazio: Bibbia ed Esercizi Spirituali.* In: *Civilta* 144: 202 Ja 16 1993
Review of: *Saint Bernard et le mystère du Christ dans le cadre de l'année liturgique* by Lemaire, Agnès. In: *Civilta* 144:199-200 Ja 16 1993
Review of: *Tu sei sacerdote oggi e sempre* by Barilla, Luigi Tirelli. In: *Civilta* 2:107-108 Ap 17 1993

Garber, Zev.
Review of: *A shared inheritance: a statement on Israel/Palestine.* In: *JEcumen Stds* 29:128-129 Wint 1992
Review of: *Beyond innocence and redemption* by Ellis, Marc H. In: *JEcumen Stds* 29:128-129 Wint 1992
Review of: *The Targum of Job* by Mangan, Céline. In: *CBQ* 55:119-120 Ja 1993
Review of: *The Targum of Proverbs* by Healey, John F. In: *CBQ* 55:119-120 Ja 1993
Review of: *The Targuym of Qohelet* by Knobel, Peters S. In: *CBQ* 55:119-120 Ja 1993
Review of: *Writing and rewriting the Holocaust* by Young, James E. In: *JEcumen Stds* 29:128-129 Wint 1992

Garcí Matubuena, Antonio.
Inculturación de la vida religiosa. *Cien Tom* 120:117-128 Ja-Ap 1993

Garcia, Emilio.
Review of: *Ojos para ver Los cristianos ante el tercer milenio* by Bühlmann, Walbert. In: *Cien Tom* 119:411-412 My-Ag 1992
Review of: *Por qué la luz no dobla las esquinas? Paisaja interior dominicano* by Solórzano Pérez, José Antonio. In: *Cien Tom* 119:625-626 S-D 1992

Garcia, Laura.
Review of: *The oldest vocation: Christian motherhood in the Middle Ages* by Atkinson, Clarissa W. In: *New Oxford Rev* 60:27-29 Je 1993

Garcia, Sheila.
Letting go. *Spir Life* 32:91-95 Sum 1993

Garcia, Victor.
Utopias y anarquismo. Madrid: Madre Tierrra, 1993. x, 220p ISBN 84-86864-08-9

Garcia-Albea, Jose E.
Mente y conducta: ensayos de psicologia cognitiva. Madrid: Trotta, 1993. x, 218p ISBN 84-87699-57-x

Garcia-Baro, Miguel.
Categorias, intencionalidad y numeros: introduccion a la filosofia primera y a los origens del pensamiento fenomenologico. Madrid: Teconos, 1993. x, 198p ISBN 84-309-2329-2

García-Mateno, Rogelio.
Universelles Vülkerrecht. *Stimm Zeit* 210:831-840 D 1992

García Ahumada, Enrique.
El catecismo en la historia de la Iglesia. *Teol Vida* 34 no 1-2:103-117 1993

Garcia Bacca, Juan David.
Sobre virtudes y vicios: tres ejercicios literario filosoficos. Madrid: Anthropos, 1993. x, 87p ISBN 84-7658-396-6

García Cordero, Maximiliano.
Los espíritus maléficos en los escritos del Nuevo Testamento. *Cien Tom* 119: 209-249 My-Ag 1992

Garcia Del Muro Solans, Juan.
Ser y conocer. Barcelona: PPU, 1993. x, 580p ISBN 84-477-0017-8

García Martínez, F. *see* Bremmer, J N, jt ed

García Prada, José María.
El retorno a la experiencis en teología: Ernst Troeltsch redivivo. *Cien Tom* 119:585-592 S-D 1992
Review of: *San Juan de la Cruz y Francisco de Yepes* by Garrido, Pablo María. In: *Cien Tom* 119:624 S-D 1992

Garcia Ruiz, Pablo.
Poder y sociedad: la sociologia en Talcott Parsons. Pamplona: Eunsa, 1993. x, 280p ISBN 84-313-1196-7

Garcia Trevijano, Carmen.
El arte de la logica. Madrid: Tecnos, 1993. x, 206p ISBN 84-309-2309-8

Gardella, Kay.
Violence on the home screen. *America* 169:4 S 11 1993

Gardiner, Thomas J.
Readers' theater for Lent. *Mod Lit* 20:18-20 Mr 1993

Gardner, M Judith.
In the mood for lent. *New Cov* 22:14-15 F 1993

Gardner, Richard A.
Psychiatrist: how possible is celibacy today? *Nat Cath Rep* 29:9 Mr 19 1993

Gareffa, Michael.
Review of: *Prodigal son/elder brother: interpretation and alterity in Augustine, Petrarch, Kafka, Levinas* by Robbins, Jill. In: *TheolStds* 54:193-194 Mr 1993

Gargan, Edward T.
Review of: *Histoire religieuse* by Durand, Jean-Dominique, and Ladous, Régis, eds. In: *CHist* 79:343-344 Ap 1993

Gargan, Edward T. *(cont'd)*
Review of: *Religion, society and politics in France since 1789* by Tallert, Frank, and Atkin, Nicholas, eds. In: *CHist* 79:342-343 Ap 1993

Gargiulo, Barbara.
Expect great things—and get them. *ReligTJ* 27:7 O 1993

Garland, David E.
Reading Matthew: a literary and theological commentary on the first Gospel. New York: The Crossroad Publishing Company, 1993. x, 269p ISBN 0-8245-1275-8 LC 92-38424

Garland, James H.
Congregation-based organizations: a church model for the 90's. *America* 169:14-16 N 13 1993

Garrett, Graeme.
Finding God in all things. *Way* 33:3-11 Ja 1993
Scripture, inspiration and the word of God. *Pacifica* 6:81-99 F 1993

Garrison, Greg.
Committee gives voice, hand to South's poor. *Nat Cath Rep* 29:5 N 20 1992
Mother Angelica's radio towers rouse static. *Nat Cath Rep* 29:8 Ja 8 1993

Garrity, Robert M.
Shame, dysfunctional families, and lack of due discretion for marriage. *Jurist* 51 no 2:364-389 1991
Spiritual and canonical values in mandatory priestly celibacy. *Stud Can* 27 no 1:217-260 1993

Garsiel, Moshe.
The story of David and Bathsheba: a different approach. *CBQ* 55:244-262 Ap 1993

Garstein, O.
Review of: *The Renaissance of the Goths in sixteenth-century Sweden: Johannes and Olaus Magnus as politicians and historians* by Johannesson, Kurt. In: *CHist* 78:654-655 O 1992

Garvais, Marcel.
Assisted suicide and legalized euthanasia. *Doctr Life* 43:308-309 My-Je 1993

Garvey, Eugenia.
Review of: *Preaching as weeping, confusion and resistance* by Smith, Christine M. In: *Sisters* 65:223-224 My 1993

Garvey, John, 1944-.
Between Dracula and Bovary: Yugoslavia's romantic nationalism. *Comm* 120:7-8 My 21 1993
The Christ of faith. *Comm* 120:7-8 Ja 29 1993
Democracy and its limits: it's wonderful; it's not enough. *Comm* 120:9-10 Ag 13 1993
An incoherent culture life after "Ozzie and Harriet". *Comm* 120:10-11 Je 18 1993
Love your enemy. *Comm* 120:10 N 19 1993
Prejudice or disagreement? Homosexuals in the military. *Comm* 120:9-10 F 26 1993
The Protestant moment? Religion in the United States. *Comm* 120:9-10 O 8 1993
A role of one's own. *Comm* 120:8-9 Mr 26 1993
We are all foreigners: religion, nation and race. *Comm* 119:8-9 D 18 1992

Garvey, Michael O.
Review of: *Against the nations: war and survival in a liberal society* by Hauerwas, Stanley Martin, 1940-. In: *Comm* 120:41-42 Ap 9 1993

Garvin, Margaret L, et al.
Holistic retreats. *Health Prog* 74:51-52+ 1993

Gass, Michael.
Abortion and moral character: a critique of Smith. *IPQ* 33:101-108 Mr 1993

Gassis, Macram Max, Bp, 1938-.
Dialogue [interview by P Mullen]. *Register* 69:1+ Je 13 1993
Sudan: a grim tragedy. *Cath Int* 4:236-237 My 1993

Gassmann, Günther.
The Church—local and Catholic: a Lutheran perspective. *Jurist* 52 no 1:518-524 1992

Gateley, Edwina.
A good Catholic girl. *Tablet* 247:851-852 Jl 3 1993
A warm, moist, salty God: women journeying towards wisdom. Trabuco Canyon: Source Books, 1993. x, 107p ISBN 0-940147-26-2 LC 93-11919

Gatta, John.
Review of: *Salem is my dwelling place: a life of Nathaniel Hawthorne* by Miller, Edwin Haviland. In: *Relig Lit* 24:91-96 Aut 1992
Review of: *The office of The scarlet letter* by Bercovitch, Sacvan. In: *Relig Lit* 24:91-96 Aut 1992

Gatta, Secondino.
I Musulmani, che Dio li protegga e li conservi!. *StudiaM* 42:271-285 1993
Un movimento religioso indigeno nelle missioni gesuitiche del Messico: la ribellione del *falso vescovo degli Acaxi (1601-1604)*. *StudiaM* 41:85-106 1992

Gaudiose, Dorothy M.
Mary's house: Mary Pyle: under the spiritual guidance of Padre Pio. New York: Society of St Paul, 1993. x, 189p ISBN 0-8189-0646-4 LC 92-21401

Gaudoin-Parker, Michael L.
The real presence through the ages: Jesus adored in the sacrament of the altar. New York: Alba House, 1993. x, 222p ISBN 0-8189-0662-6 LC 92-42274

Gaughan, J Anthony.
Review of: *New beginnings in ministry* by Murphy, James H, ed. In: *Studies* 82:103-105 Spr 1993

Gaughan, Norbert Felix, Bp, 1921-.
Willing to serve [interview by C Lund and J Sprague]. *Critic* 47:46-56 Sum 1993

Gaupin, Linda.
Confirmation: age, sequence, timing [interview]. *Mod Lit* 20:8-10 Je-Jl 1993
see Brooks-Leonard, John, jt auth

Gaustad, Edwin S.
Review of: *A history of Christianity in the United States and Canada* by Noll, Mark A. In: *CHist* 79:565-567 Jl 1993

Gauthier, Albert.
Review of: *Customary law in the "Corpus iuris canonici"* by McIntyre, John P. In: *Stud Can* 27 no 1:261-262 1993

Gauthier, Roland.
Review of: *Bibliographia Internationalis Spiritualitatis a Pontificio Instituto Spiritualitatis.* In: *CahiersJos* 41:130 Ja-Je 1993
Review of: *Chi è San Giuseppe, 3 vols* by Ambrosino, Michele. In: *CahiersJos* 41:136 Ja-Je 1993
Review of: *Diálogos de María y José* by Morán Clavel, Juan Antonio. In: *CahiersJos* 41:138-139 Ja-Je 1993
Review of: *El arca de tres llaves. Crónica del monasterio de Carmelitas Descalzas de San José, 1690-1990.* In: *CahiersJos* 41:131 Ja-Je 1993
Review of: *Giuseppe di Nazaret, un pellegrino nella fede* by Avanzo, Stanislao Mario. In: *CahiersJos* 41:137 Ja-Je 1993
Review of: *Il santo Rosario con Maria e Giuseppe* by Capuozzo, Gerardo. In: *CahiersJos* 41:130-131 Ja-Je 1993
Review of: *Joseph in the New Testament* by Toschi, Larry M. In: *CahiersJos* 41:134-135 Ja-Je 1993
Review of: *Notre Dame des hérétiques. Marie et Nazareth* by Maggi, Alberto. In: *CahiersJos* 41:141 Ja-Je 1993
Review of: *Responses to 101 questions on the Bible* by Brown, Raymond Edward. In: *CahiersJos* 41:140 Ja-Je 1993
Review of: *Saint Joseph dans notre vie* by Pfleger, Albert. In: *CahiersJos* 41:136 Ja-Je 1993
Review of: *San Giuseppe custode del Redentore* by Serafini, Alfredo, and Lotito, R. In: *CahiersJos* 41:137 Ja-Je 1993
Review of: *San José, del Sindicato de al madera* by Palmero Ramos, Rafael, and Carro Celada, Esteban. In: *CahiersJos* 41:133 Ja-Je 1993

Gawronski, Raymond T.
Poland at the crossroads (again). *America* 168:15-17 My 22, 1993
Why orthodox Catholics look to Zen. *New Oxford Rev* 60:13-16 Jl-Ag 1993

GBeckwith, Barbara.
Clinton, 4-1/2; pro-lifer's, zip: round two will be the Freedom of Choice Act [editorial]. *St Anth* 100:41 Mr 1993

Geach, Catherine.
Rice-wine and song. *Tablet* 247:710-711 Je 5 1993

Gebara, Ivone.
"I listen, I suspect, later I make poetry" [interview by S Rojas; tr fr *Pastoral Popular*]. *LADOC* 24:10-15 S-O 1993

Geddes, Diana.
Church hits crackdown on immigrants. *Register* 69:1+ Je 27 1993
For Catholics in France, a new public presence. *Register* 69:1+ Ap 25 1993

Gediman, Paul.
This museum is not a metaphor: confronting the hard facts of the Holocaust. *Comm* 120:13-15 Je 4 1993

Geets, Claude, et al, eds.
Hôpital et respect des personnes. *Supplement* 184:5-203 Mr-Ap 1993
Questions d'un gestinnaire d'hôpital, by P Tassin. Ce qu'être malade veut dire, by A Vannesse. La maladie comme expérience et comme condition, by C Geets. Vérité et mensonge dans la relation au malade, by C Geets. Face à l'enfant mourant, by H Hainaut. Pour une 5aethique de la fin de la vie, by C Geets. Quelques questions sur l'éthique en psychiatrie, by L Cassiers. Éthique et médicine expérimentale à l'hôpital, by J-F Malherbe. Accompagnement des familles et prévention des deuils pathologiques, by A Vanoverberghe. Comment faire Église aujourd'hui à l'hôpital?, by J-M Martou. Médicine générale et sciences humaines, by D Le Breton, and J Broussier. Légèreté ou gravité de la chair, by X Lacroix. La personne humaine et son identité morale, by E Fuchs.

Geets, Claude.
La maladie comme expérience et comme condition. *Supplement* 184:33-55 Mr-Ap 1993
Pour une éthique de la fin de la vie. *Supplement* 184:89-96 Mr-Ap 1993
Vérité et mensonge dans la relation au malade. *Supplement* 184:56-77 Mr-Ap 1993

Geiger, Virginia. see Vicchio, Stephen J, jt ed

Geisler, Norman L. see Beckwith, Francis J, jt auth

Geist, Joseph E.
Through the Psalms with Jesus: a devotional commentary on the Psalms with emphasis on their portrayal of Jesus. New York: Vantage Press, 1993. 175p ISBN 0-533-10345-2 LC 92-90851

Gelineau, Louis E, Bp.
Letter after charges involving local priest. *Origins* 23:111-112 Jl 1 1993

Gelpi, Donald L, 1934-.
Committed worship: a sacramental theology for converting Christians, v 2. Minnesota: The Liturgical Press, 1993. x, 312p ISBN 0-8146-5826-1 LC 92-40430
Committed worship: a sacramental theology for converting Christians, v I. Minnesota: The Liturgical Press, 1993. x, 278p ISBN 0-8146-5825-3 LC 92-40430

Gelpi, Donald L.
Review of: *Nature and spirit: an essay in ecstatic naturalism* by Corrington, Robert S. In: *TheolStds* 54:369-370 Je 1993

Gendron, Pierre.
La théologie comme science et la voction de savant d'après Max Weber. *Laval Theol Phil* 49:215-222 Je 1993

Genereux, Susan.
Education: encouraging parish-based programs. *Tod Parish* 25:33 Mr 1993

Genovese, M.
Review of: *Energy in the executive* by Eastland, Terry. In: *New Oxford Rev* 60:31-32 Ja-F 1993

Gilbert, Marjorie.
Helpful hints for DREs from a DRE. *Catechist* 27:66-67 S 1993

Gilbert, Paul P.
Review of: *Bernardo di Chiaravalle* by Leclerq, Jean. In: *Civilta* 3:306-307 Ag 7-21 1993

Review of: *La semplicità del principio: intorduzine alla metafisica* by Gilbert, Paul P. In: *Gregorianum* 73 No 4:775-776 1992

Review of: *Lexique de la culture* by Carrier, Hervé. In: *Gregorianum* 73 No 4:776 1992

Gildrie, R.
Review of: *The devil's dominion: magic and religion in early New England* by Godbeer, Richard. In: *CHist* 78:680-681 O 1992

Giles, James E.
Review of: *Beyond PC: toward a politics of understanding* by Aufderheide, Patricia, ed. In: *CrossCurr* 43:257 Sum 1993

Review of: *Education without impact* by Douglas, George. In: *CrossCurr* 43: 256 Sum 1993

Review of: *How professors play the cat guarding the cream* by Huber, Richard. In: *CrossCurr* 43:256 Sum 1993

Review of: *In the wake of theory* by Bové, Paul. In: *CrossCurr* 43:258-259 Sum 1993

Review of: *Jews in the American Academy, 1900-1940* by Klingenstein, Susanne. In: *CrossCurr* 43:261 Sum 1993

Review of: *Loose canons* by Gates, Henry Louis, Jr. In: *CrossCurr* 43:259-260 Sum 1993

Review of: *Multiculturalism and "the politics of recognition"* by Taylor, Charles, 1931-. In: *CrossCurr* 43:261-262 Sum 1993

Review of: *Politics by other means: higher education and group thinking* by Bromwich, David. In: *CrossCurr* 43:260 Sum 1993

Review of: *The ethics of authenticity* by Taylor, Charles, 1931-. In: *CrossCurr* 43:261-262 Sum 1993

Review of: *The idea of the university: a reexamination* by Pelikan, Jaroslav. In: *CrossCurr* 43:256-257 Sum 1993

Review of: *The myth of the university* by Shore, Paul. In: *CrossCurr* 43:255-256 Sum 1993

Review of: *The politics of liberal education* by Gless, Darryl, and Smith, Barbara Herrnstein, eds. In: *CrossCurr* 43:257-258 Sum 1993

Gilhooley, James.
Pastor extraordinary. *Tablet* 247:1063-1064 Ag 21 1993

Gill, Theodore A Gill, Jr.
The Reader's Digest and the World Council of Churches. *Ecmen Trends* 22: 1+ Mr 1993

Gillespie, Joseph P.
Truth-telling and marriage. *New Theol Rev* 6:71-73 Ag 1993

What's happening to the old magic? finding meaning in family crisis. *Liturgy* 10:35-41 Wint 1992

Gillie, Joyce.
Reaching into the past. *ReligTJ* 27:38 F 1993

Gillis, Virginia.
Sponsorship networks. *Health Prog* 74:34-37+ Ap 1993

Gillman, Florence Morgan.
The ministry of women in the early Church. *New Theol Rev* 6:89-94 My 1993

Review of: *The Book of Revelation* by Giblin, Charles Homer. In: *CBQ* 55: 367 Ap 1993

Gillman, John.
Review of: *Ephesians* by Lincoln, Andrew T. In: *CBQ* 55:165-167 Ja 1993

Gillman, Neil.
Review of: *The American Judaism of Mordecai M Kaplan* by Goldsmith, Emanuel S, et al, eds. In: *CrossCurr* 43:110-114 Spr 1993

Gillotte, Tony.
After six decades, nuns emerge in Burma. *Nat Cath Rep* 29:12 F 26 1993

Cambodian Catholics begin rebuilding church. *Nat Cath Rep* 29:13 My 14 1993

Gilmour, Peter.
The non-ordained pastor: a paradigm for future church leadership. *Listening* 28:81-90 Wint 1993

Review of: *Days of obligation* by Rodriguez, Richard, 1947-. In: *Critic* 47:71-75 Sum 1993

Review of: *Keeper of the moon* by McLaurin, Tim. In: *Critic* 47:78-82 Spr 1993

Gimello, Robert M. see Buswell, Robert E, Jr, jt ed

Ginter, Mark.
Fanning the parish flame. *New Cov* 22:12-13 Mr 1993

Giolla Chomhaill, Anraí Mac.
Review of: *Aisling agus tóir: an slánú i bhFilíocht Schomhairle MhicGill Eain* by Annracháin, Máire Ní. In: *Furrow* 44:126-127 F 1993

Giordan, Alma Roberts, 1917-.
On visiting the old neighbors. *America* 168:4-5 Ja 2-9 1993

Troutlilies for Mother's Day. *America* 168:4 My 8 1993

Giovannangeli, Daniel.
Finitude et altérité dans l'esthétique transcendantale. *RPhil Louvain* 91:14-30 F 1993

Giralt, Joan J.
El taller de mi. Barcelona: Ser Editorial, 1993. x, 315p ISBN 84-8860-401-7

Girard, René, 1923-.
Violence, difference, sacrifice [interview by R. Adams]. *Relig Lit* 25:11-33 Sum 1993

Gismondi, Angelo. see Fizzotti, Eugenio, jt auth

Gitay, Yehosua.
Review of: *"And you shall tell your son"* by Zakovitch, Yair. In: *OTA* 15:516 O 1992

Gitay, Yehosua. *(cont'd)*
Review of: *Abraham Ibn Ezra's two commentaries on the Minor Prophets* by Simon, Uriel. In: *OTA* 15:510-511 O 1992

Gittins, Anthony J, 1943-.
Bread for the journey: the mission of transformation and the transformation of mission. Maryknoll, New York: Orbis Books, 1993. x, 187p ISBN 0-88344-857-2 LC 92-42152

The memory lingers on. *New Theol Rev* 6:81-85 Ag 1993

Review of: *Paths to the power of myth* by Noel, Daniel C, ed. In: *New Theol Rev* 6:97-98 F 1993

Review of: *Toward a theology of inculturation* by Shorter, Aylward, 1932-. In: *New Theol Rev* 6:112-113 Ag 1993

Giudici, Maria Pia.
The angels: spiritual and exegetical notes. New York: Alba House, 1993. x, 151p ISBN 0-8189-0636-7 LC 93-30849

Giurlanda, Paul.
What about our Church's children? *America* 168:12-14 My 8 1993

Gladson, Jerry A.
Review of: *The sage in Israel and the Ancient Near East* by Gammie, John G, and Perdue, Leo G, eds. In: *CBQ* 55:196-197 Ja 1993

Glass, Charles.
Jewel without a crown. *Tablet* 247:1188 S 18 1993

Glavich, Kathleen.
The cross: a sign of love. *ReligTJ* 27:12-13 F 1993

Great teachers of faith. *ReligTJ* 26:15-16 Ja 1993

Journeying with Jerome. *ReligTJ* 27:52-53 S 1993

Like a fire within us. *ReligTJ* 27:32-33 Ap-My 1993

More than a carpenter. *ReligTJ* 27:28 Mr 1993

Who doesn't love Francis? *ReligTJ* 27:25 O 1993

Gleason, Philip.
The new Americanism in Catholic historiography. *US Cath Hist* 11:1-18 Sum 1993

Gledhill, Ruth.
Rosary to the rescue. *Tablet* 247:1037 Ag 14 1993

Glimm, Francis.
Review of: *Under the heel of Mary* by Petry, Nicholas, and Echeverría, Loreto. In: *CHist* 79:92 Ja 1993

Glotin, Édouard.
Claude La Colombiere le sens d'une canonisation. *NRT* 114:816-838 N-D 1992

Glouberman, Mark.
Cogito: inference and certainty. *Mod Schlmn* 70:81-98 Ja 1993

Gndara, Miguel Alvarez.
Santo Domingo: doloroso avance de la iglesia de Latinamericano. *Christus* 58:50-55 N-D 1992

Gnuse, Robert.
Review of: *Studien zum Alten Testament* by Fohrer, Georg. In: *CBQ* 55:195-196 Ja 1993

Review of: *The flowering of Old Testament theology* by Ollenburger, Ben C, et al, eds. In: *CBQ* 55:415-416 Ap 1993

Goal, Imre V.
Review of: *The theology of Canon Law, a methodological question* by Corecco, Eugenio, Bp. In: *Thomist* 57:546-549 Jl 1993

Goddijn, Walter, 1921-.
Raised hopes in Holland. *Tablet* 247:974-975 Jl 31 1993

Rumours abound as Bär resigns. *Tablet* 247:413-414 Mr 27 1993

Godfrey, Aaron W.
Review of: *Latinos* by Shorris, Earl. In: *New Oxford Rev* 60:30 Je 1993

Godin, A.
Review of: *A secret world* by Sipe, A W Richard. In: *Lumen* 48:358-359 S 1993

Review of: *Advances in the psychology of religion* by Brown, L B, ed. In: *Lumen* 48:355 S 1993

Review of: *Christian perspectives on faith development* by Astley, Jeff, and Francis, Leslie, eds. In: *Lumen* 48:355-356 S 1993

Review of: *I nuovi protagonisti: movimenti, associazioni gruppi nella Chiesa* by Secondin, Bruno. In: *Lumen* 48:119 Mr 1993

Review of: *Ignatius of Loyola: the psychology of a saint* by Meissner, William W. In: *Lumen* 48:358 S 1993

Review of: *Le livre de signes* by Jossua, Jean-Pierre. In: *Lumen* 48:235 Je 1993

Review of: *Logoterapia applicata: da una vita senza senso a un senso nella vita* by Fizzotti, Eugenio, and Carelli, Rocco. In: *Lumen* 48:118-119 Mr 1993

Review of: *Nuovi cammini dello Spirito: la spiritualità alle soglie del terzo millennio* by Secondin, Bruno. In: *Lumen* 48:119-120 Mr 1993

Review of: *Psicoanalisi, bisessualità e sacro* by Ancona, Leonardo, ed. In: *Lumen* 48:118 Mr 1993

Review of: *Psychologie et spiritualité: à la recherche d'une interface* by Richard, Réginald. In: *Lumen* 48:116-117 Mr 1993

Review of: *Psychology of religion: personalities, problems, possibilities* by Malony, H Newton, ed. In: *Lumen* 48:357-358 S 1993

Review of: *The experience of faith* by Gillespie, V Bailey. In: *Lumen* 48:356 S 1993

Review of: *The making of a mystic: seasons in the Life of Teresa of Avila* by Gross, Francis L, Jr, and Gross, Toni Perior. In: *Lumen* 48:356-357 S 1993

Review of: *Unresolved questions in the Freud/Jung debate* by Vandermeersch, Patrick. In: *Lumen* 48:359-360 S 1993

Godsey, John D.
Review of: *How to read Karl Barth: the shape of his theology* by Hunsinger, George. In: *Thomist* 57:269-275 Ap 1993

Review of: *Karl Barth: centenary essays* by Sykes, S W, ed. In: *Thomist* 57:269-275 Ap 1993

Review of: *The autonomy theme in the church dogmatics: Karl Barth and his critics* by Macken, John. In: *Thomist* 57:269-275 Ap 1993

Graff, Ann O'Hara.
Catholic feminist theologians on Catholic women in the Church. *New Theol Rev* 6:6-18 My 1993
Transforming today's church. *Chicago Stud* 32:127-142 Ag 1993

Grafton, Anthony.
The Vatican library goes to Washington [condensed fr *Rome reborn: the Vatican library and Renaissance Culture*]. *CDgst* 57:1-8 F 1993

Graham, K.
Review of: *Principle and profit: corporate responsibility in Ireland* by Reidy, Michael, and McCullough, Domhnall, eds. In: *Furrow* 44:58-59 Ja 1993

Graham, Michael.
Popish plots: Protestant fears in early colonial Maryland, 1676-1689. *CHist* 79:197-216 Ap 1993

Graham, Patrick M.
Review of: *Achaemenid imperial administration in Syria-Palestine and the missions of Ezra and Nehemiah* by Hoglund, Kenneth G. In: *OTA* 16:174 F 1993
Review of: *Der Fremde im antiken Juda* by Bultmann, Christoph. In: *OTA* 16:437-438 Je 1993
Review of: *Zur Aktualität des Alten Testaments: Festschrift für Georg Sauer zum 65* by Kreuzer, Siegfried, and Lüthi, Kurt, eds. In: *OTA* 16:155 F 1993

Graham, Robert A.
L'Apostolato e i Nazisti in Russia nel 1941. *Civilta* 144:437-444 Mr 6 1993
L'uso del diritto canonico nella seconda guerra mondiale. *Civilta* 3:238-246 Ag 7-21 1993

Graham, Ruth.
Review of: *How modernity came to a provincial town Citizens and clergy of Grasse* by Freeman, John F, and Williams, Roger L. In: *CHist* 79:542-543 Jl 1993

Graham, William C.
Review of: *A moral emergency* by Angelica, Jade C, 1952-. In: *Nat Cath Rep* 30:35 N 19 1993
Review of: *A new commandment: toward a renewed rite for the washing of feet* by Jeffrey, Peter. In: *Nat Cath Rep* 29:39 F 5 1993
Review of: *A promise of presence* by Downey, Michael, and Fragomeni, Richard, eds. In: *Nat Cath Rep* 29:39 F 5 1993
Review of: *A woman's healing song: prayers of consolation for the separated and the divorced* by Hide, Kerrie. In: *Nat Cath Rep* 29:36 S 10 1993
Review of: *A word for the day: reflections* by Talafous, Don. In: *Nat Cath Rep* 29:39 F 5 1993
Review of: *Acts of compassion* by Wuthnow, Robert. In: *Nat Cath Rep* 30:15 O 22 1993
Review of: *Adults and children in the art of celebration* by Nelson, Gertrude Mueller. In: *Nat Cath Rep* 29:40 My 28 1993
Review of: *An undivided heart* by Sammon, Sean D. In: *Nat Cath Rep* 30:36 N 19 1993
Review of: *Becoming a Catholic Christian* by Upton, Julia. In: *Nat Cath Rep* 30:36 N 19 1993
Review of: *Becoming bread: meditations on loving and transformation* by Norris, Gunilla. In: *Nat Cath Rep* 29:24 Mr 26 1993
Review of: *Befriending: a self-guided retreat for busy people* by Payne, Joseph A. In: *Nat Cath Rep* 29:25 Mr 26 1993
Review of: *Believing three ways in one God* by Lash, Nicholas. In: *Nat Cath Rep* 30:15 O 22 1993
Review of: *Beyond the myth of dominance: an alternative to a violent society* by McMahon, Edwin M, 1930-. In: *Nat Cath Rep* 29:18 Jl 16 1993
Review of: *Body theology* by Nelson, James B. In: *Nat Cath Rep* 29:18 Jl 16 1993
Review of: *Bringing churches together* by Goosen, Gideon. In: *Nat Cath Rep* 30:35 N 19 1993
Review of: *Celibacy: gift or law?* by Vogel, Heinz-Jurgen. In: *Nat Cath Rep* 30:36 N 19 1993
Review of: *Children in the assembly of the Church* by Brooks-Leonard, John, and Gaupin, Linda. In: *Nat Cath Rep* 29:40 My 28 1993
Review of: *Christian Initiation of older children* by Figgness, Sandra. In: *Nat Cath Rep* 29:40 My 28 1993
Review of: *Confessions of a celibate priest* by Graham, Mary Ann. In: *Nat Cath Rep* 30:16 O 22 1993
Review of: *Console one another* by Curley, Terence P. In: *Nat Cath Rep* 30:15 O 22 1993
Review of: *Conversations with a dying friend* by Carmody, John Tully. In: *Nat Cath Rep* 29:24 Mr 26 1993
Review of: *Crisis to wellness: meditation for a philosophy of living* by Petulla, Joseph. In: *Nat Cath Rep* 29:40 My 28 1993
Review of: *Daily meditations (with Scripture) for busy moms*. In: *Nat Cath Rep* 30:36 N 19 1993
Review of: *Desire and delight* by Miles, Margaret R. In: *Nat Cath Rep* 29:18 Jl 16 1993
Review of: *Discovering my experience of God: awareness and witness* by DeSiano, Frank, and Boyack, Kenneth. In: *Nat Cath Rep* 29:40-39 My 28 1993
Review of: *Divorce in the New Testament* by Collins, Raymond F. In: *Nat Cath Rep* 29:39 My 28 1993
Review of: *Easter in the early church* by Cantalamessa, Raniero. In: *Nat Cath Rep* 30:36 N 19 1993
Review of: *Echoing God's word: formation for catechists and homilists in a catechumenal church* by Dunning, James. In: *Nat Cath Rep* 29:18 Jl 16 1993
Review of: *Enduring grace* by Flinders, Carol Lee. In: *Nat Cath Rep* 30:16 O 22 1993
Review of: *Everybody has a guardian angel* by Finley, Mitchel B. In: *Nat Cath Rep* 29:36 S 10 1993
Review of: *Fashioning a healthier religion* by Aldworth, Thomas. In: *Nat Cath Rep* 29:40 F 5 1993
Review of: *Fathers, come home* by Swindell, Bill. In: *Nat Cath Rep* 30:16 O 22 1993
Review of: *Grief: climb toward understanding* by Davies, Phyllis. In: *Nat Cath Rep* 30:15 O 22 1993

Graham, William C. *(cont'd)*
Review of: *How to read the apocalypse* by Prevost, Jean-Pierre. In: *Nat Cath Rep* 30:15 O 22 1993
Review of: *If today you hear God's voice: biblical images of prayer for modern man and women* by Gunzel, Raymond. In: *Nat Cath Rep* 29:39 F 5 1993
Review of: *In the company of preachers*. In: *Nat Cath Rep* 29:18 Jl 16 1993
Review of: *In the presence of the wise and gentle Christ* by McNamara, James M. In: *Nat Cath Rep* 29:18 Jl 16 1993
Review of: *Inner healing for broken vessels: seven steps to a woman's way of healing* by Hollies, Linda H. In: *Nat Cath Rep* 29:25 Mr 26 1993
Review of: *Jesus acted up: a gay and lesbian manifesto* by Goss, Robert. In: *Nat Cath Rep* 30:15 O 22 1993
Review of: *Life after Easter* by Maly, Francis Susanne. In: *Nat Cath Rep* 29:36 S 10 1993
Review of: *Liturgical inculturation: sacramentals, religiosity, and catechesis* by Chupungco, Anscar J. In: *Nat Cath Rep* 29:40 F 5 1993
Review of: *Living the Catholic sacraments* by McCarthy, Michele. In: *Nat Cath Rep* 29:40 F 5 1993
Review of: *Living with the land: communities restoring the earth*. In: *Nat Cath Rep* 29:40 My 28 1993
Review of: *Looking for moral guidance* by Fisher, James T. In: *Nat Cath Rep* 29:18 Jl 16 1993
Review of: *Mandatory celibacy: a handbook for the laity* by Prince, Michele. In: *Nat Cath Rep* 29:40 F 5 1993
Review of: *May I have this dance* by Rupp, Joyce. In: *Nat Cath Rep* 29:40 F 5 1993
Review of: *Ministry in the Church* by Bernier, Paul. In: *Nat Cath Rep* 29:18 Jl 16 1993
Review of: *Ministry* by Osborne, Kenan B. In: *Nat Cath Rep* 30:15 O 22 1993
Review of: *Morals and the meaning of Jesus: reflections on the hard sayings* by Harvey, Nicholas Peter. In: *Nat Cath Rep* 29:18 Jl 16 1993
Review of: *My hands held out to you: the use of body and hands in prayer* by Moroni, Giancarlo. In: *Nat Cath Rep* 29:25 Mr 26 1993
Review of: *One minute nonsense* by Mello, Anthony De. In: *Nat Cath Rep* 29:25 Mr 26 1993
Review of: *Ordinarily sacred* by Sexson, Lynda. In: *Nat Cath Rep* 29:25 Mr 26 1993
Review of: *Pedagogy of the city* by Friere, Paulo. In: *Nat Cath Rep* 30:36 N 19 1993
Review of: *Plain prayers in a complicated world* by Brooke, Avery. In: *Nat Cath Rep* 30:36 N 19 1993
Review of: *Pseudo-Macarius: the fifty homilies and the great letter* by Maloney, George A, 1924-. In: *Nat Cath Rep* 29:25 Mr 26 1993
Review of: *Raised Catholic (can you tell?)* by Stivender, Ed. In: *Nat Cath Rep* 29:40+ F 5 1993
Review of: *Revolution of the heart* by Coly, Patrick G, ed. In: *Nat Cath Rep* 30:15 O 22 1993
Review of: *Sabbath time* by Edward, Tilden. In: *Nat Cath Rep* 29:40 My 28 1993
Review of: *Sacramental theology* by Vorgrimler, Herbert. In: *Nat Cath Rep* 29:40 My 28 1993
Review of: *Salvation outside the Church* by Sullivan, Francis Aloysius. In: *Nat Cath Rep* 29:40 F 5 1993
Review of: *Seasons and feasts of the Church Year* by Whalen, Michael D. In: *Nat Cath Rep* 29:18 Jl 16 1993
Review of: *Seeds of non-violence* by Dear, John, 1959-. In: *Nat Cath Rep* 29:18 Jl 16 1993
Review of: *Seek treasures in small fields: everyday holiness* by Puls, Joan. In: *Nat Cath Rep* 29:24 Mr 26 1993
Review of: *Seeking the heart of God: reflections on prayer* by Boyaxhiu, Teresa, Mother, 1910-, and Roger, Brother. In: *Nat Cath Rep* 29:25 Mr 26 1993
Review of: *Silent voices, sacred lives: women's readings for the liturgical year* by Bowe, Barbara E, et al, eds. In: *Nat Cath Rep* 29:40 F 5 1993
Review of: *Single in the Church* by Collier-Stone, Kay. In: *Nat Cath Rep* 29:36 S 10 1993
Review of: *Sister Thea Bowman, shooting star*. In: *Nat Cath Rep* 30:36 N 19 1993
Review of: *Spiritual fitness* by Donnelly, Doris. In: *Nat Cath Rep* 30:16 O 22 1993
Review of: *Starlight* by Shea, John B. In: *Nat Cath Rep* 29:39 F 5 1993
Review of: *Step spirit: the 12 steps as a spiritual program* by Chapman, Catherine. In: *Nat Cath Rep* 29:24 Mr 26 1993
Review of: *Strategic planning for pastoral ministry* by Balhoff, Michael J. In: *Nat Cath Rep* 29:40 F 5 1993
Review of: *Sunday morning* by Ramshaw, Gail. In: *Nat Cath Rep* 29:18 Jl 16 1993
Review of: *Tales of St Francis* by Bodo, Murray. In: *Nat Cath Rep* 29:25 Mr 26 1993
Review of: *The American Catholic hierarchy and Catholic Bishops in American politics* by Byrnes, Timothy A. In: *Nat Cath Rep* 30:36 N 19 1993
Review of: *The authentic doctrine of the Eucharist* by Whalen, Teresa. In: *Nat Cath Rep* 29:36 S 10 1993
Review of: *The beginning of the gospel* by Peatman, William. In: *Nat Cath Rep* 29:40 F 5 1993
Review of: *The case against Christianity* by Martin, Michael. In: *Nat Cath Rep* 30:15 O 22 1993
Review of: *The Celtic year* by Toulson, Shirley. In: *Nat Cath Rep* 30:15 O 22 1993
Review of: *The Church emerging from Vatican II* by Doyle, Dennis M. In: *Nat Cath Rep* 29:40 My 28 1993
Review of: *The college student's introduction to theology* by Rausch, Thomas P., ed. In: *Nat Cath Rep* 30:36 N 19 1993
Review of: *The Creed: the Apostolic faith in contemporary theology* by Marthaler, Berard L, 1927-. In: *Nat Cath Rep* 29:18 Jl 16 1993
Review of: *The Dead Sea Scrolls uncovered* by Eisenman, Robert H, and Wise, Michael. In: *Nat Cath Rep* 29:39 My 28 1993
Review of: *The equipping pastor* by Stevens, R. Paul, and Collins, Phil. In: *Nat Cath Rep* 30:15 O 22 1993

Graham, William C. *(cont'd)*
Review of: *The God who fell from heaven/the hour of the unexpected* by Shea, John B. In: *Nat Cath Rep* 29:39 F 5 1993
Review of: *The God who lives on my street: 10 views* by Beauchamp, Andre. In: *Nat Cath Rep* 29:39 F 5 1993
Review of: *The Gospel according to Deborah* by McGee, Michael. In: *Nat Cath Rep* 29:18 Jl 16 1993
Review of: *The joy of kindness* by Furey, Robert J. In: *Nat Cath Rep* 29:36 S 10 1993
Review of: *The kingdom of God is like* by Keating, Thomas. In: *Nat Cath Rep* 30:36 N 19 1993
Review of: *The ore and the dross* by Mertz, Fred. In: *Nat Cath Rep* 29:40 F 5 1993
Review of: *The phantoms of divinity* by Carlson, Edith. In: *Nat Cath Rep* 29:39 My 28 1993
Review of: *The promise of nature* by Haught, John F. In: *Nat Cath Rep* 30:36 N 19 1993
Review of: *The Psalms are yours* by Murphy, Roland E. In: *Nat Cath Rep* 30:36 N 19 1993
Review of: *The sacred world of the Christian* by Wagner, Mary Anthony. In: *Nat Cath Rep* 29:36 S 10 1993
Review of: *The soul of the world: a modern book of hours* by Cousineau, Phil, ed. In: *Nat Cath Rep* 29:18 Jl 16 1993
Review of: *The study of liturgy* by Jones, Cheslyn, et al, eds. In: *Nat Cath Rep* 29:40 My 28 1993
Review of: *The visionary leader: how anyone can learn to lead better* by Champlin, Joseph M. In: *Nat Cath Rep* 29:39 My 28 1993
Review of: *The way of a pilgrim and the pilgrim continues his way.* In: *Nat Cath Rep* 29:40 F 5 1993
Review of: *The way of marriage* by Milton, Jo Anne. In: *Nat Cath Rep* 30:16 O 22 1993
Review of: *The witness of the worshipping community* by Ingold, June. In: *Nat Cath Rep* 30:16 O 22 1993
Review of: *The word made flesh* by Marinelli, Anthony. In: *Nat Cath Rep* 30:35 N 19 1993
Review of: *Touching the holy: ordinariness, self-esteem, and friendship* by Wicks, Robert J. In: *Nat Cath Rep* 29:25 Mr 26 1993
Review of: *Toxic Christianity: healing the religious neurosis* by DeBlassie, Paul, III. In: *Nat Cath Rep* 29:40 My 28 1993
Review of: *Transforming the parish* by Forster, Patricia M, and Sweetser, Thomas P. In: *Nat Cath Rep* 30:36 N 19 1993
Review of: *Walking in two worlds: women's spiritual paths* by Vort, Kay Vander, et al, eds. In: *Nat Cath Rep* 29:24 Mr 26 1993
Review of: *What are they saying about the ministerial priesthood?* by Donovan, Daniel L. In: *Nat Cath Rep* 29:39 My 28 1993
Review of: *What are they saying about the social setting of the New Testament?* by Osiek, Carolyn. In: *Nat Cath Rep* 29:39 My 28 1993
Review of: *When Christ meets Christ: homilies on the Just Word* by Burghardt, Walter J. In: *Nat Cath Rep* 29:18 Jl 16 1993
Review of: *When God becomes a drug* by Booth, Leo. In: *Nat Cath Rep* 29:36 S 10 1993
Review of: *When the heart waits: spiritual direction for life's sacred questions* by Kid, Sue Monk. In: *Nat Cath Rep* 29:25 Mr 26 1993
Review of: *When your parent dies* by Curry, Cathleen L. In: *Nat Cath Rep* 30:15 O 22 1993
Review of: *With eyes to see in a journey from religion to spirituality* by Melville, Arthur. In: *Nat Cath Rep* 29:24 Mr 26 1993
Review of: *Woman, why do you weep? Spirituality for survivors of childhood sexual abuse* by Flaherty, Sandra M. In: *Nat Cath Rep* 29:24-25 Mr 26 1993
Review of: *Women of the gospel* by Powers, Isaias. In: *Nat Cath Rep* 29:36 S 10 1993
Review of: *Wonderfully, fearfully made* by Arpin, Robert L. In: *Nat Cath Rep* 29:18 Jl 16 1993
Review of: *Working in the Catholic Church, an attitudinal survey* by the National Association of Church Personnel Administrators. In: *Nat Cath Rep* 30:16 O 22 1993
Review of: *Yeshua: a model for moderns* by Swidler, Leonard. In: *Nat Cath Rep* 29:18 Jl 16 1993
Review of: *You can't grow up till you go back home* by Nerin, William F. In: *Nat Cath Rep* 30:15 O 22 1993

Graham, Ysenda Maxtone.
Review of: *The Church of England: a portrait* by Noy, Michael De la. In: *Tablet* 247:1234 S 25 1993

Gram, Frances. *see* Currier, Richard, jt auth

Gramick, Jeannine.
Celibacy: a feminist view. *Sisters* 65:255-262 Jl 1993
Lesbian identity: how to explain it all? *Sisters* 65:58-59 Ja 1993 *see* Nugent, Robert, jt auth

Granfield, Patrick.
Review of: *The church we believe in: one, Holy, Catholic and apostolic* by Sullivan, Francis Aloysius. In: *Jurist* 51 no 2:521-522 1991

Grant, J.
Review of: *A world mission: Canadian Protestantism and the quest for a new international order, 1918-1939* by Wright, Robert. In: *CHist* 78:694-695 O 1992

Grant, Richard D, Jr, and Miller, Andrea Wells.
Recovering connections. New York: HarperCollins, 1992. x, 205p ISBN 0-06-063386-7 LC 91-70707

Grant, Robert McQueen, 1917-.
Heresy and criticism: the search for authenticity in early literature. Louisville: John Knox Press, 1993. 180p ISBN 0-66421-971-3 LC 92-20017

Grant, Sara.
Review of: *A fearful symmetry?: the complementarity of men and women in ministry* by Allchin, A M, et al. In: *Tablet* 247:791-792 Je 19 1993

Grantham, James. *see* Loewenstein, David, jt ed

Grasmück, Ernst Ludwig. *see* Denzler, Georg, jt ed

Grassi, Joseph A.
Review of: *Pauline theology 1: Thessalonians, Philippians, Galatians, Philemon* by Bassler, Jouette M, ed. In: *Horizons (CTS)* 20:145 Spr 1993

Grasso, Kenneth L.
Review of: *Liberalism and the good* by Douglass, R Bruce, et al, eds. In: *IPQ* 33:371-373 S 1993 *see* Hunt, Robert P, jt ed

Gratton, Anthony, ed.
Rome reborn: the Vatican library and Renaissance culture. Washington, DC: Library of Congress, 1993. x, 323p ISBN 0-300-05442-4 LC 92-62275

Gray, Cecile.
Cutting the strings; An Easter fire; The Resurrection; The return. *Spirit* 57:50-53 Spr-Sum 1992

Gray, Dan.
Review of: *Long term care and the law: a legal guide for health care professionals* by Pozgar, George D. In: *Health Prog* 74:84-85 Ap 1993

Gray, Daria. *see* Bear, Jan, jt auth

Gray, Howard.
Changing structures. *Way Suppl* 76:72-84 Spr 1993
Continuing summons to renewal and reorientation. *Origins* 23:115-120 Jl 15 1993
Religious life's spirit of solidarity. *Origins* 23:173-176 Ag 12 1993
Review of: *Discerning God's will: Ignatius Loyola's teaching on Christian decision making* by Toner, Jules J. In: *TheolStds* 53:759-760 D 1992

Gray, Rosetta.
Religious education in the parish. *Furrow* 44:341-346 Je 1993

Grazer, Walt.
The church and asylum seekers. *Register* 69:5 Ag 8 1993

Grazin, Igor.
Natural law as a form of legal studies. *Amer J Juris* 37:1-16 1992

Greeley, Andrew Moran, 1928-.
But Father, they're priests! Clerical culture and pedophilia. *Critic* 47:43-51 Wint 1992
Contraception a baby among church's sins [commentary *Veritatis Splendor*]. *Nat Cath Rep* 29:18-21 O 15 1993
Veritatis Splendor (the Splendor of Truth), Encyclical letter on moral issues (1993 10 05) Commentary.
The faith we have lost. *America* 169:14-16+ O 2 1993
How serious is the problem of sexual abuse by clergy? *America* 168:6-10 Mr 20-27 1993
Magic in the age of faith. *America* 169:8-14 O 9 1993
Priests should make preaching thier number one job. *USCath* 58:13-17 D 1993
Religion not dying out around the world. *Origins* 23:49-58 Je 10 1993
Review of: *Textures of Irish America* by McCaffrey, Lawrence J. In: *CHist* 79:362-364 Ap 1993
Why does the church stand silent while women are abused? *USCath* 58:28-29 S 1993

Green, Arthur.
Fundamentalism by law. *Tablet* 247:204-205 F 13 1993

Green, Barbara.
Recasting a classic: a reconsideration of meaning in the Book of Job. *New Blckfrs* 74:213-221 Ap 1993

Green, Bernard D.
Tremors in the foundation of the US Catholic Church. *New Oxford Rev* 60:11-16 O 1993

Green, Joel B.
Review of: *Die letzten Tage Jesu: Markus und Johannes, ihre Traditionen und die historische Frage* by Myllykoski, Matti. In: *CBQ* 55:173-174 Ja 1993

Green, Thomas J.
The Church's teaching mission: some aspects of the normative role of episcopal conferences. *Stud Can* 27 no 1:23-57 1993
Review of: *An introduction to Canon Law* by Coriden, James A. In: *Horizons (CTS)* 19:344-345 Fall 1992
Review of: *Theology and canon law: the theories of Klaus Morsdorf and Eugenio Corecco* by Wijlens, Myriam. In: *TheolStds* 54:203 Mr 1993

Greenacre, Roger.
Epistola ad Romanos: an open letter to some Roman Catholic friends. *Month* 26:88-96 Mr 1993

Greene, Dana.
Review of: *The moral vision of Dorothy Day: a feminist perspective* by O'Connor, June E. In: *CrossCurr* 43:122-123 Spr 1993

Greenia, Conrad.
Cistercian laybrothers in the twelfth and twentieth centuries. *Cist Stud* 27 No 4:341-351 1992

Greenspahn, Frederick E.
Review of: *Creative Biblical exegesis: Christian and Jewish hermeneutics through the centuries* by Uffenheimer, Benjamin, and Reventlow, Henning Graf, eds. In: *CBQ* 55:421-422 Ap 1993
Review of: *Structure and form in the Babylonian Talmud* by Jacobs, Louis. In: *OTA* 16:446 Je 1993
Review of: *Students of the covenant: a history of Jewish Biblical scholarship in North America* by Sperling, S David. In: *OTA* 15:488-489 O 1992
Review of: *Studien zur Septuaginta: Robert Hanhart zu Ehren* by Fraenkel, Detlef, et al, eds. In: *OTA* 15:471-472 O 1992

Greenspoon, Leonard.
Review of: *Judaism: the key spiritual writings of the Jewish tradition* by Hertzberg, Arthur, ed. In: *OTA* 15:518 O 1992
Review of: *Symbol and theology in early Judaism* by Neusner, Jacob. In: *OTA* 15:518 O 1992
Review of: *The LXX version: a guide to the translation technique of the Septuagint* by Olofsson, Staffan. In: *CBQ* 55:127-128 Ja 1993

Grégoire, Jean-Pierre. *see* Englund, Robert K, jt auth

Grégoire, Reginald, et al. *see* Castagnari, Giancarlo, jt auth

Gregory, Celeste.
The real story in Denver. *OSV* 82:19 S 12 1993

Gregory, Russell. *see* Hauser, Alan J, jt auth

Grendler, Paul F.
Review of: *Erasmo e l'Umanesimo romano* by D'Ascia, Luca. In: *CHist* 79: 105-106 Ja 1993

Grennan, Eamon.
Review of: *The collected stories* by McGahern, John. In: *America* 169:20-22 Jl 31-Ag 7 1993

Grenz, Stanley.
Review of: *Creation—an ecumenical challenge? Reflections issuing from a study by the Institute for Ecumenical Research* by Lonning, Per. In: *JEcumen Stds* 29:489-491 Sum-Aut 1992
Review of: *God and creation: an ecumenical symposium* by Burrell, David B, and McGinn, Bernard John, 1937-. In: *JEcumen Stds* 29:489-491 Sum-Aut 1992

Greteman, James.
Creating a marriage. New York: Paulist, 1993. x, 106p ISBN 0-8091-3393-8 LC 92-42927

Grey, Mary.
Feminist theology, evangelisation and the embodiment of truth. *Month* 25: 485-490 D 1992
Review of: *Global responsibility: in search of a new world ethic* by Küng, Hans, 1928-. In: *Heythrop* 34:92-93 Ja 1993
Review of: *Stuggle to be the sun again: introducing Asian Women's theology* by Kyung, Chung Hyun. In: *Heythrop* 34:193-194 Ap 1993
Review of: *We dare to dream: doing theology as Asian Women* by Fabella, Virginia, and Park, Sun Ai Lee, eds. In: *Heythrop* 34:193-194 Ap 1993

Grib, Philip J.
The ethical foundations of judicial decision-making. *CLawyer* 35 no 1:1-55 1993

Gribbin, John. *see* White, Michael, jt auth

Gribble, Richard.
Celebrating the presentation. *OSV* 81:5 Ja 31 1993
The feast of Corpus Christi. *Emmanuel* 99:264-269 Je 1993
"O Blessed Mother, a sword has pierced your heart". *OSV* 82:5 S 12 1993

Gribomont, Pascal. *see* Gochet, Paul, jt auth

Griener, George E.
Herman Schell and the reform of the Catholic Church in Germany. *TheolStds* 54:427-454 S 1993
Review of: *Ernst Troeltsch* by Drescher, Hans-George. In: *TheolStds* 54:575-576 S 1993

Grieser, D. Jonathan.
Review of: *Zwingli* by Stephens, W Peter. In: *TheolStds* 54:598-599 S 1993

Griffin, Bertram F.
The reassignment of a cleric who has been professionally evaluated and treated for sexual misconduct with minors: canonical considerations. *Jurist* 51 no 2:326-339 1991

Griffin, Eltin.
Review of: *Death and new life: pastoral and theological reflections* by Harrington, Donal, ed. In: *Doctr Life* 43:374-375 Jl-Ag 1993

Griffin, James A, Bp, 1934-.
Blessings and challenges of the RCIA. *Origins* 22:565-572 Ja 28 1993
Blessings and challenges [excerpt fr a Pastoral Letter on the RCIA]. *Cath Int* 4:175-181 Ap 1993

Griffin, John. *see* Griffin, Kathy, jt auth

Griffin, John R.
Review of: *Thrown among strangers: John Henry Newman in Ireland* by McRedmond, Louis. In: *CHist* 79:352 Ap 1993

Griffin, Kathy, and Griffin, John.
How to spell success in marriage [condensed fr *The Tennessee Register* N 9 1992]. *CDgst* 57:67-69 Mr 1993

Griffin, Robert F.
A birthday tribute to Father Abraham. *OSV* 81:18 F 21 1993
A church that can survive being shamed. *OSV* 82:18 My 23 1993
Martians and their place at Notre Dame. *OSV* 81:14 Mr 21 1993
Mustering up unconditional parental love. *OSV* 82:18 My 16 1993
Receive from a woman, the bread of life? *OSV* 82:14 N 7 1993
Taking issue with the revisionists. *OSV* 82:18 My 30 1993
To the pope-bashers in Denver. *OSV* 82:14 Ag 8 1993

Griffin, William D.
Review of: *Daniel O'Connell, political pioneer* by O'Connell, Maurice, ed. In: *CHist* 79:347-348 Ap 1993

Griffin-Shelley, Eric.
Observations on healthy sexuality. *Priest* 49:29-33 Ja 1993

Griffioen, Arie J.
Brownson's early christology. *ABenR* 44:58-75 Mr 1993

Griffith, Lee.
The fall of the prison: biblical perspectives on prison abolition. Grand Rapids: Eerdmans, 1993. 280p ISBN 0-8028-0670-8

Griffiths, Bede, 1906-.
Christian and eastern mysticism [fr *a new vision of reality: Western science, Eastern mysticism and Christian faith*]. *Living Prayer* 26:3-8 My-Je 1993
The new consciousness [acceptance speech for the John Harriott Memorial Award]. *Tablet* 247:70 Ja 16 1993
Review of: *Monastic life in the Christian and Hindu traditions: a comparative study* by Creel, Austin B, and Narayanan, Vasudha, eds. In: *Heythrop* 34:222 Ap 1993

Griffiths, Leslie.
Aristide's ambassador. *Tablet* 247:429-430 Ap 3 1993
A poisoned chalice. *Tablet* 247:1254 O 2 1993
Preacher on Tower Hill. *Tablet* 247:135-136 Ja 30 1993
Review of: *Albania: who cares?* by Hamilton, Bill. In: *Tablet* 247:515 Ap 24 1993

Griffiths, Leslie. *(cont'd)*
A way out for Haiti. *Tablet* 247:708-709 Je 5 1993

Griffiths, Max.
The hungry heart. Kenthorts, Australia: Kangaroo Press, 1992. 176p ISBN 0-86417-486-1

Griffiths, P.
Review of: *Dissonant voices: religious pluralism and the question of truth* by Netland, Howard A. In: *Thomist* 56:723-726 O 1992

Grilli, Massimo.
Autore e lettore: il problema della comunicazione nell'ambito dell'esegesi biblica. *Gregorianum* 74 no 3:447-459 1993

Grimes, Laura M.
What not to say to a grieving parent. *USCath* 58:15-18 Ap 1993
Why good works are so good for you. *USCath* 58:31-32 N 1993

Grindel, Garcia. *see* Kellerman, Bill, jt auth

Grip, R.
Review of: *Seasons of the earth and heart* by Fitzgerald, William J. In: *Cist Stud* 27 No 4:[81] 1992

Grip, Robert.
Review of: *The silencing of Babylon* by Guimond, John. In: *Cist Stud* 28: [19]-[20] 1993

Grippo, Dan.
Flags don't belong in church. *USCath* 58:26-30 Mr 1993

Grisbrooke, W.
Review of: *A history of the liturgy of St John Chrysostom, volume IV, the Diptychs* by Taft, Robert F. In: *Worship* 67:474-475 S 1993

Grisez, Germain Gabriel, 1929-.
The way of the Lord Jesus, volume two, living a Christian life. Quincy, Illinois: Franciscan Press, 1993. x, 950p ISBN 0-8199-0961-0 LC 83-10508

Grissen, Lillian V.
A path through the sea: one woman's journey from depression to wholeness. Grand Rapids: Eerdmans, 1993. 240p ISBN 0-8028-0702-x

Groeschel, Benedict J.
Filled with pity. *New Cov* 22:14-15 Je 1993
Private revelation [condensed fr *A still, small voice* Ignatius, 1993]. *CDgst* 57:78-79 S 1993

Grogan, Geraldine.
Review of: *The Parnell split 1890-91* by Callanan, Frank. In: *Studies* 82:222-225 Sum 1993

Grom, Bernhard.
Cézannes Hochamt. *Stimm Zeit* 211:423-425 Je 1993
Review of: *Bibel-Psychologie* by Bucher, Anton A. In: *Stimm Zeit* 211:285-286 Ap 1993
Review of: *Erziehung zur Prosozialität bei Acht-bis Zehnjährigen am Lernort Religionsunterricht* by Bahr, Matthias. In: *Stimm Zeit* 211:575-576 Ag 1993
Review of: *Glaube* by Hentig, Hartmut von. In: *Stimm Zeit* 211:286 Ap 1993
Review of: *Werden wie die Kinder* by Winkler, Klaus. In: *Stimm Zeit* 211: 287-288 Ap 1993
Vom Egotrip zur Solidarität. *Stimm Zeit* 211:145-146 Mr 1993

Gronceski, Mark.
Be fair to Michael Griffin. *Register* 69:5 Je 27 1993

Grondelski, John M.
Catholicism and the "right" to die. *Linacre* 59:50-56 N 1992
The disembodiment of parenthood. *HPR* 93:30-31+ F 1993
Ethics, gag rules, and title X. *Linacre* 60:20-24 My 1993
Review of: *Fulfillment in Christ: a summary of "Christian moral principles"* by Grisez, Germain Gabriel, 1929-, and Shaw Russell. In: *HPR* 93:73-74 Mr 1993
Review of: *Just war and the Gulf war* by Johnson, James Turner, and Weigel, George. In: *HPR* 93:62 F 1993
Review of: *The concentration can* by Lejeune, Jerome. In: *HPR* 93:77-78 Je 1993
Review of:· *The good stewards* by Naughton, Michael. In: *HPR* 93:75-76 My 1993
Review of: *The meaning of consecration today: a Marian model for a secularized age* by Laurentin, René. In: *HPR* 93:75-76 F 1993
Shortcuts that short-circuit the liturgy. *Priest* 49:17-18 Ap 1993

Groome, Thomas H, 1945-.
Catechesis and religious education. *Living Light* 29:40-46 Aut 1992
Catechists: you are invaluable. *ReligTJ* 27:4-5 S 1993
Review of: *A fundamental practical theology: descriptive and strategic proposals* by Browning, Don S. In: *Horizons (CTS)* 20:162-163 Spr 1993

Gros, Hans.
Review of: *Civic politics in the Rome of Urban VIII* by Nussdorfer, Laurie. In: *CHist* 79:115-116 Ja 1993

Gros, Jeffrey, 1938-.
Review of: *A common calling* by Nickle, Keith, and Lull, Timothy, eds. In: *Worship* 67:476 S 1993
Review of: *A prophet with honor* by Martin, William. In: *Emmanuel* 99:175-177 Ap 1993
Review of: *Double belonging: interchurch families and Christian unity* by Kilcourse, George. In: *Cist Stud* 27 No 4:[109]-[110] 1992
Review of: *Fifth forum on bilateral conversations: international bilateral dialogues, 1965-1991* by Gassmann, Günther, ed. In: *JEcumen Stds* 29:267 Spr 1992
Review of: *Frontiers of Hispanic theology in the United States* by Deck, Allan Figueroa. In: *Spir Life* 39:180-181 Aut 1993
Review of: *In search of Christian unity* by Burgess, Joseph, ed. In: *New Theol Rev* 6:109-110 Ag 1993
Review of: *Living tradition: affirming Catholicism in the Anglican Church* by John, Jeffrey. In: *RRel* 52:475-476 My-Je 1993
Review of: *Martin Luther: the preservation of the church, 1532-1546* by Brecht, Martin. In: *RRel* 52:634-636 Jl-Ag 1993

Gros, Jeffrey, 1938-. *(cont'd)*
Review of: *Salvation in Christ* by Meyendorff, John, and Tobias, Robert, eds. In: *Worship* 67:476-477 S 1993
Review of: *Standing up, standing together* by Stream, Carol. In: *Emmanuel* 99:175=177 Ap 1993
Review of: *The history of Roman Catholic-United Methodist dialogue in the United States* by Russalesi, Steven D. In: *JEcumen Stds* 29:267-268 Spr 1992
Review of: *The sense of a people: toward a church for the human future* by Mudge, Lewis S. In: *Worship* 67:186-187 Mr 1993
Review of: *The Vienna dialogue: Vol. 1: Five Pro-Oriente consultations with Oriental Orthodoxy.* In: *JEcumen Stds* 29:269 Spr 1992
Review of: *The Vienna dialogue: Vol. 2: Summaries of the papers.* In: *JEcumen Stds* 29:269 Spr 1992
Towards a hermeneutics of piety for the ecumenical movement. *Ecumen Trends* 22:1-2+ Ja 1993

Groshen, Erica L. *see* Eberts, Randall W, jt ed

Gross, Adela.
On the road again. *ReligTJ* 27:54-55 S 1993
Review of: *Way of the cross* by Elizondo, Virgil, ed. In: *Sisters* 65:306-307 Jl 1993

Gross, H.
Review of: *Delinquenti e carcerati a Roma alla metà del '600* by Fornili, Carlo Cirillo. In: *CHist* 78:661-662 O 1992

Gross, Selwyn.
Review of: *Jewish prayer: the origins of Christian liturgy* by DiSante, Carmine. In: *Priests & People* 6:358-359 Ag-S 1992
Review of: *Cardinal Hume and the changing face of English Catholicism* by Stanford, Peter. In: *Priests & People* 7:207-209 My 1993

Gross, Toni Perior. *see* Gross, Francis L, Jr, jt auth

Gross-Diaz, Theresa.
Sexuality and spirituality in the European Middle Ages. *Chicago Stud* 32:32-42 Ap 1993

Grove, William Boyd, Bp.
Gifts from our brokenness: gifts from our unity. *Ecumen Trends* 22:12-14 S 1993

Groves, J A Ian.
Review of: *Verbs and numbers: a study of the frequencies of the Hebrew verbal tense forms in the Books of Samuel Kings and Chronicles* by Verheij, A J C. In: *CBQ* 54:771-772 O 1992

Groves, Peter.
Review of: *God, possibility and corporeality* by Sarot, Marcel. In: *New Blckfrs* 74:377-378 Jl-Ag 1993

Grubb, Geoffrey J.
Have you been saved? *ReligTJ* 27:34 Mr 1993
Repent and believe. *ReligTJ* 27:19 O 1993
Review of: *The Church emerging from Vatican II* by Doyle, Dennis M. In: *Living Light* 30:103 Aut 1993
Too good to be true. *ReligTJ* 27:39 F 1993
We believe in God. *ReligTJ* 27:18-19 S 1993
We can't buy forgiveness. *ReligTJ* 26:26 Ja 1993
Why a new catechism? *ReligTJ* 27:40-41 Ap-My 1993

Gruber, Hans-Günter.
Autonome Moral oder Moral der Autonomie? *Stimm Zeit* 211:691-699 O 1993

Gruen, Erich S.
Review of: *The Hasmoneans and their supporters: from Mattahias to the death of John Hyrcanus I* by Sievers, Joseph. In: *CBQ* 55:352-353 Ap 1993

Gründer, Karlfried. *see* Ritter, Joachim, jt auth

Grynn, Peter.
Review of: *The mysteries of the most holy rosary* by O'Brien, Michael. In: *Can Cath Rev* 11:27 S 1993

Grys, James Le.
The Christianization of modern philosophy according to Maurice Blondel. *TheolStds* 54:455-484 S 1993

Guarino, Mark, and Clarke, Kevin.
How volunteers are giving runaways new direction. *Salt* 13:18-22 F 1993

Guarino, Thomas.
Between foundationalism and nihilism: is phronēsis the via media for theology? *TheolStds* 54:37-54 Mr 1993
Review of: *The persistence of modernity: essays on aesthetics, ethics and postmodernism* by Wellmer, Albrecht. In: *TheolStds* 54:605 S 1993

Gudorf, Christine E.
Review of: *Eunuchs for the kingdom of God: women, sexuality, and the Catholic Church* by Ranke-Heinemann, Uta. In: *Horizons (CTS)* 20:186-187 Spr 1993
Review of: *Outercourse: the be-dazzling voyage* by Daly, Mary. In: *Nat Cath Rep* 29:37 F 5 1993
Sexual violence: it's sinful to remain silent. *Salt* 13:6-11 My 1993
Why have kids? *USCath* 58:27-29 F 1993

Guentner, Francis J.
Review of: *Mozart: traces of transcendence* by Kung, Hans, 1928-. In: *RRel* 52:623-625 Jl-Ag 1993

Guerello, Francesco.
La pedagogia della compagnia di Gesù. *Civilta* 2:254-259 My 1 1993

Guggenheim, Antoine.
Liberté et vérité selon K Wojtyla. *NRT* 115:194-210 Mr-Ap 1993

Guidan, E, et al.
Etica laica y sociedad pluralista. Madrid: Popular, 1993. x, 157p ISBN 84-7884-087-7

Guietti, Paolo.
Review of: *Augusto Del Moce* by Buttiglione, Rocco. In: *Crisis* 11:56-57 Ap 1993

Guietti, Paolo. *(cont'd)*
Review of: *La crisis della morale* by Buttiglione, Rocco. In: *Crisis* 11:52-53 My 1993

Guiliano, John.
Life after death in El Salvador [interview D.S. Toolan]. *America* 169:12-14 D 4 1993

Guimarães, Almir Ribeiro.
A família do documento de Santo Domingo. *REB* 53:40-51 Mr 1993

Guimon, Joes.
Psicoanalisis y literatura. Barcelona: Kairos, 1993. x, 329p ISBN 84-7245-259-x

Guinan, Michael D.
Instruction for life. *BibleT* 31:260-264 S 1993
Review of: *A tale of two cities: Sodom and Gomorrah in the Old Testament, early Jewish and early Christian traditions* by Loader, J A. In: *TheolStds* 54:382 Je 1993
Review of: *Let justice roll down: the Old Testament, ethics, and Christian life* by Birch, Bruce C. In: *TheolStds* 53:736-737 D 1992

Guindon, Andre.
Theologian offers Vatican-requested explanations. *Origins* 22:630-636 F 25 1993

Gula, Richard M.
A bioethics roundup. *Priest* 49:35-40 Je 1993
Review of: *A theology of compromise: a study of method in the ethics of Charles E Curran* by Grecco, Richard. In: *TheolStds* 53:788-789 D 1992

Gullekson, Justin W.
Review of: *The Catholic vision* by O'Connor, Edward D. In: *New Oxford Rev* 60:30-31 O 1993
Review of: *The mystery we proclaim: catechesis at the third millennium* by Kelly, Francis D. In: *New Oxford Rev* 60:31-32 S 1993

Gummer, John Selwyn, 1939-.
Shaking the foundations. *Tablet* 247:498 Ap 24 1993

Gunton, Colin.
Review of: *Sacrifice and redemption: Durham essays in theology* by Syukes, S W, ed. In: *New Blckfrs* 73:630-632 D 1992

Gustin, Marilyn Norquist.
Attentive to the word of God. *Liguorian* 81:56-60 Ap 1993
The eucharistic prayer. *Liguorian* 81:46-50 Ag 1993
The Lord's prayer and the sign of peace. *Liguorian* 81:18-22 O 1993
Our search for sacredness. *Liguorian* 81:20-24 Ja 1993
Prayers of penitence and praise. *Liguorian* 81:56-60 Mr 1993
Sacred symbol sacred ceremony. *Liguorian* 81:12-17 F 1993
Summing up the seasons of faith: the liturgical year. *Liguorian* 81:30-35 D 1993
Through your goodness we have these gift to offer. *Liguorian* 81:28-32 Jl 1993
We profess what we believe. *Liguorian* 81:48-53 My 1993
You can know God: Christian spirituality for daily living. Washington, D C: Liguori Publications, 1993. x, 212p ISBN 0-89243-479-1 LC 92-74594
You hear us when we call upon you. *Liguorian* 81:54-58 Je 1993

Gutmann, Joseph.
Review of: *Inculturation and Christian art: an Indian perspective* by Elavathingal, Sebastian. In: *JEcumen Stds* 29:284 Spr 1992

Gwozdz, Lee.
Today's singing child, tomorrow's singing adult. *Past Mus* 17:15-17 F-Mr 1993

H

Haak, Robert D.
Review of: *Zion's final destiny* by Seitz, Christopher R. In: *OTA* 15:505-506 O 1992

Haase, Albert.
The joy of forgiving [excerpt fr *Swimming in the sun*]. *St Anth* 101:28-35 O 1993
Swimming in the sun: discovering the Lord's prayer with Francis of Assisi and Thomas Merton. Cincinnati: St Anthony Messenger Press, 1993. 216p ISBN 0-86716-193-0

Haberman, Joshua A.
Towards a Jewish-Christian alliance [interview by R Lakind]. *Crisis* 11:32-38 F 1993
1992: a year of T'shuvah [reply by Joshu O Haberman, p 29]. *SIDIC* 25 No 2:29 1992

Habgood, John Stapylton, Abp, 1927-.
The moral baseline. *Tablet* 247:464 Ap 10-17 1993

Habiger, Robert D.
Designing the post-Vatican II worship space. *Mod Lit* 20:8-11 N 1993

Habito, Ruben L.F.
Healing breath: Zen spirituality for a wounded earth. Maryknoll: Orbis, 1993. x, 166p ISBN 0-88344-919-0 LC 93-5125

Hackett, Peter.
Art in retreat. *Month* 26:107 Mr 1993
Review of: *Right at the centre: an autobiography* by Parkinson, Cecil. In: *Tablet* 247:16-17 Ja 2 1993
Review of: *The Oxford companion to the English language* by McArthur, Tom, ed. In: *Month* 25:497 D 1992
The virtuosity of detachment: Walter Sickert. *Month* 26:26-27 Ja 1993

Haegel, Nancy M.
Review of: *The heart of the sky: travels among the Maya* by Canby, Peter. In: *Comm* 120:22-23 Mr 26 1993

Haes, René de.
Prolifération et persistance des sectes dans le milieu urbain de Kinshasa: analyse de quelques cas. *StudiaM* 41:205-224 1992

Haese, Ute.
Katholishe Kirche in der DDR zwischen Staat und Gesellschaft. *Stimm Zeit* 211:241-254 Ap 1993

Hafner, John H.
Review of: *Dear James* by Hassler, Jon. In: *America* 169:20-21 S 25 1993

Hagan, Charles H.
College education/values education. *Origins* 22:602-604 F 11 1993
Formation of the young as moral agents. *Origins* 23:430-432 N 25 1993
Review of: *College Catholics: a new counter-culture* by Hunt, Michael J. In: *Living Light* 30:104 Aut 1993

Haggith, David.
Word from the Lord?. *New Cov* 22:14-15 Jl 1993

Haglof, Anthony.
Review of: *Self and liberation: the Jung/Buddhism dialogue* by Meckel, Daniel J, and Moore, Robert L, eds. In: *Spir Life* 39:54-56 Spr 1993

Haig, Frank R.
Review of: *Science as salvation: a modern myth and its meaning* by Midgley, Mary. In: *TheolStds* 54:393-394 Je 1993

Haight, Roger.
Grace and the exercises. *Way Suppl* 76:44-52 Spr 1993
Liberation theology and middle class America: a personal reflection. *Chicago Stud* 32:64-76 Ap 1993
Review of: *Born before all time* by Kuschel, Karl-Josef. In: *TheolStds* 54:578-580 S 1993
Review of: *God for us: the Trinity and Christian life* by LaCugna, Catherine Mowry. In: *Horizons (CTS)* 20:129-132 Spr 1993

Hainaut, Hadelin.
Face a l'enfant mourant. *Supplement* 184:79-88 Mr-Ap 1993

Hainz, M.
Review of: *Grundrecht Asyl* by Tremmel, Hans. In: *Stimm Zeit* 210:862-863 D 1992

Haire, James.
Review of: *Jesus the Christ: the historical origins of christological doctrine* by Dahl, Nils Alstrup. In: *Pacifica* 6:245-247 Je 1993

Haldane, John.
Review of: *Defending the soul* by Ward, Keith. In: *Tablet* 247:720-721 Je 5 1993
Review of: *Postmodernism, reason and religion* by Gellner, Ernest. In: *New Blckfrs* 74:428-429 S 1993
Review of: *Soul: an introduction to the new cosmology—time, consciousness and God* by Tilby, Angela. In: *Tablet* 247:720-721 Je 5 1993
Review of: *The ethics of authenticity* by Taylor, Charles, 1931-. In: *Tablet* 247:213 F 13 1993

Halkes, Catharina J M, et al.
Mary: yesterday, today, tomorrow. New York: Crossroad, 1993. 88p ISBN 0-8245-1371-1 LC 93-19852

Hall, James A.
The unconscious Christian: images of God in dreams. Mahwah, New Jersey: Paulist Press, 1993. x, 113p ISBN 0-8091-3353-9 LC 92-26395

Hall, Michael G.
Review of: *The prism of piety: Catholick congregational clergy at the beginning of the Enlightenment* by Corrigan, John. In: *CHist* 79:358-359 Ap 1993

Hall, Sidney G, III.
Christian anti-Semitism and Paul's theology. Minneapolis: Fortress, 1993. x, 191p ISBN 0-8006-2654-0 LC 92-30395

Hall, Stewart J.
Review of: *Pastoral life and practice in the early Church* by Volz, Carl A. In: *Heythrop* 34:315-316 Jl 1993
Review of: *The emergence of the laity in the early Church* by Faivre, Alexandre. In: *Heythrop* 34:315-316 Jl 1993
Review of: *The making of the creeds* by Young, Frances. In: *Heythrop* 34:315-316 Jl 1993

Hallenbeck, Jan T.
Review of: *Before the Normans: southern Italy in the ninth and tenth centuries* by Kreutz, Barbara M. In: *CHist* 79:95-96 Ja 1993
Review of: *The lives of the eightth-century popes ("Liber Pontificalis")* by Davis, Raymond. In: *CHist* 79:514-515 Jl 1993

Hallett, Elaine.
Review of: *Certain women* by L'Engle, Madeleine. In: *New Oxford Rev* 60:30 Ap 1993

Hallett, Paul.
In light and shadow. *Register* 69:4 Je 11 1993
Review of: *"A historical commentary on the major Catholic works of Cardinal Newman"* by Griffin, John R. In: *Register* 69:5 Jl 25 1993
Review of: *The Second Vatican Council and religious liberty* by Davies, Michael. In: *Register* 69:5 F 21 1993

Halleux, André de.
The catholicity of the local church in the patriarchate of Antioch after Chalcedon. *Jurist* 52 no 1:109-129 1992
La Nativité et l'Épiphanie dans le dialogue unioniste du VIIe siècle. *Eph Theol Lovan* 78:5-37 Ap 1992
La première session du Concile D'Éphèse (22 Juin 431). *Eph Theol Lovan* 69:48-87 Ap 1993
Review of: *An anthology of Christian mysticism* by Egan, Harvey. In: *Eph Theol Lovan* 78:478-479 D 1992
Review of: *Ascetica e mistica nella patristica* by Viller, Marcel, and Rahner, Karl, 1904-1984. In: *Eph Theol Lovan* 78:447 D 1992
Review of: *Biblia y cristologia: unitad y diversita en la Iglesia; la interpretación de los dogmas*. In: *Eph Theol Lovan* 69:208-209 Ap 1993
Review of: *Christian unity* by Alberigo, Giuseppe, ed. In: *Eph Theol Lovan* 78:458-460 D 1992

Halleux, André de. *(cont'd)*
Review of: *Commentary on the Divine Liturgy* by Anjewec'i, Xosrov. In: *Eph Theol Lovan* 69:198 Ap 1993
Review of: *De geest, het woord en de zoon: theologische overdenkingen over geest-christologie, logos-christologie en drieëenheidsleer* by Schoonenberg, Piet. In: *Eph Theol Lovan* 69:211-213 Ap 1993
Review of: *De moribus ecclesiae catholicae et de moribus manichaeorum* by d'Ippona, Agostino. In: *Eph Theol Lovan* 78:456-457 D 1992
Review of: *Der Geist des Neuen Zeitalters* by Schiwy, Günther. In: *Eph Theol Lovan* 78:478 D 1992
Review of: *Der geist, das wort und der sohn: eine geist-Christologie* by Schoonenberg, Piet. In: *Eph Theol Lovan* 69:211-213 Ap 1993
Review of: *Der niemals gekündigte Bund: Exegetische Gedanken zum christlich-jüdischen Dialog* by Lohfink, Norbert. In: *Eph Theol Lovan* 78:444-445 D 1992
Review of: *Dominus Salvator: studien zur Christologie und Exegese der Kirchenväter* by Studer, Basil. In: *Eph Theol Lovan* 69:197-198 Ap 1993
Review of: *El dogma que libera* by Segundo, Juan Luis. In: *Eph Theol Lovan* 69:210-211 Ap 1993
Review of: *El problema del mal en Origenes* by Wörmer, Anneliese Meis. In: *Eph Theol Lovan* 69:195-196 Ap 1993
Review of: *Eugippe: Vie de saint Séverin* by Régerat, Philippe. In: *Eph Theol Lovan* 78:457-458 D 1992
Review of: *Foi et philosophies* by Léonard, André. In: *Eph Theol Lovan* 78:464-465 D 1992
Review of: *Ignacio de Antioquia, Policarpo de Esmirna: Carta* by Ayan Calvo, Juan Jose, ed. In: *Eph Theol Lovan* 78:450-451 D 1992
Review of: *L'Eglise-Fraternité* by Dujarier, Michel. In: *Eph Theol Lovan* 78:447-448 D 1992
Review of: *L'esperienza dello Spirito* by Vannini, Marco. In: *Eph Theol Lovan* 78:477-478 D 1992
Review of: *La chaîne sur la Genèse* by Petit, Françoise, ed. In: *Eph Theol Lovan* 78:448-449 D 1992
Review of: *La préparation évangélique: livres VIII-IX-X* by Eusebius Pamphili, Bp of Caesarea. In: *Eph Theol Lovan* 69:196 Ap 1993
Review of: *Le Cristologie contemporanee e le loro posizioni fondamentali al vaglio della dottrina di S Tommaso* by Ols, Daniel. In: *Eph Theol Lovan* 78:475-477 D 1992
Review of: *Le origini dell'anno liturgico* by Talley, Thomas J. In: *Eph Theol Lovan* 78:482 D 1992
Review of: *Le radici patristiche della teologia di Antonio Rosmini* by Quacquarelli, Antonio. In: *Eph Theol Lovan* 78:449 D 1992
Review of: *Les cent ans de la Faculté de théologie* by Doré, Joseph, ed. In: *Eph Theol Lovan* 69:219-220 Ap 1993
Review of: *Lettres festales* by D'Alexandrie, Cyrille. In: *Eph Theol Lovan* 78:452-454 D 1992
Review of: *Lo spirito dell'Età Nuova* by Schiwy, Günther. In: *Eph Theol Lovan* 78:478 D 1992
Review of: *Lo studio dei Padri della Chiesa oggi* by Covolo, Enrico Dal, and Triacca, Achille M, eds. In: *Eph Theol Lovan* 78:446-447 D 1992
Review of: *Origène: Commentaire sur le Cantique des Cantiques* by Brésard, Luc, and Crouzel, Henri, eds. In: *Eph Theol Lovan* 78:451-452 D 1992
Review of: *Pensare il bello* by Trombino, Mario, et al. In: *Eph Theol Lovan* 78:465-466 D 1992
Review of: *Registre des lettres, vol I* by Gregory I, The Great, Saint, Pope. In: *Eph Theol Lovan* 69:197 Ap 1993
Review of: *Russische Religionsphilosophie und Gnosis* by Koslowski, Peter, ed. In: *Eph Theol Lovan* 69:209-210 Ap 1993
Review of: *Sapientia et Caritas* by Perler, Othmar. In: *Eph Theol Lovan* 78:445-446 D 1992
Review of: *Sulle cose prime e ultime* by Bertola, Francesco. In: *Eph Theol Lovan* 78:477 D 1992
Review of: *Supplique au sujet des chrétiens et sur la résurrection des morts* by Athénagore. In: *Eph Theol Lovan* 69:195 Ap 1993
Review of: *Ter genezing van ziel en lichaam* by Groen, Basilius J. In: *Eph Theol Lovan* 78:481-482 D 1992
Review of: *The covenant never revoked: biblical reflections on Christian-Jewish dialogue* by Lohfink, Norbert. In: *Eph Theol Lovan* 78:444-445 D 1992
Review of: *The East Syrian lectionary* by Kannookadan, Pauly. In: *Eph Theol Lovan* 78:479-481 D 1992
Review of: *The Jesus of Christian history* by Goergen, Donald J. In: *Eph Theol Lovan* 69:209 Ap 1993
Review of: *The liberation of dogma* by Segundo, Juan Luis. In: *Eph Theol Lovan* 69:210-211 Ap 1993
Review of: *The origins of the liturgical year* by Talley, Thomas J. In: *Eph Theol Lovan* 78:482 D 1992

Halliday, Steve.
No night too dark: how God turns defeat into glorious triump. Sisters: Questar, 1993. x, 252p ISBN 0-88070-560-4

Halligan, John M.
Review of: *Power and politics in Palestine: the Jews and the governing of their land, 100 BC-AD 70* by McLaren, James S. In: *OTA* 16:447 Je 1993

Halloran, W Regis.
Review of: *The authentic doctrine of the Eucharist* by Whalen, Teresa. In: *Mod Lit* 20:39 Ag 1993
Review of: *Using illustrations to preach with power* by Chapell, Bryan. In: *Mod Lit* 20:41-42 N 1993

Halloway, George.
Laity must get involved in dollars and cents. *Register* 69:7 S 26 1993

Hallsted, Bill D.
Our wake-up call. *SocJust* 84:86 My-Je 1993

Halow, Joseph.
Innocent at Dachau. Newport Beach, California: Institute for Historical Review, 1993. x, 237p ISBN 0-939482-40-11

Halter, Deborah.
Editors' job at stake when bishops decide what's news. *Nat Cath Rep* 29:19 S 10 1993

Hamer, Jerome, Cardinal.
Activities of the Council of the "16" during 1991: religious life in the countries of Eastern Europe. *Con Life* 17 no 2:149-153 1992
Religious life and evanglization. *Con Life* 17 no 2:77-81 1992

Hamill, Paul C.
Review of: *When time shall be no more* by Boyer, Paul S. In: *Month* 26:145-146 Ap 1993

Hamilton, Alastair.
Review of: *Fourth Ezra: a commentary on the Book of Fourth Ezra* by Stone, Michael Edward. In: *Heythrop* 34:311 Jl 1993
Review of: *Frontiers of heresy: the Spanish Inquisition from the Basque Lands to Sicily* by Monter, William. In: *Heythrop* 34:329-331 Jl 1993
Review of: *Humanism and reform: the Church in Europe, England and Scotland, 1400-1643: essays in honour of James K Cameron* by Kirk, James, ed. In: *Heythrop* 34:213-214 Ap 1993
Review of: *Inquisition and society in the kingdom of Valencia, 1478-1834* by Haliczer, Stephen. In: *Heythrop* 34:329-331 Jl 1993
Review of: *Lucrecia's dreams: politics and prophecy in Sixteenth-Century Spain* by Kagan, Richard L. In: *Heythrop* 34:332-333 Jl 1993
Review of: *Martin Luther: shaping and defining the Reformation, 1521-1532* by Brecht, Martin. In: *Heythrop* 34:213-214 Ap 1993
Review of: *More's "Utopia"* by Baker-Smith, Dominic. In: *Heythrop* 34:328-329 Jl 1993
Review of: *The Anglican tradition: a handbook of sources* by Evans, G R, and Wright, J Robert, eds. In: *Heythrop* 34:340 Jl 1993
Review of: *The European Reformation* by Cameron, Euan. In: *Heythrop* 34:213-214 Ap 1993
Review of: *The fear of hell: images of damnation and salvation in early modern Europe* by Camporesi, Piero. In: *Heythrop* 34:331-332 Jl 1993
Review of: *The Restoration Church of England 1646-1689* by Spurr, John. In: *Heythrop* 34:340 Jl 1993
Review of: *The study of Anglicanism* by Sykes, Stephen, and Booty, John, eds. In: *Heythrop* 34:340 Jl 1993

Hamilton, Andrew.
Review of: *New evangelization* by Boff, Leonardo. In: *Pacifica* 6:347-349 O 1993
Review of: *The God of life* by Gutiérrez, Gustavo. In: *Pacifica* 6:347-349 O 1993

Hamilton, Daniel S.
Knocking at the papal door. *America* 168:16-17 Ap 24 1993

Hamilton, G.
Review of: *The study companion to Old Testament literature* by Campbell, Anthony F. In: *Can Cath Rev* 11:39 Ja 1993

Hamm, Dennis.
Review of: *Stephanos: histoire et discours d'Etienne dans les Actes des Apôtres* by Légasse, Simon. In: *CBQ* 55:377-378 Ap 1993

Hamma, Robert M.
The changing state of spirituality: 1968 and 1993. *America* 169:8-10 N 27 1993

Hamman, Adalbert.
How to read the church fathers. New York: The Crossroad Publishing Company, 1993. x, 132p ISBN 0-8245-1204-9 LC 92-42052

Hammond, Claire H.
American women and the professionalization of economics. *RSocEcon* 51:347-370 Aut 1993

Hammond, David M.
Review of: *Conscience in Newman's thought* by Grave, S A. In: *Relig Lit* 24:97-104 Aut 1992
Review of: *Newman and heresy* by Thomas, Stephen. In: *Relig Lit* 24:97-104 Aut 1992
Review of: *Newman on being a Christian* by Ker, Ian. In: *Relig Lit* 24:97-104 Aut 1992

Hampl, Patricia, 1946-.
A quest for vision [interview by E Wymard]. *Critic* 47:58-64 Spr 1993

Hanbury, Kevin M. *see* Foley, Anita M, jt auth

Hand, Geoffrey, 1931-.
Aubrey Gwynn: the person. *Studies* 81:375-384 Wint 1992

Hands, D Wade.
Review of: *The history and philosophy of social science* by Gordon, Scott. In: *RSocEcon* 51:112-115 Spr 1993

Hands, Donald R, and Fehr, Wayne L.
Spiritual wholeness for clergy. Washington: The Alban Institute, 1993. x, 159p ISBN 1-5669-107-2

Hanigan, James P.
Review of: *The moral virtues and theological ethics* by Cessario, Romanus. In: *Horizons (CTS)* 19:336-337 Fall 1992
Review of: *The primacy of love* by Wadell, Paul J. In: *Horizons (CTS)* 20:178-179 Spr 1993

Hanink, James G.
In the end, one thing matters. *Register* 69:5 O 31 1993
Left, right, or personalist? *New Oxford Rev* 60:14-20 N 1993
Moral living in a non-Christian world [review article *Living a Christian Life* by G. Grisez]. *OSV* 82:9 N 21 1993
A moratorium on rescues is a bad idea. *OSV* 82:19 O 3 1993
Nature and grace. *Register* 69:5 Ja 10 1993
The Prolife Movement: dead or alive? *New Oxford Rev* 60:10-14+ My 1993

Hanley, Boniface.
And more than a prophet. *Stud Form Spir* 14:161-174 My 1993

Hanley, Mary.
Review of: *Farming on the edge: saving family farms in Marin County, California* by Hart, John. In: *New Oxford Rev* 60:30-31 Ap 1993

Hanlon, James.
Review of: *Families encouraging faith* by Goewey, Jerrie Ann, and Goewey, Ken. In: *Can Cath Rev* 11:31 O 1993

Hanlon, James. *(cont'd)*
Review of: *Families experiencing faith* by Drey, Janet. In: *Can Cath Rev* 11:31 O 1993
Review of: *Families exploring faith* by Taylor, Audrey, and Taylor, Joe. In: *Can Cath Rev* 11:31 O 1993
Review of: *Families nurturing faith* by Kehrwald, Leif, and Kehrwald, Rene. In: *Can Cath Rev* 11:31 O 1993
Review of: *Families sharing faith* by Trokan, John, and Trokan, Nancy. In: *Can Cath Rev* 11:31 O 1993

Hanlon, Kevin.
Revealing happiness. *Month* 26:165-167 Ap 1993

Hann, John H.
Review of: *Excavations on the Franciscan frontier: archaeology at the Fig Springs Mission* by Weisman, Brent Richards. In: *CHist* 79:355-356 Ap 1993

Hann, Robert R.
Commitment, theology, and the dilemma of religious studies at the state university. *Horizons (CTS)* 19:263-276 Fall 1992
Review of: *Origins of Judaism: Judaism and Christianity in the first century* by Neusner, Jacob, ed. In: *JEcumen Stds* 29:122-123 Wint 1992

Hannan, Maryanne.
Once a charismatic. *New Cov* 22:23-24 My 1993

Hanney, James.
Review of: *Tragic method and tragic theology: evil in contemporary drama and religious thought* by Bouchard, L.D. In: *Heythrop* 34:321-322 Jl 1993

Hannon, Patrick.
The conscience of the voter and law-maker [Irish content]. *Doctr Life* 42:244-252 My-Je 1992

Hansen, Eric C.
Review of: *Representing belief: religion, art, and society in nineteenth-century France* by Driskel, Michael Paul. In: *CHist* 79:119-120 Ja 1993

Hansen, Jennie Chin.
Capitation works for long-term care. *Health Prog* 74:61 Jl-Ag 1993

Hansen, Tracy.
Review of: *Christianity and incest* by Imbens, Annie, and Jonker, Ineke. In: *Tablet* 247:407 Mr 27 1993
Review of: *Confronting the pain of child sexual abuse* by Winfield, Marlene, ed. In: *Tablet* 247:170 F 6 1993
Review of: *Female sexual abuse of children* by Elliott, Michele, ed. In: *Tablet* 247:1198-1199 S 18 1993

Hanshell, Deryck.
The shape of things to come in liturgy. *SacM* 119:15-18 Wint 1992

Hanus, Elaine.
Evaluating the director of religious education. *Momentum* 24:72-73 S-O 1993

Hanus, Jerome, Bp.
Easter took over her face. *Sisters* 65:121-125 Mr 1993
Pastoral associates guidelines. *Origins* 22:699-700 Mr 18 1993

Hanus, Jerome J, Bp.
Review of: *The idea of the university: a reexamination* by Pelikan, Jaroslav. In: *Crisis* 11:51-52 Ap 1993

Hanvey, J.
Review of: *Karl Barth: Biblical and evangelical theologian* by Torrance, Thomas F. In: *Heythrop* 34:87-88 Ja 1993

Harak, G Simon.
Review of: *Just peacemaking: transforming initiatives for justice and peace* by Stassen, Glen H. In: *TheolStds* 54:395 Je 1993

Häring, Bernard, 1912-.
Consulting the faithful. *Tablet* 247:941-942 Jl 24 1993
An interview with Bernard Häring, influential moral theologian [interview by J Tobin and W Bueche]. *Liguorian* 81:46-51 Je 1993
Law and gospel. *Tablet* 247:41-42 Ja 9 1993
Review of: *Theology and Canon Law* by Orsy, Ladislas M, 1921-. In: *Tablet* 247:41-42 Ja 9 1993

Harkulich, Joan T. *see* Kerrigan, Ruth, jt auth

Harl, Marguerite. *see* Dogniez, Cécile, jt auth

Harles, Sabine.
Frauen und Ökumene. *Stimm Zeit* 210:857-860 D 1992

Harmer, Catherine M.
Internationality: intentional or accidental. *RRel* 52:111-118 Ja-F 1993
Multiculturalism in religious life today. *RRel* 52:764-772 S-O 1993

Harmon, Maurice.
The rejection of Yeats: the case of Clarke and O'Faolain. *Studies* 82:243-256 Aut 1993
Review of: *Peninsula: poems* by Egan, Desmond. In: *Studies* 81:446-448 Wint 1992
Review of: *Selected poems* by Egan, Desmond. In: *Studies* 82:360-362 Aut 1993

Harms, Paul W F, et al.
Proclamation [exc fr *Liturgy: the art of celebration; Liturgy: ethics and justice,* etc]. *Liturgy* 10:71-76 Spr 1993

Harms, Paul W F.
Twenty-first Sunday after Pentecost. *Liturgy* 11:60-64 Sum 1993

Harries, Karsten.
The root of all evil: lessons of an epigram. *IJPS* 1:1-20 Mr 1993

Harrington, Ann M.
Japan's hidden Christians. Chicago: Loyola University Press, 1993. x, 110p ISBN 0-8294-0741-3

Harrington, Daniel J.
A Catholic reading of the Book of Revelation. *New Theol Rev* 6:53-63 Ag 1993
Matthew as a Christian Gospel. *Priests & People* 7:284-288 Jl 1993
Matthew as a Jewish book. *Priests & People* 7:240-244 Je 1993

HaSh'erit, Achad.
Review of: *Jesus' Jewishness: exploring the place of Jesus in early Judaism* by Charlesworth, James H, ed. In: *New Oxford Rev* 60:31-32 Ap 1993
Review of: *The Arab Christian* by Cragg, Kenneth. In: *New Oxford Rev* 60: 32 Je 1993

Haskins, D.
Review of: *Politics, poetics and hermeneutics in Milton's prose* by Loewenstein, David, and Grantham, James, eds. In: *Heythrop* 34:116-117 Ja 1993

Hassel, David.
Prayer: discouragement and its antidotes. *Sisters* 65:20-24 Ja 1993

Hassing, Per.
Review of: *I regnbagens tecken* by Eilert, Hakan. In: *JEcumen Stds* 29:116 Wint 1992

Hastings, Adrian, 1929-.
Battle for Bosnia. *Tablet* 247:1256-1257 O 2 1993
Give Bosnia a chance. *Tablet* 247:64+ Ja 16 1993
Review of: *The destruction of Yugoslavia: tracking the break-up 1980-92* by Magas, Branka. In: *Tablet* 247:405 Mr 27 1993

Hastings, Joanna.
The rosary: a prayer for all seasons. Collegeville:Liturgical, 1993. x, 212p ISBN 0-8146-2134-1 LC 92-43851

Hater, Robert J.
Priestly identity: a changing focus. *Priest* 49:19-22 Ap 1993

Hatt, Harold.
Review of: *The forgotten trinity. Vol 3* by Heron, Alasdair I C, ed. In: *JEcumen Stds* 29:477-478 Sum-Aut 1992

Hattis, Paul A.
Retooling for community benefit. *Health Prog* 74:38-41 1993

Hauerwas, Stanley. see Willimon, William H, jt auth

Hauerwas, Stanley Martin, 1940-.
[Veritatis splendor is unique]. *Comm* 120:16-18 O 22 1993

Haughey, John C.
Review of: *Christian initiation and baptism in the Holy Spirit* by McDonnell, Kilian, 1921-, and Montague, George T, eds. In: *Worship* 67:92-94 Ja 1993
Review of: *God—the world's future: systematic theology for a postmodern era* by Peters, Ted. In: *TheolStds* 54:582-584 S 1993
Review of: *Ultimate hope without God: the atheistic eschatology of Ernst Bloch* by West, Thomas H. In: *TheolStds* 54:391 Je 1993

Haught, John F.
Mystery and promise: a theology of revelation. Collegeville, Minnesota: The Liturgical Press, 1993. 224p ISBN 0-8146-5792-3 LC 92-46908
The promise of nature: ecology and cosmic purpose. New York: Paulist Press, 1993. x, 156p ISBN 0-8091-3396-2 LC 92-41353
Review of: *Belonging to the universe: explorations on the frontiers of science and spirituality* by Capra, Fritjof, et al. In: *Living Light* 29:94-95 Aut 1992
Review of: *The mind of God: the scientific basis for a rational world* by Davies, Paul. In: *TheolStds* 53:770-772 D 1992

Hauke, Mary C.
Evangelization through institutional sponsorship. *Health Prog* 74:48-50+ O 1993

Hauser, Richard A.
Review of: *Belonging to the universe: explorations on the frontiers of science and spirituality* by Capra, Fritjof, et al. In: *ChrWorld* 236:279-280 N-D 1993

Havran, Martin J.
Review of: *Cheap print and popular piety, 1550-1640* by Watt, Tessa. In: *CHist* 78:653-654 O 1992
Review of: *From counter-reformation to glorious revolution* by Trevor-Roper, Hugh. In: *CHist* 79:537-538 Jl 1993

Hawk, Patrick.
Authority (1): the role of the teacher in Buddhist/Christian formation. *Stud Form Spir* 14:23-29 F 1993

Hawke, Margaret.
When a loved one has Alzheimer's [condensed fr *HomeLife* Ja 1992]. *CDgst* 58:46-49 N 1993

Hawkes, Nigel.
Review of: *Einstein, a life in science* by White, Michael, and Gribbin, John. In: *Tablet* 247:1132 S 4 1993
Review of: *Heisenberg's war: the secret history of the German bomb* by Powers, Thomas. In: *Tablet* 247:789 Je 19 1993
Review of: *Taming the atom* by Baeyer, Hans Christian von. In: *Tablet* 247: 517 Ap 24 1993
Review of: *The private lives of Albert Einstein* by Highfield, Roger, and Carter, Paul. In: *Tablet* 247:1132 S 4 1993
Review of: *The unnatural nature of science* by Wolpert, Lewis. In: *Tablet* 246:1574-1575 D 12 1992

Hawkins, Jacqueline, ed.
Celibacy. *Way Suppl* 77:5-112 Sum 1993
Making sense of celibacy, by G Orchard. Celibacy as charism, by S Schneiders. Celibacy and clerical culture, by J O'Keefe. A survivor's tale, by D S Toolan. Unfinished agenda: a critical look at the history of celibacy, by M Malone. A feminist critique, by S Dowell. Celibacy and Intimacy, by B Kimmerling. Who chooses celibacy—and why?, by M A Coate. Celibacy in another tradition, by M Woodgate.

Hay, David.
Review of: *Invaded by love: an anthology of Christian conversion stories* by Backhouse, Robert, ed. In: *Tablet* 247:1199-1200 S 18 1993

Hayden, Hilary.
Review of: *Roman Catholicism yesterday and today* by Burns, Robert E, 1919-. In: *Living Light* 29:92-93 Spr 1993

Hayes, Cathy Cartier.
Behind closed doors. *OSV* 82:10-11 Je 27 1993

Hayes, Diana L.
An African American Catholic rite. *Living Light* 29:35-48 Wint 1992
A change is coming. *USCath* 58:38-40 S 1993
Deep river: the Christian vocation of the laity. *Spir Life* 39:131-136 Aut 1993
Review of: *The history of black Catholics in the United States* by Davis, Cyprian. In: *Living Light* 29:87-89 Spr 1993
To be black, Catholic, and female. *New Theol Rev* 6:55-62 My 1993
Who's afraid of multiculturalism? *Salt* 13:17 Ap 1993

Hayes, Doris K.
Unity through theology. *Priests & People* 7:27-29 Ja 1993

Hayes, Gary R, and McHugh, James, Bp.
Priest and two laymen charge abuse as teens. *Origins* 23:87-90 Je 24 1993

Hayes, John.
Can moral beliefs be embodied in law? [review article *Church, State, Morality, Law* by P Hannon]. *Doctr Life* 43:20-30 Ja 1993

Hayes, Matt.
The catechism as symphonic score. *Momentum* 24:66-69 S-O 1993
Review of: *Adult education and worldview construction* by McKenzie, Leon. In: *Living Light* 29:82-84 Aut 1992

Haynes, A W.
Alleluia, Hosanna, and Amen. *Can Cath Rev* 11:31-33 My 1993
Awasa. *Can Cath Rev* 11:31-33 Ap 1993
Chaplain's assistant. *Can Cath Rev* 11:31-32 S 1993
Climb every mountain. *Can Cath Rev* 11:33-35 Je 1993
Heaven on earth. *Can Cath Rev* 11:35-36 Jl-Ag 1993
Mercy and aid. *Can Cath Rev* 11:7-8 Mr 1993
Moral science. *Can Cath Rev* 11:32-33 O 1993

Hays, Edward.
Prayer made easy [adapted fr *Prayers for a planetary pilgrim*]. *St Anth* 100: 10-14 Mr 1993

Hays, Richard B.
Review of: *Walking between the times: Paul's moral reasoning* by Sampley, J Paul. In: *CBQ* 55:392-393 Ap 1993

Haywood, Christine Curtis.
It hurts so bad: parents grieve the death of their children. *St Anth* 101:42-45 Je 1993

Head, Thomas.
Review of: *Prophets in their own country: living saints and the making of sainthood in the later Middle Ages* by Kleinberg, Aviad M. In: *CHist* 79: 524-525 Jl 1993

Heagle, John. see Ferder, Fran, jt auth

Healey, Charles J.
Review of: *The Eucharistic mystery* by Power, David Noel. In: *RRel* 52:795-796 S-O 1993

Healey, Joseph G.
The assembly [exc fr *Liturgy: scripture and the assembly*]. *Liturgy* 10:69-70 Spr 1993

Healey, Michael J.
A covenant kept [condensed fr *Fordham* Wint 1993]. *CDgst* 57:89-93 Ag 1993

Healy, Charles J.
Review of: *The foundations of mysticism* by McGinn, Bernard John, 1937-. In: *America* 168:22-23 Ja 2-9 1993
Review of: *Unresting transformation: the theology and spirituality of Maude Petre* by Leonard, Ellen. In: *TheolStds* 54:199 Mr 1993

Healy, Jack.
In defense of the "Declaration". *HPR* 93:67-70 Jl 1993
The state, virtue, sex and chastity. *Linacre* 60:51-59 My 1993

Healy, Nicholas M.
Indirect methods in theology: Karl Rahner as an ad hoc apologist. *Thomist* 56:613-633 O 1992

Heaney, Robert P.
Does Catholic medical education have a future? [presentation given during 1992 100th birtday of Creighton University's Medical Schools]. *Health Prog* 74:67 Ja-F 1993

Heaney, Stephen J.
Abortion: a new generationof Catholic responses. Braintree, Massachusetts: The Pope John Center, 1992. x, 359p ISBN 0o-935372-35-0 LC 92-37020

Hearne, Brian.
Missio ad gentes. *AFER* 35:2-12 F 1993
New models of mission. *Furrow* 44:91-98 F 1993
Review of: *Faces of Jesus in Africa* by Schreiter, Robert J, ed. In: *Furrow* 44: 59 Ja 1993
Review of: *Transforming mission* by Bosch, David J. In: *Furrow* 44:60 Ja 1993

Heath, Angela.
Colorado: American Source Books, 1993. Colorado: American Source Books, 1993. 122p ISBN 0-9621333-9-6 LC 92-42895

Heath, Julia A, and Kiker, B F, 1937-.
Determinants of spells of poverty following divorce. *RSocEcon* 50:305-315 Fall 1992

Heath-Stubbs, John.
Review of: *The spiral staircase* by Johnson, Adam. In: *Tablet* 247:1134 S 4 1993

Hebblethwaite, B.
Review of: *Divine action* by Ward, Keith. In: *Heythrop* 34:100-101 Ja 1993

Hebblethwaite, Margaret, 1951-.
Divided we stand: "forward in faith" on the march. *Tablet* 247:597-598 My 8 1993
Hermits at the bottom of the garden. *Tablet* 247:782-783 Je 19 1993
Review of: *Director of women's organizations and groups—in churches and ecumenical bodies in Britain and Ireland* by Byrne, Lavinia, ed. In: *Tablet* 247:143 Ja 30 1993

Hebblethwaite, Margaret, 1951-. *(cont'd)*
Review of: *Discipleship of equals* by Fiorenza, Elisabeth Schüssler, 1938-. In: *Tablet* 247:1300-1301 O 9 1993
Review of: *Mother Church: what the experience of women is teaching her* by Cunneen, Sally. In: *Tablet* 247:1047 Ag 14 1993
Review of: *The women's Bible commentary* by Newsom, Carol A, and Ringe, Sharon H, eds. In: *Tablet* 247:725-726 Je 5 1993
Spiritual adventurers. *Tablet* 247:1066-1067 Ag 21 1993
Women in theology. *Tablet* 247:1115 Ag 28 1993

Hebblethwaite, Peter, 1930-.
African cardinal defends Rome synod site. *Nat Cath Rep* 29:11 Je 18 1993
Anglicans fleeing women priests will have to jump through hoops. *Nat Cath Rep* 29:13 My 7 1993
Anglicans seek new balance. *Nat Cath Rep* 29:12 S 17 1993
As Russians and Romans spat, sects surge. *Nat Cath Rep* 29:11 Ap 9 1993
Bishop-maker Baggio is dead [obit]. *Nat Cath Rep* 29:13 Ap 2 1993
The bishops' part. *Tablet* 247:609 My 15 1993
Catechism fails to convey pope's passion for peace. *Nat Cath Rep* 29:16 Ja 29 1993
Church of England accepts women priests—just. *Nat Cath Rep* 29:10 N 20 1992
Church's second millenium often contradicts the first [commentary *Veritas Splendor*]. *Nat Cath Rep* 29:15-17 O 15 1993
Veritatis Splendor (the Splendor of Truth), Encyclical Letter on moral issues (1993 10 05).
Did Vatican empower a Russian "crypto-Catholic"? *Nat Cath Rep* 29:10 Ap 9 1993
Discipline, not doctrine, is nub of pope's new encyclical. *Nat Cath Rep* 29:9 O 1 1993
Drama in Prague. *Tablet* 247:1210-1211 S 18 1993
Echoes of old showdown haunt new encyclical. *Nat Cath Rep* 29:13 Ag 27 1993
Encyclical insists intercourse is language of love (commentary: *Humanae Vitae*). *Nat Cath Rep* 29:15-16 Jl 16 1993
Episcopal papers speak a bit on economic justice. *Nat Cath Rep* 29:12 Ap 23 1993
Final report: "small but substantial changes". *Nat Cath Rep* 29:12 Ja 22 1993
For want of a miracle, Newman's cause is help up [por]. *Nat Cath Rep* 30:15 N 12 1993
In Assisi, religious leaders deplore cruelties. *Nat Cath Rep* 29:14 Ja 22 1993
Keeping sisters in their place at synod on religious. *Nat Cath Rep* 29:14 Jl 30 1993
Laying claim to Newman. *Tablet* 247:834 Je 26 1993
The limits of infallibility. *Tablet* 247:1036-1037 Ag 14 1993
Lorenzo's sister edits Catholic paper. *Nat Cath Rep* 29:17 F 26 1993
Murder in the cathedral. *Tablet* 247:713-714 Je 5 1993
Orthodox takes steps to influence Russia. *Nat Cath Rep* 29:14 O 15 1993
Pastors in a china shop. *Tablet* 247:1159-1160 S 11 1993
Paul VI and the women [excerpt fr *Paul VI, the first modern pope*]. *Tablet* 247:398-399 Mr 27 1993
Paul VI: the first modern Pope. New Jersey: Paulist Press, 1993. x, 749p ISBN 0-8091-0461-x LC 936475
Paul VI: the spirituality of a pope. *Priests & People* 7:110-113 Mr 1993
Polish church may sink government over abortion. *Nat Cath Rep* 29:16 Ja 15 1993
Pope gives interview, decries capitalism [por]. *Nat Cath Rep* 30:12 N 19 1993
Pope names officials for synod. *Nat Cath Rep* 29:15 Jl 30 1993
Pope offers olive branch to Islam. *Nat Cath Rep* 29:12 F 19 1993
Pope soldiers on, carries weight of seven decades. *Nat Cath Rep* 30:10-11 O 22 1993
Pope visits Baltics amid promise, perils. *Nat Cath Rep* 29:11-12 S 17 1993
Pope's visit confirms Albania's new status. *Nat Cath Rep* 29:13 My 7 1993
Pope, talking pluralism, lights path to polls. *Nat Cath Rep* 29:12 Je 18 1993
Postscript to a putsch. *Tablet* 247:510-511 Ap 24 1993
Prague hosts meeting of European bishops. *Nat Cath Rep* 29:8 O 1 1993
Putsch in Prague. *Tablet* 247:237-238 F 20 1993
Quoting the catechism. *Tablet* 247:71-72 Ja 16 1993
Ratzinger comments on changing papacy. *Nat Cath Rep* 29:16 F 26 1993
Review of: *The lovers* by West, Morris L. In: *Nat Cath Rep* 29:27 My 28 1993
Review of: *The thoughts of Pope John Paul II* by McDermott, John M, ed. In: *Tablet* 247:981-982 Jl 31 1993
Scandal in Rome has buffeted the church. *Nat Cath Rep* 29:16 Mr 26 1993
Secret ordinations kept Czech church alive. *Nat Cath Rep* 29:9-10 S 10 1993
Silvestrini's red hat in ring for nex pope [por]. *Nat Cath Rep* 30:11 N 19 1993
Sorry about that, Galileo, but it wasn't church's fault. *Nat Cath Rep* 29:21 N 13 1992
Timeless ethics. *Tablet* 247:1286-1288 O 9 1993
Veritatis Splendor, (the Splendor of Truth), Encyclical letter on moral issues, (1993-10-05). Commentary.
Vatican II diary. *Tablet* 247:750-751 Je 19 1993
The Vatican takes over European bishops. *Nat Cath Rep* 29:11 Mr 5 1993
Vatican's marked cards can give "dissenters" a raw deal. *Nat Cath Rep* 30:9 O 29 1993
Veritatis Splendor (the Splendor of Truth), encyclical letter on moral issues (1993 10 05) Commentary.
Westminster archbishop has good sense of Hume. *Nat Cath Rep* 29:17 Mr 19 1993
Will it breathe with two lungs? *Nat Cath Rep* 29:10 S 3 1993
World Youth Day tied to "culture of pilgrimage". *Nat Cath Rep* 29:12 Jl 2 1993

Heffern, Rich.
Our society is still giving mental illness a bum rap. *Nat Cath Rep* 29:8 Jl 2 1993

Heft, James L.
Can higher education foster moral development? *Origins* 22:557-565 Ja 28 1993

A taste for the other: the moral development of college students and young adults. *Living Light* 29:23-36 Spr 1993

Hegeman, Mary Theodore.
Review of: *"Old" is older than me: and other devotionals for the best years of your life* by Jensen, Maxine Dowd. In: *St Anth* 100:48-50 S 1993
Review of: *Prayers of the women mystics* by Chervin, Ronda De Sola, ed. In: *St Anth* 100:50-51 My 1993
Review of: *Scripture in the streets* by Padovano, Anthony T. In: *St Anth* 100:48-49 Ap 1993

Heggen, Carolyn Holderread, 1946-.
Sexual abuse in Christian homes and churches. Scottdale, Pennsylvania: Herald Press, 1993. 208p ISBN 0-83613-624-1 LC 92-32143

Hegy, Pierre M.
The church in the nineties: its legacy its future. Collegeville, Minnesota: The Liturgical Press, 1993. x, 323p ISBN 0-8146-2098-1 LC 92-45242
"The end of American Catholicism?"—another look. *America* 168:4-9 My 1 1993

Heher, Michael.
Future of pastors: woe or wonder? *Church* 9:32-35 Sum 1993

Hehir, J Bryan, 1940-.
The age of restraint. *Comm* 120:8-9 S 24 1993
Church brings rich resources to healthcare debate. *Health Prog* 74:51-52 Jl-Ag 1993
Clinton on the world stage: some clues to his perspective. *Comm* 120:5-7 Ja 29 1993
Clinton's foreign policy. *Comm* 120:7-8 N 19 1993
Health care for all: a Catholic perspective. *Comm* 120:7-9 My 7 1993
The memory and the hope. *Church* 9:16-20 Spr 1993
The "state" of "defense". *Comm* 120:9-10 Mr 26 1993

Heidkamp, Mary L, and Lund, James R.
A campaign, not a collection. *Church* 9:27-29 Aut 1993

Heidt, Edward R.
Review of: *Embracing the chaos: theological responses to AIDS* by Woodward, James, ed. In: *Can Cath Rev* 11:30-31 Ap 1993

Heil, John Paul.
Review of: *The prophetic gospel* by Hanson, Anthony Tyrrell. In: *CBQ* 54:780-781 O 1992

Heilbroner, Robert, 1919-.
Is a worldly philosophy still possible?: Adolph Lowe as analyst and visionary. *RSocEcon* 50:374-382 Wint 1992

Heimbach, Daniel R.
A Southern Baptist view. *Crisis* 11:23 O 1993

Heine, Heinrich, 1797-1856.
Children; Estinguished; Her family; Friends. *Spirit* 58:28-31 1993

Heinritz, Joann.
Review of: *The popular guide to the Mass* by Marrevee, William. In: *Mod Lit* 20:39 F 1993
Review of: *Trouble at the table: gathering the tribes for worship* by Doran, Carol, and Troeger, Thomas H. In: *Mod Lit* 20:36-37 S 1993
Review of: *The religious potential of the child* by Cavalletti, Sofia. In: *Mod Lit* 20:38 Ap 1993

Heinz, Andreas.
Im dienste der kirche und der erneuerung ihres gottesdienstes. *Notitiae* 28:586-599 S 1992

Heiser, W Charels.
Review of: *Exegetical dictionary of the New Testament, volume 3* by Balz, Horst, and Schneider, Gerhard, eds. In: *TheolDgst* 40:161 Sum 1993

Heiser, W Charles.
Review of: *"All that God had done with them"* by Maloney, Linda M. In: *TheolDgst* 39:371 Wint 1992
Review of: *"Il Gran Cardinale": Alessandro Farnese, patron of the arts* by Robertson, Clare. In: *TheolDgst* 40:84 Spr 1993
Review of: *"Not in heaven": coherence and complexity in biblical narrative* by Rosenblatt, Jason P, and Sitterson, Joseph C, Jr, eds. In: *TheolDgst* 39:376-377 Wint 1992
Review of: *"Some seed fell on good ground": the life of Edwin V O'Hara* by Dolan, Timothy Michael. In: *TheolDgst* 40:60 Spr 1993
Review of: *"Working the earth of the heart": the Messalian controversy in history, texts, and language to AD 431* by Stewart, Columba. In: *TheolDgst* 39:387 Wint 1992
Review of: *20th-century theology: God and the world in a transitional age* by Grenz, Stanley J, and Olson, Roger E. In: *TheolDgst* 40:65 Spr 1993
Review of: *A Baptist manual of polity and practice* by Maring, Norman Hill, and Hudson, Winthrop Still. In: *TheolDgst* 40:173 Sum 1993
Review of: *A bibliography on temples of the ancient Near East adn Mediterranean world arranged by subject and by author* by Parry, Donald W. In: *TheolDgst* 40:81 Spr 1993
Review of: *A biography of Msgr Benedict Joseph Flaget, 1763-1850* by Lemarie, Charles. In: *TheolDgst* 40:73 Spr 1993
Review of: *A bridge to dialogue: the story of Jewish-Christian relations* by Rousmaniere, John. In: *TheolDgst* 39:382 Wint 1992
Review of: *A brief reader on the virtues of the human heart* by Pieper, Josef. In: *TheolDgst* 39:379-380 Wint 1992
Review of: *A case for reason and faith* by Hellwig, Monika K, 1929-. In: *TheolDgst* 40:166-167 Sum 1993
Review of: *A Christian for all Christians: essays in honor of C S Lewis* by Walker, Andrew, and Patrick, James, eds. In: *TheolDgst* 40:57-58 Spr 1993
Review of: *A democratic Catholic Church* by Bianchi, Eugene C, and Ruether, Rosemary Radford, eds. In: *TheolDgst* 40:158 Sum 1993
Review of: *A dictionary of all religions and religious denominations: Jewish, heathen, Mahometan, Christian, ancient and modern* by Adams, Hannah, 1755-1831. In: *TheolDgst* 40:49 Spr 1993
Review of: *A dictionary of biblical tradition in English literature* by Jeffrey, David Lyle. In: *TheolDgst* 40:158-159 Sum 1993

Heiser, W Charles. *(cont'd)*

Review of: *A flock of shepherds* by Reese, Thomas Joseph, 1945-. In: *TheolDgst* 40:183 Sum 1993

Review of: *A history of Christianity in Asia, Vol I* by Moffett, Samuel Hugh. In: *TheolDgst* 40:77 Spr 1993

Review of: *A history of Christianity in the United States and Canada* by Noll, Mark A. In: *TheolDgst* 40:179 Sum 1993

Review of: *A history of the literature of Adam and Eve* by Stone, Michael Edward. In: *TheolDgst* 40:88-89 Spr 1993

Review of: *A hound of God: Pierre de la Palud and the fourteenth-century church* by Dunbabin, Jean. In: *TheolDgst* 39:359 Wint 1992

Review of: *A Muslim primer* by Zepp, Ira G, Jr. In: *TheolDgst* 40:94 Spr 1993

Review of: *A new handbook of Christian theology* by Musser, Donald W, and Price, Joseph L, eds. In: *TheolDgst* 40:78 Spr 1993

Review of: *A new worldly order: John Paul II and human freedom* by Weigel, George, ed. In: *TheolDgst* 39:376 Wint 1992

Review of: *A noble death: suicide and martyrdom among Christians and Jews in antiquity* by Droge, Arthur J, and Tabor, James D. In: *TheolDgst* 39:359 Wint 1992

Review of: *A popular dicitonary of Islam* by Netton, Ian Richard. In: *TheolDgst* 40:178 Sum 1993

Review of: *A Reinhold Niebuhr reader* by Niebuhr, Reinhold, 1892-1971. In: *TheolDgst* 40:179 Sum 1993

Review of: *A second look in the rearview mirror: further autobiographical reflections of a philosopher at large* by Adler, Mortimer Jerome. In: *TheolDgst* 40:49 Spr 1993

Review of: *A speechless child is the word God* by Mohler, James Aylward. In: *TheolDgst* 40:177 Sum 1993

Review of: *A study of Dōgen: his philosophy and religion* by Abe, Masao. In: *TheolDgst* 39:349 Wint 1992

Review of: *A study of Ignatius of Antioch in Syria and Asia* by Trevett, Christine. In: *TheolDgst* 40:90 Spr 1993

Review of: *A theological introduction to the New Testament* by Schweizer, Eduard. In: *TheolDgst* 40:186-187 Sum 1993

Review of: *A walk in the garden: biblical, iconographical and literary images of Eden* by Morris, Paul, and Sawyer, Deborah, eds. In: *TheolDgst* 40:91-92 Spr 1993

Review of: *Abba, Father, we long to see your face* by Galot, Jean. In: *TheolDgst* 40:163 Sum 1993

Review of: *Achaemenid imperial administration in Syria-Palestine and the missions of Ezra and Nehemiah* by Hoglund, Kenneth G. In: *TheolDgst* 40:167 Sum 1993

Review of: *Acts* by Polhill, John B. In: *TheolDgst* 39:380 Wint 1992

Review of: *African theology in its social context* by Bujo, Bénézet. In: *TheolDgst* 40:54 Spr 1993

Review of: *After Auschwitz* by Rubenstein, Richard L. In: *TheolDgst* 40:185 Sum 1993

Review of: *After Jesus: the triumph of Christianity.* In: *TheolDgst* 39:349 Wint 1992

Review of: *After nature's revolt: ecojustice and theology* by Hessel, Dieter T, ed. In: *TheolDgst* 40:49-50 Spr 1993

Review of: *After some years: reflections on the ministry of the priest* by Martini, Carlo Maria, Cardinal, 1926-. In: *TheolDgst* 39:372 Wint 1992

Review of: *After the thousand years* by Mealy, J Webb. In: *TheolDgst* 40:174-175 Sum 1993

Review of: *AIDS and the church: the second decade* by Shelp, Earl E, and Sunderland, Ronald H. In: *TheolDgst* 39:384 Wint 1992

Review of: *All things new: essays in honor of Roy A. Harrisville* by Hultgren, Arland J, et al, eds. In: *TheolDgst* 40:50 Spr 1993

Review of: *America against itself: moral vision and the public order* by Neuhaus, Richard John, 1936-. In: *TheolDgst* 40:78 Spr 1993

Review of: *America, religions and religion* by Albanese, Catherine L. In: *TheolDgst* 39:349 Wint 1992

Review of: *American Catholic arts and fictions* by Giles, Paul. In: *TheolDgst* 40:164 Sum 1993

Review of: *American religious and biblical spectaculars* by Forshey, Gerald Eugene. In: *TheolDgst* 40:162-163 Sum 1993

Review of: *An anthology of sacred texts by and about women* by Young, Serinity, ed. In: *TheolDgst* 40:149 Sum 1993

Review of: *An encyclopedia of religions in the United States: one hundred religious groups speak for themselves* by Williamson, William B, ed. In: *TheolDgst* 39:360 Wint 1992

Review of: *An introduction to Judaism: a textbook and reader* by Neusner, Jacob. In: *TheolDgst* 39:375-376 Wint 1992

Review of: *An introduction to New Testament textual criticism* by Vaganay, Léon. In: *TheolDgst* 39:391 Wint 1992

Review of: *Anabaptism revisited: essays on Anabaptist/Menonite studies in honor of C J Dyck* by Klaassen, Walter, ed. In: *TheolDgst* 39:349 Wint 1992

Review of: *Analytical key to the Old Testament, volume 2: Judges-2 Chronicles* by Owens, John Joseph. In: *TheolDgst* 40:180-181 Sum 1993

Review of: *Angelic monks and earthly men* by Milis, Ludo J R. In: *TheolDgst* 40:176 Sum 1993

Review of: *Anti-Christian polemic in early Islam: Abû 'Isâ-al Warrâq's "Against the Trinity"* by Warraq, Muhammad ibn Hârûn, ?-861?. In: *TheolDgst* 39:392 Wint 1992

Review of: *Antisemitism: the longest hatred* by Wistrich, Robert S. In: *TheolDgst* 40:93 Spr 1993

Review of: *Aquinas on human action* by McInerny, Ralph M. In: *TheolDgst* 40:173 Sum 1993

Review of: *Arabic Christianity in the monasteries of ninth-century Palestine* by Griffith, Sidney H. In: *TheolDgst* 40:165 Sum 1993

Review of: *Asbury Bible commentary* by Carpenter, Eugene E, and McCown, Wayne, eds. In: *TheolDgst* 40:150 Sum 1993

Review of: *Asian Christian spirituality: reclaiming traditions* by Fabella, Virginia, et al, eds. In: *TheolDgst* 39:350 Wint 1992

Review of: *Asking Benedict* by Kardong, Terrence G. In: *TheolDgst* 40:169 Sum 1993

Review of: *At home with God* by Lewis, Hedwig. In: *TheolDgst* 40:74 Spr 1993

Heiser, W Charles. *(cont'd)*

Review of: *Augustin Bea, the cardinal of unity* by Schmidt, Stjepan. In: *TheolDgst* 40:186 Sum 1993

Review of: *Augustine's De civitate Dei: an annotated a bibliography of modern criticism, 1960-1990* by Donnelly, Dorothy F, and Sherman, Mark A. In: *TheolDgst* 40:60-61 Spr 1993

Review of: *Balaam and his interpreters: a hermeneutical history of the Balaam traditions* by Greene, John T. In: *TheolDgst* 40:65 Spr 1993

Review of: *Beauty and revelation in the thought of Saint Augustine* by Harrison, Carol. In: *TheolDgst* 40:166 Sum 1993

Review of: *Becoming a catechist* by O'Malley, William J, 1931-. In: *TheolDgst* 40:180 Sum 1993

Review of: *Belief in God in our time: foundational theology, I* by Farrelly, M John. In: *TheolDgst* 39:361 Wint 1992

Review of: *Beliefs and holy places: a spiritual geography of the Pimería Alta* by Griffith, James S. In: *TheolDgst* 39:363 Wint 1992

Review of: *Belonging to God: a commentary on a brief statement of faith* by Placher, William Carl, and Willis-Watkins, David. In: *TheolDgst* 40:81 Spr 1993

Review of: *Beyond liberation theology* by Belli, Humberto, and Nash, Ronald H. In: *TheolDgst* 40:51-52 Spr 1993

Review of: *Bibliography of new religious movements in primal societies, v 6* by Turner, Harold W. In: *TheolDgst* 40:190 Sum 1993

Review of: *Bioethics yearbook, volume 1: 1988-1990* by Brody, Baruch A, ed. In: *TheolDgst* 39:352 Wint 1992

Review of: *Birth, suffering, and death: Catholic perspectives at the edges of life* by Wildes, Kevin William, ed. In: *TheolDgst* 40:52-53 Spr 1993

Review of: *Born before all time?* by Juschel, Karl-Josef. In: *TheolDgst* 40:171 Sum 1993

Review of: *Born from above: the anthropology of the Gospel of John* by Trumbower, Jeffrey A. In: *TheolDgst* 39:390 Wint 1992

Review of: *Born to new life* by Cyprian, Saint, ?-258. In: *TheolDgst* 40:158 Sum 1993

Review of: *Bultmann* by Ferguson, David. In: *TheolDgst* 40:80 Spr 1993

Review of: *But she said* by Fiorenza, Elisabeth Schüssler, 1938-. In: *TheolDgst* 40:86 Sum 1993

Review of: *By what law? the meaning of nómos in the letters of Paul* by Winger, Joseph Michael. In: *TheolDgst* 40:93 Spr 1993

Review of: *Cadbury, Knox, and Talbert: American contributions to the study of Acts* by Parsons, Mikeal C, and Tyson, Joseph B, eds. In: *TheolDgst* 40:55 Spr 1993

Review of: *CARA formation directory for men and women religious* by King, Eleace. In: *TheolDgst* 40:55-56 Spr 1993

Review of: *Care of the dying.* In: *TheolDgst* 40:154-155 Sum 1993

Review of: *Catalogue of English Bible translations* by Chamberlin, William J. In: *TheolDgst* 40:155-156 Sum 1993

Review of: *Catholic bishops in American politics* by Byrnes, Timothy A. In: *TheolDgst* 39:354 Wint 1992

Review of: *Catholic ministry to the addicted* by Barkley, Roy. In: *TheolDgst* 39:351 Wint 1992

Review of: *Catholic shrines and places of pilgrimage in the United States.* In: *TheolDgst* 40:155 Sum 1993

Review of: *Catholic social thought* by O'Brien, David J, 1938-, and Shannon, Thomas A, eds. In: *TheolDgst* 40:155 Sum 1993

Review of: *Celtic fire: the passionate religious vision of ancient Britain and IReland* by Weyer, Robert Van de, ed. In: *TheolDgst* 39:355 Wint 1992

Review of: *Challenging children to chastity* by Sattler, H Vernon. In: *TheolDgst* 40:85 Spr 1993

Review of: *Changing life patterns: adult development in spiritual direction* by Liebert, Elizabeth Ann. In: *TheolDgst* 39:369 Wint 1992

Review of: *Channels of healing prayer* by Heron, Benedict. In: *TheolDgst* 40:67-68 Spr 1993

Review of: *Charles Wesley, poet and theologian* by Kimbrough, S T, Jr, ed. In: *TheolDgst* 40:57 Spr 1993

Review of: *Christ spirit* by Deignan, Kathleen P. In: *TheolDgst* 40:158 Sum 1993

Review of: *Christ, our Mother of mercy: divine mercy and compassion in the theology of the Shewings of Julian of Norwich* by Palliser, Margaret Ann. In: *TheolDgst* 39:378-379 Wint 1992

Review of: *Christian discovery* by DiGiacomo, James J, and Walsh, John J. In: *TheolDgst* 40:159 Sum 1993

Review of: *Christian fantasy* by Manlove, Colin Nicholas. In: *TheolDgst* 40:173 Sum 1993

Review of: *Christian mission and interreligious dialogue* by Mojzes, Paul, and Swidler, Leonard, eds. In: *TheolDgst* 39:356 Wint 1992

Review of: *Christian perspectives on human development* by Aden, Leroy, et al, eds. In: *TheolDgst* 40:156 Sum 1993

Review of: *Church and age unite!* by Appleby, Raphael Scott. In: *TheolDgst* 40:50 Spr 1993

Review of: *Church and culture: German Catholic theology, 1860-1914* by O'Meara, Thomas Franklin. In: *TheolDgst* 39:377 Wint 1992

Review of: *Church and society: documents on the religious and social history of the Roman Catholic Archdiocese of Toronto* by Moir, John S, ed. In: *TheolDgst* 39:356 Wint 1992

Review of: *Church of churches* by Tillard, Jean Marie Roger, 1927-. In: *TheolDgst* 39:390 Wint 1992

Review of: *Churches and church membership in the United States 1990* by Bradley, Martin B, et al. In: *TheolDgst* 40:156-157 Sum 1993

Review of: *Cities and churches, and international bibliography* by Hartley, Loyde H. In: *TheolDgst* 40:67 Spr 1993

Review of: *Clement, of Alexandria, ca 150-ca 215: Stromateis: books one to three* by Ferguson, John. In: *TheolDgst* 39:356 Wint 1992

Review of: *Clergy ethics in a changing society: mapping the terrain* by Wind, James P, et al, eds. In: *TheolDgst* 39:356-357 Wint 1992

Review of: *Clothed with Christ: the example and teaching of Jesus in Romans 12.1-15.13* by Thompson, Michael B. In: *TheolDgst* 40:90 Spr 1993

Review of: *Codex Bezae: an early Christian manuscript and its text* by Parker, David C. In: *TheolDgst* 40:81 Spr 1993

Review of: *Codex Chimalpopoca.* In: *TheolDgst* 40:68 Spr 1993

Heiser, W Charles. *(cont'd)*

Review of: *Columbianism and the Knights of Columbus: a quincentenary history* by Kauffman, Christopher J. In: *TheolDgst* 40:70-71 Spr 1993

Review of: *Columbus and the ends of the earth: Europe's prophetic rhetoric as conquering ideology* by Kadir, Djelal. In: *TheolDgst* 39:367 Wint 1992

Review of: *Commentary on books 1-7* by Augustine, Saint, Bp of Hippo. In: *TheolDgst* 40:50 Spr 1993

Review of: *Commentary on books 8-13; indexes* by Augustine, Saint, Bp of Hippo. In: *TheolDgst* 40:50 Spr 1993

Review of: *Common journey, different paths: spiritual direction in a cross-cultural perspective* by Rakoczy, Susan, ed. In: *TheolDgst* 40:58 Spr 1993

Review of: *Communal reformation: the quest for salvation in sixteenth-century Germany* by Blickle, Peter. In: *TheolDgst* 40:53 Spr 1993

Review of: *Conciliar fellowship: a common goal* by Keshishian, Aram. In: *TheolDgst* 39:368 Wint 1992

Review of: *Concluding unscientific postscript to philosophical fragments, vol 1* by Kierkegaard, Soren Aabye, 1813-1855. In: *TheolDgst* 40:169-170 Sum 1993

Review of: *Confessions* by Augustine, Saint, Bp of Hippo. In: *TheolDgst* 40:50 Spr 1993

Review of: *Conscience first, tradition second: a study of young American Catholics* by McNamara, Patrick H. In: *TheolDgst* 39:370-371 Wint 1992

Review of: *Conscience, consensus, and the development of doctrine: revolutionary texts by John Henry Cardinal Newman* by Newman, John Henry, Cardinal, 1801-1890. In: *TheolDgst* 40:79 Spr 1993

Review of: *Contact with God: retreat conferences* by Mello, Anthony De. In: *TheolDgst* 39:358 Wint 1992

Review of: *Contemporary classics in philosophy of religion* by Loades, Ann, and Rue, Loyal D, eds. In: *TheolDgst* 39:357 Wint 1992

Review of: *Contemporary religions* by Harris, Ian, et al. In: *TheolDgst* 40:157 Sum 1993

Review of: *Contexts for Amos* by Carroll, Mark Daniel. In: *TheolDgst* 40:155 Sum 1993

Review of: *Conversion and text: the cases of Augustine of Hippo, Herman-Judah, and Constantine Tsatsos* by Morrison, Karl Frederick. In: *TheolDgst* 39:374 Wint 1992

Review of: *Cosmos and Theos* by Harris, Errol E, 1908-. In: *TheolDgst* 40:166 Sum 1993

Review of: *Cosmos, bios, theos* by Margenau, Henry, and Varghese, Roy Abraham, eds. In: *TheolDgst* 40:157 Sum 1993

Review of: *Countertraditions in the Bible* by Pardes, Ilana. In: *TheolDgst* 40:181 Sum 1993

Review of: *Cry of the urban poor* by Grigg, Viv. In: *TheolDgst* 40:65 Spr 1993

Review of: *Culture and control in counter-reformation Spain* by Cruz, Anne J, and Perry, Mary Elizabeth, eds. In: *TheolDgst* 39:357-358 Wint 1992

Review of: *Death in the midst of life* by Bregman, Lucy. In: *TheolDgst* 39:354 Wint 1992

Review of: *Defenders of the faith: inside ultra-Orthodox Jewry* by Heilman, Samuel. In: *TheolDgst* 39:365 Wint 1992

Review of: *Design in Puritan American literature* by Scheick, William J. In: *TheolDgst* 40:85 Spr 1993

Review of: *Dialogue on the path of initiation: an introduction to the life and thought of Karlfried Graf Dürckheim* by Goettmann, Alphonse. In: *TheolDgst* 39:359 Wint 1992

Review of: *Dictionary of modern theological German* by Ziefle, Helmut W. In: *TheolDgst* 40:193 Sum 1993

Review of: *Dietrich Bonhoeffer: a spoke in the wheel* by Wind, Renate. In: *TheolDgst* 40:93 Spr 1993

Review of: *Directory of religious organizations in the United States* by Melton, J Gordon. In: *TheolDgst* 40:76 Spr 1993

Review of: *Discovering God: life's adventure* by Scott, John M. In: *TheolDgst* 39:383 Wint 1992

Review of: *Disfiguring: art, architecture, religion* by Taylor, Mark C, 1945-. In: *TheolDgst* 39:389 Wint 1992

Review of: *Divine infinity in Greek and medieval thought* by Sweeney, Leo. In: *TheolDgst* 40:189 Sum 1993

Review of: *Divine violence: spectacle, psychosexuality, and radical Christianity in the Argentine "dirty war"* by Graziano, Frank. In: *TheolDgst* 40:64-65 Spr 1993

Review of: *Do justice: linking Christian faith and modern economic life* by Blank, Rebecca M. In: *TheolDgst* 40:53 Spr 1993

Review of: *Doing well and doing good* by Neuhaus, Richard John, 1936-. In: *TheolDgst* 40:178 Sum 1993

Review of: *Double belonging: interchurch families and Christian unity* by Kilcourse, George. In: *TheolDgst* 39:368 Wint 1992

Review of: *Early Chinese mysticism* by Kohn, Livia. In: *TheolDgst* 40:171 Sum 1993

Review of: *Early Christian baptism and the catechumenate* by Finn, Thomas Macy. In: *TheolDgst* 39:361-362 Wint 1992

Review of: *Early Christian baptism and the catechumenate* by Finn, Thomas Macy. In: *TheolDgst* 39:361-362 Wint 1992

Review of: *Early Christianity: origins and evolution to AD 600* by Hazlett, Ian, ed. In: *TheolDgst* 39:359-360 Wint 1992

Review of: *Eclipse of justice: ethics, economics, and the lost tradition of American Catholicism* by McCarthy, George E, and Rhodes, Royal W. In: *TheolDgst* 39:370 Wint 1992

Review of: *Ecumenism in transition* by Raiser, Konrad. In: *TheolDgst* 39:381 Wint 1992

Review of: *Egyptian light and Hebrew fire: theological and philosophical roots of Christendom in evolutionary perspective* by Luckert, Karl W. In: *TheolDgst* 39:369 Wint 1992

Review of: *Elijah and Elisha in socioliterary perspective* by Coote, Robert B. In: *TheolDgst* 39:360 Wint 1992

Review of: *Emotions and the Enneagram: working through your shadow life scrip* by Keyes, Margaret Frings. In: *TheolDgst* 40:70 Spr 1993

Review of: *Encyclopedia of American religions* by Melton, J Gordon. In: *TheolDgst* 40:175 Sum 1993

Review of: *Encyclopedic handbook of cults in America* by Melton, J Gordon. In: *TheolDgst* 39:372 Wint 1992

Heiser, W Charles. *(cont'd)*

Review of: *English hymns of the eighteenth century* by Arnold, Richard, ed. In: *TheolDgst* 40:160-161 Sum 1993

Review of: *Envisioning the new city: a reader on urban ministry* by Meyers, Eleanor Scott, ed. In: *TheolDgst* 40:61 Spr 1993

Review of: *Essays on world religions* by Smith, Huston. In: *TheolDgst* 40:87 Spr 1993

Review of: *Essential papers on messianic movements and personalities in Jewish history* by Saperstein, Marc, ed. In: *TheolDgst* 40:61-62 Spr 1993

Review of: *Eternal garden: mysticism, history, and politics at a South Asian Sufi center* by Ernst, Carl W. In: *TheolDgst* 40:61 Spr 1993

Review of: *Ethics and the Gulf War* by Vaux, Kenneth L. In: *TheolDgst* 40:191 Sum 1993

Review of: *Ethics in an aging society* by Moody, Harry R. In: *TheolDgst* 40:77 Spr 1993

Review of: *Ethnophilosophical and ethnolinguistic perspectives on the Huron Indian soul* by Pomedli, Michael M. In: *TheolDgst* 40:81-82 Spr 1993

Review of: *Eucharistic poetry: the search for presence in the writings of John donne, Gerard Manley Hopkins, Dylan Thomas, and Geoffrey Hill* by McNees, Eleanor J. In: *TheolDgst* 39:371 Wint 1992

Review of: *Evangelicalism in modern Britain: a history from the 1730s to the 1980s* by Bebbington, David William. In: *TheolDgst* 40:51 Spr 1993

Review of: *Exegesis and spiritual pedagogy in Maximus the Confessor: an investigation of the Quaestiones ad Thalassium* by Blowers, Paul M. In: *TheolDgst* 40:352-353 Wint 1992

Review of: *Experiencing ritual* by Turner, Edith. In: *TheolDgst* 40:190 Sum 1993

Review of: *Ezra-Nehemiah* by Throntveit, Mark A. In: *TheolDgst* 39:390 Wint 1992

Review of: *Faith and contents: volume one: selected essays and studies, 1952-1991* by Ong, Walter J. In: *TheolDgst* 39:378 Wint 1992

Review of: *Faith and contents: volume two: supplemental studies, 1946-1989* by Ong, Walter J. In: *TheolDgst* 39:378 Wint 1992

Review of: *Faith and philosophy in the writings of Paul Ricoeur* by Dornisch, Loretta. In: *TheolDgst* 39:359 Wint 1992

Review of: *Faith and the intifada: Palestinian Christian voices* by Ateek, Naim S, ed. In: *TheolDgst* 39:360-361 Wint 1992

Review of: *Faith and unbelief* by Arts, Herwig. In: *TheolDgst* 40:150 Sum 1993

Review of: *Faithful persuasion: in aid of a rhetoric of Christian theology* by Cunningham, David S. In: *TheolDgst* 40:59 Spr 1993

Review of: *Female piety in Puritan New England: the emergence of religious humanism* by Porterfield, Amanda. In: *TheolDgst* 39:380 Wint 1992

Review of: *Final writings* by Rahner, Karl, 1904-1984. In: *TheolDgst* 40:83 Spr 1993

Review of: *Flowing traces* by Sanford, James H, et al, eds. In: *TheolDgst* 40:162 Sum 1993

Review of: *Footwashing in John 13 and the Johannine community* by Thomas, John Christopher. In: *TheolDgst* 40:90 Spr 1993

Review of: *For all the peoples of Asia*. In: *TheolDgst* 40:162 Sum 1993

Review of: *For Christ and the university: the story of Intervarsity Christian Fellowship of the USA* by Hunt, Keith, and Hunt, Gladys. In: *TheolDgst* 39:365-366 Wint 1992

Review of: *Formative spirituality: volume five: traditional formation* by Kaam, Adrian L Van, 1920-. In: *TheolDgst* 40:91 Spr 1993

Review of: *Foundation guide for religious grant seekers* by Robinson, Kerry A. In: *TheolDgst* 39:362 Wint 1992

Review of: *Four anti-Pelagian writings* by Augustine, Saint, Bp of Hippo. In: *TheolDgst* 40:150 Sum 1993

Review of: *Four centuries of Jewish women's spirituality* by Umansky, Ellen M, and Ashton, Dianne, eds. In: *TheolDgst* 40:163 Sum 1993

Review of: *Free priests* by Powers, William F. In: *TheolDgst* 40:182 Sum 1993

Review of: *Freedom and its discontents: Catholicism confronts modernity* by Weigel, George. In: *TheolDgst* 40:92 Spr 1993

Review of: *Friends of God: virtues and gifts in Aquinas* by Wadell, Paul J. In: *TheolDgst* 39:392 Wint 1992

Review of: *From ash to fire* by Humphreys, Carolyn. In: *TheolDgst* 40:167-168 Sum 1993

Review of: *From counter-reformation to glorious revolution* by Trevor-Roper, Hugh. In: *TheolDgst* 40:189-190 Sum 1993

Review of: *From text to tradition* by Schiffman, Lawrence H. In: *TheolDgst* 39:383 Wint 1992

Review of: *Fundamentalism in comparative perspective* by Kaplan, Lawrence, ed. In: *TheolDgst* 39:362 Wint 1992

Review of: *Galatians* by Matera, Frank J. In: *TheolDgst* 40:185 Sum 1993

Review of: *Gay Catholics down under* by Rosser, B R Simon. In: *TheolDgst* 40:184 Sum 1993

Review of: *Generous lives* by Redmont, Jane. In: *TheolDgst* 40:183 Sum 1993

Review of: *Gentiles, Jews, Christians* by Conzelmann, Hans, 1915-1989. In: *TheolDgst* 40:59 Spr 1993

Review of: *George Fox and the Quakers* by Sharman, Cecil W. In: *TheolDgst* 39:384 Wint 1992

Review of: *Giordano Bruno and the embassy affair* by Bossy, John. In: *TheolDgst* 39:353 Wint 1992

Review of: *Giving Goliath his due* by Bierling, Neal. In: *TheolDgst* 40:152 Sum 1993

Review of: *Glad you asked: scriptural answers for our times* by Hampsch, John H. In: *TheolDgst* 39:363 Wint 1992

Review of: *God's beloved: Jesus' experience of the transcendent* by Cooke, Bernard J. In: *TheolDgst* 39:357 Wint 1992

Review of: *God's greatest gifts: commentaries on the commandments and the sacraments* by Thomas, Aquinas, Saint, 1225?-1274. In: *TheolDgst* 39:390 Wint 1992

Review of: *God's kingdom and the utopian error: discerning the biblical kingdom of God from its political conterfeits* by Beyerhaus, Peter P J. In: *TheolDgst* 40:52 Spr 1993

Review of: *God's warriors: the Christian right in twentieth-century America* by Wilcox, William Clyde. In: *TheolDgst* 39:393 Wint 1992

Review of: *God, harlem USA: the Father Divine story* by Watts, Jill. In: *TheolDgst* 39:392 Wint 1992

Heiser, W Charles. *(cont'd)*

Review of: *God, time and being* by Lafont, Gislain. In: *TheolDgst* 39:369 Wint 1992

Review of: *God—the world's future: systematic theology for a postmodern era* by Peters, Ted. In: *TheolDgst* 40:81 Spr 1993

Review of: *Goddesses and wise women: the literature of feminist spirituality, 1980-1992: an annotated bibliography* by Carson, Anne. In: *TheolDgst* 40: 56 Spr 1993

Review of: *Good things happen* by Westley, Richard John, 1928-. In: *TheolDgst* 40:92 Spr 1993

Review of: *Gospel of life: theology in the fourth gospel* by Beasley-Murray, George Raymond. In: *TheolDgst* 39:351 Wint 1992

Review of: *Gospel parallels* by Throckmorton, Burton H, Jr, ed. In: *TheolDgst* 40:152 Sum 1993

Review of: *Gospels and tradition* by Stein, Robert H. In: *TheolDgst* 39:387 Wint 1992

Review of: *Grace and disgrace* by Ormerod, Neil. In: *TheolDgst* 39:378 Wint 1992

Review of: *Grace and human freedom according to St Gregory of Nyssa* by Harrison, Verna E F. In: *TheolDgst* 40:67 Spr 1993

Review of: *Gustave Weigel, S.J., a pioneer of reform* by Collins, Patrick W, 1936-. In: *TheolDgst* 40:58 Spr 1993

Review of: *Habermas, modernity, and public theology* by Browning, Don S, and Fiorenza, Francis Schüssler, 1938-, eds. In: *TheolDgst* 40:66 Spr 1993

Review of: *Handbook of children's religious education* by Ratcliff, Donald E, ed. In: *TheolDgst* 40:66-67 Spr 1993

Review of: *Handbook of religious conversion* by Malony, H Newton, and Southard, Samuel, eds. In: *TheolDgst* 40:165 Sum 1993

Review of: *Hans Urs von Balthasar* by O'Donnell, John. In: *TheolDgst* 40:80 Spr 1993

Review of: *Harder than war* by McNeal, Patricia F. In: *TheolDgst* 39:371 Wint 1992

Review of: *Harmony among Christians* by Hastings, Brownlow C. In: *TheolDgst* 40:166 Sum 1993

Review of: *He is risen! a new reading of Mark's Gospel* by Humphrey, Hugh M. In: *TheolDgst* 40:69 Spr 1993

Review of: *Healing as a parish ministry: mending body, mind, and spirit* by Thomas, Leo, and Alkire, Jan. In: *TheolDgst* 39:390 Wint 1992

Review of: *Hell: the logic of damnation* by Walls, Jerry L. In: *TheolDgst* 40: 192 Sum 1993

Review of: *Historical directory of the Reformed Church in America, 1628-1992* by Gasero, Russell L. In: *TheolDgst* 40:63 Spr 1993

Review of: *Historical introduction, supplement, notes and index, vol 2* by Kierkegaard, Soren Aabye, 1813-1855. In: *TheolDgst* 40:169-170 Sum 1993

Review of: *History and mythology of the Aztecs: the Codex Chimalpopoca*. In: *TheolDgst* 40:68 Spr 1993

Review of: *History and the triune God: contributions to trinitarian theology* by Moltmann, Jürgen. In: *TheolDgst* 39:373-374 Wint 1992

Review of: *History of New Testament research; volume one: from deism to Tübingen* by Baird, William. In: *TheolDgst* 39:351 Wint 1992

Review of: *Holy ground: a study of the American camp meeting* by Brown, Kenneth O. In: *TheolDgst* 40:153 Sum 1993

Review of: *Hosea* by Davies, G I. In: *TheolDgst* 40:158 Sum 1993

Review of: *How did Christianity really begin? a historical-archaeological approach* by Teeple, Howard M. In: *TheolDgst* 39:389 Wint 1992

Review of: *How to pray always (without always praying)* by Fittipaldi, Silvio E. In: *TheolDgst* 40:62 Spr 1993

Review of: *How to read the church fathers* by Hamman, Adalbert. In: *TheolDgst* 40:165 Sum 1993

Review of: *How to rescue the earth without worshiping nature* by Campolo, Anthony. In: *TheolDgst* 40:154 Sum 1993

Review of: *Humanae Vitae: a generation later* by Smith, Janet E. In: *TheolDgst* 39:386 Wint 1992

Review of: *I suffer not a woman: rethinking 1 Timothy 2:11-15 in light of ancient evidence* by Kroeger, Richard Clark, and Kroeger, Catherine Clark. In: *TheolDgst* 40:72 Spr 1993

Review of: *I will follow you* by Pasquero, Fedele. In: *TheolDgst* 40:181 Sum 1993

Review of: *Idioms of the Greek New Testament* by Porter, Stanley E. In: *TheolDgst* 40:181-182 Sum 1993

Review of: *Idolatry* by Halbertal, Moshe, and Margalit, Avishai. In: *TheolDgst* 40:165 Sum 1993

Review of: *Ignatius Loyola: spiritual exercises* by Tetlow, Joseph Allen. In: *TheolDgst* 40:89-90 Spr 1993

Review of: *Ignatius of Loyola: the psychology of a saint* by Meissner, William W. In: *TheolDgst* 40:175 Sum 1993

Review of: *Images of afterlife* by MacGregor, Geddes. In: *TheolDgst* 40:173 Sum 1993

Review of: *Images of Judaism in Luke-Acts* by Tyson, Joseph B. In: *TheolDgst* 39:391 Wint 1992

Review of: *Images of sainthood in medieval Europe* by Blumenfeld-Kosinski, Renate, and Szell, Timea, eds. In: *TheolDgst* 40:168 Sum 1993

Review of: *Images of sanctity in Eddius Stephanus' Life of Bishop Wilfrid, an early English saint's life* by Foley, William Trent. In: *TheolDgst* 40:62 Spr 1993

Review of: *Imagination and authority: theological authorship int eh modern tradition* by Thiel, John E. In: *TheolDgst* 39:389-390 Wint 1992

Review of: *In the days of Paul* by Tambasco, Anthony J. In: *TheolDgst* 39: 388 Wint 1992

Review of: *In the footsteps of Muhammad: understanding the Islamic experience* by Renard, John. In: *TheolDgst* 39:381-382 Wint 1992

Review of: *In the footsteps of the mystics: a guide to the spiritual classics* by Simmons, Henry C. In: *TheolDgst* 39:385 Wint 1992

Review of: *In the shadow of history: Jews and conversos at the dawn of modernity* by Faur, José. In: *TheolDgst* 39:361 Wint 1992

Review of: *In the shadow of Moloch: the sacrifice of children and its impact on Western religions* by Bergmann, Martin S. In: *TheolDgst* 39:352 Wint 1992

Review of: *Insight: a study of human understanding* by Lonergan, Bernard J F, 1904-1984. In: *TheolDgst* 40:74-75 Spr 1993

Heiser, W Charles. *(cont'd)*

Review of: *Institutes of elenctic theology* by Turrettini, François, 1623-1687. In: *TheolDgst* 40:190 Sum 1993

Review of: *Integral formation of Catholic priests* by Maciel, Marcial. In: *TheolDgst* 40:75 Spr 1993

Review of: *Interpreting Hebrew poetry* by Petersen, David L, and Richards, Kent Harold. In: *TheolDgst* 40:181 Sum 1993

Review of: *Interpreting the sacred: ways of viewing religion* by Paden, William E. In: *TheolDgst* 39:378 Wint 1992

Review of: *Interpreting the sermon on the mount in the light of Jewish tradition as evidenced in the Palestinian targums of the Pentateuch* by Massey, Isabel Ann. In: *TheolDgst* 40:174 Sum 1993

Review of: *Intertwined worlds: medieval Islam and Bible criticism* by Lazarus-Yafeh, Hava. In: *TheolDgst* 40:72-73 Spr 1993

Review of: *Introducing Christian doctrine* by Erickson, Millard J. In: *TheolDgst* 40:160-161 Sum 1993

Review of: *Introduction to Jewish-Christian relations* by Shermis, Michael, and Zannoni, Arthur E, eds. In: *TheolDgst* 39:366 Wint 1992

Review of: *Introduction to the devout life* by Francis of Sales, Saint, 1567-1622. In: *TheolDgst* 40:163 Sum 1993

Review of: *Invitation to love* by Keating, Thomas. In: *TheolDgst* 40:169 Sum 1993

Review of: *Irony in Mark's Gospel* by Camery-Hoggatt, Jerry. In: *TheolDgst* 40:55 Spr 1993

Review of: *Is there a synopitc problem?* by Linnemann, Eta. In: *TheolDgst* 40:172 Sum 1993

Review of: *Isaac Hecker* by O'Brien, David J, 1938-. In: *TheolDgst* 40:180 Sum 1993

Review of: *Isaiah 1-12, a commentary* by Wildberger, Hans, 1910-1986. In: *TheolDgst* 39:393-394 Wint 1992

Review of: *Isaiah of Jerusalem: an introduction* by Doorly, William J. In: *TheolDgst* 40:61 Spr 1993

Review of: *Islam in a world of diverse faiths* by Cohn-Sherbok, Dan. In: *TheolDgst* 39:366-367 Wint 1992

Review of: *Islam* by Schimmel, Annemarie. In: *TheolDgst* 40:185 Sum 1993

Review of: *Islamic Da'wah in the West: Muslim missionary activity and the dynamics of conversion to Islam* by Poston, Larry. In: *TheolDgst* 40:82 Spr 1993

Review of: *Issues in a academic freedom* by Worgul, George S, Jr. In: *TheolDgst* 40:69 Spr 1993

Review of: *James and the Q sayings of Jesus* by Hartin, Patrick J. In: *TheolDgst* 40:69 Spr 1993

Review of: *Japanese religion and society: paradigms of structure and change* by Davis, Winston Bradley. In: *TheolDgst* 39:358 Wint 1992

Review of: *Jerome Nadal, SJ, 1507-1580* by Bangert, William V. In: *TheolDgst* 40:150-151 Sum 1993

Review of: *Jesuits in profile: alive and well in the US* by Boly, Craig, ed. In: *TheolDgst* 40:69 Spr 1993

Review of: *Jesus and the cosmos* by Edwards, Denis. In: *TheolDgst* 39:360 Wint 1992

Review of: *Jesus Christ for the modern world: the Christology of the Catholic Tübingen School* by McCready, Douglas. In: *TheolDgst* 39:370 Wint 1992

Review of: *Jesus in global contexts* by Pope-Levison, Priscilla, and Levison, John R. In: *TheolDgst* 40:181 Sum 1993

Review of: *Jesus weeps* by Recinos, Harold Joseph. In: *TheolDgst* 40:183 Sum 1993

Review of: *Jesus' call to discipleship* by Dunn, James D G. In: *TheolDgst* 40: 160 Sum 1993

Review of: *Jesus, Paul and the end of the world* by Witherington, Ben, III. In: *TheolDgst* 40:193 Sum 1993

Review of: *John among the gospels* by Smith, Dwight Moody. In: *TheolDgst* 39:385-386 Wint 1992

Review of: *John as storyteller* by Stibbe, Mark W G. In: *TheolDgst* 39:387 Wint 1992

Review of: *John Courtney Murray and the American civil conversation* by Hunt, Robert P, and Grasso, Kenneth L, eds. In: *TheolDgst* 40:69-70 Spr 1993

Review of: *John Oman and his doctrine of God* by Bevans, Stephen B. In: *TheolDgst* 40:52 Spr 1993

Review of: *John Paul II* by Bujak, Adam. In: *TheolDgst* 40:54 Spr 1993

Review of: *John the Baptizer and Prophet: a socio-historical study* by Webb, Robert L. In: *TheolDgst* 40:92 Spr 1993

Review of: *John: evangelist of the covenant people* by Pryor, John W. In: *TheolDgst* 40:182 Sum 1993

Review of: *Journey in the risen Christ: the "Little Mandate" of Catherine de Hueck Doherty* by Wild, Robert A. In: *TheolDgst* 39:393 Wint 1992

Review of: *Journey with the fathers, Year A* by Barnecut, Edith, ed. In: *TheolDgst* 40:169 Sum 1993

Review of: *Journey with the fathers, Year B* by Barnecut, Edith, ed. In: *TheolDgst* 40:169 Sum 1993

Review of: *Judaism from Cyrus to Hadrian: the Persian and Greek periods, v I* by Grabbe, Lester L. In: *TheolDgst* 40:64 Spr 1993

Review of: *Judaism from Cyrus to Hadrian: the Roman period, v II* by Grabbe, Lester L. In: *TheolDgst* 40:64 Spr 1993

Review of: *Judaism without Christianity* by Neusner, Jacob. In: *TheolDgst* 39:376 Wint 1992

Review of: *Judaism, human values, and the Jewish state* by Leibowtiz, Yeshayahu. In: *TheolDgst* 40:73 Spr 1993

Review of: *Judaism: practice and belief* by Sanders, E P. In: *TheolDgst* 39: 382-383 Wint 1992

Review of: *Judaism* by Küng, Hans, 1928-. In: *TheolDgst* 39:368 Wint 1992

Review of: *Julian's way: a practical commentary on Julian of Norwich* by Bradley, Ritamary. In: *TheolDgst* 40:53-54 Spr 1993

Review of: *Karl Rahner* by Dych, William V. In: *TheolDgst* 40:80 Spr 1993

Review of: *Kingdoms come: religion and politics in Brazil* by Ireland, Rowan. In: *TheolDgst* 39:366 Wint 1992

Review of: *Laws of heaven* by Gallagher, Michael Paul, 1939-. In: *TheolDgst* 40:63 Spr 1993

Review of: *Les approchjes empiriques en théologie: empirical approaches in theology*. In: *TheolDgst* 40:149-150 Sum 1993

Heiser, W Charles. (cont'd)

Review of: *Letters of Bede Jarrett* by Jarrett, Bede, 1881-1934. In: *TheolDgst* 39:367 Wint 1992

Review of: *Letters to contemplatives* by Johnston, William. In: *TheolDgst* 39:367 Wint 1992

Review of: *Liberalism, conservatism, and Catholicism* by Krason, Stephen M. In: *TheolDgst* 40:71-72 Spr 1993

Review of: *Liberation theologies: a research guide* by Musto, Ronald G. In: *TheolDgst* 40:78 Spr 1993

Review of: *Liberation theology* by Cadorette, Curt, et al, eds. In: *TheolDgst* 40:171-172 Sum 1993

Review of: *Life of the beloved* by Nouwen, Henri Josef Machiel, 1932-. In: *TheolDgst* 40:179-180 Sum 1993

Review of: *Life on the line* by Kilner, John F. In: *TheolDgst* 40:170 Sum 1993

Review of: *Living the Christian life: a guide to reformed spirituality* by Ramey, Robert Homer. In: *TheolDgst* 39:381 Wint 1992

Review of: *Logic, God and metaphysics* by Harris, James Franklin, ed. *TheolDgst* 40:74 Spr 1993

Review of: *Lonergan* by Crowe, Frederick E. In: *TheolDgst* 40:80 Spr 1993

Review of: *Lord, teach us to pray* by Boers, Arthur Paul. In: *TheolDgst* 40:152 Sum 1993

Review of: *Madonnas that maim: popular Catholicism in Italy since the fifteenth century* by Carroll, Michael P. In: *TheolDgst* 40:56 Spr 1993

Review of: *Magic, witchcraft, and paganism in America* by Melton, J Gordon, and Poggi, Isotta. In: *TheolDgst* 40:175 Sum 1993

Review of: *Major themes in the reformed tradition* by McKim, Donald K, ed. In: *TheolDgst* 39:371 Wint 1992

Review of: *Marcello Cervini and ecclesiastical government in Tridentine Italy* by Hudon, William V. In: *TheolDgst* 40:167 Sum 1993

Review of: *Mark and Luke in poststructuralist perspectives: Jesus begins to write* by Moore, Stephen D. In: *TheolDgst* 40:77 Spr 1993

Review of: *Marketing for churches and ministries* by Stevens, Robert E, and Loudon, David L. In: *TheolDgst* 40:188 Sum 1993

Review of: *Marquette University index* by Talmage, John Philip. In: *TheolDgst* 39:388 Wint 1992

Review of: *Mary in the mystery of the covenant* by Potterie, Ignace de la. In: *TheolDgst* 40:72 Spr 1993

Review of: *Mary, Mother* by Schug, John A. In: *TheolDgst* 40:86 Spr 1993

Review of: *Matters of life and death: calm answers to tough questions about abortion and euthanasia* by Beckwith, Francis J, and Geisler, Norman L. In: *TheolDgst* 39:351-352 Wint 1992

Review of: *Medieval Irish saints' lives* by Sharpe, Richard. In: *TheolDgst* 39:384 Wint 1992

Review of: *Memoir of Pierre Toussaint, born a slave in St Domingo* by Lee, Hannah Sawyer. In: *TheolDgst* 40:171 Sum 1993

Review of: *Menno Simons: a reappraisal* by Brunk, Gerald R, ed. In: *TheolDgst* 39:373 Wint 1992

Review of: *Mesopotamia: writing, reasoning, and the gods* by Bottéro, Jean. In: *TheolDgst* 40:53 Spr 1993

Review of: *Messianic ethics* by Wiebe, Ben. In: *TheolDgst* 40:193 Sum 1993

Review of: *Metaphor and composition in 1 Peter* by Martin, Troy W. In: *TheolDgst* 39:372 Wint 1992

Review of: *Militant and triumphant: William Henry O'Connell and the Catholic Church in Boston, 1859-1944* by O'Toole, James M, 1950-. In: *TheolDgst* 40:80 Spr 1993

Review of: *Ministry in the Church* by Bernier, Paul. In: *TheolDgst* 40:151 Sum 1993

Review of: *Miracles and the modern mind: a defense of biblical miracles* by Geisler, Norman L. In: *TheolDgst* 40:63 Spr 1993

Review of: *Models of adult religious education practice* by Wickett, R E Y. In: *TheolDgst* 39:393 Wint 1992

Review of: *Moral education and the liberal arts* by Mitias, Michael H, ed. In: *TheolDgst* 40:177 Sum 1993

Review of: *Morals for the heart: conversations of Shaykh Nizam ad-din Awliya recorded by Amir Hasan Sijzi* by Nizamuddin, Auliya, 1236-1325. In: *TheolDgst* 40:79 Spr 1993

Review of: *Mormon odyssey: the story of Ida Hunt Udall, plural wife* by Udall, Ida Hunt, 1858-1915. In: *TheolDgst* 40:90 Spr 1993

Review of: *Moving crucifixes in modern Spain* by Christian William A, Jr. In: *TheolDgst* 40:156 Sum 1993

Review of: *Muhammad, a biography of the prophet* by Armstrong, Karen. In: *TheolDgst* 39:350 Wint 1992

Review of: *Muslims in dialogue* by Swidler, Leonard. In: *TheolDgst* 40:178 Sum 1993

Review of: *My witness for the Church* by Häring, Bernard, 1912-. In: *TheolDgst* 39:364 Wint 1992

Review of: *Mystical prayer in ancient Judaism: an analysis of Ma'aseh Merkavah* by Swartz, Michael D. In: *TheolDgst* 39:388 Wint 1992

Review of: *Mysticism and language* by Katz, Steven T, ed. In: *TheolDgst* 40:178 Sum 1993

Review of: *Narrative asides in Luke-Acts* by Sheeley, Steven M. In: *TheolDgst* 40:187 Sum 1993

Review of: *Natural law and the theory of property: Grotius to Hume* by Buckle, Stephen. In: *TheolDgst* 39:354 Wint 1992

Review of: *Nelson's concordance of Bible phrases: a time-saving guide to some of the best-loved and most often used Bible phrases.* In: *TheolDgst* 39:375 Wint 1992

Review of: *New directions in mission and evangelization: basic statements 1974-1991* by Scherer, James A, and Bevans, Stephen B, eds. In: *TheolDgst* 40:78 Spr 1993

Review of: *New evangelization* by Boff, Leonardo. In: *TheolDgst* 39:353 Wint 1992

Review of: *New Testament Apocrypha* by Schneemelcher, Wilhelm, ed. In: *TheolDgst* 40:179 Sum 1993

Review of: *Newman and his age* by Gilley, Sheridan. In: *TheolDgst* 40:63-64 Spr 1993

Review of: *Newman: towards the second spring* by Ffinch, Michael. In: *TheolDgst* 39:361 Wint 1992

Review of: *Niebuhr and his age* by Brown, Charles Calvin. In: *TheolDgst* 40:153 Sum 1993

Heiser, W Charles. (cont'd)

Review of: *NKJV exhaustive concordance.* In: *TheolDgst* 40:179 Sum 1993

Review of: *No other gospel! Christianity among the world's religions* by Braaten, Carl E. In: *TheolDgst* 39:353 Wint 1992

Review of: *Old Testament women in western literature* by Frontain, Raymond-Jean, and Wojcik, Jan, eds. In: *TheolDgst* 39:377 Wint 1992

Review of: *Old Testament Yahweh texts in Paul's Christology* by Capes, David B. In: *TheolDgst* 39:355 Wint 1992

Review of: *On character building: the reader and the rhetoric of characterization in Luke-Acts* by Darr, John A. In: *TheolDgst* 40:60 Spr 1993

Review of: *Oneness Pentecostals and the Trinity* by Boyd, Gregory A. In: *TheolDgst* 40:53 Spr 1993

Review of: *Operation rescue: a challenge to the nation's conscience* by Lawler, Philip F. In: *TheolDgst* 40:72 Spr 1993

Review of: *Opus Dei* by Walsh, Michael J, 1937-. In: *TheolDgst* 40:192 Sum 1993

Review of: *Ordained to preach* by Miller, Charles E. In: *TheolDgst* 40:176 Sum 1993

Review of: *Origen and the life of the stars: a history of an idea* by Scott, Alan. In: *TheolDgst* 39:383 Wint 1992

Review of: *Out of every tribe and nation* by González, Justo L. In: *TheolDgst* 40:164 Sum 1993

Review of: *Parables in Midrash* by Stern, David. In: *TheolDgst* 40:187-188 Sum 1993

Review of: *Paradox lost* by Pahl, Jon. In: *TheolDgst* 40:80 Spr 1993

Review of: *Pastor, church and law* by Hammar, Richard R. In: *TheolDgst* 40:66 Spr 1993

Review of: *Pastoral care in the church* by Brister, C W. In: *TheolDgst* 39:354 Wint 1992

Review of: *Pastoral counseling* by Estadt, Barry K, et al, eds. In: *TheolDgst* 39:379 Wint 1992

Review of: *Paths to liberation: the mârga and its transformations in Buddhist thought* by Buswell, Robert E, Jr, and Gimello, Robert M, eds. In: *TheolDgst* 39:379 Wint 1992

Review of: *Paul on the mystery of Israel* by Harrington, Daniel J. In: *TheolDgst* 40:165-166 Sum 1993

Review of: *Paul struggles with his congregation: the pastoral message of the letters to the Corinthians* by Balthasar, Hans Urs Von, 1905-1988. In: *TheolDgst* 39:351 Wint 1992

Review of: *Person and religion* by Zdybicka, Zofia J. In: *TheolDgst* 40:193 Sum 1993

Review of: *Philosopher at large: an intellectual autobiography* by Adler, Mortimer Jerome. In: *TheolDgst* 40:49 Spr 1993

Review of: *Pierre Duhem: philosophy and history in the work of a believing physicist* by Martin, Russell Niall Dickson. In: *TheolDgst* 39:371 Wint 1992

Review of: *Piers Plowman and the problem of belief* by Harwood, Britton J. In: *TheolDgst* 40:67 Spr 1993

Review of: *Pilgrim's notebook* by Fleming, David A. In: *TheolDgst* 40:162 Sum 1993

Review of: *Pilgrimage in Ireland: the monuments and the people* by Harbison, Peter. In: *TheolDgst* 39:364 Wint 1992

Review of: *Pilgrimage of hope* by Braybrooke, Marcus. In: *TheolDgst* 39:353-354 Wint 1992

Review of: *Pilgrims' guide to America: US Catholic shrines and centers of devotion* by Moran, J Anthony. In: *TheolDgst* 39:374 Wint 1992

Review of: *Pillars of Paul's gospel* by O'Grady, John F. In: *TheolDgst* 40:180 Sum 1993

Review of: *Political writings* by Vitoria, Francisco de, 1486?-1546. In: *TheolDgst* 40:91 Spr 1993

Review of: *Popular voices in Latin American Catholicism* by Levine, Daniel H. In: *TheolDgst* 40:74 Spr 1993

Review of: *Power and persuasion in late antiquity* by Brown, Peter Robert Lamont. In: *TheolDgst* 40:153-154 Sum 1993

Review of: *Powers of darkness: principalities and powers in Paul's letters* by Arnold, Clinton E. In: *TheolDgst* 39:350 Wint 1992

Review of: *Practical discipleship* by Mueller, John J. In: *TheolDgst* 39:374 Wint 1992

Review of: *Praise disjoined: changing patterns of salvation in 17th-century English literature* by Shaw, William P, ed. In: *TheolDgst* 39:380 Wint 1992

Review of: *Prayer: finding the heart's true home* by Foster, Richard J. In: *TheolDgst* 40:163 Sum 1993

Review of: *Prayers of the women mystics* by Chervin, Ronda De Sola, ed. In: *TheolDgst* 40:57 Spr 1993

Review of: *Praying the Our Father today* by John, of Taizé. In: *TheolDgst* 40:70 Spr 1993

Review of: *Preachers of the Italian ghetto* by Ruderman, David B, ed. In: *TheolDgst* 40:182 Sum 1993

Review of: *Preaching through the Christian year: a comprehensive commentary on the Lectionary, Year A* by Craddock, Fred B, et al. In: *TheolDgst* 40:82 Spr 1993

Review of: *Preaching to strangers* by Willimon, William H, and Hauerwas, Stanley. In: *TheolDgst* 40:193 Sum 1993

Review of: *Preferential option* by Sherman, Amy L. In: *TheolDgst* 40:187 Sum 1993

Review of: *Priesthood today* by Rausch, Thomas P. In: *TheolDgst* 40:183 Sum 1993

Review of: *Processive revelation* by Reist, Benjamin A. In: *TheolDgst* 40:183-184 Sum 1993

Review of: *Professor Reinhold Niebuhr, a mentor to the Twentieth Century* by Stone, Ronald H. In: *TheolDgst* 40:188 Sum 1993

Review of: *Proleptic priests: priesthood in the Epistle to the Hebrews* by Scholer, John M. In: *TheolDgst* 40:86 Spr 1993

Review of: *Prologue to history* by Seters, John Van. In: *TheolDgst* 40:191 Sum 1993

Review of: *Prophet of our times* by Biffi, Franco. In: *TheolDgst* 40:152 Sum 1993

Review of: *Prophets in their own country: living saints and the making of sainthood in the later Middle Ages* by Kleinberg, Aviad M. In: *TheolDgst* 40:71 Spr 1993

Heiser, W Charles. *(cont'd)*

Review of: *Psychology of religion: classic and contemporary views* by Wulff, David M. In: *TheolDgst* 39:394 Wint 1992

Review of: *Psychology of religion: personalities, problems, possibilities* by Malony, H Newton, ed. In: *TheolDgst* 39:380-381 Wint 1992

Review of: *Quest for the absolute* by Matteo, Anthony M. In: *TheolDgst* 40:174 Sum 1993

Review of: *Reading John* by Talbert, Charles H. In: *TheolDgst* 40:89 Spr 1993

Review of: *Reading sacred texts through American eyes: biblical interpretation as cultural critique* by Mabee, Charles. In: *TheolDgst* 39:369-370 Wint 1992

Review of: *Readings in her story: women in Christian tradition* by MacHaffie, Barbara J. In: *TheolDgst* 40:75 Spr 1993

Review of: *Reclaiming the Jesus of history: christology today* by Eckardt, Arthur Roy. In: *TheolDgst* 39:360 Wint 1992

Review of: *Reconciliation* by Schreiter, Robert J. In: *TheolDgst* 40:186 Sum 1993

Review of: *Redating Matthew, Mark and Luke* by Wenham, John William. In: *TheolDgst* 39:393 Wint 1992

Review of: *Rediscovering New Testament prayer: boldness and blessing in the name of Jesus* by Koenig, John. In: *TheolDgst* 40:71 Spr 1993

Review of: *Rediscovering the sacred: perspectives on religion in contemporary society* by Wuthnow, Robert. In: *TheolDgst* 40:94 Spr 1993

Review of: *Reformed theology: a new paradigm for doing dogmatics* by Spykman, Gordon J. In: *TheolDgst* 39:386 Wint 1992

Review of: *Relaxation for Christians* by Maloney, H Newton. In: *TheolDgst* 40:75 Spr 1993

Review of: *Religion and personal autonomy: the third disestablishment in America* by Hammond, Phillip E. In: *TheolDgst* 40:66 Spr 1993

Review of: *Religion and sexuality in American literature* by Morey, Ann-Janine. In: *TheolDgst* 40:177-178 Sum 1993

Review of: *Religion and society in Russia: the sixteenth and seventeenth centuries* by Bushkovitch, Paul. In: *TheolDgst* 40:54-55 Spr 1993

Review of: *Religion and the family* by Burton, Laurel Arthur. In: *TheolDgst* 40:184 Sum 1993

Review of: *Religion in history: the word, the idea, and the reality = La religion dans l'histoire: le mot, l'idée, la réalité* by Despland, Michel, and Vallée, Gérard, eds. In: *TheolDgst* 40:83 Spr 1993

Review of: *Religion in society: a sociology of religion* by Johnstone, Ronald L. In: *TheolDgst* 40:70 Spr 1993

Review of: *Religion in the Andes: vision and imagination in early colonial Peru* by MacCormack, Sabine. In: *TheolDgst* 39:370 Wint 1992

Review of: *Religion, the independent sector, and American culture* by Cherry, Conrad, and Sherrill, Rowland A, eds. In: *TheolDgst* 39:381 Wint 1992

Review of: *Religions of South Africa* by Chidester, David. In: *TheolDgst* 39:356 Wint 1992

Review of: *Religious belief and emotional transformation* by Lauritzen, Paul. In: *TheolDgst* 40:171 Sum 1993

Review of: *Religious bodies in the United States: a directory* by Melton, J Gordon. In: *TheolDgst* 39:372-373 Wint 1992

Review of: *Religious holidays and calendars* by Kelly, Aidan, et al. In: *TheolDgst* 40:169 Sum 1993

Review of: *Religious information sources: a worldwide guide* by Melton, J Gordon, and Köszegi, Michael A. In: *TheolDgst* 39:373 Wint 1992

Review of: *Religious traditions of the world* by Earhart, H Byron, ed. In: *TheolDgst* 40:184 Sum 1993

Review of: *Remembering the poor: the history of Paul's collection for Jerusalem* by Georgi, Dieter. In: *TheolDgst* 40:63 Spr 1993

Review of: *Report on the Church: Catholicism after Vatican II* by McBrien, Richard P. In: *TheolDgst* 40:75 Spr 1993

Review of: *Responding to communalism: the task of religions and theology* by Arokiasamy, S, ed. In: *TheolDgst* 40:83-84 Spr 1993

Review of: *Responses to the signs of the times: selected documents: Catholic Bishops' Conference of the Philippines* by Josol, Abdon Ma C, ed. In: *TheolDgst* 39:382 Wint 1992

Review of: *Revealed histories: techniques for ancient Jewish and Christian historiography* by Hall, Robert G. In: *TheolDgst* 40:66 Spr 1993

Review of: *Revelation and redemption at Colossae* by Sappington, Thomas J. In: *TheolDgst* 40:85 Spr 1993

Review of: *Revelation* by Sinclair, Scott Gambrill. In: *TheolDgst* 40:187 Sum 1993

Review of: *Robert South (1634-1716)* by Reedy, Gerard. In: *TheolDgst* 40:83 Spr 1993

Review of: *Roget's thesaurus of the Bible* by Day, A Colin. In: *TheolDgst* 39:358 Wint 1992

Review of: *Rome and the Eastern Churches* by Nichols, Aidan. In: *TheolDgst* 39:376 Wint 1992

Review of: *Sacramental theology* by Vorgrimler, Herbert. In: *TheolDgst* 40:191-192 Sum 1993

Review of: *Sacred space* by Isaacs, Marie E. In: *TheolDgst* 40:168 Sum 1993

Review of: *Sacred violence: Paul's hermeneutic of the cross* by Hamerton-Kelly, Robert G. In: *TheolDgst* 39:363 Wint 1992

Review of: *Sainted women of the Dark Ages* by McNamara, Jo Ann, et al, eds. In: *TheolDgst* 40:85 Spr 1993

Review of: *Salt, leaven, and light* by Sanks, T Howland. In: *TheolDgst* 40:186 Sum 1993

Review of: *Salvation outside the church?* by Sullivan, Francis Aloysius. In: *TheolDgst* 40:188-189 Sum 1993

Review of: *Samnydsa Upanishads: Hindu scriptures on asceticism and renunciation.* In: *TheolDgst* 40:91 Spr 1993

Review of: *Satire and the Hebrew prophets* by Jemielity, Thomas. In: *TheolDgst* 40:168 Sum 1993

Review of: *Science, religion, and Mormon cosmology* by Paul, Erich Robert. In: *TheolDgst* 40:181 Sum 1993

Review of: *Search for the absent God* by Hill, William J, 1924-. In: *TheolDgst* 40:68 Spr 1993

Review of: *Secularizing the faith* by Marshall, David Brian. In: *TheolDgst* 40:173-174 Sum 1993

Heiser, W Charles. *(cont'd)*

Review of: *Self-definition and self-discovery in early Christianity: a study in changing horizons* by Hawkin, David J, and Robinson, Tom, eds. In: *TheolDgst* 40:87 Spr 1993

Review of: *Septuagint, scrolls and cognate writings* by Brooke, George J, and Lindars, Barnabas, eds. In: *TheolDgst* 39:383-384 Wint 1992

Review of: *Sex and the marriage covenant: a basis for morality* by Kippley, John F. In: *TheolDgst* 40:71 Spr 1993

Review of: *She who is* by Johnson, Elizabeth A, 1941-. In: *TheolDgst* 40:168-169 Sum 1993

Review of: *Shekhinah/Spirit* by Lodahl, Michael E. In: *TheolDgst* 40:172 Sum 1993

Review of: *Shepherding the flock of God: the pastoral theology of John Chrysostom* by Krupp, Robert A. In: *TheolDgst* 39:368 Wint 1992

Review of: *Silent lamp: the Thomas Merton story* by Shannon, William Henry, 1917-. In: *TheolDgst* 39:384 Wint 1992

Review of: *Sister Ignatia: angel of Alcoholics Anonymous* by Darrah, Mary C. In: *TheolDgst* 39:358 Wint 1992

Review of: *Sitting with Job: selected studies on the Book of Job* by Zuck, Roy B, ed. In: *TheolDgst* 39:385 Wint 1992

Review of: *Social justice: the teachings of Catholics, Protestants, Jews, and Muslims* by Horgan, James J, and Fuchs, Lucy, eds. In: *TheolDgst* 40:87-88 Spr 1993

Review of: *Society and spirit: a trinitarian cosmology* by Bracken, Joseph A. In: *TheolDgst* 39:393 Wint 1992

Review of: *Soldiers of Christ: preaching in late medieval and Reformation France* by Taylor, Larissa. In: *TheolDgst* 39:389 Wint 1992

Review of: *Soldiers of the virgin: the moral economy of a colonial Maya rebellion* by Gosner, Kevin. In: *TheolDgst* 40:64 Spr 1993

Review of: *Soul liberty: the Baptists' struggle in New England, 1630-1833* by McLoughlin, William Gerald. In: *TheolDgst* 39:370 Wint 1992

Review of: *Souls of the social order: the two-party system in American Protestantism* by Schmidt, Jean Miller. In: *TheolDgst* 40:85-86 Spr 1993

Review of: *Source book of self-discipline: a synthesis of Moralia in Job* by Peter, of Waltham, 1190-1196. In: *TheolDgst* 39:379 Wint 1992

Review of: *Spanish roots of America* by Arias, David, Bp, 1929-. In: *TheolDgst* 40:50 Spr 1993

Review of: *Spirit and beauty: an introduction to theological aesthetics* by Sherry, Patrick. In: *TheolDgst* 39:384-385 Wint 1992

Review of: *Spirit and nature: why the environment is a religious issue: an interfaith dialogue* by Rockefeller, Steven C, and Elder, John C. In: *TheolDgst* 40:88 Spr 1993

Review of: *Spiritual companions: introduction to the Christian classics* by Toon, Peter. In: *TheolDgst* 40:90 Spr 1993

Review of: *Spiritual direction and the encounter with God: a theological inquiry* by Barry, William A. In: *TheolDgst* 40:151 Sum 1993

Review of: *Spiritual space: the religious architecture of Pietro Belluschi* by Clausen, Meredith L. In: *TheolDgst* 40:58 Spr 1993

Review of: *Spirituality and history* by Sheldrake, Philip. In: *TheolDgst* 39:384 Wint 1992

Review of: *St John of the Cross* by Dombrowski, Daniel A. In: *TheolDgst* 39:358-359 Wint 1992

Review of: *Stewardship and the economy of God* by Reumann, John Henry Paul. In: *TheolDgst* 40:184 Sum 1993

Review of: *Struggles for solidarity* by Getz, Lorine M, and Costa, Ruy O, eds. In: *TheolDgst* 39:388 Wint 1992

Review of: *Studies in the Jewish background of Christianity* by Schwartz, Daniel R. In: *TheolDgst* 40:86 Spr 1993

Review of: *Studies in the theological ethics of Ernst Troeltsch* by Myers, Max A, and LaChat, Michael R, eds. In: *TheolDgst* 39:388 Wint 1992

Review of: *Surviving the sermon* by Schlafer, David J. In: *TheolDgst* 40:186 Sum 1993

Review of: *Testing the faith* by Gandolfo, Anita. In: *TheolDgst* 40:163-164 Sum 1993

Review of: *Text and concept in Leviticus 1:1-9* by Knierim, Rolf P. In: *TheolDgst* 40:170 Sum 1993

Review of: *Thérèse of Lisieux* by Theresa of Lisieux, Saint, 1873-1897. In: *TheolDgst* 40:189 Sum 1993

Review of: *That Jesus Christ was born a Jew* by Sonderegger, Katherine. In: *TheolDgst* 40:187 Sum 1993

Review of: *The absolute value of human action in the theology of Juan Luis Segundo* by Stefano, Frances. In: *TheolDgst* 39:387 Wint 1992

Review of: *The Acts of the apostles: vol 5* by Matera, Frank J. In: *TheolDgst* 40:185 Sum 1993

Review of: *The Alba House gospels: so you may believe.* In: *TheolDgst* 40:52 Spr 1993

Review of: *The Amarna letters* by Moran, William L, ed. In: *TheolDgst* 39:389 Wint 1992

Review of: *The American encounter with Buddhism, 1844-1912: Victorian culture and the limits of dissent* by Tweed, Thomas A. In: *TheolDgst* 39:390-391 Wint 1992

Review of: *The analyst and the mystic: psychoanalytic reflections on religion and mysticism* by Kakar, Sudhir. In: *TheolDgst* 40:70 Spr 1993

Review of: *The ancient wisdom of Origen* by Smith, John Clark. In: *TheolDgst* 40:187 Sum 1993

Review of: *The apocalyptic imagination in medieval literature* by Emmerson, Richard Kenneth, and Herzman, Ronald B. In: *TheolDgst* 40:160 Sum 1993

Review of: *The archaeology of the New Testament* by Finegan, Jack. In: *TheolDgst* 40:162 Sum 1993

Review of: *The art of spiritual guidance* by Gratton, Carolyn. In: *TheolDgst* 40:64 Spr 1993

Review of: *The awakened heart: living beyond addiction* by May, Gerald G. In: *TheolDgst* 39:372 Wint 1992

Review of: *The awakening church: 25 years of liturgical renewal* by Madden, Lawrence J, ed. In: *TheolDgst* 40:51 Spr 1993

Review of: *The beginning of the Gospel according to Saint John* by Mensch, James Richard. In: *TheolDgst* 40:175 Sum 1993

Review of: *The Bible and modern literary criticism: a critical assessment and annotated bibliography* by Powell, Mark Allan. In: *TheolDgst* 39:380 Wint 1992

Heiser, W Charles. *(cont'd)*

Review of: *The Bible in the Middle Ages* by Levy, Bernard S, ed. In: *TheolDgst* 40:151-152 Sum 1993

Review of: *The Bible, violence, and the sacred* by Williams, James G. In: *TheolDgst* 39:394 Wint 1992

Review of: *The Bible* by Prickett, Stephen, and Barnes, Robert. In: *TheolDgst* 40:82 Spr 1993

Review of: *The body divine: the symbol of the body in the works of Teilhard de Chardin and Râmânuja* by Hunt Overzee, Anne. In: *TheolDgst* 39:365 Wint 1992

Review of: *The books of contemplation: medieval Jewish mystical sources* by Verman, Mark. In: *TheolDgst* 39:391 Wint 1992

Review of: *The broken staff: Judaism through Christian eyes* by Manuel, Frank Edward. In: *TheolDgst* 40:75-76 Spr 1993

Review of: *The Byzantine empire* by Browning, Robert. In: *TheolDgst* 40:154 Sum 1993

Review of: *The camphor flame* by Fuller, Christopher John. In: *TheolDgst* 40:163 Sum 1993

Review of: *The Canaanites and their land* by Lemche, Niels Peter. In: *TheolDgst* 40:73-74 Spr 1993

Review of: *The Catholic Church and the politics of abortion: a view from the states* by Byrnes, Timothy A, and Segers, Mary C, eds. In: *TheolDgst* 39:355 Wint 1992

Review of: *The Catholic Church in Peru, 1821-1985* by Klaiber, Jeffrey L. In: *TheolDgst* 40:170 Sum 1993

Review of: *The Catholic vision* by O'Connor, Edward D. In: *TheolDgst* 39:377 Wint 1992

Review of: *The changing face of Jewish and Christian worship in North America* by Bradshaw, Paul F, and Hoffman, Lawrence A, eds. In: *TheolDgst* 39:355-356 Wint 1992

Review of: *The Chester mystery cycle* by Mills, David. In: *TheolDgst* 40:57 Spr 1993

Review of: *The Christian foundations of criminal responsibility: a philosophical study of legal reasoning* by Quinn, John F. In: *TheolDgst* 40:82-83 Spr 1993

Review of: *The Christian tradition beyond its European captivity* by Kitagawa, Joseph Mitsuo, 1915-1992. In: *TheolDgst* 40:170 Sum 1993

Review of: *The Church and politics in the Chilean countryside* by Stewart-Gambino, Hannah W. In: *TheolDgst* 40:88 Spr 1993

Review of: *The Church in Latin America, 1492-1992* by Dussel, Enrique, ed. In: *TheolDgst* 40:156 Sum 1993

Review of: *The Church, community of salvation* by Tavard, George Henry. In: *TheolDgst* 40:89 Spr 1993

Review of: *The churches of Rome* by Palladio, Andrea, 1508-1580. In: *TheolDgst* 40:80-81 Spr 1993

Review of: *The climax of the covenant: Christ and the law in Pauline theology* by Wright, Nicholas Thomas. In: *TheolDgst* 40:94 Spr 1993

Review of: *The complete works of Rather of Verona* by Ratherius, of Verona, 890?-974. In: *TheolDgst* 40:83 Spr 1993

Review of: *The counter-Reformation in the villages: religion and reform in the bishopric of Speyer, 1560-1720* by Forser, Marc R. In: *TheolDgst* 40:62 Spr 1993

Review of: *The death and resurrection of Jesus: a narrative-critical reading of Matthew 26-28* by Heil, John Paul. In: *TheolDgst* 39:365 Wint 1992

Review of: *The death of Herod* by Fenn, Richard K. In: *TheolDgst* 40:162 Sum 1993

Review of: *The development of early Christian pneumatology, with special reference to Luke-Acts* by Menzies, Robert Paul. In: *TheolDgst* 40:76 Spr 1993

Review of: *The dilemma of self-esteem* by McGrath, Alister E. In: *TheolDgst* 40:172-173 Sum 1993

Review of: *The diversity of religions* by DiNoia, J A. In: *TheolDgst* 40:60 Spr 1993

Review of: *The divine romance: Teresa of Avila's narrative theology* by Chorpenning, Joseph F. In: *TheolDgst* 40:57 Spr 1993

Review of: *The doctor and Christian marriage* by Dunn, H P. In: *TheolDgst* 40:160 Sum 1993

Review of: *The early Pentecostal revival* by Tyson, James L. In: *TheolDgst* 40:190 Sum 1993

Review of: *The Eastern Catholic Churches: an introduction to their worship and spirituality* by Roccasalvo, Joan L. In: *TheolDgst* 39:382 Wint 1992

Review of: *The Enneagram cats of Muir Beach* by Keyes, Margaret Frings. In: *TheolDgst* 40:71 Spr 1993

Review of: *The enneagram for youth* by Callahan, William J. In: *TheolDgst* 40:154 Sum 1993

Review of: *The Enneagram relationship workbook: a self and partnership assessment guide* by Keyes, Margaret Frings. In: *TheolDgst* 40:71 Spr 1993

Review of: *The ethics of St. Augustine* by Babcock, William S, ed. In: *TheolDgst* 40:62 Spr 1993

Review of: *The eucharist and the hunger of the world* by Hellwig, Monika K, 1929-. In: *TheolDgst* 40:166 Sum 1993

Review of: *The Eucharistic prayer of Addai and Mari* by Gelston, Anthony. In: *TheolDgst* 39:363 Wint 1992

Review of: *The expositor's Bible commentary with the new international version of the Holy Bible in twelve volumes, Deuteronomy-2 Samuel [v3]* by Gaebelein, Frank E, ed. In: *TheolDgst* 40:161 Sum 1993

Review of: *The eye of the storm* by Leech, Kenneth, 1939-. In: *TheolDgst* 40:73 Spr 1993

Review of: *The feminine face of the people of God* by Baril, Gilberte. In: *TheolDgst* 40:151 Sum 1993

Review of: *The feminist gospel: the movement to unite feminism with the church* by Kassian, Mary A. In: *TheolDgst* 39:367-368 Wint 1992

Review of: *The forms and orders of Western litgurgy from the tenth to the eighteenth century* by Harper, John. In: *TheolDgst* 39:364 Wint 1992

Review of: *The foundation and first decade of the National Catholic Welfare Council* by Slawson, Douglas J. In: *TheolDgst* 39:385 Wint 1992

Review of: *The frontiers of Catholicism* by Burnes, Gene. In: *TheolDgst* 40:154 Sum 1993

Review of: *The future of Early Christianity: essays in honor of Helmut Koester* by Pearson, Birger A, ed. In: *TheolDgst* 39:363 Wint 1992

Heiser, W Charles. *(cont'd)*

Review of: *The God of thinness: gluttony and other weighty matters* by Bringle, Mary Louise. In: *TheolDgst* 40:54 Spr 1993

Review of: *The Gospel according to Matthew* by Morris, Leon. In: *TheolDgst* 40:178 Sum 1993

Review of: *The Gospel of Thomas*. In: *TheolDgst* 40:164 Sum 1993

Review of: *The graced horizon* by Duffy, Stephen J. In: *TheolDgst* 40:159 Sum 1993

Review of: *The great angel: a study of Israel's second God* by Barker, Margaret. In: *TheolDgst* 40:151 Sum 1993

Review of: *The great ideas: a lexicon of Western thought* by Adler, Mortimer Jerome. In: *TheolDgst* 40:151 Sum 1993

Review of: *The great unknown* by Royo Marín, Antonio. In: *TheolDgst* 40:184-185 Sum 1993

Review of: *The harvest of humanism in Central Europe: essays in honor of Lewis W Spitz* by Fleischer, Manfred P, ed. In: *TheolDgst* 39:364-365 Wint 1992

Review of: *The heart of godly leadership* by Armerding, Hudson T. In: *TheolDgst* 40:150 Sum 1993

Review of: *The hidden life: hagiographic essays, meditations, spiritual texts* by Stein, Edith, 1891-1942. In: *TheolDgst* 40:88 Spr 1993

Review of: *The Holy Eucharist from the New Testament to Pope John Paul II* by Nichols, Aidan. In: *TheolDgst* 39:376 Wint 1992

Review of: *The hospitallers of Rhodes and their Mediterranean world* by Luttrell, Anthony. In: *TheolDgst* 40:172 Sum 1993

Review of: *The icon* by Quenot, Michel. In: *TheolDgst* 40:182-183 Sum 1993

Review of: *The immortality of the soul [De immortalitate animae]* by William, of Auvergne, Bp, ?-1249. In: *TheolDgst* 40:93 Spr 1993

Review of: *The impact of Christian missions on indigenous cultures: the "real people" and the unreal gospel* by Cox, James L. In: *TheolDgst* 40:59 Spr 1993

Review of: *The influence of religion on the development of international law* by Janis, Mark W, ed. In: *TheolDgst* 39:366 Wint 1992

Review of: *The Jesus of Christian history* by Goergen, Donald J. In: *TheolDgst* 40:64 Spr 1993

Review of: *The Jew in Christian theology* by Falk, Gerhard. In: *TheolDgst* 40:161-162 Sum 1993

Review of: *The Jews among Pagas and Christians in the Roman empire* by Lieu, Judith, et al, eds. In: *TheolDgst* 39:367 Wint 1992

Review of: *The Jews: a treasury of art and literature* by Keller, Sharon R. In: *TheolDgst* 40:69 Spr 1993

Review of: *The Johannine Epistles* by Schnackenburg, Rudolf. In: *TheolDgst* 40:186 Sum 1993

Review of: *The Joseph Campbell phenomenon: implications for the contemporary church* by Madden, Lawrence J, ed. In: *TheolDgst* 40:70 Spr 1993

Review of: *The labor of God, and Ignatian view of church and culture* by O'Brien, William J, ed. In: *TheolDgst* 39:368-369 Wint 1992

Review of: *The legend and cult of Upagupta* by Strong, John S. In: *TheolDgst* 40:188 Sum 1993

Review of: *The letters and instructions of Francis Xavier* by Xavier, Francis, St, 1506-1552. In: *TheolDgst* 39:362 Wint 1992

Review of: *The letters of Martin Buber: a life of dialogue* by Buber, Martin, 1878-1965. In: *TheolDgst* 40:54 Spr 1993

Review of: *The liberation of dogma* by Segundo, Juan Luis. In: *TheolDgst* 40:86-87 Spr 1993

Review of: *The little flowers of St Francis, a paraphrase* by Demaray, Donald E. In: *TheolDgst* 39:362 Wint 1992

Review of: *The liturgy of the world: Karl Rahner's theology of worship* by Skelley, Michael. In: *TheolDgst* 40:87 Spr 1993

Review of: *The living tradition of Catholic moral theology* by Curran, Charles E, 1934-. In: *TheolDgst* 40:157-158 Sum 1993

Review of: *The Lord's prayer* by Ayo, Nocholas. In: *TheolDgst* 40:51 Spr 1993

Review of: *The lordship of Christ: Ernst Käsemann's interpretation of Paul's theology* by Way, David. In: *TheolDgst* 39:393 Wint 1992

Review of: *The meaning of consecration today: a Marian model for a secularized age* by Laurentin, René. In: *TheolDgst* 40:72 Spr 1993

Review of: *The meaning of peace* by Yoder, Perry B, and Swartley, Willard M, eds. In: *TheolDgst* 40:76 Spr 1993

Review of: *The medieval Inquisition* by Shannon, Albert Clement. In: *TheolDgst* 40:87 Spr 1993

Review of: *The Midrash on proverbs* by Visotzky, Burton L. In: *TheolDgst* 39:373 Wint 1992

Review of: *The military orders: from the twelfth to the early fourteenth centuries* by Forey, Alan. In: *TheolDgst* 39:362 Wint 1992

Review of: *The minor prophets: an exegetical and expository commentary: volume 1: Hosea, Joel, and Amos* by McComiskey, Edward, ed. In: *TheolDgst* 40:76-77 Spr 1993

Review of: *The Mishnah* by Neusner, Jacob. In: *TheolDgst* 40:178-179 Sum 1993

Review of: *The modern encyclopedia of religions in Russia and the Soviet Union* by Steeves, Paul D, ed. In: *TheolDgst* 40:176-177 Sum 1993

Review of: *The monastery: a study in freedom, love, and community* by Hillery, George A. In: *TheolDgst* 40:68 Spr 1993

Review of: *The Mormon experience: a history of the Latter-day Saints* by Arrington, Leonard J, and Bitton, Davis. In: *TheolDgst* 40:50 Spr 1993

Review of: *The Muslims of America* by Haddad, Yvonne Yazbeck. In: *TheolDgst* 39:375 Wint 1992

Review of: *The mystic fable: v I: the sixteenth and seventeenth centuries* by Certeau, Michel de. In: *TheolDgst* 40:56 Spr 1993

Review of: *The new dictionary of Catholic spirituality* by Downey, Michael. In: *TheolDgst* 40:179 Sum 1993

Review of: *The Old Testament in early Christianity* by Ellis, Edward Earle. In: *TheolDgst* 40:160 Sum 1993

Review of: *The Old Testament [v 1]* by Tarazi, Paul Nadim. In: *TheolDgst* 40:189 Sum 1993

Review of: *The oldest vocation: Christian motherhood in the Middle Ages* by Atkinson, Clarissa W. In: *TheolDgst* 39:351 Wint 1992

Review of: *The one mediator, the saints, and Mary* by Anderson, H George, et al, eds. In: *TheolDgst* 40:180 Sum 1993

Heiser, W Charles. *(cont'd)*
Review of: *When time shall be no more* by Boyer, Paul S. In: *TheolDgst* 40: 153 Sum 1993
Review of: *Where is God when you need him?* by Schultz, Karl A. In: *TheolDgst* 39:383 Wint 1992
Review of: *Whispers of revelation: discovering the spirit of the poor* by Coleman, Bill, and Coleman, Patty. In: *TheolDgst* 40:58 Spr 1993
Review of: *Who's who in theology* by Bowden, John. In: *TheolDgst* 39:353 Wint 1992
Review of: *William Wake's Gallican Correspondence and related documents, vol 6* by Wake, William. In: *TheolDgst* 40:192 Sum 1993
Review of: *William Wake's Gallican Correspondence and related documents, vol 6* by Wake, William. In: *TheolDgst* 40:192 Sum 1993
Review of: *With staff and pen* by May, John Lawrence. In: *TheolDgst* 40:76 1993
Review of: *Witness* by Las Casas, Bartolome de, 1474-1566. In: *TheolDgst* 40:155 Sum 1993
Review of: *Women as interpreters of the Bible* by Demers, Patricia. In: *TheolDgst* 39:358 Wint 1992
Review of: *Word and light: seeing, hearing, and religious discourse* by Chidester, David. In: *TheolDgst* 40:57 Spr 1993
Review of: *World Council of Churches: signs of the spirit* by Kinnamon, Michael, ed. In: *TheolDgst* 40:93-94 Spr 1993
Review of: *World religion and human liberation* by Cohn-Sherbok, Dan, ed. In: *TheolDgst* 40:94 Spr 1993
Review of: *World religion: beliefs behind today's headlines: Buddhism, Christianity, Confucianism, Hinduism, Islam, Shintoism, Taoism* by Catoir, John T. In: *TheolDgst* 40:56 Spr 1993
Review of: *Worship* by Stevenson, Kenneth W. In: *TheolDgst* 40:188 Sum 1993
Review of: *Writings from ancient Israel* by Smelik, Klaas A D. In: *TheolDgst* 39:385 Wint 1992
Review of: *Writings on religion* by Hume, David, 1711-1776. In: *TheolDgst* 40:167 Sum 1993
Review of: *Zen Buddhism in the 20th century* by Dumoulin, Heinrich. In: *TheolDgst* 40:159 Sum 1993
Review of: *Zwingli* by Stephens, W Peter. In: *TheolDgst* 40:88 Spr 1993

Heisig, James W.
Meditation and prayer (2): sufficiency and satisfaction in Zen Buddhism: recovering an ancient symbolon. *Stud Form Spir* 14:57-74 F 1993

Heither, Theresia.
Origen's exegesis and Gn 24. *TheolDgst* 40:141-146 Sum 1993

Hejkal, Rita Redding.
We must not be silent. *OSV* 82:19 Ag 22 1993

Helgens, Sharon.
The perfect setting. *Liguorian* 81:60-66 D 1993

Heller, Chris.
An infant baptism program that works. *Tod Parish* 25:13-16 Ap-My 1993
Sponsors make the difference. *Tod Parish* 25:4+ N-D 1993

Hellwig, Monika K, 1929-.
Parishes shouldn't be parochial. *Salt* 13:13 N-D 1993
Review of: *The word and the Christ: an essay in analytic Christology* by Sturch, Richard. In: *TheolStds* 54:176-178 Mr 1993
What are the theologians saying now? Westminster: Christian Classics, 1993. x, 170p ISBN 0-87061-194-1

Helm, Paul.
Review of: *God, eternity and the nature of time* by Padgett, Alan G. In: *New Blckfrs* 74:287-288 My 1993

Hempel, Tricia.
Update on Somalia. *OSV* 81:3 F 21 1993

Hempton, David.
Review of: *Religion and revolution in early-industrial England: the Halévy Thesis and its critics* by Olsen, Gerald Wayne, ed. In: *CHist* 78:670-671 O 1992
Review of: *The Protestant evangelical awakening* by Ward, W. R. In: *Heythrop* 34:338-339 Jl 1993

Hemrick, Eugene F.
Cutting through multiculturalism. *Priest* 49:11-16 O 1993
The priesthood in the third millennium. *Priest* 49:22-24 Ag 1993
Strangers and aliens no longer, part one: the Hispanic presence in the church of the United States. Washington: United States Catholic Conference, 1993. 133p ISBN 1-55586-594-1
What challenges does the new evangelization hold? *Priest* 49:43-48 Ap 1993

Henderson, J Frank.
Learning from one another [exc fr *Liturgy: practicing ecumenism*]. *Liturgy* 10:8-9 Spr 1993

Henderson, Lawrence W.
The church in Angola: a river of many currents. Cleveland: The Pilgrim Press, 1992. x, 448p ISBN 0-8298-0938-4 LC 92-31494

Henderson, Leslie.
China's Catholicism with a twist twisting free? *Nat Cath Rep* 29:3 Jl 2 1993

Hendley, Steven.
Review of: *Modernity and its discontents* by Caputo, John D, et al. In: *IPQ* 33:130-131 Mr 1993

Hendricks, Kathleen.
Stay tuned!. *Tod Parish* 25:27-28 O 1993

Hendricks, Rick. *see* Kessell, John L, jt ed

Hendrickson, Dave.
The sublime quest of Jessica Powers [condensed fr *Wisconsin* Ap 11, 1993]. *CDgst* 57:50-56 Ag 1993

Hendrix, Kathleen.
Underground nuns [condensed fr *Los Angeles Times* S 21 1992]. *CDgst* 57: 121-124 F 1993

Henking, Susan.
Review of: *What women thought* by Lerner, Gerda. In: *America* 169:17-18 D 4 1993

Henn, W.
Review of: *Le primat de l'évêque de Rome* by Carrasco Rouco, Alfonso. In: *Gregorianum* 73 No 4:759-761 1992

Hennelly, Alfred T.
Review of: *The liberation of dogma* by Segundo, Juan Luis. In: *TheolStds* 54:181-182 Mr 1993

Hennesey, James.
Review of: *A history of Christianity in the United States and Canada* by Noll, Mark A. In: *ACHSR* 103:57-58 Aut 1992
Review of: *Spanish roots of America* by Arias, David, Bp, 1929-. In: *CHist* 79:355 Ap 1993

Hennessey, Lawrence R.
Sexuality, family, and the life of discipleship: some early Christian perspectives. *Chicago Stud* 32:19-31 Ap 1993

Hennessy, Anne.
Galilean perspectives on religious life. *RRel* 52:247-258 Mr-Ap 1993

Hennessy, Joan.
Cooperative learning: go for it!. *ReligTJ* 27:32-33 O 1993
How to care, share, and cooperate. *ReligTJ* 27:12-13 S 1993

Hennessy, Patrick.
Review of: *Theology and Canon Law* by Orsy, Ladislas M, 1921-. In: *Studies* 82:100-103 Spr 1993

Hennessy, Paul.
Founding charisms: past and present. *Origins* 23:169-173 Ag 12 1993

Henrici, Peter.
Le médiation philosophique des valeurs. *Gregorianum* 74 no 3:515-541 1993
see Ratzinger, Joseph, Cardinal, 1927-, jt ed

Henrie, Mark C.
Review of: *Multiculturalism and "the politics of recognition"* by Taylor, Charles, 1931-. In: *Crisis* 11:46-47 F 1993
Review of: *The politics of prudence* by Kirk, Russell, 1918-. In: *Crisis* 11:55-57 O 1993

Henriot, Peter F.
The social context of the AMECEA countries on the eve of the African Synod. *AFER* 34:340-363 D 1992

Henrix, Hans Hermann.
Dialog, nicht Proselytenmacherei. *Stimm Zeit* 211:679-690 O 1993

Henry, J.
Review of: *Science deified and science defied: the historical significance in Western culture, volume 2* by Olson, Richard. In: *Heythrop* 34:118-119 Ja 1993

Henry, Martin.
Beyond death. *Furrow* 43:678-680 D 1992

Henry, Patrick.
Review of: *To pray and to love: conversations on prayer with the early church* by Bondi, Roberta C. In: *Horizons (CTS)* 20:174-175 Spr 1993

Hensell, Eugene M.
Review of: *Colossians and Philemon* by Harris, Murray J. In: *CBQ* 54:783-784 O 1992
Review of: *Ein Gott, eine Offenbarung: Beiträge zur biblischen Exegese, Theologie, und Spiritualität* by Reiterer, Friedrich V, ed. In: *CBQ* 55:416-417 Ap 1993

Heren, Louis.
Review of: *J F K* by Cross, Robin. In: *Tablet* 246:1575-1576 D 12 1992
Review of: *Nixon* by Aitken, Jonathan. In: *Tablet* 247:212-213 F 13 1993
Review of: *Official and confidential: the secret life of J Edgar Hoover* by Summers, Anthony. In: *Tablet* 247:550-551 My 1 1993
Review of: *Ribbentrop* by Bloch, Michael. In: *Tablet* 247:48-49 Ja 9 1993

Heribert, Zingel. *see* Rüenauver, Hubert, jt auth

Herlong, Theophilus.
Easter: Christ crucified and raised. *Emmanuel* 99:134-137 Ap 1993

Hermans, Jo.
Un évangéliaire pour les célébrations avec enfants aux pays-bas et en flandre. *Notitiae* 28:682-683 O 1992

Hermes, Joan Garvey.
Five mothers who found time to be saints. *USCath* 58:28-33 My 1993
Reel winners: ten good movies that can make you better. *USCath* 58:6-14 O 1993
Twelve books every Catholic should read. *USCath* 58:14-23 Ja 1993

Hernán Errázuriz, Luis.
La necesidad humana del arte. *Teol Vida* 34 no 1-2:79-89 1993

Hernández, Ramón.
Francisco de Vitoria y Bartolomé de Las Casas. *Cien Tom* 119:433-457 S-D 1992
Review of: *Beato Francisco de Capillas: biografía* by Velasco, Salvador. In: *Cien Tom* 119:621 S-D 1992
Review of: *Diocesis de Calahorra y Santo Domingo* by Tellechea Idígoras, J Ignacio. In: *Cien Tom* 120:198-199 Ja-Ap 1993
Review of: *Dominicanos em Portugal: repertório do século XVI* by Rosário, Antonio do. In: *Cien Tom* 119:619 S-D 1992
Review of: *El arte de la Orden de Santo Domingo en la Galicia Medieval, 2 vols* by Manso Porto, Carmen. In: *Cien Tom* 119:426-427 My-Ag 1992
Review of: *Francisco Javier, su vida y su tiempo: India, 1547-1549, vol III* by Schurhammer, Georg. In: *Cien Tom* 120:197-198 Ja-Ap 1993
Review of: *Francisco Javier, su vida y su tiempo: India-Indonesia, 1541-1547, vol II* by Schurhammer, Georg. In: *Cien Tom* 120:197-198 Ja-Ap 1993
Review of: *Francisco Javier: su vida y su tiempo: Europa, 1506-1541, vol I* by Schurhammer, Georg. In: *Cien Tom* 120:197-198 Ja-Ap 1993
Review of: *Frandisco Javier, su vida y su tiempo: Japón-China, 1549-1552, vol IV* by Schurhammer, Georg. In: *Cien Tom* 120:197-198 Ja-Ap 1993

Hernández, Ramón. *(cont'd)*
Review of: *Historia del Carmelo Español, vol II: Provincias de Cataluña y Aragón y Valencia, 1563-1835* by Velasco Bayón, Balbino. In: *Cien Tom* 120:199-200 Ja-Ap 1993
Review of: *La institución matrimonial en la Hispania cristiana bajo medieval (1215-1563)* by Aznar, Federico R. In: *Cien Tom* 119:423 My-Ag 1992
Review of: *La reforma de la universidad de Salamanca a finales del siglo XVI: los estatutos de 1594* by Alejo Montes, Francisco Javier. In: *Cien Tom* 119:618 S-D 1992
Review of: *La Universidad en la América Hispánica* by Rodríguez Cruz, Agueda M. In: *Cien Tom* 120:196-197 Ja-Ap 1993
Review of: *Monumenta Catechetica Hispanoamericana (siglos XVI-XVIII)* by Guillermo Durán, Juan. In: *Cien Tom* 119:618-619 S-D 1992

Heron, Benedict.
Lessons from evangelicals. *Tablet* 247:674 My 29 1993
Review of: *Charismatic renewal: the search for a theology* by Smail, Tom, et al. In: *Tablet* 247:921-922 Jl 17 1993

Herr, Édouard.
Les rapports Nord-Sud après la chute du deuxième monde. *NRT* 114:837-851 N-D 1992

Herrera, Robert A.
Should the Catholic Church secede from the union? *F & R* 18:275-285 Aut 1992

Herring, C.
Review of: *Sharing the darkness: the spirituality of caring* by Cassidy, Sheila. In: *St Anth* 100:52-53 Ja 1993

Herron, Fred.
A mystical moment: spiritual direction and the adolescent. *RRel* 52:380-389 My-Je 1993

Herzman, Ronald B. *see* Emmerson, Richard Kenneth, jt auth

Hesburgh, T.
Review of: *The idea of the university: a reexamination* by Pelikan, Jaroslav. In: *CHist* 78:621-623 O 1992

Hesch, John B.
Orthopraxis in the sacramental initiation of unbaptized children of catechetical age: a canonical perspective. *Worship* 67:214-225 My 1993

Heschel, Abraham J.
On prayer: a private worship (2 parts). *SIDIC* 25 No 1: 2-6; 25 No 2: 15-17 1992

Hespel, Bertrand.
Review of: *Bell's theorem, quantum theory and conceptions of the universe* by Kakatos, Menás, ed. In: *RPhil Louvain* 91:522 Ag 1993
Review of: *Introduction to the philosophy of science* by O'Hear, Anthony. In: *RPhil Louvain* 91:520-521 Ag 1993
Review of: *Let Newton be!* by Fauvel, John, et al, eds. In: *RPhil Louvain* 91:474-475 Ag 1993
Review of: *Occult powers and hypotheses* by Clarke, Desmond M. In: *RPhil Louvain* 91:473-474 Ag 1993

Hess, Louise.
Review of: *Women who run with the wolves: myths and stories of the wild woman archetype* by Estés, Clarissa Pinkola. In: *St Anth* 101:51-52 O 1993

Heuser, Tom.
AIDS and hospitality. *Cath Work* 60:6 My 1993

Hewitt, Peter. *see* Ash, David, jt auth

Hewitt, Victor.
Comparisons from the North. *Studies* 82:24-34 Spr 1993

Hey, Michelle.
Assessment in action. *Health Prog* 74:54-57 Ja-F 1993
Misericordia Hospital. *Health Prog* 74:66-67 1993
Nursing's renaissance. *Health Prog* 74:26-32 O 1993

Heydt, Barbara von der.
Candles behind the wall: heroes of the peaceful revolution that shattered communism. Grand Rapids: Eerdmans, 1993. 224p ISBN 0-8028-3722-0

Heywood, John S.
Review of: *Structural changes in U.S. labor markets: causes and consequences* by Eberts, Randall W, and Groshen, Erica L, eds. In: *RSocEcon* 51:232-237 Sum 1993

Hibbert, Christopher. *see* Weinreb, Ben, jt ed

Hibbs, Thomas S.
MacIntyre's postmodern Thomism: reflections on Three rival versions of moral enquiry. *Thomist* 57:277-297 Ap 1993
Review of: *Three rival versions of moral enquiry* by MacIntyre, Alasdair, 1929-. In: *Thomist* 57:277-297 Ap 1993

Hiber, John W.
Review of: *Anger in the Old Testament* by Baloian, Bruce Edward. In: *OTA* 16:435-436 Je 1993

Hick, John.
Review of: *Dialogue with the other: the inter-religious dialogue* by Tracy, David. In: *JEcumen Stds* 29:280-281 Spr 1992

Hickey, Rita Marie.
The story of St Clare. *St Anth* 101:33 Ag 1993

Hickey, Tim S.
Fix your gaze [pilgrim icon]. *Columbia* 73:16-18 Ag 1993
New dimensions of service. *Columbia* 73:6-7 Jl 1993
Solidarity. *Columbia* 73:6-9 O 1993

Hicks, Douglas A.
The Taizé Community: fifty years of prayer and action. *JEcumen Stds* 29:202-214 Spr 1992

Hicks, Thomas H.
Mae: touched by sanctity's wing. *America* 169:6-7 O 30 1993

Higgins, George G, 1916-.
Review of: *Being Catholic: Commonweal* by Allen, Rodger Van. In: *Comm* 120:24-25 Jl 16 1993

Higgins, George G, 1916-, and Bole, William.
Organized labor and the Church: reflections of a "labor priest". New York: Paulist Press, 1993. x, 245p ISBN 0-8091-3374-1 LC 92-36139

Higgins, James J.
Cherishing the sacred. *Liguorian* 81:73 Jl 1993
The cross: our tree of life. *Liguorian* 81:73 Ap 1993
A divine instant replay. *Liguorian* 81:73 Je 1993
From matter to mind to meaning. *Liguorian* 81:73 Mr 1993
Happy the people God has made his own. *Liguorian* 81:73 Ja 1993
Light in a culture of violence. *Liguorian* 81:73 D 1993
One size does not fit all. *Liguorian* 81:73 My 1993
The Pope in Denver. *Liguorian* 81:73 Ag 1993
Review of: *1492 and all that* by Royal, Robert. In: *Liguorian* 81:68-69 My 1993
Review of: *Christmen: experience of priesthood today* by McGinnity, Gerard. In: *Liguorian* 81:69-70 Je 1993
Review of: *Daily readings in Catholic classics* by Myers, Rawley. In: *Liguorian* 81:70 S 1993
Review of: *Dangerous memories* by Lee, Bernard J, and Cowan, Michael A. In: *Liguorian* 81:68-69 Ap 1993
Review of: *Doing well and doing good* by Neuhaus, Richard John, 1936-. In: *Liguorian* 81:69-70 F 1993
Review of: *Everybody has a guardian angel* by Finley, Mitchel B. In: *Liguorian* 81:69 D 1993
Review of: *Faith experiences of Catholic converts* by Myers, Rawley. In: *Liguorian* 81:70 S 1993
Review of: *Father Scott reflections on women, family and relationships* by Scott, John M. In: *Liguorian* 81:69 D 1993
Review of: *Humanae Vitae: a generation later* by Smith, Janet E. In: *Liguorian* 81:68-69 Ja 1993
Review of: *I can pray with the saints* by Donze, Mary Terese, 1911-. In: *Liguorian* 81:70 Ja 1993
Review of: *Integral formation of Catholic priests* by Maciel, Marcial. In: *Liguorian* 81:69 Je 1993
Review of: *Martyr of brotherly love* by Balling, Adalbert Ludwig, and Abein, Reinhard. In: *Liguorian* 81:70 S 1993
Review of: *Modern fascism* by Veith, Gene Edward. In: *Liguorian* 81:69-70 O 1993
Review of: *More justice seekers, peace makers* by True, Michael, 1933-. In: *Liguorian* 81:69 F 1993
Review of: *My friend is dying* by Latela, Mary. In: *Liguorian* 81:68 D 1993
Review of: *Our Father, our Mother Mary and the faces of God* by Montague, George T. In: *Liguorian* 81:70 Ja 1993
Review of: *Parish alive* by McKnight, Felicia B. In: *Liguorian* 81:68 Ap 1993
Review of: *Parishes that excel* by Brennan, Patrick J. In: *Liguorian* 81:69 Ap 1993
Review of: *Priesthood today* by Rausch, Thomas P. In: *Liguorian* 81:69 Je 1993
Review of: *Quincentennial of evangelization: a time for reflection and action* by Herrera, Marina. In: *Liguorian* 81:69 My 1993
Review of: *Reading and praying the New Testament* by Kreeft, Peter John, 1937-. In: *Liguorian* 81:69 Jl 1993
Review of: *Responses to 101 questions on the Dead Sea Scrolls* by Fitzmyer, Joseph Augustine, 1920-. In: *Liguorian* 81:69-70 Jl 1993
Review of: *Salt, leaven and light* by Sanks, T Howland. In: *Liguorian* 81:69 Mr 1993
Review of: *Salvation outside the Church* by Sullivan, Francis Aloysius. In: *Liguorian* 81:68-69 Mr 1993
Review of: *Spanish roots of America* by Arias, David, Bp, 1929-. In: *Liguorian* 81:69 My 1993
Review of: *Starlight* by Shea, John B. In: *Liguorian* 81:40 Je 1993
Review of: *Teenage mothers: their experience, strength, and hope* by Beauchamp, Andre. In: *Liguorian* 81:69 D 1993
Review of: *The 17 Irish martyrs*. In: *Liguorian* 81:70 Mr 1993
Review of: *The Alba House gospels: so you may believe*. In: *Liguorian* 81:69 Jl 1993
Review of: *The awakening Church* by Madden, Lawrence J, ed. In: *Liguorian* 81:69-70 Mr 1993
Review of: *The beautiful gate rosary* by Gavlas, Kathleen. In: *Liguorian* 81:69 Ap 1993
Review of: *The black legends in Catholic Hispanic culture* by Caponnetto, Antonio. In: *Liguorian* 81:70 My 1993
Review of: *The Church emerging from Vatican II* by Doyle, Dennis M. In: *Liguorian* 81:70 My 1993
Review of: *The concentration can* by Lejeune, Jerome. In: *Liguorian* 81:70 O 1993
Review of: *The mystery of the incarnation* by Schönborn, Christoph von, Bp. In: *Liguorian* 81:70 Je 1993
Review of: *The mystery we proclaim: catechesis at the third millennium* by Kelly, Francis D. In: *Liguorian* 81:73 O 1993
Review of: *The people: reflections of native peoples on the Catholic experience in North America* by Hall, Suzanne E, ed. In: *Liguorian* 81:69 My 1993
Review of: *The road ultimately traveled* by Ranieri, Ralph. In: *Liguorian* 81:68 D 1993
Review of: *The ultimate church and promise of salvation* by Theisen, Jerome P. In: *Liguorian* 81:69 Mr 1993
Review of: *Toward my father's house: hope filled meditations for the terminally ill* by Mason, Mary Jane. In: *Liguorian* 81:68 D 1993
Review of: *Visiting the sick* by Normile, Patti. In: *Liguorian* 81:69 D 1993
Review of: *What are they saying about the ministerial priesthood?* by Donovan, Daniel L. In: *Liguorian* 81:68-69 Je 1993
Review of: *What Catholics really believe—setting the record straight* by Keating, Karl. In: *Liguorian* 81:70 S 1993
Review of: *What you should know about the Mass* by Altemose, Charlene. In: *Liguorian* 81:70 Jl 1993
Review of: *With staff and pen* by May, John Lawrence. In: *Liguorian* 81:70 F 1993
Speaking of family values. *Liguorian* 81:73 F 1993

Hoge, Dean.
Poll raises questions about future Catholic identity. *Nat Cath Rep* 29:26 O 8 1993

Hogg, Quinton McGarel, 1907-.
Review of: *Portraits and miniatures* by Jenkins, Roy. In: *Tablet* 247:982 Jl 31 1993

Höhn, Hans-Joachim.
Ethik in der Risikogesellschaft. *Stimm Zeit* 211:95-104 F 1993

Holden, Carol M. *see* Sweetser, Thomas P, jt auth

Hölderlin.
Three fragments of Pindar; Antigone, Act II; Oedipus at Colonus; Greece. *Spirit* 58:17-20 1993

Holladay, William L.
Review of: *The laments of Jeremiah and their contexts* by Smith, Mark S. In: *CBQ* 54:768-770 O 1992

Hollenbach, Paul W.
Review of: *The social world of Luke-Acts: models for interpretation* by Neyrey, Jerome H. In: *CBQ* 55:175-176 Ja 1993

Holleran, J Warren.
Review of: *John as storyteller* by Stibbe, Mark W G. In: *TheolStds* 54:194 Mr 1993

Holleran, Warren J.
Seeing the light a narrative reading of John 9 [part one]. *Eph Theol Lovan* 69:5-26 Ap 1993

Hollerich, M.
Review of: *Christianity and the rhetoric of empire: the development of Christian discourse* by Cameron, Averil. In: *TheolStds* 53:782 D 1992

Hollings, Michael.
Deepening our spiritual life. *Priests & People* 7:87-90 Mr 1993
Review of: *Daily readings with C.S. Lewis* by Hooper, Walter, ed. In: *Tablet* 247:1304 O 9 1993
Review of: *Finding your story: a Lent course* by Matthews, Melvyn. In: *Tablet* 247:278 F 27 1993
Review of: *Godspells* by Prickett, John. In: *Tablet* 247:1304 O 9 1993
Review of: *Lent with St Mark: forty days of prayer* by Garrard, Richard. In: *Tablet* 247:278 F 27 1993
Review of: *Light out of darkness* by O'Sullivan, Kathleen. In: *Tablet* 247:278 F 27 1993
Review of: *Oh God, why?: a journey through Lent for bruised pilgrims* by Hughes, Gerard W. In: *Tablet* 247:278 F 27 1993
Review of: *One minute nonsense* by Mello, Anthony De. In: *Tablet* 247:1303 O 9 1993
Review of: *Pray this way this Lent: daily reflections on the Our Father* by Powers, Isaias. In: *Tablet* 247:278 F 27 1993
Review of: *Preaching on the crucifixion* by Ford, Cleverley. In: *Tablet* 247:278 F 27 1993
Review of: *Progress through Lent: a course for pilgrims* by Bennet, George. In: *Tablet* 247:278 F 27 1993
Review of: *Reasons to hope: reflections on daily readings for Lent 1993* by Donders, Joseph G. In: *Tablet* 247:278 F 27 1993
Review of: *Scripture: guide for Lenten discussion* by Chenot, Dolores, and Petruzzi, Nancy. In: *Tablet* 247:278 F 27 1993
Review of: *Show me the way: readings for each day of Lent* by Nouwen, Henri Josef Machiel, 1932-. In: *Tablet* 247:278 F 27 1993
Review of: *Tested by the cross* by Carr, Wesley. In: *Tablet* 247:278 F 27 1993
Review of: *The Fount book of prayer* by Weyer, Robert Van de. In: *Tablet* 247:1303 O 9 1993
Review of: *The hidden word: your story in scripture* by Matthews, Melvyn. In: *Tablet* 247:278 F 27 1993
Review of: *The new scripture way of the cross: based on the Stations of the Cross led by Pope John Paul II* by Huebsch, Bill. In: *Tablet* 247:278 F 27 1993
Review of: *The voice from the cross: the seven words of Jesus* by Coggan, Donald. In: *Tablet* 247:278 F 27 1993
Review of: *Through the year with words of encouragement* by Cronin, Daniel P. In: *Tablet* 247:1303-1304 O 9 1993
Review of: *Words for life: forty meditations previously unpublished* by Farrar, Austin. In: *Tablet* 247:278 F 27 1993

Holm, Craig.
Managing to shift to ambulatory care. *Health Prog* 74:62 Jl-Ag 1993

Holman, Jean.
Review of: *Balduini de Forda opera* by Baldwin of Ford. In: *Cist Stud* 28:[30]-[31] 1993
Review of: *The mirror of charity* by Elred of Rievaulx. In: *Cist Stud* 28 no 2:[58]-[60] 1993

Holmes, Russell P.
Review of: *The fires of desire: erotic energies and the spiritual quest* by Halligan, Frederick R, and Shea, John J. In: *Spir Life* 39:53-54 Spr 1993

Holmes-White, Cecile.
Review of: *The black Bible chronicles* by McCary, P K. In: *Nat Cath Rep* 29:7 O 15 1993

Holton, Robert.
Catholic League gets a fighter at the helm. *OSV* 82:17 Jl 4 1993
Catholics look at Malcolm X. *OSV* 81:9 F 7 1993
Charting the future of Belize. *OSV* 82:5 My 23 1993
Child to child, reaching out to a world in need. *OSV* 82:5 S 19 1993
City of excitement and controversy. *OSV* 82:5 My 16 1993
A dangerous pattern. *OSV* 81:3 Mr 21 1993
Delays make Catechism unpublished best-seller. *OSV* 82:17 O 3 1993
Ecumenism in the wake of terrorism. *OSV* 81:21 Mr 28 1993
Eight hundred years of poverty and prayer [photos]. *OSV* 82:8-9 O 10 1993
The firm [directed by S Pollack]. *OSV* 81:8 Ap 18 1993
Funding our retired religious. *OSV* 81:17 Ja 10 1993
The gangsters of Greenville meet the brother of love [por]. *OSV* 82:6-7 N 21 1993
Is the sun going down on Fidel Castro's Cuba? *OSV* 82:17 O 17 1993
It's time for some Holy Name changes. *OSV* 82:13 S 26 1993

Holton, Robert. *(cont'd)*
The "magnificent obsession" of Bishop Donald Wuerl. *OSV* 81:10 Ja 3 1993
Robbing Peter, and Paul, too [Church Vandalism]. *OSV* 82:6 O 17 1993
To merge, or not to merge: that is the question. *OSV* 82:12-13 My 9 1993
Toward Christian reunity. *OSV* 81:6-7 Ja 24 1993
The wages of sin. *OSV* 82:10-11 O 24 1993
Where is the church's visibility? *OSV* 82:14 My 2 1993
Whose hand is that? *OSV* 81:12-13 Ap 4 1993

Hombert, P-M.
Review of: *Sapientia et Caritas* by Perler, Othmar. In: *MSR* 50:69 Ja-Mr 1993

Hommerding, Alan J.
A few questions from the Devil's Advocate. *Past Mus* 17:34-36 Ag-S 1993

Hommerding, Leroy.
Review of: *A promise of presence* by Downey, Michael. In: *Mod Lit* 20:39 Ap 1993
Review of: *Believing three ways in one God* by Lash, Nicholas. In: *Mod Lit* 20:42 N 1993
Review of: *Bodying forth: aesthetic liturgy* by Collins, Patrick W, 1936-. In: *Mod Lit* 20:37 My 1993
Review of: *Days of the Lord: the liturgical year, v 4: Ordinary Time, Year A.* In: *Mod Lit* 20:38 My 1993
Review of: *Deliver those in need.* In: *Mod Lit* 20:40 Ap 1993
Review of: *Discipling music ministry: twenty-first century directions* by Johanson, Calvin M. In: *Mod Lit* 20:41-42 Ag 1993
Review of: *Documents on the marriage liturgy* by Searle, Mark, 1941-1992, and Stevenson, Kenneth W. In: *Mod Lit* 20:39 Ap 1993
Review of: *Enriching the Christian year* by Perham, Michael V, et al. In: *Mod Lit* 20:42 Ag 1993
Review of: *Finding God wherever you are, selected spiritual writings* by Francis of Sales, Saint, 1567-1622. In: *Mod Lit* 20:41 Je-Jl 1993
Review of: *Helping skills for the nonprofessional counselor* by Moore, Joseph. In: *Mod Lit* 19:40-41 D 1992-Ja 1993
Review of: *Liturgical year: the worship of God; supplemental liturgical resource 7.* In: *Mod Lit* 20:38 My 1993
Review of: *More telling stories, compelling stories* by Bausch, William J. In: *Mod Lit* 20:39 O 1993
Review of: *Musica and liturgy: the Universa Laus document and commentary* by Duchesneau, Claude, and Veuthey, Michel. In: *Mod Lit* 20:37 My 1993
Review of: *Preaching about the Mass* by Huck, Gabe. In: *Mod Lit* 20:42 Mr 1993
Review of: *Reconciliation* by Schreiter, Robert J. In: *Mod Lit* 20:39-40 F 1993
Review of: *The Milwaukee Symposia for Church Composers: a ten-year report.* In: *Mod Lit* 20:40 S 1993
Review of: *The one mediator, the saints, and Mary* by Anderson, H George, et al, eds. In: *Mod Lit* 20:38 Je-Jl 1993
Review of: *Why, how and when to use prayerbook for engaged couples* by Fleming, Austin. In: *Mod Lit* 20:39 Ap 1993
Review of: *Wisdom of the Celtic saints* by Sellner, Edward Cletus. In: *Mod Lit* 20:40 Je-Jl 1993

Hong, Edna H. *see* Hong, Howard V, jt ed

Honner, John.
Review of: *Renaissance and reformation and the rise of science* by Nebelsick, Harold P. In: *Pacifica* 6:361-362 O 1993
Review of: *Systematic theology* by Fiorenza, Francis Schüssler, 1938-, and Galvin, John P, 1944-, eds. In: *Pacifica* 6:353-354 O 1993

Honoré, Jean, Abp.
Le catéchisme de l'Eglise Catholique. *NRT* 115:3-18 Ja-F 1993

Hooker, Morna D.
Review of: *Sacred space* by Isaacs, Marie E. In: *Heythrop* 34:309-310 Jl 1993

Hoonaert, Eduardo.
Review of: *Rosa Egipcíaca (uma santa Africana no Brasil)* by Mott, Luiz. In: *REB* 53:487-491 Je 1993

Hooper, Leon.
Review of: *John Courtney Murray and the American civil conversation* by Hunt, Robert P, and Grasso, Kenneth L, eds. In: *TheolStds* 54:184-186 Mr 1993

Hoose, Bernard.
Review of: *A morally deep world: an essay on moral significance and environmental ethics* by Johnson, Lawrence E. In: *Heythrop* 34:199-201 Ap 1993
Review of: *Anger, sex, doubt and death* by Holloway, Richard. In: *Way* 33:262 Jl 1993
Review of: *Ecology, economics, ethics: the broken circle* by Bormann, F Herbert, and Kellert, Stephen R, eds. In: *Heythrop* 34:199-201 Ap 1993
Review of: *Ethics in the sanctuary* by Battin, Margaret P. In: *Way* 33:261-262 Jl 1993
Review of: *Moral absolutes: tradition, revision and truth* by Finnis, John. In: *Heythrop* 34:463-464 O 1993
Review of: *New directions in moral theology* by Kelly, Kevin T. In: *Way* 33:261 Jl 1993
Review of: *The middle voice of ecological conscience: a chiasmic reading of responsibility in the neighbourhood of Levinas, Heidegger and others* by Llewelyn, John. In: *Heythrop* 34:199-201 Ap 1993
Review of: *Understanding war* by Gallie, W B. In: *Heythrop* 34:465-466 O 1993
Sin, power and the Church. *Month* 26:408-411 S-O 1993
Theological trends—sexual ethics: some recent developments. *Way* 33:54-62 Ja 1993

Hoover, Rose.
Unity and uniqueness: the perils of consistency. *Chicago Stud* 31:154-172 Ag 1992

Hooyman, Nancy W.
Does compassion include Euthanasia? *Health Prog* 74:44-47 Mr 1993
Review of: *Ethics in an aging society* by Moody, Harry R. In: *Health Prog* 74:85 Ap 1993

Hopkins, Diane Elizabeth. *see* Meyers, Albert, jt ed

Hopkins, Dwight N.
Shoes that fit our feet: sources for a constructive black theology. Maryknoll, New York: Orbis Books, 1993. x, 242p ISBN 0-88344-848-3 LC 92-38713

Hopkinson, Amanda.
Review of: *Guatemala* by Green, Duncan. In: *Tablet* 247:1045-1046 Ag 14 1993

Hoppe, Leslie J.
Biblical update: the aging process. *BibleT* 30:324-352 N 1992
The spiritual power of the elderly, C Burns. Aging according to wisdom literature, by R Bjornard. Lucan reflections on aging, C Jegen. Paul's theology of aging, by C Stockhausen. The strength of the elders, by H Perelmuter.
Don't bully people with the Bible. *USCath* 58:16-21 S 1993
Parables stories with double meanings. *St Anth* 101:22-27 O 1993
Review of: *A survey of the Old Testament* by Hill, Andrew E, and Walton, John H. In: *CBQ* 55:115-116 Ja 1993
Review of: *Miasto Boze w Psalmach* by Brzegowy, Tadeusz. In: *OTA* 16:175 F 1993
Review of: *Mysteries and revelations* by Collins, John J, and Charlesworth, James H, eds. In: *OTA* 15:470 O 1992
Review of: *The alien in Israelite law* by Houten, Christiana Van. In: *OTA* 16:186-187 F 1993
Review of: *The Biblical herem: a window on Israel's religious experience* by Stern, Philip D. In: *OTA* 16:188-189 F 1993
When institutions die. *BibleT* 31:213-218 Jl 1993 *see* Vawter, Bruce, jt auth

Hoppe, Leslie J, ed.
The Bible on sin. *BibleT* 31:68-93 Mr 1993
Sin, cleansing, and restoration, by J Craghan. The search for original sin, by C Stuhlmueller. Prophetic teaching on sin, by A Tambasco. Paralysis of the heart, by M McMahon. Sin and salvation in Romans, by M Getty.

Horan, Michael.
Review of: *Sharing faith* by Groome, Thomas H, 1945-. In: *CrossCurr* 43: 268-269 Sum 1993

Horgan, J.
Review of: *More kicks than pence: a life in Irish journalism* by O'Toole, Michael. In: *Doctr Life* 42:648-649 D 1992

Hornsby-Smith, Michael P, 1932-.
Catholic stocktaking. *Tablet* 247:164-165 F 6 1993
Towards 2000: the shape of the church. *Priests & People* 7:348-352 Ag-S 1993

Horowitz, Joel.
Review of: *The intervention of Argentina* by Shumway, Nicolas. In: *Cithara* 32:66-68 N 1992

Horrell, D.
Review of: *Covenant for a new creation: ethics, religion, and public policy* by Robb, Carol S, and Casebolt, Carl J, eds. In: *New Theol Rev* 6:104-104 F 1993

Houghton, William.
"Good riddance!" said grandma: love: the fruit of marriage, not the cause. *Comm* 120:21-22 Je 18 1993

Hourton Poisson, Jorge, Bp, 1926-.
Review of: *"The thought of Bartoleme de las Casas"* by Gutiérrez, Gustavo. In: *LADOC* 23:14-17 Jl-Ag 1993

Hove, Brian van.
Beyond the myth of the Inquisition: ours is "the golden age". *F & R* 28:335-358 Wint 1992
Oltre Il Mito Dell'Inquisizione I [2 parts]. *Civilta* 143:458-467 D 5; 578-588 D 19 1992

Hovenkotter, Maureen.
Shoulder to shoulder [Franciscan Enterprise]. *OSV* 81:16 F 21 1993

Hover, Margot.
Coming to terms with grief. *Tod Parish* 25:20 Ja 1993

Howard, Barbara, et al. *see* Bernier, Joan M, jt auth

Howard, Barbara.
Small Christian communities: what parish ministers need to know. *Tod Parish* 25:9-12 Ap-My 1993

Howard, Damian.
Review of: *Israel: the history of an idea* by Cohn-Sherbok, Dan. In: *Month* 25:495-496 D 1992
Review of: *The crucified Jew* by Cohn-Sherbok, Dan. In: *Month* 25:495-496 D 1992
Review of: *The final revolution* by Weigel, George. In: *Month* 26:194-195 My 1993

Howard, George S.
Impaled upon the horns of faith and reason. *America* 168:12-15 Mr 6 1993

Howard, Thomas.
Review of: *Journeybread for the shadowlands* by Jackson, Pamela E J. In: *New Oxford Rev* 60:31-32 N 1993

Howatch, Susan, 1940-.
A creative craft. *Tablet* 247:400-401 Mr 27 1993
A vision at Salisbury. *Tablet* 247:1007-1008 Ag 7 1993

Howe, Jean Marie.
Soulscape of a journey to spiritual being. *Word Sp* 15:1-11 1993

Howell, Maribeth.
Review of: *The Song of the Sea: Ex 15:1-21* by Brenner, Martin L. In: *OTA* 15:493-494 O 1992
Review of: *The Song of the Sea: Ex 15:1-21* by Brenner, Martin L. In: *CBQ* 55:103-105 Ja 1993

Howes, Robert G.
Dioceses abhor a vacuum, so offices multiply. *Nat Cath Rep* 29:22 Ja 15 1993

Hoyler, Geraldine M.
The ABCs of electronic data interchange. *Health Prog* 74:13 O 1993
Identifying charity care in financial statements. *Health Prog* 74:13-14 Ap 1993

Hoyt, Robert G.
Gays, lesbians and society. *Comm* 120:4-5 F 26 1993
Is it ideology? The agenda of real-life gays. *Comm* 120:4-5 My 21 1993

Hubbard, Howard, Bp.
What role for surrogate decision makers? *Origins* 22:576-579 F 4 1993

Hubbard, Robert L, Jr, et al, eds.
Studies in Old Testament theology: historical and contemporary images of God and God's people. Dallas: Word Publishing, 1992. 333p ISBN 0-8499-0865 LC 92-33070

Huck, Gabe.
Eucharist of the assembly. *Church* 9:7-11 Spr 1993 *see* Vance-Welsh, Mary C, jt auth

Huddleston, Mary Anne.
Almost empty: religious life as many seekers see it. *Sisters* 65:40-48 Ja 1993

Hudon, William V.
Review of: *Luther's earliest opponents: Catholic controversialists 1518-1525* by Bagchi, David V N. In: *TheolStds* 54:354-356 Je 1993

Hudson, Amanda.
Single and at home in the Catholic Church. *Liguorian* 81:33-35 Jl 1993

Hudson, Deal W.
Review of: *Human nature and eudaimonia in Aristotle* by Asselin, Dan. In: *IPQ* 33:128-130 Mr 1993
Review of: *Quest for the absolute* by Matteo, Anthony M. In: *TheolStds* 54: 168-169 Mr 1993

Hudson, Winthrop Still. *see* Maring, Norman Hill, jt auth

Huebsch, B.
Review of: *The Monday connnection: a spirituality of competence, affirmation, and support in the workplace* by Diehl, William, E. In: *New Theol Rev* 6:108-109 F 1993

Huel, Raymond.
Review of: *A snug little flock: the social origins of the Riel resistance of 1869-1870* by Pannekoek, Frits. In: *Can Cath Rev* 11:25 F 1993
Review of: *Canada's first nations: a history of founding peoples from earliest times* by Dickason, Olive Patricia. In: *Can Cath Rev* 11:22 S 1993

Huels, J.
Review of: *The monk's tale: a biography of Godfrey Diekmann, OSB* by Hughes, Kathleen. In: *Emmanuel* 98:179 Ap 1992

Huels, John M.
Review of: *Parish liturgy basics* by Belford, William. In: *New Theol Rev* 6: 118-119 Ag 1993
Review of: *Theology and canon law* by Orsy, Ladislas M, 1921-. In: *TheolStds* 54:203-204 Mr 1993
Women's role in Church law: past and present. *New Theol Rev* 6:19-31 My 1993

Huerga, Alvaro. *see* Murga, Vincente, jt auth

Huerre, Denis.
Monastic hospitality and the conversion of the monk. *ABenR* 44:249-257 S 1993

Hufgard, M Kilian.
Saint Bernard's third sermon for the feast of the Annunciation and a play from the N-town cycle. *Cist Stud* 28 no 2:167-178 1993

Huftier, M.
Review of: *L'Ecriture âme de la théologie* by Lafontaine, R, et al, eds. In: *MSR* 50:70 Ja-Mr 1993
Review of: *Le mystère de la liturgie* by Gozier, André. In: *MSR* 50:69-70 Ja-Mr 1993
Review of: *Les ambassadeurs du Christ* by Rolland, Philippe. In: *MSR* 50:70-71 Ja-Mr 1993

Huggett, Joyce, 1937-.
An oratory in motion. *Tablet* 247:303-304 Mr 6 1993
Review of: *Dance to the music of the spirit: the art of discernment* by Lonsdale, David. In: *Month* 26:147 Ap 1993

Hughes, Gerard J.
Review of: *Plato on the self-predication of forms* by Malcolm, John. In: *Heythrop* 34:216-217 Ap 1993
Review of: *Plato's Parmenides* by Meinwald, Constance C. In: *Heythrop* 34: 216-217 Ap 1993
Review of: *A history of God from Abraham to the present* by Armstrong, Karen. In: *Tablet* 247:890-891 Jl 10 1993
Review of: *Language, thought and falsehood in ancient Greek philosophy* by Denyer, Nicholas. In: *Heythrop* 34:323 Jl 1993
Review of: *Parmenides of Elea, fragments: a text and translation* by Gallop, David. In: *Heythrop* 34:323 Jl 1993

Hughes, Gerard W.
Review of: *Jesus* by Wilson, A N, 1950-. In: *Month* 26:30-31 Ja 1993
Review of: *The trial of the man who said he was God* by Harding, D E. In: *Month* 26:77 F 1993

Hughes, John Jay, 1928-.
Epistola ad fratrem Anglicanum. *Tablet* 247:715-716 Je 5 1993
A priesthood continued. *Tablet* 247:903 Jl 10 1993
Review of: *Anglicanism and the Christian Church* by Avis, Paul. In: *JEcumen Stds* 29:480 Sum-Aut 1992

Hughes, Kathleen.
Patterns for praying always. *Past Mus* 17:20-22 Je-Jl 1993
Review of: *A promise of presence* by Downey, Michael, and Fragomeni, Richard, eds. In: *Living Light* 29:93 Sum 1993

I

Iannace, F.
Review of: *Petrarch's genius: pentimento and prophesy* by Boyle, Marjory O'Rourke. In: *TheolStds* 53:784-785 D 1992

Idinopulos, Thomas.
Review of: *Holy city, holy places? Christian attitudes to Jerusalem and the Holy Land in the Fourth Century* by Walker, Peter W L. In: *JEcumen Stds* 29:487 Sum-Aut 1992

Idowu, Foluke.
Let go and live. *America* 169:20-21 Jl 3-10 1993

Ignatius, of Loyola, Saint, 1491-1556.
The autobiography of St. Ignatius Loyola. New York: Fordham University Press, 1992. x, 113p ISBN 0-8232-1480-x LC 92-32959

Iguíñiz Echeverraia.
Sobre las causas de la pobreza en América Latina y el Caribe. *Christus* 58: 32-37 N-D 1992

Iijima, Geneva Cobb.
Couples who pray together [condensed fr *Home Life* F 1993]. *CDgst* 57:64-66 Je 1993

Imbach, Jeffrey D.
Putting some soul into prayer. *Living Prayer* 26:3-6 Jl-Ag 1993

Imbelli, Robert P.
Book review [review article *She who is* by E Johnson]. *Church* 9:51-56 Aut 1993
Review of: *Are all Christians ministers?* by Collins, John N. In: *Comm* 120: 20+ Mr 12 1993
Review of: *Christology and spirituality* by Thompson, William M. In: *TheolStds* 53:776-778 D 1992
Review of: *God for us: the Trinity and Christian life* by LaCugna, Catherine Mowry. In: *Comm* 120:23-26 Ja 29 1993

Imerman, Vicky. see Bourgeois, Roy, jt auth

Impastato, Fara.
Review of: *The saints among us: how the spirituality committed are changing our world* by Gallup, George, Jr, and Jones, Timothy. In: *Sisters* 65:143 Mr 1993

Imperato, R.
Review of: *The Protest and the silence: suffering, death, and biblical theology* by Milazzo, G Tom. In: *New Theol Rev* 6:93-95 F 1993

Imperio, Vic N.
Dominion maximum. New York: Vantage Press, 1992. x, 139p ISBN 0-533-10077-1 LC 91-91242

Ingerflom, Claudio Sergio. see Boureau, Alain, jt ed

Ingham, M.
Review of: *The primacy of love* by Wadell, Paul J. In: *New Oxford Rev* 60:24 Ja-F 1993
Review of: *The priority of prudence: virtue and natural law in Thomas Aquinas and the implications for modern ethics* by Nelson, Daniel Mark. In: *New Oxford Rev* 60:24-26 Ja-F 1993

Inglis, Brian.
Review of: *The graced horizon* by Duffy, Stephen J. In: *Can Cath Rev* 11:21 S 1993

Ingram, Attraeta.
Review of: *The state and justice: an essay in political theory* by Fisk, Milton. In: *IJPS* 1:164-165 Mr 1993

Ingram, David.
Review of: *Habermas and the public sphere* by Calhoun, Craig, ed. In: *IPQ* 33:249-250 Je 1993

Ingram, Kristen Johnson.
Who killed Stutz Bearecat?: stories of finding faith after loss. San Jose: Resource Publications, 1993. 90p ISBN 0-89390-264-0 LC 93-23775

Ingrassia, V.
Review of: *New parish ministers: lay and religious on parish staffs* by Murnion, Philip J, 1938-, et al. In: *Momentum* 24:82-83 F-Mr 1993

Inkel, Maxine.
Celebrating African-American traditions. *Momentum* 24:71-72 N-D 1993
Lenten box projects. *ReligTJ* 27:19 Mr 1993
3 great ways to look forward. *ReligTJ* 27:56-57 S 1993

Inman, Anne.
This is the Lamb of God. *New Blckfrs* 74:191-197 Ap 1993

Innerarity, Daniel.
Hegel y el Romanticismo. Madrid: Tecnos, 1993. x, 212p ISBN 84-309-2331-4

Introvigne, Massimo.
Nel paese del punto esclamativo: *sette, culti, pseudo-religioni o nuove religioni? StudiaM* 41:1-26 1992

Iorio, Michele M.
The miraculous medal: a Marian apostolate-II. *ChrWorld* 38:74-77 Ja-F 1993

Irani, George Emile.
Review of: *The Arab Christian* by Cragg, Kenneth. In: *TheolStds* 54:378-379 Je 1993
Vatican forced to rethink Mideast policy. *Nat Cath Rep* 29:17 Mr 12 1993

Irarrázaval, Diego.
Procesos culturales y nuevas idenidades. *Christus* 58:15-19 My 1993

Irving, Diane Nutwell.
Scientific and philosophical expertise: an evaluation of the arguments on 'personhood'. *Linacre* 60:18-46 F 1993

Irwin, Joyce.
Review of: *In her own Rite: constructing feminist liturgical tradition* by Procter-Smith, Marjorie. In: *JEcumen Stds* 29:481-482 Sum-Aut 1992

Irwin, Joyce. (cont'd)
Review of: *In whose image? God and gender* by Clanton, Jann Aldredge. In: *JEcumen Stds* 29:481-482 Sum-Aut 1992
Review of: *Language for a Catholic: a program of study* by Groome, Thomas H, 1945-. In: *JEcumen Stds* 29:481-482 Sum-Aut 1992
Review of: *Mind your metaphors: a critique of language in the Bishops' pastoral letters on the role of women* by Aggeler, Maureen. In: *JEcumen Stds* 29:481-482 Sum-Aut 1992

Irwin, William H.
Review of: *Reading Isaiah* by Conrad, Edgar W. In: *CBQ* 55:329-330 Ap 1993

Isasi-Díaz, Ada María.
En la lucha-In the struggle: a Hispanic women's liberation theology. Minneapolis: Fortress, 1993. x, 226p ISBN 0-8006-2610-9 LC 93-9220

Isbell, Harold.
When the banks went off the rails. *Comm* 120:11-15 F 26 1993

Isnard, Clemente José Carlos.
Santo Domingo. *REB* 53:150-153 Mr 1993

Ives, Christopher. see Cobb, John B, Jr, jt ed

Iwanowski, Thomas B.
A way to evaluate, a way to plan. *Priest* 49:41-43 Mr 1993
Welcome to the table [sermon for a first communion Mass]. *ReligTJ* 26:16 Ja 1993

Izbicki, Thomas M.
Review of: *Il sacramento del potere: Il giuramento politico nella storia costituzionale dell'Occidente* by Prodi, Paolo. In: *CHist* 79:90-91 Ja 1993

J

Jabusch, Willard.
A Californian hermitage. *Tablet* 247:751-752 Je 1993
A neighbourhood in ruins. *Tablet* 247:1128 S 4 1993

Jackson, Pamela E J.
Journey for the shadowlands: the readings for the Rites of the Cat. Minnesota: The Liturgical Press, 1993. x, 171p ISBN 0-8146-2113-9

Jackson, Richard A.
Review of: *La royauté sacrée dans le monde Chrétien* by Boureau, Alain, and Ingerflom, Claudio Sergio, eds. In: *CHist* 79:498-499 Jl 1993

Jackson, Thomas M.
Review of: *Bailey's Café* by Naylor, Gloria. In: *America* 168:17-19 F 13 1993

Jacob, Philip.
What friends believe. *Furrow* 44:490-492 S 1993

Jacobs, H.
Review of: *De la Personne* by Stein, Edith, 1891-1942. In: *NRT* 115:277 Mr-Ap 1993
Review of: *Vocabulaire technique et critique de la philosophie* by Lalande, André. In: *NRT* 115:305 Mr-Ap 1993

Jacobs, Paul F.
Review of: *Recent archaeological discoveries and biblical research* by Dever, William G. In: *CBQ* 54:744-745 O 1992

Jacobs-Malina, D.
Beyond patriarchy: the images of family in Jesus. Mahwah: Paulist, 1993. x, 211p ISBN 0-8091-3421-7 LC 93-24501

Jacobson, Michael.
Now, here's a dollar source! [liquor]. *Register* 69:2 O 3 1993

Jacquet, Lou.
Between two worlds. *OSV* 82:8 Je 6 1993
Debating the fate of the diaconate. *OSV* 82:6 Je 13 1993
Finding growth through chronic pain. *OSV* 81:5 Ja 24 1993

Jacquette, Dale.
Chisholm on persons as entia successiva and the brain-microparticle hypothesis. *Mod Schlmn* 70:99-113 Ja 1993

Jaeger, David.
Bilateral talks to be productive [interview by L Pevtzow]. *Register* 69:1+ Ja 3 1993

Jaeger, Marietta Louise.
A mother's story of terror and forgiveness. *Liguorian* 81:14-18 Mr 1993

Jagdeo, Diane.
The river people. *Past Mus* 17:36-37 F-Mr 1993

Jahan, Emm. see Laurent, Ph, jt ed

Jaki, Stanley L.
Genesis 1: a cosmogenesis? *HPR* 93:28-32+ Ag-S 1993
The purpose of healing [address, 61st Annual Meeting of the National Federation of Catholic Physicians' Guilds O 1992]. *Linacre* 60:5-15 F 1993
The relationship between theology and science [interview by B Dodds]. *OSV* 81:8-9 F 14 1993

James, Lawrence.
Reflections and points for discussion: Mammon vs God. *Living Light* 29:38-39 Aut 1992

James, Liz.
Review of: *Visual polemics in the ninth-century Byzantine Psalters* by Corrigan, Kathleen. In: *CHist* 79:515-516 Jl 1993

James, S.
Review of: *Quakers and Baptists in colonial Massachusetts* by Pestana, Carla Gardina. In: *CHist* 78:679-680 O 1992

Jannesse, Alfred.
Ce qu'être malade veut dire. *Supplement* 184:21-32 Mr-Ap 1993

Janssens, Frederick.
La prise de conscience 'verte' et la question du pouvoir. *Lumen* 48:67-77 Mr 1993

John Paul II, Pope, 1920- (Karol Wojtyla) (elected 1978).
(cont'd)

John Paul II, Pope, spoke about Rome's ancient apostolic heritage and the catholicity and unity of the faith, while visiting the Church of Santa Suzanna at the Baths of Diocletian.

John Paul II, Pope (1993-10-10) Pedro Poveda. *OR(Eng)* 1311:1 O 13 1993
John Paul II, Pope, celebrated a Mass in St. Peter Square in which he beatified Pedro Poveda.

John Paul II, Pope, (1982-10-03) Litterae Apostolicae (Apostolic Letters) [Letters]. *AAS* 84:940-942 O 3 1992
Decree of beatification of Salvatore Lilli and his seven companions, martyrs.

John Paul II, Pope, (1983-01-25) Litterae Apostolicae (Apostolic Letters) [Latin]. *AAS* 84:828-830 S 8 1992
The beatification of the Trappist, Sister Maria Gabriella Sapheddu, is proclaimed by John Paul II, Pope.

John Paul II, Pope, (1984-04-14) Litterae Apostolicae (Apostolic Letters) [Latin]. *AAS* 84:830-832 S 8 1992
Decree of beatification of Pauline von Mallinckrodt, foundress of the Sisters of Christian Charity, is proclaimed by John Paul II, Pope.

John Paul II, Pope, (1985-08-15) Litterae Apostolicae (Apostolic Letters) [Latin]. *AAS* 84:1112-1115 D 5 1992
Beatification of Sister Anwarite Nengapeta, first martyr of Zaire raised to the honors of the Altar.

John Paul II, Pope, (1985-11-17) Litterae Apostolicae (Apostolic Letters) [Latin]. *AAS* 84:942-945 O 3 1992
Decree of beatification Rebecca Ar-Rayes by the Pope, John Paul II.

John Paul II, Pope, (1986-29-11) La Tierra Austral del Espiritu Santo y sus primeros pobladores. *Christus* 58:40-43 S 1993
Pope John Paul II spoke to the aborigines of Australia about the Holy Spirit and the first inhabitants of their country.

John Paul II, Pope, (1987-05-10) Litterae Apostolicae (Apostolic Letters) [Latin]. *AAS* 84:832-835 S 8 1992
Decree of beatification of Cardinal Andrea Ferrari by John Paul II, Pope.

John Paul II, Pope, (1988-09-03). *AAS* 84:1115-1117 D 5 1992
Apostolic letter placing Laura Vicuūna, Chilean, in the Catalog of the Blessed.

John Paul II, Pope, (1990-05-06) Litterae Apostolicae (Apostolic Letter for Beatification process) [Latin]. *AAS* 85:9-12 Ja 7 1993
John Paul II, Pope, gives written confirmation of the beatification of Blessed Jose Maria de Yermo y Parres.

John Paul II, Pope, (1990-06-18) Litterae Apostolicae (Apostolic Letters) [Latin]. *AAS* 84:835-838 S 8 1992
John Paul II, Pope, proclaims the beatification of Sister Elisabetta Renzi, foundress of the Sisters of Our Lady of Sorrows.

John Paul II, Pope, (1991-01-10) In perfect harmony with and filial submission to the bishops and the Pope. *Con Life* 17 no 2:1-4 1992
Pope John Paul II addressed a group of Superiors Genreal dealing with problems of the consecrated life in Latin America, January 10, 1991.

John Paul II, Pope, (1991-02-02) The witness and fertility of consecrated life. *Con Life* 17 no 2:5-7 1992
Pope John Paul II gave this discourse to men and women religious on the Feast of Presentation of Jesus at the Basilica of St Peter, February 2, 1991.

John Paul II, Pope, (1991-03-30) Constitutio Apostolica (Apostolic Constitution) [Latin]. *AAS* 84:937-938 O 3 1992
John Paul II, Pope, has set up a dew diocese in Guwahati, India.

John Paul II, Pope, (1991-04-22) Live your consecration in an exemplary and austere manner. *Con Life* 17 no 2:11-15 1992
Pope John Paul II gave this homily to the members of the Society of Jesus to celebrate the 450th anniversary of the birth of their founder April 22, 1991 in the Basilica of St Peter.

John Paul II, Pope, (1991-04-22) Renounce all in order to give all. *Con Life* 17 no 2:8-10 1992
Pope John Paul II gave this talk to the General Chapter of the Discalced Carmelites on April 22, 1991.

John Paul II, Pope, (1991-04-26) Your vocation is to respond to the missionary needs of the Church. *Con Life* 17 no 2:16-18 1992
Pope John Paul II gave this discourse to the men and women superiors general of the institutes founded by the Oblates of Mary Immaculate received in an audience April 26, 1991.

John Paul II, Pope, (1991-04-28) Be faithful to your word. *Con Life* 17 no 2:19-21 1992
Pope John Paul II spoke to the representatives of the religious families and secular institutes of Basilicata on April 28, 1991 at the Cathedral Potenza.

John Paul II, Pope, (1991-04-29) Constitutiones Apostolicae (Apostolic Constitution) [Latin]. *AAS* 85:5-6 Ja 7 1993
John Paul II, Pope, sets up the new Ecclesiastical Province and Metropolitan in Sorocabana, taken from the Province of Sao Paolo, Brazil.

John Paul II, Pope, (1991-05-16) The Gospel and the world: essential points of reference to your vocation. *Con Life* 17 no 2:22-25 1992
Pope John Paul II address the Superiors General of Women Religious of institutes of consecrated life in an audience on May 16, 1991.

John Paul II, Pope, (1991-05-25) Evangelize by charity. *Con Life* 17 no 2:28-30 1992
Pope John Paul II gave this address on the XXV anniversary of the promulgation of the decree Perfectae Cartatis, May 25, 1991.

John Paul II, Pope, (1991-05-25) Faithful to your particular charism. *Con Life* 17 no 2:26-27 1992
Pope John Paul II gave his address to the Society of the Daughters of the Heart of Mary for the bicentenary of the foundation of their religious congregation on May 25, 1991.

John Paul II, Pope, (1991-05-27) Poverty today requires authentic charity. *Con Life* 17 no 2:31-32 1992
Pope John Paul II addressed the General Assemb;y of the Daughters of Charity of St Vincent de Paul on May 27, 1991.

John Paul II, Pope, (1991-05-31) Harmonious unity between spiritual life and the apostolate. *Con Life* 17 no 2:33-34 1992

John Paul II, Pope, 1920- (Karol Wojtyla) (elected 1978).
(cont'd)

Pope John Paul II received in audience the General Chapters of the Congregation of the Priests of the Sacred Heart (Dehonians) on Mayh 31, 1991.

John Paul II, Pope, (1991-06-03) The Church has a great need today of your spirit of sacrifice. *Con Life* 17 no 2:35-40 1992
Pope John Paul II addressed men and women of all the diocese of Poland in the encounter before the cathedral of Kielce on June 3, 1991.

John Paul II, Pope, (1991-06-05) Litterae Apostolicae (Apostolic Letters) [Latin]. *AAS* 84:945-946 O 3 1992
The Polish foundress of the Congregation of the Missioanry Sisters of the holy family, Boleslawa Maria Lament, was beatified by the Pope, John Paul II.

John Paul II, Pope, (1991-07-03) St Louise, an example to follow and to propose. *Con Life* 17 no 2:47-50 1992
Pope John Paul II sent a letter to Sr Juana Elizondo, superior general, on the fourth centenary of the birth of St Louise de Marillac Foundress of the Daughters of Charity.

John Paul II, Pope, (1991-07-06) Constitutiones Apostolicae (Apostolic Constitution on Ecclesiastical Territory) [Latin]. *AAS* 85:8-9 Ja 7 1993
A Vicariate Apostolic is created by the Pope, John Paul II, in Tabuk, Philippine Islands.

John Paul II, Pope, (1991-07-06) Constitutiones Apostolicae (Apostolic Constitution) [Latin]. *AAS* 84:1055-1056 N 3 1992
John Paul II, Pope, created a new Apostolic Vicariate for Baguio in the Philippine Islands.

John Paul II, Pope, (1991-07-14) Bear witness gratuitiously and enthusiasitcally. *Con Life* 17 no 2:45-46 1992
Pope John Paul II addressed in audience the Franciscan Missionaries of Susa on July 14, 1991 on witness bearing.

John Paul II, Pope, (1991-07-14) Litterae Apostolicae (Apostolic Letter) [Latin]. *AAS* 84:947-949 O 3 1992
Decree of beatification of Eduardo Giuseppe Rosaz, Bishopo of Susa, by Pope John Paul II.

John Paul II, Pope, (1991-07-14) Litterae Apostolicae (Apostolic Letters) [Latin]. *AAS* 84:949-951 O 3 1992
In Brazil John Paul II, Pope, beatified Blessed Mother Pauline of the Heart of Jesus in Agony.

John Paul II, Pope, (1991-08-13) Itinera Apostolica (Apostolic Journey) [Polish]. *AAS* 84:873-878 S 8 1992
Homily of John Paul II, Pope, at the beatification Mass of the 20th century laywoman, Angela Salawa.

John Paul II, Pope, (1991-08-15) Itinera Apostolica (Apostolic Journey) [Polish]. *AAS* 84:878-885 S 8 1992
Homily of John Paul, Pope, at the Shrine of Czestochowa on World Youth Day, emphasizing the evangelical mission of youth today.

John Paul II, Pope, (1991-08-15) Itinera Apostolica (Apostolic Journey) [Polish]. *AAS* 84:885-892 S 8 1992
Talk of John Paul II, Pope, at meeting with members of the International Theological Congress in the monastery of Josna Gora, stressing the witness of contemporary martyrs as an essential element of theology.

John Paul II, Pope, (1991-08-16) Itinera Apostolica (Apostolic Journey) [Italian/Slovak/Hungarian]. *AAS* 84:892-897 S 8 1992
Homily of John Paul II, Pope, at Mass in the Basilica of Esztergom, Hungary, where emphasis was on our Lord's sustaining Hungary in the long years of suffering.

John Paul II, Pope, (1991-08-20) Itinera Apostolica (Apostolic Journey) [Hungarian]. *AAS* 84:903-911 S 8 1992
The final exhortation of John Paul II, Pope, to the Hungarian Bishops' Conference in Budapest, dealing with apostolic needs of the country.

John Paul II, Pope, (1991-08-20) Itinera Apostolica (Apostolic Journey) [Italian/Hungarian (??)]. *AAS* 84:897-902 S 8 1992
Homily of John Paul II, Pope, to faithful on the feast of St Stephen, seeking his inspiration in new-found freedom.

John Paul II, Pope, (1991-09-07) Hidden in Carmel be the light of the world and the salt of the earth. *Con Life* 17 no 2:51-52 1992
Pope John Paul II gave this discourse during a meeting with the Carmelite Nuns in Vicenza on September 7, 1991.

John Paul II, Pope, (1991-09-08) St Bridget of Sweden: a Saint of Europe. *Con Life* 17 no 2:60-63 1992
Pope John Paul II sent a letter to Mother Tekla Famiglietti, Abbess General of the Order of St Salvatore of St Bridge on the VI Centenary of the canonization of St Bridget of Sweden.

John Paul II, Pope, (1991-09-20) In your missionary service the Gospel message is ever new. *Con Life* 17 no 2:53-54 1992
Pope John Paul II gave this discourse to the General Chapter of the Missionary Sons of the Immaculate Heart of Mary (Claretians), September 20, 1991.

John Paul II, Pope, (1991-09-20) Strive assiduously for solidarity and up to date assistance in your missionary service. *Con Life* 17 no 2:55-57 1992
Pope John Paul II addressed the general Chapter; of the Combonian Missionaries of the Sacred Heart of Jesus, September 20, 1991.

John Paul II, Pope, (1991-09-21) In continuing formation your vocation is dynamically renewed. *Con Life* 17 no 2:58-59 1992
John Paul II addressed the Order of the Friars Minor Capuchin at Castel Gandolfo on September 21, 1991.

John Paul II, Pope, (1991-09-23) The new evangelization demands love in strict fidelity to the gospel. *Con Life* 17 no 2:64-66 1992
Pope John Paul II gave this address to the Minister Genral and the new Definitory of the Order of the Friars Minor on September 23, 1991.

John Paul II, Pope, (1991-09-30) Allocutiones (Speech for reception of credentials) [French]. *AAS* 84:848-850 S 8 1992
John Paul II, Pope, speech on receiving the diplomatic credentials of Count Roland Hugo van Limburg Stirum of the Kingdom of the Netherlands.

John Paul II, Pope, (1991-10-04) Allocutiones (Address to Science and Culture Meeting) [French]. *AAS* 84:855-860 S 8 1992
In an address to participants of a symposium the Pope, John Paul II, emphasizes the true cultural dimension of human progress must be kept in mind.

John Paul II, Pope, 1920- (Karol Wojtyla) (elected 1978).

(cont'd)

Address of John Paul II, Pope, to those attending plenary session of the Pontifical Council for Culture, urging continued work in areas of Europe, Africa and Latin America due to current crisis.

John Paul II, Pope, (1992-01-10) Allocutiones (Audience to welcome the new ambassador from Bangladesh) [English]. *AAS* 85:54-56 Ja 7 1993
During an audience John Paul II, Pope, extends welcome to the new ambassador to the Holy See from Bangladesh, Mufleh R. Osmany.

John Paul II, Pope, (1992-01-11) Allocutiones (Address to Diplomatic Corps accredited to the Holy See) [French]. *AAS* 85:62-73 Ja 7 1993
Papal address to Diplomatic Corps, summarizing events of 1991 and expressing hope for the future.

John Paul II, Pope, (1992-01-13) Allocutiones (Address to French Bishops on Ad Limina visit) [French]. *AAS* 85:73-80 Ja 7 1993
Audience in which spiritual formation of priests is emphasized to Bishops of Central France.

John Paul II, Pope, (1992-01-16) Allocutiones (Papal Address to Italian Bishops) [Italian]. *AAS* 85:130-135 F 3 1993
Exhortation of John Paul II, to Bishops of Italy's Apulia region, recommending dialogue and openness with Albanians.

John Paul II, Pope, (1992-01-18) Allocutiones (Exhortation to French Bishops) [French]. *AAS* 85:135-140 F 3 1993
Reception and address to French Bishops urging involvment in the new Evangelization.

John Paul II, Pope, (1992-01-23) Allocutiones (Address to Roman Rota) [Italian]. *AAS* 85:140-143 F 3 1993
The Holy Father, John Paul II, spoke in audience to Judges of Tribunal of the Roman Rota, stressing need of careful application of law to situations of human life.

John Paul II, Pope, (1992-01-24) Message for World Communications Day. *AFER* 34:130-133 Je 1992
Pope John Paul II in his message for the 26th World Communications Day, May 31, 1992, discussed the importance of witnessing, and said Catholic media professionals should feel the support of the Church.

John Paul II, Pope, (1992-01-24) Nuntii Scripto Dati (Papal message for World Day of Social Communication) [English]. *AAS* 84:990-993 O 3 1992
For World Day of Social Communication the Pope, John Paul II, stresses the need of Catholic presence in mass media.

John Paul II, Pope, (1992-01-25) Allocutiones (Homily to French Bishops) [French]. *AAS* 85:143-148 F 3 1993
John Paul II, Pope, spoke with Eastern French Bishops on Church's role in society.

John Paul II, Pope, (1992-02-11) Nuntii Scripto Dati (Written Papal Message) [French]. *AAS* 84:994-996 O 3 1992
Papal message to the UN Conference on trade and development (UNCTAD VII) on the right of people to development.

John Paul II, Pope, (1992-02-21) Itinera Apostolica (On apostolic journey speech to Diplomatic Corps in Senegal) [French]. *AAS* 85:153-157 F 3 1993
Addressing the Diplomatic Corps in Dakar, Senegal, the Holy Father, John Paul II, reminds them that solidarity knows no boundaries.

John Paul II, Pope, (1992-02-21) Itinera Apostolica (On apostolic trip address to Episcopal Conference of Senegal) [French]. *AAS* 85:148-153 F 3 1993
Talking with the Episcopal Conference of Senegal the Pope, John Paul II, recalls that inculturation will be a theme of the special Assembly for Africa of the Synod of Bishops.

John Paul II, Pope, (1992-02-22) Itinera Apostolica (Address to Catholics of Goree Island during apostolic trip) [French]. *AAS* 85:157-161 F 3 1993
Addressing Catholic of Goree Island the Holy Father recalls the abominable practice of slavery and to oppose new forms of slavery.

John Paul II, Pope, (1992-02-22) Itinera Apostolica (Address to Muslims of Senegal on Apostolic Journey) [French]. *AAS* 85:161-165 F 3 1993
The Pope, John Paul II, addresses Muslim leaders of Senegal during apostolic journey, speaking about common work for peace of those who believe in God.

John Paul II, Pope, (1992-02-23) Itinera Apostolica (Address to priests and religious of Zambia) [English]. *AAS* 85:165-170 F 3 1993
On arrival in Zambia, Pope John Paul II addresses priests and religious during Vespers on the need of the evangelical mission apostolate.

John Paul II, Pope, (1992-02-25) Itinera Apostolica (Address to catechists of Guinea during apostolic journey) [French]. *AAS* 85:175-178 F 3 1993
To the catechists of Guinea the Pope, John Paul II, expresses gratitude for their apostolic work and the continued need of laity in an ecclesial community.

John Paul II, Pope, (1992-02-25) Itinera Apostolica (Homily at ordination in Guinea during apostolic journey) [French]. *AAS* 85:171-175 F 3 1993
In Conakry, Guinea, the Holy Father, John Paul II ordained three priests and spoke of need of apostolic service.

John Paul II, Pope, (1992-02-29) Be proud of the name "Catholic". *TPS* 37: 321-323 N-D 1992
Address of Pope John Paul Ii on the 10th anniversary of the Catholic University of the Sacred Heart located in Milan, Italy.

John Paul II, Pope, (1992-03-06) Constitutio Apostolica (Apostolic Constitution) [Latin]. *AAS* 84:825-826 S 8 1992
Decree of John Paul II, Pope, in which he has set up a new diocese of Yamoussoukro in the Ivory Coast.

John Paul II, Pope, (1992-03-12) Nuntius Gratulatorius (Congratulatory Message) [Latin]. *AAS* 84:911-912 S 8 1992
Congratulatory message of the Pope, John Paul II, to Hans Hermann Card; Groer, on the occasion of the Golden Jubilee of his sacerdotal ordination.

John Paul II, Pope, (1992-03-17) Ad limina Apostolorum. *TPS* 37:324-328 N-D 1992
On March 17, John Paul II, Pope, received the first of the bishops of England and Wales and addressed the group about the pastoral concerns they share.

John Paul II, Pope, (1992-03-25) Pastores Daba Vobis Aspetti Psicologici Nella Formazione al celibato Sacerdotale. *Civilta* 3:359-379 S 4 1993

John Paul II, Pope, 1920- (Karol Wojtyla) (elected 1978).

(cont'd)

Apostolic Exhortation, Pastores dabo Vobis (I will give you shepherds), to the bishops clergy and faithful on the formation of priests in the circumstance of the present day. (Commentary).

John Paul II, Pope, (1992-03-25) Pastores Dabo Vobis (Part II). *TPS* 37: 329-363 N-D 1992
Apostolic Exhortation, Pastroes Dabo Vobis (I will give you shepherds), to the bishops clergy and faithful on the formation of priests in the circumstances of the present day.

John Paul II, Pope, (1992-03-25) Pastores Dabo Vobis. *AAS* 84:657-804 Ag 3 1992
Apostolic Exhortation, Pastores Dabo Vobis (I will give you shepherds), to the bishops, clergy, and faithful on the formation of priests in the circumstances of the present day.

John Paul II, Pope, (1992-03-30) Constitutio Apostolica (Apostolic Constitution) [Latin]. *AAS* 84:826-827 S 8 1992
John Paul II, Pope, has decreed the erection of a new diocese in Rwanda, in the area of Girongoro.

John Paul II, Pope, (1992-03-30) Litterae Apostolicae (Apostolic Letters) [Latin]. *AAS* 84:838-839 S 8 1992
A precious crown is ceded to the image of Our Lady of Fatima for veneration in a Cracow Church (Poland).

John Paul II, Pope, (1992-03-30) Litterae Apostolicae (Apostolic Letters) [Latin]. *AAS* 84:1056-1057 N 3 1992
John Paul II, Pope, decreed the coronation of the statue of Our Lady of Fatima in St Peter's Church, Wadowice (Poland).

John Paul II, Pope, (1992-04-14) Litterae apostolicae (Apostolic Letters) [Latin]. *AAS* 84:1117-1118 D 5 1992
Confirmation of the canonization of Saint Andrew Bobola.

John Paul II, Pope, (1992-04-17) Nuntii Televisifici (television message) [Italian]. *AAS* 84:984-985 O 3 1992
A television message of John Paul II, Pope, on Good Friday, in which he points out the cross as a sign of love.

John Paul II, Pope, (1992-04-19) Nuntii Televisifici (television message) [Italian]. *AAS* 84:985-990 O 3 1992
The Easter Greetings of peace and joy from Pope John Paul II.

John Paul II, Pope, (1992-04-25) Litterae Apostolicae (Apostolic Letter to create Minor Basilica in Raalte) [Latin]. *AAS* 85:125 F 3 1993
In the city of Raalte, the Netherlands, the Church of the Exaltation of the Holy Cross is raised to status of a Minor Basilica.

John Paul II, Pope, (1992-04-25) Litterae Apostolicae (Apostolic Letters) [Latin]. *AAS* 84:1057-1058 N 3 1992
The Holy Father, John Paul II, has raised the church of St Catherine of Alexandria in Lecce (Italy) to the rank of a Minor Basilica.

John Paul II, Pope, (1992-04-29) Annointing of the Sick. *TPS* 37:364-367 N-D 1992
In his general audience of April 29, Pope John Paul II discussed the Sacrament of the Annointing of the Sick and said its origin can be found in Jesus' concern and treatment of the sick.

John Paul II, Pope, (1992-04-30) Diversified service of catechists. *TPS* 38:1-4 Ja-F 1993
In his address to the mmebers of the congregation for the Evangelization of Peoples, Pope John Paul II focused on the importance of catechists to young churches.

John Paul II, Pope, (1992-05-02) The nobility of science. *TPS* 38:5-8 Ja-F 1993
In his address during a visit to the University of Trieste, John Paul II, Pope, spoke of the relationship of knowledge to faith.

John Paul II, Pope, (1992-05-11) Constitutiones Apostolicae (Apostolic Constitution for Ecclesiastical Territory) [Latin]. *AAS* 85:6-8 Ja 7 1993
The Pope, John Paul II, establishes the new dioceses of Parral from territory of the Archdiocese of Chihuahua, Mexico.

John Paul II, Pope, (1992-05-12) Litterae Apostolicae (Apostolic Letter creating Minor Basilica of Church of Nowy Sacz) [Latin]. *AAS* 85:126 F 3 1993
The parish church of Nowy Sacz, Diocese of Tarnow in Poland, is raised to status of Minor Basilica by Pope John Paul II.

John Paul II, Pope, (1992-05-14) Church upheld human rights of natives. *TPS* 38:9-13 Ja-F 1993
The participants in the International Symposium on the History of the Evangelization of America were received in audience by Pope John Paul II on May 14, 1992.

John Paul II, Pope, (1992-05-16) Constitutio Apostolica (Apostolic Constitution) [Latin]. *AAS* 84:938-939 O 3 1992
The Holy Father, Pope John Paul II, has established the new ecclesiastical Province of Cumaná, Venezuela.

John Paul II, Pope, (1992-05-17) Litterae Apostolicae (Apostolic Letters) [Latin]. *AAS* 84:1058-1060 N 3 1992
On May 17, 1992, Pope John Paul II promulgated the decree of beatification of Jose Maria Escriva de Balaguer.

John Paul II, Pope, (1992-05-18) Beatification of Sister Josephine Bakhita. *TPS* 37:371-373 N-D 1992
Pope John Paul II received in an audience some 300 Canossian Sisters and pilgrims.

John Paul II, Pope, (1992-05-18) Blessed Josemaría Excrivá de Balaguer. *TPS* 37:368-370 N-D 1992
Pope John Paul II addressed on May 18 a group of pilgrims who had come to Rome for the beatification of Josemaría Escrivá de Balaguer.

John Paul II, Pope, (1992-05-19) Litterae Apostolicae (Apostolic Letter establishing a Minor Basilica) [Latin]. *AAS* 85:13-14 Ja 7 1993
The Church of the Nativity of St. John the Baptist is raised to the status of a Minor Basilica in the Diocese of Milar.

John Paul II, Pope, (1992-05-22) Canon Law should renew ecclesial life. *TPS* 37:374-376 N-D 1992
Pope John Paul II met with members of the Canon Law Society of Great Britain and Ireland on May 22, 1992.

John Paul II, Pope, (1992-05-28) Santa Messa [Orig Spanish]. *Notitiae* 28: 404-410 Je 1992
Pope John Paul II celebrated Mass in the Vatican Basilica in the Hispanic-Mozarabic Rite on 1992-05-28.

John Paul II, Pope, 1920- (Karol Wojtyla) (elected 1978).
(cont'd)

John Paul II, Pope, (1992-05-29) Litterae Apostolicae (Apostolic Letter) [Latin]. *AAS* 85:14-15 Ja 7 1993

The Blessed Virgin Mary, under the title of "Our Lady of the Nativity", is named principal patroness and Saint Dominic is named secondary patron of the new State of Tocantin in Brazil.

John Paul II, Pope, (1992-05-31) A faithful servant and perfect friend. *TPS* 38:14-18 Ja-F 1993

John Paul II, Pope, solemnly canonized Blessed Claude La Colombiere on May 31, 1992.

John Paul II, Pope, (1992-06-01) Litterae Apostolicae (Apostolic Letters) [Latin]. *AAS* 84:1060-1061 N 3 1992

The Holy See established diplomatic relations at the level of Apostolic Nuntiature with the Republic of Nauru.

John Paul II, Pope, (1992-06-15) Live the spirit of Cardinal Lavigerie. *TPS* 38:21-23 Ja-F 1993

In a special audience for the members of the general chapter of the Society of Missionaries of Africa, known as "White Fathers", Pope John Paul II encourages them to continue to help build the Church in Africa.

John Paul II, Pope, (1992-06-24) Sea was path of Gospel for New World. *TPS* 38:24-26 Ja-F 1993

In a letter to Cardinal Giovanni Cansetri, Archbishop of Genoa, Pope John Paul II expresses his best wishes for the International Exhibition which was commemorating the voyages of Columbus.

John Paul II, Pope, (1992-06-25) Universal Catechism approved. *TPS* 37: 377-378 N-D 1992

On June 25, Pope John Paul II geve his official approval to the definitive text of the *Catechism of the Catholic Church* which will be used for the instruction of children, young people, and adults.

John Paul II, Pope, (1992-06-26) Ad limina apostolorum. *TPS* 38:29-33 Ja-F 1993

Pope John Paul II addressed the bishops of the Czeck and Slovak Federative Republic stressing that a strong clergy is the first priority for chruch renewal and that parish life is central to the formation of a Christian society.

John Paul II, Pope, (1992-06-26) Christian and Muslim women. *TPS* 38:27-28 Ja-F 1993

Address of Pope John Paul II to the participants of the Muslim-Christian Colloquium held in Rome, jointly organized by the Pontifical Council for Interreligious Dialogue and the Royal Academy for Islamic Civilization Research, Amman, Jordan.

John Paul II, Pope, (1992-07-03) Litterae Apostolicae (Apostolic Letter) [Latin]. *AAS* 85:15-16 Ja 7 1993

The Church of Saint Michael Archangel in the Diocese of Vilkavishkis in Lithuania is named a Minor Basilica.

John Paul II, Pope, (1992-07-06) Constitutiones Apostolicae (Apostolic Constitution to erect Diocese of Accra) [Latin]. *AAS* 85:119-120 F 3 1993

The Pope, John Paul II, establishes the new diocese of Accra, Ghana, with Dominic Kodwo Andoh the first Bishop.

John Paul II, Pope, (1992-07-06) Constitutiones Apsotolicae (Apostolic Constitution to erect Vicariate Apostolic in Philippines) [Latin]. *AAS* 85:124 F 3 1993

A new Apostolic Vicariate is constituted in Bontoc-Lagawe in the Philippines.

John Paul II, Pope, (1992-07-06) Constitutiones Apsotolicae (Apostolic Constitution to erect Diocese of Koforidua) [Latin]. *AAS* 85:120-121 F 3 1993

John Paul II, Pope, erects the new Diocese of Koforidua out of territory of Accra, in Ghana. The first bishop is Gabriel Palmer-Buckle.

John Paul II, Pope, (1992-07-06) Litterae Apostolicae (Apostolic Letter) [Latin]. *AAS* 85:16-17 Ja 7 1993

The Church of the Blessed Virgin Mary in Lausanne, Switzerland, is named a Minor Basilica.

John Paul II, Pope, (1992-07-08) Bishops are successors to the Apostles. *TPS* 38:34-36 Ja-F 1993

In a general audience in which he continues his catechesis on the mystery of the Church, Pope John Paul II explains that the apostles appointed successors so that the mission they received from Jesus could continue.

John Paul II, Pope, (1992-07-08) Litterae Apostolicae (Apostolic Letter) [Latin]. *AAS* 85:17-18 Ja 7 1993

The image of the Blessed Virgin Mary in Huelva, Spain, is to be crowned as Patroness of the Diocese under the title of "Nuestra Senora de la Cinta".

John Paul II, Pope, (1992-07-23) Litterae Apostolicae (Apostolic Letter) [Latin]. *AAS* 85:18-19 Ja 7 1993

The Parish Church of St. Lawrence Ruiz, in the Manila suburb of Binondi, is raised to the status of a Minor Basilica.

John Paul II, Pope, (1992-07-23) Litterae Apostolicae (Apostolic Letter) [Latin]. *AAS* 85:19-20 Ja 7 1993

The Church of Saint Nicholas Albena-Imperia Diocese of Italy is raised to the rank of a Minor Basilica.

John Paul II, Pope, (1992-07-25) Constitutiones Apostolicae (Apostolic Constitution to erect Diocese of Carora) [Latin]. *AAS* 85:122-123 F 3 1993

John Paul II, Pope, erects the new diocese of Arora, in Venezuela.

John Paul II, Pope, (1992-07-25) Constitutiones Apsotolicae (Apostolic Constitution) [Latin]. *AAS* 84:1053-1055 N 3 1992

The Holy Father, John Paul II, established the Diocese of Valle de la Pascua, with territory taken from the Diocese of Calaboyo (Venezuela). As bishop he appointed JOaquin Morón Hidalgo.

John Paul II, Pope, (1992-08-04) Litterae Apostolicae (Apostolic Letter) [Latin]. *AAS* 85:20-21 Ja 7 1993

The image of Our Lady of Consolation in Tarnou, Poland, is to be crowned according to the approved liturgical rite.

John Paul II, Pope, (1992-08-15) Christ offers abundant life. *TPS* 38:39-43 Ja-F 1993

In his message for 1993 World Youth Day, John Paul II, Pope, reflected on the meaning of life and the fullness of life which Jesus brings.

John Paul II, Pope, (1992-08-15) Message to the youth of the world. *Living Light* 29:19-22 Spr 1993

In his message for 1993 World Youth Day, John Paul II, Pope, reflected on the meaning of life and the fullness of life which Jesus brings.

John Paul II, Pope, 1920- (Karol Wojtyla) (elected 1978).
(cont'd)

John Paul II, Pope, (1992-08-28) Litterae Apostolicae (Apostolic Letter) [Latin]. *AAS* 85:21-22 Ja 7 1993

The Church of the Blessed Virgin Mary, commonly called Maria Radna, in Timisoara, is elevated to the rank of Minor Basilica.

John Paul II, Pope, (1992-09-08) Litterae Apostolicae (Apostolic Letter) [Italian]. *AAS* 84:1033-1053 N 3 1992

John Paul II, Pope, introduces an update of Vatican pension system, to which is added the new regulations.

John Paul II, Pope, (1992-09-09) Prayer as essential as breathing. *TPS* 38: 44-45 Ja-F 1993

In a general audience John Paul II, Pope, speaks of the importance of prayer and says that for Christians prayer is as essential as breathing.

John Paul II, Pope, (1992-09-10) prayer, message for peace. *TPS* 38:46-48 Ja-F 1993

In a letter to Cardinal Edward Idris Cassidy, President of the Pontifical Council for Promoting Christian Unity, Pope John Paul II reflects on the powre of prayer to unify and bring peace into the world.

John Paul II, Pope, (1992-09-16) Prayer's dialogue with God. *TPS* 38:49-50 Ja-F 1993

Catechesis of Pope John Paul II, in which he says Christian prayer has its roots in the Old Testament.

John Paul II, Pope, (1992-09-21) Litterae Apostolicae (Apostolic Letter to create Apostolic Nuntiature in Mexico) [Latin]. *AAS* 85:127 F 3 1993

A new Apostolic Nuntiature is established in Mexico in order to set up diplomatic relations with the Holy See on that level.

John Paul II, Pope, (1992-09-27) Beatification. *TPS* 38:57-60 Ja-F 1993

In his homily, Pope John Paul II discusses the faith of the twenty-one people beatified during the Mass.

John Paul II, Pope, (1992-10-08) Litterae Apostolicae (Apostolic Letter) [Latin]. *AAS* 85:22-23 Ja 7 1993

Statue of Our Lady of Guadalupe of Carrizal, patroness of the Diocese of Maracaibo, Venezuela, is to be crowned.

John Paul II, Pope, (1992-10-11) America, open your doors to Christ. *TPS* 38:78-83 Mr-Ap 1993

In his homily, John Paul II, Pope, calls on all sectors of Latin Americca society to work together to solve their problems.

John Paul II, Pope, (1992-10-12) Challenges facing the Latin American Church. *TPS* 38:84-102 Mr-Ap 1993

In his keynote address, John Paul II, Pope, discusses the theme of new evangelization, human development and Christian culture; he talks about the history, present and future of the Church in Latin America and the importance of catechesis.

John Paul II, Pope, (1992-10-12) Defend your identities and values. *TPS* 38: 103-106 Mr-Ap 1993

In his address, Pope John Paul II recognizes the painful history of African Americans and acknowledge the serious injustice committed against them.

John Paul II, Pope, (1992-10-15) Litterae Apostolica (Apostolic Letter to create a Minor Basilica of Our Lady in Chile) [Latin]. *AAS* 85:127-128 F 3 1993

John Paul II, Pope, raises the Sanctuary of Our Lady in Chile to the status of a Minor Basilica.

John Paul II, Pope, (1992-10-22) Litterae Apostolicae (Apostolic Letter in which cathedral of Kabgayi is made a Minor Basilica) [Latin]. *AAS* 85: 128-129 F 3 1993

The Cathedral of Kabgayi Diocese, Rwanda, is named a Minor Basilica by Pope John Paul II.

John Paul II, Pope, (1992-10-28) The apostolic mission of bishops. *TPS* 38: 107-110 Mr-Ap 1993

In his weekly catechesis on the mystery of the Church, Pope John Paul II speaks of the mission of bishops, both to the people of their dioceses and those outside the Church.

John Paul II, Pope, (1992-11-09) Vist ad limina. *TPS* 38:111-115 Mr-Ap 1993

In his address to the bishops of Croatia on the occasion of their first visit ad limina, Pope John Paul II reflects on the need for forgiveness in thier war torn country and the problems of relations with the Orthodox.

John Paul II, Pope, (1992-11-11) Fidei Depositum [English text]. *Origins* 22: 527+ Ja 14 1993

Fidei Depositum, Apostolic Constitution on the publication of the catechism of the Catholic Church prepared following Vatican Council II.

John Paul II, Pope, (1992-11-17) Statue of the Litterae Apostolicae (Apostolic Letter for coronation of the Virgin Mary in Halcnow) [Latin]. *AAS* 85:129-130 F 3 1993

The image of the Sorrowful Mother of God in the parish church of Halcnow, Poland, may now be crowned in the name and authority of the Pope.

John Paul II, Pope, (1992-11-21) the inalienable rights of the disabled. *TPS* 38:129-133 My-Je 1993

In his address to the Seventh International Conference sponsored by the Pontifical Council for Pastoral Assistance to Health Care Workers, John Paul II, Pope, spoke about the disabled in society.

John Paul II, Pope, (1992-11-22) Ready to confess Christ. *TPS* 38:134-137 My-Je 1993

In his homily, Pope John Paul II ties the Solemnity of Christ the King to the beatification of the Mexican martyrs.

John Paul II, Pope, (1992-12-01) Europe's signs of the times. *TPS* 38:138-141 My-Je 1993

In his address to the presidents of the Episcopal Conferences of Europe, Pope John Paul II stresses the need for renewed evangelical effort in Europe.

John Paul II, Pope, (1992-12-05) basic right to nutrition. *TPS* 38:142-146 My-Je 1993

In his address to the International Conference on Nutrition, Pope John Paul II praised the World Health Organization and Food and Agricultural Organization for their efforts to aid people who suffer from hunger.

John Paul II, Pope, (1992-12-05) serve life at its birth. *TPS* 38:147-149 My-Je 1993

John Paul II, Pope, 1920- (Karol Wojtyla) (elected 1978).
(cont'd)

In his address to the participants of the Italian Society of Gynecology and Obstetrics, Pope John Paul II speaks of the Church's teaching on the necessity of protecting life from conception to its natural end.

John Paul II, Pope, (1992-12-07) New Catechism is a gift to the Church. *TPS* 38:150-154 My-Je 1993
In his address at the official release of the Catechism of the Catholic Church, John Paul II, Pope, expresses his appreciation for the work done and the hope that all in the Church will benefit from this gift.

John Paul II, Pope, (1992-12-08) If you want peace, serve the poor. *TPS* 38:155-161 My-Je 1993
In his message to the world's leaders and all people of goodwill, Pope John Paul II says that poverty often incites people to violence which can lead to war, and that every country has the right to develop.

John Paul II, Pope, (1992-12-16) Peter ranks first. *TPS* 38:165-168 My-Je 1993
During a general audience, Pope John Paul II gives a catechesis on the Petrine ministry, describing Peter's role in the early Church, and his special appointment by Christ.

John Paul II, Pope, (1992-12-17) Catechism. *OR(Eng)* 1272:8 Ja 6 1993
In his message to the Bishops of Wales, John Paul II, Pope, spoke about their ministry and the help they are offered by the catechism of the Catholic Church.

John Paul II, Pope, (1992-12-19) Ad limina Apostolorum. *TPS* 38:193-200 Jl-Ag 1993
In his address to the bishops of south-western Germany during their ad limina visit, Pope John Paul II speaks of many aspects of Church and political life in Germany, including abortion, euthanasia, social communications, and political asylum.

John Paul II, Pope, (1992-12-20) Charity is an individual and social obligation. *TPS* 38:169-171 My-Je 1993
In his address to the staff, volunteers and guests at a soup kitchen run by the diocesan Caritas, John Paul II, Pope, praises their efforts and presents a brief explanation for the condition of poverty.

John Paul II, Pope, (1992-12-22) give thanks for the gift of serving. *TPS* 38:172-178 My-Je 1993
On December 22, 1962-1965, the College of Cardinals, the members of the Roman Curia, and Roman prelates gathered to exchange wishes for the Christmas season with Pope John Paul II.

John Paul II, Pope, (1992-12-22) Give thanks [orig Italian]. *OR(Eng)* 1272:6-7 Ja 6 1993
On December 22, 1992 the College of Cardinals, the members of the Roman Curia, and Roman prelates gathered to exchange wishes for Christmas season with John Paul II, Pope.

John Paul II, Pope, (1992-12-24) Light shines [orig Italian]. *OR(Eng)* 1272:5 Ja 6 1993
Christ alone brings peace was John Paul II, Pope, message at the Christmas Midnight Mass in St Peter's Basilica.

John Paul II, Pope, (1992-12-25) Come to heal [orig italian]. *OR(Eng)* 1271:1 Ja 6 1993
John Paul II, Pope, addressed the pilgrims who filled St Peter's Square on Christmas day, inviting everyone to worship the new-born King.

John Paul II, Pope, (1992-12-30) Marian devotion [orig Italian and French]. *OR(Eng)* 1272:11 Ja 6 1993
On December 30, during the General Audience, John Paul II, Pope, reflected on Vatican II's teachings on Mary.

John Paul II, Pope, (1992-12-31) Our generation [orig Italian]. *OR(Eng)* 1272:10 Ja 6 1993
On the last day of 1992 John Paul II, Pope, celebrated the Mass of Thanksgiving at Rome's Church f the Gesù preaching about God's desire for the salvation of the world.

John Paul II, Pope, (1993 06 05) Parishes. *TPS* 38:369-373 N-D 1993
John Paul II, Pope, expressed appreciation for religious and lay people who conduct "a Sunday celebration in the absence of a priest", when he spoke to bishops from Alabama, Kentucky, Louisiana and Tennessee.

John Paul II, Pope, (1993 08-03) God [Orig in English]. *OR(Eng)* 1303:14 Ag 18 1993
John Paul II, Pope, sent a message to Dr Mary Tanner, moderator of the Faith and Order Commission.

John Paul II, Pope, (1993-00-00) Genuine Spiritual renewal. *New Cov* 23:16-17 S 1993

John Paul II, Pope, (1993-01-01) God wants [orig Italian]. *OR(Eng)* 1272:3 Ja 6 1993
In the presence of most of the record number of Ambassadors accredited to the Holy See, John Paul II, Pope, celebrated Mass for the 26th World Day of Prayer for Peace.

John Paul II, Pope, (1993-01-01) Lent 1993 [English tr]. *Origins* 22:524 Ja 7 1993
In his message for the 1993 Lenten season, John Paul II, Pope, focused attention on the world's expanding desert-areas suffering from lack of water.

John Paul II, Pope, (1993-01-01) Peace through helping poor. *Nat Cath Rep* 29:12-13 Ja 8 1993
On Ja 1, 1993, John Paul, Pope, delivered his annual World Day of Peace Message.

John Paul II, Pope, (1993-01-01) Poverty and peace [abridged]. *Tablet* 247:25-26 Ja 2 1993
In the presence of most of the record number of ambassadors accredited to the Holy See, John Paul II, Pope, celebrated Mass for the 26th World Day of Prayer for Peace.

John Paul II, Pope, (1993-01-04) Moral responsibilities of psychiatrists. *TPS* 38:179-180 My-Je 1993
Address of Pope John Paul II to the members of the American Psychiatric Association and the World Psychiatric Association in which he acknowledges the importance of the psychiatrists work.

John Paul II, Pope, (1993-01-16) Diplomats [Origin French]. *Origins* 22:583-587 F 4 1993
John Paul II, Pope, reviewed world events of 1992, in his annual beginning-of-the year address to diplomats.

John Paul II, Pope, 1920- (Karol Wojtyla) (elected 1978).
(cont'd)

John Paul II, Pope, (1993-01-20) Telegram to President Clinton. *TPS* 38:201 Jl-Ag 1993
Pope John Paul II sent a telegram to President Clinton on the occasion of his inauguration, expressing his best wishes.

John Paul II, Pope, (1993-01-24) message for 27th World Communications Day. *AFER* 35:66-68 Ap 1993
In his message for World Communications Day, John Paul II, Pope, stressed the importance of modern means of mass communications, especially audiocassettes and videocassettes.

John Paul II, Pope, (1993-01-25) Christian unity is our desire. *TPS* 38:202-206 Jl-Ag 1993
In his homily at the close of the Week of Prayer for Christian Unity John Paul II, Pope, acknowledges the difficulties in achieving Christian unity but reaffirms the Catholic Church's commitment to the process; he focuses on hopes for future unity with the Orthodox Church through dialogue and prayer.

John Paul II, Pope, (1993-01-27) Bishop of Rome is Peter's successor. *TPS* 38:207-210 Jl-Ag 1993
Pope John Paul II explains that it was Christ's will that there should be successors of Peter, and that the papacy was determined by Christ's commands as well as the events of history.

John Paul II, Pope, (1993-01-29) Interpret law through tradition. *TPS* 38:211-214 Jl-Ag 1993
In his address during the annual meeting of the auditors, officials and advocates of the Roman Rota, Pope John Paul II focuses on the interpretation of canon law, noting that it is a guarantee of peace and a tool for preserving unity.

John Paul II, Pope, (1993-01-30) Promote the family. *TPS* 38:215-218 Jl-Ag 1993
In his address to the plenary assembly of the Pontifical Council for the family, Pope John Paul II states that the strength and stability of the family fabric represent favorable conditions for the soundness of the Christian community and of all society.

John Paul II, Pope, (1993-01-9) Discurso a los indigenas Latino Americanos. *Christus* 58:46-48 S 1993
Pope John Paul II spoke to the indigenous Indians of Latin America about their history, culture, and faith in Jesus Christ.

John Paul II, Pope, (1993-02-02) Change violence into acceptance. *TPS* 38:219-220 Jl-Ag 1993
In his letter to Archbishop Vinko Pulijic of Sarajevo, Pope John Paul II deplores the violence of war, and says that rape victims must find the support of understanding and solidarity in the community.

John Paul II, Pope, (1993-02-07) AIDS [Original in English]. *Origins* 22:613-614 F 18 1993
John Paul II, Pope, visited St Francis Hospital in Nsambya and asked doctros and researchers "not to delay" in search for AIDS cures and treatments.

John Paul II, Pope, (1993-02-08) Birth of Freedom [English text]. *Origins* 22:615-616 F 18 1993
John Paul II, Pope, expressed special concern at high illiteracy rates in Africa.

John Paul II, Pope, (1993-02-09) The Church in Africa. *Origins* 22:653-684 Mr 11 1993
John Paul II, Pope, released the working paper for the Synod of Bishops' Special Assembly for Africa, while he was in Uganda. The theme of the synod for Africa is "The Church in Africa and her evangelizing mission toward the year 2000: You shall be my witnesses' (Acts 1:8)".

John Paul II, Pope, (1993-02-10) Civil War [English text]. *Origins* 22:617-618 F 18 1993
John Paul, II, Pope, addressed to Sudan's president, Omar Al Bashir asking him to respect human rights.

John Paul II, Pope, (1993-02-10) Innocent victims. *TPS* 38:221-225 Jl-Ag 1993
A mass was celebrated in Khartoum's Green Square, by John Paul II, Pope, for millions of innocent victims of the war.

John Paul II, Pope, (1993-02-17) Vitality of African Christianity. *TPS* 38:226-229 Jl-Ag 1993
Address of John Paul II, Pope, on his experiences in Benin, Uganda, and the Sudan and the celebrations honoring the beatification of Josephine Bakhita.

John Paul II, Pope, (1993-02-24) Pope exercises supreme jurisdiction. *TPS* 38:232-235 Jl-Ag 1993
In his address, Pope John Paul II explains that the Successor of Peter enjoys full and supreme power of jurisdiction in faith and morals and in all that concerns the Church's governance.

John Paul II, Pope, (1993-02-26) Sharing clergy. *TPS* 38:236-239 Jl-Ag 1993
In his address to the first plenary meeting of the Commission for Clergy Distribution, John Paul II, Pope, renews his appeal for Churches with abundant priestly vocations to chare their clergy with dioceses suffering a shortage.

John Paul II, Pope, (1993-03-10) Innocent victims [Orig English]. *Origins* 22:618-620 F 18 1993
A Mass was celebrated in Khartoum's Green Square, by John Paul II, Pope, for millions of innocent victims of the war.

John Paul II, Pope, (1993-03-10) Letter to UN on refugees. *TPS* 38:240-242 Jl-Ag 1993
Letter of John Paul II, Pope, to Rene Valery Mongbe, President of the Path to Peace Foundation, expressing his support for the United Nations meeting on refugees.

John Paul II, Pope, (1993-03-11) Letter to UN Secretary General. *TPS* 38:243-244 Jl-Ag 1993
Letter of John Paul II, Pope, to Boutros Boutros-Ghali, Secretary-General of the United Nations, asking that the United Nations do all in its power to restore peace to Bosnia and Herzegovina.

John Paul II, Pope, (1993-03-17) Infallibility. *TPS* 38:257-260 S-O 1993
Address of John Paul II, Pope, in which he explains the assistance that God gives the papal Magisterium which includes the infallibility in the papal office.

John Paul II, Pope, 1920- (Karol Wojtyla) (elected 1978).
(cont'd)

John Paul II, Pope, (1993-03-21) Authentic witnesses of the Gospel. *TPS* 38: 245-248 Jl-Ag 1993
Homily of Pope John Paul II during the beatification ceremonies of John Duns Scotus and Dina Belanger.

John Paul II, Pope, (1993-03-27) Treat sinners with compassion. *TPS* 38: 261-265 S-O 1993
In his address to the Cardinal Major Penitentiary, the officials of the Apostolic Penitentiary and the confessors of Rome's patriarchal basilicas, Pope John Paul II speaks about the need for adequate doctrinal preparation and for sensitivity in dealings with penitents.

John Paul II, Pope, (1993-04-07) Gypsies at Auschwitz. *TPS* 38:266-267 S-O 1993
Letter of Pope John Paul II to the bishop of the diocese in which Oswiecim, the site of the Auschwitz Concentration was located, in which he joins in prayer for the Gypsies who were victims of genocide.

John Paul II, Pope, (1993-04-09) Letter to Auschwitz nuns. *TPS* 38:268-269 S-O 1993
John Paul II, Pope sent a letter to the Carmelite nuns in the convent at Auschwitz, Poland and asked them to be love itself in the heart of the Church.

John Paul II, Pope, (1993-04-09) Letter to the nuns. *Origins* 22:795 Ap 29 1993
John Paul II, Pope sent a letter to the Carmelite nuns in the convent at Auschwitz, Poland and asked them to be love itself in the heart of the Church.

John Paul II, Pope, (1993-04-15) Europe needs solidarity. *TPS* 38:270-274 S-O 1993
Address of John Paul II, Pope, to the Council of European Episcopal Conferences in which he discusses the history of the Council and that it must be an instrument of evangelization not only for Europe, but also for Africa, Asia, and the Americas.

John Paul II, Pope, (1993-04-25) May Albania be equal to the challenge. *TPS* 38:275-279 S-O 1993
In his address to the people of Albania gathered at Skanderberg Square, Pope John Paul II recognized persecution they have suffered and courages them in the challenges which they face in order to rebuild their economy and democratic structure; the Pope also calls upon the international community to assist the Albanians in these tasks.

John Paul II, Pope, (1993-04-28) Christian heritage in Iraq. *TPS* 38:280-282 S-O 1993
In his message Pope John Paul II expresses his wish that Christians remain in Iraq to perpetuate their ancient heritage; he also expresses sorrow for those suffering in Iraq, especially the children and elderly.

John Paul II, Pope, (1993-04-29) New Catechism is basis for local catechisms. *TPS* 38:283-286 S-O 1993
In his address to the presidents of the Episcopal Conference Commissions for Catechesis and other participants in a workshop on preparing local catechisms sponsored by the Congregation for the clergy, John Paul II, Pope, explains that the Catechism of the Catholic Church is destined for all the faithful who can read and understand it.

John Paul II, Pope, (1993-05-01) Catholic Journalists [Orig in Italian]. *OR(Eng)* 1296:13 Je 23 1993
Welcoming the editors and journalists of Avvenire, John Paul II, Pope, asked them to instill in readers a desire for freedom and the strength to withstand difficulties.

John Paul II, Pope, (1993-05-05) Priests sanctify through sacraments. *TPS* 38:287-290 S-O 1993
In his address, Pope John Paul II says that acting in the name of Christ presbyters administer the sacraments which, by the power of the Holy Spirit, bestow the new life of grace.

John Paul II, Pope, (1993-05-06) Help [Orig in French]. *OR(Eng)* 1292:3 My 26 1993
John Paul II, Pope, participated in celebration of Holy Childhood Association's 150th anniversary.

John Paul II, Pope, (1993-05-06) Holy Childhood Association's 150th anniversary. *TPS* 38:291-294 S-O 1993
In his address to the participants in the Pastoral Session and General Assembly of the Pontifical Mission-Aid Societies, Pope John II praises the role of children in the evangelization of other children.

John Paul II, Pope, (1993-05-07) Science [Orig in Italian]. *OR(Eng)* 1296:14 Je 23 1993
John Paul II, Pope, welcomers every opportunity to express appreciation and affection for the infirm and for those who care them.

John Paul II, Pope, (1993-05-08) Faith and science are gifts of God. *TPS* 38: 295-300 S-O 1993
During his visit to the Ettore Maiorana Research Centre, Pope John Paul II addressed the international scientific commentary saying that faith and science can enter into a dialogue which benefits both.

John Paul II, Pope, (1993-05-09) Faith. *OR(Eng)* 1292:6 My 26 1993
John Paul II, Pope, told the people of Caltanissetto to rediscover faith in their ancestors.

John Paul II, Pope, (1993-05-09) Get up [Orig in Italian]. *OR(Eng)* 1292:4+ My 26 1993
In his address to the young people of Sicily, John Paul II, Pope, encouraged them to rise from indifference and to continue to make a difference in their own lives.

John Paul II, Pope, (1993-05-09) Healthy business. *OR(Eng)* 1292:5 My 26 1993
On 9 May, 1993 during his Pastoral visit to Sicily, John Paul II, Pope, addressed the region's business leaders on the Church's social doctrine.

John Paul II, Pope, (1993-05-09) Repent! God will judge you. *TPS* 38:301-303 S-O 1993
In his homily, Pope John Paul II condemns criminal activity in Sicily, especially the Mafia, which afflict the peace-loving people of Sicily.

John Paul II, Pope, (1993-05-10) Ethical training [Orig in Italian]. *OR(Eng)* 1292:8 My 26 1993
John Paul II, Pope, inaugurated a new centre for the training and continuing education of health-care personel in Caltanissetta.

John Paul II, Pope, 1920- (Karol Wojtyla) (elected 1978).
(cont'd)

John Paul II, Pope, (1993-05-10) Sicily. *OR(Eng)* 1292:7 My 26 1993
John Paul II, Pope, visited the Monastery of St. Clare in Caltanissetta and addressed to all the Poor Clares nuns of Sicily.

John Paul II, Pope, (1993-05-12) Priests act in the Person of Christ. *TPS* 38:304-307 S-O 1993
In his address, Pope John Paul II explains that through ordination the priest is enabled to make present the eternal sacrifice of Christ; he will see to it that Christian formation aims at the active participation of the faithful in the Eucharistic celebration.

John Paul II, Pope, (1993-05-14) Huelva [Orig in Spanish]. *OR(Eng)* 1296:1+ Je 23 1993
During mass in Huelva John Paul, II, Pope, encourages Christian families to maintain a sense of the transcendent and share it with others.

John Paul II, Pope, (1993-05-14) Life [Orig in Italian]. *OR(Eng)* 1292:9+ My 26 1993
John Paul II, Pope, addressed the International Union of Superiors General of women religious on the problems of life issues.

John Paul II, Pope, (1993-05-15) Spain [Orig in Spanish]. *OR(Eng)* 1297:7 Je 30 1993
John Paul II, Pope, addressed the diplomatic accredited to Spain at the Apostolic Nunciature in Madrid.

John Paul II, Pope, (1993-05-15) Spirit [Orig in English]. *OR(Eng)* 1292:2 My 26 1993
John Paul II, Pope, addressed about the importance of the continuing exchange of gifts between all those who confess Jesus Christ as Lord and Redeemer to Ecumenical Commissions of the world's.

John Paul II, Pope, (1993-05-16). *TPS* 38:308-311 S-O 1993
In his homily Pope John Paul II speaks of the heroic virtues of four people who were just beatified.

John Paul II, Pope, (1993-05-19) Priest [Orig in Italian]. *OR(Eng)* 1292:11+ My 26 1993
At the General Audience of 19 May, 1993 John Paul II, Pope, discussed the presbyter's role in gathering the family of God into a fellowship of living unity.

John Paul II, Pope, (1993-05-22) Mary. *OR(Eng)* 1292:1 My 26 1993
John Paul II, Pope, received in St. Peter's Basilica Filipino familiiesfrom all over Europe, and spoke to them about the problems of their homeland.

John Paul II, Pope, (1993-05-23) Heart [Orig in Italian]. *OR(Eng)* 1294:8 Je 9 1993
John Paul II, Pope, blessed the cornerstone for the St Leo Youth Center in Arezzo, during his Pastoral visit in the area.

John Paul II, Pope, (1993-05-23) Presence [Orig in Italian]. *OR(Eng)* 1294: 6+ Je 9 1993
During a visit in Arezzo John Paul II, Pope, addressed a few words of encouragement to the priests of the Diocese of Arezzo.

John Paul II, Pope, (1993-05-23) Sacraments [Orig Italian]. *OR(Eng)* 1294:7 Je 9 1993
John Paul II, Pope, addressed to the young people of Arezzo and the Tuseau area and encouraged them to be good Christians.

John Paul II, Pope, (1993-05-23) Social dimension [Orig in Italian]. *OR(Eng)* 1294:5 Je 9 1993
During his Pastoral visit in Cortona John Paul II, Pope, reflected on the message of the 13th-century penitent, who can serve as an example of fidelity, charity and peacemaking for all.

John Paul II, Pope, (1993-05-24) Charism [Orig in Italian]. *OR(Eng)* 1300:9 Jl 21 1993
John Paul II, Pope, received in an audience the members of the General Chapter of the Congregation of the Little Missionary Sisters of Charity.

John Paul II, Pope, (1993-05-27) Catholic University of America [Orig in English]. *OR(Eng)* 1294:10 Je 9 1993
John Paul II, Pope, received in special audience the members of the Board of Trustees of the Catholic University of America.

John Paul II, Pope, (1993-05-28) God [Orig in Italian]. *OR(Eng)* 1294:4 Je 9 1993
John Paul II, Pope, addressed to the participants in the international symposium on the Post-Synodal Apostolic Exhortation, *Pastores dabo vobis.*

John Paul II, Pope, (1993-05-30) Hungary [Orig in Latin]. *OR(Eng)* 1294:2 Je 9 1993
John Paul II, Pope, wrote to the Bishops of Hungary announcing the reorganization of the ecclesiastical structures in that country.

John Paul II, Pope, (1993-05-31) Citizens [Orig in English]. *OR(Eng)* 1294:3 Je 9 1993
John Paul II, Pope, highlighted the Church's involvement in society in Zarubia during his audience with the Bishops of Zambia.

John Paul II, Pope, (1993-06-01) Eucharist [Orig in French]. *OR(Eng)* 1297: 8 Je 30 1993
On June 1, 1993, John Paul II, Pope, received in special audience Fr Norman Pelletier, Superior General of the Congregation of the Blessed Sacrament.

John Paul II, Pope, (1993-06-01) Year of the family [Orig in Italian]. *OR(Eng)* 1294:1+ Je 9 1993
John Paul II, Pope, on Trinity Sunday, has proclaimed 1994 as the International Year of the Family.

John Paul II, Pope, (1993-06-02) Priest [Orig in Italian]. *OR(Eng)* 1294:11 Je 9 1993
Speaking to pilgrims from every continent, John Paul II, Pope, stressed the need that priests have to meditate, celibrate mass and the Liturgy of the Hours, and recieve the Sacrament of Penance.

John Paul II, Pope, (1993-06-03) Christian hope [Orig in Italian]. *OR(Eng)* 1297:9 Je 30 1993
John Paul II, Pope, spoke in front of pilgrims from Berganio came to the Vatican to mark the anniversary of the death of Pope John XXIII on 3 June.

John Paul II, Pope, (1993-06-05) Parishes. *Origins* 23:127-128 Jl 15 1993
John Paul II, Pope, expressed appreciation for religious and lay people who conduct "a Sunday celebration in the absence of a priest," when he spoke to bishops from Alabama, Kentucky, Louisiana and Tennessee.

John Paul II, Pope, 1920- (Karol Wojtyla) (elected 1978).
(cont'd)

John Paul II, Pope, (1993-06-05) Social doctrine [Orig in Italian]. *OR(Eng)* 1297:9 Je 30 1993
John Paul II, Pope, spoke to the founding members of the "Centesiumus Annus-Pro Pontefice" Foundation, a new foundation established by Italian business leaders to study and spread the Church's social teaching.

John Paul II, Pope, (1993-06-05) Spiritual life. *OR(Eng)* 1295:3+ Je 16 1993
John Paul II, Pope, spoke about the role of the sacraments in the spiritual renewal of the country in front of the Bishops of Alabama, Kentucky, Louisiana adn Tennessee.

John Paul II, Pope, (1993-06-07) Official visit [original in Slovak]. *OR(Eng)* 1295:6 Je 16 1993
On June 7, 1993, John Paul II, Pope, received the President of the Republic of Slovakia, Michal Kováč.

John Paul II, Pope, (1993-06-08) Marriage and Holy Orders [Orig in English]. *OR(Eng)* 1296:11 Je 23 1993
John Paul II, Pope, met the Bishops of Arizona, etc, and talk about Catechism of the Catholic Church as basis for a spiritual renewal of the United States.

John Paul II, Pope, (1993-06-08) Republic of Romania. *OR(Eng)* 1297:8 Je 30 1993
John Paul II, Pope, received the new Ambassador of Romania to the Holy See, H E Mr Gheroghe Pancratiu Iuliu Gheorghiu.

John Paul II, Pope, (1993-06-09) Church [Orig Italian]. *OR(Eng)* 1298:5 Jl 7 1993
John Paul II, Pope, met the priests, religious and lay leaders of Macerata and spoke about the Church unity as source of better evangelization.

John Paul II, Pope, (1993-06-09) Eucharist [original in Italian]. *OR(Eng)* 1295:7 Je 16 1993
Before the Feast of Corpus Christi, John Paul II, Pope spoke about the Eucharist in the spiritual life of the priest.

John Paul II, Pope, (1993-06-10) Corpus Christi. *OR(Eng)* 1295:2 Je 16 1993
At the liturgical feast of Corpus Christi, John Paul II, Pope, celebrated Mass at an altar set up at the entrance to St John Lateran Basilica.

John Paul II, Pope, (1993-06-11) Ethiopian Orthodox Patriarch. *OR(Eng)* 1295:5 Je 16 1993
On June 11, 1993 John Paul II, Pope received in private audience His Holiness Abuna Paulos, Patriarch of the Ethiopian Orthodox Church.

John Paul II, Pope, (1993-06-11) Letter [Orig in English]. *OR(Eng)* 1297:2 Je 30 1993
John Paul II, Pope, wrote a letter to the Bishops of the USA on June 11, 1993.

John Paul II, Pope, (1993-06-11) Letter [Orig in English]. *TPS* 38:374-376 N-D 1993
John Paul II, Pope, wrote a letter to the Bishops of the USA on June 11, 1993.

John Paul II, Pope, (1993-06-12) Eucharist [Orig in Spanish]. *OR(Eng)* 1296: 5 Je 23 1993
Celebrating the Mass to Seville's sports stadium John Paul II, Pope, ordained 38 deacons to the priesthood.

John Paul II, Pope, (1993-06-12) God present among us [Orig in Spanish]. *OR(Eng)* 1296:4 Je 23 1993
Greeting the faithful from Seville, John Paul II, Pope, spoke about Eucharistic devotion outside of Mass.

John Paul II, Pope, (1993-06-12) Love and hope [Orig in Spanish]. *OR(Eng)* 1296:3 Je 23 1993
On his arrival in Spain John Paul II, Pope, gave a brief address.

John Paul II, Pope, (1993-06-13) International Eucharistic Congress [Orig in Spanish]. *OR(Eng)* 1296:6 Je 23 1993
John Paul II, Pope, addressed 150 delegates representing 180 nations, who had worked most directly in preparing the 45th International Eucharistic Congress.

John Paul II, Pope, (1993-06-14) New World [Orig in Spanish]. *OR(Eng)* 1296:8 Je 23 1993
John Paul II, Pope, visited da Rábida the most famous Franciscan house in Spain, whose Franciscan friary furnished many of the early missionaries to the New World.

John Paul II, Pope, (1993-06-14) Spain [Orig in Italian]. *OR(Eng)* 1297:3 Je 30 1993
John Paul II, Pope, addressed the pilgrims gathered to greet him in El Rocío.

John Paul II, Pope, (1993-06-15) Church [Orig in Spanish]. *OR(Eng)* 1297: 4+ Je 30 1993
John Paul II, Pope, addressed the Spanish Bishops to the headquarters of the Spanish Episcopal Conference.

John Paul II, Pope, (1993-06-15) God [Orgin Spanish]. *OR(Eng)* 1297:5 Je 30 1993
John Paul II, Pope, participated to the consecration of the new Cathedral of Madrid.

John Paul II, Pope, (1993-06-16) "art of arts" [Orig in Spanish]. *OR(Eng)* 1297:6 Je 30 1993
Joining the seminations of the Archdiocese of Madrid, for morning praise, John Paul II, Pope, reflects with them on various aspects of the priest formation.

John Paul II, Pope, (1993-06-16) Baptism, [Orig in Spanish]. *OR(Eng)* 1296: 1-2 Je 23 1993
John Paul II, Pope, challenged the Christian families of Spain to bear witness to unity and fidelity in marriage, in his Mass in which he canonized Blessed Enrique de Ossóy Cervelló.

John Paul II, Pope, (1993-06-16) Visit to Spain. *OR(Eng)* 1295:1+ Je 16 1993
Hundreds of thousands of people participated as John Paul II, Pope celebrated, Mass for the solemn close of the 45th International Eucharistic Congress.

John Paul II, Pope, (1993-06-19) Apostles [Orig in Italian]. *OR(Eng)* 1300:7 Jl 21 1993
John Paul II, Pope, received in special audience the members of the General Chapter of the Consolata Missionaries.

John Paul II, Pope, (1993-06-19) Human Life [Orig in Italian]. *OR(Eng)* 1298:6 Jl 7 1993

John Paul II, Pope, 1920- (Karol Wojtyla) (elected 1978).
(cont'd)

John Paul II, Pope, celebrated Mass in Macerata and expressed his encouragement and admiration to young people prepared to go to Loreto, site of a Marian Shrine.

John Paul II, Pope, (1993-06-20) Angela [Orig in Italian]. *OR(Eng)* 1298:7 Jl 7 1993
During the visit to Macerata and Foligno, John Paul II, Pope, honoured Angela of Foligno, 13th century laywoman.

John Paul II, Pope, (1993-06-20) Nature [Orig in Italian]. *OR(Eng)* 1296:1 Je 23 1993
John Paul II, Pope, blessed a chapel in the area of the Gran Sasso.

John Paul II, Pope, (1993-06-21) World. *OR(Eng)* 1300:5 Jl 21 1993
John Paul II, Pope, received in audience a group representing the Daughter of Mercy and encouraged them to serve the people of today with faith.

John Paul II, Pope, (1993-06-23) Seville [Orig in Italian]. *OR(Eng)* 1297:11 Je 30 1993
Speaking in Italian John Paul II, Pope, addressed the many pilgrims gathered in the Paul VI Audience Hall.

John Paul II, Pope, (1993-06-27) Rome [Orig Italian]. *OR(Eng)* 1297:1 Je 30 1993
On June 27 John Paul II, Pope, spoke about the "Book of the Synod".

John Paul II, Pope, (1993-06-29) Christian unity. *OR(Eng)* 1298:2 Jl 7 1993
John Paul II, Pope, received in audience a delegation sent by the Ecumenical Patriarch of Constantinople to attend celebrations in honour of Saints Peter and Paul.

John Paul II, Pope, (1993-06-29) Church. *OR(Eng)* 1298:1-2 Jl 7 1993
John Paul II, Pope, recalls Paul VI on 30th anniversary of his election.

John Paul II, Pope, (1993-06-29) Prayer [Orig in Italian]. *OR(Eng)* 1298:1-2 Jl 7 1993
John Paul II, Pope, celebrated a Mass in St. Peter's Basilica on 29 June, 1993 for the Solemnity of Sts. Peter and Paul.

John Paul II, Pope, (1993-06-30) Priests [Orig in Italian]. *OR(Eng)* 1298:11 Jl 7 1993
At the General Audience of 30 June, 1993, John Paul II, Pope, spoke about the role of Marian devotion in the prayer life of the clergy.

John Paul II, Pope, (1993-07-02) Ministry. *OR(Eng)* 1298:3+ Jl 7 1993
The role of the laity, especially of women, was the topic of the John Paul II, Pope's address to the sixth group of Bishops of the United States.

John Paul II, Pope, (1993-07-02) Women. *Origins* 23:124-126 Jl 15 1993
Lay ministry, women's roles, feminism and the parish were discussed by John Paul II, Pope, in an address to US Bishops.

John Paul II, Pope, (1993-07-11) Santo Stefano [Orig in Italian]. *OR(Eng)* 1300:3 Jl 21 1993
Addressing the faithful at the parish church of Santo Stefano, John Paul II, Pope, spoke on the parable of the sower.

John Paul II, Pope, (1993-07-17) Church. *OR(Eng)* 1300:11 Jl 21 1993
John Paul II, Pope, discussed the rationale behind priestly celibacy, seeing it as a sign of the presbyter's special consecration to Christ.

John Paul II, Pope, (1993-07-18) Praying [Orig Italian]. *OR(Eng)* 1300:1 Jl 21 1993
The theme of John Paul II, Pope, meditation on July 18, was restoration of Christian unity.

John Paul II, Pope, (1993-07-19) Pius XII [Orig in Italian]. *OR(Eng)* 1300:1 Jl 21 1993
John Paul II, Pope, paid tribute to the pastoral concern of Pius XII, who left Vatican City to console the faithful during after a bombing raid on July 19, 1943.

John Paul II, Pope, (1993-07-21) message to Faith and Order Conference. *Ecumen Trends* 22:2 O 1993
In his message to the World Conference on Faith and Order, Pope John Paul II praises the accomplishments of the Faith and Order Commission in moving towards Church unity.

John Paul II, Pope, (1993-07-21) Model [Orig in Italian]. *OR(Eng)* 1301:11 Jl 28 1993
At the General Audience of 21 July, 1993, John Paul II, Pope, discussed the presbyter's attitude toward material possessions.

John Paul II, Pope, (1993-07-25) Youth [Orig in Italian]. *OR(Eng)* 1301:1+ Jl 28 1993
John Paul II, Pope, called on young people to celebrate life instead of being the victims of a "culture of death" during his speech as Castel Gandolfo on 25 July, 1993.

John Paul II, Pope, (1993-07-28) Priests. *OR(Eng)* 1302:7 Ag 11 1993
At the General Audience of 28 July, 1993 John Paul II, Pope, discussed the priest's relationship with temporal affairs.

John Paul II, Pope, (1993-08-01) Music. *OR(Eng)* 1303:12 Ag 18 1993
John Paul II, Pope, expressed gratitude to the directors and musicians of the Ottorino Respighi Academy of Music at the conclusion of their concert at Castel Gandolfo.

John Paul II, Pope, (1993-08-01) Peace [Orig in Italian]. *OR(Eng)* 1302:1 Ag 11 1993
A call for peace and dialogue in the Middle East was issued by John Paul, II, Pope on 1 August, 1993, at the Castel Gandolfo.

John Paul II, Pope, (1993-08-04) Bishops [Orig in Italian]. *OR(Eng)* 1303:15 Ag 18 1993
At the General Audience of 4 August, 1993 John Paul II, Pope delivered this 68th address in the series on the mystery of the Church.

John Paul II, Pope, (1993-08-06) Migrant family [Orig in Italian]. *OR(Eng)* 1309:4 S 29 1993
John Paul II, Pope, has issued a message, which speaks of the impact migration has on the family, for World Migration Day, 1993-1994.

John Paul II, Pope, (1993-08-09) Church [Orig in English]. *OR(Eng)* 1303:1+ Ag 18 1993
At his arrival at the Norman Manley International Airport in Kingston, John Paul II, Pope, gave a short address on five centuries of evangelization.

John Paul II, Pope, (1993-08-10) Christ's love [Orig in English]. *OR(Eng)* 1303:2 Ag 18 1993
In his second day in Jamaica, John Paul II, Pope, visited Kingston's Holy Trinity Cathedral and preached a brief homily on Christ's love.

John Paul II, Pope, 1920- (Karol Wojtyla) (elected 1978).
(cont'd)
John Paul II, Pope, (1993-08-10) Hearts [Orig in English]. *OR(Eng)* 1303:5 Ag 18 1993
Young Jamaicans urged by John Paul II, Pope, to reject easy road of self-indulgence.
John Paul II, Pope, (1993-08-10) Jamaica. *OR(Eng)* 1303:3 Ag 18 1993
Kingston's National Stadium was the place of the Mass which John Paul II, Pope, celebrated with the faithful of Jamaica.
John Paul II, Pope, (1993-08-10) Truth [Orig in English]. *OR(Eng)* 1303:4 Ag 18 1993
John Paul II, Pope, participated in a prayer service with leaders of Jamaica's various religious communities in Holy Cross Parish Church in Kingston.
John Paul II, Pope, (1993-08-11) Jamaica's ideals [Orig in English]. *OR(Eng)* 1303:5 Ag 18 1993
In his farewell speech John Paul II, Pope, urged Jamaicans to rededicate to Jamaica's ideals.
John Paul II, Pope, (1993-08-12) Arrival [Origin English]. *Origins* 23:187-188 Ag 26 1993
At his arrival at Denver's Stapleton International Airport, John Paul II, Pope, made remarks on the necessity to concentrate on the well-being of the world's children and young people.
John Paul II, Pope, (1993-08-12) Denver. *OR(Eng)* 1303:6 Ag 18 1993
At his arrival at Stapleton International Airport in Denver, John Paul II, Pope, spoke about how society must instill high moral vision in young people.
John Paul II, Pope, (1993-08-12) Life. *OR(Eng)* 1303:7+ Ag 18 1993
John Paul II, Pope, urged youth to seek God by following the cross, in his speech at Mile High Stadium.
John Paul II, Pope, (1993-08-12) Young people [Orig in English]. *Origins* 23:188-190 Ag 26 1993
On his World Youth Day speeches, John Paul II, Pope, encouraged each young person to "have the courage to go and preach the good news among young people of the last part of the 20th century".
John Paul II, Pope, (1993-08-13) Bishops [Orig in English]. *Origins* 23:190-191 Ag 26 1993
John Paul II, Pope, asked the bishops from around the world gathered in Denver's Cathedral of the Immaculate Conception to be always ready to help the young people discover the transcendent elements of the Christian life.
John Paul II, Pope, (1993-08-13) Cross. *Origins* 23:191-192 Ag 26 1993
In his message to 70,000 World Youth Day participants making the stations of the cross in Denver's Mile High Stadium, John Paul II, Pope, urged the young people to take courage in the face of life's injustices.
John Paul II, Pope, (1993-08-14) Christ [Orig English]. *OR(Eng)* 1303:8-9 Ag 18 1993
During the solemn prayer vigil in Cherry Creek State Park John Paul II, Pope, addressed the young people on themes suggested by the Scripture.
John Paul II, Pope, (1993-08-14) Colorado [Origin in English]. *Origins* 23:194-195 Ag 26 1993
John Paul II, Pope, told some 18,000 Colorado Catholics in McNichols Sports Arena that the teaching of the Church is placed in a social and cultural context.
John Paul II, Pope, (1993-08-14) Forum. *Origins* 23:192-194 Ag 26 1993
John Paul II, Pope, told the World Forum participants about their place in the ecclesial community, during a Mass a Denver's Immaculate Conception Cathedral.
John Paul II, Pope, (1993-08-14) Prayer [Origin English]. *Origins* 23:182-186 Ag 26 1993
John Paul II, Pope, spoke about humanity as a whole at the start of an all-night prayer vigil in Cherry Creek State Park.
John Paul II, Pope, (1993-08-15) Celebration [Origin in English]. *Origins* 23:177+ Ag 26 1993
During the eucharistic celebration at Cherry Creek State Park in Denver, John Paul II, Pope, acknowledged hundreds of thousands of World Youth Day participants for becoming more conscious of their vocation.
John Paul II, Pope, (1993-08-15) Cherry Creek [Orig in English]. *Origins* 23:196 Ag 26 1993
John Paul II, Pope, announced that the next World Youth Day will take place in Manila, 1995.
John Paul II, Pope, (1993-08-15) Children. *Origins* 23:198-199 Ag 26 1993
John Paul II, Pope, appealed to national and international leaders to protect the rights of children.
John Paul II, Pope, (1993-08-15) Church [Orig in English]. *Origins* 23:197-198 Ag 26 1993
"Do not forget the Church in Vietnam," John Paul II, Pope, said to an estimated 10,000 participants in McNichols Sports Arena.
John Paul II, Pope, (1993-08-15) Farewell [Origin in English]. *Origins* 23:196-197 Ag 26 1993
John Paul II, Pope, described the World Youth Day as a wonderful exchange of spiritual gifts and experiences.
John Paul II, Pope, (1993-08-15) Gore. *Origins* 23:200 Ag 26 1993
John Paul II, Pope, expressed gratitude to the American people for assisting needy people around the world in his farewell remarks at Denver's Stapleton International Airport.
John Paul II, Pope, (1993-08-15) Loreto. *OR(Eng)* 1308:6-7 S 22 1993
John Paul II, Pope, sent a letter to Archbishop Pasquale Macchi in which he spoke of Mary's role in salvation history and in the spiritual life.
John Paul II, Pope, (1993-08-15) Manila. *OR(Eng)* 1303:11 Ag 18 1993
During a Mass on 15 August, 1993 John Paul II, Pope answered to the message of the International Youth Forum.
John Paul II, Pope, (1993-08-15) Talents. *OR(Eng)* 1303:1+ Ag 18 1993
John Paul II, Pope, celebrated the solemn Mass at Cherry Creek State Park a the end of the Eighth World Youth Day.
John Paul II, Pope, (1993-08-21) Joseph [Orig Italian]. *OR(Eng)* 1308:4 S 22 1993
Church needs Joseph's bold faith for new evangelization was the message of John Paul II, Pope, to the Sixth International Symposium of St. Joseph.

John Paul II, Pope, 1920- (Karol Wojtyla) (elected 1978).
(cont'd)
John Paul II, Pope, (1993-08-25) Obedience [Orig in Italian]. *OR(Eng)* 1305:7 S 1 1993
At the General Audience of 25 August, 1993 John Paul II, Pope, spoke of the need for presbyters to cooperate with their Bishops.
John Paul II, Pope, (1993-08-29) Baltic. *OR(Eng)* 1305:1 S 1 1993
At Castel Gandolfo, John Paul II, Pope, offered to pray for the spiritual welfare of Lithuania, Latvia and Estonia.
John Paul II, Pope, (1993-09-01) Cooperation [Orig in Italian]. *OR(Eng)* 1306:11 S 8 1993
At the Audience John Paul II, Pope met a group of 40 Aztecs and spoke about brotherly spirit between priests.
John Paul II, Pope, (1993-09-02) United States [Orig in English]. *OR(Eng)* 1306:10 S 8 1993
The new Ambassador of the United States of America to the Holy See, presented his credentials to John Paul II, Pope.
John Paul II, Pope, (1993-09-04) Baltic nations [Orig Lithuanian]. *OR(Eng)* 1306:1+ S 8 1993
At the Vilnius Airport, John Paul II, Pope, thanks God for the grace of his visit to the Baltic nations.
John Paul II, Pope, (1993-09-04) Mary [Orig in Lithuanian]. *OR(Eng)* 1306:3 S 8 1993
At the Marian shrine of Aušros Vartai in Vilnius, John Paul II, Pope, led the recitation of the Rosary on his first day to Lithuania.
John Paul II, Pope, (1993-09-04) Saint Stanislaus. *OR(Eng)* 1306:2 S 8 1993
There are no winners or losers, only people who need your help was John Paul II, Pope's message for the priests, religious and seminarians gathered in the Cathedral of Saint Stanislaus.
John Paul II, Pope, (1993-09-05) Basic values [Orig in Lithuanian]. *OR(Eng)* 1306:7-8 S 8 1993
In his meeting with representatives of the world of culture, John Paul II, Pope, spoke about the relation between basic values and democracy.
John Paul II, Pope, (1993-09-05) Beyond. *Origins* 23:235-237 S 16 1993
John Paul II, Pope, spoke to the members of the academic and cultural communities at the University of Vilnius, calling for a dialogue between faith and culture.
John Paul II, Pope, (1993-09-05) Freedom [Orig in French]. *OR(Eng)* 1306:5+ S 8 1993
John Paul II, Pope, met the Diplomatic Corps in Lithuania and spoke about new path of freedom and the full recognition of the human rights.
John Paul II, Pope, (1993-09-05) Independence. *Origins* 23:233 S 16 1993
Encouraging forgiveness, John Paul II, Pope, called for the rejection of vengeance when he visited Antakalnis Cemetery in Vilnius.
John Paul II, Pope, (1993-09-05) Lithuania [Orig Lithuanian]. *OR(Eng)* 1306:1+ S 8 1993
On 5 September, 1993, John Paul II, Pope, celebrated Mass in Vilnius and spoke to Lithuanians about the importance of Baptism and the need to renew the faith.
John Paul II, Pope, (1993-09-05) People [Orig in Polish]. *OR(Eng)* 1307:3 S 15 1993
During his visit in Vilnius John Paul II, Pope, addressed to Polish citizens with a message of peace.
John Paul II, Pope, (1993-09-05) The power of love [Orig in Lithuanian]. *OR(Eng)* 1306:8 S 8 1993
At the tomb of the martyrs of Lithuania, John Paul II, Pope, offered a prayer, asking Christ to grant them eternal rest.
John Paul II, Pope, (1993-09-06) Clergy [Orig in Lithuanian]. *OR(Eng)* 1307:7 S 15 1993
At his meeting with the Bishops of Lithuania John Paul II, Pope, told them to form the laity and to update the clergy.
John Paul II, Pope, (1993-09-06) Future [Orig in Lithuanian]. *OR(Eng)* 1307:4+ S 15 1993
During his meeting with young people of Lithuania, John Paul II, Pope, told them that true happiness can be found by responding to Christ and his loving call to each of them.
John Paul II, Pope, (1993-09-06) Holy Spirit [Orig in Lithuanian]. *OR(Eng)* 1306:6 S 8 1993
John Paul II, Pope, celebrated a Mass with faithful of Kaunas, Lithuania.
John Paul II, Pope, (1993-09-07) Churches [Orig in Italian]. *OR(Eng)* 1307:1-2 S 15 1993
John Paul II, Pope, sent a letter to the symposium of European Bishops' at meeting in Prague.
John Paul II, Pope, (1993-09-07) Cross [Orig in Lithuanian]. *OR(Eng)* 1307:5 S 15 1993
At the popular Shrine Hill of Crosses John Paul II, Pope, celebrated a Mass in honour of the Exaltation of the Cross.
John Paul II, Pope, (1993-09-07) Mary [Orig in Lithuanian]. *OR(Eng)* 1307:6 S 15 1993
Following the visit to the Chapel of the Apparition John Paul II, Pope, preached a homily at Marian Shrine.
John Paul II, Pope, (1993-09-08) Estonians [Orig in Estonian]. *OR(Eng)* 1307:15 S 15 1993
John Paul II, Pope, meet representatives of Estonia's small Catholic community at Tallinn's Catholic Church.
John Paul II, Pope, (1993-09-08) Grace [Orig in Latvian]. *OR(Eng)* 1307:10 S 15 1993
In Riga's Mežapark, John Paul II, Pope, celebrated Mass for the faithful of Latvia.
John Paul II, Pope, (1993-09-08) Latvia [Orig in Latvian]. *OR(Eng)* 1307:8 S 15 1993
In Riga's Catholic Cathedral, John Paul II, Pope, solemnly proclaimed and restored the centuries-old veneration of Saint Meinhard, first Bishop in Livonia.
John Paul II, Pope, (1993-09-08) Latvia. [Orig in Latvian]. *OR(Eng)* 1307:9 S 15 1993
Leaders of Latvia's Christian Churches joined John Paul II, Pope, in venerating St. Meinhard's tomb and prayed together.
John Paul II, Pope, (1993-09-08) Problems [Orig in Latvian]. *OR(Eng)* 1307:8 S 15 1993

John Paul II, Pope, 1920- (Karol Wojtyla) (elected 1978).
(cont'd)

John Paul II, Pope, emphasized positive ecumenical dimension in his first address in Latvia at Riga's airport.

John Paul II, Pope, (1993-09-09) Conscience [Orig in Latvian]. *OR(Eng)* 1307:11+ S 15 1993
During a short vist to the University of Riga, John Paul II, Pope, spoke to the cultural leaders of Latvia about the thinkers as society's criitcal conscience.

John Paul II, Pope, (1993-09-09) Language of love [Orig in Latvian]. *OR(Eng)* 1307:12 S 15 1993
John Paul II, Pope, visited Marian Shrine at Aglona and celebrated Mass in honour of the Birth of Mary.

John Paul II, Pope, (1993-09-10) Creator [Orig in Estonian]. *OR(Eng)* 1308:10 S 22 1993
Freedom of religion safeguards respect for man and the Creator was the theme of John Paul II, Pope, departure speech at the Tallinn airport.

John Paul II, Pope, (1993-09-10) Estonia [Orig in Estonian]. *OR(Eng)* 1308:5 S 22 1993
On 10 September, 1993 John Paul II, Pope, went to the Lutheran Church of St. Nicholas in Tallinn and pray for Estonians unity.

John Paul II, Pope, (1993-09-10) Estonia [Orig in Estonia]. *OR(Eng)* 1307:14 S 15 1993
At his arrival at Tallinn's Airport John Paul II, Pope, expressed his gratitude to God for the recent changes in Eastern and Central Europe.

John Paul II, Pope, (1993-09-10) Gospel [Orig in Estonian]. *OR(Eng)* 1308:9-10 S 22 1993
In front of Christians gathered in Tallinn's Municipal Square John Paul II, Pope, preached the homily.

John Paul II, Pope, (1993-09-10) Gospel. *OR(Eng)* 1307:13 S 15 1993
In his farewell address at Riga's airport John Paul II, Pope, spoke about Gospel as source of clear principles which can be shared by non-believers too.

John Paul II, Pope, (1993-09-10) Language [Orig in Estonian]. *OR(Eng)* 1308:8 S 22 1993
On 10 September, 1993 John Paul II, Pope gave to Estonia's President a message for the cultural leaders.

John Paul II, Pope, (1993-09-12) Trust [Orig in Italian]. *OR(Eng)* 1307:1 S 15 1993
Before the recitation of the Angelus on 12 September, 1993 John Paul II, Pope, expressed his deep satisfaction with the peace accord that would be signed by Israel and the PLO.

John Paul II, Pope, (1993-09-15) Baltic [Orig in Estonian]. *OR(Eng)* 1308:11 S 22 1993
At the General Audience on 15 September, 1993, John Paul II, Pope, spoke about people's devotion to the cross and to the Blessed Virgin in the Baltic nations.

John Paul II, Pope, (1993-09-16) Church's teaching [Orig English, French]. *OR(Eng)* 1308:3 S 22 1993
Receiving Bishops of Western Canada, John Paul II, Pope, urged them to ensure in every way that sound doctrine be taught throughout Canada.

John Paul II, Pope, (1993-09-17) Christ [Orig in Italian]. *OR(Eng)* 1309:8 S 29 1993
John Paul II, Pope, concluded his pilgrimage to La Verna addressing to the monks from Benedictine monastery of Camaldoli.

John Paul II, Pope, (1993-09-17) Christ [Orig in Italian]. *OR(Eng)* 1308:2 S 22 1993
From the Cliff of the Stigmata John Paul II, Pope, leaded young people in reciting the Angelus on 17 September, 1993.

John Paul II, Pope, (1993-09-17) Franciscans [Orig in Italian]. *OR(Eng)* 1308:2 S 22 1993
John Paul II, Pope, spoke to the Franciscan religious communities encouraging priests to abandon themselves to Jesus' crucifying love.

John Paul II, Pope, (1993-09-17) La Verna [Orig in Italian]. *OR(Eng)* 1308:1 S 22 1993
John Paul II, Pope, celebrated Mass in the Franciscan shrine of La Verna and preached the homily.

John Paul II, Pope, (1993-09-19) Paths [Orig in Italian]. *OR(Eng)* 1310:3 O 6 1993
John Paul II, Pope, sent a letter to Cardinal Cassidy, President of the Pontifical Council for promoting Christian Unity with the occasion of the seventh International Meeting "People and Religions," which brought together over 300 representatives of the world's religions.

John Paul II, Pope, (1993-09-21) Young [Origin English]. *OR(Eng)* 1309:5 S 29 1993
Speaking to prelates from the six states of New England, John Paul II, encouraged them to inspire young people with undiluted Gospel.

John Paul II, Pope, (1993-09-21) Youth. *Origins* 23:271-273 S 30 1993
John Paul II, Pope, spoke to New England bishops about Catholic education.

John Paul II, Pope, (1993-09-22) Priest. *OR(Eng)* 1309:11 S 29 1993
At the General Audience of 22 September, 1993, John Paul II, Pope, discussed the life and ministry of priests focusing on the presbyter's relationship with the laity.

John Paul II, Pope, (1993-09-23) Develop [Orig in Italian]. *OR(Eng)* 1310:3 O 6 1993
John Paul II, Pope, received in audience the participants in the international "Prix Italia", radio and television competition and urged them to improve the quality of their broadcasts.

John Paul II, Pope, (1993-09-24) Christian [Orig in English]. *OR(Eng)* 1309:3+ S 29 1993
John Paul II, Pope, addressed to the Bishops of Malawi on family life issues, at the conclusion of their ad limina visit.

John Paul II, Pope, (1993-09-25) Church [Orig in Italian]. *OR(Eng)* 1309:1-2 S 29 1993
During Mass in the Diocese of Asti, John Paul II, Pope, beatified the servant of God Giuseppe Marello, Bishop of Acqui and founder of the Oblates of St. Joseph.

John Paul II, Pope, (1993-09-25) Message [Orig in Italian]. *OR(Eng)* 1311:8 O 13 1993

John Paul II, Pope, 1920- (Karol Wojtyla) (elected 1978).
(cont'd)

During his visit to the Diocese of Asti, John Paul II, Pope, spoke to the religious community of the Oblates of St. Joseph.

John Paul II, Pope, (1993-09-26) Bring [Orig in Italian]. *OR(Eng)* 1311:8 O 13 1993
John Paul II, Pope, visited "Città di Asti" home for the elderly and encouraged them to unite their sufferings with Christ's sacrifice in the Mass and to focus on what is eternal.

John Paul II, Pope, (1993-09-26) Family [Italian]. *OR(Eng)* 1311:9-10 O 13 1993
John Paul II, Pope, visited the Church of St. Peter in Asti and spoke about the family's place in Religious education.

John Paul II, Pope, (1993-09-26) Never [Orig in Italian]. *OR(Eng)* 1311:9 O 13 1993
John Paul II, Pope, meet with young people from Asti at the sports centre and spoke about eternal life.

John Paul II, Pope, (1993-09-28) Ambassador [Orig in German]. *OR(Eng)* 1306:9 S 8 1993
The new Ambassador of Estonia to the Holy See, presented his credentials to John Paul II, Pope.

John Paul II, Pope, (1993-09-29) God. *OR(Eng)* 1311:11 O 13 1993
The restoration of the permanent diaconate was the theme of John Paul II, Pope, speech at the General Audience of 29 September, 1993.

John Paul II, Pope, (1993-09-29) Harvest. *OR(Eng)* 1310:7 O 6 1993
Priestly vocations were the subject of John Paul II, Pope, catechesis at the General Audience on September 29, 1993.

John Paul II, Pope, (1993-10-02) Church [Orig in English]. *OR(Eng)* 1311:3 O 13 1993
Consultative structures and the involvement of the laity in the Church's life and mission were among the topics John Paul II, Pope, treated when he spoke to United States Bishops at the Vatican.

John Paul II, Pope, (1993-10-02) Common good [Orig Italian]. *OR(Eng)* 1312:8-9 O 20 1993
"National identity, democracy and the common good" was the theme of the 42nd Italian Catholic Social Week with the occasion John Paul II, Pope, sent a message to Cardinal Camillo Ruini.

John Paul II, Pope, (1993-10-02) Structures [Orig in English]. *Origins* 23:348-350 O 21 1993
John Paul II, Pope, talked about consultative structures in the Church in front of a group of U.S. bishops from Pacific Northwest states.

John Paul II, Pope, (1993-10-03) Heart [Origin Italian]. *OR(Eng)* 1311:7 O 13 1993
On October 3, 1993, John Paul II, Pope celebrated Mass for the community of the Basilica of Santa Maria in Trastevere.

John Paul II, Pope, (1993-10-04) Healing [Orig in English]. *OR(Eng)* 1311:5 O 13 1993
Restoration of peace and encouragement to face the challenges in their countries was John Paul II, Pope, message to the Bishops of Ethiopia and Eritrea.

John Paul II, Pope, (1993-10-05) Faith [Orig in Italian]. *OR(Eng)* 1310:5 O 6 1993
John Paul II, Pope, urges priests and religious to educate the young in the great ideals of Christian life, in his address to the citizens of Asti.

John Paul II, Pope, (1993-10-05) Love. *OR(Eng)* 1310:6 O 6 1993
John Paul II, Pope, says marital love is an expression of God's faithful, fruitful and gratuitous love.

John Paul II, Pope, (1993-10-05) Veritatis Splendor. *Origins* 23:297-334 O 14 1993
Veritatis Splendor (the Splendor of Truth), Encyclical Letter on moral issues (1993-10-05). Original.

John Paul II, Pope, (1993-10-10) Aurelia Maria. *OR(Eng)* 1311:1 O 13 1993
John Paul II, Pope, celebrated a Mass in St. Peter Square in which he beatified Maria Aurelio.

John Paul II, Pope, (1993-10-10) Brother Amalio. *OR(Eng)* 1311:1 O 13 1993
John Paul II, Pope, celebrated a Mass in St. Peter Square in which he beatified Brother Amalio.

John Paul II, Pope, (1993-10-10) Brother Edmigio. *OR(Eng)* 1311:1 O 13 1993
John Paul II, Pope, celebrated a Mass in St. Peter Square in which he beatified Brother Edmigio.

John Paul II, Pope, (1993-10-10) Diego Ventaja Milan. *OR(Eng)* 1311:1 O 13 1993
John Paul II, Pope, celebrated a Mass in St. Peter Square in which he beatified Bishop Diego Ventaja Milan.

John Paul II, Pope, (1993-10-10) Evencio Ricardo. *OR(Eng)* 1311:1 O 13 1993
John Paul II, Pope, celebrated a Mass in St. Peter Square in which he beatified Evencio Ricardo.

John Paul II, Pope, (1993-10-10) Hope [Orig in Italian, Spanish]. *OR(Eng)* 1311:1+ O 13 1993
John Paul II, Pope, celebrated a Mass in which he beatified 11 martyrs of the Spanish Civil War and two women religious from Italy.

John Paul II, Pope, (1993-10-10) José Cecilio. *OR(Eng)* 1311:1 O 13 1993
John Paul II, Pope, celebrated a Mass in St. Peter Square in which he beatified José Cecilio.

John Paul II, Pope, (1993-10-10) Manuel Medina Olmos. *OR(Eng)* 1311:1 O 13 1993
John Paul II, Pope, celebrated a Mass in St. Peter Square in which he beatified Bishop Manuel Medina Olmos.

John Paul II, Pope, (1993-10-10) Maria crucified. *OR(Eng)* 1311:1 O 13 1993
John Paul II, Pope, celebrated a Mass in St. Peter Square in which he beatified Maria crucified.

John Paul II, Pope, (1993-10-10) Maria Francesca. *OR(Eng)* 1311:1 O 13 1993
John Paul II, Pope, celebrated a Mass in St. Peter Square in which he beatified Maria Francesca.

John Paul II, Pope, (1993-10-10) Teodomiro Joaquin. *OR(Eng)* 1311:1 O 13 1993
John Paul II, Pope, celebrated Mass in St. Peter Square in which he beatified Teodomiro Joaquin.

Katz, Nathan.
Perfection without God: a view from the Pāli Canon. *Stud Form Spir* 14:11-22 F 1993

Katz, Wallace.
Make Gotham, governable. *Comm* 120:5-7 N 19 1993

Kauffman, Christopher J.
The Americanization of St Sulpice; context and charism. *US Cath Hist* 11:21-34 Wint 1993
Christopher Columbus and American Catholic identity: 1880-1900. *US Cath Hist* 11:93-110 Spr 1993
Review of: *"Some seed fell on good ground": the life of Edwin V O'Hara* by Dolan, Timothy Michael. In: *ACHSR* 103:48-49 Aut 1992

Kaufman, Ben L, and Onder, Tina.
Sisters meet, recommit to collaborative efforts [Meeting of Cincinnati archdiocese, Mr 6 1993, Cincinnati, Ohio]. *Nat Cath Rep* 29:3 Mr 19 1993

Kaufman, Stephen A. see Fitzmyer, Joseph Augustine, 1920-, jt auth

Kaut, Bernd.
Missionary service [fr *Yours sincerely*]. *AFER* 34:376-381 D 1992

Kavanagh, Aidan.
Review of: *Early Christian Baptism and the catechumenate* by Finn, Thomas Macy. In: *CHist* 79:311-312 Ap 1993

Kavanaugh, John.
Ann Manganaro, S L. *Cath Work* 60:7 S 1993

Kay, Rene M.
Thirty-five parish tips for putting children and families first. *Church* 9:31-33 Spr 1993

Kazanecki, Thaddeus J.
The sanctification of their neighbor. *RRel* 52:574-583 Jl-Ag 1993

Kealey, Robert J.
Selectivity, an unfair criticism. *Tod Cath Teach* 27:9 N-D 1993
Teachers love their students. *Tod Cath Teach* 27:6 O 1993

Kealy, Catherine.
Review of: *Tutoring and mentoring* by Keim, Nancy, and Tolliver, Cindy. In: *Momentum* 24:80 N-D 1993

Kealy, Sean P, 1937-.
The end of the missions. *AFER* 35:20-26 F 1993
The end of the missions? *Doctr Life* 43:77-82 F 1993

Kearley, Carroll C.
Review of: *Dignity and decadence: Victorian art and the classical inheritance* by Jenkyns, Richard. In: *New Oxford Rev* 60:31-32 Jl-Ag 1993

Keating, Karl.
Wolves in sheep's clothing ensnare the faithful. *OSV* 82:6-7 Ag 1 1993

Keating, Thomas.
An interview with Father Thomas Keating [interview by A Vest]. *Liguorian* 81:12-17 Ja 1993

Keay, J.
Review of: *Leviathan* by Auster, Paul. In: *Tablet* 246:1576 D 12 1992

Kee, Howard Clark.
Review of: *Theios anēr and the Markan miracle traditions* by Blackburn, Barry. In: *CBQ* 54:774 O 1992

Keefe, Donald J.
Review of: *The glory of the Lord: a theological aesthetics, vol V: the realm of metaphysics in the modern age* by Balthasar, Hans Urs Von, 1905-1988. In: *Thomist* 57:308-316 Ap 1993

Keefe, Jeffrey.
Avarice, a.k.a. greed. *Catechist* 27:4 O 1993
Envy: the up-front sin. *Catechist* 27:5 N-D 1993
Facts on fat. *Catechist* 26:12-13 Ja 1993
The "noble" addiction. *Catechist* 26:19-20 Ap-My 1993
The seven deadly sins: pride, the number one sin. *Catechist* 27:8 S 1993
Sexual addiction. *Catechist* 26:11 Mr 1993
Some food for thought only. *Catechist* 26:6 F 1993

Keegan, Jeffrey.
Review of: *Desert Shield to Desert Storm: the second Gulf War* by Hiro, Dilip. In: *Tablet* 246:1573-1574 D 12 1992
Review of: *Storm command: a personal account of the Gulf War* by Billière, Peter de la. In: *Tablet* 246:1573-1574 D 12 1992

Keegan, V.
Review of: *The view from No 11* by Lawson, Nigel. In: *Tablet* 247:47-48 Ja 9 1993

Keegan, William.
Bankers and politicians. *Tablet* 247:781 Je 19 1993
Choices for the Chancellor. *Tablet* 247:298-299 Mr 6 1993
The ERM goes on holiday. *Tablet* 247:1000-1001 Ag 7 1993
The European journey. *Tablet* 246:1592 D 19-26 1992
The flaw in the budget. *Tablet* 247:358 Mr 20 1993
The "Observer's SOS". *Tablet* 247:573-574 My 8 1993
Trade put first. *Tablet* 247:973 Jl 17 1993
Which way for Europe? *Tablet* 247:36+ Ja 9 1993

Keeler, William H, Abp.
Achieving peace with justice in Bosnia-Herzegovina. *Origins* 22:546-548 Ja 21 1993
The Catholic priesthood [address, Knights of Columbus annual meeting, Ag 1993]. *Columbia* 73:10-13 O 1993
Correspondence released: abortion and the nominee surgeon general. *Origins* 23:229-230 S 9 1993
The media and the "American Catholic Story". *Origins* 23:417+ N 25 1993
Statement supporting Cardinal Bernardin. *Origins* 23:421-422 N 25 1993
Witness and action toward a well-ordered society. *Momentum* 24:6-8 N-D 1993

Keely, Kathleen.
Review of: *Early Christian texts of Jews an Judaism* by MacLennan, Robert S. In: *SIDIC* 25 No 1:32 1992

Keely, Kathleen. (cont'd)
Review of: *Introduction to Jewish-Christian realtions* by Shermis, Michael, and Zannoni, Arthur E, eds. In: *SIDIC* 26 no 1:32 1993
Review of: *The liberation of dogma* by Segundo, Juan Luis. In: *SIDIC* 26 no 1:32+ 1993
Review of: *Trends in mission toward the third millenium* by Jenkinson, William, and O'Sullivan, Helene, eds. In: *SIDIC* 26 no 1:32+ 1993
Review of: *World religion and human liberation* by Cohn-Sherbok, Dan, ed. In: *SIDIC* 26 no 1:32+ 1993

Keen, Benjamin.
Review of: *The only way* by Las Casas, Bartolome de, 1474-1566. In: *CHist* 79:138-139 Ja 1993

Keen, Suzanne.
Review of: *Covenant* by Shapiro, Alan. In: *Comm* 120:26-28 F 26 1993
Review of: *Seeing things* by Heaney, Seamus, 1939-. In: *Comm* 120:26-28 F 26 1993
Review of: *The museum of clear ideas* by Hall, Donald. In: *Comm* 120:21-23 S 24 1993
Review of: *The never-ending story: new poems* by Hudgins, Andrew. In: *Comm* 120:26-28 F 26 1993
Review of: *The top 500 poems* by Harmon, William, ed. In: *Comm* 120:26-27 My 7 1993

Keenan, James F.
The Christian's call to grow. *Church* 9:48-49 Spr 1993
Confidentiality, disclosure, and fiduciary responsibility. *TheolStds* 54:142-159 Mr 1993
The function of the principle of double effect. *TheolStds* 54:294-315 Je 1993
Goodness and rightness: Thomas Aquinas' Summa Theologia. Washington, D C: Georgetown University Press, 1992. x, 212p ISBN 0-87840-530-5 LC 92-3090
Learning the virtue of justice. *Church* 9:38-40 Aut 1993
Review of: *Varieties of moral personality: ethics and psychological realism* by Flanagan, Owen. In: *TheolStds* 54:182-184 Mr 1993
The virtue of fidelity. *Church* 9:38-39 Sum 1993
What's your worst moral argument? *America* 169:17-18+ O 2 1993

Keene, Donald.
Seeds in the heart: Japanese literature from earliest times to the late sixteenth century. New York: Henry Holt and Company, 1993. x, 1265p ISBN 0-8050-1999-5 LC 93-1082

Keevey, Thomas.
Good Friday: the passion of the earth. *Emmanuel* 99:129-134 Ap 1993

Kehl, Medard.
Kirche in der Fremde. *Stimm Zeit* 211:507-520 Ag 1993
Review of: *Das katholische Kirchenverständnis* by Wiedenhofer, Siegfried. In: *Stimm Zeit* 211:428-429 Je 1993

Kehrwald, Rene. see Kehrwald, Leif, jt auth

Keightley, Georgia Masters.
Themes of the lay life. *Origins* 22:761-764 Ap 15 1993

Keith, Judith Marie.
Mission integration preserves sponsor's values. *Health Prog* 74:38-40 Ap 1993

Kelleher, Margaret Mary.
Hermeneutics in the study of liturgical performance. *Worship* 67:292-318 Jl 1993

Kellenbach, Katharina von.
Review of: *Dietrich Bonhoeffers Kampf gegen die nationalsozialistische Verfolgung und Vernichtung der Juden* by Müller, Christine-Ruth. In: *JEcumen Stds* 29:126 Wint 1992

Keller, Albert.
Fremdenfeindlichkeit. *Stimm Zeit* 210:793-794 D 1992

Keller, Dan.
Reflections of a parish priest. *Momentum* 24:58-60 S-O 1993

Keller, Gerald C, and Blankenbaker, Ronald G.
Lack of primary care physicians: Achilles' heel of reform? *Health Prog* 74:48-49 Jl-Ag 1993

Kellerman, Bill, and Grindel, Garcia.
Politics and prayer [exc fr *Liturgy: teaching prayer*; *Liturgy: teaching prayer*]. *Liturgy* 10:29-31 Spr 1993

Kellert, Stephen R. see Bormann, F Herbert, jt ed

Kelley, Donald R, 1931-.
Renaissance humanism. Boston: Twayne Publishers, 1991. x, 176p ISBN 0-80578-606-6 LC 91-4776

Kelliher, Jermiah.
Review of: *The unity we seek* by Runcie, Robert. In: *Can Cath Rev* 11:28-29 Mr 1993

Kelly, C.
Review of: *Augustus De Morgan and the logic of relations* by Merrill, Daniel D. In: *Mod Schlmn* 70:70-73 N 1992

Kelly, Darlene.
Fathers' business: Catholic priests as Canadian writers see them. *Can Cath Rev* 11:21-29 Ja 1993
Miss Brodie on the prairies or what a novel says about teaching [fr *The voice*]. *Can Cath Rev* 11:19-22 O 1993
Review of: *Curriculum vitae: autobiography* by Spark, Muriel, 1918-. In: *Can Cath Rev* 11:22-24 Ap 1993

Kelly, Francis D.
The Catechism in context. *Living Light* 29:29-38 Sum 1993
A catechism with universal appeal [interview by Robert Lockwood]. *OSV* 81:21+ D 20 1992
The mystery we proclaim: catechesis of the third millennium. Indiana: Our Sunday Visitor, 1993. x, 134p ISBN 0-87973-554-6 LC 92-63220

Kelly, George A.
Catholic laity and social evils: a pre-Vatican II mandate. *SocJust* 84:67-76 My-Je 1993

Kelly, George A. *(cont'd)*
Review of: *How to keep your university Catholic* by Kennedy, Leonard A. In: *HPR* 93:79 Jl 1993

Kelly, James R, 1937-.
Collegium and the futures of Catholic higher education. *America* 169:15-17 S 11 1993
Pro-life and pro-choice after Reagan-Bush. *America* 168:11-15 Ja 30 1993
Review of: *The churching of America 1776-1990* by Finke, Roger, and Stark, Rodney. In: *Comm* 120:27-29 Ap 23 1993

Kelly, Joseph F.
Lay partners. *AFER* 34:382-384 D 1992

Kelly, Kevin T.
Do we believe in a church of sinners. *Way* 33:106-116 Ap 1993
A great pleasure [review article *The body in context* by G Moore]. *Priests & People* 7:361-365 Ag-S 1993
Labor's metamorphosis? The high stakes at Caterpillar. *Comm* 120:7-8 Ja 15 1993
A medical and moral dilemma. *Month* 26:138-144 Ap 1993
Midflight correction? Reregulation won't work. *Comm* 120:6-7 Je 18 1993
Rest for Tony Bland. *Tablet* 247:332-334 Mr 13 1993
Review of: *Prayers of blessing and praise for all occasions* by Porto, Humberto, and Schlesinger, Hugo. In: *SIDIC* 25 No 1:33 1992

Kelly, Pat.
Nixing women priests, Anglican clergy may join Rome. *Register* 69:1+ S 26 1993

Kelly, Patrick F.
Schools worthy of kids: Saint Angela's needs help. *Comm* 120:6-8 Ap 9 1993

Kelly, Patrick Hyde.
"The way we live now": Graham Greene on reading. *Can Cath Rev* 11:20-22 Ap 1993

Kelly, Robert.
New bishops, new spirit in Chur. *Tablet* 247:798 Je 19 1993
Worker-priests continue their mission. *Tablet* 247:1308 O 9 1993

Kelly, Shay.
Idols and false images of God: a psychoanalytical perspective. *Doctr Life* 43:13-19 Ja 1993
Review of: *Conversations on counseling between a doctor and a priest* by Lefébure, Marcus, and Schauder, Hans. In: *Doctr Life* 43:444-445 S 1993

Kelly, Tony.
A new ontology? A response to a recent suggestion [reply to J Honner]. *Pacifica* 6:189-209 Je 1993
Review of: *Dialogue with the other: the inter-religious dialogue* by Tracy, David. In: *Pacifica* 6:244-245 Je 1993
Review of: *Making Australia: exploring our national conversation* by Thornhill, John. In: *Pacifica* 6:234-236 Je 1993

Kelter, Irving A.
Paolo Foscarini's Letter to Galileo: the search for proofs of the earth's motion. *Mod Schlmn* 70:31-44 N 1992

Kenel, Mary Elizabeth.
Review of: *Formative spirituality: volume five: traditional formation* by Kaam, Adrian L Van, 1920-. In: *RRel* 52:625-626 Jl-Ag 1993

Kenel, Sally A.
Review of: *Generous lives* by Redmont, Jane. In: *Living Light* 30:107-108 Aut 1993

Kenis, L.
Review of: *Geschichtlichkeit und Glaube* by Denzler, Georg, and Grasmück, Ernst Ludwig, eds. In: *Eph Theol Lovan* 69:217-219 Ap 1993

Kennan, George F, 1904-.
American addictions [excerpt fr *Around the cragged hill: a personal and political philosophy*]. *New Oxford Rev* 60:14-25 Je 1993

Kennedy, Anne.
Why work with young people? *Priests & People* 7:269-272 Jl 1993

Kennedy, Brian P.
Review of: *Sharing the darkness: the spirituality of caring* by Cassidy, Sheila. In: *New Oxford Rev* 60:32 Mr 1993
Towards a manifesto for art and the sacred. *Studies* 82:311-322 Aut 1993

Kennedy, Eugene.
The see-no-problem, hear-no-problem, speak-no-problem problem sex abuse. *Nat Cath Rep* 29:5+ Mr 19 1993

Kennedy, Finola.
Faith and work. *Tablet* 247:330 Mr 13 1993
Young people and religion growing out of the Church in the 1960s and 1990s. *Studies* 81:417-425 Wint 1992

Kennedy, Frank.
Pinpointing the adversary. *Tablet* 247:930 Jl 17 1993

Kennedy, James M.
Review of: *Peuple parmi les peuples: dossier pour l'animation biblique* by Camponovo, O, et al. In: *CBQ* 55:408-409 Ap 1993

Kennedy, Kevin.
Review of: *The diocese of Killaloe* by Murphy, Ignatius. In: *Doctr Life* 43:317-318 My-Je 1993

Kennedy, L.
Review of: *Shattered vows* by Rice, David. In: *HPR* 93:65-67 F 1993

Kennedy, Leonard A.
Review of: *Church and age unite!* by Appleby, Raphael Scott. In: *Can Cath Rev* 11:27-28 S 1993
Review of: *FCS Proceedings 1991 (Church and state in America: Catholic questions)* by Kelly, George A, ed. In: *ChrWorld* 38:123 Mr-Ap 1993
Review of: *Humanae Vitae: a generation later* by Smith, Janet E. In: *Crisis* 11:50-52 Ja 1993
Review of: *The politics of prayer* by Hitchcock, Helen Hull, ed. In: *Crisis* 11:57-58 S 1993

Kennedy, M. J.
Review of: *Making saints: inside the Vatican: who become saints, who do not, and why* by Woodward, Kenneth L. In: *Heythrop* 34:351-352 Jl 1993

Kennedy, Marnie.
Retreats on the streets. *Way Suppl* 75:20-29 Aut 1992

Kennedy, Paul M, 1945-.
Preparing for the twenty-first century. New York: Random House, 1993. x, 428p ISBN 0-39458-443-0 LC 91-52668

Kennedy, Philip.
Schillebeeckx. Collegeville: Liturgical, 1993. x, 144p ISBN 0-8146-5502-5

Kennedy, Terence.
An Italian view of the debate on virtue. *Thomist* 57:123-130 Ja 1993
Review of: *Conscience and casuistry in early modern Europe* by Leites, Edmund, ed. In: *Gregorianum* 74 no 3:584-587 1993

Kennedy, Terrence.
Review of: *Problemi di etica: fondazione, norme, orietnamenti* by Berti, Enrico, ed. In: *Gregorianum* 74 No 1:169-172 1993

Kenner, M.
Review of: *Parents forever: you and your adult children* by Callahan, Sidney. In: *Nat Cath Rep* 29:38 F 5 1993

Kenny, Anthony John.
Catholics, Jews and the state of Israel. New York: Paulist Press, 1993. x, 157p ISBN 0-8091-3406-3 LC 93-17833

Kenny, James A.
Review of: *Lead us not into temptation* by Berry, Jason. In: *St Anth* 101:50-51 Ag 1993

Kenny, Joe.
The flood. *Register* 69:1+ Ag 1 1993
The light and dark side of NAFTA. *Register* 69:1+ Ag 15 1993

Kenny, Mary, 1936-.
Review of: *Behind palace doors* by Dempster, Nigel, and Evans, Peter. In: *Tablet* 247:889-890 Jl 10 1993
Review of: *Diana v Charles* by Whitaker, James. In: *Tablet* 247:889-890 Jl 10 1993
Review of: *Fall from grace* by Broderick, Joe. In: *Tablet* 247:516 Ap 24 1993
Review of: *Forbidden fruit* by Murphy, Annie. In: *Tablet* 247:516 Ap 24 1993
Review of: *Inheritance: a psychological history of the Royal Family* by Friedman, Dennis. In: *Tablet* 247:580 My 8 1993
Review of: *Life and how to survive it* by Skynner, Robin, and Cleese, John. In: *Tablet* 247:439 Ap 3 1993
Review of: *Not guilty: in defence of the modern man* by Thomas, David M. In: *Tablet* 247:371-372 Mr 20 1993
Review of: *Royal throne: the future of the monarchy* by Longford, Elizabeth. In: *Tablet* 247:580 My 8 1993
Review of: *The rise and fall of the House of Windsor* by Wilson, A N, 1950-. In: *Tablet* 247:889-890 Jl 10 1993
Review of: *The tarnished crown* by Holden, Anthony. In: *Tablet* 247:889-890 Jl 10 1993
Saints speak volumes. *Tablet* 247:911-913 Jl 17 1993
The tragic death of Eva Green. *Tablet* 247:158 F 6 1993

Kent, John.
Review of: *God and history: aspects of British theology 1875-1914* by Hinchliff, Peter. In: *New Blckfrs* 74:53-54 Ja 1993

Kenward, Robin Place.
Review of: *In search of the Neandertals: solving the puzzle of human origins* by Stringer, Christopher, and Gamble, Clive. In: *Tablet* 247:1102-1103 Ag 28 1993
Review of: *The Neandertals: changing the image of mankind* by Trinkhaus, Eric, and Shipman, Pat. In: *Tablet* 247:1102-1103 Ag 28 1993

Keogh, Daire.
Review of: *The fall and rise of the Irish nation: the Catholic question 1690-1830* by Bartlett, Thomas. In: *Studies* 81:457-459 Wint 1992
Review of: *The men of no property: Irish radicals and popular politics in the late 18th century* by Smyth, Jim. In: *Studies* 82:234-236 Sum 1993

Kepp, Michael.
Going all the way. *Register* 69:3 My 23 1993
In Brazil, renewal is thriving. *Register* 69:1+ Mr 7 1993

Ker, Ian.
Review of: *The convert cardinals: Newman and Manning* by Newsome, David. In: *Tablet* 247:1133-1134 S 4 1993

Kerber, Walter, 1926-, et al, eds.
Katholische Gesellschaftslehre im Überlick. Frankfurt: Knecht, 1993. x, 420p ISBN 3-7820-0623-2

Kereszty, Roch, 1933-. *see* Farmer, William R, jt auth

Kereszty, Roch A, 1933-.
"Bride" and "Mother" in the Super cantica of St Bernard: an ecclesiology for our time? *Communio* 20:415-436 Sum 1993
Historical research, theological inquiry, and the reality of Jesus: reflections on the method of J P Meier. *Communio* 19:576-600 Wint 1992

Kerins, M Roberta.
Review of: *The art of spiritual guidance* by Gratton, Carolyn. In: *Spir Life* 39:51-53 Spr 1993

Kerkhofs, Jan, 1924-.
Will the churches meet th Europeans? *Tablet* 247:1184-1187 S 18 1993

Kerlin, Michael J.
Maurice Blondel: 100 years after "L Action". *America* 168:12-15 Je 19-26 1993

Kermode, Frank. *see* Alter, Robert, jt ed

Kern, Walter O.
Review of: *Angelus meditations on the Litany of the Sacred Heart* by John Paul II, Pope, 1920- (Karol Wojtyla) (elected 1978). In: *HPR* 93:72-73 Ap 1993
Review of: *Historisches Wörterbuch der Philosophie* by Ritter, Joachim, and Gründer, Karlfried. In: *Stimm Zeit* 211:574-575 Ag 1993

Kerner, Robert J.
A father's blessing: it's ours for the asking. *New Cov* 23:26-27 Ag 1993

Kerness, Bonnie.
A wall of silence. *Cath Work* 60:1+ Mr-Ap 1993

Kerr, Fergus.
The human person: animal and spirit [by D Braine, review article]. *New Blckfrs* 74:333-337 Jl-Ag 1993
Review of: *Aquinas on mind* by Kenny, Anthony John. In: *Tablet* 247:726-727 Je 5 1993
Review of: *Church: the human story of God* by Schillebeeckx, Edward. In: *New Blckfrs* 73:571-573 N 1992
Review of: *Karl Rahner* by Dych, William V. In: *New Blckfrs* 74:279-281 My 1993
Review of: *Realism with a human face* by Putnam, Hilary. In: *Heythrop* 34:103-104 Ja 1993
Review of: *Schillebeeckx* by Kennedy, Philip. In: *Tablet* 247:1299-1300 O 9 1993
Review of: *The metaphysics of the "Tractatus"* by Carruthers, Peter. In: *Heythrop* 34:102-103 Ja 1993
Review of: *The weight of glory. A vision and practice for Christian faith: the future of liberal theology* by Hardy, D W, and Sedgwick, P H, eds. In: *New Blckfrs* 73:622-623 D 1992
Review of: *Tractarian semantics: finding sense in Wittgenstein's "Tractatus"* by Carruthers, Peter. In: *Heythrop* 34:102-103 Ja 1993
Review of: *Wittgenstein centenary essays* by Griffiths, A Phillips, ed. In: *Heythrop* 34:473-474 O 1993
The Trinity and Christian life. *Priests & People* 7:233-237 Je 1993

Kerrigan, Ruth, and Harkulich, Joan T.
A spiritual tool. *Health Prog* 74:46-49 My 1993

Kertzer, David I.
Sacrificed for honor: Italian infant abandonment and the politics of reproductive control. Boston: Beacon Press, 1993. x, 252p ISBN 0-8070-5604-9 LC 92-35169

Kessler, Diane C.
Ecumenical or interfaith? *Living Light* 30:89-92 Aut 1993

Kessler, Martin.
Review of: *Bijbelse Theologie, I,2* by Breukelman, F H. In: *OTA* 16:418 Je 1993
Review of: *Hooglied: eed praktische bijbelverklaring* by Mulder, M J. In: *OTA* 15:505 O 1992
Review of: *Inleiding in het Oude Testament* by Jagersma, H, and Vervenne, Marc, eds. In: *OTA* 15:483 O 1992
Review of: *Tekst and interpretatie: studies over getallen, teksten, verhalen en geschiedenis in het Oude Testament* by Jagersma, H. In: *OTA* 15:482 O 1992
Review of: *The documents from the Bar Kokhba period in the Cave of Letters* by Lewis, Naphtali, et al, eds. In: *OTA* 15:483-484 O 1992
Review of: *The indomitable Prophet: a biographical commentary on Jeremiah* by White, R E O. In: *OTA* 15:508 O 1992

Ketcham, Katherine. see Kurtz, Ernest, jt auth

Keyl, Timothy J.
Musicians as mourners. *Liturgy* 10:63-67 Wint 1992

Kezmoh, Heidi Schlumpf.
The family and religious life linked. *Register* 69:1+ My 2 1993
Religious leaders eye peacemaking. *Register* 69:1+ My 16 1993
The sexual revolution aftershock. *Register* 69:1+ My 2 1993
A tragic resort to arms. *Register* 69:1+ S 5 1993
What has the church done for your marriage lately? *USCath* 58:28-35 O 1993

Khan, A.
Review of: *Islamic fundamentalism and the Gulf Crisis* by Piscatori, James, ed. In: *TheolStds* 53:792-793 D 1992

Khantipalo, Bhikkhu.
Monastic formation in Buddhism. *Stud Form Spir* 14:117-127 F 1993

Kidder, Keith.
Who's who in The Last Supper? [condensed fr *Western New York Catholic* Mr 1993]. *CDgst* 57:1-3 Jl 1993

Kiely, Bartholomew.
Candidates with difficulties in celibacy: discernment, admission, formation. *Seminarium* 33:107-118 Ja-Mr 1993

Kiker, B F, 1937-. see Heath, Julia A, jt auth

Kilby, Karen.
Review of: *Bultmann* by Fergusson, David. In: *Priests & People* 7:250-251 Je 1993
Review of: *Karl Rahner* by Dych, William V. In: *Priests & People* 7:250-251 Je 1993

Kiley, P.
Review of: *Orestes A Brownson: selected writings* by Carey, Patrick W, ed. In: *RRel* 52:156 Ja-F 1993

Kilgallen, John J.
Jesus, Savior. *StudiaM* 42:41-65 1993
Reflections on charisma (ta) in the New Testament. *StudiaM* 41:289-323 1992

Killen, Patricia O'Connell.
An historian's perspective: then, now, and then? *Listening* 28:14-27 Wint 1993
The practice of theological reflection in small faith communities. *Chicago Stud* 31:189-196 Ag 1992

Kilroy, Bernard.
Priestly development for collaboration in ministry. *Doctr Life* 43:287-294 My-Je 1993

Kimaryo, Rogath.
Seminary and religious formation in an African milieu. *AFER* 35:202-208 Ag 1993

Kimbrell, Andrew.
Patents encroach upon the body. *Crisis* 11:43-48 My 1993

Kimel, Alvin F, Jr.
The trinity and feminism. *Thomist* 57:509-520 Jl 1993

Kimmerling, Ben.
Amongst women. *Furrow* 44:273-282 My 1993
Celibacy and intimacy. *Way Suppl* 77:87-96 Sum 1993

Kinast, Robert L.
Checklist for collaborative ministry. *Tod Parish* 25:13-16, 13-17 O S 1993
Getting a grip on stress and conflict. *Catechist* 27:27-29 S 1993
How much is lay ministry worth? *Origins* 23:287-292 O 7 1993
Review of: *Care of persons, care of worlds: a psychosystems approach to pastoral care and counseling* by Graham, Larry Kent. In: *TheolStds* 54:590-592 S 1993
When they ask your opinion, give it. *Emmanuel* 49:402-407 S 1993

Kindig, Eileen Silva.
Stringing pearls: making heirlooms of family stories. *St Anth* 101:10-15 O 1993

King, Eleace.
Vocations among teaching brothers. *RRel* 52:102-110 Ja-F 1993

King, Judine.
Musings on Earth Day near Lake Erie. *Sisters* 65:193-197 My 1993

King, Nicholas.
Is the Bible true? *Priests & People* 7:50-53 F 1993

King, P.
Review of: *The Cistercians in Scandinavia* by France, James. In: *Cist Stud* 27 No 4:[88]-[89] 1992

King, Philip J.
An archaeological companion. Louisville: John Knox, 1993. x, 240p ISBN 0-664-21920-9

King, Sue.
Being "church". *Way Suppl* 75:62-66 Aut 1992

King, Thomas M.
Review of: *Silent lamp: the Thomas Merton story* by Shannon, William Henry, 1917-. In: *TheolStds* 54:199-200 Mr 1993

King, U.
Review of: *Women towards priesthood: ministerial politics and feminist praxis* by Field-Bibb, Jacqueline. In: *Heythrop* 34:84-86 Ja 1993

Kinnamon, Michael.
Report from the fifth World Conference on Faith and Order. *Ecumen Trends* 22:1+ O 1993

Kinney, Dale.
Review of: *History as a visual art in the twelfth-century Renaissance* by Morrison, Karl Frederick. In: *CHist* 79:521-522 Jl 1993

Kinney, John, Bp.
NCCB establishes committee on sexual abuse. *Origins* 23:104-105 Jl 1 1993

Kirby, Peadar.
Reclaiming a radical heritage [review article *They have fooled you again* by D Carroll]. *Doctr Life* 43:343-348 Jl-Ag 1993

Kirk, Pamela.
Complexities of conversion: Latin American and European encounter—500 years. *Living Light* 29:22-34 Wint 1992
The power of the poor [exc fr *Liturgy: the power that unites*]. *Liturgy* 10:22-23 Spr 1993

Kirk, Russell, 1918-.
Review of: *Solzhenitsyn and the modern world* by Ericson, Edward E, Jr. In: *Crisis* 11:59-60 O 1993

Kirke, P.
Review of: *Search for the absent God* by Hill, William J, 1924-. In: *Doctr Life* 42:649-651 D 1992

Kirley, Kevin J.
Review of: *The book of saints: a dictionary of servants of God canonized by the Catholic Church.* In: *Can Cath Rev* 11:34 Ja 1993
Review of: *Traditions of spiritual guidance* by Byrne, Lavinia, ed. In: *Can Cath Rev* 11:24-25 N 1993

Kirp, David L, 1944-.
A sedan is not a home. *Comm* 120:4-6 F 12 1993

Kirschner, Leonard, and Willert, Joan St.
Making capitation work. *Health Prog* 74:57-58 Jl-Ag 1993

Kirwan, Michael.
God in many disguises. *Cath Work* 60:7 My 1993
Review of: *The puzzle of evil* by Vardy, Peter. In: *Month* 26:111-112 Mr 1993

Kischer, Clayton Ward.
Human development and reconsideration of ensoulment. *Linacre* 60:57-63 F 1993
In defense of human development. *Linacre* 59:68-75 N 1992

Kissener, Michael. see Lill, Rudolf, jt ed

Kistner, H.
Review of: *Discovering the first century Church: the Acts of the Apostles, Letters of Paul and the Book of Revelation* by Ralph, Margaret Nutting. In: *St Anth* 100:50-52 F 1993
Review of: *In the days of Paul* by Tambasco, Anthony J. In: *St Anth* 100:50-52 F 1993
Review of: *What are they saying about Acts?* by Powell, Mark Allan. In: *St Anth* 100:50-52 F 1993

Klaassen, Walter.
Review of: *Jesus—ein gekreuzigter Pharisäer?* by Lapide, Pinchas. In: *JEcumen Stds* 29:484-485 Sum-Aut 1992

Klami, Hannu Tapani.
Legal argument and decision theory. *Amer J Juris* 37:171-184 1992

Klarner, Anne.
Proclamation primer. *Mod Lit* 20:12-13 My 1993

Klaus, Hanna.
The existential isolation of contraception. *Linacre* 59:29-32 N 1992

Klein, Emma.
Review of: *Not a job for a nice Jewish boy* by Cohn-Sherbok, Dan. In: *Tablet* 247:1134-1135 S 4 1993
Review of: *The Nazi Holocaust* by Landau, Ronnie S. In: *Tablet* 247:948-949 Jl 24 1993
Review of: *To give them light: the legacy of Roman Vishniac* by Wiesel, Marion, ed. In: *Tablet* 247:948-949 Jl 24 1993

Klein, Terrance W.
Discerning vocations. *America* 168:10-11 My 1 1993
Institution narratives at the crossroads. *Worship* 67:407-418 S 1993

Klein, William Wade, et al, eds.
Introduction to biblical interpretation. Dallas: Word Publishing, 1993. x, 518p ISBN 0-8499-0774-8 LC 93-20099

Klejment, Anne.
Review of: *Perspectives on the American Catholic Church, 1789-1989* by Vicchio, Stephen J, and Geiger, Virginia, eds. In: *ACHSR* 103:54-55 Aut 1992

Klenicki, Leon.
The interfaith future: from the mind to the heart. *Ecumen Trends* 22:9 My 1993 see Fisher, Eugene J, jt ed

Klimon, William M.
Review of: *Holy women of Russia* by Meehan, Brenda. In: *Crisis* 11:56-57 Jl-Ag 1993
Review of: *In search of true wisdom: visits to Eastern spiritual fathers* by Bolshakoff, Sergius, and Pennington, M Basil, 1931-. In: *Crisis* 11:56-57 Jl-Ag 1993
Review of: *Rome and the Eastern Churches* by Nichols, Aidan. In: *Crisis* 11:51-52 Je 1993

Klimoski, Victor J.
The dilemma of being nice. *Church* 9:44-46 Spr 1993

Kmiec, Douglas W.
The higher law background of the Notre Dame law school. *Amer J Juris* 37:213-242 1992
The Notre Dame Law School Commencement Address—three natural law challenges for Notre Dame lawyers. *Amer J Juris* 37:359-361 1992

Knappert, Jan. *see* Rippin, Andrew, jt ed

Kneen, Brewster.
Can nature be a commodity? [fr *The ram's horn*]. *Cath Work* 60:1+ S 1993

Knight, Henry F.
Meeting Jacob at the Jabbok: wrestling with a text—a Midrash on Genesis 32:22-32. *JEcumen Stds* 29:451-460 Sum-Aut 1992

Knitter, Paul F. *see* Corless, Robert, jt ed

Knoblach, Thomas.
Mary and obedience. *HPR* 93:64-70 My 1993

Knockaert, André.
Le Catéchisme de l'Église catholique. *Lumen* 48:135-148 Je 1993

Knopp, Josephine.
Review of: *The partings of the ways between Christianity and Judaism and their significance for the character of Christianity* by Dunn, James D G. In: *JEcumen Stds* 29:485 Sum-Aut 1992

Knoppers, Gary N.
Review of: *The Books of Chronicles: a classified bibliography* by Kalimi, Isaac. In: *CBQ* 55:119 Ja 1993

Knowles, David.
Authentic teaching. *Tablet* 247:939-940 Jl 24 1993

Kobler, John F.
Review of: *The Passionists* by Mercurio, Roger. In: *Can Cath Rev* 11:32 Jl-Ag 1993

Kocan, George.
Martial arts, manly arts. *Crisis* 11:58-60 My 1993

Koch, Kurt.
Selbstverständnis und Praxis des kirchlichen Lehramts. *Stimm Zeit* 211:395-402 Je 1993
Sonntag um der Menschen willen. *Stimm Zeit* 211:155-167 Mr 1993

Koenig, Elisabeth K J.
Julian of Norwich, Mary Magdalene, and the drama of prayer. *Horizons (CTS)* 20:23-43 Spr 1993
Review of: *Spiritual exercises for today* by Dunne, Tad. In: *Horizons (CTS)* 19:332-333 Fall 1992
Review of: *Spiritual mentoring: guiding people through spiritual exercises to life decisions* by Dunne, Tad. In: *Horizons (CTS)* 19:332-333 Fall 1992

Koenig, John.
Review of: *The revelatory text: interpreting the New Testament as sacred scripture* by Schneiders, Sandra M. In: *Horizons (CTS)* 19:297-300 Fall 1992

Koenig-Bricker, Woodeene.
Eight ways to help the people you know. *Salt* 13:12-13 Ja 1993
How to really help the unemployed. *Salt* 13:8-12 Ja 1993
Oregon's health-care plan gets a "yes". *OSV* 81:17 Ap 11 1993
Why Johnny can't tell right from wrong [interview by W Koenig-Bricker]. *OSV* 82:10-11 Ag 29 1993

Koernke, Theresa F.
Review of: *Worship: city, church and renewal* by Baldovin, John F. In: *Horizons (CTS)* 19:324-325 Fall 1992
Review of: *Worship: culture and theology* by Power, David Noel. In: *Horizons (CTS)* 20:156-157 Spr 1993

Koester, Craig R.
Review of: *John as storyteller* by Stibbe, Mark W G. In: *CBQ* 55:399-401 Ap 1993

Koester, Craig R. *(cont'd)*
Review of: *Templum amicitiae: essays on the second temple presented to Ernst Bammel* by Horbury, William, ed. In: *CBQ* 54:822-824 O 1992

Koester, Helmut. *see* Bovon, François, jt auth

Köhler, Oscar.
Review of: *Deutsche Katholiken, 1918-1945* by Hürten, Heinz. In: *Stimm Zeit* 211:215 Mr 1993
Review of: *Die Geschichte des Christentums* by Mayeur, Jean-Marie. In: *Stimm Zeit* 211:213-214 Mr 1993
Review of: *Die Zeit der Konfession (1530-1620/30)* by Venard, Marc, ed. In: *Stimm Zeit* 211:69-70 Ja 1993
Review of: *Ende der Geschichte?* by Meyer, Martin. In: *Stimm Zeit* 211:719-720 O 1993
Review of: *Klara von Assisi* by Bartoli, Marco. In: *Stimm Zeit* 211:718 O 1993
Review of: *Segesser, Philipp Anton: Briefwechsel* by Conzemius, Victor. In: *Stimm Zeit* 211:141-142 F 1993
Review of: *Vaticanum I (1869-1870)* by Schatz, Klaus. In: *Stimm Zeit* 211:214 Mr 1993

Köhler, Oskar.
Joseph Bernhart. *Stimm Zeit* 211:376-384 Je 1993
Probleme einer Hagiographie heute. *Stimm Zeit* 211:641-644 S 1993
Soziologie und Theologie in Nachbarschaft. *Stimm Zeit* 211:210-212 Mr 1993

Kokolus, Cait.
Of heartwounds and hope. *Living Prayer* 26:13-16 S-O 1993

Kolarcik, Michael.
Review of: *Wisdom in revolt: metaphorical theology in the Book of Job* by Perdue, Leo G. In: *CBQ* 55:346-347 Ap 1993

Kollack, Theodore, 1911-.
Voices: Teddy Kolleck, Jerusalem's outspoken mayor [interview by L Pevtzow]. *Register* 69:1+ Ag 1 1993

Kollar, J.
Review of: *Explore poetry* by Graves, Donald. In: *Momentum* 24:84 F-Mr 1993

Kollar, Judith Ann.
Did faith make a difference this year? *Tod Parish* 25:6 Ap-My 1993
Do your meetings need help? *Tod Parish* 25:15-16 N-D 1993
Is anybody listening? *Tod Parish* 25:4-5 Mr 1993
Make your meetings count!. *Tod Parish* 25:34-35 S 1993
Review of: *How to run a successful meeting in half the time* by Frank, Milo. In: *Tod Parish* 25:34-35 S 1993
What do you know about your diocese? *Tod Parish* 25:12 O 1993

Kollar, Nathan R.
Review of: *Death in the midst of life* by Bregman, Lucy. In: *Horizons (CTS)* 20:190-191 Spr 1993
Secular fundamentalism and secular humanism: value sets for the twenty-first century. *Stud Form Spir* 14:233-246 My 1993

Kollar, Rene.
Plans for an 18th-century Benedictine settlement in western Pennsylvania: Bishop John Carroll and the English Benedictine Congregation. *Word Sp* 14:3-11 1992
Review of: *God's February: a life of Archie Craig, 1888-1985* by Templeton, Elizabeth. In: *JEcumen Stds* 29:266-267 Spr 1992
Review of: *The Celtic vision: prayers from the Outer Hebrides* by Waal, Esther de, ed. In: *Cist Stud* 28:[13] 1993

Koller, Christopher F.
An open letter: four things to keep in mind. *Comm* 120:5-6 Ap 23 1993
Review of: *If I were a rich man could I buy a pancreas?* by Caplan, Arthur L. In: *Comm* 120:34-35 Ap 9 1993

Kolp, Alan.
Traditions of spiritual guidance. The real presence a Quaker perspective on spiritual direction. *Way* 33:240-247 Jl 1993

Kolvenbach, Peter Hans.
Apology to native Americans for past mistakes. *Origins* 23:36-37 Je 3 1993

Komarica, Franjo, Bp, 1946-, et al.
"Help us while it is not too late!". *Cath Int* 4:230-231 My 1993

Komonchak, Joseph Andrew, 1939-.
The authority of the Catechism of the Catholic Church. *Living Light* 29:39-49 Sum 1993
[Four men taught me moral theology]. *Comm* 120:12 O 22 1993
The local church and the church Catholic: the contemporary theological problematic. *Jurist* 52 no 1:416-447 1992
Many models, one church. *Church* 9:12-15 Spr 1993
Review of: *Fullness of faith* by Himes, Michael J, and Himes, Kenneth R. In: *Comm* 120:27-29 S 24 1993
Review of: *Les cent ans de la Faculté de théologie* by Doré, Joseph, ed. In: *TheolStds* 54:390-391 Je 1993

Kondoleon, Theodore J.
A contradiction in Saint Thomas's teaching on creation. *Thomist* 57:51-61 Ja 1993

Kondrusiewicz, Tadeusz, Abp.
The Catholic Church in Russia. *Ecumen Trends* 22:13-15 O 1993
Critical time for the church in Russia. *Origins* 22:695-696 Mr 18 1993
Dialogue [interview by J Luxmoore]. *Register* 69:1+ F 7 1993

Konings, Johan.
Jesus ou os pobres? *Perspectiva* 25:149-161 My-Ag 1993
Review of: *A Palavra inspirada; a Bíblia à luz da ciência da linguagem* by Schökel, Luis Alonso. In: *Perspectiva* 25:110-113 Ja-Ap 1993
Review of: *Jesus e a sociedade de seu tempo* by Mateos, Juan, and Camacho, Fernando. In: *Perspectiva* 25:116-117 Ja-Ap 1993
Review of: *Traces bibliques dans la loi morale chez Kant* by Ternay, Henry d'Aviau de. In: *Perspectiva* 25:113-116 Ja-Ap 1993

Konstant, David Every, Bp, 1930-.
Understanding the catechism. *Priests & People* 7:213-219 Je 1993

Konstant, David Every, Bp, and Law, Bernard Francis, Cardinal, 1931-.
The catechism and inclusive language. *Origins* 22:628-630 F 25 1993

Konstantine, Steven. see Smart, Ninian, 1927-, jt auth

Kooij, A Van Der. see Dirksen, P B, jt ed

Kooij, Arie van der.
The story of David and Goliath the early history of its text. *Eph Theol Lovan* 78:118-131 Ap 1992

Koopman, Joop.
Their day in court. *Register* 69:2 Jl 4 1993

Kopas, Jane.
Outsiders in the Gospels: marginality as a source of knowledge. *Way* 33:117-126 Ap 1993
Review of: *Peace of the present: an unviolent way of life* by Dunne, John S, 1929-. In: *Horizons (CTS)* 19:335-336 Fall 1992

Köpe, Károly.
Letter to a seminarian. *SacM* 120:6-8 Aut 1993
You get what you deserve (a breath of fresh air?). *SacM* 120:6-8 Sum 1993

Kopek, Robert.
Picture that!. *BibleT* 31:225-230 Jl 1993

Koperski, Veronica.
Textlinguistics and the integrity of Philippians. *Eph Theol Lovan* 78:330-367 D 1992

Kopfensteiner, Thomas R.
Globalization and the autonomy of moral reasoning: an essay in fundamental moral theology. *TheolStds* 54:485-511 S 1993
Review of: *Global responsibility: in search of a new world ethic* by Küng, Hans, 1928-. In: *New Theol Rev* 6:104-106 F 1993

Korn, Barton.
Review of: *Community of faith: crafting Christian communities today* by Whitehead, Evelyn Eaton, and Whitehead, James D. In: *Mod Lit* 20:41 Ag 1993
Review of: *Do justice: linking Christian faith and modern economic life* by Blank, Rebecca M. In: *Mod Lit* 20:37-38 My 1993
Review of: *Good things happen* by Westley, Richard John, 1928-. In: *Mod Lit* 20:41 My 1993
Review of: *The new Catholic evangelization* by Boyack, Kenneth, ed. In: *Mod Lit* 20:40 F 1993

Korthals, Elaine.
Review of: *The art of spiritual guidance* by Gratton, Carolyn. In: *RRel* 52:627-628 Jl-Ag 1993

Kosicki, George.
Justice isn't enough. *Register* 69:4 Mr 7 1993
Who is Sister Faustina? *Register* 69:4 F 7 1993

Köszegi, Michael A. see Melton, J Gordon, jt auth

Kosztolnyik, Zoltan J.
In the European mainstream: Hungarian churchmen and thirteenth-century synods. *CHist* 79:413-433 Jl 1993

Koterski, J.
Review of: *Cognition* by Owens, John Joseph. In: *HPR* 94:75-77 O 1993
Review of: *The caterpillar that came to church: a story of the Eucharist* by Hooker, Irene H, et al. In: *HPR* 94:73 O 1993

Koterski, Joseph. see Flannery, Kevin L, jt auth

Kountz, P.
Review of: *Silent lamp: the Thomas Merton story* by Shannon, William Henry, 1917-. In: *CHist* 78:615-620 O 1992

Kow, James P.
Hegel, Kolb and Flay: foundationalism or anti-foundationalism? *IPQ* 33:203-218 Je 1993

Kowal, Peter.
Review of: *The icon* by Quenot, Michel. In: *Furrow* 44:453-454 Jl-Ag 1993

Koyzis, David T.
A Protestant consideration of icons. *New Oxford Rev* 60:24-25 Mr 1993

Kozah, P Makram.
"Pastores dabo vobis": perspectives orientales (Commentary: *Pastores dabo vobis*). *Seminarium* 32:518-529 O-D 1992

Kozar, Joseph Vicek.
The Gospel of John as good news. *Catechist* 26:44-50 F 1993
The Gospel of Luke as good news. *Catechist* 26:44-49 Ja 1993

Kraaebel, A T.
Review of: *Jewish communities in Asia Minor* by Trebilco, Paul R. In: *CBQ* 55:186-187 Ja 1993

Kraemer, Barbara.
Review of: *Alternative economic indicators* by Anderson, Victor. In: *RSocEcon* 51:247-249 Sum 1993
Review of: *Panama at the crossroads: economic development and political change in the Twentieth Century* by Zimbalist, Andrew, and Weeks, John. In: *RSocEcon* 51:250-252 Sum 1993

Kraft, William F.
A story of addiction and co-addiction. *RRel* 52:454-460 My-Je 1993

Krajewski, Stanislaw.
The challenge of Auschwitz today. *SIDIC* 26 no 1:21-22 1993

Kramb, Marie A.
Review of: *Teresa of Avila and the rhetoric of femininity* by Weber, Alison. In: *Relig Lit* 24:111-112 Aut 1992

Kramer, Kenneth P.
Death dreams: unveiling mysteries of the unconscious mind. New Jersey: Paulist Press, 1993. x, 288p ISBN 0-8091-3349-0 LC 92-29605

Kramer, Matthew.
Our longest lie: irreligious thoughts on the relation between metaphysics and politics. *PhilosTod* 37:89-109 Spr 1993

Kramer, Richard, and Vickers, Susan.
A system develops values-based reform policy. *Health Prog* 74:56 Jl-Ag 1993

Kramer, V.
Review of: *Evelyn Underhill: artist of the infinite life* by Greene, Dana. In: *Cist Stud* 27 No 4:[82]-[83] 1992

Krasevac, Edward L.
Review of: *Christology and spirituality* by Thompson, William M. In: *Thomist* 57:136-140 Ja 1993
Review of: *The passion of the Western mind* by Tarnas, Richard. In: *Thomist* 57:550-553 Jl 1993

Krason, Stephen M.
Catholic makers of America: biographical sketches of Catholic statesmen and political thinkers in America's first century, 1776-1876. Front Royal, Virginia: Christendom Press, 1993. 260p ISBN 0-931888-44-2
The essential elements of and conditions for a "Democratic Republic": the view prevalent at the founding and in Early American History. *F & R* 18:235-274 Aut 1992
An open letter to the federal government [editorial]. *SocJust* 84:131-132 S-O 1993
Review of: *Dumbing us down: the hidden curriculum of compulsory schooling* by Gatto, John Taylor. In: *SocJust* 84:93-94 My-Je 1993
Review of: *Jaws of death: gate of heaven* by Hildebrand, Dietrich von. In: *SocJust* 84:31 Ja-F 1993
Review of: *Paths to peace: a contribution.* In: *SocJust* 84:29 Ja-F 1993
What the Catholic finds wrong with secular social science. *SocJust* 84:5-11 Ja-F 1993

Krause, David.
The rushing up of Synge's buried fire. *Studies* 82:298-310 Aut 1993

Krause, Edward.
Abortion's aftermath. *Register* 69:4 O 3 1993
Another impressive "convert". *Register* 69:5 Je 27 1993
The experts are wrong again. *Register* 69:5 Mr 7 1993
Humanae Vitae at 25. *Register* 69:5 Mr 28 1993
IVF: it solves very little. *Register* 69:5 Je 6 1993
John Paul II in Lithuania. *Register* 69:4 S 19 1993
Separating fact and fiction. *Register* 69:5 Ja 3 1993
A warning from Holland. *Register* 69:5 My 9 1993
Why doctors are suspicious of "aid in dying" bills. *Register* 69:5 Je 13 1993

Krawczyk, Boleslaw.
XI Incontro Europeo dei segretari delle commisioni liturgiche nazionali. *Notitiae* 28:618-623 S 1992

Krawczyk, Marilyn Peters.
Review of: *Christian family celebrations: prayer services for special moments* by Goodwin, Lawrence J. In: *Mod Lit* 20:40 Ap 1993
Review of: *How to read and pray the parables* by Gustin, Marilyn Norquist. In: *Mod Lit* 20:42 Je-Jl 1993
Review of: *May I have this dance* by Rupp, Joyce. In: *Mod Lit* 20:39 My 1993
Review of: *Spiritually aware pastoral care* by Williams, Earle, and Williams, Elspeth. In: *Mod Lit* 19:42 D 1992-Ja 1993
Review of: *Together as a parish (family and parish books)* by Mortimer, Dolores A. In: *Mod Lit* 19:43 D 1992-Ja 1993

Kreeft, Peter John, 1937-.
Christianity for modern pagans. *Register* 69:5 Ap 11 1993
A day without sin. *New Cov* 23:33 Ag 1993
Death, the unsentimental fact, is our anchor to God's deeper realities. *Register* 69:1+ My 2 1993
The discernment dilemma. *New Cov* 22:10-14 My 1993
Gender and the will of God. *Crisis* 11:20-28 S 1993
God hides His presence to instruct us in humility. *Register* 69:1+ My 30 1993
He is risen!. *Register* 69:1+ Ap 11 1993
Heaven's dog. *New Cov* 22:21+ Ja 1993
How saints are relevant. *New Cov* 22:33 Je 1993
Human vanity: it's the wrong path. *Register* 69:1+ Ap 25 1993
Indifference turns the modern heart away from heaven. *Register* 69:1+ My 23 1993
Life-changing verses. *New Cov* 22:19+ My 1993
Only Christianity explains the heart of our human condition. *Register* 69:1+ Ap 18 1993
Prayer: just do it!. *New Cov* 22:19-20 Ap 1993
Prayers for busy people. *New Cov* 22:17+ F 1993
Review of: *Journeybread for the shadowlands* by Jackson, Pamela E J. In: *Register* 69:5 F 21 1993
A shorter summa: the essential philosophical passages of St Thomas Aquinas' Summa Theologica. San Francisco: Ignatius Press, 1993. ISBN 0-89870-435-9
Time: why we don't have any. *Register* 69:1+ My 16 1993
We should fear sin far more than death. *Register* 69:1+ My 9 1993
When a Christian sins. *New Cov* 22:19-20 Mr 1993
The Angelus [Advent series pt 1 of 4]. *OSV* 82:5 N 21 1993
A Christian take on politics. *Register* 69:1+ S 19 1993
Cosmology: where science and religion meet. *Register* 69:1+ S 5 1993
Ethics: the science of joy and happiness. *Register* 69:1+ S 12 1993
For Christians, faith and reason are partners. *Register* 69:1+ Ag 8 1993
Hail Mary [Advent, pt 2 of 4]. *OSV* 82:5 N 28 1993
Heart of the matter: what is man? *Register* 69:1+ Ag 29 1993
How we know truth; considering the source. *Register* 69:1+ Ag 15 1993
How we worship. *New Cov* 23:33 O 1993
Mary's blood. *New Cov* 23:33 N 1993
Metaphysics: what we believe about reality. *Register* 69:1+ Ag 22 1993
12 ways to know God. *New Cov* 23:33 S 1993

Kremer, Jacob.
Umkämpftes Ja zur Bibelwissenschaft. *Stimm Zeit* 211:75-94 F 1993

Kress, Robert.
Review of: *Die Kirche: eine Katholische ekklesiologie* by Kehl, Medard. In: *TheolStds* 54:179-181 Mr 1993

Kress, Robert. *(cont'd)*
Review of: *That they may live: power, empowerment, and leadership in the church* by Downey, Michael. In: *Horizons (CTS)* 19:327-328 Fall 1992
We the people: the American transformation of Roman Catholicism. *New Theol Rev* 6:63-88 My 1993

Krieg, Robert A.
Review of: *Jesus Christ for the modern world: the Christology of the Catholic Tübingen School* by McCready, Douglas. In: *TheolStds* 54:390 Je 1993

Krieger, Michael T.
The preservation of smaller Catholic library collections. *CLW* 64:27-29 Jl-S 1993

Kries, Douglas.
On Leo Strauss's understanding of the natural law theory of Thomas Aquinas. *Thomist* 57:215-232 Ap 1993

Kriewald, Diedra.
Week of prayer for Christian unity. *Liturgy* 11:34-37 Sum 1993

Krisman, Ron.
Liturgical music today [interview]. *Mod Lit* 20:10-11 O 1993

Kristol, William.
Dialogue [interview by P Mullen]. *Register* 69:1+ S 12 1993

Krivak, Andrew J.
Accompanying Dante. *America* 169:17-21 O 30 1993
"Gates of mystery: the art of Holy Russia". *America* 168:22-24 F 6 1993
Review of: *Dante's Inferno: translations by 20 contemporary poets* by Halpern, Daniel, ed. In: *America* 169:17-21 O 30 1993

Kroeger, Catherine Clark. *see* Kroeger, Richard Clark, jt auth

Kroeger, James H.
Becoming paschal evangelizers. *Emmanuel* 99:428-431+ O 1993
Cruciform dialogue in mission. *AFER* 35:13-19 F 1993

Kromm, Jane.
Introduction to re-thinking representation: Anselm and visual thinking. *Listening* 28:95-104 Spr 1993

Kropf, Richard.
Review of: *Imagination: a future for religious life* by Thomasis, Louis De. In: *Nat Cath Rep* 29:13-14 Mr 5 1993
Review of: *The rule of Benedict* by Chittister, Joan D. In: *Nat Cath Rep* 29:13-14 Mr 5 1993
Review of: *Word and spirit: a monastic review, 14—1992, aspects of monasticism in America.* In: *Nat Cath Rep* 29:13-14 Mr 5 1993

Kropf, Richard W.
Review of: *Jesus and the Dead Sea Scrolls* by Charlesworth, James H. In: *ChrWorld* 236:237-238 S-O 1993

Krosnicki, Thomas A.
The birth and growth of the lectionary. *Past Mus* 17:23-25 D 1992-Ja 1993
Spiritual profit from an Indonesian earthquake. *America* 168:5-6 F 13 1993

Kruger, Paul A.
The divine net in Hosea 7, 12. *Eph Theol Lovan* 78:132-136 Ap 1992

Krull, W.
Review of: *Historia de la Iglesia contemporanea* by Schatz, Klaus. In: *Perspectiva* 24:398-401 S-D 1992

Kruschwitz, Robert B.
Review of: *Being and goodness: the concept of the good in metaphysics and philosophical theology* by MacDonald, Scott, ed. In: *Thomist* 57:150-153 Ja 1993

Kselman, Thomas.
Review of: *Madonnas that maim: popular Catholicism in Italy since the fifteenth century* by Carroll, Michael P. In: *CHist* 79:505-506 Jl 1993

Kubicki, Judith Marie.
Review of: *Handbook for cantors* by Sotak, Diana Kodner. In: *Past Mus* 17:42 Je-Jl 1993
Review of: *The ministry of the cantor* by Hansen, James. In: *Past Mus* 17:41 Je-Jl 1993
Review of: *The parish cantor: helping Catholics pray in song* by Connolly, Michael. In: *Past Mus* 17:42 Je-Jl 1993

Kügler, H.
Review of: *Dämonische Gottesbilder* by Frielingsdorf, Karl. In: *Stimm Zeit* 211:287 Ap 1993

Kuharic, Franjo, Cardinal, 1919-.
Appeal to Croats and Muslims: stop fighting each other. *Origins* 23:33+ Je 3 1993
Cardinal eyes Croatia struggle [interview by Jonathan Luxmoore]. *Register* 69:1+ F 21 1993
In God's name, stop the war in the Balkans!. *OR(Eng)* 1292:1+ My 26 1993

Kuharski, Mary Ann, and Fleming, Dorothy.
A sign and a challenge. *Register* 69:5 Je 27 1993

Kuhn, George.
The good news for our neighborhood [interview by J Sammon]. *Cath Work* 60:1+ Ja-F 1993

Kuhne, Roberta.
The me God sees: celebrating your true identity. Sisters: Questar, 1993. x, 202p ISBN 0-8070-573-6

Kunert, Gunther.
Fundamentalismus und Religion. *Stimm Zeit* 211:53-64 Ja 1993

Kung, Hans, 1928-.
Credo: the Apostles' Creed explained for today. New York: Doubleday, 1993. x, 194p ISBN 0-385-47181-5 LC 93-915
Global responsibility: in search of a new world ethic. New York: Crossroad, 1991. x, 158p ISBN 0-8245-1102-6 LC 91-7956

Kunkel, Francis L.
Matthew, Mark, Luke, and John. *Sisters* 65:283-289 Jl 1993

Kuppler, B.
Review of: *Gemeinwohl und Eigennutz: wirtschaftliches Handeln in Verantwortung für die Zukunft.* In: *Civilta* 144:511-513 Mr 6 1993

Kurz, Paul Konrad.
Das beschädigte Land. *Stimm Zeit* 211:663-678 O 1993
Es geht um mehr als Christa Wolf. *Stimm Zeit* 211:352-356 My 1993
Von realer Gegenwart. *Stimm Zeit* 211:547-559 Ag 1993

Kurz, William S.
The problem with prophecy. *New Cov* 23:11-13 S 1993
Review of: *Host, guest, enemy, and friend: portraits of the Pharisees in Luke and Acts* by Gowler, David B. In: *CBQ* 55:154-155 Ja 1993
Review of: *Reading John:* by Talbert, Charles H. In: *TheolStds* 54:594 S 1993
Review of: *The farewell of the word: the Johannine call to abide* by Segovia, Fernando F. In: *TheolStds* 54:161-163 Mr 1993

Kydd, Ronald.
Approaching "sect" with care. *Ecumen Trends* 22:3-5 Mr 1993

Kysar, Robert.
John, the maverick gospel. Louisville: John Knox, 1993. x, 176p ISBN 0-664-25401-2

L

L'Engle, Madeleine.
The rock that is higher: story as truth. Wheaton, Illinois: H Shaw Publishers, 1993. 296p ISBN 0-87788-726-8 LC 92-24204

La Cocque, A.
Review of: *Circle of sovereignty: plotting politics in the Book of Daniel* by Fewell, Danna Nolan. In: *New Theol Rev* 6:91-93 F 1993

La Corte, Daniel M.
Review of: *Patristic scholarship: the edition of St Jerome* by Brady, James F, and Olin, John C, eds. In: *Cist Stud* 28 no 2:[49]-[50] 1993

La Mois, Loyd.
Review of: *Report on the Church: Catholicism after Vatican II* by McBrien, Richard P. In: *Living Light* 29:85-86 Sum 1993

Laberge, Léo.
Review of: *L'Ancien Testament: Cent ans d'exégèse à l'École Biblique* by Vesco, Jean-Luc. In: *CBQ* 54:773 O 1992

Labio, Catherine.
Review of: *The creators* by Boorstin, Daniel J. In: *America* 168:17-19 My 8 1993

Labonté, Ghislain R.
Review of: *Rethinking Genesis: the sources and authorship of the First Book of the Pentateuch* by Garrett, Duane. In: *OTA* 16:417 Je 1993

Laboure, M Catherine. *see* Lambert, Jean M, jt auth

Labrie, Ross.
Review of: *Foreign studies* by Endo, Shusaku, 1923-. In: *Can Cath Rev* 11:25-26 Jl-Ag 1993

Labriola, Albert C.
Review of: *Holy delight: typology, numerology, and autobiography in Donne's Devotions upon emergent occasions* by Frost, Kate Gartner. In: *Relig Lit* 25:75-80 Spr 1993
Review of: *Prayer and power: George Herbert and Renaissance courtship* by Schoenfeldt, Michael C. In: *Relig Lit* 25:75-80 Spr 1993
Review of: *The ludic self in seventeenth-century English Literature* by Nardo, Anna K. In: *Relig Lit* 25:75-80 Spr 1993

LaChat, Michael R. *see* Myers, Max A, jt ed

Lackner, Joseph M.
Liturgy and life: an overview. *Catechist* 27:86-93 S 1993

Lacocque, Pierre-Emmanuel. *see* LaCocque, André, jt auth

LaCoste, Catherine Louise, comp. *see* Harley, R Bruce, jt auth

Lacroix, Xavier.
Légèreté ou gravité de la chair. *Supplement* 184:175-191 Mr-Ap 1993

LaCugna, Catherine Mowry, 1952-.
Author's response [reply to four book reviews *God for us*]. *Horizons (CTS)* 20:135-142 Spr 1993
Review of: *Our idea of God: an introduction to philosophical theology* by Morris, Thomas V. In: *Horizons (CTS)* 20:152-153 Spr 1993
Review of: *The power to speak: feminism, language, God* by Chopp, Rebecca S. In: *JEcumen Stds* 29:108-109 Wint 1992
Review of: *What language shall I borrow? God-Talk in worship: a male response to feminist theology* by Wren, Brian. In: *JEcumen Stds* 29:108-109 Wint 1992

LaCugna, Catherine Mowry.
The Trinity: why it takes three persons to save one soul [Interview by the editors of U.S. Catholic (periodical)]. *USCath* 58:6-12 N 1993

Ladaria, Luis F.
Review of: *Compendio de la Gracia. La gracia, expresión de Dios en el hombre* by Galindo Rodrigo, José Antonio. In: *Gregorianum* 74 no 3:578-579 1993
Review of: *Eschatologie* by Hattrup, Dieter. In: *Gregorianum* 74 No 1:168-169 1993
Review of: *Zur Kirchlichen Erbsündenlehre* by Schönborn, Christoph von, Bp, et al. In: *Gregorianum* 74 No 1:163-164 1993

Ladd, George Eldon.
A theology of the New Testament. Grand Rapids: Eerdmans, 1993. 740p ISBN 0-8028-0680-5

Ladous, Régis. *see* Durand, Jean-Dominique, jt ed

Ladrière, Jean.
Interprétation et vérité. *Laval Theol Phil* 49:189-199 Je 1993

Laemmle, Mary Xavier.
Review of: *Seek treasures in small fields: everyday holiness* by Puls, Joan. In: *Sisters* 65:223 My 1993

Laffey, Alice L.
Review of: *No longer be silent* by Brown, Cheryl Anne. In: *CBQ* 55:359-360 Ap 1993
Review of: *Silence or suppression: attitudes towards women in the Old Testament* by Ljung, Inger. In: *CBQ* 54:751-752 O 1992
Review of: *Voices from the margin: interpreting the Bible in the Third World* by Sugirtharajah, R S. In: *CBQ* 54:828-829 O 1992

Lagges, Patrick R.
Spanish language cases and canon 1673, 4. *Jurist* 51 no 2:431-441 1991

Laghi, Pio, Cardianl.
De seminariis, universitatibus atque scholis Catholicis in America Latina a prima evangelizatione usque ad novam. *Seminarium* 32:369-473 Jl-S 1992
Los seminarios Iberoamericanos en el período Hispano-Portugués, by E Gardenas. Primeras fundaciones de colegios y universidades, by E Luque Aleaide. Educação: perspectivas históricas, by R Azzi. Los Seminarios en el proyecto de "nueva evangelización": resultados de las visitas apostólicas en América Latina, by F Bacarreza Rodriguez. Contribución de las universidades Católicas a la nueva evangelición, by A Montealegre. Teología de la liberación y evangelización: nuevas perspectivas, by J Scannone.
Formation must focus on Christ. *OR(Eng)* 1303:13-14 Ag 18 1993
"Pastores dabo vobis": presentazione [editorial]. *Seminarium* 32:505-517 O-D 1992
Commentaria in ADH Apost Pastores dabo vobis/I. *Seminarium* 32:505-636 O-D 1992
"Pastores dabo vobis":presentazione, by Cardinal P Laghi. "Pastores dabo vobis": Perspectives orientales, by M Kozah. La Pastores dabo vobis alla lude del pensiero conciliare sul sacerdozio e la formazione sacerdotale, by F Rypar. Sacerdocio ministerial y radicalismo de los consejos evangélicos, by C Pozo. Il Seminario Maggiore, by D Coletti. La formazione missionaria dei sacerdoti alla luce della "Pastores dabo vobis", by J Saraiva Martins. Anno propedeutico: vera novità del Concilio Vaticano II, by D Negro. I seminaristi provenienti dalle nuove realtà aggregative, by M Camisasca. The use of psychology as an aid to priestly formation, by T Costello.
Paedagogia caelibatus sacerdotalis. *Seminarium* 33:15-118 Ja-Mr 1993
Pédagogie du célibat dans les orientations et documents récents de l'église, by Msgr E Marcus. Il celibato di Gesù e la verginità di Maria, by Msgr D Marzotto. Der Zölibat: Formkraft priesterlicher exitenz und priesterlicher Dienstes, by Msgr L Scheffcyzk. Pedagogia formativa del celibato sacerdotale. Necessità, programma e metoda, by P Gianola. Amitiés sacerdotales et célibat, by Msgr M Gaidon. Priestly celibacy and association with women, by Card F Arinze. History: a school of humility and source of hope, by D Maruca. Candidates with difficulties in Celibacy: discernment, admission, formation, by B Kiely.

Lago Alba, Luis.
Retorna lo religioso: XX conversaciones de San Esteban. *Cien Tom* 119:599-602 S-D 1992
Review of: *Diccionario de teología dogmática* by Beinert, Wolfgang. In: *Cien Tom* 119:411 My-Ag 1992
Review of: *Doctrina social de la iglesia* by Camacho, Ildefonso. In: *Cien Tom* 119:615-616 S-D 1992
Review of: *El Dios de la vida* by Gutiérrez, Gustavo. In: *Cien Tom* 119:415-417 My-Ag 1992
Review of: *El rostro asiático de Cristo: notas para una teología asiática de la liberación* by Pieris, Aloysius, 1934-. In: *Cien Tom* 119:612 S-D 1992
Review of: *Entre la armonía y la ternura* by Moliner Fabregas del Pilar, José M. In: *Cien Tom* 119:625 S-D 1992
Review of: *Jesucristo al encuentro de las religiones* by Dupuis, Jacques. In: *Cien Tom* 119:604-606 S-D 1992
Review of: *La comunión de los santos: fundamento, esencia y estructura de la Iglesia* by Garijo-Guembe, Miguel M. In: *Cien Tom* 119:608-609 S-D 1992
Review of: *La enseñanza social de la Iglesia* by Yves Calvez, Jean. In: *Cien Tom* 119:614-615 S-D 1992
Review of: *La espiritualidad cristiana* by Espeja, Jesús. In: *Cien Tom* 119:621-623 S-D 1992
Review of: *La iglesia icono de la trinidad: breve eclesiología* by Forte, Bruno. In: *Cien Tom* 119:606-608 S-D 1992
Review of: *La teología como companía, memoria y profecía* by Forte, Bruno. In: *Cien Tom* 119:606-608 S-D 1992
Review of: *La Verdad os hará libres* by Gutiérrez, Gustavo. In: *Cien Tom* 119:415-417 My-Ag 1992
Review of: *Para comprender el ecumenismo* by Bosch, Juan. In: *Cien Tom* 119:603 S-D 1992
Review of: *Reflexiones de un monje* by Altisent, Agustín. In: *Cien Tom* 119:626 S-D 1992
Review of: *Teología de la liberción* by Gutiérrez, Gustavo. In: *Cien Tom* 119:415-417 My-Ag 1992
Review of: *Vaticano II: un concilio pastoral* by Floristan, Casiano. In: *Cien Tom* 119:413-414 My-Ag 1992
Review of: *Vita di Pio IX* by Polverari, Alberto. In: *Cien Tom* 119:619-621 S-D 1992

Lahaye, Beverly. see Lahaye, Time, jt auth

Lahaye, Time, and Lahaye, Beverly.
Against the tide: how to raise sexually pure kids in an "anything-goes" world. Sisters: Questar, 1993. x, 258p ISBN 0-88070-578-7

Laird, William.
Catechumens: addressing a failed marriage. *Origins* 23:358-359 O 28 1993

Lakeland, Paul.
(En)countering the (post)modern. *Month* 26:63-70 F 1993
Review of: *Theology and social theory: beyond secular reason* by Milbank, John. In: *Month* 26:63-70 F 1993

Lalawne, Stanislas, et al. see Aitken, Ann-Marie, jt auth

Lally, John.
An Irish priest in England. *Priests & People* 7:22-26 Ja 1993

Lama, Felix de.
Propuestas para Santo Domingo: indigenas de Panama. *Christus* 57:29-31 S 1992

Lamau, Marie-Louise.
La notion de qualité de la vie dans le champ dela santé. *MSR* 50:135-150 Ap-Je 1993
Review of: *Théologie de la maladie* by Larchet, J-C. In: *MSR* 50:75-76 Ja-Mr 1993

Lamba, R.
Review of: *Temi e simboli dell'eros* by Zuanazzi, Gianfranco. In: *Civilta* 144:613-614 Mr 20 1993

Lambert, David.
Joy in suffering: receiving your reward. Grand Rapids: Zondervan Publishing House, 1993. x, 64p ISBN 0-310-59673-4
Showing mercy: getting what you give. Grand Rapids: Zondervan Publishing House, 1993. x, 64p ISBN 0-310-59653-x

Lambert, Jean M, and Laboure, M Catherine.
A sign of God's presence. *Health Prog* 74:62+ Ap 1993

Lambiasi, F.
Review of: *Gli spigoli della memoria* by Luciani, Anna. In: *Civilta* 143:433-434 N 21 1992
Review of: *Un catechisme universel pour l'Église catholique* by Simon, Maurice. In: *Civilta* 3:311-312 Ag 7-21 1993

Lamieux, Raymond.
Review of: *Deux mille ans d'évangélisation* by Comby, Jean. In: *Laval Theol Phil* 49:148-149 F 1993

Lammer, Stephen E.
Review of: *Sister Aimee: the life of Aimee Semple McPherson* by Epstein, Daniel Mark. In: *America* 169:29 S 11 1993

Lamouille, A. see Boismard, M É, jt auth

Lamour, Jean Marie.
It's hard to play Jesus [interview by J B Feister]. *ST Anth* 101:36-43 Jl 1993

Lamoureux, Patricia Natali.
Review of: *Faith and social ministry: ten Christian perspectives* by Davidson, James O, ed. In: *New Theol Rev* 6:99-101 Ag 1993

Lampo, Jia, and Weiwen, Huang.
Father Pierre Teilhard de Chardin and I [excerpt fr *The story of Peking Man*]. *Teilhard Rev* 27:82-84 Wint 1992

LaNave, Gred.
Days of the Lord: the liturgical year; vol 3. Minnesota: The Liturgical Press, 1993. x, 364p ISBN 0-8146-1901-0 LC 90-22253

Landau, Yehezkel. see Burrell, David B, jt ed

Landy, Thomas.
A papal visit, a troubled island. *America* 169:6-8 Ag 14-21 1993

Lane, Belden C.
Sinai and Tabor: apophatic and kataphatic symbols in tension. *Stud Form Spir* 14:189-205 My 1993

Lane, Dermot A.
The challenge of inculturation. *Living Light* 29:3-21 Wint 1992

Lane, John Thomas.
Review of: *Disputed questions in the liturgy today* by Huels, John M. In: *Emmanuel* 98:177-179 Ap 1992
Review of: *Hymnal for Catholic students* by Huck, Gabe, ed. In: *Emmanuel* 99:358-359 Jl-Ag 1993
Review of: *The primacy of love* by Wadell, Paul J. In: *Emmanuel* 99:112 Mr 1993

Lane, Julia A.
Returning Gospel values to nursing education. *Health Prog* 74:30-35 Je 1993

Lane, Tom.
Celibacy again. *Furrow* 44:21-26 Ja 1993
One, good, true and beautiful. *Doctr Life* 43:411-417 S 1993

Lane, Wilbur.
Evening devotions. New York: Vantage Press, 1993. 49p ISBN 0-533-10380-0 LC 92-90962

Lang, David P.
Abortion and peace. *HPR* 93:10-19 Mr 1993
The politicization of language. *SocJust* 84:106-107 Jl-Ag 1993

Lang, Jovian P.
Review of: *A place for all: mental retardation catechesis and liturgy* by Harrington, Mary Theresa. In: *CLW* 64:38 Jl-S 1993
Review of: *Collection of Masses of the Blessed Virgin Mary, v I and II.* In: *Mod Lit* 20:38 O 1993
Review of: *Collection of Masses of the Blessed Virgin Mary, v I and II.* In: *Mod Lit* 20:38 O 1993
Review of: *Dictionary of cults, sects, religions and the occult* by Mather, George A, and Nichols, Larry A. In: *Mod Lit* 20:40-41 N 1993
Review of: *In heaven there are no thunderstorms: celebrating the liturgy with developmentally disabled people* by Okhuijsen, Gijs, and Opzeeland, Cees von. In: *CLW* 64:38 Jl-S 1993
Review of: *Jewish prayer: the origins of Christian liturgy* by DiSante, Carmine. In: *CLW* 64:37 Jl-S 1993
Review of: *More sower's seeds: second planting* by Cavanaugh, Brian. In: *Mod Lit* 20:40-41 O 1993
Review of: *Saints of the Roman Calendar* by Lodi, Enzo. In: *Mod Lit* 20:40-41 Ag 1993
Review of: *The ABCs of worship: a concise dictionary* by Stake, Donald Wilson. In: *Mod Lit* 20:39 Ag 1993

Lang, Marijke Hélène de.
The prehistory of the Griesbach hypothesis. *Eph Theol Lovan* 69:134-139 Ap 1993

Lazar, John E. (cont'd)
Review of: *Once more with love: a guide to marrying again* by Coyle-Hennessey, Bobbi. In: *Mod Lit* 20:40 Je-Jl 1993
Review of: *Parish liturgy basics* by Belford, William. In: *Mod Lit* 20:38 Ap 1993
Review of: *Scripture at weddings* by Marcheschi, Graziano. In: *Mod Lit* 20:39-40 My 1993
Review of: *The word in and out of season: homilies for the Sundays of Ordinary Time, Cycle A* by Viladesau, Richard. In: *Mod Lit* 20:38 My 1993
Review of: *With this ring* by Bartkowski, Rene. In: *Mod Lit* 20:40 My 1993
Review of: *Words that sing* by Ramshaw, Gail. In: *Mod Lit* 19:41-42 D 1992-Ja 1993

Le Voir, Paul W.
Review of: *An overview of Gregorian Chant* by Cardine, Dom Eugène. In: *SacM* 120:21-22 Spr 1993
Review of: *Cum angelis canere: essays on sacred music and pastoral liturgy in honour of Richard I Schuler* by Skeris, Robert A, ed. In: *SacM* 120:22-23 Spr 1993

Leadbetter, Frank.
Evolution today. *Teilhard Rev* 28:27 Sum 1993

Leaney, A R C.
Review of: *Irony in Mark's Gospel* by Camery-Hoggatt, Jerry. In: *New Blckfrs* 74:112 F 1993

Lear, Norman, 1922-.
The cathedral of business: the fountainhead of values in America today. *New Oxford Rev* 60:6-13 Ap 1993

Leary, Mary Ellen.
School-vouchers forces bowed, but unbeaten. *Nat Cath Rep* 30:6 N 12 1993

Leavitt, Robert F.
Bicentennial hopes for America's first seminary. *US Cath Hist* 11:119-122 Wint 1993

Lebeau, Paul.
Pour une Église en acte d'espérance. *Lumen* 48:149-159 Je 1993
Review of: *Escape from God* by Turner, Dean. In: *Lumen* 48:360 S 1993
Review of: *Les moniales bouddhistes* by Wijayaratna, Môhn. In: *NRT* 115:599-600 Jl-Ag 1993

Lecercle, Jean-Jacques.
Three-way games. *PhilosTod* 36:336-350 Wint 1992

Leckie, Judith.
The naked age. *Priests & People* 6:423-425 N 1992

Leclerq, Jean.
Journey and journeys. *Word Sp* 15:87-94 1993

Lecuit, Jean.
Qui dis-tu que je suis? (Mt 16, 15). *Lumen* 48:304-314 S 1993

Leder, Dennis.
Russia and the arts of Utopia. *America* 168:16 Ja 2-9 1993

Ledwig, Frances.
Director of volunteer ministries. *Church* 9:28-30 Sum 1993

Lee, Bernard J.
LIMEX: distance education in intentional learning communities. *Momentum* 24:7-9 F-Mr 1993

Lee, Dorothy A.
Pleasure: a biblical perspective. *Way* 33:19-33 Ja 1993
Presence or absence? the question of women disciples at the Last Supper. *Pacifica* 6:1-20 F 1993
Review of: *Towards a feminist critical reading of the Gospel according to Matthew* by Wainwright, Elaine Mary. In: *Pacifica* 6:102-104 F 1993

Lee, John P. see Suh, Young S, jt auth

Lee, Martin.
On the other hand, the priesthood—a conservative view. *Priests & People* 6:330-333 Ag-S 1992

Lee, Michael.
Review of: *Kill hole* by Highwater, Jamake. In: *Nat Cath Rep* 29:36 My 28 1993

Lee, Simon.
Abortion law: the tragic choices. *Doctr Life* 42:282-297 My-Je 1992

Leech, Kenneth, 1939-.
Is spiritual direction losing its bearings? *Tablet* 247:634 My 22 1993

Leehan, James.
Defiant hope: spirituality for survivors of family abuse. Louisville: John Knox, 1993. x, 176p ISBN 0-664-25463-2

Leeney, Robert.
Is there more to be said? *Columbia* 73:10-13 Ag 1993

Leers, Bernardino.
Review of: *Moral do matrimônio* by Vidal, Marciano. In: *REB* 53:486-487 Je 1993

Leese, Mary Sue.
Discovering creation. *Catechist* 27:72 S 1993

Lefchick, Basil.
Icons for liturgy. *Mod Lit* 19:10-11 D 1992-Ja 1993

Lefebvre, Leo D.
Christianity and religions of the world. *Chicago Stud* 31:258-270 N 1992
Preaching in interreligious contexts. *New Theol Rev* 6:64-70 Ag 1993
The Buddha and the Christ: explorations in Buddhist and Christian dialogue. Maryknoll: Orbis, 1993. x, 239p ISBN 0-88344-924-2 LC 93-7972

Lefevere, Patricia.
Canada bishops tackle free market fallout. *Nat Cath Rep* 29:12 My 28 1993
Christian unity: no deadline, but a boost in Spain. *Nat Cath Rep* 29:13 Ag 27 1993
Letter on gays draws protest. *Nat Cath Rep* 29:5 S 10 1993
Response to pastoral letter called positive. *Nat Cath Rep* 29:7 Ja 8 1993

Lefevere, Patricia. (cont'd)
Tide of evangelism may swamp religious freedoms. *Nat Cath Rep* 29:16 Je 18 1993
Vatican, Moscow pursue a "delicate" cooperation. *Nat Cath Rep* 29:2 Mr 12 1993

Lefevre, Marie Cecilia.
Saint Marguerite d'Youville. *Sisters* 65:183-186 My 1993

Legere, Thomas.
Broken, blessed. *Emmanuel* 99:450-451 O 1993

Legrand, F.
The demands of evangelization [excerpt fr pamphlet written during Vatican Council 2D]. *ChrWorld* 38:48-50 Ja-F 1993

Legrand, Hervé.
The local church and catholicity. *Jurist* 52 no 1:7-586 1992
The church—one and diverse—in service to mission, by A García y García. Development of a theology of the local church from the first to second Vatican Council, by O de Cardedal. The Catholicity of the church in the New Testament and in the early patristic period, by M Fahey, etc.
"One bishop per city": tensions around the expression of the Catholicity of the local church since Vatican II. *Jurist* 52 no 1:369-400 1992

Legrez, Jean. see Garrigues, Jean-Michel, jt auth

Lehmann, Daniel J.
Graying of the sisterhood [condensed fr *Chicago Sun-Times* My 2 1993]. *CDgst* 58:56-59 N 1993

Lehmann, Karl, Bp, 1936-, et al, eds.
The content of faith. New York: The Crossroad Publishing Company, 1993. x, 668p ISBN 0-8245-1221-9 LC 92-27765

Lehmann, Karl, Bp, 1936-.
The meaning of a new evangelization of Europe. *Communio* 19:541-548 Wint 1992

Lehrman, Lewis E.
Review of: *The Catholic ethic and the spirit of capitalism* by Novak, Michael, 1933-. In: *Crisis* 11:60-62 Jl-Ag 1993

Leichty, Joseph.
Review of: *Evangelical Protestantism in Ulster society, 1740-1890* by Hempton, David, and Hill, Myrtle. In: *Studies* 81:463-466 Wint 1992

Leifeld, Wendy.
A middle way for Catholic women. *New Cov* 22:7-9 Je 1993

Leigh, Richard. see Baigent, Michael, jt auth

Leipert, Jack.
How to stay sane in a crazy world [interview by M. Finley]. *OSV* 82:13 O 17 1993

Leite, P.
The rosary, arm of peace [fr *The Laity: Journal of Christian Thought* O-N, 1992]. *ChrWorld* 38:160-164 Mr-Ap 1993

Leites Oares, Alfredo.
Participação numa igreja constítuida hierarquicamente. *Periodica* 82 no 1:139-174 1993

Leiva-Merikakis, Erasmo.
The catechetical role of the liturgy and the quality of liturgical texts: the current ICEL translation. *Communio* 20:63-83 Spr 1993

Lejeune, Anthony.
Review of: *A flower in the desert* by Satterthwait, Walter. In: *Tablet* 247:376 Mr 20 1993
Review of: *Bad chemistry* by Kelly, Nora. In: *Tablet* 247:1136 S 4 1993
Review of: *City of dreams* by Gill, Anton. In: *Tablet* 247:1047 Ag 14 1993
Review of: *City of the horizon* by Gill, Anton. In: *Tablet* 247:1047 Ag 14 1993
Review of: *Curtains for the cardinal* by Eyre, Elizabeth. In: *Tablet* 247:51 Ja 9 1993
Review of: *Death among the dons* by Neel, Janet. In: *Tablet* 247:1136 S 4 1993
Review of: *Death and the Oxford box* by Stallwood, Veronica. In: *Tablet* 247:376 Mr 20 1993
Review of: *Dorothy L Sayers: a careless rage for life* by Coomes, David. In: *Tablet* 247:142 Ja 30 1993
Review of: *Dorothy L Sayers* by Reynolds, Barbara. In: *Tablet* 247:478-479 Ap 10-17 1993
Review of: *Hollywood vs America* by Medved, Michael, 1948-. In: *Tablet* 247:657 My 22 1993
Review of: *Murder under the kissing bough* by Myers, Amy. In: *Tablet* 247:376 Mr 20 1993
Review of: *Murder wears a cowl* by Doherty, P C. In: *Tablet* 247:51 Ja 9 1993
Review of: *Operation pax* by Innes, Michael. In: *Tablet* 247:1136 S 4 1993
Review of: *River god* by Smith, Wilbur. In: *Tablet* 247:1047 Ag 14 1993
Review of: *The doll's house* by Anthony, Evelyn. In: *Tablet* 247:376 Mr 20 1993
Review of: *The holy thief* by Peters, Ellis. In: *Tablet* 247:51 Ja 9 1993
Review of: *The iron hand of Mars* by Davis, Lindsey. In: *Tablet* 247:51 Ja 9 1993
Review of: *The Mamur Zapt and the spoils of Egypt* by Pearce, Michael. In: *Tablet* 247:376 Mr 20 1993
Review of: *The Plymouth cloak* by Sedley, Kate. In: *Tablet* 247:51 Ja 9 1993
Review of: *The poisoned chalice* by Clynes, Michael. In: *Tablet* 247:51 Ja 9 1993
Review of: *The Wyndham case* by Walsh, Jill Paton. In: *Tablet* 247:1136 S 4 1993
Review of: *To die like a gentleman* by Bastable, Bernard. In: *Tablet* 247:376 Mr 20 1993
Review of: *Yours until death* by Staalesen, Gunnar. In: *Tablet* 247:376 Mr 20 1993

Lemieux, Raymond.
Review of: *Lexique de la culture* by Carrier, Hervé. In: *Laval Theol Phil* 49:173-174 F 1993

Lemmon, Michele.
Haitian adoption leads to priest's ouster [photos]. *Nat Cath Rep* 29:10 O 15 1993

Lena, Marguerite.
The mission of Taizé [repr fr *Etudes*]. *Month* 26:46-52 F 1993

Lenkersdorf, Carlos.
Inculturar la palabra. *Christus* 58:36-59 S 1993

Lenney, Ailsa.
Review of: *Gnosis, study and commentaries on the esoteric tradition of Eastern Orthodox, 3 vols* by Mouravieff, Boris. In: *Teilhard Rev* 27:95-96 Wint 1992

Lennon, Joseph L.
The Saint of reason [condensed fr *The Providence Visitor* Ja 28 1993]. *CDgst* 57:139-141 Je 1993

Lenox-Conyngham, Andrew.
In the Catholic tradition. *Priests & People* 6:467-471 D 1992

Lent, Craig S.
Can a university be both great and Christian? *New Oxford Rev* 60:10-14 S 1993

Lenti, Vincent A.
Urban VIII and the revision of the Latin Hymnal. *SacM* 120:30-33 Aut 1993

Lentzen-Deis, Fritz Leo.
Metodi dell'esegesi tra mito, storicità e comunicasione. *Gregorianum* 73 No 4:731-737 1992

Lenzen, Verena.
Suicide in the Bible. *TheolDgst* 40:37-42 Spr 1993

León, D Muñoz. *see* Espinosa, R Rábanos, jt auth

Leonard, Ellen.
Review of: *Tradition and the critical spirit: Catholic modernist writings* by Tyrrell, George. In: *Horizons (CTS)* 20:150-151 Spr 1993
Review of: *A case for peace in reason and faith* by Hellwig, Monika K, 1929- . In: *Can Cath Rev* 11:30-31 O 1993

Leonard, George.
A plea for pruning. *Priests & People* 7:30-31 Ja 1993

Leonard, Glen M. *see* Allen, James B, jt auth

Leonard, Joan.
Review of: *On her way rejoicing: the fiction of Muriel Spark* by Randisi, Jennifer Lynn. In: *Relig Lit* 25:87-91 Spr 1993
Review of: *Vocation and identity in the fiction of Muriel Spark* by Edgecombe, Rodney Stenning. In: *Relig Lit* 25:87-91 Spr 1993

Leonard, John-Brooks. *see* Bernstein, Eleanor, jt ed

Leonard, William J.
The letter carrier. Kansas City: Sheed & Ward, 1993. x, 373p ISBN 1-55612-651-4 LC 93-18887

Leonardy, Heinz.
Éléments pour une philosophie de l'enseinement de la philosophie. *RPhil Louvain* 91:441-458 Ag 1993 *see* Franck, Robert, jt auth

Leonhardy, Lee.
Toward service to the church. *OSV* 81:6-7 F 7 1993

Lepain, Marc A.
Review of: *The sacred quest: an invitation to the study of religion* by Cunningham, Lawrence S, 1935-, et al. In: *Horizons (CTS)* 19:349-350 Fall 1992

Lepargneur, Hubert.
Morte cerebral e morte cerebral. *REB* 53:87-98 Mr 1993

Lepore, Ernest. *see* Fodor, Jerry, jt auth

Lesch, Walter.
Unterwegs zur interkulturellen Demokratie. *Stimm Zeit* 211:255-269 Ap 1993

Lethbridge, Lucy.
Review of: *The Chatto book of the Devil* by Spufford, Francis, ed. In: *Tablet* 247:480 Ap 10-17 1993

Leugers, A.
Review of: *Clemens August Graf von Galen: neue Forschungen zum Leben und Wirken des Bischofs von Münster* by Kuropka, Joachim, ed. In: *Stimm Zeit* 211:573-574 Ag 1993

LeVay, Simon.
The sexual brain. Cambridge: MIT Press, 1993. 168p ISBN 0-26212-178-6 LC 92-44691

Levi, A.H.T.
Review of: *Bossuet: politics drawn from Holy Scripture* by Riley, Patrick, ed. In: *Heythrop* 34:435 O 1993
Review of: *Territories of grace: cultural change in the Seventeenth-Century diocese of Grenoble* by Luria, Keith P. In: *Heythrop* 34:458-459 O 1993
Review of: *The noble savage: Jean-Jacques Rousseau 1754-1762* by Cranston, Maurice. In: *Heythrop* 34:472-473 O 1993

Levine, James.
Review of: *The semantic tradition from Kant to Carnap: to the Vienna station* by Coffa, J Alberto. In: *IJPS* 1:111-118 Mr 1993

Levison, John R.
Early Judaism looks at Adam. *BibleT* 30:372-377 N 1992
Review of: *A history of the Literature of Adam and Eve* by Stone, Michael Edward. In: *OTA* 16:451 Je 1993
Review of: *Heirs of the septuagint: Philo, Hellenistic Judaism and Early Christianity* by Hay, David M, et al, eds. In: *OTA* 16:446 Je 1993 *see* Pope-Levison, Priscilla, jt auth

Levy, I.
Review of: *In the beginning: biblical creation and science* by Aviezer, Nathan. In: *SIDIC* 25 No 2:33 1992
Review of: *Thinking the unthinkable: meanings of the Holocaust* by Gottlieb, Roger, ed. In: *SIDIC* 25 No 1:31-32 1992

Levy, I. *(cont'd)*
Review of: *Voices from Jerusalem: Jews and Christians reflect on the Holy Land* by Burrell, David B, and Landau, Yehezkel, eds. In: *SIDIC* 26 no 1:31-32 1993

Lewandowski, Joseph D.
Review of: *The transparent society* by Vattimo, Gianni. In: *Mod Schlmn* 70:231-234 Mr 1993

Lewandowski, Leonard M. *see* Canosa, James F, jt auth

Lewis, Eleanor V.
Review of: *Church and world: the unity of the Church and the renewal of human community.* In: *JEcumen Stds* 29:104-105 Wint 1992
Review of: *Clearing the way: en route to an ecumenical spirituality* by Cashmore, Gwen, and Puls, Joan. In: *JEcumen Stds* 29:104-105 Wint 1992
Review of: *Ecumenical testimony* by Brouwer, Arie R. In: *JEcumen Stds* 29:474-475 Sum-Aut 1992
Review of: *Let the spirit speak to the churches.* In: *JEcumen Stds* 29:104-105 Wint 1992
Review of: *One wind, many flames* by Thorogood, Bernard. In: *JEcumen Stds* 29:474-475 Sum-Aut 1992
Review of: *To the windof God's spirit: reflections on the Canberra theme* by Castro, Emilio. In: *JEcumen Stds* 29:104-105 Wint 1992
Review of: *Vancouver to Canberra, 1982-1990: report of the Central Committee of the World Council of Churches to the Seventh Assembly* by Best, Thomas F, ed. In: *JEcumen Stds* 29:104-105 Wint 1992
Review of: *Who will roll the stone away? The Ecumenical Decade of the Churches in Solidarity with Women* by Oduyoye, Mercy Amba. In: *JEcumen Stds* 29:104-105 Wint 1992

Lewis, Juliana.
The importance of Josefina. *Sisters* 65:130-131 Mr 1993

Lewis, Marilyn.
Reserving the sacrament in a shared church. *OChr* 29 no 2:176-184 1993
Review of: *Pour une plus grande gloire de Dieu: les missions jésuites* by Lécrivain, Philippe. In: *CHist* 78:626-627 O 1992

Li, Chenyang.
What-being: Chuang Tzu versus Aristotle. *IPQ* 33:341-353 S 1993

Libanio, Joao Batista.
A Igreja e sua capacidade de satisfazer às demandas religiosas projeto 'Construir a Esperança'. *Perspectiva* 24:367-374 S-D 1992
The Latin American church: balance, tensions and perspectives [fr *Voces*]. *LADOC* 24:16-24 N-D 1993
Review of: *Alteridade e vulnerabilidade* by Bingemer, Maria Clara L. In: *Perspectiva* 25:250-252 My-Ag 1993
Review of: *Breve teología fundamental* by Imbach, Josef. In: *Perspectiva* 25:240-242 My-Ag 1993
Review of: *Catequese ontem e hoje: dos primórdios a Medellín* by Santos, Luiz Pereira dos. In: *Perspectiva* 24:405-406 S-D 1992
Review of: *El sueño de Galilea: confesiones eclesiales de Pedro Casaldíga* by Cabestrero, Teófilo. In: *Perspectiva* 25:121-122 Ja-Ap 1993
Review of: *Escatología I y II* by Tornos, Andrés. In: *Perspectiva* 25:107-110 Ja-Ap 1993
Review of: *Estágios da fé: a psicologia do desenvolvimento humano e a busca de sentido* by Fowler, James W. In: *Perspectiva* 24:389-391 S-D 1992
Review of: *Evangelización, cultura y teología* by Scannone, Juan Carlos. In: *Perspectiva* 25:102-105 Ja-Ap 1993
Review of: *Making all things new* by Amaladoss, Michael. In: *Perspectiva* 25:229-233 My-Ag 1993
Review of: *Nossa fé: Teologia para universitários* by Gonzalez-Carvajal, Luis. In: *Perspectiva* 24:393-394 S-D 1992
Review of: *O trabalho de saber: cultura camponesa e escola rural* by Brandão, Carlos Rodrigues. In: *Perspectiva* 25:120-121 Ja-Ap 1993
Review of: *Para comprender la teología de la liberación* by Tamayo-Acosta, Juan José. In: *Perspectiva* 25:99-102 Ja-Ap 1993
Review of: *Pasión de Dios* by Metz, Johann Baptist, and Peters, Tiemo Ranier. In: *Perspectiva* 25:261-263 My-Ag 1993
Review of: *Raízes e histórias; A saga de viver, volume 1: a religião do povo* by Souza, José. In: *Perspectiva* 25:122-123 Ja-Ap 1993
Review of: *Sociologia do movimento de Jesus* by Theissen, Gerd. In: *Perspectiva* 25:2568-260 My-Ag 1993
Review of: *Teilhard de Chardin* by Betto, Frei. In: *Perspectiva* 24:404-405 S-D 1992
Review of: *Teologia: iniciação, leitura de Paula* by Penalva, José. In: *Perspectiva* 24:391-393 S-D 1992
VIII encontro intereclesial das CEBS (eventos no evento). *REB* 52:789-800 D 1992
25 anos: a vida e a história de uma revista [editorial]. *Perspectiva* 25:5-9 Ja-Ap 1993

O desafio das religiões [editorial]. *Perspevtiva* 25:133-136 My-Ag 1993

Liberatore, Albert.
Symbols in Rahner: a note on translation. *Louvain Stds* 18:145-158 Sum 1993

Libersat, Henry.
The priest and the permanent deacon. *Priest* 49:19-21 Ag 1993
Priests and the Catholic press. *Priest* 49:11-14 F 1993

Liboreiro, Cristina.
A forgotten history: blacks in Argentina. *LADOC* 23:15-22 My-Je 1993

Libowitz, Richard.
Review of: *The making of Jewish and Christian worship* by Bradshaw, Paul F, and Hoffman, Lawrence A, eds. In: *JEcumen Stds* 29:278 Spr 1992

Licht, Robert A.
Respect is not a right. *Crisis* 11:41-47 Jl-Ag 1993

Lickona, Thomas.
Is character education a responsibility of the public schools?: yes. *Momentum* 24:48+ N-D 1993

Liddy, Richard M.
Transforming light: intellectual conversion in the early Lonergan. Collegeville: Liturgical, 1993. x, 225p ISBN 0-8146-5839-3 LC 93-22620

Liechty, Joseph.
Sectarianism. *Doctr Life* 43:418-425 S 1993

Lienhard, Joseph J.
Review of: *Die lehre Markells von Ankyra in der darstellung seiner gegner* by Feige, Gerhard. In: *TheolStds* 54:196-197 Mr 1993

Lieu, Judith.
Review of: *Paul the Convert: the apostolate and apostasy of Saul the Pharisee* by Segal, Alan F. In: *Heythrop* 34:311-312 Jl 1993

Lieven, Anatol.
Another place, another war. *Tablet* 247:639-641 My 22 1993
Desperate straits for Russia's reformers. *Tablet* 247:424+ Ap 3 1993
The Pope in the role of progressive. *Tablet* 247:1171 S 11 1993
The Pope's balancing act. *Tablet* 247:1208-1209 S 18 1993
Yeltsin takes charge. *Tablet* 247:1252-1253 O 2 1993

Lievens de Waegh, M-L.
Review of: *Le pressoir mystique* by Alxandre-Bidon, D. In: *NRT* 115:139-140 Ja-F 1993

Liggion, Leonard P.
Review of: *The frontiers of Catholicism: the politics of ideology in a liberal world* by Burns, Gene. In: *Crisis* 11:53-54 My 1993

Light, Judi.
Family meetings do work. *St Anth* 101:10-14 Ag 1993

Likoudis, James.
How a Greek Orthodox became Catholic [interview by B O'Reilly]. *ChrWorld* 38:140-143 Mr-Ap 1993

Lillie, Betty Jane.
Review of: *Renewing the covenant: a theology for the postmodern Jew* by Borowitz, Eugene B. In: *Bib Th Bul* 23:135-136 Aut 1993
Review of: *Who knows what is good?* by Farmer, Kathleen A. In: *Bib Th Bul* 22:180-181 Wint 1992
Review of: *Who knows what is good?* by Farmer, Kathleen A. In: *Bib Th Bul* 23:82-83 Sum 1993

Lilly, Reginald.
Review of: *Phenomenology and deconstruction, v 1* by Cumming, Robert Denoon. In: *IPQ* 33:368-369 S 1993

Limburg, James.
Jonah, a commentary. Louisville: John Knox, 1993. x, 144p ISBN 0-664-21296-4

Lincoln, C Eric.
The black muslims in America. Grand Rapids: Eerdmans, 1993. 0-8028-0703-8 ISBN 0-8028-0703-8

Lincoln, Timothy D.
Spiritual growth in interdenominational families. *Ecumen Trends* 22:7-8 My 1993

Lind, Millard C.
Review of: *In quest of the past: studies on Israelite religion, literature, and prophetism* by Woude, A S van der, ed. In: *CBQ* 55:206-207 Ja 1993
Review of: *Theologie des Alten Testaments: vol 1* by Preuss, Horst Dietrich. In: *CBQ* 55:348-350 Ap 1993

Lindars, Barnabas. *see* Brooke, George J, jt ed

Lindberg, Carter.
Beyond charity: Reformation initiations for the poor. Minneapolis: Fortress Press, 1993. x, 235p ISBN 0-8006-2569-2 LC 92-29963

Lindbladh, Nils-Henrik.
The renewal of liturgical celebrations in the Swedish church. *Notitiae* 28:492-495 Jl 1992

Lindecker, Ruth C.
The Vatican and the disabled—what's next? *America* 168:10-12 Ap 17 1993

Linden, Ian.
Colombia's two faces. *Tablet* 247:881-882 Jl 10 1993
Joining the comedians: a report from Haiti. *Month* 26:308-312 Ag 1993
Reflections on Santo Domingo. *Month* 26:17-21 Ja 1993
Review of: *A theology of reconstruction: nation-building and human rights* by Villa-Vicencio, Charles. In: *Tablet* 247:439-440 Ap 3 1993

Lindley, P G. *see* Gunn, S J, jt ed

Lindquist, Mary M.
A bold new vision in mathematics education. *Momentum* 24:7-9 S-O 1993

Lindsay, Alan G.
Review of: *Mark and Luke in poststructuralist perspectives: Jesus begins to write* by Moore, Stephen D. In: *Relig Lit* 25:93-94 Spr 1993

Lindsay, Cecile.
Corporality, ethics, experimentation: Lyotard in the eighties. *PhilosTod* 36:389-401 Wint 1992

Linehan, D.
Review of: *Good news in a divided society: papers of the 1991 annual general meeting of the National Conference of Priests of Ireland.* In: *Doctr Life* 42:651-652 D 1992

Linn, Dennis, et al.
Belongings: bonds of healing and recovery. New Jersey: Paulist Press, 1993. x, 255p ISBN 0-8091-3365-2 LC 92-29855

Linn, Sheila Fabricant, et al. *see* Linn, Dennis, jt auth

Linscott, Mary.
Leadership, authority, and religious government. *RRel* 52:166-193 Mr-Ap 1993

Linssen, Michael. *see* Gelber, L, jt ed

Lipner, Julius J.
Seeking others in their otherness. *New Blckfrs* 74:152-165 Mr 1993

Lipscomb, Oscar Hugh, Abp, 1931-.
Review of: *The Confederacy's fighting chaplain: Father John B Bannon* by Tucker, Phillip Thomas. In: *CHist* 79:573-574 Jl 1993

Liptak, Dolores.
Review of: *St Stanislaus B and M Parish, Meriden, Connecticut* by Blejwas, Stanislaus A. In: *CHist* 79:576-577 Jl 1993

Lisska, Anthony J.
Dominican ideals in early America: the example of Edward Dominic Fenwick. *New Blckfrs* 74:382-392 S 1993
Review of: *The idea of Christian charity: a critique of some contemporary conceptions* by Graham, Gordon. In: *New Blckfrs* 74:51-53 Ja 1993

Lisson, Edwin L.
Review of: *Readings in moral theology no 7: natural law and theology* by Curran, Charles E, 1934-, and McCormick, Richard A, eds. In: *Horizons (CTS)* 20:182 Spr 1993

Litchfield, R Burr.
Review of: *The continuity of feudal power: the Caracciolo di Brienza in Spanish Naples* by Astarita, Tommaso. In: *CHist* 79:538-539 Jl 1993

Litecky, Catherine.
Review of: *The Sacrament of Christian life* by McGinty, Mary Peter. In: *Sisters* 65:142-143 Mr 1993

Littell, Franklin H., 1917-.
The ecumenical commitment to human rights. *JEcumen Stds* 29:383-398 Sum-Aut 1992

Little Sister Beatrice.
A meeting of elders. *Sisters* 65:181-182 My 1993

Littleton, Mark.
Fillin' up: devotional fuel for high performance living. Sisters: Questar, 1993. x, 180p ISBN 0-945564-72-4

Liu, Tai.
Review of: *Exile and kingdom: history and apocalypse in the Puritan migration to America* by Zakai, Avihu. In: *CHist* 79:111-113 Ja 1993

Livacić Gazzano, Ernesto.
La inquietud religiosa en cuatro poetas chilenos contemporáneos (Miguel Arteche, Carlos Bolton, Fidel Sepúlveda y Raúl Zurita). *Teol Vida* 33 no 3-4:299-314 1992

Lloyd, Sampson. *see* Moore, Rowan, jt auth

Lobdell, Maryann Artzer.
Dancing in my chair. *St Anth* 100:18-21 Ap 1993

Lobet, Benoît.
Le congrès européen de catéchèse de Münich (mai 1993). *Lumen* 48:350-352 S 1993

Lobinger, Fritz, Bp.
Theological adult formation in an African diocese. *AFER* 35:209-216 Ag 1993

Lockwood, Robert P.
A prejudice rooted in ignorance. *OSV* 82:19 Ag 15 1993

Lodge, John G.
Review of: *L'épître de saint Paul aux Ephésiens* by Bouttier, Michel. In: *CBQ* 55:357-358 Ap 1993

Loewe, Herbert, 1882-1940.
The concept of blessing. *SIDIC* 26 no 1:2-9 1993

Lofts, Steve.
Une nouvelle approche de la philosophie d'Ernst Cassirer. *RPhil Louvain* 90:523-538 N 1992
Review of: *The question of God in Heidegger's phenomenology* by Kovacs, George. In: *RPhil Louvain* 91:159-163 F 1993

Loftus, John. *see* Aarons, Mark, jt auth

Logan, Fidelis.
Listen read: a program for visually handicapped sisters. *Sisters* 65:53-54 Ja 1993

Loggen, W.
Review of: *Christi Himmelfahrt* by Wilcke, Karin. In: *Stimm Zeit* 210:861-862 D 1992

Logue, Judy.
The Bible and the RCIA. *BibleT* 31:41-45 Ja 1993

Lohfink, Norbert.
'Holy war' and the 'ban' in the Bible [condensed fr *Internationale katholische Zeitschrift: Communio* Mr 1989]. *TheolDgst* 38:109-114 Sum 1991
The Psalter and Christian meditation. *TheolDgst* 40:133-139 Sum 1993

Lombardi, Joseph L.
Obstetrical dilemmas and the principle of double effect. *Amer J Juris* 37:197-211 1992

London, Judy.
On the right path. *Health Prog* 74:36-38 Je 1993

Long, Burke O.
Review of: *'Our fathers have told us'* by Ska, Jean-Louis. In: *CBQ* 54:768 O 1992

Long, Fiachra.
Review of: *L'Union substantielle I: Blondel et Leibniz* by Leclerc, Marc. In: *IJPS* 1:156-158 Mr 1993

Long, Grace D Cumming.
Women views of Christian life. Louisville: John Knox, 1993. x, 176p ISBN 0-664-25408-x

Longfield, Bradley J. *see* Marsden, George M, jt ed

Longford, Frank.
Review of: *Edward Heath* by Campbell, John. In: *Tablet* 247:858 Jl 3 1993
Review of: *Tired and emotional: the life of Lord George Brown* by Paterson, Peter. In: *Tablet* 247:581 My 8 1993

Longley, Clifford.
No bar to entry. *Tablet* 247:1058 Ag 21 1993
Review of: *Cardinal Hume and the changing face of English Catholicism* by Stanford, Peter. In: *Tablet* 247:371 Mr 20 1993

Lonsdale, David.
Listening to the music of the spirit: the art of discernment. Notre Dame: Ave Maria Press, 1993. x, 174p ISBN 08-7793-508-4
Review of: *Anchorite spirituality* by Savage, Anne, et al, eds. In: *Way* 33:83 Ja 1993
Review of: *Immortality* by Kundera, Milan. In: *Month* 26:31 Ja 1993
Review of: *Jeremy Tarfor: selected works* by Carroll, Thomas K, ed. In: *Way* 33:83-84 Ja 1993
Review of: *The book of laughter and forgetting* by Kundera, Milan. In: *Month* 26:31-32 Ja 1993
Review of: *The eye of the storm* by Leech, Kenneth, 1939-. In: *Way* 33:159-160 Ap 1993
Review of: *The foundations of mysticism* by McGinn, Bernard John, 1937-. In: *Way* 33:82 Ja 1993
Review of: *The volcano lover: a romance* by Sontag, Susan. In: *Month* 26: 273-274 Jl 1993

Loomie, Albert J.
Review of: *Elizabeth I: war and politics, 1588-1603* by MacCaffrey, Wallace T. In: *CHist* 79:341-342 Ap 1993

Loon, Ralph R Van.
Acolytes as proclaimers. *Liturgy* 11:28-29 Sum 1993

Loose, H N. see Descouvement, P, jt auth

Lopez, Benito.
Dialogue [interview by P Mullen]. *Register* 69:1+ S 19 1993

López, Martín, Julián.
España: encuentro anual de delegados diocesanos de liturgia. *Notitiae* 28:425-428 Je 1992

Lopez-Gay, Jesus.
Review of: *For all the peoples of Asia. Federation of Asian Bishops' Conferences documents from 1970-1991* by Rosales, Gaudencio B, and Arevalo, Catalino G, eds. In: *Gregorianum* 74 no 3:594 1993
Review of: *Francisco Javier, su vida y su tiempo: Europa, 1506-1541, vol I* by Schurhammer, Georg. In: *Gregorianum* 74 no 3:595 1993
Review of: *Francisco Javier, su vida y su tiempo: India, 1547-1549, vol III* by Schurhammer, Georg. In: *Gregorianum* 74 no 3:595 1993
Review of: *Francisco Javier, su vida y su tiempo: India-Indonesia, 1541-1547, vol II* by Schurhammer, Georg. In: *Gregorianum* 74 no 3:595 1993
Review of: *Francisco Javier, su vida y su tiempo: Japón-China, 1549-1552, vol IV* by Schurhammer, Georg. In: *Gregorianum* 74 no 3:595 1993
Review of: *Historia de la Iglesia en Hispanoamérica y Filipinas (siglos XV-XIX)* by Borges, Pedro, ed. In: *Gregorianum* 74 no 2:395 1993
Review of: *New directions in mission and evangelization: basic statements 1974-1991* by Scherer, James A, and Bevans, Stephen B, eds. In: *Gregorianum* 74 no 3:594-595 1993

Lopez Hernandez, Eleazar.
Evangelizacion de los pueblos indigenas. *Christus* 57:19-23 S 1992
Insurgencia teologica de los pueblos indios. *Christus* 58:7-13 S 1993

Lopez Martin, Julian.
El evangeliario en Castellano. *Notitiae* 28:332-336 My 1992

Lord, Donna M.
Review of: *Sister Ignatia: angel of Alcoholics Anonymous* by Darrah, Mary C. In: *RRel* 52:471-473 My-Je 1993

Lord, Elizabeth.
Review of: *Creation and history* by Trigo, Pedro. In: *Way* 33:156-157 Ap 1993
Review of: *Faces of Jesus in Africa* by Schreiter, Robert J, ed. In: *Heythrop* 34:192-193 Ap 1993
Review of: *From theology to social theory: Juan Luis Segundo and the theology of liberation* by Hewitt, Marsha Aileen. In: *Heythrop* 34:90-92 Ja 1993
Review of: *Grace and disgrace* by Ormerod, Neil. In: *Way* 33:76 Ja 1993
Review of: *Liberation theology at the crossroads: democracy or revolution* by Sigmund, Paul E. In: *Heythrop* 34:90-92 Ja 1993
Review of: *Prophecy in South Africa* by Tutu, Desmond, Abp. In: *Way* 33: 76-77 Ja 1993
Review of: *Rethinking Catholic attitudes to sex* by Brett, Paul. In: *Way* 33: 77 Ja 1993
Review of: *Rethinking Christian attitudes of sex* by Brueggemann, Walter. In: *Way* 33:75-76 Ja 1993
Review of: *The codependent Church* by Hoffmann, Virginia Curran. In: *Way* 33:157-158 Ap 1993
Review of: *The cosmic covenant* by Murray, Robert. In: *Way* 33:75 Ja 1993
Review of: *The liturgy of the world* by Rahner, Karl, 1904-1984. In: *Way* 33: 156 Ap 1993
Review of: *The spirit of life* by Moltmann, Jürgen. In: *Way* 33:156-157 Ap 1993
Review of: *Theology, the university and the modern world* by Runcie, Robert. In: *Way* 33:76 Ja 1993

Lord, Mary Louise.
Virgil's Eclogues, Nicholas Trevet, and the harmony of the spheres. *Med Stud* 54:186-273 1992

Lorenz, Velva.
How beautiful are the feet [condensed fr *Standard* O 18 1992]. *CDgst* 58:36+ N 1993

Loretz, Oswald. see Dietrich, Manfried, jt auth

Lorizio, G.
Review of: *L'uomo in Maritain* by Rizzi, Giuseppe. In: *Civilta* 144:204-205 Ja 16 1993
Review of: *La settimana santa dei filosofi* by Tilliette, Xavier. In: *Civilta* 3: 536-537 S 18 1993

Lorscheider, Aloísio, Cardinal.
A IV conferência geral do episcopado Latino-Americano em Santo Domingo—República Dominicana. *REB* 53:19-39 Mr 1993

Löschcke, E. see Aragón, R, jt auth

Lotito, R. see Serafini, Alfredo, jt auth

Lott, Anastasia.
The relationship between evangelization and development. *AFER* 34:66-78 Ap 1992

Loud, G A. see Wood, Ian, jt ed

Loudon, David L. see Stevens, Robert E, jt auth

Loudon, Mary.
Review of: *Home truths* by Maitland, Sara. In: *Tablet* 247:657 My 22 1993

Loughlin, Gerard.
Over the ashes. *New Blckfrs* 73:605-613 D 1992
Review of: *A vision to pursue: beyond the crisis in Christianity* by Ward, Keith. In: *Heythrop* 34:442-444 O 1993
Review of: *Religious pluralism and unbelief: studies critical and comparative* by Hamnett, Ian. In: *Heythrop* 34:78-80 Ja 1993
Review of: *The body in context* by Moore, Gareth. In: *New Blckfrs* 74:370-371 Jl-Ag 1993
Review of: *The uniqueness of Christ in the Theocentric model: an elabortion and evaluation of the position of John Hick* by Carruthers, Gregory H. In: *Heythrop* 34:80-81 Ja 1993
Review of: *What is a story?* by Cupitt, Don. In: *Heythrop* 34:446-447 O 1993

Loughran, Eileen.
For DREs: challenge and hope. *Momentum* 24:64-65 S-O 1993
Team Spirit—the art of delegating. *Tod Parish* 25:36 Ap-My 1993

Louis, William Roger. see Blake, Robert, jt ed

Louth, Andrew.
Review of: *The foundations of mysticism* by McGinn, Bernard John, 1937-. In: *New Blckfrs* 74:110-111 F 1993

Lovat, Terence J. see Mitchell, Kenneth R, jt auth

Lovatt-Dolan, Elizabeth.
Review of: *The voice of the turtledove* by Brotherton, Anne, ed. In: *Living Light* 29:90-91 Sum 1993

Love, Stuart L.
The household: a major social component for gender analysis in the gospel of Matthew. *Bib Th Bul* 23:21-31 Spr 1993
Review of: *Disciples and leaders: the origins of Christian ministry in the New Testament* by O'Grady, John F. In: *CBQ* 55:389 Ap 1993

Lovrien, Peggy.
Find versatile service music that works. *Past Mus* 17:33-34 Ap-My 1993

Low, Anthony.
George Herbert: *The Best Love*. *Renascence* 45:159-177 Spr 1993

Lowery, David L.
Review of: *Care of the dying*. In: *Liguorian* 81:70 Jl 1993

Lowery, Mark.
Review of: *Guide to St Thomas Aquinas* by Pieper, Josef. In: *SocJust* 84:61-62 Mr-Ap 1993
Why Catholic orthodoxy is not "Catholic fundamentalism". *New Oxford Rev* 60:14-19 S 1993

Lowry, Douglas.
A faith perspective on ethical dilemmas: Good decisions and tough choices. *New Cov* 22:15-16 My 1993

Loya, Joseph A.
Review of: *Revolutions in Eastern Europe* by Nielsen, Niels C. In: *JEcumen Stds* 29:263-264 Spr 1992
Review of: *The spring of nations: churches in the rebirth of Central and Eastern Europe* by Bailey, J Martin. In: *JEcumen Stds* 29:263-264 Spr 1992

Lubac, Henri De, Cardinal.
At the service of the church: Henri de Lubac reflects on the circumstances that occasioned his writings. San Francisco: Ignatius Press, 1993. x, 411p ISBN 08-9870-414-6

Lubich, Chiara.
Chiara Lubich: life for unity. New York: New City Press, 1992. x, 181p ISBN 0-904287-45-91

Lubomirski, Hieczyslaw.
Review of: *Theocracy: in Paul's praxis and theology* by Georgi, Dieter. In: *Gregorianum* 74 No 1:154-156 1993

Lucchetti Bingemer, Maria Clara.
Teologia da libertação: uma opção pelos pobres? *REB* 52:917-927 D 1992

Luciani, Didier.
Paul et la Loi. *NRT* 115:40-68 Ja-F 1993

Lucker, Raymond A, Bp.
Justice for all: the church should lead by example. *USCath* 58:34-36 My 1993

Luckey, W.
Review of: *Liberalism, conservatism, and Catholicism* by Krason, Stephen M. In: *F & R* 18:309-312 Aut 1992

Luebering, Carol.
Let's open adoption records. *St Anth* 100:22-26 Ap 1993
Review of: *A dresser of sycamore trees: the finding of a ministry* by Keizer, Garret. In: *St Anth* 100:52 Ja 1993
Review of: *Parents forever: you and your adult children* by Callahan, Sidney. In: *St Anth* 100:50 Mr 1993
Review of: *The clown in the belfry: writings on faith and fiction* by Buechner, Frederick. In: *St Anth* 100:51 Ja 1993

Luka, Ronald, 1937-.
Battling for the Body of Christ. *Mod Lit* 20:13 S 1993
Fishing for inactives. *Tod Parish* 25:27 Mr 1993
The parish church: a house of prayer. *Mod Lit* 20:16-17 F 1993

Lynch, Joan D.
Review, of: *Image and likeness: religious visions in American film classics* by May, John R, ed. In: *Horizons (CTS)* 19:345-346 Fall 1992

Lynch, Robert, et al.
The common good: old idea, new urgency. *Origins* 23:81+ Je 24 1993

Lynn, David, and Lynn, Kathy.
Great fundraising ideas for youth groups. Grand Rapids: Zondervan Publishing House, 1993. x, 208p ISBN 0-310-67171-x

Lynn, Kathy. *see* Lynn, David, jt auth

Lynn, Thomas D.
Of politics, Catholics, and the social doctrine [commentary: *Centesimus Annus*]. *SocJust* 84:18-21 Ja-F 1993
Centisimus Annus (the Hundredth Year), on the social teaching and concern for the worker, the poor, and the unborn [1991 05 01]: encyclical letter of His Holiness Pope JP2.

Lyons, Kieran.
Gay Christians. *Furrow* 44:347-351 Je 1993

Lyotard, Jean-François.
Mainmise. *PhilosTod* 36:419-427 Wint 1992

Lyotard, Jean-François, and Larochelle, Gilbert.
That which resists, after all [conversation between cited authors]. *PhilosTod* 36:402-417 Wint 1992

M

Maas, Robin.
Life-changing choices. *Spir Life* 39:140-149 Aut 1993
Will the real me please stand up? *Living Light* 29:37-44 Spr 1993

Mac Conghail, Muriris.
The religious strain. *Furrow* 44:292-296 My 1993

Mac Réamoinn, Seán.
Laylines. *Doctr Life* 42:318-325 My-Je 1992
Laylines. *Doctr Life* 43:108-115 F 1993
Laylines. *Doctr Life* 43:365-368 Jl-Ag 1993

Maçaneiro, Marcial.
Direitos de vida numa cultura de morte. *REB* 53:52-71 Mr 1993
Instituto de Pastoral da Juventude/Leste II. *REB* 53:409-411 Je 1993

MacCarthy, Peter T.
Listening and liturgy. *SacM* 120:34-38 Aut 1993
Review of: *Heart of Mary, heart of the church* by Margerie, Bertrand de. In: *HPR* 94:78 N 1993
Review of: *Priesthood today* by Rausch, Thomas P. In: *HPR* 93:75 Je 1993
Review of: *Salvation outside the Church* by Sullivan, Francis Aloysius. In: *HPR* 93:77-78 Jl 1993
Review of: *The silence of Mary* by Larranaga, Ignacio. In: *HPR* 93:63 F 1993
Review of: *Theology: love's question* by Tekippe, Terry J. In: *HPR* 93:70-71 F 1993
Review of: *To know Christ Jesus* by Sheed, Frank J. In: *HPR* 93:80-81 Ag-S 1993
Review of: *Ysabella of Trastamara: first lady of the Renaissance* by Long, Elisabeth. In: *HPR* 93:76-77 F 1993

MacCarthy, Thomas.
Images of God and the richness of our faith [reply to W Harrington, 42 no 8 467-476 O 1992]. *Doctr Life* 42:629-630 D 1992

Macchi, Angelo.
L'ingresso di Clinton alla Casa Bianca. *Civilta* 144:363-369 F 20 1993
Review of: *Rebirth: a history of Europe since World War II*. In: *Civilta* 3: 325-326 Ag 7-21 1993

Macchiarola, Frank J.
Give it that old college try. *Comm* 120:9-12 S 10 1993

Macci, A.
Review of: *The Linchpin* by Friend, Julius W. In: *Civilta* 3:340-341 Ag 7-21 1993

MacClennan, Carole.
Celebrate the golden days!. *ReligTJ* 27:8 Ap-My 1993
Families: signs of God. *ReligTJ* 26:31 Ja 1993
Saints know how to listen. *ReligTJ* 27:34-35 O 1993
Turn this sorrow to joy (for early childhood class on the meaning of sin and repentance). *ReligTJ* 27:16-17 F 1993
We are windows to God. *ReligTJ* 27:47 S 1993
Which one is black? *ReligTJ* 27:38 Mr 1993

MacCormick, Chalmers.
Review of: *Denn wir sind Menschen voller Hoffnung: Gespräche mit dem XIV* by Bruück, Michael von. In: *JEcumen Stds* 29:494 Sum-Aut 1992
Review of: *Theologie des Dritten Auges: asiatische Spiritualität und christliche theologie* by Song, Choan-Seng. In: *JEcumen Stds* 29:114 Wint 1992
Review of: *Third-eye theology: theology in formation in Asian settings* by Song, Choan-Seng. In: *JEcumen Stds* 29:114 Wint 1992

MacCoull, LSB.
Review of: *Liste der koptischen Hanschriften des Neuen Testaments 1: Die sahidischen Handschriften der Evangelien 2* by Schmitz, Franz-Jürgen, and Mink, Gerd, eds. In: *CBQ* 55:180 Ja 1993

MacDonald, Burton.
Review of: *Studies in the chronology of the divided monarchy of Israel* by Barnes, William Hamilton. In: *CBQ* 55:320-321 Ap 1993

Mace, Irving B.
Addiction, recovery and God. *Living Prayer* 26:25-26 Ja-F 1993

MacEoin, Gary.
Curia faction goes for total control over CELAM IV. *Nat Cath Rep* 29:14-15 N 6 1992
"Democracy demands structural change". *Nat Cath Rep* 30:10 N 19 1993

MacEoin, Gary. *(cont'd)*
How US policy trickled down to a Sao Paulo jail. *Nat Cath Rep* 29:18 Mr 19 1993
Job discrimination worked in N. Ireland. *Nat Cath Rep* 30:10-11 O 29 1993
Northern Ireland. *Nat Cath Rep* 30:8-9 O 22 1993
Review of: *Peace without Hiroshima: secret action at the Vatican in the Spring of 1945* by Quigley, Martin S. In: *Nat Cath Rep* 29:15 F 26 1993
Review of: *Renewing the Irish church* by McVeigh, Joseph. In: *Nat Cath Rep* 29:30 S 10 1993
Rome tries, fails to recolonialize Latin church [CELAM IV]. *Nat Cath Rep* 29:10-11 N 13 1992
El Salvador [photos]. *Nat Cath Rep* 29:8-9 S 3 1993
What CELAM achieved at Santo Domingo. *Doctr Life* 43:95-99 F 1993
Youth were cheered on—but not really challenged. *Nat Cath Rep* 29:5 Ag 27 1993

MacGregor, Geddes.
Review of: *Christian uniqueness and Catholic spirituality* by Carmody, Denise Lardner, and Carmody, John Tully. In: *JEcumen Stds* 29:107-108 Wint 1992
Review of: *Christian uniqueness reconsidered* by D'Costa, Gavin, ed. In: *JEcumen Stds* 29:107-108 Wint 1992
Review of: *Dictionary of the Ecumenical Movement* by Lossky, Nicholas, et al, eds. In: *JEcumen Stds* 29:264-265 Spr 1992

Mack, Burton L.
Dialogue [interview by G Meyer]. *Register* 69:1+ My 9 1993
The lost gospel: the book of Q and Christian origins. New York: HarperCollins, 1993. x, 275p ISBN 0-06-065374-4 LC 92-53921

Mack, Elke.
Wirtschaftsethik. *Stimm Zeit* 211:713-716 O 1993

Macken, John.
Religion and culture in Irish society. *Studies* 82:123-130 Sum 1993
Review of: *Religion and culture in a dialogue* by Lane, Dermot A, ed. In: *Studies* 82:354-356 Aut 1993

MacKennon, Donald.
Review of: *The womb and the tomb: the mystery of the birth and resurrection of Jesus* by Montefiore, Hugh. In: *Tablet* 247:727-728 Je 5 1993

MacKinnon, Mary Heather.
Religious orders. *Nat Cath Rep* 29:13-14 F 19 1993

MacLeod, Allan.
Review of: *Wisdom, information, and wonder* by Midgley, Mary. In: *Can Cath Rev* 11:29-30 Mr 1993

MacLoughlin, James.
Just following orders: the politics of pedophilia. *Nat Cath Rep* 29:15 Ap 16 1993

MacMahon, Bernadette.
Young people and their religion [review article *Conscience first tradition second—a study of young Catholic Americans* by P McNamara]. *Doctr Life* 43:232-235 Ap 1993

Macmillan, Mona.
Review of: *The chronicle of a school, Roehampton-Woldingham 1842-1992* by O'Leary, April. In: *Tablet* 247:758-759 Je 1993

MacNamara, Francis.
Review of: *Through the year with George Otto Simms* by Whiteside, Lesley, ed. In: *Doctr Life* 43:124-125 F 1993

MacNamara, Frank.
Music in Church. *Furrow* 44:148-153 Mr 1993

Macnutt, Judith. *see* Macnutt, Francis, jt auth

Madden, Kathryn.
Why do women abort? *Crisis* 11:8 Ja 1993

Madden, Lawrence J, ed.
The Joseph Campbell phenomenon: implications for the contemporary church. Washington: The Pastoral Press, 1992. x, 153p ISBN 0-912405-89-9

Madden, Michael.
Seeing and believing. *HPR* 93:48-53 F 1993

Madden, Nora.
Fantastic folklore. *Tod Cath Teach* 26:41-42+ Ap 1993

Mader, S.
Review of: *Food for the journey, theological foundations of the Catholic health care ministry* by Casey, Juliana. In: *Linacre* 59:91-92 N 1992

Madges, William.
Review of: *An introduction to systematic theology* by Pannenberg, Wolfhart. In: *Horizons (CTS)* 19:318-319 Fall 1992

Madigan, Patrick.
Review of: *The diversity of religions* by DiNoia, J A. In: *Worship* 67:379-381 Jl 1993

Madigan, Shawn.
Communion ministers as proclaimers. *Liturgy* 11:71-72 Sum 1993

Madsen, Catherine.
Imagination, the poets' God. *CrossCurr* 43:47-59 Spr 1993

Maduro, Otto.
US Latinos and religion [interview by J S Torrens]. *America* 169:16-19 Ag 14-21 1993 *see* Ellis, Marc E, jt ed

Maesschalck, Marc.
Événement et destinée chez Schelling. *RPhil Louvain* 91:185-206 My 1993
L'idéalisme Allemand face à la raison théologique. *Laval Theol Phil* 49:309-320 Je 1993

Maestri, William F.
My rosary journal: the great mysteries. New York: Alba House, 1993. x, 102p ISBN 0-8189-0673-1

Magas, Branka.
Croat Catholics divided. *Tablet* 247:908-910 Jl 17 1993

Magee, Brian.
Communion under both kinds. *Furrow* 44:364-368 Je 1993

Magee, James J.
Life review, families, and older religious. *RRel* 52:226-235 Mr-Ap 1993

Magee, John.
What's in a pedigree? Alcimus Avitus, De Spir Hist Gest 2 50-52, and Juvenal, Sat 8 140-41. *Med Stud* 54:317-326 1992

Magers, Stella.
The child and me. *Sisters* 65:299-300 Jl 1993

Magesa, Laurenti.
"Am I not a human being and a brother/sister?". *AFER* 34:95-114 Ap 1992
Differences that bind the liberation of women in Africa. *AFER* 35:44-53 F 1993
Review of: *Ministry and authority in the Catholic Church* by Hill, Edmund. In: *AFER* 34:61-62 F 1992
When good things happen to "bad" people. *AFER* 35:79-90 Ap 1993

Magill, Gerard.
Interpreting moral doctrine: Newman on conscience and law. *Horizons (CTS)* 20:7-22 Spr 1993
Review of: *God and history: aspects of British theology 1875-1914* by Hinchliff, Peter. In: *TheolStds* 54:358-359 Je 1993
Review of: *Newman and heresy* by Thomas, Stephen. In: *Horizons (CTS)* 20:149-150 Spr 1993
Review of: *Newman: towards the second spring* by Ffinch, Michael. In: *RRel* 52:626-627 Jl-Ag 1993

Magnani, Paolo.
Diocesi di Treviso piano pastorale diocesano *Delebrare (1989-1991)*. *Notitiae 28:528-545 Ag 1992*

Magness, Jodi.
Review of: *Handbook of ancient Hebrew inscriptions* by Ahituv, Shmuel. In: *OTA* 16:401 Je 1993
Review of: *Mari and the early Israelite experience* by Malamat, Abraham. In: *OTA* 16:410 Je 1993
Review of: *The architecture of ancient Israel: from the prehistoric to the Persian periods* by Kempinski, Aharon, and Reich, Ronny, eds. In: *OTA* 16:155 F 1993

Magno, Josefina B.
Midwife for souls: spiritual care for the dying. Bosston: St Paul Books & Media, 1993. 111p ISBN 0-8198-4769-0 LC 93-32153

Maher, B.
Review of: *Create your own health patterns* by Fitzpatrick, John L. In: *Doctr Life* 43:58-60 Ja 1993

Maher, Eamon.
The Christian novelist in an age of transition-a case study. *Studies* 82:140-147 Sum 1993
Faith on the margins: the example of Jean Sulivan. *Doctr Life* 43:147-155 Mr 1993

Mahlmann, John J.
Calling a halt to the marginalization of the arts. *Momentum* 24:25-28 S-O 1993

Mahoney, Hildegarde Marie.
National health care legislation and the funding of abortion. *America* 169:8-9 O 16 1993

Mahoney, John.
The challenge of moral distinctions [revised lecture]. *TheolStds* 53:663-682 D 1992

Mahony, Roger Michael, Cardinal, 1936-, et al.
Los Angeles religious leaders: bridging the gaps that still divide. *Origins* 22:781+ Ap 29 1993

Mahony, Roger Michael, Cardinal, 1936-.
Film makers, film viewers: their challenges and opportunities [pastoral letter]. Boston: St Paul Books & Media, 1992. 31p ISBN 0-8198-2654-5
Homosexuals in the military: three issues. *Origins* 22:621+ F 25 1993
Immigration [address, multi-ethnic Mass, Los Angeles, CA, O 9 1993]. *Register* 69:2 O 24 1993
Views exchanged over poll of priests and nuns. *Origins* 23:399-400 N 11 1993
You have entertained angels without knowing it. *America* 169:16-18 N 27 1993

Mahy, Jean-François.
De la fascination à l'altérité. *Lumen* 48:317-323 S 1993

Maida, Adam, Abp.
Assisted-suicide ban supported. *Origins* 23:280 S 30 1993
Persons with disabilities. *Origins* 23:353+ O 28 1993

Maier, Francis X.
Review of: *The porcupine* by Barnes, Julian. In: *America* 168:22-23 Je 19-26 1993
Things Danny taught me: a father's story. *Comm* 120:11-12 Mr 26 1993

Maier, Peter.
Liturgische bewegung—noch aktuell?: Fachtagung der arbeitsgemeinschaft katholischer liturgikdozenten. *Notitiae* 28:751-755 N-D 1992

Main, William.
Review of: *The fanatics: a behavioral approach to political violence* by Taylor, Maxwell. In: *Crisis* 10:48-51 N 1992

Mairs, Nancy, 1943-.
Ordinary time: cycles in marriage, faith, and renewal. Boston: Beacon Press, 1993. x, 238p ISBN 0-8070-7056-4 LC 92-40421

Maitland, Sara, 1950-.
A feminist's path to Rome. *Tablet* 247:422 Ap 3 1993
Journey with my daughter. *Tablet* 247:1065-1066 Ag 21 1993

Majawa, Clement.
The vision of authentic ecumenism: a Catholic response. *AFER* 35:91-100 Ap 1993

Majía, Jorge María, Bp, 1923-.
Equal dignity [Speech, assembly on equality of women, Rome, O 21-22 1993]. *Register* 69:2 N 14 1993

Makarushka, I.
Review of: *Demons and the devil: moral imagination in modern Greek culture* by Stewart, Charles. In: *TheolStds* 53:792 D 1992

Makaya, Jean Florent.
La secte eglise unie du saint esprit du Congo. *StudiaM* 41:225-239 1992

Maker, William.
Review of: *Overcoming foundations: studies in systematic philosophy* by Winfield, Richard Dien. In: *IPQ* 33:132-133 Mr 1993

Maksymowicz, Virginia, and Tobia, Blaise.
Rethinking religious art. *ChrWorld* 236:244-251 N-D 1993

Malarcher, Patricia.
Art and liturgical environment: an artist's perspective. *New Theol Rev* 6:18-26 F 1993

Malchow, Bruce V.
Qoheleth and Jesus. *BibleT* 31:110-115 Mr 1993

Malcolm, Catherine.
My pilgrimage to Lourdes. *Liguorian* 81:32-35 O 1993

Maletta, Sammie L, Jr. *see* Place, Michael D, jt auth

Malherbe, Abraham J, and Meeks, Wayne A, eds.
The future of Christology: essays in honor of Leander E Keck. Minneapolis: Fortress Press, 1993. x, 265p ISBN 0-80062-728-8 LC 92-40265

Malherbe, Jean-François.
Éthique et médecine expérimentale à l'hôpital. *Supplement* 184:107-124 Mr-Ap 1993
"Saiser Dieu en son vestiaire" L'articulation théologique du sens chez Maître Eckhart. *Laval Theol Phil* 49:201-213 Je 1993

Malin, Irving.
Review of: *Indigo* by Wiley, Richard. In: *America* 169:26-27 Jl 3-10 1993
Review of: *Natural history* by Howard, Maureen. In: *Comm* 120:23 F 12 1993
Review of: *The son of laughter* by Buechner, Frederick. In: *Comm* 120:27-28 Jl 16 1993

Malina, Bruce J, 1933-.
The New Testament world: insights from cultural anthropology. Louisville, Kentucky: John Knox Press, 1993. 224p ISBN 0-664-25456-x
Review of: *Egalitarian community: ethnography and exegesis* by Atkins, Robert A, Jr. In: *CBQ* 55:137-138 Ja 1993
Time travel to ancient Judea. Louisville: Westminster, 1993. x, 208p ISBN 0-664-25457-8
Windows on the world of Jesus: time travel to ancient Judea. Louisville, Kentucky: John Knox Press, 1993. 208p ISBN 0-664-25457-8

Maller, Allen S.
Fasting: the Bible's spiritual diet. *Spir Life* 39:22-25 Spr 1993

Mallon, John.
The good news about vocations. *Register* 69:1+ O 10 1993
An "on-line" Catholic faith. *Register* 69:3 My 2 1993

Mallowe, Mike.
Good people get angry, too. *USCath* 58:14-21 My 1993
Let's be totally honest. *USCath* 58:20-25 Je 1993

Malloy, David.
The American hierarchy, the propaganda fide, and the composition of hte Baltimore catechism. *ACHSR* 103:35-46 Aut 1992

Malloy, Patrick L.
Review of: *Documents of Christian worship* by White, James F. In: *TheolStds* 54:603-604 S 1993

Malloy, Richard G.
Media violations. *America* 168:4-5 F 6 1993
Some of the best priests I know are women. *USCath* 58:30-31 Ap 1993

Malone, James, Bp.
Environmental degradation and social injustice. *Origins* 22:685+ Mr 18 1993

Malone, Mary.
The unfinished agenda of the Church: a critical look at the history of celibacy. *Way Suppl* 77:66-75 Sum 1993

Malone, Miriam.
Converting the religious educator. *Mod Lit* 20:18-20 Je-Jl 1993

Maloney, Elliot C.
Review of: *The interrelations of the gospels* by Dungan, David L, ed. In: *CBQ* 54:820-821 O 1992

Maloney, Francis J.
Review of: *Footwashing in John 13 and the Johannine community* by Thomas, John Christopher. In: *Pacifica* 6:212-214 Je 1993

Maloney, George A, 1924-.
Befilled with the fullness of God: living in the indwelling Trinity. New Rochelle, New York: New City, Press, 1993. x, 144p ISBN 1-56548-024-4 LC 92-42031
The gift of tears in the writings of St Ignatius Loyola and the Eastern Fathers. *Diakonia* 26 no 1:5-13 1993
The principle of economy a corrective of Christian mercy. *Diakonia* 26 no 2:119-133 1993
The spirit broods over the world. New York: Alba House, 1993. x, 172p ISBN 0-8189-0633-2 LC 92-40239

Maloney, Oliver.
Moral dilemmas in modern business. *Furrow* 44:12-20 Ja 1993

Mancuso, Theresa.
Let my prayer rise like incense before you. *Living Prayer* 26:7-13 Jl-Ag 1993
Prayer, memories, and God. *RRel* 52:541-547 Jl-Ag 1993
Psalms in the city. *Living Prayer* 26:16-22 Mr-Ap 1993
Review of: *Sharing the darkness: the spirituality of caring* by Cassidy, Sheila. In: *RRel* 52:147-148 Ja-F 1993
Vulnerability and strength: the paradox of spiritual maturity. *Living Prayer* 26:6-10 N-D 1993

Manelli, Stefano M.
Challenges refuted about Mary. *ChrWorld* 38:165-172 Mr-Ap 1993

Manenschijn, Gerrit.
The quest for a just economy in a new Europe: ethical implications of the social market economy. *Louvain Stds* 18:159-174 Sum 1993

Manfra, Jo Ann.
Review of: *A biography of Msgr Benedict Joseph Flaget, 1763-1850* by Lemarie, Charles. In: *CHist* 79:570-571 Jl 1993

Mangan, Charles M.
Just call me George. *HPR* 93:66-70 Je 1993
The blessing of children. *Register* 69:4 Mr 28 1993
The centrality of the Eucharist. *Register* 69:5 Je 20 1993
Death's true meaning. *Register* 69:4 O 31 1993
The feast of the Chair of Peter. *OSV* 81:14 F 21 1993
Real gratitude. *New Cov* 23:14-15 S 1993
Review of: *Catholic ministry to the addicted* by Barkley, Roy. In: *HPR* 93:77-78 Ja 1993
Review of: *Daily readings in Catholic classics* by Myers, Rawley, ed. In: *HPR* 94:76-77 O 1993
Review of: *Mary, Mother* by Schug, John A. In: *HPR* 93:78-79 Ja 1993
Review of: *Newman: towards the second spring* by Ffinch, Michael. In: *HPR* 93:76-79 Ap 1993
Review of: *Reincarnation: illusion or reality?* by Robillard, Edmond. In: *HPR* 93:71-72 Ap 1993
Review of: *The jeweler's shop* by Wojtyla, Karol. In: *HPR* 94:71-72 O 1993
Review of: *The Mary book—mother of evangelism (for the third millenium)* by Fox, Robert J. In: *HPR* 93:74-75 F 1993
Review of: *The mind and heart of the church: the proceedings of the Wethersfield Institute, volume 4* by McInerny, Ralph M, ed. In: *HPR* 93:81-82 Ag-S 1993
The spirituality of the diocesan priest [fr address by John Paul II to bishops of Central France, Ja 13 1992]. *Priest* 49:33-34 Je 1993

Mankowski, Paul V.
Advice for liturgical orphans. *America* 169:15+ Ag 28-S 4 1993
The prayer of Lady Macbeth: how the contraceptive mentality has neutered religious life. *F & R* 19:79-93 Spr 1993
Voices of wrath: when words become weapons. *Crisis* 10:22-25 D 1992

Manney, Dave.
War comes to Medjugorje. *New Cov* 23:7-11 N 1993

Manney, Jim.
Bosnia: couldn't something have been done? *OSV* 82:19 Ag 29 1993
Fanatics [editorial]. *New Cov* 22:5 My 1993
'Hard' news and good news. *Register* 69:5 F 7 1993
Hoosiers [editorial]. *New Cov* 23:5 Ag 1993
Learning from the Pope [editorial]. *New Cov* 23:5 N 1993
Open your hearts [editorial]. *New Cov* 23:5 O 1993
Six small syllables [editorial]. *New Cov* 22:5 Mr 1993
We're free people. *New Cov* 22:5 F 1993

Manney, Jim, ed.
Prayer that "works" [editorial]. *New Cov* 22:5 Je 1993
Seeds in the muck [editorial]. *New Cov* 23:5 S 1993

Manning, Martha.
Grace under pressure. *Salt* 13:45-46 N-D 1993
Jake's castle. *USCath* 58:35-37 Je 1993

Manning, Robert John Scheffler.
Kierkegaard and post-modernity: Judas as Kierdegaard's only disciple. *PhilosTod* 37:133-152 Sum 1993

Manning, Williard G, Jr. *see* Frank, Richard G, jt ed

Mannion, M Francis.
Humanae Vitae revisited [commentary Humanae Vitae]. *OSV* 82:19 Ag 1 1993
In praise of angels. *CDgst* 57:125-126 Ja 1993
Monasticism and modern culture: I hostility and hospitality—religious community and "the world". *ABenR* 44:3-21 Mr 1993
Monasticism and modern culture: II the cultural conversion of monks—liberalism and monastic life. *ABenR* 44:125-142 Je 1993
Monasticism and modern culture: III. the labor of tradition—monasticism as a cultural system. *ABenR* 44:290-307 S 1993
Sunday without a priest: what is at stake? [2 parts]. *Priest* 49:31-36 F 1993; 21-34 Mr 1993
Why churches shouldn't look like living rooms. *OSV* 82:23 N 21 1993 *see* Rosinski, Geri, jt auth

Manternach, Janaan. *see* Pfeifer, Carl J, jt auth

Manternach, Janaan, and Pfeifer, Carl J.
It's time for evaluation. *ReligTJ* 27:4-5 Ap-My 1993
Ways to pray with children. *ReligTJ* 27:4-7 Mr 1993
Dancing before the Lord. *ReligTJ* 26:4-6 Ja 1993
Three ways to be. *ReligTJ* 27:4-7 F 1993

Manuel Hurtado, Juan.
Comunidad y utopia la construccion de nuestra esperanza. *Christus* 58:47-49 N-D 1992

Manzanares, Julio.
Papal reservation and Recognitio: considerations and proposals. *Jurist* 52 no 1:228-254 1992

Manzaneo, Marcos.
Psicología y pedagogía de la edad evolutiva según Santo Tomás. *Cien Tom* 119:351-389 My-Ag 1992

Marchal, Michael.
The introductory rites: a chance to refocus. *Mod Lit* 20:18-19 My 1993

Marchesi, Giovanni.
Carisma e istituzione della chiesa nella teologia di Hans Urs Von Balthasar. *Civilta* 144:14-30 Ja 2 1993

Marchesi, Giovanni. *(cont'd)*
L'esegesi e l'evangelizzazione della nuova Europa. *Gregorianum* 73 No 4:719-730 1992
Fede e amore nei *Lager* Nazisti. *Civilta* 2:144-152 Ap 17 1993

Marconi, Gilberto.
Review of: *Giudaismo e Nuovo Testamento* by Del Verme, Marcello. In: *Gregorianum* 73 No 4:751-752 1992
Review of: *Metafore del Regno* by Weder, Hans. In: *Gregorianum* 74 No 1:152-154 1993 *see* O'Collins, Gerald, 1931-, jt ed

Marcozzi, R.
Review of: *A choir book for Advent* by Ladd, Paul R, Jr, ed. In: *Past Mus* 17:49 D 1992-Ja 1993
Review of: *A choir book for Christmas* by Ladd, Paul R, Jr, ed. In: *Past Mus* 17:49 D 1992-Ja 1993
Review of: *Fifty-nine liturgical rounds* by Tortolano, William. In: *Past Mus* 17:49-50 D 1992-Ja 1993

Marcus, Emile.
Pédagogie du célibat dans les orientations et documents écents de l'église. *Seminarium* 33:15-31 Ja-Mr 1993

Marcus, Joel.
Review of: *The beginning of Jesus' ministry according to Mark's Gospel* by Kuthirakkattel, Scaria. In: *CBQ* 55:162-163 Ja 1993

Marenbon, John.
Review of: *Boethius and Aquinas* by McInerny, Ralph M. In: *Heythrop* 34:318-319 Jl 1993

Margalit, Avishai. *see* Halbertal, Moshe, jt auth

Margaret, Madeline.
Review of: *Medicine at the crossroads* by Konner, Melvin. In: *Comm* 120:28-29 O 22 1993

Margerie, Bertrand de.
Introduction to the history of exegesis [v 3]. Petersham: Saint Bede's Publications, 1991. x, 169p ISBN 0-932506-97-6 LC 93-16067

Marget, Madeline.
Review of: *Intoxicated by my illness* by Broyard, Anatole. In: *Comm* 120:22-24 Ja 15 1993

Mari, Michael.
The accuser is the culprit: psychological projection as the key to understanding the abortion providers. *SocJust* 84:108-112 Jl-Ag 1993

Marias, Julian.
Razon de la filosofia. Madrid: Alianza, 1993. x, 294p ISBN 84-206-9658-7

Marie, Virginia.
If grain could talk. *RRel* 52:731-734 S-O 1993

Marinakos, Plato A.
Women and children first. *Health Prog* 74:34-37+ O 1993

Marinelli, Anthony.
The world made flesh: an overview of the Catholic faith. Mahwah: Paulist Press, 1993. 309p ISBN 0-8091-3391-1 LC 92-45629

Marino, Gordon D.
I think you should be responsible. *Comm* 120:13-15 F 12 1993

Marino, Joseph F.
Homework: a fresh approach to a perennial problem. *Momentum* 24:69-71 F-Mr 1993

Marins, José.
What are basic Christian communities? *Priests & People* 7:142-144 Ap 1993

Marins, José, and Chanona, Carolee, et al.
Un proceso eclesial Latinoamericano. *Christus* 58:23-28 Mr-Ap 1993

Marins, José, and Trevisan, Teolide M, et al.
Elementos para avaliar o VIII intereclesial das CEBS (S Maria, RS Brasil 8-12 Setembro 1992). *REB* 52:801-813 D 1992

Mariottini, Claude F.
Review of: *Amos* by Paul, Shalom M. In: *OTA* 15:513 O 1992
Review of: *God's people in God's land: family, land and property in the Old Testament* by Wright, Christopher J H. In: *OTA* 15:516 O 1992
Review of: *Judaism from Cyrus to Hadrian: the Persian and Greek periods, v I* by Grabbe, Lester L. In: *OTA* 16:445 Je 1993
Review of: *Judaism from Cyrus to Hadrian: the Roman Period, v II* by Grabbe, Lester L. In: *OTA* 16:445 Je 1993
Review of: *Micah, Nahum, Obadiah* by Mason, R A. In: *OTA* 15:511 O 1992
Review of: *The Books of Nahum, Habakkuk, and Zephaniah* by Robertson, O Palmer. In: *OTA* 15:511-512 O 1992
Review of: *The unity of the Twelve* by House, Paul R. In: *OTA* 15:510 O 1992

Marius, Richard, 1933-.
The reformation: too many assumptions? *Critic* 47:31-42 Wint 1992

Markham, Donna.
Review of: *An undivided heart* by Sammon, Sean D. In: *RRel* 52:788-789 S-O 1993

Markham, Flannan.
Review of: *Adventures in being* by Castarlenas, Alfredo Rubio de. In: *Furrow* 44:520 S 1993
Review of: *At home with God* by Lewis, Hedwig. In: *Furrow* 44:191-192 Mr 1993
Review of: *Grieving for change* by Arbuckle, Gerard A. In: *Furrow* 44:57 Ja 1993

Markham, Ian.
Creating options: shattering the "exclusivist, inclusivist, adn pluralist" paradigm [reply by Gavin D'Costa, pp 41-47]. *New Blckfrs* 74:33-34 Ja 1993

Marko, Robert P.
Review of: *War: a primer for Christians* by Allen, Joseph L. In: *Horizons (CTS)* 20:183-184 Spr 1993

Markovic, Matthew.
Review of: *With liberty and justice for whom? The recent evangelical debate over capitalism* by Gay, Craig M. In: *New Oxford Rev* 60:28 Jl-Ag 1993

Martinson, Paul Varo.
Review of: *The cross in the lotus world, vol 1: Jesus, the crucified people* by Song, Choan-Seng. In: *JEcumen Stds* 29:114-115 Wint 1992

Martos, Joseph.
The importance of spiritual fathering. *Liguorian* 81:4-9 Je 1993
Liturgy and life: sacraments, celebrations of our faith and life. *Catechist* 27:46-52 O 1993
Our fathers, ourselves healing men's brokenness. *Liguorian* 81:52-57 O 1993
Review of: *Confirmation* by Turner, Paul. In: *Living Light* 30:104-105 Aut 1993
Review of: *The historical Jesus* by Crossan, John Dominic. In: *Living Light* 29:87-88 Wint 1992
The sacramentality of the world. *Emmanuel* 99:4-7+ Ja-F 1993 *see* Rohr, Richard, 1943-, jt auth

Martou, Jean-Marie.
Comment faire Église aujourd'hui (à l'hôpital)? *Supplement* 184:145-166 Mr-Ap 1993

Marty, Martin E, 1928-.
Hey, Catholics, stand up for something!. *USCath* 58:36-37 S 1993
Multi-multiculturalism. *Critic* 47:37-45 Sum 1993
Review of: *This confident Church: Catholic leadership and life in Chicago, 1940-1965* by Avella, Steven M. In: *America* 24-26 Ag 14-21 1993
Review of: *Undermined establishment: church-state relations in America 1880-1920* by Handy, Robert T. In: *CHist* 78:686-687 O 1992

Maruca, Dominic.
History: a school of humility and a source of hope. *Seminarium* 33:96-106 Ja-Mr 1993
Review of: *Common journey, different paths: spiritual direction in a cross-cultural perspective* by Rakoczy, Susan, ed. In: *Gregorianum* 74 no 3:588-589 1993

Marx, Reinhard.
Ist Kirche anders? *Stimm Zeit* 211:123-130 F 1993

Marzotto, Damiano, Msgr.
Il celibato di Gesù e la verginità di Maria. *Seminarium* 33:32-47 Ja-Mr 1993

Mason, Alane Salierno.
Nancy Mair's book of hours. *Comm* 120:22-24 N 5 1993

Mason, Herbert.
Review of: *Morals of the heart* by Awliya, Nizam ad-Din. In: *TheolStds* 54:350-351 Je 1993

Mason, Mary Elizabeth.
Review of: *Renewal in late life through pastoral counseling* by Lapsley, James N. In: *Sisters* 65:226-227 My 1993

Mason, Philip, 1906-.
Peeling the onion. *Tablet* 247:1192 S 18 1993
Review of: *Edgar Allen Poe* by Meyers, Jeffrey. In: *Tablet* 247:109-110 Ja 23 1993
Review of: *Robert Louis Stevenson* by McLynn, Frank. In: *Tablet* 247:821-822 Je 26 1993
Thoughts of heaven. *Tablet* 247:543 My 1 1993
Wrestling with angels. *Tablet* 247:271 F 27 1993

Massa, Mark. *see* Viladesau, Richard, jt ed

Masserly, John.
Review of: *A thinker's guide to living well* by Bradford, Dennis E. In: *Mod Schlmn* 70:159-160 Ja 1993

Massion, John Carey.
The Christmas story: a gospel enactment. *Catechist* 27:16-18 N-D 1993
To memorize or not to memorize? *ReligTJ* 26:27-28 Ja 1993

Masson, J.
Review of: *Die Bhagavadgita in der neueren indischen Auslegung und in der Begegnung mit dem christlichen Glauben* by Huber, F. In: *NRT* 115:604 Jl-Ag 1993
Review of: *Ecclesiae memoria* by Henkel, Willi, ed. In: *NRT* 114:925-926 N-D 1992
Review of: *Histoire religieuse* by Durand, Jean-Dominique, and Ladous, Régis, eds. In: *NRT* 115:617-618 Jl-Ag 1993
Review of: *Propos d'un ermite* by Fu, Wang. In: *NRT* 115:601-602 Jl-Ag 1993
Review of: *Sagesse hindoue, mystique chrétienne* by Saux, H Le. In: *NRT* 115:603-604 Jl-Ag 1993
Review of: *Unsere Erde lebt* by Schlegelberger, B. In: *NRT* 115:607 Jl-Ag 1993

Mastrodonato, David.
In the shell of the old. *Cath Work* 60:7 Mr-Ap 1993
Lost strike? No such thing. *Cath Work* 60:7 Ja-F 1993

Mastrojeni, G.
Review of: *Diritto Internazionale* by Giuliano, Mario, and Scovazzi, Tullio, et al. In: *Civilta* 3:194-195 Jl 17 1993

Matera, Frank J.
Review of: *Mark's account of Peter's denial of Jesus: a history of its interpretation* by Herron, Robert W, Jr. In: *CBQ* 55:370-371 Ap 1993

Mathes, J Michael.
Review of: *The Spanish frontier in North America* by Weber, David J. In: *CHist* 79:562-564 Jl 1993

Mathews, Edward G.
Review of: *Chiana Lubich: a life for unity* by Zambonini, Franca. In: *Diakonia* 26 no 2:140 1993
Review of: *Ecumenism: a bibliographical overview* by Fahey, Michael A. In: *Diakonia* 26 no 2:138-139 1993
Review of: *Francis de Sales: finding God wherever you are* by Power, Joseph F, ed. In: *Diakonia* 26 no 2:141 1993
Review of: *Greek patristic theology, vol III* by Tsirpanlis, Constantine N. In: *Diakonia* 26 no 2:142-143 1993
Review of: *Greek patristic theology, vol IV* by Tsirpanlis, Constantine N. In: *Diakonia* 26 no 2:142-143 1993

Mathews, Edward G. *(cont'd)*
Review of: *John Henry Newman heart to heart* by Giese, Vincent. In: *Diakonia* 26 no 2:141-142 1993
Review of: *Journey to the light: spirituality as we mature* by Finch, Ann, ed. In: *Diakonia* 26 no 2:141 1993
Review of: *Promise of good things: the Apostolic Fathers* by Davies, Oliver, ed. In: *Diakonia* 26 no 2:140 1993
Review of: *The divine life, light, and love: euntes in mundum universum: Festschrift in honour of Petro B T Bilaniuk* by Pillinger, Renate, and Renhart, Erich, eds. In: *Diakonia* 26 no 2:139 1993

Mathews, Susan F.
On patient endurance [illus]. *BibleT* 31:305-312 S 1993
Review of: *John Paul II: a panorama of his teachings* by John Paul II, Pope, 1920- (Karol Wojtyla) (elected 1978). In: *Diakonia* 26 no 1:77-81 1993

Matovina, Timothy M.
Ministries and the servant community. *Worship* 67:351- Jl 1993
U.S. Hispanic Catholics and liturgical reform. *America* 169:18-19 N 6 1993

Mattam, Joseph.
The Our Father: the revolutionary prayer of commitment to the Kingdom of God. *AFER* 35:69-78 Ap 1993
The Sacrament of Reconciliation [repr fr *Vidyajyoti journal of theological reflection*]. *AFER* 34:293-322 O 1992

Mattei, Giampaolo.
Catholic seminary opens in Moscow. *OR(Eng)* 1309:6-7 S 29 1993

Matthews, Melvyn.
The panther and the hind. *New Blckfrs* 74:417-422 S 1993

Matthews, Victor H.
Review of: *Giving Goliath his due* by Bierling, Neal. In: *OTA* 16:402 Je 1993
Review of: *Identificatie-mogelijkheden in preken uit het Oude Testament* by Bos, Rein. In: *OTA* 16:402 Je 1993
Review of: *Property and the family in Biblical law* by Westbrook, Raymond. In: *OTA* 15:477-478 O 1992
Review of: *Studies in the Pentateuch* by Emerton, J A, ed. In: *CBQ* 55:413-414 Ap 1993
Review of: *Symbols of law: a contextual analysis of legal symbolic acts in the Old Testament* by Viberg, Ake. In: *OTA* 15:490 O 1992
Review of: *The comparative method in ancient Near Eastern and Biblical legal studies* by Malul, Meir. In: *OTA* 15:484 O 1992
Review of: *The roads and highways of ancient Israel* by Dorsey, David A. In: *CBQ* 55:331-332 Ap 1993

Matthis, Michael J.
Nietzsche as anti-naturalist. *PhilosTod* 37:170-182 Sum 1993

Matthys, Jean-Claude.
Review of: *Frère Maruice Hermans et les origines de l'Institut des Frères des Ecoles Chrétiennes*. In: *MSR* 50:163-166 Ap-Je 1993

Matual, David.
The Roman principle in the writings of Vladimir Solovyov. *Diakonia* 26 no 1:27-39 1993

Matz, Terry.
Christmas in the company of saints. *Liguorian* 81:50-55 D 1993

Maurer, Armand A, 1915-.
'In the twilight of the twentieth century' on divine sendings. *Can Cath Rev* 11:19-22 Jl-Ag 1993

Mawdesley, Anthony.
In the midst of life. *Month* 26:150-151 Ap 1993

Maxwell, Robert F.
Gettysburg. *Comm* 120:27-28 N 19 1993

May, David M.
Review of: *The Epistles to the Thessalonians: a commentary on the Greek text* by Wanamaker, Charles A. In: *Bib Th Bul* 23:41-42 Spr 1993

May, John D'Arcy.
Human rights as land rights in the Pacific. *Pacifica* 6:61-80 F 1993
Review of: *Transforming mission* by Bosch, David J. In: *JEcumen Stds* 29:470 Sum-Aut 1992

May, John R.
Movies: the struggle between art and entertainment. *ChrWorld* 236:252-257 N-D 1993
Review of: *Hollywood vs America* by Medved, Michael, 1948-. In: *ChrWorld* 236:252-257 N-D 1993

May, Todd.
The community's absence in Lyotard, Nancy, and Lacoue-Labarthe. *PhilosTod* 37:275-284 Aut 1993

May, William E.
From dissent to acceptance: realizing the full riches of Humanae Vitae. *HPR* 94:17-24 N 1993
Humanae Vitae, on the regulation of birth [1968 07 25] Commentary. The moral status of the embryo. *Linacre* 59:76-83 N 1992
Review of: *Humanae Vitae: a generation later* by Smith, Janet E. In: *Thomist* 57:155-161 Ja 1993
Review of: *The facts of life: science and the abortion controversy* by Morowitz, Harold J, and Trefil, James S. In: *New Oxford Rev* 60:24-26 O 1993
Review of: *The troubled dream of life* by Callahan, Daniel, 1930-. In: *Comm* 120:25-26 O 22 1993

Mayeksi, Marie Anne.
Review of: *Wisdom's daughter: the theology of Julian of Norwich* by Nuth, Joan M. In: *Horizons (CTS)* 20:172-173 Spr 1993
Review of: *The transformation of American Catholic sisters* by Quinonez, Lora Ann, and Turner, Mary Daniel. In: *ACHSR* 103:47-48 Aut 1992
Review of: *Holy siege* by Briggs, Kenneth A. In: *America* 168:27+ F 20 1993
Review of: *Laws of heaven* by Gallagher, Michael Paul, 1939-. In: *America* 168:27+ F 20 1993

Mayet, Melva.
My first incredible year. *ReligTJ* 27:20 S 1993

Mayos Solsona, Goncal.
Marxa I Sentit especulatius de la historia: comentaris a Hegel. Barcelona: PPU, 1993. x, 297p ISBN 84-477-0058-5

Mays, James L, et al, eds.
I and II chronicles: a commentary. Louisville: John Knox, 1993. x, 1104p ISBN 0-664-21845-8

Mazowiecki, Tadeusz.
Dialogue [interview by J Luxmoore and J Babiuch]. *Register* 69:1+ Ap 11 1993

Mazziotta, Richard.
Review of: *Catholic prayer* by Cunningham, Lawrence S, 1935-. In: *Mod Lit* 20:40 Ap 1993
Review of: *Family therapy in pastoral ministry* by Wynn, John Charles. In: *Mod Lit* 20:42 My 1993

McAleese, Dermot.
Solutions and political implications. *Studies* 82:61-72 Spr 1993

McAlister, Linda Lopez.
Edith Stein: essential differences. *PhilosTod* 37:70-77 Spr 1993

McArdle, Thomas.
White House guru. *Register* 69:3 S 12 1993

McAreavey, John.
Abortion and the Sacrament of Penance. *Furrow* 44:230-235 Ap 1993

McBride, Alfred.
The Baltimore catechism. *OSV* 81:17 F 28 1993
Born of water, spirit and light. *OSV* 82:13 O 24 1993
Confirmed by the Holy Spirit. *OSV* 82:13 O 31 1993
Even the passing of time is holy. *OSV* 82:9 O 17 1993
The four pillars of the new catechism. *Momentum* 24:49-51 S-O 1993
He is doctor of our souls and bodies. *OSV* 82:18 N 21 1993
He is really present. *OSV* 82:9 N 14 1993
The historical event of Christ's birth. *OSV* 82:9 My 30 1993
How the church is one. *OSV* 82:13 Ag 15 1993
The new Catechism of the Catholic Church conforms to the genuine tradition of the church, especially the teachings of the Second Vatican Council; December 7, 1992 (Commentary).
Images of Jesus: ten invitations to intimacy. Cincinnati: St Anthony Messenger Press, 1993. x, 239p ISBN 0-86716-180-9
Is there anyone sick among you? *OSV* 82:19 N 28 1993
The joyful mystery of reconciliation. *OSV* 82:12 S 5 1993
Mother of the church. *OSV* 82:12 Ag 29 1993
The mystery of the church. *OSV* 82:13 Ag 1 1993
The new Catechism of the Catholic Church conforms to the genuine tradition of the Second Vatican Council, December 7, 1992.
The new catechism of the Catholic Church. *OSV* 81:14 Mr 7 1993
New catechism prepares church for 21st century. *OSV* 81:9 F 21 1993
The new catechism's audience and uses. *OSV* 81:15 Mr 14 1993
Our bodies will rise!. *OSV* 82:9 S 12 1993
The priest as catechetical leader [2 pts]. *Priest* 49:15-20 Je 1993; 29-33 Jl 1993
The Resurrection makes credible all Christ taught. *OSV* 82:12 Je 27 1993
The second coming of Jesus: meditation and commentary on the Book of Revelation. Huntington: Our Sunday Visitor, 1993. 180p ISBN 0-87973-526-0 LC 92-61979
The spiritual birth of the people of God. *OSV* 82:15 Ag 8 1993
The new Catechism of the Catholic Church conforms to the genuine traditon of the Church, especially to the teachings of the Second Vatican Council, December 7, 1992, commentary.
The supper of the Lamb. *OSV* 82:16 N 7 1993
Under the influence of the Holy Spirit. *OSV* 82:7 Jl 11 1993
We know not the hour or the day. *OSV* 82:13 Jl 4 1993
Catechism of the Catholic Church (Commentary).
We shall be judged. *OSV* 82:16 S 26 1993
What happens after we die. *OSV* 82:13 S 19 1993
What liturgy is like a party. *OSV* 82:16 O 10 1993
The work of His dying. *OSV* 82:9 O 3 1993

McBride, Jack.
Public as a catechetical opportunity. *Momentum* 24:14-16 N-D 1993

McBrien, Richard P.
Celibacy, priest shortage plot may thicken. *Nat Cath Rep* 29:20 Jl 30 1993
A church is "Catholic" because it's sacramental. *Nat Cath Rep* 29:26 Ja 15 1993
Disobedience can crucify one, then or now. *Nat Cath Rep* 29:2 O 15 1993
The future of the Church and its ministries: imperatives for the twenty-first century. *New Theol Rev* 6:43-52 Ag 1993
Mary, mad as hell, at Medjugorje—now. *Nat Cath Rep* 29:18 Je 4 1993
Pius saw public opinion role. *Nat Cath Rep* 30:2 N 19 1993
Review of: *Catholic higher education, theology, and academic freedom* by Curran, Charles E, 1934-. In: *Horizons (CTS)* 20:189-190 Spr 1993
Review of: *Church of churches* by Tillard, Jean Marie Roger, 1927-. In: *Worship* 67:381-382 Jl 1993

McCabe, David.
Review of: *Liberal nationalism* by Tamir, Yael. In: *Comm* 120:28-29 My 21 1993
Review of: *Multiculturalism and "the politics of recognition"* by Taylor, Charles, 1931-. In: *Comm* 120:19-20 F 12 1993
Review of: *The ethics of authenticity* by Taylor, Charles, 1931-. In: *Comm* 120:19-20 F 12 1993

McCann, Deborah.
Of sanctity and saints. *ReligTJ* 27:14-15 O 1993
Review of: *A new vision of religious education* by Treston, Kevin. In: *ReligTJ* 27:14 S 1993
Review of: *A parent's guide to prayer* by Keire, Anita E. In: *ReligTJ* 27:9 Mr 1993
Review of: *Acting it out junior: discussion starters for 10-13 year olds* by Sturkie, Joan, and Cassady, Marsh. In: *ReligTJ* 27:14-15 O 1993

McCann, Deborah. *(cont'd)*
Review of: *Called to His supper: a preparation for first eucharist* by Leichner, Jeannine Timko. In: *ReligTJ* 26:10 Ja 1993
Review of: *Catholic customs and traditions: a popular guide* by Dues, Greg. In: *ReligTJ* 26:12 Ja 1993
Review of: *Christian family celebrations: prayer services for special moments* by Goodwin, Lawrence J. In: *ReligTJ* 27:9 Mr 1993
Review of: *Creativities: 101 creative activities for children to celebrate God's love* by Mathson, Patricia. In: *ReligTJ* 27:10-11 F 1993
Review of: *Daily readings with a modern mystic: selections from the writings of Evelyn Underhill* by Oberg, Delroy, ed. In: *ReligTJ* 27:15 S 1993
Review of: *Growing with Jesus* by Hakowski, Maryann. In: *ReligTJ* 27:14 O 1993
Review of: *Jesus: the word of God* by O'Toole, Margaret. In: *ReligTJ* 27:10 Ap-My 1993
Review of: *Learning by doing: 150 activities to enrich religion classes for children* by MacClennan, Carole. In: *ReligTJ* 27:14-15 S 1993
Review of: *Life of the beloved* by Nouwen, Henri Josef Machiel, 1932-. In: *ReligTJ* 27:10-11 Ap-My 1993
Review of: *Offering the Gospel to children* by Pritchard, Gretchen Wolff. In: *ReligTJ* 27:10 Ap-My 1993
Review of: *Praying our stories: reflections for youth ministers* by Ponsetto, Daniel. In: *ReligTJ* 27:10 Mr 1993
Review of: *Quicksilvers: ministering with junior high youth* by Goodwin, Carole. In: *ReligTJ* 27:10 Ap-My 1993
Review of: *Reconciliation services for children: 18 prayer services to celebrate God's forgiveness* by Costello, Gwen. In: *ReligTJ* 26:10 Ja 1993
Review of: *Religious dimensions (vol 1: Grades K-6)* by McGinnis, James. In: *ReligTJ* 27:14 S 1993
Review of: *Religious dimensions (vol 2 Grades 7-12)* by McGinnis, James. In: *ReligTJ* 27:14 S 1993
Review of: *Sharing the good news with children: stories for the common lectionary* by Goodhue, Thomas W. In: *ReligTJ* 27:10 F 1993
Review of: *Show me the way: readings for each day of Lent* by Nouwen, Henri Josef Machiel, 1932-. In: *ReligTJ* 27:10 F 1993
Review of: *St Francis of Assisi* by Bunson, Margaret, and Bunson, Matthew. In: *ReligTJ* 27:14 O 1993
Review of: *St Joan of Arc* by Bunson, Margaret, and Bunson, Matthew. In: *ReligTJ* 27:14 O 1993
Review of: *The Bible: God's word* by Woods, Laurie. In: *ReligTJ* 27:14 O 1993
Review of: *The Catholic family series* by Roberto, John, ed. In: *ReligTJ* 27:9 Mr 1993
Review of: *The week in daily prayer* by Trick, Barry J. In: *ReligTJ* 27:9 Mr 1993
Review of: *To taste and see: exploring incarnation and the ambiguities of faith* by Mann, Thomas W. In: *ReligTJ* 27:10 F 1993
Review of: *When kids bend the rules: 101 creative discipline ideas* by Crisci, Elizabeth Whitney. In: *ReligTJ* 27:11 F 1993

McCann, Patricia.
An identity dilemma: standing with the poor. *RRel* 52:428-431 My-Je 1993

McCarrick, Theodore Edgar, Abp, 1930-.
"On the ground" in Sarajevo [interview by T H Stahel, 1938-]. *America* 168:3-5 F 27 1993

McCarthy, Abigail Quigley.
Americans abroad: when good intentions go awry. *Comm* 120:11-12 Je 4 1993
"A civilization of love": the Pope in Denver. *Comm* 120:5-6 S 10 1993
From Bed-Sty to Israel: black teens on a Kibbutz. *Comm* 120:7-8 Jl 16 1993
Gimme shelter: a house can be a home. *Comm* 120:10-11 Ap 9 1993
Goodfellows: reinventing government. *Comm* 120:9-10 My 7 1993
It doesn't hurt to hope: Clinton is good at comebacks. *Comm* 120:7-8 F 12 1993
Religious wars and religious peace. *Comm* 120:6-7 Mr 12 1993
Some cause for hope. *Comm* 120:8-9 Ja 15 1993
There goes the neighborhood: the churches disturb the peace. *Comm* 120:9-10 O 22 1993

McCarthy, Colman.
Bishops amend Sermon on Mount: kill the killers. *Nat Cath Rep* 29:18 Je 4 1993
If Joint Chiefs have problem, let them disobey like men. *Nat Cath Rep* 29:7 F 19 1993
If you love Willy, you'll hate that hamburger. *Nat Cath Rep* 29:23 S 17 1993
Klan act offers no shelter to abortion clinics. *Nat Cath Rep* 29:2 F 5 1993
Pope's new encyclical has little to do with real world. *Nat Cath Rep* 30:22 O 29 1993
Veritatis Splendor (the Splendor of Truth), Encyclical Letter on moral issues (1993 10 05) Commentary.
Reno's death-penalty ethic mocks consistency. *Nat Cath Rep* 29:17 Ap 2 1993

McCarthy, Denis.
Review of: *Harder than war* by McNeal, Patricia F. In: *Nat Cath Rep* 29:28 S 10 1993

McCarthy, John.
La conferenza mondiale di Rio su ambiente e sviluppo. *Civilta* 143:560-577 D 19 1992
Review of: *Making moral decisions, a Christian approach to personal and social ethics* by Jersild, Paul. In: *New Theol Rev* 6:115-116 F 1993
Le sommet de Rio: rhétorique et sagesse. *Lumen* 48:23-26 Mr 1993

McCarthy, Patricia.
"Do this in memory of me". *Emmanuel* 99:309-313+ Jl-Ag 1993
Review of: *The woman with the alabaster jar* by Starbird, Margaret. In: *Nat Cath Rep* 29:29 S 10 1993

McCarthy, Tim.
Ancient Macedonia gropes for new paths [photos]. *Nat Cath Rep* 29:8-10 S 24 1993
Benedictine Fr Bede Griffiths, 86, dies in India [obituary]. *Nat Cath Rep* 29:8 My 21 1993
Croatia: where guns and roses don't mix [photos]. *Nat Cath Rep* 29:10-12 O 8 1993

McCarthy, Tim. (cont'd)
Election day hope stirs DC's hardest hit. *Nat Cath Rep* 29:18-21 N 20 1992
The future is now: from chaos to cosmos. *Nat Cath Rep* 29:5-6 Ap 16 1993
Growing up or selling out? Czechs face the future. *Comm* 120:13-16 S 24 1993
Light of Day shines yet at Catholic Worker. *Nat Cath Rep* 29:9-12 My 21 1993
Muzzling the dogs of war may be a mistake [photos]. *Nat Cath Rep* 29:10-11 O 1 1993
Papal call for chastity close to AIDS-ravaged Africa bone. *Nat Cath Rep* 29: 11 F 26 1993
Peace crumbles on the way to Sarajevo [photos]. *Nat Cath Rep* 29:14-16+ Ag 27 1993
Peace groups urge solidarity with Haitians. *Nat Cath Rep* 30:8 O 29 1993
Review of: *Aristide: an autobiography* by Aristide, Jean-Bertrand, 1953-. In: *Nat Cath Rep* 30:20 O 29 1993
Review of: *Miles from nowhere: tales from America's contemporary frontier* by Duncan, Dayton. In: *Nat Cath Rep* 29:18 Jl 30 1993
Review of: *Persuade us to rejoice: the liberating power of fiction* by Brown, Robert McAfee, 1920-. In: *Nat Cath Rep* 29:30 F 5 1993
Review of: *Strange pilgrims* by Márquez, Gabriel García. In: *Nat Cath Rep* 30:34 N 19 1993

McCartney, James J. see Trau, Jane Mary, jt auth

McCarty, Robert J.
Adolescent suicide: a minsterial response. *Momentum* 24:61-65 Ap-My 1993

McCarty, Shaun.
Review of: *Spiritual exercises for today* by Dunne, Tad. In: *New Theol Rev* 6:106-108 Ag 1993
Review of: *Spiritual mentoring: guiding people through spiritual exercises to life decisions* by Dunne, Tad. In: *New Theol Rev* 6:106-108 Ag 1993

McCaughey, Terence P.
Conscience as consciousness of the other [condensed fr *Memory and Redemption* Gill and Macmillan, 1993]. *Doctr Life* 43:166-178 Mr 1993

McClelland, V. Alan.
Review of: *A woman styled bold: the life of Cornelia Connelly, 1809-1879* by Flaxman, Radegunde. In: *Heythrop* 34:342-344 Jl 1993

McClorry, Brian B.
Review of: *A journey to Sakhalin* by Chekhov, Anton. In: *Month* 26:321-322 Ag 1993

McClory, Richard J.
Authority in the church: who makes the final call? *USCath* 58:6-13 Mr 1993

McClory, Robert.
Bishop demands end to dissent. *Nat Cath Rep* 29:4 F 26 1993

McCloskey, C. John, III.
Choosing a college. *Crisis* 11:42-44 O 1993

McCloskey, Liz Leibold.
Buzz words or principles? Ethics and health-care reform. *Comm* 120:10 S 24 1993
No ordinary museum. *Comm* 120:10-11 Je 4 1993
Plush lawns: here comes the baby. *Comm* 120:8-9 Ap 23 1993
The tissue issue: take it slow on fetal transplants. *Comm* 120:5-6 Mr 26 1993
Turning wine into vinegar: pre-Cana needs work. *Comm* 120:7-8 N 5 1993
Which abortion bill? Watch Kennedy. *Comm* 120:9-10 Jl 16 1993

McCloskey, Pat.
Review of: *A Church divided: the Vatican versus American Catholics* by Sweeney, Terrance. In: *St Anth* 101:50-51 Je 1993
Review of: *A flock of shepherds* by Reese, Thomas Joseph, 1945-. In: *ST Anth* 101:51-52 Jl 1993
Review of: *Isaac Hecker* by O'Brien, David J, 1938-. In: *St Anth* 100:50 Ja 1993
Review of: *Paul VI* by Hebblethwaite, Peter, 1930-. In: *St Anth* 101:48 O 1993
Review of: *Spiritual direction* by Morneau, Robert F, Bp, 1938-. In: *St Anth* 101:51-52 Ag 1993
Review of: *The search for God at Harvard* by Goldman, Ari. In: *St Anth* 100:52 Ap 1993
Review of: *The spirituality of imperfection: modern wisdom from classic stories* by Kurtz, Ernest, and Ketcham, Katherine. In: *St Anth* 100:52 F 1993

McCloud, H Edgar.
A river runs through it [Directed by R Redford]. *Crisis* 11:55-56 Ja 1993

McClure, Laura.
Enterprise zones have negligible history of success. *Nat Cath Rep* 29:9 N 13 1992

McConahay, Mary Jo.
Beware the demons loosed by Guatemala's coup. *Nat Cath Rep* 29:6 Je 4 1993
Corruption, not communism, rears as Guatemala democracy's bugaboo. *Nat Cath Rep* 29:10 Je 18 1993

McConica, James.
Review of: *Humanism and reform: the Church in Europe, England, and Scotland, 1400-1643: essays in honour of James K Cameron* by Kirk, James, ed. In: *CHist* 79:330-331 Ap 1993

McConnell, Frank, 1942-.
Bebop takes a hard shot: Dizzy Gillespie, RIP. *Comm* 120:17-18 F 12 1993
Follow that moose, northern exposure's pedigree. *Comm* 120:18-20 N 5 1993
It's not hell, just Limbaugh: excellence in bombast. *Comm* 120:20+ Je 4 1993
A nation of standups: starring in our own scripts. *Comm* 120:20-21 F 26 1993
Smart, hip and real: Bochco's "NYPD Blue". *Comm* 120:20-21 O 8 1993
Truly dishonest. *Comm* 120:14-16 Ja 29 1993

McConvery, Brendon.
Review of: *Alphonsus de Liguori, the Saint of Bourbon Naples 1696-1787* by Jones, Frederick M. In: *Tablet* 247:309-310 Mr 6 1993
Review of: *Jesus and politics* by Kealy, Sean P, 1937-. In: *Doctr Life* 42:652-653 D 1992

McConville, J Gordon.
Grace in the end: a study in Deuteronomic theology. Grand Rapids: Zondervan Publishing House, 1993. x, 176p ISBN 0-310-51421-5

McCoog, Thomas M.
Review of: *The Lord's house: a history of Sheffield's Roman Catholic buildings 1570-1990* by Evinson, Denis. In: *CHist* 79:144-145 Ja 1993 *see* Bangert, William V, jt auth

McCool, Gerald A.
Review of: *Church and culture: German Catholic theology, 1860-1914* by O'Meara, Thomas Franklin. In: *CHist* 79:123-124 Ja 1993
Review of: *Time past, time future: an historical study of Catholic moral theology* by Gallagher, John A. In: *CHist* 79:499-501 Jl 1993

McCord, H Richard, Jr.
Three pastoral challenges for family ministers. *Origins* 23:61-63 Je 10 1993

McCormack, William J, Bp., 1924-.
Church, Eucharist and mission. *Emmanuel* 99:424-427 O 1993

McCormick, Patrick.
Moral theology 2000: four signs and shifts. *ChrWorld* 236:212-216 S-O 1993
That they may converse: voices of Catholic social thought. *CrossCurr* 42:521-527 Wint 1992-1993
What kind of family did Jesus value? *USCath* 58:36-37 O 1993
Without economic justice, there's no wonderful life. *USCath* 58:18-19 D 1993

McCormick, Richard A. see Curran, Charles E, 1934-, jt ed

McCormick, Richard Arthur, 1922-.
Document begts many legitimate moral questions. *Nat Cath Rep* 29:17 O 15 1993
Veritatis Splendor (the Splendor of Truth), Encyclical letter on issues (1993 10 05) Commentary.
"Humanae Vitae" 25 years later. *America* 169:6-8+ Jl 17-24 1993
Review of: *My witness for the Church* by Häring, Bernard, 1912-. In: *TheolStds* 53:788 D 1992
Value variables in the health-care reform debate. *America* 168:7-13 My 29 1993
Veritatis Splendor and moral theology. *America* 169:8-11 O 30 1993
Veritatis Splendor, (the Splendor of truth), Encyclical letter on moral issues, (1993-01-05). Commentary.

McCown, Robert.
Christian Zen-cum-Ignatian meditation. *RRel* 52:507-518 Jl-Ag 1993

McCown, Wayne. see Carpenter, Eugene E, jt ed

McCoy, A.
Review of: *Faith seeking understanding: learning and the Catholic tradition* by Berthold, George C, ed. In: *Priests & People* 6:483-484 D 1992

McCrate, Elaine.
Accounting for the slowdown in the divorce rate in the 1980s: a bargaining perspective. *RSocEcon* 50:404-419 Wint 1992

McCready, Wayne O.
Review of: *The Gospel of Luke* by Johnson, Luke Timothy, 1943-. In: *Can Cath Rev* 11:30-31 N 1993
Review of: *The Gospel of Matthew* by Harrington, Daniel J. In: *Can Cath Rev* 11:29 S 1993

McCreesh, Thomas P.
Review of: *God is my rock: a study of translation technique and theological exegesis in the Septuagint* by Olofsson, Staffan. In: *OTA* 15:485-486 O 1992
Review of: *Jerusalem, the holy city* by Purvis, James D. In: *OTA* 15:487 O 1992
Review of: *Lexis Ludens: wordplay and the Book of Micah* by Petrotta, Anthony J. In: *OTA* 15:513 O 1992
Review of: *The LXX version: a guide to the translation technique of the Septuagint* by Olofsson, Staffan. In: *OTA* 15:486 O 1992
Review of: *Wealth and poverty in the Book of Proverbs* by Whybray, R N. In: *OTA* 15:504-505 O 1992
Review of: *What knows what is good?* by Farmer, Kathleen A. In: *OTA* 15:504 O 1992

McCrorie, Edward.
Deaf at the beach; after the ballet; four years; Saffo on the east side. *Spirit* 58:3-6 1993

McCullough, Domhnall. see Reidy, Michael, jt ed

McCullough, E J.
Environmental ethics: preaching or teaching? *Can Cath Rev* 11:16-18 Ja 1993

McCurry, James E, et al.
Proceedings of the forty-third National Convention of the Mariological Society of America held in Houston, Texas, My 28 and 29, 1992. *Marian Stds* 43:9-189 1992
Presidential address: Our Lady of Guadalupe: evangelizer of the Americas, by J McCurry. Fr Juniper B Carol, OFM: his mariology and scholarly achievement, by P Fehlner. Mary in Ordinary Time: Biblical references, by J Turro. Mary in the mysteries of Christ during Ordinary Time: liturgical references, by J Joncas. Theological reflection: from Marialis Cultus to mission—a new challenge in liturgy, devotions, and popular religion, by W Brennan. A survey of recent mariology, by E Carroll. The secretary's report, by T Thompson. Financial report, 1991-92, by J Samaha. Report, 1991-92: New England region, by M Morry. Report, 1991-1992: Western region, by J Samaha.

McCurry, James E.
Our Lady of Guadalupe: evangelizer of the Americas. *Marian Stds* 43:9-16 1992

McDade, John.
The death of Jesus and sin. *Month* 26:340-347 S-O 1993
The Epistle of James for Jews and Christians. *Month* 26:115-120 Mr 1993
The ministries of women [editorial]. *Month* 25:458-460 D 1992

McDaniel, Jay B. see Pinches, Charles, jt ed

McDarby, Patrick.
In the midst of the highest Christian feast. *Sisters* 65:206-208 My 1993

McDermott, Brian O.
Word become flesh: dimensions of Christology. Minnesota: The Liturgical Press, 1993. x, 302p ISBN 0-8146-5015-5 LC 92-34915

McDermott, Edwin J.
Parental choice in education. *America* 169:4-6 O 16 1993
Review of: *Choice in schooling: a case for tuition vouchers* by Kirkpatrick, David W. In: *America* 168:20-22 Ja 2-9 1993

McDermott, John M.
Review of: *Creation and scientific creativity: a study in the thought of S L Jaki* by Haffner, Paul. In: *IPQ* 33:244-246 Je 1993
Review of: *Dieu et l'être d'après Thomas D'Aquin et Hegel* by Brito, Emilio. In: *TheolStds* 53:752-753 D 1992
Review of: *Gesù crocifisso, Figlio di Dio* by Battaglia, Vincenzo. In: *Gregorianum* 74 no 3:575-577 1993
Review of: *The purpose of it all* by Jaki, Stanley L. In: *Gregorianum* 73 No 4:772-773 1992
Tensions in Lonergan's theory of conversion. *Gregorianum* 74 No 1:101-140 1993

McDermott, Karl A.
The evolution of the "investment system": Keynes' theory of employment and money revisited. *RSocEcon* 51:62-85 Spr 1993

McDermott, Philomena.
Preparing for the future church. *Priests & People* 7:61-64 F 1993

McDermott, Scott.
Review of: *Making Charisma: the social construction of Paul's public image* by Blasi, Anthony J. In: *Bib Th Bul* 23:84 Sum 1993

McDermott, T.
Review of: *The thought of Thomas Aquinas* by Davies, Brian. In: *Priests & People* 7:41-42 Ja 1993

McDonagh, Elizabeth.
Review of: *Pilgrim's notebook* by Fleming, David A. In: *Living Light* 29:96 Spr 1993

McDonagh, Enda.
Should the healing begin at Christmas. *Furrow* 43:651-655 D 1992

McDonagh, Francis.
Saving Santo Domingo. *Tablet* 247:128+ Ja 30 1993

McDonagh, Mary Ellen.
2,000 pack cathedral for nuns' memorial. *Nat Cath Rep* 29:6 N 20 1992

McDonagh, Melanie.
Aliens in their own land. *Tablet* 247:392-394 Mr 27 1993
Between two armies. *Tablet* 247:1284-1286 O 9 1993
A bishop at bay. *Tablet* 247:968+ Jl 31 1993
Desert island choice (2). *Tablet* 247:100 Ja 23 1993
Good news from Grimm. *Tablet* 246:1608 D 19-26 1992
Life in limbo. *Tablet* 247:458-459 Ap 10-17 1993
Review of: *Sex, art and American culture* by Paglia, Camille. In: *Tablet* 247:549-550 My 1 1993
Too reasonable by half. *Tablet* 247:774 Je 19 1993
What makes a republican? *Tablet* 247:636-638 My 22 1993

McDonagh, Sean.
Has the sun set on Rio? *Tablet* 247:749 Je 1993
Review of: *Buddhism and ecology* by Batchelor, Martine, and Brown, Kerry, eds. In: *Furrow* 44:120-123 F 1993
Review of: *Christianity and ecology* by Breuilly, Elizabeth, and Palmer, Martin, eds. In: *Furrow* 44:120-123 F 1993
Review of: *Hinduism and ecology* by Prime, Ranchor, ed. In: *Furrow* 44:120-123 F 1993
Review of: *Islam and ecology* by Khalkid, Fazlun, and O'Brien, Joanne, eds. In: *Furrow* 44:120-123 F 1993
Review of: *Judaism and ecology* by Rose, Aubrey, ed. In: *Furrow* 44:120-123 F 1993

McDonald, Claudette. see McDonald, Patrick J, jt auth

McDonald, John S.
A Jeffersonian Catholicism? *New Oxford Rev* 60:17-18 Ja-F 1993

McDonald, Patricia M.
Review of: *Women as interpreters of the Bible* by Demers, Patricia. In: *TheolStds* 54:194-195 Mr 1993
Review of: *Her image of salvation: female saviors and formative Christianity* by Corrington, Gail Paterson. In: *TheolStds* 54:549 S 1993
Review of: *In the days of Paul* by Tambasco, Anthony J. In: *Living Light* 29:95-96 Sum 1993
Review of: *Pillars of Paul's Gospel* by O'Grady, John F. In: *Living Light* 29:95-96 Sum 1993
Review of: *Reflections on glory: Paul's polemical use of the Moses-Doxa tradition in 2 Corinthians 3 1-18* by Belleville, Linda L. In: *CBQ* 55:140-141 Ja 1993
Review of: *Women who knew Paul* by Gillman, Florence Morgan. In: *Living Light* 29:95-96 Sum 1993

McDonald, Patrick J, and McDonald, Claudette.
Dark nights and hard days: a view of marital spirituality. *Spir Life* 39:150-159 Aut 1993

McDonnell, Dominic.
Accountability in the church. *Priests & People* 6:340-342 Ag-S 1992

McDonnell, Kilian, 1921-.
The Summae confessorum on the integrity of confession as prolegomena for Luther and Trent. *TheolStds* 54:405-426 S 1993
A year afterwards: the Vatican response to ARCIC, a slammed door? *OChr* 29 no 2:113-117 1993

McDonnell, Kilian, 1921-, ed.
Towards a new Pentecost: for a new evangelization. Collegeville:Liturgical, 1993. x, 72p ISBN 0-8146-5846-6 LC 92-46910

McDonough, Elizabeth.
Charisms and religious life. *RRel* 52:646-659 S-O 1993
Common life and houses. *RRel* 52:462-468 My-Je 1993
Common life. *RRel* 52:304-310 Mr-Ap 1993
Conciliar and postconciliar documents on consecrated life. *RRel* 52:780-786 S-O 1993
New communities. *RRel* 52:140-146 Ja-F 1993
Review of: *Religious life: a prophetic vision* by O'Murchu, Diarmuid. In: *RRel* 52:149-151 Ja-F 1993
The synod of consecrated life. *RRel* 52:626-621 Jl-Ag 1993

McDonough, John E.
Review of: *The rascal king: the life and times of James Michael Curley (1874-1958)* by Beatty, Jack. In: *Comm* 120:20-21 F 12 1993

McDonough, Richard.
Wittgenstein's doctrine of silence. *Thomist* 56:695-699 O 1992

McDougall, Ian.
Review of: *The Baltic revolution: Estonia, Latvia, Lithuania and the path to independence* by Lieven, Anatol. In: *Tablet* 247:757-758 Je 1993

McDowell, Gary L.
The limits of natural law: Thomas Rutherforth and the American legal tradition. *Amer J Juris* 37:57-81 1992

McEleney, Neil J.
Review of: *As ministers of Christ: the Christological dimension of ministry in the New Testament* by Forestell, J T. In: *CBQ* 55:149-150 Ja 1993

McEnroy, Carmel.
Review of: *Atonement and incarnation* by White, Vernon. In: *Horizons (CTS)* 20:160-161 Spr 1993

McEnvoy, James.
Amitié, attirance et amour chez S. Thomas d'Aquin. *RPhil Louvain* 91:383-408 Ag 1993
Review of: *Etudes religieuses* by Steenberghen, Fernand Van. In: *RPhil Louvain* 91:163-164 F 1993

McFadden, Sean.
But what shall we sell? *Tod Cath Teach* 26:30+ Ap 1993

McFague, Sallie.
The body of God: an ecological theology. Minneapolis: Fortress Press, 1993. x, 274p ISBN 0-8006 LC 93-6584

McGarry, Cecil.
The urgency of ongoing formation. *AFER* 34:134-145 Je 1992

McGeady, Mary Rose.
The runaways. *Momentum* 24:33-35 Ap-My 1993

McGee, J.
Review of: *Puritans and Roundheads: the Harleys of Brampton Bryan and the outbreak of the English Civil War* by Eales, Jacqueline. In: *CHist* 78:660-661 O 1992

McGettigan, Donal. see Browne, Frank, jt auth

McGill, Mary.
Building on traditions in Advent and Christmas. *Catechist* 27:32-33 N-D 1993
A family affair generous beyond measure. *Catechist* 27:74-75 S 1993
A family affair: the Feast of St. Francis of Assisi. *Catechist* 27:20-21 O 1993

McGillion, Chris.
"Propaganda" and "lies" after capture of guerrilla leader. *Tablet* 246:1580 D 12 1992
A lucky country's last gasp. *Tablet* 247:361 Mr 20 1993
Rome's next domino? *Tablet* 247:1224-1225 S 25 1993

McGinn, Bernard John, 1937-.
Mysticism and sexuality. *Way Suppl* 77:46-54 Sum 1993 see Burrell, David B, jt auth

McGlynn, Ciaran.
Review of: *Did the Greeks believe thier myths? an essay on the constitutive imagination* by Veyne, Paul. In: *IJPS* 1:169-170 Mr 1993

McGonigle, Thomas D.
Review of: *The foundations of mysticism* by McGinn, Bernard John, 1937-. In: *New Theol Rev* 6:115-116 Ag 1993

McGovern, Arthur F, 1929-.
Review of: *Eclipse of justice: ethics, economics, and the lost tradition of American Catholicism* by McCarthy, George E, and Rhodes, Royal W. In: *TheolStds* 54:186-187 Mr 1993
Review of: *The two churches: Catholicism and capitalism in the world system* by Budde, Michael L. In: *New Oxford Rev* 60:22-25 Jl-Ag 1993

McGovern, John E.
Educational standards and public policy. *Momentum* 24:47 S-O 1993
Silent money: political persuasion and public policy. *Momentum* 24:21-25 N-D 1993

McGovern, Thomas.
Return to Chesterton. *HPR* 93:47-55 Je 1993
The spiritual life of the priest. *HPR* 94:6-15 O 1993

McGowan, Cecilia.
Review of: *John of the Cross: conferences and essays by members of the Institute of Carmelite Studies and others* by Payne, Steven, ed. In: *Spir Life* 32:111-112 Sum 1993

McGowan, Joseph.
Review of: *Food not bombs: how to feed the hungry and build community* by McGowan, Joseph. In: *Nat Cath Rep* 29:19 Mr 19 1993
Take your shoes off my books: negotiating a Hindu-Catholic marriage. *Comm* 120:15-17 Je 18 1993

McGrane, Janice.
Praying our pain. *Spir Life* 32:87-90 Sum 1993

McGrath, Aidan.
Conformity of sentence in marriage nullity cases. *Stud Can* 27 no 1:5-22 1993

McGrath, Alister E.
Intellectuals don't need God and other modern myths. Grand Rapids: Zondervan Publishing House, 1993. x, 256p ISBN 0-310-59091-4
What was God doing on the cross? Grand Rapids: Zondervan Publishing House, 1993. x, 112p ISBN 0-310-59451-0

McGrath, Carol Rito.
Tips for computerizing your writing program. *Tod Cath Teach* 27:15-16 S 1993

McGrath, Helene.
Review of: *Celebrating the signs of God's love: the sacraments* by Pennock, Michael. In: *Mod Lit* 20:40 Ag 1993
Review of: *Clip art for Year A* by Erspamer, Steve. In: *Mod Lit* 20:39 Je-Jl 1993
Review of: *The Gospel according to Mary* by Winter, Miriam Therese. In: *Mod Lit* 20:40 Ag 1993

McGrath, Thomas.
The place of desires in the Ignatian exercises. *Way Suppl* 76:25-31 Spr 1993

McGregor, B.
Review of: *Salvation outside the Church* by Sullivan, Francis Aloysius. In: *Doctr Life* 43:60-61 Ja 1993

McGuckian, Bernard J.
Review of: *Father Mathew and the Irish temperance movement 1838-1849* by Kerrigan, Colm. In: *Studies* 82:108-110 Spr 1993
Review of: *The re-formed Jesuits* by Becker, Joseph M. In: *Studies* 82:217-220 Sum 1993

McGuckin, Terence.
Saint Thomas Aquinas and theological exegesis of sacred scripture. *New Blckfrs* 74:197-211 Ap 1993

McGuire, Brian Patrick.
An introduction to the Exordium Magnum Cisterciense. *Cist Stud* 27 No 4:278-297 1992
Review of: *Inventing the Middle Ages: the lives, works, and ideas of the great medievalists of the twentieth century* by Cantor, Norman F. In: *Cist Stud* 27 No 4:[85]-[87] 1992

McGuire, Patricia.
Reflections on World Youth Day: Catholic education. *Origins* 23:265+ S 30 1993

McGurn, William.
Cardinal in China: nothing doing. *Register* 69:1+ O 24 1993

McHugh, Frank.
An examination of cash and conscience. *Priests & People* 7:181-185 My 1993

McHugh, James, Bp. *see* Hayes, Gary R, jt auth

McHugh, Joseph F.
The Mass explained [condensed fr *Eucharistic Minister* S 1992]. *CDgst* 57:51-54 F 1993
The Mass explained: part four [condensed fr *Eucharistic Minister* D 1992]. *CDgst* 57:47-52 My 1993
The Mass explained: part three [condensed fr *Eucharistic Minister* N 1992]. *CDgst* 57:65-70 Ap 1993
The mass explained: part two [condensed fr *Eucharistic Minister* O 1992]. *CDgst* 57:83-87 Mr 1993

McHugh, Thomas.
Ten hints for adult educators. *Priests & People* 7:65-66 F 1993

McIlhone, James P.
The Gospels: a source for morality. *BibleT* 31:277-282 S 1993

McInerny, Ralph M.
Key query: what must I do to be saved? *Register* 69:1+ N 14 1993
Veritatis Splendor (the Splendor of Truth) Encyclical Letter on moral issues (1993 10 05) Commentary.
Mater Angelica. *Crisis* 11:19 O 1993
The question of Christian ethics. Washington, D C: Catholic University of America Press, 1990. x, 74p ISBN 0-81320-770-3 LC 92-25511
Review of: *Curriculum vitae* by Spark, Muriel, 1918-. In: *Crisis* 11:50-51 Jl-Ag 1993
Saint Evelyn Waugh. *Crisis* 10:2-3 N 1992
Second-hand straw. *Crisis* 11:15-17 My 1993
Spark of divinity. *Crisis* 11:50-51 Jl-Ag 1993

McInerny, Ralph M, ed.
Modernity and religion. Notre Dame: University of Notre Dame Press, 1994. x, 168p ISBN 0-268-01408-6

McInnes, Val Ambrose.
New visions: historical and theological perspectives on the Jewish-Christian dialogue. New York: Crossroad, 1993. x, 165p ISBN 0-8245-1246-4 LC 93-4190

McIntosh, Mark A.
Humanity in God: on reading Karl Barth in relation to mystical theology. *Heythrop* 34:22-40 Ja 1993

McIntyre, John P.
An apology for the "lesser sacraments". *Jurist* 51 no 2:390-414 1991
Review of: *Estudios juridico-canonicos: commemorativos del primer cincuentenario de la facultad de derecho canonico en Salamanca (1940-89)* by García y García, Antonio, ed. In: *Jurist* 51 no 2:512-513 1991
Review of: *Men astutely trained: a history of the Jesuits in the American century* by McDonough, Peter. In: *Thomist* 56:711-714 O 1992

McIntyre, Moni.
Review of: *Midlife women and death of mother: a study of psychohistorical and spiritual transformation* by Robbins, Martha A. In: *Horizons (CTS)* 20:175-176 Spr 1993
Sin, evil and death in the New Age. *Way* 33:210-221 Jl 1993

McKee, Arnold F.
Review of: *A century of Catholic Thought* by Weigel, George, and Royal, Robert, eds. In: *Can Cath Rev* 11:31-32 Je 1993
Review of: *Religion, wealth and poverty* by Schall, James Vincent, 1928-. In: *Can Cath Rev* 11:27-28 Mr 1993

McKeever, Henry.
Review of: *The foundations of mysticism* by McGinn, Bernard John, 1937-. In: *RRel* 52:312-313 Mr-Ap 1993

McKenna, Andrew.
Pascal, order, and difference. *Relig Lit* 25:55-75 Sum 1993

McKenna, Bill.
Responding to His call. *New Cov* 23:27 S 1993

McKenna, Catherine A.
Review of: *Dissent from Irish America* by McCarthy, John P. In: *America* 169:18-20 O 9 1993

McKenna, G. *see* Earley, C, jt auth

McKenna, Gemma.
Review of: *Experiencing community in small groups* by Westley, Richard John, 1928-. In: *Doctr Life* 43:445-447 S 1993
Review of: *Forming a small Christian community* by Currier, Richard, and Gram, Frances. In: *Doctr Life* 43:445-447 S 1993

McKenzie, Paula A.
Robert Coles: listening to stories of God in the lives of children. *Living Light* 29:65-72 Aut 1992

McKenzie, Steven L.
Review of: *El Desierto Transformado* by Navarro, Enrique Farfán. In: *OTA* 16:431 Je 1993
Review of: *Gott, König ung Tempel* by Hentschel, Georg. In: *OTA* 16:173-174 F 1993

McKeon, Thomas.
History of eucharistic congresses. *Emmanuel* 99:288-290 Je 1993

McKeown, Elizabeth.
Review of: *The foundation and first decade of the National Catholic Welfare Council* by Slawson, Douglas J. In: *CHist* 79:370-371 Ap 1993

McKevitt, Daniel.
Les amants du Pont Neuf. *Month* 26:28-29 Ja 1993
Bad lieutenant [directed by A Ferrara]. *Month* 26:108 Mr 1993
The crying game. *Month* 26:28 Ja 1993
The fencing master [directed by P Olea]. *Month* 26:316-317 Ag 1993
A kinder, gentler America. *Month* 26:108-109 Mr 1993
Love, betrayal and music. *Month* 26:74-75 F 1993
A river runs through it [directed by R Redford]. *Month* 26:108-109 Mr 1993
Sofie [directed by L Ullmann]. *Month* 26:276-277 Jl 1993
Sommersby. *Month* 26:230 Je 1993
The story of Qiu Ju [directed by Zhang Yimou]. *Month* 26:230-231 Je 1993
Tous les matins du monde [directed by A Corneau]. *Month* 26:74-75 F 1993

McKim, Donald K.
Review of: *John Oman and his doctrine of God* by Bevans, Stephen B. In: *TheolStds* 54:198-199 Mr 1993

McKnight, Christopher.
Review of: *Plato's Parmenides* by Meinwald, Constance C. In: *IJPS* 1:158-160 Mr 1993

McKnight, Peg.
Mysticism in Islamism and Christianity. *Living Prayer* 26:29-31 Ja-F 1993

McLane, Janice.
Alienation, cultura differences, and moral judgment. *PhilosTod* 37:78-88 Spr 1993

McLaughlin, Dorothy.
Talking to God? mind your manners. *CDgst* 57:30+ My 1993

McLaughlin, Janice.
The meaning of evangelization today. *RRel* 52:194-201 Mr-Ap 1993

McLaughlin, John L.
Review of: *Reason for being: a meditation on Ecclesiastes* by Ellul, Jacques. In: *CBQ* 55:109-110 Ja 1993

McLaughlin, T H.
A man for this season. *Tablet* 247:198-200 F 13 1993

McLaughlin, Thomas.
Review of: *Be friends of God* by Gregory the Great. In: *Cist Stud* 28:[21]-[22] 1993

McLean, Teresa.
Review of: *Curiosities of cricket* by Rice, Jonathan. In: *Tablet* 247:408 Mr 27 1993

McLellan, David. *see* Cohn-Sherbok, Dan, jt auth

McLeod, Annmarie.
Daring the truth to be told. *Sisters* 65:273-275 Jl 1993

McLeod, Frederick G.
Review of: *Early Christian baptism and the catechumenate* by Finn, Thomas Macy. In: *TheolStds* 54:195-196 Mr 1993
Review of: *Systematic theology* by Fiorenza, Francis Schüssler, 1938-, and Galvin, John P, 1944-, eds. In: *RRel* 52:311-312 Mr-Ap 1993
Review of: *The diversity of religions* by DiNoia, J A. In: *RRel* 52:633-634 Jl-Ag 1993
Review of: *The lives of Simeon Stylites.* In: *TheolStds* 54:597 S 1993
Review of: *The lives of the monks of Palestine* by Cyril of Scythopolis, 524?-558. In: *TheolStds* 53:782-783 D 1992

McLoughlin, David.
The hope which empowers. *Priests & People* 6:447-451 D 1992

McLoughlin, John.
Review of: *Medieval Irish saints' lives* by Sharpe, Richard. In: *Heythrop* 34:212-213 Ap 1993

McLoughlin, Marianna.
Escape to Eden. *Register* 69:2 O 31 1993
Teaching Somalia's children to sing again. *St Anth* 101:36-41 O 1993

McMahon, Donal.
Decision. *Furrow* 44:359-363 Je 1993

McMahon, Edwin M, 1930-.
Beyond the myth of dominance: an alternative to a violent society. Kansas City: Sheed & Ward, 1993. x, 271p ISBN 15-5612-563-1

McMahon, J Michael. *see* Ciferni, Andrew D, jt auth

McMahon, John.
Diving in. *Can Cath Rev* 11:38-39 Jl-Ag 1993
Entertain us. *Can Cath Rev* 11:38-39 S 1993
The final decade? *Can Cath Rev* 11:51-53 Ja 1993
The future now. *Can Cath Rev* 11:38-39 My 1993
Holidays. *Can Cath Rev* 11:38-39 F 1993
Manufacturing reality. *Can Cath Rev* 11:38-39 Ap 1993
Process and product. *Can Cath Rev* 11:38-39 O 1993
Unless we see the wounds. *Can Cath Rev* 11:38-39 Je 1993

McMahon, Kevin.
"Humanae Vitae": 25th anniversary. *Origins* 22:768-774 Ap 22 1993
Humanae Vitae, on the regulation of birth (commentary).

McMahon, Michael.
Paralysis of the heart. *BibleT* 31:85-88 Mr 1993

McMannus, E Leo.
Review of: *Religion and radical politics* by Craig, Robert H, 1942-. In: *Nat Cath Rep* 29:36 F 5 1993
Review of: *The American Catholic experience: a history from colonial times to the present* by Dolan, Jay P. In: *Nat Cath Rep* 29:36 F 5 1993
Review of: *The call of service* by Coles, Robert, 1929-. In: *Nat Cath Rep* 29: 21 S 17 1993
Review of: *The churching of America 1776-1990: winners and losers in our religious economy* by Finke, Roger, and Stark, Rodney. In: *Nat Cath Rep* 29:36 F 5 1993

McManus, Frederick R.
Editions of the book of Gospels in English. *Notitiae* 28:352-356 My 1992

McManus, James.
Flynn flaps focuses on job's substance, style. *Nat Cath Rep* 29:9 Je 18 1993

McManus, Michael J.
Maritals aids [interview by M Finley]. *OSV* 82:5 Je 6 1993

McMichael, Ralph N, Jr, ed.
Creation and liturgy. Washington: The Pastoral Press, 1993. 320p ISBN 1-562929-001-6

McMillian, Philip E.
Review of: *In search of "ancient Israel"* by Davies, Philip R. In: *OTA* 16:158 F 1993

McMunn, Richard.
Resolved [adopted resolutions]. *Columbia* 73:14-18 O 1993
Turning the vocations tide. *Columbia* 73:10-12 S 1993

McNair, Bruce G.
Albert the Great in the renaissance: Cristoforo Landino's use of Albert on the soul. *Mod Schlmn* 70:115-129 Ja 1993

McNair, J Frank.
Can I afford this? *Living Prayer* 26:27-28 Mr-Ap 1993
Contemplative businessperson. *Living Prayer* 26:27-28 Ja-F 1993
The market place. *Living Prayer* 26:26-27 My-Je 1993
The market place. *Living Prayer* 26:30-31 Jl-Ag 1993
The market place. *Living Prayer* 26:27-28 S-O 1993
The market place. *Living Prayer* 26:26-27 N-D 1993

McNamara, James M.
In the presence of the wise and gentile Christ. New York: Paulist Press, 1993. x, 156p ISBN 0-8091-3375-x LC 92-36141

McNamara, Martin.
Review of: *Law in religious communities in the Roman period: the debate over Torah and Nomos in Post-Biblical Judaism and Early Christianity* by Richardson, Peter, and Westerholm, Stephen. In: *CBQ* 55:202-203 Ja 1993

McNamara, William.
Watch out!. *USCath* 58:38-39 N 1993

McNamee, Catherine.
Educating for the third millennium [editorial]. *Momentum* 24:2+ F-Mr 1993
The public policy process. *Momentum* 24:2-4 N-D 1993
Review of: *Whole earth meditation: ecology for the spirit* by Sauro, Joan. In: *Momentum* 24:84 F-Mr 1993
Whose standards? Whose measure? [editorial]. *Momentum* 24:3-4 S-O 1993

McNamee, John P.
Diary of a city priest. Kansas City: Sheed & Ward, 1993. x, 258p ISBN 1-55612-662-x LC 93-11924

McNeill, John J.
The church and the homosexual. Boston: Beacon, 1993. x, 266p ISBN 0-8070-7931-6 LC 93-7088
Gay dimension to spiritual life. *Nat Cath Rep* 29:21-22 Mr 26 1993

McNeirney, Frank.
Eliminating a chance for redemption. *OSV* 82:19 Jl 11 1993

McNelis, Paul D.
Review of: *Doing well and doing good* by Neuhaus, Richard John, 1936-. In: *America* 168:18-19 Mr 13 1993

McNichols, William Hart.
The Dormition of the Mother of God. *America* 169:20 Ag 14-21 1993 *see* Stevens, Clifford, jt ed

McNulty, Frank J.
Review of: *Aquinas Institute of theology Faculty.* In: *Church* 9:56-57 Aut 1993

McNulty, Maurice F.
The catacombs: stones that shout. *CDgst* 57:108-112 Jl 1993
Forgotten feast days. *CDgst* 57:18+ Je 1993

McOwan, Rennie.
Review of: *St Andrews Rock: the state of the Church in Scotland* by Lamont, Stewart, ed. In: *Tablet* 247:693-694 My 29 1993

McOwan, Rennie. *(cont'd)*
Review of: *Wrestling with the Church* by Levison, Mary. In: *Tablet* 247:50 Ja 9 1993

McPartlan, Paul.
Henri de Lubac—evangeliser. *Priests & People* 6:343-346 Ag-S 1992

McPherson, Heather.
Icons, iconoclasm, and the power of images: reflections on art and society in post-Soviet Russia. *Listening* 28:159-171 Spr 1993

McQueen, Moira M. *see* Walsh, J Leo, jt auth

McRedmond, Louis.
An angry people. *Tablet* 247:327-329 Mr 13 1993
Change in Ireland, maybe. *Tablet* 247:9+ Ja 23 1993
The message of Mother Teresa. *Tablet* 247:764 Je 1993
Review of: *Class and ethnicity: Irish Catholics in England, 1880-1939* by Fielding, Steven. In: *Tablet* 247:277 F 27 1993
Review of: *John Courtney Murray and the American civil conversation* by Hunt, Robert P, and Grasso, Kenneth L, eds. In: *Doctr Life* 43:249-252 Ap 1993
Review of: *May the Lord in his mercy be kind to Belfast* by Parker, Tony. In: *Tablet* 247:788 Je 19 1993
Review of: *The Church emerging from Vatican II* by Doyle, Dennis M. In: *Furrow* 44:448-449 Jl-Ag 1993
Review of: *The use of memory* by Burns, Tom G. In: *Doctr Life* 43:379-380 Jl-Ag 1993
Stop the killing. *Tablet* 247:434 Ap 3 1993
Vatican II perspectives. *Doctr Life* 42:298-304 My-Je 1992
While Ulster burns. *Tablet* 247:1094 Ag 28 1993

McReynolds, Sally Ann.
Review of: *The moral vision of Dorothy Day: a feminist perspective* by O'Connor, June E. In: *Horizons (CTS)* 19:337-338 Fall 1992

McRobie, George.
Review of: *Environmental problems in third world cities* by Hardoy, J, et al. In: *Tablet* 247:1196 S 18 1993
Review of: *How much is enough? The consumer society, and the future of the earth* by Durning, Alan Thein. In: *Tablet* 246:1624 D 19-26 1992

McShane, Joseph M, 1949-.
"To form an elite body of laymen" Terence J Shealy, SJ, and the laymen's league, 1911-1922. *CHist* 78:557-580 O 1992

McShea, William P.
Review of: *Protestants: the birth of a revolution* by Ozment, Steven. In: *RRel* 52:791-792 S-O 1993

McSheffery, Daniel F.
Cornelia Connelly: model of Christian courage. *HPR* 93:57-60 My 1993
The permanent diaconate turns 25. *Priest* 49:12-15 Ag 1993
Sanctus Pontifex: twenty years later. *HPR* 93:63-67 Mr 1993
St. Jerome: doctor maximus. *HPR* 94:53-57 N 1993
The twin legacy of St. Ambrose. *CDgst* 57:120-123 Ag 1993

McSorley, Richard.
Yes, no—which is it? *Register* 69:4 N 14 1993

McTaggart, Bill.
Parish consolidation. *Liguorian* 81:33-35 Ag 1993

McTernan, Oliver.
Welcoming the stranger in Europe. *Month* 26:304-307 Ag 1993

McTighe, John P.
Come down, Zacchaeus!. *Liguorian* 81:56-60 F 1993

McVann, Mark.
One of the prophets: Matthew's testing narrative as a rite of passage. *Bib Th Bul* 23:14-20 Spr 1993
Review of: *Jesus: the servant-Messiah* by Jonge, Marinus de. In: *Bib Th Bul* 23:82 Sum 1993

McVerry, Peter.
The Church must take sides. *Furrow* 44:78-83 F 1993

McVey, Raymond.
Core of our discipleship [fr *Unity Acres Newsletter*]. *Cath Work* 60:8 Mr-Ap 1993

McWilliam, J.
Review of: *The hope of the Early Church: a handbook of patristic eschatology* by Daley, Brian E. In: *TheolStds* 53:746-748 D 1992

McWilliams, Wilson Carey, 1933-.
Clinton's new political geography: renewing the language of equality [adapted fr *The election of 1992: reports and interpretations*]. *Comm* 120:14-18 Ap 23 1993

Meadow, Mary Jo.
Personal growth and the Ignatian spiritual exercises. *Way Suppl* 76:13-24 Spr 1993

Meaney, Mary.
Vival El Papa. *Crisis* 11:15 S 1993

Medcalf, John.
A look into the future. *Tablet* 247:1118 S 4 1993
Review of: *Basic is beautiful* by Hebblethwaite, Margaret, 1951-. In: *Tablet* 247:758 Je 1993
Review of: *Celebrating resistance: the way of the cross in Latin America* by Soelle, Dorothee. In: *Tablet* 247:984 Jl 31 1993
A sister's ministry. *Tablet* 247:427 Ap 3 1993

Medema, Steven G.
Is there life beyond efficiency? Elements of a social law and economics. *RSocEcon* 51:138-153 Sum 1993

Medved, Michael, 1948-.
Hollywood's dirty little secrets. *Crisis* 11:18-23 Mr 1993

Meehan, A.
Review of: *New directions in moral theology* by Kelly, Kevin T. In: *Priests & People* 6:484-485 D 1992

Merrigan, Terrence.
Review of: *John Henry Newman: lover of truth* by Strolz, M K, and Binder, M, eds. In: *Louvain Stds* 18:188-190 Sum 1993
Review of: *Newman after a hundred years* by Ker, Ian, and Hill, Alan G, eds. In: *Louvain Stds* 18:188-190 Sum 1993
Review of: *The genius of John Henry Newman* by Ker, Ian, ed. In: *Louvain Stds* 18:188-190 Sum 1993
Review of: *Uniqueness* by Moran, Gabriel. In: *Eph Theol Lovan* 69:200-201 Ap 1993
Theology in an ecumenical context: on Catholic attitudes to the decision of the general synod of the Church of England. *Heythrop* 34:171-175 Ap 1993

Merriman, Brigid O'Shea.
Searching for Christ: the spirituality of Dorothy Day. Notre Dame: University of Notre Dame Press, 1992. x, 360p ISBN 0-268-01750-6 LC 93-23827

Merritt, Dick E, et al.
States pursue reform initiatives. *Health Prog* 74:45 Jl-Ag 1993

Mertens, Herman-Emiel.
Did the word of God become a human person? *Louvain Stds* 18:175-180 Sum 1993

Mertes, Klaus.
Fondamentalismo e religione. *Civilta* 2:116-129 Ap 17 1993

Merton, Thomas, 1915-1968.
The monastic journey. Kalamazoo: Cistercian Publications, 1992. x, 186p ISBN 0-87907-5333

Mertz, Donald W.
Instance ontology and Avicenna's arguments. *Mod Schlmn* 70:189-199 Mr 1993

Merziak, Regina.
Myths; Night snow. *Spirit* 58:26-27 1993

Messbarger, Paul.
Review of: *American Catholic arts and fictions* by Giles, Paul. In: *Relig Lit* 25:81-85 Spr 1993
Review of: *Testing the faith* by Gandolfo, Anita. In: *Relig Lit* 25:81-85 Spr 1993

Messina, A. see Gallard, George D, jt auth

Metz, Elinor D.
The camouflaged at-risk student: white and wealthy. *Momentum* 24:40-44 Ap-My 1993

Metz, Johann Baptist.
Die Dritte Welt und Europa. *Stimm Zeit* 211:3-9 Ja 1993

Metz, Kenneth.
Where in the world is the Catholic charismatic renewal? *New Cov* 22:8-10 Ja 1993

Metz, René.
Papal legates and the appointment of bishops. *Jurist* 52 no 1:259-284 1992

Metzger, Bruce M, and Coogan, Michael D, eds.
The Oxford companion to the Bible. New York: Oxford University Press, 1993. x, 874p ISBN 0-19-504645-5 LC 93-19315

Metzger, Richard M.
Marriage? Take it slow [condensed fr *The Catholic Times* Je 18 1993]. *CDgst* 58:24+ N 1993

Meuthen, Erich.
Nikolaus von Kues Skize einer Biographie. Münster: Aschendorff, 1992. x, 139p ISBN 3-402-03492-1

Meyer, Ben F.
The temple: symbol central to Biblical theology. *Gregorianum* 74 no 2:223-240 1993

Meyer, Gabriel.
Mary's bodily assumption. *Register* 69:5 Ag 15 1993
Review of: *Ending the Byzantine Greek schlism* by Likoudis, James. In: *Register* 69:4 Ap 18 1993
Review of: *Light of faith: the compendium of theology* by Thomas Aquinas, Saint. In: *Register* 69:4 Jl 4 1993

Meyer, John C.
Review of: *Philip Schaff: historian and ambassador* by Penzel, Klaus, ed. In: *JEcumen Stds* 29:265-266 Spr 1992

Meyer, Karl.
The biological basis of nonviolence. *Cath Work* 60:5 Ja-F 1993

Meyer, Lauree Hersch.
The reception and non-reception of Montreal's call to renewal [speech] to the North American Academy of Ecumenists, S 27 1992. *Ecumen Trends* 21:1+ D 1992

Meyer, Marvin W, et al. see Kloppenborg, John S, jt auth

Meyer, V N. see Helm, A J Vander, jt auth

Meyer, William E H, Jr.
From The sun also rises to High noon: the hypervisual great awakening in American literature and film. *Cithara* 32:39-59 N 1992

Meyers, William K.
NAFTA south of the border: high stakes, big hopes, real fears. *Comm* 120:5-7 S 24 1993

Meynell, Hugo.
Review of: *Beauty and holiness: the dialogue between aesthetics and religion* by Martin, James Alfred. In: *Heythrop* 34:117-118 Ja 1993
Review of: *Conditionals* by Jackson, Frank, eds. In: *Heythrop* 34:468 O 1993
Review of: *Free will and the Christian faith* by Anglin, W S. In: *Heythrop* 34:101-102 Ja 1993
Review of: *Lonergan* by Crowe, Frederick E. In: *New Blckfrs* 74:225-226 Ap 1993
Review of: *The dilemma of freedom and foreknowledge* by Zagzebski, Linda Trinkaus, 1946-. In: *Heythrop* 34:469 O 1993
Review of: *The glory of the Lord, a theological aesthetics, VII: theology: the New Covenant* by Balthasar, Hans Urs Von, 1905-1988. In: *Can Cath Rev* 11:28-29 Ap 1993

Meynell, Hugo. *(cont'd)*
Review of: *The non-reality of free will* by Double, Richard. In: *Heythrop* 34:220-221 Ap 1993
Review of: *Weakness of the will* by Gosling, Justin. In: *Heythrop* 34:324 Jl 1993

Michel, Thomas F.
Christian-Muslim dialogue in a changing world [address, The 36th Annual Robert Cardinal Bellarmine Lecture, St Louis Univ, S 30 1992]. *TheolDgst* 39:303-320 Wint 1992
I musulmani in Europa. *Civilta* 143:362-375 N 21 1992

Michnik, Adam.
The church and the left. Chicago: University of Chicago Press, 1993. 299p ISBN 0-226-52424-8 LC 92-20503

Mick, Lawrence E.
Entrance rites—lighten the load!. *Tod Parish* 25:33-35 N-D 1993
A fifty day celebration? *Tod Parish* 25:30-33 Ap-My 1993
Hospitality, reverence, and talking in church. *Tod Parish* 25:20-22 O 1993
Lent: a time for what? *Tod Parish* 25:31-32+ Ja 1993
Living a symphony in four movements. *Tod Parish* 25:20-22 13-17 S 1993
The three days at the center. *Tod Parish* 25:29-32 Mr 1993

Mickelsen, Alvera M. see Berkeley, A, jt auth

Micklem, Caryl, ed.
Contemporary prayers: the collected edition. Grand Rapids: Eerdmans, 1993. 176p ISBN 0-8028-1523-5

Midden, P J Van. see Ginkel, C Van, jt ed

Middleton, Frank.
Review of: *As we are one: essays and poems in honor of Bede Griffiths* by Bruteau, Beatrice, 1930-, ed. In: *CrossCurr* 42:564-565 Wint 1992-1993

Midgley, John, and Midgley, Sue.
Engagement: laying a foundation for success. *Liguorian* 81:16-20 Je 1993

Midgley, Sue. see Midgley, John, jt auth

Mier, Sebastián.
Partir de la doctrina o partir de la realidad? *Christus* 58:33-35 F 1993

Miesel, Sandra.
Becket, the martyred shepherd. *Register* 69:4 Ja 3 1993
A breed apart: the Desert Fathers. *OSV* 81:10-11 Ap 11 1993
A European hero. *Register* 69:14 O 17 1993
The first school teacher. *Register* 69:4 Ja 24 1993
A holy couple. *Register* 69:4 S 26 1993
A land of kingdoms, scholars and saints. *OSV* 81:18-19 Mr 14 1993
Looking at the dark side. *Register* 69:5 O 17 1993
Of sin and sanctity. *Register* 69:4 F 21 1993
Review of: *The politics of prayer* by Hitchcock, Helen Hull, ed. In: *Register* 69:5 Ap 18 1993
Review of: *Wisdom's daughter: the theology of Julian of Norwich* by Nuth, Joan M. In: *New Oxford Rev* 60:30-31 Jl-Ag 1993

Mietke, Gabriele, et al. see Deckers, Johannes Georg, jt auth

Migdal, Joel. see Kimmerling, Baruch, jt auth

Migliore, Daniel L, ed.
The Lord's prayer. Grand Rapids: Eerdmans, 1993. 152p ISBN 0-8028-0119-6

Mihalovici, Ionel.
Jews and christians in Spain today. *SIDIC* 25 No 2:12-14 1992

Mikhail-Ashrawi, Hanan.
The poet as diplomat: optimism isn't enough [interview by M.P. Kelly]. *Comm* 120:4-6 O 8 1993

Milani, Marcello. see Cappelletto, Gianni, jt auth

Milavec, Aaron.
Review of: *Jesus' Jewishness: exploring the place of Jesus in early Judaism* by Charlesworth, James H, ed. In: *JEcumen Stds* 29:121-122 Wint 1992

Milbank, John.
Out of the greenhouse. *New Blckfrs* 74:4-14 Ja 1993

Mildenberger, Friedrich.
Bílische Dogmatik: vol 3: Theologie als Ökonomic. Stuttgart: Kohlhammer, 1993. x, 496p ISBN 3-17-011083-7

Miles, Adell.
Healing of scars of childhood sexual abuse. *Priest* 49:42-44 Jl 1993
Population density: a hands-on geography activity. *Momentum* 24:14-15 S-O 1993

Miller, Adrienne.
The Hamlet syndrome: overthinkers who underachieve. New York: William Morrow and Company, 1989. 272p ISBN 0-688-07851-6 LC 88-30866

Miller, Andrea Wells. see Grant, Richard D, Jr, jt auth

Miller, Annabel.
Hope on the dole. *Tablet* 247:38-39 Ja 9 1993
Male and female created he them. *Tablet* 247:839 Jl 3 1993
Priests and laity promote renewal. *Tablet* 247:1205-1206 S 18 1993
Private schools examine their conscience. *Tablet* 247:151 Ja 30 1993

Miller, Charles E.
The spirituality of the eucharistic prayer. *Priest* 49:13-18 Ja 1993

Miller, Charles H.
Review of: *A century of biblical archaeology* by Moorey, P R S. In: *OTA* 16:411 Je 1993
Review of: *The Jordan valley survey, 1953* by Leonard, Albert, Jr. In: *OTA* 16:408-409 Je 1993

Miller, Donald E. see Seymour, Jack L, jt ed

Miller, E.
Review of: *Operation rescue: a challenge to the nation's conscience* by Lawler, Philip F. In: *New Oxford Rev* 60:20-21 Ja-F 1993
Review of: *Shattering the darkness: the crisis of the cross in the church today* by Foreman, Joseph Lapsley. In: *New Oxford Rev* 60:20-23 Ja-F 1993

Miller, Fred D, Jr. see Keyt, David, jt ed

Miller, J Michael.
Interior intelligibility: the use of Scripture in papal and conciliar documents. *Can Cath Rev* 11:9-18 S 1993
Life's greatest grace: why I belong to the Catholic Church. Huntington: Our Sunday Visitor, 1993. x, 160p ISBN 0-87973-471-9
Why confess venial sins? *OSV* 81:6 Ja 10 1993

Miller, John H.
Review of: *Military necessity and homosexuality* by Ray, Ronald D. In: *SocJust* 84:126 Jl-Ag 1993
Review of: *Soft porn plays hardball* by Reisman, Judith A. In: *SocJust* 84: 126-127 Jl-Ag 1993

Miller, L.
Review of: *Liberalism, conservatism, and Catholicism* by Krason, Stephen M. In: *Liguorian* 81:68-69 F 1993
Review of: *Prophet of our times* by Biffi, Franco. In: *Liguorian* 81:69 F 1993
Review of: *Social justice: the teachings of Catholics, Protestants, Jews, and Muslims* by Horgan, James J, and Fuchs, Lucy, eds. In: *Liguorian* 81:68 F 1993

Miller, Patricia F.
Sexuality education—forward or backward? *Momentum* 24:49-52 F-Mr 1993

Miller, Peggy.
Review of: *A bird on the wing* by Ure, John. In: *Tablet* 247:245-246 F 20 1993
Review of: *No other life* by Moore, Brian. In: *Tablet* 247:344 Mr 13 1993
Review of: *Odo's hanging* by Benson, Peter. In: *Tablet* 247:792 Je 19 1993
Review of: *Theory of war* by Brady, Joan. In: *Tablet* 247:344 Mr 13 1993

Miller, Richard Brian.
Interpretations of conflict: ethics, pacifism, and the just-war tradition. Chicago: University of Chicago Press, 1991. 294p ISBN 0-22652-795-6 LC 91-3044

Miller, Robert J.
Review of: *The christology of Jesus* by Witherington, Ben, III. In: *CBQ* 54: 810-811 O 1992

Miller, Robert L. see Weber, Gerard P, jt auth

Miller, Samuel J.
Review of: *Théologie et pouvoir en Sorbonne: La faculté de théologie de Paris et la bulle Unigenitus, 1714-1721* by Gres-Gayer, Jacques M. In: *CHist* 79:116-117 Ja 1993

Miller, Timothy.
Are the Moonies Latter-Day Mormons? *StudiaM* 41:67-83 1992

Miller, William T.
Review of: *Deuteronomy 1-11* by Christensen, Duane L. In: *OTA* 15:495-496 O 1992
Review of: *The trouble with Kings: the composition of the Book of Kings in the Deuteronomistic history* by McKenzie, Steven L. In: *OTA* 15:498-499 O 1992

Millet, Louis.
Review of: *Le Dieu des philosophes* by Magnard, Pierre. In: *RPhil Louvain* 91:509-510 Ag 1993

Millett, John.
The world faces Johnny Tripod. *Spirit* 58:42-44 1993

Millette, Adele M.
Through detachment to union. *Living Prayer* 26:22-26 Jl-Ag 1993

Milligan, Bryce.
Review of: *Einstein's dreams* by Lightman, Alan. In: *Nat Cath Rep* 29:35 My 28 1993

Milligan, Mary.
Review of: *Spiritual guides for today* by Callahan, Annice. In: *Horizons (CTS)* 20:168-169 Spr 1993

Mills, Mary E.
Thy Kingdom come in advent. *Priests & People* 6:473-476 D 1992

Milne, P.
Review of: *Explanation and its limits* by Knowles, Dudley, ed. In: *Heythrop* 34:104-105 Ja 1993

Milone, Michael.
Technology and the education renaissance. *Tod Cath Teach* 26:14-16+ Mr 1993

Minding, J Daniel.
Review of: *An introduction to moral theology* by May, William E. In: *Linacre* 60:91-93 F 1993

Miner, Chalise.
God the "in-control" mom. *St Anth* 101:18-20 N 1993

Minin, G.
Review of: *Jeunes non conformes* by Chicaud, M-B. In: *NRT* 115:150 Ja-F 1993

Mink, Gerd. see Schmitz, Franz-Jürgen, jt ed

Minnich, N.
Review of: *Erasmus: his life, works, and influence* by Augustin, Cornelis. In: *CHist* 78:651-653 O 1992

Minor, Mark.
Literacy-critical approaches to the Bible: an annotated bibliography. West Cornwall: Locust Hill Press, 1992. 520p ISBN 0-93395-148-5 LC 92-7469

Minor, Robert N.
Sarvepalli Radhakrishnan and religious pluralism. *StudiaM* 42:307-327 1993

Miracky, James.
Angels in America: millennium approaches. *America* 168:22-23 My 29 1993
Oleanna. *America* 168:16 My 15 1993
The Who's Tommy. *America* 169:17 O 9 1993

Miranda, Carlos Ortiz.
Reflections on the religious worker provisions of the 1990 Immigration Act. *CLawyer* 34 no 4:317-329 1993

Miranda, Caroline.
A sense of purpose. *Register* 69:5 Mr 28 1993

Miranda, Mario de Franco.
Review of: *Iniciação à prática da Teologia, tomo I: Introdução* by Lauret, Bernard, and Refoulé, François. In: *Perspectiva* 25:119-120 Ja-Ap 1993

Miscall, Peter D.
Review of: *Richterzeit und Königtum: Redaktionsgeschichtliche Studien zum Richterbuch* by Becker, Uwe. In: *CBQ* 55:101-102 Ja 1993

Misner, Barbara.
Review of: *The letters of Mother Caroline Friess, School Sisters of Notre Dame* by Brumleye, Barbara, ed. In: *CHist* 79:134-135 Ja 1993

Misner, Paul.
Review of: *Karl Adam: Catholicism in German culture* by Krieg, Robert Anthony. In: *CHist* 79:559-560 Jl 1993
Review of: *Vaticanum I (1869-1870)* by Schatz, Klaus. In: *TheolStds* 54:573-574 S 1993
Social Catholicism in nineteenth-century Europe: a review of recent historiography. *CHist* 78:581-600 O 1992

Misteravich, Daniel.
Negotiation: the art of community living. *Past Mus* 17:17-19 D 1992-Ja 1993

Mitchell, Alan C.
Review of: *Paul and the rhetoric of reconciliation: an exegetical investigation of the language and composition of 1 Corinthians* by Mitchell, Margaret M. In: *TheolStds* 54:163-165 Mr 1993
The use of rpéreiv and rhetorical propriety in Hebrews 2:10. *CBQ* 54:681-701 O 1992

Mitchell, Donald W.
A bibliographical review of books on spirituality in the Buddhist-Christian dialogue. *Stud Form Spir* 14:139-143 F 1993

Mitchell, Keith.
Review of: *Henry James: the imagination of genius* by Kaplan, Fred. In: *Tablet* 247:620-621 My 15 1993
Review of: *The invisible man: the life and liberties of H G Wells* by Coren, Michael. In: *Tablet* 247:141-142 Ja 30 1993
Review of: *Writers and their houses* by Marsh, Kate, ed. In: *Tablet* 247:1199 S 18 1993

Mitchell, Kenneth R, and Lovat, Terence J.
Permanently unconscious patients and the ethical controversies surrounding artificial nutrition and hydration: getting the facts straight. *Linacre* 60:75-90 F 1993

Mitchell, Leonel L.
Review of: *John Henry Newman* by Withey, Donald A. In: *Worship* 67:368-370 Jl 1993
Review of: *The promise of his glory: for the season from All Saints to Candlemas, commended by the House of Bishops of the General Synod of England.* In: *Worship* 67:177-179 Mr 1993
Review of: *Welcoming the light of Christ* by Perham, Michael V, and Stevenson, Kenneth W. In: *Worship* 67:177-179 Mr 1993

Mitchell, Marcia Alice.
Six steps through grief. *CDgst* 57:121-124 Ap 1993

Mitchell, Nathan D.
The amen corner. *Worship* 67:74-81 Ja 1993
The amen corner. *Worship* 67:164-173 Mr 1993 see Zapata, Dominga M, jt auth

Mitchell, Robert A.
Education was his line. *America* 168:4-5 Ja 30 1993

Mitra, Kana.
Review of: *Christian ethics and Indian ethos* by Das, Somen. In: *JEcumen Stds* 29:113-114 Wint 1992
Review of: *Jesus Christ and the Hindu community* by Staffner, Hans. In: *JEcumen Stds* 29:113-114 Wint 1992
Review of: *Women in India* by Das, Somen. In: *JEcumen Stds* 29:113-114 Wint 1992

Mittleman, A.
Review of: *Toward a theological encounter: Jewish understanding of Christianity* by Klenicki, Leon, ed. In: *New Theol Rev* 6:101-103 F 1993

Mize, Judith. see Fry, Patricia L, jt auth

Mize, Sandra Yocum.
Review of: *Sisters of Mercy: spirituality in America, 1843-1900* by Healy, Kathleen. In: *ACHSR* 103:49-50 Aut 1992

Modesto, Johannes.
Das Katholische Verständis von Evangelisierung, Konfession und Ökumene. *Catholica* 47:52-75 1993

Moen, Christine Boardman.
How to keep children active. *ReligTJ* 27:32-33 F 1993

Moga, Michael D.
A spirituality of aging. *RRel* 52:213-219 Mr-Ap 1993

Mohammed, Ovey N.
Averroes, Aristotle, and the Qur'an immortality. *IPQ* 33:37-55 Mr 1993

Mohan, Robert Paul.
Review of: *Victims and values: a history and a theory of suffering* by Amato, Joseph Anthony, 1938-. In: *CHist* 78:624-625 O 1992
Values that offer a running start on life. *Origins* 23:31-32 My 27 1993

Mohler, James Aylward.
Late have I loved you: an interpretation of Saint Augustine on human and divine relationships. New Rochelle, New York: New City Press, 1991. 159p ISBN 0-911782-86-9 LC 90-28643
The "Spiritual excercises" and spiritual direction. *Priest* 49:38-46 S 1993

Mola, Aldo A. see Benimeli, José A Ferrer, jt ed; Paracone, Corrado, jt ed

Mole, John W.
Whiter the mass? *HPR* 93:46-52 Jl 1993

Moleck, Fred.
Sing to the Lord a sturdy song. *Past Mus* 17:26-28 Ap-My 1993

Moleski, M.
Review of: *Sermons on the liturgy and the sacraments and on Christ the mediator* by Newman, John Henry, Cardinal, 1801-1890. In: *TheolStds* 53: 787-788 D 1992

Molloy, Kathy.
Review of: *Divorce in the New Testament* by Collins, Raymond F. In: *Studies* 82:356-360 Aut 1993

Molnar, Paul D.
Moltmann's post-modern messianic christology: a review discussion. *Thomist* 56:669-693 O 1992

Moloney, Francis J.
Review of: *The quest for the Messiah* by Painter, John. In: *Pacifica* 6:106-109 F 1993
Review of: *The son of man tradition* by Hare, Douglas R A. In: *Pacifica* 6: 214-216 Je 1993
Review of: *The son of the man in the Gospel of John* by Burkett, Delbert. In: *Pacifica* 6:109-112 F 1993

Moltmann, Jürgen. *see* Moltmann-Wendel, Elisabeth, jt auth

Moltmann-Wendel, Elisabeth, and Moltmann, Jürgen.
Humanity in God. Cleveland: The Pilgrim Press, 1993. x, 133p ISBN 0-8298-0670-9 LC 93-4180

Monachino, V.
Review of: *Delinquenti e carcerati a Roma alla metà del'600* by Fornili, Carlo Cirillo. In: *Civilta* 3:86-87 Jl 3 1993
Review of: *Luigi Taparelli, l'altro D'Azeglio* by Rosa, Luigi Di. In: *Civilta* 144:92-93 Ja 2 1993

Monaghan, Andrew.
Counseling as a Christian challenge. Westminster: Christian Classics, 1993. x, 183p ISBN 0-7171-1831-2

Monahan, Jim.
Healing is real. *New Cov* 22:26-27 Je 1993

Mondoni, Danilo.
Review of: *El libro del Génesis (1-11)* by Ravasi, Gianfranco. In: *Perspectiva* 25:265-266 My-Ag 1993
Review of: *Historia de la teología cristiana, III* by Vialnova, Evangelista. In: *Perspectiva* 25:248-250 My-Ag 1993
Review of: *Homilías sobre la Escritura en la época apostólica* by Grelot, Pierre. In: *Perspectiva* 25:257-258 My-Ag 1993
Review of: *Juan* by Ernst, Josef. In: *Perspectiva* 25:260-261 My-Ag 1993

Mongoven, Anne Marie.
Catechetics in the 90's: present state and future challenges. *Chicago Stud* 31: 229-243 N 1992

Montague, George T.
Freezing the fire: the death of relational language. *America* 168:5-7 Mr 13 1993
Gifts for everyone. *New Cov* 22:33 Mr 1993
Review of: *Colossians* by Pokorný, Petr. In: *CBQ* 54:796-797 O 1992
Review of: *D'un temple à l'autre: Pierre et l'Eglise primitive de Jérusalem* by Grappe, Christian. In: *CBQ* 55:155-157 Ja 1993 *see* McDonnell, Kilian, 1921-, jt ed

Montali, Larry.
Newcomers deserve a break. *Register* 69:1+ O 24 1993

Montealegre, Alberto.
Contribución de las universidades católicas a la nueva evangelición. *Seminarium* 32:452-462 Jl-S 1992

Montes, Fernando.
Santo Domingo-the IV LatinAmerican conference [repr fr *Mensaje*]. *LADOC* 23:1-7 Mr-Ap 1993

Montesano, Chris. *see* Montesano, Joan, jt auth

Montesano, Joan, and Montesano, Chris.
The Green Revolution: what we've learned. *Cath Work* 60:4 My 1993

Montgomery, John Warwick, 1931-.
Breaking trust with Cardinal Newman. *New Oxford Rev* 60:18-19 Ja-F 1993
Can a scientist pray. *New Oxford Rev* 60:22-23 Ap 1993
Did Jesus exist? *New Oxford Rev* 60:20-22 My 1993
Fido in heaven? *New Oxford Rev* 60:20+ O 1993
Gorgon theology. *New Oxford Rev* 60:20-21 Jl-Ag 1993
Lessons from the Amish. *New Oxford Rev* 60:26-27 N 1993
New light on the abortion controversy? *New Oxford Rev* 60:24-26 S 1993
When is a Jew not a Jew? *New Oxford Rev* 60:25-26 Je 1993

Moonan, Lawrence.
Attributing things to God. *Eph Theol Lovan* 78:86-117 Ap 1992

Mooney, Christopher F.
Theology and the Heisenberg uncertainty principle [2 parts]. *Heythrop* 34: 247-273 Jl; 373-386 O 1993

Mooney, Philip.
Au revoir, Saint Ex. *America* 169:14-16 Jl 31-Ag 7 1993

Moor, Geertruida, de.
Laybrothers and laysisters in Frisia and Holland: circa 1300-circa 1600. *Cist Stud* 27 No 4:329-339 1992

Moore, Carey A.
Review of: *The redaction of the Books of Esther* by Fox, Michael V. In: *CBQ* 55:334-335 Ap 1993

Moore, James. *see* Desmond, Adrian, jt auth

Moore, James Talmadge.
Review of: *Countering colonization, Native American women and Great Lakes missions, 1630-1900* by Devens, Carol. In: *CHist* 79:564-565 Jl 1993

Moore, Joe.
But will they ever come running? Reflections on youth ministry. *Living Light* 29:45-50 Spr 1993

Moore, John C, 1933-.
The Resurrection, the Church and the Bible. *America* 168:14 Ap 10 1993

Moore, Joseph.
Helping skills for the nonprofessional counselor. Cincinatti: St Anthony Press, 1993. x, 67p ISBN 0-86716-1744
Teenagers: are they losing faith? *ReligTJ* 26:12-14 Ja 1993

Moore, Michael S.
Review of: *Abiding astonishment: Psalms, modernity, and the making of history* by Brueggemann, Walter. In: *CBQ* 54:740-741 O 1992

Moore, Nina Polcyn.
Humphrey, Mary, -1992 [obit]. *Cath Work* 60:6 Ja-F 1993

Moore, Patrick.
Review of: *All shall be well* by Upjohn, Sheila. In: *Priests & People* 7:124 Mr 1993
Review of: *An anthology of Christian mysticism* by Egan, Harvey. In: *Priests & People* 7:124 Mr 1993
Review of: *Invitation to love: the way of Christian contemplation* by Keeting, Thomas. In: *Priests & People* 7:124 Mr 1993
Review of: *Meister Eckhart* by Backhouse, Halcyon. In: *Priests & People* 7: 124 Mr 1993
Review of: *Sin shall be a glory* by Mountrey, John Michael. In: *Priests & People* 7:124 Mr 1993
Review of: *The cloud of unknowing: reflections on selected texts* by Cooper, Austin. In: *Priests & People* 7:124 Mr 1993
Review of: *The prayers of Saint John of the Cross* by Ruiz, Alphonse. In: *Priests & People* 7:124 Mr 1993

Moore, Robert L.
Review of: *Zwischen synagoge und Obrigkeit: Zur historischen Situation der lukanischen Christen* by Stegemann, Wolfgang. In: *CBQ* 54:803-804 O 1992 *see* Meckel, Daniel J, jt ed

Mora Lomelí, Raúl H.
La universidad Ignaciana hoy en America Latina. *Christus* 57:43-51 S 1992

Morahan, Justin.
Leaven—listening to those who have left. *Furrow* 44:154-158 Mr 1993

Morales, José.
Tres maneras de articular fe y analisis. *Christus* 58:34-52 Ag 1993

Moran, Aidan.
Review of: *Perspectives on language and thought: interrelations in development* by Gelman, S A, and Byrnes, J P, eds. In: *IJPS* 1:165-166 Mr 1993

Moran, Anne E.
Employee benefits. *CLawyer* 34 no 4:407-422 1993

Moran, Dennis W. *see* Hudson, Deal W, jt ed

Moran, Gabriel.
Jews, Christians, and unique revelation. *CrossCurr* 42:468-486 Wint 1992-1993

Moran, J.
Review of: *Religious belief and ecclesiastical carrers in late Medieval England* by Harper-Bill, Christopher, ed. In: *CHist* 78:648-649 O 1992

Moran, William L.
Review of: *Formule di maledizione della Mesopotamia preclassica* by Pomponio, Francesco, ed. In: *CBQ* 55:348 Ap 1993

Moreno Garrido, Jaime.
La literatura mesopotámica antigua. *Teol Vida* 33 no 3-4:237-254 1992
La "Vita" de María Magdalena. *Teol Vida* 34 no 1-2:119-143 1993

Morey, Miguel.
Friederich Nietzsche: una biografia. Madrid: Archipielago, 1993. x, 126p ISBN 84-88595-00-x

Morgan, Anne Marie.
Other abortion providers. *Crisis* 11:18-19 Jl-Ag 1993
Primum non nocere. *Crisis* 11:17-25 Jl-Ag 1993
A profile of US home-schooling families. *Crisis* 11:29 Ap 1993

Morgan, James J.
Review of: *Dignity and solidarity: an introduction to peace and justice education* by Jackson, Owen R. In: *Living Light* 29:94-95 Spr 1993

Morgan, Winifred.
The forest and the trees. *Sisters* 65:12-19 Ja 1993

Mori, Geraldo Luis De.
O evangelho segundo Dona Lauricena. *Perspectiva* 25:197-227 My-Ag 1993

Moriarty, Fred L.
Review of: *Satire and the Hebrew prophets* by Jemielity, Thomas. In: *TheolStds* 54:551-552 S 1993

Morin, Douglas J.
No less zeal: a spiritual guide for Catholic lay people. New York: Alba House, 1993. x, 142p ISBN 0-8189-0631-6 LC 92-34242

Morley, Winifred.
Open door retreats. *Way Suppl* 75:49-55 Aut 1992

Morneau, Robert F, Bp, 1938-.
Are you ready for a richer life? *USCath* 58:38-40 O 1993
Preaching and poetry: George Herbert. *Emmanuel* 49:386-391 S 1993
Preaching and poetry: Gerard Manley Hopkins. *Emmanuel* 99:460-464 O 1993
Review of: *Some other morning* by Driscoll, Jeremy. In: *ST Anth* 101:52 Jl 1993
Review of: *Winter music: a life of Jessica Powers* by Leckey, Dolores R, 1933-. In: *Spir Life* 39:49-50 Spr 1993

Morreale, Ben. *see* Mangione, Jerre, jt auth

Morrell, Jill. *see* McCarthy, John, jt auth

Morris, Colin.
Battle at the BBC. *Tablet* 247:942-943 Jl 24 1993

Morris, M.
Review of: *Image and spirit in sacred and secular art* by Dillenberger, Jane. In: *Thomist* 56:738-740 O 1992

Morris, Thomas.
Review of: *International Kierkegaard commentary, vol 13: the Corsair Affair* by Perkins, Robert L, ed. In: *Heythrop* 34:111-112 Ja 1993

Morris, Thomas V.
RCIA: is this rite right for you? *Tod Parish* 25:20-22 N-D 1993

Morrisey, Francis G.
Review of: *Episcopal conferences* by Reese, Thomas Joseph, 1945-, ed. In: *Can Cath Rev* 11:30 Ap 1993
Review of: *Theology and canon law* by Orsy, Ladislas M, 1921-. In: *Jurist* 51 no 2:509-512 1991

Morrisey, Frank, and Campbell, Peter.
Canon law offers flexibility in collaborative relationships. *Health Prog* 74:53 Jl-Ag 1993

Morrisey, Michael P.
Consciousness and transcedence: the theology of Eric Voegelin. Notre Dame: University of Notre Dame Press, 1994. x, 384p ISBN 0-268-00793-4 LC 92-50159

Morrissey, Thomas.
Review of: *A labour history of Ireland 1824-1960* by O'Connor, Emmet. In: *Studies* 82:226-229 Sum 1993
Review of: *Dublin's turbulent priest: Cornelius Nary, 1658-1738* by Fagan, Patrick. In: *Studies* 81:469-475 Wint 1992

Morrow, Carol Ann.
High expectations: Denver, World Youth Day and the Pope [editorial]. *St Anth* 101:15 Ag 1993
A holy week in a Holy Land. *St Anth* 100:28-33 Ap 1993
Malcolm X: what his three lives can teach us [editorial]. *St Anth* 100:17 F 1993
Mary feminism: compatible but challenging. *St Anth* 100:10-15 My 1993
Review of: *Mourning in Bethlehem: the impact of the Gulf War on Palestine society* by White, Patrick. In: *ST Anth* 101:50-51 Jl 1993
Review of: *Voices from Jerusalem: Jews and Christians reflect on the Holy Land* by Burrell, David B, and Landau, Yehezkel, eds. In: *ST Anth* 101:50-51 Jl 1993
World Youth Day and the Pope: giant festival of faith. *St Anth* 101:28-37 N 1993

Morry, Matthew F.
Report, 1991-92: New England region of the Mariological Society of America. *Marian Stds* 43:193-194 1992

Morton, Russell.
Review of: *Metaphorik, Erzählstruktur und szenisch-dramatische Gestaltung in den Sondergutgleichnissen bei Lukas* by Heininger, Bernhard. In: *CBQ* 54:784-786 O 1992
Review of: *Paulus und das Judentum: Anthropologische Erwägungen* by Laato, Timo. In: *CBQ* 55:375-377 Ap 1993

Mortonson, M Sheila.
Review of: *Committed by choice: religious life today* by Merkle, Judith A. In: *Sisters* 65:309-310 Jl 1993

Morvan, Michael Le.
The Gospel is celebration [editorial]. *Teilhard Rev* 27:66-68 Wint 1992

Moser, Kay R.
Review of: *Every day doughnuts: a novel* by Adcroft, Patrice. In: *St Anth* 101:50 O 1993

Moses, Earl C, Jr.
An introduction to the Christian faith: a biblical perspective. New York: Vantage Press, 1993. 127p ISBN 0-533-10329-0 LC 92-90810

Moses, Paul.
Reporting religion: holiness in the ordinary. *America* 168:12-15 My 1 1993

Mosher, M.
Review of: *The Gospel in Dostoevsky.* In: *Cist Stud* 27 No 4:[112]-[113] 1992
Review of: *The Stave churches of Lomen: a mathematical analysis/Lomen Stavkirke: en Matematisk Analyse* by Jensenius, Jörgen H. In: *Cist Stud* 27 No 4:[103]-[104] 1992

Moskoff, William. *see* Jones, Anthony, jt ed

Moss, Christopher.
Review of: *Option for the poor* by Dorr, Donal, 1935-. In: *Tablet* 247:892 Jl 10 1993

Moss, David.
Costly giving: on Jean-Luc Marion's theology of the gift. *New Blckfrs* 74:393-399 S 1993
Law, change and revolution: a theological note on the finality of capitalist resurgence. *New Blckfrs* 73:614-622 D 1992

Mosser, David.
Review of: *Learning through suffering: the educational value of suffering in the New Testament and in its milieu* by Talbert, Charles H. In: *CBQ* 54:804-805 O 1992

Most, William G, 1914-.
Did the early Church ordain women to be priests? *Can Cath Rev* 11:21-24 F 1993

Mostyn, Trevor, 1946-.
The lost city. *Tablet* 247:1222-1223 S 25 1993

Mottard, François.
Review of: *Éléments de logique contemporaine* by Lepage, François. In: *Laval Theol Phil* 49:161 F 1993
Review of: *Philosophie de l'esprit et sciences du cerveau* by Missa, J-N, ed. In: *Laval Theol Phil* 49:163-164 F 1993

Motte, André.
Religion, poésie et philosophie: Les Grecs et la quête du divin. *RPhil Louvain* 91:366-382 Ag 1993

Motto, M.
Review of: *Il sistema delle relazioni internazionali* by Casadio, Franco A. In: *Civilta* 144:100-101 Ja 2 1993

Moudry, Richard P.
Converting the pastor. *Mod Lit* 20:6-8 Ap 1993

Mourneau, Robert F, Bp, 1938-.
An experience of God: reflections of a poet's journey. *Living Prayer* 26:3-7 S-O 1993

Mourvillier, François. *see* Chabert, Joëlle, jt auth

Moyer, Sylvia.
"Mom, I have AIDS" [condensed fr *The Family—A Catholic Perspective*, Mr 1993]. *CDgst* 57:49-53 Je 1993

Moynahan, Michael E.
Liturgy and catechesis: two sides of the same coin. *Living Light* 29:47-57 Aut 1992
Once upon a miracle: dramas for worship and religious education. New York: Paulist Press, 1993. x, 210p ISBN 0-8091-3361-x LC 92-41325

Moynihan, Robert.
Ratzinger prefers altar turned around again. *Nat Cath Rep* 29:7 My 28 1993

Mpoto, Basile.
Review of: *Logique: vol I: Méthodes pour l'informatique fondamentale* by Gochet, Paul, and Gribomont, Pascal. In: *RPhil Louvain* 91:521-522 Ag 1993

Mucci, Giandomenico.
Crisi Dei Valori: Una Terapia Comune Tra Laici E Cattolici? *Civilta* 143:450-457 D 5 1992
Il fenomeno delle stimmate. *Civilta* 2:217-226 My 1 1993
Religione, laicismo e postmodernità. *Civilta* 144:131-139 Ja 16 1993
Review of: *Dio che è amore: Trinità e vita in Cristo* by Zanghí, Giuseppe Maria. In: *Civilta* 144:403-404 F 20 1993
Review of: *Giuseppe Capograssi filosofo del nostro tempo* by Opocher, Enrico. In: *Civilta* 3:544-545 S 18 1993
Review of: *Il Sinodo dei Vescovi: assemblea special per l'Europa* by Caprile, Giovanni. In: *Civilta* 2:297-298 My 1 1993
Review of: *Il Sinodo dei Vescovi: interventi e documentazione* by Paul VI, Pope, 1897-1978 (Giovanni Battista Montini) (elected 1963). In: *Civilta* 2:297-298 My 1 1993
Review of: *Manzoni e i Gesuiti della "Civiltà Cattolica"* by Azzolin, Giovanni. In: *Civilta* 2:408-409 My 15 1993
Review of: *San Claudio La Colombière e servo fidele e perfetto del cuore di cristo* by Filosomi, Luigi, ed. In: *Civilta* 143:421-422 N 21 1992
Review of: *San Claudio la Colomière maestro di vita cristiana* by Filosomi, Luigi, ed. In: *Civilta* 143:421-422 N 21 1992
Review of: *San Paolo* by Cremona, Carlo. In: *Civilta* 3:97-98 Jl 3 1993
Review of: *Sono sempre in mezzo a voi: lettere ed altri scritti della Madre Fondatrice delle Suore Francescane Missionarie di Gesù Bambino* by Micarelli, Barbara. In: *Civilta* 144:203 Ja 16 1993
La rinascita dell'illuminismo dopo il 1989. *Civilta* 144:535-546 Mr 20 1993

Muckerman, Norman James, 1917-.
The Magnificat Mary's canticle of praise. *Liguorian* 81:4-8 My 1993

Mueller, J.
Review of: *A marginal Jew: rethinking the historical Jesus* by Meier, John P. In: *RRel* 52:153-154 Ja-F 1993
Review of: *The reason of following: Christology and the ecstatic I* by Scharlemann, Robert P. In: *TheolStds* 53:767-768 D 1992

Mueller, M. Jane.
Sixth-graders host Mass for parents. *Catechist* 27:34 O 1993

Mueller, Therese.
Lent. *Mod Lit* 20:34-35 N 1993
The season of Advent. *Mod Lit* 20:32-33 S 1993
Towards a Christian Christmas. *Mod Lit* 20:32-33 O 1993

Muir, Bernard. *see* Manion, Margaret, jt ed

Mullen, E Theodore.
Review of: *From Carmel to Horeb* by Hauser, Alan J, and Gregory, Russell. In: *CBQ* 54:747-748 O 1992

Mullen, P H, Jr.
The U.S. bishops get a new doctor of doctrine [por]. *OSV* 82:3 O 31 1993

Mullen, Peter.
Activist fights for school choice. *Register* 69:1+ S 19 1993
Another "objector". *Register* 69:2 Ap 18 1993
Are mass stats off? *Register* 69:1+ O 10 1993
Arts war likely to continue. *Register* 69:1+ Ja 10 1993
Body and soul. *Register* 69:1+ My 2 1993
Catholic educators adjust goals. *Register* 69:1+ Mr 14 1993
Catholics divided on NAFTA. *Register* 69:1+ O 17 1993
Courtship. *Register* 69:1+ Jl 4 1993
Curricula feel ire of parents. *Register* 69:1+ Je 20 1993
Educating Peter. *Register* 69:3 My 9 1993
Enough is enough!. *Register* 69:1+ S 5 1993
Families [conference, "Putting Children and Families First: Building Peace, Seeking Justice"]. *Register* 69:1+ Mr 21 1993
The fate of priest offenders. *Register* 69:1+ O 3 1993
A gift to the nation. *Register* 69:3 Ag 1 1993
The good fight. *Register* 69:3 Ap 11 1993
Hardball. *Register* 69:1+ Ap 18 1993
Helping the poor. *Register* 69:1+ Mr 7 1993
His and his. *Register* 69:1+ Je 13 1993
In post-Catholic Guatemala. *Register* 69:2 My 30 1993
In the army now. *Register* 69:1+ F 14 1993
Islam. *Register* 69:1+ My 23 1993
"Killing fields" no more. *Register* 69:3 O 17 1993
Losers? "not!". *Register* 69:1+ Ja 31 1993
The man won't stop 'til the world's smoke-free [por]. *Register* 69:1+ S 12 1993
Media get complaints on coverage. *Register* 69:1+ Ap 11 1993
Over there. *Register* 69:1+ Jl 25 1993
Rebuilding the Church in Eastern Europe. *Crisis* 11:26-28 F 1993
Renewing our love. *Register* 69:2 My 23 1993
The thaw. *Register* 69:1+ Je 11 1993
Watch out, America they mean business!. *Register* 69:1+ Ag 8 1993
Word wars. *Register* 69:1+ Ap 25 1993

Müller, Denis.
Une vision protestante de l'éthique sociale. *Laval Theol Phil* 49:57-67 F 1993

Müller, Hubert.
How the local church lives and affirms its catholicity. *Jurist* 52 no 1:340-364 1992

Müller, J. *see* Kerber, W, jt ed

Müller, Johannes.
Review of: *Verändert der Glaube die Wirtschaft?* by Fornet-Betancourt, Raúl. In: *Stimm Zeit* 211:142-143 F 1993
Weltweite Migrationen als politische Herausforderung Europas. *Stimm Zeit* 210:797-805 D 1992

Muller, Robert.
Spokesmen for the spiritual dimension of the world order. *Sisters* 65:202-205 My 1993

Mulrooney, Joseph.
Review of: *A century of Biblical archaeology* by Moorey, Roger. In: *Heythrop* 34:429-430 O 1993
Review of: *On humour and the comic in the Hebrew Bible* by Radday, Yehuda T, and Brenner, Athalya, eds. In: *Heythrop* 34:307-308 Jl 1993
Review of: *Shattered vows* by Rice, David. In: *Heythrop* 34:350-351 Jl 1993
Review of: *The trouble with Kings: the composition of the Book of Kings in the Deuteronomistic history* by McKenzie, Steven L. In: *Heythrop* 34:308-309 Jl 1993
Review of: *Wealth and poverty in the Book of Proverbs* by Whybray, R N. In: *Heythrop* 34:187-188 Ap 1993
Wisdom to live by. *BibleT* 31:272-276 S 1993

Mulryan, John.
Review of: *Nietzsche's case: philosophy as/and literature* by Magnus, Bernd, et al. In: *Cithara* 32:55-56 My 1993
Review of: *Vested interests: cross-dressing and cultural anxiety* by Garber, Marjorie. In: *Cithara* 32:65-66 N 1992

Munárriz, Jose Miguel.
The feminism of Jesus—women in the gospel [excerpt fr *Accion*]. *LADOC* 23:18-23 Jl-Ag 1993

Munárriz, José Miguel. *see* Antoncich, Ricardo, jt auth

Mundy, John Hine.
Review of: *Ketzer und Professoren* by Fichtenau, Heinrich. In: *CHist* 79:518-519 Jl 1993

Munitz, Joseph A.
Review of: *The making of a saint: the life, times and sanctification of Neophytos the recluse* by Galatariotou, Catia. In: *Heythrop* 34:209-212 Ap 1993

Münk, Hans J.
Genomanalysen im Versicherungs- und Gerichtswesen. *Stimm Zeit* 211:34-44 Ja 1993
Tierpatente im Kreuzfeuer der Kritik. *Stimm Zeit* 211:605-616 S 1993

Muñoz, Braulio.
Tensions in social theory: groundwork for a future moral sociology. Chicago: Loyola University Press, 1993. x, 367p ISBN 0-8294-0739-1 LC 92-26436

Muñoz, Héctor.
El encuentro '92 de la sociedad Argentina de liturgia. *Notitiae* 28:424-425 Je 1992

Munoz, Humberto.
Review of: *Cómo se pasa la vida* by Araneda Bravo, Fidel. In: *Teol Vida* 33 no 3-4:329-330 1992

Muñoz, Ronaldo F.
La teologia del catecismo de Juan Pablo II. *Christus* 58:32-33 Ag 1993

Munro, Robin. *see* Black, George, jt auth

Murad, Afonso.
Documento de Santo Domingo: princípiois hermenêuticos de leitura. *Perspectiva* 25:11-29 Ja-Ap 1993
"Povo de Deus renascendo das culturas oprimidas". *Perspectiva* 24:357-366 S-D 1992

Murad, Afonso, and Rezende Guimarães, Marcelo.
O amadurecimento litúrgico das CEBs e os sinais de uma nova espiritualidade. *REB* 52:821-832 D 1992

Muravchik, Joshua.
Bosnia's tragedy is shame of the West. *Register* 69:1+ O 10 1993

Murdick, Olin J.
Common prayer: an ecumenical bridge. *Ecumen Trends* 22:3-6 My 1993

Murdoch, John E, et al. *see* Asztalos, Monica, jt ed

Murnion, Philip J, 1938-.
New parish ministers: laity & religious on parish staffs. New York: National Pastoral Life Center, 1992. 131p ISBN 1-88130-701-8
Review of: *Christianity in the twenty-first century* by Wuthnow, Robert. In: *Comm* 120:23-24 Je 4 1993

Murphy, Anne.
Review of: *Holy listening: the art of spiritual direction* by Guenther, Margaret. In: *Sisters* 65:65-66 Ja 1993
Review of: *The English Bible and the seventeenth-century revolution* by Hill, Christopher. In: *Month* 26:377-378 S-O 1993
Review of: *The hour of the poor, the hour of women* by Golden, Renny. In: *Way* 33:78 Ja 1993
Review of: *Transforming grace: Christian tradition and women's experience* by Carr, Anne. In: *Way* 33:78 Ja 1993
Review of: *Women as interpreters of the Bible* by Demers, Patricia. In: *Way* 33:78 Ja 1993
Review of: *Women who knew Paul* by Gillman, Florence Morgan. In: *Way* 33:77-78 Ja 1993

Murphy, Anne, and Pridmore, John.
Review of: *Spirituality and history* by Sheldrake, Philip. In: *Way* 33:252 Jl 1993
Review of: *The Church in Latin America, 1492-1992* by Dussel, Enrique, ed. In: *Way* 33:253 Jl 1993

Murphy, Anne, and Pridmore, John. *(cont'd)*
Review of: *The English Bible and the seventeenth-century revolution* by Hill, Christopher. In: *Way* 33:253 Jl 1993
Review of: *The stripping of the altars* by Duffy, Eamon. In: *Way* 33:252-253 Jl 1993

Murphy, Annie.
Christian experience from the shadow side of history. *Way* 33:127-137 Ap 1993
Forbidden fruit: the true story of my secret love affair with Ireland's most powerful bishop. Boston: Little, Brown and Company, 1993. 358p ISBN 0-31659-090-8 LC 93-3239

Murphy, Brian P.
The canon of Irish cultural history: some questions concerning Roy Foster's Modern Ireland. *Studies* 82:171-184 Sum 1993

Murphy, Francis J.
Review of: *Histoire du Christianisme des origines à nos jours, volume XII: Guerres mondiales et totalitarismes (1914-1958)* by Mayeur, Jean-Marie, ed. In: *CHist* 79:307-308 Ap 1993

Murphy, Francis Xavier, 1914-.
The memoirs of Cardinal Leo Jozef Suenens. *America* 168:17-18 Je 5-12 1993
Review of: *Alphonsus de Liguori; the Saint of Bourbon Naples* by Jones, Frederick M. In: *America* 168:24-25 Ap 24 1993
Review of: *Memories and hopes* by Suenens, Leo Jozef, Cardinal, 1904-. In: *America* 168:17-18 Je 5-12 1993
Review of: *Paul VI* by Hebblethwaite, Peter, 1930-. In: *Nat Cath Rep* 29:15 Je 4 1993

Murphy, G Ronald.
Review of: *The damned and the elect: guilt in Western culture* by Ohly, Friedrich. In: *TheolStds* 54:386-387 Je 1993

Murphy, James H.
Review of: *Christianity and incest* by Imbens, Annie, and Jonker, Ineke. In: *Furrow* 44:258-259 Ap 1993
Review of: *Saint Patrick* by MacDonald, Iain, ed. In: *Furrow* 44:326-327 My 1993
Review of: *St Brendan* by MacDonald, Iain, ed. In: *Furrow* 44:326-327 My 1993
Review of: *St Bride* by MacDonald, Iain, ed. In: *Furrow* 44:326-327 My 1993
Review of: *St Columba* by MacDonald, Iain, ed. In: *Furrow* 44:326-327 My 1993
Review of: *Wisdom of the Celtic saints* by Sellner, Edward Cletus. In: *Furrow* 44:326-327 My 1993

Murphy, Jim.
Pilgrim. *New Cov* 22:21-22 My 1993
Service calls. *New Cov* 23:30 Ag 1993

Murphy, John J.
Willa Cather and the literature of Christian mystery. *Relig Lit* 24:39-56 Aut 1992

Murphy, Karen C.
Review of: *Converting the baptized* by O'Malley, William J, 1931-. In: *Living Light* 29:89-90 Spr 1993

Murphy, N Michael.
Review of: *Euthanasia is not the answer: a hospice physician's view* by Cundiff, David. In: *Health Prog* 74:94-95 Jl-Ag 1993

Murphy, Roland E.
The Psalms are yours. Mahwah: Paulist, 1993. x, 148p ISBN 0-8091-3411-x LC 93-15639
Review of: *Élie ou l'appel du silence* by Masson, Michel. In: *OTA* 15:499 O 1992
Review of: *A dictionary of Biblical interpretation* by Coggins, R J. In: *OTA* 15:479-480 O 1992
Review of: *A dictionary of biblical tradition in English literature* by Jeffrey, David Lyle. In: *OTA* 16:407 Je 1993
Review of: *A study of Job 4-5 in the light of contemporary literary theory* by Cotter, David W. In: *OTA* 15:503-504 O 1992
Review of: *Ben Sira-zwischen Judentum und Hellenismus* by Kieweler, Hans Volker. In: *OTA* 16:429 Je 1993
Review of: *Biblical theology of the Old and New Testaments* by Childs, Brevard S. In: *OTA* 16:438 Je 1993
Review of: *Character and ideology in the Book of Esther* by Fox, Michael V. In: *CBQ* 55:333-334 Ap 1993
Review of: *Das Hohelied, Klagelieder, das Buch Esther* by Müller, Hans-Peter, et al. In: *OTA* 15:484-485 O 1992
Review of: *Deuteronomy and the Deuteronmic school* by Weinfeld, Moshe. In: *OTA* 16:172 F 1993
Review of: *Dictionary of the Ecumenical Movement* by Lossky, Nicholas, et al, eds. In: *OTA* 16:161-162 F 1993
Review of: *Durch Leiden zur Vollendung: Die Elihureden im Buch Ijob (Ijob 32-37)* by Mende, Theresia. In: *OTA* 54:755-756 O 1992
Review of: *Egypt, Canaan, and Israel in ancient times* by Redford, Donald B. In: *OTA* 16:165 F 1993
Review of: *Egyptian religion* by Morenz, Siegfried. In: *OTA* 15:484 O 1992
Review of: *Elijah and Elisha in socioliterary perspective* by Coote, Robert B. In: *OTA* 15:470 O 1992
Review of: *Göttinen, Götter und Gottessymbole* by Keel, Othmar, and Uehlinger, Christoph. In: *OTA* 16:187 F 1993
Review of: *Genesis* by Scullion, John J. In: *OTA* 16:169 F 1993
Review of: *Hosea* by Davies, G I. In: *OTA* 16:182 F 1993
Review of: *Il Libro della Sapienza: introduzione-versione-commento* by Sisti, Adalberto. In: *OTA* 16:428 Je 1993
Review of: *Il libro di Qoèlet* by Bonora, Antonio. In: *OTA* 16:176 F 1993
Review of: *Internationale Zeitschriftenschau für Bibelwissenschaft un Grenzgebiete* by Lang, Bernhard, ed. In: *OTA* 16:161 F 1993
Review of: *Interpreting Hebrew poetry* by Petersen, David L, and Richards, Kent Harold. In: *OTA* 16:164 F 1993
Review of: *Isaiah 1-12, a commentary* by Wildberger, Hans, 1910-1986. In: *CBQ* 55:355 Ap 1993

Murphy, Roland E. *(cont'd)*
Review of: *Krieg und Staat im alten Israel* by Lohfink, Norbert. In: *OTA* 16: 439 Je 1993
Review of: *Love and joy: law, language and religion in ancient Israel* by Muffs, Yochanan. In: *OTA* 16:399 Je 1993
Review of: *Love and politics: a new commentary on the Song of Songs* by Stadelmann, Luis. In: *OTA* 16:428 Je 1993
Review of: *Mensch-Umwelt-Eigenwelt: Gesammelte Aufsätze zur Weisheit Israels* by Müller, Hans-Peter. In: *OTA* 16:423 Je 1993
Review of: *Micah-Malachi* by Kaiser, Walter C. In: *OTA* 16:433 Je 1993
Review of: *New horizons in hermeneutics: the theory and practice of transforming Biblical readings* by Thiselton, Anthony C. In: *OTA* 16:189 F 1993
Review of: *Old Testament story and faith: a literary and theological introduction* by Crenshaw, James L. In: *OTA* 15:480 O 1992
Review of: *Old Testament theology* by Brueggemann, Walter. In: *OTA* 16: 437 Je 1993
Review of: *Poetry and prophecy: the beginning of a literary tradition* by Kugel, James L. In: *OTA* 15:474 O 1992
Review of: *Prologue to history* by Seters, John Van. In: *OTA* 16:169 F 1993
Review of: *Psalms—Songs of Songs* by VanGemeren, William A, et al. In: *OTA* 16:166 F 1993
Review of: *Religionsgeschichte Israel in alttestamentlicher Zeit* by Albertz, Rainer. In: *OTA* 16:183 F 1993
Review of: *Religionsgeschichte Israels in alttestamentlicher Zeit* by Albertz, Rainer. In: *OTA* 16:434-435 Je 1993
Review of: *Sapientia Salomonis: Hieronymus' Exegese de Weisheitsbuches im Licht der Tradition* by Pock, Johann Ignaz. In: *OTA* 16:428 Je 1993
Review of: *Sources of the Pentateuch* by Campbell, Anthony F, and O'Brien, Mark A. In: *OTA* 16:415-416 Je 1993
Review of: *The Bible, violence, and the sacred* by Williams, James G. In: *OTA* 16:441 Je 1993
Review of: *The cosmic covenant* by Murray, Robert. In: *OTA* 15:514 O 1992
Review of: *The flowering of Old Testament theology* by Ollenburger, Ben C, et al, eds. In: *OTA* 15:515 O 1992
Review of: *The Garden of Eden and the hope of immortality* by Barr, James. In: *OTA* 16:436 Je 1993
Review of: *The Hebrew Bible, the Old Testament, and historical criticism* by Levenson, Jon D. In: *OTA* 16:409 Je 1993
Review of: *The origins of Biblical law: the Decalogues and the Book of the Covenant* by Carmichael, Calum M. In: *OTA* 16:185 F 1993
Review of: *The Pentateuch: an introduction to the first five Books of the Bible* by Blenkinsopp, Joseph. In: *OTA* 16:415 Je 1993
Review of: *The preacher sought to find pleasing words* by Schoors, Antoon. In: *OTA* 16:176-177 F 1993
Review of: *The sharpening of wisdom: Old Testament proverbs in translation* by Schneider, Théophile Robert. In: *OTA* 16:176 F 1993
Review of: *The women's Bible commentary* by Newsom, Carol A, and Ringe, Sharon H, eds. In: *OTA* 15:485 O 1992
Review of: *Theologie des Alten Testaments* by Preuss, Horst Dietrich. In: *OTA* 15:515 O 1992
Review of: *Through the ages in Palestinian archaeology* by Rast, Walter E. In: *OTA* 16:412 Je 1993
Review of: *What are the Targums?* by Grelot, Pierre. In: *OTA* 15:516 O 1992

Murphy, Séamus.
The Church in the post-socialist world. *Studies* 82:87-96 Spr 1993
"I don't support the IRA, but" semantic and psychological ambivalence. *Studies* 82:276-286 Aut 1993
What do we mean by consumerism? *Doctr Life* 43:294-300 My-Je 1993

Murphy, Thomas Austin, 1911-.
"A culture is dying": the timber crisis. *Origins* 22:765+ Ap 22 1993

Murphy, Virginia. *see* Surtz, Edward, jt ed

Murphy, Walter F.
Staggering toward the new Jerusalem of constitutional theory: a response to Ralph F Gaebler. *Amer J Juris* 37:337-357 1992

Murray, Douglas.
Vision and meditation in neoclassical English hymnody: notes toward sources and implications. *Listening* 28:105-117 Spr 1993

Murray, John C.
Review of: *Euthanasia: official statements from religious bodies and ecumenical organizations* by Melton, J Gordon. In: *JEcumen Stds* 29:262-263 Spr 1992
Review of: *Sex and family life: official statements from religious bodies and ecumenical organizations* by Melton, J Gordon. In: *JEcumen Stds* 29:262-263 Spr 1992

Murray, Paul.
The way of the void. *New Blckfrs* 74:116-130 Mr 1993

Murray, Pius.
"The challenge of peace" revisited. *Emmanuel* 99:314-317 Jl-Ag 1993

Murray, Robert.
J R R Tolkien and the art of the parable. *Month* 26:35-39 Ja 1993

Murrell, Kevin J.
Confidentiality. *Linacre* 60:75-80 Ag 1993

Murren, Philip J.
Employment issues. *CLawyer* 34 no 4:331-341 1993

Murrin, Linda.
Why one parish is home sweet home to teens. *USCath* 58:8 D 1993

Murrin, Michael.
Review of: *Political protest and prophecy under Henry VIII* by Jansen, Sharon L. In: *TheolStds* 54:389 Je 1993

Musiol, Jozef.
Reservation of the Eucharist in a religious house. *AFER* 34:115-121 Ap 1992

Musto, Ronald G.
Catholic peacemakers: a documentary history [VI]. New York: Garland Publishing, 1993. x, 818p ISBN 0-8153-0604-0 LC 92-42658
Review of: *La Cattura della fine: varizioni dell'escatologia in regime di cristianità* by Ruggieri, Giuseppe, ed. In: *CHist* 79:496-498 Jl 1993

Muto, Susan.
The spiritual journey: the way of Christian womanhood. *Word Sp* 15:95-104 1993

Myers, David.
Rocky mountain high. *Register* 69:1+ Ag 8 1993

Myers, Edith.
Some musings on marriage. *HPR* 94:47-51 O 1993

Myers, John, Bp.
Boosting vocations: time to refocus. *Register* 69:1+ O 10 1993
To reach full knowledge of the truth. *Origins* 22:593-601 F 11 1993

Myers, Kenneth A.
What's not in a name? *Crisis* 11:13-14 Je 1993

Myers, Nancy.
The time to act is now. *Register* 69:5 Ap 25 1993

Myers, Rawley.
The fearless monk. *HPR* 93:44-47 Mr 1993
Review of: *And so to God* by Zeller, Hubert Van. In: *HPR* 94:79 N 1993
Review of: *Co-workers of the truth: meditations for every day of the year* by Ratzinger, Joseph, Cardinal, 1927-. In: *HPR* 93:86-87 Ag-S 1993
Review of: *Discovering God: life's adventure* by Scott, John M. In: *HPR* 93:64-65 F 1993
Review of: *Edmund Campion* by Gardiner, Harold C. In: *HPR* 93:75 My 1993
Review of: *Saints of the Roman calendar* by Lodi, Enzo. In: *HPR* 94:76-77 N 1993

Myerscough, Angelita.
Review of: *Holy listening: the art of spiritual direction* by Guenther, Margaret. In: *RRel* 52:622-623 Jl-Ag 1993

N

Na'Aman, Nadav.
The pre-deuteronomistic story of King Saul and its historical significance. *CBQ* 54:638-658 O 1992

Nadeau, Jean-Guy.
Review of: *Temps et récit de Paul Ricoeur en débat* by Bouchindhomme, Christian, and Rochlitz, Rainer. In: *Laval Theol Phil* 49:149-155 F 1993

Naert, Émilienne.
Review of: *Philosophie de l'histoire: les promesses du temps* by Brun, Jean. In: *RPhil Louvain* 91:496-497 Ag 1993

Nagel, Eduard, and Palacios, Miguel.
La revista gottesdienst cuplió 25 años. *Notitiae* 29:304-306 My 1993

Nagler, N.
Review of: *Lexikon der Mission: Geschichte, Theologie, Ethnologie* by Rzepkowski, Horst. In: *Stimm Zeit* 210:863-864 D 1992

Nairn, Thomas A.
Review of: *Moral theology: challenges for the future* by Curran, Charles E, 1934-, ed. In: *New Theol Rev* 6:97-98 Ag 1993

Nakanose, Shigeyuki.
Josiah's passover: sociology and the liberating Bible. Maryknoll: Orbis Books, 1993. x, 192p ISBN 0-88344850-5 LC 93-18286

Nanney, Lisa.
Fetal-tissue "advances" threaten the unborn. *OSV* 81:23 F 7 1993

Napack, Mark Daniel.
Review of: *A Rabbi talks with Jesus* by Neusner, Jacob. In: *Spir Life* 39:181-182 Aut 1993

Narayanan, Vasudha. *see* Creel, Austin B, jt ed

Nardone, Richard M.
Review of: *The forms and orders of Western liturgy from the tenth to the eighteenth century* by Harper, John. In: *CHist* 79:304-305 Ap 1993

Nardoni, Enrique.
Charism in the early church since Rudolph Sohm: an ecumenical challenge. *TheolStds* 53:646-662 D 1992
The concept of charism in Paul. *CBQ* 55:68-80 Ja 1993
Review of: *From synagogue to church: public services and offices in the earliest Christian communities* by Burtchaell, James Tunstead. In: *TheolStds* 54:556-557 S 1993

Nash, James L.
A theological approach toward taxation. *Living Light* 29:27-37 Aut 1992

Nash, Kathleen.
"Let justice surge". *BibleT* 31:265-271 S 1993

Nash, Ronald H. *see* Belli, Humberto, jt auth

Natale, Maria Rosaria.
Review of: *Figures de la violence et de la modernité: essais sur la philosophie d'Éric Weil* by Kirscher, Gilbert. In: *RPhil Louvain* 90:590-592 N 1992
Review of: *Interprétations de Kant* by Weil, Cahiers Éric, III. In: *RPhil Louvain* 91:475-479 Ag 1993
La sagesse de l'histoire Jean-Baptiste Vico et la philosophie pratique. *RPhil Louvain* 91:249-258 My 1993

Nathan, Norman.
The universal waste basket; Bleak thought. *Spirit* 58:40 1993

Nau, Dale.
Publish and be damned: one practitioner's experience. *Jurist* 51 no 2:442-450 1991
Review of: *Le "divorce" du roi Henry VIII* by Bedouelle, Guy, and Gal, Patrick Le, eds. In: *Jurist* 51 no 2:519-520 1991
Review of: *The divorce tracts of Henry VIII* by Surtz, Edward, and Murphy, Virginia, eds. In: *Jurist* 51 no 2:517-519 1991

Naughton, Michael.
An essay on Jonathan Boswell's Community and the economy: the theory of public co-operation. *RSocEcon* 51:86-102 Spr 1993

Naughton, Michael. (cont'd)

Review of: *Community and the economy* by Boswell, Jonathan. In: *RSocEcon* 51:86-102 Spr 1993
Review of: *Reshaping work: the Cadbury experience* by Smith, Chris, et al. In: *RSocEcon* 50:339-341 Fall 1992
'They shall become one flesh'. *Sisters* 65:252-254 Jl 1993

Navarrete, Urbano.

Acta tribunalium S Sedis. *Periodica* 82 no 2:339-352 1993
De sensu clausulae dummodo non determinet voluntatem Can 1099. *Periodica* 81 no 3-4:469-493 1993
Review of: *Jurisprudencia matrimonial de los tribunales eclesiásticos españoles* by Acebal Luján, Juan L, and Aznar, Federico R. In: *Civilta* 144:98-99 Ja 2 1993

Navez, G.

Review of: *Charles de Foucauld: Cette chère dernière place* by Robert, A, ed. In: *NRT* 115:284 Mr-Ap 1993
Review of: *Icônes surprenantes de la Mère de Dieu* by Mathiot, J. In: *NRT* 115:155 Ja-F 1993
Review of: *Jacob ou la fraude* by Massenet, M. In: *NRT* 114:939 N-D 1992
Review of: *L'initiation chrétienne* by Fayol-Fricout, A, et al. In: *NRT* 114:905-906 N-D 1992
Review of: *La force du pardon* by Dupleix, A. In: *NRT* 115:136 Ja-F 1993
Review of: *Le pari éducatif* by Davin, J, and Petitclerc, J-M. In: *NRT* 115:118-119 Ja-F 1993
Review of: *Prier au Moyen Age* by Bériou, Nicole, et al, eds. In: *NRT* 115:126 Ja-F 1993
Review of: *Seigneur, qui es-tu?* by Estevez, J Medina, Bp. In: *NRT* 115:134-135 Ja-F 1993
Review of: *Teilhard de Chardin* by Carles, J, and Dupleix, A. In: *NRT* 115:284-285 Mr-Ap 1993

Navone, John.

Opera: the creative expression of Italy. *New Blckfrs* 74:400-407 S 1993
Scripture for Christian conversion. *New Blckfrs* 74:21-33 Ja 1993

Neal, Marianna Kane.

Review of: *Who told you that you were naked?* by Raub, John Jacob. In: *St Anth* 100:51-52 Ap 1993

Neale, Ann.

Aligning IDNs' financial interests with communities' best interests. *Health Prog* 74:14-15+ O 1993

Neckebrouck, Valeer.

Review of: *African Catholicism* by Hastings, Adrian, 1929-. In: *Louvain Stds* 18:191 Sum 1993
Review of: *African theology in its social context* by Bujo, Bénézet. In: *Eph Theol Lovan* 69:202-204 Ap 1993
Review of: *Afrikanische Theologie in ihrem gesellschaftlichen Kontext* by Bujo, Bénézet. In: *Eph Theol Lovan* 69:202-204 Ap 1993
Review of: *After patriarchy: feminist transformations of the world religions* by Cooey, Paula M, et al, eds. In: *Eph Theol Lovan* 69:204-205 Ap 1993
Review of: *Asian Christian spirituality: reclaiming traditions* by Fabella, Virginia, et al, eds. In: *Eph Theol Lovan* 69:208 Ap 1993
Review of: *Expanding the view: Gustavo Gutiérrez and the future of liberation theology* by Ellis, Marc E, and Maduro, Otto, eds. In: *Eph Theol Lovan* 78:181 Ap 1992
Review of: *Faces of Jesus in Africa* by Schreiter, Robert J, ed. In: *Eph Theol Lovan* 69:202 Ap 1993
Review of: *Liberation theology and its critics: toward an assessment* by McGovern, Arthur F. In: *Eph Theol Lovan* 69:205 Ap 1993
Review of: *Liberation theology: a documentary history* by Hennelly, Alfred T, ed. In: *Eph Theol Lovan* 78:181-182 Ap 1992
Review of: *Mission today: reflections from an Ignatian perspective* by Amaladoss, Michael. In: *Eph Theol Lovan* 69:202 Ap 1993
Review of: *Prayer in world religions* by Carmody, Denise Lardner. In: *Eph Theol Lovan* 78:182 Ap 1992
Review of: *Striving together: a way forward in Christian-Muslim relations* by Kimball, Charles. In: *Eph Theol Lovan* 78:182-183 Ap 1992
Review of: *The meaning of life at the edge of the third millennium* by Swidler, Leonard. In: *Eph Theol Lovan* 69:206 Ap 1993
Review of: *The will to arise: women, tradition and the Church in Africa* by Oduyoye, Mercy Amba, and Kanyoro, Musimbi R A, eds. In: *Eph Theol Lovan* 69:206-207 Ap 1993

Nedungatt, George.

The Eastern Code in English translation: errata corrige. *Jurist* 51 no 2:460-501 1991
Glossary of the main terms used in the code of canons of the Eastern churches. *Jurist* 51 no 2:451-459 1991

Needleman, Jacob. *see* Faivre, Antoine, jt ed

Neff, Blake J. *see* Ratcliff, Donald E, jt auth

Negro, Donato.

Anno propedeutico: vera novità del Concilio Vaticano II (commentary: *Pastores dabo vobis*). *Seminarium* 32:600-621 O-D 1992

Neill, John R W.

The Church of Ireland way. *Furrow* 44:283-287 My 1993

Neirnyck, F.

Review of: *Literary-critical approaches to the Bible* by Minor, Mark. In: *Eph Theol Lovan* 78:432-433 D 1992
Review of: *The Griesbach hypothesis and redaction criticism* by Johnson, Sherman E. In: *Eph Theol Lovan* 78:436-437 D 1992
Review of: *A bibliography of Greek New Testament manuscripts* by Elliott, J K. In: *Eph Theol Lovan* 78:161-162 Ap 1992
Review of: *De opkomst van de historische en literaire kritiek in de synoptische beschouwing van de evangeliën van Calvijn tot Griesbach* by Lang, Marijke Hélène de. In: *Eph Theol Lovan* 69:174-175 Ap 1993
Review of: *Gospels and tradition* by Stein, Robert H. In: *Eph Theol Lovan* 78:434-435 D 1992

Neirynck, F. (cont'd)

Review of: *Jewish eschatology, early Christian Christology and the testaments of the Twelve Patriarchs* by Jonge, Marinus de. In: *Eph Theol Lovan* 78:165-166 Ap 1992
Review of: *Johannesevangelium und Johannesbriefe* by Schmithals, Walter. In: *Eph Theol Lovan* 78:166-168 Ap 1992
Review of: *John among the gospels* by Smith, Dwight Moody. In: *Eph Theol Lovan* 78:442-444 D 1992
Review of: *Le Diatessaron: de Tatien à Justin* by Boismard, M É. In: *Eph Theol Lovan* 69:186-188 Ap 1993
Review of: *Let the reader understand* by Fowler, Robert M. In: *Eph Theol Lovan* 69:181-183 Ap 1993
Review of: *Mark: a commentary on his apology for the Cross* by Gundry, Robert H. In: *Eph Theol Lovan* 69:183-186 Ap 1993
Review of: *Q-Thomas reader* by Kloppenborg, John S, and Meyer, Marvin W, et al. In: *Eph Theol Lovan* 69:175-177 Ap 1993
Review of: *Redating Matthew, Mark and Luke* by Wenham, John William. In: *Eph Theol Lovan* 69:173-174 Ap 1993
Review of: *Sinossi dei quattro vangeli greco-italiano* by Poppi, Angelico. In: *Eph Theol Lovan* 78:437-439 D 1992
Review of: *Studia Neotestamentica* by Sabbe, Maurits. In: *Eph Theol Lovan* 78:162-165 Ap 1992
Review of: *The Anchor Bible dictionary* by Freedman, David Noel, ed. In: *Eph Theol Lovan* 78:428-432 D 1992
Review of: *The Bible and modern literary criticism* by Powell, Mark Allan. In: *Eph Theol Lovan* 78:432-433 D 1992
Review of: *The Catholic study Bible* by Senior, Donald, ed. In: *Eph Theol Lovan* 78:426 D 1992
Review of: *The First Gospel: an introduction to Q* by Jacobson, Arland Dean. In: *Eph Theol Lovan* 69:177-179 Ap 1993
Review of: *The First Gospel* by Riley, Harold. In: *Eph Theol Lovan* 69:179-180 Ap 1993
Review of: *The Gospel of Luke* by Johnson, Luke Timothy, 1943-. In: *Eph Theol Lovan* 78:441-442 D 1992
Review of: *The Gospel of Matthew* by Harrington, Daniel J. In: *Eph Theol Lovan* 78:439-441 D 1992
Review of: *The influence of the Gospel of Saint Matthew on Christian literature before Saint Irenaeus* by Massaux, Édouard. In: *Eph Theol Lovan* 69:172-173 Ap 1993
Review of: *The New Jerome Bible handbook* by Brown, Raymond Edward, et al, eds. In: *Eph Theol Lovan* 78:426-428 D 1992
Review of: *The problems of New Testament Gospel origins* by Deardorf, James W. In: *Eph Theol Lovan* 69:180-181 Ap 1993
Review of: *The Synoptic problem* by Stein, Robert H. In: *Eph Theol Lovan* 78:435-436 D 1992
Review of: *Un évangile pré-johannique; vol I: Jean 1,1-2,12* by Boismard, M É, and Lamouille, A. In: *Eph Theol Lovan* 69:189-192 Ap 1993

Nelson, Julie A.

Gender and economic ideologies. *RSocEcon* 51:287-301 Aut 1993

Nelson, Lance E.

Review of: *Gandhi on Christianity* by Ellsberg, Robert, ed. In: *JEcumen Stds* 29:283-284 Spr 1992

Nelson, Richard D.

Raising up a faithful priest. Louisville, Kentucky: John Knox Press, 1993. 208p ISBN 0-664-25347-3
Review of: *Prophetie im Streit vor dem Untergang Judas* by Hardmeier, Christof. In: *CBQ* 55:337-338 Ap 1993

Nemer, Lawrence.

Review of: *Albert Schweitzer: letters, 1905-1965* by Bähr, Hans Walter, ed. In: *CHist* 79:550-551 Jl 1993
Review of: *Christian uniqueness reconsidered* by D'Costa, Gavin, ed. In: *Pacifica* 6:225-227 Je 1993

Nemoianu, Virgil, 1940-.

The beauty of Balthasar. *Crisis* 11:42-46 Ap 1993

Neri, Michael Charles.

Review of: *Prominent visitors to the California missions (1786-1842)* by Weber, Francis J, comp. In: *CHist* 79:132-133 Ja 1993

Neschke-Hentschke, Ada.

Une nouvelle étude surle platonisme antique. *RPhil Louvain* 91:459-465 Ag 1993

Neuberger, Anne E.

Lent is a time for giving. *ReligTJ* 27:34 F 1993
Looking for God everywhere. *ReligTJ* 26:32-33 Ja 1993
Review of: *A new coat for Anna* by Ziefert, Harriet. In: *ReligTJ* 27:34 F 1993
Review of: *Arnie and the new kid* by Carlson, Nancy. In: *ReligTJ* 27:58 S 1993
Review of: *Augsburg Story Bible* by Aaseng, Rolf R. In: *ReligTJ* 27:17 Ap-My 1993
Review of: *Best friends for Frances* by Hoban, Russell, and Hoban, Lillian. In: *ReligTJ* 27:58-59 S 1993
Review of: *Dogger* by Hughes, Shirley. In: *ReligTJ* 27:34 F 1993
Review of: *Grandfather twilight* by Berger, Barbara Helen. In: *ReligTJ* 27:11 Mr 1993
Review of: *In dawn* by Shulevitz, Uri. In: *ReligTJ* 27:11 Mr 1993
Review of: *Jamaica tag-along* by Havill, Juanita. In: *ReligTJ* 27:58 S 1993
Review of: *Matthew and Tilly* by Jones, Rebecca C. In: *ReligTJ* 27:58 S 1993
Review of: *Old turtle* by Wood, Douglas. In: *ReligTJ* 26:32-33 Ja 1993
Review of: *On the day you were born* by Fraisers, Debra. In: *ReligTJ* 26:32 Ja 1993
Review of: *One of three* by Johnson, Angela, and Soman, David. In: *ReligTJ* 27:58 S 1993
Review of: *Owl moon* by Yolen, Jane. In: *ReligTJ* 27:11 Mr 1993
Review of: *Sam who never forgets* by Rice, Eva. In: *ReligTJ* 26:33 Ja 1993
Review of: *The beginner's Bible: timeless children's stories* by Henley, Karyn. In: *ReligTJ* 27:16 Ap-My 1993
Review of: *The Children's Bible in 165 stories* by Batchelor, Mary. In: *ReligTJ* 27:16 Ap-My 1993
Review of: *The hundred dresses* by Estes, Eleanor. In: *ReligTJ* 27:59 S 1993

Neuberger, Anne E. *(cont'd)*
Review of: *The legend of the Bluebonnet, an old tale of Texas* by DePaola, Tomie. In: *ReligTJ* 27:34 F 1993
Review of: *Tomie dePaola's book of Bible stories* by Paola, Tomie de. In: *ReligTJ* 27:16-17 Ap-My 1993
Review of: *When the sun rose* by Berger, Barbara Helen. In: *ReligTJ* 27:11 Mr 1993
Review of: *Where are you, Ernest and Celestine?* by Vincent, Gabrielle. In: *ReligTJ* 26:33 Ja 1993
We are a patchwork quilt. *ReligTJ* 27:36-37 O 1993
Which Bible is best? *ReligTJ* 27:16-17 Ap-My 1993

Neufeld, Dietmar.
Review of: *First, second, and third John* by Smith, Dwight Moody. In: *CBQ* 55:398-399 Ap 1993

Neuhaus, Richard John, 1936-, ed.
Augustine today. Grand Rapids: Eerdmans, 1993. 168p ISBN 0-8028-0216-8

Neuman, Matthias.
Praying in times of stress. *Living Prayer* 26:29-31 S-O 1993

Neuner, Peter.
Ein katholischer Vorschlag zur Eucharistiegemeinschaft. *Stimm Zeit* 211:443-450 Jl 1993

Neusner, Jacob.
A rabbi talks with Jesus: an intermillennial interfaith exchange. New York: Doubleday, 1993. x, 154p ISBN 0-385-42466-31 LC xs92-16395

Neustadt, Richard, 1919-.
Bill Clinton's bad start. *Tablet* 247:776+ Je 19 1993

Neutzling, Inácio.
O Mercosul e a integração Latino-Americana. *REB* 53:374-389 Je 1993

Neville, Robert Cummings, 1939-.
World community and religion. *JEcumen Stds* 29:368-382 Sum-Aut 1992

Newbigin, Lesslie.
Religious pluralism: a missiological approach. *StudiaM* 42:227-244 1993
Review of: *Ecumenism in transition* by Raiser, Konrad. In: *OChr* 29 no 3: 269-275 1993

Newman, Barbara.
Review of: *Elisabeth of Schönau: a twelfth-century visionary* by Clark, Anne L. In: *CHist* 79:96-98 Ja 1993

Newman, Jay.
Review of: *Jews and Christians* by Neusner, Jacob. In: *Can Cath Rev* 11:29-30 N 1993

Newmayr, George.
Review of: *"From cottage to work station: the family's search for social harmony in the industrial age"* by Carlson, Allan. In: *Register* 69:5 Jl 25 1993

Newton, Dennis.
A family business: management in religious congregations. *RRel* 52:610-615 Jl-Ag 1993

Neyreu, Jerome H.
Review of: *The Romans debate* by Donfried, Karl P, ed. In: *Bib Th Bul* 23: 87-88 Sum 1993
Review of: *Jude and the relatives of Jesus in the Early Church* by Bauckham, Richard. In: *CBQ* 55:139-140 Ja 1993
Review of: *The Corinthian women prophets: a reconstruction through Paul's rhetoric* by Wire, Antoinette Clark. In: *Horizons (CTS)* 19:311 Fall 1992
Review of: *What are the Gospels?* by Burridge, Richard A. In: *CBQ* 55:361-363 Ap 1993

Ngundu, Mick.
Review of: *Le mariage: droit canonique et coutumes africaines* by Antoine, Philippe. In: *Stud Can* 27 no 1:272-275 1993

Nicholas of Cusa, 1401-1464.
Toward a new Council of Florence. Washington, DC: Schiller Institute, 1993. x, 577p ISBN 0-9621095-8-4 LC 92-85238

Nicholl, Donald.
The ascent of love. *Tablet* 247:845-846 Jl 3 1993
My dream for the Pope. *Tablet* 247:230 F 20 1993
Rich man, poor man. *Tablet* 247:540-541 My 1 1993
Wrestling with truth. *Tablet* 247:1291-1292 O 9 1993

Nichols, Aidan.
Adrienne von Speyr and the mystery of the atonement. *New Blckfrs* 73:542-553 N 1992
On baptizing the visual arts: a friar's meditation on art. *New Blckfrs* 74:74-84 F 1993

Nichols, Bridget.
Review of: *The identity of Anglican worship* by Stevenson, Kenneth W, and Spinks, Bryan, eds. In: *Heythrop* 34:437 O 1993

Nichols, John A.
Cistercian monastic women: an introduction to Hidden Springs. *Cist Stud* 28:59-72 1993
Review of: *The medieval woman* by Ennen, Edith. In: *CHist* 79:511-512 Jl 1993

Nichols, Kevin.
The Catechism of the Catholic Church: some notes towards. *Living Light* 29: 7-12 Sum 1993

Nichols, Larry A. *see* Mather, George A, jt auth

Nicholson, Dorothy. *see* Jeff, Gordon, jt auth

Nickoloff, James B.
Church of the poor: the ecclesiology of Gustavo Gutiérrez. *TheolStds* 54:512-535 S 1993
Review of: *America against itself: moral vision and the public order* by Neuhaus, Richard John, 1936-. In: *America* 168:21-22 Ap 3 1993
Review of: *The God of life* by Gutiérrez, Gustavo. In: *Horizons (CTS)* 20: 157-158 Spr 1993

Nickoloff, James B. *(cont'd)*
Review of: *The living tradition of Catholic moral theology* by Curran, Charles E, 1934-. In: *America* 168:21-22 Ap 3 1993

Nicolòsi, Joseph.
Therapist says gay ministries subvert doctrine [interview by T Ryland, repr fr *San Diego News Notes*]. *Nat Cath Rep* 29:16-17 My 7 1993

Nida, Eugene A. *see* Waard, Jan de, jt auth

Niditch, B Z.
Sandor Woeres; Solidarity; Boston; St Petersburg; Summer house, Winter house; Katyn Forest; Prague; Gulag; Budapest; 1944; Lenin; Vilnius. *Spirit* 57:26-38 Spr-Sum 1993
To be continued; Kid's day; Murphy's law; Writer's block. *Spirit* 58:36-39 1993

Niebuhr, H Richard.
Radical monotheism and western culture: with supplemental essays. Louisville, Kentucky: John Knox Press, 1993. 112p ISBN 502-569-5043

Nielsen, Kai.
What is alive and what is dead in Marx and Marxism a la Elster. *Laval Theol Phil* 49:277-293 Je 1993

Niemeyer, Gerhart.
The Burke-Kirk phenomenon. *Crisis* 11:26 O 1993

Nigro, Samuel A.
The denaturalization of the profession of psychiatry. *SocJust* 84:104-106 Jl-Ag 1993
Review of: *Reparative therapy of male homosexuality* by Nicolosi, Joseph. In: *SocJust* 84:157 S-O 1993

Nijem, Fred.
From reform to renewal. *Mod Lit* 20:6-8 My 1993

Nijenhuis, John.
Review of: *Accents of God: selections from the World's Sacred Scriptures* by Rohani, M K, ed. In: *JEcumen Stds* 29:494-495 Sum-Aut 1992
Review of: *The prophecies of Jesus* by Sours, Michael. In: *JEcumen Stds* 29: 494-495 Sum-Aut 1992

Nilson, Jon.
A glitch or a gulf? Canterbury, Rome and reunion. *Comm* 120:6-8 F 26 1993

Nipkow, Karl, et al. *see* Fowler, James W, jt auth

Nitschke, Beverley A.
By water and the spirit—a United Methodist understanding of Baptism: a Lutheran response. *Ecumen Trends* 22:3-7 Ja 1993

Nkulikiyumukiza, Augustin.
Changements culturels et lieux d'expériences de la foi au Rwanda. *Lumen* 48: 195-206 Je 1993

Noble, Thomas F X.
Review of: *Province and empire: Brittany and the Carolingians* by Smith, Julia M H. In: *CHist* 79:314-315 Ap 1993

Noble, Valerie.
Women at the crossroads. *Priests & People* 6:312-317 Ag-S 1992

Noè, Virgilio, Cardinal.
Resonate Christ with Roman heart. *OR(Eng)* 1300:6 Jl 21 1993

Noemi Callejas, Juan.
Interrogantes sobre "Algunas cuestiones actuales de escatología". *Teol Vida* 33 no 3-4:225-235 1992
Lobre la dimensión política de la escatología cristiana; una aproximación teológico-fundamental. *Teol Vida* 34 no 1-2:145-152 1993

Noffsinger, John W.
Review of: *Dark night journey* by Cronk, Sandra. In: *Spir Life* 39:50-51 Spr 1993
Review of: *The Rule of Benedict: insights for the ages* by Chittister, Joan D. In: *New Oxford Rev* 60:32 Jl-Ag 1993

Nolan, Herman.
Father Faber and the Legion's concluding prayer [fr *Maria Legionis* v 34, no 2, 1991]. *ChrWorld* 37:372-375 N-D 1992

Nolan, Margaret.
Getting into credit together. *Priests & People* 7:178-180 My 1993

Nolan, Michael.
Church, state and theology in the European Community. *Studies* 82:148-159 Sum 1993

Noll, Mark A.
Review of: *Wesleyan University, 1831-1910* by Potts, David B. In: *CrossCurr* 43:272-273 Sum 1993

Noone, Timothy B.
Evidence for the use of Adam of Buckfield's writings at Paris: a note on New Haven, Yale University, Historical-Medical Library 12. *Med Stud* 54: 308-316 1992
Review of: *Quodlibetal questions* by William of Ockham, 1280?-1349?. In: *Thomist* 57:337-341 Ap 1993

Norman, Rose.
The representationj of religious experience in nineteenth-century American women's autobiography. *Listening* 28:128-140 Spr 1993

Normanly, Elizabeth.
Beyond seven sacraments. *RRel* 52:741-744 S-O 1993

Normile, Patti.
Secular Franciscans: a vibrant part of the Franciscan family. *St Anth* 101:36-41 Je 1993
Visiting the sick: a guide for parish ministers. Cincinatti: St Anthony Press, 1992. x, 139p ISBN 0-86716-1507

Norris, Frederick W.
The apostolic faith: Protestants and Roman Catholics. Minnesota: The Liturgical Press, 1992. x, 178p ISBN 0-8146-5029-5 LC 92-19536
Review of: *Hindus and Christians: a century of Protestant ecumenical thought* by Ariarajah, S Wesley. In: *Ecumen Trends* 22:10-13 Ap 1993
Review of: *The Bible and people of other faiths* by Ariarajah, S Wesley. In: *Ecumen Trends* 22:10-13 Ap 1993

Norris, Kathleen.
Emily Dickinson's lectio: wicked as I am, I read my Bible sometimes. *Sisters* 65:104-108 Mr 1993

Norris, Russell B., Jr.
Review of: *The World Council of Churches and politics, 1975-1986* by Vermaat, J A Emerson. In: *JEcumen Stds* 29:483 Sum-Aut 1992

Norris, Tom.
Review of: *John Henry Newman sermons 1824-1843, vol I: sermons on the liturgy and sacraments and on Christ the mediator* by Murray, Placid, ed. In: *Furrow* 44:192-193 Mr 1993
Review of: *John Henry Newman* by Withey, Donald A. In: *Furrow* 44:192-193 Mr 1993

North, Robert.
Review of: *I trattati nel mondo antico: forma, ideologia, funzione* by Canfora, Luciano, et al, eds. In: *CBQ* 55:192-193 Ja 1993

Northcott, Michael S.
New Age rites: the recovery of ritual. *Way* 33:189-198 Jl 1993
New World Order or new world enemies? *New Blckfrs* 74:316-327 Je 1993

Northcraft, Michael S.
Review of: *Visiting the sick* by Normile, Patti. In: *Mod Lit* 20:40 F 1993

Norweb, Mary Joseph.
The Carmelites: the first women religious in the original thirteen states. *Word Sp* 14:12-22 1992

Notebaart, James.
The third Sunday of Advent. *Liturgy* 11:5-8 Sum 1993

Nothomb, Dominique.
Le mariage en Afrique. *NRT* 114:852-869 N-D 1992

Nouwen, Henri Josef Machiel, 1932-.
Broken [excerpt fr *The life of the beloved*]. *Living Prayer* 26:3-7 Mr-Ap 1993
Finding a new way to get a glimpse of God. *New Oxford Rev* 60:6-8+ Jl-Ag 1993
Finding the trapeze artist in the priest. *New Oxford Rev* 60:8-14 Je 1993

Novak, David, 1941-.
Buber and Tillich. *JEcumen Stds* 29:159-174 Spr 1992

Novak, Francis A.
Pennies for heaven. *OSV* 82:12 Je 20 1993

Novak, Michael, 1933-.
Abandoned in a toxic culture: how we failed the new generation. *Crisis* 10:15-19 D 1992
An aborted presidency. *Crisis* 11:2-6 Mr 1993
After 26 years: Murray's public argument. *Crisis* 11:4-10 My 1993
The Catholic ethic and the spirit of capitalism. New York: Macmillan International, 1993. x, 334p ISBN 0-02923-235-x LC 92-32151
A Council betrayed. *Crisis* 11:6-7 O 1993
The creative person [presented as a paper at Conference on Wealth Creation in London, England, in July 1991]. *Can Cath Rev* 11:14-18 Je 20 1993
The crisis of the welfare state. *Crisis* 11:4-7 Jl-Ag 1993
Dullness of error, splendor of truth. *Crisis* 11:4-6+ S 1993
The lesson of Lent. *Crisis* 11:4-7 Ap 1993
Murder in Pensacola. *Crisis* 11:7-8 Ap 1993
Review of: *Bangladesh: reflections on the water* by Novak, James. In: *Crisis* 11:7 O 1993
Saint Thomas More. *Crisis* 11:5-10 Je 1993

Novitsky, Anthony W.
Review of: *Der absolutheitsanspruch des Christentums* by Bernhardt, Reinhold. In: *JEcumen Stds* 29:281-282 Spr 1992

Nowell, Irene.
How to pray the Psalms [interview by A Winter, condensed fr *Praying My-Je* 1993]. *CDgst* 57:121-126 O 1993
Review of: *'Now choose life': conversion as the way to life* by Barry, William A. In: *Cist Stud* 28 no 2:[42]-[43] 1993
Review of: *Mary in the mystery of the covenant* by Potterie, Ignace de la. In: *Worship* 67:286-287 My 1993
Review of: *The Gospel according to Mary* by Winter, Miriam Therese. In: *Sisters* 65:310-311 Jl 1993
Review of: *The revelatory text: interpreting the New Testament as sacred scripture* by Schneiders, Sandra M. In: *Worship* 67:281-282 My 1993

Nuechterlein, Anne Marie.
Families of alcoholics: a guide to healing and recovery. Minneapolis: Augsburg, 1993. x, 140p ISBN 0-80662-615-1 LC 92-19156

Nunes, Danillo.
Judas, betrayer or betrayed? New York: Vantage Press, 1992. x, 319p ISBN 0-533-10065-8 LC 91-912232

Nuth, Joan M.
Review of: *Christ, our Mother of mercy: divine mercy and compassion in the theology of the Shewings of Julian of Norwich* by Palliser, Margaret Ann. In: *TheolStds* 54:565-567 S 1993
Two medieval soteriologies: Anselm of Canterbury and Julian of Norwich. *TheolStds* 53:611-645 D 1992

Nutt, Kathleen.
Review of: *Idee und Weltwille: Schopenhauer als Kritiker Hegels* by Schmidt, Alfred. In: *IJPS* 1:160-162 Mr 1993

Nuttgens, Patrick, 1930-.
Review of: *Britain from the air* by Hawkes, Jason, and Struthers, Jane. In: *Tablet* 247:861 Jl 3 1993
Review of: *Cambridge architecture* by Rawle, Tim. In: *Tablet* 247:861 Jl 3 1993
Review of: *Frank Lloyd Wright* by Secrest, Meryle. In: *Tablet* 247:247-248 F 20 1993
University challenge. *Tablet* 247:783-784 Je 19 1993

Nuzzi, Ronald J.
Review of: *Are all Christians ministers?* by Collins, John N. In: *Nat Cath Rep* 29:15 Ap 23 1993
Review of: *Here comes everybody! stories of church* by Unsworth, Tim. In: *Nat Cath Rep* 30:29 N 19 1993

Nuzzi, Ronald J. *(cont'd)*
Review of: *Ministry in the Church* by Bernier, Paul. In: *Nat Cath Rep* 29:15 Ap 23 1993

Nwagwu, Gerard M.
Challenges facing women religious in the evangelization of Africa. *AFER* 34:146-157 Je 1992
Religious life in Africa today. *AFER* 35:222-239 Ag 1993
Religious life in Nigeria today. *RRel* 52:259-274 Mr-Ap 1993

Nwatu, Felix.
Africa and the return of priestcraft. *AFER* 35:240-251 Ag 1993

Nygren, David J.
Religious-leadership competencies. *RRel* 52:390-417 My-Je 1993

Nygren, David J, and Ukeritis, Miriam D.
The religious life futures project: executive summary. *RRel* 52:6-55 Ja-F 1993
Religious life: a time for assessing mission. *Health Prog* 74:55 Jl-Ag 1993

O

O'Boyle, Patrick J.
The messenger. *Liguorian* 81:24-25 Ag 1993

O'Brien, Christine.
Because we have children—a mother's reflection [repr fr *The companion magazine*]. *Furrow* 43:663-667 D 1992

O'Brien, David J, 1938-.
American culture key to understanding lay shifts. *Nat Cath Rep* 29:30-31 O 8 1993
Catholic evangelization and American culture. *US Cath Hist* 11:49-59 Spr 1993
The Catholic moment (address at the National Center for the Laity, 11-1-92, Chicago). *ACHSR* 103:1-10 Aut 1992
Review of: *Isaac T Hecker: the diary: Romantic religion in ante-bellum America* by Farina, John, ed. In: *CHist* 79:133-134 Ja 1993

O'Brien, David J, 1938-, and Buckley, Michael J, 1931-.
A collegiate conversation. *America* 169:18-23 S 11 1993

O'Brien, Dennis.
The Catechism [commentary]. *Comm* 120:15-16 My 7 1993
Review of: *Anatomy of love* by Fisher, Helen E. In: *Comm* 120:24-26 F 26 1993
Review of: *Moral imagination* by Johnson, Mark. In: *Comm* 120:26-27 O 22 1993
Review of: *Moral sense* by Wilson, James A. In: *Comm* 120:26-27 O 22 1993
Review of: *The education of an American Catholic* by Beeching, Paul Q. In: *Comm* 120:21+ S 10 1993

O'Brien, Edward C.
Review of: *The spiritual exercises of Saint Ignatius: a translation and commentary* by Ganss, George E. In: *RRel* 52:473-474 My-Je 1993

O'Brien, Ellen.
The adventures of Sister Maurina [condensed fr *The Philadelphia Inquirer* Ap 11 1993]. *CDgst* 57:44-49 Ag 1993

O'Brien, Joanne. *see* Khalkid, Fazlun, jt ed

O'Brien, Julia M.
Review of: *A historical-critical study of the Book of Zephaniah* by Zvi, Ehud Ben. In: *CBQ* 55:321-322 Ap 1993
Review of: *Countertraditions in the Bible* by Pardes, Ilana. In: *OTA* 16:411-412 Je 1993
Review of: *Ezekiel 18 and the rhetoric of moral discourse* by Matties, Gordon H. In: *CBQ* 55:121-122 Ja 1993
Review of: *Structure and the Book of Zechariah* by Butterworth, Mike. In: *OTA* 16:434 Je 1993

O'Brien, Mark A. *see* Campbell, Anthony F, jt auth

O'Brien, Niall.
Island of tears, island of hope: living the gospel in a revolutionary situation. Maryknoll: Orbis, 1993. x, 234p ISBN 0-88344-927-7 LC 73-23776

O'Brien, Patricia.
Review of: *Redating Matthew, Mark and Luke* by Wenham, John William. In: *HPR* 93:75-76 Ap 1993
There is a season. *HPR* 93:58-61 Mr 1993

O'Brien, Stephen.
Review of: *Catholic school education in the United States* by Grant, Mary C, and Hunt, Thomas C. In: *Momentum* 24:79-80 S-O 1993

O'Brien, Thomas J.
People will sing at funeral vigils and committals. *Past Mus* 17:39-40 Ap-My 1993

O'Cathain, Detta.
Faith in the world of business. *Priests & People* 7:186-190 My 1993

O'Collins, Gerald, 1931-.
All loves excelling. *Tablet* 246:1606 D 19-26 1992
Good News and old nonsense. *Tablet* 247:469 Ap 10-17 1993
A Gospel for the unemployed. *Tablet* 247:1182 S 18 1993
The new best-sellers: resurrection skeptics [interview by Desmond O'Grady]. *OSV* 81:5 Ap 11 1993
Review of: *Born before all time* by Kuschel, Karl-Josef. In: *Tablet* 247:1045 Ag 14 1993
Review of: *Credo: the Apostles' Creed explained for today* by Kung, Hans, 1928-. In: *Tablet* 247:722-723 Je 5 1993
Review of: *Foundations of theological study: a sourcebook* by Viladesau, Richard, and Massa, Mark, eds. In: *Gregorianum* 74 No 1:165-166 1993
Review of: *Lessico di teologia sistematica* by Beinert, Wolfgang, and Gianni, Francesconi. In: *Civilta* 143:430 N 21 1992
Review of: *The Anchor Bible dictionary* by Freedman, David Noel, ed. In: *Gregorianum* 74 no 3:563-565 1993
Review of: *The Christlike God* by Taylor, John V, Bp. In: *Tablet* 247:1045 Ag 14 1993

O'Collins, Gerald, 1931-. *(cont'd)*
Review of: *The use of memory* by Burns, Tom G. In: *Comm* 120:20-21 My 21 1993
Review of: *Who was Jesus?* by Wright, Nicholas Thomas. In: *Tablet* 247:245 F 20 1993 *see* *Moore, Sebastian, jt auth

O'Collins, Gerald, 1931-, and Marconi, Gilberto, eds.
Luke and Acts. New York: Paulist Press, 1993. x, 295p ISBN 0-8091-3360-1 LC 92-35226

O'Connell, David, 1940-.
François Mauriac's "Le cahier noir". *Comm* 120:22-23 Ap 23 1993
Review of: *The apprentice writer* by Green, Julian. In: *Comm* 120:26-27 S 24 1993
Review of: *The green paradise: autobiography, volume 1 (1900-1916)* by Green, Julian. In: *Comm* 120:26-27 S 24 1993

O'Connell, Gerard.
Bombings seen as plot to halt regeneration. *Tablet* 247:991 Jl 31 1993
Few Orthodox likely to attend prayers for peace. *Tablet* 247:54-55 Ja 9 1993
Patriarch Alexis criticises Rome. *Tablet* 247:316 Mr 6 1993
Pope gives thanks for peace accord, but foresees hard road. *Tablet* 247:1203 S 18 1993
A powerhouse of prayer for peace in Europe. *Tablet* 247:83 Ja 16 1993
Rights and wrongs of intervention. *Tablet* 246:1629 D 19-26 1992
Rome prepares to launch encyclical. *Tablet* 247:1270 O 2 1993

O'Connell, Irene.
Legal anthropology, Australian, Aborigines and natural law. *Amer J Juris* 37:243-258 1992

O'Connell, James.
God and being: the paradox of presence and absence. *Month* 26:188-193 My 1993
Ourselves and others: brokerage, reconciliation and process. *Month* 26:355-360 S-O 1993
Review of: *Peace is a process* by Bailey, Sydney D. In: *Tablet* 247:1235 S 25 1993
The sources of morality: function, conformity and aesthetics. *Heythrop* 34:160-170 Ap 1993

O'Connell, Kevin G. *see* Dahlberg, Bruce T, jt auth

O'Connell, Patricia A.
Review of: *From cradle to grave: the human face of poverty in America* by Freedman, Jonathan. In: *Comm* 120:35-36 N 5 1993

O'Connell, Patrick.
Review of: *The springs of contemplation* by Merton, Thomas, 1915-1968. In: *St Anth* 101:48-51 Je 1993
Review of: *Unfaithful angels: how social work abandoned its mission* by Specht, Harry, and Courtney, Mark E. In: *Comm* 120:35-36 N 5 1993
Worth pondering [commentary on Thomas Merton]. *Living Prayer* 26:11-12 N-D 1993
Worth pondering. *Living Prayer* 26:15-16 Ja-F 1993
Worth pondering. *Living Prayer* 26:14-15 Mr-Ap 1993
Worth pondering. *Living Prayer* 26:13-14 My-Je 1993
Worth pondering. *Living Prayer* 26:14-15 Jl-Ag 1993
Worth pondering. *Living Prayer* 26:11-12 S-O 1993

O'Connell, Robert J.
Review of: *Essays on the philosophy of Socrates* by Benson, Hugh H, ed. In: *IPQ* 33:366-368 S 1993

O'Connell, Timothy E.
Reconciliation renewal: healing for today's church. *Chicago Stud* 32:114-126 Ag 1993

O'Connell-Cahill, Catherine.
Anne-Marie Javouhey. *Salt* 13:31 Je 1993
Ida B Wells. *Salt* 13:31 Jl-Ag 1993
A look at holy role models: John Corridan, S.J. *Salt* 13:47 N-D 1993
Saint Birgitta. *Salt* 13:31 Ja 1993
Saint Frances of Rome. *Salt* 13:31 My 1993
Saint Moses the Black. *Salt* 13:31 Ap 1993

O'Connor, Bernard.
Like bread, their voices rise! Global women challenge the Church. Notre Dame: Ave Maria Press, 1993. 204p ISBN 0-87793-509-2 LC 93-77734

O'Connor, Brian.
Review of: *Freedom, truth and history: an introduction to Hegel's philosophy* by Houlgate, Stephen. In: *IJPS* 1:152-154 Mr 1993

O'Connor, David F.
Some ruminations on the identity of religious. *RRel* 52:418-427 My-Je 1993

O'Connor, Edward D.
Naturalistic humanism. *HPR* 93:19-26 Ap 1993

O'Connor, Francine M.
Easter is more than baskets and bunnies. *Liguorian* 81:38-42 Ap 1993

O'Connor, Jerome Murphy.
St Paul: promoter of the ministry of women. *Priests & People* 6:307-311 Ag-S 1992

O'Connor, John, Cardinal, and Weakland, Rembert G, Abp, 1927-.
The Church and women. *Origins* 22:532-536 Ja 14 1993

O'Connor, Kathleen M.
Review of: *Jahwe—ein patriarchaler Gott? Traditionelles Gottesbild und feministische Theologie* by Gerstenberger, Erhard S. In: *CBQ* 55:335-336 Ap 1993
Review of: *Klagender Gott—klagende Menschen* by Bak, Dong Hyun. In: *OTA* 16:432 Je 1993

O'Connor, Michael.
The Holy Spirit and the church in Catholic theology: a study in the ecclesiology of J-M R Tillard. *OChr* 28 no 4:331-341 1992

O'Connor, Thomas.
Review of: *Paul VI* by Hebblethwaite, Peter, 1930-. In: *Furrow* 44:383-385 Je 1993

O'Connor, Tom.
Reform of local government. *Studies* 82:323-332 Aut 1993
Something's wrong. *New Cov* 22:26-28 F 1993

O'Donnell, Christopher.
Introducing the new catechism. *Doctr Life* 43:201-207 Ap 1993

O'Donnell, John J.
Review of: *How to read Karl Barth: the shape of his theology* by Hunsinger, George. In: *Gregorianum* 74 no 3:582-583 1993
Review of: *Society and spirit: a trinitarian cosmology* by Bracken, Joseph A. In: *Gregorianum* 74 No 1:161-162 1993
Review of: *The Christian vision of humanity. Basic Christian anthropology* by Sachs, John R. In: *Gregorianum* 74 no 2:372-373 1993
Review of: *The craft of theology* by Dulles, Avery Robert, 1918-. In: *Gregorianum* 74 no 2:373-374 1993
Review of: *The glory of the Lord, a theological aesthetics, VI: theology: the Old Covenant* by Balthasar, Hans Urs Von, 1905-1988. In: *New Blckfrs* 73:573-574 N 1992
Review of: *The promise of Trinitarian theology* by Gunton, Colin E. In: *Heythrop* 34:189-190 Ap 1993

O'Donnell, Robert J.
The Church learning and the Church teaching: Vatican II and the liberal tradition of religious freedom. *JEcumen Stds* 29:399-417 Sum-Aut 1992
John Paul II on evangelization of culture in the United States. *Living Light* 30:9-22 Aut 1993

O'Donnell, Timothy.
The supernatural vision of life (an address given by Timothy O'Donnell on his installation as president of Christendom College: 11 O 1992). *F & R* 18:229-233 Aut 1992

O'Donoghue, Fergus.
Aubrey Gwynn: the Jesuit. *Studies* 81:393-398 Wint 1992

O'Donoghue, Helena.
Is the Irish Church in crisis? *Furrow* 44:67-77 F 1993
Review of: *Called by God* by Nemeck, Francis Kelly, and Coombs, Marie Theresa. In: *Furrow* 44:452-453 Jl-Ag 1993
Review of: *Practical discipleship* by Mueller, John J. In: *Furrow* 44:452-453 Jl-Ag 1993

O'Donoghue, Jo.
Historical themes, missionary endeavour and spiritual colonialism in Brian Moore's Black robe. *Studies* 82:131-139 Sum 1993

O'Donoghue, Noel D.
Focus on feeling. *Can Cath Rev* 11:16-21 Je 1993
Review of: *Carmelite studies 6: John of the Cross* by Payne, Steven, ed. In: *Can Cath Rev* 11:27-28 N 1993

O'Donoghue, Patrick.
Review of: *Cantate: cantor-friendly responsorial psalms, Year A* by Daly, Margaret. In: *Furrow* 44:188-189 Mr 1993

O'Donohue, James A.
Review of: *Faith and faithfulness* by Meilaender, Gilbert C. In: *America* 168:20-21 F 27 1993
Review of: *The shape of the good* by Layman, C Stephen. In: *America* 168:20-21 F 27 1993

O'Donovan, Jo.
Review of: *Community of faith: crafting Christian communities today.* In: *Furrow* 44:254-255 Ap 1993
Review of: *Forming a small Christian Community* by Currier, Richard, and Gram, Francis. In: *Furrow* 44:254-255 Ap 1993
Review of: *The Church, community of salvation* by Tavard, George Henry. In: *Furrow* 44:254-255 Ap 1993
Review of: *Thomas Merton: contemplative critic* by Nouwen, Henri Josef Machiel, 1932-. In: *Furrow* 44:388 Je 1993

O'Donovan, Leo J.
The city as a stage for time: Camille Pissaro's serial cityscapes. *America* 168:18-22 Ap 24 1993
Idiosyncrasy and genius: the Barnes Foundation on tour. *America* 169:16-18 Jl 17-24 1993

O'Driscoll, Mary, ed.
Catherine of Siena—passion for the truth, compassion for humanity: selected spiritual writings. New Rochelle: New City Press, 1993. 144p ISBN 1-56548-058-9 LC 93-2543

O'Gorman, Francis.
Mass for the slain street children. *Tablet* 247:1082-1083 Ag 21 1993
Review of: *T.S. Eliot and mysticism: the secret history of four quartets* by Murray, Paul. In: *Heythrop* 34:436 O 1993

O'Grady, Desmond.
Albanian portraits. *Tablet* 247:500+ Ap 24 1993
An American in Rome. *OSV* 81:13 Ja 3 1993
Americans regain St Susanna Church. *OSV* 81:3 F 28 1993
Awash in a sea of red ink [2nd of 2 pts]. *OSV* 82:10-11 Jl 4 1993
Baltic States. *OSV* 82:6-7 S 5 1993
A Boston politician comes to John Paul's court. *OSV* 82:3 Ag 22 1993
"Call me Lolek". *OSV* 81:16 Ap 18 1993
Candied limes for Galileo. *Tablet* 247:40-41 Ja 9 1993
Cardinal Carlo Martini: heir apparent? *OSV* 81:16 Mr 7 1993
Church and State, Italian-style. *OSV* 81:21 Ap 25 1993
Deficit buster [1st of two parts]. *OSV* 82:6 Je 27 1993
Five years that changed Rome. *OSV* 82:5 Je 20 1993
The flight from Egypt. *OSV* 81:12-13 Mr 28 1993
For Czechs, there are tiny signs of progress. *OSV* 81:3 F 7 1993
Italy's newest television star: the Pope. *OSV* 82:6 My 16 1993
Latvia growing stronger, but struggles remain. *OSV* 82:6-7 S 12 1993
Love thy neighbor—except in western Europe. *OSV* 81:7 Ja 3 1993
A phoenix rising from the ashes. *OSV* 81:21 Ap 4 1993
Religion in the ratings. *Tablet* 247:101 Ja 23 1993
Replaying the painful memories of persecution. *OSV* 82:8 N 28 1993
Restoring Albania's social fabric. *OSV* 81:21 Ap 18 1993

O'Grady, Desmond. *(cont'd)*
Saints riding stand by. *OSV* 82:10-11 O 31 1993
Through a daughter's eyes. *OSV* 81:16-17 F 14 1993

O'Grady, Jim.
Activists debate tactics for new world wars. *Nat Cath Rep* 29:6 Ja 29 1993

O'Grady, John F.
More about the Bible. *Chicago Stud* 31:316-324 N 1992
The present state of Christology. *Chicago Stud* 32:77-91 Ap 1993

O'Grady, Paul.
Review of: *Language, Saussure and Wittgenstein: how to play games with words* by Harris, Roy. In: *IJPS* 1:148-150 Mr 1993

O'Hagan, Daniel.
Beauty in natural stone. *Cath Work* 60:2 Je-Jl 1993

O'Hanlon, Gerard F.
Gospel values in Irish life today. *Doctr Life* 42:619-628 D 1992
A middle-class church for a working-class people. *Furrow* 44:3-11 Ja 1993
Review of: *Hans Urs von Balthasar* by O'Donnell, John. In: *Tablet* 247:723-725 Je 5 1993
Review of: *Karl Rahner* by Dych, William V. In: *Tablet* 247:723-725 Je 5 1993

O'Hara, Fred.
The third career of Sister Mary Pelagia, OP, author. *CLW* 64:40-42 Jl-S 1993

O'Hare, Colmán.
The story of Caedmon: Bede's account of the first English poet. *ABenR* 43:345-357 D 1992

O'Hare, Padraic.
Review of: *The Kohlberg legacy for the helping professions* by Kuhmerker, Lisa. In: *Horizons (CTS)* 19:342-343 Fall 1992

O'Hea, Eileen P.
Hermitage, a metaphor of life. *RRel* 52:503-506 Jl-Ag 1993

O'Heron, Edward J.
Your life story: self-discovery and beyond. Cincinnati: St Anthony Messenger Press, 1992. x, 181p ISBN 0-86716-177-9

O'Higgins, Kathleen.
Review of: *Lone parents, poverty and public policy in Ireland* by Millar, Jane, et al. In: *Studies* 82:110-112 Spr 1993

O'Higgins-O'Malley, Una.
Review of: *A case for peace in reason and faith* by Hellwig, Monika K, 1929-. In: *Furrow* 44:324-325 My 1993
Review of: *Let peace disturb you* by Buckley, Michael J, 1931-. In: *Furrow* 44:324-325 My 1993
Review of: *Solidarity: the missing link in Irish society* by Hamilton, Tim, et al. In: *Furrow* 44:55-56 Ja 1993

O'Keefe, James.
Living with compulsory celibacy. *Way Suppl* 77:37-45 Sum 1993

O'Keefe, Jane.
Review of: *Sing to the Lord an old song* by Hruby, Dolores, and Tindall, Susan F. In: *Past Mus* 18:60-61 O-N 1993
Review of: *Words that sing* by Ramshaw, Gail. In: *Past Mus* 18:59-60 O-N 1993

O'Keefe, Joseph M.
Review of: *Catholic schools and the common good* by Bryk, Anthony S, et al. In: *Nat Cath Rep* 30:19 O 29 1993

O'Keefe, Vincent O.
Review of: *Paul VI* by Hebblethwaite, Peter, 1930-. In: *Nat Cath Rep* 29:15 Je 4 1993

O'Keeffe, Brendan.
Review of: *The czar's madman* by Kross, Jaan. In: *Tablet* 247:408 Mr 27 1993

O'Leary, Dale.
Is folic acid a prolife concern? *Register* 69:5 Jl 4 1993
A warning on prenatal tests. *Register* 69:1+ My 16 1993

O'Leary, Paul.
The church leaking at the edges. *Doctr Life* 43:100-107 F 1993

O'Malley, Charles J.
Making parental choice happen. *Tod Cath Teach* 26:16-19 F 1993

O'Malley, William J, 1931-.
Catechesis for conversion [excerpt fr the book]. *Living Light* 29:55-63 Wint 1992
The Church of the faithful. *America* 168:6-10 Je 19-26 1993
Review of: *Dissent and order in the Middle Ages: the search for legitimate authority* by Russell, Jeffrey Burton. In: *TheolStds* 54:387-388 Je 1993
Review of: *Sharing faith* by Groome, Thomas H, 1945-. In: *America* 168:18-19 My 15 1993
A tolerance for ambiguity. *America* 169:7-13 O 2 1993
Warden for a week. *Living Light* 29:60-67 Spr 1993

O'Mara, Philip F.
Review of: *Wilbur's poetry: music in a scattering time* by Michelson, Bruce. In: *Cithara* 32:68-69 N 1992

O'Meara, Thomas Franklin.
The Dominican school of Salamanca and the Spanish conquest of America: some bibliographical notes. *Thomist* 56:555-582 O 1992

O'Neal, Sandra R.
Review of: *Medieval misogyny and the invention of western romantic love* by Bloch, R Howard. In: *TheolStds* 53:784 D 1992
Review of: *Prophets in their own country: living saints and the making of sainthood in the later Middle Ages* by Kleinberg, Aviad M. In: *TheolStds* 54:388-389 Je 1993

O'Neill, C.
Review of: *A history of French Louisiana: Volume V: the Company of the Indies 1723-1731* by Giraud, Marcel. In: *CHist* 78:681-684 O 1992

O'Neill, Jack.
The clergy's role in AA's fifth step. *Priest* 49:19-20 Mr 1993

O'Neill, Mary Aquin.
Review of: *Where can we find her? searching for women's identity in the new church* by Rosenblatt, Marie-Eloise, ed. In: *Horizons (CTS)* 19:330-331 Fall 1992
Review of: *Women and creativity* by Leckey, Dolores R, 1933-. In: *Horizons (CTS)* 19:330-331 Fall 1992

O'Neill, Robert K.
A museum for Catholics over 40. *CDgst* 57:59-64 Ja 1993

O'Reilly, Leo.
Review of: *1-3 John* by Thompson, Marianne Meye. In: *Furrow* 44:193 Mr 1993
Review of: *Hebrews* by Stedman, Ray C. In: *Furrow* 44:193 Mr 1993
Review of: *The nature and authority of the Bible* by Abba, Raymond. In: *Furrow* 44:516-517 S 1993

O'Reilly, Martin.
African independent churches and religious life. *AFER* 35:217-221 Ag 1993
Religious life in West Africa 1966-1990. *RRel* 52:566-573 Jl-Ag 1993

O'Reilly, Paul.
Review of: *Fearfully and wonderfully made* by Yancey, P, and Brand, P. In: *Month* 26:274-275 Jl 1993

O'Reilly, Stephan J.
Dollars dried up with move away from tradition. *Nat Cath Rep* 29:13 F 12 1993

O'Riordan, Sean.
Review of: *My witness for the Church* by Häring, Bernard, 1912-. In: *Tablet* 247:919 Jl 17 1993

O'Rourke, Edward W, Bp.
Let's add more mystery to the rosary. *USCath* 58:36-37 Ag 1993

O'Shaughnessy, Hugh.
Review of: *Land without evil: utopian journeys across the South American watershed* by Gott, Richard. In: *Tablet* 247:212 F 13 1993
A soap too far. *Tablet* 247:397 Mr 27 1993

O'Sullivan, Brian.
Collaborative ministry: not just words. *Tablet* 247:1211-1212 S 18 1993

O'Sullivan, Helene. see Jenkinson, William, jt ed

O'Sullivan, Tim.
Review of: *Grangegorman, psychiatric care in Dublin since 1815* by Reynolds, Joseph. In: *Studies* 82:362-364 Aut 1993

O'Toole, James M, 1950-.
Militant and Triumphant. Indiana: University of Notre Dame Press, 1993. x, 324p ISBN 0-268-01403-5

O'Toole, Michael.
Review of: *Alphonsus de Liguori, the Saint of Burbon Naples* by Jones, Frederick M. In: *Doctr Life* 43:247-248 Ap 1993

Ó Fiannachta, Pádraig. see McCone, Kim, jt auth

Ó Laoghaire, Diarmuid.
Review of: *Language maintenance and language shift as strategies of social reproduction* by Ó Riagáin, Pádraig, and Cliath, Baile Átha. In: *Studies* 82:368-370 Aut 1993
Review of: *The Celtic connection* by Price, Glanville, ed. In: *Studies* 82:365-368 Aut 1993

Oakes, Edward T.
Cardinal Newman on the season of Lent. *America* 168:7-12 Ap 3 1993
Review of: *Einbergung des menschen in das mysterium der dreieinigen liebe: eine trinitarische anthropologie nach Hans urs von Balthasar* by Meuffels, Hans Otmar. In: *TheolStds* 54:360-363 Je 1993
Review of: *Gotteswort im menschenwort: inhalt und form von theologie nach Hans urs von Balthasar* by Klaghofer-Treitler, Wolfgang. In: *TheolStds* 54:360-363 Je 1993
Review of: *Passio caritatis: trinitarische passiologie im werk Hans urs von Balthasars* by Krenski, Thomas Rudolf. In: *TheolStds* 54:360-363 Je 1993
Review of: *The glory of the Lord: a theological aesthetics, IV: the realm of metaphysics in Antiquity* by Balthasar, Hans Urs Von, 1905-1988. In: *America* 169:21-23 O 2 1993
Review of: *The glory of the Lord: a theological aesthetics, V: the realm of metaphysics in the modern age* by Balthasar, Hans Urs Von, 1905-1988. In: *America* 169:21-23 O 2 1993
Review of: *The glory of the Lord: a theological aesthetics, VI: theology: the Old Covenant* by Balthasar, Hans Urs Von, 1905-1988. In: *America* 169:21-23 O 2 1993
Review of: *The glory of the Lord: a theological aesthetics, VII: theology: the New Covenant* by Balthasar, Hans Urs Von, 1905-1988. In: *America* 169:22-23 O 2 1993
Review of: *The stripping of the altars* by Duffy, Eamon. In: *Comm* 120:27-28 Mr 12 1993

Oakman, Douglas E.
Review of: *Jesus und die Zöllner: Historische und neutestamentlich-exegetische Untersuchungen* by Herrenbrück, Fritz. In: *CBQ* 55:157-158 Ja 1993

Obach, Robert E.
Review of: *A generation of seekers* by Roof, Wade Clark, 1939-. In: *Nat Cath Rep* 29:26 S 10 1993
Review of: *Christianity in the twenty-first Century reflections on the challenges ahead* by Wuthnow, Robert. In: *Nat Cath Rep* 29:26 S 10 1993

Oberholzer, Felicidad.
Bereavement: until we meet again. *Liturgy* 10:47-56 Wint 1992

Obolensky, Alexander P.
From first to third millennium: the social Christianity of St Vladimir of Kiev. *CrossCurr* 43:203-211 Sum 1993

Ochs, Peter.
Borowitz and the postmodern renewal of theology. *CrossCurr* 43:164-183 Sum 1993

Oddie, William.
Populate or perish. *Crisis* 11:16-17 O 1993

Odell, William.
The "seamless garment" is woven slowly. *OSV* 81:8 Ja 17 1993
Why has the truth not prevailed? *OSV* 81:23 Ja 17 1993

Oeming, M. *see* Dohmen, C, jt auth

Oheideain, Eustas.
Review of: *Religion, education and the constitution* by Lane, Dermot A, ed.
In: *Doctr Life* 43:313 My-Je 1993

Ohki, Hideo. *see* Furuya, Yasua, jt auth

Okafor, Fidelis U.
Issues in African philosophy re-examined. *IPQ* 33:91-99 Mr 1993

Okhuijsen, Gijs.
In heaven there are no thunderstorms: celebrating the liturgy with developmentally disabled people. Collegeville:Liturgical, 1992. 136p ISBN 0-81461-999-1 LC 91-41-4407

Okoye, Chukwuma J.
The Eucharist and African culture. *AFER* 34:272-292 O 1992

Olaizola, Jose Luis.
Viaje al fondo de la esperanza. Madrid: Ediciones Rialp, 1993. x, 253p ISBN 84-321-2866-x

Olayiwola, David O.
The interaction of African independent churches with traditional religions in Nigeria. *StudiaM* 42:357-370 1993

Olert, Stephen, and Williams, Ruthann.
There's help for the sexual addict. *Sisters* 65:263-271 Jl 1993

Olin, John C.
The Catholic reformation: Savonarola to Ignatius Loyola: reform in the church, 1495-1540. New York: Fordham University Press, 1992. x, 218p ISBN 0-8232-1477-x LC 92-29865
Review of: *The correspondence of Erasmus Letters 1356-1534 to 1524*. In: *CHist* 79:337-338 Ap 1993 *see* Brady, James F, jt ed

Oliveira Ribeiro, Claudio de.
CEBs e ecumenismo: uma discussão a partir da dimensão ecumênica do oitavo intereclesial. *REB* 52:846-855 D 1992

Ollard, Richard.
Review of: *Cavaliers and roundheads: the English at war 1642-1649* by Hibbert, Christopher. In: *Tablet* 247:693 My 29 1993
Review of: *Four Caroline portraits* by Rowse, A L. In: *Tablet* 247:693 My 29 1993

Ollenburger, Ben C.
Review of: *Text und Sinn im Alten Testament: Textgeschichtliche und bibeltheologische Studien* by Schenker, Adrian. In: *CBQ* 55:205 Ja 1993

Olmstead, Bob.
Notre Dame conference gets axed. *Register* 69:1+ F 28 1993

Olsen, Glenn Warren, 1938-.
The ethics of conquest: the European background of Spain's mission in the New World. *Communio* 19:619-364 Wint 1992
Review of: *Dissent and order in the Middle Ages: the search for legitimate authority* by Russell, Jeffrey Burton. In: *CHist* 78:629-630 O 1992

Olsen, Mary B.
Mountain memories endure. *Liguorian* 81:60-61 S 1993

Olson, Carol.
Review of: *Hindus and Christians: a century of Protestant ecumenical thought* by Ariarajah, S Wesley. In: *JEcumen Stds* 29:285 Spr 1992

Olson, Roger E. *see* Grenz, Stanley J, jt auth

Olsthorrn, Martin.
Review of: *The last shall be first: the rhetoric of reversal in Luke* by York, John O. In: *CBQ* 54:812-813 O 1992

Ombres, Robert.
Praying for the dead. *Priests & People* 6:425-429 N 1992
Review of: *Sacraments: initiation, penance, anointing of the sick: commentary on canons 840-1007* by Woestman, William H. In: *Priests & People* 7:367 Ag-S 1993
Review of: *Special marriage cases* by Woestman, William H. In: *Priests & People* 7:367 Ag-S 1993
Review of: *The sacrament of Reconciliation* by Cuschieri, Andrew. In: *New Blckfrs* 74:222-223 Ap 1993
Vincent McNabb OP 1868-1943. *New Blckfrs* 74:330-332 Jl-Ag 1993

Onder, Tina. *see* Kaufman, Ben L, jt auth

Opzeeland, Cees von. *see* Okhuijsen, Gijs, jt auth

Orazzo, Antonio.
Review of: *Amore del bello: Studi sulla Filocalia, Atti del Simposio Internazionale sulla Filocalia.* In: *Civilta* 143:422-423 N 21 1992
Review of: *Commento al Cantico dei Cantici* by Saint-Thierry, Guglielmo di. In: *Civilta* 143:425 N 21 1992
Review of: *Commento al Vangelo di Giovanni, vol 7* by Bonaventura, San. In: *Civilta* 3:314-315 Ag 7-21 1993
Review of: *Sermoni domenicali* by Bonaventura, San. In: *Civilta* 3:316-317 Ag 7-21 1993

Órbe, Antonio.
Hacia la doctrina marcionítica de la redención. *Gregorianum* 74 No 1:45-74 1993

Orchard, Gillian.
Making sense of celibacy. *Way Suppl* 77:5-12 Sum 1993

Ord, David Robert. *see* Coote, Robert B, jt auth

Organ, Barbara E.
"The words are the messengers, the Word is the message": text and translation. *Can Cath Rev* 11:9-17 Mr 1993

Oro, Ari Pedro.
Podem Passar A Sacolinha. *REB* 53:301-323 Je 1993

Orsini, Jean-Francois.
Review of: *The Catholic ethic and the spirit of capitalism* by Novak, Michael, 1933-. In: *HPR* 94:72-75 N 1993
Review of: *Doing well and doing good* by Neuhaus, Richard John, 1936-. In: *HPR* 93:73-74 Ap 1993

Orsy, Ladislas, 1921-.
Bishops and universities: dominion or communion. *America* 169:11-16 N 20 1993
How to relate theology and Canon Law. *Origins* 22:549-552 Ja 21 1993
"Kenosis": the door to Christian unity. *Origins* 23:38-41 Je 3 1993
Review of: *Lonergan* by Crowe, Frederick E. In: *TheolStds* 54:392-393 Je 1993
Review of: *Salvation outside the Church* by Sullivan, Francis Aloysius. In: *TheolStds* 54:178-179 Mr 1993
Towards Christian unity through the kenosis of the churches. *Ecumen Trends* 22:6-10 Jl-Ag 1993

Orwen, Nancy.
Review of: *Pilgrim in the ruins: a life of Walker Percy* by Tolson, Jay. In: *Can Cath Rev* 11:23-24 O 1993

Osborn, Eric.
Justin Martyr and the Logos Spermatikos. *StudiaM* 42:143-159 1993
Rational faith. *Pacifica* 6:297-310 O 1993

Osborne, J.
Review of: *Catholic Emancipation: a shake to men's minds* by Hinde, Wendy. In: *CHist* 78:671-672 O 1992

Osborne, Kenan B.
Ministry: lay ministry in the Catholic Church, its history and theology. New Jersey: Paulist Press, 1993. x, 722p ISBN 0-8091-3371-7 LC 92-40299
Review of: *Oneself as another* by Ricoeur, Paul. In: *America* 169:27-28 Jl 3-10 1993

Osheim, D.
Review of: *Il Lazio meridionale tra Papato e Impero al tempo di Enrico VI: Atti del convegno internazionale, Fiuggi, Guarcino, Montecassino.* In: *CHist* 78:640-641 O 1992

Osiek, Carolyn.
Review of: *Sacred violence: Paul's hermeneutic of the cross* by Hamerton-Kelly, Robert G. In: *New Theol Rev* 6:88-90 Ag 1993
The city: center of early Christian life. *BibleT* 31:17-21 Ja 1993
Review of: *The future of Early Christianity: essays in honor of Helmut Koester* by Pearson, Birger A, ed. In: *CBQ* 55:199-201 Ja 1993
Review of: *The social setting of the ministry as reflected in the writings of Hermas, Clement, and Ignatius* by Maier, Harry O. In: *CBQ* 55:171-173 Ja 1993
Slavery in the second testament world. *Bib Th Bul* 22:174-179 Wint 1992

Ossandón, Pedro, and Rodríguez, Pedro.
El método de Orígenes. *Teol Vida* 33 no 3-4:185-191 1992

Ostdiek, Gilbert.
Here's a catechetical resource waiting to be used. *Past Mus* 17:28-30 Je-Jl 1993

Ostendorf, Paul.
The future and present mission of CLA. *CLW* 64:12-16 Jl-S 1993

Osuna, Antonio.
Bartolomé de Las Casas en el V Centenario: revisión de su figura y de su doctrina moral. *Cien Tom* 119:459-498 S-D 1992
Review of: *Rassegna di Letteratura Tomistica, vol XXV, anno 1989.* In: *Cien Tom* 119:628-629 S-D 1992
Review of: *Suma de Teología; III: Parte II-II* by Thomas Aquinas, Saint. In: *Cien Tom* 120:193-194 Ja-Ap 1993
Review of: *Tomás de Aquino* by Pesch, Otto Hermann, 1931-. In: *Cien Tom* 120:188-190 Ja-Ap 1993

Otellini, Steven.
At Christ's tomb. *Crisis* 10:53-55 N 1992

Ottensmeyer, H.
Review of: *The awakened heart: living beyond addiction* by May, Gerald G. In: *RRel* 52:148-149 Ja-F 1993

Outka, Gene, and Reeder, John P, Jr, eds.
Prospects for a common morality. Princeton, New Jersey: Princeton University Press, 1993. x, 302p ISBN 0-69107-418-6 LC 92-5681

Overberg, Kenneth R, 1944-.
AIDS: a worsening crisis challenges church and society. *St Anth* 100:22-27 Ja 1993
Mercy or murder? euthanasia, morality and public policy. Kansas City: Sheed and Ward, 1993. x, 278p ISBN 1-55612-609-3 LC 92-43734

Overfield, James H.
Review of: *Fifteenth-Century Carthusian reform: the world of Nicholas Kempf* by Martin, Dennis D. In: *CHist* 79:327-329 Ap 1993

Overman, Stephanie.
Hackers in habit. *OSV* 82:8 N 14 1993

Owen, Roger.
Hourani, Albert, -1993 [obit]. *Tablet* 247:152-153 Ja 30 1993

Owens, John Joseph.
Analytic and continental philosophies in overall perspective. *Mod Schlmn* 70:131-142 Ja 1993
Work Is the Key: a view from the dole queue. *Doctr Life* 43:227-231 Ap 1993

Oxtoby, W G. *see* Ching, J, jt ed

Ozar, Lorraine A.
Comunidades de base schools. *Momentum* 24:38-40 F-Mr 1993

P

Pace, Charlotte.
Converting the assembly. *Mod Lit* 20:10-13 F 1993
Converting the parish staff. *Mod Lit* 20:6-9 Mr 1993

Pace, Enzo. *see* Acquaviva, Sabinos, jt auth

Pacella, U.
Review of: *La religione a scuola tra obbligo e facoltátività* by Betti, Carmen.
In: *Civilta* 143:435 N 21 1992
Review of: *Scuola* by Venturini, Nello. In: *Civilta* 3:102 Jl 3 1993

Pacho, Alberto.
Review of: *Histoeria de la Congregación de las Carmelitas Misioners: Tomo I; Orígenes y primeros pasos: 1845-1885* by Pacho, Eulogio. In: *Teol Vida* 33 no 3-4:319-321 1992

Padberg, John.
Review of: *Marcello Cervini and ecclesiastical government in Tridentine Italy* by Hudon, William V. In: *RRel* 52:787-788 S-O 1993

Padberg, John W.
Review of: *The first Jesuits* by O'Malley, William J, 1931-. In: *America* 169: 26-30 O 16 1993

Padgett, Alan G.
Eternity and the special theory of relativity. *IPQ* 33:219-223 Je 1993

Padilla, Gilbert.
Indwelling trinity: source of joy and healing. *Spir Life* 39:44-46 Spr 1993

Paffett, Kate.
A carol for Tim. *Liguorian* 81:12-13 D 1993

Page, John.
Dialogue [interview by C Allen]. *Register* 69:1+ Je 11 1993

Paglia, Donald J.
Supporting families: a challenge for small Christian communities. *Tod Parish* 25:7-11 O 1993

Paige, Harry W, 1922-.
Ceremonies of innocence. *Liguorian* 81:20-25 F 1993
His brother's keeper: a memorial. *Liguorian* 81:18-21 My 1993
Home: a condition of the heart. *Liguorian* 81:30-34 S 1993
Trial by memory. *Liguorian* 81:4-8 Ja 1993
A vast confinement. *Liguorian* 81:46-50 Jl 1993
When words fail us. *Liguorian* 81:52-56 Ag 1993

Painter, John.
Review of: *Diakonia: reinterpreting the ancient sources* by Collins, J N. In: *Pacifica* 6:239-241 Je 1993

Pakaluk, Michael.
God and quantum mechanics: room for both. *Register* 69:1+ Ja 31 1993
God, the soul and Kurt Godel. *Register* 69:1+ F 14 1993
Relativity, relativism: they're not the same!. *Register* 69:1+ F 7 1993
Religious faith, scientific inquiry: do they need to be enemies? *Register* 69:1+ Ja 24 1993
Review of: *A Jewish conservative looks at pagan America* by Feder, Don. In: *Crisis* 11:52-53 Jl-Ag 1993
Scientists, God and "chaos" theory. *Register* 69:1+ F 21 1993

Palacio, Carlos.
Review of: *Filho de José? Jesus no judaísmo* by Lapide, Pinchas. In: *Perspectiva* 25:233-236 My-Ag 1993
Uma cristologia suspeita? *Perspectiva* 25:181-196 My-Ag 1993
La identidad problematica. *Christus* 58:26-38 My 1993
Um projeto cristológico: a colção "Jesus e Jesus Cristo". *Perspectiva* 24:375-387 S-D 1992
Review of: *De quién es Jesús? Su significación para judíos, cristianos y musulmanes* by Imbach, Josef. In: *Perspectiva* 24:404 S-D 1992
Review of: *Jesucristo, salvador del mundo: María en el plan salvífico de dios* by Auer, Johann. In: *Perspectiva* 25:105-106 Ja-Ap 1993
Review of: *Mulher e teologial* by Van Lunen-Chenu, Marie-Thérèse, and Gibellini, Rosino. In: *Perspectiva* 24:403 S-D 1992

Palacios, Miguel. *see* Nagel, Eduard, jt auth

Palange, Cecilia.
The signs of the times. *Sisters* 65:187 My 1993

Palliser, Michael.
Review of: *De Gaulle and Algeria 1940-1960* by Kettle, Michael. In: *Tablet* 247:1165-1166 S 11 1993

Palmer, Martin. *see* Breuilly, Elizabeth, jt ed

Palumbo, Gene.
Latin American bishops. *St Anth* 100:10-16 Ap 1993
Salvador archbishop attacks amnesty deal. *Nat Cath Rep* 29:8 Ap 2 1993
Salvadoran reactions to truth report vary. *Nat Cath Rep* 29:11 Mr 26 1993
Suspicion lingers in wake of Salvadoran bishop's murder. *Nat Cath Rep* 29: 10 Jl 16 1993

Pangallo, Don Mario.
Il posto della metafisica nel sapere umano Il pensiero di Maimonide e il suo influsso su S Tommasso d'Aquino. *Gregorianum* 74 no 2:331-352 1993

Pani, G.
Review of: *La figura e l'opera di Federico Alessandrini*. In: *Civilta* 144:412-413 F 20 1993

Panikkar, Raimundo, 1918-.
The cosmotheandric experience: emerging religious consciousness. Maryknoll, New York: Orbis Books, 1993. x, 160p ISBN 0-88344-862-9 LC 92-46195
There is no outer without inner space. *CrossCurr* 43:60-81 Spr 1993

Pankiewicz, Mary Ann.
Kindling a love for reading and reasoning. *Momentum* 24:44-46 S-O 1993

Pannenbert, Wolfhart.
Essays on science and faith. Louisville: Westminster, 1993. x, 208p ISBN 0-664-25384-9

Panzica, Ana.
The wrong colour. *Tablet* 247:1226-1227 S 25 1993

Paolis, Velasio De.
Delitti contro il sesto comandamento. *Periodica* 82 no 2:293-316 1993
Amissio status clericalis. *Periodica* 81 no 2:251-282 1992

Papeleux, Michel.
Esquisse d'un projet culturel une société performante pour tous. *Lumen* 47: 427-438 D 1992

Papineau, Andre, 1937-.
The fleshy way of God [excerpt fr *Sermons for sermon haters* 1992]. *Mod Lit* 19:16 D 1992-Ja 1993

Paprocki, Joseph.
Don't be afraid to change. *ReligTJ* 27:41 Mr 1993
Feeding your catechists? *ReligTJ* 27:63 S 1993
From dream to reality. *ReligTJ* 26:41 Ja 1993
Liturgy and catechesis. *ReligTJ* 27:40 F 1993
Looking back, looking ahead. *ReligTJ* 27:42 Ap-My 1993
When wandering is good. *ReligTJ* 27:40-41 O 1993

Paprocki, Thomas J.
Ethics in the everyday practice of law. *CLawyer* 35 no 2:169-180 1993

Parachin, Victor M.
Bishop, saint, journalist. *OSV* 81:3 F 7 1993
Four brave chaplains. *Priest* 49:15-16 F 1993
Helping people avoid bereavement mistakes. *Priest* 49:19-20 Ja 1993
How Christians can be good and angry. *New Cov* 22:24-25 Jl 1993
The Psalms: God's guide for living. *OSV* 81:5 Ap 25 1993
Saint in a soup kitchen: AD 370. *CDgst* 57:91-93 My 1993
When you're in trouble. *CDgst* 57:55-57 Ja 1993

Paradis, Steve.
Newest Marian shrine dedicated. *OR(Eng)* 1307:2 S 15 1993

Paré, U E.
Is there a balm in Gilead? Reflections on a Church in need of healing. *Can Cath Rev* 11:18-21 Ja 1993

Parens, Erik.
Kundera, Nietzsche, and politics on the questions of eternal return and responsibility. *PhilosTod* 37:285-297 Aut 1993

Parenti, Roberto. *see* Ballola, Giovanni Carli, jt auth

Pargament, Kenneth I, et al.
Religion and prevention in mental health: research, vision, and action. New York: The Haworth Press, 1992. 92-5887/x, 333p ISBN 1-56024 LC 225-6

Parham, Maggie.
Review of: *Grammar and style* by Dummett, Michael. In: *Tablet* 247:922 Jl 17 1993
Review of: *Nick, man of the heart* by Vanier, Thérèse. In: *Tablet* 247:655-656 My 22 1993

Parijs, Michel Van.
Les Églises de l'autre Europe à l'épreuve de la liberté. *Lumen* 48:339-352 S 1993

Paris, John J.
Review of: *Intensive care: medical ethics and the medical profession* by Zussman, Robert. In: *TheolStds* 54:189-190 Mr 1993

Park, Sun Ai Lee. *see* Fabella, Virginia, jt ed

Parker, Simon B.
Review of: *La trouvaille épigraphique de l'Ougarit, v II* by Cunchillos, Jesús-Luis. In: *CBQ* 55:330-331 Ap 1993

Parker, T H L.
Calvin's New Testament commentaries. Louisville: John Knox, 1993. x, 256p ISBN 0-664-25489-6

Parker Gumucio, Christán.
"A Religiosidade Urbana". *REB* 53:283-300 Je 1993

Parkhurst, Vance C.
Review of: *The trustee's guide to understanding healthcare antitrust law issues* by Tomes, Jonathan P. In: *Health Prog* 74:68 1993

Parnegg, Janee. *see* Larsen, Earnie, jt auth

Parpola, Simo. *see* Kwasman, Theodore, jt auth

Parrott, Andrew. *see* Keyte, Hugh, jt ed

Parry, Mary.
This is the army. *Tod Parish* 25:23 N-D 1993

Partos, L.
Review of: *Évangile et mystère* by Reynier, Chantal. In: *Lumen* 47:469 D 1992
Review of: *Beligique, pays de chrétienté?* In: *Lumen* 48:239 Je 1993
Review of: *Célébrations jeunes* by Schlitz, Jean-Marie. In: *Lumen* 47:465-466 D 1992
Review of: *Catherine de Sienne: le dialogue* by Portier, Lucienne, ed. In: *Lumen* 48:117 Mr 1993
Review of: *Cent ans après Rerum Novarum (1891) La tradition sociale du catholicisme français*. In: *Lumen* 48:240 Je 1993
Review of: *Christianisme et religions païennes dan le contre celse d'origène* by Fédou, Michel. In: *Lumen* 47:471-472 D 1992
Review of: *Exorciste aujourd'hui?* by Leneuf, Nicolas, and Vernette, Jean. In: *Lumen* 47:467-468 D 1992
Review of: *Fioretti de Jean XXIII* by Prieto, Moïse. In: *Lumen* 48:237 Je 1993
Review of: *François De Sales (Saint) traité de l'amour de Dieu* by Ferlay, Phillippe, ed. In: *Lumen* 48:234 Je 1993
Review of: *Indivisible amour* by Delbrêl, Madeleine. In: *Lumen* 48:233 Je 1993
Review of: *La délinquance. Coll. Que penser de?* by Davin, José. In: *Lumen* 48:240 Je 1993

Partos, L. *(cont'd)*
Review of: *La pratique des Exercices spirituels d'Ignace de Loyola actes du symposium de Bruxelles* by Gervais, Pierre, ed. In: *Lumen* 48:234 Je 1993
Review of: *La prière chrétienne* by Pinckaerts, Servais. In: *Lumen* 48:236-237 Je 1993
Review of: *Le chemin de la connaissance intérievre* by Divarkar, Parmananda R. In: *Lumen* 48:233-234 Je 1993
Review of: *Le courage du théologien dialogues publiés par Paul Imhof et Huber Biallowons* by Rahner, Karl, 1904-1984. In: *Lumen* 47:472 D 1992
Review of: *Le culte de la prudence* by Jean de Jésus Marie. In: *Lumen* 48:235 Je 1993
Review of: *Le père Dieu en son mystère* by Durrwell, François-Xavier. In: *Lumen* 47:471 D 1992
Review of: *Les constitutions apostoliques* by Metzger, Marcel. In: *Lumen* 48:115 Mr 1993
Review of: *Les fêtes de Dieu* by Talec, Pierre. In: *Lumen* 48:233 Je 1993
Review of: *Les sects: changer le monde ou changer de monde?* by Ancion, Jean. In: *Lumen* 47:467 D 1992
Review of: *Lexique de la culture* by Carrier, Hervé. In: *Lumen* 48:240 Je 1993
Review of: *Marte, Marie et les autres, les visages féminsde l'evangile* by Mourlon Beernaert, Pierre. In: *Lumen* 47:468-469 D 1992
Review of: *Mystique et pédagogie spirituelle. Ignace, Thérèse, Jean de la Croix. Colloque public du Centre sèvres: 22-23 Novembre, 1991.* In: *Lumen* 48:236 Je 1993
Review of: *Notre demeure est aux cieux. Coll. Cadeaux-Messages* by Helbich, Peter, and Rau, Hans Jürgen. In: *Lumen* 48:234-235 Je 1993
Review of: *Paroles pour prier* by Destang, Françoise. In: *Lumen* 48:233 Je 1993
Review of: *Pour l'honneur de mes frères. Témoignages Chrétines d'Amérique latine (1968-1992)* by Antoine, Charles. In: *Lumen* 48:239 Je 1993
Review of: *Pour une mémoire catéchuménale* by Thomas, Pascal. In: *Lumen* 47:468 D 1992
Review of: *Prends et mange chaque dimanche la parole* by Deleclos, Fabien. In: *Lumen* 47:470 D 1992
Review of: *Priére dans la vie: effort et don* by Carvalho Azevedo, Marcelo de. In: *Lumen* 48:117-118 Mr 1993
Review of: *Sainte Marie mère de Dieu, modle de l'Eglise.* In: *Lumen* 47:472 D 1992
Review of: *Un catechisme universel pour l'Église catholique* by Simon, Maurice. In: *Lumen* 47:466-467 D 1992
Review of: *Vie spirituelle et modernité. Entretiens ultimes avec Thérèse de Scott* by Légaut, Marcel. In: *Lumen* 48:235-236 Je 1993

Parunak, H Van Dyke.
Review of: *Chiasmus in the New Testament* by Lund, Nils Wilhelm. In: *CBQ* 55:383-384 Ap 1993
Review of: *Ezekiel* by Blenkinsopp, Joseph. In: *CBQ* 55:102-103 Ja 1993

Parvin, Manoucher.
On the synergism of gender and class exploitation: theory and practice under Islamic Rule. *RSocEcon* 51:201-216 Sum 1993

Pasco, Rowanne.
Religious broadcasting RIP. *Tablet* 247:1150 S 11 1993

Pasco, Rowanne, and Brown, Douglas.
Leonard, George, -1993 [obit]. *Tablet* 247:153-154 Ja 30 1993

Pascoe, L.
Review of: *Histoire du Christianisme des origines à nos jours, volume VI: Un temps d'épreuves (1274-1449)* by Jourdin, Michel Mollat du, and Vauchez, André, eds. In: *CHist* 78:645-646 O 1992

Pasha, M A.
The people of the book. New York: Vantage Press, 1993. 270p ISBN 0-533-10296-0 LC 92-93384

Pasqua, Hervé.
Review of: *Enjeux de philosophie politique moderne. Les violences de l'abstraction* by Terestchenko, Michel. In: *RPhil Louvain* 91:495 Ag 1993
Review of: *Europe, la voie romaine* by Brague, Rémi. In: *RPhil Louvain* 91:498-502 Ag 1993
Review of: *Hobbes ou la crise de l'État baroque* by Angouivent, Anne-Laure. In: *RPhil Louvain* 91:471-472 Ag 1993

Passano, Paolo Ferrari Da.
Considerazioni etico-giuridiche sulle dimissioni. *Civilta* 144:45-50 Ja 2 1993
Considerazioni giuridiche sulla chiamata di correo. *Civilta* 2:29-43 Ap 3 1993
Depenalizzazione. *Civilta* 2:161-164 Ap 17 1993
La riforma degli agenti di custodia. *Civilta* 144:354-362 F 20 1993

Pastor, Felix-Alejandro.
Optio praecipua pauperum: de ecclesiali pro pauperibus optione tamquam theonomae moralitatis criterio. *Periodica* 81 no 2:319-346 1992
Review of: *Dio dei cristiani* by Muñoz, Ronaldo. In: *Gregorianum* 74 No 1:193-194 1993
Review of: *Dio l'Unico. Sulla nascita del monoteismo in Israele* by Lohfink, Norbert, and Zenger, E, et al. In: *Gregorianum* 74 no 2:406 1993
Review of: *Dios es Padre* by Velasco, J Martín, et al. In: *Gregorianum* 74 no 3:583-584 1993
Review of: *El Dios de los cristianos. Estructura introductoria a la teologia de la Trinidad* by Peñamaría de LLano, Antonio. In: *Gregorianum* 74 no 2:372 1993
Review of: *El Dios del amor y de la paz. Tratado Teológico de Dios desde la reflexion sobre su Bondad* by García-Murga Vázquez, José Ramón. In: *Gregorianum* 74 no 2:371-372 1993
Review of: *God and evil: a unified theodicy/ theology/ philosophy* by Birnbaum, David. In: *Gregorianum* 73 No 4:773-774 1992
Review of: *Il Cristo di Unamuno: Con una antologia di testi* by Savignano, Armando. In: *Gregorianum* 74 No 1:188 1993
Review of: *La dottrina sociale della Chiesa* by Antoncich, Ricardo, and Munárriz, José Miguel. In: *Gregorianum* 74 No 1:193-194 1993
Review of: *No religion is an island. Abraham Joshua Heschel and interreligious dialogue* by Kasimow, Harold, and Sherwin, Byron L, eds. In: *Gregorianum* 74 no 2:408 1993

Pastor, Felix-Alejandro. *(cont'd)*
Review of: *Reconstructing the common good: theology and social order* by Dorrien, Gary J. In: *Gregorianum* 74 No 1:194 1993
Review of: *The God of life* by Gutiérrez, Gustavo. In: *Gregorianum* 74 No 1:194 1993
Review of: *Trinidad y Salvación: Estudios sobre la trilogía trinitaria de Juan Pablo II* by Aranda, Antonio. In: *Gregorianum* 74 No 1:162-163 1993

Patrick, Anne E.
Veritatis splendor [commentary]. *Comm* 120:18 O 22 1993

Patrick, James. *see* Walker, Andrew, jt ed

Patten, Christopher.
The advance of liberty. *Tablet* 247:1025-1027 Ag 7 1993

Patterson, Robert W.
In-house critics. *Crisis* 11:13-14 My 1993
Review of: *Made in America* by Horton, Michael Scott. In: *Crisis* 11:13-14 My 1993
Review of: *No God but God* by Guinness, Os, and Seel, John, eds. In: *Crisis* 11:13-14 My 1993

Pattn, Corrine L.
Review of: *In the shadow of Moloch: the sacrifice of children and its impact on Western religions* by Bergmann, Martin S. In: *Cithara* 32:61-62 N 1992

Patton, John.
Pastoral care in context. Louisville: Westminster, 1993. x, 288p ISBN 0-664-22034-7

Patuel I Puig, Jaume.
Quodlibets: reflexions escrites en Veu Alta. Barcelona: L'Aixernador Ed, 1993. x, 249p ISBN 84-8632-99-0

Pätzold, Barbara, et al. *see* Beyreuther, Gerald, jt ed

Paul, John, Bp.
Pastoral care for those living with HIV/AIDS. *Origins* 23:378-381 N 4 1993

Paul, Mary.
A little help, a lot of independence. *Health Prog* 74:43-45 My 1993

Pauley, Michael.
Getting the facts straight. *Register* 69:5 F 21 1993

Paulsell, William O.
Rules for prayer. New York: Paulist Press, 1993. 151p ISBN 0-8091-3410-1 LC 93-4387

Paulukonis, Mary Ann.
Review of: *Small Christian communities* by Kleissler, Thomas A, et al. In: *Living Light* 29:95 Spr 1993

Pavelin, Alan.
Diary of a country priest [directed by R Bresson]. *Month* 26:202-203 My 1993
My night with Maud [directed by E Rohmer]. *Month* 26:204-205 My 1993
Ordet [directed by C Dreyer]. *Month* 26:203-204 My 1993
The sacrifice [directed by A Tarkovsky]. *Month* 26:204 My 1993
Theology in the cinema. *Month* 26:202-205 My 1993

Pawlikowski, John T.
The church and Judaism: questions Catholics ask. *Chicago Stud* 31:244-257 N 1992
Miles to go [editorial]. *New Theol Rev* 6:3-5 My 1993
The original schism: how Jews and Christians came to a parting of the ways [Interview by the editors of U.S. Catholic (Periodical)]. *USCath* 58:15-21 O 1993
Remembering Noah [editorial]. *New Theol Rev* 6:3-5 Ag 1993
Review of: *Alienated minority: the Jews of medieval Latin Europe* by Stow, Kenneth R. In: *TheolStds* 54:598 S 1993
Review of: *From desolation to hope: an interreligious Holocaust memorial service* by Fisher, Eugene J, and Klenicki, Leon, eds. In: *JEcumen Stds* 29:119-120 Wint 1992
Review of: *In our time: the flowering of Jewish-Catholic dialogue* by Fisher, Eugene J, and Klenicki, Leon, eds. In: *JEcumen Stds* 29:119-120 Wint 1992
Review of: *Thank God: prayers of Jews and Christians* by Jegen, Carol Frances, and Sherwin, Byron L. In: *JEcumen Stds* 29:119-120 Wint 1992
Review of: *Uncompleted mission* by Dickson, Kwesi A. In: *CLW* 64:34-36 Jl-S 1993
Review of: *Whispers of revelation: discovering the spirit of the poor* by Coleman, Bill, and Coleman, Patty. In: *CLW* 64:37 Jl-S 1993
Seeing anew: beauty, the arts, and Christian faith [editorial]. *New Theol Rev* 5:3-5 F 1993

Paxton, F.
Review of: *Communities of Saint Martin: legend and ritual in medieval tours* by Farmer, Sharon. In: *CHist* 78:633-634 O 1992

Payeur, Joseph A.
Inculturation through small Christian communities. *AFER* 35:37-43 F 1993

Payne, David F.
The Collegeville Bible time-line. Collegeville: Liturgical, 1993. 15p ISBN 0-8146-2275-5 LC 93-19614

Payne, Joseph A.
Befriending: a self-guided retreat for busy people. New Jersey: Paulist Press, 1992. x, 165p ISBN 0-8091-3354-7 LC 92-28398
Review of: *Lessons of the heart: celebrating the rhythms of life* by Livingston, Patricia H. In: *ChrWorld* 236:279 N-D 1993

Payne, Steven.
Review of: *Mystic union: an essay in the phenomenology of mysticism* by Pike, Nelson. In: *Spir Life* 32:112-114 Sum 1993
Review of: *Mystic union: an essay in the phenomenology of mysticism* by Pike, Nelson. In: *TheolStds* 54:368-369 Je 1993

Pazola, Ron.
Can the Dead Sea Scrolls teach us about the living Jesus? *USCath* 58:13-20 N 1993
How conservative Catholics keep the faith. *USCath* 58:14-19 Je 1993
Who's been sitting in Peter's chair? *USCath* 58:34-39 Jl 1993

Pearce, Maurice.
This is how it was. *Month* 26:81-84 F 1993

Pearce, Sarah.
Review of: *The Bible* by Prickett, Stephen, and Barnes, Robert. In: *Heythrop* 34:430-431 O 1993

Pearson, Helen Bruch.
Do what you have the power to do: studies of six New Testament women. Nashville: Upper Room Books, 1992. x, 168p ISBN 08-358-0643-x LC 91-65725

Pearson, Patricia O.
We are teachers and models. *ReligTJ* 27:26-27 F 1993

Pearson, Paul M.
Review of: *Mentoring: the ministry of spiritual kinship* by Sellner, Edward Cletus. In: *Cist Stud* 28:[9]-[10] 1993

Pearson, Richard.
Review of: *Parables in Midrash* by Stern, David. In: *Relig Lit* 24:105-106 Aut 1992

Pease, Neal.
Review of: *Acta Nuntiaturae Polonae; vol II: Zacharias Ferreri (1519-1521) et nuntii minores (1522-1553)* by Wojtyska, Henricus Damianus, ed. In: *CHist* 79:334-335 Ap 1993
Review of: *Volume VI: Iulius Ruggieri (1565-1568)* by Glemma, Thaddeus, and Bogaczewicz, Stanislaus, eds. In: *CHist* 79:334-335 Ap 1993
Review of: *Volume XLI: Iulius Piazza (1706-1708), volume 1 (8 VII 1706-31 III 1707)* by Kopiec, Ioannes, ed. In: *CHist* 79:334-335 Ap 1993
Review of: *Volume XVIII: Franciscus Simonetta (1606-1612), volume 1 (21 VI 1606-30 IX 1607)* by Tygielski, Adalbertus, ed. In: *CHist* 79:334-335 Ap 1993

Peatman, Bill.
If God attacks, don't let him get away with it. *Nat Cath Rep* 29:2 Mr 19 1993
Review of: *Dear James* by Hassler, Jon. In: *Nat Cath Rep* 29:33 My 28 1993
Review of: *Voices from the holocaust* by Cargas, Harry James. In: *Nat Cath Rep* 29:14 My 21 1993

Pecht, Gerard.
Review of: *Awake in the spirit* by Pennington, M Basil, 1931-. In: *Liguorian* 81:69 Ag 1993
Review of: *Book of Catholic prayer* by Bliven, Edmond. In: *Liguorian* 81:70 Ag 1993
Review of: *Francis de Sales: finding God wherever you are* by Power, Joseph F, ed. In: *Liguorian* 81:70 Ag 1993
Review of: *Personality* by Hildebrand, Dietrich von. In: *Liguorian* 81:70 Ag 1993
Review of: *Prayer in the New Testament* by Doohan, Helen, and Doohan, Leonard. In: *Liguorian* 81:68 Ag 1993
Review of: *Praying in the Catholic tradition* by Schineller, Peter. In: *Liguorian* 81:69 Ag 1993
Review of: *Reawakenings* by Keating, Thomas. In: *Liguorian* 81:68-69 Ag 1993
Review of: *The week in daily prayer* by Trick, Barry J. In: *Liguorian* 81:69 Ag 1993
Review of: *Yielding, prayers for those in need of hope* by O'Malley, William J, 1931-. In: *Liguorian* 81:68 Ag 1993

Peck, Janice.
The gods of televangelism. Cresskill, New Jersey: Hampton Press, 1993. x, 271p ISBN 1-88130-365-9 LC 92-32476

Peddle, D.
Review of: *The political philosophy of Michael Oakeshott* by Franco, Paul. In: *Heythrop* 34:97-99 Ja 1993

Pedreirs, Jorge.
AIDs in the workplace: discrimination by ignorance. *CLawyer* 35 no 2:199-215 1993

Peel, Henry.
Review of: *The diocese of Killaloe* by Murphy, Ignatius. In: *Doctr Life* 43:121-122 F 1993

Peeters, Denise.
Pour une théologie à l'école de l'écologie. *Lumen* 48:51-65 Mr 1993
Toward an ecologically informed theology. *TheolDgst* 40:113-118 Sum 1993

Pelham, Judith C.
Integrated delivery challenges sponsors, systems. *Health Prog* 74:52 Jl-Ag 1993

Pelland, Gilles.
Incidence de l'exegese sur l'evolution du droit canonique durant la premiere partie du Moyen Age. *Periodica* 82 no 1:9-25 1993
Review of: *Athénagore, supplique au sujet des chrétiens et sur la résurrection des morts* by Pouderon, Bernard. In: *Gregorianum* 74 no 2:389-390 1993
Review of: *Commentaire sur le Cantique des Cantiques, tome I* by Origen. In: *Gregorianum* 74 no 2:388-389 1993
Review of: *Commentaire sur le Cantique des Cantiques, tome II* by Origen. In: *Gregorianum* 74 no 2:388-389 1993
Review of: *Hymnes* by Milan, Ambroise de. In: *Gregorianum* 74 no 3:590-591 1993

Pellegrino, Edmund D.
Catholic identity in medical schools. *Health Prog* 74:70-73 Ja-F 1993

Pelletier, Annette M.
Religious life—mystery or mistake? *RRel* 52:773-779 S-O 1993

Peloso, Barbara.
The Ignatian exercises in daily life: some problematic issues. *Way Suppl* 75:56-61 Aut 1992

Peltz, Carl F.
Walking in the kingdom of God: an Advent meditation for the busy Christian. Collegeville:Liturgical, 1993. 48p ISBN 0-8146-2238-0

Pelzel, Morris.
Review of: *Theological investigations XXIII. Final writings* by Rahner, Karl, 1904-1984. In: *Living Light* 29:95 Sum 1993

Pena, Raymundo, Bp.
A call to reassess Operation Blockade. *Origins* 23:372-373 N 4 1993

Peña Vanegas, Eduardo.
Un primer esbozo de Santo Domingo. *Christus* 58:11-14 Mr-Ap 1993

Penaskovic, R.
Review of: *Theology and dialogue: essays in conversation with George Lindbeck* by Marshall, Bruce D. In: *Heythrop* 34:88-89 Ja 1993

Penchansky, David.
Review of: *The tree of life: an exploration of Biblical wisdom literature* by Murphy, Roland E. In: *CBQ* 55:123-124 Ja 1993
Review of: *Tragedy and biblical narrative* by Exum, Cheryl J. In: *OTA* 16:158 F 1993

Penick, Carol Lacquement.
An encounter with Christ. *Living Prayer* 26:29 Jl-Ag 1993

Pennington, M Basil, 1931-.
The Cistercians SO in the United States at the 500 mark. *Word Sp* 14:23-32 1992
The fifteen mysteries in image and word. Huntington: Our Sunday Visitor, 1993. 165p ISBN 0-87973-499-x LC 92-61553
Why monks still matter. *OSV* 82:5 O 10 1993 *see* Bolshakoff, Sergius, jt auth

Penta, Leo J.
Resistance to the rule of time or a "post-metyphysical metaphysics": Michael Theunissen's Negative Theology of Time. *PhilosTod* 37:211-224 Sum 1993

Pepper, George B.
Review of: *Kant's philosophy of religion reconsidered* by Rossi, Philip J, and Wreen, Michael, eds. In: *CrossCurr* 43:116-117 Spr 1993

Perdue, Leo G, et al, eds.
Essays in memory of John G. Gammie. Louisville: John Knox, 1993. x, 352p ISBN 0-664-25295-8

Perdue, Leo G. *see* Gammie, John G, jt ed

Perelmuter, Hayim Goren.
Review of: *Paul and the Jewish law* by Tomson, Peter J. In: *New Theol Rev* 6:115-116 My 1993
Review of: *The changing face of Jewish and Christian worship in North America* by Bradshaw, Paul F, and Hoffman, Lawrence A, eds. In: *Worship* 67:86-87 Ja 1993
The strength of the elders. *BibleT* 30:347-352 N 1992

Pérez-Cotapos, Eduardo L.
Las parábolas; de Jesús: su sentido y adecuada interpreción. *Teol Vida* 33 no 3-4:165-178 1992
Review of: *Historia de la Literatura cirstiana primitiva* by Vielhauer, Philipp. In: *Teol Vida* 33 no 3-4:322-323 1992
Review of: *Las parábolas de Jesús* by Harnisch, Wolfgang. In: *Teol Vida* 33 no 3-4:323-324 1992
Review of: *Manual de la Biblia* by Mertens, Heinrich. In: *Teol Vida* 33 no 3-4:323 1992

Perez Gago, Santiago.
La atrición universal del viejo mundo XII Congreso internacional de estética: "La modernidad como estética". *Cien Tom* 119:593-597 S-D 1992

Pergler, Bonnie Schwartz.
Something old, something new. *Momentum* 24:10-12 F-Mr 1993

Peri, Vittorio.
Local churches and catholicity in the first millennium of the Roman tradition. *Jurist* 52 no 1:79-108 1992

Perico, Giacomo.
Stupro, aborto e anticoncezionali. *Civilta* 3:37-46 Jl 3 1993

Perini, Sergio. *see* Antoni, Dino De, jt auth

Perkins, Barbara.
A simple sign of service. *ReligTJ* 27:14 F 1993

Perkins, Pheme.
Review of: *Stony the road we trod: African American biblical interpretation* by Felder, Cain Hope, ed. In: *CrossCurr* 43:120-122 Spr 1993

Perko, F Michael.
Review of: *Mother Cabrini* by Sullivan, Mary Louise. In: *RRel* 52:790-791 S-O 1993
A short-lived spring. *Month* 26:313-314 Ag 1993

Perkovich, George.
Review of: *The Islamic threat* by Esposito, John. In: *Comm* 120:21-23 F 12 1993

Perona, Angeles J.
Entre el liberalismo y la socialdemocracia: la sociedad abierta. Barcelona: Anthropos, 1993. x, 248p ISBN 84-7658-394-x

Perry, John D.
The loving tree. *Living Prayer* 26:8-10 S-O 1993

Perry, John Michael.
Exploring the resurrection of Jesus. Kansas City: Sheed & Ward, 1993. x, 145p ISBN 1-55612-670-0 LC 93-29160

Perry, Mary Elizabeth. *see* Cruz, Anne J, jt ed

Perry, Norman.
Charting our second 100 years. *St Anth* 101:23 Je 1993
Fox, Andrew E, 1911-1992 [obit]. *St Anth* 100:1 Ja 1993

Person, James E, Jr.
Review of: *The glittering illusion: English sympathy for the Southern Confederacy* by Vanauken, Sheldon. In: *Crisis* 11:51-52 Mr 1993

Persson, Bertil, et al. *see* Ward, Gary L, jt ed

Pesch, Otto Hermann, 1931-.
Das Zweite Vatikanische Konzil. Frieburg: Echter, 1993. x, 444p ISBN 3-429-01533-2

Peter, C B.
Beyond a theology of development. *AFER* 35:54-67 F 1993

Peter-Raoul, Mar.
Review of: *Relentless persistence: nonviolent action in Latin America* by McManus, Philip, and Schlabach, Gerald, eds. In: *CrossCurr* 42:562-563 Wint 1992-1993

Peters, Ted.
Toward a theology of nature: essays on science and faith. Louisville, Kentucky: John Knox Press, 1993. 208p ISBN 0-664-25384-9

Peters, Tiemo Ranier. *see* Metz, Johann Baptist, jt auth

Peterson, Eugene H.
The contemplative pastor: returning to the art of spiritual direction. Grand Rapids: Eerdmans, 1993. 192p ISBN 0-8028-0114-5
The message: the New Testament in contemporary English. Colorado Springs: NavPress, 1993. 544p ISBN 0-08910-9787 LC 92-63203
Where your treasure is: psalms that summon you from self to community. Grand Rapids: Eerdmans, 1993. 176p ISBN 0-8028-01153

Peterson, John.
Deontologism and moral weakness. *IPQ* 33:173-181 Je 1993
God and the status of facts. *Thomist* 56:635-646 O 1992

Peterson, Wallace C, 1921-.
America's silent depression: a challenge to social economics. *RSocEcon* 51:2-13 Spr 1993

Petit, Jean-Claude.
Review of: *Festivals of interpretation, essays on Hans-Georg Gadamer's work* by Wright, Kathleen, ed. In: *Laval Theol Phil* 49:374 Je 1993
Review of: *L'interprétation infinie* by Bori, Pier Cesare. In: *Laval Theol Phil* 49:171-172 F 1993

Petit, Philip. *see* Hamlin, Alan, jt ed

Petitclerc, J-M. *see* Davin, J, jt auth

Petras, Kathryn. *see* Petras, Ross, jt ed

Petricek, Miroslav.
On history, charm, and grief. *PhilosTod* 36:304-308 Wint 1992

Petruzzi, Nancy. *see* Chenot, Dolores, jt auth

Pevtzow, Lisa.
Bethlehem U: politics is the sport. *Register* 69:1+ Ja 24 1993
Christianity examined at its source. *Register* 69:1+ Je 13 1993
Christians in Jewish army on rise. *Register* 69:1+ Ag 8 1993
Close to the source. *Register* 69:2 S 12 1993
Find sheds light on David's rule. *Register* 69:1+ Ag 22 1993
Greek clergy, Arab laity in dispute. *Register* 69:1+ F 7 1993
Holy Land archaeology is source of controversy. *Register* 69:1+ Jl 4 1993
In Israel, Christians "suspect". *Register* 69:1+ Ja 10 1993
Isaeli government helps fund Christian schools. *Register* 69:1+ Jl 25 1993
Israel, fundies share an agenda. *Register* 69:1+ My 23 1993
Israel, Rome near accord. *Register* 69:1+ O 3 1993
Israeli welcome cool to non-Jews. *Register* 69:1+ Mr 7 1993
Israeli-Arab Christians: a paradox. *Register* 69:1+ My 30 1993
Libyan "pilgrims" a fiasco. *Register* 69:1+ Je 20 1993
Local Xian anger high for Israel. *Register* 69:1+ Je 6 1993
No peace for reds and whites. *Register* 69:1+ Mr 21 1993
Palestine Christians vent steam. *Register* 69:1+ Jl 18 1993
Religion a key to terrorist. *Register* 69:1+ Ap 18 1993
Right or wrong, Demjanjuk may go free. *Register* 69:1+ Ag 15 1993
A rumor of peace. *Register* 69:1+ S 19 1993
Vatican slows talks with Israel. *Register* 69:1+ Mr 28 1993
Waiting for John Paul [Israel visit]. *Register* 69:2 F 14 1993
West Bank settlers won't go. *Register* 69:1+ Je 27 1993

Pezzali, Amalia.
Il Buddhismo e le altre religioni. *StudiaM* 42:347-356 1993

Pfaff, William.
The Pope dissents from America. *OSV* 82:23 N 14 1993

Pfeifer, Carl J. *see* Manternach, Janann, jt auth

Pfeifer, Carl J, and Manternach, Janaan.
Questions catechists ask and answers that really work. Kansas City: Sheed & Ward, 1993. 110p ISBN 1-55612-620-4

Pfeiffer, Heinrich.
La Madonna a Mosca e a Roma: teologia, arte, devozione popolare. *Civilta* 144:370-373 F 20 1993
Review of: *Kirchengeräte, Kreuze und Reliquiare der christlichen Kirchen.* In: *Gregorianum* 74 no 2:390-391 1993

Pfordresher, John.
Review of: *The Catholic religious poets from Southwell to Crashaw* by Cousins, Anthony D. In: *TheolStds* 54:599-600 S 1993

Pham, John-Peter.
Review of: *Scientist and Catholic: an essay on Pierre Duhem* by Jaki, Stanley L. In: *Crisis* 10:51-53 N 1992

Phan, Peter C.
Review of: *Does God exist? A believer and an atheist debate* by Miethe, Terry, and Flew, Antony. In: *Living Light* 29:98-99 Sum 1993
Review of: *Dynamics of theology* by Haight, Roger. In: *Living Light* 29:88-89 Sum 1993
Review of: *Exploring the feminine face of God* by Meehan, Bridget Mary. In: *Living Light* 29:95 Aut 1992
Review of: *Jesus Christ at the encounter of world religions* by Dupuis, Jacques. In: *Living Light* 29:90-91 Aut 1992
Review of: *Proclaiming justice and peace* by Walsh, Michael J, 1937-, and Davis, Brian, eds. In: *Living Light* 29:97-98 Sum 1993
Review of: *The craft of theology* by Dulles, Avery Robert, 1918-. In: *Living Light* 29:88-89 Sum 1993
Review of: *The God of life* by Gutiérrez, Gustavo. In: *Living Light* 29:98-99 Sum 1993

Phelan, Bernard C.
Where catechists build the church. *Priests & People* 7:54-57 F 1993

Phelan, Michael.
Review of: *The everyday God* by Dominian, Jack, 1929-, and Flood, Edmund. In: *Tablet* 247:551-552 My 1 1993

Philibert, Paul J.
Committed Christian secularity. *RRel* 52:350-362 My-Je 1993

Philippart, David.
Catholics should stand at the consecration. *USCath* 58:20-25 Jl 1993

Philippe, Pierre Paul, Cardinal, 1905-1984.
The Virgin Mary and the priesthood. New York: Alba House, 1993. x, 135p ISBN 0-8189-0668-5 LC 93-6682

Phillips, L Edwards. *see* Phillips, Sara Webb, jt auth

Phillips, Melanie.
The family and the left. *Tablet* 247:972-973 Jl 31 1993

Phipps, William E.
The wisdom and wit of Rabbi Jesus. Louisville: Westminster, 1993. x, 272p ISBN 0-664-25232-x

Piccolino, Alberta.
Activists allege torture in some US prisons. *Nat Cath Rep* 29:2 N 13 1992
Alternative health care looks beyond body. *Nat Cath Rep* 29:6 Je 18 1993
Maryhouse. *Cath Work* 60:2 Ja-F 1993

Pickard, Carmel.
Sunday—day of murder by gun and grenade. *Tablet* 247:989-990 Jl 31 1993

Picken, Elizabeth J.
Forum: if Christ is bridegroom, the priest must be male? [reply to S Butler, 66 no 6:498-517 N 1992]. *Worship* 67:269-278 My 1993

Pickstone, Charles.
The art of pain. *Month* 26:278-280 Jl 1993
Finding a world in a grain of sand: but is it art? *Month* 26:152-154 Ap 1993
Georgia O'Keeffe: American and modern. *Month* 26:199-201 My 1993
Sacred and profane sex: Edvard Munch at the National Gallery, Eric Gill at the Barbican. *Month* 26:22-25 Ja 1993
The sins of the fathers: decadence and despair in fin-de-siècle France. *Month* 26:391-395 S-O 1993

Pié-Ninot, Salvador.
La identidad eclesial de la teología fundamental. *Gregorianum* 74 No 1:75-99 1993

Piemontese, Angelo Michele. *see* Bautier, Robert Henri, jt auth

Pieper, Lori.
Top 10 reasons why the devil hates C.S. Lewis. *OSV* 82:10-11 N 7 1993

Pierce, Gregory F Augustine. *see* Droel, William, jt auth

Pierce, Joanne M.
Review of: *The Durham collectar* by Corrêa, Alicia, ed. In: *TheolStds* 54:597-598 S 1993

Pierce, Ted M.
Freedom: the teachings of Jesus. New York: Vantage Press, 1992. x, 225p ISBN 0-533-10182-4 LC 91-91544

Pieri, Francesco. *see* Morello, Giovanni, jt auth

Pieris, Aloysius, 1934-.
An Asian paradigm: inter-religious dialogue and theology of religions [repr fr Qoholet]. *Month* 26:129-134 Ap 1993
Interreligious dialogue and theology of religions: an Asian paradigm. *Horizons (CTS)* 20:106-114 Spr 1993
Whither new evangelism? *Pacifica* 6:327-334 O 1993

Pieronek, Tadeusz, Bp.
Dialogue [interview by Jonathan Luxmoore]. *Register* 69:1+ Jl 25 1993

Pierskala, Rudolf.
Rinnovamento del sacramento della confermazione. *Notitiae* 28:684-686 O 1992

Piil, Mary Alice.
Remembering the dead. *Mod Lit* 20:6-7 Ag 1993

Pike, Lori.
Searching for Bobby Fischer [directed by G Zaillian]. *Register* 69:5 O 3 1993
U2 is a rock band on a mission. *Register* 69:5 Ag 29 1993

Pilapil, V.
Review of: *Awakening to mission: the Philippine Catholic Church 1965-1981* by Giordano, Pasquale T. In: *CHist* 78:702-703 O 1992

Pilarczyk, Daniel Edward, Abp, 1934-.
Forgiveness and the Church. *OSV* 82:6 Jl 25 1993
God's unexplainable and mysterious love. *OSV* 82:6 Jl 18 1993
The importance of forgiveness. *OSV* 82:5 Jl 4 1993
Sin is real. *OSV* 82:9 Jl 11 1993
To forgive is both human and divine. *OSV* 82:5 Ag 1 1993

Pilarz, Scott.
Dazed and confused. *America* 169:23 N 20 1993
Someone who'll watch over me. *America* 168:17 Ap 3 1993

Pilch, John Joseph, 1936-.
Beat his ribs while he is young (Sir 30:12). *Bib Th Bul* 23:101-113 Aut 1993
Guiding principles behind the bad homilies. *Nat Cath Rep* 29:18 Ap 2 1993
House and hearth. *BibleT* 31:292-299 S 1993
Jews or Judeans: a translation challenge. *Mod Lit* 20:19 Ap 1993
The necessities of life: drinking and eating [photos]. *BibleT* 31:231-237 Jl 1993
Review of: *A child shall lead them: a guide to celebrating the Word with children* by Pottebaum, Gerard A, et al. In: *Mod Lit* 20:39 O 1993
Review of: *John's Gospel in new perspective* by Cassidy, Richard J. In: *Sisters* 65:307-308 Jl 1993
Review of: *Prorocy Amos i Micheasz wobec niesprawiedlit-wości spolecznej* by Witaszek, Gabriel. In: *OTA* 16:432-433 Je 1993
Review of: *Prorok wobec dziejów* by Chrostowski, Waldemar. In: *OTA* 16:180 F 1993
Review of: *Reading and praying the New Testament* by Kreeft, Peter John, 1937-. In: *Mod Lit* 20:42 Ag 1993
Review of: *Social science commentary on the synoptic gospels* by Malina, Bruce J, 1933-, and Rohrbaugh, Richard L. In: *Mod Lit* 20:40 O 1993
Review of: *The Gospels and the Letters of Paul: an inclusive-language edition* by Throckmorton, Burton H, Jr, ed. In: *Mod Lit* 20:41 Ap 1993

Pilch, John Joseph, 1936-. *(cont'd)*
Review of: *Windows on the gospel* by McCarthy, Flor. In: *Mod Lit* 20:40 Je-Jl 1993

Pimentel-Pinto, Francis.
Street children slaughtered in the night. *Tablet* 247:990 Jl 31 1993

Pinches, Charles, and McDaniel, Jay B, eds.
Good news for animals?: Christian approaches to animal well-being. Maryknoll, New York: Orbis Books, 1993. x, 258p ISBN 0-88344-866-1 LC 92-41682

Pinnington, Judith E.
Review of: *Struggles of faith* by Gallagher, Michael Paul, 1939-. In: *JEcumen Stds* 29:110 Wint 1992

Pinson, Jean-Pierre.
Review of: *Tonaire des pièces de la messe selon le Graduale Triplex et l'Offertoriale Triplex de Solesmes* by Guilmard, Dom Jacques-Marie. In: *Laval Theol Phil* 49:147-148 F 1993

Pipkin, Kate.
Africa: road to faith [photos]. *St Anth* 100:34-40 S 1993

Pippin, Robert B.
Hegel's original insight. *IPQ* 33:285-295 S 1993

Pirola, G.
Review of: *Cattolici e laicità della politica* by Rodano, Franco. In: *Civilta* 2:91-93 Ap 3 1993
Review of: *Dialettica dell'immagine: studi sull'imaginismo di Luigi Stefanini.* In: *Civilta* 144:514-515 Mr 6 1993
Review of: *Filosofia umana: itinerario di Alberto Caracciolo* by Moretto, Giovanni. In: *Civilta* 2:409-410 My 15 1993
Review of: *Il potere in discussione* by Vaiarelli, Giacomo, et al. In: *Civilta* 144:516-517 Mr 6 1993
Review of: *La questione dell'utilitarismo.* In: *Civilta* 2:205 Ap 17 1993
Review of: *La tolleranza religiosa: indagini storiche e riflessioni filosofiche* by Sina, Mario. In: *Civilta* 144:513-514 Mr 6 1993
Review of: *Platone, 2 voll* by Stefanini, Luigi. In: *Civilta* 144:515 Mr 6 1993

Pirro, R. *see* Langevin, G, jt ed

Piton, Jacques.
Un dossier "Renouvelons la terre" et ses fruits. *Lumen* 48:95-104 Mr 1993

Pittau, Franco. *see* Liegro, Luigi Di, jt auth

Piwowarski, Linda.
Eastern Europe: a church out of hiding [condensed fr *Cross Roads* Je 20, Jl 4, Jl 18, 1993]. *CDgst* 58:90-97 N 1993

Pixton, Paul B.
Review of: *Reform an Haupt und Gliedern* by Frech, Karl Augustin. In: *CHist* 79:318-319 Ap 1993

Pizzuti, D.
Review of: *Funzione della religione* by Luhmann, Niklas. In: *Civilta* 144:405-407 F 20 1993
Review of: *Sociologia delle religioni: problemi e prospettive* by Acquaviva, Sabinos, and Pace, Enzo. In: *Civilta* 3:342-343 Ag 7-21 1993

Place, Michael D.
Why we should not legalize euthanisa. *Health Prog* 74:39-43+ Mr 1993 *see* DeSilva, Joseph, jt auth

Place, Michael D, and Maletta, Sammie L, Jr.
Marital failure: the church's response. *Chicago Stud* 31:271-281 N 1992

Plank, Karl A.
The eclipse of difference: Merton's encounter with Judaism. *Cist Stud* 28 no 2:179-191 1993

Plant, Raymond M.
Review of: *Thomas More* by Martz, Louis L. In: *Can Cath Rev* 11:26-27 Ap 1993

Plante, Harry La.
Discussion: soul, rational soul and person in Thomism. *Mod Schlmn* 70:209-216 Mr 1993

Plass, Paul.
The metaphysical aspect of tenses in Proclus. *IPQ* 33:143-151 Je 1993

Platelle, Henri.
Review of: *Images of sainthood in medieval Europe* by Blumenfeld-Kosinski, Renate, and Szell, Timea, eds. In: *MSR* 50:56-59 Ja-Mr 1993
Review of: *Les Bibles en français* by Bogaert, Pierre-Maurice, et al, eds. In: *MSR* 50:53-56 Ja-Mr 1993
Le sens d'un colloque: moines et moniales devant la mort. *MSR* 50:49-51 Ja-Mr 1993

Pleasants, Julian R.
Aborted fetus can live if there's a pro-life volunteer to carry it. *Nat Cath Rep* 29:24 N 6 1992

Pleins, J David.
The Psalms: songs of tragedy, hope, and justice. Maryknoll: Orbis, 1993. x, 229p ISBN 0-88344-928-5 LC 93-17541

Pless, Cora Lee.
A clean plate and a hungry world. *Sisters* 65:214-216 My 1993

Plevnik, Joseph.
"All who walk by this rule" the canon of the New Testament. *Can Cath Rev* 11:12-20 F 1993
Review of: *Paul—one of the Prophets? a contribution to the apostle's self-understanding* by Sanders, Karl Olav. In: *CBQ* 55:177-178 Ja 1993

Plourde, Simonne. *see* Bélanger, Rodrigue, jt auth

Plueddemann, Carol. *see* Plueddemann, Jim, jt auth

Plueddemann, Jim, and Plueddemann, Carol.
Meekness: claiming your inheritance. Grand Rapids: Zondervan Publishing House, 1993. x, 64p ISBN 0-310-59623-8

Plumat, N.
Review of: *Bernard de Fontaines, Abbé de Clairvaux* by Vallery-Radot, I. In: *NRT* 114:927-928 N-D 1992
Review of: *Dictionnaire d'histoire et de géographie ecclésiastiques.* In: *NRT* 115:288-289 Mr-Ap 1993
Review of: *Diocesis de Calahorra y Santo Domingo* by Tellechea Idígoras, J Ignacio. In: *NRT* 115:614-615 Jl-Ag 1993
Review of: *Fin du monde et signes des temps.* In: *NRT* 115:612 Jl-Ag 1993
Review of: *Gli umiliati, le comunità degli ospizi della Svizzera italiana* by Moretti, A. In: *NRT* 115:611-612 Jl-Ag 1993
Review of: *Grosser Bildatlas der Kreuzzüge* by Riley-Smith, J, ed. In: *NRT* 115:287 Mr-Ap 1993
Review of: *Histoire et culture chrétienne* by Ledure, Y, ed. In: *NRT* 115:618 Jl-Ag 1993
Review of: *La Salette* by Stern, Jean. In: *NRT* 115:131 Ja-F 1993
Review of: *Lacordaire: son pays, ses amis et la liberté des ordres religieux* by Bedouelle, Guy, ed. In: *NRT* 114:921-922 N-D 1992
Review of: *Le mouvement social franciscain en France* by Burnod, J-M. In: *NRT* 114:916 N-D 1992
Review of: *Le sort de la Bulle Unigenitus* by Ceyssens, L. In: *NRT* 115:618-619 Jl-Ag 1993
Review of: *Les jésuites à Namur: 1610-1773.* In: *NRT* 115:141-142 Ja-F 1993
Review of: *Melanchthons: Briefwechsel* by Wetzel, R, ed. In: *NRT* 115:269-270 Mr-Ap 1993
Review of: *Nicolas Psaume 1518-1575, évêque et Comte de Verdun* by Ardura, B. In: *NRT* 114:930-931 N-D 1992
Review of: *Philipp Anton von Segesser* by Conzemius, Victor. In: *NRT* 114:934 N-D 1992
Review of: *Précis d'histoire grecque* by Durand, M de. In: *NRT* 114:918-919 N-D 1992
Review of: *Souvenirs et espérances* by Suenens, Leo Jozef, Cardinal, 1904-. In: *NRT* 115:285-286 Mr-Ap 1993
Review of: *Studi Gregoriani. Per la storia della "Libertas Ecclesiae"* by Stickler, A M, ed. In: *NRT* 115:611 Jl-Ag 1993
Review of: *Tesserae.* In: *NRT* 114:926-927 N-D 1992
Review of: *Una città, un fondatore.* In: *NRT* 114:932 N-D 1992

Plummer, Simon Scott.
Review of: *East Asia: from Chinese predominance to the rise of the Pacific Rim* by Cotterell, Arthur. In: *Tablet* 247:983-984 Jl 31 1993

Poché, Louis A.
Racial integration: did it work in Grand Coteau? *America* 169:16+ N 6 1993

Poda, Paula.
AIDS and comfort: no one deserves to die alone. *Salt* 13:18-21 Ap 1993

Podles, Leon J.
Masculinity and the military. *Crisis* 11:36-40 Jl-Ag 1993
Review of: *Fatherland* by Harris, Richard. In: *Crisis* 11:52-53 F 1993

Podles, Mary Elizabeth.
A garden of conceptual delights. *Crisis* 11:54-60 Je 1993
Home-schooling works. *Crisis* 11:27-32 Ap 1993

Podsiadlo, Jack.
Breaking away. *Momentum* 24:36-37 F-Mr 1993

Poel, Cornelius J van der.
Reflections on health care ethics. *Chicago Stud* 32:166-176 Ag 1993

Poelker, T.
Review of: *The Christian year* by Metford, J C J. In: *Past Mus* 17:50-51 D 1992-Ja 1993
Review of: *The origins of the liturgical year* by Talley, Thomas J. In: *Past Mus* 17:50-51 D 1992-Ja 1993
Review of: *The story of the Christian year* by Nardone, Richard M. In: *Past Mus* 17:50-51 D 1992-Ja 1993

Pöggeler, Otto.
The hermeneutics of the technological world: the Heidegger-Heisenberg dispute. *IJPS* 1:21-48 Mr 1993

Poggi, Isotta. *see* Melton, J Gordon, jt auth

Poggi, V.
Review of: *Arabi Cristiani e Arabi Musulmani* by Eid, Giuseppe Samir. In: *Civilta* 2:616-617 Je 19 1993
Review of: *Bishop Michael d'Herbigny SJ and Russia: a pre-ecumenical approach to Christian unity* by Tretjakewitsch, Léon. In: *Civilta* 2:405-407 My 15 1993
Review of: *Speranza nell'Islàm* by Dall'Oglio, Paolo. In: *Civilta* 3:193-194 Jl 17 1993

Pointon, Marcia. *see* Adler, Kathleen, jt ed

Pojman, Louis P.
Ethics: religious and secular. *Mod Schlmn* 70:1-30 N 1992

Polan, Gregory J.
Review of: *Dictionary of the Bible* by Mills, Watson E, ed. In: *OTA* 16:410-411 Je 1993
Review of: *Micah: a commentary* by Wolff, Hans Walter. In: *OTA* 16:433 Je 1993
Review of: *The literary guide to the Bible* by Alter, Robert, and Kermode, Frank, eds. In: *OTA* 16:393 Je 1993

Poletti, Ugo.
Work progresses on apse of St. Mary Major. *OR(Eng)* 1302:3+ Ag 11 1993

Polis, Dennis E.
Review of: *John of the Cross and the cognitive value of mysticism* by Payne, Steven, ed. In: *Mod Schlmn* 70:153-155 Ja 1993

Polish, Daniel F.
Review of: *A marginal Jew: rethinking the historical Jesus* by Meier, John P. In: *JEcumen Stds* 29:483-484 Sum-Aut 1992

Polkinghorne, John.
Not just any old world. *Tablet* 247:102-103 Ja 23 1993

Pollard, John E.
Overview: the catechism of the Catholic Church. *Origins* 23:7-11 My 20 1993
Planning the implementation of the Catechism of the Catholic Church. *Living Light* 29:74-77 Sum 1993

Power, William E.
Review of: *Empowering authority: the charisms of episcopacy and primacy in the Church today* by Howell, Patrick J, and Chamberlain, Guy, eds. In: *Can Cath Rev* 11:30-31 F 1993

Powers, Bruce R. *see* McLuhan, Marshall, jt auth

Powers, Isaias.
Women of the gospel. Mystic, Connecticut: Twenty-Third Publications, 1993. x, 153p ISBN 0-89622 LC 92-81796

Powers, Joseph M.
Review of: *Systematic theology* by Fiorenza, Francis Schüssler, 1938-, and Galvin, John P, 1944-, eds. In: *TheolStds* 54:173-175 Mr 1993

Pozo, Candido.
Sacerdocio ministerial y radicalismo de los consejos evangélicos. *Seminarium* 32:550-560 O-D 1992

Prado, Plinio Walder, Jr.
Argumentation and aesthetics: reflections on communication and the differend. *PhilosTod* 36:351-366 Wint 1992

Praetere, Thomas de.
Review of: *Traités et sermons* by Eckhart, Maître. In: *RPhil Louvain* 91:325 My 1993

Prager, Dennis.
Judaism's sexual revolution: why Judaism rejected homosexuality [fr *Ultimate Issues*]. *Crisis* 11:29-34+ S 1993

Prall, S.
Review of: *The revolutions of 1688* by Beddard, Robert, ed. In: *CHist* 78:662-663 O 1992

Prandi, Alberto. *see* Scroccaro, Luigino, jt auth

Prangemeier, Monika.
Focus on racism at the Kirchentag. *Tablet* 247:798 Je 19 1993

Pranger, Gary K.
Review of: *Philip Schaff: historian and ambassador* by Penzel, Klaus, ed. In: *CHist* 79:308-309 Ap 1993

Prato, Gian Luigi.
Review of: *Dal primo giudaismo alla Chiesa delle origini* by Russell, David Syme. In: *Civilta* 3:439-441 S 4 1993
Antico Testamento e culture coeve: dal rifiuto illusorio all'assimilazione vitale. *Gregorianum* 73 No 4:697-717 1992
Review of: *Commento ai Salmi, vol I: Sal 1-50* by Kimchi, R David. In: *Civilta* 143:525-526 D 5 1992
Review of: *Exégète à Jerusalem. Nouveaux mélanges d'histoire Religieuse (1890-1939)* by Lagrange, Marie-Joseph. In: *Gregorianum* 74 no 3:565-566 1993
Review of: *Il Giudaismo del secondo tempio* by Maier, Johann. In: *Gregorianum* 74 no 2:353-355 1993
Review of: *Il libro della Sapienza, vol I* by Scarpat, Giuseppe, ed. In: *Civilta* 144:507-508 Mr 6 1993
Review of: *In ascolto dei profeti e dei sapienti* by Cappelletto, Gianni, and Milani, Marcello. In: *Gregorianum* 74 no 2:405-406 1993
Review of: *In cammino con Israele* by Cappelletto, Gianni. In: *Gregorianum* 74 no 2:405-406 1993
Review of: *L'apocalittica giudaica e la sua storia* by Sacchi, Paolo. In: *Gregorianum* 74 No 1:141-142 1993
Review of: *L'asino del nemico* by Barbiero, Gianni. In: *Gregorianum* 74 no 2:355-358 1993
Review of: *La Biblia en su entorno.* In: *Gregorianum* 74 No 1:142-144 1993
Review of: *La mitologia ittitia* by Daddi, Franca Pecchioli, and Polvani, Anna Maria, eds. In: *Gregorianum* 74 no 3:571-572 1993
Review of: *Le Judaïsme et l'image* by Prigent, Pierre. In: *Gregorianum* 73 No 4:747-750 1992
Review of: *Sapienciales V Sabiduria* by Vílchez Lindez, José. In: *Gregorianum* 74 no 3:568-571 1993
Review of: *Storie di profeti* by Rofé, Alexander. In: *Civilta* 2:605-607 Je 19 1993
Review of: *Wurzeln der Weisheit: Die ältesten Sprüche Israels und anderer Völker* by Westermann, Claus. In: *Gregorianum* 74 No 1:149-150 1993

Pratt, Lonni Collins.
Helping the hurting: getting inside another's circle of pain. *New Cov* 22:15-16 Ap 1993
Lasting change. *New Cov* 22:16-17 Je 1993

Pravda, Joseph.
Résistances aux changements dans la Slovaquie actuelle. *Lumen* 47:417-425 D 1992

Preisler, Barry.
Review of: *Palestinians: the making of a people* by Kimmerling, Baruch, and Migdal, Joel. In: *America* 169:18-20 Jl 31-Ag 7 1993

Prendergast, Edith.
Leadership in religious education: envisioning new possibilities. *Catechist* 26:40-42 Ap-My 1993

Prendergast, William B.
Interpreting the Catholic vote in 1992. *America* 169:15+ O 16 1993

Prenna, L.
Review of: *Antonio Rosmini. Il carisma del Fondatore* by Valle, Alfeo. In: *Civilta* 3:436-438 S 4 1993
Review of: *La pedagogia greca: attualità di un progetto educativo* by Moscone, Maurizio. In: *Civilta* 2:410-411 My 15 1993

Prentice, Penelope.
Madness in Harold Pinter's plays and filmscripts: the public consequences of private madness. *Cithara* 32:31-38 N 1992

Prest, Loring A.
The Samaritan woman. *BibleT* 30:367-371 N 1992

Preston, Ronald.
Review of: *Christianity and the market* by Atherton, John. In: *Tablet* 247:276-277 F 27 1993

Preston, Ronald H.
Religion and the ambiguities of capitalism. Cleveland: The Pilgrim Press, 1993. x, 192p ISBN 0-8298-0946-5 LC 92-43014
Theological trends: business ethics and the pastoral task. *Way* 33:233-239 Jl 1993

Preston, William.
Review of: *Toward an African Christianity* by Hillman, Eugene. In: *Nat Cath Rep* 29:34 S 10 1993

Prevallet, Elaine M.
Holy ground [condensed fr *Weavings: a Journal of the Christian Spiritual Life* S/O 1992]. *CDgst* 57:33-38 Mr 1993

Prévost, Jean-Pierre.
How to read the Apocalypse. New York: The Crossroad Publishing Company, 1993. x, 118p ISBN 0-8245-1280-4 LC 93-16880
Review of: *JOb: réponse à Jung* by Amado Levy Valensi, E. In: *NRT* 115:263-264 Mr-Ap 1993
Review of: *L'homme, son développement religieux: etude de structuralisme génétique* by Gmünder, P, et al. In: *NRT* 115:272-273 Mr-Ap 1993

Price, Joseph L. *see* Musser, Donald W, jt ed

Price, Richard M.
Review of: *Christianity and the rhetoric of empire: the development of Christian discourse* by Cameron, Averil. In: *Heythrop* 34:447-448 O 1993

Price, W Wayne.
Confessions of a perfect parent. Grand Rapids: Eerdmans, 1993. 166p ISBN 0-8028-0676-7

Pridmore, John.
Review of: *Alphonsus de Liguori, the Saint of Bourbon Naples* by Jones, Frederick M. In: *Way* 33:165-166 Ap 1993
Review of: *David Watson* by Saunders, Teddy, and Sanson, Hugh. In: *Way* 33:166-167 Ap 1993
Review of: *Isaac Hecker* by O'Brien, David J, 1938-. In: *Way* 33:166-167 Ap 1993
Review of: *My witness for the Church* by Häring, Bernard, 1912-. In: *Way* 33:167-168 Ap 1993
Review of: *Silent lamp: the Thomas Merton story* by Shannon, William Henry, 1917-. In: *Way* 33:255 Jl 1993
Review of: *The shape of Catholic theology* by Nichols, Aidan. In: *Way* 33:79 Ja 1993
Review of: *Thomas Merton: spiritual master* by Cunningham, Lawrence S, 1935-. In: *Way* 33:254-255 Jl 1993
Review of: *Undiscovered ends* by Kent, Bruce. In: *Way* 33:167 Ap 1993
Review of: *What on earth? The Church in the world and the call of Christ* by Blair, Philip. In: *Month* 26:319-320 Ag 1993

Principe, Walter H.
Quaestiones concerning Christ from the first half of the thriteenth century. *Med Stud* 54:1-48 1992
Review of: *Saint Anselm* by Southern, R W. In: *TheolStds* 54:347-350 Je 1993

Pring, Richard.
All power to the centre. *Tablet* 247:201 F 13 1993
Flawed blueprint. *Tablet* 247:1062 Ag 21 1993
Flawed jewel in the crown. *Tablet* 247:72 Ja 16 1993
How to learn to teach. *Tablet* 247:918 Jl 17 1993
Schools for the real world. *Tablet* 247:394 Mr 27 1993
A test too far. *Tablet* 247:647 My 22 1993

Prior, Michael.
Review of: *Christological motives and motivated actions in Pauline Paraenesis* by Cruz, Hieronymus. In: *CBQ* 55:145-146 Ja 1993

Prizer, John.
Dave. *Register* 69:5 Je 13 1993
Indecent proposal. *Register* 69:5 My 23 1993
Jurassic Park [directed by S Spielberg]. *Register* 69:5 Je 11 1993
Made in America. *Register* 69:5 Je 20 1993
Menace II Society. *Register* 69:5 Jl 4 1993
Review of: "*Murdoch*" by Shawcross, William. In: *Register* 69:5 Je 6 1993
Review of: *Degenerate moderns* by Jones, Michael E. In: *Register* 69:3 Jl 18 1993
Sleepless in Seattle. *Register* 69:5 Jl 18 1993
The wave of the future. *Register* 69:2 Je 11 1993

Prizzell, L.
Review of: *The spirit of the ten commandments; shattering the myth of Rabbinic legalism* by Brooks, Roger. In: *SIDIC* 25 No 1:33 1992

Proctor-Smith, Marjorie, and Walton, Janet R.
Women at worship: interpretations of North American diversity. Louisville, Kentucky: John Knox Press, 1993. 272p ISBN 0-664-25253-2

Pronk, Pim.
Against nature? Types of moral argumentation regarding homosexuality. Grand Rapids: Eerdmans, 1993. 384p ISBN 0-8028-0623-6

Propp, William H.
Kinship in 2 Samuel 13. *CBQ* 55:39-53 Ja 1993

Prosen, Anthony J.
Separation of church and state. *SocJust* 84:57-60 Mr-Ap 1993

Proukou, Katherine.
Mysticism and feminism. *Living Prayer* 26:23-26 S-O 1993

Provost, James H.
Local church and catholicity in the constitution Pastor Bonus. *Jurist* 52 no 1:299-334 1992

Prpić, George J.
Review of: *The Yugoslav Auschwitz and the Vatican: the Croation massacre of the Serbs during World War II* by Dedijer, Vladimir. In: *CHist* 79:560-562 Jl 1993

Pryor, Bonnie.
Religion in your early childhood program. *Tod Cath Teach* 27:30+ O 1993

Przybilia, Carla. *see* Drummond, Thomas B, jt auth

Puca, P.
Review of: *I protagonisti della formazione: alla luce del documento Potissiumum Institutioni.* In: *Civilta* 144:104 Ja 2 1993

Pujol, C.
Vinum cui modica aqua miscenda est. *Periodica* 81 no 2:303-318 1992

Puleo, Mev.
A bishop who hears the cry of Haiti's poor. *St Anth* 100:34-41 My 1993

Puls, Joan. see Cashmore, Gwen, jt auth

Puntel, Betsy.
Review of: *Praying with Thérèse of Lisieux* by Schmidt, Joseph F. In: *Living Light* 29:94 Wint 1992

Purnell, A Patrick.
Guided prayer in parishes. *Way Suppl* 75:39-48 Aut 1992

Puskas, Charles B.
The letters of Paul: an introduction. Collegeville:Liturgical, 1993. x, 216p ISBN 0-8146-5690-0 LC 92-46909

Putti, P.
Review of: *La pena in crisi: il recente dibattito sulla funzione della pena* by Eusebi, Luciano. In: *Civilta* 144:98 Ja 2 1993

Putti, P M.
Review of: *L'altra adozione* by Sormano, Elena. In: *Civilta* 3:540-541 S 18 1993

Pylkkö, Pauli.
Eliminative naturalism and artistic meaning. *PhilosTod* 37:183-200 Sum 1993

Q

Quade, Quentin L.
Educational choice: getting there from here. *Momentum* 24:19-20 N-D 1993

Queralt, Antonio.
Review of: *Souffle de Dieu: Le Saint-Esprit dans le Nouveau Testament, Volume II* by Chevallier, Max-Alain. In: *Gregorianum* 74 No 1:150-152 1993

Quesnell, Quentin.
Review of: *The Messianic secret in Mark's Gospel* by Räisänen, Heikki. In: *CBQ* 54:798-799 O 1992
Review of: *Theology and the dialectics of history* by Doran, Robert M. In: *Horizons (CTS)* 19:319-320 Fall 1992

Quigley, George.
A response to unemployment: ten propositions. *Studies* 82:73-86 Spr 1993

Quigley, Thomas.
Overview: myths about Latin America's Church. *Origins* 23:362-368 O 28 1993

Quinette, Nancy. see Cann, Lorraine, jt auth

Quinn, Barbara. see Hughes, Kathleen, jt auth

Quinn, Francis, Bp.
The soul power a nation needs. *Origins* 22:605+ F 18 1993

Quinn, Gail.
Weakened research protections for unborn child opposed. *Origins* 22:610-611 F 18 1993

Quinn, J F. see Crawford, J M B, jt auth

Quinn, John F.
The "vagabond friar": Father Mathew's difficulties with the Irish bishops, 1840-1856. *CHist* 78:542-556 O 1992

Quinn, John Raphael, Abp, 1929-.
It is the best of times, to be a priest. *America* 169:16-17 S 18 1993
Pastoral planning for the new millennium. *Origins* 22:624-628 F 25 1993
Perspectives on "Veritatis Splendor". *Origins* 23:398-399 N 11 1993
Veritatis Splendor (the Splendor of Truth), Encyclical letter on moral issues (1993 10 05) [Commentary].
Scandals in the Church: reflections at Paschaltide. *America* 168:4-6 Ap 10 1993
A witness marked by love and humility. *Origins* 23:113+ Jl 15 1993

Quinn, Kevin P.
Review of: *The culture of disbelief* by Carter, Stephen L. In: *America* 169:19-20 N 27 1993

Quinn, Mary Jo.
Singing at the rites begins with Sunday. *Past Mus* 17:35-37 Ap-My 1993

Quinn, Patrick.
Aquinas concept of the body and out of body situations. *Heythrop* 34:387-400 O 1993

Quinn, Peggy.
Review of: *Geno* by O'Rourke, Lawrence M. In: *SocJust* 84:127 Jl-Ag 1993

Quitslund, Sonya A.
Review of: *Beyond patching: faith and feminism in the Catholic Church* by Schneiders, Sandra M. In: *JEcumen Stds* 29:260-262 Spr 1992
Review of: *Confessing conscience: churched women on abortion* by Tickle, Phyllis, ed. In: *JEcumen Stds* 29:260-262 Spr 1992
Review of: *Gender, doctrine, and God: the Shakers and contemporary theology* by Mercadante, Linda A. In: *JEcumen Stds* 29:260-262 Spr 1992
Review of: *Reformed and feminist: a challenge to the church* by Wijk-Bos, Johanna W H van. In: *JEcumen Stds* 29:260-262 Spr 1992
Review of: *Springs of water in a dry land: spiritual survival for Catholic women today* by Weaver, Mary Jo. In: *TheolStds* 54:606-607 S 1993
Review of: *The women's Bible commentary* by Newsom, Carol A, and Ringe, Sharon H, eds. In: *TheolStds* 54:339-341 Je 1993
Review of: *Women and Church: the challenge of ecumenical solidarity in an age of alienation* by May, Melanie A, ed. In: *JEcumen Stds* 29:260-262 Spr 1992

R

Rabitti, Paolo.
Lettera agli arcivescovi e vescovi residenziali della chiesa universale. *Notitiae* 28:714-731 N-D 1992

Rabkin, Jeremy A. see Crovitz, L Gordon, jt ed

Racine, Jean-François.
Review of: *The minor agreements* by Neirynck, Frans. In: *Laval Theol Phil* 49:376 Je 1993

Radano, John A.
Die Fünfte Weltkonferenz für Glauben und Kirchenverfassung. *Catholica* 47:20-37 1993
Pope John Paul II and "Faith and Order". *Ecumen Trends* 22:3-6 F 1993

Radcliffe, Fabian.
Faith in students. *Priests & People* 7:273-277 Jl 1993

Rader, Judith.
Dogs in the sheep; Green Father; Corn Maiden. *Spirit* 57:39-41 Spr-Sum 1992

Radlbeck-Ossmann, Regina.
In Drei Personen—der Trinitarische Schüsselbegriff "Person" in den Entwürfen Jürgen Moltmanns und Walter Kaspers. *Catholica* 47:38-51 1993

Rae, Scott B.
The California euthanasia initiative. *Linacre* 59:5-14 N 1992

Raemdonck, André van.
Pourquoi le Nouvel Âge fascine-t-il? *Lumen* 48:247-255 S 1993

Rafferty, Kevin.
Cardinal looks to the future in hope. *Tablet* 247:1203 S 18 1993
A deal with God. *Tablet* 247:1003-1004 Ag 7 1993
A Japanese rainbow. *Tablet* 247:1032-1033 Ag 14 1993
Journey to Peking. *Tablet* 247:1178-1179 S 11 1993
A monster revives. *Tablet* 247:568+ My 8 1993
Review of: *The end of Hong Kon: the secret diplomacy of imperial retreat* by Cottrell, Robert. In: *Tablet* 247:691 My 29 1993
Review of: *The fate of Hong Kong* by Segal, Gerald. In: *Tablet* 247:691 My 29 1993

Rafferty, Oliver.
The background to Archbishop Cranmer's thought on the royal supremacy. *Heythrop* 34:288-295 Jl 1993
The impasse in Northern Ireland [editorial]. *Month* 26:254-256 Jl 1993
Review of: *Northern Ireland: faith and faction* by Irvine, Maurice. In: *Heythrop* 34:348-350 Jl 1993
Review of: *The tragedy of belief: division, politics, and religion in Ireland* by Fulton, John. In: *Heythrop* 34:348-350 Jl 1993

Rahner, Karl, 1904-1984.
The great church year: the best of Karl Rahner's homilies, sermons, and meditations. New York: Crossroad, 1993. 396p ISBN 0-8245-1220-6 LC 93-3930 see Viller, Marcel, jt auth

Raine, Kathleen.
Review of: *On living and dying* by Krishnamurti, Jeddu, 1895-1986. In: *Tablet* 247:692-693 My 29 1993
Review of: *On relationship* by Krishnamurti, Jeddu, 1895-1986. In: *Tablet* 247:692-693 My 29 1993

Rainwater, M V.
Review of: *Truth and eros: Foucault, Lacan, and the question of ethics* by Rajchman, John. In: *IJPS* 1:167 Mr 1993

Räisänen, Heikki.
Freedom from the law in early Christianity. *TheolDgst* 40:43-48 Spr 1993

Raiser, Konrad.
Letter from WCC head on attack by magazine. *Ecumen Trends* 22:7 Mr 1993

Ralph, Margaret Nutting.
Discovering prophecy and wisdom: the books of Isaiah, Job, Proverbs, Psalms. New York: Paulist, 1993. x, 326p ISBN 08-0913-402-0 LC 93-10245

Rambachan, Anantanand.
Review of: *Christian ashrams: a new religious movement in contemporary India* by Ralston, Helen. In: *JEcumen Stds* 29:283 Spr 1992

Rambaldi, Giuseppe.
Ordinazioni Anglicane e Ecclesiologia. I. *Gregorianum* 74 no 2:277-307 1993
Review of: *Movimenti ecclesiali contemporanei* by Favale, Agostino, et al. In: *Gregorianum* 73 No 4:761-762 1992

Raming, Ida.
"The twelve apostles were men.". *TheolDgst* 40:21-25 Spr 1993

Ramirez, Ricardo, Bp.
What Cesar Chavez believed. *Origins* 23:17+ My 27 1993

Ramos, Alexis Mary.
A model missionary: episodes in the life of St Anthony Mary Claret. *ChrWorld* 38:124-134 Mr-Ap 1993

Ramos, L.
Review of: *Diccionario, patristico y de la Antigüendad Christiana.* In: *Christus* 58:82 N-D 1992

Rampersad, Arnold. see Asche, Arthur, jt auth

Ramsey, Boniface.
Addendum to Boniface Ramsey, "John Cassian: student of Augustine," CSQ 28 (1993): 5-15. *Cist Stud* 28 no 2:199-200 1993
John Cassian: student of Augustine. *Cist Stud* 28:5-15 1993
What did Jesus really look like? *America* 168:16-17 Je 19-26 1993

Ramsey, David.
Hidden treasure. *Mod Lit* 19:30 D 1992-Ja 1993

Ramshaw, Gail.
Review of: *She who is* by Johnson, Elizabeth A, 1941-. In: *Worship* 67:284-286 My 1993
Review of: *The Joseph Campbell phenomenon: implications for the contemporary church* by Madden, Lawrence J, ed. In: *Worship* 67:187-188 Mr 1993 *see* Lathrop, Gordon, jt auth

Randall, Scott J.
A psalm primer. *Mod Lit* 19:12-13 D 1992-Ja 1993
Review of: *Sacred sund and social change: liturgical music in Jewish and Christian experience* by Hoffman, Lawrence A, and Walton, Janet R, eds. In: *Mod Lit* 20:40 Ag 1993

Randazzo, Anthony J.
At Jacob's well. *Mod Lit* 20:17 Mr 1993

Ranger, Shelagh.
Building bridges. *Tablet* 247:258 F 20 1993

Rankin, David.
Review of: *The Trinity* by Augustine, Saint, Bp of Hippo. In: *Pacifica* 6:112-114 F 1993

Ranzino, Tom.
Formation of baptized candidates: what do you do? *Tod Parish* 25:15-18 Mr 1993

Raper, Mark.
Der Flüchtlingsdienst der Jesuiten. *Stimm Zeit* 211:45-52 Ja 1993

Rapien, Mary Lynne.
Review of: *Picking the "right" Bible study program* by Scott, Macrina. In: *St Anth* 100:52-53 My 1993

Rapley, E.
Review of: *Les collèges au féminin: les Ursulines: enseignement et vie consacré aux XVIIe et XVIIIe siècles* by Annaert, Phillippe. In: *CHist* 78:658 O 1992

Raposa, Michael L.
Jonathan Edwards' twelfth sign. *IPQ* 33:153-162 Je 1993
Review of: *Reading in communion: Scripture and ethics in Christian life* by Fowl, Stephen E, and Jones, L Gregory. In: *Thomist* 57:324-328 Ap 1993

Rasco, Emilio.
La *Parola vivente* (Eb 4, 12): dallo studio alla vita. *Gregorianum* 73 No 4:689-695 1992

Rashkow, Ilona N.
The phallacy of Genesis: a feminist and psychoanalytic approach. Louisville: Westminster, 1993. x, 144p ISBN 0-664-25250-8

Ratteray, Joan Davis.
An indigenous response to inner-city needs. *Momentum* 24:28-30 F-Mr 1993

Rattigan, Mary T.
Review of: *Twelve theological dilemmas* by Higgins, Gregory G, 1916-. In: *Horizons (CTS)* 20:153-154 Spr 1993

Ratzinger, Joseph, Cardinal, 1927-.
The Catechism of the Catholic Church in context. *Origins* 22:529-532 Ja 14 1993
On Sakharov and Rorty. *Crisis* 11:36-38 My 1993
Presentation of the Encyclical Letter "Veritatis Splendor". *OR(Eng)* 1310:1-2 O 6 1993
Veritatis Splendor (the Splendor of Truth), Encyclical letter on moral issues (1993-10-05) Commentary.

Rau, Hans Jürgen. *see* Helbich, Peter, jt auth

Rausch, Thomas P.
The CDF letter on Communion: reactions and reflections. *Ecumen Trends* 22:3-4 Ap 1993
Present state of Anglican-Roman Catholic relations: an assessment. *OChr* 29 no 2:118-125 1993
Review of: *Infallibility on trial: church, conciliarity and communion* by Bermejo, Luis M. In: *TheolStds* 54:376-378 Je 1993
The college student's introduction to theology. Collegeville: Liturgical, 1993. 216p ISBN 0-8146-5841-5 LC 93-1263

Rawlins, Rachel.
Churches hail vote for democracy. *Tablet* 247:828-829 Je 26 1993

Rawski, Conrad H.
Review of: *Letters of old age: rerum senilium libri I-XVIII* by Petrarch, Francis. In: *CHist* 79:324-326 Ap 1993

Raymo, Chet.
Review of: *Pi in the sky: counting, thinking, and being* by Barrow, John D. In: *Comm* 120:26-27 Ja 29 1993

Rea, Desmond. *see* Barber, Noel, jt ed

Read, Jean.
Review of: *You can know God: Christian spirituality for daily living* by Gustin, Marilyn Norquist. In: *RRel* 52:789-790 S-O 1993

Readings, Bill.
Pseudoethica epidemica: how pagans talk to the gods. *PhilosTod* 36:377-388 Wint 1992

Reagan, Charles E.
The self as an other [review artical *Oneselfas Another* by C Reagan]. *PhilosTod* 37:3-22 Spr 1993

Redditt, Paul L.
Review of: *Priest and Levite in Malachi* by O'Brien, Julia M. In: *CBQ* 54:761-762 O 1992

Reder, Violetta.
Professor Burkhard Neunheuser, OSB: Doctor Honoris Causa of the Pontifival Academy of Theology in Kraków. *Notitiae* 29:81-83 Ja-F 1993

Redhead, Brian. *see* Gumley, Frances, jt auth

Redington, James D.
Review of: *The unity of reality* by Brück, Michael von. In: *TheolStds* 54:175-176 Mr 1993

Redington, Patrick E.
Review of: *Christian discovery* by DiGiacomo, James J, and Walsh, John J. In: *Living Light* 29:96-97 Sum 1993

Redmond, Anthony.
Review of: *The Celtic way* by Bradley, Ian. In: *Doctr Life* 43:448 S 1993

Redmond, Gay.
Review of: *Yearning to breathe free: liberation theologies in the US* by Peter-Raoul, Mar, ed. In: *RRel* 52:313-314 Mr-Ap 1993

Redmont, Jane.
Review of: *Springs of water in a dry land: spiritual survival for Catholic women today* by Weaver, Mary Jo. In: *Comm* 120:25-26 Mr 12 1993

Redpath, Peter A.
Looting democratic capitalism. *Crisis* 10:8+ N 1992
Review of: *The primacy of love* by Wadell, Paul J. In: *HPR* 94:73-75 O 1993

Reece, Colleen L.
Tips for trips with older travelers [condensed fr *Vibrant Life* Jl/Ag 1992]. *CDgst* 57:81-91 Jl 1993

Reeder, John P, Jr. *see* Outka, Gene, jt ed

Reeder, Rachel. *see* Brueggemann, Walter, jt auth

Reedy, Jerry. *see* Hesburgh, Theodore M, jt ed

Rees, Frank.
Doubt in search of understanding. *Pacifica* 6:279-296 O 1993

Reese, Thomas Joseph, 1945-.
Bishops speak in public session of sexual abuse. *America* 169:4-6 Jl 3-10 1993
Woodstock Catechism Project revisited. *Living Light* 29:71-73 Sum 1993

Reeves, Marjorie.
Review of: *Sancta Birgitta: Revelaciones, Book VI* by Aili, Hans, ed. In: *CHist* 79:322-323 Ap 1993

Refoulé, François. *see* Lauret, Bernard, jt auth

Regan, David.
A "new" pastoral practice: mystagogy. *Furrow* 44:416-422 Jl-Ag 1993

Rego, Richard J.
Cum Petro et sub Petro. *HPR* 94:31-32+ N 1993

Reguzzoni, M.
Review of: *L'insegnamento scolastico della religione nella nuova* by Pajer, Flavio, ed. In: *Civilta* 144:93-95 Ja 2 1993

Reher, Margaret M.
Phantom heresy: A Twice-Told Tale. *US Cath Hist* 11:93-105 Sum 1993
Review of: *Church and age unite!* by Appleby, Raphael Scott. In: *CHist* 79:578-579 Jl 1993
Review of: *Isaac Hecker* by O'Brien, David J, 1938-. In: *ACHSR* 103:50-52 Aut 1992

Reich, Ronny. *see* Kempinski, Aharon, jt ed

Reicher, Chris.
Converting the youth minister. *Mod Lit* 20:8-12 Ag 1993

Reichman, Theda Kleinhans.
Walt Disney: he built an empire on a mouse [illus]. *CDgst* 57:91-96 S 1993

Reid, Barbara E.
The ethics of Luke [photos]. *BibleT* 31:283-291 S 1993
Review of: *Disciples and leaders: the origins of Christian ministry in the New Testament* by O'Grady, John F. In: *CLW* 64:39 Jl-S 1993
Review of: *John and his witness* by Collins, Raymond F. In: *CLW* 64:39-40 Jl-S 1993
Review of: *Loaves and fishes: the Gospel feeding narratives* by Grassi, Joseph A. In: *CLW* 64:39 Jl-S 1993
Review of: *Women who knew Paul* by Gillman, Florence Morgan. In: *New Theol Rev* 6:113-114 F 1993

Reid, Jane Davidson.
The Oxford guide to classical mythology in the arts, 1300-1990s. New York: Oxford University Press, 1993. ISBN 0-19504-998-5 LC 92-35374

Reid, Peter.
Review of: *Into the 21st century: a handbook for a sustainable future* by Burrows, Brian, et al. In: *Teilhard Rev* 28:28 Spr 1993

Reijen, Willem van.
The crisis of the subject: from Baroque to postmodern. *PhilosTod* 36:310-323 Wint 1992

Reiland, Philomene.
Having too much fun to retire. *Past Mus* 17:33-34 Je-Jl 1993

Reilly, Jeremiah P.
Controlling health costs. *Comm* 120:5-6 Mr 12 1993

Reilly, Matthew V.
Review of: *Ordained to preach* by Miller, Charles E. In: *HPR* 93:70-71 Ap 1993

Reilly, Patrick.
Strangers to ourselves. *New Blckfrs* 74:146-152 Mr 1993

Reilly, Robert.
The argument for the bans: combat is no place for women and gays. *Crisis* 11:39-41 Ap 1993
Sacrifice? We wrote the book on it!. *USCath* 58:40-41 N 1993

Reilly, Ruth Norrington.
Father Mac remembered. *Tablet* 247:89-90 Ja 16 1993

Reimers, Adrian J.
Learning from Mary. *New Cov* 23:28-29 S 1993

Reinart, Leonelle.
Brahms' lullaby. *Sisters* 65:282 Jl 1993

Reinerman, Alan J.
Review of: *19 aprile 1948, la mobilitazione delle organizzazioni cattoliche* by Casella, Mario. In: *CHist* 79:352-354 Ap 1993

Riley, David M. *(cont'd)*
Review of: *More than glue and glitter: a classroom guide for volunteer teachers* by O'Neal, Debbie Trafton. In: *Catechist* 27:17 S 1993
Review of: *Penitential services* by Crilly, Oliver, ed. In: *Catechist* 27:14 N-D 1993
Review of: *Saint Joan, Lazara, and the Baptism of Jesus and John.* In: *Catechist* 27:18 S 1993
Review of: *Singing for kinds* by Flodin, Mickey. In: *Catechist* 26:14 F 1993
Review of: *Sometimes you just have to tell somebody* by Cullen, Ruth V. In: *Catechist* 27:14-15 N-D 1993
Review of: *Teaching for faith* by Osmer, Richard Robert. In: *Catechist* 27:15 N-D 1993
Review of: *Tutoring and mentoring* by Keim, Nancy. In: *Catechist* 27:17 S 1993
Review of: *Where does God live?* by Gellman, Marc, and Hartman, Thomas. In: *Catechist* 27:17 S 1993

Riley, Patrick J.
The media elite and issues of faith. *Register* 69:5 O 31 1993
Review of: *Catechisms and controversies: religious education in the past conciliar years* by Wrenn, Michael J. In: *Emmanuel* 99:178 Ap 1993
Review of: *Companions of Jesus: the Jesuit martyrs of El Salvador* by Sobrino, John, et al. In: *Emmanuel* 99:479-480 O 1993
Review of: *Hispanic devotional piety: tracing the biblical roots* by Romero, C Gilbert. In: *Emmanuel* 99:238-239+ My 1993
Review of: *On the move: a history of the Hispanic Church in the United States* by Sandoval, Moses. In: *Emmanuel* 99:480-481 O 1993
Review of: *Telling stories, compelling stories: 35 stories of people of grace* by Bausch, William J. In: *Emmanuel* 99:297-298 Je 1993
Review of: *The education of an archbishop* by Wilkes, Paul, 1938-. In: *Emmanuel* 49:419-420 S 1993
Review of: *The fractured dream: America's divisive moral choices* by Drinan, Robert Francis, 1920-. In: *Emmanuel* 99:355-356 Jl-Ag 1993
Review of: *The future of the Catholic Church in America: major papers of the Virgil Michel Symposium.* In: *Emmanuel* 99:357-358 Jl-Ag 1993
Review of: *This confident Church: Catholic leadership and life in Chicago, 1940-1965* by Avella, Steven M. In: *Emmanuel* 49:416-418 S 1993
Review of: *Timely Homilies* by Bausch, William J. In: *Emmanuel* 99:297-298 Je 1993

Riley, Patrick J, and Shaw, Russell, eds.
Anti-Catholicism in the media. Huntington: Our Sunday Visitor, 1993. x, 256p ISBN 0-87973-551-1

Riley, Richard W.
In search of a new direction in education. *Momentum* 24:9-11 N-D 1993

Rimoldi, Antonio. *see* Caprioloi, Adriano, jt auth

Ringe, Sharon H. *see* Newsom, Carol A, jt ed

Ringwald, Christopher.
Horsepower, machines and human beings. *Cath Work* 60:4 S 1993
US Catholics ask if trade pact is a good deal. *OSV* 82:3 S 12 1993

Rippinger, Joel.
A monastic questionnaire: reflections of retired Abbots. *ABenR* 43:429-437 D 1992

Rist, Anna.
Catholic schooling: a consumer's view [2 parts]. *Can Cath Rev* 11:22-26 Je; 14-18 Jl-Ag 1993
Part 1—From ancient Greece to modern Britain. Part 2—The contemporary scene.
Study Greek and Latin! Reflections of a housewife. *Can Cath Rev* 11:12-15 Ja 1993 *see* Rist, John, jt auth

Rist, John, and Rist, Anna.
St. Augustine and marriage. *Priests & People* 7:327-334 Ag-S 1993

Rist, John M.
Review of: *In good conscience: reason and emotion in moral decision making* by Callahan, Sidney. In: *Can Cath Rev* 11:27-29 My 1993

Ristine, John. *see* Clark, Neal, jt auth

Ristine, John D.
A solitary life. *New Cov* 22:21-22 Mr 1993

Ristow, Kate.
Catechists sound off. *Catechist* 26:22-25 Ap-My 1993
Good versus evil: beliefs about angels and devils. *Catechist* 26:34-36 F 1993
It was good enough for me: teaching that old time religion. *Catechist* 26:14-17 Mr 1993
Tap your heels together three times and repeat after me: there's no place like home. *Catechist* 27:30-33; 29-31 N-D O 1993
Things every beginner should be told. *Catechist* 27:24-26 S 1993
We come to your table: DREs talk about first communion. *Catechist* 26:18-21 Ja 1993

Ritchey, Woody.
Communications technologies: new vistas for integrated care. *Health Prog* 74:59-60 Jl-Ag 1993

Ritschl, Dietrich.
The search for implicit axioms behind doctrinal texts. *Gregorianum* 74 no 2: 207-221 1993

Ritter, Werner H.
Schule—Bildung—Christlicher Glaube. *Stimm Zeit* 211:413-421 Je 1993

Rittner-Heir, Robbin M.
Preschool playgrounds. *Tod Cath Teach* 27:26-29 O 1993

Riva, Raimondo.
Il Vangelo di Marco: un annunico di salvezza nel mondo pagano. *StudiaM* 42:19-40 1993

Rizzerio, Laura.
Coup d'oeil sur la philosophie italienne contemporaine. *RPhil Louvain* 90: 539-556 N 1992
Platon, l'École de Tübingen et Giovanni Reale. *RPhil Louvain* 91:90-110 F 1993

Rizzi, A, et al. *see* Gibellini, R, jt auth

Rizzo, Patricia L.
Morals for home, morals for office: the double ethical life of a civil litigator. *CLawyer* 35 no 1:79-96 1993

Roach, John, Abp.
Letter to Patriarch Sabbah. *Origins* 23:812 My 6 1993
On US intervention in Bosnia. *Origins* 23:22-23 My 27 1993

Roach, Joseph J.
Review of: *Creating a partnership in faith: a parish planning guide* by Bright, Thomas, and Roberto, John, eds. In: *Living Light* 30:100 Aut 1993
Review of: *Faith and families: a parish program for parenting in faith growth* by Bright, Thomas, and Roberto, John, eds. In: *Living Light* 30:100 Aut 1993
Review of: *Families and young adolescents* by Drey, Janet, ed. In: *Living Light* 30:102-103 Aut 1993
Review of: *Families and young adults* by Bagley, Ronald M, ed. In: *Living Light* 30:102-103 Aut 1993
Review of: *Families and youth: a resource manual* by Kehrwald, Leif, and Roberto, John, eds. In: *Living Light* 30:102-103 Aut 1993
Review of: *Family rituals and celebrations* by Roberto, John, ed. In: *Living Light* 30:101-102 Aut 1993
Review of: *Handbook of youth ministry* by Ratcliff, Donald E, and Davies, James A, eds. In: *Living Light* 29:85-86 Spr 1993
Review of: *Media, faith, and families* by Roberto, John, ed. In: *Living Light* 30:101 Aut 1993
Review of: *Media, faith, and families* by Roberto, John, ed. In: *Living Light* 30:101 Aut 1993
Review of: *Rituals for sharing faith: a resource for parish ministers* by Roberto, John, ed. In: *Living Light* 30:101-102 Aut 1993
Review of: *The Catholic famliy series* by Roberto, John, ed. In: *Living Light* 30:100 Aut 1993

Robb, Carol S.
Review of: *What does the Lord require?* by Hart, Stephen. In: *America* 168: 18-19 F 27 1993

Robberechts, Edouard.
Review of: *L'imaginaire technocratique* by Larochelle, Gilbert. In: *RPhil Louvain* 91:489-495 Ag 1993
Review of: *La bénédiction de Babel. Vérité et communication* by Marty, François. In: *RPhil Louvain* 91:484-489 Ag 1993
Review of: *Pour un nouveau langage de la raison* by Fattal, Michel. In: *RPhil Louvain* 91:336-339 My 1993
Review of: *The evidential force of religious experience* by Davis, Caroline Franks. In: *RPhil Louvain* 91:503-507 Ag 1993
Review of: *Thomas Hobbes: un radical au service de la réaction* by Rogow, Arnold A. In: *RPhil Louvain* 91:468-471 Ag 1993

Roberson, Ron.
Dialogue [interview by G Burke]. *Register* 69:1+ My 23 1993

Roberto, John.
Get parents involved. *ReligTJ* 27:26-27 Mr 1993
Is your parish youth-friendly? *CDgst* 58:34-37 D 1993
More than token roles. *ReligTJ* 27:30-31 Ap-My 1993
Review of: *A child shall lead them: a guide to celebrating the word with children* by Pottebaum, Gerard A, et al. In: *ReligTJ* 27:30 Ap-My 1993
Working with parents. *ReligTJ* 27:36-37 F 1993 *see* Bright, Thomas, jt ed; Kehrwald, Leif, jt ed

Roberts, Augustine.
The journey of the heart in the Rule of Benedict. *Word Sp* 15:74-77 1993

Roberts, David.
A quick guide to Christianity. New York: Vantage Press, 1992. x, 102p ISBN 0-533-10327-4 LC 92-90783

Roberts, Jane.
Review of: *Latin palaeography: antiquity and the middle ages* by Bischoff, Bernhard. In: *Heythrop* 34:202-203 Ap 1993

Roberts, Jo.
The life of Muriel Lester. *Cath Work* 60:1+ Ag 1993

Roberts, Jo, and Wells, Paul.
CW: our diverse but common lives. *Cath Work* 60:4 Je-Jl 1993

Roberts, John R.
'Me thoughts I heard one calling, child!': Herbert's *The Collar. Renascence* 45:196-204 Spr 1993

Roberts, Marc J.
Health care: your money or your life [interview by J.S. Torrens]. *America* 169:6-9 O 4 1993

Roberts, Paul.
Review of: *The Sanctus in the Eucharistic prayer* by Spinks, Bryan D. In: *Heythrop* 34:196-198 Ap 1993

Robichaud, Paul.
Evangelizing America: transformations in Paulist mission. *US Cath Hist* 11: 61-78 Spr 1993

Robinson, Bernard P.
Review of: *Early Israel: a new horizon* by Coote, Robert B. In: *Heythrop* 34: 183- Ap 1993

Robinson, Geoffrey, Bp.
Do we know what justice is? *Origins* 23:423-430 N 25 1993

Robinson, Tom. *see* Hawkin, David J, jt ed

Robinson, William.
European dimensions of the abortion debate. *Doctr Life* 42:273-281 My-Je 1992

Robles, J R.
Los indigenas: sujetos prioritarios. *Christus* 57:15-18 S 1992

Rocca, Gregory.
Review of: *Speaking the Christian God: the Holy Trinity and the challenge of feminism* by Kimel, Alvin F, Jr, ed. In: *Thomist* 57:509-520 Jl 1993
Review of: *Systematic theology* by Fiorenza, Francis Schüssler, 1938-, and Galvin, John P, 1944-, eds. In: *Thomist* 57:305-308 Ap 1993

Roccasalvo, Joan L.
The role of religion in the development of the Znamenny-Rusin Chant. *Diakonia* 26 no 1:41-66 1993
The Union of Brest: a timely topic. *Diakonia* 26 no 3:161-183 1993

Rocchio, Vincent.
The fugitive [directed by A Davis]. *Register* 69:5 S 5 1993
The roots of tv violence. *Register* 69:3 Ag 15 1993

Roche, A.
Review of: *Humanae Vitae: a generation later* by Smith, Janet E. In: *Can Cath Rev* 11:43 Ja 1993

Roche, Mark W.
Inconsistencies in the abortion debate. *New Oxford Rev* 60:20-24 Mr 1993

Rochlitz, Rainer. see Bouchindhomme, Christian, jt auth

Rockefeller, John D, 1937-.
Fight the "prophets of doom". *Health Prog* 74:43-44 Jl-Ag 1993

Rocker, Steven.
Review of: *A marginal Jew: rethinking the historical Jesus* by Meier, John P. In: *St Anth* 100:48 Ap 1993

Rockett, Trish.
Mystery on the margins. *Furrow* 43:681-682 D 1992

Rodden, John, 1956-.
Anniversary letters from Berlin: west side, east side stories. *America* 169:10-15 Jl 3-10 1993

Rodenbaugh, Dana.
Religious leaders endorse "new global ethic". *Nat Cath Rep* 29:3 S 17 1993
Unique parliament of world religions celebrates diversity. *Nat Cath Rep* 29:4+ S 10 1993

Rodes, Robert E, Jr.
Review of: *The reformation of the ecclesiastical laws of England, 1552* by Spalding, James C, ed. In: *CHist* 79:339-340 Ap 1993

Rodríguez, E.
Review of: *La Biblia: los autores, los libros, el mensaje* by González Núñez, A. In: *Cien Tom* 119:409-410 My-Ag 1992
Review of: *Los métodos de la exégesis bíblica* by Stenger, Werner. In: *Cien Tom* 119:410 My-Ag 1992

Rodriguez, Gabriel Ignacio.
Un accord tendu autour du "service de la vie" La IVe Conférence des évêques latino-américains, à Saint-Dominigue. *Lumen* 48:105-111 Mr 1993

Rodriguez, Hector R.
Every child can learn. *Momentum* 24:51-52 Ap-My 1993

Rodriguez, Jeannette.
Review of: *We are a people! initiatives in Hispanic-American theology* by Goizueta, Roberto, ed. In: *RRel* 52:296-298 Mr-Ap 1993

Rodriguez, Otilio. see Kavanaugh, Kieran, jt auth

Rodriguez, Pedro.
El Opus Dei en la Iglesia. Madrid: Ediciones Rialp, 1993. x, 346p ISBN 84-321-2969-0

Rodríguez, Pedro. see Ossandón, Pedro, jt auth

Rodriguez, Richard, 1947-.
In California, hysteria hides immigration truth. *Nat Cath Rep* 29:12 S 10 1993
Military is afraid to admit "sissies" can be brave, too. *Nat Cath Rep* 29:15 F 12 1993

Rodriguez, Tarcisio.
Dialogue [interview by G Burke]. *Register* 69:1+ Je 27 1993

Rodriguez, Victorino.
Los sentidos internos. Barcelona: PPU, 1993. x, 158p ISBN 84-477-0066-6

Rodríguez Plaza, Braulio. see Alvarez, Rosendo, Bp, jt auth

Rodulfo, Lillie.
Film blasts Panama invasion myths. *Nat Cath Rep* 29:7 N 6 1992
Gloria Rodriguez [interview by Lillie Rodulfo]. *Salt* 13:4-6 Mr 1993

Roers, G M.
Review of: *Eine Tötung im Angesicht des Herrn Goethe* by Liersch, Werner. In: *Stimm Zeit* 211:646-648 S 1993
Review of: *Vom mönchischen Leben* by Werner, Johannes, ed. In: *Stimm Zeit* 211:359-360 My 1993

Roessler, Mark A.
Fetal tissue transplantation: an ethical analysis. *Linacre* 60:60-74 Ag 1993

Roger, Brother. see Boyaxhiu, Teresa, Mother, 1910-, jt auth

Rogers, David.
Honoring complexity: John T Wilcox on the Book of Job. *Spirit* 57:60-63 Spr-Sum 1992

Rogers, J.
Review of: *The bitterness of Job: a philosophical reading* by Wilcox, John T. In: *Spirit* 57:60-63 Spr-Sum 1992

Rogers, Nicholas.
Review of: *The Church and the arts: papers read at the 1990 summer meeting and the 1991 winter meeting of the ecclesiastical history society* by Wood, Diana, ed. In: *New Blckfrs* 74:334-336 Je 1993

Rogers, Patrick.
Review of: *Paul on the mystery of Israel* by Harrington, Daniel J. In: *Doctr Life* 43:316-317 My-Je 1993
Review of: *Theocracy: in Paul's praxis and theology* by Georgi, Dieter. In: *CBQ* 54:777-778 O 1992

Rogers, Terry.
Tabernacles of peace. *Cath Work* 60:4 Je-Jl 1993

Rogerson, J W.
Review of: *The cosmic covenant* by Murray, Robert. In: *Heythrop* 34:184-185 Ap 1993

Roggeveen, Dirk G.
Choice for America's poor. *Momentum* 24:26-28 N-D 1993

Rogozinski, Jacob.
Hell on earth Hannah Arendt in the face of Hitler. *PhilosTod* 37:257-274 Aut 1993

Rohr, Richard, 1943-.
Near occasions of grace. New York: Orbis Books, 1993. x, 118p ISBN 0-88344-852-1 LC 92-33193

Rohr, Richard, 1943-, and Martos, Joseph.
The love called solidarity. *SocJust* 84:23-24 Ja-F 1993
Prayer as relationship. *Living Prayer* 26:28-31 N-D 1993
The wild man's journey: reflections on male spirituality. Cincinnati: St Anthony Messenger Press, 1993. ISBN 0-86716-1280

Rohrbaugh, Richard L.
A peasant reading of the parable of the talents. *Bib Th Bul* 23:32-37 Spr 1993
The progress of the gospel. *BibleT* 31:22-27 Ja 1993
Review of: *The social history of Palestine in the Herodian period* by Fiensy, David A. In: *CBQ* 55:147-149 Ja 1993
The social location of the Marcan audience. *Bib Th Bul* 23:114-127 Aut 1993
see Malina, Bruce J, 1933-, jt auth

Röhrig, Johannes.
Francis Bacon und T S Eliot. *Stimm Zeit* 211:279-282 Ap 1993
Der fremde Spiegel. *Stimm Zeit* 211:10-20 Ja 1993
Review of: *Fremd in einem kalten Land: Ausländer in Deutschland* by Aziz, Namo. In: *Stimm Zeit* 211:503-504 Jl 1993
Review of: *Il ballo tondo* by Abate, Carmine. In: *Stimm Zeit* 211:215-216 Mr 1993

Roisel, V.
Review of: *Arnobii Iunioris opera minora* by Daur, Kl-D. In: *NRT* 115:266-267 Mr-Ap 1993
Review of: *Catalogue verborum quae in operibus Sancti Augustini inveniuntur*. In: *NRT* 114:907-908 N-D 1992
Review of: *Communion du Saint-Esprit* by Bobrinskoy, B. In: *NRT* 115:581-582 Jl-Ag 1993
Review of: *Instrumenta lexicologica Latina*. In: *NRT* 115:266-267 Mr-Ap 1993
Review of: *Instrumenta lexicologica Latina*. In: *NRT* 115:267 Mr-Ap 1993
Review of: *L'oeil de lumière* by Brock, Sebastian. In: *NRT* 114:908-909 N-D 1992
Review of: *Lo studio dei Padri della Chiesa oggi* by Covolo, Enrico Dal, and Triacca, Achille M, eds. In: *NRT* 115:289 Mr-Ap 1993
Review of: *Pascash Radberti: expositio in Psalmum XLIV* by Paulus, B, ed. In: *NRT* 115:267 Mr-Ap 1993
Review of: *Quaestiones et solutiones in Exodum I et II* by Philo of Alexandria. In: *NRT* 115:265-266 Mr-Ap 1993
Review of: *Repertorium annotatum operum et translationum S Augustini*. In: *NRT* 114:907 N-D 1992

Roley, Mary Eileen.
A new look at John of the Cross and the spiritual canticle. *Emmanuel* 98:149+ Ap 1992

Rolfes, Helmuth.
Die Messe im Fernsehen als Medienspektakel und Geschft. *Stimm Zeit* 211:331-342 My 1993

Roll, Susan K.
Reconciliation in 12 (not so easy) steps. *Doctr Life* 43:69-76 F 1993

Rolland, Philippe.
Discussions sur la chronologie paulinienne. *NRT* 114:870-889 N-D 1992

Romain, Philip, St.
Communicating love to others. *Liguorian* 81:30-35 Mr 1993

Roman, Mary.
Breaking the thought barrier. *Living Prayer* 26:37 My-Je 1993
Let us play. *Living Prayer* 26:37 N-D 1993
Olympian mystery. *Living Prayer* 26:37 Ja-F 1993
The stones will cry out. *Living Prayer* 26:29-31 Mr-Ap 1993
Trailing clouds of glory. *Living Prayer* 26:37 Jl-Ag 1993

Romaniuk, Kazimierz.
'Hiiopei ou 'Eiioiei en mc 6, 20? *Eph Theol Lovan* 69:140-141 Ap 1993
Les Thessaloniciens étaient-ils des paresseux? *Eph Theol Lovan* 69:142-144 Ap 1993

Romano, Joseph.
Review of: *Opus Dei: an investigation into the secret society struggling for power within the Roman Catholic Church* by Walsh, Michael J, 1937-. In: *ACHSR* 103:52-54 Aut 1992

Romeri, John.
How will Cycle A be different and the same? *Past Mus* 17:35-41 D 1992-Ja 1993
The rhythm of time, in practice. *Past Mus* 18:40-46 O-N 1993

Romero, Gilbert C.
Review of: *The Bible, baconism, and mastery over nature* by Wybrow, Cameron. In: *OTA* 16:441 Je 1993

Romero Y Galdamez, Oscar Arnulfo, Abp, 1917-1980.
Archbishop Oscar Romero: a shepherd's diary [tr I Hodgson]. Cincinnati: St Anthony Messenger Press, 1986. x, 542p ISBN 0-86716-170-1

Ronayne, Mary John.
In the Catholic tradition: St Catherine of Siena. *Priests & People* 7:153-157 Ap 1993

Roof, Wade Clark, 1939-.
A generation of seekers; the spiritual journeys of the baby boom generation. New York: HarperCollins Publishers, 1993. x, 294p ISBN 0-06-066963-2 LC 92-53920
Religion and values: noble lies? *Critic* 47:35-45 Spr 1993

Rooney, William R.
Chapter and verse: the life of Christ in poetry. New York: Vantage Press, 1993. x, 89p ISBN 0-533-10319-3 LC 92-90788

Roose-Evans, James.
Review of: *The Tibetan book of living and dying* by Rinpoche, Sogyal. In: *Tablet* 247:1234-1235 S 25 1993

Rorem, Paul. see Burrows, Mark Stephen, jt ed

Rosa, Susan.
Review of: *Rome and the Counter-Reformation in Scandinavia: the age of Gustavus Adolphus and Queen Christina of Sweden, 1622-1656* by Garstein, Oskar. In: *CHist* 79:83-88 Ja 1993

Rosales, Gaudencio B, and Arevalo, Catalino G, eds.
For all the peoples of Asia: documents from 1970-1991. Maryknoll, New York: Orbis Books, 1992. x, 356p ISBN 0-88344-837-8 LC 92-5033

Rose, John.
Preparing for Easter [3 parts]. *Can Cath Rev* 11:36-37 F; 36-37 Mr; 37-38 Ap 1993

Rose, Mary Carman.
Learning from animals. *Month* 26:331-335 Ag 1993

Rosemann, Philipp W.
Nova et vetera: "Le fondement de la morale" de Mgr A Léonard. *RPhil Louvain* 91:126-136 F 1993
Penser l'Autre: théologie négative et "postmodernité". *RPhil Louvain* 91:296-310 My 1993
Review of: *Ökonomie, Politik und Ethik aus Summa Theologiae* by Thomas Aquinas, Saint. In: *RPhil Louvain* 91:320-322 My 1993
Review of: *Guide bibliographique des études de philosphie* by Follon, Jacques. In: *RPhil Louvain* 91:514-517 Ag 1993
Review of: *Sinngestalten: Metaphysik in der Vielfalt menschlichen Fragens* by Muck, Otto, ed. In: *RPhil Louvain* 91:326-330 My 1993

RosenBlatt, Marie-Eloise.
Review of: *Here all dwell free* by Nelson, Gertrude Mueller. In: *RRel* 52:151-153 Ja-F 1993
Review of: *Theological hermeneutics* by Jeanrond, Werner G. In: *TheolStds* 54:393 Je 1993
Review of: *Womanspirit: reclaiming the deep feminine in our human spirituality* by Muto, Susan. In: *RRel* 52:151-153 Ja-F 1993
Review of: *The revelatory text: interpreting the New Testament as Sacred Scripture* by Schneiders, Sandra M. In: *New Theol Rev* 6:90-91 Ag 1993
Review of: *Form Apocalypse to Genesis: ecology, feminism and christianity* by Primavesi, Anne. In: *Horizons (CTS)* 20:159-160 Spr 1993

Rosica, Thomas M.
To share in the priesthood of suffering: a biblical reflection on the death of Our Lord. *Can Cath Rev* 11:14-16 Ap 1993

Rosinski, Geri, and Mannion, M Francis.
Conflicting styles of parish leadership: two responses. *New Theol Rev* 6:95-101 My 1993

Rosmann, Ron.
Salt of the earth: Ron Rosmann [interview by P Slattery]. *Salt* 13:4-5 F 1993

Ross, John.
AIDS silently spreading through Mexico [AIDS epidemic]. *Nat Cath Rep* 29:15 Mr 19 1993
Chiapas champion of poor troubles water, church. *Nat Cath Rep* 29:12 My 28 1993
Killing of Mexican cardinal raises fears for pope's safety. *Nat Cath Rep* 29:10 Jl 16 1993

Ross, Mary Ellen.
Review of: *New creation: Christian feminism and the renewal of the earth* by Halkes, Catharina J M. In: *TheolStds* 54:605-606 S 1993

Ross, Stephen-Joseph.
Review of: *Bartolomé De Las Casas: the only way* by Parish, Helen Rand, ed. In: *Spir Life* 39:177-179 Aut 1993

Ross, Susan A.
Review of: *The revelatory text: interpreting the New Testament as sacred scripture* by Schneiders, Sandra M. In: *Horizons (CTS)* 19:294-297 Fall 1992
Sacraments and women's experience. *Listening* 28:52-64 Wint 1993

Rosselli, John.
Review of: *Communism: a TLS companion* by Mount, Ferdinand, ed. In: *Tablet* 247:77 Ja 16 1993
Review of: *From bishop to witch: the system of the sacred in early modern Terra d'Otranto* by Gentilcore, David. In: *Tablet* 247:143 Ja 30 1993
Review of: *The modern movement: a TLS companion* by Gross, John, ed. In: *Tablet* 247:77 Ja 16 1993

Rosser, Donna Colwell.
The family rosary in the real world [condensed fr *The Family—a Catholic Perspective* O 1992]. *CDgst* 57:109-111 Ja 1993

Rossetti, Stephen.
Telling the whole truth [interview by W Bole]. *OSV* 82:6 Jl 11 1993

Rossi, Angela.
Christian life communities. *Priests & People* 7:238-239 Je 1993

Rossi, Giacomo.
Letture Psicanalitiche Della Bibbia. *Civilta* 143:476-487 D 5 1992
Review of: *La melanconia. Del buon uso e del cattivo uso della depressione nella vita spirituale* by Schaller, Jean Pierre. In: *Civilta* 3:546-547 S 18 1993
Review of: *Psicologia e vita spirituale: sofferenza e maturità umana* by Bissonnier, Henri. In: *Civilta* 144:411-412 F 20 1993

Roten, Johann G.
Hans Urs von Balthasar's anthropology in light of his marian thinking. *Communio* 20:306-333 Sum 1993
Review of: *The Virgin Mary in the writings of Maria Valtorta* by Roschini, Gabriel M. In: *Can Cath Rev* 11:36 Ja 1993

Roth, Robert J.
Review of: *John Dewey: religious faith and democratic humanism* by Rockefeller, Steven C. In: *IPQ* 33:117-122 Mr 1993

Roth, Wolfgang.
Disclosure at Emmaus. *BibleT* 31:46-51 Ja 1993
Moses and Matthew. *BibleT* 30:362-366 N 1992
Within the outlines of some ancient model. *BibleT* 31:103-109 Mr 1993

Rothschild, Richard D.
Practice parameters benefit all. *Health Prog* 74:24-29 1993

Rotman, Patrick. see Hamon, Herve, jt auth

Rottenberg, Isaac C, 1925-.
Christian-Jewish dialogue. *JEcumen Stds* 29:87-95 Wint 1992

Roubichou, Gerard.
Review of: *Viel: Louisiana's firstborn author with Evandre, the first literary creation of a native of the Mississippi Valley* by O'Neill, Charles Edwards. In: *CHist* 79:568-570 Jl 1993

Rourke, Francis.
Review of: *Preparing for the twenty-first century* by Kennedy, Paul M, 1945-. In: *America* 169:25-26 S 11 1993

Rouse, Richard H. see Rouse, Mary A, jt auth

Rousseau, Mary F.
The Pope and the kids in Denver. *Crisis* 11:18-21 O 1993

Rousseau, Robert.
Review of: *The Mass* by Deiss, Lucien. In: *Emmanuel* 99:112-114 Mr 1993
Review of: *Tomorrow will be too late: a life of Saint Peter Julian Eymard* by Pelletier, Norman. In: *Emmanuel* 99:114+ Mr 1993

Roussel, Jean-François.
Karl Barth et Dostoïevski. *Laval Theol Phil* 49:37-55 F 1993

Routhier, Gilles.
Review of: *L'évaluation pastorale au Québec* by Levasseur, Jean-Marie, and Turmel, André. In: *Laval Theol Phil* 49:155-157 F 1993
Review of: *Les Evêques d'Europe et la nouvelle évangélisation* by Legrand, Hervé. In: *Laval Theol Phil* 49:378-379 Je 1993

Roux, Francisco J de.
La iglesia en America Latina. *Christus* 58:38-46 N-D 1992
Recherche éthique dans un contexte de violence. *Lumen* 48:293-303 S 1993

Rowe, Noel.
Are there really angels in Carlton? Australian literature and theology. *Pacifica* 6:141-164 Je 1993

Rowell, G.
Review of: *From Newman to Congar: the idea of doctrinal development from the Victorians to the Second Vatican Council* by Nichols, Aidan. In: *New Blckfrs* 73:579-580 N 1992

Rowell, Geoffrey. see Dudley, Martin, jt ed

Rowland, Christopher.
Review of: *The cosmic covenant* by Murray, Robert. In: *Priests & People* 7:166 Ap 1993
Review of: *The great angel: a study of Israel's second God* by Barker, Margaret. In: *Priests & People* 7:166 Ap 1993

Roy, Louis.
Review of: *Bartolomé De Las Casas: the only way* by Parish, Helen Rand, ed. In: *ChrWorld* 236:236-237 S-O 1993

Roy, Lucien.
Shifting paradigm: layleadership in the Year 2000. *Listening* 28:6-13 Wint 1993

Royal, Robert.
Fight the system!. *Crisis* 11:11-12 S 1993
Health and the other Hillary. *Crisis* 11:11-12 O 1993
Mind the constitution. *Register* 69:5 N 14 1993
No more business as usual? *Crisis* 11:8 Mr 1993 see Weigel, George, jt ed

Royal, Robert, ed.
Jacques Maritain and the Jews. Notre Dame: University of Notre Dame Press, 1993. 264p ISBN 0-268-01193-1 LC 93-4633

Royle, Roger.
Mother Teresa: a life in pictures. New York: HarperSanFrancisco, 1992. x, 159p ISBN 0-06-067978-61 LC 92-52654

Ruane, Edward. see Siegfried, Regina, jt ed

Rubert de Ventos, Xavier.
Manies i afrodismes. Barcelona: Edicions 62, 1993. x, 107p ISBN 84-297-3651-4

Rubin, Alexis P, ed.
Scattered among the nations: documents affecting Jewish history, 49 to 11975. Dayton: Wall & Emerson, 1993. x, 350p ISBN 1-895131-10-3 LC 93-093216-1

Rubino, Carl A.
Review of: *La storia: five centuries of the Italian American experience* by Mangione, Jerre, and Morreale, Ben. In: *America* 168:22 My 1 1993

Rudbusch, G.
Review of: *Myth and metaphysics in Plato's Phaedo* by White, David A. In: *Thomist* 56:726-732 O 1992

Rudin, A James.
"Access to health care and allocation of health care resources: a Jewish perspective". *New Theol Rev* 6:80-86 F 1993

Rudolph, Katherine.
Descartes' discourse. *PhilosTod* 37:38-51 Spr 1993

Rue, Loyal D. see Loades, Ann, jt ed

Ruether, Rosemary Radford.
Future of liberation theology is down road to ecumenism. *Nat Cath Rep* 29: 16 Ap 9 1993
Gaia and God: an ecofeminist theology of earth healing. San Francisco: HarperSanFrancisco, 1992. 310p ISBN 0-06067-022-3 LC 91-58911
Managua parish combats cardinal over cathedral. *Nat Cath Rep* 29:16 F 26 1993
New voices, visions opening up liberation theology. *Nat Cath Rep* 29:20 Je 18 1993
Recent handshake ignored long Palestinian plight. *Nat Cath Rep* 29:24 O 15 1993
Revisionist history of virgin birth a misconception [review article *A Bishop Rethinks the Birth of Jesus* by J Spong]. *Nat Cath Rep* 29:27 Ja 15 1993
What bishop might tell her people about encyclical. *Nat Cath Rep* 30:18 N 12 1993
Veritatis Splendor (the Splendor of Truth) Encyclical Letter on moral issues (1993 10 05) (Commentary). *see* Bianchi, Eugene C, jt ed

Ruffing, Janet K.
The mixed life of Elizabeth Leseur [condensed fr *Mystic Quarterly* Mr 1993]. *CDgst* 57:111-116 Ag 1993

Ruiz, Jean-Pierre.
Review of: *Theological hermeneutics* by Jeanrond, Werner G. In: *Furrow* 44: 446-448 Jl-Ag 1993

Ruiz Jurado, Manuel.
Review of: *Dictionnaire de Spiritualité, ascétique et mystique, doctrine et histoire.* In: *Gregorianum* 74 No 1:174 1993
Review of: *Dictionnaire de Spiritualité, ascétique et mystique, doctrine et histoire.* In: *Gregorianum* 74 no 3:587-588 1993
Review of: *Juan de la Cruz, espíritu de llama* by Steggink, Otger, ed. In: *Gregorianum* 74 no 2:380-381 1993
Review of: *La pratique des Exercices Spirituels d'Ignace de Loyola.* In: *Gregorianum* 74 No 1:172-173 1993
Review of: *La Theologia Deutsch o la via per giungere a Dio* by Zambruno, Elisabetta. In: *Gregorianum* 74 No 1:166 1993
Review of: *Libro de la vida. Vivencia de Cristo* by Foligno, Angelo de. In: *Gregorianum* 74 no 2:381-382 1993
Review of: *The Ignation vision of India: a historical study* by Correia-Afonso, John. In: *Gregorianum* 74 No 1:181 1993

Ruiz Scaperlanda, Maria.
Finding new life on death row. *New Cov* 23:7-10 S 1993

Rule, Paul.
Review of: *The emptying God: a Buddhist-Jewish-Christian conversation* by Cobb, John B, Jr, and Ives, Christopher, eds. In: *Pacifica* 6:115-116 F 1993
Review of: *The meaning of Christ: a Mahayana theology* by Keenan, John P. In: *Pacifica* 6:115-116 F 1993

Rulli, Giovanni.
Lettera a un amico ebreo. *Civilta* 3:47-50 Jl 3 1993
Un rapporto internazionale su El Salvador. *Civilta* 2:395-403 My 15 1993
Review of: *Chiese e diritti umani: Documenti relativi ai diritti della persona e delle comunità* by Barberini, Giovanni, ed. In: *Civilta* 143:634-635 D 19 1992
Review of: *Lettera a un amico ebreo* by Svidercoschi, Gian Franco. In: *Civilta* 3:47-50 Jl 3 1993
Review of: *Mosca: I giorni della fine* by Volcic, Demetrio. In: *Civilta* 143:426-427 N 21 1992
Review of: *Reporting dalla lunga notte: appunti di giornalismo sugli americani e la guerra del Golfo* by Costa, Giuseppe. In: *Civilta* 144:408 F 20 1993
Un valido strumento di lavoro. *Civilta* 2:57-60 Ap 3 1993
Verso una ristesura dei diritti fondamentali dell'uomo? (Recoaro Terme, 11-13 settembre 1992). *Civilta* 143:602-611 D 19 1992

Rulter, G.
Review of: *The politics of prayer* by Hitchcock, Helen Hull, ed. In: *HPR* 94: 77-78 O 1993

Ruprecht, Louis A, Jr.
Mark's tragic vision: Gethsemane. *Relig Lit* 24:1-25 Aut 1992

Rusch, William G.
The state of the ecumenical movement. *Ecumen Trends* 22:3-6 Jl-Ag 1993

Rush, Ormond.
Reception hermeneutics and the "development" of doctrine: an alternative model. *Pacifica* 6:125-140 Je 1993

Rushen, Karen.
A descent into peace. *Living Prayer* 26:13-16 N-D 1993

Russell, Jeffrey Burton.
Dissent and order in the Middle Ages: the search for legitimate authority. New York: Twayne Publishers, 1992. x, 128p ISBN 0-80578-603-1 LC 92-5328
Review of: *Medieval heresy: popular movements from the Gregorian reform to the Reformation* by Lambert, Malcolm. In: *CHist* 79:145-146 Ja 1993
Review of: *Medieval worlds: barbarians, heretics, and artists in the Middles Ages* by Borst, Amo. In: *CHist* 78:630-631 O 1992

Russell, John F.
The RCIA and ecumenism: some correlations. *Ecumen Trends* 21:3-5 D 1992

Russell, John L.
Review of: *Galileo, Bellarmine and the Bible* by Blackwell, Richard J. In: *Heythrop* 34:335-336 Jl 1993

Russell, Kenneth C.
The adventures of Huck Finn. *Can Cath Rev* 11:40 Je 1993
The Age of Innocence, Orlando. *Can Cath Rev* 11:39 N 1993
Films reviewed: *The Age of Innocence Orlando.*
Amos and Andrew. *Can Cath Rev* 11:40 My 1993
Benny and Joon. *Can Cath Rev* 11:39-40 Jl-Ag 1993
The bodyguard. *Can Cath Rev* 11:40 F 1993
Born yesterday. *Can Cath Rev* 11:40 F 1993
Dave. *Can Cath Rev* 11:40 Jl-Ag 1993
Falling down [directed by J Schumacher]. *Can Cath Rev* 11:39-40 My 1993
A few good men. *Can Cath Rev* 11:39-40 F 1993

Russell, Kenneth C. *(cont'd)*
The firm [directed by S Pollack]. *Can Cath Rev* 11:40 S 1993
Get serious! The monastic condemnation of laughter. *RRel* 52:371-379 My-Je 1993
Groundhog Day. *Can Cath Rev* 11:39-40 Ap 1993
Hoffa. *Can Cath Rev* 11:40 Mr 1993
In the line of fire [directed by W Peterson]. *Can Cath Rev* 11:39-40 S 1993
Jurassic park. *Can Cath Rev* 11:39-40 S 1993
Lorenzo's oil. *Can Cath Rev* 11:40 Mr 1993
Lost in Yonkers. *Can Cath Rev* 11:39-40 Jl-Ag 1993
Mad dog and glory. *Can Cath Rev* 11:39-40 My 1993
Manhattan murder mystery [directed by W Allen]. *Can Cath Rev* 11:39-40 O 1993
Rising sun. *Can Cath Rev* 11:40 O 1993
The secret garden [directed by A. Holland]. *Can Cath Rev* 11:40 O 1993
Sommersby [directed by J Amiel]. *Can Cath Rev* 11:39-40 Ap 1993
A spirituality for the chronically ill. *Spir Life* 32:79-86 Sum 1993
Tous les matins du monde [directed by A Corneau]. *Can Cath Rev* 11:39-40 Je 1993

Russell, Letty M.
Church in the round: feminist interpretation of the church. Louisville: John Knox Press, 1993. 235p ISBN 0-66425-070-x LC 93-9306

Russello, Gerald.
Belles lettres. *Crisis* 11:63-64 S 1993
Learning to see. *Crisis* 11:54-55 Ja 1993
Review of: *Abuse of language, abuse of power* by Pieper, Josef. In: *Crisis* 10: 51-52 D 1992
Review of: *Progress and religion* by Dawson, Christopher. In: *F & R* 18:299-305 Aut 1992

Ruston, Roger.
Does it matter what we do with our money? *Priests & People* 7:171-177 My 1993
Review of: *Ethics in an age of technology* by Barbour, Ian. In: *New Blckfrs* 74:373-375 Jl-Ag 1993

Ruthrof, Horst.
Differend and agonistics: a transcendental argument? *PhilosTod* 36:324-335 Wint 1992
Frege's error. *PhilosTod* 37:306-317 Aut 1993

Rutler, George W.
The Fatherhood of God. *HPR* 93:18-23 Je 1993
Review of: *Faith and the human enterprise: a post-Vatican II vision* by Weakland, Rembert G, Abp, 1927-. In: *HPR* 93:76-77 Je 1993
Review of: *Isaac Hecker* by O'Brien, David J, 1938-. In: *HPR* 93:77-78 My 1993
Review of: *The spiritual journey of Newman* by Honoré, Jean, Abp. In: *HPR* 93:76 Jl 1993

Ruttan, Karl.
Review of: *Wildmen, warriors, and kings: masculine spirituality and the Bible* by Arnold, Patrick M. In: *Stud Form Spir* 14:287-289 My 1993

Rutten, Christian.
La stylométrie et la question de Métaphysique K. *RPhil Louvain* 90:486-496 N 1992

Ryan, Aidan.
Review of: *Finding faith in troubled times* by Collins, Pat. In: *Furrow* 44: 450-452 Jl-Ag 1993

Ryan, Dick.
The Gospel according to Matthew, Mark, Luke, John and Ringo. *OSV* 81:6-7 F 28 1993
Speaking for the bishops. *OSV* 82:16 My 16 1993
These are sisters for life [photos]. *OSV* 82:10-11 O 3 1993

Ryan, Ellen.
The infusion approach to sexuality education. *Momentum* 24:53-55 F-Mr 1993

Ryan, Jim.
Baby farming? *SocJust* 84:87-89 My-Je 1993

Ryan, Laurence, Bp, 1931-.
The once and future and Church—Carlow College Bicentenary Lecture. *Furrow* 44:459-471 S 1993
Review of: *Alfred O'Rahilly III: controversialist, Part I: social reformer* by Gaughan, J Anthony. In: *Furrow* 44:54-55 Ja 1993

Ryan, Mary Jean, and Barney, Steven M.
An investment in leadership. *Health Prog* 74:56-58 Je 1993

Ryan, Michael.
Review of: *The good stewards* by Naughton, Michael. In: *Can Cath Rev* 11: 29-30 F 1993

Ryan, Patrick J.
Investments in the future. *America* 169:30-31 N 6 1993
The right and the left. *America* 169:23 N 13 1993

Ryan, Ron.
Dreams of renewal. *New Cov* 23:25 Ag 1993
The power is on. *New Cov* 22:26-28 Jl 1993
Review of: *Cardinal Wolsey: church, state and art* by Gunn, S J, and Lindley, P G, eds. In: *TheolStds* 53:757-758 D 1992

Ryan, Thomas.
Disiplines for Christian living. New Jersey: Paulist Press, 1993. x, 274p ISBN 0-8091-3380-6 LC 92-42596
Review of: *The church's social teaching from Rerum Novarum to 1931* by Duncan, Bruce. In: *Pacifica* 6:117-119 F 1993

Rybolt, John E.
Review of: *Exodus* by Johnstone, W. In: *CBQ* 55:339-340 Ap 1993
Review of: *Sentido del dolor en Job* by García-Moreno, Antonio. In: *OTA* 16: 174-175 F 1993

Rybolt, Johu.
Review of: *Essai sur les origines du judaïsme* by Nodet, Étienne. In: *OTA* 16: 448 Je 1993

Rylands, Paddy.
Working with the Parish Project. *Priests & People* 7:58-60 F 1993

Rypar, Francesco.
La "Pastores dabo vobis" alla luce del pensiero conciliare sul sacerdozio e sulla formazione sacerdotale (commentary: *Pastores daba vobis*). *Seminarium* 32:530-549 O-D 1992

S

Sabatowich, Jerome.
They have life in the spirit. *ReligTJ* 26:36-37 Ja 1993
What do they value? *ReligTJ* 27:31 F 1993

Sabbah, Michael.
The always-new forms of suffering in the Holy Land. *Origins* 23:811 My 6 1993
That my people will live in a peaceful home [address, Christian Culture Series, D 6 1992]. *Can Cath Rev* 11:14-18 N 1993

Sable, Thomas F.
Review of: *The lives of Simeon Stylites*. In: *Diakonia* 26 no 2:135-138 1993

Sacco, Antonio.
III convegno diocesano di musica sacra (Foggia, 28 novembre 1992). *Notitiae* 28:759-760 N-D 1992

Sadaba, Javier.
El amor contra la moral. Madrid: Prodhufi, 1993. x, 165p ISBN 84-7954-126-1

Sage, Alan.
Teilhard and ecological spirituality. *Teilhard Rev* 28:11-14 Spr 1993

Sage, Athanase.
The religious life according to Saint Augustine. New Rochelle, New York: New City Press, 1990. 240p ISBN 0-911782-81-8 LC 90-47785

Sagovsky, Nicholas.
Review of: *Tradition and the critical spirit Catholic modernist writings* by Livingston, James C. In: *Heythrop* 34:459-460 O 1993
Review of: *Unresting transformation: the theology and spirituality of Maude Petre* by Leonard, Ellen. In: *Heythrop* 34:459-460 O 1993

Saint-Germain, Christian.
Pouvoir de la singularité: le pathos du visage dans le texte d'Emmanuel Lévinas. *Laval Theol Phil* 49:27-35 F 1993

Saitz, Christopher R.
Isaiah 1-39. Louisville: John Knox, 1993. x, 272p ISBN 0-8042-3131-1

Salado Martinez, Domingo.
La iglesia local en la inculturación del evangelio. *Cien Tom* 120:129-152 Ja-Ap 1993
Review of: *El Evangelio en nuevas culturas* by Espeja, Jesús. In: *Cien Tom* 119:623 S-D 1992

Salas Astrain, Ricardo.
Review of: *La teoría de la referencia: Strawson y la filosofía analítica* by González, Wenceslao. In: *RPhil Louvain* 91:519-520 Ag 1993
Review of: *Religión y modernidad. La crisis del individualismo religioso de Lutero a Neitzsche* by Gómez-Heras, José M.G. In: *RPhil Louvain* 91:510-511 Ag 1993

Saldarini, Anthony J.
Delegitimation of leaders in Matthew 23. *CBQ* 54:659-680 O 1992
Review of: *From text to tradition* by Schiffman, Lawrence H. In: *CBQ* 55:178-180 Ja 1993
Review of: *Parables in Midrash* by Stern, David. In: *TheolStds* 53:781 D 1992

Salerno, Dorsey Price.
Be creative in every class. *ReligTJ* 27:30-31 O 1993

Sales, Michel.
Who can utter the Name of God?—From the holiness of his name to the seriousness of all words. *Communio* 20:26-48 Spr 1993

Saliba, John A.
A Christian response to the New Age. *Way* 33:202-232 Jl 1993
Mormonism in the twenty-first century. *StudiaM* 41:49-67 1992
Review of: *Pilgrimage of hope* by Braybrooke, Marcus. In: *TheolStds* 54:190-192 Mr 1993
Review of: *Unbaptized God: the basic flaw in ecumenical theology* by Jenson, Robert W. In: *TheolStds* 54:608 S 1993

Salinas, Carlos.
Review of: *Episcopología de Puerto Rico* by Murga, Vincente, and Huerga, Alvaro. In: *Teol Vida* 34 no 1-2:157-158 1993
Review of: *Evangelización en América* by Borobio Garcia, et al. In: *Teol Vida* 33 no 3-4:328-329 1992
Review of: *La institución martrimonial en la Hispania cristiana bajomedieval (1215-1563)* by Aznar, Federico R. In: *Teol Vida* 33 no 3-4:328 1992
Review of: *Los concilios limenses en la evangelización latinoamericana* by Tineo, Primitivo. In: *Teol Vida* 33 no 3-4:324-325 1992
Review of: *Un libro inédito de Lebrón sobre diezmos en Indias* by Purroy Turrillas, Carmen. In: *Teol Vida* 33 no 3-4:327-328 1992

Salmon, J.
Review of: *Theology for a scientific age* by Peacocke, Arthur. In: *TheolStds* 53:790-791 D 1992

Salvini, Gianpaolo.
Review of: *Mattioli: Il gattopardo della banca commerciale Italiana* by Galli, Giancarlo. In: *Civilta* 3:97 Jl 3 1993
Una collaborazione ecclesiale tra Italia e America Latina: il ceial-cum. *Civilta* 2:369-376 My 15 1993
Editoria Cattolica. *Civilta* 144:468-471 Mr 6 1993
I Gesuiti e il Papato storia di un voto di obbedienza. *Civilta* 2:44-56 Ap 3 1993

Salvini, Gianpaolo. *(cont'd)*
I rapporti Nord-Sud dopo i cambiamenti nell'est dell'europa. *Civilta* 144:326-339 F 20 1993
Incontro tra Cristiani del sud. *Civilta* 144:51-54 Ja 2 1993
L'Italia in un difficile periodo di transizione. *Civilta* 3:449-461 S 18 1993
Natalità e politiche per la popolazione in Europa. *Civilta* 144:140-152 Ja 16 1993
Note per uno sviluppo umano. *Civilta* 3:491-501 S 18 1993
Review of: *Erasmo en América: entre la ortodoxia y la marginación* by Trusso, Francisco Eduardo. In: *Civilta* 2:96-97 Ap 3 1993
Review of: *Il gemito della creazione* by Panteghini, Giacomo. In: *Civilta* 3:435-436 S 4 1993
Review of: *In principio era il corpo* by Acquaviva, Sabino S. In: *Civilta* 2:3-15 Ap 3 1993
Review of: *La presenza italiana nella storia e nella cultura del Brasile* by Costa, Rovílio, ed. In: *Civilta* 143:542-543 D 5 1992
Review of: *Pequenba enciclopédia de Dottrina social da Ireja* by Avila, Fernando Bastos De. In: *Civilta* 2:303 My 1 1993
Review of: *Storia dell'industria Lombarda, 3 vols* by Zaninelli, Sergio, ed. In: *Civilta* 2:607-608 Je 19 1993
Review of: *Terzo Mondo e Quarto Potere: I continenti della crisi raccontati dalla televisione* by Marchi, Vichi De, and Ercolessi, Maria Cristina. In: *Civilta* 3:337 Ag 7-21 1993
Terzo rapporto sulla povertà in Italia. *Civilta* 3:55-62 Jl 3 1993
L'uomo e il suo destino. *Civilta* 3:256-262 Ag 7-21 1993

Salvini, Gianpaolo, ed.
'La carne è il cardine della salvezza' la concezione cristiana del corpo umano [editorial]. *Civilta* 2:3-15 Ap 3 1993
Un'epoca nuova nella storia del mondo e dell'Italia [editorial]. *Civilta* 3:3-14 Jl 3 1993
Gesù nella storia: una vita che non si chiude con la morte [editorial]. *Civilta* 2:105-115 Ap 17 1993
Gesù una personalità sorprendente [editorial]. *Civilta* 2:521-534 Je 19 1993
L'insegnamento di gesù [editorial]. *Civilta* 3:105-115 Jl 17 1993
Perché non si crede? La risposta di Dostoevskij [editorial]. *Civilta* 2:209-216 My 1 1993

Samaha, John M.
The Mariological Society of America Financial Report 1 July 1991 to 30 June 1992. *Marian Stds* 43:192 1992
Perspective on the universal catechism. *Liguorian* 81:32-34 Je 1993
Report, 1991-92: Western region. *Marian Stds* 43:195 1992
The revision and placement of Marian feasts. *Priest* 49:35-39 My 1993
We are not guests: the exodus of Christians from the Middle East. *Can Cath Rev* 11:11-13 N 1993

Sammon, Jane.
Courts rule on Haitians. *Cath Work* 60:3 Ag 1993
Do not conform yourselves to this age. *Cath Work* 60:3 My 1993

Sammon, Sean D.
An undivided heart: making sense of celibate chastity. New York: Alba House, 1993. x, 160p ISBN 0-8189-0674-x LC 93-3852

Sammon, Sean D, and Zielinski, Judith Ann.
Men vowed and sexual conversations about celibate chastity. *RRel* 52:446-453 My-Je 1993

Sampfer, Nathaniel. *see* Rumer, Jack, jt ed

Samra, Cal.
Documentary ignores Christian healing tradition. *OSV* 82:19 Jl 4 1993

Samra, Nicholas J, Bp.
The Melkites: Catholicism is Greek to them [interview by C Samra]. *OSV* 82:5 S 26 1993

Samway, Patrick H, 1939-.
John Moffitt: poet from Gorakhpur to America. *America* 168:17-22 Ap 10 1993
Review of: *A lesson before dying* by Gaines, Ernest J. In: *America* 169:22 Ag 28-S 4 1993
Review of: *A writer's reflections on the Church, writing and his own life* by Woiwode, Larry. In: *America* 168:19 Mr 20-27 1993
Review of: *Bluesman* by Dubus, Andre, III. In: *America* 169:22-23 Ag 28-S 4 1993
Review of: *Dream makers, dream breakers: the world of Justice Thurgood Marshall* by Rowan, Carl T. In: *America* 168:15 Mr 20-27 1993
Review of: *Extra innings* by Grumbach, Doris. In: *America* 169:18-19 Ag 28-S 4 1993
Review of: *Gandhi: voice of a new revolution* by Green, Martin. In: *America* 169:20 Ag 28-S 4 1993
Review of: *Hearts on fire: praying with Jesuits* by Harter, Michael, ed. In: *America* 169:21 Ag 28-S 4 1993
Review of: *Hodding Carter: the reconstruction of a racist* by Waldron, Ann. In: *America* 169:20 Ag 28-S 4 1993
Review of: *Live from Golgotha* by Vidal, Gore. In: *America* 168:18-19 Ja 16-23 1993
Review of: *Martyr of brotherly love* by Balling, Adalbert Ludwig, and Abeln, Reinhard. In: *America* 168:15+ Mr 20-27 1993
Review of: *Mercy or murder?: Euthanasia, morality and public policy* by Overberg, Kenneth R, 1944-. In: *America* 169:22 Ag 28-S 4 1993
Review of: *Mother Cabrini* by Sullivan, Mary Louise. In: *America* 168:15 Mr 20-27 1993
Review of: *My life as author and editor* by Yardley, Jonathan. In: *America* 168:15 Mr 20-27 1993
Review of: *New York days* by Morris, Willie. In: *America* 169:19 Ag 28-S 4 1993
Review of: *Rumors from the lost world* by Davis, Alan. In: *America* 169:23 Ag 28-S 4 1993
Review of: *Shenandoah and other verse plays* by Schwartz, Delmore. In: *America* 168:15 Mr 20-27 1993
Review of: *Stories from my life with other animals* by McConkey, James. In: *America* 169:19-20 Ag 28-S 4 1993
Review of: *Streets of Laredo* by McMurtry, Larry. In: *America* 169:23 Ag 28-S 4 1993

Samway, Patrick H, 1939-. *(cont'd)*
Review of: *Temptations* by Wilkes, Paul, 1938-. In: *America* 168:20 Mr 20-27 1993
Review of: *The Church and the left* by Michnik, Adam. In: *America* 168:18 Mr 20-27 1993
Review of: *The end of the twentieth century and the end of the Modern Age* by Lukacs, John, 1923-. In: *America* 168:18 Mr 20-27 1993
Review of: *The fountain of age* by Friedan, Betty. In: *America* 169:18 Ag 28-S 4 1993
Review of: *The letter carrier* by Leonard, William J. In: *America* 169:20-21 Ag 28-S 4 1993
Review of: *The oracle at Stoneleigh* by Taylor, Peter. In: *America* 168:20 Mr 20-27 1993
Review of: *The radical tradition* by Markus, Gilbert, ed. In: *America* 169:22 Ag 28-S 4 1993
Review of: *Where have you gone, Michelangelo? The loss of soul in Catholic culture* by Day, Thomas. In: *America* 169:21 Ag 28-S 4 1993

Sanchez, J.
Review of: *Moving crucifixes in modern Spain* by Christian, William A, Jr. In: *CHist* 78:672-673 O 1992

Sanchez, Victor.
Las ensenanzas de Don Carlos: aplicaciones practicas de la obra de Carlos Castaneda. Madrid: Havilah, 1993. x, 282p ISBN 84-87745-04-0

Sánchez Mielgo, Gerardo.
Transmisión de la revelación: escritura, tradición, magisterio: (A la luz de la *Dei Verbum del Concilio Vaticano II*). Cien Tom 119:251-289 My-Ag 1992

Sanchez Noriega, Jose Luis.
La mirada oblicua: materiales para reflexionar la vida cotiana. Madrid: Ediciones Madre Tierra, 1993. x, 200p ISBN 84-87169-53-8

Sand, Linda Lee.
Liz's 100 bears. *St Anth* 100:24-27 F 1993

Sanders, Annmarie.
We chose to stay. *Sisters* 65:91-95 Mr 1993

Sanders, Ivan.
Review of: *The wrath of nations* by Pfaff, William. In: *Comm* 120:26-29 N 5 1993

Sanders, Jack T.
Review of: *Zwischen Synagoge und Obrigkeit: Zur historischen Situation der lukanischen Christen* by Stegemann, Wolfgang. In: *JEcumen Stds* 29:125 Wint 1992

Sanders, Joanne Spisso.
Initiation: meeting the catechetical challenge. *Tod Parish* 25:19-21 Mr 1993

Sanders, Susan.
Review of: *Health care reform* by Keane, Philip S. In: *Nat Cath Rep* 30:26 N 19 1993

Sands, Ernest.
Review of: *Rite of Baptism for children.* In: *Tablet* 247:725 Je 5 1993
Review of: *The days of the Lord: the liturgical year* by Gantoy, Robert, and Swaeles, Romain. In: *Tablet* 247:725 Je 5 1993
Review of: *The liturgy of the world: Karl Rahner's theology of worship* by Skelley, Michael. In: *Tablet* 247:725 Je 5 1993
Review of: *The Lord is risen: the liturgy from Passiontide to Pentecost* by Crichton, J D. In: *Tablet* 247:725 Je 5 1993
Review of: *The revised common lectionary.* In: *Tablet* 247:725 Je 5 1993

Sands, Leo.
That God may be all in all. *Can Cath Rev* 11:36-37 S 1993

Sandys, Sebastian, ed.
Embracing the mystery: prayerful responses to AIDS. Minnesota: The Liturgical Press, 1993. x, 105p ISBN 0-8146-2222-4 LC 92-43238

Sanfelix, Vidarte, ed.
Acerca de Wittgenstein. Valencia: Pre-Textos, 1993. x, 202p ISBN 84-87101

Sanford, John A.
Mystical Christianity: a psychological commentary on the Gospel of John. New York: Crossroad, 1993. x, 350p ISBN 0-82451-230-8 LC 92-35577

Sanford, Ruth.
For the bride: finding your way in the first years of marriage. South Bend: Green Lawn, 1993. 136p ISBN 0-937779-24-5 LC 93-70110

Sanks, T Howland.
Review of: *The only way* by Las Casas, Bartolome de, 1474-1566. In: *TheolStds* 53:786 D 1992

Sanks, T Howland, and Coleman, John A, eds.
Reading the signs of the times: resources for social and cultural analysis. New York: Paulist Press, 1993. x, 232p ISBN 0-8091-33777-6 LC 92-42017

Sansen, Raymond.
Variations sceptiques sur le thème de la mort. *MSR* 50:83-98 Ap-Je 1993

Sanson, Hugh. *see* Saunders, Teddy, jt auth

Santa, Thomas M.
Beyond tears. *Liguorian* 81:24-25 Ap 1993
The breath of life. *Liguorian* 81:60-61 Ja 1993
A Christmas call [a five minute meditation]. *Liguorian* 81:48-49 D 1993
Losing control and loving it. *Liguorian* 81:46-47 Mr 1993
Prayer: our everyday encounter with God. *Liguorian* 81:4-7 F 1993
Review of: *Jesus and the riddle of the Dead Sea Scrolls* by Thiering, Barbara. In: *Liguorian* 81:70 Ap 1993
Review of: *My witness for the Church* by Häring, Bernard, 1912-. In: *Liguorian* 81:68 Ja 1993

Santalo, Lluis, A.
La matematica: una filosofia i una tecnica. BArcelona: Eumo, 1993. x, 147p ISBN 84-7602-807-5

Sante, Carmine Di.
Blessed art thou, o Lord: a Christian understanding of the Jewish blessing. *SIDIC* 26 no 1:10-14 1993

Santer, Mark, Bp, 1929-.
Review of: *The Church under Thatcher* by Clark, Henry. In: *Tablet* 247:1104 Ag 28 1993

Santognossi, Ansgar.
Keeping things in place. *Register* 69:5 F 28 1993

Santoni, Ronald E.
Sartre's adolescent rejection of God. *PhilosTod* 37:62-69 Spr 1993

Santos, Yolanda M, and Zipprich, John L.
Board members with a mission. *Health Prog* 74:32-36 Jl-Ag 1993

Sara, Solomon I.
Review of: *Anti-Christian polemic in early Islam: Abū Īsā al-Warrāq's against the Trinity* by Thomas, David M, ed. In: *TheolStds* 53:783 D 1992
Review of: *Islamic Da'wah in the West: Muslim missionary activity and the dynamics of conversion to Islam* by Poston, Larry. In: *TheolStds* 54:204 Mr 1993

Saraiva Martins, José.
La formazione missionaria dei sacerdoti alla luce della "Pastores dabo vobis" (commentary: *Pastores dabo vobis*). *Seminarium* 32:575-599 O-D 1992

Saranyana, Josep-Ignasi.
Review of: *La teología de Boecio en la transición del mundo clásico al mundo medieval* by Lluch-Baizauli, Miguel. In: *RPhil Louvain* 91:311-312 My 1993

Sasseen, Robert F, and Frank, William F.
Controversial student organizations. *Crisis* 11:38-41 O 1993

Sattler, John C.
Review of: *Contact with God: retreat conferences* by Mello, Anthony De. In: *Living Light* 29:92-93 Aut 1992
Review of: *Prayer: finding the heart's true home* by Foster, Richard J. In: *Living Light* 29:94-95 Sum 1993
Review of: *Through the eyes of faith* by Powell, John. In: *Living Light* 29:94-95 Wint 1992

Saunders, Kathy.
Florida health reform may offer model. *Register* 69:1+ Je 13 1993

Savater, Fernando.
Sin contemplaciones. Madrid: Libertarias, 1993. x, 292p ISBN 84-7683-232-x

Savonarola, Girolamo.
May I love you, Lord: a modern Psalm. *RRel* 52:241-246 Mr-Ap 1993

Sawyer, Deborah. *see* Morris, Paul, jt ed

Sbardella, Agapito.
L'antigiuridismo di Max Stirner. *Civilta* 2:248-251 My 1 1993
Review of: *L'antiguiridismo di Max Stirner* by Ferri, E. In: *Civilta* 2:248-251 My 1 1993

Scaiola, D.
Review of: *Bibbia traduction oecuménique de la Bible.* In: *Civilta* 144:195-196 Ja 16 1993
Review of: *Breve dizionario biblico* by Monloubou, Louis. In: *Civilta* 3:440-441 S 4 1993
Review of: *Evangelo secondo San Marco: Il paradosso della debolezza di Dio* by Attinger, Daniel. In: *Civilta* 144:197-198 Ja 16 1993
Review of: *I Salmi e gli altri scritti.* In: *Civilta* 3:545-546 S 18 1993
Review of: *I grandi temi dell'alleanza* by Beaucamp, Evode. In: *Civilta* 144:196-197 Ja 16 1993
Review of: *L'arte di raccontare Gesú Cristo: la scrittura narrativa del Vangelo di Luca* by Aletti, Jean-Noël. In: *Civilta* 2:404-405 My 15 1993
Review of: *Metafore del Regno* by Weder, Hans. In: *Civilta* 3:87-88 Jl 3 1993
Review of: *Ogni vivente dia lode al Signore: commento dei Salmi delle domeniche e delle feste, 3 voll* by Gilbert, Maurice. In: *Civilta* 143:641-642 D 19 1992
Review of: *Sinossi dei quattro Vangeli Greco-Italiano* by Poppi, Angelico. In: *Civilta* 3:441-442 S 4 1993

Scalamonti, Antonio Cavicchia. *see* Abruzzese, Alberto, jt ed

Scalco, Eugenio.
"Sacramentum Connubii" et institution nuptiale. *Eph Theol Lovan* 69:27-47 Ap 1993

Scally, John.
A child's Christmas in Roscommon. *Month* 25:491-494 D 1992

Scanlan, Michael.
Giving thanks. *New Cov* 22:26-27 My 1993
Keeping colleges Catholic. *Crisis* 11:33-37 O 1993
The Marian movement. *New Cov* 22:23-24 Mr 1993

Scannone, Juan Carlos.
Teología de la liberación y evangelización: nuevas perspectivas. *Seminarium* 32:463-473 Jl-S 1992

Scaperlanda, Anthony.
Review of: *Transfer spending, taxes and the American welfare state* by Peterson, Wallace C, 1921-. In: *RSocEcon* 51:118-122 Spr 1993

Scaperlanda, Maria Ruiz.
The Catholic Archives of Texas. *Columbia* 73:8-10 Jl 1993
Jailhouse confessions of faith [photos]. *OSV* 82:13 N 28 1993

Scarbrough, George.
The night he came. *Spirit* 58:1-2 1993

Scarisbrick, J.
Review of: *The stripping of the altars* by Duffy, Eamon. In: *Tablet* 247:211-212 F 13 1993

Schaafsma, Roberta.
A model for Israel. *BibleT* 31:208-212 Jl 1993

Schaberg, Jane.
Religious superiors defend school's Catholic identity. *Origins* 22:703-704 Mr 25 1993

Schaefer, David Lewis.
Review of: *The Christian Church in the Cold War* by Chadwick, Owen. In: *America* 169:20-22 O 9 1993

Schaefer, David Lewis. *(cont'd)*
Review of: *The final revolution* by Weigel, George. In: *America* 169:20-22 O 9 1993

Schaefer, Jeffrey C. *see* Westhoff, Lola J, jt auth

Schaefer, Vernon J.
A good shepherd [Andrew Stojar]. *HPR* 93:75-76 Ag-S 1993

Schaeffer-Duffy, Claire, and Schaeffer-Duffy, Scott.
Baking and breaking bread. *Cath Work* 60:4 My 1993

Schaeffer-Duffy, Scott. *see* Schaeffer-Duffy, Claire, jt auth

Schaeper, Thomas J.
Review of: *The fabrication of Louis XIV* by Burke, Peter. In: *Cithara* 32:53-54 My 1993

Schäfer, Stephen J.
Review of: *Society and spirit: a trinitarian cosmology* by Bracken, Joseph A. In: *TheolStds* 54:373-375 Je 1993

Schalck, Hermann.
Lettera dei ministri generali delle famiglie Francescane sulla vita liturgica [Rome]. *Notitiae* 28:546-560 Ag 1992

Schall, James Vincent, 1928-, et al.
The March for Life, 1993. *Crisis* 11:28-29 Mr 1993

Schall, James Vincent, 1928-.
American spirituality: a distinct contribution? *Living Light* 29:3-13 Aut 1992
An atheist in the sacristy: why does faith seek intelligence? *F & R* 28:315-334 Wint 1992
The begging industry. *Crisis* 11:44-45 Je 1993
Le catéchisme de l'église Catholique. *Crisis* 11:42-43 Mr 1993
The Church explains itself: the new catechism. *HPR* 93:9-17 Je 1993
The Day of the Dead. *Crisis* 10:43-45 N 1992
Grace has appeared. *Crisis* 10:44-45 D 1992
"Humanae Vitae" after 25 years. *Crisis* 11:48-49 Jl-Ag 1993
"I have come to bring division". *OR(Eng)* 1301:8-10 Jl 28 1993
Ludere est contemplari: on the unseriousness of human affairs. *ABenR* 44:99-111 Mr 1993
The Marlin factor in New York. *Crisis* 11:49 O 1993
On "abortion on the way out". *SocJust* 84:45-49 Mr-Ap 1993
On hearing Dvorak's "Stabat Mater". *Crisis* 11:43-45 Ja 1993
On making sense of the universe. *Crisis* 11:47-48 Ap 1993
On never reaching Canada. *Crisis* 11:49-50 My 1993
On teaching. *Crisis* 11:49-50 S 1993
Pensées pour le temps penitentiel. *Crisis* 11:39-41 F 1993
Review of: *1492 and all that* by Royal, Robert. In: *Crisis* 11:50-52 F 1993
Review of: *In defense of philosophy* by Pieper, Josef. In: *HPR* 93:82-86 Ag-S 1993
Review of: *Men astutely trained: a history of the Jesuits in the American century* by McDonough, Peter. In: *Crisis* 10:48-51 D 1992
Review of: *The emergence of liberation theology* by Smith, Christian. In: *CHist* 79:586-588 Jl 1993
Review of: *The Heliand: the Saxon Gospel* by Murphy, G Ronald. In: *Crisis* 11:48-50 Mr 1993
The teaching of Centesimus Annus. *Gregorianum* 74 No 1:17-43 1993
Centesimus Annus (the Hundredth Year), on the social teaching and concern for the worker, the poor and the unborn: encyclical letter of His Holiness Pope John Paul II (commentary).
Transcendent man in the limited city: the political philosophy of Charles N R McCoy. *Thomist* 57:63-95 Ja 1993
Working with Christ: the Catechism's social teaching. *Crisis* 11:27-30 Je 1993
Catechism of the Catholic Church (Commentary).

Schaller, Jeanne Lound.
Forming a circle of love: a profile of Judy Harris. *Liguorian* 81:54-58 S 1993
Homeless bishop speaks for the poor. *St Anth* 100:22-27 Mr 1993
Prayer rider. *Liguorian* 81:54-55 My 1993
Sharing as sign of Eucharist. *Living Prayer* 26:19-20 S-O 1993

Schalow, Frank.
Review of: *On Heidegger's Nazism and philosophy* by Rockmore, Tom. In: *IPQ* 33:241-243 Je 1993

Schaper, Donna.
Review of: *Blackberry season: a time to mourn, a time to heal* by Price, H H. In: *St Anth* 101:52 N 1993
Review of: *Channels of belief: religion and American commercial television* by Ferré, John P, ed. In: *St Anth* 100:51-52 S 1993

Scharper, Stephen B.
Promised "change" bombed by Clinton's Iraq attack. *Nat Cath Rep* 29:22 Jl 16 1993

Scharper, Stephen B, and Cunningham, Hilary, eds.
The green Bible. Maryknoll, New York: Orbis Books, 1993. x, 113p ISBN 0-85244-230-0 LC 92-35593

Schatz, Klaus.
Response to Claude Soetens. *Jurist* 52 no 1:183-188 1992

Schauder, Hans. *see* Lefébure, Marcus, jt auth

Scheele, Paul-Werner.
Das Studiendokument Kirche und Welt. *Catholica* 47 no 2:108-123 1993

Scheffczyk, Leo, Msgr.
Der Zölibat: Formkraft priesterlicher existenz und priesterlichen dienstes. *Seminarium* 33:48-59 Ja-Mr 1993

Scheib, J.
Review of: *A place for Baptism* by Kuehn, Regina. In: *Mod Lit* 19:42-43 D 1992-Ja 1993

Schenck, Stephen.
Catholic secondary schools and the new evangelization. *Living Light* 30:24-32 Aut 1993

Scherer, Scott.
Have faith, will travel. *Register* 69:1+ Ag 22 1993

Scherer-Edmunds, Meinrad.
Bethel Lutheran Church. *Salt* 13:6 N-D 1993
Our Lady of Peace parish. *Salt* 13:33 N-D 1993

Scherer-Edmunds, Meinrad. *(cont'd)*
St. Francis of Assisi Church. *Salt* 13:41 N-D 1993
St. Francis of Assisi Parish: Rx for rural crisis. *Salt* 13:26 N-D 1993
St. John student parish. *Salt* 13:21 N-D 1993

Scheuer, J.
Review of: *Bouddhisme-Christianisme: au-delà du dialogue?* by Cobb, John B, Jr. In: *Lumen* 48:115-166 Mr 1993
Review of: *Der Fall Sadhu Sundar Singh* by Biehl, M. In: *NRT* 115:602-603 Jl-Ag 1993
Review of: *La doctrine d'al-Ash'arî* by Gimaret, D. In: *NRT* 115:606 Jl-Ag 1993
Review of: *Matéiaux pour servir à l'étude de la controverse théologique islamo-chrétienne de langue arabe du VIIIe au XIIe siècle* by Khoury, P. In: *NRT* 115:605-606 Jl-Ag 1993
Review of: *Religion, learning and science in the Abbasid period* by Young, M J L, et al, eds. In: *NRT* 115:598-599 Jl-Ag 1993
Review of: *Scripture, canon and commentary* by Henderson, J B. In: *NRT* 115:600-601 Jl-Ag 1993
Review of: *Shiism* by Halm, H. In: *NRT* 115:606-607 Jl-Ag 1993
Review of: *The Sikhs* by Thursby, G R. In: *NRT* 115:604-605 Jl-Ag 1993
Review of: *The true meaning of the Lord of heaven (T'ien-chu Shis-i)* by Ricci, M. In: *NRT* 115:602 Jl-Ag 1993
Review of: *Introduction aux religons orientales* by Girault, René. In: *Lumen* 48:116 Mr 1993
Review of: *Mystiques d'Asie* by Masson, Joseph. In: *Lumen* 48:116 Mr 1993

Scheuring, Tom, et al, eds.
The poor and the good news: a call to evangelize. New Jersey: Paulist Press, 1993. x, 162p ISBN 0-8091-3359-8 LC 92-37976

Schiebl, Johanna.
Priestertum der Frau. *Stimm Zeit* 211:115-122 F 1993

Schiefen, R J.
Review of: *A W N Pugin and the revival of memorial brasses* by Meara, David. In: *CHist* 79:147-148 Ja 1993

Schilder, David M.
My parish behind the fence [condensed fr *The Catholic Times* n.d.]. *CDgst* 57:66-70 Ag 1993

Schillebeeckx, Edward.
Church: the human story of God. New York: Crossroad, 1993. x, 260p ISBN 0-8245-1050-x LC 90-36343

Schiller, Britt-Marie.
Review of: *Philosophy as therapy: an interpretation and defense of Wittgenstein's later philosophical project* by Peterman, James F. In: *Mod Schlmn* 70:156-159 Ja 1993

Schindler, David L.
Catholic theology, gender, and the future of Western civilization [editorial]. *Communio* 20:200-239 Sum 1993
Towards a eucharistic evangelization. *Communio* 19:549-575 Wint 1992

Schineller, Peter.
The Eucharist and the mission of the priest. *Emmanuel* 49:364-369 S 1993
The life and teaching of St Thomas Aquinas: a guide for the African Church today. *AFER* 34:18-28 F 1992

Schintz, Mary Ann.
Review of: *Against all odds: Sisters of Providence mission to the Chinese, 1920-1990* by Wolf, Ann Colette. In: *CHist* 79:381-383 Ap 1993

Schlabach, Gerald. *see* McManus, Philip, jt ed

Schlaerth, Katherine.
Adults should never hit kids. *USCath* 58:24-29 Ja 1993

Schlather, Mary Margaret Ann.
Distance learning: a practical alternative for catechist formation. *Momentum* 24:73-74 N-D 1993

Schlesinger, Hugo. *see* Porto, Humberto, jt auth

Schlichte, George A.
Politics in the purple kingdom: the derailment of Vatican II. Kansas City: Sheed & Ward, 1993. x, 133p ISBN 1-55612-607-7 LC 92-44098

Schlickenrieder, Annelies.
Mothering the Hummel children. *OSV* 82:6-7 Je 6 1993

Schlitt, D.
Review of: *Reason in religion: the foundations of Hegel's philosophy of religion* by Jaeschke, Walter. In: *Heythrop* 34:110-111 Ja 1993

Schlitt, Michael.
Wirtschaft und Umweltschutz aus ethischer Sicht. *Stimm Zeit* 210:806-818 D 1992

Schloen, J David.
Caravans, Kenites, and Casus belli: Enmity and Alliance in the Song of Deborah. *CBQ* 55:18-38 Ja 1993

Schmidt, J.
Review of: *The wild man's journey: reflections on male spirituality* by Rohr, Richard, 1943-, and Martos, Joseph. In: *Sisters* 65:60-61 Ja 1993

Schmidt, Ruth.
How do I live now? *USCath* 58:26-30 Je 1993

Schmidt, Stephen A.
Augustin Bea, the Cardinal of unity. New Rochelle, New York: New City Press, 1992. 806p ISBN 1-56548-016-3 LC 92-17612
The day I hated being a man. *USCath* 58:30-31 Je 1993

Schmidt-Leukel, Perry.
Zur Klassifikation religionstheologischer Modelle. *Catholica* 47 no 3:163-183 1993

Schmidtt, Miriam.
Review of: *Women as interpreters of the Bible* by Demers, Patricia. In: *Worship* 67:377-379 Jl 1993

Schmied, Gerhard.
US-Televangelismus in Deutschland. *Stimm Zeit* 211:633-640 S 1993

Schweizer, Paul.
Review of: *Indian philosophy of language* by Siderits, Mark. In: *IPQ* 33:373-376 S 1993

Schwer, Mary Angela.
Review of: *Christianity and the rhetoric of empire: the development of Christian discourse* by Cameron, Averil. In: *Relig Lit* 24:109-110 Aut 1992

Scibilia, Dominic P.
Review of: *Church and age unite!* by Appleby, Raphael Scott. In: *America* 169:26-27 Ag 14-21 1993

Scollard, Anselma.
Review of: *Anglo-Saxon crucifixion iconography, and the art of the monastic revival* by Raw, Barbara C. In: *Cist Stud* 27 No 4:[91]-[93] 1992
Review of: *Gateway to paradise: Basil the Great* by Davies, Oliver, ed. In: *Cist Stud* 28:[25]-[26] 1993

Scott, Charlene.
What gives a family value? *USCath* 58:32-37 Ja 1993

Scott, David.
Excavating the truth about abortion. *OSV* 82:5 My 30 1993
Humanitarian aid or armed intervention? *OSV* 81:12-13 Ap 18 1993
Minding their own business: worker ownership. *St Anth* 100:16-21 S 1993
The Pope came to Denver, preaching life against death. *OSV* 82:17 S 5 1993
A primer for the morally perplexed. *OSV* 82:10-11 Ag 8 1993
Review of: *The culture of disbelief* by Carter, Stephen L. In: *OSV* 82:3 N 7 1993
A revolution not by politics alone. *OSV* 81:15-16 F 28 1993
Seeking the lost Atlantis of Catholics and Jews [por]. *OSV* 82:6-7 S 19 1993
Ten ways to wake up city hall. *Salt* 13:6-11 Je 1993
Young American Catholics: how Catholic are they? *OSV* 81:6 Ap 25 1993

Scott, Geoffrey.
Review of: *Augustine Baker's inner light: a study in English recusant spirituality* by Gaffney, James William, 1931-. In: *Heythrop* 34:337-338 Jl 1993

Scott, John M.
Father Scott's reflections on women, family, and relationships. Indiana: Our Sunday Visitor, 1993. 139p ISBN 0-87973-530-9 LC 92-61551

Scott, Kieran, and Warren, Michael, 1935-.
Perspectives on marriage. New York: Oxford University Press, 1993. x, 441p ISBN 0-19-507804-7 LC 92-14595

Scott, Rivers.
Review of: *Brother Jacob [tr by A Born]* by Stangerup, Henrik. In: *Tablet* 247:1105 Ag 28 1993
Review of: *False gods* by Auchincloss, Louis. In: *Tablet* 247:552 My 1 1993
Review of: *Married past redemption* by Middleton, Stanely. In: *Tablet* 247:951 Jl 24 1993
Review of: *Mind the gap* by Miles, Jeremy. In: *Tablet* 247:951 Jl 24 1993
Review of: *The Judas cloth* by O'Faolain, Julia. In: *Tablet* 247:19 Ja 2 1993

Scott, Terrie, et al.
The message the media missed [interviews by J. Mallon]. *Crisis* 11:21-24 O 1993

Scovazzi, Tullio, et al. see Giuliano, Mario, jt auth

Scribner, Bob.
Review of: *The German peasants' War and Anabaptist Community of Goods* by Stayer, James M. In: *Heythrop* 34:455-456 O 1993

Scroggs, Robin.
Review of: *Theological ethics of the New Testament* by Lohse, Eduard. In: *CBQ* 55:381-382 Ap 1993

Scullion, John.
Review of: *The covenant never revoked: biblical reflections on Christian-Jewish dialogue* by Lohfink, Norbert. In: *SIDIC* 25 No 2:33 1992

Scullion, John J.
Genesis: a commentary for students, teachers, and preachers. Collegeville, Minnesota: Liturgical Press, 1992. x, 366p ISBN 0-81465-659-5 LC 92-12322

Scurani, Allesandro.
Review of: *Etica ed economia* by Sancinelli, Bruno. In: *Civilta* 3:444-445 S 4 1993
Review of: *Vigilio Federico Dalla Zuanna* by Rinaldi, Remo. In: *Civilta* 3:98-99 Jl 3 1993

Searcy, Dennis R.
Beyond the self-regulating market society: a critique of Polanyi's theory of the state. *RSocEcon* 51:217-231 Sum 1993

Seasoltz, R Kevin.
Review of: *Fritz Eichenberg* by Ellsberg, Robert, ed. In: *Worship* 67:370 Jl 1993
Review of: *Journey with the fathers, Year A* by Barnecut, Edith, ed. In: *Worship* 67:384-385 Jl 1993
Review of: *Spiritual space: the religious architecture of Pietro Belluschi* by Clausen, Meredith L. In: *Worship* 67:471-474 S 1993
Review of: *Theological investigations, vol XXIII* by Rahner, Karl, 1904-1984. In: *Worship* 67:90-92 Ja 1993

Seaver, Paul.
Review of: *Fire from heaven: life in an English town in the seventeenth century* by Underdown, David. In: *CHist* 79:539-541 Jl 1993

Sebahire, Mbonvinkebe.
Saving the earth to save life [condensed fr *Pro Mundi Vita Studies* F 1990]. *TheolDgst* 38:128-129 Sum 1991

Sebanc, Mark, 1941-1992.
J R R Tolkien: lover of the logos. *Communio* 20:84-106 Spr 1993

Seco, Atilano Rico.
Fray Luis de Granada y Erasmo. *Cien Tom* 119:549-578 S-D 1992

Secondin, Bruno.
Fundamentalism: challenges and dangers. *TheolDgst* 40:3-7 Spr 1993
Horizons of the charism of an institute: the "new" participation of the lay faithful. *Con Life* 17 no 2:83-97 1992

Secondin, Bruno. *(cont'd)*
Santo Domingo—an interpretation [excerpt fr *Sedos*]. *LADOC* 23:1-13 Jl-Ag 1993

Sed, N-J. see Jossua, Jean-Pierre, jt ed

Sedano, Maruja.
When parents are upset. *ReligTJ* 26:17 Ja 1993

Seddon, Catharine.
Serbia's holy land. *Tablet* 247:536-538 My 1 1993

Sedgwick, P H. see Hardy, D W, jt ed

Sedgwick, Sally.
Pippin on Hegel's critique of Kant. *IPQ* 33:273-283 S 1993

Seel, John. see Guinness, Os, jt ed

Seeley, David.
Jesus' Temple Act. *CBQ* 55:262-283 Ap 1993
Review of: *The Epistle to the Philippians: a commentary on the Greek text* by O'Brien, Peter T. In: *CBQ* 55:176-177 Ja 1993

Seethaler, Scott.
Can a diocesan priest be a contemplative? *HPR* 93:17-21 Ja 1993
The mystery of unanswered prayer. *New Cov* 23:25-27 N 1993
A prayer for all seasons. *New Cov* 23:22-26 S 1993
Praying on the run. *New Cov* 22:18-20 Je 1993
When should a priest say no? *HPR* 93:28+ Jl 1993

Segalla, Giuseppe.
Catechism presents Scripture as revelation of God's salvific plan. *OR(Eng)* 1294:9-10 Je 9 1993

Segers, Mary C. see Byrnes, Timothy A, jt ed

Segger, Jill.
Review of: *Mozart: traces of transcendence* by Küng, Hans, 1928-. In: *Priests & People* 7:82-83 F 1993

Séguin, Michel.
The biblical foundations of the thought of John Paul II on human sexuality. *Communio* 20:266-289 Sum 1993

Seguin, Robert.
Review of: *Whispers of revelation: discovering the spirit of the poor* by Coleman, Bill, and Coleman, Patty. In: *Can Cath Rev* 11:22-23 S 1993

Segundo, Juan Luis.
Our Lady of Guadalupe: a Liberating interpretation [tr fr *Conciencia Latinoamericana*]. *LADOC* 24:24-27 S-O 1993

Seibel, W.
Review of: *Bischofswahlen in der Schweiz.* In: *Stimm Zeit* 211:428 Je 1993
Review of: *Die Divisionäre des Papstes* by Boberski, Heiner. In: *Stimm Zeit* 211:284-285 Ap 1993
Review of: *Dokumente wachsender Übereinstimmung* by Meyer, Harding. In: *Stimm Zeit* 211:283-284 Ap 1993
Review of: *Ein Blick zurück—nach vorn: Johannes XXIII* by Alberigo, Giuseppe, and Wittstadt, Klaus, eds. In: *Stimm Zeit* 211:431-432 Je 1993
Review of: *Wir sind das Volk Gottes! Demokratisierung der Kirche* by Leuninger, Ernest. In: *Stimm Zeit* 211:285 Ap 1993

Seiden, Jerry.
Divine or distorted?: God as we understand God. San Diego, California: Recovery Publications, 1993. x, 142p ISBN 0-941405-19-2 LC 92-41854

Seidl, Lawrence G.
The value of spiritual health. *Health Prog* 74:48-50 1993

Seifert, William. see Urbine, William, jt auth

Seitz, Ron.
Song for nobody: a memory of Thomas Merton. Liguori: Triumph Books, 1993. 188p ISBN 0-89243-486-4 LC 92-43419

Sell, Alan P. see Bender, Ross T, jt ed

Sell, Alan P F.
Review of: *Form and transformation: a study in the philosophy of Plotinus* by Schroeder, Frederic M. In: *IJPS* 1:168-169 Mr 1993
Review of: *On the nature and existence of God* by Gale, Richard M. In: *IJPS* 1:143-146 Mr 1993

Sellers, Mortimer.
The actual validity of law. *Amer J Juris* 37:283-290 1992

Selling, Joseph A.
On sex and sexuality: the challenge of André Guindon. *Doctr Life* 43:31-41 Ja 1993

Sellner, Edward C.
Wisdom of the Celtic saints. Notre Dame, Indiana: Ave Maria Press, 1993. 207p ISBN 0-87793-492-4 LC 92-74778
The work our era demands of us: the recovery of lay leadership. *Listening* 28:65-80 Wint 1993

Selman, F J.
Immortality and the soul. *New Blckfrs* 73:566-571 N 1992

Selvaggi, Filippo.
Il mio itinerario filosofico. *Gregorianum* 74 no 2:309-329 1993
Review of: *Interrogativi sull'Universo (Luci del pensiero scientifico e filosofico sul mistero della Creazione)* by Arcidiacono, Vincenzo. In: *Gregorianum* 74 no 2:402-403 1993

Senécal, Bernard.
Etre catholique en Corée du Sud: la mulitple appartenance religieuse. *Lumen* 48:207-216 Je 1993

Senior, Donald.
Review of: *1 and 2 Peter, Jude* by Hillyer, Norman. In: *BibleT* 31:315 S 1993
Review of: *A dictionary of biblical tradition in English literature* by Jeffrey, David Lyle. In: *BibleT* 31:253 Jl 1993
Review of: *A Gospel for a new people* by Stanton, Graham N. In: *BibleT* 31:61-62 Ja 1993
Review of: *A marginal Jew: rethinking the historical Jesus* by Meier, John P. In: *TheolStds* 53:739-742 D 1992
Review of: *According to Luke* by Trainor, Michael. In: *BibleT* 31:317 S 1993

Senior, Donald. *(cont'd)*
Review of: *Antidocetic christology in the Gospel of John* by Schnelle, Udo. In: *BibleT* 31:255 Jl 1993
Review of: *Biblical theology of the Old and New Testaments* by Childs, Brevard S. In: *BibleT* 31:313 S 1993
Review of: *But she said* by Fiorenza, Elisabeth Schüssler, 1938-. In: *BibleT* 31:314 S 1993
Review of: *Colossians* by Pokorný, Petr. In: *BibleT* 31:316 S 1993
Review of: *Cycling through the gospels* by Sabatowich, Jerome. In: *BibleT* 31:254 Jl 1993
Review of: *Divorce in the New Testament* by Collins, Raymond F. In: *BibleT* 31:252 Jl 1993
Review of: *First, second, and third John* by Smith, Dwight Moody. In: *BibleT* 31:255 Jl 1993
Review of: *Gentiles, Jews, Christians* by Conzelmann, Hans, 1915-1989. In: *BibleT* 31:58 Ja 1993
Review of: *Gospell of life: theology in the fourth gospel* by Beasley-Murray, George Raymond. In: *BibleT* 31:58 Ja 1993
Review of: *Greeks, Romans, Jews* by Newsome, James D. In: *BibleT* 31:316 S 1993
Review of: *He is risen! a new reading of Mark's Gospel* by Humphrey, Hugh M. In: *BibleT* 31:60 Ja 1993
Review of: *Hellenists and Hebrews* by Hill, Craig C. In: *BibleT* 31:59 Ja 1993
Review of: *In the thick of his ministry* by Martini, Carlo Maria, Cardinal, 1926-. In: *BibleT* 31:253 Jl 1993
Review of: *Introducing the cultural context of the New Testament, vol II* by Pilch, John Joseph, 1936-. In: *BibleT* 31:60 Ja 1993
Review of: *Irony in Mark's Gospel* by Camery-Hoggatt, Jerry. In: *BibleT* 31:313 S 1993
Review of: *Jesus and the Dead Sea Scrolls* by Charlesworth, James H. In: *BibleT* 31:313 S 1993
Review of: *Jesus the Christ* by Hill, Brennan. In: *BibleT* 31:59 Ja 1993
Review of: *Jesus the Christ* by Hill, Brennan. In: *CBQ* 55:371-372 Ap 1993
Review of: *John among the gospels* by Smith, Dwight Moody. In: *BibleT* 31:61 Ja 1993
Review of: *John as storyteller* by Stibbe, Mark W G. In: *BibleT* 31:255 Jl 1993
Review of: *John's Gospel in new perspective* by Cassidy, Richard J. In: *BibleT* 31:251-252 Jl 1993
Review of: *Josephus and the New Testament* by Mason, Steve. In: *BibleT* 31:315-316 S 1993
Review of: *Journeys in dust and light* by DeMers, John. In: *BibleT* 31:313-314 S 1993
Review of: *Judaism: practice and belief* by Sanders, E P. In: *BibleT* 31:61 Ja 1993
Review of: *Let the reader understand* by Fowler, Robert M. In: *BibleT* 31:59 Ja 1993
Review of: *Matthew* by Hare, Douglas R A. In: *BibleT* 31:314 S 1993
Review of: *New Testament Apocrypha* by Schneemelcher, Wilhelm, ed. In: *BibleT* 31:316-317 S 1993
Review of: *Paul, women and wives* by Keener, Craig S. In: *BibleT* 31:315 S 1993
Review of: *Peter in Matthew* by Nau, Arlo J. In: *BibleT* 31:253-254 Jl 1993
Review of: *Prayer according to the Scriptures* by Laplace, Jean. In: *BibleT* 31:60 Ja 1993
Review of: *Prayer in the New Testament* by Doohan, Helen, and Doohan, Leonard. In: *BibleT* 31:59 Ja 1993
Review of: *Starlight* by Shea, John B. In: *BibleT* 31:255 Jl 1993
Review of: *Suffering and ministry in the spirit* by Hafemann, Scott J. In: *BibleT* 31:314 S 1993
Review of: *The Acts of the Apostles* by Johnson, Luke Timothy, 1943-. In: *BibleT* 31:253 Jl 1993
Review of: *The beginning of the gospel* by Collins, Adela Yarbro. In: *BibleT* 31:252 Jl 1993
Review of: *The beginning of the gospel* by Peatman, William. In: *BibleT* 31:254 Jl 1993
Review of: *The beloved disciple: a witness against anti-semitism* by Kaufman, Philip S. In: *BibleT* 31:60 Ja 1993
Review of: *The continuing voice of Jesus* by Boring, M Eugene. In: *BibleT* 31:58 Ja 1993
Review of: *The Gospel according to Mary* by Winter, Miriam Therese. In: *BibleT* 31:317 S 1993
Review of: *The Gospel according to Saint Mark* by Hooker, Morna D. In: *BibleT* 31:315 S 1993
Review of: *The Gospel according to St Paul* by Richards, Hubart. In: *BibleT* 31:61 Ja 1993
Review of: *The Gospel of Mark as a model for action* by Heil, John Paul. In: *BibleT* 31:252-253 Jl 1993
Review of: *The gospels in context* by Theissen, Gerd. In: *BibleT* 31:317 S 1993
Review of: *The hilarity of community* by Dawn, Marva J. In: *BibleT* 31:252 Jl 1993
Review of: *The Lord's prayer* by Ayo, Nicholas. In: *BibleT* 31:58 Ja 1993
Review of: *The love of enemy and nonretaliation in the New Testament* by Swartley, Willard M, ed. In: *BibleT* 31:255 Jl 1993
Review of: *The Messiah* by Charlesworth, James H. In: *BibleT* 31:252 Jl 1993
Review of: *The prayer texts of Luke-Acts* by Plymale, Steven F. In: *BibleT* 31:254 Jl 1993
Review of: *The tears of God* by Harrington, Wilfrid John. In: *BibleT* 31:59 Ja 1993
Review of: *The topical Josephus* by Rogers, Cleon L, Jr. In: *BibleT* 31:61 Ja 1993
Review of: *The way of the Lord* by Marcus, Joel. In: *BibleT* 31:315 S 1993
Review of: *Through the ages in Palestinian archaeology* by Rast, Walter E. In: *BibleT* 31:316 S 1993
Review of: *Toward a theological encounter: Jewish understanding of Christianity* by Klenicki, Leon, ed. In: *BibleT* 31:60 Ja 1993
Review of: *Uncompleted mission* by Dickson, Kwesi A. In: *BibleT* 31:58-59 Ja 1993
Review of: *Verbum caro* by O'Carroll, Michael. In: *BibleT* 31:254 Jl 1993

Senior, Donald. *(cont'd)*
Review of: *Voices from the edge* by Trainor, Michael, and Brady, Michael. In: *BibleT* 31:317 S 1993
Review of: *Way of the cross* by Elizondo, Virgil, ed. In: *BibleT* 31:314 S 1993
Review of: *What are they saying about Acts?* by Powell, Mark Allan. In: *BibleT* 31:60 Ja 1993
Review of: *Windows on the gospel* by McCarthy, Flor. In: *BibleT* 31:253 Jl 1993

Senn, Alfred Erich.
Review of: *Lithuanian religious life in America: a compendium of 150 Roman Catholic parishes and institutions; volume 1: Eastern United States* by Wolkovich-Valkavicius, William. In: *CHist* 79:368-369 Ap 1993

Senn, Frank C.
The assembly as proclaimer. *Liturgy* 11:14-15 Sum 1993
Review of: *Documents of Christian worship* by White, James F. In: *Worship* 67:371-373 Jl 1993
The witness of the worshiping community. New Jersey: Paulist Press, 1993. x, 177p ISBN 0-8091-3368-7 LC 92-34033

Senseman, Rita Burns.
The continuing confirmation debate [reply to Joseph Martos, 25:19-24 Mr 1992]. *Catechist* 26:37-40 Ja 1993

Senser, Robert A, 1921-.
Dragon in the toy factory: workers' rights in Asian plants. *Comm* 120:11-13 O 8 1993
Review of: *Labor and economic growth in five Asian countries* by Galenson, Walter. In: *Comm* 120:24-25 Ja 15 1993

Sepp, E J.
It's never too late to be chaste. *Liguorian* 81:50-53 S 1993

Sepulveda, Juan.
The liberation of creation. *LADOC* 23:23-27 My-Je 1993

Serra, Michele. see Nadin, Lucia, jt ed

Sestieri, Lea.
Why was the expulsion of the Jews from Spain so tragic? *SIDIC* 25 No 2:2-7 1992

Settle, Stephen.
The firm. *Register* 69:5 Ag 1 1993
Groundhog Day. *Register* 69:5 Mr 21 1993
In the line of fire. *Register* 69:5 Ag 8 1993
The right to bear arms? *Register* 69:5 Jl 25 1993
They will not be silent. *Register* 69:5 F 21 1993

Seubert, Xavier John.
Contemporary art and the expanded death of the human Jesus. *New Theol Rev* 6:27-39 F 1993
The trivialization of matter: development of ritual incapacity. *Worship* 67:38-53 Ja 1993

Seumois, A.
Review of: *L'Afrique des guérisons* by Rosnyh, Eric de. In: *Civilta* 144:103 Ja 2 1993

Seyer, Loretta.
A nation living on the brink. *Register* 69:3 My 30 1993

Seymour, Chris.
Clintonomics. *Nat Cath Rep* 29:4 F 12 1993

Seys, Pascale.
Review of: *Vocabulaire d'esthétique* by Souriau, Étienne. In: *RPhil Louvain* 91:513-514 Ag 1993

Shaffer, Thomas F.
Review of: *With liberty and justice for whom? The recent evangelical debate over capitalism* by Gay, Craig M. In: *Amer J Juris* 37:363-365 1992

Shalala, Donna E.
Reaching for a healthy tomorrow. *Momentum* 24:29-31 N-D 1993

Shanahan, Thomazine.
The sixth Sunday of Easter. *Liturgy* 11:47-49 Sum 1993

Shank, Michael H.
Review of: *Erde und kosmos im Mittelalter: das welbild vor Kolumbus* by Simek, Rudolf. In: *CHist* 79:329-330 Ap 1993

Shannon, Elizabeth.
Review of: *The Gonne-Yeats letters: 1893-1938* by White, Anna MacBride, and Jeffares, A Norman, eds. In: *Comm* 120:24-26 Ag 13 1993

Shannon, Mary L.
Bringing Jesus back out of the closet. *St Anth* 100:18-20 Ja 1993

Shannon, Thomas A.
It's easier to clone embryo than to figure consequences. *Nat Cath Rep* 30:19 N 12 1993
Method in ethics: a Scotistic contribution. *TheolStds* 54:272-293 Je 1993
Review of: *Celebrating peace* by Rouner, Leroy S, ed. In: *JEcumen Stds* 29:110-111 Wint 1992
Review of: *Dignity and solidarity: an introduction to peace and justice education* by Jackson, Owen R. In: *Horizons (CTS)* 19:338-339 Fall 1992
Review of: *Theology, politics, and peace* by Runyon, Theodore. In: *JEcumen Stds* 29:110-111 Wint 1992 see O'Brien, David J, 1938-, jt ed; Walter, James J, jt ed

Shannon, William H, 1917-.
Review of: *Thomas Merton as writer and monk: a cultural study, 1915-1951* by Kountz, Peter. In: *CHist* 79:137-138 Ja 1993
'The Catechism of the Catholic Church' [commentary]. *America* 168:6-10 Je 5-12 1993

Shapiro, Barbara C.
Teachers: identifying the best and the brightest. *Momentum* 24:29-32 S-O 1993

Sharp, John.
Catholicism and culture. *Priests & People* 7:219-223 Je 1993
Review of: *Ignatius (George) Spencer Passionist (1799-1864)* by Vanden Bussche, Jozef. In: *Month* 26:79 F 1993

Shaughnessy, Mary Angela.
Needed: volunteer policies. *Momentum* 24:62-64 N-D 1993

Shaw, Joseph M. *see* Franklin, R William, jt auth

Shaw, Roy.
Annie get your gun. *Tablet* 246:1578 D 12 1992
Anthony and Cleopatra. *Tablet* 247:825 Je 26 1993
Arcadia. *Tablet* 247:553 My 1 1993
As you like it. *Tablet* 247:695 My 29 1993
Barnum. *Tablet* 247:52 Ja 9 1993
The beggar's opera. *Tablet* 247:519 Ap 24 1993
Billy Liar. *Tablet* 247:52 Ja 9 1993
Carousel. *Tablet* 247:20 Ja 2 1993
The changeling. *Tablet* 247:793-794 Je 19 1993
Chatsky. *Tablet* 247:412 Mr 27 1993
City of angels. *Tablet* 247:622 My 15 1993
The comedy of errors. *Tablet* 247:80 Ja 16 1993
A Connecticut Yankee. *Tablet* 247:1106 Ag 28 1993
Crazy for you. *Tablet* 247:379 Mr 20 1993
Cyrano de Bergerac. *Tablet* 247:52 Ja 9 1993
The dearly beloved. *Tablet* 247:760 Je 1993
The deep blue sea. *Tablet* 247:145-146 Ja 30 1993
Don Giovanni. *Tablet* 247:314 Mr 6 1993
Don't fool with love. *Tablet* 247:622 My 15 1993
Dylan Thomas: return journey. *Tablet* 247:20 Ja 2 1993
Elegies for angels, punks and raging queens. *Tablet* 247:216 F 13 1993
Fires in the mirror. *Tablet* 247:484 Ap 10-17 1993
For services rendered. *Tablet* 247:589 My 8 1993
The game of love and chance. *Tablet* 247:113 Ja 23 1993
The ghost train. *Tablet* 246:1626 D 19-26 1992
The gift of the Gorgon. *Tablet* 247:113-114 Ja 23 1993
Godspell. *Tablet* 247:1080 Ag 21 1993
A going concern. *Tablet* 247:1268 O 2 1993
Greasepaint. *Tablet* 247:251 F 20 1993
Hair. *Tablet* 247:1268 O 2 1993
Hamlet. *Tablet* 247:80 Ja 16 1993
Hay fever. *Tablet* 246:1626 D 19-26 1992
Hysteria. *Tablet* 247:1201 S 18 1993
The importance of being earnest. *Tablet* 247:412 Mr 27 1993
Inadmissable evidence. *Tablet* 247:863 Jl 3 1993
The invisible man. *Tablet* 247:282 F 27 1993
A jovial crew. *Tablet* 247:658 My 22 1993
Juno and the paycock. *Tablet* 247:760-761 Je 1993
King Lear. *Tablet* 247:174 F 6 1993
King Lear. *Tablet* 247:1238 S 25 1993
The last Yankee. *Tablet* 247:216 F 13 1993
Lust. *Tablet* 247:1080 Ag 21 1993
Lysistrata. *Tablet* 247:893 Jl 10 1993
Macbeth. *Tablet* 247:519 Ap 24 1993
Madness in Valencia. *Tablet* 247:216 F 13 1993
The magic fundoshi. *Tablet* 247:346 Mr 13 1993
Misha's party. *Tablet* 247:1106 Ag 28 1993
Moll Flanders. *Tablet* 247:658-659 My 22 1993
Moonlight. *Tablet* 247:1267-1268 O 2 1993
The mountain giants. *Tablet* 247:1106 Ag 28 1993
Much ado about nothing. *Tablet* 247:953 Jl 24 1993
Murder in the cathedral. *Tablet* 247:1238 S 25 1993
La Musica. *Tablet* 247:251 F 20 1993
The neighbor. *Tablet* 247:553 My 1 1993
The odyssey. *Tablet* 247:1048-1049 Ag 14 1993
Oleanna. *Tablet* 247:925 Jl 17 1993
On the ledge. *Tablet* 247:695 My 29 1993
On the piste. *Tablet* 247:346 Mr 13 1993
Playland. *Tablet* 247:379 Mr 20 1993
Review of: *Tell them I'm on my way* by Goodman, Arnold. In: *Tablet* 247:1196-1197 S 18 1993
Review of: *The Oxford dictionary of quotations* by Partington, Angela, ed. In: *Tablet* 247:583-584 My 8 1993
Romeo and Juliet. *Tablet* 247:863 Jl 3 1993
The school of night. *Tablet* 247:589 My 8 1993
Separate tables. *Tablet* 247:952 Jl 24 1993
The showman. *Tablet* 247:760 Je 1993
Starlight express. *Tablet* 246:1578 D 12 1992
Sunset Boulevard. *Tablet* 247:1048 Ag 14 1993
Sweeney Todd. *Tablet* 247:793 Je 19 1993
Table number seven. *Tablet* 247:952-953 Jl 24 1993
The taming of the shrew. *Tablet* 247:825 Je 26 1993
The taming of the shrew. *Tablet* 247:1080 Ag 21 1993
Three hotels. *Tablet* 247:1201 S 18 1993
Time of my life. *Tablet* 247:1168-1169 S 11 1993
Translations. *Tablet* 247:825 Je 26 1993
Travels with my aunt. *Tablet* 246:1626 D 19-26 1992
Travesties. *Tablet* 247:1305 O 9 1993
Trelawney of the Wells. *Tablet* 247:20 Ja 2 1993
Trelawney of the Wells. *Tablet* 247:281-282 F 27 1993
Wallenstein. *Tablet* 247:1305-1306 O 9 1993
The winter's tale. *Tablet* 247:1048 Ag 14 1993

Shaw, Russell.
Review of: *Bishop Curtis of Wilmington.* In: *HPR* 93:71-73 F 1993
Review of: *John Courtney Murray and the American civil conversation* by Hunt, Robert P, and Grasso, Kenneth L, eds. In: *Register* 69:5 Ja 31 1993
Abortion "solutions" for 1993 begin to emerge. *OSV* 81:21 Ja 17 1993
Bishops entangled in their own Balkans morass. *OSV* 82:3 Je 6 1993
Can laity do more than hunt, shoot and entertain? [comments on book by author, pt 1 of 2]. *OSV* 82:17 N 7 1993
Christianity and the "eminent good works". *Register* 69:1+ Ja 10 1993
Christians, prayer and the "three good works". *Register* 69:1+ Ja 17 1993
Church is still fair game. *Register* 69:1+ S 26 1993
Clericalism and its discontents [comments on book by author, pt 2 of 2]. *OSV* 82:16 N 14 1993

Shaw, Russell. *(cont'd)*
Contracepting Humanae Vitae. *Columbia* 73:5 Je 1993
Humanae Vitae on the regulation of birth [1968 07 25].
A dirty little secret [statistics]. *Register* 69:5 O 10 1993
An ethical look at fetal-tissue research. *OSV* 81:16 Ap 25 1993
Fasting is the answer in an age hungry for meaning and love. *Register* 69:1+ Ja 24 1993
Finding the balance. *OSV* 81:3 Mr 14 1993
Gay agenda runs into opposition. *OSV* 82:3 Je 27 1993
Gay rights: a high-profile issue in the '90s. *OSV* 81:3 Ja 3 1993
Getting no respect [Freedom of Choice Act]. *OSV* 81:3 F 14 1993
How Catholic will the Clinton health-care plan be? *OSV* 82:17 S 19 1993
"Humanae Vitae": the "prophetic" encyclical (commentary: *Humanae Vitae*). *OSV* 82:5 Jl 25 1993
Humanae Vitae, on the regulation of birth [1968 07 25].
The importance of being Germain Grisez [por]. *OSV* 82:8-9 N 21 1993
Is the Supreme Court giving religion a little slack? *OSV* 82:3 Jl 11 1993
John Paul II has headed home—now what? [photos]. *Register* 69:1+ S 5 1993
Justice Ginsburg and the Supreme Court's course [por]. *OSV* 82:17 O 24 1993
Looking for answers. *OSV* 82:3 Jl 4 1993
Our alms: returning God's love. *Register* 69:1+ Ja 31 1993
The paradox of Catholics in Congress. *OSV* 81:3 Ja 24 1993
Pope calls for a new evangelization of America. *OSV* 82:3 Ag 8 1993
Pope John Paul answers the big questions in life. *OSV* 82:3 O 17 1993
Veritatis Splendor (the Splendor of Truth) Encyclical letter on moral issues (1993 10 05). Original.
The potential health-care nightmare. *OSV* 81:3 Mr 7 1993
Recess over, Congress to take up abortion issues. *OSV* 82:3 S 5 1993
Review of: *Redeemer* by Clark, Stephen B. In: *Register* 69:5 Ap 18 1993
Russia's need for spiritual rebirth. *OSV* 81:3 Ap 4 1993
Shifting the weight. *OSV* 81:3 Ap 11 1993
Spin doctors of theology give their take on the Pope. *OSV* 82:17 S 26 1993
Stirring a tempest in the pro-choice teapot. *OSV* 82:3 Jl 18 1993
To support, or not support, Clinton's plan. *OSV* 82:3 My 2 1993
Vocation: it's not just for priest anymore. *Columbia* 73:6-8 S 1993
Who decides how many are too many? *Columbia* 73:5 Jl 1993
Woman church. *Crisis* 11:8-9 Ja 1993 *see* Riley, Patrick J, jt ed

Shaw Russell. *see* Grisez, Germain Gabriel, 1929-, jt auth

Shawn, Stephen Joseph, 1944-.
The Catholic parish as a way-station of ethnicity and Americanization: Chicago's Germans and Italians, 1903-1939. Brooklyn: Carlson Publishers, 1991. 206p ISBN 0-92601-9554 LC 91-26847

Shay, Roy.
Review of: *Philip Larkin* by Motion, Andrew. In: *Tablet* 247:438-439 Ap 3 1993

Shea, John B.
Human rights and the new society. *SocJust* 84:100-104 Jl-Ag 1993
Starlight: beholding the Christmas miracle all year long. New York: The Crossroad Publishing Company, 1992. x, 192p ISBN 0-8245-1206-5 LC 92-15952
Wise guys [excerpt fr *Starlight: beholding the Christmas miracle all yar long*]. *Comm* 119:10-12 D 18 1992

Shea, John J. *see* Halligan, Frederick R, jt auth

Shea, Mark P.
An evangelical who discovered the real presence [interview by B Dodds]. *OSV* 82:7 Je 27 1993
Examining a Manichaean approach to abortion. *New Oxford Rev* 60:13-16+ Ap 1993
Holiness takes practice [condensed fr *Gleanings* 1991]. *CDgst* 57:40-42 F 1993
The liberalism of fools. *New Oxford Rev* 60:11-13 Ja-F 1993
Review of: *The outer limits of life* by Medina, John. In: *New Oxford Rev* 60:13-16+ Ap 1993

Shea, Mark P, and Bovenizer, David A.
Discovering the Real Presence. *Crisis* 11:45-48 O 1993

Shea, Moira C.
Evolution and morality. *Teilhard Rev* 28:9-15 Sum 1993

Shea, Nina.
Haiti's priest-president. *Register* 69:5 Ag 15 1993

Shea, William M.
Catholic higher education and the enlightenment: on borderlines and roots. *Horizons (CTS)* 20:99-105 Spr 1993

Sheehan, Jim.
When fundamentalism reduces God to a house pet [por]. *Nat Cath Rep* 30:23 O 29 1993

Sheehan, Lourdes.
The catechism of the Catholic Church. *Catechist* 26:20 Ap-My 1993

Sheehan, Michael, Abp.
An archdiocese's healing process. *Origins* 23:285-287 O 7 1993

Sheehan, Pete.
A good judge meets a bad choice on abortion. *OSV* 82:3 O 3 1993

Sheehy, Edward J.
Review of: *Facilitators of the free exercise of religion: Air Force chaplains, 1981-1990* by Groh, John E. In: *CHist* 79:376-377 Ap 1993

Sheeran, Jim.
Review of: *Beginning to pray* by Ó Caoimh, Tomás. In: *Furrow* 44:190-191 Mr 1993

Sheets, John R.
The nature and meaning of the priesthood. *Priest* 49:33-37 S 1993
Review of: *Freedom for ministry* by Neuhaus, Richard John, 1936-. In: *HPR* 93:76-77 Ja 1993
Review of: *Hans Urs von Balthasar: his life and work* by Schindler, David D, ed. In: *HPR* 93:72-73 Mr 1993

Sheets, John R. *(cont'd)*
Review of: *Models of revelation* by Dulles, Avery Robert, 1918-. In: *HPR* 93:
80 Ag-S 1993
Review of: *Spiritual direction and the encounter with God: a theological inquiry* by Barry, William A. In: *HPR* 93:78-79 My 1993

Sheldrake, Philip.
Celibacy and clerical culture. *Way Suppl* 77:26-36 Sum 1993
No salvation outside the world? praying in place. *Way Suppl* 75:3-11 Aut 1992
Review of: *All shall be well* by Upjohn, Sheila. In: *Way* 33:256 Jl 1993
Review of: *Changing life patterns: adult development in spiritual direction* by Liebert, Elizabeth Ann. In: *Way* 33:158-59 Ap 1993
Review of: *Holy listening: the art of spiritual direction* by Guenther, Margaret. In: *Way* 33:158 Ap 1993
Review of: *Langland, the mystics and the medieval English religious tradition* by Hussey, S S. In: *Way* 33:257 Jl 1993
Review of: *Sin shall be glory* by Mountney, John Michael. In: *Way* 33:256 Jl 1993
Review of: *The art of spiritual guidance* by Gratton, Carolyn. In: *Way* 33:158-159 Ap 1993

Shelley, Thomas J.
The history of St. Joseph's Seminary, New York. Westminster: Christian Classics, 1993. x, 480p ISBN 0-87061-198-4
Review of: *Richly blessed: the Diocese of Rockville Centre, 1957-1990* by Leonard, Joan de Lourdes. In: *CHist* 79:146-147 Ja 1993

Shelton, Charles M.
Review of: *Caring about morality: philosophical perspectives in moral psychology* by Wren, Thomas E. In: *TheolStds* 53:789-790 D 1992
What should I do? *Momentum* 24:60-61 N-D 1993

Shen, Louis.
Growing up in the Church: China and the USA. *America* 168:10-12 Ja 16-23 1993

Sheridan, Ann.
From conception to deception: the nazification of the feminist movement [por]. *Linacre* 60:31-39 Ag 1993

Sheridan, Daniel P.
"We who are left"—the death of a clerical student. *Furrow* 43:672-675 D 1992
Review of: *The unity of reality* by Brück, Michael von. In: *Horizons (CTS)* 20:193-194 Spr 1993

Sheridan, Stephen.
Considering healing. *New Cov* 22:14-16 Mr 1993

Sherman, Howard J.
The historical approach to political economy. *RSocEcon* 51:302-322 Aut 1993

Sherman, Mark A. *see* Donnelly, Dorothy F, jt auth

Sherrill, Julian F, Sr.
The metaphysics of higher spiritual conciousness. New York: Vantage Press, 1992. x, 264p ISBN 0-533-10214-6 LC 92-90684

Sherrill, Rowland A. *see* Cherry, Conrad, jt ed

Sherry, Gerard E.
Beating the communists was the easy part. *OSV* 82:13 O 3 1993
Mission to the desert [photos]. *OSV* 82:10-11 S 19 1993

Sherwin, Byron L. *see* Jegen, Carol Frances, jt auth; Kasimow, Harold, jt ed

Sherwin, Susan, 1947-.
No longer patient: feminist ethics and health care. Philadelphia: Temple University Press, 1992. 286p ISBN 0-87722-889-2 LC 91-14499

Shields, Brooke, 1965-.
'Things my mother taught me' [interview by J A Wintz, 1936-]. *St Anth* 100:28-32 My 1993

Shils, Edward. *see* Bockenförde, Ernst-Wolfgang, jt ed

Shimek, Michael.
Father and son retreats: discovering male spirituality. *Catechist* 26:34-36 Ap-My 1993

Shinn, Larry Dwight, 1942-.
Words, symbols, experience, and the naming of the divine. *JEcumen Stds* 29: 418-431 Sum-Aut 1992

Shipman, Pat. *see* Trinkhaus, Eric, jt auth

Shivanandan, Mary, and Geremia, Marion.
Natural family planning and family systems theory. *Linacre* 59:57-66 N 1992

Shorter, Aylward, 1932-.
Can Africa be free? *Tablet* 247:1060+ Ag 21 1993
Cooked in a Roman pot. *Tablet* 247:446-447 Ap 3 1993
Review of: *Ecclesiae memoria* by Henkel, Willi, ed. In: *Heythrop* 34:352-354 Jl 1993

Shulman, Steven.
Metaphors of discrimination: a comparison of Gunnar Myrdal and Gary Becker. *RSocEcon* 50:432-452 Wint 1992

Shuman, Nancy.
The cloistered heart. *RRel* 52:68-85 Ja-F 1993

Sicari, Antonio.
The family: a place of fraternity. *Communio* 20:290-305 Sum 1993

Sicre, José L.
L'actualité de l'idolâtrie. *Lumen* 48:277-292 S 1993

Sider, Ronald J.
One-sided Christianity? Uniting the church to heal a loot and broken world. Grand Rapids: Zondervan Publishing House, 1993. x, 256p ISBN 0-310-58761-1

Siegel, Lee.
Review of: *Double agent: the critic and society* by Dickstein, Morris. In: *Comm* 120:30 Ap 9 1993

Siegel, Lee. *(cont'd)*
Review of: *Politics by other means: higher education and group thinking* by Bromwich, David. In: *Comm* 120:30-31 Ap 9 1993
Temporal but timeless Daumier at the Met. *Comm* 120:20-21 Ap 23 1993
Too high the cornices: the Met's new galleries. *Comm* 120:21-22 O 22 1993

Siegel, Richard J.
Licinio Refice [fr *The sacred music of Licinio Refice*]. *SacM* 120:7-8 Spr 1993

Sietman, Klara.
Santo Domingo and beyond [repr fr *Sedos*]. *LADOC* 23:9-13 My-Je 1993

Sievernich, M.
Review of: *Teurer Segen [Christliche Mission und Kolonialismus]* by Paczensky, Gert. In: *Stimm Zeit* 211:501-502 Jl 1993

Sigal, Lillian.
Review of: *Jews and Christians* by Harrelson, Walter, and Falk, Randall M. In: *JEcumen Stds* 29:117-119 Wint 1992
Review of: *Time to meet: toward a deeper relationship between Jews and Christians* by Braybrooke, Marcus. In: *JEcumen Stds* 29:117-119 Wint 1992

Sigmond, R.
Review of: *Marketplace medicine: the rise of the for-profit hospital chains* by Lindorff, David. In: *Health Prog* 74:84-85 Ja-F 1993

Siker, Jeffrey S.
Review of: *Paul and the legacies of Paul* by Babcock, William S, ed. In: *CBQ* 54:815-817 O 1992
Review of: *Reading in communion: scripture and ethics in Christian life* by Fowl, Stephen E, and Jones, L Gregory. In: *CBQ* 55:150-151 Ja 1993

Silanes, Nereo. *see* Pikaza, Xavier, jt ed

Siller, Clodomiro.
Simbologia y mito en la Teologia India. *Christus* 58:28-35 S 1993

Siller, Hermann Pius.
Kirchenreform. *Stimm Zeit* 211:477-488 Jl 1993

Silva, Edson.
Os 500 anos e o Nordeste: Resgator as lutas indígenas. *REB* 53:174-183 Mr 1993

Silva, Jose' Antunes da.
Bread and wine for the Eucharist: are they negotiable? *AFER* 34:258-271 O 1992

Silva, José Ariavaldo da.
Review of: *Orientações para Ministros Extraordinários da Comunhão* by Goedert, Valter M. In: *REB* 53:485-491 Je 1993

Silva, Moises.
Review of: *Jodendom en vroeg christendom: continuïteit en discontinuïteit* by Baarda, T, et al, eds. In: *CBQ* 55:405-406 Ap 1993

Silva, Sergio G.
Dos años de labor del programa "fe, ciencia, universidad". *Teol Vida* 34 no 1-2:3-27 1993

Silva Arévalo, Eduardo.
La significacón teológica de los acontecimientos: El estatuto histórico de la teología según Marie-Dominique Chenu. *Teol Vida* 33 no 3-4:269-297 1992

Sim, David C.
The confession of the soldiers in Matthew 27:54. *Heythrop* 34:401-424 O 1993

Simian-Yofre, Horacio.
El desierto delos dioses: teologia e historia en el libro de Oseas. Cordoba: Ediciones El Alme, 1993. x, 283p ISBN 84-8005-007-1

Simkins, Ronald A.
Review of: *Early Israel: a new horizon* by Coote, Robert B. In: *Bib Th Bul* 23:85-86 Sum 1993

Simmonds, Gemma.
Review of: *Good things happen* by Westley, Richard John, 1928-. In: *Priests & People* 7:210 My 1993

Simmons, Adrienne.
Review of: *Measuring patient satisfaction for improved patient services* by Strasser, Stephen, and Davis, Rose Marie. In: *Health Prog* 74:68-69 Mr 1993

Simmons, Ed, Jr.
Hero [directed by S Frears]. *Crisis* 10:55-56 N 1992

Simmons, Henry C.
A woman gives a feast: transforming rituals in old age. *Liturgy* 10:21-30 Wint 1992

Simmons, Pat Flatley.
Bless me, Father. *Living Prayer* 26:25-26 Mr-Ap 1993

Simmons, Tracy Lee.
Review of: *Carnival culture: the trashing of taste in America* by Twitchell, James B. In: *Crisis* 11:54+ Mr 1993
Review of: *Memories of the Ford administration* by Updike, John, 1932-. In: *Crisis* 11:48-50 Ja 1993
Review of: *Pilgrim in the ruins: a life of Walker Percy* by Tolson, Jay. In: *Crisis* 10:47-48 N 1992

Simoens, Y.
Review of: *Allgemeine Moraltheologie* by Weber, H. In: *NRT* 115:115-116 Ja-F 1993
Review of: *Atti del I Simposio di Efesu su S Giovanni Apostolo* by Padovese, Luigi, ed. In: *NRT* 115:106-107 Ja-F 1993
Review of: *Comprendre l'Apocalypse* by Charlier, J-P. In: *NRT* 115:111-112 Ja-F 1993
Review of: *El Señor de la vida* by Molina, Contreras. In: *NRT* 115:113-114 Ja-F 1993
Review of: *I racconti post nel vangelo di S Giovanni* by Gangemi, A. In: *NRT* 115:110-111 Ja-F 1993
Review of: *L'évangile de Jean à la lumiére du judaïsme* by Manns, F. In: *NRT* 115:108-109 Ja-F 1993

Sloyan, Gerard S. *(cont'd)*
Review of: *A marginal Jew: rethinking the historical Jesus* by Meier, John P. In: *Horizons (CTS)* 20:143-145 Spr 1993
Review of: *Disinheriting the Jews: Abraham in early Christian controversy* by Siker, Jeffrey S. In: *CBQ* 55:396-398 Ap 1993
Review of: *Dying, we live: a new enquiry into the death of Christ in the New Testament* by Grayston, Kenneth. In: *JEcumen Stds* 29:117 Wint 1992
Review of: *The historical Jesus* by Crossan, John Dominic. In: *Horizons (CTS)* 20:143-145 Spr 1993
Review of: *The new Jerome Biblical commentary* by Brown, Raymond Edward, et al, eds. In: *JEcumen Stds* 29:273-274 Spr 1992
Review of: *Women in the genesis of Christianity* by Witherington, Ben, III. In: *Horizons (CTS)* 19:312-313 Fall 1992
What is John 17 saying to the churches? [exc fr *Liturgy: practicing ecumenism*]. *Liturgy* 10:16-18 Spr 1993

Sloyan, Virginia.
Review of: *Catholic prayer* by Cunningham, Lawrence S, 1935-. In: *Church* 9:62-63 Spr 1993
Review of: *Liturgical inculturation: sacramentals, religiosity, and catechesis* by Chupungco, Anscar J. In: *Church* 9:62-63 Spr 1993

Slusser, Michael.
Review of: *Saint Anselm* by Southern, R W. In: *Horizons (CTS)* 19:313 Fall 1992

Sly, Julie.
When victims and offenders meet face-to-face. *OSV* 81:6 F 14 1993

Smart, Ninian, 1927-.
Buddhism and Christianity: rivals and allies. Honolulu: University of Hawaii Press, 1993. ISBN 0-82481-519-x LC 92-29475

Smedes, Lewis, B.
Shame and grace. New York: HarperCollins, 1993. x, 170p ISBN 0-06-067521-7 LC 92-53897

Smiga, George M.
Pain and polemic: anti-Judaism in the gospels. New Jersey: Paulist Press, 1992. x, 210p ISBN 0-8091-3355-5 LC 92-20044

Smiles, Vincent.
Review of: *Paul on the mystery of Israel* by Harrington, Daniel J. In: *Sisters* 65:224-225 My 1993

Smith, Ann.
An experience of marriage. *Tablet* 247:1090 Ag 28 1993

Smith, B F.
Giving thanks. *Crisis* 10:45-46 N 1992
'I do'. *Crisis* 11:41-42 F 1993
Longtime companion. *Crisis* 11:50-51 My 1993

Smith, Barbara Herrnstein. see Gless, Darryl, jt ed

Smith, Brian.
Recovering a nation: who controls the past. *Comm* 120:5-6 Jl 16 1993
Review of: *The Church and politics in the Chilean countryside* by Stewart-Gambino, Hannah W. In: *TheolStds* 54:395-396 Je 1993

Smith, Christopher.
A matter of principle. *Register* 69:4 Jl 18 1993

Smith, David.
What is Christian teaching on abortion? *Doctr Life* 42:305-317 My-Je 1992

Smith, G.
Review of: *The reform of renewal* by Groeschel, Benedict J. In: *Can Cath Rev* 11:32 Ja 1993

Smith, James Bryan.
A spiritual formation workbook: small group resources for nurturing Christian growth. New York: HarperSanFrancisco, 1993. 82p ISBN 0-06-066965 LC 92-36860 see Foster, Richard J, jt ed

Smith, Janet E.
The connection between contraception and abortion. *HPR* 93:10-18 Ap 1993
[Many who do not profess]. *Comm* 120:14-15 O 22 1993
Reply to Gass [reply to M Gass, 33:101-108, 1993]. *IPQ* 33:233-238 Je 1993

Smith, John, Bp, et al.
Doctor killed at abortion clinic. *Origins* 22:701+ Mr 25 1993

Smith, Joyce L.
The dream of the seventh-day ark for sores and burns, for soul and body. New York: Vantage Press, 1993. 97p ISBN 0-533-09090-3

Smith, Karen Sue.
Do's and don'ts for eucharistic ministers. *Church* 9:38-40 Spr 1993
Review of: *College Catholics: a new counter-culture* by Hunt, Michael J. In: *Church* 9:59 Sum 1993
Review of: *Fritz Eichenberg* by Ellsberg, Robert, ed. In: *Church* 9:57 Sum 1993
Review of: *Il Duce's other woman* by Cannistraro, Philip V, and Sullivan, Brian R. In: *Comm* 120:23-24 O 8 1993
Waiting in the wings: will laypeople take a leading role in the church? [a reader's survey]. *USCath* 58:6-13 F 1993

Smith, Lewis.
Review of: *Jesus* by Wilson, A N, 1950-. In: *New Blckfrs* 74:227-228 Ap 1993

Smith, Marianne, and Buckwalter, Kathleen C.
Mental healthcare for rural seniors. *Health Prog* 74:52-56+ Mr 1993

Smith, Mark M.
Review of: *The goddess Anat in Ugaritic myth* by Walls, Neal H. In: *OTA* 16:414 Je 1993

Smith, Mark S.
Review of: *A grammar of Biblical Hebrew* by Joüon, Paul. In: *CBQ* 55:116-119 Ja 1993
Review of: *Curse tablets and binding spells from the ancient world* by Gager, John G, ed. In: *OTA* 16:405 Je 1993
Review of: *Psalms and story: inset hymns in Hebrew narrative* by Watts, James W. In: *OTA* 16:415 Je 1993
Review of: *Ruth Amiran volume* by Eitan, E, et al, eds. In: *OTA* 16:151-152 F 1993

Smith, Mark S. *(cont'd)*
Review of: *The Aramaic of Daniel in the light of Old Aramaic* by Stefanovic, Zdravko. In: *OTA* 15:509-510 O 1992
Review of: *The Bible in Aramaic based on Old Manuscripts and Hebrew texts* by Sperber, Alexander. In: *OTA* 15:519-520 O 1992
Review of: *The Book of Isaiah—Le Livre d'Isaïe* by Vermeylen, Jacques R, ed. In: *OTA* 16:429-430 Je 1993
Review of: *The great angel: a study of Israel's second God* by Barker, Margaret. In: *OTA* 16:184 F 1993
Review of: *The Old Testament of the Old Testament: patriarchal narratives and Mosaic Yahwism* by Moberly, R W L. In: *OTA* 15:493 O 1992
Review of: *The revised psalms of the New American Bible*. In: *OTA* 15:486-487 O 1992
Review of: *The roads and highways of ancient Israel* by Dorsey, David A. In: *OTA* 15:481 O 1992
Review of: *Under every green tree: popular religion in sixth-century Judah* by Ackermann, Susan. In: *OTA* 16:434 Je 1993
Review of: *W M L de Wette, founder of modern Biblical criticism: an intellectual biography* by Rogerson, John W. In: *OTA* 15:488 O 1992
Review of: *Yigael Yadin Memorial volume* by Ben-Tor, Amnon, et al, eds. In: *OTA* 16:149-151 F 1993
Review of: *The proto-Cuneiform texts from Jemdet Nasr. I* by Englund, Robert K, and Grégoire, Jean-Pierre. In: *OTA* 16:405 Je 1993

Smith, Matt.
Guadalupe icon comes to US. *Nat Cath Rep* 29:3 Ja 29 1993
Mexican political parties fight for Catholic votes. *Nat Cath Rep* 29:5 S 3 1993
Pope's visit to Mexico renews ties severed 130 years ago. *Nat Cath Rep* 29:7 Ag 27 1993

Smith, Pamela.
Life after Easter. New Jersey: Paulist Press, 1993. x, 88p ISBN 0-8091-3379-2 LC 92-21195

Smith, Patricia.
Commitment: reflections on women at a tomb. *Sisters* 65:132-136 Mr 1993

Smith, Paul R.
Is it okay to call God mother?: considering the feminine face of God. Peabody: Hendrickson Publishers, 1993. 273p ISBN 1-56563-013-0 LC 93-25810

Smith, Quentin.
Reply to Craig: the possible infinitude of the past [reply to W L Craig, 31 no 4:387-410 1991]. *IPQ* 33:109-115 Mr 1993

Smith, Richard F.
The Hare Krishna movement. *StudiaM* 41:107-126 1992

Smith, Robin.
Review of: *Blindspots* by Sorensen, Roy A. In: *Mod Schlmn* 70:73-75 N 1992

Smith, Russell, E.
Review of: *Matters of life and death* by Cobb, John B, Jr. In: *Linacre* 59:86-88 N 1992
Health care rationing: a theologian's perspective. *Linacre* 60:20-29 Ag 1993

Smith, Russell, E, ed.
Symposium on the twentieth anniversary of Encyclical Humanae. Braintree, Massachusetts: The Pope John Center, 1991. x, 384p ISBN 0-935372-30-x LC 91-20331

Smith, Sean Mayne. see Jamie, Kathleen, jt auth

Smith, T. Allan.
Review of: *Theology and church* by Kasper, Walter. In: *Can Cath Rev* 11:26 Jl-Ag 1993
Review of: *Eastern Christianity: the Byzantine tradition* by Cross, Lawrence. In: *Can Cath Rev* 11:27 O 1993

Smith, Virginia.
The last gospel [condensed fr *Catholic Update* 1992]. *CDgst* 57:137-142 My 1993

Smither, James R.
Review of: *Beneath the cross: Catholics and Huguenots in sixteenth-century France* by Diefendorf, Barbara S. In: *CHist* 79:109-110 Ja 1993

Smolarski, Dennis C.
Pastoral paradigms for public prayer. *Mod Lit* 20:16-18 N 1993

Smolenski, Stanley.
Fatima's consecration: the Soviet collapse. *HPR* 93:8-16 Ja 1993

Smolich, Thomas H.
Catechetics in an at-risk community. *Momentum* 24:7-10 Ap-My 1993

Smyth, Damian.
Review of: *Now parish ministers: laity and religious on parish staffs* by Murnion, Philip J, 1938-, et al. In: *Mod Lit* 20:37-38 S 1993
Review of: *Prayer-book for engaged couples* by Fleming, Austin. In: *Mod Lit* 20:38-39 S 1993
Review of: *Welcome: tools and techniques for new member ministry* by Weeks, Andrew D. In: *Mod Lit* 20:36 My 1993

Smyth, Geraldine Marie.
Between the flood and the rainbow: encountering God in the living community of creation. *Doctr Life* 43:216 Ap 1993

Smythe, Harry.
Mascall, Eric Lionel, 1905-1993 [obit]. *Tablet* 247:256-257 F 20 1993

Smythe, William E.
Review of: *Jesus, the liberator of desire* by Moore, Sebastian. In: *Can Cath Rev* 11:32-33 Je 1993

Sneck, William J.
Review of: *Ignatius of Loyola: the psychology of a saint* by Meissner, William W. In: *RRel* 52:469-471 My-Je 1993

Snyder, John J.
Review of: *On divorce [tr by N Davidson]* by Ronald, Louis de. In: *Can Cath Rev* 11:30-31 S 1993

Snyder, Margaret.
Malcolm after Mecca: East Africa, 1964. *Comm* 119:6-7 D 18 1992

Snyder, Martin.
Review of: *From conquest to struggle* by Batstone, David. In: *Pacifica* 6:344-346 O 1993

Snyder, Mary Hembrow.
Review of: *Mother church: what the experience of women is teaching her* by Cunneen, Sally. In: *Horizons (CTS)* 19:329-330 Fall 1992
Review of: *Religious woman: contemporary reflections on eastern texts* by Lardner, Denise. In: *Horizons (CTS)* 19:347-348 Fall 1992
Review of: *The window of vulnerability: a political spirituality* by Soelle, Dorothee. In: *CrossCurr* 42:549-550 Wint 1992-1993

Soane, Brendan.
Review of: *New directions in moral theology* by Kelly, Kevin T. In: *Tablet* 247:311 Mr 6 1993

Soards, Marion L.
Review of: *Metaphorik und mythos im Neuen Testament* by Kertelge, Karl, ed. In: *CBQ* 54:826-827 O 1992

Sobel, A. see Benedikt, B, jt ed

Sobo, Elizabeth.
American foreign aid is now in the condom biz. *Register* 69:1+ Je 20 1993
At Dakar conference "fix was in" [UN regional conference on population control, D 5-12, 1992, Dakar, Senegal]. *Register* 69:1+ Ja 17 1993
Bishops united against population-control efforts. *Register* 69:1+ Ja 3 1993
CARE for a contraceptive, lady? *Register* 69:2 Mr 21 1993

Sobran, Joseph.
The dangerous Rush Limbaugh. *Crisis* 11:18-21 My 1993
Sexually challenged. *Crisis* 11:41-43 Je 1993

Sobrero, Alberto A. see Banfi, Emanuele, jt ed; Lavinio, Cristina, jt auth

Sobreroca I Ferrer, Lluis Antoni.
Dominar el pas dels anys. Barcelona: Scripta, 1993. x, 272p ISBN 84-85205-29-4

Sobrino, John.
Boff-an "apostolic and pastoral crisis" [fr *Sal Terrae*]. *LADOC* 24:16-23 S-O 1993
Los vientos que soplaron en Santo Domingo. *Christus* 58:29-39 Mr-Ap 1993
Misereor super turbas. *Christus* 58:36-38 F 1993

Soden, Wolfram von.
Introduction to the ancient world. Grand Rapids: Eerdmans, 1993. 256p ISBN 0-8028-0142-0

Söding, Thomas.
Erweis des Geistes und der Kraft. *Catholica* 47 no 3:184-209 1993
Das Wortfeld der Liebe im Paganen und Biblischen Griechisch. *Eph Theol Lovan* 78:284-330 D 1992

Soelle, Dorothee.
Moses, Jesus, and Marx: utopians in search of justice. *CrossCurr* 42:528-535 Wint 1992-1993
On earth as in heaven. Louisville: Westminster, 1993. x, 96p ISBN 0-664-25494-2
Stations of the cross: a Latin American pilgrimage. Minneapolis: Fortress Press, 1993. x, 146p ISBN 0-80062-688-5 LC 92-34220

Soetens, Claude.
The Holy See and the promotion of an indigenous clergy from Leo XIII to Pius XII. *Jurist* 52 no 1:162-182 1992 see Lamberigts, Matthieu, jt ed

Sokolwski, Robert, 1934-.
Splitting the faithful: inclusive language is wrong biblically, pastorally, and doctrinally. *Crisis* 11:24-27 Mr 1993

Solberg, Winton U.
Review of: *The secularization of the academy* by Marsden, George M, and Longfield, Bradley J, eds. In: *CHist* 79:369-370 Ap 1993

Solheim, James.
National Council of Churches denies observer status to UFMCC. *Ecumen Trends* 22:13 Ja 1993
Roman Catholic bishops of Britain set guidelines for Anglican converts. *Ecumen Trends* 22:16 My 1993
Roman Catholics and Episcopalians release statement on 25 years of dialogue. *Ecumen Trends* 22:16 Mr 1993

Solomon, Jonathan.
The golden curtain. *Tablet* 247:186 F 13 1993

Solomon, Norman.
Christian-Jewish relations in a new Europe. *Month* 26:9-16 Ja 1993 see Cohen, Jeff, jt auth

Soman, David. see Johnson, Angela, jt auth

Sommavilla, Guido.
Robert Musil: da Nietzsche alla mistica. *Civilta* 3:129-142 Jl 17 1993

Sommerfeldt, John R, ed.
Bernardus Magister: in celebration of the nonacentary of the birth of Saint Bernard of Clairvaux: 1090-1990. Massachusetts: Cistercian Publications, 1992. x, 578p ISBN 0-87907-635-6 LC 92-13334

Sondag, John.
Guarding our children's eternity. *Register* 69:5 Mr 7 1993

Sonn, Tamara.
Review of: *Journeys in holy lands: the evolution of the Abraham-Ishmael legends in Islamic exegesis* by Firestone, Reuven. In: *JEcumen Stds* 29:129-130 Wint 1992

Sonzini, E.
Review of: *Alla scuola del "ladrone" penitente* by Ledrus, Michel. In: *Civilta* 3:202-203 Jl 17 1993
Review of: *Bruno il Santo della Ceriota: dio risponde nel deserto* by Papàsogli, Giorgio. In: *Civilta* 2:412 My 15 1993

Sonzini, E. *(cont'd)*
Review of: *Maria e la debolezza di Dio. Il messaggio' spirituale di Grignion de Montfort* by Morinay, Jean. In: *Civilta* 2:107 Ap 17 1993

Soons, Alan.
Alvaro Alonso Barba's Art of metallurgy: from the poetical to the technological. *Cithara* 32:3-12 My 1993

Sorci, Pietro.
L'accoglienza nella comunità ecclesiale il rito dell'iniziazione cristiana degli adulti a vent'anni dalla promulgazione. *Notitiae* 29:84-87 Ja-F 1993

Sorensen, Kathleen M.
Rebuilding broken lives. *Momentum* 24:20-25 Ap-My 1993

Sorge, Bartolomeo.
Battere La Mafia Uiti Si Può. *Civilta* 143:468-475 D 5 1992

Sorokowski, Andrew.
Cornerstone or stumbling-block? *America* 169:15-17 O 23 1993

Sosa, Juan J.
Hospitality for and by musicians: melody and text. *Past Mus* 17:18-21 F-Mr 1993

Soskice, Janet Martin.
"The truth looks different from here". *New Blckfrs* 73:528-542 N 1992
Women's problems. *Priests & People* 6:301-306 Ag-S 1992

Sosoe, Lukas. see Renault, Alain, jt auth

Southard, Samuel. see Malony, H Newton, jt ed

Spaeth, Robert L, 1935-.
Hope in the White House. *Crisis* 11:9 F 1993
The leaning tower of truth. *Comm* 120:6-7 Mr 26 1993
Review of: *Rome reborn: the Vatican Library and Renaissance culture* by Grafton, Anthony, ed. In: *Comm* 120:26-27 My 21 1993

Spalding, Thomas W.
Review of: *Isaac Hecker* by O'Brien, David J, 1938-. In: *CHist* 79:571-573 Jl 1993

Spann, Shirley A.
Stepping out on faith. Boston: Deluxe Publications, 1992. 70p ISBN 0-9632239-0-9

Spanneut, Michel.
Review of: *Bardesane d'Edesse la première philosophie syriaque* by Teixidor, Javier. In: *MSR* 50:152-154 Ap-Je 1993
Review of: *Institutions divines* by Lactantius. In: *MSR* 50:151-152 Ap-Je 1993
Review of: *Les écrits des Pères apostoliques*. In: *MSR* 50:76-77 Ja-Mr 1993

Sparr, Arnold.
Chesterton and Catholic moments: some reflections on Catholic revivals, past and present. *ACHSR* 103:11-22 Aut 1992

Specktor, Mordecai.
American Indians, panel discuss religious laws. *Nat Cath Rep* 29:4 Mr 26 1993

Spector, Sheila A.
Blake's Milton as kabbalistic vision. *Relig Lit* 25:19-33 Spr 1993

Speeten, Joseph Van Der.
Prier et chanter chacun dans sa propre langue. *Notitiae* 28:755-759 N-D 1992

Spencer, F Scott.
The Ethiopian eunuch and his bible: a social-science analysis. *Bib Th Bul* 22:155-165 Wint 1992

Spencer, R.
Review of: *Ending the Byzantine Greek schism* by Likoudis, James. In: *HPR* 93:67-69 F 1993

Sperling, David S.
Review of: *Die Sprache der Ahiqarsprüche* by Kottsieper, Ingo. In: *CBQ* 55:340-342 Ap 1993

Speyr, Adrienne von, 1902-1967.
The birth of the church: meditations of John 18-21. San Francisco: Ignatius Press, 1991. 443p ISBN 0-89870-368-9 LC 90-85550
Mary in the Church [fr *Handmaid of the Lord* tr by E.A. Nelson]. *Communio* 20:451-456 Sum 1993

Spidlik, Thomas.
Drinking from the hidden fountain: a patristic breviary. London: New City, 1992. 447p ISBN 0-904287-39-4
Review of: *Dialoghi al monastero* by Tsatsos, Constantinos. In: *Civilta* 3:200 Jl 17 1993
Review of: *Il battesimo delle russe: bilancio di un millennio* by Graciotti, Sante, ed. In: *Civilta* 2:95-96 Ap 3 1993
Review of: *Nel deserto accanto ai fratelli: vite di Gerasimo e di Giorgio di Choziba* by Segni, Campagnano Di, ed. In: *Civilta* 2:308-309 My 1 1993
Review of: *Storia del monachesimo, vol I: le origini orientali: da sant'Antonio a san Basilio* by Gobry, Ivan. In: *Civilta* 2:411 My 15 1993
Review of: *Storia del monachesimo, vol II: Il tempo dell'espansione da san Colombano a san Bonifacio* by Gobry, Ivan. In: *Civilta* 2:411 My 15 1993
Review of: *Dalla Russia con fede, vol I: Vie dell'originalità cristiana russa* by Joos, André. In: *Civilta* 144:198-199 Ja 16 1993
San Sergio di Radonež en San Francesco di Assisi. *Civilta* 143:596-601 D 19 1992

Spielmann, Richard M.
Review of: *Catholics, Anglicans, and Puritans* by Trevor-Roper, Hugh. In: *JEcumen Stds* 29:106 Wint 1992

Spinetta, Pat Deasy, and Collins, Denis E.
Ministry to the chronically ill child. *Momentum* 24:28-30+ Ap-My 1993

Spinks, Bryan. see Stevenson, Kenneth W, jt ed

Spinks, Bryan D.
Review of: *Worship, culture and theology* by Power, David Noel. In: *Heythrop* 34:195-196 Ap 1993

Spinks, Bryan D. *(cont'd)*
Review of: *Worship: city, church and renewal* by Baldovin, John F. In: *Heythrop* 34:195-196 Ap 1993

Spinks, J.
Review of: *The Jewish roots of Christian liturgy* by Fisher, Eugene J, ed. In: *Heythrop* 34:81-82 Ja 1993

Spoerl, Joseph S.
Peter Singer on famine, affluence, and morality: a Christian response. *Amer J Juris* 37:113-133 1992

Spohn, William C.
The magisterium and morality. *TheolStds* 54:95-111 Mr 1993
Review of: *The Bible and the moral life* by Sleeper, C Freeman. In: *TheolStds* 54:594-595 S 1993

Sponshiado, Breno A.
10 anos do instituto de teologia e pastoral de Passo Fundo. *REB* 53:184-187 Mr 1993

Spreafico, Ambrogio. *see* Deiana, Giovanni, jt auth

Squires, John.
Review of: *Hellenists and Hebrews* by Hill, Craig C. In: *Pacifica* 6:341-342 O 1993

Squires, Susan E. *see* Angell, Jeannette L, jt auth

St. Louis, Ralph.
Review of: *The sacred world of the Christian* by Wagner, Mary Anthony. In: *New Oxford Rev* 60:27-30 N 1993

St Lawrence, Brenda.
Review of: *The politics of peace* by Frost, Brian. In: *SIDIC* 26 no 1:32 1993

St Leger, Moya Frenz.
God and the unconscious mind: the Eugen Drewermann case. *Doctr Life* 43:323-332 Jl-Ag 1993
On the one hand, women and ordination—time for dialogue? *Priests & People* 6:327-329 Ag-S 1992
Review of: *New beginnings in ministry* by Murphy, James H, ed. In: *Furrow* 44:189-190 Mr 1993

St Romain, Philip.
Cultivating healthy boundaries. *Liguorian* 81:25-29 S 1993
God's loving spirit in our hearts. *Liguorian* 81:4-8 Jl 1993
The journey toward self-esteem. *Liguorian* 81:12-16 My 1993
We are created to love. *Liguorian* 81:54-59 Ja 1993

Staalsett, Gunnar.
Entering ecumenism's reception phase. *Origins* 23:744-746 Ap 8 1993

Stacey, Tom.
Review of: *Living dangerously* by Graef, Roger. In: *Tablet* 247:141 Ja 30 1993
Review of: *Living with Beelzebub* by Mayo, Gael Elton. In: *Tablet* 246:1623-1624 D 19-26 1992
Review of: *Young offenders* by Longford, Francis Aungier Packenham, 1905-. In: *Tablet* 247:1263 O 2 1993

Stack, George J.
Nietzsche's earliest essays: translation of and commentary on "Fate and History" and "Freedom of Will and Fate". *PhilosTod* 37:153-169 Sum 1993

Stackhouse, Max L.
Review of: *Religious aesthetics: a theological study of making and meaning* by Brown, Frank Burch. In: *CrossCurr* 43:123-124 Spr 1993

Stafford, Francis J, Abp.
Denver is a mirror of the future [interview by S P Lovett]. *OR(Eng)* 1301:5 Jl 28 1993
Eucharistic foundation of sacerdotal celibacy. *Origins* 23:211-216 S 2 1993
A man for this season. *New Cov* 23:29 O 1993

Stafford, Geraldine.
What Catholic teens need to know about sex. *HPR* 94:52-54 O 1993

Stafford, J Francis, Abp, 1939-.
Dialogue [interview by C Mason]. *Register* 69:1+ Ag 15 1993
Moral reason is basis of virtue. *OR(Eng)* 1311:10 O 13 1993
Veritatis Splendor (the splendor of truth), Encyclical Letter on the moral issues (1993-10-05). Commentary.
Nuptiality and priesthood. *Register* 69:2 O 10 1993
Praying with Peter [excerpts fr a pastoral letter to the Church of Denver]. *Crisis* 11:26-31 Jl-Ag 1993

Stafford, W.
Review of: *The theology of John Fisher* by Rex, Richard. In: *CHist* 78:650-651 O 1992

Stage, Elizabeth K. *see* Hoffman, Kenneth M, jt auth

Stahel, Thomas H, 1938-.
Review of: *Dead man walking* by Prejean, Helen. In: *America* 169:2 Jl 17-24 1993
CNN does it again. *America* 168:16-17 My 1 1993
New Emmys and new season. *America* 169:24-25 O 16 1993
Of many things. *America* 168:2 Ja 2-9 1993
Of new programs and other matters, like well, you know. *America* 168:24-25 F 20 1993
The "real Catholic story": U.S. Bishops meet. *America* 169:4-5 D 4 1993
Review of: *Enduring grace: living portraits of seven women mystics* by Flinders, Carol Lee. In: *America* 169:2 Jl 17-24 1993
Review of: *The letters and instructions of Francis Xavier*. In: *America* 168:2 My 29 1993
Review of: *The spiritual conquest, accomplished by the religious of the Society of Jesus in the Provinces of Paraguay, Parana, Uruguay, and Tape* by Montoya, Antonio Ruiz de. In: *America* 168:2 My 29 1993
Television as service: asking the right questions. *America* 169:22-23 Jl 3-10 1993

Staley, Jeffrey L.
Review of: *Let the reader understand* by Fowler, Robert M. In: *CBQ* 55:152-154 Ja 1993

Stamschror, Robert P.
Review of: *Catechesis and controversies: religious education in the postconciliar years* by Wrenn, Michael J. In: *Living Light* 29:81-82 Aut 1992

Stamwitz, Alicia von.
Blessed Josephine Bakhita: woman of faith and forgiveness. *Liguorian* 81:46-53 F 1993
The legacy of Archbishop James Lyke. *Liguorian* 81:46-53 Ap 1993

Stamwitz, Alicia Von.
Review of: *Sharing the good news with children* by Goodhue, Thomas W. In: *Liguorian* 81:70 Ap 1993

Stamwitz, Alicia von.
Saint Aloysius Gonzaga: patron of youth. *Liguorian* 81:26-32 Ag 1993

Standún, Pádraig.
Priestly options in a retrenching Church. *Furrow* 44:84-87 F 1993

Stanfield, Jacqueline B.
Family policy in America: a continuing controversy. *RSocEcon* 50:420-431 Wint 1992

Stanfield, James Ronald.
Economy and society at the close of the American century: an introduction. *RSocEcon* 50:366-373 Wint 1992
Review of: *The rise and fall of capitalism* by Brenner, Y S. In: *RSocEcon* 51:378-380 Aut 1993

Stanford, Peter.
No joy for Jerry. *Tablet* 247:1257-1258 O 2 1993
Perils of the God-slot. *Tablet* 246:1558 D 12 1992 *see* Saunders, Kate, jt auth

Stankicwicz, Antonius.
De curatoris porcessualis designatione pro mente infirmis. *Periodica* 81 no 3-4:495-520 1992
De nullitate sententiae iudicialis propter absolutam iudicis incompetentiam. *Periodica* 81 no 3-4:535-552 1992

Stanley, Charles.
A touch of his peace. Grand Rapids: Zondervan Publishing House, 1993. x, 144p ISBN 0-310-54558-7

Stanley, Teresa.
Meeting mission challenges in IDNs. *Health Prog* 74:28-31+ Jl-Ag 1993

Stanton, Graham N.
A gospel for a new people: studies in Matthew. Louisville, Kentucky: John Knox Press, 1993. 424p ISBN 0-664-25499-3

Stanton, Timothy.
Prayer and work, mostly in South Africa. *RRel* 52:553-565 Jl-Ag 1993

Stark, Rodney. *see* Finke, Roger, jt auth

Starkloff, Carl.
Attention verses distraction: beyond the Quincentennial of Columbus. *TheolDgst* 40:119-131 Sum 1993

Starosta, William J, and Chaudhary, Anju G.
"I can wait 40 or 400 years": Gandhian Satyagraha West and East. *IPQ* 33:163-172 Je 1993

Starr, Bill.
When words shape reality. *SocJust* 84:80-83 My-Je 1993

Stasiak, Susan A.
The little red house. *Spir Life* 39:160-163 Aut 1993

Staunton, William.
"Music" [fr *Dictionary of the Church*]. *SacM* 120:13-14 Spr 1993

Stavans, Ilan.
The journey of Richard Rodriguez. *Comm* 120:20-22 Mr 26 1993
Review of: *Days of obligation* by Rodriguez, Richard, 1947-. In: *Comm* 120:20-22 Mr 26 1993
Review of: *Hunger of memory* by Rodriguez, Richard, 1947-. In: *Comm* 120:20-22 Mr 26 1993

Stead, Julian.
Review of: *Vatican II, theophany and the phenomenon of man* by Kobler, John F. In: *Crisis* 11:59-61 S 1993

Stebbins, J.
Review of: *The dilemma of freedom and foreknowledge* by Zagzebski, Linda Trinkaus, 1946-. In: *Thomist* 56:714-718 O 1992

Stebbins, Michael.
Review of: *The case for Christian humanism* by Franklin, R William, and Shaw, Joseph M. In: *New Oxford Rev* 60:26-27 Jl-Ag 1993

Stedler, Richard.
The Jewish nun. *Sisters* 65:212-213 My 1993

Stedman, Rick.
Lou Holtz man with a winning message. *Liguorian* 81:14-17 O 1993

Steel, G.
Review of: *Catholic rites today: abridged texts for students* by Bouley, Allan, ed. In: *Priests & People* 7:40-41 Ja 1993

Steele, James. *see* Barlett, Donald, jt auth

Steele, Michael L.
Mediating the Catechism of the Catholic Church. *Living Light* 30:84-87 Aut 1993

Steenberghen, Fernand, Van.
Review of: *Waarheid als weg* by Decorte, Jos. In: *RPhil Louvain* 91:315-316 My 1993
École Saint-Thomas. *RPhil Louvain* 91:1-4 F 1993
Review of: *Étienne Gilson* by Shook, Laurence K. In: *RPhil Louvain* 90:589-590 N 1992

Steenberghen, Fernand Van. *(cont'd)*
Review of: *Dictionnaire des Lettres françaises* by Grente, Georges, Cardinal, ed. In: *RPhil Louvain* 91:312-313 My 1993
Review of: *Dizionario enciclipedico del pensiero di san Tommaso d'Aquino* by Mondin, Battista. In: *RPhil Louvain* 91:322-323 My 1993
Review of: *Figure medievali della teologia, volumo primo* by Biffi, Inos. In: *RPhil Louvain* 91:319-320 My 1993
Review of: *Filosofia e religione* by Marchesi, Angelo. In: *RPhil Louvain* 91:152-153 F 1993
Review of: *Il "Dio de filosofi"* by Berti, Enrico. In: *RPhil Louvain* 91:152-154 F 1993
Review of: *Le livre du gentil et des trois sages* by Lulle, Raymond. In: *RPhil Louvain* 91:324-425 My 1993
Review of: *Méthodologies informatiques et nouveaux horizons dans les recherches médiévales* by Hamesse, Jacqueline, ed. In: *RPhil Louvain* 91:314-315 My 1993
Review of: *Pensiero medioevale e pensiero contemporaneo* by Marchesi, Angelo. In: *RPhil Louvain* 91:316-317 My 1993
Review of: *Rencontres de cultures dans la philosophie médiévale* by Hamesse, Jacqueline, and Fattori, Marta, eds. In: *RPhil Louvain* 91:313-314 My 1993

Stefan, Bonaventure.
Making the rounds with a hospital chaplain. *OSV* 82:12 O 31 1993

Steffen, Lloyd.
Review of: *The reason of following: Christology and the ecstatic I* by Scharlemann, Robert P. In: *CrossCurr* 43:114-116 Spr 1993

Stegmann, Franz Josef.
Soziale Marktwirtschaft—was ist das? *Stimm Zeit* 211:291-302 My 1993

Steichen, Donna.
Are we all feminists now? *SocJust* 84:11-15 Ja-F 1993
Review of: *The politics of prayer* by Hitchcock, Helen Hull, ed. In: *SocJust* 84:62 Mr-Ap 1993

Steif, William.
Aristide's possible return raises Haiti hopes. *Nat Cath Rep* 29:15 Ja 29 1993

Stein, Waltraut J H.
Politics and mystery: the integration of Judaism and Christianity in Edith Stein. *Spir Life* 32:104-110 Sum 1993

Steinacker, Hans.
Peter Wimsey—Ein Lord braucht seinen Mord. *Stimm Zeit* 211:403-412 Je 1993

Steinfels, Margaret O'Brien, 1941-.
The laity and the leadership crisis. *Comm* 120:8+ S 10 1993
The virtues of Sarajevo: reflections of a city dweller. *Comm* 120:4-5 Je 18 1993
The worst of the "Times" some news doesn't fit. *Comm* 120:4-5 Mr 12 1993

Steinfels, Peter, 1941-.
Review of: *Lead us not into temptation* by Berry, Jason. In: *Comm* 120:16-18 Mr 12 1993

Steinhaus, Barbara J.
Review of: *Dementia and aging: ethics, values, and policy choices* by Binstock, Robert H., et al, eds. In: *Health Prog* 74:71 O 1993

Stelzmann, Rainulf A.
Das Problem der Heiligkeit in unserer Zeit. *Stimm Zeit* 211:489-500 Jl 1993

Stempien, Theresa L.
Technology framework. *Health Prog* 74:58-62 Ja-F 1993

Stempsey, William E.
The big blue van and the little children. *America* 168:8-12 Mr 13 1993

Stenger, Werner.
Introduction to New Testament exegesis. Grand Rapids: Eerdmans, 1993. 240p ISBN 0-8028-0138-2

Stenstad, Gail.
Merleau-Ponty's logos: the sens-ing of flesh. *PhilosTod* 37:52-61 Spr 1993

Stephens, F.
Review of: *Stained glass: an illustrated history* by Brown, Sarah. In: *Tablet* 246:1625 D 19-26 1992

Stephenson, Joan.
Breathless: all about emphysema [condensed from *Harvard Health Letter* D 1992]. *CDgst* 57:8-12 Ag 1993

Sterling, Gregory E.
Review of: *The romans debate* by Donfried, Karl P, ed. In: *CBQ* 55:409-411 Ap 1993

Stern, Ephraim, ed.
The new encyclopedia of archaeological excavations in the Holy Land. New York: Simon & Schuster, 1993. 64p ISBN 0-13-276288-9

Stevens, Barbara.
The miracle of San Luis. *OSV* 81:10-11 Ja 10 1993

Stevens, Bernard.
Sur la spécificité philosophique du Japon. *RPhil Louvain* 91:275-295 My 1993

Stevens, Clifford, and McNichols, William Hart, eds.
Aloysius. Huntington: Our Sunday Visitor, 1993. x, 160p ISBN 0-87973-528-7

Stevens, Maryanne.
Review of: *Befriending the earth: a theology of reconciliation between humans and the earth* by Berry, Thomas. In: *Horizons (CTS)* 20:158-159 Spr 1993

Stevens, Richard G.
Review of: *Energy in the executive* by Eastland, Terry. In: *Crisis* 11:53-55 Jl-Ag 1993
Review of: *Restoration* by Will, George. In: *Crisis* 11:53-56 Je 1993

Stevenson, Jane.
Review of: *Literacy and power in Anglo-Saxon literature* by Lerer, Seth. In: *Heythrop* 34:450-451 O 1993

Stevenson, Kenneth W. *see* Perham, Michael V, jt auth; Searle, Mark, 1941-1992, jt auth

Stewart, Columba.
The monastic journey according to John Cassian. *Word Sp* 15:29-40 1993

Stewart, Stanley.
Investigating Herbert criticism. *Renascence* 45:131-158 Spr 1993

Steyn, Richard.
Mandela in waiting. *Tablet* 247:811-812 Je 26 1993
Negotiating a revolution. *Tablet* 247:263-264 F 27 1993
South Africa on the edge. *Tablet* 247:1152+ S 11 1993

Stikker, Allerd.
Teilhard today. *Teilhard Rev* 28:23-27 Spr 1993

Stock, Ann.
Converting the school. *Mod Lit* 20:12-14 O 1993

Stocker, Mark.
Review of: *Imagining the Pacific: in the wake of the Cook voyages* by Smith, Bernard. In: *Tablet* 247:1167 S 11 1993
Review of: *Town and country* by Girouard, Mark. In: *Tablet* 247:142-143 Ja 30 1993

Stockhausen, Carol Kern.
Paul's theology of aging. *BibleT* 30:341-346 N 1992

Stoeber, Michael.
From proclamation to interreligious dialogue. *Living Light* 30:32-41 Aut 1993

Stoecklin, Carol.
An invitation to dance: towards a spirituality of education. *Living Light* 29:58-64 Aut 1992

Stoesz, Willis.
The universal attitude of Shinto as expressed in the Shinto sect Kurozumikyō. *JEcumen Stds* 29:215-229 Spr 1992

Stoever, William K B.
Review of: *Paradox lost* by Pahl, Jon. In: *CHist* 79:356-357 Ap 1993

Stokes, Richard.
Review of: *God's dominion: a sceptic's quest* by Graham, Ron. In: *Can Cath Rev* 11:26-27 Je 1993

Stone, Elaine Murray.
Elizabeth Bayley Seton: an American saint. New York: Paulist Press, 1993. 86p ISBN 0-8091-6609-7 LC 92-42020

Stone, Howard W.
Crisis counseling. Minneapolis: Fortress, 1993. x, 96p ISBN 0-8006-2760-1 LC 92-39489

Stone, M.
Review of: *Freedom and the end of reason: on the moral foundation of Kant's critical philosophy* by Velkley, Richard L. In: *Heythrop* 34:109-110 Ja 1993

Stoneman, W.
Review of: *The cult of the Virgin Mary in Anglo-Saxon England* by Clayton, Mary. In: *CHist* 78:631-632 O 1992

Stoney, Brian.
Place and retreat. *Way Suppl* 75:12-19 Aut 1992

Stookey, Laurence Hull.
One bread, one cup [exc fr *Liturgy: putting on Christ; Liturgy: covenant with the world*]. *Liturgy* 10:4-6 Spr 1993

Storck, Thomas.
Aristotle, your garden and your body. *HPR* 93:24-29 F 1993
Distributing America. *New Oxford Rev* 60:6-10 My 1993

Storey, Eileen.
"American-Salaam-Iraqi". *Cath Work* 60:8 Ja-F 1993

Storey, Tony.
Our Easter hope and my priesthood. *Priests & People* 7:145-147 Ap 1993

Stourton, Edward.
Maastricht: dead or alive? *Tablet* 247:936-937 Jl 24 1993

Stout, Nancy T.
Review of: *Earthsongs: praying with nature* by Simsic, Wayne. In: *St Anth* 101:52-53 Ag 1993
Review of: *Encounters with angels: the interplay of psyche and spirit in the counseling situation* by Patterson, Richard B. In: *ST Anth* 101:52-53 Jl 1993
Review of: *Natural prayer: encountering God in nature* by Simsic, Wayne. In: *St Anth* 101:52-53 Ag 1993
Review of: *Seek treasures in small fields: everyday holiness* by Puls, Joan. In: *St Anth* 101:50-51 O 1993

Stovall, Dennis. *see* King, Laurie, jt auth

Straeten, J van der.
Review of: *Studien zur Überlieferungsgeschichte der lateinischen Legenda aurea* by Fleith, B. In: *NRT* 115:278 Mr-Ap 1993

Strajek, Martin.
Review of: *Die vielen Gesichter des einen Gottes: Christen und Juden im Gespräch* by Neudecker, Reinhard. In: *JEcumen Stds* 29:121 Wint 1992

Strange, Roderick.
Here I am in the classroom. *Tablet* 247:202-203 F 13 1993

Stransky, Thomas F.
Vatican-Israel diplomatic relations. *America* 169:4-9 N 6 1993

Stratton, Florence.
Vested interests in Somalia. *Cath Work* 60:3 Ja-F 1993

Stratton, Robin.
The purification of desire by means of desire in Dante's 'Purgatorio'. *Spir Life* 39:34-36 Spr 1993

Stratton-Lake, Philip.
Reason, appropriateness and hope: sketch of a kantian account of a finite rationality. *IJPS* 1:61-80 Mr 1993

Strauss, Gerald.
Review of: *The harvest of humanism in Central Europe: essays in honor of Lewis W Spitz* by Fleischer, Manfred P, ed. In: *CHist* 79:106-108 Ja 1993

Stravinskas, Peter.
All is found in the "Our Father". *Register* 69:1+ O 31 1993
The creed, like a reliable map, will lead us to heaven. *Register* 69:1+ My 30 1993
The data don't lie. *Register* 69:5 Mr 28 1993
Dialogue [interview by P Mullen]. *Register* 69:1+ Ja 24 1993
A gospel guide to the season. *Register* 69:1+ F 21 1993
The Holy Spirit is everywhere you are. *Register* 69:1+ O 10 1993
Introducing the newest and most up-to-date Catholic dictionary. Huntington: Our Sunday Visitor, 1993. x, 500p ISBN 0-87973-507-4
Jesus and a paralytic: the lesson. *Register* 69:1+ Mr 14 1993
Jesus feeds a hungry multitude and prefigures the life-giving Eucharist. *Register* 69:1+ Mr 21 1993
Jesus meets Nicodemus and the Samaritan woman. *Register* 69:1+ Mr 7 1993
John, theologian and poet, traces the signs of Christ's divine identity. *Register* 69:1+ F 28 1993
The marks of the church [commentary]. *Register* 69:1+ O 17 1993
The new Catechism of the Catholic Church conforms to the genuine tradition of the Church, especially to the teachings of the Second Vatican Council, December 7, 1992.
The new universal catechism: a renewed content, traditional form. *Register* 69:1+ My 2 1993
The new universal catechism: why it's vitally necessary. *Register* 69:1+ Ap 25 1993
On heaven, hell and judgment. *Register* 69:1+ O 24 1993
Our Lord cures the blind man. *Register* 69:1+ Mr 28 1993
Truth reaffirmed about creation and humanity's fall. *Register* 69:1+ My 23 1993
When we witness Christ's glory, we share His divine life. *Register* 69:5 Ap 11 1993
Why the creed is the heart of our faith. *Register* 69:1+ My 9 1993
Why we need the creeds. *Register* 69:1+ My 16 1993

Stretch, John J. *see* Szwabo, Peggy, jt auth

Strobel, Lee.
Inside the mind of unchurched Harry and Mary. Grand Rapids: Zondervan Publishing House, 1993. x, 224p ISBN 0-310-37561-4

Strohl, Lydia.
Icon painters in Pennsylvania [condensed fr *Pittsburgh*, F 1993]. *CDgst* 57:14-18 My 1993

Strong, Lee.
They heard a second call [condensed fr *Catholic Courier* Ap 29 1993]. *CDgst* 57:120-124 S 1993

Struckhoff, Charlotte, and Winters, Anne Marie.
The continuing confirmation debate [replies to J Martos, 25:19 Mr 1992; 56-60 Ap/My 1992]. *Catechist* 26:31-33 F 1993

Strukelj, Anton.
Man and woman under God: the dignity of the human being according to Hans Urs von Balthasar. *Communio* 20:377-388 Sum 1993

Strusinski, Robert.
Now that we've rearranged the furniture, how do things look? *Past Mus* 17:30-33 Ag-S 1993

Struthers, Jane. *see* Hawkes, Jason, jt auth

Stuart, Elizabeth.
Chosen: gay Catholic priests tell their stories. New York: Chapman, 1993. / ISBN 02-256-6682-0 LC 92-34966

Stuhlmueller, Carroll.
Review of: *2 Kings* by Long, Burke O. In: *BibleT* 31:119-120 Mr 1993
Review of: *A declaration on peace* by Gwyn, Douglas, et al. In: *BibleT* 30:381 N 1992
Review of: *A Muslim primer* by Zepp, Ira G, Jr. In: *BibleT* 31:122 Mr 1993
Review of: *Almanac of the Bible* by Wigoder, Geoffrey Bernard, 1922-, et al, eds. In: *BibleT* 31:250 Jl 1993
Review of: *At the start Genesis made new* by Korsak, Mary Phil. In: *BibleT* 31:119 Mr 1993
Review of: *Chattel or person? The status of women in the Mishnah* by Wegner, Judith Romney. In: *BibleT* 31:248 Jl 1993
Review of: *Citations and allusions to Jewish Scripture in early Christian and Jewish writings through 180 C E* by McLean, Bradley H. In: *BibleT* 31:247-248 Jl 1993
Review of: *Come close to the Lord* by Lesser, R H. In: *BibleT* 31:55 Ja 1993
Review of: *Creation and history* by Trigo, Pedro. In: *BibleT* 31:57 Ja 1993
Review of: *Discovering Old Testament origins* by Ralph, Margaret Nutting. In: *BibleT* 31:121 Mr 1993
Review of: *Ecclesiastes* by Murphy, Roland E. In: *BibleT* 31:248 Jl 1993
Review of: *Exploring scripture* by Cunningham, Philip J. In: *BibleT* 30:380-381 N 1992
Review of: *Exploring the Bible* by Tooma, Lynn. In: *BibleT* 30:383 N 1992
Review of: *Exploring the story of Israel* by Nelson, Yvette. In: *BibleT* 31:55 Ja 1993
Review of: *Ezra-Nehemiah* by Throntveit, Mark A. In: *BibleT* 30:383 N 1992
Review of: *Finding the lost: cultural keys to Luke 15* by Bailey, Kenneth E. In: *BibleT* 31:122 Mr 1993
Review of: *Four views on hell* by Crockett, William, ed. In: *BibleT* 31:245-246 Jl 1993
Review of: *From Jewish prophet to Gentile God* by Casey, Maurice. In: *BibleT* 31:123 Mr 1993
Review of: *Galatians* by Matera, Frank J. In: *BibleT* 31:125 Mr 1993
Review of: *Galileo, Bellarmine and the Bible* by Blackwell, Richard J. In: *BibleT* 31:244 Jl 1993
Review of: *Genesis: an introduction* by Westermann, Claus. In: *BibleT* 31:250 Jl 1993
Review of: *Genesis* by Scullion, John J. In: *BibleT* 31:249 Jl 1993
Review of: *Glad you asked: scriptural answers for our times* by Hampsch, John H. In: *BibleT* 31:54 Ja 1993

Stuhlmueller, Carroll. *(cont'd)*
Review of: *God's surprising presence: praying with the Hebrew Scriptures* by Fritz, Maureena. In: *BibleT* 31:119 Mr 1993
Review of: *Heresy and criticism: the search for authenticity in early Christian literature* by Grant, Robert McQueen, 1917-. In: *BibleT* 31:246 Jl 1993
Review of: *How to read the church fathers* by Hamman, Adalbert. In: *BibleT* 31:246 Jl 1993
Review of: *How to teach with the lectionary* by McBrien, Philip J. In: *BibleT* 31:247 Jl 1993
Review of: *In defense of revolution: the Elohist history* by Coote, Robert B. In: *BibleT* 30:380 N 1992
Review of: *In the beginning: a humorous survey of the Bible* by Lambin, Helen Reichert. In: *BibleT* 30:381 N 1992
Review of: *In the beginning: creation and the priestly history* by Coote, Robert B, and Ord, David Robert. In: *BibleT* 30:380 N 1992
Review of: *In the company of preachers* by Siegfried, Regina, and Ruane, Edward, eds. In: *BibleT* 31:249 Jl 1993
Review of: *International kosher cookbook* by Plotch, Batia, and Cobe, Patricia. In: *BibleT* 31:56 Ja 1993
Review of: *Interpreting Hebrew poetry* by Petersen, David L, and Richards, Kent Harold. In: *BibleT* 31:120 Mr 1993
Review of: *Introducing the cultural context of the Old Testament, vol I* by Pilch, John Joseph, 1936-. In: *BibleT* 30:381-382 N 1992
Review of: *Introduction to the scripture read in worship* by Sydnor, William. In: *BibleT* 30:383 N 1992
Review of: *Isaiah 1-12, a commentary* by Wildberger, Hans, 1910-1986. In: *BibleT* 30:383 N 1992
Review of: *Jeremiah* by Jones, Douglas Rawlinson. In: *BibleT* 31:55 Ja 1993
Review of: *Jesus and the riddle of the Dead Sea Scrolls* by Thiering, Barbara. In: *BibleT* 31:126 Mr 1993
Review of: *Jesus: a gospel portrait* by Senior, Donald. In: *BibleT* 31:121-122 Mr 1993
Review of: *Judaism without Christianity* by Neusner, Jacob. In: *BibleT* 31:55-56 Ja 1993
Review of: *Just a sister away* by Weems, Renita J. In: *BibleT* 31:57 Ja 1993
Review of: *Let's pray together (volume II)* by Pfeifer, Alice Ann. In: *BibleT* 31:120 Mr 1993
Review of: *Leviticus* by Hartley, John E. In: *BibleT* 31:57 Ja 1993
Review of: *Listening with the heart.* In: *BibleT* 31:247 Jl 1993
Review of: *Love and politics: a new commentary on the Song of Songs* by Stadelmann, Luis. In: *BibleT* 31:249-250 Jl 1993
Review of: *Major Hindu festivals: a Christian appreciation* by Subhash, Anand. In: *BibleT* 31:53 Ja 1993
Review of: *Mary in the mystery of the covenant* by Potterie, Ignace de la. In: *BibleT* 31:124 Mr 1993
Review of: *Muhammad, a biography of the prophet* by Armstrong, Karen. In: *BibleT* 31:118 Mr 1993
Review of: *New Adam* by Culbertson, Philip. In: *BibleT* 31:54 Ja 1993
Review of: *No greater love* by Binz, Stephen J. In: *BibleT* 31:118 Mr 1993
Review of: *No longer be silent* by Brown, Cheryl Anne. In: *BibleT* 31:53 Ja 1993
Review of: *Old Testament theology* by Brueggemann, Walter. In: *BibleT* 31:245 Jl 1993
Review of: *Paul and John* by Dicharry, Warren. In: *BibleT* 31:124 Mr 1993
Review of: *Pauline theology I: Thessalonians, Philippians, Galatians, Philemon* by Bassler, Jouette M, ed. In: *BibleT* 31:122-123 Mr 1993
Review of: *People of the body* by Eilberg-Schwartz, Howard, ed. In: *BibleT* 31:246 Jl 1993
Review of: *Perseverance in trials* by Martini, Carlo Maria, Cardinal, 1926-. In: *BibleT* 31:247 Jl 1993
Review of: *Pillars of Paul's Gospel* by O'Grady, John F. In: *BibleT* 31:125 Mr 1993
Review of: *Preaching the revised common lectionary: year A: Advent, Christmas, Epiphany* by Soards, Marionn L, et al. In: *BibleT* 30:383 N 1992
Review of: *Prologue to history* by Seters, John Van. In: *BibleT* 31:250 Jl 1993
Review of: *Psalm services for group prayer* by Cleary, William. In: *BibleT* 31:245 Jl 1993
Review of: *Psalms 51-100* by Tate, Marvin E. In: *BibleT* 31:57 Ja 1993
Review of: *Psalms for contemplation* by Valles, Carlos G. In: *New Theol Rev* 6:113-114 My 1993
Review of: *Reading John* by Talbert, Charles H. In: *BibleT* 31:126 Mr 1993
Review of: *Reconciliation* by Schreiter, Robert J. In: *BibleT* 30:382 N 1992
Review of: *Redeemer* by Clark, William B. In: *BibleT* 31:119 Mr 1993
Review of: *Sacred violence: Paul's hermeneutic of the cross* by Hamerton-Kelly, Robert G. In: *BibleT* 31:124-125 Mr 1993
Review of: *Satire and the Hebrew prophets* by Jemielity, Thomas. In: *BibleT* 31:55 Ja 1993
Review of: *Scientific malpractice: the creation/evolution debate* by Zabilka, Ivan L. In: *BibleT* 31:251 Jl 1993
Review of: *Scripture reflections* by Donders, Joseph G. In: *BibleT* 31:54 Ja 1993
Review of: *Seasons of friendship: Naomi and Ruth as a pattern* by Bankson, Marjory Zoet. In: *BibleT* 31:53 Ja 1993
Review of: *Sennacherib's "palace without rival" at Nineveh* by Russell, John Malcolm. In: *BibleT* 30:382 N 1992
Review of: *So the woman went her way* by Bundesen, Lynne. In: *BibleT* 31:245 Jl 1993
Review of: *So you mean to read the Bible* by Sloyan, Gerard S. In: *BibleT* 31:249 Jl 1993
Review of: *Sources of the Pentateuch* by Campbell, Anthony F, and O'Brien, Mark A. In: *BibleT* 31:245 Jl 1993
Review of: *Stewardship and the economy of God* by Reumann, John Henry Paul, 1927-. In: *BibleT* 31:125-126 Mr 1993
Review of: *Swords into plowshares: theological reflections on peace* by Burggraeve, Roger, and Vervenne, Marc, eds. In: *BibleT* 31:123 Mr 1993
Review of: *Targum Neofiti 1: Genesis.* In: *BibleT* 30:379-380 N 1992
Review of: *Targum pseudo-Jonathan: Genesis.* In: *BibleT* 30:379-380 N 1992
Review of: *Tell me the Bible* by Chabert, Joëlle, and Mourvillier, François. In: *BibleT* 31:53 Ja 1993

Stuhlmueller, Carroll. *(cont'd)*
Review of: *The Anchor Bible dictionary* by Freedman, David Noel, ed. In: *BibleT* 30:379 N 1992
Review of: *The Bible and the moral life* by Sleeper, C Freeman. In: *BibleT* 31:249 Jl 1993
Review of: *The Book of Psalms* by Craven, Toni. In: *BibleT* 31:119 Mr 1993
Review of: *The creationl of feminist consciousness from the middle ages to eighteen seventy* by Lerner, Gerda. In: *BibleT* 31:247 Jl 1993
Review of: *The Gospel according to Matthew* by Morris, Leon. In: *BibleT* 31:125 Mr 1993
Review of: *The gospel of peace* by Mauser, Ulrich. In: *BibleT* 31:125 Mr 1993
Review of: *The Holy Land* by Murphy-O'Connor, Jerome. In: *BibleT* 31:248 Jl 1993
Review of: *The Johannine Epistles* by Schnackenburg, Rudolf. In: *BibleT* 31:126 Mr 1993
Review of: *The liberation of dogma* by Segundo, Juan Luis. In: *BibleT* 31:121 Mr 1993
Review of: *The literature of destruction: Jewish responses to catastrophe* by Roskies, David G, ed. In: *BibleT* 31:248 Jl 1993
Review of: *The meaning of peace* by Yoder, Perry B, and Swartley, Willard M, eds. In: *BibleT* 31:250-251 Jl 1993
Review of: *The mystery and the passion* by Buttrick, David G. In: *BibleT* 31:123 Mr 1993
Review of: *The New Jerome Bible handbook* by Brown, Raymond Edward, et al, eds. In: *BibleT* 31:118-119 Mr 1993
Review of: *The nonviolent coming of God* by Douglass, James W. In: *BibleT* 31:124 Mr 1993
Review of: *The Old Testament of the Old Testament: patriarchal narratives and Mosaic Yahwism* by Moberly, R W L. In: *BibleT* 31:120 Mr 1993
Review of: *The Old Testament story* by Tullock, John H. In: *BibleT* 31:57 Ja 1993
Review of: *The Old Testament: a bibliography* by Zannoni, Arthur E. In: *BibleT* 31:251 Jl 1993
Review of: *The people of nowhere* by Rubinstein, Danny. In: *BibleT* 31:56 Ja 1993
Review of: *The Psalms in inclusive language* by Arackal, Joseph J. In: *BibleT* 31:244 Jl 1993
Review of: *The Psalms, New American Bible 1991.* In: *BibleT* 31:121 Mr 1993
Review of: *The Psalms, New American Bible 1991.* In: *BibleT* 31:121 Mr 1993
Review of: *The Schocken guide to Jewish books* by Holtz, Barry W, ed. In: *BibleT* 31:54-55 Ja 1993
Review of: *The Talmud* by Steinsaltz, Adin. In: *BibleT* 31:122 Mr 1993
Review of: *The will to arise: women, tradition and the Church in Africa* by Oduyoye, Mercy Amba, and Kamyoro, Musimbi R A, eds. In: *BibleT* 31:56 Ja 1993
Review of: *The woman's Bible commentary* by Newsom, Carol A, and Ringe, Sharon H, eds. In: *BibleT* 31:56 Ja 1993
Review of: *The word made clear* by McIlhone, James P. In: *BibleT* 30:381 N 1992
Review of: *Treatise on the passover and dialogue of Origen with Heraclides* by Origène. In: *BibleT* 31:56 Ja 1993
Review of: *Under every green tree: popular religion in sixth-century Judah* by Ackermann, Susan. In: *BibleT* 31:244 Jl 1993
Review of: *Understanding Scripture* by Berkeley, A, and Mickelsen, Alvera M. In: *BibleT* 31:120 Mr 1993
Review of: *Understanding the Bible* by Harris, Stephen L. In: *BibleT* 30:381 N 1992
Review of: *Understanding the Dead Sea Scrolls* by Shanks, Hershel, ed. In: *BibleT* 31:126 Mr 1993
Review of: *What are the Targums?* by Grelot, Pierre. In: *BileT* 31:54 Ja 1993
Review of: *What has archaeology to do with faith?* by Charlesworth, James H, and Weaver, Walter P, eds. In: *BibleT* 31:123-124 Mr 1993
Review of: *Where is God when you need him?* by Schultz, Karl A. In: *BibleT* 30:382 N 1992
Review of: *Women as interpreters of the Bible* by Demers, Patricia. In: *BibleT* 31:54 Ja 1993
Review of: *Women of the gospels* by Powers, Isaias. In: *BibleT* 31:120-121 Mr 1993
Review of: *Word and presence: a commentary on the book of Deuteronomy* by Cairns, Ian. In: *BibleT* 30:380 N 1992
Review of: *Writings from ancient Israel* by Smelik, Klaas A D. In: *BibleT* 31:57 Ja 1993
Review of: *Zealots for zion* by Friedman, Robert I. In: *BibleT* 31:246 Jl 1993
Review of: *Zion's final destiny* by Seitz, Christopher R. In: *BibleT* 30:382-383 N 1992
The search for original sin. *BibleT* 31:73-78 Mr 1993

Stuhmueller, Carroll.
Review of: *Braided streams: Esther and a woman's way of growing* by Bankson, Marjory Zoet. In: *BibleT* 31:53 Ja 1993

Stultz, Newell M.
Review of: *High noon in Southern Africa: making peace in a rough neighborhood* by Crocker, Chester A. In: *America* 168:19-20+ Je 19-26 1993

Sturzl, Jo Ann. see Williams, Donna Reilly, jt auth

Suarez, Federico.
La pasion de nuestro senor Jesucristo. Madrid: Rialp, 1993. x, 311p ISBN 84-321-3001-x

Suazo, Fernando.
Cultura occidental y culturas indígenas. *Cien Tom* 120:101-115 Ja-Ap 1993

Suenens, Leo-Jozef, Cardinal, 1904-.
"Most Holy Father: I hope to avoid the shock that your decision would cause" [Letter to PP VI to protect the infant charismatic renewal]. *New Cov* 22:7-9 Ap 1993

Sugirtharajah, R S, ed.
Asian faces of Jesus. Maryknoll: Orbis Books, 1993. x, 267p ISBN 0-88344-833-5 LC 93-536

Suh, Young S, and Lee, John P.
The "how-to" of integrated delivery. *Health Prog* 74:48 Jl-Ag 1993

Sullivan, Andrew.
"I'm here" [interview by T H Stahel, 1938-]. *America* 168:5-11 My 8 1993

Sullivan, Brian R. see Cannistraro, Philip V, jt auth

Sullivan, Francis Aloysius.
Response to Wolfgang Beinert. *Jurist* 52 no 1:484-489 1992
Review of: *The Catholic doctrine of non-Christian religious according to the Second Vatican Council* by Ruokanen, Miika. In: *TheolStds* 54:201 Mr 1993
The "secondary object" of infallibility. *TheolStds* 54:536-550 S 1993

Sullivan, George R.
The Congress in transition: act II, scene I. *America* 168:6-8 Ja 2-9 1993

Sullivan, James A.
Review of: *Stanford White's New York* by Lowe, David Garrard. In: *Crisis* 11:58-60 Ap 1993
Review of: *The future of Thomism* by Hudson, Deal W, and Moran, Dennis W, eds. In: *HPR* 94:75-76 N 1993
Review of: *The politics of prudence* by Kirk, Russell, 1918-. In: *Can Cath Rev* 11:30 Je 1993
The sickening smile of Jesus; the jetty. *Spirit* 58:23-25 1993

Sullivan, Jay.
I remember Covenant House [condensed fr *Fordham* Wint 1993]. *CDgst* 57:94-97 Ag 1993

Sullivan, John.
Review of: *Meister Eckhart: mystical theologian* by Davies, Oliver. In: *Heythrop* 34:434 O 1993
Review of: *Morality and modernity* by Poole, Ross. In: *Heythrop* 34:464-465 O 1993

Sullivan, John L.
Review of: *L'asino del nemico* by Barbiero, Gianni. In: *CBQ* 55:100-101 Ja 1993

Sullivan, Joseph M, Bp, 1930-.
An opportunity for positive change. *Health Prog* 74:56-59+ 1993

Sullivan, Robert E.
Review of: *Paul VI* by Hebblethwaite, Peter, 1930-. In: *America* 168:18+ My 1 1993

Sullivan, Thomas D, and Atkinson, Gary.
Malum Vitandum: the role of intentions in first-order morality. *IJPS* 1:99-110 Mr 1993

Sullivan, Walter Francis, Bp, 1928-.
"The challenge of peace"—10 years later. *OSV* 82:23 My 16 1993

Sullivan, William M.
Review of: *The spirit of community* by Etizioni, Amitai. In: *Comm* 120:22-23 My 7 1993

Sulmasy, Daniel P.
The fullness of life. *Health Prog* 74:76-78 Ja-F 1993

Sulyk, Stephen.
Present situation of the Ukrainian Catholic Church in Ukraine. *Diakonia* 26 no 3:149-160 1993

Sun, Henry T C.
Review of: *Deuteronomy* by Miller, Patrick D. In: *CBQ* 54:757-758 O 1992
Review of: *Die Kompositionsgeschichte des Bundesbuches Exodus 20* by Osumi, Yuichi. In: *CBQ* 55:343-344 Ap 1993

Sunderland, Edwin S S.
Roman canon law in Reformation England: a review [review article *Roman canon law in Reformation England* by R Helmholz]. *Jurist* 51 no 2:415-422 1991

Sunderland, Ronald H. see Shelp, Earl E, jt auth

Sundermeier, Michael, and Egan, Desmond, eds.
Gerard Manley Hopkins annual 1993. Omaha: Creighton University Press, 1993. x, 123p ISBN 1-881871-07-x

Sunshine, Edward R.
Sexual morality from a social perspective. *Chicago Stud* 31:301-315 N 1992

Suquiía, Goicoechea Angel, Cardinal, 1916-.
The church—one and diverse—in service to mission. *Jurist* 52 no 1:7-10 1992
The new evangelization: some tasks and risks of the present [address to the Spanish Episcopal Conference Plenary Assembly (May 18, 1992)]. *Communio* 19:515-540 Wint 1992

Sussman, Cornelia Silver, 1914-.
The novel as spiritual guide. *Living Prayer* 26:18-22 Ja-F 1993

Sutcliffe, Tom.
Women priests and Anglo-Catholics. *Month* 26:53-56 F 1993

Sutera, Judith.
Benedictine nuns in the United States. *Word Sp* 14:33-40 1992
Review of: *Radical Christian communities* by Rausch, Thomas P. In: *Cist Stud* 28:[29]-[30] 1993

Suther, Eleanor.
Review of: *Sharing faith* by Groome, Thomas H, 1945-. In: *Worship* 67:373-375 Jl 1993

Suttner, Ernst Chr.
Das Ökumenismusdekret des Konzils. *Stimm Zeit* 211:303-317 My 1993
Die Unterdrückung der Ukrainischen Unierten Kirche unter Stalin und das Moskauer Patriarchat. *Stimm Zeit* 211:560-512 Ag 1993

Sutton, Alphonsus M.
Current errors and their refutation: confessors and spiritual directors. *ChrWorld* 38:51-55 Ja-F 1993
Current errors and their refutation: respect the charisms God has given Holy Doctors and the Magisterium. *ChrWorld* 38:144-152 Mr-Ap 1993

Svoboda, Melannie.
Beyond stable and straw. *Liguorian* 81:45-47 D 1993
Discipline: more goals than rules. *ReligTJ* 27:4-6 O 1993
Journal of a novice director. *RRel* 52:602-609 Jl-Ag 1993

Svoboda, Melannie. *(cont'd)*
The penance of inconvenience. *Liguorian* 81:26-29 F 1993
Seven common mistakes—and how to fix them. *Catechist* 27:65-66 S 1993
Talents for living in community. *RRel* 52:131-139 Ja-F 1993

Swaeles, Romain. *see* Gantoy, Robert, jt auth

Swain, Lionel.
Reading the Easter gospels. Collegeville, Minnesota: The Liturgical Press, 1993. 131p ISBN 0-81465-699-4 LC 92-40432

Swan, Darlis J. *see* Ford, John T, jt ed

Swan, Melanie M. *see* Berkowitz, David A, jt auth

Swan, Peter.
Review of: *The Catholic families* by Bence-Jones, Mark. In: *Can Cath Rev* 11:24-25 S 1993

Swanston, Hamish F G.
Review of: *Mozart: traces of transcendence* by Kung, Hans, 1928-. In: *New Blckfrs* 74:285-287 My 1993
Review of: *Wolf in the sheepfold: the Bible as a problem for Christianity* by Carroll, Robert P. In: *New Blckfrs* 73:576-578 N 1992

Swartley, Willard M. *see* Yoder, Perry B, jt ed

Swartz, Michael D. *see* Schiffman, Lawrence H, jt auth

Sweeney, Eileen C.
Thomas Aquinas' double metaphysics of simplicity and infinity. *IPQ* 33:297-317 S 1993

Sweeney, James.
The Decade of Evangelisation: has Catholicism changed? *Month* 25:461-466 D 1992

Sweeney, Jim.
Descent into hell. *OSV* 82:10-11 Ag 15 1993
Holy fragments. *OSV* 82:10-11 Jl 11 1993
Rome reborn: the Vatican library and renaissance culture. *OSV* 81:12-13 F 7 1993

Sweeney, John.
La cultura y sus dinamismos. *Christus* 58:12-14 My 1993

Sweeney, Marvin A.
Review of: *Biblical names: a literary study of Midrashic derivations and Puns* by Garsiel, Moshe. In: *OTA* 16:158-159 F 1993
Review of: *The Book of Amos* by Rösel, Hartmut N. In: *CBQ* 54:762-763 O 1992

Sweeney, Patricia James.
Review of: *The quality school: managing students without coercion* by Glasser, William. In: *Momentum* 24:78-79 S-O 1993

Sweet, Leonard I, ed.
Communication and change in American religious history. Grand Rapids: Eerdmans, 1993. 400p ISBN 0-8028-0682-1

Sweet, W.
Review of: *Hobbes* by Tuck, Richard. In: *Heythrop* 34:107-108 Ja 1993

Sweetland, Dennis M.
Review of: *Adam Christology as the exegetical and theological substructure of 2 Corinthians 4:7-f:21* by Pate, C Marvin. In: *CBQ* 55:389-391 Ap 1993
Review of: *He is risen! a new reading of Mark's Gospel* by Humphrey, Hugh M. In: *Bib Th Bul* 23:43 Spr 1993
Review of: *The mission of Christ and His church: studies in christology and ecclesiology* by Meier, John P. In: *Bib Th Bul* 23:86-87 Sum 1993

Sweetman, Brendan.
Review of: *God without being* by Marion, Jean-Luc. In: *New Oxford Rev* 60:25-26 Jl-Ag 1993
Review of: *Mystic union: an essay in the phenomenology of mysticism* by Pike, Nelson. In: *New Oxford Rev* 60:28-30 O 1993

Sweetser, Thomas P. *see* Forster, Patricia M, jt auth

Sweetser, Thomas P, and Forster, Patricia M.
A Festschrift on small faith communities [symposium, Institute of Pastoral Studies of Loyola University, Jl 1991]. *Chicago Stud* 31:173-181 Ag 1992

Sweetser, Thomas P, and Holden, Carol M.
Leadership in a successful parish. Kansas City: Sheed & Ward, 1992. x, 203p ISBN 1-55612-564-x LC 92-20718

Swetnam, James.
Review of: *Der Brief an die Hebräer* by Weiss, Hans-Friedrich. In: *CBQ* 55:187-189 Ja 1993
Review of: *Proleptic priests: priesthood in the Epistle to the Hebrews* by Scholer, John M. In: *CBQ* 54:799-800 O 1992

Swidler, Arlene.
Homosexuality and world religions. Philadelphia: Trinity Press International, 1993. 232p ISBN 1-56338-051-x LC 93-6848
Review of: *Generous lives* by Redmont, Jane. In: *St Anth* 101:48 Je 1993

Swidler, Leonard.
Islam and the trialogue of Abrahamic religions. *CrossCurr* 42:444-452 Wint 1992-1993 *see* Mojzes, Paul, jt ed

Swindell, Bill.
Fathers come home: a wake-up call for busy dads. South Bend, Indiana: Greenlawn Press, 1992. x, 101p ISBN 0-937779-23-7 LC 92-75551

Swindle, Donna. *see* Weyant, Jennie, jt auth

Sykes, Charles J.
The future that works: Milwaukee's School choice revolution. *Crisis* 11:28-32 Ja 1993

Sylva, Douglas.
'Whatever is original, spare, strange'. *America* 168:4 Je 5-12 1993

Symondson, Anthony.
Review of: *The architecture of George Pace* by Pace, Peter. In: *Month* 26:78 F 1993

Synan, Edward A.
Review of: *The Church and the Jews in the XIIIth century: volume II, 1254-1314* by Grayzel, Solomon. In: *CHist* 79:99-100 Ja 1993

Szafranski, Richard T.
Show more faith in your prayers. *USCath* 58:36-37 Mr 1993

Szczepanowski, Richard.
She teaches American liberation theology. *Nat Cath Rep* 30:18 O 29 1993

Szell, Timea. *see* Blumenfeld-Kosinski, Renate, jt ed

Szentmártoni, Mihály.
Review of: *Prevenire le crisi: Un contributo della logoterapia* by Lukas, Elisabeth. In: *Gregorianum* 74 No 1:189 1993

Szura, John Paul.
Review of: *A theology of force and violence* by Mayhew, Peter. In: *New Theol Rev* 6:118-119 My 1993

Szwabo, Peggy, and Stretch, John J.
Autonomy and care for the frail elderly. *Health Prog* 74:50-51+ My 1993

Szyszkiewicz, Tom.
Dead Sea Scroll scholars discuss latest findings. *Register* 69:1+ My 23 1993

T

Taber, D.
Review of: *Between church and state: the lives of four French prelates in the late Middle Ages* by Guenée, Bernard. In: *TheolStds* 53:755-757 D 1992

Tabet, Paul F.
Intervene to protect innocent. *OR(Eng)* 1309:10 S 29 1993

Tabor, James D. *see* Droge, Arthur J, jt auth

Taborda, Francisco.
Cristianismo e culturas indígenas. *REB* 53:259-282 Je 1993
Nueva evangelizacion promocion humana cultura Cristiana. *Christus* 58:40-47 Mr-Ap 1993
Review of: *Celebar o Deus da vida* by Barros Souza, Marcelo de. In: *Perspectiva* 25:252-255 My-Ag 1993
Review of: *Como vi e vivi Santo Domingo* by Nery, Israel José. In: *Perspectiva* 25:264-265 My-Ag 1993
Review of: *Nosso Credo* by Codina, Victor. In: *Perspectiva* 25:258 My-Ag 1993
Review of: *O segredo feminino do Mistéro* by Bingemer, Maria Clara L. In: *Perspectiva* 25:242-245 My-Ag 1993
Review of: *Santo Domingo: Bajo el signo de la esperanza* by Salvatierra, Angel. In: *Perspectiva* 25:263-264 My-Ag 1993
Review of: *Tomás de Aquino* by Pesch, Otto Hermann, 1931-. In: *Perspectiva* 25:237-238 My-Ag 1993

Tackett, Timothy.
Review of: *The Huguenots and French opinion, 1685-1787: the Enlightenment debate on toleration* by Adams, Geoffrey. In: *CHist* 79:541-542 Jl 1993

Tada, Joni Eareckson. *see* Newman, Gene, jt auth

Taeubner, Stefan.
Obdachlosigkeit in Deutschland. *Stimm Zeit* 211:187-196 Mr 1993

Tagerud, Yael. *see* Sigurdson, Jon, jt ed

Takagi, Takako Frances.
Inculturation and adaptation in Japan before and after Vatican Council II. *CHist* 79:2467-267 Ap 1993

Talar, C J T.
Conspiracy to commit heresy: The Anti-Americanist Polemic of Canon Henri Delassus. *US Cath Hist* 11:77-92 Sum 1993

Talbert, Charles H.
Review of: *Luke-Acts: Scandinavian perspectives* by Luomanen, Petri, ed. In: *CBQ* 55:198 Ja 1993

Talley, Thomas J.
Review of: *L'anafora eucaristica* by Mazza, Enrico. In: *Worship* 67:375-377 Jl 1993
Review of: *The anaphoras of St Basil and St James* by Fenwick, John R K. In: *Worship* 67:480-481 S 1993

Tallon, Andrew.
The heart in Rahner's philosophy of mysticism. *TheolStds* 53:700-728 D 1992
Review of: *Karl Rahner* by Dych, William V. In: *TheolStds* 54:392 Je 1993

Tamames, Ramon.
La Reconquista del Paraiso. Barcelona: Temas de Hoy, 1993. x, 203p ISBN 84-7880-231-2

Tambasco, Anthony J.
Prophetic teaching on sin. *BibleT* 31:79-84 Mr 1993
Quodlibetalia biblica. *Chicago Stud* 31:282-289 N 1992

Tamburello, Dennis E.
Bernard of Clairvaux in the thought of Meister Eckhart. *Cist Stud* 28:73-91 1993

Tan, Amy, 1952-.
Live, on stage with Amy Tan [interview by E Wymard]. *Critic* 47:77-83 Wint 1992

Tang, Edmond, and Wiest, Jean-Paul, eds.
The Catholic Church in modern China: perspectives. Maryknoll: Orbis, 1993. x, 260p ISBN 0-88344-834-3 LC 93-14944

Tanghe, Vincent.
Lilit in Edom (Jes 34, 5-15). *Eph Theol Lovan* 69:125-133 Ap 1993

Tanner, Kathryn, 1957-.
The politics of God: Christian theologies and social justice. Minneapolis: Fortress Press, 1992. 262p ISBN 0-80062-613-3 LC 92-19360

Tanner, Mary, et al.
Towards koinonia/communion in faith, life and witness: revised discussion paper for the Fifth World Conference on Faith and Order. *Ecumen Trends* 22:1-24 Je 1993

Tanner, Mary.
"God unites—in Christ a new creation". *OChr* 28 no 4:300-306 1992
The time has come: a vision for the Fifth World Conference on Faith and Order [fr *The Ecumenical review*]. *Cath Int* 4:239-244 My 1993

Tanner, Norman P.
Do North Americans understand the Middle Ages better than Europeans? *America* 169:5-6 O 2 1993
Medieval Christendom and the restoration of a Christian society. *Month* 25: 467-472 D 1992
Review of: *Intellectual life in the middle ages: essays presented to Margaret Gibson* by Smith, Lesley, and Ward, Benedicta, eds. In: *New Blckfrs* 74: 331-333 Je 1993
Sin in the Middle Ages. *Month* 26:372-375 S-O 1993

Tanner, R E S.
African traditional religions and their reactions to other faiths. *StudiaM* 42: 371-394 1993

Tapuerca Ceballos, Jesús.
Hacia el protagonismo de los pueblos indígenas de América. *Cien Tom* 120: 57-77 Ja-Ap 1993

Tassi, Aldo.
Person as the mask of being. *PhilosTod* 37:201-210 Sum 1993

Tassin, Paul.
Questions d'un gestionnaire d'hôpital. *Supplement* 184:7-19 Mr-Ap 1993

Tastard, Terry.
Review of: *What is the new age saying to the church* by Drane, John. In: *Way* 33:85-86 Ja 1993

Tataryn, Myroslaw.
Review of: *Perspectives orthodoxes sur l'Église Communion* by Baillargeon, Gaëtan. In: *JEcumen Stds* 29:472-473 Sum-Aut 1992

Tate, Daniel L.
Review of: *Beyond Hegel and dialectic: speculation, cult, and comedy* by Desmond, William. In: *Cithara* 32:58-60 My 1993

Taubitz, Ronald.
Teaching narrative prose. *Tod Cath Teach* 27:34+ S 1993

Tauran, Jean-Louis, Abp.
World cannot survive without justice, peace and development. *OR(Eng)* 1301:4 Jl 28 1993

Tavard, George Henry.
"Communion" in a time of estrangement. *Ecumen Trends* 22:1+ My 1993
Review of: *Chair de l'Eglise, chair du Christ* by Tillard, Jean Marie Roger, 1927-. In: *TheolStds* 54:200 Mr 1993
Review of: *Les idéalites casuistiques* by Cariou, Pierre. In: *TheolStds* 54:600 S 1993
Review of: *Salvation outside the Church* by Sullivan, Francis Aloysius. In: *CHist* 79:89-90 Ja 1993
Review of: *Systematic theology, vol 1* by Pannenberg, Wolfhart. In: *OChr* 28 no 4:387-392 1992
Sor Juana and evangelization in New Spain. *US Cath Hist* 11:21-27 Spr 1993
The work of ARC-USA: reflections post-factum. *OChr* 29 no 3:247-259 1993

Taylor, Audrey. see Taylor, Joe, jt auth

Taylor, Joe. see Taylor, Audrey, jt auth

Taylor, Mark C, 1945-.
Nots. Chicago: University of Chicago Press, 1993. x, 275p ISBN 02-2679-130-0 LC 92-38702
Review of: *Gaia and God: a new theology for a renewed earth* by Ruether, Rosemary Radford. In: *America* 168:26-27+ My 29 1993

Taylor, Mary Sue.
Prayer for daybreak and day's end, vol II: January through June. Cincinnati: St Anthony Messenger Press, 1993. 428p ISBN 0-86716-147-7
Prayer for daybreak and day's end, vol III: July through December. Cincinnati: St Anthony Messenger Press, 1993. 432p ISBN 0-86716-148-5

Taylor, Pam.
They taught me love. *Sisters* 65:55-57 Ja 1993

Taylor, Patrick.
Review of: *Borders* by Hobhouse, Penelope. In: *Tablet* 247:375 Mr 20 1993
Review of: *Climbers and wall plants for year round colour* by Taylor, Jane. In: *Tablet* 247:375 Mr 20 1993
Review of: *Containers and baskets for year round colour* by McHoy, Peter. In: *Tablet* 247:375 Mr 20 1993
Review of: *Lawns and ground cover* by Lacey, Stephen. In: *Tablet* 247:375 Mr 20 1993
Review of: *Oxford book of garden verse* by Hunt, John Dixon. In: *Tablet* 247:375 Mr 20 1993
Review of: *Perennials* by Rix, Martyn. In: *Tablet* 247:375 Mr 20 1993
Review of: *The container garden* by Tarling, Thomasina. In: *Tablet* 247:375 Mr 20 1993
Review of: *The flower garden* by Dillon, Helen. In: *Tablet* 247:375 Mr 20 1993
Review of: *The formal garden* by Laird, Mark. In: *Tablet* 247:480-481 Ap 10-17 1993
Review of: *The glasshouse garden* by Watkins, John. In: *Tablet* 247:375 Mr 20 1993
Review of: *The grafter's handbook* by Garner, R J. In: *Tablet* 247:375 Mr 20 1993
Review of: *The mystic garden* by Swinscow, Douglas. In: *Tablet* 247:375 Mr 20 1993
Review of: *The Royal Horticultural Society encyclopaedia of gardening.* In: *Tablet* 247:375 Mr 20 1993
Review of: *The secret gardens of France* by Osler, Mirabel. In: *Tablet* 247: 375 Mr 20 1993
Review of: *The shady garden* by Taylor, Jane. In: *Tablet* 247:375 Mr 20 1993
Review of: *Wall plants and climbers* by Buchan, Ursula. In: *Tablet* 247:375 Mr 20 1993

Taylor, Terri.
The pebble in my pocket. *Liguorian* 81:58-59 O 1993

Teasdale, Wayne.
Dom Bede Griffiths: symbol of the marriage of East and West (1906-1993). *Living Prayer* 26:17-18 S-O 1993
A gathering of the faiths: Chicago 1993. *Living Prayer* 26:29-30 My-Je 1993

Tegeder, V.
Review of: *House of stone: the Duluth Benedictines* by Boo, Mary Richard. In: *CHist* 78:687-689 O 1992

Tekippe, Patricia.
Haiti, Sarajevo, peacemaking among topics at Pax Christi USA's assembly. *Nat Cath Rep* 29:2 Ag 27 1993

Tekippe, Terry J.
A note on Roger Haight's spirit Christology. *HPR* 93:53-59 Jl 1993

Temple, Katharine.
Home by another way. *Cath Work* 60:1+ Ja-F 1993
Paying to lose our jobs. *Cath Work* 60:6 Mr-Ap 1993
Transformed by the renewal of the mind. *Cath Work* 60:3 My 1993

Tepedino, Ana María.
Carta aos Membros da Associação Ecumênica de Teólogos do Terceiro Mundo (ASETT) na América Latina. *REB* 53:188-192 Mr 1993

Terry, Randall.
Dialogue [interview by M Meehan]. *Register* 69:1+ F 21 1993

TeSelle, Eugene, 1931-.
Review of: *Convenantal theology: the Eucharistic order of history (two volumes)* by Keefe, Donald J. In: *America* 168:19+ My 8 1993

Tesfai, Yacob.
Concepts of division and unity in the ecumenical movement. *Ecumen Trends* 22:9-15 Mr 1993
An overview of the ecumenical landscape: identifying some signposts. *OChr* 28 no 4:342-356 1992

Teske, Roland J.
Review of: *"Creatio," "Conversio," "Formatio" Chez S Augustin* by Vannier, Marie-Anne. In: *TheolStds* 53:748-749 D 1992
Review of: *Augustine's love wisdom* by Bourke, Vernon J. In: *Mod Schlmn* 70:237-238 Mr 1993
Review of: *Augustine: Confessions, commentary on Books 1-7; vol 2* by O'Donnell, James J, ed. In: *TheolStds* 54:563-565 S 1993
Review of: *Augustine: Confessions, commentary on Books 8-13; vol 3* by O'Donnell, James J, ed. In: *TheolStds* 54:563-565 S 1993
Review of: *Augustine: Confessions, introduction and text; vol 1* by O'Donnell, James J, ed. In: *TheolStds* 54:563-565 S 1993
Review of: *Christian friendship in the fourth century* by White, Carolinne. In: *TheolStds* 54:596 S 1993
Review of: *Desire and delight: a new reading of Augustine's Confessions* by Miles, Margaret R. In: *TheolStds* 54:196 Mr 1993

Tetlow, Joseph A.
Review of: *Men astutely trained: a history of the Jesuits in the American century* by McDonough, Peter. In: *CHist* 79:289-301 Ap 1993
At the heart of the Eucharist. *RRel* 52:735-740 S-O 1993
The emergence of an American Catholic spirituality. *TheolDgst* 40:27-36 Spr 1993

Thanawala, Kishor.
Poverty and development: economics and reality. *RSocEcon* 50:258-268 Fall 1992

Thavis, John.
Bishops ask pope to allow married priests. *Nat Cath Rep* 29:7 O 1 1993
China calls, Vatican responds. *Nat Cath Rep* 29:15 S 24 1993
Italian bishops bash "irregular" liaisons. *Nat Cath Rep* 30:7 O 22 1993
Pope: reject "extreme" feminism. *Nat Cath Rep* 29:7 Jl 16 1993
15-year papacy sets direction for church for years to come. *Nat Cath Rep* 30: 11 O 22 1993

Theobald, Robert.
The future ain't what it used to be [interview by Salt editors]. *Salt* 13:6-11 Jl-Ag 1993

Thiboudeau, Victor.
Review of: *Philosophie de l'éducation* by Morin, Lucien, and Brunet, Louis. In: *Laval Theol Phil* 49:357-359 Je 1993

Thiel, John E.
Review of: *Faithful persuasion: in aid of a rhetoric of Christian theology* by Cunningham, David S. In: *TheolStds* 54:366-368 Je 1993

Thiele, Gloria.
Mary Mauren healer of hearts. *St Anth* 100:40-43+ Ja 1993
Michelangelo's Four Pieta's [photos]. *CDgst* 57:1-6 Ag 1993
Tomb of St Francis. *CDgst* 57:1-2+ O 1993

Thiessen, Gesa.
Faith into art: religion and Vincent van Gogh. *Doctr Life* 43:267-274 My-Je 1993
Review of: *Art is my life, a tribute to James White* by Kennedy, Brian P. In: *Studies* 81:454-456 Wint 1992
Review of: *The Church, community of salvation* by Tavard, George Henry. In: *Studies* 82:207-210 Sum 1993

Thigpen, Paul.
His open arms welcomed me. *New Cov* 23:18-21 S 1993

Thiry, Joan.
What every teacher needs to know about copyright. *Momentum* 24:65-67 N-D 1993

Thomas, Christopher.
Review of: *Sex, art, and American culture* by Paglia, Camille. In: *Comm* 120: 25-26 Je 4 1993

Thomas, D.
Review of: *The Celtic world* by Cunliffe, Barry. In: *Tablet* 246:1576 D 12 1992
Review of: *The princes in the Tower* by Weir, Alison. In: *Tablet* 247:17 Ja 2 1993

Thomas, David M.
Marriage and daily life: adult learning that really matters. *Tod Parish* 25:20-22 Ap-My 1993

Thomas, Denis.
Review of: *The tower of London: an artist's portrait* by Casson, Hugh, and White, Richard T. In: *Tablet* 247:440 Ap 3 1993

Thomas, Ellen Lamar.
The eleventh commandment: listen!. *CDgst* 57:78-81 Ap 1993

Thomas, Janna.
The blessings of loving-kindness. *Living Prayer* 26:20-21 Jl-Ag 1993
Many mansions. *Living Prayer* 26:17-18 N-D 1993

Thomas, Joseph R.
Review of: *Opus Dei* by Walsh, Michael J, 1937-. In: *St Anth* 100:50 My 1993

Thomas, Patricia.
How much can you help your heart? [condensed from *Harvard Health New Letter* S 1992]. *CDgst* 57:10-13 Mr 1993

Thomas Aquinas, Saint.
Light of faith: the compenduine of theology. Manchester: Sophia Institute Press, 1993. x, 412p ISBN 0-918477-15-8 LC 93-6793

Thompson, David, Bp.
Synod convoked for Charleston Diocese. *Origins* 22:509+ Ja 7 1993

Thompson, Donna.
John Paul delivers goods in Denver. *Register* 69:1+ Ag 29 1993
Nun issues warning [breast cancer]. *Register* 69:3 O 24 1993
Salt of the earth: Donna Thompson [interview by M Ervin]. *Salt* 13:4-5 Je 1993

Thompson, Geraldine.
A fortnight lasts forever. *Can Cath Rev* 11:9-12 Ja 1993
Review of: *From nuns to sisters* by Neal, Mari Augusta. In: *Can Cath Rev* 11:39-40 Ja 1993

Thompson, J Milburn.
Review of: *Active nonviolence: a way of personal peace* by Vanderhaar, Gerard A. In: *Emmanuel* 99:179-180 Ap 1993
Review of: *Harvesting peace: the arms race and human need* by Simon, Arthur. In: *Emmanuel* 99:179-180 Ap 1993
Review of: *Iraq: military victory, moral defeat* by Fox, Thomas C. In: *Emmanuel* 99:116+ Mr 1993
Review of: *Natural prayer: encountering God in nature* by Simsic, Wayne. In: *Emmanuel* 99:236-237 My 1993

Thompson, John.
A Presbyterian viewpoint. *Furrow* 44:399-402 Jl-Ag 1993

Thompson, Margaret Susan.
Service as sacrament: sisters and the meaning of American Catholicism. *Sisters* 65:82-90 Mr 1993

Thompson, Stephanie.
Being with those who mourn [photographs]. *BibleT* 31:95-101 Mr 1993

Thompson, Thomas L.
Review of: *Il contributo del Movimento dei focolari alla koinonia ecumenica* by Back, Joan Patricia. In: *JEcumen Stds* 29:479-480 Sum-Aut 1992
Review of: *Mary for all Christians* by Macquarrie, John. In: *Can Cath Rev* 11:34-35 Ja 1993
The secretary's report. *Marian Stds* 43:190-191 1992

Thompson, William M.
Review of: *The revelatory text: interpreting the New Testament as sacred scripture* by Schneiders, Sandra M. In: *Horizons (CTS)* 19:288-294 Fall 1992

Thomson, Clarence.
Review of: *Adventures in medialand* by Cohen, Jeff, and Solomon, Norman. In: *Nat Cath Rep* 30:35 N 19 1993
Review of: *Future of the body: explorations into the further evolution of human nature* by Murphy, Michael. In: *Nat Cath Rep* 29:17 Ja 22 1993

Thoren, Ken.
Carny priest. *OSV* 82:10-11 Je 13 1993

Thorn, William.
Young, pregnant, and valued [condensed fr *Columbia* Ap 1993]. *CDgst* 57:37-39 Ag 1993

Thornhill, John.
A wholesome agnosticism and Christianity's coming dialogue with the world religions. *Pacifica* 6:265-277 O 1993

Thornton, Lawrence, 1937-.
Bearing witness [interview by P Gilmour]. *Critic* 47:84-94 Wint 1992

Thorpe, Doug.
A celebration of Denise Levertov's comings and goings. *CrossCurr* 43:247-252 Sum 1993

Thunder, James.
Until death do they part? *Register* 69:5 F 14 1993

Thurian, Max.
Eucharist and blessing. *SIDIC* 26 no 1:19-20 1993
Review of: *Eucharist* by Bouyer, Louis. In: *SIDIC* 26 no 1:19-20 1993

Thurston, Anne.
The ministry of women: gift or threat to the churches? *Doctr Life* 43:387-395 S 1993
On the margin. *Tablet* 247:534 My 1 1993
The spiritual life of children. *Doctr Life* 42:594-599 D 1992
What do women want? *Furrow* 43:668-671 D 1992

Thurston, Bonnie.
Review of: *Ace of freedoms: Thomas Merton's Christ* by Kilcourse, George. In: *America* 169:22 S 18 1993

Tichy, George J, II.
The Age Discrimination in Employment Act of 1967. *CLawyer* 34 no 4:373-384 1993

Tichy, George J, II. *(cont'd)*
The Americans with Disabilities Act of 1990. *CLawyer* 34 no 4:343-361 1993
The Drug-Free Workplace Act of 1988. *CLawyer* 34 no 4:363-371 1993

Tiefel, Hans O.
Review of: *The call to personhood* by McFadyen, Alistair I. In: *America* 168:18+ Mr 6 1993
Review of: *Valuing life* by Kleinig, John. In: *America* 168:18+ Mr 6 1993

Tierney, Mark.
Review of: *The diocese of Killaloe* by Murphy, Ignatius. In: *Studies* 82:210-214 Sum 1993

Tierney, Michael.
The songs we would have sung to him [fr *The family worker*]. *Cath Work* 60:4 Mr-Ap 1993

Tierney, Stephen.
Almost a million at Mass in Madrid. *Tablet* 247:828 Je 26 1993

Tierney, Terrence E.
Annulment: do you have a case? New York: Alba House, 1993. x, 142p ISBN 0-8189-0667-7 LC 93-7090

Tighe, William J.
Review of: *The Huguenots in England: immigration and settlement, c 1550-1700* by Cottret, Bernard. In: *CHist* 79:529-530 Jl 1993

Tihon, M. A.
Review of: *Si tu connaissais* by Guelluy, Robert. In: *Lumen* 48:234 Je 1993

Tihon, Paul.
Cinq siècles d'Amérique Latine (editorial). *Lumen* 47:367-368 D 1992
Review of: *Garder espoir: Écrits sur la réforme de l'Eglise* by Küng, Hans, 1928-. In: *Lumen* 48:114 Mr 1993
Review of: *Jésus en Amérique latine: sa signification pour la foi et la christologie* by Sobrino, John. In: *Lumen* 48:114-115 Mr 1993
Review of: *L'histoire des hommes récit de Dieu* by Schillebeeckx, Edward. In: *Lumen* 48:232 Je 1993
Review of: *Les approches empiriques en théologie* by Pelchat, Marc. In: *Lumen* 48:113 Mr 1993
Review of: *Libération et progressisme* by Duquoc, Christian. In: *Lumen* 47:470-471 D 1992
Review of: *Un racisme pas si ordinaire* by Ancion, Jean. In: *Lumen* 48:239 Je 1993

Tilby, Angela.
The medium and the message. *Tablet* 247:269-270 F 27 1993
Review of: *Sexuality and spiritual growth* by Timmerman, Joan. In: *Way* 33:84 Ja 1993
Review of: *The body in context* by Moore, Gareth. In: *Way* 33:85-85 Ja 1993
Soul: God, self and the new cosmology. New York: Doubleday, 1993. x, 310p ISBN 0-385-47125-4 LC 93-12994

Tillard, Jean Marie Roger, 1927-.
Build community or die. *Priests & People* 7:129-199 Ap 1993
Concrete koinonia. *Tablet* 247:1146-1147 S 4 1993
The local church within catholicity. *Jurist* 52 no 1:448-454 1992
Reception—communion. *OChr* 28 no 4:307-322 1992

Tiller, Ken.
Review of: *Old English poetry in medieval Christian perspective* by Garde, Judith N. In: *Relig Lit* 25:95-96 Spr 1993

Tilley, Maureen A.
Review of: *Disinheriting the Jews: Abraham in early Christian controversy* by Siker, Jeffrey S. In: *Horizons (CTS)* 20:146-149 Spr 1993

Tilley, Terrence W.
Review of: *What are they saying about God and evil?* by Whitney, Barry L. In: *Horizons (CTS)* 19:322-323 Fall 1992

Tillier, A-M. see Hublin, J-J, jt ed

Tilliette, Xavier.
Il centenario de *L'Action* di M. Blondel. *Civilta* 3:388-393 S 4 1993
Review of: *Filosofia e trascendenza. Con due Saggi di Emmanuel Levinas* by Levinas, Emmanuel. In: *Gregorianum* 74 no 3:598 1993
Review of: *Fondamento ed esasperazione. Saggio sul pensare di Emmanuel Lévinas* by Petrosino, Silvano. In: *Gregorianum* 74 no 3:598 1993
Review of: *Idealismo e Nichilismo. La Lettera di Jacobi u Fichte* by Iacovacci, Alberto. In: *Gregorianum* 74 no 3:597 1993
Review of: *Leiblichkeit als Lebendigkeit. Michel Henrys Leben-sphänomenologie absoluter Subjektivität als Affektivität* by Kühn, Rolf. In: *Gregorianum* 74 no 3:596-597 1993
Review of: *Relazione, regola e diritto: l'intersoggettività giuridica nella prospettiva di Joseph de Finance* by Savarese, Paolo. In: *Civilta* 144:617 Mr 20 1993
Review of: *Scritti kantiani* by Jacobi, F H. In: *Gregorianum* 74 no 3:597 1993

Timbie, Janet.
Review of: *The transcendent God of Eugnostos* by Trakatellis, Demetrios. In: *CBQ* 55:401-402 Ap 1993

Timbrell, Charles.
French pianism: an historical perspective. White Plains: Pro/Am Music Resources, 1992. x, 288p ISBN 0-912483-89-x

Timko, Philip.
Pray at fixed times, pray always: patterns of monastic prayer. *ABenR* 43:395-413 D 1992

Timmerman, Joan H.
Review of: *Building bridges: gay and lesbian reality and the Catholic Church* by Nugent, Robert, and Gramick, Jeannine. In: *Horizons (CTS)* 20:187-188 Spr 1993
Lancelot Andrewes and T S Eliot: the making of histories. *ABenR* 44:76-98 Mr 1993

Tindall, Susan F. see Hruby, Dolores, jt auth

Tipton, Paul.
Review of: *Conduct unbecoming: gays and lesbians in the US military* by Shilts, Randy. In: *Register* 69:5 Je 6 1993

Tipton, Paul. *(cont'd)*
Review of: *Politics by other means: higher education and group thinking* by Bromwich, David. In: *Register* 69:4 My 23 1993

Tiso, Francis V.
The Karma Kagyupa Tibetan Buddhists. *StudiaM* 41:145-167 1992

Titone, Margaret.
How to handle the rage within. *Liguorian* 81:52-55 Jl 1993

Tobia, Blaise. *see* Maksymowicz, Virginia, jt auth

Tobias, Robert. *see* Meyendorff, John, jt ed

Tobie, Pierre.
Le cours de religion à l'école un débat de société. *Lumen* 48:223-229 Je 1993

Tobin, Thomas H.
Controversy and continuity in Romans 1:18-3:20. *CBQ* 55:298-318 Ap 1993
Review of: *The spurious texts of Philo of Alexandria* by Royse, James R. In: *OTA* 16:193-194 F 1993

Tock, Jean-François.
Review of: *Montaigne et la mélancolie, La sagesse des Essais* by Screech, Michaël A. In: *RPhil Louvain* 91:467-468 Ag 1993
Review of: *Pascal et la philosophie* by Carraud, Vincent. In: *RPhil Louvain* 91:472-473 Ag 1993
Review of: *Pascal, la clé du chiffre* by Magnard, Pierre. In: *RPhil Louvain* 91:472 Ag 1993

Todd, J.
Review of: *The new creation in Christ* by Griffiths, Bede, 1906-. In: *Tablet* 247:76 Ja 16 1993

Tolhurst, James.
A concise catechism for Catholics. Grand Rapids: Eerdmans, 1993. 80p ISBN 0-8028-0122-6

Tolhurst, Joseph.
Review of: *A new guide to the debate about God* by Prozesky, Martin. In: *Priests & People* 7:168 Ap 1993
Review of: *Systematic theology, Roman Catholic perspective* by Fiorenza, Francis Schüssler, 1938-, and Galvin, John P, 1944-, eds. In: *Priests & People* 6:360 Ag-S 1992
Review of: *The craft of theology* by Dulles, Avery Robert, 1918-. In: *Priests & People* 7:84 F 1993

Tolliver, Cindy. *see* Keim, Nancy, jt auth

Tomalak, Ann.
One inner city parish community. *Priests & People* 7:138-144 Ap 1993

Tomar Romero, Francisca.
Persona y amor: el personalismo de Jaime Bofill. Lleida: PPU, 1993. x, 364p ISBN 84-477-011301

Tombes, Jonathan.
Listening to Cecilia. *Crisis* 11:52-54 Mr 1993

Tombes, Jonathan, and Tucker, Jeffrey.
Deforming the liturgy. *Crisis* 10:20-24 N 1992

Toner, Roisin.
A young person's view. *Priests & People* 7:251-268 Jl 1993

Toner, W.
Review of: *Life on the dole*. In: *Studies* 82:220-222 Sum 1993
Review of: *Our view at last* by Brennan, Keith, et al. In: *Studies* 82:220-222 Sum 1993
Review of: *Telling it like it is* by O'Neill, Cathleen. In: *Studies* 82:220-222 Sum 1993

Toolan, David S.
Chicago's Parliament of the World's Religions. *America* 169:3-4 S 25 1993
Of lingering eyes and talking things: Adorno and Deleuze on philosophy since Auschwitz. *PhilosTod* 37:227-246 Aut 1993
Review of: *Fighting for life: contest, sexuality, and consciousness* by Ong, Walter J. In: *Church* 9:55-58 Spr 1993
Review of: *Fire in the belly: on being a man* by Keen, Sam. In: *Church* 9:55-58 Spr 1993
Review of: *Iron John: a book about men* by Bly, Robert. In: *Church* 9:55-58 Spr 1993
Review of: *The wild man's journey: reflections on male spirituality* by Rohr, Richard, 1943-, and Martos, Joseph. In: *Church* 9:55-58 Spr 1993
Review of: *Wildmen, warriors, and kings: masculine spirituality and the Bible* by Arnold, Patrick M. In: *Church* 9:55-58 Spr 1993
Second thoughts on the population bomb. *America* 168:16-17 Mr 6 1993
A survivor's tale. *Way Suppl* 77:55-65 Sum 1993

Toolan, Suzanne.
Tis a gift to be simple [interview]. *Mod Lit* 19:6-9 D 1992-Ja 1993

Toomey, Philippa.
Review of: *Cleopatra's sister* by Lively, Penelope. In: *Tablet* 247:824 Je 26 1993
Review of: *Docklands* by Williams, Stephanie. In: *Tablet* 247:373 Mr 20 1993
Review of: *Exploring rural France* by Sanger, Andrew. In: *Tablet* 247:373 Mr 20 1993
Review of: *Exploring rural Ireland* by Sanger, Andrew. In: *Tablet* 247:373 Mr 20 1993
Review of: *Felidae* by Pirincci, Akif. In: *Tablet* 247:1015 Ag 7 1993
Review of: *How to break bad news* by Buckman, Robert. In: *Tablet* 247:585 My 8 1993
Review of: *Howard Carter and the discovery of the tomb of Tutankhamun* by Winstone, H V F. In: *Tablet* 247:373 Mr 20 1993
Review of: *New York* by Barnard, Josie. In: *Tablet* 247:373 Mr 20 1993
Review of: *Paris* by Cullen, Catherine. In: *Tablet* 247:373 Mr 20 1993
Review of: *Rome* by Belford, Ros. In: *Tablet* 247:373 Mr 20 1993
Review of: *The condition of the working class in England* by Engels, Friedrich. In: *Tablet* 247:585 My 8 1993
Review of: *The Grasmere journals* by Wordsworth, Dorothy. In: *Tablet* 247:585-586 My 8 1993
Review of: *The lost continent; travels in small town America* by Bryson, Bill. In: *Tablet* 247:373 Mr 20 1993

Toomey, Philippa. *(cont'd)*
Review of: *When the summer ended* by Bogle, Joanna, and Wolkowinska, Cecylia. In: *Tablet* 247:585 My 8 1993
Review of: *Wilfred Owen* by Stallworthy, Jon. In: *Tablet* 247:585 My 8 1993

Toomey, Stephana.
Death and grief in murals [photographs]. *Liturgy* 10:58-62 Wint 1992

Toomey, V. *see* Finan, T, jt ed

Toon, Peter.
The art of meditating on scripture. Grand Rapids: Zondervan Publishing House, 1993. x, 176p ISBN 0-310-57761-6

Topel, John.
Review of: *Christus Faber: the master builder and the house of God* by Meyer, Ben F. In: *TheolStds* 54:552-554 S 1993
Review of: *Faith and history: essays in honor of Paul W Meyer* by Carroll, John T, et al, eds. In: *CBQ* 54:818-819 O 1992

Torly, V.
Review of: *Dieu en son Royaume* by Desroussilles, Dupuigrenet. In: *NRT* 115:139 Ja-F 1993

Torraco, Stephen F.
"Listening" to nature: the significance of Leon Kass for Catholic moral theology. *Linacre* 60:40-55 Ag 1993

Torralba Rossello, Francese.
Geographia de l'absurd. Lerida: Pages, 1993. 149p ISBN 84-7935-132-2
Amor y diferencia. Barcelona: PPU, 1993. x, 383p ISBN 84-477-0118-2

Torrello Cascante, Ramon, Abp.
A year of T'shuvah [statement made to Central Conference of American Rabbis (March 26, 1992: Toledo)]. *SIDIC* 25 No 2:28-29 1992

Torrens, James S.
Best of friends. *America* 168:23 Ap 24 1993
A birthday party and the Jesuit case. *America* 168:3-4 My 15 1993
Blood brothers. *America* 169:18 S 18 1993
A fundamentalist Nicaragua? *America* 168:6-9 Ja 16-23 1993
"The Greek miracle". *America* 168:18 Ap 3 1993
Kiss of the Spider woman. *America* 169:21 N 20 1993
The last Yankee. *America* 168:16 F 27 1993
Of many things. *America* 169:2 Jl 3-10 1993
A perfect Ganesh. *America* 169:22 Ag 14-21 1993
Refugees in the limelight. *America* 168:6 Ap 3 1993
Review of: *A framework for survival: health, human rights, and humanitarian assistance in conflicts and disasters* by Cahill, Kevin Michael, 1936-, ed. In: *America* 168:2 Je 19-26 1993
Shakespeare for my father. *America* 169:18 S 18 1993
The song of Jacob Zulu. *America* 168:18 Je 19-26 1993
Time to let out the secret. *America* 169:4 O 23 1993
"The waking dream" photography's first century. *America* 168:18-19 My 22, 1993
The years. *America* 168:16 F 27 1993

Torrens, Paul R.
Health care reform: now for the hard part!. *America* 168:14-15 Ap 3 1993
When social responsibility pays. *America* 169:5 Jl 17-24 1993

Torres, Hector.
Santo Domingo—an interpretation. *LADOC* 23:1-8 My-Je 1993

Tortolano, W.
Review of: *A new hymnal for colleges and schools* by Rowthorn, Jeffery, and Schulz-Widmar, Russell, eds. In: *Past Mus* 17:47-48 D 1992-Ja 1993

Torvend, Samuel.
The visual proclamation of Christian worship. *Liturgy* 11:39-44 Sum 1993
see Lathrop, Gordon, jt auth

Totah, Mary David.
Review of: *What are they saying about Acts?* by Powell, Mark Allan. In: *Cist Stud* 28:[21] 1993

Toubeau, A.
Review of: *Aimer la Bible avec Élisabeth de la Trinité* by Févotte, P-M. In: *NRT* 115:306-307 Mr-Ap 1993
Review of: *Aux frontières du Royaume* by Pommeraye, R de la. In: *NRT* 115:131-132 Ja-F 1993
Review of: *Briefe an Roman Ingarden* by Stein, Edith, 1891-1942. In: *NRT* 114:936-937 N-D 1992
Review of: *Cent ans de catholicisme social dans la région du Nord*. In: *NRT* 114:916-917 N-D 1992
Review of: *Chair de l'Eglise, chair du Christ* by Tillard, Jean Marie Roger, 1927-. In: *NRT* 114:901-902 N-D 1992
Review of: *Court traité de l'existence chrétienne* by Cattin, Y. In: *NRT* 115:132 Ja-F 1993
Review of: *Der Streit um Drewermann* by Benedikt, B, and Sobel, A, eds. In: *NRT* 115:292-293 Mr-Ap 1993
Review of: *Edith Stein: Einführung in die Philosophie* by Gelber, L, et al, eds. In: *NRT* 115:276-277 Mr-Ap 1993
Review of: *Eugen Drewermann-Bibliographie* by Sobel, A. In: *NRT* 115:293 Mr-Ap 1993
Review of: *Faith in the world of work* by Erlander, L. In: *NRT* 114:923-924 N-D 1992
Review of: *Introduzione al Nuovo Testamento* by Migliore, Fr. In: *NRT* 115:296 Mr-Ap 1993
Review of: *Jesus und seine Schüler* by Stuhlhofer, Fr. In: *NRT* 114:942-943 N-D 1992
Review of: *L'Église dans la transformation actuelle de l'Amérique Latine à la lumière du Concile Vatican II.* In: *NRT* 115:291-292 Mr-Ap 1993
Review of: *L'action caritative du Saint-Siège en faveur des prisonniers de guerre (1939-1945)* by Papeleux, L. In: *NRT* 114:924-925 N-D 1992
Review of: *L'anatomia dell'anima* by Bergamo, Mino. In: *NRT* 114:910-911 N-D 1992
Review of: *La liturgie aujourd'hui* by Adam, Adolf. In: *NRT* 114:903 N-D 1992
Review of: *La Rivelazione* by Schmitz, J. In: *NRT* 114:898 N-D 1992

Toubeau, A. *(cont'd)*
Review of: *Les Églises face à l'entreprise: cent ans de pensée sociale* by Laurent, Ph, and Jahan, Emm, eds. In: *NRT* 114:915-916 N-D 1992
Review of: *Neanche Dio può stare solo* by Turoldo, D M. In: *NRT* 115:135-136 Ja-F 1993
Review of: *Peuple de prêtres?* by Dentin, P. In: *NRT* 115:300 Mr-Ap 1993
Review of: *Pour lire l'Apocalypse* by Prevost, Jean-Pierre. In: *NRT* 114:941-942 N-D 1992
Review of: *Religionskritik* by Weger, K-H. In: *NRT* 115:302-303 Mr-Ap 1993
Review of: *Sulle tracce del Concilio.* In: *NRT* 115:297-298 Mr-Ap 1993
Review of: *Thérèse et Lisieux* by Descouvement, P, and Loose, H N. In: *NRT* 115:283 Mr-Ap 1993
Review of: *The open door* by Theissen, Gerd. In: *NRT* 114:944 N-D 1992
Review of: *Unerbittliches Licht* by Gerl, H-B. In: *NRT* 114:935-936 N-D 1992
Review of: *Virgo Liber Verbi* by Calaguig, I M, ed. In: *NRT* 115:136-137 Ja-F 1993

Tourneau, Dominique Le.
Review of: *Diritto di associazione e associazioni di fedeli* by Navarro, Luis. In: *Stud Can* 27 no 1:269-271 1993
Review of: *El dolo en el matrimonio canónico* by Jusdado Ruiz-Capillas, Miguel Angel. In: *Stud Can* 27 no 1:267-268 1993
Review of: *Il "munus docendi Ecclesia": diritti e doveri dei fedeli* by Errázuriz Mackenna, Carlos José. In: *Stud Can* 27 no 1:264-265 1993
Review of: *Introducción al derecho canónico* by Larrainzar González, Carlos. In: *Stud Can* 27 no 1:268-269 1993
Review of: *Le Pape et le gouvernement de l'Église* by D'Onorio, Joël-Benoît. In: *Stud Can* 27 no 1:276-278 1993
Review of: *Tempus otii: fragmentos sobre los orígenes y el uso primitivo de los términos "praelatus" y "praelatura"* by Hervada, Javier. In: *Stud Can* 27 no 1:275-276 1993
Review of: *Territorialidad y personalidad en la organización eclesiástica: el caso de los ordinariatos militares* by Viana, Antonio. In: *Stud Can* 27 no 1:271-272 1993
Review of: *Vetera et nova: cuestiones de derecho canónico y afines (1958-1991), 2 vols* by Hervada, Javier. In: *Stud Can* 27 no 1:266-267 1993

Tous Ral, Jose M.
Compartamiento social y dinamica de groupos. Barcelona: PPU, 1993. x, 379p ISBN 84-477-0140-9

Tov, Emmanuel. *see* Fishbane, Michael, jt auth

Townsend, John Rowe.
Review of: *Elizabeth Gaskell: a habit of stories* by Uglow, Jenny. In: *Tablet* 247:343-344 Mr 13 1993
Review of: *The descent of manners* by St George, Andrew. In: *Tablet* 247:1105 Ag 28 1993
Review of: *The people in the playground* by Opie, Iona. In: *Tablet* 247:621 My 15 1993
Review of: *The Victorian governess* by Hughes, Kathleen. In: *Tablet* 247:789-790 Je 19 1993

Townsend, John T.
Review of: *From text to tradition* by Schiffman, Lawrence H. In: *New Theol Rev* 6:117-118 My 1993

Townsend, Mark.
Review of: *From synagogue to church: public services and offices in the earliest Christian communities* by Burtchaell, James Tunstead. In: *Furrow* 44:454-455 Jl-Ag 1993
Review of: *The beloved disciple: witness against anti-Semitism* by Kaufman, Philip S. In: *Furrow* 44:187-188 Mr 1993

Tozzi, Eugene.
Review of: *Sharing faith* by Groome, Thomas H, 1945-. In: *Church* 9:59-60 Spr 1993

Traboulay, D.
Review of: *Francisco de Vitoria zu Krieg und Frieden* by Justenhoven, Heinz-Gerhard. In: *TheolStds* 53:786-787 D 1992

Tracy, Thomas F.
Review of: *Types of Christian theology* by Frei, Hans W, 1922-1988. In: *America* 168:19-20 Je 5-12 1993

Trainor, Michael.
Review of: *Theological approaches to Christian education* by Seymour, Jack L, and Miller, Donald E, eds. In: *New Theol Rev* 6:100-101 F 1993
Review of: *Inheriting the earth: the Pauline basis of a spirituality for our time* by Byrne, Brendan. In: *New Theol Rev* 6:98-99 Ag 1993

Transferetti, José Antonio.
Review of: *No coração da Amazônia: juruá, o rio que chora* by Derickx, João, and Transferetti, José Antonio. In: *REB* 53:239-241 Mr 1993 *see* Derickx, João, jt auth

Trau, Jane Mary, and McCartney, James J.
In the best interest of the patient. *Health Prog* 74:50-56 Ap 1993

Traube, Patrick.
La nouvelle distinction stéréotypes et perceptions respectives des chrétiens et des athées. *Lumen* 47:377-390 D 1992

Traviss, Mary Peter.
Review of: *Why Johnny can't tell right from wrong* by Kilpatrick, William. In: *Momentum* 24:77-78 S-O 1993

Traylen, Mary Anne.
Review of: *A history of God from Abraham to the present* by Armstrong, Karen. In: *Month* 26:320-321 Ag 1993
Review of: *The mind of God: science and the search for ultimate meaning* by Davies, Paul. In: *Month* 26:235 Je 1993

Traylen, Maryanne.
Hero of the sewers. *Tablet* 247:1290 O 9 1993
Review of: *Fallen angels* by Jones, Robin Lloyd. In: *Tablet* 247:1075 Ag 21 1993

Trebolle Barrera, Julio.
La Biblia Judia y la Biblia Cristiana. Madrid: Trotta, 1993. x, 670p ISBN 84-87699-55-3

Trefil, James S. *see* Morowitz, Harold J, jt auth

Tremblay, Donald.
Review of: *Au-delà de son rêve: Délia Tétreault* by Raguin, Yves. In: *CHist* 79:378-379 Ap 1993

Treston, Kevin.
Ways to approach the Bible. *ReligTJ* 27:8-10 O 1993
What should you teach? *ReligTJ* 27:9-11 S 1993

Trevijano, Ramon.
Response to Michael Fahey. *Jurist* 52 no 1:71-78 1992

Trevisan, Teolide M, et al. *see* Marins, José, jt auth

Triacca, Achille M.
Il biennio di formazione all'istituto superiore d'arte sacre beato angelico alla minerva di Roma. *Notitiae* 28:227-228 Mr 1992
Review of: *Il santorale di Paolo VI* by Bonetti, Angelo, ed. In: *Notitiae* 28:624 S 1992
Sfondo "liturgico-vitale" del catechismo della chiesa Cattolica. *Notitiae* 29:34-47 Ja-F 1993 *see* Covolo, Enrico Dal, jt ed

Trible, Phyllis.
Review of: *Jonah: a new translation, with introduction, commentary, and interpretation* by Sasson, Jack M. In: *CBQ* 55:131-133 Ja 1993

Trifogli, Cecilia.
Giles of Rome on natural motion in the void. *Med Stud* 54:136-161 1992

Trigilio, John P.
Liturgical despots. *HPR* 93:66-69 Ja 1993

Trigo, Pedro.
La asamblea y el documento. *Christus* 58:48-61 Mr-Ap 1993
Del imaginario alternativo al imaginario vigente y al revolucionario. *Christus* 57:23-41 O 1992
El mundo como mercado significado y juicio. *Christus* 58:25-31 N-D 1992

Tripp, D.
Review of: *The forms and orders of Western liturgy from the tenth to the eighteenth century* by Harper, John. In: *Worship* 67:87-89 Ja 1993

Troccio, Julie. *see* Forschner, Brian, jt auth

Troeger, Thomas H. *see* Doran, Carol, jt auth

Tröger, Karl-Wolfgang.
Peace and Islam [condensed fr *Islam and Christian Muslim Relations* Je, 1990]. *TheolDgst* 38:115-118 Sum 1991

Troiano, Edna M. *see* Johnson, Pegram, III, jt auth

Trokan, Nancy, John. *see* Trokan, John, jt auth

Trost, Frederick. *see* Trost, Louise, jt auth

Trost, Louise, and Trost, Frederick.
Readers as proclaimers of the word. *Liturgy* 11:45-46 Sum 1993

Trotta, Carmen.
Crimes laid bare. *Cath Work* 60:5 Mr-Ap 1993
Gratuitous suffering. *Cath Work* 60:8 Ja-F 1993

True, Michael, 1933-.
Live the revolution now!. *Cath Work* 60:8 Ag 1993

Truitt, Gordon E.
How you keep them singing. *Past Mus* 17:13-17 Ag-S 1993

Truitt, Gordon E, ed.
The Sacramentary revisited. *Past Mus* 17:16-25+ Je-Jl 1993
The Sacramentary's introductory materials: worth a second look, by M R Francis. Patterns for praying always, K Hughes. Why don't our presiders chant?, R J Batastini. Here's a catechetical resource waiting to be used, by G Ostdiek.

Trujillo, Alfonso López, Cardinal.
The family is sanctuary of life. *OR(Eng)* 1305:4-5 S 1 1993

Trujillo, López.
Church and rights of the family. *OR(Eng)* 1301:6-7 Jl 28 1993

Tsuchida, Christina.
Jesus and the way of childhood. *Living Prayer* 26:19-20 N-D 1993

Tsumuraya, Katsuko.
Review of: *Le jardin d'Éden: mythe fondateur de l'Occident* by Louys, Daniel. In: *OTA* 16:167-168 F 1993

Tuck, Mary.
What are prisons for? *Tablet* 247:1157-1158 S 11 1993

Tucker, Jeffrey. *see* Tombes, Jonathan, jt auth

Tuckett, C M.
The four Gospels 1992. *Eph Theol Lovan* 78:385-396 D 1992

Tuffy, Edward. *see* Leonard, Seán, jt auth

Tull, Charles J.
Review of: *The Coughlin-Fahey connection: Father Charles E Coughlin, Father Denis Fahey, CSSp, and religious Anti-Semitism in the United States* by Athans, Mary Christine. In: *CHist* 79:371-373 Ap 1993

Tuohey, John F.
Mercy: an insufficient motive for euthanasia. *Health Prog* 74:51-53 O 1993
Review of: *No way out? pastoral care of the divorced and remarried* by Häring, Bernard, 1912-. In: *Jurist* 51 no 2:525-526 1991

Tuohy, John.
There's no such thing as a childhood on the streets. *USCath* 58:18-25 Mr 1993

Tuohy, Patrice J.
Religious symbols belong in your home. *USCath* 58:19-24 Ap 1993

Turmel, André. *see* Levasseur, Jean-Marie, jt auth

Turner, Geoffrey.
Evangelisation and the ghost of Lessing. *Month* 25:473-478 D 1992
The Qumran Scrolls: Christian or Jewish? *Month* 26:247-252 Je 1993

Vandergrift, Nicki Verploegen.
Stewardship and the disposition of reverence. *Stud Form Spir* 14:219-231 My 1993

Vandergrift, Ray.
Review of: *Papal pronouncements: a guide 1740-1978, 2 volumes* by Carlen, Claudia. In: *Living Light* 29:95 Wint 1992

VanderKam, James C.
Review of: *A tribute to Geza Vermes: essays on Jewish and Christian literature and history* by Davies, Philip R, and White, Richard T, eds. In: *CBQ* 55:193-195 Ja 1993

Vandervelde, George.
Koinonia ecclesiology—ecumenical breakthrough? *OChr* 29 no 2:126-142 1993

Vanek, Elizabeth-Anne.
Inner journeying: the hero's quest. *Emmanuel* 98:158-163 Ap 1992
Prodigal Father. *Emmanuel* 99:96-100 Mr 1993

Vanhoyne, Albert.
Passé et présent de la commission biblique. *Gregorianum* 74 no 2:261-275 1993

Vanier, Therese.
Review of: *Disciplines for Christian living: interfaith perspectives* by Ryan, Thomas. In: *Tablet* 247:950-951 Jl 24 1993

Vanneste, A.
Review of: *Antropologia del hombre caido: el pecado original* by Sayes, José Antonio. In: *Eph Theol Lovan* 69:213-214 Ap 1993
Review of: *Third World theologies: commonalities and divergences* by Abraham, K C, ed. In: *Eph Theol Lovan* 78:179-180 Ap 1992
Review of: *Uncompleted mission* by Dickson, Kwesi A. In: *Eph Theol Lovan* 78:468-469 D 1992
Review of: *Vie monastique et inculturation à la lumière des traditions et situations africaines.* In: *Eph Theol Lovan* 78:183-184 Ap 1992

Vanni, Ugo.
Il *Padre Nostro* I. *Civilta* 3:345-358 S 4 1993
Il regno millenario di Cristo e dei suoi (Apos 20, 1-10). *StudiaM* 42:67-95 1993

Vanoverberghe, Arlette.
Accompagnement des familles et prévention des deuils pathologiques. *Supplement* 184:125-144 Mr-Ap 1993

Vanzan, Piersandro.
Review of: *Se non diventerete come donne: simboli religiosi del femminile* by Gentili, Antonio. In: *Civilta* 143:528-529 D 5 1992
Review of: *Si vous ne devenez comme des femmes: symboles religieux du féminin* by Gentili, Antonio. In: *Civilta* 143:528-529 D 5 1992
Crisi e recupero del teocentrismo trinitario. *Civilta* 3:143-146 Jl 17 1993
Italo Mancini: un profeta sotto la toga dell'accademico. *Civilta* 2:351-364 My 15 1993
La nuova evangelizzazione alla IV Conferenza Generale dell'Episcopato Latinoamericano. *Civilta* 3:462-476 S 18 1993
Review of: *Cristo nella vita della famiglia* by Scabini, Pino. In: *Civilta* 2:195-196 Ap 17 1993
Review of: *Donne in chiaroscuro: un processo penale nella Teramo di fine '800* by Nicola, Giulia Paola Di, ed. In: *Civilta* 2:93-94 Ap 3 1993
Review of: *Il canto del pane* by Arslan, Antonio. In: *Civilta* 2:608-609 Je 19 1993
Review of: *Il fascino del Sacro nella cultura moderna* by Gamba, Ulderico, ed. In: *Civilta* 3:312-313 Ag 7-21 1993
Review of: *Il tempo dell'utopia: itinerari al femminile: simboli, realtà, profezia* by Nicola, Giulia Paola Di, ed. In: *Civilta* 2:93-94 Ap 3 1993
Review of: *L'uomo e il futuro, vol I: È possibile il futuro dell'uomo?* by Palumbieri, Sabino. In: *Civilta* 3:537-539 S 18 1993
Review of: *Per essere liberi: logoterapia quotidiana* by Fizzotti, Eugenio. In: *Civilta* 2:99-100 Ap 3 1993
Review of: *Se non io, chi per me?* by Gozzini, Vilma Occhipinti. In: *Civilta* 3:195-196 Jl 17 1993
La teologia del XX secolo. *Civilta* 2:566-568 Je 19 1993

Varacalli, Joseph A.
Catholics and politics in post-world war II America: some key questions. *SocJust* 84:78-83 My-Je 1993

Vardy, P.
Review of: *Søren Kierkegaard: "eighteen upbuilding discourses"* by Hong, Howard V, and Hong, Edna H, eds. In: *Heythrop* 34:112-113 Ja 1993

Varg, Paul A.
Review of: *United States attitudes and policies toward China* by Neils, Patricia, ed. In: *CHist* 79:581-582 Jl 1993

Varghese, Roy Abraham. *see* Margenau, Henry, jt ed

Varley, Virginia.
Culture and current practice. *Way Suppl* 76:32-43 Spr 1993

Varriale, E.
Review of: *La famiglia ritrovata* by Volpi, Claudio, and Gallotta, Nino. In: *Civilta* 2:414-415 My 15 1993
Review of: *La grande mutazione: il PCI* by Pilieri, Antonio. In: *Civilta* 144:416 F 20 1993

Vatavuk, William M.
Novel Catholicism: Waugh and Greene [condensed fr *Catholic Twin Circle* D 27 1992-Ja 31 1993]. *CDgst* 57:42-47 O 1993

Vatter, Harold Goodhue, 1910-, and Walker, John F.
Orthodox investment vs. government spending: two contrasting models for the 1990s. *RSocEcon* 51:154-173 Sum 1993

Vauchez, André.
The laity in the Middle Ages: religious practices and experiences. Notre Dame: University of Notre Dame, 1993. x, 350p ISBN 0-268-01297-0 LC 92-53746 *see* Jourdin, Michel Mollat du, jt ed

Vaughan, Judy.
Faith in contemporary society. *Chicago Stud* 31:197-200 Ag 1992

Vecchi, Ernesto.
La celebrazione del matrimonio. *Notitiae* 28:201-221 Mr 1992

Ven, Joao Henrique Van de.
Delcaração da dlegação de Pax Christi Internacional para a IV Conferência Geral do Episcopado Latino-Americano. *REB* 53:163-166 Mr 1993

Venard, Marc.
Ultramontaine or Gallican? The French eposcopate at the end of the sixteenth century. *Jurist* 52 no 1:42-161 1992

Ventline, Lawrence M.
Five cries of parish. *Priest* 49:17-21 F 1993
Five ways to put out the welcome mat at mass. *Emmanuel* 99:8-11 Ja-F 1993
Review of: *Love affair: a prayer journal* by Greeley, Andrew Moran, 1928-. In: *Emmanuel* 99:237-239+ My 1993
Review of: *Love in a fearful land: a Guatemalan story* by Nouwen, Henri Josef Machiel, 1932-. In: *Emmanuel* 99:359-360 Jl-Ag 1993
Review of: *My witness for the Church* by Häring, Bernard, 1912-. In: *St Anth* 100:50-51 Mr 1993
Review of: *Near occasions of grace* by Rohr, Richard, 1943-. In: *St Anth* 100:48 S 1993
Review of: *Report on the Church: Catholicism after Vatican II* by McBrien, Richard P. In: *St Anth* 100:50 F 1993
Review of: *Sermons for sermon haters* by Papineau, Andre, 1937-. In: *St Anth* 100:51 Ja 1993
Review of: *Sermons for sermon haters* by Papineau, Andre, 1937-. In: *Emmanuel* 99:298+ Je 1993

Venturini, Mary. *see* O'Collins, Gerald, 1931-, jt auth

Venturini, Nereo.
Il vi centenario della morte di San Sergio di Radonež. *Civilta* 143:589-596 D 19 1992

Vercruysse, Jos E.
Review of: *L'Église et monde.* In: *Civilta* 3:446-447 S 4 1993
Review of: *Molte Chiese cristiane* by Cereti, Giovanni. In: *Civilta* 3:307-308 Ag 7-21 1993
Review of: *A concise dictionary of theology* by O'Collins, Gerald, 1931-, and Farrugia, Edward G. In: *Eph Theol Lovan* 78:178 Ap 1992
Review of: *Christian unity* by Alberigo, Giuseppe, ed. In: *Gregorianum* 73 No 4:768-770 1992
Review of: *Giovanni Calvino: Il riformatore e la sua influenza sulla cultura occidentale* by McGrath, Alister E. In: *Gregorianum* 74 No 1:181-182 1993
Review of: *L'unità della Chiesa: un dibattito e un progetto* by Sartori, Luigi. In: *Eph Theol Lovan* 78:179 Ap 1992
Review of: *La Lettera ai Romani (1515-1516)* by Lutero, Martin. In: *Eph Theol Lovan* 78:461-462 D 1992
Review of: *La riforma protestante nell'Italia del Cinquecento* by Caponetto, Salvatore. In: *Gregorianum* 74 no 2:394 1993
Review of: *Salvation outside the Church* by Sullivan, Francis Aloysius. In: *Eph Theol Lovan* 69:198-200 Ap 1993

Verdonck, C.
Review of: *Éterniser sa vie* by Evely, L. In: *NRT* 115:120 Ja-F 1993
Review of: *La vie la mort* by Mertens, C. In: *NRT* 115:119-120 Ja-F 1993

Verheyden, Jacques R.
Review of: *"Arkandisziplin", Allegorese, Mystagogie* by Jacob, Christoph. In: *Eph Theol Lovan* 78:454-456 D 1992
Une prière pour le renouveau de Jérusalem le Psaume 51. *Eph Theol Lovan* 78:257-283 D 1992

Vernette, Jean.
Les sectes, nouveaux mouvements religieux, et la nouvelle religiosité en Europe. *Lumen* 47:439-450 D 1992 *see* Leneuf, Nicolas, jt auth

Vervenne, Marc.
Review of: *A Greek-English lexicon of the septuagint* by Lust, Johan, et al, eds. In: *Eph Theol Lovan* 69:118-124 Ap 1993
Review of: *Exodus vertaald en verklaard, vol 2* by Houtman, C. In: *Eph Theol Lovan* 78:407-409 D 1992
Review of: *Exodus vertaald en verklaard, vol I* by Houtman, C. In: *Eph Theol Lovan* 78:407-409 D 1992 *see* Burggraeve, Roger, jt ed; Jagersma, H, jt ed

Veto, M.
Review of: *La créatin selon Schelling* by Brito, Emilio. In: *Eph Theol Lovan* 78:175-176 Ap 1992

Veuthey, Michel. *see* Duchesneau, Claude, jt auth

Veverka, Fayette Breaux.
The Education of American Catholics: shaping the third millenium. *Listening* 28:28-40 Wint 1993

Viau, Marcel.
Le discours théologique et son objet: perspectives neo-pragmatistes. *Laval Theol Phil* 49:233-248 Je 1993

Vickers, Susan. *see* Kramer, Richard, jt auth

Victor, Jeffrey S.
Satanic panic: the creation of a contemporary legend. Chicago: Open Court, 1993. x, 408p ISBN 08-1269-191-1 LC 93-995

Vidal, Marciano.
Moral fundamental en el nuevo catecismo. *Christus* 58:42-50 Je 1993

Vidulich, Dorothy.
If underground, women's press mulitiplies. *Nat Cath Rep* 29:2 Ja 15 1993
Institute offers revenue, revival for neighborhoods. *Nat Cath Rep* 29:7 Mr 5 1993
Mahony preaches life as "seamless garment" to pro-life marchers. *Nat Cath Rep* 29:3-4 F 5 1993
News at Pantex bittersweet. *Nat Cath Rep* 29:6 F 26 1993
Old guard hangs in there at meeting on church future. *Nat Cath Rep* 29:3 O 1 1993
The price of helping the poor. *Nat Cath Rep* 29:4 Ap 9 1993

Vidulich, Dorothy. *(cont'd)*
Small church communities wax. *Nat Cath Rep* 29:4 Jl 16 1993
Social ministers ask Congress to consider families [Social ministry gathering, F 28-Mr 3 1993, Washington, DC]. *Nat Cath Rep* 29:3 Mr 12 1993
Some Roman Catholic women who won't take no for an answer. *Nat Cath Rep* 29:7 Mr 26 1993
Stewardship also requires greenbacks, critic says. *Nat Cath Rep* 29:9 Ja 8 1993
Texas university aids migrants [photos]. *Nat Cath Rep* 30:16-17 O 29 1993 *see* Jones, Arthur C, 1936-, jt auth

Vigil, José María.
Que queda de la opcion por los pobres? *Christus* 58:7-19 Ag 1993 *see* Casaldáliga, Pedro, Bp, 1928-, jt auth

Viladesau, Richard.
Review of: *Systematic theology, vol 1* by Pannenberg, Wolfhart. In: *TheolStds* 54:171-173 Mr 1993

Villa, Federica. *see* Casetti, Francesco, jt ed

Villano, Mark.
The world of film. *ChrWorld* 236:270-275 N-D 1993

Villegas, Beltrán M.
El hombre Jesús. *Teol Vida* 34 no 1-2:29-38 1993
Redaccón y tradici5aon en Ef 2, 11-22. *Teol Vida* 33 no 3-4:179-184 1992

Vincent, Francis T.
A view of Oxfordshire and St Edmund Campion. *America* 168:4-5 Ap 24 1993

Vincie, Catherine.
The liturgical assembly: review and reassessment. *Worship* 67:123-144 Mr 1993

Vincie, Catherine, and Doss, Joe Morris.
Victims of violence [exc fr *Liturgy: ritual and reconciliation; Liturgy: ethics and justice*]. *Liturgy* 10:24-26 Spr 1993

Vinh, Alphonse.
Probing Russian Orthodox spirituality. *New Oxford Rev* 60:17-20 My 1993

Virkler, Henry A.
Broken promises: understanding, healing and preventing affairs in Christian marriage. Dallas: Word Publishing, 1992. x, 306p ISBN 0-8499-0838-8 LC 91-39489

Visotzky, Burton L.
Review of: *Parables in Midrash* by Stern, David. In: *CBQ* 55:183-184 Ja 1993

Visser, Dirk.
Worsening crisis in the Dutch Church. *Tablet* 247:797-798 Je 19 1993

Vivian, Tim.
Reading the saints: early monastic texts and resources available in English. *Cist Stud* 28:17-58 1993
Review of: *Seeds of non-violence* by Dear, John, 1959-. In: *Cist Stud* 27 No 4:[114]-[115] 1992
Review of: *The eye of the storm* by Leech, Kenneth, 1939-. In: *Cist Stud* 28 no 2:[44]-[45] 1993
Review of: *The glowing mind: prayer in some Caroline Divines* by Byrom, John. In: *Cist Stud* 27 No 4:[81] 1992
Review of: *The mind in the heart: Michael Ramsey: theologian and man of prayer* by Kendall, Lorna. In: *Cist Stud* 27 No 4:[109] 1992

Viviano, Benedict.
Eight beatitudes from Qumran [photos]. *BibleT* 31:219-224 Jl 1993

Vogel, Carl.
Is there room for justice in your backyard? *Salt* 13:6-11 Ap 1993

Vogels, Walter A.
Review of: *'n Narratologiese ondersoek van die boek Jona* by Potgieter, J H. In: *OTA* 16:182 F 1993
Review of: *Beobachtungen zu der Plagenerzählung in Exodus* by Schmidt, Ludwig. In: *CBQ* 55:350-351 Ap 1993
Review of: *Kol haddĕbārîm hā'ēlleh* by Bauer, Uwe F W. In: *OTA* 15:493 O 1992
Review of: *La théophanie du Sinaï, Ex 19-24: exégèse et théologie* by Renaud, Bernard. In: *CBQ* 55:130-131 Ja 1993
Review of: *Pentateuchal and Deuteronomistic studies* by Brekelmans, Chris, and Lust, Johan, eds. In: *CBQ* 54:817-818 O 1992

Vogue, Albert de.
From the coenobium to solitude: the history of a monastic vocation. *Word Sp* 15:51-68 1993
The life of St Benedict: Gregory the Great. Petersham: St Bede's Publications, 1993. x, 186p ISBN 0-932506-77-1 LC 93-420

Volf, Miroslav.
Catholicity of "two or three": free church reflections on the catholicity of the local church. *Jurist* 52 no 1:525-546 1992
Exclusion and embrace: theological reflections in the wake of "ethnic cleansing". *JEcumen Stds* 29:230-248 Spr 1992

Vollaro, Daniel R.
Review of: *Organized labor and the Church* by Higgins, George G, 1916-. In: *Nat Cath Rep* 29:14 S 3 1993

Volpe, L.
Review of: *Aufbrüche in eine neue Verantwortung* by Hunold, G W, and Kappes, C, eds. In: *NRT* 115:117-118 Ja-F 1993
Review of: *Doctrina social de la Iglesia* by Camacho, Ildefonso. In: *NRT* 114:917 N-D 1992
Review of: *Donna in questione* by Militello, C. In: *NRT* 115:584-585 Jl-Ag 1993
Review of: *Imparare a credere* by Ardusso, Franco. In: *NRT* 115:578 Jl-Ag 1993
Review of: *Impegno cristiano* by Frosini, G. In: *NRT* 115:578 Jl-Ag 1993
Review of: *Jours du Seigneur*. In: *NRT* 114:904-905 N-D 1992
Review of: *L'Église catholique pour ou contre le libéralisme?* by Baboin-Jaubert, A. In: *NRT* 114:914 N-D 1992
Review of: *L'évangile de Marc* by Hervieux, J. In: *NRT* 114:941 N-D 1992
Review of: *L'identità cristiana oggi*. In: *NRT* 115:594 Jl-Ag 1993

Volpe, L. *(cont'd)*
Review of: *La cause des pauvres* by Durand, A. In: *NRT* 115:147 Ja-F 1993
Review of: *La dérive totalitaire du libéralisme* by Schooyans, Michel. In: *NRT* 114:913-914 N-D 1992
Review of: *Liturgia* by Augé, M. In: *NRT* 115:578 Jl-Ag 1993
Review of: *Llengua i catecisme de Mallorca: entre la pastoral i la politica* by Batle, J Amengual I. In: *NRT* 114:905 N-D 1992
Review of: *Psicopedagogia e agire cristiano* by Colonna, F S. In: *NRT* 115:150-151 Ja-F 1993
Review of: *Séparés, divorcés, une possible espérance* by Salaün, P. In: *NRT* 115:117 Ja-F 1993
Review of: *Solidarité et développement: l'engagement de l'Église catholique.* In: *NRT* 115:146-147 Ja-F 1993
Review of: *Soziales Denken in einer zerrissenen Welt* by Kerber, W, and Müller, J, eds. In: *NRT* 114:917-918 N-D 1992
Review of: *Sterbehilfe und Menschenwürde* by Schockenhoff, E. In: *NRT* 115:119 Ja-F 1993
Review of: *Une pensée sociale catholique* by Cuche, Fr-X. In: *NRT* 114:914-915 N-D 1992

Voyé, Liliane.
Response to Hervé Legrand. *Jurist* 52 no 1:401-410 1992

Vree, Dale.
Review of: *Vocation of peace* by Zahn, Gordon C. In: *New Oxford Rev* 60:30 O 1993
Review of: *Works of mercy* by Eichenberg, Fritz. In: *New Oxford Rev* 60:31-32 Je 1993
Why was Christ a male? *Register* 69:5 Ja 10 1993

Vree, Maria Valencia.
Review of: *Disposable people? The plight of refugees* by Mayotte, Judy. In: *New Oxford Rev* 60:27-28 Jl-Ag 1993
Review of: *The concentration can* by Lejeune, Jerome. In: *New Oxford Rev* 60:29-30 Je 1993

W

Waal, Esther de.
Coming home: encountering the Rule of St. Benedict. *Word Sp* 15:78-86 1993
Review of: *Candle inthe darkness: Celtic spirituality from Wales* by Thomas, Patrick. In: *Tablet* 247:1302 O 9 1993
Review of: *God failed to enfold me: praying in the Celtic tradition* by Calvert, Mary. In: *Tablet* 247:1302-1303 O 9 1993
Review of: *The Celtic way* by Bradley, Ian. In: *Tablet* 247:1302 O 9 1993
Review of: *The Celtic year* by Toulson, Shirley. In: *Tablet* 247:1302-1303 O 9 1993
Review of: *The elements of Celtic Christianity* by Duncan, Anthony. In: *Tablet* 247:1302 O 9 1993
Review of: *Wisdom of the Celtic saints* by Sellner, Edward Cletus. In: *Tablet* 247:1302 O 9 1993

Waal, Victor A de.
Review of: *Spiritual direction and the encounter with God: a theological inquiry* by Barry, William A. In: *Cist Stud* 28:[4]-[5] 1993

Wagner, Christine.
Review of: *Generous lives* by Redmont, Jane. In: *Sisters* 65:138 Mr 1993

Wagner, David.
Can abortion be curbed? A report from Saint Louis. *Crisis* 11:18-19 Ap 1993
Sorry, the numbers were cooked. *Register* 69:5 Ap 25 1993

Wagner, Harald.
Ekklesiologische optionen Evangelischer Theologie als Mögliche Leitbilder der Okumene. *Catholica* 47 no 2:124-141 1993

Wagner, Marion.
Ein Kirchen bild für unsere Zeit? *Stimm Zeit* 211:533-546 Ag 1993
The new Catechism of the Catholic Church conforms to the genuine tradition of the Church, especially to the teachings of the Second Vatican Council, December 7, 1992 (Commentary).

Wagner, Mary Anthony.
The sacred world of the Christian: sensed in faith. Minnesota: The Order of St Benedict, 1993. v, 147p ISBN 0-8146-2102-3 LC 92-40431

Wagner, Nick.
Converting the liturgist. *Mod Lit* 20:12-14 N 1993

Wagner, Roseann.
The contribution of the widowed seminarian/priest. *Priest* 49:53-55 Ag 1993

Wahl, Thomas P.
The Lord's song in a foreign land [in three parts]. *Worship* 67:53-74 Ja; 194-213 My; 318-332 Jl 1993

Wainwright, Elaine.
Review of: *Women and the Genesis of Christianity* by Witherington, Ben, III. In: *Pacifica* 6:219-221 Je 1993

Wako, Gabriel Zubeir, Abp, et al.
Making dialogue work. *Origins* 23:72-76 Je 17 1993

Waldegrave, Caroline. *see* Leith, Prue, jt auth

Walden, Mary.
Annulments healing the wounds of divorce. *Liguorian* 81:20-26 Mr 1993

Waldenfels, Hans.
China im Wandel. *Stimm Zeit* 211:385-394 Je 1993

Waldron, Thomas.
As I see it—Holy Week meditations. *Furrow* 44:215-218 Ap 1993

Walgenbach, Mary David.
Our deepening relationships. *Sisters* 65:2-7 Ja 1993

Walker, David A.
Trinity and creation in the theology of St. Thomas Aquinas. *Thomist* 57:443-455 Jl 1993

Walker, Don.
Media literacy: the Vatican echoes McLuhan. *America* 168:4-5 Mr 6 1993

Walker, John F. see Vatter, Harold Goodhue, 1910-, jt auth

Walker, Margaret Urban.
Review of: *Ludwig Wittgenstein: the duty of genius* by Monk, Ray. In: *IPQ* 33:370-371 S 1993

Walker, Wyatt Tee.
The soul of black worship [exc fr *Liturgy: in daily life*]. *Liturgy* 10:56-58 Spr 1993

Wall, Barbara.
E J Oliver. *Tablet* 246:1586 D 12 1992

Wall, John N.
Review of: *Robert South (1634-1716)* by Reedy, Gerard. In: *TheolStds* 54: 600-601 S 1993
Review of: *The scale of perfection* by Hilton, Walter. In: *TheolStds* 53:785-786 D 1992

Wallace, James A, 1944-.
Enchanted April. *Liguorian* 81:43 F 1993
The funeral liturgy communicating peace and hope. *Liguorian* 81:53 Mr 1993
Lorenzo's oil. *Liguorian* 81:35 Je 1993
Love field. *Liguorian* 81:51 Jl 1993
Malcolm X [directed by S Lee]. *Liguorian* 81:43 Ap 1993
Media education at home. *Liguorian* 81:49 S 1993
Not just another political speech. *Liguorian* 81:51 Ja 1993
Passion fish. *Liguorian* 81:51 Jl 1993
The promise of Easter. *Liguorian* 81:4-7 Ap 1993
Reconciliation: restored to full health and grace. *Liguorian* 81:4-9 Mr 1993
Reconsidering the parish mission. *Worship* 67:340-351 Jl 1993
Review of: *Amusing ourselves to death* by Postman, Neil. In: *Liguorian* 81:43 O 1993
Review of: *New Adam* by Culbertson, Philip. In: *New Theol Rev* 6:104-105 Ag 1993
Review of: *Seasons of faith and conscience: kairos, confession, liturgy* by Kellermann, Bill Wylie. In: *New Theol Rev* 6:99-100 F 1993
Review of: *The electronic golden calf: images, religion and the making of meaning* by Goethals, Gregor T. In: *Liguorian* 81:43 O 1993
Review of: *The inference that makes science* by McMullin, Ernan. In: *Thomist* 57:131-132 Ja 1993
Sommersby. *Liguorian* 81:35 Je 1993
Truly, madly deeply. *Liguorian* 81:43 F 1993
TV mothers and fathers. *Liguorian* 81:45 My 1993
TV sweeps and stats. *Liguorian* 81:51 Ag 1993

Wallace, Ruth A.
Catholic women more open to change than Catholic men. *Nat Cath Rep* 29: 28 O 8 1993

Wallis, Joe L.
Integrating the ideas of dissenting economists into a theory of transforamational leadership. *RSocEcon* 51:14-39 Spr 1993

Walls, Alma Marie.
Review of: *Touching the holy: ordinariness, self-esteem, and friendship* by Wicks, Robert A. In: *Sisters* 65:226 My 1993

Walls, Roland.
Review of: *The radical tradition* by Markus, Gilbert, ed. In: *Priests & People* 7:83-84 F 1993

Walmsley, G.
Review of: *Lonergan workshop, v VI* by Lawrence, Fred, ed. In: *Heythrop* 34: 113-114 Ja 1993

Walsh, A.
Review of: *Isabel of Spain: the Catholic queen* by Carroll, Warren H. In: *SocJust* 84:30-31 Ja-F 1993

Walsh, Brian.
Review of: *A place for all—American essays in liturgy* by Harrington, Mary Theresa. In: *Priests & People* 7:125-126 Mr 1993
Review of: *In heaven there are no thunderstorms—celebrating the liturgy with developmentally disabled people* by Okhuijsen, Gijs, and Opzeeland, Cees von. In: *Priests & People* 7:125-126 Mr 1993

Walsh, Catherine.
Bang the drum—not: Women-Church in the desert. *Comm* 120:6-7 Je 4 1993
Carnage in the Balkans. *St Anth* 100:32-33 Mr 1993
Catholic relief services. *St Anth* 100:41 S 1993
Peter Lynch: applying Wall Street wizardry to Catholic schools. *St Anth* 100: 16-22 My 1993
Stage is set for Aristide's return. *St Anth* 101:42 Ag 1993

Walsh, David.
Newman on the secular need for religious education. *F & R* 28:359-385 Wint 1992

Walsh, Denis.
Review of: *The universe story* by Swimme, Brian, and Berry, Thomas. In: *CrossCurr* 43:107-110 Spr 1993

Walsh, J Leo, and McQueen, Moira M.
Law, ethics, and language: the House of Lords and Tony Bland. *Can Cath Rev* 11:6-8 Jl-Ag 1993

Walsh, James L.
Review of: *Who lives? who dies? ethical criteria in patient selection* by Kilner, John F. In: *Linacre* 60:94-95 Ag 1993

Walsh, Jerome T.
Review of: *"Had God not been on my side": an examination of the narrative technique of the story of Jacob and Laban, Genesis 29, 1-32, 2* by Sherwood, Stephen K. In: *CBQ* 54:767 O 1992

Walsh, Jill Paton.
Review of: *A responsible man* by Kee, Cynthia. In: *Tablet* 247:440 Ap 3 1993
Review of: *Einstein's dreams* by Lightman, Alan. In: *Tablet* 247:518 Ap 24 1993
Review of: *The Green Knight* by Murdoch, Iris. In: *Tablet* 247:1236 S 25 1993

Walsh, John E.
Peter and the ghost. *HPR* 93:24-28 My 1993

Walsh, John J. see DiGiacomo, James J, jt auth

Walsh, Joseph L.
Review of: *Isaac Hecker* by O'Brien, David J, 1938-. In: *CrossCurr* 42:542-545 Wint 1992-1993

Walsh, Julia A. see Warren, Jeffrey A, jt auth

Walsh, Katherine.
Aubrey Gwynn—the scholar. *Studies* 81:385-392 Wint 1992

Walsh, Liam G.
Anglican/Roman Catholic dialogue: where we stand now. *Doctr Life* 43:3-12 Ja 1993
Thomas the thinker [review article *The thought of Thomas Acquinas* by B Davies]. *Doctr Life* 43:156-161 Mr 1993

Walsh, Michael J, 1937-.
At the top of the class. *Tablet* 247:994-995 Jl 31 1993
Review of: *A view from Rome on the eve of the MOdernist crisis* by Schultenover, David G. In: *Tablet* 247:1006-1007 Ag 7 1993
Review of: *City steeple, city streets: saints' tales from Granada and a changing Spain* by Slater, Candace. In: *Heythrop* 34:215 Ap 1993
Review of: *Mary Magdalen* by Haskins, Susan. In: *Tablet* 247:1296 O 9 1993
Review of: *The victory of the cross* by O'Grady, Desmond. In: *Tablet* 247:173 F 6 1993
Schools at the crossroads. *Tablet* 247:226 F 13 1993
Those English liberals. *Tablet* 247:1006-1007 Ag 7 1993

Walsh, Michael J, 1937-, and Wijngaards, John.
Europe's new religions. *Tablet* 247:448-449 Ap 3 1993

Walsh, Richard.
Between classes: a time to reach out. *Catechist* 26:18+ Mr 1993
Let's hear it for doctrine. *ReligTJ* 27:38-39 Ap-My 1993
On the front line: who's minding the door? *Priest* 49:19-20 Jl 1993

Walsh, Terrance G.
Review of: *Hegel and the Spirit* by Olson, Alan M. In: *TheolStds* 54:571-573 S 1993

Walter, James J.
Review of: *A theology of compromise: a study of method in the ethics of Charles E Curran* by Grecco, Richard. In: *Horizons (CTS)* 20:188-189 Spr 1993

Walter, Vogels.
Review of: *The protest and the silence: suffering, death, and biblical theology* by Milazzo, G Tom. In: *OTA* 16:439 Je 1993

Walter Scott.
Ever old, yet ever new. *Register* 69:5 F 7 1993

Walters, Hugh.
Mary Magdalene. *Doctr Life* 43:363-365 Jl-Ag 1993
Review of: *Ethics and the environment* by Taylor, C G W. In: *New Blckfrs* 73:578-579 N 1992
Review of: *The earth beneath—a critical guide to green theology* by Ball, Ian, et al, eds. In: *New Blckfrs* 73:578-579 N 1992

Walters, Michael.
Church courts weigh the history of a marriage. *Register* 69:1+ S 19 1993
Church tribunals look after the supreme good of souls. *Register* 69:1+ S 26 1993
On the letter and the spirit of church law. *Register* 69:1+ S 5 1993
What God has joined. *Register* 69:1+ S 12 1993

Walthall, Barbara.
Art comes to life at St Ann School. *Momentum* 24:56-57 F-Mr 1993

Walton, James.
Cliffhanger [directed by R Harlin]. *Tablet* 247:864 Jl 3 1993
Madame Bovary [directed by C Chabrol]. *Tablet* 247:760 Je 1993
Review of: *Alfred Gregory's Everest*. In: *Tablet* 247:584 My 8 1993
Review of: *Ancient land: sacred ritual* by Lowenstein, Tom. In: *Tablet* 247:584 My 8 1993
Review of: *Balooning over Everest* by Dickinson, Leo. In: *Tablet* 247:584 My 8 1993
Review of: *Beyond Ararat* by Selby, Bettina. In: *Tablet* 247:584 My 8 1993
Review of: *Caught ina mirror: reflections of Japan* by Martineau, Lisa. In: *Tablet* 247:584 My 8 1993
Review of: *Falling off the map* by Iyer, Pico. In: *Tablet* 247:584 My 8 1993
Review of: *Inshallah* by Fallaci, Oriana. In: *Tablet* 247:312 Mr 6 1993
Review of: *It's all true* by Rambali, Paul. In: *Tablet* 247:584 My 8 1993
Review of: *Jonathan Carver's travels through America 1766-68* by Gelb, Norman, ed. In: *Tablet* 247:584-585 My 8 1993
Review of: *Light* by Lindgren, Torgny. In: *Tablet* 247:792 Je 19 1993
Review of: *The autonomous region* by Jamie, Kathleen, and Smith, Sean Mayne. In: *Tablet* 247:584 My 8 1993
Review of: *The captain's wife: South American journals of Martha Graham 1821-3* by Mavor, Elizabeth. In: *Tablet* 247:584 My 8 1993
Review of: *The last elephant* by Gavron, Jeremy. In: *Tablet* 247:584 My 8 1993
Review of: *The taming of eagles* by Edwards-Jones, Imogen. In: *Tablet* 247: 584 My 8 1993

Walton, Janet R. see Hoffman, Lawrence A, jt ed; Proctor-Smith, Marjorie, jt auth

Walton, John H. see Hill, Andrew E, jt auth

Walton, Rivkah.
Beyond sentimentality: consciousful design of ceremonial objects. *CrossCurr* 43:82-91 Spr 1993

Wangler, Joan Norman.
Forgiving an ex-spouse who walked out. *Liguorian* 81:49-51 O 1993

Wangler, Thomas E.
Americanist beliefs and papal orthodoxy: 1884-1899. *US Cath Hist* 11:37-52 Sum 1993

Wankenne, A.
Review of: *À ciel ouvert sur les ailes de l'Ange.* In: *NRT* 115:156 Ja-F 1993
Review of: *À prix d'or* by Kraus, H. In: *NRT* 115:138-139 Ja-F 1993
Review of: *Les saints patrons des métiers en Belgique* by Heirwegh, J-J, and Belle, J-L van. In: *NRT* 115:137 Ja-F 1993

Wanous, Suzanne.
Learning prayers by heart. *Catechist* 27:40-41 O 1993

Wansbrough, Henry.
Review of: *Chambers dictionary of beliefs and religion* by Goring, Rosemary, ed. In: *Tablet* 247:950 Jl 24 1993
Review of: *Did Jesus know he was God?* by Dreyfus, Francois. In: *Priests & People* 6:437-438 N 1992
Review of: *From Jewish prophet to Gentile God* by Casey, Maurice. In: *Priests & People* 6:437-438 N 1992
Review of: *James and the Q sayings of Jesus* by Hartin, Patrick J. In: *Priests & People* 6:439 N 1992
Review of: *Jesus and the oral gospel tradition* by Wansbrough, Henryenry, ed. In: *Priests & People* 6:437-438 N 1992
Review of: *Matthew, evangelist and teacher* by Frances, R T. In: *Priests & People* 6:435 N 1992
Review of: *Persuasive artistry* by Watson, Duane F, ed. In: *Priests & People* 6:435-436 N 1992
Review of: *Picking the "right" Bible study program* by Scott, Macrina. In: *Priests & People* 6:486 D 1992
Review of: *Possessions and the life of faith, a reading of Luke-Acts* by Gillman, John. In: *Priests & People* 6:435-436 N 1992
Review of: *Responses to 101 questions on the Dead Sea Scrolls* by Fitzmyer, Joseph Augustine, 1920-. In: *Tablet* 247:721-722 Je 5 1993
Review of: *The art of performance: towards a theology of Holy Scripture* by Young, Frances. In: *Heythrop* 34:188-189 Ap 1993
Review of: *The Book of Revelation* by Giblin, Charles Homer. In: *Priests & People* 6:486 D 1992
Review of: *The climax of the covenant* by Wright, Nicholas Thomas. In: *Priests & People* 6:439 N 1992
Review of: *The Dead Sea scrolls deception* by Baigent, Michael, and Leigh, Richard. In: *Priests & People* 6:440 N 1992
Review of: *The Dead Sea Scrolls uncovered* by Eisenman, Robert H, and Wise, Michael. In: *Tablet* 247:721-722 Je 5 1993
Review of: *The Gospel according to Saint Mark* by Hooker, Morna D. In: *Priests & People* 6:435-436 N 1992
Review of: *The gospel and the gospels* by Stuhlmacher, P, ed. In: *Priests & People* 6:437-438 N 1992
Review of: *The historical Jesus* by Crossan, John Dominic. In: *Priests & People* 6:437-438 N 1992
Review of: *The interpretation of the New Testament 1861-1986* by Neill, Stephen, and Wright, Tom. In: *Priests & People* 6:485-486 D 1992
Review of: *The Messianic secret in Mark's Gospel* by Räisänen, Heikki. In: *Priests & People* 6:435-436 N 1992
Review of: *The passion of Jesus in the Gospel of John* by Senior, Donald. In: *Priests & People* 6:435-436 N 1992
Review of: *The pre-Christian Paul* by Hengel, Martin. In: *Priests & People* 6:439 N 1992
Review of: *The prophetic gospel* by Hanson, Anthony Tyrrell. In: *Priests & People* 6:435-436 N 1992
Review of: *The theology of the Letter to the Hebrews* by Lindars, Barnabas. In: *Priests & People* 6:439 N 1992
Review of: *The theology of the second letter to the Corinthians* by O'Connor, Jerome Murphy. In: *Priests & People* 6:439 N 1992
Review of: *Understanding the Dead Sea Scrolls* by Shanks, Hershel, ed. In: *Tablet* 247:721-722 Je 5 1993
Review of: *Understanding the Fourth Gospel* by Ashton, John. In: *Priests & People* 6:435-436 N 1992
Review of: *What are they saying about John?* by Sloyan, Gerard S. In: *Priests & People* 6:486 D 1992

Ward, Anthony.
The Codex Pagesianus: witness to church renewal. *ABenR* 44:308-333 S 1993

Ward, Benedicta. see Smith, Lesley, jt ed

Ward, Donald.
A cautionary tale. *Can Cath Rev* 11:6-8 Ja 1993
Our Lady of Bellevue [editorial]. *Can Cath Rev* 11:2-4 O 1993

Ward, Graham.
George Steiner and the theology of culture. *New Blckfrs* 74:98-105 F 1993
Review of: *God without being* by Marion, Jean-Luc. In: *New Blckfrs* 74:55-56 Ja 1993
Tragedy as subclause: George Steiner's dialogue with Donald MacKinnon. *Heythrop* 34:274-287 Jl 1993

Ward, Hannah.
Boundary-dwellers. *Way* 33:97-105 Ap 1993

Ward, Hannah, and Lord, Elizabeth.
Review of: *An easier yoke? a perspective on Christian ministry* by Rowe, Trevor. In: *Way* 33:164 Ap 1993
Review of: *Living the vision: religious vows in the age of change* by Fiand, Barbara. In: *Way* 33:165 Ap 1993
Review of: *New beginnings in ministry* by Murphy, James H, ed. In: *Way* 33:164-165 Ap 1993

Ward, Hannah, and Wild, Jennifer.
Review of: *Changing women, changing church* by Uhr, Marie Louise. In: *Way* 33:258 Jl 1993
Review of: *Refusing holy orders* by Sahgal, Gita, and Yuval-Davis, Nira. In: *Way* 33:257 Jl 1993
Review of: *The voice of the turtledove* by Brotherton, Anne, ed. In: *Way* 33:258 Jl 1993
Review of: *They call her pastor* by Wallace, Ruth A. In: *Way* 33:259 Jl 1993
Review of: *Wives of Catholic clergy* by Fichter, Joseph H. In: *Way* 33:259 Jl 1993

Ward, Keith.
Review of: *An introduction to the philosophy of religion* by Davies, Brian. In: *New Blckfrs* 74:430 S 1993

Ward, Keith. *(cont'd)*
Review of: *Revelation: from metaphor to analogy* by Swinburne, Richard. In: *New Blckfrs* 74:47-49 Ja 1993

Ward, Sheila.
The role of women in the evolutionary process. *Teilhard Rev* 28:25-26 Sum 1993

Ward, W. R.
Review of: *Cane Ridge: America's Pentecost* by Conkin, Paul K. In: *Heythrop* 34:344-345 Jl 1993

Wardlaw, Harry.
Review of: *Christian theology and inter-religious dialogue* by Wiles, Maurice. In: *Pacifica* 6:355-357 O 1993

Wardle, Lynn D, 1947-.
Conscience clauses offer little protection [excerpt fr *Journal of logal medicine*]. *Health Prog* 74:79-83 Jl-Ag 1993

Ware, Ann Patrick.
Review of: *Springs of water in a dry land: spiritual survival for Catholic women today* by Weaver, Mary Jo. In: *Nat Cath Rep* 29:23 Mr 26 1993

Warner, Ed.
Review of: *George F Kennan and the making of American foreign policy, 1947-1950* by Miscamble, Wilson D. In: *Crisis* 11:55-56 My 1993

Warren, Jeffrey A, and Walsh, Julia A.
Portal to the community. *Health Prog* 74:37-40 Jl-Ag 1993

Warren, Michael, 1935-.
Celebration, judgment, practice. *Furrow* 44:199-207 Ap 1993
Faith, culture, and the worshipping community: shaping the practice of the local church. Washington, DC: The Pastoral Press, 1993. x, 194p ISBN 1-56929-002-4
The local church and its practice of the gospel: the materiality of discipleship in a catechesis of liberation. *Worship* 67:433-460 S 1993
Youth evangelization and counter-evangelization. *Living Light* 30:42-52 Aut 1993 see Scott, Kieran, jt auth

Washington, Harold C.
Review of: *Judith—eine Frau im Spannungsfeld von Autonomie und göttlicher Führung* by Hellmann, Monika. In: *OTA* 16:422 Je 1993

Waskow, Arthur.
Review of: *Boys will be boys: breaking the link between masculinity and violence* by Miedzian, Myriam. In: *CrossCurr* 42:539-542 Wint 1992-1993

Waters, John.
Can the Church reclaim our common conscience? *Furrow* 44:263-272 My 1993

Waters, William R.
A review of the troops: social economics in the twentieth century. *RSocEcon* 51:262-286 Aut 1993
Review of: *Opportunity knocks: American economic policy after Gorbachev* by Solo, Robert A. In: *RSocEcon* 51:103-105 Spr 1993

Watkins, Clare.
Collaborators, informers and secret service. *New Blckfrs* 74:263-279 My 1993

Watley, William D.
Singing the Lord's song in a strange land: the African-American churches and ecumenism. Grand Rapids: Eerdmans, 1993. 188p ISBN 0-8028-0711-9

Watson, Gordon.
Review of: *The Göttingen dogmatics: instruction in the Christian religion, vol I* by Barth, Karl, 1886-1968. In: *Pacifica* 6:236-239 Je 1993

Watson, Nigel.
Review of: *The climax of the covenant* by Wright, Nicholas Thomas. In: *Pacifica* 6:337-340 O 1993
Review of: *The Gospel according to Saint Matthew, volume II* by Davies, W D, and Allison, Dale C. In: *Pacifica* 6:104-106 F 1993

Watson, Wilfred G E.
Review of: *The Bible in the light of cuneiform literature: scripture in context III* by Hallo, William W, et al, eds. In: *CBQ* 54:821-822 O 1992

Watt, William Montgomery.
Islamic attitudes to other religions. *StudiaM* 42:245-255 1993
Islamic fundamentalism. *StudiaM* 41:241-252 1992

Watté, Pierre.
Anthropologie et philosophie: un double retour au fondement. *RPhil Louvain* 91:207-227 My 1993

Wauck, Mark A.
The Alba House Gospels: so you may believe. New York: Society of St Paul, 1992. x, 92p ISBN 0-8189-0625-1 LC 91-40303

Wawrykow, Joseph.
Review of: *Thomas Aquinas: an evangelical appraisal* by Geisler, Norman L. In: *Thomist* 57:529-532 Jl 1993

Wayman, Alex.
The Buddhist attitude toward Hinduism. *StudiaM* 42:329-345 1993

Weafer, John A.
A Church in recession—three national surveys, 1974-1992. *Furrow* 44:219-225 Ap 1993

Weakland, Rembert G, Abp, 1927-.
A challenge of peace: North-South dialogue. *Origins* 23:292-296 O 7 1993
Faith and the human enterprise: a post-Vatican II vision. Maryknoll: Orbis Books, 1992. 168p ISBN 0-88344-835-1 LC 92-32884
Herald of hope [repr fr the *Catholic Herald*]. *LADOC* 23:23-24 Mr-Ap 1993
The song of the Church. *Origins* 23:12-16 My 20 1993 see O'Connor, John, Cardinal, jt auth

Weakland, Rembert G, Abp, 1927-, and Eastman, Theodore, Bp.
Reconciling unity and plurality. *Origins* 22:587-588 F 4 1993

Weales, Gerald, 1925-.
Angels in America. *Comm* 120:19-20 Jl 16 1993
Faith healer. *Comm* 120:16 Mr 12 1993
Fool moon. *Comm* 120:24 Ap 9 1993

Whalen, C.
Review of: *Losing time: the industrial policy debate* by Graham, Otis L, Jr. In: *RSocEcon* 50:348-353 Fall 1992

Whalen, Michael.
Review of: *Building bridges: gay and lesbian reality and the Catholic Church* by Nugent, Robert, and Gramick, Jeannine. In: *Living Light* 29:90-91 Wint 1992
Review of: *The story of the Christian year* by Nardone, Richard M. In: *Living Light* 29:88-89 Aut 1992

Whalen, William J.
Hinduism: what do you know about the world's oldest religion? *USCath* 58: 25-29 Ap 1993
What do Southern Baptists believe? *USCath* 58:22-27 S 1993

Whalon, Michael D.
Seasons and feasts of the church year. New York: Paulist Press, 1993. 180p ISBN 0-8091-3346-6 LC 92-24215

Whalon, Pierre W.
A response to Chris Barrigar's social theory, language, and the crisis in Anglican pluralism. *JEcumen Stds* 29:461-465 Sum-Aut 1992

Wheeler, Edward T.
Review of: *Arcadia* by Crace, Jim. In: *Comm* 120:26-27 Je 18 1993
Review of: *English music* by Ackroyd, Peter. In: *Comm* 120:25 Mr 26 1993

Whelan, Joseph P.
How I pray now [a conversation with Thomas H. Stahel]. *America* 169:17-20 N 20 1993

Whelan, Michael.
When anomalies consistently appear at the interface between learning and experience we must act. *Stud Form Spir* 14:271-285 My 1993

White, Barry.
Public life in Northern Ireland. *Furrow* 43:656-662 D 1992

White, Benton J.
Taking the Bible seriously. Louisville: Westminster, 1993. x, 192p ISBN 0-664-25452-7

White, Faye E.
A monastic and a firefighter. *Sisters* 65:30-34 Ja 1993

White, Graham.
William of Ockham andAdam Wodeham. *Heythrop* 34:296-302 Jl 1993

White, Harry. see Gillen, Gerard, jt ed

White, Jane H.
Antitrust law may be a barrier to collaboration. *Health Prog* 74:22-24+ Jl-Ag 1993
Basic health benefits: deciding what to cover. *Health Prog* 74:8-10 Je 1993
Cutting through the confusion of managed competition. *Health Prog* 74:10-12+ Mr 1993
Global budgets: a key to Clinton's reform strategy? *Health Prog* 74:10-12 Ap 1993
Hospital-physician relationships: a hurdle on the road to reform. *Health Prog* 74:12-13+ 1993
A postelection look at healthcare reform. *Health Prog* 74:12-15 Ja-F 1993
What will healthcare reform cost? *Health Prog* 74:15-17+ My 1993

White, John L.
Review of: *The purpose of Romans: a comparative letter structure investigation* by Jervis, L Ann. In: *CBQ* 55:158-160 Ja 1993

White, Joseph M.
The diocesan seminary and the community of faith: reflections from the American experience [photos]. *US Cath Hist* 11:1-20 Wint 1993

White, Kevin.
Three previously unpublished chapters from St Thomas Aquinas's commentary on Aristotle's Meteora: Sentencia Super Meteora 2 13-15. *Med Stud* 54:49-93 1993

White, Leland J.
If ministers switched to private practice? *Nat Cath Rep* 29:17-19 Ja 15 1993

White, Leland J, ed.
Helping people cope with Robertson, Ratzinger, et al [editorial]. *Bib Th Bul* 22:146-148 Wint 1992
Our adversaries are not simpleminded: people need best in biblical scholarship to meet challenge [editorial]. *Bib Th Bul* 23:2-3 Spr 1993
What if our only witness happens to be blind? [editorial]. *Bib Th Bul* 23:90 Aut 1993

White, Norm.
Review of: *The corporate reapers: the book of agribusiness* by Krebs, A. V. In: *Nat Cath Rep* 29:24 F 19 1993

White, Patricia A.
How Mary became my mother. *Liguorian* 81:46-48 O 1993

White, Patrick.
Voices in the wilderness. *Tablet* 246:1594-1596 D 19-26 1992

White, Richard.
My sad history in math. *Tod Cath Teach* 27:10 N-D 1993

White, Richard T. see Casson, Hugh, jt auth; Davies, Philip R, jt ed

White, Susan J.
Taking differences seriously [exc fr *Liturgy: practicing ecumenism*]. *Liturgy* 10:7 Spr 1993

Whitehair, M.
Review of: *Channels of healing prayer* by Heron, Benedict. In: *Sisters* 65:67 Ja 1993

Whitehead, Charles.
The disturbing charismatic renewal. *New Cov* 23:29 N 1993
It's safe to fail. *New Cov* 22:29 Jl 1993

Whitehead, Evelyn Eaton. see Whitehead, James D, jt auth

Whitehead, Evelyn Eaton, and Whitehead, James D.
Christians and their passions. *RRel* 52:702-711 S-O 1993

Whitehead, F.
Review of: *La vida loca: gang days in LA* by Rodriguez, Luis J. In: *Nat Cath Rep* 29:6 Ja 8 1993

Whitehead, James D, et al, eds.
Being a priest today. Collegeville, Minnesota: The Liturgical Press, 1992. 206p ISBN 0-81465-032-5 LC 92-4819

Whitehead, James D. see Whitehead, Evelyn Eaton, jt auth

Whitehead, Sharon.
Teaching as a vocation in the public school. *Momentum* 24:22-25 F-Mr 1993

Whitmore, Todd David.
Moral methodology and pastoral responsiveness: the case of abortion and the care of children. *TheolStds* 54:316-338 Je 1993
Review of: *The primacy of love* by Wadell, Paul J. In: *New Theol Rev* 6:117-118 Ag 1993

Whitney, Barry L.
Review of: *Society and spirit: a trinitarian cosmology* by Bracken, Joseph A. In: *Horizons (CTS)* 19:320-321 Fall 1992

Whitney, Sally.
Minority museum: fighting hatred, instilling dignity. *St Anth* 100:34-39 Ap 1993

Whyte, Gerry.
Abortion and the law. *Doctr Life* 42:253-272 My-Je 1992
Amending constitutional policy on abortion [Ireland]. *Doctr Life* 42:600-607 D 1992

Wickenhauser, Timothy.
Review of: *Mead and Merleau-Ponty: toward a common vision* by Rosenthal, Sandra B, and Bourgeois, Patrick L. In: *Mod Schlmn* 70:155-156 Ja 1993

Wicker, Brian.
After Kuwait the deluge. *New Blckfrs* 74:85-98 F 1993

Wickham, Lionel.
Response to De Halleux and Van Esbroeck. *Jurist* 52 no 1:130-137 1992

Wicks, J.
Review of: *Bartolomé De Las Casas: the only way* by Parish, Helen Rand, ed. In: *Gregorianum* 73 No 4:770-771 1992

Wicks, Robert J.
Encountering God in the third Christian millennium: a spirituality of contradiction and mystery. *ChrWorld* 236:223-226 S-O 1993

Wicks, Robert J, and Estadt, Barry K, eds.
Pastoral counseling in a global church: voices from the field. Maryknoll, New York: Orbis Books, 1993. x, 169p ISBN 0-88344-865-3 LC 93-22082

Wickstrom, John B.
Review of: *Church and chronicle in the Middle Ages: essays presented to John Taylor* by Wood, Ian, and Loud, G A, eds. In: *CHist* 79:100-101 Ja 1993

Widener, Katie.
We have been gifted. *ReligTJ* 27:33-34 Ap-My 1993

Widner, Thomas C.
The Ukrainian Catholic Church: up from the underground. *America* 169:12-15 O 23 1993

Wiebe, Donald.
Review of: *Types of Christian theology* by Frei, Hans W, 1922-1988. In: *Cithara* 32:56-58 My 1993

Wieder, Laurence, 1945-. see Atwan, Robert, jt ed

Wiegand, Ginny.
Sister Mary of the streets [condensed fr *The Philadelphia Inquirer* N 22 1992]. *CDgst* 57:34-47 Ap 1993

Wiel, C van de.
Review of: *El itinerario jurídico del Opus Dei: Historia y defensa de un carisma* by Fuenmayor, Amadeo de, et al. In: *Eph Theol Lovan* 78:492-493 D 1992
Review of: *L'itinéraire juridique de l'Opus Dei* by Fuenmayor, Amadoe de, et al. In: *Eph Theol Lovan* 78:492-493 D 1992
Review of: *Legislazione sugli ordinariati castrensi* by Baura, Eduardo. In: *Eph Theol Lovan* 78:491-492 D 1992

Wielocx, R.
Review of: *Collectanea Augustiniana: mélanges T J van Bavel* by Bruning, B, et al, eds. In: *Eph Theol Lovan* 69:146-155 Ap 1993

Wiemeyer, Joachim.
Politische Ethick und Politikverdrossenheit. *Stimm Zeit* 211:363-375 Je 1993

Wiest, J.
Review of: *La croix et le glaive: L'Eglise Catholique et l'occupation Américaine d'Haïti, 1915-1934* by Pamphile, Léon Denius. In: *CHist* 78: 698-700 O 1992
Review of: *Monaci nella tormenta: La "Passio" dei monaci trappisti di Yan-Kia-ping e di Liese testimoni della fede nella Cina di Mao-Tze-Tung* by Quattrocchi, Paolino Beltrame. In: *CHist* 78:701-702 O 1992

Wiest, Jean-Paul. see Tang, Edmond, jt ed

Wight, Jonathan C.
Preaching and the under-20 set. *HPR* 93:60-66 Jl 1993

Wigoder, Geoffrey Bernard, 1922-.
After the handshake. *Tablet* 247:1220-1221 S 25 1993
Can there be peace in Israel? *Tablet* 247:840-841 Jl 3 1993
Rabin and Arafat brave radical wrath. *Tablet* 247:1120-1121 S 4 1993

Wijngaards, John.
God's feminine touch. *Tablet* 247:683-684 My 29 1993 see Walsh, Michael J, 1937-, jt auth

Wilcken, John.
Review of: *Banyo studies* by Byrne, Neil, ed. In: *Pacifica* 6:121-122 F 1993

Wilcox, Patricia.
Influences; Influences Flood; International Folk Sing. *Spirit* 57:18-20 Spr-Sum 1992

Wilcox, William H.
Review of: *How judges reason: the logic of adjudication* by Levin, Joel. In: *Amer J Juris* 37:373-379 1992

Wild, Robert A.
Review of: *Hebrews 1-8; Hebrews 9-13* by Lane, William L. In: *CBQ* 55:163-165 Ja 1993

Wildavsky, Aaron.
Assimilation vs separation: Joseph the Administrator and the politics of religion in biblical Israel. New Brunswick, New Jersey: Transaction Publishers, 1993. x, 236p ISBN 1-56000-081-3 LC 92-20151

Wilderink, Vital Joao G.
O mosaico de Santo Domingo. *REB* 53:154-157 Mr 1993

Wiles, Maruice.
Review of: *Credo: the Apostles' Creed explained for today* by Kung, Hans, 1928-. In: *New Blckfrs* 74:422-425 S 1993

Wiles, Maurice.
Review of: *Believing three ways in one God* by Lash, Nicholas. In: *New Blckfrs* 74:422-425 S 1993

Wiley, Juli Loesch.
Why feminists and prolifers need each other. *New Oxford Rev* 60:9-14 N 1993

Wilfred, Felix.
Leave the temple: Indian paths to human liberation. Maryknoll, New York: Orbis Books, 1992. x, 199p ISBN 0-88344-794-0 LC 92-20801

Wilgenbusch, Sandra.
Let the arts come alive!. *Tod Cath Teach* 27:30-33 Ag 1993

Wilhauck, Susan.
Review of: *By what authority: a conversation on teaching among United Methodists* by Price, Elizabeth Box, and Foster, Charles R, eds. In: *Living Light* 30:105-106 Aut 1993

Wilhelmsen, Frederick D, 1923-.
Mr. Conservative. *Crisis* 11:28 O 1993

Wilken, Robert L.
Review of: *The broken staff: Judaism through Christian eyes* by Manuel, Frank Edward. In: *Comm* 120:21-22 Ja 15 1993

Wilkes, Paul, 1938-.
The forging of a freelance writer [interview by J Deedy]. *Critic* 47:22-30 Wint 1992
Harry John was not your average American Catholic [photos]. *Nat Cath Rep* 29:13-20 S 17 1993
Mostar man: "Let my son be last sacrifice". *Nat Cath Rep* 29:7-12 Ja 29 1993

Wilkins, Mark.
Review of: *Catholics and the New Age* by Pacwa, Mitch. In: *St Anth* 100:52 Mr 1993
Review of: *Recovering Catholics: what to do when religion comes between you and God* by Larsen, Earnie, and Parnegg, Janee. In: *St Anth* 100:51-52 Mr 1993
Review of: *The idea of the university: a reexamination* by Pelikan, Jaroslav. In: *St Anth* 100:50-51 S 1993
Review of: *After Jesus: the triumph of Christianity.* In: *St Anth* 101:48-49 O 1993

Wilkins, Roger, 1932-.
The "Brown" decision: 40 years later. *America* 169:4-5 Jl 17-24 1993

Wilkins, Sally.
Thomas Merton: monk and mystic. *Liguorian* 81:14-20 D 1993

Wilkinson, Gertrude A.
Listening. *Living Prayer* 26:1 Mr-Ap 1993
Reflections of a pilgrim [editorial]. *Living Prayer* 26:1 Ja-F 1993

Wilkinson, Paul.
Review of: *To the ends of the earth* by Yallop, David. In: *Tablet* 247:619 My 15 1993

Willard, Dallas.
In search of guidance: developing a conversational relationship with God. New York: HarperSanFrancisco, 1993. x, 247p ISBN 0-06-069520-x LC 92-56406

Willcock, C.
Review of: *Tonal allegory in the vocal music of J S Bach* by Chafe, Eric. In: *TheolStds* 53:760-761 D 1992

Willert, Joan St. see Kirschner, Leonard, jt auth

Willey, David.
All change in Italy. *Tablet* 247:808+ Je 26 1993
God's politician: Pope John Paul II, the Catholic Church, and the new world order. New York: St Martin's Press, 1993. x, 258p ISBN 0-31208-798-5 LC 92-36031
Italy at the cleaners. *Tablet* 247:360-361 Mr 20 1993
Looking for rain in a spiritual desert. *Tablet* 247:95-96 Ja 23 1993
Word faiths for peace. *Tablet* 247:1276-1277 O 2 1993

Willey, Eldred.
The new churches. *Tablet* 247:165-166 F 6 1993
On the streets of London. *Tablet* 247:611-612 My 15 1993 see Willey, Petroc, jt auth

Willey, Petroc, and Willey, Eldred.
The earth as a gift. *New Blckfrs* 74:60-74 F 1993

Willhauck, Susan.
Review of: *Handbook of children's religious education* by Ratcliff, Donald E, ed. In: *Living Light* 29:77-79 Wint 1992

William, Thomas Stafford, Cardinal, 1930-.
Evangelization and the Church's social teaching. *Cath Int* 4:210-214 Mv 1993

Williams, Alison.
Christians and the New Age. *Teilhard Rev* 27:88-94 Wint 1992
Review of: *A Christian in the New Age* by Spink, Peter. In: *Teilhard Rev* 27:89-91 Wint 1992
Review of: *God and the Aquarian age: the new era of the kingdom* by Smith, Adrian B. In: *Teilhard Rev* 27:91-94 Wint 1992
Review of: *Jottings: historical and political* by Pryer, Peter. In: *Teilhard Rev* 27:97-98 Wint 1992
Review of: *Science of the Gods: reconciling mystery and matter* by Ash, David, and Hewitt, Peter. In: *Teilhard Rev* 28:29-31 Sum 1993
Review of: *The emerging New Age* by Simmons, F L. In: *Teilhard Rev* 27:88-89 Wint 1992
Review of: *The notebooks of Paul Brunton: perspectives* by Brunton, Paul. In: *Teilhard Rev* 28:31-33 Sum 1993
Review of: *The reform of the United Nations, a volume in the series annual review of UN affairs, vol I* by Muller, Joachim W. In: *Teilhard Rev* 27:96-97 Wint 1992

Williams, Donna Reilly.
Christmas mourning: reaching out to the grief stricken. *Mod Lit* 19:14-15 D 1992-Ja 1993

Williams, Elspeth. see Williams, Earle, jt auth

Williams, Ian S.
Review of: *Remembering esperanza: a cultural-political theology of North American praxis* by Taylor, Mark K. In: *Pacifica* 6:228-231 Je 1993

Williams, James G.
Review of: *Biblical criticism in crisis?* by Brett, Mark G. In: *CBQ* 55:325-327 Ap 1993

Williams, Joan.
The feast of hospitality. *ReligTJ* 27:25 Ap-My 1993
Review of: *A case for peace in reason and faith* by Hellwig, Monika K, 1929-. In: *Living Prayer* 26:32-33 My-Je 1993
Review of: *A grammar of consent: the existence of God in Christian tradition* by Nichols, Aidan. In: *Living Prayer* 26:33 Ja-F 1993
Review of: *Archbishop Oscar Romero: a shepherd's diary [tr by I B Hodgson]* by Romero Y Galdamez, Oscar Arnulfo, Abp, 1917-1980. In: *Living Prayer* 26:32 S-O 1993
Review of: *Care of the soul: a guide for cultivating depth and sacredness in everyday life* by Moore, Thomas. In: *Living Prayer* 26:32 My-Je 1993
Review of: *Convergence: a reconciliation of Judaism and Christianity in the life of one woman* by Bruder, Judith. In: *Living Prayer* 26:33 N-D 1993
Review of: *Dark night journey* by Cronk, Sandra. In: *Living Prayer* 26:32 Ja-F 1993
Review of: *Generous lives* by Redmont, Jane. In: *Living Prayer* 26:33 Jl-Ag 1993
Review of: *Life of the beloved* by Nouwen, Henri Josef Machiel, 1932-. In: *Living Prayer* 26:32 Mr-Ap 1993
Review of: *Living with wisdom: a life of Thomas Merton* by Forest, Jim. In: *Living Prayer* 26:32-33 Mr-Ap 1993
Review of: *Spirituality and history* by Sheldrake, Philip. In: *Living Prayer* 26:32-33 S-O 1993
Review of: *Starlight* by Shea, John B. In: *Living Prayer* 26:32-33 N-D 1993
Review of: *The collected works of St John of the Cross* by Kavanaugh, Kieran, and Rodriguez, Otilio. In: *Living Prayer* 26:32 Ja-F 1993
Review of: *The Noah paradox: time as burden, time as blessing* by Ochs, Carol. In: *Living Prayer* 26:32-33 Jl-Ag 1993
Review of: *The recovery of love: Christian mysticism and the addictive society* by Imbach, Jeffrey D. In: *Living Prayer* 26:32 Jl-Ag 1993
Review of: *The vigil: keeping watch in the season of Christ's coming* by Wright, Wendy M. In: *Living Prayer* 26:32 N-D 1993
Review of: *Twenty-two gathering prayers* by Arackal, Joseph J. In: *Living Prayer* 26:33 Mr-Ap 1993
Review of: *What are they saying about the theology of suffering?* by Richard, Lucien. In: *Living Prayer* 26:33 My-Je 1993
Review of: *Winter music: a life of Jessica Powers* by Leckey, Dolores R, 1933-. In: *Living Prayer* 26:33 Mr-Ap 1993

Williams, John Allen.
Review of: *Pandemonium: ethnicity in international politics* by Moynihan, Daniel Patrick. In: *America* 169:24-25 N 6 1993

Williams, John R.
Review of: *Bioethics and secular humanism: the search for a common morality* by Engelhardt, H Tristram, Jr. In: *Heythrop* 34:221-222 Ap 1993

Williams, Melvin G.
Taming a parish nightmare. *Tod Parish* 25:12+ N-D 1993

Williams, Monty.
Review of: *Spiritual intimacy and community* by English, John. In: *Can Cath Rev* 11:28-29 N 1993

Williams, Rhys H. see Demerath, N J, III, jt auth

Williams, Roger L. see Freeman, John F, jt auth

Williams, Rowan.
T.S. Eliot and mysticism: a discussion. *Doctr Life* 43:396-401 S 1993

Williams, Ruthann. see Olert, Stephen, jt auth

Williams, Shirley, 1930-.
The end of the road. *Tablet* 247:676 My 29 1993
Review of: *Fighting all the way* by Castle, Barbara. In: *Tablet* 247:948 Jl 24 1993

Williamson, Clark M.
Post-holocaust church theology. Louisville: John Knox, 1993. x, 352p ISBN 0-664-254-54-3

Williamson, David.
Homosexual people in the church. *Priests & People* 7:335-339 Ag-S 1993

Willie, Caroljean.
The first Christmas. *Tod Cath Teach* 27:28 N-D 1993

Willis, John T.
Review of: *Studien zur literarkritischen Methode* by Werlitz, Jürgen. In: *OTA* 16:430-431 Je 1993

Willis, Timothy M.
Review of: *The Lucianic manuscripts of 1 Reigns: Vol 1, Majority Text* by Taylor, Bernard A. In: *OTA* 16:421 Je 1993

Willis, Wendell.
Review of: *The pre-Christian Paul* by Hengel, Martin. In: *CBQ* 55:368-370 Ap 1993

Willis-Watkins, David. see Placher, William Carl, jt auth

Willumsen, K.
Review of: *Sharing faith* by Groome, Thomas H, 1945-. In: *TheolStds* 53:791 D 1992

Wilmer, Gary G.
Responding to the goodness of God. *Momentum* 24:45-47 N-D 1993

Wilmore, Gayraud S. see Cone, James H, jt ed

Wilsnack, Dorie. see Weinberg, Bill, jt auth

Wilson, Chip.
Mainstreaming. *Register* 69:1+ Je 20 1993
Showing the way home. *Register* 69:2 Je 27 1993

Wilson, Clyde N.
Review of: *America's British culture* by Kirk, Russell, 1918-. In: *Crisis* 11:57-58 O 1993

Wilson, Desmond.
Public life in Northern Ireland—another view. *Furrow* 44:140-147 Mr 1993

Wilson, James Q.
Culture and the moral sense [fr *The moral sense*]. *Crisis* 11:8+ O 1993

Wilson, Richard.
Preaching: the not so good news. *Priests & People* 7:72-73 F 1993
The root of all evil. *Priests & People* 7:194-195 My 1993
The sins of the flesh. *Priests & People* 7:346-347 Ag-S 1993

Wilson-Smith, Timothy.
Review of: *Shakespeare: the evidence* by Wilson, Ian. In: *Tablet* 247:1264-1265 O 2 1993

Wiltshire, Peter.
Seeking discernment. *Living Prayer* 26:24-25 My-Je 1993

Wimmer, Joseph F.
Review of: *Let justice roll down: the Old Testament, ethics, and Christian life* by Birch, Bruce C. In: *OTA* 15:514 O 1992
Review of: *Nahum, Habakkuk and Zephaniah* by Roberts, J J M. In: *OTA* 15:511 O 1992
Review of: *Pre-exilic prophecy: words of warning, dreams of hope, spirituality of pre-exilic prophets* by Sklba, Richard J. In: *OTA* 15:505 O 1992
Review of: *The Pentateuch* by Guinan, Michael D. In: *OTA* 15:492 O 1992

Windsor, Patricia.
Does the church mishandle its cultural treasures? *USCath* 58:14-20 F 1993
Review of: *Generous lives* by Redmont, Jane. In: *Comm* 119:20-21 D 18 1992

Wingenbach, Gregory C.
Koinonia ecclesiology: a response [reply to G. Vandervelde, pp 126-142]. *OChr* 29 no 2:143-148 1993

Winifred, Mary. see Wallace, Patricia F, jt auth

Winkels, Frank.
Converting the musician. *Mod Lit* 20:10-11 My 1993

Winkler, Jude.
Review of: *Jesus and the future* by Tiede, David. In: *CBQ* 54:788-789 O 1992
Review of: *Jesus as teacher* by Perkins, Pheme. In: *CBQ* 54:788-789 O 1992
Review of: *The world of Jesus: first century Judaism in crisis* by Riches, John. In: *CBQ* 54:788-789 O 1992
Review of: *Theological ethics of the New Testament* by Lohse, Eduard. In: *Living Light* 29:90 Aut 1992
Review of: *What can we know about Jesus?* by Kee, Howard Clark. In: *CBQ* 54:788-789 O 1992

Winkworth, Margaret.
Gertrude of Helfta: the herald of divine love. New York: Paulist Press, 1993. x, 259p ISBN 0-8091-0458-x LC 92-20663

Winston, David.
Review of: *Il libro della Sapienza, vol I* by Scarpat, Giuseppe, ed. In: *CBQ* 54:764-765 O 1992

Winter, Harry.
Bridge builders. *New Cov* 22:7-9 My 1993

Winter, Miriam Therese.
The gospel according to Mary: a New Testament for women. New York: The Crossroad Publishing Company, 1993. x, 143p ISBN 0-8245-1174-3 LC 92-403531

Winters, Anne Marie. see Struckhoff, Charlotte, jt auth

Winther-Nielsen, Nicolai.
Review of: *Josuaboken: en programskrift för davidisk restauration* by Ottosson, Magnus. In: *CBQ* 55:345-346 Ap 1993

Wintz, Jack Alton, 1936-.
Clare of Assisi lives today! [photos]. *St Anth* 101:28-35 Ag 1993
The Franciscan Missions of Florida a lost history is found again. *St Anth* 101:28-35 Je 1993
Guatemala: land of beauty and sorrow. *ST Anth* 101:28-34 Jl 1993

Wirpsa, Leslie.
Amid shortage of food, Cuba forages for future. *Nat Cath Rep* 29:11-12 Je 4 1993
CELAM IV "bottom line" its own statement. *Nat Cath Rep* 29:9 N 20 1992
Church and state circle warily as faith flourishes. *Nat Cath Rep* 29:13-14 Je 4 1993
Colombia confronts the sword [photos]. *Nat Cath Rep* 29:8-9 Ap 9 1993
Cuba: "a strange new hybrid" feeling for its roots. *Nat Cath Rep* 29:9-10+ Je 4 1993
Curia ignites angry protest at CELAM IV. *Nat Cath Rep* 29:12-13 N 6 1992
Hints of ecclesial self-criticism disappear. *Nat Cath Rep* 29:13 Ja 22 1993

Wirpsa, Leslie. *(cont'd)*
Life-form patents are "shady aspect" of NAFTA. *Nat Cath Rep* 29:16 Mr 19 1993
Medellín spirit lives, no thanks to Vatican. *Nat Cath Rep* 29:11-13 O 15 1993
Pope and US juggle agendas. *Nat Cath Rep* 29:16 Jl 30 1993
Refugees blaze more hopeful shining path in Peru. *Nat Cath Rep* 29:12 O 1 1993

Wise, Christopher.
The whatness of Loulou: allegories of Thomism in Flaubert. *Relig Lit* 25:35-49 Spr 1993

Wise, Michael. see Eisenman, Robert H, jt auth

Wiseman, James A.
"I have experienced God": religious experience in the theology of Karl Rahner. *ABenR* 44:22-57 Mr 1993
Review of: *Spirituality and emptiness: the dynamics of spiritual life in Buddhism and Christianity* by Mitchell, Donald W. In: *Cist Stud* 27 No 4: [111]-[112] 1992
Review of: *The mystic fable: v I: the sixteenth and seventeenth centuries* by Certeau, Michel de. In: *CHist* 79:535-537 Jl 1993
Traditions of spiritual guidance: John Ruusbroec as spiritual guide. *Way* 33: 148-155 Ap 1993

Wisman, Jon D.
Review of: *Why aren't economists as important as garbagemen?* by Colander, David. In: *RSocEcon* 51:374-378 Aut 1993

Wister, Robert J.
Dialogue [interview by Peter Mullen]. *Register* 69:1+ F 28 1993
Reflections on the priesthood in contemporary America. *US Cath Hist* 11: 126-129 Wint 1993
Review of: *Spanish roots of America* by Arias, David, Bp, 1929-. In: *Momentum* 24:82 F-Mr 1993

Witczak, Michael G.
Review of: *The banquet's wisdom* by Macy, Gary. In: *Living Light* 29:97 Spr 1993

Witek, John W.
Review of: *Documentos del Japón, 1547-1557* by Ruiz-de-Medina, Juan, ed. In: *CHist* 79:379-381 Ap 1993
Review of: *Sino-Vatican relations: problems in conflicting authority, 1976-1986* by Leung, Beatrice. In: *TheolStds* 54:363-365 Je 1993

Witherup, Ronald D.
The "intellectual" formation of priests. *Priest* 49:46-52 Ag 1993
Preaching the passion with sensitivity to Judaism. *Priest* 49:12-16 Ap 1993
Review of: *Judaism: practice and belief* by Sanders, E P. In: *OTA* 15:519 O 1992
Review of: *Old Testament Yahweh texts in Paul's Christology* by Capes, David B. In: *OTA* 15:517 O 1992
Review of: *Studies in the Jewish background of Christianity* by Schwartz, Daniel R. In: *OTA* 16:450 Je 1993
Review of: *The beloved disciple: a witness against anti-semitism* by Kaufman, Philip S. In: *CBQ* 54:801-802 O 1992
Review of: *The passion of Jesus in the Gospel of John* by Senior, Donald. In: *CBQ* 54:801-802 O 1992
Review of: *The way of the Lord* by Marcus, Joel. In: *OTA* 16:447-448 Je 1993
Review of: *What are they saying about John?* by Sloyan, Gerard S. In: *CBQ* 54:801-802 O 1992

Witter, Jacqueline.
Reaching yound adults: ask them and they will come. *Tod Parish* 25:7-10 S 1993

Wittstadt, Klaus. see Alberigo, Giuseppe, jt ed

Wodding, C A M.
Review of: *Gods of earth* by Jordan, Michael. In: *Month* 26:32-33 Ja 1993

Woeger, William.
Converting the artist. *Mod Lit* 20:10-11 S 1993

Wogaman, J Philip.
Christian ethics: a historical introduction. Louisville: John Knox, 1993. x, 352p ISBN 0-664-25163-3

Woiwode, Larry.
Acts: a writer's reflections on the church, writing, and his own acts. San Francisco: HarperSanFrancisco, 1993. 244p ISBN 0-06069-404-1 LC 92-52503

Wojcicki, Ed.
Catholics should learn to say no to their parish. *USCath* 58:21-25 N 1993
Do I really have to sell all I have? *USCath* 58:32-33 Je 1993
A great place for dialogue: reflections of a former newspaper editor. *America* 168:12-15 F 27 1993

Wojcik, Jan. see Frontain, Raymond-Jean, jt ed

Wolanin, Adam.
Review of: *Inculturation and ecclesial communion: culture and church in the teaching of Pope John Paul II* by George, Francis E. In: *Gregorianum* 73 No 4:762-763 1992
Review of: *Lexikon der Mission: Geschichte, Theologie, Ethnologie* by Rzepkowski, Horst. In: *Civilta* 2:300-301 My 1 1993
Review of: *Uncompleted mission* by Dickson, Kwesi A. In: *Gregorianum* 74 no 2:395-399 1993

Wolcott, John.
Becoming whole again. *OSV* 81:5 Ja 3 1993

Wolfe, Gregory.
The Catholic as Conservative: Russell Kirk's Christian humanism. *Crisis* 11: 25-32 O 1993
Review of: *Acts* by Woiwode, Larry. In: *Register* 69:5 O 3 1993
Review of: *The patron Saint of Liars* by Patchett, Ann. In: *Crisis* 11:56-58 My 1993

Wolfe, Michael.
The conversion of Henri IV: politics, power, and religious belief in early modern France. Cambridge: Harvard University Press, 1993. 253p ISBN 0-67417-031-8 LC 92-24881

Wolff, Pierre.
Discernment. Missouri: Triumph Books, 1993. x, 145p ISBN 0-89243-485-6 LC 93-7922

Wolff, Tatiana.
Review of: *Before the revolution: a view of Russia under the last Tsar* by FitzLyon, Kyril, and Browning, Tatiana. In: *Tablet* 247:275 F 27 1993

Wolff, Tobias.
Review of: *Strange Gods* by Cornwell, John. In: *Tablet* 247:984-985 Jl 31 1993

Wolkowinska, Cecylia. *see* Bogle, Joanna, jt auth

Wollemborg, Leo J.
Finita la commedia: the fix is out. *Comm* 120:7-9 Je 18 1993

Wolterstorff, Nicholas P.
Review of: *Faith and reason from Plato to Plantinga* by Hoitenga, Dewey J, Jr. In: *Thomist* 57:542-546 Jl 1993

Wong, Pamela Pearson.
The death of dreams: coping with the loss of an unborn child. *St Anth* 100:36-39 Ja 1993

Wood, Charles.
Activists and charismatics: stronger ties and shared respect. *New Cov* 23:8-12 O 1993
A biblical view of human nature. *OSV* 81:19 Ja 10 1993
An example of substantial lay responsibility [Minnesota Parish]. *Priest* 49:42-45 My 1993
I want to know if you love my Lord (includes a photo essay by Steven P Smith). *USCath* 58:26- Jl 1993
Not just any port in a storm [photos]. *OSV* 81:12-13 Ja 24 1993
A prayerful parish. *New Cov* 22:8-10 Mr 1993
Review of: *Imagination and authority: theological authorship in the modern tradition* by Thiel, John E. In: *TheolStds* 53:768-770 D 1992
Teens can offer your parish more than car washes. *USCath* 58:6+ D 1993
This parish's education program puts faith in its families. *OSV* 81:6-7 Mr 7 1993

Wood, Derek. *see* Bertodano, Teresa de, jt auth

Wood, Steve.
Dialogue [interview by Jan Slattery]. *Register* 69:1+ Jl 18 1993

Wood, Susan.
Review of: *God for us: the Trinity and Christian life* by LaCugna, Catherine Mowry. In: *Horizons (CTS)* 20:127-129 Spr 1993
Review of: *The craft of theology* by Dulles, Avery Robert, 1918-. In: *RRel* 52:629-630 Jl-Ag 1993
Review of: *The papacy* by Schimmelpfennig, Bernhard. In: *TheolStds* 54:384 Je 1993

Woodcock, Evelyn.
World without frontiers. *Teilhard Rev* 27:85-87 Wint 1992

Woodcock, John.
Review of: *The white hole in time: our future evolution and the meaning of now* by Russell, Peter. In: *Teilhard Rev* 28:28 Spr 1993

Wooden, Cindy.
Seminary "product" still scarce. *Nat Cath Rep* 29:2 S 17 1993

Woodgate, Michael.
Celibacy in another tradition. *Way Suppl* 77:106-112 Sum 1993

Woodrow, Alain.
Broadcast and be saved. *Tablet* 247:9-10 Ja 2 1993
Review of: *Genet* by White, Edmund. In: *Tablet* 247:1044-1045 Ag 14 1993
Sacking the Socialists. *Tablet* 247:395-396 Mr 27 1993

Woods, Laurie.
The Bible: God's world. Minnesota: The Liturgical Press, 1993. 92p ISBN 0-8146-2276-3

Woods, Richard.
New age spiritualities: how are we to talk of God? *New Blckfrs* 74:76-191 Ap 1993
Review of: *A priest on trial* by Lynch, Bernard. In: *Tablet* 247:246-247 F 20 1993
Review of: *Julian's way: a practical commentary on Julian of Norwich* by Bradley, Ritamary. In: *New Blckfrs* 74:281-282 My 1993
What is new age spirituality? *Way* 33:176-188 Jl 1993

Woodward, Kenneth L.
Catholic higher education: what happened? *Comm* 120:13-16+ Ap 9 1993
Review of: *Thinking out loud* by Quindlen, Anna. In: *Comm* 120:17-18+ My 21 1993

Woofenden, Graham.
The ancient cathedral office and today's needs. *Worship* 67:388-405 S 1993

Woolf, James Dudley.
The search for self: a study of the poetic mind. New York: Vantage Press, 1993. 320p ISBN 0-533-10364-9 LC 92-90889

Woolfenden, Graham.
"Let us offer each other the sign of peace"—an enquiry. *Worship* 67:239-252 My 1993
The sacraments and evangelisation. *Month* 26:121-126 Mr 1993

Worcester, Thomas.
History as caveat and consolation. *America* 169:13-15 Jl 17-24 1993

Worland, Stephen T.
Review of: *Doing faithjustice: an introduction to Catholic social thought* by Kammer, Fred. In: *RSocEcon* 51:380-387 Aut 1993
Review of: *Doing well and doing good* by Neuhaus, Richard John, 1936-. In: *Crisis* 11:54-56 Ap 1993
Review of: *The political theory of liberation theology* by Pottenger, John R. In: *RSocEcon* 50:353-358 Fall 1992

Worlock, Derek, Abp, 1920-.
A nearly great biography [review article *Paul VI, the first modern Pope* by P. Hebblethwaite]. *Priests & People* 7:294-298 Jl 1993

Worth, Robert.
Review of: *A suitable boy* by Seth, Vikram. In: *Comm* 120:25-26 My 21 1993

Wreen, Michael. *see* Rossi, Philip J, jt ed

Wright, A D.
Review of: *Heresy and mysticism in Sixteenth-Century Spain: the Alumbrados* by Hamilton, Alastair. In: *CHist* 79:525-526 Jl 1993
Review of: *Jerome Nadal, SJ, 1507-1580* by Bangert, William V. In: *CHist* 79:110-111 Ja 1993

Wright, Benjamin G, III.
Review of: *God is my rock: a study of translation techinque and theological exegesis in the Septuagint* by Olofsson, Staffan. In: *CBQ* 55:126-127 Ja 1993

Wright, H Norman.
Crisis counseling: what to do during the first 72 hours. Ventura: Regal Books, 1993. 335p ISBN 0-8307-1611-4 LC 93-10514
Questions women ask in private. Ventura, California: Regal Books, 1993. 426p ISBN 0-8307-1522-3 LC 93-913

Wright, J Robert.
The Genesis of a book: readings for the daily office from the early church. *Worship* 67:144-155 Mr 1993
Review of: *Handbook of patrology* by Hamell, Patrick J. In: *Cist Stud* 28:[22]-[23] 1993 *see* Evans, G R, jt ed

Wright, John H.
Review of: *She who is* by Johnson, Elizabeth A, 1941-. In: *TheolStds* 54:371-373 Je 1993
Review of: *The vigilant God: providence in the thought of Augustine, Aquinas, Calvin and Barth* by Davies, Horton. In: *TheolStds* 54:596-597 S 1993
Roger Haight's spirit Christology [reply to Roger Haight, pp 257-287 Je 1992]. *TheolStds* 53:729-735 D 1992

Wright, John W.
Review of: *Das Image der Nomaden im Alten Israel und in der lkonographie seiner sesshaften Nachbarn* by Staubli, Thomas. In: *OTA* 15:489 O 1992
Review of: *Exégète à Jérusalem: Nouveaux mélanges d'histoire Religieuse (1890-1939)* by Lagrange, Marie-Joseph. In: *CBQ* 55:414-415 Ap 1993
Review of: *Ezra-Nehemiah* by Throntveit, Mark A. In: *OTA* 15:500 O 1992
Review of: *Forms of deformity* by Holden, Lyn. In: *OTA* 16:159 F 1993

Wright, P.
Review of: *More by accident* by Greenhill, Denis. In: *Tablet* 247:79 Ja 16 1993

Wright, Tom. *see* Neill, Stephen, jt auth

Wrightson, K.
Review of: *A rural society after the Black Death: Essex 1350-1525* by Poos, L R. In: *CHist* 78:647-648 O 1992

Wroe, Ann.
A church off the street. *Tablet* 247:262 F 27 1993
On the bright side. *Tablet* 247:390 Mr 27 1993
A pair of shoes. *Tablet* 247:538 My 1 1993
Review of: *Some other rainbow* by McCarthy, John, and Morrell, Jill. In: *Tablet* 247:654 My 22 1993
Review of: *The Vatican and Zionism: conflict in the Holy Land, 1895-1925* by Minerbi, Sergio I. In: *Heythrop* 34:119-120 Ja 1993
A sacred landscape. *Tablet* 247:192-193 F 13 1993

Wuerl, Donald William, Bp, 1941-.
The diocesan Bishop's perspective on implementing the Catechism. *Living Light* 30:73-78 Aut 1993
The fifth commandment. *Columbia* 73:19 Ag 1993
The fourth commandment. *Columbia* 73:15 Jl 1993
The sixth commandment. *Columbia* 73:13 S 1993
The third commandment. *Columbia* 73:21 Je 1993
Though painful, Pittsburgh reorganization draws praise. *Register* 69:1+ O 31 1993

Wukas, Mark.
Ministry potential discerner. *Columbia* 73:12-14 Jl 1993

Würtele, Hélène.
Review of: *Saint Jean de la Croix* by Longchamp, Max Huot de. In: *Laval Theol Phil* 49:171 F 1993

Wuthnow, Robert.
Christianity in the twenty-first century: reflections on the challenges ahead. New York: Oxford University Press, 1993. x, 251p ISBN 0-19507-957-4 LC 92-28689
Your money or your faith. *CDgst* 57:92-98 Jl 1993

Wycliff, Don.
Review of: *Lure and loathing: essays on race, identity, and the ambivalences of assimilation* by Early, Gerald, ed. In: *Comm* 120:22-23 My 21 1993
Review of: *The culture of disbelief* by Carter, Stephen L. In: *Comm* 120:22-23 O 8 1993

Wyneken, Cherise.
A rose is a rose is a rose. *Spir Life* 39:47-48 Spr 1993

Wynn, Mark.
Review of: *Spirit and beauty: an introduction to theological aesthetics* by Sherry, Patrick. In: *New Blckfrs* 74:375-376 Jl-Ag 1993

Wyschogrod, Edith.
Killing the cat: sacrifice and beauty in Genet and Mishima. *Relig Lit* 25:107-119 Sum 1993

Wyschogrod, Michael.
Review of: *Das christliche Bekenntnis zu Jesus, dem Juden* by Marquardt, Friedrich-Wilhelm. In: *JEcumen Stds* 29:275-276 Spr 1992
Review of: *Das christliche Bekenntnis zu Jesus, dem Juden* by Friedrich-Wilhelm, Marquardt. In: *JEcumen Stds* 29:275-276 Spr 1992
Review of: *The lonely man of faith* by Soloveitchik, Joseph B, 1903-. In: *Comm* 120:26 Ja 15 1993

Wysocki, Paul.
The sign of the star; the sign of the cross. *Emmanuel* 99:51-52 Ja-F 1993

Y

Yablonka, Marc Phillip.
St Joseph's Hospital. *Sisters* 65:209-211 My 1993

Yarbrough, Stephen R, and Adams, John C.
Delightful conviction: Jonathan Edwards and the rhetoric of conversion. Westport: Greenwood Press, 1993. x, 208p ISBN 0-313-27582-3

Yarnold, Edward John, 1926-.
The Annunciation: pivotal moment of history. *Month* 26:237-239 Je 1993
The Church as communion. *Tablet* 246:1564-1565 D 12 1992
Review of: *A separate God: the Christian origins of gnosticism* by Pétrement, Simone. In: *New Blckfrs* 73:625-626 D 1992
Review of: *Peter and Paul in the Church of Rome: the ecumenical potential of a forgotten perspective* by Farmer, William R, and Kereszty, Roch, 1933-. In: *Can Cath Rev* 11:33-34 F 1993
Review of: *Regnum Caelorum: patterns of future hope in early Christianity* by Hill, Charles E. In: *New Blckfrs* 74:327-329 Je 1993
Review of: *Rome and the Eastern Churches* by Nichols, Aidan. In: *Month* 26:110-111 Mr 1993
Review of: *Saint Anselm* by Southern, R W. In: *Month* 26:378-379 S-O 1993
A way past Apostolicae Curae. *Tablet* 247:874 Jl 10 1993

Yasutake, Michael.
Salt of the earth: Rev Michael Yasutake [interview by M Scherer-Emunds]. *Salt* 13:4-5 Jl-Ag 1993

Yeager, D M.
"I saw a Kingfisher": grace and ruin in Golding's the spire. *Horizons (CTS)* 20:44-66 Spr 1993

Yee, Gale A.
Review of: *Far more precious than jewels: perspectives on Biblical women* by Darr, Katheryn Pfisterer. In: *OTA* 15:480 O 1992

Yepes Stork, Ricardo.
La doctrina del acto en Aristoteles. Pamplona: Eunsa, 1993. x, 1993 ISBN 84-313-1231-9

Yevics, Philip E.
Review of: *Il matrimonio in Oriente e Occidente* by Prader, Joseph. In: *Diakonia* 26 no 1:67-76 1993

Ying, Yu-Wen. see Muñoz, Ricardo F, jt auth

Yip, Ka-Chi.
Review of: *Sino-Vatican relations: problems in conflicting authority, 1976-1986* by Leung, Beatrice. In: *CHist* 79:383-384 Ap 1993

Yoest, Charmaine Crouse.
The Murphy Brown factor at work. *Register* 69:5 S 5 1993

Yoshida, Gregory.
Incense: a user's guide. *Mod Lit* 20:16-18 Ap 1993

Yound, York.
A young pilgrim's notebook. *OSV* 82:9 S 5 1993

Young, E.
Review of: *She who is* by Johnson, Elizabeth A, 1941-. In: *Nat Cath Rep* 29:10 F 12 1993
Review of: *Taking off the patriarchal glasses* by Cypser, Cora Elizabeth. In: *Nat Cath Rep* 29:10 F 12 1993

Young, Frances.
Virtuoso theology: the Bible and interpretation. Cleveland: The Pilgrim Press, 1990. x, 198p ISBN 0-8298-0948-1 LC 92-43008

Young, John.
Body and soul. *HPR* 94:60-63+ O 1993
The priest as resident theologian. *HPR* 93:29-32 Mr 1993

Young, Lorna.
Review of: *Class and idol in the English hymn* by Adey, Lionel. In: *Can Cath Rev* 11:32 F 1993

Young, Robert V.
Herbert and the Real Presence. *Renascence* 45:179-195 Spr 1993
The quatercentenary of George Herbert, 1593-1993. *Renascence* 45:131-204 Spr 1993
Investigating Herbert criticism, by S. Stewart. George Herbert: the best love, by A. Low. Herbert and the Real Presence, by R.V. Young. Me thoughts I heard one calling, Child!: Herbert's "The Collar", by J.R. Roberts.

Young, Serinity, ed.
An anthology of sacred texts by and about women. New York: Crossroad, 1993. x, 452p ISBN 0-8245-1143-3 LC 92-36343

Young, York.
A pilgrim of hope comes preaching new life. *OSV* 82:3 Ag 29 1993
A retreat in motion. *OSV* 82:6 My 23 1993
Trying to live as God sees fit. *OSV* 82:19 S 12 1993

Younger, Lawson K, Jr.
Review of: *Hittite myths* by Hoffner, Harry A. In: *CBQ* 55:339 Ap 1993
Review of: *Josua 13-21: ein priesterschriftlicher Abschnitt im deuteronomistischen Geschichtswerk* by Cortese, Enzo. In: *CBQ* 55:105-106 Ja 1993

Yuval-Davis, Nira. see Sahgal, Gita, jt auth

Yzermans, Vincent A.
First evangelizer of the first diocese. *US Cath Hist* 11:1-19 Spr 1993

Z

Zaccaria, Sante.
XXVI congresso nazionale ceciliano (Bologna, 16-20 settembre 1992). *Notitiae* 28: 736-740 N-D 1992

Zaffi, Maria Cecilia.
Review of: *IX centenário do Nascimento de S Bernardo. Encontros de Alcobaça e Simpósio de Lisboa.* In: *Gregorianum* 74 no 2:391-393 1993
Review of: *Melliflui Doctoris opera* by Cataldi, Riccardo. In: *Gregorianum* 74 no 3:591-592 1993
Review of: *I tre fondatori di Cîteaux* by Damme, Jean-Baptiste Van. In: *Gregorianum* 74 No 1:179-181 1993

Zagano, Phyllis.
Woman to woman: an anthology of women's spiritualities. Collegeville: Liturgical, 1993. x, 115p ISBN 0-8146-5025-2 LC 93-18865

Zaggelski, Linda Trinkaus, 1946-, ed.
Rational faith: Catholic responses to reformed epistemology. Indiana: Notre Dame Press, 1993. x, 290p ISBN 0-268-01643-7 LC 92-537-42

Zagzebski, Linda.
Review of: *Time and eternity* by Leftow, Brian. In: *New Oxford Rev* 60:30 S 1993

Zahn, Gordon C.
Review of: *The end of the twentieth century and the end of the Modern Age* by Lukacs, John, 1923-. In: *New Oxford Rev* 60:24-26+ My 1993
Zahn, Gordon C. *America* 168:5-7 My 15 1993

Zalatorius, Genevieve.
Our Lady of Siluva. *Register* 69:2 Mr 28 1993

Zalba, Marcelino.
Review of: *La vida cristiana. Curso de teología moral fundamental* by García de Haro, Ramon. In: *Gregorianum* 74 no 2:378-380 1993

Zalewska, Georgette.
Confirmation: a grass-roots theological reflection process. *Living Light* 29:51-59 Spr 1993

Zambonini, Franca.
Teresa of Calcutta: a pencil in God's hand. New York: Alba House, 1993. 189p ISBN 0-8189-0670-7 LC 93-1046

Zaner, Richard M.
Troubled voices: stories of ethics and illness. Cleveland: Pilgrim Press, 1993. x, 161p ISBN 0-8298-0964-3 LC 93-3823

Zanghjeratti, Massimiliano M.
A Marian missionary venture [review article *The Franciscan Legend of the Immaculate* by I Cammi]. *ChrWorld* 38:41-47 Ja-F 1993

Zannoni, Arthur E. see Shermis, Michael, jt ed

Zapata, Dominga M, and Mitchell, Nathan D.
Prayer is life [exc fr *Liturgy: rhythms of prayer*]. *Liturgy* 10:42-46 Spr 1993

Zech, Charles E.
The Catholic Church, resource allocation and the priest shortage. *RSocEcon* 50:297-304 Fall 1992

Zeender, John.
Review of: *Deutsche Bischöfe im Ersten Weltkrieg* by Scheidgen, Hermann-Joseph. In: *CHist* 79:551-555 Jl 1993

Zeitlin, Ariel.
Sisters who cherish the dying [condensed fr *Lear's* F 1993]. *CDgst* 57:64-70 My 1993

Zen, Joseph Er-jwun.
Did Chinese Catholics die for a secondary truth? *Origins* 22:714-716 Mr 25 1993

Zenger, E, et al. see Lohfink, Norbert, jt auth

Zepp, Ira G, Jr.
A Muslim primer: beginner's guide to Islam. Westminster, Maryland: Wakefield Editions, 1992. x, 292p ISBN 0-87061-188-7 LC 91-73300

Zeps, Michael J.
Review of: *From prejudice to persecution: a history of Austrian anti-Semitism* by Pauley, Bruce F. In: *CHist* 79:125 Ja 1993

Zhang, Ellen Y.
Review of: *God without being* by Marion, Jean-Luc. In: *CrossCurr* 43:273-277 Sum 1993

Ziegler, Elena.
Finding the religious dimension in family life. *Momentum* 24:78-79 F-Mr 1993

Zielinski, Judith Ann. see Sammon, Sean D, jt auth

Zielinski, Martin.
The American Catholic and Chicago response to Rerum Novarum [commentary *Rerum Novarum*]. *Chicago Stud* 31:142-153 Ag 1992

Zilonka, Paul.
Review of: *A body broken for people: Eucharist in the New Testament* by Moloney, Francis J. In: *CBQ* 54:793 O 1992

Zimbelman, Joel.
Theology, praxis, and ethics in the thought of Juan Luis Segundo, SJ. *Thomist* 57:233-267 Ap 1993

Zimmerman, Anthony.
"Did Jesus know he was God?" revisited. *Priest* 49:11-14 S 1993
I begin at the beginning. *Linacre* 60:86-92 Ag 1993
The priest: why celibate? *Priest* 49:12-20+ My 1993
Purification before the beatific vision. *HPR* 93:23-30 Ja 1993

Zimmerman, Mark.
How St. Claudine persevered [condensed fr *Catholic Standard* Jl 15 1993]. *CDgst* 58:88-91 D 1993

BOOK TITLE
INDEX

Abandonment to divine providence. Caussade, Jean Pierre de, -1751. New York: Doubleday, 1975. x, 119p ISBN 0-385-24937-3 LC 74-2827

Abortion: a new generation of Catholic responses. Heaney, Stephen J. Braintree, Massachusetts: The Pope John Center, 1992. x, 359p ISBN 0o-935372-35-0 LC 92-37020

According to Paul: studies in the theology of the Apostle. Fitzmyer, Joseph Augustine, 1920-. New York: Paulist, 1993. x, 177p ISBN 08-0913-390-3 LC 93-20453

Acerca de Wittgenstein. Sanfelix, Vidarte, ed. Valencia: Pre-Textos, 1993. x, 202p ISBN 84-87101

Actividades de conceptuacion: materiales de didactica de la filosofia sobre supuestos constructivistas. Benavente, Jose W. Madrid: Akal, 1993. x, 136p ISBN 84-460-0166-7

Acts: a writer's reflections on the church, writing, and his own acts. Woiwode, Larry. San Francisco: HarperSanFrancisco, 1993. 244p ISBN 0-06069-404-1 LC 92-52503

Advent and psychic birth. Burke, Mariann. New York: Paulist, 1993. x, 164p ISBN 0-8091-3431-4 LC 93-19318

After Jesus: the triumph of Christianity. . Pleasantville, New York: Reader's Digest, 1993. 352p ISBN 0-89577-9

Against nature? Types of moral argumentation regarding homosexuality. Pronk, Pim. Grand Rapids: Eerdmans, 1993. 384p ISBN 0-8028-0623-6

Against the tide: how to raise sexually pure kids in an 'anything-goes' world. Lahaye, Time, and Lahaye, Beverly. Sisters: Questar, 1993. x, 258p ISBN 0-88070-578-7

The Alba House Gospels: so you may believe. Wauck, Mark A. New York: Society of St Paul, 1992. x, 92p ISBN 0-8189-0625-1 LC 91-40303

Alcoholism: a guide to diagnosis, intervention, and treatment. Gallant, Donald M, 1929-. New York: Norton, 1987. x, 256p ISBN 0-39370-043-7 LC 87-23966

Aloysius. Stevens, Clifford, and McNichols, William Hart, eds. Huntington: Our Sunday Visitor, 1993. x, 160p ISBN 0-87973-528-7

Alphonsus de Liguori: the Saint of Bourbon Naples, 1696-1787. Jones, Frederick M. Westminster: Christian Classics, 1992. x, 532p ISBN 08-7061-195-x LC 92-73646

The American Catholic heritage: reflections on the growth and influence of the Catholic Church in the United States. Burghardt, Walter J, et al. Rome: Pontifical North American College, 1992. 131p ISBN 1-55586-544-5

American Catholic laity in a changing church. D'Antonio, William V, et al. Kansas City: Sheed and Ward, 1989. x, 193p ISBN 1-55612-247-0 LC 88-60114

El amor contra la moral. Sadaba, Javier. Madrid: Prodhufi, 1993. x, 165p ISBN 84-7954-126-1

Amor y diferencia. Torralba Rossello, Francese. Barcelona: PPU, 1993. x, 383p ISBN 84-477-0118-2

Angela of Foligno: complete works. Angela, of Foligno, 1248?-1309. New York: Paulist Press, 1993. x, 424p ISBN 0-8091-0460-1 LC 92-38830

The angels and us. Adler, Mortimer Jerome. New York: Macmillan, 1982. x, 205p ISBN 0-02-030065-4 LC 93-1377

The angels: spiritual and exegetical notes. Giudici, Maria Pia. New York: Alba House, 1993. x, 151p ISBN 0-8189-0636-7 LC 93-30849

Annulment: do you have a case? Tierney, Terrence E. New York: Alba House, 1993. x, 142p ISBN 0-8189-0667-7 LC 93-7090

An anthology of sacred texts by and about women. Young, Serinity, ed. New York: Crossroad, 1993. x, 452p ISBN 0-8245-1143-3 LC 92-36343

Anti-Catholicism in the media. Riley, Patrick J, and Shaw, Russell, eds. Huntington: Our Sunday Visitor, 1993. x, 256p ISBN 0-87973-551-1

Any room for Christ in Asia? Boff, Leonardo, and Elizondo, Virgil, eds. Maryknoll, New York: Orbis Books, 1993. ISBN 0-88344-870-x

The apostles' creed: a faith to live by. Cranfield, C E B. Grand Rapids: Eerdmans, 1993. 72p ISBN 0-8028-0709-7

The Apostle's dialogue with American culture. Jewett, Robert. Louisville: Westminster, 1993. x, 192p ISBN 0-664-25482-9

The apostolic faith: Protestants and Roman Catholics. Norris, Frederick W. Minnesota: The Liturgical Press, 1992. x, 178p ISBN 0-8146-5029-5 LC 92-19536

Arator on the Acts of the Apostles. Hillier, Richard. New York: Oxford University Press, 1993. x, 224p ISBN 0-814786-4

An archaeological companion. King, Philip J. Louisville: John Knox, 1993. x, 240p ISBN 0-664-21920-9

Archbiship Oscar Romero: a shepherd's diary. Romero, Oscar Arnulfo, Abp. Cincinnati: St Anthony Messenger Press, 1993. 542p ISBN 0-86716-170-1

Are all Christian ministers? Collins, John N. Collegeville: The Liturgical Press, 1992. x, 168p ISBN 0-8146-2168-6 LC 92-9599

Aristide: an autobiography. Aristide, Jean-Bertrand, 1953-. Maryknoll, New York: Orbis Books, 1993. 205p ISBN 0-88344-845-9 LC 92-34558

The art of meditating on scripture. Toon, Peter. Grand Rapids: Zondervan Publishing House, 1993. x, 176p ISBN 0-310-57761-6

El arte de la logica. Garcia Trevijano, Carmen. Madrid: Tecnos, 1993. x, 206p ISBN 84-309-2309-8

Asian faces of Jesus. Sugirtharajah, R S, ed. Maryknoll: Orbis Books, 1993. x, 267p ISBN 0-88344-833-5 LC 93-536

Assimiliation vs separation: Joseph the Administrator and the politics of religion in biblical Israel. Wildavsky, Aaron. New Brunswick, New Jersey: Transaction Publishers, 1993. x, 236p ISBN 1-56000-081-3 LC 92-20151

At pure heart: the window to God. Hummel, Charles, and Hummel, Anne. Grand Rapids: Zondervan Publishing House, 1993. x, 64p ISBN 0-310-59643-2

At the service of the church: Henri de Lubac reflects on the circumstances that occasioned his writings. Lubac, Henri De, Cardinal. San Francisco: Ignatius Press, 1993. x, 411p ISBN 08-9870-414-6

At the start: Genesis made new. . New York: Doubleday, 1992. x, 237p ISBN 0-385-47180-7 LC 93-916

Athens and Jerusalem: the role of philosophy in theology. Bonsor, Jack A. Mahwah: Paulist Press, 1993. 192p ISBN 0-8091-3398-9

August Benzinger: international portrait painter. Benzinger, Mariel. Kansas City: Sheed & Ward, 1993. 355p ISBN 1-55612-614-x LC 93-19230

Augustin Bea, the Cardinal of unity. Schmidt, Stephen A. New Rochelle, New York: New City Press, 1992. 806p ISBN 1-56548-016-3 LC 92-17612

Augustine today. Neuhaus, Richard John, 1936-, ed. Grand Rapids: Eerdmans, 1993. 168p ISBN 0-8028-0216-8

Author's response [reply to four book reviews, The Revelatory Text]. Schneiders, Sandra M. Horizons (CTS) 19:303-309 Fall 1992.

The autobiography of St. Ignatius Loyola. Ignatius, of Loyola, Saint, 1491-1556. New York: Fordham University Press, 1992. x, 113p ISBN 0-8232-1480-x LC 92-32959

Backgrounds of early Christianity. Ferguson, Everett. Grand Rapids: Eerdmans, 1993. 608p ISBN 0-8028-0669-4

Backpack meditations for Lent. Schneider, Valerie. New York: Paulist Press, 1990. 57p ISBN 0-8091-3195-1 LC 90-41230

Baptism in water and Baptism in the spirit: a biblical, liturgical, and theological exposition. Larere, Philippe. Collegeville: Liturgical, 1993. 94p ISBN 0-8146-2225-9 LC 93-10845

The Barna report, volume 3, 1993-94: absolute confusion. Beacon, George. Ventura: Regal Books, 1993. x, 309p ISBN 0-8307-1641-6

Becoming a Catholic Christian: a pilgrim's guide to the Rite of Christian Initiation of Adults. Upton, Julia. Washington: The Pastoral Press, 1993. 84p ISBN 1-56929-004-0

Becoming married: family living in pastoral perspective. Anderson, Herbert, and Fite, Cotton R. Louisville: Westminster, 1993. x, 160p ISBN 0-664-25126-9

Befilled with the fullness of God: living in the indwelling Trinity. Maloney, George A, 1924-. New Rochelle, New York: New City, Press, 1993. x, 144p ISBN 1-56548-024-4 LC 92-42031

Befriending: a self-guided retreat for busy people. Payne, Joseph A. New Jersey: Paulist Press, 1992. x, 165p ISBN 0-8091-3354-7 LC 92-28398

Being a priest today. Whitehead, James D, et al, eds. Collegeville, Minnesota: The Liturgical Press, 1992. 206p ISBN 0-81465-032-5 LC 92-4819

Being Catholic: Commonweal from the seventies to the nineties. Allen, Rodger Van. Chicago: Loyola University Press, 1993. x, 203p ISBN 0-8294-0744-8 LC 92-40701

Belongings: bonds of healing and recovery. Linn, Dennis, et al. New Jersey: Paulist Press, 1993. x, 255p ISBN 0-8091-3365-2 LC 92-29855

Bernardus Magister: in celebration of the nonacentary of the birth of Saint Bernard of Clairvaux: 1090-1990. Sommerfeldt, John R, ed. Massachusetts: Cistercian Publications, 1992. x, 578p ISBN 0-87907-635-6 LC 92-13334

Beyond charity: Reformation initiations for the poor. Lindberg, Carter. Minneapolis: Fortress Press, 1993. x, 235p ISBN 0-8006-2569-2 LC 92-29963

Beyond patriarchy: the images of family in Jesus. Jacobs-Malina, D. Mahwah: Paulist, 1993. x, 211p ISBN 0-8091-3421-7 LC 93-24501

Beyond the darkness, into the light: thinking about sin and forgiveness today. Caserta, Thomas G. Boston: St Paul Books & Media, 1993. 67p ISBN 0-8198-1142 LC 93-19167

Beyond the myth of dominance: an alternative to a violent society. McMahon, Edwin M, 1930-. Kansas City: Sheed & Ward, 1993. x, 271p ISBN 15-5612-563-1

The Bible for today's family. . Nashville: American Bible Society, 1991. x, 758p ISBN

The Bible: God's world. Woods, Laurie. Minnesota: The Liturgical Press, 1993. 92p ISBN 0-8146-2276-3

Biblia del peregrino; vol 1: tento de la Biblia; vol 2; notas exegeticas. Schokel, Luis Alonso. Bilbao: Ege-Mensajero, 1993. x, 2700p ISBN 84-7726-074-5

La Biblia Judia y la Biblia Cristiana. Trebolle Barrera, Julio. Madrid: Trotta, 1993. x, 670p ISBN 84-87699-55-3

Biblical faith and natural theology. Barr, James. New York: Oxford University Press, 1993. x, 256p ISBN 0-826205-1

The bicentennials history of Georgetown University: from academy to university, 1789-1982, v1. Curran, Robert. Washington: Georgetown University Press, 1993. 445p ISBN 0-87840-485-6 LC 92-47499

Bilische Dogmatik: vol 3: Theologie als Ökonomic. Mildenberger, Friedrich. Stuttgart: Kohlhammer, 1993. x, 496p ISBN 3-17-011083-7

Bind us together. Weber, Gerard P, and Miller, Robert L. Chicago: ACTA Publications, 1993.

The birth lottery: prenatal diagnosis and selective abortion. Boss, Judith A. Chicago: Loyola University Press, 1993. 326p ISBN 0-8294-0740-5 LC 92-49738

The birth of the church: meditations of John 18-21. Speyr, Adrienne von, 1902-1967. San Francisco: Ignatius Press, 1991. 443p ISBN 0-89870-368-9 LC 90-85550

The birth of the New Testament: the origin and development of the first Christian generation. Collins, Raymond F. New York: Crossroad, 1993. x, 324p ISBN 0-8245-1276-6 LC 93-16647

Black Bible chronicles: book one: from Genesis to the promised land. . New York: African American Family Press, 1993. 190p ISBN 1-56977-000-x LC 93-071549

The black muslims in America. Lincoln, C Eric. Grand Rapids: Eerdmans, 1993. 0-8028-0703-8 ISBN 0-8028-0703-8

Black theology: a documentary history, vol I, 1966-1979. Cone, James H, and Wilmore, Gayraud S, eds. Maryknoll: Orbis Books, 1993. 462p ISBN 0-88344-853-x LC 92-44927

Black theology: a documentary history, vol II, 1980-1992. Cone, James H, and Wilmore, Gayraud S, eds. Maryknoll: Orbis Books, 1993. x, 450p ISBN 0-88344-773-8 LC 79-12747

The body of God: an ecological theology. McFague, Sallie. Minneapolis: Fortress Press, 1993. x, 274p ISBN 0-8006 LC 93-6584

Bodying forth: aesthetic liturgy. Collins, Patrick W, 1936-. New Jersey: Paulist Press, 1992. x, 187p ISBN 0-8091-3352-0 LC 92-28045

The book of common worship, daily prayer. . Louisville: John Knox, 1993. x, 512p ISBN 0-664-22032-0

Book of common worship, pastoral edition. . Louisville: John Knox, 1993. x, 368p ISBN 0-664-22033-9

The book of daily prayers. Webber, Robert. Grand Rapids: Eerdmans, 1993. 544p ISBN 0-8028-3753-0

Born to life. Davies, Oliver, ed. New Rochelle, New York: New City Press, 1992. 127p ISBN 1-56548-006-6 LC 92-14860

Bread for the journey: the mission of transformation and the transformation of mission. Gittins, Anthony J, 1943-. Maryknoll, New York: Orbis Books, 1993. x, 187p ISBN 0-88344-857-2 LC 92-42152

Breathing deeply of God's new life. Boyer, Mark G. Cincinnati: St Anthony Messenger Press, 1993. x, 170p ISBN 0-86716-163-9

Broken promises: understanding, healing and preventing affairs in Christian marriage. Virkler, Henry A. Dallas: Word Publishing, 1992. x, 306p ISBN 0-8499-0838-8 LC 91-39489

The Buddha and the Christ: explorations in Buddhist and Christian dialogue. Lefebvre, Leo D. Maryknoll: Orbis, 1993. x, 239p ISBN 0-88344-924-2 LC 93-7972

Buddhism and Christianity: rivals and allies. Smart, Ninian, 1927-. Honolulu: University of Hawaii Press, 1993. ISBN 0-82481-519-x LC 92-29475

Building the free society: democracy, capitalism, and Catholic Social Teaching. Weigel, George, and Royal, Robert, eds. Grand Rapids: Eerdmans, 1993. 232p ISBN 0-8028-0129-x

Bultmann. Ferguson, David. Collegeville: The Liturgical Press, 1992. x, 154p ISBN 0-8146-5037-6

But she said: feminist practices of biblical interpretation. Fiorenza, Elisabeth Schüssler, 1938-. Boston: Beacon, 1992. x, 261p ISBN 0-8070-1214-9

Calendar of documents and related historical materials in the Archival Center, Archdiocese of Los Angeles. . Mission Hills: Saint Francis Historical Society, 1993. //x, 79p ISBN

Called to the mountains: the autobiography of Reverend Ralph W. Beiting and the Christian Appalachian project. Beiting, Ralph W. Lancaster: Christian Appalachian Project, 1993. //x, 112p ISBN

Calvin's New Testament commentaries. Parker, T H L. Louisville: John Knox, 1993. x, 256p ISBN 0-664-25489-6

Can virtue be taught? Darling-Smith, Barbara. Notre Dame: University of Notre Dame Press, 1993. x, 224p ISBN 0-268-00799-3 LC 93-4578

Candles behind the wall: heroes of the peaceful revolution that shattered communism. Heydt, Barbara von der. Grand Rapids: Eerdmans, 1993. 224p ISBN 0-8028-3722-0

Categorias, intencionalidad y numeros: introduccion a la filosofia primera y a los origens del pensamiento fenomenologico. Garcia-Baro, Miguel. Madrid: Tecnos, 1993. x, 198p ISBN 84-309-2329-2

Catherine of Siena—passion for the truth, compassion for humanity: selected spiritual writings. O'Driscoll, Mary, ed. New Rochelle: New City Press, 1993. 144p ISBN 1-56548-058-9 LC 93-2543

The Catholic Church in modern China: perspectives. Tang, Edmond, and Wiest, Jean-Paul, eds. Maryknoll: Orbis, 1993. x, 260p ISBN 0-88344-834-3 LC 93-14944

The Catholic ethic and the spirit of capitalism. Novak, Michael, 1933-. New York: Macmillan International, 1993. x, 334p ISBN 0-02923-235-x LC 92-32151

Catholic makers of America: biographical sketches of Catholic statesmen and political thinkers in America's first century, 1776-1876. Krason, Stephen M. Front Royal, Virginia: Christendom Press, 1993. 260p ISBN 0-931888-44-2

The Catholic parish as a way-station of ethnicity and Americanization: Chicago's Germans and Italians, 1903-1939. Shawn, Stephen Joseph, 1944-. Brooklyn: Carlson Publishers, 1991. 206p ISBN 0-92601-9554 LC 91-26847

Catholic peacemakers: a documentary history [VI]. Musto, Ronald G. New York: Garland Publishing, 1993. x, 818p ISBN 0-8153-0604-0 LC 92-42658

The Catholic reformation: Savonarola to Ignatius Loyola: ·reform in the church, 1495-1540. Olin, John C. New York: Fordham University Press, 1992. x, 218p ISBN 0-8232-1477-x LC 92-29865

The Catholic religious poets from Southwell to Crashaw. Cousins, Anthony D. Westminster: Christian Classics, 1993. x, 224p ISBN 0-7220-1570-4

Catholics, Jews and the state of Israel. Kenny, Anthony John. New York: Paulist Press, 1993. x, 157p ISBN 0-8091-3406-3 LC 91-17833

Celebration of the word. Deiss, Lucien. Collegeville: Liturgical, 1993. x, 145p ISBN 0-8146-2090-6 LC 93-15193

Chapter and verse: the life of Christ in poetry. Rooney, William R. New York: Vantage Press, 1993. x, 89p ISBN 0-533-10319-3 LC 92-90788

Chapters into verse: poetry in English inspired by the Bible [vol I: Genesis to Malachi]. Atwan, Robert, and Wieder, Laurence, 1945-, eds. New York: Oxford University Press, 1993. x, 481p ISBN 0-19-506913-7 LC 92-37206

Chapters into verse: poetry in English inspired by the Bible [vol II: Gospels to Revelation]. Atwan, Robert, and Wieder, Laurence, 1945-, eds. New York: Oxford University Press, 1993. x, 391p ISBN 0-19-508305-9 LC 92-37206

Chiara Lubich: life for unity. Lubich, Chiara. New York: New City Press, 1992. x, 181p ISBN 0-904287-45-91

Chinese religious. Ching, Julia. Maryknoll: Orbis, 1993. x, 275p ISBN 0-88344-875-0 LC 93-2896

Chosen: gay Catholic priests tell their stories. Stuart, Elizabeth. New York: Chapman, 1993. / ISBN 02-256-6682-0 LC 92-34966

Christendom and Christianity in the Middle Ages. Bredero, Adriaan H. Grand Rapids: Eerdmans, 1993. 448p ISBN 0-8028-3692-5

Christian anti-Semitism and Paul's theology. Hall, Sidney G, III. Minneapolis: Fortress, 1993. x, 191p ISBN 0-8006-2654-0 LC 92-30395

Christian ethics: a historical introduction. Wogaman, J Philip. Louisville: John Knox, 1993. x, 352p ISBN 0-664-25163-3

Christian perspectives on religious knowledge. Evans, C Stephen, and Westphal, eds. Grand Rapids: Eerdmans, 1993. 288p ISBN 0-8028-0679-1

Christianity in the twenty-first century: reflections on the challenges ahead. Wuthnow, Robert. New York: Oxford University Press, 1993. x, 251p ISBN 0-19507-957-4 LC 92-28689

Christmas literature from writers ancient and modern. Johnson, Pegram, III, and Troiano, Edna M. Louisville: Westminster, 1993. x, 352p ISBN 0-664-22030-4

Christology in dialogue. Berkey, Robert F, and Edwards, Sarah A, eds. Cleveland: The Pilgrim Press, 1993. 390p ISBN 0-8298-0956-2 LC 47004

The Church and morality: an ecumenical and Catholic approach. Curran, Charles E, 1934-. Minneapolis: Fortress Press, 1993. 126p ISBN 0-8006-2756-3 LC 92-47448

The church and the American teenager: what works and doesn't work in youth ministry. Campolo, Tony. Grand Rapids: Zondervan Publishing House, 1993. x, 224p ISBN 0-310-52471-7

The church and the homosexual. McNeill, John J. Boston: Beacon, 1993. x, 266p ISBN 0-8070-7931-6 LC 93-7088

The church and the left. Michnik, Adam. Chicago: University of Chicago Press, 1993. 299p ISBN 0-226-52424-8 LC 92-20503

A church historian's odyssey. Davies, Horton. Grand Rapids: Eerdmans, 1993. 218p ISBN 0-8028-0712-7

The church in Angola: a river of many currents. Henderson, Lawrence W. Cleveland: The Pilgrim Press, 1992. x, 448p ISBN 0-8298-0938-4 LC 92-31494

The church in the nineties: its legacy its future. Hegy, Pierre M. Collegeville, Minnesota: The Liturgical Press, 1993. x, 323p ISBN 0-8146-2098-1 LC 92-45242

Church in the round: feminist interpretation of the church. Russell, Letty M. Louisville: John Knox Press, 1993. 235p ISBN 0-66425-070-x LC 93-9306

Church: the human story of God. Schillebeeckx, Edward. New York: Crossroad, 1993. x, 260p ISBN 0-8245-1050-x LC 90-36343

Collaborative ministry: communion, contention, commitment. Cooper, Norman P. New York: Paulist Press, 1993. x, 200p ISBN 0-8091-3376-8 LC 92-38074

Collected works of G K Chesterton VI 14: short stories, fairytales, mystery, and illustrations. Chesterton, Gilbert Keith, 1874-1936. San Francisco: Ignatius Press, 1993. ISBN 0-89870-401-4

College Catholics: a new counter-culture. Hunt, Michael J. New Jersey: Paulist Press, 1993. x, 172p ISBN 0-8091-3362-8 LC 92-37378

The college student's introduction to theology. Rausch, Thomas P, ed. Collegeville: Liturgical, 1993. 216p ISBN 0-8146-5841-5 LC 93-1263

The Collegeville Bible time-line. Payne, David F. Collegeville: Liturgical, 1993. 15p ISBN 0-8146-2275-5 LC 93-19614

Colorado: American Source Books, 1993. Heath, Angela. Colorado: American Source Books, 1993. 122p ISBN 0-9621333-9-6 LC 92-42895

Committed worship: a sacramental theology for converting Christians, v 2. Gelpi, Donald L, 1934-. Minnesota: The Liturgical Press, 1993. x, 312p ISBN 0-8146-5826-1 LC 92-40430

Committed worship: a sacramental theology for converting Christians, v I. Gelpi, Donald L, 1934-. Minnesota: The Liturgical Press, 1993. x, 278p ISBN 0-8146-5825-3 LC 92-40430

Communication and change in American religious history. Sweet, Leonard I, ed. Grand Rapids: Eerdmans, 1993. 400p ISBN 0-8028-0682-1

Companions in grace: a handbook for directors of the spiritual exercises of St. Ignatius of Loyola. Cowan, Marion, and Futrell, John Carroll. Kansas City: Sheed & Ward, 1993. x, 246p ISBN 1-55612-667-0 LC 93-6194

Compartamiento social y dinamica de groupos. Tous Ral, Jose M. Barcelona: PPU, 1993. x, 379p ISBN 84-477-0140-9

Complete works. Angela, of Foligno, 1248?-1309. New York: Paulist Press, 1993. x, 424p ISBN 0-80910-460 LC 92-38830

El concejo y consejeros del principe. Furio Ceriol, Fadrique. Madrid: Tecnos, 1993. x, 178p ISBN 84-309-2278-4

Concili Ecumenic Vatica 2: Constitucions, Decrets, Declaracions. . Barcelona: Claret, 1993. x, 495p ISBN 84-7263-839-1

A concise catechism for Catholics. Tolhurst, James. Grand Rapids: Eerdmans, 1993. 80p ISBN 0-8028-0122-6

Conferencia episcopal Catalona, malgrat tot. Bardulet, Salvador. Barcelona: Llibres de L'Index, 1993. x, 99p ISBN 84-87561-46-2

Confessions of a perfect parent. Price, W Wayne. Grand Rapids: Eerdmans, 1993. 166p ISBN 0-8028-0676-7

Confirmation: the baby in Solomon's court. Turner, Paul. New Jersey: Paulist Press, 1993. x, 188p ISBN 0-8091-3370-9 LC 92-320094

Consciousness and transcedence: the theology of Eric Voegelin. Morrisey, Michael P. Notre Dame: University of Notre Dame Press, 1994. x, 384p ISBN 0-268-00793-4 LC 92-50159

Console one another: a guide for Christian funerals. Curley, Terence P. Kansas City: Sheed & Ward, 1993. 100p ISBN 1-55612-600-x LC 93-3540

The contemplative pastor: returning to the art of spiritual direction. Peterson, Eugene H. Grand Rapids: Eerdmans, 1993. 192p ISBN 0-8028-0114-5

Contemporary prayers: the collected edition. Micklem, Caryl, ed. Grand Rapids: Eerdmans, 1993. 176p ISBN 0-8028-1523-5

The content of faith. Lehmann, Karl, Bp, 1936-, et al, eds. New York: The Crossroad Publishing Company, 1993. x, 668p ISBN 0-8245-1221-9 LC 92-27765

Contra el tiempo. Carcia Calvo, Agustin. Zamora: Lucina, 1993. x, 302p ISBN 84-85708-5

The conversion of Henri IV: politics, power, and religious belief in early modern France. Wolfe, Michael. Cambridge: Harvard University Press, 1993. 253p ISBN 0-67417-031-8 LC 92-24881

The cosmotheandric experience: emerging religious consciousness. Panikkar, Raimundo, 1918-. Maryknoll, New York: Orbis Books, 1993. x, 160p ISBN 0-88344-862-9 LC 92-46195

Counseling as a Christian challenge. Monaghan, Andrew. Westminster: Christian Classics, 1993. x, 183p ISBN 0-7171-1831-2

Creating a marriage. Greteman, James. New York: Paulist, 1993. x, 106p ISBN 0-8091-3393-8 LC 92-42927

Creation and liturgy. McMichael, Ralph N, Jr, ed. Washington: The Pastoral Press, 1993. 320p ISBN 1-562929-001-6

Creation in Biblical traditions. Clifford, Richard J, ed. Washington: The Catholic Biblical Association of America, 1992. 151p ISBN 0-915170-23-x LC 92-20268

Credo: the Apostles' Creed explained for today. Kung, Hans, 1928-. New York: Doubleday, 1993. x, 194p ISBN 0-385-47181-5 LC 93-915

Crisis counseling. Stone, Howard W. Minneapolis: Fortress, 1993. x, 96p ISBN 0-8006-2760-1 LC 92-39489

Crisis counseling: what to do during the first 72 hours. Wright, H Norman. Ventura: Regal Books, 1993. 335p ISBN 0-8307-1611-4 LC 93-10514

A crisis of conscience: a Catholic doctor speaks out for reform. Barber, Hugh R K. New York: Carol Publishing Group, 1993. 22p ISBN 1-55972-162-6 LC 92-39827

Critica del lenguaje ordinario. . Madrid: Libertarias, 1993. x, 780p ISBN 84-7683-252-2

The cutting edge: how churches speak on social and ethical issues. Ellingsen, Mark. Grand Rapids: Eerdmans, 1993. 400p ISBN 0-8028-0710-0

Days of the Lord, vol 5, ordinary time: year B. . Collegeville: Liturgical, 1993. 376p ISBN 0-8146-1903-7 LC 90-22253

Days of the Lord: the liturgical year; vol 2. Beaumont, Madeleine. Minnesota: The Liturgical Press, 1990. x, 274p ISBN 0-8146-1900-2 LC 90-22253

Days of the Lord: the liturgical year; vol 3. LaNave, Gred. Minnesota: The Liturgical Press, 1993. x, 364p ISBN 0-8146-1901-0 LC 90-22253

The Dead Sea Scrolls uncovered: the first complete translation and interpretation of 50 key documents withheld for over 35 years. Eisenman, Robert H. Rockport: Element, 1992. 286p ISBN 1-85230-368-9

The Dead Sea Scrolls, Vol I, rules: rules of the community and related documents. Charlesworth, James H. Louisville: John Knox, 1993. x, 300p ISBN 0-664-21994-4

The Dead Sea Scrolls, vol II, rules: Damascus document, war scroll, and related documents. Charlesworth, James H. Louisville: John Knox, 1993. x, 300p ISBN 0-664-22037-1

Death and destiny in the Bible. Wensing, Michael G. Minnesota: The Order of St Benedict, 1993. x, 83p ISBN 0-8146-2093-0 LC 92-27237

Death dreams: unveiling mysteries of the unconscious mind. Kramer, Kenneth P. New Jersey: Paulist Press, 1993. x, 288p ISBN 0-8091-3349-0 LC 92-29605

Deciding who lives: fateful choices in the intensive care nursery. Anspach, Renée R. Berkeley: University of California Press, 1993. x, 303p ISBN 0-520-05268-4 LC 91-44245

Defiant hope: spirituality for survivors of family abuse. Leehan, James. Louisville: John Knox, 1993. x, 176p ISBN 0-664-25463-2

Degenerate moderns. Jones, Michael E. San Francisco: Ignatius Press, 1993. ISBN 0-89810-447-2

Delightful conviction: Jonathan Edwards and the rhetoric of conversion. Yarbrough, Stephen R, and Adams, John C. Westport: Greenwood Press, 1993. x, 208p ISBN 0-313-27582-3

A democratic Catholic Church: in a reconstruction of Roman Catholicism. Bianchi, Eugene C, and Ruether, Rosemary Radford, eds. New York: Crossroad, 1993. x, 262p ISBN 0-8245-1186-7 LC 92-7920

The depleted self: sin in a narcissistic age. Capps, Donald. Minneapolis: Fortress Press, 1993. x, 176p ISBN 0-80062-587-0 LC 92-7931

El desierto delos dioses: teologia e historia en el libro de Oseas. Simian-Yofre, Horacio. Cordoba: Ediciones El Alme, 1993. x, 283p ISBN 84-8005-007-1

Devotional classics: selected readings for individuals and groups. Foster, Richard J, and Smith, James Bryan, eds. New York: HarperSanFrancisco, 1993. 353p ISBN 0-06-066966-7 LC 92-53912

Dialogue about Catholic's sexual teaching. Curran, Charles E, 1934-, and McCormick, Richard A, eds. Mahwah: Paulist, 1993. x, 601p ISBN 0-8091-3414-4 LC 93-12460

Diary of a city priest. McNamee, John P. Kansas City: Sheed & Ward, 1993. x, 258p ISBN 1-55612-662-x LC 93-11924

Dioniso dormido sobre un tigre: a traves de Nietzchey su teoria del lenguaje. Lynch, Enrique. Barcelona: Destino, 1993. x, 400p ISBN 84-233-2269-6

El dios de los dioses: ciencia del arte. Galan, Ilia. Madríd: Líbertarias, 1993. x, 237p ISBN 84-7954-116-4

The discerning heart: discovering a personal God. Conroy, Maureen. Chicago: Loyola University Press, 1993. x, 272p ISBN 0-8294-0752-9 LC 93-12508

Discernment. Wolff, Pierre. Missouri: Triumph Books, 1993. x, 145p ISBN 0-89243-485-6 LC 93-7922

Disciples at the crossroads: perspectives on worship and church leadership. Bernstein, Eleanor, ed. Collegeville:Liturgical, 1993. x, 153p ISBN 0-8146-2146-5 LC 93-591

Discipleship of equals: a critical feminist ecology of liberation. Fiorenza, Elisabeth Schüssler, 1938-. New York: Crossroad, 1993. x, 372p ISBN 0-82451-244-8 LC 92-31264

Discovering prophecy and wisdom: the books of Isaiah, Job, Proverbs, Psalms. Ralph, Margaret Nutting. New York: Paulist, 1993. x, 326p ISBN 08-0913-402-0 LC 93-10245

Discusiones sobre la metafisica. Armesto, Indalecio. Santiago: Universidad, 1993. x, 360p ISBN 84-7191-968-0

Disiplines for Christian living. Ryan, Thomas. New Jersey: Paulist Press, 1993. x, 274p ISBN 0-8091-3380-6 LC 92-42596

Dissent and order in the Middle Ages: the search for legitimate authority. Russell, Jeffrey Burton. New York: Twayne Publishers, 1992. x, 128p ISBN 0-80578-603-1 LC 92-5328

Divine or distorted?: God as we understand God. Seiden, Jerry. San Diego, California: Recovery Publications, 1993. x, 142p ISBN 0-941405-19-2 LC 92-41854

Do what you have the power to do: studies of six New Testament women. Pearson, Helen Bruch. Nashville: Upper Room Books, 1992. x, 168p ISBN 08-358-0643-x LC 91-65725

La doctrina del acto en Aristoteles. Yepes Stork, Ricardo. Pamplona: Eunsa, 1993. x, 1993 ISBN 84-313-1231-9

Dominar el pas dels anys. Sobreroca I Ferrer, Lluis Antoni. Barcelona: Scripta, 1993. x, 272p ISBN 84-85205-29-4

Dominion maximum. Imperio, Vic N. New York: Vantage Press, 1992. x, 139p ISBN 0-533-10077-1 LC 91-91242

Dorothy L Sayers: the centenary celebration. Dale, Alzina Stone. New York: Walker and Co, 1993. 166p ISBN 0-80273-224-0 LC 92-44894

The dream of the seventh-day ark for sores and burns, for soul and body. Smith, Joyce L. New York: Vantage Press, 1993. 97p ISBN 0-533-09090-3

Drinking from the hidden fountain: a patristic breviary. Spidlik, Thomas. London: New City, 1992. 447p ISBN 0-904287-39-4

Easter in the early church: an anthology of Jewish and early Christian texts. Cantalamessa, Raniero. Collegeville: The Liturgical, 1993. x, 254p ISBN 0-8146-2164-3 LC 92-43999

Educating in faith. Boys, Mary C. Kansas City: Sheed & Ward, 1989. 230p ISBN 1-55612-668-9

Education for ministry: reform and renewal in theological education. Schner, George P, 1946-. Kansas City: Sheed & Ward, 1993. x, 195p ISBN 15-5612-566-6 LC 92-32958

The education of an American Catholic. Beeching, Paul Q. Chicago: The Thomas More Press, 1993. x, 405p ISBN 0-88347-275-9

Elizabeth Ann Seton: a woman of prayer. Celeste, Marie. New York: Alba House, 1993. 134p ISBN 0-8189-0650-2 LC 92-44978

Elizabeth Bayley Seton: an American saint. Stone, Elaine Murray. New York: Paulist Press, 1993. 86p ISBN 0-8091-6609-7 LC 92-44027

Embracing the mystery: prayerful responses to AIDS. Sandys, Sebastian, ed. Minnesota: The Liturgical Press, 1993. x, 105p ISBN 0-8146-2222-4 LC 92-43238

The emperor and the Gods. Schowalter, Daniel N. Minneapolis: Fortress, 1993. 164p ISBN 0-8006-7082-5 LC 90-40141

Enneagram companions: growing in relationships and spiritual direction. Zuercher, Suzanne. Notre Dame: Ave Maria Press, 1993. 181p ISBN 0-87793-510-6 LC 93-71263

Enough is enough: grace for the restless heart. Westfall, John F. New York: HarperSanFrancisco, 1993. x, 165p ISBN 0-06-069289-8 LC 91-58990

Las ensenanzas de Don Carlos: aplicaciones practicas de la obra de Carlos Castaneda. Sanchez, Victor. Madrid: Havilah, 1993. x, 282p ISBN 84-87745-04-0

Entre el liberalismo y la socialdemocracia: la sociedad abierta. Perona, Angeles J. Barcelona: Anthropos, 1993. x, 248p ISBN 84-7658-394-x

Entrevista sobre el fundador del Opus Dei, realizada por Cesare Cavallieri. Portillo, Alvaro del. Madrid: Rialp, 1993. x, 252p ISBN 84-321-2972-0

Eros and the Jews: from biblical Israel to contemporary America. Biale, David. New York: Basic Books, 1992. 319p ISBN 0-4650-2033-x

Essays in memory of John G. Gammie. Perdue, Leo G, et al, eds. Louisville: John Knox, 1993. x, 352p ISBN 0-664-25295-8

Essays on science and faith. Pannenbert, Wolfhart. Louisville: Westminster, 1993. x, 208p ISBN 0-664-25384-9

Etica laica y sociedad pluralista. Guidan, E, et al. Madrid: Popular, 1993. x, 157p ISBN 84-7884-087-7

The Eucharist, our sanctification. Cantalamessa, Raniero. Minnesota: The Order of St Benedict, 1993. x, 89p ISBN 0-8146-2075-2 LC 92-404-433

Eucharist: celebrating its rhythms in our lives. Bernier, Paul. Indiana: Ave Maria Press, 1993. 160p ISBN 0-87793-506-8 LC 92-75342

The Eucharistic mystery: revitalizing the tradition. Power, David Noel. New York: The Crossroad Publishing Company, 1992. x, 370p ISBN 0-8245-1220-0 LC 92-29777

Evangelical Kernels: a theological spirituality of the religious life. Billy, Dennis J. New York: Alba House, 1993. ISBN

Evening devotions. Lane, Wilbur. New York: Vantage Press, 1993. 49p ISBN 0-533-10380-0 LC 92-90962

Ever ancient, ever new: Villanova University, 1842-1992 [photos]. Contosta, David R, and Gallagher, Dennis J. Virginia Beach: The Donning Company, 1992. 120p ISBN 0-89865-870-0 LC 92-24373

The everlasting man. Chesterton, Gilbert Keith, 1874-1936. San Francisco: Ignatius Press, 1993. ISBN 0-89870-444-8

Everybody has guardian angel: and other lasting lessons I learned in Catholic School. Finley, Mitchel B. New York: The Crossroad Publishing Company, 1993. 188p ISBN 0-8245-1268-5 LC 92-39443

Everything I needed to know about success, I learned in the Bible (and so can you!). Briley, Richard Gaylord. New Hampshire: The publisher-In-The-Glen, 1993. x, 144p ISBN 1-882988-05-1

Explorations in theology, VI III: creator spirit. Balthasar, Hans Urs Von, 1905-1988. San Francisco: Ignatius Press, 1993. ISBN 0-89870-437-5

Exploring the resurrection of Jesus. Perry, John Michael. Kansas City: Sheed & Ward, 1993. x, 145p ISBN 1-55612-670-0 LC 93-29160

The faces of the gods: vodou and Roman Catholicism in Haiti. Desmangles, Leslie Gèrald. Chapel Hill: The University of North Carolina Press, 1992. 218p ISBN 0-80782-059-8 LC 92-53625

Facilitating for growth: a guide for Scripture groups and small Christian communities. Fleischer, Barbara J. Collegeville: Liturgical, 1993. 160p ISBN 0-8146-2170-8 LC 93-1341

Facing the abusing God: a theology of protest. Blumenthal, David Reuben, 1938-. Louisville: John Knox, 1993. x, 208p ISBN 0-664-25464-0

Facts, myths and maybes: everything you think you know about Catholicism. Deedy, John G, 1933-. Chicago: The Thomas More Press, 1993. 320p ISBN 0-88347-272-4

Faith and the human enterprise: a post-Vatican II vision. Weakland, Rembert G, Abp, 1927-. Maryknoll: Orbis Books, 1992. 168p ISBN 0-88344-835-1 LC 92-32884

Faith, culture, and the worshipping community: shaping the practice of the local church. Warren, Michael, 1935-. Washington, DC: The Pastoral Press, 1993. x, 194p ISBN 1-56929-002-4

Faith without dogma: the place of religion in postmodern societies. Ferrarotti, Franco. New Jersey: Transaction Publishers, 1993. x, 181p ISBN 1-56000-074-0 LC 92-17835

Faith without prejudice: rebuilding Christian attitudes toward Judaism. Fisher, Eugene J. New York: The Crossroad Publishing Company, 1993. x, 208p ISBN 0-8245-1266-9 LC 92-36342

The fall of the prison: biblical perspectives on prison abolition. Griffith, Lee. Grand Rapids: Eerdmans, 1993. 280p ISBN 0-8028-0670-8

Families of alcoholics: a guide to healing and recovery. Nuechterlein, Anne Marie. Minneapolis: Augsburg, 1993. x, 140p ISBN 0-80662-615-1 LC 92-19156

Father Scott's reflections on women, family, and relationships. Scott, John M. Indiana: Our Sunday Visitor, 1993. 139p ISBN 0-87973-530-9 LC 92-61551

Fathers come home: a wake-up call for busy dads. Swindell, Bill. South Bend, Indiana: Greenlawn Press, 1992. x, 101p ISBN 0-937779-23-7 LC 92-75551

A feminist model for pastoral psychology. DeMarinis, Valerie M. Louisville: John Knox, 1993. x, 208p ISBN 0-664-22041-x

The fifteen mysteries in image and word. Pennington, M Basil, 1931-. Huntington: Our Sunday Visitor, 1993. 165p ISBN 0-87973-499-x LC 92-61553

Fillin' up: devotional fuel for high performance living. Littleton, Mark. Sisters: Questar, 1993. x, 180p ISBN 0-945564-72-4

Film makers, film viewers: their challenges and opportunities [pastoral letter]. Mahony, Roger Michael, Cardinal, 1936-. Boston: St Paul Books & Media, 1992. 31p ISBN 0-8198-2654-5

Fire bearer: evoking a priestly humanity. Dwinell, Michael. Liguori: Triumph Books, 1993. x, 198p ISBN 0-89243-531-3 LC 92-43418

The first step for people in relationships with addicts. Hunter, Mic. Minneapolis: CompCare Publishers, 1989. x, 122p ISBN 0-89638-163-3 LC 89-15709

For all the peoples of Asia: documents from 1970-1991. Rosales, Gaudencio B, and Arevalo, Catalino G, eds. Maryknoll, New York: Orbis Books, 1992. x, 356p ISBN 0-88344-837-8 LC 92-5033

For the bride: finding your way in the first years of marriage. Sanford, Ruth. South Bend: Green Lawn, 1993. 136p ISBN 0-937779-24-5 LC 93-70110

Forbidden fruit: the true story of my secret love affair with Ireland's most powerful bishop. Murphy, Annie. Boston: Little, Brown and Company, 1993. 358p ISBN 0-31659-090-8 LC 93-3239

Forever faithful: the unfolding of God's promise to creation. Reiser, William, 1943-. Collegeville:Liturgical, 1993. 98p ISBN 0-8146-5849-0 LC 93-15191

Forming a small Christian community: a personal journey. Currier, Richard. Mystic: Twenty-Third Publications, 1992. 178p ISBN 0-89622-511-9 LC 91-68557

Francis de Sales: finding God wherever you are. Power, Joseph F. New York: New City Press, 1993. 159p ISBN 1-56548-021-x LC 92-44973

Freedom and creation in three traditions. Burrell, David B. Notre Dame: University of Notre Dame Press, 1993. x, 224p ISBN 0-268-00987-2 LC 92-53745

Freedom: the teachings of Jesus. Pierce, Ted M. New York: Vantage Press, 1992. x, 225p ISBN 0-533-10182-4 LC 91-91544

French pianism: an historical perspective. Timbrell, Charles. White Plains: Pro/Am Music Resources, 1992. x, 288p ISBN 0-912483-89-x

Friederich Nietzsche: una biografia. Morey, Miguel. Madrid: Archipielago, 1993. x, 126p ISBN 84-88595-00-x

From victim to Victor: a biblical guide for turning hurting into healing. Martinez, Yvonne. San Diego: Recovery Publications, 1993. x, 127p ISBN 0-941405-24-9 LC 93-13946

Fullness of faith: the public significance of theology. Himes, Michael J, and Himes, Kenneth R. New York: Paulist Press, 1993. x, 213p ISBN 0-8091-3372-5 LC 92-36140

The future of Christology: essays in honor of Leander E Keck. Malherbe, Abraham J, and Meeks, Wayne A, eds. Minneapolis: Fortress Press, 1993. x, 265p ISBN 0-80062-728-8 LC 92-40265

Gaia and God: an ecofeminist theology of earth healing. Ruether, Rosemary Radford. San Francisco: HarperSanFrancisco, 1992. 310p ISBN 0-06067-022-3 LC 91-58911

Galatians without tears. Dalton, William J. Collegeville, Minnesota: The Liturgical Press, 1992. 75p ISBN 0-8146-2227-5 LC 93-18782

The Garden of Eden and the hope of immortality. Barr, James. Minneapolis: Fortress Press, 1993. 146p ISBN 0-80062-744-x LC 92-27037

The gardeners of God: an encounter with five million Bahá'ís. Gouvion, Colette, and Jouvion, Philippe. Oxford: Oneworld, 1993. x, 223p ISBN 1-85168-052-7

The gate of glory. Carey, George Leonard, Abp of Canterbury, 1935-. Grand Rapids: Eerdmans, 1993. 256p ISBN 0-8028-3724-7

Gateway to paradise: Basil the Great. Davies, Oliver, ed. New Rochelle, New York: New City Press, 1992. 125p ISBN 1-56548-0023 LC 91-34259

Genesis 12-50: Abraham and all the families of the earth. Janzen, J Gerald. Grand Rapids: Eerdmans, 1993. 230p ISBN 0-8028-0148-x

Genesis, creation, and creationism. Bailey, Lloyd R. New Jersey: Paulist Press, 1993. x, 259p ISBN 0-8091-3255-9 LC 92-33185

The genesis of God: a theological genealogy. Altizer, Thomas J J. Louisville: John Knox, 1993. x, 208p ISBN 0-664-21996-9

Genesis: a commentary for students, teachers, and preachers. Scullion, John J. Collegeville, Minnesota: Liturgical Press, 1992. x, 366p ISBN 0-81465-659-5 LC 92-12322

Geographia de l'absurd. Torralba Rossello, Francesc. Lerida: Pages, 1993. 149p ISBN 84-7935-132-2

Gerard Manley Hopkins annual 1993. Sundermeier, Michael, and Egan, Desmond, eds. Omaha: Creighton University Press, 1993. x, 123p ISBN 1-881871-07-x

Gertrude of Helfta: the herald of divine love. Winkworth, Margaret. New York: Paulist Press, 1993. x, 259p ISBN 0-8091-0458-x LC 92-20663

Geschichte der religiösen Ideen: 5 vols. Eliade, Mircea, 1907-1985. Freiburg: Herder, 1993. x, 2200p ISBN 3-451-04200-2

Global responsibility: in search of a new world ethic. Kung, Hans, 1928-. New York: Crossroad, 1991. x, 158p ISBN 0-8245-1102-6 LC 91-7956

The gods of televangelism. Peck, Janice. Cresskill, New Jersey: Hampton Press, 1993. x, 271p ISBN 1-88130-365-9 LC 92-32476

God's passionate and our desire response. Barry, William A. Indiana: Ave Maria Press, 1993. x, 143p ISBN 0-87793-501-7 LC 92-75346

God's politician: Pope John Paul II, the Catholic Church, and the new world order. Willey, David. New York: St Martin's Press, 1993. x, 258p ISBN 0-31208-798-5 LC 92-36031

Good news for animals?: Christian approaches to animal well-being. Pinches, Charles, and McDaniel, Jay B, eds. Maryknoll, New York: Orbis Books, 1993. x, 258p ISBN 0-88344-866-1 LC 92-41682

Goodness and rightness: Thomas Aquinas' Summa Theologia. Keenan, James F. Washington, D C: Georgetown University Press, 1992. x, 212p ISBN 0-87840-530-5 LC 92-3090

The Gospel according to John: a literary and theological commentary. Brodia, Thomas L. New York: Oxford University, 1993. x, 625p ISBN 0-19-505800-3 LC 91-38200

The gospel according to Mary: a New Testament for women. Winter, Miriam Therese. New York: The Crossroad Publishing Company, 1993. x, 143p ISBN 0-8245-1174-3 LC 92-403531

A gospel for a new people: studies in Matthew. Stanton, Graham N. Louisville, Kentucky: John Knox Press, 1993. 424p ISBN 0-664-25499-3

Gott Suchen sich Selbst Erkennen. Cassian, Johannes. Freiburg: Herder, 1993. x, 480p ISBN 3-451-23246-4

Grace in the end: a study in Deuteronomic theology. McConville, J Gordon. Grand Rapids: Zondervan Publishing House, 1993. x, 176p ISBN 0-310-51421-5

The great church year: the best of Karl Rahner's homilies, sermons, and meditations. Rahner, Karl, 1904-1984. New York: Crossroad, 1993. 396p ISBN 0-8245-1220-6 LC 93-3930

Great fundraising ideas for youth groups. Lynn, David, and Lynn, Kathy. Grand Rapids: Zondervan Publishing House, 1993. x, 208p ISBN 0-310-67171-x

The green Bible. Scharper, Stephen B, and Cunningham, Hilary, eds. Maryknoll, New York: Orbis Books, 1993. x, 113p ISBN 0-85244-230-0 LC 92-35593

Guiding your parish through the Christian initiation process: a handbook for leaders. Bruns, William R. Cincinnati: St Anthony Messenger Press, 1993. 152p ISBN 0-86716-188-4

The Hail Mary: a verbal icon of Mary. Ayo, Nicholas. Notre Dame: University of Notre Dame Press, 1994. x, 256p ISBN 0-268-01101-x LC 93-24743

The Hamlet syndrome: overthinkers who underachieve. Miller, Adrienne. New York: William Morrow and Company, 1989. 272p ISBN 0-688-07851-6 LC 88-30866

A handbook for coping. Gaddy, Welton C. Louisville: Westminster, 1993. x, 128p ISBN 0-664-25458-6

The hastening that waits. Biggar, Nigel. New York: Oxford University Press, 1993. x, 208p ISBN 0-826457-7

Healing breath: Zen spirituality for a wounded earth. Habito, Ruben L.F. Maryknoll: Orbis, 1993. x, 166p ISBN 0-88344-919-0 LC 93-5125

Hegel y el Romanticismo. Innerarity, Daniel. Madrid: Tecnos, 1993. x, 212p ISBN 84-309-2331-4

Hellfire and lighting rods: liberating science, technology, and religion. Ferré, Frederick. Maryknoll, New York: Orbis Books, 1993. 92-39488 ISBN 0-88344-856-4 LC 92-39488

Helping skills for the nonprofessional counselor. Moore, Joseph. Cincinatti: St Anthony Press, 1993. x, 67p ISBN 0-86716-1744

Here comes everybody!: stories of church. Unsworth, Tim. New York: Crossroad, 1993. x, 226p ISBN 0-8245-1231-6 LC 93-4699

Heresy and criticism: the search for authenticity in early literature. Grant, Robert McQueen, 1917-. Louisville: John Knox Press, 1993. 180p ISBN 0-66421-971-3 LC 92-20017

The hiddennes of God. Law, David R. New York: Oxford University Press, 1993. x, 256p ISBN 0-826336-8

Hildegard of Bingen: mystic healer, companion of the angels. Ulrich, Ingeborg. Collegeville: Liturgical, 1990. 258p ISBN 0-8146-2132-5 LC 93-19848

Historical atlas of the Middle East. Freeman-Grenville, G S P. New York: Simon & Schuster, 1993. x, 144p ISBN 0-13-3-390915-8

The history of St. Joseph's Seminary, New York. Shelley, Thomas J. Westminster: Christian Classics, 1993. x, 480p ISBN 0-87061-198-4

The Holy Spirit and the Christian life: the library of theological ethics. Barth, Karl, 1886-1968. Louisville: John Knox, 1993. x, 96p ISBN 0-664-25325-3

El hombre es imagen de Dios. Dolby Mugica, Maria del Carmen. Pamplona: Eunsa, 1993. x, 274p ISBN 84-313-1223-8

Homosexuality and world religions. Swidler, Arlene. Philadelphia: Trinity Press International, 1993. 232p ISBN 1-56338-051-x LC 93-6848

Horizons for Catholic feminist theology. Conn, Joann Wolski, and Conn, Walter E, eds. Washington, D C: Georgetown University Press, 1992. x, 207p ISBN 0-87840-534-8 LC 92-30435

Horrific traumata: a pastoral response to the post-traumatic stress disorder. Sinclair, N Duncan. Binghamton, New York: The Haworth Pastoral Press, 1993. x, 118p ISBN 1-56024-294-9 LC 92-4194

How to handle trouble. Carmody, John Tully. New York: Doubleday, 1993. x, 226p ISBN 0-385-47120-3 LC 93-16848

How to read the Apocalypse. Prévost, Jean-Pierre. New York: The Crossroad Publishing Company, 1993. x, 118p ISBN 0-8245-1280-4 LC 93-16880

How to read the church fathers. Hamman, Adalbert. New York: The Crossroad Publishing Company, 1993. x, 132p ISBN 0-8245-1204-9 LC 92-42052

Human sexuality: an all-embracing gift. Coleman, Gerald D. New York: Alba House, 1992. x, 441p ISBN 0-81890-643-x LC 92-20661

Humanity in God. Moltmann-Wendel, Elisabeth, and Moltmann, Jürgen. Cleveland: The Pilgrim Press, 1993. x, 133p ISBN 0-8298-0670-9 LC 93-4180

The hungry heart. Griffiths, Max. Kenthorts, Australia: Kangaroo Press, 1992. 176p ISBN 0-86417-486-1

I and II chronicles: a commentary. Mays, James L, et al, eds. Louisville: John Knox, 1993. x, 1104p ISBN 0-664-21845-8

I sit listening to the wind: woman's encounter within herself. Duerk, Judith. San Diego: LuraMedia, 1993. x, 103p ISBN 0-931055-98-9 LC 93-991

La ilustracion olvidada. Condorcet, de Gouges, de Lamberty y Otros. Madrid: Anthropos, 1993. x, 176p ISBN 84-7658-408-3

Images of Jesus: ten invitations to intimacy. McBride, Alfred. Cincinnati: St Anthony Messenger Press, 1993. x, 239p ISBN 0-86716-180-9

In heaven there are no thunderstorms: celebrating the liturgy with developmentally disabled people. Okhuijsen, Gijs. Collegeville:Liturgical, 1992. 136p ISBN 0-81461-999-1 LC 91-41-4407

In search of guidance: developing a conversational relationship with God. Willard, Dallas. New York: HarperSanFrancisco, 1993. x, 247p ISBN 0-06-069520-x LC 92-56406

In the company of preachers. . Minnesota: The Liturgical Press, 1993. x, 227p ISBN 0-8146-2091-4 LC 92-32646

In the presence of the wise and gentile Christ. McNamara, James M. New York: Paulist Press, 1993. x, 156p ISBN 0-8091-3375-x LC 92-36141

Incarnation: contemporary writers on the New Testament. Corn, Alfred, ed. New York: Penguin Books, 1991. x, 361p ISBN 0-14011-583-8 LC 90-21991

Innocent at Dachau. Halow, Joseph. Newport Beach, California: Institute for Historical Review, 1993. x, 237p ISBN 0-939482-40-11

Inside the mind of unchurched Harry and Mary. Strobel, Lee. Grand Rapids: Zondervan Publishing House, 1993. x, 224p ISBN 0-310-37561-4

Intellectuals don't need God and other modern myths. McGrath, Alister E. Grand Rapids: Zondervan Publishing House, 1993. x, 256p ISBN 0-310-59091-4

Interactional morality: a foundation for moral discernment in Catholic pastoral ministry. Poorman, Mark L. Washington: Georgetown University Press, 1993. 157p ISBN 0-87840-536-4 LC 93-3803

Interpretations of conflict: ethics, pacificism, and the just-war tradition. Miller, Richard Brian. Chicago: University of Chicago Press, 1991. 294p ISBN 0-22652-795-6 LC 91-3044

Interwoven destinies: Jews and Christians through the ages. Fisher, Eugene J. New Jersey: Paulist Press, 1993. x, 154p ISBN 0-8091-8363-6 LC 92-37707

Intimate bedfellows: love, sex, and the Catholic Church. Finn, Thomas, and Finn, Donna. Boston: St. Paul Books & Media, 1993. 85p ISBN 0-8198-3667-2 LC 92-42622

Introducing the newest and most up-to-date Catholic dictionary. Stravinskas, Peter. Huntington: Our Sunday Visitor, 1993. x, 500p ISBN 0-87973-507-4

Introduction to biblical interpretation. Klein, William Wade, et al, eds. Dallas: Word Publishing, 1993. x, 518p ISBN 0-8499-0774-8 LC 93-20099

Introduction to New Testament exegesis. Stenger, Werner. Grand Rapids: Eerdmans, 1993. 240p ISBN 0-8028-0138-2

Introduction to systematic theology. Slavens, Thomas Paul. Maryland: University Press of America, 1992. x, 71p ISBN 0-8191-8228-1 LC 91-10147

Introduction to the ancient world. Soden, Wolfram von. Grand Rapids: Eerdmans, 1993. 256p ISBN 0-8028-0142-0

An introduction to the Christian faith: a biblical perspective. Moses, Earl C, Jr. New York: Vantage Press, 1993. 127p ISBN 0-533-10329-0 LC 92-90810

Introduction to the history of exegesis [v 3]. Margerie, Bertrand de. Petersham: Saint Bede's Publications, 1991. x, 169p ISBN 0-932506-97-6 LC 93-16067

Is it okay to call God mother?: considering the feminine face of God. Smith, Paul R. Peabody: Hendrickson Publishers, 1993. 273p ISBN 1-56563-013-0 LC 93-25810

Isaiah 1-39. Saitz, Christopher R. Louisville: John Knox, 1993. x, 272p ISBN 0-8042-3131-1

Isaiah and urban possibility. Brueggemann, Walter. Louisville: Westminster, 1993. x, 96p ISBN 0-664-25460-8

Islam and the west: the making of an image. Daniel, Norman. Oxford: Oneworld, 1993. x, 467p ISBN 1-85168-043-8

Island of tears, island of hope: living the gospel in a revolutionary situation. O'Brien, Niall. Maryknoll: Orbis, 1993. x, 234p ISBN 0-88344-927-7 LC 73-23776

Jacques Maritain and the Jews. Royal, Robert, ed. Notre Dame: University of Notre Dame Press, 1993. 264p ISBN 0-268-01193-1 LC 93-4633

Japan's hidden Christians. Harrington, Ann M. Chicago: Loyola University Press, 1993. x, 110p ISBN 0-8294-0741-3

The Jesuit assassinations. . Kansas City: Sheed and Ward, 1990. x, 158p ISBN 1-55612-409-0

Jesus acted up: a gay and lesbian manifesto. Goss, Robert. New York: HarperSanFrancisco, 1993. x, 240p ISBN 0-06-063318-2 LC 92-56415

Jesus and the Dead Sea Scrolls. Charlesworth, James H. New York: Doubleday, 1992. x, 370p ISBN 0-385-24863-6 LC 92-2617

Jesus and the forgotten city: new light on Sepphoris and the urban world of Jesus. Batey, Richard A. Grand Rapids: Baker Book House, 1991.

Jesus: der neue Mensch. Borg, Marcus J. Frieburg: Herder, 1993. x, 240p ISBN 3-451-23093-3

John Henry Newman: heart to heart. Giese, Vincent. New York: New City Press, 1993. x, 96p ISBN 1-56548-023-6 LC 92-42030

John Paul II. Bujak, Adam. Krakow: Parol Company, 1992. x, 111p ISBN 0-89870-424-13 LC 92-71934

John, the maverick gospel. Kysar, Robert. Louisville: John Knox, 1993. x, 176p ISBN 0-664-25401-2

Jonah, a commentary. Limburg, James. Louisville: John Knox, 1993. x, 144p ISBN 0-664-21296-4

The Joseph Campbell phenomenon: implications for the contemporary church. Madden, Lawrence J, ed. Washington: The Pastoral Press, 1992. x, 153p ISBN 0-912405-89-9

Joseph Fletcher: memoir of an ex-radical: reminiscence and reappraisal. Fletcher, Joseph. Louisville: John Knox, 1993. x, 96p ISBN 0-664-25372-5

Josiah's passover: sociology and the liberating Bible. Nakanose, Shigeyuki. Maryknoll: Orbis Books, 1993. x, 192p ISBN 0-88344850-5 LC 93-18286

Journey for the shadowlands: the readings for the Rites of the Cat. Jackson, Pamela E J. Minnesota: The Liturgical Press, 1993. x, 171p ISBN 0-8146-2113-9

Journey in dust and light: a modern pilgrimage through the life and letters of Paul. DeMers, John. Minnesota: The Liturgical Press, 1993. x, 112p ISBN 0-8146-5701-x LC 92-40482

Journey of love: God moving in our hearts and lives. Conroy, Maureen. Mahwah: The Paulist Press, 1993. 82p ISBN 0-8091-3413-6 LC 93-979

Journey with the Fathers: commentaries on the Sunday gospels, Year A. Barnecot, Edith, ed. New York: New City Press, 1992. 168p ISBN 1-56548-013-9 LC 92-20685

Journey with the Fathers; commentaries on the Sunday gospels, Year B. Barnecut, Edith, ed. New Rochelle: New City Press, 1993. 160p ISBN 1-56548-056-2 LC 92-20685

Joy in suffering: receiving your reward. Lambert, David. Grand Rapids: Zondervan Publishing House, 1993. x, 64p ISBN 0-310-59673-4

The joy of kindness. Furey, Robert J. New York: The Crossroad Publishing Company, 1993. x, 155p ISBN 0-8245-1269-3 LC 92-38935

Juan de Zumarraga y su "Regla Cristiana breve". Alejos-Grau, Carmen Jose. Vitoria: Gobierno Vasco, 1993. x, 242p ISBN 84-457-0129-0

Judas, betrayer or betrayed? Nunes, Danillo. New York: Vantage Press, 1992. x, 319p ISBN 0-533-10065-8 LC 91-912232

Julian's way: a practical commentary on Julian of Norwich. Bradley, Ritamary. London: HarperCollins Religious, 1992. x, 231p ISBN 0-00-599275-3

Just a moment: life matters with Father Tom. Hartman, Thomas. Liguori: Triumph Books, 1993. 222p ISBN 0-89243-530-5 LC 92-43420

Karl Barth: his life from letters and autobiographical texts. Busch, Eberhard. Grand Rapids: Eerdmans, 1993. 600p ISBN 0-8028-0708-9

Katholische Gesellschaftslehre im Überlick. Kerber, Walter, 1926-, et al, eds. Frankfurt: Knecht, 1993. x, 420p ISBN 3-7820-0623-2

Kleines credo fur Verunsicherte. Beinert, Wolfgang, et al. Freiburg: Herder, 1993. x, 144p ISBN 3-451-23245-6

En la lucha-In the struggle: a Hispanic women's liberation theology. Isasi-Díaz, Ada María. Minneapolis: Fortress, 1993. x, 226p ISBN 0-8006-2610-9 LC 93-9220

The laity in the Middle Ages: religious practices and experiences. Vauchez, André. Notre Dame: University of Notre Dame, 1993. x, 350p ISBN 0-268-01297-0 LC 92-53746

Late have I loved you: an interpretation of Saint Augustine on human and divine relationships. Mohler, James Aylward. New Rochelle, New York: New City Press, 1991. 159p ISBN 0-911782-86-9 LC 90-28643

Leadership in a successful parish. Sweetser, Thomas P, and Holden, Carol M. Kansas City: Sheed & Ward, 1992. x, 203p ISBN 1-55612-564-x LC 92-20718

Leave the temple: Indian paths to human liberation. Wilfred, Felix. Maryknoll, New York: Orbis Books, 1992. x, 199p ISBN 0-88344-794-0 LC 92-20801

The letter carrier. Leonard, William J. Kansas City: Sheed & Ward, 1993. x, 373p ISBN 1-55612-651-4 LC 93-18887

The letters of Paul: an introduction. Puskas, Charles B. Collegeville: Liturgical, 1993. x, 216p ISBN 0-8146-5690-0 LC 92-46909

Letting God free us: meditations on Ignatian Spiritual Exercises. Martini, Carlo Maria, Cardinal, 1926-. New Rochelle: New City Press, 1993. 128p ISBN 1-56548-053-8 LC 93-15187

Liberation theology: an introductory guide. Brown, Robert McAfee, 1920-. Louisville: John Knox Press, 1993. x, 143p ISBN 0-66425-424-1 LC 92-30934

Libre de familia: dotze germans I deu escubas. . Barcelona: Deriva, 1993. x, 147p ISBN 84-97981-05-4

Life after Easter. Smith, Pamela. New Jersey: Paulist Press, 1993. x, 88p ISBN 0-8091-3379-2 LC 92-21195

The life of St Benedict: Gregory the Great. Vogue, Albert de. Petersham: St Bede's Publications, 1993. x, 186p ISBN 0-932506-77-1 LC 93-420

The life of the venerable servant of God Vincent de Paul: founder and first superior general of the Congregation of the Mission (book one). Abelly, Louis. New Rochelle, New York: New City Press, 1993. 403p ISBN 1-56548-052-x LC 93-9446

Life's greatest grace: why I belong to the Catholic Church. Miller, J Michael. Huntington: Our Sunday Visitor, 1993. x, 160p ISBN 0-87973-471-9

Light in the Lord. Hume, George Basil, Cardinal, 1923-. Minnesota: The Liturgical Press, 1991. x, 174p ISBN 0-8146-2142-2 LC 92-43998

Light of faith: the compenduine of theology. Thomas Aquinas, Saint. Manchester: Sophia Institute Press, 1993. x, 412p ISBN 0-918477-15-8 LC 93-6793

Like bread, their voices rise! Global women challenge the Church. O'Connor, Bernard. Notre Dame: Ave Maria Press, 1993. 204p ISBN 0-87793-509-2 LC 93-77734

Listening to the music of the spirit: the art of discernment. Lonsdale, David. Notre Dame: Ave Maria Press, 1993. x, 174p ISBN 08-7793-508-4

A litany of saints. Ball, Ann. Indiana: Our Sunday Visitor, 1993. 244p ISBN 0-879973 LC 92-61546

Literacy-critical approaches to the Bible: an annotated bibliography. Minor, Mark. West Cornwall: Locust Hill Press, 1992. 520p ISBN 0-93395-148-5 LC 92-7469

Literary stategy in the Epistle of Jude. Daryl, Charles J. Scranton: University of Scranton Press, 1993. 258p ISBN 0-94086-616-1 LC 91-66129

The liturgical dictionary of Eastern Christianity. Day, Peter D. Collegeville: Liturgical, 1993. x, 334p ISBN 0-8146-5848-2 LC 93-20377

Liturgy and personality: the healing power of formal prayer. Hildebrand, Dietrich von. Manchester: Sophia Institute Press, 1993. x, 165p ISBN 0-918477-13-1 LC 29-19821

Living free in Christ. Anderson, Neil T. Ventura: Gospel Light, 1993. 310p ISBN 0-8307-1604-1 LC 93-7358

The living water will quench your thirst. Canada, Allie C. New York: Vantage Press, 1993. x, 74p ISBN 0-533-10338-x LC 92-90826

La locura compartida. Rendueles Olmedo, Guillermo. Asturias: Belladona, 1993. x, 1993 ISBN 84-604-5959-4

Logica, Plenguatge i matematica. Graell i Deniel, Ferran. Barcelona: Anthropos, 1993. x, 377p ISBN 84-7658-399-0

Looking for Jesus. Carlisle, Thomas John. Grand Rapids: Eerdmans, 1993. 180p ISBN 0-8028-0667-8

Looking for moral guidance: dilemma and the Bible. Fischer, James A. New York: Paulist Press, 1992. x, 152p ISBN 0-8091-3170-6 LC 92-35933

The Lord's prayer. Migliore, Daniel L, ed. Grand Rapids: Eerdmans, 1993. 152p ISBN 0-8028-0119-6

The Lord's Supper: towards an ecumenical understanding of the Eucharist. Larere, Philippe. Collegeville: Liturgical, 1993. x, 94p ISBN 0-8146-2226-7 LC 98-010816

Los sentidos internos. Rodriguez, Victorino. Barcelona: PPU, 1993. x, 158p ISBN 84-477-0066-6

The lost gospel: the book of Q and Christian origins. Mack, Burton L. New York: HarperCollins, 1993. x, 275p ISBN 0-06-065374-4 LC 92-53921

Love's mind: an essay on contemplative life. Dunne, John S, 1929-. Notre Dame: University of Notre Dame Press, 1993. x, 208p ISBN 0-268-01303-9 LC 93-13910

Luke and Acts. O'Collins, Gerald, 1931-, and Marconi, Gilberto, eds. New York: Paulist Press, 1993. x, 295p ISBN 0-8091-3360-1 LC 92-35226

Major works/Margaret Ebner. Hindsley, Leonard P, ed. Mahwah: Paulist, 1993. x, 209p ISBN 0-8091-0462-8 LC 92-46650

Making peace: resolving personal conflicts. Hummel, Charles, and Hummel, Anne. Grand Rapids: Zondervan Publishing House, 1993. x, 64p ISBN 0-310-59653-x

Manies i afrodismes. Rubert de Ventos, Xavier. Barcelona: Edicions 62, 1993. x, 107p ISBN 84-297-3651-4

Marriage and sacrament: a theology of Christian marriage. Lawler, Michael G. Collegeville: Liturgical, 1993. x, 122p ISBN 0-8146-5051-1 LC 93-22619

Martha, Mary, and Jesus: weaving action and contemplation in daily life. Carter, Nancy Corson. Minnesota: The Order of St Benedict, 1992. x, 134p ISBN 0-8146-2119-8 LC 92-23586

Marxa I Sentit especulatius de la historia: comentaris a Hegel. Mayos Solsona, Goncal. Barcelona: PPU, 1993. x, 297p ISBN 84-477-0058-5

Mary: yesterday, today, tomorrow. Halkes, Catharina J M, et al. New York: Crossroad, 1993. 88p ISBN 0-8245-1371-1 LC 93-19852

Mary's day—Saturday: meditations for Marian celebrations. Boyer, Mark G. Minnesota: The Liturgical Press, 1993. x, 116p ISBN 0-8146-2092-2 LC 92-39441

Mary's house: Mary Pyle: under the spiritual guidance of Padre Pio. Gaudiose, Dorothy M. New York: Society of St Paul, 1993. x, 189p ISBN 0-8189-0646-4 LC 92-21401

La matematica: una filosofia i una tecnica. Santalo, Lluis, A. BArcelona: Eumo, 1993. x, 147p ISBN 84-7602-807-5

The me God sees: celebrating your true identity. Kuhne, Roberta. Sisters: Questar, 1993. x, 202p ISBN 0-8070-573-6

Measuring the days. Eifrig, Gail McGrew. Grand Rapids: Zondervan Publishing House, 1993. x, 400p ISBN 0-06-069248-0

Meditations on Mary. Cooke, Terence. New York: Alba House, 1993. x, 132p ISBN 0-8189-0683-9 LC 93-26373

Medjugorje day by day: a daily meditation book based on the messages of Our Lady of Medjugorje. Beyer, Richard J. Indiana: Ave Maria Press, 1993. [265] leaves ISBN 0-87793-494-0 LC 92-74779

Meekness: claiming your inheritance. Plueddemann, Jim, and Plueddemann, Carol. Grand Rapids: Zondervan Publishing House, 1993. x, 64p ISBN 0-310-59623-8

Meeting each other in doctrine, liturgy, and government. Meeter, Daniel. Grand Rapids: Eerdmans, 1993. 240p ISBN 0-8028-0717-8

Memoirs of a philosopher. Copleston, Frederick C. Kansas City: Sheed & Ward, 1993. 228p ISBN 1-55612-570-4 LC 93-7810

Mente y conducta: ensayos de psicologia cognitiva. Garcia-Albea, Jose E. Madrid: Trotta, 1993. x, 218p ISBN 84-87699-57-x

Mercy or murder? euthanasia, morality and public policy. Overberg, Kenneth R, 1944-. Kansas City: Sheed and Ward, 1993. x, 278p ISBN 1-55612-609-3 LC 92-43734

The message: the New Testament in contemporary English. Peterson, Eugene H. Colorado Springs: NavPress, 1993. 544p ISBN 0-08910-9787 LC 92-63203

Messiah: the Gospel according to Handel's Oratorio. Bullard, Roger A. Grand Rapids: Eerdmans, 1993. 152p ISBN 0-8028-0125-0

The metaphysics of higher spiritual conciousness. Sherrill, Julian F, Sr. New York: Vantage Press, 1992. x, 264p ISBN 0-533-10214-6 LC 92-90684

Midwife for souls: spiritual care for the dying. Magno, Josefina B. Bosston: St Paul Books & Media, 1993. 111p ISBN 0-8198-4769-0 LC 93-32153

Militant and Triumphant. O'Toole, James M, 1950-. Indiana: University of Notre Dame Press, 1993. x, 324p ISBN 0-268-01403-5

A minister's handbook of mental disorders. Ciarrocchi, Joseph W. Mahwah: Paulist, 1993. x, 221p ISBN 0-8091-3403-9 LC 93-11092

Ministry and the American legal system: a guide for clergy, lay workers, and congregations. Couser, Richard B. Minneapolis: Fortress Press, 1993. 356p ISBN 0-8006-2603-6 LC 92-34214

The ministry of consolation: the parish guide for comforting the bereaved. Curley, Terence P. New York: Alba House, 1993. 70p ISBN 0-8189-0651-0 LC 93-10315

Ministry: lay ministry in the Catholic Church, its history and theology. Osborne, Kenan B. New Jersey: Paulist Press, 1993. x, 722p ISBN 0-8091-3371-7 LC 92-40299

Eine Minute Unsinn. DeMello, Anthony, 1931-. Frieburg: Herder, 1993. x, 224p ISBN 3-451-23053-4

La mirada oblicua: materiales para reflexionar la vida cotiana. Sanchez Noriega, Jose Luis. Madrid: Ediciones Madre Tierra, 1993. x, 200p ISBN 84-87169-53-8

Mission and ministry in the global church. Bellagamba, Anthony. Maryknoll, New York: Orbis Books, 1992. x, 150p ISBN 0-88344-813-0 LC 92-19820

El mite de l'expulsio des paradis o els auguris de l'home boig: cartes a l'academia. Dala Pujolras, Joaquim. Barcelona: Edicions, 1993. x, 222p ISBN 84-297-3609-3

Modernismo y Teosofia. Larrea Lopez, Juan Felix. Madrid: Libertarias, 1993. x, 400p ISBN 84-7954-122-9

Modernity and religion. McInerny, Ralph M, ed. Notre Dame: University of Notre Dame Press, 1994. x, 168p ISBN 0-268-01408-6

Möglichkeiten und Grenzen einer Christologie, von unten. Kaiser, Alfred, 1872-1917. Munster: Aschendorff, 1992. x, 334p ISBN 3-402-03161-2

The monastic journey. Merton, Thomas, 1915-1968. Kalamazoo: Cistercian Publications, 1992. x, 186p ISBN 0-87907-5333

A moral emergency: breaking the cycle of child sexual abuse. Angelica, Jade C, 1952-. Kansas City: Sheed & Ward, 1993. x, 161p ISBN 15-5612-617-4 LC 93-939

Morality and youth: fostering Christian identity. DiGiacomo, James J. Kansas City: Sheed & Ward, 1993. x, 156p ISBN 1-55612-652-2 LC 93-938

Morals and the meaning of Jesus: reflections on the hard sayings. Harvey, Nicholas Peter. Cleveland: The Pilgrim Press, 1993. x, 112p ISBN 0-8298-0947-3 LC 94-41216

Mother Teresa: a life in pictures. Royle, Roger. New York: HarperSanFrancisco, 1992. x, 159p ISBN 0-06-067978-61 LC 92-52654

Mother Teresa: a woman in love. Joly, Edward Le. Indiana: Ave Maria Press, 1993. 190p ISBN 0-877793-7 LC 92-75249

Mourning: the prelude to laughter. Bruno, Bonnie. Grand Rapids: Zondervan Publishing House, 1993. x, 64p ISBN 0-310-59613-0

Music and morals. Cole, Basil. New York: Alba House, 1993. x, 158p ISBN 0-8189-0660-x LC 92-36135

A Muslim primer: beginner's guide to Islam. Zepp, Ira G, Jr. Westminster, Maryland: Wakefield Editions, 1992. x, 292p ISBN 0-87061-188-7 LC 91-73300

My rosary journal: the great mysteries. Maestri, William F. New York: Alba House, 1993. x, 102p ISBN 0-8189-0673-1

My work: in retrospect. Balthasar, Hans Urs Von, 1905-1988. San Francisco: Ignatius Press, 1993. ISBN 0-89870-435-9

Mysterium paschale: the mystery of Easter. Balthasar, Hans Urs Von, 1905-1988. Grand Rapids: Eerdmans, 1993. 168p ISBN 0-8028-0216-8

Mystery and promise: a theology of revelation. Haught, John F. Collegeville, Minnesota: The Liturgical Press, 1993. 224p ISBN 0-8146-5792-3 LC 92-46908

The mystery of Christ and why we don't get it. Capon, Robert Farrar. Grand Rapids: Eerdmans, 1993. 192p ISBN 0-8028-0121-8

The mystery of the incarnation. Schönborn, Christoph von, Bp. San Francisco: Ignatius Press, 1992. x, 67p ISBN 0-89870-393-x LC 92-73690

The mystery we proclaim: catechesis of the third millennium. Kelly, Francis D. Indiana: Our Sunday Visitor, 1993. x, 134p ISBN 0-87973-554-6 LC 92-63220

Mystical Christianity: a psychological commentary on the Gospel of John. Sanford, John A. New York: Crossroad, 1993. x, 350p ISBN 0-82451-230-8 LC 92-35577

Mythological woman: contemporary reflections on ancient religious stories. Carmody, Denise Lardner. New York: The Crossroad Publishing Company, 1992. x, 160p ISBN 0-8245-1217-0 LC 92-26086

Native American religions: an introduction. Carmody, Denise Lardner, and Carmody, John Tully. Mahwah: Paulist, 1993. 270p ISBN 0-8091-3404-7 LC 93-15547

Near occasions of grace. Rohr, Richard, 1943-. New York: Orbis Books, 1993. x, 118p ISBN 0-88344-852-1 LC 92-33193

Nelson's quick-reference Bible questions and answers. . Nashville: Thomas Nelson Publishers, 1987. x, 374p ISBN 0-8407-6905-9 LC 92-47030

A new commandment: toward a renewed rite for the washing of feet. Jeffery, Peter, 1953-. Collegeville, Minnesota: The Liturgical Press, 1992. 80p ISBN 0-81462-004-3 LC 92-17174

The new dictionary of Catholic spirituality. Downey, Michael, ed. Minnesota: The Order of St Benedict, 1993. x, 1083p ISBN 0-8146-5525-4 LC 92-40959

The new encyclopedia of archaeological excavations in the Holy Land. Stern, Ephraim, ed. New York: Simon & Schuster, 1993. 64p ISBN 0-13-276288-9

A new introduction to the Spiritual exercises of St. Ignatius. Dister, John E. Collegeville: Liturgical, 1993. x, 114p ISBN 0-8146-5844-x LC 93-20553

New parish ministers: laity & religious on parish staffs. Murnion, Philip J, 1938-. New York: National Pastoral Life Center, 1992. 131p ISBN 1-88130-701-8

New Testament commentary survey. Carson, D A. Grand Rapids: Baker Book House, 1993. 92p ISBN 0-80102-579-6 LC 93-12051

The New Testament is in Greek: a short course for exegetes. Countryman, L William. Grand Rapids: Eerdmans, 1993. 205p ISBN 0-8028-0665-1

The New Testament world: insights from cultural anthropology. Malina, Bruce J, 1933-. Louisville, Kentucky: John Knox Press, 1993. 224p ISBN 0-664-25456-x

New visions: historical and theological perspectives on the Jewish-Christian dialogue. McInnes, Val Ambrose. New York: Crossroad, 1993. x, 165p ISBN 0-8245-1246-4 LC 93-4190

Nikolaus von Kues Skize einer Biographie. Meuthen, Erich. Münster: Aschendorff, 1992. x, 139p ISBN 3-402-03492-1

No less zeal: a spiritual guide for Catholic lay people. Morin, Douglas J. New York: Alba House, 1993. x, 142p ISBN 0-8189-0631-6 LC 92-34242

No longer patient: feminist ethics and health care. Sherwin, Susan, 1947-. Philadelphia: Temple University Press, 1992. 286p ISBN 0-87722-889-2 LC 91-14499

No night too dark: how God turns defeat into glorious triump. Halliday, Steve. Sisters: Questar, 1993. x, 252p ISBN 0-88070-560-4

Not of this world: the life and teaching of Fr Seraphim Rose, pathfinder to the heart of ancient Christianity. Christensen, Damascene, 1961-. Forestville: Fr Seraphim Rose Foundation, 1993. x, 1042p ISBN 09-386-3552-2 LC 93-83654

Nots. Taylor, Mark C, 1945-. Chicago: University of Chicago Press, 1993. x, 275p ISBN 02-2679-130-0 LC 92-38702

O Susan!: looking forward with hope after the death of a child. Angell, James W. Pasadena: Hope, 1990. 115p ISBN 0-932727-401-9 LC 90-4699

La obscenidad. Castilla del Pino, Carlos. Madrid: Alianza, 1993. x, 156p ISBN 84-206-2744-5

The oil of gladness: annointing in the Christian tradition. Dudley, Martin, and Rowell, Geoffrey, eds. Collegeville: Liturgical, 1993. x, 221p ISBN 0-8146-2245-3

On cover: based on the new Jerome biblical commentary. Brown, Raymond Edward, et al, eds. London: G Chapman, 1992. x, 456p ISBN 0-22566-642-1 LC 92-44543

On earth as in heaven. Soelle, Dorothee. Louisville: Westminster, 1993. x, 96p ISBN 0-664-25494-2

On life and love: a guide to Catholic teaching on marriage and family. Urbine, William, and Seifert, William. Mystic: Twenty-Third, 1993. x, 128p ISBN 08-9622-570-4

Once upon a miracle: dramas for worship and religious education. Moynahan, Michael E. New York: Paulist Press, 1993. x, 210p ISBN 0-8091-3361-x LC 92-41325

The one mediator, the saints, and Mary. Anderson, H George, et al, eds. Minneapolis: Augsburg Fortress, 1992. x, 397p ISBN 0-8066-2579-1 LC 91-40822

One-sided Christianity? Uniting the church to heal a loot and broken world. Sider, Ronald J. Grand Rapids: Zondervan Publishing House, 1993. x, 256p ISBN 0-310-58761-1

The ongoing feast: table fellowship and eschatology. Just, Arthur A., Jr. Collegeville: Liturgical, 1993. x, 307p ISBN 0-8146-6013-4 LC 93-595

El Opus Dei en la Iglesia. Rodriguez, Pedro. Madrid: Ediciones Rialp, 1993. x, 346p ISBN 84-321-2969-0

Ordinary time: cycles in marriage, faith, and renewal. Mairs, Nancy, 1943-. Boston: Beacon Press, 1993. x, 238p ISBN 0-8070-7056-4 LC 92-40421

Organized labor and the Church: reflections of a 'labor priest'. Higgins, George G, 1916-, and Bole, William. New York: Paulist Press, 1993. x, 245p ISBN 0-8091-3374-1 LC 92-36139

Origen y decadencia del logos. Aragay Tusell, Narcis. Barcelona: Anthropos, 1993. x, 284p ISBN 84-7658-383-4

Overcoming fear between Jews and Christians. Charlesworth, James H. New York: Crossroad, 1993. x, 198p ISBN 0-8245-1265-0 LC 92-31262

The Oxford companion to the Bible. Metzger, Bruce M, and Coogan, Michael D, eds. New York: Oxford University Press, 1993. x, 874p ISBN 0-19-504645-5 LC 93-19315

The Oxford guide to classical mythology in the arts, 1300-1990s. Reid, Jane Davidson. New York: Oxford University Press, 1993. ISBN 0-19504-998-5 LC 92-35374

Pain and polemic: anti-Judaism in the gospels. Smiga, George M. New Jersey: Paulist Press, 1992. x, 210p ISBN 0-8091-3355-5 LC 92-00044

Papers originally presented at a symposium: the Church: salvation and mission. LaVerdiere, Eugene Armand, 1936-, ed. Collegeville, Minnesota: The Liturgical Press, 1993. 104p ISBN 0-8146-2141-4 LC 93-9678

Para una ciencia del sujeto: investigacion de la persona. Fierro, Alfredo. Barcelona: Anthropos, 1993. x, 494p ISBN 84-7658-387-7

Paradojas del individualismo. Camps, Victoria. Barcelona: Critica, 1993. x, 201p ISBN 84-7423-591-x

Partners with the poor: an emerging approach to relief and development. Aaker, Jerry. New York: Friendship Press, 1993. x, 158p ISBN 0-377-00252-6 LC 93-35591

La pasion de nuestro senor Jesucristo. Suarez, Federico. Madrid: Rialp, 1993. x, 311p ISBN 84-321-3001-x

A passion for the possible: a message to U.S. churches. Coffin, William Sloane. Louisville: John Knox, 1993. x, 96p ISBN 0-664-25428-4

Pastoral care in context. Patton, John. Louisville: Westminster, 1993. x, 288p ISBN 0-664-22034-7

Pastoral counseling in a global church: voices from the field. Wicks, Robert J, and Estadt, Barry K, eds. Maryknoll, New York: Orbis Books, 1993. x, 169p ISBN 0-88344-865-3 LC 93-22082

Pastoral response to sexual ethics. Arnold, William V. Louisville, Kentucky: John Knox, 1993. 176p ISBN 0-66425420-0

A path through the sea: one woman's journey from depression to wholeness. Grissen, Lillian V. Grand Rapids: Eerdmans, 1993. 240p ISBN 0-8028-0702-x

The path to hope: fragments from a theologian's journey. Boff, Leonardo. Maryknoll, New York: Orbis Books, 1993. x, 134p ISBN 0-88344-815-7 LC 92-35823

Paul VI: the first modern Pope. Hebblethwaite, Peter, 1930-. New Jersey: Paulist Press, 1993. x, 749p ISBN 0-8091-0461-x LC 936475

Pelagius on St Paul's Epistle to the Romans. Bruyn, Theodore de, ed. New York: Oxford University Press, 1993. x, 248p ISBN 0-814399-0

Pennsylvania Dutch. Wentz, Richard E, ed. New York: Paulist Press, 1993. x, 329p ISBN 0-8091-0439-3 LC 92-33184

Pentecostal unity: recurring frustration and enduring hopes. Crowe, Terrence Robert. Chicago: Loyola University Press, 1993. x, 282p ISBN 0-8294-0746 LC 93-20683

The people of the book. Pasha, M A. New York: Vantage Press, 1993. 270p ISBN 0-533-10296-0 LC 92-93384

Perseverance in trials: reflections on Job. Martini, Carlo Maria, Cardinal, 1927-. Minnesota: The Order of St Benedict, 1992. x, 141p ISBN 0-8146-2060-4 LC 92-19276

Persona y amor: el personalismo de Jaime Bofill. Tomar Romero, Francisca. Lleida: PPU, 1993. x, 364p ISBN 84-477-011301

Perspectives on marriage. Scott, Kieran, and Warren, Michael, 1935-. New York: Oxford University Press, 1993. x, 441p ISBN 0-19-507804-7 LC 92-14595

The phallacy of Genesis: a feminist and psychoanalytic approach. Rashkow, Ilona N. Louisville: Westminster, 1993. x, 144p ISBN 0-664-25250-8

The pilgrim's guide to Rome's principal churches. Tylenda, Joseph N. Minnesota: The Liturgical Press, 1993. x, 380p ISBN 0-8146-5016-3 LC 92-42870

Poder y sociedad: la sociologia en Talcott Parsons. Garcia Ruiz, Pablo. Pamplona: Eunsa, 1993. x, 280p ISBN 84-313-1196-7

Politics in the purple kingdom: the derailment of Vatican II. Schlichte, George A. Kansas City: Sheed & Ward, 1993. x, 133p ISBN 1-55612-607-7 LC 92-44098

The politics of God: Christian theologies and social justice. Tanner, Kathryn, 1957-. Minneapolis: Fortress Press, 1992. 262p ISBN 0-80062-613-3 LC 92-19360

Pontius Pilate: Book II [novel]. Babb, Charles E. New York: Vantage Press, 1992. x, 369p ISBN 0-533-10149 LC 91-91527

The poor and the good news: a call to evangelize. Scheuring, Tom, et al, eds. New Jersey: Paulist Press, 1993. x, 162p ISBN 0-8091-3359-8 LC 92-37976

The Pope speaks to the American Church: John Paul II's homilies, speeches, and letters to Catholics in the United States. John Paul II, Pope, 1920- (Karol Wojtyla) (elected 1978). San Francisco: HarperSanFrancisco, 1992. 512p ISBN 0-06064-211-4 LC 91-55298

Possessed: the true story of an exorcism. Allen, Thomas B. New York: Doubleday, 1993. 259p ISBN 0-385-42034-x LC 92-42038

Post-holocaust church theology. Williamson, Clark M. Louisville: John Knox, 1993. x, 352p ISBN 0-664-254-54-3

A practical guide to community ministry. Bos, A David. Louisville, Kentucky: John Knox Press, 1993. 112p ISBN 0-694-25045-5

Prayer for daybreak and day's end, vol II: January through June. Taylor, Mary Sue. Cincinnati: St Anthony Messenger Press, 1993. 428p ISBN 0-86716-147-7

Prayer for daybreak and day's end, vol III: July through December. Taylor, Mary Sue. Cincinnati: St Anthony Messenger Press, 1993. 432p ISBN 0-86716-148-5

Prayer in the New Testament. Doohan, Helen. Collegeville: Liturgical, 1992. 143p ISBN 0-81465-007-4 LC 91-35750

Praying the passion: living the Gospel-scriptural reflections for adult believers. Cornwell, Malcolm. Collegeville:Liturgical, 1993. 76p ISBN 0-8146-2220-8 LC 92-40656

Preparing for the twenty-first century. Kennedy, Paul M, 1945-. New York: Random House, 1993. x, 428p ISBN 0-39458-443-0 LC 91-52668

Preparing for worship: Sundays and feast days. Donovan, Daniel L. Mahwah: Paulist, 1993. x, 211p ISBN 0-8091-3424-1 LC 93-13704

Prescribing our future: ethical challenges in genetic counseling. Bartels, Dianne M, et al, eds. New York: Aldine de Gruyter, 1993. 186p ISBN 0-20230-452-3 LC 92-21469

Presente y futuro del hombre. Polo, Leonardo. Madrid: Rialp, 1993. x, 208p ISBN 84-321-2977-1

Promise of good things: the Apostolic Fathers. Davies, Oliver, ed. New Rochelle, New York: New City Press, 1993. 115p ISBN 1-56548-019-8 LC 92-42033

The promise of nature: ecology and cosmic purpose. Haught, John F. New York: Paulist Press, 1993. x, 156p ISBN 0-8091-3396-2 LC 92-41353

Promises for the graduate. Richards, Larry. Grand Rapids: Zondervan Publishing House, 1993. x, 128p ISBN 0-310-39700-6

Prospects for a common morality. Outka, Gene, and Reeder, John P, Jr, eds. Princeton, New Jersey: Princeton University Press, 1993. x, 302p ISBN 0-69107-418-6 LC 92-5681

The Psalms are yours. Murphy, Roland E. Mahwah: Paulist, 1993. x, 148p ISBN 0-8091-3411-x LC 93-15639

The Psalms in inclusive language. Arakal, Joseph J. Minnesota: The Liturgical Press, 1993. x, 150p ISBN 0-8146-2024-8 LC 92-32647

The Psalms: songs of tragedy, hope, and justice. Pleins, J David. Maryknoll: Orbis, 1993. x, 229p ISBN 0-88344-928-5 LC 93-17541

Psalter for the Christian people: an inclusive-language revision of the Psalter of the Book of common prayer 1979. Lathrop, Gordon, and Ramshaw, Gail. Collegeville: Liturgical, 1993. x, 199p ISBN 0-8146-6134-3 LC 93-10817

Psicoanalisis y literatura. Guimon, Joes. Barcelona: Kairos, 1993. x, 329p ISBN 84-7245-259-x

The question of Christian ethics. McInerny, Ralph M. Washington, D C: Catholic University of America Press, 1990. x, 74p ISBN 0-81320-770-3 LC 92-25511

Questions catechists ask and answers that really work. Pfeifer, Carl J, and Manternach, Janaan. Kansas City: Sheed & Ward, 1993. 110p ISBN 1-55612-620-4

Questions women ask in private. Wright, H Norman. Ventura, California: Regal Books, 1993. 426p ISBN 0-8307-1522-3 LC 93-913

A quick guide to Christianity. Roberts, David. New York: Vantage Press, 1992. x, 102p ISBN 0-533-10327-4 LC 92-90783

Quodlibets: reflexions escrites en Veu Alta. Patuel I Puig, Jaume. Barcelona: L'Aixernador Ed, 1993. x, 249p ISBN 84-8632-99-0

The quotable Johnson. Danckert, Stephen C. San Francisco: Ignatius Press, 1992. x, 148p ISBN 0-89870-415-5 LC 92-71942

A rabbi talks with Jesus: an intermillennial interfaith exchange. Neusner, Jacob. New York: Doubleday, 1993. x, 154p ISBN 0-385-42466-31 LC xs92-16395

Radical monotheism and western culture: with supplemental essays. Niebuhr, H Richard. Louisville, Kentucky: John Knox Press, 1993. 112p ISBN 502-569-5043

Radical optimism: rooting ourselves in reality. Bruteau, Beatrice, 1930-. New York: The Crossroad Publishing Company, 1993. x, 119p ISBN 0-8245-1354 LC 92-39444

Raising up a faithful priest. Nelson, Richard D. Louisville, Kentucky: John Knox Press, 1993. 208p ISBN 0-664-25347-3

Rational faith: Catholic responses to reformed epistemology. Zaggelski, Linda Trinkaus, 1946-, ed. Indiana: Notre Dame Press, 1993. x, 290p ISBN 0-268-01643-7 LC 92-537-42

Razing the bastions: on the church in this age. Balthasar, Hans Urs Von, 1905-1988. San Francisco: Ignatius Press, 1993. ISBN 0-89870-428-6

Razon de la filosofia. Marias, Julian. Madrid: Alianza, 1993. x, 294p ISBN 84-206-9658-7

Reading Matthew: a literary and theological commentary on the first Gospel. Garland, David E. New York: The Crossroad Publishing Company, 1993. x, 269p ISBN 0-8245-1275-8 LC 92-38424

Reading the Easter gospels. Swain, Lionel. Collegeville, Minnesota: The Liturgical Press, 1993. 131p ISBN 0-81465-699-4 LC 92-40432

Reading the signs of the times: resources for social and cultural analysis. Sanks, T Howland, and Coleman, John A, eds. New York: Paulist Press, 1993. x, 232p ISBN 0-8091-33777-6 LC 92-42017

The real presence through the ages: Jesus adored in the sacrament of the altar. Gaudoin-Parker, Michael L. New York: Alba House, 1993. x, 222p ISBN 0-8189-0662-6 LC 92-42274

La Reconquista del Paraiso. Tamames, Ramon. Barcelona: Temas de Hoy, 1993. x, 203p ISBN 84-7880-231-2

Recover and heal: meditations on the twelve steps. Albertus, Karen. Cincinatti: St Anthony Press, 1993. x, 308p ISBN 0-86716-1531

Recovering connections. Grant, Richard D, Jr, and Miller, Andrea Wells. New York: HarperCollins, 1992. x, 205p ISBN 0-06-063386-7 LC 91-70707

Reel power: spiritual growth through film. Sinetar, Marsha. Missouri: Triumph Books, 1993. x, 179p ISBN 0-89243-529-1 LC 92-44676

Rekindling the passion. Jorgensen, Susan S. San Jose: Resource Publications, Inc, 1993. x, 251p ISBN 0-89390-236-5 LC 92-32396

Religion and prevention in mental health: research, vision, and action. Pargament, Kenneth I, et al. New York: The Haworth Press, 1992. 92-5887/x, 333p ISBN 1-56024 LC 225-6

Religion and the ambiguities of capitalism. Preston, Ronald H. Cleveland: The Pilgrim Press, 1993. x, 192p ISBN 0-8298-0946-5 LC 92-43014

The religious life according to Saint Augustine. Sage, Athanase. New Rochelle, New York: New City Press, 1990. 240p ISBN 0-911782-81-8 LC 90-47785

Renaissance humanism. Kelley, Donald R, 1931-. Boston: Twayne Publishers, 1991. x, 176p ISBN 0-80578-606-6 LC 91-4776

Responde la iglesia a los desafios de hoy?: cartas pastorales. Castellanos, Nicholas. Madrid: Grupo Libros, 1993. x, 666p ISBN 84-7906-202-9

Resurrection love-life. Dent, Barbara. Mahwah: Paulist, 1993. x, 189p ISBN 0-8091-3405-5 LC 93-11006

Revelation. Harrington, Wilfrid John. Collegeville: Liturgical, 1993. x, 271p ISBN 0-8146-5818-0 LC 93-15197

The revolution of the glory; introduction and part I; fundamental theology. Beeck, Frans Jozef van. Collegeville: Liturgical, 1993. x, 360p ISBN 0-8146-5498-3

Richard Rohr: Illuminations of his life and work. Ebert, Andreas, and Brockman, Patricia C, eds. New York: The Crossroad Publishing Company, 1993. x, 200p ISBN 0-8245-1270-7 LC 93-20130

The rise and fall of the United States. Farrall, Harold J. New York: Vantage Press, 1992. x, 175p ISBN 0-533-10224-3 LC 92-93307

Risen indeed: a Christian philosophy of resurrection. Davis, Stephen T. Grand Rapids: Eerdmans, 1993. 232p ISBN 0-8028-0126-9

Road to Emmaus: a new model for catechesis. Ashkar, Dominic. Sant Jose: Resource Publications, 1993. x, 194p ISBN 0-89390-266-7 LC 93-17566

The rock that is higher: story as truth. L'Engle, Madeleine. Wheaton, Illinois: H Shaw Publishers, 1993. 296p ISBN 0-87788-726-8 LC 92-24204

The Roman Catholics. Carey, Patrick W. Westport: Greenwood Press, 1993. x, 375p ISBN 0-313-25439-7 LC 93-20125

Rome reborn: the Vatican library and Renaissance culture. Gratton, Anthony, ed. Washington, DC: Library of Congress, 1993. x, 323p ISBN 0-300-05442-4 LC 92-62275

The rosary: a prayer for all seasons. Hastings, Joanna. Collegeville:Liturgical, 1993. x, 212p ISBN 0-8146-2134-1 LC 92-43851

El rostre de l'altre: passeig filosoficper l'obra d'Emmanuel Levinas. Antich, Xavier. Valencia: Edicions 314, 1993. x, 149p ISBN 84-7502-374-6

The rule of Benedict: insights for the ages. Chittister, Joan D. New York: The Crossroad Publishing Company, 1992. x, 180p ISBN 0-8245-2503-5 LC 92-17161

Rules for prayer. Paulsell, William O. New York: Paulist Press, 1993. 151p ISBN 0-8091-3410-1 LC 93-4387

Rupert Mayer: der verstummte Prophet. Bleistein, Roman, 1928-. Frankfurt: Knecht, 1993. x, 480p ISBN 3-7620-0664-x

The sacred world of the Christian: sensed in faith. Wagner, Mary Anthony. Minnesota: The Order of St Benedict, 1993. v, 147p ISBN 0-8146-2102-3 LC 92-40431

Sacrificed for honor: Italian infant abandonment and the politics of reproductive control. Kertzer, David I. Boston: Beacon Press, 1993. x, 252p ISBN 0-8070-5604-9 LC 92-35169

Saint Patrick's world. . Notre Dame: University of Notre Dame Press, 1993. x, 355p ISBN 0-268-01749-2 LC 93-21717

Saint Paul at the movies: the apostle's dialogue with American culture. Jewett, Robert. Louisville, Kentucky: John Knox Press, 1993. 192p ISBN 0-664-25482-9

Satanic panic: the creation of a contemporary legend. Victor, Jeffrey S. Chicago: Open Court, 1993. x, 408p ISBN 08-1269-191-1 LC 93-995

Scattered among the nations: documents affecting Jewish history, 49 to 11975. Rubin, Alexis P, ed. Dayton: Wall & Emerson, 1993. x, 350p ISBN 1-895131-10-3 LC 93-093216-1

Schillebeeckx. Kennedy, Philip. Collegeville: Liturgical, 1993. x, 144p ISBN 0-8146-5502-5

Science, knowledge and mind: a study in the philosophy of C S Peirce. Delaney, Cornelius F, 1938-. Indiana: University of Notre Dame Press, 1993. x, 183p ISBN 0-268-01748-4 LC 92-53743

The search for self: a study of the poetic mind. Woolf, James Dudley. New York: Vantage Press, 1993. 320p ISBN 0-533-10364-9 LC 92-90889

Search for the absent God: tradition and modernity in religious understanding. Hill, William J, 1924-. New York: Crossroad, 1992. x, 224p ISBN 0-82451-111-4-x LC 91-30773

Searching for Christ: the spirituality of Dorothy Day. Merriman, Brigid O'Shea. Notre Dame: University of Notre Dame Press, 1992. x, 360p ISBN 0-268-01750-6 LC 93-23827

Seasons and feasts of the church year. Whalon, Michael D. New York: Paulist Press, 1993. 180p ISBN 0-8091-3346-6 LC 92-24215

Seasons of the feminine divine: Christian feminist prayers for the liturgical cycle. Schmitt, Mary Kathleen Speegle. New York: The Crossroad Publishing Company, 1993. 129p ISBN 0-8245-1279-0 LC 93-588

The second coming of Jesus: meditation and commentary on the Book of Revelation. McBride, Alfred. Huntington: Our Sunday Visitor, 1993. 180p ISBN 0-87973-526-0 LC 92-61979

Secularization, rationalism, and sectarianism: essays in honour of Bryan R Wilson. Barker, Eileen, et al, eds. New York: Oxford University Press, 1993. x, 322p ISBN 0-19-827721-0 LC 92-41458

Seeds in the heart: Japanese literature from earliest times to the late sixteenth century. Keene, Donald. New York: Henry Holt and Company, 1993. x, 1265p ISBN 0-8050-1999-5 LC 93-1082

Seeking the heart of God: reflections on prayer. Boyaxhiu, Teresa, Mother, 1910-. New York: HarperCollins, 1992. x, 100p ISBN 0-06-068238-8 LC 92-54257

Ser y conocer. Garcia Del Muro Solans, Juan. Barcelona: PPU, 1993. x, 580p ISBN 84-477-0017-8

Sexual abuse in Christian homes and churches. Heggen, Carolyn Holderread, 1946-. Scottdale, Pennsylvania: Herald Press, 1993. 208p ISBN 0-83613-624-1 LC 92-32143

The sexual brain. LeVay, Simon. Cambridge: MIT Press, 1993. 168p ISBN 0-26212-178-6 LC 92-44691

Sexual character: beyond technique to intimacy. Dawn, Marva J. Grand Rapids: Eerdmans, 1993. 192p ISBN 0-8028-0700-3

Shame and grace. Smedes, Lewis, B. New York: HarperCollins, 1993. x, 170p ISBN 0-06-067521-7 LC 92-53897

Share the good news. Bertolucci, John. Boston: St Paul Books & Media, 1993. 28p ISBN 0-8198-6885-x

Shoes that fit our feet: sources for a constructive black theology. Hopkins, Dwight N. Maryknoll, New York: Orbis Books, 1993. x, 242p ISBN 0-88344-848-3 LC 92-40437

A shorter summa: the essential philosophical passages of St Thomas Aquinas' Summa Theologica. Kreeft, Peter John, 1937-. San Francisco: Ignatius Press, 1993. ISBN 0-89870-435-9

Showing mercy: getting what you give. Lambert, David. Grand Rapids: Zondervan Publishing House, 1993. x, 64p ISBN 0-310-59653-x

Sida, impuls de vida?: experiencia de Joan Ferrer Sisquella. Bovet, Joan M. Barcelona: Claret, 1993. x, 135p ISBN 84-7263-837-5

Sin contemplaciones. Savater, Fernando. Madrid: Libertarias, 1993. x, 292p ISBN 84-7683-232-x

Singing the Lord's song in a strange land: the African-American churches and ecumenism. Watley, William D. Grand Rapids: Eerdmans, 1993. 188p ISBN 0-8028-0711-9

Sobre virtudes y vicios: tres ejercicios literario filosoficos. Garcia Bacca, Juan David. Madrid: Anthropos, 1993. x, 87p ISBN 84-7658-396-6

Somebodyness: Martin Luther King, Jr., and the theory of dignity. Baker-Fletcher, Garth. Minneapolis: Fortress, 1993. x, 193p ISBN 0-8006-7087-6 LC 93-19847

Son of man: a new life of Christ. Drane, John. Grand Rapids: Eerdmans, 1993. 160p ISBN 0-8028-3710-7

Song for nobody: a memory of Thomas Merton. Seitz, Ron. Liguori: Triumph Books, 1993. 188p ISBN 0-89243-486-4 LC 92-43419

Soul: God, self and the new cosmology. Tilby, Angela. New York: Doubleday, 1993. x, 310p ISBN 0-385-47125-4 LC 93-12994

Wild creatures discovering the theological plain. Johnson, Ken, and Coe, John. Grand Rapids: Zondervan Publishing House, 1993. x, 112p ISBN 0-310-57681-4

The wild man's journey: reflections on male spirituality. Rohr, Richard, 1943-, and Martos, Joseph. Cincinnati: St Anthony Messenger Press, 1993. ISBN 0-86716-1280

Windows in heaven. Burton, Grace Oakes. New York: Vantage Press, 1993. 58p ISBN 0-533-10339-8 LC 92-90825

Windows on the world of Jesus: time travel to ancient Judea. Malina, Bruce J, 1933-. Louisville, Kentucky: John Knox Press, 1993. 208p ISBN 0-664-25457-8

The wisdom and wit of Rabbi Jesus. Phipps, William E. Louisville: Westminster, 1993. x, 272p ISBN 0-664-25232-x

Wisdom for the graduate. Richards, Larry. Grand Rapids: Zondervan Publishing House, 1993. 128p ISBN 0-310-39710-3

Wisdom of the Celtic saints. Sellner, Edward C. Notre Dame, Indiana: Ave Maria Press, 1993. 207p ISBN 0-87793-492-4 LC 92-74778

With Christ in the school and ministry of praying. Fomum, Zacharias Tanee. New York: Vantage Press, 1992. x, 235p ISBN 0-533-09575-1 LC 91-90888

Within context: essays on Jews and Judaism in the New Testament. Efroymson, David P, et al, eds. Collegeville, Minnesota: The Liturgical Press, 1993. x, 160p ISBN 0-8146-5033-3 LC 92-34914

The witness of the worshiping community. Senn, Frank C. New Jersey: Paulist Press, 1993. x, 177p ISBN 0-8091-3368-7 LC 92-34033

Witnesses to the faith: community, infallibility, and the ordinary. Gaillardetz, Richard R. New Jersey: Paulist Press, 1992. x, 238p ISBN 0-8091-3350-4 LC 92-280431

Woman to woman: an anthology of women's spiritualities. Zagano, Phyllis. Collegeville: Liturgical, 1993. x, 115p ISBN 0-8146-5025-2 LC 93-18865

Women at worship: interpretations of North American diversity. Proctor-Smith, Marjorie, and Walton, Janet R. Louisville, Kentucky: John Knox Press, 1993. 272p ISBN 0-664-25253-2

Women, earth, and creator spirit. Johnson, Elizabeth A, 1941-. New York: Paulist Press, 1993. x, 79p ISBN 0-8091-3415-2 LC 92-42018

Women in the vanishing cloister: organizational decline in Catholic religious orders in the United States. Ebaugh, Helen Rose Fuchs. New Brunswick: Rutgers University Press, 1993. 191p ISBN 0-81351-865-2 LC 92-8035

Women of the gospel. Powers, Isaias. Mystic, Connecticut: Twenty-Third Publications, 1993. x, 153p ISBN 0-89622 LC 92-81796

Women views of Christian life. Long, Grace D Cumming. Louisville: John Knox, 1993. x, 176p ISBN 0-664-25408-x

Wonderfully, fearfully made. Arpin, Robert L. New York: HarperSanFrancisco, 1992. x, 207p ISBN 0-060075-6 LC 92-53906

Word become flesh: dimensions of Christology. McDermott, Brian O. Minnesota: The Liturgical Press, 1993. x, 302p ISBN 0-8146-5015-5 LC 92-34915

The word in the desert: scripture and the quest for holiness in early Christian monasticism. Burton-Christie, Douglas. New York: Oxford University Press, 1993. 336p ISBN 0-19-506614-6 LC 91-4150

Working in the Catholic Church: NACP attitudinal survey. . Kansas City: Sheed & Ward, 1993. 164p ISBN 1-55612-568-2 LC 93-19042

The world made flesh: an overview of the Catholic faith. Marinelli, Anthony. Mahwah: Paulist Press, 1993. 309p ISBN 0-8091-3391-1 LC 92-45629

You can know God: Christian spirituality for daily living. Gustin, Marilyn Norquist. Washington, D C: Liguori Publications, 1993. x, 212p ISBN 0-89243-479-1 LC 92-74594

Your life story: self-discovery and beyond. O'Heron, Edward J. Cincinnati: St Anthony Messenger Press, 1992. x, 181p ISBN 0-86716-177-9

Your wedding workbook. Belting, Natalia, and Hine, James R. Danville: Interstate Publishers, 1993. 121p ISBN 0-8134-2953-6

Das Zweite Vatikanische Konzil. Pesch, Otto Hermann, 1931-. Frieburg: Echter, 1993. x, 444p ISBN 3-429-01533-2

1944. Camping, Harold. New York: Vantage Press, 1992. x, 551p ISBN 0-533-10368-1 LC 92-90269

BOOK
REVIEW
INDEX

A

Aarons, Mark, and Loftus, John.
Unholy trinity: how the Vatican's Nazi networks betrayed western intelligence to the Soviets. St Martin's Press, 1991.
Lapomarda, V. CHist 78:675-677 O 1992.

Aaseng, Rolf R.
Augsburg Story Bible. Augsberg Fortress Publishers, n.d.
Neuberger, Anne E. ReligTJ 27:17 Ap-My 1993.

Abate, Carmine.
Il ballo tondo. Malik, 1992.
Röhrig, Johannes. Stimm Zeit 211:215-216 Mr 1993.

Abba, Raymond.
The nature and authority of the Bible. James Clarke & Co, n.d.
O'Reilly, Leo. Furrow 44:516-517 S 1993.

Abe, Masao.
A study of Dôgen: his philosophy and religion. State University of New York Press, 1992.
Heiser, W Charles. TheolDgst 39:349 Wint 1992.

Abela, Anthony M.
Changing youth culture in Malta. Diocesan Youth Commission, 1992.
Anon. Gregorianum 74 no 2:412 1993.

Abraham, K C, ed.
Third World theologies: commonalities and divergences. Orbis, 1990.
Vanneste, A. Eph Theol Lovan 78:179-180 Ap 1992.

Abruzzese, Alberto, and Scalamonti, Antonio Cavicchia, eds.
La felicità eterna: la rappresentazione della morte nella TV e nei media. RAI-Nuovo ERI, 1992.
Baragli, Enrico. Civilta 3:336-337 Ag 7-21 1993.

Accornero, Pier Giuseppe.
Il pioniere Leonardo Murialdo tra giovani e mondo operaio. Ed Paoline, 1992.
Mellinato, Giuseppe. Civilta 2:612 Je 19 1993.

Acebal Luján, Juan L, and Aznar, Federico R.
Jurisprudencia matrimonial de los tribunales eclesiásticos españoles. Universidad Pontificia, 1991.
Navarrette, U. Civilta 144:98-99 Ja 2 1993.

Achenbach, Reinhard.
Israel zwischen Verheissung und Gebot. Lang, 1991.
Begg, Christopher T. OTA 15:495 O 1992.

Ackermann, Susan.
Under every green tree: popular religion in sixth-century Judah. Scholars, 1992.
Stuhlmueller, Carroll. BibleT 31:244 Jl 1993.
Smith, Mark S. OTA 16:434 Je 1993.

Ackroyd, Peter.
English music. Alfred A Knopf, n.d.
Wheeler, Edward T. Comm 120:25 Mr 26 1993.

Acquaviva, Sabino S.
In principio era il corpo. Borla, 1977.
Salvini, Gianpaolo. Civilta 2:3-15 Ap 3 1993.

Acquaviva, Sabinos, and Pace, Enzo.
Sociologia delle religioni: problemi e prospettive. La Nuova Italia Scientifica, 1992.
Pizzuti, D. Civilta 3:342-343 Ag 7-21 1993.

Adam, Adolf.
Foundations of liturgy. Liturgical Press, 1992.
Brown, Daniel A. Mod Lit 20:36 My 1993.
Skublics, Ernest. Can Cath Rev 11:36-37 My 1993.
La liturgie aujourd'hui. Brepols, 1991.
Toubeau, A. NRT 114:903 N-D 1992.

Adams, Geoffrey.
The Huguenots and French opinion, 1685-1787: the Enlightenment debate on toleration. Wilfred Laurier University Press, 1991.
Tackett, Timothy. CHist 79:541-542 Jl 1993.

Adams, Hannah, 1755-1831.
A dictionary of all religions and religious denominations: Jewish, heathen, Mahometan, Christian, ancient and modern. Scholars Press, 1992.
Heiser, W Charles. TheolDgst 40:49 Spr 1993.

Adams, James Luther, and Bense, Walter F, eds.
Ernst Troeltsch: religion in history. T. and T. Clark, 1991.
Chapman, Mark D. Heythrop 34:461-463 O 1993.

Adams, Walter, and Brock, James W.
Antitrust economics on trial: a dialogue on the New Laissez-Faire. Princeton University Press, 1991.
Dugger, William M. RSocEcon 50:346-348 Fall 1992.

Adcroft, Patrice.
Every day doughnuts: a novel. St. Martin's Press, n.d.
Moser, Kay R. St Anth 101:50 O 1993.

Addinall, Peter.
Philosophy and biblical interpretation. Cambridge University, 1991.
Reuscher, J. TheolStds 53:781 D 1992.

Aden, Leroy, et al, eds.
Christian perspectives on human development. Baker Book House, 1992.
Heiser, W Charles. TheolDgst 40:156 Sum 1993.

Adey, Lionel.
Class and idol in the English hymn. University of British Columbia Press, n.d.
Young, Lorna. Can Cath Rev 11:32 F 1993.

Adinolfi, M.
Ellenismo e Bibbia. Dehoniane, 1991.
Harvengt, A. NRT 114:943-944 N-D 1992.
Il Verbo uscito dal silenzio. Dehoniane, 1992.
Anon. NRT 115:621-622 Jl-Ag 1993.

Adler, Kathleen, and Pointon, Marcia, eds.
The body imaged: the human form and visual cultural since the REnaissance. Cambridge University Press, n.d.
Reyntiens, Patrick. Tablet 247:582 My 8 1993.

Adler, Mortimer Jerome.
The great ideas: a lexicon of Western thought. Macmillan, 1992.
Heiser, W Charles. TheolDgst 40:49 Spr 1993.
Haves without have-nots: essays for the 21st century on democracy and socialism. Macmillan, 1991.
Bruyn, Severyn T. RSocEcon 51:105-108 Spr 1993.
Philosopher at large: an intellectural autobiography. Macmillan, 1992.
Heiser, W Charles. TheolDgst 40:49 Spr 1993.
A second look in the rearview mirror: further autobiographical reflections of a philosopher at large. Macmillan, 1992.
Heiser, W Charles. TheolDgst 40:49 Spr 1993.

Adriányi, Gabriel.
Geschichte der Kirche Osteuropas im 20: Jahrhundert. Ferdinand Schöningh, 1992.
Lukacs, John, 1923-. CHist 79:143 Ja 1993.

After Jesus: the triumph of Christianity.
Reader's Digest, 1992.
Heiser, W Charles. TheolDgst 39:349 Wint 1992.
Wilkins, Mark M. St Anth 101:48-49 O 1993.

Aggeler, Maureen.
Mind your metaphors: a critique of language in the Bishops' pastoral letters on the role of women. Paulist, 1991.
Irwin, Joyce. JEcumen Stds 29:481-482 Sum-Aut 1992.

Ahituv, Shmuel.
Handbook of ancient Hebrew inscriptions. Biblical Encyclopedia, 1992.
Magness, Jodi. OTA 16:401 Je 1993.

Aili, Hans, ed.
Sancta Birgitta: Revelaciones, Book VI. Almqvist & Wiksell International, 1991.
Reeves, Marjorie. CHist 79:322-323 Ap 1993.

Aitken, Jonathan.
Nixon. Weidenfeld and Nicolson, n.d.
Heren, Louis. Tablet 247:212-213 F 13 1993.

Akizuki, Ryōmin.
Mahāyāna: Buddhism for a post-modern world. Asian Humanities Press, 1990.
Cobb, John B, Jr. JEcumen Stds 29:285-286 Spr 1992.

Al-Assiouty, Sarwat Anis.
Recherches comparées sur le Christianisme primitif et l'Islâm premier: Jésus le non-Juif, vol II. Letouzey & Ané, 1987.
Renard, John. JEcumen Stds 29:132-133 Wint 1992.
Recherches comparées sur le Christianisme primitif et l'Islâm premier: Origines, vol III. Letouzey & Ané, 1989.
Renard, John. JEcumen Stds 29:132-133 Wint 1992.
Recherches comparées sur le Christianisme primitif et l'Islâm premier: Théorie des sources, vol I. Letouzey & Ané, 1987.
Renard, John. JEcumen Stds 29:132-133 Wint 1992.

The Alba House gospels: so you may believe.
Alba House, 1992.
Heiser, W Charles. TheolDgst 40:52 Spr 1993.
Higgins, James J. Liguorian 81:69 Jl 1993.

Albanese, Catherine L.
America, religions and religion. Wadsworth Publishing Co, 1992.
Heiser, W Charles. TheolDgst 39:349 Wint 1992.

Alberigo, Giuseppe, ed.
Christian unity. Peeters, 1991.
Vercruysse, Jos E. Gregorianum 73 No 4:768-770 1992.
Halleux, André de. Eph Theol Lovan 78:458-460 D 1992.
Christianson, Gerald. CHist 79:326-327 Ap 1993.
Davis, Leo Donald. TheolStds 54:351-354 Je 1993.

Alberigo, Giuseppe and Wittstadt, Klaus, eds.
Ein Blick zurück—nach vorn: Johannes XXIII. Echter, 1992.
Seibel, W. Stimm Zeit 211:431-432 Je 1993.

Albertus, Karen.
Recover and heal. St Anthony Messenger Press, n.d.
Dollen, Charles. Priest 49:48 Ja 1993.

Albertz, Rainer.
Religionsgeschichte Israel in alttestamentlicher Zeit. Vandenhoeck & Ruprecht, 1992.
Murphy, Roland E. OTA 16:183 F 1993.
Murphy, Roland E. OTA 16:434-435 Je 1993.

Aldworth, Thomas.
Fashioning a healthier religion. Thomas Aldworth, n.d.
Graham, William C. Nat Cath Rep 29:40 F 5 1993.

Alejo Montes, Francisco Javier.
La reforma de la universidad de Salamanca a finales del siglo XVI: los estatutos de 1594. Historia de la Universidad 51, 1990.
Hernández, Ramón. Cien Tom 119:618 S-D 1992.

Alessandria, Cirillo di.
Commento alla lettera ai Romani. Città Nuova, 1991.
Ferrua, Antonio. Civilta 144:96-97 Ja 2 1993.
Dialoghi sulla Trinità. Citta Nuova, 1991.
Ferrua, Antonio. Civilta 3:313-314 Ag 7-21 1993.

Alessi, Adr.
Filosofia della religione. LAS, 1991.
Evrard, P. NRT 115:274 Mr-Ap 1993.

Aletti, Jean-Noël.
L'arte di raccontare Gesú Cristo: la scrittura narrativa del Vangelo di Luca. Queriniana, 1991.
Scaiola, D. Civilta 2:404-405 My 15 1993.

Alexander, J H.
Le Tabernacle ou l'Évangile selon Moïse. Ligue pour la Lecture de la Bible, 1992.
　　Renard, L J. *NRT* 114:939 N-D 1992.

Alexander, Loveday, ed.
Images of empire. Sheffield, 1991.
　　Harrington, Daniel J. *CBQ* 55:191-192 Ja 1993.

Alfred Gregory's Everest.
Constable, n.d.
　　Walton, James. *Tablet* 247:584 My 8 1993.

Alison, James.
Knowing Jesus. SPCK, n.d.
　　Campbell, James. *Month* 26:198 My 1993.

Allchin, A M, et al.
A fearful symmetry?: the complementarity of men and women in ministry. SPCK, n.d.
　　Grant, Sara. *Tablet* 247:791-792 Je 19 1993.

Allen, Bob.
On foot in Snowdonia. Michael Joseph, n.d.
　　Braybrooke, Neville. *Tablet* 247:583 My 8 1993.

Allen, Brigid.
The soup book. Papermac, n.d.
　　Poole, Shona Crawford. *Tablet* 247:373 Mr 20 1993.

Allen, James B, and Leonard, Glen M.
The story of the Latter-day Saints. Deseret Book, 1992.
　　Heiser, W Charles. *TheolDgst* 40:149 Sum 1993.

Allen, Joseph L.
War: a primer for Christians. Abington Press, 1991.
　　Marko, Robert P. *Horizons (CTS)* 20:183-184 Spr 1993.

Allen, Karen Lawrence, and Allen, Gary Gene.
Roots and wings. Pilgrim Press, n.d.
　　Apathy, Andy. *Nat Cath Rep* 29:16 S 24 1993.

Allen, Leslie C.
Ezekiel 20-48. Word, 1990.
　　Gossai, Hemchand. *CBQ* 54:736-737 O 1992.
Ezekiel 20-48. Word Books, 1990.
　　Lust, Johan. *Eph Theol Lovan* 69:158-159 Ap 1993.

Allen, Rodger Van.
Being Catholic: Commonweal. Loyola University Press, n.d.
　　Higgins, George G, 1916-. *Comm* 120:24-25 Jl 16 1993.

Allsopp, Michael E, and Burke, R R, eds.
John Henry Newman—Theology and reform. Garland, 1992.
　　Arkins, Brian. *Studies* 82:347-350 Aut 1993.

Alston, William P.
Perceiving God. Cornell University Press, 1991.
　　Davies, Brian. *IPQ* 33:124-127 Mr 1993.

Altemose, Charlene.
What you should know about the Mass. Liguori Publications, n.d.
　　Higgins, James J. *Liguorian* 81:70 Jl 1993.

Alter, Robert.
The world of Biblical literature. Basic Books, 1992.
　　Harrington, Daniel J. *America* 168:26-27 F 6 1993.
　　Di Lella, Alexander A. *OTA* 15:478 O 1992.
　　Heiser, W Charles. *TheolDgst* 40:149 Sum 1993.

Alter, Robert, and Kermode, Frank, eds.
The literary guide to the Bible. Harvard University Press, 1987.
　　Polan, Gregory J. *OTA* 16:393 Je 1993.

Altisent, Agustín.
Reflexiones de un monje. Ed Sígueme, 1990.
　　Lago Alba, Luis. *Cien Tom* 119:626 S-D 1992.

Álvarez Lázaro, Pedro.
Libero pensiero e Massoneria. Gangemi, 1991.
　　Caprile, Giovanni. *Civiltà* 2:610-611 Je 19 1993.

Alxandre-Bidon, D.
Le pressoir mystique. Cerf, 1990.
　　Lievens de Waegh, M-L. *NRT* 115:139-140 Ja-F 1993.

Amado Levy Valensi, E.
JOb: réponse à Jung. Éd du Cerf, 1991.
　　Prévost, Jean-Pierre. *NRT* 115:263-264 Mr-Ap 1993.

Amaladoss, Michael.
Making all things new. Gujarat Sahitya Prakash, 1990.
　　LIbanio, Joao Batista. *Perspectiva* 25:229-233 My-Ag 1993.
Mission today: reflections from an Ignatian perspective. Centrum Ignatianum Spiritualitatis, 1989.
　　Neckebrouck, Valeer. *Eph Theol Lovan* 69:202 Ap 1993.

Amato, Joseph Anthony, 1938-.
Victims and values: a history and a theory of suffering. Praeger, 1990.
　　Mohan, Robert Paul. *CHist* 78:624-625 O 1992.

Amazing buildings.
Dorling Kindersley, n.d.
　　Braybrooke, Neville. *Tablet* 247:374 Mr 20 1993.

Ambrose, Stephen E.
Nixon, Kissinger and moral 'pragmatism' Nixon: ruin and recovery 1973-1990. Simon and Schuster, 1991.
　　Egan, A. *Month* 25:497-499 D 1992.

Ambrosino, Michele.
Chi è San Giuseppe, 3 vols. Edizioni Dehoniane, 1991.
　　Gauthier, Roland. *CahiersJos* 41:136 Ja-Je 1993.

Amore del bello: Studi sulla Filocalia, Atti del Simposio Internazionale sulla Filocalia.
Qiqajon-Comunità, 1991.
　　Orazzo, Antonio. *Civiltà* 143:422-423 N 21 1992.

Anaximandre.
Fragments et Témoignages. PUF, 1991.
　　Escole, R. *NRT* 115:303-304 Mr-Ap 1993.

Anbar, Moshé.
Josué et l'Alliance de Sichem. Lang, 1992.
　　Begg, Christopher T. *OTA* 16:420-421 Je 1993.

Ancion, Jean.
Pour un christianisme de resistance. Liège, où va ton Église? Hollogne-aux-Pierres, 1992.
　　Anon. *NRT* 115:635 Jl-Ag 1993.
Un racisme pas si ordinaire. Hollogne-aux-Pierres, 1992.
　　Tihon, Paul. *Lumen* 48:239 Je 1993.
Les sects: changer le monde ou changer de monde? Édition de l'Auteur, 1991.
　　Partos, L. *Lumen* 47:467 D 1992.

Ancona, Leonardo, ed.
Psicoanalisi, bisessualità e sacro. Teda Edizioni, 1991.
　　Godin, A. *Lumen* 48:118 Mr 1993.

Anderson, F I, and Freedman, D N.
A new translation with introduction and commentary. Doubleday, 1989.
　　Lust, Johan. *Eph Theol Lovan* 78:156-157 Ap 1992.

Anderson, H George, et al, eds.
The one mediator, the saints, and Mary. Fortress, 1992.
　　Hommerding, Leroy. *Mod Lit* 20:38 Je-Jl 1993.
　　Heiser, W Charles. *TheolDgst* 40:180 Sum 1993.

Anderson, Victor.
Alternative economic indicators. Chapman and Hall, 1991.
　　Kraemer, Barbara. *RSocEcon* 51:247-249 Sum 1993.

Anella, Steven.
This confident church: Catholic leadership and life in Chicago, 1940-1965. University of Notre Dame Press, n.d.
　　Costello, Gerald M, 1931-. *USCath* 58:48-51 Jl 1993.

Angel, Hans-Gerd.
Christliche Moral zwischen Vernunft und Offenbarung. Verlag Friedrich Pustet, 1992.
　　Étienne, Jacques. *Eph Theol Lovan* 69:215-216 Ap 1993.

Angelica, Jade C, 1952-.
A moral emergency. Sheed & Ward, n.d.
　　Graham, William C. *Nat Cath Rep* 30:35 N 19 1993.

Anglin, W S.
Free will and the Christian faith. Clarendon Press, 1990.
　　Meynell, Hugo. *Heythrop* 34:101-102 Ja 1993.

Angouivent, Anne-Laure.
Hobbes ou la crise de l'État baroque. Presses universitaires de France, 1992.
　　Pasqua, Hervé. *RPhil Louvain* 91:471-472 Ag 1993.

Anjewec'i, Xosrov.
Commentary on the Divine Liturgy. St Vartan Press, 1991.
　　Halleux, André de. *Eph Theol Lovan* 69:198 Ap 1993.

Annaert, Phillippe.
Les collèges au féminin: les Ursulines: enseignement et vie consacré aux XVIIe et XVIIIe siècles. Vie consacrée, 1992.
　　Rapley, E. *CHist* 78:658 O 1992.

Annracháin, Máire Ní.
Aisling agus tóir: an slánú i bhFilíocht Schomhairle MhicGill Eain. An Sagart, n.d.
　　Giolla Chomhaill, Anraí Mac. *Furrow* 44:126-127 F 1993.

Anthony, Evelyn.
The doll's house. Bantam, n.d.
　　Lejeune, Anthony. *Tablet* 247:376 Mr 20 1993.

Antoine, Charles.
Pour l'honneur de mes frères. Témoignages Chrétines d'Amérique latine (1968-1992). Karthala, 1991.
　　Partos, L. *Lumen* 48:239 Je 1993.

Antoine, Philippe.
Le mariage: droit canonique et coutumes africaines. Beauchesne, 1992.
　　Ngundu, Mick. *Stud Can* 27 no 1:272-275 1993.

Antonazzi, Giovanni, ed.
L'enciclica Rerum Novarum: testo autentico e redazioni preparatori dai documenti originali. Storia e Letteratura, 1991.
　　Mellinato, Giuseppe. *Civiltà* 2:299-300 My 1 1993.

Antoncich, Ricardo.
La Encíclica "centesimus annus" en la nueva evangelización de América Latina. CEP, 1992.
　　Camacho, Ildefonso. *Perspectiva* 24:406-407 S-D 1992.

Antoncich, Ricardo, and Munárriz, José Miguel.
La dottrina sociale della Chiesa. Cittadella Editrice, 1991.
　　Pastor, Felix-Alejandro. *Gregorianum* 74 No 1:193-194 1993.

Antoni, Dino De, and Perini, Sergio.
Diocesi di Chioggia. Giuta Regionale del Veneto Gregoriana, 1992.
　　Mellinato, Giuseppe. *Civiltà* 3:93-94 Jl 3 1993.

L'Apocalyptique.
Médisèvres, 1991.
　　Simoens, Y. *NRT* 115:107-108 Ja-F 1993.

Appelhof, Mary.
Worms eat my garbage. Flowerfield Enterprises, n.d.
　　Gonzalez, Paula. *Tod Parish* 25:18-19 Ap-My 1993.

Appleby, Raphael Scott.
Church and age unite! University of Notre Dame Press, 1992.
　　Heiser, W Charles. *TheolDgst* 40:50 Spr 1993.
　　Scibilia, Dominic P. *America* 169:26-27 Ag 14-21 1993.
　　Kennedy, Leonard A. *Can Cath Rev* 11:27-28 S 1993.
　　Reher, Margaret Mary. *CHist* 79:578-579 Jl 1993.
Glimpses of God: prayer for young adults. Kevin Mayhew, n.d.
　　Forrester, David. *Tablet* 247:728 Je 5 1993.

Les approchjes empiriques en théologie: empirical approaches in theology.
Université Laval, 1992.
　　Heiser, W Charles. *TheolDgst* 40:149-150 Sum 1993.

Appy, Christian G.
Working-class war. University of North Carolina Press, n.d.
　　Polner, Murray. *Comm* 120:29-30 Ap 23 1993.

Après la Shoa: Juifs et chrétiens s'interrogent.
Centre d'Études Istina, 1991.
　Renard, L J. *NRT* 115:148-149 Ja-F 1993.
Aquinas Institute of theology Faculty.
The Liturgical Press, 1993.
　McNulty, Frank J. *Church* 9:56-57 Aut 1993.
Aquino, Mariá Pilar.
Nuestro clamor por la vida: teología Latinoamericana desde la perspectiva de la mujer. Editorial Dei, 1992.
　Burgaleta, Claudio. *RRel* 52:295-296 Mr-Ap 1993.
Arackal, Joseph J.
The Psalms in inclusive language. The Liturgical Press, 1993.
　Stuhlmueller, Carroll. *BibleT* 31:244 Jl 1993.
Twenty-two gathering prayers. Sheed and Ward, 1992.
　Williams, Joan. *Living Prayer* 26:33 Mr-Ap 1993.
Aragón, R, and Löschcke, E.
La Iglesia de los pobres en Nicaragua: Historia y perspectivas. no publisher given, n.d.
　Espeja, Jesús. *Cien Tom* 120:187 Ja-Ap 1993.
Aranda, Antonio.
Trinidad y Salvación: Estudios sobre la trilogía trinitaria de Juan Pablo II. Ediciones Universidad de Navarra, 1990.
　Pastor, Felix-Alejandro. *Gregorianum* 74 No 1:162-163 1993.
Araneda Bravo, Fidel.
Cómo se pasa la vida. Instituto Professional de Estudios Superiores, 1991.
　Munoz, Humberto. *Teol Vida* 33 no 3-4:329-330 1992.
Arango, E.
Un camino de formación inicial en la vida religiosa. Verbo Divino, 1992.
　Anon. *NRT* 115:636 Jl-Ag 1993.
Arbuckle, Gerard A.
Grieving for change. Geoffrey, Chapman, n.d.
　Markham, Flannan. *Furrow* 44:57 Ja 1993.
El arca de tres llaves. Crónica del monasterio de Carmelitas Descalzas de San José, 1690-1990.
Editorial Cochrane, 1989.
　Gauthier, Roland. *CahiersJos* 41:131 Ja-Je 1993.
Arcidiacono, Vincenzo.
Interrogativi sull'Universo (Luci del pensiero scientifico e filosofico sul mistero della Creazione). ESUR-Ignatianum, 1992.
　Selvaggi, Filippo. *Gregorianum* 74 no 2:402-403 1993.
Ardura, B.
Nicolas Psaume 1518-1575, évêque et Comte de Verdun. Cerf, 1990.
　Plumat, N. *NRT* 114:930-931 N-D 1992.
Ardusso, Franco.
Gesù Christo, Figlio Dio Vivente. no publisher given, 1992.
　Giachi, Gualberto. *Civilta* 2:301-302 My 1 1993.
Imparare a credere. Ed Paoline, 1992.
　Giachi, Gualberto. *Civilta* 2:301-302 My 1 1993.
　Volpe, L. *NRT* 115:578 Jl-Ag 1993.
Arendt, Hannah.
Auschwitz et Jérusalem. Éditions Deuxtemps Tierce, 1991.
　Ponton, Lionel. *Laval Theol Phil* 49:345-346 Je 1993.
Juger, sur la philosophie politique de Kant. Éditions du Seuil, 1991.
　Ponton, Lionel. *Laval Theol Phil* 49:343-344 Je 1993.
La nature du totalitarisme. Bibliothèque philosophique Payot, 1990.
　Ponton, Lionel. *Laval Theol Phil* 49:344-345 Je 1993.
Arens, E, ed.
Habermas e La Teologia. Queriniana, 1992.
　Brena, Gian Luigi. *Civilta* 3:51-54 Jl 3 1993.
Ariarajah, S Wesley.
The Bible and people of other faiths. The World Council of Churches, 1985.
　Norris, Frederick W. *Ecumen Trends* 22:10-13 Ap 1993.
Hindus and Christians: a century of Protestant ecumenical thought. Eerdmans, 1991.
　Norris, Frederick W. *Ecumen Trends* 22:10-13 Ap 1993.
　Olson, Carol. *JEcumen Stds* 29:285 Spr 1992.
Arias, David, Bp, 1929-.
Spanish roots of America. Our Sunday Visitor, 1992.
　Wister, Robert J. *Momentum* 24:82 F-Mr 1993.
　Higgins, James J. *Liguorian* 81:69 My 1993.
　Hennesey, James. *CHist* 79:355 Ap 1993.
　Heiser, W Charles. *TheolDgst* 40:50 Spr 1993.
Aristide, Jean-Bertrand, 1953-.
Aristide: an autobiography. Orbis, n.d.
　McCarthy, Tim. *Nat Cath Rep* 30:20 O 29 1993.
Arkins, Brian.
Desmond Egan. Milestone Press, n.d.
　Goodby, John. *Studies* 82:105-108 Spr 1993.
Armerding, Hudson T.
The heart of godly leadership. Crossway Books, 1992.
　Heiser, W Charles. *TheolDgst* 40:150 Sum 1993.
Armstrong, A H.
Hellenic and Christian studies. Variorum, 1990.
　Edwards, M J. *Heythrop* 34:203-204 Ap 1993.
Armstrong, Karen.
A history of God from Abraham to the present. Heinemann, 1993.
　Hughes, Gerard J. *Tablet* 247:890-891 Jl 10 1993.
　Traylen, Mary Anne. *Month* 26:320-321 Ag 1993.
Muhammad, a biography of the prophet. Harper and Row, 1991.
　Stuhlmueller, Carroll. *BibleT* 31:118 Mr 1993.
Muhammad, a biography of the prophet. HarperSanFrancisco, 1992.
　Heiser, W Charles. *TheolDgst* 39:350 Wint 1992.
Arnaiz, Francisco.
San Ignacio de Loyola por dentro. G Arevalo, n.d.
　Caprile, Giovanni. *Civilta* 2:612 Je 19 1993.

Arnold, Clinton E.
Powers of darkness: principalities and powers in Paul's letters. InterVarsity Press, 1992.
　Heiser, W Charles. *TheolDgst* 39:350 Wint 1992.
Arnold, John.
The quality of mercy: fresh look at the sacrament of reconciliation. St Pauls, n.d.
　Forrester, David. *Tablet* 247:586 My 8 1993.
Arnold, Patrick M.
Wildmen, warriors, and kings: masculine spirituality and the Bible. Crossroad, 1991.
　Finley, Mitchel B. *St Anth* 100:14-15 Ja 1993.
　Toolan, David S. *Church* 9:55-58 Spr 1993.
　Ruttan, Karl. *Stud Form Spir* 14:287-289 My 1993.
　Schwan, Paul Mark. *Cist Stud* 28:[13]-[15] 1993.
　Endres, John C. *Horizons (CTS)* 20:166-167 Spr 1993.
Arnold, Richard, ed.
English hymns of the eighteenth century. Peter Lang, 1991.
　Heiser, W Charles. *TheolDgst* 40:160-161 Sum 1993.
Arokiasamy, S, ed.
Responding to communalism: the task of religions and theology. Gujarat Sahitya Prakash, 1991.
　Heiser, W Charles. *TheolDgst* 40:83-84 Spr 1993.
Arpin, Robert L.
Wonderfully, fearfully made. HarperSanFrancisco, n.d.
　Graham, William C. *Nat Cath Rep* 29:18 Jl 16 1993.
Arrington, Leonard J, and Bitton, Davis.
The Mormon experience: a history of the Latter-day Saints. University of Illinois Press, 1992.
　Heiser, W Charles. *TheolDgst* 40:50 Spr 1993.
Arslan, Antonio.
Il canto del pane. Guerini e Associati, 1993.
　Vanzan, Piersandro. *Civilta* 2:608-609 Je 19 1993.
Artom, Guido.
I giorni del mondo. Morcelliana, 1991.
　Flumeri, E. *Civilta* 143:637-638 D 19 1992.
Arts, Herwig.
Faith and unbelief. Liturgical, 1992.
　Heiser, W Charles. *TheolDgst* 40:150 Sum 1993.
Arzubialde, S.
Ejercicios Espirituales de S Ignacio. Sal Terrae, 1991.
　Renard, L J. *NRT* 115:127-128 Ja-F 1993.
Asche, Arthur, and Rampersad, Arnold.
Days of grace: a memoir. Knopf, n.d.
　Costello, Gerard M, 1931-. *USCath* 58:48-51 N 1993.
Asciutto, Liborio.
Eve e le sue sorelle. Ed. Dehoniane, 1992.
　Ferrua, Antonio. *Civilta* 3:442-445 S 4 1993.
Ash, David, and Hewitt, Peter.
Science of the Gods: reconciling mystery and matter. Gateway Books, 1990.
　Williams, Alison. *Teilhard Rev* 28:29-31 Sum 1993.
Ashton, John.
Understanding the Fourth Gospel. Oxford University Press, 1991.
　Wansbrough, Henry. *Priests & People* 6:435-436 N 1992.
　Brown, Raymond Edward. *TheolStds* 53:744-746 D 1992.
　Harrington, Daniel J. *America* 168:33-34 F 6 1993.
　Heiser, W Charles. *TheolDgst* 39:350 Wint 1992.
Asselin, Dan.
Human nature and eudaimonia in Aristotle. Peter Lang, 1989.
　Hudson, Deal W. *IPQ* 33:128-130 Mr 1993.
Assmann, Hugo, and Hinkelammert, Franz J.
A idolatria do mercado: ensaio sobre economia e teologia. Vozes, 1989.
　Gonzalez Faus, José Ignacio. *Perspectiva* 24:387-389 S-D 1992.
Astarita, Tommaso.
The continuity of feudal power: the Caracciolo di Brienza in Spanish Naples. Cambridge University Press, 1992.
　Litchfield, R Burr. *CHist* 79:538-539 Jl 1993.
Astley, Jeff, and Francis, Leslie, eds.
Christian perspectives on faith development. Gracewing Fowler Wright, 1992.
　Godin, A. *Lumen* 48:355-356 S 1993.
Asztalos, Monica, and Murdoch, John E, et al, eds.
Knowledge and the sciences in medieval philosophy, vol I. Acta Philosophica Fennica, 1990.
　Unguru, Sebetai. *Heythrop* 34:325-326 Jl 1993.
Ateek, Naim S, ed.
Faith and the intifada: Palestinian Christian voices. Orbis Books, 1991.
　Heiser, W Charles. *TheolDgst* 39:360-361 Wint 1992.
Athans, Mary Christine.
The Coughlin-Fahey connection: Father Charles E Coughlin, Father Denis Fahey, CSSp, and religious Anti-Semitism in the United States. Peter Lang, 1991.
　Tull, Charles J. *CHist* 79:371-373 Ap 1993.
Athénagore.
Supplique au sujet des chrétiens et sur la résurrection des morts. Éd du Cerf, 1992.
　Halleux, André de. *Eph Theol Lovan* 69:195 Ap 1993.
Atherton, John.
Christianity and the market. SPCK, n.d.
　Preston, Ronald. *Tablet* 247:276-277 F 27 1993.
Athill, Diana.
Make believe. Sinclair Stevenson, n.d.
　Berridge, Elizabeth. *Tablet* 247:621 My 15 1993.
Atkins, Robert A, Jr.
Egalitarian community: ethnography and exegesis. University of Alabama, 1991.
　Malina, Bruce J, 1933-. *CBQ* 55:137-138 Ja 1993.

Atkinson, Clarissa W.
The oldest vocation: Christian motherhood in the Middle Ages. Cornell
University Press, 1991.
Heiser, W Charles. *TheolDgst* 39:351 Wint 1992.
Garcia, Laura. *New Oxford Rev* 60:27-29 Je 1993.

Atkinson, David.
The message of Job: suffering and grace. Inter-Varsity, 1991.
Urbrock, William J. *OTA* 16:423 Je 1993.

Atti del IX Congresso Tomistico Intrnazionale.
Libreria Editrice Vaticana, 1991, 1992.
Evrard, P. *NRT* 115:274-276 Mr-Ap 1993.

Attinger, Daniel.
Evangelo secondo San Marco: Il paradosso della debolezza di Dio. Nuove
Frontiere, 1991.
Scaiola, D. *Civilta* 144:197-198 Ja 16 1993.

Attridge, Harold W, et al, eds.
*Of scribes and scrolls: studies on the Hebrew Bible, Intertestamental Ju-
daism, and Christian Origins.* University Press of America, 1990.
Endres, John C. *CBQ* 54:814-815 O 1992.

Attridge, Harold W.
The epistle to the Hebrews: a commentary on the Epistle to the Hebrews.
Fortress Press, 1989.
Ashton, John. *Heythrop* 34:77-78 Ja 1993.

Auchincloss, Louis.
False gods. Constable, n.d.
Scott, Rivers. *Tablet* 247:552 My 1 1993.

Auer, Johann.
Jesucristo, salvador del mundo: María en el plan salvífico de dios. Herder,
1990.
Palacio, Carlos. *Perspectiva* 25:105-106 Ja-Ap 1993.

Aufderheide, Patricia, ed.
Beyond PC: toward a politics of understanding. Graywolf Press, 1992.
Giles, James E. *CrossCurr* 43:257 Sum 1993.

Augé, M.
Liturgia. Ed Paoline, 1992.
Volpe, L. *NRT* 115:578 Jl-Ag 1993.

Augustin, Cornelis.
Erasmus: his life, works, and influence. University of Toronto Press, 1991.
Minnich, N. *CHist* 78:651-653 O 1992.

Augustine, Saint, Bp of Hippo.
Commentary on books 1-7. Clarendon Press, 1992.
Heiser, W Charles. *TheolDgst* 40:50 Spr 1993.
Commentary on books 8-13; indexes. Clarendon Press, 1992.
Heiser, W Charles. *TheolDgst* 40:50 Spr 1993.
Confessions. Clarendon Press, 1992.
Heiser, W Charles. *TheolDgst* 40:50 Spr 1993.
Four anti-Pelagian writings. Catholic University of America, 1992.
Heiser, W Charles. *TheolDgst* 40:150 Sum 1993.
The Trinity. New City Press, 1990.
Rankin, David. *Pacifica* 6:112-114 F 1993.

Aujoud'hui dimanche.
Ed. du Cerf, 1992.
Anon. *NRT* 115:631-632 Jl-Ag 1993.

Auneau, Joseph, ed.
Les Psaumes et les autres Écrits. Desclée, 1990.
Eynikel, E. *Eph Theol Lovan* 78:161 Ap 1992.

Auster, Paul.
Leviathan. Faber, n.d.
Keay, J. *Tablet* 246:1576 D 12 1992.

Austin, Gerard, ed.
Fountain of life. The Pastoral Press, 1991.
Dean, Stephen. *Priests & People* 6:356-357 Ag-S 1992.
Driscoll, Michael S. *Worship* 67:184-186 Mr 1993.

Avanzo, Stanislao Mario.
Giuseppe di Nazaret, un pellegrino nella fede. Edizioni Cantagalli, 1991.
Gauthier, Roland. *CahiersJos* 41:137 Ja-Je 1993.

Avella, Steven M.
This confident Church: Catholic leadership and life in Chicago, 1940-1965.
University of Notre Dame Press, 1992.
Marty, Martin E, 1928-. *America* 169:24-26 Ag 14-21 1993.
Riley, Patrick J. *Emmanual* 49:416-418 S 1993.

Aviezer, Nathan.
In the beginning: biblical creation and science. KTAV Publishing House, n.d.
Levy, I. *SIDIC* 25 No 2:33 1992.

Avila, Fernando Bastos De.
Pequenba enciclopédia de Dottrina social da Ireja. Ed Loyola, 1991.
Salvini, Gianpaolo. *Civilta* 2:303 My 1 1993.

Avis, Paul.
Anglicanism and the Christian Church. Fortress, 1989.
Hughes, John Jay, 1928-. *JEcumen Stds* 29:480 Sum-Aut 1992.

Awliya, Nizam ad-Din.
Morals of the heart. Paulist Press, 1992.
Mason, Herbert. *TheolStds* 54:350-351 Je 1993.

Ayan Calvo, Juan Jose, ed.
Ignacio de Antioquia, Policarpo de Esmirna: Carta. Ciudad Nueva, 1991.
Halleux, André de. *Eph Theol Lovan* 78:450-451 D 1992.

Ayo, Nicholas.
The Lord's prayer. Notre Dame Press, 1992.
Senior, Donald. *BibleT* 31:58 Ja 1993.
Dollen, Charles. *Priest* 49:56 Ag 1993.

Ayo, Nocholas.
The Lord's prayer. Notre Dame Press, 1992.
Heiser, W Charles. *TheolDgst* 40:51 Spr 1993.

Aziz, Namo.
Fremd in einem kalten Land: Ausländer in Deutschland. Herder, 1992.
Röhrig, Johannes. *Stimm Zeit* 211:503-504 Jl 1993.

Aznar, Federico R.
*La institución martrimonial en la Hispania cristiana bajomedieval (1215-
1563).* Salamanca, 1989.
Salinas, Carlos. *Teol Vida* 33 no 3-4:328 1992.
Hernández, Ramón. *Cien Tom* 119:423 My-Ag 1992.

Azzolin, Giovanni.
Manzoni e i Gesuiti della "Civiltà Cattolica". UCIM, 1992.
Mucci, Giandomenico. *Civilta* 2:408-409 My 15 1993.

B

Baarda, T, et al, eds.
Jodendom en vroeg christendom: continuïteit en discontinuïteit. Kok, 1991.
Silva, Moises. *CBQ* 55:405-406 Ap 1993.

Babcock, William S, ed.
The ethics of St. Augustine. Scholars Press, 1991.
Heiser, W Charles. *TheolDgst* 40:62 Spr 1993.
Paul and the legacies of Paul. Southern Methodist University, 1990.
Siker, Jeffrey S. *CBQ* 54:815-817 O 1992.

Babin, Pierre.
The new era in religious communication. Fortress Press, 1991.
Zukowski, Angela Ann. *Momentum* 24:80-81 F-Mr 1993.

Baboin-Jaubert, C.
L'Église catholique pour ou contre le libéralisme? Lyon, 1991.
Volpe, L. *NRT* 114:914 N-D 1992.

Bach, Steven.
Marlene Dietrich: life and legend. Morrow, n.d.
Coren, Michael. *Can Cath Rev* 11:4-6 F 1993.

Back, Joan Patricia.
Il contributo del Movimento dei focolari alla koinonia ecumenica. Citta
Nuova Editrice, 1988.
Thompson, Thomas. *JEcumen Stds* 29:479-480 Sum-Aut 1992.

Backhouse, Halcyon.
Meister Eckhart. Hodder & Stoughton Christian Classics, 1992.
Moore, Patrick. *Priests & People* 7:124 Mr 1993.

Backhouse, Robert, ed.
Invaded by love: an anthology of Christian conversion stories. Marshall
Pickering, n.d.
Hay, David. *Tablet* 247:1199-1200 S 18 1993.

Bacovcin, Helen.
The way of a pilgrim. Doubleday Image, n.d.
Cunningham, Lawrence S, 1935-. *Comm* 120:26 Mr 26 1993.

Baeyer, Hans Christian von.
Taming the atom. Viking, n.d.
Hawkes, Nigel. *Tablet* 247:517 Ap 24 1993.

Bagchi, David V N.
Luther's earliest opponents: Catholic controversialists 1518-1525. Fortress
Press, 1992.
Hudon, William V. *TheolStds* 54:354-356 Je 1993.

Bagley, Ronald M, ed.
Families and young adults. no publisher given, n.d.
Roach, Joseph J. *Living Light* 30:102-103 Aut 1993.

Bähr, Hans Walter, ed.
Albert Schweitzer: letters, 1905-1965. Macmillan, 1992.
Nemer, Lawrence. *CHist* 79:550-551 Jl 1993.

Bahr, Matthias.
*Erziehung zur Prosozialität bei Acht-bis Zehnjährigen am Lernort Religion-
sunterricht.* Eos, 1992.
Grom, Bernhard. *Stimm Zeit* 211:575-576 Ag 1993.

Baigent, Michael, and Leigh, Richard.
The Dead Sea scrolls deception. Jonathan Cape, 1991.
Wansbrough, Henry. *Priests & People* 6:440 N 1992.

Bailey, J Martin.
*The spring of nations: churches in the rebirth of Central and Eastern
Europe.* Friendship Press, 1991.
Loya, Joseph A. *JEcumen Stds* 29:263-264 Spr 1992.

Bailey, James L, and Broek, Lyle D Vander.
Literary forms in the New Testament: a handbook. Westminster, 1992.
Johnson, Luke Timothy, 1943-. *CBQ* 55:356-357 Ap 1993.

Bailey, Kenneth E.
Finding the lost: cultural keys to Luke 15. Concordia Publishing House,
1992.
Stuhlmueller, Carroll. *BibleT* 31:122 Mr 1993.

Bailey, Sydney D.
Peace is a process. Quaker Home Service and Woodbrook College, n.d.
O'Connell, James. *Tablet* 247:1235 S 25 1993.

Baillargeon, Gaëtan.
Perspectives orthodoxes sur l'Église Communion. Médiaspaul, 1989.
Tataryn, Myroslaw. *JEcumen Stds* 29:472-473 Sum-Aut 1992.

Baird, William.
History of New Testament research; volume one: from deism to Tübingen.
Fortress Press, 1992.
Heiser, W Charles. *TheolDgst* 39:351 Wint 1992.

Bak, Dong Hyun.
Klagender Gott—klagende Menschen. de Gruyter, 1990.
Biddle, Mark E. *CBQ* 55:108-109 Ja 1993.
O'Connor, Kathleen M. *OTA* 16:432 Je 1993.

Baker, David L.
*Two Testaments, one Bible: a study of the theological relationship between
the Old and New Testaments.* InterVarsity, 1991.
Hilber, John W. *OTA* 16:183-184 F 1993.

Baker-Smith, Dominic.
More's "Utopia". HarperCollins Academic, 1991.
Hamilton, Alastair. *Heythrop* 34:328-329 Jl 1993.

Baldock, Robert.
Pablo Casals. Gollancz, n.d.
Amis, John. *Tablet* 247:172-173 F 6 1993.

Baldovin, John F.
Worship: city, church and renewal. Pastoral Press, 1991.
Koernke, Theresa F. *Horizons (CTS)* 19:324-325 Fall 1992.
Spinks, Bryan D. *Heythrop* 34:195-196 Ap 1993.

Baldwin of Ford.
Balduini de Forda opera. Brepols, 1991.
Holman, Jean. *Cist Stud* 28:[30]-[31] 1993.

Balhoff, Michael J.
Strategic planning for pastoral ministry. Pastoral Press, n.d.
Graham, William C. *Nat Cath Rep* 29:40 F 5 1993.
Clayton-Lea, Paul. *Furrow* 44:124-125 F 1993.

Ball, Ian, et al, eds.
The earth beneath—a critical guide to green theology. SPCK, 1992.
Walters, Hugh. *New Blckfrs* 73:578-579 N 1992.

Ball, William Bentley, ed.
In search of a national morality: a manifesto for evangelicals and Catholics.
Ignatius Press, n.d.
Baker, Kenneth. *HPR* 93:78 Je 1993.

Ballestero, Anastasio.
Dio, l'uomo e la preghiera. SEI, 1991.
Forlizzi, G. *Civilta* 2:201 Ap 17 1993.

Balling, Adalbert Ludwig, and Abein, Reinhard.
Martyr of brotherly love. Crossroad, n.d.
Higgins, James J. *Liguorian* 81:70 S 1993.

Balling, Adalbert Ludwig, and Abein, Reinhard.
Martyr of brotherly love. Crossroad, n.d.
Samway, Patrick H, 1939-. *America* 168:15+ Mr 20-27 1993.
Cunningham, Lawrence S, 1935-. *Comm* 120:28 Je 4 1993.

Ballola, Giovanni Carli, and Parenti, Roberto.
Mozart. Rusconi, 1990.
Arledler, G. *Civilta* 143:639 D 19 1992.

Baloian, Bruce Edward.
Anger in the Old Testament. Lang, 1992.
Hiber, John W. *OTA* 16:435-436 Je 1993.

Balquière, Georgette.
L'Évangile de Marie. Éditions du Lion de Juda, 1986.
Bedard, Mariette. *CahiersJos* 41:139 Ja-Je 1993.

Balthasar, Hans Urs Von, 1905-1988.
Credo. Méditations sur le Symbole des Apôtres. Nouvelle Cite, 1992.
Beenaert, P. Mourlon. *Lumen* 48:232-233 Je 1993.
Explorations in theology 2: spouse of the word. Ignatius, 1991.
Dulles. *TheolStds* 53:763-765 D 1992.
The glory of the Lord, a theological aesthetics, VI: theology: the Old Covenant. T and T Clark, 1991.
Gerhart, Mary. *Relig Lit* 25:67-74 Spr 1993.
Keefe, Donald J. *Thomist* 57:308-316 Ap 1993.
O'Donnell, John J. *New Blckfrs* 73:573-574 N 1992.
Oakes, Edward T. *America* 169:22-23 O 2 1993.
The glory of the Lord, a theological aesthetics, VII: theology: the New Covenant. Ignatius, 1989.
Gerhart, Mary. *Relig Lit* 25:67-74 Spr 1993.
Meynell, Hugo. *Can Cath Rev* 11:28-29 Ap 1993.
Oakes, Edward T. *America* 169:21-23 O 2 1993.
The glory of the Lord: a theological aesthetics, IV: the realm of metaphysics in Antiquity. Ignatius, 1989.
Gerhart, Mary. *Relig Lit* 25:67-74 Spr 1993.
Oakes, Edward T. *America* 169:21-23 O 2 1993.
The glory of the Lord: a theological aesthetics, V: the realm of metaphysics in the modern age. Ignatius, 1991.
Gerhart, Mary. *Relig Lit* 25:67-74 Spr 1993.
Oakes, Edward T. *America* 169:21-23 O 2 1993.
Homo creatus est. Morcelliana, 1991.
Fisichella, Rino. *Gregorianum* 74 No 1:157-158 1993.
Paul struggles with his congregation: the pastoral message of the letters to the Corinthians. Ignatius Press, 1992.
Heiser, W Charles. *TheolDgst* 39:351 Wint 1992.
Simplicité chrétienne. Desclée, 1992.
Renard, L J. *NRT* 115:316 Mr-Ap 1993.
Theo-drama: theological dramatic theory, vol 1: Prologomena. Ignatius Press, 1988.
Gerhart, Mary. *Relig Lit* 25:67-74 Spr 1993.
Theo-drama: theological dramatic theory, vol 2: Dramatis personae: man in God. Ignatius Press, 1990.
Gerhart, Mary. *Relig Lit* 25:67-74 Spr 1993.
Theologie der drei Tage. Johannes Verlag, 1990.
Fisichella, Rino. *Gregorianum* 73 No 4:756 1992.
Two sisters in the Spirit: Thérèse of Lisieux and Elizabeth of the Trinity.
Ignatius Press, 1992.
Anon. *Spir Life* 39:188 Aut 1993.

Balz, Horst, and Schneider, Gerhard, eds.
Exegetical dictionary of the New Testament, volume 3. Eerdmans, 1993.
Heiser, W Charels. *TheolDgst* 40:161 Sum 1993.

Banfi, Emanuele, and Sobrero, Alberto A, eds.
Il linguaggio giovanile degli anni Novanta. Laterza, 1992.
Baragli, Enrico. *Civilta* 3:334-335 Ag 7-21 1993.

Bangert, William V.
Jerome Nadal, SJ, 1507-1580. Loyola University Press, 1992.
Wright, A D. *CHist* 79:110-111 Ja 1993.
Heiser, W Charles. *TheolDgst* 40:150-151 Sum 1993.
Cohen, Thomas V. *TheolStds* 54:567-569 S 1993.

Bangert, William V, and McCoog, Thomas M.
Jerome Nadal, S.J., 1507-1580. Loyola University Press, n.d.
Endean, Philip, and Lonsdale, David. *Way* 33:250-251 Jl 1993.

Bankson, Marjory Zoet.
Braided streams: Esther and a woman's way of growing. LuraMedia, 1985.
Stuhmueller, Carroll. *BibleT* 31:53 Ja 1993.
Seasons of friendship: Naomi and Ruth as a pattern. LuraMedia, 1987.
Stuhlmueller, Carroll. *BibleT* 31:53 Ja 1993.

Banville, John.
Ghosts. Secker & Warburg, 1993.
Cremins, Robert. *Studies* 82:370-374 Aut 1993.

Baptism, Eucharist and ministry 1982-1990: report on the process and responses.
WCC Publications, 1990.
Falardeau, Ernest R, 1928-. *Emmanuel* 98:176-177 Ap 1992.

Baracco, Lino.
Ritrovare le radici. no publisher given, 1991.
Caprile, Giovanni. *Civilta* 2:198-199 Ap 17 1993.

Barasch, Moshe.
Icon: studies in the history of an idea. New York University Press, 1992.
Ettlinger, Gerard H. *CHist* 79:303-304 Ap 1993.

Barberini, Giovanni, ed.
Chiese e diritti umani: Documenti relativi ai diritti della persona e delle comunità. Ed Scientifiche Italiane, 1991.
Rulli, Giovanni. *Civilta* 143:634-635 D 19 1992.

Barbiero, Gianni.
L'asino del nemico. Editrice Pontificio, 1991.
Sullivan, John L. *CBQ* 55:100-101 Ja 1993.
Prato, Gian Luigi. *Gregorianum* 74 no 2:355-358 1993.

Barbour, Ian.
Ethics in an age of technology. SCM Press, 1992.
Ruston, Roger. *New Blckfrs* 74:373-375 Jl-Ag 1993.
Religion in an age of science: the Gifford lectures, vol I. Harper and Row, 1990.
Conway, Pierre. *HPR* 93:77-79 F 1993.

Bareham, Lindsey.
Celebration of soup. Michael Joseph, n.d.
Poole, Shona Crawford. *Tablet* 247:373 Mr 20 1993.

Baret, G.
Le défi des Témoins de Jéhovah. La Maison de la Bible, 1992.
Anon. *NRT* 115:629-630 Jl-Ag 1993.

Baril, Gilberte.
The feminine face of the people of God. Liturgical, 1992.
Heiser, W Charles. *TheolDgst* 40:151 Sum 1993.

Barilla, Luigi Tirelli.
Tu sei sacerdote oggi e sempre. Ares-Dante Alighieri, 1991.
Ganzi, I M. *Civilta* 2:107-108 Ap 17 1993.

Baring, Anne, and Cashford, Jules.
The myth of the goddess. Penguin, n.d.
Bromberg, Judith. *Nat Cath Rep* 30:27 N 19 1993.

Barker, Margaret.
The great angel: a study of Israel's second God. SPCK, 1992.
Smith, Mark S. *OTA* 16:184 F 1993.
Rowland, Christopher. *Priests & People* 7:166 Ap 1993.
Heiser, W Charles. *TheolDgst* 40:151 Sum 1993.

Barkley, Roy.
Catholic ministry to the addicted. Our Sunday Visitor, 1992.
Mangan, Charles M. *HPR* 93:77-78 Ja 1993.
Heiser, W Charles. *TheolDgst* 39:351 Wint 1992.

Barlett, Donald, and Steele, James.
America: what went wrong. Universal Press Syndicate Co, 1992.
Beseda, David. *Cath Work* 60:6 Je-Jl 1993.

Barnard, Josie.
New York. Virago, n.d.
Toomey, Philippa. *Tablet* 247:373 Mr 20 1993.

Barnecut, Edith, ed.
Journey with the fathers, Year A. New City Press, 1992.
Brown, Daniel A. *Mod Lit* 20:38 My 1993.
Seasoltz, R Kevin. *Worship* 67:384-385 Jl 1993.
Heiser, W Charles. *TheolDgst* 40:169 Sum 1993.
Journey with the fathers, Year B. New City Press, 1993.
Heiser, W Charles. *TheolDgst* 40:169 Sum 1993.

Barnes, Julian.
The porcupine. Knopf, n.d.
Maier, Francis X. *America* 168:22-23 Je 19-26 1993.

Barnes, William Hamilton.
Studies in the chronology of the divided monarchy of Israel. Scholars, 1991.
MacDonald, Burton. *CBQ* 55:320-321 Ap 1993.

Barnhardt, Wilton.
Gospel. St. Martin's Press, n.d.
Bartelme, Elizabeth. *Comm* 120:26-27 O 8 1993.

Barone, Michael.
The almanac of American politics 1994. National Journal, n.d.
Hunt, George W, 1937-. *America* 169:2 Ag 28-S 4 1993.

Barr, James.
Biblical faith and natural theology. Oxford, 1993.
  Davies, Brian. *New Blckfrs* 74:367-369 Jl-Ag 1993.
The Garden of Eden and the hope of immortality. Fortress, 1992.
  Murphy, Roland E. *OTA* 16:436 Je 1993.
  Burns, Camilla. *TheolStds* 54:593-594 S 1993.
Barratt, Alexandra.
The herald of God's loving kindness, books one and two. Cistercian Publications, n.d.
  Meredith, Anthony, et al. *Way* 33:163 Ap 1993.
Barros Souza, Marcelo de.
Celebar o Deus da vida. Loyola, 1992.
  Taborda, Francisco. *Perspectiva* 25:252-255 My-Ag 1993.
Barrow, John D.
Pi in the sky: counting, thinking, and being. Oxford University Press, n.d.
  Raymo, Chet. *Comm* 120:26-27 Ja 29 1993.
Barry, William A.
"Now choose life": conversion as the way to life. Paulist Press, 1990.
  Nowell, Irene. *Cist Stud* 28 no 2:[42]-[43] 1993.
Spiritual direction and the encounter with God: a theological inquiry. Paulist, 1992.
  Behnen, Josue. *Sisters* 65:143-144 Mr 1993.
  Waal, Victor A de. *Cist Stud* 28:[4]-[5] 1993.
  Sheets, John R. *HPR* 93:78-79 My 1993.
  Heiser, W Charles. *TheolDgst* 40:151 Sum 1993.
Barry, William A, and Conolly, William J.
Pratica della direzione spirituale. OR, 1990.
  Mellinato, Giuseppe. *Civilta* 3:198-200 Jl 17 1993.
Barth, Karl, 1886-1968.
The Göttingen dogmatics: instruction in the Christian religion, vol I. Eerdmans, 1991.
  Godsey, John D. *Thomist* 57:269-275 Ap 1993.
  Watson, Gordon. *Pacifica* 6:236-239 Je 1993.
Barthélemy, D.
Critique textuelle de l'Ancien Testament. Vandenhoeck and Ruprecht, 1992.
  Ska, Jean Louis. *NRT* 115:258-259 Mr-Ap 1993.
Barthélemy, D, ed.
Études et Documents sur l'histoire de l'Université de Fribourg. Éd Universitaires, 1991.
  Anon. *NRT* 114:922-923 N-D 1992.
Bartholomäus, Lore.
Camillo de Lellis. Citta Nuova, 1992.
  Mellinato, Giuseppe. *Civilta* 2:612 Je 19 1993.
Bartkowski, Rene.
With this ring. Liguori Publications, 1992.
  Lazar, John E. *Mod Lit* 20:40 My 1993.
Bartlett, Thomas.
The fall and rise of the Irish nation: the Catholic question 1690-1830. Gill and Macmillan, 1992.
  Keogh, Daire. *Studies* 81:457-459 Wint 1992.
Bartoli, Marco.
Klara von Assisi. Coelde, 1993.
  Köhler, Oscar. *Stimm Zeit* 211:718 O 1993.
Bartoszewski, Wladyslaw T.
The convent at Auschwitz. Bowerdean Press, 1990.
  Bramlett, Bruce R. *JEcumen Stds* 29:279-280 Spr 1992.
Basilica Patriarcale in Venezia San Marco: I mosaici; vol I.
Fabbri, 1990-1991.
  Capizzi, Carmelo. *Civilta* 3:329-330 Ag 7-21 1993.
Bassler, Jouette M, ed.
Pauline theology 1: Thessalonians, Philippians, Galatians, Philemon. Fortress, 1991.
  Grassi, Joseph A. *Horizons (CTS)* 20:145 Spr 1993.
  Stuhlmueller, Carroll. *BibleT* 31:122-123 Mr 1993.
Bastable, Bernard.
To die like a gentleman. Macmillan, n.d.
  Lejeune, Anthony. *Tablet* 247:376 Mr 20 1993.
Batchelor, Martine, and Brown, Kerry, eds.
Buddhism and ecology. Cassell, n.d.
  McDonagh, Sean. *Furrow* 44:120-123 F 1993.
Batchelor, Mary.
The Children's Bible in 165 stories. Lion Publishing, n.d.
  Neuberger, Anne E. *ReligTJ* 27:16 Ap-My 1993.
Batle, J Amengual I.
Llengua i catecisme de Mallorca: entre la pastoral i la politica. Institut d'Estudis Baleàrics, 1991.
  Volpe, L. *NRT* 114:905 N-D 1992.
Batsdorff, Susanne M, ed.
Edith Stein: selected writings, with comments, reminiscences and translations. Templegate, 1990.
  Jessey, Cornelia. *Cist Stud* 28:[16]-[18] 1993.
Batstone, David.
From conquest to struggle. State University of New York, 1991.
  Snyder, Martin. *Pacifica* 6:344-346 O 1993.
Battaglia, Vincenzo.
Gesù crocifisso, Figlio di Dio. Pontificium Athenaeum Antonianum, 1991.
  McDermott, John M. *Gregorianum* 74 no 3:575-577 1993.
Battin, Margaret P.
Ethics in the sanctuary. Yale University Press, n.d.
  Hoose, Bernard. *Way* 33:261-262 Jl 1993.
Batto, Bernard F.
Slaying the dragon. Westminster, 1992.
  Harrington, Daniel J. *America* 168:28-29 F 6 1993.
  Gossai, Hemchand. *OTA* 16:436 Je 1993.

Bauckham, Richard.
Jude and the relatives of Jesus in the Early Church. T & T Clark, 1990.
  Neyrey, Jerome H. *CBQ* 55:139-140 Ja 1993.
Baudiquey, Paul.
Vangelo secondo Rembrandt. SEI, 1991.
  Caprile, Giovanni. *Civilta* 3:328-329 Ag 7-21 1993.
Bauer, Uwe F W.
Kol haddĕbārîm hā'ēlleh. Lang, 1991.
  Vogels, Walter A. *OTA* 15:493 O 1992.
Baura, Eduardo.
Legislazione sugli ordinariati castrensi. Giuffré, 1992.
  Wiel, C van de. *Eph Theol Lovan* 78:491-492 D 1992.
Bausch, William J.
More telling stories, compelling stories. Twenty-Third, 1993.
  Hommerding, Leroy. *Mod Lit* 20:39 O 1993.
Telling stories, compelling stories: 35 stories of people of grace. Twenty-Third, 1991.
  Riley, Patrick J. *Emmanuel* 99:297-298 Je 1993.
Timely Homilies. Twenty-Third Publications, 1990.
  Riley, Patrick J. *Emmanuel* 99:297-298 Je 1993.
Bautier, Robert Henri, and Piemontese, Angelo Michele.
La comunicazione nella storia. SEAT/STET, 1992.
  Baragli, Enrico. *Civilta* 3:338 Ag 7-21 1993.
Baylor, Michael G, ed.
The radical Reformation. Cambridge University Press, 1992.
  Dipple, Geoffrey L. *CHist* 79:526-527 Jl 1993.
Bayon, Balbino Velasco.
Historia del Carmelo Español, vol 1: Desde los orígenes hasta finalizar el concilio de Trento, c 1265-1563. Institutum Carmelitanum, 1990.
  Egan, Keith J. *CHist* 78:644-645 O 1992.
Beard, Henry, and Cerf, Christopher.
The official politically correct dictionary and handbook. Grafton, n.d.
  Aitken, Tom. *Tablet* 247:406-407 Mr 27 1993.
Beasley-Murray, George Raymond.
Gospel of life: theology in the fourth gospel. Hendrickson Publishers, 1991.
  Heiser, W Charles. *TheolDgst* 39:351 Wint 1992.
  Henderickson Publishers, 1991. Senior, Donald. *BibleT* 31:58 Ja 1993.
Beatty, Jack.
The rascal king: the life and times of James Michael Curley (1874-1958). Addison Wesley, n.d.
  McDonough, John E. *Comm* 120:20-21 F 12 1993.
Beaucamp, Evode.
Igrandi temi dell'alleanza. Borla, 1991.
  Scaiola, D. *Civilta* 144:196-197 Ja 16 1993.
Livre de la consolation d'Israël Is XL-LV. Cerf, 1991.
  Galot, Jean. *Gregorianum* 73 No 4:752-753 1992.
  Renard, L J. *NRT* 114:940-941 N-D 1992.
  Begg, Christopher T. *OTA* 15:506 O 1992.
Beauchamp, Andre.
The God who lives on my street: 10 views. Twenty-Third Publications, n.d.
  Graham, William C. *Nat Cath Rep* 29:39 F 5 1993.
Teenage mothers: their experience, strength, and hope. Resource, 1993.
  Higgins, James J. *Liguorian* 81:69 D 1993.
Beauman, Nicola.
Morgan: a biography of E M Forster. Hodder & Stoughton, n.d.
  Elborn, Geoffrey. *Tablet* 247:1013-1014 Ag 7 1993.
Bebbington, David William.
Evangelicalism in modern Britain: a history from the 1730s to the 1980s. Baker Book House, 1992.
  Heiser, W Charles. *TheolDgst* 40:51 Spr 1993.
Becher, Jeanne, ed.
Women, religion and sexuality: studies on the impact of religious teachings on women. WCC Publications, 1990.
  Field-Bibb, J. *Heythrop* 34:82 Ja 1993.
Becker, Joseph M.
The re-formed Jesuits. Baker Book House, 1992.
  Heiser, W Charles. *TheolDgst* 40:51 Spr 1993.
The re-formed Jesuits. Ignatius Press, 1992.
  McGuckian, Bernard J. *Studies* 82:217-220 Sum 1993.
Becker, Uwe.
Richterzeit und Königtum: Redaktionsgeschichtliche Studien zum Richterbuch. de Gruyter, 1990.
  Miscall, Peter D. *CBQ* 55:101-102 Ja 1993.
Beckett, Wendy.
Art and the sacred. Rider, n.d.
  Reyntiens, Patrick. *Tablet* 247:407-408 Mr 27 1993.
Becking, Bob.
Een magisch Ritueel in Jahwistisch Perspectief. Rijksuniversiteit Utrecht, 1992.
  Begg, Christopher T. *OTA* 16:422 Je 1993.
Beckwith, Francis J, and Geisler, Norman L.
Matters of life and death: calm answers to tough questions about abortion and euthanasia. Baker Book House, 1991.
  Heiser, W Charles. *TheolDgst* 39:351-352 Wint 1992.
Beddard, Robert, ed.
The revolutions of 1688. Clarendon Press, 1991.
  Prall, S. *CHist* 78:662-663 O 1992.
Bede, the Venerable, Saint.
Homilies on the Gospels, 2 vols. Cistercian, 1991.
  Barker, Bede M. *Cist Stud* 28:[23]-[25] 1993.
Bedouelle, Guy, ed.
Lacordaire: son pays, ses amis et la liberté des ordres religieux. Cerf, 1991.
  Plumat, N. *NRT* 114:921-922 N-D 1992.
Bedouelle, Guy, and Gal, Patrick Le, eds.
Le "divorce" du roi Henry VIII. Libraire Droz, S A, 1987.
  Nau, Dale. *Jurist* 51 no 2:519-520 1991.

Beeching, Paul Q.
The education of an American Catholic. Thomas More Press, n.d.
O'Brien, Dennis. *Comm* 120:21+ S 10 1993.

Beinert, Wolfgang.
Diccionario de teología dogmática. Editorial Herder, 1990.
Lago Alba, Luis. *Cien Tom* 119:411 My-Ag 1992.

Beinert, Wolfgang, and Gianni, Francesconi.
Lessico di teologia sistematica. Queriana, 1990.
O'Collins, Gerald, 1931-. *Civilta* 143:430 N 21 1992.

Beit-Hallahmi, Benjamin.
Original sins: reflections on the history of Zionism and Israel. Pluto Press, n.d.
Adams, Michael. *Tablet* 247:309 Mr 6 1993.

Bélanger, Rodrigue, and Plourde, Simonne.
Actualiser la morale, mélanges offerts à René Simon. Cerf, 1992.
Boissinot, Christian. *Laval Theol Phil* 49:331-334 Je 1993.

Belford, Ros.
Rome. Virago, n.d.
Toomey, Philippa. *Tablet* 247:373 Mr 20 1993.

Belford, William.
Parish liturgy basics. Pastoral, 1992.
Lazar, John E. *Mod Lit* 20:38 Ap 1993.
Huels, John M. *New Theol Rev* 6:118-119 Ag 1993.

Beligique, pays de chrétienté?
ISCP-CDD, 1991.
Partos, L. *Lumen* 48:239 Je 1993.

Bell, Keith.
Complete catalogue of paintings of Stanley Spencer. Phaidon, n.d.
Reyntiens, Patrick. *Tablet* 247:581 My 8 1993.

Bellah, Robert Neely, 1927-.
The broken covenant. University of Chicago Press, 1992.
Davis, Thomas X. *Cist Stud* 28 no 2:[60]-[62] 1993.

Belleville, Linda L.
Reflections on glory: Paul's polemical use of the Moses-Doxa tradition in 2 Corinthians 3 1-18. Sheffield, 1991.
McDonald, Patricia M. *CBQ* 55:140-141 Ja 1993.

Belli, Humberto, and Nash, Ronald H.
Beyond liberation theology. Baker Book House, 1992.
Heiser, W Charles. *TheolDgst* 40:51-52 Spr 1993.

Beloch, Julius.
Campania: storia e topografia della Napoli antica e dei suoi dintorni. Bibliopolis, 1989.
Ferrua, Antonio. *Civilta* 3:100 Jl 3 1993.

Ben-Tor, Amnon, et al, eds.
Yigael Yadin Memorial volume. The Hebrew University, 1989.
Smith, Mark S. *OTA* 16:149-151 F 1993.

Ben-Tor, Amnon.
The archaeology of Ancient Israel. Yale University Press, 1992.
Harrington, Daniel J. *America* 168:27 F 6 1993.
Edelman, Diana V. *OTA* 16:157 F 1993.

Bence-Jones, Mark.
The Catholic families. Constable, n.d.
Swan, Peter. *Can Cath Rev* 11:24-25 S 1993.

Bender, Ross T, and Sell, Alan P, eds.
Baptism, peace, and the state in the Reformed and Mennonite traditions. Wilfred Laurier, 1991.
Friesen, Jon. *JEcumen Stds* 29:475-476 Sum-Aut 1992.

Benedikt, B, and Sobel, A, eds.
Der Streit um Drewermann. Verlag A Sobel, 1992.
Toubeau, A. *NRT* 115:292-293 Mr-Ap 1993.

Benelli, Gian Carlo.
La gnosi; Il volto oscuro della storia. Mondadori, 1991.
Forlizzi, G. *Civilta* 144:509-511 Mr 6 1993.

Benimeli, José A Ferrer, and Mola, Aldo A, eds.
La Massoneria oggi. Bastogi, 1991.
Caprile, Giovanni. *Civilta* 2:207 Ap 17 1993.

Benker, G.
Loslassen können—die Liebe finden. Matthias-Grünewald-Verlag, 1991.
Renard, L J. *NRT* 115:129-130 Ja-F 1993.

Bennet, George.
Progress through Lent: a course for pilgrims. The Canterbury Press, n.d.
Hollings, Michael. *Tablet* 247:278 F 27 1993.

Benson, Hugh H, ed.
Essays on the philosophy of Socrates. Oxford University Press, 1992.
O'Connell, Robert J. *IPQ* 33:366-368 S 1993.

Benson, Peter.
Odo's hanging. Hodder & Stoughton, n.d.
Miller, Peggy. *Tablet* 247:792 Je 19 1993.

Bentley, James, ed.
Some corner of a foreign field: poetry of the Great War. Little Brown, n.d.
Blythe, Ronald. *Tablet* 247:310-311 Mr 6 1993.

Bentley, Peter, et al.
Faith without the church? Nominalism in Australian Christianity. Christian Research Association, 1992.
Balycomb, John. *Pacifica* 6:359-361 O 1993.

Berardino, Angelo Di, ed.
Encyclopedia of the early Church. Oxford University Press, n.d.
Harrington, Daniel J. *America* 168:35 F 6 1993.

Bercovitch, Sacvan.
The office of The scarlet letter. The Johns Hopkins University Press, 1991.
Gatta, John. *Relig Lit* 24:91-96 Aut 1992.

Bergamo, Mino.
L'anatomia dell'anima. Il Mulino, 1991.
Toubeau, A. *NRT* 114:910-911 N-D 1992.
Mellinato, Giuseppe. *Civilta* 3:202 Jl 17 1993.

Bergan, Jacqueline Syrup, and Schwan, Marie.
Praying with Ignatius of Loyola. St Mary's Press, n.d.
Endean, Philip, and Lonsdale, David. *Way* 33:250 Jl 1993.

Berger, Barbara Helen.
Grandfather twilight. Philomel Books, n.d.
Neuberger, Anne E. *ReligTJ* 27:11 Mr 1993.
When the sun rose. Philomel Books, n.d.
Neuberger, Anne E. *ReligTJ* 27:11 Mr 1993.

Berger, Klaus.
Synopse des Vierten Buches Esra und der Syrischen Baruch Apolalypse. Franke, 1992.
Begg, Christopher T. *OTA* 16:442 Je 1993.

Berger, Teresa.
Theologie in Hymnen? Telos Verlag, 1989.
Bussche, J. *Eph Theol Lovan* 78:485-486 D 1992.

Berger, Thomas, and Berger, Petra.
The Easter craft book. Floris, n.d.
Braybrooke, Neville. *Tablet* 247:374 Mr 20 1993.

Bergmann, Martin S.
In the shadow of Moloch: the sacrifice of children and its impact on Western religions. Columbia University Press, 1992.
Pattn, Corrine L. *Cithara* 32:61-62 N 1992.
Heiser, W Charles. *TheolDgst* 39:352 Wint 1992.

Bergonzi, Bernard, 1929-.
Wartime and aftermath: English literature and its background, 1939-1960. Oxford University Press, n.d.
Berridge, Elizabeth. *Tablet* 247:822-823 Je 26 1993.

Bergson, Henri.
Leçons de morale, psychologie et métaphysique au lycée Henri-IV. Presses universitaires de France, 1992.
Étienne, Jacques. *RPhil Louvain* 90:583-586 N 1992.

Bériou, Nicole, et al, eds.
Prier au Moyen Age. Brepols, 1991.
Navez, G. *NRT* 115:126 Ja-F 1993.
Galot, Jean. *Gregorianum* 74 no 3:589 1993.

Berkeley, A, and Mickelsen, Alvera M.
Understanding Scripture. Hendrickson Publishers, 1992.
Stuhlmueller, Carroll. *BibleT* 31:120 Mr 1993.

Berlingò, Salvatore.
Enti e beni religiosi in Italia. Il Mulino, 1992.
Da Passano, P. *Civilta* 144:99-100 Ja 2 1993.

Berman, Constance Hoffman.
Medieval agriculture, the southern French countryside, and the early Cistercians. American Philosophical Society, 1986.
Callahan, Daniel, 1930-. *CHist* 78:636-640 O 1992.

Berman, Paul.
Debating PC: the controversy over political correctness on college campuses. Laurel, 1992.
Gerber, Leslie E. *CrossCurr* 43:118-120 Spr 1993.

Bermejo, Luis M.
Infallibility on trial: church, conciliarity and communion. Christian Classics, 1992.
Rausch, Thomas P. *TheolStds* 54:376-378 Je 1993.

Bernard, Charles-André, ed.
Teologia spirituale. AVE, 1991.
Clarot, B. *NRT* 115:133 Ja-F 1993.

Bernauer, James W.
Michel Foucault's force of flight: toward an ethics of thought. Humanities Press International, 1990.
Babich, Babette E. *IJPS* 1:135-137 Mr 1993.

Bernhardt, Reinhold.
Der absolutheitsanspruch des Christentums. Gütersloher Verlagshaus Gerd Mohn, 1990.
Novitsky, Anthony W. *JEcumen Stds* 29:281-282 Spr 1992.

Bernier, Paul.
Ministry in the Church. Twenty-Third, 1992.
Nuzzi, Ronald J. *Nat Cath Rep* 29:15 Ap 23 1993.
Falardeau, Ernest R, 1928-. *Emmanuel* 99:296 Je 1993.
Byrne, Pat. *Mod Lit* 20:38 Je-Jl 1993.
Burkhard, John J. *Living Light* 29:86 Sum 1993.
Graham, William C. *Nat Cath Rep* 29:18 Jl 16 1993.
Heiser, W Charles. *TheolDgst* 40:151 Sum 1993.

Bernstein, Eleanor.
Disciples at the crossroads. The Liturgical Press, n.d.
Anon. *Church* 9:42 Aut 1993.

Bernstein, Eleanor, and Leonard, John-Brooks, eds.
Children in the assembly of the church. Liturgy Training Pubs, 1992.
Lazar, John E. *Mod Lit* 20:40 O 1993.

Berrigan, Daniel.
Tulips in the prison yard. Dedalus Press, n.d.
Egan, Desmond. *Tablet* 247:248 F 20 1993.

Berry, Jason.
Lead us not into temptation. Doubleday, n.d.
Steinfels, Peter, 1941-. *Comm* 120:16-18 Mr 12 1993.
Costello, Gerald M, 1931-. *USCath* 58:48-51 Mr 1993.
Kenny, James A. *St Anth* 101:50-51 Ag 1993.

Berry, Thomas.
Befriending the earth: a theology of reconciliation between humans and the earth. Twenty-Third Publications, 1991.
Stevens, Maryanne. *Horizons (CTS)* 20:158-159 Spr 1993.

Berryman, Jerome.
Godly play: a way of religious education. Harper, 1991.
Dash, Millicent A. *Living Light* 29:84-85 Aut 1992.

Berselli, Constante, ed.
Hymns to Christ and a concert of miniatures. Saint Paul Publications, n.d.
Dougherty, Josephine. *Can Cath Rev* 11:31 N 1993.

Berthold, George C, ed.
Faith seeking understanding: learning and the Catholic tradition. Saint Anselm College Press, 1991.
    McCoy, A. *Priests & People* 6:483-484 D 1992.
    Buijs, Joseph A. *Can Cath Rev* 11:30 Jl-Ag 1993.

Berti, Enrico.
Il 'Dio de filosofi'. Edizioni universitarie Zara, 1992.
    Steenberghen, Fernand Van. *RPhil Louvain* 91:152-154 F 1993.

Berti, Enrico, ed.
Problemi di etica: fondazione, norme, orietnamenti. Gregoriana Libreria Editrice-Fondazione Lanza, 1992.
    Kennedy, Terrence. *Gregorianum* 74 No 1:169-172 1993.

Bertodano, Teresa de, and Wood, Derek.
Through the year with Joyce Huggett. Eagle, n.d.
    Forrester, David. *Tablet* 247:728 Je 5 1993.

Bertola, Francesco.
Sulle cose prime e ultime. Augustinus, 1991.
    Halleux, André de. *Eph Theol Lovan* 78:477 D 1992.

Beseghi, Emi, and Faeti, Antonio, eds.
La scala a chiocciola. Paura, horror, finzioni. Dal romanzo gotico a Dylan Dog. La Nuova Italia, 1993.
    Flumeri, E. *Civilta* 3:543-544 S 18 1993.

Best, Ernest.
The temptation and the passion: the Markan soteriology, second edition. Cambridge University Press, 1990.
    Brown, Raymond Edward. *Heythrop* 34:73-74 Ja 1993.

Best, Thomas F, ed.
Vancouver to Canberra, 1982-1990: report of the Central Committee of the World Council of Churches to the Seventh Assembly. WCC Publications, 1990.
    Lewis, Eleanor V. *JEcumen Stds* 29:104-105 Wint 1992.

Besutti, P Giuseppe M.
Virgo liber verbi. Edizioni Marianum, 1991.
    Galot, Jean. *Gregorianum* 74 no 2:370-371 1993.

Betti, Carmen.
La religione a scuola tra obbligo e facoltãtività. Manzuoli, 1989.
    Pacella, U. *Civilta* 143:435 N 21 1992.

Betto, Frei.
Teilhard de Chardin. Letras e Letras, 1992.
    Libanio, Joao Batista. *Perspectiva* 24:404-405 S-D 1992.

Beutler, Johannes, and Fortna, Robert T, eds.
The shepherd discourse of John 10 and its context: studies by members of the Johannine writings seminar. Cambridge University Press, 1991.
    Ashton, John. *Heythrop* 34:76-77 Ja 1993.

Bevans, Stephen B.
John Oman and his doctrine of God. Cambridge University Press, 1992.
    McKim, Donald K. *TheolStds* 54:198-199 Mr 1993.
    Heiser, W Charles. *TheolDgst* 40:52 Spr 1993.

Beyerhaus, Peter P J.
God's kingdom and the utopian error: discerning the biblical kingdom of God from its political conterfeits. Crossway Books, 1992.
    Heiser, W Charles. *TheolDgst* 40:52 Spr 1993.

Beyreuther, Gerald, and Pätzold, Barbara, et al, eds.
Fürstinnen und Städterinnen. Herder, 1993.
    Brieskorn, Norbert. *Stimm Zeit* 211:717-718 O 1993.

Biallas, Leonard J.
World religions: a story approach. Twenty-Third Publications, 1991.
    Chapple, Christopher. *Horizons (CTS)* 20:191-192 Spr 1993.

Bianchi, Eugene C, and Ruether, Rosemary Radford, eds.
A democratic Catholic Church. Crossroad, 1992.
    Cunningham, Lawrence S, 1935-. *Comm* 120:28-29 Mr 26 1993.
    Heiser, W Charles. *TheolDgst* 40:158 Sum 1993.

Bibbia traduction oecuménique de la Bible.
LDC, 1992.
    Scaiola, D. *Civilta* 144:195-196 Ja 16 1993.

La Biblia en su entorno.
Editorial Verbo Divino, 1990.
    Prato, Gian Luigi. *Gregorianum* 74 No 1:142-144 1993.

Biblia Patristica.
CNRS, 1991.
    Anon. *NRT* 115:153 Ja-F 1993.

Biblia y cristologia: unitad y diversitad en la Iglesia; la interpretación de los dogmas.
Instituto Teológico Francescano, 1992.
    Halleux, André de. *Eph Theol Lovan* 69:208-209 Ap 1993.

Bibliographia Internationalis Spiritualitatis a Pontificio Instituto Spiritualitatis.
Edizione del Teresianum, 1992.
    Gauthier, Roland. *CahiersJos* 41:130 Ja-Je 1993.

Biddle, Mark E.
A redaction history of Jeremiah 2:1-4:2. Theologischer Verlag, 1990.
    Berridge, John M. *CBQ* 55:323-324 Ap 1993.

Biehl, M.
Der Fall Sadhu Sundar Singh. P. Lang, 1990.
    Scheuer, J. *NRT* 115:602-603 Jl-Ag 1993.

Bierling, Neal.
Giving Goliath his due. Baker, 1992.
    Heiser, W Charles. *TheolDgst* 40:152 Sum 1993.
    Matthews, Victor H. *OTA* 16:402 Je 1993.

Bifet, J Esquerda.
Pastorale per una Chiesa missionaria. Università Urbaniana, 1991.
    Anon. *NRT* 115:294 Mr-Ap 1993.

Biffi, Franco.
Prophet of our times. New City Press, 1992.
    Miller, L. *Liguorian* 81:69 F 1993.
    Heiser, W Charles. *TheolDgst* 40:152 Sum 1993.

Biffi, Inos.
Figure medievali della teologia, volumo primo. Jaca Book, 1992.
    Steenberghen, Fernand Van. *RPhil Louvain* 91:319-320 My 1993.

Billière, Peter de la.
Storm command: a personal account of the Gulf War. HarperCollins, n.d.
    Keegan, Jeffrey. *Tablet* 246:1573-1574 D 12 1992.

Bingemer, Maria Clara L.
Alteridade e vulnerabilidade. Loyola, 1993.
    Libanio, Joao Batista. *Perspectiva* 25:250-252 My-Ag 1993.
O segredo feminino do Mistério. Vozes, 1991.
    Cavalcanti, Tereza. *REB* 52:1002-1003 D 1992.
    Taborda, Francisco. *Perspectiva* 25:242-245 My-Ag 1993.

Binstock, Robert H., et al, eds.
Dementia and aging: ethics, values, and policy choices. Johns Hopkins University Press, 1992.
    Steinhaus, Barbara J. *Health Prog* 74:71 O 1993.

Binz, Stephen J.
No greater love. The Liturgical Press, 1992.
    Stuhlmueller, Carroll. *BibleT* 31:118 Mr 1993.

Birch, Bruce C.
Let justice roll down: the Old Testament, ethics, and Christian life. John Knox, 1991.
    Guinan, Michael D. *TheolStds* 53:736-737 D 1992.
    Wimmer, Joseph F. *OTA* 15:514 O 1992.

Birnbaum, David.
God and evil: a unified theodicy/ theology/ philosophy. Klay Publishing House, 1989.
    Pastor, Felix-Alejandro. *Gregorianum* 73 No 4:773-774 1992.

Bischoff, Bernhard.
Latin palaeography: antiquity and the middle ages. Cambridge University Press, 1990.
    Roberts, Jane. *Heythrop* 34:202-203 Ap 1993.

Bischofswahlen in der Schweiz.
NZN, 1992.
    Seibel, W. *Stimm Zeit* 211:428 Je 1993.

Bishop Curtis of Wilmington.
Tan Books and Publishers, 1991.
    Shaw, Russel. *HPR* 93:71-73 F 1993.

Bissonnier, Henri.
Psicologia e vita spirituale: sofferenza e maturità umana. Città Nuova, 1991.
    Rossi, Giacomo. *Civilta* 144:411-412 F 20 1993.

Black, George, and Munro, Robin.
Black hands of Beijing: lives of defiance in China's democracy movement. Wiley, n.d.
    Breen, Lawrie. *Tablet* 247:1132-1133 S 4 1993.

Blackburn, Barry.
Theios anēr and the Markan miracle traditions. Mohr, 1991.
    Kee, Howard Clark. *CBQ* 54:774 O 1992.

Blackwell, Richard J.
Galileo, Bellarmine and the Bible. University of Notre Dame, 1991.
    Conway, Pierre. *HPR* 93:76-79 Mr 1993.
Galileo, Bellarmine and the Bible. University of Notre Dame Press, 1992.
    Dollen, Charles. *Priest* 49:48 Mr 1993.
    Stuhlmueller, Carroll. *BibleT* 31:244 Jl 1993.
    Russell, John L. *Heythrop* 34:335-336 Jl 1993.

Blair, Philip.
What on earth? The Church in the world and the call of Christ. Lutterworth, 1993.
    Pridmore, John. *Month* 26:319-320 Ag 1993.

Blake, Robert, and Louis, William Roger, eds.
Churchhill. Oxford University Press, n.d.
    Hodgkin, E C. *Tablet* 247:478 Ap 10-17 1993.

Blanch, Santiago Alcolea.
Museo del Prado. Rizzoli, 1992.
    Ferrua, Antonio. *Civilta* 3:331-332 Ag 7-21 1993.

Blanchette, Oliva.
The perfection of the universe according to Aquinas: a theological cosmology. Pennsylvania State University Press, 1992.
    Heiser, W Charles. *TheolDgst* 39:352 Wint 1992.
    Clarke, W Norris. *TheolStds* 54:167-168 Mr 1993.

Blandino, G, et al.
Un discussion sur Le ethica del felicitate. Servicio de Libros UMI, 1991.
    Anon. *NRT* 115:143-144 Ja-F 1993.

Blandre, Bernard.
Les témoins de Jéhovah. Brépols, 1991.
    Debarge, Louis. *MSR* 50:65-66 Ja-Mr 1993.

Blank, Rebecca M.
Do justice: linking Christian faith and modern economic life. United Church Press, 1992.
    Korn, Barton. *Mod Lit* 20:37-38 My 1993.
    Heiser, W Charles. *TheolDgst* 40:53 Spr 1993.

Blanquart, Fabien.
Le premier jour. Cerf, 1991.
    Simoens, Y. *NRT* 115:109-110 Ja-F 1993.
    Galot, Jean. *Gregorianum* 74 no 2:365-366 1993.

Blasberg-Kuhnke, Martina.
Erwachsene glauben. Eos, 1992.
    Bleistein, Roman, 1928-. *Stimm Zeit* 211:646 S 1993.

Blasi, Anthony J.
Making Charisma: the social construction of Paul's public image. Transaction Publishers, 1991.
    McDermott, Scott. *Bib Th Bul* 23:84 Sum 1993.

Blejwas, Stanislaus A.
St Stanlislaus B and M Parish, Meriden, Connecticut. Central Connecticut State University, 1991.
    Liptak, Dolores. *CHist* 79:576-577 Jl 1993.

Blenkinsopp, Joseph.
Ezekiel. John Knox, 1990.
Parunak, H Van Dyke. *CBQ* 55:102-103 Ja 1993.
The Pentateuch: an introduction to the first five Books of the Bible. Doubleday, 1992.
Murphy, Roland E. *OTA* 16:415 Je 1993.

Blickle, Peter.
Communal reformation: the quest for salvation in sixteenth-century Germany. Humanities Press, 1992.
Edwards, Mark U, Jr. *CHist* 79:332-333 Ap 1993.
Heiser, W Charles. *TheolDgst* 40:53 Spr 1993.

Bliven, Edmond.
Book of Catholic prayer. Oregon Catholic Press, n.d.
Pecht, Gerard. *Liguorian* 81:70 Ag 1993.

Bloch, Michael.
Ribbentrop. Bantam, n.d.
Heren, Louis. *Tablet* 247:48-49 Ja 9 1993.

Bloch, R Howard.
Medieval misogyny and the invention of western romantic love. University of Chicago, 1991.
O'Neal, Sandra R. *TheolStds* 53:784 D 1992.

Bloch-Smith, Elizabeth.
Judahite burial practices and beliefs about the dead. JSOT, 1992.
Edelman, Diana V. *OTA* 15:478 O 1992.

Blodgett, Harriet, ed.
The Englishwoman's diary. Fourth Estate, n.d.
Lawson, Sarah. *Tablet* 247:111 Ja 23 1993.

Blowers, Paul M.
Exegesis and spiritual pedagogy in Maximus the Confessor: an investigation of the Quaestiones ad Thalassium. University of Notre Dame Press, 1991.
Heiser, W Charles. *TheolDgst* 39:352-353 Wint 1992.

Blumenfeld-Kosinski, Renate, and Szell, Timea, eds.
Images of sainthood in medieval Europe. Cornell University Press, 1991.
Meisel, Sandra. *New Oxford Rev* 60:30-31 Jl-Ag 1993.
Heiser, W Charles. *TheolDgst* 40:168 Sum 1993.
Platelle, H. *MSR* 50:56-59 Ja-Mr 1993.

Blumes, Teresa.
La contabilidad en las Reducciones guaranies. Centro de Estudios antropológicos, Universidad Católica, 1992.
Carbonell De Masy, Rafael. *Gregorianum* 74 no 3:592 1993.

Bly, Robert.
Iron John: a book about men. Addison Wesley, n.d.
Toolan, David S. *Church* 9:55-58 Spr 1993.

Boberski, Heiner.
Die Divisionäre des Papstes. Otto Müller, 1992.
Seibel, W. *Stimm Zeit* 211:284-285 Ap 1993.

Bobrinskoy, B.
Communion du Saint-Esprit. Abbaye de Bellefontaine, 1992.
Roisel, V. *NRT* 115:581-582 Jl-Ag 1993.

Bockenförde, Ernst-Wolfgang, and Shils, Edward, eds.
Jews and Christians in a pluralistic world. St Martin's Press, 1991.
Byles, Mary. *CrossCurr* 42:562 Wint 1992-1993.

Bodéüs, Richard.
Aristote et la théologie des vivants immortels. Les Belles Lettres, 1992.
Ponton, Lionel. *Laval Theol Phil* 49:176-177 F 1993.

Bodo, Murray.
Tales of St Francis. St Anthony Messenger Press, n.d.
Graham, William C. *Nat Cath Rep* 29:25 Mr 26 1993.
Dollen, Charles. *Priest* 49:48 My 1993.
Anon. *Church* 9:43 Aut 1993.

Boecker, Hans Jochen.
Mose 25, 12-37, 1. Isaak und Jakob. Theologischer V., 1992.
Begg, Christopher T. *OTA* 16:418-419 Je 1993.

Boers, Arthur Paul.
Lord, teach us to pray. Herald Press, 1992.
Heiser, W Charles. *TheolDgst* 40:152 Sum 1993.

Boff, Leonardo.
Faith on the edge: religion and marginalized existence. Harper and Row, 1989.
Bevans, Stephen. *New Theol Rev* 6:118-119 F 1993.
New evangelization. Orbis Books, 1992.
Heiser, W Charles. *TheolDgst* 39:353 Wint 1992.
Dupuis, Jacques. *Gregorianum* 74 no 2:383-384 1993.
New evangelization. Collins Dove, 1992.
Hamilton, Andrew. *Pacifica* 6:347-349 O 1993.

Bogaert, Pierre-Maurice, et al, eds.
Les Bibles en français. Brepols, 1991.
Platelle, Henri. *MSR* 50:53-56 Ja-Mr 1993.

Boggio, G.
Fioele; Baruc, Abdia, Aggeo, Zaccaria, Malachia. Queriniana, 1991.
Ska, Jean Louis. *NRT* 115:296 Mr-Ap 1993.

Bogle, Joanna, and Wolkowinska, Cecylia.
When the summer ended. Gracewing, n.d.
Toomey, Philippa. *Tablet* 247:585 My 8 1993.

Bogliolo, Luigi.
Pío IX: profilo spirituale. Città del Vaticano, 1989.
Barrado, J. *Cien Tom* 120:194-195 Ja-Ap 1993.

Bohman, James.
New philosophy of social science. MIT Press, 1991.
Marler, J. *Mod Schlmn* 70:63-66 N 1992.

Boismard, M É.
Le Diatessaron: de Tatien à Justin. Gabalda, 1992.
Neirynck, F. *Eph Theol Lovan* 69:186-188 Ap 1993.

Boismard, M É, and Lamouille, A.
Un évangile pré-johannique; vol I: Jean 1,1-2,12. Gabalda, 1993.
Neirynck, F. *Eph Theol Lovan* 69:189-192 Ap 1993.

Boland, T P.
James Duhig. University of Queensland Press, 1986.
Byrne, N. *CHist* 78:700-701 O 1992.

Bolshakoff, Sergius, and Pennington, M Basil, 1931-.
In search of true wisdom: visits to Eastern spiritual fathers. Alba House, n.d.
Klimon, William M. *Crisis* 11:56-57 Jl-Ag 1993.

Boly, Craig, ed.
Jesuits in profile: alive and well in the US. Loyola University Press, 1992.
Heiser, W Charles. *TheolDgst* 40:69 Spr 1993.

Bonald, Louis de.
On divorce. Transaction Publishers, 1992.
Bergin, Martin J, Jr. *CHist* 79:344-345 Ap 1993.

Bonaventura, San.
Commento al Vangelo di Giovanni, vol 7. Citta Nuova, 1990-1991.
Orazzo, Antonio. *Civilta* 3:314-315 Ag 7-21 1993.
Sermoni domenicali. Citta Nuova, 1992.
Orazzo, Antonio. *Civilta* 3:316-317 Ag 7-21 1993.

Bondi, Roberta C.
To pray and to love: conversations on prayer with the early church. Fortress Press, 1991.
Henry, Patrick. *Horizons (CTS)* 20:174-175 Spr 1993.

Bonetti, Angelo, ed.
Il santorale di Paolo VI. Editrice Ancora, 1990.
Triacca, Achille M. *Notitiae* 28:624 S 1992.

Bonhoeffer, Dietrich.
La parole de la prédication. Labor et Fides, 1992.
Joós, Ernest. *Laval Theol Phil* 49:157-159 F 1993.
Le parole de la prédication. Labor et Fides, 1992.
Anon. *NRT* 115:631 Jl-Ag 1993.

Bonora, Antonio.
Il libro di Qoèlet. Città Nuova, 1992.
Murphy, Roland E. *OTA* 16:176 F 1993.

Boo, Mary Richard.
House of stone: the Duluth Benedictines. St Scholastica Priory Books, 1991.
Tegeder, V. *CHist* 78:687-689 O 1992.

The book of saints: a dictionary of servants of God canonized by the Catholic Church.
A and C Black, n.d.
Kirley, K. *Can Cath Rev* 11:34 Ja 1993.

Boorstin, Daniel J.
The creators. Random House, n.d.
Labio, Catherine. *America* 168:17-19 My 8 1993.

Booth, Leo.
When God becomes a drug. Tarcher-Perigee, n.d.
Graham, William C. *Nat Cath Rep* 29:36 S 10 1993.

Borbone, Pier Giorgio.
Il libro del Profeta Osea: Edizione critica del testo ebraico. Silvio Zamorani, 1990.
Cresko, John F. *CBQ* 54:737-738 O 1992.

Borges, Pedro, ed.
Historia de la Iglesia en Hispanoamérica y Filipinas (siglos XV-XIX). Biblioteca de Autores Cristianos, 1992.
Lopez-Gay, Jesus. *Gregorianum* 74 no 2:395 1993.
Schwaller, John F. *CHist* 79:584-585 Jl 1993.

Bori, Pier Cesare.
L'interprétation infinie. Cerf, 1991.
Petit, Jean-Claude. *Laval Theol Phil* 49:171-172 F 1993.

Boring, M Eugene.
The continuing voice of Jesus. Westminster, 1991.
Senior, Donald. *BibleT* 31:58 Ja 1993.
Buchanan, George Wesley. *CBQ* 55:141-143 Ja 1993.

Bormann, F Herbert, and Kellert, Stephen R, eds.
Ecology, economics, ethics: the broken circle. Yale University Press, 1991.
Hoose, Bernard. *Heythrop* 34:199-201 Ap 1993.

Borobio Garcia, et al.
Evangelización en América. Colección Salamanca, 1988.
Salinas, Carlos. *Teol Vida* 33 no 3-4:328-329 1992.

Borowitz, Eugene B.
Renewing the covenant: a theology for the postmodern Jew. Jewish Publication Society, 1991.
Berenbaum, Michael. *TheolStds* 53:774-775 D 1992.
Lillie, Betty Jane. *Bib Th Bul* 23:135-136 Aut 1993.

Borst, Amo.
Medieval worlds: barbarians, heretics, and artists in the Middles Ages. University of Chicago Press, 1992.
Russell, Jeffrey Burton. *CHist* 78:630-631 O 1992.

Bos, Rein.
Identificatie-mogelijkheden in preken uit het Oude Testament. Kok, 1992.
Matthews, Victor H. *OTA* 16:402 Je 1993.

Bosch, David J.
Transforming mission. Orbis Books, 1991.
Hearne, Brian. *Furrow* 44:60 Ja 1993.
Bevans, Stephen. *New Theol Rev* 6:106-108 F 1993.
May, John D'Arcy. *JEcumen Stds* 29:470 Sum-Aut 1992.

Bosch, Juan.
Para comprender el ecumenismo. Editorial Verbo divino, 1991.
Lago Alba, Luis. *Cien Tom* 119:603 S-D 1992.

Bosco, Giovanni.
Scritti editi e inediti. Libreria Ateneo Salesiano, 1991.
DiGiovanni, Stephen M. *CHist* 79:350 Ap 1993.

Bosetti, Elena.
La tenda e il bastone. Paoline, 1992.
Anon. *Gregorianum* 74 no 3:601-602 1993.
Begg, Christopher T. *OTA* 16:436-437 Je 1993.

Bosi, Roberto.
Monasteri italiani. Calderini, 1992.
Caprile, Giovanni. *Civilta* 3:101-102 Jl 3 1993.

Bosk, Charles L.
All God's mistakes: genetic counseling in a pediatric hospital. University of Chicago Press, n.d.
  Lanham, Richard J. *New Oxford Rev* 60:32 S 1993.

Bosman, H L, et al, eds.
Plutocrats and paupers: wealth and poverty in the Old Testament. Schaik, 1991.
  Harrison, Robert. *OTA* 16:437 Je 1993.

Bossy, John.
Giordano Bruno and the embassy affair. Yale University Press, 1991.
  Heiser, W Charles. *TheolDgst* 39:353 Wint 1992.

Boswell, Jonathan.
Community and the economy. Routledge, 1991.
  Naughton, Michael. *RSocEcon* 51:86-102 Spr 1993.

Botha, J Eugene.
Jesus and the samaritan woman. E.J. Brill, 1991.
  Collins, Raymond F. *Louvain Stds* 18:187-188 Sum 1993.

Botkin, Daniel.
Discordant harmonies: a new ecology for the twenty-first century. Oxford University Press, 1990.
  Burton-Christie, Douglas. *Horizons (CTS)* 20:163-165 Spr 1993.

Bottéro, Jean.
Mesopotamia: writing, reasoning, and the gods. University of Chicago Press, 1992.
  Heiser, W Charles. *TheolDgst* 40:53 Spr 1993.

Bouchard, Constance Brittain.
Holy entrepreneurs: Cistercians, knights, and economic exchange in twelfth-century Burgundy. Cornell University Press, 1991.
  Callahan, Daniel, 1930-. *CHist* 78:636-640 O 1992.

Bouchard, Gary M.
Femmes et pouvoir dans la cité philosophique: relire l'Utopie de Thomas More. Éditions Logiques, 1992.
  Allard, G. *Laval Theol Phil* 49:175-176 F 1993.

Bouchard, L.D.
Tragic method and tragic theology: evil in contemporary drama and religious thought. Pennsylvania State University Press, 1989.
  Hanney, James. *Heythrop* 34:321-322 Jl 1993.

Bouchindhomme, Christian, and Rochlitz, Rainer.
Temps et récit de Paul Ricoeur en débat. Cerf, 1990.
  Nadeau, Jean-Guy. *Laval Theol Phil* 49:149-155 F 1993.

Boulay, F R H Du.
The England of Piers Plowman: William Langland and his vision of the fourteenth century. Boydell and Brewer, 1991.
  Day, John. *TheolStds* 53:785 D 1992.

Bouley, Allan, ed.
Catholic rites today: abridged texts for students. Liturgical Press, 1992.
  Steel, G. *Priests & People* 7:40-41 Ja 1993.

Boureau, Alain, and Ingerflom, Claudio Sergio, eds.
La royauté sacrée dans le monde Chrétien. Éditions de l'École des Hautes Études en Sciences Sociales, 1992.
  Jackson, Richard A. *CHist* 79:498-499 Jl 1993.

Bourgeois, Bernard.
Études hégéliennes: raison et décision. Presses Universitaires de France, 1992.
  Ponton, Lionel. *Laval Theol Phil* 49:350-351 Je 1993.

Bourke, Vernon J.
Augustine's love of wisdom. Purdue University Press, 1992.
  Clark, Mary T. *IPQ* 33:376-377 S 1993.
  Teske, Roland J. *Mod Schlmn* 70:237-238 Mr 1993.

Bouttier, Michel.
L'épître de saint Paul aux Ephésiens. Labor et Fides, 1991.
  Lodge, John G. *CBQ* 55:357-358 Ap 1993.
  Galot, Jean. *Gregorianum* 73 No 4:753-754 1992.

Bouyer, Louis.
Cosmos: the world and the glory of God. Saint Bede's Publications, n.d.
  Reitan, Eric A. *Can Cath Rev* 11:32-33 F 1993.
Eucharist. Notre Dame University Press, 1968.
  Thurian, Max. *SIDIC* 26 no 1:19-20 1993.
Women mystics. Ignatius Press, 1993.
  Anon. *Spir Life* 39:188 Aut 1993.

Bové, Paul.
In the wake of theory. Wesleyan University Press, 1992.
  Giles, James E. *CrossCurr* 43:258-259 Sum 1993.

Bovon, François, and Koester, Helmut.
Genèse de l'écriture chrétienne. Brepols, 1991.
  Galot, Jean. *Gregorianum* 74 no 2:363 1993.

Bowden, Henry Warner.
Church history in an age of uncertainty: historiographical patterns in the United States, 1906-1990. Southern Illinois University Press, 1991.
  Lukacs, John. *CHist* 78:689-690 O 1992.

Bowden, John.
Who's who in theology. Crossroad, 1992.
  Cunningham, Lawrence S, 1935-. *Comm* 120:25-26 F 12 1993.
  Heiser, W Charles. *TheolDgst* 39:353 Wint 1992.

Bowe, Barbara E, et al, eds.
Silent voices, sacred lives: women's readings for the liturgical year. Paulist, 1992.
  Graham, William C. *Nat Cath Rep* 29:40 F 5 1993.
  Anon. *Church* 9:43 Sum 1993.
  Grady, Margaret Northcraft. *Mod Lit* 20:39 Ag 1993.
  Covino, Paul. *Past Mus* 17:52-53 Ag-S 1993.
  Cunningham, Lawrence S, 1935-. *Comm* 120:29-30 O 8 1993.

Bowen, David G, ed.
The Satanic verses: Bradford responds. Bradford & Ilkley Community College, n.d.
  Campbell, James. *Month* 26:322 Ag 1993.

Boyack, Kenneth, ed.
The new Catholic evangelization. Paulist Press, 1992.
  Korn, Barton. *Mod Lit* 20:40 F 1993.

Boyaxhiu, Teresa, Mother, 1910-, and Roger, Brother.
Seeking the heart of God: reflections on prayer. HarperSanFrancisco, n.d.
  Graham, William C. *Nat Cath Rep* 29:25 Mr 26 1993.

Boyd, Gregory A.
Oneness Pentecostals and the Trinity. Baker Book House, 1992.
  Heiser, W Charles. *TheolDgst* 40:53 Spr 1993.
Trinity and process. Peter Lang, 1992.
  Heiser, W Charles. *TheolDgst* 40:153 Sum 1993.

Boyer, Paul S.
When time shall be no more. Harvard University Press, 1992.
  Hamill, Paul C. *Month* 26:145-146 Ap 1993.
  Heiser, W Charles. *TheolDgst* 40:153 Sum 1993.
  Di Lella, Alexander A. *OTA* 16:429 Je 1993.

Boyle, Marjory O'Rourke.
Petrarch's genius: pentimento and prophesy. University of California, 1991.
  Iannace, F. *TheolStds* 53:784-785 D 1992.

Bozak, Barbara A.
Life "Anew": a literary-theological study of Jer 30-31. Biblical Institute, 1991.
  Biddle, Mark E. *CBQ* 55:324-325 Ap 1993.

Braaten, Carl E.
No other gospel! Christianity among the world's religions. Fortress Press, 1992.
  Heiser, W Charles. *TheolDgst* 39:353 Wint 1992.

Bracken, Joseph A.
Society and spirit: a trinitarian cosmology. Susquehanna University Press, 1991.
  Whitney, Barry L. *Horizons (CTS)* 19:320-321 Fall 1992.
  O'Donnell, John J. *Gregorianum* 74 No 1:161-162 1993.
  Heiser, W Charles. *TheolDgst* 39:393 Wint 1992.
  Schäfer, Stephen J. *TheolStds* 54:373-375 Je 1993.

Braden, Suzanne G, and Clement, Shirley F.
Caring evangelism: a visitation program for congregations. Discipleship Resources, 1991.
  Alfred, Joseph R. *Mod Lit* 20:36 My 1993.
Leader's guide. Discipleship Resources, 1991.
  Alfred, Joseph R. *Mod Lit* 20:36 My 1993.
Participant's workbook. Discipleship Resources, 1991.
  Alfred, Joseph R. *Mod Lit* 20:36 My 1993.

Bradford, Dennis E.
A thinker's guide to living well. Open Court, 1990.
  Masserly, John. *Mod Schlmn* 70:159-160 Ja 1993.

Bradley, Ian.
The Celtic way. Darton Longman and Todd, 1992.
  Redmond, Anthony. *Doctr Life* 43:448 S 1993.
  Waal, Esther de. *Tablet* 247:1302 O 9 1993.

Bradley, Martin B, et al.
Churches and church membership in the United States 1990. Glenmary Research Center, 1992.
  Heiser, W Charles. *TheolDgst* 40:156-157 Sum 1993.

Bradley, Ritamary.
Julian's way: a practical commentary on Julian of Norwich. HarperSanFrancisco, 1992.
  Heiser, W Charles. *TheolDgst* 40:53-54 Spr 1993.
  Woods, Richard. *New Blckfrs* 74:281-282 My 1993.
  Cunningham, Lawrence S, 1935-. *Comm* 120:29-30 Ag 13 1993.

Bradshaw, Paul F.
The search for the origins of Christian worship. SPCK; Oxford University Press, 1992.
  Baldovin, John F. *TheolStds* 54:557-559 S 1993.

Bradshaw, Paul F, and Hoffman, Lawrence A, eds.
The changing face of Jewish and Christian worship in North America. University of Notre Dame Press, 1992.
  Perelmuter, Hayim Goren. *Worship* 67:86-87 Ja 1993.
  Heiser, W Charles. *TheolDgst* 39:355-356 Wint 1992.
The making of Jewish and Christian worship. University of Notre Dame Press, 1991.
  Libowitz, Richard. *JEcumen Stds* 29:278 Spr 1992.

Brady, James F, and Olin, John C, eds.
Patristic scholarship: the edition of St Jerome. University of Toronto Press, 1992.
  Bietenholz, Peter G. *CHist* 79:336-337 Ap 1993.
  La Corte, Daniel M. *Cist Stud* 28 no 2:[49]-[50] 1993.

Brady, Joan.
Theory of war. André Deutsch, n.d.
  Miller, Peggy. *Tablet* 247:344 Mr 13 1993.

Brague, Rémi.
Europe, la voie romaine. Idées, 1992.
  Pasqua, Hervé. *RPhil Louvain* 91:498-502 Ag 1993.
Saint Bernard et la philosophie. Presses universitaires de France, 1993.
  Bedouelle, Thierry. *RPhil Louvain* 91:318-319 My 1993.

Brambilla, Rosa.
Gesù Cristo nella narrativa italiana del'900. Pro Civitate Christiana, 1992.
  Flumeri, E. *Civilta* 2:308 My 1 1993.

Brandão, Carlos Rodrigues.
O trabalho de saber: cultura camponesa e escola rural. FTD, 1990.
  Libanio, Joao Batista. *Perspectiva* 25:120-121 Ja-Ap 1993.

Brandmüller, Walter.
Galileo la Chiesa, ossia il diritto ad errare. Lib Ed Vaticana, 1992.
  Casanovas, J. *Civilta* 3:310-311 Ag 7-21 1993.

Brantschen, J B.
Hoffnung fur Zeit und Ewigkeit. Herder, 1992.
  Renard, L.-J. *NRT* 115:591 Jl-Ag 1993.

Bratcher, Robert G, and Reyburn, William D.
A translator's handbook on the Book of Psalms. United Bible Societies, 1991.
  Cresko, Anthony R. *CBQ* 54:738-740 O 1992.

Bratton, Susan Power.
Christianity, wilderness, and wildlife: the original desert solitaire. Associated University Presses, n.d.
  Caldecott, Stratford. *Tablet* 247:1233-1234 S 25 1993.

Braulik, Georg.
Die deuteronomischen Gesetze und der Dekalog. Katholisches Bibelwerk, 1991.
  Begg, Christopher T. *OTA* 16:171 F 1993.
Deuteronomium II. Echter, 1992.
  Begg, Christopher T. *OTA* 16:171 F 1993.

Braybrooke, Marcus.
Pilgrimage of hope. Crossroad, 1992.
  Heiser, W Charles. *TheolDgst* 39:353-354 Wint 1992.
  Barnes, Michael R. *Way* 33:168 Ap 1993.
  Saliba, John A. *TheolStds* 54:190-192 Mr 1993.
Time to meet: toward a deeper relationship between Jews and Christians. SCM Press, 1990.
  Sigal, Lillian. *JEcumen Stds* 29:117-119 Wint 1992.

Breach of trust/breach of faith: child sexual abuse in the Church and society.
Publications Service Canadian Conference of Catholic Bishops, n.d.
  Campbell, Joe. *Can Cath Rev* 11:30-31 My 1993.

Brecht, Martin.
Martin Luther: shaping and defining the Reformation, 1521-1532. Fortress Press, 1990.
  Hamilton, Alastair. *Heythrop* 34:213-214 Ap 1993.
Martin Luther: the preservation of the church, 1532-1546. Fortress Press, 1993.
  Gros, Jeffrey, 1938-. *RRel* 52:634-636 Jl-Ag 1993.

Bredin, Eamonn.
Rediscovering Jesus: challenge of discipleship. Claretian Publications, 1990.
  Dupuis, Jacques. *Gregorianum* 74 No 1:192 1993.

Bregman, Lucy.
Death in the midst of life. Baker, 1992.
  Heiser, W Charles. *TheolDgst* 39:354 Wint 1992.
  Kollar, Nathan R. *Horizons (CTS)* 20:190-191 Spr 1993.

Brekelmans, Chris, and Lust, Johan, eds.
Pentateuchal and Deuteronomistic studies. Leuven University Press, 1990.
  Vogels, Walter A. *CBQ* 54:817-818 O 1992.
  Schoors, A. *Eph Theol Lovan* 78:148-149 Ap 1992.

Bremmer, J N, and García Martínez, F, eds.
Sacred history and sacred texts in early Judaism. Kok Pharos, 1992.
  Lust, Johan. *Eph Theol Lovan* 69:156-157 Ap 1993.

Brennan, Keith, et al.
Our view at last. Tallaght Centre for the Unemployed, 1992.
  Toner, W. *Studies* 82:220-222 Sum 1993.

Brennan, Patrick J.
Parishes that excel. The Crossroad Publishing Company, n.d.
  Higgins, James J. *Liguorian* 81:69 Ap 1993.

Brennan, Troyen.
Just doctoring: medical ethics in the United States. University of California Press, n.d.
  Benestad, J Brian. *America* 168:20+ My 22, 1993.

Brenner, Martin L.
The Song of the Sea: Ex 15:1-21. Gruyter, 1991.
  Howell, Maribeth. *OTA* 15:493-494 O 1992.
  Howell, Maribeth. *CBQ* 55:103-105 Ja 1993.

Brenner, Y S.
The rise and fall of capitalism. Edward Elgar, 1991.
  Stanfield, James Ronald. *RSocEcon* 51:378-380 Aut 1993.

Brereton, Virginia Lieson.
From sin to salvation: stories of women's conversions, 1800 to the present. Indiana University Press, 1991.
  Porterfield, Amanda. *Horizons (CTS)* 20:165-166 Spr 1993.

Brésard, Luc, and Crouzel, Henri, eds.
Origène: Commentaire sur le Cantique des Cantiques. no publisher given, 1991.
  Halleux, André de. *Eph Theol Lovan* 78:451-452 D 1992.

Brett, Mark G.
Biblical criticism in crisis? Cambridge University Press, 1991.
  Williams, James G. *CBQ* 55:325-327 Ap 1993.

Brett, Paul.
Rethinking Catholic attitudes to sex. Center for the study of theology in the University of Essen, n.d.
  Lord, Elizabeth. *Way* 33:77 Ja 1993.

Breuilly, Elizabeth, and Palmer, Martin, eds.
Christianity and ecology. Cassell, n.d.
  McDonagh, Sean. *Furrow* 44:120-123 F 1993.

Breukelman, F H.
Bijbelse Theologie, I,2. Kok, 1992.
  Kessler, Martin. *OTA* 16:418 Je 1993.

Bria, Ion.
The sense of ecumenical tradition. WCC Publications, 1991.
  Bundy, Lester I. *JEcumen Stds* 29:472 Sum-Aut 1992.

Brichto, Herbert C.
Toward a grammar of biblical poetics: tales of the prophets. Oxford University, 1992.
  Boadt, Lawrence. *TheolStds* 54:160-161 Mr 1993.

Briend, Jacques.
Dieu dans l'Ecriture. Cerf, 1992.
  Begg, Christopher T. *OTA* 16:184-185 F 1993.

Briend, Jacques, and Cothenet, E, eds.
DBSup 11, 1057-1420. Sarepta, 1991.
  Begg, Christopher T. *OTA* 16:403 Je 1993.
DBSup 12, 1-256. Scribes, 1992.
  Begg, Christopher T. *OTA* 16:403 Je 1993.

Briggs, Kenneth A.
Holy siege. HarperSanFranciso, n.d.
  Mayeski, Mary Anne. *America* 168:27+ F 20 1993.

Briggs, Robin.
Communities of belief: cultural and social tensions in early modern France. Clarendon Press, 1989.
  Schneider, R. *CHist* 78:655-657 O 1992.

Bright, Thomas, and Roberto, John, eds.
Creating a partnership in faith: a parish planning guide. No publisher given, n.d.
  Roach, Joseph J. *Living Light* 30:100 Aut 1993.
Faith and families: a parish program for parenting in faith growth. No publisher given, n.d.
  Roach, Joseph J. *Living Light* 30:100 Aut 1993.

Brill, Norman Q.
America's psychic malignancy: the problem of crime, substance abuse, poverty and welfare—identifying causes with possible remedies. Charles C Thomas, 1993.
  Anon. *Health Prog* 74:68 My 1993.

Bringle, Mary Louise.
The God of thinness: gluttony and other weighty matters. Abingdon Press, 1992.
  Heiser, W Charles. *TheolDgst* 40:54 Spr 1993.

Brinkman, Johan.
The perception of space in the Old Testament. Kok Pharos, 1992.
  Begg, Christopher T. *OTA* 15:494 O 1992.

Briquel-Chatonnet, F.
Les relations entre les cités de la côte phenicienne et les royaumes d'Israël et de Juda. Peeters, 1992.
  Edelman, Diana V. *OTA* 16:394 Je 1993.

Brister, C W.
Pastoral care in the church. HarperSanFrancisco, 1992.
  Heiser, W Charles. *TheolDgst* 39:354 Wint 1992.

Brito, Emilio.
La créatin selon Schelling. Peeters, 1987.
  Veto, M. *Eph Theol Lovan* 78:175-176 Ap 1992.
Dieu et l'être d'après Thomas D'Aquin et Hegel. Press Universitaires de France, 1991.
  McDermott, John M. *TheolStds* 53:752-753 D 1992.

Brock, David.
"The real Anita Hill: the untold story". Free Press, n.d.
  Farrell, Regina. *Register* 69:5 Je 20 1993.

Brock, Sebastian.
The luminous eye: the spiritual world vision of Saint Ephrem the Syrian. Cistercian, 1992.
  Davis, Thomas X. *Cist Stud* 28:[38] 1993.
L'oeil de lumière. Abbaye de Bellefontaine, 1991.
  Roisel, V. *NRT* 114:908-909 N-D 1992.

Brockington, J L.
Hinduism and Christianity. St. Martin's, 1992.
  Carpenter, David. *TheolStds* 54:607-608 S 1993.

Broderick, Joe.
Fall from grace. Bandon, n.d.
  Kenny, Mary, 1936-. *Tablet* 247:516 Ap 24 1993.

Brodeur, Raymond.
Les catéchismes au Québec 1702-1963. Editions du Centre National de la Recherche Scientifique, 1990.
  Marthaler, Berard L, 1927-. *CHist* 79:377-378 Ap 1993.

Brody, Baruch A, ed.
Bioethics yearbook, volume 1: 1988-1990. Academic Publishers, 1991.
  Heiser, W Charles. *TheolDgst* 39:352 Wint 1992.

Bromberg, Judith.
The spirit of community. Crown, n.d.
  Bromberg, Judith. *Nat Cath Rep* 29:27 S 10 1993.

Bromwich, David.
Politics by other means: higher education and group thinking. Yale University Press, 1992.
  Siegel, Lee. *Comm* 120:30-31 Ap 9 1993.
  Tipton, Paul. *Register* 69:4 My 23 1993.
  Giles, James E. *CrossCurr* 43:260 Sum 1993.

Brooke, Avery.
Plain prayers in a complicated world. Cowley, n.d.
  Graham, William C. *Nat Cath Rep* 30:36 N 19 1993.

Brooke, George J, and Lindars, Barnabas, eds.
Septuagint, scrolls and cognate writings. Scholars Press, 1992.
  Heiser, W Charles. *TheolDgst* 39:383-384 Wint 1992.

Brooker, Jewel Spears, ed.
The placing of T S Eliot. University of Missouri Press, 1991.
  Campbell, James. *Relig Lit* 24:107-108 Aut 1992.

Brookner, Anita.
A family romance. Cape, n.d.
  Delay, Jill. *Tablet* 247:951 Jl 24 1993.
Fraud. Random House, n.d.
  Bromberg, Judith. *Nat Cath Rep* 29:28 My 28 1993.

Brooks, James A.
The New Testament text of Gregory of Nyssa. Scholars, 1991.
  Brogan, John J. *CBQ* 55:143-145 Ja 1993.

Brooks, Roger.
The spirit of the ten commandments; shattering the myth of Rabbinic legalism. Harper and Row, 1990.
  Prizzell, L. *SIDIC* 25 No 1:33 1992.

Brooks-Leonard, John, and Gaupin, Linda.
Children in the assembly of the Church. Liturgy Training Publications, n.d.
  Graham, William C. *Nat Cath Rep* 29:40 My 28 1993.

Broshi, Magen, ed.
The Damascus document reconsidered. The Shrine of the Book, Israel Museum, 1992.
  Fitzgerald, Aloysius. *OTA* 15:469 O 1992.

Brotherton, Anne, ed.
The voice of the turtledove. Paulist, 1992.
  Lovatt-Dolan, Elizabeth. *Living Light* 29:90-91 Sum 1993.
  Ward, Hannah, and Wild, Jennifer. *Way* 33:258 Jl 1993.
  Heiser, W Charles. *TheolDgst* 40:191 Sum 1993.

Brouwer, Arie R.
Ecumenical testimony. William B. Eerdmans, 1991.
  Lewis, Eleanor V. *JEcumen Stds* 29:474-475 Sum-Aut 1992.

Brown, Charles Calvin.
Niebuhr and his age. Trinity Press International, 1992.
  Heiser, W Charles. *TheolDgst* 40:153 Sum 1993.

Brown, Cheryl Anne.
No longer be silent: first century Jewish portraits of biblical women. Westminster, 1992.
  Franke, Chris. *OTA* 16:442 Je 1993.
  Stuhlmueller, Carroll. *BibleT* 31:53 Ja 1993.
  Laffey, Alice L. *CBQ* 55:359-360 Ap 1993.

Brown, Frank Burch.
Religious aesthetics: a theological study of making and meaning. Princeton University Press, 1992.
  Stackhouse, Max L. *CrossCurr* 43:123-124 Spr 1993.

Brown, Kenneth O.
Holy ground: a study of the American camp meeting. Garland, 1992.
  Heiser, W Charles. *TheolDgst* 40:153 Sum 1993.

Brown, L B, ed.
Advances in the psychology of religion. Pergamon, 1985.
  Godin, A. *Lumen* 48:355 S 1993.

Brown, Malcolm.
The Imperial War Museum book of the First World War: a great conflict recalled in previously unpublished letters, diaries, and memoirs. Sidgwick and Jackson, n.d.
  Blythe, Ronald. *Tablet* 247:654-655 My 22 1993.

Brown, Neil.
Spirit of the world: the moral basis of Christian spirituality. Catholic Institute of Sydney, 1990.
  Casey, Michael. *Pacifica* 6:224-225 Je 1993.

Brown, Paul B.
In and for the world: bringing the contemporary into Christian worship. Fortress Press, 1992.
  Gollob, Timothy. *Mod Lit* 20:37-38 Je-Jl 1993.

Brown, Peter Robert Lamont.
Power and persuasion in late antiquity: towards a Christian empire. University of Wisconsin Press, 1992.
  Bankston, Carl L, III. *Comm* 120:28-29 Ap 9 1993.
  Heiser, W Charles. *TheolDgst* 40:153-154 Sum 1993.

Brown, Ralph.
Marriage annulment in the Catholic church. Third Edition, 1990.
  Fellhauer, David E. *Jurist* 51 no 2:524-525 1991.

Brown, Raymond Edward, et al, eds.
The New Jerome Bible handbook. The Liturgical Press, 1992.
  Neirynck, F. *Eph Theol Lovan* 78:426-428 D 1992.
  Stuhlmueller, Carroll. *BibleT* 31:118-119 Mr 1993.
The new Jerome Biblical commentary. Prentice-Hall, 1990.
  Sloyan, Gerard S. *JEcumen Stds* 29:273-274 Spr 1992.

Brown, Raymond Edward.
Responses to 101 questions on the Bible. Paulist, 1990.
  Gauthier, Roland. *CahiersJos* 41:140 Ja-Je 1993.

Brown, Richard.
Church and state in modern Britain 1700-1850. Routledge, 1991.
  Butler, Perry. *Heythrop* 34:460-461 O 1993.

Brown, Robert McAfee, 1920-.
Persuade us to rejoice: the liberating power of fiction. John Knox Press, n.d.
  McCarthy, Tim. *Nat Cath Rep* 29:30 F 5 1993.

Brown, Sarah.
Stained glass: an illustrated history. Studio Editions, n.d.
  Stephens, F. *Tablet* 246:1625 D 19-26 1992.

Browning, Don S.
A fundamental practical theology: descriptive and strategic proposals. Fortress, 1991.
  Barenbaum, M. *TheolStds* 53:772-775 D 1992.
  Groome, Thomas H, 1945-. *Horizons (CTS)* 20:162-163 Spr 1993.

Browning, Don S, and Fiorenza, Francis Schüssler, 1938-, eds.
Habermas, modernity, and public theology. Crossroad, 1992.
  Heiser, W Charles. *TheolDgst* 40:66 Spr 1993.

Browning, Robert.
The Byzantine empire. Catholic University of America Press, 1992.
  Heiser, W Charles. *TheolDgst* 40:154 Sum 1993.

Broyard, Anatole.
Intoxicated by my illness. Clarkson Potter, n.d.
  Marget, Madeline. *Comm* 120:22-24 Ja 15 1993.

Brück, Michael von.
The unity of reality. Paulist Press, 1991.
  Redington, James D. *TheolStds* 54:175-176 Mr 1993.
  Sheridan, Daniel P. *Horizons (CTS)* 20:193-194 Spr 1993.

Bruder, Judith.
Convergence: a reconciliation of Judaism and Christianity in the life of one woman. Doubleday, 1993.

Bruder, Judith. *(cont'd)*
  Casteel, John L. *RRel* 52:631-632 Jl-Ag 1993.
  Williams, Joan. *Living Prayer* 26:33 N-D 1993.
  Golan, Joan Marlow. *America* 169:22+ N 6 1993.

Brueggemann, Walter.
Abiding astonishment: Psalms, modernity, and the making of history. John Knox, 1991.
  Moore, Michael S. *CBQ* 54:740-741 O 1992.
Old Testament theology. Fortress, 1992.
  Harrington, Daniel J. *America* 168:26 F 6 1993.
  Stuhlmueller, Carroll. *BibleT* 31:245 Jl 1993.
  Murphy, Roland E. *OTA* 16:437 Je 1993.
Power, providence, and personality: biblical insight into life and ministry. John Knox, 1990.
  Craig, Kenneth M, Jr. *CBQ* 54:741-742 O 1992.
The prophetic imagination. Fortress Press, 1978.
  Brummel, M. *USCath* 58:6-13 Ja 1993.
Rethinking Christian attitudes of sex. Center for the study of theology in the University of Essen, n.d.
  Lord, Elizabeth. *Way* 33:75-76 Ja 1993.

Bruguès, Jean-Louis.
Fecondazione artificiale: una scelta etica? SEI, 1991.
  Cultrera, Francesco. *Civilta* 143:423-425 N 21 1992.

Brumleye, Barbara, ed.
The letters of Mother Caroline Friess, School Sisters of Notre Dame. School Sisters of Notre Dame, 1991.
  Misner, Barbara. *CHist* 79:134-135 Ja 1993.

Brun, Jean.
Philosophie de l'histoire: les promesses du temps. Stock, 1990.
  Naert, Émilienne. *RPhil Louvain* 91:496-497 Ag 1993.

Bruning, B, et al, eds.
Collectanea Augustiniana: mélanges T J van Bavel. Peeters, 1990.
  Wielocx, R. *Eph Theol Lovan* 69:146-155 Ap 1993.

Brunk, Gerald R, ed.
Menno Simons: a reappraisal. Eastern Mennonite College, 1992.
  Heiser, W Charles. *TheolDgst* 39:373 Wint 1992.

Brunner-Traut, Emma, ed.
Die groben Religionen des Alten Orients und der Antike. Kohlhammer, 1992.
  Begg, Christopher T. *OTA* 16:403-404 Je 1993.

Brunton, Paul.
The notebooks of Paul Brunton: perspectives. Larson, 1984.
  Williams, Alison. *Teilhard Rev* 28:31-33 Sum 1993.

Bruteau, Beatrice, 1930-, ed.
As we are one: essays and poems in honor of Bede Griffiths. Philosophers' Exchange, 1991.
  Middleton, Frank. *CrossCurr* 42:564-565 Wint 1992-1993.

Brutton, Philip.
Ensign in Italy: a platoon commander's story. Leo Cooper, n.d.
  Aitken, Tom. *Tablet* 247:759 Je 1993.

Bruück, Michael von.
Denn wir sind Menschen voller Hoffnung: Gespräche mit dem XIV. Kaiser Verlag, 1988.
  MacCormick, Chalmers. *JEcumen Stds* 29:494 Sum-Aut 1992.

Bryk, Anthony S, et al.
Catholic schools and the common good. Harvard University Press, n.d.
  O'Keefe, Joseph M. *Nat Cath Rep* 30:19 O 29 1993.

Bryson, Bill.
The lost continent; travels in small town America. Abacus, n.d.
  Toomey, Philippa. *Tablet* 247:373 Mr 20 1993.

Bryson, John M, and Crosby, Barbara C.
Leadership for the common good: tackling public problems in a shared-power world. Jossey-Bass, 1992.
  Anon. *Health Prog* 74:67 Je 1993.

Brzegowy, Tadeusz.
Miasto Boze w Psalmach. Polskie Towarzystwo Teologiczne, 1989.
  Hoppe, Leslie J. *OTA* 16:175 F 1993.

Buber, Martin, 1878-1965.
The letters of Martin Buber: a life of dialogue. Schocken Books, 1991.
  Heiser, W Charles. *TheolDgst* 40:54 Spr 1993.

Buchan, Ursula.
Wall plants and climbers. Pavilion Books, n.d.
  Taylor, Patrick. *Tablet* 247:375 Mr 20 1993.

Bucher, Anton A.
Bibel-Psychologie. Kohlhammer, 1992.
  Grom, Bernhard. *Stimm Zeit* 211:285-286 Ap 1993.

Buchwald, W, et al.
Dictionnaire des auteurs latins et grecs de l'Antiquité et du Moyen Âge. Brepols, n.d.
  Anon. *NRT* 115:152-153 Ja-F 1993.

Buckle, Stephen.
Natural law and the theory of property: Grotius to Hume. Oxford University Press, 1991.
  Heiser, W Charles. *TheolDgst* 39:354 Wint 1992.

Buckley, Michael J, 1931-.
Let peace disturb you. St Paul Publications, n.d.
  O'Higgins-O'Malley, Una. *Furrow* 44:324-325 My 1993.

Buckman, Robert.
How to break bad news. Papermac, n.d.
  Toomey, Philippa. *Tablet* 247:585 My 8 1993.

Budde, Michael L.
The two churches: Catholicism and capitalism in the world system. Duke University Press, 1992.
  McGovern, Arthur F, 1929-. *New Oxford Rev* 60:22-25 Jl-Ag 1993.
  Heiser, W Charles. *TheolDgst* 40:54 Spr 1993.

Budwig, Robert.
The vegetable market cookbook. Rosendale Press, n.d.
  Poole, Shona Crawford. *Tablet* 247:373 Mr 20 1993.

Buechner, Frederick.
The clown in the belfry: writings on faith and fiction. HarperSanFrancisco, n.d.
    Luebering, Carol. *St Anth* 100:51 Ja 1993.
The son of laughter. HarperSanFrancisco, n.d.
    Feister, John Bookser. *Nat Cath Rep* 29:37 My 28 1993.
    Malin, Irving. *Comm* 120:27-28 Jl 16 1993.

Bugnion-Secretan, P.
La mère Angélique Arnauld, 1591-1661. Cerf, 1991.
    Renard, L J. *NRT* 114:931-932 N-D 1992.

Bühlmann, Walbert.
Ojos para ver Los cristianos ante el tercer milenio. Herder, 1990.
    Garcia, Emilio. *Cien Tom* 119:411-412 My-Ag 1992.

Bujak, Adam.
John Paul II. Ignatius Press, 1992.
    Heiser, W Charles. *TheolDgst* 40:54 Spr 1993.

Bujanda, Jesus M de, ed.
Index d'Anvers, 1569, 1570, 1571. Éditions de l'Université de Sherbrooke, 1988.
    Coppens, Christian. *CHist* 79:532-534 Jl 1993.

Bujo, Bénézet.
African theology in its social context. Orbis Books, 1992.
    Neckebrouck, Valeer. *Eph Theol Lovan* 69:202-204 Ap 1993.
    Blaszczak, Gerald R. *TheolStds* 54:396 Je 1993.
    Heiser, W Charles. *TheolDgst* 40:54 Spr 1993.
Afrikanische Theologie in ihrem gesellschaftlichen Kontext. Patmos, 1986.
    Neckebrouck, Valeer. *Eph Theol Lovan* 69:202-204 Ap 1993.

Bultmann, Christoph.
Der Fremde im antiken Juda. Vandenhoeck & Ruprecht, 1992.
    Graham, Patrick M. *OTA* 16:437-438 Je 1993.

Bundesen, Lynne.
So the woman went her way. Simon & Schuster Publishers, 1993.
    Stuhlmueller, Carroll. *BibleT* 31:245 Jl 1993.

Bunson, Margaret, and Bunson, Matthew.
St Francis of Assisi. Our Sunday Visitor, n.d.
    McCann, Deborah. *ReligTJ* 27:14 O 1993.
St Joan of Arc. Our Sunday Visitor, n.d.
    McCann, Deborah. *ReligTJ* 27:14 O 1993.

Bur, J.
Pour comprendre la Vierge Marie dans le mystère du Christ et de l'Église. Ed du Cerf, 1992.
    Renard, L-J. *NRT* 115:589 Jl-Ag 1993.

Burgess, Anthony.
A mouthful of air. Hutchinson, n.d.
    Braybrooke, Neville. *Tablet* 247:48 Ja 9 1993.

Burgess, Joseph, ed.
In search of Christian unity. Fortress, 1991.
    Gros, Jeffrey, 1938-. *New Theol Rev* 6:109-110 Ag 1993.

Burggraeve, Roger, and Vervenne, Marc, eds.
Swords into plowshares: theological reflections on peace. Peeters Press, 1991.
    Stuhlmueller, Carroll. *BibleT* 31:123 Mr 1993.

Burghardt, Walter J.
Dare to be Christ: homilies for the nineties. Paulist Press, n.d.
    Cylwicki, Albert. *Can Cath Rev* 11:29 My 1993.
When Christ meets Christ: homilies on the Just Word. Liturgical, n.d.
    Graham, William C. *Nat Cath Rep* 29:18 Jl 16 1993.

Burgmann, Hans.
Der "Sitz im Leben" in den Josuafluch-Texten, in 4 Q 379 22 II und 4 Q Testimonia. Enigma, 1990.
    Fitzmyer, Joseph Augustine, 1920-. *OTA* 16:190 F 1993.

Burke, Peter.
The fabrication of Louis XIV. Yale University Press, 1992.
    Schaeper, Thomas J. *Cithara* 32:53-54 My 1993.

Burkett, Delbert.
The son of the man in the Gospel of John. JSOT, 1991.
    Moloney, Francis J. *Pacifica* 6:109-112 F 1993.
    Boer, Martinus C de. *CBQ* 55:360-361 Ap 1993.

Burnes, Gene.
The frontiers of Catholicism. University of California Press, 1992.
    Heiser, W Charles. *TheolDgst* 40:154 Sum 1993.

Burnod, J-M.
Le mouvement social franciscain en France. Franciscaines, 1991.
    Plumat, N. *NRT* 114:916 N-D 1992.

Burns, Gene.
The frontiers of Catholicism: the politics of ideology in a liberal world. University of California Press, n.d.
    Liggion, Leonard P. *Crisis* 11:53-54 My 1993.

Burns, Robert E, 1919-.
Foundations of Crusader Valencia: revolt and recovery, 1257-1264: diplomatarium of the Crusader Kingdom of Valencia. Princeton University Press, 1991.
    Hillgarth, J. *CHist* 78:642-643 O 1992.
Roman Catholicism yesterday and today. Loyola University Press, 1992.
    Hayden, Hilary. *Living Light* 29:92-93 Spr 1993.

Burns, Tom G.
The use of memory: publishing and further pursuits. Sheed & Ward, n.d.
    Bull, George, 1929-. *Tablet* 247:341-342 Mr 13 1993.
    Campbell, James. *Month* 26:198 My 1993.
    O'Collins, Gerald, 1931-. *Comm* 120:20-21 My 21 1993.
    McRedmond, Louis. *Doctr Life* 43:379-380 Jl-Ag 1993.
    Bailey, Bede. *New Blckfrs* 74:372-373 Jl-Ag 1993.

Burrell, David B, and McGinn, Bernard John, 1937-.
God and creation: an ecumenical symposium. Notre Dame, 1990.
    Grenz, Stanley. *JEcumen Stds* 29:489-491 Sum-Aut 1992.

Burrell, David B, and Landau, Yehezkel, eds.
Voices from Jerusalem: Jews and Christians reflect on the Holy Land. Paulist Press, 1992.

Burrell, David B, and Landau, Yehezkel, eds. *(cont'd)*
    Heiser, W Charles. *TheolDgst* 39:391 Wint 1992.
    Levy, I. *SIDIC* 26 no 1:31-32 1993.
    Morrow, Carol Ann. *ST Anth* 101:50-51 Jl 1993.

Burridge, Richard A.
What are the Gospels? Cambridge University Press, 1992.
    Fiore, Benjamin. *TheolStds* 53:780-781 D 1992.
    Davies, Meg. *New Blckfrs* 74:109-110 F 1993.
    Heiser, W Charles. *TheolDgst* 39:354 Wint 1992.
    Neyrey, Jerome H. *CBQ* 55:361-363 Ap 1993.

Burrows, Brian, et al.
Into the 21st century: a handbook for a sustainable future. Adamantine Press, 1992.
    Reid, Peter. *Teilhard Rev* 28:28 Spr 1993.

Burrows, Mark Stephen.
Jean Gerson and De consolatione theologiae (1418). Mohr, 1991.
    Brown, Catherine D. *TheolStds* 53:754-755 D 1992.
    Martin, Dennis D. *CHist* 79:101-102 Ja 1993.

Burrows, Mark Stephen, and Rorem, Paul, eds.
Biblical hermeneutics in historical perspective. Eerdmans, 1991.
    Mercer, Calvin. *CBQ* 55:407-408 Ap 1993.

Burtchaell, James Tunstead.
From synagogue to church: public services and offices in the earliest Christian communities. Cambridge University Press, 1992.
    Townsend, Mark. *Furrow* 44:454-455 Jl-Ag 1993.
    Nardoni, Enrique. *TheolStds* 54:556-557 S 1993.
The giving and taking of life: essays ethical. University of Notre Dame Press, 1989.
    Barry, R. *Thomist* 56:733-738 O 1992.

Burton, Anthony.
The railway builders. John Murray, n.d.
    Forrest, Denys. *Tablet* 247:173 F 6 1993.

Burton, Laurel Arthur.
Religion and the family. Haworth Press, 1992.
    Heiser, W Charles. *TheolDgst* 40:184 Sum 1993.

Burton-Christie, Douglas.
The Word in the desert: scripture and the quest for holiness in early Christian monasticism. Oxford University Press, n.d.
    Cunningham, Lawrence S, 1935-. *Comm* 120:28-29 Ag 13 1993.

Bushkovitch, Paul.
Religion and society in Russia: the sixteenth and seventeenth centuries. Oxford University Press, 1992.
    Heiser, W Charles. *TheolDgst* 40:54-55 Spr 1993.

Busse, Heribert.
Die theologischen Beziehungen des Islams zu Judentum und Christentum. Wissenschaftliche Buchgesellschaft, 1988.
    Biechler, James E. *JEcumen Stds* 29:131-132 Wint 1992.

Buswell, Robert E, Jr.
The Zen monastic experience: Buddhist practice in contemporary Korea. Princeton University Press, 1992.
    Heiser, W Charles. *TheolDgst* 40:55 Spr 1993.

Buswell, Robert E, Jr, and Gimello, Robert M, eds.
Paths to liberation: the mârga and its transformations in Buddhist thought. University of Hawaii Press, 1992.
    Heiser, W Charles. *TheolDgst* 39:379 Wint 1992.

But was it just? Reflections on the morality of the Persian Gulf War.
Doubleday, 1992.
    Joblin, Joseph, 1920-. *Civilta* 2:302 My 1 1993.

Butler, Jon.
Awash in a sea of faith: Christianizing the American people. Harvard University Press, 1990.
    Burton, David H. *Heythrop* 34:223-224 Ap 1993.
    Burton, David H. *Heythrop* 34:341-342 Jl 1993.

Butterworth, Mike.
Structure and the Book of Zechariah. Sheffield, 1992.
    O'Brien, Julia M. *OTA* 16:434 Je 1993.

Buttiglione, Rocco.
Augusto Del Moce. Piemme, n.d.
    Guietti, Paolo. *Crisis* 11:56-57 Ap 1993.
La crisis della morale. Dino Editore, n.d.
    Guietti, Paolo. *Crisis* 11:52-53 My 1993.

Buttrick, David G.
The mystery and the passion. Fortress Press, 1992.
    Harrington, Daniel J. *America* 168:32-33 F 6 1993.
    Stuhlmueller, Carroll. *BibleT* 31:123 Mr 1993.

Byatt, A S.
Angels and insects. Chatto & Windus, n.d.
    Delay, Jill. *Tablet* 247:79 Ja 16 1993.

Byrne, Brendan.
Inheriting the earth: the Pauline basis of a spirituality for our time. Alba House, 1990.
    Trainor, Michael. *New Theol Rev* 6:98-99 Ag 1993.

Byrne, Lavinia, ed.
Director of women's organizations and groups—in churches and ecumenical bodies in Britain and Ireland. Council of Churches for Britain and Ireland, n.d.
    Hebblethwaite, Margaret, 1951-. *Tablet* 247:143 Ja 30 1993.
Traditions of spiritual guidance. Liturgical, n.d.
    Kirley, Kevin J. *Can Cath Rev* 11:24-25 N 1993.

Byrne, Neil, ed.
Banyo studies. Pius XII Seminary, 1992.
    Wilcken, John. *Pacifica* 6:121-122 F 1993.

Byrnes, Timothy A.
The American Catholic hierarchy and Catholic Bishops in American politics. Princeton University Press, n.d.
    Graham, William C. *Nat Cath Rep* 30:36 N 19 1993.

Byrnes, Timothy A. *(cont'd)*
Catholic bishops in American politics. Princeton University Press, 1991.
  Benestad, J Brian. *CHist* 78:691-693 O 1992.
  Heiser, W Charles. *TheolDgst* 39:354 Wint 1992.

Byrnes, Timothy A, and Segers, Mary C, eds.
The Catholic Church and the politics of abortion: a view from the states.
  Westview Press, 1992.
  Heiser, W Charles. *TheolDgst* 39:355 Wint 1992.

Byrom, John.
The glowing mind: prayer in some Caroline Divines. SLG, 1991.
  Vivian, Tim. *Cist Stud* 27 No 4:[81] 1992.

Byron, Brother.
Sacrifice and symbol. Catholic Institute of Sydney, 1991.
  Renwart, Léon. *NRT* 115:585-586 Jl-Ag 1993.

C

Cabestrero, Teófilo.
El sueño de Galilea: confesiones eclesiales de Pedro Casaldíga. Publicaciones
  Clarentianas, 1992.
  Libanio, Joao Batista. *Perspectiva* 25:121-122 Ja-Ap 1993.

Cabie, Robert.
L'histoire de la messe des origines à nos jours. Desclée, 1990.
  Rey, Bernard. *MSR* 50:77-78 Ja-Mr 1993.
History of the Mass. Pastoral Press, 1992.
  Brown, Daniel A. *Mod Lit* 20:37 Je-Jl 1993.

Cabre, Agustin.
Mariano o la fuerza de Dios. no publisher given, n.d.
  Barrios Villegos, Marciano. *Teol Vida* 34 no 1-2:161-162 1993.

Cadorette, Curt, et al, eds.
Liberation theology. Orbis Books, 1992.
  Burns, Paul. *Tablet* 247:726 Je 5 1993.
  Anon. *NRT* 115:625-626 Jl-Ag 1993.
  Heiser, W Charles. *TheolDgst* 40:171-172 Sum 1993.

Cahill, Kevin Michael, 1936-, ed.
*A framework for survival: health, human rights, and humanitarian assistance
  in conflicts and disasters.* HarperCollins, n.d.
  Torrens, James S. *America* 168:2 Je 19-26 1993.

Cahill, Lisa Sowle.
Women and sexuality. Paulist Press, n.d.
  Anon. *Furrow* 44:62 Ja 1993.

Cairns, Ian.
Word and presence: a commentary on the book of Deuteronomy. William B
  Eerdmans Publishing Company, 1992.
  Stuhlmueller, Carroll. *BibleT* 30:380 N 1992.

Calabria bizantina: testimonianze d'arte e strutture di territori.
  Rubbettino, 1991.
  Capizzi, Carmelo. *Civilta* 143:538-539 D 5 1992.

Calaguig, I M, ed.
Virgo Liber Verbi. Ed Marianum, 1991.
  Toubeau, A. *NRT* 115:136-137 Ja-F 1993.

Calhoun, Craig, ed.
Habermas and the public sphere. MIT Press, 1992.
  Ingram, David. *IPQ* 33:249-250 Je 1993.

Calian, Carnegie Samuel.
*Theology without boundaries: encounter of Eastern Orthodoxy and Western
  tradition.* John Knox Press, 1992.
  Antoci, Peter. *Living Light* 29:89-90 Wint 1992.
  Heiser, W Charles. *TheolDgst* 39:355 Wint 1992.

Callahan, Annice.
Spiritual guides for today. Crossroad, 1992.
  Milligan, Mary. *Horizons (CTS)* 20:168-169 Spr 1993.
  Downey, Michael. *Cist Stud* 28 no 2:[41]-[42] 1993.
  Bevans, Stephen. *CLW* 64:36 Jl-S 1993.

Callahan, Daniel, 1930-.
The troubled dream of life. Simon & Schuster, n.d.
  May, William E. *Comm* 120:25-26 O 22 1993.
What kind of life: the limits of medical progress. Simon & Schuster, 1990.
  Barnet, Robert J. *Linacre* 60:93-94 Ag 1993.

Callahan, Sidney.
In good conscience: reason and emotion in moral decision making. Harper,
  1991.
  Rist, John M. *Can Cath Rev* 11:27-29 My 1993.
  Allsopp, Michael E. *Month* 26:376-377 S-O 1993.
Parents forever: you and your adult children. Crossroad, 1992.
  Kenner, M. *Nat Cath Rep* 29:38 F 5 1993.
  Luebering, Carol. *St Anth* 100:50 Mr 1993.
  Good, Mary O'Neill. *Church* 9:58-59 Sum 1993.

Callahan, William J.
The enneagram for youth. Loyola University Press, 1992.
  Heiser, W Charles. *TheolDgst* 40:154 Sum 1993.

Callanan, Frank.
The Parnell split 1890-91. Cork University Press, 1992.
  Grogan, Geraldine. *Studies* 82:222-225 Sum 1993.

Callard, David.
The case of Anna Kavan. Peter Owen, n.d.
  English, Isobel. *Tablet* 247:694 My 29 1993.

Calliari, Paoli.
Servire la Chiesa: Il venerabile Pio Bruno Lanteri (1759-1830). Krenon, 1989.
  Mellinato, Giuseppe. *Civilta* 143:533-534 D 5 1992.

Callow, Philip.
Walt Whitman. Allison and Busby, n.d.
  Braybrooke, Neville. *Tablet* 247:213-214 F 13 1993.

Calvert, Mary.
God failed to enfold me: praying in the Celtic tradition. Grail, n.d.
  Waal, Esther de. *Tablet* 247:1302-1303 O 9 1993.

Calvez, Jean-Yves.
Questions venues de l'Est. Ed Ouvrieres, 1992.
  Joblin, Joseph, 1920-. *Civilta* 3:341 Ag 7-21 1993.

Camacho, Ildefonso.
Doctrina social de la Iglesia. Paulinas, 1991.
  Volpe, L. *NRT* 114:917 N-D 1992.
  Lago Alba, Luis. *Cien Tom* 119:615-616 S-D 1992.

Cameron, Averil.
*Christianity and the rhetoric of empire: the development of Christian dis-
  course.* University of California, 1991.
  Hollerich, M. *TheolStds* 53:782 D 1992.
  Schwer, Mary Angela. *Relig Lit* 24:109-110 Aut 1992.
  Price, Richard M. *Heythrop* 34:447-448 O 1993.

Cameron, Euan.
The European Reformation. Oxford University Press, 1991.
  Hamilton, Alastair. *Heythrop* 34:213-214 Ap 1993.
  Bast, Robert J. *CHist* 79:331-332 Ap 1993.

Camery-Hoggatt, Jerry.
Irony in Mark's Gospel. Cambridge University Press, 1992.
  Leaney, A R C. *New Blckfrs* 74:112 F 1993.
  Heiser, W Charles. *TheolDgst* 40:55 Spr 1993.
  Senior, Donald. *BibleT* 31:313 S 1993.

Campbell, Anthony F.
The study companion to Old Testament literature. The Liturgical Press, n.d.
  Hamilton, G. *Can Cath Rev* 11:39 Ja 1993.

Campbell, Anthony F, and O'Brien, Mark A.
Sources of the Pentateuch. Fortress, 1993.
  Stuhlmueller, Carroll. *BibleT* 31:245 Jl 1993.
  Murphy, Roland E. *OTA* 16:415-416 Je 1993.

Campbell, John.
Edward Heath. Cape, n.d.
  Longford, Frank. *Tablet* 247:858 Jl 3 1993.

Campbell, Margaret.
Henry Purcell—glory of his age. Hutchinson, n.d.
  Amis, John. *Tablet* 247:585 My 8 1993.

Campion, Francis X.
Grand rounds on medical malpractice. American Medical Association, 1990.
  Barton, Ellen L. *Health Prog* 74:68 Mr 1993.

Campolo, Anthony.
How to rescue the earth without worshiping nature. Thomas Nelson, 1992.
  Heiser, W Charles. *TheolDgst* 40:154 Sum 1993.

Camponovo, O, et al.
Peuple parmi les peuples: dossier pour l'animation biblique. Labor et Fides,
  1990.
  Kennedy, James M. *CBQ* 55:408-409 Ap 1993.

Camporesi, Piero.
The fear of hell: images of damnation and salvation in early modern Europe.
  Polity Press, 1991.
  Hamilton, Alastair. *Heythrop* 34:331-332 Jl 1993.

Canby, Peter.
The heart of the sky: travels among the Maya. HarperCollins, n.d.
  Haegel, Nancy M. *Comm* 120:22-23 Mr 26 1993.

Cane, Bill.
Circles of hope: breathing life and spirit into a wonderful world. Orbis, 1992.
  Evans, Bernard F. *Sisters* 65:221 My 1993.

Canfora, Luciano, et al, eds.
I trattati nel mondo antico: forma, ideologia, funzione. L'Erma, 1990.
  North, Robert. *CBQ* 55:192-193 Ja 1993.

Cannistraro, Philip V, and Sullivan, Brian R.
Il Duce's other woman. William Morrow & Co., n.d.
  Smith, Karen Sue. *Comm* 120:23-24 O 8 1993.

Canobbio, G.
Laici o cristiani? Morcelliana, 1992.
  Anon. *NRT* 115:624 Jl-Ag 1993.

Cantalamessa, Raniero.
Easter in the early church. Liturgical, n.d.
  Graham, William C. *Nat Cath Rep* 30:36 N 19 1993.
The Eucharist: our sanctification. The Liturgical Press, n.d.
  Dollen, Charles. *Priest* 49:48 Je 1993.
Mary, mirror of the Church. The Liturgical Press, n.d.
  Flanagan, Donald. *Furrow* 44:189 Mr 1993.

Cantimpré, Thomas de.
Vie de sainte Lutgarde. Presses universitaires de Namur.
  Renard, L J. *NRT* 115:305 Mr-Ap 1993.

Cantisani, Antonio.
Va e grida: le prediche del Ven. Domenico Lentini. Vivarium, 1992.
  Capizzi, Carmelo. *Civilta* 3:324-325 Ag 7-21 1993.

Cantor, Norman F.
*Inventing the Middle Ages: the lives, works, and ideas of the great medieval-
  ists of the twentieth century.* William Morrow, 1991.
  McGuire, Brian Patrick. *Cist Stud* 27 No 4:[85]-[87] 1992.

Caparros, E, et al, eds.
*University of Navarre-Saint Paul University, Code of Canon Law annotated:
  Latin-English edition of the Code of Canon Law.* Wilson & Lafleur, 1993.
  Galles, Duane L C M. *SacM* 120:39-40 Aut 1993.

Caparros, E.
Code de droit canonique: édition bilingue et annotée. Wilson and Lafleur,
  1990.
  Burns, Brian A. *Jurist* 51 no 2:508 1991.

Capes, David B.
Old Testament Yahweh texts in Paul's Christology. Mohr, 1992.
  Witherup, Ronald D. *OTA* 15:517 O 1992.
  Heiser, W Charles. *TheolDgst* 39:355 Wint 1992.

Caplan, Arthur L.
If I were a rich man could I buy a pancreas? Indiana University Press, n.d.
Koller, Christopher F. *Comm* 120:34-35 Ap 9 1993.

Capobianco, Paolo.
Il vento che li portò a Gaeta. Gaetagrafiche, 1991.
Caprile, Giovanni. *Civilta* 3:93 Jl 3 1993.

Caponetto, Salvatore.
La riforma protestante nell'Italia del Cinquecento. Claudiana, 1992.
Vercruysse, Jos E. *Gregorianum* 74 no 2:394 1993.

Caponnetto, Antonio.
The black legends in Catholic Hispanic culture. Catholic Central Verein of America, n.d.
Higgins, James J. *Liguorian* 81:70 My 1993.

Cappelletto, Gianni.
In cammino con Israele. Edizioni Messaggero, 1991.
Prato, Gian Luigi. *Gregorianum* 74 no 2:405-406 1993.

Cappelletto, Gianni, and Milani, Marcello.
In ascolto dei profeti e dei sapienti. Edizioni Messaggero, 1992.
Prato, Gian Luigi. *Gregorianum* 74 no 2:405-406 1993.

Cappelli, Piero.
Communicazione: crisi della Chiesa. Marietti, 1992.
Baragli, Enrico. *Civilta* 3:337-338 Ag 7-21 1993.

Capra, Fritjof, et al.
Belonging to the universe: explorations on the frontiers of science and spirituality. HarperSanFrancisco, 1991.
Haught, John F. *Living Light* 29:94-95 Aut 1992.
Hauser, Richard A. *ChrWorld* 236:279-280 N-D 1993.

Caprile, Giovanni.
Il Sinodo dei Vescovi: assemblea special per l'Europa. La Civilita Cattolica, 1992.
Mucci, Giandomenico. *Civilta* 2:297-298 My 1 1993.

Caprioloi, Adriano, and Rimoldi, Antonio.
Diocesi di Milano. La Scuola, 1990.
Mellinato, Giuseppe. *Civilta* 3:93-94 Jl 3 1993.

Capuozzo, Gerardo.
Il santo Rosario con Maria e Giuseppe. Santuario di S. Giuseppe, 1988.
Gauthier, Roland. *CahiersJos* 41:130-131 Ja-Je 1993.

Caputo, John D, et al.
Modernity and its discontents. Fordham University Press, 1992.
Hendley, Steven. *IPQ* 33:130-131 Mr 1993.

Carbognano, Cosimo Comidas De.
Descrizione Topografica dello Stato Presente di Costantinopoli arricchita di figure. Pont 1st Orientale, 1992.
Capizzi, Carmelo. *Civilta* 2:97-98 Ap 3 1993.

Carbonell de Masy, Rafael.
Estrategias de desarrollo rural en los pueblos Guaraníes (1609-1767). Instituto de Estudios Fiscales-Instituto de Cooperación Iberoamericana, 1992.
Anon. *Gregorianum* 74 no 3:605-606 1993.

Carbray, Richard J.
Prophets of human solidarity. Krohn and Associates, 1992.
Belisle, Jennifer. *Cath Work* 60:6 S 1993.

Carden, John.
A world at prayer: the new ecumenical prayer cycle. Twenty-Third Publications, 1990.
Covino, Paul. *Past Mus* 17:49 Ap-My 1993.

Il cardinale Pericle Felici.
Editrice Vaticana, 1992.
Caprile, Giovanni. *Civilta* 3:95-96 Jl 3 1993.

Cardine, Dom Eugène.
An overview of Gregorian Chant. Paraclete Press, 1992.
Le Voir, Paul W. *SacM* 120:21-22 Spr 1993.

Care of the dying.
The Catholic Health Association, 1993.
Lowery, David L. *Liguorian* 81:70 Jl 1993.
Catholic Health Association, 1993.
Heiser, W Charles. *TheolDgst* 40:154-155 Sum 1993.

Carey, George Leonard, Abp of Canterbury, 1935-.
The gate of glory. Hodder and Stoughton, n.d.
Anon. *Furrow* 44:62 Ja 1993.

Carey, Patrick W, ed.
Orestes A Brownson: selected writings. Paulist, 1991.
Kiley, P. *RRel* 52:156 Ja-F 1993.

Cargas, Harry James.
Voices from the holocaust. University Press of Kentucky, n.d.
Peatman, Bill. *Nat Cath Rep* 29:14 My 21 1993.

Cariou, Pierre.
Les idéalites casuistiques. Presses Universitaires de France, 1992.
Tavard, George Henry. *TheolStds* 54:600 S 1993.

Carlen, Claudia.
Papal pronouncements: a guide 1740-1978, 2 volumes. Pierian Press, 1990.
Vandergrift, Ray. *Living Light* 29:95 Wint 1992.

Carles, J, and Dupleix, A.
Teilhard de Chardin. Centurion, 1991.
Navez, G. *NRT* 115:284-285 Mr-Ap 1993.

Carlson, Allan.
"From cottage to work station: the family's search for social harmony in the industrial age". Ignatius Press, n.d.
Newmayr, George. *Register* 69:5 Jl 25 1993.

Carlson, Edith.
The phantoms of divinity. Prometheus Books, n.d.
Graham, William C. *Nat Cath Rep* 29:39 My 28 1993.

Carlson, Nancy.
Arnie and the new kid. Viking, n.d.
Neuberger, Anne E. *ReligTJ* 27:58 S 1993.

Carmichael, Calum M.
The origins of Biblical law: the Decalogues and the Book of the Covenant. Cornell University, 1992.
Murphy, Roland E. *OTA* 16:185 F 1993.

Carmody, Denise Lardner.
Prayer in world religions. Orbis, 1990.
Neckebrouck, Valeer. *Eph Theol Lovan* 78:182 Ap 1992.

Carmody, Denise Lardner, and Carmody, John Tully.
Christian uniqueness and Catholic spirituality. Paulist Press, 1990.
MacGregor, Geddes. *JEcumen Stds* 29:107-108 Wint 1992.
The republic of many mansions: foundations of American religious thought. Paragon, 1990.
Kaminski, Phyllis H. *Horizons (CTS)* 19:316-317 Fall 1992.

Carmody, John Tully.
Conversations with a dying friend. Paulist, n.d.
Graham, William C. *Nat Cath Rep* 29:24 Mr 26 1993.
Hill, Brennan R. *Horizons (CTS)* 19:323-324 Fall 1992.

Carmody, John Tully, and Carmody, Denise Lardner.
Catholic spirituality and the history of religions. Paulist Press, 1991.
Cunningham, Lawrence S, 1935-. *Cist Stud* 28 no 2:[40] 1993.
Christian uniqueness and Catholic spirituality. Paulist Press, 1990.
DiNoia, J A. *Living Light* 29:85-86 Aut 1992.

Caron, Jacques.
Angoisse et communication chez S Kierkegaard. Odense University Press, 1992.
Blanc, Louis-Charles de. *Laval Theol Phil* 49:359-365 Je 1993.

Carothers, Thomas.
In the name of democracy: US policy toward Latin America in the Reagan years. University California Press, n.d.
Wells, Allen. *America* 168:24-26 My 29 1993.

Carpenter, Eugene E, and McCown, Wayne, eds.
Asbury Bible commentary. Zondervan, 1992.
Heiser, W Charles. *TheolDgst* 40:150 Sum 1993.

Carpenter, Humphrey.
La vita di J R R Tolkien. Ares, 1991.
Flumeri, E. *Civilta* 143:431-432 N 21 1992.

Carr, Anne.
Transforming grace: Christian tradition and women's experience. T and T Clark, n.d.
Murphy, Anne. *Way* 33:78 Ja 1993.

Carr, David.
Educating the virtues. Routledge, 1991.
Casey, Gerard. *IJPS* 1:163 Mr 1993.

Carr, David McLain.
From D to Q. Scholars Press, 1991.
Lust, Johan. *Eph Theol Lovan* 78:413-414 D 1992.

Carr, Wesley.
Tested by the cross. Harper Collins Fount, n.d.
Hollings, Michael. *Tablet* 247:278 F 27 1993.

Carrasco Rouco, Alfonso.
Le primat de l'évêque de Rome. Éditions Universitaires, 1990.
Henn, W. *Gregorianum* 73 No 4:759-761 1992.

Carraud, Vincent.
Pascal et la philosophie. Presses universitaires de France, 1992.
Tock, Jean-François. *RPhil Louvain* 91:472-473 Ag 1993.

Carré, John le.
The night manager. Hodder & Stoughton, n.d.
Denniston, Robin. *Tablet* 247:1014-1015 Ag 7 1993.

Carretto, Carlo.
The desert journal. Orbis Books, n.d.
Dollen, Charles. *Priest* 49:48 Mr 1993.
The desert journal. Fount, n.d.
Forrester, David. *Tablet* 247:728 Je 5 1993.

Carrier, Hervé.
Lexique de la culture. Desclee, 1992.
Gilbert Paul P. *Gregorianum* 73 No 4:776 1992.
Lemieux, Raymond. *Laval Theol Phil* 49:173-174 F 1993.
Partos, L. *Lumen* 48:240 Je 1993.
Nouveau regard sur la doctrine sociale de l'Église. Cité du Vatican, 1990.
Menin, G. *NRT* 115:145-146 Ja-F 1993.

Carroll, John T, et al, eds.
Faith and history: essays in honor of Paul W Meyer. Scholars, 1990.
Topel, John. *CBQ* 54:818-819 O 1992.

Carroll, Mark Daniel.
Contexts for Amos. JSOT, 1992.
Gossai, Hemchand. *OTA* 15:513 O 1992.
Heiser, W Charles. *TheolDgst* 40:155 Sum 1993.

Carroll, Michael O.
Verbum caro: an encyclopedia on Jesus the Christ. The Liturgical Press, n.d.
Campbell, James. *Month* 26:236 Je 1993.

Carroll, Michael P.
Madonnas that maim: popular Catholicism in Italy since the fifteenth century. The John Hopkins University Press, 1992.
Heiser, W Charles. *TheolDgst* 40:56 Spr 1993.
Kselman, Thomas. *CHist* 79:505-506 Jl 1993.

Carroll, Robert P.
Wolf in the sheepfold: the Bible as a problem for Christianity. SPCK, 1991.
Swanston, Hamish F G. *New Blckfrs* 73:576-578 N 1992.

Carroll, Thomas K, ed.
Jeremy Tarfor: selected works. Paulist Press, n.d.
Lonsdale, David. *Way* 33:83-84 Ja 1993.

Carroll, Warren H.
Isabel of Spain: the Catholic queen. Christendom Press, 1991.
Walsh, A. *SocJust* 84:30-31 Ja-F 1993.

Carruthers, Annette.
Edward Barnsley and his workshop: arts and crafts in the twentieth century. White Cockade Publishing, n.d.
Crawford, Alan. *Tablet* 247:214 F 13 1993.

Carruthers, Gregory H.
The uniqueness of Christ in the Theocentric model: an elabortion and evaluation of the position of John Hick. University Press of America, 1990.
Loughlin, Gerard. *Heythrop* 34:80-81 Ja 1993.

Carruthers, Peter.
The metaphysics of the "Tractatus". Cambridge University Press, 1990.
Kerr, Fergus. *Heythrop* 34:102-103 Ja 1993.
Tractarian semantics: finding sense in Wittgenstein's "Tractatus". Basil Blackwell, 1989.
Kerr, Fergus. *Heythrop* 34:102-103 Ja 1993.

Carson, Anne.
Goddesses and wise women: the literature of feminist spirituality, 1980-1992: an annotated bibliography. The Crossing Press, 1992.
Heiser, W Charles. *TheolDgst* 40:56 Spr 1993.

Carter, Guy, and Eyden, René van, et al, eds.
Bonhoeffer's ethics: old Europe and new frontiers. Kok Pharos, 1991.
Étienne, Jacques. *Eph Theol Lovan* 78:483-484 D 1992.

Carter, Stephen L.
The culture of disbelief. Basic, n.d.
Wycliff, Don. *Comm* 120:22-23 O 8 1993.
Hunt, George W, 1937-. *America* 169:2 O 30 1993.
Scott, David. *OSV* 82:3 N 7 1993.
Quinn, Kevin P. *America* 169:19-20 N 27 1993.

Carter, Tim.
Music in the late renaissance and early baroque. Amadeus Press, 1992.
Schuler, Richard Joseph, 1920-. *SacM* 120:22 Spr 1993.

Carvalho Azevedo, Marcelo de.
Priére dans la vie: effort et don. Centurion, 1989.
Partos, L. *Lumen* 48:117-118 Mr 1993.

Cary-Elwes, Columba.
Work and prayer—the rule of St Benedict for lay people. Burns and Oates, 1992.
Butlin, M. *Priests & People* 7:40 Ja 1993.

Casadio, Franco A.
Il sistema delle relazioni internazionali. Cedam, 1991.
Motto, M. *Civilta* 144:100-101 Ja 2 1993.

Casaldáliga, Pedro, Bp, 1928-, and Vigil, José María.
Espiritualidad de la liberación. no publisher given, 1993.
Bravo Gallardo, Carlos. *Christus* 58:59 My 1993.

Cascioli, Lino.
Il Figlio dell'Uomo. Il Parnaso, 1991.
Caprile, Giovanni. *Civilta* 143:642 D 19 1992.

Casella, Mario.
19 aprile 1948, la mobilitazione delle organizzazioni cattoliche. Congedo, 1992.
Reinerman, Alan J. *CHist* 79:352-354 Ap 1993.

Casetti, Francesco, and Villa, Federica, eds.
La storia commune: funzioni, forma e generi della fiction televisiva. Nuova ERI, 1992.
Flumieri, E. *Civilta* 2:415-416 My 15 1993.

Casey, Juliana.
Food for the journey, theological foundations of the Catholic health care ministry. St Louis Catholic Health Association, 1991.
Mader, S. *Linacre* 59:91-92 N 1992.

Casey, Maurice.
From Jewish prophet to Gentile God. John Knox Press, 1991.
Wansbrough, Henry. *Priests & People* 6:437-438 N 1992.
Stuhlmueller, Carroll. *BibleT* 31:123 Mr 1993.

Casey, Michael.
Towards God: the western traditon of contemplation. Collins Dove, 1991.
Harris, Luke. *Cist Stud* 28:[15]-[16] 1993.
What are we at? Columba Press, 1992.
Burns, Roger. *Priests & People* 7:250 Je 1993.

Cashmore, Gwen, and Puls, Joan.
Clearing the way: en route to an ecumenical spirituality. WCC Publications, 1990.
Lewis, Eleanor V. *JEcumen Stds* 29:104-105 Wint 1992.

Cassidy, Richard J.
John's Gospel in new perspective. Orbis Books, 1992.
Pilch, John Joseph, 1936-. *Sisters* 65:307-308 Jl 1993.
Senior, Donald. *BibleT* 31:251-252 Jl 1993.

Cassidy, Sheila.
Sharing the darkness: the spirituality of caring. Orbis, 1991.
Herring, C. *St Anth* 100:52-53 Ja 1993.
Mancuso, Theresa. *RRel* 52:147-148 Ja-F 1993.
Kennedy, Brian P. *New Oxford Rev* 60:32 Mr 1993.
Dell, Mary Lynn. *New Theol Rev* 6:102-104 Ag 1993.

Cassola, Mimmi.
Due felicissimi anni. Jaca Book, 1992.
Flumeri, E. *Civilta* 3:206 Jl 17 1993.

Casson, Hugh, and White, Richard T.
The tower of London: an artist's portrait. The Herbert Press, n.d.
Thomas, Denis. *Tablet* 247:440 Ap 3 1993.

Castagnari, Giancarlo, and Grégoire, Reginald, et al.
Miscellanea della storia della carta. Pia Universita dei Cartai, 1991.
Baragli, Enrico. *Civilta* 3:319-320 Ag 7-21 1993.

Castarlenas, Alfredo Rubio de.
Adventures in being. Gracewing, n.d.
Markham, Flannan. *Furrow* 44:520 S 1993.

Castelli, Elizabeth A.
Imitating Paul: a discourse of power. John Knox Press, 1991.
Aichele, George. *CrossCurr* 43:130 Spr 1993.

Castelluccio, Giuseppe.
L'antropologia di Gregorio Nisseno. Levante, 1992.
Cremascoli, G. *Civilta* 144:402-403 F 20 1993.

Castle, Barbara.
Fighting all the way. Macmillan, n.d.
Williams, Shirley, 1930-. *Tablet* 247:948 Jl 24 1993.

Castro, Emilio.
To the windof God's spirit: reflections on the Canberra theme. WCC Publications, 1990.
Lewis, Eleanor V. *JEcumen Stds* 29:104-105 Wint 1992.

Castro, F Pérez.
El códice de profetas de el Cairo. Departamento de filología bíblica y de oriente antiguo, 1992.
Begg, Christopher T. *OTA* 16:177-178 F 1993.

Castro, Gaetano Lo.
Le prelature personali. Profili giurdici. Dott. A. Giuffre, 1988.
Celeghin, Adriano. *Gregorianum* 74 no 2:386-388 1993.

Cataldi, Riccardo.
Mellifui Doctoris opera. Abbazia di Casamari, 1992.
Zaffi, Maria Cecilia. *Gregorianum* 74 no 3:591-592 1993.

Catalogue verborum quae in operibus Sancti Augustini inveniuntur.
Thesaurus Linguae Augustinianae, 1990.
Roisel, V. *NRT* 114:907-908 N-D 1992.

La catequesis de la comunidad.
Edice, 1990.
Gonzales Roser, Antonio. *Christus* 58:60 Ag 1993.

La Catequesis en la Iglesia.
Central Catequistica Salesiana, 1991.
Gonzales Roser, Antonio. *Christus* 58:60 Ag 1993.

Catholic shrines and places of pilgrimage in the United States.
United States Catholic Conference, 1992.
Heiser, W Charles. *TheolDgst* 40:155 Sum 1993.

Catholicisme: hier aujourd'hui demain.
Letouzy et Ané, 1992.
Renard, L J. *NRT* 115:288 Mr-Ap 1993.

Catoir, John T.
World religion: beliefs behind today's headlines: Buddhism, Christianity, Confucianism, Hinduism, Islam, Shintoism, Taoism. Alba House, 1992.
Heiser, W Charles. *TheolDgst* 40:56 Spr 1993.
Fisher, Eugene J. *CLW* 64:36-37 Jl-S 1993.

Cattin, Y.
Court traité de l'existence chrétienne. Cerf, 1992.
Toubeau, A. *NRT* 115:132 Ja-F 1993.

Cavalletti, Sofia.
The religious potential of the child. Liturgy Training Publications, 1992.
Heinritz, Joanne. *Mod Lit* 20:38 Ag 1993.
Covino, Paul. *Past Mus* 17:49-50 Ap-My 1993.

Cavanaugh, Brian.
More sower's seeds: second planting. Paulist, 1992.
Lang, Jovian P. *Mod Lit* 20:40-41 O 1993.

Cavatas, Natale.
The ecumenical movement today. Editorale Eco, 1991.
Bundy, Lester I. *JEcumen Stds* 29:472 Sum-Aut 1992.

Ceccarini, Luigi.
Il mito in Platone. Marietti, 1991.
Brena, Gian Luigi. *Civilta* 2:410 My 15 1993.

Cecolin, Romano, ed.
Sacerdozio e mediazioni: dimensioni della mediazione nell'esperienza della Chiesa. Messaggero-Abbazia di Santa Giustina, 1991.
Ferraro, Giuseppe. *Civilta* 143:526-528 D 5 1992.

Cent ans après Rerum Novarum (1891) La tradition sociale du catholicisme français.
Mediasevres, 1991.
Partos, L. *Lumen* 48:240 Je 1993.

Cent ans de catholicisme social dans la région du Nord.
No publisher given, 1991.
Toubeau, A. *NRT* 114:916-917 N-D 1992.

Il Centrismo dopo De Gasperi: Da Pella a Loli; Vol XVIII, 1959-1963.
Nuovo Cei, 1991-1992.
Caprile, Giovanni. *Civilta* 143:531-532 D 5 1992.

Il Centrismo: Apogeo e caduta di DeGasperi Vol XVII: 1954-1958.
Nuova Cei, 1991-1992.
Caprile, Giovanni. *Civilta* 143:531-532 D 5 1992.

Cerceda, Enrique de la Lama.
J A Llorente, un ideal de burguesía: su vida y su obra hasta el exilio en Francia (1756-1813). Ediciones Universidad de Navarra, 1991.
Callahan, William J. *CHist* 79:118-119 Ja 1993.

Cereti, Giovanni.
Molte Chiese cristiane. Queriniana, 1992.
Vercruysse, J E. *Civilta* 3:307-308 Ag 7-21 1993.

Cerini, Marisa.
Dieu amour dans l'expérience et al pensée de Chiara Lubich. Nouvelle Cité, 1992.
Renard, L-J. *NRT* 115:595 Jl-Ag 1993.
Dio Amore nell'esperienza e nel pensiero di Chiara Lubich. Citta Nuova, 1991.
Forlizzi, G. *Civilta* 3:197-198 Jl 17 1993.

Certeau, Michel de.
The mystic fable: v I: the sixteenth and seventeenth centuries. University of Chicago Press, n.d.
Cunningham, Lawrence S, 1935-. *Comm* 120:30 My 7 1993.
Heiser, W Charles. *TheolDgst* 40:56 Spr 1993.
Wiseman, James A. *CHist* 79:535-537 Jl 1993.

Cervelli, Amedeo.
Fonti di diritto nella perdonanza aquilana. Colacchi, 1991.
   Castelli, Ferdinando. *Civilta* 2:99 Ap 3 1993.
Cessario, Romanus.
The moral virtues and theological ethics. University of Notre Dame Press, 1991.
   Hanigan, James P. *Horizons (CTS)* 19:336-337 Fall 1992.
   Bagileo, Nick. *Crisis* 11:48-49 F 1993.
Ceyssens, L.
Le sort de la Bulle Unigenitus. Peeters, 1992.
   Plumat, N. *NRT* 115:618-619 Jl-Ag 1993.
Chabert, Joëlle, and Mourvillier, François.
Tell me the Bible. The Liturgical Press, 1991.
   Stuhlmueller, Carroll. *BibleT* 31:53 Ja 1993.
Chadwick, Owen.
The Christian Church in the cold war. The Penguin Press, n.d.
   Dollen, Charles. *Priest* 49:48 Mr 1993.
   Lavelle, Michael. *Comm* 120:39-40 Ap 9 1993.
   Schaefer, David Lewis. *America* 169:20-22 O 9 1993.
Chafe, Eric.
Tonal allegory in the vocal music of J S Bach. University of California, 1991.
   Willcock, C. *TheolStds* 53:760-761 D 1992.
Chamberlin, William J.
Catalogue of English Bible translations. Greenwood Press, 1991.
   Heiser, W Charles. *TheolDgst* 40:155-156 Sum 1993.
Champlin, Joseph M.
The visionary leader: how anyone can learn to lead better. Crossroad, n.d.
   Graham, William C. *Nat Cath Rep* 29:39 My 28 1993.
Chandler, Paul, ed.
The land of Carmel: essays in honor of Joachim Smet. Institutum Carmelitanum, 1991.
   Jurado, M. *Gregorianum* 73 No 4:765-766 1992.
Chapell, Bryan.
Using illustrations to preach with power. Zondervan, 1992.
   Halloran, W Regis. *Mod Lit* 20:41-42 N 1993.
Chapman, Catherine.
Step spirit: the 12 steps as a spiritual program. Paulist, 1992.
   Graham, William C. *Nat Cath Rep* 29:24 Mr 26 1993.
   Fehringer, Clara. *Sisters* 65:313 Jl 1993.
Charles, Prince of Wales, 1948-, and Cover, Charles.
Highgrove: portrait of an estate. Chapmans, n.d.
   Forrest, Denys. *Tablet* 247:1103-1104 Ag 28 1993.
Charlesworth, James H.
Graphic concordance to the Dead Sea Scrolls. John Knox Press, 1992.
   Dennis, A-M. *NRT* 115:262-263 Mr-Ap 1993.
   Fitzmyer, Joseph Augustine, 1920-. *CBQ* 55:328-329 Ap 1993.
   Lust, Johan. *Louvain Stds* 18:185-186 Sum 1993.
Jesus and the Dead Sea Scrolls. Doubleday, 1992.
   Senior, Donald. *BibleT* 31:313 S 1993.
   Kropf, Richard W. *ChrWorld* 236:237-238 S-O 1993.
The Messiah. Fortress Press, 1992.
   Senior, Donald. *BibleT* 31:252 Jl 1993.
Charlesworth, James H, ed.
Jesus' Jewishness: exploring the place of Jesus in early Judaism. The Crossroad Publishing Company, 1991.
   HaSh'erit, Achad. *New Oxford Rev* 60:31-32 Ap 1993.
   Milavec, Aaron. *JEcumen Stds* 29:121-122 Wint 1992.
The Messiah. Fortress, n.d.
   Harrington, Daniel J. *America* 168:30 F 6 1993.
Charlesworth, James H, and Weaver, Walter P, eds.
What has archaeology to do with faith? Trinity Press International, 1992.
   Stuhlmueller, Carroll. *BibleT* 31:123-124 Mr 1993.
   Heiser, W Charles. *TheolDgst* 40:192-193 Sum 1993.
Charlier, J-P.
Comprendre l'Apocalypse. Cerf, 1991.
   Simoens, Y. *NRT* 115:111-112 Ja-F 1993.
Charmley, John.
Churchill: the end of glory. Hodder and Stoughton, n.d.
   Hodgkin, E C. *Tablet* 247:275-276 F 27 1993.
Charron, Régine.
Concordance des textes de Nag Hammadi. Les Presses de l'Université Laval, 1992.
   Desjardins, Michel. *Laval Theol Phil* 49:376-377 Je 1993.
Chauvet, P, et al.
Pour une théologie du sacerdoce. Mame, 1992.
   Anon. *NRT* 115:623-624 Jl-Ag 1993.
Chavannes, Henry.
The analogy between God and the world in St Thomas Aquinas and Karl Barth. Vantage Press, n.d.
   Carroll, Denis. *Furrow* 44:256-258 Ap 1993.
Chazan, Robert.
Barcelona and beyond: the Disputation of 1263 and its aftermath. University of California Press, 1992.
   Burns, Robert E, 1919-. *CHist* 79:488-495 Jl 1993.
Chekhov, Anton.
A journey to Sakhalin. Ian Faulkner, 1993.
   McClorry, Brian B. *Month* 26:321-322 Ag 1993.
Chenis, C.
Fondamenti teorici dell'arte sacra. LAS, 1991.
   Menin, G. *NRT* 115:155 Ja-F 1993.
Chenot, Dolores, and Petruzzi, Nancy.
Scripture: guide for Lenten discussion. Twenty-Third Publications, n.d.
   Hollings, Michael. *Tablet* 247:278 F 27 1993.
Chenu, Br.
La trace d'un visage. Centurian, 1992.
   Renard, L J. *NRT* 115:300-301 Mr-Ap 1993.

Cherry, Conrad, and Sherrill, Rowland A, eds.
Religion, the independent sector, and American culture. Scholars Press, 1992.
   Heiser, W Charles. *TheolDgst* 39:381 Wint 1992.
Chervin, Ronda De Sola, ed.
Prayers of the women mystics. Servant Publications, 1992.
   Egan, Eileen. *Cath Work* 60:6 Mr-Ap 1993.
   Hegeman, Mary Theodore. *St Anth* 100:50-51 My 1993.
   Heiser, W Charles. *TheolDgst* 40:57 Spr 1993.
Chevalier, Jacques.
Histoire de la pensée, v I. Ed Universitaires, 1992.
   Wéry, Ccile. *RPhil Louvain* 91:137-138 F 1993.
   Debarge, Louis. *MSR* 50:161-163 Ap-Je 1993.
Chevalier, Yves.
L'antisémitisme. Cerf, 1988.
   Debarge, Louis. *MSR* 50:66-68 Ja-Mr 1993.
Chevallier, Max-Alain.
Souffle de Dieu: Le Saint-Esprit dans le Nouveau Testament, Volume II. Beauchesne, 1990.
   Queralt, Antonio. *Gregorianum* 74 No 1:150-152 1993.
Chi dite che io sia?
Ed Dehoniane, 1992.
   Dupuis, Jacques. *Civilta* 3:103 Jl 3 1993.
Chicaud, M-B.
Jeunes non conformes. Desclee, 1990.
   Minin, G. *NRT* 115:150 Ja-F 1993.
Chidester, David.
Religions of South Africa. Routledge, 1992.
   Heiser, W Charles. *TheolDgst* 39:356 Wint 1992.
Word and light: seeing, hearing, and religious discourse. University of Illinois Press, 1992.
   Heiser, W Charles. *TheolDgst* 40:57 Spr 1993.
Childs, Brevard S.
Biblical theology of the Old and New Testaments. Fortress, 1993.
   Senior, Donald. *BibleT* 31:313 S 1993.
   Murphy, Roland E. *OTA* 16:438 Je 1993.
Chilton, Bruce.
The temple of Jesus. Pennsylvania State University Press, 1992.
   Heiser, W Charles. *TheolDgst* 40:156 Sum 1993.
Chimirri, Giovanni.
Pensare dio: introduzione all religione. Logos, 1992.
   Blandino, G. *Civilta* 144:518-519 Mr 6 1993.
Ching, J, and Oxtoby, W G, eds.
Discovering China. University of Rochester Press, 1992.
   Anon. *NRT* 115:628 Jl-Ag 1993.
Chittister, Joan D.
The Rule of Benedict: insights for the ages. Crossroad Publishing Company, n.d.
   Noffsinger, John W. *New Oxford Rev* 60:32 Jl-Ag 1993.
   Kropf, Richard. *Nat Cath Rep* 29:13-14 Mr 5 1993.
   Zuercher, Suzanne. *RRel* 52:792-793 S-O 1993.
Chiyo, Uno.
The story of a single woman. Peter Owen, n.d.
   Billington, Rachel, 1942-. *Tablet* 247:19 Ja 2 1993.
Cholvy, Gérard, et al.
Jeunesses chrétiennes au XXe siècle. Ouvrières, 1991.
   Debarger, Louis. *MSR* 50:59-61 Ja-Mr 1993.
Chomsky, Noam.
Illusioni necessarie: mass media e democrazia. Eleuthera, 1992.
   Baragli, Enrico. *Civilta* 3:336 Ag 7-21 1993.
Chopp, Rebecca S.
The power to speak: feminism, language, God. Crossroad, 1989.
   Graff, A. *New Theol Rev* 6:114-115 F 1993.
   LaCugna, Catherine Mowry, 1952-. *JEcumen Stds* 29:108-109 Wint 1992.
Chorpenning, Joseph F.
The divine romance: Teresa of Avila's narrative theology. Loyola University Press, 1992.
   Cunningham, Lawrence S, 1935-. *Comm* 120:24-25 F 12 1993.
   Luti, J Mary. *TheolStds* 54:197 Mr 1993.
   Heiser, W Charles. *TheolDgst* 40:57 Spr 1993.
   Dreyer, Elizabeth. *Spir Life* 39:176-177 Aut 1993.
Chorpenning, Joseph F, ed.
Just man, husband of Mary, guardian of Christ. St Joseph's Press, 1993.
   Anon. *Spir Life* 39:183 Aut 1993.
Christensen, Bryce J.
Utopia against the family: the problems and politics of the American family. Ignatius Press, 1990.
   Bullert, Gary. *SocJust* 84:92-93 My-Je 1993.
Christensen, Duane L.
Deuteronomy 1-11. Word, 1991.
   Miller, William T. *OTA* 15:495-496 O 1992.
Christiaens, Louis.
Travail, cultures, religions. L'Encyclique sociale du Pape Jean Paul II Centesimus annus. IIES, 1992.
   Joblin, Joseph, 1920-. *Civilta* 3:445 S 4 1993.
Christian faith and the world economy today: a study document from the World Council of Churches.
World Council of Churches Publications, n.d.
   Campbell, James. *Month* 26:80 F 1993.
Christian, William A, Jr.
Moving crucifixes in modern Spain. Princeton University Press, 1992.
   Sanchez, J. *CHist* 78:672-673 O 1992.
Christian William A, Jr.
Moving crucifixes in modern Spain. Princeton University Press, 1992.
   Heiser, W Charles. *TheolDgst* 40:156 Sum 1993.

Corless, Robert, and Knitter, Paul F, eds.
Buddhist emptiness and Christian trinity: essays and explorations. Paulist Press, 1990.
Benavidas, Gustavo. *Horizons (CTS)* 20:194-196 Spr 1993.

Cormier, Robert.
Tunes for bears to dance to. Delacorte Press, n.d.
Hines, Susan C. *St Anth* 100:53 My 1993.

Cornwell, John.
Strange Gods. Simon & Schuster, n.d.
Wolff, Tobias. *Tablet* 247:984-985 Jl 31 1993.

Corpus orationum.
Brepols, 1992.
Evenou, Jean. *Notitiae* 29:307-308 My 1993.

Corral Prieto, Luis.
Los católicos y la no-violencia. no publisher given, 1992.
Joblin, Joseph, 1920-. *Gregorianum* 74 no 2:398-399 1993.

Corrêa, Alicia, ed.
The Durham collectar. Boydell & Brewer, 1992.
Pierce, Joanne M. *TheolStds* 54:597-598 S 1993.

Correia-Afonso, John.
The Ignation vision of India: a historical study. Gujarat Sahitya Prakash, 1991.
Ruiz Jurado, Manuel. *Gregorianum* 74 No 1:181 1993.

The correspondence of Erasmus Letters 1356-1534 to 1524.
University of Toronty Press, 1992.
Olin, John C. *CHist* 79:337-338 Ap 1993.

Corrigan, John.
The prism of piety: Catholick Congregational clergy at the beginning of the Enlightenment. Oxford University Press, 1991.
Heiser, W Charles. *TheolDgst* 39:357 Wint 1992.
Hall, Michael G. *CHist* 79:358-359 Ap 1993.

Corrigan, Kathleen.
Visual polemics in the ninth-century Byzantine Psalters. Cambridge University Press, 1992.
James, Liz. *CHist* 79:515-516 Jl 1993.

Corrington, Gail Paterson.
Her image of salvation: female saviors and formative Christianity. John Knox, 1992.
McDonald, Patricia M. *TheolStds* 54:549 S 1993.

Corrington, Robert S.
Nature and spirit: an essay in ecstatic naturalism. Fordham University Press, 1992.
Gelpi, Donald L. *TheolStds* 54:369-370 Je 1993.

Cortese, Enzo.
Josua 13-21: ein priesterschriftlicher Abschnitt im deuteronomistischen Geschichtswerk. Vandenhoeck & Ruprecht, 1990.
Younger, Lawson K, Jr. *CBQ* 55:105-106 Ja 1993.

Corvalan, G N V.
Conversation de fond avec Carlos Castaneda. Éd du Cerf, 1992.
Anon. *NRT* 115:629 Jl-Ag 1993.

Cossé-Durlin, J.
Sartulaire de Saint-Nicaise de Reims. CNRS, 1991.
Harvengt, A. *NRT* 114:919-920 N-D 1992.

Costa, Giuseppe.
Reporting dalla lunga notte: appunti di giornalismo sugli americani e la guerra del Golfo. Sciascia, 1991.
Rulli, Giovanni. *Civilta* 144:408 F 20 1993.

Costa, Rovílio, ed.
La presenza italiana nella storia e nella cultura del Brasile. Fondazione, 1991.
Salvini, Gianpaolo. *Civilta* 143:542-543 D 5 1992.

Costello, Gwen.
Reconciliation services for children: 18 prayer services to celebrate God's forgiveness. Twenty-Third Publications, n.d.
McCann, Deborah. *ReligTJ* 26:10 Ja 1993.

Côte, Gh.
Le Cénacle. Beauchesne, 1991.
Renard, L J. *NRT* 115:311 Mr-Ap 1993.

Cotter, David W.
A study of Job 4-5 in the light of contemporary literary theory. Scholars, 1992.
Murphy, Roland E. *OTA* 15:503-504 O 1992.
Beuken, W A M. *Eph Theol Lovan* 69:165-166 Ap 1993.

Cotter, Theresa.
Christ is coming: celebrating Advent, Christmas and Epiphany. St. Anthony Messenger, 1992.
Ebrom, John Martin. *Mod Lit* 20:41 N 1993.
Riley, David M. *Catechist* 27:14 N-D 1993.

Cotterell, Arthur.
East Asia: from Chinese predominance to the rise of the Pacific Rim. John Murray, n.d.
Plummer, Simon Scott. *Tablet* 247:983-984 Jl 31 1993.

Cottiaux, Jean.
Sainte Julienne de Cornillon, promotrice de la Fête-Dieu. Carmel de Cornillon-Sanctuaire de Sainte Julienne, 1991.
Galot, Jean. *Gregorianum* 74 No 1:176-177 1993.

Cottier, G.
Consacrés dans la vérité. Mame, 1992.
Anon. *NRT* 115:637 Jl-Ag 1993.

Cottin, Jérôme.
Jésus-Christ en écriture d'images. Labor et Fides, 1990.
Espinel, J Luis. *Cien Tom* 119:408 My-Ag 1992.

Cottrell, Robert.
The end of Hong Kon: the secret diplomacy of imperial retreat. John Murray, n.d.
Rafferty, Kevin. *Tablet* 247:691 My 29 1993.

Cottret, Bernard.
The Huguenots in England: immigration and settlement, c 1550-1700. Cambridge University Press, 1992.
Tighe, William J. *CHist* 79:529-530 Jl 1993.

Cousineau, Phil, ed.
The soul of the world: a modern book of hours. HarperSanFrancisco, n.d.
Graham, William C. *Nat Cath Rep* 29:18 Jl 16 1993.

Cousins, Anthony D.
The Catholic religious poets from Southwell to Crashaw. Sheed & Ward, 1991.
Pfordresher, John. *TheolStds* 54:599-600 S 1993.
Davidson, Peter. *Heythrop* 34:456-458 O 1993.

Covolo, Enrico Dal, and Triacca, Achille M, eds.
Lo studio dei Padri della Chiesa oggi. LAS, 1991.
Halleux, André de. *Eph Theol Lovan* 78:446-447 D 1992.
Roisel, V. *NRT* 115:289 Mr-Ap 1993.

Cowan, Rick, ed.
The next marketing handbook for independent schools. National Association of Independent Schools, 1991.
Burke, Mariann. *Momentum* 24:83-84 F-Mr 1993.

Cowe, S Peter.
The Armenian verson of Daniel. Scholars, 1992.
Blanshard, Monica J. *OTA* 16:181-182 F 1993.

Cox, James L.
The impact of Christian missions on indigenous cultures: the "real people" and the unreal gospel. The Edwin Mellen Press, 1991.
Heiser, W Charles. *TheolDgst* 40:59 Spr 1993.

Coyle-Hennessey, Bobbi.
Once more with love: a guide to marrying again. Ave Maria Press, 1993.
Lazar, John E. *Mod Lit* 20:40 Je-Jl 1993.

Crabtree, H.
The Christian life: traditional metaphors and contemporary theologies. Fortress Press, 1992.
Harvengt, A. *NRT* 115:593-594 Jl-Ag 1993.

Crace, Jim.
Arcadia. Atheneum, n.d.
Wheeler, Edward T. *Comm* 120:26-27 Je 18 1993.

Craddock, Fred B, et al.
Preaching through the Christian year: a comprehensive commentary on the Lectionary, Year A. Trinity Press International, 1992.
Heiser, W Charles. *TheolDgst* 40:82 Spr 1993.

Cragg, Kenneth.
The Arab Christian. John Knox Press, 1991.
Beggiani, Seely. *Living Light* 29:91-93 Wint 1992.
HaSh'erit, Achad. *New Oxford Rev* 60:32 Je 1993.
Irani, George Emile. *TheolStds* 54:378-379 Je 1993.

Craghan, John Francis, 1936-.
Lenten guide for parish leaders. Twenty-Third Publications, 1990.
Ebrom, John Martin. *Mod Lit* 20:39 My 1993.

Craig, Mary.
Candles in the dark: seven modern martyrs. Hodder & Stoughton, n.d.
Forrester, David. *Tablet* 247:728 Je 5 1993.

Craig, Robert H, 1942-.
Religion and radical politics. Temple University Press, n.d.
McMannus, E Leo. *Nat Cath Rep* 29:36 F 5 1993.
Cochran, Clarke E. *Comm* 120:25-27 Jl 16 1993.

Cranston, Maurice.
The noble savage: Jean-Jacques Rousseau 1754-1762. The Penguin Press, 1991.
Levi, A H T. *Heythrop* 34:472-473 O 1993.

Craven, Toni.
The Book of Psalms. Michael Glazier Books, 1992.
Stuhlmueller, Carroll. *BibleT* 31:119 Mr 1993.

Crawford, J M B, and Quinn, J F.
The Christian foundations of criminal responsibility: a philosophical study of legal reasoning. The Edwin Mellen Press, 1991.
Brenner, Susan W. *Amer J Juris* 37:367-371 1992.

Creel, Austin B, and Narayanan, Vasudha, eds.
Monastic life in the Christian and Hindu traditions: a comparative study. The Edwin Mellen Press, 1990.
Griffiths, Bede, 1906-. *Heythrop* 34:222 Ap 1993.

Cremona, Carlo.
San Paolo. Rusconi, 1993.
Mucci, Giandomenico. *Civilta* 3:97-98 Jl 3 1993.

Crenshaw, James L.
Old Testament story and faith: a literary and theological introduction. Hendrickson, 1992.
Murphy, Roland E. *OTA* 15:480 O 1992.

Crichton, J D.
The Lord is risen: the liturgy from Passiontide to Pentecost. Kevin Mayhew, n.d.
Sands, Ernest. *Tablet* 247:725 Je 5 1993.

Crilly, Oliver, ed.
Penitential services. Twenty-Third, n.d.
Riley, David M. *Catechist* 27:14 N-D 1993.

Crisci, Elizabeth Whitney.
When kids bend the rules: 101 creative discipline ideas. Accent Books, 1992.
McCann, Deborah. *ReligTJ* 27:11 F 1993.

La crisi jugoslava: Posizione e azione della Santa Sede (1991-1992).
Libreria Editrice Vaticana, 1992.
Caprile, Giovanni. *Civilta* 143:434 N 21 1992.

Cristianesimo e religione.
Glossa, 1992.
Anon. *NRT* 115:627 Jl-Ag 1993.

D

D'Costa, Gavin, ed. *(cont'd)*
Biallas, Leonard J. *Horizons (CTS)* 19:346-347 Fall 1992.
MacGregor, Geddes. *JEcumen Stds* 29:107-108 Wint 1992.
Nemer, Lawrence. *Pacifica* 6:225-227 Je 1993.

d'Ippona, Agostino.
De moribus ecclesiae catholicae et de moribus manichaeorum. Augustinus, 1991.
Halleux, André de. *Eph Theol Lovan* 78:456-457 D 1992.

D'Onorio, Joël-Benoît.
Jean-Paul II et l'éthique politique. Ed Universitaires, 1992.
Joblin, Joseph, 1920-. *Civilta* 3:205 Jl 17 1993.
La liberté religieuse dans le monde: analyse doctrinale et politique. Ed Universitaires, 1991.
Joblin, Joseph, 1920-. *Civilta* 2:102 Ap 3 1993.
La morale et la guerre. Téqui, 1992.
Joblin, Joseph, 1920-. *Civilta* 3:205 Jl 17 1993.
Le Pape et le gouvernement de l'Eglise. Tardy, 1992.
Tourneau, Dominique Le. *Stud Can* 27 no 1:276-278 1993.
Joblin, Joseph, 1920-. *Gregorianum* 74 no 2:385-386 1993.

Daddi, Franca Pecchioli, and Polvani, Anna Maria, eds.
La mitologia ittitia. Paideia, 1990.
Prato, Gian Luigi. *Gregorianum* 74 no 3:571-572 1993.

Dahl, Nils Alstrup.
Jesus the Christ: the historical origins of christological doctrine. Fortress Press, 1991.
Haire, James. *Pacifica* 6:245-247 Je 1993.

Dahlberg, Bruce T, and O'Connell, Kevin G.
Tell el-Hesi: the site and the expedition. Eisenbrauns, 1989.
Bloch-Smith, Elizabeth. *CBQ* 55:106-107 Ja 1993.

Daily meditations (with Scripture) for busy moms.
ACTA, n.d.
Graham, William C. *Nat Cath Rep* 30:36 N 19 1993.

Daily Roman missal.
Scepter Publishers, n.d.
Burke, Greg. *Register* 69:5 N 14 1993.

Daino, Peter.
Mary: mother of sorrows, mother of defiance. Orbis Books, n.d.
Dollen, Charles. *Priest* 49:48 Je 1993.

Dalbesio, A.
Quello che abbiamo udito e veduto. EDB, 1990.
Simoens, Y. *NRT* 115:114-115 Ja-F 1993.

Dales, Richard C.
Medieval discussions of the eternity of the world. E J Brill, 1990.
Welten, Willibrord. *Gregorianum* 74 No 1:187-188 1993.

Daley, Brian E.
The hope of the Early Church: a handbook of patristic eschatology. Cambridge University, 1991.
McWilliam, J. *TheolStds* 53:746-748 D 1992.
Meredith, Anthony. *Heythrop* 34:314-315 Jl 1993.

Dalkins, Arthur Burton.
Totus tuus. Academy of the Immaculate Conventual Franciscans, n.d.
Dollen, Charles. *Priest* 49:52 Ap 1993.

Dall'Oglio, Paolo.
Speranza nell'Islàm. Marietti, 1991.
Poggi, V. *Civilta* 3:193-194 Jl 17 1993.

Dallmayr, Fred.
Between Freiburg and Frankfurt: toward a critical ontology. University of Massachusetts Press, 1991.
Braaten, Jane. *IPQ* 33:246-249 Je 1993.

Dalton, William J.
Christ's proclamation to the spirits: a study of 1 Peter 3:18-4:6. Pontifical Biblical Institute, 1989.
Elliot, John H. *Bib Th Bul* 23:135 Aut 1993.

Daly, Margaret.
Cantate: cantor-friendly responsorial psalms, Year A. Veritas, n.d.
O'Donoghue, Patrick. *Furrow* 44:188-189 Mr 1993.

Daly, Mary.
Outercourse: the be-dazzling voyage. HarperSanFrancisco, n.d.
Gudorf, Christine E. *Nat Cath Rep* 29:37 F 5 1993.

Daly, Robert J.
Origen: on the Passover and dialogue with Heraclides. Paulist Press, n.d.
Meredith, Anthony, and Lonsdale, David, et al. *Way* 33:161-162 Ap 1993.

Damascius.
Traité des premiers principes, vol I. Les Belles Lettres, 1986.
Destrée, Pierre. *RPhil Louvain* 91:148-150 F 1993.
Traité des premiers principes, vol II. Les Belles Lettres, 1989.
Destrée, Pierre. *RPhil Louvain* 91:148-150 F 1993.
Traité des premiers principes, vol III. Les Belles Lettres, 1991.
Destrée, Pierre. *RPhil Louvain* 91:148-150 F 1993.

Damblon, Dieter.
Die Bedeutung der katholischen Jugendverbände für die auberschulische Jugenbildung in der gegenwärtigen Jugendsituation. Lang, 1992.
Bleistein, Roman, 1928-. *Stimm Zeit* 211:213 Mr 1993.

Dameron, George W.
Episcopal power and Florentine society, 1000-1320. Harvard University Press, 1991.
Bourdua, Louise. *Heythrop* 34:326-327 Jl 1993.

Damiani, Peter.
Peter Damiani: Letters 61-90. Catholic University of America Press, 1992.
Cowdrey, H E J. *CHist* 79:315-316 Ap 1993.

Damme, Jean-Baptiste Van.
I tre fondatori di Cîteaux. Borla, 1991.
Zaffi, MariaCecilia. *Gregorianum* 74 No 1:179-181 1993.

Daniels, Dwight R, et al, eds.
Ernten was man sät. Neukirchener, 1991.
Begg, Christopher T. *OTA* 16:151 F 1993.

Darblay, Jerome, and D'Arnoux, Alexandra.
Seaside houses. Ebury, n.d.
Braybrooke, Neville. *Tablet* 247:583 My 8 1993.

Darr, John A.
On character building: the reader and the rhetoric of characterization in Luke-Acts. John Knox Press, 1992.
Heiser, W Charles. *TheolDgst* 40:60 Spr 1993.
Karris, Robert J. *CBQ* 55:363-364 Ap 1993.

Darr, Katheryn Pfisterer.
Far more precious than jewels: perspectives on Biblical women. John Knox Press, 1991.
Yee, Gale A. *OTA* 15:480 O 1992.

Darrah, Mary C.
Sister Ignatia: angel of Alcoholics Anonymous. Loyola University Press, 1992.
Callahan, Nelson J. *CHist* 79:143-144 Ja 1993.
Heiser, W Charles. *TheolDgst* 39:358 Wint 1992.
Lord, Donna M. *RRel* 52:471-473 My-Je 1993.

Das, Somen.
Christian ethics and Indian ethos. ISPCK, 1989.
Mitra, Kana. *JEcumen Stds* 29:113-114 Wint 1992.
Women in India. ISPCK, 1989.
Mitra, Kana. *JEcumen Stds* 29:113-114 Wint 1992.

Daur, Kl-D.
Arnobii Iunioris opera minora. Brepols, 1992.
Roisel, V. *NRT* 115:266-267 Mr-Ap 1993.

Davidson, James D, ed.
Faith and social ministry: ten Christian perspectives. Loyola University Press, 1990.
Lamoureux, Patricia Natali. *New Theol Rev* 6:99-101 Ag 1993.

Davidson, Maxwell J.
Angels at Qumran. Sheffield, 1992.
Launderville, Dale. *OTA* 16:443 Je 1993.

Davidson, Robert.
A beginner's guide to the Old Testament. St Andrew, 1992.
Begg, Christopher T. *OTA* 16:157-158 F 1993.
Wisdom and worship. Trinity, 1990.
Clifford, Richard J. *CBQ* 54:742-743 O 1992.

Davies, Brian.
An introduction to the philosophy of religion. Oxford University Press, 1993.
Ward, Keith. *New Blckfrs* 74:430 S 1993.
The thought of Thomas Aquinas. Clarendon, 1992.
McDermott, T. *Priests & People* 7:41-42 Ja 1993.
Heiser, W Charles. *TheolDgst* 40:60 Spr 1993.

Davies, G I.
Hosea. Eerdmans, 1992.
Murphy, Roland E. *OTA* 16:182 F 1993.
Heiser, W Charles. *TheolDgst* 40:158 Sum 1993.

Davies, Gaius.
Genius and grace. Hodder and Stoughton, n.d.
Anon. *Month* 25:499 D 1992.

Davies, Gordon F.
Israel in Egypt: reading Exodus 1-2. JSOT, 1992.
Di Lella, Alexander A. *OTA* 16:169-170 F 1993.

Davies, Horton.
The vigilant God: providence in the thought of Augustine, Aquinas, Calvin and Barth. Lang, 1992.
Wright, John H. *TheolStds* 54:596-597 S 1993.

Davies, Michael.
The Second Vatican Council and religious liberty. Neumann, 1992.
Hallett, Paul. *Register* 69:5 F 21 1993.
Baker, Kenneth. *HPR* 93:76-77 Jl 1993.

Davies, Oliver.
Cyprian of Carthage: born to new life. New City, n.d.
Meredith, Anthony, and Lonsdale, David, et al. *Way* 33:162 Ap 1993.
Meister Eckhart: mystical theologian. SPCK, 1991.
Reynolds, P L. *New Blckfrs* 74:165-168 Mr 1993.
Sullivan, John. *Heythrop* 34:434 O 1993.

Davies, Oliver, ed.
Gateway to paradise: Basil the Great. New City, 1992.
Scollard, Anselma. *Cist Stud* 28:[25]-[26] 1993.
Meredith, Anthony, et al. *Way* 33:162 Ap 1993.
Promise of good things: the Apostolic Fathers. New City Press, 1993.
Mathews, Edward G. *Diakonia* 26 no 2:140 1993.

Davies, Paul.
The mind of God: science and the search for ultimate meaning. Penguin, n.d.
Traylen, Mary Anne. *Month* 26:235 Je 1993.
The mind of God: the scientific basis for a rational world. Simon and Schuster, 1992.
Haught, John F. *TheolStds* 53:770-772 D 1992.

Davies, Philip R.
In search of "ancient Israel". JSOT, 1992.
McMillian, Philip E. *OTA* 16:158 F 1993.

Davies, Philip R, and White, Richard T, eds.
A tribute to Geza Vermes: essays on Jewish and Christian literature and history. Sheffield, 1990.
VanderKam, James C. *CBQ* 55:193-195 Ja 1993.

Davies, Phyllis.
Grief: climb toward understanding. Sunnybank, n.d.
Graham, William C. *Nat Cath Rep* 30:15 O 22 1993.

Davies, W D, and Allison, Dale C.
The Gospel according to Saint Matthew, volume II. T and T Clark, 1991.
Watson, Nigel. *Pacifica* 6:104-106 F 1993.

Davin, J, and Petitclerc, J-M.
Le pari éducatif. Centurion, 1991.
Navez, G. *NRT* 115:118-119 Ja-F 1993.

DePaola, Tomie.
The legend of the Bluebonnet, an old tale of Texas. G P Putnam's Sons, n.d.
Neuberger, Anne E. *ReligTJ* 27:34 F 1993.

Derickx, João, and Transferetti, José Antonio.
No coração da Amazônia: juruá, o rio que chora. Ed Vozes, 1992.
Transferetti, José Antonio. *REB* 53:239-241 Mr 1993.

Desclos, Jean.
Une morale pour la vie: catégories principales et petit vocabulaire de l'éthique. Médiaspaul, 1992.
Chénard, Gabriel. *Laval Theol Phil* 49:173 F 1993.

Descouvement, P, and Loose, H N.
Thérèse et Lisieux. Novalis, 1991.
Toubeau, A. *NRT* 115:283 Mr-Ap 1993.

DeSiano, Frank, and Boyack, Kenneth.
Discovering my experience of God: awareness and witness. Paulist Press, n.d.
Graham, William C. *Nat Cath Rep* 29:40-39 My 28 1993.

Desmond, Adrian, and Moore, James.
Darwin: the life of a tormented evolutionist. Warner, n.d.
Coren, Michael. *Can Cath Rev* 11:4-6 F 1993.

Desmond, William.
Beyond Hegel and dialectic: speculation, cult, and comedy. State University of New York Press, 1992.
Tate, Daniel L. *Cithara* 32:58-60 My 1993.

Despland, Michel, and Vallée, Gérard, eds.
Religion in history: the word, the idea, and the reality = La religion dans l'histoire: le mot, l'idée, la réalité. Canadian Corporation for Studies in Religion, 1992.
Heiser, W Charles. *TheolDgst* 40:83 Spr 1993.

Desroches, H.
Hommes et religions. no publisher given, 1992.
Anon. *NRT* 115:627-628 Jl-Ag 1993.

Desroussilles, Dupuigrenet.
Dieu en son Royaume. Cerf, 1991.
Torly, V. *NRT* 115:139 Ja-F 1993.

Destang, Françoise.
Paroles pour prier. Se Seneve, 1991.
Partos, L. *Lumen* 48:233 Je 1993.

Le Deuxième Concile du Vatican (1959-1965).
Ecole Française de Rome, 1989.
Chappin, Marcel. *Gregorianum* 74 No 1:185-187 1993.

Devens, Carol.
Countering colonization, Native American women and Great Lakes missions, 1630-1900. University of California Press, 1991.
Moore, James Talmadge. *CHist* 79:564-565 Jl 1993.

Dever, William G.
Recent archaeological discoveries and biblical research. University of Washington, 1990.
Jacobs, Paul F. *CBQ* 54:744-745 O 1992.

Devitt, Patrick M.
How adult is adult religious education? Gabriel Moran's contribution to adult religious education. Veritas, 1991.
Clark, Anthony. *Heythrop* 34:201-202 Ap 1993.
That you may believe. A brief history of religious education. Dominican Publications, 1992.
Marthaler, Berard L, 1927-. *Living Light* 29:92 Sum 1993.

Dialettica dell'immagine: studi sull'imaginismo di Luigi Stefanini.
Marietti, 1991.
Pirola, G. *Civilta* 144:514-515 Mr 6 1993.

Diamond, Philip.
Covent Garden fish book. Kyle Cathie, n.d.
Poole, Shona Crawford. *Tablet* 247:374 Mr 20 1993.

Diccionario patristico y de la Antigüedad Cristiana.
Ed Sígueme, 1991.
Celeada, Gregorio. *Cien Tom* 119:418-420 My-Ag 1992.

Diccionario, patristico y de la Antigüedad Christiana.
Ediciones Sígueme, 1992.
Ramos, L. *Christus* 58:82 N-D 1992.

Dicharry, Warren.
Paul and John. The Liturgical Press, 1992.
Stuhlmueller, Carroll. *BibleT* 31:124 Mr 1993.

Dickason, Olive Patricia.
Canada's first nations: a history of founding peoples from earliest times. McClelland and Stewart, n.d.
Huel, Raymond. *Can Cath Rev* 11:22 S 1993.

Dickinson, Leo.
Balooning over Everest. Cape, n.d.
Walton, James. *Tablet* 247:584 My 8 1993.

Dickson, Kwesi A.
Uncompleted mission. Orbis, 1991.
Senior, Donald. *BibleT* 31:58-59 Ja 1993.
Vanneste, A. *Eph Theol Lovan* 78:468-469 D 1992.
Wolanin, Adam. *Gregorianum* 74 no 2:395-399 1993.
Pawlikowski, John T. *CLW* 64:34-36 Jl-S 1993.

Dickstein, Morris.
Double agent: the critic and society. Oxford University Press, n.d.
Siegel, Lee. *Comm* 120:30 Ap 9 1993.

Dictionnaire de Spiritualité, ascétique et mystique, doctrine et histoire.
Beauchesne, 1992.
Renard, L J. *NRT* 115:153-154 Ja-F 1993.
Ruiz Jurado, Manuel. *Gregorianum* 74 No 1:174 1993.

Dictionnaire de Spiritualité, ascétique et mystique, doctrine et histoire.
Beauchesne, 1992.
Ruiz Jurado, Manuel. *Gregorianum* 74 no 3:587-588 1993.

Dictionnaire d'histoire et de géographie ecclésiastiques.
Letouzey et Ané, 1990-1992.
Plumat, N. *NRT* 115:288-289 Mr-Ap 1993.

Diefendorf, Barbara S.
Beneath the cross: Catholics and Huguenots in sixteenth-century France. Oxford University Press, 1991.
Smither, James R. *CHist* 79:109-110 Ja 1993.

Diehl, William, E.
The Monday connnection: a spirituality of competence, affirmation, and support in the workplace. HarperCollins, 1991.
Huebsch, B. *New Theol Rev* 6:108-109 F 1993.

Dierkens, Al, ed.
Apparitions et miracles. Éditions de l'Université Libre de Bruxelles, 1991.
Bernard, J. *NRT* 115:608-609 Jl-Ag 1993.

Dietrich, Manfried, and Loretz, Oswald.
'Jahwe und seine Áschera'. Ugarit-Verlag, 1992.
Fitzgerald, Aloysius. *OTA* 16:185-186 F 1993.

Dietrich, Walter.
David, Saul und die Propheten. Kohlhammer, 1992.
Begg, Christopher T. *OTA* 16:173 F 1993.

Una difficile transizione Verso il Centro-Sinistra.
Nuova Cei, 1991-1992.
Caprile, Giovanni. *Civilta* 143:531-532 D 5 1992.

DiGiacomo, James J, and Walsh, John J.
Christian discovery. Orbis Books, 1992.
Redington, Patrick E. *Living Light* 29:96-97 Sum 1993.
Heiser, W Charles. *TheolDgst* 40:159 Sum 1993.

Dilenge, Giovanni.
Dermi divini nelle religioni: Induismo, Buddhismo, Religiostà cinese, Islam. Porfidio, 1991.
De Rosa, G. *Civilta* 144:101-102 Ja 2 1993.

Diliberto, Gioia.
Hadley. Thomas Allen & Sons, n.d.
Coren, Michael. *Can Cath Rev* 11:4-6 F 1993.

Dilke, Annabel.
Present from the past. Deutsch, André, n.d.
Delay, Jill. *Tablet* 247:248 F 20 1993.

Dillenberger, Jane.
Image and spirit in sacred and secular art. Cross, 1990.
Morris, M. *Thomist* 56:738-740 O 1992.

Dillon, Helen.
The flower garden. Conran Octopus, n.d.
Taylor, Patrick. *Tablet* 247:375 Mr 20 1993.

DiNoia, J A.
The diversity of religions. Catholic University of America Press, 1992.
Borelli, John. *Living Light* 29:93-94 Spr 1993.
Heiser, W Charles. *TheolDgst* 40:60 Spr 1993.
McLeod, Frederick G. *RRel* 52:633-634 Jl-Ag 1993.
Madigan, Patrick. *Worship* 67:379-381 Jl 1993.
D'Costa, Gavin. *Thomist* 57:524-528 Jl 1993.

La diocesi di Roma 1991-92.
Editoriale Italiana, 1992.
Caprile, Giovanni. *Civilta* 143:640-641 D 19 1992.

Dios es padre.
Secretariado Trinitario, 1991.
Escol, R. *NRT* 114:898-899 N-D 1992.

Dirksen, P B, and Kooij, A Van Der, eds.
Abraham Kuenen. Brill, 1993.
Begg, Christopher T. *OTA* 16:394 Je 1993.

DiSante, Carmine.
Jewish prayer: the origins of Christian liturgy. Paulist, 1991.
Gross, S. *Priests & People* 6:358-359 Ag-S 1992.
Lang, Jovian P. *CLW* 64:37 Jl-S 1993.

Divarkar, Parmananda R.
Le chemin de la connaissance intérievre. Mediaspaul, 1993.
Partos, L. *Lumen* 48:233-234 Je 1993.

Dobroczyński, Grzegorz.
Einsicht und Bekehrung. Ausgangspunkt der Fundamentaltheologie bei Bernard Longergan. Peter Lang, 1992.
Fisichella, Rino. *Gregorianum* 74 no 2:366-367 1993.

La doctrine de la revelation divine de Saint Thomas D'Aquin: actes du symposium sur la pensée de Saint Thomas d'Aquin.
Libreria Editrice Vaticana, 1990.
D'Amécourt, Joseph. *Thomist* 57:141-146 Ja 1993.

Dodd, Christine.
Called to mission—a workbook for the Decade of Evangelization. Chapman, 1991.
Anon. *Furrow* 44:63 Ja 1993.

Doeuff, Michèle Le.
Hipparchia's choice, an essay concerning women, philosophy, etc. Basil Blackwell, n.d.
Ainley, Alison. *IJPS* 1:137-140 Mr 1993.

Dogniez, Cécile, and Harl, Marguerite.
Le Deutéronome. Cerf, 1992.
Begg, Christopher T. *OTA* 16:171-172 F 1993.
Lust, Johan. *Eph Theol Lovan* 78:411-413 D 1992.

Dogniez, Cécile, and Harl, Margurite, eds.
La Bible d'Alexandrie: le Deutéronome. Éd du Cerf, 1992.
Ska, Jean Louis. *NRT* 115:253-254 Mr-Ap 1993.

Doherty, James.
They made me a priest. Columba Press, 1992.
  Burns, Roger. *Priests & People* 7:209-210 My 1993.
Doherty, P C.
Murder wears a cowl. Headline, n.d.
  Lejeune, Anthony. *Tablet* 247:51 Ja 9 1993.
Dohmen, C, and Oeming, M.
Biblischer Kanon: Warum und Wozu? Herder, 1992.
  Ska, Jean Louis. *NRT* 115:247-248 Mr-Ap 1993.
Dolan, Jay P.
The American Catholic experience: a history from colonial times to the present. University of Notre Dame Press, n.d.
  McMannus, E Leo. *Nat Cath Rep* 29:36 F 5 1993.
Dolan, Timothy Michael.
"Some seed fell on good ground": the life of Edwin V O'Hara. The Catholic University of America Press, 1992.
  Bovée, David S. *CHist* 79:373-374 Ap 1993.
  Heiser, W Charles. *TheolDgst* 40:60 Spr 1993.
  Kauffman, Christopher J. *ACHSR* 103:48-49 Aut 1992.
Dombrowski, Bruno W W.
An annotated translations of Miqsât Ma'aseh ha-ha-Torâ. no publisher given, 1992.
  Fitzmyer, Joseph Augustine, 1920-. *OTA* 16:191 F 1993.
Dombrowski, Daniel A.
St John of the Cross. University of New York Press, 1992.
  Heiser, W Charles. *TheolDgst* 39:358-359 Wint 1992.
St John of the Cross. State University of New York Press, 1992.
  Charron, Donna. *Mod Schlmn* 70:238-242 Mr 1993.
Dominian, Jack, 1929-, and Flood, Edmund.
The everyday God. Geoffrey Chapman, n.d.
  Phelan, Michael. *Tablet* 247:551-552 My 1 1993.
Donadeo, Maria.
Inno Acatisto in onore della Madre di Dio. Marietti, 1991.
  Cremascoli, G. *Civilta* 3:308-310 Ag 7-21 1993.
Donadio, Berengario di.
Vita di Chiara da Montefalco. Città Nuova, 1991.
  Forlizzi, G. *Civilta* 143:534-535 D 5 1992.
Donaldson, Scott.
Archibald Macleish. Thomas Allen & Sons, n.d.
  Coren, Michael. *Can Cath Rev* 11:4-6 F 1993.
Donders, Joseph G.
Reasons to hope: reflections on daily readings for Lent 1993. CAFOD, n.d.
  Hollings, Michael. *Tablet* 247:278 F 27 1993.
Scripture reflections. Twenty-Third Publications, 1992.
  Stuhlmueller, Carroll. *BibleT* 31:54 Ja 1993.
Donfried, Karl P.
The Romans debate. Hendrickson, 1991.
  Byrne, Brendan. *Pacifica* 6:216-218 Je 1993.
Donfried, Karl P, ed.
The Romans debate. Hendrickson Publishers, 1991.
  Neyreu, Jerome H. *Bib Th Bul* 23:87-88 Sum 1993.
  Sterling, Gregory E. *CBQ* 55:409-411 Ap 1993.
Donnelly, Doris.
Spiritual fitness. HarperSanFrancisco, n.d.
  Graham, William C. *Nat Cath Rep* 30:16 O 22 1993.
Donnelly, Dorothy F, and Sherman, Mark A.
Augustine's De civitate Dei: an annotated a bibliography of modern criticism, 1960-1990. Peter Lang, 1991.
  Heiser, W Charles. *TheolDgst* 40:60-61 Spr 1993.
Donovan, Daniel L.
What are they saying about the ministerial priesthood? Paulist, 1992.
  Graham, William C. *Nat Cath Rep* 29:39 My 28 1993.
  Gaillardetz, Richard R. *TheolStds* 54:200-201 Mr 1993.
  Higgins, James J. *Liguorian* 81:68-69 Je 1993.
  Heiser, W Charles. *TheolDgst* 40:159 Sum 1993.
Donze, Mary Terese, 1911-.
I can pray with the saints. Liguori Publications, n.d.
  Higgins, James J. *Liguorian* 81:70 Ap 1993.
Doohan, Helen, and Doohan, Leonard.
Prayer in the New Testament. Liturgical, 1992.
  Senior, Donald. *BibleT* 31:59 Ja 1993.
  Pecht, Gerard. *Liguorian* 81:68 Ag 1993.
Doolittle, Robert.
Homemade youth retreats. St. Mary's Press, n.d.
  Riley, David M. *Catechist* 27:15 N-D 1993.
Doorly, William J.
Isaiah of Jerusalem: an introduction. Paulist, 1992.
  Begg, Christopher T. *OTA* 16:178 F 1993.
  Heiser, W Charles. *TheolDgst* 40:61 Spr 1993.
Doran, Carol, and Troeger, Thomas H.
Trouble at the table: gathering the tribes for worship. Abingdon Press, 1992.
  Heinritz, Joann. *Mod Lit* 20:36-37 S 1993.
Doran, Robert M.
Theology and the dialectics of history. University of Toronto Press, 1990.
  Quesnell, Quentin. *Horizons (CTS)* 19:319-320 Fall 1992.
Doré, Joseph, ed.
Les cent ans de la Faculté de théologie. Beauchesne, 1992.
  Halleux, André de. *Eph Theol Lovan* 69:219-220 Ap 1993.
  Komonchak, Joseph Andrew, 1939-. *TheolStds* 54:390-391 Je 1993.
Introduction à l'étude de la théologie. Desclee, 1992.
  Escol, R. *NRT* 114:897-898 N-D 1992.
  Escol, R. *NRT* 115:577 Jl-Ag 1993.

Dornisch, Loretta.
Faith and philosophy in the writings of Paul Ricoeur. The Edwin Mellen Press, 1990.
  Heiser, W Charles. *TheolDgst* 39:359 Wint 1992.
Dorp, Jacob van.
Josia. Rijksuniversiteit, 1991.
  Beuken, W A M. *Eph Theol Lovan* 78:414-415 D 1992.
Dorr, Donal, 1935-.
Option for the poor. Gill & Macmillan, n.d.
  Moss, Christopher. *Tablet* 247:892 Jl 10 1993.
The social justice agenda: justice, ecology, power, and the church. Orbis, 1991.
  Elsbernd, M. *Cist Stud* 27 No 4:[115]-[116] 1992.
Dorrien, Gary J.
Reconstructing the common good: theology and social order. Orbis Books, 1990.
  Pastor, Felix-Alejandro. *Gregorianum* 74 No 1:194 1993.
Dorsey, David A.
The roads and highways of ancient Israel. John Hopkins University, 1991.
  Smith, Mark S. *OTA* 15:481 O 1992.
  Matthews, Victor H. *CBQ* 55:331-332 Ap 1993.
Dotolo, Carmelo.
Sulle trace di Dio. Lineamenti di Teologia fondamentale. Messagero, 1992.
  Anon. *Gregorianum* 74 no 2:412-413 1993.
Double, Richard.
The non-reality of free will. Oxford University Press, 1991.
  Meynell, Hugo. *Heythrop* 34:220-221 Ap 1993.
Doucet, Hubert.
Al fiume del silenzio. SEI, 1992.
  Cultrera, Francesco. *Civilta* 3:203-204 Jl 17 1993.
Douglas, George.
Education without impact. Birch Lane Press, 1992.
  Giles, James E. *CrossCurr* 43:256 Sum 1993.
Douglass, James W.
The nonviolent coming of God. Orbis, 1991.
  Cudahy, R. *Cist Stud* 27 No 4:[116]-[118] 1992.
  Stuhlmueller, Carroll. *BibleT* 31:124 Mr 1993.
  Downey, Michael. *Spir Life* 32:117-119 Sum 1993.
Douglass, R Bruce, et al, eds.
Liberalism and the good. Routledge, 1991.
  Grasso, Kenneth L. *IPQ* 33:371-373 S 1993.
Downey, Michael.
The new dictionary of Catholic spirituality. Liturgical, 1993.
  Dollen, Charles. *Priest* 49:48 Jl 1993.
  Heiser, W Charles. *TheolDgst* 40:179 Sum 1993.
  Jordan, Chris. *St Anth* 101:50-52 N 1993.
That they may live: power, empowerment, and leadership in the church. Crossroad, 1991.
  Kress, Robert. *Horizons (CTS)* 19:327-328 Fall 1992.
Downey, Michael, and Fragomeni, Richard, eds.
A promise of presence. Pastoral Press, 1992.
  Graham, William C. *Nat Cath Rep* 29:39 F 5 1993.
  Hommerding, Leroy. *Mod Lit* 20:39 Ap 1993.
  Hughes, Kathleen. *Living Light* 29:93 Sum 1993.
Doyle, Dennis M.
The Church emerging from Vatican II. Twenty-Third, 1992.
  Gollob, Timothy. *Mod Lit* 20:40 My 1993.
  Higgins, James J. *Liguorian* 81:70 My 1993.
  Graham, William C. *Nat Cath Rep* 29:40 My 28 1993.
  McRedmond, Louis. *Furrow* 44:448-449 Jl-Ag 1993.
  Grubb, Geoffrey J. *Living Light* 30:103 Aut 1993.
Drane, John.
What is the new age saying to the church. Marshall Pickering, n.d.
  Tastard, Terry. *Way* 33:85-86 Ja 1993.
Drescher, Hans-George.
Ernst Troeltsch. Vandenhoeck and Ruprecht, 1991.
  Renwart, Léon. *NRT* 115:282-283 Mr-Ap 1993.
Ernst Troeltsch. Fortress, 1993.
  Griener, George E. *TheolStds* 54:575-576 S 1993.
Drey, Janet.
Families experiencing faith. Don Bosco Multimedia, n.d.
  Hanlon, James. *Can Cath Rev* 11:31 O 1993.
Drey, Janet, ed.
Families and young adolescents. no publisher given, n.d.
  Roach, Joseph J. *Living Light* 30:102-103 Aut 1993.
Dreyfus, Francois.
Did Jesus know he was God? Mercier Press, Cork, 1991.
  Wansbrough, Henry. *Priests & People* 6:437-438 N 1992.
Drèze, J.
Raison d'État, raison de Dieu. Beauchesne, 1991.
  Renard, L J. *NRT* 114:928-929 N-D 1992.
Driancourt-Ginod, J.
Ainsi priaient les luthériens. Éd du Cerf, 1992.
  Clarot, B. *NRT* 115:613-614 Jl-Ag 1993.
Drijvers, Jan Willem.
Helena Augusta: the mother of Constantine the Great and the legend of her finding the True Cross. E J Brill, 1992.
  Drake, H A. *CHist* 79:508-509 Jl 1993.
Drilling, Peter.
Trinity and ministry. Fortress Press, 1991.
  Heiser, W Charles. *TheolDgst* 40:61 Spr 1993.
Drinan, Robert Francis, 1920-.
The fractured dream: America's divisive moral choices. Crossroads Publishing Company, 1991.
  Riley, Patrick J. *Emmanuel* 99:355-356 Jl-Ag 1993.

Driscoll, Jeremy.
The Ad monachos of Evagrius Ponticus. Pont Ateneo S Anselmo, 1991.
  Ferrua, Antonio. *Civilta* 143:432-433 N 21 1992.
Some other morning. Story Line Press, Inc, n.d.
  Morneau, Robert F, Bp, 1938-. *ST Anth* 101:52 Jl 1993.

Driskel, Michael Paul.
Representing belief: religion, art, and society in nineteenth-century France.
  The Pennsylvania State University Press, 1992.
  Hansen, Eric C. *CHist* 79:119-120 Ja 1993.

Droge, Arthur J, and Tabor, James D.
A noble death: suicide and martyrdom among Christians and Jews in antiquity. HarperSanFrancisco, 1991.
  Heiser, W Charles. *TheolDgst* 39:359 Wint 1992.

Dubus, Andre, III.
Bluesman. Faber & Faber, n.d.
  Samway, Patrick H, 1939-. *America* 169:22-23 Ag 28-S 4 1993.

Duchesneau, Claude, and Veuthey, Michel.
Musica and liturgy: the Universa Laus document and commentary. Pastorl Press, 1992.
  Hommerding, Leroy. *Mod Lit* 20:37 My 1993.

Ducornet, E.
Matteo Ricci, le lettré d'Occident. Éd du Cerf, 1992.
  Anon. *NRT* 115:305-306 Mr-Ap 1993.

Dues, Greg.
Catholic customs and traditions: a popular guide. Twenty-Third Publications, n.d.
  McCann, Deborah. *ReligTJ* 26:12 Ja 1993.
  Riley, David M. *Catechist* 26:15 F 1993.

Duffy, Eamon.
The stripping of the altars. Yale University Press, 1993.
  Scarisbrick, J. *Tablet* 247:211-212 F 13 1993.
  Oakes, Edward T. *Comm* 120:27-28 Mr 12 1993.
  Murphy, Anne, and Pridmore, John. *Way* 33:252-253 Jl 1993.
  Heiser, W Charles. *TheolDgst* 40:159 Sum 1993.
  Bernard, G W. *Heythrop* 34:452-455 O 1993.

Duffy, Stephen J.
The graced horizon. Liturgical, 1992.
  Dollen, Charles. *Priest* 49:48 Ja 1993.
  Dych, William V. *TheolStds* 54:375-376 Je 1993.
  Anon. *NRT* 115:625 Jl-Ag 1993.
  Inglis, Brian. *Can Cath Rev* 11:21 S 1993.
  Heiser, W Charles. *TheolDgst* 40:159 Sum 1993.

Duggan, Michael.
The consuming fire: a Christian introduction to the Old Testament. Ignatius, 1991.
  Anon. *ChrWorld* 37:383+ N-D 1992.
  Boadt, Lawrence. *OTA* 16:404 Je 1993.

Dujarier, Michel.
L'Église-Fraternité, vol I. Cerf, 1991.
  Galot, Jean. *Gregorianum* 74 no 2:407 1993.
  Beenaert, P. Mourlon. *Lumen* 48:232 Je 1993.
L'Église-Fraternité. Cerf, 1991.
  Halleux, André de. *Eph Theol Lovan* 78:447-448 D 1992.

Dulles, Avery Robert, 1918-.
The craft of theology. Crossroad, n.d.
  Cooke, Bernard. *America* 168:19+ Ja 16-23 1993.
  Tolhurst, Joseph. *Priests & People* 7:84 F 1993.
  Corkery, James. *Studies* 82:97-100 Spr 1993.
  O'Donnell, John J. *Gregorianum* 74 no 2:373-374 1993.
  Phan, Peter C. *Living Light* 29:88-89 Sum 1993.
  Wood, Susan. *RRel* 52:629-630 Jl-Ag 1993.
Models of revelation. Orbis Books, 1992.
  Sheets, John R. *HPR* 93:80 Ag-S 1993.

Dumais, Monique.
Les droits des femmes. Paulines and Médiaspaul, 1992.
  Bouchard, Gary M. *Laval Theol Phil* 49:174-175 F 1993.

Dummett, Michael.
Grammar and style. Duckworth, n.d.
  Parham, Maggie. *Tablet* 247:922 Jl 17 1993.

Dumont, R, ed.
L'Église démantelée. EPO, 1990.
  Anon. *NRT* 115:293-294 Mr-Ap 1993.

Dumoulin, Heinrich.
Zen Buddhism in the 20th century. Weatherhill, 1992.
  Heiser, W Charles. *TheolDgst* 40:159 Sum 1993.

Dunbabin, Jean.
A hound of God: Pierre de la Palud and the fourteenth-century church. Oxford University PRess, 1991.
  Heiser, W Charles. *TheolDgst* 39:359 Wint 1992.

Duncan, Anthony.
The elements of Celtic Christianity. Element, n.d.
  Waal, Esther de. *Tablet* 247:1302 O 9 1993.

Duncan, Bruce.
The church's social teaching from Rerum Novarum to 1931. Collins Dove, 1991.
  Ryan, Thomas. *Pacifica* 6:117-119 F 1993.

Duncan, Dayton.
Miles from nowhere: tales from America's contemporary frontier. Viking, n.d.
  McCarthy, Tim. *Nat Cath Rep* 29:18 Jl 30 1993.

Dungan, David L, ed.
The interrelations of the gospels. Peeters, 1990.
  Maloney, Elliot C. *CBQ* 54:820-821 O 1992.

Dunn, H P.
The doctor and Christian marriage. Alba House, 1992.
  Heiser, W Charles. *TheolDgst* 40:160 Sum 1993.

Dunn, James D G.
Jesus' call to discipleship. Cambridge University Press, 1992.
  Heiser, W Charles. *TheolDgst* 40:160 Sum 1993.
The partings of the ways between Christianity and Judaism and their significance for the character of Christianity. Trinity, 1991.
  Knopp, Josephine. *JEcumen Stds* 29:485 Sum-Aut 1992.

Dunn, John, ed.
Democracy. Oxford University Press, n.d.
  Deneen, Patrick J. *Comm* 120:35-36 Ap 9 1993.

Dunne, John S, 1929-.
Peace of the present: an unviolent way of life. University of Notre Dame Press, 1991.
  Kopas, Jane. *Horizons (CTS)* 19:335-336 Fall 1992.

Dunne, Tad.
Spiritual exercises for today. Harper, 1991.
  Koenig, Elisabeth K J. *Horizons (CTS)* 19:332-333 Fall 1992.
  McCarty, Shaun. *New Theol Rev* 6:106-108 Ag 1993.
Spiritual mentoring: guiding people through spiritual exercises to life decisions. Harper, 1991.
  Koenig, Elisabeth K J. *Horizons (CTS)* 19:332-333 Fall 1992.
  McCarty, Shaun. *New Theol Rev* 6:106-108 Ag 1993.

Dunning, James.
Echoing God's word: formation for catechists and homilists in a catechumenal church. Liturgy Training Publications, n.d.
  Graham, William C. *Nat Cath Rep* 29:18 Jl 16 1993.

Dupleix, A.
La force du pardon. Nouvelle Cité, 1990.
  Navez, G. *NRT* 115:136 Ja-F 1993.

Dupuis, Jacques.
Introduzione alla cristologia. Piemme, 1993.
  Anon. *Gregorianum* 74 no 3:602-603 1993.
Jésus-Christ à la rencontre des religions. Desclée, 1989.
  Bruyn, P-H De. *NRT* 115:595-596 Jl-Ag 1993.
Jesus Christ at the encounter of world religions. Orbis Books, 1991.
  D'Costa, Gavin. *Thomist* 56:719-723 O 1992.
  Phan, Peter C. *Living Light* 29:90-91 Aut 1992.
Jeuscristo al encuentro de las religiones. Paulinas, 1991.
  Bruyn, P-H De. *NRT* 115:595-596 Jl-Ag 1993.
  Lago Alba, Luis. *Cien Tom* 119:604-606 S-D 1992.

Duquoc, Christian.
Libération et progressisme. Cerf, 1987.
  Tihon, Paul. *Lumen* 47:470-471 D 1992.

Durand, A.
La cause des pauvres. Cerf, 1991.
  Volpe, L. *NRT* 115:147 Ja-F 1993.

Durand, Guillaume.
Evèque de Mende (1230-1296). Edit du C N R S, 1992.
  Évenou, Jean. *Notitiae* 29:307 My 1993.

Durand, Jean-Dominique, and Ladous, Régis, eds.
Histoire religieuse. Beauchesne, 1992.
  Gargan, Edward T. *CHist* 79:343-344 Ap 1993.
  Masson, J. *NRT* 115:617-618 Jl-Ag 1993.

Durand, M de.
Précis d'histoire grecque. Cerf, 1991.
  Plumat, N. *NRT* 114:918-919 N-D 1992.

Durbin, Paul T.
Europe, America and technology: philosophical perspectives. Kluwer Academic Publishers, 1991.
  Wennemann, D. *Mod Schlmn* 70:77-78 N 1992.

Durcan, Paul.
A snail in my prime. Harvill, n.d.
  Campbell, James. *Month* 26:381 S-O 1993.

Durning, Alan Thein.
How much is enough? The consumer society, and the future of the earth. Earthscan, n.d.
  McRobie, George. *Tablet* 246:1624 D 19-26 1992.

Durrwell, François-Xavier.
Le père Dieu en son mystère. Cerf, 1987.
  Partos, L. *Lumen* 47:471 D 1992.

Dussel, Enrique, ed.
The Church in Latin America, 1492-1992. Burns and Oates, n.d.
  Murphy, Anne, and Pridmore, John. *Way* 33:253 Jl 1993.
The Church in Latin America, 1492-1992. Orbis Books, 1992.
  Heiser, W Charles. *TheolDgst* 40:156 Sum 1993.

Dworkin, Ronald.
Life's dominion. Alfred A Knopf, n.d.
  Callahan, Daniel, 1930-. *Comm* 120:23-24 S 24 1993.

Dych, William V.
Karl Rahner. Chapman, 1992.
  Endean, Philip. *Month* 26:76-77 F 1993.
  O'Hanlon, Gerard F. *Tablet* 247:723-725 Je 5 1993.
  Tallon, Andrew. *TheolStds* 54:392 Je 1993.
  Heiser, W Charles. *TheolDgst* 40:80 Spr 1993.
  Kerr, Fergus. *New Blckfrs* 74:279-281 My 1993.
  Kilby, Karen. *Priests & People* 7:250-251 Je 1993.
  Endean, Philip. *Heythrop* 34:440-442 O 1993.

E

Eales, Jacqueline.
Puritans and Roundheads: the Harleys of Brampton Bryan and the outbreak of the English Civil War. Cambridge University Press, 1990.
McGee, J. *CHist* 78:660-661 O 1992.

Earhart, H Byron, ed.
Religious traditions of the world. San Francisco, 1992.
Heiser, W Charles. *TheolDgst* 40:184 Sum 1993.

Earley, C, and McKenna, G.
Partners in faith: a programme of adult faith development. Columba Press, n.d.
Cahill, F. *Furrow* 44:56-57 Ja 1993.

Early, Gerald, ed.
Lure and loathing: essays on race, identity, and the ambivalences of assimilation. The Penguin Press, n.d.
Wycliff, Don. *Comm* 120:22-23 My 21 1993.

Eastland, Terry.
Energy in the executive. The Free Press, n.d.
Genovese, M. *New Oxford Rev* 60:31-32 Ja-F 1993.
Stevens, Richard G. *Crisis* 11:53-55 Jl-Ag 1993.

Eberts, Randall W, and Groshen, Erica L, eds.
Structural changes in U.S. labor markets: causes and consequences. Armonk, 1991.
Heywood, John S. *RSocEcon* 51:232-237 Sum 1993.

Echegaray, Joaquín González.
El Creciente fértil y la Biblia. Verbo Divino, 1991.
Althann, Robert. *CBQ* 55:110-111 Ja 1993.

Echlin, Edward P, 1930-.
The deacon and creation. The Church Union, 1992.
Jones, D. *Priests & People* 6:359 Ag-S 1992.

Eckardt, Arthur Roy.
Reclaiming the Jesus of history: christology today. Fortress Press, 1992.
Heiser, W Charles. *TheolDgst* 39:360 Wint 1992.
Johnson, Elizabeth A, 1941-. *TheolStds* 54:580-581 S 1993.

Eckhart, Maître.
Traités et sermons. Flammarion, 1993.
Praetere, Thomas de. *RPhil Louvain* 91:325 My 1993.

Les écrits des Pères apostoliques.
Cerf, 1990.
Spanneut, Michel. *MSR* 50:76-77 Ja-Mr 1993.

L'Écriture âme de la théologie.
Institut d'Études Théologiques, 1990.
Farahian, Edmond. *Gregorianum* 74 No 1:144-146 1993.

Edelman, Diana Vikander, ed.
The fabric of history. Sheffield, 1991.
Schoors, A. *Eph Theol Lovan* 78:402-403 D 1992.
Dearman, J Andrew. *CBQ* 55:411-413 Ap 1993.

Edgecombe, Rodney Stenning.
Vocation and identity in the fiction of Muriel Spark. University of Missouri Press, 1990.
Leonard, Joan. *Relig Lit* 25:87-91 Spr 1993.

Edgerton, W Dow.
The passion of interpretation. Westminster, 1992.
Begg, Christopher T. *OTA* 16:405 Je 1993.

Edward, Tilden.
Sabbath time. Upper Room Books, n.d.
Graham, William C. *Nat Cath Rep* 29:40 My 28 1993.

Edwards, David L.
The real Jesus. Fount, n.d.
Galvin, John P, 1944-. *Tablet* 246:1575 D 12 1992.

Edwards, Denis.
Jesus and the cosmos. Paulist Press, 1991.
Heiser, W Charles. *TheolDgst* 39:360 Wint 1992.

Edwards, Owain Tudor.
Matins, Lauds, and Vespers for St David's Day. D.S. Brewer, 1990.
Davies, Oliver. *Heythrop* 34:327-328 Jl 1993.

Edwards, Ruth B.
The case for women's ministry. SPCK, 1989.
Porter, Muriel. *Pacifica* 6:221-223 Je 1993.

Edwards-Jones, Imogen.
The taming of eagles. Weidenfeld & Nicolson, n.d.
Walton, James. *Tablet* 247:584 My 8 1993.

Egan, Desmond.
Peninsula: poems. Kavanagh Press, 1992.
Harmon, Maurice. *Studies* 81:446-448 Wint 1992.
Selected poems. Goldsmith, 1992.
Harmon, Maurice. *Studies* 82:360-362 Aut 1993.

Egan, Eileen, and Egan, Kathleen, eds.
Blessed are you: Mother Teresa and the Beatitudes. Fount, n.d.
Forrester, David. *Tablet* 247:728 Je 5 1993.

Egan, Harvey.
An anthology of Christian mysticism. Liturgical, 1991.
Halleux, André de. *Eph Theol Lovan* 78:478-479 D 1992.
Moore, Patrick. *Priests & People* 7:124 Mr 1993.
Cooper, Austin. *Pacifica* 6:243-244 Je 1993.

Eggensperger, T, et al, eds.
Verröhnung: Versuche zu ihrer Geschichte und Zukunft. Matthias-Grünewald-Verlag, 1991.
De Luis Carballada, R. *Cien Tom* 119:412-413 My-Ag 1992.

L'Église dans la transformation actuelle de l'Amérique Latine à la lumière du Concile Vatican II.
Éd du Cerf, 1992.
Toubeau, A. *NRT* 115:291-292 Mr-Ap 1993.

L'Église et monde.
Cerf, 1993.
Vercruysse, J.E. *Civilta* 3:446-447 S 4 1993.

Ehr, Marie Louise, ed.
Changing women, changing church. Millennium Books, 1992.
Porter, Muriel. *Pacifica* 6:231-234 Je 1993.

Eichenberg, Fritz.
Works of mercy. Orbis Books, n.d.
Vree, Dale. *New Oxford Rev* 60:31-32 Je 1993.

Eid, Giuseppe Samir.
Arabi Cristiani e Arabi Musulmani. NED, 1991.
Poggi, V. *Civilta* 2:616-617 Je 19 1993.

Eilberg-Schwartz, Howard, ed.
People of the body. State University of New York Press, 1992.
Stuhlmueller, Carroll. *BibleT* 31:246 Jl 1993.

Eilert, Hakan.
I regnbagens tecken. Verbum, 1989.
Hassing, Per. *JEcumen Stds* 29:116 Wint 1992.

Der eine Gott und die Göttin.
Herder, 1991.
Renard, L J. *NRT* 114:938-939 N-D 1992.

Eisenman, Robert H, and Wise, Michael.
The Dead Sea Scrolls uncovered. Element, 1992.
Crampsey, James A. *Month* 26:146-147 Ap 1993.
Graham, William C. *Nat Cath Rep* 29:39 My 28 1993.
Wansbrough, Henry. *Tablet* 247:721-722 Je 5 1993.

Eitan, E, et al, eds.
Ruth Amiran volume. Israel Exploration Society, 1990.
Smith, Mark S. *OTA* 16:151-152 F 1993.

Elavathingal, Sebastian.
Inculturation and Christian art: an Indian perspective. Urbaniana University Press, 1990.
Gutmann, Joseph. *JEcumen Stds* 29:284 Spr 1992.

Elders, Leo J.
The philosophical theology of St Thomas Aquinas. E J Brill, 1990.
Carabine, Deirdre. *IJPS* 1:164 Mr 1993.

Eliade, Mircea, 1907-1986, and Couliano, Ioan P.
The Eliade guide to world religions. HarperSanFrancisco, 1991.
Powell, Jouett L. *JEcumen Stds* 29:281 Spr 1992.

Elizondo, Virgil, ed.
Way of the cross. Orbis, 1992.
Gross, Adela. *Sisters* 65:306-307 Jl 1993.
Senior, Donald. *BibleT* 31:314 S 1993.

Ellacuría, Ignacio.
Conversione della Chiesa al Regno di Dio. Per annunciarlo e realizzarlo nella storia. Queriniana, 1992.
Babolin, A. *Civilta* 3:438-439 S 4 1993.

Eller, Cynthia.
Living in the lap of the goddess. Crossroad, n.d.
Bromberg, Judith. *Nat Cath Rep* 30:27 N 19 1993.

Elliott, J K.
A bibliography of Greek New Testament manuscripts. Cambridge University Press, 1989.
Neirynck, F. *Eph Theol Lovan* 78:161-162 Ap 1992.

Elliott, John H.
A home for the homeless: a social-scientific criticism of I Peter. Fortress, 1990.
Burnett, Fred. *CBQ* 55:364-365 Ap 1993.

Elliott, Michele, ed.
Female sexual abuse of children. Longman, n.d.
Hansen, Tracy. *Tablet* 247:1198-1199 S 18 1993.

Ellis, Edward Earle.
The Old Testament in early Christianity. Baker Book House, 1992.
Heiser, W Charles. *TheolDgst* 40:160 Sum 1993.

Ellis, Marc E, and Maduro, Otto, eds.
Expanding the view: Gustavo Gutiérrez and the future of liberation theology. Orbis, 1990.
Neckebrouck, Valeer. *Eph Theol Lovan* 78:181 Ap 1992.

Ellis, Marc H.
Beyond innocence and redemption. Harper & Row, 1990.
Garber, Zev. *JEcumen Stds* 29:128-129 Wint 1992.

Ellsberg, Robert, ed.
Dorothy Day. Orbis, n.d.
Cunningham, Lawrence S, 1935-. *Comm* 120:26 F 12 1993.
Fritz Eichenberg. Orbis, 1992.
Feister, John Bookser. *St Anth* 101:50 Je 1993.
Smith, Karen Sue. *Church* 9:57 Sum 1993.
Seasoltz, R Kevin. *Worship* 67:370 Jl 1993.
Gandhi on Christianity. Orbis Books, 1991.
Dupuis, Jacques. *Gregorianum* 74 No 1:193 1993.
Nelson, Lance E. *JEcumen Stds* 29:283-284 Spr 1992.

Ellsburg, Robert, ed.
Dorothy Day. Orbis, n.d.
Dollen, Charles. *Priest* 49:52 F 1993.

Ellul, Jacques.
Reason for being: a meditation of Ecclesiastes. Eerdmans, 1990.
Marlin, Randal. *Can Cath Rev* 11:30-31 Ja 1993.
McLaughlin, John L. *CBQ* 55:109-110 Ja 1993.
The technological bluff. William B Eerdmans, n.d.
Marlin, Randal. *Can Cath Rev* 11:30-31 Ja 1993.

Elred of Rievaulx.
The life of Saint Edward King and Confessor. St Edward's Press, 1990.
  Dutton, Marsha L. *Cist Stud* 28 no 2:[53]-[57] 1993.
The mirror of charity. Cistercian Publications, 1990.
  Holman, Jean. *Cist Stud* 28 no 2:[58]-[60] 1993.

Elvins, Mark.
Catholic trivia. HarperCollins, n.d.
  Braybrooke, Neville. *Tablet* 247:374 Mr 20 1993.

Emanuel, Ezekiel J.
The ends of human life: medical ethics in a liberal polity. Harvard University Press, n.d.
  Lanham, Richard J. *New Oxford Rev* 60:30-31 Ja-F 1993.

Emeis, Dieter.
Mit den Sakramenten leben. Herder, 1993.
  Bleistein, Roman, 1928-. *Stimm Zeit* 211:575 Ag 1993.

Emerton, J A, ed.
Studies in the Pentateuch. Brill, 1990.
  Matthews, Victor H. *CBQ* 55:413-414 Ap 1993.

Emery, Norman.
The coalminers of Durham. Alan Sutton, n.d.
  Forrest, Denys. *Tablet* 246:1622 D 19-26 1992.

Emmerson, Grace I.
Isaiah 56-66. Sheffield, 1992.
  Begg, Christopher T. *OTA* 16:431-432 Je 1993.

Emmerson, Richard Kenneth, and Herzman, Ronald B.
The apocalyptic imagination in medieval literature. University of Pennsylvania Press, 1992.
  Heiser, W Charles. *TheolDgst* 40:160 Sum 1993.

Enchiridion Vaticanum, vol 12.
Ed Dehoniane, 1992.
  Caprile, Giovanni. *Civilta* 144:415-416 F 20 1993.

Enciclopedia delle scienze fisiche, vol I.
Instituto della Enciclopedia Italiana, 1992.
  Artuso, P. *Civilta* 2:407-408 My 15 1993.

The encyclopaedia of seashells.
Hale, n.d.
  Braybrooke, Neville. *Tablet* 247:374 Mr 20 1993.

Endo, Shusaku, 1923-.
The final martyrs. Peter Owen, n.d.
  Bull, George, 1929-. *Tablet* 247:1077 Ag 21 1993.
Foreign studies. Sceptre, n.d.
  Labrie, Ross. *Can Cath Rev* 11:25-26 Jl-Ag 1993.

Engelhardt, H Tristram, Jr.
Bioethics and secular humanism: the search for a common morality. SCM Press, 1991.
  Williams, John R. *Heythrop* 34:221-222 Ap 1993.

Engels, Friedrich.
The condition of the working class in England. Oxford University Press, n.d.
  Toomey, Philippa. *Tablet* 247:585 My 8 1993.

Engh, Michael E.
Frontier faiths: church, temple, and synagogue in Los Angeles, 1846-1888. University of New Mexico Press, 1992.
  Weber, Francis J. *CHist* 78:684-685 O 1992.

English, John.
Spiritual intimacy and community. DLT, n.d.
  Endean, Philip, and Lonsdale, David. *Way* 33:251-252 Jl 1993.
Spiritual intimacy and community. Paulist, n.d.
  Williams, Monty. *Can Cath Rev* 11:28-29 N 1993.

Englund, Robert K, and Grégoire, Jean-Pierre.
The proto-Cuneiform texts from Jemdet Nasr. I. Mann, 1991.
  Smith, Marks. *OTA* 16:405 Je 1993.

Ennen, Edith.
The medieval woman. Basil Blackwell, 1989.
  Nichols, John A. *CHist* 79:511-512 Jl 1993.

Epstein, Daniel Mark.
Sister Aimee: the life of Aimee Semple McPherson. Harcourt Brace Jovanovich, n.d.
  Lammer, Stephen E. *America* 169:29 S 11 1993.

Erickson, Millard J.
Introducing Christian doctrine. Baker Book House, 1992.
  Heiser, W Charles. *TheolDgst* 40:160-161 Sum 1993.

Erickson, Victoria Lee.
Where silence speaks. Fortress, n.d.
  Bromberg, Judith. *Nat Cath Rep* 30:27 N 19 1993.

Ericson, Edward E, Jr.
Solzhenitsyn and the modern world. Regnery Gateway, n.d.
  Kirk, Russell, 1918-. *Crisis* 11:59-60 O 1993.

Erlander, L.
Faith in the world of work. Uppsala, 1991.
  Toubeau, A. *NRT* 114:923-924 N-D 1992.

Ernst, Carl W.
Eternal garden: mysticism, history, and politics at a South Asian Sufi center. State University of New York Press, 1992.
  Heiser, W Charles. *TheolDgst* 40:61 Spr 1993.

Ernst, Josef.
Juan. Herder, 1992.
  Mondoni, Danilo. *Perspectiva* 25:260-261 My-Ag 1993.

Errázuriz Mackenna, Carlos José.
Il 'munus docendi Ecclesia': diritti e doveri dei fedeli. Giuffrè, 1991.
  Tourneau, Dominique Le. *Stud Can* 27 no 1:264-265 1993.

Erspamer, Steve.
Clip art for Year A. Liturgy Training Publications, 1992.
  McGrath, Helene. *Mod Lit* 20:39 Je-Jl 1993.

Espeja, Jesús.
La espiritualidad cristiana. Ed Verbo Divino, 1992.
  Lago Alba, Luis. *Cien Tom* 119:621-623 S-D 1992.
El Evangelio en nuevas culturas. Editorial Verbo Divino, 1992.
  Salado Martinez, Domingo. *Cien Tom* 119:623 S-D 1992.

Espinosa, R Rábanos, and León, D Muñoz.
Bibliografia Joanica. Conseio Superior de Investigaciones Científicas, 1990.
  Simoeus, Y. *NRT* 115:105 Ja-F 1993.

Esponera Cerdán, Alfonso.
Los dominicos y la evangelización del Uruguay. Ed San Esteban, 1992.
  Barrado, G. *Cien Tom* 119:424-425 My-Ag 1992.

Esposito, John.
The Islamic threat. Oxford University Press, n.d.
  Perkovich, George. *Comm* 120:21-23 F 12 1993.

Estadt, Barry K, et al, eds.
Pastoral counseling. Prentice Hall, 1991.
  Heiser, W Charles. *TheolDgst* 39:379 Wint 1992.

Estés, Clarissa Pinkola.
Women who run with the wolves: myths and stories of the wild woman archetype. Ballantine Books, n.d.
  Hess, Louise. *St Anth* 101:51-52 O 1993.

Estes, Eleanor.
The hundred dresses. Harcourt, Brace, Jovanovich, n.d.
  Neuberger, Anne E. *ReligTJ* 27:59 S 1993.

Estevez, J Medina, Bp.
Seigneur, qui es-tu? Desclée, 1991.
  Navez, G. *NRT* 115:134-135 Ja-F 1993.

Ethique et communication, Actes du Colluque.
IRCOM, 1991.
  Baragli, Enrico. *Civilta* 2:201-202 Ap 17 1993.

L'etica nei comitati di bioetica: atti del 3 seminario di etica professionale: 4-8 giugno 1990.
Edi Oftes, 1991.
  Cultrera, Francesco. *Civilta* 2:303-304 My 1 1993.

Etizioni, Amitai.
The spirit of community. Crown Publishers, n.d.
  Sullivan, William M. *Comm* 120:22-23 My 7 1993.

Eugen, Paul.
Geschichte der christlichen Erziehung, vol 1. Herder, 1993.
  Bleistein, Roman, 1928-. *Stimm Zeit* 211:717 O 1993.

Eusebi, Luciano.
La pena in crisi: il recente dibattito sulla funzione della pena. Morcelliana, 1990.
  Putti, P. *Civilta* 144:98 Ja 2 1993.

Eusebius Pamphili, Bp of Caesarea.
La préparation évangélique: livres VIII-IX-X. Éd du Cerf, 1991.
  Halleux, André de. *Eph Theol Lovan* 69:196 Ap 1993.

Evans, Craig A, 1952-.
Noncanonical writings and the New Testament. Hendrickson, 1992.
  Begg, Christopher T. *OTA* 16:443 Je 1993.

Evans, G R.
Problems of authority in the Reformation debates. Cambridge University Press, 1992.
  Ferme, Brian. *New Blckfrs* 74:333-334 Je 1993.

Evans, G R, and Wright, J Robert, eds.
The Anglican tradition: a handbook of sources. SPCK, 1991.
  Hamilton, Alastair. *Heythrop* 34:340 Jl 1993.

Evely, L.
Éterniser sa vie. Centurion, 1991.
  Verdonck, C. *NRT* 115:120 Ja-F 1993.

Everson, Stephen, ed.
Psychology. Cambridge University Press, 1991.
  Dillon, John. *IJPS* 1:140-142 Mr 1993.

Evinson, Denis.
The Lord's house: a history of Sheffield's Roman Catholic buildings 1570-1990. Sheffield Academic Press, 1991.
  McCoog, Thomas M. *CHist* 79:144-145 Ja 1993.

Exum, Cheryl J.
Tragedy and biblical narrative. Cambridge University, 1992.
  Penchansky, David. *OTA* 16:158 F 1993.
Tragedy and biblical narrative. Cambridge University Press, 1992.
  Heiser, W Charles. *TheolDgst* 40:161 Sum 1993.

Eynikel, Erik, ed.
Wie wijsheid zoekt, vindt het Leven. Katholieke Bibjel Stichting, 1991.
  Begg, Christopher T. *OTA* 15:502 O 1992.

Eyre, Elizabeth.
Curtains for the cardinal. Headline, n.d.
  Lejeune, Anthony. *Tablet* 247:51 Ja 9 1993.

F

Fabella, Virginia, et al, eds.
Asian Christian spirituality: reclaiming traditions. Orbis Books, 1992.
  Heiser, W Charles. *TheolDgst* 39:350 Wint 1992.
  Neckebrouck, Valeer. *Eph Theol Lovan* 69:208 Ap 1993.
  Dupuis, Jacques. *Gregorianum* 74 no 3:589-590 1993.

Fabella, Virginia, and Park, Sun Ai Lee, eds.
We dare to dream: doing theology as Asian Women. Orbis Books, 1989.
  Grey, Mary. *Heythrop* 34:193-194 Ap 1993.

Fackenheim, Emil L.
The Jewish Bible after the Holocaust. Indiana University Press, 1990.
  Craig, Kenneth M, Jr. *JEcumen Stds* 29:127-128 Wint 1992.

Fagan, Patrick.
Dublin's turbulent priest: Cornelius Nary, 1658-1738. RIA, 1991.
  Morrissey, Thomas. *Studies* 81:469-475 Wint 1992.

Fagerberg, David W.
What is liturgical theology? Liturgical, 1992.
Dollen, Charles. *Priest* 49:52 Ap 1993.
Skublics, Ernest. *Can Cath Rev* 11:37 My 1993.
Empereur, James L. *TheolStds* 54:589-590 S 1993.

Faherty, William Barnaby.
American Catholic heritage: stories of growth. Sheed and Ward, 1991.
Crews, Clyde F. *ACHSR* 103:55-56 Aut 1992.

Fahey, Michael A.
Ecumenism: a bibliographical overview. Greenwood Press, 1992.
Mathews, Edward G. *Diakonia* 26 no 2:138-139 1993.

Fahy, Catherine, comp.
The James Joyce—Paul Leon papers. National Library of Ireland, n.d.
Costello, Peter. *Studies* 81:452-454 Wint 1992.

Fahy, Patrick S.
Faith in Catholic classrooms. St. Paul, 1992.
Brusselmans, A. *Lumen* 48:354 S 1993.

Faivre, Alexandre.
The emergence of the laity in the early Church. Paulist Press, 1990.
Hall, Stewart J. *Heythrop* 34:315-316 Jl 1993.

Faivre, Antoine, and Needleman, Jacob, eds.
Modern esoteric spirituality: world spirituality: an encyclopdic history of the Religious quest. Crossroads, n.d.
Bromberg, L. *Nat Cath Rep* 29:35 F 5 1993.

Fales, F M, and Postgate, J N.
Imperial administrative records. Helsinki University Press, 1992.
Fitzgerald, Aloysius. *OTA* 16:408 Je 1993.

Falk, Gerhard.
The Jew in Christian theology. McFarland, 1992.
Heiser, W Charles. *TheolDgst* 40:161-162 Sum 1993.

Falla, Terry C.
A key to the Peshitta Gospels: vol 1, Ālaph-Dālath. Brill, 1991.
Attridge, Harold W. *CBQ* 55:146-147 Ja 1993.

Fallaci, Oriana.
Inshallah. Chatto and Windus, n.d.
Walton, James. *Tablet* 247:312 Mr 6 1993.

Falsini, R, ed.
L'iniziazione cristiana degli adulti. O.R., 1992.
Anon. *NRT* 115:632-633 Jl-Ag 1993.

Fanti, Aldo.
Parole feriali. Marietta, 1992.
Caprile, Giovanni. *Civilta* 3:201-202 Jl 17 1993.

Farina, John, ed.
Isaac T Hecker: the diary: Romantic religion in ante-bellum America. Paulist Press, 1988.
O'Brien, David J, 1938-. *CHist* 79:133-134 Ja 1993.

Farinelli, Giuseppe.
Dal Manzoni alla Scapigliatura. IPL, 1991.
Bortone, G. *Civilta* 143:633-34 D 19 1992.

Farmer, Kathleen A.
What knows what is good? Handsel, 1991.
McCreesh, Thomas P. *OTA* 15:504 O 1992.
Asma, Lawrence F. *CBQ* 54:745-746 O 1992.
Lillie, Betty Jane. *Bib Th Bul* 22:180-181 Wint 1992.
Lillie, Betty Jane. *Bib Th Bul* 23:82-83 Sum 1993.

Farmer, Sharon.
Communities of Saint Martin: legend and ritual in medieval tours. Cornell University Press, 1991.
Paxton, F. *CHist* 78:633-634 O 1992.

Farmer, William R, and Kereszty, Roch, 1933-.
Peter and Paul in the Church of Rome: the ecumenical potential of a forgotten perspective. Paulist Press, n.d.
Yarnold, Edward John, 1926-. *Can Cath Rev* 11:33-34 F 1993.

Farnham, Suzanne, et al.
Listening hearts: discerning call in community. Morehouse Publishing, 1991.
Anon. *Spir Life* 39:189 Aut 1993.

Farr, Evelyn.
The world of Fanny Burney. Peter Owen, n.d.
Forrest, Denys. *Tablet* 247:1200 S 18 1993.

Farrar, Austin.
Words for life: forty meditations previously unpublished. SPCK, n.d.
Hollings, Michael. *Tablet* 247:278 F 27 1993.

Farrar, Cynthia.
The origins of democratic thinking. Cambridge University Press, 1989.
Destrée, Pierre. *RPhil Louvain* 91:140-141 F 1993.

Farrelly, M John.
Belief in God in our time: foundational theology, I. Michael Glazier Books, 1992.
Heiser, W Charles. *TheolDgst* 39:361 Wint 1992.

Farronato, Gabriele.
Crespano del grappa. Moro, 1992.
Mellinato, Giuseppe. *Civilta* 2:413-414 My 15 1993.

Farson, Daniel.
The gilded gutter life of Francis Bacon. Century, n.d.
Reyntiens, Patrick. *Tablet* 247:691-692 My 29 1993.

Fattal, Michel.
Pour un nouveau langage de la raison. Beauchesne, 1987.
Robberechts, Edouard. *RPhil Louvain* 91:336-339 My 1993.

Fattorini, Emma.
Germania e Santa Sede: le nunziature di Pacelli fra la Grande guerra e la Repubblica di Weimar. Societa editrice il Mulino, 1992.
Conway, John S. *CHist* 79:555-557 Jl 1993.

Fatula, Mary Ann.
Thomas Aquinas: preacher and friend. Liturgical Press, 1993.
Anon. *Spir Life* 39:185 Aut 1993.

Faur, José.
In the shadow of history: Jews and conversos at the dawn of modernity. University of New York Press, 1992.
Heiser, W Charles. *TheolDgst* 39:361 Wint 1992.

Faustini, Gianni.
Il sistema dell'informazione e la deontonologia, Vol II. Ordine dei Giornalista-Consiglio Nazionales, 1991.
Baragli, Enrico. *Civilta* 2:201-202 Ap 17 1993.

Fauvel, John, et al, eds.
Let Newton be!. Oxford University Press, 1988.
Hespel, Bertrand. *RPhil Louvain* 91:474-475 Ag 1993.

Favale, Agostino, et al.
Movimenti ecclesiali contemporanei. Bibliotecadi Scienze Religiose, 1991.
Rambaldi, Giuseppe. *Gregorianum* 73 No 4:761-762 1992.

Fayol-Fricout, A, et al.
L'initiation chrétienne. Desclée, 1991.
Navez, G. *NRT* 114:905-906 N-D 1992.

Fearghail, Fearghus O.
The introduction to Luke-Acts. Biblical Institute, 1991.
Gowler, David B. *CBQ* 55:381-389 Ap 1993.

Fechter, Friedrich.
Bewältigung der Katastrophe: Untersuchungen zu ausgewählten Fremdvölkersprüchen im Ezekielbuch. W de Gruyter, 1992.
Lust, Johan. *Eph Theol Lovan* 69:159-160 Ap 1993.

Fedalto, Giorgio.
Acta Eugenii papae IV (1431-1447) e Vaticanis aliisque regestis collegit notisque illustravit. Fontes, 1990.
Capizzi, Carmelo. *Civilta* 144:193-194 Ja 16 1993.
Rufino di Concordia tra Oriente e Occidente. Città Nuova, 1990.
Capizzi, Carmelo. *Civilta* 143:636 D 19 1992.

Feder, Don.
A Jewish conservative looks at pagan America. Huntington House, n.d.
Pakaluk, Michael. *Crisis* 11:52-53 Jl-Ag 1993.

Fédou, Michel.
Christianisme et religions païennes dan le contre celse d'origène. Beauchesne, 1989.
Partos, L. *Lumen* 47:471-472 D 1992.

Feige, Gerhard.
Die lehre Markells von Ankyra in der darstellung seiner gegner. Benno, 1991.
Lienhard, Joseph J. *TheolStds* 54:196-197 Mr 1993.

Feinstein, Elaine.
Lawrence's women: the intimate life of D H Lawrence. HarperCollins, n.d.
Bergonzi, Bernard, 1929-. *Tablet* 247:246 F 20 1993.

Felder, Cain Hope, ed.
Stony the road we trod: African American biblical interpretation. Fortress Press, 1991.
Perkins, Pheme. *CrossCurr* 43:120-122 Spr 1993.

Feldman, David.
When did wild poodles roam the earth? HarperCollins, n.d.
Hunt, George W, 1937-. *America* 168:2 F 13 1993.

Felici, Sergio.
La Mariologia nella catechesi dei Padri. LAS, 1991.
Galot, Jean. *Gregorianum* 74 no 2:369-370 1993.

Felici, Sergio, ed.
"Humanitas" classica e "Sapientia" cristiana. LAS, 1992.
Hilaire, S. *NRT* 115:619-620 Jl-Ag 1993.

Fenn, Richard K.
The death of Herod. Cambridge University Press, 1992.
Heiser, W Charles. *TheolDgst* 40:162 Sum 1993.

Fenwick, John R K.
The anaphoras of St Basil and St James. Pontificium Institutum Orientale, 1992.
Talley, Thomas J. *Worship* 67:480-481 S 1993.

Ferder, Fran, and Heagle, John.
Your sexual self: pathways to authentic intimacy. Ave Maria Press, 1992.
Christantiello, Phillip D. *RRel* 52:315-316 Mr-Ap 1993.

Ferguson, David.
Bultmann. The Liturgical Press, 1992.
Heiser, W Charles. *TheolDgst* 40:80 Spr 1993.

Ferguson, John.
Clement, of Alexandria, ca 150-ca 215: Stromateis: books one to three. The Catholic University of America Press, 1991.
Heiser, W Charles. *TheolDgst* 39:356 Wint 1992.

Fergusson, David.
Bultmann. Chapman, 1992.
Kilby, Karen. *Priests & People* 7:250-251 Je 1993.

Ferlay, Phillipe, ed.
François De Sales (Saint) traité de l'amour de Dieu. Mediaspaul, 1992.
Partos, L. *Lumen* 48:234 Je 1993.

Ferlita, Ernest.
The paths of life: reflections on the readings for Sundays and holy days. Alba House, 1992.
Heiser, W Charles. *TheolDgst* 40:62 Spr 1993.

Fernández, Miguel Pérez.
La lengua de los sabios. Verbo Divino, 1992.
Begg, Christopher T. *OTA* 16:448-449 Je 1993.

Ferrari, Giuseppe.
Giordano Dell'Amore. Rusconi, 1989.
Giachi, Gualberto. *Civilta* 2:611-612 Je 19 1993.

Ferrari, Giuseppe.
Alle origini di Soriano Calabro. Mapograf, 1990.
Capizzi, Carmelo. *Civilta* 144:410-411 F 20 1993.

Ferraro, Giuseppe.
Nel nome del Padre: commento esegetico alle letture festive. Piemme, 1992.
Simon, Michele. *Civilta* 143:635 D 19 1992.

Ferré, John P, ed.
Channels of belief: religion and American commercial television. Iowa State University Press, n.d.
Schaper, Donna. *St Anth* 100:51-52 S 1993.

Ferri, E.
L'antiguiridismo di Max Stirner. Giuffré, 1991.
Sbardella, Agapito. *Civilta* 2:248-251 My 1 1993.

Ferris, Elizabeth G.
Beyond borders. World Council of Churches, n.d.
Broderick, John J. *Nat Cath Rep* 29:31 S 10 1993.

Ferry, Jean-Marc.
Les puissances de l'expérience. Cerf, 1991.
Fuchs, Eric. *Supplement* 184:193-203 Mr-Ap 1993.

Feshbach, Murray, and Friendly, Alfred, Jr.
Ecocide in the USSR. Basic Books, 1992.
Brown, William S. *RSocEcon* 51:244-246 Sum 1993.

Fessard, Gaston.
Hegel, le christianisme et l'histoire. Presses universitaires de France, 1990.
Gérard, Gilbert. *RPhil Louvain* 91:481-482 Ag 1993.

Feuillet, A.
La primauté de Pierre. Desclée, 1992.
Anon. *NRT* 115:623 Jl-Ag 1993.

Févotte, P-M.
Aimer la Bible avec Élisabeth de la Trinité. Cerf, 1991.
Toubeau, A. *NRT* 115:306-307 Mr-Ap 1993.

Février, James G.
Storia della scrittura. ECIG, 1992.
Baragli, Enrico. *Civilta* 2:203-204 Ap 17 1993.

Fewell, Danna Nolan.
Circle of sovereignty: plotting politics in the Book of Daniel. Abingdon Press, 1991.
La Cocque, A. *New Theol Rev* 6:91-93 F 1993.

Ffinch, Michael.
Newman: towards the second spring. Ignatius Press, 1992.
Mangan, Charles M. *HPR* 93:76-79 Ap 1993.
Heiser, W Charles. *TheolDgst* 39:361 Wint 1992.
Newman: towards the second spring. Weindenfeld & Nicholson, 1992.
Jelly, Frederick M. *TheolStds* 54:197-198 Mr 1993.
Magill, Gerard. *RRel* 52:626-627 Jl-Ag 1993.

Fiand, Barbara.
Living the vision: religious vows in the age of change. Crossroad, n.d.
Ward, Hannah, and Lord, Elizabeth. *Way* 33:165 Ap 1993.

Fichte, Johann Gottlieb.
Nachgelassene Schriften 1804-1805. Frommann-Holzboog, 1989.
Depré, Olivier. *RPhil Louvain* 90:564-570 N 1992.

Fichtenau, Heinrich.
Ketzer und Professoren. Verlag C H Beck, 1992.
Mundy, John Hine. *CHist* 79:518-519 Jl 1993.

Fichter, Joseph H.
The pastoral provisions: married Catholic priests. Sheed & Ward, 1989.
Butler, Sara. *JEcumen Stds* 29:269-270 Spr 1992.
Wives of Catholic clergy. Sheed and Ward, n.d.
Gibeau, Dawn. *Nat Cath Rep* 29:16 N 6 1992.
Ward, Hannah, and Wild, Jennifer. *Way* 33:259 Jl 1993.

Field-Bibb, Jacqueline.
Women towards priesthood: ministerial politics and feminist praxis. Cambridge University Press, 1991.
King, U. *Heythrop* 34:84-86 Ja 1993.
Donovan, Daniel. *TheolStds* 54:379-381 Je 1993.

Fielding, Steven.
Class and ethnicity: Irish Catholics in England, 1880-1939. Open University Press, n.d.
McRedmond, Louis. *Tablet* 247:277 F 27 1993.

Fiensy, David A.
The social history of Palestine in the Herodian period. Mellen, 1991.
Heiser, W Charles. *TheolDgst* 39:361 Wint 1992.
Rohrbaugh, Richard L. *CBQ* 55:147-149 Ja 1993.

Fiévet, Michel.
Giovanni Battista de La Salle. Città Nuova, 1991.
Forlizzi, G. *Civilta* 2:310-311 My 1 1993.

Fifield, Christopher.
True artist and true friend. Oxford University Press, n.d.
Amis, John. *Tablet* 247:585 My 8 1993.

Figgness, Sandra.
Christian Initiation of older children. The Liturgical Press, n.d.
Graham, William C. *Nat Cath Rep* 29:40 My 28 1993.

Figuerora, Allan, ed.
Frontiers of Hispanic theology in the United States. Orbis, n.d.
Cunningham, Lawrence S, 1935-. *Comm* 120:30-31 O 8 1993.

La figura e l'opera di Federico Alessandrini.
Consiglio Relgionale delle Marche, 1992.
Pani, G. *Civilta* 144:412-413 F 20 1993.

Filibeck, Giorgio.
Les droits de l'homme dans l'enseignement de l'Eglise: De Jean XXIII à Jean-Paul II. Libr Ed Vaticana, 1992.
Joblin, Joseph, 1920-. *Civilta* 2:614 Je 19 1993.

Filoramo, Giovanni.
A history of Gnosticism. Basil Blackwell, 1990.
Edwards, M J. *Heythrop* 34:204-205 Ap 1993.

Filosomi, Luigi, ed.
San Claudio La Colombière e servo fidele e perfetto del cuoredi cristo. ivi, 1992.
Mucci, Giandomenico. *Civilta* 143:421-422 N 21 1992.
San Claudio la Colomière maestro di vita cristiana. ADP, 1992.
Mucci, Giandomenico. *Civilta* 143:421-422 N 21 1992.

Fimrite, Ron, ed.
Birth of a fan. Macmillan, n.d.
DiGiacomo, James J. *America* 168:17 Ap 17 1993.

Fin du monde et signes des temps.
Privat, 1992.
Plumat, N. *NRT* 115:612 Jl-Ag 1993.

Finan, T, and Toomey, V, eds.
The relationship between neoplatonism and Christianity. Four Courts, 1992.
Arkins, Brian. *Studies* 82:351-354 Aut 1993.

Finance, Joseph de.
En balbutiant l'Indicible. Editrice Pontificia Università Gregoriana, 1992.
Anon. *Gregorianum* 74 No 1:197 1993.
Personne et Valeur. Editrice Pontificia Università Gregoriana, 1992.
Anon. *Gregorianum* 74 No 1:198 1993.

Finch, Ann, ed.
Journey to the light: spirituality as we mature. New City Press, 1993.
Mathews, Edward G. *Diakonia* 26 no 2:141 1993.

Finegan, Jack.
The archaeology of the New Testament. Princeton University Press, 1992.
Cunningham, Lawrence S, 1935-. *Comm* 120:27 Je 4 1993.
Heiser, W Charles. *TheolDgst* 40:162 Sum 1993.

Finke, Roger, and Stark, Rodney.
The churching of America 1776-1990: winners and losers in our religious economy. Rutgers University Press, n.d.
McMannus, E Leo. *Nat Cath Rep* 29:36 F 5 1993.
The churching of America 1776-1990. Rutgers University Press, n.d.
Kelly, James R, 1937-. *Comm* 120:27-29 Ap 23 1993.

Finley, Mitchel B.
Everybody has a guardian angel. Crossroad, 1993.
Graham, William C. *Nat Cath Rep* 29:36 S 10 1993.
Higgins, James J. *Liguorian* 81:69 D 1993.
Living scripture (Cycle A): reproducible lectioanry-based reflections on Sunday scriptures. Sheed and Ward, 1992.
Borgia, Francis. *Mod Lit* 20:39 Je-Jl 1993.
Your family in focus. Ave Maria Press, n.d.
Dollen, Charles. *Priest* 49:48 Je 1993.
Apathy, Andy. *Nat Cath Rep* 29:16 S 24 1993.

Finn, Jerome K.
Building youth ministry in the parish. St Mary's Press, 1993.
Anon. *Church* 9:42 Sum 1993.

Finn, Thomas Macy.
Early Christian Baptism and the catechumenate. The Liturgical Press, 1992.
Duffy, Regis A. *Worship* 67:181-182 Mr 1993.
Johnson, Maxwell E. *Worship* 67:182-184 Mr 1993.
Heiser, W Charles. *TheolDgst* 39:361-362 Wint 1992.
Heiser, W Charles. *TheolDgst* 39:361-362 Wint 1992.
McLeod, Frederick G. *TheolStds* 54:195-196 Mr 1993.
Kavanagh, Aidan. *CHist* 79:311-312 Ap 1993.

Finnegan, William.
A complicated war: the harrowing of Mozambique. University of California Press, n.d.
Cooper, Rand Richards. *Comm* 119:18-20 D 18 1992.

Finnis, John.
Moral absolutes: tradition, revision and truth. Catholic University of America Press, 1991.
Hartley, J. *Linacre* 59:88-91 N 1992.
Bradley, Gerard V. *New Oxford Rev* 60:30-31 S 1993.
Hoose, Bernard. *Heythrop* 34:463-464 O 1993.

Fiorenza, Elisabeth Schüssler, 1938-.
But she said. Beacon, 1992.
Coll, Regina. *Nat Cath Rep* 29:27 F 5 1993.
Harrington, Daniel J. *America* 168:35 F 6 1993.
Bergant, Dianne. *TheolStds* 54:344-345 Je 1993.
Heiser, W Charles. *TheolDgst* 40:86 Spr 1993.
Senior, Donald. *BibleT* 31:314 S 1993.
Discipleship of equals. SCM, n.d.
Hebblethwaite, Margaret, 1951-. *Tablet* 247:1300-1301 O 9 1993.
Revelation, vision of a just world. Fortress, 1991.
Bernas, Casimir. *Cist Stud* 27 No 4:[84]-[85] 1992.
Harrington, Daniel J. *America* 168:35 F 6 1993.
Simoens, Y. *NRT* 115:113 Ja-F 1993.

Fiorenza, Francis Schüssler, 1938-, and Galvin, John P, 1944-, eds.
Systematic theology, Roman Catholic perspective. Gill and Macmillan, 1992.
Tolhurst, Joseph. *Priests & People* 6:360 Ag-S 1992.
Draper, Anthony. *Doctr Life* 43:56-58 Ja 1993.
Systematic theology. Fortress Press, 1991.
McLeod, Frederick G. *RRel* 52:311-312 Mr-Ap 1993.
Powers, Joseph M. *TheolStds* 54:173-175 Mr 1993.
Rocca, Gregory. *Thomist* 57:305-308 Ap 1993.
Galot, Jean. *Gregorianum* 74 no 3:579-580 1993.
Systematic theology. Gill and Macmillan, 1991.
Honner, John. *Pacifica* 6:353-354 O 1993.

Firestone, Reuven.
Journeys in holy lands: the evolution of the Abraham-Ishmael legends in Islamic exegesis. State University of New York Press, 1990.
Sonn, Tamara. *JEcumen Stds* 29:129-130 Wint 1992.

Fischer, Bonifatius.
Die lateinischen Evangelien bis zum 10. Jahrhundert. Herder, 1991.
Cody, Aelred. *CBQ* 55:366-367 Ap 1993.

Fishbane, Michael, and Tov, Emmanuel.
Sha'arei Talmon: studies in Hebrew Bible. Eisenbrauns, 1992.
Lust, Johan. *Eph Theol Lovan* 78:404-406 D 1992.

Fisher, Eugene J, ed.
The Jewish roots of Christian liturgy. Paulist Press, 1990.
Spinks, J. *Heythrop* 34:81-82 Ja 1993.

Fritsch, Albert.
Eco-Church. Resource Publications, 1992.
Covino, Paul. *Past Mus* 17:52 Ag-S 1993.

Fritz, Maureena.
God's surprising presence: praying with the Hebrew Scriptures. Saint Mary's Press, 1992.
Stuhlmueller, Carroll. *BibleT* 31:119 Mr 1993.

Frölich, Walter.
The letters of St Anselm of Canterbury, vol I. Cistercian Publications, n.d.
Meredith, Anthony, et al. *Way* 33:163 Ap 1993.

From pain to hope.
Publications Service Canadian Conference of Catholic Bishops, n.d.
Campbell, Joe. *Can Cath Rev* 11:30-31 My 1993.

Frontain, Raymond-Jean, and Wojcik, Jan, eds.
Old Testament women in western literature. University of Central Arkansas Press, 1991.
Heiser, W Charles. *TheolDgst* 39:377 Wint 1992.

Frosini, G.
Impegno cristiano. Ed Paoline, 1992.
Volpe, L. *NRT* 115:578 Jl-Ag 1993.

Frossard, André.
Il mondo di Giovanni Paolo II. Piemme, 1992.
Caprile, Giovanni. *Civilta* 3:101 Jl 3 1993.

Frost, Brian.
The politics of peace. Darton, Longman & Todd, 1991.
St Lawrence, Brenda. *SIDIC* 26 no 1:32 1993.

Frost, David.
An autobiography: part 1. HarperCollins, n.d.
Arnold-Foster, Val. *Tablet* 247:1197-1198 S 18 1993.

Frost, Kate Gartner.
Holy delight: typology, numerology, and autobiography in Donne's Devotions upon emergent occasions. Princeton University Press, 1990.
Labriola, Albert C. *Relig Lit* 25:75-80 Spr 1993.

Fryer, Jonathan.
Eye of the camera: a life of Christopher Isherwood. Allison & Busby, n.d.
Bergonzi, Bernard, 1929-. *Tablet* 247:1074-1075 Ag 21 1993.

Fu, Wang.
Propos d'un ermite. Ed du Cerf, 1992.
Masson, J. *NRT* 115:601-602 Jl-Ag 1993.

Fuchs, Lucy.
Gifts and giving. Alba House, 1991.
Chen, Sheryl Frances. *Cist Stud* 28 no 2:[41] 1993.

Fuenmayor, Amadeo de, et al.
El itinerario jurídico del Opus Dei: Historia y defensa de un carisma. EUNSA, 1982.
Wiel, C van de. *Eph Theol Lovan* 78:492-493 D 1992.

Fuenmayor, Amadoe de, et al.
L'itinéraire juridique de l'Opus Dei. Desclée, 1992.
Wiel, C van de. *Eph Theol Lovan* 78:492-493 D 1992.

Fujita, Neil S.
Japan's encounter with Christianity: the Catholic mission in pre-modern Japan. Paulist Press, 1991.
Cooper, Michael. *Heythrop* 34:334-335 Jl 1993.

Fuller, Christopher John.
The camphor flame. Princeton University Press, 1992.
Heiser, W Charles. *TheolDgst* 40:163 Sum 1993.

Fulton, John.
The tragedy of belief: division, politics, and religion in Ireland. Oxford Clarendon Press, 1991.
Rafferty, Oliver. *Heythrop* 34:348-350 Jl 1993.

Fung, Raymond.
Evangelistically yours. World Council of Churches, 1992.
Bowes, Keith. *Pacifica* 6:363-365 O 1993.

Funk, Charles Earle:
Heavens to Betsy! and other curious sayings. Perennial, n.d.
Hunt, George W, 1937-. *America* 168:2 F 27 1993.

Furey, Robert J.
The joy of kindness. Crossroad, n.d.
Graham, William C. *Nat Cath Rep* 29:36 S 10 1993.

Furuya, Yasua, and Ohki, Hideo.
Nihon no shingaku. Jordan Press, 1989.
Drummond, Richard H. *JEcumen Stds* 29:115-116 Wint 1992.

Fussell, Edwin Sill, 1922-.
The Catholic side of Henry James. Cambridge University Press, 1993.
Chervin, Ronda. *New Oxford Rev* 60:30-31 N 1993.

The future of the Catholic Church in America: major papers of the Virgil Michel Symposium.
The Liturgical Press, 1991.
Riley, Patrick J. *Emmanuel* 99:357-358 Jl-Ag 1993.

G

Gaboriau, Florent.
Progrès de la théologie: a quelles conditions? FAC-Editions, 1991.
Galot, Jean. *Gregorianum* 74 No 1:167 1993.

Gabriele, Edward F.
Prayers for dawn and dusk. St Mary's Press, 1992.
Borgia, Francis. *Mod Lit* 19:41 D 1992-Ja 1993.

Gaebelein, Frank E, ed.
The expositor's Bible commentary with the new international version of the Holy Bible in twelve volumes, Deuteronomy-2 Samuel [v3]. Zondervan Publishing House, 1992.
Heiser, W Charles. *TheolDgst* 40:161 Sum 1993.

Gaffney, James William, 1931-.
Augustine Baker's inner light: a study in English recusant spirituality. University of Scranton Press, 1989.
Scott, Geoffrey. *Heythrop* 34:337-338 Jl 1993.

Gafo, Javier, ed.
Etica y ecología. UPCO, 1991.
Cultrera, Francesco. *Civilta* 144:508-509 Mr 6 1993.

Gager, John G, ed.
Curse tablets and binding spells from the ancient world. Oxford University Press, 1992.
Smith, Mark S. *OTA* 16:405 Je 1993.

Gaines, Ernest J.
A lesson before dying. Knopf, 1993.
Samway, Patrick H, 1939-. *America* 169:22 Ag 28-S 4 1993.

Gairdner, William D.
North of the border. Stoddart Publishing, n.d.
Farrell, Michael J. *Register* 69:5 Mr 21 1993.
The war against the family. Stoddart, n.d.
Eady, Robert. *Can Cath Rev* 11:25-26 S 1993.

Gal, Zvi.
Lower Galilee during the Iron Age. Eisenbrauns, 1992.
Edelman, Diana V. *OTA* 16:406 Je 1993.

Galambush, Julie.
Jerusalem in the Book of Ezekiel. Scholars, 1992.
Gossai, Hemchand. *OTA* 16:180 F 1993.
Lust, Johan. *Eph Theol Lovan* 69:161 Ap 1993.

Galatariotou, Catia.
The making of a saint: the life, times and sanctification of Neophytos the recluse. Cambridge University Press, 1991.
Munitz, Joseph A. *Heythrop* 34:209-212 Ap 1993.

Galbraith, John Kenneth, 1908-.
The culture of contentment. Houghton Mifflin, 1992.
Dugger, William M. *RSocEcon* 51:108-111 Spr 1993.

Gale, Richard M.
On the nature and existence of God. Cambridge University Press, 1991.
Sell, Alan P F. *IJPS* 1:143-146 Mr 1993.
Dodds, Michael J. *Thomist* 57:317-321 Ap 1993.

Galea, Michael, and Ciarlò, Canon John, eds.
St. Paul in Malta. Veritas, 1992.
Farrugia, E G. *Civilta* 3:196-197 Jl 17 1993.

Galenson, Walter.
Labor and economic growth in five Asian countries. Praeger, n.d.
Senser, Robert A, 1921-. *Comm* 120:24-25 Ja 15 1993.

Galerón, Soledad, et al, eds.
Prophetic vision: pastoral reflections on the national pastoral plan for Hispanic ministry. MACC, 1992.
Davis, Kenneth. *RRel* 52:299 Mr-Ap 1993.
Vision profetica/prophetic vision. Sheed and Ward, 1992.
Feliciano, Teo. *Church* 9:61 Spr 1993.

Galgan, Gerald J.
God and subjectivity. Peter Lang, 1990.
Martinez, Roy. *Laval Theol Phil* 49:166-167 F 1993.

Galimard, Pierre.
Da 6 a 11 anni: Sviluppo dell intelligenza, maturazione affettiva, scoperta della vita sociale, confronti familiari. Ancora, 1991.
Baragli, Enrico. *Civilta* 144:102 Ja 2 1993.

Galin, Alice, ed.
American Catholic higher education: essential documents, 1967-1990. University of Notre Dame Press, n.d.
Fussell, Edwin, 1922-. *New Oxford Rev* 60:26-30 S 1993.

Galindo, Florencio.
El protestantismo fundamentalista. Verbo Divino, 1992.
Anon. *Teol Vida* 34 no 1-2:158-159 1993.
Valle, Luis del. *Christus* 58:63 S 1993.

Galindo Rodrigo, José Antonio.
Compendio de la Gracia. La gracia, expresión de Dios en el hombre. Ediciones Edicep, 1991.
Ladaria, Luis F. *Gregorianum* 74 no 3:578-579 1993.

Galino Carrillo, Ángeles, et al.
Personalización educativa. Génesis y estado actual. Ediciones Rialp, 1991.
Lasala, Fernando de. *Gregorianum* 74 no 2:400-402 1993.

Gall, Robert Le.
La messe au fil de ses rites. no publisher given, n.d.
Anon. *Notitiae* 29:87-88 Ja-F 1993.

Gallagher, John A.
Time past, time future: an historical study of Catholic moral theology. Paulist, 1990.
McCool, Gerald A. *CHist* 79:499-501 Jl 1993.

Gallagher, Michael Paul, 1939-.
Laws of heaven. Ticknor & Fields, 1992.
Mayeski, Mary Anne. *America* 168:27+ F 20 1993.
Heiser, W Charles. *TheolDgst* 40:63 Spr 1993.
Losing God. Twenty-Third Publications, n.d.
Cunningham, Lawrence S, 1935-. *Comm* 120:26 Mr 26 1993.
Struggles of faith. The Columba Press, 1990.
Pinnington, Judith E. *JEcumen Stds* 29:110 Wint 1992.

Galli, Giancarlo.
Mattioli: Il gattopardo della banca commerciale Italiana. Rizzoli, 1991.
Salvini, Gianpaola. *Civilta* 3:97 Jl 3 1993.

Gallie, W B.
Understanding war. Routledge, 1991.
Hoose, Bernard. *Heythrop* 34:465-466 O 1993.

Gallop, David.
Parmenides of Elea, fragments: a text and translation. University of Toronto Press, 1991.
Hughes, Gerard J. *Heythrop* 34:323 Jl 1993.

Gallup, George, Jr, and Jones, Timothy.
The saints among us: how the spirituality committed are changing our world.
Morehouse Publishing, 1992.
Impastato, Fara. *Sisters* 65:143 Mr 1993.

Galot, Jean.
Abba, Father, we long to see your face. Alba House, 1992.
Heiser, W Charles. *TheolDgst* 40:163 Sum 1993.
Abba, father. Alba House, 1992.
Dollen, Charles. *Priest* 49:48 Ja 1993.
Anon. *Gregorianum* 74 No 1:196 1993.
Il cuore di Cristo. Seconda edizione. Desclée de Brouwer, 1953.
Anon. *Gregorianum* 74 no 2:411 1993.
Saint Joseph. Editions Sursum, 1991.
Bedard, Mariette. *CahiersJos* 41:137-138 Ja-Je 1993.

Gamba, Ulderico, ed.
Il fascino del Sacro nella cultura moderna. Gregoriana, 1992.
Vanzan, Piersandro. *Civilta* 3:312-313 Ag 7-21 1993.

Gambero, Luigi.
Maria nel pensiero dei Padri della Chiesa. Ed Paoline, 1991.
Caprile, Giovanni. *Civilta* 144:202-203 Ja 16 1993.

Gammie, John G, and Perdue, Leo G, eds.
The sage in Israel and the Ancient Near East. Eisenbrauns, 1990.
Gladson, Jerry A. *CBQ* 55:196-197 Ja 1993.

Gandolfo, Anita.
Testing the faith. Greenwood Press, 1992.
Messbarger, Paul. *Relig Lit* 25:81-85 Spr 1993.
Heiser, W Charles. *TheolDgst* 40:163-164 Sum 1993.

Gandt, François de, et Souffrin, Pierre, eds.
La physique d'Aristote et les conditions d'une science de la nature. Vrin, 1991.
Destrée, Pierre. *RPhil Louvain* 91:143-145 F 1993.

Gangemi, A.
I racconti post nel vangelo di S Giovanni. Galatea Editrice, 1989.
Simoens, Y. *NRT* 115:110-111 Ja-F 1993.

Ganss, George E.
The spiritual exercises of Saint Ignatius: a translation and commentary. Loyola University Press, 1992.
O'Brien, Edward C. *RRel* 52:473-474 My-Je 1993.

Gantoy, Robert, and Swaeles, Romain.
The days of the Lord: the liturgical year. Liturgical Press, n.d.
Sands, Ernest. *Tablet* 247:725 Je 5 1993.

Garber, Marjorie.
Vested interests: cross-dressing and cultural anxiety. Routledge, Chapman and Hall, 1992.
Mulryan, John. *Cithara* 32:65-66 N 1992.

García-Dominiguez, L M.
Las afecciones desordenadas. Sal Terrae, 1992.
Renard, L-J. *NRT* 115:593 Jl-Ag 1993.

García-Moreno, Antonio.
Sentido del dolor en Job. Seminario Conciliar, 1990.
Schoors, A. *Eph Theol Lovan* 78:424 D 1992.
Rybolt, John E. *OTA* 16:174-175 F 1993.
Galot, Jean. *Gregorianum* 74 no 2:406 1993.

García-Murga Vázquez, José Ramón.
El Dios del amor y de la paz. Tratado Teológico de Dios desde la reflexion sobre su Bondad. UPCO Departamento de Publicaciones Universidad Comillas, 1991.
Pastor, Felix-Alejandro. *Gregorianum* 74 no 2:371-372 1993.

García Archilla, Aurelio A.
The theology of history and apologetic historiography in Heinrich Bullinger. Mellen Research University Press, 1992.
Heiser, W Charles. *TheolDgst* 40:164 Sum 1993.

García de Haro, Ramon.
La vida cristiana. Curso de teología moral fundamental. Universidad de Navarra, 1992.
Zalba, Marcelino. *Gregorianum* 74 no 2:378-380 1993.

García Martínez, Florentino.
Qumran and Apocalyptic: studies on the Aramaic texts from Qumran. E J Brill, 1992.
Lust, Johan. *Eph Theol Lovan* 69:169-170 Ap 1993.
Textos de Qumrán. Editorial Trotta, 1992.
Lust, Johan. *Eph Theol Lovan* 69:170-171 Ap 1993.

García y García, Antonio, ed.
Estudios juridico-canonicos: commemorativos del primer cincuentenario de la facultad de derecho canonico en Salamanca (1940-89). Publicaciones Universidad Pontificia, 1991.
McIntyre, John P. *Jurist* 51 no 2:512-513 1991.

Garde, Judith N.
Old English poetry in medieval Christian perspective. D S Brewer, 1991.
Tiller, Ken. *Relig Lit* 25:95-96 Spr 1993.

Gardía-Lomas, J M, ed.
Ejercicios espirituales y mondo de hoy. Sal Terrae, 1992.
Renard, L-J. *NRT* 115:592-593 Jl-Ag 1993.

Gardies, Jean-Louis.
Le raisonnement par l'absurde. Presses universitaires de France, 1991.
Kalianowski, Georges. *RPhil Louvain* 91:517-519 Ag 1993.

Gardiner, Harold C.
Edmund Campion. Ignatius Press, 1992.
Myers, Rawley. *HPR* 93:75 My 1993.

Garijo-Guembe, Miguel M.
La comunión de los santos: fundamento, esencia y estructura de la Iglesia. Editorial Herder, 1991.
Lago Alba, Luis. *Cien Tom* 119:608-609 S-D 1992.

Garner, R J.
The grafter's handbook. Cassell, n.d.
Taylor, Patrick. *Tablet* 247:375 Mr 20 1993.

Garrard, Richard.
Lent with St Mark: forty days of prayer. Kevin Mayhew, n.d.
Hollings, Michael. *Tablet* 247:278 F 27 1993.

Garrett, Duane.
Rethinking Genesis: the sources and authorship of the First Book of the Pentateuch. Baker, 1991.
Labonté, Ghislain R. *OTA* 16:417 Je 1993.

Garrido, Pablo María.
San Juan de la Cruz y Francisco de Yepes. Sígueme, 1989.
García Prada, José María. *Cien Tom* 119:624 S-D 1992.

Garrigues, Jean-Michel, and Legrez, Jean.
Moines dans l'assemblée des Fidèles. Beauchesne, 1992.
Kardong, Terence G. *CHist* 79:94-95 Ja 1993.

Garsiel, Moshe.
Biblical names: a literary study of Midrashic derivations and Puns. BarIlan University, 1991.
Sweeney, Marvin A. *OTA* 16:158-159 F 1993.

Garstein, Oskar.
Rome and the Counter-Reformation in Scandinavia: the age of Gustavus Adolphus and Queen Christina of Sweden, 1622-1656. E J Brill, 1992.
Rosa, Susan. *CHist* 79:83-88 Ja 1993.

Garzonio, Ghiara Lucia.
Senza vaotarsi indietro: vita di S Agnese d'Assisi. LEF, 1991.
Forlizzi, G. *Civilta* 143:534 D 5 1992.

Gasero, Russell L.
Historical directory of the Reformed Church in America, 1628-1992. Eerdmans, 1992.
Heiser, W Charles. *TheolDgst* 40:63 Spr 1993.

De Gasperi e la scelta occidentale: La strategia del Centrismo; Vol; XVV: 1950-1953.
Nuova Cei, 1991-1992.
Caprile, Giovanni. *Civilta* 143:531-532 D 5 1992.

Gasser, Ulrich.
Ot, Der Diener Gottes Peter Rigler (1796-1873): Beiträge zu einer Lebensbeschreibung. Konferenzblatt, 1989.
Bacher, Alfred. *Gregorianum* 74 No 1:182-184 1993.

Gassmann, Günther, ed.
Fifth forum on bilateral conversations: international bilateral dialogues, 1965-1991. World Council of Churches Publications, 1992.
Gros, Jeffrey, 1938-. *JEcumen Stds* 29:267 Spr 1992.

Gates, Henry Louis, Jr.
Loose canons. Oxford University Press, 1992.
Castronovo, David. *Comm* 119:22-23 D 18 1992.
Giles, James E. *CrossCurr* 43:259-260 Sum 1993.

Gatto, John Taylor.
Dumbing us down: the hidden curriculum of compulsory schooling. New Society Publishers, 1992.
Krason, Stephen M. *SocJust* 84:93-94 My-Je 1993.

Gaudiose, Dorothy M.
Mary's house. Alba House, n.d.
Dollen, Charles. *Priest* 49:48 Je 1993.

Gaudoin-Parker, Michael L.
The real presence through the ages. Alba House, n.d.
Dollen, Charles. *Priest* 49:56 Ag 1993.

Gaughan, J Anthony.
Alfred O'Rahilly III: controversialist, Part I: social reformer. Kingdom Books, n.d.
Ryan, Laurence, Bp, 1931-. *Furrow* 44:54-55 Ja 1993.

Gauvreau, Gustave.
Une belle église. Deusxième édition. Paroisse Saint-Joseph, 1989.
Bedard, Mariette. *CahiersJos* 41:131-133 Ja-Je 1993.
Paroisse St-Joseph. 100 ans 1892-1992. Fabrique Saint-Joseph, 1992.
Bedard, Mariette. *CahiersJos* 41:132-133 Ja-Je 1993.

Gauvreau, Michael.
The evangelical century: college and creed in English Canada from the Great Revival to the Great Depression. McGill-Queen's University Press, 1991.
Marshall, David B. *CHist* 79:583-584 Jl 1993.

Gavlas, Kathleen.
The beautiful gate rosary. Our Sunday Visitor, n.d.
Higgins, James J. *Liguorian* 81:69 Ap 1993.

Gavron, Jeremy.
The last elephant. HarperCollins, n.d.
Walton, James. *Tablet* 247:584 My 8 1993.

Gay, Craig M.
With liberty and justice for whom? The recent evangelical debate over capitalism. Eerdmans, 1991.
Shaffer, Thomas F. *Amer J Juris* 37:363-365 1992.
Markovic, Matthew. *New Oxford Rev* 60:28 Jl-Ag 1993.

Geisler, Norman L.
Miracles and the modern mind: a defense of biblical miracles. Baker Book House, 1991.
Heiser, W Charles. *TheolDgst* 40:63 Spr 1993.
Thomas Aquinas: an evangelical appraisal. Baker Book House, 1991.
Wawrykow, Joseph. *Thomist* 57:529-532 Jl 1993.

Gelabert Ballester, Martín.
Vivir como Cristo: antropología teológica. Ed San Pio X, 1992.
Espeja, Jesús. *Cien Tom* 119:610 S-D 1992.

Gelander, Shamai.
David and his God: religious ideas as reflected in Biblical historiography and literature. Simor, 1991.
Begg, Christopher T. *OTA* 15:498 O 1992.

Gelb, Norman, ed.
Jonathan Carver's travels through America 1766-68. Wiley, n.d.
Walton, James. *Tablet* 247:584-585 My 8 1993.

Gelber, L, et al, eds.
Edith Stein: Einführung in die Philosophie. Herder, 1991.
Toubeau, A. *NRT* 115:276-277 Mr-Ap 1993.

Gelber, L, and Linssen, Michael, eds.
The hidden life: essays/meditations/spiritual texts the collected works of Edith Stein. ICS Publications, n.d.
Slanina, Mary Gerarda. *Can Cath Rev* 11:28-29 Jl-Ag 1993.

Gellman, Marc, and Hartman, Thomas.
Where does God live? Triumph Books, n.d.
Riley, David M. *Catechist* 27:17 S 1993.

Gellner, Ernest.
Postmodernism, reason and religion. Routledge, 1992.
Haldane, John. *New Blckfrs* 74:428-429 S 1993.

Gelman, S A, and Byrnes, J P, eds.
Perspectives on language and thought: interrelations in development. Cambridge University Press, 1992.
Moran, Aidan. *IJPS* 1:165-166 Mr 1993.

Gelston, Anthony.
The Eucharistic prayer of Addai and Mari. Oxford University Press, 1992.
Heiser, W Charles. *TheolDgst* 39:363 Wint 1992.
Cutrone, Emmanuel J. *Worship* 67:282-284 My 1993.

Gemeinwohl und Eigennutz: wirtschaftliches Handeln in Veranwortung für die Zukunft.
Mohn, 1991.
Kuppler, B. *Civilta* 144:511-513 Mr 6 1993.

Gentilcore, David.
From bishop to witch: the system of the sacred in early modern Terra d'Otranto. Manchester University Press, n.d.
Rosselli, John. *Tablet* 247:143 Ja 30 1993.

Gentili, Antonio.
Se non diventerete come donne: simboli religiosi del femminile. Ancora, 1991.
Vanzan, P. *Civilta* 143:528-529 D 5 1992.
Si vous ne devenez comme des femmes: symboles religieux du féminin. Ed Paulines, 1991.
Vanzan, P. *Civilta* 143:528-529 D 5 1992.

Gentles, Ian, ed.
A time to choose life: women, abortion, and human rights. Stoddart Publishing, n.d.
Campbell, Joe. *Can Cath Rev* 11:26 F 1993.

George, Francis E.
Inculturation and ecclesial communion: culture and church in the teaching of Pope John Paul II. Urbaniana University Press, 1990.
Wolanin, Adam. *Gregorianum* 73 No 4:762-763 1992.

Georgi, Dieter.
Remembering the poor: the history of Paul's collection for Jerusalem. Abingdon Press, 1992.
Heiser, W Charles. *TheolDgst* 40:63 Spr 1993.
Theocracy: in Paul's praxis and theology. Fortress Press, 1991.
Rogers, Patrick. *CBQ* 54:777-778 O 1992.
Lubomirski, Hieczyslaw. *Gregorianum* 74 No 1:154-156 1993.

Gerhart, Mary.
Genre choices, gender questions. University of Oklahoma Press, n.d.
Appleyard, Joseph A. *America* 169:27-28 S 11 1993.

Gerl, H-B.
Unerbittliches Licht. Matthias-Grünewald-Verlag, 1991.
Toubeau, A. *NRT* 114:935-936 N-D 1992.

Gersh, Stephen, and Kannengiesser, Charles, eds.
Platonism in late antiquity. University of Notre Dame Press, 1992.
Barnes, Michel R. *Cist Stud* 28 no 2:[48]-[49] 1993.

Gerstenberger, Erhard S.
Jahwe—ein patriarchaler Gott? Traditionelles Gottesbild und feministische Theologie. Kohlhammer, 1988.
O'Connor, Kathleen M. *CBQ* 55:335-336 Ap 1993.

Gerstenmaier, Brigitte, and Gerstenmaier, Eugene.
Zwei können widerstehen. Bouvier, 1992.
Bleistein, Roman, 1928-. *Stimm Zeit* 211:143-144 F 1993.

Gervais, Pierre, ed.
La pratique des Exercices spirituels d'Ignace de Loyola actes du symposium de Bruxelles. Editions de l'Institut d'etudes theologiques, 1991.
Partos, L. *Lumen* 48:234 Je 1993.

Die Geschichte des Kartäuserordens, 2 vols.
Edwin Mellen Press, 1991.
Renard, L J. *NRT* 115:309-310 Mr-Ap 1993.

Gesteira, Manuel.
La eucaristía misterio de comunión. Ed Sígueme, 1992.
Bandera, Armando. *Cien Tom* 119:414-415 My-Ag 1992.

Gesy, Lawrence.
Today's destructive cults and movements. Our Sunday Visitor, n.d.
Dollen, Charles. *Priest* 49:48 O 1993.

Getz, Lorine M, and Costa, Ruy O, eds.
Struggles for solidarity. Fortress Press, 1992.
Heiser, W Charles. *TheolDgst* 39:388 Wint 1992.
Anon. *NRT* 115:626 Jl-Ag 1993.

Ghini, Emanuela.
Lettera ai Colosei: commento pastorale. Edizioni Dehoniane, 1990.
Farahian, Edmond. *Gregorianum* 73 No 4:754-755 1992.

Giammusso, Salvatore.
Lettere dalla Sicilia a S Alfonso. Collegium S Alfonsi de Urbe, 1991.
Caprile, Giovanni. *Civilta* 143:539-540 D 5 1992.

Giannantonio, Pompeo, ed.
Alfonso M de'Liguori e la società civile del suo tempo: Atti del Convegno internazionale per il Bicentenario della morte del santo. Leo S Olschki Editore, 1990.
Dooley, B. *CHist* 78:664-665 O 1992.

Gianni, Andrea.
L'istruzione religiosa nelle scuole italiane. Ed Paoline, 1991.
Brunetta, Giuseppe. *Civilta* 2:206-207 Ap 17 1993.

Giannino, Alfonso.
La fiera dei ricordi: Cortometraggi su Mussomeli e mussomelesi. Lussografica, 1990.
Capizzi, Carmelo. *Civilta* 2:618-619 Je 19 1993.

Gibbs, Robert.
Correlations in Rosenzweig and Levinas. Princeton University Press, 1992.
Barber, Michael D. *Mod Schlmn* 70:234-236 Mr 1993.

Gibellini, R, and Rizzi, A, et al.
Teologie della liberazione. Editrice AVE, 1991.
Galot, Jean. *Gregorianum* 74 no 2:408 1993.

Gibert, P.
Petite histoire de l'exégèse biblique. Cerf, 1992.
Harvengt, A. *NRT* 115:246-247 Mr-Ap 1993.
Le récit biblique de rêve. Profac, 1990.
Anon. *NRT* 114:943 N-D 1992.

Giblin, Charles Homer.
The Book of Revelation. Liturgical, 1991.
Wansbrough, Henry. *Priests & People* 6:486 D 1992.
Aune, David E. *TheolStds* 54:342-344 Je 1993.
Gillman, Florence Morgan. *CBQ* 55:367 Ap 1993.

Gielen, Marlis.
Tradition und Theologie neutestamentlicher Haustafelethik. Hain, 1990.
Elliott, John H. *CBQ* 54:779-780 O 1992.

Giese, Vincent.
John Henry Newman heart to heart. New City Press, 1993.
Mathews, Edward G. *Diakonia* 26 no 2:141-142 1993.

Gil, Federico R Aznar.
La institucion matrimonial en la Hispania Cristiana bajo-medieval (1215-1563). Caja Salamanca, 1989.
Brundage, James A. *Jurist* 51 no 2:515-517 1991.

Gilbert, Ann, et al.
Liturgy models. Center for Learning, 1991.
Brown, David O. *Mod Lit* 20:36 My 1993.

Gilbert, Maurice.
Les louanges du Seigneur. Edime International, 1991.
Renard, L J. *NRT* 114:904 N-D 1992.
Ogni vivente dia lode al Signore: commento dei Salmi delle domeniche e delle feste, 3 voll. ADP, 1991-1992.
Scaiola, D. *Civilta* 143:641-642 D 19 1992.

Gilbert, Paul P.
Introduzione alla teologia medievale. Piemme, 1992.
Anon. *Gregorianum* 74 no 2:411 1993.
La semplicità del principio: intorduzine alla metafisica. Piemme, 1992.
Gilbert Paul P. *Gregorianum* 73 No 4:775-776 1992.

Gildea, Joseph.
Source book of self-discipline: a synthesis of moralia. Peter Lang Publishers, 1991.
Davies, Thomas X. *Cist Stud* 28 no 2:[51]-[52] 1993.

Gildea, Joseph, ed.
Peter of Waltham, remediarium conversorum. Associated University Presses, 1984.
Davis, Thomas X. *Cist Stud* 28 no 2:[51]-[52] 1993.

Giles, Paul.
American Catholic arts and fictions. Cambridge University Press, 1992.
Bankston, Carl L, III. *Comm* 120:28-30 F 26 1993.
Brogan, Jacqueline Vaught. *America* 168:19 My 15 1993.
Messbarger, Paul. *Relig Lit* 25:81-85 Spr 1993.
Heiser, W Charles. *TheolDgst* 40:164 Sum 1993.

Gill, Anton.
City of dreams. Bloomsbury, n.d.
Lejeune, Anthony. *Tablet* 247:1047 Ag 14 1993.
City of the horizon. Bloomsbury, n.d.
Lejeune, Anthony. *Tablet* 247:1047 Ag 14 1993.

Gillen, Gerard, and White, Harry, eds.
Music and the Church. Irish Academic Press, n.d.
Egan-Buffet, Maire. *Furrow* 44:321-322 My 1993.

Gillespie, V Bailey.
The experience of faith. Religious Education Press, 1988.
Godin, A. *Lumen* 48:356 S 1993.

Gilley, Sheridan.
Newman and his age. Christian Classics, 1991.
Heiser, W Charles. *TheolDgst* 40:63-64 Spr 1993.

Gillman, Florence Morgan.
Women who knew Paul. Liturgical, 1992.
Reid, Barbara E. *New Theol Rev* 6:113-114 F 1993.
Murphy, Anne. *Way* 33:77-78 Ja 1993.
McDonald, Patricia M. *Living Light* 29:95-96 Sum 1993.

Gillman, John.
Possessions and the life of faith, a reading of Luke-Acts. Collegeville, 1991.
Wansbrough, Henry. *Priests & People* 6:435-436 N 1992.

Gimaret, D.
La doctrine d'al-Ash'arî. Ed du Cerf, 1990.
Scheuer, J. *NRT* 115:606 Jl-Ag 1993.

Ginkel, C Van, and Midden, P J Van, eds.
Psalmenstudie Prof Nic Ridderbos en het boek der Psalmen. Kok Pharos, 1991.
Begg, Christopher T. *OTA* 15:501 O 1992.

Giordano, Pasquale T.
Awakening to mission: the Philippine Catholic Church 1965-1981. New Day Publishers, 1988.
Pilapil, V. *CHist* 78:702-703 O 1992.

Giorgianni, Gianni.
Gesù a rischio: un confronto con la radicalità del Vangelo. Ed Paoline, 1992.
Giachi, Gualberto. *Civilta* 144:408-409 F 20 1993.

Girard, René, 1923-.
A theater of envy: William Shakespeare. Oxford University Press, 1991.
Cox, John D. *Relig Lit* 24:85-90 Aut 1992.

Girardi, Mario.
Gioia: una città nella storia e civiltà di Puglia. Schena, 1992.
Ferrua, Antonio. *Civilta* 3:320 Ag 7-21 1993.

Giraud, Marcel.
A history of French Louisiana: Volume V: the Company of the Indies 1723-1731. Louisiana State University Press, 1991.
O'Neill, C. *CHist* 78:681-684 O 1992.

Girault, René.
Introduction aux religions orientales. Droguet et Ardant, 1991.
Evrard, P. *NRT* 115:597-598 Jl-Ag 1993.
Scheurer, J. *Lumen* 48:116 Mr 1993.

Girouard, Mark.
Town and country. Yale University Press, n.d.
Stockers, Mark. *Tablet* 247:142-143 Ja 30 1993.

Girzone, Joseph F.
Joshua in the Holy Land. Macmillan, 1987.
Finley, Mitchel B. *St Anth* 100:14 Ja 1993.
Feister, John Bookser. *Nat Cath Rep* 29:37 My 28 1993.
Harter, Michael. *America* 169:21 N 6 1993.

Gitay, Yehoshua.
Isaiah and his audience. Van Gorcum, 1991.
Franke, Chris. *OTA* 16:178 F 1993.

Giuliano, Mario, and Scovazzi, Tullio, et al.
Diritto Internazionale. Giuffre, 1991.
Mastrojeni, G. *Civilta* 3:194-195 Jl 17 1993.

Giusta o inquista? Considerazioni sol carattere morale della guerra del Golfo.
Anabasi, 1992.
Joblin, Joseph, 1920-. *Civilta* 2:302 My 1 1993.

Giustinelli, Franco.
Razzismo, scuola, società. La Nuova Italia, 1991.
Katunarich, S.M. *Civilta* 3:445-446 S 4 1993.

Glasser, William.
The quality school: managing students without coercion. HarperCollins, 1992.
Sweeney, Patricia James. *Momentum* 24:78-79 S-O 1993.

Glassner, Gottfried.
Vision eines auf Verheissung gegründeten Jerusalem: textanalytische Studien zu Jesaja 54. Osterreichische Katholisches Bibelwerk, 1991.
Begg, Christopher T. *OTA* 15:507-508 O 1992.

Glazebrook, Philip.
The road to Khiva. Harvill, n.d.
Hodgkin, E C. *Tablet* 246:1625 D 19-26 1992.

Gleason, Norma.
Proverbs from around the world. Citadel, n.d.
Hunt, George W, 1937-. *America* 169:2 O 2 1993.

Glemma, Thaddeus, and Bogaczewicz, Stanislaus, eds.
Volume VI: Iulius Ruggieri (1565-1568). Institutem Historicum Polonicum Romae, 1991.
Pease, Neal. *CHist* 79:334-335 Ap 1993.

Glendinning, Victoria.
Trollope. Random House, n.d.
Coren, Michael. *Can Cath Rev* 11:4-6 F 1993.

Gless, Darryl, and Smith, Barbara Herrnstein, eds.
The politics of liberal education. Duke University Press, 1992.
Giles, James E. *CrossCurr* 43:257-258 Sum 1993.

Glueckert, Leopold G.
Between two amnesties: former political prisoners and exiles in the Roman revolution of 1848. Garland Publishing, Inc, 1991.
Cummings, Raymond L. *CHist* 79:145 Ja 1993.

Gmünder, P, et al.
L'homme, son développement religieux: etude de structuralisme génétique. Ed du Cerf, 1991.
Prévost, Jean-Pierre. *NRT* 115:272-273 Mr-Ap 1993.

Gobry, Ivan.
Pythagore. Ed Universitaires, 1992.
Baudry, Gérard-Henry. *MSR* 50:72-73 Ja-Mr 1993.
Storia del monachesimo, vol I: le origini orientali: da sant'Antonio a san Basilio. Città Nuova, 1991.
Spidlik, Thomas. *Civilta* 2:411 My 15 1993.
Storia del monachesimo, vol II: Il tempo dell'espansione da san Colombano a san Bonifacio. Città Nuova, 1991.
Spidlik, Thomas. *Civilta* 2:411 My 15 1993.

Gochet, Paul, and Gribomont, Pascal.
Logique: vol I: Méthodes pour l'informatique fondamentale. Hermès, 1990.
Mpoto, Basile. *RPhil Louvain* 91:521-522 Ag 1993.

Godbeer, Richard.
The devil's dominion: magic and religion in early New England. Cambridge University Press, 1992.
Gildrie, R. *CHist* 78:680-681 O 1992.

Goedert, Valter M.
Orientações para Ministros Extraordinários da Comunhão. Edições Paulinas, 1992.
Silva, José Ariavaldo da. *REB* 53:485-491 Je 1993.

Goergen, Donald J.
The Jesus of Christian history. Liturgical Press, 1992.
Halleux, André de. *Eph Theol Lovan* 69:209 Ap 1993.
Heiser, W Charles. *TheolDgst* 40:64 Spr 1993.

Goergen, Donald J, ed.
Being a priest today. Liturgical, 1992.
Bedford, William J. *Church* 9:60-61 Spr 1993.
Brady, Ray. *Furrow* 44:381-383 Je 1993.
Candon, Cyprian. *Doctr Life* 43:375-376 Jl-Ag 1993.

Goethals, Gregor T.
The electronic golden calf: images, religion and the making of meaning. Cowley, n.d.
Wallace, James A, 1944-. *Liguorian* 81:43 O 1993.

Goettmann, Alphonse.
Dialogue on the path of initiation: an introduction to the life and thought of Karlfried Graf Dürckheim. Globe Press Books, 1992.
Heiser, W Charles. *TheolDgst* 39:359 Wint 1992.

Goewey, Jerrie Ann, and Goewey, Ken.
Families encouraging faith. Don Bosco Multimedia, n.d.
Hanlon, James. *Can Cath Rev* 11:31 O 1993.

Goff, Jacques Le.
Your money or your life. MIT Press, 1988.
Charron, Donna Card. *Mod Schlmn* 70:230-231 Mr 1993.

Goizueta, Roberto, ed.
We are a people! initiatives in Hispanic-American theology. Fortress Press, 1992.
Rodriguez, Jeannette. *RRel* 52:296-298 Mr-Ap 1993.

Golden, Renny.
The hour of the poor, the hour of women. Crossroad, n.d.
Murphy, Anne. *Way* 33:78 Ja 1993.

Golden, Stephanie.
The women outside: meanings and myths of homelessness. University of California Press, n.d.
Meehan, Bridget Mary. *New Oxford Rev* 60:31-32 My 1993.

Goldenberg, Naomi R.
Returning words to flesh: feminism, psychoanalysis, and the resurrection of the body. Beacon Press, 1992.
Craft, Carolyn M. *CrossCurr* 42:554-559 Wint 1992-1993.

Goldingay, John E.
Daniel. no publisher given, 1989.
Lust, Johan. *Eph Theol Lovan* 69:162 Ap 1993.

Goldman, Ari.
The search for God at Harvard. Ballantine Books, n.d.
McCloskey, Pat. *St Anth* 100:52 Ap 1993.

Goldman, Yohanan.
Prophétie et royauté au retour de l'exil. Vandehoeck and Ruprecht, 1992.
Begg, Christopher T. *OTA* 16:179 F 1993.

Goldsmith, Emanuel S, et al, eds.
The American Judaism of Mordecai M Kaplan. New York University Press, 1990.
Gillman, Neil. *CrossCurr* 43:110-114 Spr 1993.

Gómez-Heras, José M.G.
Religión y modernidad. La crisis del individualismo religioso de Lutero a Neitzsche. Monte de Piedad, 1986.
Salas Astrain, Ricardo. *RPhil Louvain* 91:510-511 Ag 1993.

Gómez García, Vito Tomás.
El Cardenal Fr Manuel García y Gil, OP Obispo de Badajoz y Arzobispo de Zaragoza (1802-1881). Valencia, 1990.
Barrado, J. *Cien Tom* 119:425-426 My-Ag 1992.

Gonen, Rivka.
Burial patterns and cultural diversity in late Bronze Age. Eisenbrauns, 1992.
Edelman, Diana V. *OTA* 16:406 Je 1993.

González, Justo L.
Out of every tribe and nation. Abingdon Press, 1992.
Heiser, W Charles. *TheolDgst* 40:164 Sum 1993.

González, Wenceslao.
La teoría de la referencia: Strawson y la filosofía analítica. Murcie, 1986.
Salas Astrain, Ricardo. *RPhil Louvain* 91:519-520 Ag 1993.

Gonzalez-Carvajal, Luis.
Nossa fé: Teologia para universitários. Loyola, 1992.
Libanio, Joao Batista. *Perspectiva* 24:393-394 S-D 1992.

González Faus, José Ignacio.
Ningún obispo impuesto. Santander, 1992.
Anon. *Christus* 58:91 Mr-Ap 1993.

González Núñez, A.
La Biblia: los autores, los libros, el mensaje. Ediciones Paulings, 1989.
Rodríguez, E. *Cien Tom* 119:409-410 My-Ag 1992.

Good news in a divided society: papers of the 1991 annual general meeting of the National Conference of Priests of Ireland.
Dominican Publications, 1992.
Linehan, D. *Doctr Life* 42:651-652 D 1992.

Goodhue, Thomas W.
Sharing the good news with children: stories for the common lectionary. St Anthony Messenger Press, n.d.
McCann, Deborah. *ReligTJ* 27:10 F 1993.
Sharing the good news with children. St Anthony Messenger Press, n.d.
Stamwitz, Alicia Von. *Liguorian* 81:70 Ap 1993.

Goodman, Arnold.
Tell them I'm on my way. Chapmans, n.d.
Shaw, Roy. *Tablet* 247:1196-1197 S 18 1993.

Goodman, Billy.
A kid's guide to how to save the planet. Avon Books, 1990.
Riley, David M. *Catechist* 26:14 F 1993.

Goodman, Lenn.
On justice: an essay in Jewish philosophy. L.E. Goodman, 1991.
Dougherty, Jude P, 1930-. *Crisis* 11:52-55 O 1993.

Goodwin, Carole.
Quicksilvers: ministering with junior high youth. Crossroad, n.d.
McCann, Deborah. *ReligTJ* 27:10 Ap-My 1993.
Dotterweich, Kass. *Liguorian* 81:68 S 1993.

Goodwin, Lawrence J.
Christian family celebrations: prayer services for special moments. Our Sunday Visitor, 1992.
McCann, Deborah. *ReligTJ* 27:9 Mr 1993.
Krawczyk, Marilyn Peters. *Mod Lit* 20:40 Ap 1993.

Goosen, Gideon.
Bringing churches together. Sheed & Ward, n.d.
Graham, William C. *Nat Cath Rep* 30:35 N 19 1993.

Gordon, Scott.
The history and philosophy of social science. Routledge, n.d.
Hands, D Wade. *RSocEcon* 51:112-115 Spr 1993.

Görg, Manfred.
Aegyptiaca-Biblica: Notizen und Beiträge zu den Beziehungen zwischen Ägypten und Israel. Harrassowitz, 1991.
Begg, Christopher T. *OTA* 15:472-473 O 1992.
Josua. Echter, 1991.
Begg, Christopher T. *OTA* 15:496-497 O 1992.

Goring, Rosemary, ed.
Chambers dictionary of beliefs and religion. Chambers, n.d.
Wansbrough, Henry. *Tablet* 247:950 Jl 24 1993.

Gosling, Justin.
Weakness of the will. Routledge Press, 1990.
Meynell, Hugo. *Heythrop* 34:324 Jl 1993.

Gosner, Kevin.
Soldiers of the virgin: the moral economy of a colonial Maya rebellion. The University of Arizona Press, 1992.
Gerhard, Peter. *CHist* 79:141-142 Ja 1993.
Soldiers of the virgin: the moral economy of a colonial Maya rebellion. University of Arizona Press, 1992.
Heiser, W Charles. *TheolDgst* 40:64 Spr 1993.

The Gospel in Dostoevsky.
Plough, 1988.
Mosher, M. *Cist Stud* 27 No 4:[112]-[113] 1992.

The Gospel of Thomas.
HarperSanFrancisco, 1992.
Heiser, W Charles. *TheolDgst* 40:164 Sum 1993.

Goss, Robert.
Jesus acted up: a gay and lesbian manifesto. HarperSanFrancisco, n.d.
Graham, William C. *Nat Cath Rep* 30:15 O 22 1993.

Gott, Richard.
Land without evil: utopian journeys across the South American watershed. Verso, n.d.
O'Shaughnessy, Hugh. *Tablet* 247:212 F 13 1993.

Gottlieb, Roger, ed.
Thinking the unthinkable: meanings of the Holocaust. Paulist Press, n.d.
Levy, I. *SIDIC* 25 No 1:31-32 1992.

Gougaud, Louis.
Christianity in Celtic lands. Four Courts Press, 1992.
Dollard, James. *Furrow* 44:517-518 S 1993.

Goulder, Michael.
The prayers of David (Psalms 51-72): Studies in the Psalter, II. JSOT Press, 1990.
Althann, Robert. *Heythrop* 34:186-187 Ap 1993.

Gourgues, Michel.
Jean, de l'exégèse à la prédication, Vol I: carême et Pâques. Cerf, 1993.
Beenaert, P. Mourlon. *Lumen* 48:231 Je 1993.

Gowler, David B.
Host, guest, enemy and friend: portraits of the Pharisees in Luke and Acts. Lang, 1991.
Elliott, John H. *Bib Th Bul* 23:42-43 Spr 1993.
Host, guest, enemy, and friend: portraits of the Pharisees in Luke and Acts. Lang, 1991.
Kurz, William S. *CBQ* 55:154-155 Ja 1993.

Goyard-Fabre, Simone.
Les fondements de l'ordre juridique. Presses Universitaires de France, 1992.
Ponton, Lionel. *Laval Theol Phil* 49:354-355 Je 1993.

Gozier, André.
Le mystère de la liturgie. Cerf, 1990.
Huftier, M. *MSR* 50:69-70 Ja-Mr 1993.
Le regard intérieur. Mame, 1991.
Renard, L J. *NRT* 115:310 Mr-Ap 1993.

Gozzelino, Giorgio.
Il mistero dell'uomo in Cristo. Editrice Elle Di Ci, 1991.
Galot, Jean. *Gregorianum* 74 no 3:577-578 1993.

Gozzini, Vilma Occhipinti.
Se non io, chi per me? Pegaso, 1991.
Vanzan, Piersandro. *Civilta* 3:195-196 Jl 17 1993.

Grabbe, Lester L.
Judaism from Cyrus to Hadrian: the Persian and Greek periods, v I. Fortress Press, 1991.
Heiser, W Charles. *TheolDgst* 40:64 Spr 1993.
Judaism from Cyrus to Hadrian: the Persian and Greek periods, v I. Fortress, 1992.
Mariottini, Claude F. *OTA* 16:445 Je 1993.
Judaism from Cyrus to Hadrian: the Roman period, v II. Fortress Press, 1991.
Heiser, W Charles. *TheolDgst* 40:64 Spr 1993.
Judaism from Cyrus to Hadrian: the Roman Period, v II. Fortress, 1992.
Mariottini, Claude F. *OTA* 16:445 Je 1993.

Graciotti, Sante, ed.
Il battesimo delle russe: bilancio di un millennio. Olschki, 1991.
Spidlik, Thomas. *Civilta* 2:95-96 Ap 3 1993.

Graef, Roger.
Living dangerously. HarperCollins, n.d.
Stacey, Tom. *Tablet* 247:141 Ja 30 1993.

Graff, Gerald.
Beyond the culture wars: how teaching the conflicts can revitalize American education. Norton, n.d.
Devine, Philip E. *New Oxford Rev* 60:22-24 My 1993.

Grafton, Anthony, ed.
Rome reborn, the Vatican Library and Renaissance culture. Yale University Press, n.d.
Reyntiens, Patrick. *Tablet* 247:582 My 8 1993.

Grafton, Anthony, ed. *(cont'd)*
Rome reborn: the Vatican Library and Renaissance culture. Yale University Press, n.d.
Spaeth, Robert L. *Comm* 120:26-27 My 21 1993.

Gragg, Larry Dale.
The Salem witch crisis. Praeger, 1992.
Heiser, W Charles. *TheolDgst* 40:164-165 Sum 1993.

Graham, Gordon.
The idea of Christian charity: a critique of some contemporary conceptions. University of Notre Dame Press, 1990.
Lisska, Anthony J. *New Blckfrs* 74:51-53 Ja 1993.

Graham, Larry Kent.
Care of persons, care of worlds: a psychosystems approach to pastoral care and counseling. Abingdon, 1992.
Kinast, Robert L. *TheolStds* 54:590-592 S 1993.

Graham, Mary Ann.
Confessions of a celibate priest. University Editions, n.d.
Graham, William C. *Nat Cath Rep* 30:16 O 22 1993.

Graham, Otis L, Jr.
Losing time: the industrial policy debate. Harvard University Press, n.d.
Whalen, C. *RSocEcon* 50:348-353 Fall 1992.

Graham, Ron.
God's dominion: a sceptic's quest. McClelland & Stewart, n.d.
Stokes, Richard. *Can Cath Rev* 11:26-27 Je 1993.

Graham, W S.
Aimed at nobody. Faber, n.d.
Bergonzi, Bernard, 1929-. *Tablet* 247:170-171 F 6 1993.

Granada, Miguel.
Cosmología, religión y política en el Renacimiento. Anthropos, 1988.
Astrain, Ricardo Salas. *RPhil Louvain* 91:466-467 Ag 1993.

Granfield, David.
Heightened consciousness: the mystical difference. Paulist Press, 1991.
Downey, Michael. *Horizons (CTS)* 20:170-172 Spr 1993.
Egan, Harvey D. *TheolStds* 54:394-395 Je 1993.

Grant, Mary C, and Hunt, Thomas C.
Catholic school education in the United States. Garland, 1992.
O'Brien, Stephen. *Momentum* 24:79-80 S-O 1993.
Corry, Emmett. *CLW* 64:30-32 Jl-S 1993.

Grant, Robert McQueen, 1917-.
Heresy and criticism: the search for authenticity in early Christian literature. John Knox Press, 1993.
Stuhlmueller, Carroll. *BibleT* 31:246 Jl 1993.

Grappe, Christian.
D'un temple à l'autre: Pierre et l'Eglise primitive de Jérusalem. Press Universitaires de France, 1992.
Montague, George T. *CBQ* 55:155-157 Ja 1993.

Grassi, Joseph A.
Loaves and fishes: the Gospel feeding narratives. Liturgical, 1991.
Reid, Barbara E. *CLW* 64:39 Jl-S 1993.
The secret identity of the beloved disciple. Paulist, 1992.
Bruns, Edgar J. *CBQ* 55:367-368 Ap 1993.

Grasso, E.
Lieve clown. Colomba, 1991.
Renard, L J. *NRT* 114:906 N-D 1992.
Il vangelo sulle strade dell'uomo. Missionaria Italiana, 1992.
Anon. *NRT* 115:634-635 Jl-Ag 1993.

Gratton, Carolyn.
The art of spiritual guidance. Crossroad, 1992.
DeWaal, E. *Cist Stud* 27 No 4:[83]-[84] 1992.
Kerins, M Roberta. *Spir Life* 39:51-53 Spr 1993.
Sheldrake, Philip. *Way* 33:158-159 Ap 1993.
Heiser, W Charles. *TheolDgst* 40:64 Spr 1993.
Korthals, Elaine. *RRel* 52:627-628 Jl-Ag 1993.

Grave, S A.
Conscience in Newman's thought. Clarendon Press, 1989.
Hammond, David M. *Relig Lit* 24:97-104 Aut 1992.
Gambra, Irene. *RPhil Louvain* 90:577-581 N 1992.

Graves, Donald.
Explore poetry. Heinemann, 1992.
Kollar, J. *Momentum* 24:84 F-Mr 1993.

Gravio, Dario Di.
I problemi del concordato preventivo. De Cristofaro, 1991.
Fratto, A. *Civilta* 3:545 S 18 1993.

Grayston, Kenneth.
Dying, we live: a new enquiry into the death of Christ in the New Testament. Oxford University Press, 1990.
Sloyan, Gerard S. *JEcumen Stds* 29:117 Wint 1992.

Grayzel, Solomon.
The Church and the Jews in the XIIIth century: volume II, 1254-1314. Wayne State University Press, 1989.
Synan, Edward A. *CHist* 79:99-100 Ja 1993.

Graziano, Frank.
Divine violence: spectacle, psychosexuality, and radical Christianity in the Argentine "dirty war". Westview Press, 1992.
Heiser, W Charles. *TheolDgst* 40:64-65 Spr 1993.

Grecco, Richard.
A theology of compromise: a study of method in the ethics of Charles E Curran. Lang, 1991.
Gula, Richard M. *TheolStds* 53:788-789 D 1992.
Walter, James J. *Horizons (CTS)* 20:188-189 Spr 1993.

Greeley, Andrew Moran, 1928-.
The Catholic myth: the behavior and beliefs of American Catholics. Charles Scribner's Sons, 1990.
Finley, Mitchel B. *St Anth* 100:12 Ja 1993.
Fall from grace. G.P. Putnam's Sons, n.d.
Finley, Mitchel B. *St Anth* 101:53 N 1993.
Love affair: a prayer journal. Crossroad, 1992.
Finley, Mitchel B. *St Anth* 100:52-53 F 1993.

Greeley, Andrew Moran, 1928-. *(cont'd)*
Ventline, Lawrence M. *Emmanuel* 99:237-239+ My 1993.
Religion in der Popkultur. Styria, 1993.
Bleistein, Roman, 1928-. *Stimm Zeit* 211:429-430 Je 1993.
Wages of sin. G P Putnam's Sons, n.d.
Finley, Mitchel B. *St Anth* 100:52-53 F 1993.

Green, Duncan.
Guatemala. Latin America Bureau, n.d.
Hopkinson, Amanda. *Tablet* 247:1045-1046 Ag 14 1993.

Green, Julian.
The apprentice writer. Marion Boyars Publishers, n.d.
O'Connell, David, 1940-. *Comm* 120:26-27 S 24 1993.
The green paradise: autobiography, volume 1 (1900-1916). Marion Boyars
Publishers, n.d.
O'Connell, David, 1940-. *Comm* 120:26-27 S 24 1993.

Green, Martin.
Gandhi: voice of a new revolution. Continuum, n.d.
Samway, Patrick H, 1939-. *America* 169:20 Ag 28-S 4 1993.

Green, Ronald M.
Kierkegaard and Kant: the hidden debt. State University of New York Press,
1992.
Westphal, Merold. *TheolStds* 54:389-390 Je 1993.

Greenblatt, Stephen.
Marvelous possessions: the wonder of the New World. University of Chicago
Press, 1991.
Kadir, Djelal. *Cithara* 32:62-63 N 1992.
Deen, Leonard. *Comm* 120:25-26 O 8 1993.

Greene, Dana.
Evelyn Underhill: artist of infinite life. Darton, Longman and Todd, 1991.
Bowie, Fiona. *Heythrop* 34:347-348 Jl 1993.
Evelyn Underhill: artist of the infinite life. Crossroad, 1990.
Kramer, V. *Cist Stud* 27 No 4:[82]-[83] 1992.
Bradley, Ritamary. *Relig Lit* 24:79-84 Aut 1992.

Greene, John T.
*Balaam and his interpreters: a hermeneutical history of the Balaam tradi-
tions.* Scholars Press, 1992.
Heiser, W Charles. *TheolDgst* 40:65 Spr 1993.

Greenhill, Denis.
More by accident. Wilton, n.d.
Wright, P. *Tablet* 247:79 Ja 16 1993.

Greer, Rowan A.
Broken lights and mended lives: theology and common life in the Church.
Pennsylvania State University Press, 1986.
Berthold, George C. *Thomist* 57:328-330 Ap 1993.

Gregory the Gret: the life of Saint Benedict.
St. Bede's Publication, 1993.
Cannon, Howard. *Word Sp* 15:105-106 1993.

Gregory I, The Great, Saint, Pope.
Registre des lettres, vol I. Éd du Cerf, 1991.
Halleux, André de. *Eph Theol Lovan* 69:197 Ap 1993.

Gregory the Great.
Be friends of God. Cowley, 1990.
McLaughlin, Thomas. *Cist Stud* 28:[21]-[22] 1993.

Gréil, Michael Mac, ed.
Monsignor James Horan, memoirs: 1911-1986. Brandon Books, 1992.
Simpson, Anne. *Doctr Life* 43:122-124 F 1993.

Greisch, Jean, ed.
Penser la religion. Beauchesne, 1991.
Brito, Emilio. *Eph Theol Lovan* 78:463-464 D 1992.

Grelot, Pierre.
Homilías sobre la Escritura en la época apostólica. Herder, 1991.
Mondoni, Danilo. *Perspectiva* 25:257-258 My-Ag 1993.
What are the Targums? Liturgical Press, 1992.
Stuhlmueller, Carroll. *BileT* 31:54 Ja 1993.
Murphy, Roland E. *OTA* 15:516 O 1992.

Grente, Georges, Cardinal, ed.
Dictionnaire des Lettres françaises. Fayard, 1992.
Steenberghen, Fernand Van. *RPhil Louvain* 91:312-313 My 1993.

Grenz, Stanley J, and Olson, Roger E.
20th-century theology: God and the world in a transitional age. Inter-Varsity
Press, 1992.
Heiser, W Charles. *TheolDgst* 40:65 Spr 1993.

Gres-Gayer, Jacques M.
*Théologie et pouvoir en Sorbonne: La faculté de théologie de Paris et la
bulle Unigenitus, 1714-1721.* Klincksieck, 1991.
Miller, Samuel J. *CHist* 79:116-117 Ja 1993.
Joassart, Bernard. *NRT* 115:615 Jl-Ag 1993.

Grey, Mary.
The wisdom of fools? SPCK, n.d.
Clague, Julie. *Tablet* 247:1301-1302 O 9 1993.

Gribble, Richard.
The history and devotion of the rosary. Our Sunday Visitor, n.d.
Dollen, Charles. *Priest* 49:52 F 1993.

Grieco, Gianfranco, and Del Preite, Mariano.
Gennaro, il Santo di Napoli. VELAR, 1992.
Caprile, Giovanni. *Civilta* 3:323 Ag 7-21 1993.

Griffin, Emilie.
The reflective executive: a spirituality of business and enterprise. Crossroads,
n.d.
Harter, Michael. *America* 169:20 N 6 1993.

Griffin, John R.
*"A historical commentary on the major Catholic works of Cardinal New-
man".* Peter Lang Press, n.d.
Hallett, Paul. *Register* 69:5 Jl 25 1993.

Griffith, James S.
Beliefs and holy places: a spiritual geography of the Pimería Alta. The
University of Arizona Press, 1992.
Heiser, W Charles. *TheolDgst* 39:363 Wint 1992.
Polzer, Charles W. *CHist* 79:360 Ap 1993.

Griffith, Sidney H.
Arabic Christianity in the monasteries of ninth-century Palestine. Ashgate
Publishing, 1992.
Heiser, W Charles. *TheolDgst* 40:165 Sum 1993.

Griffiths, A Phillips, ed.
Wittgenstein centenary essays. Cambridge University Press, 1991.
Kerr, Fergus. *Heythrop* 34:473-474 O 1993.

Griffiths, Bede, 1906-.
The new creation in Christ. Darton, Longman & Todd, 1992.
Freeman, Laurence. *Tablet* 246:1604 D 19-26 1992.
Todd, J. *Tablet* 247:76 Ja 16 1993.

Griffiths, Paul J.
An apology for apologetics: a study in the logic of interreligious dialogue.
Orbis Books, 1991.
D'Costa, Gavin. *Thomist* 56:719-723 O 1992.
Dupuis, Jacques. *Gregorianum* 74 No 1:175 1993.

Grigg, Viv.
Cry of the urban poor. MARC, 1992.
Heiser, W Charles. *TheolDgst* 40:65 Spr 1993.

Grindel, J A.
Wither the U S church? Orbis Books, 1991.
Anon. *NRT* 115:292 Mr-Ap 1993.

Grisez, Germain Gabriel, 1929-, and Shaw Russell.
Fulfillment in Christ: a summary of "Christian moral principles". University
of Notre Dame Press, 1991.
Grondelski, John M. *HPR* 93:73-74 Mr 1993.

Gritella, Gianfranco.
La Certosa di S Stefano del Bosco a Serra S Bruno. L'Artistica Savigliano,
1991.
Capizzi, Carmelo. *Civilta* 3:321-322 Ag 7-21 1993.

Groen, Basilius J.
Ter genezing van ziel en lichaam. Deutscher Studien Verlag, 1991.
Halleux, André de. *Eph Theol Lovan* 78:481-482 D 1992.

Groeschel, Benedict J.
The reform of renewal. Ignatius Press, n.d.
Smith, G. *Can Cath Rev* 11:32 Ja 1993.
A still small voice. Ignatius Press, 1993.
DeLong, Allen. *RRel* 52:636-637 Jl-Ag 1993.
Dollen, Charles. *Priest* 49:48 Jl 1993.

Groh, John E.
Facilitators of the free exercise of religion: Air Force chaplains, 1981-1990.
United States Air Force, 1991.
Sheehy, Edward J. *CHist* 79:376-377 Ap 1993.

Grom, Bernhard.
Religionspsychologie. Vandenhoeck and Ruprescht, 1992.
Goller, H. *Stimm Zeit* 211:71-72 Ja 1993.

Groome, Thomas H, 1945-.
Language for a Catholic: a program of study. Sheed and Ward, 1991.
Irwin, Joyce. *JEcumen Stds* 29:481-482 Sum-Aut 1992.
Sharing faith. Harper, 1991.
Willumsen, K. *TheolStds* 53:791 D 1992.
Tozzi, Eugene. *Church* 9:59-60 Spr 1993.
Marthaler, Bernard L, 1927-. *Living Light* 29:86-87 Spr 1993.
O'Malley, William J, 1931-. *America* 168:18-19 My 15 1993.
Horan, Michael. *CrossCurr* 43:268-269 Sum 1993.
Suther, Eleanor. *Worship* 67:373-375 Jl 1993.

Gross, Francis L, Jr, and Gross, Toni Perior.
The making of a mystic: seasons in the Life of Teresa of Avila. State
University of New York Press, 1993.
Godin, A. *Lumen* 48:356-357 S 1993.

Gross, John, ed.
The modern movement: a TLS companion. Harvill, n.d.
Rosselli, John. *Tablet* 247:77 Ja 16 1993.

Gross, Philip.
The all-nite café. Faber & Faber, n.d.
Lawson, Sarah. *Tablet* 247:1015 Ag 7 1993.

Grossi, Manzoni.
*Atti del XIV Congresso Nazionale di Studi Manzoniani (Lecco, 10-14 ottobre
1990) tomo I.* Centro Nazionale Studi Manzoniani, 1991.
Bortone, G. *Civilta* 3:539-540 S 18 1993.

Gruber, Mayer I.
The motherhood of God and other studies. Scholars, 1992.
Begg, Christopher T. *OTA* 16:395 Je 1993.

Grumbach, Doris.
Extra innings. W. W. Norton, n.d.
Samway, Patrick H, 1939-. *America* 169:18-19 Ag 28-S 4 1993.

Guccione, Eugenio, ed.
*Gioacchino Ventura e il pensiero politico d'ispirazione cristiana
dell'Ottocento.* Leo S Olschki Editore, 1991.
Coppa, Frank J. *CHist* 79:348-349 Ap 1993.

Gudorf, Christine E.
Victimization: examining Christian complicity. Trinity Press International,
1992.
Heiser, W Charles. *TheolDgst* 40:65 Spr 1993.

Guelluy, Robert.
Si tu connaissais. Duculot, 1991.
Étienne, Jacques. *Eph Theol Lovan* 78:185-186 Ap 1992.
Renard, L J. *NRT* 115:313-314 Mr-Ap 1993.
Tihon, M. A. *Lumen* 48:234 Je 1993.

Guenée, Bernard.
Between church and state: the lives of four French prelates in the late Middle Ages. University of Chicago, 1991.
Taber, D. *TheolStds* 53:755-757 D 1992.

Guenther, Margaret.
Holy listening: the art of spiritual direction. Cowley Publications, 1992.
Murphy, Anne. *Sisters* 65:65-66 Ja 1993.
Sheldrake, Philip. *Way* 33:158 Ap 1993.
Myerscough, Angelita. *RRel* 52:622-623 Jl-Ag 1993.

Guillermo Durán, Juan.
Monumenta Catechetica Hispanoamericana (siglos XVI-XVIII). Universidad Católica de Santa María de los Buenos Aires, 1990.
Hernández, Ramón. *Cien Tom* 119:618-619 S-D 1992.

Guillou, M-J Le.
Du scandale du mal à la rencontre de Dieu. Éd Saint-Paul, 1991.
Renard, L J. *NRT* 115:133-134 Ja-F 1993.

Guilmard, Dom Jacques-Marie.
Tonaire des pièces de la messe selon le Graduale Triplex et l'Offertoriale Triplex de Solesmes. Etudes Grégoriennes, 1991.
Pinson, Jean-Pierre. *Laval Theol Phil* 49:147-148 F 1993.

Guimond, John.
The silencing of Babylon. Paulist, 1991.
Grip, Robert. *Cist Stud* 28:[19]-[20] 1993.

Guinan, Michael D.
The Pentateuch. Liturgical Press, 1990.
Wimmer, Joseph F. *OTA* 15:492 O 1992.
Bailey, Randall C. *CBQ* 55:111-113 Ja 1993.

Guindon, Andre.
The sexual creators. University Press of America, 1986.
Couture, Denise. *Laval Theol Phil* 49:321-329 Je 1993.

Guinness, Os, and Seel, John, eds.
No God but God. Moody Press, 1992.
Patterson, Robert W. *Crisis* 11:13-14 My 1993.

Gumley, Frances, and Redhead, Brian.
Protestors for paradise: the story of Christian reformers from the thirteenth to the twenty-first century. BBC Books, n.d.
Craig, Mary. *Tablet* 247:517-518 Ap 24 1993.

Gundry, Robert H.
Mark: a commentary on his apology for the Cross. Eerdmans, 1993.
Neirynck, F. *Eph Theol Lovan* 69:183-186 Ap 1993.

Gunn, David M, ed.
Narrative and novella in Samuel: studies by Hugo Gressmann and other scholars, 1906-1923. Almond, 1991.
Humphrey, W Lee. *CBQ* 54:746-747 O 1992.

Gunn, S J, and Lindley, P G, eds.
Cardinal Wolsey: church, state and art. Cambridge University Press, 1991.
Ryan, Ron. *TheolStds* 53:757-758 D 1992.
Rex, R. *CHist* 78:607-614 O 1992.

Gunneweg, Antonius H J.
Sola Scriptura. Vandenhoeck and Ruprecht, 1992.
Begg, Christopher T. *OTA* 16:153 F 1993.

Gunton, Colin E.
The promise of Trinitarian theology. T and T Clark, 1991.
Bracken, Joseph A. *Horizons (CTS)* 19:321-322 Fall 1992.
O'Donnell, John J. *Heythrop* 34:189-190 Ap 1993.

Gunzel, Raymond.
If today you hear God's voice: biblical images of prayer for modern man and women. Sheed and Ward, n.d.
Graham, William C. *Nat Cath Rep* 29:39 F 5 1993.

Gurtler, Gary M.
Plotinus: the experience of unity. Peter Lang, 1989.
Clarke, W Norris. *IPQ* 33:123-124 Mr 1993.

Gustin, Marilyn Norquist.
How to read and pray the parables. Liguori Publications, 1992.
Krawczyk, Marilyn Peters. *Mod Lit* 20:42 Je-Jl 1993.
You can know God: Christian spirituality for daily living. Liguori Publications, 1993.
Read, Jean. *RRel* 52:789-790 S-O 1993.

Gutiérrez, Gustavo.
El Dios de la vida. Sígueme, 1992.
Lago Alba, Luis. *Cien Tom* 119:415-417 My-Ag 1992.
The God of life. Orbis, 1991.
Dorr, Donal, 1935-. *Furrow* 43:706-708 D 1992.
Pastor, Felix-Alejandro. *Gregorianum* 74 No 1:194 1993.
Renard, L J. *NRT* 115:313 Mr-Ap 1993.
Nickoloff, James B. *Horizons (CTS)* 20:157-158 Spr 1993.
Phan, Peter C. *Living Light* 29:98-99 Sum 1993.
Hamilton, Andrew. *Pacifica* 6:347-349 O 1993.
Teología de la liberción. Sígueme, 1990.
Lago Alba, Luis. *Cien Tom* 119:415-417 My-Ag 1992.
"*The thought of Bartoleme de las Casas*". CEP, n.d.
Hourton Poisson, Jorge, Bp, 1926-. *LADOC* 23:14-17 Jl-Ag 1993.
La Verdad os hará libres. Sígueme, 1990.
Lago Alba, Luis. *Cien Tom* 119:415-417 My-Ag 1992.

Guzzetti, Giovanni Battista.
Cristianesimo ed economia, vol II. Massimo, 1992.
Cultrera, Francesco. *Civilta* 143:529-530 D 5 1992.
L'insegnamento sociale della chiesa: L'insegnamento socioeconomico. LDC, 1991.
Cultrera, Francesco. *Civilta* 143:529-530 D 5 1992.

Gwyn, Douglas, et al.
A declaration on peace. Herald Press, 1991.
Stuhlmueller, Carroll. *BibleT* 30:381 N 1992.

Gwyn, Peter.
The king's cardinal: the life and death of Thomas Wolsey. Barrie, 1990.
Rex, R. *CHist* 78:607-614 O 1992.

Gwynn, Aubrey.
The Irish Church in the eleventh and twelfth centuries. Four Courts Press, 1992.
Dollard, James. *Furrow* 44:517-518 S 1993.

Gyr, M.
Laissez-vous renouveler par l'Esprit. Pneumathèque, 1991.
Renard, L J. *NRT* 115:314 Mr-Ap 1993.

H

Haag, Ernst.
Vom Sabbat zum Sonntag. Paulinus, 1991.
Chilton, Bruce. *CBQ* 55:336-337 Ap 1993.

Hacker, Andrew.
Two nations. Charles Scribner's Sons, 1992.
Altschuler, Glenn C. *CrossCurr* 42:545-549 Wint 1992-1993.

Haddad, Yvonne Yazbeck.
The Muslims of America. Oxford University Press, 1991.
Heiser, W Charles. *TheolDgst* 39:375 Wint 1992.

Hafemann, Scott J.
Suffering and ministry in the spirit. William B Eerdmans, 1990.
Senior, Donald. *BibleT* 31:314 S 1993.

Haffner, Paul.
Creation and scientific creativity: a study in the thought of S L Jaki. Christendom Press, 1991.
McDermott, John M. *IPQ* 33:244-246 Je 1993.
Anon. *Gregorianum* 74 no 3:604-605 1993.

Hafner, Julian.
The end of marriage: why monogamy isn't working. Century, n.d.
Billington, Rachel, 1942-. *Tablet* 247:1232-1233 S 25 1993.

Hagen, K, ed.
Augustine, the harvest, and theology (1200-1650). E J Brill, 1990.
Escol, R. *NRT* 114:909-910 N-D 1992.

Hagstrom, D H.
The coherence of the Book of Micah. Scholars Press, 1988.
Lust, Johan. *Eph Theol Lovan* 78:159-160 Ap 1992.

Hagstrum, Jean H.
Esteem enlivened by desire. University of Chicago Press, n.d.
Lasch, Christopher, 1932-. *Comm* 120:22-24 F 26 1993.

Haight, Roger.
Dynamics of theology. Paulist Press, 1990.
Phan, Peter C. *Living Light* 29:88-89 Sum 1993.
Buggert, Donald W. *New Theol Rev* 6:93-95 Ag 1993.

Hakowski, Maryann.
Growing with Jesus. Ave Maria Press, n.d.
Riley, David M. *Catechist* 27:17-18 S 1993.
McCann, Deborah. *ReligTJ* 27:14 O 1993.

Halberstam, David.
The fifties. Villard, n.d.
Costello, Gerald M, 1931-. *USCath* 58:40-43 D 1993.

Halbertal, Moshe, and Margalit, Avishai.
Idolatry. Harvard University Press, 1992.
Barker, Margaret. *Month* 26:196-197 My 1993.
Heiser, W Charles. *TheolDgst* 40:165 Sum 1993.

Haliczer, Stephen.
Inquisition and society in the kingdom of Valencia, 1478-1834. University of California Press, 1990.
Hamilton, Alastair. *Heythrop* 34:329-331 Jl 1993.

Halkes, Catharina J M.
New creation: Christian feminism and the renewal of the earth. John Knox, 1991.
Ross, Mary Ellen. *TheolStds* 54:605-606 S 1993.

Hall, Basil.
Humanists and Protestants, 1500-1900. T & T Clark Ltd, 1990.
Atkins, Anselm. *JEcumen Stds* 29:112-113 Wint 1992.

Hall, Christine, ed.
The deacon's ministry. GraceWing Books, 1991.
Jones, D. *Priests & People* 6:359 Ag-S 1992.
Gollob, Timothy. *Mod Lit* 20:38 Je-Jl 1993.

Hall, Donald.
The museum of clear ideas. Ticknor & Fields, n.d.
Keen, Suzanne. *Comm* 120:21-23 S 24 1993.

Hall, Robert G.
Revealed histories: techniques for ancient Jewish and Christian historiography. Sheffield, 1991.
Lust, Johan. *Eph Theol Lovan* 69:168-169 Ap 1993.
Heiser, W Charles. *TheolDgst* 40:66 Spr 1993.

Hall, Stuart G.
Doctrine and practice in the early Church. SPCK, 1991.
Gould, Graham. *Heythrop* 34:432-433 O 1993.

Hall, Suzanne E, ed.
The people: reflections of native peoples on the Catholic experience in North America. National Catholic Educational Association, n.d.
Higgins, James J. *Liguorian* 81:69 My 1993.

Halligan, Frederick R, and Shea, John J.
The fires of desire: erotic energies and the spiritual quest. Crossroad, n.d.
Holmes, Russell P. *Spir Life* 39:53-54 Spr 1993.

Hallo, William W, et al, eds.
The Bible in the light of cuneiform literature: scripture in context III. Mellen, 1990.
Watson, Wilfred G E. *CBQ* 54:821-822 O 1992.

Halm, H.
Shiism. Edinburgh University Press, 1992.
Scheuer, J. *NRT* 115:606-607 Jl-Ag 1993.

Halpern, Daniel, ed.
Dante's Inferno: translations by 20 contemporary poets. Ecco Press, n.d.
 Krivak, Andrew J. *America* 169:17-21 O 30 1993.

Hamell, Patrick J.
Handbook of patrology. Alba, 1991.
 Wright, J Robert. *Cist Stud* 28:[22]-[23] 1993.

Hamerton-Kelly, Robert G.
Sacred violence: Paul's hermeneutic of the cross. Fortress, 1992.
 Stuhlmueller, Carroll. *BibleT* 31:124-125 Mr 1993.
 Heiser, W Charles. *TheolDgst* 39:363 Wint 1992.
 Osick, Carolyn. *New Theol Rev* 6:88-90 Ag 1993.

Hamesse, Jacqueline, ed.
Méthodologies informatiques et nouveaux horizons dans les recherches médiévales. Brepols, 1992.
 Steenberghen, Fernand Van. *RPhil Louvain* 91:314-315 My 1993.

Hamesse, Jacqueline, and Fattori, Marta, eds.
Rencontres de cultures dans la philosophie médiévale. Università degli studi, 1990.
 Steenberghen, Fernand Van. *RPhil Louvain* 91:313-314 My 1993.

Hamilton, Alastair.
Heresy and mysticism in Sixteenth-Century Spain: the Alumbrados. James Clarke, 1992.
 Brinkman, B.R. *Heythrop* 34:333-334 Jl 1993.
 Wright, A D. *CHist* 79:525-526 Jl 1993.

Hamilton, Bill.
Albania: who cares? Autumn House Press, n.d.
 Griffiths, Leslie. *Tablet* 247:515 Ap 24 1993.

Hamilton, Ian.
Keepers of the flame. Hutchinson, n.d.
 Braybrooke, Neville. *Tablet* 247:311-312 Mr 6 1993.

Hamilton, Tim, et al.
Solidarity: the missing link in Irish society. Jesuit Centre for Faith and Justice, n.d.
 O'Higgins-O'Malley, Una. *Furrow* 44:55-56 Ja 1993.

Hamilton, Victor P.
The Book of Genesis, Chapters 1-17. Eerdmans, 1990.
 Brueggemann, Walter. *CBQ* 55:113-115 Ja 1993.

Hamilton, Vivien.
Boudin at Trouville. John Murray, n.d.
 Reyntiens, Patrick. *Tablet* 247:582 My 8 1993.

Hamlin, Alan, and Petit, Philip, eds.
The good polity: normative analysis of the state. Basil Blackwell, 1991.
 Archard, David. *IJPS* 1:146-148 Mr 1993.

Hamman, Adalbert.
How to read the church fathers. Crossroad, 1993.
 Stuhlmueller, Carroll. *BibleT* 31:246 Jl 1993.
 Heiser, W Charles. *TheolDgst* 40:165 Sum 1993.

Hammar, Richard R.
Pastor, church and law. Christian Ministry Resources, n.d.
 Heiser, W Charles. *TheolDgst* 40:66 Spr 1993.

Hammond, Phillip E.
Religion and personal autonomy: the third disestablishment in America. University of South Carolina Press, 1992.
 Heiser, W Charles. *TheolDgst* 40:66 Spr 1993.

Hamnett, Ian.
Religious pluralism and unbelief: studies critical and comparative. Routledge, 1990.
 Loughlin, Gerard. *Heythrop* 34:78-80 Ja 1993.

Hamon, Herve, and Rotman, Patrick.
You see, I haven't forgotten. Random House, n.d.
 Coren, Michael. *Can Cath Rev* 11:4-6 F 1993.

Hampl, Patricia, 1946-.
Virgin time: in search of the contemplative life. Farrar, Straus, Giroux, n.d.
 Donavin, Denise Perry. *ST Anth* 101:53 Jl 1993.
 Donovan, M. *America* 168:18-20 Ja 2-9 1993.
 Costello, Gerald M, 1931-. *USCath* 58:48-49 S 1993.

Hampsch, John H.
Glad you asked: scriptural answers for our times. Our Sunday Visitor, 1992.
 Stuhlmueller, Carroll. *BibleT* 31:54 Ja 1993.
 Heiser, W Charles. *TheolDgst* 39:363 Wint 1992.

Hands, John.
Darkness at dawn. HarperCollins, n.d.
 Rich, Vera. *Tablet* 247:1167 S 11 1993.

Handy, Robert T.
Undermined establishment: church-state relations in America 1880-1920. Princeton University Press, 1991.
 Marty, Martin E. *CHist* 78:686-687 O 1992.
 Heiser, W Charles. *TheolDgst* 39:363-364 Wint 1992.
 Drinan, Robert Francis, 1920-. *Horizons (CTS)* 20:152 Spr 1993.

Hanegraaff, D J.
Met de Torah is het begonnen. Vol 3: Rondom de mondelinge. G. F. Callenbach, 1990.
 Bohen, Marian. *JEcumen Stds* 29:274 Spr 1992.

Hank, Thich Nhat.
Peace is every step. Bantam, n.d.
 Harter, Michael. *America* 169:21 N 6 1993.

Hannon, Patrick.
Church, state, morality, and law. Christian Classics, n.d.
 Cochran, Clarke E. *Comm* 120:25-27 Jl 16 1993.

Hansen, James.
The ministry of the cantor. The Liturgical Press, 1985.
 Kubicki, Judith Marie. *Past Mus* 17:41 Je-Jl 1993.

Hanson, Anthony Tyrrell.
The prophetic gospel. T and T Clark, 1991.
 Wansbrough, Henry. *Priests & People* 6:435-436 N 1992.
 Heil, John Paul. *CBQ* 54:780-781 O 1992.

Hapgood, Marilyn Oliver.
Wallpaper and the artist: from Dürer to Warhol. Abbeville Press, n.d.
 Reyntiens, Patrick. *Tablet* 247:581-582 My 8 1993.

Harbison, Peter.
Pilgrimage in Ireland: the monuments and the people. Syracuse University Press, 1992.
 Bitel, L. *CHist* 78:625-626 O 1992.
 Heiser, W Charles. *TheolDgst* 39:364 Wint 1992.

Harbison, Robert.
The Shell guide to English parish churches. André Deutsch, n.d.
 Hartman, John F, 1921-. *Tablet* 247:18-19 Ja 2 1993.

Härdelin, Alf, ed.
In quest of the kingdom: ten papers on Medieval monastic spirituality. Biblioteca Theologie Practicae, 1991.
 France, J. *Cist Stud* 27 No 4:[89]-[91] 1992.

Harding, D E.
The trial of the man who said he was God. Arkana Penguin, 1992.
 Hughes, Gerard W. *Month* 26:77 F 1993.

Hardmeier, Christof.
Prophetie im Streit vor dem Untergang Judas. Gruyter, 1990.
 Nelson, Richard D. *CBQ* 55:337-338 Ap 1993.

Hardoy, J, et al.
Environmental problems in third world cities. Earthscan, n.d.
 McRobie, George. *Tablet* 247:1196 S 18 1993.

Hardy, D W, and Sedgwick, P H, eds.
The weight of glory. A vision and practice for Christian faith: the future of liberal theology. T & T Clark, 1991.
 Kerr, Fergus. *New Blckfrs* 73:622-623 D 1992.
 Chapman, Mark D. *Heythrop* 34:319-320 Jl 1993.

Hare, Douglas R A.
Matthew. John Knox Press, 1993.
 Senior, Donald. *BibleT* 31:314 S 1993.
The son of man tradition. Fortress Press, 1990.
 Adam, Andrew K M. *CBQ* 54:782-783 O 1992.
 Moloney, Francis J. *Pacifica* 6:214-216 Je 1993.

Häring, Bernard, 1912-.
My witness for the Church. Paulist Press, 1992.
 Santa, Thomas M. *Liguorian* 81:68 Ja 1993.
 McCormick, Richard Arthur, 1922-. *TheolStds* 53:788 D 1992.
 Ventline, Lawrence M. *St Anth* 100:50-51 Mr 1993.
 Heiser, W Charles. *TheolDgst* 39:364 Wint 1992.
 Pridmore, John. *Way* 33:167-168 Ap 1993.
 Rigali, Norbert J. *Horizons (CTS)* 20:181 Spr 1993.
 O'Riordan, Sean. *Tablet* 247:919 Jl 17 1993.
No way out? pastoral care of the divorced and remarried. St Paul Publications, 1990.
 Tuohey, John F. *Jurist* 51 no 2:525-526 1991.
La théologie morale: idées maîtresses. Cerf, 1992.
 Chénard, Gabriel. *Laval Theol Phil* 49:172-173 F 1993.

Harl, Marguerite.
La langue de Japhet. Cerf, 1992.
 Lust, Johan. *Eph Theol Lovan* 78:406-407 D 1992.

Harley, R Bruce, and LaCoste, Catherine Louise, comp.
Readings in diocesan heritage, volume XI: Most Rev Charles Francis Buddy: first Bishop of San Diego, 1936-1966. The Diocese of San Diego, 1991.
 Weber, Francis J. *CHist* 79:135-137 Ja 1993.

Harmon, William, ed.
The top 500 poems. Columbia University Press, n.d.
 Keen, Suzanne. *Comm* 120:26-27 My 7 1993.

Harmsen, T H B M, ed.
John Gee's "Foot out of the snare" (1624). Cicero Press, 1992.
 Clancy, Thomas H. *CHist* 79:113-114 Ja 1993.

Harnisch, Wolfgang.
Las parábolas de Jesús. Ed Sigueme, 1989.
 Pérez-Cotapos, Eduardo L. *Teol Vida* 33 no 3-4:323-324 1992.

Harper, John.
The forms and orders of Western litgurgy from the tenth to the eighteenth century. Clarendon Press, 1991.
 Heiser, W Charles. *TheolDgst* 39:364 Wint 1992.
 Tripp, D. *Worship* 67:87-89 Ja 1993.
 Nardone, Richard M. *CHist* 79:304-305 Ap 1993.

Harper-Bill, Christopher, ed.
Religious belief and ecclesiastical careers in late Medieval England. Boydell and Brewer, 1991.
 Dunstan, G R. *Heythrop* 34:451-452 O 1993.
 Moran, J. *CHist* 78:648-649 O 1992.

Harrelson, Walter, and Falk, Randall M.
Jews and Christians. Abingdon Press, 1990.
 Sigal, Lillian. *JEcumen Stds* 29:117-119 Wint 1992.

Harrington, Ann M.
Japan's hidden Christians. Loyola University Press, n.d.
 DeCoursey, Vincent W, Jr. *Nat Cath Rep* 29:19 Je 18 1993.

Harrington, Daniel J.
The Gospel of Matthew. Liturgical, 1991.
 Neirynck, F. *Eph Theol Lovan* 78:439-441 D 1992.
 McCready, Wayne O. *Can Cath Rev* 11:29 S 1993.

Higgins, George G, 1916-. *(cont'd)*
Vollaro, Daniel R. *Nat Cath Rep* 29:14 S 3 1993.
Cort, John C. *Comm* 120:26-27 Ag 13 1993.
DeCosse, David E. *America* 169:18-20 S 25 1993.

Higgins, Gregory G, 1916-.
Twelve theological dilemmas. Paulist, 1991.
Rattigan, Mary T. *Horizons (CTS)* 20:153-154 Spr 1993.

Higgins, Michael, et al, eds.
Catholic education: transforming our world a Canadian perspective. Novalis, n.d.
D'Souza, M O. *Can Cath Rev* 11:23-24 S 1993.

Highfield, Roger, and Carter, Paul.
The private lives of Albert Einstein. Faber, n.d.
Hawkes, Nigel. *Tablet* 247:1132 S 4 1993.

Highfield, Ron.
Barth and Rahner in dialogue. Lang, 1989.
Brito, Emilio. *Eph Theol Lovan* 78:471-472 D 1992.

Highwater, Jamake.
Kill hole. Grove Press, n.d.
Lee, Michael. *Nat Cath Rep* 29:36 My 28 1993.

Hilberg, Raul.
Perpetrators victims bystanders; the Jewish catastrophe 1933-1945. Harper-Collins, n.d.
Costello, Gerald M, 1931-. *USCath* 58:48-51 F 1993.

Hildebrand, Dietrich von.
Jaws of death: gate of heaven. Sophia Institute Press, 1980.
Krason, Stephen M. *SocJust* 84:31 Ja-F 1993.
Liturgy and personality. Sophia Institute, 1993.
Dollen, Charles. *Priest* 49:48 Jl 1993.
Baker, Kenneth. *HPR* 94:71-72 N 1993.
Man and woman: love and the meaning of intimacy. Sophia Institute Press, 1992.
Baker, Kenneth. *HPR* 93:74 My 1993.
Personality. Sophia Institute Press, n.d.
Pecht, Gerard. *Liguorian* 81:70 Ag 1993.
What is philosophy? Routledge, 1991.
Gorvan, Patrick. *IJPS* 1:170-171 Mr 1993.

Hill, Andrew E, and Walton, John H.
A survey of the Old Testament. Zondervan, 1991.
Hoppe, Leslie J. *CBQ* 55:115-116 Ja 1993.

Hill, Brennan.
Jesus the Christ. Twenty-Third, 1991.
Senior, Donald. *BibleT* 31:59 Ja 1993.
Senior, Donald. *CBQ* 55:371-372 Ap 1993.

Hill, Charles E.
Regnum Caelorum: patterns of future hope in early Christianity. Clarendon Press, 1992.
Skeris, Robert A. *F & R* 28:415-418 Wint 1992.
Yarnold, Edward John, 1926-. *New Blckfrs* 74:327-329 Je 1993.

Hill, Christopher.
The English Bible and the seventeenth-century revolution. Penguin, n.d.
Coren, Michael. *Can Cath Rev* 11:5-6 Je 20 1993.
Murphy, Anne, and Pridmore, John. *Way* 33:253 Jl 1993.
Murphy, Anne. *Month* 26:377-378 S-O 1993.

Hill, Craig C.
Hellenists and Hebrews. Fortress, 1992.
Senior, Donald. *BibleT* 31:59 Ja 1993.
Squires, John. *Pacifica* 6:341-342 O 1993.

Hill, Edmund.
Ministry and authority in the Catholic Church. Geoffrey Chapman, 1988.
Magesa, Laurenti. *AFER* 34:61-62 F 1992.

Hill, William J, 1924-.
Search for the absent God. Crossroad, 1992.
Kirke, P. *Doctr Life* 42:649-651 D 1992.
Heiser, W Charles. *TheolDgst* 40:68 Spr 1993.
Burrell, David B. *Thomist* 57:521-524 Jl 1993.

Hillers, Delbert R.
Lamentations: a new translation with introduction and commentary. Doubleday, 1992.
Begg, Christopher T. *OTA* 16:179 F 1993.

Hillery, George A.
The monastery: a study in freedom, love, and community. Praeger, 1992.
Heiser, W Charles. *TheolDgst* 40:68 Spr 1993.

Hillman, Eugene.
Toward an African Christianity. Paulist, n.d.
Preston, William. *Nat Cath Rep* 29:34 S 10 1993.

Hillyer, Norman.
1 and 2 Peter, Jude. Hendrickson, 1992.
Senior, Donald. *BibleT* 31:315 S 1993.

Hilton, Walter.
The scale of perfection. Paulist, 1991.
Wall, John N. *TheolStds* 53:785-786 D 1992.

Himes, Michael J, and Himes, Kenneth R.
Fullness of faith. Paulist, n.d.
Carmody, John Tully. *Nat Cath Rep* 29:19 Jl 30 1993.
Komonchak, Joseph Andrew, 1939-. *Comm* 120:27-29 S 24 1993.

Hinchliff, Peter.
God and history: aspects of British theology 1875-1914. Clarendon Press, 1992.
Kent, John. *New Blckfrs* 74:53-54 Ja 1993.
God and history: aspects of British theology 1875-1914. Clarendon, 1992.
Magill, Gerard. *TheolStds* 54:358-359 Je 1993.

Hinde, Wendy.
Catholic Emancipation: a shake to men's minds. Blackwell, 1992.
Osborne, J. *CHist* 78:671-672 O 1992.

Hines, Joanna.
Dora's room. Hodder & Stoughton, n.d.
Delay, Jill. *Tablet* 247:759 Je 1993.

Hinnells, John R, ed.
Who's who of world religions. Simon and Schuster, 1992.
Biallas, Leonard J. *Horizons (CTS)* 20:192-193 Spr 1993.

Hiro, Dilip.
Desert Shield to Desert Storm: the second Gulf War. Paladin, n.d.
Keegan, Jeffrey. *Tablet* 246:1573-1574 D 12 1992.

Historia de la evangelización de América: Trayectoria, identidad y esperanza de continente.
Libreria Editrice Vaticana, 1992.
Barrios Villegos, Marciano. *Teol Vida* 34 no 1-2:163 1993.

History and mythology of the Aztecs: the Codex Chimalpopoca.
The University of Arizona Press, 1992.
Heiser, W Charles. *TheolDgst* 40:68 Spr 1993.

Hitchcock, Helen Hull, ed.
The politics of prayer. Ignatius, 1992.
Steichen, Donna. *SocJust* 84:62 Mr-Ap 1993.
Miesel, Sandra. *Register* 69:5 Ap 18 1993.
Kennedy, Leonard A. *Crisis* 11:57-58 S 1993.
Rulter, G. *HPR* 94:77-78 O 1993.

Hoban, Russell, and Hoban, Lillian.
Best friends for Frances. Harper and Row, n.d.
Neuberger, Anne E. *ReligTJ* 27:58-59 S 1993.

Hobbs, T R.
A time for war: a study of warfare in the Old Testament. Michael Glazier, 1989.
Bergant, Dianne. *New Theol Rev* 6:114-115 My 1993.

Hobhouse, Penelope.
Borders. Pavilion Books, n.d.
Taylor, Patrick. *Tablet* 247:375 Mr 20 1993.

Hodgson, Irene B.
Archbishop Oscar Romero: a shepherd's diary. St Anthony's Messenger Press, 1993.
Anon. *Spir Life* 39:185-186 Aut 1993.

Hoffman, Lawrence A, and Walton, Janet R, eds.
Sacred sund and social change: liturgical music in Jewish and Christian experience. University of Notre Dame Press, 1992.
Randall, Scott J. *Mod Lit* 20:40 Ag 1993.

Hoffmann, Virginia Curran.
The codependent Church. Crossroad, n.d.
Lord, Elizabeth. *Way* 33:157-158 Ap 1993.

Hoffner, Harry A.
Hittite myths. Scholars, 1990.
Younger, Lawson K, Jr. *CBQ* 55:339 Ap 1993.

Hofmann, Karl.
Eine katholische Generation zwischen Kirche und Welt. Wissner, 1992.
Bleistein, Roman, 1928-. *Stimm Zeit* 211:70-71 Ja 1993.

Hofstra, Marilyn M.
Voices: Native American hymns and worship resources. Discipleship Resources, n.d.
Gibson, F. *Mod Lit* 19:40 D 1992-Ja 1993.

Hogg, J.
La certosa di Trisulti. Institut für Anglistik und Amerikanistik, 1991.
Anon. *NRT* 115:308 Mr-Ap 1993.

Hoglund, Kenneth G.
Achaemenid imperial administration in Syria-Palestine and the missions of Ezra and Nehemiah. Scholars, 1992.
Graham, Patrick M. *OTA* 16:174 F 1993.
Heiser, W Charles. *TheolDgst* 40:167 Sum 1993.

Hoitenga, Dewey J, Jr.
Faith and reason from Plato to Plantinga. State University of New York Press, 1991.
Wolterstorff, Nicholas P. *Thomist* 57:542-546 Jl 1993.

Holden, Anthony.
The tarnished crown. Bantam Press, n.d.
Kenny, Mary, 1936-. *Tablet* 247:889-890 Jl 10 1993.

Holden, Lyn.
Forms of deformity. JSOT, 1991.
Wright, John W. *OTA* 16:159 F 1993.

Hollermann, Ephrem.
The reshaping of a tradition; American Benedictine women 1852-1881. UMI Dissertation Service, n.d.
Anon. *ABenR* 44:112-113 Mr 1993.

Hollies, Linda H.
Inner healing for broken vessels: seven steps to a woman's way of healing. Upper Room Books, n.d.
Graham, William C. *Nat Cath Rep* 29:25 Mr 26 1993.

Hollings, Michael.
Love heals: prayers in a violent world. McCrimmon, n.d.
Forrester, David. *Tablet* 247:586 My 8 1993.

Holloway, Richard.
Anger, sex, doubt and death. SPCK, n.d.
Hoose, Bernard. *Way* 33:262 Jl 1993.

Holmes, Richard.
Fatal avenue: a traveller's history of the battlefields of northern France and Flanders, 1346-1945. Cape, n.d.
Blythe, Ronald. *Tablet* 247:108-109 Ja 23 1993.

Holmes, Stephen.
The anatomy of antiliberalism. Harvard University Press, 1993.
Elshtain, Jean Bethke, 1941-. *Comm* 120:30-32 N 5 1993.

Holtz, Barry W, ed.
The Schocken guide to Jewish books. Schocken Books, 1992.
Stuhlmueller, Carroll. *BibleT* 31:54-55 Ja 1993.

Homo imago et amicus Dei.
Pont Collegium Croaticum Sancti Hieronymi, 1991.
Caprile, Giovanni. *Civilta* 2:614-615 Je 19 1993.

Hong, Howard V, and Hong, Edna H, eds.
Søren Kierkegaard: "eighteen upbuilding discourses". Princeton University Press, 1990.
Vardy, P. *Heythrop* 34:112-113 Ja 1993.

Honoré, Jean, Abp.
The spiritual journey of Newman. Alba House, 1992.
Dollen, Charles. *Priest* 49:52 Ap 1993.
Rutler, George W. *HPR* 93:76 Jl 1993.

Hood, Robert E.
Must God remain Greek? Afro cultures and God-talk. Fortress, 1990.
Bevans, Stephen. *New Theol Rev* 6:95-96 Ag 1993.

Hooker, Irene H, et al.
The caterpillar that came to church: a story of the Eucharist. Our Sunday Visitor, 1993.
Koterski, J. *HPR* 94:73 O 1993.

Hooker, Morna D.
The Gospel according to Saint Mark. Hendrickson, 1991.
Wansbrough, Henry. *Priests & People* 6:435-436 N 1992.
Senior, Donald. *BibleT* 31:315 S 1993.

Hooper, Walter, ed.
Daily readings with C.S. Lewis. Fount, n.d.
Hollings, Michael. *Tablet* 247:1304 O 9 1993.

Hoover, Robert G.
Creating an effective parish pastoral council. Liturgical, n.d.
Weathers, Barbara. *CLW* 64:32-33 Jl-S 1993.

Hopkins, D N, and Cummings, G C L, eds.
Cut loose your stammering tongue. Orbis Books, 1991.
Anon. *NRT* 115:628-629 Jl-Ag 1993.

Hopper, David H.
Technology, theology, and the idea of progress. John Knox, 1991.
Casey, Stephen J. *Horizons (CTS)* 19:341-342 Fall 1992.

Hopper, Stanley Romaine, 1907-1991.
The way of transfiguration: religious imagination as theopoiesis. John Knox Press, 1992.
Heiser, W Charles. *TheolDgst* 40:68 Spr 1993.

Horbury, William, ed.
Templum amicitiae: essays on the second temple presented to Ernst Bammel. JSOT, 1991.
Koester, Craig R. *CBQ* 54:822-824 O 1992.

Horgan, James J, and Fuchs, Lucy, eds.
Social justice: the teachings of Catholics, Protestants, Jews, and Muslims. St Leo's College Press, 1992.
Miller, L. *Liguorian* 81:68 F 1993.
Heiser, W Charles. *TheolDgst* 40:87-88 Spr 1993.

Horovitz, Michael, ed.
Grandchildren of Albion. New Departures, n.d.
Aitken, Tom. *Tablet* 247:51 Ja 9 1993.

Horst, P W van der.
Ancient Jewish epitaphs. Kok Pharos Publishing House, 1991.
Schoors, A. *Eph Theol Lovan* 78:403-404 D 1992.

Horst, Ulrich.
Evangelische ARmut und Kirche: Thomas von Aquin und die Armutskontroversen des 13 und gebinnenden 14 Jahrhunderts. Akademie Verlag, 1992.
Bandera, Armando. *Cien Tom* 120:195-196 Ja-Ap 1993.

Horton, Michael Scott.
Made in America. Baker, 1991.
Patterson, Robert W. *Crisis* 11:13-14 My 1993.

Houlden, J L.
Bible and belief. SPCK, 1991.
Fergusson, David. *New Blckfrs* 74:50-51 Ja 1993.

Houlden, Leslie, ed.
Austin Farrer: the essential sermons. SPCK, n.d.
Donaldson, Terence L. *Can Cath Rev* 11:31 F 1993.

Houlgate, Stephen.
Freedom, truth and history: an introduction to Hegel's philosophy. Routledge, 1991.
O'Connor, Brian. *IJPS* 1:152-154 Mr 1993.

Hourcade, J.
Pourquoi la femme? Desclée, 1992.
Anon. *NRT* 115:299-300 Mr-Ap 1993.

Hours, Bernard.
Madame Louise, princesse au Carmel (1737-1787). Les Editions du Cerf, 1987.
Farnham, J. *CHist* 78:665-666 O 1992.

House, Paul R.
The unity of the Twelve. Almond, 1990.
Lust, Johan. *Eph Theol Lovan* 78:156 Ap 1992.
Mariottini, Claude F. *OTA* 15:510 O 1992.

House, Paul R, ed.
Beyond form criticism: essays in Old Testament literary criticism. Eisenbrauns, 1992.
Begg, Christopher T. *OTA* 16:154 F 1993.

Houten, Christiana Van.
The alien in Israelite law. JSOT, 1991.
Hoppe, Leslie J. *OTA* 16:186-187 F 1993.

Houtman, C.
Exodus vertaald en verklaard, vol 2. J H Kok, 1989.
Vervenne, Marc. *Eph Theol Lovan* 78:407-409 D 1992.
Exodus vertaald en verklaard, vol I. J H Kok, 1986.
Vervenne, Marc. *Eph Theol Lovan* 78:407-409 D 1992.

Hover, Margot.
Caring for yourself when caring for others. Twenty-Third, 1993.
Anon. *Health Prog* 74:68 1993.

Howard, Maureen.
Natural history. Norton, n.d.
Malin, Irving. *Comm* 120:23 F 12 1993.

Howell, Patrick J, and Chamberlain, Guy, eds.
Empowering authority: the charisms of episcopacy and primacy in the Church today. Sheed and Ward, n.d.
Power, William E. *Can Cath Rev* 11:30-31 F 1993.

Hruby, Dolores, and Tindall, Susan F.
Sing to the Lord an old song. Pastoral Press, n.d.
O'Keefe, Jane. *Past Mus* 18:60-61 O-N 1993.

Hsia, Po-chia R.
Trent 1475. Yale University Press, 1992.
Heiser, W Charles. *TheolDgst* 40:167 Sum 1993.

Huber, F.
Die Bhagavadgita in der neueren indischen Auslegung und in der Begegnung mit dem christlichen Glauben. Verlag der ev.-luth, 1991.
Masson, J. *NRT* 115:604 Jl-Ag 1993.

Huber, Richard.
How professors play the cat guarding the cream. Mason University Press, 1992.
Giles, James E. *CrossCurr* 43:256 Sum 1993.

Hublin, J-J, and Tillier, A-M, eds.
Aux origines d'Homo sapiens. PUF, 1991.
Anon. *NRT* 115:294-295 Mr-Ap 1993.

Huck, Gabe.
Preaching about the Mass. Liturgy Training Publications, 1992.
Hommerding, Leroy. *Mod Lit* 20:42 Mr 1993.
The three days: parish prayer in the Paschal Triduum. Liturgy Training Publications, 1992.
Gollob, Timothy. *Mod Lit* 19:40 D 1992-Ja 1993.

Huck, Gabe, ed.
Hymnal for Catholic students. Liturgy Training Publications, 1989.
Lane, John Thomas. *Emmanuel* 99:358-359 Jl-Ag 1993.

Hudgins, Andrew.
The never-ending story: new poems. Houghton Mifflin Company, n.d.
Keen, Suzanne. *Comm* 120:26-28 F 26 1993.

Hudon, William V.
Marcello Cervini and ecclesiastical government in Tridentine Italy. Illinois University Press, 1992.
Cesareo, Francesco C. *CHist* 79:338-339 Ap 1993.
Padberg, John. *RRel* 52:787-788 S-O 1993.
Heiser, W Charles. *TheolDgst* 40:167 Sum 1993.

Hudson, Deal W, and Moran, Dennis W, eds.
The future of Thomism. University of Notre Dame Press, 1992.
Sullivan, James A. *HPR* 94:75-76 N 1993.

Huebsch, Bill.
The new scripture way of the cross: based on the Stations of the Cross led by Pope John Paul II. Twenty-Third Publications, n.d.
Hollings, Michael. *Tablet* 247:278 F 27 1993.

Huels, John M.
Disputed questions in the liturgy today. Liturgy Training Publication, 1988.
Lane, John Thomas. *Emmanuel* 98:177-179 Ap 1992.

Hughes, Gerard W.
Oh God, why?: a journey through Lent fo bruised pilgrims. The Bible Reading Fellowship, n.d.
Anon. *Month* 26:114 Mr 1993.
Oh God, why?: a journey through Lent for bruised pilgrims. Bible Reading Fellowship, n.d.
Hollings, Michael. *Tablet* 247:278 F 27 1993.

Hughes, Jeremy.
Secrets of the times. JSOT, 1990.
Lust, Johan. *Eph Theol Lovan* 78:413 D 1992.

Hughes, Kathleen.
The monk's tale: a biography of Godfrey Diekmann, OSB. Liturgical Press, 1991.
Huels, J. *Emmanuel* 98:179 Ap 1992.
The Victorian governess. Hambledon Press, n.d.
Townsend, John Rowe. *Tablet* 247:789-790 Je 19 1993.

Hughes, Robert.
Culture of complaint: the fraying of America. Oxford University Press, n.d.
Power, Michael. *Can Cath Rev* 11:25-26 O 1993.

Hughes, Shirley.
Dogger. William Morrow Co, n.d.
Neuberger, Anne E. *ReligTJ* 27:34 F 1993.

Hultgren, Arland J, et al eds.
All things new: essays in honor of Roy A. Harrisville. Luther Northwestern Theological Seminary, 1992.
Heiser, W Charles. *TheolDgst* 40:50 Spr 1993.

Human sexuality: a Catholic perspective for education and lifelong learning.
United States Catholic Conference Office for Publishing, n.d.
Campbell, Joe. *Can Cath Rev* 11:30-31 My 1993.

Hume, David, 1711-1776.
Writings on religion. Open Court, 1992.
Heiser, W Charles. *TheolDgst* 40:167 Sum 1993.

Hume, George Basil, Cardinal, 1923-.
Light in the Lord. The Liturgical Press, n.d.
Dollen, Charles. *Priest* 49:48 My 1993.

Humphrey, Hugh M.
He is risen! a new reading of Mark's Gospel. Paulist Press, 1992.
Senior, Donald. *BibleT* 31:60 Ja 1993.
Sweetland, Dennis M. *Bib Th Bul* 23:43 Spr 1993.
Anon. *Furrow* 44:127-128 F 1993.
Heiser, W Charles. *TheolDgst* 40:69 Spr 1993.

Humphreys, Carolyn.
From ash to fire. New City Press, 1992.
Heiser, W Charles. *TheolDgst* 40:167-168 Sum 1993.

Hunger, Hermann.
Astrological reports to Assyrian kings. Helsinki University Press, 1992.
Fitzgerald, Aloysius. *OTA* 16:408 Je 1993.

Jervis, L Ann.
The purpose of Romans: a comparative letter structure investigation. Sheffield, 1991.
White, John L. *CBQ* 55:158-160 Ja 1993.

Les jésuites à Namur: 1610-1773.
Namur Presses universitaires, 1991.
Plumat, N. *NRT* 115:141-142 Ja-F 1993.

Jésus et la violence.
no publisher given, n.d.
Anon. *NRT* 115:637-638 Jl-Ag 1993.

Joblin, Joseph, 1920-.
La iglesia y la guerra: conciencia, violencia y poder. Herder, 1990.
Junges, J. *Perspectiva* 24:395-398 S-D 1992.

Johannesson, Kurt.
The Renaissance of the Goths in sixteenth-century Sweden: Johannes and Olaus Magnus as politicians and historians. University of California Press, 1991.
Garstein, O. *CHist* 78:654-655 O.1992.

Johanson, Calvin M.
Discipling music ministry: twenty-first century directions. Hendrickson Pubs, 1992.
Hommerding, Leroy. *Mod Lit* 20:41-42 Ag 1993.

John, Jeffrey.
Living tradition: affirming Catholicism in the Anglican Church. Cowley Publications, 1992.
Gros, Jeffrey, 1938-. *RRel* 52:475-476 My-Je 1993.

John, of Taizé.
Praying the Our Father today. The Pastoral Press, 1992.
Heiser, W Charles. *TheolDgst* 40:70 Spr 1993.

John Paul II, Pope, 1920- (Karol Wojtyla) (elected 1978).
Angelus meditations on the Litany of the Sacred Heart. Our Sunday Visitor, n.d.
Kern, Walter O. *HPR* 93:72-73 Ap 1993.
Dieci comandamenti. Ed Paoline, 1991.
Caprile, Giovanni. *Civilta* 2:305-306 My 1 1993.
John Paul II: a panorama of his teachings. New City Press, 1989.
Mathews, Susan F. *Diakonia* 26 no 1:77-81 1993.
The pope speaks to the American church: John Paul II's homilies, speeches, and letters to Catholics in the United States. HarperSanFrancisco, 1992.
Heiser, W Charles. *TheolDgst* 40:70 Spr 1993.

Johnson, Adam.
The spiral staircase. Acumen Publications, n.d.
Heath-Stubbs, John. *Tablet* 247:1134 S 4 1993.

Johnson, Angela, and Soman, David.
One of three. Franklin Watts, n.d.
Neuberger, Anne E. *ReligTJ* 27:58 S 1993.

Johnson, Denis.
Jesus' son. Farrar, Straus and Giroux, n.d.
Donnelly, Daria. *Comm* 120:23-24 Ag 13 1993.

Johnson, Elizabeth A, 1941-.
She who is. Crossroad, 1992.
Donovan, M. *America* 168:18-20 Ja 2-9 1993.
Young, E. *Nat Cath Rep* 29:10 F 12 1993.
Johnson, Luke Timothy, 1943-. *Comm* 120:17-22 Ja 29 1993.
Ramshaw, Gail. *Worship* 67:284-286 My 1993.
Wright, John H. *TheolStds* 54:371-373 Je 1993.
Boys, Mary C. *CrossCurr* 43:269-272 Sum 1993.
Heiser, W Charles. *TheolDgst* 40:168-169 Sum 1993.

Johnson, Evelyn M R, and Bower, Bobbie.
Building a great children's ministry. Abingdon Press, 1992.
Gallagher, Miriam J. *Mod Lit* 20:41 Je-Jl 1993.

Johnson, James Turner, and Weigel, George.
Just war and the Gulf war. Ethics and Public Policy Center, 1991.
Grondelski, John M. *HPR* 93:62 F 1993.
Just war and the Gulf War. Ethics and Public Policy Center, 1991.
Pope, Stephen J. *America* 168:26-27+ Ap 24 1993.

Johnson, Lawrence E.
A morally deep world: an essay on moral significance and environmental ethics. Cambridge University Press, 1991.
Hoose, Bernard. *Heythrop* 34:199-201 Ap 1993.

Johnson, Luke Timothy, 1943-.
The Acts of the Apostles. Liturgical, 1991.
Harrington, Daniel J. *America* 168:34-35 F 6 1993.
Senior, Donald. *BibleT* 31:253 Jl 1993.
The Gospel of Luke. Liturgical, 1992.
Harrington, Jay M. *Louvain Stds* 18:181-183 Sum 1993.
Neirynck, F. *Eph Theol Lovan* 78:441-442 D 1992.
McCready, Wayne O. *Can Cath Rev* 11:30-31 N 1993.

Johnson, Mark.
Moral imagination. University of Chicago, n.d.
O'Brien, Dennis. *Comm* 120:26-27 O 22 1993.

Johnson, Marshall D.
The purpose of the Biblical genealogies with special reference to the setting of the genealogies of Jesus. Cambridge University Press, 1988.
Bedard, Mariette. *CahiersJos* 41:139-140 Ja-Je 1993.

Johnson, Sherman E.
The Griesbach hypothesis and redaction criticism. Scholars Press, 1991.
Neirnyck, F. *Eph Theol Lovan* 78:436-437 D 1992.

Johnston, William.
Letters to contemplatives. Orbis Books, 1991.
Cummings, Charles. *Cist Stud* 28:[1] 1993.
Heiser, W Charles. *TheolDgst* 39:367 Wint 1992.

Johnstone, Ronald L.
Religion in society: a sociology of religion. Prentice Hall, 1992.
Heiser, W Charles. *TheolDgst* 40:70 Spr 1993.

Johnstone, W.
Exodus. Sheffield, 1990.
Rybolt, John E. *CBQ* 55:339-340 Ap 1993.

Jonas, Hans.
Le principe responsabilité, une éthique pour la civilisation technologique. Cerf, 1990.
Boissinot, Christian. *Laval Theol Phil* 49:334-339 Je 1993.

Jones, Anthony, and Moskoff, William, eds.
The great market debate in Soviet economics: an anthology. M.E. Sharpe, 1991.
Rider, Christine. *RSocEcon* 51:252-257 Sum 1993.

Jones, Arthur C, 1936-.
Capitalism and Christians: tough gospel challenges in a troubled world economy. Paulist Press, n.d.
Dunne, George M. *Nat Cath Rep* 29:16 Ap 2 1993.

Jones, Cheslyn, et al, eds.
The study of liturgy. SPCK, n.d.
Graham, William C. *Nat Cath Rep* 29:40 My 28 1993.

Jones, Douglas Rawlinson.
Jeremiah. Eerdmans, 1992.
Stuhlmueller, Carroll. *BibleT* 31:55 Ja 1993.
Gossai, Hemchand. *OTA* 15:508 O 1992.

Jones, Frederick M.
Alphonsus de Liguori, the Saint of Bourbon Naples 1696-1787. Gill and Macmillan, 1992.
McConvery, Brendon. *Tablet* 247:309-310 Mr 6 1993.
Devlin, Brendan P. *Furrow* 43:704-706 D 1992.
Pridmore, John. *Way* 33:165-166 Ap 1993.
Karrer, Walter. *Liguorian* 81:68 O 1993.
O'Toole, Michael. *Doctr Life* 43:247-248 Ap 1993.
Twomey, Vincent. *Studies* 82:214-217 Sum 1993.
Murphy, Francis Xavier, 1914-. *America* 168:24-25 Ap 24 1993.
Cunningham, Lawrence S, 1935-. *Comm* 120:28-29 My 7 1993.

Jones, Michael E.
Degenerate moderns. Ignatius Press, n.d.
Prizer, John. *Register* 69:3 Jl 18 1993.

Jones, Pamela M.
Ambrosiana: art patronage and reform in seventeenth-century Milan. Cambridge University Press, n.d.
Reyntiens, Patrick. *Tablet* 247:582 My 8 1993.

Jones, Rebecca C.
Matthew and Tilly. Dutton Children's Books, n.d.
Neuberger, Anne E. *ReligTJ* 27:58 S 1993.

Jones, Robin Lloyd.
Fallen angels. Canongate, n.d.
Traylen, Maryanne. *Tablet* 247:1075 Ag 21 1993.

Jong, Stephan de.
Het verhaal van Hizkia en Sanherib. Centrale Huisdrukkerij V U, 1992.
Begg, Christopher T. *OTA* 15:499-500 O 1992.

Jonge, Marinus de.
Jesus, the servant-Messiah. Yale University Press, 1991.
Evans, Craig A, 1952-. *CBQ* 54:775-776 O 1992.
McVann, Mark. *Bib Th Bul* 23:82 Sum 1993.
Jewish eschatology, early Christian Christology and the testaments of the Twelve Patriarchs. Brill, 1991.
Neirynck, F. *Eph Theol Lovan* 78:165-166 Ap 1992.

Joos, André.
Dalla Russia con fede, vol I: Vie dell'originalità cristiana russa. Vivere in, 1991.
Spidlik, Tomas. *Civilta* 144:198-199 Ja 16 1993.

Jordan, Anthony J.
Major John MacBride. Historical Society, n.d.
Fogarty, Tom. *Studies* 82:229-230 Sum 1993.

Jordan, Michael.
Gods of earth. Bantam Press, 1992.
Wodding, C A M. *Month* 26:32-33 Ja 1993.

Jorgensen, Susan S.
Rekindling the passion. Resource Publications, 1993.
Dollen, Charles. *Priest* 49:52 Ap 1993.
Cassidy, Mary. *Furrow* 44:518-519 S 1993.

Josipovici, Gabriel.
In a hotel garden. Carcanet, n.d.
Cooke, Judy. *Tablet* 247:985 Jl 31 1993.

Josol, Abdon Ma C, ed.
Responses to the signs of the times: selected documents: Catholic Bishops' Conference of the Philippines. Redemptorist Publications, 1991.
Heiser, W Charles. *TheolDgst* 39:382 Wint 1992.

Jossua, Jean-Pierre.
Le livre de signes. Cerf, 1993.
Godin, A. *Lumen* 48:235 Je 1993.

Jossua, Jean-Pierre, and Sed, N-J, ed.
Interpréter. Ed du Cerf, 1992.
Anon. *NRT* 115:298-299 Mr-Ap 1993.

Joüon, Paul.
A grammar of Biblical Hebrew. Biblical Institute, 1991.
    Smith, Mark S. *CBQ* 55:116-119 Ja 1993.

Jourdin, Michel Mollat du, and Vauchez, André, eds.
Histoire du Christianisme des origines à nos jours, volume VI: Un temps d'épreuves (1274-1449). Desclée-Fayard, 1990.
    Pascoe, L. *CHist* 78:645-646 O 1992.

Jours du Seigneur.
Brepols, 1991.
    Volpe, L. *NRT* 114:904-905 N-D 1992.

Juan De La Cruz, San.
Obras comletas, a cargo de Maximiliano Herráiz. Sígueme, n.d.
    Bandera, Armando. *Cien Tom* 119:420 My-Ag 1992.

Jueller, David L.
Foundation of Karl Barth's doctrine of reconciliation: Jesus Chrsit crucified and risen. Toronto Studies in Theology, 1990.
    Fackre, G. *TheolStds* 53:762-763 D 1992.

Jungmann, Josef Andreas.
Breve storia della preghiera cristiana. no publisher given, 1991.
    Mellinato, Giuseppe. *Civilta* 3:198-200 Jl 17 1993.

Juschel, Karl-Josef.
Born before all time? Crossroad, 1992.
    Heiser, W Charles. *TheolDgst* 40:171 Sum 1993.

Jusdado Ruiz-Capillas, Miguel Angel.
El dolo en el matrimonio canónico. Bosch, 1991.
    Tourneau, Dominique Le. *Stud Can* 27 no 1:267-268 1993.

Justenhoven, Heinz-Gerhard.
Francisco de Vitoria zu Krieg und Frieden. Bachem, 1991.
    Traboulay, D. *TheolStds* 53:786-787 D 1992.

K

Kaam, Adrian L Van, 1920-.
Formative spirituality: volume five: traditional formation. Crossroad, 1992.
    Heiser, W Charles. *TheolDgst* 40:91 Spr 1993.
    Kenel, Mary Elizabeth. *RRel* 52:625-626 Jl-Ag 1993.

Kadir, Djelal.
Columbus and the ends of the earth: Europe's prophetic rhetoric as conquering ideology. University of California Press, 1992.
    Heiser, W Charles. *TheolDgst* 39:367 Wint 1992.
    West, Delno C. *Cithara* 32:52-53 My 1993.

Kagan, Richard L.
Lucrecia's dreams: politics and prophecy in Sixteenth-Century Spain. University of California Press, 1990.
    Hamilton, Alastair. *Heythrop* 34:332-333 Jl 1993.

Kaiser, Otto.
Grundrib der Einleitung in die kanonischen und deuteronkanonischen Schriften des Alten Testaments. Mohr, 1992.
    Begg, Christopher T. *OTA* 16:159-160 F 1993.

Kaiser, Walter C.
Micah-Malachi. Word, 1992.
    Murphy, Roland E. *OTA* 16:433 Je 1993.

Kakar, Sudhir.
The analyst and the mystic: psychoanalytic reflections on religion and mysticism. University of Chicago Press, 1992.
    Heiser, W Charles. *TheolDgst* 40:70 Spr 1993.

Kakatos, Menás, ed.
Bell's theorem, quantum theory and conceptions of the universe. D. Reidel, 1989.
    Hespel, Bertrand. *RPhil Louvain* 91:522 Ag 1993.

Kalimi, Isaac.
The Books of Chronicles: a classified bibliography. Simor, 1990.
    Knoppers, Gary N. *CBQ* 55:119 Ja 1993.

Kammer, Fred.
Doing faithjustice: an introduction to Catholic social thought. Paulist, 1991.
    Weber, Leonard J. *Horizons (CTS)* 19:340-341 Fall 1992.
    Worland, Stephen T. *RSocEcon* 51:380-387 Aut 1993.

Kannookadan, Pauly.
The East Syrian lectionary. Mar Thoma Yogam, 1991.
    Halleux, André de. *Eph Theol Lovan* 78:479-481 D 1992.

Kapera, Zdizislaw J.
Qumran Cave IV and MMT. Enigma, 1991.
    Fitzmyer, Joseph Augustine, 1920-. *OTA* 16:192-193 F 1993.

Kaplan, Fred.
Henry James: the imagination of genius. Hodder & Stoughton, n.d.
    Mitchell, Keith. *Tablet* 247:620-621 My 15 1993.

Kaplan, Lawrence, ed.
Fundamentalism in comparative perspective. The University of Massachusetts Press, 1992.
    Heiser, W Charles. *TheolDgst* 39:362 Wint 1992.

Kardong, Terrence G.
Asking Benedict. Assumption Abbey Press, 1992.
    Heiser, W Charles. *TheolDgst* 40:169 Sum 1993.

Karris, Robert J.
Jesus and the marginalized in John's Gospel. The Liturgical Press, 1990.
    Boys, Mary C. *CBQ* 54:786-787 O 1992.

Kasimow, Harold, and Sherwin, Byron L, eds.
No religion is an island. Abraham Joshua Heschel and interreligious dialogue. Orbis Books, 1991.
    Pastor, Felix-Alejandro. *Gregorianum* 74 no 2:408 1993.

Kasper, Walter.
Theology and church. The Crossroad Publishing Company, n.d.
    Smith, T. Allan. *Can Cath Rev* 11:26 Jl-Ag 1993.

Kassian, Mary A.
The feminist gospel: the movement to unite feminism with the church. Crossway Books, 1992.
    Heiser, W Charles. *TheolDgst* 39:367-368 Wint 1992.

Kasteel, Annemarie.
Francis Janssens, 1843-1897: a Dutch-American prelate. The Center for Louisiana Studies, 1992.
    Frange, Jonathan De. *CHist* 79:365-366 Ap 1993.
    Chappin, Marcel. *Gregorianum* 74 no 3:593 1993.

Katafiasz, Karen.
Celebrate-your-womanhood therapy. Abbey Press, n.d.
    Dangel, Mary Jo. *St Anth* 100:52-53 Mr 1993.

Katz, Steven T, ed.
Mysticism and language. Oxford University Press, 1992.
    Cunningham, Lawrence S, 1935-. *Comm* 120:28 Ag 13 1993.
    Heiser, W Charles. *TheolDgst* 40:178 Sum 1993.

Kauffman, Christopher J.
Columbianism and the Knights of Columbus: a quincentenary history. Simon & Schuster, 1992.
    Heiser, W Charles. *TheolDgst* 40:70-71 Spr 1993.
Faith and fraternalism: the history of the Knights of Columbus. Simon and Schuster, 1992.
    Crews, Clyde F. *Living Light* 30:109-110 Aut 1993.
Mission to rural America: the story of W Howard Bishop, founder of Glenmary. Paulist, 1991.
    Allitt, Patrick. *ChrWorld* 236:236+ S-O 1993.

Kaufman, Philip S.
The beloved disciple: a witness against anti-semitism. The Liturgical Press, 1991.
    Senior, Donald. *BibleT* 31:60 Ja 1993.
    Witherup, Ronald D. *CBQ* 54:801-802 O 1992.
The beloved disciple: witness against anti-Semitism. The Liturgical Press, 1991.
    Townsend, Mark. *Furrow* 44:187-188 Mr 1993.

Kavanaugh, John F.
Following Christ in a consumer society: the spirituality of cultural resistance. Orbis Books, 1991.
    Bretzke, J. *Gregorianum* 73 No 4:763-764 1992.

Kavanaugh, Kieran.
God speaks in the night: the life, times, and teaching of St John of the Cross. Institute of Carmelite Studies, 1991.
    Egan, Keith J. *Horizons (CTS)* 19:315 Fall 1992.

Kavanaugh, Kieran, and Rodriguez, Otilio.
The collected works of St John of the Cross. ICS Publications, 1991.
    Williams, Joan. *Living Prayer* 26:32 Ja-F 1993.

Kazantzis, Judith.
The rabbit magician plate. Sinclair-Stevenson, n.d.
    Lawson, Sarah. *Tablet* 247:1015 Ag 7 1993.

Kazhdan, Alexander P.
The Oxford dictionary of Byzantium 1-3. Oxford University, 1991.
    Dennis, George T. *TheolStds* 53:749-752 D 1992.

Kealy, Sean P, 1937-.
Jesus and politics. The Liturgical Press, 1990.
    McConvery, Brendon. *Doctr Life* 42:652-653 D 1992.
    Boys, Mary C. *CBQ* 54:786-787 O 1992.

Keane, Philip S.
Health care reform. Paulist, n.d.
    Sanders, Susan. *Nat Cath Rep* 30:26 N 19 1993.

Keating, Karl.
What Catholics really believe—setting the record straight. Servant Publications, n.d.
    Higgins, James J. *Liguorian* 81:70 S 1993.

Keating, Thomas.
Invitation to love. Element, 1992.
    Heiser, W Charles. *TheolDgst* 40:169 Sum 1993.
The kingdom of God is like. Crossroad, n.d.
    Graham, William C. *Nat Cath Rep* 30:36 N 19 1993.
Reawakenings. Crossroad, n.d.
    Campbell, Charles M. *St Anth* 100:53 Mr 1993.
    Pecht, Gerard. *Liguorian* 81:68-69 Ag 1993.

Kee, Cynthia.
A responsible man. Chatto & Windus, n.d.
    Walsh, Jill Paton. *Tablet* 247:440 Ap 3 1993.

Kee, Howard Clark.
What can we know about Jesus? Cambridge University, 1990.
    Winkler, Jude. *CBQ* 54:788-789 O 1992.

Keefe, Donald J.
Convenantal theology: the Eucharistic order of history (two volumes). University Press of America, n.d.
    TeSelle, Eugene, 1931-. *America* 168:19+ My 8 1993.

Keel, Othmar.
Das Recht der Bilder gesehen zu werden. Vandehoeck & Ruprecht, 1992.
    Fitzgerald, Aloysius. *OTA* 16:407 Je 1993.

Keel, Othmar, and Uehlinger, Christoph.
Göttinen, Götter und Gottessymbole. Herder, 1992.
    Murphy, Roland E. *OTA* 16:187 F 1993.
    Ska, Jean Louis. *NRT* 115:260-261 Mr-Ap 1993.

Keel-Leu, Hildi.
Vorderasiatische Stempelsiegel. Vandenhoeck and Ruprecht, 1992.
    Fitzgerald, Aloysius. *OTA* 16:160 F 1993.

Keen, Sam.
Fire in the belly: on being a man. Bantam, n.d.
    Toolan, David S. *Church* 9:55-58 Spr 1993.

Keenan, Brian.
An evil cradling. Hutchinson, n.d.
    FitzGerald, Barbara. *Furrow* 44:119 F 1993.

Keenan, John P.
The meaning of Christ: a Mahayana theology. Orbis Books, 1989.
 Rule, Paul. *Pacifica* 6:115-116 F 1993.
Keener, Craig S.
Paul, women and wives. Hendrickson, 1992.
 Senior, Donald. *BibleT* 31:315 S 1993.
Keeting, Thomas.
Invitation to love: the way of Christian contemplation. Element, 1992.
 Moore, Patrick. *Priests & People* 7:124 Mr 1993.
Kehl, Medard.
Die Kirche: eine Katholische ekklesiologie. Echter, 1992.
 Kress, Robert. *TheolStds* 54:179-181 Mr 1993.
Kehrwald, Leif, and Kehrwald, Rene.
Families nurturing faith. Don Bosco Multimedia, n.d.
 Hanlon, James. *Can Cath Rev* 11:31 O 1993.
Kehrwald, Leif, and Roberto, John, eds.
Families and youth: a resource manual. no publisher given, n.d.
 Roach, Joseph J. *Living Light* 30:102-103 Aut 1993.
Keim, Nancy.
Tutoring and mentoring. Resource Publications, 1993.
 Riley, David M. *Catechist* 27:17 S 1993.
Keim, Nancy, and Tolliver, Cindy.
Tutoring and mentoring. Resource Publications, 1993.
 Kealy, Catherine. *Momentum* 24:80 N-D 1993.
Keire, Anita E.
A parent's guide to prayer. Curriculm Development Associates, n.d.
 McCann, Deborah. *ReligTJ* 27:9 Mr 1993.
Keizer, Garret.
A dresser of sycamore trees: the finding of a ministry. Viking, n.d.
 Luebering, Carol. *St Anth* 100:52 Ja 1993.
Keller, Philip.
A layman looks at the Love of God: a devotional study of 1 Corinthians 13. Marshall Pickering, n.d.
 Forrester, David. *Tablet* 247:728 Je 5 1993.
Keller, Sharon R.
The Jews: a treasury of art and literature. Hugh Lauter Levin Associates, 1992.
 Heiser, W Charles. *TheolDgst* 40:69 Spr 1993.
Kellermann, Bill Wylie.
Seasons of faith and conscience: kairos, confession, liturgy. Orbis, 1991.
 Wallace, James A, 1944-. *New Theol Rev* 6:99-100 F 1993.
Kelley, Page H.
Biblical Hebrew: an introductory grammar. Eerdmans, 1992.
 Dempsey, Deirdre A. *OTA* 16:160-161 F 1993.
Kelly, Aidan, et al.
Religious holidays and calendars. Omnigraphics, 1993.
 Heiser, W Charles. *TheolDgst* 40:169 Sum 1993.
Kelly, Francis D.
The mystery we proclaim: catechesis at the third millennium. Our Sunday Visitor, n.d.
 Gullekson, Justin W. *New Oxford Rev* 60:31-32 S 1993.
 Higgins, James J. *Liguorian* 81:73 O 1993.
Kelly, George A, ed.
FCS Proceedings 1991 (Church and state in America: Catholic questions). St John's University, 1992.
 Kennedy, Leonard A. *ChrWorld* 38:123 Mr-Ap 1993.
Kelly, Joseph F.
The concise dictionary of early Christianity. Liturgical, n.d.
 Dollen, Charles. *Priest* 49:52 F 1993.
 Campbell, James. *Month* 26:236 Je 1993.
Kelly, Kevin T.
New directions in moral theology. Geoffrey Chapman, 1992.
 Meehan, A. *Priests & People* 6:484-485 D 1992.
 Hogan, Linda. *Doctr Life* 43:61-62 Ja 1993.
 Harvey, Nicholas Peter. *Month* 26:33-34 Ja 1993.
 Soane, Brendan. *Tablet* 247:311 Mr 6 1993.
 Curran, Charles E, 1934-. *Heythrop* 34:198 Ap 1993.
New directions in moral theology. Geoffrey Chapman, n.d.
 Hoose, Bernard. *Way* 33:261 Jl 1993.
Kelly, Nora.
Bad chemistry. Collins Crime Club, n.d.
 Lejeune, Anthony. *Tablet* 247:1136 S 4 1993.
Kelly, Patrick Hyde.
Locke on money vol I, II. Clarendon Press, 1991.
 Chisholm, John E. *IJPS* 1:154-156 Mr 1993.
Kempinski, Aharon, and Reich, Ronny, eds.
The architecture of ancient Israel: from the prehistoric to the Persian periods. Israel Exploration Society, 1992.
 Magness, Jodi. *OTA* 16:155 F 1993.
Kendall, Lorna.
The mind in the heart: Michael Ramsey: theologian and man of prayer. SLG, 1991.
 Vivian, Tim. *Cist Stud* 27 No 4:[109] 1992.
Kennedy, Brian P.
Art is my life, a tribute to James White. The National Gallery of Ireland, n.d.
 Thiessen, Gesa. *Studies* 81:454-456 Wint 1992.
Kennedy, Leonard A.
Ethics for high schools. Life Ethics Centre, n.d.
 Callam, Daniel. *Can Cath Rev* 11:28-29 F 1993.
How to keep your university Catholic. Life Ethics Centre, n.d.
 Callam, Daniel. *Can Cath Rev* 11:28-29 F 1993.
How to keep your university Catholic. Veritas, 1992.
 Kelly, George A. *HPR* 93:79 Jl 1993.
Saint Thomas Aquinas: his importance today. Life Ethics Centre, n.d.
 Callam, Daniel. *Can Cath Rev* 11:28 F 1993.

Kennedy, Paul M, 1945-.
Preparing for the twenty-first century. HarperCollins, n.d.
 Hartley, Anthony. *Tablet* 247:477-478 Ap 10-17 1993.
 Schroth, Raymond A, 1933-. *Nat Cath Rep* 29:14 Ap 16 1993.
 Rourke, Francis. *America* 169:25-26 S 11 1993.
Kennedy, Philip.
Schillebeeckx. Geoffrey Chapman, n.d.
 Kerr, Fergus. *Tablet* 247:1299-1300 O 9 1993.
Kenny, Anthony John.
Aquinas on mind. Routledge, n.d.
 Kerr, Fergus. *Tablet* 247:726-727 Je 5 1993.
The Catholic-Jewish dialogue and the state of Israel. Council of Christians and Jews, 1991.
 Fisher, Eugene J. *SIDIC* 25 No 1:32-33 1992.
Kenny, James.
Loving and learning: a guide to practical parenting. St Anthony Messenger, n.d.
 Dotterweich, Kass. *Liguorian* 81:69 S 1993.
Kent, Bruce.
Undiscovered ends. HarperCollins, n.d.
 Pridmore, John. *Way* 33:167 Ap 1993.
Keppes, Steven.
The text as thou. Indiana University Press, n.d.
 Cunningham, Lawrence S, 1935-. *Comm* 120:28 O 8 1993.
Ker, Ian.
Newman on being a Christian. University of Notre Dame Press, 1990.
 Hammond, David M. *Relig Lit* 24:97-104 Aut 1992.
Ker, Ian, ed.
The genius of John Henry Newman. Clarendon, 1989.
 Merrigan, Terrence. *Louvain Stds* 18:188-190 Sum 1993.
Ker, Ian, and Hill, Alan G, eds.
Newman after a hundred years. Clarendon, 1990.
 Merrigan, Terrence. *Louvain Stds* 18:188-190 Sum 1993.
Newman after hundred years. Clarendon, 1990.
 Evrard, P. *NRT* 114:932-933 N-D 1992.
Kerber, W, ed.
Das Absolute in der Ethik. Kindt Verlag, 1991.
 Anon. *NRT* 115:143 Ja-F 1993.
Menschenrechte und kulturelle Identität. Kindt Verlag, 1991.
 Menin, G. *NRT* 115:125 Ja-F 1993.
Wie tolerant ist der Islam? Kindt Verlag, 1991.
 Anon. *NRT* 115:629 Jl-Ag 1993.
Kerber, W, and Müller, J, eds.
Soziales Denken in einer zerrissenen Welt. Herder, 1991.
 Volpe, L. *NRT* 114:917-918 N-D 1992.
Kerr, Fergus.
La théologie après Wittgenstein. Cerf, 1991.
 Brito, Emilio. *Eph Theol Lovan* 78:469-470 D 1992.
Theology after Wittgenstein. Blackwell, 1986.
 Brito, Emilio. *Eph Theol Lovan* 78:469-470 D 1992.
Kerrigan, Colm.
Father Mathew and the Irish temperance movement 1838-1849. Cork University Press, 1992.
 Slevin, Gerard. *Doctr Life* 43:120-121 F 1993.
 McGuckian, Bernard J. *Studies* 82:108-110 Spr 1993.
Fr Mathew and the Irish temperance movement 1838-1849. Cork University Press, 1992.
 Campbell, Patrick J. *Furrow* 43:703-704 D 1992.
Kertelge, Karl, ed.
Metaphorik and mythos im Neuen Testament. Herder, 1990.
 Soards, Marion L. *CBQ* 54:826-827 O 1992.
Keshishian, Aram.
Conciliar fellowship: a common goal. WCC Publications, 1992.
 Heiser, W Charles. *TheolDgst* 39:368 Wint 1992.
Kessell, John L, and Hendricks, Rick, eds.
By force of arms: the journals of Don Diego de Vargas, New Mexico, 1691-1693. University of New Mexico Press, 1992.
 Espinosa, J Manuel. *CHist* 79:360-362 Ap 1993.
Kettle, Michael.
De Gaulle and Algeria 1940-1960. Quartet, n.d.
 Palliser, Michael. *Tablet* 247:1165-1166 S 11 1993.
Keyes, Margaret Frings.
Emotions and the Enneagram: working through your shadow life scrip. Molysdatur Publications, 1992.
 Heiser, W Charles. *TheolDgst* 40:70 Spr 1993.
The Enneagram cats of Muir Beach. Molysdatur Publications, 1992.
 Heiser, W Charles. *TheolDgst* 40:71 Spr 1993.
The Enneagram relationship workbook: a self and partnership assessment guide. Molysdatur Publications, 1992.
 Heiser, W Charles. *TheolDgst* 40:71 Spr 1993.
Keyt, David, and Miller, Fred D, Jr, eds.
A companion to Aristotle's Politics. Basil Blackwell, 1991.
 Hyland, Eddie. *IJPS* 1:119-128 Mr 1993.
Keyte, Hugh, and Parrott, Andrew, eds.
The new Oxford book of carols. Oxford University Press, n.d.
 Schuler, Richard Joseph, 1920-. *SacM* 119:24 Wint 1992.
Khalkid, Fazlun, and O'Brien, Joanne, eds.
Islam and ecology. Cassell, n.d.
 McDonagh, Sean. *Furrow* 44:120-123 F 1993.
Khoury, P.
Matéiaux pour servir à l'étude de la controverse théologique islamo-chrétienne de langue arabe du VIIIe au XIIe siècle. Oros-Verlag, 1991.
 Scheuer, J. *NRT* 115:605-606 Jl-Ag 1993.
Kid, Sue Monk.
When the heart waits: spiritual direction for life's sacred questions. HarperSanFrancisco, n.d.
 Graham, William C. *Nat Cath Rep* 29:25 Mr 26 1993.

Kidd, Reggie M.
Wealth and beneficence in the pastoral Epistles: a "bourgeois" form of early Christianity? Scholars, 1990.
   Karris, Robert J. *CBQ* 54:789-790 O 1992.

Kienzle, William X.
Dead wrong. Andrew and McMeel, n.d.
   Callam, Daniel. *Can Cath Rev* 11:27 Jl-Ag 1993.

Kierkegaard, Soren Aabye, 1813-1855.
Concluding unscientific postscript to philosophical fragments, vol 1. Princeton University Press, 1992.
   Heiser, W Charles. *TheolDgst* 40:169-170 Sum 1993.
Historical introduction, supplement, notes and index, vol 2. Princeton University Press, 1992.
   Heiser, W Charles. *TheolDgst* 40:169-170 Sum 1993.

Kieweler, Hans Volker.
Ben Sira-zwischen Judentum und Hellenismus. Lang, 1992.
   Murphy, Roland E. *OTA* 16:429 Je 1993.

Kilcourse, George.
Ace of freedoms: Thomas Merton's Christ. University of Notre Dame Press, n.d.
   Thurston, Bonnie. *America* 169:22 S 18 1993.
Double belonging: interchurch families and Christian unity. Paulist, 1992.
   Gros, Jeffrey, 1938-. *Cist Stud* 27 No 4:[109]-[110] 1992.
   Heiser, W Charles. *TheolDgst* 39:368 Wint 1992.
   Falardeau, Ernest R, 1928-. *Emmanuel* 99:177-178 Ap 1993.
   Bramlett, Bruce R. *JEcumen Stds* 29:478-479 Sum-Aut 1992.

Kilner, John F.
Life on the line. Eerdmans, 1992.
   Heiser, W Charles. *TheolDgst* 40:170 Sum 1993.
Life on the line. William B. Eerdmans, 1992.
   Dunklee, Larry. *Health Prog* 74:70-71 O 1993.
Who lives? who dies? ethical criteria in patient selection. Yale University Press, n.d.
   Walsh, James L. *Linacre* 60:94-95 Ag 1993.

Kilpatrick, William.
Why Johnny can't tell right from wrong. Simon & Schuster, 1992.
   Traviss, Mary Peter. *Momentum* 24:77-78 S-O 1993.

Kimball, Charles.
Striving together: a way forward in Christian-Muslim relations. Orbis, 1991.
   Neckebrouck, Valeer. *Eph Theol Lovan* 78:182-183 Ap 1992.

Kimbrough, S T, Jr, ed.
Charles Wesley, poet and theologian. Abingdon Press, 1992.
   Heiser, W Charles. *TheolDgst* 40:57 Spr 1993.

Kimchi, R David.
Commento ai Salmi, vol I: Sal 1-50. Città Nuova, 1991.
   Prato, Gian Luigi. *Civilta* 143:525-526 D 5 1992.

Kimel, Alvin F, Jr, ed.
Speaking the Christian God: the Holy Trinity and the challenge of feminism. Eerdmans, 1992.
   Johnson, Luke Timothy, 1943-. *Comm* 120:17-22 Ja 29 1993.
   Rocca, Gregory. *Thomist* 57:509-520 Jl 1993.

Kimmerling, Baruch, and Migdal, Joel.
Palestinians: the making of a people. The Free Press, n.d.
   Preisler, Barry. *America* 169:18-20 Jl 31-Ag 7 1993.

Kinberger, Mary Kay.
Lonergan on conversion: applications for religious reformation. American University Studies, 1992.
   Anon. *Spir Life* 39:189 Aut 1993.

King, Eleace.
CARA formation directory for men and women religious. Center for Applied Reasearch in the Apostolate, 1992.
   Heiser, W Charles. *TheolDgst* 40:55-56 Spr 1993.

King, Laurie, and Stovall, Dennis.
Classroom publishing: a practical guide to enhancing student literacy. Blue Heron Publishing, 1992.
   Vander Meer, Elizabeth. *Momentum* 24:78-79 N-D 1993.

King, Martin Luther.
Io ho un sogno. Scritti e discorsi che hanno cambiato il mondo. SEI, 1993.
   Flumeri, E. *Civilta* 3:542-543 S 18 1993.

King, Thomas M.
Merton: mystic at the center of America. Liturgical, 1992.
   Hart, Patrick. *Cist Stud* 28:[34]-[35] 1993.

Kingsbury, Jack Dean.
Conflict in Luke: Jesus, authorities, disciples. Fortress, 1991.
   Danker, Frederick. *CBQ* 54:790-791 O 1992.

Kinnamon, Michael, ed.
World Council of Churches: signs of the spirit. Eerdmans, 1992.
   Heiser, W Charles. *TheolDgst* 40:93-94 Spr 1993.

Kinney, Lisa F.
Lobby for your library. American Library Association, 1992.
   Weathers, Barbara. *CLW* 64:33-34 Jl-S 1993.

Kippley, John F.
Sex and the marriage covenant: a basis for morality. The Couple to Couple League International, 1991.
   Heiser, W Charles. *TheolDgst* 40:71 Spr 1993.

Kirchengeräte, Kreuze und Reliquiare der christlichen Kirchen.
K. G. Saur, 1992.
   Pfeiffer, Heinrich. *Gregorianum* 74 no 2:390-391 1993.

Kirk, Andrew.
Loosing the chains. Hodder and Stoughton, n.d.
   Barnes, Michael R. *Way* 33:169 Ap 1993.

Kirk, James, ed.
Humanism and reform: the Church in Europe, England and Scotland, 1400-1643: essays in honour of James K Cameron. Basil Blackwell, 1990.
   Hamilton, Alastair. *Heythrop* 34:213-214 Ap 1993.
Humanism and reform: the Church in Europe, England, and Scotland, 1400-1643: essays in honour of James K Cameron. Blackwell Publishers, 1991.
   McConica, James. *CHist* 79:330-331 Ap 1993.

Kirk, John M.
Politics and the Catholic Church in Nicaragua. University Press of Florida, n.d.
   Deck, Allan Figueroa. *America* 169:24-26 N 20 1993.

Kirk, Russell, 1918-.
America's British culture. Transaction, n.d.
   Wilson, Clyde N. *Crisis* 11:57-58 O 1993.
The politics of prudence. Intercollegiate Studies Institute, n.d.
   Sullivan, James A. *Can Cath Rev* 11:30 Je 1993.
   Henrie, Mark C. *Crisis* 11:55-57 O 1993.

Kirkpatrick, David W.
Choice in schooling: a case for tuition vouchers. Loyola University Press, n.d.
   McDermott, Edwin J. *America* 168:20-22 Ja 2-9 1993.

Kirscher, Gilbert.
Figures de la violence et de la modernité: essais sur la philosophie d'Éric Weil. Presses universitaires de Lille, 1992.
   Natale, Maria Rosaria. *RPhil Louvain* 90:590-592 N 1992.

Kitagawa, Joseph Mitsuo, 1915-1992.
The Christian tradition beyond its European captivity. Trinity Press International, 1992.
   Heiser, W Charles. *TheolDgst* 40:170 Sum 1993.

Klaasen, Walter, ed.
Anabaptism revisited: essays on Anabaptist/Menonite studies in honor of C J Dyck. Herald Press, 1992.
   Heiser, W Charles. *TheolDgst* 39:349 Wint 1992.

Klaghofer-Treitler, Wolfgang.
Gotteswort im menschenwort: inhalt und form von theologie nach Hans urs von Balthasar. Tyrolia, 1992.
   Oakes, Edward T. *TheolStds* 54:360-363 Je 1993.

Klaiber, Jeffrey L.
The Catholic Church in Peru, 1821-1985. Catholic University of America Press, 1992.
   Heiser, W Charles. *TheolDgst* 40:170 Sum 1993.
   Cleary, Edward L. *America* 169:19+ O 23 1993.

Klasvogt, P.
Leben zur Verherrlichung Gottes. Borengässer, 1992.
   Anon. *NRT* 115:633 Jl-Ag 1993.

Klauck, Hans-Josef.
Der erste Johannesbrief. Neukirchener, 1991.
   Forestell, Terence. *CBQ* 55:374-375 Ap 1993.

Kleinberg, Aviad M.
Prophets in their own country: living saints and the making of sainthood in the later Middle Ages. University of Chicago Press, 1992.
   O'Neal, Sandra R. *TheolStds* 54:388-389 Je 1993.
   Heiser, W Charles. *TheolDgst* 40:71 Spr 1993.
   Head, Thomas. *CHist* 79:524-525 Jl 1993.

Kleinig, John.
Valuing life. Princeton University Press, n.d.
   Tiefel, Hans O. *America* 168:18+ Mr 6 1993.
   Devine, Philip E. *New Oxford Rev* 60:29-30 Jl-Ag 1993.

Kleissler, Thomas A, et al.
Small Christian communities. Paulist Press, 1991.
   Paulukonis, Mary Ann. *Living Light* 29:95 Spr 1993.

Klenicki, Leon, ed.
Toward a theological encounter: Jewish understanding of Christianity. Paulist Press, 1991.
   Senior, Donald. *BibleT* 31:60 Ja 1993.
   Mittleman, A. *New Theol Rev* 6:101-103 F 1993.

Klingenstein, Susanne.
Jews in the American Academy, 1900-1940. Yale University Press, 1991.
   Giles, James E. *CrossCurr* 43:261 Sum 1993.

Klocker, Harry.
William of Ockham and the divine freedom. Marquette University Press, 1992.
   Bourke, Vernon J. *Mod Schlmn* 70:160-162 Ja 1993.
   Brinkman, B.R. *Heythrop* 34:470-472 O 1993.

Kloppenborg, John S, and Meyer, Marvin W, et al.
Q-Thomas reader. Polebridge Press, 1990.
   Neirynck, F. *Eph Theol Lovan* 69:175-177 Ap 1993.

Knierim, Rolf P.
Text and concept in Leviticus 1:1-9. J C B Mohr, 1992.
   Heiser, W Charles. *TheolDgst* 40:170 Sum 1993.

Knight, George William.
The pastoral epistles. The Paternoster Press, 1992.
   Heiser, W Charles. *TheolDgst* 40:170-171 Sum 1993.

Knitter, Paul.
Nessun altro nome? Un esame critico degli atteggiamenti cristiani verso le religioni mondiali. Orbis Books, 1985.
   Dupuis, Jacques. *Gregorianum* 74 No 1:175-176 1993.

Knobel, Peters S.
The Targuym of Qohelet. Liturgical Press, 1991.
   Garber, Zev. *CBQ* 55:119-120 Ja 1993.

Knowles, Dudley, ed.
Explanation and its limits. Cambridge University Press, 1990.
   Milne, P. *Heythrop* 34:104-105 Ja 1993.

Knowlton, Stephen R.
Popular politics and the Irish Catholic Church: the rise and fall of the Independent Irish Party, 1850-1859. Garland Publishing, Inc, 1991.
   Larkin, Emmet. *CHist* 79:122-123 Ja 1993.

Kobler, John F.
Vatican II, theophany and the phenomenon of man. Peter Lang, n.d.
   Stead, Julian. *Crisis* 11:59-61 S 1993.
   Dhondt, U. *Can Cath Rev* 11:29 O 1993.

Koch, Carl.
Created God's image: meditating on our body. St Mary's Press, 1992.
   Christantiello, Phillip D. *RRel* 52:315-316 Mr-Ap 1993.

Küng, Hans, 1928-. *(cont'd)*
Heiser, W Charles. *TheolDgst* 39:368 Wint 1992.
Mozart: traces of transcendence. SCM Press, 1992.
Turner, Geoffrey. *Month* 25:496 D 1992.
Clayton-Lea, Paul. *Furrow* 44:58 Ja 1993.
Segger, Jill. *Priests & People* 7:82-83 F 1993.
Swanston, Hamish F G. *New Blckfrs* 74:285-287 My 1993.
Guentner, Francis J. *RRel* 52:623-625 Jl-Ag 1993.
Forsythe, Basil. *Can Cath Rev* 11:31 N 1993.
Theology for the third millennium. HarperCollins, 1992.
Flanagan, Donald. *Doctr Life* 43:190-191 Mr 1993.

Kupke, Raymond J, ed.
American Catholic preaching and piety in the time of John Carroll. The University Press of America, 1991.
Curran, R Emmett. *CHist* 79:567-568 Jl 1993.

Kurelek, William.
A northern nativity. Christmas dreams of a prairie boy. Tundra Books, 1984.
Bedard, Mariette. *CahiersJos* 41:141-142 Ja-Je 1993.

Kuropka, Joachim, ed.
Clemens August Graf von Galen: neue Forschungen zum Leben und Wirken des Bischofs von Münster. Regensberg, 1992.
Leugers, A. *Stimm Zeit* 211:573-574 Ag 1993.

Kurtz, Ernest, and Ketcham, Katherine.
The spirituality of imperfection: modern wisdom from classic stories. Bantam Books, n.d.
McCloskey, Pat. *St Anth* 100:52 F 1993.

Kuschel, Karl-Josef.
Born before all time. SCM, 1992.
Harrington, Wilfrid J. *Furrow* 44:322-324 My 1993.
O'Collins, Gerald, 1931-. *Tablet* 247:1045 Ag 14 1993.
Haight, Roger. *TheolStds* 54:578-580 S 1993.
Brinkman, B.R. *Heythrop* 34:437-440 O 1993.
Acton, Charles. *Priests & People* 7:126 Mr 1993.

Kushner, Lawrence.
God was in this place and I, I did not know. Jewish Lights, 1991.
Blumenthal, David Reuben, 1938-. *CrossCurr* 42:551-554 Wint 1992-1993.

Kuthirakkattel, Scaria.
The beginning of Jesus' ministry according to Mark's Gospel. Biblical Institute, 1990.
Marcus, Joel. *CBQ* 55:162-163 Ja 1993.

Kwasman, Theodore, and Parpola, Simo.
Legal transactions of the royal court of Nineveh. Helsinki University Press, 1992.
Fitzgerald, Aloysius. *OTA* 16:408 Je 1993.

Kymlicka, Will.
Contemporary political philosophy: an introduction. Clarendon, 1990.
Pourtois, Hervé. *RPhil Louvain* 91:483-484 Ag 1993.

Kyung, Chung Hyun.
Stuggle to be the sun again: introducing Asian Women's theology. SCM Press, 1991.
Grey, Mary. *Heythrop* 34:193-194 Ap 1993.

L

L'Engle, Madeleine.
Certain women. Farrar Straus & Giroux, n.d.
Hallett, Elaine. *New Oxford Rev* 60:30 Ap 1993.
Burlin, Katrin. *America* 169:19+ O 2 1993.

Laato, Timo.
Paulus und das Judentum: Anthropologische Erwägungen. Abo Akademi, 1991.
Morton, Russell. *CBQ* 55:375-377 Ap 1993.

Labourdette, Marie-Michel.
Un maître en théologie. École de Théologie, 1992.
Fueyo Suárez, Bernardo. *Cien Tom* 119:616-617 S-D 1992.

Lacey, Stephen.
Lawns and ground cover. Pavilion Books, n.d.
Taylor, Patrick. *Tablet* 247:375 Mr 20 1993.

LaCocque, André.
The feminine unconventional: four subversive figures in Israel's tradition. Fortress, 1990.
Bergant, Dianne. *Horizons (CTS)* 19:310-311 Fall 1992.
Subversives ou un Pentateuque de femmes. Cerf, 1992.
Begg, Christopher T. *OTA* 16:161 F 1993.
Ska, Jean Louis. *NRT* 115:259-260 Mr-Ap 1993.

LaCocque, André, and Lacocque, Pierre-Emmanuel.
Jonah: a psycho-religious approach to the prophet. University of South Carolina Press, 1990.
Jeffers, Ann. *Heythrop* 34:72-73 Ja 1993.

Lactantius.
Institutions divines. Éd du Cerf, 1992.
Spanneut, Michel. *MSR* 50:151-152 Ap-Je 1993.

LaCugna, Catherine Mowry.
God for us: the Trinity and Christian life. HarperCollins, 1992.
Imbelli, Robert P. *Comm* 120:23-26 Ja 29 1993.
Culpepper, Gary. *Living Light* 29:85-87 Wint 1992.
Wood, Susan. *Horizons (CTS)* 20:127-129 Spr 1993.
Haight, Roger. *Horizons (CTS)* 20:129-132 Spr 1993.
Donovan, Mary Ann. *Horizons (CTS)* 20:132-133 Spr 1993.

LaCugna, Catherine Mowry. *(cont'd)*
Finan, Barbara A. *Horizons (CTS)* 20:134-135 Spr 1993.
God for us: the Trinity and Christian life. HarperCollins, 1992.
Anon. *USCath* 58:6-12 N 1993.

Ladany, Laszlo.
Law and legality in China. Hurst, n.d.
Breen, Laurie. *Tablet* 247:49 Ja 9 1993.

Ladaria, L F.
Introduzione alla Antropologia teologica. Piemme, 1992.
Anon. *NRT* 115:624-625 Jl-Ag 1993.

Ladd, Paul R, Jr, ed.
A choir book for Advent. GIA Publications, 1990.
Marcozzi, R. *Past Mus* 17:49 D 1992-Ja 1993.

Laffey, Alice L.
Wives, harlots and concubines. SPCK, 1990.
Jeffers, Ann. *Heythrop* 34:71-72 Ja 1993.

Lafitte, Nicholas.
Near Calvary: selected poems 1959-1970. The Many Press, n.d.
Egan, Desmond. *Tablet* 247:248 F 20 1993.

Lafont, Gislain.
God, time and being. Saint Bede's Publications, 1992.
Heiser, W Charles. *TheolDgst* 39:369 Wint 1992.

Lafontaire, R, et al, eds.
L'Ecriture âme de la théologie. Brepols, 1990.
Huftier, M. *MSR* 50:70 Ja-Mr 1993.

Lagrange, Marie-Joseph.
Exégète à Jérusalem: Nouveaux mélanges d'histoire Religieuse (1890-1939). Gabalda, 1991.
Wright, John W. *CBQ* 55:414-415 Ap 1993.
Exégète à Jerusalem. Nouveaux mélanges d'histoire Religieuse (1890-1939). Gabalda, 1991.
Prato, Gian Luigi. *Gregorianum* 74 no 3:565-566 1993.

Laird, Mark.
The formal garden. Thames & Hudson, n.d.
Taylor, Patrick. *Tablet* 247:480-481 Ap 10-17 1993.

Lalande, André.
Vocabulaire technique et critique de la philosophie. PUF, 1991.
Jacobs, H. *NRT* 115:305 Mr-Ap 1993.
Follon, Jacques. *RPhil Louvain* 91:512-513 Ag 1993.

Lamattina, Gaetano.
Carmine Donatello Crocco: "Il partigiano del Re". Greco, 1992.
Ferrua, Antonio. *Civilta* 2:96 Ap 3 1993.

Lamb, Richard.
Churchill as war leader. Bloomsbury, n.d.
Hodgkin, E C. *Tablet* 247:478 Ap 10-17 1993.
War in Italy 1943-45: a brutal story. John Murray, n.d.
Aitken, Tom. *Tablet* 247:920 Jl 17 1993.

Lamberigts, Matthieu, and Soetens, Claude, eds.
A la veille du Concile Vatican II. Bibliotheek van de Faculteit der Godgeleerdheid, 1992.
Boudens, R. *Eph Theol Lovan* 78:487-488 D 1992.

Lambert, Malcolm.
Medieval heresy: popular movements from the Gregorian reform to the Reformation. Blackwell, 1992.
Russell, Jeffrey Burton. *CHist* 79:145-146 Ja 1993.

Lambin, Helen Reichert.
In the beginning: a humorous survey of the Bible. ACTA , 1991.
Stuhlmueller, Carroll. *BibleT* 30:381 N 1992.
Bernas, Casimir. *Cist Stud* 28 no 2:[47]-[48] 1993.

Lambrecht, Jan.
Out of the treasure. Eerdmans, n.d.
Harrington, Daniel J. *America* 168:33 F 6 1993.

Lameri, A.
L'attività di promozione liturgica dell'Opera della Regalità. O.R., 1992.
Anon. *NRT* 115:634 Jl-Ag 1993.

Lamont, Stewart, ed.
St Andrews Rock: the state of the Church in Scotland. Bellew Publishing, n.d.
McOwan, Rennie. *Tablet* 247:693-694 My 29 1993.

Lanciani, Rodolfo.
Storia degli scavi di Roma. Quasar, 1992.
Ferrua, Antonio. *Civilta* 3:332-333 Ag 7-21 1993.

Landau, Ronnie S.
The Nazi Holocaust. I. B. Tauris, n.d.
Klein, Emma. *Tablet* 247:948-949 Jl 24 1993.

Lane, Dermot A.
Christ at the centre: selected issues in Christology. Veritas Publications, 1990.
Dupuis, Jacques. *Gregorianum* 73 No 4:758 1992.

Lane, Dermot A, ed.
Religion and culture in a dialogue. Columba, 1993.
Campbell, James. *Month* 26:381 S-O 1993.
Macken, John. *Studies* 82:354-356 Aut 1993.
Oheideain, Eustas. *Doctr Life* 43:313 My-Je 1993.

Lane, William L.
Hebrews 1-8; Hebrews 9-13. Word Books, 1991.
Wild, Robert A. *CBQ* 55:163-165 Ja 1993.

Lang, Bernhard, ed.
Internationale Zeitschriftenschau für Bibelwissenschaft un Grenzgebiete. Patmos, 1992.
Murphy, Roland E. *OTA* 16:161 F 1993.

Lang, Marijke Hélène de.
De opkomst van de historische en literaire kritiek in de synoptische be-schouwing van de evangeliën van Calvijn tot Griesbach. Faculteit der Godgeleerdheid, 1993.
Neirynck, F. Eph Theol Lovan 69:174-175 Ap 1993.

Langan, John P, et al.
Catholic universities in church and society. Georgetown University Press, n.d.
Hunt, John F, and Saunders, Paul C. Comm 120:24-26 N 19 1993.

Langevin, G, and Pirro, R, eds.
Le Christ et les cultures dans le monde et l'histoire. Bellarmin, 1991.
Evrard, P. NRT 114:900-901 N-D 1992.

Langlois, Claude, and Laplanche, François, eds.
La science catholique: L'"Encyclopédie théologique" de Migne (1844-1873) entre apologétique et vulgarisation. Editions du Cerf, 1992.
Costigan, Richard F. CHist 79:351-352 Ap 1993.

Langmuir, Gavin I.
Toward a definition of Antisemitism. University of California Press, 1990.
Davies, Alan. JEcumen Stds 29:126-127 Wint 1992.

Lapide, Pinchas.
Filho de José? Jesus no judaísmo. Loyola, 1993.
Palacia, Carlos. Perspectiva 25:233-236 My-Ag 1993.
Jesus—ein gekreuzigter Pharisäer? Gütersloher Verlagshaus Gerd Mohn, 1990.
Klaassen, Walter. JEcumen Stds 29:484-485 Sum-Aut 1992.

Laplace, Jean.
Prayer according to the Scriptures. Veritas Publications, 1991.
Senior, Donald. BibleT 31:60 Ja 1993.

Lapsley, James N.
Renewal in late life through pastoral counseling. Paulist Press, 1992.
Mason, Mary Elizabeth. Sisters 65:226-227 My 1993.

Larchet, J-C.
Théologie de la maladie. Cerf, 1991.
Lamau, Marie-Louise. MSR 50:75-76 Ja-Mr 1993.

Lardner, Denise.
Religious woman: contemporary reflections on eastern texts. Crossroad, 1991.
Snyder, Mary Hembrow. Horizons (CTS) 19:347-348 Fall 1992.

Laroche, M.
La vie en son nom. Ed Présence, 1992.
Renard, L-J. NRT 115:588 Jl-Ag 1993.

Larochelle, Gilbert.
L'imaginaire technocratique. Boréal, 1990.
Robberechts, Edouard. RPhil Louvain 91:489-495 Ag 1993.

Larrainzar González, Carlos.
Introducción al derecho canónico. Editorial IDECSA, 1991.
Tourneau, Dominique Le. Stud Can 27 no 1:268-269 1993.

Larranaga, Ignacio.
The silence of Mary. Books & Media, 1991.
MacCarthy, Peter T. HPR 93:63 F 1993.
Heiser, W Charles. TheolDgst 39:369 Wint 1992.

Larsen, Earnie, and Parnegg, Janee.
Recovering Catholics: what to do when religion comes between you and God. HarperSanFrancisco, 1992.
Wilkins, Mark. St Anth 100:51-52 Mr 1993.
Anon. USCath 58:31-35 Mr 1993.

Las Casas, Bartolome de, 1474-1566.
The only way. Paulist Press, 1992.
Sanks, T Howland. TheolStds 53:786 D 1992.
Keen, Benjamin. CHist 79:138-139 Ja 1993.
Witness. Orbis Books, 1992.
Heiser, W Charles. TheolDgst 40:155 Sum 1993.

Lash, Nicholas.
Believing three ways in one God. SCM, 1992.
Gallagher, Peter. Month 26:318-319 Ag 1993.
Hommerding, Leroy. Mod Lit 20:42 N 1993.
Dulles. Tablet 247:1296-1297 O 9 1993.
Wiles, Maurice. New Blckfrs 74:422-425 S 1993.
Graham, William C. Nat Cath Rep 30:15 O 22 1993.

Latela, Mary.
My friend is dying. Liguori, 1993.
Higgins, James J. Liguorian 81:68 D 1993.

Latourelle, Rene, et al, eds.
Diccionario de teología fundamental. Ed Paulinas, 1992.
Bentué, Antonio. Teol Vida 34 no 1-2;161 1993.
Dictionnaire de théologie fondamentale. Ed du Cerf, 1992.
Escol, R. NRT 115:286-287 Mr-Ap 1993.

Lattke, Michael.
Hymnus: Materialen zu einer Geschichte der antiken Hymnologie. Vanden-hoeck and Ruprecht, 1991.
Franzmann, Majella. Pacifica 6:210-212 Je 1993.

Laurent, Ph, and Jahan, Emm, eds.
Les Églises face à l'entreprise: cent ans de pensée sociale. Centurion, 1991.
Toubeau, A. NRT 114:915-916 N-D 1992.

Laurentin, René.
The meaning of consecration today: a Marian model for a secularized age. Ignatius Press, 1992.
Grondelski, John M. HPR 93:75-76 F 1993.
Heiser, W Charles. TheolDgst 40:72 Spr 1993.
Retour à Dieu avec Marie. OEIL, 1991.
Renard, L J. NRT 115:135 Ja-F 1993.

Laurentini, Giuliano.
La biblioteca dei cappuccini di Livorno. Bibl Prov Cappuccini, 1992.
Carlini, G. Civilta 3:320-321 Ag 7-21 1993.

Lauret, Bernard, and Refoulé, François.
Iniciação à prática da Teologia, tomo I: Introdução. Loyola, 1992.
Miranda, Mario de Franco. Perspectiva 25:119-120 Ja-Ap 1993.

Lauritzen, Paul.
Religious belief and emotional transformation. Bucknell University Press, 1992.
Heiser, W Charles. TheolDgst 40:171 Sum 1993.

Lavinio, Cristina, and Sobrero, Alberto A.
La lingua degli studenti universitari. La Nuovo Italita, 1991.
Baragli, Enrico. Civilta 2:203 Ap 17 1993.

Il lavoro. Diritto e avventura dell'uomo.
Libr. Ed. Vaticana, 1992.
Joblin, Joseph, 1920-. Civilta 3:444 S 4 1993.

Lawler, Michael.
Ecumenical marriage and remarriage: gifts and challenges to the churches. Twenty-Third Publications, 1990.
Butler, Sara. JEcumen Stds 29:269-270 Spr 1992.

Lawler, Philip F.
Operation rescue: a challenge to the nation's conscience. Our Sunday Visitor, 1992.
Miller, E. New Oxford Rev 60:20-21 Ja-F 1993.
Heiser, W Charles. TheolDgst 40:72 Spr 1993.

Lawrence, Bruce C, ed.
Nizam Ad-Din Awliya: morals for the heart: conversations of Shaykh Nizam ad-Din Awliya recorded by Amir Hasan Sijzi. Paulist, 1992.
Bell, D. Cist Stud 27 No 4:[110]-[111] 1992.

Lawrence, Fred, ed.
Lonergan workshop, v VI. Scholars' Press, 1986.
Walmsley, G. Heythrop 34:113-114 Ja 1993.
Lonergan workshop. Scholars' Press, 1990.
Brito, Emilio. Eph Theol Lovan 78:470 D 1992.

Lawson, Nigel.
The view from No 11. Bantam, n.d.
Keegan, V. Tablet 247:47-48 Ja 9 1993.

Layman, C Stephen.
The shape of the good. University of Notre Dame Press, n.d.
O'Donohue, James A. America 168:20-21 F 27 1993.

Layton, Scott C.
Archaic features of Canaanite personal names in the Hebrew Bible. Scholars, 1990.
Fulco, William J. CBQ 54:749-751 O 1992.

Lazarus-Yafeh, Hava.
Intertwined worlds: medieval Islam and Bible criticism. Princeton University Press, 1992.
Heiser, W Charles. TheolDgst 40:72-73 Spr 1993.

Il Lazio meridionale tra Papato e Impero al tempo di Enrico VI: Atti del convegno internazionale, Fiuggi, Guarcino, Montecassino.
Ministero per i Beni Culturali e Ambientali, 1991.
Osheim, D. CHist 78:640-641 O 1992.

Leach, William.
Land of desire. Pantheon, n.d.
Blackburn, Thomas E. Nat Cath Rep 29:17 S 24 1993.

Leckey, Dolores R, 1933-.
Winter music: a life of Jessica Powers. Sheed & Ward, 1992.
Williams, Joan. Living Prayer 26:33 Mr-Ap 1993.
Women and creativity. Paulist, 1991.
O'Neill, Mary Aquin. Horizons (CTS) 19:330-331 Fall 1992.
Winter music: a life of Jessica Powers. Sheed & Ward, 1992.
Morneau, Robert F, Bp, 1938-. Spir Life 39:49-50 Spr 1993.

Leclerc, Marc.
L'Union substantielle I: Blondel et Leibniz. Culture et Vérité, 1991.
Long, Fiachra. IJPS 1:156-158 Mr 1993.

Leclerq, Jean.
Bernardo di Chiaravalle. Vita e Pensiero, 1992.
Gilbert, Paul P. Civilta 3:306-307 Ag 7-21 1993.

Lécrivain, Philippe.
Pour une plus grande gloire de Dieu: les missions jésuites. Découvertes Galimard, 1991.
Lewis, Marilyn. CHist 78:626-627 O 1992.

Leddy, Mary Jo, et al.
In the eye of the Catholic storm: the Church since Vatican II. HarperCollins Publishers Ltd, 1992.
Anon. Sisters 65:63-64 Ja 1993.

Leddy, Mary Jo.
Reweaving religious life. Twenty-Third Publications, n.d.
Barrins, Aine. Furrow 44:387-388 Je 1993.

Lederer, Richard.
The miracle of language. Pocket Books, n.d.
Hunt, George W, 1937-. America 169:2 Jl 31-Ag 7 1993.
More anguished English. Delacorte, n.d.
Hunt, George W, 1937-. America 169:2 O 9 1993.

Ledrus, Michel.
Alla scuola del "ladrone" penitente. AdP, 1992.
Sonzini, E. Civilta 3:202-203 Jl 17 1993.

Ledure, Y, ed.
Histoire et culture chrétienne. Beauchesne, 1992.
Plumat, N. NRT 115:618 Jl-Ag 1993.

Lee, Bernard J.
The Galilean Jewishness of Jesus: retrieving the Jewish origins of Christian-ity. Paulist Press, 1988.
Dupuis, Jacques. Gregorianum 73 No 4:757-758 1992.

Lee, Bernard J, and Cowan, Michael A.
Dangerous memories. Sheed and Ward, n.d.
Higgins, James J. Liguorian 81:68-69 Ap 1993.

Lee, Hannah Sawyer.
Memoir of Pierre Toussaint, born a slave in St Domingo. Western Hemi-sphere Cultural Society, 1992.
Heiser, W Charles. TheolDgst 40:171 Sum 1993.

Leech, Kenneth, 1939-.
The eye of the storm. HarperCollins, 1992.
Durbin, J. Sisters 65:66-67 Ja 1993.

Leech, Kenneth, 1939-. *(cont'd)*
The eye of the storm. DL T, n.d.
  Campbell-Johnston, Michael. *Tablet* 247:110 Ja 23 1993.
The eye of the storm. DLT, n.d.
  Lonsdale, David. *Way* 33:159-160 Ap 1993.
The eye of the storm. HarperCollins, 1992.
  Heiser, W Charles. *TheolDgst* 40:73 Spr 1993.
  Vivian, Tim. *Cist Stud* 28 no 2:[44]-[45] 1993.

Lefebure, Leo D.
Towards a contemporary wisdom Christology: a study of Karl Rahner and Norman Pittenger. University Press of America, 1988.
  Galvin, John P, 1944-. *Heythrop* 34:191-192 Ap 1993.

Lefébure, Marcus, and Schauder, Hans.
Conversations on counseling between a doctor and a priest. T & T Clark, 1990.
  Kelly, Shay. *Doctr Life* 43:444-445 S 1993.

Lefebvre, Patricia.
Les pouvoirs de la parole: L'Église et Rousseau (1762-1848). Éd du Cerf, 1992.
  Hilaire, S. *NRT* 115:615-616 Jl-Ag 1993.

Lefort, Claude.
Écrire—à l'épreuve du politique. Calmann-Lévy, 1992.
  Ponton, Lionel. *Laval Theol Phil* 49:346-348 Je 1993.

Leftow, Brian.
Time and eternity. Cornell University Press, n.d.
  Zagzebski, Linda. *New Oxford Rev* 60:30 S 1993.

Lega, Carlo.
Mannuale di bioetica e deontologia medica. Giuffrè, 1991.
  Cultrera, Francesco. *Civilta* 144:91-92 Ja 2 1993.

Legarde, Claude.
Au nom des Pères. La Bible pour la prière. Mame, 1992.
  Beenaert, P. Mourlon. *Lumen* 48:231 Je 1993.

Légasse, Simon.
Stephanos: histoire et discours d'Etienne dans les Actes des Apôtres. Cerf, 1992.
  Galot, Jean. *Gregorianum* 73 No 4:753 1992.
  Hamm, Dennis. *CBQ* 55:377-378 Ap 1993.

Légaut, Marcel.
Vie spirituelle et modernité. Entretiens ultimes avec Thérèse de Scott. Centurion/Duculot, 1992.
  Partos, L. *Lumen* 48:235-236 Je 1993.

Legrand, Hervé, et al, eds.
Iglesias locales y catolicidad. Universidad Pontificia, 1992.
  Bandera, Armando. *Cien Tom* 119:610-611 S-D 1992.

Legrand, Hervé.
Les Évêques d'Europe et la nouvelle évangélisation. Les Éditions du Cerf, 1991.
  Routhier, Gilles. *Laval Theol Phil* 49:378-379 Je 1993.

Lehmann, L K, and Schnackenburg, R.
Brauchen wir noch Zeugen? Herder, 1992.
  Anon. *NRT* 115:636-637 Jl-Ag 1993.

Leibniz, Gottfried Wilhelm.
Allgemeiner politischer und historischer Briefwechsel. Akademie Verlag, 1990.
  Deschepper, Jean Pierre. *RPhil Louvain* 90:560-564 N 1992.

Leibowtiz, Yeshayahu.
Judaism, human values, and the Jewish state. Harvard University Press, 1992.
  Heiser, W Charles. *TheolDgst* 40:73 Spr 1993.

Leichner, Jeannine Timko.
Called to His supper: a preparation for first eucharist. Our Sunday Visitor, n.d.
  McCann, Deborah. *ReligTJ* 26:10 Ja 1993.

Leites, Edmund, ed.
Conscience and casuistry in early modern Europe. Cambridge University Press, 1988.
  Kennedy, Terence. *Gregorianum* 74 no 3:584-587 1993.

Leith, Prue, and Waldegrave, Caroline.
Leith's vegetarian cookery. Bloomsbury, n.d.
  Poole, Shona Crawford. *Tablet* 247:373 Mr 20 1993.

Lejeune, Anthony.
White's: the first three hundred years. A & C Black, n.d.
  Usborne, Richard. *Tablet* 247:860-861 Jl 3 1993.

Lejeune, Jerome.
The concentration can. Ignatius, n.d.
  Grondelski, John M. *HPR* 93:77-78 Je 1993.
  Vree, Maria Valencia. *New Oxford Rev* 60:29-30 Je 1993.
  Higgins, James J. *Liguorian* 81:70 O 1993.

Lemaire, Agnès.
Saint Bernard et le mystère du Christ dans le cadre de l'année liturgique. no publisher given, 1991.
  Ganzi, I M. *Civilta* 144:199-200 Ja 16 1993.

Lemarie, Charles.
A biography of Msgr Benedict Joseph Flaget, 1763-1850. The Flaget-LeMarie Group, Ltd, 1992.
  Heiser, W Charles. *TheolDgst* 40:73 Spr 1993.
A biography of Msgr Benedict Joseph Flaget, 1763-1850. The Flaget-Lemarie Group, 1992.
  Manfra, Jo Ann. *CHist* 79:570-571 Jl 1993.

Lemche, Niels Peter.
The Canaanites and their land. Academic Press, 1991.
  Lust, Johan. *Eph Theol Lovan* 78:151-152 Ap 1992.
  Heiser, W Charles. *TheolDgst* 40:73-74 Spr 1993.

Lemcio, Eugene E.
The past of Jesus in the gospels. Cambridge University Press, 1991.
  Black, Clifton C. *CBQ* 55:378-379 Ap 1993.

Lemoine, M, ed.
Hugues de Saint-Victor: l'art de lire. Éd du Cerf, 1991.
  Hilarie, S. *NRT* 115:268 Mr-Ap 1993.

Leneuf, Nicolas, and Vernette, Jean.
Exorciste aujourd'hui? Mulhouse, 1991.
  Partos, L. *Lumen* 47:467-468 D 1992.

Lentini, Anselmo.
Te Decet hymnus, l'Innario della "Liturgia Horarum". Typis Polyglottis Vaticanis, 1984.
  Schuler, Richard Joseph, 1920-. *SacM* 120:22 Spr 1993.

Leonard, Albert, Jr.
The Jordan valley survey, 1953. Eisenbrauns, 1992.
  Miller, Charles H. *OTA* 16:408-409 Je 1993.

Léonard, André.
Foi et philosophies. Culture et Vérité, 1991.
  Halleux, André de. *Eph Theol Lovan* 78:464-465 D 1992.
  Escol, R. *NRT* 115:303 Mr-Ap 1993.

Leonard, Ellen.
Unresting transformation: the theology and spirituality of Maude Petre. University Press of America, 1991.
  Marlin, Hilda. *Can Cath Rev* 11:27-28 Ap 1993.
  Healy, Charles J. *TheolStds* 54:199 Mr 1993.
  Sagovsky, Nicholas. *Heythrop* 34:459-460 O 1993.

Leonard, George.
Here and now: a spirituality for the redeemed. Hodder & Stoughton, n.d.
  Brown, Douglas. *Tablet* 247:1102 Ag 28 1993.

Leonard, Joan de Lourdes.
Richly blessed: the Diocese of Rockville Centre, 1957-1990. Diocese of Rockville Centre, 1991.
  Shelley, Thomas J. *CHist* 79:146-147 Ja 1993.

Leonard, Seán, and Tuffy, Edward.
St. Joseph, quiet man of God. Irish Messenger Publications, 1991.
  Bedard, Mariette. *CahiersJos* 41:133-134 Ja-Je 1993.

Leonard, William J.
The letter carrier. Sheed & Ward, n.d.
  Samway, Patrick H, 1939-. *America* 169:20-21 Ag 28-S 4 1993.

Leonardi, Ruggero.
Nella giungla di Salgari. Ed Paoline, 1992.
  Flumeri, E. *Civilta* 144:409-410 F 20 1993.

Lepage, François.
Eléments de logique contemporaine. Les Presses, 1991.
  Mottard, François. *Laval Theol Phil* 49:161 F 1993.

Lerer, Seth.
Literacy and power in Anglo-Saxon literature. University of Nebraska Press, 1991.
  Stevenson, Jane. *Heythrop* 34:450-451 O 1993.

Lerner, Gerda.
The creationl of feminist consciousness from the middle ages to eighteen seventy. Oxford University Press, 1993.
  Stuhlmueller, Carroll. *BibleT* 31:247 Jl 1993.
What women thought. Oxford University Press, n.d.
  Henking, Susan. *America* 169:17-18 D 4 1993.

Leskov, Nikolai.
On the edge of the world. St. Vladimir's Seminary, 1992.
  Rexine, John E. *Diakonia* 26 no 3:197-199 1993.

Lesser, R H.
Come close to the Lord. St Paul Publications, 1991.
  Stuhlmueller, Carroll. *BibleT* 31:55 Ja 1993.

Let the spirit speak to the churches.
  WCC Publications, 1990.
  Lewis, Eleanor V. *JEcumen Stds* 29:104-105 Wint 1992.

The letters and instructions of Francis Xavier.
  Institute of Jesuit Sources, n.d.
  Stahel, Thomas H, 1938-. *America* 168:2 My 29 1993.
  Dollen, Charles. *Priest* 49:48 O 1993.

Leung, Beatrice.
Sino-Vatican relations: problems in conflicting authority, 1976-1986. Cambridge University Press, 1992.
  Yip, Ka-Chi. *CHist* 79:383-384 Ap 1993.
  Witek, John W. *TheolStds* 54:363-365 Je 1993.

Leuninger, Ernest.
Wir sind das Volk Gottes! Demokratisierung der Kirche. Knecht, 1992.
  Seibel, W. *Stimm Zeit* 211:285 Ap 1993.

Leutzsch, Martin.
Die wahrnehmung sozialer Wirklichkeit im Hirten des Hermas. Vandenhoeck a Ruprecht, 1989.
  Chappin, Marcel. *Gregorianum* 73 No 4:766-767 1992.

Levasseur, Jean-Marie, and Turmel, André.
L'évaluation pastorale au Québec. Pastor, 1992.
  Routhier, Gilles. *Laval Theol Phil* 49:155-157 F 1993.

Levenson, Jon D.
The Hebrew Bible, the Old Testament, and historical criticism. Westminster, 1993.
  Murphy, Roland E. *OTA* 16:409 Je 1993.

Levertov, Denise.
New and selected essays. New Directions, n.d.
  Martinez, Demetria. *Nat Cath Rep* 29:31 S 10 1993.

Levi, Peter.
Tennyson. Macmillan, n.d.
  Marshall, Judith. *Tablet* 247:372-373 Mr 20 1993.

Levin, Bernard.
If you want my opinion. Cape, n.d.
  Aitken, Tom. *Tablet* 247:77-78 Ja 16 1993.

Levin, Joel.
How judges reason: the logic of adjudication. Peter Lang, 1992.
  Wilcox, William H. *Amer J Juris* 37:373-379 1992.

Levinas, Emmanual.
Filosofia e trascendenza. Con due Saggi di Emmanuel Levinas. Casa Editrice Marietti, 1992.
  Tilliette, Xavier. *Gregorianum* 74 no 3:598 1993.

Levine, Amy-Jill, ed.
"Women like this": new perspectives on Jewish women in the Greco-Roman world. Scholars, 1991.
  Doran, Robert. *CBQ* 54:827-828 O 1992.

Levine, Daniel H.
Popular voices in Latin American Catholicism. Princeton University Press, 1992.
  Heiser, W Charles. *TheolDgst* 40:74 Spr 1993.
  Campbell-Johnson, Michael. *Month* 26:379-380 S-O 1993.

Levison, Mary.
Wrestling with the Church. Arthur James, n.d.
  McOwan, Rennie. *Tablet* 247:50 Ja 9 1993.

Levy, Bernard S, ed.
The Bible in the Middle Ages. Medieval & Renaissance texts and studies, 1992.
  Heiser, W Charles. *TheolDgst* 40:151-152 Sum 1993.

Levy, Steven.
Artificial life. Pantheon, n.d.
  Lanham, Richard J. *New Oxford Rev* 60:26-28 Mr 1993.

Lewer, Nick.
Physicians and the peace movement. Frank Cass, n.d.
  Rich, Vera. *Tablet* 247:405-406 Mr 27 1993.

Lewis, Alan.
Pundemoniam. Paul Watkins Publishing, 1992.
  Martin, David. *Priests & People* 7:252 Je 1993.

Lewis, Anthony.
Make no law. Random House, n.d.
  Donnelly, Samuel J M. *America* 168:16-17 F 13 1993.

Lewis, Hedwig.
At home with God. Gujart Sahitya Prakask, 1991.
  Markham, Flannan. *Furrow* 44:191-192 Mr 1993.
  Heiser, W Charles. *TheolDgst* 40:74 Spr 1993.

Lewis, Naphtali, et al, eds.
The documents from the Bar Kokhba period in the Cave of Letters. The Shrine of the Book, 1989.
  Kessler, Martin. *OTA* 15:483-484 O 1992.

Liderbach, Daniel.
Why do we suffer? new ways of understanding. Paulist, 1992.
  Cummings, Owen F. *Living Light* 30:107 Aut 1993.

Lieb, Michael.
The visionary made. Cornell University Press, 1991.
  Heiser, W Charles. *TheolDgst* 40:172 Sum 1993.

Liebert, Elizabeth Ann.
Changing life patterns: adult development in spiritual direction. Paulist Press, 1992.
  Heiser, W Charles. *TheolDgst* 39:369 Wint 1992.
  Sheldrake, Philip. *Way* 33:158-59 Ap 1993.

Liegro, Luigi Di, and Pittau, Franco.
Per conoscere l'islàm: Cristiani e musulmani nel mondo di oggi. Piemme, 1991.
  Caprile, Giovanni. *Civilta* 144:413-414 F 20 1993.

Liersch, Werner.
Eine Tötung im Angesicht des Herrn Goethe. Neues Leben, n.d.
  Roers, G M. *Stimm Zeit* 211:646-648 S 1993.

Lieu, Judith, et al, eds.
The Jews among Pagas and Christians in the Roman empire. Routlege, 1992.
  Heiser, W Charles. *TheolDgst* 39:367 Wint 1992.

Lieven, Anatol.
The Baltic revolution: Estonia, Latvia, Lithuania and the path to independence. Yale University Press, n.d.
  McDougall, Ian. *Tablet* 247:757-758 Je 1993.

Lieven, Dominic.
Nicholas II, Emperor of all the Russias. John Murray, n.d.
  FitzLyon, April. *Tablet* 247:820-821 Je 26 1993.

Life on the dole.
Tallaght Centre of the Unemployed, 1991.
  Toner, W. *Studies* 82:220-222 Sum 1993.

Lifschitz, D.
Je bénirai le Seigneur en tout temps: Psaume 34. Droguet-Ardant, 1992.
  Ska, Jean Louis. *NRT* 115:255-256 Mr-Ap 1993.

Lifschitz, Daniel.
Perché Signore, Te ne stai Lontano? Elle Di Ci, 1992.
  Begg, Christopher T. *OTA* 16:427 Je 1993.

Lightman, Alan.
Einstein's dreams. Bloomsbury, n.d.
  Walsh, Jill Paton. *Tablet* 247:518 Ap 24 1993.
  Milligan, Bryce. *Nat Cath Rep* 29:35 My 28 1993.

Likoudis, James.
Ending the Byzantine Greek schism. United for the Faith, 1992.
  Spencer, R. *HPR* 93:67-69 F 1993.

Lill, Rudolf, and Kissener, Michael, eds.
Hochverrat? Universitätsverlag, 1993.
  Bleistein, Roman, 1928-. *Stimm Zeit* 211:718-719 O 1993.

Lillo, Pasquale.
Concordato, "accordi" e "intese" tra lo stato e la chiesa cattolica. Giuffré, 1990.
  Ferrari da Passano, Paolo. *Civilta* 144:615-616 Mr 20 1993.

Lincoln, Andrew T.
Ephesians. Word Books, 1990.
  Gillman, John. *CBQ* 55:165-167 Ja 1993.

Lindars, Barnabas.
The theology of the Letter to the Hebrews. CUP, 1991.
  Wansbrough, Henry. *Priests & People* 6:439 N 1992.

Lindgren, Torgny.
Light. Harvill, n.d.
  Walton, James. *Tablet* 247:792 Je 19 1993.

Lindorff, David.
Marketplace medicine: the rise of the for-profit hospital chains. Bantam Books, 1992.
  Sigmond, R. *Health Prog* 74:84-85 Ja-F 1993.

Lindvall, Michael.
The good news from North Haven. Doubleday, n.d.
  Lang, Stephanie. *St Anth* 100:50-51 Ap 1993.

Lingenfelter, Sherwood G.
Transforming culture: a challenge for Christian mission. Baker Book House, 1992.
  Heiser, W Charles. *TheolDgst* 40:74 Spr 1993.

Linn, Dennis, and Linn, Sheila Fabricant, et al.
Belonging: bonds of healing and recovery. Paulist Press, 1993.
  Renner, Maranatha. *Sisters* 65:308-309 Jl 1993.

Linnemann, Eta.
Is there a synopitc problem? Baker Book House, 1992.
  Heiser, W Charles. *TheolDgst* 40:172 Sum 1993.

Listening with the heart.
The Liturgical Press, 1992.
  Stuhlmueller, Carroll. *BibleT* 31:247 Jl 1993.

Liturgical year: the worship of God; supplemental liturgical resource 7.
John Knox Press, 1992.
  Hommerding, Leroy. *Mod Lit* 20:38 My 1993.

Lively, Penelope.
Cleopatra's sister. Viking, n.d.
  Toomey, Philippa. *Tablet* 247:824 Je 26 1993.

The lives of Simeon Stylites.
Cistercian, 1992.
  Sable, Thomas F. *Diakonia* 26 no 2:135-138 1993.
  McLeod, Frederick G. *TheolStds* 54:597 S 1993.

Living with the land: communities restoring the earth.
New Society Publishers, n.d.
  Graham, William C. *Nat Cath Rep* 29:40 My 28 1993.

Livingston, James C.
Tradition and the critical spirit Catholic modernist writings. Fortress, 1991.
  Sagovsky, Nicholas. *Heythrop* 34:459-460 O 1993.

Livingston, Patricia H.
Lessons of the heart: celebrating the rhythms of life. Ave Maria, 1992.
  Domeier, Renée. *Sisters* 65:141 Mr 1993.
  Payne, Joseph A. *ChrWorld* 236:279 N-D 1993.

Ljung, Inger.
Silence or suppression: attitudes towards women in the Old Testament. Almqvist and Wiksell, 1989.
  Laffey, Alice L. *CBQ* 54:751-752 O 1992.

Llewelyn, John.
The middle voice of ecological conscience: a chiasmic reading of responsibility in the neighbourhood of Levinas, Heidegger and others. Macmillan, 1991.
  Hoose, Bernard. *Heythrop* 34:199-201 Ap 1993.

Lloyd, A C.
The anatomy of neoplatonism. Clarendon Press, 1990.
  Edwards, M J. *Heythrop* 34:217-218 Ap 1993.

Lluch-Baizauli, Miguel.
La teología de Boecio en la transición del mundo clásico al mundo medieval. Ediciones Universidad de Navarra, 1990.
  Saranyana, Josep-Ignasi. *RPhil Louvain* 91:311-312 My 1993.

Loader, J A.
A tale of two cities: Sodom and Gomorrah in the Old Testament, early Jewish and early Christian traditions. Kok, 1990.
  Bundy, David. *CBQ* 54:752-753 O 1992.
  Lust, Johan. *Eph Theol Lovan* 69:157-158 Ap 1993.
  Guinan, Michael D. *TheolStds* 54:382 Je 1993.

Loades, Ann, and Rue, Loyal D, eds.
Contemporary classics in philosophy of religion. Open Court, 1991.
  Heiser, W Charles. *TheolDgst* 39:357 Wint 1992.

Lockhart, James.
Nahuas and Spaniards: postconquest Central Mexican history and philology. Stanford University Press, 1991.
  Schrocoler, S. *CHist* 78:695-696 O 1992.

Lodahl, Michael E.
Shekhinah/Spirit. Paulist, 1992.
  Heiser, W Charles. *TheolDgst* 40:172 Sum 1993.

Lodi, Enzo.
Saints of the Roman Calendar. Alba House, 1992.
  Lang, Jovian P. *Mod Lit* 20:40-41 Ag 1993.
Saints of the Roman calendar. Alba House, 1992.
  Myers, Rawley. *HPR* 94:76-77 N 1993.

Loewenstein, David, and Grantham, James, eds.
Politics, poetics and hermeneutics in Milton's prose. Cambridge University Press, 1990.
  Haskins, D. *Heythrop* 34:116-117 Ja 1993.

Lohfink, Norbert.
The covenant never revoked: biblical reflections on Christian-Jewish dialogue. Paulist Press, 1991.
  Dupuis, Jacques. *Gregorianum* 73 No 4:750 1992.
  Scullion, John. *SIDIC* 25 No 2:33 1992.
  Halleux, André de. *Eph Theol Lovan* 78:444-445 D 1992.
  Harrington, Daniel J. *CBQ* 54:753 O 1992.
  Buren, Paul Matthews van, 1924-. *JEcumen Stds* 29:122 Wint 1992.

Lohfink, Norbert. *(cont'd)*
Krieg und Staat im alten Israel. Institut für Theologie und Frieden, 1992.
  Murphy, Roland E. *OTA* 16:439 Je 1993.
Lobgesänge der Armen: Studien zum Magnifikat, den HJodajot von Qumran und einigen späten Psalmen. Katholisches Bibelwerk, 1990.
  Adler, William. *CBQ* 55:380-381 Ap 1993.
Der niemals gekündigte Bund: Exegetische Gedanken zum christlich-jüdischen Dialog. Herder, 1989.
  Halleux, André de. *Eph Theol Lovan* 78:444-445 D 1992.
Studien zum Deuteronomium und zur deuteronomistischen Literatur II. Katholisches Bibelwerk, 1991.
  Begg, Christopher T. *OTA* 15:496 O 1992.
Lohfink, Norbert, and Zenger, E, et al.
Dio l'Unico. Sulla nascita del monoteismo in Israele. Morcelliana, 1991.
  Pastor, Felix-Alejandro. *Gregorianum* 74 no 2:406 1993.
Lohse, Eduard.
Etica teologica del nuovo testamento. Paideia, 1991.
  Cultrera, Francesco. *Civiltà* 143:631-633 D 19 1992.
Theological ethics of the New Testament. Fortress, 1991.
  Winkler, Jude. *Living Light* 29:90 Aut 1992.
  Scroggs, Robin. *CBQ* 55:381-382 Ap 1993.
Lombardi, Donald N.
Progressive health care management strategies. American Hospital Publishing, 1992.
  Anon. *Health Prog* 74:68 My 1993.
Lonergan, Bernard J F, 1904-1984.
Insight: a study of human understanding. University of Toronto Press, 1992.
  Heiser, W Charles. *TheolDgst* 40:74-75 Spr 1993.
Long, Asphodel P.
In a chariot drawn by lions: the search for the female deity. The Women's Press, n.d.
  Boss, Sarah. *Tablet* 247:1297-1299 O 9 1993.
Long, Burke O.
2 Kings. William B Eerdmans Publishing Company, 1991.
  Stuhlmueller, Carroll. *BibleT* 31:119-120 Mr 1993.
Long, Elisabeth.
Ysabella of Trastamara: first lady of the Renaissance. Alhamar Publishing, Inc, 1992.
  MacCarthy, Peter T. *HPR* 93:76-77 F 1993.
Longchamp, Albert.
Ignazio di Loyola: Breve profilo spirituale. Città Nuova, 1990.
  Mellinato, Giuseppe. *Civiltà* 143:533-534 D 5 1992.
Longchamp, Max Huot de.
Saint Jean de la Croix. FAC, 1992.
  Würtele, Hélène. *Laval Theol Phil* 49:171 F 1993.
  Renard, L J. *NRT* 115:129 Ja-F 1993.
  Adnès, Pierre. *Gregorianum* 74 No 1:172 1993.
Longenecker, Bruce W.
Eschatology and the covenant: a comparison of 4 Ezra and Romans 1-11. Sheffield, 1991.
  Crawford, Barry S. *CBQ* 55:167-169 Ja 1993.
Longenecker, Richard N.
Galatians. Word, 1990.
  Tyler, Ronald. *CBQ* 54:791-792 O 1992.
Longford, Elizabeth.
Royal throne: the future of the monarchy. Hodder & Stoughton, n.d.
  Kenny, Mary, 1936-. *Tablet* 247:580 My 8 1993.
Longford, Francis Aungier Packenham, 1905-.
Young offenders. Chapmans, n.d.
  Stacey, Tom. *Tablet* 247:1263 O 2 1993.
Longley, Michael.
Gorse fires. Secker and Warburg, 1991.
  Goodby, John. *Studies* 81:448-452 Wint 1992.
Longman, Tremper.
Fictional Akkadian autobiography: a generic and comparative study. Eisenbrauns, 1991.
  Edelman, Diana V. *OTA* 16:409-410 Je 1993.
Longshore, George F.
Top docs: managing the search for physician leaders. American College of Physician Executives, 1992.
  Anon. *Health Prog* 74:94 Jl-Ag 1993.
Lonning, Per.
Creation—an ecumenical challenge? Reflections issuing from a study by the Institute for Ecumenical Research. Mercer University Press, 1989.
  Grenz, Stanley. *JEcumen Stds* 29:489-491 Sum-Aut 1992.
Lonsdale, David.
Dance to the music of the spirit: the art of discernment. DLT, n.d.
  Huggett, Joyce, 1937-. *Month* 26:147 Ap 1993.
López Amat, Alfredo.
La vita consacrata, Le varie forme dalle origini ad oggi. Città Nuova, 1991.
  Barruffo, A. *Civiltà* 144:200 Ja 16 1993.
Lossky, Nicholas, et al, eds.
Dictionary of the Ecumenical Movement. Eerdmans, 1991.
  Murphy, Roland E. *OTA* 16:161-162 F 1993.
  MacGregor, Geddes. *JEcumen Stds* 29:264-265 Spr 1992.
Louf, André.
Tuning in to grace: a quest for God. DLT, 1992.
  Lansdale, David. *Way* 33:160 Ap 1993.
  Justice, Cornelius. *Cist Stud* 28 no 2:[43]-[44] 1993.
Louys, Daniel.
Le jardin d'Éden: mythe fondateur de l'Occident. Cerf, 1992.
  Tsumuraya, Katsuko. *OTA* 16:167-168 F 1993.
  Ska, Jean Louis. *NRT* 115:252 Mr-Ap 1993.
Lovell, James Blair.
Anastasia, the lost princess. Robson Books, n.d.
  FitzLyon, April. *Tablet* 246:1622-1623 D 19-26 1992.

Lowe, David Garrard.
Stanford White's New York. Doubleday, n.d.
  Sullivan, James A. *Crisis* 11:58-60 Ap 1993.
Lowenstamm, Samuel E.
From Babylon to Canaan. Hebrew University Press, 1992.
  Begg, Christopher T. *OTA* 16:397-398 Je 1993.
Lowenstein, Tom.
Ancient land: sacred ritual. Bloomsbury, n.d.
  Walton, James. *Tablet* 247:584 My 8 1993.
Lubac, Henri de, Cardinal, 1896-.
Auf den Wegen Gottes. Johannes Verlag Einsiedeln, 1992.
  Anon. *NRT* 115:620-621 Jl-Ag 1993.
Lubsczyk, Hans.
Die Einheit der Schrift: Gesammelte Aufsätze. St Benno, 1989.
  Begg, Christopher T. *OTA* 15:474-475 O 1992.
Lucas, John.
Reggie. Julia MacRae, n.d.
  Amis, John. *Tablet* 247:585 My 8 1993.
Luciani, Alfredo.
Catechismo sociale cristiano. Monadori, 1992.
  Joblin, Joseph, 1920-. *Gregorianum* 74 no 2:399 1993.
Luciani, Anna.
Gli spigoli della memoria. Ellemme, 1991.
  Lambiasi, F. *Civiltà* 143:433-434 N 21 1992.
Luckert, Karl W.
Egyptian light and Hebrew fire: theological and philosophical roots of Christendom in evolutionary perspective. State University of New York Press, 1992.
  Heiser, W Charles. *TheolDgst* 39:369 Wint 1992.
Luhmann, Niklas.
Funzione della religione. Morcelliana, 1991.
  Pizzuli, D. *Civiltà* 144:405-407 F 20 1993.
Lukacs, John, 1923-.
The end of the 20th century and the end of the modern age. Ticknor & Fields, n.d.
  Crilly, Scholastica. *Register* 69:4 Je 27 1993.
  Samway, Patrick H, 1939-. *America* 168:18 Mr 20-27 1993.
  Zahn, Gordon C. *New Oxford Rev* 60:24-26+ My 1993.
Lukas, Elisabeth.
Prevenire le crisi: Un contributo della logoterapia. Herder, 1989.
  Szentmártoni, Mihály. *Gregorianum* 74 No 1:189 1993.
Lukefather, Oscar.
A Catholic guide to the Bible. Liguori Publications, n.d.
  Kaler, Patrick. *Liguorian* 81:68-69 Jl 1993.
Lulle, Raymond.
Il libro dell'Amico e dell'Amato. Dialoghi mistici. Città Nuova, 1991.
  Feruzzi, G. *Civiltà* 2:196 Ap 17 1993.
Le livre du gentil et des trois sages. Éditions du Cerf, 1993.
  Steenberghen, Fernand Van. *RPhil Louvain* 91:324-425 My 1993.
Lund, Nils Wilhelm.
Chiasmus in the New Testament. Hendrickson, 1992.
  Parunak, H Van Dyke. *CBQ* 55:383-384 Ap 1993.
Lundquist, John M.
The temple. Thames & Hudson, n.d.
  Braybrooke, Neville. *Tablet* 247:790 Je 19 1993.
Luomanen, Petri, ed.
Luke-Acts: Scandinavian perspectives. Vandenhoeck & Ruprecht, 1991.
  Talbert, Charles H. *CBQ* 55:198 Ja 1993.
Luria, Keith P.
Territories of grace: cultural change in the Seventeenth-Century diocese of Grenoble. University of California Press, 1991.
  Levi, A.H.T. *Heythrop* 34:458-459 O 1993.
Lust, Johan, et al, eds.
A Greek-English lexicon of the Septuagint. Deutsche Bibelgesellschaft, 1992.
  Di Lella, Alexander A. *OTA* 16:162 F 1993.
  Vervenne, Marc. *Eph Theol Lovan* 69:118-124 Ap 1993.
Lustiger, Jean-Marie, Cardinal, 1926-.
Nous avons rendez-vous avec l'Europe. Mame, 1991.
  Clarot, B. *NRT* 115:120-121 Ja-F 1993.
Lutero, Martin.
La Lettera ai Romani (1515-1516). Paoline, 1991.
  Vercruysse, Jos E. *Eph Theol Lovan* 78:461-462 D 1992.
Luttrell, Anthony.
The hospitallers of Rhodes and their Mediterranean world. Ashgate Publishing, 1992.
  Heiser, W Charles. *TheolDgst* 40:172 Sum 1993.
Luzbetak, Louis J.
Chiesa e cultura. EMI, n.d.
  Dupuis, Jacques. *Civiltà* 3:208 Jl 17 1993.
Luzi, Pietro.
La passione del Nome di Dio nella storia della salvezza. LDC, 1991.
  Ganzi, I M. *Civiltà* 2:200-201 Ap 17 1993.
Lynch, Bernard.
A priest on trial. Bloomsbury, n.d.
  Woods, Richard. *Tablet* 247:246-247 F 20 1993.

M

Mabee, Charles.
Reading sacred texts through American eyes: biblical interpretation as cultural critique. Mercer University Press, 1991.
  Heiser, W Charles. *TheolDgst* 39:369-370 Wint 1992.

MacCaffrey, Wallace T.
Elizabeth I: war and politics, 1588-1603. Princeton University Press, 1992.
Loomie, Albert J. *CHist* 79:341-342 Ap 1993.

Maccarrone, Michele, ed.
Il primato del vescovo di Roma nel primo millennio: Ricerche e testimonianze: Atti del Symposium storico-teologico, Roma 9-13 ottobre 1989. Libreria Ed Vaticana, 1991.
Capizzi, Carmelo. *Civilta* 144:407-408 F 20 1993.

MacClennan, Carole.
Learning by doing: 150 activities to enrich religion classes for children. Twenty-Third, n.d.
McCann, Deborah. *ReligTJ* 27:14-15 S 1993.

MacCormack, Sabine.
Religion in the Andes: vision and imagination in early colonial Peru. Princeton University Press, 1991.
Gagliano, Joseph A. *CHist* 79:139-140 Ja 1993.
Heiser, W Charles. *TheolDgst* 39:370 Wint 1992.

MacDonald, Alan.
The essential Easter book. Lion, n.d.
Braybrooke, Neville. *Tablet* 247:374 Mr 20 1993.

MacDonald, Iain, ed.
Saint Patrick. Floris, n.d.
Murphy, James H. *Furrow* 44:326-327 My 1993.
St Brendan. Floris, n.d.
Murphy, James H. *Furrow* 44:326-327 My 1993.
St Bride. Floris, n.d.
Murphy, James H. *Furrow* 44:326-327 My 1993.
St Columba. Floris, n.d.
Murphy, James H. *Furrow* 44:326-327 My 1993.

MacDonald, Scott, ed.
Being and goodness: the concept of the good in metaphysics and philosophical theology. Cornell University Press, 1991.
Kruschwitz, Robert B. *Thomist* 57:150-153 Ja 1993.

MacGregor, A J.
Fire and light in the Western Triduum: their use at Tenebrae and at the Paschal Vigil. The Liturgical Press, 1992.
Brown, Daniel A. *Mod Lit* 20:40 Ag 1993.

MacGregor, Geddes.
Images of afterlife. Paragon House, 1992.
Heiser, W Charles. *TheolDgst* 40:173 Sum 1993.

MacHaffie, Barbara J.
Readings in her story: women in Christian tradition. Fortress Press, 1992.
Heiser, W Charles. *TheolDgst* 40:75 Spr 1993.

Maciel, Marcial.
Integral formation of Catholic priests. Alba House, 1992.
Higgins, James J. *Liguorian* 81:69 Je 1993.
Heiser, W Charles. *TheolDgst* 40:75 Spr 1993.

MacIntyre, Alasdair, 1929-.
Three rival versions of moral enquiry. University of Notre Dame Press, 1990.
Hibbs, Thomas S. *Thomist* 57:277-297 Ap 1993.

Macken, John.
The autonomy theme in the church dogmatics: Karl Barth and his critics. Cambridge University Press, 1990.
Godsey, John D. *Thomist* 57:269-275 Ap 1993.

MacKenzie, Norman H, ed.
The early poetic manuscripts and note-books of Gerard Manley Hopkins in facsimile. Garland Publishing, 1991.
Endean, Philip. *Month* 26:148-149 Ap 1993.
The later poetic manuscripts of Gerard Manley Hopkins in facsimile. Garland Publishing, 1991.
Endean, Philip. *Month* 26:148-149 Ap 1993.

MacLennan, Robert S.
Early Christian texts of Jews an Judaism. Scholars Press, 1990.
Keely, Kathleen. *SIDIC* 25 No 1:32 1992.
Early Christian texts on Jews and Judaism. Scholars Press, 1990.
Frank, Sue. *JEcumen Stds* 29:124-125 Wint 1992.

MacNeil, Robert.
Burden of desire. Doubleday, n.d.
Hurley, Karen. *Ant Anth* 100:50 Ja 1993.

Macnutt, Francis, and Macnutt, Judith.
Tessuto nel grembo: Guida alla preghiera per genitori in attesa. Ancora, 1991.
Discepolo, S. *Civilta* 144:201 Ja 16 1993.

Macquarrie, John.
Mary for all Christians. William B Eerdmans, n.d.
Thompson, Thomas L. *Can Cath Rev* 11:34-35 Ja 1993.
Mary for all Christians. Eerdmans, 1990.
Gaggney, J Patrick. *JEcumen Stds* 29:271-272 Spr 1992.
Mary for all Christians. Collins, 1990.
Cadwallader, Alan H. *Pacifica* 6:349-352 O 1993.

Macy, Gary.
The banquet's wisdom. Paulist Press, 1992.
Witczak, Michael G. *Living Light* 29:97 Spr 1993.
The banquet's wisdom. Paulist, 1992.
Austin, G. *Worship* 67:477-478 S 1993.

Madden, Lawrence J, ed.
The awakening church: 25 years of liturgical renewal. The Liturgical Press, 1992.
Heiser, W Charles. *TheolDgst* 40:51 Spr 1993.
The awakening Church. Liturgical, 1992.
Higgins, James J. *Liguorian* 81:69-70 Mr 1993.
The awakening church. Liturgical, 1992.
Donovan, Kevin. *Month* 26:112-113 Mr 1993.
The Joseph Campbell phenomenon: implications for the contemporary church. The Pastoral Press, 1992.
Ramshaw, Gail. *Worship* 67:187-188 Mr 1993.
Heiser, W Charles. *TheolDgst* 40:70 Spr 1993.

Madden, Peter.
A raw deal: trade and the world's poor. Christian Aid, n.d.
Anon. *Month* 25:499 D 1992.

Madelin, Henri.
La menace idéologique. Cerf, 1988.
Debarge, Louis. *MSR* 50:74-75 Ja-Mr 1993.

Madonia, Nicolò.
Ermeneutica et cristologia in Walter Kasper. Augustinus, 1990.
Brito, Emilio. *Eph Theol Lovan* 78:473-474 D 1992.

Madre, Ph.
Aspirez aux charismes. Pneumathèque, 1992.
Renard, L J. *NRT* 115:314 Mr-Ap 1993.

Maduro, Otto, ed.
Judaism, Christianity, and liberation—an agenda for dialogue. Orbis, 1991.
Bossman, David M. *Horizons (CTS)* 19:339-340 Fall 1992.
Aronowicz, Annette. *CrossCurr* 43:125-127 Spr 1993.

Maeckelberghe, Els.
Desperately seeking Mary: a feminist appropriation of a traditional religious symbol. Kok Pharos, 1992.
Cunneen, Sally. *CrossCurr* 43:134-135 Spr 1993.
Britt, John. *Horizons (CTS)* 20:155-156 Spr 1993.

Maesschalck, Marc.
Raison et pouvoir. Les impasses de la pensée politique postmoderne. Facultés universitaires Saint-Louis, 1992.
Joblin, Joseph, 1920-. *Gregorianum* 74 no 3:598-599 1993.

Magas, Branka.
The destruction of Yugoslavia: tracking the break-up 1980-92. Verso, n.d.
Hastings, Adrian, 1929-. *Tablet* 247:405 Mr 27 1993.

Maggi, Alberto.
Notre Dame des hérétiques. Marie et Nazareth. Editions Pauline, 1990.
Gauthier, Roland. *CahiersJos* 41:141 Ja-Je 1993.

Maggi, Giuseppe.
Pompei città non città. Loffredo, 1991.
Caprile, Giovanni. *Civilta* 2:617-618 Je 19 1993.

Maggio, Stefano.
Lo spirito di Don Bosco nel cuore del Beato Don Rinaldi. Torino, 1990.
Mellinato, Giuseppe. *Civilta* 143:543-544 D 5 1992.

Maggioni, Bruno.
Cristianesimo quotidiano. OR, 1991.
Ganzi, I M. *Civilta* 2:199 Ap 17 1993.

Magnano, Pasquale.
Syracusana Ecclesia, vol I: Appunti di storia sulla Chiesa siracusana, vol I. Archivio Storica della Curia, 1992.
Ferrua, Antonio. *Civilta* 3:322-323 Ag 7-21 1993.

Magnante, Antonio.
La teologia dell'esodo nei Salmi. Edizioni Dehoniane, 1991.
Begg, Christopher T. *OTA* 16:426 Je 1993.

Magnard, Pierre.
Le Dieu des philosophes. Mame, 1992.
Millet, Louis. *RPhil Louvain* 91:509-510 Ag 1993.
Pascal, la clé du chiffre. Editions universitaires, 1991.
Tock, Jean-François. *RPhil Louvain* 91:472 Ag 1993.

Magnus, Bernd, et al.
Nietzsche's case: philosophy as/and literature. Routledge, 1993.
Mulryan, John. *Cithara* 32:55-56 My 1993.

Magocsi, Paul Robert, ed.
Morality and reality: the life and times of Andrei Sheptyts'kyi. University of Alberta, 1989.
Bohachevsky-Chomiak, M. *CHist* 78:677-679 O 1992.

Magrassi, Mariano.
Maria, stella sul nostro commino. no publisher given, 1991.
Caprile, Giovanni. *Civilta* 3:201-202 Jl 17 1993.
Per me vivere è Cristo. La Scala, 1991.
Caprile, Giovanni. *Civilta* 3:201-202 Jl 17 1993.

Maguire, Daniel C.
The moral core of Judaism and Christianity. Fortress, n.d.
Dietrich, Donald J. *America* 169:15-17 D 4 1993.

Maher, Mary.
The devil's card. St Martin's Press, n.d.
Costello, Gerald M, 1931-. *USCath* 58:49-50 S 1993.

Mahoney, Donna Tiernan.
Touching the face of God—intimacy and celibacy in priestly life. Mercier Press, n.d.
Anon. *Furrow* 44:63 Ja 1993.

Maier, Harry O.
The social setting of the ministry as reflected in the writings of Hermas, Clement, and Ignatius. Wilfrid Laurier University, 1991.
Osiek, Carolyn. *CBQ* 55:171-173 Ja 1993.

Maier, Johann.
Il Giudaismo del secondo tempio. Paideia Editrice, 1991.
Prato, Gian Luigi. *Gregorianum* 74 no 2:353-355 1993.

Main, John.
Word made flesh. Darton, Longman & Todd, n.d.
Forrester, David. *Tablet* 247:1304 O 9 1993.

Maisonneuve, D de la.
L'hébreu biblique par les textes, Vol 2. Desclee, 1991.
Ska, Jean Louis. *NRT* 115:249-250 Mr-Ap 1993.

Maitland, Sara.
Home truths. Chatto and Windus, n.d.
Loudon, Mary. *Tablet* 247:657 My 22 1993.

Majello, Carlo.
L'arte di communicare. Angeli, 1991.
Baragli, Enrico. *Civilta* 2:203 Ap 17 1993.

Makiya, Kanan.
Cruelty and silence. Cape, n.d.
Hodgkin, E C. *Tablet* 247:618 My 15 1993.

Malamat, Abraham.
Mari and the early Israelite experience. Oxford University Press, 1992.
  Magness, Jodi. *OTA* 16:410 Je 1993.

Malcolm, John.
Plato on the self-predication of forms. Clarendon Press, 1991.
  Hughes, Gerald. *Heythrop* 34:216-217 Ap 1993.

Malina, Bruce J, 1933-, and Rohrbaugh, Richard L.
Social science commentary on the synoptic gospels. Fortress, 1992.
  Pilch, John Joseph, 1936-. *Mod Lit* 20:40 O 1993.

Maloney, George A, 1924-.
Pseudo-Macarius: the fifty homilies and the great letter. Paulist, n.d.
  Graham, William C. *Nat Cath Rep* 29:25 Mr 26 1993.

Maloney, H Newton.
Relaxation for Christians. Ballantine Books, 1992.
  Heiser, W Charles. *TheolDgst* 40:75 Spr 1993.

Maloney, Linda M.
"All that God had done with them". Peter Lang, 1991.
  Heiser, W Charles. *TheolDgst* 39:371 Wint 1992.

Malony, H Newton, ed.
Psychology of religion: personalities, problems, possibilities. Baker Book House, 1991.
  Heiser, W Charles. *TheolDgst* 39:380-381 Wint 1992.
  Godin, A. *Lumen* 48:357-358 S 1993.

Malony, H Newton, and Southard, Samuel, eds.
Handbook of religious conversion. Religious Education Press, 1992.
  Conn, Walter E. *Living Light* 29:87-88 Sum 1993.
  Heiser, W Charles. *TheolDgst* 40:165 Sum 1993.

Malul, Meir.
The comparative method in ancient Near Eastern and Biblical legal studies. Neukirchener V, 1990.
  Matthews, Victor H. *OTA* 15:484 O 1992.

Maly, Francis Susanne.
Life after Easter. Paulist Press, n.d.
  Graham, William C. *Nat Cath Rep* 29:36 S 10 1993.

Manaranche, A.
J'aime mon Église. Fayard, 1991.
  Clarot, B. *NRT* 115:583-584 Jl-Ag 1993.

Manathodath, Jacob.
Culture dialogue, and the Church. Intercultural, 1990.
  Baum, Gregory. *JEcumen Stds* 29:491-492 Sum-Aut 1992.

Manes, Emma Luppino.
L'Agesilao di Senofonte tra commiato ed encomio. Jaca, 1992.
  Ferrua, Antonio. *Civilta* 3:317-318 Ag 7-21 1993.

Manfrin, Renzo.
Il fascino di un volto Biografia di San Leopoldo. Deganello, 1992.
  Mellinato, Giuseppe. *Civilta* 2:612 Je 19 1993.

Mangan, Célione.
The Targum of Job. Liturgical Press, 1991.
  Garber, Zev. *CBQ* 55:119-120 Ja 1993.

Mangione, Jerre, and Morreale, Ben.
La storia: five centuries of the Italian American experience. HarperCollins, n.d.
  Rubino, Carl A. *America* 168:22 My 1 1993.

Manion, Margaret, and Muir, Bernard, eds.
Medieval texts and images: studies of manuscripts from the Middle Ages. Harwood, 1991.
  Barker, Bede M. *Cist Stud* 27 No 4:[105]-[108] 1992.

Manlove, Colin Nicholas.
Christian fantasy. University of Notre Dame, 1992.
  Dollen, Charles. *Priest* 49:52 F 1993.
  Heiser, W Charles. *TheolDgst* 40:173 Sum 1993.

Mann, Thomas W.
To taste and see: exploring incarnation and the ambiguities of faith. Pilgrim Press, n.d.
  McCann, Deborah. *ReligTJ* 27:10 F 1993.

Manns, F.
L'évangile de Jean à la lumiére du judaïsme. Franciscan Printing Press, 1991.
  Simoens, Y. *NRT* 115:108-109 Ja-F 1993.

Mansfield, Bruce.
Man on his own: interpretations of Erasmus, c 1750-1920. University of Toronto Press, 1992.
  DeMolen, Richard L. *CHist* 79:502-505 Jl 1993.

Manso Porto, Carmen.
El arte de la Orden de Santo Domingo en la Galicia Medieval, 2 vols. Universidad Complutense, 1991.
  Hernández, Ramón. *Cien Tom* 119:426-427 My-Ag 1992.

Manuel, Frank Edward.
The broken staff: Judaism through Christian eyes. Harvard University Press, 1992.
  Wilken, Robert L. *Comm* 120:21-22 Ja 15 1993.
  Heiser, W Charles. *TheolDgst* 40:75-76 Spr 1993.

Maraini, Dacia.
Isolina [tr S. Williams]. Peter Owen, n.d.
  Dorrell, Fleur. *Tablet* 247:1266 O 2 1993.

Maraval, P.
Les persécutions des chrétines durant les quatre premiers siècles. Desclée, 1992.
  Joassart, Bernard. *NRT* 115:610-611 Jl-Ag 1993.

Marchadour, A.
L'évangile de Jean. Novalis, 1992.
  Renard, L J. *NRT* 115:297 Mr-Ap 1993.

Marcheschi, Graziano.
Scripture at weddings. Liturgy Training Publications, 1992.
  Lazar, John E. *Mod Lit* 20:39-40 My 1993.

Marchesi, Angelo.
Filosofia e religione. Edizioni Unicopli, 1991.
  Steenberghen, Fernand Van. *RPhil Louvain* 91:152-153 F 1993.
Pensiero medioevale e pensiero contemporaneo. CUSL, 1992.
  Steenberghen, Fernand Van. *RPhil Louvain* 91:316-317 My 1993.

Marchi, Cesare.
In punta di lingua. Rizzoli, 1992.
  Baragli, Enrico. *Civilta* 3:334-335 Ag 7-21 1993.

Marchi, Vichi De, and Ercolessi, Maria Cristina.
Terzo Mondo e Quarto Potere: I continenti della crisi raccontati dalla televisione. RAI-Nuova ERI, 1991.
  Salvini, Gianpaolo. *Civilta* 3:337 Ag 7-21 1993.

Marcolini, Egidio.
Storie e leggende di 100 Paesi. Piemme, 1993.
  Flumeri, E. *Civilta* 2:613 Je 19 1993.

Marconcini, B, et al.
Angeli e Demoni. Dehoniane, 1991.
  Anon. *NRT* 115:621 Jl-Ag 1993.

Marconi, Gilberto.
Il dio da vedere. Racconti lucani del giorno di Pasqua. Stamperia d'arte Ribichini, 1992.
  Anon. *Gregorianum* 74 no 2:411-412 1993.

Marcozzi, Vittorio.
Alla ricerca di nostri predecessori: compendio di paleoantropologia. Ed Paoline, 1992.
  Allessandri, M. *Civilta* 143:523-524 D 5 1992.

Marcus, Joel.
The way of the Lord. John Knox, 1992.
  Senior, Donald. *BibleT* 31:315 S 1993.
The way of the Lord. Westminster, 1992.
  Witherup, Ronald D. *OTA* 16:447-448 Je 1993.

Marcy, Gary.
The banquet's wisdom. Paulist Press, n.d.
  Gibbons, Robin. *Way* 33:260 Jl 1993.

Mardones, José Ma.
Fe y politica. Sal Terrae, 1992.
  Bravo, Gallardo Carlos. *Christus* 58:62 S 1993.

Maresca, Adolfo.
Dizionario giuridico diplomatico. Giiuffrè, 1991.
  Joblin, Joseph, 1920-. *Civilta* 143:639-640 D 19 1992.

Margenau, Henry, and Varghese, Roy Abraham, eds.
Cosmos, bios, theos. Open Court, 1992.
  Heiser, W Charles. *TheolDgst* 40:157 Sum 1993.

Margerie, B de.
Histoire doctrinale du culte au Couer de Jésus. Mame, 1992.
  Renard, L-J. *NRT* 115:587-588 Jl-Ag 1993.

Margerie, Bertrand de.
Heart of Mary, heart of the church. AMI Press, 1992.
  MacCarthy, Peter T. *HPR* 94:78 N 1993.

Margolis, Jonathan.
Cleese encounters. McClelland and Stewart, n.d.
  Coren, Michael. *Can Cath Rev* 11:3-4 Ja 1993.

Maria Icona della tenerezza del Padre.
  Ed Augustinus, 1992.
  Renard, L-J. *NRT* 115:590-591 Jl-Ag 1993.

Marinelli, Anthony.
The word made flesh. Paulist, n.d.
  Graham, William C. *Nat Cath Rep* 30:35 N 19 1993.

Maring, Norman Hill, and Hudson, Winthrop Still.
A Baptist manual of polity and practice. Judson Press, 1991.
  Heiser, W Charles. *TheolDgst* 40:173 Sum 1993.

Marion, Jean-Luc.
Dieu sans l'être. Presses Universitaires de France, 1991.
  Galot, Jean. *Gregorianum* 74 no 3:577 1993.
  Schmitz, Kenneth L. *Thomist* 57:495-508 Jl 1993.
  Ward, Graham. *New Blckfrs* 74:55-56 Ja 1993.
  Sweetman, Brendan. *New Oxford Rev* 60:25-26 Jl-Ag 1993.
  Zhang, Ellen Y. *CrossCurr* 43:273-277 Sum 1993.
  Richardson, William J. *TheolStds* 54:576-578 S 1993.

Maritain, R.
OEuvres complètes. Éd Saint-Paul, 1991.
  Escole, R. *NRT* 115:304-305 Mr-Ap 1993.

Markus, Gilbert, ed.
The radical tradition. Darton Longman & Todd, 1992.
  Walls, Roland. *Priests & People* 7:83-84 F 1993.
  Samway, Patrick H, 1939-. *America* 169:22 Ag 28-S 4 1993.

Markus, R A.
The end of ancient Christianity. Cambridge University Press, n.d.
  Buckley, L. *Can Cath Rev* 11:36-37 Ja 1993.

Marquardt, Friedrich-Wilhelm.
Das christliche Bekenntnis zu Jesus, dem Juden. Verlag, 1990.
  Wyschogrod, Michael. *JEcumen Stds* 29:275-276 Spr 1992.

Márquez, Gabriel García.
Strange pilgrims. Alfred A. Knopf, n.d.
  McCarthy, Tim. *Nat Cath Rep* 30:34 N 19 1993.

Marrevee, William.
The popular guide to the Mass. Pastoral Press, 1992.
  Heinritz, Joann. *Mod Lit* 20:39 F 1993.

Marris, Robin.
Reconstructing Keynesian economics with imperfect competition. Edward Elgar, n.d.
  Duitt, Amitava Krishna. *RSocEcon* 51:393-395 Aut 1993.

Marsden, George M, and Longfield, Bradley J, eds.
The secularization of the academy. Oxford University Press, 1992.
   Solberg, Winton U. *CHist* 79:369-370 Ap 1993.

Marsden, John Joseph.
Marxian and Christian utopianism. Monthly Review, 1991.
   Bancroft, Nancy. *JEcumen Stds* 29:492-493 Sum-Aut 1992.

Marsh, Kate, ed.
Writers and their houses. Hamish Hamilton, n.d.
   Mitchell, Keith. *Tablet* 247:1199 S 18 1993.

Marshall, Bruce D.
Theology and dialogue: essays in conversation with George Lindbeck. University of Notre Dame Press, 1990.
   Penaskovic, R. *Heythrop* 34:88-89 Ja 1993.

Marshall, Cynthia.
Last things and last plays: Shakespearan eschatology. Southern Illinois University Press, 1991.
   Cox, John D. *Relig Lit* 24:85-90 Aut 1992.

Marshall, David Brian.
Secularizing the faith. Toronto University Press, 1992.
   Heiser, W Charles. *TheolDgst* 40:173-174 Sum 1993.

Marthaler, Berard L, 1927-.
The Creed: the Apostolic faith in contemporary theology. Twenty-Third, n.d.
   Graham, William C. *Nat Cath Rep* 29:18 Jl 16 1993.
   Cunningham, Lawrence S, 1935-. *Comm* 120:29 O 8 1993.

Martin, Dennis D.
Fifteenth-Century Carthusian reform: the world of Nicholas Kempf. E J Brill, 1992.
   Overfield, James H. *CHist* 79:327-329 Ap 1993.

Martin, Henry-Jean.
Storia e potere della scrittura. Laterza, 1990.
   Baragli, Enrico. *Civilta* 2:203-204 Ap 17 1993.

Martin, James Alfred.
Beauty and holiness: the dialogue between aesthetics and religion. Princeton University Press, 1990.
   Meynell, Hugo. *Heythrop* 34:117-118 Ja 1993.

Martin, Michael.
The case against Christianity. Temple University Press, n.d.
   Graham, William C. *Nat Cath Rep* 30:15 O 22 1993.

Martin, Russell Niall Dickson.
Pierre Duhem: philosophy and history in the work of a believing physicist. Open Court, 1991.
   Heiser, W Charles. *TheolDgst* 39:371 Wint 1992.

Martin, Troy W.
Metaphor and composition in 1 Peter. Scholars Press, 1992.
   Heiser, W Charles. *TheolDgst* 39:372 Wint 1992.

Martin, William.
A prophet with honor. William Morrow, 1991.
   Gros, Jeffrey, 1938-. *Emmanuel* 99:175-177 Ap 1993.

Martineau, Lisa.
Caught ina mirror: reflections of Japan. Macmillan, n.d.
   Walton, James. *Tablet* 247:584 My 8 1993.

Martínez, Felícismo.
Iglesia sacerdotal, Iglesia prof5aetica. Sígueme.
   Bandera, Armando. *Cien Tom* 119:420-421 My-Ag 1992.

Martínez, Florentino García.
Qumran and Apocalyptic: studies on the Aramaic texts from Qumran. Brill, 1992.
   Fitzmyer, Joseph Augustine, 1920-. *OTA* 16:190 F 1993.

Martinez, Florentino García.
Textos de Qumrán. Trotta, 1992.
   Fitzmyer, Joseph Augustine, 1920-. *OTA* 16:444 Je 1993.

Martini, Carlo Maria, Cardinal, 1926-.
After some years: reflections on the ministry of the priest. Veritas, 1991.
   Heiser, W Charles. *TheolDgst* 39:372 Wint 1992.
In the thick of his ministry. The Liturgical Press, 1990.
   Senior, Donald. *BibleT* 31:253 Jl 1993.
Perseverance in trials. The Liturgical Press, 1992.
   Stuhlmueller, Carroll. *BibleT* 31:247 Jl 1993.

Martini, Carlo Maria, Cardinal, 1927-.
David et le Christ. Brepolis, 1991.
   Renard, L J. *NRT* 115:312 Mr-Ap 1993.
Prêtres, quelques années après. Éd du Cerf, 1992.
   Renard, L J. *NRT* 115:316-317 Mr-Ap 1993.
What am I that you care for me? Liturgical Press, n.d.
   Harrington, Daniel J. *America* 168:29 F 6 1993.

Martinich, Aloysius P.
The two gods of Leviathan. Cambridge University Press, 1992.
   Heiser, W Charles. *TheolDgst* 40:174 Sum 1993.

Martins, Sebastião.
Caminhos de Minas: apresentação de Francisco Iglésias. Editoração Publicações e Comunicações, 1992.
   Campolina Martins, Antonio Henrique. *REB* 53:238-239 Mr 1993.

Martorell, J.
Oyentes de la Palabra. STJ, n.d.
   Anon. *NRT* 115:632 Jl-Ag 1993.

Marty, F, and Dhôtel, J-C, eds.
L'expérience spirituelle et théologique. Médiasèvres, 1992.
   Renard, L J. *NRT* 115:311 Mr-Ap 1993.

Marty, François.
La bénédiction de Babel. Vérité et communication. Cerf, 1990.
   Robberechts, Edouard. *RPhil Louvain* 91:484-489 Ag 1993.

Martz, Louis L.
Thomas More. Yale University Press, n.d.
   Plant, Raymond M. *Can Cath Rev* 11:26-27 Ap 1993.

Mascellani, Elisa.
Prudens dispensator verbi: Romani 5, 12-21 nell' esegesi di Clemente Alessandrino e Origene. La Nuova Italia Editrice, 1990.
   Bundy, David. *Eph Theol Lovan* 78:171-172 Ap 1992.

Mason, Mary Jane.
Toward my father's house: hope filled meditations for the terminally ill. Liguori, 1993.
   Higgins, James J. *Liguorian* 81:68 D 1993.

Mason, R A.
Micah, Nahum, Obadiah. JSOT, 1991.
   Mariottini, Claude F. *OTA* 15:511 O 1992.

Mason, Steve.
Josephus and the New Testament. Hendrickson, 1992.
   Senior, Donald. *BibleT* 31:315-316 S 1993.

Massaro, Matteo.
Epigrafia metrica latina di età repubblicana. Instituto di Latino dell'Università degli Studi, 1992.
   Ferrua, Antonio. *Civilta* 2:412-413 My 15 1993.

Massaux, Édouard.
The influence of the Gospel of Saint Matthew on Christian literature before Saint Irenaeus. Mercer, 1990.
   Neirynck, F. *Eph Theol Lovan* 69:172-173 Ap 1993.

Massenet, M.
Jacob ou la fraude. Cerf, 1991.
   Navez, G. *NRT* 114:939 N-D 1992.

Massengale, Jean Montague.
Jean-Honoré Fragonard. Thames & Hudson, n.d.
   Reyntiens, Patrick. *Tablet* 247:582 My 8 1993.

Masseroni, Enrico.
Agape: Un cammino sulla carità alla scuola del Nuovo Testamento. Ed Paoline, 1991.
   Ganzi, I M. *Civilta* 144:200-201 Ja 16 1993.

Massey, Isabel Ann.
Interpreting the sermon on the mount in the light of Jewish tradition as evidenced in the Palestinian targums of the Pentateuch. Edwin Mellen Press, 1991.
   Heiser, W Charles. *TheolDgst* 40:174 Sum 1993.

Masson, Joseph.
Mystiques d'Asie. Desclée de Brouwer, 1992.
   Scheurer, J. *Lumen* 48:116 Mr 1993.
   Renard, L-J. *NRT* 115:595-597 Jl-Ag 1993.

Masson, Michel.
Élie ou l'appel du silence. Cerf, 1992.
   Murphy, Roland E. *OTA* 15:499 O 1992.

Mastroianni, F F.
Maria nella Civiltà dell'Amore. Ed T D C, 1991.
   Anon. *NRT* 115:313 Mr-Ap 1993.

Masugi, Ken, ed.
Interpreting Tocqueville's Democracy in America. Rowman and Littlefield, 1991.
   Marler, J C. *Mod Schlmn* 70:225-227 Mr 1993.

Masullo, Aldo.
Filosofie del soggetto e diritto del senso. Marietti, 1991.
   Ciaramelli, Fabio. *RPhil Louvain* 91:330-333 My 1993.

Matagne, C.
Répertoire des ouvrages du XVIIIe siècle de la bibliothèque du CDRR (1651-1700). Centre de Documentation et de Recherche Religieuses, 1992.
   Harvengt, A. *NRT* 115:290 Mr-Ap 1993.

Mateos, Juan, and Camacho, Fernando.
Jesus e a sociedade de seu tempo. Paulinas, 1992.
   Konings, Johan. *Perspectiva* 25:116-117 Ja-Ap 1993.

Matera, Frank J.
The Acts of the apostles: vol 5. Liturgical, 1992.
   Heiser, W Charles. *TheolDgst* 40:185 Sum 1993.
Galatians. Liturgical, 1992.
   Harrington, Daniel J. *America* 168:35 F 6 1993.
   Stuhlmueller, Carroll. *BibleT* 31:125 Mr 1993.
   Heiser, W Charles. *TheolDgst* 40:185 Sum 1993.

Mathei, Mauro.
Esbozo de un Santoral latinoamericano. Paulinas, 1992.
   Barrios Villegos, Marciano. *Teol Vida* 34 no 1-2:162 1993.

Mather, George A, and Nichols, Larry A.
Dictionary of cults, sects, religions and the occult. Zondervan, 1993.
   Lang, Jovian P. *Mod Lit* 20:40-41 N 1993.

Mathiot, J.
Icônes surprenantes de la Mère de Dieu. Éd Paulines, 1990.
   Navez, G. *NRT* 115:155 Ja-F 1993.

Mathson, Patricia.
Creativities: 101 creative activities for children to celebrate God's love. Ave Maria Press, 1992.
   McCann, Deborah. *ReligTJ* 27:10-11 F 1993.
   Riley, David M. *Catechist* 26:14 F 1993.

Mattai, Giuseppe.
Oltre le sabbie mobili. SEI, 1992.
   Cultrera, Francesco. *Civilta* 3:202-203 Jl 17 1993.

Matteo, Anthony M.
Quest for the absolute. Northern Illinois University, 1992.
   Hudson, Deal W. *TheolStds* 54:168-169 Mr 1993.
   Heiser, W Charles. *TheolDgst* 40:174 Sum 1993.

Matthews, Melvyn.
Finding your story: a Lent course. Darton, Longman and Todd, n.d.
   Hollings, Michael. *Tablet* 247:278 F 27 1993.
The hidden word: your story in scripture. Darton, Longman and Todd, n.d.
   Hollings, Michael. *Tablet* 247:278 F 27 1993.

McGinn, Bernard John, 1937-.
The foundations of mysticism. Crossroad, 1991.
Healy, Charles J. *America* 168:22-23 Ja 2-9 1993.
McKeever, Henry. *RRel* 52:312-313 Mr-Ap 1993.
Bouyer, Louis. *CHist* 79:93 Ja 1993.
The foundations of mysticism. Crossroads, 1991.
Lonsdale, David. *Way* 33:82 Ja 1993.
The foundations of mysticism. Crossroad, 1992.
Louth, Andrew. *New Blckfrs* 74:110-111 F 1993.
Dupré, Louis. *Thomist* 57:133-135 Ja 1993.
The foundations of mysticism. Crossroad, 1991.
McGonigle, Thomas D. *New Theol Rev* 6:115-116 Ag 1993.
The presence of God: a history of Western Christian mysticism. Crossroad, 1991.
Cavadini, John C. *Horizons (CTS)* 20:146-149 Spr 1993.

McGinnis, James.
Educating for peace and justice religious dimensions K-6. Institute for Peace and Justice, 1993.
Jurski, Joan. *Momentum* 24:79-80 N-D 1993.
Religious dimensions (vol 1: Grades K-6). Institute for Peace and Justice, n.d.
McCann, Deborah. *ReligTJ* 27:14 S 1993.
Religious dimensions (vol 2 Grades 7-12). Institute for Peace and Justice, n.d.
McCann, Deborah. *ReligTJ* 27:14 S 1993.

McGinnity, Gerard.
Christmen: experience of priesthood today. Christian Classics, n.d.
Higgins, James J. *Liguorian* 81:69-70 Je 1993.

McGinty, Mary Peter.
The Sacrament of Christian life. Thomas More Press, 1992.
Litecky, Catherine. *Sisters* 65:142-143 Mr 1993.
The sacrament of Christian life. Thomas More Press, 1992.
Heiser, W Charles. *TheolDgst* 40:75 Spr 1993.

McGonagall, William.
The world's worst poet. Templegate, n.d.
Hunt, George W, 1937-. *America* 168:2 Je 5-12 1993.

McGovern, Arthur F.
Liberation theology and its critics: toward an assessment. Orbis Books, 1989.
Neckebrouck, Valeer. *Eph Theol Lovan* 69:205 Ap 1993.

McGowan, Joseph.
Food not bombs: how to feed the hungry and build community. New Society Publishers, n.d.
McGowan, Joseph. *Nat Cath Rep* 29:19 Mr 19 1993.

McGrath, Alister E.
The dilemma of self-esteem. Crossway Books, 1992.
Heiser, W Charles. *TheolDgst* 40:172-173 Sum 1993.
Giovanni Calvino: Il riformatore e la sua influenza sulla cultura occidentale. Basil Blackwell, 1990.
Vercruysse, Jos E. *Gregorianum* 74 No 1:181-182 1993.

McHoy, Peter.
Containers and baskets for year round colour. Cassell, n.d.
Taylor, Patrick. *Tablet* 247:375 Mr 20 1993.

McIlhone, James P.
The word made clear. Thomas More Press, 1992.
Stuhlmueller, Carroll. *BibleT* 30:381 N 1992.

McInerny, Ralph M.
Aquinas on human action. Catholic University of America Press, 1992.
Davies, Brian. *IPQ* 33:239-240 Je 1993.
Heiser, W Charles. *TheolDgst* 40:173 Sum 1993.
Boethius and Aquinas. Catholic University of America, 1990.
Marenbon, John. *Heythrop* 34:318-319 Jl 1993.

McInerny, Ralph M, ed.
The mind and heart of the church: the proceedings of the Wethersfield Institute, volume 4. Ignatius Press, 1991.
Mangan, Charles M. *HPR* 93:81-82 Ag-S 1993.

McIntosh, Marjorie Keniston.
A community tranformed: the manor and liberty of Havring, 1500-1620. Cambridge University Press, 1992.
Poos, L R. *CHist* 79:104-105 Ja 1993.

McIntyre, Anthony Osler.
Medieval Tuscany and Umbria. Penguin Books, n.d.
Adams, Michael. *Tablet* 247:1076-1077 Ag 21 1993.

McIntyre, John P.
Customary law in the "Corpus iuris canonici". Mellen Research University Press, 1990.
Gauthier, Albert. *Stud Can* 27 no 1:261-262 1993.

McKenzie, Leon.
Adult education and worldview construction. Krieger Publishing, 1991.
Hayes, Matt. *Living Light* 29:82-84 Aut 1992.

McKenzie, Steven L.
The trouble with Kings: the composition of the Book of Kings in the Deuteronomistic history. Brill, 1991.
Miller, William T. *OTA* 15:498-499 O 1992.
Mulrooney, Joseph. *Heythrop* 34:308-309 Jl 1993.

McKim, Donald K, ed.
Major themes in the reformed tradition. Eerdmans, 1992.
Heiser, W Charles. *TheolDgst* 39:371 Wint 1992.

McKnight, Felicia B.
Parish alive. The Crossroad Publishing Company, n.d.
Higgins, James J. *Liguorian* 81:68 Ap 1993.

McKnight, Scott.
A light among the Gentiles: Jewish missionary activity in the Second Temple period. Fortress Press, 1991.
Chesnutt, Randall D. *CBQ* 55:169-170 Ja 1993.

McLaren, James S.
Power and politics in Palestine: the Jews and the governing of their land, 100 BC-AD 70. Sheffield, 1992.
Bergren, Theodore A. *CBQ* 55:384-385 Ap 1993.
Halligan, John M. *OTA* 16:447 Je 1993.

McLaurin, Tim.
Keeper of the moon. Anchor Books, 1991.
Gilmour, Peter. *Critic* 47:78-82 Spr 1993.

McLean, Bradley H.
Citations and allusions to Jewish Scripture in early Christian and Jewish writings through 180 C E. Mellen, 1992.
Harrington, Daniel J. *CBQ* 55:170-171 Ja 1993.
Stuhlmueller, Carroll. *BibleT* 31:247-248 Jl 1993.

McLoughlin, William Gerald.
Soul liberty: the Baptists' struggle in New England, 1630-1833. Brown University Press, 1991.
Heiser, W Charles. *TheolDgst* 39:370 Wint 1992.

McLuhan, Marshall, and Powers, Bruce R.
Il villaggio globale. XXI secolo. Sugar Co, 1992.
Baragli, Enrico. *Civilta* 3:335 Ag 7-21 1993.

McLynn, Frank.
Robert Louis Stevenson. Hutchinson, n.d.
Mason, Philip, 1906-. *Tablet* 247:821-822 Je 26 1993.

McMahon, Edwin M, 1930-.
Beyond the myth of dominance: an alternative to a violent society. Sheed & Ward, n.d.
Graham, William C. *Nat Cath Rep* 29:18 Jl 16 1993.

McManus, Philip, and Schlabach, Gerald, eds.
Relentless persistence: nonviolent action in Latin America. New Society Publishers, 1990.
Peter-Raoul, Mar. *CrossCurr* 42:562-563 Wint 1992-1993.

McMullin, Ernan.
The inference that makes science. Marquette University Press, 1992.
Wallace, James A, 1944-. *Thomist* 57:131-132 Ja 1993.

McMurtry, Larry.
Streets of Laredo. Simon & Schuster, n.d.
Samway, Patrick H, 1939-. *America* 169:23 Ag 28-S 4 1993.

McNamara, James M.
In the presence of the wise and gentle Christ. Paulist Press, n.d.
Graham, William C. *Nat Cath Rep* 29:18 Jl 16 1993.

McNamara, Jo Ann, et al, eds.
Sainted women of the Dark Ages. Duke University Press, 1992.
Cunningham, Lawrence S, 1935-. *Comm* 120:26 F 12 1993.
Heiser, W Charles. *TheolDgst* 40:85 Spr 1993.

McNamara, Patrick H.
Conscience first, tradition second: a study of young American Catholics. State University of New York Press, 1992.
Heiser, W Charles. *TheolDgst* 39:370-371 Wint 1992.

McNamee, John P.
Diary of a city priest. Sheed & Ward, n.d.
Unsworth, Tim. *Nat Cath Rep* 30:25-26 N 19 1993.

McNeal, Patricia F.
Harder than war. Rutgers University Press, 1992.
Heiser, W Charles. *TheolDgst* 39:371 Wint 1992.
Pope, Stephen J. *America* 168:26-27+ Ap 24 1993.
McCarthy, Denis. *Nat Cath Rep* 29:28 S 10 1993.

McNees, Eleanor J.
Eucharistic poetry: the search for presence in the writings of John donne, Gerard Manley Hopkins, Dylan Thomas, and Geoffrey Hill. Bucknell University Press, 1992.
Heiser, W Charles. *TheolDgst* 39:371 Wint 1992.

McPartlan, Paul.
The Eucharist makes the Church: Henri de Lubac and John Zizioulas join in dialogue. T & T Clark, n.d.
Chadwick, Henry. *Tablet* 247:1135-1136 S 4 1993.

McPartlan, Paul, ed.
One in 2000? Towards Catholic-Orthodox unity: agreed statements and parish papers. St Pauls, n.d.
Chadwick, Henry. *Tablet* 247:1135-1136 S 4 1993.

McRedmond, Louis.
Thrown among strangers: John Henry Newman in Ireland. Verias Press, 1990.
Griffin, John R. *CHist* 79:352 Ap 1993.

McVeigh, Joseph.
Renewing the Irish church. Mercier Press, n.d.
MacEoin, Gary. *Nat Cath Rep* 29:30 S 10 1993.

Mead, Lawrence M.
The new politics of poverty. Basic Books, 1992.
Altschuler, Glenn C. *CrossCurr* 42:545-549 Wint 1992-1993.

Mealy, J Webb.
After the thousand years. Cornell University Press, 1992.
Heiser, W Charles. *TheolDgst* 40:174-175 Sum 1993.

Meara, David.
A W N Pugin and the revival of memorial brasses. Mansell Publishing Limited, 1991.
Schiefen, R J. *CHist* 79:147-148 Ja 1993.

Meckel, Daniel J, and Moore, Robert L, eds.
Self and liberation: the Jung/Buddhism dialogue. Paulist Press, n.d.
Haglof, Anthony. *Spir Life* 39:54-56 Spr 1993.

Meddi, Dotolo e Luciano.
Adulti nella Fede. Itinerari per la formazione del Catechsita degli adulti. Dehoniane, 1992.
Anon. *Gregorianum* 74 no 2:413 1993.

Medici, Lorenza de'.
Tuscany: the beautiful cookbook. Simon & Schuster, n.d.
Poole, Shona Crawford. *Tablet* 247:374 Mr 20 1993.

Medici, Priscilla Grazioli.
Medici, marmorari romani. Libr Editrice Vaticana, 1992.
Ferrua, Antonio. *Civilta* 3:325 Ag 7-21 1993.

Medina, John.
The outer limits of life. Oliver-Nelson, n.d.
Shea, Mark P. *New Oxford Rev* 60:13-16+ Ap 1993.

Medina, Jorge.
Juan Diego y la Santísma Virgen María de Guadalupe. Patris y Universidad Gabriela Mistral, 1992.
Barrios Villegos, Marciano. *Teol Vida* 34 no 1-2:162-163 1993.

Medved, Michael, 1948-.
Hollywood vs America. HarperCollins, 1992.
Lejeune, Anthony. *Tablet* 247:657 My 22 1993.
Baker, Kenneth. *HPR* 93:87-89 Ag-S 1993.
Attarian, John. *Crisis* 11:55-57 S 1993.
May, John R. *ChrWorld* 236:252-257 N-D 1993.
Holywood vs America. HarperCollins, .
Costello, Gerald M, 1931-. *USCath* 58:48-50 Je 1993.

Meehan, Brenda.
Holy women of Russia. HarperSanFrancisco, n.d.
Klimon, William M. *Crisis* 11:56-57 Jl-Ag 1993.

Meehan, Bridget Mary.
Exploring the feminine face of God. Sheed and Ward, 1991.
Phan, Peter C. *Living Light* 29:95 Aut 1992.

Meier, John P.
A marginal Jew: rethinking the historical Jesus. Doubleday, 1991.
Mueller, J. *RRel* 52:153-154 Ja-F 1993.
Senior, Donald. *TheolStds* 53:739-742 D 1992.
Rocker, Steven. *St Anth* 100:48 Ap 1993.
Sloyan, Gerard S. *Horizons (CTS)* 20:143-145 Spr 1993.
Donahue, John R. *CBQ* 55:385-387 Ap 1993.
Polish, Daniel F. *JEcumen Stds* 29:483-484 Sum-Aut 1992.
The mission of Christ and His church: studies in christology and ecclesiology. Michael Glazier, 1990.
Sweetland, Dennis M. *Bib Th Bul* 23:86-87 Sum 1993.

Meier, Kurt.
Kreuz und Hakenkreuz. Deutscher Taschenbuch Verlag, 1992.
Boberach, H. *Stimm Zeit* 211:357-358 My 1993.

Meilaender, Gilbert C.
Faith and faithfulness: basic themes in Christian ethics. University of Notre Dame Press, 1991.
Daurio, Janice. *New Oxford Rev* 60:29+ Mr 1993.
Faith and faithfulness. University of Notre Dame Press, 1991.
Vacek, E. *TheolStds* 53:789 D 1992.
O'Donohue, James A. *America* 168:20-21 F 27 1993.
Battaglia, Anthony. *Horizons (CTS)* 20:179-181 Spr 1993.

Meinwald, Constance C.
Plato's Parmenides. Oxford University Press, 1991.
Hughes, Gerald. *Heythrop* 34:216-217 Ap 1993.
McKnight, Christopher. *IJPS* 1:158-160 Mr 1993.

Meissner, William W.
Ignatius of Loyola: the psychology of a saint. Yale University Press, 1992.
Marluca, Dominic. *Tablet* 247:16 Ja 2 1993.
Cunningham, Lawrence S, 1935-. *Comm* 120:27 Mr 26 1993.
Sneck, William J. *RRel* 52:469-471 My-Je 1993.
Appleby, George W. *New Oxford Rev* 60:30-31 Je 1993.
Endean, Philip. *Way* 33:249-250 Jl 1993.
Heiser, W Charles. *TheolDgst* 40:175 Sum 1993.
Godin, A. *Lumen* 48:358 S 1993.
Ignatius of Loyola. Yale University Press, 1992.
Andrews, Paul. *Studies* 82:198-206 Sum 1993.

Melchiorre, Virgilio, ed.
Maschio-femmina: nuovi padri e nuove madri. Ed Paoline, 1992.
Flumeri, E. *Civilta* 144:614-615 Mr 20 1993.

Mello, Anthony De.
Contact with God: retreat conferences. Loyola University Press, 1991.
Sattler, John C. *Living Light* 29:92-93 Aut 1992.
Heiser, W Charles. *TheolDgst* 39:358 Wint 1992.
One minute nonsense. Loyola University Press, n.d.
Graham, William C. *Nat Cath Rep* 29:25 Mr 26 1993.
One minute nonsense. Gujarat Sahitya, n.d.
Hollings, Michael. *Tablet* 247:1303 O 9 1993.

Melton, J Gordon.
Directory of religious organizations in the United States. Gale Research, 1992.
Heiser, W Charles. *TheolDgst* 40:76 Spr 1993.
Encyclopedia of American religions. Gale Research, 1993.
Heiser, W Charles. *TheolDgst* 40:175 Sum 1993.
Encyclopedic handbook of cults in America. Garland Publishing, 1992.
Heiser, W Charles. *TheolDgst* 39:372 Wint 1992.
Euthanasia: official statements from religious bodies and ecumenical organizations. Gale Research Inc., 1991.
Murray, John C. *JEcumen Stds* 29:262-263 Spr 1992.
Religious bodies in the United States: a directory. Garland Publishing, 1992.
Heiser, W Charles. *TheolDgst* 39:372-373 Wint 1992.
Sex and family life: official statements from religious bodies and ecumenical organizations. Gale Research Inc., 1991.
Murray, John C. *JEcumen Stds* 29:262-263 Spr 1992.

Melton, J Gordon, and Köszegi, Michael A.
Religious information sources: a worldwide guide. Garland Publishing, 1992.
Heiser, W Charles. *TheolDgst* 39:373 Wint 1992.

Melton, J Gordon, and Poggi, Isotta.
Magic, witchcraft, and paganism in America. Garland Publishing, 1992.
Heiser, W Charles. *TheolDgst* 40:175 Sum 1993.

Melville, Arthur.
With eyes to see in a journey from religion to spirituality. Stillpoint, n.d.
Graham, William C. *Nat Cath Rep* 29:24 Mr 26 1993.

Memoriam Sanctorum venerantes.
Istituto di Archeologia Cristiana, 1992.
Ferrua, Antonio. *Civilta* 3:329 Ag 7-21 1993.

Mende, Theresia.
Durch Leiden zur Vollendung: Die Elihureden im Buch Ijob (Ijob 32-37). Paulinus, 1990.
Murphy, Roland E. *CBQ* 54:755-756 O 1992.

Mensch, Elizabeth, and Freeman, Alan.
The politics of virtue: is abortion debatable? Duke University Press, n.d.
Callahan, Daniel, 1930-. *Comm* 120:23-24 S 24 1993.
Elshtain, Jean Bethke, 1941-. *Comm* 120:24-25 S 24 1993.

Mensch, James Richard.
The beginning of the Gospel according to Saint John. Peter Lang, 1992.
Heiser, W Charles. *TheolDgst* 40:175 Sum 1993.

Menzies, Robert Paul.
The development of early Christian pneumatology, with special reference to Luke-Acts. JSOT Press, 1991.
Heiser, W Charles. *TheolDgst* 40:76 Spr 1993.

Mercadante, Linda A.
Gender, doctrine, and God: the Shakers and contemporary theology. Abingdon Press, 1990.
Quitslund, Sonya A. *JEcumen Stds* 29:260-262 Spr 1992.

Mercurio, Roger.
The Passionists. The Liturgical Press, n.d.
Kobler, John F. *Can Cath Rev* 11:32 Jl-Ag 1993.

Merkle, Judith A.
Committed by choice: religious life today. The Liturgical Press, 1992.
Mortonson, M Sheila. *Sisters* 65:309-310 Jl 1993.

Merrill, Daniel D.
Augustus De Morgan and the logic of relations. Kluwer Academic Publishers, 1990.
Kelly, C. *Mod Schlmn* 70:70-73 N 1992.

Mertens, C.
La vie la mort. Beauchesne, 1991.
Verdonck, C. *NRT* 115:119-120 Ja-F 1993.

Mertens, Heinrich.
Manual de la Biblia. Herder, 1989.
Pérez-Cotapos, Eduardo L. *Teol Vida* 33 no 3-4:323 1992.

Merton, Thomas, 1915-1968.
The springs of contemplation. Farrar, Straus, Giroux, 1992.
O'Connell, Patrick. *St Anth* 101:48-51 Je 1993.
Heiser, W Charles. *TheolDgst* 40:175-176 Sum 1993.
Thomas Merton. Paulist, 1992.
Heiser, W Charles. *TheolDgst* 40:176 Sum 1993.

Mertz, Fred.
The ore and the dross. Richshaw Publications, n.d.
Graham, William C. *Nat Cath Rep* 29:40 F 5 1993.

Messori, Vittorio.
Un italiano serio: il beato Francesco Faà di Bruno. Ed Paoline, 1990.
Mellinato, Giuseppe. *Civilta* 143:429-430 N 21 1992.
Sergio Paronetto: libertà d'iniziativa e giustizia sociale. Studium, 1991.
Mellinato, Giuseppe. *Civilta* 143:429-430 N 21 1992.

Meštrović, Stjepan G, et al.
The road from paradise. University Press of Kentucky, 1993.
Chalupa, V. *SocJust* 84:154-157 S-O 1993.

Metford, J C J.
The Christian year. Crossroad Publishing, 1991.
Poelker, T. *Past Mus* 17:50-51 D 1992-Ja 1993.

Metz, Johann Baptist, and Peters, Tiemo Ranier.
Pasión de Dios. Herder, 1992.
Libanio, Joao Batista. *Perspectiva* 25:261-263 My-Ag 1993.

Metzger, Bruce Manning.
The text of the New Testament: its transmission, corruption, and restoration. Oxford University Press, 1992.
Heiser, W Charles. *TheolDgst* 39:373 Wint 1992.

Metzger, Marcel.
Les constitutions apostoliques. Cerf, 1992.
Partos, L. *Lumen* 48:115 Mr 1993.

Metzler, Josef.
America pontificia primi saeculi evangelizationis 1493-1592: documenta pontificia ex registris et minutis praesertim.$. Liberia Editrice Vaticana, 1991.
Poole, Shona Crawford. *CHist* 78:601-606 O 1992.

Meuffels, Hans Otmar.
Einbergung des menschen in das mysterium der dreienigen liebe: eine trinitarische anthropologie nach Hans urs von Balthasar. Echter, 1991.
Oakes, Edward T. *TheolStds* 54:360-363 Je 1993.

Meyendorff, John.
Imperial unity and Christian divisions: the Church 450-680 A.D. St Vladimir's Seminary Press, 1989.
Bilaniuk, Petro B T. *CHist* 79:510-511 Jl 1993.

Meyendorff, John, and Tobias, Robert, eds.
Salvation in Christ. Augsburg, 1992.
Gros, Jeffrey, 1938-. *Worship* 67:476-477 S 1993.

Meyer, Ben F.
Christus Faber: the master builder and the house of God. Pickwick, 1992.
Topel, John. *TheolStds* 54:552-554 S 1993.

Meyer, Hans Bernhard.
Eucharistie. Geschichte, Theologie, pastoral. Verlag Fridrich Pustet, 1989.
Galot, Jean. *Gregorianum* 74 no 2:407 1993.

Meyer, Harding.
Dokumente wachsender Übereinstimmung. Bonifatius, Lembeck, 1992.
Seibel, W. *Stimm Zeit* 211:283-284 Ap 1993.

Meyer, Martin.
Ende der Geschichte? Hauser, 1993.
Köhler, Oscar. *Stimm Zeit* 211:719-720 O 1993.

Mitias, Michael H, ed.
Moral education and the liberal arts. Greenwood Press, 1992.
  Heiser, W Charles. *TheolDgst* 40:177 Sum 1993.

Moberly, R W L.
From Eden to Golgotha. Scholars, 1992.
  Begg, Christopher T. *OTA* 16:155-156 F 1993.
The Old Testament of the Old Testament: patriarchal narratives and Mosaic Yahwism. Fortress, 1992.
  Stuhlmueller, Carroll. *BibleT* 31:120 Mr 1993.
  Smith, Mark S. *OTA* 15:493 O 1992.
  Endres, John C. *TheolStds* 54:381-382 Je 1993.

Moffett, Samuel Hugh.
A history of Christianity in Asia, Vol I. HarperCollins, 1992.
  Heiser, W Charles. *TheolDgst* 40:77 Spr 1993.
  Cunningham, Lawrence S, 1935-. *Comm* 120:27-28 Je 4 1993.

Mohler, James Aylward.
A speechless child is the word God. New City Press, 1992.
  Heiser, W Charles. *TheolDgst* 40:177 Sum 1993.

Moioli, G.
L'esperienza spirituale. Glossa, 1992.
  Anon. *NRT* 115:635-636 Jl-Ag 1993.
Temi cristiani maggiori. no publisher given, 1992.
  Anon. *NRT* 115:636 Jl-Ag 1993.

Moir, John S, ed.
Church and society: documents on the religious and social history of the Roman Catholic Archdiocese of Toronto. The Archdiocese of Toronto, 1991.
  Heiser, W Charles. *TheolDgst* 39:356 Wint 1992.

Mojzes, Paul.
Religious liberty in Eastern Europe and the USSR before and after the great transformation. East European Monographs, 1992.
  Dunn, Dennis J. *CHist* 79:354-355 Ap 1993.

Mojzes, Paul, and Swidler, Leonard, eds.
Christian mission and interreligious dialogue. The Edwin Mellen Press, 1990.
  Heiser, W Charles. *TheolDgst* 39:356 Wint 1992.
  Baum, Gregory. *JEcumen Stds* 29:491-492 Sum-Aut 1992.

Mokah, Abou.
Les confessions d'un Arabe catholique. Centurion, 1991.
  Renard, L J. *NRT* 114:937-938 N-D 1992.

Mola, Aldo A.
L'amministrazione communale di Cuneo dal Settecento ai giorni nostri. Artigrafiche Corall, 1991.
  Caprile, Giovanni. *Civilta* 3:102-103 Jl 3 1993.

Molette, Ch.
La Vierge Marie dans la piéte du peuple chrétien depuis Vatican II. Médiaspaul, 1992.
  Renard, L-J. *NRT* 115:588-589 Jl-Ag 1993.

Molina, Contreras.
El Señor de la vida. Ed Sígueme, 1991.
  Simoens, Y. *NRT* 115:113-114 Ja-F 1993.

Molinaro, A, et al.
La verità: quali vie? Éd Augustinus, 1991.
  Anon. *NRT* 115:301 Mr-Ap 1993.

Moliner Fabregas del Pilar, José M.
Entre la armonía y la ternura. Ed Sígueme, 1990.
  Lago Alba, Luis. *Cien Tom* 119:625 S-D 1992.

Molla, S.
Les idées noires de Martin Luther King. Labor et Fides, 1992.
  Renard, L-J. *NRT* 115:616-617 Jl-Ag 1993.

Moloney, Francis J.
A body broken for people: Eucharist in the New Testament. Dove, 1990.
  Zilonka, Paul. *CBQ* 54:793 O 1992.

Moltmann, Jürgen.
History and the triune God: contributions to trinitarian theology. Crossroad, 1992.
  Bracken, Joseph A. *TheolStds* 53:765 D 1992.
  Heiser, W Charles. *TheolDgst* 39:373-374 Wint 1992.
The spirit of life. SCM, 1992.
  Lord, Elizabeth. *Way* 33:156-157 Ap 1993.
  Heiser, W Charles. *TheolDgst* 40:177 Sum 1993.
The way of Jesus Christ. HarperSanFrancisco, 1990.
  Chapman, G Clarke. *JEcumen Stds* 29:477-478 Sum-Aut 1992.

Moltmann-Wendel, Elisabeth, and Moltmann, Jürgen.
God—his and hers. SCM Press, 1991.
  D'Costa, Gavin. *New Blckfrs* 73:627-628 D 1992.

Mondin, Battista.
Dizionario enciclipedico del pensiero di san Tommaso d'Aquino. Edizioni Studio Domenicano, 1991.
  Steenberghen, Fernand Van. *RPhil Louvain* 91:322-323 My 1993.

Monk, Ray.
Ludwig Wittgenstein: the duty of genius. Penguin, 1991.
  Walker, Margaret Urban. *IPQ* 33:370-371 S 1993.

Monloubou, Louis.
Breve dizionario biblico. Queriniana, 1992.
  Scaiola, D. *Civilta* 3:440-441 S 4 1993.

Montague, George T.
Our Father, our Mother Mary and the faces of God. Franciscan University Press, n.d.
  Higgins, James J. *Liguorian* 81:70 Ja 1993.

Montani, M.
Filosofia della cultura. Biblioteca di Scienze Religiose, 1991.
  Anon. *NRT* 115:156-157 Ja-F 1993.

Montefiore, Hugh.
Reclaiming the high ground: a Christian response to secularism. St Martin's Press, 1990.
  Atkins, Anselm. *JEcumen Stds* 29:112-113 Wint 1992.

Montefiore, Hugh. *(cont'd)*
The womb and the tomb: the mystery of the birth and resurrection of Jesus. Fount, n.d.
  MacKennon, Donald. *Tablet* 247:727-728 Je 5 1993.

Monter, William.
Frontiers of heresy: the Spainish Inquisition from the Basque Lands to Sicily. Cambridge University Press, 1990.
  Hamilton, Alastair. *Heythrop* 34:329-331 Jl 1993.

Montfiore, Hugh, ed.
The gospel and contemporary culture. Mowbray, 1992.
  Richards, Michael. *Priests & People* 6:357-358 Ag-S 1992.

Montini, Giovanni Battista.
Interventi nella Commissione Centrale Preparatoria del Concilio Ecumenico Vaticano II (gennaio-Giugno 1962). Instituto Paolo VI, 1992.
  Caprile, Giovanni. *Civilta* 3:317 Ag 7-21 1993.

Montoya, Antonio Ruiz de.
The spiritual conquest, accomplished by the religious of the Society of Jesus in the Provinces of Paraguay, Parana, Uruguay, and Tape. Institute of Jesuit Sources, n.d.
  Stahel, Thomas H, 1938-. *America* 168:2 My 29 1993.
  Dollen, Charles. *Priest* 49:56 S 1993.

Moody, Harry R.
Ethics in an aging society. The Johns Hopkins University Press, 1992.
  Hooyman, Nancy W. *Health Prog* 74:85 Ap 1993.
  Heiser, W Charles. *TheolDgst* 40:77 Spr 1993.

Moor, Johannes C de.
The rise of Yahwism: the roots of Israelite monotheism. Peeters, 1990.
  Schoors, A. *Eph Theol Lovan* 78:400-402 D 1992.

Moore, Brian.
Manto nero (Blackrobe). Piemme, 1992.
  Baragli, Enrico. *Civilta* 2:307 My 1 1993.
No other life. André Deutsch, n.d.
  Miller, Peggy. *Tablet* 247:344 Mr 13 1993.
  Slavin, J P. *Nat Cath Rep* 29:18 Ag 27 1993.
  Elie, Paul, 1965-. *Comm* 120:25-26 N 5 1993.

Moore, Gareth.
The body in context. SCM, 1992.
  Tilby, Angela. *Way* 33:85-85 Ja 1993.
  Loughlin, Gerard. *New Blckfrs* 74:370-371 Jl-Ag 1993.

Moore, James Talmadge.
Through fire and flood: the Catholic Church in frontier Texas, 1836-1900. Texas A & M University Press, 1992.
  Heiser, W Charles. *TheolDgst* 40:77 Spr 1993.

Moore, Joseph.
Choice. Paulist Press, n.d.
  Anon. *Church* 9:42 Aut 1993.
Helping skills for the nonprofessional counselor. St Anthony Messenger Press, 1992.
  Hommerding, Leroy. *Mod Lit* 19:40-41 D 1992-Ja 1993.

Moore, Michael S.
The Balaam traditions, their character and development. Drew University, 1987.
  Lust, Johan. *Eph Theol Lovan* 78:417 D 1992.

Moore, Rick Dale.
God saves: lessons from the Elisha stories. Sheffield, 1990.
  Lust, Johan. *Eph Theol Lovan* 78:153 Ap 1992.
  Futato, Mark D. *CBQ* 55:342-343 Ap 1993.

Moore, Rowan, and Lloyd, Sampson.
Panoramas of London. Weidenfeld & Nicholson, n.d.
  Barker, Felix. *Tablet* 247:1076 Ag 21 1993.

Moore, Sebastian.
Jesus, the liberator of desire. Crossroad Publishing Company, n.d.
  Smythe, William E. *Can Cath Rev* 11:32-33 Je 1993.

Moore, Stephen D.
Literary criticism and the gospels: the theoretical challenge. Yale University Press, 1989.
  Aichele, George. *CrossCurr* 42:558-561 Wint 1992-1993.
Mark and Luke in poststructuralist perspectives: Jesus begins to write. Yale University Press, 1992.
  Lindsay, Alan G. *Relig Lit* 25:93-94 Spr 1993.
  Heiser, W Charles. *TheolDgst* 40:77 Spr 1993.

Moore, Thomas.
Care of the soul: a guide for cultivating depth and sacredness in everyday life. HarperCollins, 1992.
  Williams, Joan. *Living Prayer* 26:32 My-Je 1993.
Care of the soul. HarperCollins, n.d.
  Costello, Gerald M, 1931-. *USCath* 58:48-50 Ag 1993.

Moorey, P R S.
A century of biblical archaeology. Westminster, 1991.
  Harrington, Daniel J. *America* 168:28 F 6 1993.
  Miller, Charles H. *OTA* 16:411 Je 1993.

Moorey, Roger.
A century of Biblical archaeology. Lutterworth, 1991.
  Mulrooney, Joseph. *Heythrop* 34:429-430 O 1993.

Mora, Vincent.
La symbolique de la création dans l'évangile de Matthieu. Les Editions du Cerf, 1991.
  Farahian, Edmond. *Gregorianum* 74 no 3:573-575 1993.

Moraldi, Luigi.
Vangelo Arabo aprocrifo dell'Apostolo Giovanni da un manuscrito della Biblioteca Ambrosiana. Editorale Jaca Book, 1991.
  Bundy, David. *Eph Theol Lovan* 78:168-169 Ap 1992.

Morales, José.
Newman (1801-1890). Ed Rialp, 1990.
  Renard, L J. *NRT* 114:933-934 N-D 1992.

Moran, Gabriel.
Uniqueness. Orbis Books, 1992.
    Merrigan, Terrence. *Eph Theol Lovan* 69:200-201 Ap 1993.
    Heiser, W Charles. *TheolDgst* 40:177 Sum 1993.

Moran, J Anthony.
Pilgrims' guide to America: US Catholic shrines and centers of devotion. Our Sunday Visitor, 1992.
    Heiser, W Charles. *TheolDgst* 39:374 Wint 1992.

Moran, Sally.
A woman for all seasons. Twenty-Third Publications, n.d.
    Dollen, Charles. *Priest* 49:56 Ag 1993.

Moran, William L, ed.
The Amarna letters. The Johns Hopkins University Press, 1992.
    Fitzgerald, Aloysius. *OTA* 16:163 F 1993.
    Heiser, W Charles. *TheolDgst* 39:389 Wint 1992.

Morán Clavel, Juan Antonio.
Diálogos de María y José. Sociedad Centroamericana de Investigación y Divulgación de San José, 1991.
    Gauthier, Roland. *CahiersJos* 41:138-139 Ja-Je 1993.

Morandin, Adriano.
Vasco di Carbonera: storia, arte, ambiente. San Vito, 1992.
    Mellinato, Giuseppe. *Civilta* 2:413-414 My 15 1993.

Morello, Giovanni, and Pieri, Francesco.
Documenti Pontifici sullo scautismo. Ancora, 1991.
    Caprile, Giovanni. *Civilta* 144:207 Ja 16 1993.

Morenz, Siegfried.
Egyptian religion. Cornell, 1992.
    Murphy, Roland E. *OTA* 15:484 O 1992.

Moretti, A.
Gli umiliati, le comunità degli ospizi della Svizzera italiana. Ed. Helbing & Lichtenhahn, 1992.
    Plumat, N. *NRT* 115:611-612 Jl-Ag 1993.

Moretto, Giovanni.
Filosofia umana: itinerario di Alberto Caracciolo. Morcelliana, 1992.
    Pirola, G. *Civilta* 2:409-410 My 15 1993.

Morey, Ann-Janine.
Religion and sexuality in American literature. Cambridge University Press, 1992.
    Heiser, W Charles. *TheolDgst* 40:177-178 Sum 1993.

Morin, Lucien, and Brunet, Louis.
Philosophie de l'éducation. De Boeck-Wesmael, 1992.
    Thiboudeau, Victor. *Laval Theol Phil* 49:357-359 Je 1993.

Morinay, Jean.
Maria e la debolezza di Dio. Il messaggio' spirituale di Grignion de Montfort. Città Nuova, 1991.
    Sonzini, E. *Civilta* 2:107 Ap 17 1993.

Morley, Janet.
Bread of tomorrow. SPCK Christian aid, n.d.
    Gibbons, Robin. *Way* 33:260-261 Jl 1993.

Morneau, Robert F, Bp, 1938-.
Spiritual direction. Crossroad Publishing Company, n.d.
    McCloskey, Pat. *St Anth* 101:51-52 Ag 1993.

Moro, Walter.
Isegnare TV a scuola. La Nuova Italia, 1991.
    Baragli, Enrico. *Civilta* 2:102-103 Ap 3 1993.
Lettura e didattica del racconto visivo. no publisher given, 1991.
    Baragli, Enrico. *Civilta* 2:102-103 Ap 3 1993.

Moroni, Giancarlo.
My hands held out to you: the use of body and hands in prayer. Paulist, n.d.
    Graham, William C. *Nat Cath Rep* 29:25 Mr 26 1993.

Morowitz, Harold J, and Trefil, James S.
The facts of life: science and the abortion controversy. Oxford University Press, n.d.
    May, William E. *New Oxford Rev* 60:24-26 O 1993.

Morris, Leon.
The Gospel according to Matthew. Eerdmans, 1992.
    Stuhlmueller, Carroll. *BibleT* 31:125 Mr 1993.
    Heiser, W Charles. *TheolDgst* 40:178 Sum 1993.

Morris, Paul, and Sawyer, Deborah, eds.
A walk in the garden: biblical, iconographical and literary images of Eden. JSOT Press, 1992.
    Heiser, W Charles. *TheolDgst* 40:91-92 Spr 1993.

Morris, Thomas H.
Walking together in faith: a handbook for sponsors of Christian initiation. Paulist Press, n.d.
    Cahill, F. *Furrow* 44:56-57 Ja 1993.

Morris, Thomas Q, ed.
Taking charge of graduate medical education: to meet the nation's needs in the 21st century. Josiah Macy, Jr Foundation, 1992.
    Anon. *Health Prog* 74:94 Jl-Ag 1993.

Morris, Thomas V.
Our idea of God: an introduction to philosophical theology. University of Notre Dame Press, 1991.
    LaCugna, Catherine Mowry, 1952-. *Horizons (CTS)* 20:152-153 Spr 1993.

Morris, Willie.
New York days. Little, Brown, n.d.
    Samway, Patrick H, 1939-. *America* 169:19 Ag 28-S 4 1993.

Morrison, Karl Frederick.
Conversion and text: the cases of Augustine of Hippo, Herman-Judah, and Constantine Tsatsos. University Press of Virginia, 1992.
    Heiser, W Charles. *TheolDgst* 39:374 Wint 1992.
History as a visual art in the twelfth-century Renaissance. Princeton University Press, 1990.
    Kinney, Dale. *CHist* 79:521-522 Jl 1993.
Understanding conversion. University Press of Virginia, 1992.
    Heiser, W Charles. *TheolDgst* 39:374 Wint 1992.

Morrissey, Thomas.
A man called Hughes, the life and times of Seamus Hughes, 1881-1943. Veritas, 1991.
    D'Arcy, Fergus. *Studies* 81:482-484 Wint 1992.

Mortimer, Dolores A.
Together as a parish (family and parish books). Ave Maria Press, n.d.
    Krawczyk, Marilyn Peters. *Mod Lit* 19:43 D 1992-Ja 1993.

Morton, F L.
"Pro-Choice vs prolife: abortion and the courts in Canada". University of Oklahoma Press, n.d.
    Farrell, Regina. *Register* 69:5 Jl 25 1993.

Moscati, Sabatino.
Gli adoratori di Moloch. Jaca Book, 1991.
    Ferrua, Antonio. *Civilta* 3:541-542 S 18 1993.

Moscone, Maurizio.
La pedagogia greca: attualità di un progetto educativo. Janua, 1990.
    Prenna, L. *Civilta* 2:410-411 My 15 1993.

Moseley, Fred.
The falling rate of profit in the postwar United States economy. St. Martins, 1991.
    Devine, James. *RSocEcon* 51:387-392 Aut 1993.

Moser, Georg.
Täglich Grund zur Hoffnung. Herder, 1992.
    Bleistein, Roman, 1928-. *Stimm Zeit* 211:283 Ap 1993.

Motion, Andrew.
Philip Larkin. Faber, n.d.
    Shay, Roy. *Tablet* 247:438-439 Ap 3 1993.

Mott, Luiz.
Rosa Egipcíaca (uma santa Africana no Brasil). Editora bertrand Brasil, 1993.
    Hoonaert, Eduardo. *REB* 53:487-491 Je 1993.

Motto, F.
Giovanni Bosco: scritti editi e inediti. LAS, 1991.
    Renard, L J. *NRT* 115:280-281 Mr-Ap 1993.

Mount, Ferdinand.
The subversive family: an alternative history of love and marriage. Free Press, n.d.
    Baumann, Paul. *Comm* 120:28 Je 18 1993.

Mount, Ferdinand, ed.
Communism: a TLS companion. Harvill, n.d.
    Rosselli, John. *Tablet* 247:77 Ja 16 1993.

Mountney, John Michael.
Sin shall be glory. DLT, n.d.
    Sheldrake, Philip. *Way* 33:256 Jl 1993.

Mountrey, John Michael.
Sin shall be a glory. DLT, 1992.
    Moore, Patrick. *Priests & People* 7:124 Mr 1993.

Mouravieff, Boris.
Gnosis, study and commentaries on the esoteric tradition of Eastern Orthodox, 3 vols. Praxis Institute Press, n.d.
    Lenney, Ailsa. *Teilhard Rev* 27:95-96 Wint 1992.

Mourlon Beernaert, Pierre.
Marte, Marie et les autres, les visages féminsde l'evangile. Lumen Vitae, 1992.
    Partos, L. *Lumen* 47:468-469 D 1992.

Mouw, Richard D.
Uncommon decency: Christian civility in an uncivil world. Varsity Press, n.d.
    Costello, Gerald M, 1931-. *USCath* 58:48-51 Ap 1993.

Mouw, Richard J.
Uncommon decency: Christian civility in an uncivil world. Varsity Press, n.d.
    Decker, Christopher W. *New Oxford Rev* 60:28-29 Jl-Ag 1993.

Mowinckel, Sigmund.
The psalms in Israel's worship. JSOT, 1992.
    Begg, Christopher T. *OTA* 15:501 O 1992.

Moyers, Bill.
Healing of the mind. Doubleday, n.d.
    Costello, Gerald M, 1931-. *USCath* 58:48-50 Ag 1993.

Moynihan, Daniel Patrick.
Pandemonium: ethnicity in international politics. Oxford University Press, n.d.
    Williams, John Allen. *America* 169:24-25 N 6 1993.

Muck, Otto, ed.
Sinngestalten: Metaphysik in der Vielfalt menschlichen Fragens. Tyrolia-Verlag, 1989.
    Rosemann, Philipp W. *RPhil Louvain* 91:326-330 My 1993.

Mudge, Lewis S.
The sense of a people: toward a church for the human future. Trinity Press International, 1992.
    Gros, Jeffrey, 1938-. *Worship* 67:186-187 Mr 1993.

Mueller, John J.
Practical discipleship. Liturgical, 1992.
    Heiser, W Charles. *TheolDgst* 39:374 Wint 1992.
    O'Donoghue, Helena. *Furrow* 44:452-453 Jl-Ag 1993.
Valuing our differences: the history of African-American Catholics in the United States. Brown-ROA, 1993.
    Heiser, W Charles. *TheolDgst* 40:77 Spr 1993.

Muffs, Yochanan.
Love and joy: law, language and religion in ancient Israel. Harvard University Press, 1992.
    Murphy, Roland E. *OTA* 16:399 Je 1993.

Muir, Richard.
The coastlines of Britain. Macmillan, n.d.
    Braybrooke, Neville. *Tablet* 247:583 My 8 1993.

Muir, T E.
Stonyhurst College 1593-1993. James & James, n.d.
    Burns, Tom G. *Tablet* 247:108 Ja 23 1993.
    Anon. *Month* 26:114 Mr 1993.

Mukherjee, Pr, and Estin, C.
Contes et fêtes du Bengale. Beauchesne, 1991.
Anon. *NRT* 115:157 Ja-F 1993.

Mulder, M J.
Hooglied: eed praktische bijbelverklaring. Kok, 1991.
Kessler, Martin. *OTA* 15:505 O 1992.

Mullarney, Máire.
What about me? Town House and Country House, n.d.
Barrins, Aine. *Furrow* 44:449-450 Jl-Ag 1993.

Müller, Christine-Ruth.
Dietrich Bonhoeffers Kampf gegen die nationalsozialistische Verfolgung und Vernichtung der Juden. Chr Kaiser Verlag, 1990.
Kellenbach, Katharina von. *JEcumen Stds* 29:126 Wint 1992.

Muller, Gerhard Ludwig.
La celebración eucarística: un camino con Cristo. Herder, 1991.
Anon. *Perspectiva* 25:124-125 Ja-Ap 1993.

Müller, Hans-Peter, et al.
Das Hohelied, Klagelieder, das Buch Esther. Vandenhoeck and Ruprecht, n.d.
Murphy, Roland E. *OTA* 15:484-485 O 1992.

Müller, Hans-Peter.
Mensch-Umwelt-Eigenwelt: Gesammelte Aufsätze zur Weisheit Israels. Kohlhammer, 1992.
Murphy, Roland E. *OTA* 16:423 Je 1993.

Muller, Joachim W.
The reform of the United Nations, a volume in the series annual review of UN affairs, vol I. Oceana Publications, Inc, 1992.
Williams, Alison. *Teilhard Rev* 27:96-97 Wint 1992.

Müller, Karl.
Teologia della missione. EMI, 1992.
Dupuis, Jacques. *Civilta* 3:206-207 Jl 17 1993.

Mullins, Michael.
Called to be saints: Christian living in first-century Rome. Veritas, 1992.
Benko, S. *CHist* 78:627-628 O 1992.

Muñoz, Ricardo F, and Ying, Yu-Wen.
The prevention of depression. Johns Hopkins University Press, 1993.
Anon. *Health Prog* 74:70-71 O 1993.

Muñoz, Ronaldo.
Dio dei cristiani. Cittadella Editrice, 1990.
Pastor, Felix-Alejandro. *Gregorianum* 74 No 1:193-194 1993.
The God of Christians. Orbis Books, 1990.
Dupuis, Jacques. *Gregorianum* 74 no 2:382-383 1993.

Murata, Sachiko.
The Tao of Islam: a sourcebook on gender relationships in Islamic thought. State University of New York Press, 1992.
Heiser, W Charles. *TheolDgst* 39:374 Wint 1992.

Muratore, S, ed.
Teologia e filosofia. AVE, 1990.
Evrard, P. *NRT* 115:273 Mr-Ap 1993.

Murdoch, Iris.
The Green Knight. Chatto & Windus, n.d.
Walsh, Jill Paton. *Tablet* 247:1236 S 25 1993.
Metaphysics as a guide to morals. The Penguin Press, n.d.
Allen, Diogenes. *Comm* 120:24-25 Ap 23 1993.
Barnes, Michael R. *Month* 26:272-273 Jl 1993.
Delaney, Hubert. *Studies* 82:339-346 Aut 1993.

Murga, Vincente, and Huerga, Alvaro.
Episcopología de Puerto Rico. Universidad Católica de Puerto Rico, 1987-1990.
Salinas, Carlos. *Teol Vida* 34 no 1-2:157-158 1993.

Murnion, Philip J, 1938-, et al.
New parish ministers: lay and religious on parish staffs. National Pastoral Life Center, 1992.
Ingrassia, V. *Momentum* 24:82-83 F-Mr 1993.
Smyth, Damian. *Mod Lit* 20:37-38 S 1993.

Murphy, Annie.
Forbidden fruit. Little, Brown, n.d.
Kenny, Mary, 1936-. *Tablet* 247:516 Ap 24 1993.

Murphy, Daniel.
Tolstoy and education. Irish Academic Press, 1992.
Costello, Peter. *Studies* 81:478-482 Wint 1992.

Murphy, Frederick J.
The religious world of Jesus: an introduction to Second Temple Palestinian Judaism. Abingdon Press, 1991.
Heiser, W Charles. *TheolDgst* 39:374-375 Wint 1992.

Murphy, G Ronald.
The Heliand: the Saxon Gospel. Oxford University Press, n.d.
Schall, James Vincent, 1928-. *Crisis* 11:48-50 Mr 1993.

Murphy, Ignatius.
The diocese of Killaloe. Four Courts Press, 1991.
Peel, Henry. *Doctr Life* 43:121-122 F 1993.
Jones, Frederick M. *Furrow* 44:186-187 Mr 1993.
Kennedy, Kevin. *Doctr Life* 43:317-318 My-Je 1993.
Tierney, Mark. *Studies* 82:210-214 Sum 1993.

Murphy, James H, ed.
New beginnings in ministry. The Columba Press, 1992.
St Leger, Moya Frenz. *Furrow* 44:189-190 Mr 1993.
Ward, Hannah, and Lord, Elizabeth. *Way* 33:164-165 Ap 1993.
Gaughan, J Anthony. *Studies* 82:103-105 Spr 1993.

Murphy, Martin.
St Gregory's College, Seville 1592-1767. Catholic Record Society, 1992.
Bellord, Julia. *Priests & People* 7:42 Ja 1993.

Murphy, Michael.
Future of the body: explorations into the further evolution of human nature. Jeremy P Tarcher, n.d.
Thomson, Clarence. *Nat Cath Rep* 29:17 Ja 22 1993.

Murphy, Roland E.
Ecclesiastes. Word Publishing, 1992.
Stuhlmueller, Carroll. *BibleT* 31:248 Jl 1993.
The Psalms are yours. Paulist, n.d.
Graham, William C. *Nat Cath Rep* 30:36 N 19 1993.
The Song of Songs: a commentary on the Book of Canticles or the Song of Songs. Fortress, 1990.
Pope, Marvin H. *CBQ* 54:758-761 O 1992.
The tree of life: an exploration of Biblical wisdom literature. Doubleday, 1990.
Penchansky, David. *CBQ* 55:123-124 Ja 1993.

Murphy, Sheila.
A delicate dance: sexuality, celibacy, and relationships among Catholic clergy and religious. Crossroad, 1992.
Wedl, Lois. *Sisters* 65:139-140 Mr 1993.

Murphy-O'Connor, Jerome.
The Holy Land. Oxford University Press, 1992.
Stuhlmueller, Carroll. *BibleT* 31:248 Jl 1993.

Murray, Les.
Translations from the natural world. Carcanet, n.d.
Egan, Desmond. *Tablet* 247:949 Jl 24 1993.

Murray, Paul.
T.S. Eliot and mysticism: the secret history of four quartets. Macmillan, 1991.
O'Gorman, Francis. *Heythrop* 34:436 O 1993.

Murray, Placid.
John Henry Newman, sermons 1824-1843, volume I: sermons on the liturgy and sacraments on Christ the mediator. Clarendon Press, 1991.
Ford, J Massynbaerde. *Worship* 67:84-85 Ja 1993.
Norris, Tom. *Furrow* 44:192-193 Mr 1993.

Murray, Robert.
The cosmic covenant. Sheed & Ward, 1992.
Harrington, Daniel J. *America* 168:29 F 6 1993.
Lord, Elizabeth. *Way* 33:75 Ja 1993.
Murphy, Roland E. *OTA* 15:514 O 1992.
Rogerson, J W. *Heythrop* 34:184-185 Ap 1993.
Rowland, Christopher. *Priests & People* 7:166 Ap 1993.
Beuken, W A M. *Eph Theol Lovan* 69:167-168 Ap 1993.
Fretheim, Terence E. *TheolStds* 54:341-342 Je 1993.

The musical notation of Latin liturgical chants.
Paraclete Press, 1991.
Farrell, Gerard. *SacM* 120:30-33 Sum 1993.

Musser, Donald W, and Price, Joseph L, eds.
A new handbook of Christian theology. The Lutterworth Press, n.d.
Campbell, James. *Month* 26:34 Ja 1993.
Heiser, W Charles. *TheolDgst* 40:78 Spr 1993.

Musto, Ronald G.
The Catholic peace tradition. Orbis, 1986.
Elsbernd, M. *Cist Stud* 27 No 4:[118]-[119] 1992.
Liberation theologies: a research guide. Garland Publishing, 1991.
Heiser, W Charles. *TheolDgst* 40:78 Spr 1993.

Mutis, Alvaro.
Maqroll. Picador, n.d.
Billington, Rachel, 1942-. *Tablet* 247:892 Jl 10 1993.

Muto, Susan.
Womanspirit: reclaiming the deep feminine in our human spirituality. Crossroad, 1991.
RosenBlatt, Marie-Eloise. *RRel* 52:151-153 Ja-F 1993.
Anon. *Word Sp* 15:95-104 1993.

Myers, Amy.
Murder under the kissing bough. Headline, n.d.
Lejeune, Anthony. *Tablet* 247:376 Mr 20 1993.

Myers, Max A, and LaChat, Michael R, eds.
Studies in the theological ethics of Ernst Troeltsch. Edward Mellen Press, 1991.
Heiser, W Charles. *TheolDgst* 39:388 Wint 1992.

Myers, Rawley.
Daily readings in Catholic classics. Ignatius, 1992.
Dollen, Charles. *Priest* 49:48 Mr 1993.
Mangan, Charles M. *HPR* 94:76-77 O 1993.
Higgins, James J. *Liguorian* 81:70 S 1993.
Faith experiences of Catholic converts. Our Sunday Visitor, n.d.
Higgins, James J. *Liguorian* 81:70 S 1993.

Myllykoski, Matti.
Die letzten Tage Jesu: Markus und Johannes, ihre Traditionen und die historische Frage. Suomalainen Tiedeakatemia, 1991.
Green, Joel B. *CBQ* 55:173-174 Ja 1993.

Mystique et pédagogie spirituelle. Ignace, Thérèse, Jean de la Croix. Colloque public du Centre sèvres: 22-23 Novembre, 1991.
Mediasevres, 1992.
Partos, L. *Lumen* 48:236 Je 1993.

N

Nadin, Lucia, and Serra, Michele, eds.
La lingua come strumento di libertà. IRRSAE, 1990.
　Baragli, Enrico. *Civilta* 143:639 D 19 1992.

Nagel, Thomas.
Equality and partiality. Oxford University Press, 1991.
　Baker, John F. *IJPS* 1:129-133 Mr 1993.

Nardo, Anna K.
The ludic self in seventeenth-century English Literature. University of New York Press, 1991.
　Labriola, Albert C. *Relig Lit* 25:75-80 Spr 1993.

Nardone, Richard M.
The story of the Christian year. Paulist Press, 1991.
　Poelker, T. *Past Mus* 17:50-51 D 1992-Ja 1993.
　Whalen, Michael. *Living Light* 29:88-89 Aut 1992.
　Heiser, W Charles. *TheolDgst* 39:375 Wint 1992.

Natali, Carlo.
La sagezza di Aristotele. Bibliopolis, 1989.
　Destrée, Pierre. *RPhil Louvain* 91:142-143 F 1993.

Nau, Arlo J.
Peter in Matthew. Michael Glazier Books, 1992.
　Senior, Donald. *BibleT* 31:253-254 Jl 1993.

Naughton, Michael.
The good stewards. University Press of America, 1992.
　Grondelski, John M. *HPR* 93:75-76 My 1993.
　Ryan, Michael. *Can Cath Rev* 11:29-30 F 1993.
　Danner, Peter L. *RSocEcon* 51:122-123 Spr 1993.

Naumann, Thomas.
Hoseas Erben: Strukturen der Nachinterpretation im Buch Hosea. Kohlhammer, 1991.
　Begg, Christopher T. *OTA* 15:512 O 1992.

Navarro, Enrique Farfán.
El Desierto Transformado. Biblical Institute, 1992.
　McKenzie, Steven L. *OTA* 16:431 Je 1993.

Navarro, Luis.
Diritto di associazione e associazioni di fedeli. Giuffrè, 1991.
　Schouppe, J. *Eph Theol Lovan* 78:490-491 D 1992.
　Tourneau, Dominique Le. *Stud Can* 27 no 1:269-271 1993.

Naylor, Gloria.
Bailey's Café. Harcourt Brace Jovanovich, n.d.
　Jackson, Thomas M. *America* 168:17-19 F 13 1993.

Nayrozov, Andrei.
The gingerbread race. Picador, n.d.
　FitzLyon, April. *Tablet* 247:1263-1264 O 2 1993.

Neal, Mari Augusta.
From nuns to sisters. Twenty-Third Publications, n.d.
　Thompson, Geraldine. *Can Cath Rev* 11:39-40 Ja 1993.

Neale, David A.
None but the sinners: religious categories in the Gospel of Luke. JSOT Press, 1991.
　Bode, Edward L. *Bib Th Bul* 23:183-184 Sum 1993.

Nebel, R.
Santa María Tonantzin Virgen de Guadalupe. Neue Zeitschrift für Missionswissenschaft, 1992.
　Evrard, P. *NRT* 115:589-590 Jl-Ag 1993.

Nebelsick, Harold P.
Renaissance and reformation and the rise of science. T & T Clark, 1992.
　Honner, John. *Pacifica* 6:361-362 O 1993.

Neckebrouck, Valeer.
De stomme duivelen: het anti-missinair syndroom in de westerse Kerk. Brugge, Tabor, 1990.
　Boudens, R. *Eph Theol Lovan* 78:184-185 Ap 1992.

Neel, Janet.
Death among the dons. Constable, n.d.
　Lejeune, Anthony. *Tablet* 247:1136 S 4 1993.

Nefontaine, L.
La franc-maçonnerie. Éd Cerf, 1990.
　Anon. *NRT* 115:295 Mr-Ap 1993.

Neill, Stephen, and Wright, Tom.
The interpretation of the New Testament 1861-1986. OUP, 1988.
　Wansbrough, Henry. *Priests & People* 6:485-486 D 1992.

Neils, Patricia, ed.
United States attitudes and policies toward China. M E Sharpe, 1990.
　Varg, Paul A. *CHist* 79:581-582 Jl 1993.

Neirynck, Frans.
The minor agreements. Presses Universitaires de Louvain, 1991.
　Racine, Jean-François. *Laval Theol Phil* 49:376 Je 1993.

Nelson, C Ellis.
Helping teenagers grow morally. John Knox, 1992.
　Anon. *Church* 9:42 Sum 1993.

Nelson, Daniel Mark.
The priority of prudence: virtue and natural law in Thomas Aquinas and the implications for modern ethics. Pennsylvania State University, 1992.
　Ingham, M. *New Oxford Rev* 60:24-26 Ja-F 1993.
　Heiser, W Charles. *TheolDgst* 39:375 Wint 1992.
　Porter, Jean. *TheolStds* 54:202-203 Mr 1993.

Nelson, Gertrude Mueller.
Adults and children in the art of celebration. no publisher given, n.d.
　Graham, William C. *Nat Cath Rep* 29:40 My 28 1993.
Here all dwell free: stories to heal the wounded feminine. Doubleday, 1991.
　Craft, Carolyn M. *CrossCurr* 42:554-558 Wint 1992-1993.

Nelson, Gertrude Mueller. *(cont'd)*
Here all dwell free. Doubleday, 1992.
　RosenBlatt, Marie-Eloise. *RRel* 52:151-153 Ja-F 1993.
　Burke, Mariann. *ChrWorld* 236:238-239 S-O 1993.

Nelson, James B.
Body theology. John Knox Press, n.d.
　Graham, William C. *Nat Cath Rep* 29:18 Jl 16 1993.

Nelson, Yvette.
Celebrating the Eucharist. St Mary's Press, 1992.
　Gollob, Timothy. *Mod Lit* 19:40 D 1992-Ja 1993.
Exploring the story of Israel. Saint Mary's Press, 1992.
　Stuhlmueller, Carroll. *BibleT* 31:55 Ja 1993.

Nelson's concordance of Bible phrases: a time-saving guide to some of the best-loved and most often used Bible phrases.
Thomas Nelson Publishers, 1992.
　Heiser, W Charles. *TheolDgst* 39:375 Wint 1992.

Nemeck, Francis Kelly, and Coombs, Marie Theresa.
Called by God. Liturgical Press, n.d.
　O'Donoghue, Helena. *Furrow* 44:452-453 Jl-Ag 1993.

Nerin, William F.
You can't grow up till you go back home. Crossroad, n.d.
　Graham, William C. *Nat Cath Rep* 30:15 O 22 1993.

Nery, Israel José.
Como vi e vivi Santo Domingo. Vozes, 1993.
　Taborda, Francisco. *Perspectiva* 25:264-265 My-Ag 1993.

Netland, Howard A.
Dissonant voices: religious pluralism and the question of truth. Eerdmans, 1991.
　Griffiths, P. *Thomist* 56:723-726 O 1992.

Netton, Ian Richard.
A popular dicitonary of Islam. Humanities Press International, 1992.
　Heiser, W Charles. *TheolDgst* 40:178 Sum 1993.

Netzer, Ehud.
Masada III: the Yigael Yadin excavations 1963-65, final reports. The Hebrew University of Jerusalem, 1991.
　Fitzgerald, Aloysius. *OTA* 16:164 F 1993.

Neuberger, Julia.
The things that matter. Kyle Cathie, n.d.
　Braybrooke, Neville. *Tablet* 247:374 Mr 20 1993.

Neudecker, Reinhard.
Die vielen Gesichter des einen Gottes: Christen und Juden im Gespräch. Chr Kaiser Verlad, 1989.
　Strajek, Martin. *JEcumen Stds* 29:121 Wint 1992.

Neuhaus, Richard John, 1936-.
America against itself: moral vision and the public order. University of Notre Dame Press, 1992.
　Baker, Kenneth. *HPR* 93:69-70 F 1993.
　Nickoloff, James B. *America* 168:21-22 Ap 3 1993.
　Heiser, W Charles. *TheolDgst* 40:78 Spr 1993.
Doing well and doing good. Doubleday, 1992.
　Higgins, James J. *Liguorian* 81:69-70 F 1993.
　McNelis, Paul D. *America* 168:18-19 Mr 13 1993.
　Orsini, Jean-Francois. *HPR* 93:73-74 Ap 1993.
　Worland, Stephen T. *Crisis* 11:54-56 Ap 1993.
　Bayer, Richard C. *TheolStds* 54:187-189 Mr 1993.
　Hurley, Karen. *St Anth* 101:52 Ag 1993.
　Heiser, W Charles. *TheolDgst* 40:178 Sum 1993.
Freedom for ministry. Eerdmans, 1992.
　Sheets, John R. *HPR* 93:76-77 Ja 1993.
　Byrne, Harry M. *RRel* 52:630-631 Jl-Ag 1993.

Neumann, Kenneth J.
The authenticity of the Pauline Epistles in the light of stylostatistical analysis. Scholars, 1990.
　Bergren, Theodore A. *CBQ* 54:795-796 O 1992.

Neusner, Jacob.
An introduction to Judaism: a textbook and reader. John Knox Press, 1992.
　Heiser, W Charles. *TheolDgst* 39:375-376 Wint 1992.
Jews and Christians: the myth of a common tradition. SCM Press, 1991.
　Frank, Sue. *JEcumen Stds* 29:124-125 Wint 1992.
　Newman, Jay. *Can Cath Rev* 11:29-30 N 1993.
Judaism without Christianity. KTAV Publishing House, 1991.
　Stuhlmueller, Carroll. *BibleT* 31:55-56 Ja 1993.
　Heiser, W Charles. *TheolDgst* 39:376 Wint 1992.
The Mishnah. Trinity Press International, 1992.
　Heiser, W Charles. *TheolDgst* 40:178-179 Sum 1993.
A Rabbi talks with Jesus. Doubleday Books, 1993.
　Napack, Mark Daniel. *Spir Life* 39:181-182 Aut 1993.
Symbol and theology in early Judaism. Fortress, 1991.
　Greenspoon, Leonard. *OTA* 15:518 O 1992.
The transformation of Judaism: from philosophy to religion. University of Illinois Press, 1992.
　Heiser, W Charles. *TheolDgst* 40:78 Spr 1993.

Neusner, Jacob, ed.
Origins of Judaism: Judaism and Christianity in the first century. Garland Publishing, Inc, 1990.
　Hann, Robert R. *JEcumen Stds* 29:122-123 Wint 1992.

Neusner, Jacob, and Dupuis, J, eds.
The Christian faith: doctrinal documents of the Catholic Church. Harper Collins, n.d.
　Anon. *Month* 25:499 D 1992.

Nevin, Thomas R.
Simone Weil: protrait of a self-exiled Jew. University of North Carolina Press, n.d.
　Cunningham, Lawrence S, 1935-. *Comm* 120:25 F 12 1993.

The New Jerome Bible Handbook.
Liturgical, 1992.
  Begg, Christopher T. *OTA* 16:164 F 1993.

Newbigin, Lesslie.
The Gospel in a pluralist society. World Council of Churches Publications, 1989.
  Boisclair, Regina A. *JEcumen Stds* 29:282-283 Spr 1992.
Truth to tell: the Gospel as public truth. William B Eerdmans, n.d.
  Baldner, Steven. *Can Cath Rev* 11:26-28 F 1993.

Newman, Gene, and Tada, Joni Eareckson.
All God's children: ministry with disabled persons. Zondervan, 1993.
  Gallagher, Miriam J. *Mod Lit* 20:38 O 1993.

Newman, John Henry, Cardinal, 1801-1890.
Conscience, consensus, and the development of doctrine: revolutionary texts by John Henry Cardinal Newman. Doubleday, 1992.
  Heiser, W Charles. *TheolDgst* 40:79 Spr 1993.
Sermons 1824-1843. Clarendon Press, 1991.
  Detienne, P. *NRT* 114:912-913 N-D 1992.
Sermons on the liturgy and the sacraments and on Christ the mediator. Oxford Clarendon, 1991.
  Moleski, M. *TheolStds* 53:787-788 D 1992.

Newsom, Carol A, and Ringe, Sharon H, eds.
The woman's Bible commentary. John Knox, 1992.
  Stuhlmueller, Carroll. *BibleT* 31:56 Ja 1993.
  Harrington, Daniel J. *America* 168:26 F 6 1993.
  Murphy, Roland E. *OTA* 15:485 O 1992.
  Hebblethwaite, Margaret, 1951-. *Tablet* 247:725-726 Je 5 1993.
  Quitslund, Sonya A. *TheolStds* 54:339-341 Je 1993.

Newsome, David.
The convert cardinals: Newman and Manning. John Murray, n.d.
  Ker, Ian. *Tablet* 247:1133-1134 S 4 1993.

Newsome, James D.
Greeks, Romans, Jews. Trinity Press, 1992.
  Senior, Donald. *BibleT* 31:316 S 1993.

Neyrey, Jerome H.
The social world of Luke-Acts: models for interpretation. Hendrickson, 1991.
  Hollenbach, Paul W. *CBQ* 55:175-176 Ja 1993.

Niccacci, Alviero.
Lettura sintattica della prosa ebraico-biblica: principi e applicazioni. Franciscan Printing, 1991.
  Fulco, William F. *CBQ* 55:125 Ja 1993.
Un profeta tra oppressori e oppressi. Franciscan Printing Press, 1989.
  Lust, Johan. *Eph Theol Lovan* 78:420-421 D 1992.

Nicholas of Cusa, 1401-1464.
Opera omnia. XVI: Sermones I (1430-1441). Felix Meiner, 1991.
  Biecheler, James E. *JEcumen Stds* 29:272-273 Spr 1992.

Nichols, Aidan.
From Newman to Congar: the idea of doctrinal development from the Victorians to the Second Vatican Council. T and T Clark, 1990.
  Rowell, G. *New Blckfrs* 73:579-580 N 1992.
A grammar of consent: the existence of God in Christian tradition. University of Notre Dame Press, 1991.
  Williams, Joan. *Living Prayer* 26:33 Ja-F 1993.
The Holy Eucharist from the New Testament to Pope John Paul II. Ignatius Press, 1991.
  Heiser, W Charles. *TheolDgst* 39:376 Wint 1992.
The Holy Eucharist. Veritas, 1991.
  Boulding, Mary Cecily. *New Blckfrs* 73:574-576 N 1992.
The panther and the hind: a theological history of Anglicanism. T & T Clark, n.d.
  Chadwick, Henry. *Tablet* 247:342-343 Mr 13 1993.
  Barbour, Brian. *New Oxford Rev* 60:22-23 O 1993.
Rome and the Eastern Churches. The Liturgical Press, 1992.
  Heiser, W Charles. *TheolDgst* 39:376 Wint 1992.
  Yarnold, Edward John, 1926-. *Month* 26:110-111 Mr 1993.
  Klimon, William M. *Crisis* 11:51-52 Je 1993.
  Dennis, George T. *CHist* 79:302-303 Ap 1993.
The shape of Catholic theology. T and T Clark, n.d.
  Pridmore, John. *Way* 33:79 Ja 1993.
Yves Congar. Morehouse-Barlow, n.d.
  Donovan, Daniel. *Can Cath Rev* 11:33 Jl-Ag 1993.

Nicholson, Peter P.
The political philosophy of the British idealists. Cambridge University Press, 1990.
  Harris, Errol E, 1908-. *Heythrop* 34:94-97 Ja 1993.

Nickle, Keith, and Lull, Timothy, eds.
A common calling. Augsburg, 1992.
  Gros, Jeffrey, 1938-. *Worship* 67:476 S 1993.

Nicodème-Annuel formation chrétienne des adultes.
Assas Éditions et CNER, 1992.
  Fossion, André. *Lumen* 47:465 D 1992.

Nicola, Giulia Paola Di, ed.
Donne in chiaroscuro: un processo penale nella Teramo di fine '800. Demian, 1992.
  Vanzan, Piersandro. *Civilta* 2:93-94 Ap 3 1993.
Il tempo dell'utopia: itinerari al femminile: simboli, realtà, profezia. Ed Dehoniane, 1992.
  Vanzan, Piersandro. *Civilta* 2:93-94 Ap 3 1993.

Nicolai, Vincenzo Fiocchi.
La catacomba di S Savinilla a Nepi. Pont Commissione di Archeologia Sacra, 1992.
  Ferrua, Antonio. *Civilta* 3:330-331 Ag 7-21 1993.

Nicolosi, Joseph.
Reparative therapy of male homosexuality. Jason Aronson, 1991.
  Nigro, Samuel A. *SocJust* 84:157 S-O 1993.

Niditch, Susan.
Text and tradition: the Hebrew Bible and folklore. Scholars, 1990.
  Day, Peggy L. *CBQ* 55:198-199 Ja 1993.

Niebuhr, Reinhold, 1892-1971.
A Reinhold Niebuhr reader. Trinity Press International, 1992.
  Heiser, W Charles. *TheolDgst* 40:179 Sum 1993.

Niehoff, Maren.
The figure of Joseph in post-biblical Jewish literature. Brill, 1992.
  Dougherty, Edward. *TheolStds* 54:383-384 Je 1993.

Nielsen, Eduard.
Abrahams historie:en historisk-kritisk kommentar til Genesis 11, 26-25, 11. Museum Tusculanums Forlag, 1992.
  Begg, Christopher T. *OTA* 16:419 Je 1993.

Nielsen, Niels C.
Revolutions in Eastern Europe. Orbis Books, 1991.
  Menin, G. *NRT* 115:148 Ja-F 1993.
  Loya, Joseph A. *JEcumen Stds* 29:263-264 Spr 1992.

Nissenson, Marilyn.
The ubiquitous pig. Weidenfeld, n.d.
  Braybrooke, Neville. *Tablet* 247:374 Mr 20 1993.

Nizamuddin, Auliya, 1236-1325.
Morals for the heart: conversations of Shaykh Nizam ad-din Awliya recorded by Amir Hasan Sijzi. Paulist Press, 1992.
  Heiser, W Charles. *TheolDgst* 40:79 Spr 1993.

NKJV exhaustive concordance.
Thomas Nelson, 1993.
  Heiser, W Charles. *TheolDgst* 40:179 Sum 1993.

Noce, Celestino.
Didimo il cieco: Lo Spirito Santo. Città Nuova, 1990.
  Cattaneo, E. *Civilta* 144:404-405 F 20 1993.

Noddings, Nel.
Women and evil. The University of California Press, n.d.
  Cunningham, A. *Can Cath Rev* 11:40-41 Ja 1993.

Nodet, Étienne.
Essai sur les origines du judaïsme. Cerf, 1992.
  Rybolt, Johu. *OTA* 16:448 Je 1993.

Noel, Daniel C, ed.
Paths to the power of myth. Crossroad, 1990.
  Gittins, Anthony J, 1943-. *New Theol Rev* 6:97-98 F 1993.

Noll, Mark A.
A history of Christianity in the United States and Canada. William B Eerdmans Publishing Company, 1992.
  Hennesey, James. *ACHSR* 103:57-58 Aut 1992.
  Heiser, W Charles. *TheolDgst* 40:179 Sum 1993.
  Gaustad, Edwin S. *CHist* 79:565-567 Jl 1993.

Nolthenius, Helene.
Un uomo dalla valle di Spoleto: Francesco tra i suoi contemporanei. Messaggero, 1991.
  Forlizzi, G. *Civilta* 143:535-536 D 5 1992.

Nordheim, Eckhard von.
Die Selbstbehauptung Israels in der Welt des Alten Orients. Vandenhoeck and Ruprecht, 1992.
  Begg, Christopher T. *OTA* 16:156 F 1993.

Normile, Patti.
Visiting the sick. St Anthony Messenger Press, 1992.
  Northcraft, Michael S. *Mod Lit* 20:40 F 1993.
  Heiser, W Charles. *TheolDgst* 40:79 Spr 1993.
  Higgins, James J. *Liguorian* 81:69 D 1993.

Normingotn, Susan.
Napoleon's children. Alan Sutton, n.d.
  Forrest, Denys. *Tablet* 247:1200 S 18 1993.

Norris, Gunilla.
Becoming bread: meditations on loving and transformation. Crown, n.d.
  Graham, William C. *Nat Cath Rep* 29:24 Mr 26 1993.

Norris, Kathleen.
Dakota: a spiritual geography. Ticknor & Fields, n.d.
  Anon. *ABenR* 44:112-113 Mr 1993.
  Bartelme, Elizabeth. *Comm* 120:23-24 My 7 1993.
  Badaracco, Claire M. *America* 169:23-24 Ag 14-21 1993.

Noske, Frits.
Saints and sinners. The Latin musical dialogue in the seventeenth century. Oxford University Press, 1992.
  Schuler, Richard Joseph, 1920-. *SacM* 120:39 Aut 1993.

Noth, Martin.
The Deuteronomistic history. Sheffield, 1991.
  Lust, J. *Eph Theol Lovan* 78:149 Ap 1992.

Nothomb, P.
Les tuniques d'aveugle. La Différence/La Longue Vue, 1990.
  Ska, Jean Louis. *NRT* 115:252-253 Mr-Ap 1993.

Nouwen, Henri Josef Machiel, 1932-.
In the name of Jesus: reflections on Christian leadership. Crossroad Publishing Co, 1991.
  Sinwell, Joseph P. *Living Light* 29:93 Aut 1992.
Life of the beloved. Crossroad, 1992.
  Williams, Joan. *Living Prayer* 26:32 Mr-Ap 1993.
  Aloysia, M. *Sisters* 65:141-142 Mr 1993.
  McCann, Deborah. *ReligTJ* 27:10-11 Ap-My 1993.
  Heiser, W Charles. *TheolDgst* 40:179-180 Sum 1993.
Love in a fearful land: a Guatemalan story. Ave Maria Press, n.d.
  Ventline, Lawrence M. *Emmanuel* 99:359-360 Jl-Ag 1993.
The return of the prodigal son: a meditation on fathers, brothers, and sons. Doubleday, 1992.
  Heiser, W Charles. *TheolDgst* 40:79 Spr 1993.
Show me the way: readings for each day of Lent. Crossroad, n.d.
  McCann, Deborah. *ReligTJ* 27:10 F 1993.

Nouwen, Henri Josef Machiel, 1932-. *(cont'd)*
  Hollings, Michael. *Tablet* 247:278 F 27 1993.
Thomas Merton: contemplative critic. Triumph Books, 1991.
  O'Donovan, Jo. *Furrow* 44:388 Je 1993.
Novak, David, 1941-.
Jewish social ethics. Oxford University Press, 1992.
  Dougherty, Jude P, 1930-. *Crisis* 11:52-55 O 1993.
Jewish-Christian dialogue: a Jewish justification. Oxford University Press, 1989.
  Schwartz, D. *SocJust* 84:29-30 Ja-F 1993.
Novak, James.
Bangladesh: reflections on the water. Indiana University Press, n.d.
  Novak, Michael, 1933-. *Crisis* 11:7 O 1993.
Novak, Michael, 1933-.
The Catholic ethic and the spirit of capitalism. Free Press, 1993.
  Blackburn, Thomas E. *Nat Cath Rep* 29:16 Ap 2 1993.
  Dionne, E J, Jr. *Comm* 120:9-12 My 21 1993.
  Lehrman, Lewis E. *Crisis* 11:60-62 Jl-Ag 1993.
  Cviic, Christopher. *Tablet* 247:1012-1013 Ag 7 1993.
  Bayer, Richard C. *TheolStds* 54:592-593 S 1993.
  Orsini, Jean-Francios. *HPR* 94:72-75 N 1993.
Il Novantesimo della presenza salesiana in Schio 1901-1991.
  Dalla Costa, 1991.
  Mellinato, Giuseppe. *Civilta* 143:543-544 D 5 1992.
Novitas et veritas vitae: Aux sources du renouveau de la morale chrétienne.
  Ed Univeristaires - Cerf, 1991.
  Cultrera, Francesco. *Civilta* 2:304-305 My 1 1993.
Nowell, Iris.
Hot breakfast for sparrows: my life with Harold Town. Stoddart, n.d.
  Coren, Michael. *Can Cath Rev* 11:4-6 F 1993.
Noy, Michael De la.
The Church of England: a portrait. Simon & Schuster, n.d.
  Graham, Ysenda Maxtone. *Tablet* 247:1234 S 25 1993.
Nugent, Robert, and Gramick, Jeannine.
Building bridges: gay and lesbian reality and the Catholic Church. Twenty-Third Publications, 1992.
  Whalen, Michael. *Living Light* 29:90-91 Wint 1992.
  Timmerman, Joan H. *Horizons (CTS)* 20:187-188 Spr 1993.
Nussbaum, Martha Craven.
The fragility of goodness. Cambridge University Press, 1986.
  Destrée, Pierre. *RPhil Louvain* 91:138-140 F 1993.
Nussdorfer, Laurie.
Civic politics in the Rome of Urban VIII. Princeton University Press, 1992.
  Gros, Hans. *CHist* 79:115-116 Ja 1993.
Nuth, Joan M.
Wisdom's daughter: the theology of Julian of Norwich. Crossroad, 1991.
  Miesel, Sandra. *New Oxford Rev* 60:30-31 Jl-Ag 1993.
  Mayeksi, Marie Anne. *Horizons (CTS)* 20:172-173 Spr 1993.

O

O'Brien, Conor Cruise.
The great melody: a thematic biography of Edmund Burke. Sinclair Stevenson, 1992.
  Bull, George, 1929-. *Tablet* 247:618-619 My 15 1993.
  Barry, Kevin. *Studies* 82:333-339 Aut 1993.
O'Brien, David J, 1938-.
Isaac Hecker. Paulist, 1992.
  McCloskey, Pat. *St Anth* 100:50 Ja 1993.
  Walsh, Joseph L. *CrossCurr* 42:542-545 Wint 1992-1993.
  Rutler, George W. *HPR* 93:77-78 My 1993.
  Pridmore, John. *Way* 33:166-167 Ap 1993.
  Portier, William J. *TheolStds* 54:356-357 Je 1993.
  Reher, Margaret Mary. *ACHSR* 103:50-52 Aut 1992.
  Heiser, W Charles. *TheolDgst* 40:180 Sum 1993.
  Spalding, Thomas W. *CHist* 79:571-573 Jl 1993.
O'Brien, David J, 1938-, and Shannon, Thomas A, eds.
Catholic social thought. Orbis Books, 1992.
  Heiser, W Charles. *TheolDgst* 40:155 Sum 1993.
O'Brien, John.
Theology and the option for the poor. Liturgical Press, 1992.
  Dorr, Donal, 1935-. *Furrow* 43:706-708 D 1992.
O'Brien, Julia M.
Priest and Levite in Malachi. Scholars, 1990.
  Redditt, Paul L. *CBQ* 54:761-762 O 1992.
O'Brien, Kate.
Teresa of Avila. Mercier Press, n.d.
  Campbell, James. *Month* 26:381 S-O 1993.
O'Brien, Michael.
The mysteries of the most holy rosary. The White Horse Press, n.d.
  Grynn, Peter. *Can Cath Rev* 11:27 S 1993.
O'Brien, Peter T.
The Epistle to the Philippians: a commentary on the Greek text. Eerdmans, 1991.
  Seeley, David. *CBQ* 55:176-177 Ja 1993.
O'Brien, William J, ed.
The labor of God, and Ignatian view of church and culture. Georgetown University Press, 1991.
  Heiser, W Charles. *TheolDgst* 39:368-369 Wint 1992.
O'Carroll, Michael.
Verbum caro: an encyclopedia on Jesus, the Christ. The Liturgical Press, 1992.

O'Carroll, Michael. *(cont'd)*
  Heiser, W Charles. *TheolDgst* 39:377 Wint 1992.
Verbum caro. Michael Glazier Books, 1992.
  Senior, Donald. *BibleT* 31:254 Jl 1993.
O'Collins, Gerald, 1931-, and Farrugia, Edward G.
A concise dictionary of theology. Paulist Press, 1991.
  Vercruysse, Jos E. *Eph Theol Lovan* 78:178 Ap 1992.
  Collinge, William J. *Living Light* 29:85 Wint 1992.
O'Collins, Gerald, 1931-, and Venturini, Mary.
Believing. HarperCollins, n.d.
  Edwards, David L. *Tablet* 247:859-860 Jl 3 1993.
O'Connell, Colin B.
A study of Heinrich Ott's theological development. Lang, 1991.
  Fakre, Gabriel. *TheolStds* 54:601 S 1993.
O'Connell, Maurice, ed.
Daniel O'Connell, political pioneer. Institute of Public Administration, 1991.
  Griffin, William D. *CHist* 79:347-348 Ap 1993.
O'Connor, Edward C.
The Catholic vision. Our Sunday Visitor Books, n.d.
  Finley, Mitchel B. *St Anth* 100:53 Ja 1993.
O'Connor, Edward D.
The Catholic vision. Our Sunday Visitor, 1992.
  Heiser, W Charles. *TheolDgst* 39:377 Wint 1992.
  Gullekson, Justin W. *New Oxford Rev* 60:30-31 O 1993.
O'Connor, Emmet.
A labour history of Ireland 1824-1960. Gill and Macmillan, 1992.
  Morrissey, Thomas. *Studies* 82:226-229 Sum 1993.
O'Connor, Jerome Murphy.
The theology of the second letter to the Corinthians. no publisher given, n.d.
  Wansbrough, Henry. *Priests & People* 6:439 N 1992.
O'Connor, June E.
The moral vision of Dorothy Day: a feminist perspective. Crossroad, 1991.
  McReynolds, Sally Ann. *Horizons (CTS)* 19:337-338 Fall 1992.
  Greene, Dana. *CrossCurr* 43:122-123 Spr 1993.
O'Donnell, James J, ed.
Augustine: Confessions, commentary on Books 1-7; vol 2. Oxford University Press, 1992.
  Teske, Roland J. *TheolStds* 54:563-565 S 1993.
Augustine: Confessions, commentary on Books 8-13; vol 3. Oxford University Press, 1992.
  Teske, Roland J. *TheolStds* 54:563-565 S 1993.
Augustine: Confessions, introduction and text; vol 1. Oxford University Press, 1992.
  Teske, Roland J. *TheolStds* 54:563-565 S 1993.
O'Donnell, John.
Hans Urs von Balthasar. Liturgical, 1992.
  O'Hanlon, Gerard F. *Tablet* 247:723-725 Je 5 1993.
  Heiser, W Charles. *TheolDgst* 40:80 Spr 1993.
O'Donnell, John J.
Hans Urs von Balthasar. Liturgical, 1992.
  Chapp, Larry. *TheolStds* 54:602 S 1993.
  Endean, Philip. *Heythrop* 34:440-442 O 1993.
O'Donoghue, Noel D.
Mystics for our time. Liturgical, n.d.
  Anon. *Can Cath Rev* 11:19-21 N 1993.
O'Donovan, Oliver.
Résurrection et expérience morale. Presses universitaires de France, 1992.
  Bedouelle, Thierry. *RPhil Louvain* 91:507-509 Ag 1993.
O'Faolain, Julia.
The Judas cloth. Sinclair-Stevenson, n.d.
  Scott, Rivers. *Tablet* 247:19 Ja 2 1993.
O'Grady, Desmond.
The victory of the cross. HarperCollins, n.d.
  Walsh, Michael J, 1937-. *Tablet* 247:173 F 6 1993.
  Campbell, Patrick J. *Furrow* 44:123 F 1993.
O'Grady, John F.
Disciples and leaders: the origins of Christian ministry in the New Testament. Paulist, 1991.
  Reid, Barbara E. *CLW* 64:39 Jl-S 1993.
  Love, Stuart L. *CBQ* 55:389 Ap 1993.
Pillars of Paul's Gospel. Paulist Press, 1992.
  Stuhlmueller, Carroll. *BibleT* 31:125 Mr 1993.
  McDonald, Patricia M. *Living Light* 29:95-96 Sum 1993.
  Heiser, W Charles. *TheolDgst* 40:180 Sum 1993.
O'Hanlon, Gerard F.
The immutability of God in the theology of Hans Urs von Balthasar. Cambridge University Press, 1990.
  Brito, Emilio. *Eph Theol Lovan* 78:470-471 D 1992.
  Dupuis, Jacques. *Gregorianum* 74 No 1:160-161 1993.
Cambridge University Press, 1992.
  Flanagan, Donald. *Doctr Life* 43:252-254 Ap 1993.
O'Hear, Anthony.
Introduction to the philosophy of science. Clarendon, 1989.
  Hespel, Bertrand. *RPhil Louvain* 91:520-521 Ag 1993.
O'Heron, Edward J.
Your life story. St Anthony Messenger Press, n.d.
  Dollen, Charles. *Priest* 49:48 Jl 1993.
O'Leary, April.
The chronicle of a school, Roehampton-Woldingham 1842-1992. Woldingham School, n.d.
  Macmillan, Mona. *Tablet* 247:758-759 Je 1993.
O'Malley, William J, 1931-.
Becoming a catechist. Paulist, 1992.
  Di Giacomo, J. *America* 168:22-23 Ja 16-23 1993.
  Weishaar, Patricia A. *Sisters* 65:220-221 My 1993.
  Anon. *Church* 9:42 Sum 1993.

Opocher, Enrico.
Giuseppe Capograssi filosofo del nostro tempo. Giuffrè, 1991.
Mucci, Giandomenico. *Civilta* 3:544-545 S 18 1993.

Origen.
Commentaire sur le Cantique des Cantiques, tome I. Cerf, 1991.
Pelland, Gilles. *Gregorianum* 74 no 2:388-389 1993.
Commentaire sur le Cantique des Cantiques, tome II. Cerf, 1992.
Pelland, Gilles. *Gregorianum* 74 no 2:388-389 1993.

Origène.
Treatise on the passover and dialogue of Origen with Heraclides. Paulist Press, 1992.
Stuhlmueller, Carroll. *BibleT* 31:56 Ja 1993.

Origine et postérité de l'évangile de Jean.
Cerf, 1990.
Simoeus, Y. *NRT* 115:105-106 Ja-F 1993.

Ormerod, Neil.
Grace and disgrace. Morehouse Publishing, 1992.
Lord, Elizabeth. *Way* 33:76 Ja 1993.
Heiser, W Charles. *TheolDgst* 39:378 Wint 1992.

Orsy, Ladislas M, 1921-.
Theology and Canon Law. Liturgical Press, 1992.
Häring, Bernard, 1912-. *Tablet* 247:41-42 Ja 9 1993.
Morrisey, Francis G. *Jurist* 51 no 2:509-512 1991.
Huels, John M. *TheolStds* 54:203-204 Mr 1993.
Hennessy, Patrick. *Studies* 82:100-103 Spr 1993.
Davey, Theodore. *Month* 26:232-233 Je 1993.
Heiser, W Charles. *TheolDgst* 40:80 Spr 1993.

Ortiz, Elisabeth Lambert.
The encyclopedia of herbs, spices and flavourings. Dorling Kindersley, n.d.
Poole, Shona Crawford. *Tablet* 247:373-374 Mr 20 1993.

Ortoleva, Peppino.
Per una storia dei media. Anicia, 1992.
Baragli, Enrico. *Civilta* 3:333-334 Ag 7-21 1993.

Osborne, Kenan B.
Ministry. Paulist, n.d.
Dollen, Charles. *Priest* 49:56 S 1993.
Doyle, Dennis M. *Comm* 120:26-28 S 10 1993.
Graham, William C. *Nat Cath Rep* 30:15 O 22 1993.

Osiek, Carolyn.
What are they saying about the social setting of the New Testament? Paulist Press, n.d.
Graham, William C. *Nat Cath Rep* 29:39 My 28 1993.

Osler, Mirabel.
The secret gardens of France. Pavilion Books, n.d.
Taylor, Patrick. *Tablet* 247:375 Mr 20 1993.

Osmer, Richard Robert.
Teaching for faith. John Knox, n.d.
Riley, David M. *Catechist* 27:15 N-D 1993.

Ostrom, Elinor.
Crafting institution for self-governing irrigation systems. Institute for Contemporary Studies, 1992.
Jonish, James. *RSocEcon* 51:116-118 Spr 1993.

Osumi, Yuichi.
Die Kompositionsgeschichte des Bundesbuches Exodus 20. Vandenhoeck & Ruprecht, 1991.
Sun, Henry T C. *CBQ* 55:343-344 Ap 1993.

Otranto, Giorgio.
Italia meridionale e PUglia paleocristiane. Edipuglia, 1991.
Boudens, R. *Eph Theol Lovan* 78:449-450 D 1992.

Ottosson, Magnus.
Josuaboken: en programskrift för davidisk restauration. Almqvist and Wiksell, 1991.
Begg, Christopher T. *OTA* 15:497 O 1992.
Josuaboken: en programskrift för davidisk restauration. Almqvist & Wiksell, 1991.
Winther-Nielsen, Nicolai. *CBQ* 55:345-346 Ap 1993.

Ouspensky, Leonid.
Theology of the icon, 2 vols. St. Vladimir's Seminary, 1992.
Rexine, John E. *Diakonia* 26 no 3:201-206 1993.

Overberg, Kenneth R, 1944-.
Mercy or murder?: Euthanasia, morality and public policy. Sheed & Ward, n.d.
Samway, Patrick H, 1939-. *America* 169:22 Ag 28-S 4 1993.

Overman, J Andrew.
Matthew's Gospel and formative Judaism. Fortress, 1990.
Doyle, B Rod. *Pacifica* 6:335-337 O 1993.

Owens, John Joseph.
Analytical key to the Old Testament, volume 2: Judges-2 Chronicles. Baker Book House, 1992.
Heiser, W Charles. *TheolDgst* 40:180-181 Sum 1993.
Cognition. University of St Thomas, 1992.
Koterski, J. *HPR* 94:75-77 O 1993.

Ozment, Steven.
Protestants: the birth of a revolution. Doubleday, 1992.
McShea, William P. *RRel* 52:791-792 S-O 1993.

P

Pace, Peter.
The architecture of George Pace. B T Batsford Ltd, 1991.
Symondson, Anthony. *Month* 26:78 F 1993.

Pacho, Eulogio.
Histoeria de la Congregación de las Carmelitas Misioners: Tomo I; Orígenes y primeros pasos: 1845-1885. Burgos, 1991.
Pacho, Alberto. *Teol Vida* 33 no 3-4:319-321 1992.

Paco, L, ed.
I preti da 2,000 anni memori di Cristo tra gli uomini. Piemme, 1991.
Anon. *NRT* 115:149 Ja-F 1993.

Pacwa, Mitch.
Catholics and the New Age. Servant, 1992.
Wilkins, Mark. *St Anth* 100:52 Mr 1993.
Berbusse, Edward J. *F & R* 28:419-424 Wint 1992.

Paczensky, Gert.
Teurer Segen [Christliche Mission und Kolonialismus]. Knaus, 1991.
Sievernich, M. *Stimm Zeit* 211:501-502 Jl 1993.

Paden, William E.
Interpreting the sacred: ways of viewing religion. Beacon Press, 1992.
Heiser, W Charles. *TheolDgst* 39:378 Wint 1992.

Padgett, Alan G.
God, eternity and the nature of time. St Martin's Press, 1992.
Helm, Paul. *New Blckfrs* 74:287-288 My 1993.

Padoux, André.
Vāc, the concept of the word in selected Hindu Tantras. State University of New York Press, 1990.
Couture, André. *Laval Theol Phil* 49:168-169 F 1993.

Padovano, Anthony T.
Scripture in the streets. Paulist Press, n.d.
Hegeman, Mary Theodore. *St Anth* 100:48-49 Ap 1993.

Padovese, Luigi.
I sacerdoti dei primi secoli. Piemme, 1992.
Renard, L J. *NRT* 115:316 Mr-Ap 1993.
Ferrua, Antonio. *Civilta* 3:315-316 Ag 7-21 1993.

Padovese, Luigi, ed.
Atti del I simposio di Efeso su S Giovanni Apostolo. Instituto Francescano di Spiritualità, 1991.
Ferraro, Giuseppe. *Gregorianum* 74 No 1:156-157 1993.
Atti del I Simposio di Efesu su S Giovanni Apostolo. Instituto Francescano di Spiritualità, 1991.
Simoens, Y. *NRT* 115:106-107 Ja-F 1993.

Paglia, Camille.
Sex, art and American culture. Viking, n.d.
McDonagh, Melanie. *Tablet* 247:549-550 My 1 1993.
Thomas, Christopher. *Comm* 120:25-26 Je 4 1993.

Pahl, Jon.
Paradox lost. Johns Hopkins University Press, 1992.
Stoever, William K B. *CHist* 79:356-357 Ap 1993.
Heiser, W Charles. *TheolDgst* 40:80 Spr 1993.

Painter, John.
The quest for the Messiah. T and T Clark, 1991.
Moloney, Francis J. *Pacifica* 6:106-109 F 1993.

Pajer, Flavio, ed.
L'insegnamento scolastico della religione nella nuova. LDc, 1991.
Reguzzoni, M. *Civilta* 144:93-95 Ja 2 1993.

Palazzi, Antonella.
The great book of vegetables. Simon & Schuster, n.d.
Poole, Shona Crawford. *Tablet* 247:373 Mr 20 1993.

Palazzi, Fernando, and Folena, Gianfranco.
Dizionario della lingua italiana. Loescher, 1992.
Capizzi, Carmelo. *Civilta* 2:194-195 Ap 17 1993.

Palladio, Andrea, 1508-1580.
The churches of Rome. Medieval & Renaissance Texts & Studies, 1991.
Heiser, W Charles. *TheolDgst* 40:80-81 Spr 1993.

Palliser, Margaret Ann.
Christ, our Mother of mercy: divine mercy and compassion in the theology of the Shewings of Julian of Norwich. Gruyter, 1992.
Heiser, W Charles. *TheolDgst* 39:378-379 Wint 1992.
Nuth, Joan M. *TheolStds* 54:565-567 S 1993.

Palmer, Andrew.
Monk and mason on the Tigris frontier. University of Cambridge Oriental Publications 39, 1990.
Davis, Thomas X. *Cist Stud* 28:[36]-[37] 1993.

Palmer, Martin.
Coming of age: an exploration of Christianity and the New Age. Aquarian, n.d.
Caldecott, Stratford. *Tablet* 247:790-791 Je 19 1993.
What should we teach? WCC, 1991.
Boisclair, Regina A. *JEcumen Stds* 29:493-494 Sum-Aut 1992.

Palmero Ramos, Rafael, and Carro Celada, Esteban.
San José, del Sindicato de al madera. Edit. Monte Carmelo, 1990.
Gautier, Roland. *CahiersJos* 41:133 Ja-Je 1993.

Palumbieri, Sabino.
L'uomo e il futuro, vol I: È possibile il futuro dell'uomo? Editione Dehoniane, 1991.
Vanzan, Piersandro. *Civilta* 3:537-539 S 18 1993.

Pamphile, Léon Denius.
La croix et le glaive: L'Eglise Catholique et l'occupation Américaine d'Haïti, 1915-1934. Editions des Antilles S A, 1991.
Wiest, J. *CHist* 78:698-700 O 1992.

Pangallo, Don Mario.
L'essere come atto nel tomismo essenziale di Cornelio Fabro. Libreria Editrice Vaticana, 1987.
Derousseaux, Louis. *MSR* 50:158-161 Ap-Je 1993.
La libertà di Dio in S. Tommaso e in Duns Scoto. Libreria Editrice Vaticana, 1992.
Anon. *Gregorianum* 74 no 3:604 1993.

Pannekoek, Frits.
A snug little flock: the social origins of the Riel resistance of 1869-1870.
Watson & Dwyer, n.d.
Huel, Raymond. *Can Cath Rev* 11:25 F 1993.

Pannenberg, Wolfhart.
An introduction to systematic theology. Eerdmans, 1991.
Madges, William. *Horizons (CTS)* 19:318-319 Fall 1992.
Systematic theology, vol 1. Eerdmans, 1991.
Tavard, George Henry. *OChr* 28 no 4:387-392 1992.
Viladesau, Richard. *TheolStds* 54:171-173 Mr 1993.
Systematische theologie, vol I. Vandehoeck and Ruprecht, 1988.
Brito, Emilio. *Eph Theol Lovan* 78:462-463 D 1992.
Teologia sistematica, vol 1. Queriniana, 1990.
Brito, Emilio. *Eph Theol Lovan* 78:462-463 D 1992.

Panteghini, Giacomo.
Il gemito della creazione. Messaggeto, 1992.
Salvini, Gianpaolo. *Civilta* 3:435-436 S 4 1993.

Panzeri, F, and Righetto, R, eds.
Racconta il too Dio. Mondadori, 1993.
Castelli, Ferdinando. *Civilta* 2:563-565 Je 19 1993.

Paola, Tomie de.
Tomie dePaola's book of Bible stories. G P Putnam Sons, n.d.
Neuberger, Anne E. *ReligTJ* 27:16-17 Ap-My 1993.

Paor, Liam de, 1926-.
St Patrick's world. Four Courts Press, 1993.
Corish, Patrick J. *Furrow* 44:386 Je 1993.

Papàsogli, Giorgio.
Bruno il Santo della Ceriota: dio risponde nel deserto. Città Nuova, 1991.
Sonzini, E. *Civilta* 2:412 My 15 1993.

Papeleux, L.
L'action caritative du Saint-Siège en faveur des prisonniers de guerre (1939-1945). Institut Historiue Belge de Rome, 1991.
Toubeau, A. *NRT* 114:924-925 N-D 1992.

Papineau, Andre, 1937-.
Sermons for sermon haters. Resource Publications, 1992.
Ventline, Lawrence M. *St Anth* 100:51 Ja 1993.
Ventline, Lawrence M. *Emmanuel* 99:298+ Je 1993.

Paracone, Corrado, and Mola, Aldo A, eds.
Per una scuola che funzioni: dal mito delle riforme alla ricerca dell'efficacia. Armando, 1991.
Femminis, A. *Civilta* 2:415 My 15 1993.

Pardes, Ilana.
Countertraditions in the Bible. Harvard University Press, 1992.
Heiser, W Charles. *TheolDgst* 40:181 Sum 1993.
O'Brien, Julia M. *OTA* 16:411-412 Je 1993.

Pargament, Kenneth I, et al.
Religion and prevention in mental health: research, vision, and action. Haworth Press, 1993.
Anon. *Health Prog* 74:67 Je 1993.

Parini, Jay.
The last station, a novel of Tolstoy's last year. HarperCollins, n.d.
FitzLyon, April. *Tablet* 247:481 Ap 10-17 1993.

Parish, Helen Rand, ed.
Bartolomé De Las Casas: the only way. Paulist, 1992.
Wicks, J. *Gregorianum* 73 No 4:770-771 1992.
Dollen, Charles. *Priest* 49:52 F 1993.
Ross, Stephen-Joseph. *Spir Life* 39:177-179 Aut 1993.
Roy, Louis. *ChrWorld* 236:236-237 S-O 1993.

Parker, David C.
Codex Bezae: an early Christian manuscript and its text. Cambridge University Press, 1992.
Heiser, W Charles. *TheolDgst* 40:81 Spr 1993.

Parker, Michael.
Hello down there. Scribner's, n.d.
Wendling, Ronald. *America* 169:20 Jl 17-24 1993.

Parker, Steve.
The body atlas. Dorling Kindersley, n.d.
Braybrooke, Neville. *Tablet* 247:582 My 8 1993.

Parker, Tony.
May the Lord in his mercy be kind to Belfast. Jonathan Cape, n.d.
McRedmond, Louis. *Tablet* 247:788 Je 19 1993.
Campbell, James. *Month* 26:275 Jl 1993.

Parkinson, Cecil.
Right at the centre: an autobiography. Weidenfeld & Nicolson, n.d.
Hackett, Peter. *Tablet* 247:16-17 Ja 2 1993.

Parks, Tim.
Goodness. Grove Press, n.d.
Schroth, Raymond A, 1933-. *Nat Cath Rep* 29:34 My 28 1993.
Juggling the stars. Grove Press, n.d.
Schroth, Raymond A, 1933-. *Nat Cath Rep* 29:34 My 28 1993.

Il Parlamento italiano 1861-198, vol XV: 1948-1949.
Nuova Cei, 1991-1992.
Caprile, Giovanni. *Civilta* 143:531-532 D 5 1992.

Parry, Donald W.
A bibliography on temples of the ancient Near East adn Mediterranean world arranged by subject and by author. The Edwin Mellen Press, 1992.
Heiser, W Charles. *TheolDgst* 40:81 Spr 1993.

Parsons, Mikeal C, and Tyson, Joseph B, eds.
Cadbury, Knox, and Talbert: American contributions to the study of Acts. Scholars Press, 1992.
Heiser, W Charles. *TheolDgst* 40:55 Spr 1993.

Partington, Angela, ed.
The Oxford dictionary of quotations. Oxford University Press, n.d.
Shaw, Roy. *Tablet* 247:583-584 My 8 1993.

Pascal, Robert Anthony, et al.
The collected works of Eric Voegelin, volume 27: the nature of the law and related legal writings. Louisiana State University Press, 1991.
Marnell, Michael M. *Jurist* 51 no 2:514-515 1991.

Pasquero, Fedele.
I will follow you. Alba House, 1992.
Heiser, W Charles. *TheolDgst* 40:181 Sum 1993.

Patchett, Ann.
The patron Saint of Liars. Houghton Mifflin, 1992.
Costello, Gerald M, 1931-. *USCath* 58:48-51 Ja 1993.
Wolfe, Gregory. *Crisis* 11:56-58 My 1993.

Pate, C Marvin.
Adam Christology as the exegetical and theological substructure of 2 Corinthians 4:7-f:21. University Press of America, 1991.
Sweetland, Dennis M. *CBQ* 55:389-391 Ap 1993.

Patel, Raj, et al.
Equal partners? Theological training and racial justice. CCBI Publications, n.d.
Campbell, James. *Month* 26:34 Ja 1993.

Paterson, Peter.
Tired and emotional: the life of Lord George Brown. Chatto & Windus, n.d.
Longford, Frank. *Tablet* 247:581 My 8 1993.

Paths to peace: a contribution.
Liturgical Publications, 1987.
Krason, Stephen M. *SocJust* 84:29 Ja-F 1993.

Patkus, Ronald D, ed.
From generation to generation II: stories in Catholic history from the archives of the Archdiocese of Boston. Christopher Publishing House, 1992.
Casey, Thomas F. *CHist* 79:575-576 Jl 1993.

Patocka, Jan.
Le monde naturel et le mouvement de l'existence humaine. Kluwer Academic Publishers, 1988.
Bourke, Vernon J. *Mod Schlmn* 70:68-70 N 1992.

Pattel-Gray, Anne.
Cry for justice: the aborginal and islander contribution to the World Council of Churches 7th Assembly. Aboriginal and Islander Commission of the Australian Council of Churches, 1991.
Fernández-Calienes, Raúl. *Pacifica* 6:120-121 F 1993.
Through aboriginal eyes. World Council of Churches, 1991.
Dutney, Andrew. *Pacifica* 6:119-120 F 1993.

Patterson, Richard B.
Encounters with angels: the interplay of psyche and spirit in the counseling situation. Loyola University Press, n.d.
Stout, Nancy T. *ST Anth* 101:52-53 Jl 1993.

Pattison, Robert.
The great dissent: John Henry Newman and the liberal heresy. Oxford University Press, 1991.
Ferreira, M Jamie. *Thomist* 57:331-336 Ap 1993.
Begley, Ronald. *Can Cath Rev* 11:23-24 Jl-Ag 1993.

Paul VI et la vie internationale.
Instituto Paolo VI—Studium, 1992.
Caprile, Giovanni. *Civilta* 3:327-328 Ag 7-21 1993.

Paul, Erich Robert.
Science, religion, and Mormon cosmology. University of Illinois Press, 1992.
Heiser, W Charles. *TheolDgst* 40:181 Sum 1993.

Paul, Shalom M.
Amos. Fortress, 1991.
Clifford, Richard J. *TheolStds* 53:737-739 D 1992.
Mariottini, Claude F. *OTA* 15:513 O 1992.
Gossai, Hemchand. *CBQ* 55:128-129 Ja 1993.
Conroy, Charles. *Gregorianum* 74 no 2:358-362 1993.

Paul VI, Pope, 1897-1978 (Giovanni Battista Montini) (elected 1963).
Il Sinodo dei Vescovi: interventi e documentazione. Instituto Paolo VI Studium, 1992.
Mucci, Giandomenico. *Civilta* 2:297-298 My 1 1993.

Pauley, Bruce F.
From prejudice to persecution: a history of Austrian anti-Semitism. The University of North Carolina Press, 1992.
Zeps, Michael J. *CHist* 79:125 Ja 1993.

Paulus, B, ed.
Pascash Radberti: expositio in Psalmum XLIV. Brepols, 1991.
Roisel, V. *NRT* 115:267 Mr-Ap 1993.

Paulus, Engelbert.
Liebe—das Geheimnis der Welt. Echter Verlag, 1990.
Brito, Emilio. *Eph Theol Lovan* 78:473 D 1992.

Paverd, Frans, van de.
St John Chrysostom, the Omilies on the statues: an introduction. Pontificium Institutum Studiorum Orientalium, 1991.
Ferrua, Antonio. *Civilta* 144:97 Ja 2 1993.

Pavese, A.
Sai Baba. Piemme, 1992.
Renard, L-J. *NRT* 115:607-608 Jl-Ag 1993.

Pawlikowski, John T.
When Catholics speak about Jesus. Liturgy Training Press, 1987.
Anon. *USCath* 58:15-21 O 1993.

Payne, Joseph A.
Befriending: a self-guided retreat for busy people. Paulist, n.d.
Graham, William C. *Nat Cath Rep* 29:25 Mr 26 1993.

Payne, Steven, ed.
Carmelite studies 6: John of the Cross. ICS Publications, n.d.
O'Donoghue, Noel D. *Can Cath Rev* 11:27-28 N 1993.
John of the Cross and the cognitive value of mysticism. Kluwer Academic Publishers, 1990.
Polis, Dennis E. *Mod Schlmn* 70:153-155 Ja 1993.
John of the Cross: conferences and essays by members of the Institute of Carmelite Studies and others. ICS Publications, n.d.
McGowan, Cecilia. *Spir Life* 32:111-112 Sum 1993.

Pazdan, Mary Margaret.
The Son of Man: a metaphor for Jesus in the Fourth Gospel. Liturgical, 1991.
Christie, Dolores L. *Emmanual* 49:418-419 S 1993.

Peacocke, Arthur.
Theology for a scientific age. Blackwell, 1990.
Salmon, J. *TheolStds* 53:790-791 D 1992.

Pearce, Michael.
The Mamur Zapt and the spoils of Egypt. Collins Crime Club, n.d.
Lejeune, Anthony. *Tablet* 247:376 Mr 20 1993.

Pearson, Birger A, ed.
The future of Early Christianity: essays in honor of Helmut Koester. Fortress Press, 1991.
Heiser, W Charles. *TheolDgst* 39:363 Wint 1992.
Osiek, Carolyn. *CBQ* 55:199-201 Ja 1993.

Pearson, T R.
Cry me a river. Henry Holt, n.d.
Dufresne, Bethe. *Comm* 120:37-38 Ap 9 1993.

Peatman, William.
The beginning of the gospel. Liturgical Press, 1992.
Graham, William C. *Nat Cath Rep* 29:40 F 5 1993.
The beginning of the gospel. Liturgical, 1992.
Senior, Donald. *BibleT* 31:254 Jl 1993.

Peck, M Scott.
Meditations from the road. Rider, n.d.
Forrester, David. *Tablet* 247:1304 O 9 1993.

Pecorari, Paolo, ed.
Giseppe Toniolo tra economia e società. Del Blanco, 1990.
Mellinato, Giuseppe. *Civilta* 143:429-430 N 21 1992.

Peffer, R G.
Marxism, morality and social justice. Princeton University Press, 1990.
Marsden, J. *Heythrop* 34:93-94 Ja 1993.

Pelagius, 360-420.
The letters of Pelagius and his followers. Boydell, 1991.
Hunter, David G. *TheolStds* 54:385 Je 1993.

Pelchat, Marc.
Les approches empiriques en théologie. Université Laval, 1992.
Tihon, Paul. *Lumen* 48:113 Mr 1993.

Pelikan, Jaroslav.
Confessor between east and west: a portrait of Ukrainian Cardinal Josyf Slipyj. William B Eerdmans Publishing Co, 1990.
Cholij, R. *Heythrop* 34:121 Ja 1993.
The idea of the university: a reexamination. Yale University Press, 1992.
Hesburgh, T. *CHist* 78:621-623 O 1992.
Pouncey, P. *America* 168:19-20 Ja 30 1993.
Lash, Nicholas. *Tablet* 247:171-172 F 6 1993.
Hanus, Jerome J, Bp. *Crisis* 11:51-52 Ap 1993.
Dulles. *IPQ* 33:240-241 Je 1993.
Giles, James E. *CrossCurr* 43:256-257 Sum 1993.
Wilkins, Mark. *St Anth* 100:50-51 S 1993.

Pelletier, Francis Jeffrey.
Parmenides, Plato, and the semantics of not-being. University of Chicago Press, 1990.
Marler, J. *Mod Schlmn* 70:66-68 N 1992.

Pelletier, Norman.
Tomorrow will be too late: a life of Saint Peter Julian Eymard. Emmanuel Publications, 1992.
Rousseau, Robert. *Emmanuel* 99:114+ Mr 1993.

Penalva, José.
Teologia: iniciação, leitura de Paula. Ave Maria, 1992.
Libanio, Joao Batista. *Perspectiva* 24:391-393 S-D 1992.

Peñamaría de LLano, Antonio.
El Dios de los cristianos. Estructura introductoria a la teologia de la Trinidad. Sociedad de Educación Atenas, 1990.
Pastor, Felix-Alejandro. *Gregorianum* 74 no 2:372 1993.

Pennington, M Basil, 1931-.
Awake in the spirit. Crossroad Publishing Company, n.d.
Pecht, Gerard. *Liguorian* 81:69 Ag 1993.
A retreat with Thomas Merton. Element Books, 1991.
Blunden, Stephen. *Priests & People* 7:81-82 F 1993.

Pennock, Michael.
Celebrating the signs of God's love: the sacraments. Ave Maria Press, 1993.
McGrath, Helene. *Mod Lit* 20:40 Ag 1993.

Le Pentateuque en question.
Labor et Fides, 1989.
Ska, Jean Louis. *NRT* 115:250-251 Mr-Ap 1993.

Penzel, Klaus, ed.
Philip Schaff: historian and ambassador. Mercer University Press, 1991.
Pranger, Gary K. *CHist* 79:308-309 Ap 1993.
Meyer, John C. *JEcumen Stds* 29:265-266 Spr 1992.

Pepler, Stephen.
Stephen's history of saints. Cardozo Kindersley, n.d.
Braybrooke, Neville. *Tablet* 247:374 Mr 20 1993.

Perdue, Leo G.
Wisdom in revolt: metaphorical theology in the Book of Job. Sheffield, 1991.
Lust, Johan. *Eph Theol Lovan* 69:164-165 Ap 1993.
Kolarcik, Michael. *CBQ* 55:346-347 Ap 1993.

Peretto, E, ed.
La mariologia nell'organizzazione delle discipline teologiche. Marianum, 1992.
Renard, L-J. *NRT* 115:582 Jl-Ag 1993.

Perham, Michael V, et al.
Enriching the Christian year. Liturgical Press, 1993.
Hommerding, Leroy. *Mod Lit* 20:42 Ag 1993.
Gibbons, Robin. *Way* 33:261 Jl 1993.

Perham, Michael V, and Stevenson, Kenneth W.
Welcoming the light of Christ. The Liturgical Press, 1991.
Mitchell, Leonel L. *Worship* 67:177-179 Mr 1993.

Perkins, Pheme.
Jesus as teacher. Cambridge University, 1990.
Winkler, Jude. *CBQ* 54:788-789 O 1992.

Perkins, Robert L, ed.
International Kierkegaard commentary, vol 13: the Corsair Affair. Mercer University Press, 1990.
Morris, Thomas. *Heythrop* 34:111-112 Ja 1993.

Perler, Othmar.
Sapientia et Caritas. Universitäts, 1990.
Halleux, André de. *Eph Theol Lovan* 78:445-446 D 1992.
Hombert, P-M. *MSR* 50:69 Ja-Mr 1993.

Pernet, Henry.
Mirages du masque. Labor et Fides, 1988.
Debarge, Louis. *MSR* 50:73-74 Ja-Mr 1993.

Perrier, J.
Nous partons pour la Terre Sante. Presses Universitaires de France, 1992.
Harvengt, A. *NRT* 115:291 Mr-Ap 1993.

Perrin, Luc.
Il caso Lefebvre. Marietti, 1991.
Caprile, Giovanni. *Civilta* 143:434-435 N 21 1992.

Perry, Richard.
Mexico's fortress monasteries. Espadaña Press, 1992.
Baird, Joseph A. *CHist* 79:140-141 Ja 1993.

Pesch, Otto Hermann, 1931-.
Tomás de Aquino. Herder, 1992.
Arteaga Manieu, Andrés. *Teol Vida* 34 no 1-2:159-160 1993.
Osuna, Antonio. *Cien Tom* 120:188-190 Ja-Ap 1993.
Taborda, Francisco. *Perspectiva* 25:237-238 My-Ag 1993.

Pestana, Carla Gardina.
Quakers and Baptists in colonial Massachusetts. Cambridge University Press, 1991.
James, S. *CHist* 78:679-680 O 1992.

Peter, of Waltham, 1190-1196.
Source book of self-discipline: a synthesis of Moralia in Job. Peter Lang, 1991.
Heiser, W Charles. *TheolDgst* 39:379 Wint 1992.

Peter-Raoul, Mar, ed.
Yearning to breathe free: liberation theologies in the US. Orbis Books, 1990.
Redmond, Gay. *RRel* 52:313-314 Mr-Ap 1993.

Peterkiewicz, Jerzy.
In the scales of fate: an autobiography. Marion Boyars, n.d.
Craig, Mary. *Tablet* 247:1235-1236 S 25 1993.

Peterman, James F.
Philosophy as therapy: an interpretation and defense of Wittgenstein's later philosophical project. SUNY Press, 1992.
Schiller, Britt-Marie. *Mod Schlmn* 70:156-159 Ja 1993.

Peters, Ellis.
The holy theif. Headline, n.d.
Lejeune, Anthony. *Tablet* 247:51 Ja 9 1993.

Peters, Ted.
God—the world's future: systematic theology for a postmodern era. Fortress, 1992.
Heiser, W Charles. *TheolDgst* 40:81 Spr 1993.
Haughey, John C. *TheolStds* 54:582-584 S 1993.

Petersen, David L, and Richards, Kent Harold.
Interpreting Hebrew poetry. Fortress, 1992.
Murphy, Roland E. *OTA* 16:164 F 1993.
Stuhlmueller, Carroll. *BibleT* 31:120 Mr 1993.
Interpreting Hebrew poetry. Fortress Press, 1992.
Heiser, W Charles. *TheolDgst* 40:181 Sum 1993.

Peterson, Michael L, ed.
The problem of evil: selected readings. University of Notre Dame Press, 1992.
Heiser, W Charles. *TheolDgst* 40:82 Spr 1993.

Peterson, Wallace C, 1921-.
Transfer spending, taxes and the American welfare state. Kluwer Academic Publishers, 1991.
Scaperlanda, Anthony. *RSocEcon* 51:118-122 Spr 1993.

Le petit guide de la Bible.
Médiaspaul, 1992.
Renard, L J. *NRT* 115:142 Ja-F 1993.

Petit, Françoise, ed.
La chaîne sur la Genèse. Peeters, 1991.
Halleux, André de. *Eph Theol Lovan* 78:448-449 D 1992.
Ska, Jean Louis. *NRT* 115:295-296 Mr-Ap 1993.

Petit, Ian.
Your sins are forgiven. Darton, Longman & Todd, n.d.
Forrester, David. *Tablet* 247:586 My 8 1993.

Petit, Jean-Claude.
Jésus: Christ universel? Éditions Fides, 1990.
Brito, Emilio. *Eph Theol Lovan* 78:474-475 D 1992.

Petrà, B.
Tra cielo e terra. EDB, 1992.
Harvengt, A. *NRT* 115:116-117 Ja-F 1993.

Petrarch, Francis.
Letters of old age: rerum senilium libri I-XVIII. Johns Hopkins University Press, 1992.
Rawski, Conrad H. *CHist* 79:324-326 Ap 1993.

Petras, Ross, and Petras, Kathryn, eds.
The 776 stupidest things ever said. Doubleday, n.d.
Hunt, George W, 1937-. *America* 168:2 My 22, 1993.

Pétrement, Simone.
A separate God: the Christian origins of gnosticism. Longman and Todd, 1991.
Yarnold, Edward John, 1926-. *New Blckfrs* 73:625-626 D 1992.

Petrosino, Silvano.
Fondamento ed esasperazione. Saggio sul pensare di Emmanuel Lévinas. Casa Editrice Marietti, 1992.
Tilliette, Xavier. *Gregorianum* 74 no 3:598 1993.

Petrotta, Anthony J.
Lexis Ludens: wordplay and the Book of Micah. Lang, 1991.
McCreesh, Thomas P. *OTA* 15:513 O 1992.

Petry, Nicholas, and Echeverría, Loreto.
Under the heel of Mary. Routledge, 1988.
Glimm, Francis. *CHist* 79:92 Ja 1993.

Pettegre, Andrew, ed.
The early Reformation in Europe. Cambridge University Press, n.d.
Cunningham, Lawrence S, 1935-. *Comm* 120:29 Je 4 1993.

Pettinati, Guido.
I santi canonizzati del giorno, 12 voll: Gennaio-Dicembre. Segno, 1991-1993.
Giachi, Gualberto. *Civilta* 144:519 Mr 6 1993.

Petulla, Joseph.
Crisis to wellness: meditation for a philosophy of living. Community Resource Institute Press, n.d.
Graham, William C. *Nat Cath Rep* 29:40 My 28 1993.

Pfaff, William.
The wrath of nations. Simon & Schuster, 1993.
Sanders, Ivan. *Comm* 120:26-29 N 5 1993.

Pfeifer, Alice Ann.
Let's pray together (volume II). Hi-Time Publishers, Inc, 1992.
Stuhlmueller, Carroll. *BibleT* 31:120 Mr 1993.

Pfleger, Albert.
Saint Joseph dans notre vie. Maison des Frères Maristes, 1991.
Gauthier, Roland. *CahiersJos* 41:136 Ja-Je 1993.

Philips, Dirk, 1504-1568.
The writings of Dirk Philips, 1504-1568. Herald Press, 1992.
Heiser, W Charles. *TheolDgst* 39:379 Wint 1992.

Phillips, Sara Webb, and Phillips, L Edwards.
Leading public prayer. Discipleship Resources, 1992.
Gallagher, Miriam J. *Mod Lit* 20:41-42 My 1993.

Philo of Alexandria.
Quaestiones et solutiones in Exodum I et II. Cerf, 1992.
Roisel, V. *NRT* 115:265-266 Mr-Ap 1993.
Questiones et solutiones in Exodus I et II. Cerf, 1992.
Begg, Christopher T. *OTA* 16:449 Je 1993.

Piccinelli, Aldo.
L'esperienza spirituale di Itala Mela. Abbazia San Paolo, 1991.
Ganzi, I M. *Civilta* 3:200-201 Jl 17 1993.

Piccoli Catello, Marisa.
Il Presepe napoletano. Guida, 1991.
Caprile, Giovanni. *Civilta* 143:636 D 19 1992.

Pie I Minot, Salvador.
Tratado de teología fundamental. Ed Secretariado Trinitario, 1991.
Bentué, Antonio. *Teol Vida* 34 no 1-2:160-161 1993.

Pieper, Jeanne.
The Catholic woman: difficult choices in a modern world. Contemporary, n.d.
Bromberg, Judith. *Nat Cath Rep* 30:27 N 19 1993.

Pieper, Josef.
Abuse of language, abuse of power. Ignatius, n.d.
Russello, Gerald. *Crisis* 10:51-52 D 1992.
A brief reader on the virtues of the human heart. Ignatius Press, 1991.
Heiser, W Charles. *TheolDgst* 39:379-380 Wint 1992.
Guide to St Thomas Aquinas. Ignatius Press, 1991.
Lowery, Mark. *SocJust* 84:61-62 Mr-Ap 1993.
In defense of philosophy. Ignatius Press, 1992.
Schall, James Vincent, 1928-. *HPR* 93:82-86 Ag-S 1993.

Pieris, Aloysius, 1934-.
El rostro asiático de Cristo: notas para una teología asiática de la liberación. Ed Sígueme, 1991.
Lago Alba, Luis. *Cien Tom* 119:612 S-D 1992.

Pietrantonio, Ugo.
Considerazioni e osservazioni su alcune Opere di Storia del Molise recenti e passate. Enne, 1992.
Ferrua, Antonio. *Civilta* 3:326 Ag 7-21 1993.

Pikaza, Xavier, and Silanes, Nereo, eds.
Diccionario teológico: El Dios cristiano. Secretariado Trinitario, 1992.
Bandera, Armando. *Cien Tom* 120:190 Ja-Ap 1993.

Pike, Nelson.
Mystic union: an essay in the phenomenology of mysticism. Cornell University Press, 1992.
Payne, Steven. *Spir Life* 32:112-114 Sum 1993.
Payne, Steven. *TheolStds* 54:368-369 Je 1993.
Sweetman, Brendan. *New Oxford Rev* 60:28-30 O 1993.

Pilch, John Joseph, 1936-.
Introducing the cultural context of the New Testament, vol II. Paulist Press, 1991.
Senior, Donald. *BibleT* 31:60 Ja 1993.
Craghan, John F. *Bib Th Bul* 22:180 Wint 1992.
Introducing the cultural context of the Old Testament, vol I. Paulist Press, 1991.
Stuhlmueller, Carroll. *BibleT* 30:381-382 N 1992.
Craghan, John F. *Bib Th Bul* 22:180 Wint 1992.

Pilieri, Antonio.
La grande mutazione: il PCI. Vallecchi, 1991.
Varriale, E. *Civilta* 144:416 F 20 1993.

Pillinger, Renate, and Renhart, Erich, eds.
The divine life, light, and love: euntes in mundum universum: Festschrift in honour of Petro B T Bilaniuk. Andreas Schnider Verlages-Arelier, 1992.
Mathews, Edward G. *Diakonia* 26 no 2:139 1993.

Pinckaerts, Servais.
La parola e la coscienza. SEI, 1991.
Cultrera, Francesco. *Civilta* 144:610-611 Mr 20 1993.
La prière chrétienne. Editions Universitaires, 1989.
Partos, L. *Lumen* 48:236-237 Je 1993.

Piolanti, A.
La comunione dei santi e la vita eterna. Libreria Editrice Vaticana, 1992.
Renwart, Léon. *NRT* 114:902-903 N-D 1992.

Piovesana, G.
Storia del pensiero filosofico russo (988-1988). Ed Paoline, 1992.
Simon, Michelef. *Civilta* 144:153-157 Ja 16 1993.

Pipino, Cristina.
Un'amicizia massonica: Carteggio Lemmi-Carducci con documenti inediti. Bastogi, 1991.
Caprile, Giovanni. *Civilta* 2:101 Ap 3 1993.

Pirincci, Akif.
Felidae. Fourth Estate, n.d.
Toomey, Philippa. *Tablet* 247:1015 Ag 7 1993.

Pirotte, Jean, and Derroitte, Henri.
Eglises et santé dans le tiers monde: hier et aujourd'hui. E J Brill, 1991.
Joblin, Joseph, 1920-. *Gregorianum* 73 No 4:771-773 1992.

Piscatori, James, ed.
Islamic fundamentalism and the Gulf Crisis. University of Chicago, 1991.
Khan, A. *TheolStds* 53:792-793 D 1992.

Placher, William Carl, and Willis-Watkins, David.
Belonging to God: a commentary on a brief statement of faith. John Knox Press, 1992.
Heiser, W Charles. *TheolDgst* 40:81 Spr 1993.

Pléthon, Georges Gémiste.
Traité des vertus. E J Brill, 1988.
Destrée, Pierre. *RPhil Louvain* 91:150-151 F 1993.

Plimpton, George, ed.
The writer's chapbook. Penguin, n.d.
Hunt, George W, 1937-. *America* 168:2 F 20 1993.

Plongeron, Bernard.
L'Abbé Grégoire (1750-1831) ou l'Arche de la Fraternité. Letouzey et Ané.
Van Kley, D. *CHist* 78:667-670 O 1992.

Plotch, Batia, and Cobe, Patricia.
International kosher cookbook. Ballantine Books, 1992.
Stuhlmueller, Carroll. *BibleT* 31:56 Ja 1993.

Plotin.
Traité sur la liberté et la volonté de 'Un. Vrin, 1990.
Destrée, Pierre. *RPhil Louvain* 91:146-148 F 1993.

Plymale, Steven F.
The prayer texts of Luke-Acts. Peter Lang Publishing, 1991.
Senior, Donald. *BibleT* 31:254 Jl 1993.

Pock, Johann Ignaz.
Sapientia Salomonis: Hieronymus' Exegese de Weisheitsbuches im Licht der Tradition. Technische Universität Graz, 1992.
Murphy, Roland E. *OTA* 16:428 Je 1993.

Pocock, Tom.
Rider Haggard and the lost empire. Weidenfeld & Nicolson, n.d.
Usborne, Richard. *Tablet* 247:1164-1165 S 11 1993.

Pohlmann, Karl-Friedrich.
Ezechielstudien. Gruyter, 1992.
Lust, Johan. *Eph Theol Lovan* 78:418-419 D 1992.
Dempsey, Deirdre A. *OTA* 16:181 F 1993.

Pokorný, Petr.
Colossians. Hendrickson, 1991.
Montague, George T. *CBQ* 54:796-797 O 1992.
Senior, Donald. *BibleT* 31:316 S 1993.

Polhill, John B.
Acts. Broadman Press, 1992.
Heiser, W Charles. *TheolDgst* 39:380 Wint 1992.

Poliziano, Angelo.
Stanze, Orfeo, Rime. Garzanti, 1992.
Ferrua, Antonio. *Civilta* 2:306-307 My 1 1993.

Pollack, Aharon.
Al Hasetumot Bamizmor. Nezer, 1991.
Hillmer, Mark. *OTA* 16:426-427 Je 1993.

Polverari, Alberto.
Vita di Pio IX. Citta del Vaticano, 1986.
Lago Alba, Luis. *Cien Tom* 119:619-621 S-D 1992.

Pomedli, Michael M.
Ethnophilosophical and ethnolinguistic perspectives on the Huron Indian soul. The Edwin Mellen Press, 1991.
Heiser, W Charles. *TheolDgst* 40:81-82 Spr 1993.

Pommeraye, R de la.
Aux frontières du Royaume. Centurion, 1992.
Toubeau, A. *NRT* 115:131-132 Ja-F 1993.

Pomponio, Francesco, ed.
Formule di maledizione della Mesopotamia preclassica. Paideia, 1990.
Moran, William L. *CBQ* 55:348 Ap 1993.

Ponsetto, Daniel.
Praying our stories: reflections for youth ministers. St Mary's Press, n.d.
McCann, Deborah. *ReligTJ* 27:10 Mr 1993.
Anon. *Church* 9:42 Sum 1993.

Poole, Ross.
Morality and modernity. Routledge, 1991.
Sullivan, John. *Heythrop* 34:464-465 O 1993.

Poos, L R.
A rural society after the Black Death: Essex 1350-1525. Cambridge University Press, 1991.
Wrightson, K. *CHist* 78:647-648 O 1992.

Pope-Levison, Priscilla, and Levison, John R.
Jesus in global contexts. John Knox Press, 1992.
Heiser, W Charles. *TheolDgst* 40:181 Sum 1993.

Poppi, Angelico.
Sinossi dei quattro vangeli greco-italiano. Edizioni Messaggero, 1992.
Neirynck, F. *Eph Theol Lovan* 78:437-439 D 1992.
Sinossi dei quattro Vangeli Greco-Italiano. Messaggero, 1992.
Scaiolo, D. *Civilta* 3:441-442 S 4 1993.

Porter, Stanley E.
Idioms of the Greek New Testament. JSOT Press, 1992.
    Heiser, W Charles. *TheolDgst* 40:181-182 Sum 1993.

Porterfield, Amanda.
Female piety in Puritan New England: the emergence of religious humanism.
Oxford University Press, 1992.
    Heiser, W Charles. *TheolDgst* 39:380 Wint 1992.

Portier, Lucienne, ed.
Catherine de Sienne: le dialogue. Cerf, 1992.
    Partos, L. *Lumen* 48:117 Mr 1993.

Porto, Humberto, and Schlesinger, Hugo.
Prayers of blessing and praise for all occasions. Twenty-third Publications, 1987.
    Kelly, Kevin T. *SIDIC* 25 No 1:33 1992.

Postel, Sandra.
Last oasis: facing water scarcity. W W Norton and Company, n.d.
    Decoursey, Vincent W, Jr. *Nat Cath Rep* 29:18 Mr 12 1993.

Postman, Neil.
Amusing ourselves to death. Penguin, n.d.
    Wallace, James A, 1944-. *Liguorian* 81:43 O 1993.

Poston, Larry.
Islamic Da'wah in the West: Muslim missionary activity and the dynamics of conversion to Islam. Oxford University Press, 1992.
    Sara, Solomon I. *TheolStds* 54:204 Mr 1993.
    Heiser, W Charles. *TheolDgst* 40:82 Spr 1993.

Potgieter, J H.
'n Narratologiese ondersoek van die boek Jona. The University of Pretoria, 1991.
    Vogels, Walter A. *OTA* 16:182 F 1993.

Pottebaum, Gerard A, et al.
A child shall lead them: a guide to celebrating the word with children.
Treehaus Communications, n.d.
    Roberto, John. *ReligTJ* 27:30 Ap-My 1993.
    Pilch, John Joseph, 1936-. *Mod Lit* 20:39 O 1993.

Pottebaum, Gerard A.
The rites of people. Pastoral Press, 1992.
    Schumacher, Theresa. *Sisters* 65:309 Jl 1993.
    Brown, David O. *Mod Lit* 20:42 Ag 1993.
    Van Hoomissen, G. *Lumen* 48:354-355 S 1993.

Pottenger, John R.
The political theory of liberation theology. State University of New York Press, 1989.
    Worland, Stephen T. *RSocEcon* 50:353-358 Fall 1992.

Potterie, Ignace de la.
Mary in the mystery of the covenant. Alba House, 1992.
    Stuhlmueller, Carroll. *BibleT* 31:124 Mr 1993.
    Nowell, Irene. *Worship* 67:286-287 My 1993.
    Heiser, W Charles. *TheolDgst* 40:72 Spr 1993.
    Brennan, Walter T. *CLW* 64:38-39 Jl-S 1993.

Potts, David B.
Wesleyan University, 1831-1910. Yale University Press, 1992.
    Noll, Mark A. *CrossCurr* 43:272-273 Sum 1993.

Pouderon, Bernard.
Athénagore, supplique au sujet des chrétiens et sur la résurrection des morts.
Les Éditions du Cerf, 1992.
    Pelland, Gilles. *Gregorianum* 74 no 2:389-390 1993.

Poupard, Paul, Cardinal, 1930-.
What will give us happiness? Veritas Publications, n.d.
    Campbell, James. *Month* 26:80 F 1993.
    Joyce, Patricia. *Furrow* 44:256 Ap 1993.

Pour une lecture du Catéchisme de l'Église catholique.
Mame, 1993.
    Anon. *NRT* 115:632 Jl-Ag 1993.

Pourtois, Jean-Pierre, and Desmet, Huguette.
Epistemología e instrumentación en ciencias humanas. Ed Herder, 1992.
    Fueyo Suárez, Bernardo. *Cien Tom* 119:627-628 S-D 1992.

Povilus, Judith M.
United in his name. New City Press, 1992.
    Heiser, W Charles. *TheolDgst* 40:182 Sum 1993.

Powell, James M.
Albertanus of Brescia: the pursuit of happiness in the early thirteenth century. University of Pennsylvania Press, 1992.
    Banker, James R. *CHist* 79:321-322 Ap 1993.

Powell, James M, ed.
Muslims under Latin rule, 1100-1300. Princeton University Press, n.d.
    Amprimoz, A. *Can Cath Rev* 11:33 Ja 1993.

Powell, John.
Through the eyes of faith. Tabor Publishing Co, 1992.
    Sattler, John C. *Living Light* 29:94-95 Wint 1992.

Powell, Mark Allan.
The Bible and modern literary criticism: a critical assessment and annotated bibliography. Greenwood Press, 1992.
    Heiser, W Charles. *TheolDgst* 39:380 Wint 1992.
The Bible and modern literary criticism. Greenwood Press, 1992.
    Neirynck, F. *Eph Theol Lovan* 78:432-433 D 1992.
What are they saying about Acts? Paulist, 1991.
    Senior, Donald. *BibleT* 31:60 Ja 1993.
    Kistner, H. *St Anth* 100:50-52 F 1993.
    Totah, Mary David. *Cist Stud* 28:[21] 1993.
    Heiser, W Charles. *TheolDgst* 40:82 Spr 1993.
What are they saying about Luke? Paulist Press, 1989.
    Esler, Philip F. *Bib Th Bul* 23:84-85 Sum 1993.

Power, David Noel.
The Eucharistic mystery. Crossroad, 1992.
    Healey, Charles J. *RRel* 52:795-796 S-O 1993.
    Cunningham, Lawrence S., 1935-. *Comm* 120:28-29 O 8 1993.

Power, David Noel. *(cont'd)*
Worship, culture and theology. Pastoral Press, 1990.
    Spinks, Bryan D. *Heythrop* 34:195-196 Ap 1993.
    Koernke, Theresa F. *Horizons (CTS)* 20:156-157 Spr 1993.

Power, Joseph F, ed.
Francis de Sales: finding God wherever you are. New City Press, 1993.
    Mathews, Edward G. *Diakonia* 26 no 2:141 1993.
    Pecht, Gerard. *Liguorian* 81:70 Ag 1993.

Powers, Isaias.
Pray this way this Lent: daily reflections on the Our Father. Twenty-Third Publications, 1993.
    Hollings, Michael. *Tablet* 247:278 F 27 1993.
Women of the gospel. Twenty-Third Publications, 1992.
    Dollen, Charles. *Priest* 49:52 Ap 1993.
    Graham, William C. *Nat Cath Rep* 29:36 S 10 1993.
    Stuhlmueller, Carroll. *BibleT* 31:120-121 Mr 1993.

Powers, Thomas.
Heisenberg's war: the secret history of the German bomb. Cape, n.d.
    Hawkes, Nigel. *Tablet* 247:789 Je 19 1993.

Powers, William F.
Free priests. Loyola University Press, 1992.
    Cleary, W. *Nat Cath Rep* 29:38 F 5 1993.
    Heiser, W Charles. *TheolDgst* 40:182 Sum 1993.

Pozgar, George D.
Long term care and the law: a legal guide for health care professionals.
Aspen Publishers, 1992.
    Gray, Dan. *Health Prog* 74:84-85 Ap 1993.

Prader, Joseph.
Il matrimonio in Oriente e Occidente. Pontificium Institutum Orientalium, 1992.
    Yevics, Philip E. *Diakonia* 26 no 1:67-76 1993.

La pratique des Exercices Spirituels d'Ignace de Loyola.
Editions de l'Institut d'Etudes Théologiques, 1991.
    Ruiz Jurado, Manuel. *Gregorianum* 74 No 1:172-173 1993.

Pratzner, Ferdinand, ed.
I congressi Eucaristici Internazionali per una nuova evangelizzazione.
Libreria Editrice Vaticana, 1991.
    Caprile, Giovanni. *Civilta* 143:638 D 19 1992.

Pregare con Ignazio: Bibbia ed Esercizi Spirituali.
Apostolato della Preghiera, 1991.
    Ganzi, I M. *Civilta* 144:202 Ja 16 1993.

Pregent, Carol.
When a child dies. Ave Maria Press, n.d.
    Dollen, Charles. *Priest* 49:48 Ja 1993.

Preghiere di marito e moglie.
Gribauda, 1991.
    Caprile, Giovanni. *Civilta* 2:198-199 Ap 17 1993.

Prejean, Helen.
Dead man walking. Random House, n.d.
    Stahel, Thomas H, 1928-. *America* 169:2 Jl 17-24 1993.
    Schroth, Raymond A, 1933-. *America* 169:20 S 18 1993.
    Hochman, Hilary. *Comm* 120:30-31 N 19 1993.

Preuss, Horst Dietrich.
Theologie des Alten Testaments: vol 1. Kohlhammer, 1991.
    Lind, Millard C. *CBQ* 55:348-350 Ap 1993.
    Murphy, Roland E. *OTA* 15:515 O 1992.

Prevost, Jean-Pierre.
How to read the apocalypse. Crossroad, n.d.
    Graham, William C. *Nat Cath Rep* 30:15 O 22 1993.
Pour lire l'Apocalypse. Cerf, 1991.
    Toubeau, A. *NRT* 114:941-942 N-D 1992.

Prezzolini, Giuseppe.
L'arte di persuadere. Liguori, 1991.
    Baragli, Enrico. *Civilta* 3:207 Jl 17 1993.

Price, Elizabeth Box, and Foster, Charles R, eds.
By what authority: a conversation on teaching among United Methodists.
Abingdon, 1991.
    Wilhauck, Susan. *Living Light* 30:105-106 Aut 1993.

Price, Glanville, ed.
The Celtic connection. Colin Smythe, 1992.
    Ó Laoghaire, Diarmuid. *Studies* 82:365-368 Aut 1993.

Price, H H.
Blackberry season: a time to mourn, a time to heal. Luramedia, n.d.
    Schaper, Donna. *St Anth* 101:52 N 1993.

Prickett, John.
Godspells. The Book Guild, n.d.
    Hollings, Michael. *Tablet* 247:1304 O 9 1993.

Prickett, Stephen, and Barnes, Robert.
The Bible. Cambridge University Press, 1991.
    Heiser, W Charles. *TheolDgst* 40:82 Spr 1993.
    Pearce, Sarah. *Heythrop* 34:430-431 O 1993.

Priestland, Gerald.
My pilgrim way. Mowbray, n.d.
    Furlong, Monica, 1930-. *Tablet* 247:1265-1266 O 2 1993.

Prieto, Moïse.
Fioretti de Jean XXIII. Centurion, 1992.
    Partos, L. *Lumen* 48:237 Je 1993.

Prigent, Pierre.
Le Judaïsme et l'image. J C B Mohr, 1990.
    Prato, Gian Luigi. *Gregorianum* 73 No 4:747-750 1992.

Primatt, Humphry.
The duty of mercy: and the sin of cruelty to brute animals. Centaur Press, n.d.
    Caldecott, Stratford. *Tablet* 247:1233-1234 S 25 1993.

Primavesi, Anne.
From Apocalypse to Genesis: ecology, feminism and christianity. Fortress Press, 1991.
Rosenblatt, Mary-Eloise. *Horizons (CTS)* 20:159-160 Spr 1993.
From Apocalypse to Genesis: ecology, feminism and Christianity. Tunbridge Wells, Burns and Oates, 1991.
Jeffers, Ann. *Heythrop* 34:444-445 O 1993.

Prime, Ranchor, ed.
Hinduism and ecology. Cassell, n.d.
McDonagh, Sean. *Furrow* 44:120-123 F 1993.

Prince, Michele.
Mandatory celibacy: a handbook for the laity. New Paradigm Books, n.d.
Graham, William C. *Nat Cath Rep* 29:40 F 5 1993.

Prini, Pietro.
Il corpo che siame: introduzione all'antropologia etica. SEI, 1991.
Valori, J. *Civilta* 144:515-516 Mr 6 1993.

Pritchard, Gretchen Wolff.
Offering the Gospel to children. Cowley Publications, n.d.
McCann, Deborah. *ReligTJ* 27:10 Ap-My 1993.

Privitera, Salvatore.
Il volto morale dell'uomo. Edi Oftes, 1991.
Cultrera, Francesco. *Civilta* 3:89-91 Jl 3 1993.

Procter-Smith, Marjorie.
In her own Rite: constructing feminist liturgical tradition. Abingdon Press, 1990.
Irwin, Joyce. *JEcumen Stds* 29:481-482 Sum-Aut 1992.

Prodi, Paolo.
Il sacramento del potere: Il giuramento politico nella storia costituzionale dell'Occidente. Società editrice il Mulino, 1992.
Izbicki, Thomas M. *CHist* 79:90-91 Ja 1993.

The promise of his glory: for the season from All Saints to Candlemas, commended by the House of Bishops of the General Synod of England.
The Liturgical Press, 1991.
Mitchell, Leonel L. *Worship* 67:177-179 Mr 1993.

Prozesky, Martin.
A new guide to the debate about God. SCM, 1992.
Tolhurst, Joseph. *Priests & People* 7:168 Ap 1993.
Gallagher, Michael Paul, 1939-. *Tablet* 247:823-824 Je 26 1993.

Pryer, Peter.
Jottings: historical and political. Arthur H Stockwell Ltd, 1991.
Williams, Alison. *Teilhard Rev* 27:97-98 Wint 1992.

Pryor, John W.
John: evangelist of the covenant people. InterVarsity Press, 1992.
Heiser, W Charles. *TheolDgst* 40:182 Sum 1993.

The Psalms, New American Bible 1991.
The Liturgical Press, 1992.
Stuhlmueller, Carroll. *BibleT* 31:121 Mr 1993.

Pseudo-Palladio.
Le geni dell'India e i Brahmani. Citta Nuova, 1992.
Ferrua, Antonio. *Civilta* 3:232-324 Ag 7-21 1993.

Puls, Joan.
Seek treasures in small fields: everyday holiness. Twenty-Third, 1993.
Graham, William C. *Nat Cath Rep* 29:24 Mr 26 1993.
Laemmle, Mary Xavier. *Sisters* 65:223 My 1993.
Stout, Nancy T. *St Anth* 101:50-51 O 1993.

Puritz, Gerd.
Elisabeth Schumann. Andre Deutsch, n.d.
Amis, John. *Tablet* 247:585 My 8 1993.

Purroy Turrillas, Carmen.
Un libro inédito de Lebrón sobre diezmos en Indias. Ediciones Universicad de Navarra, 1991.
Salinas, Carlos. *Teol Vida* 33 no 3-4:327-328 1992.

Purvis, James D.
Jerusalem, the holy city. The Scarecrow Press, 1991.
McCreesh, Thomas P. *OTA* 15:487 O 1992.

Pury, Albert De, ed.
Le Pentateuque en question. Labor et Fides, 1991.
Begg, Christopher T. *OTA* 16:167 F 1993.

Putnam, Hilary.
Realism with a human face. Harvard University Press, 1990.
Kerr, Fergus. *Heythrop* 34:103-104 Ja 1993.

Putti, Joseph.
Theology as hermeneutics. Kristu Jyoti Publications, n.d.
Corbett, Thomas. *Furrow* 44:126 F 1993.

Q

Quacquarelli, Antonio.
Le radici patristiche della teologia di Antonio Rosmini. Edipuglia, 1991.
Halleux, André de. *Eph Theol Lovan* 78:449 D 1992.

Quando Karol aveva 18 anni.
Ed Paoline, 1992.
Caprile, Giovanni. *Civilta* 2:612-613 Je 19 1993.

Quattrocchi, Paolino Beltrame.
Monaci nella tormenta: La "Passio" dei monaci trappisti di Yan-Kia-ping e di Liese testimoni della fede nella Cina di Mao-Tze-Tung. Abbaye de Cîteaux, 1991.
Wiest, J. *CHist* 78:701-702 O 1992.
Posso darti del tu, Signore? Note di Catechesi sulla preghiera, vol I. Piemme, 1991.
Caprile, Giovanni. *Civilta* 2:198-199 Ap 17 1993.

Quenot, Michel.
The icon. St Vladimir's Seminary Press, 1991.
Kowal, Peter. *Furrow* 44:453-454 Jl-Ag 1993.
Heiser, W Charles. *TheolDgst* 40:182-183 Sum 1993.

La questione dell'utilitarismo.
Marietti, 1991.
Pirola, G. *Civilta* 2:205 Ap 17 1993.

Quigley, Martin S.
Peace without Hiroshima: secret action at the Vatican in the Spring of 1945.
Madison Books, n.d.
MacEoin, Gary. *Nat Cath Rep* 29:15 F 26 1993.

Quill, Timothy E.
Death and dignity. W W Norton, n.d.
Jordan, Patrick. *Comm* 120:22-23 Jl 16 1993.

Quindlen, Anna.
Thinking out loud. Random House, n.d.
Woodward, Kenneth L. *Comm* 120:17-18+ My 21 1993.

Quiney, Anthony, and Meers, Nick.
Panorama of English villages. Weidenfeld & Nicholson, n.d.
Blythe, Ronald. *Tablet* 247:891 Jl 10 1993.

Quinn, John F.
The Christian foundations of criminal responsibility: a philosophical study of legal reasoning. The Edwin Mellen Press, 1991.
Heiser, W Charles. *TheolDgst* 40:82-83 Spr 1993.

Quinonez, Lora Ann, and Turner, Mary Daniel.
The transformation of American Catholic sisters. Temple University Press, 1992.
Bland, Joan. *CHist* 79:375-376 Ap 1993.
Mayeski, Marie Ann. *ACHSR* 103:47-48 Aut 1992.

R

Rabaté, J-M, and Wetzel, M, eds.
L'éthique du don. Transition, 1992.
Boissinot, Christian. *Laval Theol Phil* 49:339-342 Je 1993.

Racca, Giorgio.
Paola pio Perazzo: Il ferroviere santo. Messaggero, 1991.
Ganzi, I M. *Civilta* 143:536 D 5 1992.

Radday, Yehuda T, and Brenner, Athalya, eds.
On humour and the comic in the Hebrew Bible. Almond, 1990.
Culley, Robert C. *CBQ* 55:201-202 Ja 1993.
Mulrooney, Joseph. *Heythrop* 34:307-308 Jl 1993.

Rademacher, William J.
Lay ministry: a theological, spiritual, and pastoral handbook. Crossroad Continuum, n.d.
Dutka, Joanna. *Can Cath Rev* 11:29-30 Jl-Ag 1993.

Radi, Luciano.
La grande maestra: la Tv tra politica e società. Cinque Lune, 1991.
Baragli, Enrico. *Civilta* 144:102-103 Ja 2 1993.

Rae, John.
Delusions of grandeur. HarperCollins, n.d.
Denniston, Robin. *Tablet* 247:479-480 Ap 10-17 1993.

Raffaelli, Sergio.
La lingua filmata: Didascalie e dialoghi nel cinema italiano. Le Lettere, 1992.
Baragli, Enrico. *Civilta* 144:102 Ja 2 1993.

Raffelt, A.
Proseminar theologie. Herder, 1992.
Harvengt, A. *NRT* 115:289-290 Mr-Ap 1993.

Rafferty, Oliver, ed.
Reconciliation. Essays in honour of Michael Hurley. Columba Press, n.d.
Carroll, Denis. *Furrow* 44:514-515 S 1993.

Raguin, Yves.
Au-delà de son rêve: Délia Tétreault. Fides Editions, 1991.
Tremblay, Donald. *CHist* 79:378-379 Ap 1993.

Rahner, Karl, 1904-1984.
Le courage du théologien dialogues publiés par Paul Imhof et Huber Biallowons. Cerf, 1985.
Partos, L. *Lumen* 47:472 D 1992.
Final writings. Crossroad, 1992.
Heiser, W Charles. *TheolDgst* 40:83 Spr 1993.
The liturgy of the world. The Liturgical Press, n.d.
Lord, Elizabeth. *Way* 33:156 Ap 1993.
Theological investigations XXII. Crossroad, 1992.
Cunningham, Lawrence S, 1935-. *Cist Stud* 28:[2]-[3] 1993.
Pelzel, Morris. *Living Light* 29:95 Sum 1993.
Cunningham, Lawrence S, 1935-. *Cist Stud* 28:[2]-[3] 1993.
Seasoltz, R Kevin. *Worship* 67:90-92 Ja 1993.
Endean, Philip. *Month* 26:76-77 F 1993.

Raine, Kathleen.
Living with myster: poems 1987-91. Golgonooza Press, n.d.
Jennings, Elizabeth, 1926-. *Tablet* 247:824 Je 26 1993.

Räisänen, Heikki.
The Messianic secret in Mark's Gospel. Clark, 1990-.
Wansbrough, Henry. *Priests & People* 6:435-436 N 1992.
Quesnell, Quentin. *CBQ* 54:798-799 O 1992.

Raiser, Konrad.
Ecumenism in transition. WCC, 1991.
Heiser, W Charles. *TheolDgst* 39:381 Wint 1992.

Raiser, Konrad. *(cont'd)*
Finger, Thomas. *Ecumen Trends* 22:5-9 Ap 1993.
Ellingsen, Mark. *JEcumen Stds* 29:470-472 Sum-Aut 1992.
Newbigin, Lesslie. *OChr* 29 no 3:269-275 1993.

Rajchman, John.
Truth and eros: Foucault, Lacan, and the question of ethics. Routledge, 1991.
Rainwater, M V. *IJPS* 1:167 Mr 1993.

Rakoczy, Susan, ed.
Common journey, different paths: spiritual direction in a cross-cultural perspective. Orbis Books, 1992.
Heiser, W Charles. *TheolDgst* 40:58 Spr 1993.
Maruca, Dominic. *Gregorianum* 74 no 3:588-589 1993.
Burke, Christine E. *Pacifica* 6:357-359 O 1993.

Rakover, Nahum.
The multi-language bibliography of Jewish law. The Jewish Legal Heritage Society, 1990.
Begg, Christopher T. *OTA* 15:487 O 1992.

Ralph, Margaret Nutting.
Discovering Old Testament origins. Paulist Press, 1992.
Begg, Christopher T. *OTA* 16:164 F 1993.
Stuhlmueller, Carroll. *BibleT* 31:121 Mr 1993.
Discovering the first century Church: the Acts of the Apostles, Letters of Paul and the Book of Revelation. Paulist Press, n.d.
Kistner, H. *St Anth* 100:50-52 F 1993.

Ralston, Helen.
Christian ashrams: a new religious movement in contemporary India. Edwin Mellen Press, 1987.
Baker, John F. *Can Cath Rev* 11:31 Mr 1993.
Rambachan, Anantanand. *JEcumen Stds* 29:283 Spr 1992.

Rambali, Paul.
It's all true. Heinemann, n.d.
Walton, James. *Tablet* 247:584 My 8 1993.

Ramet, Pedro, ed.
Cross and commissar: the politics of religion in Eastern Europe and the USSR. Indiana University Press, 1987.
Hull, Henry Lane. *CHist* 79:126-128 Ja 1993.
Eastern Christianity and politics in the twentieth century. Duke University Press, 1988.
Hull, Henry Lane. *CHist* 79:126-128 Ja 1993.

Ramet, Sabrina Petra, ed.
Religious policy in the Soviet Union. Cambridge University Press, n.d.
Bourdeaux, Michael, 1934-. *Tablet* 247:3-4 Ja 2 1993.

Ramey, Robert Homer.
Living the Christian life: a guide to reformed spirituality. John Knox Press, 1992.
Heiser, W Charles. *TheolDgst* 39:381 Wint 1992.

Ramírez, Iacobus M.
De gratia Dei: in I-II Summae theologiae divi Thomae expositio. Ed San Esteban, 1992.
Bandera, Armando. *Cien Tom* 120:191-193 Ja-Ap 1993.

Ramon, Brother.
Forty days and forty nights: a guide for spending time alone with God. Marshall Pickering, n.d.
Forrester, David. *Tablet* 247:586 My 8 1993.

Ramsey, Nigel, et al, eds.
St Dunstan. The Boydell Press, 1992.
John, Eric. *CHist* 79:517-518 Jl 1993.

Ramshaw, Gail.
Sunday morning. Liturgy Training Publications, n.d.
Graham, William C. *Nat Cath Rep* 29:18 Jl 16 1993.
Words that sing. Liturgy Training Publications, 1992.
Lazar, John E. *Mod Lit* 19:41-42 D 1992-Ja 1993.
Field, Anne. *Worship* 67:179-181 Mr 1993.
O'Keefe, Jane. *Past Mus* 18:59-60 O-N 1993.

Ramsland, Katherine.
Prism of the night: a biography of Anne Rice. McClelland & Stewart, n.d.
Coren, Michael. *Can Cath Rev* 11:4-6 F 1993.

Randisi, Jennifer Lynn.
On her way rejoicing: the fiction of Muriel Spark. The Catholic University of America Press, 1991.
Leonard, Joan. *Relig Lit* 25:87-91 Spr 1993.

Ranieri, Ralph.
The road ultimately traveled. Liguori, 1993.
Higgins, James J. *Liguorian* 81:68 D 1993.

Ranke-Heinemann, Uta.
Eunuchs for the kingdom of God: women, sexuality and the Catholic Church. Doubleday, 1990.
Kappler, Sheila. *Can Cath Rev* 11:28 O 1993.
Gudorf, Christine E. *Horizons (CTS)* 20:186-187 Spr 1993.

Rashkow, Ilona N.
Upon the dark places: anti-Semitism and sexism in English Renaissance Biblical translation. Almond, 1990.
Begg, Christopher T. *OTA* 15:487-488 O 1992.
Heiser, W Charles. *TheolDgst* 39:381 Wint 1992.

Raspanti, Antonino.
Filosofia, teologia, religione. Edi Oftes, 1991.
Brito, Emilio. *Eph Theol Lovan* 78:460 D 1992.

Rassegna di Letteratura Tomistica, vol XXV, anno 1989.
Editrice Domenicana Italiana, 1992.
Osuna, Antonio. *Cien Tom* 119:628-629 S-D 1992.

Rast, Walter E.
Through the ages in Palestinian archaeology. Trinity, 1992.
Senior, Donald. *BibleT* 31:316 S 1993.
Murphy, Roland E. *OTA* 16:412 Je 1993.

Ratcliff, Donald E, ed.
Handbook of children's religious education. Religious Education Press, 1992.
Willhauck, Susan. *Living Light* 29:77-79 Wint 1992.
Heiser, W Charles. *TheolDgst* 40:66-67 Spr 1993.

Ratcliff, Donald E, and Neff, Blake J.
The complete guide to religious educational vouchers. Religious Education Press, 1992.
Brown, Anne. *Momentum* 24:78 N-D 1993.

Ratcliff, Donald E, and Davies, James A, eds.
Handbook of youth ministry. REP Books, 1991.
Roach, Joseph J. *Living Light* 29:85-86 Spr 1993.

Ratherius, of Verona, 890?-974.
The complete works of Rather of Verona. Medieval & Renaissance texts & studies, 1991.
Heiser, W Charles. *TheolDgst* 40:83 Spr 1993.

Ratushinskaya, Irina.
Dance with a shadow. Bloodaxe, n.d.
Bergonzi, Bernard, 1929-. *Tablet* 247:170-171 F 6 1993.

Ratzinger, Joseph, Cardinal, 1927-.
Co-workers of the truth: meditations for every day of the year. Ignatius Press, n.d.
Myers, Rawley. *HPR* 93:86-87 Ag-S 1993.
Église et théologie. Mame, 1992.
Anon. *NRT* 115:622 Jl-Ag 1993.

Ratzinger, Joseph, Cardinal, 1927-, and Henrici, Peter, eds.
Credo. Communio, 1992.
Anon. *NRT* 115:620 Jl-Ag 1993.

Raub, John Jacob.
Who told you that you were naked? Crossroad Publishing Company, n.d.
Neal, Marianna Kane. *St Anth* 100:51-52 Ap 1993.

Raudive, Zenta Maurina.
Dostoevskij: creatore di uomini e cercatore di Dio. Ed Paoline, 1992.
Flumeri, E. *Civilta* 3:341-342 Ag 7-21 1993.

Rausch, David A.
A legacy of hatred: why Christians must not forget the Holocaust. Baker Book House, 1990.
Davies, Alan. *JEcumen Stds* 29:126-127 Wint 1992.

Rausch, Thomas P., ed.
The college student's introduction to theology. Liturgical, n.d.
Graham, William C. *Nat Cath Rep* 30:36 N 19 1993.

Rausch, Thomas P.
Priesthood today. Paulist, 1992.
MacCarthy, Peter T. *HPR* 93:75 Je 1993.
Higgins, James J. *Liguorian* 81:69 Je 1993.
Heiser, W Charles. *TheolDgst* 40:183 Sum 1993.
Collins, Raymond F. *Louvain Stds* 18:190 Sum 1993.
Radical Christian communities. Liturgical, 1990.
Sutera, Judith. *Cist Stud* 28:[29]-[30] 1993.

Ravasi, Gianfranco.
El libro del Génesis (1-11). Herder, 1992.
Mondoni, Danilo. *Perspectiva* 25:265-266 My-Ag 1993.

Raw, Barbara C.
Anglo-Saxon crucifixion iconography, and the art of the monastic revival. Cambridge University Press, 1990.
Scollard, Anselma. *Cist Stud* 27 No 4:[91]-[93] 1992.

Rawle, Tim.
Cambridge architecture. André Deutsch, n.d.
Nuttgens, Patrick, 1930-. *Tablet* 247:861 Jl 3 1993.

Ray, Ronald D.
Military necessity and homosexuality. USMCR, 1992.
Miller, John H. *SocJust* 84:126 Jl-Ag 1993.

Rayburn, William D.
A handbook on the Book of Job. United Bible Societies, 1992.
Begg, Christopher T. *OTA* 16:424 Je 1993.

Raymo, Chet.
The dork of Cork. Warner Books, n.d.
Collins, Clare. *Comm* 120:23-24 Jl 16 1993.

Read, Piers Paul.
Ablaze—the story of Chernobyl. Secker & Warburgh, n.d.
Rich, Vera. *Tablet* 247:756-757 Je 1993.

Rebirth: a history of Europe since World War II.
Westview, 1992.
Macchi, Angelo. *Civilta* 3:325-326 Ag 7-21 1993.

Recinos, Harold Joseph.
Jesus weeps. Abingdon Press, 1992.
Heiser, W Charles. *TheolDgst* 40:183 Sum 1993.

Redaelli, Carlo Roberto M.
Il concetto di diritto della chiesa nella riflessione canonistica tra concilio e codice. Glossa, 1991.
Chirlanda, G. *Civilta* 143:524-525 D 5 1992.

Redford, Donald B.
Egypt, Canaan, and Israel in ancient times. Princeton University, 1992.
Murphy, Roland E. *OTA* 16:165 F 1993.

Reding, José.
Traversées. Vie Ouvrière, 1992.
Foisson, A. *Lumen* 48:112-113 Mr 1993.

Redmont, Jane.
Generous lives. William Morrow, 1992.
Windsor, Patriciag. *Comm* 119:20-21 D 18 1992.
Wagner, Christine. *Sisters* 65:138 Mr 1993.
Cinnici, Rosemary. *America* 168:18-19 Ap 17 1993.
Cunneen, Sally. *CrossCurr* 43:128-129 Spr 1993.
Swidler, Arlene. *St Anth* 101:48 Je 1993.

Redmont, Jane. *(cont'd)*
Williams, Joan. *Living Prayer* 26:33 Jl-Ag 1993.
Heiser, W Charles. *TheolDgst* 40:183 Sum 1993.
Kenel, Sally A. *Living Light* 30:107-108 Aut 1993.

Reeder, Ray.
The Bach English-title index. Fallen Leaf Press, 1993.
Schuler, Richard Joseph, 1920-. *SacM* 120:40 Aut 1993.

Reedy, Gerard.
Robert South (1634-1716). Cambridge University Press, 1992.
Heiser, W Charles. *TheolDgst* 40:83 Spr 1993.
Wall, John N. *TheolStds* 54:600-601 S 1993.

Rees, Nigel.
Epitaphs. Bloomsbury, n.d.
Braybrooke, Neville. *Tablet* 247:374 Mr 20 1993.

Reese, Thomas Joseph, 1945-.
A flock of shepherds. Sheed & Ward, 1992.
Byrnes, Timothy A. *Comm* 120:28-29 Ja 29 1993.
Cooke, Bernard. *America* 169:20-21 Jl 17-24 1993.
McCloskey, Pat. *ST Anth* 101:51-52 Jl 1993.
Heiser, W Charles. *TheolDgst* 40:183 Sum 1993.

Reese, Thomas Joseph, 1945-, ed.
Episcopal conferences. Georgetown University Press, n.d.
Morrisey, Francis G. *Can Cath Rev* 11:30 Ap 1993.

Régerat, Philippe.
Eugippe: Vie de saint Séverin. Cerf, 1991.
Halleux, André de. *Eph Theol Lovan* 78:457-458 D 1992.

Reid, Gordon.
The wind from the stars: through the year with George MacDonald. Harper-
Collins, n.d.
Forrester, David. *Tablet* 247:728 Je 5 1993.

Reidy, Michael, and McCullough, Domhnall, eds.
Principle and profit: corporate responsibility in Ireland. Columba Press, n.d.
Graham, K. *Furrow* 44:58-59 Ja 1993.

Reilly, Robin.
Josiah Wedgwood. Macmillan, n.d.
Cooke, Judy. *Tablet* 247:277-278 F 27 1993.

Reinerman, Alan J.
*Austria and the Papacy in the Age Metternich, volume 2: revolution and
reaction, 1830-1838.* Catholic University of America Press, 1989.
Bertier de Sauvigny, G de. *CHist* 79:546-547 Jl 1993.

Reisman, Judith A.
Soft porn plays hardball. Huntington House, n.d.
Miller, John H. *SocJust* 84:126-127 Jl-Ag 1993.

Reist, Benjamin A.
Processive revelation. John Knox Press, 1992.
Heiser, W Charles. *TheolDgst* 40:183-184 Sum 1993.

Reiterer, Friedrich V, ed.
*Ein Gott, eine Offenbarung: Beiträge zur biblischen Exegese, Theologie, und
Spiritualität.* Echter, 1991.
Hensell, Eugene M. *CBQ* 55:416-417 Ap 1993.

La religion de ma mère: Les femmes et la transmission de la foi.
Cerf, 1992.
Gibson, Ralph. *CHist* 79:306-307 Ap 1993.

Renard, John.
In the footsteps of Muhammad: understanding the Islamic experience. Paul-
ist Press, 1992.
Heiser, W Charles. *TheolDgst* 39:381-382 Wint 1992.

Renaud, Bernard.
La théophanie du Sinaï, Ex 19-24: exégèse et théologie. Gabalda, 1991.
Vogels, Walter A. *CBQ* 55:130-131 Ja 1993.

Renault, Alain, and Sosoe, Lukas.
Philosophie du droit. Presses Universitaires de Frances, 1991.
Ponton, Lionel. *Laval Theol Phil* 49:352-354 Je 1993.

Rendsburg, Gary A.
Linguistic evidence for the Northern origin of selected Psalms. Scholars
Press, 1990.
Schoors, A. *Eph Theol Lovan* 78:423-424 D 1992.

Repertorium annotatum operum et translationum S Augustini.
Augustinus Verlag, 1992.
Roisel, V. *NRT* 114:907 N-D 1992.

Reumann, John Henry Paul, 1927-.
Stewardship and the economy of God. William B Eerdmans Publishing Co,
1992.
Stuhlmueller, Carroll. *BibleT* 31:125-126 Mr 1993.

Reumann, John Henry Paul.
Stewardship and the economy of God. The Ecumenical Center for Steward-
ship Studies, 1992.
Heiser, W Charles. *TheolDgst* 40:184 Sum 1993.
Variety and unity in New Testament thought. Oxford University Press, 1991.
Bode, Edward L. *Bib Th Bul* 23:136 Aut 1993.

Reumann, John Henry Paul, ed.
The promise and practice of Biblical theology. Fortress, 1991.
Adam, Andrew K M. *CBQ* 55:417-418 Ap 1993.

Reuther, Rosemary Radford.
Gaia and God: an ecofeminist theology of earth healing. HarperCollins, n.d.
Coll, Regina. *Nat Cath Rep* 29:27 F 5 1993.

The revised common lectionary.
Canterbury Press, n.d.
Sands, Ernest. *Tablet* 247:725 Je 5 1993.

The revised psalms of the New American Bible.
Catholic Book, 1992.
Smith, Mark S. *OTA* 15:486-487 O 1992.

The revised Psalms of the New American Bible.
Catholic Book Publishing Co, 1992.
Heiser, W Charles. *TheolDgst* 40:52 Spr 1993.

Rex, Richard.
The theology of John Fisher. Cambridge University Press, 1991.
Stafford, W. *CHist* 78:650-651 O 1992.
Evrard, P. *NRT* 114:929-930 N-D 1992.

Reyburn, William D.
A handbook on lamentations. United Bible Societies, 1992.
Begg, Christopher T. *OTA* 16:432 Je 1993.

Reymond, B.
Entre la grâce et la foi. Labor et Fides, 1992.
Evrard, P. *NRT* 115:121-122 Ja-F 1993.

Reynier, Chantal.
Évangile et mystère. Cerf, 1992.
Partos, L. *Lumen* 47:469 D 1992.
L'évangile selon saint Jean. Médiasèvres, 1991.
Simoens, Y. *NRT* 115:108 Ja-F 1993.

Reynolds, Barbara.
Dorothy L Sayers. Hodder & Stoughton, n.d.
Lejeune, Anthony. *Tablet* 247:478-479 Ap 10-17 1993.

Reynolds, Joseph.
Grangegorman, psychiatric care in Dublin since 1815. Institute of Public
Administration, 1991.
O'Sullivan, Tim. *Studies* 82:362-364 Aut 1993.

Rhodes, Anthony.
The Vatican in the age of the Cold War 1945-1980. Michael Russell, n.d.
Cviic, Christopher. *Tablet* 247:1012-1013 Ag 7 1993.

Ricci, M.
The true meaning of the Lord of heaven (T'ien-chu Shis-i). Institut Ricci,
1985.
Scheuer, J. *NRT* 115:602 Jl-Ag 1993.

Rice, David.
Shattered vows. Triumph Books, 1992.
Kennedy, L. *HPR* 93:65-67 F 1993.
Shattered vows. Michael Joseph, 1990.
Mulrooney, Joseph. *Heythrop* 34:350-351 Jl 1993.

Rice, Eva.
Sam who never forgets. Greenwillow Books, 1977.
Neuberger, Anne E. *ReligTJ* 26:33 Ja 1993.

Rice, Jonathan.
Curiosities of cricket. Pavilion Press, n.d.
McLean, Teresa. *Tablet* 247:408 Mr 27 1993.

Richard, Lucien.
What are they saying about the theology of suffering? Paulist Press, 1992.
Williams, Joan. *Living Prayer* 26:33 My-Je 1993.
Anon. *Health Prog* 74:68 My 1993.

Richard, Réginald.
Psychologie et spiritualité: à la recherche d'une interface. Presses de
l'Université Laval, 1992.
Godin, A. *Lumen* 48:116-117 Mr 1993.

Richards, E Randolph.
The secretary in the letters of Paul. Mohr, 1991.
Fiore, Benjamin. *CBQ* 55:391-392 Ap 1993.

Richards, Fiona V.
Scarab seals from a middle to late Bronze Age tomb at Pella in Jordan.
Vandenhoeck and Ruprecht, 1992.
Fitzgerald, Aloysius. *OTA* 16:165 F 1993.

Richards, Hubart.
The Gospel according to St Paul. The Liturgical Press, 1990.
Senior, Donald. *BibleT* 31:61 Ja 1993.

Richardson, Peter, and Westerholm, Stephen.
*Law in religious communities in the Roman period: the debate over Torah
and Nomos in Post-Biblical Judaism and Early Christianity.* Wilfrid Laurier University, 1991.
McNamara, Martin. *CBQ* 55:202-203 Ja 1993.

Richardson, Rosamond.
The long shadow: inside Stalin's family. Little, Brown & Co, n.d.
Fitzlyon, April. *Tablet* 247:920-921 Jl 17 1993.

Riches, John.
The world of Jesus: first century Judaism in crisis. Cambridge University,
1990.
Winkler, Jude. *CBQ* 54:788-789 O 1992.

Ricoeur, Paul.
Lectures 1: autour du politique. Éditions du Seuil, 1991.
Ponton, Lionel. *Laval Theol Phil* 49:348-350 Je 1993.
Oneself as another. University of Chicago Press, n.d.
Osborne, Kenan B. *America* 169:27-28 Jl 3-10 1993.

Ridley, Jasper.
Maximilian and Juarez. Constable, n.d.
Latham-Koenig, Alfred. *Tablet* 247:1014 Ag 7 1993.

Rigal, J.
Le mystère de l'Église. Ed du Cerf, 1992.
Renard, L-J. *NRT* 115:582-583 Jl-Ag 1993.

Riley, Harold.
The First Gospel. Mercer University Press, 1992.
Neirynck, F. *Eph Theol Lovan* 69:179-180 Ap 1993.

Riley, Patrick, ed.
Bossuet: politics drawn from Holy Scripture. Cambridge University Press,
1991.
Levi, A.H.T. *Heythrop* 34:435 O 1993.

Riley-Smith, J, ed.
Grosser Bildatlas der Kreuzzüge. Herder, 1992.
Plumat, N. *NRT* 115:287 Mr-Ap 1993.

Rinaldi, Remo.
Vigilio Federico Dalla Zuanna. Colibrì, 1992.
Scurani, Allesandro. *Civilta* 3:98-99 Jl 3 1993.

Rinpoche, Sogyal.
The Tibetan book of living and dying. Rider, n.d.
Roose-Evans, James. *Tablet* 247:1234-1235 S 25 1993.

Rinser, Luise.
Diario del carcere. Piemme, 1991.
Flumeri, E. *Civilta* 144:617-618 Mr 20 1993.
Rippin, Andrew, and Knappert, Jan, eds.
Textual sources for the study of Islam. The University of Chicago Press, 1990.
Burrell, David B. *Horizons (CTS)* 19:348-349 Fall 1992.
Risse, Günter.
Gott ist Christus der Sohn der Maria. Borengässer, 1989.
Bent, Ans J van der. *JEcumen Stds* 29:489 Sum-Aut 1992.
Rite of Baptism for children.
Geoffrey Chapman, n.d.
Sands, Ernest. *Tablet* 247:725 Je 5 1993.
Ritter, Joachim, and Gründer, Karlfried.
Historisches Wörterbuch der Philosophie. Schwabe, 1992.
Kern, Walter O. *Stimm Zeit* 211:574-575 Ag 1993.
A ritual for laypersons.
The Liturgical Press, n.d.
Anon. *Church* 9:42 Aut 1993.
Rivera, Luis N.
A violent evangelism: the political and religious conquest of the Americas.
John Knox, 1992.
Dodd, Thomas. *TheolStds* 54:569-571 S 1993.
Cleary, Edward L. *America* 169:19+ O 23 1993.
Rix, Martyn.
Perennials. Pan, n.d.
Taylor, Patrick. *Tablet* 247:375 Mr 20 1993.
Rizzi, Giuseppe.
L'uomo in Maritain. Logos, 1990.
Lorizio, G. *Civilta* 144:204-205 Ja 16 1993.
Robb, Carol S, and Casebolt, Carl J, eds.
Covenant for a new creation: ethics, religion, and public policy. Orbis Books, 1991.
Horrell, D. *New Theol Rev* 6:104-104 F 1993.
Di Domizio, Daniel. *Living Light* 29:87-88 Aut 1992.
Robbins, Jill.
Prodigal son/elder brother: interpretation and altereity in Augustine, Petrarch, Kafka, Levinas. University of Chicago Press, 1991.
Gareffa, Michael. *TheolStds* 54:193-194 Mr 1993.
Robbins, Martha A.
Midlife women and death of mother: a study of psychohistorical and spiritual transformation. Peter Lang, 1990.
McIntyre, Moni. *Horizons (CTS)* 20:175-176 Spr 1993.
Robelin, Jean.
Maïmonide et le langage religieux. PUF, 1991.
Valevičius, Andrius. *Laval Theol Phil* 49:374-375 Je 1993.
Robert, A, ed.
Charles de Foucauld: Cette chère dernière place. Éd du Cerf, 1991.
Navez, G. *NRT* 115:284 Mr-Ap 1993.
Roberto, John, ed.
The Catholic family series. Multimedia, 1992.
McCann, Deborah. *ReligTJ* 27:9 My 1993.
Roach, Joseph J. *Living Light* 30:100 Aut 1993.
Family rituals and celebrations. Don Bosco Multimedia, 1993.
Borgia, Francis. *Mod Lit* 20:38 Ap 1993.
Roach, Joseph J. *Living Light* 30:101-102 Aut 1993.
Media, faith, and families. No publisher given, n.d.
Roach, Joseph J. *Living Light* 30:101 Aut 1993.
Roach, Joseph J. *Living Light* 30:101 Aut 1993.
Rituals for sharing faith: a resource for parish ministers. No publisher given, n.d.
Roach, Joseph J. *Living Light* 30:101-102 Aut 1993.
Roberts, J J M.
Nahum, Habakkuk and Zephaniah. John Knox, 1991.
Wimmer, Joseph F. *OTA* 15:511 O 1992.
Robertson, Clare.
"Il Gran Cardinale": Alessandro Farnese, patron of the arts. Yale University Press, 1992.
Coffin, David R. *CHist* 79:108-109 Ja 1993.
Heiser, W Charles. *TheolDgst* 40:84 Spr 1993.
Robertson, O Palmer.
The Books of Nahum, Habakkuk, and Zephaniah. Eerdmans, 1990.
Mariottini, Claude F. *OTA* 15:511-512 O 1992.
Robillard, Edmond.
Reincarnation: illusion or reality? Alba House, 1992.
Mangan, Charles M. *HPR* 93:71-72 Ap 1993.
Robinson, Fred Miller.
The man in the bowler hat, his history and iconography. University of North Carolina Press, n.d.
Anon. *Tablet* 247:1161 S 11 1993.
Robinson, I R.
The Papacy, 1073-1198: continuity and innovation. Cambridge University Press, 1990.
Dunstan, G R. *Heythrop* 34:205-208 Ap 1993.
Robinson, Kerry A.
Foundation guide for religious grant seekers. Scholars Press, 1992.
Heiser, W Charles. *TheolDgst* 39:362 Wint 1992.
Robinson, Neal.
Christ in Islam and Christianity. New York Press, 1991.
Burrell, David B. *Horizons (CTS)* 20:196-197 Spr 1993.
Rocca, Tommaso La, ed.
Thomas Müntzer e la rivoluzione dell'uomo comune. Claudiana, 1990.
Boudens, R. *Eph Theol Lovan* 78:172-173 Ap 1992.
Roccasalvo, Joan L.
The Eastern Catholic Churches: an introduction to their worship and spirituality. The Liturgical Press, 1992.
Heiser, W Charles. *TheolDgst* 39:382 Wint 1992.

Rockefeller, Steven C.
John Dewey: religious faith and democratic humanism. Columbia University Press, 1991.
Roth, Robert J. *IPQ* 33:117-122 Mr 1993.
Rockefeller, Steven C, and Elder, John C.
Spirit and nature: why the environment is a religious issue: an interfaith dialogue. Farrar, Straus & Giroux, 1992.
Heiser, W Charles. *TheolDgst* 40:88 Spr 1993.
Rockmore, Tom.
On Heidegger's Nazism and philosophy. University of Californial Press, 1992.
Schalow, Frank. *IPQ* 33:241-243 Je 1993.
Rockmore, Tom, and Singer, Beth J, eds.
Antifoundationalism old and new. Temple University Press, 1992.
Colapietro, Vincent M. *IPQ* 33:251-254 Je 1993.
Rodano, Franco.
Cattolici e laicità della politica. Editori Riuniti, 1992.
Pirola, G. *Civilta* 2:91-93 Ap 3 1993.
Rodríguez, Luis J.
La vida loca: gang days in LA. Curbstone Press, n.d.
Whitehead, F. *Nat Cath Rep* 29:6 Ja 8 1993.
Rodríguez, Petrus.
Catechismus Romanus seu Catechismus ex decreto Concilii Tridentini ad parochos Pii quinti Pont. Ediciones Universidad de Navarra, 1989.
Simon, Michele. *Eph Theol Lovan* 78:173-175 Ap 1992.
Rodriguez, Richard, 1947-.
Days of obligation. Viking, 1992.
Stavans, Ilan. *Comm* 120:20-22 Mr 26 1993.
Gilmour, Peter. *Critic* 47:71-75 Sum 1993.
Hunger of memory. Bantam, n.d.
Stavans, Ilan. *Comm* 120:20-22 Mr 26 1993.
Rodríguez, S.
Pasado y futuro de al Teología de la Liberación. Verbo Divino, 1992.
Anon. *NRT* 115:626-627 Jl-Ag 1993.
Rodríguez, Valentín.
Evolución de la Iglesia según J González Arintero. Fundación Universitaria Española, 1992.
Bandera, Armando. *Cien Tom* 120:190-191 Ja-Ap 1993.
Rodríguez Cruz, Agueda M.
La Universidad en la América Hispánica. Editorial MAPFRE, 1992.
Hernández, Ramón. *Cien Tom* 120:196-197 Ja-Ap 1993.
Roepke, Wilhelm.
The social crisis of our time. Transaction, 1992.
Karsten, Siegfried G. *RSocEcon* 51:371-374 Aut 1993.
Rofé, Alexander.
Storie di profeti. Paidei, 1991.
Prato, Gian Luigi. *Civilta* 2:605-607 Je 19 1993.
Rogers, Cleon L, Jr.
The topical Josephus. Zondervan, 1992.
Senior, Donald. *BibleT* 31:61 Ja 1993.
Begg, Christopher T. *OTA* 16:193 F 1993.
Heiser, W Charles. *TheolDgst* 40:84 Spr 1993.
Rogers, Mary Beth.
Cold anger: a story of faith and power politics. University of North Texas Press, 1990.
Finks, P David. *CrossCurr* 42:563-564 Wint 1992-1993.
Rogerson, John W.
W M L de Wette, founder of modern Biblical criticism: an intellectual biography. JSOT, 1992.
Smith, Mark S. *OTA* 15:488 O 1992.
Rogow, Arnold A.
Thomas Hobbes: un radical au service de la réaction. Presses universitaires de France, 1990.
Robberechts, Edouard. *RPhil Louvain* 91:468-471 Ag 1993.
Rohani, M K, ed.
Accents of God: selections from the World's Sacred Scriptures. Oneworld, 1991.
Nijenhuis, John. *JEcumen Stds* 29:494-495 Sum-Aut 1992.
Rohr, Richard, 1943-.
Near occasions of grace. Orbis, 1993.
Weber, Bernadette. *Sisters* 65:311-312 Jl 1993.
Ventline, Lawrence M. *St Anth* 100:48 S 1993.
Radical grace. St. Anthony Messenger Press, n.d.
Dollen, Charles. *Priest* 49:48 O 1993.
Simplicity: the art of living. Crossroad, 1990.
Johnson, Timothy. *Cist Stud* 28:[8]-[9] 1993.
Rohr, Richard, 1943-, and Martos, Joseph.
The wild man's journey: reflections on male spirituality. St Anthony Messenger, 1992.
Schmidt, J. *Sisters* 65:60-61 Ja 1993.
Toolan, David S. *Church* 9:55-58 Spr 1993.
Carmody, John Tully. *Horizons (CTS)* 20:167-168 Spr 1993.
Röhrig, Johannes.
Worte in der Fremde. Verlag A Lehmann, 1992.
Mennekes, F. *Stimm Zeit* 211:358-359 My 1993.
Rolland, Philippe.
Les ambassadeurs du Christ. Cerf, 1991.
Poutain, Thomas R. *Laval Theol Phil* 49:365-369 Je 1993.
Farahian, Edmond. *Gregorianum* 74 no 3:572-573 1993.
Huftier, M. *MSR* 50:70-71 Ja-Mr 1993.
Romanato, Gianpaolo.
Pio X: la vita di papa Sarto. Rusconi, 1992.
Mellinato, Giuseppe. *Civilta* 143:533-534 D 5 1992.
Romero, C Gilbert.
Hispanic devotional piety: tracing the biblical roots. Orbis Books, 1991.
Riley, Patrick J. *Emmanuel* 99:238-239+ My 1993.

Romero Y Galdamez, Oscar Arnulfo, Abp, 1917-1980.
Archbishop Oscar Romero: a shepherd's diary [tr by I B Hodgson]. St Anthony Messenger Press, 1993.
    Williams, Joan. *Living Prayer* 26:32 S-O 1993.

Ronald, Louis de.
On divorce [tr by N Davidson]. Transaction Publishers, n.d.
    Snyder, John J. *Can Cath Rev* 11:30-31 S 1993.

Ronsisvalle, Vanni.
Venerina. Camunia, 1993.
    Flumeri, E. *Civilta* 3:338-339 Ag 7-21 1993.

Roof, Wade Clark, 1939-.
A generation of seekers. HarperSanFrancisco, n.d.
    Anon. *America* 168:3 My 1 1993.
    Obach, Robert E. *Nat Cath Rep* 29:26 S 10 1993.
    Weber, Peggy. *St Anth* 101:50 N 1993.

Roohizadegan, Olya.
Olya's story. Oneworld Publications, n.d.
    Hodgkin, E C. *Tablet* 247:1014 Ag 7 1993.

Rooney, Lucy, and Faricy, Robert.
Signore Gesù insegnami a pregare. Corso di preghiera personale in sette settimane. Ancora, 1991.
    Caprile, Giovanni. *Civilta* 2:198-199 Ap 17 1993.

Rorty, Amelie Oksenberg.
Mind in action: essays in the philosophy of mind. Beacon Press, 1988.
    Churchill, John. *Thomist* 57:533-542 Jl 1993.

Rosa, Luigi Di.
Luigi Taparelli, l'altro D'Azeglio. Cisalpino, 1991.
    Monachino, V. *Civilta* 144:92-93 Ja 2 1993.

Rosa, Mario.
Clero e società nell'Italia contemporanea. Laterza, 1992.
    Armando, G. *Civilta* 3:318-319 Ag 7-21 1993.

Rosales, Gaudencio B, and Arevalo, Catalino G, eds.
For all the peoples of Asia. Federation of Asian Bishops' Conferences documents from 1970-1991. Orbis Books, 1992.
    Lopez-Gay, Jesus. *Gregorianum* 74 no 3:594 1993.

Rosales, Raul, and De Ferari, Jose Manuel, eds.
Breve Diccionario Teológico Latinoamericano. Ed Rehue, 1992.
    Bentué, Antonio. *Teol Vida* 34 no 1-2:158 1993.

Rosário, Antonio do.
Dominicanos em Portugal: repertório do século XVI. Instituto Historico Dominicano, 1991.
    Hernández, Ramón. *Cien Tom* 119:619 S-D 1992.

Roschini, Gabriel M.
The Virgin Mary in the writings of Maria Valtorta. Kolbe's Publications Inc, n.d.
    Roten, Johann G. *Can Cath Rev* 11:36 Ja 1993.

Rose, Aubrey, ed.
Judaism and ecology. Cassell, n.d.
    McDonagh, Sean. *Furrow* 44:120-123 F 1993.

Rösel, Hartmut N.
The Book of Amos. University of Haifa, 1990.
    Sweeney, Marvin A. *CBQ* 54:762-763 O 1992.

Rosenblatt, Jason P, and Sitterson, Joseph C, Jr, eds.
'Not in heaven': coherence and complexity in biblical narrative. Indiana University Press, 1991.
    Heiser, W Charles. *TheolDgst* 39:376-377 Wint 1992.
    Humphreys, Lee W. *CBQ* 55:419-420 Ap 1993.

Rosenblatt, Marie-Eloise, ed.
Where can we find her? searching for women's identity in the new church. Paulist, 1991.
    O'Neill, Mary Aquin. *Horizons (CTS)* 19:330-331 Fall 1992.

Rosenfield, Denis L.
Du mal: essai pour introduire en philosophie le concept du mal. Aubier, 1989.
    Pourtois, Hervé. *RPhil Louvain* 91:497 Ag 1993.

Rosenthal, Sandra B, and Bourgeois, Patrick L.
Mead and Merleau-Ponty: toward a common vision. Albany State University of New York Press, 1991.
    Wickenhauser, Timothy. *Mod Schlmn* 70:155-156 Ja 1993.

Roskies, David G, ed.
The literature of destruction: Jewish responses to catastrophe. Jewish Publication Society, 1989.
    Stuhlmueller, Carroll. *BibleT* 31:248 Jl 1993.

Rosnyh, Eric de.
L'Afrique des guérisons. Karthala, 1992.
    Seumois, A. *Civilta* 144:103 Ja 2 1993.

Rosser, B R Simon.
Gay Catholics down under. Praeger, 1992.
    Heiser, W Charles. *TheolDgst* 40:184 Sum 1993.

Rossi, Philip J, and Wreen, Michael, eds.
Kant's philosophy of religion reconsidered. Indiana University Press, 1991.
    Pepper, George B. *CrossCurr* 43:116-117 Spr 1993.

Rosswurm, Steve, ed.
The CIO's left-led unions. Rutgers University Press, n.d.
    Cort, John C. *Comm* 120:26-27 Ag 13 1993.

Un rostro nuevo para la Catequesis.
no publisher given, 1992.
    Gonzales Roser, Antonio. *Christus* 58:61 Ag 1993.

Roth, Philip.
Operation Shylock: a confession. Cape, n.d.
    Aitken, Tom. *Tablet* 247:552 My 1 1993.

Rouner, Leroy S, ed.
Celebrating peace. University of Notre Dame Press, 1990.
    Shannon, Thomas A. *JEcumen Stds* 29:110-111 Wint 1992.

Rouse, Mary A, and Rouse, Richard H.
Authentic witnesses: approaches to Medieval texts and manuscripts. University of Notre Dame Press, 1992.
    Amos, Thomas. *CHist* 79:313-314 Ap 1993.

Rousmaniere, John.
A bridge to dialogue: the story of Jewish-Christian relations. Paulist Press, 1991.
    Heiser, W Charles. *TheolDgst* 39:382 Wint 1992.

Rowan, Carl T.
Dream makers, dream breakers: the world of Justice Thurgood Marshall. Little, Brown, n.d.
    Samway, Patrick H, 1939-. *America* 168:15 Mr 20-27 1993.

Rowe, Trevor.
An easier yoke? a perspective on Christian ministry. SCM Press, n.d.
    Ward, Hannah, and Lord, Elizabeth. *Way* 33:164 Ap 1993.

Rowland, Beth, ed.
Esteem builders for children's ministry. Group Pub, 1992.
    Borgia, Francis. *Mod Lit* 20:41 O 1993.

Rowse, A L.
Four Caroline portraits. Duckworth, n.d.
    Ollard, Richard. *Tablet* 247:693 My 29 1993.

Rowthorn, Jeffery, and Schulz-Widmar, Russell, eds.
A new hymnal for colleges and schools. Yale University Press, n.d.
    Tortolano, W. *Past Mus* 17:47-48 D 1992-Ja 1993.

The Royal Horticultural Society encyclopaedia of gardening.
Dorling Kindersley, n.d.
    Taylor, Patrick. *Tablet* 247:375 Mr 20 1993.

Royal, Robert.
1492 and all that: political manipulations of history. Ethics and Public Policy Center, 1992.
    Poole, Stafford. *CHist* 79:501-502 Jl 1993.
    Schall, James Vincent, 1928-. *Crisis* 11:50-52 F 1993.
    Higgins, James J. *Liguorian* 81:68-69 My 1993.

Royo Marín, Antonio.
The great unknown. Western Hemisphere Cultural Society, 1991.
    Heiser, W Charles. *TheolDgst* 40:184-185 Sum 1993.

Royse, James R.
The spurious texts of Philo of Alexandria. Brill, 1991.
    Tobin, Thomas H. *OTA* 16:193-194 F 1993.

Royster, Dmitri, Bp.
The kingdom of God: the sermon on the mount. St. Vladimir's Seminary, 1992.
    Rexine, John E. *Diakonia* 26 no 3:196-197 1993.

Rubenstein, Richard L.
After Auschwitz. John Hopkins University Press, 1992.
    Heiser, W Charles. *TheolDgst* 40:185 Sum 1993.

Rubin, Miri.
Corpus Christi: the Eucharist in late medieval culture. Cambridge University Press, 1991.
    Burr, David. *CHist* 79:522-524 Jl 1993.

Rubinstein, Danny.
The people of nowhere. Random House, 1991.
    Stuhlmueller, Carroll. *BibleT* 31:56 Ja 1993.

Ruderman, David B, ed.
Preachers of the Italian ghetto. University of California Press, 1992.
    Heiser, W Charles. *TheolDgst* 40:182 Sum 1993.

Rudoni, Antonio.
Dizionario dei nomi geografici italiani e stranieri. Don Bosco, 1992.
    Baragli, Enrico. *Civilta* 144:616-617 Mr 20 1993.

Rüenauver, Hubert, and Heribert, Zingel.
Den Sonntag feiern. Kösel, 1992.
    Bleistein, Roman, 1928-. *Stimm Zeit* 210:861 D 1992.

Ruether, Rosemary Radford.
Gaia and God: a new theology for a renewed earth. HarperSanFrancisco, n.d.
    Taylor, Mark C, 1945-. *America* 168:26-27+ My 29 1993.

Ruffato, Francesco, ed.
Tracce di umanità nei lager nazisti: testimonianze raccolte dal Centro Culturale P M Kolbe di Venezia-Mestre. Ed Dehoniane, 1991.
    Forlizzi, G. *Civilta* 143:540 D 5 1992.

Ruffinengo, Pier Paolo.
Le cose, il pensiero, l'essere. Marietti, 1988.
    Côté, Antoine. *RPhil Louvain* 91:333-336 My 1993.

Ruggieri, Giuseppe, ed.
La Cattura della fine: varizioni dell'escatologia in regime di cristianità. Casa Editrice Marietti, 1992.
    Musto, Ronald G. *CHist* 79:496-498 Jl 1993.

Ruiz, Alphonse.
The prayers of Saint John of the Cross. New City Press, 1992.
    Moore, Patrick. *Priests & People* 7:124 Mr 1993.

Ruiz, Ramón Eduardo.
Triumphs and tragedy: a history of the Mexican people. Norton, n.d.
    Wells, Allen. *America* 169:25-26 Jl 3-10 1993.

Ruiz-de-Medina, Juan, ed.
Documentos del Japón, 1547-1557. Instituto Historico de la Compañía de Jesús, 1990.
    Witek, John W. *CHist* 79:379-381 Ap 1993.

Ruiz de la Peña, Juan Luis.
El don de Dios. Editorial Sal Terrae, 1991.
    Mees, Leonardo. *REB* 53:237-238 Mr 1993.
    Renwart, Léon. *NRT* 115:586-587 Jl-Ag 1993.

Ruiz De Montoya, Antonio, 1585-1652.
The spiritual conquest accomplished by the religious of the Society of Jesus in the provinces of Paraguay, Parand, Uruguay, and Tape. Institute of Jesuit Sources, 1993.
    Heiser, W Charles. *TheolDgst* 40:84 Spr 1993.

The rule of Benedict.
Crossroad Publishing Company, n.d.
    Anon. *Church* 9:43 Aut 1993.

The Rule of the Templars: the French text of the Rule of the Order of the Knights Templar.
Boydell, 1992.
    Elkins, Sharon. *TheolStds* 54:386 Je 1993.

The Rule of the Templars: the French text of the rule of the Order of the Knights Templar.
The Boydell Press, 1992.
    Menache, Sophia. *CHist* 79:519-520 Jl 1993.

Rumer, Jack, and Sampfer, Nathaniel, eds.
So that your values live on: ethical wills and how to prepare them. Jewish Lights, 1991.
    Frizzell, Lawrence E. *SIDIC* 25 No 2:11 1992.

Runcie, Robert.
Theology, the university and the modern world. Center for the Study of Theology in the University of Essen, n.d.
    Lord, Elizabeth. *Way* 33:76 Ja 1993.
The unity we seek. Darton, Longman and Todd, n.d.
    Kelliher, Jermiah. *Can Cath Rev* 11:28-29 Mr 1993.

Runyon, Theodore.
Theology, politics, and peace. Orbis Books, 1989.
    Shannon, Thomas A. *JEcumen Stds* 29:110-111 Wint 1992.

Ruokanen, Miika.
The Catholic doctrine of non-Christian religious according to the Second Vatican Council. Brill, 1992.
    Sullivan, Francis Aloysius. *TheolStds* 54:201 Mr 1993.

Rupp, Joyce.
May I have this dance. Ave Maria Press, 1992.
    Graham, William C. *Nat Cath Rep* 29:40 F 5 1993.
    Krawczyk, Marilyn Peters. *Mod Lit* 20:39 My 1993.

Ruppert, Lothar.
Genesis: ein kritischer und tehologischer Kommentar. Echter, 1992.
    Begg, Christopher T. *OTA* 16:168 F 1993.

Russalesi, Steven D.
The history of Roman Catholic-United Methodist dialogue in the United States. University Microfilms, 1992.
    Gros, Jeffrey, 1938-. *JEcumen Stds* 29:267-268 Spr 1992.

Russell, David Syme.
Dal primo giudaismo alla Chiesa delle origini. Paideia, 1991.
    Prata, Gian Luigi. *Civilta* 3:439-441 S 4 1993.
Divine disclosure: an introduction to Jewish apocalyptic. SCM, 1992.
    Day, John. *New Blckfrs* 74:170-172 Mr 1993.
    Begg, Christopher T. *OTA* 16:439-440 Je 1993.

Russell, Jeffrey Burton.
Dissent and order in the Middle Ages: the search for legitimate authority. Twayne, 1992.
    Olsen, Glenn Warren, 1938-. *CHist* 78:629-630 O 1992.
    O'Malley, William J, 1931-. *TheolStds* 54:387-388 Je 1993.

Russell, John Malcolm.
Sennacherib's "palace without rival" at Nineveh. University of Chicago.
    Stuhlmueller, Carroll. *BibleT* 30:382 N 1992.

Russell, Peter.
The white hole in time: our future evolution and the meaning of now. Aquarian, 1992.
    Woodcock, John. *Teilhard Rev* 28:28 Spr 1993.

Ryan, John.
Irish monasticism. Four Courts Press, 1992.
    Dollard, James. *Furrow* 44:517-518 S 1993.

Ryan, Thomas.
Disciplines for Christian living: interfaith perspectives. Paulist Press, n.d.
    Vanier, Therese. *Tablet* 247:950-951 Jl 24 1993.

Rygier, Maria.
La Franc-Maçonnerie italienne devant la guerre et devant le fascisme. Forni, 1990.
    Caprile, Giovanni. *Civilta* 143:537-538 D 5 1992.

Rzepkowski, Horst.
Lexikon der Mission: Geschichte, Theologie, Ethnologie. Styria, 1992.
    Nagler, N. *Stimm Zeit* 210:863-864 D 1992.
    Wolanin, Adam. *Civilta* 2:300-301 My 1 1993.

S

Sabatowich, Jerome.
Cycling through the gospels. Resource Publications, 1992.
    Senior, Donald. *BibleT* 31:254 Jl 1993.

Sabbe, Maurits.
Studia Neotestamentica. Peeters, 1991.
    Neirynck, F. *Eph Theol Lovan* 78:162-165 Ap 1992.

Sacchi, Paolo.
L'apocalittica giudaica e la sua storia. Paideia, 1990.
    Prata, Gian Luigi. *Gregorianum* 74 No 1:141-142 1993.
    Bernas, Casimir. *CBQ* 55:203-204 Ja 1993.

Sachs, Jeffrey.
Poland's jump to the market economy. MIT Press, n.d.
    Byrnes, Timothy A. *Comm* 120:29-31 N 19 1993.

Sachs, John R.
The Christian vision of humanity. Basic Christian anthropology. The Liturgical Press, 1991.
    O'Donnell, John J. *Gregorianum* 74 no 2:372-373 1993.

Safire, William.
The first dissident: the book of Job in today's politics. Random House, n.d.
    Farrell, Michael J. *Nat Cath Rep* 29:25-26 F 5 1993.

Sagne, J-C.
Traité de théologie spirituelle. Ed du Chalet, 1992.
    Renard, L-J. *NRT* 115:587 Jl-Ag 1993.

Sahgal, Gita, and Yuval-Davis, Nira.
Refusing holy orders. Virago Press, n.d.
    Ward, Hannah, and Wild, Jennifer. *Way* 33:257 Jl 1993.

Sailhamer, John H.
The Pentateuch as narrative: a biblical-theological commentary. Zondervan Publishing House, 1992.
    Heiser, W Charles. *TheolDgst* 40:84-85 Spr 1993.

Sainsbury, Mark.
Logical forms. Blackwell, 1991.
    Casey, Gerard. *IJPS* 1:168 Mr 1993.

Saint Joan, Lazara, and the Baptism of Jesus and John.
GIA Publications, n.d.
    Riley, David M. *Catechist* 27:18 S 1993.

Le Saint Prophète Élie d'après les Pères de l'Église.
Abbaye de Bellefontaine, 1992.
    Harvengt, A. *NRT* 115:591-592 Jl-Ag 1993.

Saint-Thierry, Guglielmo di.
Commento al Cantico dei Cantici. Qiqajon-Comunità di Bose, 1991.
    Orazzo, Antonio. *Civilta* 143:425 N 21 1992.

Sainte Marie mère de Dieu, modle de l'Eglise.
Le Centurion, 1987.
    Partos, L. *Lumen* 47:472 D 1992.

Sainted women of the dark ages.
Duke University Press, 1992.
    Cunningham, Lawrence S, 1935-. *TheolStds* 54:385-386 Je 1993.

Saisons bibliques.
Éd. du Cerf, 1992.
    Anon. *NRT* 115:631 Jl-Ag 1993.

Salaün, P.
Séparés, divorcés, une possible espérance. Nouvelle Cité, 1990.
    Volpe, L. *NRT* 115:117 Ja-F 1993.

Salem, Jean.
Tel un dieu parmi les hommes. Vrin, 1989.
    Destrée, Pierre. *RPhil Louvain* 91:145-146 F 1993.

Salinas, Maximiliano.
Canto a lo divino y religión del oprimido en Chile. Ediciones Rehue, n.d.
    Galleguillos Guzmán, Juan. *Teol Vida* 33 no 3-4:327 1992.

Salvatierra, Angel.
Santo Domingo: Bajo el signo de la esperanza. EDICAY, 1993.
    Taborda, Francisco. *Perspectiva* 25:263-264 My-Ag 1993.

Samartha, S J.
One Christ—many religions: toward a revised christology. Orbis Books, 1991.
    DiNoia, J A. *Living Light* 29:85-86 Aut 1992.

Sammon, Sean D.
An undivided heart. Alba House, 1993.
    Markham, Donna. *RRel* 52:788-789 S-O 1993.
    Graham, William C. *Nat Cath Rep* 30:36 N 19 1993.

Samnydsa Upanishads: Hindu scriptures on asceticism and renunciation.
Oxford University Press, 1992.
    Heiser, W Charles. *TheolDgst* 40:91 Spr 1993.

Sampley, J Paul.
Walking between the times: Paul's moral reasoning. Fortress, 1991.
    Hays, Richard B. *CBQ* 55:392-393 Ap 1993.

Sancinelli, Bruno.
Etica ed economia. Ares, 1992.
    Scurani, Allesandro. *Civilta* 3:444-445 S 4 1993.

Sanders, E P.
Jewish law from Jesus to the Mishnah: five studies. SCM Press, 1990.
    Riches, John. *Heythrop* 34:431-432 O 1993.
Judaism: practice and belief. Trinity, 1992.
    Senior, Donald. *BibleT* 31:61 Ja 1993.
    Harrington, Daniel J. *America* 168:31 F 6 1993.
    Witherup, Ronald D. *OTA* 15:519 O 1992.
    Heiser, W Charles. *TheolDgst* 39:382-383 Wint 1992.
    Feldman, Louis H. *CBQ* 55:393-394 Ap 1993.

Sanders, Karl Olav.
Paul—one of the Prophets? a contribution to the apostle's self-understanding. Mohr, 1991.
    Plevnik, Joseph. *CBQ* 55:177-178 Ja 1993.

Sandin, Robert T.
The rehabilitation of virtue. Praeger, 1992.
    Heiser, W Charles. *TheolDgst* 40:185 Sum 1993.

Sandoval, Moses.
On the move: a history of the Hispanic Church in the United States. Orbis, 1990.
    Riley, Patrick J. *Emmanuel* 99:480-481 O 1993.

Sands, Jack, and Gammons, Peter.
Coming apart at the seams. Macmillan, n.d.
    DiGiacomo, James J. *America* 168:17 Ap 17 1993.

Sanford, James H, et al, eds.
Flowing traces. Princeton University Press, 1992.
    Heiser, W Charles. *TheolDgst* 40:162 Sum 1993.

Sanford, John A.
Mystical Christianity: a psychological commentary on the Gospel of John. Crossroads Publishing Company, 1993.
    Anon. *Spir Life* 39:187-188 Aut 1993.

Sanger, Andrew.
Exploring rural France. Helm, n.d.
    Toomey, Philippa. *Tablet* 247:373 Mr 20 1993.
Exploring rural Ireland. Helm, n.d.
    Toomey, Philippa. *Tablet* 247:373 Mr 20 1993.

Sanks, T Howland.
Salt, leaven and light. Crossroad, 1992.
    Higgins, James J. *Liguorian* 81:69 Mr 1993.
    Cunningham, Lawrence S, 1935-. *Comm* 120:29 Mr 26 1993.
    Heiser, W Charles. *TheolDgst* 40:186 Sum 1993.

Sanks, T Howland, and Coleman, John A, eds.
Reading the signs of the times. Paulist, 1993.
    Basler, Howard B. *Church* 9:56 Aut 1993.
    Brown, David O. *Mod Lit* 20:37 O 1993.
    Harter, Michael. *America* 169:20 N 6 1993.

Sant, Carmel.
Bible translation and language. Essays into the history of Bible translation in Maltese. Faculty of Theology University of Malta, 1992.
    Abela, Anthony M. *Gregorianum* 74 no 3:567-568 1993.

Sante, Carmine Di.
Jewish prayer: the origins of Christian liturgy. Paulist, 1991.
    Hoffman, L. *New Theol Rev* 6:95-97 F 1993.
    Boisclair, Regina A. *JEcumen Stds* 29:486-487 Sum-Aut 1992.
    Sloyan, Gerald S. *Worship* 67:287-288 My 1993.

Santos, Luiz Pereira dos.
Catequese ontem e hoje: dos primórdios a Medellín. Paulinas, 1987.
    Libanio, Joao Batista. *Perspectiva* 24:405-406 S-D 1992.

Saperstein, Marc, ed.
Essential papers on messianic movements and personalities in Jewish history. New York University Press, 1992.
    Heiser, W Charles. *TheolDgst* 40:61-62 Spr 1993.

Sapienza, Leonardo.
Pregare per le vocazioni. Rogate, 1991.
    Caprile, Giovanni. *Civilta* 2:199-200 Ap 17 1993.

Sappington, Thomas J.
Revelation and redemption at Colossae. JSOT, 1991.
    Heiser, W Charles. *TheolDgst* 40:85 Spr 1993.
    Elliott, Niel. *CBQ* 55:395-396 Ap 1993.

Sarot, Marcel.
God, possibility and corporeality. Kok Pharos, 1992.
    Groves, Peter. *New Blckfrs* 74:377-378 Jl-Ag 1993.

Sartori, Luigi.
L'unità della Chiesa: un dibattito e un progetto. Queriniana, 1989.
    Vercruysse, Jos E. *Eph Theol Lovan* 78:179 Ap 1992.

Sasson, Jack M.
Jonah: a new translation, with introduction, commentary, and interpretation. Doubleday, 1989.
    Trible, Phyllis. *CBQ* 55:131-133 Ja 1993.

Satterthwait, Walter.
A flower in the desert. Collins Crime Club, n.d.
    Lejeune, Anthony. *Tablet* 247:376 Mr 20 1993.

Sattler, H Vernon.
Challenging children to chastity. Catholic Central Verein of America, 1991.
    Heiser, W Charles. *TheolDgst* 40:85 Spr 1993.
    Diamond, Eugene F. *Linacre* 60:96 Ag 1993.

Saunders, Kate, and Stanford, Peter.
Catholics and sex. Heinemann, 1992.
    Fisher, Anthony. *Priests & People* 6:354-356 Ag-S 1992.

Saunders, Teddy, and Sanson, Hugh.
David Watson. Hodder and Stoughton, n.d.
    Pridmore, John. *Way* 33:166-167 Ap 1993.

Sauro, Joan.
Whole earth meditation: ecology for the spirit. Lura Media, 1992.
    McNamee, Catherine. *Momentum* 24:84 F-Mr 1993.

Saux, H Le.
Sagesse hindoue, mystique chrétienne. Centurion, 1991.
    Masson, J. *NRT* 115:603-604 Jl-Ag 1993.

Savage, Anne, et al, eds.
Anchorite spirituality. Paulist, n.d.
    Lonsdale, David. *Way* 33:83 Ag 1993.
    Cunningham, Lawrence S, 1935-. *Comm* 120:30 Ag 13 1993.

Savarese, Paolo.
Relazione, regola e diritto: l'intersoggettività giuridica nella prospettiva di Joseph de Finance. Giuffre, 1990.
    Tilliette, Xavier. *Civilta* 144:617 Mr 20 1993.

Savignano, Armando.
Il Cristo di Unamuno: Con una antologia di testi. Queriniana, 1990.
    Pastor, Felix-Alejandro. *Gregorianum* 74 No 1:188 1993.

Sayes, José Antonio.
Antropologia del hombre caido: el pecado original. Biblioteca de Autores Cristianos, 1991.
    Vanneste, A. *Eph Theol Lovan* 69:213-214 Ap 1993.
    Renwart, Léon. *NRT* 114:899-900 N-D 1992.
    Galot, Jean. *Gregorianum* 74 No 1:165 1993.

Scabini, Pino.
Cristo nella vita della famiglia. Ed Paoline, 1992.
    Vanzan, Piersandro. *Civilta* 2:195-196 Ap 17 1993.

Scalabrin, C, ed.
Bibliografia Filosofica Italiana: 1989 and 1990. L S Olschki, 1991, 1992.
    Escol, R. *NRT* 115:277-278 Mr-Ap 1993.

Scannone, Juan Carlos.
Evangelización, cultura y teología. Guadalupe, 1990.
    Libanio, Joao Batista. *Perspectiva* 25:102-105 Ja-Ap 1993.

Scarpat, Giuseppe, ed.
Il libro della Sapienza, vol I. Paideia, 1989.
    Winston, David. *CBQ* 54:764-765 O 1992.
    Prato, Gian Luigi. *Civilta* 144:507-508 Mr 6 1993.

Schall, James Vincent, 1928-.
Religion, wealth and poverty. The Fraser Institute, n.d.
    McKee, Arnold F. *Can Cath Rev* 11:27-28 Mr 1993.
What is God like? The Liturgical Press, n.d.
    Dollen, Charles. *Priest* 49:48 My 1993.
    Campbell, James. *Month* 26:149 Ap 1993.

Schaller, Jean-Pierre.
Un bouquet spirituel. Beauchesne, 1992.
    Anon. *NRT* 115:315-316 Mr-Ap 1993.

Schaller, Jean Pierre.
La melanconia. Del buon uso e del cattivo uso della depressione nella vita spirituale. Gribaudi, 1991.
    Rossi, Giacomo. *Civilta* 3:546-547 S 18 1993.

Scharlemann, Robert P.
The reason of following: Christology and the ecstatic I. University of Chicago, 1991.
    Mueller, J. *TheolStds* 53:767-768 D 1992.
    Steffen, Lloyd. *CrossCurr* 43:114-116 Spr 1993.

Schatz, Klaus.
Historia de la Iglesia contemporanea. Herder, 1992.
    Krull, W. *Perspectiva* 24:398-401 S-D 1992.
    Barrios, Marciano. *Teol Vida* 33 no 3-4:330 1992.
La primauté du Pape. Ed du Cerf, 1992.
    Joassart, Bernard. *NRT* 115:609-610 Jl-Ag 1993.
Vaticanum I (1869-1870). Schoningh, 1992.
    Köhler, Oscar. *Stimm Zeit* 211:214 Mr 1993.
    Misner, Paul. *TheolStds* 54:573-574 S 1993.

Scheick, William J.
Design in Puritan American literature. University Press of Kentucky, 1992.
    Heiser, W Charles. *TheolDgst* 40:85 Spr 1993.

Scheidgen, Hermann-Joseph.
Deutsche Bischöfe im Ersten Weltkrieg. Böhlau Verlag, 1991.
    Zeender, John. *CHist* 79:551-555 Jl 1993.

Schelling, Friedrich Wilhelm Joseph.
Einleitung in die Philosophie. Frommann-Holzboog, 1989.
    Depré, Olivier. *RPhil Louvain* 90:570-571 N 1992.

Schenk, Richard.
Die gnade vollendeter endlichkeit: zur transzendentaltheologischen auslegung der thomanischen anthropologie. Herder, 1989.
    Alberg, Jeremiah L. *Thomist* 57:321-323 Ap 1993.

Schenker, Adrian.
Text und Sinn im Alten Testament: Textgeschichtliche und bibeltheologische Studien. Vandenhoeck & Ruprecht, 1991.
    Ollenburger, Ben C. *CBQ* 55:205 Ja 1993.

Scherer, James A, and Bevans, Stephen B, eds.
New directions in mission and evangelization: basic statements 1974-1991. Orbis Books, 1992.
    Heiser, W Charles. *TheolDgst* 40:78 Spr 1993.
    Lopez-Gay, Jesus. *Gregorianum* 74 no 3:594-595 1993.

Schibler, Daniel.
Le livre de Michée. Edifac, 1989.
    Lust, Johan. *Eph Theol Lovan* 78:159 Ap 1992.

Schiffman, Lawrence H.
From text to tradition. Ktav Publishing House, 1991.
    Heiser, W Charles. *TheolDgst* 39:383 Wint 1992.
    Townsend, John T. *New Theol Rev* 6:117-118 My 1993.
    Saldarini, Anthony J. *CBQ* 55:178-180 Ja 1993.

Schiffman, Lawrence H, and Swartz, Michael D.
Hebrew and Aramaic incantation texts from the Cairo Genizah. JSOT, 1992.
    Fitzgerald, Aloysius. *OTA* 16:165-166 F 1993.

Schillebeeckx, Edward.
Church: the human story of God. SCM, 1990.
    Kerr, Fergus. *New Blckfrs* 73:571-573 N 1992.
    Hilkert, Mary Catherine. *Horizons (CTS)* 19:325-326 Fall 1992.
L'histoire des hommes récit de Dieu. Cerf, 1992.
    Tihon, Paul. *Lumen* 48:232 Je 1993.

Schilling, Heinz.
Civic Calvinism in Northwestern Germany and the Netherlands: sixteenth to nineteenth centuries. Sixteenth Century Journal Publishers, 1991.
    Benedict, Philip. *CHist* 79:530-532 Jl 1993.

Schimmel, Annemarie.
Islam. State University of New York Press, 1992.
    Heiser, W Charles. *TheolDgst* 40:185 Sum 1993.

Schimmelpfennig, Bernhard.
The papacy. Columbia University Press, 1992.
    Wood, Susan. *TheolStds* 54:384 Je 1993.
    Heiser, W Charles. *TheolDgst* 40:186 Sum 1993.

Schindler, David D, ed.
Hans Urs von Balthasar: his life and work. Ignatius Press, 1992.
    Sheets, John R. *HPR* 93:72-73 Mr 1993.

Schineller, Peter.
Praying in the Catholic tradition. Liguori Publications, 1992.
    Borgia, Francis. *Mod Lit* 20:39 My 1993.
    Pecht, Gerard. *Liguorian* 81:69 Ag 1993.

Schipani, Daniel S.
Religious education encounters liberation theology. The Religious Education Press, n.d.
    Chater, Mark. *Doctr Life* 43:125-126 F 1993.

Schiwy, Günther.
Der Geist des Neuen Zeitalters. Kösel, 1987.
    Halleux, André de. *Eph Theol Lovan* 78:478 D 1992.
Lo spirito dell'Età Nuova. Queriniana, 1991.
    Halleux, André de. *Eph Theol Lovan* 78:478 D 1992.

Schlafer, David J.
Surviving the sermon. Cowley Publications, 1992.
    Heiser, W Charles. *TheolDgst* 40:186 Sum 1993.

Schlegelberger, B.
Unsere Erde lebt. Neue Zeitschrift für Missionswissenschaft, 1992.
Masson, J. *NRT* 115:607 Jl-Ag 1993.
Schley, D G.
Shiloh: a Biblical city in tradition and history. Academic Press, 1989.
Lust, Johan. *Eph Theol Lovan* 78:152 Ap 1992.
Schlitz, Jean-Marie.
Célébrations jeunes. Lumen Vitae, 1992.
Partos, L. *Lumen* 47:465-466 D 1992.
Schmidt, Alfred.
Idee und Weltwille: Schopenhauer als Kritiker Hegels. Carl Hanser Verlag, 1988.
Nutt, Kathleen. *IJPS* 1:160-162 Mr 1993.
Schmidt, Jean Miller.
Souls of the social order: the two-party system in American Protestantism. Carlson Publishing, 1991.
Heiser, W Charles. *TheolDgst* 40:85-86 Spr 1993.
Schmidt, Joseph F.
Praying with Thérèse of Lisieux. Saint Mary's Press, 1992.
Puntel, Betsy. *Living Light* 29:94 Wint 1992.
Schmidt, Ludwig.
Beobachtungen zu der Plagenerzählung in Exodus. Brill, 1990.
Vogels, Walter A. *CBQ* 55:350-351 Ap 1993.
Schmidt, Stjepan.
Augustin Bea, the cardinal of unity. New City Press, 1992.
Heiser, W Charles. *TheolDgst* 40:186 Sum 1993.
Schmithals, Walter.
Johannesevangelium und Johannesbriefe. Gruyter, 1992.
Neirynck, F. *Eph Theol Lovan* 78:166-168 Ap 1992.
Schmitz, Franz-Jürgen, and Mink, Gerd, eds.
Liste der koptischen Hanschriften des Neuen Testaments 1: Die sahidischen Handschriften der Evangelien 2. de Gruyter, 1991.
MacCoull, LSB. *CBQ* 55:180 Ja 1993.
Schmitz, J.
La Rivelazione. Queriniana, 1991.
Toubeau, A. *NRT* 114:898 N-D 1992.
Schnackenburg, Rudolf.
Dios ha enviado a su Hijo? El misterio de la navidad. Herder, 1992.
Anon. *Perspectiva* 25:124 Ja-Ap 1993.
The Johannine Epistles. The Crossroad Publishing Company, 1992.
Harrington, Daniel J. *America* 168:34 F 6 1993.
Stuhlmueller, Carroll. *BibleT* 31:126 Mr 1993.
The Johannine Epistles. New City Press, 1992.
Heiser, W Charles. *TheolDgst* 40:186 Sum 1993.
Schneemelcher, Wilhelm, ed.
New Testament Apocrypha. Westminster, 1991.
Collins, Adela Yarbro. *CBQ* 55:180-182 Ja 1993.
Senior, Donald. *BibleT* 31:316-317 S 1993.
Heiser, W Charles. *TheolDgst* 40:179 Sum 1993.
Fitzmyer, Joseph Augustine, 1920-. *TheolStds* 54:554-556 S 1993.
Schneider, Théophile Robert.
The sharpening of wisdom: Old Testament proverbs in translation. University of South Africa, 1990.
Murphy, Roland E. *OTA* 16:176 F 1993.
Schneiders, Sandra M.
Beyond patching: faith and feminism in the Catholic Church. Paulist Press, 1991.
Quitslund, Sonya A. *JEcumen Stds* 29:260-262 Spr 1992.
The revelatory text: interpreting the New Testament as sacred scripture. Harper, 1992.
Ross, Susan A. *Horizons (CTS)* 19:294-297 Fall 1992.
Koenig, John. *Horizons (CTS)* 19:297-300 Fall 1992.
Gerhart, Mary. *Horizons (CTS)* 19:300-302 Fall 1992.
Thompson, William M. *Horizons (CTS)* 19:288-294 Fall 1992.
Nowell, Irene. *Worship* 67:281-282 My 1993.
Barta, Karen A. *TheolStds* 54:165-166 Mr 1993.
Rosenblatt, Marie Eloise. *New Theol Rev* 6:90-91 Ag 1993.
Schnelle, Udo.
Antidocetic christology in the Gospel of John. Fortress Press, 1992.
Senior, Donald. *BibleT* 31:255 Jl 1993.
Schockenhoff, E.
Sterbehilfe und Menschenwürde. Pustet, 1991.
Volpe, L. *NRT* 115:119 Ja-F 1993.
Schoenfeldt, Michael C.
Prayer and power: George Herbert and Renaissance courtship. The University of Chicago Press, 1991.
Labriola, Albert C. *Relig Lit* 25:75-80 Spr 1993.
Schökel, Luis Alonso.
A Palavra inspirada; a Bíblia à luz da ciência da linguagem. Loyola, 1992.
Konings, Johan. *Perspectiva* 25:110-113 Ja-Ap 1993.
Scholer, John M.
Proleptic priests: priesthood in the Epistle to the Hebrews. JSOT, 1991.
Swetnam, James. *CBQ* 54:799-800 O 1992.
Heiser, W Charles. *TheolDgst* 40:86 Spr 1993.
Schon, Isabel.
A Hispanic heritage, series IV: a guide to juvenile books about Hispanic people and cultures. Scarecrow, 1991.
Weathers, Barbara. *CLW* 64:33 Jl-S 1993.
Schönberger, R.
Was ist Scholastik? Bernward, 1991.
Escol, R. *NRT* 115:302 Mr-Ap 1993.

Schönborn, Christoph Von, Bp, et al.
Zur Kirchlchen Erbsündenlehre. Johannes Verlag, 1991.
Renwart, Léon. *NRT* 114:899-900 N-D 1992.
Schönborn, Christoph von, Bp, et al.
Zur Kirchlichen Erbsündenlehre. Johannes Verlag, 1991.
Ladaria, Luis F. *Gregorianum* 74 No 1:163-164 1993.
Schönborn, Christoph von, Bp.
Un homme pris par le mystère de Dieu. Mame, 1992.
Renard, L J. *NRT* 115:307 Mr-Ap 1993.
The mystery of the incarnation. Ignatius Press, n.d.
Higgins, James J. *Liguorian* 81:70 Je 1993.
Schoonenberg, Piet.
De geest, het woord en de zoon: theologische overdenkingen over geest-christologie, logos-christologie en drieëenheidsleer. J H Kok, 1991.
Halleux, André de. *Eph Theol Lovan* 69:211-213 Ap 1993.
Halleux, André de. *Eph Theol Lovan* 69:211-213 Ap 1993.
Schoors, Antoon.
The preacher sought to find pleasing words: a study of the language of Qohelet. Peeters, 1992.
Lust, Johan. *Eph Theol Lovan* 69:166-167 Ap 1993.
The preacher sought to find pleasing words. Peeters and Departement Orientalistiek, 1992.
Murphy, Roland E. *OTA* 16:176-177 F 1993.
Schooyans, Michel.
Aborto e Politica. Ed Vaticana, 1991.
Caprile, Giovanni. *Civilta* 3:204-205 Jl 17 1993.
La dérive totalitaire du libéralisme. Éditions Universitaires, 1991.
Volpe, L. *NRT* 114:913-914 N-D 1992.
Joblin, James, 1920-. *Civilta* 3:340 Ag 7-21 1993.
Schreckenberg, Heinz, and Schubert, Kurt.
Jewish historiography and iconography in early and medieval Christianity. Fortress, 1992.
Feldman, Louis H. *OTA* 16:449-450 Je 1993.
Schreiner, Josef.
Leben nach der Weisung Gottes. Echter, 1992.
Begg, Christopher T. *OTA* 16:399-400 Je 1993.
Schreiter, Robert J.
In water and in blood. Crossroad, 1988.
Falardeau, Ernest R, 1928-. *Emmanuel* 99:356 Jl-Ag 1993.
Falardeau, Ernest R, 1928-. *Emmanuel* 99:478-479 O 1993.
Reconciliation. Orbis, 1992.
Stuhlmueller, Carroll. *BibleT* 30:382 N 1992.
Hommerding, Leroy. *Mod Lit* 20:39-40 F 1993.
Heiser, W Charles. *TheolDgst* 40:186 Sum 1993.
Schreiter, Robert J, ed.
Faces of Jesus in Africa. SCM Press, 1992.
Hearne. Brian. *Furrow* 44:59 Ja 1993.
Dupuis, Jacques. *Gregorianum* 74 No 1:159-160 1993.
Lord, Elizabeth. *Heythrop* 34:192-193 Ap 1993.
Neckebrouck, Valeer. *Eph Theol Lovan* 69:202 Ap 1993.
Schroeder, Frederic M.
Form and transformation: a study in the philosophy of Plotinus. McGill-Queen's University Press, 1992.
Sell, Alan P F. *IJPS* 1:168-169 Mr 1993.
Schug, John A.
Mary, Mother. St Francis Chapel Press, 1992.
Mangan, Charles M. *HPR* 93:78-79 Ja 1993.
Heiser, W Charles. *TheolDgst* 40:86 Spr 1993.
Schultenover, David G.
A view from Rome on the eve of the MOdernist crisis. Fordham University Press, n.d.
Walsh, Michael J, 1937-. *Tablet* 247:1006-1007 Ag 7 1993.
Schultz, Karl A.
Where is God when you need him? Alba House, 1991.
Stuhlmueller, Carroll. *BibleT* 30:382 N 1992.
Heiser, W Charles. *TheolDgst* 39:383 Wint 1992.
Chen, Sheryl Frances. *Cist Stud* 28 no 2:[40]-[41] 1993.
Schulz-Flügel, E, ed.
Vetus Latina Die Reste der altlateinischen Bibel. Herder, 1992.
Ska, Jean Louis. *NRT* 115:256-257 Mr-Ap 1993.
Schunck, Klaus-Dietrich, and Auigustin, Matthias, eds.
Goldene Äpfel in silbernen Schalen. Lang, 1992.
Begg, Christopher T. *OTA* 16:156 F 1993.
Schüngel-Straumann, Helen.
Rûah bewegt die Welt. Katholisches Bibelwerk, 1992.
Begg, Christopher T. *OTA* 16:440 Je 1993.
Schurhammer, Georg.
Francisco Javier, su vida y su tiempo: Europa, 1506-1541, vol I. Herder, 1955.
Lopez-Gay, Jesus. *Gregorianum* 74 no 3:595 1993.
Francisco Javier, su vida y su tiempo: India, 1547-1549, vol III. Herder, 1955.
Hernández, Ramón. *Cien Tom* 120:197-198 Ja-Ap 1993.
Lopez-Gay, Jesus. *Gregorianum* 74 no 3:595 1993.
Francisco Javier, su vida y su tiempo: India-Indonesia, 1541-1547, vol II. Herder, 1955.
Hernández, Ramón. *Cien Tom* 120:197-198 Ja-Ap 1993.
Lopez-Gay, Jesus. *Gregorianum* 74 no 3:595 1993.
Francisco Javier, su vida y su tiempo: Japón-China, 1549-1552, vol IV. Herder, 1955.
Lopez-Gay, Jesus. *Gregorianum* 74 no 3:595 1993.
Francisco Javier: su vida y su tiempo: Europa, 1506-1541, vol I. Herder,

Schurhammer, Georg. *(cont'd)*
1955.
Hernández, Ramón. *Cien Tom* 120:197-198 Ja-Ap 1993.
Frandisco Javier, su vida y su tiempo: Japón-China, 1549-1552, vol IV. Herder, 1955.
Hernández, Ramón. *Cien Tom* 120:197-198 Ja-Ap 1993.

Schussler, Elisabeth.
Discipleship of equals. Crossroad, n.d.
Bromberg, Judith. *Nat Cath Rep* 30:27 N 19 1993.

Schützeichel, Harald, ed.
Die Messe: ein kirchenmusicalishes handbuch. Patmos-Verlag, 1991.
Jaschinski, Eckhard. *Past Mus* 17:53 Ag-S 1993.

Schwartz, Daniel R.
Studies in the Jewish background of Christianity. Mohr, 1992.
Heiser, W Charles. *TheolDgst* 40:86 Spr 1993.
Witherup, Ronald D. *OTA* 16:450 Je 1993.

Schwartz, Delmore.
Shenandoah and other verse plays. BOA Editions, n.d.
Samway, Patrick H, 1939-. *America* 168:19 Mr 20-27 1993.

Schwartz, Regina, ed.
The book and the text: the Bible and literary theory. Basil Blackwell, 1990.
Aichele, George. *CrossCurr* 42:558-561 Wint 1992-1993.

Schwehn, Mark R.
Exiles from Eden: religion and the academic vocation in America. Oxford University Press, n.d.
Gaffney, Edward McGlynn, Jr, 1941-. *Comm* 120:26-28 Ap 9 1993.

Schweizer, Eduard.
A theological introduction to the New Testament. Abingdon Press, 1991.
Heiser, W Charles. *TheolDgst* 40:186-187 Sum 1993.

Schwienhorst-Schönberger, Ludger.
Das Bundesbuch (Ex 20, 22-23, 33): Studien zu seiner Enstehung und Theologie. de Gruyter, 1990.
Dozeman, Thomas B. *CBQ* 54:765-766 O 1992.

Scola, Angelo.
Hans Urs von Balthasar: uno stile teologico. Jaca Book, 1991.
Fisichella, Rino. *Gregorianum* 74 no 3:581-582 1993.

Scopello, M.
Les gnostiques. Cerf-Fides, 1991.
Renard, L J. *NRT* 115:142-143 Ja-F 1993.

Scott, Alan.
Origen and the life of the stars: a history of an idea. Oxford University Press, 1991.
Heiser, W Charles. *TheolDgst* 39:383 Wint 1992.

Scott, Dom Geoffrey.
Gothic rage undone: English monks in the Age of Enlightenment. Downside Abbey, n.d.
Anon. *Word Sp* 15:107 1993.

Scott, Johanna.
Science and language links classroom implications. Heinemann Educational Books, 1993.
Brennan, Jim. *Momentum* 24:77 N-D 1993.

Scott, John M.
Discovering God: life's adventure. Our Sunday Visitor, 1992.
Myers, Rawley. *HPR* 93:64-65 F 1993.
Heiser, W Charles. *TheolDgst* 39:383 Wint 1992.
Father Scott reflections on women, family and relationships. Our Sunday Visitor, 1993.
Higgins, James J. *Liguorian* 81:69 D 1993.

Scott, Kieran, and Warren, Michael, 1935-.
Perspectives on marriage. Oxford University Press, n.d.
Billington, Rachel, 1942-. *Tablet* 247:1232-1233 S 25 1993.

Scott, Macrina.
Picking the "right" Bible study program. ACTA Publications, n.d.
Wansbrough, Henry. *Priests & People* 6:486 D 1992.
Rapien, Mary Lynne. *St Anth* 100:52-53 My 1993.

Screech, Michaël A.
Montaigne et la mélancolie, La sagesse des Essais. Presses universitaires de France, 1992.
Tock, Jean-François. *RPhil Louvain* 91:467-468 Ag 1993.

Scroccaro, Luigino, and Prandi, Alberto.
Un paese nel Veneto. Comune, 1991.
Mellinato, Giuseppe. *Civilta* 2:413-414 My 15 1993.

Scullion, John J.
Genesis. Liturgical, 1992.
Murphy, Roland E. *OTA* 16:169 F 1993.
Stuhlmueller, Carroll. *BibleT* 31:249 Jl 1993.

Scurani, Alessandro.
Pensieri per i giorni di festa. ADP, 1992.
Giachi, Gualberto. *Civilta* 3:339-340 Ag 7-21 1993.

Se-Mang, Peter Kim.
Parish councils on missin: coresponsibility and authority among pastors and parishioners. Beniah Publisher, n.d.
Dalton, William J. *Furrow* 44:125-126 F 1993.

Seager, Richard Hughes, ed.
The dawn of religious pluralism: voices from The World's Parliament of Religions, 1893. Open Court, 1993.
Richesin, L Dale. *Ecumen Trends* 22:7-12 S 1993.

Searle, Mark, 1941-1992, and Stevenson, Kenneth W.
Documents on the marriage liturgy. Liturgical Press, 1992.
Hommerding, Leroy. *Mod Lit* 20:39 Ap 1993.

Sebass, Horst.
Herrscherverheissungen im Alten Testament. Neukirchener, 1992.
Begg, Christopher T. *OTA* 16:187-188 F 1993.

Sebastián, Luis de.
Mundo rico, mundo pobre: Pobreza y solidaridad en el mundo de hoy. Santander, 1992.
Anon. *Christus* 58:91 Mr-Ap 1993.

Secondin, Bruno.
I nuovi protagonisti: movimenti, associazioni gruppi nella Chiesa. Edizioni Paoline, 1991.
Godin, A. *Lumen* 48:119 Mr 1993.
Nuovi cammini dello Spirito: la spiritualità alle soglie del terzo millennio. Ed Paoline, 1990.
Godin, A. *Lumen* 48:119-120 Mr 1993.

Secrest, Meryle.
Frank Lloyd Wright. Knopf, n.d.
Nuttgens, Patrick, 1930-. *Tablet* 247:247-248 F 20 1993.
Coren, Michael. *Can Cath Rev* 11:4-6 F 1993.

Sedley, Kate.
The Plymouth cloak. Collins Crime Club, n.d.
Lejeune, Anthony. *Tablet* 247:51 Ja 9 1993.

Segal, Alan F.
Paul the Convert: the apostolate and apostasy of Saul the Pharisee. Yale University Press, 1990.
Lieu, Judith. *Heythrop* 34:311-312 Jl 1993.
Boisclair, Regina A. *JEcumen Stds* 29:276-277 Spr 1992.

Segal, Gerald.
The fate of Hong Kong. Simon & Schuster, n.d.
Rafferty, Kevin. *Tablet* 247:691 My 29 1993.

Segalla, Giuseppe.
Carisma e istituzione e servizio della carità negli Atti degli Apostoli. Gregoriana Libreria Editrice, 1991.
Farahian, Edmond. *Gregorianum* 74 no 2:366 1993.

Segbroeck, F Van, et al, eds.
The four gospels 1992: Festschrift Frans Neirynck. Leuven University Press, 1992.
Collins, Raymond F. *Louvain Stds* 18:186-187 Sum 1993.

Segni, Campagnano Di, ed.
Nel deserto accanto ai fratelli: vite di Gerasimo e di Giorgio di Choziba. Qiqajon-Comunità di Bose, 1991.
Spidlik, Thomas. *Civilta* 2:308-309 My 1 1993.

Segovia, Fernando F.
The farewell of the word: the Johannine call to abide. Fortress Press, 1991.
Cummings, Charles. *Cist Stud* 28:[18]-[19] 1993.
Kurz, William S. *TheolStds* 54:161-163 Mr 1993.

Segundo, Juan Luis.
El dogma que libera. Editorial Sal Terrae, 1989.
Halleux, André de. *Eph Theol Lovan* 69:210-211 Ap 1993.
The liberation of dogma. Orbis, 1992.
Stuhlmueller, Carroll. *BibleT* 31:121 Mr 1993.
Hennelly, Alfred T. *TheolStds* 54:181-182 Mr 1993.
Keely, Kathleen. *SIDIC* 26 no 1:32+ 1993.
Halleux, André de. *Eph Theol Lovan* 69:210-211 Ap 1993.
Heiser, W Charles. *TheolDgst* 40:86-87 Spr 1993.
Colombo, J.A. *Living Light* 30:108-109 Aut 1993.
Signs of the times: theological reflections. Orbis, n.d.
Harter, Michael. *America* 169:20 N 6 1993.

Seitz, Christopher R.
Zion's final destiny. Fortress Press, 1991.
Stuhlmueller, Carroll. *BibleT* 30:382-383 N 1992.
Haak, Robert D. *OTA* 15:505-506 O 1992.

Selbourne, David.
The spirit of the age. Sinclair-Stevenson, n.d.
Hartley, Anthony. *Tablet* 247:477-478 Ap 10-17 1993.

Selby, Bettina.
Beyond Ararat. John Murray, n.d.
Walton, James. *Tablet* 247:584 My 8 1993.

Self, Donald R, ed.
Public mental health marketing. Haworth Press, 1993.
Anon. *Health Prog* 74:70 O 1993.

Sellner, Edward Cletus.
Mentoring: the ministry of spiritual kinship. Notre Dame University Press, 1990.
Pearson, Paul M. *Cist Stud* 28:[9]-[10] 1993.
Wisdom of the Celtic saints. Ave Maria Press, 1993.
Dollen, Charles. *Priest* 49:48 My 1993.
Hommerding, Leroy. *Mod Lit* 20:40 Je-Jl 1993.
Murphy, James H. *Furrow* 44:326-327 My 1993.
Waal, Esther de. *Tablet* 247:1302 O 9 1993.

Senior, Donald.
Jesus: a gospel portrait. Paulist Press, 1992.
Stuhlmueller, Carroll. *BibleT* 31:121-122 Mr 1993.
The passion of Jesus in the Gospel of John. Liturgical, 1991.
Wansbrough, Henry. *Priests & People* 6:435-436 N 1992.
Witherup, Ronald D. *CBQ* 54:801-802 O 1992.

Senior, Donald, ed.
The Catholic study Bible. Oxford University Press, 1990.
Neirynck, F. *Eph Theol Lovan* 78:426 D 1992.

Senn, Frank C.
The witness of the worshipping community: liturgy and the practice of evangelism. Paulist, 1993.
Byrne, Pat. *Mod Lit* 20:36 S 1993.

Sennott, Charles M.
Broken Covenant. Simon and Schuster, n.d.
Costello, Gerald M, 1931-. *USCath* 58:48-51 Mr 1993.

Serafini, Alfredo, and Lotito, R.
San Giuseppe custode del Redentore. Febbraio, 1991.
Gauthier, Roland. *CahiersJos* 41:137 Ja-Je 1993.

Serrin, William.
Homestead: the glory and tragedy of an American steel town. Random House, n.d.
Zon, Calivin G. *Nat Cath Rep* 29:14 Ap 9 1993.

Seters, John Van.
Prologue to history. John Knox, 1992.
    Murphy, Roland E. *OTA* 16:169 F 1993.
    Stuhlmueller, Carroll. *BibleT* 31:250 Jl 1993.
    Heiser, W Charles. *TheolDgst* 40:191 Sum 1993.
Seth, Vikram.
A suitable boy. Orion, n.d.
    Elborn, Geoffrey. *Tablet* 247:518 Ap 24 1993.
    Worth, Robert. *Comm* 120:25-26 My 21 1993.
Seward, Desmond.
The dancing sun: jouneys to the miracle shrines. Macmillan, n.d.
    Craig, Mary. *Tablet* 247:820 Je 26 1993.
Sexson, Lynda.
Ordinarily sacred. University Press of Virginia, n.d.
    Graham, William C. *Nat Cath Rep* 29:25 Mr 26 1993.
Seymour, Jack L, and Miller, Donald E, eds.
Theological approaches to Christian education. Abingdon Press, 1990.
    Trainor, M. *New Theol Rev* 6:100-101 F 1993.
Seymour, Miranda.
Ottoline Morrell. Hoddor and Stoughton, n.d.
    English, Isobel. *Tablet* 246:1573 D 12 1992.
Shaffrey, Maura.
Irish cottages. Weidenfeld & Nicholson, n.d.
    Braybrooke, Neville. *Tablet* 247:583 My 8 1993.
Shanks, Hershel, et al.
The Dead Sea Scrolls after forty years. Biblical Archaeology Society, 1991.
    Fitzmyer, Joseph Augustine, 1920-. *OTA* 16:194 F 1993.
Shanks, Hershel, ed.
Understanding the Dead Sea Scrolls. Random House, 1992.
    Stuhlmueller, Carroll. *BibleT* 31:126 Mr 1993.
    Wansbrough, Henry. *Tablet* 247:721-722 Je 5 1993.
    Chen, Sheryl Frances. *Cist Stud* 28 no 2:[46]-[47] 1993.
    Heiser, W Charles. *TheolDgst* 40:190-191 Sum 1993.
Shanks, Hershel, and Cole, Dan P, eds.
Archaeology and the Bible: the best of BAR. Biblical Archaeology Society, 1990.
    Edelman, Diana V. *OTA* 15:475-476 O 1992.
Shannon, Albert Clement.
The medieval Inquisition. The Liturgical Press, 1991.
    Heiser, W Charles. *TheolDgst* 40:87 Spr 1993.
Shannon, William Henry, 1917-.
Silence on fire: the prayer of awareness. Crossroad, 1991.
    Downey, Michael. *Cist Stud* 28:[11]-[12] 1993.
Silent lamp: the Thomas Merton story. Crossroad, 1992.
    Kountz, P. *CHist* 78:615-620 O 1992.
    Cunningham, Lawrence S, 1935-. *Comm* 120:24 F 12 1993.
    Hart, Patrick. *Cist Stud* 28:[35]-[36] 1993.
    Heiser, W Charles. *TheolDgst* 39:384 Wint 1992.
    King, Thomas M. *TheolStds* 54:199-200 Mr 1993.
    Campbell, James. *Month* 26:198 My 1993.
    Brady, Ray. *Furrow* 44:325-326 My 1993.
    Pridmore, John. *Way* 33:255 Jl 1993.
Shapiro, Alan.
Covenant. University of Chicago Press, n.d.
    Keen, Suzanne. *Comm* 120:26-28 F 26 1993.
Shapiro, Joseph P.
No pity. Random House, n.d.
    DeCoursey, Vincent W, Jr. *Nat Cath Rep* 29:22 O 15 1993.
A shared inheritance: a statement on Israel/Palestine.
Council of Churches for Britain & Ireland, 1990.
    Garber, Zev. *JEcumen Stds* 29:128-129 Wint 1992.
Sharman, Cecil W.
George Fox and the Quakers. Friends United Press, 1991.
    Heiser, W Charles. *TheolDgst* 39:384 Wint 1992.
Sharpe, Richard.
Medieval Irish saints' lives. Oxford University Press, 1991.
    McLoughlin, John. *Heythrop* 34:212-213 Ap 1993.
    Heiser, W Charles. *TheolDgst* 39:384 Wint 1992.
Shaw, William P, ed.
Praise disjoined: changing patterns of salvation in 17th-century English literature. Peter Lang, 1991.
    Heiser, W Charles. *TheolDgst* 39:380 Wint 1992.
Shawcross, William.
"Murdoch". Simon & Schuster, n.d.
    Prizer, John. *Register* 69:5 Je 6 1993.
Shea, John B.
The God who fell from heaven/the hour of the unexpected. Thomas More Press, n.d.
    Graham, William C. *Nat Cath Rep* 29:39 F 5 1993.
Starlight. Crossroad, 1992.
    Graham, William C. *Nat Cath Rep* 29:39 F 5 1993.
    Higgins, James J. *Liguorian* 81:40 Je 1993.
    Senior, Donald. *BibleT* 31:255 Jl 1993.
    Williams, Joan. *Living Prayer* 26:32-33 N-D 1993.
Sheed, Frank J.
To know Christ Jesus. Ignatius Press, 1992.
    MacCarthy, Peter T. *HPR* 93:80-81 Ag-S 1993.
Sheeley, Steven M.
Narrative asides in Luke-Acts. Cornell University Press, 1992.
    Heiser, W Charles. *TheolDgst* 40:187 Sum 1993.
Sheldon, Garrett Ward.
The political philosophy of Thomas Jefferson. The Johns Hopkins University Press, 1991.
    Crout, Robert Rhodes. *Cithara* 32:63-65 N 1992.

Sheldon, Michael.
Orwell. HarperCollins, n.d.
    Bazyn, Barbara. *New Oxford Rev* 60:28-30 Ap 1993.
Sheldrake, Philip.
Spirituality and history. Crossroad, 1992.
    Downey, Michael. *TheolStds* 53:778-780 D 1992.
    Heiser, W Charles. *TheolDgst* 39:384 Wint 1992.
    Conn, Joann Wolski. *Horizons (CTS)* 20:173-174 Spr 1993.
    Murphy, Anne, and Pridmore, John. *Way* 33:252 Jl 1993.
    Williams, Joan. *Living Prayer* 26:32-33 S-O 1993.
Sheldrake, Rupert.
The rebirth of nature: the greeming of science and God. Bantam, 1991.
    Burton-Christie, Douglas. *Horizons (CTS)* 20:163-165 Spr 1993.
Shelp, Earl E, and Sunderland, Ronald H.
AIDS and the church: the second decade. John Knox Press, 1992.
    Heiser, W Charles. *TheolDgst* 39:384 Wint 1992.
Shelton, Charles M.
Morality and the adolescent: a pastoral psychology approach. Crossroad, 1989.
    Anon. *Church* 9:42 Sum 1993.
Shelton, James B.
Mighty in word and deed: the role of the Holy Spirit in Luke-Acts. Hendrickson, 1991.
    Karris, Robert J. *CBQ* 55:182-183 Ja 1993.
Shepherd, Linda Jean.
Lifting the veil. Shambhala Publications, n.d.
    Zoretich, Frank. *Nat Cath Rep* 29:34 S 10 1993.
Sherman, Amy L.
Preferential option. Eerdmans, 1992.
    Heiser, W Charles. *TheolDgst* 40:187 Sum 1993.
Sherman, V Clayton.
Creating the new American hospital: a time for greatness. Jossey-Bass, 1993.
    Anon. *Health Prog* 74:94 Jl-Ag 1993.
Shermis, Michael, and Zannoni, Arthur E, eds.
Introduction to Jewish-Christian realtions. Paulist Press, 1991.
    Keely, Kathleen. *SIDIC* 26 no 1:32 1993.
    Heiser, W Charles. *TheolDgst* 39:366 Wint 1992.
Sherry, Patrick.
Spirit and beauty: an introduction to theological aesthetics. Clarendon, 1992.
    Heiser, W Charles. *TheolDgst* 39:384-385 Wint 1992.
    Wynn, Mark. *New Blckfrs* 74:375-376 Jl-Ag 1993.
    Feeney, Joseph J. *TheolStds* 54:603-605 S 1993.
Sherwood, Stephen K.
"Had God not been on my side": an examination of the narrative technique of the story of Jacob and Laban, Genesis 29, 1-32, 2. Lang, 1990.
    Walsh, Jerome T. *CBQ* 54:767 O 1992.
Shilts, Randy.
Conduct unbecoming: gays and lesbians in the US military. St Martin's Press, n.d.
    Tipton, Paul. *Register* 69:5 Je 6 1993.
    Fisher, James T. *Comm* 120:6-7 My 21 1993.
Shook, Laurence K.
Étienne Gilson. Jaca Book, 1991.
    Steenberghen, Fernand Van. *RPhil Louvain* 90:589-590 N 1992.
Shore, Paul.
The myth of the university. University Press of America, 1992.
    Giles, James E. *CrossCurr* 43:255-256 Sum 1993.
Shorris, Earl.
Latinos. Norton, n.d.
    Cleary, Edward L. *Comm* 120:23-24 Mr 26 1993.
    Godfrey, Aaron W. *New Oxford Rev* 60:30 Je 1993.
Shorter, Aylward, 1932-.
Toward a theology of inculturation. Orbis, 1989.
    Gittins, Anthony J, 1943-. *New Theol Rev* 6:112-113 Ag 1993.
    Falardeau, Ernest R, 1928-. *Emmanuel* 99:478 O 1993.
Shrader-Frechette, Kr, ed.
Nuclear energy and ethics. WCC Publications, 1991.
    Menin, G. *NRT* 115:151-152 Ja-F 1993.
Shulevitz, Uri.
In dawn. Farrar, Straus and Giroux, n.d.
    Neuberger, Anne E. *ReligTJ* 27:11 Mr 1993.
Shumway, Nicolas.
The intervention of Argentina. University of California Press, 1991.
    Horowitz, Joel. *Cithara* 32:66-68 N 1992.
Sibilio, Vincenzo.
I Gesuiti e la Calabria. Atti del Convegno: Reggio Calabria, 27-28 febbraio 1991. Laruffa, 1992.
    Castelli, Ferdinando. *Civilta* 3:547 S 18 1993.
Siderits, Mark.
Indian philosophy of language. Kluwer, 1991.
    Schweizer, Paul. *IPQ* 33:373-376 S 1993.
Sieben, Hermann-Josef.
Origenes. Herder, 1991.
    Frohnhofen, H. *Stimm Zeit* 211:142 F 1993.
Siegfried, Regina, and Ruane, Edward, eds.
In the company of preachers. The Liturgical Press, 1993.
    Stuhlmueller, Carroll. *BibleT* 31:249 Jl 1993.
Sievernich, Michael, et al, eds.
Conquista und Evangelisation. Grünewald, 1992.
    Brieskorn, Norbert. *Stimm Zeit* 211:430-431 Je 1993.
Sievers, Joseph.
The Hasmoneans and their supporters: from Mattahias to the death of John Hyrcanus I. Scholars, 1990.
    Gruen, Erich S. *CBQ* 55:352-353 Ap 1993.

Sigmund, Paul E.
Liberation theology at the crossroads: democracy or revolution. Oxford University Press, 1990.
   Lord, Elizabeth. *Heythrop* 34:90-92 Ja 1993.

Sigurdson, Jon, and Tagerud, Yael, eds.
The intelligent corporation: the privatisation of intelligence. Taylor Graham, 1992.
   Hunter, Gregory. *CLW* 64:34 Jl-S 1993.

Siker, Jeffrey S.
Disinheriting the Jews: Abraham in early Christian controversy. John Knox, 1991.
   Tilley, Maureen A. *Horizons (CTS)* 20:146-149 Spr 1993.
   Sloyan, Gerard S. *CBQ* 55:396-398 Ap 1993.
   Berenbaum, Michael. *JEcumen Stds* 29:485-486 Sum-Aut 1992.

Silburn, Lilian.
Instant et cause: le discontinu dans la pensée philosophique de l'Inde. De Boccard, 1989.
   Couture, André. *Laval Theol Phil* 49:168 F 1993.

Silva, Custódio Augusto Ferreira, da.
Informatica e diritti umani. Ed Dehoniane, 1991.
   Baragli, Enrico. *Civilta* 144:103-104 Ja 2 1993.

Silva, Valmor da.
Segunda Epístola aos Tessalonicenses. Editora Vozes Ltda, 1992.
   Gorgulho, Maria Laura. *REB* 53:479-485 Je 1993.

Silva Henriquez, Raul.
Memorias. Ediciones Copygraph, n.d.
   Barrios, Marciano. *Teol Vida* 33 no 3-4:325-326 1992.

Silverman, William A.
Human experimentation: a guided step into the unknown. Oxford University Press, 1985.
   Barnet, Robert J. *Linacre* 60:90-92 My 1993.

Simek, Rudolf.
Erde und kosmos im Mittelalter: das welbild vor Kolumbus. Verlag C H Beck, 1992.
   Shank, Michael H. *CHist* 79:329-330 Ap 1993.

Simmons, F L.
The emerging New Age. Bear and Company, 1990.
   Williams, Alison. *Teilhard Rev* 27:88-89 Wint 1992.

Simmons, Henry C.
In the footsteps of the mystics: a guide to the spiritual classics. Paulist Press, 1992.
   Heiser, W Charles. *TheolDgst* 39:385 Wint 1992.

Simon, Arthur.
Harvesting peace: the arms race and human need. Sheed and Ward, 1990.
   Thompson, J Milburn. *Emmanuel* 99:179-180 Ap 1993.

Simon, Maurice.
Un catechisme universel pour l'Église catholique. Peeters, 1992.
   Partos, L. *Lumen* 47:466-467 D 1992.
   Lambiasi, F. *Civilta* 3:311-312 Ag 7-21 1993.
   Marthaler, Berard L, 1927-. *TheolStds* 54:587-589 S 1993.

Simon, Uriel.
Abraham Ibn Ezra's two commentaries on the Minor Prophets. Bar-Ilan University, 1989.
   Gitay, Yehosua. *OTA* 15:510-511 O 1992.
Four approaches to the Book of Pslams: from Saadia Gaon to Abraham Ibn Ezra. State University of New York Press, 1991.
   Cooper, Alan. *CBQ* 55:353-354 Ap 1993.

Simon, Yves R, 1903-1961.
Philosophy of democratic government. University of Chicago Press, 1951.
   Schram, Glenn N. *New Oxford Rev* 60:13-17 Ja-F 1993.

Simoni, Enrico.
Bibliografia della Massoneria in Italia. Bastogi, 1992.
   Caprile, Giovanni. *Civilta* 3:95 Jl 3 1993.

Simsic, Wayne.
Earthsongs: praying with nature. Saint Mary's Press, n.d.
   Stout, Nancy T. *St Anth* 101:52-53 Ag 1993.
Natural prayer: encountering God in nature. Saint Mary's Press, 1992.
   Thompson, J Milburn. *Emmanuel* 99:236-237 My 1993.
   Stout, Nancy T. *St Anth* 101:52-53 Ag 1993.

Simundson, Daniel J.
Faith under fire: how the Bible speaks to us in times of suffering. Harper, 1990.
   Bernas, Casimir. *Cist Stud* 28:[20] 1993.

Sina, Mario.
La tolleranza religiosa: indagini storiche e riflessioni filosofiche. Vita e Pensiero, 1991.
   Pirola, G. *Civilta* 144:513-514 Mr 6 1993.

Sinclair, Scott Gambrill.
Revelation. Bibal Press, 1992.
   Heiser, W Charles. *TheolDgst* 40:187 Sum 1993.

Sipe, A W Richard.
A secret world. Brunner/Mazel, 1990.
   Repicky, Robert A. *Can Cath Rev* 11:31 Je 1993.
   Godin, A. *Lumen* 48:358-359 S 1993.

Sister Thea Bowman, shooting star.
   St. Mary's Press, n.d.
   Graham, William C. *Nat Cath Rep* 30:36 N 19 1993.

Sisti, Adalberto.
Il Libro della Sapienza: introduzione-versione-commento. Porziuncola, 1992.
   Murphy, Roland E. *OTA* 16:428 Je 1993.

Ska, Jean-Louis.
"Our fathers have told us". Biblical Institute, 1990.
   Long, Burke O. *CBQ* 54:768 O 1992.
   Lust, Johan. *Eph Theol Lovan* 78:151-152 Ap 1992.

Skelley, Michael.
The liturgy of the world: Karl Rahner's theology of worship. Pueblo, n.d.
   Sands, Ernest. *Tablet* 247:725 Je 5 1993.
   Heiser, W Charles. *TheolDgst* 40:87 Spr 1993.
   Byrne, Pat. *Mod Lit* 20:39 S 1993.

Skeris, Robert A, ed.
Cum angelis canere: essays on sacred music and pastoral liturgy in honour of Richard I Schuler. Catholic Church Music Associates, 1993.
   Le Voir, Paul W. *SacM* 120:22-23 Spr 1993.

Sklba, Richard J.
Pre-exilic prophecy: words of warning, dreams of hope, spirituality of pre-exilic prophets. Liturgical, 1990.
   Wimmer, Joseph F. *OTA* 15:505 O 1992.
   Bailey, Randall C. *CBQ* 55:111-113 Ja 1993.

Skynner, Robin, and Cleese, John.
Life and how to survive it. Methuen, n.d.
   Kenny, Mary, 1936-. *Tablet* 247:439 Ap 3 1993.

Slade, Herbert.
Contemplative intimacy. Darton, Longman & Todd, n.d.
   Chapman, Vera. *Teilhard Rev* 28:28 Sum 1993.

Slater, Candace.
City steeple, city streets: saints' tales from Granada and a changing Spain. University of California Press, 1990.
   Walsh, Michael J, 1937-. *Heythrop* 34:215 Ap 1993.

Slater, Nigel.
Real fast food. Michael Joseph, n.d.
   Poole, Shona Crawford. *Tablet* 247:374 Mr 20 1993.

Slawson, Douglas J.
The foundation and first decade of the National Catholic Welfare Council. Catholic University of America Press, 1992.
   Heiser, W Charles. *TheolDgst* 39:385 Wint 1992.
   McKeown, Elizabeth. *CHist* 79:370-371 Ap 1993.

Sleeper, C Freeman.
The Bible and the moral life. John Knox, 1993.
   Stuhlmueller, Carroll. *BibleT* 31:249 Jl 1993.
   Spohn, William C. *TheolStds* 54:594-595 S 1993.

Sloyan, Gerard S.
So you mean to read the Bible!. Liturgical Press, 1992.
   Durken, Daniel. *Sisters* 65:64-65 Ja 1993.
   Stuhlmueller, Carroll. *BibleT* 31:249 Jl 1993.
What are they saying about John? Paulist Press, 1991.
   Wansbrough, Henry. *Priests & People* 6:486 D 1992.
   Witherup, Ronald D. *CBQ* 54:801-802 O 1992.

Smail, Tom, et al.
Charismatic renewal: the search for a theology. SPCK, n.d.
   Heron, Benedict. *Tablet* 247:921-922 Jl 17 1993.

Smart, Ninian, 1927-, and Konstantine, Steven.
Christian systematic theology in a world context. Fortress, 1991.
   Schreiter, Robert. *TheolStds* 53:775-776 D 1992.

Smelik, Klaas A D.
Converting the past: studies in ancient Israelite and Moabite historiography. Brill, 1992.
   Edelman, Diana V. *OTA* 15:476 O 1992.
Writings from ancient Israel. John Knox Press, 1992.
   Stuhlmueller, Carroll. *BibleT* 31:57 Ja 1993.
   Harrington, Daniel J. *America* 168:27-28 F 6 1993.
   Heiser, W Charles. *TheolDgst* 39:385 Wint 1992.

Smiga, George M.
Pain and polemic: anti-Judaism in the Gospels. Paulist, 1992.
   Harrington, Daniel J. *New Theol Rev* 6:87-88 Ag 1993.

Smith, Adrian B.
God and the Aquarian age: the new era of the kingdom. McCrimmons, 1990.
   Williams, Alison. *Teilhard Rev* 27:91-94 Wint 1992.

Smith, Bernard.
Imagining the Pacific: in the wake of the Cook voyages. Yale University Press, n.d.
   Stocker, Mark. *Tablet* 247:1167 S 11 1993.

Smith, Chris, et al.
Reshaping work: the Cadbury experience. Cambridge, n.d.
   Naughton, Michael. *RSocEcon* 50:339-341 Fall 1992.

Smith, Christian.
The emergence of liberation theology. University of Chicago Press, 1991.
   Schall, James Vincent, 1928-. *CHist* 79:586-588 Jl 1993.

Smith, Christine M.
Preaching as weeping, confusion and resistance. John Knox Press, 1992.
   Garvey, Eugenia. *Sisters* 65:223-224 My 1993.

Smith, Dwight Moody.
First, second, and third John. John Knox, 1991.
   Senior, Donald. *BibleT* 31:255 Jl 1993.
   Neufeld, Dietmar. *CBQ* 55:398-399 Ap 1993.
John among the gospels. Fortress Press, 1992.
   Senior, Donald. *BibleT* 31:61 Ja 1993.
   Neirynck, F. *Eph Theol Lovan* 78:442-444 D 1992.
   Heiser, W Charles. *TheolDgst* 39:385-386 Wint 1992.

Smith, Huston.
Essays on world religions. Paragon Press, 1992.
   Heiser, W Charles. *TheolDgst* 40:87 Spr 1993.
The world's religions. HarperSanFrancisco, 1991.
   Heiser, W Charles. *TheolDgst* 39:386 Wint 1992.

Smith, Janet E.
Humanae Vitae: a generation later. The Catholic University of America Press, 1991.
   Higgins, James J. *Liguorian* 81:68-69 Ja 1993.

Spurr, John.
The Restoration Church of England 1646-1689. Yale University Press, 1991.
    Hamilton, Alastair. *Heythrop* 34:340 Jl 1993.

Spykman, Gordon J.
Reformed theology: a new paradigm for doing dogmatics. Eerdmans, 1992.
    Heiser, W Charles. *TheolDgst* 39:386 Wint 1992.

Squires, John T.
The plan of God in Luke-Acts. Cambridge University Press, 1993.
    Johnson, Luke Timothy. *New Blckfrs* 74:426-428 S 1993.

St George, Andrew.
The descent of manners. Chatto & Windus, n.d.
    Townsend, John Rowe. *Tablet* 247:1105 Ag 28 1993.

Staal, Frits.
Jouer avec le feu: pratique et théorie du rituel védique. l'Institut de Civilization Indienne, 1990.
    Couture, André. *Laval Theol Phil* 49:169-170 F 1993.

Staalesen, Gunnar.
Yours until death. Constable, n.d.
    Lejeune, Anthony. *Tablet* 247:376 Mr 20 1993.

Stachniewski, John.
The persecutory imagination: English Puritanism and the literature of religous despair. Oxford University Press, 1991.
    Heiser, W Charles. *TheolDgst* 39:386 Wint 1992.

Stadelmann, Luis.
Love and politics: a new commentary on the Song of Songs. Paulist, 1992.
    Stuhlmueller, Carroll. *BibleT* 31:249-250 Jl 1993.
    Murphy, Roland E. *OTA* 16:428 Je 1993.

Staffner, Hans.
Jesus Christ and the Hindu community. Gujarat Sahitya Prakash, 1987.
    Mitra, Kana. *JEcumen Stds* 29:113-114 Wint 1992.

Stählin, W.
Le mystère de Dieu. Ed du Cerf, 1991.
    Renwart, Léon. *NRT* 115:579-580 Jl-Ag 1993.

Stake, Donald Wilson.
The ABCs of worship: a concise dictionary. John Knox Press, 1992.
    Lang, Jovian P. *Mod Lit* 20:39 Ag 1993.

Stallwood, Veronica.
Death and the Oxford box. Macmillan, n.d.
    Lejeune, Anthony. *Tablet* 247:376 Mr 20 1993.

Stallworthy, Jon.
Wilfred Owen. Oxford University Press, n.d.
    Toomey, Philippa. *Tablet* 247:585 My 8 1993.

Stanford, Peter.
Cardinal Hume and the changing face of English Catholicism. Geoffrey Chapman, 1992.
    Longley, Clifford. *Tablet* 247:371 Mr 20 1993.
    Gross, Selwyn. *Priests & People* 7:207-209 My 1993.
The seven deadly sins: stories on human weakness and virtue. Triumph Books, n.d.
    Finley, Mitchel B. *St Anth* 100:52 My 1993.

Stangerup, Henrik.
Brother Jacob [tr by A Born]. Marion Boyars, n.d.
    Scott, Rivers. *Tablet* 247:1105 Ag 28 1993.

Stannard, Martin.
Evelyn Waugh: the later years 1939-1966. Norton, 1992.
    Donohue, John W, 1917-. *America* 168:8-10 Ap 10 1993.

Stanton, Graham N.
A Gospel for a new people. T & T Clark, 1992.
    Senior, Donald. *BibleT* 31:61-62 Ja 1993.
    Harrington, Daniel J. *America* 168:33 F 6 1993.

Starbird, Margaret.
The woman with the alabaster jar. Bear, n.d.
    McCarthy, Patricia. *Nat Cath Rep* 29:29 S 10 1993.

Staring, Adrianus, ed.
Medieval Carmelite heritage: early reflections on the nature of the order. Institutum Carmelitanum, 1989.
    Egan, Keith J. *CHist* 78:641-642 O 1992.

Stassen, Glen H.
Just peacemaking: transforming initiatives for justice and peace. John Knox Press, 1992.
    Harak, G Simon. *TheolStds* 54:395 Je 1993.

Staubli, Thomas.
Das Image der Nomaden im Alten Israel und in der Ikonographie seiner sesshaften Nachbarn. Vandenhoeck and Ruprecht, 1991.
    Wright, John W. *OTA* 15:489 O 1992.

Stayer, James M.
The German peasants' War and Anabaptist Community of Goods. McGill-Queens University Press, 1991.
    Scribner, Bob. *Heythrop* 34:455-456 O 1993.

Stead, Julian.
Saint Benedict, a Rule for beginners. St. Bede's Publications, 1993.
    Cannon, Howard. *Word Sp* 15:105-106 1993.

Steck, Odil Hannes.
Gottesknecht und Zion. Mohr, 1992.
    Begg, Christopher T. *OTA* 16:178-179 F 1993.
Studien zu Tritojesaja. Gruyter, 1991.
    Begg, Christopher T. *OTA* 15:477 O 1992.

Stedman, Ray C.
Hebrews. Inter Varsity Press, n.d.
    O'Reilly, Leo. *Furrow* 44:193 Mr 1993.

Steenberghen, Fernand Van.
Études religieuses. Ed F.X. de Guibert, 1991.
    McEvoy, James. *RPhil Louvain* 91:163-164 F 1993.

Steeves, Paul D, ed.
The modern encyclopedia of religions in Russia and the Soviet Union. Academic International Press, 1988.
    Heiser, W Charles. *TheolDgst* 40:176-177 Sum 1993.

Stefanini, Luigi.
Platone, 2 voll. Istituto di Storia della Filosofia dell'Università degli Studi, 1991.
    Pirola, G. *Civilta* 144:515 Mr 6 1993.

Stefano, Frances.
The absolute value of human action in the theology of Juan Luis Segundo. University Press of America, 1992.
    Heiser, W Charles. *TheolDgst* 39:387 Wint 1992.

Stefano, Gianni di.
Annali Selinuntini. Accademia Selinuntina di Scienze Lettere ed Arti, 1991.
    Ferrua, Antonio. *Civilta* 2:208 Ap 17 1993.

Stefanovic, Zdravko.
The Aramaic of Daniel in the light of Old Aramaic. JSOT, 1992.
    Smith, Mark S. *OTA* 15:509-510 O 1992.
    Lust, Johan. *Eph Theol Lovan* 69:162-163 Ap 1993.

Stegemann, Wolfgang.
Zwischen synagoge und Obrigkeit: Zur historischen Situation der lukanischen Christen. Vandenhoeck and Ruprecht, 1991.
    Moore, Robert L. *CBQ* 54:803-804 O 1992.
    Sanders, Jack T. *JEcumen Stds* 29:125 Wint 1992.

Steggink, Otger, ed.
Juan de la Cruz, espíritu de llama. Kok Pharos Publishing House, 1991.
    Ruiz Jurado, Manuel. *Gregorianum* 74 no 2:380-381 1993.

Steichen, Donna.
Ungodly rage: the hidden face of Catholic feminism. Ignatius Press, n.d.
    DeCock, M. *Can Cath Rev* 11:41-42 Ja 1993.

Stein, Edith, 1891-1942.
Briefe an Roman Ingarden. Herder, 1991.
    Toubeau, A. *NRT* 114:936-937 N-D 1992.
The hidden life: hagiographic essays, meditations, spiritual texts. ICS Publications, 1992.
    Beha, Marie, 1926-. *RRel* 52:152-153 Ja-F 1993.
    Heiser, W Charles. *TheolDgst* 40:88 Spr 1993.
De la Personne. Ed du Cerf, 1992.
    Jacobs, H. *NRT* 115:277 Mr-Ap 1993.

Stein, Robert H.
Gospels and tradition. Baker, 1991.
    Neirynck, F. *Eph Theol Lovan* 78:434-435 D 1992.
    Heiser, W Charles. *TheolDgst* 39:387 Wint 1992.
The Synoptic problem. Baker, 1987.
    Neirynck, F. *Eph Theol Lovan* 78:435-436 D 1992.

Stein, Stephen J.
The Shaker experience in America: a history of the United Society of Believers. Yale University Press, 1992.
    Heiser, W Charles. *TheolDgst* 39:387 Wint 1992.

Steinsaltz, Adin.
The Talmud. Random House, 1991.
    Stuhlmueller, Carroll. *BibleT* 31:122 Mr 1993.

Stemberger, Günter.
Il Giudaismo classico. Città Nuova, 1991.
    Katunarich, S M. *Civilta* 3:92-93 Jl 3 1993.
Studien zum rabbinischen Judentum. Katholisches Bibelwerk, 1990.
    Begg, Christopher T. *OTA* 16:450-451 Je 1993.

Stendahl, Krister, and Charlesworth, James H, eds.
The Scrolls and the New Testament. Crossroad, 1992.
    Fitzmyer, Joseph Augustine, 1920-. *OTA* 15:520 O 1992.

Stenger, Werner.
Los métodos de la exégesis bíblica. Herder, 1990.
    Rodríguez, E. *Cien Tom* 119:410 My-Ag 1992.
Metodologia biblica. Queriniana, 1991.
    Simoens, Y. *NRT* 115:246-247 Mr-Ap 1993.

Stenoniana.
Ed Universitaires, Pérolles, 1991.
    Renard, L J. *NRT* 115:306 Mr-Ap 1993.

Stephens, W Peter.
Zwingli. Oxford University Press, 1992.
    Heiser, W Charles. *TheolDgst* 40:88 Spr 1993.
    Grieser, D. Jonathan. *TheolStds* 54:598-599 S 1993.

Stern, David.
Parables in Midrash. Harvard University Press, 1991.
    Saldarini, Anthony J. *TheolStds* 53:781 D 1992.
    Pearson, Richard. *Relig Lit* 24:105-106 Aut 1992.
    Visotzky, Burton L. *CBQ* 55:183-184 Ja 1993.
    Heiser, W Charles. *TheolDgst* 40:187-188 Sum 1993.

Stern, Jean.
La Salette. Cerf, 1991.
    Caprile, Giovanni. *Civilta* 143:544-545 D 5 1992.
    Plumat, N. *NRT* 115:131 Ja-F 1993.

Stern, Philip D.
The Biblical herem: a window on Israel's religious experience. Scholars, 1991.
    Hoppe, Leslie J. *OTA* 16:188-189 F 1993.

Stevens, Clifford, and McNichols, William Hart, eds.
Aloysius. Our Sunday Visitor, n.d.
    Dollen, Charles. *Priest* 49:56 S 1993.

Stevens, R. Paul, and Collins, Phil.
The equipping pastor. Alban Institute, n.d.
    Graham, William C. *Nat Cath Rep* 30:15 O 22 1993.

Stevens, Robert E, and Loudon, David L.
Marketing for churches and ministries. Haworth Press, 1992.
    Heiser, W Charles. *TheolDgst* 40:188 Sum 1993.

Stevenson, Kenneth W.
The first rites. Liturgical, 1989.
    Foley, Edward. *New Theol Rev* 6:108-109 Ag 1993.
Worship: wonderful and sacred mystery. The Pastoral Press, n.d.
    Gibbons, Robin. *Way* 33:260 Jl 1993.

Stevenson, Kenneth W. *(cont'd)*
Worship. Pastoral Press, 1992.
Brown, David O. *Mod Lit* 20:39 F 1993.
Heiser, W Charles. *TheolDgst* 40:188 Sum 1993.

Stevenson, Kenneth W, and Spinks, Bryan, eds.
The identity of Anglican worship. Mowbray, 1991.
Nichols, Bridget. *Heythrop* 34:437 O 1993.

Stewart, Charles.
Demons and the devil: moral imagination in modern Greek culture. Princeton University, 1991.
Makarushka, I. *TheolStds* 53:792 D 1992.

Stewart, Columba.
"Working the earth of the heart": the Messalian controversy in history, texts, and language to AD 431. Clarendon Press, 1991.
Blowers, Paul M. *Cist Stud* 28:[26]-[29] 1993.
Heiser, W Charles. *TheolDgst* 39:387 Wint 1992.

Stewart-Gambino, Hannah W.
The Church and politics in the Chilean countryside. Westview, 1992.
Smith, Brian. *TheolStds* 54:395-396 Je 1993.
Heiser, W Charles. *TheolDgst* 40:88 Spr 1993.

Stibbe, Mark W G.
John as storyteller. Cambridge University Press, 1992.
Heiser, W Charles. *TheolDgst* 39:387 Wint 1992.
Holleran, J Warren. *TheolStds* 54:194 Mr 1993.
Senior, Donald. *BibleT* 31:255 Jl 1993.
Koester, Craig R. *CBQ* 55:399-401 Ap 1993.

Stickler, A M, ed.
Studi Gregoriani. Per la storia della "Libertas Ecclesiae". LAS, 1991.
Plumat, N. *NRT* 115:611 Jl-Ag 1993.

Stivender, Ed.
Raised Catholic (can you tell?). August House, n.d.
Graham, William C. *Nat Cath Rep* 29:40+ F 5 1993.
Hurley, Karen. *St Anth* 101:52 N 1993.

Stock, K.
Jésus, la bonté de Dieu. Desclée, 1992.
Renard, L J. *NRT* 115:296-297 Mr-Ap 1993.

Stone, Michael Edward.
Fourth Ezra: a commentary on the Book of Fourth Ezra. Fortress Press, 1990.
Hamilton, Alastair. *Heythrop* 34:311 Jl 1993.
A history of the literature of Adam and Eve. Scholars, 1992.
Heiser, W Charles. *TheolDgst* 40:88-89 Spr 1993.
Levison, John R. *OTA* 16:451 Je 1993.

Stone, Ronald H.
Professor Reinhold Niebuhr, a mentor to the Twentieth Century. Westminister, 1992.
Heiser, W Charles. *TheolDgst* 40:188 Sum 1993.

Storr, Anthony.
Music and the mind. HarperCollins, n.d.
Amis, John. *Tablet* 246:1624 D 19-26 1992.

Stow, Kenneth R.
Alienated minority: the Jews of medieval Latin Europe. Harvard University Press, 1992.
Pawlikowski, John T. *TheolStds* 54:598 S 1993.

Strange, W A.
The problem of the text of Acts. Cambridge University Press, 1992.
Heiser, W Charles. *TheolDgst* 40:89 Spr 1993.

Strasser, Stephen, and Davis, Rose Marie.
Measuring patient satisfaction for improved patient services. American Healthcare Executives, 1991.
Simmons, Adrienne. *Health Prog* 74:68-69 Mr 1993.

Stratmann, Martina.
Hinkmar von Reims als Verwalter von Bistum und Kirchenprovinz. Jan Thorbecke Verlag, 1991.
Contreni, J. *CHist* 78:632-633 O 1992.

Straw, Carole.
Gregory the Great: perfection in imperfection. University of California Press, 1988.
Cusack, P. *Cist Stud* 27 No 4:[93]-[95] 1992.

Stream, Carol.
Standing up, standing together. National Association of Evangelicals, 1992.
Gros, Jeffrey, 1938-. *Emmanuel* 99:175=177 Ap 1993.

Stringer, Christopher, and Gamble, Clive.
In search of the Neandertals: solving the puzzle of human origins. Thames & Hudson, n.d.
Kenward, Robin Place. *Tablet* 247:1102-1103 Ag 28 1993.

Stritch, Thomas.
My Notre Dame: memories and reflections of sixty years. University of Notre Dame Press, 1991.
Burns, Jeffrey M. *CHist* 79:148 Ja 1993.

Strolz, M K, and Binder, M, eds.
John Henry Newman: lover of truth. Urbaniana Press, 1991.
Merrigan, Terrence. *Louvain Stds* 18:188-190 Sum 1993.

Strong, John S.
The legend and cult of Upagupta. Princeton University Press, 1992.
Heiser, W Charles. *TheolDgst* 40:188 Sum 1993.

Strosbert, Martin, et al, eds.
Rationing America's medical care: the Oregon plan and beyond. The Brookings Institute, 1992.
Barnet, Robert J. *Linacre* 60:92-94 My 1993.

Strübind, Kim.
Tradition als Interpretation in der Chronik. S de Gruyter, 1991.
Lust, Johan. *Eph Theol Lovan* 78:415-416 D 1992.
Begg, Christopher T. *OTA* 15:500 O 1992.

Stuart, Elizabeth.
Chosen: gay Catholic priests tell their stories. Geoffrey Chapman, 1993.
Callaghan, Brendan. *Tablet* 247:550 My 1 1993.
Cunliffe, C R A. *Priests & People* 7:366-367 Ag-S 1993.

Studer, Basil.
Dominus Salvator: studien zur Christologie und Exegese der Kirchenväter. Pontificio Ateneo S Anselmo, 1992.
Halleux, André de. *Eph Theol Lovan* 69:197-198 Ap 1993.

Stuhlhofer, Fr.
Jesus und seine Schüler. Brunnen Verlag, 1991.
Toubeau, A. *NRT* 114:942-943 N-D 1992.

Stuhlmacher, P, ed.
The gospel and the gospels. Fowler Wright, 1991.
Wansbrough, Henry. *Priests & People* 6:437-438 N 1992.

Sturch, Richard.
The word and the Christ: an essay in analytic Christology. Oxford University Press, 1991.
Galvin, John P, 1944-. *Heythrop* 34:190-191 Ap 1993.
Hellwig, Monika K, 1929-. *TheolStds* 54:176-178 Mr 1993.

Sturkie, Joan, and Cassady, Marsh.
Acting it out junior: discussion starters for 10-13 year olds. Resource Publications, n.d.
McCann, Deborah. *ReligTJ* 27:14-15 O 1993.

Style, Sue.
Honey. Pavillion, n.d.
Forrest, Denys. *Tablet* 247:173 F 6 1993.

Subhash, Anand.
Major Hindu festivals: a Christian appreciation. St Paul Publications, 1991.
Stuhlmueller, Carroll. *BibleT* 31:53 Ja 1993.

Suenens, Leo Jozef, Cardinal, 1904-.
Memories and hopes. Veritas, 1992.
Hurley, Mark Joseph, Bp, 1919-. *CHist* 79:130-131 Ja 1993.
Murphy, Francis Xavier, 1914-. *America* 168:17-18 Je 5-12 1993.
Souvenirs et espérances. Fayard, 1991.
Plumat, N. *NRT* 115:285-286 Mr-Ap 1993.
Caprile, Giovanni. *Civilta* 3:91-92 Jl 3 1993.

Suggs, M Jack, et al, eds.
The Oxford Study Bible. Revised English Bible with the Apocrypha. Oxford University Press, 1992.
Gibson, James E. *JEcumen Stds* 29:273 Spr 1992.

Sugirtharajah, R S.
Voices from the margin: interpreting the Bible in the Third World. Orbis, 1991.
Bergant, Dianne. *New Theol Rev* 6:90-91 F 1993.
Laffey, Alice L. *CBQ* 54:828-829 O 1992.
Dupuis, Jacques. *Gregorianum* 74 no 3:566-567 1993.

Sulle tracce del Concilio.
Seminario Vscovile di Bergamo, 1991.
Toubeau, A. *NRT* 115:297-298 Mr-Ap 1993.

Sullivan, Francis Aloysius.
The church we believe in: one, Holy, Catholic and apostolic. Paulist Press, 1988.
Granfield, Patrick. *Jurist* 51 no 2:521-522 1991.
Salvation outside the Church. Paulist Press, 1992.
McGregor, B. *Doctr Life* 43:60-61 Ja 1993.
Graham, William C. *Nat Cath Rep* 29:40 F 5 1993.
Higgins, James J. *Liguorian* 81:68-69 Mr 1993.
Tavard, George Henry. *CHist* 79:89-90 Ja 1993.
Anon. *Gregorianum* 74 No 1:196 1993.
Orsy, Ladislas, 1921-. *TheolStds* 54:178-179 Mr 1993.
MacCarthy, Peter T. *HPR* 93:77-78 Jl 1993.
Vercruysse, Jos E. *Eph Theol Lovan* 69:198-200 Ap 1993.
Endean, Philip. *Way* 33:249 Jl 1993.
Escol, R. *NRT* 115:584 Jl-Ag 1993.
Heiser, W Charles. *TheolDgst* 40:188-189 Sum 1993.

Sullivan, Francis P.
All eyes and blind: parable stories for Sunday Scripture—Cycle B. Sheed & Ward, n.d.
Cylwicki, Albert. *Can Cath Rev* 11:30 S 1993.

Sullivan, Mary Louise.
Mother Cabrini. Center Migration Studies, 1992.
Samway, Patrick H, 1939-. *America* 168:15 Mr 20-27 1993.
Weisgram, Jane. *Sisters* 65:222-223 My 1993.
Perko, F Michael. *RRel* 52:790-791 S-O 1993.

Summers, Anthony.
Official and confidential: the secret life of J Edgar Hoover. Gollancz, n.d.
Heren, Louis. *Tablet* 247:550-551 My 1 1993.

Sur les litanies de saint Joseph.
Dominique Martin Morin, 1991.
Bedard, Mariette. *CahiersJos* 41:135 Ja-Je 1993.

Surin, Kenneth.
Christ, ethics and tragedy essays in honor of Donald MacKinnon. Cambridge University Press, 1989.
Brinkman, B.R. *Heythrop* 34:437-438 O 1993.

Surtz, Edward, and Murphy, Virginia, eds.
The divorce tracts of Henry VIII. Moreana, 1988.
Nau, Dale. *Jurist* 51 no 2:517-519 1991.

Sutela, Pekka.
Economic thought and economic reform in the Soviet Union. Cambridge University Press, 1991.
Rider, Christine. *RSocEcon* 51:252-257 Sum 1993.

Sutera, Judith.
"Stewardship and the kingdom in RB 31-33". American Benedictine Review 41, 1990.
Baumstein, P. *Cist Stud* 27 No 4:[95]-[96] 1992.

Sutton, Agneta.
Infertility and assisted conception. The Catholic Bishops' Joint Committee on Bio-Ethical Issues, n.d.
Marshall, John. *Tablet* 247:823 Je 26 1993.

Svidercoschi, Gian Franco.
Lettera a un amico ebreo. Mondadori, 1993.
Rulli, Giovanni. *Civilta* 3:47-50 Jl 3 1993.

Swafford, Jan.
The new guide to classical music. Macmillan Papermac, n.d.
Amis, John. *Tablet* 247:585 My 8 1993.

Swartley, Willard M, ed.
The love of enemy and nonretaliation in the New Testament. John Knox Press, 1992.
Senior, Donald. *BibleT* 31:255 Jl 1993.

Swartz, Michael D.
Mystical prayer in ancient Judaism: an analysis of Ma'aseh Merkavah. JCB Mohr, 1992.
Heiser, W Charles. *TheolDgst* 39:388 Wint 1992.

Sweeney, Leo.
Divine infinity in Greek and medieval thought. Lang, 1992.
Bracken, Joseph A. *TheolStds* 54:365-366 Je 1993.
Heiser, W Charles. *TheolDgst* 40:189 Sum 1993.

Sweeney, Terrance.
A Church divided: the Vatican versus American Catholics. Prometheus Books, n.d.
McCloskey, Pat. *St Anth* 101:50-51 Je 1993.

Swidler, Leonard, et al, eds.
Bursting the bonds? A Jewish-Christian dialogue on Jesus and Paul. Orbis Books, 1990.
Dupuis, Jacques. *Gregorianum* 74 no 2:367-369 1993.
Brawley, Robert L. *JEcumen Stds* 29:277-278 Spr 1992.

Swidler, Leonard.
The meaning of life at the edge of the third millennium. Paulist Press, 1992.
Neckebrouck, Valeer. *Eph Theol Lovan* 69:206 Ap 1993.
Muslims in dialogue. Edwin Mellen Press, 1992.
Heiser, W Charles. *TheolDgst* 40:178 Sum 1993.
Yeshua: a model for moderns. Sheed & Ward, n.d.
Graham, William C. *Nat Cath Rep* 29:18 Jl 16 1993.

Swidler, Leonard, ed.
Human rights: Christians, Marxists, and others in dialogue. Paragon, 1991.
Bancroft, Nancy. *JEcumen Stds* 29:493 Sum-Aut 1992.

Swimme, Brian, and Berry, Thomas.
The universe story. HarperSanFrancisco, 1992.
Blewitt, J. *Nat Cath Rep* 29:28-29 F 5 1993.
Walsh, Denis. *CrossCurr* 43:107-110 Spr 1993.

Swinburne, Richard.
Revelation: from metaphor to analogy. Clarendon Press, 1991.
Ward, Keith. *New Blckfrs* 74:47-49 Ja 1993.

Swindell, Bill.
Fathers, come home. Greenlawn Press, n.d.
Graham, William C. *Nat Cath Rep* 30:16 O 22 1993.

Swinscow, Douglas.
The mystic garden. Halsgrove Press, n.d.
Taylor, Patrick. *Tablet* 247:375 Mr 20 1993.

Sydnor, William.
Introduction to the scripture read in worship. Morehouse Publishing, 1991.
Stuhlmueller, Carroll. *BibleT* 30:383 N 1992.

Sykes, Charles J.
A nation of victims. Saint Martin's Press, n.d.
Crocker, H W, III. *Crisis* 11:50-51 Mr 1993.

Sykes, S W, ed.
Karl Barth: centenary essays. Cambridge University Press, 1989.
Godsey, John D. *Thomist* 57:269-275 Ap 1993.
Sacrifice and redemption. Cambridge University Press, 1991.
Renwart, Léon. *NRT* 115:584 Jl-Ag 1993.

Sykes, Stephen, and Booty, John, eds.
The study of Anglicanism. SPCK, 1988.
Hamilton, Alastair. *Heythrop* 34:340 Jl 1993.

Synan, Vinson.
The Spirit said 'grow'. MARC, 1992.
Heiser, W Charles. *TheolDgst* 40:89 Spr 1993.

Syukes, S W, ed.
Sacrifice and redemption: Durham essays in theology. Cambridge University Press, 1991.
Gunton, Colin. *New Blckfrs* 73:630-632 D 1992.

Szentmártoni, Mihály.
Introduzione alla teologia pastorale. Piemme, 1992.
Anon. *Gregorianum* 74 no 3:603-604 1993.

Szpek, Heidi M.
Translation technique in the Peshitta to Job. Scholars, 1992.
Di Lella, Alexander A. *OTA* 16:424 Je 1993.

T

Taatz, Irene.
Frühjüdische briefe: die paulinischen Briefe im Rahmen der offiziellen religiösen Briefe des Frühjudentums. Vandenhoeck & Ruprecht, 1991.
Bowe, Barbara E. *CBQ* 55:185-186 Ja 1993.

Taft, Robert F.
The Byzantine Rite. Liturgical, 1992.
Brown, Daniel A. *Mod Lit* 20:36 S 1993.
A history of the liturgy of St John Chrysostom, volume IV, the Diptychs. Pontificium Institution Orientale, 1991.

Taft, Robert F. *(cont'd)*
Grisbrooke, W. *Worship* 67:474-475 S 1993.
La Liturgie des Heures en Orient et en Occident. Brepols, 1991.
Evenou, Jean. *Notitiae* 28:761-762 N-D 1992.

Talafous, Don.
A word for the day: reflections. Liturgical Press, n.d.
Graham, William C. *Nat Cath Rep* 29:39 F 5 1993.

Talbert, Charles H.
Learning through suffering: the educational value of suffering in the New Testament and in its milieu. Liturgical, 1991.
Mosser, David. *CBQ* 54:804-805 O 1992.
Reading John:. Crossroad, 1992.
Kurz, William S. *TheolStds* 54:594 S 1993.
Harrington, Daniel J. *America* 168:34 F 6 1993.
Stuhlmueller, Carroll. *BibleT* 31:126 Mr 1993.
Heiser, W Charles. *TheolDgst* 40:89 Spr 1993.

Talec, Pierre.
Les fêtes de Dieu. Centurion, 1991.
Partos, L. *Lumen* 48:233 Je 1993.

Tallert, Frank, and Atkin, Nicholas, eds.
Religion, society and politics in France since 1789. The Hambledon Press, 1991.
Gargan, Edward T. *CHist* 79:342-343 Ap 1993.

Talley, Thomas J.
Les origines de l'année liturgique. Cerf, 1990.
Anon. *NRT* 115:630-631 Jl-Ag 1993.
Le origini dell'anno liturgico. Queriniana, 1991.
Halleux, André de. *Eph Theol Lovan* 78:482 D 1992.
The origins of the liturgical year. Liturgical Press, 1991.
Poelker, T. *Past Mus* 17:50-51 D 1992-Ja 1993.
Halleux, André de. *Eph Theol Lovan* 78:482 D 1992.
Worship: reforming tradition. The Pastoral Press, 1990.
Covino, Paul. *Past Mus* 17:48-49 Ap-My 1993.

Talmage, John Philip.
Marquette University index. United States Catholic Conference, 1991.
Heiser, W Charles. *TheolDgst* 39:388 Wint 1992.

Talmon, Shemaryahu.
The world of Qumran from within. Brill, 1989.
Launderville, Dale. *OTA* 15:520-521 O 1992.

Talmon, Shemaryahu, ed.
Jewish civilization in the Hellenistic-Roman period. Trinity International, 1991.
Fitzmyer, Joseph Augustine, 1920-. *OTA* 16:451-452 Je 1993.

Tamayo-Acosta, Juan José.
Para comprender la teología de la liberación. Editorial Verbo Divino, 1991.
Libanio, Joao Batista. *Perspectiva* 25:99-102 Ja-Ap 1993.

Tambasco, Anthony J.
In the days of Paul. Paulist Press, 1992.
Kistner, H. *St Anth* 100:50-52 F 1993.
Heiser, W Charles. *TheolDgst* 39:388 Wint 1992.
McDonald, Patricia M. *Living Light* 29:95-96 Sum 1993.

Tamir, Yael.
Liberal nationalism. Princeton University Press, n.d.
McCabe, David. *Comm* 120:28-29 My 21 1993.

Tang, Edmond, and Wiest, Jean-Paul, eds.
The Catholic Church in modern China. Orbis, n.d.
Breen, Lawrie. *Tablet* 247:1262-1263 O 2 1993.

Tang, Shui Yan.
Institutions and collective action: self-governance in irrigation. Institute for Contemporary Studies, 1992.
Jonish, James. *RSocEcon* 51:116-118 Spr 1993.

Tanner, Kathryn, 1957-.
The politics of God: Christian theologies and social justice. Fortress Press, 1992.
Egan, Anthony. *Month* 26:234 Je 1993.

Tappy, Ron E.
The archaeology of Israelite Samaria, vol. 1. Scholars, 1992.
Edelman, Diana V. *OTA* 16:412 Je 1993.

Taradach, Madeleine.
El Midrash: introducció a la literatura midràshica, als targumim i als midrashim. Herder, 1989.
Lust, Johan. *Eph Theol Lovan* 78:160-161 Ap 1992.
Le Midrash: introduction à la littérature midrashique. Labor et Fides, 1991.
Lust, Johan. *Eph Theol Lovan* 78:160-161 Ap 1992.

Tarazi, Paul Nadim.
The Old Testament [v 1]. St Vladimir's Seminary, 1991.
Heiser, W Charles. *TheolDgst* 40:189 Sum 1993.

Targonski, Francesco.
Teologia morale et mentalità scientifica. Editrice Miscellanea Francescana, 1985.
Étienne, Jacques. *Eph Theol Lovan* 78:482-483 D 1992.

Targum Neofiti 1: Genesis.
Michael Glazier Books, 1992.
Stuhlmueller, Carroll. *BibleT* 30:379-380 N 1992.

Targum pseudo-Jonathan: Genesis.
Michael Glazier Books, 1992.
Stuhlmueller, Carroll. *BibleT* 30:379-380 N 1992.

Tarling, Thomasina.
The container garden. Conran Octopus, n.d.
Taylor, Patrick. *Tablet* 247:375 Mr 20 1993.

Tarnas, Richard.
The passion of the Western mind. Crown Publishers, 1991.
Krasevac, Edward L. *Thomist* 57:550-553 Jl 1993.

Tate, Marvin E.
Psalms 51-100. Word, 1991.
Stuhlmueller, Carroll. *BibleT* 31:57 Ja 1993.

Tauler, Jean.
Sermons. Cerf, 1991.
Breton, Jean-Claude. *Laval Theol Phil* 49:170-171 F 1993.

Tavard, George Henry.
The Church, community of salvation. Liturgical, 1992.
Coulombe, Charles. *New Oxford Rev* 60:28 Mr 1993.
O'Donovan, Jo. *Furrow* 44:254-255 Ap 1993.
Daly, Bernard M. *Can Cath Rev* 11:29 Je 1993.
Heiser, W Charles. *TheolDgst* 40:89 Spr 1993.
Thiessen, Gesa. *Studies* 82:207-210 Sum 1993.
Anon. *NRT* 115:622-623 Jl-Ag 1993.
Merkle, Judith A. *TheolStds* 54:584-585 S 1993.

Taylor, Audrey, and Taylor, Joe.
Families exploring faith. Don Bosco Multimedia, n.d.
Hanlon, James. *Can Cath Rev* 11:31 O 1993.

Taylor, Bernard A.
The Lucianic manuscripts of 1 Reigns: Vol 1, Majority Text. Scholars, 1992.
Willis, Timothy M. *OTA* 16:421 Je 1993.

Taylor, C G W.
Ethics and the environment. Oxford, 1992.
Walters, Hugh. *New Blckfrs* 73:578-579 N 1992.

Taylor, Charles, 1931-.
The ethics of authenticity. Harvard University Press, 1992.
Haldane, John. *Tablet* 247:213 F 13 1993.
McCabe, David. *Comm* 120:19-20 F 12 1993.
Giles, James E. *CrossCurr* 43:261-262 Sum 1993.
Devine, Philip E. *New Oxford Rev* 60:32 O 1993.
Multiculturalism and "the politics of recognition". Princeton University Press, n.d.
McCabe, David. *Comm* 120:19-20 F 12 1993.
Multiculturalism and "the politics of recognition". Princeton University Press, 1992.
Henrie, Mark C. *Crisis* 11:46-47 F 1993.
Giles, James E. *CrossCurr* 43:261-262 Sum 1993.

Taylor, Elisabeth Russell.
Pillion riders. Peter Owen, n.d.
Delay, Jill. *Tablet* 247:922 Jl 17 1993.

Taylor, Jane.
Climbers and wall plants for year round colour. Cassell, n.d.
Taylor, Patrick. *Tablet* 247:375 Mr 20 1993.
The shady garden. Conran Octopus, n.d.
Taylor, Patrick. *Tablet* 247:375 Mr 20 1993.

Taylor, Joe, and Taylor, Audrey.
Families exploring faith: a parent's guide to the older adolescent years. John Bosco Multimedia, n.d.
Dotterweich, Kass. *Liguorian* 81:68-69 S 1993.

Taylor, John V, Bp.
The Christlike God. SCM, n.d.
Endean, Philip. *Way* 33:248 Jl 1993.
O'Collins, Gerald, 1931-. *Tablet* 247:1045 Ag 14 1993.
Gallagher, Peter. *Month* 26:318-319 Ag 1993.

Taylor, Larissa.
Soldiers of Christ: preaching in late medieval and Reformation France. Oxford University Press, 1992.
Farge, James K. *CHist* 79:103-104 Ja 1993.
Heiser, W Charles. *TheolDgst* 39:389 Wint 1992.

Taylor, Marion Ann.
The Old Testament in the old Princeton school. Mellen Research University, 1992.
Begg, Christopher T. *OTA* 16:412-413 Je 1993.

Taylor, Mark C, 1945-.
Disfiguring: art, architecture, religion. University of Chicago Press, 1992.
Heiser, W Charles. *TheolDgst* 39:389 Wint 1992.

Taylor, Mark K.
Remembering esperanza: a cultural-political theology of North American praxis. Orbis Books, 1990.
Williams, Ian S. *Pacifica* 6:228-231 Je 1993.

Taylor, Maxwell.
The fanatics: a behavioral approach to political violence. Brassey's, n.d.
Main, William. *Crisis* 10:48-51 N 1992.

Taylor, Peter.
The oracle at Stoneleigh. Knopf, n.d.
Samway, Patrick H, 1939-. *America* 168:20 Mr 20-27 1993.

Taylor, Telford.
The anatomy of the Nuremberg Trials: a personal memoir. Bloomsbury, n.d.
Hodgkin, E C. *Tablet* 247:515-516 Ap 24 1993.

Teeple, Howard M.
How did Christianity really begin? a historical-archaeological approach. Religion and Ethics Institute, 1992.
Heiser, W Charles. *TheolDgst* 39:389 Wint 1992.

Teixidor, Javier.
Bardesane d'Edesse la première philosophie syriaque. Éd du Cerf, 1992.
Spanneut, Michel. *MSR* 50:152-154 Ap-Je 1993.

Tekippe, Terry J.
Theology: love's question. University Press of America, 1992.
MacCarthy, Peter T. *HPR* 93:70-71 F 1993.

Tellechea Idígoras, J Ignacio.
Diocesis de Calahorra y Santo Domingo. Instituto Español de Historia Eclesiástica, 1991.
Hernández, Ramón. *Cien Tom* 120:198-199 Ja-Ap 1993.
Plumat, N. *NRT* 115:614-615 Jl-Ag 1993.

Témoins sans frontières.
Éd du Lion de Juda, 1992.
Renard, L J. *NRT* 115:307-309 Mr-Ap 1993.

Templeton, Elizabeth.
God's February: a life of Archie Craig, 1888-1985. British Coundil of Churches, 1991.
Kollar, Rene. *JEcumen Stds* 29:266-267 Spr 1992.

Terestchenko, Michel.
Enjeux de philosophie politique moderne. Les violences de l'abstraction. Presses universitaires de France, 1992.
Pasqua, Hervé. *RPhil Louvain* 91:495 Ag 1993.

Ternay, Henry d'Aviau de.
Traces bibliques dans la loi morale chez Kant. Beauchesne, 1986.
Konings, Johan. *Perspectiva* 25:113-116 Ja-Ap 1993.

Terrasse, Jean.
De mentor à orphée, essais sur les écrits pédagogiques de Rousseau. Éditions Hurtubise HMH.
Larochelle, Élaine. *Laval Theol Phil* 49:373-374 Je 1993.

Tesserae.
Aschendorffsche Verlagsbuchhandlung, 1991.
Plumat, N. *NRT* 114:926-927 N-D 1992.

Tetlow, Joseph Allen.
Ignatius Loyola: spiritual exercises. Crossroad, 1992.
Harter, Michael G. *RRel* 52:474-475 My-Je 1993.
Heiser, W Charles. *TheolDgst* 40:89-90 Spr 1993.
Endean, Philip, and Lonsdale, David. *Way* 33:251 Jl 1993.

Theisen, Jerome P.
The ultimate church and promise of salvation. The Liturgical Press, n.d.
Higgins, James J. *Liguorian* 81:69 Mr 1993.

Theissen, Gerd.
The gospels in context. Fortress, 1991.
Senior, Donald. *BibleT* 31:317 S 1993.
The open door. Fortress, 1991.
Toubeau, A. *NRT* 114:944 N-D 1992.
Sociologia do movimento de Jesus. Sinodal/Vozes, 1989.
Libanio, Joao Batista. *Perspectiva* 25:2568-260 My-Ag 1993.

Theresa of Lisieux, Saint, 1873-1897.
Nella Chiesa io sarò l'amore. Citta Nuova, 1991.
Mellinato, Giuseppe. *Civilta* 3:198-200 Jl 17 1993.
Preghiere. Queriniana, 1991.
Mellinato, Giuseppe. *Civilta* 3:198-200 Jl 17 1993.
Thérèse of Lisieux. New City Press, 1992.
Heiser, W Charles. *TheolDgst* 40:189 Sum 1993.

Thérèse de l'Enfant-Jésus, Docteur de l'Amour.
Éd du Carmel, 1991.
Renard, L J. *NRT* 115:130 Ja-F 1993.

Therese, Miriam.
Winter, womanwitness: a feminist lectionary and psalter: women of the Hebrew Scriptures, Part 2. Crossroad, 1992.
Chen, Sheryl Frances. *Cist Stud* 27 No 4:[119]-[110] 1992.

Thévenot, Xavier.
Compter sur Dieu, etude de théologie morale. Les Éditions du Cerf, 1992.
Chénard, Gabriel. *Laval Theol Phil* 49:377-378 Je 1993.

Thiel, John E.
Imagination and authority: theological authorship in the modern tradition. Fortress, 1991.
Wood, Charles. *TheolStds* 53:768-770 D 1992.
Lash, Nicholas. *Heythrop* 34:445-446 O 1993.
Heiser, W Charles. *TheolDgst* 39:389-390 Wint 1992.

Thiering, Barbara.
Jesus and the riddle of the Dead Sea Scrolls. HarperCollins, 1992.
Stuhlmueller, Carroll. *BibleT* 31:126 Mr 1993.
Santa, Thomas M. *Liguorian* 81:70 Ap 1993.

Thils, Gustave.
La communion ecclésiale dans le cadre juridique de l'État moderne. Peeters, 1993.
Étienne, Jacques. *Eph Theol Lovan* 69:216-217 Ap 1993.
L'État moderne non-confessionnel et le message chrétien. Peeters, 1992.
Étienne, Jacques. *Eph Theol Lovan* 78:484 D 1992.
Anon. *NRT* 115:151 Ja-F 1993.
Primauté et infaillibilité du Pontife romain à Vatican I et autres études d'ecclésiologie. Peeters, 1989.
Simon, Michele. *Eph Theol Lovan* 78:176-177 Ap 1992.
La profession de foi et le serment de fidélité. Publications de la Faculté de théologie, 1989.
Simon, Michele. *Eph Theol Lovan* 78:177-178 Ap 1992.

Thiselton, Anthony C.
New horizons in hermeneutics: the theory and practice of transforming Biblical readings. Zondervan, 1992.
Murphy, Roland E. *OTA* 16:189 F 1993.

Thomas, Aquinas, Saint, 1225?-1274.
God's greatest gifts: commentaries on the commandments and the sacraments. Sophia Institute Press, 1992.
Heiser, W Charles. *TheolDgst* 39:390 Wint 1992.

Thomas, David M.
Not guilty: in defence of the modern man. Weidenfeld & Nicolson, n.d.
Kenny, Mary, 1936-. *Tablet* 247:371-372 Mr 20 1993.

Thomas, David M, ed.
Anti-Christian polemic in early Islam: Abū Īsā al-Warrāq's against the Trinity. Cambridge University, 1992.
Sara, Solomon I. *TheolStds* 53:783 D 1992.

Thomas, George M.
Revivalism and social change: Christianity, nation building and the market in the nineteenth-century United States. University of Chicago Press, 1989.
Aspinwall, Bernard. *Heythrop* 34:345-346 Jl 1993.

Thomas, John Christopher.
Footwashing in John 13 and the Johannine community. Cornell University Press, 1991.
Heiser, W Charles. *TheolDgst* 40:90 Spr 1993.
Maloney, Francis J. *Pacifica* 6:212-214 Je 1993.

Thomas, Leo, and Alkire, Jan.
Healing as a parish ministry: mending body, mind, and spirit. Ave Maria Press, 1992.
Brown, David O. *Mod Lit* 19:42 D 1992-Ja 1993.
Heiser, W Charles. *TheolDgst* 39:390 Wint 1992.

Thomas, M M.
My ecumenical journey: 1947-1975. Ecumenical Publishing Centre Private Ltd, 1990.
Bent, Ans J van der. *JEcumen Stds* 29:105-106 Wint 1992.

Thomas, Pascal.
Pour une mémoire catéchuménale. Service National du Catéchuménat, 1992.
Partos, L. *Lumen* 47:468 D 1992.

Thomas, Patrick.
Candle inthe darkness: Celtic spirituality from Wales. Gomer Press, n.d.
Waal, Esther de. *Tablet* 247:1302 O 9 1993.

Thomas, R S.
Mass for hard times. Bloodaxe, n.d.
Bergonzi, Bernard, 1929-. *Tablet* 247:170-171 F 6 1993.

Thomas, Robert.
Passer de soi-même à Dieu, Sainte-Foy. Sigier, 1990.
Ganzi, I M. *Civilta* 144:199-200 Ja 16 1993.
La Vierge Marie: homélies des Pères Cisterciens. Ann Sigier, 1989.
Barker, Bede M. *Cist Stud* 28:[32]-[34] 1993.
Vita di S Bernardo. Borla, 1991.
Forlizzi, G. *Civilta* 2:309-310 My 1 1993.

Thomas, Stephen.
Newman and heresy. Cambridge University Press, 1991.
Detienne, P. *NRT* 114:911-912 N-D 1992.
Hammond, David M. *Relig Lit* 24:97-104 Aut 1992.
Magill, Gerard. *Horizons (CTS)* 20:149-150 Spr 1993.

Thomas Aquinas, Saint.
Light of faith: the compendium of theology. Sophia Institute Press, n.d.
Meyer, Gabriel. *Register* 69:4 Jl 4 1993.
Dollen, Charles. *Priest* 49:56 S 1993.
Ökonomie, Politik und Ethik aus Summa Theologiae. Verlag Wirtschaft und Finanzen, 1991.
Rosemann, Philipp W. *RPhil Louvain* 91:320-322 My 1993.
Suma de Teología; III: Parte II-II. Biblioteca de Autores Cristianos, 1991.
Osuna, Antonio. *Cien Tom* 120:193-194 Ja-Ap 1993.

Thomasis, Louis De.
Imagination: a future for religious life. Metanoia Group, 1992.
Kropf, Richard. *Nat Cath Rep* 29:13-14 Mr 5 1993.
Davies, Julian A. *Sisters* 65:306 Jl 1993.

Thomasma, David C.
Human life in the balance. John Knox, 1990.
Di Domizio, Daniel. *Living Light* 29:87-88 Aut 1992.

Thompson, Leslie M, et al, eds.
Perspectives on life-threatening illness for allied health professionals. Haworth Press, 1993.
Anon. *Health Prog* 74:68-69 1993.

Thompson, Marianne Meye.
1-3 John. Inter Varsity Press, n.d.
O'Reilly, Leo. *Furrow* 44:193 Mr 1993.

Thompson, Michael B.
Clothed with Christ: the example and teaching of Jesus in Romans 12.1-15.13. JSOT Press, 1991.
Heiser, W Charles. *TheolDgst* 40:90 Spr 1993.

Thompson, Thomas L.
Early history of the Israelite people: from the written and archaeological sources. Brill, 1992.
Edelman, Diana V. *OTA* 16:413 Je 1993.

Thompson, William M.
Christology and spirituality. Crossroad, 1991.
Imbelli, Robert P. *TheolStds* 53:776-778 D 1992.
Krasevac, Edward L. *Thomist* 57:136-140 Ja 1993.
Cook, Michael L. *Horizons (CTS)* 20:154-155 Spr 1993.
Galot, Jean. *Gregorianum* 74 no 2:369 1993.

Thornhill, John.
Making Australia: exploring our national conversation. Millenium Books, 1992.
Kelly, Tony. *Pacifica* 6:234-236 Je 1993.

Thorogood, Bernard.
One wind, many flames. WCC, 1991.
Lewis, Eleanor V. *JEcumen Stds* 29:474-475 Sum-Aut 1992.

Throckmorton, Burton H, Jr, ed.
Gospel parallels. Thomas Nelson, 1992.
Heiser, W Charles. *TheolDgst* 40:152 Sum 1993.
The Gospels and the Letters of Paul: an inclusive-language edition. Pilgrim Press, 1992.
Pilch, John Joseph, 1936-. *Mod Lit* 20:41 Ap 1993.

Throntveit, Mark A.
Ezra-Nehemiah. John Knox Press, 1992.
Stuhlmueller, Carroll. *BibleT* 30:383 N 1992.
Wright, John W. *OTA* 15:500 O 1992.
Heiser, W Charles. *TheolDgst* 39:390 Wint 1992.

Thurian, Max.
Una vita per l'unita. Piemme, 1991.
Mellinato, Giuseppe. *Civilta* 143:533-534 D 5 1992.
Clarot, B. *NRT* 114:937 N-D 1992.

Thursby, G R.
The Sikhs. E. J. Brill, 1992.
Scheuer, J. *NRT* 115:604-605 Jl-Ag 1993.

Thwaite, Anthony, ed.
Selected letters of Philip Larkin 1940-1985. Faber and Faber, 1992.
Marshall, Oliver. *Studies* 82:230-234 Sum 1993.

Tickle, Phyllis, ed.
Confessing conscience: churched women on abortion. Abingdon Press, 1990.
Quitslund, Sonya A. *JEcumen Stds* 29:260-262 Spr 1992.

Tiede, David.
Jesus and the future. Cambridge University, 1990.
Winkler, Jude. *CBQ* 54:788-789 O 1992.

Tierney, Terrence E.
Annulment. Alba House, n.d.
Dollen, Charles. *Priest* 49:48 O 1993.

Tilby, Angela.
Science and the soul. SPCK, 1992.
Hodgson, Peter. *New Blckfrs* 74:168-170 Mr 1993.
Endean, Philip. *Way* 33:248 Jl 1993.
Soul: an introduction to the new cosmology—time, consciousness and God. BBC Education, n.d.
Haldane, John. *Tablet* 247:720-721 Je 5 1993.

Tillard, Jean Marie Roger, 1927-.
Chair de l'Eglise, chair du Christ. Cerf, 1992.
Toubeau, A. *NRT* 114:901-902 N-D 1992.
Tavard, George Henry. *TheolStds* 54:200 Mr 1993.
Church of churches. The Liturgical Press, 1992.
Heiser, W Charles. *TheolDgst* 39:390 Wint 1992.
Falardeau, Ernest R, 1928-. *Emmanuel* 99:357 Jl-Ag 1993.
McBrien, Richard P. *Worship* 67:381-382 Jl 1993.
Iglesia de iglesias: Eclesiología de comunión. Sígueme, 1991.
Bandera, Armando. *Cien Tom* 119:613-614 S-D 1992.

Tillich, P.
La dimension religieuse de la culture. Presses de l'Université Laval, 1990.
Evrard, P. *NRT* 115:270-272 Mr-Ap 1993.

Tilliette, G.
Jésus en ses mystères. Desclée, 1992.
Renard, L J. *NRT* 115:312 Mr-Ap 1993.

Tilliette, Xavier.
Le Christ de la philosophie. Éditiones du Cerf, 1990.
Brito, Emilio. *RPhil Louvain* 91:154-156 F 1993.
La semaine Sainte des philosophes. Desclée, 1992.
Brito, Emilio. *RPhil Louvain* 91:156-159 F 1993.
La settimana santa dei filosofi. Morcelliana, 1992.
Lorizio, G. *Civilta* 3:536-537 S 18 1993.

Timmer, John.
Once upon a time: story sermons for children. Zondervan Publishing House, 1992.
Alfred, Joseph R. *Mod Lit* 20:40-41 Je-Jl 1993.

Timmerman, Joan.
Sexuality and spiritual growth. Crossroad, n.d.
Tilby, Angela. *Way* 33:84 Ja 1993.

Tineo, Primitivo.
Los concilios limenses en la evangelización latinoamericana. Ediciones Universidad de Navarra, 1990.
Salinas, Carlos. *Teol Vida* 33 no 3-4:324-325 1992.

Tinsley, B C.
History and polemics in the reformation. Associated University Press, 1992.
Evrard, P. *NRT* 115:613 Jl-Ag 1993.

Toibin, Colm.
The heather blazing. St Martin's Press, n.d.
Costello, Gerald M, 1931-. *USCath* 58:50-51 S 1993.

Tolson, Jay.
Pilgrim in the ruins: a life of Walker Percy. Simon & Schuster, n.d.
Simmons, Tracy Lee. *Crisis* 10:47-48 N 1992.
Orwen, Nancy. *Can Cath Rev* 11:23-24 O 1993.

Tomberg, Valentin.
Covenant of the heart: meditations of a Christian hermeticist on the mysteries of tradition. Element Books, n.d.
Caldecott, Stratford. *Tablet* 247:790-791 Je 19 1993.

Tomes, Jonathan P.
The trustee's guide to understanding healthcare antitrust law issues. Healthcare Financial Management Association, 1992.
Parkhurst, Vance C. *Health Prog* 74:68 1993.

Tomizza, Fulvio.
Heavenly supper: the story of Maria Janis. The University of Chicago Press, 1991.
Astarita, Tommaso. *CHist* 79:114-115 Ja 1993.

Tompkins, Peter, and Bird, Christopher.
Secrets of the soil. Penguin Books, n.d.
Anon. *Teilhard Rev* 27:98-99 Wint 1992.

Tomson, Peter.
Paul and the Jewish law. Fortress, 1990.
Turro, James C. *CBQ* 54:805-806 O 1992.

Tomson, Peter J.
Paul and the Jewish law. Fortress, 1990.
Perelmuter, Hayim Goren. *New Theol Rev* 6:115-116 My 1993.

Toner, James Hugh.
The sword and the cross. Praeger, 1992.
Heiser, W Charles. *TheolDgst* 40:189 Sum 1993.

Toner, Jules J.
Discerning God's will: Ignatius Loyola's teaching on Christian decision making. Institute of Jesuit Sources, 1991.
Gray, Howard. *TheolStds* 53:759-760 D 1992.

Tooma, Lynn.
Exploring the Bible. St Mary's Press, 1990.
Stuhlmueller, Carroll. *BibleT* 30:383 N 1992.

Toon, Peter.
Spiritual companions: introduction to the Christian classics. Baker Book House, 1992.
Heiser, W Charles. *TheolDgst* 40:90 Spr 1993.

Tornos, Andrés.
Escatología I y II. Publicaciones de la Universidad Pontificia Comillas, 1991.
Libanio, Joao Batista. *Perspectiva* 25:107-110 Ja-Ap 1993.

Torrance, Thomas F.
Karl Barth: Biblical and evangelical theologian. T and T Clark, 1990.
Hanvey, J. *Heythrop* 34:87-88 Ja 1993.

Torre, Michael D, ed.
Freedom in the modern world: Maritain, Simon, Adler. American Maritain Association, 1989.
Brinkman, B R. *Heythrop* 34:470-472 O 1993.

Tortolano, William.
Fifty-nine liturgical rounds. GIA Publications, 1990.
Marcozzi, R. *Past Mus* 17:49-50 D 1992-Ja 1993.

Toschi, Larry M.
Joseph in the New Testament. St. Joseph's House of Studies, 1991.
Gauthier, Roland. *CahiersJos* 41:134-135 Ja-Je 1993.

Toulson, Shirley.
The Celtic year. Element, n.d.
Waal, Esther de. *Tablet* 247:1302-1303 O 9 1993.
Graham, William C. *Nat Cath Rep* 30:15 O 22 1993.

Tournay, Raymond Jacques.
Seeing and hearing God with the Psalms: the prophetic liturgy of the Second Temple. Sheffield, 1991.
Lust, Johan. *Eph Theol Lovan* 69:163-164 Ap 1993.
Voir et entendre Dieu avec les Psaumes, ou la liturgie prophétique du second temple à Jérusalem. Gabalda, 1988.
Lust, Johan. *Eph Theol Lovan* 69:163-164 Ap 1993.

Tov, Emanuel.
Textual criticism of the Hebrew Bible. Fortress, 1992.
Di Lella, Alexander A. *OTA* 16:413-414 Je 1993.

Tracy, David.
Dialogue with the other: the inter-religious dialogue. Peeters Press, 1990.
Hick, John. *JEcumen Stds* 29:280-281 Spr 1992.
Kelly, Tony. *Pacifica* 6:244-245 Je 1993.

Trainor, Michael.
According to Luke. CollinsDove, 1992.
Senior, Donald. *BibleT* 31:317 S 1993.

Trainor, Michael, and Brady, Michael.
Voices from the edge. CollinsDove, 1992.
Senior, Donald. *BibleT* 31:317 S 1993.

Trakatellis, Demetrios.
The transcendent God of Eugnostos. Holy Cross Orthodox, 1991.
Timbie, Janet. *CBQ* 55:401-402 Ap 1993.

Trebilco, Paul R.
Jewish communities in Asia Minor. Cambridge University, 1991.
Kraaebel, A T. *CBQ* 55:186-187 Ja 1993.

Tremmel, Hans.
Grundrecht Asyl. Herder, 1992.
Hainz, M. *Stimm Zeit* 210:862-863 D 1992.

Treston, Kevin.
A new vision of religious education. Twenty-Third, n.d.
McCann, Deborah. *ReligTJ* 27:14 S 1993.

Tretjakewitsch, Léon.
Bishop Michael d'Herbigny SJ and Russia: a pre-ecumenical approach to Christian unity. Augustinus, 1990.
Poggi, V. *Civilta* 2:405-407 My 15 1993.
Bishop Michel d'Herbigny SJ and Russia: a pre-ecumenical approach to Christian unity. Augustinus, 1990.
Hull, Henry Lane. *CHist* 79:128-129 Ja 1993.

Trettel, Giulio.
La Vergine Maria in s cromazio. Giulia, 1991.
Cremascoli, G. *Civilta* 144:95-96 Ja 2 1993.

Trevett, Christine.
A study of Ignatius of Antioch in Syria and Asia. The Edwin Mellen Press, 1992.
Heiser, W Charles. *TheolDgst* 40:90 Spr 1993.

Trevor-Roper, Hugh.
Catholics, Anglicans, and Puritans. The University of Chicago Press, 1988.
Spielmann, Richard M. *JEcumen Stds* 29:106 Wint 1992.
From counter-reformation to glorious revolution. University of Chicago Press, 1992.
Heiser, W Charles. *TheolDgst* 40:189-190 Sum 1993.
Havran, Martin J. *CHist* 79:537-538 Jl 1993.

Triboulet, R.
Gaston de Renty: 1611-1649. Beauchesne, 1991.
Renard, L J. *NRT* 115:279 Mr-Ap 1993.

Trick, Barry J.
The week in daily prayer. The Liturgical Press, n.d.
McCann, Deborah. *ReligTJ* 27:9 Mr 1993.
Pecht, Gerard. *Liguorian* 81:69 Ag 1993.

Trigo, Pedro.
Creation and history. Orbis, 1991.
Stuhlmueller, Carroll. *BibleT* 31:57 Ja 1993.
Lord, Elizabeth. *Way* 33:156-157 Ap 1993.
Carroll, Denis. *Furrow* 44:385-386 Je 1993.

Trillin, Calvin.
Remembering Denny. Farrar, Straus & Giroux, n.d.
Hunt, George W, 1937-. *America* 168:2 My 8 1993.

Trinkhaus, Eric, and Shipman, Pat.
The Neandertals: changing the image of mankind. Cape, n.d.
Kenward, Robin Place. *Tablet* 247:1102-1103 Ag 28 1993.

Troia, Pasquale, ed.
La musica e la Bibbia: atti del Convegno Internazionale di Studi (Siena 24-26 agosto 1992). Garamond, 1992.
Arledler, G. *Civilta* 144:100 Ja 2 1993.

Trokan, John, and Trokan, Nancy.
Families sharing faith. Don Bosco Multimedia, n.d.
Hanlon, James. *Can Cath Rev* 11:31 O 1993.

Trombino, Mario, et al.
Pensare il bello. Augustinus, 1991.
Halleux, André de. *Eph Theol Lovan* 78:465-466 D 1992.
Fisichella, Rino. *Gregorianum* 74 no 2:408-409 1993.

Trotta, Giuseppe.
Il sabato nella tradizione ebraica. Morcelliana, 1991.
Katunarich, S M. *Civilta* 2:100-101 Ap 3 1993.

True, Michael, 1933-.
More justice seekers, peace makers. Twenty-Third, 1992.
Higgins, James J. *Liguorian* 81:69 F 1993.
To construct peace. Twenty-Third, 1992.
Belisle, Jennifer. *Cath Work* 60:6 S 1993.

Trumbower, Jeffrey A.
Born from above: the anthropology of the Gospel of John. C B Mohr, 1992.
Heiser, W Charles. *TheolDgst* 39:390 Wint 1992.

Trusso, Francisco Eduardo.
Erasmo en América: entre la ortodoxia y la marginación. Troquel, 1991.
Salvini, Gianpaolo. *Civilta* 2:96-97 Ap 3 1993.

Trutwin, Werner, and Breuning, Klaus, eds.
Amare il prossimo: corso di etica. Brescia, 1991.
Cultrera, Francesco. *Civilta* 144:192-193 Ja 16 1993.

Trutwin, Werner, and Francesconi, Gianni, eds.
Credere in Dio. Corso di teologia. Queriniana, 1991.
Ferrari, M. *Civilta* 3:543 S 18 1993.

Tsatsos, Constantinos.
Dialoghi al monastero. Le Lettere, 1991.
Spidlik, Thomas. *Civilta* 3:200 Jl 17 1993.

Tsirpanlis, Constantine N.
Greek patristic theology, vol III. E O Press, 1987.
Mathews, Edward G. *Diakonia* 26 no 2:142-143 1993.
Greek patristic theology, vol IV. E O Press, 1990.
Mathews, Edward G. *Diakonia* 26 no 2:142-143 1993.
Introduction to eastern patristic and Orthodox theology. Liturgical, 1991.
Fox, Christina. *Pacifica* 6:343-344 O 1993.

Tuck, Richard.
Hobbes. Oxford University Press, 1989.
Sweet, W. *Heythrop* 34:107-108 Ja 1993.

Tucker, Phillip Thomas.
The Confederacy's fighting chaplain: Father John B Bannon. University of Alabama Press, 1992.
Lipscomb, Oscar Hugh, Abp, 1931-. *CHist* 79:573-574 Jl 1993.

Tuell, Jack M, and Fjeld, Roger W, eds.
Episcopacy: Lutheran-United Methodist dialogue II. Augsburg, 1991.
Diener, Paul W. *JEcumen Stds* 29:268 Spr 1992.

Tufano, Victoria M.
Celebrating the rites of adult initiation: pastoral reflections. Liturgy Training Publications, 1992.
Berthelot, M. *Mod Lit* 20:39 F 1993.

Tugwell, Simon.
Human immortality and the redemption of death. Templegate, n.d.
Callam, Daniel. *Can Cath Rev* 11:42 Ja 1993.

Tullock, John H.
The Old Testament story. Prentice-Hall, 1992.
Stuhlmueller, Carroll. *BibleT* 31:57 Ja 1993.

Tunstead, James.
From synagogue to church: public services and offices in the earliest Christian communities. Cambridge University Press, 1992.
Gordon, Charles B. *Priests & People* 7:166-168 Ap 1993.

Tupini, Giorgio.
De Gasperi: una testimonianza. Il Mulino, 1992.
Mellinato, Giuseppe. *Civilta* 143:536-537 D 5 1992.

Turner, Dean.
Escape from God. Hope Publishing House, 1991.
Lebeau, Paul. *Lumen* 48:360 S 1993.

Turner, Edith.
Experiencing ritual. University of Pennsylvania Press, 1992.
Heiser, W Charles. *TheolDgst* 40:190 Sum 1993.

Turner, Harold W.
Bibliography of new religious movements in primal societies, v 6. G K Hall, 1992.
Heiser, W Charles. *TheolDgst* 40:190 Sum 1993.

Turner, Laurence A.
Announcements of Plot in Genesis. Scheffield, 1990.
Carr, David. *CBQ* 55:133-134 Ja 1993.

Turner, Paul.
Confirmation. Paulist, 1993.
Brown, Daniel A. *Mod Lit* 20:36 S 1993.
Gibeau, Dawn. *Nat Cath Rep* 29:15 O 1 1993.
Martos, Joseph. *Living Light* 30:104-105 Aut 1993.

Turnley, David C.
The Russian heart: days of crisis and hope. Phaidon Press, n.d.
FitzLyon, April. *Tablet* 247:76-77 Ja 16 1993.

Turoldo, D M.
Neanche Dio può stare solo. Piemme, 1991.
Toubeau, A. *NRT* 115:135-136 Ja-F 1993.

Turow, Scott.
Pleading guilty. Farrar, Straus & Giroux, n.d.
Wexler, Joyce. *America* 169:22 N 27 1993.

Turrettini, François, 1623-1687.
Institutes of elenctic theology. Presbyterian and Reformed, 1992.
Heiser, W Charles. *TheolDgst* 40:190 Sum 1993.

Turtledove, Harry.
The guns of the South: a novel of the Civil War. Ballantine Books, n.d.
Arbery, Glenn. *Crisis* 11:58-59 Jl-Ag 1993.

U

V

Varillon, Brother.
Vivre le christianisme. Centurion, 1992.
Renard, L.-J. *NRT* 115:594-595 Jl-Ag 1993.

Vattimo, Gianni.
The transparent society. Johns Hopkins University Press, 1992.
Lewandowski, Joseph D. *Mod Schlmn* 70:231-234 Mr 1993.

Vaux, Kenneth L.
Ethics and the Gulf War. Westview Press, 1992.
Heiser, W Charles. *TheolDgst* 40:191 Sum 1993.

Vawter, Bruce, and Hoppe, Leslie J.
A new heart: a commentary on the Book of Ezekiel. Eerdsmans, 1991.
Duguid, Iain M. *CBQ* 54:770 O 1992.

Veith, Gene Edward.
Modern fascism. Concordia, n.d.
Higgins, James J. *Liguorian* 81:69-70 O 1993.

Velasco, J Martín, et al.
Dios es Padre. Ediciones Secretariado Trinitario, 1991.
Pastor, Felix-Alejandro. *Gregorianum* 74 no 3:583-584 1993.

Velasco, Salvador.
Beato Francisco de Capillas: biografía. Imprenta Provincial, 1989.
Hernández, Ramón. *Cien Tom* 119:621 S-D 1992.

Velasco Bayón, Balbino.
Historia del Carmelo Español, vol II: Provincias de Cataluña y Aragón y Valencia, 1563-1835. Institutum Carmelitanum, 1992.
Hernández, Ramón. *Cien Tom* 120:199-200 Ja-Ap 1993.

Velkley, Richard L.
Freedom and the end of reason: on the moral foundation of Kant's critical philosophy. University of Chicago Press, 1989.
Stone, M. *Heythrop* 34:109-110 Ja 1993.

Venard, Marc, ed.
Die Zeit der Konfession (1530-1620/30). Herder, 1992.
Köhler, Oscar. *Stimm Zeit* 211:69-70 Ja 1993.

Venturini, Nello.
Scuola. La Nuova Cultura, 1992.
Pacella, U. *Civilta* 3:102 Jl 3 1993.

Verheij, A J C.
Verbs and numbers: a study of the frequencies of the Hebrew verbal tense forms in the Books of Samuel Kings and Chronicles. Van Gorcum, 1990.
Groves, J A Ian. *CBQ* 54:771-772 O 1992.

Vermaat, J A Emerson.
The World Council of Churches and politics, 1975-1986. Freedom House, 1989.
Norris, Russell B., Jr. *JEcumen Stds* 29:483 Sum-Aut 1992.

Verman, Mark.
The books of contemplation: medieval Jewish mystical sources. State University of New York, 1992.
Heiser, W Charles. *TheolDgst* 39:391 Wint 1992.

Vermeylen, Jacques R, ed.
The Book of Isaiah—Le Livre d'Isaïe. Peeters, 1989.
Smith, Mark S. *OTA* 16:429-430 Je 1993.

Verso la pace.
LDC, 1992.
Joblin, Joseph, 1920-. *Civilta* 3:443-444 S 4 1993.

Vesco, Jean-Luc.
L'Ancien Testament: Cent ans d'exégèse à l'École Biblique. Gabalda, 1990.
Laberge, Léo. *CBQ* 54:773 O 1992.

Veyne, Paul.
Did the Greeks believe thier myths? an essay on the constitutive imagination. The University of Chicago Press, 1988.
McGlynn, Ciaran. *IJPS* 1:169-170 Mr 1993.

Via, Dan O, Jr.
Self-deception and wholeness in Paul and Matthew. Fortress, 1990.
Getty, Mary Ann. *CBQ* 54:806-807 O 1992.

Vialnova, Evangelista.
Historia de la teología cristiana, III. Herder, 1992.
Mondoni, Danilo. *Perspectiva* 25:248-250 My-Ag 1993.

Viana, Antonio.
Territorialidad y personalidad en la organización eclesiástica: el caso de los ordinariatos militares. Servicio de publicaciones de la Universidad de Navarra, 1991.
Tourneau, Dominique Le. *Stud Can* 27 no 1:271-272 1993.

Viberg, Ake.
Symbols of law: a contextual analysis of legal symbolic acts in the Old Testament. Almqvist and Wiksell International, 1992.
Matthews, Victor H. *OTA* 15:490 O 1992.

Vicchio, Stephen J, and Geiger, Virginia, eds.
Perspectives on the American Catholic Church, 1789-1989. Christian Classics, 1989.
Klejment, Anne. *ACHSR* 103:54-55 Aut 1992.

Vidal, Gore.
Live from Golgotha. Random House, n.d.
Samway, Patrick H, 1939-. *America* 168:18-19 Ja 16-23 1993.

Vidal, Marciano.
L'etica cristiana. Borla, 1992.
Cultrera, Francesco. *Civilta* 2:192-193 Ap 17 1993.
Moral do matrimônio. Editora Vozes, 1992.
Leers, Bernardino. *REB* 53:486-487 Je 1993.

Vie monastique et inculturation à la lumière des traditions et situations africaines.
Archidiocèse de Kinshasa et Aide Inter-Monastères, 1989.
Vanneste, A. *Eph Theol Lovan* 78:183-184 Ap 1992.

Vielhauer, Philipp.
Historia de la Literatura cirstiana primitiva. Biblioteca de Estudios Bíblicos 72, 1991.
Pérez-Cotapos, Eduardo L. *Teol Vida* 33 no 3-4:322-323 1992.

Viellard-Baron, Jean-Louis.
Bergson. Presses universitaires de France, 1991.
Etienne, Jacques. *RPhil Louvain* 90:586-587 N 1992.

The Vienna dialogue: Vol. 1: Five Pro-Oriente consultations with Oriental Orthodoxy.
Pro Oriente, 1990.
Gros, Jeffrey, 1938-. *JEcumen Stds* 29:269 Spr 1992.

The Vienna dialogue: Vol. 2: Summaries of the papers.
Pro Oriente, 1991.
Gros, Jeffrey, 1938-. *JEcumen Stds* 29:269 Spr 1992.

Vigeur, Jean-Claude Maire, and Bagliani, Agostino Paravicini, eds.
La parola all'accusato. Sellerio Editore, 1991.
Brundage, James A. *CHist* 79:319-320 Ap 1993.

Viladesau, Richard.
The word in and out of season: homilies for the Sundays of Ordinary Time, Cycle A. Paulist Press, 1992.
Lazar, John E. *Mod Lit* 20:38 My 1993.

Viladesau, Richard, and Massa, Mark, eds.
Foundations of theological study: a sourcebook. Paulist Press, 1991.
O'Collins, Gerald, 1931-. *Gregorianum* 74 No 1:165-166 1993.
Draper, Anthony. *Doctr Life* 43:248-249 Ap 1993.

Vilanova, Evangelista.
Historia de la teología cristiana, vol III: Siglos XVIII, XIX, XX. Herder, 1992.
Celada, Gregorio. *Cien Tom* 120:200-202 Ja-Ap 1993.

Vílchez Lindez, José.
Sapienciales V Sabiduria. Editorial Verbo Divino, 1990.
Prato, Gian Luigi. *Gregorianum* 74 no 3:568-571 1993.

Villa-Vicencio, Charles.
A theology of reconstruction: nation-building and human rights. Cambridge University Press, n.d.
Linden, Ian. *Tablet* 247:439-440 Ap 3 1993.

Villar, José R.
Teologia de la Iglesia particular. Ediciones Universidad de Salamanca, 1989.
Schouppe, J. *Eph Theol Lovan* 78:488-490 D 1992.

Viller, Marcel, and Rahner, Karl, 1904-1984.
Ascetica e mistica nella patristica. Queriniana, 1991.
Halleux, André de. *Eph Theol Lovan* 78:447 D 1992.

Vincent, Gabrielle.
Where are you, Ernest and Celestine? Greenwillow Books, 1977.
Neuberger, Anne E. *ReligTJ* 26:33 Ja 1993.

Visotzky, Burton L.
The Midrash on proverbs. Yale University Press, 1992.
Heiser, W Charles. *TheolDgst* 39:373 Wint 1992.

Vitek, John M.
A companion way: mentoring youth in searching faith. St Mary's Press, 1992.
Riley, David M. *Catechist* 26:15 F 1993.
Anon. *Church* 9:42 Sum 1993.

Vitoria, Francisco de, 1486?-1546.
Political writings. Cambridge University Press, 1991.
Heiser, W Charles. *TheolDgst* 40:91 Spr 1993.

Vogel, Heinz-Jurgen.
Celibacy: gift or law? Alba House, n.d.
Cornwell, Peter. *Tablet* 247:1073-1074 Ag 21 1993.
Graham, William C. *Nat Cath Rep* 30:36 N 19 1993.

Volcic, Demetrio.
Mosca: I giorni della fine. Mondadori, 1992.
Rulli, Giovanni. *Civilta* 143:426-427 N 21 1992.

Volf, Miroslav.
Working in the spirit: toward a theology for work. Oxford University Press, n.d.
Markovic, Matthew. *New Oxford Rev* 60:31-32 O 1993.

Volpi, Claudio, and Gallotta, Nino.
La famiglia ritrovata. BM Italiana, 1992.
Varriale, E. *Civilta* 2:414-415 My 15 1993.

Volz, Carl A.
Pastoral life and practice in the early Church. Augsburg Fortress, 1990.
Hall, Stewart J. *Heythrop* 34:315-316 Jl 1993.

Voorhees, Don.
The book of totally useless information. Citadel, n.d.
Hunt, George W, 1937-. *America* 169:2 Ag 14-21 1993.

Voors, Robert E Van.
The ascents of James: history and theology of a Jewish-Christian community. Scholars Press, 1989.
Frank, Sue. *JEcumen Stds* 29:124-125 Wint 1992.

Vorgrimler, Herbert.
Sacramental theology. Liturgical, 1992.
Dollen, Charles. *Priest* 49:48 Ja 1993.
Graham, William C. *Nat Cath Rep* 29:40 My 28 1993.
Skublics, Ernest. *Can Cath Rev* 11:36-37 My 1993.
Heiser, W Charles. *TheolDgst* 40:191-192 Sum 1993.
Bevans, Stephen. *CLW* 64:33 Jl-S 1993.
Duffy, Regis A. *TheolStds* 54:585 S 1993.

Vort, Kay Vander, et al, eds.
Walking in two worlds: women's spiritual paths. North Star Press, n.d.
Graham, William C. *Nat Cath Rep* 29:24 Mr 26 1993.

Vukšić, Tomo.
I rapporti tra i cattolici e gli ortodossi nella Bosnia ed Erzegovina dal 1878 al 1903: uno studio storico-teologico. Pont Collegio Croato di San Girolamo, 1991.
Caprile, Giovanni. *Civilta* 2:298-299 My 1 1993.

W

Waal, Esther de, ed.
The Celtic vision: prayers from the Outer Hebrides. St Bede's, 1990.
Kollar, Rene. *Cist Stud* 28:[13] 1993.

Waard, Jan de, and Nida, Eugene A.
A translator's handbook on the Book of Ruth. United Bible Societies, 1992.
Gossai, Hemchand. *OTA* 15:497-498 O 1992.

Waddams, S M.
Law, politics and the Church of England: the career of Stephen Lushington, 1782-1873. Cambridge University Press, 1992.
Ellens, J P. *CHist* 79:346-347 Ap 1993.

Wadell, Paul J.
Friends of God: virtues and gifts in Aquinas. Peter Lang, 1991.
Heiser, W Charles. *TheolDgst* 39:392 Wint 1992.
The primacy of love. Paulist, 1992.
Ingham, M. *New Oxford Rev* 60:24 Ja-F 1993.
Lane, John Thomas. *Emmanuel* 99:112 Mr 1993.
Pope, Stephen J. *TheolStds* 54:202 Mr 1993.
Hanigan, James P. *Horizons (CTS)* 20:178-179 Spr 1993.
Bretzke, James T. *Gregorianum* 74 no 2:376-378 1993.
Whitmore, Todd David. *New Theol Rev* 6:117-118 Ag 1993.
Redpath, Peter A. *HPR* 94:73-75 O 1993.

Wagner, Mary Anthony.
The sacred world of the Christian. Liturgical, 1993.
Graham, William C. *Nat Cath Rep* 29:36 S 10 1993.
Borgia, Francis. *Mod Lit* 20:37-38 O 1993.
St. Louis, Ralph. *New Oxford Rev* 60:27-30 N 1993.

Wainwright, Elaine Mary.
Towards a feminist critical reading of the Gospel according to Matthew. Walter de Gruyter, 1991.
Lee, Dorothy A. *Pacifica* 6:102-104 F 1993.

Wake, William.
William Wake's Gallican Correspondence and related documents, vol 6. Peter Lang, 1992.
Heiser, W Charles. *TheolDgst* 40:192 Sum 1993.
Heiser, W Charles. *TheolDgst* 40:192 Sum 1993.

Wal, Adri van der.
Micah: a classified bibliography. Free University Press, 1990.
Lust, Johan. *Eph Theol Lovan* 78:158-159 Ap 1992.

Waldron, Ann.
Hodding Carter: the reconstruction of a racist. Algonquin Books, n.d.
Samway, Patrick H, 1939-. *America* 169:20 Ag 28-S 4 1993.

Waldron, John D.
The Quakers and the salvationists. The Salvation Army Supplies, 1990.
Heiser, W Charles. *TheolDgst* 39:392 Wint 1992.

Walker, Andrew, and Patrick, James, eds.
A Christian for all Christians: essays in honor of C S Lewis. Regnery Gateway, 1992.
Vanauken, Sheldon. *Crisis* 11:47-48 Ja 1993.
Heiser, W Charles. *TheolDgst* 40:57-58 Spr 1993.

Walker, Martin.
The Cold War. Fourth Estate, n.d.
Hodgkin, E C. *Tablet* 247:1164 S 11 1993.

Walker, Peter W L.
Holy city, holy places: Christian attitudes to Jerusalem and the Holy Land in the fourth century. Clarendon Press, 1990.
Cameron, A. *Heythrop* 34:114-116 Ja 1993.
Idinopulos, Thomas. *JEcumen Stds* 29:487 Sum-Aut 1992.

Walker, Randi Jones.
Protestantism in the Sangre de Cristos, 1850-1920. University of New Mexico Press, 1991.
Deutsch, S. *CHist* 78:685-686 O 1992.

Wallace, Patricia F, and Winifred, Mary.
Using the 12 steps to grow spiritually. Dimension Books, 1992.
Fehringer, Clara. *Sisters* 65:313 Jl 1993.

Wallace, Ruth A.
They call her pastor. State University of New York Press, 1992.
Arnold, Linda. *Living Light* 29:81-82 Wint 1992.
Ward, Hannah, and Wild, Jennifer. *Way* 33:259 Jl 1993.
Heiser, W Charles. *TheolDgst* 40:192 Sum 1993.

Walls, Jerry L.
Hell: the logic of damnation. University of Notre Dame Press, 1992.
Heiser, W Charles. *TheolDgst* 40:192 Sum 1993.

Walls, Neal H.
The goddess Anat in Ugaritic myth. Scholars, 1992.
Smith, Mark M. *OTA* 16:414 Je 1993.

Walsh, Jill Paton.
The Wyndham case. Hodder & Stoughton, n.d.
Lejeune, Anthony. *Tablet* 247:1136 S 4 1993.

Walsh, Michael J, 1937-.
Opus Dei: an investigation into the secret society struggling for power within the Roman Catholic Church. Harper, 1992.
Dinter, Paul E. *Comm* 120:22+ Mr 12 1993.
Romano, Joseph. *ACHSR* 103:52-54 Aut 1992.
Thomas, Joseph R. *St Anth* 100:50 My 1993.
Crilly, Scholastica. *Register* 69:4 My 2 1993.
Heiser, W Charles. *TheolDgst* 40:192 Sum 1993.
Cohalan, F. *HPR* 94:67-71 O 1993.

Walsh, Michael J, 1937-, and Davies, Brian.
Proclaiming justice and peace. Twenty-Third Publications, 1991.
Anon. *Furrow* 44:128 F 1993.

Walsh, Michael J, 1937-, and Davis, Brian, eds.
Proclaiming justice and peace. Twenty-Third Publications, 1991.
Phan, Peter C. *Living Light* 29:97-98 Sum 1993.

Walter, James J, and Shannon, Thomas A, eds.
Quality of life: the new medical dilemma. Paulist Press, 1990.
Boyle, John P. *Horizons (CTS)* 20:177-178 Spr 1993.

Walzer, Michael.
What it means to be an American. Marsilio, n.d.
Douglass, R Bruce. *Comm* 120:32-33 Ap 9 1993.

Wanamaker, Charles A.
The Epistles to the Thessalonians: a commentary on the Greek text. Paternoster Press, 1990.
May, David M. *Bib Th Bul* 23:41-42 Spr 1993.

Wanger, Walter.
Ragman and other cries of faith. Hodder & Stoughton, n.d.
Campbell, James. *Month* 26:381 S-O 1993.

Wansbrough, Henry, ed.
Jesus and the oral gospel tradition. Sheffield, 1991.
Boring, Eugene M. *CBQ* 55:422-423 Ap 1993.

Wansbrough, Henryenry, ed.
Jesus and the oral gospel tradition. Sheffield, 1991.
Wansbrough, Henry. *Priests & People* 6:437-438 N 1992.

Ward, Benedicta.
Donne del deserto. Qiqajon-Comunità di Bose, 1993.
Flumeri, E. *Civilta* 2:205 Ap 17 1993.

Ward, Gary L, and Persson, Bertil, et al, eds.
Independent bishops: an international directory. Apogee Books, 1990.
Cogan, Patrick. *Stud Can* 27 no 1:263-264 1993.

Ward, James M.
Thus says the Lord: the message of the prophets. Abingdon Press, 1991.
Heiser, W Charles. *TheolDgst* 39:392 Wint 1992.

Ward, Keith.
Defending the soul. One World, n.d.
Haldane, John. *Tablet* 247:720-721 Je 5 1993.
Divine action. Collins, 1990.
Hebblethwaite, B. *Heythrop* 34:100-101 Ja 1993.
A vision to pursue: beyond the crisis in Christianity. SCM Press, 1991.
Loughlin, Gerard. *Heythrop* 34:442-444 O 1993.

Ward, W. R.
The Protestant evangelical awakening. Cambridge University Press, 1992.
Hempton, David. *Heythrop* 34:338-339 Jl 1993.

Warden, Michael.
The practical youth ministry. Group Pub., 1993.
Gallagher, Miriam J. *Mod Lit* 20:40 O 1993.

Warner, Martin, ed.
Religion and philosophy. Cambridge University Press, 1992.
Chappell, T D J. *New Blckfrs* 74:106-109 F 1993.

Warraq, Muhammad ibn Hârûn, ?-861?
Anti-Christian polemic in early Islam: Abû 'Isâ-al Warrâq's "Against the Trinity". Cambridge University Press, 1992.
Heiser, W Charles. *TheolDgst* 39:392 Wint 1992.

Warren, Allen, ed.
A church for the nation? Essays on the future of Anglicanism. Gracewing, n.d.
Cornwell, Peter. *Tablet* 247:619-620 My 15 1993.

Warren, Michael, 1935-.
Communications and cultural analysis. Greenwood Publishing Group, 1992.
Francis, Mark R. *Worship* 67:478-480 S 1993.

Watkin, Pamela.
Joyce's Ockenden. Broadmead Press, n.d.
Craig, Mary. *Tablet* 247:1104 Ag 28 1993.

Watkins, John.
The glasshouse garden. Conran Octopus, n.d.
Taylor, Patrick. *Tablet* 247:375 Mr 20 1993.

Watson, Duane F, ed.
Persuasive artistry. JSOT, 1991.
Wansbrough, Henry. *Priests & People* 6:435-436 N 1992.
Burnett, Fred W. *CBQ* 54:830-831 O 1992.

Watt, David Harrington.
A transforming faith: explorations of twentieth-century American evangelicalism. Rutgers University Press, 1991.
Bratt, J. *CHist* 78:690-691 O 1992.

Watt, Tessa.
Cheap print and popular piety, 1550-1640. Cambridge University Press, 1991.
Havran, Martin J. *CHist* 78:653-654 O 1992.

Watts, Dorothy.
Christians and pagans in Roman Britain. Routledge, 1991.
Francis, Louis. *Heythrop* 34:448-450 O 1993.

Watts, James W.
Psalms and story: inset hymns in Hebrew narrative. Sheffield, 1992.
Smith, Mark S. *OTA* 16:415 Je 1993.

Watts, Jill.
God, harlem USA: the Father Divine story. University of California Press, 1992.
Heiser, W Charles. *TheolDgst* 39:392 Wint 1992.

The way of a pilgrim and the pilgrim continues his way.
Doubleday, n.d.
Graham, William C. *Nat Cath Rep* 29:40 F 5 1993.

Way, David.
The lordship of Christ: Ernst Käsemann's interpretation of Paul's theology. Oxford University Press, 1991.
Heiser, W Charles. *TheolDgst* 39:393 Wint 1992.

Weakland, Rembert G, Abp, 1927-.
Faith and the human enterprise: a post-Vatican II vision. Orbis Books, 1992.
    Doyle, Dennis M. *Comm* 120:18-20 Mr 12 1993.
    Rutler, George W. *HPR* 93:76-77 Je 1993.
    Ribando, William. *Sisters* 65:312 Jl 1993.
Weaver, Mary Jo.
Springs of water in a dry land: spiritual survival for Catholic women today.
Beacon Press, 1993.
    Redmont, Jane. *Comm* 120:25-26 Mr 12 1993.
    Ware, Ann Patrick. *Nat Cath Rep* 29:23 Mr 26 1993.
    Quitslund, Sonya A. *TheolStds* 54:606-607 S 1993.
Webb, Robert L.
John the Baptizer and Prophet: a socio-historical study. JSOT, 1991.
    Harrington, Daniel J. *CBQ* 54:807-808 O 1992.
    Heiser, W Charles. *TheolDgst* 40:92 Spr 1993.
Weber, Alison.
Teresa of Avila and the rhetoric of femininity. Princeton University Press,
1990.
    Kramb, Marie A. *Relig Lit* 24:111-112 Aut 1992.
    Cammarata, Joan F. *CrossCurr* 43:113-114 Spr 1993.
Weber, David J.
The Spanish frontier in North America. Yale University Press, 1992.
    Mathes, J Michael. *CHist* 79:562-564 Jl 1993.
Weber, Francis J, comp.
Prominent visitors to the California missions (1786-1842). The Archival
Center, 1991.
    Neri, Michael Charles. *CHist* 79:132-133 Ja 1993.
Weber, H.
Allgemeine Moraltheologie. Styria, 1991.
    Simoens, Y. *NRT* 115:115-116 Ja-F 1993.
Weder, Hans.
Metafore del Regno. Paideia, 1991.
    Marconi, Gilberto. *Gregorianum* 74 No 1:152-154 1993.
    Scaiola, D. *Civilta* 3:87-88 Jl 3 1993.
Weeks, Andrew D.
Welcome: tools and techniques for new member ministry. Alban Institute,
1992.
    Smyth, Damian. *Mod Lit* 20:36 My 1993.
Weems, Renita J.
Just a sister away. LuraMedia, 1988.
    Stuhlmueller, Carroll. *BibleT* 31:57 Ja 1993.
Weger, K-H.
Religionskritik. Styria, 1991.
    Toubeau, A. *NRT* 115:302-303 Mr-Ap 1993.
Wegner, Judith Romney.
Chattel or person? The status of women in the Mishnah. Oxford University
Press, 1988.
    Stuhlmueller, Carroll. *BibleT* 31:248 Jl 1993.
Weigel, George.
The final revolution. Oxford University Press, n.d.
    Lavelle, Michael. *Comm* 120:39-40 Ap 9 1993.
    Luxmoore, Jonathan, and Babiuch, Jolanta. *New Oxford Rev* 60:27-28
Ap 1993.
    Howard, Damian. *Month* 26:194-195 My 1993.
    Cviic, Christopher. *Tablet* 247:1012-1013 Ag 7 1993.
    Schaefer, David Lewis. *America* 169:20-22 O 9 1993.
    Corley, Felix. *Can Cath Rev* 11:25-26 N 1993.
Freedom and its discontents: Catholicism confronts modernity. Ethics and
Public Policy Center, 1991.
    Heiser, W Charles. *TheolDgst* 40:92 Spr 1993.
Weigel, George, ed.
A new worldly order: John Paul II and human freedom. Ethics and Public
Policy Center, 1991.
    Heiser, W Charles. *TheolDgst* 39:376 Wint 1992.
Weigel, George, and Royal, Robert, eds.
A century of Catholic social thought. Ethics and Public Policy Center, n.d.
    Hunt, Robert P. *Crisis* 11:52-54 Ja 1993.
A century of Catholic Thought. Ethics and Public Policy Center, n.d.
    McKee, Arnold F. *Can Cath Rev* 11:31-32 Je 1993.
Weil, Cahiers Éric, III.
Interprétations de Kant. Presses universitaires de Lille, 1992.
    Natale, Maria Rosaria. *RPhil Louvain* 91:475-479 Ag 1993.
Weinfeld, Moshe.
Deuteronomy 1-11. Doubleday, 1991.
    Lust, Johan. *Eph Theol Lovan* 78:410-411 D 1992.
    Ska, Jean Louis. *NRT* 115:254-255 Mr-Ap 1993.
Deuteronomy and the Deuteronmic school. Eisenbrauns, 1992.
    Murphy, Roland E. *OTA* 16:172 F 1993.
Weinreb, Ben, and Hibbert, Christopher, eds.
The London encylopaedia. Macmillan, n.d.
    Barker, Felix. *Tablet* 247:1076 Ag 21 1993.
Weir, Alison.
The princes in the Tower. Bodley Head, n.d.
    Thomas, D. *Tablet* 247:17 Ja 2 1993.
Weisman, Brent Richards.
*Excavations on the Franciscan frontier: archaeology at the Fig Springs
Mission.* University Press of Florida, 1992.
    Hann, John H. *CHist* 79:355-356 Ap 1993.
Weiss, Hans-Friedrich.
Der Brief an die Hebräer. Vandenhoeck & Ruprecht, 1991.
    Swetnam, James. *CBQ* 55:187-189 Ja 1993.
Weiss, Raymond L.
Maimonides' ethics: the encounter of philosophic and religious morality.
University of Chicago Press, 1991.
    Berenbaum, Michael. *TheolStds* 54:387 Je 1993.
Welch, Robert, ed.
Irish writers and religion. Colin Smythe Ltd, 1992.
    Duffy, Hugh P. *Studies* 81:443-446 Wint 1992.

Welch, Sharon D.
A feminist ethic of risk. Fortress Press, 1990.
    Allsopp, Michael E. *Month* 26:233-234 Je 1993.
Wellmer, Albrecht.
*The persistence of modernity: essays on aesthetics, ethics and postmodern-
ism.* MIT, 1991.
    Guarino, Thomas. *TheolStds* 54:605 S 1993.
Wenham, John William.
Redating Matthew, Mark and Luke. InterVarsity Press, 1992.
    O'Brien, Patricia. *HPR* 93:75-76 Ap 1993.
    Heiser, W Charles. *TheolDgst* 39:393 Wint 1992.
    Neirynck, F. *Eph Theol Lovan* 69:173-174 Ap 1993.
Werlitz, Jürgen.
Studien zur literarkritischen Methode. Gruyter, 1992.
    Willis, John T. *OTA* 16:430-431 Je 1993.
Werner, Johannes, ed.
Vom mönchischen Leben. Josel, 1992.
    Roers, G M. *Stimm Zeit* 211:359-360 My 1993.
Wessels, A.
Immagini di Gesù nelle culture non europee. Queriniana, 1992.
    Renard, L-J. *NRT* 115:581 Jl-Ag 1993.
West, Gerald O.
*Biblical hermeneutics of liberation: modes of reading the Bible in the South
African context.* Cluster, 1991.
    Bergant, Dianne. *CBQ* 55:189-190 Ja 1993.
West, Morris L.
The lovers. no publisher given, n.d.
    Hebblethwaite, Peter, 1930-. *Nat Cath Rep* 29:27 My 28 1993.
West, Thomas H.
Ultimate hope without God: the atheistic eschatology of Ernst Bloch. Lang,
n.d.
    Haughey, John C. *TheolStds* 54:391 Je 1993.
Westbrook, Raymond.
Property and the family in Biblical law. JSOT, 1991.
    Matthews, Victor H. *OTA* 15:477-478 O 1992.
Westermann, Claus.
Genesis: an introduction. Fortress Press, 1992.
    Stuhlmueller, Carroll. *BibleT* 31:250 Jl 1993.
The living Psalms. T and T Clark, 1989.
    Anderson, Robert A. *Pacifica* 6:100-101 F 1993.
Wurzeln der Weisheit: Die ältesten Sprüche Israels und anderer Völker.
Vandenhoeck and Ruprecht, 1990.
    Prato, Gian Luigi. *Gregorianum* 74 No 1:149-150 1993.
Westheimer, Ruth.
The art of arousal. Abbeville Press, n.d.
    Reyntiens, Patrick. *Tablet* 247:1046-1047 Ag 14 1993.
Westley, Richard John, 1928-.
Experiencing community in small groups. Twenty-Third Publications, 1992.
    McKenna, Gemma. *Doctr Life* 43:445-447 S 1993.
Good things happen. Twenty-Third, 1992.
    Korn, Barton. *Mod Lit* 20:41 My 1993.
    Anon. *Furrow* 44:254-255 Ap 1993.
    Simmonds, Gemma. *Priests & People* 7:210 My 1993.
    Heiser, W Charles. *TheolDgst* 40:92 Spr 1993.
Westphal, Merold.
Hegel, freedom, and modernity. SUNY Press, 1992.
    Flay, Joseph C. *IPQ* 33:365-366 S 1993.
Wetzel, R, ed.
Melanchthons: Briefwechsel. Fromann-Holzboog, 1991.
    Plumat, N. *NRT* 115:269-270 Mr-Ap 1993.
Wevers, John William.
Text history of the Greek Exodus. Vandenhoeck and Ruprecht, 1992.
    Di Lella, Alexander A. *OTA* 16:170-171 F 1993.
Weyer, Robert Van de.
The fount book of prayer. HarperCollins, n.d.
    Campbell, James. *Month* 26:236 Je 1993.
The Fount book of prayer. Fount, n.d.
    Hollings, Michael. *Tablet* 247:1303 O 9 1993.
Weyer, Robert Van de, ed.
Celtic fire: the passionate religious vision of ancient Britain and IReland.
Doubleday, 1991.
    Heiser, W Charles. *TheolDgst* 39:355 Wint 1992.
Wezeman, Phyllis Vos, and Fournier, Jude Dennis.
Joy to the world. Ave Maria Press, n.d.
    Riley, David M. *Catechist* 27:14 N-D 1993.
Whalen, Michael D.
Seasons and feasts of the Church Year. Paulist, 1993.
    Dooley, Katherine. *Living Light* 29:92 Sum 1993.
    Graham, William C. *Nat Cath Rep* 29:18 Jl 16 1993.
    Brown, David O. *Mod Lit* 20:39 S 1993.
Whalen, Teresa.
The authentic doctrine of the Eucharist. Sheed & Ward, 1993.
    Halloran, W Regis. *Mod Lit* 20:39 Ag 1993.
    Graham, William C. *Nat Cath Rep* 29:36 S 10 1993.
What are the Targums? selected texts.
The Liturgical Press, 1992.
    Heiser, W Charles. *TheolDgst* 40:92 Spr 1993.
***What can you do for your country: a report on national and commu-
nity service.***
U.S. Government Printing Office, 1993.
    Haser, Kathleen. *Momentum* 24:77-78 N-D 1993.
When others must choose: deciding for patients without capacity.
Health Education Services, 1992.
    Finder, Stuart G. *Health Prog* 74:66-68 Je 1993.
Whitaker, James.
Diana v Charles. Signet, n.d.
    Kenny, Mary, 1936-. *Tablet* 247:889-890 Jl 10 1993.

Williams, C J F.
Being identity and truth. Clarendon Press, 1992.
Charlton, William. *New Blckfrs* 74:329-331 Je 1993.

Williams, David S.
Stylometrical authorship studies in Flavius Josephus and related literature. Mellen, 1992.
Begg, Christopher T. *OTA* 16:194 F 1993.

Williams, Donna Reilly, and Sturzl, Jo Ann.
Grief ministry. Resource Publications, 1992.
Riley, David M. *Catechist* 26:14 F 1993.
Brennan, Dermot. *Doctr Life* 43:447-448 S 1993.

Williams, Earle, and Williams, Elspeth.
Spiritually aware pastoral care. Paulist Press, 1992.
Krawczyk, Marilyn Peters. *Mod Lit* 19:42 D 1992-Ja 1993.

Williams, James G.
The Bible, violence, and the sacred. HarperSanFrancisco, 1992.
Heiser, W Charles. *TheolDgst* 39:394 Wint 1992.
Murphy, Roland E. *OTA* 16:441 Je 1993.

Williams, Rowan.
Teresa of Avila. Morehouse, 1991.
Egan, Keith J. *Horizons (CTS)* 19:314 Fall 1992.

Williams, Stephanie.
Docklands. Phaidon, n.d.
Toomey, Philippa. *Tablet* 247:373 Mr 20 1993.

Williamson, William B, ed.
An encyclopedia of religions in the United States: one hundred religious groups speak for themselves. Crossroad, 1991.
Heiser, W Charles. *TheolDgst* 39:360 Wint 1992.

Willimon, William H, and Hauerwas, Stanley.
Preaching to strangers. John Knox Press, 1992.
Heiser, W Charles. *TheolDgst* 40:193 Sum 1993.

Wilson, A N, 1950-.
Jesus. Sinclair Stevenson, 1992.
Hughes, Gerard W. *Month* 26:30-31 Ja 1993.
Allen, Charlotte. *Crisis* 11:30-35 Mr 1993.
Smith, Lewis. *New Blckfrs* 74:227-228 Ap 1993.
Doyle, Ailín. *Furrow* 44:455-456 Jl-Ag 1993.
The rise and fall of the House of Windsor. Sinclair-Stevenson, n.d.
Kenny, Mary, 1936-. *Tablet* 247:889-890 Jl 10 1993.
The vicar of sorrows. Sinclair Stevenson, n.d.
Fitzgerald, Penelope. *Tablet* 247:1266 O 2 1993.

Wilson, Bryan.
The social dimensions of Sectarianism: sects and new religious movements in contemporary society. Clarendon Press, 1990.
Beckford, J. *Heythrop* 34:120-121 Ja 1993.

Wilson, Derek.
The Astors. Weidenfeld & Nicolson, n.d.
Forrest, Denys. *Tablet* 247:343 Mr 13 1993.

Wilson, Edmund.
The sixties: the last journal, 1960-72. Farrar, Straus & Giroux, n.d.
Castronovo, David. *Comm* 120:29-30 O 22 1993.

Wilson, Ian.
Shakespeare: the evidence. Headline, n.d.
Wilson-Smith, Timothy. *Tablet* 247:1264-1265 O 2 1993.

Wilson, James A.
Moral sense. Free Press, n.d.
O'Brien, Dennis. *Comm* 120:26-27 O 22 1993.

Wilson-Smith, Timothy.
Delacroix: a life. Constable, n.d.
Latham-Koenig, Alfred. *Tablet* 247:110-111 Ja 23 1993.

Wimbush, Vincent L, ed.
Ascetic behavior in Greco-Roman antiquity: a sourcebook. Fortress, 1990.
Finn, Thomas Macy. *CBQ* 54:808-810 O 1992.

Wind, James P, et al, eds.
Clergy ethics in a changing society: mapping the terrain. John Knox Press, 1991.
Heiser, W Charles. *TheolDgst* 39:356-357 Wint 1992.

Wind, Renate.
Dietrich Bonhoeffer: a spoke in the wheel. Eerdmans, 1992.
Heiser, W Charles. *TheolDgst* 40:93 Spr 1993.

Winfield, Marlene, ed.
Confronting the pain of child sexual abuse. Family Service Units, n.d.
Hansen, Tracy. *Tablet* 247:170 F 6 1993.

Winfield, Richard Dien.
Overcoming foundations: studies in systematic philosophy. Columbia University Press, 1989.
Maker, William. *IPQ* 33:132-133 Mr 1993.

Winger, Joseph Michael.
By what law? the meaning of nómos in the letters of Paul. Scholars Press, 1992.
Heiser, W Charles. *TheolDgst* 40:93 Spr 1993.

Winkler, Jude.
The gift of Christmas. Catholic Book Publishers, 1992.
Allen, Juanita. *Mod Lit* 20:40 N 1993.

Winkler, Klaus.
Werden wie die Kinder. Matthias Grünewald, 1992.
Grom, Bernhard. *Stimm Zeit* 211:287-288 Ap 1993.

Winstone, H V F.
Howard Carter and the discovery of the tomb of Tutankhamun. Constable, n.d.
Toomey, Philippa. *Tablet* 247:373 Mr 20 1993.

Winter, Miriam Therese.
The Gospel according to Mary. Crossroad, 1993.
Nowell, Irene. *Sisters* 65:310-311 Jl 1993.
McGrath, Helene. *Mod Lit* 20:40 Ag 1993.
Coffey, Kathy. *Momentum* 24:76 S-O 1993.
Senior, Donald. *BibleT* 31:317 S 1993.

Wire, Antoinette Clark.
The Corinthian women prophets: a reconstruction through Paul's rhetoric. Fortress, 1990.
Neyrey, Jerome H. *Horizons (CTS)* 19:311 Fall 1992.

Wissink, J B M.
The eternity of the world in thought of Thomas Aquinas and his contemporaries. E J Brill, 1990.
Baldner, Steven. *Thomist* 57:146-149 Ja 1993.

Wister, Robert J, ed.
Priest: identity and ministry. The Liturgical Press, n.d.
Fuerth, Patrick W. *Can Cath Rev* 11:34 Jl-Ag 1993.

Wistrich, Robert S.
Antisemitism: the longest hatred. Pantheon Books, 1992.
Heiser, W Charles. *TheolDgst* 40:93 Spr 1993.

Witaszek, Gabriel.
Prorocy Amos i Micheasz wobec niesprawiedlit-wości społecznej. Redemptorystów, 1992.
Pilch, John Joseph, 1936-. *OTA* 16:432-433 Je 1993.

Witherington, Ben, III.
The christology of Jesus. Fortress, 1990.
Miller, Robert J. *CBQ* 54:810-811 O 1992.
Jesus, Paul and the end of the world. InterVarsity Press, 1992.
Heiser, W Charles. *TheolDgst* 40:193 Sum 1993.
Women and the Genesis of Christianity. Cambridge University Press, 1990.
Wainwright, Elaine. *Pacifica* 6:219-221 Je 1993.
Sloyan, Gerard S. *Horizons (CTS)* 19:312-313 Fall 1992.

Withey, Donald A.
John Henry Newman. Sheed and Ward, 1992.
Norris, Tom. *Furrow* 44:192-193 Mr 1993.
Mitchell, Leonel L. *Worship* 67:368-370 Jl 1993.

Woestman, William H.
Sacraments: initiation, penance, anointing of the sick: commentary on canons 840-1007. St Paul University, 1992.
Ombres, Robert. *Priests & People* 7:367 Ag-S 1993.
Special marriage cases. St. Paul University, 1992.
Ombres, Robert. *Priests & People* 7:367 Ag-S 1993.

Woiwode, Larry.
Acts. HarperCollins, n.d.
Wolfe, Gregory. *Register* 69:5 O 3 1993.
A writer's reflections on the Church, writing and his own life. HarperSanFrancisco, n.d.
Samway, Patrick H, 1939-. *America* 168:19 Mr 20-27 1993.

Wojtyla, Karol.
The jeweler's shop. Ignatius, 1992.
Mangan, Charles M. *HPR* 94:71-72 O 1993.

Wojtyska, Henricus Damianus, ed.
Acta Nuntiaturae Polonae; vol II: Zacharias Ferreri (1519-1521) et nuntii minores (1522-1553). Institutem Historicum Polonicum Romae, 1992.
Pease, Neal. *CHist* 79:334-335 Ap 1993.

Wolf, Ann Colette.
Against all odds: Sisters of Providence mission to the Chinese, 1920-1990. Sisters of Providence, 1990.
Schintz, Mary Ann. *CHist* 79:381-383 Ap 1993.

Wolff, Hans Walter.
Micah: a commentary. Augsburg, 1990.
Polan, Gregory J. *OTA* 16:433 Je 1993.

Wolff, Pierre.
Discernment. Triumph Books, 1993.
Dollen, Charles. *Priest* 49:48 Je 1993.
Anon. *Spir Life* 39:188-189 Aut 1993.

Wolff-Salin, Mary.
The shadow side of community and the growth of the self. Crossroad, 1988.
Fehringer, Clara. *Sisters* 65:61-62 Ja 1993.

Wolffe, John.
The Protestant crusade in Great Britain, 1829-1860. Oxford University Press, 1991.
Arnstein, Walter L. *CHist* 79:120-122 Ja 1993.

Wolin, Richard, ed.
The Heidegger controversy. MIT Press, n.d.
Marlin, Randal. *Can Cath Rev* 11:29-30 O 1993.

Wolkovich-Valkavicius, William.
Lithuanian religious life in America: a compendium of 150 Roman Catholic parishes and institutions; volume 1: Eastern United States. Lithuanian Religious Life in America, 1991.
Senn, Alfred Erich. *CHist* 79:368-369 Ap 1993.

Wolpert, Lewis.
The unnatural nature of science. Faber, n.d.
Hawkes, Nigel. *Tablet* 246:1574-1575 D 12 1992.

Wonneberger, Reinhard.
Redaktion: Studien zur Textforschung im Alten Testament, entwickelt am Beispiel der Samuel-Überlieferung. Vandenhoeck & Ruprecht, 1992.
Begg, Christopher T. *OTA* 16:421 Je 1993.

Wood, Bryant G.
The sociology of pottery in ancient Palestine. JSOT, 1990.
Edelman, Diana V. *OTA* 15:491 O 1992.

Wood, Diana, ed.
The Church and the arts: papers read at the 1990 summer meeting and the 1991 winter meeting of the ecclesiastical history society. Blackwell for the Ecclesiastical History Society, 1992.
Rogers, Nicholas. *New Blckfrs* 74:334-336 Je 1993.

Wood, Douglas.
Old turtle. Pfeifer Hamilton Publications, 1992.
Neuberger, Anne E. *ReligTJ* 26:32-33 Ja 1993.

Wood, Ian, and Loud, G A, eds.
Church and chronicle in the Middle Ages: essays presented to John Taylor. The Hambleton Press, 1991.
Wickstrom, John B. *CHist* 79:100-101 Ja 1993.

X

Y

Yunker, James A.
Socialism revised and modernized: the case for pragmatic market socialism.
Praeger, 1992.
Elliot, John E. *RSocEcon* 51:241-244 Sum 1993.

Yves Calvez, Jean.
La enseñanza social de la Iglesia. Editorial Herder, 1991.
Lago Alba, Luis. *Cien Tom* 119:614-615 S-D 1992.

Z

Zabilka, Ivan L.
Scientific malpractice: the creation/evolution debate. Bristol House, 1992.
Stuhlmueller, Carroll. *BibleT* 31:251 Jl 1993.

Zagano, Phyllis.
Woman to woman. Liturgical, n.d.
Bromberg, Judith. *Nat Cath Rep* 30:27 N 19 1993.

Zagzebski, Linda Trinkaus, 1946-.
The dilemma of freedom and foreknowledge. Oxford University Press, 1991.
Stebbins, J. *Thomist* 56:714-718 O 1992.
Meynell, Hugo. *Heythrop* 34:469 O 1993.

Zaharopoulos, Dimitri Z.
Theodore of Mopsuestia on the Bible. Paulist, 1989.
Urbrock, William J. *OTA* 15:491-492 O 1992.

Zahn, Gordon C.
Vocation of peace. Fortkamp, n.d.
Vree, Dale. *New Oxford Rev* 60:30 O 1993.

Zakai, Avihu.
Exile and kingdom: history and apocalypse in the Puritan migration to America. Cambridge University Press, 1992.
Liu, Tai. *CHist* 79:111-113 Ja 1993.

Zakovitch, Yair.
"And you shall tell your son". Magnes, 1991.
Gitay, Yehosua. *OTA* 15:516 O 1992.
Ruth: introduction and commentary. Magnes, 1990.
Zvi, Ehud Ben. *CBQ* 55:134-135 Ja 1993.

Zambonini, Franca.
Chiana Lubich: a life for unity. New City Press, 1992.
Mathews, Edward G. *Diakonia* 26 no 2:140 1993.

Zambruno, Elizabetta.
La Theologia Deutsch o la via per giungere a Dio. Vita e Pensiero, 1991.
Renard, L J. *NRT* 115:126-127 Ja-F 1993.
Ruiz Jurado, Manuel. *Gregorianum* 74 No 1:166 1993.

Zamora, Daisy.
Clean slate. Clubstone Press, n.d.
Martinez, Demetria. *Nat Cath Rep* 29:31 S 10 1993.

Zanghí, Giuseppe Maria.
Dio che è amore: Trinità e vita in Cristo. Città Nuova, 1991.
Mucci, Giandomenico. *Civilta* 144:403-404 F 20 1993.

Zaninelli, Sergio, ed.
Storia dell'industria Lombarda, 3 vols. Il Polifilo, 1988-1992.
Salvini, Gianpaolo. *Civilta* 2:607-608 Je 19 1993.

Zannini, Gian Ludovico Masetti.
Quel che passava il convento: Tavola e cucina dei monasteri femminili nei secoli XVI-XVIII in Romagna. Romagna Arte e Storia, 1991.
Caprile, Giovanni. *Civilta* 144:205-206 Ja 16 1993.

Zannoni, Arthur E.
The Old Testament: a bibliography. Michael Glazier Books, 1992.
Stuhlmueller, Carroll. *BibleT* 31:251 Jl 1993.

Zannotti, Luciano.
Stato sociale, edilizia di culto e pluralismo religioso: contributo allo studio della problematica del dissenso religioso. Giuffre, 1990.
Ferrari da Passano, Paolo. *Civilta* 144:618-619 Mr 20 1993.

Zarlenga, Angelico Rinaldo.
Art and the Word of God: arte e la Parola di dio. Fra Angelico Art Foundation Dominicans, 1990.
Ciappi, M L. *Civilta* 144:414-415 F 20 1993.

Zdybicka, Zofia J.
Person and religion. Peter Lang, 1991.
Heiser, W Charles. *TheolDgst* 40:193 Sum 1993.

Zeller, Hubert Van.
And so to God. St Bede's Publications, 1992.
Forrester, David. *Tablet* 247:586 My 8 1993.
And so to God. St. Bede's Publications, 1992.
Myers, Rawley. *HPR* 94:79 N 1993.

Zenger, Er.
Ich will die Morgenröte wecken. Herder, 1991.
Harvengt, A. *NRT* 114:939-940 N-D 1992.

Zepp, Ira G, Jr.
A Muslim primer. Christian Classics, 1992.
Stuhlmueller, Carroll. *BibleT* 31:122 Mr 1993.
Heiser, W Charles. *TheolDgst* 40:94 Spr 1993.

Ziefert, Harriet.
A new coat for Anna. Alfred A Knopf, n.d.
Neuberger, Anne E. *ReligTJ* 27:34 F 1993.

Ziefle, Helmut W.
Dictionary of modern theological German. Baker Book House, 1993.
Heiser, W Charles. *TheolDgst* 40:193 Sum 1993.

Zimbalist, Andrew, and Weeks, John.
Panama at the crossroads: economic development and political change in the Twentieth Century. University of California, 1991.
Kraemer, Barbara. *RSocEcon* 51:250-252 Sum 1993.

Zimdars-Swartz, Sandra L.
Encountering Mary: from La Salette to Medjugorje. Princeton University Press, 1991.
Johnson, Elizabeth A, 1941-. *Horizons (CTS)* 19:317 Fall 1992.

Žitnik, Maksimilijan.
Sacramenta. Bibliographia internationalis, 4 vols. Pontificia Università Gregoriana, 1992.
Anon. *Gregorianum* 74 no 3:603 1993.
Sacramenta: Biliographia internationalis, vol I: A-G, 1-17 583. Pont University Gregoriana, 1992.
Ferraro, Giuseppe. *Civilta* 143:432 N 21 1992.

Zoffoli, Enrico.
Dizionario del cristianesimo. Synopsis, 1992.
Ferrua, Antonio. *Civilta* 144:205 Ja 16 1993.

Zuanazzi, Gianfranco.
Temi e simboli dell'eros. Citta Nuova, 1991.
Lamba, R. *Civilta* 144:613-614 Mr 20 1993.

Zuck, Roy B, ed.
Sitting with Job: selected studies on the Book of Job. Baker, 1992.
Begg, Christopher T. *OTA* 15:502-503 O 1992.
Heiser, W Charles. *TheolDgst* 39:385 Wint 1992.

Zuckerman, Bruce.
Job the silent: a study in historical counterpoint. Oxford University, 1991.
Vall, Gregory. *CBQ* 55:135-137 Ja 1993.

Zussman, Robert.
Intensive care: medical ethics and the medical profession. University of Chicago Press, 1992.
Paris, John J. *TheolStds* 54:189-190 Mr 1993.
Post, Stephen G. *America* 169:26-29 N 20 1993.

Zvi, Ehud Ben.
A historical-critical study of the Book of Zephaniah. Gruyter, 1992.
Lust, Johan. *Eph Theol Lovan* 78:421-422 D 1992.
O'Brien, Julia M. *CBQ* 55:321-322 Ap 1993.

Zwaanstra, Henry.
Catholicity and secession. William B. Eerdmans, 1991.
Friesen, John. *JEcumen Stds* 29:475-476 Sum-Aut 1992.

1

The 17 Irish martyrs.
Veritas Publications, n.d.
Higgins, James J. *Liguorian* 81:70 Mr 1993.

LIST OF PERIODICALS INDEXED

Includes for each periodical the full
title, abbreviation used, address, frequency,
number of volumes per year,
rate of annual subscription, and ISSN.

ACTA APOSTOLICAE SEDIS - AAS, Libreria Editrice Vaticana, 00120 Vatican City (irregular 1 v Ja) $40 VC 0001-5199.

AFRICAN ECCLESIAL REVIEW - AFER, Gaba Publications, P.O. Box 4002, Eldoret, Kenya (bi-m 1 v Ja) $15 surface, $25 air KE 0001-1134.

AMERICA - 106 W. 56th St., New York, NY 10019 (w, except 1st w of Ja and alternate weeks Jl-Ag2 v Ja, Jl) $33 US 0002-7049.

AMERICAN BENEDICTINE REVIEW - ABenR, Assumption Abbey, Richardton, ND 58652 (q 1 v Mr) $15 US 0002-7650.

AMERICAN CATHOLIC HISTORICAL SOCIETY RECORDS - ACHSR, American Catholic Historic Society of Philadelphia, 263 S. 4th St., Philadelphia, PA 19106 (q 1 v Mr) $10 US 0002-7790.

AMERICAN CATHOLIC PHILOSOPHICAL QUARTERLY - ACPAP, Catholic University of America, Washington, DC 20064 (annual 1 v) $4 US 0065-7638.

AMERICAN CATHOLIC PHILOSOPHICAL ASSOCIATION PROCEEDINGS - ACPAP, Catholic University of America, Washington, DC 20064 (annual 1 v) $4 US 0065-7628.

AMERICAN JOURNAL OF JURISPRUDENCE - Amer J Juris Law Building, Notre Dame, IN 46556 (annual) $11 US 0069-8995.

AUGUSTINIAN STUDIES - Augustin Stud, Villanova University, Villanova, PA 19085 (annual) $15 US 0094-5323.

BIBLE TODAY - BibleT, Liturgical Press, St. John's Abbey, Collegeville, MN 56321 (6 x yr) $18 US 0006-0836.

THE BIBLICAL ARCHAEOLOGIST - Bibl Archaeol, The American Schools of Oriental Research, 4243 Spruce St., Philadelphia PA 19104 (q 1 v F) $19, US 0006-0895.

BIBLICAL THEOLOGY BULLETIN - Bib Th Bul, Seton Hall University, South Orange, NJ 07079-2696 (q 1 v F) $15 0146 1079

CAHIERS DE JOSEPHOLOGIE - CahiersJos, Centre de Recherche 3800 Chemin Reine-Marie Montreal, H3V, Canada 1H6 (2 x yr 1 v Ja-Je) $20 CN 0007-9774.

THE CANADIAN CATHOLIC REVIEW - Can Cath Rev, 1437 College Drive, Saskatoon, Saskatchewan, Canada S74 OW6 (11 x yr 1 v Ja) $20 Canada, $25 US CN 0714-7724.

CATHECHIST, Peter Li, Inc., 2451 E. River Rd., Dayton, OH 45439 (m through school yr, except D, 1 v S) $18 US 0008-7726.

CATHOLIC BIBLICAL QUARTERLY - CBQ, Catholic Biblical Association of America, Catholic University of America, Washington, DC 20064 (q 1 v Ja) $15 US 0008-7912.

CATHOLIC DIGEST - CDgst, P.O. 1812, Des Moines. IA 50336 (m 1 v N) $13.97 US 0008-7998.

CATHOLIC HISTORICAL REVIEW - CHist, American Catholic Historic Association, Catholic University of America, Washington, DC 20064 (q 1 v Ap) $25 US 0008-8080.

CATHOLIC INTERNATIONAL - Cath Inst, Novalis, P.O. Box 31, Little Silver, NJ 07739 (bi weekly) $60 1 153197.

THE CATHOLIC LAWYER - CLawyer, St. Thomas More Institute for Legal Research, St. John's University School of Law, Fromkes Hall, Grand Central & Utopia Parkways, Jamaica, NY 11439 (q 1 v w) $5 US 0008-8137.

CATHOLIC LIBRARY WORLD - CLW, Catholic Library Association, 461 W. Lancaster Ave., Haverford, PA. 19041 (bi-m) $45 US 0008-820x.

CATHOLIC THEOLOGICAL SOCIETY OF AMERICA PROCEEDINGS - CTSAP, Santa Clara University, Santa Clara, CA 95053 (annual) US 0069-1267.

CATHOLIC WORKER - Cath Work, 36 East First St., New York, NY 10003 (m. bi-m Mr-Ap, Jl Ag, O-N 1 v Ja) $.25 US 0008-8463.

CATHOLICA, Aschendorffsche Verlagbuchhandlung, Postfach 1124, W-4400 Munster (q 1 v Ja) 68 DM GW 0008-8501.

CHICAGO STUDIES - Chicago Stds, P.O. Box 665, Mundelin, IL 60060 (3 x yr 1 v Ap) $14.50, US 0009-3718.

CHRIST TO THE WORLD - ChrWorld, Via di Propaganda 1-c, 00187 Rome, Italy (bi-m 1 v Ja) $16 IT 0011-1465.

CHRISTUS [Mexico] - Christus, Centro de Reflexion Teologica, Augosto Rodin 355, Apartado 19213, 03730 Mexico, D.F. (m 1 v F) $35 MX 0009-5842.

CHURCH, National Pastoral Life Center, 299 Elizabeth St., New York, NY 10012 (q 1 v Sp) $28 US 0883-5667.

CIENCIA TOMISTA - CIEN TOM, Estudio Teologico de San Esteban, Plaza del Concilio de Trento, 4, Apartado 17, Salamanca, Spain (3 x yr 1 v Ja) $35 SP 0210-0398.

CISTERCIAN STUDIES - Cist Stud, Saint Joseph's Abbey, Spencer, MA 01562 (q 1 v) $20 BE 0578-3224.

CITHARA, St. Bonaventure University, St. Bonventure, NY 14778 (semi-annual 1 v N) $6 US 0009-7527.

LA CIVILTA CATTOLICA - Civilta, Via di Porta Pinciana, 1-00187 Rome, Italy (semi-monthly) $100 IT 009-8167.

COLUMBIA, Dept. 18, P.O. Drawer 1670, New Haven, CT 06507 (m 1 v Ja) $6 US 0010-1869.

COMMONWEAL - Comm, 15 Dutch St., New York, NY 10038 (bi-w except m Christmas-New Year's, Jl & Ag 1 v Ja) $32 US 0010-33

COMMUNICATIONES, Pontificial Commission for the Revision of the Code of Canon Law, Piazza Pio XII, 10, 00193 Rome, Italy (semi-annual 1 v Ja) $18 IT 0393-0327.

COMMUNIO: INTERNATIONAL CATHOLIC REVIEW - Communio, P.O. Box 1046, Notre Dame, IN 46556 (q 1 v Sp) $26 US 0094-2065.

CONSECRATED LIFE - Con Life, Institute on Religious Life, 4200 North Austin Ave., Chicago, IL 60634 (q 1 v Sp) $15 US 0884-7010.

CRISIS, Brownson Institute, P.O. Box 1006, Notre Dame, IN 46556 (m, bi-m Jl-Ag) $25 US 0084-1705.

CRITIC, The Thomas More Association, 205 W. Monroe St., Chicago, IL 60606-5097 (q 1 v Fall) $17 US 0011-149X.

CROSS CURRENTS - CrossCurr, Box 147, Pearl River, NY 10965-9940 (q 1 v W) $22.50 US 0011-1953.

DIAKONIA, University of Scranton, Scranton, PA 18510-4507 (3 x yr 1 v Ap) $16 US 0012-1959.

DOCTRINE AND LIFE - Doctr Life, Dominican Publications, Saviors, Upper Dorset St., Dublin 1, Ireland (m. except My/Je, Jl/Ag) $18 IE 0012-446X.

LA DOCUMENTATION CATHOLIQUE - Doc Cath, Bayard Presse, 5 Rue Bayard, 75393 Paris Cedex 8, France (semi-m 1 v Ja) 270 FR 0012-4613.

EAST ASIAN PASTORAL REVIEW - EAPR, East Asian Pastoral Institute, P.O. Box 1815, Manila, Phillippines (q 1 v Ja) $12 surface, $31 air PH 0040-0564.

ECUMENICAL TRENDS - Ecumen Trends, Graymoor Ecumenical Institute, Garrison, NY 10524 (11 x yr, m except Ag, 1 v Ja) $10 US 0360-9073.

EMMANUEL, 5384 Wilson Mills Rd., Cleveland, OH 44143-3092 (m, bi-m Ja/F, Jl/Ag) $18.95 US 0013-6719.

ENVOY, Institute of Formative Spirituality, Duquesne University, Pittsburgh, PA 15282 (bi-m 1 v Ja) $7 US 0013-9408.

EPHEMERIDES THEOLOGICAE LOVANIENSES - Eph Theol Lovan, Bondgenotenlaan 153, BP 41, B-3000 Leuven, Belgium (q) 2000 F BE 0013-9513.

FAITH AND REASON - F & R, Christendom College, Route 3, Front Royal, VA 22630 (q 1 v Sp) $20 US 0098-5449.

FURROW, St. Patrick's College, Maynooth, County Kildare, Ireland (m 1 v Ja) $26 surface, $35 air IE 0016-3120.

GREGORIANUM, Pontificia Universita Gregoriana, Piazza della Pilotta, 35, 00187 Rome, Italy (q 1 v) $60 IT 0017-4114.

HEALTH PROGRESS - Health Prog, 4455 Woodson Rd., St. Louis, MO 63134-3797 (10 x yr 1 v Ja) $40.

HEYTHROP JOURNAL - Heythrop, Heythrop College (University of London), 11 Cavendish Square, London W1M OAN England (q 1 v Ja) $30 UK 0018-1196.

HOMILETIC AND PASTORAL REVIEW - HPR, Catholic Polls, Inc., 86 Riverside Dr., New York, NY 10024 (m, bi-m Ag-S 1 v O) $20 US 0018-4268.

HORIZONS; JOURNAL OF THE COLLEGE THEOLOGY SOCIETY - Horizons (CTS), Council on the Study of Religion, Executive Office, Wilfried Laurier University, Waterloo, Ontario, Canada N2L 3C5 (semi-annual 1 v Sp) $28 US 0360-9669.

INTERNATIONAL JOURNAL OF PHILOSOPHICAL STUDIES - IJPS, Cheriton House, North Way, Andover, Hants SP 10 5 BE,UK

INTERNATIONAL PHILOSOPHICAL QUARTERLY - IPQ, Fordham University, Bronx, NY 10458 (q 1 v Mr) $30 US 0019-0365.

JOURNAL OF ECUMENICAL STUDIES - JEcumen Stds, Temple University, 1936 N. Broad St., Philadelphia, PA 19122 (q 1 v W) $20 US 0022-0558.

JOURNAL OF INTERDISCIPLINARY STUDIES - J Interdisc St, Third St., Suite 11, Santa Monica, CA 90405 (annual) $15 US 0890-0132.

JURIST, Catholic University of America, Washington, DC 20064 (semi-annual) $20 US 0022-6858.

LATIN AMERICAN DOCUMENTATION - LADOC, Latinamerica Press, Apartado 5594, Lima 100, Peru (bi-m) $18 PE 0360-3350.

LAVAL THEOLOGIQUE ET PHILOSOPHIQUE - Laval Theol Phil, Faculte de Philosophie, Universite Laval, Quebec 10, Canada (3 x yr 1 v F) $28 CN 0023-9054.

LIGUORIAN, 1 Liguori Dr., Liguori, MO 63057 (m 1 v Ja) $15 US 0022-3450.

LINACRE QUARTERLY - Linacre, 850 Elm Grove Rd., Elm Grove, WI 53122 (q 1 v F) $24 US 0024-3639.

LISTENING, Lewis University, Box 1108, Rt. 53, Romeoville, IL 60441-2298 (3 x yr 1 v W) $11.50 US 0024-4414.

LITURGY, The Liturgical Conference, 810 Rhode Island Ave., NE, Washington, DC 20018 (q 1 v) $35 US 0458-063X.

LIVING LIGHT, U.S. Catholic Conference, 3211 4th Ave., NE, Washington, DC 20001 (1 v O) $18.50 US 0024-5275.

LIVING PRAYER, Beckley Hill, Rural Route 2, Box 4784. Barre, VT 05641 (bi-m) $17 US 0890-5568.

LOUVAIN STUDIES - Louvain Stds, Faculty of Theology, University of Louvain, Naamsestraat 100, B 3000, Louvain, Belgium (semi-annual Sp & Fall 1 v biennially) $18 BE 0024-6964.

LUMEN VITAE - Lumen,184, Rue Washington, 1050 Brussels, Belgium, Aquinas Subscription Agency, 561 Fort Road, St. Paul, MN 55102 (q 1 v Mr) $27.50 BE 0024-7324.

MANUSCRIPTA, St. Louis University Library, St. Louis, MO 63131 (3 x yr 1 v Mr) $11 US 0025-2603.

MARIAN STUDIES - Marian Stds, Marian Library, University of Dayton, Dayton, OH 45469 (annual) $10 US 0464-9680.

MEDIAEVAL STUDIES - Med Stud, Pontifical Institute of Mediaeval Studies, 59 Queen's Park Crescent East, Toronto, Ontario, Canada M5S 2C4 (annual) $31 CN 0076-5872.

MELANGES DE SCIENCE RELIGIEUSE - MSR, Universite de Lille, 60 Boulevard Vauban, 59046 Lille, France (q 1 v Mr) 106 FR.

MID-AMERICA - MidAm, Loyol University Chicago, 6525 N. Sheridan Road, Chicago, IL 60626 (3xyr) & 9 US 0026-2927.

MODERN LITURGY - Mod Lit, Resource Publications, Inc., 160 E. Virginia St., #290, San Jose, CA 95112.

MODERN SCHOOLMAN - Mod Schlmn, St. Louis University, 221 North Grance Blvd., St. Louis, MO 63103 (q 1 v N) $26 US 0026-8402.

MOMENTUM, National Catholic Educational Association, Suite 100, 1077 30th St., NW, Washington, DC 20007 (q 1 v F) $20 US 0026-914X.

MONTH, 114 Mount St., London W1Y 6AH, England (m except Ag 1 v Ja) $30 UK 0027-0172.

NATIONAL CATHOLIC REGISTER - Register, 12700 Ventura Blvd., Suite 2000, Studio City, CA 91604 (w 1 v) $25 US 0027-8920.

NATIONAL CATHOLIC REPORTER - Nat Cath Rep, P.O. Box 281, Kansas City, MO 64141 (w S-My except 1 w in Ja, bi-w Je-Ag 1 v O) $27 US 0027-8939.

NEW BLACKFRIARS - New Blckfrs, Oxford OX1 3LY, England (m 1 v Ja) $27 UK 0028-4289.

NEW COVENANT - New Cov, 840 Airport Blvd., P.O. Box 7009, Ann Arbor, MI 48107 (m 1 v Jl) $17.95 US 0744-8589.

NEW OXFORD REVIEW - New Oxford Rev, New Oxford Review, Inc., 1069 Kains Ave., Berkeley, CA 94706 (m except Ja-F and Jl-Ag) $19 US 0149-4244.

NEW THEOLOGY REVIEW - New Theol Rev, Liturgical Press, St. John's Abbey, Collegeville, MN 56321 (q 1 v F) $22 0896-4297.

NOTITIAE, Sacred Congregation for the Sacraments and Divine Worship, 10 Piazza Pio XII, 00913 Rome, Italy (m 1 v Ja) $25 VC 0029-4306.

NOUVELLE REVUE TRHEOLOGIQUE - NRT, Rue de Bruxelles 61, 500 Namur, Belgium, F.W. Faxon Company, Inc., 15 Southwest Park, Westwood, MA 02090 (bi-m 1 v Ja) $60 BE 0029-4845.

OLD TESTAMENT ABSTRACTS - OTA, Catholic University of America, 414 Administration Bldg., Washingoton, DC 20064 (3 x a yr.) $14 US 0364-8591.

ONE IN CHRIST - OChr, Turvey Abbey, Turvey, Bedfordshire MK43 8DE, England (q 1 v Ja) $34 UK 0030-252X.

ORIGINS, National Catholic News Service, 1312 Massachusetts Ave., NW, Washington, DC 20005 (w, bi-w Jl & Ag 1 v My) $87 US 0093-609X.

L'OSSERVATORE ROMANO (ENGLISH EDITION) - OR (Eng), Vatican City (w) $55 surface, $75 air VC 0030-6312.

OUR SUNDAY VISITOR - OSV, Our Sunday Visitor, Inc. Noll Plaza, Huntington, IN 46750 (w 1 v My) $26 US 0030-6979.

PACIFICA, P.O. Box 271, Brunswick East, Victoria 3057, Australia (3 x a yr) $31 AU 1030-570X.

PASTORAL MUSIC - Past Mus, National Association of Pastoral Musicians, 225 Sheridan St., NW. Washington, DC 20011 (bi-m 1 v O-N) $24 US 0363-6569.

PERIODICA DE RE MORALI CANONICA LITURGICA - Periodica, Gregorian University, Piazza della Pilotta, 4, Rome 00187 Italy (q) $50 IT 0031-529X.

PERSPECTIVA TEOLOGICA - Perspectiva, Caixa Posta 5047, 31611 - Belo Horizonte, MG, Brazil BL 0102-4469.

PHILOSOPHICAL STUDIES - PhilosStuds, Department of Philosophy, University College Dublin, Dublin 4, Ireland (annual) $35 IE 0554-0739.

PHILOSOPHY TODAY - PhilosTod, DePaul University, 25 E Jackson Blvd., Chicago, IL 60604 (q 1 v Sp) $18 US 0031-8256.

THE POPE SPEAKS - TPS, Our Sunday Visitor, Inc., 200 Noll Plaza Huntington, IN 46750 (q 1 v W) $18 US 0032-4353.

PRIEST, Our Sunday Visitor, Inc., Noll Plaza, Huntington, IN 46750 (m except Jl 1 v Ja) $30 US 0032-8200.

PRIESTS & PEOPLE - The Tablet Publishing Co. Ltd. 1 King Street Cloisters, Clifton Walk, London W6 0QZ, England (11 x a yr) $37 UK 0009-8736.

RELIGION AND LITERATURE - Relig Lit, Department of English, University of Notre Dame, Notre Dame, IN 46556 (3 x yr 1 v W) $15 US 0029-4500.

RELIGION TEACHER'S JOURNAL - ReligTJ, Twenty-Third Publications, P.O. Box 180, West Mystic, CT 06355 (m S-My bi-m N-D 1 v F) $14 US 0034-401X.

REVIEW FOR RELIGIOUS - RRel, Room 428, 3601 Lindell Blvd., St. Louis, MO 63108 (bi-m 1 v Ja) $15 US 0034-639X.

REVIEW OF SOCIAL ECONOMY - RSocEcon, Peter L. Danner, Department of Economics, Marquette University, Milwaukee, WI 53233 (3 x yr 1 v Ap) $35 US 0034-6764.

REVISTA ECLESIASTICA BRASILEIRA - REB, Editora Vozes Ltda, Matriz Rua Frel Luis, 100, Caixa Postal 90023 B, 25689 Petraopollis - RJ, Brazil (q 1 v Mr) $80.

REVUE PHILOSOPHIQUE DE LOUVAIN - RPhil Louvain, Institute Superieure de Philosophie, College Thomas More (SH3), Chemin Aristote, 1, B-1348 Louvain-la-Neuve, Belgium, Subs. Editions Peeters, BP 41, B-3000 Louvain, Belgium (q 1 v F) $40 1,250 BF, including Repertoire Bibliographique 1,900 BE 0035-3841.

REVUE THEOLOGIQUE DE LOUVAIN -RTheol Louvain, College Albert Descamps, Grand Place, 45 B-1348 Louvain-la-Neuve, Belgium (q 1 v Mr) $22 BE 0080-2654.

SACRED MUSIC - SacM, 548 Lafond Ave., St. Paul, MN 55103 (q 1 v Sp) $12.50 US 0036-2255.

ST. ANTHONY MESSENGER - St Anth, 1615 Republic St., Cincinnati, OH 45210 (m 1 v Je) $16 US 0036-276X.

SALT, 205 W. Monroe, Chicago, IL 60606 (10 x yr 1 v Ja) $15 US 0883-2587.

SCRIPTURE BULLETIN - ScriptB, Catholic Biblical Association, 8 Holly Hill Close, Southampton S01 7EU, England (semi-annual 1 v Sp) $10 UK 0036-9780.

SEMINARIUM, Sacred Congregation for Catholic Education, 00120 Vatican City) q 1 v Ja-Mr) $35 VC 0582-6314.

SIDIC: SERVICE INTERNATIONAL DE DOCUMENTATION JUDÉO-CHRÉTIENNE - SIDIC, Via de Plebiscito 112, 00816 Rome, Italy, Dr. Eugene Fisher, Secretariat for Catholic-Jewish Relations, 3211 4th St., NE, Washington, DC 20017-1194 (3 x yr) $7.50 surface, $9.50 air.

SISTERS TODAY - Sisters, St. John's Abbey, Collegeville, MN 56321 (m except Jl and Ag 1 v S) $15 US 0037-590X.

SOCIAL JUSTICE REVIEW - SocJust, 3835 Westminster Pl., St, Louis MO 63108 (m, bi-m Jl-Ag 1 v Ap) $15 US 0037-7767.

SOCIAL THOUGHT - SocThought, National Conference of Catholic Charities, 1319 F Street NW, Washington, DC 20004 (q 1 v Sp) $18 US 0099-183X.

SPIRIT, Seton Hall University, South Orange, NJ 07079 (bi-annual 1 v Sp) $4 US 0038-7584.

SPIRITUAL LIFE - Spir Life, 2131 Lincoln Rd., NE, Washington, DC 20002-1199 (q 1 v Sp) $9 US 0038-7630.

SPIRITUALITY TODAY - Spir Tod, 3642 Lindell Blvd., St. Louis, MO 63108-3396 (q 1 v Mr) US 0162-6760.

STIMMEN DER ZEIT - Stimm Zeit, Zuccalistrasse 16, 8000 Munchen 19, Germany (m 2 v Ja Jl)) 61.80 DM 6 months GW 0039-1492.

STUDIA CANONICA - Stud Can, Universite Saint-Paul, 223 rue Main, Ottawa, Ontario K1S 1C4, Canada (semi-annual 1 v) $25 CN 0039-310X.

STUDIA MISSIONALIA - StudiaM, Gregorian University, Plaza della Pilotta, 4, 00187 Rome, Italy (annual) $30 IT 0080-3987.

STUDIES, 35 Lower Leeson, St., Dublin, Ireland (q 1 v Sp) $30 IE 0039-3495.

STUDIES IN FORMATIVE SPIRITUALITY - Stud Form Spir, Institute of Formative Spirituality, Duquesne University, Pittsburgh, PA 15282 (3 x yr 1 v F) $18 US 0193-2748.

LE SUPPLEMENT - Supplement, Les Editions du Cerf, 29 Blvd Latour-Maubourg, 75340 Paris, Cedex 7, France (q) 220 FF FR 0750-1455.

TABLET, 1 King Street Cloisters, Clifton Walk, London W60QZ, England (w) UK 0039-8837.

THE TEILHARD REVIEW - Teilhard Rev, The Teilhard Centre for the Future of Man, 23 Kensington Square, London 1W8 5HN, England (3 x yr v F) $30 UK 0050-2184.

TEOLOGIA Y VIDA - Teol Vida, Facultad de Teologia, Universidad Catolica de Chile, Diagonal Oriente 3300, Casilla 114D, Santiago, Chile (q 1 v Ja) $25 CL 0049-3449.

THEOLOGICAL STUDIES - TheolStds, P.O. Box 64002, Baltimore, MD 2126 (q 1 v Mr) $17 US 0040-5639.

THEOLOGY DIGEST - TheolDgst, P.O. Box 6036, Duluth, MN 55806 (q 1 v Ja) $12 US 0040-5728.

THOMIST, 487 Michigan Ave., NE, Washington, DC 20017-1585 (q 1 v Ja) $35 US 0040-6325.

THOUGHT, Fordham University Press, 441 East Fordham Rd., Bronx, NY 10458 (q 1 v Sp) $17.50 US 0040-6457.

TODAY'S CATHOLIC TEACHER - Tod Cath Teach, Peter Li, Inc., 2451 East River Rd., Dayton, OH 45439 (m during school year, except D 1 v S) $14.95 US 0040-8441.

TODAY'S PARISH - Tod Parish, Twenty-Third Publications, P.O. Box 180, 185 Willow St., West Mystic, CT 06355 (m except bi-m N-D 1 v S) $22 US 0041-8459.

U.S. CATHOLIC - USCath, 205 W. Monroe St., Chicago, IL 60606-9963 (m 1 v My) $15 US 0041-7548.

U.S. CATHOLIC HISTORIAN - US Cath Hist, P.O. Box 16229, Baltimore, MD 21210 (q) $30 US 0735-8318.

THE WAY - Way, 114 Mount Street, London, W1Y 6AN, England (q 1 v Ja) $26.50 UK 0043-1575.

WAY SUPPLEMENT - Way Suppl, 114 Mount Street, London, W1Y 6AN, England (3 x yr) $26.

WORD & SPIRIT - Word Sp, St. Bede's Publications, Petersham, MA 01366 (annual) US 0193-9211.

WORSHIP, St. John's Abbey, Collegeville, MN 56321 (bi-m 1 v Ja) $22 US 0043-941X.